International GAAP® 2010

Generally Accepted Accounting Practice
under International Financial Reporting Standards

Mike Bonham

Richard Crisp

Matthew Curtis

Mike Davies

Pieter Dekker

Tim Denton

Lindy Ellis

Meredith Lloyd

James Luke

Robert McCracken

Richard Moore

Robert Overend

Hedy Richards

Tim Rogerson

Matt Williams

Quality In Everything We Do

A John Wiley and Sons, Ltd, Publication

This edition first published in 2010 by John Wiley & Sons Ltd.

Cover, cover design and content copyright © 2010 Ernst & Young LLP.

The United Kingdom firm of Ernst & Young LLP is a member of Ernst & Young Global.

International GAAP® is a registered trademark of Ernst & Young LLP.

http://www.internationalgaap.com

Registered office

John Wiley & Sons Ltd, The Atrium, Southern Gate, Chichester, West Sussex, PO19 8SQ, United Kingdom

For details of our global editorial offices, for customer services and for information about how to apply for permission to reuse the copyright material in this book please see our website at www.wiley.com

Wiley also publishes its books in a variety of electronic formats. Some content that appears in print may not be available in electronic books.

Designations used by companies to distinguish their products are often claimed as trademarks. All brand names and product names used in this book are trade names, service marks, trademarks or registered trademarks of their respective owners. The publisher is not associated with any product or vendor mentioned in this book. This publication is designed to provide accurate and authoritative information in regard to the subject matter covered. It is sold on the understanding that the publisher is not engaged in rendering professional services. If professional advice or other expert assistance is required, the services of a competent professional should be sought.

This publication has been carefully prepared, but it necessarily contains information in summary form and is therefore intended for general guidance only, and is not intended to be a substitute for detailed research or the exercise of professional judgement. The publishers, Ernst & Young LLP, Ernst & Young Global or any of its Member Firms or partners or staff can accept no responsibility for loss occasioned to any person acting or refraining from action as a result of any material in this publication. On any specific matter, reference should be made to the appropriate adviser.

ISBN 978-0-470-68800-7

[Ernst & Young personnel only ISBN 978-0-470-68971-4]

A catalogue record for this book is available from the British Library.

Printed in Great Britain by CPI William Clowes Ltd, Beccles, Suffolk, NR34 7TL

This book is printed on acid-free paper responsibly manufactured from sustainable forestry in which at least two trees are planted for each one used for paper production.

About this book

This 2010 edition of International GAAP has increased in length by approximately 100 pages since the last edition, due to the fact that it has been revised and expanded in order to:

- deal with all new and amended authoritative pronouncements, including guidance on applying the recent revisions to IAS 1 (Presentation of Financial Statements), IAS 23 (Borrowing Costs), IAS 27 (Consolidated and Separate Financial Statements) and IFRS 3 (Business Combinations) along with the recently issued IFRIC Interpretations and the revisions to other standards;

- provide insight and guidance on the interpretation and practical application of IFRS from a truly global perspective, based on the experience of the book's authors in dealing with recent day-to-day practical issues; and

- explain the many current initiatives that are presently being pursued by the IASB and IFRIC and that will lead to changes in accounting requirements. In particular recently issued discussion papers on Revenue Recognition and Leases and recently issued exposure drafts on Financial Instruments, Consolidation, Income Taxes and Joint Ventures may all significantly impact present accounting practices.

The book is published in two volumes, comprising 43 Chapters, three indexes, and over 100 pages of detailed contents. These are set out over the two volumes as follows:

Volume 1
- Complete set of detailed contents
- Chapters 1 to 25
- Index of extracts from financial statements
- Index of standards
- Index

Volume 2
- Complete set of detailed contents
- Chapters 26 to 43
- Index of extracts from financial statements
- Index of standards
- Index

Foreword

Philip Laskawy

Vice Chairman of the Trustees
International Accounting Standards Committee
Foundation

When I wrote the foreword to the 2009 edition of this book I commented on the speed with which International Financial Reporting Standards (IFRSs) had emerged as the leading financial reporting framework and commented on the prospect of IFRSs being the one language of accounting in major capital markets within a few years. However the fallout from the financial crisis has meant that the last twelve months have been challenging ones for accounting standard-setters. Various commentators have, wrongly in my view, blamed IFRSs and their alleged pro-cyclicality for exacerbating the financial crisis. At the same time, following the change of administration in the US, others have questioned the US's commitment to IFRS adoption, bringing the IASB's convergence strategy into question. Finally concerns have once again surfaced about the extent of political influence over the standard setting process.

However whilst it has been a difficult and stressful year for the IASB it is important to remember that a recurrent theme of those that have commented on the financial crisis and its aftermath has been the critical importance of achieving a single set of high quality globally converged financial reporting standards. The absence of a common internationally accepted set of standards provides opportunities for regulatory arbitrage and imposes unnecessary costs on users and preparers of accounts. It is my strong belief that only IFRSs, established by an independent IASB, can be this set of standards. Therefore I very much support the continuing efforts of the IASB's Chairman, Sir David Tweedie, and others to achieve that end.

Important progress has been made during the past year. A roadmap for the adoption of IFRSs in Japan was approved in June 2009 and in the many other jurisdictions where the decision to adopt IFRSs had already been made preparations for the adoption of IFRS continued. The establishment of a formal public accountability link for the IASC Foundation to leading public capital market authorities has and will continue to enhance the legitimacy of IFRSs whilst ensuring the continuing independence of the standard setting process. Developments in the US are therefore critical – convergence efforts with the US Financial Accounting Standards Board (FASB) and a commitment to a single set of high-quality, global standards in the US are essential to achieving the IASB's global mission.

Of course the purpose of having a single set of high quality globally converged financial reporting standards is to ensure consistent, unbiased, transparent and relevant information whatever the location of the reporting entity. This can only be achieved if IFRSs are interpreted and applied consistently around the world. It therefore remains my view that the single most important challenge now facing all those involved in the adoption of IFRSs including national standard setters, other accounting bodies and regulators is to ensure that the application of IFRSs leads to a truly single set of standards used worldwide, and that 'national variations' in the interpretation and application of IFRS do not emerge. I have no doubt that calls will be made for even greater consistency and clarity in the application of IFRSs – both within individual industries and countries, and across industries and national borders. Consequently, I believe that if country-specific variations of IFRSs develop, they will be a substantial hindrance to IFRSs becoming a truly global tool of financial communication.

In this regard I warmly welcome the publication of the 2010 edition of this book, as I believe that it has an important part to play in the process of promoting consistent, comparable and high quality financial reporting under IFRSs. Because IFRSs are based upon principles, there is an enormous need for a book such as this; a book that not only provides an analysis of the requirements of the standards and the principles that they expound, but also presents a clear explanation of how the standards should be interpreted and applied in practice. It addresses the main issues in International GAAP by explaining thoroughly the technical aspects of each standard, and providing a detailed analysis of possible solutions to the complex practical issues the application of each standard raises. All this is accompanied by worked examples, a comprehensive discussion of the possible alternative solutions available, and practical illustrations taken from the actual financial statements of companies that report under IFRSs.

October 2009   *Philip Laskawy*

Preface

International accounting standards have come a long way since Henry Benson led the way to the creation, first, of the Accountants International Study Group in 1967 and, thereafter, of the International Accounting Standards Committee in 1973. Perhaps most remarkable is the pace at which the globalisation of accounting standards has moved: from the position only a few years ago where numerous disparate national systems existed, to the position today where, despite some recent hiccups, there is a realistic prospect that within a few years IFRS will be the globally recognised accounting language in the major capital markets.

This represents a considerable achievement by all concerned: the European Union, whose leaders had the vision to set the agenda for a common financial reporting regime across the EU; the former Board of the International Accounting Standards Committee (IASC), who undertook the core standards programme that laid the groundwork for global acceptance of international standards; the many countries throughout the world whose standard-setters have contributed to the work of the IASC and the International Accounting Standards Board (IASB); the members of the IASB, who have worked assiduously under the unstinting leadership of Sir David Tweedie; and the large number of governments that have recognised the value of a common financial reporting regime, and adopted IFRS.

This past year has clearly been a very difficult one for the global economy. There are different views on the part that financial reporting requirements may have played in the recent turbulent times that we have experienced. Some argue that accounting standards and requirements have exacerbated these market difficulties. We do not agree with this view. We do however welcome the rapid actions that the IASB has undertaken to review a number of the areas of commonly recognised complexity and difficulty. The benefits derived from having a single set of globally applied, high quality financial reporting standards would be considerable. It is encouraging that constituents still recognise these benefits and continue to press the IASB and FASB to move forward. In this regard we await the SEC's imminent announcement of its intention on the 'Roadmap' to adoption of IFRS with great interest.

We are also encouraged that there is general recognition of the need for standard setters to be both independent and accountable. We therefore welcome the recent changes the IASCF trustees have made to try and achieve this. Crucially we should not allow recent difficulties to derail the significant progress that has been made to date. Rather, we should take heart from how far we have come, and stay focused on the bigger picture and the substantial benefits that would be realised from a single global accounting language.

****

We are deeply indebted to many of our colleagues within the global organisation of Ernst & Young for their selfless assistance and support in the publication of this book. It has been a truly international effort, with valuable contributions from Ernst & Young people around the globe.

Our thanks go particularly to those who reviewed and edited drafts, most notably: Justine Belton, Doug Cameron, Garth Coppin, Tai Danmola, Lucineia Donnelly, Michael Elliot, Charlie Feeney, Rob Gaillard, John Guess, Sven Hayn, Paul Hebditch, Michiel van der Lof, John O'Grady, Eric Ohlund, Danita Ostling, Tatiana Pavlova, Ruth Picker, Gerard van Santen, Alison Spivey, Matthew Sutton, Leo van der Tas, Lynda Tomkins, and Paul Wallek. Within the Financial Reporting Group itself, our thanks go to everyone who directly and indirectly contributed to the book's creation: Elizer Baltazar, Denise Brand, Robin Chatterjee, Larissa Connor, Bernd Kremp, Margaret Pankhurst, Megan Price, Inayatullah Qureshi, Claire Taylor and Lawrence Wong. We also thank Jeremy Gugenheim for his assistance with the production technology throughout the period of writing.

As authors, however, we take responsibility for all the opinions expressed in the book, and the blame for all its faults.

London,

October 2009

	Mike Bonham	James Luke
	Richard Crisp	Robert McCracken
	Matthew Curtis	Richard Moore
	Mike Davies	Robert Overend
	Pieter Dekker	Hedy Richards
	Tim Denton	Tim Rogerson
	Lindy Ellis	Matt Williams
	Meredith Lloyd	

List of chapters

Volume 1

The list of chapters in Volume 2 follows overleaf.

Volume 2

Detailed contents: Volume 1

CHAPTER 2   THE QUEST FOR A CONCEPTUAL FRAMEWORK FOR FINANCIAL REPORTING

CHAPTER 4   NON-CURRENT ASSETS HELD FOR SALE AND DISCONTINUED OPERATIONS

CHAPTER 5   FIRST-TIME ADOPTION

CHAPTER 6   CONSOLIDATED FINANCIAL STATEMENTS

CHAPTER 7   CONSOLIDATION PROCEDURES AND NON-CONTROLLING INTERESTS

CHAPTER 8   SEPARATE AND INDIVIDUAL FINANCIAL STATEMENTS

CHAPTER 9   BUSINESS COMBINATIONS

CHAPTER 10   COMMON CONTROL BUSINESS COMBINATIONS

CHAPTER 13   FOREIGN EXCHANGE

CHAPTER 14   HYPERINFLATION

CHAPTER 15   INTANGIBLE ASSETS

CHAPTER 17   INVESTMENT PROPERTY

CHAPTER 18   IMPAIRMENT OF FIXED ASSETS AND GOODWILL

CHAPTER 19   CAPITALISATION OF BORROWING COSTS

CHAPTER 20   INVENTORIES

CHAPTER 25   REVENUE RECOGNITION

The detailed table of contents of Volume 2 follows overleaf.

Detailed contents: Volume 2

CHAPTER 27   SHARE-BASED PAYMENT

CHAPTER 28   EMPLOYEE BENEFITS

CHAPTER 29   FINANCIAL INSTRUMENTS: INTRODUCTION

CHAPTER 31   FINANCIAL INSTRUMENTS: FINANCIAL LIABILITIES AND EQUITY

CHAPTER 32   FINANCIAL INSTRUMENTS: MEASUREMENT

CHAPTER 34   FINANCIAL INSTRUMENTS: DISCLOSURES

CHAPTER 36   EARNINGS PER SHARE

CHAPTER 39   STATEMENT OF CASH FLOWS

CHAPTER 40   INTERIM FINANCIAL REPORTING

CHAPTER 41 AGRICULTURE

CHAPTER 42   EXTRACTIVE INDUSTRIES

CHAPTER 43   INSURANCE CONTRACTS

Abbreviations

The following abbreviations are used in this book:

Professional and regulatory bodies:

AASB	Australian Accounting Standards Board
AICPA	American Institute of Certified Public Accountants
APB	Accounting Principles Board (of the AICPA, predecessor of the FASB)
ARC	Accounting Regulatory Committee of representatives of EU Member States
ASB	Accounting Standards Board in the UK
ASC	Accounting Standards Committee (the predecessor of the ASB)
CESR	Committee of European Securities Regulators, an independent committee whose members comprise senior representatives from EU securities regulators
CICA	Canadian Institute of Chartered Accountants
EC	European Commission
EFRAG	European Financial Reporting Advisory Group
EITF	Emerging Issues Task Force in the US
EU	European Union
FAF	Financial Accounting Foundation
FASB	Financial Accounting Standards Board in the US
G4+1	The (now disbanded) group of four plus 1, actually with six members, that comprised an informal 'think tank' of staff from the standard setters from Australia, Canada, New Zealand, UK, and USA, plus the IASC
IASB	International Accounting Standards Board
IASC	International Accounting Standards Committee. The former Board of the IASC was the predecessor of the IASB
IASCF	International Accounting Standards Committee Foundation
ICAEW	Institute of Chartered Accountants in England and Wales
ICAS	Institute of Chartered Accountants of Scotland
IFRIC	International Financial Reporting Interpretations Committee of the IASB
IGC	Implementation Guidance Committee on IAS 39 (now disbanded)

IOSCO   International Organisation of Securities Commissions

JWG   Joint Working Group of Standard-setters that comprised representatives from the IASC, the FASB, and eight other international bodies. The purpose of the (now disbanded) group was to develop an integrated and harmonised standard on financial instruments – a task they were unable to complete

SAC   Standards Advisory Council, which provides advice to the IASB on a wide range of issues

SEC   Securities and Exchange Commission (the US securities regulator)

SIC   Standing Interpretations Committee of the IASC (replaced by IFRIC)

Accounting related terms:

ADS   American Depositary Shares

AFS   Available-for-sale investment

ARB   Accounting Research Bulletins (issued by the AICPA)

ARS   Accounting Research Studies (issued by the APB)

CGU   Cash Generating Unit

CIS   Comprehensive Income Statement, as developed by the G4+1 group of accounting standard-setters, and published in June 1999 in the ASB Discussion Paper *Reporting Financial Performance: Proposals for Change*

CU   Currency Unit

CULS   Convertible Unsecured Loan Stock

DPF   Discretionary Participation Feature

E   Exposure Draft (of an IAS)

EBIT   Earnings Before Interest and Taxes

EBITDA   Earnings Before Interest, Taxes, Depreciation and Amortisation

ED   Exposure Draft

EPS   Earnings per Share

FAS   Financial Accounting Standards (issued by the FASB)

FC   Foreign currency

FIFO   First-In, First-Out basis of valuation

FRS   Financial Reporting Standard (issued by the ASB)

FTA   First-time Adoption

GAAP   Generally accepted accounting practice (as it applies under IFRS), or generally accepted accounting principles (as it applies to the US)

HTM   Held-to-maturity investment

IAS   International Accounting Standard (issued by the former board of the IASC)

IBNR	Incurred but not reported claims
IFAC	International Federation of Accountants
IFRS	International Financial Reporting Standard (issued by the IASB)
IPO	Initial Public Offering
IPR&D	In-process Research and Development
IRR	Internal Rate of Return
JV	Joint Venture
LAT	Liability Adequacy Test
LC	Local Currency
LIBOR	London Inter Bank Offered Rate
LIFO	Last-In, First-Out basis of valuation
NBV	Net Book Value
NRV	Net Realisable Value
PP&E	Property, Plant and Equipment
R&D	Research and development
SFAC	Statement of Financial Accounting Concepts (issued by the FASB as part of its conceptual framework project)
SFAS	Statement of Financial Accounting Standards (issued by the FASB)
SPE	Special Purpose Entity
TSR	Total Shareholder Return
VIU	Value In Use
WACC	Weighted Average Cost of Capital

References to IFRSs, IASs, Interpretations and supporting documentation:

AG	Application Guidance
AV	Alternative View
B, BCZ	Basis for Conclusions on IASs
BC	Basis for Conclusions on IFRSs and IASs
DO	Dissenting Opinion
IE	Illustrative Examples on IFRSs and IASs
IG	Implementation Guidance
IN	Introduction to IFRSs and IASs

Authoritative literature

The content of this book takes into account all accounting standards and other relevant rules issued up to September 2009. Consequently, it covers the IASB's *Framework for the Preparation and Presentation of Financial Statements* and authoritative literature listed below.

Unless otherwise indicated therein, all references in footnotes to the extant pronouncements below are to the versions of those pronouncements as approved and included in the Bound Volume of International Financial Reporting Standards at 1 January 2009 published by the IASB (ISBN 978-1-905590-90-2).

Effective 1 July 2009 US GAAP accounting standards that are issued by various standard setters are now organised by a comprehensive Accounting Standards Codification scheme, which is now the single source of authoritative US GAAP. For purposes of this publication we still refer to the previously issued, and still commonly referred to, US GAAP pronouncements, even though these are now deemed to be non-authoritative.

† The standards and interpretations marked with a dagger have been withdrawn or superseded.

IASB Framework
Framework for the Preparation and Presentation of Financial Statements

International Financial Reporting Standards	
IFRS 1	First-time Adoption of International Financial Reporting Standards
IFRS 2	Share-based Payment
IFRS 3	Business Combinations
IFRS 4	Insurance Contracts
IFRS 5	Non-current Assets Held for Sale and Discontinued Operations
IFRS 6	Exploration for and Evaluation of Mineral Resources
IFRS 7	Financial Instruments: Disclosures
IFRS 8	Operating Segments

International Accounting Standards	
IAS 1	Presentation of Financial Statements
IAS 2	Inventories
IAS 7	Statement of Cash Flows
IAS 8	Accounting Policies, Changes in Accounting Estimates and Errors
IAS 10	Events after the Reporting Period

International Financial Reporting Interpretations Committee Interpretations

IFRIC 15	Agreements for the Construction of Real Estate
IFRIC 16	Hedges of a Net Investment in a Foreign Operation
IFRIC 17	Distributions of Non-cash Assets to Owners
IFRIC 18	Transfer of Assets from Customers

Standing Interpretations Committee Interpretations

SIC-7	Introduction of the Euro
SIC-10	Government Assistance – No Specific Relation to Operating Activities
SIC-12	Consolidation – Special Purpose Entities
SIC-13	Jointly Controlled Entities – Non-Monetary Contributions by Venturers
SIC-15	Operating Leases – Incentives
SIC-21	Income Taxes – Recovery of Revalued Non-Depreciable Assets
SIC-25	Income Taxes – Changes in the Tax Status of an Entity or its Shareholders
SIC-27	Evaluating the Substance of Transactions Involving the Legal Form of a Lease
SIC-29	Service Concession Arrangements: Disclosures
SIC-31	Revenue – Barter Transactions Involving Advertising Services
SIC-32	Intangible Assets – Web Site Costs

Other IASB publications

Amendments to IFRS 1 First-time Adoption of International Financial Reporting Standards

Improving Disclosures about Financial Instruments (Amendments to IFRS 7 Financial Instruments: Disclosures)

Embedded Derivatives (Amendments to IFRIC 9 and IAS 39)

Group Cash-settled Share-Based Payment Transactions (Amendments to IFRS 2)

Improvements to IFRSs (issued 16 April 2009)

International Financial Reporting Standard (IFRS) for Small and Medium-sized Entities (SMEs)

IASB Exposure Drafts

ED 9	Joint Arrangements
	Amendments to IAS 37 Provisions, Contingent Liabilities and Contingent Assets and IAS 19 Employee Benefits
	An Improved Conceptual Framework for Financial Reporting –
	Chapter 1: The Objective of Financial Reporting
	Chapter 2: Qualitative Characteristics and Constraints of Decision-useful Financial Reporting Information
	Simplifying Earnings per Share – Proposed Amendments to IAS 33
	Discontinued Operations – Proposed Amendments to IFRS 5
ED 10	Consolidated Financial Statements
	Relationships with the State (Proposed Amendments to IAS 24)
ED/2009/1	Post-implementation Revisions to IFRIC Interpretations (Proposed amendments to IFRIC 9 and IFRIC 16)
ED/2009/2	Income Tax

IFRIC Exposure Drafts

Chapter 1

The development of International GAAP

1   THE EVOLUTION OF THE INTERNATIONAL ACCOUNTING STANDARDS BOARD

Globalisation is the removal of barriers to free trade and the closer integration of national economies.[1] With globalisation has come the increasing integration of world markets for goods, services and capital – with the result that companies that traditionally were reliant on their domestic capital markets for financing now have substantially increased access to debt and equity capital both inside and outside their national borders.

Yet – perhaps not entirely surprisingly the world of financial reporting has historically been slow to respond reflecting, no doubt, a widespread 'nationalism' in respect of countries' own standards. However, more rapid progress has now started to be made. This is particularly well illustrated by the recent activities of the US Securities and Exchange Commission (SEC).

In November 2007 the SEC voted unanimously to remove the requirement for a reconciliation to US GAAP from financial statements prepared in accordance with International Financial Reporting Standards (IFRSs) issued by the International Accounting Standards Board (IASB). The SEC's removal of the reconciliation requirement for IFRS reporters is discussed more fully at 3.3.4 below.

More recently in August 2008 the SEC approved for public comment its 'roadmap' relating to the eventual use of IFRSs by US companies. The proposed 'roadmap' anticipates mandatory reporting under IFRSs beginning in 2014, 2015 or 2016 depending on the size of the company. The SEC's proposed Roadmap is discussed more fully at 3.3.6 below.

The key question at the time of writing is whether this progress can be maintained. Following a change in administration in the US, and the fallout from the financial crisis (discussed below at 3.6) the way forward with the Roadmap seems rather less clear. Although there are indications that the SEC remains committed to IFRS, nevertheless the momentum does seem to have been lost from the process. So much so that, speaking at the American Accounting Association's annual meeting in 2009, David Tweedie, Chairman of the IASB, is quoted as saying 'Where is the USA. That is a question I am asked around the world…My view is that the US needs to commit by 2011 one way or another'.

Undoubtedly, one of the main advantages of a single set of global accounting standards is that it would enable the international capital markets to assess and compare inter-company performance in a much more meaningful, effective and efficient way than is presently possible. This should increase companies' access to global capital and ultimately reduce the cost thereof; yet it is only in the last five to ten years or so that this has been seen as even a realistic possibility – a possibility that has come about largely as a result of bold action on the part of the European Commission.

The European Heads of Government, the Commission announced in June 2000 that it would present proposals to introduce the requirement that all listed EU companies report in accordance with IAS by 2005. This requirement – which was finally adopted in an EU Regulation in 2002[2] – has changed fundamentally not only the face of European financial reporting, but global reporting as well. Largely following Europe's lead, scores of countries have either already adopted IFRS directly, or have aligned their national standards with IFRS, or have committed to do so in the foreseeable future.

Although the European Union is almost certainly the IASB's most significant single constituency for the time being, there are also a number of other economically developed countries that either have already adopted – or will be adopting – IFRS as their primary system of GAAP. Notable examples are Canada, which has announced that Canadian GAAP will be replaced by IFRS from 2011 onwards[3], and Japan where, in June 2009 the Business Accounting Council (a key advisory body for the Financial Services Agency) approved a roadmap for the adoption of IFRS in Japan, subject to a final decision in 2012. This latter decision follows an agreement in August 2007 between the Accounting Standards Board of Japan and the IASB to accelerate convergence between Japanese GAAP and IFRSs, with the aim of removing all differences on or before 30 June 2011. Significantly also, countries such as Brazil, China, India and Korea have made significant progress towards the adoption of IFRS, whilst countries such as Australia and South Africa have already aligned their national standards with IFRS (see section 6 below).

The European Commission's decision to adopt IFRS as the basis of financial reporting for all listed EU companies coincided also with the restructuring of the former International Accounting Standards Committee and the formation on 1 April 2001 of the present day International Accounting Standards Board (IASB), as discussed in section 2 below. Since then, the IASB and the US Financial Accounting Standards Board (FASB) have become increasingly committed to the convergence of IFRS and US GAAP. This is evidenced by the October 2002 Norwalk Agreement and the February 2006 Memorandum of Understanding between the FASB and the

IASB, both of which are discussed at 3.3 below. Most significantly, the IASB and FASB have now largely aligned their agendas to the extent that many major projects – such as consolidations, impairment, income taxes, revenue recognition and employee benefit accounting – are now undertaken jointly.

The result is that in recent years global financial reporting has ceased to be characterised by numerous disparate national systems to the point at which there are today essentially only two – IFRS and US GAAP. Furthermore, it had come to seem highly likely that a single set of global accounting standards would be achieved in the foreseeable future. Whilst the fallout from the financial crisis and the apparent loss of momentum on the SEC's Roadmap, alluded to above, may have raised some doubts about that final outcome, huge progress has nevertheless been made. This chapter is devoted to outlining how this has been achieved.

1.1   The Accountants International Study Group

Whilst many remarkable individuals have featured in the past 40 years' evolution of international accounting, perhaps the single person that stands out as the visionary behind the formation of the International Accounting Standards Committee (IASC) – the predecessor to today's International Accounting Standards Board – is Lord Benson, former President of the Institute of Chartered Accountants in England and Wales (ICAEW) and senior partner in Cooper Brothers & Co.[4] Henry Benson foresaw the importance of international accounting standards and, as President of the ICAEW, pioneered the practical steps that led to the creation, first, of the Accountants International Study Group in 1967 and, ultimately, of the International Accounting Standards Committee in 1973. Henry Benson was the first Chairman of the IASC, serving from 1973 to 1975.

The idea of the Accountants International Study Group was publicly unveiled by Henry Benson during his term as President of the ICAEW, at the Annual Conference of the Canadian Institute of Chartered Accountants (CICA), held in August 1966. Following further discussions with the Presidents of the CICA and the American Institute of Certified Public Accountants (AICPA), the three institutes announced in January 1967 that agreement had been reached for the formation of the Study Group, with AICPA President Robert Trueblood appointed as its first Chairman.

It seems that the formation of the Group may well have been driven by Henry Benson's early conviction of the essential need for harmonised accounting and auditing rules and procedures. The first indication of Henry Benson's understanding of the need for international harmonisation may be found in the Terms of Reference of the Study Group, which read as follows: 'To institute comparative studies as to accounting thought and practice in participating countries, to make reports from time to time, which, subject to the prior approval of the sponsoring Institutes, would be issued to members of those Institutes'.[5] Thus, it seems that Henry Benson believed that the UK, US and Canada should not each be operating in their own technical vacuums without considering developments in the other two.

The Study Group lasted for ten years, and was wound up in 1977. During its existence, it published 20 documents covering a wide range of accounting and auditing topics. These publications were, in effect, comparative studies of existing accepted practice, and the opinions expressed therein were termed 'conclusions'.

1.2   The International Accounting Standards Committee (IASC)

The origins of the IASC can be traced back to the 10th World Congress of Accountants, which was held in September 1972 in Sydney. It was here that Henry Benson – who had been asked by the major accounting Institutes to create an international accounting body based on the Accountants International Study Group – proposed the formation of a new body that would be responsible for the formulation of international accounting standards. Following further meetings between the Presidents of the AICPA, CICA, ICAEW and The Institute of Chartered Accountants of Scotland (ICAS) it was agreed to broaden the participation of countries in the formation of an international accounting body beyond the 'three nations' of the Study Group. Accordingly, invitations were extended to the accounting bodies in Australia, France, Germany, Japan, Mexico and the Netherlands to attend a meeting in London in March 1973.

This meeting led to the formation in June 1973 of the International Accounting Standards Committee as an independent private-sector body through an agreement made by professional accountancy bodies from Australia, Canada, France, Germany, Japan, Mexico, the Netherlands, the United Kingdom and Ireland and the United States of America. From 1983, the IASC's members included all the professional accountancy bodies that were members of the International Federation of Accountants (IFAC). At the time when the Board of the IASC was dissolved in 2001, there were 153 members from 112 countries.

The IASC was founded to formulate and publish, in the public interest, International Accounting Standards (IAS) to be observed in the presentation of published financial statements and to promote their worldwide acceptance and observance.[6] It was envisaged that IAS should be capable of worldwide acceptance and contribute to a significant improvement in the quality and comparability of corporate disclosure.[7]

Although the composition of the IASC Board changed over time, during the last part of its life the business of the IASC was conducted by a Board comprising representatives of accountancy bodies in thirteen countries (or combinations of countries) appointed by the Council of IFAC, and up to four other organisations with an interest in financial reporting. Each Board Member was permitted to nominate up to two representatives and a technical adviser to attend Board meetings. The IASC encouraged each Board Member to include in its delegation at least one person working in industry and one person who was directly involved in the work of the national standard setting body.[8] The Board also had a number of observer members (including representatives of the European Commission, the International Organisation of Securities Commissions (IOSCO) and the FASB) who participated in the debate but did not vote. In 1998, the People's Republic of China became a member of IFAC and joined the IASC Board as an observer member. In 1999, IASC Board meetings were opened up to public observation.

The IASC Board established an international Consultative Group in 1981 that included representatives of international organisations of preparers and users of financial statements, stock exchanges and securities regulators. The Consultative Group met periodically to discuss the technical issues in IASC projects, the IASC's work programme and its strategy. This group played an important part in the IASC's due process for the setting of International Accounting Standards and in gaining acceptance for the resulting standards.

In 1995, the IASC established a high-level international Advisory Council, made up of individuals in senior positions from the accountancy profession, business and the other users of financial statements. The Advisory Council was responsible for the oversight of the IASC, including finances, and was expected to promote generally the acceptability of International Accounting Standards and enhance the credibility of the IASC's work.

1.2.1　*The IASC's Standing Interpretations Committee (SIC)*

The IASC Board formed a Standing Interpretations Committee (SIC) in 1997 to consider, on a timely basis, accounting issues that were likely to receive divergent or unacceptable treatment in the absence of authoritative guidance. Its consideration was within the context of existing International Accounting Standards and the IASC *Framework*. In developing interpretations, the SIC consulted similar national committees that had been nominated for that purpose by Member Bodies. The SIC had up to twelve voting members from various countries, including individuals from the accountancy profession, preparer groups, user groups and accounting academics. The European Commission and IOSCO had observer seats. In 2000, SIC meetings were opened up to public observation.

The SIC considered the following criteria for taking issues onto its agenda:

- the issue should involve an interpretation of an existing Standard within the context of the IASC *Framework*;
- the issue should have practical and widespread relevance;
- the issue should relate to a specific fact pattern; and
- significantly divergent interpretations must either be emerging or already exist in practice.

SIC interpretations were published initially in draft form for public comment (usually 60 days), and if no more than three of its voting members voted against an interpretation, the SIC asked the Board to approve the final interpretation for issue; as was the case for International Accounting Standards, this required three-quarters of the Board to vote in favour. The SIC dealt with issues of reasonably widespread importance, not issues of concern to only a small number of businesses. The interpretations that were issued covered both mature issues, where there was unsatisfactory practice within the scope of existing International Accounting Standards, and emerging issues relating to topics not considered when the standards were developed.

The SIC was reconstituted as the International Financial Reporting Interpretations Committee (IFRIC) in December 2001 (see 2.2.8 below).

1.2.2   The IASC's comparability/improvements project

When International Accounting Standards were first issued, they permitted several alternative accounting treatments. The principal reason for this was that the IASC viewed its initial function as prohibiting undesirable accounting practices, whilst acknowledging that there might be more than one acceptable solution to a specific accounting issue.

In 1993, the Board of the IASC completed a major project (known as the comparability/improvements project), which had set out to reduce many of the permitted alternative accounting options. This project took four years to complete and culminated in the publication of a package of ten revised international standards, which became operative for accounting periods beginning on or after 1 January 1995. Unfortunately, this project was less successful than many had hoped it would be, and although the number of permitted alternative options was reduced, not all were eliminated; this meant that international standards still incorporated 'benchmark' treatments and 'allowed alternative' treatments. However, as discussed more fully below, the new International Accounting Standards Board (IASB), through its own Improvements Project, did eliminate a number of the alternative accounting treatments. Where an IAS retains alternative treatments, the IASB removed virtually all references to 'benchmark treatment' and 'allowed alternative treatment', instead using descriptive references, such as 'cost model' and 'revaluation model'.

1.3   The IASC/IOSCO agreement

An increasingly global marketplace brings with it increasing interdependence among regulators. There must be strong links between regulators and the capacity to give effect to those links. Created in 1983, the International Organisation of Securities Commissions (IOSCO) is the world's primary forum of international cooperation for securities regulatory agencies. Its membership comprises national regulatory bodies that have day-to-day responsibility for securities regulation and the administration of securities laws in their countries. The objectives of IOSCO's members are:[9]

- to cooperate together to promote high standards of regulation in order to maintain just, efficient and sound markets;
- to exchange information on their respective experiences in order to promote the development of domestic markets;
- to unite their efforts to establish standards and an effective surveillance of international securities transactions; and
- to provide mutual assistance to promote the integrity of the markets by a rigorous application of the standards and by effective enforcement against offences.

In 1989, IOSCO prepared a report entitled *International Equity Offers*, which noted that cross-border offerings would be facilitated by the development of internationally accepted accounting standards. Rather than attempt to develop those standards itself, IOSCO focused on the efforts of the IASC to provide acceptable international accounting standards for use in multinational securities offerings.

In 1993, IOSCO wrote to the IASC detailing the necessary components of a reasonably complete set of standards to create a comprehensive body of principles for business entities undertaking cross-border securities offerings. In 1994, IOSCO completed a review of the then-current IASC standards and identified a number of issues that would have to be addressed, as well as standards that the IASC would have to improve, before IOSCO could consider recommending IASC standards for use in cross-border listings and offerings. IOSCO divided the issues into three categories:

- issues that required a solution prior to consideration by IOSCO of an endorsement of the IASC standards;

- issues that would not require resolution before IOSCO could consider endorsement, although individual jurisdictions might specify treatments that they would require if those issues were not addressed satisfactorily in the IASC standards; and

- areas where improvements could be made, but that the IASC did not need to address prior to consideration of the IASC standards by IOSCO.

In July 1995, the Board of the IASC and IOSCO's Technical Committee announced that an important milestone had been reached in the development of IAS. The Board had developed a work plan (to become known as 'the core standards work programme') that the Technical Committee agreed would result, upon successful completion, in IAS comprising a comprehensive core set of standards. Completion of comprehensive core standards that were acceptable to the Technical Committee would allow the Technical Committee to recommend the endorsement of IAS by IOSCO for cross-border capital raising and listing purposes in all global markets. IOSCO had already endorsed IAS 7 – *Cash Flow Statements* – and had indicated to the IASC that fourteen of the existing international standards did not require additional improvement, provided that the other core standards were successfully completed.[10]

Both the IASC and IOSCO agreed that there was a compelling need for high quality, comprehensive IAS. The goal of both bodies in reaching this agreement was that financial statements prepared in accordance with IAS could be used worldwide in cross border offerings and listings as an alternative to the use of national accounting standards.

The IASC Board worked extraordinarily hard over the ensuing four and a half years to fulfil its side of the IOSCO agreement. Board meetings were increased both in terms of frequency and duration, several new Steering Committees were formed and several major new projects were placed on the Board's agenda. The Board completed its revised core set of standards at its December 1998 meeting, at which IAS 39 – *Financial Instruments: Recognition and Measurement* – was approved for issue. As a result, the IOSCO review of these core standards began in 1999. In the meantime, IOSCO announced that it wished the issue of accounting for investment properties to be added to the list of core standards, and this matter was dealt with in a new standard, IAS 40 – *Investment Property* – which was approved for issue by the IASC Board at its March 2000 meeting.

So all that remained outstanding was for the IOSCO Technical Committee to announce the result of its assessment of the IASC core standards. However, at the time, many observers felt that the US Securities and Exchange Commission (SEC) was unlikely to allow IOSCO to endorse IASC standards unconditionally unless they corresponded closely to existing US standards. A more likely scenario was that some or all of the IASC standards would be accepted by the SEC only on the basis of additional disclosures and other conditions. Such an attitude was likely to have been reinforced by a FASB publication that claimed to have identified 255 differences between US GAAP and IASC standards.[11]

1.4   The SEC Concept Release on International Accounting Standards

Whilst the financial reporting world was waiting for IOSCO's Technical Committee to complete its assessment of the IASC's core standards and to declare its likely attitude towards recognising the new body of IAS without requiring reconciliation to national standards, the US Securities and Exchange Commission (SEC) appeared to pre-empt what was to come by publishing in February 2000 a 'Concept Release' on International Accounting Standards.[12]

The Concept Release set out the hurdles IAS would have to clear if they were to be deemed acceptable for US filing purposes. The document was mainly in the form of a series of questions apparently seeking opinions about, and experiences of using, IAS. However, although it claimed to be seeking input to determine under what conditions the SEC 'should accept financial statements of foreign private issuers that are prepared using the standards promulgated by the International Accounting Standards Committee', it also set out far broader conditions than the quality of accounting standards for accepting IAS financial statements without reconciliation to US GAAP, including the quality of auditing standards, audit quality assurance, regulation and enforcement.

There is little doubt that the SEC would argue that its Release was objective and fair-minded. Indeed, it started out in a noble enough manner: 'The globalisation of the securities markets has challenged securities regulators around the world to adapt to meet the needs of market participants while maintaining the current high levels of investor protection and market integrity'. This sentence contained two main statements; first, the challenge for securities regulators to adapt and, second, an assertion that, in general, levels of investor protection and market integrity were considered to be high.

However, what followed these encouraging statements was an elaborate exposition of why the SEC should not itself adapt in order to help realise the globalisation aim. Furthermore, it seemed to follow from the SEC's views about the need for changes (i.e. improvements) in what it called 'infrastructure support' that the SEC did not in fact believe that there were high levels of investor protection and market integrity outside the US.

Of course, the essential issue at hand was whether the SEC should accept financial statements prepared under IAS. Instead of responding directly to this question and looking for ways of adapting its own approach as a basis for embracing IAS, the SEC's view seemed to be that the world should adopt its philosophy of regulation. However, it made no suggestions as to how this should be done, or by whom. Although the SEC at one point stated that it was not focusing on differences between IAS and US GAAP, elsewhere it made it clear that differences between IAS and US GAAP were less than desirable, and clearly implied that the benchmark that IAS needed to meet was US GAAP.

Unfortunately, this posture led some commentators to the inescapable conclusion that the SEC was in favour of adaptation – but by everyone except the SEC. It seemed that countries that wished to adapt and progress in relation to IAS should do so separately and apart from the SEC.

The phrase 'high quality' was a recurring theme throughout the Release. No one would disagree with the need for high quality accounting standards in the context of the global financial markets. However, the Release seemed to be based on the premise that the US model met the criteria for high quality, and that any other model, being different, by definition did not. The inference inevitably to be drawn by readers of the Release was that US standards were high quality standards; the US system of formulating and explaining standards was best; any standards that were different, or differently formulated and explained, were lesser quality standards; US standards gave better investor protection than other standards; and regulation and enforcement of standards and the auditing profession was better in the US than anywhere else.

The SEC position centred on investor protection and the pre-eminence of US GAAP, and the regulatory and enforcement regime by which it was underpinned. Therefore, the clear message was that companies had to continue to use US GAAP if they wished to raise capital in the US – at least companies had to produce a US GAAP reconciliation, which was tantamount to the same thing – or else investors would be at risk.

The Concept Release attracted numerous letters of response, many of which expressed views that questioned the general thrust of the document. Although there was never any follow-up to the Release by the SEC, it nevertheless appeared to set the scene for what was to come three months later in IOSCO's Assessment Report on IAS.

1.5 The IOSCO Assessment Report on International Accounting Standards

The IOSCO assessment should be seen in the context of the situation at that time regarding the acceptance of IAS by the international capital markets. The reality was that many of the world's stock exchanges – including the European Union exchanges, Sydney and Zurich – already accepted IAS financial statements for cross-border listing purposes without reconciliation to national GAAP. The only significant exceptions were the exchanges in Canada and the USA. Consequently, a large part of the IOSCO effort was directed towards gaining the acceptance of the North American securities regulators.

In May 2000, IOSCO announced the completion of its assessment of the IASC's core standards through the publication by IOSCO's Technical Committee of a report that summarised its assessment work.[13] In view of the SEC Concept Release that had been issued three months earlier (see 1.4 above), the outcome of the Technical Committee's assessment of the IASC's core standards was perhaps not unexpected. Nevertheless, its content was a great disappointment to many observers and those that had been involved in the core standards programme, who believed that the IASC Board had, in good faith, fulfilled all its obligations under the IOSCO agreement.

The report stated that IOSCO had assessed 30 IASC standards, including their related interpretations (termed 'the IASC 2000 standards'), and considered their suitability for use in cross-border offerings and listings. Although the report recommended that IOSCO members should permit incoming multinational issuers to use the IASC 2000 standards to prepare their financial statements for cross-border offerings and listings, this recommendation was made subject to a significant proviso. The proviso was that each IOSCO member, in deciding how to implement the IASC 2000 standards in its jurisdiction, could choose to mandate one or more of the following 'supplemental treatments':

- *Reconciliation:* this would require reconciliation of the treatment specified in an IASC 2000 standard to another specified accounting treatment (which may be a host country national accounting treatment). This reconciliation would be expected to be presented in a footnote to the financial statements and would quantify the effect of applying the specified alternative accounting treatment;

- *Supplemental disclosure:* this would require supplemental disclosure, either in the form of:
    - more detailed footnote disclosure than an IASC 2000 standard requires; or
    - additional detail on the face of the primary financial statements (e.g. income statement or balance sheet line items) that would have to be presented.

- *Interpretation:* this would require a specific application of an IASC 2000 standard, either:
    - in cases where an IASC 2000 standard permitted different approaches to an issue, generally with one approach identified as a 'benchmark' and another as an 'allowed alternative', specifying which approach (the 'benchmark' or 'allowed alternative') was accepted in a host jurisdiction; or
    - to clarify ambiguity or address silence in an IASC 2000 standard, by specifying a particular interpretation of the IASC 2000 standard that should be used in a host jurisdiction.

If the specified treatment was not followed, it was expected that an IOSCO member would require reconciliation to the specified treatment.

In an Appendix running to more than 100 pages, the report identified numerous 'concerns' raised by IOSCO members during the assessment of the IASC 2000 standards. These 'concerns' included an analysis of outstanding substantive issues relating to the standards, specifying supplemental treatments that might be required in a particular jurisdiction to address each of these concerns.

The effect of this report by the Technical Committee of IOSCO was to negate the intention of the IASC/IOSCO agreement. Its impact was to perpetuate the existing position whereby a company faced the possibility of having to comply with more than one reporting regime in order to obtain a cross-border listing, thereby doing nothing to remove duplication, complication and expense.

Thus, the long-awaited 'endorsement' from IOSCO was, in fact, only a qualified acceptance of IAS that still allowed IOSCO members to request any supplemental treatment that they considered necessary. Whilst one could accept that different regulatory jurisdictions might require additional note disclosures in line with local circumstances, the imposition of any reconciliation requirement mandating different recognition and measurement rules was clearly contrary to any notion of accounting harmonisation. It therefore seemed at the time that any such unconditional endorsement of IAS by IOSCO for cross-border capital raising and listing purposes in all global markets was a long way off, and would require substantial further effort on all sides.

In fact – as discussed at 3.3.4 below – that endorsement has come much quicker than most people expected, with the SEC agreeing in November 2007 to accept from foreign private issuers financial statements prepared in accordance with IFRS as issued by the IASB without reconciliation to US GAAP.[14]

2   THE RECONSTITUTION OF THE IASC

2.1   Shaping IASC for the future

Few would disagree that since its formation in 1973, the IASC had achieved a great deal within the limitations of its structure. However, with the globalisation of the world's capital markets, the increasing complexity of business transactions and the growing pressure for a single set of internationally harmonised accounting standards, the IASC Board believed that structural changes were needed for it to anticipate and meet effectively the new challenges that it faced.

Consequently, the IASC Board saw the completion of its core standards programme as an appropriate moment to undertake a review of its strategy. As a result, in 1998 it appointed a Strategy Working Party to conduct a general review of the strategy of the IASC.

The Working Party published its proposals in December 1998 in a Discussion Paper entitled 'Shaping IASC for the future'.[15] The Working Party's proposals were fairly radical, but were framed within the rather nebulous notion of a 'partnership with national standard setters'.[16] The rationale behind this was that the IASC should enter into a partnership with national standard setters enabling the IASC to work with them to accelerate convergence between national standards and International Accounting Standards. However, in order to form this 'partnership', the Working Party proposed the abolition of the IASC Board structure and the establishment of a bicameral system in its place. Under this system, power would be concentrated in a Standards Development Committee (SDC), comprising a small group of select full-time standard setters. It was also proposed that the SDC would replace the IASC's Steering Committee system, under which Standards had been developed. The Working Party's recommendations covered a number of other areas, including the IASC's system of due process, implementation, education, enforcement and funding.

Perhaps not surprisingly, the Working Party's proposals met with considerable opposition, both from within the IASC Board and outside. The principal criticisms of the proposals centred on the bicameral system and the concept of the SDC. One general perception was that the Discussion Paper was aimed at further entrenching the position of the G4+1 group of Anglo-Saxon accounting standard setters.[17]

However, many considered the biggest single failing of the Working Party's proposals to be that they did not address adequately the key issue of legitimacy among the IASC's constituencies. So, whilst there was agreement with the objectives identified by the Working Party, there was less support for the structure that was proposed in order to achieve them, since the proposed structure would not have ensured legitimacy. The Discussion Paper contained little elaboration on the details of the proposed 'partnership with national standard setters' and other key constituencies, with the result that their role under the proposed structure was unclear.

Particular concern was expressed also about the representation of users and preparers of accounts in any new standard setting structure. Ultimately, the long-term credibility of International Accounting Standards would depend on their acceptance by the preparer and user communities as well as the international capital markets. Consequently there had to be full participation by all the key players in the marketplace in order to secure the future of IAS.

The IASC Board had a joint meeting on 30 June 1999 with the Strategy Working Party to discuss the comments received on the Discussion Paper. The discussion indicated that the proposed bicameral/SDC system should be abandoned in favour of a single Board structure. There was a general consensus that this single Board should comprise a blend of full and part-time members, although the overall size of the Board and precise proportion of full and part-timers was not agreed. The Strategy Working Party met again during July 1999 in order to develop a new proposal along the lines of its discussions with the IASC Board.

2.2   The new IASC structure

In November 1999, the IASC's Strategy Working Party presented its final report – *Recommendations on Shaping IASC for the Future* – to the IASC Board.[18] In fact, the report was delivered somewhat as a *fait accompli*, and it was clear to the members of the IASC Board that there was little room for discussion: they could either take it or leave it. It seemed to many observers that the process had become highly politicised, and that the influence of the US SEC could be detected in ensuring that the IASB would be constituted as closely as possible in the image of the FASB. Although the Strategy Working Party had seemingly dealt with the objections raised concerning its original bi-cameral structure, a number of fundamental difficulties that many observers and commentators had raised had not been resolved.

From a European perspective, these difficulties surrounded the issue of legitimacy and political accountability that were considered to be vital elements in order to ensure maximum commitment from those constituencies who would have to implement, regulate and enforce the system. The link between legitimacy and enforcement exists because broad support from the key constituencies involved makes it significantly more likely that standards will be applied and enforced, which in turn gives them credibility. However, there was a clear tension between this 'representative' model that was clearly preferred in Europe and elsewhere on the one hand, and the SEC/FASB 'expert' model on the other.

In any event, the Strategy Working Party's proposal was presented to the IASC Board as a non-negotiable agreement with the SEC. This meant that the Board, left with no room to manoeuvre, adopted unanimously the recommendations of the Strategy Working Party. These were then approved by the member bodies of the International Federation of Accountants, under whose patronage the IASC Board operated. The new structure adopted is outlined below.

2.2.1   The IASC Foundation (IASCF)

The governance of the IASC organisation rests with the Trustees of the IASC Foundation who, in turn, act under the terms of the IASC Foundation Constitution.[19] The first Board of Trustees was appointed during the second half of 2000 by a Nominating Committee that was set up for that sole purpose under the Chairmanship of the then US SEC Chairman, Mr. Arthur Levitt. Initially, the Board comprised nineteen Trustees, under the Chairmanship of Mr. Paul A. Volcker, a Former Chairman of the US Federal Reserve Board. However, the number of Trustees was increased to twenty-two, following a review of the Constitution in 2005. It is a requirement of the IASC Foundation Constitution that, in order to ensure a broad international basis, there must be:[20]

- six Trustees appointed from North America;
- six Trustees appointed from Europe;
- six Trustees appointed from the Asia/Oceania region; and
- four Trustees appointed from any area, subject to establishing overall geographical balance.

The appointment of all subsequent Trustees to fill vacancies caused by routine retirement or other reasons is the responsibility of the existing Trustees. The appointment of the Trustees is normally for a term of three years, renewable once.[21]

The IASC Foundation Constitution requires that the Trustees should comprise individuals that, as a group, provide an appropriate balance of professional backgrounds, including auditors, preparers, users, academics, and other officials serving the public interest. Two of the Trustees will normally be senior partners of prominent international accounting firms. To achieve such a balance, Trustees are selected after consultation with national and international organisations of auditors (including the International Federation of Accountants), preparers, users and academics. The Trustees are required to establish procedures for inviting suggestions for appointments from these relevant organisations and for allowing individuals to put forward their own names, including advertising vacant positions.[22]

The Constitution provides that 'all Trustees shall be required to show a firm commitment to the IASC Foundation and the IASB as a high quality global standard-setter, to be financially knowledgeable, and to have an ability to meet the time commitment. Each Trustee shall have an understanding of, and be sensitive to the challenges associated with the adoption and application of high quality global accounting standards developed for use in the world's capital markets and by other users.'[23]

The first act of the Board of Trustees in 2000 was to appoint Sir David Tweedie (who had just completed a highly distinguished period of ten years as the Chairman of the UK's Accounting Standards Board) as the first Chairman of the new International Accounting Standards Board (IASB) with effect from 1 January 2001. Subsequently, in January 2001, the Trustees appointed the thirteen other members of the IASB. In December 2005, the Trustees announced that Sir David Tweedie had been re-appointed as IASB Chairman for a further five year term.

The Trustees are responsible also for appointing the members of the International Financial Reporting Interpretations Committee (IFRIC) and Standards Advisory Council (SAC).[24] In addition, their duties include the following:[25]

- assuming responsibility for establishing and maintaining appropriate financing arrangements;

- reviewing annually the strategy of the IASC Foundation and the IASB and their effectiveness, including consideration, but not determination, of the IASB's agenda;

- approving annually the budget of the IASC Foundation and determining the basis for funding;

- reviewing broad strategic issues affecting accounting standards, promoting the IASC Foundation and its work and promoting the objective of rigorous application of International Accounting Standards and International Financial Reporting Standards (the Trustees are, however, excluded from involvement in technical matters relating to accounting standards);

- establishing and amending operating procedures, consultative arrangements and due process for the IASB, the IFRIC and the SAC;

- approving amendments to the Constitution after following a due process, including consultation with the SAC and publication of an Exposure Draft for public comment;

- exercising all powers of the IASC Foundation except for those expressly reserved to the IASB, IFRIC and the SAC; and

- publishing an annual report on the IASC Foundation's activities, including audited financial statements and priorities for the coming year.

With effect from 1 April 2001, the IASB assumed international accounting standard setting responsibilities from its predecessor body, the IASC.

The IASB structure has the following main features: the IASC Foundation is an independent organisation having two main bodies, the Trustees and the IASB, as well as a Standards Advisory Council and the International Financial Reporting Interpretations Committee. The IASC Foundation Trustees appoint the IASB Members, exercise oversight and raise the funds needed, whereas the IASB has sole responsibility for setting accounting standards.

The IASC Foundation has developed four principles for a funding system. Those principles are that it should be:

- Broad based;

- Compelling;

- Open ended; and

- Country specific.

The Trustees believe that from 2008 they have been successful in establishing national funding regimes consistent with these principles in a number of countries. Historically the major funders of the IASC Foundation have been the international accounting firms, the US, Japan and the UK.

Set out below is a graphical representation of the IASC Foundation structure:[26]

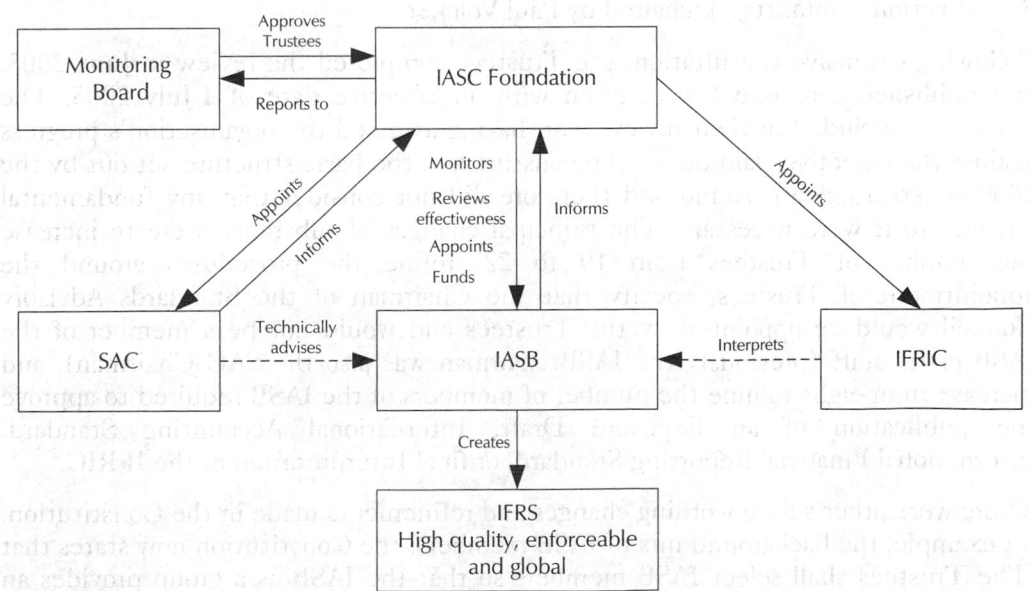

2.2.2   *The IASC Foundation Constitution*[27]

The IASC Foundation Constitution was approved in its original form by the Board of the former International Accounting Standards Committee (IASC) in March 2000 and by the members of IASC at a meeting in Edinburgh on 24 May 2000. At its meeting in December 1999, the IASC Board had appointed a Nominating Committee to select the first Trustees. These Trustees took office in May 2000 as a result of the approval of the Constitution. In execution of their duties under the Constitution, the Trustees formed the International Accounting Standards Committee Foundation on 6 February 2001. The Foundation was formed as a not-for-profit corporation incorporated in the State of Delaware, USA, and is the parent entity of the IASB, which is based in London.

Each Trustee is required to act in the public interest. In addition, the Trustees are required to undertake, at regular intervals, a review of the entire structure of the IASC Foundation and its effectiveness. These reviews are to include consideration of changing the geographical distribution of Trustees in response to changing global economic conditions, and the proposals of each review are required to be published for public comment. The first such review was required to commence three years after the coming into force of the Constitution, with the objective of implementing any agreed changes by February 2006, five years after the coming into force of the Constitution. Thereafter, the Trustees are required to undertake a similar review every five years.[28]

In accordance with the above commitment, on 12 November 2003, the Trustees announced that they had initiated a review of the Foundation's constitutional arrangements that govern the operating procedures of the Foundation and the IASB. In launching this, the Trustees emphasised that they were willing to examine any aspect of the Constitution and would be consulting a wide range of organisations. To coordinate the process, the Trustees established an internal committee (the 'Constitution Committee'), chaired by Paul Volcker.

Following extensive consultation, the Trustees completed the review in June 2005, and published a revised Constitution with an effective date of 1 July 2005. The Trustees concluded in their review that, having assessed the organisation's progress against the objectives laid out in the constitution, the basic structure set out by the 2000 constitution was sound and therefore did not consider that any fundamental changes to it were necessary. The principal changes of substance were to increase the number of Trustees from 19 to 22, refine the procedures around the appointment of Trustees, specify that the Chairman of the Standards Advisory Council would be appointed by the Trustees and would not be a member of the IASB or its staff (previously the IASB chairman was also the SAC Chairman), and increase from eight to nine the number of members of the IASB required to approve the publication of an Exposure Draft, International Accounting Standard, International Financial Reporting Standard, or final Interpretation of the IFRIC.[29]

There were other subtle wording changes and refinements made in the Constitution, for example, the background mix of IASB members: the Constitution now states that 'The Trustees shall select IASB members so that the IASB as a group provides an appropriate mix of recent practical experience among auditors, preparers, users and academics',[30] whereas previously the requirement was for minimums of five practising auditors, three preparers of financial statements, three users of financial statements, and one academic.

The Constitution sets out the basic structural and procedural framework for the various bodies of the IASC Organisation. Article 2 of the Constitution sets the objectives of the IASC Foundation as follows:[31]

(a)   to develop, in the public interest, a single set of high quality, understandable and enforceable global accounting standards that require high quality, transparent and comparable information in financial statements and other financial reporting to help participants in the world's capital markets and other users make economic decisions;

(b)   to promote the use and rigorous application of those standards;

(c)   in fulfilling the objectives associated with (a) and (b), to take account of, as appropriate, the special needs of small and medium-sized entities and emerging economies; and

(d)   to bring about convergence of national accounting standards and International Accounting Standards and International Financial Reporting Standards to high quality solutions.

In December 2005, the Trustees announced that Mr. Tommaso Padoa-Schioppa, a founding member of the Executive Board of the European Central Bank, would replace Paul Volcker as Chairman of the Board of Trustees of the IASC Foundation, effective 1 January 2006. Mr. Volcker retired from the Board of Trustees, leaving behind an important legacy as its first Chairman.

Unfortunately, Mr. Padoa-Schioppa's term of office as Chairman of the Board of Trustees lasted only until May 2006, when he stepped down following his appointment to a position in the Government of Italy. Mr. Philip Laskawy, a retired Chairman and CEO of Ernst & Young International, was then appointed as a caretaker Chairman during the search for a new high-profile chair. Subsequently, Mr. Gerrit Zalm, the former Deputy Prime Minister and Finance Minister of the Netherlands became the next Chairman of Trustees for a three-year term beginning on 1 January 2008. Mr. Laskawy became Vice Chairman of the Trustees from that date.

2.2.3   Second constitution review

As IFRSs become more widely adopted by countries as their system of financial reporting, and used throughout the world's capital markets, so has it become necessary to strengthen the institutional framework and accountability of the whole IASC organisation, including the Trustees and the IASB. Consequently, in recent times, the calls for greater governance and accountability around the IASCF have become louder and more frequent. Following their meeting at the end of October 2007, the Trustees announced proposals to enhance the IASB's governance arrangements and reinforce the organisation's public accountability.[32] The enhanced governance proposals proposed by the Trustees were as follows:[33]

- Establish a formal reporting link to official organisations: The Trustees should establish a link to a representative group of official organisations, including securities regulators. This body would approve Trustee appointments and review Trustee oversight activities, including the adequacy of the annual funding arrangements as well as the overall budget. The establishment of this 'representative group of official organisations' is discussed below;

- Develop a multi-layered, multi-faceted approach to accountability beyond the formal link to official organisations: The Trustees should intensify and deepen their engagement with key stakeholder groups and develop mechanisms for the Trustees to receive input outside formalised procedures. This would necessarily include mechanisms for meeting with official organisations and policymakers and private sector institutions. Furthermore, such accountability would require consideration of the role and structure of the Standards Advisory Council in the organisation's accountability;

- Create a mechanism for public input to the Trustees outside regularly scheduled meetings with specific stakeholder groups: The Trustees should establish enhanced mechanisms for input from interested parties who wish to comment on the IASC Foundation's and the IASB's policies, processes, and procedures;

- Continue efforts towards a sustained, broad-based funding regime: Having already significantly broadened the funding base through the new approach adopted in 2006, the Trustees should continue their work to broaden the funding base further.

In April 2008 the Trustees formally launched the second constitution review. The full review should be completed by 2010. However, the Trustees wished to deal with two issues earlier; the governance and public accountability of the IASC Foundation (the creation of a Monitoring Board) and the size and composition of the IASB. Following a period of consultation the constitution was amended to address these two issues in January 2009. The Monitoring Board is discussed further at 2.2.4 below and the size and composition of the IASB at 2.2.5.

The second phase of the second constitution review was launched in December 2008 with the publication of a discussion document which was intended to obtain comments on all the other elements of the constitution. To stimulate debate the discussion paper included a series of questions such as:

- Is the definition of the primary objective of the IASC Foundation still appropriate?

- Should the constitution make specific reference to its principle-based approach?

- Should the remit be extended to include not-for-profit organisations and the public sector?

- Is the current fixed geographical basis for appointment of Trustees still appropriate?

- How effective are the Trustees in their oversight of the IASB?

- Should there be a separate fast track procedure for changes in IFRSs which are 'urgent'?

Responses to the discussion paper were due by March 2009 and the Trustees have subsequently been developing their thinking. The Trustees have clearly sought to provide the opportunity for constituents to provide feedback on all areas of concern but it will be surprising if any radical changes in the constitution emerge at the end of this second phase.

2.2.4   *The Monitoring Board*

A constant criticism of the IASB and of the IASC Foundation has been of its lack of 'accountability' and apparent lack of responsiveness to the concerns of its constituents. This criticism has increased as the level of international acceptance of IFRSs has grown.

The IASCF Trustees have recognised this concern. In a 2008 consultation paper on the constitution they noted that they understood that the IASC Foundation's unique structure makes demonstrating public accountability more challenging than it would be for a national standard setter, which normally reports to national regulators, governments or parliaments.[34]

The response to these concerns has been the creation of a Monitoring Board to provide a formal link between the Trustees and public authorities. This relationship seeks to replicate, on an international basis, the link between accounting standard-setters and those public authorities that have generally overseen accounting standard-setters.[35]

The responsibilities of the Monitoring Board are to:

- Participate in the process for appointing Trustees and approve the appointment of Trustees;

- Review and provide advice to the Trustees on the fulfilment of their responsibilities – there is an obligation on the Trustees to report annually to the Monitoring Board;

- Meet with the Trustees or a sub-group thereof at least annually. The Monitoring Group have the authority to request meetings with the Chairman of the Trustees and with the Chairman of the IASB to discuss any area of the work of the IASCF or the IASB.[36]

The Monitoring Board initially comprises:

(a)   the responsible member of the European Commission;

(b)   the chair of the IOSCO Emerging Markets Committee;

(c)   the chair of the IOSCO Technical Committee;

(d)   the commissioner of the Japan Financial Services Agency;

(e)   the chairman of the US SEC; and

(g)   as an observer, the chairman of the Basel Committee on Banking Supervision.[37]

A Charter for the Monitoring Board has been agreed. The Charter notes that the Monitoring Board's mission is:

- To cooperate to promote the continued development of International Financial Reporting Standards as a high quality set of global accounting standards;

- To monitor and reinforce the public interest oversight function of the IASCF, while preserving the independence of the IASB. In that regard;

- To participate in the selection and approval of the IASCF Trustee appointments;

- To advise the IASCF Trustees with respect to the fulfilment of their responsibilities, in particular with respect to regulatory legal and policy developments that are pertinent to the IASCF's oversight of the IASB and appropriate sources of IASCF funding; and

- To discuss issues and share view relating to International Financial Reporting Standards, as well as regulatory and market developments affecting the development and functioning of these standards.[38]

To support the effective operation of the Monitoring Board a Memorandum of Understanding (MoU) has also been agreed between the Monitoring Group and the Trustees, which sets out how the oversight process will work in practice.

When the Trustees originally proposed the Monitoring Board, a number of commentators expressed concerns that it could threaten the independence of the IASB and lead to greater 'political interference' if the Monitoring Board began to influence specific decisions. Concerns about political interference in standard setting have also increased because of the way that both the FASB and IASB were seen to react to political pressure during the financial crisis. This goes to the heart of a very difficult balancing exercise. Most observers want the Trustees and the IASB to be responsive to constituents' concerns but they also support the principle of 'independent standard setting' – how do you achieve both?

As regards the role and influence of the Monitoring Board, the Trustees were satisfied that because its role was restricted to oversight of the Trustees' fulfilment of their responsibilities there was no risk to the independence of the IASB. Furthermore the preservation of the independence of the IASB is, as noted above, part of the mission of the Monitoring Board. However, the MoU provides a wide remit for the Monitoring Board, including the following statement:

'The IASCF Monitoring Board may refer accounting issues to and will confer regarding those issues with, the Trustees and the IASB Chair. (i) The Trustees will work with the IASB to ensure these issues are addressed in a timely manner. (ii) If the IASB determines that consideration of the issue(s) identified by the IASCF Monitoring Board are not advisable or that the issue(s) cannot be resolved within the timeframe suggested by the Monitoring Board, the Trustees should: (1) call on the IASB to undertake all reasonable efforts to consider issues(s) in a manner that is consistent with the public interest taking account the protection of investors (2) call on the IASB to explain its position on the issue(s) and (3) promptly notify the IASCF Monitoring Board of the IASB's position.' [39]

Accordingly a final conclusion as to whether the revised structure will achieve the desired outcome of increasing accountability whilst maintaining the independence of the IASB will only be possible once there has been an opportunity to see how it operates in practice.

2.2.5   *The International Accounting Standards Board (IASB)*

At the time of writing the IASB comprises fifteen members, however the constitution requires that this should be increased to sixteen by no later than 1 July 2012. Up to three members may be part time and the remainder full time.[40] The members of the IASB are appointed by the Trustees. The main qualifications for membership of the IASB are professional competence and practical experience.[41]

The Trustees are required to select IASB members so that the IASB as a group provides an appropriate mix of recent practical experience among auditors, preparers, users and academics.[42] Furthermore, the IASB is, in consultation with the Trustees, expected to establish and maintain liaison with national standard-setters and other official bodies concerned with standard-setting in order to promote the convergence of national accounting standards and IFRSs.[43]

Prior to the second constitution review the selection of IASB members was not based on geographical considerations. However, the constitution has now been so that in order to ensure a broad international basis, by July 2012 the IASB will normally be required to comprise:

(a)   four members from Asia/Oceania;

(b)   four members form Europe;

(c)   four members from North America ;

(d)   one member from Africa;

(e)   one member from South America; and

(f)   two members appointed from any area, subject to maintaining overall geographical balance.[44]

The responsibilities of the IASB are listed in Article 37 of the Constitution. Its primary role is to have complete responsibility for all IASB technical matters including the preparation and issuing of International Accounting Standards, International Financial Reporting Standards and Exposure Drafts, each of which shall include any dissenting opinions, and final approval of Interpretations by the IFRIC.[45]

Approval by at least nine members of the IASB is required for the publication of an Exposure Draft, International Accounting Standard, International Financial Reporting Standard, or final Interpretation of the IFRIC, if there are fewer than sixteen members of the IASB. If there are sixteen members that approval is required by at least ten members.[46] Other decisions of the IASB, including the publication of a discussion paper, require a simple majority of the members of the IASB present at a meeting that is attended by at least 60% of the members of the IASB.[47] The IASB has full discretion over its technical agenda and over project assignments on technical matters. It must, however, consult the SAC on major projects, agenda decisions and work priorities.[48]

The IASB (whose meetings are open to the public) met in technical session for the first time in April 2001. During this meeting, it approved a resolution to adopt the pre-existing body of International Accounting Standards and Interpretations issued by the former IASC Board and the SIC respectively. The IASB announced also that the IASC Foundation Trustees had agreed that the accounting standards issued by the IASB would be designated 'International Financial Reporting Standards (IFRS)'. The pre-existing pronouncements, however, continue to be designated 'International Accounting Standards (IAS)'.

2.2.6 The IASB's Due Process Handbook

The Trustees of the IASC Foundation have set up a committee – the Trustees' Procedures Committee – with the task of regularly reviewing and, if necessary, amending the procedures of due process in the light of experience and comments from the IASB and constituents. The Committee reviews proposed procedures for the IASB's due process on new projects and the composition of working groups and ensures that their membership reflects a diversity of views and expertise. The 'Due Process Handbook for the IASB' describes the consultative arrangements of the IASB. It is based on the previously existing framework of due process laid out in the Constitution of the IASC Foundation and the *Preface to International Financial Reporting Standards* issued by the IASB. It also reflects the public consultation conducted by the IASB in 2004 and 2005. The Trustees approved the Handbook in March 2006, following two rounds of public consultations, review by the Standards Advisory Council, and public debate by the Trustees.[49]

The procedures described in the Handbook address the following requirements:[50]

- transparency and accessibility;
- extensive consultation and responsiveness; and
- accountability.

In accordance with the IASC Foundation's Constitution, the IASB has full discretion in developing and pursuing its technical agenda and in organising the conduct of its work. In order to gain a wide range of views from interested parties throughout all stages of a project's development, the Trustees and the IASB have established consultative procedures to govern the standard-setting process.[51]

The IASB's standard-setting process comprises the following six stages, with the Trustees having the opportunity to ensure compliance at various points throughout the process:[52]

- Stage 1: Setting the agenda;
- Stage 2: Project Planning;
- Stage 3: Development and publication of a discussion paper;
- Stage 4: Development and publication of an exposure draft;

- Stage 5: Development and publication of an IFRS; and
- Stage 6: Procedures after an IFRS is issued.

It is important to note that the IASB's due process requirements are separated into mandatory and non-mandatory steps under the IASCF Constitution. The following due process steps are mandatory:[53]

- developing and pursuing the IASB's technical agenda;
- preparing and issuing standards and exposure drafts, each of which is to include any dissenting opinions;
- establishing procedures for reviewing comments made within a reasonable period on documents published for comment;
- consulting the SAC on major projects, agenda decisions and work priorities; and
- publishing bases for conclusions with standards and exposure drafts.

The steps specified in the Constitution as being 'non-mandatory' include:[54]

- publishing a discussion document (e.g. a discussion paper);
- establishing working groups or other types of specialist advisory groups;
- holding public hearings; and
- undertaking field tests (both in developed countries and in emerging markets).

If the IASB decides not to undertake any of the non-mandatory steps defined by the Constitution, it is required by the Constitution to state its reasons (known as the 'comply or explain' approach). Explanations are normally made at IASB meetings, and are published in the decision summaries and in the basis for conclusions with the exposure draft or standard in question.[55]

Although not mandatory the IASB has started to make extensive use of public meetings and roundtables to ensure that it has appropriate input from its constituents.

As discussed further below there has been a criticism of the IASB during its attempts to respond to the financial crisis for its failure to follow 'due process'. This criticism relates to a failure to issue an exposure draft (in the case of the October 2008 amendment to IAS 39 dealing with reclassification of financial assets) and more generally for only providing a short period for constituents to respond to proposals rather than the more normal three months. As a consequence the IASB is looking to develop a 'fast track' process which can be applied in 'urgent' situations. Inevitably there will be questions as to what constitutes an urgent issue, but there appears to be a general agreement that such a process would be useful. Potential principles for this process were discussed at the Standards Advisory Council meeting in June 2009. The main themes to emerge were that the process:

- should be applied in extremely rare cases;
- should involve a minimum 30 day consultation period; and
- could usefully include consultation with the Trustees and/or the SAC.

The maintenance of the independence of the IASB was also seen as an important consideration as 'urgent' issues will almost inevitably be ones where there is the greatest risk of external pressure on the IASB to arrive at a desired outcome.

The IASB and the Trustees will finalise their thinking in due course. It is perhaps worth noting that the IASB may be drawing a wider definition of urgent issues than some of those involved in the SAC discussions – at its July meeting it issued two proposals with only a 30 day comment period.

2.2.7 The Standards Advisory Council (SAC)

The primary objective of the SAC (whose members are appointed by the Trustees) is to provide a forum for participation by organisations and individuals with an interest in international financial reporting, having diverse geographical and functional backgrounds, with the objective of:

- Giving advice to the IASB on agenda decisions and priorities in the IASB's work;

- Informing the IASB on the views of the organisations and individuals on the council on major standard-setting projects; and

- Giving other advice to the IASB or the Trustees.[56]

The SAC comprises 'thirty or more members, having a diversity of geographical and professional backgrounds, appointed for renewable terms of three years'.[57] The Chairman of the Council is appointed by the Trustees, and may not be a member of the IASB or a member of its staff.[58] The SAC normally meets at least three times a year, and its meetings are open to the public. The SAC is required to be consulted by the IASB in advance of IASB decisions on major projects and by the Trustees in advance of any proposed changes to the IASC Foundation Constitution.[59]

Originally appointments to the SAC were made on an individual basis, however from 2009 the Trustees have decided that nominations to the SAC will primarily be on the basis of representation of relevant organisations. The Trustees felt that this would allow the IASB to receive views reflecting a wider range of interested parties and will give greater authority to the views received. The newly reconstituted SAC met for the first time in February 2009 under its new chairman, Paul Cherry, a former chairman of the Canadian Accounting Standards Board.

2.2.8 The International Financial Reporting Interpretations Committee (IFRIC)

The International Financial Reporting Interpretations Committee (IFRIC) assists the IASB in improving financial reporting through timely identification, discussion and resolution of financial reporting issues within the framework of IFRSs. The IFRIC was established in December 2001 by the Trustees of the International Accounting Standards Committee Foundation, when it replaced the previous interpretations committee, the SIC (see 1.2.1 above). Mr. Robert Garnett, an IASB member, is the non-voting chairman of the IFRIC. The IFRIC currently has fourteen voting members, with the European Commission and IOSCO having observer status. The quorum for a meeting of the IFRIC is ten members, and approval of Draft or final Interpretations requires that not more than four voting members vote against the Draft or final Interpretation.

Initially, the responsibilities and *modus operandi* of the IFRIC were set out in the *Preface to International Financial Reporting Interpretations*. On its own initiative, but with the Trustees' support, the IFRIC undertook an internal review of its operations. In March 2005 the IASC Foundation published for public comment a consultation paper *IFRIC Review of Operations*. In the light of its consideration of the comments received, the IFRIC developed a draft handbook of its due process. Subsequently, the Trustees considered an analysis of the comment letters, the IFRIC's recommendations and a draft of the handbook. In May 2006, the IASC Foundation published the IFRIC Due Process Handbook in draft for public comment. The final version of the Handbook – which supersedes the *Preface to International Financial Reporting Interpretations* – was approved by the Trustees in January 2007 and published in February 2007.[60]

The IFRIC meets six times a year. All technical decisions are taken at sessions that are open to public observation. The IFRIC reviews newly identified financial reporting issues not specifically addressed in IFRSs or issues where unsatisfactory or conflicting interpretations have developed, or seem likely to develop in the absence of authoritative guidance, with a view to reaching a consensus on the appropriate treatment.[61]

A　　The IFRIC's system of due process

The IFRIC due process comprises the following seven stages:[62]

Stage 1: Identification of issues

The primary responsibility for identifying issues to be considered by the IFRIC is that of its members and appointed observers. Preparers, auditors and others with an interest in financial reporting are encouraged to refer issues to the IFRIC when they believe that divergent practices have emerged regarding the accounting for particular transactions or circumstances or when there is doubt about the appropriate accounting treatment and it is important that a standard treatment is established.

Stage 2: Setting the agenda

The IFRIC decides after debate in a public meeting whether or not to add an issue to its agenda. The Committee assesses proposed agenda items against the criteria listed below. An issue does not have to satisfy all the criteria to qualify for addition to the agenda.

(a)　The issue is widespread and has practical relevance;

(b)　The issue indicates that there are significantly divergent interpretations (either emerging or already existing in practice). The IFRIC will not add an item to its agenda if IFRSs are clear, with the result that divergent interpretations are not expected in practice;

(c)   Financial reporting would be improved through elimination of the diverse reporting methods;

(d)   The issue can be resolved efficiently within the confines of existing IFRSs and the *Framework*, and the demands of the interpretation process. The issue should be sufficiently narrow in scope to be capable of interpretation, but not so narrow that it is not cost-effective for the IFRIC and its constituents to undertake the due process associated with an Interpretation;

(e)   It is probable that the IFRIC will be able to reach a consensus on the issue on a timely basis;

(f)   If the issue relates to a current or planned IASB project, there is a pressing need to provide guidance sooner than would be expected from the IASB's activities. The IFRIC will not add an item to its agenda if an IASB project is expected to resolve the issue in a shorter period than the IFRIC requires to complete its due process.

A consultative period applies to issues that are not added to the agenda. The draft reason for not adding an item to the agenda is published in *IFRIC Update* and electronically on the IASB Website with a comment period of not less than 30 days. The comments received are placed on the public record, unless confidentiality is specifically requested by the commentator (supported by good reason such as commercial confidence), and form part of the deliberation that takes place at the next available IFRIC meeting. At that meeting the IFRIC decides whether to add the issue to its agenda.

A simple majority of IFRIC members present at the meeting can agree to add any issue to the IFRIC agenda. The reasons for not adding an item to the IFRIC agenda are posted on the IASB Website as a historical record of decisions taken. That record is not updated as standards are amended and does not form part of IFRSs.

As a result of this approach, a significant amount of IFRIC meeting time is devoted to discussing whether or not issues should be added to its agenda. In the majority of cases, the decision is not to add items and often results in lengthy debates between IFRIC members and IASB staff over the formulation of the reasons for such decisions. These decisions are formally titled *Agenda Decisions* but have become known as 'rejection notices'.

To ensure that the IFRIC considers only issues on which timely guidance can be provided, over the course of a project it reassesses from time to time whether the issues can be addressed appropriately within the mandate. If an issue has been considered at three meetings and there is still no consensus in prospect for either a draft or final Interpretation, the IFRIC considers whether it should be removed from the agenda. The IFRIC may extend consideration of the issue for an additional period, normally not more than one or two meetings. If the IFRIC has concluded that it will not be able to reach a consensus, it will discontinue work on the issue, inform the IASB and publish the fact that work has been discontinued. The IFRIC may recommend that the matter be taken up by the IASB.

Stage 3: IFRIC meetings and voting

The IFRIC meets in public and follows procedures similar to the IASB's general policy for its Board meetings.

The quorum for a meeting of the IFRIC is ten members, and the approval of Draft or final Interpretations requires that not more than four voting members vote against the Draft or final Interpretation.

Stage 4: Development of a draft Interpretation

The IFRIC reaches its conclusions on the basis of information contained in Issue Summaries that are prepared under the supervision of IASB staff. An Issue Summary describes the issue to be discussed and provides the information necessary for IFRIC members to gain an understanding of the issue and make decisions about it. An Issue Summary is developed for the IFRIC's consideration after a thorough review of the authoritative accounting literature and possible alternatives, including consultation where appropriate with national standard-setters.

Stage 5: The IASB's role in the release of a draft Interpretation

IASB members have access to all IFRIC agenda papers. They are expected to comment on technical matters as the issues are being considered, particularly if they have concerns about alternatives the IFRIC is considering. Thereafter, IASB members are informed when the IFRIC reaches a consensus on a draft Interpretation. The draft Interpretation is released for public comment unless four or more IASB members object within a week of being informed of its completion.

If a draft Interpretation is not released because of IASB members' objections, the issue will be considered at the next IASB meeting. On the basis of discussion at the meeting, the IASB will decide whether the draft Interpretation should be published or whether the matter should be referred back to the IFRIC, added to its own agenda or not be the subject of any further action.

Stage 6: Comment period and deliberation

Draft Interpretations are made available for public comment for not less than 60 days. All comments received during the comment period are considered by the IFRIC before an Interpretation is finalised. Comment letters are made publicly available unless confidentiality is requested by the commentator (supported by good reason such as commercial confidence). A staff summary and analysis of the comment letters are provided to the IFRIC.

If the proposed Interpretation is changed significantly, the IFRIC will consider whether it should be re-exposed. Re-exposure is not required automatically and will depend on the significance of the changes contemplated, whether they were raised in the Basis for Conclusions on the draft Interpretation or in questions posed by the IFRIC, their significance for practice, and what might be learned by the IFRIC from re-exposure.

Stage 7: The IASB's role in an Interpretation

When the IFRIC has reached a consensus on an Interpretation, the Interpretation is put to the IASB for ratification, in a public meeting, before being issued. Approval by the IASB requires at least nine IASB members to be in favour. The IASB votes on the Interpretation as submitted by the IFRIC. If an Interpretation is not approved by the IASB, the IASB provides the IFRIC with an analysis of the objections and concerns of those voting against the Interpretation. On the basis of this analysis, the IASB will decide whether the matter should be referred back to the IFRIC, added to its own agenda or not be the subject of any further action. All approved Interpretations are issued by the IASB.

B   The Authority of IFRIC Interpretations[63]

IFRIC Interpretations set out the consensus that entities are required to apply if their financial statements are described as being prepared in accordance with IFRSs. The authoritative text of a draft Interpretation or an Interpretation is that published by the IASB in the English language. IFRIC Interpretations usually apply to periods beginning on or after a specified effective date (usually three months from the date of issue). However, the IFRIC may choose to vary that approach. Transitional provisions that apply on initial application of an IFRIC consensus are specified in the Interpretation. In keeping with IFRSs, the presumption is that IFRIC Interpretations will be applied retrospectively in accordance with IAS 8 – *Accounting Policies, Changes in Accounting Estimates and Errors*. The IFRIC also considers the effect of the transitional provisions on first-time adopters of IFRSs, including the interaction of the transitional provisions with those of IFRS 1 – *First-time Adoption of International Financial Reporting Standards*. An IFRIC Interpretation is withdrawn when an IFRS or other authoritative document issued by the IASB that overrides or confirms a previously issued IFRIC consensus becomes effective. The IFRIC Interpretations that would be affected by an authoritative IASB document are identified in the exposure draft of that document.

3   THE IASB'S TECHNICAL AGENDA AND GLOBAL CONVERGENCE

3.1   An initial agenda of twenty-five technical projects

In contemplation of the handover of its functions to the new IASB, the Board of the former International Accounting Standards Committee approved a public Statement at its December 2000 meeting.[64] The purpose of the Statement was to comment on the IASC Board's current work-in-progress and record some of the thinking of the Board resulting from its work on agenda items in progress and other discussions.

In the light of this, and after consultation with the SAC, national accounting standard setters, regulators and other interested parties, the IASB determined an initial agenda of nine technical projects. These were divided into three broad categories:

- Projects intended to provide leadership and promote convergence, which comprised the following:
    - Accounting for insurance contracts;
    - Business combinations;
    - Reporting financial performance; and
    - Accounting for share based payments.
- Projects intended to provide for easier application of International Financial Reporting Standards, which comprised the following:
    - Guidance on first-time application of IFRSs;
    - Activities of financial institutions: disclosure and presentation; and
- Projects intended to improve existing standards, which comprised the following:
    - Preface to IFRSs;
    - Improvements to existing IASs (see 3.2 below); and
    - Amendments to IAS 39.

In addition to these, sixteen other issues were adopted as 'partner projects' by one or more of the IASB's national standard setting partners. The IASB announced that it would be working with these partners, or at least monitoring their efforts, in order to ensure that any differences between national standard setters or with the IASB would be identified and resolved as quickly as possible. The issues concerned were as follows:

- accounting measurement;
- accounting by extractive industries;
- accounting for financial instruments (i.e. the comprehensive full fair value project);
- accounting for leases;
- accounting by small and medium entities and emerging economies;
- accounting for taxes on income (i.e. dealing with issues of convergence between IAS 12 – *Income Taxes* – and certain national standards such as the UK standard FRS 19 – *Deferred Tax*);
- business combinations;
- consolidation policy;
- definitions of elements of financial statements;
- derecognition issues, other than those addressed in IAS 39;
- employee benefits (dealing with issues of convergence between IAS 19 – *Employee Benefits* – and certain national standards such as the UK standard FRS 17 – *Retirement Benefits*);
- impairment of assets;
- intangible assets;
- liabilities and revenue recognition;

- Management's Discussion and Analysis (an area not currently dealt with in the IASC literature); and
- revaluation of certain assets.

3.2   The Improvements Project

In April 2001, the IASB announced the launch of its 'Improvements Project' and called for suggestions as to how existing standards could be improved. The objective of the project was to add clarity and consistency to the requirements of existing IASs issued by the former IASC Board. The specific topics that were addressed came from information already provided to the IASB by sources such as IOSCO, national standard setters, the SIC, major accounting firms and other commentators. The issues addressed were those identified as narrow issues of substance whose resolution could improve the quality of an IAS and/or increase convergence of national and international standards. The Board wished to address these issues immediately, so that companies adopting IAS for the first time would not be faced with significant additional change thereafter.

An Improvements Sub-Committee comprising four Board members was established to consider all the suggestions made for improvement and to make recommendations to the full Board. In May 2002, the Board issued an Exposure Draft proposing amendments to thirteen standards and the withdrawal of one (IAS 15 – *Information reflecting the effect of changing prices*). Eventually, in December 2003, the Board issued the thirteen revised standards in final form, together with 'consequential amendments' to a further seventeen standards. In fact, many of the 'consequential amendments' were somewhat more in the nature of substantive changes (for example, the definition of 'joint control' in IAS 31 – *Interests in Joint Ventures*) – raising questions about the Board's due process. The Improvements Project eliminated some of the alternative accounting treatments in these 'improved' standards. Where an IAS retains alternative treatments, the IASB removed virtually all references to 'benchmark treatment' and 'allowed alternative treatment', instead using descriptive references, such as 'cost model' and 'revaluation model'.

Introducing the revised standards, Sir David Tweedie commented as follows: 'The Improvements Project has raised the quality and enhanced the consistency of international accounting standards. The Board has devoted much time and resources during its first two years of operation to ensuring that we have a solid base on which we can build. From this improved set of standards, we shall move forward on the many complex issues facing accounting today and pursue our longer-term goal of global convergence'.[65]

In reality, the improvements project took more time than originally envisaged (almost three years) to complete, with the result that the Board was not able to devote sufficient time either to dealing with fundamental issues such as measurement, revenue recognition, performance reporting and accounting for common control transactions, or to resolving crucial industry issues such as those relating to the insurance and extractive industries. Consequently, the 2005 landmark of adoption of IFRS by the EU (discussed further in section 5 below) was reached with significant gaps in the IASB's authoritative literature, which has, on occasion, required preparers and their auditors to exercise a considerable degree of judgement in determining the appropriate accounting.

3.3   IFRS/US GAAP convergence

'Convergence' is a term used to describe the coming together of national systems of financial reporting and IFRSs. Since its formation in 2001, the IASB has made great strides toward achieving global accounting convergence, with the result that the global acceptance of IFRS is rapidly becoming a reality. All listed EU companies are already required to prepare their consolidated financial statements in accordance with adopted IFRSs. Elsewhere, scores of non-EU countries have either adopted or are in the process of adopting IFRSs or are aligning their national standards with them. For example, in January 2006, Canada's Accounting Standards Board ratified a five-year plan to converge Canadian GAAP with IFRS,[66] and Brazil, China, India, Japan and Korea are committed to convergence within a similar time frame (see section 6 below).

3.3.1   *Convergence with US GAAP: The Norwalk Agreement*

For many years, the co-operation between the IASC/IASB and national standard setters had happened – mostly at an informal level – through a variety of bodies such as the G4+1 and the Joint Working Group of Standard Setters.[67] In the US, support for convergence has grown steadily, and in October 2002 the IASB and FASB issued a memorandum of understanding that marked a significant step towards the two Boards formalising their commitment to the convergence of IFRS and US GAAP.[68]

This agreement was reached at a joint meeting held at the FASB's offices in Norwalk, Connecticut, USA in September 2002, where the two Boards each acknowledged their commitment to the development of high-quality, compatible accounting standards that could be used for both domestic and cross-border financial reporting. At that meeting, both Boards pledged to use their best efforts to (a) make their existing financial reporting standards fully compatible as soon as is practicable and (b) to coordinate their future work programmes to ensure that once achieved, compatibility is maintained.[69]

To achieve compatibility, the two Boards agreed, as a matter of high priority, to:
*   undertake a short-term project aimed at removing a variety of individual differences between US GAAP and IFRS;
*   remove other differences between IFRSs and US GAAP that would remain at 1 January 2005, through coordination of their future work programmes; that is, through the mutual undertaking of discrete, substantial projects that both Boards would address concurrently;
*   continue progress on the joint projects that they were currently undertaking; and
*   encourage their respective interpretative bodies to coordinate their activities.[70]

The Boards agreed to commit the necessary resources to complete such a major undertaking and to start deliberating differences identified for resolution in the short-term project with the objective of achieving compatibility by identifying common, high-quality solutions. Both Boards agreed also to use their best efforts to issue an exposure draft of proposed changes to US GAAP or IFRSs that reflected common solutions to some, and perhaps all, of the differences identified for inclusion in the short-term project during 2003.[71]

3.3.2   US GAAP convergence and the SEC reconciliation requirement for foreign private issuers: the 2009 'roadmap'

A significant proportion of the world's largest non-US companies are listed on the New York Stock Exchange in addition to their domestic stock exchanges, and are therefore subject to SEC regulation. For those that file a Form 20-F, there had been a requirement to provide reconciliations from National GAAP to US GAAP for both income and equity.

Consequently, the Norwalk Agreement was warmly welcomed around the world – particularly by those SEC-registered foreign private issuer companies that were required to provide US GAAP reconciliations, who saw this as a means of removing the reconciliation requirement. In addition, a European Commission statement welcomed the IASB/FASB commitment to achieving real convergence between their respective accounting standards by 2005, when listed EU companies would be required to apply IFRS. The EU statement made the point that the announcement heralded a major step towards a global system of accounting standards and hoped that it would, in particular, help the SEC to accept financial statements prepared by EU companies in accordance with IFRS, without reconciliation to US GAAP, for the purposes of listing on the US markets.

In April 2005, the then SEC Chairman William Donaldson met with EU Internal Markets Commissioner Charlie McCreevy to discuss a range of topics of mutual interest between the SEC and the EU, including the importance of compatible approaches to furthering investor protection and expanding the use of high-quality global accounting standards. At this meeting, SEC Chairman Donaldson tabled a 'roadmap' developed by SEC staff that highlighted the steps needed to eliminate the US GAAP reconciliation requirement for SEC-registered foreign private issuers that apply IFRSs. The roadmap established a goal of eliminating the requirement as early as possible and by 2009 at the latest. However, it was made clear that achieving this goal would, amongst other things, depend on a detailed analysis of the faithfulness and consistency of the application and interpretation of IFRS in financial statements across companies and jurisdictions, and continued progress on the IASB-FASB convergence project.[72]

Further confirmation that the SEC remained committed to the 'roadmap' was received in the form of a joint statement issued by the SEC Chairman Christopher Cox and EU Internal Markets Commissioner Charlie McCreevy on the occasion of Commissioner McCreevy's visit to Washington in February 2006. In re-affirming the SEC's commitment to the roadmap, SEC Chairman Cox stated the following: 'The

SEC is working diligently toward the goal of eliminating the existing IFRS to US GAAP reconciliation requirement. Achieving that goal depends on various factors, as discussed in the April 2005 roadmap, including the effective implementation of IFRS in practice. The ultimate success of IFRS for the benefit of the global capital markets depends on the contributions of many parties, including investors, regulators, auditors, issuers and standard setters.'[73] Again, this statement emphasised the importance that the SEC was placing on its assessment of how effectively IFRSs are applied in practice.

Nonetheless, as a highly significant sign that the goals of the 'roadmap' have almost been achieved, the SEC agreed in November 2007 to accept from foreign private issuers financial statements prepared in accordance with IFRS as issued by the IASB without reconciliation to US GAAP (see 3.3.4 below).

3.3.3 Memorandum of Understanding between the FASB and the IASB[74]

On 27 February 2006, the FASB and the IASB published a Memorandum of Understanding (MOU) that reaffirmed the two Boards' shared objective of developing high quality, common accounting standards for use in the world's capital markets. The MOU was a further elaboration of the objectives and principles first described in the Boards' Norwalk Agreement published in October 2002 (see 3.3.1 above). While the document did not represent a change in the boards' convergence work programme, it did reflect the context of the 2009 'roadmap' for the removal of the reconciliation requirement for non-US companies that use IFRSs and are registered with the SEC in the United States (see 3.3.2 above). It also reflected the work undertaken by the Committee of European Securities Regulators (CESR) to identify areas for improvement of accounting standards.

Both the FASB and the IASB noted in the MOU that removing the current reconciliation requirements would require continued progress on the two Boards' convergence programme. Accordingly, the MOU set out milestones that the FASB and the IASB believed were achievable by 2008.

The Boards agreed that trying to eliminate differences between their respective standards when both were in need of significant improvement was not the best use of resources – instead, new common standards should be developed. Consistent with that principle, convergence work would continue to proceed on the following two tracks:

- first, the Boards would reach a conclusion about whether major differences in focused areas should be eliminated through one or more short-term standard-setting projects, and, if so, would aim to complete or substantially complete work in those areas by 2008; and

- second, the FASB and the IASB would seek to make continued progress on joint projects in other areas identified by both boards where current accounting practices under US GAAP and IFRSs were regarded as candidates for improvement (eleven areas were identified in the MOU).

The boards pointed out that their work programmes are not limited to the items listed in the MOU. The FASB and the IASB would follow their normal due process when adding items to their agendas.

Topics for short-term convergence included the following:

To be examined by the FASB	To be examined by the IASB
Fair value option*	Borrowing costs
Impairment (jointly with the IASB)	Impairment (jointly with the FASB)
Income tax (jointly with the IASB)	Income tax (jointly with the FASB)
Investment properties**	Government grants
Research and development	Joint ventures
Subsequent events	Segment reporting
FASB Note: * On the active agenda at 1 July 2005. ** To be considered by the FASB as part of the fair value option project.	*IASB Note:* Topics are part of or to be added to the IASB's short-term convergence project, which is already on the agenda.

Progress on the various projects can perhaps be described as mixed. Certainly progress has been slower than was anticipated and a number of the areas to be addressed have proved intractable for the boards. Nevertheless the boards concluded during 2008 that most of the milestones had been reached or were due to be reached during 2008, and as a result there was little guidance on prioritisation of projects on the board's active agenda.[75] Given the number of jurisdictions that have announced their intention to adopt or converge with IFRS in the next five years the chairmen of the two boards agreed to extend the timetable of the existing MOU through to 2011, to better direct the work plan of the two boards during that period. This was discussed at a joint meeting of the boards in April 2008 and again at the IASB's June 2008 meeting after which an updated workplan was issued.

These developments took place in the expectation that the SEC would be announcing plans for the adoption of IFRSs in the US. In August 2008 the SEC approved for public comment its proposed 'roadmap' relating to the eventual use of IFRSs by US companies (see 3.3.6 below). It was clear that the SEC saw the continued progress of the IASB and FASB on convergence as being an important condition for progress on the Roadmap.

In September 2008 the two Boards published a short memorandum *Completing the February 2006 Memorandum of Understanding: A progress report and timetable for completion.* However, progress against the expectations set out in that memorandum has been adversely affected by the time the Boards have had to spend during 2008 and 2009 dealing with the implications of the financial crisis.

3.3.4 SEC acceptance of IFRS financial statements without reconciliation to US GAAP

Under SEC rules, the term 'foreign private issuer' includes a corporation or other organisation incorporated or organised under the laws of any foreign country. Foreign private issuers that register securities with the SEC are currently required to present audited statements of income, financial position, changes in shareholders' equity and cash flows for each of the past three financial years. Up until 2007, all foreign private issuers were required to reconcile to US GAAP the financial statements that they file with the SEC if the financial statements were prepared using any basis of accounting other than US GAAP.

In one of the most significant moves towards convergence and mutual recognition in recent times, the SEC issued in July 2007 a consultative document that proposed amendments to Form 20-F to accept – without reconciliation to US GAAP – financial statements prepared in accordance with IFRS as issued by the IASB.[76] This proposal was approved by the SEC in November 2007, and applied to financial statements covering years ended after 15 November 2007.[77] The changes apply to an eligible issuer regardless of whether it is required to prepare such IFRS financial statements by its home country regulator or securities exchange, or whether it simply chooses to do so for the purpose of its Form 20-F.[78]

However, it is important to note that, whilst the SEC's rule change in November 2007 allows a foreign private issuer to file financial statements prepared in accordance with IFRS as issued by the IASB without reconciliation to US GAAP, the SEC has not changed existing reconciliation requirements for foreign private issuers that file their financial statements under other sets of accounting standards, or that are not in full compliance with IFRS as issued by the IASB. According to the SEC, 'the purpose of the requirement to use the IASB-approved version is to encourage the development of IFRS as a uniform global standard, not a divergent set of standards applied differently in every nation.'[79] Consequently, in order to be eligible to omit the reconciliation, an issuer will be required, in a prominent footnote to its financial statements, to state unreservedly and explicitly that its financial statements are in compliance with IFRS as issued by the IASB. In addition, in its report, the independent auditor will be required to opine similarly on whether or not those financial statements comply with IFRS as issued by the IASB.[80]

This means that the proposed amendments will not be available to an issuer that files financial statements that include deviations from IFRS as issued by the IASB. A foreign private issuer that does not state unreservedly and explicitly that its financial statements are in compliance with IFRS as issued by the IASB, or for which the auditor's report contains any qualification relating to the application of IFRS as issued by the IASB, will continue to be required to provide the US GAAP reconciliation under current rules. Similarly, an issuer that files its financial statements using a set of generally accepted accounting principles of another jurisdiction also will continue to reconcile to US GAAP as under current rules when preparing its financial statements for inclusion in a registration statement or annual report.

Consequently, it seems clear that the proposed amendments will not apply to issuers using a jurisdictional or other variation of IFRS – for example, where an EU company prepares it financial statements in accordance with IFRS as adopted in the EU, where this differs from full IFRS. However, it will be acceptable under the SEC's proposals for an issuer to state compliance with both IFRS as issued by the IASB and a jurisdictional variation of IFRS, and for an audit firm to opine that financial statements comply with IFRS as issued by the IASB and a jurisdictional variation of IFRS, so long as the statement relating to the former was unreserved and explicit.[81]

3.3.5   SEC Concept Release on allowing US issuers to prepare financial statements in accordance with IFRS

The SEC's July 2007 proposal to accept IFRS financial statements without reconciliation to US GAAP raised the question as to whether it also should accept financial statements prepared in accordance with IFRSs from US issuers. Consequently, in August 2007, the SEC published a Concept Release to obtain information about the extent and nature of the public's interest in allowing US issuers to prepare financial statements in accordance with IFRSs for purposes of complying with the rules and regulations of the SEC.[82]

According to the SEC, it had identified at least two market forces that might provide incentives for some market participants to request in the future that the SEC accepts from US issuers financial statements prepared in accordance with IFRSs.[83]

First, as a growing number of jurisdictions move to IFRS, more non-US companies will report their financial results in accordance with IFRS. If a critical mass of non-US companies in a certain industry sector or market reports in accordance with IFRS, then there might be pressure for US issuers in that industry sector or market to likewise report in accordance with IFRS to enable investors to compare US issuers' financial results more efficiently with those of their competitors.

Second, as more jurisdictions accept financial statements prepared in accordance with IFRS for local regulatory or statutory filing purposes, US issuers' subsidiaries based in these jurisdictions might be preparing and filing their local financial statements using IFRS as their basis of accounting. If US issuers have a large number of subsidiaries reporting in this manner, then these US issuers – most likely large, multinational corporations – might incur lower costs in preparing their consolidated financial statements using IFRS rather than US GAAP.

The Commission anticipated that not all US issuers would have incentives to use IFRS. For example, US issuers without significant customers or operations outside the United States – which might tend to be smaller public companies – might not have the market incentives to prepare IFRS financial statements for the foreseeable future. Additionally, the Commission recognised that there might be significant consequences to allowing US issuers to prepare their financial statements in accordance with IFRSs. If the Commission were to accept financial statements prepared in accordance with IFRSs from US issuers, then investors and market participants would have to be able to understand and work with both IFRS and US GAAP when comparing among US issuers, because not all US issuers would be likely to elect to prepare IFRS financial statements. On a more practical level, a US issuer might have contracts such as loan agreements that include covenants based on US GAAP financial measures or leases for which rental payments are a function of revenue as determined under US GAAP. Similarly, US issuers might use their financial statements as the basis for filings with other regulators and authorities (for example, local and federal tax authorities, supervisory regulators) that might require US GAAP financial information.

Consequently, the SEC consultation around the Concept Release focused on such matters as:

- Whether market participants believe that the SEC should allow US issuers to prepare financial statements in accordance with IFRS;
- What the effect would be on the US capital markets of some US issuers reporting in accordance with IFRS and others in accordance with US GAAP;
- What effect the change would have on cost of capital;
- Whether comparative advantages would be conferred on those US issuers who move to IFRS versus those that do not;
- What the effect would be on the US capital markets of not affording the opportunity for US issuers to report in accordance with either IFRS or US GAAP; and
- What immediate, short-term or long-term incentives would a US issuer have to prepare IFRS financial statements and what immediate, short-term or long-term barriers would a US issuer encounter in seeking to prepare IFRS financial statements.

Comments on the Concept release were required by 13 November 2007 and in December 2007 the SEC held two roundtables; one on IFRS in the US markets and one on the practical issues surrounding the use of IFRS in the US. The roundtables indicated strong support for a single set of high quality globally accepted accounting standards, and a recognition that the rest of the word is already heading in this direction and that the end point will be IFRS not US GAAP. This seems to mark the point of a significant change in opinion in the US away from support for an option to adopt IFRS towards support for a requirement to do so. Subsequently in August 2008 the SEC approved for public comment its Roadmap relating to the eventual use of IFRSs by US companies.

3.3.6 *The proposed Roadmap*

The SEC approved for public comment a proposed Roadmap outlining the milestones and conditions that, if met, could lead to the use of IFRS in the US.

The Roadmap anticipates that IFRS reporting would be phased in between 2014 and 2016 depending on the size and status of the company.

The Roadmap outlines what companies would need to provide in their first set of IFRS financial statement filed with the SEC. Three years of audited financial statements would be required in the first year of IFRS reporting. Assuming a 2014 conversion date this means a calendar year company would need to include in its filings for 2014: balance sheets as of 31 December 2014 and 2013 and income statements, cash flow statements and statements of changes in equity for the years ended 31 December 2014, 2013 and 2012. In addition, IFRS 1 would require the presentation of the 'opening balance sheet' as of the date of transition to IFRS (in this example – 1 January 2012).

This transition approach would be different from what the SEC required of FPIs in their initial IFRS filings. For those filings, the SEC provided transition relief by requiring only two years of income statements, cash flow statements and statements of changes in equity.

The Roadmap also includes the following milestones and conditions:

> Improvements in accounting standards: The SEC expects the FASB and the IASB to continue to work together and progress towards convergence of IFRS and US GAAP. The updated Memorandum of Understanding between the FASB and the IASB is discussed at 3.3.3 above.

> Accountability and funding of IASCF: To date, the International Accounting Standards Committee Foundation (IASCF) has financed IASB operations largely through voluntary contributions from companies, accounting firms, international organisations and central banks. The Roadmap would require the IASCF to develop a funding mechanism that will enable it to remain a stand-alone, private-sector organization with the necessary resources to conduct its work in a timely fashion.

> Improvement in the use of interactive data (XBRL) for IFRS: The SEC has invested heavily in XBRL and expects that IFRS information will be capable of being provided to the SEC in interactive data format. The IASCF has issued a version of an IFRS taxonomy, which the SEC will consider in evaluating the status of this milestone.

> Improvements in IFRS education and training: Before making a final decision to move towards IFRS, the SEC will consider the state of preparedness of US issuers, auditors and users, including the extent and availability of IFRS education and training.

The Roadmap contains a provision that would permit certain US companies meeting specified criteria to file IFRS financial statements with the SEC for years ending on or after 15 December 2009. Based on a preliminary assessment, the SEC expects that approximately 110 companies across 34 industries would qualify for this provision. In order to be eligible for this provision, a US issuer must meet the following criteria:

> Be one of the 20 largest companies (based on global market capitalisation in its industry; and

> Participate in an industry in which the use of IFRS is more prevalent then any other basis of accounting.

For companies that meet these criteria, the SEC will require either a one-year reconciliation of the issuer's financial statements from IFRS to US GAAP, in accordance with IFRS 1, or an unaudited three-year reconciliation of the issuer's financial statements from IFRS to US GAAP until such time as the use of IFRS becomes mandatory. The proposed Roadmap will seek public comment on these two alternatives.

In the proposed Roadmap the SEC stated that it expected to make its final decision regarding the mandatory use of IFRS in 2011 based on whether, in the SEC's view, adoption of IFRS is in the public interest and would benefit investors. The SEC believes this timing would give companies sufficient notice to begin producing IFRS information for internal purposes in 2012.

The SEC has now received comments on the Roadmap and there has also been a change of administration and the subsequent appointment of Mary Schapiro as Chairman of the SEC.

The SEC received approximately 200 comment letters, which were submitted by a wide range of constituents including preparers, investors, auditors and academics. Comments varied widely so it is difficult to identify a common thread or whether there is a preference for mandating IFRS in the US. Perhaps inevitably there was general support for the goal of a single set of high quality accounting standards. However many respondents expressed concern at the SEC's approach and felt that the Roadmap did not adequately address the complexity and cost of any transition. A number of respondents argued that the goal might best be achieved through further convergence of US GAAP and IFRS over a 'reasonable' timescale. Many respondents challenged whether the timetable for the completion of the current phase of convergence was achievable without compromising the quality of the resultant standards. Concerns were also expressed about the funding and independence of the IASB and how IFRS standards with less interpretive guidance would operate in the US regulatory environment. The Financial Accounting Foundation (the body which has oversight of the FASB) submitted a response calling on the SEC to conduct a thorough analysis of the issues raised by the Roadmap, including an analysis of possible conversion approaches such as convergence through continued convergence of standards over a longer period.

During her confirmation hearings Mary Schapiro made it clear that whilst she supported the goal of a single set of global accounting standards she did not feel bound by the proposed Roadmap.

These developments have led to a growing doubt amongst many observers that the Roadmap will proceed as originally envisaged. Such uncertainty is clearly very unhelpful and it is to be hoped that the SEC will be able to clarify its position as quickly as possible.

3.3.7   The future for convergence

Although one of the ways forward suggested in the US is further convergence of standards over a longer timescale we doubt whether that is a realistic prospect. In July 2009 the Federation of European Accountants (FEE) issued a call for a new approach to setting global financial reporting standards. FEE argues that convergence has delivered many benefits including the elimination of the SEC's reconciliation requirement. However, it believes that there are now diminishing returns from convergence due to the rapid increase in complexity with little benefit to users which arises from seeking to eliminate increasingly smaller differences. FEE therefore believes that the IASB should change its strategy to focus on major improvements and simplifications to IFRS and that it should work with standard setters from around the world in doing so. Such a change would lead to a significant reduction in the number of IASB projects.

We suspect that FEE's comments will have some resonance amongst the IASB's constituents. For example there was very little enthusiasm for a proposed amendment to IAS 33 – *Earnings per Share* which was part of the convergence agenda and the Board now seems to have put that project on hold. There has been a similar lack of enthusiasm for a convergence-based proposed amendment to IAS 12, particularly once the FASB effectively dropped their corresponding project. Furthermore constituents have been commenting for some time on the length of the IASB's agenda.

It would appear that this issue has been recognised by the Board. Speaking at the American Accounting Association's 2009 annual meeting David Tweedie made the following observations;

'The European Federation of Accountancy Bodies has just talked about how the point has been reached where there have been diminishing returns from convergence with US GAAP, particularly as more and more countries, including major economies such as Japan and India move towards direct adoption of full IFRS, and the IASB should change its strategy and concentrate exclusively on major improvements and simplifications of IFRS for the short term. We think that's wrong. If you're going to have global standards we need the US, but it cannot go on indefinitely...My view is we must keep going. But to be blunt if the US turns down IFRS or does not even put a date certain – it does not matter when it is to be, 2017 who cares, if they don't commit, I think it will be impossible to continue this after 2011.'

It would therefore seem that we are at an important point in the search for a single set of high quality international financial reporting standards. All interested parties express their desire for such an outcome, it is to be hoped that continued progress can be achieved.

3.4   The IASB's current agenda

The IASB's current agenda includes the following:[84]

- **Financial Crisis related projects**
  - Classification of rights issues;
  - Consolidation;
  - Credit risk and liability measurement;
  - Derecognition;
  - Fair value measurement guidance;

- Financial instruments;
  - Classification and measurement;
  - Impairment;
  - Hedging.
- **Memorandum of understanding projects**
  - Financial statement presentation;
  - Financial instruments with characteristics of equity;
  - Income taxes;
  - Joint ventures;
  - Leases;
  - Post employment benefits;
  - Discount rate;
  - Recognition and presentation;
  - Revenue recognition.
- **Other Projects**
  - Annual improvements;
  - Discontinued operations (IFRS 5);
  - Emission trading schemes;
  - Amendment to IFRC 14;
  - Insurance contracts;
  - Liabilities (IAS 37);
  - Management commentary;
  - Rate regulated activities;
  - Related party disclosures.
- **Conceptual Framework**
  - Phase A: Objectives and qualitative characteristics;
  - Phase B: Elements and recognition;
  - Phase C: Measurement;
  - Phase D: Reporting entity.
- **Research Agenda**
  - Common control;
  - IAS 33.

The length of the IASB's agenda and its expected completion remain daunting. As already noted some observers and indeed some of the board have questioned whether the IASB will be able to achieve its target. However, to the extent that SEC acceptance of IFRS for US companies is felt to be dependent upon the finalisation of some of this agenda it is likely and perhaps understandable that the IASB will devote resources to those projects.

The difficulty is that there is a risk that other projects which are of great importance to some stakeholders may be squeezed in this process, either by being delayed or, which in some ways could be worse, having the time available for proper review and consideration of the issues reduced. Balancing these competing demands on its time and making progress on its agenda will continue to be a major challenge of the IASB over the next few years.

3.5   The IASB's 'Annual Improvements Process'

During 2007, the IASB adopted an annual process to deal with 'non-urgent, minor amendments to IFRSs' (the 'Annual Improvements Process'). Issues dealt with in this process are expected to arise from matters raised by the IFRIC and suggestions from IASB staff or practitioners, and are likely to focus on areas of inconsistency in IFRSs or where clarification of wording is required.

It seems that the premise behind the annual improvements process is to streamline the IASB's standard-setting process. If a number of minor amendments are processed together, there will be benefits both to constituents and the IASB. Agenda proposals and proposed solutions will be presented by IASB staff to the Board in the course of the year. The Board will discuss the proposals and make decisions about the proposed solutions. Subsequently, the decisions of the Board will be published in IASB *Update*, and once the Board has reviewed the amendments, a final draft of these amendments would be published on the IASB Website.

3.6   The impact of the financial crisis

The financial crisis has had a significant impact on the IASB and on the development of IFRS in 2008 and 2009. At a basic level the time the Board has had to spend discussing issues arising from the crisis has caused delays in other projects, but more fundamentally it has put pressure on the Board's working relationship with the FASB, it has raised again questions about the quality of some of the Board's standards and has probably had an impact on the credibility of the Board itself.

There is a detailed description of the chronology of the Board's responses to the financial crisis in Chapter 29 at 1.6. Rather than repeat that here it is perhaps more useful to consider, at a high level, some of the key events and try to draw out their implications.

The Financial Stability Forum (now the Financial Stability Board) was established to enhance cooperation amongst the various national and international regulatory bodies. In 2008 it raised concerns about the difficulty of valuing financial instruments in markets which had become illiquid. The IASB responded by the appointment of an Expert Advisory Panel which proceeded to produce valuation guidance. Subsequently the IASB and FASB worked hard to ensure that there was consistency of guidance between IFRS and US GAAP.

Later in 2008 the EU expressed considerable concern that European financial institutions should not be at a disadvantage compared to their US peer group. Eventually, under pressure from the EU, this led to the publication, without due process, of the reclassification amendment to IAS 39. There was considerable criticism of the Board's decision to act without due process, although there was an understanding of the position the Board found itself in. Differences in guidance between US GAAP and IFRS inevitably remained even after those changes.

The current requirements of IFRS in relation to financial instruments has been repeatedly challenged during the crisis leading to an amendment to IFRS 7 – *Financial Instruments: Disclosures* – to improve the quality of fair value disclosures and to the more fundamental revision (discussed further in Chapter 29) which the Board is progressing at the time of writing.

In October 2008 the FASB and IASB announced the creation of the Financial Crisis Advisory Group (FCAG). The remit of this group was to consider how improvements in financial reporting could enhance investor confidence in financial markets and to identify significant accounting issues that require the urgent attention of the Boards as well as issues for longer term consideration. In July 2009 the FCAG issued a report to the two Boards which was also sent to the G20. In the report the FCAG noted that general purpose financial reporting plays a critical role in the financial system and outlined four principles for financial reporting:

- Effective financial reporting – this depends on high quality standards, consistently applied. Users must have confidence in the transparency and integrity of financial reporting;

- Limitations of financial reporting – all users need to recognise the limitations of financial reporting. Financial reporting can only provide a snapshot of performance not perfect insight into the effects of macro-economic developments;

- Convergence of accounting standards – it is critically important to achieve a single set of high quality globally converged standards; and

- Standard setter independence and accountability – standard setters must enjoy a high degree of independence from commercial and political pressures, but they must be accountable and they must follow appropriate due process.

Various thoughts arise from this brief summary. Firstly that standard setting remains susceptible to political pressure and that the application of due process together with appropriate governance structures for the standard setters are a key defence against that. Secondly whilst US GAAP and IFRS remain as separate bodies of guidance there remains the risk that at times of stress there will be pressure to converge to the 'weaker' standard, what some have called a 'race to the bottom'. Thirdly it is important to recognise the validity of the FCAG's observations on the limitations of financial reporting. Financial reporting is important, there was and is scope for improving standards on financial instruments, but weaknesses in those standards did not cause the financial crisis as some have claimed and any search for perfection in standard setting is ultimately doomed because of the inherent limitations the FCAG explains. Finally however it is worth noting that there appears still to be common ground that a single set of high quality financial reporting standards is a desirable goal. It is to be hoped that the IASB and others are able to deliver that.

4   FINANCIAL REPORTING IN COMPLIANCE WITH INTERNATIONAL FINANCIAL REPORTING STANDARDS

4.1   Statement of compliance with IFRS

The year 2005 was a watershed for IFRS with a significant number of countries adopting IFRS as their principal financial reporting regime – either directly (as in the case of the 27 Member States of the European Union), or by aligning their national standards with IFRS (for example, Australia and South Africa).

The main document setting out the basis on which financial statements should be presented under IFRSs, and the required contents of those financial statements, is IAS 1 – *Presentation of Financial Statements*.[85] An entity whose financial statements comply with IFRSs 'shall make an explicit and unreserved statement of such compliance in the notes'.[86] IFRS compliance involves complying with all the recognition, measurement and disclosure provisions of the standards and interpretations. For this reason, IAS 1 states that 'financial statements shall not be described as complying with IFRSs unless they comply with all the requirements of IFRSs'.[87] The IASB has therefore established unambiguously the principle that full application of its standards and related interpretations is necessary for a company to be able to assert that its financial statements comply with IFRS. This requirement means also that it is not acceptable to omit any of the required disclosures of IFRSs on the basis that the information is commercially sensitive or potentially detrimental to the entity.

4.2   Fair presentation and compliance with IFRS

Paragraph 15 of IAS 1 states that 'financial statements shall present fairly the financial position, financial performance and cash flows of an entity'. It goes on to state that fair presentation requires the faithful representation of the effects of transactions, other events and conditions in accordance with the definitions and recognition criteria for assets, liabilities, income and expenses set out in the *Framework*. The application of IFRSs, with additional disclosure when necessary, is presumed to result in financial statements that achieve a fair presentation.[88]

IAS 1 states that in virtually all circumstances, a fair presentation is achieved by compliance with applicable IFRSs.[89] A fair presentation under IFRS also requires an entity:

(a)   to select and apply accounting policies in accordance with IAS 8 which sets out a hierarchy of authoritative guidance that management considers in the absence of a Standard or an Interpretation that specifically applies to an item;

(b)   to present information, including accounting policies, in a manner that provides relevant, reliable, comparable and understandable information; and

(c)   to provide additional disclosures when compliance with the specific requirements in IFRSs is insufficient to enable users to understand the impact of particular transactions, other events and conditions on the entity's financial position and financial performance.[90]

4.3   The fair presentation override

IAS 1 makes it clear that inappropriate accounting policies are not rectified either by disclosure of the accounting policies used or by notes or explanatory material.[91] For this reason, IAS 1 had to cater for those situations where compliance with a standard or interpretation would distort fair presentation. Consequently, the standard provides that in the extremely rare circumstances in which management concludes that compliance with a requirement in a Standard or an Interpretation would be so misleading that it would conflict with the objective of financial statements set out in the *Framework*, the entity shall depart from that requirement if the relevant regulatory framework requires, or otherwise does not prohibit, such a departure.[92]

When an entity applies this fair presentation override in these circumstances, it must disclose the following:[93]

(a)   that management has concluded that the financial statements present fairly the entity's financial position, financial performance and cash flows;

(b)   that it has complied with applicable Standards and Interpretations, except that it has departed from a particular requirement to achieve a fair presentation;

(c)   the title of the Standard or Interpretation from which the entity has departed, the nature of the departure, including the treatment that the Standard or Interpretation would require, the reason why that treatment would be so misleading in the circumstances that it would conflict with the objective of financial statements set out in the *Framework*, and the treatment adopted; and

(d)   for each period presented, the financial impact of the departure on each item in the financial statements that would have been reported had the treatment required by the Standard or Interpretation been applied.

When an entity has departed from a requirement of a Standard or an Interpretation in a prior period, and that departure affects the amounts recognised in the financial statements for the current period, the standard requires it to make the disclosures set out in (c) and (d) above.[94] Set out below is an example of the application of the fair presentation override, together with all the related disclosures:

Extract 1.1: National Express Group plc (2006)
NOTES TO THE CONSOLIDATED ACCOUNTS
FOR THE YEAR ENDED 31 DECEMBER 2006 [extract]

2   ACCOUNTING POLICIES [extract]

Basis of preparation [extract]

The financial statements have been prepared under the historical cost convention, except for the recognition of derivative financial instruments and available for sale investments detailed below.

As noted above, the Group has taken the extremely rare decision to depart from the requirement of IAS 19 'Retirement Benefits' so as to present fairly its financial performance, position and cash flows in respect of its obligation for the RPS. The details of this departure and impact on the Group's accounts are set out in note 35.

A summary of the Group's accounting policies applied in preparing the accounts for the year ended 31 December 2006 is set out below.

The preparation of accounts in conformity with generally accepted accounting principles requires the use of estimates and assumptions that affect the reported amounts of assets and liabilities at the date of the accounts and the reported amounts of revenues and expenses during the reporting period. Although these estimates are based on management's best knowledge, actual results ultimately may differ from those estimates.

The key sources of estimation uncertainty that have a significant risk of causing material adjustments to the carrying amounts of assets and liabilities within the next financial year are the measurement and impairment of indefinite life intangible assets (including goodwill) and measurement of defined benefit pension obligations. The measurement of intangible assets other than goodwill on a business combination involves estimation of future cash flows and the selection of a suitable discount rate. The Group determines whether indefinite life intangible assets are impaired on an annual basis and this requires an estimation of the value in use of the cash generating units to which the intangible assets are allocated. This requires estimation of future cash flows and choosing a suitable discount rate (see note 14). Measurement of defined benefit pension obligations requires estimation of future changes in salaries and inflation, as well as mortality rates, the expected return on assets and the choice of a suitable discount rate (see note 35).

35   PENSIONS AND OTHER POST-EMPLOYMENT BENEFITS [extract]
b)   **Accounting for the Railways Pension Scheme**

The majority of employees of the UK Train companies are members of the appropriate section of the RPS, a funded defined benefit scheme. The RPS is a shared cost scheme, which means that costs are formally shared 60% employer and 40% employee. To date, the Group has experienced five changes of UK Train franchise ownership where the current owner has funded the scheme during the franchise term and the pension deficit at franchise exit has transferred to the new owner, without cash settlement. However, although the Group's past experience has proven otherwise, our legal advisers have opined that in certain situations, the liability for the deficit on the relevant sections of the RPS could theoretically crystallise for funding by an individual TOC at the end of the franchise. By entering into the franchise contract, the TOC becomes the designated employer for the term of the contract and under the rules of the RPS must fund its share of the pension liability in accordance with the schedule of contributions agreed with the Scheme trustees and actuaries and for which there is no funding cap set out in the franchise contract. We understand that franchise contracts entered into in the future will clarify that RPS pension deficits and surpluses will not be the responsibility of the outgoing franchisee following exit.

To comply with IAS 19, the Group is required to account of its legal obligation under the formal terms of the RPS and its constructive obligation that arises under the terms of each franchise agreement.

In determining the appropriate accounting policy for the RPS to ensure that the Group's accounts present fairly its financial position, financial performance and cash flows, management has consulted with TOC industry peers and has concluded that the Group's constructive but not its legal RPS defined benefit obligations should be accounted for in accordance with IAS 19. This accounting policy, which in all other respects is consistent with that set out in this note for the Group's other defined benefit schemes, means that the Group's accounts reflect that element of the deficits anticipated to be settled by the Group during the franchise term and will prevent gains arising on transfer of the existing RPS deficits to a new owner at franchise exit.

In calculating the Group's constructive obligations in respect of the RPS, the Group has calculated the total pension deficits in each of the RPS sections in accordance with IAS 19 and the assumptions set out above. These deficits are reduced by a 'franchise adjustment' which is that portion of the deficit projected to exist at the end of the franchise and for which the Group will not be required to fund. The franchise adjustment, which has been calculated by the Group's actuaries, is offset against the present value of the RPS liabilities so as to fairly present the financial performance, position and cash flows of the Group's obligations.

The franchise adjustment decreased from £71.0m at 31 December 2005 to £44.4m at 31 December 2006. The decrease is caused by interest on the franchise adjustment of £2.5m offset by net actuarial movements in scheme liabilities of £6.7m and by £22.4m relating to the franchise exits. In the prior year, the franchise adjustment increased by £3.4m from £67.6m at 1 January 2005 to £71.0m at 31 December 2005. The increase was caused by interest on the franchise adjustment of £3.6m offset by net actuarial movements in scheme liabilities of £0.2m.

If the Group had accounted for its legal obligation in respect of the RPS instead of the constructive obligation, the following adjustments would have been made to the financial information:

	2006 £m	2005 £m
Balance sheet		
Defined benefit pension deficit	(44.4)	(71.0)
Deferred tax asset	13.6	20.1
Intangible asset	3.3	3.4
Net reduction in net assets	(27.5)	(47.5)
Statement of recognised income and expense		
Actuarial gains/(losses)	6.7	0.2
Tax on actuarial gains and losses	(0.3)	0.3
Net increase in actuarial gains	6.4	0.5
Income statement		
Interest on franchise adjustment	(2.5)	(3.6)
Curtailment gain on franchise exit	22.4	–
Intangible asset amortisation	0.2	1.1
Deferred tax credit/(charge)	(6.2)	0.3
Net increase in income	13.9	(2.2)

It should be noted that the fair presentation override is a requirement (not an option) of IAS 1 to be applied only in the extremely rare circumstances in which management concludes – as in the case set out above – that compliance with a requirement in a Standard or an Interpretation would be so misleading that it would conflict with the objective of financial statements set out in the *Framework*.

However, at the same time, the IASB has introduced a somewhat contradictory twist to the application of the override. As noted above, the override can be applied only if 'the relevant regulatory framework requires, or otherwise does not prohibit' its use. This means that the Board has built into IAS 1 the possibility of regulatory intervention in its application. Paragraph 23 of IAS 1 provides for the situation where 'the relevant regulatory framework' prohibits departure from a requirement in a particular standard or interpretation. In such cases, the standard requires an entity, to the maximum extent possible, to reduce the perceived misleading aspects of compliance by disclosing:[95]

(a)   the title of the Standard or Interpretation in question, the nature of the requirement, and the reason why management has concluded that complying with that requirement is so misleading in the circumstances that it conflicts with the objective of financial statements set out in the *Framework*; and

(b)   for each period presented, the adjustments to each item in the financial statements that management has concluded would be necessary to achieve a fair presentation.

This seems to contradict the clear statement in paragraph 18 of IAS 1 that 'inappropriate accounting policies are not rectified either by disclosure of the accounting policies used or by notes or explanatory material'.[96]

Nevertheless, in our view, the fair presentation override is an important element of financial reporting under IFRSs, as we believe that in any financial reporting regime it is necessary to cater for those extremely rare situations where compliance with a standard or interpretation would distort fair presentation. Interestingly, though, this view is not shared by the staff of the SEC. In a report on the 'Adoption by the United States Financial Reporting System of a Principles-Based Accounting System', the SEC staff states that they do not consider the override to be an appropriate component of principles-bases standard-setting. This view is expressed in the following terms:[97]

'While we believe that it is important for preparers and auditors to determine that the financial statements clearly and transparently provide information to investors that allows them to evaluate the company's financial position, results of operations, and cash flows, we do not believe that a "true and fair override" is a necessary component of a principles-based or objectives-oriented standard setting system. In fact, we would expect that an objectives-oriented standard setting regime should reduce legitimate concerns about the established standards not providing appropriate guidance, as the standards should be based on objectives that would almost certainly not be met by a presentation that was not "true and fair".'

Whilst we can see the logic of the SEC staff's view that in a truly principles-based or objectives-oriented regime the override would not be necessary, the reality is that any system of GAAP will inevitably include a degree of rules-based requirements.

5   THE MOVE TO IFRS IN THE EUROPEAN UNION

5.1   Historical differences in European accounting

European accounting has historically been the product of disparate social, economic and political factors, which have resulted in a number of deep-rooted differences in financial reporting practice throughout the region. The factors that have caused these differences include a variety of legal and tax systems, the perceived objectives of financial reporting and the significance of different sources of finance.

Prior to the adoption of IFRS there was no common broad-based statement of generally accepted theoretical principles that underpinned financial reporting across the individual Member States of the European Union (EU). Clearly, though, it was not the lack of a conceptual framework that caused the differences in European financial reporting practices. European accounting evolved over many centuries, and the differences that exist throughout Europe were shaped by the conditions in each European country.

Until the adoption of IFRS, the principal mechanism employed by the European Union to reduce these differences was the adoption of Directives under its company law harmonisation programme. These Directives are not laws that apply directly to companies, but instructions to Member States to alter their own national legislation, if necessary, so as to ensure compliance with the provisions of the Directive. In most cases, the Directives lay down minimum requirements only, so that there is nothing to prevent a Member State from imposing supplementary requirements of a more stringent nature, provided that these are not incompatible with the Directives.

The most significant Directives in the area of financial reporting are the Fourth and Seventh, which were adopted into national legislation by most EU countries during the 1980s.[98] The principal objective of the Fourth Directive was to achieve harmonisation in respect of formats, valuation rules and note disclosure, whilst the Seventh established a requirement for EU companies to prepare consolidated accounts on a common basis.

However, in negotiating the Fourth and Seventh Directives with the EU Member States, the Commission found that the deep-rooted differences in European accounting could be reconciled only through compromise. For example, in the case of the Fourth Directive, this involved a compromise between the German and French desire for certainty and precision in accounts (as reflected in the compulsory charts of accounts in France and the mandatory formats for the balance sheet and profit and loss account in Germany), and the Anglo-Saxon/Dutch desire for a more pragmatic approach requiring the accounts taken as a whole to present a true and fair view. In the case of the Seventh Directive, there was a compromise struck between the economic and legal concepts of a group.

5.2   Harmonisation achieved by the Fourth and Seventh Directives

Historically, the objectives of financial reporting have varied in different countries, and this fact is reflected in the relative importance given to the various parties who have an interest in accounting information. For example, financial reporting in certain countries, such as the UK and The Netherlands, has developed on the basis that shareholders are the most important group entitled to receive financial information. This approach arose from the situation where businesses had historically obtained a substantial proportion of their funds from the public generally and where responsibility for the conduct of the operations of the business was divorced from ownership. Consequently, investors required regular reports to assess the performance achieved by management and future prospects, and annual accounts ensured that the stewardship function was being exercised properly.

In other countries the primary purpose of financial reporting has historically been to provide information for the tax authorities and other government bodies interested in national economic planning. The assessment of liabilities to tax had to be based on standard rules regarding the recognition of income, deduction of expenses and measurement of assets; in this way, all businesses would be subject to tax on the same basis. In Belgium, France, Germany, Greece, Italy, Luxembourg and Portugal, standardised accounts have been used mainly to measure taxable profits. Although in Germany company law has been the principal authority for financial reporting measurement practices, it has historically been based on principles of historical cost and tax-based depreciation.

These contrasting attitudes to the purpose of financial reporting adversely affected the harmonisation of accounting law and practice in the EU, such that the harmonisation programme under the Directives has only been partially successful. This is clearly evidenced by the fact that harmonisation has not been achieved in the areas of recognition and measurement – both of which are fundamental to comparability in financial reporting. Nevertheless, it is clear that the Fourth and Seventh Directives have provided a base level for harmonisation of financial reporting in the EU, and have undoubtedly led to improvements in the quality and comparability of company accounts throughout the Union over the last twenty-five years. They have contributed also to improving the conditions for cross-border business and have allowed the mutual recognition of financial statements for the purposes of quotations on securities exchanges throughout the EU. Moreover, a further important contribution of the Directives has been in the area of creditor protection through the public availability of financial information. In contrast to the US, where only SEC registrant companies are required to publish financial statements, all limited liability companies in the EU are required to produce and publish financial information.

5.3   The European Commission's 1995 Communication on international harmonisation

In 1995 the European Commission issued a Communication (i.e. policy statement)[99] stating that, while EU legislation had improved considerably the quality of financial reporting in the Union, the Directives did not provide answers to all the problems that faced preparers and users of accounts and accounting standard setters. In the Commission's view, the most urgent problem that needed to be addressed concerned European companies with an 'international vocation' (the so-called 'global players') and the need to facilitate the access of such European global players to the international capital markets. The accounts prepared by those companies in accordance with their national legislation (based on the Accounting Directives) were not acceptable for international capital market purposes. These companies were therefore obliged to prepare two sets of accounts, one set which was in conformity with the Accounting Directives and another set required by the international capital markets.

The Commission examined several possible approaches to dealing with the issue of 'upgrading' EU accounting legislation. After careful consideration, the Commission suggested that a closer cooperation between the EU and the IASC, with the objective of ultimately adopting International Accounting Standards at the EU level, was the preferred solution. Referring to the 1995 agreement between IOSCO and the IASC to produce a core set of international accounting standards which would be endorsed by IOSCO (see 1.3 above), the Commission concluded that 'rather than amend the existing Directives, the proposal is to improve the present situation by associating the EU with the efforts undertaken by IASC and IOSCO towards a broader international harmonisation of accounting standards'.

This policy statement of the Commission paved the way for the acceptance of IAS by the EU. Unfortunately, the Commission could not anticipate in 1995 that the ultimate endorsement of IAS by IOSCO in May 2000 would only be a qualified acceptance of the standards. As it turned out, one of the main objectives of the Commission in moving towards IAS (access of European companies to international capital markets without having to provide reconciliations to any National GAAP) was only partly achieved.

5.4   The European Commission's Financial Services Action Plan

Meanwhile, certain EU Member States set about making it easier for their multinational companies to gain access to the international capital markets. In February 1998, new legislation was enacted in Germany to the effect that International Accounting Standards (or indeed other 'internationally recognised accounting principles' such as US GAAP) could be used in the consolidated financial statements of listed groups instead of German law and accounting principles. There was an added proviso that the financial statements must also be 'consistent with' the EU Accounting Directives.

Similar amended legislation was enacted in France in April 1998, allowing French companies whose securities were traded on a regulated market to use IAS or another body of international standards as the sole basis for their consolidated accounts. A number of other European countries (including Italy, Austria, Luxembourg, Belgium and Spain) followed suit. At the time, these were revolutionary changes, and demonstrated the influence of Anglo-American accounting philosophies, at least on those companies that wished either to seek access to the international capital markets, or to achieve greater transparency in their financial reporting. It also raised the stakes for the European Commission, emphasising the need for the Commission to deliver on the strategy set out in its 1995 Communication.

As part of its strategy to embrace IAS, and in response to the growing use of IAS by EU multinational companies, the Commission carried out an ongoing examination of the conformity between the Accounting Directives and IASs and SIC Interpretations.[100] Generally, these comparisons concluded that (with the exception of IAS 39 – see below) there are few conflicts between the Accounting Directives and IAS. Those minor conflicts that did exist would be addressed by the Commission in the context of the modernisation of the Accounting Directives that took place during the next two years or so. The Commission's programme of modernising the Accounting Directives not only removed existing conflicts between IAS and the Directives, but ensured also that all the options then available under IAS would be available to EU companies.

In May 1999, the Commission issued its Financial Services Action Plan.[101] The plan confirmed the Commission's position that comparable, transparent and reliable financial information is fundamental to an efficient and integrated EU capital market, and that International Accounting Standards seemed the most appropriate benchmark for a single set of financial reporting requirements that would be the catalyst for the development of a single EU capital market.

This initiative was given further impetus by the summit of the European Heads of Government held in Lisbon in March 2000, where it was agreed that a single European capital market should be developed as a matter of priority. It was acknowledged further that the adoption of a single financial reporting framework for the European Union was a vital element in that process. The summit conclusions stressed the need to accelerate completion of the internal market for financial services and set a deadline of 2005 to implement the Commission's Financial Services Action Plan.

Following this lead by the European Heads of Government, the Commission announced in June 2000 that it would present proposals to:

- introduce the requirement that all listed EU companies report in accordance with IAS by 2005; and
- modernise the EU Accounting Directives to reduce potential conflicts with IAS and bring the Directives into line with modern accounting developments.[102]

Meanwhile, EU companies reporting at the time under IAS faced an immediate problem as IAS 39, which was due to become operative for 2001 financial statements, required certain financial instruments to be recorded at fair value, in some cases with the changes in fair value being recorded in the profit and loss account. These requirements meant that there was a significant conflict between an IAS and the Accounting Directives, with the result that EU companies would not be able to continue to apply IAS unless significant amendments were made to the Directives.

Accordingly, the Commission put forward a proposal to amend the Fourth and Seventh Directives in order to enable EU companies to comply with IAS 39, and therefore prepare their financial statements in conformity with IAS. This was approved by the Council and by the European Parliament in May 2001 in the form of a Directive (the 'Fair Value' Directive) that amended the Fourth, Seventh and Bank Accounts Directives.[103]

Although the Commission wanted to provide more flexibility in the Fair Value Directive in order to anticipate future developments in accounting for financial instruments, the EU Member States insisted on including certain restrictions in the Directive in order to make it as close as possible to the then current version of IAS 39. Unfortunately, as a result, these restrictions meant that the IASB's extension of the fair value provisions in IAS 39 (the 'full fair value option') created new conflicts with the Fourth Directive, which have had to be addressed through further amendments to the Directive. The amendments were published on 16 August 2006 in the Official Journal of the European Union in the form of a new Directive 2006/46/EC, which amended the Fourth and Seventh Company Law Directives, as well as the accounting directives for banks and insurance undertakings.[104] This new Directive deals with a number of financial reporting matters, including:

- establishing collective responsibility of the members of the company body that is responsible for the preparation of the company's financial reports for ensuring that the company's annual report gives a true and fair view;

- requiring companies to provide disclosure about off balance sheet arrangements and related party transactions;

- requiring publicly traded companies to include a corporate governance statement in their annual reports; and

- enabling individual EU Member States to either permit or require companies to apply the relevant IFRSs that deal with financial instruments. This amendment thus deals with the existing conflicts between the Directives and IAS 39, and means that future amendments to any of the IFRSs that address financial instruments will not create any future conflicts with the Directives. In particular, this means that IAS 39's full fair value option is now compatible with the Directives.

EU Member States were required to enact the provisions of the new Directive into their national legislation by 5 September 2008 at the latest.

5.5   The European Commission's Regulation on the application of IAS in the European Union

On 13 February 2001, the European Commission published a draft EU Regulation[105] that would require publicly traded EU incorporated companies[106] to prepare, by 2005 at the latest, their consolidated accounts under IAS 'adopted' (see below) for application within the EU. This was adopted unanimously by the Council, and on 12 March 2002, by a vote of 492 for, 5 against and 29 abstentions, the European Parliament endorsed this proposal. This was adopted as Regulation No. 1606/2002 of the European Parliament and of the Council on 19 July 2002.[107]

An EU Regulation has direct effect on companies, without the need for national legislation. However, the Regulation also provides an option for Member States to permit or require the application of adopted IAS in the preparation of annual (unconsolidated) accounts and to permit or require the application of adopted IAS by unlisted companies. This means that Member States can require the uniform application of adopted IAS by important sectors such as banking or insurance, regardless of whether or not companies are listed.

The Regulation established also the basic rules for the creation of an endorsement mechanism for the adoption of IAS, the timetable for implementation and a review clause to permit an assessment of the overall approach proposed. The endorsement mechanism is discussed below.

Internal Market Commissioner, Frits Bolkestein, commented as follows on the adoption of the Regulation by the Council: 'I am delighted that the IAS Regulation has been adopted in a single reading and am grateful for the positive attitude of both the Parliament and the Council. I believe IAS are the best standards that exist. Applying them throughout the EU will put an end to the current Tower of Babel in financial reporting. It will help protect us against malpractice. It will mean investors and other stakeholders will be able to compare like with like. It will help European firms to compete on equal terms when raising capital on world markets. What is more, during my recent visit to the US, I saw hopeful signs that the US will now work with us towards full convergence of our accounting standards.'

There are currently approximately 7,000 companies listed on EU regulated markets that are subject to the Regulation. Only about 275 of these companies applied IAS prior to 2005.

5.6   The EU endorsement mechanism

The Regulation (see 5.5 above) defines the EU endorsement mechanism, which was already foreseen in the Commission's June 2000 Communication. The Commission took the view that an endorsement mechanism was needed to provide the necessary public oversight. The Commission considered also that it was not appropriate, politically or legally, to delegate accounting standard setting unconditionally and irrevocably to a private organisation over which the EU had no influence. In addition, the endorsement mechanism is responsible for examining whether the standards adopted by the IASB satisfy relevant EU public policy criteria.

The role of the endorsement mechanism is not to reformulate or replace IFRSs, but to oversee the adoption of new standards and interpretations, intervening only when these contain material deficiencies or have failed to cater for features specific to the EU economic or legal environments. The central task of this mechanism is to confirm that IFRSs provide a suitable basis for financial reporting by listed EU companies. The mechanism is based on a two-tier structure, combining a regulatory level with an expert level, to assist the Commission in its endorsement role.

The recitals to the Regulation state that the endorsement mechanism should act expeditiously in relation to proposed international accounting standards and also be a means to deliberate, reflect and exchange information on international accounting standards among the main parties concerned, in particular national accounting standard setters, supervisors in the fields of securities, banking and insurance, central banks including the European Central Bank (ECB), the accounting profession and users and preparers of accounts. The mechanism should be a means of fostering common understanding of adopted international accounting standards in the Community.[108]

There are three criteria set out in the Regulation on the application of IAS in the EU with which any individual IAS must comply if it is to be adopted:[109]

- the standard should not be contrary to the principle of true and fair in conformity with the Accounting Directives;

- the standard should be conducive to the European public good; and

- the standard should meet basic criteria as to the quality of information required for financial statements to be useful to users.

These criteria, although wide, do not appear unreasonable or overly burdensome in the light of the substantial power the EU has effectively vested in the IASB, a body not accountable to the EU electorate. It is important to note that although a standard or interpretation can only be adopted if all three criteria are met, this does not mean that if all three criteria are met a standard or interpretation must necessarily be adopted. However, if a standard or interpretation is not adopted, EU companies are free to apply it, other than in those cases where such application would be in conflict with an accounting standard that has been adopted or with EU law.

Concerns have been expressed on occasions about the speed of the EU endorsement process but to date, apart from the carve out from IAS 39, all IASB standards to have gone through the process have ultimately been endorsed albeit that a number of IFRIC interpretations have had delayed application dates under the endorsement. However, the discussions in relation to IFRS 8 – *Operating Segments* – were particularly difficult and as a consequence the EU has enacted Regulation 297/2008 which gives the Parliament a greater involvement in the endorsement process.

5.6.1 The regulatory level of the endorsement mechanism: The Accounting Regulatory Committee

The Accounting Regulatory Committee (ARC) was set up by the European Commission in accordance with the requirements contained in Article 6 of the EC's IAS Regulation (EC/1606/2002). The ARC is composed of representatives from EU Member States and is chaired by the Commission. The function of the Committee is a regulatory one and consists of providing an opinion on Commission proposals to adopt (endorse) an international accounting standard as envisaged under Article 3 of the IAS Regulation. The ARC operates on the basis of appropriate institutional arrangements and under existing comitology[110] rules that will ensure full transparency and accountability towards the Council and the European Parliament.

Under these rules, the Commission presents to the ARC a report that is required to identify the relevant international accounting standard and examine both its conformity with the conditions set out in the Regulation and its suitability as a basis for financial reporting in the EU. The ARC must decide, on the basis of qualified majority voting, whether to recommend to the European Commission that it should adopt or reject the standard for application in the EU. The same procedure applies to the adoption of amendments to previously adopted Standards and of IFRIC Interpretations.

5.6.2   *The European Financial Reporting Advisory Group (EFRAG)*

The European Financial Reporting Advisory Group (EFRAG), a private-sector initiative, was established by ten key constituents interested in financial reporting in Europe, including the European Federation of Accountants (FEE), Business Europe, the European Round Table, the European Banking Federation (EBF), and the Comité Européen des Assurances (CEA).

EFRAG is a two-tier organisation, comprising:

- a group of twelve highly qualified experts (the EFRAG Technical Expert Group), to carry out the technical work; and

- a Supervisory Board of European Organisations (the EFRAG Supervisory Board), to guarantee representation of the full European interest and to enhance the legitimacy and credibility of EFRAG.

The 12 voting members of the Technical Expert Group (TEG) were selected from throughout Europe and come from a variety of backgrounds. The chairmen of the French, German and UK Standard Setters are non-voting members of TEG, and representatives of the European Commission, CESR and the IASB attend TEG meetings as observers.

The members of TEG are appointed by the Supervisory Board, with the assistance of a Nominating Committee, following an open call for candidates. The Supervisory Board looks primarily to the qualifications of the TEG candidates in terms of knowledge and experience and endeavours to ensure a broad geographical balance together with experience from preparers, the accounting profession, users and academics.

The principal aim of EFRAG is to provide proactive input into the work of the IASB. EFRAG advises the European Commission on the technical assessment of IFRSs and Interpretations, for application in the EU. The technical work of EFRAG is carried out by TEG on the basis of a wide consultation process. National standard setters of Europe have access to EFRAG through a number of routes. In common with other consultative organisations, they receive regular updates of EFRAG agenda items and decisions. Additionally, they comprise EFRAG's Consultative Forum, meeting at least twice a year to engage in technical debate on matters arising from the EFRAG agenda.

TEG was set up by EFRAG on 26 June 2001. Its role is to provide the private sector support and expertise needed to assess the standards and interpretations developed by the IASB on a timely basis. It also has the responsibility to provide input into the IASB standard setting process at all stages of a particular project, and particularly in the early phases. TEG ensures that EU users and preparers are involved in the preparatory discussions of the standards at the international level, and in the technical assessment of the standards, before their adoption by the EU. The role of users has recently received greater prominence through the establishment of a User Panel to assist TEG in its work by providing input from the user community on its comment letters and endorsement advice. In addition the Panel provides input on the long-term proactive work carried out by EFRAG itself. When appropriate, the Panel also assists the user representatives in the various EFRAG working groups.[111]

In an initiative designed to enable Europe as a whole to participate more effectively in the global accounting debate, EFRAG and the European national standard setters agreed to pool some of their resources and work together more closely. It was agreed that this initiative should start by concentrating on long-term pro-active work with the objective of stimulating debate on important items on the IASB agenda at an early stage in the standard-setting process, before the IASB formally issues its proposals. This initiative is known as the 'Proactive Accounting Activities in Europe' (or PAAinE) initiative and has the joint ambitions of representing a European point of view and exercising greater influence on the standard-setting process.

Work carried out under the PAAinE initiative can take a number of different forms and the full objectives of the initiative are:

- to stimulate, carry out and manage pro-active development activities designed to encourage the debate in Europe on accounting matters and to enhance the quality of the pro-active input to the IASB;

- to co-ordinate and resource monitoring work of IASB and FASB projects; and

- to try to ensure, as far as is practicable, that the views that Europe conveys to the IASB are consistent.[112]

With the increasing adoption of IFRS there has been a recognition within Europe that there is a need to reorganise EFRAG to ensure that there are sufficient resources and expertise devoted to representing European views and interests in the IASB standard setting process. In July 2008 a proposal to enhance the governance structure and resource of EFRAG was announced.

This reorganisation will not change the basic objectives of EFRAG which remain to advise the European Commission and to articulate Europe views on IASB proposals. It is however anticipated that the greater resources will enable it to operate more effectively.

The revised structure of EFRAG is as set out below:

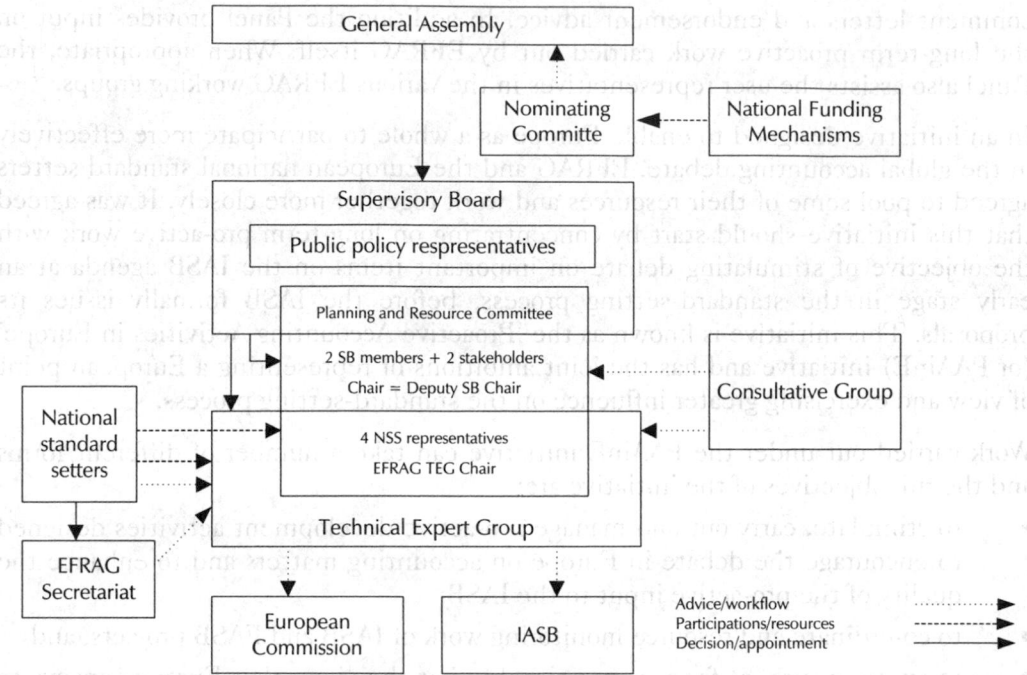

5.6.3 Standards Advice Review Group

In July 2006 the European Commission announced the formation of a Standards Advice Review Group for the purpose of ensuring objectivity and proper balance of EFRAG opinions. The Commission appoints the members of the Group from independent experts whose experience and competence in accounting, in particular in financial reporting issues, are widely recognised. The members are appointed in a personal capacity and will advise the Commission independently of any outside influence. The Group's task is to assess whether or not the endorsement advice given by the EFRAG is well balanced and objective. The group is expected to deliver its advice to the Commission within three weeks of EFRAG publishing its endorsement advice.[113]

5.7   Roundtable for the consistent application of IFRS in the EU

In February 2006, the European Commission formed a temporary Roundtable on Consistent Application of IFRSs. The Roundtable met for the first time in May 2006. The function of the Roundtable is set out in its Terms of Reference as follows:[114]

'The function of the Roundtable is to act as a simple and efficient forum for European accounting experts to identify, at an early stage, emerging and potentially problematic accounting issues in relation to consistent application. The Roundtable will thereby complete the existing European infrastructure contributing to a proper and consistent application of IFRS. The Roundtable would gather views in Member States through audit firms, standard setters and other bodies. It could then identify and group together those issues where it is felt there is a real risk of divergence and recommend which of those should be taken up by IFRIC as a matter of urgency. As such the Roundtable would also act as a filter mechanism. It should be underlined that the Roundtable will not be making any interpretations or guidance under IFRS. This is the task of IFRIC. When allowed to do so by their statutory working rules, EU national enforcers of financial information grouped within CESR/EECS[115] will inform the Roundtable about enforcement decisions taken under the Transparency and Prospectus Directives in relation to financial reporting based on IFRS.'

The Roundtable is chaired by the European Commission, and includes all the key EU stakeholders. However, the Commission recognises that for the Roundtable to function effectively, it is vital that the absolute number of participants should be kept as low as practically possible. Of course, a balance must be struck between having, on one hand, a manageable number of participants and, on the other, the need to include the relevant stakeholders. Consequently, in addition to Commission representatives, the Roundtable comprises a total of seventeen representatives from the IASB, CESR, EFRAG, FEE, Business Europe, the audit firms, National-Standard Setters and preparers. However, in addition to the three representatives from the EU National Standard-Setters (France, Germany and the UK), any other national standard-setter can participate by advance notice to the Commission.

It is important to note that the Roundtable is neither a decision-making nor interpretative body. Its function is limited to informal discussion on key topics and it will not develop into any form of interpretative authority on accounting standards. Issues discussed by the Roundtable will, if considered appropriate, be developed into technical papers. Thereafter, if the Roundtable believes that a particular technical paper has highlighted an issue of common concern, the issue will be submitted to IFRIC for consideration.

The output of the meetings of the Roundtable takes the form of a brief, publicly available summary of the meeting by the Chair, setting out the key issues that were discussed and those issues on which common concern was expressed and which therefore warranted referral to the IFRIC.

More recently the Roundtable has fallen into disuse due to the limited number of issues being brought forward.

5.8   Enforcement and regulation in an integrated European capital market

The European Commission set an ambitious agenda for the European Union to establish an integrated financial and capital market by 2010. However, progress with European capital market integration – a vital ingredient of this agenda – has so far been slow. Nevertheless, the economic gains to be derived from an integrated pan-European financial and capital market are considerable. European companies will have greater access to a deep and liquid market at lower costs of capital; and European consumers will enjoy wider investment choice and increasing net returns on their investments. The macroeconomic benefits could be substantial also, as increased investment implies stronger job creation and GDP growth.

However, the basic structures needed for an integrated market are not yet in place. In Europe, trans-national companies have to report to regulators in twenty-seven member states. They face a wide variety of different rules and regulations and investors have to negotiate fragmented markets that frustrate cross-border trading. Taken together with the differences in regulation, enforcement, taxation, legal systems and bankruptcy laws, this gives a situation that Baron Alexandre Lamfalussy described as 'a remarkable cocktail of Kafkaesque inefficiency that serves no-one – neither consumers, nor investors, nor SMEs, nor large companies, nor governments.' By contrast, the US capital markets provide clear evidence that efficiencies are forced upon businesses when their performances are easily comparable; without these pressures, inefficiency can go unnoticed.

Consequently, the greatest challenge facing Europe in delivering an efficient single capital market is the task of efficient regulation and enforcement. The absence of an effective and coordinated enforcement mechanism severely limits the credibility of any financial reporting regime. Clearly, the adoption of IFRS in Europe will improve the functioning of the securities markets only when it is properly and rigorously enforced. This means that the supervisors of the European capital markets have a crucial role to play in ensuring that companies comply with financial reporting requirements. In our view, this can be achieved only through the establishment of an efficient and lean Europe-wide regulatory system. This implies the co-operative development and implementation of a common EU approach to regulation that would establish a level playing field for EU financial reporting, maintained by rigorous enforcement that will prevent regulatory arbitrage.

In introducing the IAS Regulation, the European Commission stated that one of its key actions would be the development of an enforcement infrastructure that would ensure the rigorous application of IAS by listed companies in the EU. The focus of this initiative would be on disseminating implementation guidance, encouraging high quality auditing, and reinforcing coordinated regulatory oversight. A coordinating body was set up, as described below.

5.8.1   The Committee of European Securities Regulators (CESR)

The Committee of European Securities Regulators (CESR) was established by the European Commission Decision of June 2001.[116] This decision was taken in the light of the recommendation of the Report of the Committee of Wise Men on the Regulation of European Securities Markets (the Lamfalussy Report) as endorsed by the European Council and the European Parliament.[117] CESR is an independent Committee whose members comprise senior representatives from national public authorities competent in the field of securities. CESR has set out its own operational arrangements in its Charter.[118]

The CESR Chair and Vice-Chair are elected from among the Members for a period of two years. The Committee meets at least four times a year. CESR works with the support of a secretariat headed by a Secretary General. A representative of the European Commission is entitled to participate actively in all discussions held by CESR.

CESR submits an Annual Report to the European Commission, which is also sent to the European Parliament and the Council. The Chair of CESR reports regularly to the European Parliament and maintains strong links with the European Securities Committee.

The main tasks of CESR are to:

- advise the European Commission on securities policy issues, either at the European Commission's request or on its own initiative;

- prepare implementing measures as requested by the European Commission;

- foster and review common and uniform day-to-day implementation and application of Community legislation;

- issue guidelines, recommendations and standards that the CESR members introduce in their regulatory practices on a voluntary basis;

- undertake reviews of regulatory and supervisory practices within the single market; for that purpose a Review Panel has been established under the terms specified in a protocol attached to the Charter;

- develop effective operational network mechanisms to enhance day-to-day consistent supervision and enforcement of the Single Market for financial services. The Committee contributes to supervisory convergence through a Mediation Mechanism, established under the terms specified in a protocol attached to the Charter; and

- observe and assess the evolution of financial markets and the global trends in securities regulation and their impact on the regulation of the Single Market for financial services.

In addition, CESR established a sub-group of experts in the field of accounting and auditing, known as CESR-Fin. The principal challenges facing CESR-Fin are to reinforce cooperation among EU national regulators enforcing compliance with IFRS and to deepen the relationship with securities regulators in major third countries on financial reporting matters. This latter challenge is driven by the need to work on the global acceptance of IFRS financial statements prepared by EU entities that are subject to supervision both within and outside Europe.

The tasks of CESR-Fin are set out in its terms of reference as follows:[119]

- to coordinate the operational activities of EU National Enforcers in relation to the enforcement of compliance with IFRS. This includes:

    - the analysis and discussion of individual enforcement decisions under IFRS and emerging financial reporting issues under IFRS;

    - the identification of issues that are not covered by financial reporting standards or which may be affected by conflicting interpretations for referral to standard setting or interpretive bodies such as IASB or IFRIC;

    - the exchange of views and experiences on methods for supervising the financial information of companies offering publicly securities and/or having these securities listed on an EU regulated market;

- to monitor pro-actively and influence the regulatory developments in the area of accounting and auditing, including an active monitoring of the EU endorsement processes of international standards and the work of relevant EU accounting and/or auditing Committees;

- to identify issues in relation to the areas covered above that should be addressed by CESR through appropriate measures such as standards, guidelines or recommendations. CESR-Fin can also make proposals on best enforcement practices or for peer reviews among enforcers;

- to advise other CESR groups, such as the Prospectus Contact Group or the Transparency Expert Group, on technical accounting and auditing issues raised by these groups in relation to their area of activity or as a result of implementation issues identified in connection with CESR-Fin activities;

- to establish and maintain the appropriate relationship with securities regulators from major capital markets outside Europe, in order to foster the operational cooperation between EU and non-EU regulators in the area of financial reporting.

5.8.2   CESR Standard No. 1

During the seventh meeting of CESR held in Paris in March 2003, the first CESR standard on *Financial Information: Enforcement of standards on financial information in Europe*, was approved.[120] The standard represents a significant part of CESR's contribution to the task of developing and implementing a common approach to the enforcement of IFRS in Europe.

The standard sets down 21 principles on which, in CESR's view, harmonisation of the institutional oversight systems in Europe may be achieved. In particular, a definition of enforcement of standards on financial information, its scope, the selection techniques applicable by the enforcers and the responsibilities of the different parties involved are outlined.

The standard states that for financial information other than prospectuses, ex-post enforcement is the normal procedure, whilst for prospectuses ex-ante approval is the norm. Enforcement of all financial information should normally be achieved by selecting a number of issuers and documents to be examined. The preferred models for selecting financial information for enforcement purposes are mixed models whereby a risk-based approach is combined with a rotation and/or a sampling approach.[121]

Where a material misstatement in the financial information is detected, enforcers are required to take appropriate actions to achieve an appropriate disclosure and where relevant, public correction of misstatement.[122] Enforcers should periodically report to the public on their activities providing, as a minimum, information on the enforcement policies adopted and decisions taken in individual cases including accounting and disclosure matters.[123]

5.8.3 CESR Standard No. 2

In April 2004, CESR issued a standard on the organisation of greater co-ordination of enforcement activities by supervisors of financial information in Europe.[124] The standard's aim is further to contribute to the creation within Europe of robust and consistent enforcement of IFRS. The key principles introduced by Standard no. 2 include:

- discussion of enforcement decisions and experiences within a formalised structure;

- the principle that all supervisors should take into account existing decisions taken by EU National Enforcers; and

- the development of a database as a practical reference tool that sets out decisions taken by EU National Enforcers to provide a record of previous decisions reached in particular cases.

The CESR database has now been established, and provides EU securities regulators with the means of sharing with each other their regulatory activity and experiences. In principle, this is a positive development as it will help to promote consistency in the regulation and enforcement of IFRS financial reporting throughout the EU – something that is crucial in the development of an integrated EU capital market.

In addition, extracts from EECS's database of enforcement decisions are now made public on the CESR website.

5.8.4 CESR/SEC joint work plan

In August 2006 – as part of their ongoing regulatory dialogue – CESR and the SEC published a joint work plan that focuses on three key issues. For each of the following three items, the work plan includes a description of the project goal and the next steps to be taken:[125]

A Implementation of IFRS and US GAAP by internationally active issuers

What this means in practical terms is that, as part of their regular review of corporate filings, the staff of the SEC will review foreign private issuers' implementation of IFRS. Similarly, staff of CESR Members will continue to review US GAAP implementation by US issuers in the European Union. Under the work plan, the output of these reviews will be used in the following ways:

- The staff of the SEC and CESR-Fin will share information about areas of IFRS and US GAAP that are troublesome in terms of high-quality and consistent application; and

- Where appropriate, the staff of the SEC and the staff of CESR Members will consult on issuer-specific matters regarding the application of US GAAP and IFRS in order to facilitate a solution that contributes to the consistent application of US GAAP or IFRS by companies that are both listed in the EU and registered with the SEC. Protocols for the sharing of this confidential information between the staff of individual CESR members (e.g. in the UK and Germany) and the staff of the SEC have been established.

These two levels of discussion are aimed at helping to ensure that high standards are maintained and consistent financial reporting is achieved. In addition, they are aimed at ensuring that a single regulator does not act unilaterally or that two individual regulators do not act in an inconsistent manner in relation to companies whose financial statements are subject to review by both.

B   Modernisation of financial reporting and disclosure

The goal here is to evaluate and identify information technology solutions for disclosure and electronic storage of corporate information (including financial information). The plan is for SEC staff and the relevant CESR expert group (in this case, the Transparency Expert Group, CESR-Tech) to exchange views on policies favouring the use of technology and IT networks in the disclosure and storage of financial information, including the use of interactive data.

C   Discussion of risk management practices

In this case, Staff of the SEC and CESR will discuss methodology and tools for prioritising risks they confront as regulators, the risks that have been identified and ranked as high-priority, and the methodology that has resulted in the categorisation of these risks as high-priority. Once common risks are identified, the SEC and CESR will discuss approaches to managing those risks.

6   THE ADOPTION OF IFRS OUTSIDE THE EUROPEAN UNION

A body of generally high quality International Financial Reporting Standards has now been promulgated, and approximately 100 countries have either already adopted IFRS directly, or have aligned their national standards with IFRS, or have committed to do so in the foreseeable future – albeit in many of these 100 countries IFRS is either required only for certain companies (for example, listed companies or financial institutions), or permitted rather than required.

Although the European Union is almost certainly the IASB's most significant single constituency for the time being, there are also a number of other countries that either have already adopted – or will be adopting – IFRS as their primary system of GAAP. Set out below is a brief summary of the basis on which just some of these countries have adopted IFRS.

6.1   Australia

The Australian Financial Reporting Council (FRC) is a statutory body established under the *Australian Securities and Investments Commission Act 2001, as amended by the Corporate Law Economic Reform Program (Audit Reform and Corporate Disclosure) Act 2004*. The FRC is responsible for providing broad oversight of the process for setting accounting and auditing standards as well as monitoring the effectiveness of auditor independence requirements in Australia and providing the Australian Government with reports and advice on these matters. It comprises key stakeholders from the business community, the professional accounting bodies, governments and regulatory agencies.

In July 2002, the Chairman of the FRC announced that the FRC had formalised its support for the adoption by Australia of international accounting standards by 1 January 2005. In accordance with this strategic directive, the Australian Accounting Standards Board (AASB) issued Australian equivalents to IFRSs (AIFRS) on 15 July 2004. Australian Accounting Standards have the force of law for Australian corporations, and therefore the standards issued by the IASB are required to be issued as Australian standards by the AASB. The implementation of the Australian equivalents to international standards has achieved the FRC's strategic directive of ensuring that the financial statements of for-profit entities applying AASB standards are also in compliance with IASB standards.

In adopting the IASB's standards, the AASB's initial approach was to adopt the content and wording of the standards. Words were changed only where there was a need to accommodate the Australian legislative environment. At the time of initial adoption in 2005, in certain AIFRS Standards the AASB permitted only one of certain optional treatments available in the equivalent IASB standards, and retained a number of specific disclosures from domestic GAAP in addition to the disclosure requirements of IFRS. On 30 April 2007, the AASB issued AASB 2007-4 *Amendments to Australian Accounting Standards arising from ED 151 and Other Amendments*. This new standard is a result of an AASB decision that, in principle, Australian equivalents to IFRSs should reflect to the maximum extent possible the requirements and wording of IFRS. AASB 2007-4 was effective for reporting periods beginning on or after 1 July 2007, and had the effect of incorporating all remaining IFRS accounting policy options into AIFRS and removing almost all Australian-specific disclosure requirements from AIFRS.

In some cases, existing AASB standards contained commentary that was not included in the equivalent IASB standards. The AASB has removed all this guidance that was not part of the standards, except where the guidance deals with situations that are commonly encountered in the Australian environment but which are not catered for in the IASB standards.

In 2007, the Australian Auditing and Assurance Standards Board (AUASB) issued a revised auditing standard requiring the auditor to opine on the entity's statement of compliance with IFRS made in accordance with the Australian equivalent of paragraph 14 of IAS 1, if such statement has been made.

The AASB plans to continue to work to maintain consistency with the IASB's standards in order that the FRC's strategic directive continues to be met. IFRS also applies to public sector organisations such that no 'local GAAP' remains

6.2   Brazil

In Brazil, the 'Comissão de Valores Mobiliários' (CVM) is the body responsible for the regulation of the financial statements of publicly listed companies, with the exception of companies in the financial services sector. These financial statements are currently required to be prepared in accordance with Brazilian Corporate Law and local accounting standards. In July 2007, following a period of public consultation, the CVM issued Instruction No. 457, which requires publicly listed companies to publish their consolidated financial statements in accordance with IFRS for periods ending on or after 1 January 2010, with earlier adoption being permitted. Banks and financial institutions are regulated by the Brazilian Central Bank which has also announced the objective of requiring the adoption of IFRS by 2010.[126]

6.3   Canada

In Canada the body charged with the responsibility for establishing standards of accounting and reporting for Canadian companies and not-for-profit organisations is the Accounting Standards Board (AcSB). The AcSB derives its authority from the Canadian Institute of Chartered Accountants (CICA). The AcSB is supported in its standard setting role by the Accounting Standards Oversight Committee (AcSOC), which was established in 2000.

In January 2006 the AcSB ratified a new Strategic Plan outlining its direction for financial reporting in Canada for the period 2006 to 2011. Under this plan the AcSB set out its intent to pursue separate strategies for each of the major categories of reporting entities in Canada, which are:

• publicly accountable enterprises;

• non-publicly accountable enterprises; and

• not-for-profit organisations.

In so doing, the AcSB recognised that it may not be possible to address the divergent needs of different categories of reporting entities properly within a single strategy.

For publicly accountable enterprises, the AcSB has decided to converge Canadian GAAP with IFRSs over a transitional period to a changeover date of January 1, 2011. From that date forward, Canadian GAAP for publicly accountable enterprises will be IFRS as issued by the IASB. However, the Canadian Securities Administrators will accept applications from publicly accountable enterprises for early adoption of IFRS. The term 'publicly accountable enterprises' encompasses public companies and some other classes of enterprise that have relatively large or diverse classes of financial statement users. However, as part of its implementation plan, the AcSB is considering the need for a revised definition of a publicly accountable enterprise. For non-publicly accountable enterprises and not-for-profit organizations the AcSB has undertaken to develop and propose new bases of accounting that are based on Canadian rather than International Standards, although IFRS also will be available for use by those entities on a voluntary basis.

In its plans for publicly accountable enterprises, the AcSB has taken into account the experiences of the European Union and the other jurisdictions that have already converted to IFRSs so as to minimise the disruption to business arising from the conversion. The key features of its convergence plan are the relatively long transitional period and a phased adoption of IFRS throughout the transitional period and at the changeover date. However, since IFRS reporting will commence from the first quarter of 2011, many publicly accountable enterprises will select their new IFRS policies and prepare opening balance sheets during 2010.

In its strategy document the AcSB explained that its plans for converging Canadian GAAP to IFRSs include:

- adopting standards newly developed by the International Accounting Standards Board (IASB) that are converged with standards issued by the FASB, as these new global standards are issued;

- replacing other Canadian standards with corresponding IFRSs already issued, in accordance with a separate convergence implementation plan developed in consultation with affected stakeholders;

- working with both the IASB and the FASB to ensure that the Canadian perspective is taken into account in their deliberations; and

- working to promote the further convergence of IASB and FASB standards.

The adoption of IFRSs in Canada for publicly accountable enterprises will mean that the AcSB will effectively cease to make final decisions on most matters affecting the technical content and timing of implementation of standards applied to publicly accountable enterprises in Canada. The AcSB has stated that it will continue to assess and monitor the application of IFRS in Canada. While the AcSB retains the power to modify or add to the requirements of IFRSs, it intends to avoid changing IFRSs when adopting them as Canadian GAAP. Accordingly, the AcSB does not expect to eliminate any options within existing IFRSs. As issues relevant to Canadian users of financial information arise in future the AcSB will work to resolve them through IFRIC – the IASB's interpretive body or the IASB – and, in the event that this is not possible, it will stand ready to develop additional temporary guidance.

6.4   China and Hong Kong

6.4.1   China

The developments in IFRS have been playing an important role in the development of accounting standards and practices in China. The Ministry of Finance (the MOF) – through its Accounting Regulatory Department – is responsible for the promulgation of accounting standards. In 1993, the MOF started a work programme to develop a set of *Accounting Standards for Business Enterprises* (ASBE). Before 2006, China had promulgated and implemented ASBE – *Basic Standard*, with 16 specific ASBE, as well as *Accounting System for Business Enterprises*, *Accounting System for Financial Institutions* and *Accounting System for Small Business Enterprises* which are applicable to various business enterprises.

Representatives of the China Accounting Standards Committee (CASC) – which falls under the Accounting Regulatory Department of the MOF – and the IASB met in Beijing in November 2005 to discuss a range of issues relating to the convergence of Chinese accounting standards with IFRSs. That meeting followed a series of CASC-IASB staff meetings in Beijing in October. At the conclusion of the meeting in November, the two delegations released a joint statement setting out key points of agreement, including the following:

- China stated that convergence is one of the fundamental goals of their standard-setting programme, with the intention that an enterprise applying ASBE should produce financial statements that are the same as those of an enterprise that applies IFRSs; and

- The delegation acknowledged that convergence with IFRSs will take time and how to converge with IFRSs is a matter for China to determine.

In February 2006, the MOF issued a series of new and revised ASBE which included the revised *Basic Standard*, 22 newly-promulgated accounting standards and 16 revised accounting standards. The new and revised ASBE were effective from 1 January 2007 for listed companies. Other companies are also encouraged to adopt them.

The new and revised ASBE, to a large extent, represent convergence with IFRS, with due consideration being given to specific situations in China. The ASBE cover the recognition, measurement, presentation and disclosure of most transactions and events, financial reporting, and nearly all the topics covered by the current IFRS literature. Most of the new and revised ASBE are substantially in line with the corresponding IFRS. For instance, the requirements set out in the standards on revenue, income tax, financial instruments and consolidated financial statements are very similar to those in IAS 18 – *Revenue*, IAS 12 – *Income taxes*, IAS 39 – *Financial Instruments: Recognition and Measurement*, and IAS 27 – *Consolidated and Separate Financial Statements* – respectively. However, there are accounting standards that do not have an IFRS equivalent, such as that on non-monetary transactions, and there are a few standards with requirements that may not be entirely in line with IFRS. A notable example is the accounting standard on impairment of assets, which prohibits the reversal of an impairment loss for long-lived assets. Another example is the standard on investment property under which the fair value model can be used only when certain strict criteria are met.

Although at present, only listed companies and certain entities in the finance industry are required to apply it, the publication of the new and revised ASBE is an important milestone in the convergence process. Thus, although a few exceptions are still acknowledged in certain areas between local and international practices, the convergence process has begun to narrow the gap, particularly over the last few years when significant progress has been made.

6.4.2   *Hong Kong*

The Hong Kong Institute of Certified Public Accountants (HKICPA), a statutory body established under the Professional Accountants Ordinance, is the principal source of accounting principles in Hong Kong. These include a series of Hong Kong Financial Reporting Standards (HKFRS), accounting standards referred to as Hong Kong Accounting Standards (HKAS) and Interpretations issued by the HKICPA. The term 'Hong Kong Financial Reporting Standards' is deemed to include all of the foregoing. While HKFRS have no direct legal force, they derive their authority from the HKICPA, which may take disciplinary action against any of its members responsible, as preparer or as auditor, for financial statements that do not follow the requirements of the pronouncements.

In 2001, the HKICPA Council mandated a strategy of achieving convergence between its accounting standards and IFRSs issued by the IASB. HKFRSs were fully converged with IFRS with effect from 1 January 2005. The HKICPA Council supports the integration of its standard setting process with that of the IASB.

Although the HKICPA Council has a policy of maintaining convergence of HKFRSs with IFRSs, the HKICPA Council may consider it appropriate to include additional disclosure requirements in a HKFRS or, in some exceptional cases, to deviate from an IFRS. Each HKFRS issued by Council contains information about the extent of compliance with the equivalent IFRS. Where the requirements of a HKFRS and an IFRS differ, the HKFRS should be followed by entities reporting within the area of application of the HKFRSs. However in practice, exceptions to IFRSs are few and relate to certain transitional provisions.

6.5   India

The issue of convergence with IFRS has gained significant momentum in India. At present, the Accounting Standards Board (ASB) of the Institute of Chartered Accountants of India (ICAI) formulates Accounting Standards based on IFRS; however, these standards remain sensitive to local conditions, including the legal and economic environments. Accordingly, the Accounting Standards issued by the ICAI depart from the corresponding IFRSs in order to ensure consistency with the legal, regulatory and economic environments of India. However, it is worth noting that, in some cases, departures are also made on account of conceptual differences with the treatments prescribed in IFRSs.

Although the ICAI is the principal standard-setter, regulators have also set standards for their respective constituencies. The Reserve Bank of India formulates accounting requirements for banks; the Securities and Exchange Board of India, which regulates listed companies, formulates accounting requirements for mutual funds as well as presentation formats for quarterly disclosures by listed companies; it has also formulated accounting rules for employee stock options, which are required to be followed by all listed companies; and the Insurance Regulatory and Development Authority of India formulates accounting requirements for insurance companies. Financial statement presentation requirements are set out in the Companies Act, which also includes other accounting requirements, such as the minimum depreciation rate and accounting for foreign exchange differences.

At its meeting held in May 2006, the Council of the ICAI expressed the view that full IFRS may be adopted at a future date, at least for listed and large entities. The ASB, at its meeting held in August 2006, considered the matter and supported the Council's view that there would be several advantages of converging with IFRS. As a result, in view of the extent of differences between IFRSs and Indian Accounting Standards as well as the fact that convergence with IFRS would be an important policy decision, the ASB decided to form an IFRS Task Force. The objectives of this Task Force were to: (i) explore the approach for achieving convergence with IFRSs, and (ii) lay down a road map for achieving convergence with IFRSs with a view to making India IFRS-compliant.

Based on the recommendations of the IFRS Task Force, the Council of the ICAI has decided to adopt a 'big bang' approach and fully converge Indian Accounting Standards with IFRSs issued by the IASB for accounting periods commencing on or after 1 April 2011.

During 2009 the Ministry of Corporate Affairs has set up a high powered group comprising various stakeholders. This core group is supported by two sub groups. The first sub-group will identify changes required in various laws, regulations and accounting standards for convergence with IFRS and prepare a clear road map for achieving the same. The second sub-group will interact with various stakeholders in order to understand their concerns on the issue of convergence with IFRS, identify problem areas and ascertain the preparedness of the stakeholders for such convergence. In the first joint meeting of all the groups held on August 6, 2009, the discussions were encouraging and indicated strong support for convergence from all participants in the meeting.

6.6   Japan[127]

In August 2007, Ikuo Nishikawa, Chairman of the Accounting Standards Board of Japan (ASBJ), and Sir David Tweedie, Chairman of the IASB, jointly announced an agreement (known as 'The Tokyo Agreement') to accelerate convergence between Japanese GAAP and IFRSs, a process that was started in March 2005.

As part of the agreement the two boards will seek to eliminate by 2008 major differences between Japanese GAAP and IFRSs, with the remaining differences being removed on or before 30 June 2011. Whilst the target date of 2011 does not apply to any major new IFRSs now being developed that will become effective after 2011, both boards will work closely to ensure the acceptance of the international approach in Japan when new standards become effective.

Both the ASBJ and IASB share the belief that convergence towards high quality accounting standards will greatly benefit capital markets around the world. They therefore launched a joint project in March 2005 with the final goal of accomplishing convergence between Japanese GAAP and IFRSs. In their discussions in this joint project, the boards identified differences between the two sets of standards and have already made progress towards eliminating those differences.

The ASBJ and the IASB will proceed with the projects in the light of the changing environment surrounding global convergence of accounting standards and will enhance co-operation to facilitate greater input in the international standard-setting process from Japan. For this purpose, in addition to the joint meeting between representatives of the ASBJ and the IASB held semi-annually since 2005, both boards will establish working groups led by project directors in order to discuss further the major issues emerging in the development of accounting standards in a practical manner.

In September 2007, the ASBJ and the IASB held their first two-day meeting since the announcement of 'The Tokyo Agreement'. This meeting had two objectives: first, to review the convergence programme and the shared goal of eliminating major differences between IFRSs and Japanese GAAP by 2008, with the remaining differences being removed on or before 30 June 2011; and, second, to discuss the arrangements for the ASBJ to input its views into the IASB's current work programme. The discussions included a review of short-term convergence projects, where major differences are to be eliminated towards the goal of 2008.[128]

In June 2009 the Business Advisory Council (BAC) a key advisory body to the Financial Services Agency approved a roadmap for the adoption of IFRS in Japan. The key points of this roadmap are:

- Option of voluntary adoption of IFRS from fiscal years ending after 31 March 2010 for companies with global financial or operating activities; and

- Decision on the mandatory adoption of IFRS to be made in 2012. If IFRS were mandatorily adopted the likely application date is either 2015 or 2016.

Although this roadmap is obviously completely independent of the SEC's process discussed earlier it will be interesting to see whether developments in the US impact on these Japanese proposals.

6.7 South Africa

At present all South African companies are required to prepare annual financial statements which are to be audited. For this purpose, companies use accounting standards issued by the South African standard setting body, the Accounting Practices Board (APB).

From 1994 to 2003 the APB issued accounting standards that were generally the same as the equivalent international standards, but with a few minor differences.

In 2004 all IFRS in issue at that time were adopted in South Africa, thus removing the remaining differences, other than historic differences in effective dates, between IFRS and South African standards. Since then, to date, all IASB standards and interpretations have been adopted in South Africa without any changes.

With effect from periods beginning on or after 1 January 2005 the South African securities exchange, JSE Limited, required listed companies to prepare financial statements under IFRS. Other companies, except as noted below, either use IFRS or South African Generally Accepted Accounting Practice, which is IFRS affected by some historical effective date differences and the non application of IFRS 1.

The Companies Act, together with its Fourth Schedule and the stock exchange's listing requirements, has certain disclosure requirements that are additional to those contained in IFRS. For example, the JSE Listings Requirements require the calculation of headline earnings per share and disclosure of a detailed reconciliation of headline earnings to the earnings numbers used in the calculation of basic earnings per share in accordance with the requirements of IAS 33.[129] The securities exchange has a GAAP Monitoring Panel which investigates complaints of non compliance with accounting standards and its disclosure requirements.

South Africa has issued its own interpretations on four issues, as a result of the IASB deciding not to issue opinions on issues that were considered to be specific to South

Africa. These deal with an additional tax payable when dividends are declared, the meaning of substantively enacted tax rates and tax laws in a South African context, accounting for black economic empowerment transactions (which deals with certain issues specific to these types of transactions that are not dealt with in IFRIC 8 – *Scope of IFRS 2)* and the application of IFRIC 14 in a South African environment.

Amendments to the Companies Act promulgated in 2007 made provision for legal backing to accounting standards. It also required certain companies (mainly listed companies and their subsidiaries) to use accounting standards that were in accordance with IFRS, but allowed certain unlisted companies to use accounting standards that were not necessarily in accordance with IFRS. As a result the APB issued the IASB's then exposure draft on IFRS for SMEs as a standard for these companies. When the final IASB standard on IFRS for SMEs was adopted in South Africa in 2009, the APB extended the scope of entities which could use this standard, to include some subsidiaries of listed companies.

A new Companies Act was promulgated in 2009 which is expected to be become effective in the second half of 2010. In terms of regulations which have not yet been published, certain companies will not be required to issue audited financial statements and different accounting standards could apply to different categories of companies, thus still requiring some companies to comply with standards that are consistent with IFRS. A Financial Reporting Standards Council as required by this act is to replace the APB.

7   WHAT CONSTITUTES INTERNATIONAL GAAP?

7.1   Generally Accepted Accounting Practice

It is clear that 2005 was a watershed year for IFRS with a significant number of countries adopting it as their principal financial reporting regime. In the years since other countries have decided to adopt IFRS. At the same time the work of regulators, the IFRIC and the general development of consensus amongst preparers and users as to what constitute acceptable practices has led to a reduction in the diversity in practice that inevitably attended the initial widespread adoption of IFRS. As such it may be felt that IFRS has now emerged as an *International GAAP*. However, as discussed earlier in this chapter there remain pressures on the standard setting process and local interpretations of IASB standards remain. As such there are clearly limits to its 'general acceptance'.

7.2   Principles vs. rules[130]

The question whether accounting standards should be principles or rules-based has been debated for decades. Views are often influenced by historical tradition, legal and regulatory environments and prejudice. However, with IFRS in the process of becoming the accepted global financial reporting framework, and with the growing emphasis on convergence between US GAAP and IFRS, this debate is once again at the forefront of the standard-setting agenda.

The distinction between the two approaches lies precisely where their respective descriptions suggest: principles-based standards are based on a clear hierarchy of overarching principles, contain few or no 'bright line' provisions and rely heavily on the exercise of judgement as to what constitutes fair presentation; rules-based standards are characterised by 'bright line' and anti-abuse provisions and allow relatively less scope for the exercise of judgement in their application. An example of this distinction lies in the requirements for lease classification under IFRS and US GAAP respectively, in so far as IFRS requires a judgement to be formed as to where the risks and rewards incidental to ownership of an asset lie, whereas US GAAP sets down a checklist of rules that must be applied in making this determination. This is not to say that IFRS does not also have rules-based standards, since IAS 39 – *Financial Instruments: Recognition and Measurement* and IFRS 2 – *Share-based Payment* – are highly rules-based and not to say that US GAAP does not contain principles.

In fact, IAS 39 provides an instructive example of the differences between rules and principles.[131] In accounting for the hedging of financial risk, a guiding principle might be that the performance statement should reflect the reduction of volatility achieved economically by the hedge. Intuitively, if a company has mitigated the effects of a particular risk – foreign exchange fluctuations for example – it makes sense that this reduction in volatility should flow through to the performance statement in the form of a neutral profit and loss impact (or something which is close to neutral depending on the efficacy of the hedge). It is interesting to note that IAS 39 does not embody such a principle. Rather, there are complex rules that determine whether or not it is acceptable to flow the impact of the hedge and hedged item through profit or loss in the same period; and, because the rules include onerous documentation and effectiveness testing requirements, profit and loss neutrality is an outcome that is effectively optional. In other words, if the hedge is not documented and/or the effectiveness tests are not performed, hedge accounting cannot be applied. As a result, it is perfectly possible for the performance statement to report volatility even though economically none exists because a company is hedged perfectly over the term of the hedged instrument.

Whether or not IFRS develops into a truly principles-based system will depend largely on the attitudes and approaches of all the participants in the financial reporting process including standard-setters, preparers, auditors, users and regulators. Whilst US GAAP is clearly principles-based (though not based on the same principles throughout, which creates its own problems), it seems that the rules have grown over a number of years due to the demands of preparers and auditors for more detailed guidance and certainty, and the demands from regulators for consistency. There seems, therefore, to be a natural tension between the desire for comparability and the quest for a principles-based system,[132] and it is essential that IFRS does not suffer the growth of rules as US GAAP has. In our view, it is necessary to recognise that complete comparability is never possible in accounting. Instead, more emphasis needs to be placed on explaining the key judgements made by preparers of financial statements, including the sensitivities around those judgements. However, the danger for IFRS is that the demand for implementation guidance may increase as IFRSs become more widely applied and more detailed rules are called for.

Interestingly, the staff of the SEC seem to have come to the view that rules-based standards often provide a vehicle for circumventing the intention of the standards. In a report on the 'Adoption by the United States Financial Reporting System of a Principles-Based Accounting System', the SEC staff have recommended that those involved in the standard-setting process should more consistently develop standards on a principles-based or objectives-oriented basis. In the view of the SEC staff, an optimal accounting standard involves a concise statement of substantive accounting principles with few, if any, exceptions or conceptual inconsistencies in the standard.[133] In this report, the SEC staff made the following observations on the relationship between comparability and principles-based standards:[134]

'We believe that, overall, the movement to an objectives-oriented approach to standard setting should result in increased comparability in terms of economic substance. Indeed, the comparability arguably associated with a rules-based regime is often illusory. This is for four reasons.

'First, complex financial engineering stimulated by and designed to circumvent a rules-based regime reduces transparency and, correspondingly, may reduce genuine comparability of underlying economic circumstances.

'Second, a uniformity of accounting treatment may only result in a superficial kind of comparability if guidance is inappropriately rigid and thereby forces unlike arrangements into the same accounting treatment.

'Third, the clustering of underlying transactions on either side of bright-line rules associated with a rules-based regime results in different accounting treatment being given to arrangements that are fundamentally the same.

'Fourth, it should be noted, of course, that under an objectives-oriented regime, comparability can be achieved as long as there is transparency of method used through disclosure, albeit not necessarily at the same cost to the investor or analyst as under a rules-based regime.

'That being said, there may be some instances in which objectives-oriented accounting standards result in the loss of some degree in the precision of comparability of financial statements across firms and industries in some narrow application contexts, or at least render it more expensive to achieve comparability. That is, in certain applications, the extra guidance and greater detail provided under a rules-based regime may result in a greater uniformity.'

This clearly highlights the tension between the advantages claimed for rules and those claimed for principles when it comes to how standards should be formulated. At heart, a principles-based system must be underpinned by a degree of trust in the participants, as well as rigorous enforcement. For example, the view is sometimes expressed that standards are set on the basis that Finance Directors or Chief Financial Officers cannot be trusted and need to be policed.[135] Whether or not this is the case, a pre-requisite of principles-based standards is that regulators have to be prepared to accept a range of judgement-based outcomes.[136] Regulators need to trust preparers and auditors, who in turn must be capable of exercising judgement in an appropriate manner. Acceptance of different judgements implies also that the IASB will need to review fundamentally the basis on which note disclosures are presented, and will need to place substantially more emphasis on the provision of information in the notes to the accounts that explains the judgements made by management, together with ranges of possible outcomes and sensitivity analyses. It may be necessary also for regulators and legislators to provide some protection for preparers and auditors against exposure to litigation in the event that disclosed assumptions fail to materialise.

7.3   Practical interpretations of IFRS

In 2005 IFRS became the global standard for financial reporting in the world's capital markets outside North America virtually overnight; therefore, significant questions of interpretation have inevitably arisen. Many of these are issues of precedent and will have cross-border implications. The biggest challenge facing regulators is to ensure that national variations in the interpretation and application of IFRS do not emerge. Although IFRIC exists as the IASB's interpretations arm, IFRIC is neither able, nor should it be expected, to deal with issues of interpretation that will arise on a day-to-day basis. The need to apply due process and the need to avoid descending into a rules-based system mean that companies cannot expect either IFRIC or the IASB to provide immediate answers to every practical issue that arises.

In reality, the day-to-day issues of interpretation will be decided, initially, by company managements and their auditors. Thereafter, regulators may become influential to a greater or lesser extent. The role of IFRIC and the IASB will principally be to monitor the practical application of standards and, if deemed necessary, issue an interpretation or amend a standard in response to what they consider to be the development of unacceptable treatments or inappropriate practices.

This means that all those involved with the development of IFRS into a global financial reporting framework bear a considerable responsibility to ensure that the development is evolutionary and based on a broad consensus. For the EU in particular, cross-border consistency in regulation and enforcement is essential. Consequently, one of the interesting aspects of financial reporting during the next decade will be to observe how the process of acceptance and implementation of IFRS across the world generally, and the EU in particular, develops.

7.4   Who 'owns' International GAAP?

The adoption of IFRS in the European Union as the single financial reporting framework for listed companies, combined with the move to IFRS in many other countries such as Australia, Brazil, Canada, China, India, Japan, South Africa and Switzerland, means that the question of the 'ownership' of International GAAP has inevitably arisen, and who, therefore, is the ultimate authority when the inevitable differences of opinion and judgement occur. The IASCFs constitutional review (discussed at 2.2.3 to 2.2.5 above) with its focus on improved governance and geographical balance is a manifestation of that.

This issue has a number of practical implications for companies applying IFRS; for example, what happens in cases where:

- different (and potentially conflicting) interpretations of the same standard are given by different regulators? or

- there is uncertainty about who has jurisdiction in cases of conflict between two parties on the question of the conformity of a specific set of financial statements with IFRS? For example, what are the roles of the national courts, the European Court of Justice, National Regulators, the IASB, IFRIC etc.?

There is, moreover, the possibility of an even greater level of uncertainty being created as the custom and practice that are an essential part of any GAAP begin to accrue. Hitherto, all standard setting bodies have been given their legitimacy by, and have operated within, national legislative frameworks; by contrast, the IASB is a private sector body, with no political accountability. In theory at least, all it does is set the standards; issues of compliance and enforcement are outside its frame of reference. There is no supreme legislative body or regulator that can decide, for all concerned with applying International GAAP, what does and does not constitute conformity with International GAAP. Rather, pronouncements, rulings, and interpretations issued by others outside the IASB organisation will inevitably become part of International GAAP, although in our view the IASB should make strenuous efforts to monitor and, where relevant, challenge these.

Therefore, it seems that it will only be a matter of time before the ultimate ownership and authority of International GAAP is tested. Paradoxically it may be that the more successful International GAAP becomes as a global financial reporting system, the more its interpretation, integrity and meaning will be disputed.

8   CONCLUSION

International Accounting Standards have come a long way in the 40 years since the establishment of the Accountants International Study Group by Henry Benson in 1967. When International Accounting Standards were first issued by the former Board of the IASC, some of them permitted alternative accounting treatments. The principal reason for this was that the IASC viewed its initial function as prohibiting undesirable accounting practices, whilst acknowledging that there might be more than one acceptable solution to a specific accounting issue. Today, the focus is on removal of options, consistency and comparability.

The European Commission's Regulation requiring all EU companies listed on a regulated market to prepare their consolidated financial statements in accordance with IFRSs means that the much-discussed notion of globally harmonised financial reporting under a single set of accounting standards is now a real possibility. Europe's decision has encouraged many other countries to adopt a similar path.

The challenge for the next few years is therefore to ensure that the much talked about goal of a single set of high quality converged financial reporting standards applied throughout the world, which everyone seems to agree is a desirable outcome is actually achieved. The IASB will clearly have a critical role in this.

References

1 Joseph Stiglitz, *Globalization and its discontents*, Penguin Books, 2002, page ix.
2 European Union, *Regulation of the European Parliament and of the Council on the application of international accounting standards*, Regulation No. 1606/2002, 19 July 2002.
3 Chartered Accountants of Canada, Media Release, *Canada's Accounting Standards Board ratifies its strategic plan: Approves convergence with international reporting standards*, Toronto, January 10, 2006.
4 Henry Alexander Benson was a Chartered Accountant who was born and educated in South Africa. He served on the Council of the ICAEW between 1956 and 1975, and as President in 1966-67. He was advisor to the Governor of the Bank of England from 1975 to 1983 and served as Chairman, Royal Commission on Legal Services 1976 to 1979. In his Obituary published in *The Times* on 7 March 1995 it was stated that 'Few men outside Whitehall can have had more influence on public affairs in post-war Britain than Henry Benson. As senior partner in the firm of Coopers & Lybrand, he built up an international reputation as one of the most formidable accountants of his time.' Henry Benson died on 5 March 1995, aged 85.
5 Foreword to *Accounting and Auditing Approaches to Inventories in Three Nations: Stock in Trade and Work in Progress in Canada, the United Kingdom and the United States: a survey*, Accountants International Study Group, Institute of Chartered Accountants in England and Wales, January 1968.
6 IASC, *Preface to Statements of International Accounting Standards*, para. 2.
7 IASC, *Shaping IASC for the future: A Discussion Paper issued for comment by the Strategy Working Party of the International Accounting Standards Committee*, IASC, 7 December 1998, para. 2.
8 At the time of its dissolution on 1 April 2001, the IASC Board members were: Australia, Canada, France, Germany, India, Japan, Malaysia, Mexico, Netherlands, Nordic Federation of Public Accountants, South Africa, United Kingdom, United States of America and representatives of the International Council of Investment Associations (ICIA), the Federation of Swiss Industrial Holding Companies and the International Association of Financial Executives Institutes (IAFEI). The Indian delegation included a representative from Sri Lanka and the South African delegation included a representative from Zimbabwe. Representatives of the European Commission, the United States Financial Accounting Standards Board (FASB), the International Organisation of Securities Commissions (IOSCO), and the People's Republic of China attended Board meetings as observers.
9 IOSCO Annual Report 2006.
10 IASC Board and IOSCO Technical Committee, *Joint Press Release*, Paris, July 9, 1995.
11 *The IASC-U.S. Comparison Project: A Report on the Similarities and Differences between IASC Standards and U.S. GAAP*, FASB, November 1996.
12 U.S. Securities And Exchange Commission, *SEC Concept Release: International Accounting Standards*, Release Nos. 33-7801, 34-42430; International Series No. 1215 Washington, 18 February 2000.
13 IOSCO, Report of the Technical Committee of the International Organisation of Securities Commissions, *IASC Standards – Assessment Report*, May 2000.
14 Press Release, *SEC Takes Action to Improve Consistency of Disclosure to U.S. Investors in Foreign Companies*, U.S. Securities and Exchange Commission, 2007-235, November 15, 2007. The SEC's reference to IFRS as issued by the IASB is significant, as it excludes those versions of IFRS that contain 'local variations' to the official IASB text of IFRS.
15 IASC, *Shaping IASC for the future: A Discussion Paper issued for comment by the Strategy Working*

Party of the International Accounting Standards Committee, IASC, 7 December 1998, para. 2.

16 IASC, *Shaping IASC for the future: A Discussion Paper issued for comment by the Strategy Working Party of the International Accounting Standards Committee*, para. 115 *et seq.*

17 The G4+1 was an informal grouping of staff members of the standard-setting bodies of Australia, Canada, New Zealand, the United Kingdom, the United States of America and the IASC. From time to time, the G4+1 published position papers on accounting topics of current interest. These papers did not necessarily reflect the official views of any of the standard-setting bodies represented. At a meeting of the G4+1 held in January 2001, the Group discussed whether its activities should continue given the imminent commencement of activities by the new International Accounting Standards Board (IASB) and agreed to disband and cancel its planned future activities.

18 Report of the IASC's Strategy Working Party, *Recommendations on shaping IASC for the future*, November 1999.

19 IASC Foundation Constitution, approved by the Members of IASC at a meeting in Edinburgh, Scotland on 24 May 2000 and revised by the IASC Foundation Trustees on 5 March 2002, 8 July 2002, 21 June 2005, 31 October 2007 and 15 January 2009.

20 IASC Foundation Constitution, Article 6.

21 IASC Foundation Constitution, Article 8. To provide continuity, some of the initial Trustees served staggered terms so as to retire after four or five years.

22 IASC Foundation Constitution, Article 7.

23 IASC Foundation Constitution, Article 6.

24 IASC Foundation Constitution, Article 15(b).

25 IASC Foundation Constitution, Articles 13 and 15.

26 The IASC Foundation structure is taken from 'Who we are and what we do' available on the IASB website at: www.iasb.org/About+Us.htm

27 As part of the governance arrangements of the IASCF, the original Constitution required that the Trustees of the IASC Foundation should undertake a review of the entire structure of the IASC Foundation and its effectiveness. The Constitution specified that this review should commence three years after the coming into force of the Constitution, with the objective of implementing any agreed changes five years after the coming into force of the Constitution (i.e. 6 February 2006).

At a meeting on 4 November 2003, the Trustees discussed the need to consult interested parties on the full range of issues raised by the Constitution, and agreed on various aspects of the review, including the procedures for conducting the review, the extent of consultation, staffing, and the issues to be discussed. On 12 November 2003, the Trustees announced that they had initiated a review of the Foundation's constitutional arrangements that govern the operating procedures of the Foundation and the IASB. In launching this, the Trustees emphasised that they were willing to examine any aspect of the Constitution and would be consulting a wide range of organisations. To coordinate the process, the Trustees established an internal committee (the 'Constitution Committee'), chaired by Paul Volcker.

Following extensive consultation, the Trustees completed the review in June 2005, and published a revised Constitution with an effective date of 1 July 2005. The Constitution was further revised in October 2007 and January 2009.

28 IASC Foundation Constitution, Article 17.

29 IASC Foundation Constitution, Article 36.

30 IASC Foundation Constitution, Article 27.

31 IASC Foundation Constitution, Article 2.

32 International Accounting Standards Committee Foundation, Press Release, *Trustees announce strategy to enhance governance, report on conclusions at Trustees' meeting*, 6 November 2007.

33 International Accounting Standards Committee Foundation, Press Release, *Trustees announce strategy to enhance governance, report on conclusions at Trustees' meeting*, pages 1 and 2.

34 Review of the Constitution, IASCF, July 2008, para. 12

35 IASC Foundation Constitution, Article 18.

36 IASC Foundation Constitution, Article 19.

37 IASC Foundation Constitution, Article 21.

38 Charter of the IASCF Monitoring Board.

39 Monitoring Board Memorandum of Understanding para. 9B.

40 IASC Foundation Constitution, Article 24.

41 IASC Foundation Constitution, Article 25.

42 IASC Foundation Constitution, Article 27.

43 IASC Foundation Constitution, Article 28.

44 IASC Foundation Constitution, Article 26.

45 IASC Foundation Constitution, Article 37(a).

46 IASC Foundation Constitution, Article 36.

47 IASC Foundation Constitution, Article 36.

48 IASC Foundation Constitution, Article 37(d)(iii).
49 Due Process Handbook for the IASB, Approved by the Trustees March 2006, paras. 1 to 3.
50 Due Process Handbook for the IASB, para. 9.
51 Due Process Handbook for the IASB, para. 6.
52 Due Process Handbook for the IASB, paras. 18 to 51.
53 Due Process Handbook for the IASB, para. 110.
54 Due Process Handbook for the IASB, para. 111.
55 Due Process Handbook for the IASB, para. 112.
56 IASC Foundation Constitution, Article 44.
57 IASC Foundation Constitution, Article 45.
58 IASC Foundation Constitution, Article 45.
59 IASC Foundation Constitution, Article 46.
60 Due Process Handbook for the International Financial Reporting Interpretations Committee, International Accounting Standards Committee Foundation, February 2007, para. 2.
61 Due Process Handbook for the International Financial Reporting Interpretations Committee, para. 5.
62 Due Process Handbook for the International Financial Reporting Interpretations Committee, paras. 17 to 43.
63 Due Process Handbook for the International Financial Reporting Interpretations Committee, paras. 44 to 46.
64 Statement by the Board of the International Accounting Standards Committee, December 2000.
65 IASB Press Release, *International Accounting Standards Board issues wide-ranging improvements to Standards*, 18 December 2003.
66 Chartered Accountants of Canada, Media Release, *Canada's Accounting Standards Board ratifies its strategic plan: Approves convergence with international reporting standards*, Toronto, January 10, 2006.
67 The Joint Working Group of Standard Setters comprised representatives from the IASC, the FASB and eight other international bodies. The purpose of the Group was to develop an integrated and harmonised standard on financial instruments – a task that they were unable to complete.
68 FASB and IASB joint Press Release, *FASB and IASB Agree to Work Together toward Convergence of Global Accounting Standards*, London, 29 October 2002.
69 Memorandum of Understanding – the Norwalk Agreement.
70 Memorandum of Understanding – the Norwalk Agreement.
71 Memorandum of Understanding – the Norwalk Agreement.
72 U.S. Securities and Exchange Commission, Chairman Donaldson Meets with EU Internal Market Commissioner McCreevy, Washington, D.C., April 21, 2005.
73 U.S. Securities and Exchange Commission, Accounting Standards: SEC Chairman Cox and EU Commissioner McCreevy Affirm Commitment to Elimination of the Need for Reconciliation Requirements, Washington, D.C., Feb. 8, 2006.
74 See FASB and IASB Press Release: 'US FASB and IASB reaffirm commitment to enhance consistency, comparability and efficiency in global capital markets', 27 February 2006 and 'A Roadmap for Convergence between IFRSs and US GAAP – 2006-2008: Memorandum of Understanding between the FASB and the IASB', 27 February 2006.
75 *IASB Update*, April 2008.
76 Securities and Exchange Commission, 17 CFR Parts 210, 230, 239 and 249, [Release Nos. 33-8818; 34-55998; International Series Release No. 1302; File No. S7-13-07], RIN 3235-AJ90, *Acceptance from Foreign Private Issuers of financial statements prepared in accordance with International Financial Reporting Standards without reconciliation to U.S. GAAP*.
77 Press Release, *SEC Takes Action to Improve Consistency of Disclosure to U.S. Investors in Foreign Companies*, U.S. Securities and Exchange Commission, 2007-235, November 15, 2007.
78 Securities and Exchange Commission, 17 CFR Parts 210, 230, 239 and 249, [Release Nos. 33-8818; 34-55998; International Series Release No. 1302; File No. S7-13-07], RIN 3235-AJ90, *Acceptance from Foreign Private Issuers of financial statements prepared in accordance with International Financial Reporting Standards without reconciliation to U.S. GAAP*, page 39.
79 Press Release, *SEC Takes Action to Improve Consistency of Disclosure to U.S. Investors in Foreign Companies*, U.S. Securities and Exchange Commission, 2007-235, November 15, 2007.
80 Securities and Exchange Commission, 17 CFR Parts 210, 230, 239 and 249, [Release Nos. 33-8818; 34-55998; International Series Release No. 1302; File No. S7-13-07], RIN 3235-AJ90, *Acceptance from Foreign Private Issuers of financial statements prepared in accordance with International Financial Reporting Standards without reconciliation to U.S. GAAP*, page 39.

81 Securities and Exchange Commission, 17 CFR Parts 210, 230, 239 and 249, [Release Nos. 33-8818; 34-55998; International Series Release No. 1302; File No. S7-13-07], RIN 3235-AJ90, *Acceptance from Foreign Private Issuers of financial statements prepared in accordance with International Financial Reporting Standards without reconciliation to U.S. GAAP*, pages 39 and 40.

82 Securities and Exchange Commission, 17 CFR Parts 210, 228, 229, 230, 239, 240 and 249 [Release No. 33-8831; 34-56217; IC-27924; File No. S7-20-07] RIN 3235-AJ93, Concept Release on allowing U.S. issuers to prepare financial statements in accordance with International Financial Reporting Standards, August 7, 2007. The comment date of this Concept Release was 13 November 2007.

83 Securities and Exchange Commission, 17 CFR Parts 210, 228, 229, 230, 239, 240 and 249 [Release No. 33-8831; 34-56217; IC-27924; File No. S7-20-07] RIN 3235-AJ93, Concept Release on allowing U.S. issuers to prepare financial statements in accordance with International Financial Reporting Standards, pages 12 and 13.

84 Prepared on the basis of: *IASB Work Plan – projected timetable as at 1 August 2009.*

85 IAS 1, *Presentation of financial statements*, IASB.

86 IAS 1, para. 16.

87 IAS 1, para. 16.

88 IAS 1, para. 15.

89 IAS 1, para. 17.

90 IAS 1, para. 17.

91 IAS 1, para. 18.

92 IAS 1, para. 19.

93 IAS 1, para. 20.

94 IAS 1, para. 21.

95 IAS 1, para. 23.

96 IAS 1, para. 18.

97 Study Pursuant to Section 108(d) of the Sarbanes-Oxley Act of 2002 on the Adoption by the United States Financial Reporting System of a Principles-Based Accounting System. Submitted to Committee on Banking, Housing, and Urban Affairs of the United States Senate and Committee on Financial Services of the United States House of Representatives, Office of the Chief Accountant Office of Economic Analysis United States Securities and Exchange Commission, Section III. Components of Objectives-Oriented Standard Setting, G. No True and Fair Override

98 Fourth Council Directive 78/660/EEC of 25 July 1978 based on Article 54 (3) (g) of the Treaty on the annual accounts of certain types of companies; Seventh Council Directive 83/349/EEC of 13 June 1983 based on the Article 54 (3) (g) of the Treaty on consolidated accounts.

99 Communication from the European Commission, *Accounting harmonisation: a new strategy vis-à-vis international harmonisation*, 1995.

100 See for example, European Commission, *Examination of the conformity between International Accounting Standards applicable to accounting periods beginning before 1 July 1999 and the European Accounting Directives*, February 2000; European Commission, *Examination of the Conformity between SIC-1 to SIC-25 and the European Accounting Directives*, February 2001. The full set of these comparisons may be found on the EC website: http://europa.eu.int/comm/internal_market/en/company/account/index.htm

101 European Commission, COM(1999) 232 final of 11.05.1999, *Financial Services: Implementing the Framework for Financial Markets: Action Plan*, May 1999.

102 European Commission, *EU Financial Reporting Strategy: the way forward*, June 2000.

103 European Union, *Directive of the European Parliament and of the Council amending Directives 78/660/EEC, 83/349/EEC and 86/635/EEC as regards the valuation rules for the annual accounts and consolidated accounts of certain types of companies as well as of banks and other financial institutions*, PE-CONS 3624/01, Brussels, 22 May 2001.

104 Directive 2006/46/EC of the European Parliament and of the Council of 14 June 2006 amending Council Directives 78/660/EEC on the annual accounts of certain types of companies, 83/349/EEC on consolidated accounts, 86/635/EEC on the annual accounts and consolidated accounts of banks and other financial institutions and 91/674/EEC on the annual accounts and consolidated accounts of insurance undertakings.

105 European Commission, *Proposal for a Regulation of the Parliament and of the Council on the Application of International Accounting Standards*, COM(2001) 80, February 2001.

106 This means those with their securities admitted to trading on a regulated market within the meaning of Article 1(13) of Council Directive 93/22/EEC (on investment services in the securities field) or those offered to the public in view of their

admission to such trading under Council Directive 80/390/EEC (co-ordinating the requirements for the drawing up, scrutiny and distribution of the listing particulars to be published for the admission of securities to official stock exchange listing).

107 European Union, *Regulation of the European Parliament and of the Council on the application of international accounting standards*, Regulation No. 1606/2002, 19 July 2002.

108 EU IAS Regulation, Recital 11.

109 EU IAS Regulation, Article 3.

110 The term 'comitology' is essentially jargon meaning 'committee procedure'. It describes a process under which the European Commission, when implementing EU law, has to consult special advisory committees made up of experts from the EU Member States.

111 EFRAG, User Panel: Terms of Reference, 20 August 2006.

112 www.efrag.org/content/default.asp?id=4109

113 European Commission, Accounting: new Commission expert group to ensure balanced advice on accounting standards, Brussels, 17 July 2006.

114 European Commission Internal Market and Services DG, 'Consistent IFRS application: Roundtable'.

115 EECS refers to 'European Enforcers Coordination Sessions', which includes CESR members and non-CESR members who have competences in the enforcement of compliance with IFRS.

116 Commission of the European Communities, *Establishing the Committee of European Securities Regulators*, Commission Decision of 6 June 2001.

117 The Lamfalussy Report, *Final Report of the Committee of Wise Men on The Regulation of European Securities Markets*, Brussels, 15 February 2001.

118 The Committee of European Securities Regulators, *Charter of the Committee of European Securities Regulators*. The Charter took effect on 11 September 2001, and was amended in July 2006.

119 The Committee of European Securities Regulators, Terms of Reference on the Organisation and Functioning of CESR-Fin, 17 May 2006, para. 1.

120 The Committee of European Securities Regulators, Standard No. 1 on Financial Information: *Enforcement of standards on financial information in Europe*, CESR/03-073, 12 March 2003.

121 CESR Standard No.1, Principles 11 to 13.

122 CESR Standard No.1, Principle 16.

123 CESR Standard No.1, Principle 21.

124 The Committee of European Securities Regulators, Standard No. 2, *Co-ordination of Enforcement Activities*, CESR/03-317c, 22 April 2004.

125 US Securities and Exchange Commission: SEC and CESR Launch Work Plan Focused on Financial Reporting: Developing Cross Atlantic Financial Markets, Washington, D.C., Aug. 2, 2006.

126 Brazilian Central Bank, Communication 14.259/06.

127 Press Release, *The ASBJ and the IASB announce Tokyo Agreement on achieving convergence of accounting standards by 2011*, IASB, 8 August 2007.

128 International Accounting Standards Board, Press Release, *ASBJ and IASB make continued progress towards goal of convergence in accounting standards by 2011*, 2 October 2007.

129 The South African Institute of Chartered Accountants, *Headline Earnings*, Circular 8/2007, July 2007. 'Headline earnings' is an additional earnings number that is permitted by IAS 33. The starting point is earnings as determined in IAS 33, excluding certain '*separately identifiable re-measurements*', net of related tax (both current and deferred) and minority interest. An example of an item that would be excluded in the calculation of headline earnings is any impairment and subsequent reversal of an impairment covered by IAS 36.

130 This section draws heavily from 'Rules Not Principles – A Question of Judgement', The Institute of Chartered Accountants of Scotland, April 2006. This document was published by the Technical Policy Board of The Institute of Chartered Accountants of Scotland (ICAS). The views expressed in this document are those of the members of the Principles versus Rules Working Group and do not necessarily represent the views of the Board or of the Council of the Institute.

131 This example is taken from The Institute of Chartered Accountants of Scotland, 'Rules Not Principles – A Question of Judgement', page 6.

132 A view expressed also by The Institute of Chartered Accountants of Scotland in 'Rules Not Principles – A Question of Judgement', page 5.

133 *Study Pursuant to Section 108(d) of the Sarbanes-Oxley Act of 2002 on the Adoption by the United States Financial Reporting System of a Principles-Based Accounting System.* Submitted to

Committee on Banking, Housing, and Urban Affairs of the United States Senate and Committee on Financial Services of the United States House of Representatives, Office of the Chief Accountant Office of Economic Analysis United States Securities and Exchange Commission, Executive Summary.

134 *Study Pursuant to Section 108(d) of the Sarbanes-Oxley Act of 2002 on the Adoption by the United States Financial Reporting System of a Principles-Based Accounting System.* Submitted to Committee on Banking, Housing, and Urban Affairs of the United States Senate and Committee on Financial Services of the United States House of Representatives, Office of the Chief Accountant Office of Economic Analysis United States Securities and Exchange Commission, Section V, Economic and Policy Analysis: H Comparability Issues.

135 See, for example, The Institute of Chartered Accountants of Scotland, 'Rules Not Principles – A Question of Judgement', page 10.

136 This is one of the 10 recommendations of The Institute of Chartered Accountants of Scotland, 'Rules Not Principles – A Question of Judgement', page 3.

Chapter 2

The quest for a conceptual framework for financial reporting

1 INTRODUCTION

There have been numerous attempts over many decades to define the purpose and nature of accounting. These are to be found in countless writings on accounting theory, the authors of which have considered many of the conceptual issues that require resolution in the development of a conceptual framework for financial reporting. Perhaps not surprisingly, most of the earlier studies were carried out by individual academics and academic committees in the US; for example, the writings in 1940 of Paton and Littleton[1] were intended to present a framework of accounting theory that would be regarded as a coherent and consistent foundation for the development of accounting standards, whilst the studies carried out over the years by various committees of the American Accounting Association have made a significant contribution to accounting theory.[2] In addition to the research carried out by individuals and academic committees, professional accounting bodies around the world have also, from time to time, issued statements that deal with various aspects of accounting theory. These can be seen as the first attempts at developing some form of conceptual framework, some of which are discussed later in this chapter.

However, the position today is very different from that which existed even ten years ago: with the globalisation of business and the increased access to the world's capital markets that goes with it, there are essentially only two global-scale systems of financial reporting – IFRS and US GAAP. As these two systems converge, it is logical to think that the development of a single agreed conceptual framework is a precondition for the convergence of the two systems. Whilst discussing the many international endeavours undertaken over the past 50 years in the quest for a conceptual framework for financial reporting, this chapter focuses on the existing conceptual frameworks of the IASB and FASB, as well as their joint project currently under way to develop a single agreed conceptual framework for global financial reporting.

1.1   What is a conceptual framework?

In general terms, a conceptual framework is a statement of generally accepted theoretical principles which form the frame of reference for a particular field of enquiry. In terms of financial reporting, these theoretical principles provide the basis for both the development of new reporting practices and the evaluation of existing ones. Since the financial reporting process is concerned with the provision of information that is useful in making business and economic decisions, a conceptual framework will form the theoretical basis for determining which events should be accounted for, how they should be measured and how they should be communicated to the user. Therefore, although it is theoretical in nature, a conceptual framework for financial reporting has a highly practical end in view.

1.2   Why is a conceptual framework necessary?

A conceptual framework for financial reporting should therefore be a theory of accounting against which practical problems can be tested objectively, the utility of which is decided by the adequacy of the practical solutions it provides. However, the various standard-setting bodies around the world initially often attempted to resolve practical accounting and reporting problems through the development of accounting standards, without such an accepted theoretical frame of reference. The end result was that standard-setters determined the form and content of external financial reports, without resolving such fundamental issues as:

- what are the objectives of these reports?
- who are the users of these reports?
- what are the informational needs of these users?
- what types of report will best satisfy their needs?

Consequently, standards were often produced on a haphazard and 'fire-fighting' basis with the danger of mutual inconsistencies. On the other hand, if an agreed framework were to exist, the role of the standard-setters would be changed from that of fireman to that of architect, as the framework would provide them with a basis for designing external financial reports that meet the needs of the user.

Perhaps the word 'agreed' is the key qualification in this argument. The IASB's conceptual framework was clearly derived from the FASB framework, which was developed much earlier. Not surprisingly therefore, the IASB framework (although substantially less detailed) has many aspects in common with the FASB equivalent. The resulting underlying similarity between the FASB and IASB conceptual frameworks is explained within this chapter. However, the way these principles are translated into detailed rules within the accounting standards issued by each of the standard-setters can result in very different financial reports.[3]

Furthermore, the existence of a given conceptual framework can be used as a lever to alter the basis of actual financial reporting towards the type of measurement base chosen in that framework – the full implications of which may not be understood by accountants generally.

Equally, experience of the last thirty years shows that, in the absence of an agreed comprehensive conceptual framework, the same theoretical issues are revisited on numerous occasions by different standard-setting working parties. This inevitably sometimes resulted in the development of standards that were internally inconsistent and inconsistent with each other, or which were founded on incompatible concepts. For example, inconsistencies and conflicts have existed between and within individual standards concerning the emphasis placed on substance versus form; matching versus prudence; and whether earnings should be determined through balance sheet measurements or by matching costs and revenue. Some standard-setters have permitted two or more methods of accounting for the same set of circumstances, whilst others permitted certain accounting practices to be followed on an arbitrary or unspecified basis. These inconsistencies and irrationalities perhaps reflect the difficulty of determining what is 'true and fair'.

There have been differences also in the tactics adopted by standard setters concerning how the tenets of a conceptual framework become realised in actual financial reports. There are significant differences between the tactics adopted by the FASB on the one hand, and the IASB on the other. In the US the FASB, in spite of its pioneering work on a conceptual framework, has also produced a large number of highly detailed accounting rules. Clearly, the proliferation of accounting standards in the US stems from many factors, including the legal and regulatory environment; however, a more satisfactory conceptual framework might reduce the need for such a large number of highly detailed standards, since more emphasis could be placed on general principles rather than specific rules. Indeed this change of emphasis has been specifically considered by the US authorities following the reporting problems that led to the creation of the Sarbanes-Oxley Act and the setting up of the Public Company Accounting Oversight Board in the US. This is not to say that the more 'general principles' based IASB approach to standard setting is necessarily more satisfactory than the FASB's; rather that the legal and regulatory environment within which non-US businesses habitually work is quite different from that of the USA.

The political and economic environment not only influences the approach taken to standard setting, but also the nature of the conceptual framework on which standards are based. Following the European Union's decision to require listed entities to apply adopted IFRS in their consolidated financial statements and the widespread incorporation of IFRS into the national GAAPs of many other countries, the IASB is faced with a considerable number and variety of stakeholders. These different stakeholders are likely to express differing views on proposals issued by the IASB and will certainly want their views to be taken into account. Under these circumstances, an agreed conceptual framework is of great value, though standard-setters' best bulwark against undue interference in the standard-setting process is the capital markets' need for financial reporting that is a sound basis for decision making, which in turn implies relevance, reliability, practicality and understandability. While it is probable that these characteristics are more likely to be achieved using a sound theoretical foundation, the converse also applies: namely that the framework must result in standards that account appropriately for actual business practice and economic reality. Otherwise how, for example, is an industry to be persuaded that a particular accounting treatment perceived as adversely affecting its economic interests is better than one which does not?[4]

An agreed framework is therefore not the panacea for all accounting problems. Nor does it obviate the need for judgement to be exercised in the process of resolving accounting issues. What it can provide is a framework within which those judgements can be made. Indeed this is happening, as the principles expressed in the IASB's *Framework for the Preparation and Presentation of Financial Statements* are frequently referred to in IFRSs and during the process of their development. Unfortunately there is clear evidence also of the IASB issuing standards that contravene its own conceptual framework. For example IAS 38 – *Intangible Assets* – requires the capitalisation of goodwill as an asset, despite the fact that goodwill does not meet the definition of an asset in the IASB's conceptual framework. Similarly IAS 12 – *Income Taxes* – requires recognition of deferred tax assets and liabilities that do not meet the asset and liability definitions under the framework.

As discussed more fully in section 5 of this chapter, the IASB and the FASB are currently engaged in the development of a new joint conceptual framework.

1.3   Accounting and the globalisation of economic activity

A further dimension to any consideration of the development of a conceptual framework must be the economic background to this process. Globalisation – the global interdependence, cultural homogeneity, integration of ownership and use, and depersonalisation of economic assets – is a term now frequently used, when even a decade ago it was relatively rare. The process of globalisation has been happening for centuries if not millennia – arguably since the first empires started to spread their core cultural and economic systems. However, it has now become obvious that since the 1960s the huge growth in telecommunications; the ease, speed and low cost of physical travel; the economic growth experienced by many countries throughout the world together with the spread of the 'western' business culture, has resulted in globalisation on an unprecedented scale.

Financial reporting has not been insulated from this process. As discussed below, during the last fifty years the development of a conceptual framework has increasingly preoccupied standard-setting bodies. To start with, these were mainly single-country initiatives, the first modern work being undertaken in the US in the 1970s and 80s. The FASB framework subsequently formed the basis of the framework developed by the former board of the IASC (which was adopted in 2001 by the IASB), as well as the frameworks of various national standard-setters, such as those of the UK, Canada, Australia and New Zealand.

Reflecting economic globalisation, the world now finds itself with only two principal sets of accounting standards: IFRS and US GAAP, a state of affairs that seemed unlikely even 10 years ago. With the benefit of hindsight it seems obvious that globalisation would require harmonisation of financial reporting; nevertheless the speed with which it has occurred has been remarkable, greatly assisted by the European Union's bold decision to harmonise financial reporting for listed EU entities under the IFRS umbrella. Furthermore, the integration process has not stopped, as in September 2002 the FASB and the IASB signed the Norwalk Agreement that commits both standard setters further to converge and harmonise their respective regimes. Since that time a number of IASB standards have indeed been (or are in the process of being) altered to align them with their US equivalents and similarly changes have been made to FASB statements. The objectives and principles of the Norwalk Agreement have since been re-affirmed and elaborated upon in a Memorandum of Understanding that was entered into by the IASB and the FASB in February 2006 which was in turn further updated in 2008 (see Chapter 1 at 3.3.3).

These developments illustrate the paradoxical nature of the search for a conceptual framework. The idea of a framework is to have a set of principles that guide the detailed requirements of individual standards, yet those principles are influenced by practical global economic and political reality. Ultimately, economic forces and the needs of the capital markets for useful information will be the context in which standard-setters operate. Arguably, their frameworks, or even as seems possible now, their framework, will always be as much practice into theory, as the reverse.

2   THE DEVELOPMENT OF A US CONCEPTUAL FRAMEWORK

2.1   Accounting Research Studies

The Accounting Principles Board (APB) of the American Institute of Certified Public Accountants (AICPA) was formed in 1959 to replace the former Committee on Accounting Procedure and the Committee on Terminology. During its existence, the Committee on Accounting Procedure had issued a series of Accounting Research Bulletins (ARBs). In 1953, the first 42 ARBs (eight of which dealt solely with terminology) were revised and restated as a consolidated ARB No. 43 and Accounting Terminology Bulletin No. 1; thereafter, a further eight ARBs were issued. The ARBs were supposedly aimed at the development of generally accepted accounting principles; however, the Committee met with considerable criticism over its failure to deal with contemporary accounting issues (such as leasing and business combinations), which could not be solved from precedents and required the development of accounting principles through pure accounting research.

As a direct response to this, the President of the AICPA set up the Special Committee on Research Program in 1957; in 1958 the Committee recommended the formation of the APB, and the appointment of a director of research with a permanent research staff. The Special Committee also recommended that 'an immediate project of the accounting research staff should be a study of the basic postulates underlying accounting principles generally, and the preparation of a brief statement thereof. There should be also a study of the broad principles of accounting. ... The results of these, as adopted by the [Accounting Principles] Board, should serve as the foundation for the entire body of future pronouncements by the Institute on accounting matters, to which each new release should be related.'[5]

This, therefore, was probably the first mandate given by a professional body for the development of a conceptual framework. The AICPA appointed Maurice Moonitz as its first Director of Accounting Research; Moonitz started work on the postulates study, and appointed Robert Sprouse to work with him on the study of broad accounting principles. The products of the research were contained in Accounting Research Study No. 1 – *The Basic Postulates of Accounting*[6] – and Accounting Research Study No. 3 – *A Tentative Set of Broad Accounting Principles for Business Enterprises* – which were published in 1961 and 1962 respectively.[7]

These studies, however, caused a storm of controversy. Instead of establishing a sound foundation of accounting theory through rigorous argument based on deductive reasoning, Moonitz and Sprouse attempted to persuade the accounting profession to accept a new system of financial reporting based on current values. Furthermore, the realisation principle was discarded on the basis of the assertion that 'profit is attributable to the whole process of business activity, not just to the moment of sale.'[8] This was reflected, for example, in the statement that 'inventories which are readily saleable at known prices with negligible costs of disposal, or with known or readily predictable costs of disposal, should be measured at net realizable value.'[9]

However, the criticism that was levelled at these studies appeared to be based more on the fear of the unknown, rather than on any intellectual shortcomings. Consequently, they were viewed as being too radically different from contemporary generally accepted accounting practice to be accepted, and were rejected by the APB. This resulted in the commissioning of Grady's Accounting Research Study No. 7 – *Inventory of Generally Accepted Accounting Principles for Business Enterprises* – which was published in 1965 and which catalogued the various accounting methods that had been approved by ARBs, APB Opinions or some other precedent.

In all, 15 Accounting Research Studies were published during the life of the APB. However, following the rejection of ARS Nos. 1 and 3, the studies tended to be carried out on an ad hoc basis and without the support of a common foundation. Furthermore, the recommendations contained in the research studies appeared to have been largely ignored in the drafting of the 31 Opinions that the APB issued between 1962 and 1973. Consequently, generally accepted accounting principles in the US were continuing to be formulated without the benefit of research or the foundation of an agreed theoretical framework and, to all intents and purposes, the APB slowly resorted to the position of its predecessor, the Committee on Accounting Procedure.

2.2   APB Statement No. 4

In 1965 the APB made a further attempt to provide a basis for guiding the future development of accounting by establishing a committee to carry out a study that could be used as a basis for understanding the broad fundamentals of accounting. In 1970, the APB approved Statement No. 4 – *Basic Concepts and Accounting Principles Underlying Financial Statements of Business Enterprises*.[10] The statement contained a description of (1) the environment of financial accounting, (2) the objectives of financial statements, (3) the basic features and basic elements of financial accounting and (4) a summary of existing generally accepted accounting principles.

Therefore, it was (on its own admission)[11] a descriptive statement, not prescriptive. For example, assets and liabilities were defined as economic resources and obligations 'that are recognised and measured in conformity with generally accepted accounting principles',[12] which meant that the definitions failed to provide a theoretical basis for the development of generally accepted principles. As a result APB No. 4 was deficient as a theory of accounting and did not respond to the problems that were facing the profession at the time and which had been brought about by the inconsistencies and inadequacies of financial reporting practice.

2.3   The Wheat and Trueblood Committees

In 1971, in response to continued criticism from both within the profession and from the SEC about its inability to establish sound accounting principles, the AICPA announced the formation of two study groups: the *Study Group on Establishment of Accounting Principles*, to be chaired by Francis Wheat, and the *Study Group on Objectives of Financial Statements*, to be chaired by Robert Trueblood. The Wheat Committee published its report in 1972, resulting in the establishment of the Financial Accounting Standards Board (FASB) in 1973 as the successor to the APB. This had the effect of taking the responsibility for setting accounting standards away from the accounting profession and placing it in the hands of an independent body in the private sector. The FASB comprised seven members appointed by the Financial Accounting Foundation (FAF), and was funded by the sale of publications and from contributions made to the FAF. The Board of Trustees of the FAF was appointed by its eight sponsoring organisations, which include, inter alia, the American Accounting Association, the AICPA and two organisations which represent government.

The study carried out by the Trueblood Committee represents the next significant step in the attempt to develop a conceptual framework. In setting the terms of reference of the study group, the Board of Directors of the AICPA stated that the main purpose of the study was 'to refine the objectives of financial statements'.[13] They went on to suggest that APB Statement No. 4 would be a logical starting point for the study, whilst at the same time noting that APB 4 'contains objectives in terms of what is considered acceptable today rather than in terms of what is needed and what is attainable to meet these needs.'[14] The study group was asked to consider at least the following questions:

- Who needs financial statements?
- What information do they need?
- How much of the needed information can be provided by accounting?
- What framework is required to provide the needed information?[15]

The Trueblood Report[16] was published in October 1973 and developed twelve objectives of financial statements. The principal objective was stated in the following terms: 'the basic objective of financial statements is to provide information useful for making economic decisions.'[17] Having established its twelve objectives of financial statements, the report then discussed seven qualitative characteristics which information contained in financial statements should possess in order to satisfy the needs of users.[18] As will be seen below, the Trueblood Report's objectives of financial statements formed the basis for the development of the FASB's first concepts statement, whilst the qualitative characteristics identified were amongst those discussed in the second concepts statement.

2.4   The FASB conceptual framework

The Trueblood Committee was at work on its report when the FASB came into existence. Consequently, the Trueblood Report was effectively passed on to the FASB for consideration, thus signalling the beginnings of the FASB's Conceptual Framework Project. The FASB duly considered the report and in June 1974 published a Discussion Memorandum – *Conceptual Framework for Accounting and Reporting: Consideration of the Report of the Study Group on the Objectives of Financial Statements* – which asked for comments on the issues raised.[19] A public hearing was held during September 1974, and in December 1976 the FASB published its *Tentative Conclusions on Objectives of Financial Statements of Business Enterprises*. In December 1976 the FASB also published a paper – *Scope and Implications of the Conceptual Framework Project* – which summarised its aims for the project, the expected benefits to be derived and the main areas which were expected to be covered.[20]

Following the criticism and eventual replacement of first the Committee on Accounting Procedure, followed by the APB, the FASB was seen by many commentators to be the last opportunity of keeping accounting standard-setting in the private sector. The FASB was clearly aware that accounting standards had to regain the credibility of public opinion which had been lost as a result of the many perceived abuses of financial reporting during the 1960s. The FASB referred to this lack of public confidence, and the possible consequences thereof, as follows: 'scepticism about financial reporting has adverse effects on businesses, on business leaders, and on the public at large. One of these effects is the risk of imposition of government reporting and other regulatory requirements that are not justified – requirements that are not in the public interest because the perceived benefits do not exist or are more than offset by costly interference with the orderly operation of the economy. Scepticism creates adverse public opinion, which may be the antecedent of unjustified government regulation. Every company, every industry stands to suffer because of scepticism about financial reporting.'[21] The FASB, therefore, saw its conceptual framework project as the means of enhancing the credibility of financial statements in the eyes of the public.

The FASB also recognised that although there had been many attempts by individuals and organisations (such as the American Accounting Association) to develop a theory of accounting, none of these individual theories had become universally accepted or relied on in practice. They therefore expressed a need for a '*constitution*, a coherent system of interrelated objectives and fundamentals that can lead to consistent standards and that prescribes the nature, function, and limits of financial accounting and financial statements.'[22] The conceptual framework was expected to:

(a)   guide the body responsible for establishing standards;

(b)   provide a frame of reference for resolving accounting questions in the absence of a specific promulgated standard;

(c)   determine bounds for judgement in preparing financial statements;

(d)   increase financial statement users' understanding of and confidence in financial statements; and

(e)   enhance comparability.[23]

To date the FASB has issued seven concepts statements, of which one (SFAC No. 4) deals with the objectives of financial reporting by non-business organisations and is beyond the scope of this book, whilst another (SFAC No. 3 – *Elements of Financial Statements of Business Enterprises*) dealt with elements of financial statements by business enterprises, and was superseded by SFAC No. 6 – *Elements of Financial Statements* – which expanded the scope of SFAC No. 3 to encompass not-for-profit organisations. The remaining five are discussed in the sections which follow.

2.5   The objectives of financial reporting

The first phase of the FASB's conceptual framework project was to develop a statement of the objectives of financial reporting. Clearly, some pioneering work in this area had been done by the Trueblood Committee (see 2.3 above), and this formed the basis of the FASB's first concepts statement. Nevertheless, it was not until 1978 that the FASB finally published this statement.

SFAC No. 1 – *Objectives of Financial Reporting by Business Enterprises* – starts off by making the point that financial reporting includes not only financial statements, but also incorporates other means of communicating financial and non-financial information; this may be achieved, for example, through the medium of stock exchange documents, news releases, management forecasts etc.[24] Having said this, the statement stresses that 'financial reporting is not an end in itself but is intended to provide information that is useful in making business and economic decisions.'[25] This, however, is no new revelation; it is the type of broad generalisation that has characterised numerous previous attempts at establishing a conceptual framework. On the other hand, what it does do is raise all the same issues which the Trueblood Committee had been asked to consider seven years previously, such as: For whom is this information intended? What types of 'business and economic decisions' do they make? What information do they need to enable them to make these decisions? What framework is required to provide this needed information?

The statement details an extensive list of potential users, distinguishing between those with a direct interest and those with an indirect interest in the information provided by financial reporting.[26] The groups of user which have a direct interest include owners, management, creditors and employees; whilst user groups such as financial analysts and advisers, journalists, regulatory authorities and trade unions are deemed to have an indirect interest, since they advise or represent those who have a direct interest. However, having identified this wide range of users, the statement focuses on the information needs of investors and creditors. These are encompassed in the first of three primary objectives identified in the statement: 'financial reporting should provide information that is useful to present and potential investors and creditors and other users in making rational investment, credit, and similar decisions.'[27]

This objective leads to the first of the two most significant and far-reaching conclusions in the statement, namely that 'financial reporting should provide information to help investors, creditors, and others assess the amounts, timing, and uncertainty of prospective net cash inflows to the related enterprise.'[28] The statement articulated its reasoning behind this conclusion as follows: 'Potential users of financial information most directly concerned with a particular business enterprise are generally interested in its ability to generate favourable cash flows, because their decisions relate to amounts, timing, and uncertainties of expected cash flows. To investors, lenders, suppliers, and employees, a business enterprise is a source of cash in the form of dividends or interest and perhaps appreciated market prices, repayment of borrowing, payment for goods or services, or salaries and wages. They invest cash, goods, or services in an enterprise and expect to obtain sufficient cash in return to make the investment worthwhile. They are directly concerned with the ability of the enterprise to generate favourable cash flows and may also be concerned with how the market's perception of that ability affects the relative prices of its securities. To customers, a business enterprise is a source of goods or services, but only by obtaining sufficient cash to pay for the resources it uses and to meet its other obligations can the enterprise provide those goods or services. To managers, the cash flows of a business enterprise are a significant part of their management responsibilities, including their accountability to directors and owners. Many, if not most, of their decisions have cash flow consequences for the enterprise. Thus, investors, creditors, employees, customers, and managers significantly share a common interest in an enterprise's ability to generate favourable cash flows. Other potential users of financial information share the same interest, derived from investors, creditors, employees, customers, or managers whom they advise or represent or derived from an interest in how those groups (and especially stockholders) are faring.'[29]

In reaching this conclusion, the FASB was aware of the fact that it might precipitate an adverse reaction leading to the possible rejection of the statement through what might have been seen as an objective that would ultimately result in companies being required to present cash flow, management forecast or current value information. The FASB pre-empted this potential adverse reaction by stating that 'the objective focuses on the purpose for which information provided should be useful ... rather than the kinds of information that may be useful for that purpose. The objective neither requires nor prohibits "cash flow information", "current value information", "management forecast information", or any other specific information. Conclusions about "current value information" and "management forecast information" are beyond the scope of this Statement. Paragraphs 42-44 [of SFAC No. 1] note that information about cash receipts and disbursements is not usually considered to be the most useful information for the purposes described in this objective.'[30]

The second fundamental conclusion reached in SFAC No. 1 that has far-reaching implications for the future development of accounting standards is concerned with the primary focus of financial reporting. During the early stages of the development of accounting rules in the first half of this century, the primary focus of financial statements was based on the principle of 'stewardship'. This arose from the fact that the management of an enterprise were primarily seen to be accountable to the owners for safeguarding the assets which had been entrusted to them, leading to a balance sheet emphasis in financial reporting. However, the focus has gradually shifted away from the notion of the balance sheet reporting on the custodianship of assets, to an earnings emphasis based on the principle that the income statement should present 'decision-useful' information. This is encapsulated in the statement in SFAC No. 1 that 'the primary focus of financial reporting is information about an enterprise's performance provided by measures of earnings and its components. Investors, creditors, and others who are concerned with assessing the prospects for enterprise net cash inflows are especially interested in that information.'[31]

SFAC No. 1 still recognises the fact that financial reporting should provide information about how the management of an enterprise has discharged its stewardship responsibility.[32] However, it goes on to say that 'earnings information is commonly the focus for assessing management's stewardship or accountability. Management, owners, and others emphasize enterprise performance or profitability in describing how management has discharged its stewardship accountability.'[33]

In other words, the statement is asserting that the measurement of earnings in the income statement should take precedence over the measurement of assets and liabilities in the balance sheet. This is an important principle which should have had an important impact on the principles laid down in the development of future accounting standards. However, as will be seen below, the FASB's subsequent concepts statements have essentially avoided the issue of how to determine net income. Furthermore, more recent statements issued by the FASB tend to suggest an uncertainty as to whether an earnings or balance sheet approach should be followed (for example, SFAS 109 – *Accounting for Income Taxes* – would appear to view the balance sheet as the primary statement).

This tension between income statement and balance sheet primacy has swayed towards the balance sheet, at least as far as recent IASB standards indicate. As is more fully described at 3 below, the IASB's conceptual framework adopts a balance sheet approach to recognition, whereby all the elements of financial statements are defined in terms of assets and liabilities, with the consequence that income recognition is a function of increases and decreases in net assets rather than the completion of acts of performance.

Consequently, despite the focus of the capital markets on performance measurement, the conceptual underpinning for financial reporting adopted by the FASB and the IASB appears to be focusing principally on the recognition and derecognition of assets and liabilities.

2.6   The qualitative characteristics of accounting information

The FASB's second Concepts Statement – *Qualitative Characteristics of Accounting Information* – examines the characteristics that make accounting information useful to the users of that information. The statement views these characteristics as 'a hierarchy of accounting qualities', which then form the basis for selecting and evaluating information for inclusion in financial reports. The hierarchy is represented in Figure 2.1 below:[34]

Figure 2.1

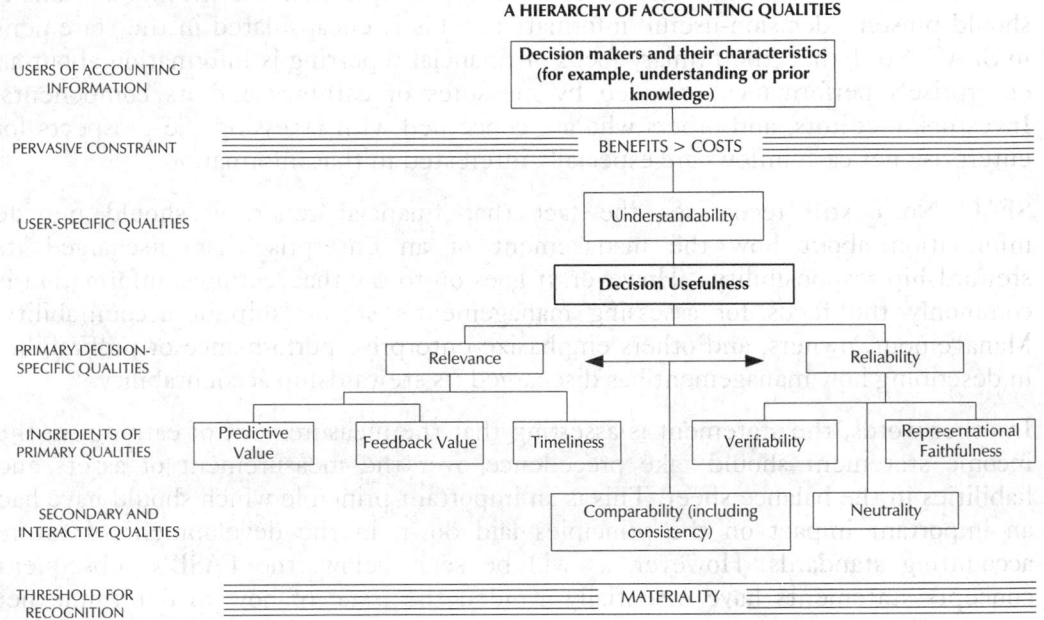

A HIERARCHY OF ACCOUNTING QUALITIES

USERS OF ACCOUNTING INFORMATION — Decision makers and their characteristics (for example, understanding or prior knowledge)

PERVASIVE CONSTRAINT — BENEFITS > COSTS

USER-SPECIFIC QUALITIES — Understandability

Decision Usefulness

PRIMARY DECISION-SPECIFIC QUALITIES — Relevance ↔ Reliability

INGREDIENTS OF PRIMARY QUALITIES — Predictive Value | Feedback Value | Timeliness | Verifiability | Representational Faithfulness

SECONDARY AND INTERACTIVE QUALITIES — Comparability (including consistency) | Neutrality

THRESHOLD FOR RECOGNITION — MATERIALITY

2.6.1   The decision-makers

The decision-makers (users) appear at the top of the hierarchy against the background of their own specific characteristics. Whilst usefulness for decision-making is the most important quality that accounting information should possess, each decision-maker has to judge what information is useful for a specific decision. This judgement would be based on such factors as the nature of the decision to be made, the information already in the individual's possession or available from other sources, the decision-making process employed and the decision maker's capacity to process all the information obtained.

2.6.2   The cost/benefit constraint

Since information should be provided only if the benefits to be derived from that information outweigh the costs of providing it, the cost/benefit constraint pervades the hierarchy. However, the application of this constraint may cause a certain amount of difficulty, since the costs of providing financial information are normally borne by the enterprise (and ultimately passed on to its customers), whilst the users reap the benefits. For this reason, the normal forces of demand and supply will not prevail in the market of financial information, since the external user will almost always view the benefits of additional information as outweighing the costs.

2.6.3 Understandability

The hierarchy depicts understandability as being the key quality for accounting information to achieve 'decision usefulness'. SFAC No. 1 stated that the information provided by financial reporting 'should be comprehensible to those who have a reasonable understanding of business and economic activities and are willing to study the information with reasonable diligence.'[35] Information, whilst it may be relevant, will be wasted if it is provided in a form which cannot be understood by the users for whom it was intended. SFAC No. 1 elaborated on the relationship between useful information and understandability as follows: 'financial information is a tool and, like most tools, cannot be of much direct help to those who are unable or unwilling to use it or who misuse it. Its use can be learned, however, and financial reporting should provide information that can be used by all – non-professionals as well as professionals – who are willing to learn to use it properly. Efforts may be needed to increase the understandability of financial information. Cost-benefit considerations may indicate that information understood or used by only a few should not be provided. Conversely, financial reporting should not exclude relevant information merely because it is difficult for some to understand or because some investors or creditors choose not to use it.'[36]

2.6.4 Relevance and reliability

The qualities that distinguish 'better' (more useful) information from 'inferior' (less useful) information are primarily the qualities of relevance and reliability, with some other characteristics that those qualities imply. SFAC No. 2 identifies relevance and reliability as 'the two primary qualities that make accounting information useful for decision making. Subject to constraints imposed by cost and materiality, increased relevance and increased reliability are the characteristics that make information a more desirable commodity – that is, one useful in making decisions.'[37] However, this was not new – the qualitative characteristics of relevance and reliability had been discussed in several preceding studies (such as the Trueblood and Corporate Reports). What was new (and probably the most significant aspect of SFAC No. 2), was the explicit recognition of the fact that 'reliability and relevance often impinge on each other'.[38] Consequently, whenever accounting standards are set, decisions have to be made concerning the relative importance of these two characteristics, often resulting in trade-offs being made between them.

In today's context, where standard-setting bodies seem intent on replacing the historical cost system by an income and measurement system based on fair values, deciding the relative weight to be attributed to relevance and to reliability when presenting information is increasingly pertinent. It is worth noting, therefore, that in their joint conceptual framework project, the FASB and IASB are proposing to remove reliability as a primary quality for decision-useful information.

A   Relevance

SFAC No. 2 defines relevant accounting information as being information that is 'capable of making a difference in a decision by helping users to form predictions about the outcomes of past, present, and future events or to confirm or correct prior expectations.'[39] The statement further describes 'timeliness' as an 'ancillary aspect of relevance. If information is not available when it is needed or becomes available only so long after the reported events that it has no value for future action, it lacks relevance and is of little or no use.'[40] Therefore, in the context of financial reporting, the characteristic of timeliness means that information must be made available to users before it loses its capacity to influence their decisions. However, while timeliness alone cannot make information relevant, a lack of timeliness can result in information losing a degree of relevance which it once had.[41] On the other hand, in many instances there also has to be a trade-off between timeliness and reliability, since generally the more timely the information the less reliable it is.

The hierarchy identifies 'predictive value' and 'feedback value' as the other components of relevance on the basis that 'information can make a difference to decisions by improving decision makers' capacities to predict or by confirming or correcting their earlier expectations'.[42] Predictive value is defined as 'the quality of information that helps users to increase the likelihood of correctly forecasting the outcome of past or present events',[43] whilst feedback value is defined as 'the quality of information that enables users to confirm or correct prior expectations.'[44] Clearly, however, in saying that accounting information has predictive value, it is not suggesting that it is itself a prediction.

B   Reliability

Reliability is the second of the primary qualities, and is ascribed three attributes in the hierarchy. The statement asserts that the 'reliability of a measure rests on the faithfulness with which it represents what it purports to represent, coupled with an assurance for the user, which comes through verification, that it has that representational quality.'[45] This definition gives rise to the three subsidiary qualities of 'representational faithfulness', 'verifiability', and 'neutrality'. Representational faithfulness essentially means that information included in financial reports should represent what it purports to represent. In other words, financial reporting should be truthful. For example, if a group's consolidated balance sheet discloses cash and bank balances, users would be justified in assuming that, in the absence of any statement to the contrary, the financial statements were truthful, and that these represented cash resources freely available to the group; however, if the reality of the situation was that the cash resources were situated in countries which had severe exchange control restrictions, and were, therefore, not available to the group, some might hold the view that the financial statements would not be entirely 'representationally faithful'.

Reliable information should also be verifiable and neutral so that neither measurement nor measurer bias results in the information being presented in such a way that it unjustifiably influences the particular decision being made. Verifiability is a quality of representational faithfulness in that it excludes the possibility of measurement bias, whilst neutrality implies the provision of all relevant and reliable information – irrespective of the effects that the information will have on the entity or a particular user group.

2.6.5 Comparability

The hierarchy lists comparability as an additional quality that financial information should possess in order to achieve relevance and reliability. The quality of comparability includes the fundamental accounting concept of consistency, since the usefulness of information is greatly enhanced if it is prepared on a consistent basis from one period to the next, and can be compared with corresponding information of the same enterprise for some other period, or with similar information about some other enterprise.

2.6.6 Materiality

All the qualitative criteria discussed in SFAC No. 2 are subject to a materiality threshold, since only material information will have an impact on the decision-making process. However, the statement provides no quantitative guidelines for materiality, and it will be a matter of judgement for the providers of information to determine whether or not an item of information has crossed the materiality threshold for recognition. Materiality is closely related to the characteristic of relevance, since both are defined in terms of what influences or makes a difference to an investor or other decision-maker. On the other hand, the two concepts can be distinguished; a decision by management not to disclose certain information may be made because users have no interest in that kind of information (i.e. it is not relevant to their specific needs), or because the amounts involved are too small to make a difference to the users' decisions (i.e. they are not material).

However, if the preparers of financial statements are to decide on what to include in their reporting package, they must have a clear understanding of the users of their reports and their specific information and decision-making needs. In so doing, they should be aware of the types of information likely to influence their decisions (i.e. relevance) as well as the associated magnitude of this information (i.e. materiality). Consequently, financial reporting will focus generally on information that is regarded as relevant, and specifically on that which is material. The principal difficulty with this, however, is that the materiality thresholds of users vary from class to class and amongst individual users in the same class.

2.6.7 Conservatism

SFAC No. 2 includes an interesting discussion on the convention of 'conservatism' (i.e. prudence).[46] In so doing, it draws a distinction between the 'deliberate, consistent understatement of net assets and profits',[47] and the practice of ensuring that 'uncertainties and risks inherent in business situations are adequately considered'.[48] The statement recognised the fact that, in the eyes of bankers and other lenders, deliberate understatement of assets was desirable, since it increased their margin of safety on assets pledged as security for debts. On the other hand, it was also recognised that consistent understatement was difficult to maintain over a period of any length, and that understated assets would clearly lead to overstated income in later periods when the assets were ultimately realised. Consequently, unwarranted and deliberate conservatism in financial reporting would lead to a contravention of certain of the qualitative characteristics, such as neutrality and representational faithfulness. The new IASB-FASB conceptual framework project, discussed at 5 below, has further elevated representational faithfulness and downgraded conservatism as a qualitative characteristic of financial statements.

2.7   The elements of financial statements

SFAC No. 6 was issued in 1985 as a replacement to SFAC No. 3 having expanded its scope to encompass non-profit organisations. The statement defines ten 'elements' of financial statements that are directly related to the measurement of performance and financial status of an entity. However, the elements are very much interrelated, as six of them are arithmetically derived from the definitions of assets and liabilities.

2.7.1   Assets

Assets are defined as being 'probable future economic benefits obtained or controlled by a particular entity as a result of past transactions or events.'[49] However, the statement then goes on to say that the kinds of items that qualify as assets under this definition are also commonly called 'economic resources'. They are the scarce means that are useful for carrying out economic activities, such as consumption, production and exchange.[50] The common characteristic possessed by all assets is 'service potential' or 'future economic benefit' which eventually results in net cash inflows to the enterprise.[51]

Under historical cost accounting a non-monetary asset is no more than a deferred cost; a cost which has been incurred before the balance sheet date and, in terms of the accruals concept, relates to future periods beyond the balance sheet date, thereby justifying it being carried forward as an asset. This applies to all non-monetary assets that are recognised in an historical cost balance sheet – whether they be tangible fixed assets, inventory, prepayments or deferred development expenditure. Consequently, there are certain occasions when items will be recognised as assets under the traditional historical cost system, but which will not fit the SFAC No. 6 definition of an asset. For example the spreading of certain pension-related expenses over the service lives of employees is seemingly in conflict with this definition because an unexpensed pension cost, if carried forward in the balance sheet, would fail to conform to the 'economic resource with future benefits' definition of an asset.

The selection of this definition has also embedded a deep-rooted problem within the FASB's existing conceptual framework. First, as far as SFAC No. 6 is concerned, since most of the elements defined in the statement are derived from the definition of an asset, any inadequacy in this definition inevitably affects the validity of the definitions of other elements. Second, in identifying the elements of financial statements before addressing the fundamental issues of how they are to be measured and on what basis of capital maintenance profit is to be determined, the FASB seriously limited its ability to address the issues of recognition and measurement properly. The result of this is that SFAC No. 5 – *Recognition and Measurement in Financial Statements of Business Enterprises* – has serious shortcomings (see 2.8 below).

2.7.2   *Liabilities*

Liabilities are defined as 'probable future sacrifices of economic benefits arising from present obligations of a particular entity to transfer assets or provide services to other entities in the future as a result of past transactions or events.'[52] The statement goes on to say that a liability has three essential characteristics:

(a)   it embodies a present duty or responsibility to one or more other entities that entails settlement by probable future transfer or use of assets at a specified or determinable date, on occurrence of a specified event, or on demand;

(b)   the duty or responsibility obligates the entity, leaving it little or no discretion to avoid the future sacrifice; and

(c)   the transaction or other event obligating the entity has already happened.[53]

Thus, in terms of this definition, liabilities represent the amounts of obligations – giving rise to a problem similar to that outlined above in respect of the definition of assets. There are certain items which have traditionally been recognised as liabilities, but which do not meet the statement's definition. This is because they are deferred credits awaiting recognition in the profit and loss account, rather than obligations to other entities. This has led to quite tortuous methods of accounting for what are straightforward matters under traditional historic cost accounting.

2.7.3   *Equity*

Equity is defined as 'the residual interest in the assets of an entity that remains after deducting its liabilities.'[54] This is a somewhat tautological definition arising from the accounting equation that assets minus liabilities equals equity, but it avoids the potential problem of having non-equity items that are neither assets nor liabilities. Equity is, in fact, the sum of the equity investments made by the entity's owners, and the entity's earnings retained from its profit-making activities. Because of the way in which the definitions of the various elements are interrelated, it might appear to some that the FASB have taken the easy route in defining equity as net assets, rather than in terms of capital contributions plus retained earnings; a possible explanation for this might be that it enabled the FASB to define income in terms of changes in equity.

2.7.4   *Investments by owners*

Investments by owners are defined as being 'increases in equity of a particular business enterprise resulting from transfers to it from other entities of something valuable to obtain or increase ownership interests (or equity) in it.'[55] The statement goes on to say that although investments by owners are most commonly made in the form of assets, the investments can also be represented by services, or the settlement or conversion of liabilities of the enterprise.[56]

2.7.5   *Distributions to owners*

Distributions to owners are defined as 'decreases in equity of a particular business enterprise resulting from transferring assets, rendering services, or incurring liabilities by the enterprise to owners.'[57] Distributions to owners, therefore, incorporate all forms of capital distributions which result in a decrease in net assets.

2.7.6   *Comprehensive income*

Comprehensive income is defined as 'the change in equity of a business enterprise during a period from transactions and other events and circumstances from nonowner sources. It includes all changes in equity during a period except those resulting from investments by owners and distributions to owners.'[58] On its own, the term 'comprehensive income' is somewhat meaningless; for example, how does it tie in with the statement in SFAC No. 1[59] that 'the primary focus of financial reporting is information about an enterprise's performance provided by measures of earnings and its components'? Clearly, the FASB was keeping its options open by not defining earnings; in fact, it explained (in a footnote to SFAC No. 6) that whilst 'comprehensive income' is the term used in the statement for the concept that was called 'earnings' in SFAC No. 1, SFAC No. 5 had described earnings for a period as excluding certain cumulative accounting adjustments and other non-owner changes in equity that are included in comprehensive income for a period.[60]

The FASB issued a standard on this topic in June 1997, SFAS 130 – *Reporting Comprehensive Income* – however a generally accepted standard based on the concept continues to elude standard-setters. The IASB in 2003 decided to postpone its project to produce an exposure draft on the topic, and at the IASB-FASB joint meeting in April 2004 the joint boards gave every impression that the difficulties of defining and accounting for comprehensive income continue to remain formidable.

2.7.7   *Revenues, expenses, gains and losses*

SFAC No. 6 identifies the remaining four elements as those which constitute the basic components of 'comprehensive income':

Revenues, which are 'inflows or other enhancements of assets of an entity or settlements of its liabilities (or a combination of both) from delivering or producing goods, rendering services, or other activities that constitute the entity's ongoing major central operations.'[61]

Expenses, which are 'outflows or other using up of assets or incurrences of liabilities (or a combination of both) from delivering or producing goods, rendering services, or carrying out other activities that constitute the entity's ongoing major or central operations.'[62]

Gains, which are 'increases in equity (net assets) from peripheral or incidental transactions of an entity and from all other transactions and other events and circumstances affecting the entity except those that result from revenues or investments by owners.'[63]

Losses, which are 'decreases in equity (net assets) from peripheral or incidental transactions of an entity and from all other transactions and other events and circumstances affecting the entity except those that result from expenses or distributions to owners.'[64]

Therefore, comprehensive income equals revenues minus expenses plus gains minus losses; however, although the statement states that revenues, expenses, gains and losses can be combined in various ways to obtain various measures of enterprise performance,[65] it fails to define net income.

The difficulty surrounding the FASB's definitions of the ten elements is that they are so interrelated, that in attempting to piece them together into a meaningful accounting framework, one gets caught up in a tautology of terms which all lead back to the definitions of assets and liabilities. Essentially, what the FASB is saying is that assets minus liabilities equals equity and comprehensive income equals changes in equity (excluding transactions with owners), therefore comprehensive income equals the change in net assets. Consequently, the definition of comprehensive income would incorporate items such as capital contributions from non-owners, government grants for capital expenditure and unrealised holding gains. This would be all very well, if the issues of measurement and capital maintenance had already been settled. However, this is not the case, with the result that the FASB is either restricting itself in the future development of different accounting models for different purposes, or it might have to develop different definitions of the elements of financial statements as different models are developed.

In fact it now seems that the FASB and IASB have concluded that the definitions of the elements of financial statements are, indeed, deficient and require reconsideration. This view was confirmed by the IASB announcement in July 2001 that it has placed the definitions of the elements of financial statements on its agenda of technical projects. Further confirmation is provided by the decision taken at the April 2004 FASB/IASB joint board meeting to begin work on a new conceptual framework project, Phase B of which is addressing elements.

2.8   Recognition and measurement

Throughout the framework project, the FASB had avoided dealing with certain fundamental issues on the basis that they were the 'subject of another project'.[66] The result was the publication in December 1984 of SFAC No. 5 which attempted to deal with all the previously unresolved issues. However, the statement was somewhat inconclusive – possibly as a consequence of both its self-imposed restrictions discussed above, and the need to reach compromises in order to complete this phase of the project. The statement tends to describe practices current at the time, rather than indicate preferences or propose improvements; for example, in dealing with the issue of measurement attributes, the statement merely states that 'items currently reported in financial statements are measured by different attributes, depending on the nature of the item and the relevance and reliability of the attribute measured.'[67] Then, instead of either prescribing a particular measurement attribute, or discussing the circumstances under which particular attributes should apply, the statement discusses five different attributes which 'are used in present practice' – historical cost, current cost, current market value, net realisable value and present value of future cash flows – and concludes that 'the use of different attributes will continue'.[68] Furthermore, the statement fails to prescribe a particular concept of capital maintenance that should be adopted by an entity, although the FASB bases its discussions on the concept of financial capital maintenance.[69]

The statement defines recognition as 'the process of formally recording or incorporating an item into the financial statements of an entity as an asset, liability, revenue, expense, or the like.'[70] It goes on to discuss four 'fundamental recognition criteria' which any item should meet in order for it to be recognised in the financial statements of an entity. These criteria, which are subject to a cost-benefit constraint and a materiality threshold, are described as follows:

Definitions – the item meets the definition of an element of financial statements.

Measurability – the item has a relevant attribute measurable with sufficient reliability.

Relevance – the information about the item is capable of making a difference in user decisions.

Reliability – the information is representationally faithful, verifiable and neutral.[71]

Although it was probably worth setting out these criteria, they are no more than an encapsulation of certain criteria already contained in Concepts Statements 2 and 6.

SFAC No. 5 does make some progress in distinguishing between comprehensive income, earnings and net income. It states that the concept of earnings is similar to net income in present practice, and that a statement of earnings will be much like a present income statement, although 'earnings' does not include the cumulative effect of certain accounting adjustments of earlier periods that are recognised in the current period.[72] However, the statement goes on to say that the FASB 'expects the concept of earnings to be subject to the process of gradual change or evolution that has characterised the development of net income.'[73] Whilst many would agree with the principle that gradual change is the best approach towards gaining general acceptance, one of the problems with SFAC No. 5 is that the FASB does not indicate what it considers to be the desirable direction for this gradual change to follow. Furthermore, the FASB seems to be saying that concepts will evolve as accounting standards are developed – instead of the other way around.

In an evaluation of the FASB's conceptual framework, Professor David Solomons (who, incidentally, was the principal author of SFAC No. 2) took a distinctly critical view of this 'evolutionary' view of the emergence of concepts, stating the following: 'These appeals to evolution should be seen as what they are – a cop-out. If all that is needed to improve our accounting model is reliance on evolution ... why was an expensive and protracted conceptual framework project necessary in the first place? ... And, for that matter, if progress is simply a matter of waiting for evolution, who needs the FASB?'[74] Professor Solomons came to the following conclusions about SFAC No. 5: 'Under a rigorous grading system I would give Concepts Statement No. 5 an F and require the board to take the course over again – that is, to scrap the statement and start afresh.'[75] This led Solomons to conclude ultimately that 'my judgment of the project as a whole must be that it has failed.'[76]

Interestingly, the FASB's own special report on its conceptual framework makes the point that although SFAC No. 5's name implies that it gives conceptual guidance on recognition and measurement, its conceptual contributions to financial reporting are not really in those areas.[77] The report goes on to say that 'as a result of compromises necessary to issue it, much of Concepts Statement 5 merely describes present practice and some of the reasons that have been used to support or explain it but provides little or no conceptual basis for analyzing and attempting to resolve the controversial issues of recognition and measurement about which accountants have disagreed for years.'[78] The concluding sentence of the FASB's report sums up elegantly the views that have long been expressed by critics of SFAC No. 5: 'Concepts Statement 5 does make some noteworthy conceptual contributions – they are just not on recognition and measurement.'[79]

2.9   Using cash flow information in accounting measurements (discounting)

In February 2000 the FASB issued a new Statement of Financial Accounting Concepts, SFAC 7 – *Using cash flow information and present value in accounting measurements.* The finalised statement resulted from drafts published in 1999 and 1997. The purpose of the statement is to provide a framework for using future cash flows as the basis for accounting measurement. It aims to provide general principles governing the use of present value, especially when the amounts of future cash flows and/or their timing are uncertain. The proposals are limited to issues of measurement and do not address recognition questions.

Present values are used to incorporate the time value of money in a measurement. In their simplest form, present value techniques capture the amount that an entity demands (or that others demand from it) for money that it will receive (or pay) in the future.[80] The FASB's objective of using present value in an accounting measurement is to capture, to the extent possible, the economic difference between sets of estimated future cash flows, taking into account their uncertainty as well as their timing differences. Normal discounting distinguishes between a cash flow of €1,000 due in one day and a cash flow of €1,000 due in ten years, although both have an undiscounted measurement of €1,000. SFAC 7 seeks to distinguish additionally between cash flows based upon their different risks. For example to distinguish between two identical inflows due in (say) five years time, but which have different risks attached to them because of the relative uncertainties of their being received. Consequently, SFAC 7 postulates that a present value measurement which incorporates the uncertainty in estimated future cash flows always provides more relevant information than a measurement based on the undiscounted sum of those cash flows or a discounted measurement that ignores uncertainty.[81]

Any combination of cash flows and interest rates could be used to compute a present value, at least in the broadest sense of the term. However, present value is not an end in itself. Simply applying an arbitrary interest rate to a series of cash flows provides limited information to financial statement users, and may mislead rather than assist. To provide relevant information in financial reporting, present value must represent some observable measurement attribute of assets or liabilities. The statement identifies the following characteristics of a present value measurement that would capture fully the economic differences between various future cash flows:

- An estimate of the future cash flow;

- Expectations about possible variations in amount or timing of those cash flows;

- The time value of money, represented by the risk free rate of interest;

- The price for bearing the uncertainty inherent in the asset or liability; and

- Other, sometimes unidentifiable, factors including illiquidity and market imperfections.[82]

SFAC 7 selects fair value as the sole measurement attribute that incorporates all the above aspects, and rejects the possible alternatives of value in use, effective settlement and cost-accumulation as being less satisfactory. The FASB holds that each of the rejected measurement attributes (a) adds factors that are not contemplated in the price of a market transaction for the asset or liability in question, (b) inserts assumptions made by the entity's management in the place of those the market would make, and/or (c) excludes factors that would be contemplated in the price of a market transaction. Consequently fair value represents a price and, as such, provides an unambiguous objective for the development of the cash flows and interest rates used in present value measurement.[83]

The statement sets out the following four general principles that, it considers, govern any application of present value techniques in measuring assets:

- To the extent possible, estimated cash flows and interest rates should reflect assumptions about all future events and uncertainties that would be considered in deciding whether to acquire an asset or group of assets in an arm's-length transaction for cash;

- Interest rates used to discount cash flows should reflect assumptions that are consistent with those inherent in the estimated cash flows. Otherwise, the effect of some assumptions will be double counted or ignored. For example, an interest rate of 12 per cent might be applied to contractual cash flows of a loan. That rate reflects expectations about future defaults from loans with particular characteristics. That same 12 per cent rate should not be used to discount expected cash flows because those cash flows already reflect assumptions about future defaults;

- Estimated cash flows and interest rates should be free from both bias and factors unrelated to the asset or group of assets in question. For example, deliberately understating estimated net cash flows to enhance the apparent future profitability of an asset introduces a bias into the measurement; and

- Estimated cash flows or interest rates should reflect the range of possible outcomes rather than a single most likely, minimum, or maximum possible amount.[84]

The stance adopted by SFAC 7 on the measurement of liabilities is consistent with its conclusion on assets. Thus fair value is the single measurement objective when present value is to be used in measuring liabilities, although the statement is not particularly specific as to how fair value is to be determined, stating that the measurement of liabilities 'may require different techniques in arriving at fair value'. However it does state that the objective of using present value techniques to estimate the fair value of a liability is to estimate the value of assets required currently to (a) settle the liability or (b) transfer the liability to an entity of comparable credit standing.[85] The difficulty of defining and identifying fair value remains a problem for any conceptual framework that relies upon the notion, and is further discussed at 3 below in relation to the IASB's framework.

The most significant element of SFAC 7 as concerns liabilities, centres around the incorporation of the entity's own credit standing into the measurement. Fair value in settlement as described above implies that the credit standing of the entity must be taken into account in arriving at the fair value of its liabilities. Accordingly, the fair value in settlement of an entity's liability should assume settlement with an entity of comparable, rather than superior, credit standing. Consequently, as the entity's credit standing affects the interest rate at which it borrows in the market place, it therefore affects the fair value of its liabilities.

This view entails the FASB adopting a quite complex form of discounting in SFAC 7, to facilitate which it has defined for its purposes a number of terms that are not necessarily used in their normal everyday sense. Instead of discounting the best estimate of any future cash flow (i.e. the most likely amount), the statement insists that the 'expected' cash flows should be discounted. The 'expected' cash flow to be used is defined as the sum of probability-weighted amounts in a range of possible estimated amounts.[86] Therefore, SFAC 7 requires the estimation of the likelihood of a range of outcomes (for example, for the repayment of a debt); the probability weighting of each; the calculation of each probability weighted amount; their summation and finally the calculation of the present value of that derived total. The statement does not define the rate to be used in any discounting but appears to indicate that a risk free rate is often the appropriate rate to use.

The inclusion of the credit standing of entities in the calculations can produce unwanted results. The lower the credit rating of a business, the higher the interest rate it will have to pay. Therefore, after discounting, the obligation of a low credit rated firm (using the higher discount rate its higher borrowing rate implies) will produce a lower net present value than that of a firm with an identical obligation and a better credit rating. This produces the extraordinary result whereby a poorer credit-rated, less safe firm, shows a significantly lower liability than a higher rated, safer firm – despite the fact that both have an identical settlement payment to make. Nevertheless, this is the position that the IASB has taken in its standard on the recognition and measurement of financial instruments, IAS 39 – *Financial Instruments: Recognition and Measurement*. This standard requires that, in determining the fair value of its liabilities, an entity should take account of its own credit risk.[87]

All in all, SFAC 7 comes across as no more than an overview of the issues surrounding the use of present values in accounting measurement. In spite of choosing fair values as the sole allowable measurement base, it leaves the door open to a fairly wide range of discounting practices, which can be applied as and when the FASB so decides. It is unfortunate that the statement contains no explanation in plain English of what its practical ramifications are and where, if it were to be adopted, financial reporting would be heading.

2.10   Concluding remarks on the FASB conceptual framework

In order to be able to assess the success or failure of the FASB's conceptual framework project, one must refer back to the originally perceived benefits of the project and evaluate whether or not any of them has been achieved (see 2.4 above). Perhaps the acid test may be found in analysing the extent to which the FASB has used the framework in the development of accounting standards. Possibly the best example of where the framework has been used as the basis for an accounting standard is in the development of SFAS 95 – *Statement of Cash Flows* – however the linkages have not always been so clear.

The weakness of the FASB's conceptual framework project may be attributed to a number of factors; however, the most significant reason will probably be shown to be the Board's failure to deal with the fundamental issues of recognition and measurement. To a certain extent, the FASB has fallen into the same trap as the AICPA did in APB Statement No. 4, in that SFAC No. 5 is a descriptive rather than a prescriptive statement; a statement of accounting concepts should provide a frame of reference for the formulation of financial reporting practice, and not be a description of what current reporting practices are. In the words of Professor Stephen Zeff, 'the FASB's conceptual framework failed to fulfil expectations that it might constitute a powerful intellectual force for improving financial reporting.'[88]

Underlying the entire issue of developing a conceptual framework is the unspoken yet pervasive view of the project's authors that the logical structure for the framework should be a highly deductive one whereby the entire schema follows from a number of definitional assertions. To the practically minded accountant the problem of (for instance) ensuring worthless research and development expenditure is not carried forward, is one of determining whether the expenditure in question is likely to result in profitable sales in the future. By contrast, this precise problem is cited in the FASB special report as a prime reason for adopting a definition that excludes all deferred charges. This desire for an entirely deductive system amounts to a view of what accounting is that may not coincide with reality. Accounting is an activity born out of the needs of society (principally the needs of industrialised nations) that responds to those needs as and when conditions alter. The fact that the framework project has not obviously impinged upon the thinking behind a number of standards seems to be evidence for this view. It may not be a fault that accounting lacks a set of principles that accurately and inescapably predict the future in the way that scientific laws do; rather it may be a necessary attribute of accounting continuing to be useful to society.[89]

This is not to say that the FASB's project has been ineffective; it contains some outstanding work, particularly in the area of qualitative characteristics, and has fundamentally influenced the thinking and output of other standard setters, most notably the Board of the IASC and its successor, the IASB. As discussed below, the definitions adopted in the conceptual framework of the IASB are taken essentially unchanged from the FASB's concept statements. Thus, intentionally or not, the FASB's framework project has created a global language and definitional structure used by the only two standard-setting bodies currently involved with global-scale financial reporting.

However, both for the FASB and for the IASB, if the deductive model is to be maintained, a way must be found to address the fundamental issues of recognition and measurement that does not involve both attempting to maintain the truth of the framework's definitions while quietly compromising them when events require it. As discussed in 5 below, the IASB and the FASB are in the process of formulating a new joint Framework and it is to be hoped that the opportunity will be taken both to acknowledge and address the inconsistencies and difficulties that currently exist.

3   THE IASB'S CONCEPTUAL FRAMEWORK

3.1   Introduction

In May 1988, the Board of the IASC (before it was reconstituted as the IASB) issued an exposure draft – *Framework for the Preparation and Presentation of Financial Statements* – which set out its understanding of 'the conceptual framework that underlies the preparation and presentation of financial statements'.[90] This was converted without major change into a final statement in September 1989, although it is stressed within the statement that it will be revised from time to time in the light of the Board's experience in working with it.[91] The statement is not an accounting standard and does not override any specific international accounting standard or interpretation.[92] Whilst it therefore has much the same status as the FASB's concepts statements, unlike those statements, the IASB's framework does have a formal place in the IFRS hierarchy to which reference should be made when selecting accounting policies in the absence of a specific standard or interpretation. This is set out in paragraph 11 of IAS 8 – *Accounting Policies, Changes in Accounting Estimates and Errors* – and is discussed in Chapter 3.

In April 2001 the newly constituted IASB formally adopted the Framework, and it is the most recently published version of it that is referred to in this section. The Framework is a short document at 35 pages and 110 numbered paragraphs, and clearly is derived from the FASB's first six concepts statements. It is therefore open to the same criticisms and contains the same flaws as the FASB's concepts, which are discussed at 2.4 to 2.10 above.

The IASB and the FASB are currently undertaking the development of a new joint framework. A number of preliminary documents have been published and discussions have taken place at IASB open meetings, though it does not appear that any fundamentally new approach is being contemplated. The joint IASB-FASB framework project is discussed at 5 below.

3.2   The contents of the IASB's Framework

The Framework sets out in its introduction that its purpose is to:

'(a)   assist the Board of IASC in the development of future International Accounting Standards and in its review of existing International Accounting Standards;

(b)   assist the Board of IASC in promoting harmonisation of regulations, accounting standards and procedures relating to the presentation of financial statements by providing a basis for reducing the number of alternative accounting treatments permitted by International Accounting Standards;

(c)   assist national standard-setting bodies in developing national standards;

(d)   assist preparers of financial statements in applying International Accounting Standards and in dealing with topics that have yet to form the subject of an International Accounting Standard;

(e)   assist auditors in forming an opinion as to whether financial statements conform with International Accounting Standards;

(f)   assist users of financial statements in interpreting the information contained in financial statements prepared in conformity with International Accounting Standards; and

(g)   provide those who are interested in the work of IASC with information about its approach to the formulation of International Accounting Standards.'[93]

The Board accepts that there may be conflicts between the Framework and the provisions of individual standards, but states that these are expected to diminish over time as standards are reviewed or replaced.

Perhaps inevitably the reporting status quo seems to be taken as read by the Framework; as evidenced, for example, by the statement in the introduction to the effect that financial statements normally include a balance sheet, a profit and loss statement, a statement of changes in financial position and notes.[94] The document is then devoted to applying its discussion to this traditional financial reporting package, without, for example, following or apparently even considering the possibility of an entirely new package.

Following the Introduction, the IASB's *Framework* is divided into the following seven major sections that are discussed below:

- The objective of financial statements;
- Underlying assumptions;
- Qualitative characteristics of financial statements;
- The elements of financial statements;
- Recognition of the elements of financial statements;
- Measurement of the elements of financial statements; and
- Concepts of capital and capital maintenance.

3.2.1 *The objective and underlying assumptions of financial statements*

The objective of financial statements set out in the IASB's Framework is described in terms of decision-usefulness and will be quite familiar to readers of the FASB equivalent:

> 'to provide information about the financial position, performance and changes in financial position of an enterprise that is useful to a wide range of users in making economic decisions.'[95]

Stewardship is specifically referred to in a paragraph elaborating upon the objective of financial statements, and refers to the fact that there are decisions to be made by users of financial statements that require the management's stewardship to be assessed. The framework states this objective as follows:

> 'Financial statements also show the results of the stewardship of management, or the accountability of management for the resources entrusted to it. Those users who wish to assess the stewardship or accountability of management do so in order that they may make economic decisions; these decisions may include, for example, whether to hold or sell their investment in the entity or whether to reappoint or replace the management.'[96]

Users are listed in the Introduction as investors, employees, lenders, suppliers and trade creditors, customers, governments and their agencies, and the public – a list that excludes nobody; however, it has to be admitted that the needs of all these groups cannot be met. Therefore financial statements that meet the needs of investors who 'are providers of risk capital' are stated to satisfy also 'most of the needs of other users that financial statements can satisfy'.[97] Perhaps it may be indicative of the derivative nature of the Framework that the phrase 'that financial statements can satisfy' is used. If an examination of a subject starts with preconceptions of what can and cannot be done, it is unlikely that much in the way of new insights or approaches will emerge. In any event, the investor's perspective is chosen as the one most likely to be useful in the preparation of what will remain general purpose financial statements.

The remainder of this part of the Framework contains a range of assertions, also quite familiar, covering how users need to know about the performance, financial position, cash generation, and liquidity and solvency of an entity, including changes in them.

The Framework sets out two 'underlying assumptions': the accruals basis of accounting and the going concern basis. Accruals is described as follows, significantly omitting matching from the concept:

> 'effects of transactions and other events are recognised when they occur (and not as cash or its equivalent is received or paid) and they are recorded in the accounting records and reported in the financial statements of the periods to which they relate.'[98]

Later on in the Framework, in the section on recognition, the point is specifically made that 'the application of the matching concept under this framework does not allow the recognition of items in the balance sheet which do not meet the definition of assets and liabilities.'[99] Equally significantly, prudence is not an underlying assumption of the Framework, but is relegated to being a subsidiary quality of reliability.

The going concern assumption is quite conventionally stated as follows:

> 'financial statements are normally prepared on the assumption that an enterprise is a going concern and will continue in operation for the foreseeable future. Hence, it is assumed that the enterprise has neither the intention nor the need to liquidate or curtail materially the scale of its operations.'[100]

3.2.2   *The qualitative characteristics of financial statements*

The Framework explains that qualitative characteristics are the attributes that make the information provided in financial statements useful to users.[101] The qualitative characteristics set out in the document are also taken directly from the FASB conceptual framework project. The familiar list of understandability, relevance, reliability and comparability is advanced.

A   Understandability

One of the factors that all framework attempts have sought to address is understandability, which is dealt with in its entirety in the IASB's Framework as follows:

> 'An essential quality of the information provided in financial statements is that it is readily understandable by users. For this purpose, users are assumed to have a reasonable knowledge of business and economic activities and accounting and a willingness to study the information with reasonable diligence. However, information about complex matters that should be included in the financial statements because of its relevance to the economic decision-making needs of users should not be excluded merely on the grounds that it may be too difficult for certain users to understand.'[102]

The Framework has advanced as an essential quality in the above paragraph that the 'information provided in financial statements ... is readily understandable by users'; however, this is significantly different from financial statements actually *being* understood. The paragraph goes on to specify the required capabilities of users as having 'a reasonable knowledge of business and economic activities and accounting and a willingness to study the information with reasonable diligence.' This assertion, whilst similar to those in other frameworks, avoids the understandability problem in two ways.

First the phrase 'reasonable knowledge ... of accounting' is entirely open-ended. It is highly unlikely that this could possibly be interpreted to mean 'a complete technical understanding of all the nuances involved with the intricacies of the many accounting rules and regulations', for example. However, if that is the case there remains a danger that some of the requirements of IFRSs will be difficult for the non-specialist accountant to understand.

Second, the capabilities required would probably reduce the 'allowable' users to a small set of professional analysts, accountants, academics, and the odd graduate of the subject. When this constituency is contrasted with the many types of people who actually own shares, the extremely diverse individual capabilities of even this 'providers of risk capital' user group, and with the very wide definition of users in the Framework, it becomes apparent that the issue of understandability remains considerable and cannot comfortably be defined away in the manner attempted.

B   Relevance

Relevance is the second principal qualitative characteristic put forward. The Framework asserts that 'Information has the quality of relevance when it influences the economic decisions of users by helping them evaluate past, present or future events or confirming, or correcting, their past evaluations.'[103] The predictive value of relevant information is emphasised. Not that financial statements should be predictions in the sense of forecasts, but that the information they contain should be relevant to predictions that users might make for themselves about the 'ability of the enterprise to take advantage of opportunities and its ability to react to adverse situations.'[104]

Materiality is discussed as a subsection of relevance, in terms of providing a threshold point below which relevance does not exist. Information is stated to be material 'if its omission or misstatement could influence the economic decisions of users taken on the basis of the financial statements.'[105] The important question, however, is against which yardstick information should be judged to be material or immaterial, and for whom, but the Framework provides no further discussion of, or guidance about, identifying material items. In practice materiality is both a qualitative as well as a quantitative concept, mere small size would not necessarily make an item immaterial. Thus in this matter the Framework seems more superficial than would be expected.

C   Reliability

Reliability is the third primary qualitative characteristic. Information is reliable if 'it is free from material error and bias and can be depended upon by users to represent faithfully that which it either purports to represent or could reasonably be expected to represent.'[106] Importantly, the Framework highlights the trade-off between reliability and relevance, stating that 'information may be relevant but so unreliable in nature or representation that its recognition may be potentially misleading.'[107] This is significant as the IASB and FASB have decided, as part of their joint framework project, to remove reliability – once thought of by both boards as a primary decision-specific quality – from the framework (see 5.2.2 below).

Faithful representation is used by the Framework as a term that can explain and clarify the notion of reliability. It states that 'Most financial information is subject to some risk of being less than a faithful representation of that which it purports to portray.'[108] This is a considerable admission and either is an overstatement of the case (i.e. there is no material risk in most cases) or if considered true, calls into question why the IASB has accepted it as a satisfactory state of affairs. More importantly, 'faithful representation' assumes satisfactory answers exist to fundamental questions. In particular, answers about what a given item in a set of financial statements might 'purport to represent'. Fundamentally this is taking as solved and understood the entire set of difficulties that the accounting profession and the many framework attempts have, and are still, grappling with.

Substance over form, neutrality, prudence and completeness are cited as four other characteristics that along with representational faithfulness, contribute to the principal qualitative characteristic of reliability. Essentially, substance over form relies upon accepting the possibility that the economic reality of a transaction can be disguised by its legal form. This doctrine means that any transactions structured to give a legal form that does not reflect the underlying economic reality, should be accounted for in accordance with that economic reality rather than the legal form. Thus a sale of a property would not be considered to result in an immediate profit to an entity if the entity simultaneously entered into a leasing agreement that had all the characteristics of a secured loan on that property.

The Framework defines neutrality as freedom from bias. There is no discussion of neutrality in the Framework, other than the statement that 'financial statements are not neutral if, by the selection or presentation of information, they influence the making of a decision or judgement in order to achieve a predetermined result or outcome.'[109]

Prudence (conservatism) is dealt with slightly more fully. Prudence is characterised as follows:

> 'Prudence is the inclusion of a degree of caution in the exercise of the judgements needed in making the estimates required under conditions of uncertainty, such that assets or income are not overstated and liabilities or expenses are not understated. However, the exercise of prudence does not allow, for example, the creation of hidden reserves or excessive provisions, the deliberate understatement of assets or income, or the deliberate overstatement of liabilities or expenses, because the financial statements would not be neutral and, therefore, not have the quality of reliability.'[110]

Prudence is characterised here as (a) to be exercised only when uncertainty exists, and (b) not to include 'income smoothing' – characterised as overstatement of provisions or liabilities or understatement of assets. Under an historical cost system this is not what prudence means. Rather it means the necessary caution, once thought fundamental to financial reporting, whereby profit is not taken until it is earned. Under the prudence concept, revenue and profits are not anticipated but are recognised by inclusion in the profit and loss account only when realised in the form of cash or of other assets the ultimate cash realisation of which can be assessed with reasonable certainty. On the other hand, provision is made for all known liabilities whether the amount of these is known with certainty or is a best estimate in the light of the information available.

Completeness, the fourth sub-characteristic of reliability, means 'the financial statements must be complete within the bounds of materiality and cost.'[111]

D   Comparability

Comparability is the fourth principal qualitative characteristic in the Framework, which is an uncontroversial characteristic shared by all conceptual frameworks. Additionally, the IASB includes in the discussion the importance of disclosing accounting policies as an essential part of comparability:

> 'An important implication of the qualitative characteristic of comparability is that users be informed of the accounting policies employed in the preparation of the financial statements, any changes in those policies and the effects of such changes. Users need to be able to identify differences between the accounting policies for like transactions and other events used by the same enterprise from period to period and by different enterprises.'[112]

The point is made, however, that comparability does not extend to preventing the improvement of accounting standards. Comparability also entails the provision of comparative figures for the corresponding preceding accounting periods.

There follows a discussion under the heading 'Timeliness' that recognises that there is an element of conflict between two of the principal qualitative characteristics: relevance and reliability:

> 'To provide information on a timely basis it may often be necessary to report before all aspects of a transaction or other event are known, thus impairing reliability. Conversely, if reporting is delayed until all aspects are known, the information may be highly reliable but of little use to users who have had to make decisions in the interim.'[113]

The Framework indicates that this conflict is to be resolved by considering 'how best to satisfy the economic decision-making needs of users'[114] although how these are to be identified in any particular case is not discussed. Paragraph 45 of the Framework acknowledges that a 'trade-off between qualitative characteristics is often necessary' and that their relative importance 'is a matter of professional judgement'.

3.2.3   The elements of financial statements

A   Assets

The section of the Framework that deals with the elements of financial statements is also derived from its FASB equivalent. Assets are defined as:

'(a)   An asset is a resource controlled by the enterprise as a result of past events and from which future economic benefits are expected to flow to the enterprise.'[115]

The definition of an asset used by the Framework is adopted wholesale from the FASB framework, with one important difference. Under SFAC 6 the discussion is in the context of benefits 'obtained or controlled', while the Framework definition refers solely to resources 'controlled' by the enterprise. This is a fundamental difference that has significant implications in practice – for example goodwill falls within the definition of an asset under the FASB concepts, but falls outside the definition under the IASB's Framework, as it fails to meet the 'controlled' requirement. The problem the IASB's Framework therefore has is that it fails to include within its asset definition an asset that all accountants in practice, and the IASB itself, acknowledge *is* an asset. The same problem occurred in the UK's framework project (see 4.6 below for a further discussion of this point).

This definition also has to contend with the problem that future economic benefits may not materialise. Consequently, for an item to be recognised as an asset it must be 'probable that any future economic benefit associated with the item will flow to … the enterprise.'[116] The question therefore arises: what is a future economic benefit? Future economic benefits are obviously other items of property, near cash such as debtors, or cash itself. The logical problem in the absence of any other meaning being given to the phrase 'future economic benefits' is that the asset definition is completely circular. It has no explanatory power, but is precisely logically equivalent to: 'an asset is a resource controlled by the enterprise from which assets are expected to be gained by the enterprise in the future'.

Thus both the FASB and the IASB have a flawed definition at the heart of their conceptual frameworks. If the definition of assets is flawed the entire logical structure derived from it is too, including all the remaining definitions of the elements of financial statements that depend upon the asset definition.

Paragraph 50 of the Framework makes it clear that because something meets the definition of an asset or liability, it does not imply it will necessarily be included ('recognised') in the balance sheet. That is, meeting the definition is a necessary but not a sufficient condition for inclusion in the financial statements. The IASB's recognition criteria are discussed in the following section. Once again, and importantly, the Framework emphasises that:

> 'In assessing whether an item meets the definition of an asset, liability or equity, attention needs to be given to its underlying substance and economic reality and not merely its legal form.'[117]

B   Liabilities

In the IASB's Framework a liability is defined as:

> 'a present obligation of the enterprise arising from past events, the settlement of which is expected to result in an outflow from the enterprise of resources embodying economic benefits.'[118]

The 'present obligation arising from a past event' definition of a liability is also adopted from the FASB equivalent, with the same consequences for recognising provisions which, if based solely on the basis of a management decision, will not qualify under this definition. For example, IAS 37 – *Provisions, Contingent Liabilities and Contingent Assets* – relies heavily on this definition to restrict severely the circumstances under which provisions can be recognised. This is because provisions are not seen as a separate element of financial statements and, instead, are defined as being a subset of liabilities (see Chapter 24). The concept of the 'constructive obligation' used in IAS 37 as a sub-set of the term present obligation, is not referred to in the Framework.

Assets and liabilities are therefore characterised as rights and obligations – rights to receive future economic benefits in the form of cash inflows and obligations to transfer out economic benefits in the form of cash outflows. The remaining definitions are derived from these definitions of assets and liabilities.

C　Equity

Equity is defined as follows:

> 'Equity is the residual interest in the assets of the enterprise after deducting all its liabilities.'[119]

Again the wording is similar to that used in SFAC 6. The logic of the definition is identical, and follows from the equation that assets minus liabilities equals equity.

D　Income and expenses

Income and expenses definitions rely directly upon the balance sheet approach outlined above., and are defined in terms of the changes to assets and liabilities as follows:

> 'Income is increases in economic benefits during the accounting period in the form of inflows or enhancements of assets or decreases of liabilities that result in increases in equity, other than those relating to contributions from equity participants.

> 'Expenses are decreases in economic benefits during the accounting period in the form of outflows or depletions of assets or incurrences of liabilities that result in decreases in equity, other than those relating to distributions to equity participants.'[120]

Although income and expenses are defined in terms of balance sheet recognition criteria in the same manner as adopted by the FASB, the Framework has adopted a simpler approach as it uses a single element to cover what SFAC 6 describes separately as revenues and gains (see 2.7.7 above). The distinction is that the US definitions differentiate between gains arising from central operations and those which do not, whereas the IASB Framework uses a single definition for both. This is explained as follows: 'Gains represent other items that meet the definition of income and may, or may not, arise in the course of the ordinary activities of an entity. Gains represent increases in economic benefits and as such are no different in nature from revenue. Hence, they are not regarded as constituting a separate element in this Framework.'[121]

Similarly, the definition of expenses embraces both expenses and losses[122] as the terms are used in SFAC 6 (see 2.7.7 above).

The realisation principle is not discussed in the Framework, except to the extent that it is made clear that income and expenses include both realised and unrealised gains and losses. This is expressed as follows: 'The definition of income also includes unrealised gains; for example, those arising on the revaluation of marketable securities and those resulting from increases in the carrying amount of long-term assets. ... The definition of expenses also includes unrealised losses, for example, those arising from the effects of increases in the rate of exchange for a foreign currency in respect of the borrowings of an entity in that currency.'[123]

3.2.4 *Recognition of the elements of financial statements*

The recognition criteria adopted in the Framework are also entirely familiar from other conceptual framework projects. Thus an asset will be recognised if 'it is probable that the future economic benefits will flow to the enterprise and the asset has a cost or value that can be measured reliably.'[124] A liability is recognised 'when it is probable that an outflow of resources embodying economic benefits will result from the settlement of a present obligation and the amount at which the settlement will take place can be measured reliably.'[125] As with its US equivalents, the recognition criteria for income and expenses are derived by deduction from these definitions.

The balance sheet approach to income and expense recognition is absolutely explicit in the Framework, as demonstrated by paragraph 92:

> 'Income is recognised in the income statement when an increase in future economic benefits related to an increase in an asset or a decrease of a liability has arisen that can be measured reliably. This means, in effect, that recognition of income occurs simultaneously with the recognition of increases in assets or decreases in liabilities.'

Paragraph 94 contains similar wording relating to expense recognition.

3.2.5 *Measurement of the elements of financial statements*

This is the third stage of the IASB's process of inclusion of an item into the financial statements. First there is definition (e.g. of an asset); if an item meets the definition, then comes recognition; if an item can be recognised (i.e. it is probable that economic benefits will come to the enterprise and that cost or value can be measured reliably); the final stage is measurement. However, despite the importance of measurement to any conceptual framework, the IASB's framework provides no conceptual guidance whatsoever in this area.

Measurement is defined as:

> 'the process of determining the monetary amounts at which the elements of the financial statements are to be recognised and carried in the balance sheet and income statement. This involves the selection of the particular basis of measurement.'[126]

The Framework lists four 'basis of measurement' possibilities: historical cost; current cost; realisable (settlement) value; and present value. Present value means that assets are carried at the present value of their expected future cash flows, while liabilities are carried at the present value of the amount that will be required to settle the liability in the future. In spite of its frequent use in the IASB's standards, fair value is not among the measurement bases listed in the Framework and is not in fact mentioned in it at all. However, in its current standards the IASB defines fair value as 'the amount for which an asset could be exchanged between knowledgeable, willing parties in an arm's length transaction', which essentially means that the term fair value has been adopted to mean what the Framework refers to as realisable value.

There is no further discussion of which measurement basis might be preferable. The subject is dealt with in its entirety in a solely descriptive manner in three paragraphs, and ends with the statement that historical cost is most commonly adopted.

3.2.6　*Concepts of capital and capital maintenance*

Finally, there is a short section dealing with concepts of capital maintenance. This summarises the concepts of physical and financial capital maintenance as follows:

> 'Under a financial concept of capital, such as invested money or invested purchasing power, capital is synonymous with the net assets or equity of the enterprise. Under a physical concept of capital, such as operating capability, capital is regarded as the productive capacity of the enterprise based on, for example, units of output per day.'[127]

No attempt is made to examine or discuss the adequacy of each concept or how their use might contribute to improving financial reporting. Even recommending one or the other is avoided by the customary and in effect empty formula of 'selection of the appropriate concept of capital by an enterprise should be based on the needs of the users of its financial statements'.[128]

This final section ends with the statement that the Framework is applicable to any chosen accounting model, in that it is 'applicable to a range of accounting models and provides guidance on preparing and presenting the financial statements constructed under the [any] chosen model.'[129] This is unlikely to be the case as, for example, even a brief reading of section 4 below shows that there are a number of alternative conceptual framework possibilities in respect of which the IASB's Framework would have little or no obvious application or relevance. Finally the Framework ends on a rather open ended note as follows:

> 'At the present time, it is not the intention of the Board of IASC to prescribe a particular model other than in exceptional circumstances, such as for those enterprises reporting in the currency of a hyperinflationary economy. This intention will, however, be reviewed in the light of world developments.'[130]

3.3　　Assessment of the IASB's Framework

There is no really fundamental difference in substance between the IASB and FASB conceptual frameworks, apart from the fact that the FASB statements are more voluminous and detailed than the IASB equivalent. The IASB document clearly derives from the original FASB work embodied in its concepts statements, and in truth the IASB's Framework is little more than a synopsis of the FASB conceptual statements and shares their shortcomings. It is perhaps unfortunate, and certainly was a lost opportunity, that the IASB did not take the chance presented by the publication of a conceptual framework document to explore more fundamentally the questions posed by such an endeavour. A conceptual framework should be more than an *ex post facto* justification of an already chosen approach, in our view.

The fundamental problem with the Framework is that we do not believe that it is possible to develop general purpose rules on the recognition of elements of financial statements, whilst simultaneously leaving open the questions of how they are to be measured and against what capital maintenance yardstick profit is to be determined. We do not suggest that any one system is necessarily superior to another, but it is not possible to fit all possible systems of accounting into one framework of rules on the elements of financial statements and their recognition. We believe that lack of clarity on this point has led to constant confusion on accounting concepts, where ideas which belong in discrete methodologies are used interchangeably and lead to a result that lacks any cohesion. It should be the role of a conceptual framework study to unravel this tangle, but in this respect at least we believe that the IASB Framework document simply compounds the confusion by failing to distinguish the essential features that make different approaches mutually incompatible.

4   OTHER FRAMEWORK ENDEAVOURS

For those concerned with understanding the process by which the IASB has arrived at many of its standards, or with making a contribution to the development of future IFRSs through Exposure Draft responses, an understanding of how the profession has moved from uncritical use of historical cost in the 1960s to a mix of cost and fair value today, is valuable. The IASB and many national equivalents developed their views in response to the appearance of practical financial reporting problems that caused users and others to require change. In the past this imperative triggered fundamental work by a number of accounting bodies and standard setters from different nations, and their contributions to the development of financial reporting are outlined below. This work taken together, has contributed consciously or not to the development of the IASB's own framework, and the thinking that underlies it.

4.1   The Corporate Report

The first real attempt by the accounting profession in Europe to develop a conceptual framework is to be found in a discussion paper issued by the UK accounting profession in 1975 by the then-styled Accounting Standards Steering Committee and entitled *The Corporate Report*.[131]

The discussion paper dealt with 'the fundamental aims of published financial reports and the means by which these aims can be achieved'[132] and used the term 'corporate report' to mean 'the comprehensive package of information of all kinds which most completely describes an organisation's economic activity.'[133] It was suggested that this 'comprehensive package' should include more than the 'basic financial statements' (i.e. the balance sheet, profit and loss account and funds statement), and should incorporate additional narrative and descriptive statements.[134] The discussion paper centred on three main elements: 'the types of organisation which should be expected to publish regular financial information; the main users of such information and their needs; and the form of report which will best meet those needs.'[135]

The discussion paper followed the basic approach that corporate reports should seek to satisfy, as far as possible, the information needs of users.[136] The Committee argued that every economic entity of significant size has an implicit responsibility to report publicly, and concluded that general purpose reports designed for general purpose use are the primary means by which this public accountability is fulfilled. Users were defined 'as those having a reasonable right to information concerning the reporting entity',[137] a right that arises from the entity's public accountability.

The paper identified seven user groups[138] as having a reasonable right to information, and discussed the basis of the rights of each group and their information needs. Not surprisingly, the Committee identified a considerable overlap of interest between each of the user groups, including items such as 'evaluating the performance of the entity', 'estimating the future prospects of the entity', 'evaluating managerial performance', 'assessing the liquidity of the entity, its present or future requirements for additional fixed or working capital, and its ability to raise long and short term finance.'[139]

On this basis the Committee concluded that 'the fundamental objective of corporate reports is to communicate economic measurements of and information about the resources and performance of the reporting entity useful to those having reasonable rights to such information.'[140] They went on to say that in order to fulfil this objective and be useful, corporate reports should be relevant, understandable, reliable, complete, objective, timely and comparable[141] (these qualitative characteristics identified were similar to those discussed in the Trueblood Report).

The discussion paper then reviewed the conventional thinking on the aim of published reports together with the then-existing features of published financial statements of UK companies. The Committee also conducted a survey of corporate objectives amongst the chairmen of 300 of the largest UK listed companies, and concluded that 'distributable profit can no longer be regarded as the sole or premier indicator of performance.'[142] Consequently, it was suggested that there was a need for additional indicators of performance in the corporate reports of all entities.[143]

Part II of the study considered the 'measurement and method' of achieving the above aims. Since the Committee had concluded that current reporting practices did not fully satisfy the needs of users, it was suggested that the following additional statements should be published in the corporate report: a statement of value added, an employment report, a statement of money exchanges with government, a statement of transactions in foreign currency, a statement of future prospects and a statement of corporate objectives.[144] In addition, the Committee recommended further study into methods of social accounting as well as the disaggregation of certain financial information.[145]

Finally, the Committee discussed the concepts and measurements employed in the 'basic financial statements'. In considering the purpose of profit measurement, it concluded that income statements 'should be concerned with the measurement of performance although they may also be used in the measurement of capital maintenance and income distributability.'[146] It was, however, recognised that this dual purpose of income statements often gave rise to conflict in the application of accounting concepts – particularly the fundamental concepts of prudence and matching. Various measurement bases were then discussed in the context of the inadequacies of the historical cost system. The Committee stated that 'the usefulness of financial statements in fulfilling user needs is restricted at the present time because of the defects of the basis of measurement generally used. Historical cost accounting fails, in times of rapidly changing prices and values, to ensure that sufficient provision is made for capital maintenance.'[147]

The committee then briefly surveyed several bases of measurement, including historical cost, current purchasing power (CPP) and various current value bases such as replacement cost and net realisable value. The conclusion reached was that no one system of measurement is capable of satisfying the user needs identified in the study, and that, therefore, research should be undertaken into the feasibility of multi-column reporting, as well as into the development of a standardised system of current value accounting.[148]

It is probable that the business community were concerned about the possibility of their reporting responsibility being extended through the development of the Committee's concept of public accountability. Although this aspect of the Corporate Report has largely been absent from all further conceptual framework documents, arguably it was a far-sighted approach. The rise of public interest in, and of academic research into, alternative reports dealing with areas such as the environment and corporate social responsibility, may indicate that the public accountability aspect of corporate reporting will have to become more formally recognised. Indeed, this is the case already with the prominence now being attached to corporate governance disclosures by a number of listing authorities.

4.2   Financial reporting in times of high inflation

Through most of the 1970s and early 1980s, inflation was an intractable problem in the UK and in certain other countries, with rates of inflation well above 10% common, and on occasion over 20%. Inflation poses insoluble problems for historical cost based financial statements because the buying-power of a monetary unit from one accounting period to the next is so different. Outlining the findings of a UK Government committee set up to consider this problem provides a useful way of considering the alternative systems of accounting that have been put forward, as opposed to the more evolutionary nature of the FASB's approach.

The UK Government announced the creation of an Inflation Accounting Committee, subsequently referred to as the Sandilands Committee after its chairman, 'to consider whether, and if so how, company accounts should allow for changes (including relative changes) in costs and prices'.[149] The Sandilands Report is dealt with here in some detail, as it was, and remains, the most comprehensive summary of the many different approaches that have been taken by academic and professional accountants, prompted by a variety of economic conditions, to solving the problems that have surrounded the development of a conceptual framework.

The Sandilands Report followed a similar approach to that of the Corporate Report to the extent that it focused on the information needs of users. The report stated that 'the requirements of users of accounts should be the fundamental consideration in deciding the information to be disclosed in company accounts.'[150]

The report proposed the development of a system of accounting for inflation that would evolve towards a system of current cost accounting, the essential features of which are:

(a) money is the unit of measurement (as opposed to the 'current purchasing power' basis of expressing financial information in terms of a unit of measurement of constant value when prices change);

(b) assets and liabilities should be shown in the balance sheet at their 'value to the business'; and

(c) operating profit (to be known as 'current cost profit') would be calculated after charging the 'value to the business' of the assets consumed during the period, thereby excluding holding gains and showing them separately.[151]

4.2.1 *Current Purchasing Power accounting*

In formulating its system of current cost accounting, the Committee examined three alternative accounting systems that had been developed in an attempt to overcome the deficiencies of historical cost accounting. The first of these systems studied was a 'current purchasing power' (CPP) method of inflation accounting, whereby supplementary information would be given in addition to the historical cost financial statements. The main features of the CPP approach were:

(a) companies would continue to keep their records and present their basic annual accounts in historical pounds, i.e. in terms of the value of the pound at the time of each transaction or revaluation;

(b) in addition, all listed companies should present to their shareholders a supplementary statement in terms of the value of the pound at the end of the period to which the accounts relate;

(c) the conversion of the figures in the basic accounts into the figures in the supplementary statement should be by means of a general index of the purchasing power of the pound;[152] and

(d) the directors would be required to provide in a note to the supplementary statement an explanation of the basis on which it has been prepared and it was considered desirable that directors should comment on the significance of the figures.[153]

The Committee concluded that the CPP method 'does not remedy the main deficiencies of historic cost accounting during a time of changing costs and prices and we do not recommend it as the best long-term solution to the problem of accounting for inflation.'[154] Numerous arguments were put forward to support this conclusion, for example:

- since, during a period of changing prices, historical cost figures expressed in terms of monetary units do not show the 'value to the business' of assets, a CPP supplementary statement will show the historic cost figures restated in units of current purchasing power, not the 'value to the business' of assets.[155] Thus, a major deficiency of historical cost accounts would not be overcome;

- since companies were required to express their CPP supplementary statements in terms of the current purchasing power of the pound at the closing balance sheet date, the unit of measurement in the supplementary statement would change from year to year. This was likely to cause confusion, compounded by the fact that companies which had different accounting dates would be preparing supplementary statements in terms of different units, resulting in a lack of comparability;[156] and

- since a unit of measurement with an absolute value through time is unattainable, there is no advantage in preparing financial statements in CPP units rather than in units of money.[157]

4.2.2   Value accounting

The Committee then examined three forms of 'value accounting' – a term used to describe a wide range of different accounting systems which measure net assets by reference to their 'value' rather than their cost. The three value accounting systems examined were: replacement cost accounting; present value accounting; and continuously contemporary accounting.

A   Replacement cost accounting based on current entry values

'Replacement cost' is the price which will have to be paid to replace an asset used or given up in exchange for another asset. Consequently, the basic principle underlying replacement cost accounting is that, since a business has to replace its assets over time in order to continue in operational existence, charges for the consumption or exchange of an asset should be based on the cost of replacing it. Consequently, assets are valued at the balance sheet date by reference to the price which would have to be paid at that date to purchase a similar asset in a similar condition – i.e. the replacement cost of the assets. This system, therefore, adopts a method of income determination that reflects changes in capital both at the point of realisation of assets and, before realisation, while holding assets.

The pioneers of an income and value model based on replacement costs (entry values) were Edwards and Bell,[158] who attempted to interpret accounting concepts in terms of economic concepts. Their theory abandoned both the realisation principle and the idea of the 'unitary income statement' which does not separate operating profit from holding gains. They introduced a new concept of 'business profit', which was made up of current operating profit of the current period, realised holding gains of the same period and unrealised holding gains.

A major disadvantage of the replacement cost model is the difficulty and subjectivity involved in assigning replacement costs; for example, are replacement costs based on identical or equivalent replacements, and how is technological obsolescence dealt with? However, the Sandilands Committee took the view that this disadvantage was far outweighed by the usefulness of the information provided by the system in the form of meaningful balance sheet values and a segregated business profit figure. The Sandilands Committee concluded that the replacement cost accounting system 'comes close to meeting the dominant requirements of users of accounts and the Committee's own proposals have many similarities with certain forms of this system of accounting.'[159]

B   *Present value accounting*

Present value accounting is based on the economic concept of income, and values an asset on the basis of the present value of the cash flows that are expected to be derived from that asset. In order to maintain the capital of the entity, an amount at least equal to the original investment should be reinvested, whilst the remaining cash flows are treated as realised. For example, if the discounted net present value of all expected future cash flows of an entity are €100,000 at the beginning of the year and €115,000 at the end of the year, and if the net cash flows arising during the year were €10,000, then the profit for the year will be €25,000, since this amount could be distributed whilst maintaining the original capital base of €100,000.

Whilst this approach might have some degree of theoretical soundness, the Sandilands Committee considered it to be totally impracticable. The Committee believed that issues such as risk, the determination of discount rates, changes in interest rates and the uncertainty of future cash flows presented virtually insurmountable problems. The Sandilands Committee therefore rejected present value accounting on the grounds that use of economic value as the basis of valuation of an asset would not meet the needs of users, as it would only be in comparatively few cases that this would represent the value of an asset to a business.[160]

C   *Continuously Contemporary Accounting (CoCoA)*

The current value income model based on exit prices or realisable market values was first advocated by MacNeal in a book published by him in 1939 which dealt, inter alia, with the ethical issue of 'truth' in accounting.[161] MacNeal maintained that financial statements could only present the 'truth' if assets were stated at their current value and the profit and losses accruing from the changes in these values are included in income, and classified as either realised or unrealised. MacNeal did, however, concede that under certain circumstances the use of net realisable values was not appropriate, and that in such cases current replacement costs should be used.

The system known as continuously contemporary accounting (CoCoA) was formally introduced by Chambers in a book published in 1966,[162] and the case for exit value accounting was further developed by Sterling.[163] Chambers' theory is based on the premise that entities must be able to choose between alternative courses of action and, because resources are limited, they need to know what resources are available to enable them to engage in exchanges. Consequently, Chambers asserts that this capacity to engage in exchanges is measured by the opportunity cost of holding assets in their existing form, and that this opportunity cost is represented by the current cash equivalent of assets – which Chambers defines as being their current sales value. Initially, Chambers did not apply this principle rigorously and proposed that stocks should be valued at current replacement cost. However, he subsequently amended his view and advocated that exit values should be applied to the valuation of all assets. A difference in the theories of Chambers and Sterling is, for example, that Chambers believed that net realisable values should be based on the assumption that assets are realised in an orderly manner based on sensible adaptations to changing circumstances; Sterling, on the other hand, believed that net realisable values should be based on immediate liquidation prices.

The capital maintenance concept adopted by CoCoA is based on the preservation of the purchasing power of shareholders' equity (using the monetary unit as the unit of measurement, and not the current purchasing power unit used in CPP accounting). Consequently, since all assets (both monetary and non-monetary) are measured at net realisable value, income is defined as the difference between opening and closing equity after maintaining the purchasing power or cash equivalent of such equity. Income for the year, therefore, will comprise (1) the net profit/loss on business operations, (2) the accrued profit/loss arising from the change in the current cash equivalent of assets and (3) the effect on the capital of the entity brought about by the change in the purchasing power of money.

However, despite the widespread publication of his theories, Chambers failed to gain any measure of support for CoCoA outside academic circles.

There is no doubt that there are some compelling theoretical arguments for the presentation of financial statements based on net realisable values; for example, they provide useful information in the assessment of liquidity and financial flexibility. However, net realisable value is unlikely to reflect an asset's 'value to the business', since, for instance, an item of plant might have negligible net realisable value but substantial use value. Therefore, whilst the disclosure of net realisable values might provide useful supplementary information, the arguments in favour of CoCoA as the primary basis of accounting are unconvincing. CoCoA was rejected by the Sandilands Committee on the basis that, as a whole, it did not satisfy the information needs of users which they had identified.[164] It is, however, noteworthy that in its discussion document – *Making Corporate Reports Valuable* – the Research Committee of the ICAS advocated a reporting system based on net realisable values[165] (see 4.4 below). Rather interestingly, the measurement ideas underlining the FASB's standard on fair value measurement, SFAS 157, published in 2006, bear a striking resemblance to Chambers' ideas. SFAS 157 is further discussed at 6.2 below.

4.2.3 Cash flow accounting

Finally the Sandilands Committee considered cash flow accounting. The principal proponents of cash flow reporting were Lee[166] and Lawson,[167] although there are several other advocates of various approaches to cash flow reporting. Lee's system of cash flow reporting relied heavily on exit value theory and aimed to report both actual and potential cash flows. Assets are classified according to their realisability, based on Chambers' principle of orderly liquidation. If a sale price does not exist, assets are to be accounted for as having a zero cash equivalent.[168] Lee suggested the following four asset classifications for his statement of financial position:

1.   realised assets (e.g. bank balances);

2.   readily-realisable assets (i.e. assets which have a ready market and sale price, such as listed securities, debtors and stocks of finished goods);

3.   non-readily-realisable assets (i.e. assets which do have a market and sale price, but which would not be quickly realised because of the limited nature of the market, such as certain items of plant and work-in-progress); and

4.   not-realisable assets (i.e. assets which have no known sales price and no market, and would therefore be ascribed a zero value, such as highly specialised or obsolete plant).[169]

Liabilities are classified according to maturity, in line with conventional accounting practice.

Lee proposed that, in addition to a 'statement of financial position', the cash flow reporting system should present a 'statement of realised cash flow', a 'statement of realisable earnings' and a 'statement of changes in financial position'.[170] The statement of realised cash flow would report an entity's actual cash inflows and outflows during a particular period; it is noteworthy that the information contained in this statement would be broadly equivalent to that which would be presented in a statement of cash flows under IAS 7 – *Cash Flow Statements* (see Chapter 39). The statement of realisable earnings would report periodic profit similar to that provided by a net realisable value accounting system, except that it is described in terms of realised and realisable cash flows. The statement would provide an analysis of realised earnings (derived from the entity's operating cash flow), and unrealised earnings (which represent potential cash flows that have accrued during the period as a result of changes in the realisable values of assets, net of the changes in liabilities). The statement of changes in financial position was effectively a conventional funds statement presented on an exit value basis.

Although there are a number of practical accounting and disclosure problems in cash flow reporting, it does have considerable merit. However, one difficulty which does exist is caused by the artificial 12 month reporting period and the necessity to measure 'profitability' over that period and from one period to the next. The principal reason for the development of the accrual basis of accounting was that financial statements prepared on a cash basis (which was probably the oldest form of presentation) provided distorted profit figures from one period to the next.

Although the Sandilands Committee stated that there was 'much of value in the cash flow accounting principle',[171] it was felt that cash flow accounting would rekindle all the 'old difficulties of assessing the profit or loss for the year when the accounting system does not match revenues against costs incurred in their generation.'[172] The Committee therefore concluded that the abandonment of the existing concept of the profit and loss account in favour of a cash flow statement would result in the information needs of users not being met. Clearly, however, the Committee had not considered the possibility of the presentation of a 'statement of realisable earnings' as advocated by Lee, which would provide a more stable basis for reporting profit than the statement of receipts and payments the Committee apparently envisaged. Lee, however, recognised the problems created by the traditional 12 month reporting period, and suggested that a solution might be found in the use of multi-period aggregates for analysis purposes.

4.2.4   *Current cost accounting (CCA)*

The Sandilands Committee recommended the development of a system of current cost accounting that used the monetary unit as the unit of measurement and dealt with the effects of specific price changes (as opposed to changes in the general purchasing power of money) on individual businesses. The Committee recommended that the balance sheet should present the 'value to the business' of the company's assets, which was equated with the amount of the loss that would be suffered by an entity if the asset were to be lost or destroyed. Whilst it was stated that the 'value to the business' of an asset might, under certain circumstances, be its net realisable value or economic value, it would normally be based on its replacement cost. Because the Committee recommended that financial statements be drawn up in terms of the monetary unit, no adjustment would be made for monetary items.[173] However, it is arguable that current cost accounting does not produce a balance sheet which seeks to be a statement of values of the resources of the company; it simply updates the costs at which they are recorded. This distinction can be illustrated by looking at the financial statements of an oil and gas exploration company. Even on a current cost basis, the carrying value of its principal assets is still based on the (backward-looking) cost of exploration expenditure incurred, not the (forward-looking) value of the oil and gas it has found.

Under the Sandilands system, an entity's 'current cost profit' for a period would be calculated by charging against income 'the value to the business' of assets consumed during the year. In simple terms, therefore, the current cost profit could be derived from the historical cost profit by means of an adjustment to depreciation and a cost of sales adjustment. The Committee also recommended the presentation of a summary statement of total gains or losses for the period, which would present the entity's total gains/losses in terms of three classifications: operating gains/losses (i.e. current cost profit/loss), extraordinary gains/losses and holding gains/losses. An interesting observation regarding these two statements recommended by the Committee is that they are based on a different capital maintenance concepts. The calculation of current cost profit was based on the concept of physical capital maintenance, whilst the summary statement of total gains was concerned with the maintenance of financial capital. However, because the calculation of current cost profit subsequently received greater prominence than the summary of total gains, it is generally thought that the Sandilands proposals were based on the concept of physical capital maintenance.[174]

The Committee recommended that current cost accounting should replace historical cost accounting, and that its proposals should be incorporated in an accounting standard. Its recommendations met with little support, which was attributed at the time to the fact that there was considerable objection to the replacement of historical cost accounting by a new untested system; the proposals were considered too complicated; and the profit figure was considered misleading without adjustment for monetary items.

Subsequently, a further UK study – The Hyde Guidelines – recommended that three adjustments should be made to the historical cost results: in addition to the depreciation and cost of sales adjustments proposed by Sandilands, it was recommended that a 'gearing adjustment' be made as an interim solution to dealing with monetary items in inflation-adjusted financial statements. Since no account of the existence of borrowings was taken in calculating current cost operating profit, the implication was that operating capability had to be maintained entirely out of the generation of revenues. However, the reality is clearly that this could be financed partly by borrowings; consequently, the gearing adjustment was designed to take account of the extent to which fixed assets and working capital were financed by borrowings.

Following these efforts a standard, SSAP 16 – *Current cost accounting* – was issued in the UK in 1980 that:[175]

(a)   introduced a fourth adjustment, called the 'monetary working capital adjustment', which effectively extended the cost of sales adjustment (which allowed for increases in the investment needed to maintain stocks when prices were increasing) to the other working capital items. Consequently, the monetary working capital adjustment represented an estimate of the extra investment in debtors, creditors and liquid resources required to maintain operations when prices were increasing;

(b)   proposed the presentation of a current cost balance sheet, in which fixed assets and stock would be measured on a current cost basis; and

(c)   proposed that listed companies disclose current cost earnings per share.

SSAP 16 perpetuated the concept of current cost operating profit based on the maintenance of physical capital, which had been extended to monetary working capital through the monetary working capital adjustment. The associated gearing adjustment probably arose as a result of the need to compromise with critics of the entire process in order to find an acceptable solution – as opposed to having any theoretically sound justification.

It is worthy of note, given our view that ultimately any accounting theoretical framework will be subject to the rigorous test of whether it is applicable and useful in practice, that SSAP 16 suffered a very low level of compliance until it was eventually withdrawn.

It might be argued that the activities described in this section provide evidence for the view that accounting standard setting is a process of establishing convention in response to the needs of the times. The high inflation rates of the late 1970s and early 1980s drove both practitioners and academics to undertake various studies and produce a number of recommendations. Since inflation has ceased to be as significant a concern, interest in this problem has, perhaps inevitably, noticeably waned.

4.3   Canada: The Stamp Report

In 1980, Professor Edward Stamp produced a research study primarily for the Canadian Institute of Chartered Accountants which was 'intended to provide a Canadian solution to the problem of improving the quality of corporate financial reporting standards.'[176] Stamp adopted a similar approach to that of other studies (such as the Corporate Report and Trueblood) by looking at users, their needs, their rights to information and the qualitative characteristics of that information. Stamp identified a more detailed list of users (15 in all) than did, for example, the Corporate or Sandilands Reports.

Stamp developed a set of 20 qualitative criteria which could be used as yardsticks whereby standard-setters, as well as the preparers and users of published financial statements, can decide whether or not the financial statements are meeting the objectives of financial reporting and the needs of users. An interesting rider to this aspect of Stamp's study was that he subsequently used his list of qualitative criteria as the basis of an empirical study of the relative importance of each of the criteria.[177] Stamp supplied each member of the UK's standard setting body (the ASC at that time) with a copy of Chapter 7 of his CICA research study in which the significance and meaning of each of the 20 criteria were discussed. He also gave them each a questionnaire in which they were asked to rank the 20 criteria in order of importance.[178] Although the ranking revealed 'relevance' as the most important criterion and 'conservatism' as the least important, this in itself was not the most significant aspect of Stamp's study. The real significance was that he demonstrated it would be possible to establish rankings of characteristics of accounting information for each category of user.

In his CICA research study, Stamp also devoted a considerable amount of effort towards discussing certain fundamental conceptual issues such as problems of allocation, income measurement, capital maintenance, the proprietary versus the entity theory, and the question of which attribute accounting should measure.[179] These issues are all fundamental to the development of a conceptual framework for financial reporting; yet they have not been resolved unequivocally by the conceptual frameworks of the two most influential global standard setting bodies – the FASB and the IASB.

4.4   Discussion document: 'Making Corporate Reports Valuable'

4.4.1   Background

This discussion document, which was issued in 1988, was the product of a major research project undertaken by the Research Committee of the Institute of Chartered Accountants of Scotland, and included David Tweedie (now Sir David Tweedie, Chairman of the IASB) among its project members. The reason why this paper was so refreshing at the time was principally because the research committee started from the basis of a 'clean sheet'. In other words, the members were able to ignore existing laws, accounting rules, terminology and all other constraints in order to try and achieve what they believed to be the best result. The Committee started off by explaining what motivated it to reconsider the nature of corporate reporting. The reasons which were given included the following basic conclusions:

- all financial reports ought to reflect economic reality;

- the information which investors need is the same in kind, but not in volume, as the information which managements need to run their entities;

- some of the information that management has but does not normally communicate comes out into the open when management wants something – such as additional capital or to be able to defend a hostile take-over bid;

- present-day financial reports are deficient in that they are based on legal form rather than economic substance, on cost rather than value, on the past rather than the future, and on 'profit' rather than 'wealth';

- there is no consistent conceptual basis underlying the production of either the profit and loss account or the balance sheet, and some of the concepts used appear to defy normal understanding of financial affairs;

- corporate reports are not made public sufficiently speedily; and

- the audit report is insufficiently informative and is often incomprehensible to non-auditors.[180]

The Committee then discussed various bases for applying values to assets, focusing on historical cost, current replacement cost, current net realisable values and economic values. Having discussed what it saw as the deficiencies of historical cost and economic value, the Committee noted that current replacement cost and net realisable value both met its criteria of economic reality and 'additivity' (i.e. the total number in a statement should not mean something different in kind from its constituent numbers). Nevertheless, the Committee expressed a preference for net realisable value as the basis for applying values to assets, 'principally because it is value-based whereas replacement cost is cost-based',[181] and it was felt that 'value rather than cost is important in assessing financial wealth.'[182]

4.4.2   The proposed information package

The Committee proposed what was then an entirely new information package, using net realisable values as the basis of valuation. In order to present the financial wealth of an entity, the Committee proposed that the following four basic statements should replace the existing financial statements:

(a)   *Assets and Liabilities Statement*, which would present the assets and liabilities of the entity at the reporting date, each stated at its net realisable value. Net realisable values would normally be determined according to the principle of orderly disposal, unless the entity is in financial trouble, in which case 'a more appropriate method' (such as break-up values) should be used;[183]

(b)   *Operations Statement*, which calculates the financial wealth added to the entity by trading and by its operations generally. It differs from the present form of profit and loss account in that:

(i)   there would be no depreciation charge;

(ii)   the stock would be accounted for at net realisable value; and

(iii) the only exceptional or extraordinary items would be those arising out of unusual events of a revenue nature; exceptional or extraordinary gains or losses on fixed assets would be dealt with in the Statement of Changes in Financial Wealth outlined at (c) below;[184]

(c) *Statement of Changes in Financial Wealth*, which shows the change in the worth of the business for the period under consideration, such change being split into its main components with an indication of how each of these arose. The Committee proposed that the change in wealth would be measured in terms of year-end pounds, although 'in times of significant inflation it may be helpful if investors can be given an indication of the real change in financial wealth over the period concerned by applying the retail price index';[185] and

(d) *Distributions Statement*, which reflects the distributable change in financial wealth for the period plus any surpluses retained from previous periods, less dividends paid and proposed. In times of rising prices the 'real value' of capital should be maintained by an inflation adjustment which should be shown in the distributions statement and might be computed by applying the retail price index to the value of shareholders' contributed capital as at the start of the period. The paper went on to say that entities wishing to maintain their operating capability in physical terms could make a further appropriation to maintain the asset portfolio or to provide for the replacement of the services which these assets have been supplying.[186]

In addition to the four basic statements and information relating to corporate objectives and future financial plans, the Committee suggested the inclusion of the following additional information in the reporting package:

(a) a cash flow statement;

(b) segmental information;[187]

(c) information on related parties;

(d) information on accounting areas subject to uncertainty, for example management's view on the margin of error in accounting estimates;

(e) a statement on relative innovation which would illustrate the stance that the company is adopting in relation to innovation;

(f) information on effectiveness and lead-time of research and development;

(g) information on the economic environment within which the entity operates, including an analysis of facts such as market share, market strength, market size, the activities of competitors etc.;

(h) comparative operational statistics contrasting the reporting firm with its competitors;[188]

(i) information on staff resources; and

(j) information on ownership, management and their responsibilities.

4.4.3 Conclusion

At the time this was one of the boldest, most innovative and refreshing discussion documents ever to be published by a professional accounting body anywhere in the world. Of course it had flaws and can be criticised for either failing to address or inadequately addressing certain issues; however, it should be seen for what it was – a document designed to stimulate discussion, experimentation and further research. Although there was always the danger that the document would be regarded as too revolutionary in its approach, and be dismissed as an amusing intellectual exercise, it is now clear that the IASB's agenda of accounting change and development draws heavily on MCRV. For example the list of supplementary information above no longer looks innovative because so much of its suggested contents now appears in the financial reports of companies.

4.5   The Solomons Report

In May 1987, the Research Board of the ICAEW announced that it had decided to sponsor a project to address the need for guidelines for decisions in financial reporting. Professor David Solomons, a recently retired academic who in his lifetime was president of both the American Accounting Association and the British Accounting Association, agreed to carry out the study.

Solomons followed an approach to the subject that was almost identical to that taken by the FASB (see 2 above), perhaps not surprisingly considering that he acted as consultant to the FASB on its conceptual framework project and was principal author of SFAC No. 2. He started by examining the purposes of financial reporting, identifying users and how their needs were at present being met. His report then discussed the elements of financial statements and decided upon the asset and liability, rather than the revenue and expense, approach to financial accounting.[189]

Solomons' principal argument against the revenue and expense view of income determination was that it 'opens the door to all kinds of income smoothing'[190] and that it 'threatens the integrity of the balance sheet and its value as a useful financial statement. Its value is maximized if it can be seen as a statement of financial position; but it can only be that if all the items in it are truly assets, liabilities, and equity, and not other bits left over from the profit and loss account, and if all such items that are capable of being recognised are included in it.'[191] This attitude of Solomons has obviously been influential in the thinking of the IASB subsequently.

Solomons then set about defining the elements of financial statements on much the same basis as was done in SFAC No. 6 (see 2.4 above). Assets are defined as 'resources or rights incontestably controlled by an entity at the accounting date that are expected to yield it future economic benefits',[192] whilst liabilities are defined as 'obligations of an entity at the accounting date to make future transfers of assets or services (sometimes uncertain as to timing and amount) to other entities.'[193] As with the FASB and IASB concepts, all the other elements are then derived from these basic definitions; for example, owners' equity comprises net assets and income is the change in net assets.[194]

The Report focused attention on the issues of recognition and measurement and the choice of an accounting model for use in preparing general purpose financial statements. In view of the fact that Solomons' guidelines are based on the asset and liability view, it is not surprising that his recognition criteria concentrate on these two elements. Consequently, under Solomons' approach, an item should only be recognised in financial statements if:

'(a)   it conforms to the definition of an asset or liability or of one of the sub-elements derived therefrom; and

(b)   its magnitude as specified by the accounting model being used can be measured and verified with reasonable certainty; and

(c)   the magnitude so arrived at is material in amount.'[195]

Solomons, having rejected the historical cost model generally in use at the time, set about devising an improved model for general purpose financial reporting, and listed the following five criteria that such an improved model should possess:

(a)   the balance sheet should be a true and fair statement of an entity's financial condition, showing all its assets and liabilities that satisfy the above recognition criteria and conform with the asset and liability definitions;

(b)   the entity's assets and liabilities should be carried in the balance sheet at their value to a going concern at the balance sheet date;

(c)   profits or losses should mean increases or decreases of real financial capital as compared with the amount at the beginning of the year;

(d)   the results shown by the financial statements should be measured consistently and should therefore be comparable from year to year, both in periods of fluctuating prices and stable prices; and

(e)   all the information given by the financial statements should be verifiable and cost-effective.[196]

(In a subsequent posthumous publication entitled *Commentary: criteria for choosing an accounting model*[197] the number of criteria is expanded to seven, the extra two being essentially clarifications of the meanings of the original five.)

Solomons then attempted to prove that the model that best satisfies these requirements rests on two concepts: value to the business (as espoused by the Corporate Report and Sandilands Committee) and the maintenance of real financial capital. Although these may have some intellectual appeal, it is difficult to see whether either of them has any practical meaning. Solomons identified an asset's value to the business as being the loss that the business would suffer if it were deprived of the asset. He argued that since if deprived of an asset, the business would normally seek to replace it, replacement cost would determine value to the business.

However, Solomons recognised that circumstances exist where an asset's value to the business might be less than its replacement cost; for example, in the circumstances where a plant asset is technologically inferior to an equivalent new asset, the current cost of replacing the services rendered by the existing asset should be used. Furthermore, where an asset would not be replaced by a business if it were lost, its value to the business would be its recoverable amount, which is the higher of the asset's present value and its net realisable value. Therefore, Solomons' final formula for 'value to the business' is that it is equal to 'current cost or recoverable amount, if that is lower.'[198] It is interesting to note that this approach is almost identical to the criteria specified in IAS 36 – *Impairment of assets* – for identifying if an asset is impaired (see Chapter 18).

In the case of liabilities, the Solomons' equivalent to an asset's deprival value is a liability's relief value. In other words, liabilities would be valued at the amount that the entity 'could currently raise by the issue of a precisely similar debt security or the cost of discharging the liability by the most economical means, whichever is the higher.'[199] The view advanced in the late 1990s by the G4+1, is very similar to the Solomons approach and is clearly still influential in the thinking of the IASB today.

As mentioned above, Solomons' model is based on the maintenance of real financial capital, with income being defined in terms of the change in net worth. He took the view that because of the uncertainty surrounding the measurement and verification of intangible assets, the changes in such assets cannot be recognised in financial statements; consequently, income will only include changes in recognised tangible assets minus changes in recognised liabilities.[200] This view seems untenable today in view of the important role intangibles play in business and commerce, and provides another interesting example of the influence that business practice has on accounting theory, as at the time Solomons wrote, his views on the recognition of intangibles were not considered obviously flawed.

Solomons recommended a 'current-cost-constant-purchasing-power model' that recognised both changes in the general level of prices and changes in specific prices, and was based on the maintenance of real financial capital, not operating capacity.[201] The following pro forma profit and loss account illustrates how Solomons' version of real income is derived:[202]

Pro forma profit and loss account as proposed by Solomons

	£
Sales revenue	×××
Current cost (or lower recoverable amount) of goods sold	×××
	×××
Depreciation at current cost	×××
Other expenses	×××
	×××
Current operating profit	×××
Add:	
Holding gains less losses on non-monetary assets (net of inflation)	×××
Purchasing power gains on monetary liabilities less purchasing power losses on monetary assets	×××
	×××
Real income	×××

However it is the views expressed by Solomons on pensions that seem extraordinarily prescient and influential to the present day reader. For example he recommended if all or most of the assets of a pension plan can be moved freely back to the employer from the plan by a vote of the trustees, then the affairs of the plan should be consolidated with those of the employer. This approach is based on the view that a pension fund is, in effect, an off balance sheet vehicle set up to meet a company's future obligations. Solomons' proposal was extremely close to the approach adopted by the IASB in IAS 19 (Revised) – *Employee Benefits* – which is discussed in Chapter 28.

On the subject of goodwill, Solomons states that non-purchased goodwill should not be recognised; his reason for this being that 'determining the value of goodwill where it is not the subject of a purchase and sale transaction and in the presence of a highly imperfect market is too subjective to yield a reliable measure for the purpose of recognition.'[203] What he is saying is that since non-purchased goodwill does not have an historical cost, it is not possible to update an unknown cost in order to determine its current cost. The same argument applies to all internally generated intangibles, such as brand names. This remains a considerable problem for standard setters, in view of the commercial importance of intangible assets.

4.6   The UK's conceptual framework

The United Kingdom's conceptual framework document is interesting as it was the most recently published and also because the then Chairman of the UK's Accounting Standards Board, Sir David Tweedie, is currently Chairman of the IASB. The finalised version of the UK's Accounting Standards Board's *Statement of Principles for Financial Reporting* was published in December 1999 and the abbreviation 'SoP' is used hereafter.[204] The SoP is now somewhat redundant in the context of EU reporting under IFRS, and is therefore very briefly outlined below; although in view of the involvement of Sir David Tweedie, and its relatively recent publication, it may subsequently be seen as having been influential on the new IASB-FASB framework project's outcome.

The SoP comprised a compendium of eight 'chapters', with titles that owe much to the US and IASC's framework projects:

1. The objective of financial statements;
2. The reporting entity;
3. The qualitative characteristics of financial information;
4. The elements of financial statements;
5. Recognition in financial statements;
6. Measurement in financial statements;
7. Presentation of financial information; and
8. Accounting for interests in other entities.

The ASB acknowledged that, in drafting the SoP it was drawing heavily on the work of previous projects in other countries, notably the FASB concept statements discussed at 2 above and the IASC Framework discussed at 3 above. The objectives ascribed to financial statements are therefore quite familiar.[205]

As in the IASB's Framework, the investor's perspective is deemed to represent the user's needs. Having established this generalisation, the SoP then goes on to assert that investors need information about the generation and use of cash in order to assess the entity's: liquidity and solvency; the relationship between profits and cash flows; the implications that financial performance has for future cash flows; and other aspects of financial adaptability.[206] Therefore, the academic stance that predicting future cash flows is the objective of reporting is endorsed.

The SoP also selects relevance and reliability as the two primary characteristics of accounting information, and again recognises that they are sometimes in conflict, so as to require a trade-off between them. In this case the choice is to be resolved as follows:

> 'if a choice exists between relevant and reliable approaches that are mutually exclusive, the approach chosen needs to be the one that results in the relevance of the information provided being maximised.'[207]

Therefore, the SoP takes the view that relevance takes priority over reliability and states that relevant information has the ability to 'influence the economic decisions of users and is provided in time to influence those decisions.'[208] This assertion of the priority of relevance over reliability was a substantial departure from the traditional view of prudence (conservatism), and was a harbinger of what has emerged from the first stage of the joint IASB-FASB framework project (discussed at 5.2 below). However it is a departure that is not altogether surprising, given the move towards fair value accounting that is predicated on the view that fair values are more relevant than cost, even if they may be less reliable. This view overlooks that fact that users find information relevant only if it is reliable, and there is a threshold of reliability below which relevance ceases.

Thereafter the discussion of qualitative characteristics follows closely the IASB's Framework discussed above, including the unsatisfactory defining away of the problem of understandability.

Seven elements of financial statements are defined: Assets, Liabilities, Ownership Interest, Gains, Losses, Contributions from Owners, Distributions to Owners. The definitions and their deductive structure closely follow the IASB's Framework, starting with a near-identical asset definition. A definitional refinement is added however, namely that for a future economic benefit to be an asset it must also be 'controlled independently of the business as a whole.'[209] This new concept of independence from the business as a whole is only illustrated, not defined, although examples are given: 'market share, superior management or good labour relations ... cannot be controlled independently of the business as a whole.'[210] In this way, the SoP intends to prevent certain types of expenditure from being deferred and carried forward in the balance sheet as an asset.

Revenue recognition (which is not characterised as such) is referred to as follows:

> 'In a transaction involving the provision of services or goods for a net gain, the recognition criteria described above [i.e. the asset/liability criteria above] will be met on the occurrence of the critical event in the operating cycle involved.'[211]

By including this paragraph, the UK framework document seems to be fending off any potential criticism of its asset/liability approach to revenue recognition. In defending the approach that gains and losses are merely increases and decreases in net assets, other than those resulting from transactions with shareholders, the ASB is attempting to assert that both an asset/liability approach and a critical event approach to revenue recognition end up with the same answer. What the above paragraph is saying is that a net gain that is recognised on the basis of the critical event approach will necessarily result in an increase in net assets, with the result that the asset/liability recognition criteria will also be met.

However, while this is so, the converse is not. The implication is that irrespective of whether one follows a balance sheet approach to income recognition or a transactions-based income statement approach, one will always get to the same end-result. This is patently not true. Just because all revenue recognised under an income statement based transactions system will satisfy the asset/liability recognition criteria, it does not follow that all increases and decreases in net assets relate to revenue arising 'on the occurrence of the critical event in the operating cycle involved'. Revenue recognition criteria are more demanding than those for recognising changes in assets and liabilities, since in our view they should embody the concept of the revenue having been earned, based on performance by the reporting company. The issue of revenue recognition is discussed in detail in Chapter 25.

The SoP settles for a traditional approach to the statements that should be included in financial reports. However its discussion of how to account for investments in other entities acknowledges a difficulty inherent in both the UK's and IASB's framework documents. This difficulty is that the definition of assets excludes goodwill (because goodwill cannot meet the 'controlled' part of the definition), which creates a particular problem for the presentation of group accounts. This is acknowledged in the SoP, which seeks to justify the departure from the principle as follows:

> 'Purchased goodwill ... is not an asset in itself ... [but] if the parent's investment is to be fully reflected in the group's financial statements and the parent is to be held accountable for its investment ... purchased goodwill needs to be recognised as if it were an asset.'[212]

Perhaps this admission illustrates how standard setters often will, when practical considerations require it, quietly ignore the fundamental principles their standards are stated to rest upon.

4.7   Conclusion

It can be seen that much of the academic and professionally sponsored research described above has been influential in shaping the underlying thinking in, and the practical requirements of, the IASB's accounting standards. Equally it is clear that much of this research has been influenced by the economic circumstances of the periods in which it took place. For example, inflation is no longer a preoccupation either of the profession or of economists, yet it was the phenomenon that drove much of the work described above. Somewhat paradoxically, historical cost accounting with its inherent simplicity, certainty and understandability, although easily dismissed as inadequate in inflationary times, becomes increasingly viable in the current low-inflation environment. It is one of those historical 'what-if' questions, but whether fair value concepts would be so important in current thinking had the current low-inflationary economic environment existed for the last 40 years, is an interesting moot point.

It is also interesting to note that a number of concepts used in current IASB standards (e.g. fair value, value in use) are really applications of concepts already extant in the academic literature. Value to the business as described by Solomons (see 4.5 above) equates to value in use; while fair value, as used by the IASB, is really sometimes an entry value, as discussed by Edwards and Bell (see 4.2.2 A above) and sometimes an exit value as discussed by Chambers, Sterling and Lee (see 4.2.2 C and 4.2.3 above).

5   CONVERGENCE AND THE IASB-FASB FRAMEWORK PROJECT

5.1   Introduction

The IASB and the FASB have a stated policy of working towards the convergence of International GAAP and US GAAP. This had been happening at an informal level for many years through a variety of bodies such as the G4+1 and the Joint Working Group on Financial Instruments. However, as described in Chapter 1, in September 2002 at a meeting between the IASB and the FASB, held at Norwalk, Connecticut, USA, this cooperation was placed on a more formal footing. Consequently in April 2004 at a joint meeting the FASB and the IASB agreed that their underlying conceptual frameworks should be revisited and, if possible, an agreed single conceptual framework produced. This endeavour is now a formal IASB-FASB joint project and is in progress.

The joint framework project is planned to be developed over a number of phases as follows:

Phase A:	Objectives and Qualitative Characteristics
Phase B:	Definition of elements, recognition and derecognition
Phase C:	Measurement
Phase D:	Reporting entity concept
Phase E:	Boundaries of financial reporting, and Presentation and Disclosure
Phase F:	Purpose and status of the framework
Phase G:	Application of the framework to Not-for-Profit Entities
Phase H:	Remaining issues, if any

Phase A was published by both the IASB and the FASB as an Exposure Draft in May 2008 and the final chapter is currently due to be published in the third quarter of 2009. A discussion paper on Phase D was also published in May 2008, and the subsequent exposure draft is expected in the third quarter of 2009. Discussion papers are expected in relation to Phase B in the second half of 2010 and in relation to Phase C in the final quarter of 2009. All of these timescales have slipped over the past twelve months reflecting the extent to which the boards have had to devote time to addressing issues arising from the financial crisis. When combined with the fact that the other phases are not currently active this suggests that the finalisation of the Conceptual Framework may not occur for some time.

5.2   IASB-FASB Exposure Draft – An improved conceptual framework for financial reporting

In May 2008 the IASB published an exposure draft – *An improved conceptual framework for financial reporting.*[213]

The core of the exposure draft is the first two chapters of a new conceptual framework:

Chapter 1:   The Objective of Financial Reporting

Chapter 2:   Qualitative Characteristics of Decision-useful Financial Reporting Information.

In addition, it contains an explanatory preface setting out why the Boards are undertaking the project. The Boards have elected not to conduct a full review of their existing versions, as explained in the Preface:

> 'The boards concluded that a comprehensive reconsideration of all concepts would not be an efficient use of their resources. Many aspects of their frameworks are consistent with each other and do not seem to need fundamental revision. Instead, the boards adopted an approach that focuses mainly on improving their existing frameworks and achieving their convergence, giving priority to issues that are likely to yield standard-setting benefits in the near term.'[214]

Interestingly the preface also notes that the boards have not yet agreed on the status that will be accorded to the new conceptual framework. Under IFRS entities are required to consider the current IASB framework when there is no standard or interpretation that specifically applies to a transaction, but there is no similar requirement under US GAAP. Both boards have however agreed that the framework will not have the status of a financial reporting standard and will not override existing standards, including those that are inconsistent with the framework.[215]

The boards have also decided that they will each finalise the framework as chapters are completed. A number of commentators have argued that the framework should only be finalised once all elements have been completed to ensure that all issues have been appropriately considered before final conclusions are reached. The boards have decided not to follow that approach but they acknowledge that as a consequence 'later phases of the project may include consequential amendments to parts of the framework that were completed in earlier phases'.[216]

The two draft chapters of the new IASB-FASB conceptual framework are discussed in the following sections.

5.2.1   *The objective of financial reporting*

The exposure draft proposes the following statement of the objective of financial reporting:

> 'The objective of general purpose external financial reporting is to provide financial information about the reporting entity that is useful to present and potential equity investors, lenders and other creditors in making decisions in their capacity as capital providers. Information that is decision-useful to capital providers may be useful to other users of financial reporting who are not capital providers.'[217]

This definition has been changed from that proposed in the original discussion paper which had focused simply on investment and similar resource allocation decisions. In response to comments that this focus was too narrow the boards concluded that the objectives of financial reporting should be broad enough to encompass all of the decisions that are made by capital providers.[218]

The exposure draft notes that general purpose financial reporting is directed to the needs of a wide range of users rather than only to the needs of a single group. It arises from the needs of those who cannot prescribe all the financial information they need from an entity. The boards believe that general purpose financial information should focus on the needs of capital providers, specifically present and potential equity investors, lenders and other creditors. 'An entity obtains economic resources from capital providers in exchange for claims on those resources. By virtue of those claims, capital providers have the most critical and immediate need for general purpose financial information about the economic resources of the entity.'[219]

This wider perspective has also led the boards to conclude that general purpose financial reporting should reflect the perspective of the entity rather than that of the entity's equity investors or any other group of capital providers.[220] The exposure draft discusses the differences between the 'entity perspective' and the 'proprietary perspective' and concludes that the entity perspective is more consistent with the way businesses are now conducted.

The meaning of the phrase 'decision-useful' is further clarified as follows:

> 'Capital providers are interested in financial reporting because it provides information that is useful for making decisions. The decisions that capital providers make include whether and how to allocate their resources to a particular entity (i.e. whether and how to provide capital) and whether and how to protect and enhance their investments. When making those decisions, capital providers are interested in assessing the entity's ability to generate net cash inflows and management's ability to protect and enhance the capital providers' investments.'[221]

Again this marks something of a change from the discussion paper which had focused solely on enabling users to assess the future cash flow prospects.

The exposure draft notes that general purpose financial reporting is only one of the sources of information available to users of financial reports and notes that users of general purpose financial statements need to be aware of the characteristics and limitations of such financial statements.

As already alluded to Chapter 1 emphasises that financial reporting should provide information about the economic resources of the entity (its assets) and the claims on those resources (its liabilities). Financial reporting should also explain which transactions or other events have caused the economic resources and claims to change. The boards believe that together this information provides useful information to allow capital providers to assess the entity's ability to generate cash flows and management's effectiveness in fulfilling its stewardship role. The ability of users to interpret general purpose financial reporting will be improved by the inclusion of management's explanations of the information in the financial reports. This is particularly true where the financial reporting is affected by management's estimates and judgements.[222]

A   Stewardship

The exclusion from the original discussion paper of a separate stewardship objective had been one of the proposals that triggered most comments from respondents. The boards had essentially argued that there was no need for a stewardship objective because the decision useful information about future cash flows that allowed users to make investment and credit decisions would also meet the stewardship objective. There was not universal agreement on this point. Indeed even at the time two members of the IASB put forward an alternative view. They noted that whilst information relevant to predicting future economic benefit is relevant to the stewardship process it will not provide a complete set of information for stewardship purposes, because stewardship may require more focus on past rather than future transactions. They believed that stewardship and decision-usefulness for investors are parallel but different objectives.

Although the exposure draft does not establish a separate objective for stewardship the boards have modified the objective to make it broader and have articulated two aspects of decision usefulness, usefulness in assessing cash flow prospects and usefulness in assessing stewardship. Whilst these changes do not go as far as some might like they do serve to reinforce that assessment of stewardship is an important part of general purpose financial reporting which will be welcomed by many.

B   The 'Entity Perspective'

A number of commentators on the initial discussion paper had questioned whether it was appropriate for the boards to determine that the entity perspective was the appropriate reporting model in advance of reaching final conclusions on other stages of the framework. In the exposure draft the boards have sought to explain their preference for the model. They do however acknowledge that this will need to be considered in later phases as follows:

> 'Although the boards decided to adopt the entity perspective as it pertains to the objective of financial reporting , they have not yet considered all of the possible implications of that decision on future phases of the framework. The boards have not yet considered the effect that adopting the entity perspective

in Chapter 1 will have on phases that have yet to be deliberated, and therefore have not yet decided whether there are implications for decisions to be made in those phases'.[223]

It will be interesting to see how this issue develops in the later stages of the framework.

C   *Financial performance*

The draft framework makes it explicit that financial performance is secondary to, and derived from, balance sheet changes between the start and end of an accounting period, 'Information about an entity's financial performance during a period *reflected by changes in its resources and the claims on those resources, other than changes resulting from financing transactions*, is also useful in assessing the entity's past and future ability to generate net cash inflows'[224] (emphasis added).

This statement confirms and makes entirely explicit the Boards' commitment to the balance sheet approach to measuring performance, the acceptance of which is critical to the justification and adoption of the Boards' fair value measurement agenda (see 6 below). A definition of performance in terms of changes in wealth between t1 and t2, logically implies that current valuations are required – otherwise the data would not be comparable. The Boards are thus explicitly rejecting in their new framework document other measures of financial performance, such as one that would require a sales transaction, or a realised profit.

5.2.2   *The qualitative characteristics of decision-useful financial reporting information*

Chapter 2 of the draft framework deals with qualitative characteristics. The exposure draft identifies two 'fundamental qualitative characteristics' of decision-useful financial reporting information:

- relevance;
- faithful representation.[225]

It then goes on to identify four 'enhancing qualitative characteristics':

- comparability;
- verifiability;
- timeliness; and
- understandability.[226]

There are two 'pervasive constraints' which limit the information provided by financial reporting:

- materiality; and
- costs.[227]

It is quite revealing to compare this outline with the discussion of qualitative characteristics in the current IASB framework. Many of the words used are of course the same – only verifiability has been added. However, whereas the current framework identifies the four principle characteristics as understandability, relevance, reliability and comparability[228] and states that the relative importance of those characteristic in different cases is a matter of professional judgements,[229] the exposure draft is quite clear that relevance and faithful representation (which is only a sub-element of reliability in the current framework) are the fundamental characteristics.

Under the new proposal for financial information to be useful it must posses the two fundamental characteristics of relevance and faithful representation. The other enhancing characteristics are complementary to the fundamental characteristics and distinguish more useful information from less useful information.[230]

Although many of the concepts have been brought forward essentially unchanged the most significant proposed change – and one which triggered many responses when proposed in the discussion paper – is the replacement of the characteristic of reliability with faithful representation.

The IASB's existing framework document states that 'information has the quality of reliability when it is free from material error and bias and can be depended upon by users to represent faithfully that which it either purports to represent or could reasonably be expected to represent.'[231] It goes on to state that 'information may be relevant but so unreliable in nature or representation that its recognition may be potentially misleading.'[232] However, the IASB has decided that the existing framework does not convey 'the meaning of reliability clearly enough to avoid misunderstandings',[233] and is therefore proposing to remove reliability from the framework and to replace it with the qualitative characteristic of 'faithful representation'.

A number of commentators have observed that if there is misunderstanding about the meaning of the word 'reliable' the boards could perhaps have sought to improve the definition. The boards have however rejected these arguments:

> 'Many respondents to the discussion paper commented unfavourably on the boards preliminary decision to replace reliability with faithful representation. However, in those comments, each respondent described reliability differently from how the boards described reliability in their existing frameworks. Furthermore, many respondents' descriptions of reliability more closely resembled the boards' notion of verifiability than reliability. These comments led the boards to affirm their decision to replace the term reliability with faithful representation.' [234]

The Exposure Draft discusses faithful representation in the following terms:

> 'Faithful representation – the faithful depiction in financial reports of economic phenomena – is essential if information is to be decision-useful. To represent economic phenomena faithfully, accounting representations must be complete, neutral and free from material error. Accordingly the boards proposed that faithful representation encompasses all the key qualities that the previous frameworks included as aspects of reliability.' [235]

A   Verifiability

Verifiability is defined in the Exposure Draft as:

> 'a quality of information that helps assure users that information faithfully represents the economic phenomena that it purports to represent. Verifiability implies that different knowledgeable and independent observers could reach general consensus, although not necessarily agreement that either; (a) the information represents the economic phenomena that it purports to represent without material error or bias; or (b) an appropriate recognition or measurement method has been applied without material error or bias.'[236]

Concerns have been expressed that this definition with its focus on consensus between observers and the use of methodologies may permit the recognition of items which might not previously have been regarded as 'reliable'. The boards have however not accepted the concerns and the only change between the discussion paper and the Exposure Draft is that whereas verifiability was originally included as a component of faithful representation it is now included as a separate enhancing characteristic.

B   Neutrality and conservatism

The current IASB framework recognises prudence as a sub-element of reliability being the inclusion of a degree of caution in the exercise of the judgements needed in making estimates in conditions of uncertainty so that assets and income are not overstated and liabilities and costs are not understated. However, the boards have concluded that an admonition to be prudent would of itself introduce bias into financial reporting[237] and that would be inconsistent with the concept of neutrality, which in turn is a critical part of 'faithful representation'.

C   Understandability

The increasing length and complexity of financial reporting have led to concerns that users are finding financial reports increasingly difficult to understand. Some therefore look for greater simplicity in financial reporting. The difficulty is that the activities and transactions entered into by businesses are increasingly complex and for financial information to be relevant those transactions have to be appropriately presented. It is therefore perhaps understandable that the boards have a rather different perspective on complexity. The exposure draft expresses a view that whilst appropriate presentation of information can help users, understanding that information fundamentally depends on the users themselves and they are assumed to have a reasonable knowledge of business and be able to read financial reports. Where necessary they may need to seek the help of an advisor.[238] It may well be that the key to this intractable issue lies in appropriate management discussions and disclosure.

D   Substance over form

The notion of 'substance over form' – such a powerful inhibitor of synthetic schemes to hide the real extent of an entity's obligations – has been omitted from the draft framework, even though it has considerable prominence in the IASB's current document. The justification is as follows:

'To represent legal form that differs from the economic substance of the underlying economic phenomenon could not result in a faithful representation. Accordingly, the proposed framework does not identify *substance over form* as a component of faithful representation because to do so would be redundant.'[239]

Whilst the boards may see no need for the inclusion of the concept in the framework we continue to believe that its inclusion would be helpful.

5.2.3   *Further considerations by the Boards*

The boards have considered the exposure draft further in the light of comments received. The discussions to date indicate that most if not all of the key principles in the exposure draft will be reconfirmed in the final chapter when published. Interestingly at the March 2009 joint meeting of the two boards it was agreed that each framework will maintain its current hierarchical status which if applied would appear to perpetuate the difference in the status of the framework under IFRS and US GAAP discussed at 5.2 above.[240]

5.3   IASB-FASB Discussion Paper – An improved conceptual framework for financial reporting

In May 2008 the IASB published a Discussion Paper –*Preliminary Views on an improved Conceptual Framework for Financial Reporting – The Reporting Entity.*[241] The discussion paper is divided into four sections. The first section addresses the reporting entity concept, section 2 considers the group reporting entity and how best to circumscribe the area of business activity which comprises the reporting entity, section 3 discusses parent entity financial reporting and the final section addresses control issues. Each of the sections are discussed in turn below.

5.3.1   *The reporting entity concept*

The boards note that there is no reporting entity concept in their existing conceptual frameworks, which therefore had no clear starting point. Their preliminary view is that there is no need to develop a precise definition of a reporting entity, however there is an issue as to what the boundaries of the reporting entity might be.[242] In particular there are some people who would argue that the reporting entity must be a legal entity. Having discussed the issues arising from the question the boards conclude that a reporting entity should not be limited to business activities that are structured as legal entities. Instead the reporting entity should be described as being a circumscribed area of business activity.[243] This could encompass a sole trader a trust or partnership or a group of entities. The boards noted a concern that this definition might be seen as too vague and have expanded the proposed definition slightly to 'a circumscribed area of business activity of interest to present and potential equity investors, lenders and other capital providers'.[244]

This broad definition would appear to facilitate the preparation of 'combined' and 'carve out' financial statements both of which can cause difficulties under the current IASB standards (this is discussed in more detail in 3.4 and 3.5 of Chapter 6).

5.3.2   Group reporting entity

In the second section the boards consider three possible ways to define the boundaries of the group:

- the controlling entity model
- the common control model
- the risks and rewards model.

The chapter discusses the concept of control in the light of current accounting literature. The boards' preliminary view is that control should not be based solely on power but should also include the concept of obtaining benefit from that power. If one entity has power over another but not the ability to benefit from that power it seems unlikely that the two entities together meet the boards' definition of a reporting entity discussed in 5.3.1 above.[245] The boards have developed a working definition of control as follows;

> 'Control of an entity is the ability to direct the financing and operating policies of an entity, so as to access benefits from that entity (or to reduce the incidence of losses) and increase, maintain or protect the amount of those benefits (or reduce the amount of those losses)'.[246]

Under the controlling entity model the circumscribed area of business activity is defined by the extent of an entity's control. The reporting entity is thus the traditional parent and subsidiaries structure.

Under the common control model the circumscribed area of business activity is defined by entities under the control of the same controlling entity.

The risks and rewards model is an approach which requires the combination of two entities when the activities of the second affect the wealth of the residual shareholders of the first.[247]

The boards have tentatively concluded that the risks and rewards model is based on too broad a concept and therefore does not provide a conceptually robust basis for determining the composition of the group.[248] In particular they note that the nature of residual interest is such that the activities of virtually every other entity with which an entity conducts business has the potential to affect that entity. It could lead to the inclusion of major suppliers and customers in an entity's financial statements.[249]

Of the two control models the boards conclude that the controlling entity model is more consistent with the objectives of financial reporting, however there may be circumstances where combined financial statements of commonly controlled entities would provide useful information to equity investors, lenders and other capital providers of the controlled entities. For this to be the case, as well as the entities being under common control, other circumstances will need to exist to support the conclusion that the entities do constitute an appropriate circumscribed area of business activity.[250]

5.3.3   *Parent entity financial reporting*

The boards' consideration of reporting by the parent entity reaches two perhaps not very surprising conclusions. Firstly, that where one entity has control of another, consolidated financial statements are those which are consistent with the objective of general purpose financial reporting.[251] However, whilst opinions as to the value of parent entity only financial statements are mixed there appears to be no reason to preclude their presentation as long as they are included in the same report as the consolidated accounts.[252]

5.3.4   *Control Issues*

In the final section the boards consider issues relating to the control concept:

(a)   determining when one legal entity has control over another;

(b)   control other than by legal rights;

(c)   latent control and the treatment of options;

(d)   power is not shared with others; and

(e)   control, joint control and significant influence.[253]

The Boards' tentative conclusions are that:

(a)   establishing whether control exists involves assessing all the existing facts and circumstances and there are no single facts and circumstances that, in all cases, evidence that one entity has control over another;

(b)   the concept of control should include situations in which control exists but might be temporary;

(c)   control should not be limited to circumstances in which the entity has sufficient voting rights to direct the financing and operating policies of another but should be a broad concept encompassing similar circumstances;

(d)   having options over voting rights which would give control if exercised does not of itself establish control;

(e)   control cannot exist if an entity must obtain the agreement of others; and

(f)   significant influence is not sufficient to establish control.

5.3.5   *Further consideration by the Boards*

The boards have considered the discussion paper further in the light of comments received. The decisions to date do not suggest there will be major changes when the exposure draft is published in the third quarter of 2009. However, in January 2009 the IASB did tentatively decide to revise and widen the description of a reporting entity to 'a circumscribed area of economic activity whose financial information has the potential to be useful to present and potential equity investors, lenders and other capital providers for decisions in their capacity as capital providers'. It also agreed to clarify that an entity can be a reporting entity even if currently inactive.[254]

5.4   Phase C – Measurement

As discussed at 5.1 above it is expected that the IASB will publish a Discussion Paper on Phase C – Measurement in the final quarter of 2009. The aim of the Discussion Paper and ultimately of the final chapter is to describe the factors the Boards should consider when making their decisions about measurement methods in future standards.

Discussions by the Board to date suggest that the proposed conceptual framework will be based on five measurement factors. These factors are:

- Method of value realisation
- Cost of preparing and using measures
- Relative level of confidence in different measures
- Use of consistent measures for similar items and items used together
- Separability of changes in measures.

The paper will discuss the relationship of those factors to the objectives of financial reporting and the characteristics of decision useful information already discussed in Phase A. The Board has also tentatively decided to include a discussion of three possible measurement methods:

- Actual or estimated current prices (which will become past prices in future periods if an item is not remeasured)
- Actual past entry prices adjusted for interest accruals, depreciation, amortisation, impairments and similar things
- Other proscribed computations based on discounted or undiscounted estimates of future cash flows (which would include value in use and fair value based measurements, amongst other things).

By definition any decision that a standard setter makes on the most appropriate measurement basis must balance the sometimes conflicting needs of users and preparers of financial statements whilst recognising cost and benefit issues. It is to be hoped that the result of Phase C is appropriately balanced guidance which recognises that different measurement bases will continue to be appropriate in different circumstances.

5.5   Phase B – Elements

The Discussion Paper on Phase B is currently expected to be published in the second half of 2010. The objective of this phase is to refine and converge the two Boards' frameworks so as to clarify the definitions of asset and liability, to resolve differences regarding other elements and to revise recognition criteria concepts.

As discussed earlier in this chapter the definition of asset and liability are of fundamental importance to financial reporting and shortcomings in the current definitions have caused difficulties. In their discussions to date the Boards have identified a number of problems with the current definitions of both asset and liability and have tentatively agreed revised definitions.

As regards assets the Boards believe that the current definition has led users to believe that there must be a high likelihood of future economic benefits for an asset to be recognised. Similarly they believe that too much emphasis is placed on the future flow of economic benefits rather than the item that currently exists – the economic resource. Finally they believe that the terms control and past transaction have been misunderstood.

All of this has led to a proposed working definition – 'An asset of an entity is a present economic resource to which the entity has a right or other access that others do not have'.

The Boards have similar concerns about the current definition of liability and have adopted a working definition – 'A liability of an entity is a present economic obligation for which the entity is the obligor'.

Both definitions will be supported by accompanying text which will explain and amplify the various components of the definitions.

The Boards have expended considerable effort on these new definitions as befits their fundamental importance to any financial reporting framework and the revised definitions appear to address some of the concerns articulated in this chapter. However the full implications of Phase B will have to be considered once the Discussion Paper is published

5.6   The status of the framework

Progress on the revised conceptual framework has, perhaps inevitably, been slow, made slower by the Boards' focus on the financial crisis in 2008 and 2009. The Boards intend to finalise Phases as they complete them. However, with a number of the Phases currently inactive it is likely to be some considerable time before there is a fully articulated revised framework. This will continue to be a source of disappointment to those who believe that a conceptually strong framework is essential to an effective future standard setting process.

5.7   Exposure Draft – Management Commentary

Although not explicitly part of the initial Conceptual Framework project it is perhaps worth noting that in June 2009 the IASB published an exposure draft on Management Commentary. In the introduction to the exposure draft the IASB makes the following observation:

'The exposure draft is prepared on the basis that management commentary lies within the boundaries of financial reporting and, therefore, is within the scope of the conceptual framework for financial reporting. In developing its proposals for management commentary, the Board took into account its recent work on the objective and qualitative characteristics of financial reporting.'[255]

As discussed earlier in this chapter management commentary can help to explain the financial statements and can assist users in understanding the financial position, performance and cash flows of reporting entities. The exposure draft is intended to set out a broad framework for the preparation of management commentaries which accompany financial statements prepared under IFRS.

The Board does not propose to develop an IFRS; rather the intention is that the non-binding framework will be applied by management of individual reporting entities to their own specific circumstances.

The Exposure Draft sets out three basic principles which the IASB believe underpin decision useful management commentary:

- it provides management's view of the entities performance, position and development
- it supplements and complements information presented in the financial statements; and
- it has an orientation to the future. [256]

The IASB emphasises that the management commentary must have the qualitative characteristics discussed in Phase A of the Conceptual Framework project. In other words it must be relevant and a faithful representation of what it seeks to describe and in addition comparability, verifiability, timeliness and understandability should be maximised. [257]

Although the Board envisages that the broad framework will be implemented differently by different managements it does believe that there are certain elements of content which will be included in all management commentaries:

- the nature of the business
- management's objectives and strategies for meeting those objectives
- the entity's most significant resources risks and relationships
- the results of operations and prospects; and
- the critical performance measures and indicators that management use to evaluate the entity's performance against stated objectives. [258]

Whether this guidance will be finalised remains open to question. A number of IASB Board members opposed its publication for a variety of reasons. An interesting alternative view put forward by some Board members is that the management commentary must inevitably reflect management's view and therefore cannot be neutral as defined in Phase A. This is presumably based on a view that even if management endeavour to be even handed and balanced the management commentary remains their view and therefore not neutral. Other issues raised include concerns that the publication of non-authoritative guidance would not lead to an improvement in financial reporting, and that the project is not an appropriate use of IASB resources. It is difficult not to have some sympathy with this latter concern, given the heavy workload currently facing the IASB, particularly given that it could be argued that there is little new in the IASB's proposals (for example the guidance in Reporting Statement 1 issued by the UK ASB covers much similar ground). However it may well be that constituents will find the guidance and the framework provided by the IASB helpful.

6   MEASUREMENT

Measurement – how to express in monetary terms an asset or liability depicted in financial statements – is perhaps the most fundamental aspect of accounting currently under consideration. For many decades historical cost, or modified historical cost, has been used as the basis for measuring assets or liabilities. Gradually over the last decade or so, this has changed as more complex types of financial instruments and methods of financing businesses have emerged. Currently, most financial statements contain assets and liabilities that are measured using a variety of measurement methods, depending upon the type of asset or liability concerned. A typical modern financial statement in compliance with IFRS might include, for example, assets measured in all of the following ways: historical cost, depreciated historical cost, market value, calculated fair value, valuations by actuaries or other specialists, and measurements modified by impairment tests.

The use and potential increase in use, of fair value in financial reporting has provoked considerable debate in recent years. The recent financial crisis has added to that debate with some observers going so far as to blame the crisis on the use of fair values for financial instruments. Whilst we would disagree with those who seek to blame the crisis on the use of fair values it is clearly appropriate to include a discussion of fair value in this chapter.

Three publications on the subject of measurement – an IASB discussion paper on measurement; a FASB standard on fair value measurement; and an IASB Exposure Draft developed from that FASB standard – are discussed at 6.1, 6.2 and 6.3 below.

6.1   Discussion paper: Measurement bases for financial accounting – measurement on initial recognition

In November 2005 the IASB published a Discussion Paper entitled *Measurement bases for financial accounting – measurement on initial recognition*. This paper represents the output of a research project that was undertaken by the staff of the Canadian Accounting Standards Board at the request of the IASB and on the basis of input from, and discussions with, individual members of the IASB and their staff. However, its content was not formally deliberated by the IASB.

'Measurement' in the context of this paper refers to whether the actual cost, or fair value, or some other method is the best measurement basis to use in considering the values at which assets are to be recognised initially and carried in the balance sheet. The paper is quite extensive, running to some 140 pages, and contains the following major sections:

Summary

Part I: Measurement bases project

Chapter 1	Purpose of project and scope
Chapter 2	Criteria for evaluation

Part II: Measurement on initial recognition

The purpose of the project is stated as follows:

'The project is intended to provide the International Accounting Standards Board (IASB) and national standard setters with a sound conceptual basis for:

(a)   revising and expanding the measurement aspects of their conceptual frameworks; and

(b)   improving the measurement requirements of their financial reporting standards.

'In regard to (a), the IASB and the Financial Accounting Standards Board (FASB) in the United States have initiated a joint project to converge and improve their conceptual frameworks, including the measurement aspects. For the IASB, the discussion paper represents the first step of its due process for the measurement aspects within the broader conceptual framework project.'[259]

The project was undertaken 'because existing measurement standards and practices are inconsistent, and a number of major measurement issues remain unsettled. Some existing standards reflect more or less arbitrary mixed measurement compromises, pending resolution of conflicting views on appropriate measurement bases. The coverage of the measurement component of existing conceptual frameworks is very limited and out of date. Major developments have taken place since these frameworks were put in place that have significant implications for accounting measurement. These include developments in finance theory and capital markets, the application of present value and statistical probability principles, fair value measurement practices, and computer and information technology.'[260]

6.1.1   *The 'cash-equivalent expectations attribute' of assets and liabilities*

The analysis in the paper starts with a discussion of the evaluation criteria that should be applied to each possible measurement basis and 'proceeds on the basis that these criteria should be developed from, and be consistent with, the objectives of financial reporting, qualitative characteristics, and definitions of the elements of financial statements that are contained in the existing conceptual frameworks of accounting standard setters.'[261] Consequently, the paper provides a brief analysis based mainly on the IASB's conceptual framework, with the aim of establishing the necessary 'evaluation criteria'.

The conclusion of this analysis is that the primary criteria for evaluating possible measurement bases, derived from the conceptual frameworks, are:[262]

(a)   Decision usefulness;

(b)   Qualitative characteristics of useful information:

- Understandability;

- Relevance – predictive value, feedback value, timeliness;

- Reliability – representational faithfulness, neutrality, verifiability;

- Comparability.

(c)   Concepts of assets and liabilities:

- How the expected cash-equivalent flow attribute of assets and liabilities is measured.

(d)   Cost/benefit considerations.

The paper concludes that these aspects of the frameworks 'narrow the rationally acceptable possibilities, but they are not sufficient, in themselves, for achieving agreement on a single measurement basis or how to choose between different bases in different circumstances.'[263] Since the existing IASB Framework makes no attempt to relate measurement to other parts of the framework, but simply lists indiscriminately some of the measurement bases that are employed in financial statements, we do not believe the Framework can even be said to 'narrow the rationally acceptable possibilities'.

Nevertheless, whilst the paper's analysis of the IASB Framework provides no great conceptual insight, the authors of the paper use it to conclude that 'the information on the amounts (value), timing and uncertainty of cash-equivalent flows is considered to be the primary focus of financial accounting.'[264] This leads to the statement 'that "assets" (economic resources ultimately reflecting expected direct or indirect cash flows or cash-equivalent benefits) and "liabilities" (present obligations reflecting expected outflows of economic resources, ultimately cash or cash-equivalent outflows) are the basic subject matter of financial accounting measurement. Since it is the cash-equivalent expectations attribute of assets and liabilities that is the primary focus of business activities, it seems appropriate to conclude that this attribute should be the primary focus of accounting measurement.'[265] As will be seen below, the premise that 'the cash-equivalent expectations attribute of an asset is the primary focus of accounting measurement' enables the paper to conclude that fair value is the most relevant measure of an asset or liability on initial recognition.

6.1.2   *Possible bases for measurement on initial recognition*

The paper analyses possible bases of measurement for assets and liabilities on initial recognition only – i.e. when assets and liabilities are first recognised in the financial statements of an entity. Issues relating to re-measurement, including impairment, will be dealt with in subsequent papers. The conclusions reached are described as being 'tentative' and will be re-assessed when their potential implications for re-measurement are considered in subsequent papers.

The paper does not deal generally with the timing of when initial recognition of an asset or a liability should occur. The paper does, however, propose that initial measurement should be determined as at the date of initial recognition. This has important implications. For example, if prices change between the date when a fixed cash price is negotiated and the initial recognition of the asset acquired, then, in accordance with some measurement bases, the asset would be measured based on prices at the later date. Furthermore, the paper proposes that the initial recognition of a non-contractual asset that is developed over a period of time should be considered to occur, for purposes of initial measurement, when the asset becomes ready to contribute to the generation of future cash flows.

The paper proposes that the following are the possible bases for measurement on initial recognition, and proposes working definitions, based as a starting reference point on those currently being used in IFRSs:[266]

(a) *Historical cost*: Assets are recorded at the fair value of the consideration given to acquire them at the time of their acquisition. Liabilities are recorded at the fair value of the consideration received in exchange for incurring the obligations at the time they were incurred.

     This is based on the definition of historical cost in the IASB *Framework* at paragraph 100(a), with the following changes:

     (i)   The IASB definition states that 'Assets are recorded at the amount of cash or cash equivalents paid or the fair value of the consideration given ...', whilst the paper asserts that the words 'cash or cash equivalents paid' are redundant because the amount of cash or cash equivalents paid should always equal the fair value of consideration given;

     (ii) The IASB definition states that 'Liabilities are recorded at the amount of proceeds received in exchange for the obligation.' In the Discussion Paper, the words 'amount of proceeds' are replaced by 'fair value of the consideration'. This change is made ostensibly in order to be more precise and consistent with the definition of historical cost for assets;

     (iii) The IASB definition goes on to add that '... or in some circumstances (for example, income taxes), at the amounts of cash or cash equivalents to be paid to satisfy the liability in the normal course of business.' This phrase has been omitted from the above definition because it seems – to the paper's authors – to be describing an expected value measurement rather than one that is consistent with the historical cost objective.

(b) *Current Cost – Reproduction Cost and Replacement Cost:* The reproduction cost of an asset is defined as 'the most economic current cost of replacing an existing asset with an identical one', whilst the replacement cost of an asset is defined as 'the most economic current cost of replacing an existing asset with an asset of equivalent productive capacity or service potential.'[267]

     International accounting standards had formerly defined replacement cost as '... the current acquisition cost of a similar asset, new or used, or of an equivalent productive capacity or service potential.'[268] This is commonly known as 'current cost'. Current cost is defined for the purposes of the paper as the most economic cost of an asset or of its equivalent productive capacity or service potential. This definition embodies reproduction cost and replacement cost, which are usually separately defined in the authoritative literature of other standard setters.

The liability equivalent of replacement and reproduction cost is not defined in IFRSs. However, for the purposes of the paper, it has been presumed to be 'the fair value of the consideration that the owing entity would have received if the liability had been incurred by it on the measurement date';[269]

(c) *Net realizable value (of an asset):* The estimated selling price in the ordinary course of business less the estimated costs of completion and the estimated costs necessary to make the sale.

This is the definition found in IAS 2 – *Inventories*. Again, the equivalent liability definition does not seem to have formally been defined in accounting literature, but the paper proposes that it may be defined as 'the estimated amount that would be incurred in the ordinary course of business to be released from the liability on the measurement date plus the estimated costs necessary to secure that release';[270]

(d) *Value in use (of an asset):* The present value of estimated future cash flows expected to arise from the continuing use of an asset and from its disposal at the end of its useful life. This is the definition found in IAS 36. This definition does not state whose expectations should be the basis for determining value in use, although it is clear from IAS 36 that the objective is to reflect the reporting entity management's best estimates of future cash flows;

(e) *Fair value*: The amount for which an asset or liability could be exchanged between knowledgeable, willing parties in an arm's length transaction. This is the existing IFRS definition that is consistently used in its standards (for example, in IAS 39), with one change. The IFRS definition states '... asset could be exchanged, or a liability settled ...', whereas the definition above defines fair value in terms of the amount for which either an asset or a liability could be exchanged. In the view of the paper's authors, this change avoids the implication that the fair value of a liability is necessarily the amount for which it could be settled, that is, its exit value. In other words, the paper – in the view of its authors – adopts a working definition of the fair value measurement basis expressed in neutral terms as the amount that could be exchanged for an asset or liability, without seeming to be limited to an exit, as opposed to an entry, market price;[271]

(f) *Deprival value:* The loss that an entity would suffer if it were deprived of an asset. It is the lower of replacement cost and recoverable amount on the measurement date, with recoverable amount being the higher of value in use and net realizable value.[272] The paper notes that some people do not consider deprival value to be a separate measurement basis, but rather a decision rule for selecting between three of the above measurement bases (replacement cost, net realizable value, and value in use). However, the paper argues that deprival value is based on an overarching theory of management behaviour that adds an important dimension that integrates the three bases into a distinct measurement approach.[273]

The paper explains that 'present value' does not appear on this list of measurement bases because it is not a measurement basis in itself. Rather, it is a measurement technique that can be applied to make estimates under several of the above measurement bases. The present value measurement technique is important because it provides the mathematical structure for valuing expected future cash flows, taking into account the time value of money and attendant risks.[274]

6.1.3 *Market vs. entity-specific measurement objectives*

The paper proposes that differences between bases for measuring assets and liabilities on initial recognition arise from two fundamental sources:

- Market versus entity-specific measurement objectives; and
- Differences in defining the properties that affect the values of assets and liabilities.

The market value measurement objective is to measure an asset or liability at the price for which it would be exchanged under competitive market conditions, reflecting the market's expectations as to the amounts, timing and uncertainty of future cash flows discounted at market rates of return for commensurate risk. The paper analyses the essential properties of market value, and addresses its relationship to fair value.

An entity-specific measurement objective looks to the expectations of the reporting entity, which may differ significantly from those implicit in a market price. Any measure of an asset or liability that differs from its market value must be based, explicitly or implicitly, on entity-specific expectations that differ from those of the market.

The paper concludes that, for external financial reporting purposes, the market measurement objective has important qualities that make it superior to entity-specific measurement objectives, at least on initial recognition. In particular, the paper asserts that the more relevant financial statement measurement objective on initial recognition for investors and other external users is that entities be measured against market values and subject to the discipline of the marketplace, rather than to entities' individual expectations.

However, this proposed conclusion presumes the existence of a market for an asset or liability on initial recognition, or failing the existence of an observable market, the ability to estimate reliably what the market price would be if a market did exist. It is proposed that the objective of the fair value measurement basis is to represent the properties of market value.

In fact, in the absence of any evaluation of the relative merits of the two approaches, the discussion in the paper provides at least as much support for the views of those who favour an entity-specific approach as it does for those who favour a market-based approach. The paper states that its conclusion that the market value objective is superior to an entity specific measurement has been reached 'on the basis of [the paper's] conceptual analysis.'[275] We are not necessarily convinced. The limited 'conceptual analysis' that the paper does contain in fact points to 'the cash-equivalent expectations attribute of assets and liabilities' being more appropriately reflected in the measurement of cash generating units on the basis of value to the business (VTB), rather than on the basis of an exit value for individual assets and liabilities, which would in most cases be calculated based on the assumptions of a hypothetical market comprising hypothetical buyers and sellers.

6.1.4   *Value-affecting properties of assets and liabilities*

The paper argues that, traditionally, measurement bases have been classified and evaluated in terms of whether they are 'entry' or 'exit' values. An entry value is a measure of the amount for which an asset could be bought or a liability could be incurred. An exit value is a measure of the amount for which an asset could be realized or a liability could be settled.

However, the paper presents an entirely different perspective of the entry-exit value debate, and argues that the market value measurement objective does not envisage that there could be different entry and exit market (fair) values for the same asset or liability at the same time. We believe that this assertion is open to challenge. For example, the replacement cost (entry value) of a specialised production asset may well be different from its net realisable (exit) value – for example, in the case of an oil refinery. Nevertheless, the paper asserts that differences between apparent market values of seemingly identical assets or liabilities, for example between their exit and entry values, may be attributable to one or both of the following sources:

(a)   Differences between the assets and liabilities traded in different markets. Apparently different entry and exit prices for an asset or liability may be due to, sometimes subtle, differences between the asset or liability that is traded in an 'entry' market and the asset or liability that is traded in an 'exit' market;

(b)   Entity-specific charges or credits. Some differences between exit and entry values of assets and liabilities are due to entity-specific charges or credits. Under the market value measurement objective, these would be treated as expenses or income (or perhaps, in some cases, as direct charges or credits to equity) on recognition. Under an entity-specific measurement objective, they might qualify for inclusion in the measurement of the asset or liability depending on management's expectations, intentions, and assumptions. An example of this might be transaction costs, which the paper believes should be expensed and not included in the initial measurement of an asset.

6.1.5   *Fair value*

Having put forward the proposition that the market value measurement objective provides superior information, the paper (almost inevitably) concludes that fair value is more relevant than the other identified bases on initial recognition. This determination is made on the basis of the assertion that all of the alternative measurement bases other than fair value directly or indirectly incorporate entity-specific measurements. For this reason, the paper proposes that fair value should be used to measure assets and liabilities on initial recognition, provided it can be measured reliably.

Nevertheless, the paper does acknowledge that significant measurement uncertainty in measuring fair value exists in some common situations. Some of the problems identified include determining what constitutes a market and understanding what data inputs market participants would likely use when a market does not exist for the item in question.

The paper then considers which measurement bases are acceptable substitutes for fair value when fair value cannot be measured reliably on initial recognition. Consistent with the fundamental proposition that the market value measurement objective provides superior information, the paper proposes that the alternative measurement basis used should be the one that is most consistent with the market value measurement objective, provided it can be measured reliably and, when cost bases are used, the amount is expected to be recoverable.

In evaluating cost bases as possible substitutes for fair value on initial recognition, replacement cost is considered to be more relevant than reproduction cost, and both are considered more relevant than historical cost.

Net realizable value and value in use are considered and rejected as substitutes for fair value on initial recognition. However, redefined concepts of realizable value and present value, applied as consistently as possible with the fair value measurement objective, are considered as possible estimates of, or substitutes for, fair value. The analysis indicates that replacement cost is unlikely to be capable of reliable estimation in many cases, and that reproduction cost may be reliably estimable in some situations in which replacement cost is not. The paper asserts that there are also significant reliability limitations with historical cost measurements, notably the indeterminacy inherent in any one-to-many cost allocations, and the failure to include costs that were incurred before the asset or liability qualified for initial recognition. Nonetheless, the paper accepts that historical cost can be an appropriate substitute in some cases. The paper acknowledges that deprival value overcomes some of the potential weaknesses of each of its component measurement bases evaluated individually and proposes a refinement of the deprival value decision rule in light of the analysis of the alternative measurement bases.

On the basis of this analysis, the paper proposes a four-level measurement hierarchy for assets and liabilities when they are initially recognized:[276]

Level 1 – observable market prices; any adjustments are consistent with those that market participants can be expected to make;

Level 2 – accepted valuation models or techniques; all significant inputs are consistent with those that market participants can be expected to use;

Level 3 – current cost (i.e. reproduction cost and replacement cost); with the possibility of substituting historical cost, provided a reliable estimate can be made and the amount can be expected to be recoverable;

Level 4 – models and techniques that use entity-specific inputs only; when unavoidable and when not demonstrably inconsistent with those that market participants can be expected to use.

The paper notes that only Level 1 and 2 measurements should be described as 'fair value'. Level 3 and 4 measurement bases have sufficient relevance and reliability to be used as substitutes for fair value, but are not sufficiently based on market expectations to be described as 'fair value'. Importantly, the paper notes that if none of the above measurement alternatives is feasible, the item in question fails to meet the conditions for recognition as an asset or liability.

It is worth noting that this proposed hierarchy differs in some important respects from the fair value hierarchy in the FASB draft standard on fair value measurements (see 6.2 below).

6.1.6   *Efficient market price*

The paper includes lengthy discussion and analysis of market and entity-specific measurement objectives and a comparison of the two. The discussion and analysis is almost entirely based on finance literature and assumes that an 'efficient market price' (unaffected by entity-specific factors) can be determined for all assets and liabilities. Indeed, the Paper refers to an 'a priori expectation reasoned from the market value measurement objective … that there can be only one fair value for a particular asset or liability on a measurement date.'[277] However, in the real world few assets and liabilities are traded on active markets and therefore few assets and liabilities have real market values.

Furthermore, we have no confidence that a deductive approach to the practice of financial reporting will yield satisfactory outcomes when those deductions are based upon *a priori*, rather than *a posteriori*, premises. The paper claims that a deductive approach will be 'most useful in developing conceptual theories and hypotheses concerning the various possible measurement bases', and it expects 'inductive analysis' to act as a 'reality check'.[278] We are not convinced that the methodology adopted by the authors has, in fact, included such a reality check in practice.

The paper takes this further, stating that 'competitive market forces work to resolve diverse expectations of various entities' managements to a single price that impartially reflects all publicly available information… .'[279] Therefore, where there is more than one market in which an asset or liability is traded, the problem of different prices is to be dealt with by the simple expedient of '…[excluding the differences] from the determination of fair value.'[280] This assumes that it is possible firstly to identify the nature and then to quantify the effect of the particular differences that are responsible for causing the market price in a particular market to deviate from pure fair value and that when these differences are stripped away, the one fair value of similar assets or liabilities will be revealed. We do not believe this to be realistic.

Similarly, the paper goes on to presume that if a market does not exist, it is nevertheless possible to estimate reliably what the market price would be were a market to exist, which seems contradictory and illogical. Since, according to the paper, it takes competitive market forces to resolve diverse expectations of various entities' managements to a single price,[281] how can there be such a single price for a particular asset or liability if there is no market with 'competitive market forces'? If there is no market, how can such a market be assumed to exist and how could anyone arrive at a single price that is reliable? In short, in the absence of a market it becomes extremely difficult either to identify the fair value from a range of possible options or to prove that the value selected is the 'true' one.

The analysis in the paper is based solely on the premise that this 'one fair value' characteristic 'gives [market value] measurements a quality of comparability over time and as between entities' whereas 'an entity-specific measurement ... is subject to the vagaries of individual entity expectations, intentions and assumptions'[282] and is therefore less relevant. As we believe there is neither in theory nor in practice 'one fair value' that can be demonstrated logically to be such in the face of alternative fair values, we believe that the analysis in the paper is fundamentally flawed.

In our view, the conceptual analysis on which the paper is based is simplistic. It adopts a dualistic approach under which every market imperfection or inefficiency is attributed to 'entity-specific' factors. However, whilst it is true that markets will tend to 'work to resolve diverse expectations ... to a single price', it is also the very essence of dynamic markets that new diverse expectations are constantly being created based on new information or differences in the information known to market participants. This will particularly be the case with assets and liabilities that are not actively traded because there are insufficient knowledgeable, willing buyers and willing sellers to arbitrage away price differences.

We are therefore not necessarily convinced that market value measurement in practice has the qualities of reliability and relevance that the paper claims, except where there is an efficient market for the asset or liability *and* where market value measurement provides the most useful insight into the value, timing and uncertainty of cash-equivalent flows. The items for which the efficient market and usefulness criteria are met include some financial instruments and investment properties, which are already required or permitted to be measured at market value in IFRS financial statements. It is to be hoped that the Discussion paper on Phase C of the Conceptual Framework will enable these issues to be further explored.

6.2 The FASB Statement of Financial Accounting Standards No.157 – Fair Value Measurements

In September 2006 the FASB published Statement of Financial Accounting Standards No. 157 – *Fair value measurements*.[283] This statement becomes effective for financial statements issued for fiscal years beginning after 15 November 2007 and interim periods within those years. The statement provides guidance on how to arrive at fair values under those FASB standards that already require a fair value measurement to be made; it does not extend the scope of fair value measurement in US GAAP. This FASB standard is significant for IFRS, as the IASB issued it unchanged in November 2006 in the form of a Discussion Paper.

The changes to current US practice that will result from the application of SFAS 157 relate to the definition of fair value, the methods used to measure fair value, and the expanded disclosures about fair value measurements.

The SFAS clarifies that the meaning it ascribes to fair value is an exit price:

> 'The definition of fair value retains the exchange price notion in earlier definitions of fair value. This Statement clarifies that the exchange price is the price in an orderly transaction between market participants to sell the asset or transfer the liability in the market in which the reporting entity would transact for the asset or liability, that is, the principal or most advantageous market for the asset or liability. The transaction to sell the asset or transfer the liability is a hypothetical transaction at the measurement date, considered from the perspective of a market participant that holds the asset or owes the liability. Therefore, the definition focuses on the price that would be received to sell the asset or paid to transfer the liability (an exit price), not the price that would be paid to acquire the asset or received to assume the liability (an entry price).'[284]

The SFAS states further that:[285]

- fair value is a market measurement, not an entity-specific one (consistent with the stance taken in the measurement paper discussed at 6.1 above). Therefore, a fair value measurement should be determined based on the assumptions that market participants would use in pricing the asset or liability. As a basis for considering market participant assumptions in fair value measurements, SFAS 157 establishes a fair value hierarchy (see below) that distinguishes between (1) market participant assumptions developed based on market data obtained from sources independent of the reporting entity (observable inputs) and (2) the reporting entity's own assumptions about market participant assumptions developed based on the best information available in the circumstances (unobservable inputs). The notion of unobservable inputs is intended to allow for situations in which there is little, if any, market activity for the asset or liability at the measurement date. In those situations, the reporting entity need not undertake all possible efforts to obtain information about market participant assumptions. However, the reporting entity must not ignore information about market participant assumptions that is reasonably obtainable without undue cost and effort;

- market participant assumptions must include assumptions about risk (for example, the risk inherent in using a valuation technique to measure fair value rather than an observable market price) and/or the risk inherent in the inputs to the valuation technique. A fair value measurement should include an adjustment for risk if market participants would include one in pricing the related asset or liability, even if the adjustment is difficult to determine. Therefore, a measurement (for example, a 'mark-to-model' measurement) that does not include an adjustment for risk would not represent a fair value measurement if market participants would include one in pricing the related asset or liability;

- market participant assumptions must also include assumptions about the effect of a restriction on the sale or use of an asset. A fair value measurement for a restricted asset should consider the effect of the restriction if market participants would consider the effect of the restriction in pricing the asset;

- a fair value measurement for a liability must reflect its non-performance risk (the risk that the obligation will not be fulfilled). Because non-performance risk includes the reporting entity's credit risk, the reporting entity should consider the effect of its credit risk (credit standing) on the fair value of the liability in all periods in which the liability is measured at fair value under other accounting pronouncements (such as FAS 133). Whilst this requirement has the counterintuitive effect of producing 'gains' when an entity's credit worthiness deteriorates – because the liability is reduced – and 'losses' when it improves – because the liability increases, it should be noted that it is already a requirement under IAS 39 that the credit risk relating to a financial liability is included in the fair value measurement of that liability.[286]

Fair value is defined in the standard as 'the price that would be received to sell an asset or paid to transfer a liability in an orderly transaction between market participants at the measurement date.'[287] The fair value arrived at must take into consideration the condition and location of the asset at the measurement date,[288] which means that entity-specific considerations must play a part, although the SFAS states that fair value is not an entity specific measurement.[289] Market participants are defined as 'buyers and sellers in the principal (or most advantageous) market … that are:

a.　Independent of the reporting entity; that is, they are not related parties

b.　Knowledgeable, having a reasonable understanding about the asset or liability and the transaction based on all available information, including information that might be obtained through due diligence efforts that are usual and customary

c.　Able to transact for the asset or liability

d.　Willing to transact for the asset or liability; that is, they are motivated but not forced or otherwise compelled to do so.'[290]

The SFAS states that a fair value measurement assumes that the transaction to sell the asset or transfer the liability occurs in the principal market, or in the absence of a principal market in the most advantageous market.[291] The principal market is 'the market in which the reporting entity would sell the asset or transfer the liability with the greatest volume and level of activity for the asset or liability'.[292] The most advantageous market is the market in which the reporting entity would sell the asset of transfer the liability with the price that maximises the amount that would be received for the asset or minimises the amount to be paid to transfer the liability considering transaction costs. If there is a principal market, the fair value measurement shall represent the price in that market, even if the price in a different market is potentially more advantageous.[293]

The SFAS includes the concept of 'highest and best use'. One reason this is necessary is because often an asset is used in conjunction with others and its worth on its own is not representative of its worth within the asset group. The SFAS states that 'In broad terms, highest and best use refers to the use of an asset by market participants that would maximize the value of the asset or group of assets within which the asset would be used'.[294] The measurement to determine fair value must take into account both the use to which the asset is being put or will be put by the entity (fair value in-use), and the most advantageous price that could be obtained for that asset if its use were to be changed (fair value in-exchange). This is explained as follows:

'The highest and best use of the asset establishes the valuation premise used to measure the fair value of the asset. Specifically:

   a.   *In-use*. The highest and best use of the asset is in-use if the asset would provide maximum value to market participants principally through its use in combination with other assets as a group (as installed or otherwise configured for use). For example, that might be the case for certain nonfinancial assets. If the highest and best use of the asset is in-use, the fair value of the asset shall be measured using an in-use valuation premise. When using an in-use valuation premise, the fair value of the asset is determined based on the price that would be received in a current transaction to sell the asset assuming that the asset would be used with other assets as a group and that those assets would be available to market participants. Generally, assumptions about the highest and best use of the asset should be consistent for all of the assets of the group within which it would be used.

   b.   *In-exchange*. The highest and best use of the asset is in-exchange if the asset would provide maximum value to market participants principally on a standalone basis. For example, that might be the case for a financial asset. If the highest and best use of the asset is in-exchange, the fair value of the asset shall be measured using an in-exchange valuation premise. When using an in-exchange valuation premise, the fair value of the asset is determined based on the price that would be received in a current transaction to sell the asset standalone.'[295]

The notion of 'highest and best use' is not an easy one to explain in principle, and it is not completely obvious how it should be identified or used in practice. It appears to imply a partial acceptance of entity-specific considerations, as the group of assets to be taken into account in an in-use valuation will in many cases be those actually being used by the entity in conjunction with the asset being valued.

The SFAS states that valuation techniques consistent with a market approach, an income approach or a cost approach shall be used to measure fair value.[296] These are, respectively in brief, actual market prices, or prices modelled on market data; discounted future cash flows or option pricing models such as the Black-Scholes-Merton formula or a binomial model; and the cost of what would be required to replace the service capacity of an asset (current replacement cost).[297]

There is a section of the SFAS that deals with the 'inputs' that may be used to arrive at fair value. These are (i) observable inputs: i.e. inputs that reflect the assumptions market participants would use in pricing assets or liabilities based on market data obtained from sources independent of the reporting entity; and (ii) unobservable inputs: i.e. inputs that reflect the entity's own assumptions about the assumptions market participants would use in pricing the asset or liability.[298] To further clarify this notion, the SFAS includes a fair value hierarchy, which is illustrated in Figure 2 below:

Figure 2.2

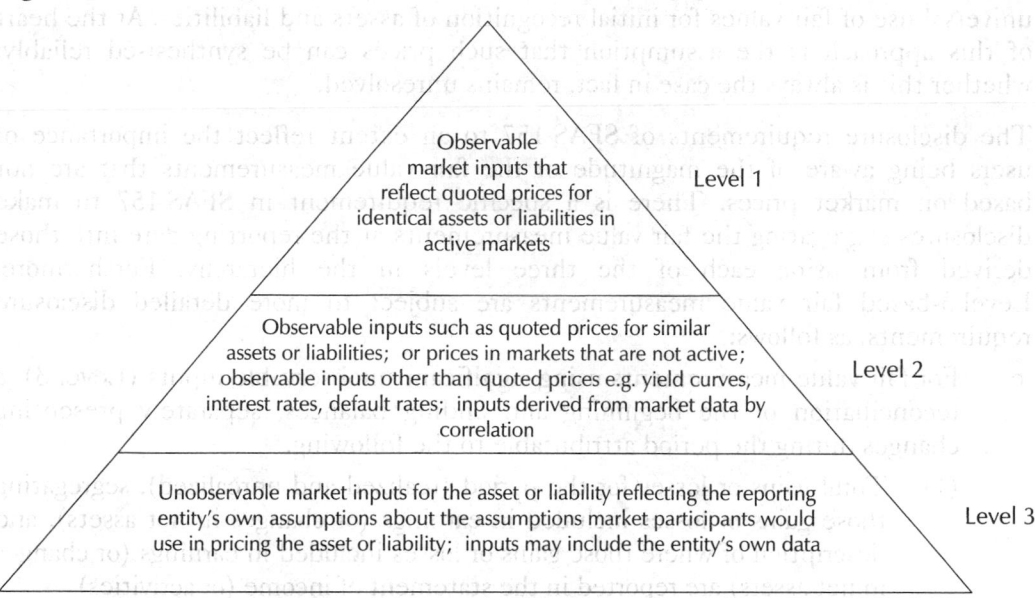

Level 1 inputs represent quoted market prices for identical assets; level 2 inputs are either quoted market prices for similar assets or liabilities, or market inputs such as interest rates, yield curves and default rates.[299] Level 3 unobservable market inputs are less clear, and the SFAS explains them as follows:

> 'Unobservable inputs shall be used to measure fair value to the extent that observable inputs are not available, thereby allowing for situations in which there is little, if any, market activity for the asset or liability at the measurement date. However, the fair value measurement objective remains the same, that is, an exit price from the perspective of a market participant that holds the asset or owes the liability. Therefore, unobservable inputs shall reflect the reporting entity's own assumptions about the assumptions that market participants would use in pricing the asset or liability (including assumptions about risk). Unobservable inputs shall be developed based on the best information available in the circumstances, which might include the reporting entity's own data. In developing unobservable inputs, the reporting entity need not undertake all possible efforts to obtain information about market participant assumptions. However, the reporting entity shall not ignore information about market participant assumptions that is reasonably available without undue cost and effort. Therefore, the reporting entity's own data used to develop unobservable inputs shall be adjusted if information is reasonably available without undue cost and effort that indicates that market participants would use different assumptions.'[300]

The difficulty is that market prices do not exist for a number of the assets and liabilities that are required to be measured at fair value by existing FASB standards, which in turn requires the use of unobservable market inputs that result in a less reliable measurement of fair value. This difficulty is similar to that faced by the

Measurement discussion paper considered at 6.1 above, which recommends the universal use of fair values for initial recognition of assets and liabilities. At the heart of this approach is the assumption that such prices can be synthesised reliably; whether this is always the case in fact, remains unresolved.

The disclosure requirements of SFAS 157 to an extent reflect the importance of users being aware of the magnitude of the fair value measurements that are not based on market prices. There is a specific requirement in SFAS 157 to make disclosures segregating the fair value measurements at the reporting date into those derived from using each of the three levels in the hierarchy. Furthermore, Level 3-based fair value measurements are subject to more detailed disclosure requirements, as follows:

'c.   For fair value measurements using significant unobservable inputs (Level 3), a reconciliation of the beginning and ending balances, separately presenting changes during the period attributable to the following:

(1)   Total gains or losses for the period (realized and unrealized), segregating those gains or losses included in earnings (or changes in net assets), and description of where those gains or losses included in earnings (or changes in net assets) are reported in the statement of income (or activities)

(2)   Purchases, sales, issuances, and settlements (net)

(3)   Transfers in and/or out of Level 3 (for example, transfers due to changes in the observability of significant inputs)

d.   The amount of the total gains or losses for the period in subparagraph (c)(1) above included in earnings (or changes in net assets) that are attributable to the change in unrealized gains or losses relating to those assets and liabilities still held at the reporting date and a description of where those unrealized gains or losses are reported in the statement of income (or activities)'.[301]

The SFAS includes substantial implementation guidance and discussion of present value techniques in its appendices.

6.2.1   The conceptual significance of FAS 157

The importance of SFAS 157 for a discussion of conceptual frameworks is twofold: (i) it codifies the way one influential standard setter considers that a fair value can be synthesised reliably in the absence of market prices; and (ii) it thereby opens the way for an extension of the application of fair value measurements to a more general use, as most assets and liabilities do not have observable market prices.

It is instructive to note that the basis of valuation put forward in SFAS 157 is in fact almost identical to that advanced by Chambers in the 1960s as set out in 4.2.2 C above. Chambers advocated 'continuously contemporary accounting' (CoCoA). The theory was based on the premise that entities must be able to choose between alternative courses of action and, because resources are limited, they need to know what resources are available to enable them to engage in exchanges. The theory further stated that this capacity to engage in exchanges is measured by the opportunity cost of holding assets in their existing form, and that this opportunity cost is represented by the current cash equivalent of assets – which Chambers defined as being their current sales value. He advocated further that exit values should be determined on the assumption that assets are realised in an orderly manner, based on sensible adaptations to changing circumstances. This notion is seemingly identical to SFAS 157's notion of the highest and best use.

Whether such a measurement basis is accurately described as a fair value, and whether it is suitable for general use throughout financial reporting, are matters that we consider should be addressed specifically and agreed upon. As already discussed Phase C of the Conceptual Framework project should provide the opportunity for that discussion

6.3   Exposure Draft – Fair Value Measurement

In May 2009 the IASB issued an exposure draft on Fair Value Measurement. The exposure draft seeks to define fair value, to establish a framework for measuring fair value and requires disclosures about fair value measurement. The purpose of the exposure draft is not to extend the use of fair value, rather to provide a single complete source of guidance on fair value. Accordingly it also proposes consequential changes to other standards which currently address fair value. The Board's stated objectives in publishing the exposure draft are:

- to establish a single source of guidance for all fair value measurements required or permitted by IFRS to reduce the complexity and improve consistency in their application;
- to clarify the definition of fair value and related guidance in order to communicate the measurement objective more clearly; and
- to enhance disclosures about fair value to enable users of financial statements to assess the extent to which fair value is used and to inform them about the inputs used to determine those fair values.

The exposure draft is based on a core principle that fair value is the price that would be received to sell an asset or paid to transfer a liability in an orderly transaction between market participants at the measurement date, in other words it is explicitly an exit price model. In the absence of actual transactions the fair value assumes a hypothetical transaction in the most advantageous market for the asset or liability.

The IASB has considered whether this definition of fair value is consistent with its intentions in all those cases where the term fair value is currently used in its literature. It has concluded that, with three specific exceptions which it intends to deal with separately that it is.

The fair value measurement proposed requires that the entity determine:

- the asset or liability which is the subject of measurement (consistent with its unit of account);
- the valuation premise that is appropriate for the measurement (consistent with its highest and best use);
- the most advantageous market;
- the appropriate valuation technique, considering the availability of data with which to develop inputs that represent the assumptions the market participants would use in pricing the asset or liability and the level of the fair value hierarchy within which the inputs are categorised.[302]

The core principle of the Exposure Draft is then broken down with a discussion of:

- the asset or liability;
- the transaction;
- market participants;
- the price;
- application to assets;
- application to liabilities;
- application to equity instruments.[303]

Fair value measurement needs to consider the characteristics of the asset or liability if a market participant would consider them when determining a price for them.[304] It should assume that the transaction occurs in the most advantageous market, that is the market which maximises the amount to be received for an asset (after allowing for transaction costs and any costs of transport.[305]

Market participants must be deemed to be independent, knowledgeable, able to enter into the transaction and willing to do so, but not forced to do so.

The fair value measurement assumes that the market participant will use the asset for its highest and best use. Highest and best use means the use of the asset which maximises the value of the asset having regard to uses of the asset which are physically possible, legally permissible and financially feasible.[306] This requires consideration of whether the asset should be valued 'in use', that is if the highest value would be obtained through use of the asset in combination with other assets or 'in exchange' if the highest value would be obtained on a stand alone basis.[307]

The Exposure Draft includes a discussion of various valuation techniques which may be applicable and includes a three level valuation hierarchy consistent with that in FAS 157.

As can be seen from the brief summary of the Exposure Draft above it is very much based on FAS 157 (albeit that there are some differences which the IASB is specifically seeking feedback on as part of the consultation process).

The proposals to provide a single source of guidance are reasonable and should serve to promote consistency in practice. The key question remains in what circumstances is the exit price fair value model set out in the Exposure Draft an appropriate measurement basis for the purposes of financial reporting.

6.4   Measurement: current state

As already noted considerable heat has been generated in discussions about fair value and its application to financial reporting and it may well be that the publication of the Exposure Draft on Fair Value Measurement discussed in 6.3 above will stimulate further discussion. However in many ways the key issue is not so much whether fair value as defined in the Exposure Draft is an appropriate measure – in certain cases including many financial instruments we believe it is. We do not agree with those who have sought to argue that the use of fair value has in some way caused the recent financial crisis. Rather the issue is which of the various possible measurement approaches should be applied to which assets and liabilities and in what circumstances so as to provide the most useful information to users of financial statements. We hope that the publication of the Discussion Paper on Phase C of the conceptual framework will provide the opportunity for a full debate of that.

7   CONCLUSION

This chapter provides an outline of the immense amount of energy that has been expended (both on the part of individuals and by specifically constituted committees) in attempting to establish an agreed conceptual framework for financial reporting. It has also highlighted the irreconcilable differences and logical difficulties that exist in the various accounting theories that have been developed over the years.

The existence of such framework documents might have raised the prospect of a degree of rigour and consistency being applied to accounting standards issued by the various standard-setting bodies. In practice, however, standard setters have made more use of these documents to prevent practices they dislike, and framework documents have, on occasion, been conveniently ignored when a standard is required that conflicts with them. Inconsistencies of this nature are probably inevitable whilst matters that are fundamental to their resolution remain unresolved. Since Edwards and Bell and Maurice Moonitz (see 4.2.2A and 2.1 above respectively) published their work in the early 1960s, there has been controversy over, and disagreement about, the valuation basis to be used in financial reporting. These disagreements have been over whether current values should be used in place of historical costs at all, and if so what type of current value system is to be used. Further disagreement surrounds the way current values are to be determined even if a given system is selected.

Against this background and given the number of jurisdictions that are committed to adopting, or converging with, IFRS in the near term we continue to support the IASB/FASB joint conceptual framework initiative. We hope that it leads to the development of a new framework that will support standard setters in the future.

References

1 W. A. Paton and A. C. Littleton, *An Introduction to Corporate Accounting Standards*, Monograph No. 3, American Accounting Association, 1940.

2 See, for example: American Accounting Association, Executive Committee, 'A Tentative Statement of Accounting Principles Affecting Corporate Reports', *Accounting Review*, June 1936, pp. 187-191; American Accounting Association, Executive Committee, 'Accounting Principles Underlying Corporate Financial Statements', *Accounting Review*, June 1941, pp. 133-139; American Accounting Association, Committee to Prepare a Statement of Basic Accounting Theory, *A Statement of Basic Accounting Theory*, 1966; American Accounting Association, Committee on Concepts and Standards for External Financial Reports, *Statement on Accounting Theory and Theory Acceptance*, 1977. The 1977 report concluded that closure on the debate was not feasible, which is perhaps indicative of the complexity of the problem.

3 As can be seen, for example, in the way that asset impairment is measured and accounted for under IFRS and US GAAP. It is for this reason that the IASB and FASB have embarked on a project to develop an agreed single conceptual framework – see section 5 of this chapter.

4 For a full discussion on the politicisation of accounting see: David Solomons, 'The Politicization of Accounting', Journal of Accountancy, November 1978, p. 71.

5 Maurice Moonitz, *The Basic Postulates of Accounting*, Accounting Research Study No. 1, AICPA, 1961, Preface.

6 The basic postulates of accounting.

7 Robert T. Sprouse and Maurice Moonitz, *A Tentative Set of Broad Accounting Principles for Business Enterprises*, Accounting Research Study No. 3, AICPA, 1962.

8 A Tentative Set of Broad Accounting Principles for Business Enterprises, p. 14.

9 A Tentative Set of Broad Accounting Principles for Business Enterprises, p. 27.

10 APB Statement No. 4, *Basic Concepts and Accounting Principles Underlying Financial Statements of Business Enterprises*, AICPA, October 1970.

11 APB Statement No. 4, para. 3.

12 APB Statement No. 4, para. 132.

13 Report of the Study Group on the Objectives of Financial Statements, *Objectives of Financial Statements*, AICPA, October 1973, p. 65.

14 *Objectives of Financial Statements*, AICPA.

15 *Objectives of Financial Statements*, AICPA.

16 *Objectives of Financial Statements*, AICPA.

17 *Objectives of Financial Statements*, AICPA p. 13.

18 *Objectives of Financial Statements*, AICPA pp. 57-60.

19 FASB Discussion Memorandum, *Conceptual Framework for Accounting and Reporting: Consideration of the Report of the Study Group on the Objectives of Financial Statements*, FASB, June 6, 1974.

20 FASB, Scope and Implications of the Conceptual Framework Project, FASB, December 2, 1976.

21 FASB, Scope and Implications of the Conceptual Framework Project, p. 5.

22 FASB, Scope and Implications of the Conceptual Framework Project, p. 2.

23 FASB, Scope and Implications of the Conceptual Framework Project, pp. 5 and 6.

24 SFAC No. 1, *Objectives of Financial Reporting by Business Enterprises*, FASB, November 1978, para. 7.

25 SFAC No. 1, para. 9.

26 SFAC No. 1, para. 24.

27 SFAC No. 1, para. 34.

28 SFAC No. 1, para. 37.

29 SFAC No. 1, para. 24.

30 SFAC No. 1, footnote 6.

31 SFAC No. 1, para. 43.

32 SFAC No. 1, para. 50.

33 SFAC No. 1, para. 51.

34 SFAC No. 2, *Qualitative Characteristics of Accounting Information*, FASB, May 1980, Figure 1.

35 SFAC No. 1, para. 34.

36 SFAC No. 2, para. 36.

37 SFAC No. 2, p. x.

38 SFAC No. 2, para. 90.

39 SFAC No. 2, p. xi.

40 SFAC No. 2, para. 56.

41 SFAC No. 2.

42 SFAC No. 2, para. 51.

43 SFAC No. 2, p. xvi.

44 SFAC No. 2.

45 SFAC No. 2, para. 59.

46 SFAC No. 2, paras. 91-97.

47 SFAC No. 2, para. 93.

48 SFAC No. 2, para. 95.

49 SFAC No. 6, *Elements of Financial Statements*, a replacement of FASB Concepts Statement No. 3, FASB, December 1985, para. 25.

50 SFAC No. 6, para. 27.

51 SFAC No. 6, para. 28.

52 SFAC No. 6, para. 35.

53 SFAC No. 6, para. 36.

54 SFAC No. 6, para. 49.

55 SFAC No. 6, para. 66.

56 SFAC No. 6.

57 SFAC No. 6, para. 67.

58 SFAC No. 6, para. 70.

59 SFAC No. 1, para. 43.

60 SFAC No. 6, p. 1, footnote 1.

61 SFAC No. 6, para. 78.

62 SFAC No. 6, para. 80.

63 SFAC No. 6, para. 82.

64 SFAC No. 6, para. 83.

65 SFAC No. 6, para. 77.

66 See, for example, SFAC No. 3, *Elements of Financial Statements of Business Enterprises*, FASB, December 1980, para. 58.

67 SFAC No. 5, *Recognition and Measurement in Financial Statements of Business Enterprises*, FASB, December 1984, para. 66.

68 SFAC No. 5, paras. 66-70.

69 SFAC No. 5, paras. 45-48.

70 SFAC No. 5, para. 58.

71 SFAC No. 5, para. 63.

72 SFAC No. 5, paras. 33 and 34.

73 SFAC No. 5, para. 35.

74 David Solomons, 'The FASB's Conceptual Framework: An evaluation', Journal of Accountancy, June 1986, pp. 114-124, at p. 122.

75 The FASB's Conceptual Framework: An evaluation, p. 124.

76 The FASB's Conceptual Framework: An evaluation.

77 Special Report: The Framework of Financial Accounting Concepts and Standards, p. 158.

78 Special Report: The Framework of Financial Accounting Concepts and Standards, p. 158.

79 Special Report: The Framework of Financial Accounting Concepts and Standards, p. 160.

80 Statement of Financial Accounting Concepts 7, *Using Cash Flow Information and Present Value in Accounting Measurements*, FASB, February 2000, para. 19.

81 SFAC No. 7, para. 21.

82 SFAC No. 7, para. 23.

83 SFAC No. 7, paras. 31 and 37.

84 SFAC No. 7, para. 41.

85 SFAC No. 7, para. 75.

86 SFAC No. 7, Glossary of terms.

87 IAS 39, *Financial Instruments: Recognition and Measurement*, IASB, December 2003 (amended March 2004), para. BC89.

88 Stephen A. Zeff, Accounting Horizons, 'A Perspective on the U.S. Public/Private-Sector Approach to the Regulation of Financial Reporting', Vol. 9 No. 1, March 1995, p. 60.

89 See Steinar Sars Kvifte, *The Usefulness of the Asset-Liability View – An Analysis of Conceptual Frameworks and the Implications for Norwegian Accounting Regulation*. PhD Dissertation in Accounting, The Norwegian School of Economics and Business Administration, the Department of Accounting, Auditing and Law, Bergen, Norway. In this dissertation, Dr. Kvifte provides substantial evidence to support the conclusion that the asset/liability definitions of the FASB conceptual framework have been ineffective tools in accounting standard-setting in the US. Similar evidence is provided in the case of the IASB Framework.

90 Exposure Draft, *Framework for the Preparation and Presentation of Financial Statements*, IASC, May 1988.

91 *Framework for the Preparation and Presentation of Financial Statements*, IASB, September 1989, para. 4.

92 Framework, para. 2.

93 Framework, para. 1.

94 Framework, para. 7.

95 Framework, para. 12.

96 Framework, para. 14.

97 Framework, para. 10.

98 Framework, para. 22.

99 Framework, para. 95.

100 Framework, para. 23.

101 Framework, para. 24.

102 Framework, para. 25.

103 Framework, para. 26.

104 Framework, para. 27.

105 Framework, para. 30.

106 Framework, para. 31.

107 Framework, para. 32.

108 Framework, para. 34.

109 Framework, para. 36.

110 Framework, para. 37.

111 Framework, para. 38.

112 Framework, para. 40.

113 Framework, para. 43.

114 Framework, para. 43.

115 Framework, para. 49.

116 Framework, para. 83.

117 Framework, para. 51.

118 Framework, para. 49.

119 Framework, para. 49.

120 Framework, para. 70.

121 Framework, para. 75.

122 Framework, para. 79.

123 Framework, paras. 76 and 79.

124 Framework, para. 83.

125 Framework, para. 91.

126 Framework, para. 99.

127 Framework, para. 102.

128 Framework, para. 103.

129 Framework, para. 110.

130 Framework, para. 110.

131 *The Corporate Report*, A discussion paper published for comment by the Accounting Standards Steering Committee, London, 1975.

132 The Corporate Report, para. 0.1.

133 The Corporate Report, para. 0.2.

134 The committee's recommended package of information which should be contained in the annual corporate reports of business enterprises is listed in Appendix 2 of the discussion paper.

135 The Corporate Report, para. 0.3.

136 The Corporate Report, para. 1.1.

137 The Corporate Report, para. 1.8.

138 The Corporate Report, para. 1.9. The seven user groups identified were: (a) the equity investor group, (b) the loan creditor group, (c) the employee group, (d) the analyst-adviser group, (e) the business contact group, (f) the government and (g) the public.

139 The Corporate Report, paras. 2.1-2.40.

140 The Corporate Report, para. 3.2.

141 The Corporate Report, para. 3.3.

142 The Corporate Report, para. 4.30.

143 The Corporate Report, para. 4.40.

144 The Corporate Report, para. 6.56.

145 The Corporate Report, paras. 6.56 and 6.57.

146 The Corporate Report, para. 7.4.

147 The Corporate Report, para. 7.15.

148 The Corporate Report, paras. 7.40 and 7.43.

149 Report of the Inflation Accounting Committee, *Inflation Accounting*, Cmnd. 6225, London: HMSO, 1975, (the Sandilands Report), p. iv.

150 Inflation Accounting, para. 144.

151 Inflation Accounting, Chapter 12.

152 SSAP 7 (Provisional) *Accounting for the changes in the purchasing power of money*, May 1974 recommended that the RPI should be used for this purpose.

153 SSAP 7, para. 12.

154 The Sandilands Report, para. 20.

155 The Sandilands Report, para. 422.

156 The Sandilands Report, paras. 411 and 412.

157 The Sandilands Report, para. 415.

158 Edwards and Bell have made significant contributions in the areas of income determination and value measurement – however, it is beyond the scope of this book to provide a detailed analysis of their theories. Their case for income and value measurement based on replacement costs may be found in their classic work: E. O. Edwards and P. W. Bell, *The Theory and Measurement of Business Income*, University of California Press, 1961.

159 The Sandilands Report, para. 453.

160 The Sandilands Report, para. 499.

161 Kenneth MacNeal, *Truth in Accounting*, Philadelphia: University of Pennsylvania Press, 1939.

162 R. J. Chambers, *Accounting, Evaluation and Economic Behaviour*, Prentice-Hall, 1966.

163 R. R. Sterling, *Theory of the Measurement of Enterprise Income*, University of Kansas Press, 1970.

164 The Sandilands Report, para. 510.

165 The Institute of Chartered Accountants of Scotland, *Making Corporate Reports Valuable*, London: Kogan Page, 1988, paras. 6.20-6.23.

166 Lee has published numerous papers on the subject of cash flow accounting, the ideas of which have been drawn together in his book: Tom Lee, *Cash Flow Accounting*, Wokingham, Van Nostrand Reinhold (UK), 1984.

167 Lawson has published widely on the subject of cash flow accounting – see, for example: G. H. Lawson, '*Cash-flow Accounting*', The Accountant, October 28th, 1971, pp. 586-589; G. H. Lawson, '*The Measurement of Corporate Profitability on a Cash-flow Basis*', The International Journal of Accounting Education and Research, Vol. 16, No. 1, pp. 11-46.

168 Tom Lee, *op. cit.*, p. 51.

169 Tom Lee, *op. cit.*, pp. 51-52.

170 Lee presents a quantified example of his proposed cash flow reporting system, Tom Lee, *op. cit.*, pp. 57-72.

171 The Sandilands Report, para. 518.

172 The Sandilands Report, para. 517.

173 The Sandilands Report, para. 537.

174 For a detailed discussion of the capital maintenance concepts which apply in the Sandilands proposals, see: H. C. Edey, '*Sandilands and the Logic of Current Cost*', Accounting and Business Research, Volume 9, No. 35, Summer 1979, pp. 191-200.

175 SSAP 16, *Current cost accounting*, March 1980, para. 9.

176 Edward Stamp, *Corporate Reporting: Its Future Evolution*, a research study published by the Canadian Institute of Chartered Accountants, 1980, (the Stamp Report), Ch. 1, para. 3.

177 Edward Stamp, '*First steps towards a British conceptual framework*', Accountancy, March 1982, pp. 123-130.

178 Stamp's qualitative criteria were ranked (from most important to least important) by the ASC members as follows ('*First steps towards a British conceptual framework*', Accountancy, March 1982, Figure 2, p. 126): relevance, clarity, substance over form, timeliness, comparability, materiality, freedom from bias, objectivity, rationality, full disclosure, consistency, isomorphism, verifiability, cost/benefit effectiveness, non-arbitrariness, data availability, flexibility, uniformity, precision, conservatism.

179 The Stamp Report, Chapter 2.

180 Making Corporate Reports Valuable, paras. 1.1-1.20, *passim*.

181 Making Corporate Reports Valuable, para. 6.36.

182 Making Corporate Reports Valuable, para. 6.36.

183 Making Corporate Reports Valuable, paras. 7.12-7.20, *passim*.

184 Making Corporate Reports Valuable, para. 7.21.

185 Making Corporate Reports Valuable, paras. 7.23-7.26, *passim*.

186 Making Corporate Reports Valuable, paras. 7.27-7.32, *passim*.

187 Making Corporate Reports Valuable, para. 7.39.

188 Making Corporate Reports Valuable, para. 5.44.

189 David Solomons, *Guidelines for Financial Reporting Standards*, A Paper Prepared for The Research Board of the Institute of Chartered Accountants in England and Wales and addressed to the Accounting Standards Committee, ICAEW, 1989, (the Solomons Report), p. 17.

190 Guidelines for Financial Reporting Standards, p. 18.

191 Guidelines for Financial Reporting Standards, p. 18.

192 Guidelines for Financial Reporting Standards, p. 20.

193 Guidelines for Financial Reporting Standards, p. 21.

194 Guidelines for Financial Reporting Standards, pp. 23-28.

195 Guidelines for Financial Reporting Standards, p. 43.

196 Guidelines for Financial Reporting Standards, pp. 51-52.

197 Accounting Horizons, vol. 9 no. 1, pp. 42-51.

198 Guidelines for Financial Reporting Standards, p. 53.

199 Guidelines for Financial Reporting Standards, p. 53.

200 Guidelines for Financial Reporting Standards, p. 54.

201 Guidelines for Financial Reporting Standards, p. 55.

202 Guidelines for Financial Reporting Standards, p. 56.

203 Guidelines for Financial Reporting Standards, p. 69.

204 Statement of Principles for Financial Reporting, ASB, December 1999.

205 Statement of Principles for Financial Reporting Chapter 1, Principles.

206 Statement of Principles for Financial Reporting para. 1.18

207 Statement of Principles for Financial Reporting Chapter 3, Principles.

208 Statement of Principles for Financial Reporting Chapter 3, Principles.

209 Statement of Principles for Financial Reporting para. 4.21.

210 Statement of Principles for Financial Reporting para. 4.21.

211 Statement of Principles for Financial Reporting Chapter 5, Principles.

212 Statement of Principles for Financial Reporting para. 8.13.

213 *An improved conceptual framework for financial reporting*, IASB, May 2008. ('Framework ED')

214 Framework ED, para. P8.

215 Framework ED, para. P14.

216 Framework ED, para. P15.

217 Framework ED, para. OB2.

218 Framework ED, para. BC1.29.

219 Framework ED, para OB6.

220 Framework ED, para. OB5.

221 Framework ED, para. OB9 .

222 Framework ED, paras. OB25, OB21 and OB24.

223 Framework ED, para. BC1.16.

224 Framework ED, para. OB21.

225 Framework ED, para. QC2.

226 Framework ED, para. QC15.

227 Framework ED, para QC 27.

228 Framework, para. 24.

229 Framework, para. 45.

230 Framework exposure draft QC15.

231 Framework, para. 31.

232 Framework, para. 32.

233 Framework ED, para BC2.11.

234 Framework ED, para. BC2.16.

235 Framework ED, para. BC2.15.

236 Framework ED, para. QC20.

237 Framework ED, para. BC2.21.

238 Framework ED, para. QC24.

239 Framework ED, para. BC2.19.

240 The Boards current thinking is summarised on its website www.iasb.org.uk.

241 Preliminary Views, *An improved conceptual framework for financial reporting*, IASB, May 2008.
242 Preliminary Views, para. 14
243 Preliminary Views, para. 22
244 Preliminary Views, para. S2
245 Preliminary Views, para. 48
246 Preliminary Views, para. 49
247 Preliminary Views, para. 97
248 Preliminary Views, para. 104
249 Preliminary Views, para. 98
250 Preliminary Views, para. 93
251 Preliminary Views, para. 136
252 Preliminary Views, para. 140
253 Preliminary Views, para. 141
254 The Boards current thinking is summarised on its website www.iasb.org.uk.
255 Exposure Draft Management Commentary, IASB ('ED Management Commentary), Introduction
256 ED Management Commentary, para 13
257 ED Management Commentary, para 20
258 ED Management Commentary, para 24
259 Discussion paper, *Measurement bases for financial accounting – measurement on initial recognition*, IASB, November 2005, Introduction p6.
260 Measurement bases for financial accounting – measurement on initial recognition, Summary, p7.
261 Measurement bases for financial accounting – measurement on initial recognition, para. 29.
262 Measurement bases for financial accounting – measurement on initial recognition, para. 54.
263 Measurement bases for financial accounting – measurement on initial recognition, para. 55.
264 Measurement bases for financial accounting – measurement on initial recognition, para. 48.
265 Measurement bases for financial accounting – measurement on initial recognition, para. 48.
266 Measurement bases for financial accounting – measurement on initial recognition, paras. 69 to 96.
267 Measurement bases for financial accounting – measurement on initial recognition, para. 81.
268 IAS 15, para. 13. IAS 15 was withdrawn by the IASB with effect from 1 January, 2005, with the result that, as of that date, the term is no longer defined in IASB standards.
269 Measurement bases for financial accounting – measurement on initial recognition, para. 83.
270 Measurement bases for financial accounting – measurement on initial recognition, para. 85.
271 Measurement bases for financial accounting – measurement on initial recognition, para. 89.
272 Measurement bases for financial accounting – measurement on initial recognition, para. 94.
273 Measurement bases for financial accounting – measurement on initial recognition, para. 73.
274 Measurement bases for financial accounting – measurement on initial recognition, para. 71.
275 Measurement bases for financial accounting – measurement on initial recognition, para. 128.
276 Measurement bases for financial accounting – measurement on initial recognition, Chapters 7 and 8 generally.
277 Measurement bases for financial accounting – measurement on initial recognition, para. 135.
278 Measurement bases for financial accounting – measurement on initial recognition, para. 26.
279 Measurement bases for financial accounting – measurement on initial recognition, para. 128.
280 Measurement bases for financial accounting – measurement on initial recognition, para. 180.
281 Measurement bases for financial accounting – measurement on initial recognition, para. 128.
282 Measurement bases for financial accounting – measurement on initial recognition, para. 128.
283 Statement of Financial Accounting Standards No.157 – *Fair Value Measurements*, FASB, September 2006.
284 SFAS 157, Summary.
285 SFAS 157, Summary.
286 IAS 39, AG82.
287 SFAS 157, para. 5.
288 SFAS 157, para. 6.
289 SFAS 157, Summary.
290 SFAS 157, para. 10.
291 SFAS 157, para. 8.
292 SFAS 157, para. 8.
293 SFAS 157, para. 10.
294 SFAS 157, para. 12.
295 SFAS 157, para. 13.
296 SFAS 157, para. 18.
297 SFAS 157, para. 18.
298 SFAS 157, para. 21.
299 SFAS 157, paras. 24-29.
300 SFAS 157, para. 30.
301 SFAS 157, para. 32.
302 Exposure Draft Fair Value Measurement, IASB ('ED Fair Value Measurement'), Introduction
303 ED Fair Value Measurement, para 4.
304 ED Fair Value Measurement, para 5.
305 ED Fair Value Measurement, para 8.
306 EDFair Value Measurement, para 17.
307 ED Fair Value Measurement, paras 20 and 21.

Chapter 3   Presentation of financial statements and accounting policies

1   INTRODUCTION

There is no single standard dealing with the form, content and structure of financial statements and the accounting policies to be applied in their preparation. Of course, all international accounting standards specify some required disclosures and many mention the level of prominence required (such as on the face of a primary statement rather than in the notes). The subject of just what financial statements are, their purpose, contents and presentation is addressed principally by three standards.

IAS 1 – *Presentation of Financial Statements* – is the main standard dealing with the overall requirements for the presentation of financial statements, including their purpose, form, content and structure.[1] IAS 8 – *Accounting Policies, Changes in Accounting Estimates and Errors* – deals with the requirements for the selection and application of accounting policies.[2] It also deals with the requirements as to when changes in accounting policies should be made, and how such changes should be accounted for and disclosed. This chapter deals with the requirements of IAS 1 and IAS 8, including the requirements of the latter dealing with changes in accounting estimates and errors. Chapter 4 discusses the requirements of IFRS 5 – *Non-current Assets Held for Sale and Discontinued Operations*.[3] That standard principally deals with the classification and presentation of non-current assets held for sale in the balance sheet, and the presentation of the results of discontinued operations, although it also sets out the measurement requirements for such items.

1.1   IAS 1

1.1.1   *Background to IAS 1*

In August 1997, the IASC issued IAS 1 (revised) – *Presentation of Financial Statements* – which consolidated and replaced IAS 1 – *Disclosure of Accounting Policies* (originally published in 1974), IAS 5 – *Information to be Disclosed in Financial Statements* (originally published in 1974), and IAS 13 – *Presentation of Current Assets and Current Liabilities* (originally published in 1979). In December 2003 the standard was updated as part of the IASB's improvements project and some further revisions were made in March 2004 by IFRS 5.

In December 2004 a revision to IAS 19 – *Employee Benefits* – relating to the recognition of actuarial gains and losses made consequential amendments to IAS 1. In August 2005, IFRS 7 – *Financial Instruments: Disclosures* – was published by the IASB. This made some minor consequential amendments to IAS 1.

In September 2007 the IASB published a revised IAS 1. Whilst the revision constituted a major re-write of the standard in terms of the ordering of paragraphs and the terminology used, the bulk of the content was unchanged. The principal changes introduced in 2007 were as follows:

- The terms 'balance sheet' and 'cash flow statement' were changed to 'statement of financial position' and 'statement of cash flows' respectively. However, the new names are not mandatory;

- An additional balance sheet and related notes are to be presented as at the beginning of the earliest period presented, but only in periods when the comparatives have been changed;

- The revised standard requires a statement of comprehensive income to include all 'non-owner' changes in equity. However, the title of the statement is not mandatory and it may also be presented as two distinct statements – an income statement and a statement of comprehensive income. This is to be presented in addition to a statement of changes in equity containing changes arising from transactions with owners and other changes;

- A new requirement to disclose income tax and reclassification adjustments relating to each component of other comprehensive income; and

- Distributions to owners may now only be presented in the statement of changes in equity.

The revised standard applies to periods beginning on or after 1 January 2009. Early adoption is permitted if it is disclosed. This Chapter presents an analysis and discussion of the revised IAS 1. The previous edition of this book, *International GAAP 2009* provides a more detailed analysis of the differences between the current standard and its predecessor.

As noted above, the new terminology for the primary statements is not mandatory. Furthermore, there remains a choice of presenting one statement of comprehensive income or a separate income statement and statement of other comprehensive income. We suspect that many entities will be reluctant to give up the familiar balance sheet and income statement until such time as it is mandatory. For this reason International GAAP 2010 discusses all areas of IFRS in these familiar terms.

IAS 1 was further amended in

- February 2008 as a consequence of the revision to IAS 32 – *Financial Instruments: Presentation* – allowing a special balance sheet presentation for 'puttable financial instruments' (see 3.1.6 below);

- In May 2008, a revised IAS 27 – *Consolidated and Separate Financial Statements* – was published which made amendments to the requirements of IAS 1 relating to the structure of the statement of changes in equity (see 3.3 below);

- May 2008 also saw the publication of the IASB's annual improvement project, which contained some minor updates to IAS 1; and

- April 2009 by the IASB's annual improvement project clarifying the distinction between current and non-current liabilities when the liabilities may be settled in equity.

IAS 1 deals with the components of financial statements, fair presentation, fundamental accounting concepts, disclosure of accounting policies, the structure and content of financial statements and the statement of changes in equity.

1.1.2 Objective and scope of IAS 1

IAS 1 applies to what it calls 'general purpose financial statements' (financial statements), that is those intended to meet the needs of users who are not in a position to require an entity to prepare reports tailored to meet their particular information needs, and it should be applied to all such financial statements prepared in accordance with International Financial Reporting Standards.[4] Although International Financial Reporting Standards (IFRSs) is probably a self explanatory phrase, both IAS 1 and IAS 8 define it as 'Standards and Interpretations adopted by the International Accounting Standards Board (IASB). They comprise:

(a)   International Financial Reporting Standards;

(b)   International Accounting Standards; and

(c)   Interpretations developed by the International Financial Reporting Interpretations Committee (IFRIC) or the former Standing Interpretations Committee (SIC).[5]

An important point here is that implementation guidance for standards issued by the IASB does not form part of those standards, and therefore does not contain requirements for financial statements.[6] Accordingly, the often voluminous implementation guidance accompanying standards is not, strictly speaking, part of 'IFRS'. We would generally be surprised, though, at entities not following such guidance without valid reason.

The standard applies equally to all entities including those that present consolidated financial statements and those that present separate financial statements, as defined in IAS 27 (discussed in Chapter 6).[7] IAS 1 does not apply to the structure and content of condensed interim financial statements prepared in accordance with

IAS 34 – *Interim Financial Reporting* (discussed in Chapter 40),[8] although its provisions relating to fair presentation, compliance with IFRS and fundamental accounting principles do apply to interims.[9] These provisions of IAS 1 are discussed at 4.1 below.

The objective of the standard is to prescribe the basis for presentation of general purpose financial statements, and by doing so to ensure comparability both with the entity's financial statements of previous periods and with the financial statements of other entities. The standard sets out overall requirements for the presentation of financial statements, guidelines for their structure and minimum requirements for their content. The recognition, measurement and disclosure of specific transactions and other events are dealt with in other standards and in interpretations.[10]

IAS 1 is primarily directed at profit oriented entities (including public sector business entities), and this is reflected in the terminology it uses and its requirements. It acknowledges that entities with not-for-profit activities in the private sector, public sector or government may want to apply the standard and that such entities may need to amend the descriptions used for particular line items in the financial statements and for the financial statements themselves.[11] Furthermore, IAS 1 is a general standard that does not address issues specific to particular industries. It does observe, though, that entities without equity (such as some mutual funds) or whose share capital is not equity (such as some co-operative entities) may need to adapt the presentation of members' or unit holders' interests.[12]

1.2   IAS 8

1.2.1   Background to IAS 8

IAS 8 has a long history, dating back to 1976. The standard in its current form and with its current title was published in December 2003 as part of the IASB's improvements project.

1.2.2   Objective and scope of IAS 8

IAS 8 applies to selecting and applying accounting policies, and accounting for changes in accounting policies, changes in accounting estimates and corrections of prior period errors.[13] Its objective is to prescribe the criteria for selecting and changing accounting policies, together with the accounting treatment and disclosure of changes in accounting policies, changes in accounting estimates and corrections of errors. The standard's intention is to enhance the relevance and reliability of an entity's financial statements and the comparability of those financial statements over time and with the financial statements of other entities.[14]

Two particular issues which one might expect to be dealt with regarding the above are discussed in other standards and cross-referred to by IAS 8:

- disclosure requirements for accounting policies, except those for changes in accounting policies, are dealt with in IAS 1;[15] and

- accounting and disclosure requirements regarding the tax effects of corrections of prior period errors and of retrospective adjustments made to apply changes in accounting policies are dealt with in IAS 12 – *Income Taxes* (discussed in Chapter 26).[16]

2   THE PURPOSE AND COMPOSITION OF FINANCIAL STATEMENTS

What financial statements are and what they are for are clearly important basic questions for any body of accounting literature, and answering them is the main purpose of IAS 1.

2.1   The purpose of financial statements

IAS 1 describes financial statements as a structured representation of the financial position and financial performance of an entity. It states that the objective of financial statements is to provide information about the financial position, financial performance and cash flows of an entity that is useful to a wide range of users in making economic decisions. A focus on assisting decision making by the users of financial statements is seeking (at least in part) a forward looking or predictive quality. This is reflected by some requirements of accounting standards (for example, the disclosure of discontinued operations (discussed in Chapter 4), and the use of profit from continuing operations as the control number in calculating diluted earnings per share (discussed at 6.3.1 in Chapter 36)) and also the desire of some entities to present performance measures excluding what they see as unusual, infrequent or just historic items (discussed at 3.2.6 below).

IAS 1 also acknowledges a second important role of financial statements. That is, that they also show the results of management's stewardship of the resources entrusted to it. To meet this objective, IAS 1 requires financial statements provide information about an entity's:

(a)   assets;

(b)   liabilities;

(c)   equity;

(d)   income and expenses, including gains and losses;

(e)   contributions by owners and distributions to owners in their capacity as owners (owners being defined as holders of instruments classified as equity);[17] and

(f)   cash flows.

The standard observes that this information, along with other information in the notes, assists users of financial statements in predicting the entity's future cash flows and, in particular, their timing and certainty.[18]

2.2   Frequency of reporting and period covered

IAS 1 requires that a complete set of financial statements (including comparative information, see 2.4 below) be presented 'at least annually'. Whilst this drafting is not exactly precise, it does not seem to mean that financial statements must never be more than a year apart (which is perhaps the most natural meaning of the phrase). This is because the standard goes on to mention that the end of an entity's reporting period may change, and that the annual financial statements are therefore presented for a period *longer* or shorter than one year. When this is the case, IAS 1 requires disclosure of, in addition to the period covered by the financial statements:

(a)   the reason for using a longer or shorter period; and

(b)   the fact that amounts presented in the financial statements are not entirely comparable.[19]

Normally financial statements are consistently prepared covering a one year period. Some entities, particularly in the retail sector, traditionally present financial statements for a 52-week period. IAS 1 does not preclude this practice.[20]

2.3   The components of a complete set of financial statements

A complete set of financial statements under IAS 1 comprises the following, each of which should be presented with equal prominence:[21]

(a)   a balance sheet as at the end of the period (IAS 1 uses the phrase 'statement of financial position', but indicates that other titles may be used);

(b)   a statement of comprehensive income for the period to be presented either as:

(i)   one single statement of comprehensive income; or

(ii)   a separate income statement and statement of comprehensive income. In this case, the former must be presented immediately before the latter;[22]

(c)   a statement of changes in equity for the period;

(d)   a statement of cash flows for the period;

(e)   notes, comprising a summary of significant accounting policies and other explanatory information; and

(f)   a balance sheet as at the beginning of the earliest comparative period when:

(i)   an accounting policy has been applied retrospectively; or

(ii)   a retrospective restatement has been made; or

(iii)   items have been reclassified.[23]

The standard explains that notes contain information in addition to that presented in the primary statements above, and provide narrative descriptions or disaggregations of items presented in those statements and information about items that do not qualify for recognition in those statements.[24]

In addition to information about the reporting period, IAS 1 also requires information about the preceding period. Comparative information is discussed at 2.4 below.

Financial statements are usually published as part of a larger annual report, with the accompanying discussions and analyses often being more voluminous than the financial statements themselves. IAS 1 acknowledges this, but makes clear that such reports and statements (including financial reviews, environmental reports and value added statements) presented outside financial statements are outside the scope of IFRSs.[25]

Notwithstanding that this type of information is not within the scope of IFRSs, IAS 1 devotes two paragraphs to discussing what this information may comprise, observing that:

- a financial review by management may describe and explain the main features of the entity's financial performance and financial position and the principal uncertainties it faces and that it may include a review of:

  - the main factors and influences determining financial performance, including changes in the environment in which the entity operates, the entity's response to those changes and their effect, and the entity's policy for investment to maintain and enhance financial performance, including its dividend policy;

  - the entity's sources of funding and its targeted ratio of liabilities to equity (since 2007 IAS 1 itself has in fact required certain disclosures about capital. These are discussed at 5.4 below); and

  - the entity's resources not recognised in the balance sheet in accordance with IFRS.[26]

- reports and statements such as environmental reports and value added statements may be presented, particularly in industries in which environmental factors are significant and when employees are regarded as an important user group.[27]

It strikes us as strange that an accounting standard would concern itself with a discussion of matters outside its scope in this way. However, discursive reports accompanying financial statements are not just common (indeed, required by most markets) but also clearly useful, so perhaps the IASB's discussion is attempting to encourage and support their preparation. In October 2005 the IASB published a discussion paper on management commentary. The paper assesses the role the IASB could play in improving the quality of the management commentary that frequently accompanies financial statements. The IASB sets out its view that management commentary is widely regarded as an important part of companies' annual reports and many jurisdictions have developed requirements or principles on management commentary. The Paper reviews those requirements and offers recommendations on how the IASB might promote the wider adoption of best practice in the interests of investors and others who use financial reports. The paper does not properly address the key question as to whether financial statements can achieve a 'fair presentation' on their own, or whether a management commentary is needed to do so.

At its December 2007 meeting, the IASB voted to move the management commentary project from its research agenda to its active agenda. The Board decided that work on the project should result in the production of a guidance document based on the Management Commentary discussion paper issued in October 2005. This resulted in the publication by the IASB of an exposure draft titled *Management Commentary* in June 2009. The comment period ends on 1 March 2010 and the Board expects to publish completed guidance by the second half of 2010.[28]

The IASB's proposals are intended to provide a basis for the development of good management commentary. The Board's intention is to offer a non-binding framework and limited guidance on its application, which could be adapted to the legal and economic circumstances of individual jurisdictions. The exposure draft focuses on publicly traded entities however, the Board's view is that, if applicable, it may be a useful tool for non-exchange traded entities, for example, privately held and state-owned enterprises.[29]

Notwithstanding the clear usefulness of management commentaries, we believe that it has historically been recognised that financial statements can stand alone and achieve a fair presentation without a supporting commentary. Accordingly, we question the IASB's mandate to develop guidance in this area.

2.4   Comparative information

IAS 1 requires, except when IFRSs permit or require otherwise, comparative information to be disclosed in respect of the previous period for all amounts reported in the current period's financial statements.[30] If any information is voluntarily presented, there will by definition be no standard or interpretation providing a dispensation from comparatives. Accordingly, comparative information is necessary for any voluntarily presented current period disclosure.

The above requirement represents the minimum which is required in all circumstances: two complete sets of primary statements and notes. However, further comparative information is required in certain circumstances. Whenever an entity:

(a)   applies an accounting policy retrospectively; or

(b)   makes a retrospective restatement; or

(c)   reclassifies items in its financial statements

an additional balance sheet and related notes is required as at the beginning of the earliest period presented.[31]

The above requirement indicates that whenever one of (a) to (c) above occurs, an additional balance sheet and notes thereto is required without exception. This would therefore seem to apply even if there has been no change to the balance sheet concerned. In this regard it is worth noting that the exposure draft preceding the revised standard proposed an additional balance sheet in all cases. In explaining the change to require it only in the above circumstances the Board said the following.

'By adding a statement of financial position as at the beginning of the earliest comparative period, the exposure draft proposed that an entity should present three statements of financial position and two of each of the other statements. Considering that financial statements from prior years are readily available for financial analysis, the Board decided to require only two statements of financial position, except when the financial statements have been affected by retrospective application or retrospective restatement, as defined in IAS 8 Accounting Policies, Changes in Accounting Estimates and Errors, or when a reclassification has been made. In those circumstances three statements of financial position are required.'[32]

In light of the above and also the provisions of the standard relating to materiality (discussed at 4.1.5 below), we think that in practice many entities will consider the requirement immaterial to the extent that additional information is unchanged from that previously published. On that basis, when any of (a) to (c) above apply:

- an additional balance sheet as at the beginning of the earliest period presented would be needed only if it is different from how it was originally published; and

- if such an additional balance sheet is presented, judgment (including an assessment of materiality) will be required in determining which notes related to the additional balance sheet are required to be presented.

It is important to note that 'reclassifies' as that word is used by IAS 1 in this context (at (c) above) is not referring to a 'reclassification adjustment'. 'Reclassification adjustments' is a term defined by IAS 1 which describes the recognition of items in profit or loss which were previously recognised in other comprehensive income (often referred to as 'recycling'). IAS 1 applies this definition when setting out the required presentation and disclosure of such items (see 3.2.4 B below). 'Reclassifications' are discussed further below.

Comparative information is also required for narrative and descriptive information when it is relevant to an understanding of the current period's financial statements.[33] The standard illustrates the current year relevance of the previous year's narratives with a legal dispute, the outcome of which was uncertain at the previous period and is yet to be resolved (the disclosure of contingent liabilities is discussed in Chapter 24). It observes that users benefit from information that the uncertainty existed at the end of the previous period, and about the steps that have been taken during the period to resolve the uncertainty.[34]

Another example would be the required disclosure of material items, which would include items commonly called exceptional items, although that expression is not used by the standard (see 3.2.6 below). IAS 1 requires that the nature and amount of such items be disclosed separately.[35] Often a simple caption or line item heading will be sufficient to convey the 'nature' of material items. Sometimes, though a more extensive description in the notes may be needed to do this. In that case, the same information is likely to be relevant the following year.

As noted at 1.1.2 above, one of the objectives of IAS 1 is to ensure the comparability of financial statements with previous periods. The standard notes that enhancing the inter-period comparability of information assists users in making economic decisions, especially by allowing the assessment of trends in financial information for predictive purposes.[36] Requiring the presentation of comparatives allows such a comparison to be made within one set of financial statements. For a comparison to be meaningful, the amounts for prior periods need to be reclassified whenever the presentation or classification of items in the financial statements is amended. When this is the case, disclosure is required of the nature, amount and reasons for the reclassification.[37]

The standard acknowledges, though, that in some circumstances it is impracticable to reclassify comparative information for a particular prior period to achieve comparability with the current period. For these purposes, reclassification is impracticable when it cannot be done after making every reasonable effort to do so.[38] An example given by the standard is that data may not have been collected in the prior period(s) in a way that allows reclassification, and it may not be practicable to recreate the information.[39] When it proves impracticable to reclassify comparative data, IAS 1 requires disclosure of the reason for this and also the nature of the adjustments that would have been made if the amounts had been reclassified.[40]

As well as reclassification to reflect current period classifications as required by IAS 1, a change to comparatives as they were originally reported could be necessary:

(a)   following a change in accounting policy (discussed at 4.4 below);

(b)   to correct an error discovered in previous financial statements (discussed at 4.6 below); or

(c)   in relation to non-current assets held for sale, disposal groups and discontinued operations (discussed in Chapter 4).

2.5   Identification of the financial statements and accompanying information

2.5.1   *Identification of financial statements*

It is commonly the case that financial statements will form only part of a larger annual report, regulatory filing or other document. As IFRSs only apply to financial statements, it is important that the financial statements are clearly identified so that users of the report can distinguish information that is prepared using IFRSs from other information that may be useful but is not the subject of those requirements.[41]

When IAS 1 was revised in 2007, the way in which the above was expressed was subtly changed. The word 'necessarily' was introduced to the earlier version as follows. 'IFRSs apply only to financial statements, and not *necessarily* to other information ...' It is not entirely clear what the IASB was trying to achieve with this amendment. One possibility is that the IASB is referring to IFRS compliant data re-presented outside the actual financial statements.

As well as requiring that the financial statements be clearly distinguished, IAS 1 also requires that each financial statement and the notes be identified clearly. Furthermore, the following is required to be displayed prominently, and repeated when that is necessary for the information presented to be understandable:

(a)   the name of the reporting entity or other means of identification, and any change in that information from the end of the preceding period;

(b)   whether the financial statements are of an individual entity or a group of entities;

(c)   the date of the end of the reporting period or the period covered by the set of financial statements or the notes (presumably whichever is appropriate to that component of the financial statements);

(d)   the presentation currency, as defined in IAS 21 – *The Effects of Changes in Foreign Exchange Rates* (discussed in Chapter 13); and

(e)   the level of rounding used in presenting amounts in the financial statements.[42]

These requirements are met by the use of appropriate headings for pages, statements, notes, and columns etc. The standard notes that judgement is required in determining the best way of presenting such information. For example, when the financial statements are presented electronically, separate pages are not always used; the above items then need to be presented to ensure that the information included in the financial statements can be understood.[43] IAS 1 considers that financial statements are often made more understandable by presenting information in thousands or millions of units of the presentation currency. It considers this acceptable as long as the level of rounding in presentation is disclosed and material information is not omitted.[44]

2.5.2   Statement of compliance with IFRS

As well as identifying which particular part of any larger document constitutes the financial statements, IAS 1 also requires that financial statements complying with IFRSs make an explicit and unreserved statement of such compliance in the notes.[45] As this statement itself is required for full compliance, its absence would render the whole financial statements non-compliant, even if there was otherwise full compliance. In a curious twist, the standard goes on to say that 'an entity shall not describe financial statements as complying with IFRSs unless they comply with all the requirements of IFRSs.'[46] It is one thing for a standard setter to say what is necessary to comply with its rules. However, it is quite another thing to try and prescribe what an entity (which is, by definition, *not* complying with its rules) may or may not say.

3   THE STRUCTURE OF FINANCIAL STATEMENTS

As noted at 2.3 above, a complete set of financial statements under IAS 1 comprises the following, each of which should be presented with equal prominence:[47]

(a)   a balance sheet as at the end of the period (IAS 1 uses the phrase 'statement of financial position', but indicates that other titles may be used);

(b)   a statement of comprehensive income for the period to be presented either as:

  (i)   one single statement of comprehensive income; or

  (ii)   a separate income statement and statement of comprehensive income. In this case, the former must be presented immediately before the latter;[48]

(c)   a statement of changes in equity for the period;

(d)   a statement of cash flows for the period;

(e)   notes, comprising a summary of significant accounting policies and other explanatory information; and

(f)   a balance sheet as at the beginning of the earliest comparative period in certain circumstances.[49]

The standard adopts a generally permissive stance, by setting out minimum levels of required items to be shown in each statement (sometimes specifically on the face of the statement, and sometimes either on the face or in the notes) whilst allowing great flexibility of order and layout.[50] The standard notes that sometimes it uses the term 'disclosure' in a broad sense, encompassing items 'presented in the financial statements'. It observes that other IFRSs also require disclosures and that, unless specified to the contrary, they may be made 'in the financial statements'.[51] This begs the question: if not in 'the financial statements' then where else could they be made? We suspect this stems from, or is reflective of, an ambiguous use of similar words and phrases. In particular, 'financial statements' appears to be restricted to the 'primary' statements (balance sheet, income statement, statement of changes in equity and statement of cash flows) when describing what a 'complete set of financial statements' comprises (see 2.3 above). This is because a complete set also includes notes. For the purposes of specifying where a particular required disclosures should be made, we consider the term 'in the financial statements' is intended to mean *anywhere* within the 'complete set of financial statements' – in other words the primary statements or notes.

IAS 1 observes that cash flow information provides users of financial statements with a basis to assess the ability of the entity to generate cash and cash equivalents and the needs of the entity to utilise those cash flows. Requirements for the presentation of the statement of cash flows and related disclosures are set out IAS 7 – *Statement of Cash Flows*.[52] Statements of cash flows are discussed in Chapter 39; each of the other primary statements listed above is discussed in the following sections.

3.1   The balance sheet (or statement of financial position)

3.1.1   *The distinction between current/non-current assets and liabilities*

A   General

In most situations (but see the exception discussed below, and the treatment of non-current assets held for sale discussed in Chapter 4) IAS 1 requires balance sheets to distinguish current assets and liabilities from non-current ones.[53] The standard uses the term 'non-current' to include tangible, intangible and financial assets of a long-term nature. It does not prohibit the use of alternative descriptions as long as the meaning is clear.[54] A common alternative description seen in practice is the term fixed assets.

The standard explains the requirement to present current and non-current items separately by observing that when an entity supplies goods or services within a clearly identifiable operating cycle, separate classification of current and non-current assets and liabilities on the face of the balance sheet will provide useful information by distinguishing the net assets that are continuously circulating as working capital from those used in long-term operations. Furthermore, the analysis will also highlight assets that are expected to be realised within the current operating cycle, and liabilities that are due for settlement within the same period.[55] The distinction between current and non-current items therefore depends on the length of the entity's operating cycle. The standard states that the operating cycle of an entity is the time between the acquisition of assets for processing and their realisation in cash or cash equivalents. However, when the entity's normal operating cycle is not clearly identifiable, it is assumed to be twelve months.[56]

Once assets have been classified as non-current they should not normally be reclassified as current assets until they meet the criteria to be classified as held for sale in accordance with IFRS 5 (see Chapter 4). However, with effect for periods beginning on or after 1 January 2009, an entity which routinely sells items of property plant and equipment previously held for rental should transfer such items to inventory when they cease to be rented and become held for sale.[57] Assets of a class that an entity would normally regard as non-current that are acquired exclusively with a view to resale also should not be classified as current unless they meet those criteria.[58]

The basic requirement of the standard is that current and non-current assets, and current and non-current liabilities, should be presented as separate classifications on the face of the balance sheet.[59] The standard defines current assets and current liabilities (discussed at 3.1.3 and 3.1.4 below), with the non-current category being the residual.[60] Example 3.1 at 3.1.7 below provides an illustration of a balance sheet presenting this classification.

An exception to this requirement is when a presentation based on liquidity provides information that is reliable and is more relevant. When that exception applies, all assets and liabilities are required to be presented broadly in order of liquidity.[61] The reason for this exception given by the standard is that some entities (such as financial institutions) do not supply goods or services within a clearly identifiable operating cycle, and for these entities a presentation of assets and liabilities in increasing or decreasing order of liquidity provides information that is reliable and more relevant than a current/non-current presentation.[62]

The standard also makes clear that an entity is permitted to present some of its assets and liabilities using a current/non-current classification and others in order of liquidity when this provides information that is reliable and more relevant. It goes on to observe that the need for a mixed basis of presentation might arise when an entity has diverse operations.[63]

Whichever method of presentation is adopted, IAS 1 requires for each asset and liability line item that combines amounts expected to be recovered or settled:

(a)   no more than twelve months after the balance sheet date; and

(b)   more than twelve months after the balance sheet date;

disclosure of the amount expected to be recovered or settled after more than twelve months.[64]

The standard explains this requirement by noting that information about expected dates of realisation of assets and liabilities is useful in assessing the liquidity and solvency of an entity. In this vein, IAS 1 contains a reminder that IFRS 7 requires disclosure of the maturity dates of financial assets (including trade and other receivables) and financial liabilities (including trade and other payables) – see Chapter 34 (formerly these were requirements of IAS 32). This assertion in IAS 1 is not strictly correct, as IFRS 7 in fact only requires a maturity *analysis* (rather than maturity dates) and only requires this for financial liabilities. IFRS 7 is discussed in Chapter 34. Similarly, IAS 1 views information on the expected date of recovery and settlement of non-monetary assets and liabilities such as inventories and provisions as also useful, whether assets and liabilities are classified as current or as non-current. An example of this given by the standard is that an entity should disclose the amount of inventories that are expected to be recovered more than twelve months after the balance sheet date.[65]

B   Classification of derivatives to which hedge accounting is not applied

The classification of assets and liabilities as current is discussed at 3.1.3 and 3.1.4 below.

IAS 1 was amended in May 2008 by the IASB's annual improvements project, with effect from periods beginning on or after 1 January 2009. Prior to this there was a degree of confusion regarding the classification of derivatives to which hedge accounting was not applied.

The unamended IAS 1 required that derivative assets and liabilities be classified as current if they were 'held primarily for the purpose of being traded'. For current assets, this was reiterated in the non-bold explanatory text. However, for current liabilities the non-bold explanatory text included 'Examples [of items held primarily for trading] include financial liabilities classified as held for trading in accordance with IAS 39 …' As discussed in Chapter 29, derivatives are classified as held for trading if they fail to qualify for hedge accounting. This could be for a number of reasons, for example:

(a)   the entity is genuinely actively trading in derivatives;

(b)   the entity has achieved an effective economic hedge but chooses not to apply hedge accounting, perhaps on the grounds that the requirements for designation, documentation and effectiveness testing are considered overly onerous;

(c)   whilst the entity expects some degree of economic hedge, the derivative is not expected to be 'highly effective' in accordance with IAS 39 – *Financial Instruments: Recognition and Measurement*; or

(d)   the derivative is embedded in another instrument and, whilst not qualifying for hedge accounting, was taken out for commercial reasons unrelated to speculative trading.

Based on the natural meaning of the words 'held primarily for trading' (b), (c) and (d) could be viewed as not being so held, as that was not the entity's motive for entering into them. However, they certainly are *classified* as such in accordance with IAS 39. The ambiguity in the standard inevitably resulted in a variety of practice. Many entities opted to present as current all derivatives which are not accounted for as hedges. Others took the view that derivatives which do not qualify for hedge accounting need not necessarily be regarded as held primarily for trading.

The IASB resolved this conflict by making it clear that being classified as held for trading under IAS 39 does not, of itself, mean the derivative is current for IAS 1 purposes. The discussions at 3.1.3 and 3.1.4 below reflect the revised standard.

An example of a company classifying some such items as non-current and others as current is shown in the extract below.

Extract 3.1: Suez Group (2005)

Note 1 Summary of significant accounting policies [extract]

M. Derivatives and hedge accounting [extract]

4. Derivative instruments not qualifying for hedge accounting: recognition and presentation [extract]

These items mainly concern derivative financial instruments used in economic hedges that have not been – or are no longer – documented, as well as derivatives entered into by the Group in connection with proprietary energy trading activities and energy trading on behalf of its customers.

When a derivative financial instrument does not qualify or no longer qualifies for hedge accounting, changes in fair value are recognized directly in income, under "Changes in fair value of commodity derivative instruments," in operating income for derivative instruments with nonfinancial assets as the underlying, and in financial income or expense for currency, interest rate and equity derivatives.

Derivative instruments used by the Group in connection with proprietary energy trading activities and energy trading on behalf of customers and other derivatives expiring in less than 12 months are recognized in the consolidated balance sheet in current assets and liabilities. All other derivative financial instruments are recognized in non-current assets and liabilities.

C   Settlement of a liability by issuing of equity

As discussed at 3.1.4 below, a liability will fall to be classified as current if an entity does not have an unconditional right to defer settlement for at least twelve months after the balance sheet date. For periods beginning before 1 January 2010, IAS 1 does not elaborate further the meaning of 'settlement' and in particular does not restrict the word to mean only those forms of settlement which involve a net outflow of resources. Furthermore, the Framework indicates that the conversion of a liability into equity is a form of settlement.[66] One consequence of this is that if the conversion option in convertible debt is exercisable by the holder at any time then the liability component would fall to be classified as current even if the maturity for cash settlement is greater than one year. The accounting treatment for convertible debt is discussed in Chapter 31.

The IASB considered this issue and in particular considered the relevance of equity settlement to the notion in the Framework that information about liquidity and solvency is useful to users of financial statements. The Board concluded that classifying liabilities based on the requirements to transfer cash or other assets better reflects the liquidity and solvency position of an entity. Accordingly, the IASB set out to amend IAS 1 as part of the 2007 annual improvements process. The proposed amendment was to clarify that an entity needs an unconditional right to defer settlement *by the transfer of cash or other assets* for more than a year in order to classify a liability as non-current.[67] The proposed revision was, however, not proceeded with until the 2008 improvement project which was published in April 2009. For periods beginning on or after 1 January 2010 the provision discussed above is supplemented with the following. 'Terms of a liability that could, at the option of the counterparty, result in its settlement by the issue of equity instruments do not affect its classification'.[68] Early application is allowed if disclosed.[69]

3.1.2   Non-current assets and disposal groups held for sale

The general requirement to classify balance sheet items as current or non-current (or present them broadly in order of liquidity) is overlaid with further requirements by IFRS 5 regarding non-current assets held for sale and disposal groups (discussed in Chapter 4). IFRS 5's aim is that entities should present and disclose information that enables users of the financial statements to evaluate the financial effects of disposals of non-current assets (or disposal groups).[70] In pursuit of this aim, IFRS 5 requires:

- non-current assets classified as held for sale and the assets of a disposal group classified as held for sale to be presented separately from other assets in the balance sheet; and

- the liabilities of a disposal group classified as held for sale to be presented separately from other liabilities in the balance sheet.

These assets and liabilities should not be offset and presented as a single amount. In addition:

(a)   major classes of assets and liabilities classified as held for sale should generally be separately disclosed either on the face of the balance sheet or in the notes (see 3.1.6 below). However, this is not necessary for a disposal group if it is a subsidiary that met the criteria to be classified as held for sale on acquisition; and

(b)   any cumulative income or expense recognised in other comprehensive income relating to a non-current asset (or disposal group) classified as held for sale should be presented separately.[71]

3.1.3   Current assets

IAS 1 was amended in May 2008 by the IASB's annual improvements project, with effect from periods beginning on or after 1 January 2009. The amendment relates to a potential conflict regarding derivatives *classified* as held for trading under IAS 39. The issue is discussed at 3.1.1 B above. The discussion below reflects the amended IAS 1.

IAS 1 requires an asset to be classified as current when it satisfies any of the following criteria, with all other assets classified as non-current. The criteria are:

(a)   it is expected to be realised in, or is intended for sale or consumption in, the entity's normal operating cycle (discussed at 3.1.1 above);

(b)   it is held primarily for the purpose of trading;

(c)   it is expected to be realised within twelve months after the end of the reporting period; or

(d)   it is cash or a cash equivalent (as defined in IAS 7, discussed in Chapter 39) unless it is restricted from being exchanged or used to settle a liability for at least twelve months after the end of the reporting period.[72]

As an exception to this, deferred tax assets are never allowed to be classified as current.[73]

Current assets include assets (such as inventories and trade receivables) that are sold, consumed or realised as part of the normal operating cycle even when they are not expected to be realised within twelve months after the balance sheet date. Current assets also include assets held primarily for the purpose of being traded (for example, some financial assets classified as held for trading in accordance with IAS 39 discussed in Chapter 29 at 7.1.1) and the current portion of non-current financial assets.[74]

3.1.4   Current liabilities

IAS 1 was amended in May 2008 by the IASB's annual improvements project, with effect from periods beginning on or after 1 January 2009. The amendment relates to a potential conflict regarding derivatives *classified* as held for trading under IAS 39. The issue is discussed at 3.1.1 B above. The discussion below reflects the amended IAS 1.

IAS 1 requires a liability to be classified as current when it satisfies any of the following criteria, with all other liabilities classified as non-current. The criteria are:

(a)   it is expected to be settled in the entity's normal operating cycle (discussed at 3.1.1 above);

(b)   it is held primarily for the purpose of trading;

(c)   it is due to be settled within twelve months after the end of the reporting period; or

(d)   the entity does not have an unconditional right to defer settlement of the liability for at least twelve months after the end of the reporting period.[75]

As an exception to this, deferred tax liabilities are never allowed to be classified as current.[76]

For periods beginning on or after 1 January 2010 (d) above has been modified in relation to liabilities which the counter party could require to be settled in equity. This is discussed at 3.1.1C above.

The standard notes that some current liabilities, such as trade payables and some accruals for employee and other operating costs, are part of the working capital used in the entity's normal operating cycle. Such operating items are classified as current liabilities even if they are due to be settled more than twelve months after the end of the reporting period.[77]

However, neither IAS 19 nor IAS 1 specifies where in the balance sheet an asset or liability in respect of a defined benefit plan should be presented, nor whether such balances should be shown separately on the face of the balance sheet or only in the notes – this is left to the judgement of the reporting entity (see 3.1.5 below). When the format of balance sheet distinguishes current assets and liabilities from non-current ones, the question arises as to whether this split needs also to be made for defined benefit plan balances. IAS 19 does not specify whether such a split should be made, on the grounds that it may sometimes be arbitrary.[78]

Some current liabilities are not settled as part of the normal operating cycle, but are due for settlement within twelve months after the end of the reporting period or held primarily for the purpose of being traded. Examples given by the standard are some (but not necessarily all) financial liabilities classified as held for trading in accordance with IAS 39, bank overdrafts, and the current portion of non-current financial liabilities, dividends payable, income taxes and other non-trade payables. Financial liabilities that provide financing on a long-term basis (i.e. are not part of the working capital used in the entity's normal operating cycle) and are not due for settlement within twelve months after the end of the reporting period are non-current liabilities.[79]

The assessment of a liability as current or non-current is applied very strictly in IAS 1. In particular, a liability should be classified as current:

(a)   when it is due to be settled within twelve months after the end of the reporting period, even if:

    (i)   the original term was for a period longer than twelve months; and

    (ii)   an agreement to refinance, or to reschedule payments, on a long-term basis is completed after the period end and before the financial statements are authorised for issue (although disclosure of the post period end refinancing would be required);[80] or

(b)   when an entity breaches a provision of a long-term loan arrangement on or before the period end with the effect that the liability becomes payable on demand. This is the case even if the lender agreed, after the period end and before the authorisation of the financial statements for issue, not to demand payment as a consequence of the breach (although the post period end agreement would be disclosed). The meaning of the term 'authorised for issue' is discussed in Chapter 37 at 2.1. The standard explains that the liability should be classified as current because, at the period end, the entity does not have an unconditional right to defer its settlement for at least twelve months after that date.[81] However, the liability would be classified as non-current if the lender agreed by the period end to provide a period of grace ending at least twelve months after the balance sheet date, within which the entity can rectify the breach and during which the lender cannot demand immediate repayment.[82]

The key point here is that for a liability to be classified as non-current requires that the entity has *at the end of the reporting period* an unconditional right to defer its settlement for at least twelve months thereafter. Accordingly, the standard explains that liabilities would be non-current if an entity expects, and has the discretion, to refinance or roll over an obligation for at least twelve months after the period end under an existing loan facility, even if it would otherwise be due within a shorter period. However, when refinancing or rolling over the obligation is not at the discretion of the entity the obligation is classified as current.[83]

3.1.5   Information required on the face of the balance sheet

IAS 1 does not contain a prescriptive format or order for the balance sheet.[84] Rather, it contains two mechanisms which require certain information to be shown on the face of the balance sheet. First, it contains a list of specific items for which this is required, on the basis that they are sufficiently different in nature or function to warrant separate presentation.[85] Second, it stipulates that additional line items, headings and subtotals should be presented on the face of the balance sheet when such presentation is relevant to an understanding of the entity's financial position.[86] Clearly this is a highly judgemental decision for entities to make when preparing a balance sheet, and allows a wide variety of possible presentations. The judgement as to whether additional items should be presented separately is based on an assessment of:

(a)   the nature and liquidity of assets;

(b)   the function of assets within the entity; and

(c)   the amounts, nature and timing of liabilities.[87]

IAS 1 indicates that the use of different measurement bases for different classes of assets suggests that their nature or function differs and, therefore, that they should be presented as separate line items. For example, different classes of property, plant and equipment can be carried at cost or revalued amounts in accordance with IAS 16 – *Property, Plant and Equipment*.[88]

As a minimum, the face of the balance sheet should include line items that present the following amounts:[89]

(a)   property, plant and equipment;

(b)   investment property;

(c)   intangible assets;

(d)   financial assets (excluding amounts shown under (e), (h) and (i));

(e)   investments accounted for using the equity method;

(f)   biological assets;

(g)   inventories;

(h)   trade and other receivables;

(i)   cash and cash equivalents;

(j)   the total of assets classified as held for sale and assets included in disposal groups classified as held for sale in accordance with IFRS 5;

(k)   trade and other payables;

(l)   provisions;

(m)   financial liabilities (excluding amounts shown under (k) and (l));

(n)   liabilities and assets for current tax, as defined in IAS 12;

(o)   deferred tax liabilities and deferred tax assets, as defined in IAS 12;

(p)   liabilities included in disposal groups classified as held for sale in accordance with IFRS 5;

(q)   non-controlling interests, presented within equity; and

(r)   issued capital and reserves attributable to owners of the parent.

The standard notes that items above represent a list of items that are sufficiently different in nature or function to warrant separate presentation on the face of the balance sheet. In addition:

(a)   line items should be included when the size, nature or function of an item or aggregation of similar items is such that separate presentation is relevant to an understanding of the entity's financial position; and

(b)   the descriptions used and the ordering of items or aggregation of similar items may be amended according to the nature of the entity and its transactions, to provide information that is relevant to an understanding of the entity's financial position. For example, a financial institution may amend the above descriptions to provide information that is relevant to the operations of a financial institution.[90]

3.1.6   *Information required either on the face of the balance sheet or in the notes*

IAS 1 requires further sub-classifications of the line items shown on the face of the balance sheet to be presented either on the face of the balance sheet or in the notes. The requirements for these further sub-classifications are approached by the standard in a similar manner to those for line items on the face of the balance sheet. There is a prescriptive list of items required (see below) and also a more general requirement that the sub-classifications should be made in a manner appropriate to the entity's operations.[91] The standard notes that the detail provided in sub-classifications depends on the requirements of IFRSs (as numerous disclosures are required by other standards) and on the size, nature and function of the amounts involved.[92]

Aside of the specific requirements, deciding what level of detailed disclosure is necessary is clearly a judgemental exercise. As is the case for items on the face of the balance sheet, IAS 1 requires that the judgement as to whether additional items should be presented separately should be based on an assessment of:

(a)   the nature and liquidity of assets;

(b)   the function of assets within the entity; and

(c)   the amounts, nature and timing of liabilities.[93]

The disclosures will also vary for each item, examples given by the standard are:

(a)   items of property, plant and equipment are disaggregated into classes in accordance with IAS 16;

(b)   receivables are disaggregated into amounts receivable from trade customers, receivables from related parties, prepayments and other amounts;

(c)   inventories are disaggregated, in accordance with IAS 2 – *Inventories*, into classifications such as merchandise, production supplies, materials, work in progress and finished goods;

(d)   provisions are disaggregated into provisions for employee benefits and other items; and

(e)   equity capital and reserves are disaggregated into various classes, such as paid-in capital, share premium and reserves.[94]

IAS 1 specifically requires the following information regarding equity and share capital to be shown either on the face of the balance sheet or in the notes:

(a)   for each class of share capital:

   (i)   the number of shares authorised;

   (ii)   the number of shares issued and fully paid, and issued but not fully paid;

   (iii) par value per share, or that the shares have no par value;

   (iv)   a reconciliation of the number of shares outstanding at the beginning and at the end of the period;

   (v)   the rights, preferences and restrictions attaching to that class including restrictions on the distribution of dividends and the repayment of capital;

   (vi)   shares in the entity held by the entity or by its subsidiaries or associates; and

   (vii) shares reserved for issue under options and contracts for the sale of shares, including the terms and amounts; and

(b)   a description of the nature and purpose of each reserve within equity.[95]

An entity without share capital (such as a partnership or trust) should disclose information equivalent to that required by (a) above, showing changes during the period in each category of equity interest, and the rights, preferences and restrictions attaching to each category of equity interest.[96]

With effect for periods beginning on or after 1 January 2009, IAS 32 allows two specific classes of liabilities to be reported as equity. These are:

*   puttable financial instruments; and

*   instruments that impose on the entity an obligation to deliver to another party a pro rata share of the net assets of the entity only on liquidation.

Both terms are defined and discussed at length in IAS 32 (see Chapter 31 at 3.2.2).

If an entity reclassifies one of these items between financial liabilities and equity, IAS 1 requires disclosure of:

*   the amount reclassified into and out of each category (financial liabilities or equity); and

*   the timing and reason for that reclassification.[97]

3.1.7   *Illustrative balance sheets*

The implementation guidance accompanying IAS 1 provides an illustration of a balance sheet presented to distinguish current and non-current items. It makes clear that other formats may be equally appropriate, as long as the distinction is clear.[98] As discussed in Chapter 4, IFRS 5 provides further guidance relating to the presentation of non-current assets and disposal groups held for sale.

Example 3.1:   Illustrative balance sheet[99]

XYZ GROUP – BALANCE SHEET AS AT 31 DECEMBER 2010

(in thousands of Euros)

	2010	2009
ASSETS		
Non-current assets		
Property, plant and equipment	350,700	360,020
Goodwill	80,800	91,200
Other intangible assets	227,470	227,470
Investments in associates	100,150	110,770
Available-for-sale investments	142,500	156,000
	901,620	945,460
Current assets		
Inventories	135,230	132,500
Trade receivables	91,600	110,800
Other current assets	25,650	12,540
Cash and cash equivalents	312,400	322,900
	564,880	578,740
Total assets	1,466,500	1,524,200
EQUITY AND LIABILITIES		
Equity attributable to owners of the parent		
Share capital	650,000	600,000
Retained earnings	243,500	161,700
Other components of equity	10,200	21,200
	903,700	782,900
Non-controlling interests	70,050	48,600
Total equity	973,750	831,500
Non-current liabilities		
Long-term borrowings	120,000	160,000
Deferred tax	28,800	26,040
Long-term provisions	28,850	52,240
Total non-current liabilities	177,650	238,280
Current liabilities		
Trade and other payables	115,100	187,620
Short-term borrowings	150,000	200,000
Current portion of long-term borrowings	10,000	20,000
Current tax payable	35,000	42,000
Short-term provisions	5,000	4,800
Total current liabilities	315,100	454,420
Total liabilities	492,750	692,700
Total equity and liabilities	1,466,500	1,524,200

3.2   The statement of comprehensive income and the income statement

As noted at 1.1.1 above, IAS 1 was substantially amended in September 2007, with effect for periods beginning on or after 1 January 2009. Perhaps the most significant change relates to performance reporting, with the familiar income statement and statement of changes in equity (or statement of recognised income and expense) replaced with a statement of comprehensive income. This section deals with the latest version of the standard. Differences between these requirements and those of the previous version of the standard are discussed in the previous edition of this book, *International GAAP 2009*.

3.2.1   *Profit and loss, and comprehensive income*

The IASB regards all changes in net assets (other than the introduction and return of capital) and not just more traditional realised profits, as 'performance' in its widest sense. Accordingly, IAS 1 requires a performance statement showing such changes and calls it a statement of comprehensive income.

Total comprehensive income is defined by IAS 1 as the change in equity during a period resulting from transactions and other events, other than those changes resulting from transactions with owners in their capacity as owners. It comprises all components of 'profit or loss' and of 'other comprehensive income'. These two terms are defined as follows:

*   profit or loss is the total of income less expenses, excluding the components of other comprehensive income; and

*   other comprehensive income comprises items of income and expense (including reclassification adjustments) that are not recognised in profit or loss as required or permitted by other IFRSs.[100]

IAS 1 does not define 'income' or 'expenses', which leaves these two definitions somewhat incomplete. However, in our view it is clear that 'income and expense' means the same as 'total comprehensive income' in this context. This is also clear from the discussion of income and expense in the Framework, discussed in Chapter 2 at 3.2.3. The use of a variety of terminology is recognised by IAS 1 which notes the following. 'Although this Standard uses the terms "other comprehensive income", "profit or loss" and "total comprehensive income", an entity may use other terms to describe the totals as long as the meaning is clear. For example, an entity may use the term "net income" to describe profit or loss.'[101]

What this means is that profit and loss is the default category – all comprehensive income is part of profit and loss unless IFRSs say it is or may be 'other' comprehensive income.[102]

IAS 1 sets out the following items which are included in other comprehensive income:

(a)   changes in revaluation surplus relating to property, plant and equipment and intangible assets (discussed in Chapters 16 and 15 respectively);

(b)   actuarial gains and losses on defined benefit plans when these are recognised outside of profit and loss as permitted by IAS 19 (discussed in Chapter 28);

(c)   gains and losses arising from translating the financial statements of a foreign operation (discussed in Chapter 13);

(d)   gains and losses on remeasuring available-for-sale financial assets (discussed in Chapter 32); and

(e)   the effective portion of gains and losses on hedging instruments in a cash flow hedge (discussed in Chapter 33).[103]

IAS requires that all items of income and expense be presented either:

(a)   in a single statement of comprehensive income; or

(b)   in two separate statements:

    (i)   an income statement (containing components of profit and loss); and

    (ii)   a statement of comprehensive income beginning with profit and loss and containing components of other comprehensive income.[104]

If the approach in (b) is followed, the income statement must be displayed immediately before the statement of comprehensive income.[105]

In addition to this fundamental choice, IAS 1 provides that different titles may be used for these statements.[106] This means that, should they wish, entities could continue to use familiar titles like income statement and statement of recognised income and expense.

We think it likely that many entities will continue to present a separate income statement, and this section is structured in these terms. However, the requirements are the same whether total comprehensive income is presented in one or two statements.

IAS 1 adopts an essentially permissive approach to the format of the income statement and statement of comprehensive income. It observes that, because the effects of an entity's various activities, transactions and other events differ in frequency, potential for gain or loss and predictability, disclosing the components of financial performance assists users in understanding the financial performance achieved and in making projections of future performance.[107] In other words, some analysis of the make-up of net profit and other comprehensive income is needed, but a wide variety of presentations would all be acceptable. The general rule is that income and expense items are not offset unless certain criteria are met; this is discussed at 4.1.5 B below.

Whether one or two statements are presented, IAS 1 requires certain specific items to appear on the face of the statement(s) and then supplements this with a more general requirement that:

- additional line items be presented on the face of the statement(s); and
- the descriptions used and the ordering of items be amended;

when this is relevant to an understanding of the entity's financial performance.[108] The standard explains that additional line items should be included, and the descriptions used and the ordering of items amended when this is necessary to explain the elements of financial performance. Factors to be considered would include materiality and the nature and function of the items of income and expense. An example of this is that a financial institution may amend the descriptions to provide information that is relevant to the operations of a financial institution.[109]

3.2.2 Information required on the face of the income statement

As is the case for the balance sheet, IAS 1 sets out certain items which must appear on the face of the income statement and other required disclosures which may be made either on the face or in the notes.

As a minimum, the face of the income statement should include line items that present the following amounts (although as noted above, the order and description of the items should be amended as necessary):

(a)   revenue;

(b)   finance costs;

(c)   share of the profit or loss of associates and joint ventures accounted for using the equity method;

(d)   tax expense;

(e)   a single amount comprising the total of:

    (i)   the post-tax profit or loss of discontinued operations; and

    (ii)   the post-tax gain or loss recognised on the measurement to fair value less costs to sell or on the disposal of the assets or disposal group(s) constituting the discontinued operation;

(f)   profit or loss;[110] and

(g)   the following as allocations of profit or loss for the period:

    (i)   profit or loss attributable to non-controlling interests; and

    (ii)   profit or loss attributable to owners of the parent.[111]

As discussed at 3.2.3 below, an analysis of expenses is required based either on their nature or their function. IAS 1 encourages, but does not require this to be shown on the face of the income statement.[112]

The current IAS 1 has omitted the requirement in the 1997 version to disclose the results of operating activities as a line item on the face of the income statement. The reason given for this in the Basis for Conclusions to the standard is that 'Operating activities' are not defined in the standard, and the Board decided not to require disclosure of an undefined item.[113]

The Basis for Conclusions to IAS 1 goes on to state that 'The Board recognises that an entity may elect to disclose the results of operating activities, or a similar line item, even though this term is not defined. In such cases, the Board notes that the entity should ensure the amount disclosed is representative of activities that would normally be considered to be "operating".

'In the Board's view, it would be misleading and would impair the comparability of financial statements if items of an operating nature were excluded from the results of operating activities, even if that had been industry practice. For example, it would be inappropriate to exclude items clearly related to operations (such as inventory write-downs and restructuring and relocation expenses) because they occur irregularly or infrequently or are unusual in amount. Similarly, it would be inappropriate to exclude items on the grounds that they do not involve cash flows, such as depreciation and amortisation expenses.'[114]

The implementation guidance accompanying the standard provides an illustrative example of an income statement (see Example 3.3 at 3.2.3 B below).

3.2.3   *Classification of expenses recognised in profit or loss by nature or function*

IAS 1 states that components of financial performance may differ in terms of frequency, potential for gain or loss and predictability, and requires that expenses should be sub-classified to highlight this.[115] To achieve this, the standard requires the presentation of an analysis of expenses (but only those recognised in profit or loss) using a classification based on either their nature or their function within the entity, whichever provides information that is reliable and more relevant.[116] It is because each method of presentation has merit for different types of entities, that the standard requires management to make this selection.[117] As noted at 3.2.2 above IAS 1 encourages, but does not require the chosen analysis to be shown on the face of the income statement.[118] This means that entities are permitted to disclose the classification on the face on a mixed basis, as long as the required classification is provided in the notes. Indeed, the IASB itself produces an example of such an income statement in an appendix to IAS 7.[119]

The standard also notes that the choice between the function of expense method and the nature of expense method will depend on historical and industry factors and the nature of the entity. Both methods provide an indication of those costs that might vary, directly or indirectly, with the level of sales or production of the entity. However, because information on the nature of expenses is useful in predicting future cash flows, additional disclosure is required when the function of expense classification is used (see B below).[120]

A   *Analysis of expenses by nature*

For some entities, 'more reliable and relevant information' may be achieved by aggregating expenses for display in profit or loss according to their nature (for example, depreciation, purchases of materials, transport costs, employee benefits and advertising costs), and not reallocating them among various functions within the entity. IAS 1 observes that this method may be simple to apply because no allocations of expenses to functional classifications are necessary. The standard illustrates a classification using the nature of expense method is as follows:

Example 3.2:   Example of classification of expenses by nature[121]

Revenue		×
Other income		×
Changes in inventories of finished goods and work in progress	×	
Raw materials and consumables used	×	
Employee benefits expense	×	
Depreciation and amortisation expense	×	
Other expenses	×	
Total expenses		(×)
Profit before tax		×

The implementation guidance accompanying the standard provides a further example of an income statement analysing expenses by nature. Whilst very similar to the above, it is expanded to show further captions as follows:[122]

Example 3.3:   Illustrative income statement

XYZ GROUP – INCOME STATEMENT FOR THE YEAR ENDED 31 DECEMBER 2010

(in thousands of Euro)

	2010	2009
Revenue	390,000	355,000
Other income	20,667	11,300
Changes in inventories of finished goods and work in progress	(115,100)	(107,900)
Work performed by the entity and capitalised	16,000	15,000
Raw material and consumables used	(96,000)	(92,000)
Employee benefits expense	(45,000)	(43,000)
Depreciation and amortisation expense	(19,000)	(17,000)
Impairment of property, plant and equipment	(4,000)	–
Other expenses	(6,000)	(5,500)
Finance costs	(15,000)	(18,000)
Share of profit of associates	35,100	30,100
Profit before tax	161,667	128,000
Income tax expense	(40,417)	(32,000)
Profit for the year from continuing operations	121,250	96,000
Loss for the year from discontinued operations	–	(30,500)
Profit for the year	121,250	65,500
Profit attributable to:		
Owners of the parent	97,000	52,400
Non controlling interests	24,250	13,100
	121,250	65,500
Earnings per share (€)		
Basic and diluted	0.46	0.30

A footnote to the illustrative examples explains that 'share of profits of associates' means share of the profit attributable to the owners of the associates and hence is after tax and non-controlling interests.

B   Analysis of expenses by function

For some entities, 'reliable and more relevant information' may be achieved by aggregating expenses for display purposes according to their function for example, as part of cost of sales, the costs of distribution or administrative activities. Under this method, IAS 1 requires as a minimum, disclosure of cost of sales separately from other expenses (although it does not specify whether this should be on the face of the statement or in the notes). The standard observes that this method can provide more relevant information to users than the classification of expenses by nature, but that allocating costs to functions may require arbitrary allocations and involve considerable judgement. An example of classification using the function of expense method given by the standard set out below. A second example is given as the 'income statement' section of a combined statement of comprehensive income, see Example 3.5 below.

Example 3.4:   Example of classification by function[123]

Revenue	×
Cost of sales	(×)
Gross profit	×
Other income	×
Distribution costs	(×)
Administrative expenses	(×)
Other expenses	(×)
Profit before tax	×

The guidance notes that the line item relating to associates means the share of associates' profit attributable to owners of the associates, i.e. it is after tax and non-controlling interests in the associates.

Entities classifying expenses by function are required by IAS 1 to disclose additional information on the nature of expenses, and this must include depreciation and amortisation expense and employee benefits expense.[124] This requirement of IAS 1 strikes us as unnecessary as the disclosure of these items (broken down into their components) is specifically required by IAS 16, IAS 19 and IAS 38 – *Intangible Assets*.

3.2.4   The statement of comprehensive income

A   The face of the statement of comprehensive income

Whether presented as a separate statement or as section of a combined statement (see 3.2.1 above), the face of the statement of comprehensive income should set out the following:[125]

(a)   profit or loss (if two statements are presented this will be a single line item. If one combined statement is presented this will be the final line item of the 'income statement' section of it);

(b)   each component of comprehensive income, classified by nature, which include:

(i)   changes in revaluation surplus relating to property, plant and equipment and intangible assets (discussed in Chapters16 and 15 respectively);

(ii)   actuarial gains and losses on defined benefit plans when these are recognised outside of profit and loss as permitted by IAS 19 (discussed in Chapter 28);

(iii)   gains and losses arising from translating the financial statements of a foreign operation (discussed in Chapter 13);

(iv)   gains and losses on remeasuring available-for-sale financial assets (discussed in Chapter 32);

(v)   the effective portion of gains and losses on hedging instruments in a cash flow hedge (discussed in Chapter 33);[126] and

(vi)   the aggregate amount of tax relating to components of comprehensive income, unless the components are shown individually net of tax (see 3.2.4 below);[127]

(c)   share of other comprehensive income of associates and joint ventures accounted for using the equity method;

(d)   reclassification adjustments, unless the components of comprehensive income are shown after any related reclassification adjustments (see B below);[128] and

(e)   total comprehensive income.

In a separate statement of other comprehensive income IAS 1 also requires an analysis of total comprehensive income for the period between that attributable to:

(a)   non-controlling interests, and

(b)   owners of the parent.[129]

In a combined statement of total comprehensive income, the equivalent analysis of profit and loss would also be required as would earnings per share disclosures (discussed in Chapter 36). When two separate statements are presented, these would appear on the income statement.[130]

IAS 1 provides an illustration of both the 'one statement' and 'two statement' approach in its implementation guidance. The illustration of a single statement of comprehensive income is reproduced in Example 3.5 below. The illustration of a separate income statement is reproduced in Example 3.4 above and the illustrative separate statement of other comprehensive income is reproduced in Example 3.7 below.

Example 3.5:   *Presentation of comprehensive income in one statement and the classification of expenses by nature*[131]

XYZ GROUP –STATEMENT OF COMPREHENSIVE INCOME FOR THE YEAR ENDED 31 DECEMBER 2010

(in thousands of Euro)

	2010	2009
Revenue	390,000	355,000
Other income	20,667	11,300
Changes in inventories of finished goods and work in progress	(115,100)	(107,900)
Work performed by the entity and capitalised	16,000	15,000
Raw material and consumables used	(96,000)	(92,000)
Employee benefits expense	(45,000)	(43,000)
Depreciation and amortisation expense	(19,000)	(17,000)
Impairment of property, plant and equipment	(4,000)	–
Other expenses	(6,000)	(5,500)
Finance costs	(15,000)	(18,000)
Share of profit of associates	35,100	30,100
Profit before tax	161,667	128,000
Income tax expense	(40,417)	(32,000)
Profit for the year from continuing operations	121,250	96,000
Loss for the year from discontinued operations	–	(30,500)
Profit for the year	121,250	65,500
Other comprehensive income:		
Exchange differences on translating foreign operations	5,334	10,667
Available-for-sale financial assets	(24,000)	26,667
Cash flow hedges	(667)	(4,000)
Gains on property revaluation	933	3,367
Actuarial gains (losses) on defined benefit pension plans	(667)	1,333
Share of other comprehensive income of associates	400	(700)
Income tax relating to components of other comprehensive income	4,667	(9,334)
Other comprehensive income for the year, net of tax	(14,000)	28,000
Total comprehensive income for the year	107,250	93,500
Profit attributable to:		
Owners of the parent	97,000	52,400
Non-controlling interests	24,250	13,100
	121,250	65,500
Total comprehensive income attributable to:		
Owners of the parent	85,800	74,800
Non-controlling interests	21,450	18,700
	107,250	93,500
Earnings per share (€)		
Basic and diluted	0.46	0.30

The illustrative examples in the standard all use the option, which is discussed at B below, to present components of other comprehensive income net of related reclassifications. The disclosure of those reclassifications in a note is reproduced in Example 3.6 below. This note also demonstrates a 'reclassification' not to profit and loss but to the balance sheet (as a result of cash flow hedging, see Chapter 33). Whilst not addressed explicitly by the standard, evidently these items (like reclassifications to profit or loss) need not be shown on the face of the statement.

B   *Reclassification adjustments*

'Reclassification adjustments' are items recognised in profit or loss which were previously recognised in other comprehensive income (commonly referred to as 'recycling') and IAS 1 requires their disclosure.[132] Examples include adjustments arising in relation to:

- the disposal of a foreign operation;

- the derecognition of available-for-sale financial assets; and

- hedged forecast transactions affecting profit or loss.

The standard allows a choice of how reclassification adjustments are presented. They may either be presented 'gross' on the face of the statement, or alternatively shown in the notes. In the latter case, components of comprehensive income on the face of the statement are shown net of any related reclassification adjustments.[133]

IAS 1 illustrates this requirement as follows:

Example 3.6:   Note disclosure of components of other comprehensive income[134]

XYZ Group
Disclosure of components of other comprehensive income (a)
Notes
Year ended 31 December 2010
(in thousands of currency units)

	2010		2009	
Other comprehensive income				
Exchange differences on translating foreign operations(b)		5,334		10,667
Available-for-sale financial assets:				
Gains arising during the year	1,333		30,667	
Less: reclassification adjustments for gains included in profit or loss	(25,333)	(24,000)	(4,000)	26,667
Cash flow hedges:				
Gains (losses) arising during the year	(4,667)		(4,000)	
Less: reclassification adjustments for gains (losses) included in profit or loss	3,333			
Less: adjustments for amounts transferred to initial carrying of hedged items	667	(667)	–	(4,000)

	2010	2009
Gains on property revaluation	933	3,367
Actuarial gains (losses) on defined benefit pension plans	(667)	1,333
Share of other comprehensive income of associates	400	(700)
Other comprehensive income	(18,667)	37,334
Income tax relating to components of other comprehensive income(c)	4,667	(9,334)
Other comprehensive income for the year	(14,000)	28,000

(a)   When an entity chooses an aggregated presentation in the statement of comprehensive income, the amounts for reclassification adjustments and current year gain or loss are presented in the notes.

(b)   There was no disposal of a foreign operation. Therefore, there is no reclassification adjustment for the years presented.

(c)   The income tax relating to each component of other comprehensive income is disclosed in the notes.

Some IFRSs require that gains and losses recognised in other comprehensive income should not be 'recycled' to profit and loss, and hence will not give rise to reclassification adjustments. IAS 1 gives the following examples:

(a)   revaluation surpluses for revalued property, plant and equipment, and intangible assets; and

(b)   actuarial gains and losses on defined benefit plans.

The standard observes that whilst items in (a) are not reclassified to profit or loss they may be transferred to retained earnings as the assets concerned are used or derecognised.[135]

C   *Tax on items of other comprehensive income*

IAS 1 requires disclosure of the amount of income tax relating to each component of other comprehensive income, including reclassification adjustments, either on the face of the statement or in the notes.[136] This may be done by presenting the components of other comprehensive income either:

(a)   net of related tax effects; or

(b)   before related tax effects with one amount shown for the aggregate amount of income tax relating to those components.[137]

The reference to reclassification adjustments here and in the definition of other comprehensive income (see 3.2.1 above) seems to suggest that such adjustments are themselves 'components' of other comprehensive income. That would mean that the standard requires disclosure of tax related to reclassification adjustments. The implementation guidance, however, suggests this is not required because the note illustrating the presentation in (b) above allocates tax only to items of comprehensive income themselves net of related reclassification adjustments.

IAS 1 provides an illustration of both approaches in its implementation guidance.

The illustrative statement of comprehensive income and related note analysing tax is reproduced in Example 3.7 below.

Example 3.7:   *Statement of comprehensive income illustrating the presentation of comprehensive income in two statements (separate income statement shown in Example 3.3 above) with note disclosure of the tax effects relating to components of other comprehensive income[138]*

XYZ GROUP – STATEMENT OF COMPREHENSIVE INCOME FOR THE YEAR ENDED 31 DECEMBER 2010

(in thousands of Euro)

	2010	2009
Profit for the year	121,250	65,500
Other comprehensive income:		
Exchange differences on translating foreign operations	4,000	8,000
Available-for-sale financial assets	(18,000)	20,000
Cash flow hedges	(500)	(3,000)
Gains on property revaluation	600	2,700
Actuarial gains (losses) on defined benefit pension plans	(500)	1,000
Share of other comprehensive income of associates	400	(700)
Other comprehensive income for the year, net of tax	(14,000)	28,000
TOTAL COMPREHENSIVE INCOME FOR THE YEAR	107,250	93,500
Total comprehensive income attributable to:		
Owners of the parent	85,800	74,800
Non-controlling interests	21,450	18,700
	107,250	93,500

XYZ Group
Disclosure of tax effects relating to each component of other comprehensive income
Notes
Year ended 31 December 2010

(in thousands of currency units)

	2010			2009		
	Before-tax account	Tax (expense) benefit	Net-of-tax amount	Before-tax amount	Tax (expense) benefit	Net-of-tax amount
Exchange differences on translating foreign operations	5,334	(1,334)	4,000	10,667	(2,667)	8,000
Available-for-sale financial assets	(24,000)	6,000	(18,000)	26,667	(6,667)	20,000
Cash flow hedges	(667)	167	(500)	(4,000)	1,000	(3,000)
Gains on property revaluation	933	(333)	600	3,367	(667)	2,700

Actuarial gains (losses) on defined benefit pension plans	(667)	167	(500)	1,333	(333)	1,000
Share of other comprehensive income of associates	400	–	400	(700)	–	(700)
Other comprehensive income	(18,667)	4,667	(14,000)	37,334	(9,334)	28,000

3.2.5   Discontinued operations

As discussed in Chapter 4, IFRS 5 requires the presentation of a single amount on the face of the income statement relating to discontinued operations, with further analysis either on the face of the income statement or in the notes.

3.2.6   Material, exceptional and extraordinary items

A   Exceptional or material items

IAS 1 does not use the phrase exceptional items. However, it does require that when items of income or expense (a term covering both profit and loss, and other comprehensive income) are material, their nature and amount should be disclosed separately.[139] Materiality is discussed at 4.1.5 A below. The standard goes on to suggest that circumstances that would give rise to the separate disclosure of items of income and expense include:

(a)   write-downs of inventories to net realisable value or of property, plant and equipment to recoverable amount, as well as reversals of such write-downs;

(b)   restructurings of the activities of an entity and reversals of any provisions for the costs of restructuring;

(c)   disposals of items of property, plant and equipment;

(d)   disposals of investments;

(e)   discontinued operations;

(f)   litigation settlements; and

(g)   other reversals of provisions.[140]

This information may be given on the face of the income statement, on the face of the statement of comprehensive income or in the notes. In line with the permissive approach taken to the format of the performance statements discussed above, the level of prominence given to such items is left to the judgement of the entity concerned. However, regarding (e) above, IFRS 5 requires certain information to be presented on the face of the income statement (see Chapter 4).

B   Ordinary activities and extraordinary items

There is a certain amount of tension (or at least of ongoing evolution) in the IFRS literature concerning results from ordinary activities, and in particular the categorisation of certain items as not falling within them – that is extraordinary items.

The IASB's *Framework* seems to consider the distinction a useful one, and states 'Income and expenses may be presented in the income statement in different ways so as to provide information that is relevant for economic decision-making. For example, it is common practice to distinguish between those items of income and expenses that arise in the course of the ordinary activities of the enterprise and those that do not. This distinction is made on the basis that the source of an item is relevant in evaluating the ability of the enterprise to generate cash and cash equivalents in the future; for example, incidental activities such as the disposal of a long-term investment are unlikely to recur on a regular basis. When distinguishing between items in this way consideration needs to be given to the nature of the enterprise and its operations. Items that arise from the ordinary activities of one enterprise may be unusual in respect of another.'[141] This was reflected in the requirement in the pre-December 2003 version of IAS 8 to present this distinction on the face of the income statement supported by a definition of ordinary activities and extraordinary items.[142]

In 2003, the IASB's improvements project took a different view of the ordinary/extraordinary distinction, perhaps due to a feeling that it was being abused. Accordingly, IAS 1 and IAS 8 were amended to prohibit entities making this distinction, IAS 1 now stating that an entity 'shall not present any items of income or expense as extraordinary items, in the statement of comprehensive income or the separate income statement (if presented), or in the notes.'[143]

3.3   The statement of changes in equity

For periods beginning on or after 1 July 2009, IAS 1 requires the presentation of a statement of changes in equity showing on the face of the statement:[144]

(a)   total comprehensive income for the period (comprising profit and loss and other comprehensive income – see 3.2.1 above) showing separately the total amounts attributable to owner of the parent and to non-controlling interests;

(b)   for each component of equity, the effects of retrospective application or retrospective restatement recognised in accordance with IAS 8 (discussed at 4.4 and 4.6 below); and

(c)   for each component of equity, a reconciliation between the carrying amount at the beginning and the end of the period, separately disclosing changes resulting from:

    (i)   profit or loss;

    (ii)   each item of other comprehensive income; and

    (iii)   transactions with owners in their capacity as owners, showing separately contributions by and distributions to owners and changes in ownership interests in subsidiaries that do not result in a loss of control.

It can be seen that (a) above is effectively a sub-total of all the items required by (c)(i) and (c)(ii).

For these purposes, 'components' of equity include each class of contributed equity, the accumulated balance of each class of other comprehensive income and retained earnings.[145]

This analysis reflects the focus of the IASB on the balance sheet – whereby any changes in net assets (aside of those arising from transactions with owners) are gains and losses, regarded as performance. In this vein, IAS 1 observes that changes in an entity's equity between two balance sheet dates reflect the increase or decrease in its net assets during the period. Except for changes resulting from transactions with owners acting in their capacity as owners (such as equity contributions, reacquisitions of the entity's own equity instruments and dividends) and transaction costs directly related to such transactions, the overall change in equity during a period represents the total amount of income and expenses, including gains and losses, generated by the entity's activities during that period.[146]

After taking account of total gains and losses and owner transactions in this way, any other changes in equity will result from the restatement of prior periods. Point (b) above reflects this. IAS 8 requires retrospective adjustments to effect changes in accounting policies, to the extent practicable, except when the transitional provisions in another IFRS require otherwise. IAS 8 also requires that restatements to correct errors are made retrospectively, to the extent practicable. IAS 1 observes that retrospective adjustments and retrospective restatements 'are not changes in equity but they are adjustments to the opening balance of retained earnings, except when an IFRS requires retrospective adjustment of another component of equity.' Point (b) above therefore requires disclosure in the statement of changes in equity of the total adjustment to each component of equity resulting, separately, from changes in accounting policies and from corrections of errors. These adjustments should be disclosed for each prior period and the beginning of the period.[147]

The requirements above apply to periods beginning on or after 1 July 2009, and reflect a subtle change to the requirements as originally published in 2007. The change came about through an amendment consequential to IAS 27 (as amended in 2008) (discussed in Chapter 6). If IAS 27 (as amended in 2008) is applied to earlier periods, then so must its consequential amendment to IAS 1. Before that amendment, the standard expressed the requirements in (c) above slightly differently, as follows:

- the amounts of transactions with owners in their capacity as owners, showing separately contributions by and distributions to owners; and

- for each component of equity, a reconciliation between the carrying amount at the beginning and the end of the period, separately disclosing each change.

As can be seen, the new requirements require a more detailed analysis of changes in the components of equity. In particular, the latest version of the standard requires separate disclosure of profit or loss and each item of comprehensive income. Whilst the main text of IAS 1 was amended to introduce this requirement, the illustrative examples accompanying the standard were not. Somewhat regrettably, this means the illustrative examples fail to comply with the standard. In August 2009 the IASB issued an exposure draft of proposing various amendments to IFRS. The exposure draft proposes amending IAS 1 to allow the information in (a)-(c) above to be shown either on the face of the statement or in the notes.[148]

The illustrative statement from implementation guidance accompanying IAS 1 is set out below.

Example 3.8:   *Combined statement of all changes in equity*[149]

XYZ Group – Statement of changes in equity for the year ended 31 December 2010
(in thousands of currency units)

	Share capital	Retained earnings	Translation of foreign operations	Available-for-sale financial assets	Cash flow hedged	Re-valuation surplus	Total	Non-controlling interest	Total equity
Balance at 1 January 2009	600,000	118,100	(4,000)	1,600	2,000	–	717,700	29,800	747,500
Changes in accounting policy	–	400	–	–	–	–	400	100	500
Restated balance	600,000	118,500	(4,000)	1,600	2,000	–	718,100	29,900	748,000
Changes in equity for 2009									
Dividends	–	(10,000)	–	–	–	–	(10,000)	–	(10,000)
Total comprehensive income for the year (a)	–	53,200	6,400	16,000	(2,400)	1,600	74,800	18,700	93,500
Balance at 31 December 2009	600,000	161,700	2,400	17,600	(400)	1,600	782,900	48,600	831,500
Changes in equity for 2010									
Issue of share capital	50,000	–	–	–	–	–	50,000	–	50,000
Dividends	–	(15,000)	–	–	–	–	(15,000)	–	(15,000)
Total comprehensive income for the year (b)	–	96,600	3,200	(14,400)	(400)	800	85,800	21,450	107,250
Transfer to retained earnings	–	200	–	–	–	200	–	–	–
Balance at 31 December 2010	650,000	243,500	5,600	3,200	(800)	2,220	903,700	70,959	973,750

(a)   The amount included in retained earnings for 2009 of 53,200 represents profit attributable to owners of the parent of 52,400 plus actuarial gains on defined benefit pension plans of 800 (1,333, less tax 333, less non-controlling interest 200).

The amount included in the translation, available-for-sale and cash flow hedge reserves represent other comprehensive income for each component, net of tax and non-controlling interest, e.g. other comprehensive income related to available-for-sale financial assets for 2009 of 16,000 is 26,667, less tax 6,667, less non-controlling interest 4,000. The amount included in the revaluation surplus of 1,600 represents the share of other comprehensive income of associates of (700) plus gains on property revaluation of 2,300 (3,367, less tax 667, less non-controlling interest 400). Other comprehensive income of associates relates solely to gains or losses on property revaluation.

(b)   The amount included in retained earnings of 2010 of 96,600 represents profit attributable to owners of the parent of 97,000 plus actuarial losses on defined benefit pension plans of 400 (667, less tax 167, less non-controlling interest 100).
The amount included in the translation, available-for-sale and cash flow hedge reserves represent other comprehensive income for each component, net of tax and non-controlling interest, e.g. other comprehensive income related to the translation of foreign operations for 2010 of 3,200 is 5,334, less tax 1,334, less non-controlling interest 800. The amount included in the revaluation surplus of 800 represents the share of other comprehensive income of associates of 400 plus gains on property revaluation of 400 (933, less tax 333, less non-controlling interest 200). Other comprehensive income of associates relates solely to gains or losses on property revaluation,

3.4   The notes to the financial statements

IAS 1 requires the presentation of notes to the financial statements that:

(a)   present information about the basis of preparation of the financial statements and the specific accounting policies used (see 5.1 below);

(b)   disclose the information required by IFRSs that is not presented on the face of the primary statements; and

(c)   provide additional information that is not presented on the face of the primary statements, but is relevant to an understanding of any of them.[150]

The notes should, as far as practicable, be presented in a systematic manner. Each item on the face of the primary statements should be cross-referenced to any related information in the notes.[151]

The notes are normally presented in the following order, which is intended to assist users in understanding the financial statements and comparing them with financial statements of other entities:

(a)   a statement of compliance with IFRSs (see 5.1 below);

(b)   a summary of significant accounting policies applied (see 5.1 below);

(c)   supporting information for items presented on the face of the primary statements, in the order in which each statement and each line item is presented; and

(d)   other disclosures, including:

     (i)   contingent liabilities (discussed in Chapter 24) and unrecognised contractual commitments; and

     (ii)   non-financial disclosures, e.g. the entity's financial risk management objectives and policies (discussed in Chapter 34).[152]

However, the standard allows that notes providing information about the basis of preparation of the financial statements and specific accounting policies may be presented as a separate component of the financial statements.[153]

Although the above represents the normal arrangement of the notes, in some circumstances it may be necessary or desirable to vary the ordering of specific items within the notes. An example given by the standard is that information on changes in fair value recognised in profit or loss may be combined with information on maturities of financial instruments, although the former disclosures relate to profit or loss and the latter relate to the balance sheet. Nevertheless, a systematic structure for the notes should be retained as far as practicable.[154]

4　ACCOUNTING POLICIES

The selection and application of accounting policies is obviously crucial in the preparation of financial statements. As a general premise, the whole purpose of accounting standards is to specify required accounting policies, presentation and disclosure. However, judgement will always remain; many standards may allow choices to accommodate different views, and no body of accounting literature could hope to prescribe precise treatments for all possible situations.

In the broadest sense, accounting policies are discussed by both IAS 1 and IAS 8. Whilst, as its title suggest, IAS 8 deals explicitly with accounting policies, IAS 1 deals with what one might describe as overarching or general principles.

4.1　General principles

IAS 1 deals with some general principles relating to accounting policies, with IAS 8 discussing the detail of selection and application of individual accounting policies and their disclosure.

The general principles discussed by IAS 1 can be described as follows:

- fair presentation and compliance with accounting standards;
- going concern;
- the accrual basis of accounting;
- consistency;
- materiality and aggregation;
- offsetting; and
- profit or loss for the period.

These are discussed in the sections that follow.

4.1.1　Fair presentation

A　Fair presentation and compliance with IFRS

Consistent with its objective and statement of the purpose of financial statements, IAS 1 requires that financial statements present fairly the financial position, financial performance and cash flows of an entity. Fair presentation for these purposes requires the faithful representation of the effects of transactions, other events and conditions in accordance with the definitions and recognition criteria for assets, liabilities, income and expenses set out in the Framework (discussed in Chapter 2).

The main premise of the standard is that application of IFRSs, with additional disclosure when necessary, is presumed to result in financial statements that achieve a fair presentation.[155] As noted at 1.1.2 above, an important point here is that implementation guidance for standards issued by the IASB does not form part of those standards (unless they are explicitly 'scoped-in'), and therefore does not contain requirements for financial statements.[156] Accordingly, the often voluminous implementation guidance accompanying standards is not, strictly speaking, part of 'IFRS'. We would generally be surprised, though, at entities not following such guidance without valid reason. The presumption that application of IFRS (with any necessary additional disclosure) results in a fair presentation is potentially rebuttable, as discussed at B below.

To reflect this presumption, as discussed at 2.5.2 above, the standard requires an explicit and unreserved statement of compliance to be included in the notes. A fair presentation also requires an entity to:

(a)   select and apply accounting policies in accordance with IAS 8, which also sets out a hierarchy of authoritative guidance that should be considered in the absence of an IFRS that specifically applies to an item (see 4.3 below);

(b)   present information, including accounting policies, in a manner that provides relevant, reliable, comparable and understandable information; and

(c)   provide additional disclosures when compliance with the specific requirements in IFRSs is insufficient to enable users to understand the impact of particular transactions, other events and conditions on the entity's financial position and financial performance.[157]

However, the standard makes clear that inappropriate accounting policies are not rectified either by disclosure of the accounting policies used or by notes or explanatory material.[158] We support this position, however the IASB has (admittedly only in rare situations) essentially delegated standard setting to the authors of 'relevant regulatory frameworks' in this regard. As discussed at B below, it is possible that a rare circumstance arises where departure from a provision of IFRS is needed to achieve fair presentation. This is only allowed by IAS 1, however, if permitted by such a regulatory framework. If it is not, then it seems the fairest presentation politically possible for the IASB is indeed achieved through additional disclosure in the face of inappropriate accounting policies.

B   The fair presentation override

The presumption that the application of IFRSs, with additional disclosure when necessary, results in financial statements that achieve a fair presentation is a rebuttable one, although the standard makes clear that in virtually all situations a fair presentation is achieved through compliance.[159]

The standard observes that an item of information would conflict with the objective of financial statements when it does not represent faithfully the transactions, other events and conditions that it either purports to represent or could reasonably be expected to represent and, consequently, it would be likely to influence economic decisions made by users of financial statements. When assessing whether complying with a specific requirement in an IFRS would be so misleading that it would conflict with the objective of financial statements, IAS 1 requires consideration of:

(a)   why the objective of financial statements is not achieved in the particular circumstances; and

(b)   how the entity's circumstances differ from those of other entities that comply with the requirement. If other entities in similar circumstances comply with the requirement, there is a rebuttable presumption that the entity's compliance with the requirement would not be so misleading that it would conflict with the objective of financial statements.[160]

In the extremely rare circumstances in which management concludes that compliance with a requirement in an IFRS would be so misleading that it would conflict with the objective of financial statements, IAS 1 requires departure from that requirement. However, this is only permitted if the 'relevant regulatory framework requires, or otherwise does not prohibit, such a departure', which is discussed further below.[161]

When the relevant regulatory framework allows a departure, an entity should make it and also disclose:

(a)   that management has concluded that the financial statements present fairly the entity's financial position, financial performance and cash flows;

(b)   that it has complied with applicable IFRSs, except that it has departed from a particular requirement to achieve a fair presentation;

(c)   the title of the IFRS from which the entity has departed, the nature of the departure, including:

　　　　(i)   the treatment that the IFRS would require;

　　　　(ii)   the reason why that treatment would be so misleading in the circumstances that it would conflict with the objective of financial statements set out in the Framework; and

　　　　(iii)   the treatment adopted;

(d)   for each period presented, the financial impact of the departure on each item in the financial statements that would have been reported in complying with the requirement; and

(e)   when there has been a departure from a requirement of an IFRS in a prior period, and that departure affects the amounts recognised in the financial statements for the current period, the disclosures set out in (c) and (d) above.[162]

Regarding (e) above, the standard explains that the requirement could apply, for example, when an entity departed in a prior period from a requirement in an IFRS for the measurement of assets or liabilities and that departure affects the measurement of changes in assets and liabilities recognised in the current period's financial statements.[163]

An example of a company adopting the fair presentation override is shown in Extract 1.1 in Chapter 1.

When the relevant regulatory framework does not allow a departure from IFRS, IAS 1 accepts that, notwithstanding the failure to achieve fair presentation, that it should not be made. Although intended to occur only in extremely rare circumstances, this is a very important provision of the standard as it allows a 'relevant regulatory framework' to override a requirement of IFRS which is specifically necessary to achieve a fair presentation. In that light, it is perhaps surprising that there is no definition or discussion in the standard of what a relevant regulatory framework is.

When a departure otherwise required by IAS 1 is not allowed by the relevant regulatory framework, the standard requires that the perceived misleading aspects of compliance are reduced, to the maximum extent possible, by the disclosure of:

(a)   the title of the IFRS in question, the nature of the requirement, and the reason why management has concluded that complying with that requirement is so misleading in the circumstances that it conflicts with the objective of financial statements set out in the Framework; and

(b)   for each period presented, the adjustments to each item in the financial statements that management has concluded would be necessary to achieve a fair presentation.[164]

Overall, this strikes us as a fairly uncomfortable compromise. However, the rule is reasonably clear and in our view such a circumstance will indeed be a rare one.

4.1.2 *Going concern*

When preparing financial statements, IAS 1 requires management to make an assessment of an entity's ability to continue as a going concern. This term is not defined, but its meaning is implicit in the requirement of the standard that financial statements should be prepared on a going concern basis unless management either intends to liquidate the entity or to cease trading, or has no realistic alternative but to do so. The standard goes on to require that when management is aware, in making its assessment, of material uncertainties related to events or conditions that may cast significant doubt upon the entity's ability to continue as a going concern, those uncertainties should be disclosed. When financial statements are not prepared on a going concern basis, that fact should be disclosed, together with the basis on which the financial statements are prepared and the reason why the entity is not regarded as a going concern.[165]

In assessing whether the going concern assumption is appropriate, the standard requires that all available information about the future, which is at least, but is not limited to, twelve months from the end of the reporting period should be taken into account. The degree of consideration required will depend on the facts in each case. When an entity has a history of profitable operations and ready access to financial resources, a conclusion that the going concern basis of accounting is appropriate may be reached without detailed analysis. In other cases, management may need to consider a wide range of factors relating to current and expected profitability, debt repayment schedules and potential sources of replacement financing before it can satisfy itself that the going concern basis is appropriate.[166]

There is no guidance in the standard concerning what impact there should be on the financial statements if it is determined that the going concern basis is not appropriate. Accordingly, entities will need to consider carefully their individual circumstances to arrive at an appropriate basis.

4.1.3   *The accrual basis of accounting*

IAS 1 requires that financial statements be prepared, except for cash flow information, using the accrual basis of accounting.[167] No definition of this is given by the standard, but an explanation is presented that 'When the accrual basis of accounting is used, items are recognised as assets, liabilities, equity, income and expenses (the elements of financial statements) when they satisfy the definitions and recognition criteria for those elements in the Framework.'[168]

The Framework itself is a little more helpful, explaining the accruals basis as follows. 'Under this basis, the effects of transactions and other events are recognised when they occur (and not as cash or its equivalent is received or paid) and they are recorded in the accounting records and reported in the financial statements of the periods to which they relate. Financial statements prepared on the accrual basis inform users not only of past transactions involving the payment and receipt of cash but also of obligations to pay cash in the future and of resources that represent cash to be received in the future. Hence, they provide the type of information about past transactions and other events that is most useful to users in making economic decisions.'[169]

The requirements of the framework are discussed in more detail in Chapter 2.

4.1.4   *Consistency*

As noted at 1.1.2 and 1.2.2 above, one of the objectives of both IAS 1 and IAS 8 is to ensure the comparability of financial statements with those of previous periods. To this end, each standard addresses the principle of consistency.

IAS 1 requires that the 'presentation and classification' of items in the financial statements be retained from one period to the next unless:

(a)   it is apparent, following a significant change in the nature of the entity's operations or a review of its financial statements, that another presentation or classification would be more appropriate having regard to the criteria for the selection and application of accounting policies in IAS 8 (see 4.3 below); or

(b)   an IFRS requires a change in presentation.[170]

The standard goes on to amplify this by explaining that a significant acquisition or disposal, or a review of the presentation of the financial statements, might suggest that the financial statements need to be presented differently. An entity should change the presentation of its financial statements only if the changed presentation provides information that is reliable and is more relevant to users of the financial statements and the revised structure is likely to continue, so that comparability is not impaired. When making such changes in presentation, an entity will need to reclassify its comparative information as discussed at 2.4 above.[171]

IAS 8 addresses consistency of accounting policies and observes that users of financial statements need to be able to compare the financial statements of an entity over time to identify trends in its financial position, financial performance and cash flows. For this reason, the same accounting policies need to be applied within each period and from one period to the next unless a change in accounting policy meets certain criteria (changes in accounting policy are discussed at 4.4 below).[172] Accordingly, the standard requires that accounting policies be selected and applied consistently for similar transactions, other events and conditions, unless an IFRS specifically requires or permits categorisation of items for which different policies may be appropriate. If an IFRS requires or permits such categorisation, an appropriate accounting policy should be selected and applied consistently to each category.[173]

4.1.5   Materiality, aggregation and offset

A   Materiality and aggregation

Financial statements result from processing large numbers of transactions or other events that are aggregated into classes according to their nature or function. The final stage in the process of aggregation and classification is the presentation of condensed and classified data, which form line items in the financial statements, or in the notes.[174] The extent of aggregation versus detailed analysis is clearly a judgemental one, with either extreme eroding the usefulness of the information.

IAS 1 resolves this issue with the concept of materiality, by requiring:

- each material class of similar items to be presented separately in the financial statements; and

- items of a dissimilar nature or function to be presented separately unless they are immaterial.[175]

Materiality is defined by both IAS 1 and IAS 8 as follows. 'Omissions or misstatements of items are material if they could, individually or collectively, influence the economic decisions that users make on the basis of the financial statements. Materiality depends on the size and nature of the omission or misstatement judged in the surrounding circumstances. The size or nature of the item, or a combination of both, could be the determining factor.'[176] At a general level, applying the concept of materiality means that a specific disclosure required by an IFRS need not be provided if the information is not material.[177]

IAS 1 and IAS 8 go on to observe that assessing whether an omission or misstatement could influence economic decisions of users, and so be material, requires consideration of the characteristics of those users. For these purposes users are assumed to have a reasonable knowledge of business and economic activities and accounting and a willingness to study the information with reasonable diligence. Therefore, the assessment of materiality needs to take into account how users with such attributes could reasonably be expected to be influenced in making economic decisions.[178]

Regarding the presentation of financial statements, IAS 1 requires that if a line item is not individually material, it should be aggregated with other items either on the face of those statements or in the notes. The standard also states that an item that is not sufficiently material to warrant separate presentation on the face of those statements may nevertheless be sufficiently material for it to be presented separately in the notes.[179]

B   Offset

IAS 1 considers it important that assets and liabilities, and income and expenses, are reported separately. This is because offsetting in the income statement or statement of comprehensive income or the balance sheet, except when offsetting reflects the substance of the transaction or other event, detracts from the ability of users both to understand the transactions, other events and conditions that have occurred and to assess the entity's future cash flows. It clarifies, though, that measuring assets net of valuation allowances – for example, obsolescence allowances on inventories and doubtful debts allowances on receivables – is not offsetting.[180]

Accordingly, IAS 1 requires that assets and liabilities, and income and expenses, should not be offset unless required or permitted by an IFRS.[181]

Just what constitutes offsetting, particularly given the rider noted above of 'reflecting the substance of the transaction' is, not always obvious. IAS 1 expands on its meaning as follows. It notes that:

(a)   IAS 18 – *Revenue* – defines revenue and requires it to be measured at the fair value of the consideration received or receivable, taking into account the amount of any trade discounts and volume rebates allowed by the entity – in other words a notional 'gross' revenue and a discount should not be shown separately, but should be 'offset'. Revenue is discussed in Chapter 25;

(b)   entities can undertake, in the course of their ordinary activities, other transactions that do not generate revenue but are incidental to the main revenue-generating activities. The results of such transactions should be presented, when this presentation reflects the substance of the transaction or other event, by netting any income with related expenses arising on the same transaction. For example:

(i)   gains and losses on the disposal of non-current assets, including investments and operating assets, should be reported by deducting from the proceeds on disposal the carrying amount of the asset and related selling expenses; and

(ii)   expenditure related to a provision that is recognised in accordance with IAS 37 – *Provisions, Contingent Liabilities and Contingent Assets* – and reimbursed under a contractual arrangement with a third party (for example, a supplier's warranty agreement) may be netted against the related reimbursement;[182] and

(c)   gains and losses arising from a group of similar transactions should be reported on a net basis, for example, foreign exchange gains and losses or gains and losses arising on financial instruments held for trading. However, such gains and losses should be reported separately if they are material.[183]

The offset of finance items in the income statement was discussed in 2006 by IFRIC and then by the IASB. IFRIC asked the Board to consider an apparent conflict between the requirements of IAS 1 and IFRS 7 regarding the presentation of finance costs. IFRIC observed that paragraphs 32 and (at that time) 81 (now paragraph 82) of IAS 1 precluded presenting 'net finance costs' on the face of the income statement without showing separately the finance costs and finance revenue included in the net amount. However, paragraph IG13 of IFRS 7 stated that total interest income and total income expense are components of finance costs. This indicates a net presentation in the income statement. The Board decided to resolve this conflict by amending paragraph IG13. An amendment to IFRS 7 was made as part of the Board's 2007 annual improvements project to clarify that finance income and expense may not be offset.[184]

4.1.6   Profit or loss for the period

The final provision of IAS 1 which we term a general principle is a very important one. It is that, unless an IFRS requires or permits otherwise, all items of income and expense recognised in a period should be included in profit or loss.[185] This is the case whether one combined statement of comprehensive income is presented or whether a separate income statement is presented (discussed at 3.2.1 above).

Income and expense are not defined by the standard, but they are defined by the Framework as follows:

(a)   income is increases in economic benefits during the accounting period in the form of inflows or enhancements of assets or decreases of liabilities that result in increases in equity, other than those relating to contributions from equity participants; and

(b)   expenses are decreases in economic benefits during the accounting period in the form of outflows or depletions of assets or incurrences of liabilities that result in decreases in equity, other than those relating to distributions to equity participants.[186]

This clearly indicates to us that the terms do not have what many would consider their natural meaning, as they encompass all gains and losses (for example, capital appreciation in a non-current asset like property). As discussed at 6 below, how to present financial performance, including all gains and losses, is currently being debated by the Board and key to this is the meaning of 'profit or loss'. As things stand now, there is a somewhat awkward compromise with various gains and losses either required or permitted to bypass profit or loss and be reported instead in 'other comprehensive income'. Importantly, as discussed at 3.2.1 above, profit and loss, and other comprehensive income may each be reported as a separate statement.

IAS 1 notes that normally, all items of income and expense recognised in a period are included in profit or loss, and that this includes the effects of changes in accounting estimates. However, circumstances may exist when particular items may be excluded from profit or loss for the current period. IAS 8 deals with two such circumstances: the correction of errors and the effect of changes in accounting policies (discussed at 4.4 and 4.6 below).[187] Other IFRSs deal with items that may meet the Framework's definitions of income or expense but are usually excluded from profit or loss. Examples include:

(a)   changes in revaluation surplus relating to property, plant and equipment and intangible assets (discussed in Chapters 16 and 15);

(b)   actuarial gains and losses on defined benefit plans when these are recognised outside of profit and loss as permitted by IAS 19 (discussed in Chapter 28);

(c)   gains and losses arising from translating the financial statements of a foreign operation (discussed in Chapter 13);

(d)   gains and losses on remeasuring available-for-sale financial assets (discussed in Chapter 32); and

(e)   the effective portion of gains and losses on hedging instruments in a cash flow hedge (discussed in Chapter 33).[188]

4.2   The distinction between accounting policies and accounting estimates

IAS 8 defines accounting policies as 'the specific principles, bases, conventions, rules and practices applied by an entity in preparing and presenting financial statements.'[189] In particular, IAS 8 considers a change in 'measurement basis' to be a change in accounting policy (rather than a change in estimate).[190] Although not a defined term, IAS 1 (when requiring disclosure of them) gives examples of measurement bases as follows:

- historical cost;
- current cost;
- net realisable value;
- fair value; and
- recoverable amount.[191]

'Accounting estimates' is not a term defined directly by the standards. However, it is indirectly defined by the definition in IAS 8 of a change in an accounting estimate as follows. A change in accounting estimate is an adjustment of the carrying amount of an asset or a liability, or the amount of the periodic consumption of an asset, that results from the assessment of the present status of, and expected future benefits and obligations associated with, assets and liabilities. Changes in accounting estimates result from new information or new developments and, accordingly, are not corrections of errors.[192] Examples given by the IASB are estimates of bad debts and the estimated useful life of, or the expected pattern of consumption of the future economic benefits embodied in, a depreciable asset.[193]

The standard also notes that corrections of errors should be distinguished from changes in accounting estimates. Accounting estimates by their nature are approximations that may need revision as additional information becomes known. For example, the gain or loss recognised on the outcome of a contingency is not the correction of an error.[194]

The distinction between an accounting policy and an accounting estimate is particularly important because a very different treatment is required when there are changes in accounting policies or accounting estimates (discussed at 4.4 and 4.5 below). When it is difficult to distinguish a change in an accounting policy from a change in an accounting estimate, IAS 8 requires the change to be treated as a change in an accounting estimate.[195]

4.3   The selection and application of accounting policies

Entities complying with IFRS (which is a defined term, discussed at 1.1.2 above) do not have a free hand in selecting accounting policies, indeed the very purpose of a body of accounting literature is to confine such choices.

IFRS set out accounting policies that the IASB has concluded result in financial statements containing relevant and reliable information about the transactions, other events and conditions to which they apply.[196]

To this end, IAS 8's starting point is that when an IFRS specifically applies to a transaction, other event or condition, the accounting policy or policies applied to that item should be determined by applying the IFRS and considering any relevant implementation guidance issued by the IASB for the IFRS.[197] This draws out the distinction that IFRS must be *applied* whereas implementation guidance (which, as discussed at 1.1.2 above, is not part of IFRS) must be *considered*. As noted earlier, though, we would generally be surprised at entities not following such guidance without good reason.

Those policies need not be applied when the effect of applying them is immaterial. However, it is inappropriate to make, or leave uncorrected, immaterial departures from IFRSs to achieve a particular presentation of an entity's financial position, financial performance or cash flows.[198] The concept of materiality is discussed at 4.1.5 above.

There will be circumstances where a particular event, transaction or other condition is not specifically addressed by IFRS. When this is the case, IAS 8 sets out a hierarchy of guidance to be considered in the selection of an accounting policy.

The primary requirement of the standard is that management should use its judgement in developing and applying an accounting policy that results in information that is:

(a)   relevant to the economic decision-making needs of users; and

(b)   reliable, in that the financial statements:

  (i)   represent faithfully the financial position, financial performance and cash flows of the entity;

(ii)   reflect the economic substance of transactions, other events and conditions, and not merely the legal form;

(iii)   are neutral, i.e. free from bias;

(iv)   are prudent; and

(v)   are complete in all material respects.[199]

There is, in our view, clearly a tension between (b) (iii) and (b) (iv) above. Prudence and neutrality are not defined or otherwise discussed by IAS 8. However, the Framework discusses them and goes some way to addressing this tension as follows. 'To be reliable, the information contained in financial statements must be neutral, that is, free from bias. Financial statements are not neutral if, by the selection or presentation of information, they influence the making of a decision or judgement in order to achieve a predetermined result or outcome.

'The preparers of financial statements do, however, have to contend with the uncertainties that inevitably surround many events and circumstances, such as the collectability of doubtful receivables, the probable useful life of plant and equipment and the number of warranty claims that may occur. Such uncertainties are recognised by the disclosure of their nature and extent and by the exercise of prudence in the preparation of the financial statements. Prudence is the inclusion of a degree of caution in the exercise of the judgements needed in making the estimates required under conditions of uncertainty, such that assets or income are not overstated and liabilities or expenses are not understated. However, the exercise of prudence does not allow, for example, the creation of hidden reserves or excessive provisions, the deliberate understatement of assets or income, or the deliberate overstatement of liabilities or expenses, because the financial statements would not be neutral and, therefore, not have the quality of reliability.'[200]

In support of this primary requirement, the standard gives guidance on how management should apply this judgement. This guidance comes in two 'strengths' – certain things which management is required to consider, and others which it 'may' consider, as follows.

In making this judgement, management *should* refer to, and consider the applicability of, the following sources in descending order:

(a)   the requirements and guidance in IFRSs dealing with similar and related issues; and

(b)   the definitions, recognition criteria and measurement concepts for assets, liabilities, income and expenses in the Framework;[201] and

in making this judgement, management *may* also consider the most recent pronouncements of other standard-setting bodies that use a similar conceptual framework to develop accounting standards, other accounting literature and accepted industry practices, to the extent that these do not conflict with the sources in (a) and (b) above.[202]

4.4   Changes in accounting policies

As discussed at 4.1.4 above, consistency of accounting policies and presentation is a basic principle in both IAS 1 and IAS 8. Accordingly, IAS 8 only permits a change in accounting policies if the change:

(a)   is required by an IFRS; or

(b)   results in the financial statements providing reliable and more relevant information about the effects of transactions, other events or conditions on the entity's financial position, financial performance or cash flows.[203]

IAS 8 addresses changes of accounting policy arising from three sources:

(a)   the initial application (including early application) of an IFRS containing specific transitional provisions;

(b)   the initial application of an IFRS which does not contain specific transitional provisions; and

(c)   voluntary changes in accounting policy.

Policy changes under (a) should be accounted for in accordance with the specific transitional provisions of that IFRS.

A change of accounting policy under (b) or (c) should be applied retrospectively, that is applied to transactions, other events and conditions as if it had always been applied.[204] The standard goes on to explain that retrospective application requires adjustment of the opening balance of each affected component of equity for the earliest prior period presented and the other comparative amounts disclosed for each prior period presented as if the new accounting policy had always been applied.[205] The standard observes that the amount of the resulting adjustment relating to periods before those presented in the financial statements (which is made to the opening balance of each affected component of equity of the earliest prior period presented) will usually be made to retained earnings. However, it goes on to note that the adjustment may be made to another component of equity (for example, to comply with an IFRS). IAS 8 also makes clear that any other information about prior periods, such as historical summaries of financial data, should be also adjusted.[206]

Frequently it will be straightforward to apply a change in accounting policy retrospectively. However, the standard accepts that sometimes it may be impractical to do so. Accordingly, retrospective application of a change in accounting policy is not required to the extent that it is impracticable to determine either the period-specific effects or the cumulative effect of the change.[207] This is discussed further at 4.7 below. As noted at 4.3 above, in the absence of a specifically applicable IFRS an entity may apply an accounting policy from the most recent pronouncements of another standard-setting body that use a similar conceptual framework. The standard makes clear that a change in accounting policy reflecting a change in such a pronouncement is a voluntary change in accounting policy which should be accounted for and disclosed as such.[208]

Perhaps unnecessarily, the standard clarifies that the following are not changes in accounting policy:

- the application of an accounting policy for transactions, other events or conditions that differ in substance from those previously occurring; and

- the application of a new accounting policy for transactions, other events or conditions that did not occur previously or were immaterial.[209]

More importantly, the standard requires that a change to a policy of revaluing intangible assets or property plant and equipment in accordance with IAS 38 and IAS 16 respectively is not to be accounted for under IAS 8 as a change in accounting policy. Rather, such a change should be dealt with as a revaluation in accordance with the relevant standards (discussed in Chapter 15 and Chapter 16).[210] What this means is that it is not permissible to restate prior periods for the carrying value and depreciation charge of the assets concerned. Aside of this particular exception, the standard makes clear that a change in measurement basis is a change in an accounting policy, and not a change in an accounting estimate. However, when it is difficult to distinguish a change in an accounting policy from a change in an accounting estimate, the standard requires it to be treated as a change in an accounting estimate, discussed in 4.5 below.[211]

4.5   Changes in accounting estimates

The making of estimates is a fundamental feature of financial reporting reflecting the uncertainties inherent in business activities. IAS 8 notes that the use of reasonable estimates is an essential part of the preparation of financial statements and it does not undermine their reliability. Examples of estimates given by the standard are:

- bad debts;

- inventory obsolescence;

- the fair value of financial assets or financial liabilities;

- the useful lives of, or expected pattern of consumption of the future economic benefits embodied in, depreciable assets; and

- warranty obligations.[212]

Of course there are many others, some of the more subjective relating to share-based payments and post-retirement benefits.

Estimates will need revision as changes occur in the circumstances on which they are based or as a result of new information or more experience. The standard observes that, by its nature, the revision of an estimate does not relate to prior periods and is not the correction of an error.[213] Accordingly, IAS 8 requires that changes in estimate be accounted for prospectively;[214] defined as recognising the effect of the change in the accounting estimate in the current and future periods affected by the change.[215] The standard goes on to explain that this will mean (as appropriate):

- adjusting the carrying amount of an asset, liability or item of equity in the balance sheet in the period of change; and

- recognising the change by including it in profit and loss in:
  - the period of change, if it affects that period only (for example, a change in estimate of bad debts); or
  - the period of change and future periods, if it affects both (for example, a change in estimated useful life of a depreciable asset or the expected pattern of consumption of the economic benefits embodied in it).[216]

4.6   Correction of errors

Errors can arise in respect of the recognition, measurement, presentation or disclosure of elements of financial statements. IAS 8 states that financial statements do not comply with IFRS if they contain errors that are:

(a)   material; or

(b)   immaterial but are made intentionally to achieve a particular presentation of an entities financial position, financial performance or cash flows.[217]

The concept in (b) is a little curious. As discussed at 4.1.5 above, an error is material if it could influence the economic decisions of users taken on the basis of the financial statements. We find it difficult to imagine a scenario where an entity would deliberately seek to misstate its financial statements to achieve a particular presentation of its financial position, performance or cash flows but only in such a way that *did not* influence the decisions of users. In any event, and perhaps somewhat unnecessarily, IAS 8 notes that potential current period errors detected before the financial statements are authorised for issue should be corrected in those financial statements. This requirement is phrased so as to apply to all potential errors, not just material ones.[218] The standard notes that corrections of errors are distinguished from changes in accounting estimates. Accounting estimates by their nature are approximations that may need revision as additional information becomes known. For example, the gain or loss recognised on the outcome of a contingency is not the correction of an error.[219]

As with all things, financial reporting is not immune to error and sometimes financial statements can be published which, whether by accident or design, contain errors. IAS 8 defines prior period errors as omissions from, and misstatements in, an entity's financial statements for one or more prior periods (including the effects of mathematical mistakes, mistakes in applying accounting policies, oversights or misinterpretations of facts, and fraud) arising from a failure to use, or misuse of, reliable information that:

(a)   was available when financial statements for those periods were authorised for issue; and

(b)   could reasonably be expected to have been obtained and taken into account in the preparation and presentation of those financial statements.[220]

When it is discovered that material prior period errors have occurred, IAS 8 requires that they be corrected in the first set of financial statements prepared after their discovery.[221] The correction should be excluded from profit or loss for the period in which the error is discovered. Rather, any information presented about prior periods (including any historical summaries of financial data) should be restated as far back as practicable.[222] This should be done by:

(a)   restating the comparative amounts for the prior period(s) presented in which the error occurred; or

(b)   if the error occurred before the earliest prior period presented, restating the opening balances of assets, liabilities and equity for the earliest prior period presented.[223]

This process is described by the standard as retrospective restatement, which it also defines as correcting the recognition, measurement and disclosure of amounts of elements of financial statements as if a prior period error had never occurred.[224]

The implementation guidance accompanying the standard provides an example of the retrospective restatement of errors as follows.

Example 3.9:   Retrospective restatement of errors[225]

During 2010, Beta Co discovered that some products that had been sold during 2009 were incorrectly included in inventory at 31 December 2009 at €6,500.

Beta's accounting records for 2010 show sales of €104,000, cost of goods sold of €86,500 (including €6,500 for the error in opening inventory), and income taxes of €5,250.

In 2009, Beta reported:

	€
Sales	73,500
Cost of goods sold	(53,500)
Profit before income taxes	20,000
Income taxes	(6,000)
Profit	14,000

The 2009 opening retained earnings was €20,000 and closing retained earnings was €34,000.

Beta's income tax rate was 30 per cent for 2010 and 2009. It had no other income or expenses.

Beta had €5,000 of share capital throughout, and no other components of equity except for retained earnings. Its shares are not publicly traded and it does not disclose earnings per share.

Beta Co
Extract from the statement of comprehensive income

	2010 €	(restated) 2009 €
Sales	104,000	73,500
Cost of goods sold	(80,000)	(60,000)
Profit before income taxes	24,000	13,500
Income taxes	(7,200)	(4,050)
Profit	16,800	9,450

Beta Co
Statement of Changes in Equity

	Share capital €	Retained earnings €	Total €
Balance at 31 December 2008	5,000	20,000	25,000
Profit for the year ended 31 December 2009 as restated	–	9,450	9,450
Balance at 31 December 2009	5,000	29,450	34,450
Profit for the year ended 31 December 2010	–	16,800	16,800
Balance at 31 December 2010	5,000	46,250	51,250

Extracts from the Notes

1. Some products that had been sold in 2009 were incorrectly included in inventory at 31 December 2009 at €6,500. The financial statements of 2009 have been restated to correct this error. The effect of the restatement on those financial statements is summarised below. There is no effect in 2010.

	Effect on 2009 €
(Increase) in cost of goods sold	(6,500)
Decrease in income tax expense	1,950
(Decrease) in profit	(4,550)
(Decrease) in inventory	(6,500)
Decrease in income tax payable	1,950
(Decrease) in equity	(4,550)

As is the case for the retrospective application of a change in accounting policy, retrospective restatement for the correction of prior period material errors is not required to the extent that it is impracticable to determine either the period-specific effects or the cumulative effect of the error.[226] This is discussed further at 4.7 below.

4.7   Impracticability of restatement

As noted at 4.4 and 4.6 above, IAS 8 does not require the restatement of prior periods following a change in accounting policy or the correction of material errors if such a restatement is impracticable.

The standard devotes a considerable amount of guidance to discussing what 'impracticable' means for these purposes.

The standard states that applying a requirement is impracticable when an entity cannot apply it after making every reasonable effort to do so. It goes on to note that, for a particular prior period, it is impracticable to apply a change in an accounting policy retrospectively or to make a retrospective restatement to correct an error if:

(a)   the effects of the retrospective application or retrospective restatement are not determinable;

(b)   the retrospective application or retrospective restatement requires assumptions about what management's intent would have been in that period; or

(c)   the retrospective application or retrospective restatement requires significant estimates of amounts and it is impossible to distinguish objectively information about those estimates that:

    (i)   provides evidence of circumstances that existed on the date(s) as at which those amounts are to be recognised, measured or disclosed; and

    (ii)   would have been available when the financial statements for that prior period were authorised for issue,

from other information.[227]

An example of a scenario covered by (a) above given by the standard is that in some circumstances it may impracticable to adjust comparative information for one or more prior periods to achieve comparability with the current period because data may not have been collected in the prior period(s) in a way that allows either retrospective application of a new accounting policy (or its prospective application to prior periods) or retrospective restatement to correct a prior period error, and it may be impracticable to recreate the information.[228]

IAS 8 observes that it is frequently necessary to make estimates in applying an accounting policy and that estimation is inherently subjective, and that estimates may be developed after the balance sheet date. Developing estimates is potentially more difficult when retrospectively applying an accounting policy or making a retrospective restatement to correct a prior period error, because of the longer period of time that might have passed since the affected transaction, other event or condition occurred.

However, the objective of estimates related to prior periods remains the same as for estimates made in the current period, namely, for the estimate to reflect the circumstances that existed when the transaction, other event or condition occurred.[229] Hindsight should not be used when applying a new accounting policy to, or correcting amounts for, a prior period, either in making assumptions about what management's intentions would have been in a prior period or estimating the amounts recognised, measured or disclosed in a prior period. For example, if an entity corrects a prior period error in measuring financial assets previously classified as held-to-maturity investments in accordance with IAS 39, it should not change their basis of measurement for that period if management decided later not to hold them to maturity. In addition, if an entity corrects a prior period error in calculating its liability for employees' accumulated sick leave in accordance with IAS 19, it would disregard information about an unusually severe influenza season during the next period that became available after the financial statements for the prior period were authorised for issue. However, the fact that significant estimates are frequently required when amending comparative information presented for prior periods does not prevent reliable adjustment or correction of the comparative information.[230]

Therefore, retrospectively applying a new accounting policy or correcting a prior period error requires distinguishing information that:

(a)   provides evidence of circumstances that existed on the date(s) as at which the transaction, other event or condition occurred; and

(b)   would have been available when the financial statements for that prior period were authorised for issue,

from other information. The standard states that for some types of estimates (e.g. an estimate of fair value not based on an observable price or observable inputs), it is impracticable to distinguish these types of information. When retrospective application or retrospective restatement would require making a significant estimate for which it is impossible to distinguish these two types of information, it is impracticable to apply the new accounting policy or correct the prior period error retrospectively.[231]

IAS 8 addresses the impracticability of restatement separately (although similarly) for changes in accounting policy and the correction of material errors.

4.7.1   *Impracticability of restatement for a change in accounting policy.*

When retrospective application of a change in accounting policy is required, the change in policy should be applied retrospectively except to the extent that it is impracticable to determine either the period-specific effects or the cumulative effect of the change.[232] When an entity applies a new accounting policy retrospectively, the standard requires it to be applied to comparative information for prior periods as far back as is practicable. Retrospective application to a prior period is not practicable for these purposes unless it is practicable to determine the cumulative effect on the amounts in both the opening and closing balance sheets for that period.[233]

When it is impracticable to determine the period-specific effects of changing an accounting policy on comparative information for one or more prior periods presented, the new accounting policy should be applied to the carrying amounts of assets and liabilities as at the beginning of the earliest period for which retrospective application is practicable and a corresponding adjustment to the opening balance of each affected component of equity for that period should be made. The standard notes that this may be the current period.[234]

When it is impracticable to determine the cumulative effect, at the beginning of the current period, of applying a new accounting policy to all prior periods, the standard requires an adjustment to the comparative information to apply the new accounting policy prospectively from the earliest date practicable.[235] Prospective application is defined by the standard as applying the new accounting policy to transactions, other events and conditions occurring after the date as at which the policy is changed.[236] This means that the portion of the cumulative adjustment to assets, liabilities and equity arising before that date is disregarded. Changing an accounting policy is permitted by IAS 8 even if it is impracticable to apply the policy prospectively for any prior period.[237]

The implementation guidance accompanying the standard illustrates the prospective application of a change in accounting policy as follows.

Example 3.10: *Prospective application of a change in accounting policy when retrospective application is not practicable*[238]

During 2010, Delta Co changed its accounting policy for depreciating property, plant and equipment, so as to apply much more fully a components approach, whilst at the same time adopting the revaluation model.

In years before 2010, Delta's asset records were not sufficiently detailed to apply a components approach fully. At the end of 2009, management commissioned an engineering survey, which provided information on the components held and their fair values, useful lives, estimated residual values and depreciable amounts at the beginning of 2010. However, the survey did not provide a sufficient basis for reliably estimating the cost of those components that had not previously been accounted for separately, and the existing records before the survey did not permit this information to be reconstructed.

Delta's management considered how to account for each of the two aspects of the accounting change. They determined that it was not practicable to account for the change to a fuller components approach retrospectively, or to account for that change prospectively from any earlier date than the start of 2010. Also, the change from a cost model to a revaluation model is required to be accounted for prospectively (see 4.4 above). Therefore, management concluded that it should apply Delta's new policy prospectively from the start of 2010.

Additional information:

Delta's tax rate is 30 per cent.

	€
Property, plant and equipment at the end of 2009:	
Cost	25,000
Depreciation	(14,000)
Net book value	11,000
Prospective depreciation expense for 2010 (old basis)	1,500
Some results of the engineering survey:	
Valuation	17,000
Estimated residual value	3,000
Average remaining asset life (years)	7
Depreciation expense on existing property, plant and equipment for 2010 (new basis)	2,000

Extract from the Notes

1   From the start of 2010, Delta changed its accounting policy for depreciating property, plant and equipment, so as to apply much more fully a components approach, whilst at the same time adopting the revaluation model. Management takes the view that this policy provides reliable and more relevant information because it deals more accurately with the components of property, plant and equipment and is based on up-to-date values. The policy has been applied prospectively from the start of 2010 because it was not practicable to estimate the effects of applying the policy either retrospectively, or prospectively from any earlier date. Accordingly, the adoption of the new policy has no effect on prior years. The effect on the current year is to increase the carrying amount of property, plant and equipment at the start of the year by €6,000; increase the opening deferred tax provision by €1,800; create a revaluation reserve at the start of the year of €4,200; increase depreciation expense by €500; and reduce tax expense by €150.

4.7.2   Impracticability of restatement for a material error

IAS 8 requires that a prior period error should be corrected by retrospective restatement except to the extent that it is impracticable to determine either the period-specific effects or the cumulative effect of the error.[239]

When it is impracticable to determine the period-specific effects of an error on comparative information for one or more prior periods presented, the opening balances of assets, liabilities and equity should be restated for the earliest period for which retrospective restatement is practicable (which the standard notes may be the current period).[240]

When it is impracticable to determine the cumulative effect, at the beginning of the current period, of an error on all prior periods, the comparative information should be restated to correct the error prospectively from the earliest date practicable.[241] The standard explains that this will mean disregarding the portion of the cumulative restatement of assets, liabilities and equity arising before that date.[242]

5   DISCLOSURE REQUIREMENTS

5.1   Disclosures relating to accounting policies

5.1.1   Disclosure of accounting policies

A   Summary of significant accounting policies

IAS 1 makes the valid observation that it is important for users to be informed of the measurement basis or bases used in the financial statements (for example, historical cost, current cost, net realisable value, fair value or recoverable amount) because the basis on which the financial statements are prepared significantly affects their analysis.[243]

Accordingly, the standard requires disclosure in a summary of significant accounting policies of:

(a)   the measurement basis (or bases) used in preparing the financial statements; and

(b)   the other accounting policies used that are relevant to an understanding of the financial statements.[244]

When more than one measurement basis is used in the financial statements, for example when particular classes of assets are revalued, it is sufficient to provide an indication of the categories of assets and liabilities to which each measurement basis is applied.[245]

It is clearly necessary to apply judgement when deciding on the level of detail required in a summary of accounting policies. However, the general tone of IAS 1 suggests a quite detailed analysis is necessary. Of particular note, is that the decision as to whether to disclose a policy should not just be a function of the magnitude of the sums involved. The standard states that an accounting policy may be significant because of the nature of the entity's operations even if amounts for current and prior periods are not material. It is also appropriate to disclose each significant accounting policy that is not specifically required by IFRSs, but is selected and applied in accordance with IAS 8 (discussed at 4.3 above).[246]

In deciding whether a particular accounting policy should be disclosed, IAS 1 requires consideration of whether disclosure would assist users in understanding how transactions, other events and conditions are reflected in the reported financial performance and financial position. Disclosure of particular accounting policies is especially useful to users when those policies are selected from alternatives allowed in standards and interpretations. An example is disclosure of whether a venturer recognises its interest in a jointly controlled entity using proportionate consolidation or the equity method (discussed in Chapter 12). Some standards specifically require disclosure of particular accounting policies, including choices made by management between different policies they allow. For example:

- IAS 16 – *Property, Plant and Equipment* – requires disclosure of the measurement bases used for classes of property, plant and equipment (discussed in Chapter 16); and

- IAS 23 – *Borrowing Costs* – requires disclosure of whether borrowing costs are recognised immediately as an expense or capitalised as part of the cost of qualifying assets (for periods beginning before 1 January 2009. For subsequent periods the option of immediate expense recognition has been withdrawn).[247]

Each entity is required to consider the nature of its operations and the policies that the users of its financial statements would expect to be disclosed for that type of entity. For example:

- an entity subject to income taxes would be expected to disclose its accounting policies for income taxes, including those applicable to deferred tax liabilities and assets; and

- when an entity has significant foreign operations or transactions in foreign currencies, disclosure of accounting policies for the recognition of foreign exchange gains and losses would be expected.[248]

B   Judgements made in applying accounting policies

The process of applying an entity's accounting policies requires various judgements, apart from those involving estimations, that can significantly affect the amounts recognised in the financial statements. For example, judgements are required in determining:

(a)   whether financial assets are held-to-maturity investments;

(b)   when substantially all the significant risks and rewards of ownership of financial assets and lease assets are transferred to other entities;

(c)   whether, in substance, particular sales of goods are financing arrangements and therefore do not give rise to revenue; and

(d)   whether the substance of the relationship between the entity and a special purpose entity indicates that the special purpose entity is controlled by the entity.[249]

IAS 1 requires disclosure, in the summary of significant accounting policies or other notes, of the judgements (apart from those involving estimations, see 5.2.1 below) management has made in the process of applying the entity's accounting policies that have the most significant effect on the amounts recognised in the financial statements.[250]

Some of these disclosures are required by other standards. For example:

- IAS 27 requires an entity to disclose the reasons why the entity's ownership interest does not constitute control, in respect of an investee that is not a subsidiary even though more than half of its voting or potential voting power is owned directly or indirectly through subsidiaries; and

- IAS 40 – *Investment Property* – requires disclosure of the criteria developed by the entity to distinguish investment property from owner-occupied property and from property held for sale in the ordinary course of business, when classification of the property is difficult.[251]

5.1.2   Disclosure of changes in accounting policies

IAS 8 distinguishes between accounting policy changes made pursuant to the initial application of an IFRS from voluntary changes in accounting policy (discussed at 4.4 above). It sets out different disclosure requirements for each, as set out in A and B below. Also, if an IFRS is in issue but is not yet effective and has not been applied certain disclosures of its likely impact are required. These are set out in C below.

A   *Accounting policy changes pursuant to the initial application of an IFRS*

When initial application of an IFRS has an effect on the current period or any prior period, would have such an effect except that it is impracticable to determine the amount of the adjustment, or might have an effect on future periods, an entity should disclose:

(a)   the title of the IFRS;

(b)   when applicable, that the change in accounting policy is made in accordance with its transitional provisions;

(c)   the nature of the change in accounting policy;

(d)   when applicable, a description of the transitional provisions;

(e)   when applicable, the transitional provisions that might have an effect on future periods;

(f)   for the current period and each prior period presented, to the extent practicable, the amount of the adjustment:

   (i)   for each financial statement line item affected; and

   (ii)   if IAS 33 – *Earnings per Share* – applies to the entity, for basic and diluted earnings per share;

(g)   the amount of the adjustment relating to periods before those presented, to the extent practicable; and

(h)   if retrospective application required by IAS 8 is impracticable for a particular prior period, or for periods before those presented, the circumstances that led to the existence of that condition and a description of how and from when the change in accounting policy has been applied.

Impracticability of restatement is discussed at 4.7 above. Financial statements of subsequent periods need not repeat these disclosures.[252]

B   Voluntary changes in accounting policy

When a voluntary change in accounting policy has an effect on the current period or any prior period, would have an effect on that period except that it is impracticable to determine the amount of the adjustment, or might have an effect on future periods, an entity should disclose:

(a)   the nature of the change in accounting policy;

(b)   the reasons why applying the new accounting policy provides reliable and more relevant information;

(c)   for the current period and each prior period presented, to the extent practicable, the amount of the adjustment:

    (i)   for each financial statement line item affected; and

    (ii)   if IAS 33 applies to the entity, for basic and diluted earnings per share;

(d)   the amount of the adjustment relating to periods before those presented, to the extent practicable; and

(e)   if retrospective application is impracticable for a particular prior period, or for periods before those presented, the circumstances that led to the existence of that condition and a description of how and from when the change in accounting policy has been applied.

Financial statements of subsequent periods need not repeat these disclosures.[253]

Impracticability of restatement is discussed at 4.7 above. Example 3.8 therein illustrates the above disclosure requirements.

C   Future impact of a new IFRS

When an entity has not applied a new IFRS that has been issued but is not yet effective, it should disclose:

(a)   that fact; and

(b)   known or reasonably estimable information relevant to assessing the possible impact that application of the new IFRS will have on the financial statements in the period of initial application.[254]

In producing the above disclosure, the standard requires that an entity should consider disclosing:

(a)   the title of the new IFRS;

(b)   the nature of the impending change or changes in accounting policy;

(c)   the date by which application of the IFRS is required;

(d)   the date as at which it plans to apply the IFRS initially; and

(e)   either:

(i)   a discussion of the impact that initial application of the IFRS is expected to have on the entity's financial statements; or

(ii) if that impact is not known or reasonably estimable, a statement to that effect.[255]

5.2   Disclosure of estimation uncertainty and changes in estimates

5.2.1 Sources of estimation uncertainty

Determining the carrying amounts of some assets and liabilities requires estimation of the effects of uncertain future events on those assets and liabilities at the balance sheet date. Examples given by IAS 1 are that, in the absence of recently observed market prices used to measure them, the following assets and liabilities require future-oriented estimates to measure them:

- the recoverable amount of classes of property, plant and equipment;
- the effect of technological obsolescence on inventories;
- provisions subject to the future outcome of litigation in progress; and
- long-term employee benefit liabilities such as pension obligations.

These estimates involve assumptions about such items as the risk adjustment to cash flows or discount rates used, future changes in salaries and future changes in prices affecting other costs.[256]

In light of this, IAS 1 requires disclosure of information about the assumptions concerning the future, and other major sources of estimation uncertainty at the balance sheet date, that have a significant risk of resulting in a material adjustment to the carrying amounts of assets and liabilities *within the next financial year*. In respect of those assets and liabilities, the notes must include details of:

(a)   their nature; and

(b)   their carrying amount as at the balance sheet date.[257]

IAS 1 goes on to observe that these assumptions and other sources of estimation uncertainty relate to the estimates that require management's most difficult, subjective or complex judgements. As the number of variables and assumptions affecting the possible future resolution of the uncertainties increases, those judgements become more subjective and complex, and the potential for a consequential material adjustment to the carrying amounts of assets and liabilities normally increases accordingly.[258]

The disclosures are required to be presented in a manner that helps users of financial statements to understand the judgements management makes about the future and about other key sources of estimation uncertainty. The nature and extent of the information provided will vary according to the nature of the assumption and other circumstances. Examples given by the standard of the types of disclosures to be made are:

(a)   the nature of the assumption or other estimation uncertainty;

(b)   the sensitivity of carrying amounts to the methods, assumptions and estimates underlying their calculation, including the reasons for the sensitivity;

(c)   the expected resolution of an uncertainty and the range of reasonably possible outcomes within the next financial year in respect of the carrying amounts of the assets and liabilities affected; and

(d)   an explanation of changes made to past assumptions concerning those assets and liabilities, if the uncertainty remains unresolved.[259]

The disclosure of some of these key assumptions is required by other standards. IAS 1 notes the following examples:

- IAS 37 requires disclosure, in specified circumstances, of major assumptions concerning future events affecting classes of provisions;

- IFRS 7 requires disclosure of significant assumptions used in estimating the fair values of financial assets and financial liabilities that are carried at fair value (formerly required by IAS 32); and

- IAS 16 requires disclosure of significant assumptions used in estimating fair values of revalued items of property, plant and equipment.[260]

Other examples would include:

- IAS 19 requires disclosure of actuarial assumptions;

- IFRS 2 – *Share-based Payment* – requires disclosure, in certain circumstances, of: the option pricing model used, and the method used and the assumptions made to incorporate the effects of early exercise; and

- IAS 36 – *Impairment of Assets* – requires disclosure, in certain circumstances, of each key assumption on which management has based its cash flow projections.

These assumptions and other sources of estimation uncertainty are not required to be disclosed for assets and liabilities with a significant risk that their carrying amounts might change materially within the next financial year if, at the balance sheet date, they are measured at fair value based on recently observed market prices. This is because, whilst their fair values might change materially within the next financial year those changes would not arise from assumptions or other sources of estimation uncertainty at the balance sheet date.[261] Also, it is not necessary to disclose budget information or forecasts in making the disclosures.[262] Furthermore, the disclosures of particular judgements management made in the process of applying the entity's accounting policies (discussed at 5.1.1 B above) do not relate to the disclosures of sources of estimation uncertainty.[263]

When it is impracticable to disclose the extent of the possible effects of a assumption or another source of estimation uncertainty at the balance sheet date, the entity should disclose that it is reasonably possible, based on existing knowledge, that outcomes within the next financial year that are different from assumptions could require a material adjustment to the carrying amount of the asset or liability affected. In all cases, the entity should disclose the nature and carrying amount of the specific asset or liability (or class of assets or liabilities) affected by the assumption.[264]

In our view, these requirements of IAS 1 represent potentially highly onerous disclosures. The extensive judgements required in deciding the level of detail to be given has resulted in a wide variety of disclosure in practice. The Basis for Conclusions to the standard reveals that the Board was aware that the requirement could potentially require quite extensive disclosures and explains its attempt to limit this as follows. 'IAS 1 limits the scope of the disclosures to items that have a significant risk of causing a material adjustment to the carrying amounts of assets and liabilities *within the next financial year*. The longer the future period to which the disclosures relate, the greater the range of items that would qualify for disclosure, and the less specific are the disclosures that could be made about particular assets or liabilities. A period longer than the next financial year might obscure the most relevant information with other disclosures.'[265]

5.2.2   Changes in accounting estimates

IAS 8 requires disclosure of the nature and amount of a change in an accounting estimate that has an effect in the current period or is expected to have an effect in future periods, except for the disclosure of the effect on future periods when it is impracticable to estimate that effect.[266] If the amount of the effect in future periods is not disclosed because estimating it is impracticable, that fact should be disclosed.[267]

5.3   Disclosure of prior period errors

When correction has been made for a material prior period error, IAS 8 requires disclosure of the following:

(a)   the nature of the prior period error;

(b)   for each prior period presented, to the extent practicable, the amount of the correction:

   (i)   for each financial statement line item affected; and

   (ii)   if IAS 33 applies to the entity, for basic and diluted earnings per share;

(c)   the amount of the correction at the beginning of the earliest prior period presented; and

(d)   if retrospective restatement is impracticable for a particular prior period, the circumstances that led to the existence of that condition and a description of how and from when the error has been corrected.

Financial statements of subsequent periods need not repeat these disclosures.[268]

Example 3.9 at 4.6 above illustrates these disclosure requirements.

5.4   Disclosures about capital

5.4.1   General capital disclosures

The IASB believes that the level of an entity's capital and how it manages it are important factors for users to consider in assessing the risk profile of an entity and its ability to withstand unexpected adverse events. Furthermore, the level of capital might also affect the entity's ability to pay dividends.[269] For these reasons, IAS 1 requires disclosure of information that enables users of financial statements to evaluate an entity's objectives, policies and processes for managing capital.[270]

To achieve this, IAS 1 requires disclosure of the following, which should be based on the information provided internally to the entity's key management personnel:[271]

(a) qualitative information about its objectives, policies and processes for managing capital, including:

(i) a description of what it manages as capital;

(ii) when an entity is subject to externally imposed capital requirements, the nature of those requirements and how those requirements are incorporated into the management of capital; and

(iii) how it is meeting its objectives for managing capital;

(b) summary quantitative data about what it manages as capital;

Some entities regard some financial liabilities (e.g. some forms of subordinated debt) as part of capital. Other entities regard capital as excluding some components of equity (e.g. components arising from cash flow hedges);

(c) any changes in (a) and (b) from the previous period;

(d) whether during the period it complied with any externally imposed capital requirements to which it is subject; and

(e) when the entity has not complied with such externally imposed capital requirements, the consequences of such non-compliance.

IAS 1 observes that capital may be managed in a number of ways and be subject to a number of different capital requirements. For example, a conglomerate may include entities that undertake insurance activities and banking activities, and those entities may also operate in several jurisdictions. When an aggregate disclosure of capital requirements and how capital is managed would not provide useful information or distorts a financial statement user's understanding of an entity's capital resources, the standard requires disclosure of separate information for each capital requirement to which the entity is subject.[272]

Examples 3.12 and 3.13 below are based on the illustrative examples of capital disclosures contained in the implementation guidance accompanying IAS 1.

Example 3.11:   Illustrative capital disclosures: An entity that is not a regulated financial institution[273]

The following example illustrates the application of the requirements discussed above for an entity that is not a financial institution and is not subject to an externally imposed capital requirement. In this example, the entity monitors capital using a debt-to-adjusted capital ratio. Other entities may use different methods to monitor capital. The example is also relatively simple. An entity should decide, in the light of its circumstances, how much detail to provide.

Facts

Group A manufactures and sells cars. It includes a finance subsidiary that provides finance to customers, primarily in the form of leases. Group A is not subject to any externally imposed capital requirements.

Example disclosure

The Group's objectives when managing capital are:

- to safeguard the entity's ability to continue as a going concern, so that it can continue to provide returns for shareholders and benefits for other stakeholders; and

- to provide an adequate return to shareholders by pricing products and services commensurately with the level of risk.

The Group sets the amount of capital in proportion to risk. The Group manages the capital structure and makes adjustments to it in the light of changes in economic conditions and the risk characteristics of the underlying assets. In order to maintain or adjust the capital structure, the Group may adjust the amount of dividends paid to shareholders, return capital to shareholders, issue new shares, or sell assets to reduce debt.

Consistently with others in the industry, the Group monitors capital on the basis of the debt-to-adjusted capital ratio. This ratio is calculated as net debt ÷ adjusted capital. Net debt is calculated as total debt (as shown in the statement of financial position) less cash and cash equivalents. Adjusted capital comprises all components of equity (i.e. share capital, share premium, non-controlling interests, retained earnings, and revaluation reserve) other than amounts recognised in equity relating to cash flow hedges, and includes some forms of subordinated debt.

During 2010, the Group's strategy, which was unchanged from 2009, was to maintain the debt-to-adjusted capital ratio at the lower end of the range 6:1 to 7:1, in order to secure access to finance at a reasonable cost by maintaining a BB credit rating. The debt-to-adjusted capital ratios at 31 December 2010 and at 31 December 2009 were as follows:

	2010 €million	2009 €million
Total debt	1,000	1,100
Less: cash and cash equivalents	(90)	(150)
Net debt	910	950
Total equity	110	105
Add: subordinated debt instruments	38	38
Less: amounts recognised in equity relating to cash flow hedges	(10)	(5)
Adjusted capital	138	138
Debt-to-adjusted capital ratio	6.6	6.9

The decrease in the debt-to-adjusted capital ratio during 2010 resulted primarily from the reduction in net debt that occurred on the sale of subsidiary Z. As a result of this reduction in net debt, improved profitability and lower levels of managed receivables, the dividend payment was increased to €2.8 million for 2010 (from €2.5 million for 2009).

Example 3.12:   Illustrative capital disclosures: An entity that has not complied with externally imposed capital requirements[274]

The following example illustrates the application of the requirement to disclose when an entity has not complied with externally imposed capital requirements during the period. Other disclosures would be provided to comply with the other requirements relating to capital.

Facts

Entity A provides financial services to its customers and is subject to capital requirements imposed by Regulator B. During the year ended 31 December 2010, Entity A did not comply with the capital requirements imposed by Regulator B. In its financial statements for the year ended 31 December 2010, Entity A provides the following disclosure relating to its non-compliance.

Example disclosure

Entity A filed its quarterly regulatory capital return for 30 September 2010 on 20 October 2010. At that date, Entity A's regulatory capital was below the capital requirement imposed by Regulator B by $1 million. As a result, Entity A was required to submit a plan to the regulator indicating how it would increase its regulatory capital to the amount required. Entity A submitted a plan that entailed selling part of its unquoted equities portfolio with a carrying amount of $11.5 million in the fourth quarter of 2010. In the fourth quarter of 2010, Entity A sold its fixed interest investment portfolio for $12.6 million and met its regulatory capital requirement.

5.4.2   Puttable financial instruments classified as equity

With effect for periods beginning on or after 1 January 2009, IAS 32 allows certain liabilities called 'puttable financial instruments' to be classified as equity. Puttable financial instrument is a term defined and discussed at length in IAS 32 (see Chapter 31 at 3.2.2). The IASB observes that 'Financial instruments classified as equity usually do not include any obligation for the entity to deliver a financial asset to another party. Therefore, the Board concluded that additional disclosures are needed in these circumstances.'[275]

The required disclosure for puttable financial instruments classified as equity instruments is as follows:

(a)   summary quantitative data about the amount classified as equity;

(b)   its objectives, policies and processes for managing its obligation to repurchase or redeem the instruments when required to do so by the instrument holders, including any changes from the previous period;

(c)   the expected cash outflow on redemption or repurchase of that class of financial instruments; and

(d)   information about how the expected cash outflow on redemption or repurchase was determined.[276]

5.5   Other disclosures

IAS 1 also requires disclosure:

(a)   in the notes of:

(i)   the amount of dividends proposed or declared before the financial statements were authorised for issue but not recognised as a distribution to owners during the period, and the related amount per share; and

(ii)   the amount of any cumulative preference dividends not recognised;[277]

(b)   in accordance with IAS 10 – *Events After the Reporting Period* – the following non-adjusting events in respect of loans classified as current liabilities, if they occur between the balance sheet date and the date the financial statements are authorised for issue (see Chapter 37):

(i)   refinancing on a long-term basis;

(ii)   rectification of a breach of a long-term loan arrangement; and

(iii)   the granting by the lender of a period of grace to rectify a breach of a long-term loan arrangement ending at least twelve months after the balance sheet date;[278]

(c)   the following, if not disclosed elsewhere in information published with the financial statements:

(i)   the domicile and legal form of the entity, its country of incorporation and the address of its registered office (or principal place of business, if different from the registered office);

(ii)   a description of the nature of the entity's operations and its principal activities;

(iii)   the name of the parent and the ultimate parent of the group; and

(iv)   (with effect for periods beginning on or after 1 January 2009) if it is a limited life entity, information regarding the length of its life.[279]

6   FUTURE DEVELOPMENTS

6.1   The IASB's joint project on financial statement presentation

6.1.1   Overview of the project

The IASB is currently pursuing a project which it terms 'financial statement presentation'. Although the project began as a consideration of the presentation of gains and losses, it has evolved to have a much wider scope. The current intention of the IASB is to pursue the project jointly with the FASB. The IASB/FASB Boards' stated objectives in this project are to present information in the individual financial statements (and among the financial statements) in ways that improve the ability of investors, creditors, and other financial statement users to:

(a)   understand an entity's present and past financial position;

(b)   understand the past operating, financing, and other activities that caused an entity's financial position to change and the components of those changes; and

(c)   use that financial statement information (along with information from other sources) to assess the amounts, timing, and uncertainty of an entity's future cash flows.

The project is divided into the following three phases:

• Phase A addressed what constitutes a complete set of financial statements and requirements to present comparative information. The IASB and FASB have completed deliberations on this phase;

• Phase B addresses more fundamental issues for presentation of information on the face of the financial statements; and

• Phase C (which has not yet begun) will address interim financial reporting in US GAAP. The IASB may reconsider the requirements in IAS 34.[280] IAS 34 is discussed in Chapter 40.

Phases A and B are discussed further at 6.1.2 and 6.1.3 below.

6.1.2 *Financial statement presentation project Phase A*

Phase A of the project resulted in the publication in March 2006 of an exposure draft of proposed amendments to IAS 1.[281] In September 2007 the revised standard was published, it applies to annual periods beginning on or after 1 January 2009. Earlier application is permitted but must be disclosed. This Chapter reflects the latest requirements in the revised version. The differences between the current and previous versions are discussed in International GAAP 2009.

6.1.3 *Financial statement presentation project Phase B*

Phase B of the project (the current phase) addresses more fundamental issues. This phase of the project resulted in the publication of a Discussion Paper in October 2008 entitled *Preliminary Views on Financial Statement Presentation*. This is expected to be followed by an exposure draft in 2010 and a final standard in 2011.[282]

The IASB summarises its proposals as follows.

The proposed presentation model requires an entity to present information about the way it creates value (its business activities) separately from information about the way it funds or finances those business activities (its financing activities).

(a) An entity should further separate information about its business activities by presenting information about its operating activities separately from information about its investing activities.

(b) An entity should present information about the financing of its business activities separately depending on the source of that financing. Specifically, information about non-owner sources of finance (and related changes) should be presented separately from owner sources of finance (and related changes).

(c) An entity should present information about its discontinued operations separately from its continuing business and financing activities.

(d) An entity should present information about its income taxes separately from all other information in the statements of financial position and cash flows. In its statement of comprehensive income, an entity should separately present information about its income tax expense (benefit) related to:

(i) income from continuing operations (the total of its income or loss from business and financing activities);

(ii) discontinued operations; and

(iii) other comprehensive income items.[283]

6.2   Statement of changes in equity

As discussed at 3.3 above, the IASB is proposing to amend IAS 1. The proposed amendment is to allow the detailed analysis currently required on the face of the statement of changes in equity to be shown in the notes.

6.3   IFRS for private entities

Shortly after its inception in 2001, the IASB began a project to develop accounting standards suitable for small and medium-sized entities (SMEs). The Board set up a Working Group of experts to provide advice on the issues and alternatives and potential solutions.[284] In June 2004, the Board published a discussion paper called Preliminary Views on Accounting Standards for Small and Medium-sized Entities setting out, and inviting comments on, the Board's approach.[285]

This was followed by an exposure of a proposed IFRS for small and medium-sized entities in February 2007.

A final standard was issued by the IASB on 9 July 2009 entitled International Financial Reporting Standard for Small and Medium-sized Entities (IFRS for SMEs).

7   CONCLUSION

IAS 1 and IAS 8 deal with overlapping issues and together run to nearly 200 detailed paragraphs, along with extensive further material in appendices. In our view their usefulness could be greatly enhanced by combining them in one standard and reducing repetition. Notwithstanding this and the occasional lack of clarity, they provide a workable backbone for IFRS.

References

1 IAS 1, *Presentation of Financial Statements*, IASB.
2 IAS 8, *Accounting Policies, Changes in Accounting Estimates and Errors*, IASB.
3 IFRS 5, *Non-current Assets Held for Sale and Discontinued Operations*, IASB.
4 IAS 1, paras. 2 and 7.
5 IAS 1, para. 7 and IAS 8, para. 5.
6 IAS 8, para. 9.
7 IAS 27, *Consolidated and Separate Financial Statements*, IASB.
8 IAS 34, *Interim Financial Reporting*, IASB.
9 IAS 1, para. 4.
10 IAS 1, paras. 1 and 3.
11 IAS 1, para. 5.
12 IAS 1, para. 6.
13 IAS 8, para. 3.
14 IAS 8, para. 1.
15 IAS 8, para. 2.
16 IAS 8, para. 4.
17 IAS 8, para. 7.
18 IAS 1, para. 9.
19 IAS 1, para. 36.
20 IAS 1, para. 37.
21 IAS 1, para. 11.
22 IAS 1, para. 12.
23 IAS 1, para. 10.
24 IAS 1, para. 7.
25 IAS 1, para. 14.
26 IAS 1, para. 13.
27 IAS 1, para. 14.
28 Project Update: Management Commentary, IASB website, August 2009.
29 Project Update: Management Commentary, IASB website, August 2009.
30 IAS 1, para. 38.
31 IAS 1, para. 39.
32 IAS 1, para. BC 32.
33 IAS 1, para. 38.
34 IAS 1, para. 40.
35 IAS 1, para. 97.
36 IAS 1, para. 43.
37 IAS 1, para. 41.
38 IAS 1, para. 7.
39 IAS 1, para. 430.
40 IAS 1, para. 42.
41 IAS 1, paras. 49-50.

42 IAS 1, para. 51.
43 IAS 1, para. 52.
44 IAS 1, para. 53.
45 IAS 1, para. 16.
46 IAS 1, para. 16.
47 IAS 1, paras. 10 and 11.
48 IAS 1, para. 12.
49 IAS 1, para. 10.
50 IAS 1, para. 48.
51 IAS 1, para. 48.
52 IAS 1, para. 111.
53 IAS 1, para. 60.
54 IAS 1, para. 67.
55 IAS 1, para. 62.
56 IAS 1, paras. 68 and 70.
57 *Improvements to IFRSs*, IASB, May 2008, IAS 16, *Property Plant and Equipment*, IASB, para. 68A.
58 IFRS 5, para. 3.
59 IAS 1, para. 60.
60 IAS 1, paras. 66 and 69.
61 IAS 1, para. 60.
62 IAS 1, para. 63.
63 IAS 1, para. 64.
64 IAS 1, para. 61.
65 IAS 1, para. 65.
66 *Framework for the preparation and presentation of financial statements*, IASB, para 62(e).
67 Near final draft of amendment to IAS 1 – Classification of the liability component of a convertible instrument, IASB, website version July 2007.
68 *Improvements to IFRSs*, April 2009, IAS 1, para. 69.
69 *Improvements to IFRSs*, April 2009, IAS 1, para. 139D.
70 IFRS 5, para. 30.
71 IFRS 5, paras. 38-39.
72 IAS 1, para. 66.
73 IAS 1, para. 56.
74 *Improvements to IFRSs*, May 2008, IAS 1, para. 68.
75 IAS 1, para. 69.
76 IAS 1, para. 56.
77 IAS 1, para. 70.
78 IAS 19, *Employee Benefits*, IASB, paras. 118 and BC81.
79 IAS 1, para. 71 as amended May 2008.
80 IAS 1, paras. 72 and 76.
81 IAS 1, paras. 74 and 76.
82 IAS 1, para. 75.
83 IAS 1, para. 673.
84 IAS 1, para. 57.
85 IAS 1, paras. 54 and 57.
86 IAS 1, para. 55.
87 IAS 1, para. 58.
88 IAS 1, para. 59.
89 IAS 1, para. 54.
90 IAS 1, para. 57.
91 IAS 1, para. 77.
92 IAS 1, para. 78.
93 IAS 1, paras. 58 and 78.
94 IAS 1, para. 78.
95 IAS 1, para. 79.
96 IAS 1, para. 80.
97 Amendments to IAS 32 *Financial Instruments: Presentation and IAS 1 Presentation of Financial Statements Puttable Financial Instruments and Obligations Arising on Liquidation*, IAS 1, para. 80A), IASB, February 2008.
98 IAS 1, para. IG3.
99 IAS 1, para. Implementation Guidance: Part I.
100 IAS 1, para. 7.
101 IAS 1, para. 8.
102 IAS 1, para. 88.
103 IAS 1, para. 7.
104 IAS 1, para. 81.
105 IAS 1, para. 12.
106 IAS 1, para. 10.
107 IAS 1, para. 86.
108 IAS 1, paras. 85 and 86.
109 IAS 1, para. 86.
110 IAS 1, para. 82.
111 IAS 1, para. 83.
112 IAS 1, paras. 99 and 100.
113 IAS 1, para. BC55.
114 IAS 1, para. BC56.
115 IAS 1, para. 101.
116 IAS 1, para. 99.
117 IAS 1, para. 105.
118 IAS 1, para. 100.
119 IAS 7, *Statement of Cash flows*, IASB, Appendix A.
120 IAS 1, para. 105.
121 IAS 1, para. 102.
122 IAS 1, para. IG6.
123 IAS 1, para. 103.
124 IAS 1, para. 104.
125 IAS 1, paras. 81 and 82.
126 IAS 1, para. 7.
127 IAS 1, para. 91.
128 IAS 1, para. 94.
129 IAS 1, para. 83.
130 IAS 1, para. 84 and IAS 33, *Earnings per Share*, IASB, para. 67A.
131 IAS 1, para. IG6.
132 IAS 1, paras. 7, 92, 93 and 95.
133 IAS 1, para. 94.
134 IAS 1, para. IG6.
135 IAS 1, para. 96.
136 IAS 1, para. 90.
137 IAS 1, para. 91.
138 IAS 1, para. IG6.
139 IAS 1, para. 97.

140 IAS 1, para. 98.
141 *Framework for the Preparation and Presentation of Financial Statements*, IASB, para. 72.
142 IAS 8 (revised 1993), *Net Profit or Loss for the period, Fundamental Errors and Changes in Accounting Policies*, IASC, December 1993, paras. 6 and 10-15.
143 IAS 1, para. 87.
144 IAS 1, para. 106.
145 IAS 1, para. 108.
146 IAS 1, para. 109.
147 IAS 1, para. 110.
148 Exposure Draft ED/2009/11, *Improvements to IFRS*, IASB, August 2009.
149 IAS 1, para. IG6.
150 IAS 1, para. 112.
151 IAS 1, para. 113.
152 IAS 1, para. 114.
153 IAS 1, para. 116.
154 IAS 1, para. 115.
155 IAS 1, para. 15.
156 IAS 8, para. 8.
157 IAS 1, para. 17.
158 IAS 1, para. 18.
159 IAS 1, para. 19.
160 IAS 1, para. 24.
161 IAS 1, para. 19.
162 IAS 1, paras. 20-21.
163 IAS 1, para. 22.
164 IAS 1, para. 23.
165 IAS 1, para. 25.
166 IAS 1, para. 26.
167 IAS 1, para. 27.
168 IAS 1, para. 28.
169 *Framework*, para. 22.
170 IAS 1, para. 45.
171 IAS 1, para. 46.
172 IAS 8, para. 15.
173 IAS 8, para. 13.
174 IAS 1, para. 30.
175 IAS 1, para. 29.
176 IAS 1, para. 7 and IAS 8, para. 5.
177 IAS 1, para. 31.
178 IAS 1, para. 7 and IAS 8, para. 6.
179 IAS 1, para. 30.
180 IAS 1, para. 33.
181 IAS 1, para. 32.
182 IAS 1, para. 34.
183 IAS 1, para. 35.
184 *Improvements to IFRSs*, May 2008, IFRS 7, para. IG13.
185 IAS 1, para. 88.
186 *Framework*, para. 70.
187 IAS 1, para. 89.
188 IAS 1, paras. 7 and 89.
189 IAS 8, para. 5.
190 IAS 8, para. 35.
191 IAS 1, para. 118.
192 IAS 8, para. 5.
193 IAS 8, para. 38.
194 IAS 8, para. 48.
195 IAS 8, para. 35.
196 IAS 8, para. 8.
197 IAS 8, para. 7.
198 IAS 8, para. 8.
199 IAS 8, para. 10.
200 *Framework*, paras. 36-37.
201 IAS 8, para. 11.
202 IAS 8, para. 12.
203 IAS 8, para. 14.
204 IAS 8, paras. 5 and 19-20.
205 IAS 8, para. 22.
206 IAS 8, para. 26.
207 IAS 8, para. 23.
208 IAS 8, para. 21.
209 IAS 8, para. 16.
210 IAS 8, paras. 17-18.
211 IAS 8, para. 35.
212 IAS 8, paras. 32-33.
213 IAS 8, para. 34.
214 IAS 8, para. 36.
215 IAS 8, para. 5.
216 IAS 8, paras. 36-38.
217 IAS 8, para. 41.
218 IAS 8, para. 41.
219 IAS 8, para. 48.
220 IAS 8, para. 5.
221 IAS 8, para. 42.
222 IAS 8, para. 46.
223 IAS 8, para. 42.
224 IAS 8, para. 5.
225 IAS 8, Implementation Guidance, Example 1.
226 IAS 8, para. 43.
227 IAS 8, para. 5.
228 IAS 8, para. 50.
229 IAS 8, para. 51.
230 IAS 8, para. 53.
231 IAS 8, para. 52.
232 IAS 8, para. 23.
233 IAS 8, para. 26.
234 IAS 8, para. 24.
235 IAS 8, para. 25.
236 IAS 8, para. 5.
237 IAS 8, para. 27.
238 IAS 8, Implementation Guidance, Example 3.
239 IAS 8, para. 43.
240 IAS 8, para. 44.
241 IAS 8, para. 45.
242 IAS 8, para. 47.
243 IAS 1, para. 118.
244 IAS 1, para. 117.
245 IAS 1, para. 118.
246 IAS 1, para. 121.
247 IAS 1, para. 119.

248 IAS 1, para. 120.
249 IAS 1, para. 123.
250 IAS 1, para. 122.
251 IAS 1, para. 124.
252 IAS 8, para. 28.
253 IAS 8, para. 29.
254 IAS 8, para. 30.
255 IAS 8, para. 31.
256 IAS 1, para. 126.
257 IAS 1, para. 125.
258 IAS 1, para. 127.
259 IAS 1, para. 129.
260 IAS 1, para. 133.
261 IAS 1, para. 128.
262 IAS 1, para. 130.
263 IAS 1, para. 132.
264 IAS 1, para. 131.
265 IAS 1, para. BC84.
266 IAS 8, para. 39.
267 IAS 8, para. 40.
268 IAS 8, para. 49.
269 IAS 1, para BC86.
270 IAS 1, para 134.
271 IAS 1, para 135.
272 IAS 1, para 136.
273 IAS 1, Implementation Guidance, para IG10.
274 IAS 1, Implementation Guidance, para IG11.
275 Amendments to IAS 32 *Financial Instruments: Presentation* and IAS 1 *Presentation of Financial Statements Puttable Financial Instruments and Obligations Arising on Liquidation*, IAS 1, para. BC100B, IASB, February 2008.
276 IAS 1, para 136A.
277 IAS 1, para. 137.
278 IAS 1, para. 76.
279 Amendments to IAS 32 *Financial Instruments: Presentation and IAS 1 Presentation of Financial Statements Puttable Financial Instruments and Obligations Arising on Liquidation*, IAS 1, para. 138 and 139B, IASB, February 2008.
280 *IASB website project summary*, IASB, July 2008.
281 IAS 1 (ED), *Exposure draft of proposes amendments to IAS 1 Presentation of Financial Statements: A Revised Presentation*, IASB, March 2006.
282 *IASB website project summary*, IASB, July 2008.
283 Discussion paper: Preliminary Views on Financial Statement Presentation, IASB, October 2008, Para. S4.
284 Exposure Draft of a proposed IFRS for Small and Medium-sized Entities, IASB, February 2007, para. BC2.
285 Exposure Draft of a proposed IFRS for Small and Medium-sized Entities, IASB, February 2007.

Chapter 4　　Non-current assets held for sale and discontinued operations

1　INTRODUCTION

1.1　Background to IFRS 5

The IASC issued IAS 35 – *Discontinuing Operations* – in June 1998, which was concerned with the presentation and disclosures relating to *discontinuing* operations. It contained no recognition or measurement rules of its own. In March 2004 IAS 35 was replaced by IFRS 5 – *Non-current Assets Held for Sale and Discontinued Operations*.[1]

IFRS 5 was developed as part of the IASB's convergence project and arises from the IASB's consideration of FASB Statement No. 144 – *Accounting for the Impairment or Disposal of Long-Lived Assets* (SFAS 144), which was issued in 2001.[2] SFAS 144 addresses three areas:

(a) the impairment of long-lived assets to be held and used;

(b) the classification, measurement and presentation of long-lived assets held for sale; and

(c) the classification and presentation of discontinued operations.

The IASB concluded that there were extensive differences between IFRSs and US GAAP as regards (a) above, which it did not think capable of resolution in a relatively short time. However, convergence on the other two areas was thought to be worth pursuing within the context of the short-term convergence project.[3] Accordingly, IFRS 5 was published, which achieves substantial convergence with the requirements of SFAS 144 relating to assets held for sale, the timing of the classification of operations as discontinued and the presentation of such operations.[4] However, there are still differences between the two. For example, the definition of a discontinued operation in IFRS 5 is narrower. The IASB used a different definition to the one contained in SFAS 144 on the grounds that the size of the operation which would meet SFAS 144's definition was too small and that this was causing practical problems. Accordingly, the IASB intends to work with the FASB to arrive at a converged definition.[5] The Board's proposals are discussed at 6.1 below.

IFRS 5 was amended in May 2008 as part of the IASB's 2007 annual improvements project – *Improvements to IFRSs*. The revision is discussed at 2.1.3 below.

The standard was amended in November 2008 by IFRIC 17 – *Distribution of Non-cash Assets to Owners* (see 2.1.2 below) and again in April 2009 by the IASB's 2008 improvements project (see 2.2.2 below).

In August 2009 the IASB published a proposed amendment to IFRS 5. The proposal is to clarify that the loss of significant influence or joint control of an investment brings it into the scope of IFRS 5.[6]

1.2   Objective and scope of IFRS 5

The objective of IFRS 5 is to specify the accounting for assets held for sale, and the presentation and disclosure of discontinued operations. In particular, the standard requires that non-current assets (and, in a 'disposal group', liabilities and current assets, discussed at 2.1.1 below) meeting its criteria to be classified as held for sale:

(a)   be measured at the lower of carrying amount and fair value less costs to sell, with depreciation on them ceasing; and

(b)   be presented separately on the face of the balance sheet with the results of discontinued operations presented separately in the income statement.[7]

The classification and presentation requirements apply to all recognised non-current assets and disposal groups, while there are certain exceptions to the measurement provisions of the standard.[8] These issues are discussed further at 2.2 below.

With effect for periods beginning on or after 1 July 2009 the classification, presentation and measurement requirements of IFRS 5 applicable to assets (or disposal groups) classified as held for sale also apply also to those classified as held for distribution to owners acting in their capacity as owners.[9] This is discussed at 2.1.2 below.

1.3   Effective date and transitional provisions

As noted at 3.2 below, IFRS 5 was amended in January 2008 to require disclosure of the amount of income from continuing operations and discontinued operations attributable to owners of the parent. This applies to periods beginning on or after 1 July 2009. If an entity applies IAS 27 – *Consolidated and Separate Financial Statements* (as amended in January 2008) for an earlier period, it must also apply the amendments to IFRS 5.[10]

The IASB's improvements to IFRSs (published in May 2008) clarified the requirements for sale transactions resulting in loss of control of a subsidiary. This is discussed at 2.1.3 below. These improvements to IFRS 5 apply for annual periods beginning on or after 1 July 2009. Earlier application is permitted if it is disclosed. If the amendment is applied early the revisions made to IAS 27 as part of the improvements project in May 2008 (discussed in Chapter 8) must also be applied.

As discussed at 2.2.1 below, IFRIC 17 extended the classification, presentation and measurement provisions of IFRS 5 to items held for distribution to owners. Those amendments apply prospectively to non-current assets (or disposal groups) classified as held for distribution to owners in periods beginning on or after 1 July 2009. Retrospective application is not permitted. Earlier application is permitted. If an entity applies the amendments for a period beginning before 1 July 2009 it should disclose that fact and also apply IFRS 3 (as revised in 2008) – *Business Combinations*, IAS 27 (as amended in May 2008) – *Consolidated and separate financial statements* – and IFRIC 17.[11]

As discussed at 2.2.2 below, in April 2009 *Improvements to IFRSs* changed the disclosure requirements to be applied to items within the scope of IFRS 5. That applies prospectively for annual periods beginning on or after 1 January 2010. Earlier application is allowed if it is disclosed.[12]

2 NON-CURRENT ASSETS (AND DISPOSAL GROUPS) HELD FOR SALE

2.1 Classification of non-current assets (and disposal groups) held for sale or held for distribution to owners

IFRS 5 frequently refers to current assets and non-current assets. It provides a definition of each term as follows:

'An entity shall classify an asset as current when:

(a) it expects to realise the asset, or intends to sell or consume it in its normal operating cycle;

(b) it holds the asset primarily for the purpose of trading;

(c) it expects to realise the asset within twelve months after the reporting period; or

(d) the asset is cash or a cash equivalent (as defined in IAS 7 *Statement of Cash Flows*) unless the asset is restricted from being exchanged or used to settle a liability for at least twelve months after the reporting period.'

A non-current asset is 'an asset that does not meet the definition of a current asset.'[13]

These definitions are the same as those in IAS 1 – *Presentation of Financial Statements* (discussed in Chapter 3 at 3.1.1).

2.1.1 *The concept of a disposal group*

As its title suggests, IFRS 5 addresses the accounting treatment of non-current assets held for sale, that is assets whose carrying amount will be recovered principally through sale rather than continuing use in the business.[14] However, the standard also applies to certain liabilities and current assets where they form part of a 'disposal group'.

The standard observes that sometimes an entity will dispose of a group of assets, possibly with some directly associated liabilities, together in a single transaction.[15] A common example would be the disposal of a subsidiary. For these circumstances, IFRS 5 introduces the concept of a disposal group, which it defines as 'a group of assets to be disposed of, by sale or otherwise, together as a group in a single transaction, and liabilities directly associated with those assets that will be transferred in the transaction. The group includes goodwill acquired in a business combination if the group is a cash-generating unit to which goodwill has been allocated in accordance with the requirements of paragraphs 80-87 of IAS 36 – *Impairment of Assets* (as revised in 2004) or if it is an operation within such a cash-generating unit.'[16]

The use of the phrase 'together in a single transaction' indicates that the only liabilities that can be included in the group are those assumed by the purchaser. Accordingly, any borrowings of the entity which are to be repaid out of the sales proceeds would be excluded from the disposal group.

The standard goes on to explain that a disposal group:

- may be a group of cash-generating units, a single cash-generating unit, or part of a cash-generating unit. However, once the cash flows from an asset or group of assets are expected to arise principally from sale rather than continuing use, they become less dependent on cash flows arising from other assets, and a disposal group that was part of a cash-generating unit becomes a separate cash-generating unit; and

- may include any assets and any liabilities of the entity, including current assets, current liabilities and assets outside the scope of the measurement requirements of IFRS 5 (see 2.2 below).[17]

Discontinued operations are discussed at 3 below. As noted there, it seems highly unlikely that the definition of a discontinued operation would ever be met by a single non-current asset. Accordingly, a discontinued operation will also be a disposal group.

2.1.2 Classification as held for sale or as held for distribution to owners

IFRS 5 requires a non-current asset (or disposal group) to be classified as held for sale if its carrying amount will be recovered principally through a sale transaction rather than through continuing use.[18] For these purposes, sale transactions include exchanges of non-current assets for other non-current assets when the exchange has commercial substance in accordance with IAS 16 – *Property, Plant and Equipment* (discussed in Chapter 16).[19] For assets classified according to a liquidity presentation (see Chapter 3 at 3.1.1), non-current assets are taken to be assets that include amounts expected to be recovered more than twelve months after the balance sheet date.[20]

Determining whether (and when) an asset stops being recovered principally through use and becomes recoverable principally through sale is clearly the critical distinction, and much of the standard is devoted to explaining how to make the determination.

For an asset (or disposal group) to be classified as held for sale:

(a)   it must be available for immediate sale in its present condition, subject only to terms that are usual and customary for sales of such assets (or disposal groups);

(b)   its sale must be highly probable;[21] and

(c)   it must genuinely be sold, not abandoned.[22]

These criteria are discussed further below. If an asset (or disposal group) has been classified as held for sale, but these criteria cease to be met, an entity should cease to classify the asset (or disposal group) as held for sale.[23] Changes in plan are discussed at 2.2.5 below.

Slightly different criteria apply when an entity acquires a non-current asset (or disposal group) exclusively with a view to its subsequent disposal. In that case it should only classify the non-current asset (or disposal group) as held for sale at the acquisition date if:

• the 'one-year requirement' is met subject to its one exception (this is part of being 'highly probable', discussed at B below); and

• it is highly probable that any other criteria in (a) and (b) above that are not met at that date will be met within a short period following the acquisition (usually within three months).[24]

The standard also makes it clear that the criteria in (a) and (b) above must be met at the balance sheet date for a non-current asset (or disposal group) to be classified as held for sale in those financial statements when issued. However, if those criteria are met after the balance sheet date but before the authorisation of the financial statements for issue, the standard requires certain additional disclosures (discussed at 5 below).[25]

With effect for periods beginning on or after 1 July 2009 the classification, presentation and measurement requirements of IFRS 5 applicable to assets (or disposal groups) classified as held for sale also apply also to those classified as held for distribution to owners acting in their capacity as owners.[26] This applies when an entity is committed to distribute the asset (or disposal group) to its owners. For this to be the case, the assets must be available for immediate distribution in their present condition and the distribution must be highly probable.

For the distribution to be highly probable, actions to complete the distribution must have been initiated and should be expected to be completed within one year from the date of classification. Actions required to complete the distribution should indicate that it is unlikely that significant changes to the distribution will be made or that the distribution will not be completed. The probability of shareholders' approval (if this is required) should be considered as part of the assessment of whether the distribution is highly probable.[27]

A   *Meaning of available for immediate sale*

To qualify for classification as held for sale, a non-current asset (or disposal group) must be available for immediate sale in its present condition subject only to terms that are usual and customary for sales of such assets (or disposal groups). This is taken to mean that an entity currently has the intention and ability to transfer the asset (or disposal group) to a buyer in its present condition. The standard illustrates this concept with the following examples.

Example 4.1:   Non-current assets and disposal groups available for immediate sale[28]

1   Disposal of a headquarters building

An entity is committed to a plan to sell its headquarters building and has initiated actions to locate a buyer.

(a)   The entity intends to transfer the building to a buyer after it vacates the building. The time necessary to vacate the building is usual and customary for sales of such assets. The criterion of being available for immediate sale would therefore be met at the plan commitment date.

(b)   The entity will continue to use the building until construction of a new headquarters building is completed. The entity does not intend to transfer the existing building to a buyer until after construction of the new building is completed (and it vacates the existing building). The delay in the timing of the transfer of the existing building imposed by the entity (seller) demonstrates that the building is not available for immediate sale. The criterion would not be met until construction of the new building is completed, even if a firm purchase commitment for the future transfer of the existing building is obtained earlier.

2   Sale of a manufacturing facility

An entity is committed to a plan to sell a manufacturing facility and has initiated actions to locate a buyer. At the plan commitment date, there is a backlog of uncompleted customer orders.

(a)   The entity intends to sell the manufacturing facility with its operations. Any uncompleted customer orders at the sale date will be transferred to the buyer. The transfer of uncompleted customer orders at the sale date will not affect the timing of the transfer of the facility. The criterion of being available for immediate sale would therefore be met at the plan commitment date.

(b)   The entity intends to sell the manufacturing facility, but without its operations. The entity does not intend to transfer the facility to a buyer until after it ceases all operations of the facility and eliminates the backlog of uncompleted customer orders. The delay in the timing of the transfer of the facility imposed by the entity (seller) demonstrates that the facility is not available for immediate sale. The criterion would not be met until the operations of the facility cease, even if a firm purchase commitment for the future transfer of the facility were obtained earlier.

3   Land and buildings acquired through foreclosure

An entity acquires through foreclosure a property comprising land and buildings that it intends to sell.

(a)   The entity does not intend to transfer the property to a buyer until after it completes renovations to increase the property's sales value. The delay in the timing of the transfer of the property imposed by the entity (seller) demonstrates that the property is not available for immediate sale. The criterion of being available for immediate sale would therefore not be met until the renovations are completed.

(b)   After the renovations are completed and the property is classified as held for sale but before a firm purchase commitment is obtained, the entity becomes aware of environmental damage requiring remediation. The entity still intends to sell the property. However, the entity does not have the ability to transfer the property to a buyer until after the remediation is completed. The delay in the timing of the transfer of the property imposed by others *before* a firm purchase commitment is obtained demonstrates that the property is not available for immediate sale (different requirements could apply if this happened *after* a firm commitment is obtained, as illustrated in scenario (b) of Example 4.2 below). The criterion would not continue to be met. The property would be reclassified as held and used in accordance with the requirements discussed at 2.2.5 below.

B   Meaning of highly probable

Many observers may consider the meaning of 'highly probable' to be reasonably self-evident, albeit highly judgemental. However, IFRS 5 provides extensive discussion of the topic. As a first step, the term is defined by the standard as meaning 'significantly more likely than probable'. This is supplemented by a second definition – probable is defined as 'more likely than not'.[29] Substituting the latter into the former leads to a definition of highly probable as meaning 'significantly more likely than more likely than not'. This is reassuringly close to (but, a little surprisingly, not the same as) the meaning given to the term in IAS 39 – *Financial Instruments: Recognition and Measurement* – which observes that 'the term "highly probable" indicates a much greater likelihood of happening than the term "more likely than not".[30]

In the particular context of classification as held for sale, the IASB evidently did not consider that 'significantly more likely than more likely than not' was an adequate definition of the phrase, so the standard goes on to elaborate as follows.

For the sale to be highly probable:

*   the appropriate level of management must be committed to a plan to sell the asset (or disposal group);

*   an active programme to locate a buyer and complete the plan must have been initiated;

*   the asset (or disposal group) must be actively marketed for sale at a price that is reasonable in relation to its current fair value;

*   the sale should be expected to qualify for recognition as a completed sale within one year from the date of classification (although in certain circumstances this period may be extended as discussed below); and

*   actions required to complete the plan should indicate that it is unlikely that significant changes to the plan will be made or that the plan will be withdrawn.[31]

As noted above, with effect for periods beginning on or after 1 July 2009 the classification, presentation and measurement requirements of IFRS 5 applicable to assets (or disposal groups) classified as held for sale also apply also to those classified as held for distribution to owners acting in their capacity as owners.[32] This classification is subject to certain conditions, including that the distribution must be highly probable.

For the distribution to be highly probable, actions to complete the distribution must have been initiated and should be expected to be completed within one year from the date of classification. Actions required to complete the distribution should indicate that it is unlikely that significant changes to the distribution will be made or that the distribution will not be completed. The probability of shareholders' approval (if this is required) should be considered as part of the assessment of whether the distribution is highly probable.[33]

The basic rule above that for qualification as held for sale the sale should be expected to qualify for recognition as a completed sale within one year from the date of classification (the 'one year rule') is applied quite strictly by the standard. In particular, that criterion would not be met if:

(a)   an entity that is a commercial leasing and finance company is holding for sale or lease equipment that has recently ceased to be leased and the ultimate form of a future transaction (sale or lease) has not yet been determined;

(b)   an entity is committed to a plan to 'sell' a property that is in use, and the transfer of the property will be accounted for as a sale and finance leaseback.[34]

In (a), the entity does not yet know whether the asset will be sold at all and hence may not presume that it will be sold within a year. In (b), whilst in legal form the asset has been sold it will not be *recognised* as sold in the financial statements.

As indicated above, the standard contains an exception to the one year rule. It states that events or circumstances may extend the period to complete the sale beyond one year. Such an extension would not preclude an asset (or disposal group) from being classified as held for sale if the delay is caused by events or circumstances beyond the entity's control and there is sufficient evidence that the entity remains committed to its plan to sell the asset (or disposal group). This will be the case in the following situations:[35]

(a)   at the date an entity commits itself to a plan to sell a non-current asset (or disposal group) it reasonably expects that others (not a buyer) will impose conditions on the transfer of the asset (or disposal group) that will extend the period required to complete the sale; and:

   (i)   actions necessary to respond to those conditions cannot be initiated until after a firm purchase commitment is obtained; and

   (ii)   a firm purchase commitment is highly probable within one year;

(b)   an entity obtains a firm purchase commitment and, as a result, a buyer or others unexpectedly impose conditions on the transfer of a non-current asset (or disposal group) previously classified as held for sale that will extend the period required to complete the sale; and:

   (i)   timely actions necessary to respond to the conditions have been taken; and

   (ii)   a favourable resolution of the delaying factors is expected;

(c)   during the initial one year period, circumstances arise that were previously considered unlikely and, as a result, a non-current asset (or disposal group) previously classified as held for sale is not sold by the end of that period; and

   (i)   during the initial one year period the entity took action necessary to respond to the change in circumstances;

   (ii)   the non-current asset (or disposal group) is being actively marketed at a price that is reasonable, given the change in circumstances; and

(iii)   the non-current asset (or disposal group) remains available for immediate sale and the sale is highly probable.[36]

Firm purchase commitment is a defined term in IFRS 5, meaning an agreement with an unrelated party, binding on both parties and usually legally enforceable, that:

• specifies all significant terms, including the price and timing of the transactions; and

• includes a disincentive for non-performance that is sufficiently large to make performance highly probable.[37]

The word 'binding' in this definition seems to envisage an agreement still being subject to contingencies. The standard provides an example where a 'firm purchase commitment' exists but is subject to regulatory approval (see scenario (a) in Example 4.2 below). In our view, to be 'binding' in this sense a contingent agreement should be only subject to contingencies outside the control of both parties.

The standard illustrates each of these exceptions to the one year rule with the following examples.

Example 4.2:   *Exceptions to the 'one year rule'*

Scenario illustrating (a) above[38]

An entity in the power generating industry is committed to a plan to sell a disposal group that represents a significant portion of its regulated operations. The sale requires regulatory approval, which could extend the period required to complete the sale beyond one year. Actions necessary to obtain that approval cannot be initiated until after a buyer is known and a firm purchase commitment is obtained. However, a firm purchase commitment is highly probable within one year. In that situation, the conditions for an exception to the one year requirement would be met.

Scenario illustrating (b) above[39]

An entity is committed to a plan to sell a manufacturing facility in its present condition and classifies the facility as held for sale at that date. After a firm purchase commitment is obtained, the buyer's inspection of the property identifies environmental damage not previously known to exist. The entity is required by the buyer to make good the damage, which will extend the period required to complete the sale beyond one year. However, the entity has initiated actions to make good the damage, and satisfactory rectification of the damage is highly probable. In that situation, the conditions for an exception to the one year requirement would be met.

Scenario illustrating (c) above[40]

An entity is committed to a plan to sell a non-current asset and classifies the asset as held for sale at that date.

(a)   During the initial one year period, the market conditions that existed at the date the asset was classified initially as held for sale deteriorate and, as a result, the asset is not sold by the end of that period. During that period, the entity actively solicited but did not receive any reasonable offers to purchase the asset and, in response, reduced the price. The asset continues to be actively marketed at a price that is reasonable given the change in market conditions, and the criteria regarding availability for immediate sale which is highly probable are therefore met. In that situation, the conditions for an exception to the one year requirement would be met. At the end of the initial one year period, the asset would continue to be classified as held for sale.

(b)   During the following one year period, market conditions deteriorate further, and the asset is not sold by the end of that period. The entity believes that the market conditions will improve and has not further reduced the price of the asset. The asset continues to be held for sale, but at a price in excess of its current fair value. In that situation, the absence of a price reduction demonstrates that the asset is not available for immediate sale. In addition, to meet the condition that a sale be highly probable also requires an asset to be marketed at a price that is reasonable in relation to its current fair value. Therefore, the conditions for an exception to the one year requirement would not be met. The asset would be reclassified as held and used in accordance with the requirements discussed at 2.2.5 below.

C   *Abandonment*

IFRS 5 stipulates that a non-current asset (or disposal group) that is to be abandoned should not be classified as held for sale. This includes non-current assets (or disposal groups) that are to be used to the end of their economic life and non-current assets (or disposal groups) that are to be closed rather than sold. The standard explains that this is because its carrying amount will be recovered principally through continuing use.[41]

If the disposal group to be abandoned meets the criteria for being a discontinued operation the standard requires it to be treated as such in the income statement and relevant notes.[42] This is discussed at 3.1 below. However, a non-current asset that has been temporarily taken out of use should not be accounted for as if it had been abandoned.[43] An example given by the standard is of a manufacturing plant that ceases to be used because demand for its product has declined but which is maintained in workable condition and is expected to be brought back into use if demand picks up. The plant is not regarded as abandoned.[44] However, in these circumstances an impairment loss may need to be recognised in accordance with IAS 36 (discussed in Chapter 18).

2.1.3   *Partial disposals of operations*

The IASB amended IFRS 5 as part of the 2007 annual improvements project, published in May 2008. With effect for periods beginning on or after 1 July 2009, the revised standard provides that when an entity is committed to a sale plan involving loss of control of a subsidiary it should classify all the assets and liabilities of that subsidiary as held for sale when the relevant criteria are met (see 2.1 above), regardless of whether it will retain a non-controlling interest in the former subsidiary after the sale.[45] If the subsidiary in question meets the definition of a discontinued operation, the standard's presentation and disclosure requirements for discontinued operations apply (see 3.2 below).[46]

Before its amendment in May 2008, IFRS 5 provided no guidance relating to a partial disposal of an operation for determining whether the definition of held for sale is met. The key here is exactly what is meant by the phrase 'carrying amount will be recovered principally through a sale transaction rather than through continuing use.' An entity could sell some, but not all, of its interest in an operation such that the balance retained is:

(a)   still a subsidiary;

(b)   an available for sale investment accounted for under IAS 39;

(c) an associate or jointly controlled entity accounted for using the equity method; or

(d) a joint venture accounted for by proportionate consolidation.

The question arises as to whether, other things aside, it is appropriate to consider the operation's assets and liabilities to be held for sale.

The two extremes (a) and (b) above are not contentious. If the operation remains a subsidiary (and the assets and liabilities of it therefore remain fully consolidated) it is hard to argue that the assets and liabilities are recovered principally though sale. If the stake retained is a simple minority investment (subsequently carried at fair value as an available for sale investment) it is equally clear that the assets and liabilities concerned have indeed been recovered principally through sale. The doubt lies in the middle of these extremes where the selling entity's share of the assets and liabilities are still reflected in its balance sheet, either as one line or through proportionate consolidation. In particular, if the original stake in a subsidiary is less than 100% the proportion of that stake disposed of may be less than 50% – arguably the natural meaning of 'principally' in the phrase 'recovered principally through a sale transaction'.

There seems to be no obvious conclusion to deal satisfactorily with the various issues discussed above. In light of this and the lack of clarity in the standard we expect that for periods beginning before 1 July 2009 a variety of approaches are acceptable, based on the individual facts and circumstances and on the judgement of the entity concerned.

For periods beginning on or after 1 July 2009, the amendment to IAS 27 makes it clear that any investment retained in a former subsidiary should be recognised at fair value.[47]

2.2 Measurement of non-current assets (and disposal groups) held for sale

2.2.1 Scope of the measurement requirements

IFRS 5's classification and presentation requirements apply to all recognised non-current assets (which is defined in the same way as in IAS 1, discussed at 2.1 above) and disposal groups. However, the measurement provisions of the standard do not apply to the following assets (which remain covered by the standards listed) either as individual assets or as part of a disposal group:[48]

(a) deferred tax assets (dealt with in IAS 12 – *Income Taxes*);

(b) assets arising from employee benefits (dealt with in IAS 19 – *Employee Benefits*);

(c) financial assets within the scope of IAS 39;

(d) non-current assets that are accounted for in accordance with the fair value model in IAS 40 – *Investment Property*;

(e) non-current assets that are measured at fair value less costs to sell in accordance with IAS 41 – *Agriculture*; and

(f) contractual rights under insurance contracts as defined in IFRS 4 – *Insurance Contracts*.

2.2.2   Measurement of non-current assets and disposal groups held for sale

A   Measurement on initial classification as held for sale

IFRS 5 requires that immediately before the initial classification of an asset (or disposal group) as held for sale, the carrying amount of the asset (or all the assets and liabilities in the group) should be measured in accordance with applicable IFRSs.[49] In other words, an entity should apply its usual accounting policies up until the criteria for classification as held for sale are met.

Thereafter a non-current asset (or disposal group) classified as held for sale should be measured at the lower of its carrying amount and fair value less costs to sell.[50] Fair value is defined as 'the amount for which an asset could be exchanged, or a liability settled, between knowledgeable, willing parties in an arm's length transaction.' Costs to sell are defined as 'the incremental costs directly attributable to the disposal of an asset (or disposal group), excluding finance costs and income tax expense.'[51] When the sale is expected to occur beyond one year, the costs to sell should be measured at their present value. Any increase in the present value of the costs to sell that arises from the passage of time should be presented in profit or loss as a financing cost.[52] For disposal groups, the standard adopts a portfolio approach. It requires that if a non-current asset within the scope of its measurement requirements is part of a disposal group, the measurement requirements should apply to the group as a whole, so that the group is measured at the lower of its carrying amount and fair value less costs to sell.[53] It will still be necessary to apportion any write down to the underlying assets of the disposal group, but no element is apportioned to items outside the scope of the standard's measurement provisions. This is discussed further at 2.2.3 below.

Items held for distribution to owners should be measured at the lower of carrying amount and fair value less costs to distribute. Costs to distribute are incremental costs directly attributable to the distribution, excluding finance costs and income tax expense.[54]

If a newly acquired asset (or disposal group) meets the criteria to be classified as held for sale (which, as discussed at 2.1.2 above are subtly different for assets acquired exclusively with a view to subsequent disposal), applying the above requirements will result in the asset (or disposal group) being measured on initial recognition at the lower of its carrying amount had it not been so classified (for example, cost) and fair value less costs to sell. This means that, if the asset (or disposal group) is acquired as part of a business combination, it will be measured at fair value less costs to sell.[55]

The implementation guidance accompanying the standard provides the following illustration of a subsidiary acquired with a view to sale.

Example 4.3:   Measuring and presenting subsidiaries acquired with a view to sale and classified as held for sale[56]

Entity A acquires an entity H, which is a holding company with two subsidiaries, S1 and S2. S2 is acquired exclusively with a view to sale and meets the criteria to be classified as held for sale. Accordingly, S2 is also a discontinued operation (see 3.1 below).

The estimated fair value less costs to sell of S2 is €135. A accounts for S2 as follows:

- initially, A measures the identifiable liabilities of S2 at fair value, say at €40;

- initially, A measures the acquired assets as the fair value less costs to sell of S2 (€135) plus the fair value of the identifiable liabilities (€40), i.e. at €175;

- at the balance sheet date, A remeasures the disposal group at the lower of its cost and fair value less costs to sell, say at €130. The liabilities are remeasured in accordance with applicable IFRSs, say at €35. The total assets are measured at €130 + €35, i.e. at €165;

- at the balance sheet date, A presents the assets and liabilities separately from other assets and liabilities in its consolidated financial statements as illustrated in Example 4.5 at 2.2.4 below; and

- in the income statement, A presents the total of the post-tax profit or loss of S2 and the post-tax gain or loss recognised on the subsequent remeasurement of S2, which equals the remeasurement of the disposal group from €135 to €130.

Further analysis of the assets and liabilities or of the change in value of the disposal group is not required.

The final sentence in the IASB's above example is somewhat misleading. It is true to say that IFRS 5 requires no further disclosures that would involve further analysis. However, for periods beginning before 1 January 2010 there are other accounting standards where the disclosure requirements have not been 'switched-off' and accordingly still apply. For example, disclosures for the whole entity would still appear to be required in respect of financial instruments, income tax and pensions. It is fair to say that some confusion exists in practice in this area. In particular, some IFRS reporters consider that the various disclosures required by other standards should reflect only the continuing operations of the group. In response to this, the IASB amended IFRS 5 to make clear that disclosures in other IFRSs do not apply to non-current assets (or disposal groups) classified as held for sale or discontinued operations unless those IFRSs require:

- specific disclosures in respect of non-current assets (or disposal groups) classified as held for sale or discontinued operations; or

- disclosures about the measurement of assets and liabilities within a disposal group that are not within the scope of the measurement requirement of IFRS 5 and such disclosures are not already provided in the other notes to the financial statements.

The standard goes on to say that additional disclosures about non-current assets (or disposal groups) classified as held for sale or discontinued operations may be necessary to comply with the general requirements of IAS 1, in particular paragraphs 15 and 125 of that Standard.[57] Those provisions deal with fair presentation and estimation uncertainty and are discussed in Chapter 3 at 4.1.1 and 5.2.1.

Furthermore, a detailed purchase price analysis and tracking of the acquired entity is still needed, notwithstanding a partial relaxation of what is required to be disclosed by IFRS 5. This is needed not just for the disclosures in other standards but also to be able to determine the split between gross assets and liabilities and how movements in the carrying amounts are reflected in profit or loss, or other comprehensive income.

B　Subsequent remeasurement

While a non-current asset is classified as held for sale or while it is part of a disposal group classified as held for sale it should not be depreciated or amortised. Interest and other expenses attributable to the liabilities of a disposal group classified as held for sale should continue to be recognised.[58]

On subsequent remeasurement of a disposal group, the standard requires that the carrying amounts of any assets and liabilities that are not within the scope of its measurement requirements, be remeasured in accordance with applicable IFRSs before the fair value less costs to sell of the disposal group is remeasured.[59]

2.2.3　Impairments and reversals of impairment

The requirement to measure a non-current asset or disposal group held for sale at the lower of carrying amount less costs to sell may give rise to a write down in value (impairment loss) and possibly its subsequent reversal. As noted above, the first step is to account for any items outwith the scope of the standard's measurement rules in the normal way. After that, any excess of carrying value over fair value less costs to sell should be recognised as an impairment.[60]

Any subsequent increase in fair value less costs to sell of an asset up to the cumulative impairment loss previously recognised either in accordance with IFRS 5 or in accordance with IAS 36 should be recognised as a gain.[61] In the case of a disposal group, any subsequent increase in fair value less costs to sell should be recognised:

(a)　to the extent that it has not been recognised under another standard in relation to those assets outside the scope of IFRS 5's measurement requirements; but

(b)　not in excess of the cumulative amount of losses previously recognised under IFRS 5 or before that under IAS 36 in respect of the non-current assets in the group which are within the scope of the measurement rules of IFRS 5.[62]

Any impairment loss (or any subsequent gain) recognised for a disposal group should be allocated to the non-current assets in the group that are within the scope of the measurement requirements of IFRS 5. The order of allocation should be:

- first, to reduce the carrying amount of any goodwill in the group; and
- then, to the other non-current assets of the group pro rata on the basis of the carrying amount of each asset in the group.[63]

This is illustrated by the standard with the following example.

Example 4.4:   *Allocation of impairment loss to the components of a disposal group*[64]

An entity plans to dispose of a group of its assets (as an asset sale). The assets form a disposal group, and are measured as follows:

	Carrying amount at the reporting date before classification as held for sale €	Carrying amount as remeasured immediately before classification as held for sale €
Goodwill	1,500	1,500
Property, plant and equipment (carried at revalued amounts)	4,600	4,000
Property, plant and equipment (carried at cost)	5,700	5,700
Inventory	2,400	2,200
Available for sale financial assets	1,800	1,500
Total	16,000	14,900

The entity recognises the loss of €1,100 (€16,000 – €14,900) immediately before classifying the disposal group as held for sale. The entity estimates that fair value less costs to sell of the disposal group amounts to €13,000. Because an entity measures a disposal group classified as held for sale at the lower of its carrying amount and fair value less costs to sell, the entity recognises an impairment loss of €1,900 (€14,900 – €13,000) when the group is initially classified as held for sale. The impairment loss is allocated to non-current assets to which the measurement requirements of the IFRS are applicable. Therefore, no impairment loss is allocated to inventory and AFS financial assets. The loss is allocated to the other assets in the order of allocation described above.

The allocation can be illustrated as follows:

First, the impairment loss reduces any amount of goodwill. Then, the residual loss is allocated to other assets pro rata based on the carrying amounts of those assets.

	Carrying amount as remeasured immediately before classification as held for sale €	Allocated impairment loss €	Carrying amount after allocation of impairment loss €
Goodwill	1,500	(1,500)	–
Property, plant and equipment (carried at revalued amounts)	4,000	(165)	3,835
Property, plant and equipment (carried at cost)	5,700	(235)	5,465
Inventory	2,200	–	2,200
AFS financial assets	1,500	–	1,500
Total	14,900	(1,900)	13,000

In the first table of this example, it is not particularly clear what the meaning and purpose of the left hand column is. The fact that some of the figures are different in each column, seems to indicate that the column header 'Carrying amount at the reporting date before classification as held for sale' is referring to the opening balance sheet at the beginning of the period in which the classification is made. As noted at 2.2.2 A above, an entity is required to remeasure the assets as normal under the relevant standards immediately before classifying them as held for sale. This would mean the difference of €1,100 reflects routine accounting entries (such as depreciation and revaluation) from the start of the period to the date of classification as held to sale. Also worthy of note is that the example does not say where the entity recognises the loss of €1,100. Given that the disposal group contains available for sale financial assets, some of this amount would probably be recorded in other comprehensive income rather than in profit or loss. Similarly, movements in property plant and equipment held at revalued amounts may fall to be recorded directly in other comprehensive income.

The standard contains a reminder that requirements relating to derecognition are set out in IAS 16 for property, plant and equipment (discussed in Chapter 16), and IAS 38 – *Intangible Assets* – for intangible assets (discussed in Chapter 15) and notes that a gain or loss not previously recognised by the date of the sale of a non-current asset (or disposal group) should be recognised at the date of derecognition.[65]

One thing which the example above fails to illustrate is a logical flaw in the standard's measurement requirements. It is quite possible that the required impairment exceeds the carrying value of the non-current assets within the scope of the standard's measurement rules. IFRS 5 is silent on what to do in such circumstances. Possible approaches would be:

(a)   to apply the impairment to current assets;

(b)   to apply the impairment to non-current assets outside the scope of the standard's measurement rules; or

(c)   to recognise a separate provision.

For the present, entities will need to apply judgement based on individual circumstances. This issue was brought to the attention of IFRIC which referred it to the IASB. The IASB intends to address the issue through a future amendment to IFRS 5. The Board decided tentatively to consider amending IFRS 5 as a matter of priority and to work with the FASB to ensure IFRS 5 remains aligned with US GAAP.[66]

2.2.4   *Balance sheet presentation of non-current assets and disposal groups held for sale*

The general requirement, discussed in Chapter 3 at 3.1.1, to classify balance sheet items as current or non-current (or present them broadly in order of liquidity) is overlaid with further requirements by IFRS 5 regarding non-current assets held for sale and disposal groups. IFRS 5's aim is that entities should present and disclose information that enables users of the financial statements to evaluate the financial effects of disposals of non-current assets (or disposal groups).[67] In pursuit of this aim, IFRS 5 requires:

•   non-current assets classified as held for sale and the assets of a disposal group classified as held for sale to be presented separately from other assets in the balance sheet; and

•   the liabilities of a disposal group classified as held for sale to be presented separately from other liabilities in the balance sheet.

These assets and liabilities should not be offset and presented as a single amount. In addition:

(a)   major classes of assets and liabilities classified as held for sale should generally be separately disclosed either on the face of the balance sheet or in the notes. However, this is not necessary for a disposal group if it is a subsidiary that met the criteria to be classified as held for sale on acquisition; and

(b)   any cumulative income or expense recognised directly in other comprehensive income relating to a non-current asset (or disposal group) classified as held for sale should be presented separately.[68]

The requirement in (b) was included in response to comments made to the IASB during the development of the standard. The Board describes the development as follows. 'Respondents to ED 4 noted that the separate presentation within equity of amounts relating to assets and disposal groups classified as held for sale (such as, for example, unrealised gains and losses on available-for-sale assets and foreign currency translation adjustments) would also provide useful information. The Board agreed and has added such a requirement to the IFRS.'[69] On that basis, it might be considered that any non-controlling (or minority) interest within equity relating to non-current assets (or disposal groups) held for sale should also be presented separately as it would seem to represent equally useful information about amounts within equity. However, such disclosure of non-controlling (or minority) interests is not specifically required by the standard so would remain voluntary. As noted at 3.2 below, the IASB introduced (for periods beginning on or after 1 July 2009) a requirement to analyse the income for the period attributable to owners between continuing and discontinued operations.

IFRS 5 is silent as to whether the information specified in (b) above should be on the face of the balance sheet or in a note. However, the implementation guidance to IFRS 5 shows a caption called 'Amounts recognised in other comprehensive income and accumulated in equity in relation to non-current assets held for sale' and illustrates the requirements as follows.

Example 4.5:   *Presenting non-current assets or disposal groups classified as held for sale*[70]

At the end of 2010, an entity decides to dispose of part of its assets (and directly associated liabilities). The disposal, which meets the criteria to be classified as held for sale, takes the form of two disposal groups, as follows:

	Carrying amount after classification as held for sale	
	Disposal group I €	Disposal group II €
Property, plant and equipment	4,900	1,700
AFS financial asset	*1,400	–
Liabilities	(2,400)	(900)
Net carrying amount of disposal group	3,900	800

*   An amount of €400 relating to these assets has been recognised in other comprehensive income and accumulated in equity.

The presentation in the entity's balance sheet of the disposal groups classified as held for sale can be shown as follows:

	2010 €	2009 €
ASSETS		
Non-current assets		
AAA	×	×
BBB	×	×
CCC	×	×
	×	×
Current assets		
DDD	×	×
EEE	×	×
	×	×
Non-current assets classified as held for sale	8,000	–
Total assets	×	×
EQUITY AND LIABILITIES		
Equity attributable to equity holders of the parent		
FFF	×	×
GGG	×	×
Amounts recognised in other comprehensive income and accumulated in equity relating to non-current assets held for sale	400	
	×	×
Non-controlling (or minority) interests	×	×
Total equity	×	×
Non-current liabilities		
HHH	×	×
III	×	×
JJJ	×	×
	×	×
Current liabilities		
KKK	×	×
LLL	×	×
MMM	×	×
	×	×
Liabilities directly associated with non-current assets classified as held for sale	3,300	–
	×	×
Total liabilities	×	×
Total equity and liabilities	×	×

The presentation requirements for assets (or disposal groups) classified as held for sale at the end of the reporting period do not apply retrospectively. The comparative balance sheets for any previous periods are therefore not re-presented.

Once assets have been classified as non-current they should not be reclassified as current assets until they meet the criteria to be classified as held for sale in accordance with IFRS 5. Assets of a class that an entity would normally regard as non-current that are acquired exclusively with a view to resale also should not be classified as current unless they meet those criteria.[71]

The treatment of comparatives when the classification as held for sale commences or ceases is discussed at 4 below.

2.2.5　*Changes to a plan of sale*

An asset (or disposal group) should cease to be classified as held for sale if the criteria discussed in 2.1.2 are no longer met.[72]

If an individual asset or liability is removed from a disposal group classified as held for sale, the remaining assets and liabilities of the disposal group to be sold should only continue to be measured as a group if the group still meets these criteria. Otherwise, the remaining non-current assets of the group that individually meet the criteria should be measured individually at the lower of their carrying amounts and fair values less costs to sell at that date. Any that do not meet the criteria should cease to be classified as held for sale.[73]

A non-current asset that ceases to be classified as held for sale (or ceases to be included in a disposal group classified as held for sale) should be measured at the lower of:

(a)　its carrying amount before the asset (or disposal group) was classified as held for sale, adjusted for any depreciation, amortisation or revaluations that would have been recognised had the asset (or disposal group) not been classified as held for sale; and

(b)　its recoverable amount at the date of the subsequent decision not to sell.

Regarding (b) above, the standard notes that if the non-current asset is part of a cash-generating unit, its recoverable amount is the carrying amount that would have been recognised after the allocation of any impairment loss arising on that cash-generating unit in accordance with IAS 36.[74] Recoverable amount is defined as the higher of:

- an asset's fair value less costs to sell; and
- its value in use.

Value in use is defined as 'the present value of estimated future cash flows expected to arise from the continuing use of an asset and from its disposal at the end of its useful life.'[75]

Any required adjustment to the carrying amount of a non-current asset that ceases to be classified as held for sale should be included:

- in income from continuing operations in the period in which the criteria are no longer met (unless the asset had been revalued in accordance with IAS 16 or IAS 38 before classification as held for sale, in which case the adjustment should be treated as a revaluation increase or decrease); and

- in the same income statement (or statement of comprehensive income) caption used to present any gain or loss recognised in relation to remeasuring non-current assets (or disposal groups) held for sale but not meeting the definition of a discontinued operation.[76]

3   DISCONTINUED OPERATIONS

As discussed at 3.2 below, IFRS 5 requires the presentation of a single amount on the face of the income statement relating to discontinued operations, with further analysis either on the face of the income statement or in the notes.

3.1   Definition of a discontinued operation

IFRS 5 defines a discontinued operation as 'a component of an entity that either has been disposed of, or is classified as held for sale, and

(a)   represents a separate major line of business or geographical area of operations;

(b)   is part of a single co-ordinated plan to dispose of a separate major line of business or geographical area of operations; or

(c)   is a subsidiary acquired exclusively with a view to resale.'[77]

Classification as held for sale is discussed at 2.1 above. For the purposes of the above definition, a 'component of an entity' is also defined by the standard as comprising 'operations and cash flows that can be clearly distinguished, operationally and for financial reporting purposes, from the rest of the entity. In other words, a component of an entity will have been a cash-generating unit or a group of cash-generating units while being held for use.'[78] IFRS 5 defines cash generating unit in the same way as IAS 36, that is as 'the smallest identifiable group of assets that generates cash inflows that are largely independent of the cash inflows from other assets or groups of assets.'[79] Cash generating units are discussed in Chapter 18.

It seems highly unlikely that this definition of a discontinued operation would ever be met by a single non-current asset. Accordingly, a discontinued operation will also be a 'disposal group' which is a group of assets to be disposed of, by sale or otherwise, together as a group in a single transaction, and liabilities directly associated with those assets that will be transferred in the transaction (discussed at 2.1.1 above). In our view, the definition of a discontinued operation is somewhat vague, and in particular much will depend on the interpretation of 'a separate major line of business or geographical area of business'. We think this will inevitably mean different things to different people, and that comparability in financial reporting will suffer as a result. However, it is only an interim measure. The IASB used this definition in preference to the one contained in SFAS 144, on the grounds that the size of the operation which would meet SFAS 144's definition was too small and that this was causing practical problems. Accordingly, the IASB noted in the standard that it 'intends to work with the FASB to arrive at a converged definition within a relatively short time.'[80] In April 2007, the IASB agreed to add to its agenda a project to re-consider the definition of discontinued operations through a joint project with the FASB.[81] This project is discussed at 6.3 below.

As discussed at 2.1.2 C above, IFRS 5 stipulates that a non-current asset (or disposal group) that is to be abandoned should not be classified as held for sale. This includes non-current assets (or disposal groups) that are to be used to the end of their economic life and non-current assets (or disposal groups) that are to be closed rather than sold. However, if the disposal group to be abandoned meets the criteria above for being a discontinued operation the standard requires it to be treated as such in the income statement and relevant notes 'at the date on which it ceases to be used.'[82] In other words, the treatment as discontinued in the income statement only starts in the period when abandonment actually occurs (see Example 4.6 below).

A non-current asset that has been temporarily taken out of use should not be accounted for as if it had been abandoned.[83] Accordingly it would not be disclosed as a discontinued operation. The standard provides an illustration of a discontinued operation arising from abandonment upon which the following example is based.

Example 4.6:   Discontinued operation arising from abandonment[84]

In October 2010 an entity decides to abandon all of its cotton mills, which constitute a major line of business. All work stops at the cotton mills during the year ended 31 December 2011. In the financial statements for the year ended 31 December 2010, results and cash flows of the cotton mills are treated as continuing operations. In the financial statements for the year ended 31 December 2011, the results and cash flows of the cotton mills are treated as discontinued operations and the entity makes the disclosures required (see 3.2 below).

3.2   Presentation of discontinued operations

IFRS 5 requires the presentation of a single amount on the face of the income statement (or statement of comprehensive income if a separate income statement is not presented) comprising:

(a)   the post-tax profit or loss of discontinued operations; and

(b)   the post-tax gain or loss recognised on the measurement to fair value less costs to sell or on the disposal of the assets or disposal group(s) constituting the discontinued operation.[85]

This single amount should be further analysed (either on the face of the statement or in the notes) into:

(a)   the revenue, expenses and pre-tax profit or loss of discontinued operations;

(b)   the gain or loss recognised on the measurement to fair value less costs to sell or on the disposal of the assets or disposal group(s) constituting the discontinued operation; and

(c)   separately for each of (a) and (b) the related income tax expense as required by IAS 12 (see Chapter 26).

The analysis is not required for disposal groups that are newly acquired subsidiaries that meet the criteria to be classified as held for sale on acquisition (see 2.2.2 above).[86] However, in either case it should be remembered that any disclosures that might be required by other IFRSs about amounts recognised in the income statement need to include any relevant amounts relating to the discontinued operations. This is subject to certain reductions for periods beginning on or after 1 January 2010 and is discussed at 2.2.2 above.

If the required analysis is presented on the face of the income statement it should be presented in a section identified as relating to discontinued operations, i.e. separately from continuing operations. The standard also makes clear that any gain or loss on the remeasurement of a non-current asset (or disposal group) classified as held for sale that does not meet the definition of a discontinued operation should not be included within these amounts for discontinued operations, but be included in profit or loss from continuing operations.[87]

With effect for periods beginning on or after 1 July 2009, IFRS 5 requires disclosure of the amount of income from continuing operations and discontinued operations attributable to owners of the parent. This may be given either in the notes or on the face of the income statement (or statement of comprehensive income).[88]

IFRS 5 requires that all the above disclosures be re-presented for prior periods presented in the financial statements so that the disclosures relate to all operations that have been discontinued by the balance sheet date for the latest period presented.[89] Accordingly, adjustments to the comparative information as originally reported will be necessary for those disposal groups categorised as discontinued operations. Comparative information relating to discontinued operations is discussed further at 4 below.

The implementation guidance accompanying IFRS 5 provides the following illustration of the presentation of discontinued operations.

Example 4.7:   Presenting discontinued operations[90]

> *XYZ GROUP – STATEMENT OF COMPREHENSIVE INCOME FOR THE YEAR ENDED 31 DECEMBER 2010 (illustrating the classification of expenses by function)*

(in thousands of Euros)

	2010	2009
Continuing operations		
Revenue	×	×
Cost of sales	(×)	(×)
Gross profit	×	×
Other income	×	×
Distribution costs	(×)	(×)
Administrative expenses	(×)	(×)
Other expenses	(×)	(×)
Finance costs	(×)	(×)
Share of profit of associates	×	×
Profit before tax	×	×
Income tax expense	(×)	(×)
Profit for the period from continuing operations	×	×
Discontinued operations		
Profit for the period from discontinued operations*	×	×
Profit for the period	×	×

Attributable to:

Owners of the parent		
Profit for the period from continuing operations	×	×
Profit for the period from discontinued operations	×	×
Profit for the period attributable to owners of the parent	×	×
Non-controlling interest		
Profit for the period from continuing operation	×	×
Profit for the period from discontinued operations	×	×
Profit for the period attributable to non-controlling interests	×	×
	×	×

* The required analysis would be given in the notes.

The entity did not recognise any components of other comprehensive income in the periods presented.

The above reflects the requirement to disclose the amount of income from continuing operations and discontinued operations attributable to owners of the parent. It is noteworthy that the standard's illustrative example goes beyond what is strictly required by also giving an equivalent analysis for income attributable to non-controlling interests.

Adjustments in the current period to amounts previously presented in discontinued operations that are directly related to the disposal of a discontinued operation in a prior period should be classified separately in discontinued operations. The nature and amount of the adjustments should be disclosed. Examples given by the standard of circumstances in which these adjustments may arise include the following:

(a)   the resolution of uncertainties that arise from the terms of the disposal transaction, such as the resolution of purchase price adjustments and indemnification issues with the purchaser;

(b)   the resolution of uncertainties that arise from and are directly related to the operations of the component before its disposal, such as environmental and product warranty obligations retained by the seller; and

(c)   the settlement of employee benefit plan obligations, provided that the settlement is directly related to the disposal transaction.[91]

In addition, IFRS 5 requires disclosure of the net cash flows attributable to the operating, investing and financing activities of discontinued operations. The standard allows that these disclosures may be presented either in the notes or on the face of the financial statements. It is not readily clear what 'on the face of the financial statements' is intended to mean, but it seems likely that this data would be presented on the face of the cash flow statement. These disclosures are not required for disposal groups that are newly acquired subsidiaries that meet the criteria to be classified as held for sale on acquisition (see 2.2.2 above).[92]

As a discontinued operation will also be a disposal group, the balance sheet presentation for disposal groups (discussed at 2.2.4 above) also apply to discontinued operations.

3.3   Trading between continuing and discontinued operations

Notwithstanding the one line income statement presentation discussed above, discontinued operations remain consolidated in group financial statements. That means any transactions between discontinued and continuing operations are eliminated as usual in the consolidation. As a consequence, the amounts ascribed to the continuing and discontinued operations will be income and expense only from transactions with counterparties external to the group. Importantly, this means the results presented on the face of the income statement will not necessarily represent the activities of the operations as individual entities, particularly when there has been significant trading between the continuing and discontinued operations. Some might consider the results for the continuing and discontinued operations on this basis to be of little use to readers of accounts. An argument could be made that allocating external transactions to or from the discontinued operation would yield more meaningful information.

One approach would be to fully eliminate transactions for the purpose of presenting the income statement then provide supplementary information. This is illustrated in the following extract:

Extract 4.1: BP p.l.c. (2006)

Notes to the Financial Statements [extract]

7   Segmental analysis [extract]

By business	Exploration and production	Refining and Marketing	Gas, Power and Re-newables	Other businesses and corporate	Consolid-ation adjustment and elimin-ations	Total group	Innovene operations	Consolid-ation adjustment and elimin-ations[a]	$million 2005 Total continuing operations
Sales and other operating revenues									
Segment sales and other operating revenues	47,210	213,326	25,696	21,295	(55,359)	252,168	(20,627)	8,251	239,792
Less: sales between businesses	(32,606)	(11,407)	(3,095)	(8,251)	55,359	–	8,251	(8,251)	–
Third party sales	14,604	201,919	22,601	13,044	–	252,168	(12,376)	–	239,792
Equity-accounted earnings	3,232	249	62	(14)	–	3,529	14	–	3,543
Segment revenues	17,836	202,168	22,663	13,030	–	255,697	(12,362)	–	243,335
Interest and other revenues	–	–	–	–	689	689	(76)	–	613
Total revenues	17,836	202,168	22,663	13,030	689	256,386	(12,438)	–	243,948

Segment results									
Profit (loss) before interest and tax	25,502	6,926	1,172	(569)	(208)	32,823	(668)	527	32,682
Finance costs and other finance expense	–	–	–	–	(758)	(758)	(3)	–	(761)
Profit (loss) before taxation	25,502	6,296	1,172	(569)	(966)	32,065	(671)	527	31,921
Taxation	–	–	–	–	(9,433)	(9,433)	133	(173)	(9,473)
Profit (loss) for the year	25,502	6,926	1,172	(569)	(10,399)	22,632	(538)	354	22,448

[a]In the circumstances of discontinued operations, IFRS requires that the profits earned by the discontinued operations, in this case the Innovene operations, on sales to the continuing operations be eliminated on consolidation from the discontinued operations and attributed to the continuing operations and vice versa. This adjustment has two offsetting elements: the net margin on crude refined by Innovene as substantially all crude for its refineries was supplied by BP and most of the refined products manufactured were taken by BP; and the margin on sales of feedstock from BP's US refineries to Innovene's manufacturing plants. The profits attributable to individual segments are not affected by this adjustment. This representation does not indicate the profits earned by continuing or Innovene operations, as if they were standalone entities, for past periods or likely to be earned in future periods.

4   COMPARATIVE INFORMATION

As discussed in Chapter 3 at 2.4, IAS 1 requires the presentation of comparative information. IFRS 5 deals with the particular requirements for non-current assets held for sale (and disposal groups) and discontinued operations. However, in our view, the way it does so is somewhat muddled.

Entities will need to consider whether any (and if so what) changes are necessary to comparative information as previously reported whenever:

- non-current assets or disposal groups first become classified as such; and
- that classification ceases.

This will need to be considered in terms of both the income statement (or statement of comprehensive income) and balance sheet and separately (for the income statement) for those components falling to be treated as discontinued operations.

4.1   Treatment of comparative information on initial classification as held for sale

4.1.1   The income statement (or combined statement of comprehensive income)

For non-current assets and disposal groups not qualifying as discontinued operations there are no special requirements relating to income statement presentation, accordingly no restatement of comparative amounts would be relevant.

When a component of an entity becomes classified as a discontinued operation, separate presentation of the total of its results for the period and any gain or loss on remeasurement is required on the face of the statement (see 3.2 above). IFRS 5 requires that these disclosures be re-presented for prior periods presented in the financial statements so that the disclosures relate to all operations that have been discontinued by the balance sheet date for the latest period presented.[93] Accordingly, adjustments to the comparative information as originally reported will be necessary for those disposal groups categorised as discontinued operations.

4.1.2   The balance sheet

IFRS 5 states that 'An entity shall not reclassify or re-present amounts presented for non-current assets or for the assets and liabilities of disposal groups classified as held for sale in the balance sheets for prior periods to reflect the classification in the balance sheet for the latest period presented.'[94] The implementation guidance accompanying the standard contains an example of a disposal group becoming classified as held for sale (see Example 4.5 at 2.2.4 above), and states that the presentation requirements for assets (or disposal groups) classified as held for sale at the end of the reporting period do not apply retrospectively. The comparative balance sheets for any previous periods are therefore not re-presented.[95] In our view, comparatives should not be re-presented when the classification as held for sale ceases.

The standard has no separate requirements relating to the balance sheet for a disposal group also qualifying as a discontinued operation and accordingly comparatives are not adjusted.

4.2   Treatment of comparative information on the cessation of classification as held for sale

4.2.1   General requirements

As discussed at 2.2.5 above, when a non-current asset ceases to be classified as held for sale the measurement basis for it reverts to what it would have been if it had not been so classified at all (or recoverable amount if lower). Typically this would require a 'catch-up' depreciation charge as depreciation would not have been accounted for while it was held for sale. The standard explicitly requires this to be a current year charge.[96] This seems to indicate that for non-current assets and disposal groups ceasing to be so classified the *measurement* of items in comparative information (income statement and balance sheet) should not be revisited. This requirement applies equally to discontinued operations. However, as discussed at 4.2.2 below, this is not the case for associates and joint ventures.

Regarding the treatment of discontinued operations in the income statement, the standard states that if an entity ceases to classify a component as held for sale, the results of operations of the component previously presented in discontinued operations should be reclassified and included in income from continuing operations for all periods presented. The amounts for prior periods should be described as having been re-presented.[97]

As discussed at 4.1.2 above, the amounts presented for non-current assets or for the assets and liabilities of disposal groups classified as held for sale in the comparative balance sheet should not be reclassified or re-presented.

4.2.2   *The treatment of associates and joint ventures*

Somewhat perplexingly, both IAS 28 – *Investments in Associates* – and IAS 31 – *Interests in Joint Ventures* – require a different approach to that discussed above. When an investment in an associate or an interest in a jointly controlled entity previously classified as held for sale (and hence accounted for in accordance with IFRS 5) ceases to be so classified they are required to be accounted for using the equity method or proportionate consolidation (as appropriate) *as from the date of classification as held for sale.*[98] Both standards also state that financial statements for the periods since classification as held for sale should be amended accordingly.

5   DISCLOSURE REQUIREMENTS

5.1   Requirements of IFRS 5

As discussed at 2.2.4 and 3.2 above, IFRS 5 sets out detailed requirements for the prominent presentation of amounts relating to non-current assets held for resale, disposal groups and discontinued operations. In addition, disclosure is required in the notes in the period in which a non-current asset (or disposal group) has been either classified as held for sale or sold of:

(a)   a description of the non-current asset (or disposal group);

(b)   a description of the facts and circumstances of the sale, or leading to the expected disposal, and the expected manner and timing of that disposal;

(c)   the gain or loss recognised as a result of measuring the non-current asset (or disposal group) at fair value less costs to sell (discussed at 2 above) and, if not separately presented on the face of the income statement, the caption in the income statement that includes that gain or loss; and

(d)   if applicable, the segment in which the non-current asset (or disposal group) is presented in accordance with IFRS 8 – *Operating segments* (discussed in Chapter 35 at 2.3.1).[99]

If a non-current asset (or disposal group) meets the criteria to be classified as held for sale after the balance sheet date but before the financial statements are authorised for issue, the information specified in (a), (b) and (d) above should also be disclosed in the notes.[100]

Further, should:

•   a non-current asset (or disposal group) cease to be classified as held for sale; or

•   an individual asset or liability be removed from a disposal group,

IFRS 5 requires disclosure, in the period of the decision to change the plan to sell the non-current asset (or disposal group), a description of the facts and circumstances leading to the decision and the effect of the decision on the results of operations for the period and any prior periods presented.[101]

5.2   Requirements of other standards

For periods beginning on or after 1 January 2010 IFRS 5 addresses, and to an extent restricts, disclosure requirements contained in other standards. This is discussed at 2.2.2 above.

6   FUTURE DEVELOPMENTS

6.1   Joint project with the FASB

The IASB is conducting a joint project with the FASB to reconsider the definition of discontinued operations.

The IASB issued an exposure draft in September 2008.

The key proposal in the exposure draft is to change the definition of discontinued operations as follows.

A discontinued operation is a component of an entity that:

(a)   is an operating segment and either has been disposed of or is classified as held for sale; or

(b)   is a business that meets the criteria to be classified as held for sale on acquisition.[102]

Operating segments are discussed in Chapter 35 at 2.3.

Entities not subject to the requirements of IFRS 8 would not otherwise need to determine what constitutes an operating segment. In order to comply with IFRS 5 this determination will now be required for all entities with a discontinued operation.

Under IFRS 8 segment data may be presented other than in accordance with IFRS. Even if this is the case, the IFRS 5 disclosures must be in accordance with IFRS.[103]

The Board discussed matters arising from responses to the exposure draft in July 2009, and decided tentatively:

- that the standard should continue to require an entity to present discontinued operations on the face of the statement of comprehensive income;

- to define a discontinued operation as:

    (a)   a reportable segment disposed of or classified as held for sale; or

    (b)   a business that meets the criteria to be classified as held for sale on acquisition.

- that re-exposure of these proposals is unnecessary; and

- that the staff should investigate further the disclosure requirements in US GAAP for components of an entity that have been disposed of or classified as held for sale.[104]

The IASB currently expects to publish a revised standard by the end of 2009.[105]

6.2   Allocation of impairment losses

As noted at 2.2.3 above, IFRS 5 contains a logical flaw in its measurement requirements. It is quite possible that a required impairment exceeds the carrying value of the non-current assets within the scope of the standard's measurement rules. IFRS 5 is silent on what to do in such circumstances.

This issue was brought to the attention of IFRIC which referred it to the IASB. The IASB intends to address the issue through a future amendment to IFRS 5. The Board decided tentatively to consider amending IFRS 5 as a matter of priority and to work with the FASB to ensure IFRS 5 remains aligned with US GAAP.[106]

6.3   Classification of associates and jointly controlled ventures as held for sale

In August 2009 the IASB published a proposed amendment to IFRS 5. The proposal is to clarify that when an entity is committed to a sale plan involving loss of significant influence of an associate or loss of joint control of a jointly controlled entity all of those interests should be classified as held for sale when the standard's criteria (discussed at 2.1 above) are met. This is the case regardless of whether the entity will retain a non-controlling interest.[107]

7   CONCLUSION

Our original conclusion on the publication of IFRS 5 was that it was not particularly well drafted nor well conceived. This seems to be reflected in the numerous recent amendments to it – three changes of substance within one 12 month period and two more expected soon.

The current definition of a discontinued operation is vague, and in particular the meaning of 'a separate major line of business' will inevitably mean different things to different people. The requirement not to depreciate assets which are still actively used (for periods which could exceed a year) introduces a conflict with how assets which are not intended to be sold are treated – although the requirements for impairment and the use of current price residuals may limit the practical impact of this on the balance sheet. Also, the portfolio approach to measuring disposal groups conflicts with the general requirements for separate determination used elsewhere in IFRS and sits particularly awkwardly with the components approach of IAS 16.

References

1 IFRS 5, *Non-current Assets Held for Sale and Discontinued Operations*, IASB, para. 45.
2 IFRS 5, paras. IN2-IN3.
3 IFRS 5, para. IN4.
4 IFRS 5, para. IN5.
5 IFRS 5, paras. BC67-BC71.
6 Exposure Draft ED/2009/11, *Improvements to IFRS*, IASB, August 2009.

period of first-time application.'³ It became clear shortly after SIC-8 was issued that, although theoretically sound, the approach taken by the interpretation could give rise to substantial practical difficulties for entities adopting IFRSs for the first time. For example, it required all prior business combinations to be restated on an IFRSs basis, which would have been wholly impracticable.

1.1.2   The need for IFRS 1

The spotlight was placed firmly on first-time adoption of IFRSs when the European Commission proposed to require all publicly traded EU incorporated companies to prepare their consolidated accounts under IFRSs, by 2005 at the latest. After the IASB had been made aware of the considerable practical difficulties surrounding first-time application under SIC-8, it announced that it would undertake a separate project on this subject. Consequently, in July 2002, the IASB published ED 1 – *First-time Application of International Financial Reporting Standards*.⁴ The Board made significant changes to the exposure draft before finalising it in June 2003 as IFRS 1 – *First-time Adoption of International Financial Reporting Standards*.

In the introduction to the original version of IFRS 1, the IASB cited the following reasons for replacing SIC-8 by IFRS 1:⁵

- SIC-8 required full retrospective application that could cause costs that exceeded the likely benefits for users of financial statements;

- although SIC-8 did not require retrospective application when this would be impracticable, it did not define 'impracticable' leaving it unclear whether it should be interpreted as a high hurdle or a low hurdle;

- SIC-8 could require a first-time adopter to apply two different versions of a Standard if a new version were introduced during the periods covered by its first financial statements prepared under IASs and the new version prohibited retrospective application;

- SIC-8 did not state clearly whether a first-time adopter should use hindsight in applying recognition and measurement decisions retrospectively; and

- there was some doubt about how SIC-8 interacted with specific transitional provisions in individual Standards.

IFRS 1 offers many significant improvements over SIC-8, but it also has a number of weaknesses. Firstly, given the IASB's worldwide constituency, IFRS 1 had to be written in a way that completely ignores a first-time adopter's previous GAAP. One of the IASB's aims in developing IFRS 1 was 'to find solutions that would be appropriate for any entity, in any part of the world, regardless of whether adoption occurs in 2005 or at a different time'.⁶ Consequently, first-time adoption exemptions are made available to all first-time adopters, including those first-time adopters whose previous GAAP was very close to IFRSs. A first-time adopter will be able to make considerable adjustments to its opening IFRS balance sheet, using the available exemptions in IFRS 1, even if the difference between its previous GAAP and IFRSs was only minor. It may also be required to make considerable adjustments due to the exemptions and exceptions in the standard.

Secondly, in its basis for conclusions, the IASB notes that ideally a regime for the first-time adoption of IFRSs would achieve comparability between the financial statements of an entity over time, between different first-time adopters, and between first-time adopters and entities already applying IFRSs.[7] Inevitably there are tensions between these three objectives. SIC-8 gave priority to ensuring comparability between a first-time adopter and entities already reporting under IFRSs. The IASB reconsidered this in developing IFRS 1 and decided to give priority to achieving 'comparability over time within a first-time adopter's first IFRS financial statements and between different entities adopting IFRSs for the first time at a given date; thus, achieving comparability between first-time adopters and entities that already apply IFRSs is a secondary objective.'[8]

1.1.3   IFRS 1 (as revised in 2008)

Whenever it issues a new standard the IASB considers whether a first-time adopter should apply that standard retrospectively or prospectively. In the limited number of cases that the IASB considers prospective application more appropriate it will amend IFRS 1.[9]

The IASB's desire to ensure that IFRS 1 comprises all first-time adoption rules has meant that the original IFRS 1 had been amended by standards and interpretations that the Board has subsequently issued. This approach always carried the risk that its complexity might eventually overwhelm its practical application. Therefore, it was perhaps not surprising when the Board directed its staff in February 2007 to draft a restructured version of IFRS 1 to deal with the issues arising from the fact that 'IFRS 1 has been amended several times to accommodate first-time adoption requirements resulting from new standards or amendments to standards. Because of the way IFRS 1 is structured, such amendments are making the standard more complex and less clear. As more amendments become necessary, this problem will become worse.'[10]

In November 2008, the IASB issued IFRS 1 (as revised in 2008) – *First-Time Adoption of International Financial Reporting Standards*, which retains the substance of the previous version of the standard but within a changed structure.[11] The revised standard no longer includes any of the wording related to exemptions that were only available to entities adopting IFRSs before 1 July 2009.

1.1.4   Terminology and references

This chapter only deals with IFRS 1 (as revised in 2008), which is effective for periods beginning on or after 1 July 2009 (see 2.1 below). In the remainder of this chapter any reference to IFRS 1 should be read as a reference to IFRS 1 (as revised in 2008), the previous version of the standard is referred to as IFRS 1 (2008 Bound Volume).

1.2   Objective

The underlying principle in IFRS 1 is that a first-time adopter should prepare financial statements as if it had always applied IFRSs, but there are a number of exemptions and exceptions that allow or require a first-time adopter to deviate from the general rule. The objective of IFRS 1 is to ensure that an entity's first IFRS financial statements and its first IFRS interim financial statements contain high quality financial information that:[12]

(a)   is transparent for users and comparable over all periods presented;

(b)   provides a suitable starting point for accounting in accordance with IFRSs; and

(c)   can be generated at a cost that does not exceed the benefits to users.

1.3   Scope and definitions

1.3.1   *Who is a first-time adopter?*

Clearly, given the differing regimes applicable to first-time adopters and entities already using IFRSs, what counts as first-time adoption is a question of some importance. The standard defines an entity's first IFRS financial statements as being the first annual financial statements in which an entity adopts IFRSs by an 'explicit and unreserved statement' of compliance with IFRSs in those financial statements.[13] The decisive factor is whether or not the entity made that explicit and unreserved statement. An entity is *not* considered to be a first-time adopter if it departed from certain IFRS (whether recognition, measurement or disclosure) in its previous financial statements but still made an explicit and unreserved statement of compliance. An entity that is not a first-time adopter cannot apply IFRS 1 to changes in its accounting policies. Instead, such an entity should apply:[14]

•   the requirements of IAS 8 – *Accounting Policies, Changes in Accounting Estimates and Errors*; and

•   specific transitional requirements in other IFRSs.

IFRS 1 states that an entity's first IFRS financial statements will be subject to IFRS 1 even if it presented its most recent previous financial statements in conformity with IFRSs in all respects except that they did not contain an explicit and unreserved statement.[15] An entity's financial statements are considered its first IFRS financial statements, and thus fall within the scope of IFRS 1, when it:

'(a)   presented its most recent previous financial statements:

(i)   in accordance with national requirements that are not consistent with IFRSs in all respects;

(ii)   in conformity with IFRSs in all respects, except that the financial statements did not contain an explicit and unreserved statement that they complied with IFRSs;

(iii) containing an explicit statement of compliance with some, but not all, IFRSs;

(iv)   in accordance with national requirements inconsistent with IFRSs, using some individual IFRSs to account for items for which national requirements did not exist; or

(v)   in accordance with national requirements, with a reconciliation of some amounts to the amounts determined in accordance with IFRSs;

(b)   prepared financial statements in accordance with IFRSs for internal use only, without making them available to the entity's owners or any other external users;

(c) prepared a reporting package in accordance with IFRSs for consolidation purposes without preparing a complete set of financial statements as defined in IAS 1 – *Presentation of Financial Statements* (as revised in 2007); or

(d) did not present financial statements for previous periods.'[16]

Therefore, an entity whose most recent previous financial statements contained an explicit and unreserved statement of compliance with IFRSs can never be considered a first-time adopter. This is the case even in the following circumstances:

- the entity issued financial statements claiming to comply both with national GAAP and IFRSs, and subsequently drops the national GAAP compliance claim; or

- the entity issued financial statements containing an explicit and unreserved statement of compliance with IFRSs despite the fact that the auditors issued a qualified audit report on those IFRS financial statements; or

- the entity stops presenting a separate set of financial statements under national requirements, which was presented in addition to its IFRS financial statements.[17]

The IASB could have introduced special rules that would have required an entity that significantly departed from IFRSs to apply IFRS 1. However, the IASB considered that such rules would lead to 'complexity and uncertainty'.[18] In addition, this would have given entities applying 'IFRS-lite' (i.e. entities not applying IFRSs rigorously in all respects) an option to side step the requirements of IAS 8.[19]

It is clear that the scope of IFRS 1 is very much rule-based, which, as the example below illustrates, can lead to different answers in similar situations and sometimes to counter-intuitive answers.

Example 5.1:   Scope of application of IFRS 1

Entity A applied IFRSs in its previous financial statements, but stated that it 'applied IFRSs except for SIC-12 – *Consolidation – Special Purpose Entities*.'

Entity A is a first-time adopter because its financial statements did not contain an unreserved statement of compliance with IFRSs. It is irrelevant whether the auditors' report was qualified or not.

Entity B applied IFRSs in its previous financial statements and stated that the 'financial statements are prepared in conformity with IFRSs.' Despite that statement, entity B had not applied SIC-12.

Entity B is not a first-time adopter because its financial statements contained an unreserved statement of compliance with IFRSs. Even if the auditors had qualified their report, the entity would still not be a first-time adopter.

Example 5.2:   Entity applying national GAAP and IFRSs

Entity C prepares two sets of financial statements, one set of financial statements based on its national GAAP and the other set based on IFRSs. The IFRS financial statements contained an explicit and unreserved statement of compliance with IFRSs and were made available externally. From 2010 onwards, entity C stops presenting financial statements based on its national GAAP.

Entity C is not a first-time adopter because it already published financial statements that contained an explicit and unreserved statement of compliance with IFRSs.

*Example 5.3:   Repeated application of IFRS 1 when an entity does not apply IFRSs
for one year*

Entity D prepared IFRS financial statements for 2007 and 2008 that contained an unreserved statement of compliance with IFRSs. However, in 2009 Entity D did not make an unreserved statement of compliance with IFRSs.

Entity D would be considered a first-time adopter for the purposes of its 2010 financial statements because its most recent financial statements did not contain an unreserved statement of compliance with IFRSs. This is the case even though Entity D produced IFRS financial statements before 2009.

There is no requirement under IFRS 1 for entity D to base its first IFRS financial statements in 2010 on the IFRS information that it produced before 2009. Therefore, entity D is able to apply the IFRS 1 exemptions without regard to the election it made in its first IFRS financial statements in 2007. In fact, entity D is unable to apply certain IFRS 1 exemptions by reference to the date of transition that it used in its 2007 financial statements.

In July 2009, the IASB issued the *International Financial Reporting Standard for Small and Medium-sized Entities* (IFRS for SMEs) which states that 'an entity can be a first-time adopter of the *IFRS for SMEs* only once. If an entity using the *IFRS for SMEs* stops using it for one or more reporting periods and then is required, or chooses, to adopt it again later, the special exemptions, simplifications and other requirements in this section do not apply to the re-adoption.'[20] Unlike the IFRS for SMEs, IFRS 1 does not prohibit an entity from applying IFRS 1 more than once and, in fact, requires it in some cases.[21]

*Example 5.4:   First IFRS financial statements outside the annual report or statutory
financial statements*

Entity E prepared financial statements under its previous GAAP for the period ending 31 December 2009. In connection with its initial public offering, entity E published an offering document that includes IFRS financial statements that contain an unreserved statement of compliance with IFRSs. The date of transition to IFRSs for the purposes of those financial statements, which cover the most recent three financial years, was 1 January 2007.

Entity E's annual report (or statutory financial statements) are prepared under IFRSs for the first time for the period ending 31 December 2010.

The IFRS financial statements included in entity E's offering document were its first IFRS financial statements. Entity E should not apply IFRS 1 in its first annual financial statements (or statutory financial statements) prepared under IFRSs as it is not a first-time adopter. Although not required by IFRSs, entity E may want to repeat information about its transition to IFRSs in its annual financial statement.

If, however, entity E had included financial statements in its offering document that did not contain an unreserved statement of compliance with IFRSs (e.g. combined financial statements) then the annual financial statements for 2010 (or statutory financial statements) would need to be prepared in accordance with IFRS 1. If those financial statements only included comparative information for the year ended 31 December 2009 then E's the date of transition would be 1 January 2009.

1.3.2   When should IFRS 1 be applied?

An entity that presents its first IFRS financial statements is a first-time adopter[22] and should apply IFRS 1 in preparing those financial statements.[23] It should also apply the standard in each interim financial report that it presents under IAS 34 – *Interim Financial Reporting* – for a part of the period covered by its first IFRS financial statements.[24] However, IFRS 1 does not apply when a first-time adopter issues a 'trading statement' at its interim reporting date that is not described as complying with IAS 34 or IFRSs.[25]

1.3.3 Defined terms

IFRS 1 defines the following terms in connection with the transition to IFRSs:[26]

Date of transition to IFRSs: The beginning of the earliest period for which an entity presents full comparative financial statements under IFRSs in its first IFRS financial statements.

First IFRS financial statements: The first annual financial statements in which an entity adopts International Financial Reporting Standards, by an explicit and unreserved statement of compliance with IFRSs.

First IFRS reporting period: The latest reporting period covered by an entity's first IFRS financial statements.

Opening IFRS statement of financial position (i.e. opening IFRS balance sheet): An entity's statement of financial position (i.e. balance sheet) at the date of transition to IFRSs.

International Financial Reporting Standards: Standards and Interpretations adopted by the International Accounting Standards Board (IASB). They comprise:

(a)   International Financial Reporting Standards;

(b)   International Accounting Standards; and

(c)   Interpretations developed by the International Financial Reporting Interpretations Committee (IFRIC) or the former Standing Interpretations Committee (SIC).

Previous GAAP: The basis of accounting that a first-time adopter used immediately before adopting IFRSs.

A   Determining the previous GAAP

An entity may prepare two complete sets of financial statements, e.g. one set of financial statements based on its national GAAP and another set for distribution to foreign investors based on US GAAP. Applying the definition of 'previous GAAP' (i.e. 'the basis of accounting that a first-time adopter used immediately before adopting IFRSs'[27]) to such a dual reporting entity is not straight forward, as the examples below illustrate:

(a)   *a dual reporting entity adopts IFRSs and at the same time stops presenting financial statements under its national GAAP and US GAAP:* Both national GAAP and US GAAP meet the definition of 'previous GAAP'. However, the entity can only present one set of IFRS financial statements. Therefore, the entity must choose a 'previous GAAP'. While, at least in theory, this appears to be a free choice there are a number of limiting constraints that should be taken into account:

      (i)   national legislation and regulatory requirements may restrict an entity's options and require either national GAAP or US GAAP to be designated as the previous GAAP;

(ii)   comparability with other entities in the same jurisdiction may be increased if all entities in that jurisdiction use the same GAAP as their previous GAAP; and

(iii) one set of financial statements is considered to be the 'main' set of financial statements, for example:

- if the national GAAP financial statements received very limited circulation then they are clearly not the entity's 'main' financial statements. Conversely, if the US GAAP financial statements are only prepared for a specific purpose (e.g. to obtain a bank loan) then they may not be the entity's 'main' financial statements; or

- the relative dominance of shareholder groups might form an indication as to which set of financial statements is considered to be the 'main' set of financial statements.

An entity should apply judgement when the constraints above do not all identify the same GAAP as the previous GAAP.

IFRS 1 only requires disclosure of reconciliations between an entity's previous GAAP and IFRSs. However, it will be advisable for an entity to provide disclosures, on a voluntary basis, that contain sufficient information to enable users to understand the material reconciling items between the IFRS financial statements and the financial statements that were not prepared under its previous GAAP. Some national regulators (e.g. the US Securities and Exchange Commission), in fact, expect such disclosures.[28]

(b)   *a dual reporting entity adopts IFRSs and at the same time continues to present financial statements under its national GAAP but stops presenting financial statements under US GAAP:* While one might expect US GAAP to be treated as the previous GAAP, both national GAAP and US GAAP meet the definition of 'previous GAAP'. An entity should therefore consider the criteria (i) to (iv) under (a) above in determining its previous GAAP.

If an entity treats its national GAAP as its previous GAAP then it may want or need to present an explanation of the differences between US GAAP and IFRSs to aid former users of the US GAAP financial statements.

As illustrated in Extract 5.1 below, when Infosys adopted IFRSs it treated Indian GAAP as its previous GAAP even though it continued to report under Indian GAAP for statutory purposes. However, Infosys did provide additional reconciliations between US GAAP and its previous GAAP.

(c)   *a dual reporting entity adopts IFRSs and at the same time stops presenting financial statements under US GAAP, several years later it stops presenting financial statements under its national GAAP:* If the entity treated US GAAP as its previous GAAP when it adopted IFRSs then under paragraph 4(a) of IFRS 1 the entity is not a first-time adopter when it ceases to present financial statements under its national GAAP. However, the entity may want or need to present an explanation of the differences between its national GAAP and IFRSs to aid former users of its national GAAP financial statements.

Extract 5.1: Infosys Technologies Limited (2009)

2 Notes to the consolidated financial statements [extract]

2.1 Transition to IFRS reporting [extract]

The financial statements of Infosys Technologies Limited and its subsidiaries have been prepared in accordance with IFRS. Infosys Technologies Limited and its subsidiaries adopted all IFRS standards and the adoption was carried out in accordance to IFRS 1, using April 1, 2007 as the transition date. The transition was carried out from Indian GAAP, which was considered as the Previous GAAP. The effect of adopting IFRS has been summarized in the reconciliations provided. The transition to IFRS reporting has resulted in changes in the reported financial statements, notes thereto and accounting principles compared to what had been presented previously. Until the adoption of IFRS, the financial statements included in the Annual Reports on Form 20-F and Quarterly Reports on Form 6-K were prepared in accordance with accounting principles generally accepted in the United States of America (U.S. GAAP) under the historical cost convention on the accrual basis. However, for the purposes of the transition, such transition was carried out from Indian GAAP, which has been considered as the Previous GAAP. The reconciliation statements provided in Note 2.2 describe the differences between IFRS and Indian GAAP. In addition, reconciliations from U.S. GAAP to Indian GAAP have been provided in Note 2.3 for the periods presented.

The Group's financial statements for the year ending March 31, 2009 are the first annual financial statements to comply with IFRS.

2.3 The following voluntary reconciliations provide a quantification of reconciliation items between U.S. GAAP and Previous GAAP: [extract]

• equity as at April 1, 2007 (Note 2.3.1)

• equity as at March 31, 2008 (Note 2.3.2)

• equity as at March 31, 2009 (Note 2.3.3)

• net income for the year ended March 31, 2008 (Note 2.3.4)

• net income for the year ended March 31, 2009 (Note 2.3.5)

B   Transition to IFRSs from a similar GAAP

One consequence of the ongoing harmonisation of accounting standard around the world is that many national GAAPs are now virtually identical to IFRSs. However, differences between these national GAAPs and IFRSs often exist regarding the scope, transitional provisions, effective dates and actual wording of standards. In addition, some national GAAPs contain accounting alternatives not permitted by IFRSs.

When an entity reporting under such a national GAAP adopts IFRSs there will often not be any major changes required in its accounting policies to comply with IFRSs. However, as discussed at 1.3.1 above, IFRS 1 does not require an assessment of whether a previous GAAP was very similar to IFRSs. Therefore, regardless of the absence of real differences in accounting policies, that entity would be a first-time adopter when it includes an explicit and unreserved statement of compliance with IFRSs for the first time. So even if the entity's accounting policies were already fully compliant with IFRSs:

(a)   it would be permitted to apply the IFRS 1 exemptions;

(b)   it would need to restate items for which the applicable first-time adoption exemptions differ from the transitional rules applicable to ongoing reporters (e.g. deferred taxation, defined benefit plans and currency translation);

(c)   it would not be permitted to apply different versions of IFRSs that were effective at earlier dates; and

(d)   it would need to explain the transition to IFRSs.

While an entity might benefit from being able to apply the IFRS 1 exemptions, the requirement to apply current IFRSs retrospectively (see (b) and (c) above) may cause real problems as it may force the entity to make certain adjustments that would not have been necessary if their previous GAAP financial statements had also been described as being in compliance with IFRSs. An entity that prepares financial statements under its national GAAP using accounting policies that are identical to IFRSs should consider carefully what the impact would be if it decided, or was required to, make a dual statement of compliance with both its national GAAP and IFRSs as issued by the IASB.

1.3.4   *Defined terms: First-time adoption timeline*

An entity's first IFRS financial statements must include at least three statements of financial position (i.e. balance sheets), two statements of comprehensive income, two separate income statements (if presented), two statements of cash flows and two statements of changes in equity and related notes, including comparative information.[29] The beginning of the earliest comparative period for which the entity presents full comparative information under IFRSs will be treated as its date of transition to IFRSs. The diagram below shows how for an entity with a December year-end the above terms are related:

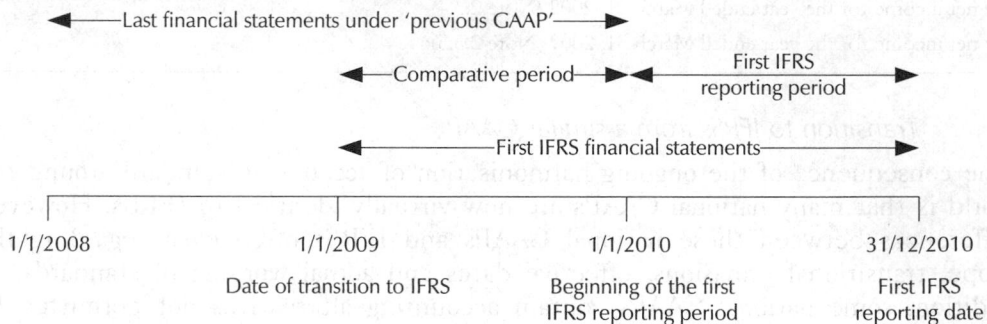

The diagram above also illustrates that there is a period of overlap, for the financial year 2009, which is reported first under the entity's previous GAAP and then as a comparative period under IFRSs. The following example illustrates how an entity should determine its date of transition to IFRSs.

Example 5.5:   Determining the date of transition to IFRSs

Entity A's year-end is 31 December and it presents financial statements that include one comparative period. Entity A is required (e.g. by national legislation) to produce IFRS financial statements for the first accounting period starting on or after 1 January 2010.

A's first IFRS financial statements are for the period ending on 31 December 2010. Its date of transition to IFRSs is 1 January 2009, which is the beginning of the first comparative period included in its IFRS financial statements.

Entity B's year-end is 31 July and it presents financial statements that include two comparative periods. Entity B is required to produce IFRS financial statements for the first accounting period starting on or after 1 January 2010.

B's first IFRS financial statements are for the period ending on 31 July 2011. Its date of transition to IFRSs is 1 August 2008, which is the beginning of the earliest comparative period included in its IFRS financial statements.

Entity C's most recent financial statements, under its previous GAAP are for the period from 1 July 2008 to 31 December 2009. Entity C presents its first IFRS financial statements for the period ending 31 December 2010.

C's date of transition is 1 July 2008. While paragraph 21 of IFRS 1 and paragraph 36 of IAS 1 require presentation of at least one comparative period, IFRSs do not require the comparative period to be a 12-month period. Thus, the entity's date of transition will be the beginning of the first comparative period, irrespective of the length of that period. However, paragraph 36 of IAS 1 would require disclosure of the reason why the comparative period is not 12 months and disclosure of the fact that the periods presented are not entirely comparable.

Similarly, it is generally not considered to be a problem if the current or comparative period in an entity's first IFRS financial statements only covers a 52-week period, because IAS 1 does not preclude the practice of presenting financial statements for 52-week financial periods.[30]

1.3.5 Defined terms: Fair value and deemed cost

Some exemptions in IFRS 1 refer to 'fair value' and 'deemed cost', which the standard defines as follows:[31]

Deemed cost: An amount used as a surrogate for cost or depreciated cost at a given date. Subsequent depreciation or amortisation assumes that the entity had initially recognised the asset or liability at the given date and that its cost was equal to the deemed cost.

Fair value: The amount for which an asset could be exchanged, or a liability settled, between knowledgeable, willing parties in an arm's length transaction.

In determining the fair value of items, a first-time adopter should apply the definition of fair value in Appendix A of IFRS 1 and any more specific guidance in other IFRSs on the determination of fair values for the asset or liability in question.[32] The fair values determined by a first-time adopter should reflect the conditions that existed at the date for which they were determined,[33] i.e. the first-time adopter should not apply hindsight in measuring the fair value at an earlier date.

2 EFFECTIVE DATE

2.1 First-time adoption under IFRS 1 (as revised in 2008)

IFRS 1 (as revised in 2008) should be applied to an entity's first IFRS financial statements for a period beginning on or after 1 July 2009, earlier application is permitted.[34] In theory it is possible for an entity to apply IFRS 1 (as revised in 2008) before its effective date of 1 July 2009 while not applying any of the standards or amendments below, which have the same effective date and also permit early adoption:[35]

Standard or interpretation	Main amendments to IFRS 1
IAS 23 (as revised in 2007) – *Borrowing Costs*	IFRS 1.D23
IFRS 3 (as revised in 2008) – *Business Combinations*	IFRS 1.19, C1, C4(f)-(g)
IAS 27 (as amended in 2008) – *Consolidated and Separate Financial Statements*	IFRS 1.B7
Amendments to IFRS 1 First-time Adoption of International Financial Reporting Standards and IAS 27 Consolidated and Separate Financial Statements: Cost of an Investment in a Subsidiary, Jointly Controlled Entity or Associate	IFRS 1.31 and D14-D15
Amendments to IFRS 5 Non-current Assets Held for Sale and Discontinued Operations	IFRS 1.B7

This chapter does not deal with the first-time adoption of the earlier versions of the above standards (i.e. the version before the above revisions and amendments). A detailed discussion of the first-time adoption of the earlier versions of those standards can be found in Chapter 5 of the previous edition of this book, *International GAAP 2009*.

2.1.1   Amendments to IFRS 1

In July 2009 the IASB published an amendment to IFRS 1 – *Additional Exemptions for First-time Adopters* (Amendments to IFRS 1), which added paragraphs 31A, D8A, D9A and D21A and amended paragraph D1(c), (d) and (l). These amendments, which are discussed in sections 5.5.4, 5.6.2 B, 5.14.2 and 6.5.3 below, should be applied for annual periods beginning on or after 1 January 2010. Earlier application is permitted. If an entity applies the amendments for an earlier period it should disclose that fact.[36]

2.2   First-time adoption under IFRS 1 (Bound Volume 2008)

An entity that adopts IFRSs for a period beginning before 1 July 2009, and does not adopt IFRS 1 (as revised in 2008) early, should apply IFRS 1 (Bound Volume 2008) – *First-Time Adoption of International Financial Reporting Standards*. A detailed discussion of that standard can be found in Chapter 5 of the previous edition of this book, *International GAAP 2009*.

3   RECOGNITION AND MEASUREMENT

3.1   Opening IFRS balance sheet and accounting policies

At the date of transition to IFRSs (e.g. 1 January 2009 for an entity presenting one year of comparative figures and reporting at 31 December 2010) an entity should prepare and present an opening IFRS balance sheet that is the starting point for its accounting under IFRSs.[37]

The requirement to prepare an opening IFRS balance sheet and 'reset the clock' at that date poses a number of challenges for first-time adopters. Even a first-time adopter that already applies a standard that is directly based on IFRSs may decide to restate items in its opening IFRS balance sheet (see 1.3.3 B above). This happens, for example, in the case of an entity applying a pension standard that is based on

IAS 19 – *Employee Benefits* – before an entity's date of transition to IFRSs because the transitional rules in the standard differ from those in IFRS 1.

IFRS 1 requires a first-time adopter to use the same accounting policies in its opening IFRS balance sheet and for all periods presented in its first IFRS financial statements. However, this may not be straightforward, since to achieve this, the entity should comply with each IFRSs effective at the end of its first IFRS reporting period, and should take into account a number of allowed exemptions from certain IFRSs and mandatory exceptions to retrospective application of other IFRSs in accordance with IFRS 1 (see 3.3 below).[38] In other words, the fundamental principle of IFRS 1 is to require full retrospective application of the standards in force at the end of an entity's first IFRS reporting period, but with limited exceptions. The IASB initially entertained a suggestion to restrict retrospective application of IFRSs to a limited 'look back' period of three to five years – to avoid the cost of investigating very old transactions – but concluded that this approach could lead to the omission of material assets or liabilities from an entity's opening IFRS balance sheet.[39] The diagram below shows how the process of selecting IFRS accounting policies operates.

The requirement to apply the same accounting policies to all periods also prohibits a first-time adopter from applying previous versions of standards that were effective at earlier dates.[40] The IASB believes that this:

- enhances comparability because the first IFRS financial statements are prepared on a consistent basis over time;

- gives users comparative information that is based on IFRSs that are superior to superseded versions of those standards; and

- avoids unnecessary costs.[41]

For similar reasons, IFRS 1 also permits an entity to apply a new standard that is not yet mandatory if that standard allows early application.[42] Users of financial statements should be aware that, depending on the end of an entity's first IFRS reporting period, it may or may not have the option to choose which version of a particular standard it may apply, as can be seen in the example below.

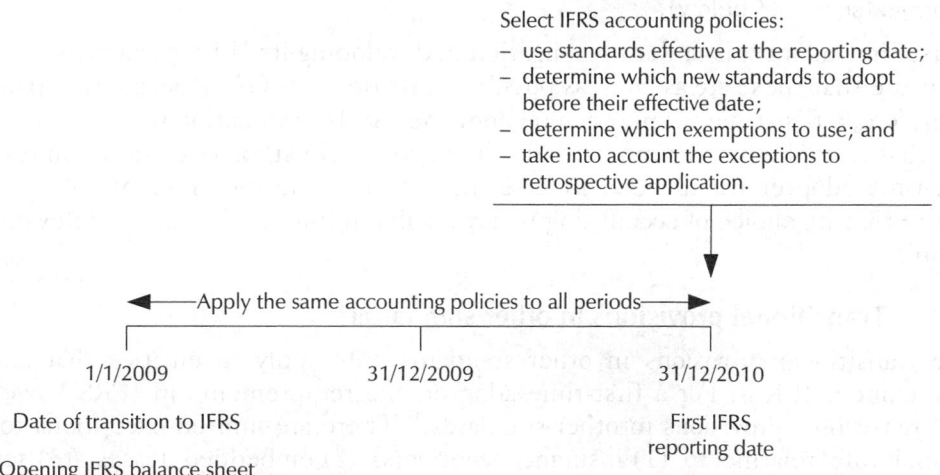

Select IFRS accounting policies:
– use standards effective at the reporting date;
– determine which new standards to adopt before their effective date;
– determine which exemptions to use; and
– take into account the exceptions to retrospective application.

◀——Apply the same accounting policies to all periods——▶

1/1/2009   31/12/2009   31/12/2010

Date of transition to IFRS   First IFRS
                                                         reporting date

Opening IFRS balance sheet

Example 5.6:   Prohibition from applying superseded standards

Entity A's date of transition to IFRSs is 1 January 2009 and its first IFRS reporting period ends 31 December 2010. Should entity B account for business combinations under IFRS 3 (2007 Bound Volume) – *Business Combinations* – or IFRS 3 (as revised in 2008) – *Business Combinations* – in its first IFRS financial statements?

IFRS 1 requires entity A to apply IFRS 3 (as revised in 2008) because IFRS 3 (as revised in 2008) is effective at the end of its first IFRS reporting period. Since IFRS 1 prohibits an entity from applying IFRS 3 (2007 Bound Volume) to the period before 1 July 2009 while applying IFRS 3 (as revised in 2008) in the remainder of 2009 and 2010, Entity A has to apply IFRS 3 (as revised 2008) for all periods presented.[43] *Note however that entity A does not need to apply IFRS 3 (as revised in 2008) to business combinations before its date of transition (see 5.2 below).*

Apart from when the exceptions at 3.3 below apply, an entity should in preparing its opening IFRS balance sheet:

'(a)   recognise all assets and liabilities whose recognition is required by IFRSs;

(b)   not recognise items as assets or liabilities if IFRSs do not permit such recognition;

(c)   reclassify items that it recognised in accordance with previous GAAP as one type of asset, liability or component of equity, but are a different type of asset, liability or component of equity in accordance with IFRSs; and

(d)   apply IFRSs in measuring all recognised assets and liabilities.'[44]

Any change in accounting policies on adoption of IFRSs may cause changes in the amounts previously recorded in respect of events and transactions that occurred before the date of transition. The effects of these changes should be recognised at the date of transition to IFRSs in retained earnings or, if appropriate, in another category of equity.[45] For example, an entity that applies the IAS 16 – *Property, Plant and Equipment* – revaluation model (see Chapter 16 at 4.1) in its first IFRS financial statements would recognise the difference between cost and the revalued amount of property, plant and equipment in a revaluation reserve. Conversely, an entity that had applied a revaluation model under its previous GAAP, but decided to apply the cost model under IAS 16, would reallocate the revaluation reserve to retained earnings (see 7.5.3 below).

A first-time adopter is under no obligation in developing its IFRS accounting policies to ensure that these are as close as possible to its previous GAAP accounting policies. Therefore, a first-time adopter could adopt the IAS 16 revaluation model despite the fact that it applied a cost model under its previous GAAP or vice versa. However, a first-time adopter would need to take into account the requirements of IAS 8 to ensure that its choice of accounting policy results in information that is relevant and reliable.[46]

3.2   Transitional provisions in other standards

The transitional provisions in other standards only apply to entities that already report under IFRSs. For a first-time adopter, the requirements in IFRS 1 override the transitional provisions in other standards.[47] There are limited exceptions to this general rule relating to (1) insurance contracts, (2) embedded leases, (3) service concessions, and (4) borrowing costs. In these cases IFRS 1 specifically requires application of the transitional rules in the relevant standard (see 5.4, 5.6, 5.13 and 5.14 below, respectively).

It is important to note that the transition rules for first-time adopters and entities that already report under IFRSs may differ significantly.

The IASB considers on a 'case by case when it issues a new IFRS whether a first-time adopter should apply that IFRS retrospectively or prospectively. The Board expects that retrospective application will be appropriate in most cases, given its primary objective of comparability over time within a first-time adopter's first IFRS financial statements. However, if the Board concludes in a particular case that prospective application by a first-time adopter is justified, it will amend the IFRS on first-time adoption of IFRSs.'[48]

In October 2004, the IFRIC considered whether first-time adopters, which cannot apply a requirement after making every reasonable effort to do so, are permitted to use the 'impracticability' exception under IAS 8. The IFRIC agreed 'that there were potential issues, especially with respect to "old" items, such as property, plant and equipment. However, those issues could usually be resolved by using one of the transition options available in IFRS 1'.[49]

3.3　Departures from full retrospective application

The IASB's *Framework* recognises the necessity to balance the cost and benefit of information as a constraint that may limit the provision of relevant and reliable information in financial reporting.[50] In developing IFRS 1, the IASB specifically considered this cost-benefit constraint, which resulted in a number of exceptions from the general principle of retrospective application. It is worthwhile noting that the IASB 'expects that most first-time adopters will begin planning on a timely basis for the transition to IFRSs. Accordingly, in balancing benefits and costs, the Board took as its benchmark an entity that plans the transition well in advance and can collect most information needed for its opening IFRS balance sheet at, or very soon after, the date of transition to IFRSs.'[51]

IFRS 1 establishes two types of departure from the principle of full retrospective application of standards in force at the end of the first IFRS reporting period:[52]

- it prohibits retrospective application of some aspects of other standards (see 3.3.1 below);[53] and

- it grants a number of optional exemptions from some of the requirements of other standards (see 3.3.2 below).[54]

3.3.1　*Exceptions to retrospective application of other IFRS*

IFRS 1 defines a number of mandatory *exceptions* that prohibit 'retrospective application of IFRSs in some areas, particularly where retrospective application would require judgements by management about past conditions after the outcome of a particular transaction is already known.'[55] The mandatory *exceptions* in the standard cover the following situations:[56]

(a)　estimates (see 4.2 below);

(b)　derecognition of financial assets and financial liabilities (see 4.3 below);

(c)   hedge accounting (see 4.4 below); and

(d)   non-controlling interests (see 4.5 below).

The reasoning behind the first three exceptions is that retrospective application of IFRSs in these situations could easily result in an unacceptable use of hindsight and lead to arbitrary or biased restatements, which would be neither relevant nor reliable.

3.3.2   Exemptions from other IFRS

In addition to the mandatory *exceptions* noted above, IFRS 1 grants limited *exemptions* from the general requirement of full retrospective application of the standards in force at the end of an entity's the first IFRS reporting period 'where the cost of complying with them would be likely to exceed the benefits to users of financial statements.'[57] The standard establishes exemptions in relation to:[58]

- business combinations (see 5.2 below);

- share-based payment transactions (see 5.3 below);

- insurance contracts (see 5.4 below);

- deemed cost (see 5.5 below);

- leases (see 5.6 below);

- employee benefits (see 5.7 below);

- cumulative translation differences (see 5.8 below);

- investments in subsidiaries, jointly controlled entities and associates (see 5.9 below);

- assets and liabilities of subsidiaries, associates and joint ventures (see 5.10 below);

- compound financial instruments (see 5.11 below);

- designation of previously recognised financial instruments (see 5.12 below);

- fair value measurement of financial assets or financial liabilities at initial recognition (see 5.13 below);

- decommissioning liabilities included in the cost of property, plant and equipment (see 5.14 below);

- financial assets or intangible assets accounted for in accordance with IFRIC 12 – *Service Concession Arrangements* (see 5.15 below);

- borrowing costs (see 5.16 below); and

- transfers of assets from customers (see 5.17 below).[59]

It is specifically prohibited under IFRS 1 to apply these exemptions by analogy to other items.[60]

Application of these exemptions is entirely optional, i.e. a first-time adopter can pick and choose the exemptions that it wants to apply. Importantly, the IASB did not establish a hierarchy of exemptions. Therefore, when an item is covered by more than one exemption, a first-time adopter has a free choice in determining the order in which it applies the exemptions.

Example 5.7:   *Order of application of exemptions*

Entity A acquired a building in a business combination. If entity A were to apply the business combinations exemption it would have to value the building at €120. However, if it were to use the fair value as the deemed cost of the building it would have to value it at €150. Which value should entity A use?

A can choose whether it wants to value the building at €120 or €150 in its opening IFRS balance sheet. The fact that entity A uses the business combinations exemption does not prohibit it from applying the 'fair value as deemed cost' exemption in relation to the same assets.

4   EXCEPTIONS TO RETROSPECTIVE APPLICATION OF OTHER IFRSs

4.1   Introduction

As noted at 3.3.1 above, IFRS 1 provides a number of mandatory *exceptions* that specifically prohibit retrospective application of IFRSs in the following situations:[61]

(a)   estimates (see 4.2 below);

(b)   derecognition of financial assets and financial liabilities (see 4.3 below);

(c)   hedge accounting (see 4.4 below); and

(d)   non-controlling interests (see 4.5 below).

Each of these exceptions is explained in detail below.

4.2   Estimates

IFRS 1 requires an entity to use estimates under IFRSs that are consistent with the estimates made for the same date under its previous GAAP – after adjusting for any difference in accounting policy – unless there is objective evidence that those estimates were in error.[62] IAS 8 defines prior period errors as:

> '... omissions from, and misstatements in, the entity's financial statements for one or more prior periods arising from a failure to use, or misuse of, reliable information that:
>
> (a)   was available when financial statements for those periods were authorised for issue; and
>
> (b)   could reasonably be expected to have been obtained and taken into account in the preparation and presentation of those financial statements.
>
> Such errors include the effects of mathematical mistakes, mistakes in applying accounting policies, oversights or misinterpretations of facts, and fraud.'[63]

Under IFRS 1 an entity cannot apply hindsight and make 'better' estimates when it prepares its first IFRS financial statements. This also means that an entity is not allowed to consider subsequent events that provide evidence of conditions that existed at that date, but that came to light after the date of its previous GAAP financial statements were finalised. The IASB considers that although some of those events might qualify as adjusting events in accordance with IAS 10 – *Events After the Reporting Period* – 'if the entity made those estimates on a basis consistent with IFRSs ... it would be more helpful to users – and more consistent with IAS 8 – to recognise the revision of those estimates as income or expense in the period when the entity made the revision, rather than in preparing the opening IFRS balance sheet.'[64] Effectively, the IASB wishes to prevent entities from using hindsight to 'clean up' their balance sheets as part of the opening IFRS balance sheet exercise. In addition, the exception also ensures that a first-time adopter need not conduct a search for, and change the accounting for, events that might have otherwise qualified as adjusting events.

As discussed at 4.4.2 A in relation to measurement of derivative financial instruments, IFRS 1 requires an entity that is unable to determine whether a particular portion of an adjustment is a transitional adjustment or a change in estimate, to treat that portion as a change in accounting estimate under IAS 8, with appropriate disclosures as required by paragraphs 32 to 40 of IAS 8.[65] The distinction between changes in accounting policies and changes in accounting estimates is discussed in detail in Chapter 3 at 4.2.

The requirement that an entity should use estimates consistent with those made under its previous GAAP applies both to estimates made in respect of the date of transition to IFRSs and to those in respect of the end of any comparative period.[66] IFRS 1 provides the following guidance on how an entity should put this requirement into practice:

- When an entity receives information after the relevant date about estimates that it had made under previous GAAP, it treats this information in the same way as a non-adjusting event after the reporting period under IAS 10.[67] An entity can be in one of the following two positions:[68]

  - its previous GAAP accounting policy was consistent with IFRSs, in which case the adjustment is reflected in the period in which the revision is made; or

  - its previous GAAP accounting policy was not consistent with IFRSs, in which case it adjusts the estimate for the difference in accounting policies.

  In both situations, if an entity later adjusts those estimates, it accounts for the revisions to those estimates as events in the period in which it makes the revisions;[69]

- When an entity needs to make estimates under IFRSs at the relevant date that were not required under its previous GAAP, those estimates should be consistent with IAS 10 and reflect conditions that existed at the relevant date. This means, for example, that estimates of market prices, interest rates or foreign exchange rates should reflect market conditions at that date;[70] and

- IFRS 1 does not override the requirements in other IFRSs that base classifications or measurements on circumstances existing at a particular date, such as for example:

  - the distinction between finance leases and operating leases;

  - the restrictions in IAS 38 – *Intangible Assets* – that prohibit capitalisation of expenditure on an internally generated intangible asset if the asset did not qualify for recognition when the expenditure was incurred; and

  - the distinction between financial liabilities and equity instruments.[71]

The flowchart below shows the decision-making process that an entity needs to apply in dealing with estimates under its previous GAAP.

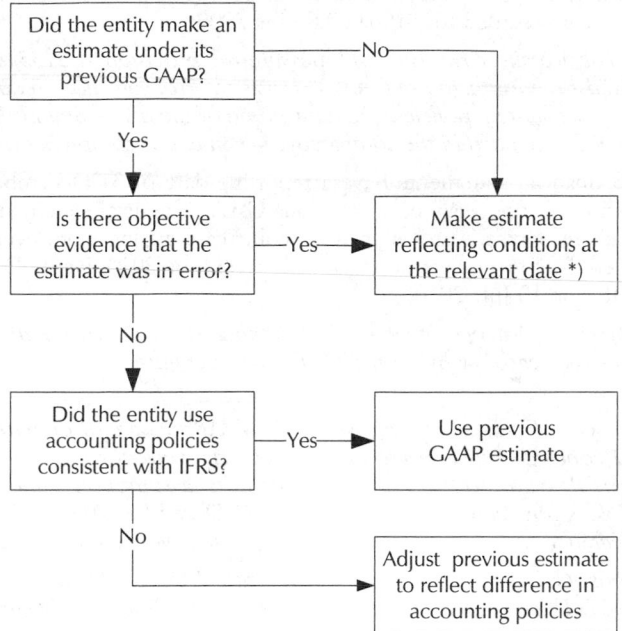

*) the relevant date is the date to which the estimate relates

If a first-time adopter concludes that estimates under previous GAAP were made in error, it should distinguish the correction of those errors from changes in accounting policies in its reconciliations from previous GAAP to IFRSs (see 6.4 below).[72]

The example below illustrates how an entity should deal with estimates under its previous GAAP.[73]

Example 5.8:   Application of IFRS 1 to estimates

Entity A previously accounted for its pension plan on a cash basis. However, under IAS 19 the plan is classified as a defined benefit plan and actuarial estimates are required.

A will need to make estimates under IFRSs at the relevant date that reflect conditions that existed at the relevant date. This means, for example, that it needs to use a discount rate that would have been used at that time, ignoring any developments after that date.

Entity B accounted for inventories at the lower of cost and net realisable value under its previous GAAP. B's accounting policy is consistent with the requirements of IAS 2 – *Inventories*. Under previous GAAP, the goods were accounted for at a price of £1.25/kg. Due to changes in market circumstances, entity B ultimately could only sell the goods in the following period for £0.90/kg.

Assuming that B's estimate of the net realisable value was not in error, it will account for the goods at £1.25/kg upon transition to IFRSs and will make no adjustments because the estimate was not in error and its accounting policy was consistent with IFRSs. The effect of selling the goods for £0.90/kg will be reflected in the period in which they were sold.

Entity C's first IFRS financial statements have a reporting date of 31 December 2010 and include comparative information for one year. In its previous GAAP financial statements for 31 December 2008, Entity C accounted for a provision of $150,000 in connection with a court case. Entity C's accounting policy was consistent with the requirements of IAS 37 – *Provisions, Contingent Liabilities and Contingent Assets*, except for the fact that Entity C did not discount the provision for the time value of money. The discounted value of the provision at 31 December 2008 would have been $135,000. The case was settled for $190,000 during 2009.

In its opening IFRS balance sheet Entity C will measure the provision at $135,000. IFRS 1 does not permit an entity to adjust the estimate itself, unless it was in error, but does require an adjustment to reflect the difference in accounting policies. The unwinding of the discount and the adjustment due to the under-provision will be included in the comparative statement of comprehensive income for 2009.

Entity D's first IFRS financial statements have a reporting date of 31 December 2010 and include comparative information for one year. In its previous GAAP financial statements for 31 December 2009, Entity D did not recognise a provision for a court case arising from events that occurred in September 2009. When the court case was concluded on 30 June 2010, Entity D was required to pay €1,000,000 and paid this on 10 July 2010.

In preparing its comparative balance sheet at 31 December 2009, the treatment of the court case at that date depends on the reason why Entity D did not recognise a provision under its previous GAAP at that date.

Scenario 1 – Previous GAAP was consistent with IAS 37. At the date of preparing its 2009 financial statements, Entity D concluded that the recognition criteria were not met. In this case, Entity D's assumptions under IFRSs are to be consistent with its assumptions under previous GAAP. Therefore, Entity A does not recognise a provision at 31 December 2009 and the effect of settling the court case is reflected in the 2010 statement of comprehensive income.

Scenario 2 – Previous GAAP was not consistent with IAS 37. Therefore, Entity D develops estimates under IAS 37. Under IAS 37, an entity determines whether an obligation exists at the end of the reporting period by taking account of all available evidence, including any additional evidence provided by events after the end of the reporting period. Similarly, under IAS 10, the resolution of a court case after the end of the reporting period is an adjusting event if it confirms that the entity had a present obligation at that date. In this instance, the resolution of the court case confirms that Entity D had a liability in September 2009 (when the events occurred that gave rise to the court case). Therefore, Entity D recognises a provision at 31 December 2009. Entity D measures that provision by discounting the €1,000,000 paid on 10 July 2010 to its present value, using a discount rate that complies with IAS 37 and reflects market conditions at 31 December 2009.

4.3   Derecognition of financial assets and liabilities

A first-time adopter should apply the derecognition requirements in IAS 39 – *Financial Instruments: Recognition and Measurement* – prospectively to transactions occurring on or after 1 January 2004. Therefore, if a first-time adopter derecognised non-derivative financial assets or non-derivative financial liabilities under its previous GAAP as a result of a transaction that occurred before 1 January 2004, it should not recognise those assets and liabilities under IFRSs (unless they qualify for recognition as a result of a later transaction or event).[74] A first-time adopter that wants to apply the derecognition requirements in IAS 39 retrospectively from a date of the entity's choosing can only do so 'provided that the information needed to apply IAS 39 to financial assets and financial liabilities derecognised as a result of past transactions was obtained at the time of initially accounting for those transactions.'[75] This will effectively prevent most first-time adopters from restating transactions that occurred before 1 January 2004.

A first-time adopter that derecognised non-derivative financial assets and liabilities under its previous GAAP before 1 January 2004 will not have to recognise these items under IFRSs even if they meet the IAS 39 recognition criteria.[76] However,

SIC-12 – *Consolidation – Special Purpose Entities* – contains no specific transitional or first-time adoption provisions. Accordingly, its requirements with regard to the consolidation of SPEs should be applied fully retrospective by first-time adopters. For example, an entity may have derecognised, under its previous GAAP, non-derivative financial assets and liabilities when they were transferred to another entity. If that entity is considered to be an SPE under SIC-12, those assets and liabilities will be re-recognised on transition to IFRSs by way of consolidation of the SPE rather than through application of IAS 39. Of course, if the SPE itself then subsequently achieved derecognition of the items concerned under the entity's previous GAAP (other than by transfer to a second SPE or member of the entity's group), then the items remain derecognised on transition.

IFRS 1 acknowledges that some arrangements for the transfer of assets, particularly securitisations, may last for some time, with the result that transfers might be made both before and on or after 1 January 2004 under the same arrangement. IFRS 1 clarifies that transfers made under such arrangements fall within the first-time adoption provisions only if they occurred before 1 January 2004. Transfers on or after 1 January 2004 are subject to the full requirements of IAS 39.[77]

4.4 Hedge accounting

Hedge accounting is dealt with comprehensively in Chapter 33. The first-time adoption issues relating to hedge accounting are discussed below.

4.4.1 Hedge accounting: Prohibition on retrospective application

IFRS 1 explains that entities are prohibited from designating retrospectively as a hedge a transaction that was entered into before the date of transition to IFRSs.[78] In the basis for conclusions, it is explained that:

'...it is unlikely that most entities would have adopted IAS 39's criteria for (a) documenting hedges at their inception and (b) testing the hedges for effectiveness, even if they intended to continue the same hedging strategies after adopting IAS 39. Furthermore, retrospective designation of hedges (or retrospective reversal of their designation) could lead to selective designation of some hedges to report a particular result.[79]

'To overcome these problems, the transitional requirements in [the original version of] IAS 39 require an entity already applying IFRS to apply the hedging requirements prospectively when it adopts IAS 39. As the same problems arise for a first-time adopter, the IFRS requires prospective application by a first-time adopter.'[80]

Unfortunately, there is only a limited amount of guidance in IFRS 1 regarding hedge accounting and therefore it is not entirely clear what applying these requirements of IAS 39 'prospectively' actually involves, especially insofar as the opening IFRS balance sheet is concerned. However, the basis for conclusions continues:

'ED 1 [*First-time Application of International Financial Reporting Standards*] included a redrafted version of the transitional provisions in IAS 39 and related Questions and Answers (Q&As) developed by the IAS 39 Implementation Guidance Committee. The Board confirmed in the Basis for Conclusions published with ED 1 that it did not intend the redrafting to create substantive changes. However, in the light of responses to ED 1, the Board decided in finalising IFRS 1 that the redrafting would not make it easier for first-time adopters and others to understand and apply the transition provisions and Q&As. However, the project to improve IAS 32 and IAS 39 resulted in certain amendments to the transition requirements. In addition, this project incorporated selected other Q&As (i.e. not on transition) into IAS 39. The Board therefore took this opportunity to consolidate all the guidance for first-time adopters in one place, by incorporating the Q&As on transition into IFRS 1.[81]

This indicates that the transitional provisions set out in the original version of IAS 39 and IGC Q&As, ED 1 and IFRS 1 are intended to be broadly consistent. Consequently, the fact that all three sources are expressed in different ways can be useful in interpreting this aspect of IFRS 1. These documents are referred to at 4.4.2 below where they assist in understanding the requirements set out in IFRS 1.

4.4.2   Hedge accounting: opening IFRS balance sheet

A   Measurement of derivatives and elimination of deferred gains and losses

Under its previous GAAP an entity's accounting policies might have included a number of accounting treatments for derivatives that formed part of a hedge relationship. For example, accounting policies might have included those where the derivative was:

- not explicitly recognised as an asset or liability (e.g. in the case of a forward contract used to hedge an expected but uncontracted future transaction);

- recognised as an asset or liability but at an amount different from its fair value (e.g. a purchased option recognised at its original cost, perhaps less amortisation; or an interest rate swap accounted for by accruing the periodic interest payments and receipts); or

- subsumed within the accounting for another asset or liability (e.g. a foreign currency denominated monetary item and a matching forward contract or swap accounted for as a 'synthetic' functional currency denominated monetary item).

Whatever the previous accounting treatment, a first-time adopter should isolate and separately account for all derivatives in its opening IFRS balance sheet as assets or liabilities measured at fair value.[82]

The implementation guidance explains that all derivatives, other than those that are financial guarantee contracts or designated and effective hedging instruments, are classified as held for trading. Accordingly, the difference between the previous carrying amount of a derivative (which may have been zero) and its fair value should be recognised as an adjustment of the balance of retained earnings at the beginning of the financial year in which IFRS 1 is initially applied (other than for a derivative that is a financial guarantee contract or a designated and effective hedging instrument).[83] In addition, IFRS 1 requires an entity that is unable to determine whether a particular portion of an adjustment is a transitional adjustment or a change in estimate, to treat that portion as a change in accounting estimate under IAS 8, with appropriate disclosures as required by paragraphs 32 to 40 of IAS 8.[84] The distinction between changes in accounting policies and changes in accounting estimates is discussed in detail in Chapter 3 at 4.2.

Hedge accounting policies under an entity's previous GAAP might also have included one or both of the following accounting treatments:

- derivatives were measured at fair value but, to the extent they were regarded as hedging future transactions, the gain (or loss) arising was reported as a liability (or asset) such as deferred (or accrued) income;

- realised gains or losses arising on the termination of a previously unrecognised derivative used in a hedge relationship (such as an interest rate swap hedging a borrowing) were included in the balance sheet as deferred or accrued income and amortised over the remaining term of the hedged exposure.

In all cases, an entity is required to eliminate deferred gains and losses arising on derivatives 'that were reported in accordance with previous GAAP as if they were assets or liabilities'.[85] Essentially, this is because deferred gains and losses do not meet the definition of assets or liabilities under the IASB's *Framework*. In contrast to adjustments made to restate derivatives at fair value, the implementation guidance does not specify in general terms how to deal with adjustments to eliminate deferred gains or losses, i.e. whether they should be taken to retained earnings or a separate component of equity.

The requirement to eliminate deferred gains and losses does not appear to extend to those that have been included in the carrying amount of other assets or liabilities that will continue to be recognised under IFRSs. For example, under an entity's previous GAAP, the carrying amount of non-financial assets such as inventories or property, plant and equipment might have included the equivalent of a basis adjustment (i.e. hedging gains or losses were considered an integral part of the asset's cost). In fact, carrying forward this treatment into an entity's first set of IFRS financial statements would be consistent with the transitional provisions of the December 2003 version of IAS 39. Of course, entities should also consider any other provisions of IFRS 1 that apply to those hedged items.

The way in which an entity accounts for these adjustments will, to a large extent, dictate how its existing hedge relationships will be reflected in its ongoing IFRS financial statements. Particularly, an entity's future results will be different depending on whether the adjustments are taken to retained earnings or to a separate component of equity – in the latter case they would be reclassified from equity to profit or loss at a later date but would not in the former. Similarly, its future results would be affected if the carrying amounts of related assets or liabilities are changed to reflect these adjustments (as opposed to the adjustments being made to retained earnings).

For short-term hedges (e.g. of sales and inventory purchases) these effects are likely to work their way out of the IFRS financial statements relatively quickly. However, for other hedges (e.g. of long term borrowings) an entity's results may be affected for many years. The question of which hedge relationships should be reflected in an entity's opening IFRS balance sheet is dealt with at B to D below.

B   Hedge relationships reflected in the opening IFRS balance sheet

The standard states that a first-time adopter *should not* reflect a hedging relationship in its opening IFRS balance sheet if that hedging relationship is of a type that *does not* qualify for hedge accounting under IAS 39. As examples of this it cites many hedging relationships where the hedging instrument is a cash instrument or written option; where the hedged item is a net position; or where the hedge covers interest risk in a held-to-maturity investment.[86] If the hedge effectiveness assessments under previous GAAP were not compliant with IAS 39 then that does not mean that the hedge relationships themselves should be viewed as ones that do not qualify for hedge accounting under IAS 39.

However, if an entity had designated a net position as a hedged item under its previous GAAP, the IASB decided that an individual item within that net position *may* be designated as a hedged item under IFRSs, provided that it does so no later than the date of transition to IFRSs.[87] In other words, such designation could allow the hedge relationship to be reflected in the opening IFRS balance sheet.

Further, a first-time adopter is not permitted to designate hedges retrospectively in relation to transactions entered into before the date of transition to IFRSs.[88] This would appear to prevent an entity from reflecting hedge relationships in its opening balance sheet that it did not identify as such under its previous GAAP. It does not however, prevent such designation if planned and documented prior to the date of transition.

It might seem to follow that a hedge relationship designated under an entity's previous GAAP *should* be reflected in its opening IFRS balance sheet if that hedging relationship *is* of a type that *does* qualify for hedge accounting under IAS 39. In fact, if an entity was allowed not to reflect such a hedge in its opening IFRS balance sheet this would effectively allow the retrospective reversal of the hedge designation. As noted at A above, this is something the IASB has sought to avoid.[89] However, while such a 'principle' seems to be implied by the implementation guidance (see C and D below), the IASB has not actually articulated it in these terms.

There are, perhaps, a number of reasons for the IASB's reticence. For example, under an entity's previous GAAP, it might not have been clear whether a derivative instrument was actually designated as a hedge. Further, even if it were clear that a derivative had previously been designated as a hedge, the hedged item might not have been identified with sufficient specificity to allow the effects of the hedge to be reflected in the opening IFRS balance sheet and/or, thereafter, to be 'unwound' at the appropriate time. Nevertheless, if (1) a hedge relationship can be specifically identified under an entity's previous GAAP and (2) that hedge relationship is eligible for hedge accounting under IFRSs then, in our opinion, the entity should account for the hedge relationship upon transition, regardless of whether or not the hedge relationship is effective. However, if the hedge relationship does not meet the requirements in IAS 39 prospectively then hedge discontinuation rules in that standard apply immediately after transition.

C   *Reflecting cash flow hedges in the opening IFRS balance sheet*

The implementation guidance to IFRS 1 explains that a first-time adopter may, under its previous GAAP, have deferred gains and losses on a cash flow hedge of a forecast transaction. If at the date of transition to IFRSs the hedged forecast transaction is not highly probable, but is expected to occur, the entire deferred gain or loss should be recognised in equity.[90] To be consistent, this would be included in the same component of equity an entity would use to accumulate future gains and losses on cash flow hedges.

This raises the question of how to deal with such a hedge if, at the date of transition to IFRSs, the forecast transaction *was* highly probable. It would make no sense if the former was required to be reflected in the opening IFRS balance sheet, but the latter (which is clearly a 'better' hedge) was not. Therefore, it must follow that a cash flow hedge should be reflected in the opening IFRS balance sheet in the way set out above if the hedged item is a forecast transaction that is highly probable. Similarly, it follows that a cash flow hedge of the variability in cash flows attributable to a particular risk associated with a recognised asset or liability (such as all or some future interest payments on variable rate debt) should also be reflected in the opening balance sheet.

If, at the date of transition to IFRSs, the forecast transaction was *not* expected to occur, this would be a relationship of a type that does not qualify for hedge accounting under IAS 39. Therefore the hedging relationship should not be reflected in the opening IFRS balance sheet. In fact ED 1 was explicit on this point.[91]

There are various ways in which gains or losses might have been deferred under an entity's previous GAAP. ED 1 explained that, in this context, deferral included:

• treating deferred gains as if they were liabilities and deferred losses as if they were assets; and

• not recognising changes in the fair value of the hedging instrument.[92]

Even though this explanation was not incorporated into IFRS 1, at a conceptual level there is scarce reason why it should not apply under the standard. However, it is possible to read parts of the implementation guidance as preventing this treatment if the hedge has not been designated in an effective hedge under IAS 39 by the date of transition. The following example highlights this issue.

Example 5.9:   Unrecognised gains and losses on existing cash flow hedge

Entity A has the euro as its functional currency. In September 2008 it entered into a forward currency contract to sell dollars for euros in twelve months to hedge dollar denominated sales it forecasts are highly probable to occur in September 2009. Entity A will apply IAS 39 from 1 January 2009 its date of transition to IFRSs. The historical cost of the forward contract is €nil and at the date of transition it had a positive fair value of €100.

Case 1: Gains and losses deferred

Under entity A's previous GAAP, until the sales occurred the forward contract was recognised in the balance sheet at its fair value and the resulting gain or loss was deferred in the balance sheet as a liability or asset. When the sale occurred, any deferred gain or loss was recognised in profit or loss as an offset to the revenue recognised on the hedged sales.

Case 2: Gains and losses unrecognised

Under entity A's previous GAAP the contract was not recognised in the balance sheet. When the sale occurred, any unrecognised gain or loss was recognised in profit or loss as an offset to the revenue recognised on the hedged sales.

In Case 1 the relationship can clearly be reflected in entity A's opening IFRS balance sheet whether or not it is designated as an effective hedge in accordance with IAS 39 at the date of transition: there is no restriction on transferring the deferred gain to a separate component of equity and there is no adjustment to the carrying amount of the forward contract.

Case 2 is slightly more problematic. As noted at A above, the implementation guidance explains that the difference between the previous carrying amount of a derivative and its fair value should be recognised as an adjustment of the balance of retained earnings (other than for a derivative that is a financial guarantee contract or a designated and effective hedging instrument).[93] Read literally, this implementation guidance could prevent the relationship from being reflected in entity A's opening IFRS balance sheet, if it had not designated the relationship as an effective hedge in accordance with IAS 39 at the date of transition. This is because the adjustment to the carrying amount of the forward would be recorded in retained earnings rather than a separate component of equity.

Such an interpretation would allow entity A to choose not to designate (in accordance with IAS 39) certain cash flow hedges, say those that are in a loss position, until one day after its date of transition, thereby allowing associated hedging losses to bypass profit or loss completely. However, this would effectively result in the retrospective de-designation of hedges to achieve a desired result, thereby breaching this general principle of IFRS 1. Arguably this general principle of the standard should take precedence over the implementation guidance.

D   Reflecting fair value hedges in the opening IFRS balance sheet

The implementation guidance to IFRS 1 explains that a first-time adopter may, under its previous GAAP, have deferred or not recognised gains and losses on a fair value hedge of a hedged item that is not measured at fair value. For such a fair value hedge, the entity should adjust the carrying amount of the hedged item at the date of transition to IFRSs. The adjustment, which is essentially the effective part of the hedge that was not recognised in the carrying amount of the hedged item under the previous GAAP, should be calculated as the lower of:

(a)   that portion of the cumulative change in the fair value of the hedged item that reflects the designated hedged risk and was not recognised under previous GAAP; and

(b)   that portion of the cumulative change in the fair value of the hedging instrument that reflects the designated hedged risk and, under previous GAAP, was either (i) not recognised or (ii) deferred in the balance sheet as an asset or liability.[94]

This requirement is consistent with the requirement in the original version of IAS 39 (and the proposals in ED 1) under which any balance sheet positions in fair value hedges of existing assets and liabilities would be accounted for in the opening balance sheet in (broadly) the same manner as above.[95]

Available-for-sale assets are measured at fair value, so the guidance above would not appear to apply to fair value hedges of such instruments. However, it would be logical to apply an equivalent adjustment to the cost or amortised cost of such assets.

E   *Reflecting foreign net investment hedges in the opening IFRS balance sheet*

IFRS 1 does not provide explicit guidance on reflecting foreign net investment hedges in the opening IFRS balance sheet. However, paragraph 102 of IAS 39 requires that ongoing IFRS reporting entities account for those hedges similarly to cash flow hedges. It can therefore be argued that the first-time adoption provisions regarding cash flow hedges (see C above) also apply to hedges for foreign net investments.

A first-time adopter that applies the exemption to reset cumulative translation differences to zero (see 5.8 below) should not reclassify pre-transition gains and losses on the hedging instruments that were recognised in equity to profit or loss upon disposal of a foreign operation. Instead, those pre-transition gains and losses should be recognised in the opening balance of retained earnings to avoid a disparity between the treatment of the gains and losses on the hedged item and the hedging instrument. In other words, the requirement to reset the cumulative translation differences also applies to related gains and losses on hedging instruments.

4.4.3   *Hedge accounting: subsequent treatment*

The implementation guidance explains that hedge accounting can be applied prospectively only from the date the hedge relationship is fully designated and documented. Therefore, if the hedging instrument is still held at the date of transition to IFRSs, the designation and documentation of a hedge relationship must be completed on or before that date if the hedge relationship is to qualify for hedge accounting on an ongoing basis from that date.[96]

Although not addressed explicitly in the standard, where the necessary designation and documentation is in place by the date of transition to IFRSs, in our view this need not be considered a de-designation of the previous GAAP hedge relationship and re-designation under IAS 39. Consequently, the assessment of hedge effectiveness may be performed on the assumption that the hedge relationship started on the same date that it did under previous GAAP, possibly avoiding some of the pitfalls associated with hedging instruments that have a non-zero fair value at the time of designation.[97] However, if an entity did not apply hedge accounting under its previous GAAP then it is not appropriate to include fair value movements before the date of transition in the retrospective hedge effectiveness test.

An entity may, before the date of transition to IFRSs, have designated a transaction as a hedge that does not meet the conditions for hedge accounting in IAS 39. In these cases it should follow the general requirements in IAS 39 for discontinuing hedge accounting – these are dealt with in Chapter 33 at 4.1.3 for fair value hedges and in Chapter 33 at 4.2.3 for cash flow hedges.[98]

For cash flow hedges, any net cumulative gain or loss that was reclassified to equity on initial application of IAS 39 (see 4.4.2 C above) should remain in equity until:

(a)   the forecast transaction subsequently results in the recognition of a non-financial asset or non-financial liability;

(b)   the forecast transaction affects profit or loss; or

(c)   subsequently circumstances change and the forecast transaction is no longer expected to occur, in which case any related net cumulative gain or loss that had been reclassified to equity on initial application of IAS 39 is reclassified to profit or loss.[99]

The requirements above do little more than reiterate the general requirements of IAS 39, i.e. that hedge accounting can only be applied prospectively if the qualifying conditions are met, and entities should experience few interpretative problems in dealing with this aspect of the hedge accounting requirements.

4.4.4   Hedge accounting: examples

The following examples illustrate the guidance considered at 4.4.1 to 4.4.3 above.

Example 5.10:   Pre-transition cash flow hedges

Case 1: All hedge accounting conditions met from date of transition and thereafter

In 2001 entity A borrowed €10m from a bank. The terms of the loan provide that a coupon of 3 month LIBOR plus 2% is payable quarterly in arrears and the principal is repayable in 2016. In 2004, entity A decided to 'fix' its coupon payments for the remainder of the term of the loan by entering into a twelve-year pay-fixed, receive-floating interest rate swap. The swap has a notional amount of €10m and the floating leg resets quarterly based on 3 month LIBOR.

In entity A's final financial statements prepared under its previous GAAP, the swap was clearly identified as a hedging instrument in a hedge of the loan and was accounted for as such. The fair value of the swap was not recognised in entity A's balance sheet and the periodic interest settlements were accrued and recognised as an adjustment to the loan interest expense. On 1 January 2009, entity A's date of transition to IFRSs, the loan and the swap were still in place and the swap had a positive fair value of €1m and a €nil carrying amount. In addition, entity A met all the conditions in IAS 39 to permit the use of hedge accounting for this arrangement throughout 2009 and 2010.

In its opening IFRS balance sheet entity A should:

• recognise the interest rate swap as an asset at its fair value of €1m; and

• credit €1m to a separate component of equity, to be reclassified to profit or loss as the hedged transactions (future interest payments on the loan) affect profit or loss.

In addition, hedge accounting would be applied throughout 2009 and 2010.

Case 2: Hedge terminated prior to date of transition

The facts are as in Case 1 except that in April 2008 entity A decided to terminate the hedge and the interest rate swap was settled for its then fair value of €1.5m. Under its previous GAAP, entity A's stated accounting policy in respect of terminated hedges was to defer any realised gain or loss on terminated hedging instruments where the hedged exposure remained. These gains or losses would be recognised in profit or loss at the same time as gains or losses on the hedged exposure. At the end of December 2008, A's balance sheet included a liability (unamortised gain) of €1.4m.

IFRS 1 does not explicitly address hedges terminated prior to the date of transition but we see no reason why these relationships should not be reflected in an entity's opening IFRS balance sheet in the same way as other cash flow hedges that are reflected in an entity's closing balance sheet under its previous GAAP. Accordingly, in its opening IFRS balance sheet entity A should:

- remove the deferred gain of €1.4m from the balance sheet; and

- credit €1.4m to a separate component of equity, to be reclassified to profit or loss as the hedged transactions (future interest payments on the loan) affect profit or loss.

Example 5.11:   Existing fair value hedges

Case 1: All hedge accounting conditions met from date of transition and thereafter (1)

On 15 November 2008, entity B entered into a forward contract to sell 50,000 barrels of crude oil to hedge all changes in the fair value of certain inventory. Entity B will apply IAS 39 from 1 January 2009, its date of transition to IFRSs. The historical cost of the forward contract is $nil and at the date of transition the forward had a negative fair value of $50.

In entity B's final financial statements prepared under its previous GAAP, the forward was clearly identified as a hedging instrument in a hedge of the inventory and was accounted for as such. The contract was recognised in the balance sheet as a liability at its fair value and the resulting loss was deferred in the balance sheet as an asset. In the period between 15 November 2008 and 1 January 2009 the fair value of the inventory increased by $47. In addition, entity B met all the conditions in IAS 39 to permit the use of hedge accounting for this arrangement throughout 2009 until the forward expired.

In its opening IFRS balance sheet entity B should:

- continue to recognise the forward contract as a liability at its fair value of $50;

- derecognise the $50 deferred loss on the forward contract;

- recognise the crude oil inventory at its historical cost plus $47 (the lower of the change in fair value of the crude oil inventory, $47, and that of the forward contract, $50); and

- record the net adjustment of $3 in retained earnings.

In addition, hedge accounting would be applied throughout 2009 until the forward expired.

Case 2: All hedge accounting conditions met from date of transition and thereafter (2)

In 2001 entity C borrowed €10m from a bank. The terms of the loan provide that a coupon of 8% is payable quarterly in arrears and the principal is repayable in 2016. In 2004, entity C decided to alter its coupon payments for the remainder of the term of the loan by entering into a twelve-year pay-floating, receive-fixed interest rate swap. The swap has a notional amount of €10m and the floating leg resets quarterly based on 3 month LIBOR.

In entity C's final financial statements prepared under its previous GAAP, the swap was clearly identified as a hedging instrument in a hedge of the loan and accounted for as such. The fair value of the swap was not recognised in entity C's balance sheet and the periodic interest settlements on the swap were accrued and recognised as an adjustment to the loan interest expense.

On 1 January 2009, entity C's date of transition to IFRSs, the loan and the swap were still in place and the swap had a negative fair value of €1m and a €nil carrying amount. The cumulative change in the fair value of the loan attributable to changes in 3 month LIBOR was €1.1m, although this change was not recognised in entity C's balance sheet because the loan was accounted for at cost. In addition, entity C met all the conditions in IAS 39 to permit the use of hedge accounting for this arrangement throughout 2009 and 2010.

In its opening IFRS balance sheet entity C should:

- recognise the interest rate swap as a liability at its fair value of €1m; and

- reduce the carrying amount of the loan by €1m (the lower of the change in its fair value attributable to the hedged risk, €1.1m, and that of the interest rate swap, $1m).

In addition, hedge accounting would be applied throughout 2009 and 2010.

Case 3: Hedge terminated prior to date of transition

The facts are as in Case 2 above except that in April 2008 entity C decided to terminate the hedge and the interest rate swap was settled for its then negative fair value of €1.5m. Under its previous GAAP, entity C's stated accounting policy in respect of terminated hedges was to defer any gain or loss on the hedging instrument as a liability or an asset where the hedged exposure remained and this gain or loss was recognised in profit or loss at the same time as the hedged exposure. At the end of December 2008 the unamortised loss recognised as an asset in entity C's balance sheet was €1.4m. In 2008 the cumulative change in the fair value of the loan attributable to changes in 3 month LIBOR that had not been recognised was €1.6m.

In its opening IFRS balance sheet entity C should:

- remove the deferred loss of €1.4m from the balance sheet; and
- reduce the carrying amount of the loan by €1.4m (the lower of the change in its fair value attributable to the hedged risk, €1.6m, and the change in value of the interest rate swap that was deferred in the balance sheet, €1.4m).

The €1.4m adjustment to the loan would be amortised to profit or loss over its remaining term.

Case 4: Documentation completed after the date of transition

The facts are as in Case 2 above except that, at the date of transition, entity C had not prepared documentation that would allow it to apply hedge accounting under IAS 39. Hedge documentation was subsequently prepared as a result of which the hedge qualified for hedge accounting with effect from the beginning of July 2009 and throughout 2010.

As in Case 2, in its opening IFRS balance sheet entity C should:

- recognise the interest rate swap as a liability at its fair value of €1m; and
- reduce the carrying amount of the loan by €1m (the lower of the change in its fair value attributable to the hedged risk, €1.1m, and that of the interest rate swap, €1m), because the loan was clearly identified as a hedged item.

For the period from January 2009 to June 2009, hedge accounting would not be available. Accordingly, the interest rate swap would be remeasured to its fair value and any gain or loss would be recognised in profit or loss with no offset from remeasuring the loan. With effect from July 2009 hedge accounting would be applied prospectively.

4.5   Non-controlling interests

A first-time adopter that applies IAS 27 (as amended in 2008) – *Consolidated and Separate Financial Statements*, should apply the standard retrospectively, with the exception of the following requirements of IAS 27 (as amended in 2008) that apply prospectively from its date of transition to IFRSs:[100]

(a)   the requirement in paragraph 28 that total comprehensive income is attributed to the owners of the parent and to the non-controlling interests even if this results in the non-controlling interests having a deficit balance;

(b)   the requirements in paragraphs 30 and 31 on accounting for changes in the parent's ownership interest in a subsidiary that do not result in a loss of control; and

(c)   the requirements in paragraphs 34 to 37 on accounting for a loss of control over a subsidiary, and the related requirements of paragraph 8A of IFRS 5 – *Non-current Assets Held for Sale and Discontinued Operations*.

The above exceptions from the requirement to apply IFRSs fully retrospectively are based on the transitional rules in IAS 27 (as amended in 2008) for existing IFRS reporting entities.[101] As explained at 5.2.1 below, if a first-time adopter restates any business combination prior to its date of transition to comply with IFRS 3 (as revised in 2008) – *Business Combinations* – it must also apply IAS 27 (as amended in 2008) from that date onwards.[102]

5   VOLUNTARY EXEMPTIONS FROM THE REQUIREMENTS OF CERTAIN IFRSs

5.1   Introduction

As noted at 3.3.2 above, IFRS 1 grants limited *exemptions* from the general requirement of full retrospective application of the standards in force at the end of an entity's the first IFRS reporting period.[103] Each of these exemptions is explained in detail below.

5.2   Business combinations and acquisitions of associates and joint ventures

The business combinations exemption in IFRS 1 is probably the single most important exemption in the standard, as it permits a first-time adopter not to restate business combinations prior to its date of transition to IFRSs. The detailed guidance on the application of the business combinations exemption is contained in Appendix C to IFRS 1 and is organised as follows in the sections below:[104]

- option to restate business combinations retrospectively (see 5.2.1 below);

- classification of business combinations (see 5.2.2 below);

- recognition and measurement of assets and liabilities (see 5.2.3 below);

- restatement of goodwill (see 5.2.4 below);

- currency adjustments to goodwill (see 5.2.5 below);

- previously unconsolidated subsidiaries (see 5.2.6 below);

- previously consolidated entities that are not subsidiaries (see 5.2.7 below); and

- measurement of deferred taxation and non-controlling interests (see 5.2.8 below).

5.2.1   *Option to restate business combinations retrospectively*

A first-time adopter must account for business combinations after its date of transition to IFRSs under IFRS 3 (as revised in 2008), i.e. any business combinations during the comparative periods need to be restated in accordance with IFRSs. An entity may elect not to apply IFRS 3 (as revised in 2008) to business combinations before the date of transition. However, if a first-time adopter does restate a business combination prior to its date of transition to comply with IFRS 3 (as revised in 2008) it must also restate any subsequent business combinations under IFRS 3 (as revised in 2008) and apply IAS 27 (as amended in 2008) from that date onwards.[105] In other words, as shown on the time line below, a first-time adopter is allowed to choose any date in the past and account for business combinations going forward under IFRS 3 (as revised in 2008) without having to restate business combinations prior to the earliest IFRS 3 (as revised in 2008) restatement.

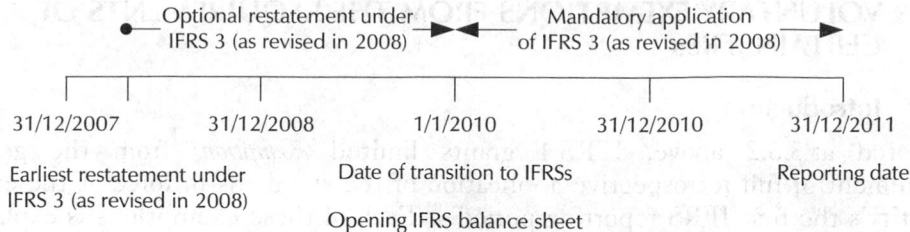

Even if a first-time adopter elects not to restate certain business combinations, it may need to restate the carrying amounts of the acquired assets and liabilities as described at 5.2.3 below.

Extracts 5.9 and 5.10 at 6.3 below illustrate the typical disclosure made by entities that opted not to restate business combinations before their date of transition to IFRSs, while Extract 5.2 below illustrates an entity that chose to restate business combinations from a date earlier than its date of transition.

Extract 5.2: ICON plc (2007)

Statement of Accounting Policies [extract]

Business combinations [extract]

The purchase method of accounting is employed in accounting for the acquisition of subsidiaries by the Group. The Group has availed of the option to restate business combinations which occurred prior to the transition date of 1 June 2004. The Group has chosen to restate all business combinations which occurred on or after 1 June 2001 and accordingly goodwill has not been amortised from this date but has been carried forward at its net book value and has been subject to impairment testing in accordance with IAS 36 *Impairment of Assets*.

Originally, the IASB proposed not to permit restatement of business combinations prior to the date of transition to IFRSs as this 'could require an entity to recreate data that it did not capture at the date of a past business combination and make subjective estimates about conditions that existed at that date. These factors could reduce the relevance and reliability of the entity's first IFRS financial statements.'[106] However, the IASB considered that – especially where the information is more likely to be available – it would be conceptually preferable to restate business combinations as the 'effects of business combination accounting can last for many years' and 'previous GAAP may differ significantly from IFRSs'.[107] Therefore, the IASB concluded that although it could not require restatement of business combinations for cost-benefit reasons, it should at least permit restatement on condition that all subsequent business combinations are also restated.[108]

Existing IFRS-reporting entities cannot apply IFRS 3 (as revised in 2008) retrospectively at all, although they can early adopt it for annual periods starting on or after 30 June 2007.[109] However, there is no comparable restriction that prevents retrospective adoption of IFRS 3 (as revised in 2008) by first-time adopters. Nevertheless, in our opinion, a first-time adopter should not restate business combinations under IFRS 3 (as revised in 2008) before the date of transition when this would require undue use of hindsight, even though this is not specifically prohibited.

A   Associates and joint ventures

The exemption for past business combinations applies also to past acquisitions of associates and interests in joint ventures. However, it is important to note that the date selected for the first restatement of business combinations will also be applied to the restatement of acquisitions of associates and interests in joint ventures.[110]

5.2.2   Classification of business combinations

IFRS 3 (as revised in 2008) mandates that a business combination should be accounted for as an acquisition or reverse acquisition. An entity's previous GAAP may be based on a different definition of, for example, a business combination, an acquisition, a merger and a reverse acquisition. An important benefit of the business combinations exemption is that a first-time adopter will not have to determine the classification of past business combinations in accordance with IFRSs.[111] For example, a transaction that was accounted for as a merger or uniting of interests using the pooling-of-interests method under an entity's previous GAAP will not have to be reclassified and accounted for under the acquisition method or purchase method. However, an entity may still elect to do so if it so wishes – subject, of course, to the conditions set out under 5.2.1 above.

The business combinations exemption applies only to 'business combinations that the entity recognised before the date of transition to IFRSs.'[112] While the business combinations exemption applies to the acquisition of businesses as defined under IFRS 3 (as revised in 2008) (see A below), it does not apply to a transaction that IFRS considers to be an acquisition of an asset (see B below).

A   Definition of a 'business' under IFRSs

A first-time adopter needs to consider whether past transactions would qualify as business combinations under IFRS 3 (as revised in 2008). That standard defines a business combination as 'a transaction or other event in which an acquirer obtains control of one or more businesses. Transactions sometimes referred to as "true mergers" or "mergers of equals" are also business combinations as that term is used in this IFRS.'[113] A business is defined as 'an integrated set of activities and assets that is capable of being conducted and managed for the purpose of providing a return in the form of dividends, lower costs or other economic benefits directly to investors or other owners, members or participants.'[114] In addition, IFRS 3 (as revised in 2008) states that 'if the assets acquired are not a business, the reporting entity shall account for the transaction or other event as an asset acquisition' (see B below).[115]

Finally, the scope of the business combinations exemption is broader than that of IFRS 3 (as revised in 2008) as it also applies to common control business combinations.[116]

B   Asset acquisitions

As discussed under A above, IFRS 3 (as revised in 2008) provides a very specific definition of what is a business combination. Therefore, it is possible that under some national GAAPs, transactions that are not business combinations (e.g. asset acquisitions), may have been accounted for as if they were business combinations. A first-time adopter will need to restate any transactions that it accounted for as business combinations under its previous GAAP, but which are not business combinations under IFRSs.

Example 5.12:   Acquisition of assets

Entity A acquired a holding company that held a single asset at the time of acquisition. That holding company had no employees and the asset itself was not in use at the date of acquisition. Entity A accounted for the transaction under its previous GAAP using the purchase method, which resulted in goodwill. Can entity A apply the business combinations exemption to the acquisition of this asset?

If entity A concludes that the asset is not a business as defined in IFRS 3 (as revised in 2008), it will not be able to apply the business combinations exemption. Instead, entity A should account for such transactions as asset acquisitions.

5.2.3   Recognition and measurement of assets and liabilities

A   Derecognition of assets and liabilities

A first-time adopter should exclude from its opening IFRS balance sheet any items it recognised under its previous GAAP that do not qualify for recognition as an asset or liability under IFRSs. If the first-time adopter previously recognised an intangible asset, as part of a business combination, that does not qualify for recognition as an asset under IAS 38, it should reclassify that item and the related deferred tax and non-controlling interests with an offsetting change to goodwill (unless it previously deducted goodwill directly from equity under its previous GAAP) (see 5.2.4 below). All other changes resulting from derecognition of such assets and liabilities should be accounted for as adjustments of retained earnings.[117]

B   Recognition of assets and liabilities

In its opening IFRS balance sheet, a first-time adopter should recognise all assets and liabilities that were acquired or assumed in a past business combination, with the exception of:[118]

- certain financial assets and liabilities that were derecognised and that fall under the derecognition exception (see 4.3 above); and

- assets (including goodwill) and liabilities that were not recognised in the acquirer's consolidated balance sheet under its previous GAAP that would not qualify for recognition under IFRSs in the separate balance sheet of the acquiree (see Example 5.18 below).

The change resulting from the recognition of such assets and liabilities should be accounted for as an adjustment of retained earnings or another category of equity, if appropriate. However, if the change results from the recognition of an intangible asset that was previously subsumed in goodwill, it should be accounted for as an adjustment of that goodwill (see 5.2.4 A below).[119] As indicated at E below, the recognition of such intangibles will be rare.

The following examples, which are based on the guidance on implementation of IFRS 1, illustrate how a first-time adopter would apply these requirements. Further examples can be found at E below.

Example 5.13:   Finance lease not capitalised under previous GAAP[120]

Background

Parent A's date of transition to IFRSs is 1 January 2009. Parent A acquired subsidiary B on 15 January 2006 and did not capitalise subsidiary B's finance leases. If subsidiary B prepared separate financial statements under IFRSs, it would recognise finance lease obligations of £300 and leased assets of £250 at 1 January 2009.

Application of requirements

In its consolidated opening IFRS balance sheet, parent A recognises finance lease obligations of £300 and leased assets of £250, and charges £50 to retained earnings.

Example 5.14:   Restructuring provision[121]

Background

Parent C's first IFRS financial statements are for a period that ends on 31 December 2010 and include comparative information for 2009 only. It chooses not to restate previous business combinations under IFRSs. On 1 July 2008, parent C acquired 100 per cent of subsidiary D. Under its previous GAAP, parent C recognised an (undiscounted) restructuring provision of ¥100 that would not have qualified as an identifiable liability under IFRSs. The recognition of this restructuring provision increased goodwill by ¥100. At 31 December 2008 (date of transition to IFRSs), parent C:

(a)   had paid restructuring costs of ¥60; and

(b)   estimated that it would pay further costs of ¥40 in 2009, and that the effects of discounting were immaterial. At 31 December 2008, those further costs did not qualify for recognition as a provision under IAS 37.

Application of requirements

In its opening IFRS balance sheet, parent C:

(a)   does not recognise a restructuring provision.

(b)   does not adjust the amount assigned to goodwill. However, parent C tests the goodwill for impairment under IAS 36 – *Impairment of Assets*, and recognises any resulting impairment loss.

(c)   as a result of (a) and (b), reports retained earnings in its opening IFRS balance sheet that are higher by ¥40 (before income taxes, and before recognising any impairment loss) than in the balance sheet at the same date under previous GAAP.

C   *Subsequent measurement under IFRSs not based on cost*

IFRSs require subsequent measurement of some assets and liabilities on a basis other than original cost, such as fair value. When a first-time adopter does not apply IFRS 3 (as revised in 2008) retrospectively to a business combination, such assets and liabilities must be measured on that other basis in its opening IFRS balance sheet. Any change in the carrying amount of those assets and liabilities should be accounted for as an adjustment of retained earnings, or other appropriate category of equity, rather than as an adjustment of goodwill.[122]

Example 5.15:   Items not measured at original cost

Entity A acquired in a business combination a trading portfolio of equity securities and a number of investment properties. Under its previous GAAP, entity A initially measured these assets at cost (i.e. their fair value at the date of acquisition).

Upon adoption of IFRSs, entity A measures the trading portfolio of equity securities and the investment properties (under the IAS 40 – *Investment Properties* – fair value model) at fair value in its opening IFRS balance sheet. The resulting adjustment to these assets at the date of transition is reflected in retained earnings.

D   Subsequent measurement on a cost basis under IFRSs

For assets and liabilities that are accounted for on a cost basis under IFRSs, the standard stipulates that 'immediately after the business combination, the carrying amount in accordance with previous GAAP, of assets acquired and liabilities assumed in that business combination shall be their deemed cost in accordance with IFRSs at that date. If IFRSs require a cost-based measurement of those assets and liabilities at a later date, that deemed cost shall be the basis for cost-based depreciation or amortisation from the date of the business combination.'[123]

Cost basis, being based on previous GAAP, might be considered as inconsistent with the requirements of IFRSs for assets and liabilities that were *not* acquired in a business combination. However, the IASB did not identify any situations in which 'it would not be acceptable to bring forward cost-based measurements made in accordance with previous GAAP.'[124]

Example 5.16:   Items measured on a cost basis

Entity A applies the business combination exemption under IFRS 1. In a business combination entity A acquired property, plant and equipment, inventory and accounts receivable. Under its previous GAAP, entity A initially measured these assets at cost (i.e. their fair value at the date of acquisition).

Upon adoption of IFRSs, entity A determines that its accounting policy for these assets under its previous GAAP complied with the requirements of IFRSs. Therefore, property, plant and equipment, inventory and accounts receivable are not adjusted, but recognised in the opening IFRS balance sheet at the carrying amount under the previous GAAP.

I   Meaning of 'immediately after the business combination'

The standard does not specifically define 'immediately after a business combination', but it is commonly understood that this takes account of the final determination of the purchase price allocation and final completion of purchase accounting. In other words, a first-time adopter would not use the provisionally determined fair values of assets acquired and liabilities assumed in applying the business combinations exemption.

Example 5.17:   Provisionally determined fair values

Parent B acquired subsidiary C in August 2008 and made a provisional assessment of subsidiary C's identifiable net assets in its 31 December 2008 consolidated financial statements under its previous GAAP. In its 31 December 2009 consolidated financial statements – its last financial statements under previous GAAP – parent B completed the initial accounting for the business combination and adjusted the provisional values of the identifiable net assets and the corresponding goodwill. Upon first-time adoption of IFRSs, parent B elects not to restate past business combinations.

In preparing its opening IFRS balance sheet, parent B should use the adjusted carrying amounts of the identifiable net assets as determined in its 2009 financial statements rather than the provisional carrying amounts of the identifiable net assets and goodwill at 31 December 2009.

IFRS 1 is silent as to whether the relevant carrying amounts of the identifiable net assets and goodwill are those that appeared in the financial statements drawn up immediately before the transition date (i.e. 31 December 2008 in the example above) or any restated balance appearing in a later set of previous GAAP accounts. Since the adjustments that were made under previous GAAP effectively resulted in a restatement of the balances at the transition date in a manner that is consistent with the approach permitted by IFRSs, it is in our opinion appropriate to reflect those adjustments in the opening IFRS balance sheet. Since the adjustments are effectively made as at the transition date it is also appropriate to use the window period permitted by previous GAAP provided that this does not extend into the first IFRS reporting period since any restatements in that period can only be made in accordance with IFRS 3 (as revised in 2008). In effect, the phrase 'immediately after the business combination' in paragraph C4(e) of IFRS 1 should be interpreted as including a window period that ends at the earlier of the end of the window period allowed by the previous GAAP and the beginning of the first IFRS reporting period.

II   *In-process research and development*

IFRS 1 makes clear that in-process research and development (IPR&D) that was included within goodwill under an entity's previous GAAP should not be recognised separately upon transition to IFRSs unless it qualifies for recognition under IAS 38 in the financial statement of the acquiree.[125] However, IFRS 1 is silent on the treatment of IPR&D that was identified separately by an entity under the business combinations accounting standard of its previous GAAP, but which was immediately written off to profit or loss.

There are two possible situations. If the standard under previous GAAP that requires IPR&D to be written off is an integral part of purchase method under that GAAP then the carrying amount of IPR&D 'immediately after the business combination' would be zero. However, if that standard is not an integral part of the purchase method (e.g. it merely requires accelerated amortisation) then the carrying amount 'immediately after the business combination' would be the amount allocated to IPR&D by the business combinations standard under previous GAAP.

The above distinction may be largely irrelevant if the business combination takes place several years before the transition to IFRSs because, in practice, the IPR&D may have been amortised or may be impaired before the date of transition.

E   *Measurement of items not recognised under previous GAAP*

An asset acquired or a liability assumed in a past business combination may not have been recognised under the entity's previous GAAP. However, this does not mean that such items have a deemed cost of zero in the opening IFRS balance sheet. Instead, the acquirer recognises and measures those items in its opening IFRS balance sheet on the basis that IFRSs would require in the balance sheet of the acquiree.[126] Also, if the acquirer had not recognised a contingent liability under its previous GAAP that still exists at the date of transition to IFRSs, the acquirer should recognise that contingent liability at that date unless IAS 37 – *Provisions, Contingent Liabilities and Contingent Assets* – would prohibit its recognition in the financial statements of the acquiree.[127] The change resulting from the recognition of such assets and liabilities should be accounted for as an adjustment of retained earnings or another category of equity, if appropriate. The IASB included this requirement to avoid 'an unjustifiable departure from the principle that the opening IFRS balance sheet should include all assets and liabilities.'[128]

A first-time adopter that restates previous business combinations under IFRSs will recognise the intangible assets held by acquired subsidiaries. However, intangible assets acquired as part of a business combination that were not recognised under a first-time adopter's previous GAAP, will rarely be recognised in the opening IFRS balance sheet of a first-time adopter that applies the business combinations exemption because either (1) they cannot be capitalised in the acquiree's own balance sheet or (2) capitalisation would require the use of hindsight which is not permitted under IAS 38 (see 7.16 below).

Example 5.18:   Items not recognised under previous GAAP

Entity A acquired Entity B but did not capitalise B's finance leases and internally generated customer lists under its previous GAAP.

Upon first-time adoption of IFRSs, entity A recognises the finance leases in its opening IFRS balance sheet using the amounts that entity B would recognise in its opening IFRS balance sheet. The resulting adjustment to the net assets at the date of transition is reflected in retained earnings; goodwill is not restated to reflect the net assets that would have been recognised at the date of acquisition (see 5.2.4 below). However, entity A does not recognise the customer lists in its opening IFRS balance sheet, because entity B is not permitted to capitalise internally generated customer lists. Any value that might have been attributable to the customer lists would remain subsumed in goodwill in A's opening IFRS balance sheet.

Entity C acquired Entity D but did not recognise D's brand name as a separate intangible asset under its previous GAAP.

Upon first-time adoption of IFRSs, entity C will not recognise D's brand name in its opening IFRS balance sheet because entity D would not have been permitted under IAS 38 to recognise it as an asset in its own separate balance sheet. Again, any value that might have been attributable to the brand name would remain subsumed in goodwill in C's opening IFRS balance sheet.

F   Example of recognition and measurement requirements

The following example, which is based on one within the implementation guidance in IFRS 1 illustrates many of the requirements discussed above.

Example 5.19:   Business combination example[129]

Background

Parent A's first IFRS financial statements are for a reporting period that ends on 31 December 2010 and include comparative information for 2009 only. On 1 July 2006, parent A acquired 100 per cent of subsidiary B. Under its previous GAAP, parent A:

(a) classified the business combination as an acquisition by parent A;

(b) measured the assets acquired and liabilities assumed at the following amounts under previous GAAP at 31 December 2008 (date of transition to IFRSs):

    (i) identifiable assets less liabilities for which IFRSs require cost-based measurement at a date after the business combination: €200 (with a tax base of €150 and an applicable tax rate of 30 per cent);

    (ii) pension liability (for which the present value of the defined benefit obligation measured under IAS 19 is €130 and the fair value of plan assets is €100): €nil (because parent A used a pay-as-you-go cash method of accounting for pensions under its previous GAAP). The tax base of the pension liability is also €nil;

    (iii) goodwill: €180;

(c) did not, at the date of acquisition, recognise deferred tax arising from temporary differences associated with the identifiable assets acquired and liabilities assumed.

Application of requirements

In its opening (consolidated) IFRS balance sheet, parent A:

(a) classifies the business combination as an acquisition by parent A even if the business combination would have qualified under IFRS 3 (as revised in 2008) as a reverse acquisition by subsidiary B (paragraph C4(a) of IFRS 1);

(b) does not adjust the accumulated amortisation of goodwill. Parent A tests the goodwill for impairment under IAS 36 and recognises any resulting impairment loss, based on conditions that existed at the date of transition to IFRSs. If no impairment exists, the carrying amount of the goodwill remains at €180 (paragraph C4(g) of IFRS 1);

(c) for those net identifiable assets acquired for which IFRSs require cost-based measurement at a date after the business combination, treats their carrying amount under previous GAAP immediately after the business combination as their deemed cost at that date (paragraph C4(e) of IFRS 1);

(d) does not restate the accumulated depreciation and amortisation of the net identifiable assets in (c) above, unless the depreciation methods and rates under previous GAAP result in amounts that differ materially from those required under IFRSs (for example, if they were adopted solely for tax purposes and do not reflect a reasonable estimate of the asset's useful life under IFRSs). If no such restatement is made, the carrying amount of those assets in the opening IFRS balance sheet equals their carrying amount under previous GAAP at the date of transition to IFRSs (€200) (paragraph IG7 of IFRS 1);

(e) if there is any indication that identifiable assets are impaired, tests those assets for impairment, based on conditions that existed at the date of transition to IFRSs (see IAS 36);

(f) recognises the pension liability, and measures it, at the present value of the defined benefit obligation (€130) less the fair value of the plan assets (€100), giving a carrying amount of €30, with a corresponding debit of €30 to retained earnings (paragraph C4(d) of IFRS 1). However, if subsidiary B had already adopted IFRSs in an earlier period, parent A would measure the pension liability at the same amount as in subsidiary B's separate financial statements (paragraph D17 of IFRS 1 and IG Example 9);

(g) recognises a net deferred tax liability of €6 (€20 at 30 per cent) arising from:

    (i) the taxable temporary difference of €50 (€200 less €150) associated with the identifiable assets acquired and non-pension liabilities assumed; less

    (ii) the deductible temporary difference of €30 (€30 less €nil) associated with the pension liability.

Parent A recognises the resulting increase in the deferred tax liability as a deduction from retained earnings (paragraph C4(k) of IFRS 1). If a taxable temporary difference arises from the initial recognition of the goodwill, entity A does not recognise the resulting deferred tax liability (paragraph 15(a) of IAS 12 – *Income Taxes*).

5.2.4   *Restatement of goodwill*

A   *Mandatory adjustments of goodwill*

Under the business combinations exemption, a first-time adopter takes the carrying amount of goodwill under its previous GAAP at the date of transition to IFRSs as a starting point and only adjusts it as follows:[130]

(a) A first-time adopter increases goodwill at the date of transition by an amount equal to the carrying amount of an item that it recognised as an intangible asset acquired in a business combination under its previous GAAP (less any related deferred tax and non-controlling interests), but which does not meet the recognition criteria under IFRSs. That is, the first-time adopter accounts for the change in classification prospectively and does not, for example, reverse the cumulative amortisation on the item that it recognised as an intangible asset under its previous GAAP;

(b) If a first-time adopter is required to recognise an intangible asset under IFRSs that was subsumed in goodwill under its previous GAAP, it decreases goodwill accordingly and adjusts deferred tax and non-controlling interests (see 5.2.3 E above);

(c) 'Regardless of whether there is any indication that the goodwill may be impaired, the first-time adopter shall apply IAS 36 [*Impairment of Assets*] in testing the goodwill for impairment at the date of transition to IFRSs and in recognising any resulting impairment loss in retained earnings (or, if so required by IAS 36, in revaluation surplus). The impairment test shall be based on conditions at the date of transition to IFRSs.'[131]

As noted at 5.2.1 A above, the business combinations exemption also applies to associates and joint ventures. Therefore a transition impairment review should be carried out on the entire carrying amount of investments in associates and joint ventures that comprise an element of goodwill.

Application of the above guidance may sometimes be more complicated than expected as is illustrated in the example below.

Example 5.20:   *Recognition and derecognition of acquired intangible assets*

Entity A acquired an online retailer, entity B, before its date of transition to IFRSs. Under its previous GAAP, entity A recognised an intangible asset of ¥1,200 related to 'deferred marketing costs', which does not meet the recognition criteria under IFRSs. Entity A also acquired customer relationships with a fair value of ¥900 that do meet the recognition criteria under IFRS 3 (as revised in 2008), but which it did not recognise as an intangible asset under its previous GAAP.

Upon adoption of IFRSs, entity A is required to derecognise the 'deferred marketing costs' intangible asset and increase the carrying amount of goodwill for a corresponding amount. Nevertheless, the customer relationship intangible asset that is subsumed in goodwill cannot be recognised as its carrying amount in the balance sheet of the acquiree, entity B, would have been nil.

In economic terms it may be argued that the 'deferred marketing costs' intangible asset in the example above comprises the value that would have been attributable under IFRSs to the acquired customer relationships. However, unless entity A concluded that not recognising a customer relationship intangible asset was an error under its previous GAAP, it would not be able to recognise a customer relationship intangible asset upon adoption of IFRSs.

Under IFRS 1, assets acquired and liabilities assumed in a business combination prior to the date of transition to IFRSs are not necessarily valued on a basis that is consistent with IFRSs. This can lead to 'double counting' in the carrying amount of assets and goodwill as is illustrated in the example below.

Example 5.21:   *Impairment testing of goodwill on first-time adoption*

Entity C acquired a business before its date of transition to IFRSs. The cost of acquisition was €530 and entity C allocated the purchase price as follows:

	€
Properties, at carry-over cost	450
Liabilities, at amortised cost	(180)
Goodwill	260
Purchase price	530

The goodwill under entity C's previous GAAP relates entirely to the properties that had a fair value at date of acquisition that was significantly in excess of their value on a carry-over cost basis. In entity C's opening IFRS balance sheet the same assets, liabilities and goodwill are valued as follows:

	€
Properties, at fair value	750
Liabilities, at amortised cost	(180)
Provisional IFRS goodwill (before impairment test)	260
Total carrying amount	830

Entity C used the option to measure the properties at fair value at its date of transition in its opening IFRS balance sheet. However, IFRS 1 does not permit goodwill to be adjusted to reflect the extent to which the increase in fair value relates to the time of the acquisition. The total carrying amount of the acquired net assets including goodwill of €830 may now exceed the recoverable amount. When entity C tests the 'provisional IFRS goodwill' for impairment on first-time adoption of IFRSs, the recoverable amount of the business is determined to be €620. Accordingly, it will have to recognise an impairment of goodwill of €210 and disclose this impairment under IFRS 1.

In some cases the write-off will completely eliminate the goodwill and thereby any 'double counting'. However, in this particular case the remaining goodwill of €50 in truth represents goodwill that was internally generated between the date of acquisition and the date of transition to IFRSs.

The IASB accepted that IFRS 1 'does not prevent the implicit recognition of internally generated goodwill that arose after the date of the business combination. However, the Board concluded that an attempt to exclude such internally generated goodwill would be costly and lead to arbitrary results.'[132]

B   Prohibition of other adjustments of goodwill

The IASB concluded that 'to avoid costs that would exceed the likely benefits to users', IFRS 1 should prohibit restatement of goodwill for most other adjustments reflected in the opening IFRS balance sheet, unless a first-time adopter elects to apply IFRS 3 (as revised in 2008) retrospectively.[133] Therefore, a first-time adopter electing not to apply IFRS 3 (as revised in 2008) retrospectively is not permitted to make any adjustments to goodwill other than those described at A above. For example, such a first-time adopter should not restate the carrying amount of goodwill:[134]

(i)   to exclude in-process research and development acquired in that business combination (unless the related intangible asset would qualify for recognition under IAS 38 in the balance sheet of the acquiree);

(ii)   to adjust previous amortisation of goodwill;

(iii)   to reverse adjustments to goodwill that IFRS 3 (as revised in 2008) would not permit, but were made under previous GAAP because of adjustments to assets and liabilities between the date of the business combination and the date of transition to IFRSs.

Although IFRS 1 specifically prohibits other adjustments to goodwill, differences between the goodwill amount in the opening IFRS balance sheet and that in the financial statements under previous GAAP may arise because:

(a) goodwill may have to be restated as a result of a retrospective application of IAS 21 – *The Effects of Changes in Foreign Exchange Rates* (see 5.2.5 below);

(b) goodwill in relation to previously unconsolidated subsidiaries will have to be recognised (see 5.2.6 below);

(c) goodwill in relation to transactions that do not qualify as business combinations under IFRSs must be derecognised (see 5.2.2 above); and

(d) 'negative goodwill' that may have been included within goodwill under previous GAAP should be derecognised under IFRSs (see C below).

Example 5.22: Adjusting goodwill

Entity A acquired Entity B but under its previous GAAP it did not recognise the following items:

- B's customer lists which had a fair value of ¥1,100 at the date of the acquisition and ¥1,500 at the date of transition to IFRSs; and

- Deferred tax liabilities related to the fair value adjustment of B's property, plant and equipment, which amounted to ¥9,500 at the date of the acquisition and ¥7,800 at the date of transition to IFRSs.

What adjustment should entity A make to goodwill to account for the customer lists and deferred tax liabilities at its date of transition to IFRSs?

As explained at 5.2.3 E above, entity A cannot recognise the customer lists when it uses the business combinations exemption. Accordingly, entity A cannot adjust goodwill for the customer lists.

A must recognise the deferred tax liability at its date of transition under IAS 12 because there is no exemption from recognising deferred taxation under IFRS 1. However, entity A is not permitted to adjust goodwill for the deferred tax liability that would have been recognised at the date of acquisition. Instead, entity A should recognise the change in deferred tax of ¥7,800 in retained earnings or other category of equity, if appropriate.

C   Derecognition of negative goodwill

Although IFRS 1 does not specifically address accounting for negative goodwill recognised under a previous GAAP, negative goodwill should be derecognised by a first-time adopter because it is not permitted to 'recognise items as assets or liabilities if IFRSs do not permit such recognition'.[135] Negative goodwill clearly does not meet the definition of a liability under the IASB's *Framework* and its recognition is not permitted under IFRS 3 (as revised in 2008). While not directly applicable to a first-time adopter, the transitional provisions of IFRS 3 (as revised in 2008) specifically require that any negative goodwill is derecognised upon adoption (see Chapter 9 at 4.2.2).[136]

D   Goodwill previously deducted from equity

If a first-time adopter deducted goodwill from equity under its previous GAAP then it should not recognise that goodwill in its opening IFRS balance sheet. Also, it should not reclassify that goodwill to profit or loss if it disposes of the subsidiary or if the investment in the subsidiary becomes impaired.[137] Effectively, under IFRSs such goodwill ceases to exist.

Example 5.23:   Goodwill deducted from equity and treatment of related intangible assets[138]

Entity A acquired a subsidiary before the date of transition to IFRSs. Under its previous GAAP, entity A:

(a)   recognised goodwill as an immediate deduction from equity;

(b)   recognised an intangible asset of the subsidiary that does not qualify for recognition as an asset under IAS 38; and

(c)   did not recognise an intangible asset of the subsidiary that would qualify under IAS 38 for recognition as an asset in the financial statements of the subsidiary. The subsidiary held the asset at the date of its acquisition by entity A.

In its opening IFRS balance sheet, entity A:

(a)   does not recognise the goodwill, as it did not recognise the goodwill as an asset under previous GAAP;

(b)   does not recognise the intangible asset that does not qualify for recognition as an asset under IAS 38. Because entity A deducted goodwill from equity under its previous GAAP, the elimination of this intangible asset reduces retained earnings (see 5.2.3 A above); and

(c)   recognises the intangible asset that qualifies under IAS 38 for recognition as an asset in the financial statements of the subsidiary, even though the amount assigned to it under previous GAAP in A's consolidated financial statements was nil (see 5.2.3 E above). The recognition criteria in IAS 38 include the availability of a reliable measurement of cost and entity A measures the asset at cost less accumulated depreciation and less any impairment losses identified under IAS 36 (see 7.14 below). Because entity A deducted goodwill from equity under its previous GAAP, the recognition of this intangible asset increases retained earnings. However, if this intangible asset had been subsumed in goodwill recognised as an asset under previous GAAP, entity A would have decreased the carrying amount of that goodwill accordingly (and, if applicable, adjusted deferred tax and non-controlling interests) (see 5.2.4 A above).

The prohibition to reinstate goodwill that was deducted from equity may have a significant impact on first-time adopters that hedge their foreign net investments.

Example 5.24:   Goodwill related to foreign net investments

Entity B, which uses the euro (€) as its functional currency, acquired a subsidiary in the United States whose functional currency is the US dollar ($). The goodwill on the acquisition of $2,100 was deducted from equity. Under its previous GAAP Entity B hedged the currency exposure on the goodwill because it would be required to recognise the goodwill as an expense upon disposal of the subsidiary.

IFRS 1 does not permit reinstatement of goodwill deducted from equity nor does it permit transfer of goodwill to profit or loss upon disposal of the investment in the subsidiary. Under IFRSs, goodwill deducted from equity ceases to exist and entity B can no longer hedge the currency exposure on that goodwill. Therefore, exchange gains and losses relating to the hedge will no longer be classified in currency translation difference but recognised in profit and loss upon adoption of IFRSs.

If a first-time adopter deducted goodwill from equity under its previous GAAP then adjustments resulting from the subsequent resolution of a contingency affecting the purchase consideration should be recognised in retained earnings.[139] Effectively, the adjustment is being accounted for in the same way as the original goodwill that arose on the acquisition, rather than having to be accounted for in accordance with IFRS 3 (as revised in 2008). This requirement could affect, for example, the way a first-time adopter accounts for earn-out clauses relating to business combinations prior to its date of transition to IFRSs.

Example 5.25:   Earn-out clause in acquisition

Entity C acquired a business before its date of transition to IFRSs and agreed to make an initial payment to the seller together with further payments based on a multiple of future profits of the acquiree. The fair value of the earn-out, which is contingent on future profits, changes after the date of transition to IFRSs. Under entity C's previous GAAP any goodwill was written off against equity as incurred.

After its date of transition to IFRSs, entity C will account for changes in the fair value of the earn-out as a change in purchase consideration and recognise it in retained earnings.[140]

5.2.5   Currency adjustments to goodwill

A first-time adopter need not apply IAS 21 'retrospectively to fair value adjustments and goodwill arising in business combinations that occurred before the date of transition to IFRSs.'[141] This exemption is different from the 'cumulative translation differences' exemption, which is discussed at 5.8 below.

IAS 21 requires that 'any goodwill arising on the acquisition of a foreign operation and any fair value adjustments to the carrying amounts of assets and liabilities arising on the acquisition of that foreign operation shall be treated as assets and liabilities of the foreign operation.'[142] For a first-time adopter it may be impracticable, especially after a corporate restructuring, to determine retrospectively the currency in which goodwill and fair value adjustments should be expressed. If IAS 21 is not applied retrospectively, a first-time adopter should treat such fair value adjustments and goodwill 'as assets and liabilities of the entity rather than as assets and liabilities of the acquiree. Therefore, those goodwill and fair value adjustments either are already expressed in the entity's functional currency or are non-monetary foreign currency items, which are reported using the exchange rate applied in accordance with previous GAAP.'[143]

If a first-time adopter chooses not to take the full exemption, it must apply IAS 21 retrospectively to fair value adjustments and goodwill arising in either:[144]

(a)   all business combinations that occurred before the date of transition to IFRSs; or

(b)   all business combinations that the entity elects to restate to comply with IFRS 3 (as revised in 2008).

In practice the exemption may be of limited use for a number of reasons.

First, the exemption permits 'goodwill and fair value adjustments' to be treated as assets and liabilities of the entity rather than as assets and liabilities of the acquiree. Implicit in the exemption is the requirement to treat goodwill and fair value adjustments consistently. However, the IASB apparently did not consider that many first-time adopters, under their previous GAAP, will have treated fair value adjustments as assets or liabilities of the acquiree, while at the same time treating goodwill as an asset of the acquirer. As the exemption under IFRS 1 did not foresee this particular situation, those first-time adopters will need to restate either their goodwill or fair value adjustments. In many cases restatement of goodwill is less onerous than restatement of fair value adjustments.

Secondly, the paragraphs in IFRS 1 that introduce the exemption were drafted at a later date than the rest of the Appendix that they form part of. Instead of referring to 'first-time adopter' these paragraphs refer to 'entity'. Nevertheless, it is clear from the context that 'entity' should be read as 'first-time adopter'. This means that the exemption only permits goodwill and fair value adjustments to be treated as assets of the first-time adopter (i.e. ultimate parent). In practice, however, many groups have treated goodwill (and fair value adjustments) as an asset of an intermediate parent. Where the intermediate parent has a functional currency that is different from that of the ultimate parent or the acquiree, it will be necessary to restate goodwill (and fair value adjustments).

The decision to treat goodwill and fair value adjustments as either items denominated in the parent's or the acquiree's functional currency will also affect the extent to which the net investment in those foreign subsidiaries can be hedged (see also 5.2.4 D above).

5.2.6   *Previously unconsolidated subsidiaries*

Under its previous GAAP a first-time adopter may not have consolidated a subsidiary acquired in a past business combination. In that case, a first-time adopter applying the business combinations exemption should adjust the carrying amounts of the subsidiary's assets and liabilities to the amounts that IFRSs would require in the subsidiary's balance sheet. The deemed cost of goodwill 'equals the difference at the date of transition to IFRSs between:

(i)   the parent's interest in those adjusted carrying amounts; and

(ii)   the cost in the parent's separate financial statements of its investment in the subsidiary.'[145]

The cost of a subsidiary in the parent's separate financial statements will depend on which option the parent has taken to measure the cost under IFRS 1 (see 5.9.2 below). A first-time adopter is precluded from calculating what the goodwill would have been at the date of the original acquisition. The deemed cost of goodwill will, however, be capitalised as an asset in the opening IFRS balance sheet. The following example, which is based on one within the guidance on implementation of IFRS 1, illustrates this requirement.

Example 5.26:   Subsidiary not consolidated under previous GAAP[146]

Background

Parent A's date of transition to IFRSs is 1 January 2009. Under its previous GAAP, parent A did not consolidate its 75 per cent interest in subsidiary B, which it acquired in a business combination on 15 July 2006. On 1 January 2009:

(a)   the cost of parent A's investment in subsidiary B is $180.

(b)   under IFRSs, subsidiary B would measure its assets at $500 and its liabilities (including deferred tax under IAS 12) at $300. On this basis, subsidiary B's net assets are $200 under IFRSs.

Application of requirements

Parent A consolidates subsidiary B. The consolidated balance sheet at 1 January 2009 includes:

(a)   subsidiary B's assets at $500 and liabilities at $300;

(b)   non-controlling interests of $50 (25 per cent of [$500 − $300]); and

(c)   goodwill of $30 (cost of $180 less 75 per cent of [$500 − $300]). Parent A tests the goodwill for impairment under IAS 36 and recognises any resulting impairment loss, based on conditions that existed at the date of transition to IFRSs.

If the cost of the subsidiary (as measured under IFRS 1) is lower than the net asset value at the date of transition to IFRSs, the difference is taken to retained earnings.

Slightly different rules apply to all other subsidiaries (i.e. those not acquired in a business combination) that an entity did not consolidate under its previous GAAP, the main difference being that goodwill should not be recognised in relation to those subsidiaries (see 5.9 below).

The above example from IFRS 1 seems to be clear; a first-time adopter that applies IFRS 3 (as revised in 2008) cannot recognise goodwill relating to the non-controlling interest in subsidiaries that it did not consolidate under its previous GAAP.

Note that if a first-time adopter, in its separate financial statements, does not opt to measure its cost of investment in a subsidiary at its fair value at the date of transition, it is required to calculate the deemed cost of the goodwill by comparing the cost of the investment to its share of the carrying amount of the net assets determined on a different date. In the case of a highly profitable subsidiary this could give rise to the following anomaly:

Example 5.27:   Calculation of deemed goodwill

Parent C acquired subsidiary D before the date of transition for $500. The net assets of entity D would have been $220 under IFRSs at the date of acquisition. Subsidiary D makes on average an annual net profit of $60, which it does not distribute to entity C.

At the date of transition to IFRSs, the cost of entity C's investment in subsidiary D is still $500. However, the net assets of subsidiary D have increased to $460. Therefore, under IFRS 1 the deemed cost of goodwill is $40.

The deemed goodwill is much lower than the goodwill that was paid at the date of acquisition because subsidiary D did not distribute its profits. In fact, if subsidiary D had distributed a dividend to its parent just before its date of transition, the deemed goodwill would have been significantly higher.

5.2.7   Previously consolidated entities that are not subsidiaries

A first-time adopter may have consolidated an investment under its previous GAAP that does not meet the definition of a subsidiary under IFRSs. In this case the entity should first determine the appropriate classification of the investment under IFRSs and then apply the first-time adoption rules in IFRS 1. Generally such previously consolidated investments should be accounted for as either:

- *an associate:* First-time adopters applying the business combinations exemption should also apply that exemption to past acquisitions of investments in associates. If the business combinations exemption is not applicable or the entity did not acquire the investment in the associate, IAS 28 – *Investments in Associates* – should be applied retrospectively;

- *a joint venture:* First-time adopters applying the business combinations exemption should also apply that exemption to past acquisitions of investments in joint ventures. If the business combinations exemption is not applicable or the entity did not acquire the investment in the joint venture, IAS 31 – *Interests in Joint Ventures* – should be applied retrospectively;

- *an investment under IAS 39* (see 5.12 below); or

- *an executory contract or service concession arrangement:* There are no first-time adoption exemptions that apply; therefore, IFRSs should be applied retrospectively.

5.2.8 Measurement of deferred taxation and non-controlling interests

Deferred taxation is calculated based on the difference between the carrying amount of assets and liabilities and their respective tax base. Therefore, deferred taxation should be calculated after all assets acquired and liabilities assumed have been adjusted under IFRS 1.[147]

IAS 27 (as amended in 2008) defines non-controlling interest as 'the equity in a subsidiary not attributable, directly or indirectly, to a parent'.[148] Non-controlling interests related to subsidiaries acquired in a business combination should be calculated after all assets acquired, liabilities assumed and deferred taxation have been adjusted under IFRS 1.[149]

Any resulting change in the carrying amount of deferred taxation and non-controlling interests should be recognised by adjusting retained earnings (or, if appropriate, another category of equity), unless they relate to adjustments to intangible assets that are adjusted against goodwill.

Example 5.28:   Restatement of intangible assets, deferred tax and non-controlling interests[150]

Entity A's first IFRS financial statements are for a period that ends on 31 December 2010 and include comparative information for 2009 only. On 1 July 2006, entity A acquired 75% of subsidiary B. Under its previous GAAP, entity A assigned an initial carrying amount of £200 to intangible assets that would not have qualified for recognition under IAS 38. The tax base of the intangible assets was £nil, giving rise to a deferred tax liability (at 30%) of £60. Entity A measured non-controlling interests as their share of the fair value of the identifiable net assets acquired. Goodwill arising on the acquisition was capitalised as an asset in A's consolidated financial statements.

On 1 January 2009 (the date of transition to IFRSs), the carrying amount of the intangible assets under previous GAAP was £160, and the carrying amount of the related deferred tax liability was £48 (30% of £160).

Under IFRS 1, entity A reclassifies intangible assets that do not qualify for recognition as separate assets under IAS 38, together with the related deferred tax liability of £48 and non-controlling interests, as part of goodwill (see 5.2.4 A above). The related non-controlling interests amount to £28 (25% of £112 (£160 minus £48)). Entity A makes the following adjustment in its opening IFRS balance sheet:

Goodwill	£84
Deferred tax liability	£48
Non-controlling interests	£28
Intangible assets	£160

A tests the goodwill for impairment under IAS 36 and recognises any resulting impairment loss, based on conditions that existed at the date of transition to IFRSs.

Under IFRS 1, a first-time adopter is required to 'adjust opening retained earnings if, on transition to IFRSs, it recognises for the first time a deferred tax liability relating to an acquired intangible asset recognised in accordance with its previous GAAP. In contrast, if the entity had subsumed the intangible asset in recognised goodwill in accordance with its previous GAAP, it would be required to decrease the carrying amount of goodwill accordingly and, if applicable, adjust deferred tax and minority interests.'[151] The IASB discussed this issue in October 2005, but decided not to propose an amendment to address this inconsistency.

5.3   Share-based payment transactions

IFRS 2 – *Share-based Payment* – applies to accounting for the acquisition of goods or services in equity-settled share-based payment transactions, cash-settled share-based payment transactions and transactions in which the entity or the counter-party has the option to choose between settlement in cash or equity. IFRS 1 contains the following exemptions and requirements regarding share-based payment transactions:

(a)   if a first-time adopter 'has disclosed publicly the fair value of those equity instruments, determined at the measurement date, as defined in IFRS 2' then it is encouraged to apply IFRS 2 to:[152]

    (i)   equity instruments that were granted on or before 7 November 2002 (i.e. the date the IASB issued ED 2 – *Share-based Payment*);

    (ii)   equity instruments that were granted after 7 November 2002 but vested before the date of transition to IFRSs.

Many first-time adopters will not have published the fair value of equity instruments granted and are, therefore, not allowed to apply IFRS 2 retrospectively to those share-based payment transactions;

(b)   for all grants of equity instruments to which IFRS 2 has not been applied a first-time adopter shall nevertheless disclose the information required by paragraphs 44 and 45 of IFRS 2;[153] and

(c)   if a first-time adopter modifies the terms or conditions of a grant of equity instruments to which IFRS 2 has not been applied, the entity is not required to apply paragraphs 26-29 of IFRS 2 if the modification occurred before the date of transition to IFRSs.[154]

Furthermore, for share-based payment transaction that give rise to liabilities:[155]

(d)   a first-time adopter is 'encouraged, but not required, to apply IFRS 2 to liabilities arising from share-based payment transactions that were settled before the date of transition to IFRSs'; and

(e)   IFRS 1 provides additional transitional exemptions that are no longer relevant as they apply to liabilities that were settled before 1 January 2005.

There are a number of interpretation issues concerning these exemptions and requirements:

*   *Meaning of 'disclosed publicly' under (a) above*

    IFRS 1 only permits retrospective application of IFRS 2 to the extent that the entity has 'disclosed publicly' the fair value of the equity instruments concerned, but IFRSs do not define what is meant by 'disclosed publicly'. The basis for conclusions to IAS 40 – *Investment Properties*, which also uses the phrase 'disclosed publicly', states that 'there is a risk that restatement of prior periods might allow entities to manipulate their reported profit or loss for the period by selective use of hindsight in determining fair values in prior periods. Accordingly, the Board decided to prohibit restatement in the fair value model, except where an entity has already publicly disclosed fair values for prior periods ...'.[156] It is therefore likely that the IASB introduced the same wording in relation to share-based payment transactions to ensure that only entities that contemporaneously calculated and publicly disclosed the fair value of their share-based payment transactions would be able to apply IFRS 2 retrospectively.

Although IFRS 1 does not specifically require public disclosure of the fair value of an entity's share-based payment transactions in its previous financial statements, in our opinion it is clear that IFRS 1 requires fair value to have been published contemporaneously. In our view, the requirements in IFRS 1 to disclose publicly the fair value of share-based payment transactions can be met even if the fair value is only disclosed in aggregate rather than for individual awards.

- *Specific rules for first-time adopters under (a)(ii) and (d) above*

  Although the transitional rules for first-time adopters are based on the transitional rules in IFRS 2 for existing IFRS reporting entities, the IASB specifically added for first-time adopters the exemptions under (a)(ii) and (d) above.[157] The 'date of transition to IFRSs' to which those exemptions refer is the first day of the earliest comparative period presented in a first-time adopter's first set of IFRS financial statements. In our view, this allows an entity to accelerate the vesting of an award that was otherwise due to vest after the date of transition to IFRSs in order to avoid applying IFRS 2 to that award.

- *Consistent selection of the exemptions under (a), (d) and (e) above*

  A first-time adopter can choose which of the exemptions under (a), (d) and (e) it wants to apply, i.e. there is no specific requirement to select the exemptions in a consistent manner. However, the qualitative characteristics of financial statements as set out in the *Framework* would seem to dictate that a first-time adopter should apply the above exemptions in a consistent manner.[158]

- *Meaning of 'encouraged' under (a) and (d) above*

  Under IFRS 1 a first-time adopter is 'encouraged', but not required, to apply IFRS 2 to certain categories of share-based payment transactions (see (a) and (d) above). That raises the question whether a first-time adopter might interpret 'encouraged' literally and, for example, decide to apply IFRS 2 only to some share-based payment transactions granted before 7 November 2002. Keeping in mind the qualitative characteristics of financial statements as set out in the *Framework* it is acceptable that a first-time adopter only applies IFRS 2 to share-based payment transactions:[159]

  (1) after a certain date (e.g. 1 January 2001), while not applying it to earlier transactions;

  (2) for which fair values were disclosed publicly.

  Although IFRS 1 does not specifically prohibit a literal reading of 'encouraged', we believe that it would generally not be appropriate for a first-time adopter to determine the scope of application of IFRS 2 using criteria other than those outlined under (1) and (2) above.

- *Treatment of modifications, cancellations and settlements under (c) above*

  There is a slight ambiguity concerning the interpretation of the exemption under (c) above, because paragraph D2 of IFRS 1 refers only to the *modification* of awards. This could allow a literal argument that IFRS 2 and IFRS 1 do not prescribe any specific treatment when an entity cancels or settles (as opposed to modifying) an award falling within (a) above. However, paragraph D2 also require an entity to apply paragraphs 26-29 of IFRS 2 to 'modified' awards. Paragraphs 26-29 deal not only with modification but also with cancellation and settlement, and indeed paragraphs 28 and 29 are not relevant to *modification* at all. This makes it clear, in our view, that the IASB intended IFRS 2 to be applied not only to modification, but also to any cancellation or settlement of an award falling within (a) above, unless the modification, cancellation or settlement occurs before the date of transition to IFRSs.[160]

- *Transactions where the counterparty has a choice of settlement method under (c) above*

  These are not specifically addressed in the first-time adoption rules. It therefore appears that, where such transactions give rise to recognition of both an equity component and a liability component, the equity component is subject to the transitional rules for equity-settled transactions and the liability component to those for cash-settled transactions. This could well mean that the liability component of such a transaction is recognised in the financial statements, whilst the equity component is not.

- *Application of IFRS 2 to cash-settled transactions settled before the date of transition to IFRSs under (d) above*

  It is not entirely clear what lies behind this exemption, since a first-time adopter would never be required to report a share-based payment transaction (or indeed any transaction) settled before the date of transition.

Extract 5.3 from Armour Group provides an illustration of typical disclosures made by entities that applied the share-based payments exemption.

Extract 5.3: Armour Group plc (2008)

Notes to the Consolidated Financial Statements [extract]

1 Accounting Policies [extract]

Changes in Accounting Policies

First-time Adoption

IFRS 1 "First-time Adoption of International Financial Reporting Standards" permits certain transitional exemptions when first adopting IFRS. The Company has elected to apply the following exemptions:

- ...

- IFRS 2: Share-based Payments has not been applied to share-based payments granted prior to 7 November 2002. The consolidated financial statements for the year ended 31 August 2007, which were prepared by the Company under UK GAAP, adopted FRS 20: Share-based Payments and therefore no additional adjustment is required on conversion to IFRS.

Extract 5.4 from SAP provides an illustration of a company that did not apply the share-based payments exemption.

Extract 5.4: SAP AG (2007)

NOTES TO THE CONSOLIDATED FINANCIAL STATEMENTS 2007 [extract]

A. Basis of Presentation [extract]

(1) General [extract]

(1F) Share-Based Compensation Programs

Under U.S. GAAP, we have accounted for share-based compensation programs using the intrinsic value-based method according to Accounting Principles Board Opinion 25 Accounting for Stock Issued to Employees until December 31, 2005. As of January 1, 2006, we started applying the fair value recognition provisions of Statements of Financial Accounting Standards 123 (revised 2004) Share-based Payment (SFAS 123R).

Under IFRS, all share-based payment programs are recorded at fair value. Equity-settled programs are recorded based on grant-date fair value, while liabilities for cash-settled programs are adjusted to current fair value at each reporting date. From January 1, 2006, onwards, the method of accounting for our share-based compensation programs is essentially the same under U.S. GAAP and IFRS.

For our cash-settled and equity-settled share-based payment arrangements we have not used the exemption of IFRS 1 in our opening balance sheet but adopted IFRS 2 Share-based payment retrospectively. As a result, the difference between the intrinsic value method and the fair value method was recorded in the opening balance sheet increasing retained earnings by €42 million. Due to the fact that certain cash-settled share-based payment programs have been hedged, the increase in liabilities resulted in a €27 million offset, net of tax, of the recognized portion of the hedge instrument in Other components of equity.

5.3.1 Use of previously published fair values

There is no explicit requirement in IFRS 1 or IFRS 2 that any voluntary retrospective application of IFRS 2 must be based on the fair value previously published. This might appear to allow a first-time adopter the flexibility of using a different valuation for IFRS 2 purposes than that previously used for disclosure purposes. However, the requirements of IFRS 1 in relation to estimates under previous GAAP (see 4.2 above) mean that the assumptions used in any different accounting model must be consistent with those used in the originally disclosed valuation. The entity will also need to consider the implications of the assertion, in effect, that there is more than one fair value for the same transaction.

5.3.2 Restatement of costs recognised under previous GAAP

A first-time adopter may elect to take advantage of the transitional provisions in IFRS 1 which allow it not to apply IFRS 2 to certain share-based payment transactions whether or not it recognised a cost for those transactions in accordance with its previous GAAP. Neither IFRS 1 nor IFRS 2 clearly indicates the appropriate treatment of the costs of share-based payment transactions that were recognised under the previous GAAP. In practice, either of the following approaches is considered acceptable, provided that the treatment chosen is disclosed in the financial statements if the previously recognised costs are material:

- *recognise previous GAAP share-based payment expense* – For transactions covered by the share-based payments exemption, a share-based payment expense determined in accordance with the previous GAAP is recognised in the first IFRS financial statements; or

- *recognise no share-based payment expense* – No share-based payment expense is recognised for those transactions that are covered by the share-based payments exemption.

Under both approaches the comparability between reporting periods is somewhat limited. Full comparability can only be achieved if the first-time adopter does not use the share-based payment exemption or once all share-based payment transactions that are not accounted for under IFRS 2 have vested, have been exercised or lapsed.

5.4   Insurance contracts

A first-time adopter may apply the transitional provisions in IFRS 4 – *Insurance Contracts*.[161] That standard limits an insurer to changing 'its accounting policies for insurance contracts if, and only if, the change makes the financial statements more relevant to the economic decision-making needs of users and no less reliable, or more reliable and no less relevant to those needs. An insurer shall judge relevance and reliability by the criteria in IAS 8.'[162]

The claims development information (see Chapter 43 at 10.2.5) need not be disclosed for claims development that occurred more than five years before the end of the first IFRS reporting period. For entities taking advantage of this relief, the claims development information will be built up from five to ten years in the five years following adoption of IFRSs. Additionally, if it is 'impracticable' for a first-time adopter to prepare information about claims development that occurred before the beginning of the earliest period for which full comparative information is presented, this fact should be disclosed.[163]

IFRS 1 and IFRS 4 provide additional transitional exemptions from the requirements to provide comparative information that are no longer of any practical relevance as they apply to annual periods beginning before 1 January 2005.[164]

5.5   Deemed cost

5.5.1   Background

IFRS 1 requires full retrospective application of standards extant at the end of a first-time adopter's first IFRS reporting period. Therefore, in the absence of the deemed cost exemption, the requirements of, for example, IAS 16, IAS 38, IAS 40, and IFRS 6 – *Exploration for and Evaluation of Mineral Resources* – would have to be applied as if the first-time adopter had always applied these standards. This could be quite onerous because:

- these items are long-lived which means that accounting records for the period of acquisition may not be available anymore. In the case of formerly state-owned businesses, the required accounting records possibly never even existed;

- the entity may have revalued the items in the past as a matter of accounting policy or because this was required under national law; or

- even if the items were carried at depreciated cost, the accounting policy for recognition and depreciation may not have been IFRSs compliant.

Given the significance of items like property, plant and equipment in the balance sheet of most first-time adopters (and the sheer number of transactions affecting property, plant and equipment), restatement is not only difficult but would often also involve undue cost and effort. Nevertheless, a first-time adopter needs a cost basis for those assets in its opening IFRS balance sheet. Therefore, the IASB decided to introduce the notion of a 'deemed cost' that is not the 'true' IFRS compliant cost basis of an asset, but a surrogate that is deemed to be a suitable starting point.

In its deliberations on IFRS 1, the IASB noted that 'reconstructed cost data might be less relevant to users, and less reliable, than current fair value data. ... Therefore, the IFRS permits an entity to use fair value as deemed cost in some cases without any need to demonstrate undue cost or effort.'[165]

There are four separate types of deemed cost exemptions in IFRS 1:

- fair value or revaluation as deemed cost (see 5.5.2 below);

- event-driven fair value measurement as deemed cost (see 5.5.3 below);

- deemed cost for oil and gas assets (see 5.5.4 below); and

- deemed cost in determining the cost of an investment in a subsidiary, jointly controlled entity or associate (see 5.9.2 below).

5.5.2 *Fair value or revaluation as deemed cost*

A   *Scope of 'fair value or revaluation as deemed cost' exemption*

To deal with the problem of restatement of long-lived assets upon first-time adoption of IFRSs, the standard permits a first-time adopter – for the categories of assets listed below – to measure an item in its opening IFRS balance sheet using an amount that is based on its deemed cost:[166]

- property, plant and equipment (see 7.5);[167]

- investment property, if an entity elects to use the cost model in IAS 40. The fact that the exemption can only be applied to investment property accounted for under the cost model will not pose any problems in practice as the fair value model under IAS 40 requires an entity to measure its investment property at fair value at its date of transition to IFRSs;[168] and

- intangible assets (see 7.16) that meet:

  - the recognition criteria in IAS 38 (including reliable measurement of original cost); and

  - the criteria in IAS 38 for revaluation (including the existence of an active market).[169]

A first-time adopter cannot use a deemed cost approach for any other assets or liabilities.[170]

The use of fair value or revaluation as deemed cost for intangible assets will be very limited in practice because of the very restrictive definition of an active market in IAS 38 (see Chapter 15 at 2.4.2 A).[171] It is therefore unlikely that a first-time adopter will be able to apply this exemption to any intangible assets.

It is important to note that this exemption does not take classes or categories of assets as its unit of measure, but refers to 'an item of property, plant and equipment'.[172] The same exemption is available for investment property and intangible assets. IAS 16 does not 'prescribe the unit of measure for recognition, i.e. what constitutes an item of property, plant and equipment. Thus, judgement is required in applying the recognition criteria to an entity's specific circumstances' (see Chapter 15 at 2.3.2).[173] A first-time adopter can therefore apply the deemed cost exemption to only some of its assets. For example, it could apply the exemption only to:

- a selection of properties;
- part of a factory; or
- some of the assets leased under a single finance lease.

The IASB argued that it is not necessary to restrict application of the exemption to classes of assets to prevent selective revaluations, because 'IAS 36 requires an impairment test if there is any indication that an asset is impaired. Thus, if an entity uses fair value as deemed cost for assets whose fair value is above cost, it cannot ignore indications that the recoverable amount of other assets may have fallen below their carrying amount. Therefore, the IFRS does not restrict the use of fair value as deemed cost to entire classes of asset.'[174] Nevertheless, it seems doubtful that the quality of financial information would benefit from a revaluation of a haphazard selection of items of property, plant and equipment. Therefore, a first-time adopter should exercise judgment in selecting the items to which it believes it is appropriate to apply the exemption.

Extracts 5.5 and 5.6 below are typical disclosures of the use of the 'fair value or revaluation as deemed cost' exemption.

Extract 5.5: Publicis Groupe SA (2005)

Notes to the consolidated financial statements [extract]

Note 32.2 Accounting options related to first-time application of IFRS [extract]

Measurement of certain tangible assets at fair value as deemed cost

Publicis opted to revalue its building at 133, avenue des Champs Elysées in Paris at its fair value and to consider this value as being the deemed cost at the transition date. The fair value of this building at the transition date amounts to €164 M, which represents an adjustment of €159 M compared to its carrying amount under previous accounting standards. The valuation was performed by an independent expert using the rent capitalization method.

Extract 5.6: DaimlerChrysler AG (2006)

Notes to Consolidated Financial Statements [extract]

2. Explanation of transition to IFRS [extract]

Introduction [extract]

Fair value or revaluation as deemed cost. The Group elected to measure certain real estate properties at fair value as of January 1, 2005 and to use that estimate as deemed cost. The effects of that election are presented below. DaimlerChrysler has not elected a general accounting policy to revalue long-lived assets.

(in millions of €)	Adjustment recorded	Carrying amount
Property, plant and equipment	(387)	974

B   Determining deemed cost

The deemed cost that a first-time adopter uses is either:

(a) the fair value of the item at the date of transition to IFRSs (see 1.3.5 above); or[175]

(b) a previous GAAP revaluation at or before the date of transition to IFRSs, if the revaluation was, at the date of the revaluation, broadly comparable to:[176]

    (i)   fair value; or

    (ii)   cost or depreciated cost in accordance with IFRSs, adjusted to reflect, for example, changes in a general or specific price index.

The revaluations referred to in (b) above need only be 'broadly comparable to fair value or reflect an index applied to a cost that is broadly comparable to cost determined in accordance with IFRSs' (e.g. an impairment write-down might result in a carrying amount that is broadly comparable to fair value).[177] It appears that in the interest of practicality the IASB is allowing a good deal of flexibility in this matter. The IASB explains in the basis for conclusions that 'it may not always be clear whether a previous revaluation was intended as a measure of fair value or differs materially from fair value. The flexibility in this area permits a cost-effective solution for the unique problem of transition to IFRSs. It allows a first-time adopter to establish a deemed cost using a measurement that is already available and is a reasonable starting point for a cost-based measurement.'[178]

IFRS 1 describes the revaluations referred to in (b) above as a 'previous GAAP revaluation'. Therefore, such revaluations can only be used as the basis for deemed cost under IFRS 1 if they were recognised in the first-time adopter's previous GAAP financial statements.

A first-time adopter that uses the exemption is required to disclose the resulting IFRS 1 adjustment separately (see 6.5.1 below).

C   Deemed cost determined before the date of transition to IFRSs

If the deemed cost of an asset was determined before the date of transition to IFRSs then an IFRS accounting policy needs to be applied to that deemed cost in the intervening period to determine what the carrying amount of the asset is in the opening IFRS balance sheet. In other words, when a first-time adopter uses a fair value or a revaluation as the deemed cost of an item of property, plant and equipment it will need to start depreciating the item 'from the date for which the entity established the fair value measurement or revaluation' and not from its date of transition to IFRSs.[179] The example below illustrates the application of this requirement.

Example 5.29:   Deemed cost of property, plant and equipment

Entity A used to revalue items of property, plant and equipment to fair value under its previous GAAP, but changed its accounting policy on 1 January 2003 when it adopted a different accounting policy. Under that accounting policy, entity A did not depreciate the asset and only recognised the maintenance costs as an expense. Entity A's date of transition to IFRSs is 1 January 2009.

In its balance sheet under previous GAAP the carrying amount of the asset is £80 at the date of transition to IFRSs, which is equal to the last revaluation. Entity A can use the last revalued amount as the deemed cost of the asset on 1 January 2003. However, Entity A will need to apply IAS 16 to the period after 1 January 2003 because the accounting policy under its previous GAAP is not permitted under IFRSs. Assuming that the economic life of the asset is 40 years and that the residual value is nil, Entity A would account for the asset at £68 in its opening IFRS balance sheet, which represents the deemed cost minus 6 years of depreciation.

D   Conclusion

At its date of transition to IFRSs, a first-time adopter is allowed under IFRS 1 to measure property, plant and equipment, investment properties and intangible assets at an amount based on either:

- historical cost determined in accordance with IAS 16, IAS 38 and IAS 40;
- fair value at the date of transition to IFRSs;
- a revalued amount that is equal to:
  - fair value at the date of revaluation;
  - cost adjusted for changes in a general or specific index; or
  - an event-driven fair value, for example, at the date of an initial public offering or privatisation (see 5.5.3 below); or
- in the case of an item acquired in a business combination (see 5.2 above):
  - carrying amount under previous GAAP immediately after acquisition; or
  - if the item was not recognised under previous GAAP, the carrying amount on the basis that IFRSs would require in the separate balance sheet of the acquiree.

The fact that IFRS 1 offers so many different bases for valuation does not disturb the IASB as it reasons that 'cost is generally equivalent to fair value at the date of acquisition. Therefore, the use of fair value as the deemed cost of an asset means that an entity will report the same cost data as if it had acquired an asset with the same remaining service potential at the date of transition to IFRSs. If there is any lack of comparability, it arises from the aggregation of costs incurred at different dates, rather than from the targeted use of fair value as deemed cost for some assets. The Board regarded this approach as justified to solve the unique problem of introducing IFRSs in a cost-effective way without damaging transparency.'[180] Although this is valid, it still means that an individual first-time adopter can greatly influence its future reported performance by carefully selecting a first-time adoption policy for the valuation of its assets. Users of the financial statements of a first-time adopter should therefore be mindful that historical trends under the previous GAAP might no longer be present in an entity's IFRS financial statements.

5.5.3 *Event-driven fair value measurement as deemed cost*

'A first-time adopter may have established a deemed cost in accordance with previous GAAP for some or all of its assets and liabilities by measuring them at their fair value at one particular date because of an event such as a privatisation or initial public offering.'[181] A first-time adopter may use such event-driven fair value measurements as deemed cost for IFRSs at the date of that measurement.

IFRS 1 describes the revaluations above as 'deemed cost in accordance with previous GAAP'. Therefore, such revaluations can only be used as the basis for deemed cost under IFRS 1 if they were recognised in the first-time adopter's previous GAAP financial statements.

The 'fair value or revaluation as deemed cost' exemption discussed at 5.5.2 above, only applies to items of property, plant and equipment, investment property and certain intangible assets.[182] The event-driven deemed cost exemption is broader in scope because it states when a first-time adopter 'established a deemed cost in accordance with previous GAAP *for some or all of its assets and liabilities* [emphasis added] by measuring them at their fair value at one particular date ... It may use such event-driven fair value measurements as deemed cost for IFRSs at the date of that measurement.'[183] Similarly, the Basis for Conclusions to IFRS 1 states that the standard 'permits an entity to use amounts determined using previous GAAP as deemed cost for IFRSs in the following cases ... if an entity established a deemed cost in accordance with previous GAAP for some or all assets and liabilities by measuring them at their fair value at one particular date because of an event such as a privatisation or initial public offering'.[184]

There are two important limitations in the scope of the event-driven deemed cost exemption:

- While the exemption applies, in principle, to all assets and liabilities of an entity, it does not override the recognition criteria in IFRSs.[185] Consequently, a first-time adopter should derecognise goodwill, assets (e.g. certain intangible assets such as brand names and research) and liabilities that do not qualify for recognition under IFRSs in the balance sheet of the entity; and

- The exemption cannot be used if the event-driven revaluation did not result in a remeasurement to full fair value (i.e. it cannot be used in the case of a partial step-up towards fair value).

Finally, although a first-time adopter may use the event-driven fair value measurements as deemed cost for any asset or liability, it does not have to use them for all assets and liabilities.[186]

A   *'Push down' accounting*

Under some previous GAAPs an entity may have prepared its financial statements using 'push down' accounting, that is, the carrying amount of its assets and liabilities is based on their fair value at the date it became a subsidiary of its parent. If such a subsidiary subsequently adopts IFRSs, it will often require a very significant effort to determining the carrying amount of those assets and liabilities on a historical costs basis at the date of transition to IFRSs.

The event-driven deemed cost exemption applies to events 'such as a privatisation or initial public offering.'[187] This list of events is clearly not meant to be exhaustive, but rather describes events that result in re-measurement of some or all assets and liabilities at their fair value. An acquisition that results in an entity becoming a subsidiary is a change of control event similar to a privatisation or an initial public offering. In our view, the application of 'push down' accounting results in an event-driven fair value measurement that may be used as deemed cost for IFRSs at the date of that measurement.[188]

As noted above however, the event-driven deemed cost exemption can only be used if the application of 'push down' accounting resulted in recognition of assets and liabilities at their fair value. For example, previous GAAP may not have required remeasurement to full fair value in the case of a partial acquisition or a step-acquisition, or if there was a bargain purchase.

B   'Fresh start' accounting

Some previous GAAPs require an entity that emerges from bankruptcy to apply 'fresh start' accounting, which involves recognition of assets and liabilities at their fair value at that date.

As noted at A above, the list of events in paragraph D8 of IFRS 1 is clearly not meant to be exhaustive, but rather describes certain events that result in re-measurement of some or all assets and liabilities at their fair value. In our view, the application of 'fresh start' accounting results in an event-driven fair value measurement that may be used as deemed cost for IFRSs at the date of that measurement.[189]Also, as discussed above, the use of such exemption is limited to instances that resulted in the recognition of the related assets and liabilities at their full fair value (i.e. it cannot be used in the case of a partial step-up towards fair value).

C   Future developments

In August 2009, the IASB published the exposure draft *Improvements to IFRSs*, which proposes to amend the guidance on event-driven fair values.[190] As discussed above, the current exemption permits a first-time adopter to use a revaluation basis as deemed cost when an event such as a privatisation triggered a revaluation at or before the date of transition to IFRSs. The Board concluded that its reasons for granting this exemption 'were equally valid for such events that occurred after the date of transition to IFRSs but during the periods covered by the first-time adopter's first IFRS financial statements'.[191] The Board therefore proposes to replace the final sentence of paragraph D8 of IFRS 1 as follows:

> '...If the measurement date is before the end of the first IFRS reporting period, the first-time adopter may use such event-driven fair value measurements as deemed cost for IFRSs at the date of that measurement. If the measurement date is after the first-time adopter's date of transition to

IFRSs, the entity may elect a deemed cost at the date of transition that meets the criteria in paragraphs D5-D7. The event-driven fair value measurement within the entity's first IFRS reporting period is recognised as deemed cost when the event occurs.'[192]

The Board explicitly considered whether or not to allow a first-time adopter 'to establish the deemed cost on the date of transition to IFRSs using the revaluation amounts subsequently obtained on the date of measurement, adjusted to exclude any depreciation, amortisation or impairment between the date of transition to IFRSs and the date of that measurement'.[193] Instead, the Board decided:

'...to require an entity to establish the deemed cost as of the event-driven fair value measurement date and, for the periods before that date, present historical costs or other amounts already permitted by IFRS 1. The Board notes that this proposed presentation overcomes the use of hindsight. It also presents supportable carrying amounts for such assets on the date of transition that are broadly consistent with the existing requirements of IFRS 1 and with the principle of the transition. Because any significant adjustments related to an event that triggers such a revaluation would already be highlighted in the first IFRS financial statements and disclosures, the proposed presentation clearly identifies the effects of any significant difference in depreciation or amortisation between the periods before and after the date of measurement.'[194]

The proposed amendment is expected to be effective for annual periods beginning on or after 1 January 2011. If an entity applies the amendment for an earlier period, it should disclose that fact.[195] In addition, the Board is proposing that 'if an entity had first applied IFRSs in an earlier period, the entity is permitted to apply the amendment to paragraph D8 in the first annual period after the amendment is effective as if it had been available in that earlier period.'[196]

5.5.4 Deemed cost for oil and gas assets

It is common practice in some countries to account (e.g. under the 'full cost accounting' method) for exploration and development costs for properties in development or production in cost centres that include all properties in a large geographical area. However, this method of accounting generally uses a unit of account that is much larger than is acceptable under IFRSs. Applying IFRSs fully retrospectively would pose significant problems for first-time adopters because it would also require amortisation 'to be calculated (on a unit of production basis) for each year, using a reserves base that has changed over time because of changes in factors such as geological understanding and prices for oil and gas. In many cases, particularly for older assets, this information may not be available.'[197] Even when such information is available the effort and cost to determine the opening balances at the date of transition would usually be very high.

The fair value or revaluation as deemed cost exemption (see 5.5.2 above), however, was not considered to be suitable because:

'...Determining the fair value of oil and gas assets is a complex process that begins with the difficult task of estimating the volume of reserves and resources. When the fair value amounts must be audited, determining significant inputs to the estimates generally requires the use of qualified external experts. For entities with many oil and gas assets, the use of this fair value as deemed cost alternative would not meet the Board's stated intention of avoiding excessive cost ...'[198]

The IASB, therefore, decided to introduce an exemption for first-time adopters that accounted under their previous GAAP for 'exploration and development costs for oil and gas properties in the development or production phases ... in cost centres that include all properties in a large geographical area'.[199] Under the exemption, a first-time adopter may elect to measure oil and gas assets at the date of transition to IFRSs on the following basis:

'(a)   exploration and evaluation assets at the amount determined under the entity's previous GAAP; and

(b)   assets in the development or production phases at the amount determined for the cost centre under the entity's previous GAAP. The entity shall allocate this amount to the cost centre's underlying assets pro rata using reserve volumes or reserve values as of that date.'[200]

For the purposes of this exemption, oil and gas assets comprise only those assets used in the exploration, evaluation, development or production of oil and gas.

A first-time adopter that uses the exemption under (b) should disclose that fact and the basis on which carrying amounts determined under previous GAAP were allocated.[201]

To avoid the use of deemed costs resulting in an oil and gas asset being measured at more than its recoverable amount, the Board decided that oil and gas assets that were valued using this exemption should be tested for impairment at the date of transition to IFRSs as follows:[202]

• exploration and evaluation assets should be test for impairment under IFRS 6; and

• assets in the development and production phases should be tested for impairment under IAS 36.

The deemed cost amounts should be reduced to take account of any impairment charge.

This exemption, which was introduced in July 2009 when the IASB published an amendment to IFRS 1, should be applied for annual periods beginning on or after 1 January 2010. Earlier application is permitted, provided that all other amendments to IFRS 1 that were introduced in July 2009 are also applied (see 2.1.1 above).[203]

Finally, when a first-time adopter applies the deemed cost exemption for oil and gas assets, it should also apply the IFRIC 1 – *Changes in Existing Decommissioning, Restoration and Similar Liabilities* – exemption for oil and gas assets at deemed cost (see 5.14.2 below).

5.6   Leases

5.6.1   IAS 17 and SIC-15

IFRS 1 does not include any specific exemption from the retrospective application of IAS 17 – *Leases* – and SIC-15 – *Operating Leases – Incentives*. Therefore, a first-time adopter is required to classify leases as operating or finance leases under IAS 17 based on the circumstances existing at the inception of the lease and not those existing at the date of transition to IFRSs.[204] However, if 'at any time the lessee and the lessor agree to change the provisions of the lease, other than by renewing the lease, in a manner that would have resulted in a different classification of the lease … if the changed terms had been in effect at the inception of the lease, the revised agreement is regarded as a new agreement over its term.'[205] In other words, an entity classifies a lease based on the lease terms that are in force at its date of transition to IFRSs; the lease classification is not based on lease terms that are no longer in force.

A first-time adopter should apply SIC-15 – *Operating Leases – Incentives (amended 2003)* – retrospectively to all leases, regardless of their starting date.[206]

5.6.2   IFRIC 4

A   IFRIC 4 transitional provisions

IFRIC 4 – *Determining whether an Arrangement contains a Lease* – contains specific transitional provisions for existing IFRS-reporting entities that address the practical difficulties in going back potentially many years and making a meaningful assessment of whether the arrangement satisfied the criteria at that time. First-time adopters may apply the same transitional provisions, which allow them to apply IFRIC 4 to arrangements existing at their date of transition on the basis of facts and circumstances existing at that date.[207] The example below from the implementation guidance in IFRS 1 illustrates this exemption.

Example 5.30:   Determining whether an arrangement contains a lease[208]

Entity A's first IFRS financial statements are for a period that ends on 31 December 2010 and include comparative information for 2009 only. Its date of transition to IFRSs is 1 January 2009.

On 1 January 2001, entity A entered into a take-or-pay arrangement to supply gas. On 1 January 2004, there was a change in the contractual terms of the arrangement.

On 1 January 2009, entity A may determine whether the arrangement contains a lease under IFRIC 4 on the basis of facts and circumstances existing on that date. Alternatively, the entity applies the criteria in IFRIC 4 on the basis of facts and circumstances existing on 1 January 2001 and reassesses the arrangement on 1 January 2004.

B   Arrangements assessed for leases under previous GAAP

A first-time adopter may have adopted a standard under its previous GAAP that had the same effect as the requirements of IFRIC 4 and that had the same transitional provisions. Such an entity may therefore already 'apply requirements having the same effect as the requirements of IFRIC 4 to some or all arrangements (even if the wording of those requirements is not identical)', although possibly using a different starting date than IFRIC 4.[209] Before the amendment, which was introduced in July 2009 when the IASB published an amendment to IFRS 1 – *Additional Exemptions for*

First-time Adopters (Amendments to IFRS 1), IFRS 1 required such an entity to reassess that accounting upon first-time adoption on the basis of facts and circumstances existing at transition date.

To prevent such first-time adopters from having to incur additional costs, with no obvious benefits, the IASB introduced the following exemption:

> 'If a first-time adopter made the same determination of whether an arrangement contained a lease in accordance with previous GAAP as that required by IFRIC 4 but at a date other than that required by IFRIC 4, the first-time adopter need not reassess that determination when it adopts IFRSs. For an entity to have made the same determination of whether the arrangement contained a lease in accordance with previous GAAP, that determination would have to have given the same outcome as that resulting from applying IAS 17 *Leases* and IFRIC 4.'[210]

While this exemption only applies to arrangements that were assessed under previous GAAP in the same manner as required by IFRIC 4, a first-time adopter is permitted to apply the IFRIC 4 exemption under A above to arrangements that were not assessed in such a manner.[211]

This exemption should be applied for annual periods beginning on or after 1 January 2010. Earlier application is permitted, provided that all other amendments to IFRS 1 that were introduced in July 2009 are also applied (see 2.1.1 above).[212]

5.7   Employee benefits

IAS 19 allows an entity to use a 'corridor' approach that leaves some actuarial gains and losses on defined benefit plans unrecognised.[213] To calculate the net cumulative unrecognised gains or losses at the date of transition to IFRSs, a first-time adopter would need to determine actuarial gains or losses for each year since inception (or later date of acquisition of the subsidiary to which the defined benefit plan relates) of each defined benefit plan. It is obvious that a full retrospective application of IAS 19 would be costly (if not impossible to achieve) and not benefit users of the financial statements.[214] Therefore, the IASB introduced an exemption that allows a first-time adopter 'to recognise all cumulative actuarial gains and losses at the date of transition to IFRSs, even if it uses the corridor approach for later actuarial gains and losses'.

If a first-time adopter uses the above exemption it will have to apply it to all its defined benefit plans.[215] However, the exemption applicable to a parent (or investor) that becomes a first-time adopters after its subsidiary (or associates and joint ventures) (see 5.10.2 below) would not allow the 'corridor' to be reset at the parent's (or investor's) date of transition for defined benefit plans of those subsidiaries (or associates and joint ventures).

In the extract below Norsk Hydro discloses that it used the employee benefits exemption in IFRS 1.

> *Extract 5.7: Norsk Hydro ASA (2007)*
>
> NOTE 47 Conversion to IFRS [extract]
>
> **Employee benefits**
>
> IFRS 1 allows for all cumulative actuarial gains and losses at the date of transition to be recognized as of the date of transition as an alternative to full retrospective application of IAS 19 Employee Benefits. Hydro has chosen to adopt this transition policy, and has recognized all 1 January 2006 cumulative actuarial gains and losses at the date of transition with the effect posted directly against equity. Hydro applies the same economic and actuarial assumptions under IFRS as applied under US GAAP, and will continue to use the corridor approach when accounting for actuarial gains and losses on an ongoing basis.

5.7.1 Full actuarial valuations

An entity's first IFRS financial statements reflect its defined benefit liabilities or assets on at least three different dates, that is, the end of the first IFRS reporting period, the end of the comparative period and the date of transition to IFRSs. An entity that presents two comparative periods would have to calculate its defined benefits obligations at four different dates. Clearly, it is quite costly to require a first-time adopter to perform three, or possibly even four, actuarial valuations. However, the IASB decided against permitting 'an entity to use a single actuarial valuation, based, for example, on assumptions valid at the reporting date, with service costs and interest costs based on those assumptions for each of the periods presented.'[216] The IASB's main objection to such an exemption was that it 'would conflict with the objective of providing understandable, relevant, reliable and comparable information for users.'[217] Nevertheless, the IASB agreed to the compromise position that if an entity obtains a full actuarial valuation at one or two dates, it is allowed to roll forward (or roll back) to another date but only as long as the roll forward (or roll back) reflects material transactions and other material events between those dates (including changes in market prices and interest rates).[218]

5.7.2 Actuarial assumptions

A first-time adopter's actuarial assumptions at its date of transition to IFRSs should be consistent with the ones it used for the same date under its previous GAAP, unless there is objective evidence that those assumptions were in error (see 4.2 above). The impact of any later revisions to those assumptions is an actuarial gain or loss of the period in which the entity makes the revisions.[219] If a first-time adopter needs 'to make actuarial assumptions at the date of transition to IFRSs that were not necessary in accordance with its previous GAAP' these actuarial assumptions should 'not reflect conditions that arose after the date of transition to IFRSs. In particular, discount rates and the fair value of plan assets at the date of transition to IFRSs reflect market conditions at that date. Similarly, the entity's actuarial assumptions at the date of transition to IFRSs about future employee turnover rates do not reflect a significant increase in estimated employee turnover rates as a result of a curtailment of the pension plan that occurred after the date of transition to IFRSs.'[220]

5.7.3   Unrecognised past service costs

While the employee benefits exemption applies to unrecognised actuarial gains or losses, it does not apply to unrecognised past service costs that relate to unvested benefits. The IASB decided that an exemption for past service cost was not justified because a full retrospective application of IAS 19 to unrecognised past service costs 'is less onerous than the retrospective application of the corridor for actuarial gains and losses because it does not require the recreation of data since the inception of the plan.'[221] A first-time adopter therefore needs to look at periods before its date of transition to IFRSs to determine the amount of unrecognised past service costs that relate to unvested benefits in accordance with IAS 19.

5.7.4   Exemption from presenting historical summary information

When IAS 19 was amended in December 2004, the IASB introduced a requirement in paragraph 120A(p) of IAS 19 to disclose the following amounts for the current annual period and previous four annual periods of (see Chapter 28 at 7.2):

- the present value of the defined benefit obligation, the fair value of the plan assets and the surplus or deficit in the plan; and
- the experience adjustments arising on:
  - the plan liabilities expressed either as (1) an amount or (2) a percentage of the plan liabilities at the balance sheet date; and
  - the plan assets expressed either as (1) an amount or (2) a percentage of the plan assets at the balance sheet date.

Obviously, an entity that applied the employee benefits exemption above will not be able to comply with this requirement for periods prior to its date of transition. An entity is therefore permitted to disclose the above information for each accounting period prospectively from the transition date.[222]

5.8   Cumulative translation differences

IAS 21 requires that, on disposal of a foreign operation, the cumulative amount of the exchange differences deferred in the separate component of equity relating to that foreign operation (which includes, for example, the cumulative translation difference for that foreign operation, the exchange differences arising on certain translations to a different presentation currency and any gains and losses on related hedges) should be recognised in profit or loss when the gain or loss on disposal is recognised.[223] This also applies to exchange differences arising on monetary items that form part of a reporting entity's net investment in a foreign operation.[224]

Full retrospective application of IAS 21 would require a first-time adopter to restate all financial statements of its foreign operations to IFRSs from their date of inception or later acquisition onwards, and then determine the cumulative translation differences arising in relation to each of these foreign operations. The costs of this restatement are likely to exceed the benefits to users of financial statements. For this reason 'a first-time adopter need not comply with these requirements for cumulative translation differences that existed at the date of transition to IFRSs. If a first-time adopter uses this exemption:

(a)   the cumulative translation differences for all foreign operations are deemed to be zero at the date of transition to IFRSs; and

(b)   the gain or loss on a subsequent disposal of any foreign operation shall exclude translation differences that arose before the date of transition to IFRSs and shall include later translation differences.'[225]

If a first time adopter chooses to use this exemption, it should apply it to all foreign operations at its date of transition to IFRSs (i.e. even those foreign operations that became first-time adopters before their parent). Any existing separate component of the first-time adopter's equity relating to such translation differences should be transferred to retained earnings at the date of transition.

An entity may present its financial statements in a presentation currency that differs from its functional currency. IFRS 1 is silent on whether the cumulative translation differences exemption should be applied to all translation differences or possibly separately to differences between the parent's functional currency and the presentation currency. However, IAS 21 does not distinguish between (1) the translation differences arising on translation of subsidiaries into the functional currency of the parent and (2) those arising on the translation from the parent's functional currency to the presentation currency. In our opinion, the exemption should therefore be applied consistently to both types of translation differences.

Since there is no requirement to justify the use of the exemption on grounds of impracticality or undue cost or effort, an entity that already has a separate component of equity and the necessary information to determine how much of it relates to each foreign operation in accordance with IAS 21 (or can do so without much effort) is still able to use the exemption. Accordingly, an entity that has cumulative exchange losses in respect of foreign operations, may consider it advantageous to use the exemption so as to avoid having to recognise these losses in the event of the foreign operation being sold at some time in the future.

The extract below illustrates how companies typically disclose the fact that they have made use of this exemption.

Extract 5.8: Norsk Hydro ASA (2007)

NOTE 47 Conversion to IFRS [extract]

Cumulative translation differences

IFRS 1 offers the first-time adopter of IFRS the option to reset the cumulative translation differences that existed at the date of adoption (i.e. the US GAAP translation differences) to zero as of the date of transition to IFRS as an alternative to establishing a cumulative translation difference as if the accounting and translation principles in IAS 21 The Effects of Changes in Foreign Exchange Rates had always been used and the measurement of assets and liabilities had been as required by currently implemented IFRS. Hydro has elected to utilize this option, and has reset the cumulative translation differences for all foreign operations to zero as of 1 January 2006. Future gains or losses on a subsequent disposal of any foreign operation will therefore exclude translation differences that arose before 1 January 2006.

5.8.1   Gains and losses arising on related hedges

Unfortunately, IFRS 1 is not entirely clear whether this concession extends to similar gains and losses arising on related hedges. Paragraph D13, which contains the concession, explains that a first-time adopter need not comply with 'these requirements'.[226] The requirements referred to are those summarised in paragraph D12 which explain that IAS 21 requires an entity

(a)   to recognise some translation differences as other comprehensive income and accumulate these in a separate component of equity; and

(b)   on disposal of a foreign operation, to reclassify the cumulative translation difference for that foreign operation (*including, if applicable, gains and losses on related hedges*) from equity to profit or loss as part of the gain or loss on disposal.[227]

The problem arises because paragraph D12 does not refer to the recognition of hedging gains or losses in comprehensive income and accumulation in a separate component of equity (only the subsequent reclassification thereof). Accordingly, a very literal reading of the standard might suggest that an entity *is* required to identify historical gains and losses on such hedges. However, even if this position is accepted, on what basis this might be done is not at all clear. For example, it is quite likely that such hedges would not have met the conditions for hedge accounting in IAS 39 and, other than in paragraph D12, IFRS 1 does not specifically address net investment hedges at all.

It is clear that the reasons cited by the IASB for including this concession apply as much to related hedges as they do to the underlying exchange differences. The fact that IFRS 1 can be read otherwise might be seen as little more than poor drafting. In fact there is already clear evidence that paragraph D12 was not subject to the most rigorous scrutiny before publication – it is IAS 39, not IAS 21, that deals with the reclassification of gains and losses recognised in other comprehensive income in a net investment hedge from equity to profit or loss. Accordingly, we believe it is entirely appropriate for this concession to be applied to net investment hedges as well as the underlying gains and losses.

5.9   Investments in subsidiaries, jointly controlled entities and associates

5.9.1   Consolidated financial statements: Subsidiaries and Special Purpose Entities

A first-time adopter should consolidate all subsidiaries and Special Purpose Entities, except when IAS 27 requires otherwise.[228] First-time adoption of IFRSs may therefore result in the consolidation for the first time of a subsidiary not consolidated under previous GAAP, either because the subsidiary was not regarded as such under previous GAAP, or because the parent did not prepare consolidated financial statements under previous GAAP. If a first-time adopter did not consolidate a subsidiary under its previous GAAP, it should recognise the assets and liabilities of that subsidiary in its consolidated financial statements at the date of transition at either:[229]

(a)   if the subsidiary adopted IFRSs, the same carrying amounts as in the separate IFRS financial statements of the subsidiary, after adjusting for consolidation procedures and for the effects of the business combination in which it acquired the subsidiary;[230] or

(b)   if the subsidiary did not adopted IFRSs, the carrying amounts that IFRSs would require in the subsidiary's separate balance sheet.[231]

If the newly-consolidated subsidiary was acquired in a business combination before the date of the parent's transition to IFRSs, the parent calculates goodwill as the difference between the carrying amount determined under either (a) or (b) above and the cost in the parent's separate financial statements of its investment in the subsidiary (see 5.2.6 above).[232] Therefore, if the first-time adopter accounted for the investment as an associate under its previous GAAP, it cannot use the notional goodwill previously calculated under the equity method as the basis for goodwill under IFRSs.

It should be noted that 'goodwill' calculated as described above is no more than a pragmatic 'plug' that facilitates the consolidation process but that does not represent the true goodwill that might have been recorded if IFRSs had been applied at the date of the original business combination.

If the parent did not acquire the subsidiary, but established it, it does not recognise goodwill.[233] Any difference between the carrying amount of the subsidiary and the net identifiable assets as determined in (a) or (b) above would be treated as an adjustment to equity, representing the accumulated profits or losses that would have been recognised as if the subsidiary had always been consolidated.

The adjustment of the carrying amounts of assets and liabilities of a first-time adopter's subsidiaries may affect non-controlling interests and deferred tax.[234]

5.9.2   Separate financial statements: Cost of an investment in a subsidiary, jointly controlled entity or associate

In May 2008, the IASB issued *Amendments to IFRS 1 First-time Adoption of International Financial Reporting Standards and IAS 27 Consolidated and Separate Financial Statements: Cost of an Investment in a Subsidiary, Jointly Controlled Entity or Associate*. The amendments address the various difficulties that can arise from a fully retrospective application of the cost method under IAS 27 in separate financial statements. For example, if a parent holds an investment in a subsidiary for many years then it is often costly and difficult (and perhaps even impossible) to:[235]

• measure the fair value of the consideration given at the date of acquisition; and

• determine whether any dividends received from a subsidiary after its acquisition were paid out of pre-acquisition retained earnings.

After the amendments, IAS 27 still requires a first-time adopter to account for its investments in subsidiaries, jointly controlled entities and associates either:[236]

• at cost; or

• in accordance with IAS 39.

However, if a first-time adopter measures such an investment at cost then it can now elect to measure that investment at one of the following amounts in its separate opening IFRS statement of financial position:

'(a)   cost determined in accordance with IAS 27 or

(b)   deemed cost. The deemed cost of such an investment shall be its:

  (i)   fair value (determined in accordance with IAS 39) at the entity's date of transition to IFRSs in its separate financial statements or

  (ii)   previous GAAP carrying amount at that date.

  A first-time adopter may choose either (i) or (ii) above to measure its investment in each subsidiary, jointly controlled entity or associate that it elects to measure using a deemed cost.'[237]

The above exemption is applicable for annual periods beginning on or after 1 July 2009, but earlier application is permitted.[238]

A first-time adopter that applies the exemption should disclose certain additional information in its financial statements (see 6.5.2 below).

5.10   Assets and liabilities of subsidiaries, associates and joint ventures

Within groups, some subsidiaries, associates and joint ventures may have a different date of transition to IFRSs than the parent/investor (for example, national legislation required IFRSs after, or prohibited IFRSs at, the date of transition to IFRSs of the parent/investor). This could result in permanent differences between the IFRS figures in a subsidiary's own financial statements and those it reports to its parent. In turn this could force a subsidiary to keep two parallel sets of accounting records based on different dates of transition to IFRSs.[239] To mitigate this difficulty, the IASB introduced a special exemption regarding the assets and liabilities of subsidiaries, associates and joint ventures.

IFRS 1 contains detailed guidance on the approach to be adopted when a parent adopts IFRSs before its subsidiary (see 5.10.1 below) and also on when a subsidiary adopts IFRSs before its parent (see 5.10.2 below). These provisions also apply when IFRSs are adopted at different dates by:

- an investor in an associate and the associate; or

- a venturer in a jointly controlled entity and the jointly controlled entity.[240]

In the discussion that follows 'parent' should be therefore read as including an investor in an associate or a venturer in a jointly controlled entity, and 'subsidiary' as including an associate or a jointly controlled entity. Additionally, references to consolidation adjustments should be read as including similar adjustments made when applying equity accounting or proportionate consolidation.

IFRS 1 also addresses the requirements for a parent that adopts IFRSs at different dates for the purposes of its consolidated and its separate financial statements (see 5.10.4 below).

5.10.1 Subsidiary becomes a first-time adopter later than its parent

If a subsidiary becomes a first-time adopter later than its parent, it should in its financial statements measure its assets and liabilities at either:

'(a)   the carrying amounts that would be included in the parent's consolidated financial statements, based on the parent's date of transition to IFRSs, if no adjustments were made for consolidation procedures and for the effects of the business combination in which the parent acquired the subsidiary; or

(b)   the carrying amounts required by the rest of [IFRS 1], based on the subsidiary's date of transition to IFRSs. These carrying amounts could differ from those described in (a):

   (i)   when the exemptions in this IFRS result in measurements that depend on the date of transition to IFRSs;

   (ii)   when the accounting policies used in the subsidiary's financial statements differ from those in the consolidated financial statements. For example, the subsidiary may use as its accounting policy the cost model in IAS 16 *Property, Plant and Equipment*, whereas the group may use the revaluation model.'[241]

A similar election is available to an associate or joint venture that becomes a first-time adopter later than an entity that has significant influence or joint control over it.[242] The following example, which is taken from the guidance on implementation of IFRS 1, illustrates how an entity should apply these requirements.

Example 5.31:   Parent adopts IFRSs before subsidiary[243]

Background

Parent A presents its (consolidated) first IFRS financial statements in 2008. Its foreign subsidiary B, wholly owned by parent A since formation, prepares information under IFRSs for internal consolidation purposes from that date, but subsidiary B will not present its first IFRS financial statements until 2010.

Application of requirements

If subsidiary B applies paragraph D16(a) of IFRS 1, the carrying amounts of its assets and liabilities are the same in both its opening IFRS balance sheet at 1 January 2009 and parent A's consolidated balance sheet (except for adjustments for consolidation procedures) and are based on parent A's date of transition to IFRSs.

Alternatively, subsidiary B may, under paragraph D16(b) of IFRS 1, measure all its assets or liabilities based on its own date of transition to IFRSs (1 January 2009). However, the fact that subsidiary B becomes a first-time adopter in 2010 does not change the carrying amounts of its assets and liabilities in parent A's consolidated financial statements.

Under option (b) a subsidiary would prepare its own IFRS financial statements, completely ignoring the IFRS reports that its parent uses in preparing its consolidated financial statements. Under option (a) the numbers in a subsidiary's IFRS financial statements will be as close to those used by its parent as possible. However, differences other than those arising from consolidation procedures and business combinations will still exist in many cases, for example:

• a subsidiary may have hedged an exposure by entering into a transaction with a fellow subsidiary. Such transaction could qualify for hedge accounting in the subsidiary's own financial statements but not in the parent's consolidated financial statements; or

• a pension plan may have to be classified as a defined contribution plan from the subsidiary's point of view, but is accounted for as a defined benefit plan in the parent's consolidated financial statements.

The IASB seems content with the fact that the exemption 'will ease some practical problems',[244] though it will rarely succeed in achieving more than a moderate reduction of the number of reconciling differences between a subsidiary's own reporting and the numbers used by its parent.

Application of option (a) would be more difficult when a parent and its subsidiary (joint venture or associate) have different financial years. In that case, IFRS 1 would seem to require the IFRS information for the subsidiary (joint venture or associate) to be based on the parent's date of transition to IFRSs, which may not even coincide with an interim reporting date of the subsidiary (joint venture or associate).

A subsidiary may become a first-time adopter later than its parent, because it previously prepared a reporting package under IFRSs for consolidation purposes but did not present a full set of financial statements under IFRSs. The above election may be 'relevant not only when a subsidiary's reporting package complies fully with the recognition and measurement requirements of IFRSs, but also when it is adjusted centrally for matters such as review of events after the reporting period and central allocation of pension costs.'[245] Adjustments made centrally to an unpublished reporting package are not considered to be corrections of errors for the purposes of the disclosure requirements in IFRS 1. However, a subsidiary is not permitted to ignore misstatements that are immaterial to the consolidated financial statements of its parent but material to its own financial statements.

If a subsidiary was acquired after the parent's date of transition to IFRSs, it seems that the subsidiary cannot apply option (a) because 'the carrying amounts that would be included in the parent's consolidated financial statements, based on the parent's date of transition to IFRSs' would not exist.[246]

The exemption is also available to associates and joint ventures. This means that in many cases an associate or joint venture that wants to apply option (a) will need to choose which shareholder it considers its 'parent' for IFRS 1 purposes and determine the IFRS carrying amount of its assets and liabilities by reference to that parent's date of transition to IFRSs.

5.10.2 Parent becomes a first-time adopter later than its subsidiary

If an entity becomes a first-time adopter later than its subsidiary, associate or joint venture the entity should 'in its consolidated financial statements, measure the assets and liabilities of the subsidiary (or associate or joint venture) at the same carrying amounts as in the financial statements of the subsidiary (or associate or joint venture), after adjusting for consolidation and equity accounting adjustments and for the effects of the business combination in which the entity acquired the subsidiary.'[247]

Unlike other first-time adoption exemptions, this exemption does not offer a choice between different accounting alternatives. In fact, whereas a subsidiary can choose to prepare its first IFRS financial statements by reference to its own date of transition to IFRSs or that of its parent, the parent itself *must* use the IFRS measurements already used in the subsidiary's separate financial statements, except to adjust for consolidation procedures and for the effects of the business combination in which the parent acquired the subsidiary.[248]

The following example, which is taken from the guidance on implementation of IFRS 1, illustrates how an entity should apply these requirements.

Example 5.32:   Subsidiary adopts IFRSs before parent[249]

Background

Parent C presents its (consolidated) first IFRS financial statements in 2010. Its foreign subsidiary D, wholly owned by parent C since formation, presented its first IFRS financial statements in 2008. Until 2010, subsidiary D prepared information for internal consolidation purposes under parent C's previous GAAP.

Application of requirements

The carrying amounts of subsidiary D's assets and liabilities at 1 January 2009 are the same in both parent C's (consolidated) opening IFRS balance sheet and subsidiary D's own financial statements (except for adjustments for consolidation procedures) and are based on subsidiary D's date of transition to IFRSs. The fact that parent C becomes a first-time adopter in 2010 does not change the carrying amounts of subsidiary D's assets and liabilities.

IFRS 1 does not elaborate on exactly what constitute 'consolidation adjustments' but in our view it would encompass adjustments required in order to harmonise D's accounting policies with those of C as well as purely 'mechanical' consolidation adjustments such as the elimination of intragroup balances, profits and losses.

When a subsidiary adopts IFRSs before its parent, this will limit the parent's ability to choose first-time adoption exemptions in IFRS 1 freely as related to that subsidiary, as illustrated in the example below.

Example 5.33:   Limited ability to choose first-time adoption exemptions

Parent E will adopt IFRSs for the first time in 2010 and its date of transition is 1 January 2009. Subsidiary F adopted IFRSs in 2007 and its date of transition was 1 January 2006:

(a) Subsidiary F and parent E both account for their property, plant and equipment at historical cost under IAS 16. Upon first-time adoption, parent E may only adjust carrying amounts of subsidiary F's assets and liabilities to adjust for the effects of consolidation, equity accounting and business combinations. Parent E can therefore not apply the exemption to use fair value as deemed cost of subsidiary F's property, plant and equipment as at its own date of transition (1 January 2009);

(b) Subsidiary F accounts for its property, plant and equipment at revalued amounts under IAS 16, while parent E accounts for its property, plant and equipment at historical cost under IAS 16. In this case, parent E would not be allowed to apply the exemption to use fair value as deemed cost of subsidiary F's property, plant and equipment because paragraph D17 of IFRS 1 would only permit adjustments for the effects of consolidation, equity accounting and business combinations Although a consolidation adjustment would be necessary, this would only be to adjust Subsidiary F's revalued amounts to figures based on historical cost.

However, this does not mean that the parent's ability to choose first-time adoption exemptions will always be limited, for example:

• Subsidiary F may have deemed the cumulative translation difference for all its foreign subsidiaries to be zero at its date of transition (i.e. 1 January 2006). When Parent E adopts IFRSs it can deem subsidiary F's cumulative translation differences to be zero at its date of transition (1 January 2009), because paragraph D13 of IFRS 1 specifically states that under the option 'the cumulative translation differences for *all* [emphasis added] foreign operations are deemed to be zero at the date of transition to IFRSs'; and

• Subsidiary F may have elected to recognise all cumulative actuarial gains and losses at its date of transition (i.e. 1 January 2006). A literal reading of IFRS 1 would be that paragraph D17 prevents parent E from applying the exemption in paragraph D10 because it cannot reset the actuarial gains and losses related to subsidiary F. Another acceptable reading of the requirements of IFRS 1 is that while parent E may not reset the actuarial gains and losses related to subsidiary F, it does have the option to reset all other actuarial gains and losses that are not covered by the requirements of paragraph D17.

5.10.3 Implementation guidance on accounting for assets and liabilities of subsidiaries, associates and joint ventures

When an entity applies the requirements discussed under 5.10.1 and 5.10.2 above, these do not override the following requirements of IFRS 1:[250]

- the business combinations exemption in Appendix C to IFRS 1 applies in respect of assets and liabilities of a subsidiary acquired and assumed in a business combination that occurred before the parent's date of transition to IFRSs. The rules summarised at 5.10.2 above (parent adopting IFRSs after subsidiary) apply only to assets and liabilities acquired and assumed by the subsidiary after the business combination and still held and owed by it at the parent's date of transition to IFRSs;

- the requirements in IFRS 1 apply in full to assets and liabilities to which the provisions summarised in paragraphs D16 and D17 of IFRS 1 are not relevant; and

- a first-time adopter must give all the disclosures required by IFRS 1 as of its own date of transition to IFRSs.

5.10.4 Adoption of IFRSs on different dates in separate and consolidated financial statements

If a parent becomes a first-time adopter for its separate financial statements earlier or later than for its consolidated financial statements, it must measure its assets and liabilities at the same amounts in both financial statements, except for consolidation adjustments.[251] As drafted, the requirement is merely that the 'same' basis be used, without being explicit as to which set of financial statements should be used as the benchmark. However, it seems clear from the context that the IASB intends that the measurement basis used in whichever set of financial statements first comply with IFRSs must also be used when IFRSs are subsequently adopted in the other set.

5.11   Compound financial instruments

IAS 32 – *Financial Instruments: Presentation* – requires compound financial instruments (e.g. convertible bonds) to be split at inception into separate equity and liability components. If the liability component is no longer outstanding, a full retrospective application of IAS 32 would involve identifying two components, one representing the original equity component and the other representing the cumulative interest on the liability component, both of which are accounted for in equity (see Chapter 31 at 8). A first-time adopter does not need to make this allocation if the liability component is no longer outstanding at the date of transition to IFRSs.[252] For example, in the case of a convertible bond that has been converted into equity, it is not necessary to make this split.

A first-time adopter applying this exemption can therefore avoid the possibly complex allocation process that would be involved. However, if the liability component of the compound instrument is still outstanding at the date of transition to IFRSs then a split will need to be made (see Chapter 31).[253]

This transitional exemption is slightly interesting in that it refers to a 'requirement' in IAS 32 to credit the equity component arising on initial recognition of a compound instrument to a separate component of equity. We are unable to identify such a requirement – IAS 32 requires merely that the amount be credited to equity (Chapter 31 at 4.3.1). Moreover, IFRS 1 implies a further requirement that the amount originally credited to the equity component must remain in that separate component permanently. However, this is arguably contradicted by the application guidance to IAS 32 which, on conversion of a convertible bond, allows a transfer within equity of the amount originally credited there in respect of the equity component (see Chapter 31 at 4.4.1). Thus, even if, on initial recognition of a compound instrument, the entity had been required to credit the equity component to a separate component of equity, on final conversion or settlement it could, on subsequent conversion of the instrument, notionally have transferred the separately recognised component of equity to another component of equity (e.g. retained earnings), so that no further adjustment would be required on transition to IFRSs.

This transitional exemption is of limited value in practice because the number of different compound financial instruments that were outstanding before the date of transition to IFRSs is bound to be limited for any given first-time adopter.

5.12   Designation of previously recognised financial instruments

5.12.1 *Available-for-sale financial assets*

Subject to the criteria in IAS 39, an entity can designate a financial asset (typically one that would otherwise be classified as loans and receivables) upon initial recognition as an *available-for-sale financial asset* (see Chapter 29 at 7.4). However, a first-time adopter is allowed to designate such an asset as available-for-sale at the date of transition to IFRSs,[254] although it would need to make certain additional disclosures (see 6.4 below).[255]

Retrospective designation of financial instruments as available-for-sale financial assets 'requires a first-time adopter to recognise the cumulative fair value changes in a separate component of equity in the opening IFRS balance sheet, and transfer those fair value changes to the income statement on subsequent disposal or impairment of the asset'. The IASB recognised that this could give rise to a selective approach, whereby first-time adopters would only designate financial instruments with cumulative gains as available-for-sale, but it noted that a first-time adopter could achieve similar results by selectively disposing of some financial assets before the date of transition to IFRSs. Therefore, IFRS 1 does not impose any additional restrictions on a first-time adopters regarding the designation of financial instruments as available-for-sale financial assets at its date of transition to IFRSs.[256]

5.12.2 *Financial asset or financial liability at fair value through profit or loss*

Although IAS 39 permits a financial instrument to be designated only on initial recognition as a financial asset or financial liability at fair value through profit or loss, a first-time adopter is permitted to designate, at its date of transition to IFRSs, any financial asset or financial liability as at fair value through profit or loss provided the asset or liability meets the criteria in paragraph 9(b)(i), 9(b)(ii) or 11A of IAS 39 at that date.[257] It is clear from the transitional requirements in IFRS 1 (2008) that first-time adopters with a date of transition to IFRSs on or after 1 September 2005 should complete the designation by their date of transition.[258] In other words, designation should be made contemporaneously and cannot be documented retrospectively.

A first-time adopter that applies this exemption needs to make certain additional disclosures (see 6.4 below).[259]

5.12.3 *Implementation guidance on other categories of financial instruments*

The implementation guidance to IFRS 1 clarifies how, in preparing its opening IFRS balance sheet, an entity should apply the criteria in IAS 39 to identify those financial assets and financial liabilities that are measured at fair value and those that are measured at amortised cost.[260]

A   *Held-to-maturity investments*

The standard explains that 'classification of financial assets as held-to-maturity investments relies on a designation made by the entity in applying IAS 39 reflecting the entity's intention and ability at the date of transition to IFRSs.'[261] In other words, sales or transfers of held-to-maturity investments before the date of transition to IFRSs do not trigger the 'tainting' rules in IAS 39.

B   *Financial assets or financial liabilities at fair value through profit or loss*

Except for those financial assets that are designated as at fair value through profit or loss at the date of transition (see 5.12.2 above), non-derivative financial instruments are included within the opening IFRS balance sheet as at fair value through profit or loss only if the asset or liability was:[262]

- acquired or incurred principally for the purpose of sale or repurchase in the near term; or

- at the date of transition to IFRSs, part of a portfolio of identified financial instruments that were managed together and for which there was evidence of a recent actual pattern of short-term profit taking.

These instruments would be classified as held for trading rather than being designated at fair value through profit and loss.

C   *Loans and receivables*

In assessing whether or not a financial asset meets the definition of loans and receivables at the date of transition to IFRSs a first-time adopter should consider the circumstances that existed when it first met the recognition criteria in IAS 39.[263]

D   *Financial assets and financial liabilities measured at amortised cost*

The cost of financial assets and financial liabilities measured at amortised cost in the opening IFRS balance sheet should be determined on the basis of circumstances existing when the assets and liabilities first satisfied the recognition criteria in IAS 39, unless they were acquired in a past business combination in which case their carrying amount under previous GAAP immediately following the business combination is their deemed cost under IFRSs at that date.[264]

To determine amortised cost using the effective interest method, it is necessary to determine the transaction costs incurred when the instrument was originated. During the development of IFRS 1, some argued that determining these transaction costs could involve undue cost or effort for financial instruments originated long before the date of transition to IFRSs and argued for concessions to be made, e.g. by allowing transaction costs to be ignored.[265] However, the IASB believes that the unamortised portion of transaction costs at the date of transition to IFRSs is unlikely to be material for most financial instruments. Further, even where the unamortised portion may be material, reasonable estimates are believed possible. Therefore, no exemption was granted in this area.[266]

E   *Available-for-sale financial assets*

In addition to those financial assets that are designated as available-for-sale at the date of transition (see 5.12.1 above), this category includes those non-derivative financial assets that are not in any of the other categories identified by IAS 39.[267]

Where, upon initial application of IFRSs, an investment is classified as available-for-sale, any previous revaluation gain is recognised in a separate component of equity. Subsequently, the entity recognises gains and losses on the available-for-sale financial asset in other comprehensive income and accumulates the cumulative gains and losses in that separate component of equity until the investment is impaired, sold, collected or otherwise disposed of. On subsequent derecognition or impairment of the available-for-sale financial asset, the first-time adopter reclassifies to profit or loss the cumulative gain or loss remaining in equity.[268]

During the development of IFRS 1, some suggested that the cost of determining the amount to be included in a separate component of equity would exceed the benefits. However, the IASB noted that these costs would be minimal if a first-time adopter carried the available-for-sale financial assets under previous GAAP at cost or the lower of cost and market value. They acknowledged that these costs might be more significant if they were carried at fair value, but in that case those assets might well be classified as held for trading. Therefore, the requirement that a first-time adopter should apply IAS 39 retrospectively to available-for-sale financial assets was retained in the standard.[269]

Given the requirements in respect of impairments of available-for-sale equity instruments full retrospective application in this area may not be as straightforward as the IASB thinks. However, this does not change the fact that no exceptions have been made in this respect.

F   Derivatives

All derivatives, except for those that are financial guarantee contracts or designated and effective hedging instruments, are classified as held for trading under IAS 39. Therefore, the difference between their fair value and their previous carrying amount should be recognised as an adjustment to retained earnings at the beginning of the financial year in which IAS 39 is initially applied (other than for a derivative that is a financial guarantee contract or a designated and effective hedging instrument).[270]

G   Embedded derivatives

Under IAS 39, some embedded derivatives are accounted for separately at fair value. Some argued that retrospective application of this requirement would be costly and suggested either an exemption from retrospective application of this requirement, or a requirement or option to use the fair value of the host instrument at the date of transition to IFRSs as the deemed cost of the instrument at that date should be introduced.[271]

Although the IASB recognised that an option not to account separately for some pre-existing embedded derivatives was provided when the equivalent US GAAP requirements became mandatory, it concluded that the failure to measure embedded derivatives at fair value would diminish the relevance and reliability of an entity's first IFRS financial statements. It also observed that IAS 39 addresses an inability to measure an embedded derivative and the host contract separately (in such cases, the entire combined contract is measured at fair value).[272] Accordingly, no exception was granted in this area.

Consequently, when an entity is required to separate an embedded derivative from a host contract, the initial carrying amounts of the components at the date the instrument first satisfied the recognition criteria in IAS 39 should reflect circumstances that existed at that date. If the initial carrying amounts of the embedded derivative and host contract cannot be determined reliably, the entire combined contract should be designated at fair value through profit or loss.[273]

Further guidance is provided by IFRIC 9 – *Reassessment of Embedded Derivatives* – which states that, on first-time adoption, an entity should make an assessment of whether an embedded derivative is required to be separated from the host contract and accounted for as a derivative on the basis of conditions that existed at the later of the date it first became party to the contract and the date a reassessment is required (see Chapter 29 at 5.4.1).[274]

5.12.4 Loan impairments

An entity's estimates of loan impairments at the date of transition to IFRSs should be consistent with estimates made for the same date under previous GAAP (after adjustments to reflect any difference in accounting policies), unless there is objective evidence that those assumptions were in error. Any later revisions to those estimates should be treated as impairment losses (or reversals of impairment losses) of the period in which the entity makes the revisions.[275]

In the context of the detailed requirements for loan impairments, it is unclear where the dividing line between estimates and accounting policies lies. Therefore, for entities with material impairment provisions, such as banks and similar financial institutions, this requirement overlooks a very important point of detail.

5.13   Fair value measurement of financial assets or financial liabilities at initial recognition

First-time adopters are given some transitional relief in respect of the day 1 profit requirements of IAS 39 – in fact this is the same as was available to existing IFRS reporters.[276] Consequently, first-time adopters may apply the requirements of paragraphs AG76 and AG76A of IAS 39 in any of the following ways:[277]

(a)   retrospectively;

(b)   prospectively to transactions entered into after 25 October 2002; or

(c)   prospectively to transactions entered into after 1 January 2004.

It is important to note that the latter dates are fixed and do not change according to an entity's date of transition.

The second option was added in the light of concerns of the IASB's constituents that 'retrospective application would diverge from the requirements of US GAAP'.[278] Although these US GAAP requirements have now been superseded, the option remains.

5.14   Decommissioning liabilities included in the cost of property, plant and equipment

5.14.1 IFRIC 1 exemption

Under IAS 16 the cost of an item of property, plant and equipment includes 'the initial estimate of the costs of dismantling and removing the item and restoring the site on which it is located, the obligation for which an entity incurs either when the item is acquired or as a consequence of having used the item during a particular period for purposes other than to produce inventories during that period.'[279] Therefore, a first-time adopter needs to ensure that cost includes an item representing the decommissioning provision as determined under IAS 37.[280]

An entity should apply IAS 16 in determining the resulting amount included in the cost of the asset, before depreciation and impairment losses. Items such as depreciation and impairment losses cause differences between the carrying amount of the liability and the amount related to decommissioning costs included in the carrying amount of the asset. An entity accounts for changes in decommissioning provisions in accordance with IFRIC 1 but IFRS 1 provides an exemption for changes that occurred before the date of transition to IFRSs and prescribes an alternative treatment if the exemption is used.[281] In such cases, a first-time adopter should:

'(a)   measure the [decommissioning] liability as at the date of transition to IFRSs in accordance with IAS 37;

(b)   to the extent that the liability is within the scope of IFRIC 1, estimate the amount that would have been included in the cost of the related asset when the liability first arose, by discounting the liability to that date using its best estimate of the historical risk-adjusted discount rate(s) that would have applied for that liability over the intervening period; and

(c)   calculate the accumulated depreciation on that amount, as at the date of transition to IFRSs, on the basis of the current estimate of the useful life of the asset, using the depreciation policy adopted by the entity in accordance with IFRSs.'[282]

Example 5.34:   *Decommissioning component in property, plant and equipment*

Entity A's date of transition to IFRSs is 1 January 2009 and the end of its first IFRS reporting period is 31 December 2010. Entity A built a factory that was completed and ready for use on 1 January 2004. Under its previous GAAP, Entity A accrued a decommissioning provision over the expected life of the plant. The facts can be summarised as follows:

Cost of the plant	€1,400
Residual value	€200
Economic life	20 years
Original estimate of decommissioning cost in year 20	€175
Revised estimate in 2006 of decommissioning cost in year 20	€300
Discount rate applicable to decommissioning liability	
(the discount rate is assumed to be constant)	5.65%
Discounted value of original decommissioning liability on 1 January 2004	€58
Discounted value of revised decommissioning liability on 1 January 2004	€100
Discounted value of revised decommissioning liability on 1 January 2009	€131

If entity A applies the exemption from full retrospective application, what are the carrying amounts of the factory and the decommissioning liability in A's opening IFRS balance sheet?

The tables below show how entity A accounts for the decommissioning liability and the factory under its previous GAAP, under IFRS 1 using the exemption and under IFRS 1 applying IFRIC 1 retrospectively.

	Decommissioning liability		
	Previous GAAP	*Exemption IFRS 1*	*Retrospective application of IFRIC 1*
1 January 2004	–	100	58
Decommissioning costs €175 ÷ 20 years × 2 =	17.5		
Decommissioning costs €100 × (1.0565² – 1) =		12	
Decommissioning costs €58 × (1.0565² – 1) =			7
1 January 2006	17.5	112	65
Revised estimate of decommissioning provision	12.5		47
1 January 2006	30	112	112
Decommissioning costs €300 ÷ 20 years × 3 =	45		
Decommissioning costs €112 × (1.0565³ – 1) =		19	
Decommissioning costs €112 × (1.0565³ – 1) =			19
1 January 2009	75	131	131
Decommissioning costs €300 ÷ 20 years × 2 =	30		
Decommissioning costs €131 × (1.0565² – 1) =		16	
Decommissioning costs €131 × (1.0565² – 1) =			16
31 December 2010	105	147	147

In calculating the decommissioning provision, it makes no difference whether entity A goes back in time and tracks the history of the decommissioning provision or whether it just calculates the decommissioning provision at its date of transition to IFRSs. This is not the case for the calculation of the related asset, as can be seen below.

	Factory		
	Previous GAAP	*Exemption IFRS 1*	*Retrospective application of IFRIC 1*
1 January 2004	1,400	1,500	1,458
Depreciation (€1,400 – €200) ÷ 20 years × 2 =	(120)		
Depreciation (€1,500 – €200) ÷ 20 years × 2 =		(130)	
Depreciation (€1,458 – €200) ÷ 20 years × 2 =			(126)
1 January 2006			1,332
Revised estimate of decommissioning provision			47
1 January 2006			1,379
Depreciation (€1,400 – €200) ÷ 20 years × 3 =	(180)		
Depreciation (€1,500 – €200) ÷ 20 years × 3 =		(195)	
Depreciation (€1,379 – €200) ÷ 18 years × 3 =			(197)
1 January 2009	1,100	1,175	1,182
Depreciation (€1,400 – €200) ÷ 20 years × 2 =	(120)		
Depreciation (€1,500 – €200) ÷ 20 years × 2 =		(130)	
Depreciation (€1,379 – €200) ÷ 18 years × 2 =			(131)
31 December 2010	980	1,045	1,051

As can be seen above, a full retrospective application of IFRIC 1 would require an entity to go back in time and account for each revision of the decommissioning provision in accordance with IFRIC 1. In the case of a long-lived asset there could be a significant number of revisions that a first-time adopter would need to account for. It should also be noted that despite the significant revision of the decommissioning costs, the impact on the carrying amount of the factory is quite modest.

At its date of transition to IFRSs (1 January 2009), entity A makes the following adjustments:

- the decommissioning liability is increased by €56 (= €131 – €75) to reflect the difference in accounting policy, irrespective of whether entity A applies the exemption or not; and

- if entity A applies the exemption it increases the carrying amount of the factory by €75. Whereas if entity A applies IFRIC 1 retrospectively, the carrying amount of the factory would increase by €82.

It is important to note that in both cases the decommissioning component of the factory will be significantly lower than the decommissioning liability itself.

From the above example it is clear that the exemption reduces the amount of effort required to restate items of property, plant and equipment with a decommissioning component. In many cases the difference between the two methods will be insignificant, except where an entity had to make major adjustments to the estimate of the decommissioning costs near the end of the life of the related assets.

5.14.2 IFRIC 1 exemption for oil and gas assets at deemed cost

A first-time adopter that applies the deemed cost exemption for oil and gas assets (see 5.5.4 above) should not apply the IFRIC 1 exemption in paragraph D21 of IFRS 1 (see 5.14.1 above) or IFRIC 1 itself, but instead:

'(a) measure decommissioning, restoration and similar liabilities as at the date of transition to IFRSs in accordance with IAS 37; and

(b) recognise directly in retained earnings any difference between that amount and the carrying amount of those liabilities at the date of transition to IFRSs.'[283]

The IASB introduced this requirement because it believed that the existing IFRIC 1 exemption would require detailed calculations that would not be practicable for entities that apply the deemed cost exemption for oil and gas assets.[284]

This exemption, which was introduced in July 2009 when the IASB published an amendment to IFRS 1, should be applied for annual periods beginning on or after 1 January 2010. Earlier application is permitted, provided that all other amendments to IFRS 1 that were introduced in July 2009 are also applied (see 2.1.1 above).[285]

5.15 Financial assets or intangible assets accounted for in accordance with IFRIC 12

Service concession arrangements are contracts between the government and the private sector to attract private sector participation in the development, financing, operation and maintenance of public infrastructure (e.g. roads, bridges, hospitals, water distribution facilities, energy supply and telecommunication networks).[286]

A first-time adopter may apply the transitional provision in IFRIC 12.[287] That interpretation requires retrospective application unless it is, for any particular service arrangement, impracticable for the operator to apply IFRIC 12 retrospectively at the start of the earliest period presented, in which case it should:

'(a) recognise financial assets and intangible assets that existed at the start of the earliest period presented;

(b) use the previous carrying amounts of those financial and intangible assets (however previously classified) as their carrying amounts as at that date; and

(c) test financial and intangible assets recognised at that date for impairment, unless this is not practicable, in which case the amounts shall be tested for impairment as at the start of the current period.'[288]

5.16 Borrowing costs

Full retrospective application of IAS 23 (as revised in 2007) – *Borrowing Costs* – would be problematic as the adjustment would be required in respect of all assets held that would, at any point in the past, have satisfied the criteria for capitalisation of borrowing costs. To avoid this problem, IFRS 1 allows a first-time adopter to apply a modified form of the transitional provisions set out in IAS 23 (as revised in 2007), which means that:[289]

- it capitalises borrowing costs relating to qualifying assets for which the commencement date for capitalisation is on or after 1 July 2009 or the date of transition to IFRSs, whichever is later; or

- it may elect to designate any date before 1 July 2009 or the date of transition to IFRSs, whichever is later, and to capitalise borrowing costs relating to all qualifying assets for which the commencement date for capitalisation is on or after that date.

In December 2008, the IASB decided to change the effective date of IFRS 1 (as revised in 2008) from 1 January 2009 to 1 July 2009.[290] A consequential amendment was made to the reference date in the first-time adoption exemption for borrowing costs in IFRS 1, but not to the Implementation Guidance in paragraph IG23 of IFRS 1.[291] As the Implementation Guidance is not part of IFRS 1, but only accompanies it, first-time adopters can ignore this minor inconsistency.

If a first-time adopter established a deemed cost for an asset (see 5.5 above) then it cannot capitalise borrowing costs incurred before the measurement date of the deemed cost.[292]

5.17   Transfers of assets from customers

IFRIC 18 – *Transfers of Assets from Customers* – deals with the accounting for items of property, plant and equipment, received from customers, that the entity must then use either to connect those customers to a network and/or to provide those customers with ongoing access to a supply of goods or services (see Chapter 16 at 3.2.1 H). Applying IFRIC 18 retrospectively would require an entity to establish a carrying amount for assets that had been transferred in the past. The IFRIC concluded that retrospective application may be impracticable and that IFRIC 18 should therefore require prospective application to transfers received after its effective date.[293]

The IFRIC introduced similar transitional relief into IFRS 1, which allows first-time adopters to apply IFRIC 18 prospectively to transfers of assets from customers received on or after 1 July 2009 or the date of transition to IFRSs, whichever is later. In addition, a first-time adopter may 'designate any date before the date of transition to IFRSs and apply IFRIC 18 to all transfers of assets from customers received on or after that date'.[294] Therefore, unlike existing IFRS-reporting entities, a first-time adopter is permitted to apply IFRIC 18 to past transfers even if the valuations and other information required to apply the interpretation were not obtained contemporaneously.

6   PRESENTATION AND DISCLOSURE

IFRS 1 does not exempt a first-time adopter from any of the presentation and disclosure requirements in other standards,[295] with the exception of certain disclosures regarding:

- claims development information under IFRS 4 (see 5.4 above); and
- actuarial experience adjustments under IAS 19 (see 5.7.4 above).

6.1   Comparative information

IAS 1 requires (except where a standard or interpretation permits or requires otherwise) comparative information in respect of the previous period for all amounts reported in the financial statements and for narrative and descriptive information when it is relevant to an understanding of the current period's financial statements.[296]

To comply with IAS 1 (as revised in 2007), an entity's first IFRS financial statements should include 'at least three statements of financial position, two statements of comprehensive income, two separate income statements (if presented), two statements of cash flows and two statements of changes in equity and related notes, including comparative information'.[297]

6.2   Non-IFRS comparative information and historical summaries

Normally IFRSs require comparative information that is prepared on the same basis as information relating to the current reporting period. However, when an entity presents historical summaries of selected data for periods before the first period for which they present full comparative information under IFRSs, the standard does not require such summaries to comply with the recognition and measurement requirements of IFRSs.[298]

As an entity is only allowed to apply IFRS 1 in its first IFRS financial statements, a literal reading of IFRS 1 would seem to suggest that the above exemption is not available to an entity that prepares its second IFRS financial statements. In practice this is not likely to cause a significant problem because this type of information is generally presented outside the financial statements where it is not covered by the requirements of IFRSs.

If an entity presents comparative information under its previous GAAP in addition to the comparative information required by IFRSs it should:

'(a)   label the previous GAAP information prominently as not being prepared in accordance with IFRSs; and

(b)   disclose the nature of the main adjustments that would make it comply with IFRSs. An entity need not quantify those adjustments.'[299]

Although IFRS 1 does not specifically require disclosure of this information when the historical summaries are presented outside the financial statements, such disclosure would be of benefit to users of such historical summaries.

6.3   Explanation of transition to IFRSs

A first-time adopter is required to explain how the transition from its previous GAAP to IFRSs affected its reported financial position, financial performance and cash flows.[300] The IASB decided 'that such disclosures are essential ... because they help users understand the effect and implications of the transition to IFRSs and how they need to change their analytical models to make the best use of information presented using IFRSs.'[301]

As indicated at 3.3.2 above, IFRS 1 offers a wide range of exemptions that a first-time adopter may elect to apply. However, somewhat curiously, the standard does not explicitly require an entity to disclose which exemptions it has applied and how it applied them. In the case of, for example, the exemptions relating to employee benefits and cumulative translation differences, it will be rather obvious whether or not an entity has chosen to apply the exemption. In other cases, users will have to rely on a first-time adopter disclosing those transitional accounting policies that are 'relevant to an understanding of the financial statements'.[302] In practice most first-time adopters voluntarily disclose which IFRS 1 exemptions they elected to apply and which exceptions apply to them, as is illustrated below by Extracts 5.9 and 5.10.

Extract 5.9: Infosys Technologies Limited (2009)

2 Notes to the consolidated financial statements [extract]

2.1.1 Exemptions from retrospective application

Following are the optional exemptions which we have opted to apply / not to apply :

1. *Business combinations exemption* – The company has applied the exemption as provided in IFRS 1 on non-application of IFRS 3, Business Combinations to business combinations consummated prior to April 1, 2007 (Transition Date). Pursuant to which goodwill arising from business combinations have been stated at the carrying amount under Indian GAAP in IFRS financial statements as at the date of transition. Further, intangible assets and related deferred tax assets which were subsumed in goodwill were not recognized in the opening balance sheet as at April 1, 2007 as those did not qualify for recognition in the separate balance sheet of the acquired entity.

2. *Fair value as deemed cost exemption* – The company has not elected to measure any item of property, plant and equipment at its fair value at the date of transition; property, plant and equipment have been measured at cost in accordance with IFRS.

3. *Employee benefits exemption* – The company has elected not to apply the exemption as provided in IFRS 1 relating to application of the corridor approach. Under Indian GAAP the company recognized all actuarial gains / losses immediately in the income statement. The accounting treatment has not undergone any change upon adoption of IFRS. Further, the company has elected to apply the exemption provided in IFRS 1 relating to the disclosure of amounts representing the present value of defined benefit obligation, fair value of plan assets, surplus or deficit in the plan and experience adjustments, if any, for the previous four annual periods. Accordingly, the company is providing the required disclosures for each accounting period prospectively from the date of transition to IFRS.

4. *Cumulative translation differences exemption* – The company had accumulated foreign exchange translation gains and losses on subsidiaries in a separate component of equity under Indian GAAP. IAS 21, The Effects of Changes of Foreign Exchange Rates, require exchange differences arising on net investments in subsidiaries to be classified as equity until disposal. Upon transition to IFRS, the treatment of recording translation differences on subsidiaries in equity did not undergo any change and consequently the optional exemption of setting cumulative translation reserve to zero as at April 1, 2007 was not required to be applied.

5. *Compound financial instruments* – The company does not have any compound financial instrument as on the date of transition. Consequently, upon adoption of IFRS the optional exemption allowed of non-segregation of the liability component if such component was no longer outstanding on the date of transition is not applicable to the company.

6. *Assets and liabilities of subsidiaries, associates and joint ventures exemption* – All entities of the Group are transitioning to IFRS on the same date; consequent to which this exemption is not required to be applied.

7. *Share-based payment transaction exemption* – The company has elected to apply the share-based payment exemption available under IFRS 1 on application of IFRS 2, to only grants made after November 7, 2002 and remained unvested as at the Transition Date. Consequent to which fair value of such grants have been recognized in the Income Statement from the Transition Date.

8. *Fair value measurement of financial assets or liabilities at initial recognition* – The company has not applied the amendment offered by the revision of IAS 39 on the initial recognition of the financial instruments measured at fair value through profit or loss where there is no active market.

9. *Designation of financial assets and financial liabilities exemption* – The company does not have any financial assets or liabilities which required to be designated and which meet the required criteria given in IFRS 1, as financial asset or financial liability at fair value through profit or loss or available-for-sale as at the Transition Date.

10. *Changes in decommissioning liabilities included in the cost of property, plant and equipment exemption* – The company does not have material decommissioning, restoration and similar liabilities in the cost of property, plant and equipment and hence the exemption is not applicable.

11. *Leases exemption* – The company has no arrangements containing a lease as defined under IFRIC 4, *Determining whether an Arrangement contains a Lease*, as of the Transition Date and hence this exemption has not been applicable to the company.

12. *Financial asset or an intangible asset accounted for in accordance with IFRIC 12, Service Concession Arrangements exemption* – The company has no arrangements which would be classified under service concession arrangements.

13. *Borrowing costs* – The company has not taken any loans and hence this Standard and the related exemption is not applicable.

2.1.2 Exceptions from full retrospective application

1. *Derecognition of financial assets and liabilities exception* – Financial assets and liabilities derecognized before January 1, 2004 are not re-recognized under IFRS. The company has chosen not to apply the IAS 39 derecognition criteria to an earlier date. No arrangements were identified that had to be assessed under this exception.

2. *Hedge accounting exception* – The company has not identified any hedging relationships. Hence, this exception of not reflecting in its opening IFRS balance sheet a hedging relationship of a type that does not qualify for hedge accounting under IAS 39, is not applicable.

3. *Estimates exception* – Upon an assessment of the estimates made under Indian GAAP, the company has concluded that there was no necessity to revise the estimates under IFRS except where estimates were required by IFRS and not required by Indian GAAP.

4. *Assets classified as held for sale and discontinued operations* – The company did not have any assets classified as held for sale and hence this exemption is not applicable.

Extract 5.10: Norsk Hydro ASA (2007)

NOTE 47 Conversion to IFRS [extract]

Each year since around 1986, Hydro has presented financial statements under US GAAP, up to and including the fiscal year ending 31 December 2006. As of 1 January 2007, Hydro converted to IFRS and now uses IFRS for all financial reporting for the group. Hydro's transition date to IFRS is 1 January 2006.

This footnote presents Hydro's IFRS financial statements for the IFRS transition period. The IFRS information included in this footnote is reconciled to the previously reported US GAAP 2006 income statement and the 1 January 2006 and 31 December 2006 US GAAP balance sheets, as well as to the US GAAP shareholders' equity as of 1 January 2006 and 31 December 2006. This footnote also discloses the IFRS transition principles adopted by Hydro and includes a discussion of the principle differences between IFRS and US GAAP for Hydro. See note 1 Summary accounting principles and reporting entity for information related to Hydro's IFRS accounting policies. Additional information related to our US GAAP reporting is available in Hydro's Annual Report 2006.

Transition to IFRS – IFRS 1 elected exemptions

Hydro's transition to IFRS follows the regulation in IFRS 1 First-time Adoption of International Financial Reporting Standards (IFRS 1). IFRS 1 offers the possibility to utilize certain exemptions from retrospective implementation of IFRS as if always applied. Hydro has evaluated the options available in IFRS 1, and has elected to adopt transition implementation policies in the areas of business combinations, employee benefits, cumulative translation differences, designation of previously recognized financial instruments, share-based payment transactions and asset retirement obligations. A summary of these transition accounting policies is given below. Transition policies available in IFRS 1 that are not material for Hydro are not included in the discussion.

Business combinations

IFRS 3 Business Combinations (IFRS 3) deviates in certain respects when compared to the US GAAP standards applicable for accounting for business combinations. The implementation guidance for the current US GAAP standards gives, for certain acquisitions, a different result compared to full retrospective implementation of IFRS 3.

Hydro has elected to utilize the option in IFRS 1 to not apply IFRS 3 retrospectively to past business combinations completed as of 1 January 2006. The impact of this policy decision is that all prior business combinations will continue to be accounted for as they originally were under US GAAP, including the allocation of acquisition cost. This includes the recognition of any goodwill identified in these transactions.

Employee benefits

IFRS 1 allows for all cumulative actuarial gains and losses at the date of transition to be recognized as of the date of transition as an alternative to full retrospective application of IAS 19 Employee Benefits. Hydro has chosen to adopt this transition policy, and has recognized all 1 January 2006 cumulative actuarial gains and losses at the date of transition with the effect posted directly against equity. Hydro applies the same economic and actuarial assumptions under IFRS as applied under US GAAP, and will continue to use the corridor approach when accounting for actuarial gains and losses on an ongoing basis.

Cumulative translation differences

IFRS 1 offers the first-time adopter of IFRS the option to reset the cumulative translation differences that existed at the date of adoption (i.e. the US GAAP translation differences) to zero as of the date of transition to IFRS as an alternative to establishing a cumulative translation difference as if the accounting and translation principles in IAS 21 The Effects of Changes in Foreign Exchange Rates had always been used and the measurement of assets and liabilities had been as required by currently implemented IFRS. Hydro has elected to utilize this option, and has reset the cumulative translation differences for all foreign operations to zero as of 1 January 2006. Future gains or losses on a subsequent disposal of any foreign operation will therefore exclude translation differences that arose before 1 January 2006.

Designation of previously recognized financial instruments

Marketable and non-marketable trading shares as defined under US GAAP are classified as financial assets at fair value through profit and loss under IFRS. Shares held for trading are classified as part of Short-term investments. Hydro has elected that non-marketable shares previously classified under US GAAP as not held for trading are classified as available-for-sale under IFRS with changes in fair value booked against equity. The shares are presented in the balance sheet as part of Financial Assets. Non-marketable shares in the US GAAP balance sheet were classified as Prepaid pension, investment and other non-current assets, and measured at cost.

Share-based payment transactions

Hydro adopted IFRS 2 Share-based Payment (IFRS 2) as of 1 January 2006. IFRS 1 encourages first-time adopters of IFRS to apply IFRS 2 to equity instruments granted on or before 7 November 2002. Hydro has applied IFRS 2 to all share-based payments, including the share appreciation rights granted prior to 7 November 2002.

Asset retirement obligations

IFRS 1 allows for a simplified treatment of historic changes when estimating the asset retirement obligations between the initial inception of the liability and the adoption of IFRS. Hydro has elected to utilize this option. The asset retirement obligations have been calculated as of Hydro's 1 January 2006 transition date in accordance with IAS 37 Provisions using the best estimate of removal cost and timing, and the risk free interest rates for the relevant currencies and expected life of the asset as of the date of estimation. The IFRS estimate resulted in an increase in recognized asset retirement obligations of NOK 3,040 million as of 1 January 2006. The estimated amount that would have been included in the historical cost of the asset, based on historical interest rates and accumulated depreciation based on that amount, have been calculated. That estimated amount is only insignificantly different from the asset value recognized under US GAAP. Hydro has therefore not recognized any difference in historical cost or carrying value of the related fixed assets in connection with the transition to IFRS.

If a first-time adopter did not present financial statements for previous periods this fact should be disclosed.[303] For example, in practice this disclosure is sometimes made by entities that did not prepare consolidated accounts under their previous GAAP. In such cases and others, an explanation of how the transition to IFRSs affected the entity's reported financial position, financial performance and cash flows cannot be presented, because relevant comparative information under the entity's previous GAAP does not exist.

6.3.1   Disclosure of reconciliations

A first-time adopter is required to present:

- reconciliations of its equity reported under previous GAAP to its equity under IFRSs at:[304]
  - the date of transition to IFRSs; and
  - the end of the latest period presented in the entity's most recent annual financial statements under previous GAAP;
- a reconciliation to its total comprehensive income under IFRSs for the latest period in the entity's most recent annual financial statements. The starting point for that reconciliation should be total comprehensive income under previous GAAP for the same period or, if an entity did not report such a total, profit or loss under previous GAAP;[305] and
- an explanation of the material adjustments to the statement of cash flows, if it presented one under its previous GAAP.[306]

First-time adopters should not apply the requirements of IAS 8 relating to the disclosure of changes in accounting policies because that standard 'does not deal with changes in accounting policies that occur when an entity first adopts IFRSs.'[307]

The example below illustrates how these requirements apply to an entity whose first IFRS financial statements are for the period ending on 31 December 2010 and whose date of transition to IFRSs is 1 January 2009.

Example 5.35:   Reconciliations to be presented in first IFRS financial statements

Entity A's date of transition to IFRSs is 1 January 2009 and the end of it first IFRS reporting period is 31 December 2010. Which primary financial statements and reconciliations should entity A present in its first IFRS financial statements?

	1 January 2009	31 December 2009	31 December 2010
Balance sheet	●	●	●
Reconciliation of equity	●	●	
For the period ending			
Statement of comprehensive income *			●
Statement of cash flows			●
Statement of changes in equity			●
Reconciliation of comprehensive income †			●
Explanation of material adjustments to the statement of cash flows			●

---

* alternatively the entity should present two statements: an income statement and a statement of comprehensive income

† if an entity did not report comprehensive income then a reconciliation from profit or loss under previous GAAP to comprehensive income under IFRSs should be presented

These reconciliations should be sufficiently detailed to enable users to understand the material adjustments to the balance sheet, income statement and statement of comprehensive income and the entity should distinguish between the correction of errors and changes in accounting policies.[308] While the standard does not prescribe a layout for these reconciliations, the implementation guidance contains an example of a line-by-line reconciliation of the balance sheet, statement of comprehensive income and income statement.[309] Such a presentation may be particularly appropriate when a first-time adopter needs to make transitional adjustments that affect a significant number of line items in the primary financial statements. If the adjustments are less pervasive a straightforward reconciliation of equity, comprehensive income and/or profit or loss may be able to provide an equally effective explanation of how the adoption of IFRSs affects the reported financial position, financial performance and cash flows.

6.3.2 Line-by-line reconciliations and detailed explanations

The extract below from the 2005 financial statements of Vodafone complies with the versions of IFRS 1 and IAS 1 that were effective in 2005. However, it provides a good example of an entity that not only provides summary reconciliations of equity and profit or loss, but also line-by-line reconciliations, as suggested by the Implementation Guidance, and detailed explanations of the reconciling items.

Extract 5.11: Vodafone Group Plc (2005)

Notes to the Consolidated Financial Statements [extract]

40   Transition to IFRS on first-time adoption [extract]

Basis of preparation of IFRS financial information

The Group's Annual Report for the year ended 31 March 2006 is the first annual Consolidated Financial Statements that comply with IFRS. The Consolidated Financial Statements have been prepared in accordance with the significant accounting policies described in note 2. The Group has applied IFRS 1, "First-time Adoption of International Financial Reporting Standards" in preparing these statements.

IFRS 1 exemptions

IFRS 1 sets out the procedures that the Group must follow when it adopts IFRS for the first time as the basis for preparing its Consolidated Financial Statements. The Group is required to establish its IFRS accounting policies as at 31 March 2006 and, in general, apply these retrospectively to determine the IFRS opening balance sheet at its date of transition, 1 April 2004. This standard provides a number of optional exemptions to this general principle. These are set out below, together with a description in each case of the exemption adopted by the Group.

Business combinations that occurred before the opening IFRS balance sheet date (IFRS 3, "Business Combinations")

The Group has elected not to apply IFRS 3 retrospectively to business combinations that took place before the date of transition. As a result, in the opening balance sheet, goodwill arising from past business combinations remains as stated under UK GAAP at 31 March 2004.

If the Group had elected to apply IFRS 3 retrospectively, the purchase consideration would have been allocated to the following major categories of acquired intangible assets and liabilities based on their fair values: licence and spectrum fees, brands, customer bases, and deferred tax liabilities. Goodwill would have been recognised as the excess of the purchase consideration over the fair values of acquired assets and liabilities – retrospective application may have resulted in an increase or decrease to goodwill. The fair values of the acquired intangible assets would have been amortised over their respective useful lives.

Employee benefits – actuarial gains and losses (IAS 19, "Employee Benefits")

The Group has elected to recognise all cumulative actuarial gains and losses in relation to employee benefit schemes at the date of transition.

Share-based payments (IFRS 2, "Share-based Payment")

The Group has elected to apply IFRS 2 to all relevant share-based payment transactions granted but not fully vested at 1 April 2004.

Financial instruments (IAS 39, "Financial Instruments: Recognition and Measurement" and IFRS 7, "Financial Instruments: Disclosures")

The Group has applied IAS 32 and IAS 39 for all periods presented and has therefore not taken advantage of the exemption in IFRS 1 that would enable the Group to only apply these standards from 1 April 2005.

Cumulative translation differences (IAS 21, "The Effects of Changes in Foreign Exchange Rates")

The Group has deemed the cumulative translation differences at the date of transition to IFRS to be zero. As a result, the gain or loss of a subsequent disposal of any foreign operation will exclude the translation differences that arose before the date of transition to IFRSs.

If the Group had not applied the exemption, the gain or loss on any disposals after the transition date would include additional cumulative transaction differences relating to the business disposed of.

Fair value or revaluation as deemed cost (IAS 16, "Property, Plant and Equipment" and IAS 38, "Intangible Assets")

The Group has not elected to measure any item of property, plant and equipment or intangible asset at the date of transition to IFRS at its fair value.

Impact of transition to IFRS

The following is a summary of the effects of the differences between IFRS and UK GAAP on the Group's total equity shareholders' funds and profit for the financial year for the years previously reported under UK GAAP following the date of transition to IFRS.

Total equity shareholders' funds

	Note	1 April 2004 £m	31 March 2005 £m
Total equity shareholders' funds (UK GAAP)		111,924	99,317
Measurement and recognition differences:			
Intangible assets	a	(164)	13,986
Proposed dividends	b	728	1,395
Financial instruments	c	385	350
Share-based payments	d	12	63
Defined benefit pension schemes	e	(257)	(361)
Deferred and current taxes	f	(1,011)	(774)
Other		(66)	(176)
Total equity shareholders' funds (IFRS)		111,551	113,800

Profit for the year ended 31 March 2005	Note	£m
Loss on ordinary activities after taxation (UK GAAP)		(6,938)
Measurement and recognition differences:		
Intangible assets	a	14,263
Financial instruments	c	(174)
Share-based payments	d	(91)
Defined benefit pension schemes	e	7
Deferred and current taxes	f	10
Other		(130)
Presentation differences:		
Presentation of equity accounted investments	g	(45)
Presentation of joint ventures	h	(384)
Profit for the financial year (IFRS)		6,518

There were no significant differences between IFRS and UK GAAP on the Group's cash flow statement for the year ended 31 March 2005.

Measurement and recognition differences

a. Intangible assets

IAS 38, "Intangible Assets" requires that goodwill is not amortised. Instead it is subject to an annual impairment review. As the Group has elected not to apply IFRS 3 retrospectively to business combinations prior to the opening balance sheet date under IFRS, the UK GAAP goodwill balance, after adjusting for items including the impact of proportionate consolidation of joint ventures, at 31 March 2004 (£78,753 million) has been included in the opening IFRS consolidated balance sheet and is no longer amortised.

Under IAS 38, capitalised payments for licences and spectrum fees are amortised on a straight line basis over their useful economic life. Amortisation is charged from the commencement of service of the network. Under UK GAAP, the Group's policy was to amortise such costs in proportion to the capacity of the network during the start up period and then on a straight-line basis thereafter.

b. Proposed dividends

IAS 10, "Events after the Balance Sheet Date" requires that dividends declared after the balance sheet date should not be recognised as a liability at that balance sheet date as the liability does not represent obligation as defined by IAS 37, "Provisions, Contingent Liabilities and Contingent Assets".

c. Financial instruments

IAS 32, "Financial Instruments: Disclosure and Presentation" and IAS 39, "Financial Instruments: Recognition and Measurement" address the accounting for, and reporting of, financial instruments. IAS 39 sets out detailed accounting requirements in relation to financial assets and liabilities.

All derivative financial instruments are accounted for at fair market value whilst other financial instruments are accounted for either at amortised cost or at fair value depending on their classification. Subject to certain criteria, financial assets and financial liabilities may be designated as forming hedge relationships as a result of which fair value changes are offset in the income statement or charged/credited to equity depending on the nature of the hedge relationship.

d. Share-based payments

IFRS 2, "Share-based Payment" requires that an expense for equity instruments granted be recognised in the financial statements based on their fair value at the date of grant. This expense, which is primarily in relation to employee option and performance share schemes, is recognised over the vesting period of the scheme.

While IFRS 2 allows the measurement of this expense to be calculated only on options granted after 7 November 2002, the Group has applied IFRS 2 to all instruments granted but not fully vested as at 1 April 2004. The Group has adopted the binomial model for the purposes of calculating fair value under IFRS, calibrated using a Black-Scholes framework.

e.   Defined benefit pension schemes

The Group elected to adopt early the amendment to IAS 19, "Employee Benefits" issued by the IASB on 16 December 2004 which allows all actuarial gains and losses to be charged or credited to equity.

The Group's opening IFRS balance sheet at 1 April 2004 reflects the assets and liabilities of the Group's defined benefit schemes totalling a net liability of £154 million. The transitional adjustment of £257 million to opening reserves comprises the reversal of entries in relation to UK GAAP accounting under SSAP 24 less the recognition of the net liabilities of the Group's and associated undertakings' defined benefit schemes.

f.   Deferred and current taxes

The scope of IAS 12, "Income Taxes" is wider than the corresponding UK GAAP standards, and requires deferred tax to be provided on all temporary differences rather than just timing differences under UK GAAP.

As a result, taxes in the Group's IFRS opening balance sheet at 1 April 2004 were adjusted by £1.0 billion. This includes an additional deferred tax liability of £1.8 billion in respect of the differences between the carrying value and tax written down value of the Group's investments in associated undertakings and joint ventures. This comprises £13 billion in respect of differences that arose when US investments were acquired and £0.5 billion is respect of undistributed earnings of certain associated undertakings and joint ventures, principally Vodafone Italy. UK GAAP does not permit deferred tax to be provided on the undistributed earnings of the Group's associated undertakings and joint ventures until there is a binding obligation to distribute those earnings.

IAS 12 also requires deferred tax to be provided in respect of the Group's liabilities under its post employment benefit arrangements and on other employee benefits such as share and share option schemes.

g.   Presentation of equity accounted investments

Under IFRS, in accordance with IAS 1, "Presentation of Financial Statements", "Tax on profit" on the face of the consolidated income statement comprises the tax charge of the Company, its subsidiaries and its share of the tax charge of joint ventures. The Group's share of its associated undertakings' tax charges is shown as part of "Share of result in associated undertakings" rather than being disclosed as part of the tax charge under UK GAAP.

In respect of the Verizon Wireless partnership, the line "Share of result in associated undertakings" includes the Group's share of pre-tax partnership income and the Group's share of the post-tax income attributable to corporate entities (as determined for US corporate income tax purposes) held by the partnership. The tax attributable to the Group's share of allocable partnership income is included as part of "Tax on profit" in the consolidated income statement. This treatment reflects the fact that tax on allocable partnership income is, for US corporate income tax purposes, a liability of the partners and not the partnership. Under UK GAAP, the Group's share of minority interests in associated undertakings was reported in minority interests, under IFRS this is reported within investments in associated undertakings.

h.   Presentation of joint ventures

IAS 31, "Interests in Joint Ventures" defines a jointly controlled entity a an entity where unanimous consent over the strategic financial and operating decisions is required between the parties sharing control. Control is defined as the power to govern the financial and operating decisions of an entity so as to obtain economic benefit from it.

The Group has reviewed the classification of its investments and concluded that the Group's 76.9% (31 March 2005: 76.8%) interest in Vodafone Italy, classified as a subsidiary undertaking under UK GAAP, should be accounted for as a joint venture under IFRS. In addition, the Group's interests in South Africa, Poland, Kenya and Fiji, which were classified as associated undertakings under UK GAAP, have been classified as joint ventures under IFRS as a result of the contractual rights held by the Group. The Group's interest in Romania was classified as a joint venture until the acquisition of the controlling stake from Telesystem International Wireless Inc. of Canada completed on 31 May 2005. The Group has adopted proportionate consolidation as the method of accounting for these six entities.

Under UK GAAP, the revenue, operating profit, net financing costs and taxation of Vodafone Italy were consolidated in full in the income statement with a corresponding allocation to minority interest. Under proportionate consolidation, the Group recognises its share of all income statement lines with no allocation to minority interest. There is no effect on the result for a financial period from this adjustment.

Under UK GAAP, the Group's interests in South Africa, Poland, Romania, Kenya and Fiji were accounted for under the equity method, with the Group's share of operating profit, interest and tax being recognised separately in the consolidated income statement. Under proportionate consolidation, the Group recognises its share of all income statement lines. There is no effect on the result for a financial period from this adjustment.

Under UK GAAP, the Group fully consolidated the cash flows of Vodafone Italy, but did not consolidate the cash flows of its associated undertakings. The IFRS consolidated cash flow statement reflects the Group's share of cash flows relating to its joint ventures on a line by line basis, with a corresponding recognition of the Group's share of net debt for each of the proportionately consolidated entities.

Other differences

i. Reclassification of non-equity minority interests to liabilities

The primary impact of the implementation of IAS 32 is the reclassification of the $1.65 billion preferred shares issued by the Group's subsidiary. Vodafone Americas Inc., from non-equity minority interests to liabilities. The reclassification at 1 April 2004 was £875 million. Dividend payments by this subsidiary, which were previously reported in the Group's income statement as non-equity minority interests, have been reclassified to financing costs.

j. Fair value of available-for-sale financial assets

The Group has classified certain of its cost-based investments as available-for-sale financial assets as defined in IAS 39. This classification does not reflect the intentions of management in relation to these investments. These assets are measured at fair value at each reporting date with movements in fair value taken to equity. At 1 April 2004, a cumulative increase of £233 million in the fair value over the carrying value of these investments was recognised.

Reconciliation of the UK GAAP consolidated profit and loss account to the IFRS consolidated income statement

Year ended 31 March 2005

UK GAAP format	UK GAAP £m	Presentation differences £m	Measurement and recognition differences £m	Discontinued operations £m	IFRS £m	IFRS format
Turnover	34,133	–	(60)	(7,395)	26,678	Revenue
Cost of sales	(20,733)	–	(711)	5,664	(15,800)	Cost of sales
Gross profit	13,380	–	(771)	(1,731)	10,878	Gross profit
Selling and distribution costs	(2,031)	–	(15)	397	(1,649)	Selling and distribution expenses
Administrative expenses	(16,653)	315	12,812	670	(2,856)	Administrative expenses
		404	1,576	–	1,980	Share of result in associated undertakings
		(315)	(160)	–	(475)	Other income and expense
Operating loss	(5,304)	404	13,442	(664)	7,878	Operating profit
Share of result in associated undertakings	1,193	(1,193)				
Exceptional non-operating items	13	(13)				
		8	(2)	(13)	(7)	Non-operating income and expense
		324	(21)	(9)	294	Investment income
Net interest payable and similar items	(604)	(113)	(183)	20	(880)	Financing costs
Loss on ordinary activities before taxation	(4,702)	(583)	13,236	(666)	7,285	Profit before taxation
Tax on loss on ordinary activities	(2,236)	538	265	(436)	(1,869)	Tax on profit

Loss on ordinary activities after taxation	(6,938)	(45)	13,501	(1,102)	5,416	Profit on ordinary activities after taxation from continuing operations
	–		–	1,102	1,102	Profit on ordinary activities after taxation from discontinued operations
	(6,938)	(45)	13,501	–	6,518	Profit for the financial year
Minority interest	(602)	45	449	–	(108)	Profit for the financial year attributable to minority interests
Loss for the financial year	(7,540)	–	13,950	–	6,410	Profit for the financial year attributable to equity shareholders

Reconciliation of the UK GAAP consolidated balance sheet to the IFRS consolidated balance sheet 1 April 2004

UK GAAP format	UK GAAP £m	Presentation differences £m	Measurement and recognition differences £m	IFRS £m	IFRS format
Fixed assets:					Non-current assets:
Intangible assets	93,622	–	1,002	94,624	Intangible assets
Tangible assets	18,083	–	(971)	17,112	Property, plant and equipment
Investments in associated undertakings	21,226	–	(800)	20,426	Investments in associated undertakings
Other investments	1,049	–	233	1,282	Other investments
		671	136	807	Deferred tax assets
		221	(9)	212	Trade and other receivables
	133,980	892	(409)	134,463	
Current assets:					Current assets:
Stocks	458	–	10	468	Inventory
Debtors	6,901	(6,901)			
		372	(103)	269	Taxation recoverable
		5,148	305	5,453	Trade and other receivables
Investments	4,381	(4,381)			
Cash at bank and in hand	1,409	4,381	61	5,851	Cash and cash equivalents
	13,149	(1,381)	273	12,041	
Total assets	147,129	(489)	(136)	146,504	Total assets
Capital and reserves:					Equity:
Called up share capital	4,280	–	–	4,280	Called up share capital
Share premium account	52,154	–	–	52,154	Share premium account
Own shares held	(1,136)	–	–	(1,136)	Own shares held
Other reserve	99,640	–	310	99,950	Additional paid-in capital
		–	233	233	Other reserve
Profit and loss account	(43,014)	–	(916)	(43,930)	Retained losses
Total equity shareholders' funds	111,924	–	(373)	111,551	Total equity shareholders' funds
Minority interests	3,007	–	(2,198)	809	Minority interests
	114,931	–	(2,571)	112,360	
Creditors – amounts falling due after more than one year	12,975	(12,975)			Non-current liabilities
		12,224	1,859	14,083	Long-term borrowings
		3,314	1,421	4,735	Deferred tax liabilities
		(73)	227	154	Post employment benefits
Provisions for liabilities and charges	4,197	(3,858)	5	344	Provisions for liabilities and charges
		751	(449)	302	Trade and other payables
	17,172	(617)	3,063	19,618	

Creditors – amounts falling due within one year	15,026	(15,026)			Current liabilities:
		2,054	788	2,842	Short-term borrowings
		4,275	(356)	3,919	Current taxation liabilities
		8,643	(1,068)	7,575	Trade and other payables
					Provisions for liabilities and
		182	8	190	charges
	15,026	128	(628)	14,526	
	147,129	(489)	(136)	146,504	Total equity and liabilities

31 March 2005

UK GAAP format	UK GAAP £m	Presentation differences £m	Measurement and recognition differences £m	IFRS £m	IFRS format
Fixed assets:					Non-current assets:
		68,673	12,326	80,999	Goodwill
Intangible assets	83,464	(68,673)	1,358	16,149	Other intangible assets
Tangible assets	18,398	–	(956)	17,442	Property, plant and equipment
Investments in associated undertakings	19,398	–	836	20,234	Investment in associated undertakings
Other investment	852	–	329	1,181	Other investments
		1,084	100	1,184	Deferred tax assets
		12	–	12	Post employment benefits
		613	(28)	585	Trade and other receivables
	122,112	1,709	13,965	137,786	
Current assets:					Current assets:
Stocks	430	–	10	440	Inventory
Debtors	7,698	(7,698)			
		268	(230)	38	Taxation receivables
		5,049	115	5,164	Trade and other receivables
Investments	816	(816)			
Cash at bank and in hand	2,850	816	103	3,759	Cash and cash equivalents
	11,794	(2,381)	(2)	9,411	
	133,906	(672)	13,963	147,197	Total assets
Capital and reserves:					Equity:
Called up share capital	4,286	–	–	4,286	Called up share capital
Share premium account	52,284	–	–	52,284	Share premium account
Own shares held	(5,121)	–	–	(5,121)	Own shares held
Other reserve	99,556	–	525	100,081	Additional paid-in capital
		–	1,781	1,781	Accumulated other recognised income and expense
Profit and loss account	(51,688)	–	12,177	(39,511)	Retained losses
Total equity shareholders' funds	99,317	–	14,483	113,800	Total equity shareholders' funds
Minority interests	2,818	–	(2,970)	(152)	Minority interests
	102,135	–	11,513	113,648	
Creditors – amounts falling due after more than one year	12,382	(12,382)			Non-current liabilities:
		11,613	1,577	13,190	Long-term borrowings
		3,481	1,368	4,849	Deferred tax liabilities
		(171)	307	136	Post employment benefits
Provisions for liabilities and charges	4,552	(4,235)	2	319	Provisions for other liabilities and charges
		797	(359)	438	Trade and other payables
	16,934	(897)	2,895	18,932	

Creditors – amounts falling due within one year	14,837	(14,837)			Current liabilities:
		392	1,611	2,003	Short-term borrowings
		4,759	(406)	4,353	Current taxation liabilities
		9,717	(1,694)	8,033	Trade and other payables
					Provisions for other liabilities
		194	34	228	and charges
	14,837	225	(445)	14,617	
	133,906	(672)	13,963	147,196	Total equity and liabilities

6.3.3   Recognition and reversal of impairments

If a first-time adopter recognised or reversed any impairment losses on transition to IFRSs it should disclose the information that IAS 36 would have required if the entity had recognised those impairment losses or reversals in the period beginning with the date of transition to IFRSs (see Chapter 18 at 4).[310] The purpose of this disclosure requirement is that while 'there is inevitably subjectivity about impairment losses [the] disclosure provides transparency about impairment losses recognised on transition to IFRSs. These losses might otherwise receive less attention than impairment losses recognised in earlier or later periods.'[311]

6.3.4   Inclusion of IFRS 1 reconciliations by cross reference

The reconciliation disclosures required by IFRS 1 are generally quite lengthy. While IFRS 1 allows certain of these disclosures to be included in an entity's first interim report under IAS 34 by way of cross-reference to another published document, there is no corresponding exemption regarding an entity's first annual IFRS financial statements.[312] Therefore, a first-time adopter should include all disclosures required by IFRS 1 within its first IFRS financial statements in the same way it would need to include other lengthy disclosures such as those on business combinations, financial instruments and employee benefits. Notwithstanding this requirement, any additional voluntary information regarding the conversion to IFRSs that was previously published but that is not specifically required by IFRS 1 need not be repeated in the first IFRS financial statements.

6.4   Designation of financial instruments

IAS 39 permits a financial instrument to be designated on initial recognition as a *financial asset or financial liability at fair value through profit or loss* or as an *available-for-sale financial asset*, subject to the criteria in that standard.[313] If a first-time adopter designates a previously recognised financial asset or financial liability as a 'financial asset or financial liability at fair value through profit or loss' or a financial asset as available-for-sale (see 5.12 above), it should disclose for each category:[314]

- the fair value of any financial assets or financial liabilities designated into it at the date of designation; and

- their classification and carrying amount in the previous financial statements.

The extract below illustrates the above disclosure requirement.

Extract 5.12: Aegon N.V. (2005)

Notes to the consolidated financial statements of AEGON Group [extract]

56 First-time adoption of IFRS [extract]

DESIGNATION OF FINANCIAL ASSETS AND FINANCIAL LIABILITIES AS FINANCIAL ASSETS OR FINANCIAL LIABILITIES AT FAIR VALUE THROUGH PROFIT OR LOSS OR AS AVAILABLE-FOR-SALE FINANCIAL ASSET

The following table provides a summary of the fair value of financial assets and financial liabilities designated into each of these categories as at January 1, 2004, and their classification and carrying amount in the previous financial statements:

FINANCIAL ASSETS DESIGNATED AS AT FAIR VALUE THROUGH PROFIT OR LOSS AT JANUARY 1, 2004

	Carrying value under DAP	Fair value 1 January 2004
CLASSIFICATION UNDER DAP		
General account investments		
Other financial investments	9,489	9,803
Investments for account of policyholders	99,868	99,868
	109,357	109,671

FINANCIAL LIABILITIES DESIGNATED AS AT FAIR VALUE THROUGH PROFIT OR LOSS AT JANUARY 1, 2004

	Carrying value under DAP	Fair value 1 January 2004
CLASSIFICATION UNDER DAP		
General account liabilities		
Technical provisions	638	638
Technical provisions with investments for account of policyholders	42,506	42,539
	43,144	43,177

FINANCIAL ASSETS CLASSIFIED AS AVAILABLE-FOR-SALE AT JANUARY 1, 2004

	Carrying value under DAP	Fair value 1 January 2004
CLASSIFICATION UNDER DAP		
General account investments		
Other financial investments	88,183	91,831
	88,183	91,831

6.5   Disclosures regarding deemed cost

6.5.1   *Use of fair value as deemed cost*

If a first-time adopter uses 'fair value in its opening IFRS balance sheet as deemed cost for an item of property, plant and equipment, an investment property or an intangible asset' (see 5.5.2 above), it should disclose for each line item in the opening IFRS balance sheet:[315]

- the aggregate of those fair values; and

- the aggregate adjustment to the carrying amounts reported under previous GAAP.

This disclosure is illustrated in Extracts 5.5 and 5.6 at 5.5.2 above.

6.5.2   Use of deemed cost for investments in subsidiaries, jointly controlled entities and associates

If a first-time adopter measures its investments in subsidiaries, jointly controlled entities or associates at deemed cost in the parent company's opening IFRS balance sheet (see 5.9.2 above), the entity's first IFRS separate financial statements should disclose:

'(a)   the aggregate deemed cost of those investments for which deemed cost is their previous GAAP carrying amount;

(b)   the aggregate deemed cost of those investments for which deemed cost is fair value; and

(c)   the aggregate adjustment to the carrying amounts reported under previous GAAP.'[316]

6.5.3   Use of deemed cost for oil and gas assets

If a first-time adopter uses the exemption in paragraph D8A(b) of IFRS 1 for oil and gas assets (see 5.5.4 above), it should disclose that fact and the basis on which carrying amounts determined under previous GAAP were allocated.[317]

6.6   Interim financial reports

If a first-time adopter presents an interim financial report under IAS 34 for part of the period covered by its first IFRS financial statements, that report includes:[318]

(a)   a reconciliation of its equity under previous GAAP at the end of that comparable interim period to its equity under IFRSs at that date;

(b)   a reconciliation to its total comprehensive income under IFRSs for that comparable interim period (current and year to date). The starting point for that reconciliation is total comprehensive income under previous GAAP for that period or, if an entity did not report such a total, profit or loss under previous GAAP; and

(c)   the reconciliations described at 6.3.1 above or a cross-reference to another published document that includes these reconciliations.

For an entity presenting annual financial statements under IFRSs, it is not compulsory to prepare interim financial reports under IAS 34. Therefore, the above requirements only apply to first-time adopters that prepare interim reports under IAS 34 on a voluntary basis or that are required to do so by a regulator or other party.[319]

Examples 5.37 and 5.38 below show which reconciliations should be included in half-year reports and quarterly reports, respectively.

Example 5.36:   Reconciliations to be presented in IFRS half-year reports

As in Example 5.35 at 6.3.1 above, Entity A's date of transition to IFRSs is 1 January 2009, the end of it first IFRS reporting period is 31 December 2010 and it publishes a half-year report as at 30 June 2010 under IAS 34. Which primary financial statements and reconciliations should entity A present in its first IFRS half-year report?

	1 January 2009	30 June 2009	31 December 2009	30 June 2010
Balance sheet			●	●
Reconciliation of equity	● ‡	●	● ‡	
For the period ending				
Statement of comprehensive income *			●	●
Statement of cash flows			●	●
Statement of changes in equity			●	●
Reconciliation of comprehensive income †			●	● ‡
Explanation of material adjustments to the statement of cash flows				● ‡

* alternatively the entity should present two statements: an income statement and statement of comprehensive income
† if an entity did not report comprehensive income then a reconciliation from profit or loss under previous GAAP to comprehensive income under IFRSs should be presented
‡ these additional reconciliations are required under paragraph 24 of IFRS 1

The IAS 34 requirements regarding the disclosure of primary financial statements in interim reports are discussed in Chapter 40.

As can be seen from the tables in Example 5.36, the additional reconciliations and explanations required under (c) above would be presented out of context, i.e. without the balance sheet, income statement, statement of comprehensive income and statement of cash flows to which they relate. For this reason, a first-time adopter may want to consider either (1) to include the primary financial statements to which these reconciliations relate or (2) to refer to another document that includes these reconciliations.

Example 5.37: *Reconciliations to be presented in IFRS quarterly reports*[320]

Entity B's date of transition to IFRSs is 1 January 2009, the end of it first IFRS reporting period is 31 December 2010 and it publishes quarterly reports under IAS 34. Which reconciliations should entity B present in its 2010 interim reports and in its first IFRS financial statements?

	Reconciliation of equity	Reconciliation of comprehensive income or profit or loss †	Explanation of material adjustments to cash flow statement
First quarter			
1 January 2009	○		
31 December 2009	○	○	○
31 March 2009			
– 3 months ending	●	●	
Second quarter			
30 June 2009			
– 3 months ending		●	
– 6 months ending	●	●	

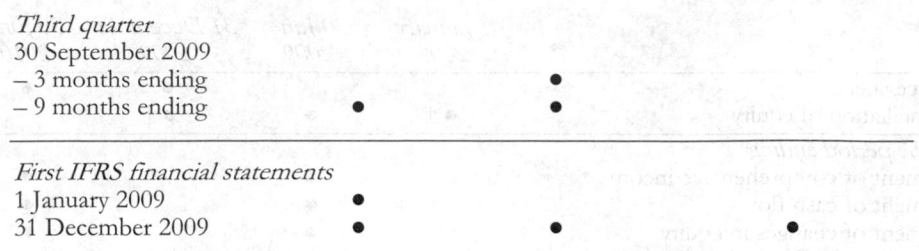

Third quarter
30 September 2009
– 3 months ending
– 9 months ending

First IFRS financial statements
1 January 2009
31 December 2009

● Mandatory disclosures required to be included in the interim report.

○ These reconciliations are only required to be presented in an entity's *first* interim financial report under IAS 34 and may be included by way of a cross-reference to another published document in which these reconciliations are presented.

† A first-time adopter should present a reconciliation of comprehensive income or, if it did not did not report comprehensive income, a reconciliation from profit or loss under previous GAAP to comprehensive income under IFRSs should be presented.

Interim financial reports under IAS 34 contain considerably less detail than annual financial statements because they 'are based on the assumption that users of the interim financial report also have access to the most recent annual financial statements.'[321] Therefore, a first-time adopter will have to ensure that its first interim financial report contains sufficient information about events or transactions that are material to an understanding of the current interim period. A first-time adopter must include significantly more information in its first IFRS interim report than it would normally include in an interim report; alternatively, it could cross refer to another published document that includes such information.[322] For example, a first-time adopter will need to disclose its IFRS accounting policies and, to the extent information was not provided under previous GAAP, any disclosures that material to an understanding of the current interim period.

6.7   Disclosure of IFRS information before adoption of IFRSs

As the adoption of IFRSs may have a significant impact on their financial statements many entities will want to provide information on the expected impact of IFRSs. There are certain difficulties that arise as a result of IFRS 1 when an entity decides to quantify the impact of the adoption of IFRSs. In particular, IFRS 1 requires an entity to draw up an IFRS opening balance sheet at its date of transition based on the standards that are effective at the reporting date for its first IFRS financial statements. Therefore, it is not possible to prepare IFRS financial information – and assess the full impact of IFRSs – until an entity knows (1) its date of transition to IFRSs and (2) exactly which standards will be effective at the first reporting date.

If an entity wants to quantify the impact of the adoption of IFRSs before its date of transition, it would not be able to do this in accordance with IFRS 1. While an entity would be able to select a date and apply by analogy the requirements of IFRS 1 to its previous GAAP financial information as of that date, it would not be able to claim that such additional information complied with IFRSs. An entity should avoid presenting such additional information if it believed that the information, despite being clearly marked as not IFRS compliant, would be misleading or misunderstood.

If an entity wants to quantify the impact of the adoption of IFRSs in advance of the release of its first IFRS reporting date but after its date of transition, there may still be some uncertainty regarding the standards that apply. If so, an entity should disclose the nature of the uncertainty as is illustrated by the extract below from BSkyB Group's IFRS announcement and consider describing the information as 'preliminary' IFRS information.

Extract 5.13: BSkyB Group plc (2005)

Restated financial information for the year ended 30 June 2005 under International Financial Reporting Standards ("IFRS") [extract]

Part 1 [extract]

NOTE 1 [extract]

Basis of preparation

The attached financial information has been prepared in accordance with the accounting standards and interpretations that the Group expects to be in effect at 30 June 2006, the date of the Group's first full financial statements prepared on an IFRS basis. However, there remains some uncertainty as to whether the International Accounting Standards Board ("IASB") and other related bodies will issue new or revised standards, which, subject to their endorsement by the European Commission, may or may not be mandatory for the Group's 30 June 2006 financial statements, and which the Group may or may not adopt early on a voluntary basis. It is possible that the restated information for 2005 presented in this document may be subject to change before its inclusion in the 2006 Annual Report and Accounts, which will contain the Group's first full financial statements prepared in accordance with IFRS.

---

7   ACCOUNTING POLICIES AND PRACTICAL APPLICATION ISSUES

The exceptions and exemptions of IFRS 1 were explained at 4 and 5 above, respectively. This section provides an overview of the detailed application guidance in IFRS 1 (to the extent that it is not covered in sections 4 and 5 above) and some of the practical application issues that are not directly related to any of the exceptions or exemptions. These issues are discussed on a standard by standard basis as follows:

- IAS 7 – *Statement of Cash Flows* (see 7.1 below);
- IAS 8 – *Accounting Policies, Changes in Accounting Estimates and Errors* (see 7.2 below);
- IAS 11 – *Construction Contracts* (see 7.3 below);
- IAS 12 – *Income Taxes* (see 7.4 below);
- IAS 16 – *Property, Plant and Equipment* (see 7.5 below);
- IAS 17 – *Leases* (see 7.6 below);
- IAS 18 – *Revenue Recognition* (see 7.7 below);
- IAS 19 – *Employee Benefits* (see 7.8 below);
- IAS 21 – *The Effects of Changes in Foreign Exchange Rates* (see 7.9 below);
- IAS 23 – *Borrowing Costs* (see 7.10 below);
- IAS 28 – *Investments in Associates* (see 7.11 below);
- IAS 29 – *Financial Reporting in Hyperinflationary Economies* (see 7.12 below);
- IAS 31 – *Interests in Joint Ventures* (see 7.13 below);
- IAS 36 – *Impairment of Assets* (see 7.14 below);

- IAS 37 – *Provisions, Contingent Liabilities and Contingent Assets* (see 7.15 below); and

- IAS 38 – *Intangible Assets* (see 7.16 below).

7.1   IAS 7 – Statement of cash flows

A statement of cash flows prepared under IAS 7 – *Statement of Cash Flows* – may differ in the following ways from the one prepared under an entity's previous GAAP:

- The definition of cash under IAS 7 may well differ from the one used under previous GAAP. In particular, IAS 7 includes with cash and cash equivalents those bank overdrafts that are repayable on demand and that form an integral part of an entity's cash management;[323]

- The layout and definition of the categories of cash flows (i.e. operating, investing and financing) is often different from previous GAAP. In addition, IAS 7 contains specific requirements about the classification of interest, dividends and taxes; and

- Differences in accounting policies between IFRSs and previous GAAP often have a consequential impact on the statement of cash flows.

IFRS 1 requires disclosure of an explanation of the material adjustments to the statement of cash flows, if it presented one under its previous GAAP (see 6.3.1 above). The extract below illustrates how an IFRS statement of cash flows may differ from the one under previous GAAP.

Extract 5.14: Scottish Power plc (2006)

Notes to the Group Accounts [extract]

42   Reconciliation of previously reported financial statements under UK GAAP to IFRS [extract]

(d)   Reconciliation of the group cash flow under UK GAAP to IFRS as at 31 March 2005

The consolidated statement of cash flows prepared in accordance with FRS 1 'Cash flow statements' presents substantially the same information as that required under IFRS. Under IFRS, however, there are certain differences from UK GAAP with regard to the classification of items within the cash flow statement and with regard to the definition of cash and cash equivalents.

Under UK GAAP, cash flows were presented separately for operating activities, dividends received from joint ventures and associates, returns on investments and servicing of finance, taxation, capital expenditure and financial investment, acquisitions and disposals, equity dividends paid, management of liquid resources and financing. Under IFRS, only three categories of cash flow activity are reported: operating activities, investing activities and financing activities.

Under IFRS, items which under UK GAAP would have been included within management of liquid resources fall within the definition of cash and cash equivalents.

The requirements of IAS 38 state that certain non-current assets, namely capitalised software and hydro relicensing costs, previously included within tangible assets, are reclassified as intangible assets. This has resulted in £54.6 million being reclassified from the purchase of property, plant and equipment to the purchase of intangible assets. A further £1.2 million has been reclassified from the purchase of property, plant and equipment to the proceeds from the sale of intangible assets.

IFRIC 4 contains guidance on the identification of lease arrangements. The group's arrangements have been assessed against the criteria contained in IAS 17 to determine, firstly, whether any arrangements qualify for lease accounting and, secondly, whether the leases should be categorised as operating or finance leases. The identification of additional finance leases has resulted in £11.7 million being reclassified from cash generated from operations to interest paid (£8.8 million) and proceeds from borrowings (£2.9 million).

7.2 IAS 8 – Accounting policies, changes in accounting estimates and errors

7.2.1 Changes in IFRS accounting policies before first IFRS financial statements

Some first-time adopters find that they need to change their IFRS accounting policies after they have prepared an IFRS interim report but before their first IFRS financial statements. Such a change in accounting policies could relate either to the ongoing IFRS accounting policies or to the selection of IFRS 1 exemptions. Normally when an entity changes an accounting policy, it should apply IAS 8 to such a change. However, IFRS 1 specifically states that 'IAS 8 does not deal with changes in accounting policies that occur when an entity first adopts IFRSs.'[324] Instead, the standard requires that a first-time adopter should apply the same accounting policies in its opening IFRS balance sheet and throughout all periods presented in its first IFRS financial statements.[325] Therefore, the change in accounting policies should be treated as a change in the entity's IFRS opening balance sheet and the policy should be applied consistently in all periods presented under IFRSs. In our view, additional disclosures about the nature of the change in accounting policies would generally be appropriate under IAS 1.

The distinction between changes in accounting policies and changes in accounting estimates is discussed in detail in Chapter 3 at 4.2.

A   Future developments

The issue above was specifically considered by the IASB as part of its annual improvements project. Consequently, in August 2009, the IASB published the exposure draft *Improvements to IFRSs*, which specifically states that 'IAS 8 does not apply to the changes in accounting policies an entity makes when it adopts IFRSs or changes in those policies until it presents its first IFRS financial statements.'[326] Therefore, 'if during the period covered by its first IFRS financial statements an entity changes its accounting policies or its use of the exemptions contained in this IFRS', it should explain the changes in accordance with paragraph 23 of IFRS 1 (see 6.3 below) and update the reconciliations required by paragraphs 24(a) and (b) of IFRS 1 (see 6.3.1 below).[327] A similar requirement would apply to the disclosures in a first-time adopter's interim financial reports (see 6.6 below).[328] The proposed amendment is expected to be effective for annual periods beginning on or after 1 January 2011. If an entity applies the amendment for an earlier period, it should disclose that fact.[329]

7.2.2 Changes in estimates and correction of errors

An entity that adopts IFRSs needs to assess carefully the impact of information that has become available since it prepared its most recent previous GAAP financial statements because the new information:

- may be a new estimate that should be accounted for prospectively (see 4.2 above); or

- may expose an error in the previous GAAP financial statements due to mathematical mistakes, mistakes in applying accounting policies, oversights or misinterpretations of facts, and fraud. In the reconciliation from previous GAAP to IFRSs such errors should be disclosed separate from the effect of changes in accounting policies (see 6.3.1 above).

7.3   IAS 11 – Construction contracts

IFRS 1 contains no specific requirements or exemptions with regard to IAS 11. There are no exemptions from the application of IAS 11's measurement rules as at the date of transition. Therefore, the standard has to be applied with full retrospective application as at the entity's first reporting date under IFRSs.

In many jurisdictions entities are permitted to use the completed contract method for some or all construction contracts. Under this method, revenue is only recognised when the contract is complete or substantially complete and until this point costs and amounts billed to the customer are recorded in the balance sheet. This accounting may not be appropriate under IAS 11. Although IAS 11 is primarily concerned with recording contract activity it also affects the balances carried forward to the extent that profits and losses have been recognised on individual contracts in previous periods. Therefore, entities will be required first to determine the appropriate manner of recognising revenue for construction contracts under IAS 11 and second to review all such contracts as at transition to ensure that their carrying amounts have been recorded in a manner that is appropriate for IAS 11. Considerable care needs to be taken to avoid undue use of hindsight in applying IAS 11 retrospectively.

7.4   IAS 12 – Income taxes

There are no particular provisions in IFRS 1 with regard to the first-time adoption of IAS 12, although the implementation guidance notes that IAS 12 requires entities to provide for deferred tax on temporary differences measured by reference to enacted or substantively enacted legislation.[330]

The full retrospective application of IAS 12 as required by IFRS 1 poses several problems that may not be immediately obvious at first sight. First of all, IAS 12 does not require an entity to account for all temporary differences. For example, an entity is not required under IAS 12 to recognise deferred tax for temporary differences relating to:

- the initial recognition of goodwill;[331] and
- the initial recognition of an asset or liability in a transaction that is not a business combination and that affected neither accounting profit nor taxable profit.[332]

In addition, a change in deferred tax should be accounted for in other comprehensive income or equity, instead of profit or loss, when the tax relates to an item that was originally accounted for in other comprehensive income.

Therefore, full retrospective application of IAS 12 requires a first-time adopter to establish the history of the items that give rise to temporary differences because, depending on the type of transaction, it may not be necessary to account for deferred tax, or changes in the deferred tax may need to be accounted for in other comprehensive income or equity.

The main issue for many first-time adopters of IFRSs will be that their previous GAAP either required no provision for deferred tax, or required provision under a timing difference approach. They also need to be aware that many of the other adjustments made to the transition balance sheet will also have a deferred tax effect that must be accounted for. Entities that also report under US GAAP must also bear in mind that IAS 12, though derived from FAS 109 – *Accounting for Income Taxes*, is different in a number of important respects.

7.4.1 Previously revalued plant, property and equipment treated as deemed cost on transition

In some cases IFRS 1 allows an entity, on transition to IFRSs, to treat the carrying amount of plant, property or equipment revalued under its previous GAAP as a deemed cost for the purposes of IFRSs (see 5.5.2 above).

Where an asset is carried at deemed cost on transition to IFRSs, but the tax base of the asset remains at original cost (or an amount based on original cost), the previous GAAP revaluation will give rise to a temporary difference (typically, a taxable temporary difference) associated with the asset. IAS 12 requires deferred tax to be recognised on any such temporary difference at transition.

If, after transition, the deferred tax is required to be remeasured (e.g. because of a change in tax rate, or a re-basing of the asset for tax purposes), and the asset concerned was revalued outside profit or loss under previous GAAP, the question arises as to whether the resulting deferred tax income or expense should be recognised in, or outside, profit or loss.

The argument for recognising such income or expense in profit or loss is essentially that the reference in paragraph 61A of IAS 12 to the tax effects of 'items recognised outside profit or loss' must mean items recognised outside profit or loss under IFRSs, not under previous GAAP. An asset carried at deemed cost on transition is not otherwise treated as a revalued asset for the purposes of IFRSs. For example, any impairment of such an asset must be accounted for in profit or loss. By contrast, any impairment of plant, property or equipment treated as a revalued asset under IAS 16 would be accounted for outside profit or loss – in other comprehensive income – up to the amount of the cumulative revaluation gain previously recognised.

The argument for recognising such income or expense outside profit or loss is essentially that the reference in paragraph 61A of IAS 12 to the tax effects of 'items recognised outside profit or loss' need not be read as referring only to items recognised outside profit or loss equity under IFRSs. Those who hold this view may do so in the context that the entity's previous GAAP required tax income and expense to be allocated between profit or loss, other comprehensive income and equity in a manner similar to that required by IAS 12. It is argued that it is inappropriate that the effect of transitioning from pre-transition GAAP to IFRSs should be to require recognition in profit or loss of an item that would have been recognised outside profit or loss under the ongoing application of either previous GAAP or IFRSs. The counter-argument to this is that there are a number of other similar inconsistencies under IFRS 1.

A more persuasive argument for the latter view might be that, whilst IFRSs do not regard such an asset as having been revalued, it does allow the revalued amount to stand. IFRSs are therefore recognising an implied contribution by owners in excess of the original cost of the asset which, although it is not a 'revaluation' under IFRSs, would nevertheless have been recognised in equity on an ongoing application of IFRSs.

In our view, either approach is acceptable, so long as it is applied consistently.

7.4.2　Share-based payment transactions subject to transitional provisions of IFRS 1 and IFRS 2

While IFRS 1 provides exemptions from applying IFRS 2 to certain share-based payment transactions, there are no corresponding exemptions from the provisions of IAS 12 relating to share-based payment transactions. Therefore the provisions of IAS 12 relating to share-based payments apply to all share-based payment transactions, whether they are accounted for in accordance with IFRS 2 or not. A tax-deductible share-based payment is treated as having a carrying amount equivalent to the total cumulative expense recognised in respect of it, irrespective of how, or indeed whether, the share-based payment is itself accounted for.

This means that on transition to IFRSs, and subject to the restrictions on recognition of deferred tax assets (see Chapter 26 at 4.2.3), a deferred tax asset should be established for all share-based payment transactions outstanding at that date, including those not accounted for under the transitional provisions.

Where such an asset is remeasured or recognised after transition to IFRSs, the general rule regarding the 'capping' of the amount of any tax relief recognised in profit or loss to the amount charged to the profit or loss applies. Therefore, if there was no profit or loss charge for share-based payment transactions under the previous GAAP, all tax effects of share-based payment transactions not accounted for under IFRS 2 should be dealt with in other comprehensive income.

7.4.3　Retrospective restatements or applications

IAS 8 requires retrospective restatements or retrospective applications arising from corrections of errors and changes in accounting policy to be accounted for as an adjustment to equity in the period in which the retrospective restatement or application occurs.

IAS 12 therefore requires the tax effect of a retrospective restatement or application to be dealt with as an adjustment to equity also. However, as drafted, IAS 12 can also be read as requiring any subsequent remeasurement of such tax effects to be accounted for in equity also. This would give rise to a rather surprising result, as illustrated by Example 5.38 below.

Example 5.38:　Remeasurement of deferred tax liability recognised as the result of retrospective application

An entity's date of transition to IFRSs was 1 January 2004. As a result of the adoption of IAS 37 – *Provisions, Contingent Liabilities and Contingent Assets*, its first IFRS financial statements (prepared for the year ended 31 December 2005) show an additional liability for environmental remediation costs of €5 million as an adjustment to opening reserves, together with an associated deferred tax asset at 40% of €2 million.

The environmental liability does not change substantially over the next few accounting periods, but during the year ended 31 December 2010 the tax rate falls to 30%. This requires the deferred tax asset to be remeasured to €1.5 million giving rise to tax expense of €500,000. Should this expense be recognised in profit or loss for the period or in equity?

If read literally, IAS 12 can be construed as requiring this expense to be accounted for in equity, as being a remeasurement of an amount originally recognised in equity. However, we question whether this was really the intention of IAS 12. There is a fundamental difference between an item that by its nature would always be recognised *directly* outside profit or loss (e.g. certain foreign exchange differences or revaluations of plant, property and equipment) and an item which in the normal course of events would be accounted for in profit or loss, but when recognised for the first time as the result of a change in accounting policy (such as in Example 5.38 above) is dealt with as a 'catch up' adjustment to opening equity.

Such a 'catch up' adjustment is necessary only because the entity is not presenting comparative information for all periods since it first commenced business. If it had done so, all the charge for environmental costs (and all the related deferred tax) would have been reflected in profit or loss in previous income statements. In our view, once such items have been recognised as a 'catch up' adjustment, any subsequent changes should in principle be accounted for in profit or loss as if the new accounting policy had always been in force.

7.4.4 Defined benefit pension plans

IAS 19 – *Employee Benefits* – permits an entity, in accounting for a defined benefit post-employment benefit plan, to recognise actuarial gains and losses relating to the plan in full in other comprehensive income. At the same time, a calculated current service cost and finance income and expense relating to any plan assets are recognised in profit or loss.

In many jurisdictions, tax relief for post-employment benefits is given on the basis of cash contributions paid to the plan fund (or benefits paid when a plan is unfunded).

This significant difference between the way in which defined plans are treated for tax and financial reporting purposes can make the allocation of tax relief for them between profit or loss and other comprehensive income somewhat arbitrary, as illustrated by Example 5.39 below.

Example 5.39:   Tax relief for defined benefit pension plans

At 1 January 2009 an entity that pays tax at 40% has a fully-funded defined benefit pension scheme. During the year ended 31 December 2009 it records a total cost of €1 million, of which €800,000 is allocated to profit or loss and €200,000 to other comprehensive income. In January 2010 it makes a funding payment of €450,000, tax relief on which is received through the current tax charge for the year ended 31 December 2010.

Assuming that the entity is able to recognise a deferred tax asset for the entire €1 million charged in 2009, it will record the following entry for income taxes in 2009.

	€	€
Deferred tax asset [€1,000,000 @ 40%]	400,000	
Deferred tax income (profit or loss) [€800,000 @ 40%]		320,000
Deferred tax income (other comprehensive income) [€200,000 @ 40%]		80,000

When the funding payment is made, the accounting deficit on the fund is reduced by €450,000. This gives rise to deferred tax expense of €180,000 (€450,000 @ 40%), as some of the deferred tax asset at 31 December 2009 is released, and current tax income of €180,000. The difficulty is how to allocate this movement between profit or loss and other comprehensive income, as it is ultimately a matter of arbitrary allocation as to whether the funding payment is regarded as making good (for example):

- €450,000 of the €800,000 deficit previously accounted for in profit or loss;
- the whole of the €200,000 of the deficit previously accounted for in other comprehensive income and €250,000 of the €800,000 deficit previously accounted for in profit or loss; or
- a pro-rata share of those parts of the total deficit accounted for in profit or loss and other comprehensive income.

For an entity that has adopted the transitional provision of IFRS 1 that allows all cumulative actuarial gains and losses to be recognised on transition to IFRSs, it will be quite impossible to determine how much of those cumulative gains and losses would have been accounted for in the profit or loss, and how much in other comprehensive income, if IFRSs has always been applied.

The issue raised above is of particular importance when a first-time adopter has large funding shortfalls on its defined benefit schemes and at the same can only recognise part of its deferred tax assets. In such a situation the method of allocation may well affect the after tax profit in a given year.

In our view (see Chapter 26 at 6.1.7), these are instances of the exceptional circumstances envisaged by IAS 12 when a strict allocation of tax between profit or loss and other comprehensive income is not possible. Accordingly, any reasonable method of allocation may be used, provided that it is applied on a consistent basis.

One approach might be to compare the funding payments made to the scheme in the previous few years with the charges made to profit or loss under IAS 19 in those periods. If, for example, it is found that the payments were equal to or greater than the charges to profit or loss, it could reasonably be concluded that any surplus or deficit on the balance sheet is broadly represented by items that have been accounted for in other comprehensive income.

7.5   IAS 16 – Property, plant and equipment

The implementation guidance discussed in this section applies to property, plant and equipment as well as investment properties that are accounted for under the cost model in IAS 40.[333]

7.5.1   Depreciation method and rate

If a first-time adopter's depreciation methods and rates under its previous GAAP are acceptable under IFRSs then it accounts for any change in estimated useful life or depreciation pattern prospectively from when it makes that change in estimate (see 4.2 above). However, if the depreciation methods and rates are not acceptable under IFRSs and the difference has a material impact on the financial statements, a first-time adopter should adjust the accumulated depreciation in its opening IFRS balance sheet retrospectively.[334] Additional differences may arise from the requirement in IAS 16 to review the residual value and the useful life of an asset at least each financial year end,[335] which may not be required under a first-time adopter's previous GAAP.

If a restatement of the depreciation methods and rates would be too onerous, a first-time adopter could opt instead to use fair value as the deemed cost. However, application of the deemed cost exemption is not always the only approach available. In practice, many first-time adopters have found that, other than buildings, there are generally few items of property, plant and equipment that still have a material carrying amount after more than 30 or 40 years of use. Therefore, the carrying value that results from a fully retrospective application of IAS 16 may not differ much from the carrying amount under an entity's previous GAAP.

7.5.2   Estimates of useful life and residual value

An entity may use fair value as deemed cost for an item of property, plant and equipment that it had depreciated to zero under its previous GAAP (i.e. the asset has already reached the end of its originally assessed economic life). Although IFRS 1 requires an entity to use estimates made under its previous GAAP, paragraph 51 of IAS 16 would require the entity to re-assess the remaining useful life and residual value at least annually. Therefore, the asset's deemed cost should be depreciated over its re-assessed economic life and taking into account its re-assessed residual value.

The same applies when an entity does not use fair value or revaluation as deemed cost. If there were indicators in the past that the useful life or residual value changed but those changes were not required to be recognised under previous GAAP, the IFRS carrying amount as of the date of transition should be determined by taking into account the re-assessed economic life and the re-assessed residual value.

7.5.3   Revaluation model

A first-time adopter that chooses to account for some or all classes of property, plant and equipment under the revaluation model needs to present the cumulative revaluation surplus as a separate component of equity. However, IFRS 1 requires that 'the revaluation surplus at the date of transition to IFRSs is based on a comparison of the carrying amount of the asset at that date with its cost or deemed cost.'[336] If revaluations under previous GAAP did not satisfy the criteria in IFRS 1 (see 5.5.2 B above), a first-time adopter measures the revalued assets in its opening IFRS balance sheet on one of the following bases:[337]

(a)   cost (or deemed cost) less any accumulated depreciation and any accumulated impairment losses under the cost model in IAS 16;

(b)   deemed cost, being the fair value at the date of transition to IFRSs; or

(c)   revalued amount, if the entity adopts the revaluation model in IAS 16 as its accounting policy under IFRSs for all items of property, plant and equipment in the same class.

A first-time adopter that uses fair value as the deemed cost for those classes of property, plant and equipment would be required to reset the cumulative revaluation surplus to zero. Therefore any previous GAAP revaluation surplus related to assets valued at deemed cost cannot be used to offset a subsequent impairment or revaluation loss under IFRSs.

7.5.4   Parts approach

IAS 16 requires a 'parts approach' to the recognition of property, plant and equipment. Thus a large item such as an aircraft is recognised as a series of 'parts' that may have different useful lives. An engine of an aircraft may be a part. IAS 16 does not prescribe the physical unit of measure (the 'part') for recognition or what constitutes an item of property, plant and equipment.[338] Instead the standard relies on judgement 'in applying the recognition criteria to an entity's specific circumstances.'[339] However, the standard does require an entity to:

- apply a very restrictive definition of maintenance costs (or costs of day-to-day servicing) which it describes as 'primarily the costs of labour and consumables, and may include the cost of small parts. The purpose of these expenditures is often described as for the "repairs and maintenance" of the item of property, plant and equipment';[340]

- derecognise the carrying amount of the parts that are replaced; and[341]

- depreciate separately each part of an item of property, plant and equipment with a cost that is significant in relation to the total cost of the item.[342]

Based on this, it is reasonable to surmise that parts can be relatively small units. Therefore, it is possible that even if a first-time adopter's depreciation methods and rates are acceptable under IFRSs, it may have to restate property, plant and equipment because its unit of measure was based on physical units significantly larger than IAS 16's parts.

In practice, however, there is seldom a need to account for every single part of an asset separately. Very often there is no significant difference in the reported amounts once all significant parts have been identified. Furthermore, as explained in Chapter 16 at 7.1, an entity may not actually need to identify the parts of an asset until it incurs the replacement expenditure.

7.6   IAS 17 – Leases

Other than the IFRIC 4 exemption (see 5.6 above) there are no exemptions regarding lease accounting available to a first-time adopter.

7.6.1   *Assets held under finance leases*

A first-time adopter should recognise all assets held under finance leases on its balance sheet. If those assets were not recognised previously, the first-time adopter needs to determine the following:

(a)   the fair value of the assets or, if lower, the present value of the minimum lease payments at the date of inception of the lease;

(b)   the carrying amount of the assets at the date of transition to IFRSs by applying IFRS accounting policies to their subsequent measurement;

(c)   the interest rate implicit in the lease; and

(d)   the carrying amount of the lease liability in accordance with IAS 17.

When determining the information under (b) above is impracticable, a first-time adopter may want to apply the deemed cost exemption to those assets (see 5.5.2 above). However, no corresponding exemption exists regarding the lease liability.

7.7   IAS 18 – Revenue recognition

A first-time adopter that has received amounts that do not yet qualify for recognition as revenue under IAS 18 (e.g. the proceeds of a sale that does not qualify for revenue recognition) should recognise those amounts as a liability in its opening IFRS balance sheet.[343] It is therefore possible that revenue that was already recognised under a first-time adopter's previous GAAP will need to be deferred in its opening IFRS balance sheet and recognised again (this time under IFRSs) as revenue at a later date.

Conversely, it is possible that revenue deferred under a first-time adopter's previous GAAP cannot be recognised as deferred revenue in the opening IFRS balance sheet. A first-time adopter would not be able to report such revenue deferred under its previous GAAP as revenue under IFRSs at a later date.

7.8   IAS 19 – Employee benefits

7.8.1   *Cumulative amount of actuarial gains and losses recognised in other comprehensive Income*

If a first-time adopter adopts a policy of recognising actuarial gains and losses in other comprehensive income in the period in which they occur, it would be required by paragraph 120A(i) of IAS 19 to disclose the *cumulative amount* of actuarial gains and losses recognised in other comprehensive income. In practice many first-time adopters are unable to determine the cumulative amount of actuarial gains and losses recognised in other comprehensive income and make a disclosure similar to the one found in the financial statements of Carillon.

Extract 5.15: Carillon plc (2008)

Notes to the consolidated financial statements [extract]

33. Retirement benefit obligations [extract]

The cumulative amount of actuarial gains and losses recognised since 1 January 2004 in the Group statement of recognised income and expense is £(9.6) million (2007: £97.8 million). The Group is unable to determine how much of the pension scheme deficit recognised on transition to IFRS of £85.2 million and taken directly to total equity is attributable to actuarial gains and losses since inception of the schemes. Therefore, the Group is unable to determine the amount of actuarial gains and losses that would have been recognised in the Group statement of recognised income and expense before 1 January 2004.

7.9   IAS 21 – The effects of changes in foreign exchange rates

7.9.1   *Functional currency*

A first-time adopter needs to confirm whether all entities included within the financial statements have appropriately determined their functional currency. IAS 21 defines an entity's functional currency as 'the currency of the primary economic environment in which the entity operates' and contains detailed guidance on determining the functional currency.[344]

If the functional currency of an entity is not readily identifiable, IAS 21 requires consideration of 'whether the activities of the foreign operation are carried out as an extension of the reporting entity, rather than being carried out with a significant degree of autonomy'.[345] This requirement often leads to the conclusion under IFRSs that intermediate holding companies, treasury subsidiaries and foreign sales offices have the same functional currency as their parent.

Many national GAAPs do not specifically define the concept of functional currency, or they may contain guidance on identifying the functional currency that differs from that in IAS 21. Consequently, a first-time adopter that measured transactions in a currency that was not its functional currency will need to restate its financial statements. Full retrospective application of IAS 21 is extremely onerous as it affects measurement of all non-monetary items in a first-time adopter's opening IFRS balance sheet. The exemption that allows a first-time adopter to reset the cumulative exchange differences in equity to zero cannot be applied to assets or liabilities (see 5.8 above). In October 2004, the IFRIC considered whether 'a specific exception should be granted to first-time adopters to permit entities to translate all assets and liabilities at the transition date exchange rate rather than applying the functional currency approach in IAS 21 ... The IFRIC agreed that the position under IFRS 1 and IAS 21 was clear, and that there was no scope for an Interpretation on this topic that would provide any relief.'[346]

A first-time adopter would need to restate its financial statements because IFRS 1 does not contain an exemption that would allow it to use a currency other than the functional currency in determining the cost of assets and liabilities in its opening IFRS balance sheet. The principal difficulty relates to non-monetary items that are measured on the basis of historical cost, particularly property, plant and machinery, since these will need to be re-measured in terms of the IAS 21 functional currency at the rates of exchange applicable at the date of acquisition of the assets concerned, and recalculating cumulative depreciation or amortisation charges accordingly. It may be that to overcome this difficulty an entity should consider using the option in IFRS 1 whereby the fair value of such assets at the date of transition is treated as being their deemed cost (see 5.5.2 above).

7.10   IAS 23 – Borrowing costs

While IAS 23 (as revised in 2007) was intended to converge the accounting for capitalised borrowing costs under IFRSs with US GAAP, full convergence was not achieved. The standard lists a number of areas in which it continues to differ from US GAAP:

- the definition of 'borrowing costs' in IAS 23 (as revised in 2007) differs from the term 'interest cost' under US GAAP (e.g. borrowing costs may include certain exchange differences on foreign currency borrowings);[347]

- the definition of 'qualifying asset' in IAS 23 (as revised in 2007) differs from US GAAP in regards of (1) the length of the construction period required, (2) assets measured at fair value, (3) investments accounted for under the equity method and (4) assets acquired with gifts or grants; and[348]

- the treatment of funds borrowed specifically for the purpose of obtaining a qualifying assets and determination of the capitalisation rate.[349]

Similar differences are likely to exist between IFRSs and previous GAAPs other than US GAAP. If a first-time adopter had previously capitalised borrowing costs in a way that does not comply with IAS 23 (as revised in 2007), it might not want to apply IAS 23 (as revised in 2007) fully retrospectively and instead rely on the borrowing costs exemption (see 5.16 above).

7.11 IAS 28 – Investments in associates

7.11.1 General

There are a number of first-time adoption exemptions that impact the accounting for investments in associates:

- the business combinations exemption, which also applies to past acquisitions of investments in associates (see 5.2.1 A above);

- an exemption in respect of determining the cost of an associate within any separate financial statements that an entity may prepare (see 5.9 above); and

- there are separate rules that deal with situations in which an investor adopts IFRSs before or after an associate does so (see 5.10 above).

Otherwise there are no specific first-time adoption provisions in IAS 28, which means that a first-time adopter of IFRSs is effectively required to apply IAS 28 as if it had always done so. For some first-time adopters, this may mean application of the equity method for the first time. For the majority of first time adopters, however, the issue is likely that they are already applying the equity method under their national GAAP, and will now need to identify the potentially significant differences between the methodology of the equity method under their previous GAAP and under IAS 28.

In particular there may be differences between:

- the criteria used to determine which investments are associates;

- the elimination of transactions between investors and associates;

- the treatment of loss-making associates;

- the permitted interval between the reporting dates of an investor and an associate with non-coterminous year-ends;

- the treatment of investments in entities formerly classified as associates; and

- the requirement for uniform accounting policies between the investor and investee.

7.11.2 Transition impairment review

A first-time adopter of IFRSs is required by IFRS 1 to apply an impairment test in accordance with IAS 36 to any goodwill recognised at the date of transition to IFRSs, regardless of whether there is any indication of impairment.[350] IFRS 1 specifically notes that its provisions with regard to past business combinations apply also to past acquisitions of investments in associates.[351] Therefore, a transition impairment review must be undertaken in accordance with the requirements of paragraphs C4(g) and C4(h) of IFRS 1 for investments in associates whose carrying value includes an element of goodwill. This impairment review will, however, need to be carried out on the basis required by IAS 28 as described in Chapter 11 at 4.

7.12   IAS 29 – Financial reporting in hyperinflationary economies

The IASB decided not to exempt first-time adopters from retrospective application of IAS 29 – *Financial Reporting in Hyperinflationary Economies*. Although the cost of restating financial statements for the effects of hyperinflation in periods before the date of transition to IFRSs might exceed the benefits, particularly if the currency is no longer hyperinflationary, the IASB concluded that a full retrospective 'restatement should be required, because hyperinflation can make unadjusted financial statements meaningless or misleading.'[352]

In preparing its opening IFRS balance sheet a first-time adopter should apply IAS 29 to any periods during which the economy of the functional currency or presentation currency was hyperinflationary.[353] To make the restatement process less onerous, a first-time adopter may want to consider using fair value as deemed cost for long-lived assets such as property, plant and equipment, investment properties and certain intangible assets (see 5.5.2 above).[354] If a first-time adopter applies the exemption to use fair value or a revaluation as deemed cost, it applies IAS 29 to periods after the date for which the revalued amount or fair value was determined.[355]

7.13   IAS 31 – Interests in joint ventures

The first-time adoption exemptions that are available for investments in associates can also be applied to investments in jointly controlled entities, regardless of whether they are accounted for under the equity method or proportionately consolidated (see 7.11 above).

The requirements for 'jointly controlled operations' and 'jointly controlled assets' may well result in the 're-recognition' of assets that were not recognised under previous GAAP, so as to reflect the requirement of IAS 31 to treat assets used in such joint ventures as assets of the venturers themselves rather than of the venture.

7.14   IAS 36 – Impairment of assets

As far as goodwill is concerned, first time adopters of IFRSs are required by IFRS 1 to subject all goodwill carried in the balance sheet at the date of transition to an impairment test, regardless of whether there are any indicators of impairment (see 5.2.4 above).[356]

IFRS 1 does not specifically call for an impairment test of other assets, but such an impairment test might be appropriate if a first-time adopter makes use of the deemed cost exemption. In arguing that it is not necessary to restrict application of that exemption to classes of assets to prevent selective revaluations, the IASB effectively relies on IAS 36 to avoid overvaluations:

> 'IAS 36 requires an impairment test if there is any indication that an asset is impaired. Thus, if an entity uses fair value as deemed cost for assets whose fair value is above cost, it cannot ignore indications that the recoverable amount of other assets may have fallen below their carrying amount. Therefore, IFRS 1 does not restrict the use of fair value as deemed cost to entire classes of asset.'[357]

The estimates used to determine whether a first-time adopter recognises an impairment loss or provision at the date of transition to IFRSs should be consistent with estimates made for the same date under previous GAAP (after adjustments to reflect any difference in accounting policies), unless there is objective evidence that those estimates were in error.[358] If a first-time adopter needs to make estimates for that date that were not necessary under its previous GAAP, such estimates and assumptions should not reflect conditions that arose after the date of transition to IFRSs.[359]

If a first-time adopter's opening IFRS balance sheet reflects impairment losses, it recognises any later reversal of those impairment losses in profit or loss unless IAS 36 requires that reversal to be treated as a revaluation. This applies to both impairment losses recognised under previous GAAP and additional impairment losses recognised on transition to IFRSs.[360]

A first-time adopter needs to make certain disclosure regarding any impairment losses that it recognised or reversed on transition to IFRSs (see 6.3.3 above).

7.15 IAS 37 – Provisions, contingent liabilities and contingent assets

The main issue for a first-time adopter in applying IAS 37 is that IFRS 1 prohibits retrospective application of some aspects of IFRSs relating to estimates (see 4.2 above). IFRS 1 notes that the estimates used to determine whether an entity recognises a provision under IAS 37 (and to measure any such provision) at the date of transition to IFRSs are to be consistent with estimates made for the same date under previous GAAP (after adjustments to reflect any difference in accounting policies) unless there is objective evidence that those estimates were in error. The entity has to report the impact of any later revisions to those estimates as an event of the period in which it makes the revisions.[361]

Also, in assessing whether it needs to recognise a provision under IAS 37 (and in measuring any such provision) at the date of transition to IFRSs, an entity may need to make estimates for that date that were not necessary under its previous GAAP. Such estimates and assumptions do not reflect conditions that arose after the date of transition to IFRSs.[362]

These requirements also apply to provisions at the end of the comparative period presented in an entity's first IFRS financial statements.[363] Accordingly, an entity cannot use hindsight in determining the provisions under IAS 37 to be included within its opening IFRS balance sheet (and at the end of the comparative period).

Finally, when application of IAS 37 changes the way an entity accounts for provisions it needs to consider whether there are any consequential changes, for example:

- derecognition of a provision for general business risks may mean that assets in the related cash-generating unit are impaired;
- derecognition of a provision for general credit risks may indicate that the carrying amount of related financial assets need to be adjusted to take account of existing credit losses; and
- remeasurement of a decommissioning provision may indicate that the decommissioning component of the corresponding asset needs to be reconsidered.

The above list is not exhaustive and a first-time adopter should carefully consider whether changes in other provisions have a consequential impact.

7.16   IAS 38 – Intangible assets

An intangible asset is only capable of capitalisation under IAS 38 if it is probable that the future economic benefits attributable to the asset will flow to the entity and the cost of the asset can be measured reliably.[364] Accordingly, an entity's opening IFRS balance sheet:[365]

(a)   excludes all intangible assets and other intangible items that do not meet the criteria for recognition under IAS 38 at the date of transition to IFRSs; and

(b)   includes all intangible assets that meet the recognition criteria in IAS 38 at that date, except for intangible assets acquired in a business combination that were not recognised in the acquirer's consolidated balance sheet under previous GAAP and also would not qualify for recognition under IAS 38 in the separate balance sheet of the acquiree.

IAS 38 imposes a number of additional criteria that further restrict capitalisation of internally generated intangible assets. An important restriction is the prohibition from using hindsight to conclude retrospectively that the recognition criteria are met, thereby capitalising an amount previously recognised as an expense.[366] A first-time adopter of IFRSs must be particularly careful that, in applying IAS 38 retrospectively as at the date of transition, it does not capitalise costs incurred before the standard's recognition criteria were met. Therefore, a first-time adopter is only permitted to capitalise the costs of internally generated intangible assets when it:[367]

(a)   concludes, based on an assessment made and documented at the date of that conclusion, that it is probable that future economic benefits from the asset will flow to the entity; and

(b)   has a reliable system for accumulating the costs of internally generated intangible assets when, or shortly after, they are incurred.

In other words, it is not permitted under IFRS 1 to reconstruct retrospectively the costs of intangible assets. If an internally generated intangible asset qualifies for recognition at the date of transition to IFRSs, a first-time adopter recognises the asset in its opening IFRS balance sheet even if it had recognised the related expenditure as an expense under its previous GAAP.[368] However, first-time adopters that did not capitalise internally generated intangible assets are unlikely to have the type of documentation and systems required by IFRS 1 and will therefore not be able to capitalise these items in their opening IFRS balance sheet. Furthermore, if the asset does not qualify for recognition under IAS 38 until a later date, its cost is the sum of the expenditure incurred from that later date.[369] Nonetheless, going forward, first-time adopters will need to implement the internal systems and procedures that enable them to determine whether or not any future internally generated intangible assets should be capitalised (for example, in the case of development costs).

Capitalisation of separately acquired intangible assets will generally be easier because contemporaneous documentation that was prepared to support the investment decisions often exists.[370] However, if an entity did not recognise an intangible asset acquired in a business combination under its previous GAAP, it would only be able to do so upon first-time adoption if the intangible asset met the IAS 38 recognition criteria in the balance sheet of the acquiree (see 5.2.3 E above).[371]

If a first-time adopter's 'amortisation methods and rates in accordance with previous GAAP would be acceptable in accordance with IFRSs, the entity does not restate the accumulated amortisation in its opening IFRS balance sheet. Instead, the entity accounts for any change in estimated useful life or amortisation pattern prospectively from the period when it makes that change in estimate ... However, in some cases, an entity's amortisation methods and rates in accordance with previous GAAP may differ from those that would be acceptable in accordance with IFRSs ... If those differences have a material effect on the financial statements, the entity adjusts the accumulated amortisation in its opening IFRS balance sheet retrospectively so that it complies with IFRSs.'[372]

The residual value and the useful life of an intangible asset should be reviewed at least each financial year end under IAS 38,[373] which is often something that is not required under a first-time adopter's previous GAAP.

8 REGULATORY ISSUES

8.1 First-time adoption by foreign private issuers that are SEC registrants

8.1.1 SEC guidance

A foreign private issuer that is registered with the US Securities and Exchange Commission (SEC) is normally required to present two comparative periods for its statement of comprehensive income (or income statement), statement of cash flows and statement of changes in equity. Converting two comparative periods to IFRSs was considered to be a considerable burden to companies. Therefore, in April 2005, the SEC published amendments to Form 20-F that provided for a limited period a two-year accommodation for foreign private issuers that were first-time adopters of IFRSs.[374] In March 2008, the SEC extended indefinitely the two-year accommodation to all foreign private issuers that are first-time adopters of IFRSs as issued by the IASB.[375]

The amendment states that 'An issuer that changes the body of accounting principles used in preparing its financial statements presented pursuant to Item 8.A.2 ("Item 8.A.2") to International Financial Reporting Standards ("IFRS") issued by the International Accounting Standards Board ("IASB") may omit the earliest of three years of audited financial statements required by Item 8.A.2 if the issuer satisfies the conditions set forth in this Instruction G. For purposes of this instruction, the term "financial year" refers to the first financial year beginning on or after January 1 of the same calendar year.'[376] The accommodation only applies to an issuer that (a) adopts IFRSs for the first time by an explicit and unreserved statement of compliance with IFRS as issued by the IASB and (b) the issuer's most recent audited financial statements are prepared in accordance with IFRSs.

First-time adopters that rely on the accommodation are allowed, but not required, to include any financial statements, discussions or other financial information based on their previous GAAP. If first-time adopters do include such information, they should prominently disclose cautionary language to avoid inappropriate comparison with information presented under IFRSs. The SEC did not mandate a specific location for any previous GAAP information but did prohibit presentation of previous GAAP information in a side-by-side columnar format with IFRS financial information.

In addition, the accommodation only requires entities to provide selected historical financial data based on IFRSs for the two most recent financial years. Selected historical financial data based on US GAAP would continue to be required for the five most recent financial years. Although the SEC does not prohibit entities from including selected financial data based on previous GAAP in their annual reports, side-by-side presentation of data prepared under IFRSs and data prepared under previous GAAP is prohibited.

Where a narrative discussion of its financial condition is provided, the accommodation requires management to focus on the financial statements prepared under IFRSs as issued by the IASB for the past two financial years.

IFRS 1 requires a first-time adopter to present a reconciliation from its previous GAAP to IFRSs in the notes to its financial statements and allows certain exceptions from full retrospective application of IFRSs in deriving the relevant data. Under the SEC's accommodation, any issuer relying on any of the elective or mandatory exceptions from IFRSs that are contained within IFRS 1 will have to disclose additional information which includes:[377]

- to the extent the primary financial statements reflect the use of exceptions permitted or required by IFRS 1:
  - detailed information for each exception used, including:
    - an indication of the items or class of items to which the exception was applied; and
    - a description of what accounting principle was used and how it was applied; and
  - where material, qualitative disclosure of the impact on financial condition, changes in financial condition and results of operations that the treatment specified by IFRSs would have had absent the election to rely on the exception.

8.1.2   IPTF guidance

In November 2008, the Center for Audit Quality SEC Regulations Committee's International Practices Task Force ('IPTF') provided guidance as to the reconciliation requirements of an SEC foreign private issuer the first time it presents IFRS financial statements in its Form 20-F, when that issuer previously used US GAAP for its primary financial statements filed with the SEC. The IPTF guidance addresses the concern that the reconciliations called for by IFRS 1, which are prepared using the issuer's local GAAP rather than US GAAP, would not have sufficient information to help US investors to bridge from the prior US GAAP financial statements filed with the SEC to IFRS. Accordingly, the IPTF guidance requires additional detailed reconciliations in these circumstances from US GAAP to IFRS either in a one step or a two step format.

The reconciliation requirements for each of the scenarios are described below:

- *SEC Foreign Private Issuers who currently report under their local GAAP and provide a reconciliation from their local GAAP to US GAAP* –In the year of adoption of IFRS, these entities will be allowed to file two years rather than three years of statements of income, shareholders' equity and cash flows prepared in accordance with IFRS. As part of the IFRS transition, these entities will provide the disclosures and reconciliations required under IFRS 1 including:

  - an equity reconciliation as at the transition balance sheet date and as at the comparative year-end balance sheet date;

  - a comprehensive income (or income statement) reconciliation for the comparative year; and

  - an explanation of material adjustments to the statement of cash flows for the comparative year.

  If the IFRS 1 disclosures and reconciliations are prepared using the local GAAP as the issuer's previous GAAP rather than US GAAP, no additional US GAAP to IFRS or US GAAP to local GAAP reconciliations will be required.

- *SEC foreign private issuers that currently report under US GAAP only* – Some SEC foreign private issuers currently use US GAAP as their primary GAAP in both their home jurisdiction and the United States without reconciliation. These registrants would also be eligible to file two years rather than three years of statements of comprehensive income, shareholders' equity and cash flows in their first set of IFRS financial statements. In the year of adoption of IFRS, these entities will be required to provide the IFRS 1 disclosures and reconciliations described above. Such disclosures will be prepared using US GAAP as the issuer's previous GAAP.

- *SEC foreign private issuers that currently report under local GAAP for local reporting and under US GAAP in their SEC Form 20-F filings (assuming these issuers adopt IFRS in the current period for both local and SEC reporting purposes)* –. These registrants would also be eligible to file two years rather than three years of statements of comprehensive income, shareholders' equity and cash flows in their first set of IFRS financial statements. Under IFRS 1, such entities might conclude their local GAAP is their previous GAAP and their IFRS 1 disclosures and reconciliations would be prepared on that basis. As a reconciliation from their local GAAP to US GAAP was not previously provided, the SEC will require additional disclosure in the Form 20-F to enable US investors to understand material reconciling items between US GAAP and IFRS in the year of adoption. Two possible forms of disclosure are acceptable:

  - *One-Step Format* – Registrants can provide an analysis of the differences between US GAAP and IFRS in a tabular format (consistent with Item 17 of Form 20-F) for the same time period and dates that the IFRS 1 reconciliations are required. The registrant must provide this disclosure for equity as at the beginning and end of the most recent comparative period to the year of adoption and of comprehensive income (or profit or loss) for the most recent comparative year. A description of the differences between US GAAP and IFRS for the statement of cash flows is not necessary because registrants are not required to reconcile IAS 7 cash flow statements to those prepared under US GAAP.

- *Two-Step Format* – Registrants can choose to disclose a two-step reconciliation which would include a quantitative analysis of the differences between US GAAP and their local GAAP and between their local GAAP to IFRS. The registrant must provide these reconciliations for equity as of the beginning and end of the most recent comparative period to the year of adoption of IFRS and for comprehensive income (or profit or loss) for the most recent comparative year. Registrants will also be required to provide an explanation of the material differences between the cash flow statement under US GAAP and the cash flow statement under their local GAAP for the most recent comparative period to the year of adoption of IFRS.

- *SEC foreign private issuers that currently report under IFRS for local reporting and under US GAAP in their SEC Form 20-F filings (assuming these issuers adopted IFRS for local reporting in a period that preceded the earliest period for which audited financial statements are required in their SEC filing)* – These registrants would not be eligible to file two years of statements of comprehensive income, shareholders' equity and cash flows the first time they file IFRS financial statements with the SEC, since they are not first-time adopters of IFRS. Rather, they are required to present a complete set of IFRS financial statements for all periods required by the Form 20-F. In addition, these issuers will be required to present a reconciliation that enables US investors to bridge their previous US GAAP to IFRS. Such a reconciliation will be similar to the One-Step Format described above, except that the periods presented will be for equity as of the most recent comparative period presented and for comprehensive income (or profit or loss) for the two most recent comparative periods. However, if the issuers are required to present a balance sheet as of the end of the earliest comparative period, the reconciliation will also be required of the equity as of the end of that period.

8.2   Disclosure of IFRS information in financial statements for periods prior to an entity's first IFRS reporting period

8.2.1   CESR recommendation

In December 2003, the Committee of European Securities Regulators (CESR) published a recommendation that encourages European listed companies 'to provide markets with appropriate and useful information during the transition phase from local accounting standards to International Financial Reporting Standards', which a first-time adopter may want to follow or use as a starting point in developing its own disclosures.[378] The recommendation provides helpful guidance about disclosures that an entity may want to include in its financial statements and interim reports just before and just after its transition to IFRSs. The key recommendations are as follows:

- in its previous GAAP financial statements for the period prior to its date of transition, an entity should disclose its plan and degree of achievement in its move towards IFRSs;

- in its last financial statements under its previous GAAP an entity should present the reconciliations from previous GAAP to IFRSs and an explanatory note to explain the effect of the transition;

- in its IFRS interim reporting before its first full IFRS financial statements, an entity should present the primary financial statements for the most recent comparative period both under IFRSs and its previous GAAP (the so-called 'bridge approach'); and

- in its first IFRS financial statements, an entity should present the disclosures required by IFRS 1 (see 6.3 above). In addition, CESR also considers the 'bridge approach' equally acceptable for the annual financial statements.

8.2.2   IFRS guidance

Although IFRS 1 provides detailed rules on disclosures to be made in an entity's first IFRS financial statements and in interim reports covering part of its first IFRS reporting period, it does not provide any guidance on presenting a reconciliation to IFRSs in financial reports before the start of the first IFRS reporting period. An entity wishing to disclose information on the impact of IFRSs in its last financial statements under its previous GAAP cannot claim that such information is prepared and presented in accordance with IFRSs because it does not disclose all information required in full IFRS financial statements and it does not disclose comparative information.

As the extract below illustrates, in practice, some entities get around this problem by disclosing pro forma IFRS information and stating that the pro forma information does not comply with IFRSs.

Extract 5.16: ARINSO International SA (2003)

2003 IFRS Consolidated Financial Information [extract]

1. OPENING BALANCE AT JANUARY 1, 2003 [extract]

In 2003, ARINSO decided to anticipate the adoption of the International Financial Reporting Standards (earlier called International Accounting Standards (IAS)). These standards will become mandatory in 2005 for the consolidated financial statements of all companies listed on stock exchanges within the European Union.

As of 2004 ARINSO will publish quarterly reports in full compliance with IFRS. In order to have comparable figures as requested by IFRS, the 2003 financial statements were already prepared on an IFRS basis. In 2003, the impact of the IFRS conversion on the quarterly figures was published in our press releases.

The main differences between Belgian Generally Accepted Accounting Principles (GAAP) and IFRS as well as a reconciliation of the equity to IFRS at the date of conversion are presented hereunder.

---

3. IFRS VALUATION RULES [extract]

3.2 Adoption of the IFRS

The IFRS standards will be adopted for the first time in the consolidated financial statements for the year ended December 31, 2004. The standard for the first time application of the IFRS, published by the IASB in June 2003, was utilized in the pro forma consolidated IFRS balance sheet, income statement and cash flow statement published for the year ended December 31, 2003.

The information related to accounting year 2003 was converted from Belgian GAAP to IFRS in view of the comparison of information next year. The 2004 annual report will include all necessary comparable information.

Free translation of the Statutory Auditor's Report submitted to the shareholders, originally prepared in Dutch, on the restatement of the consolidated balance sheet, the profit and loss account and cash flow statement from accounting principles generally accepted in Belgium into IFRS [extract]

The financial statements provided, which do not include all notes to the financial statements in accordance with IFRS, have been prepared under the responsibility of the company's management, and do not comply with IFRS.

---

9   FUTURE DEVELOPMENTS

9.1   Consequential amendments

The IASB is currently pursuing a number of projects that are likely to result in certain amendments to IFRS 1:

- in March 2009, the IASB issued the exposure draft *Income Tax*, which proposes certain exceptions and exemptions to avoid full retrospective application of IAS 12;[379]

- in March 2009, the IASB issued the exposure draft *Derecognition (proposed amendments to IAS 39 and IFRS 7)*, which proposes to amend the exception on derecognition of financial assets and financial liabilities. The amendment proposes to permit prospective application of the new guidance on derecognition and provides transitional relief regarding the disclosures required by IFRS 7 – *Financial Instruments: Disclosures*;[380]

- in May 2009, the IASB issued the exposure draft *Fair Value Measurement*, which proposes minor consequential amendments to IFRS 1;[381]

- in July 2009, the IASB issued the exposure draft *Financial Instruments: Classification and Measurement*, which proposes consequential amendments to the exemptions relating to the classification of financial instruments;[382] and

- in August 2009, the IASB issued the exposure draft *Improvements to IFRSs*, which proposes two amendments to IFRS 1 that deal with:[383]

  - accounting policy changes in the year of adoption (see 7.2.1 A above); and

  - revaluation basis as deemed cost (see 5.5.3 C above).

9.2   Transitional relief for newly converting countries

While the IASB took account of the requests for relief from its European constituency in developing IFRS 1, it is now discussing issues that arise from the differences between IFRSs and the GAAPs of countries that will convert in the near future.

Accordingly, in September 2008, the IASB published the exposure draft *Additional Exemptions for First-time Adopters: Proposed amendments to IFRS 1*, which addressed a several issues that Canadian entities would be likely to face in adopting IFRSs. In July 2009, this resulted in the IASB issuing an amendment to IFRS 1 – *Additional Exemptions for First-time Adopters* (Amendments to IFRS 1) – that deals with (1) the measurement of oil and gas assets, (2) leases and (3) decommissioning provisions.[384]

The amendment regarding rate-regulated entities, which was included in the exposure draft, was deferred in May 2009 by the Board and became part of the rate-regulated activities project.[385] In July 2009, the IASB published the exposure draft *Rate-regulated Activities*, which proposes to add the following exemption for rate-regulated activities to IFRS 1:

> 'Entities with rate-regulated activities as defined in [draft] IFRS X Rate-regulated Activities may hold, or have previously held, items of property, plant and equipment or intangible assets for use in those activities. The carrying amount of such items sometimes includes amounts that were included in accordance with previous GAAP that would be recognised separately as regulatory assets in accordance with [draft] IFRS X. If this is the case, a first-time adopter may elect to use the carrying amount of such an item at the date of transition to IFRSs as deemed cost. An entity may use this election or that relating to borrowing costs in paragraph D23 but not both.'[386]

At the time of writing the IASB expected to issue a final standard on rate-regulated activities in the second quarter of 2010.[387]

10   CONCLUSION

It was always clear that a first-time adoption standard driven by the desire to avoid undue cost and effort would have to include exemptions that would permit first-time adopters to apply IFRSs in a practical manner. The objectives that the IASB sets out in the standard are to ensure that an entity's first IFRS financial statements and its first IFRS interim financial reports contain high quality financial information that:

'(a)   is transparent for users and comparable over all periods presented;

(b)   provides a suitable starting point for accounting in accordance with IFRS; and

(c)   can be generated at a cost that does not exceed the benefits to users.'[388]

It seemed unavoidable that these objectives would be subject to practical reality. Inevitably, the range of options available in IFRS 1 has meant that similar entities have produced dissimilar IFRS financial statements. For example, the first-time adoption rules on business combination, hedge accounting, derecognition and estimates have resulted in financial statements that still owe much to the first-time adopter's previous

GAAP. Nevertheless, the effect of these exemptions and exceptions fades quickly once an entity has been reporting under IFRSs for a few years.

In the long run, only the effect of the business combinations and 'fair value or revaluation as deemed cost' exemptions will be enduring. However, even the impact of those exemptions will be relatively insignificant compared with, for example, the effect an acquisition can have on the comparability of financial statements from one period to another.

IFRS 1 has made the transition to IFRSs much more straightforward than would ever have been possible under the theoretically pure, but practically unworkable, SIC-8. Still, some first-time adopters of IFRSs will have concerns about, for example, the complexity of the first-time adoption exemption for share-based payments. Others will complain about the unfairness of a business combination exemption that does not allow any adjustment to goodwill for items other than intangible assets and impairments.

IFRS 1 continues to be a living document as is evidenced by the structural changes made to it over the past twelve months. IFRS 1 (as revised in 2008) which was published in November 2008 (see 1.1.3 above) is a welcome improvement over the previous version of the standard, which had become too complex and unclear. Similarly the amendment to IFRS 1 – *Additional Exemptions for First-time Adopters* (Amendments to IFRS 1), which addresses several issues that Canadian entities would be likely to face in adopting IFRSs, is both helpful and timely.

We hope that the IASB will continue to take a practical approach to first-time adoption that steers a reasonable course between practicality and theoretical perfection.

References

1 IFRS 1, *First-Time Adoption of International Financial Reporting Standards*, IASB.

2 Regulation (EC) No 1606/2002 of the European Parliament and of the Council of 19 July 2002 on the application of international accounting standards, article 4 defines these companies as follows: 'For each financial year starting on or after 1 January 2005, companies governed by the law of a Member State shall prepare their consolidated accounts in conformity with the international accounting standards adopted in accordance with the procedure laid down in Article 6(2) if, at their balance sheet date, their securities are admitted to trading on a regulated market of any Member State within the meaning of Article 1(13) of Council Directive 93/22/EEC of 10 May 1993 on investment services in the securities field.'

3 SIC-8, *First-Time Application of IASs as the Primary Basis of Accounting*, SIC, July 1998, para. 3.

4 ED 1, *First-time Application of International Financial Reporting Standards*, IASB, July 2002.

5 IFRS 1 (2008), *First-time Adoption of International Financial Reporting Standards*, IASB, 2008 Bound Volume, para. IN1.

6 IFRS 1, para. BC3.

7 IFRS 1, para. BC9.

8 IFRS 1, para. BC10.

9 IFRS 1, para. BC14.

10 *IASB Update*, IASB, February 2007, p. 3.

11 IFRS 1, para. IN2.

12 IFRS 1, para. 1.
13 IFRS 1, para. 3 and Appendix A.
14 IFRS 1, para. 5.
15 IFRS 1, para. 3.
16 IFRS 1, para. 3.
17 IFRS 1, para. 4.
18 IFRS 1, para. BC5.
19 IFRS 1, para. BC6.
20 IFRS for SMEs, *International Financial Reporting Standard for Small and Medium-sized Entities*, IASB, July 2009, para. 35.2.
21 IFRS 1, para. 3(a).
22 IFRS 1, Appendix A.
23 IFRS 1, para. 2(a).
24 IFRS 1, para. 2(b).
25 IAS 34, *Interim Financial Reporting*, IASB, para. 3.
26 IFRS 1, Appendix A.
27 IFRS 1, Appendix A.
28 *International Practices Task Force – November 25, 2008 – Highlights*, Center for Audit Quality Washington Office, 25 November 2008, pp. 2-10.
29 IFRS 1, para. 21.
30 IAS 1, *Presentation of Financial Statements*, IASB, para. 37.
31 IFRS 1, Appendix A.
32 IFRS 1, para. 19.
33 IFRS 1, para. 19.
34 IFRS 1, para. 34.
35 IFRS 1, paras. 35-39.
36 Amendments to IFRS 1, *Additional Exemptions for First-time Adopters*, IASB, July 2009, para. 39A.
37 IFRS 1, para. 6.
38 IFRS 1, para. 7.
39 IFRS 1, paras. BC17-BC18.
40 IFRS 1, para. 8.
41 IFRS 1, para. BC11.
42 IFRS 1, para. 8.
43 *IFRIC Update*, IFRIC, May 2009, p. 3.
44 IFRS 1, para. 10.
45 IFRS 1, para. 11.
46 IAS 8, *Accounting Policies, Changes in Accounting Estimates and Errors*, IASB, paras. 10-12.
47 IFRS 1, para. 9.
48 IFRS 1, para. BC14.
49 *IFRIC Update*, IFRIC, October 2004, p. 3.
50 Framework, *Framework for the Preparation and Presentation of Financial Statements*, para. 44.
51 IFRS 1, para. BC27.
52 IFRS 1, para. 12.
53 IFRS 1, para. 13.
54 IFRS 1, para. D1.
55 IFRS 1, para. IN5.
56 IFRS 1, paras. 13 and B1.
57 IFRS 1, para. IN5.
58 IFRS 1, para. D1.
59 IFRIC 18, *Transfers of Assets from Customers*, para. A1 (para. D1).
60 IFRS 1, para. D1.
61 IFRS 1, para. B1.
62 IFRS 1, para. 14.
63 IAS 8, para. 5.
64 IFRS 1, para. BC84.
65 IFRS 1, para. IG58B.
66 IFRS 1, para. 17.
67 IFRS 1, paras. 15 and IG2.
68 IFRS 1, para. IG3.
69 IFRS 1, para. IG3.
70 IFRS 1, paras. 16 and IG3.
71 IFRS 1, para. IG4.
72 IFRS 1, para. 26.
73 IFRS 1, IG Example 1.
74 IFRS 1, para. B2.
75 IFRS 1, para. B3.
76 IFRS 1, paras. IG53-IG54.
77 IFRS 1, para. IG53.
78 IFRS 1, para. B1(b).
79 IFRS 1, para. BC75.
80 IFRS 1, para. BC76.
81 IFRS 1, para. BC77.
82 IFRS 1, para. B4.
83 IFRS 1, para. IG58A.
84 IFRS 1, para. IG58B.
85 IFRS 1, para. B4.
86 IFRS 1, para. B5.
87 IFRS 1, para. B5.
88 IFRS 1, para. B6.
89 IFRS 1, para. BC75.
90 IFRS 1, para. IG60B.
91 ED 1, para. C3(c)(i).
92 ED 1, para. C4.
93 IFRS 1, para. IG58A.
94 IFRS 1, para. IG60A.
95 IAS 39 (amended 2000), *Financial Instruments: Recognition and Measurement*, IASB, December 1998 (amended 2000), para. 172(e) and ED 1, para. C3(b).
96 IFRS 1, para. IG60.
97 IAS 39, *Financial Instruments: Recognition and Measurement*, IASB, para. F.4.2.
98 IFRS 1, para. B6.
99 IFRS 1, para. IG60B.
100 IFRS 1, para. B7.
101 IAS 27, *Consolidated and Separate Financial Statements*, IASB, para. 45.
102 IFRS 1, paras. B7 and C1.
103 IFRS 1, para. D1.
104 IFRS 1, para. 13 and Appendix C.
105 IFRS 1, para. C1.
106 IFRS 1, para. BC32.
107 IFRS 1, paras. BC33-BC34.
108 IFRS 1, para. BC34.

109 IFRS 3, *Business Combinations*, IASB, para. 64.
110 IFRS 1, para. C5.
111 IFRS 1, para. C4(a).
112 IFRS 1, Appendix C.
113 IFRS 3, Appendix A.
114 IFRS 3, Appendix A.
115 IFRS 3, para. 3.
116 IFRS 3, para. 2(c).
117 IFRS 1, para. C4(c).
118 IFRS 1, para. C4(b).
119 IFRS 1, paras. C4(b) and C4(g)(i).
120 IFRS 1, IG Example 7.
121 IFRS 1, IG Example 3.
122 IFRS 1, para. C4(d).
123 IFRS 1, para. C4(e).
124 IFRS 1, para. BC36.
125 IFRS 1, para. C4(h)(i).
126 IFRS 1, para. C4(f).
127 IFRS 1, para. C4(f).
128 IFRS 1, para. BC35.
129 IFRS 1, IG Example 2.
130 IFRS 1, para. C4(g).
131 IFRS 1, para. C4(g).
132 IFRS 1, para. BC39.
133 IFRS 1, para. BC38.
134 IFRS 1, para. C4(h).
135 IFRS 1, para. 10.
136 IFRS 3, para. B69(e).
137 IFRS 1, para. C4(i).
138 IFRS 1, IG Example 5.
139 IFRS 1, para. C4(i).
140 IFRS 1, para. C4(i)(ii).
141 IFRS 1, paras. C2 and IG21A.
142 IAS 21, *The Effects of Changes in Foreign Exchange Rates*, IASB, para. 47.
143 IFRS 1, para. C2.
144 IFRS 1, para. C3.
145 IFRS 1, para. C4(j).
146 IFRS 1, IG Example 6.
147 IFRS 1, para. C4(k).
148 IAS 27, para. 4.
149 IFRS 1, para. C4(k).
150 IFRS 1, IG Example 4.
151 *IASB Update*, IASB, October 2005, p. 1.
152 IFRS 1, para. D2.
153 IFRS 1, para. D2.
154 IFRS 1, para. D2.
155 IFRS 1, para. D3.
156 IAS 40, *Investment Property*, IASB, para. B67(h).
157 IFRS 1, para. BC63B.
158 Framework, paras. 25-28.
159 Framework, paras. 25-28.
160 IFRS 1, para. D2 and IFRS 2, *Share-Based Payments*, IASB , paras. 26-29.
161 IFRS 1, para. D4.
162 IFRS 4, *Insurance Contracts*, IASB, para. 22.
163 IFRS 4, para. 44.
164 IFRS 4, paras. 42-43.
165 IFRS 1, para. BC42.
166 IFRS 1, paras. D5-D6.
167 IFRS 1, para. D5.
168 IFRS 1, para. D7.
169 IFRS 1, para. D7.
170 IFRS 1, para. D7.
171 IFRS 1, para. IG50.
172 IFRS 1, para. D5.
173 IAS 16, *Property, Plant and Equipment*, IASB, para. 9.
174 IFRS 1, para. BC45.
175 IFRS 1, para. D5.
176 IFRS 1, para. D6.
177 IFRS 1, para. BC47.
178 IFRS 1, para. BC47.
179 IFRS 1, paras. IG8-IG9.
180 IFRS 1, para. BC43.
181 IFRS 1, para. D8.
182 IFRS 1, paras. D5-D7.
183 IFRS 1, para. D8.
184 IFRS 1, para. BC46.
185 IFRS 1, para. 10.
186 IFRS 1, para. D8.
187 IFRS 1, para. D8.
188 IFRS 1, para. D8.
189 IFRS 1, para. D8.
190 *Exposure Draft – Improvements to IFRSs: Proposed amendments to IFRS 1 First-Time Adoption*, IASB, August 2009, pp. 11-12 (IFRS 1, para. D8).
191 *Exposure Draft – Improvements to IFRSs: Proposed amendments to IFRS 1 First-Time Adoption*, p. 14 (IFRS 1, para. BC4).
192 *Exposure Draft – Improvements to IFRSs: Proposed amendments to IFRS 1 First-Time Adoption*, pp. 11-12 (IFRS 1, para. D8).
193 *Exposure Draft – Improvements to IFRSs: Proposed amendments to IFRS 1 First-Time Adoption*, p. 14 (IFRS 1, para. BC5).
194 *Exposure Draft – Improvements to IFRSs: Proposed amendments to IFRS 1 First-Time Adoption*, p. 14 (IFRS 1, para. BC6).
195 *Exposure Draft – Improvements to IFRSs: Proposed amendments to IFRS 1 First-Time Adoption*, p. 11 (IFRS 1, para. 39B).
196 *Exposure Draft – Improvements to IFRSs: Proposed amendments to IFRS 1 First-Time Adoption*, p. 11 (IFRS 1, para. 39B).
197 Amendments to IFRS 1, para. BC47A.
198 Amendments to IFRS 1, para. BC47B.
199 Amendments to IFRS 1, para. D8A.
200 Amendments to IFRS 1, para. D8A.
201 Amendments to IFRS 1, para. 31A.
202 Amendments to IFRS 1, para. D8A.
203 Amendments to IFRS 1, para. 39A.
204 IFRS 1, para. IG14.

205 IAS 17, *Leases*, para. 13.
206 IFRS 1, para. IG16.
207 IFRIC 4, *Determining whether an Arrangement contains a Lease*, para. 17 and IFRS 1, paras. D9, IG204-IG205 and BC63D.
208 IFRS 1, IG Example 202.
209 Amendments to IFRS 1, para. BC63DA.
210 Amendments to IFRS 1, para. D9A.
211 Amendments to IFRS 1, para. IG206.
212 Amendments to IFRS 1, para. 39A.
213 IFRS 1, para. D10.
214 IFRS 1, para. BC48.
215 IFRS 1, paras. D10 and IG18.
216 IFRS 1, paras. BC50-BC51.
217 IFRS 1, para. BC51.
218 IFRS 1, paras. BC51 and IG21.
219 IFRS 1, para. IG19.
220 IFRS 1, para. IG20.
221 IFRS 1, para. BC52.
222 IFRS 1, para. D11.
223 IAS 21, para. 48 and IFRS 1, para. D12.
224 IAS 21, paras. 32 and 39 and IFRS 1, para. D12.
225 IFRS 1, para. D13.
226 IFRS 1, para. D13.
227 IFRS 1, para. D12.
228 IFRS 1, para. IG26.
229 IFRS 1, para. IG27(a).
230 IFRS 1, para. D17.
231 IFRS 1, para. C4(j).
232 IFRS 1, paras. C4(j) and IG27(b).
233 IFRS 1, para. IG27(c).
234 IFRS 1, para. IG28.
235 IFRS 1, paras. BC58A-BC58C.
236 IFRS 1, para. D14.
237 IFRS 1, para. D15.
238 IFRS 1, para. 38.
239 IFRS 1, para. BC59.
240 IFRS 1, paras. D16-D17.
241 IFRS 1, para. D16.
242 IFRS 1, para. D16.
243 IFRS 1, IG Example 8.
244 IFRS 1, para. BC62.
245 IFRS 1, para. IG31.
246 IFRS 1, para. D16.
247 IFRS 1, para. D17.
248 IFRS 1, para. BC63.
249 IFRS 1, IG Example 9.
250 IFRS 1, para. IG30.
251 IFRS 1, para. D17.
252 IFRS 1, para. D18.
253 IFRS 1, paras. IG35-IG36.
254 IFRS 1, para. D19(a).
255 IFRS 1, para. 29.
256 IFRS 1, paras. BC81-BC82.
257 IFRS 1, para. D19(b).
258 IFRS 1 (2008), para. 25A(b) to (d).
259 IFRS 1, para. 29.

260 IFRS 1, para. IG56.
261 IFRS 1, para. IG56(a).
262 IFRS 1, paras. IG56(d)(i) and (ii).
263 IFRS 1, para. IG56(b).
264 IFRS 1, para. IG57.
265 IFRS 1, para. BC72.
266 IFRS 1, para. BC73.
267 IFRS 1, para. IG56(e).
268 IFRS 1, para. IG59.
269 IFRS 1, para. BC83.
270 IFRS 1, para. IG56(c) and IG58A.
271 IFRS 1, para. BC65.
272 IFRS 1, para. BC66.
273 IFRS 1, para. IG55. The implementation guidance says the entire combined contract should be treated as held for trading (not designated at fair value through profit or loss). This reflects an earlier version of IAS 39 as the implementation guidance was not updated to reflect a subsequent amendment.
274 IFRIC 9, *Reassessment of Embedded Derivatives*, para. 8.
275 IFRS 1, para. IG58.
276 IFRS 1, para. BC83A.
277 IFRS 1, para. D20.
278 IFRS 1, para. BC83A.
279 IAS 16, para. 16(c).
280 IFRS 1, para. IG13.
281 IFRS 1, paras. IG 13 and IG201-IG203.
282 IFRS 1, para. D21.
283 Amendments to IFRS 1, para. D21A.
284 Amendments to IFRS 1, para. BC63CA.
285 Amendments to IFRS 1, para. 39A.
286 IFRIC 12, *Service Concession Arrangements*, paras. 1 and 2.
287 IFRS 1, para. D22.
288 IFRIC 12, paras. 29 and 30.
289 IAS 23, para. 27 and IFRS 1, paras. D23 and IG23.
290 *IASB Update*, IASB, December 2008, p. 4.
291 IFRS 1, paras. D23 and IG23.
292 IFRS 1, para. IG23.
293 IFRIC 18, para. BC25.
294 IFRIC 18, para. A2 (IFRS 1, para. D24).
295 IFRS 1, para. 20.
296 IAS 1, para. 38.
297 IFRS 1, para. 21.
298 IFRS 1, para. 22.
299 IFRS 1, para. 22.
300 IFRS 1, para. 23.
301 IFRS 1, para. BC91.
302 IAS 1, para. 108.
303 IFRS 1, para. 28.
304 IFRS 1, para. 24.
305 IFRS 1, para. 24.
306 IFRS 1, para. 25.
307 IFRS 1, para. 27.

308 IFRS 1, paras. 25-26.
309 IFRS 1, para. IG63.
310 IFRS 1, para. 24.
311 IFRS 1, para. BC94.
312 IFRS 1, paras. 32-33.
313 IAS 39, para. 9.
314 IFRS 1, para. 29.
315 IFRS 1, para. 30.
316 IFRS 1, para. 31.
317 Amendments to IFRS 1, para. 31A.
318 IFRS 1, para. 32.
319 IFRS 1, para. IG37(b).
320 IFRS 1, IG Example 10.
321 IFRS 1, para. 33.
322 IFRS 1, para. 33.
323 IAS 7, *Statement of Cash Flows*, para. 8.
324 IFRS 1, paras. 5 and 27.
325 IFRS 1, para. 7.
326 *Exposure Draft – Improvements to IFRSs: Proposed amendments to IFRS 1 First-Time Adoption*, p. 10 (IFRS 1, para. 27).
327 *Exposure Draft – Improvements to IFRSs: Proposed amendments to IFRS 1 First-Time Adoption*, p. 10 (IFRS 1, para. 27A).
328 *Exposure Draft – Improvements to IFRSs: Proposed amendments to IFRS 1 First-Time Adoption*, p. 11 (IFRS 1, para. 32(c)).
329 *Exposure Draft – Improvements to IFRSs: Proposed amendments to IFRS 1 First-Time Adoption*, p. 11 (IFRS 1, para. 39B).
330 IFRS 1, paras. IG5-IG6.
331 IAS 12, *Income Taxes*, IASB, para. 15.
332 IAS 12, paras. 15 and 24.
333 IFRS 1, para. IG62.
334 IFRS 1, para. IG7.
335 IAS 16, para. 51.
336 IFRS 1, para. IG10.
337 IFRS 1, para. IG11.
338 IFRS 1, para. IG12.
339 IAS 16, para. 9.
340 IAS 16, para. 12.
341 IAS 16, para. 13.
342 IAS 16, para. 43.
343 IFRS 1, para. IG17.
344 IAS 21, paras. 8-14.
345 IAS 21, para. 11.
346 *IFRIC Update*, IFRIC, October 2004, p. 3.
347 IAS 23, para. BC20.
348 IAS 23, para. BC22.
349 IAS 23, paras. BC23-BC24.
350 IFRS 1, para. C4(g)(ii).
351 IFRS 1, para. C5.
352 IFRS 1, para. BC67.
353 IFRS 1, para. IG32.
354 IFRS 1, para. IG33.
355 IFRS 1, para. IG34.
356 IFRS 1, para. C4(g)(ii).
357 IFRS 1, para. BC45.

358 IFRS 1, para. IG40.
359 IFRS 1, para. IG41.
360 IFRS 1, para. IG43.
361 IFRS 1, para. IG40.
362 IFRS 1, para. IG41.
363 IFRS 1, paras. 14-17.
364 IAS 38, para. 21. and IFRS 1, para. IG45.
365 IFRS 1, para. IG44.
366 IAS 38, para. 71.
367 IFRS 1, para. IG46.
368 IFRS 1, para. IG47.
369 IFRS 1, para. IG47.
370 IFRS 1, para. IG48.
371 IFRS 1, para. IG49.
372 IFRS 1, para. IG51.
373 IAS 38, *Intangible Assets*, IASB, para. 104.
374 Release No. 33-8567, *First-Time Application of International Financial Reporting Standards*, Securities and Exchange Commission (SEC), 12 April 2005.
375 Release No. 33-8879, *Acceptance from Foreign Private Issuers of Financial Statements Prepared in Accordance with International Financial Reporting Standards without Reconciliation to U.S. GAAP*, Securities and Exchange Commission, 4 March 2008.
376 Release No. 33-8879.
377 Release No. 33-8567.
378 *European Regulation on the Application of IFRS in 2005 – Recommendation for Additional Guidance Regarding the Transition to IFRS (CESR/03-323e)*, Committee of European Securities Regulators (CESR), December 2003.
379 *Exposure Draft: Income Tax*, IASB March 2009, pp. 50 and 51.
380 *Exposure Draft: Derecognition (proposed amendments to IAS 39 and IFRS 7)*, IASB, March 2009, pp. 47 and 51.
381 *Exposure Draft: Fair Value Measurement*, IASB May 2009, pp. 50, 51 and 61.
382 *Exposure Draft: Financial Instruments: Classification and Measurement – Draft amendments to other IFRSs and guidance*, IASB, July 2009, pp. 4 and 5.
383 *Exposure Draft – Improvements to IFRSs: Proposed amendments to IFRS 1 First-Time Adoption*, p. 9.
384 *Additional Exemptions for First-time Adopters: amendments to IFRS 1*, IASB, July 2009.
385 *IASB Update*, IASB, May 2009, pp. 2-3.
386 *Exposure Draft: Rate-regulated Activities*, IASB, July 2009, p. 24.
387 *IASB Work Plan – projected timetable as at 1 August 2009*, IASB, www.iasb.org.uk, 7 September 2009.
388 IFRS 1, para. 1.

Chapter 6

Consolidated financial statements

1   THE CONCEPT OF A GROUP

1.1   Background

It is a commercial practice of long standing for an entity to conduct its business not only directly but also through strategic investments in other entities. IFRS, and most national GAAPs, broadly distinguish three types of such strategic investment:

- entities controlled by the reporting entity (subsidiaries). These include entities that, although not owned by the reporting entity, are operating for its benefit (special purpose entities);

- entities jointly controlled by the reporting entity and one or more third parties (joint ventures);[1] and

- entities that, while not controlled or jointly controlled by the reporting entity, are subject to significant influence by it (associates).

This raises the question of how such strategic investments should be accounted for. There is a consensus that it is not adequate to account for such entities merely by recording income received from them, and that some mechanism is required to reflect their activities directly in the financial statements of reporting entities that hold them. Under IFRS:

- an entity and its subsidiaries are collectively referred to as a 'group', and accounted for in accordance with IAS 27 (as amended in 2008) – *Consolidated and Separate Financial Statements* – or IAS 27 (2007) – *Consolidated and Separate Financial Statements* – using consolidated financial statements (which are addressed in the remainder of this chapter). As discussed in more detail at 6 below, the amendments made in 2008 to IAS 27 should be applied for annual periods beginning on or after 1 July 2009;[2]

- associates are accounted for in accordance with IAS 28 – *Investments in Associates* – using equity accounting (which is addressed in Chapter 11); and

- joint ventures are accounted for in accordance with IAS 31 – *Interests in Joint Ventures* – using a variety of methods, depending on their structure (see Chapter 12).

IFRS also acknowledges that entities may wish (or be obliged by local legal requirements) to present additional financial statements in which such strategic investments are accounted for on some other basis, such as cost or valuation. Whilst IFRS does not require the preparation of such additional financial statements (referred to as 'separate financial statements'), it does prescribe the accounting treatment to be followed where they are prepared and stated to be in compliance with IFRS.[3] Separate financial statements are discussed in Chapter 8.

1.2   The objectives of consolidated financial statements

Consolidated financial statements are designed to extend the reporting entity so as to embrace other entities which are subject to its control. They involve treating the net assets and activities of subsidiaries held by a reporting entity as if they were part of the holding entity's own net assets and activities. The overall aim is to present the results and state of affairs of the reporting entity and its subsidiaries (referred to as a group) as if they were those of a single entity.

As noted above, the standard dealing with this topic under IFRS is IAS 27, which requires a parent (i.e. an entity with one or more subsidiaries)[4] to present consolidated financial statements in which all subsidiaries are included.[5]

1.3   What is a subsidiary?

The definition of a subsidiary is fundamental to any discussion of consolidated financial statements, since this determines the scope and extent of the reporting entity which is the subject of the consolidated financial statements. When the concept of consolidated financial statements was originally introduced in the first half of the last century, the question of whether or not an entity was a subsidiary was generally determined by legal ownership. In other words, any entity in which the reporting entity held more than half the equity would be regarded as subject to the reporting entity's control (and therefore a subsidiary), whereas any entity in which the reporting entity held half or less of the equity would be regarded as not subject to the reporting entity's control (and therefore a not subsidiary).

However, this 'ownership' model proved increasingly inadequate, particularly with the growth of 'off-balance sheet' financing from the 1970s onwards. It proved relatively easy for a reporting entity to set up another entity in which it had little or no legal ownership interest, but which it effectively controlled (for example, because the shares were owned by parties who could be expected to act in accordance with the reporting entity's wishes). It became common for companies to use such entities as vehicles for undertaking borrowings that did not appear in the consolidated financial statements, because the borrowing entity, although controlled by the reporting entity, did not meet the definition of a subsidiary under the ownership model.

As a result, there emerged a new concept: the question of whether or not an entity is a subsidiary for consolidation purposes should be determined not by legal ownership, but by the existence of economic control. The first major codification of an 'economic control' model for consolidated financial statements was in the EU Seventh Company Law Directive in 1983.

However, the concept of economic control in the Seventh Directive was widely drawn. For example, the Directive allowed (but did not require) consolidation of an entity by a shareholder that in practice appointed the majority of the board, even if it did not have the majority of the voting rights. This was to cater with the situation where, due to the wide dispersal of the majority of shareholdings, a significant minority shareholder can exercise *de facto* control. The Directive also permitted, but did not require, a further extension of the 'economic control' model to so-called 'horizontal' groups – i.e. entities with no shareholding relationship but under common control (e.g. because they are owned by the same individual). IAS 27 does not require consolidation of 'horizontal' groups (see 3.4 below), but the treatment of entities over which there is *de facto* control is somewhat more ambiguous (see 2.1.3 below).

The consolidation model in IAS 27 is based primarily on the legal and contractual rights of shareholders, rather than on a pure 'ownership' model or 'economic control' model. However, aspects of an 'economic control' model are also in evidence, particularly in the SIC interpretation SIC-12 – *Consolidation – Special Purpose Entities* (see 2.2 below).[6]

1.4 Development of IAS 27

IAS 27 was originally issued in April 1989 and has since been subject to various amendments. In December 2003, as part of the IASB's improvements project, the previous version of IAS 27 was withdrawn and superseded by a substantially revised version, which reduced the number of alternatives in accounting for subsidiaries in consolidated financial statements and in accounting for investments in the separate financial statements of a parent, venturer or investor.[7] In January 2008, IAS 27 was amended as part of the second phase of the business combinations project, which primarily changed the accounting for non-controlling interests and the loss of control of a subsidiary,[8] and in May 2008, the IABS issued *Cost of an Investment in a Subsidiary, Jointly Controlled Entity or Associate*, which deals with accounting in separate financial statements.

The IASB has a number of projects on its agenda that may result in changes to IAS 27 that are discussed at 7 below.

1.5 How consolidated and separate financial statements are dealt with in Chapters 6 to 8

The subject matter of this and the next two chapters is the requirement to prepare consolidated financial statements, the consolidation procedures to be applied, accounting for non-controlling (or minority) interests and the guidance concerning the preparation of separate financial statements. More specifically, these chapters address the requirements of IAS 27 (as amended in 2008), IAS 27 (2007) and SIC-12. The requirements of IFRS 3 (as revised in 2008) – *Business Combinations* – and IFRS 3 (2007) – *Business Combinations* – are discussed in Chapters 9 and 10.

The chapters dealing with consolidated and separated financial statements, and the topics covered by each, are as follows:

Chapter 6 – *Consolidated financial statements*

- the concept of a group
- development of IAS 27
- definition of a subsidiary
- requirement to prepare consolidated financial statements
- scope of consolidated financial statements
- disclosures in consolidated financial statements
- transitional issues

Chapter 7 – *Consolidation procedures and non-controlling interests*

- consolidation procedures
- accounting for changes in ownership interests (other than business combinations and common control transactions, which are dealt with in Chapters 9 and 10, respectively)
- accounting for non-controlling (or minority) interests
- accounting for call and put options over non-controlling (or minority) interests
- first-time adoption issues

Chapter 8 – *Separate and individual financial statements*

- requirements of separate financial statements
- disclosure requirements for separate financial statements
- individual financial statements

While the IASB made significant amendments to IAS 27 in 2008, many things have remained the unchanged. Hence, to the extent that the requirements of IAS 27 (as amended in 2008) and IAS 27 (2007) are similar or identical, they are discussed together and the standard is referred to as 'IAS 27'. However, where significant differences exist the requirements of both versions of IAS 27 are discussed separately in this chapter.

It should be noted that differences exist between the definitions and treatment of 'non-controlling interests' in IAS 27 (as amended in 2008) and 'minority interests' in IAS 27 (2007). However, in contexts where the terms 'non-controlling interests' and 'minority interests' are synonymous reference is made to 'non-controlling (or minority) interests'.

2   DEFINITION OF SUBSIDIARY

As indicated at 1.3 above, the definition of 'subsidiary' is fundamental to any discussion of consolidated financial statements. The question is also relevant to the subject of off-balance sheet financing, because frequently this definition determines whether the group balance sheet should include the accounts of an entity which holds certain assets and liabilities which management may not wish to include in the consolidated financial statements.

IAS 27 uses the following definition of subsidiary and related terms.

A *parent* is an entity with one or more subsidiaries.[9]

A *subsidiary* is an entity, including an unincorporated entity such as a partnership, that is controlled by another entity (known as the parent).[10]

A *group* is a parent and all its subsidiaries.[11]

Control is the power to govern the financial and operating policies of an entity so as to obtain benefits from its activities.[12]

2.1   Control

As can be seen, the definition of control effectively underpins the definition of parent and subsidiary, and IAS 27 therefore elaborates on it further.

2.1.1   *Primary indicators of control*

IAS 27 states that control is presumed to exist if the parent owns, directly or indirectly through subsidiaries, more than half of the voting power of an entity unless, in exceptional circumstances, it can be clearly demonstrated that such ownership does not constitute control. In assessing the existence of control, an entity should ignore any indirect interest over which it cannot exercise control, for example, because they are held via an associate or joint venture. Control is also considered to exist even when the parent does not own a majority of the voting rights when there is:

(a)   power over more than half of the voting rights by virtue of an agreement with other investors;

(b)   power to govern the financial and operating policies of the entity under a statute or an agreement;

(c)   power to appoint or remove the majority of the members of the board of directors or equivalent governing body and control of the entity is by that board or body; or

(d)   power to cast the majority of votes at meetings of the board of directors or equivalent governing body and control of the entity is by that board or body.[13]

IAS 27 does not elaborate on the situations in which it might be 'clearly demonstrated' that ownership of more than half the voting power does not constitute control. The most obvious, and common, example will be where, by virtue of one or more of (a) to (d) above, an entity is a subsidiary of another shareholder owning half or less of the voting power. Similarly, if another party has veto rights over, or the ability to block, substantive decisions of the majority holder that may mean that the majority holder effectively cannot exercise control. In this context, substantive decisions are the significant decisions made in the ordinary course of business that are normally expected to arise in directing and carrying out the entity's current business activities (e.g. the approval of the annual operating budget is expected to be in the ordinary course of business, and therefore the minority party's ability to veto that decision is likely to provide them with effective participation, provided that the right is substantive and that such veto results in the entity having to redraft and re-propose a new budget).

In complex situations where minority shareholders have rights of veto or approval over certain issues, it may be helpful to have regard to the analysis, for the purposes of US GAAP, in EITF 96-16 – *Investor's Accounting for an Investee When the Investor Has a Majority of the Voting Interest but the Minority Shareholder or Shareholders Have Certain Approval or Veto Rights*.[14] Broadly, EITF 96-16 draws a distinction between minority rights that essentially exist to protect the minority from potentially damaging actions by the majority shareholders (which would not normally impact on the control exercised by majority shareholders) and minority rights that result in active participation in day-to-day decisions of the entity (which may result in a rebuttal of the presumption that the majority shareholder has control). Whether the rights of non-controlling shareholders are protective or participative can be complex and will often require careful judgement. In some cases, the effect might be that the entity is in fact a joint venture between the majority and minority shareholder which should be accounted for in accordance with IAS 31 (see Chapter 12).

As discussed at 7.2.1 D below, in ED 10 – *Consolidated Financial Statements* – the IASB proposes to include guidance similar to EITF 96-16 in a future consolidation standard because 'the guidance is widely accepted and incorporating it in the proposed IFRS would help with international convergence.'[15]

The extract below from the financial statements of Vodafone illustrates how the existence of substantive participating rights held by non-controlling (or minority) shareholders may sometimes prevent the majority shareholder from exercising control.

Extract 6.1: Alliance Pharma plc (2008)

Notes to the financial statements [extract]

for year ended 31 December 2008

33. JOINT VENTURE [extract]

Name	Principal activity	Country of incorporation	% owned
Unigreg Ltd	Distribution of pharmaceutical products	British Virgin Islands	60

The Group considered the existence of substantive participating rights held by the minority shareholder which provide that shareholder with a veto right over the significant financial and operating policies of Unigreg Ltd and determined that, as a result of these rights, the Group does not have control over the financial and operating policies of Unigreg Ltd, despite the Group's 60% ownership interest.

The implementation guidance to IAS 27 notes that it is inherent in the definition of control than an entity cannot be controlled by more than one party (although it might be jointly controlled by more than one party). Accordingly, when two or more entities each hold significant voting rights (whether actual rights or potential rights – see 2.1.2 below), the factors in (a) to (d) above should be reassessed into order to determine which entity (if any) actually has control.[16]

IAS 27 emphasises that the reference to 'power' in the definition of 'control' above means the ability to do or affect something. Consequently, an entity has control over another entity when it currently has the ability to exercise that power, regardless of whether control is actively demonstrated or is passive in nature.[17] Passive control may be exercised over another entity through potential voting rights (see 2.1.2 below).

2.1.2   Potential voting rights

An entity may own share warrants, share call options, debt or equity instruments that are convertible into ordinary shares, or other similar instruments that have the potential, if exercised or converted, to give the entity voting power or reduce another party's voting power over the financial and operating policies of another entity (potential voting rights).[18]

IAS 27 requires an entity to consider the existence and effect of potential voting rights that are currently exercisable or convertible, including potential voting rights held by another entity (see B below), when assessing whether an entity has the power to govern the financial and operating policies of another entity.[19] As discussed further at B below, IAS 27 takes a very strict and, some might argue, rather form-based approach to determining what potential voting rights should be taken into account for this purpose.

A   Interaction with IAS 28 and IAS 31

IAS 28 and IAS 31 also require the existence and effect of potential voting rights to be taken into account in assessing whether an entity has, respectively, significant influence over, or joint control of, another entity. Accordingly, the guidance in IAS 27 on this issue, summarised below, is also relevant to IAS 28 and IAS 31.[20] However, IAS 27 notes that its guidance may be less relevant to IAS 31, since the issue of whether or not an entity is a joint venture depends primarily on the contractual relationship between the parties[21] (which would not typically be affected by the existence of potential voting rights).

B   What rights are 'currently exercisable'?

Potential voting rights are not currently exercisable or convertible when they cannot be exercised or converted until a future date or until the occurrence of a future event.[22] The effect of this requirement is illustrated by Example 6.1 below.

Example 6.1:   *Potential voting rights (1)*

An entity (A) holds 40% of another entity (B), together with loan notes in B convertible, at A's option, into further shares in B which, if issued, would give A a 60% interest in B. A can require conversion of its loan notes into shares at any time on or after the fifth anniversary of their issue.

Until that fifth anniversary occurs, A cannot exercise its conversion rights. They are therefore ignored, such that B would not (absent other circumstances) be a subsidiary of A. Once the fifth anniversary has occurred, A can exercise its option to convert and is therefore regarded as having the majority of the voting rights of B, such that B would (absent exceptional circumstances) become a subsidiary of A for the purposes of IAS 27.

A literal reading of IAS 27 might suggest that unless the potential voting right is exercisable immediately, it should be ignored in assessing control. In practice, however, many potential voting rights are not exercisable immediately but rather only exercisable after giving notice (e.g. options over the shares of unlisted entities often include a notice period of several days or a week). In our opinion the existence of a short notice period should be ignored in assessing whether rights are 'currently exercisable' and judgement should be exercised in determining whether potential voting rights are 'currently exercisable'.

The implementation guidance indicates that potential voting rights include not only those actually held by an entity (as in the example above), but also those to which the entity currently has the right of access, as illustrated by Example 6.2 below.[23]

Example 6.2:   *Potential voting rights (2)*

Entities A, B and C own 25%, 35% and 40% respectively of the ordinary shares that carry voting rights at a general meeting of shareholders of entity D. B and C also have share warrants that are exercisable at any time at a fixed price and provide potential voting rights. A has a call option to purchase these share warrants at any time for a nominal amount. If the call option is exercised, A would have the potential to increase its ownership interest, and thereby its voting rights, in D to 51% and dilute B's and C's interests to 23% and 26% respectively.

Although the share warrants are not owned by A, they are considered in assessing control because they are currently exercisable by B and C. Normally, if an action (e.g. purchase or exercise of another right) is required before an entity has ownership of a potential voting right, the potential voting right is not regarded as held by the entity. However, the share warrants are, in substance, held by A, because the terms of the call option are designed to ensure A's position. The combination of the call option and share warrants gives A the power to set the operating and financial policies of D, because A could currently exercise the option and share warrants.

Example 6.2 also illustrates the requirement of IAS 27 that the reporting entity must have regard not only to its own potential voting rights in an investee, but also to those of other shareholders. A potential practical issue here is that, in some more secretive jurisdictions, it might be difficult to obtain information about the potential voting power of other shareholders.

C   *Management intention and ability to exercise potential ownership rights*

IAS 27 adds some further points of clarification. In assessing whether potential voting rights contribute to control, an entity must examine all facts and circumstances (including the terms of exercise of the potential voting rights and any other contractual arrangements whether considered individually or in combination) that affect potential voting rights, except the intention of management and the financial ability to exercise or convert.[24]

The implementation guidance expands on this point at some length, but in the process adds some confusion. On the one hand, it gives some illustrative examples (the substance of which is reproduced as Examples 6.3 to 6.5 below) which suggest that this requirement is to be interpreted very strictly.[25]

Example 6.3:   *Potential voting rights (3)*

Entities A and B own 80% and 20% respectively of the ordinary shares that carry voting rights at a general meeting of shareholders of entity C. A sells one half of its interest to D and buys call options from D that are exercisable at any time at a premium to the market price when issued and, if exercised, would return to A its original 80% ownership interest and voting rights. Although the options are out of the money, they are currently exercisable and give A the power to continue to set the operating and financial policies of C, because A could exercise its options now. The existence of the potential voting rights is considered, and it is determined (absent other special circumstances) that A controls C.

Example 6.4:   *Potential voting rights (4)*

Entities A, B and C each own one third of the ordinary shares that carry voting rights at a general meeting of shareholders of entity D. A, B and C each have the right to appoint two directors to the board of D. A also owns call options that are exercisable at a fixed price at any time and, if exercised, would give it all the voting rights in D. The management of A does not intend to exercise the call options, even if B and C do not vote in the same manner as A. The existence of the potential voting rights is considered and it is determined (absent other special circumstances) that A controls D. The intention of A's management does not influence the assessment.

Example 6.5:   *Potential voting rights (5)*

Entities A and B own 55% and 45% respectively of the ordinary shares that carry voting rights at a general meeting of shareholders of entity C. B also holds debt instruments that are convertible into ordinary shares of C. The debt can be converted, on payment of a substantial exercise price in comparison with B's net assets, at any time and, if converted, would require B to borrow additional funds to make the payment. If the debt were to be converted, B would hold 70% of the voting rights and A's interest would reduce to 30%. Although the debt instruments are convertible at a substantial price, they are currently convertible and the conversion feature gives B the power to set the operating and financial policies of C. The existence of the potential voting rights, as well as the other factors described at 2.1.1 above, is considered and it is determined (absent other special circumstances) that B, not A, controls C. The financial ability of B to pay the conversion price does not influence the assessment.

On the other hand, the guidance states, somewhat contradictorily, that potential voting rights should be ignored where they lack economic substance '(e.g. where the exercise price is set in a manner that precludes exercise in any feasible scenario).'[26] The use of the word 'feasible' is rather curious, but may have been used in deliberate distinction from the more expected 'foreseeable' – in other words exercise has to be almost impossible rather than merely highly unlikely. However, this is somewhat contradicted by Example 6.5 above, which stresses that B's financial inability to exercise its conversion rights is irrelevant, and by the overall emphasis on the importance of there being a currently exercisable right.

This almost casual reference to economic substance in the implementation guidance together with the requirement in the main body of IAS 27 (and IAS 28) to examine 'all facts and circumstances' surrounding potential voting rights is no doubt in part an attempt to prevent potential abuses by the use of contrived agreements to deconsolidate loss-making or highly-geared subsidiaries.

However, in our view, the IASB has been so preoccupied by an understandable anxiety to prevent deconsolidation of subsidiaries through contrived sales (as in Example 6.3 above) that it has, particularly through the explicit prohibition on having regard to 'the intention of management and the financial ability to exercise or convert', created the real risk of entities achieving deconsolidation through contrived option arrangements, as illustrated in Example 6.6 below.

Example 6.6:   *Potential voting rights (6)*

A parent (P) wishes to deconsolidate its loss-making subsidiary (S). It grants immediately exercisable options at an uneconomically high price to a friendly third party (F) which, if exercised, would give F ownership of more than half of the voting power of S. Although the options do not lack economic substance entirely, it is known by all concerned that F has no intention of actually exercising its options, and that it would not be in its financial interest to do so. Yet IAS 27 appears to require P to ignore these very pertinent facts in its assessment of whether or not S should continue to be treated as a subsidiary of P.

However, this is not the end of the matter. It might well be that P would continue to be regarded as the parent on the basis that it had an (unwritten) agreement with F that F would never actually exercise its options, thus falling within condition (a) in 2.1.1 above. Moreover, the provisions of SIC-12 could well be relevant (see 2.2 below). Most importantly perhaps, F would be unlikely to enter into such a transaction if it were subject to IAS 27 or a broadly comparable national standard.

Whilst fully exercisable potential voting rights may give rise to situations where an entity becomes (or ceases to be) a subsidiary, the proportion of the entity that is accounted for depends on the actual ownership interests at each reporting date (see Chapter 7 at 2.2).

2.1.3   De facto control

De facto control over an entity by a minority shareholder may arise in a number of ways. Two common examples are when other shareholdings are widely dispersed, or when a sufficient number of other shareholders regularly fail to exercise their rights as shareholders (e.g. to vote at general meetings) that the minority shareholder wields the majority of votes actually cast.

In our view IAS 27 as currently drafted would not necessarily require consolidation of entities subject only to *de facto* control since the definition of control refers to the 'power' to govern the financial and operating policies of an entity (see 2 above) and power is explained as representing the ability to do or effect something, whether actively or passively (see 2.1.1 above). In our view, this wording, as reinforced by the implementation guidance in the standard, refers to powers arising from the contractual rights of shareholders in relation to the entity and to each other, rather than to an ability to control arising as a result of particular circumstances.

A IASB statement on de facto control

In October 2005 it was reported in *IASB Update* that the IASB had recently become aware of differences in how IAS 27 might be applied in the circumstances in which an entity owns less than half the voting power in an entity. As result the IASB discussed the definition of control in IAS 27 and decided to make a statement outlining its views on *de facto* control, in the following terms:

'IAS 27 contemplates that there are circumstances in which one entity can control another entity without owning more than half the voting power.[27]

'During its deliberations on its control project, the Board confirmed its view that an entity holding a minority interest can control another entity in the absence of any formal arrangements that would give it a majority of the voting rights. For example, control is achievable if the balance of holdings is dispersed and the other shareholders have not organised their interests in such a way that they exercise more votes than the minority holder. This is sometimes referred to as "de facto control".

'During those deliberations, the Board has made it clear that, in its view, the control concept in IAS 27 includes de facto control. The Board also acknowledged that professional skill and judgement is required in applying the control concept including determining if de facto control exists. The Board has recently become aware that some who apply IFRSs hold the view that, in the circumstances described, IAS 27 requires an entity to have legal control over a majority of the voting rights to consolidate another entity.

'The Board accepts that it would have been helpful if IAS 27 had included guidance to assist preparers in exercising the judgement to apply the control concept. Without that guidance there is a greater risk that two entities faced with the same set of circumstances might reach different conclusions on whether they control another entity. The Board is aware that differences in the application of IAS 27 might also be influenced by the practices followed in jurisdictions before adopting IFRSs.'[28]

B Implications of the IASB's statement

In our view, any determination of whether *de facto* control exists will always have to be based on the particular circumstances and it is unlikely to be sufficiently certain that *de facto* control exists until actions have been taken that provide evidence of control – i.e. control must have been actively exercised. In general, the more the legal or contractually-based powers that are held in relation to an entity fall short of 50% of the total, the greater will be the need for evidence of actively exercised de facto control.

As noted at 2 above, IAS 27 defines control as 'the power to govern the financial and operating policies of an entity so as to obtain benefits from its activities.' It follows from this definition that control involves the ability:

- to make decisions without the support or consent of other shareholders; and
- to give directions with respect to the operating and financial policies of the entity concerned, with which directions the entity's directors are obliged to comply.

Accordingly, a parent-subsidiary relationship does not exist where an investor must obtain the consent of one or more other shareholders in order to govern the policies of the investee.

In order to have the ability to govern the financial and operating policies of an entity, an investor must be able to hold the management of the entity accountable. It is therefore unlikely that *de facto* control over an entity can exist unless the investor has the power to appoint and remove a majority of its governing body (i.e. normally the board of directors in the case of a company). This power is normally exercisable by holders of the voting shares in general meeting.

In practice, *de facto* control is most likely to be evidenced where a minority voting interest holder is able to have its chosen candidates (re)nominated for election to an entity's board of directors and its votes exceed 50% of the votes typically cast in the entity's election of directors. For example, if only 70% of the eligible votes are typically cast on resolutions for the appointment of directors, a minority holding of 40% might give *de facto* control. For this to be the case, however, the remaining shares would have to be widely held, such that no party has an interest of sufficient size to block, either by itself or with a small number of others, the wishes of the minority voting interest holder.

The question may also arise as to whether *de facto* control can exist where a minority voting interest represents less than 50% of votes typically cast in elections of directors, for example a voting interest of 30% where, typically, 70% of the eligible votes are cast in elections. This is highly unlikely to be the case. As control is unilateral, no account should be taken in assessing whether *de facto* control exists of the possibility that other shareholders will cast their votes in the same way as the holder of a substantial minority interest.

Determining when an entity is subject to *de facto* control is not easy in practice. Consistency demands that the investment in an entity does not unnecessarily 'yo-yo' in and out of consolidation – resulting in a series of business combinations and disposals – where a more careful judgement would have avoided it.

As the IASB has acknowledged, until such time as the IASB issues guidance to assist preparers in exercising the judgement required to apply the control concept, there will be differences in how IAS 27 is applied. Accordingly, we do not believe that the IASB's statement on *de facto* control obliged companies to change any pre-existing accounting policy with regard to the scope of the consolidated financial statements. As discussed at 7.2.1 C below, ED 10 proposes that a reporting entity holding less than a majority of voting rights may still have the power to direct the activities of another.

One practical issue that will need to be addressed by any guidance that the IASB may issue in due course is the accounting treatment required when an entity shifts between being under the *de facto* control of the investor (and therefore a subsidiary) and being subject only to the investor's significant influence (and therefore an associate).

The extract below from the financial statements of Xstrata provides an example of an accounting policy that considers *de facto* control in assessing whether or not an investment should be consolidated.

Extract 6.2: Xstrata plc (2008)

Notes to the Financial Statements [extract]

6. Principal Accounting Policies [extract]

Basis of consolidation

The financial statements consolidate the financial statements of Xstrata plc (the Company) and its subsidiaries (the Group). All inter-entity balances and transactions, including unrealised profits and losses arising from intra-Group transactions, have been eliminated in full. The results of subsidiaries acquired or sold are consolidated for the periods from or to the date on which control passes. Control is achieved where the Group has the power to govern the financial and operating policy of an entity so as to obtain benefits from its activities. This occurs when the Group has more than 50% voting power through ownership or agreements, except where minority rights are such that a minority shareholder is able to prevent the Group from exercising control. In addition control may exist without having more than 50% voting power through ownership or agreements, or in the circumstances of enhanced minority rights, as a consequence of de facto control. De facto control is control without the legal right to exercise unilateral control, and involves decision making ability that is not shared with others and the ability to give directions with respect to the operating and financial policies of the entity concerned. Where there is a loss of control of a subsidiary, the financial statements include the results for the part of the reporting period during which Xstrata plc has control. Subsidiaries use the same reporting period and same accounting policies as Xstrata plc.

2.1.4 Investments held in a fiduciary capacity

An entity (A) such as a fund-manager may hold, on behalf of investors in a fund, an interest in another entity (B) that either on its own or when combined with any interest held by A on its own account, gives A control of the majority of the voting rights in, or the ability to appoint or remove a majority of the members of the board of, B. This raises the question of whether B should be regarded as a subsidiary of A.

In our view, it generally should not. IAS 27 defines control as 'the power to govern the financial and operating policies of an entity *so as to obtain benefits from its activities*' (our emphasis added). A trustee or other fiduciary exercises any decision making powers relating to assets under its management so as obtain benefits not for itself but for those on whose behalf it exercises the powers.

Determining whether an entity is the owner of an investment or merely holds an interest in a fiduciary capacity requires a careful assessment of the facts. As illustrated in Example 6.7 below, consolidation is still required if an entity legally owns and controls an investment, even if the risks and rewards have been passed on to a third party.

Example 6.7:   Control over investment vehicle by an insurance company

An insurance company makes certain investments on behalf of unit-linked contract holders. One of those investments is an interest of more than 50% in an investment fund. Should the insurance company consolidate the investment fund?

The unit-linked contract holders are not the legal owner of the investment in the fund. Also, the insurance company is under no obligation to return the shares in the underlying investment to the unit-linked contract holders upon termination of the contract. The insurance company is the legal owner and the unit-linked contract holders have no direct relationship with (and decision-making powers over) the investment fund. In other words, the unit-linked contracts do not diminish the insurance company's ability to control the investment fund. Therefore, the presumption is that the insurance company should consolidate the investment fund unless it can be demonstrated that it does not have control as defined in paragraph 13 of IAS 27.

While the insurance company in the example above holds a matched position of units in the investment fund and unit-linked contracts, they are under no obligation to hold an investment in the units of the investment fund. Conversely, the unit-linked contract holders have no direct legal rights that entitle them to the units in the investment fund that are owned by the insurance company. In other words, the insurance company does not hold the units in the investment fund in a fiduciary capacity.

2.2   Special Purpose Entities

Like many national standard setters before it, the IASB (strictly, its predecessor the IASC) has had to address the issue of an entity conducting its affairs through a vehicle that, though not meeting the definition of a subsidiary, is still controlled by the entity. In principle, there should be less need for such guidance under IFRS (which defines a subsidiary simply as a controlled entity) as compared to other national GAAPs where subsidiary is defined by reference to a number of more specific, or more legally framed, indicators (so that further guidance is required in order to establish an over-riding control test).

In practice, however, the off-balance sheet industry proved no less active under IFRS than elsewhere, so that the SIC felt compelled to issue SIC-12. This requires an entity to consolidate a 'special purpose entity' ('SPE') when the substance of the relationship between them indicates that the entity controls the SPE.[29]

2.2.1   Definition of SPE

SIC-12 is in fact careful *not* to define an SPE, so as to minimise the possibility of avoiding its requirements through exploitation of a loophole in the drafting. Instead an SPE is described as an entity 'created to accomplish a narrow and well-defined objective (e.g. to effect a lease, research and development activities or a securitisation of financial assets).' An SPE may take the form of a corporation, trust, partnership or unincorporated entity. SPEs are often created with legal arrangements that impose strict and sometimes permanent limits on the decision-making powers of their governing board, trustee or management over the operations of the SPE that cannot be modified, other than perhaps by the creator or sponsor of the SPE (i.e. they operate on 'autopilot').[30]

This description is extremely wide and could, in our view, include not only a separate legal entity, but also an economic entity represented by a parcel of 'ring fenced' assets and liabilities within a larger legal entity, such as a cell in a protected cell entity (see Chapter 12 at 2.5), or a portfolio of securitised assets and the related borrowings.

The sponsor (or entity on whose behalf the SPE was created) frequently transfers assets to the SPE, obtains the right to use assets held by the SPE or performs services for the SPE, while other parties ('capital providers') may provide the funding to the SPE. An entity that engages in transactions with an SPE (frequently the creator or sponsor) may in substance control the SPE.[31] A beneficial interest in an SPE may, for example, take the form of a debt instrument, an equity instrument, a participation right, a residual interest or a lease. Some beneficial interests may simply provide the holder with a fixed or stated rate of return, while others give the holder rights or access to other future economic benefits of the SPE's activities. In most cases, the creator or sponsor (or the entity on whose behalf the SPE was created) retains a significant beneficial interest in the SPE's activities, even though it may own little or none of the SPE's equity.[32]

SIC-12 does not apply to post-employment benefit plans or other long-term employee benefit plans accounted for under IAS 19 – *Employee Benefits*. It does, however, apply to share-based payment plans.[33] The accounting for share-based payment plans and post-employment plans is dealt with in Chapters 27 and 28, respectively.

2.2.2 Determining whether an entity is an SPE

SIC-12 notes that control of an SPE may arise through the predetermination of its activities so that it operates on 'autopilot', or otherwise. It emphasises those provisions of IAS 27 that indicate that an entity has control over another entity, even though it owns one half or less (or even none) of the voting power in that other entity (see 2.1 above).[34]

In particular, SIC-12 points out that, under IAS 27, control of an entity comprises the ability to control the entity's decision making with a view to obtaining benefits from the entity. The ability to control decision-making alone is not sufficient to establish control for accounting purposes, but must be accompanied by the objective of obtaining benefits from the entity's activities.[35]

These reminders are doubtless made in the context that the first line of defence for those seeking to establish an off-balance sheet SPE tends to be to argue that some third party (such as a charitable trust) owns all the voting rights. However, if the trust (as is typically the case) does not obtain any real benefit from the SPE, this indicates that it is not the SPE's parent for accounting purposes.

SIC-12 states that determining whether or not an entity controls an SPE is a matter of judgement on the facts of each case. However, one or more of the circumstances set out in (a) to (d) below may indicate that an entity controls an SPE:[36]

(a)   In substance, the activities of the SPE are being conducted on behalf of the entity according to its specific business needs so that the entity obtains benefits from the SPE's operation. This is particularly likely to be the case where the SPE was directly or indirectly created by the reporting entity. Examples are where the SPE:

(i)   is principally engaged in providing a source of long-term capital to an entity or funding to support an entity's ongoing major or central operations; or

(ii)   provides a supply of goods or services that is consistent with an entity's ongoing major or central operations which, without the existence of the SPE, would have to be provided by the entity itself.

However, economic dependence of an entity on the reporting entity (such as the relationship of a supplier to a significant customer) does not, by itself, lead to control;

(b)   In substance, the entity has the decision-making powers (including those coming into existence after the formation of the SPE) to obtain the majority of the benefits of the activities of the SPE or, by setting up an 'autopilot' mechanism, the entity has delegated these decision-making powers. Examples of such powers are:

(i)   power unilaterally to dissolve an SPE; or

(ii)   power to change, or veto proposed changes to, the SPE's charter or bylaws.

(c)   In substance, the entity has the rights to obtain the majority of the benefits of the SPE and therefore may be exposed to risks incident to the activities of the SPE. These rights may arise through a statute, contract, agreement, or trust deed, or any other scheme, arrangement or device. Such rights to benefits in the SPE may be indicators of control when they are specified in favour of an entity that is engaged in transactions with an SPE and that entity stands to gain those benefits from the financial performance of the SPE. Examples are:

(i)   rights to a majority of any economic benefits distributed by an entity in the form of future net cash flows, earnings, net assets, or other economic benefits; or

(ii)   rights to majority residual interests in scheduled residual distributions or in a liquidation of the SPE.

(d)   In substance, the entity retains the majority of the residual or ownership risks related to the SPE or its assets in order to obtain benefits from its activities. Frequently, the reporting entity guarantees a return or credit protection directly or indirectly through the SPE to outside investors who provide substantially all of the capital to the SPE. As a result of the guarantee, the entity retains residual or ownership risks and the investors are, in substance, only lenders because their exposure to gains and losses is limited. Examples are:

(i)   the capital providers do not have a significant interest in the underlying net assets of the SPE;

(ii)   the capital providers do not have rights to the future economic benefits of the SPE;

(iii) the capital providers are not substantively exposed to the inherent risks of the underlying net assets or operations of the SPE; or

(iv)   in substance, the capital providers receive mainly consideration equivalent to a lender's return through a debt or equity interest.

In November 2006, the IFRIC was asked to consider whether a relative weight should be given to the various indicators in paragraph 10 of SIC-12 in determining who should consolidate an SPE. The IFRIC noted that 'the factors set out in paragraph 10 of SIC-12 are indicators only and not necessarily conclusive' because the circumstances vary case by case. The IFRIC decided not to take the issue onto its agenda because in its view 'SIC-12 requires that the party having control over an SPE should be determined through the exercise of judgement and skill in each case, after taking into account all relevant factors.'[37]

2.2.3   Practical interpretation issues

A   Securitisation transactions

SPEs are most commonly found in, but are not unique to, the financial services sector, where they are used as vehicles for securitisation of financial assets such as mortgages or credit card receivables. The effect of SIC-12, combined with the derecognition provisions of IAS 39 – *Financial Instruments: Recognition and Measurement* – may be that:

- a securitisation transaction qualifies as a sale of the financial asset concerned (which is thus, in principle, derecognised, or removed from the financial statements); but

- the 'buyer' is an SPE, so that the asset is immediately re-recognised through consolidation of the SPE.

This is discussed further in Chapter 30 at 4.

B   Majority of the benefits and risks

In our view, the reference to the majority of benefits and risks in criteria (c) and (d) at 2.2.2 above should be read as referring to the majority of benefits and risks that are likely to arise in practice rather than to the majority of all theoretically possible benefits and risks as illustrated by Example 6.8 below.

Example 6.8:   Assessment of majority of benefits and risks of an SPE

An SPE is established to undertake a securitisation of financial assets. The SPE has only nominal equity, but issues €1,000 of debt – €100 subordinated debt to the reporting entity and €900 senior debt to a financial institution. The SPE buys €1,000 of receivables from the reporting entity.

The terms of the two classes of debt have the effect that the reporting entity bears the first €100 of any credit losses and the financial institution the remainder. This could suggest that the financial institution is bearing the majority of the risks, since it has €900 of the possible €1,000 bad debt risk. However, if (as is likely to be the case) bad debt risk is in the order of, say, 5% to 7%, all the losses that are in fact likely to occur will be borne by the reporting entity as the holder of the subordinated debt. This would lead to the conclusion that the SPE should be consolidated by the reporting entity.

This analysis is consistent with the approach to assessing risks and benefits under the rules for the derecognition of financial assets in IAS 39, where more weight is required to be given to those risks and benefits that are more likely to occur (see Chapter 30 at 4.5).

C   Benefits not necessarily financial

As discussed at 2.2.2 above, the first of the indicators of whether an entity is an SPE is that its activities are being conducted on behalf of the entity according to its specific business needs so that the entity obtains benefits from the SPE's operation. In our view this does not necessarily require that the reporting entity has any direct financial benefit, as illustrated by Example 6.9 below.

Example 6.9:   SPE with no direct financial benefit for the reporting entity

The reporting entity wishes to issue debt, the coupons on which are linked to the price of a commodity (to which the entity's revenue is strongly correlated), to a provider of finance that wants to lend fixed rate debt. The solution in most cases would be for the entity to issue fixed rate debt to the lender and then hedge it by entering into a swap under which it pays index-linked interest and receives fixed rate interest.

Such a swap would not qualify as a hedging instrument under IAS 39 and would therefore, if entered into directly by the entity, be required to be recorded at fair value through profit or loss, resulting in potentially significant volatility in the financial statements. To avoid this, the entity sets up an SPE, to which it issues floating rate debt. The SPE then issues fixed rate debt to the lender and enters into a pay index-linked/receive fixed interest rate swap on arm's-length terms with a third party.

The financial risks and rewards of the SPE are shared by the lender and the counterparty to the swap. The entity might therefore argue that, as it has no financial risks or rewards, it should not consolidate the SPE. However, in our view, it could be argued that the SPE was set up according to the entity's business needs – i.e. to achieve financial 'engineering', by avoiding the potential volatility that would arise from accounting for the swap under IAS 39 – and should therefore be consolidated by the reporting entity.

An argument that the SPE was set up for the benefit of the lender – on the grounds that this enables it to lend fixed rate rather than the index-linked rate required by the entity – does not, in our view, have merit. If, as is likely, there is no shortage of potential borrowers seeking to borrow at fixed rate, the SPE is not required in order to fulfil the lender's commercial needs.

The extract below from the financial statements of Barclays illustrates some of the accounting issues discussed above.

Extract 6.3: Barclays PLC (2008)

Significant Accounting Policies [extract]

4. Consolidation [extract]

Subsidiaries [extract]

The consolidated financial statements combine the financial statements of Barclays PLC and all its subsidiaries, including certain special purpose entities (SPEs) where appropriate, made up to 31st December. Entities qualify as subsidiaries where the Group has the power to govern the financial and operating policies of the entity so as to obtain benefits from its activities, generally accompanying a shareholding of more than one half of the voting rights. The existence and effect of potential voting rights that are currently exercisable or convertible are considered in assessing whether the Group controls another entity. Details of the principal subsidiaries are given in Note 41.

SPEs are consolidated when the substance of the relationship between the Group and that entity indicates control. Potential indicators of control include, amongst others, an assessment of the Group's exposure to the risks and benefits of the SPE.

---

29 Securitisations

The Group was party to securitisation transactions involving Barclays residential mortgage loans, business loans and credit card balances. In addition, the Group acts as a conduit for commercial paper, whereby it acquires static pools of residential mortgage loans from other lending institutions for securitisation transactions.

In these transactions, the assets, or interests in the assets, or beneficial interests in the cash flows arising from the assets, are transferred to a special purpose entity, or to a trust which then transfers its beneficial interests to a special purpose entity, which then issues floating rate debt securities to third-party investors.

Securitisations may, depending on the individual arrangement result in continued recognition of the securitised assets and the recognition of the debt securities issued in the transaction; lead to partial continued recognition of the assets to the extent of the Group's continuing involvement in those assets or to derecognition of the assets and the separate recognition, as assets or liabilities, of any rights and obligations created or retained in the transfer. Full derecognition only occurs when the Group transfers both its contractual right to receive cash flows from the financial assets, or retains the contractual rights to receive the cash flows, but assumes a contractual obligation to pay the cash flows to another party without material delay or reinvestment, and also transfers substantially all the risks and rewards of ownership, including credit risk, prepayment risk and interest rate risk.

The following table shows the carrying amount of securitised assets, stated at the amount of the Group's continuing involvement where appropriate, together with the associated liabilities, for each category of asset in the balance sheet:

	2008		2007	
	Carrying amount of assets £m	Associated liabilities £m	Carrying amount of assets £m	Associated liabilities £m
Loans and advances to customers				
Residential mortgage loans	12,754	(13,172)	16,000	(16,786)
Credit card receivables	1,888	(2,109)	4,217	(3,895)
Other personal lending	212	(256)	422	(485)
Wholesale and corporate loans and advances	7,702	(8,937)	8,493	(8,070)
Total	22,556	(24,474)	29,132	(29,236)
Assets designated at fair value through profit or loss				
Retained interest in residential mortgage loans	316	–	895	–

Retained interests in residential mortgage loans are securities which represent a continuing exposure to the prepayment and credit risk in the underlying securitised assets. The total amount of the loans was £31,734m (2007:£23,097m). The retained interest is initially recorded as an allocation of the original carrying amount based on the relative fair values of the portion derecognised and the portion retained.

42 Other entities [extract]

There are a number of entities that do not qualify as subsidiaries under UK Law but which are consolidated when the substance of the relationship between the Group and the entity (usually a Special Purpose Entity (SPE)) indicates that the entity is controlled by the Group. Such entities are deemed to be controlled by the Group when relationships with such entities gives rise to benefits that are in substance no different from those that would arise were the entity a subsidiary.

The consolidation of such entities may be appropriate in a number of situations, but primarily when:

– the operating and financial policies of the entity are closely defined from the outset (i.e. it operates on an 'autopilot' basis) with such policies being largely determined by the Group;

– the Group has rights to obtain the majority of the benefits of the entity and/or retains the majority of the residual or ownership risks related to the entity; or

– the activities of the entity are being conducted largely on behalf of the Group according to its specific business objectives.

> Such entities are created for a variety of purposes including securitisation, structuring, asset realisation, intermediation and management.
>
> Entities may have a different reporting date from that of the parent of 31st December. Dates may differ for a variety of reasons including local reporting regulations or tax laws. In accordance with our accounting policies, for the purpose of inclusion in the consolidated financial statements of Barclays PLC, entities with different reporting dates are made up until 31st December.
>
> Entities may have restrictions placed on their ability to transfer funds, including payment of dividends and repayment of loans, to their parent entity.
>
> Reasons for the restrictions include:
>
> – Central bank restrictions relating to local exchange control laws.
>
> – Central bank capital adequacy requirements.
>
> – Company law restrictions relating to treatment of the entities as going concerns.
>
> Although the Group's interest in the equity voting rights in certain entities exceeds 50%, or it may have the power to appoint a majority of their Boards of Directors, they are excluded from consolidation because the Group either does not direct the financial and operating policies of these entities, or on the grounds that another entity has a superior economic interest in them. Consequently, these entities are not deemed to be controlled by Barclays.

D   Subsequent reassessment of SIC-12 conditions

The question whether an entity should assess its relationship with an SPE not only at inception but also in subsequent periods has recently received much attention. Also, accounting for SPEs is one of the key factors driving the IASB's consolidation project (see 7.2 below). SIC-12 requires consolidation of an SPE when 'the substance of the relationship between an entity and the SPE indicates that the SPE is controlled by that entity'.[38] However, SIC-12 is silent on whether there should be a reassessment of who should consolidate an SPE, after inception. Nevertheless, as SIC-12 is an interpretation of IAS 27, reassessment is required under certain circumstances, since consolidation is required by IAS 27 whenever an entity controls another entity. In our view, under SIC-12, the consolidation decision would need to be evaluated whenever:

(a)   there is a change in the contractual arrangements between the parties to the SPE; or

(b)   any of the parties take steps to strengthen its position and, in doing so, acquires a greater level of control.

The extract below from the financial statement of Barclays lists some of the reasons for reassessing the substance of the relationship between an entity and an SPE.

> *Extract 6.4: Barclays PLC (2008)*
>
> **Financial review** [extract]
>
> **Additional financial disclosure** [extract]
>
> **Off-balance sheet arrangements** [extract]
>
> **Special purpose entities** [extract]
>
> Transactions entered into by the Group may involve the use of SPEs. SPEs are entities that are created to accomplish a narrow and well defined objective. There are often specific restrictions or limits around their on-going activities.

Transactions with SPEs take a number of forms, including:

- The provision of financing to fund asset purchases, or commitments to provide finance for future purchases.
- Derivative transactions to provide investors in the SPE with a specified exposure.
- The provision of liquidity or backstop facilities which may be drawn upon if the SPE experiences future funding difficulties.
- Direct investment in the notes issued by SPEs.

Depending on the nature of the Group's resulting exposure, it may consolidate the SPE on to the Group's balance sheet. The consolidation of SPEs is considered at inception, based on the arrangements in place and the assessed risk exposures at that time. In accordance with IFRS, SPEs are consolidated when the substance of the relationship between the Group and the entity indicates control. Potential indicators of control include, amongst others, an assessment of the Group's exposure to the risks and benefits of the SPE. The initial consolidation analysis is revisited at a later date if:

(i)   the Group acquires additional interests in the entity;

(ii)   the contractual arrangements of the entity are amended such that the relative exposures to risks and rewards change; or if

(iii)   the Group acquires control over the main operating and financial decisions of the entity.

A number of the Group's transactions have recourse only to the assets of unconsolidated SPEs. Typically, the majority of the exposure to these assets is borne by third parties and the Group's risk is mitigated through over-collateralisation, unwind features and other protective measures. The Group's involvement with unconsolidated third party conduits, collateralised debt obligations and structured investment vehicles is described further below.

A potential example of the situation described under (b) above is that if commercial paper cannot be reissued for longer than a certain period of time, the agreement governing the structure may require the assets to be liquidated. The liquidity provider, knowing that a sale of the assets in the present environment is likely to result in losses, might decide to extend the life of the structure by buying the new issue of commercial paper. This was not an action that was anticipated in the original agreement and may mean that the liquidity provider, by doing this, has changed the relative contractual positions of the various parties to the SPE and taken effective control.

While it is possible that the substance in the relationship between an entity and an SPE changes due to specific actions taken by one of the parties, it is equally possible that the nature of the relationship is altered by other events such as changes in the risk profile of each party that has entered into transactions with the SPE. What if such changes result from market conditions and not through any action taken by those parties (e.g. impairment of the assets owned by an SPE)? So long as the initial SIC-12 assessment is not called into question (e.g. because it was based on incomplete or inaccurate information), the fact that the losses incurred by the SPE exceed the capital provided to it, such that the residual risk now lies with another party, (for example the SPE sponsor), does not of itself necessarily mean that there has been any transfer of control between the parties to the structure. However, in many cases the party bearing the residual risk will take steps to protect its position that would trigger a reassessment of whether it controls and should therefore consolidate the SPE. Further, SIC-12 requires consideration not only of who has the residual risks but also on whose behalf the activities of the SPE are (now) being conducted and who, in substance, has the decision-making powers to control the SPE. If it is considered necessary to reassess the consolidation, there is no requirement in SIC-12 to incorporate the market's view of risk – the entity would be permitted to use its own forecasts of the losses likely to arise.

Reassessment of who should consolidate an SPE is a difficult issue and each individual situation will need to be assessed, based on the particular facts and the circumstances.

3   REQUIREMENT TO PREPARE CONSOLIDATED FINANCIAL STATEMENTS

IAS 27 requires a parent to prepare consolidated financial statements – i.e. financial statements of a group presented as those of a single economic entity,[39] unless it avails itself the exemption discussed at 3.1 below.[40] The consolidated financial statements of a parent that is an investor in an associate must also comply with IAS 28 (see Chapter 11), and the consolidated financial statements of a parent that is a venturer in a jointly controlled entity must also comply with IAS 31 (see Chapter 12).[41]

3.1   Exemption from preparing consolidated financial statements

A parent should present consolidated financial statements in which it consolidates its investments in subsidiaries in accordance with IAS 27.[42] A parent need not present consolidated financial statements if and only if:[43]

(a)   the parent is itself a wholly-owned subsidiary, or is a partially-owned subsidiary of another entity and its other owners, including those not otherwise entitled to vote, have been informed about, and do not object to, the parent not presenting consolidated financial statements;

(b)   the parent's debt or equity instruments are not traded in a public market (a domestic or foreign stock exchange or an over-the-counter market, including local and regional markets);

(c)   the parent did not file, nor is it in the process of filing, its financial statements with a securities commission or other regulatory organisation for the purpose of issuing any class of instruments in a public market; and

(d)   the ultimate or any intermediate parent of the parent produces consolidated financial statements available for public use that comply with International Financial Reporting Standards.

Where an entity avails itself of this exemption, it may, but is not required, to prepare separate financial statements (see Chapter 8) as its only financial statements.[44] If separate financial statements are prepared, however, they must comply with the provisions of IAS 27 for such statements.[45]

The conditions for exemption from preparing consolidated financial statements, although mostly self-explanatory, raise a number of detailed issues of interpretation as follows.

3.1.1 Condition (a) – consent of non-controlling (or minority) shareholders

IAS 27 requires that, where the parent is itself a partly-owned subsidiary, any non-controlling (or minority) shareholders are actively informed of the parent's intention not to prepare consolidated financial statements. The non-controlling (or minority) shareholders do not have to give explicit consent – the absence of dissent is sufficient. Interestingly, however, IAS 27 sets no limit on when the non-controlling (or minority) shareholders can register any objection. Thus, in principle, it would be open to non-controlling (or minority) shareholders to object to a parent's election not to prepare consolidated financial statements not merely at the eleventh hour before the accounts are printed but even after they have been issued. Furthermore, condition (a) refers to 'shareholders', which means that approval should also be obtained from the holders of preference shares. Parents that are partly-owned subsidiaries and wish to take the exemption from preparing consolidated financial statements might therefore be well-advised to obtain explicit written consent from non-controlling (or minority) shareholders in advance.

IAS 27 also requires all non-controlling (or minority) owners 'including those not otherwise entitled to vote' to be informed of the parent's intention not to prepare consolidated financial statements. Thus, for example, any the holders of any non-voting preference shares must be notified of, and consent (or not object) to, the entity's intention to take the exemption.

As drafted, the requirement to inform the non-controlling (or minority) shareholders where the parent 'is a partially-owned subsidiary of another entity' is slightly ambiguous, as illustrated by Examples 6.10 and 6.11 below.

Example 6.10:   Consent for not preparing consolidated financial statements (1)

A parent wishing to claim the exemption (P) is owned 60% by entity A and 40% by entity B. Entity A and entity B are both wholly-owned by entity C. In this case, in our view, P would not be obliged to inform its non-controlling (or minority) shareholder B of any intention not to prepare consolidated financial statements since, although it is a partly-owned subsidiary of A, it is a wholly-owned subsidiary of C (and therefore satisfies condition (a) without regard to its immediate owners).

Example 6.11:   Consent for not preparing consolidated financial statements (2)

The facts are as in Example 6.10 above, except that A and B were both owned by an individual (Mr X). P is not a wholly-owned subsidiary of any other entity, and therefore the rules applicable to partly-owned subsidiaries apply. Thus, it appears that in such a case IAS 27 requires P to inform B of any intention not to prepare consolidated financial statements.

3.1.2 Condition (b) – securities not traded in a public market

The potential source of confusion here is what exactly constitutes a 'public market'. It is clear that, where quoted prices are available for any of the parent's securities on a generally recognised stock exchange, it cannot avoid the requirement to prepare consolidated financial statements. However, what is the position of a parent with securities for which there are no quoted prices but which are occasionally traded, for example on a matched bargain basis, through an exchange (as opposed to by private treaty between individual buyers and sellers)?

It is clear from the Basis for Conclusions for IAS 27 that the IASB regarded conditions (b) and (c) above as linked, in other words that an entity would fall within (c) before falling within (b).[46] It will be seen that condition (c) refers to the filing of financial statements with a securities commission or regulator as a precursor to public listing of securities. In our view, therefore, it may reasonably be inferred that any security that is traded in circumstances where it is necessary to have filed financial statements with a securities commission or regulator should be regarded as 'traded in a public market' for the purposes of condition (b).

3.1.3   Condition (c) – no filing of financial statements for the purpose of listing securities

The difficulties here arise from the less than clear drafting.

Firstly, it is not clear whether the 'financial statements' referred to are only those prepared under IFRS or include those prepared in pursuance of local requirements. In our view, the phrase is intended to mean any financial statements filed in connection with the public trading of securities. This is because the Basis for Conclusions for IAS 27 makes clear the IASB's view that the information needs of users of financial statements of entities whose debt or equity instruments are traded in a public market are best served when investments in subsidiaries, associates and jointly controlled entities are accounted for in accordance with IAS 27, IAS 28 and IAS 31. The Board therefore decided that the exemption from preparing such consolidated financial statements should not be available to such entities or to entities in the process of issuing instruments in a public market.[47] In other words, the key test is that the entity's securities are, or are about to be, publicly traded.

Secondly, IAS 27 allows an exemption from preparing consolidated financial statements only to an entity that 'did' not file financial statements in connection with the public trading of securities, without any reference to the period to which those financial statements relate. Thus, if read literally, IAS 27 would deny the exemption to any parent that has ever had publicly traded securities, which would include those hundreds of previously listed entities that are now wholly-owned subsidiaries as a result of takeover activity or group reorganisations. This, we suggest, is a nonsense that the IASB cannot have intended. On the other hand, the use of the word 'did' means that, again if read literally, IAS 27 cannot be referring to already filed financial statements for the current period, since an entity that had already prepared its financial statements for the current period would have no reason to be considering IAS 27 in respect of that period. In our view, condition (c) makes sense only if 'did' is regarded as a drafting slip for 'does'. In other words, the test is whether the entity currently has, or shortly will have, an ongoing obligation to file financial statements with a regulator in connection with the public trading of any of its securities.

3.1.4   Condition (d) – IFRS financial statements of parent's parent publicly available

A possible issue here might be whether the exemption can be claimed only where a parent of the parent prepares consolidated financial statements under IFRS that are publicly available through some form of national or regional public filing requirement, or whether it also applies where those consolidated financial statements are available on request.

The disclosure requirements in respect of entities that have taken advantage of the exemption from preparing consolidated financial statements make it clear that either route is acceptable, provided that the source for obtaining the consolidated financial statements of the relevant parent of the parent is disclosed (see Chapter 8 at 3.1).

3.2   Entity no longer a parent at the end of the reporting period

IAS 27 simply states that a parent must prepare consolidated financial statements (unless exempt under the criteria discussed at 3.1 above). By contrast, national law, or other regulations, may require an entity that is a parent at the end of it reporting period to prepare consolidated financial statements. This begs the question of whether IAS 27 requires an entity to prepare consolidated financial statements only if it is a parent at the end of the reporting period, or also if it was a parent at any time during the period.

In our view, the requirement of IAS 27 for a parent to consolidate a subsidiary until the date on which the parent ceases to control the subsidiary (see Chapter 7 at 3.2 and 3.3) indicates that consolidated financial statements should be prepared by an entity that was a parent during the period, even if it is no longer at the end of the reporting period, for example because it has disposed of all its subsidiaries. This will mean that, if a parent does not prepare consolidated financial statements in these circumstances pursuant to a concession in local law – see 3.3 below), it will not be able present separate financial statements in purported compliance with IFRS.

Likewise, we believe that an entity not preparing consolidated financial statements which had an associate, or in interest in a joint venture, during the reporting period but no longer does so at the year end should apply IAS 28 or IAS 31, as the case may be, to those investments in its financial statements for the period, if not otherwise exempt from doing so.

3.3   Interaction of IAS 27 and EU law

For entities incorporated in the European Union (EU), there may in some cases be a subtle interaction between the requirements of IAS 27 and the EU Regulation on International Accounting Standards which can affect:

- whether separate financial statements can be published before the consolidated financial statements (see Chapter 8 at 1.2.1); and

- the scope of the EU Regulation on International Accounting Standards (see Chapter 8 at 1.2.2

3.4   Combined financial statements

Combined financial statements are sometimes prepared under IFRS for a reporting 'entity' that does not comprise a group under IAS 27. Examples might be:

- two or more legal entities under common control of the same individual or group of individuals (e.g. 'horizontal' groups); or

- a group of business units that are intended to become a group for the purposes of IAS 27 in the future (e.g. following an initial public offering or demerger).

This raises the question as to whether such financial statements, even if they comply fully with all other aspects of IFRS, can be stated to be in compliance with IFRS, on the basis that they are prepared in respect of a reporting entity not recognised as such by IFRS.

In our view, there are very limited circumstances in which such combined financial statements can give a true and fair view in accordance with IFRS. As a minimum it would be necessary for there to be:

- a common ownership structure for all entities within the whole 'group';

- a common board of directors for all material operational, financing and investing decisions; and

- evidence of the integration of the 'group' for operational purposes (e.g. budgetary control purposes, financing structure, operation as an unified business).

This is not an exclusive 'checklist' and it would be necessary for each such 'group' to be considered on its own merits. We also consider it essential that the combined financial statements of such a 'group' include:

- all entities that are part of the 'group' for operational purposes (including any associates and joint ventures);

- all normal consolidation entries (such as elimination of 'intra-group' transactions and 'intra-group' profits and losses);

- a comprehensive list of all entities that have been combined in the financial statements and the beneficial ownership of these entities; and

- comprehensive related party disclosures.

In those very rare cases where full compliance with IFRS is possible, the reporting entity would effectively be invoking the fair presentation override in IAS 1 – *Presentation of Financial Statements* (see Chapter 3 at 4.1.1 B), so as to prepare consolidated financial statements for an entity not considered a group under IAS 27.

In most cases this will not be justified, but it may well be possible to assert that the various financial statements included in the combined financial statements individually comply with IFRS, and then explain the basis on which they have been combined.

Although this reflects our view of the position under current IFRS the Board is developing a broader concept of the reporting entity as part of its discussion of the conceptual framework (see 7.1 below) and the recently issued standard for small and medium-sized entities (see A below) specifically permits the preparation of combined accounts so it is possible that IFRS guidance in this area will change.

A   Small and medium-size entities

In July 2009, the IASB issued the *International Financial Reporting Standard for Small and Medium-sized Entities (IFRS for SMEs)*, which defines combined financial statements as 'a single set of financial statements of two or more entities controlled by a single investor'.[48] Unlike IAS 27 (as amended in 2008), the *IFRS for SMEs* permits – but does not require – combined financial statements to be prepared.[49]

If an investor (i.e. not a parent) prepares combined financial statements and describes them as conforming to the *IFRS for SMEs*, those statements should comply with all of the requirements of that IFRS. That means that:[50]

- intercompany transactions and balances should be eliminated;
- profits or losses resulting from intercompany transactions that are recognised in assets such as inventory and property, plant and equipment should be eliminated;
- the financial statements of the entities included in the combined financial statements should be prepared as of the same reporting date unless it is impracticable to do so; and
- uniform accounting policies should be followed for like transactions and other events in similar circumstances.

The *IFRS for SMEs* requires the following disclosures in combined financial statements:[51]

- the fact that the financial statements are combined financial statements;
- the reason why combined financial statements are prepared;
- the basis for determining which entities are included in the combined financial statements;
- the basis of preparation of the combined financial statements; and
- the related party disclosures required by Section 33 of the *IFRS for SMEs*.

However, an entity that applies IAS 27 (as amended in 2008) cannot apply by analogy the above guidance from the *IFRS for SMEs*.

3.5   Carve-out financial statements

Entities sometimes prepare financial statements that include parts of certain legal entities. An example might be a group of business units, some of which may be legal entities while others are parts of entities, that are intended to become a group for the purposes of IAS 27 (e.g. in an initial public offering or demerger). These are often known as 'carve-out' financial statements. This raises the question as to whether such carve-out financial statements, even if they comply fully with all other aspects of IFRS, can be stated to be in compliance with IFRS, given that they do not include all the profits or losses, assets, liabilities and equity of the legal entities they comprise. For example, IAS 27 requires consolidation of all subsidiaries and does not permit exclusion of certain subsidiaries or certain assets and liabilities of those subsidiaries from consolidation. Also, assets and liabilities are defined in the

Framework by reference to an entity rather than the business that they are part of. That, again, suggests that financial statements under IFRS should include all assets and liabilities of the entities that are consolidated, rather than a subset of those.

While stock exchange regulators frequently require presentation of historical financial information prepared on a carve-out basis, there is no guidance under IFRS that describes how such information should be prepared. Unfortunately, IFRS does not contain a definition of 'entity' or 'reporting entity', which might help in answering the question: what are the assets, liabilities, income and expenses of the carved-out entity? That means that there are additional practical issues that arise when preparing financial statements on a carve-out basis:

- *Management judgement and hindsight*: Absent clear legal boundaries, determining whether certain items are part of a business often requires significant management judgement and possibly use of hindsight. In addition, the risk exists that comparative information is prepared on a basis that reflects the impact of events before they actually occur (e.g. disposals of assets);

- *Allocation of overhead costs*: Businesses that are part of a larger legal entity often benefit from certain overheads (e.g. legal or administrative);

- *Transfers of assets*: The legal entity that owns the business may have undergone a reorganisation that resulted in the transfer of assets between its businesses, which raises question about recognising gains or losses on disposals and the appropriate cost basis of assets acquired;

- *Funding costs*: While it may be relatively straight forward to identify which assets are used in a business, it is often not clear to what extent a legal entity's liabilities and equity should be attributed to the individual business that it owns. The individual businesses may differ considerably in nature, e.g. a legal entity may own both a low-risk established business and a high-risk new venture. Therefore, it is not clear how interest expenses and other aspects of an entity's funding structure (e.g. embedded derivatives and compound financial instruments) should be allocated;

- *Taxation and pensions*: Carved out businesses often do not file their own tax returns, which raises questions about the allocation of tax charges and tax liabilities. As tax liabilities are generally those of legal entities it would be necessary to consider whether (1) the carved out business remains within that legal entity or whether (2) the business' assets and liabilities are transferred to a new owner. Similar issues arise in respect of defined benefit plans; and

- *Designation*: To some extent accounting under IFRS relies on management's stated intent and other designations (e.g. financial instrument and hedge designations, intent regarding assets held for sale and designation of groups of cash-generating units). There is often no clear way of reflecting management's intent and designations in carve-out financial statements.

There is clearly a risk that an inappropriate allocation could result in a set of financial statements that does not offer a 'true and fair view' of the reporting entity (e.g. the reporting entity might appear more profitable or have more favourable balance sheet ratios). While some of the issues listed above would also apply to legal entities within a larger group (i.e. a legal entity might not represent a business that could exist independently without support from the group), at least in those cases it is possible to identify clearly the (legal) boundaries of the reporting entity.

Applying a carve-out basis of preparation of accounting under IFRS raises significant concerns under the *Framework* about the reliability, comparability, understandability and completeness of such financial statements. The basis of preparation typically requires numerous departures from the requirements of specific standards (e.g. accounting for income taxes and non-consolidation of subsidiaries). Furthermore, in jurisdictions that require the preparation of carve-out financial statements, usually a local regulator will have issued more detailed guidance on its preparation and/or will decide on a case-by-case basis whether the resulting financial statements are appropriate.

Preparation of financial information on a carve-out basis generally requires a substantial number of adjustments and allocations to be made, draws heavily on pronouncements of other standard-setting bodies that are referred to by the hierarchy of authoritative guidance in IAS 8 – *Accounting Policies, Changes in Accounting Estimates and Errors* – and requires certain departures from IFRS.

Absent clarification by the IASB or IFRIC, diversity in practice will continue to exist. In our view, however, the basis of preparation should not contain an explicit and unreserved statement of compliance with IFRS, but disclose:

* which accounting standards have been applied;

* the significant accounting judgements that were made including the carve-out adjustments and allocations; and

* explain in which respects they do not comply with IFRS as issued by the IASB (e.g. non-compliance with paragraph 13 of IAS 27).

4 SCOPE OF CONSOLIDATED FINANCIAL STATEMENTS

Consolidated financial statements must include all subsidiaries of the parent,[52] including SPEs (see 2.2 above). An accounting policy stating that 'all material subsidiaries are consolidated' or 'all subsidiaries are consolidated except for immaterial subsidiaries' would not be in accordance with IFRS, because materiality is not an accounting policy. However, materiality can be invoked in applying accounting policies (i.e. financial statements might still be in compliance with IFRS if certain immaterial subsidiaries are not consolidated).

Although consolidated financial statements must include all subsidiaries of the parent, if on acquisition a subsidiary meets the criteria to be classified as held for sale in accordance with IFRS 5 – *Non-current Assets Held for Sale and Discontinued Operations*, it is accounted for in accordance with IFRS 5 (see Chapter 4),[53] rather than following the consolidation procedures discussed in Chapter 7.

4.1   Venture capital organisations and similar entities

IAS 27 specifically notes that a subsidiary is not excluded from consolidation simply because the investor is a venture capital organisation, mutual fund, unit trust or similar entity.[54] The intention here is to emphasise that, although certain associates and joint ventures held by such investors are exempt from the general requirements of IAS 28 and IAS 31 (see Chapters 11 and 12), there is no such exemption for investments in subsidiaries under IAS 27.

A number of commentators on the exposure draft of the improved IAS 27 expressed the view that it was inconsistent to allow venture capitalists and similar entities to use fair value accounting for their portfolio investments in associates and joint ventures, but not for their investments in subsidiaries. The IASB rejects this view at some length in the Basis for Conclusions by drawing what it saw as a clear distinction between investments in controlled entities (i.e. subsidiaries) and those in uncontrolled entities. Essentially, the IASB sees the fact that a subsidiary is controlled as more significant than the fact that it may be held as part of a portfolio of investments, and believes that a consistent accounting approach (i.e. consolidation) should be applied to all controlled entities by all investors, irrespective of their industry, or the strategy for holding the investment.[55]

4.2   Subsidiaries with dissimilar activities

A subsidiary cannot be excluded from consolidation because its business activities are dissimilar from those of the other entities within the group. Instead, relevant information is provided by consolidating such subsidiaries and disclosing additional information in the consolidated financial statements about the different business activities of subsidiaries. IAS 27 clarifies that the disclosures required by IFRS 8 – *Operating Segments* (see Chapter 35) help to explain the significance of different business activities within the group.[56]

4.3   Subsidiaries subject to restrictions

It is noted in the Basis for Conclusions to IAS 27 that an entity is not permitted to exclude from consolidation an entity that it continues to control simply because that entity is operating under severe long-term restrictions that significantly impair its ability to transfer funds to the parent. Control must be lost for exclusion to occur.[57]

In fact, such a requirement does not appear explicitly in the main body of IAS 27, but it is broadly consistent with the fact that the standard notes that a parent loses control when it loses the power to govern the financial and operating policies of an investee so as to obtain benefit from its activities. The loss of control can occur with or without a change in absolute or relative ownership levels. It could occur, for example, when a subsidiary becomes subject to the control of a government, court, administrator or regulator. It could also occur as a result of a contractual agreement.[58]

However, there is a certain lack of clarity as to the IASB's precise intentions here. On the one hand, the previous paragraph suggests that control of a subsidiary is lost (other than through disposal or reduction of ownership) only when a third party actively manages the subsidiary. However, the basic definition of a subsidiary is an entity that is subject to control, defined as the power to govern the financial and operating policies of an entity 'so as to obtain benefits from its activities'. If an investor is unable through exchange controls or other restrictions to obtain any benefits from another entity – even an entity that it owns and manages on a day-to-day basis – is there not an argument that, since the investor is unable 'to obtain benefits from its activities', the investor does not have control of the entity as defined by IAS 27?

Perhaps the distinction that the IASB is intending to draw is between:

- restrictions, that 'significantly impair' the ability of a subsidiary to transfer funds to its parent (which do not result in a loss of control as defined in IAS 27), such as

  - exchange controls; or

  - in the case of a US-registered subsidiary, filing for protection from creditors under Chapter 11 of the United States Bankruptcy Code (and similar arrangements in other jurisdictions); and

restrictions which completely prevent such transfers, such as arrangements in which administrators are appointed to take on the decision-making abilities of the previous board, which do result in a loss of control as defined in IAS 27.

5 DISCLOSURE IN CONSOLIDATED FINANCIAL STATEMENTS

The following disclosures are required in consolidated financial statements:[59]

(a) the nature of the relationship between the parent and a subsidiary when the parent does not own, directly or indirectly through subsidiaries, more than half of the voting power (see Extract 6.5 below);

(b) the reasons why the ownership, directly or indirectly through subsidiaries, of more than half of the voting or potential voting power of an investee does not constitute control (see Extract 6.1 above);

(c) where the reporting date or period of the financial statements of a subsidiary used to prepare consolidated financial statements is different from the reporting date or period of the parent (see Extract 6.6 below):

  (i) the reporting date of that subsidiary's financial statements; and

  (ii) the reason for using a different reporting date or period; and

(d) the nature and extent of any significant restrictions (e.g. resulting from borrowing arrangements or regulatory requirements) on the ability of subsidiaries to transfer funds to the parent in the form of cash dividends or to repay loans or advances (see Extracts 6.8 and 6.9 below).

An entity that applies IAS 27 (as amended in 2008) should also disclose:[60]

(e)   a schedule that shows the effects of any changes in a parent's ownership interest in a subsidiary that do not result in a loss of control on the equity attributable to owners of the parent; and

(f)   if control of a subsidiary is lost, the parent should disclose the gain or loss, if any, recognised in accordance with paragraph 34 of IAS 27 (see Chapter 7 at 3.2.1), and:

(i)   the portion of that gain or loss attributable to recognising any investment retained in the former subsidiary at its fair value at the date when control is lost; and

(ii)   the line item(s) in the statement of comprehensive income in which the gain or loss is recognised (if not presented separately in the statement of comprehensive income).

Extract 6.5 below illustrates the requirement under (a) above to disclose the nature of the relationship between the parent and a subsidiary when the parent does not own more than half of the voting power:

Extract 6.5: HSBC Holdings plc (2008)

Notes on the Financial Statements [extract]

24 Investments in subsidiaries [extract]

Subsidiaries excluding SPEs where HSBC owns less than 50 per cent of the voting rights

Subsidiary	HSBC's interest in equity capital %	Description of relationship that gives HSBC control
2008		
HSBC Private Equity Fund 3	38.8	HSBC has control under IAS 27 because it is the investment adviser/manager of the fund and has a significant equity interest.
2007		
HSBC Private Equity Fund 3	38.8	HSBC has control under IAS 27 because it is the investment adviser/manager of the fund and has a significant equity interest.

Extract 6.6 below from the 31 March 2007 financial statements of SABMiller illustrates the disclosures required under (c) above.

Extract 6.6: SABMiller plc (2008)

Notes to the consolidated financial statements [extract]

1. Accounting policies [extract]

e) Basis of consolidation [extract]

(i) Subsidiaries [extract]

Some of the company's subsidiaries have a local statutory accounting reference date of 31 December. These are consolidated using management prepared information on a basis coterminous with the company's accounting reference date.

Extracts 6.7 and 6.8 below illustrate the requirement under (d) above to disclose significant restrictions on the ability of subsidiaries to transfer funds to the parent.

Extract 6.7: Fortis SA/NV and Fortis N.V. (2007)

General Notes [extract]

4 Shareholders' equity [extract]

4.6 Dividend [extract]

The companies comprising Fortis are subject to legal restrictions regarding the amount of dividend they may pay to their shareholders. The Netherlands Civil Code stipulates that a Dutch company may pay dividends only if the net equity of that company exceeds the total of the paid-up and called-up capital and the reserves required by law or by the company's Articles of Association.

Under the Belgian Companies Code, 5% of a company's annual net profit must be placed in a reserve fund until this fund reaches 10% of the share capital. No dividends may be paid if the value of the company's net assets falls below, or following payment of dividend would fall below, the sum of its paid-up capital and non-distributable reserves.

Belgian and Dutch subsidiaries are also subject to dividend restrictions arising from minimum capital and solvency requirements imposed by regulators in the countries in which those subsidiaries operate.

Extract 6.8: Cairn Energy PLC (2007)

RISK FACTORS [extract]

Exchange Rates, Interest Rates, Currency Controls and Fiscal Regulation [extract]

The Group's financing costs may be significantly affected by interest rate volatility. Furthermore, the GoI [Government of India] currently operates certain controls on currency exports which restrict the transfer from India of Rupees. While the policy and practice of the GoI has been to relax many of these controls and no restrictions are in place at present that would prevent free remittance of dividends from Cairn India to the Company, there is a risk that controls may be re-imposed in future. Indian law further restricts the ability of the Company to dispose of certain of its shares in Cairn India until three years after the IPO.

Notes to the Accounts [extract]

18. Investments [extract]

There is a restriction in the ability of some Group companies to distribute profits to Cairn Energy PLC, the ultimate parent company, as a result of negative distributable reserves in Cairn Energy Holdings Limited, an intermediate holding company.

---

6   TRANSITIONAL PROVISIONS

IAS 27 (2007) was effective for annual periods beginning on or after 1 January 2005. Entities were encouraged to adopt IAS 27 (2007) for earlier periods, but were required to disclose that they had done so.[61] There were no transitional provisions, so that an existing IFRS user had to apply IAS 27 (2007) with full retrospective effect.

The amendments made in 2008 to paragraphs 4, 18, 19, 26 to 37 and 41(e) and (f) of IAS 27 should be applied for annual periods beginning on or after 1 July 2009. Entities are permitted to adopt IAS 27 (as amended in 2008) for earlier periods, but are required to disclose that they have done so.[62] However, an entity should not apply these amendments for annual periods beginning before 1 July 2009 unless it also applies IFRS 3 (as revised in 2008). An entity should apply the 2008 amendments to IAS 27 retrospectively, with the following exceptions:[63]

(a)   the amendment to paragraph 28 of IAS 27 (as amended in 2008) for attributing total comprehensive income to the owners of the parent and to the non-controlling interests even if this results in the non-controlling interests having a deficit balance. Therefore, an entity should not restate any profit or loss attribution for reporting periods before the amendment is applied (see Chapter 7 at 4.4.2);

(b)   the requirements in paragraphs 30 and 31 of IAS 27 (as amended in 2008) for accounting for changes in ownership interests in a subsidiary after control is obtained. Therefore, the requirements in paragraphs 30 and 31 do not apply to changes that occurred before an entity applies the amendments (see Chapter 7 at 3.2.2); and

(c)   the requirements in paragraphs 34 to 37 of IAS 27 (as amended in 2008) for the loss of control of a subsidiary. An entity must not restate the carrying amount of an investment in a former subsidiary if control was lost before it applies those amendments. In addition, an entity is not permitted to recalculate any gain or loss on the loss of control of a subsidiary that occurred before the amendments are applied (see Chapter 7 at 3.2.1).

The Board concluded that the implementation difficulties and costs associated with applying the above amendments retrospectively would have outweighed the benefit of improved comparability of financial information.[64]

7   FUTURE DEVELOPMENTS

The IASB and IFRIC are engaged in several projects that will affect the accounting treatment of subsidiaries:

- IASB's Framework: Phase D Reporting entity (see 7.1 below); and
- Consolidation project (see 7.2 below).

7.1   IASB's Framework: Phase D Reporting entity

At a joint meeting in April 2004 the FASB and the IASB agreed that their underlying conceptual frameworks should be revisited and, if possible, an agreed single conceptual framework produced.

The joint framework project is planned to be developed over a number of phases (see Chapter 2 at 5), one of which – Phase D – deals with the reporting entity. In May 2008, the IASB issued the discussion paper *Preliminary Views on an improved Conceptual Framework for Financial Reporting: The Reporting Entity*, which considers issues relevant in developing a reporting entity concept for the Board's common conceptual framework.[65] The Discussion Paper is subdivided into four sections:

- *The reporting entity concept* – The Board's preliminary view is that the conceptual framework should broadly describe rather than precisely define a reporting entity as a circumscribed area of business activity of interest to present and potential equity investors, lenders and other capital providers. Furthermore, a reporting entity should not just be limited to business activities that are structured as legal entities;[66]

- *Group reporting entity* – Section 2 of the document discusses when the relationship between one entity and another is such that the boundary between the two entities should be disregarded, and the two entities instead presented as a single unit.[67] The Board's preliminary views are that:

  '(a)   if control is used to determine the composition of a group reporting entity, then control should be defined at the conceptual level.

   (b)   control over another entity entails both power over that entity and the ability to obtain benefits.

   (c)   determining whether one entity has control over another involves an assessment of all the existing facts and circumstances.'[68]

  The Discussion Paper considers three approaches to determining the composition of a group reporting entity: the controlling entity model, the common control model and the risks and rewards model.[69] The preliminary view is that the controlling entity model should be used as the primary basis for determining the composition of a group reporting entity. The common control model may also provide useful information to users; therefore use of that approach would be determined at the standards level;[70]

- *Parent entity financial reporting* – The Board's preliminary view is that consolidated financial statements should be presented from the perspective of the group reporting entity (i.e. not from the perspective of the parent company's shareholders), which is consistent with the decision in the first phase of the conceptual framework project to adopt the entity perspective and also consistent with amendments introduced by IAS 27 (as amended in 2008). However, this does not preclude inclusion of financial reports information that is primarily directed to the needs of a particular group of capital providers.[71] The IASB also concluded that the conceptual framework should not preclude the presentation of parent-only financial statements, provided that they are included in the same financial report as consolidated financial statements;[72] and

- *Control issues* – Section 4 of the document considers difficult issues such as latent control and the treatment of options over voting rights.[73]

In January 2009, the Board discussed some of the issues arising from responses to the Discussion Paper and tentatively decided 'to state that a reporting entity is a circumscribed area of economic activity whose financial information has the potential to be useful to present and potential equity investors, lenders and other capital providers for decisions in their capacity as capital providers'.[74] In addition , the Board affirmed that (1) a reporting entity need not be a legal entity, (2) a legal entity could, but would not necessarily, meet the description of a reporting entity and (3) a branch or segment of a legal entity could, but would not necessarily, meet the description of a reporting entity. The Board also tentatively decided that:

- 'if the reporting entity controls other entities, it should present consolidated financial statements using the controlling entity model.

- when the controlling entity is not a reporting entity, it may be useful to present combined financial statements of entities under common control.

- an assessment of risks and rewards might be useful for implementing the controlling entity model in some circumstances, but should not replace control as the basis for identifying the entities to be consolidated.

- parent-only financial statements should not be mandatory but may provide useful information if they are presented together with consolidated financial statements.'[75]

Furthermore, in March 2009, the Board decided tentatively that:[76]

- the concept of control of an entity should be discussed at a high level in the conceptual framework;

- the relationship referred to as 'significant influence' does not constitute control of an entity; and

- the forthcoming exposure draft should not discuss proportionate consolidation.

Also, the Board instructed its staff to start drafting an exposure draft, but cautioned that reversions might be needed as a result of the Board's discussion of the responses to ED 10 (see 7.2 below). At the time of writing the Board expected the exposure draft to be published in the third quarter of 2009, with a view to publishing the final chapter of the conceptual framework on this topic in the second half of 2010.[77]

7.2   Consolidation project

7.2.1   *Overview of ED 10: Consolidated Financial Statements*

In June 2003 the IASB added a project on consolidation to its agenda, the ultimate aim of which is to issue a new IFRS to replace IAS 27 and SIC-12. In December 2008, the Board published ED 10, which is discussed in detail below.

A   *Definition of control of an entity*

A new definition of control of an entity is proposed in ED 10 that would apply to all types of investment structures. Under ED 10, control is 'the power of a reporting entity to direct the activities of another entity to generate returns for the reporting entity'.[78] The definition consists of three elements:

- *Power*, which refers to the 'ability to direct the activities of another'. Power to 'govern the strategic operating and financing policies' as referred to today is only one way in which this control can be achieved, therefore potentially more entities may be caught;[79]

- *Returns*, which may be positive or negative and must vary according to the activities of the controlled entity; and[80]

- *Link between power and benefits*, the power held by the reporting entity should be commensurate with the returns that the reporting entity is exposed to. The underlying assumption in ED 10 is that the entity receiving the greatest returns from another entity is likely to have the greatest power over that entity.[81]

ED 10 proposes that control must be current and must be reassessed on a continuous basis, concepts on which IAS 27 (as amended in 2008) is silent.[82]

B   Currently exercisable options and convertible instruments

Simply holding currently exercisable options that, if exercised, would give the reporting entity more than half of the voting rights in the entity is not sufficient to demonstrate control of that entity. Instead, ED 10 proposes that entities holding such options, need to assess whether, when taken with other arrangements in place, they have the power to direct the activities of another entity.[83]

C   De facto control

ED 10 proposes that a reporting entity holding less than a majority of voting rights may still have the power to direct the activities of another. The exposure draft proposes additional guidance to determine whether power exists in such cases. In particular, it proposes that an entity has power to direct the activities of another entity, if:[84]

- it has more voting rights than any other party; and
- its voting rights are sufficient to give it the ability to determine the strategic operating and financing policies.

To determine if the voting rights are sufficient, ED 10 proposes numerous factors that could be considered, similar to the other arrangements that are evaluated when considering if currently exercisable options and convertible instruments give sufficient power. This will therefore require an assessment of all facts and circumstances in each situation.

D   Approval or veto rights of other parties

ED 10 proposes that a reporting entity can still control another entity even though other parties have protective rights in that other entity. The protective rights must however be limited to rights that do not affect the reporting entity's ability to direct the strategic operating and financing policies of the entity.[85]

The Basis for Conclusions notes the following in this context: 'Some asked the Board to incorporate guidance similar to that in the US EITF No. 96-16 *Investor's Accounting for an Investee When the Investor Has a Majority of the Voting Interest but the Minority Shareholder or Shareholders Have Certain Approval or Veto Rights*. The Board decided that such an approach was appropriate because the guidance is widely accepted and incorporating it in the proposed IFRS would help with international convergence.'[86]

E   Agency arrangements

ED 10 specifically notes that a reporting entity does not control an entity if it is acting as an agent on behalf of another party.[87] Additional guidance is proposed to evaluate the role of 'kick-out rights' of managers and the receipt of variable fee as remuneration. Unconditional rights to remove the entity from a management control function indicate that another entity (the principal) has retained the power to direct the activities of the entity (therefore an agency relationship exists). However, the right to remove the entity only in exceptional circumstances such as bankruptcy or breach of contract is indicative of having only protective rights.[88] Similarly, when an entity receives a fee that is commensurate with the services provided or in the case of performance fee arrangements, there is no requirement to repay fees already received if the value of the portfolio of assets decreases in a subsequent period, indicates that the entity is acting as an agent.[89]

In situations where a reporting entity acts simultaneously in the role of a principal and agent, such as where a fund manager holds investments on its own account and within funds that it manages, ED 10 proposes to put the onus on the reporting entity to demonstrate that it does not use the power it has as an agent for its own benefits.

F   Structured entities

The exposure draft introduces a new term 'structured entities' to replace 'special purpose entities'. A structured entity is an entity whose activities are restricted to the extent that they are not directed by a governing body.

ED 10 does not propose bright line requirements setting out when a reporting entity should consolidate a structured entity. Rather, an entity needs to consider all facts and circumstances to determine whether it has the power to direct the activities that cause the returns of the structured entity to vary, for example:[90]

- what is the purpose and design of the structured entity?
- what returns does the reporting entity earn from its involvement with the structured entity?
- to what extent are the activities of the structured entity predetermined?
- does the reporting entity have the ability to change the restrictions or predetermined strategic policies of the structured entity?
- what is the effect of any related arrangements?
- is the entity is acting as an agent in its relationship with the structured entity?

G   Disclosures

ED 10 proposes significant new disclosure requirements including:[91]

- a description of the judgements made in deciding whether or not an entity controls another entity;
- any restrictions that are a consequence of assets and liabilities being held by subsidiaries including the extent to which non-controlling interests can restrict the activities of such subsidiaries; and

- in the case of structured entities that a reporting entity does not control, disclosures regarding the nature and risks associated with the reporting entity's involvement.

  Involvement in this context includes both contractual and non-contractual arrangements that expose the reporting entity to risk. This includes disclosure of the value of assets transferred to structured entities at the date of transfer, income earned from the reporting entity's involvement with structured entities, and a description of the type of income. This information would be disclosed by relevant category (determined based on the risk). It is proposed that this quantitative information is disclosed for the current period and the preceding two reporting periods. It is also proposed that the maximum exposure to losses from involvement with a structured entity is disclosed and the basis on which this exposure is determined.

H   Transitional provisions

ED 10 proposes that entities should apply the new IFRS prospectively. As such, if at the date of adoption a reporting entity identifies an entity which should now be consolidated, the reporting entity will need to account for it as a business combination. Similarly if a reporting entity considers that it no longer controls a subsidiary, it will need to account for it as a disposal at that date.[92]

7.2.2   Some observations about ED 10

We support the Board's decision to attempt to develop one consolidation principle, based on control, that would be applicable to all types of entities. We believe that the existence today of two different models under IAS 27 (as revised in 2008) and SIC-12 can cause tension when assessing whether one entity has control of another entity.

However, we have significant concerns that ED 10, as it is currently drafted, does not achieve that objective. In particular, we have concerns that in a number of places, the exposure draft is not operational and will create diversity in practice. As such, we do not think that the proposals provide 'clearer guidance' than the current IAS 27 (as revised in 2008) and SIC-12 for determining when one entity controls another. This arises primarily from the lack of clearly articulated principles and contradictory requirements in the exposure draft. In summary, our key areas of concern are:

- the link between power and returns is not clear and could lead to differing interpretations;
- the principles to identify agency relationships are not clear and do not address the fundamental issue of whether it is necessary to have removal rights or not to identify such relationships;
- the principles and guidance about power to direct without a majority of the voting rights are not clear, and we believe it will lead to consolidation of entities where control does not exist;
- the assessment of options that when exercised give the holder a majority of the voting rights is likewise unclear and contradictory;

- the requirements, in a number of places, appear to deem control to exist due to the inaction/action of others – referred to as the 'ability to be in control'. However, it is our belief that this is not actual control. We believe control means that the party has the ability to 'force' decisions/actions regardless of the inaction/action of others;

- the definition of 'returns' is not clear, and the principles are contradictory; and

- the separation of structured entities and non-structured entities for the purposes of determining control is potentially dangerous and we believe it will perpetuate the confusion between two models.

We also believe that, as drafted, a number of structures that are consolidated when applying IAS 27 (as revised in 2008) and SIC-12 will no longer be consolidated when applying the ED 10.

We are also disappointed that the IASB and FASB did not develop a common standard on consolidation with the FASB, particularly as the FASB has also been revising the requirements for variable-interest-entities. We believe that the issue of consolidation and control of an entity is an area which would benefit significantly from a converged standard issued by both Boards.

Due to the above factors, we do not believe that the Board should proceed with this amendment. Rather, we believe that the Board should pursue a short term solution to amend only the disclosure requirements of the current IAS 27 (as revised in 2008) and SIC-12, thereby improving the disclosures around consolidated and non-consolidated entities. As a longer term project, we urge the IASB and FASB to work together to develop a common consolidation standard with clear principles upon which control is assessed. Although retaining two models in IFRS is not ideal, we believe that practice has developed in such a way that the current models are applied relatively consistently.

In this context, we are also concerned that the disclosure requirements proposed in ED 10 are too extensive and will overwhelm both the preparers and the users.

Whether the Boards go ahead with this proposal, and/or pursue a longer-term project with the FASB, we also believe the Board should:

- include examples illustrating the application of the principles to a broad range of structures and investments; and

- conduct field tests as to the application of the consolidation principles and disclosure requirements.

7.2.3   Current developments

In July 2009, the Board began its deliberations of the proposals in ED 10, taking into account the comments and information received from respondents to the exposure draft and from participants at the round table meetings held in Toronto, Tokyo and London. The Board decided tentatively that:

- 'control, defined to require a reporting entity to have both the power to direct the activities and the ability to benefit from that power, is the only basis for consolidation.

- exposure to risks and rewards alone does not constitute control. Exposure to risks and rewards is an indicator of control because the greater a reporting entity's exposure to risks and rewards from its involvement with an entity, the greater the incentive for the reporting entity to obtain rights sufficient to give it the power to direct the activities of an entity.

- reputational risk does not give a reporting entity the power to direct the activities of an entity. However, the existence of reputational risk can give a reporting entity an incentive to control another entity.

- if a reporting entity holds less than half of the voting rights of an entity, the reporting entity can have the power to direct the activities of that entity, depending on the circumstances.

- if a reporting entity holds options or convertible instruments to obtain voting rights in an entity, the reporting entity can have the power to direct the activities of that entity.'[93]

The Board continue its deliberations of issues raised by respondents to the exposure draft and, at the time of writing, expects to publish a final standard in the second half of 2009.[94]

References

1 A joint venture need not take the form of a separate entity (see Chapter 12).
2 IAS 27, *Consolidated and Separate Financial Statements*, IASB, para. 1 and IAS 27 (2007), *Consolidated and Separate Financial Statements*, IASB, 2007 Bound Volume, para. 1.
3 IAS 27, para. 3 and IAS 27 (2007), para. 3.
4 IAS 27, para. 4 and IAS 27 (2007), para. 4.
5 IAS 27, paras. 9 and 12 and IAS 27 (2007), paras. 9 and 12.
6 SIC-12, *Consolidation – Special Purpose Entities*, IASB.
7 IAS 27, para. IN1.
8 IAS 27, para. IN2.
9 IAS 27, para. 4 and IAS 27 (2007), para. 4.
10 IAS 27, para. 4 and IAS 27 (2007), para. 4.
11 IAS 27, para. 4 and IAS 27 (2007), para. 4.
12 IAS 27, para. 4 and IAS 27 (2007), para. 4.
13 IAS 27, para. 13 and IAS 27 (2007), para. 13.
14 EITF 96-16, *Investor's Accounting for an Investee When the Investor Has a Majority of the Voting Interest but the Minority Shareholder or Shareholders Have Certain Approval or Veto Rights*, EITF, July 1998.
15 ED 10, *Exposure Draft: Consolidated Financial Statements*, IASB, December 2008, para. BC61.
16 IAS 27, para. IG4 and IAS 27 (2007), para. IG4.
17 IAS 27, para. IG2 and IAS 27 (2007), para. IG2.
18 IAS 27, para. 14 and IAS 27 (2007), para. 14.
19 IAS 27, paras. 14 and IG1-IG4 and IAS 27 (2007), paras. 14 and IG1-IG4.
20 IAS 27, paras. 14 and IG1 and IAS 27 (2007), paras. 14 and IG1.
21 IAS 27, para. IG3 and IAS 27 (2007), para. IG3.
22 IAS 27, para. 14 and IAS 27 (2007), para. 14.
23 IAS 27, para. IG8 (Example 3) and IAS 27 (2007), para. IG8 (Example 3).
24 IAS 27, para. 15 and IAS 27 (2007), para. 15.
25 IAS 27, para. IG8 (Examples 1, 4 and 5).

26 IAS 27, para. IG2 and IAS 27 (2007), para. IG2.
27 For example, IAS 27 requires disclosure of the reason for consolidating an entity in which the reporting entity does not own more than one-half of the voting power.
28 *IASB Update*, IASB, October 2005, p. 2.
29 SIC-12, para. 8.
30 SIC-12, para. 1.
31 SIC-12, para. 2.
32 SIC-12, para. 3.
33 SIC-12, paras. 6 and paras. 15A to 15E.
34 SIC-12, para. 9.
35 SIC-12, para. 13.
36 SIC-12, para. 10 and Appendix.
37 *IFRIC Update*, IFRIC, November 2006, p. 11.
38 SIC-12, para. 8.
39 IAS 27, para. 4 and IAS 27 (2007), para. 4.
40 IAS 27, para. 10 and IAS 27 (2007), para. 10.
41 IAS 27, para. 5 and IAS 27 (2007), para. 5.
42 IAS 27, para. 9 and IAS 27 (2007), para. 9.
43 IAS 27, para. 10 and IAS 27 (2007), para. 10.
44 IAS 27, para. 8 and IAS 27 (2007), para. 8.
45 IAS 27, para. 11 and IAS 27 (2007), para. 11.
46 IAS 27, para. BC15 and IAS 27 (2007), para. BC10.
47 IAS 27, para. BC15 and IAS 27 (2007), para. BC10.
48 IFRS for SMEs, *International Financial Reporting Standard for Small and Medium-sized Entities (IFRS for SMEs)*, IASB, July 2009, para. 9.28.
49 IFRS for SMEs, para. 9.28.
50 IFRS for SMEs, para. 9.29.
51 IFRS for SMEs, para. 9.30.
52 IAS 27, para. 12 and IAS 27 (2007), para. 12.
53 IFRS 5, *Non-current Assets Held for Sale and Discontinued Operations*, IASB, paras. 15-18 and 39.
54 IAS 27, para. 16 and IAS 27 (2007), para. 19.
55 IAS 27, paras. BC21-BC27 and IAS 27 (2007), paras. BC16-BC22.
56 IAS 27, para. 17 and IAS 27 (2007), para. 20.
57 IAS 27, para. BC20 and IAS 27 (2007), para. IN9.
58 IAS 27, para. 32 and IAS 27 (2007), para. 21.
59 IAS 27, para. 41 and IAS 27 (2007), para. 40.
60 IAS 27, para. 41.
61 IAS 27 (2007), para. 43.
62 IAS 27, para. 45.
63 IAS 27, para. 45.
64 IAS 27, para. BC73.
65 Discussion Paper, *Preliminary Views on an improved Conceptual Framework for Financial Reporting: The Reporting Entity*, IASB, May 2008, para. S1.
66 Discussion Paper, para. S2.
67 Discussion Paper, para. S3.
68 Discussion Paper, para. S4.
69 Discussion Paper, para. S5.
70 Discussion Paper, para. S6.
71 Discussion Paper, para. S8.
72 Discussion Paper, para. S9.
73 Discussion Paper, para. S10.
74 *IASB Update*, IASB, January 2009, p. 3.
75 *IASB Update*, IASB, January 2009, p. 3.
76 *IASB Update*, IASB, March 2009, p. 2.
77 *IASB Work Plan – projected timetable as at 1 August 2009*, IASB, www.iasb.org.uk, 10 August 2009.
78 ED 10, para. 4.
79 ED 10, paras. 8 and 9.
80 ED 10, paras. 10 and 11.
81 ED 10, para. 13.
82 ED 10, para. 15.
83 ED 10, para. B13.
84 ED 10, paras. 26-29.
85 ED 10, paras. B1 and B2.
86 ED 10, para. BC61.
87 ED 10, para. B3.
88 ED 10, para. B4.
89 ED 10, paras. B5-B8.
90 ED 10, paras. 30-38.
91 ED 10, paras. 48 and B30-B49.
92 ED 10, paras. 52-53.
93 *IASB Update*, IASB, July 2009, p. 1.
94 *IASB Work Plan – projected timetable as at 1 August 2009*, IASB, www.iasb.org.uk, 10 August 2009.

Chapter 7

Consolidation procedures and non-controlling interests

1 INTRODUCTION

1.1 Background

The concepts underlying consolidation and the requirement to prepare consolidated financial statements are discussed in Chapter 6. This chapter deals with:

- consolidation procedures (see 2 below);
- accounting for changes in ownership interests (see 3 below);
- accounting for non-controlling interests (see 4 below);
- call and put options over non-controlling interests (see 5 below); and
- transitional issues (see 6 below).

1.2 Consolidating partly owned subsidiaries

In preparing consolidated financial statements, an entity combines the financial statements of the parent and its subsidiaries in order that the consolidated financial statements present financial information about the group as that of a single economic entity. Various alternative ways of looking at a group become relevant when there are subsidiary companies which are not wholly owned by the parent. The particular matters which are affected are:

- the elimination of the effects of intragroup transactions;
- the calculation and treatment of non-controlling (or minority) interests, i.e. the interests of shareholders other than the controlling shareholder; and
- the treatment of changes in stake in the subsidiary.

There are two widely accepted concepts, referred to respectively as the entity concept and the proprietary concept, although the latter has a number of further variants.

1.2.1   The entity concept

The entity concept focuses on the existence of the group as an economic unit, rather than looking at it only through the eyes of the dominant shareholder group. It concentrates on the resources controlled by the entity, and regards the identity of owners with claims on these resources as being of secondary importance. It therefore makes no distinction between the treatment given to different classes of shareholders, whether they are shareholders in the parent or shareholders in a subsidiary, and all transactions between the shareholders are regarded as internal to the group.

1.2.2   The proprietary (parent entity) concept

The proprietary concept emphasises ownership through a controlling shareholding interest, and regards the consolidated financial statements as being principally for the information of the shareholders of the parent. Its primary concern is not to present financial statements which are relevant to shareholders of subsidiaries. This is achieved either by treating the non-controlling shareholders as 'outsiders' and reflecting their interests as quasi-liabilities or by leaving them out of the group financial statements entirely, thereby consolidating only the parent's percentage interest in the assets and liabilities of the subsidiary (the 'proportionate consolidation' method). The proprietary concept is sometimes referred to as the 'parent entity' concept, and there is a variant of it known as the 'parent entity extension' concept, which leans more towards the entity concept described above.

1.2.3   Different concepts of a group allowed under IFRS

IFRS 3 (2007) – *Business Combinations* – and IAS 27 (2007) – *Consolidated and Separate Financial Statements* – contain elements of the entity, parent entity and hybrid entity concept rather than following any one on a consistent basis.

	Section	Entity concept	Parent entity concept	Hybrid entity concept *)
IAS 27 (2007) and IFRS 3 (2007)				
Elimination of intragroup transactions	2.4	●		
Decrease in ownership interest without loss of control	3.3.2	●	●	●
Increase in ownership interest	3.3.3	●	●	●
Accounting for goodwill upon acquisition	4.1.3		●	
Presentation of minority interest	4.3	●		
Accounting for losses in partly-owned subsidiaries	4.4.2		●	

*) Under this method, the difference between the cost of the additional interest in the subsidiary and the minority interest's share of the assets and liabilities reflected in the consolidated balance sheet at the date of the acquisition of the minority interest is reflected partly as goodwill and partly as an equity transaction (see 3.3.2 A below).

In IFRS 3 (as revised in 2008) – *Business Combinations* – and IAS 27 (as amended in 2008) – *Consolidated and Separate Financial Statements* – the IASB has effectively aligned IFRS to the entity concept.

	Section	Entity concept	Parent entity concept
IAS 27 (as amended in 2008) and IFRS 3 (as revised in 2008)			
Elimination of intragroup transactions	2.4	●	
Decrease in ownership interest without loss of control	3.2.2	●	
Increase in ownership interest	3.2.2	●	
Accounting for goodwill upon acquisition	4.1.3	●	●
Presentation of non-controlling interest	4.3	●	
Accounting for losses in partly-owned subsidiaries	4.4.1	●	

However, IFRS still effectively allows a choice between the entity concept and the parent entity concept in accounting for goodwill on acquisition of a subsidiary. IFRS 3 (as revised in 2008) permits an acquirer to measure any non-controlling interest in an acquiree at the acquisition date either at fair value or as the non-controlling interest's proportionate share of the acquiree's net identifiable assets, on a transaction-by-transaction basis.[1] The Basis for Conclusions to IFRS 3 (as revised in 2008) observes that the 'IASB reluctantly concluded that the only way the revised IFRS 3 would receive sufficient votes to be issued was if it permitted an acquirer to measure a non-controlling interest either at fair value or at its proportionate share of the acquiree's identifiable net assets, on a transaction-by-transaction basis'.[2]

1.2.4 Comparison between the different concepts of a group

The distinction between the different methods in practice can best be illustrated by an example:

Example 7.1: *Comparison between the different concepts of a group*

Assume that entity A buys 75% of entity B for €1,200 when entity B has total net assets with a fair value of €1,000 and a carrying amount of €800. The fair value of the 25% minority interest is €400. Under the various concepts described above, the consolidated balance sheet of entity A would incorporate the effects of the acquisition calculated as follows:

	Entity concept €	Proprietary concept €	Parent entity extension concept €
Net assets of B	1,000	950	1,000
Goodwill	600	450	450
	1,600	1,400	1,450
Investor interest	1,200	1,200	1,200
Non-controlling (or minority) interest	400	200	250
	1,600	1,400	1,450

Entity concept

Both the net identifiable assets and goodwill are reported in the balance sheet at the full amount of their fair value as determined by the transaction involving the majority shareholder. These amounts are then apportioned between the controlling and non-controlling shareholders.

Proprietary concept

The proprietary concept leaves the non-controlling (or minority) interest unaffected by the transaction of the controlling shareholder. It is shown simply as their proportionate share of the carrying values of the net assets of the entity. This means that the goodwill is stated at a figure which represents the difference between the cost of the 75% investment (€1,200) and 75% of the fair value of the assets (€750). Perhaps more disturbingly, the assets are carried on a mixed basis which represents 75% of their fair value and 25% of their book value.

This feature is eliminated if proportionate consolidation is adopted, since the non-controlling (or minority) interest is disregarded altogether, being set against the assets and liabilities of the subsidiary on a line by line basis, so that only the controlling investor's share of the subsidiary's assets is consolidated. This would result in the consolidation of assets of €750 and goodwill of €450, representing the total of the investment of €1,200. However, IFRS does not allow proportionate consolidation for subsidiaries, although it is currently one of the permitted treatments for certain types of joint venture (see Chapter 12).

Parent entity extension concept

The mixed basis for the carrying amount of net identifiable assets is also avoided in the parent entity extension concept, which includes the net identifiable assets at the whole amount of their fair value and apportions that between the controlling shareholder's interest and the non-controlling (or minority) interests, but includes goodwill only as it relates to the controlling investor.

A   Intragroup transactions

The different concepts are also relevant to the calculation of the adjustments made to eliminate the effects of intragroup transactions (i.e. those between entities within the same group). If entity A in Example 7.1 sold an item of inventory to entity B for a profit of €100, and entity B still held the inventory at the year end, it would be necessary to make an adjustment on consolidation to eliminate what was an unrealised profit from the group point of view.

Under the proprietary concept, the non-controlling shareholders are regarded as outsiders, and therefore there is a case for saying that 25% of the profit *has* been realised; this would be done by limiting the elimination of intragroup profit to €75.

Under the proportionate consolidation method, only 75% of the inventory would appear in the consolidated balance sheet in the first place, so the adjustment would simply be to deduct €75 from both the group profit and loss account and from the inventory.

Under the entity concept, as it is the parent which has made the sale, the whole write-down of inventory of €100 would be charged against the group profit and loss account, with no amount attributed to the non-controlling (or minority) interest. This is the approach adopted in IAS 27.

B   *Loss-making subsidiaries*

A further practical situation where differences between the concepts emerge is when a partly-owned subsidiary makes losses which put it into overall deficit. Under the entity concept, the consolidated financial statements would continue to account for these losses and apportion them between the controlling and non-controlling (or minority) shareholders in proportion to their holdings, even if this created a debit balance for the non-controlling (or minority) interest in the balance sheet.

A proprietary concept would not normally permit the non-controlling (or minority) interest to be shown as a debit balance, because it could not usually be regarded as a recoverable asset (except to the extent that the minority has a binding obligation and is able to make an additional investment to cover the losses) from the point of view of the majority interest, which is the orientation of the financial statements under the proprietary concept. This is the approach required by IAS 27 (2007). However, IAS 27 (as amended in 2008) requires that total comprehensive income be attributed to the owners of the parent and to the non-controlling interests even if this results in the non-controlling interests having a deficit balance (see 4.4 below).

1.3   Terminology: non-controlling interests versus minority interests

The 2008 amendments to IAS 27 changed the term 'minority interest' to 'non-controlling interest'. There are some differences between the definitions of 'non-controlling interests' and 'minority interests' in IAS 27 (as amended in 2008) and IAS 27 (2007), respectively, which are discussed in detail at 4.1 below. However, in contexts where the terms 'non-controlling interests' and 'minority interests' are synonymous this chapter refers to 'non-controlling (or minority) interests'.

While the IASB made significant amendments to IAS 27 in 2008, many things have remained unchanged. Hence, to the extent that the requirements of IAS 27 (as amended in 2008) and IAS 27 (2007) are similar or identical, they are discussed together and the standard is referred to as 'IAS 27'. However, where significant differences exist the requirements of both versions of IAS 27 are discussed separately in this chapter.

2   CONSOLIDATION PROCEDURES

It is beyond the scope of this chapter to discuss the detailed mechanics of the consolidation process, for which reference should be made to the various specialised texts which give a full exposition of this subject. The analysis below essentially deals only with those areas where IAS 27 (as amended in 2008) and IAS 27 (2007) prescribe one of a number of possible treatments.

This section deals with the following practical aspects of consolidation:

* basic principles (see 2.1 below);
* acquisition of a subsidiary that is not a business (see 2.1.1 below);
* proportionate consolidated (see 2.2 below);
* method of consolidation (see 2.3 below);

- intragroup eliminations (see 2.4 below);
- non-coterminous accounting periods (see 2.5 below); and
- consistent accounting policies (see 2.6 below).

2.1   Basic principles

In preparing consolidated financial statements, an entity first combines the financial statements of the parent and its subsidiaries on a 'line-by-line' basis by adding together like items of assets, liabilities, equity, income and expenses. In order that the consolidated financial statements present financial information about the group as that of a single economic entity, the following adjustments are made:

(a)   the carrying amount of the parent's investment in each subsidiary and the parent's portion of equity of each subsidiary are eliminated. Any difference (representing either goodwill if positive or, if negative, the excess of the acquirer's interest in the net fair value of the acquiree's identifiable assets, liabilities and contingent liabilities over cost) is accounted for in accordance with IFRS 3 (see Chapter 9);

(b)   non-controlling (or minority) interests in the profit or loss of consolidated subsidiaries for the reporting period are identified; and

(c)   non-controlling (or minority) interests in the net assets of consolidated subsidiaries are identified separately from the parent's ownership interests in them. Non-controlling (or minority) interests in the net assets consist of:

(i)   the amount of those non-controlling (or minority) interests at the date of the original combination calculated in accordance with IFRS 3; and

(ii)   the non-controlling (or minority) interests' share of changes in equity since the date of the combination.[3]

Non-controlling interest is defined as the equity in a subsidiary not attributable, directly or indirectly, to a parent.[4] While minority interest is defined as that portion of the profit or loss and net assets of a subsidiary attributable to equity interests that are not owned, directly or indirectly through subsidiaries, by the parent.[5] The accounting treatment for non-controlling (or minority) interests is discussed in more detail at 4 below.

2.1.1   Acquisition of a subsidiary that is not a business

The above basic principles should also be applied when a parent acquires an interest in an entity that is not a business, as illustrated in the example below.

Example 7.2:   Acquisition of a majority interest in a single asset entity

Entity A pays £160,000 to acquire an 80% controlling interest in entity B, which holds a single property that does not constitute a business. The remaining 20% interest is held by an unrelated third party. How should entity A account for its interest in entity B?

Under IAS 27, entity A is required to consolidate entity B and recognise a non-controlling (or minority) interest in accordance with IFRS 3.[6] The latter standard states that when an entity acquires a group of assets or net assets that does not constitute a business, it should allocate the cost of the group between the individual identifiable assets and liabilities in the group based on their relative fair values at the date of acquisition.[7] Therefore, after entity A allocates its purchase consideration to the individual assets acquired, it notionally grosses up those assets and recognises the difference as non-controlling (or minority) interest:

	£m	£m
Investment property (£160,000 ÷ 80%)	200,000	
Non-controlling (or minority) interest (£200,000 × 20%)		40,000
Cash		160,000

The non-controlling (or minority) interests are stated at their proportion of the relative fair values of the assets. Tax effects, if any, have been ignored in this example.

If, however, in the above example there was an arrangement between entity A and the non-controlling (or minority) interest resulting in joint control, IAS 31 – *Interests in Joint Ventures* – would be applied (see Chapter 12 at 3.3), and the investment in entity B would be recognised and measured using proportionate consolidation or the equity method.

2.2   Proportion consolidated

As discussed in Chapter 6 at 2.1.2, IAS 27 (as amended in 2008) and IAS 27 (2007) require that, where an investor has currently exercisable contingent rights over shares (such as options or conversion rights) in another entity, those rights should be taken into account in determining whether or not the investor controls that other entity.

However, when potential voting rights exist, the proportions of profit or loss and changes in equity allocated to the parent and non-controlling (or minority) interests are determined on the basis of present ownership interests and do not reflect the possible exercise or conversion of potential voting rights.[8] These provisions are equally applicable to determining what share of an associate or joint venture should be accounted for under, respectively IAS 28 – *Investments in Associates* – and IAS 31.[9]

The basic principle is illustrated by Example 7.3 below.

Example 7.3:   Potential voting rights

Entities A and B hold 40% and 60% respectively of the equity of entity C. A also holds a currently exercisable option over one third of B's shares, which, if exercised, would give A a 60% interest in C. This would, absent exceptional circumstances, lead to the conclusion that C was a subsidiary of A. However, in preparing its consolidated financial statements, A would attribute 60% of the results and net assets of C to non-controlling (or minority) interests.

However, simply to allocate the proportions of profit or loss and changes in equity on the basis of present legal ownership interests might not always be appropriate. The implementation guidance to IAS 27 (as amended in 2008) and IAS 27 (2007) clarifies that, in determining the level of present ownership interest, an entity should have regard to the eventual exercise of potential rights and other derivatives that give the entity access to the economic benefits at present.[10]

The treatment in Example 7.3 above will be appropriate if the options contain one or more of the following features:

- the option price has not yet been determined;

- the option price is based on the expected future results or net assets of the subsidiary at the date of exercise; or

- it has been agreed between A and B that, prior to the exercise of the option, all retained profits may be freely distributed to the existing shareholders according to their current shareholdings.

It may well be that, as part of a business combination, put and call options are created over non-controlling (or minority) interests. The issues raised by such arrangements are discussed further at 5 below. Finally, the proportion consolidated might be different when cumulative preference shares are held by non-controlling (or minority) interests (see 4.5 below) or under IAS 27 (2007) when a subsidiary is loss-making (see 4.4 below).

2.2.1   Interaction with IAS 39

Interests in subsidiaries, associates or joint ventures are normally accounted for in accordance with, respectively, IAS 27, IAS 28 and IAS 31, while derivatives over such interests are normally accounted for in accordance with IAS 39 – *Financial Instruments: Recognition and Measurement* (see Chapter 29 at 3.1). Where, however, the effect of a derivative is taken into account in determining not merely the existence of control (or of significant influence or joint control) but also the share of the investment to be accounted for, it ceases to be within the scope of IAS 39.[11] This is entirely appropriate, since, if IAS 39 continued to be applied, there would clearly be an element of double counting by an entity that accounted both for changes in the fair value of such a derivative under IAS 39 and for the effective interest created by the derivative in the underlying investment under IAS 27, IAS 28 or IAS 31.

2.3   Method of consolidation

IAS 27 (as amended in 2008) and IAS 27 (2007) do not specifically address the question whether consolidated accounts should be prepared using the direct method or the step-by-step method. IFRIC 16 – *Hedges of a Net Investment in a Foreign Operation* – defines these methods as follows:[12]

- *Direct method* – The financial statements of the foreign operation are translated directly into the functional currency of the ultimate parent; and

- *Step-by-step method* – The financial statements of the foreign operation are first translated into the functional currency of any intermediate parent(s) and then translated into the functional currency of the ultimate parent (or the presentation currency if different).

With the exception of the determination of currency translation differences that arise upon consolidation both methods produce exactly the same outcomes. The Basis for Conclusions to IFRIC 16 explains that 'the difference becomes apparent in the determination of the amount of the foreign currency translation reserve that is subsequently reclassified to profit or loss. An ultimate parent entity using the direct method of consolidation would reclassify the cumulative foreign currency translation reserve that arose between its functional currency and that of the foreign operation. An ultimate parent entity using the step-by-step method of consolidation might reclassify the cumulative foreign currency translation reserve reflected in the financial statements of the intermediate parent, i.e. the amount that arose between the functional currency of the foreign operation and that of the intermediate parent, translated into the functional currency of the ultimate parent.'[13]

IFRIC 16 notes that in the case of a disposal of a subsidiary by an intermediate parent 'the use of the step-by-step method of consolidation may result in the reclassification to profit or loss of an amount different from that used to determine hedge effectiveness. This difference may be eliminated by determining the amount relating to that foreign operation that would have arisen if the direct method of consolidation had been used. Making this adjustment is not required by IAS 21 – *The Effects of Changes in Foreign Exchange Rates*. However, it is an accounting policy choice that should be followed consistently for all net investments.'[14]

IFRIC 16 is discussed in more detail in Chapter 13 at 3.3.5 and 3.3.6 and Chapter 33 at 3.6.

2.4   Intragroup eliminations

IAS 27 (as amended in 2008) and IAS 27 (2007) require intragroup balances, transactions, income, expenses and dividends to be eliminated in full.[15] Profits and losses resulting from intragroup transactions that are recognised in assets, such as inventory and fixed assets, are eliminated in full.[16]

Example 7.4:   Transactions with a partly owned subsidiary

A parent entity sells a 100% owned subsidiary to another subsidiary in which it holds only an 80% interest. The fair value of the consideration received is in excess of the carrying amount of the net assets of the 100% subsidiary that it sold. Should the parent entity eliminate the gain in its consolidated accounts?

Under the proprietary (parent entity) concept, the non-controlling (or minority) shareholders are regarded as outsiders, and hence it might be thought that there is a case for saying that 20% of the gain has been realised (see 1.2.4 A above). However, the transaction is not a transaction with non-controlling (or minority) interests as there has been no issue, transfer or purchase of shares or other equity instruments to or from non-controlling (or minority) interests. Accordingly, the transaction cannot be considered to be a partial disposal of an interest in a subsidiary and accounted for as such (see 3.2.2 and 3.3.2 below). Instead, irrespective of whether the parent applies the entity concept or the proprietary concept, IAS 27 (as amended in 2008) and IAS 27 (2007) specifically require gains on intragroup transactions to be eliminated in full. As a consequence, no gain or loss is recognised in the consolidated income statement.

Although losses on intragroup transactions are to be eliminated in full, such losses may indicate an impairment that requires recognition in the consolidated financial statements.[17] For example, if one member of a group sells a property to another at a price intended to replicate an arm's-length price which is lower than the carrying value of the asset, the transfer may well indicate that the property is no longer part of a larger cash-generating unit whose value in use is not sensitive to the shortfall in the individual asset's fair value. The property may now be impaired from the perspective of the consolidated financial statements (see Chapter 18).

Moreover, intragroup transactions, although eliminated, may, under IAS 12 – *Income Taxes* – give rise to a tax charge or credit in the consolidated financial statements if they result in a change in the tax base of the item that is the subject of the transaction.[18] This is discussed in Chapter 26 at 5.5.

2.5   Non-coterminous accounting periods

It is implicit in the objective of consolidated financial statements (i.e. that they should be prepared as if the group were a single entity) that the financial statements of the various members of the group incorporated in the consolidated financial statements should cover the same accounting period.

Accordingly, IAS 27 (as amended in 2008) and IAS 27 (2007) require the financial statements of the parent and its subsidiaries used in the preparation of the consolidated financial statements to be prepared as at the same reporting date. When the end of the reporting period of the parent is different from that of a subsidiary, the subsidiary prepares, for consolidation purposes, additional financial statements as of the same date as the financial statements of the parent unless it is impracticable to do so.[19] IAS 27 (as amended in 2008) and IAS 27 (2007) do not clarify what is meant by 'impracticable' in this context, but it may reasonably be assumed that the IASB intended the same meaning as in IAS 1 – *Presentation of Financial Statements*, i.e. that the entity cannot comply with the requirement after making every effort to do so (see Chapter 3 at 2.4).[20]

When the financial statements of a subsidiary used in the preparation of consolidated financial statements are prepared as of a date different from that of the parent's financial statements, adjustments must be made for the effects of significant transactions or events that occur between that date and the date of the parent's financial statements (e.g. dividends paid by the subsidiary or a significant impairment loss on assets). In any case, the difference between the end of the reporting period of the subsidiary and that of the parent must be no more than three months. The length of the reporting periods and any difference between the ends of the reporting periods must be the same from period to period.[21] This implies that where a subsidiary previously consolidated on the basis of non-coterminous financial statements is consolidated using coterminous financial statements, it is necessary to restate comparative information so that financial information in respect of the subsidiary is included in the consolidated financial statements for an equivalent period in each period presented.

IAS 27 (as amended in 2008) and IAS 27 (2007) require merely that a non-coterminous accounting period of a subsidiary used for consolidation purposes ends within three months of that of the parent. It is not necessary (as in some current national GAAPs) for such a period to end before that of the parent.

The accounting policy of Prudential illustrates the treatment of entities with non-coterminous year-ends.

Extract 7.1: Prudential plc (2008)

Notes on the Group financial statements [extract]

A: Background and accounting policies [extract]

A4: Significant accounting policies [extract]

c Other assets, liabilities, income and expenditure [extract]

Basis of consolidation [extract]

The consolidated financial statements of the Group include the assets, liabilities and results of the Company and subsidiary undertakings in which Prudential has a controlling interest, using accounts drawn up to 31 December 2008 except where entities have non-coterminous year ends. In such cases, the information consolidated is based on the accounting period of these entities and is adjusted for material changes up to 31 December. Accordingly, the information consolidated is deemed to cover the same period for all entities throughout the Group. The results of subsidiaries are included in the financial statements from the date acquired to the effective date of disposal. All inter-company transactions are eliminated on consolidation. Results of asset management activities include those for managing internal funds.

2.6   Consistent accounting policies

The objective that consolidated financial statements should be prepared as if the group were a single entity also implies that the financial statements being aggregated in the consolidation process have been compiled on a consistent basis and, therefore, that uniform accounting policies have been adopted by all the members of the group. Of course, local reporting requirements for each subsidiary might dictate that different policies must be used for domestic purposes. Where this occurs it is necessary to ensure that appropriate adjustments are made in the course of the consolidation process to eliminate the effects of such differences.

IAS 27 (as amended in 2008) and IAS 27 (2007) require consolidated financial statements to be prepared using uniform accounting policies for like transactions and other events in similar circumstances.[22] Accordingly, if a member of the group uses accounting policies other than those adopted in the consolidated financial statements for like transactions and events in similar circumstances, appropriate adjustments must be made to its financial statements in preparing the consolidated financial statements.[23]

3   ACCOUNTING FOR CHANGES IN OWNERSHIP INTERESTS

3.1   Commencement of consolidation

It is inherent in the definition of a subsidiary (i.e. an entity controlled by the parent) that it should be consolidated from the date on which the parent first achieves control to the date on which control is lost. While IAS 27 (as amended in 2008) and IAS 27 (2007) deal with methods of accounting for business combinations and their effects on consolidation, the determination of the date of acquisition (i.e. the date on which control is first obtained) is governed by IFRS 3 (see Chapter 9 at 2 and 3).[24]

IAS 27 (as amended in 2008) and IAS 27 (2007) note that the income and expenses of a subsidiary are included from the date of acquisition until the date on which the parent ceases to control the subsidiary.[25] This also applies to a subsidiary held for sale accounted for under IFRS 5 – *Non-current Assets Held for Sale and Discontinued Operations* (see Chapter 4). If a parent loses control over a subsidiary, it cannot restate its comparative information relating to that subsidiary using the equity method.

IAS 27 (as amended in 2008) explains that income and expense of a subsidiary should be based on the values of the assets and liabilities recognised in the parent's consolidated financial statements at the acquisition date. For example, depreciation expense recognised in the consolidated statement of comprehensive income is based on the fair values of the related depreciable assets recognised in the consolidated financial statements at the acquisition date.[26]

3.2   IAS 27 (as amended in 2008)

A parent can lose control of a subsidiary because of a transaction that changes its absolute or relative ownership level. Alternatively, a parent might lose control without a change in absolute or relative ownership levels as a result of a contractual agreement or when, for example, the subsidiary becomes subject to the control of a government, court, administrator or regulator.[27]

3.2.1   Accounting for a loss of control

Upon loss of control the previous parent-subsidiary relationship ceases to exist. Hence, when a parent loses control of a subsidiary it:

'(a)   derecognises the assets (including any goodwill) and liabilities of the subsidiary at their carrying amounts at the date when control is lost;

(b)   derecognises the carrying amount of any non-controlling interests in the former subsidiary at the date when control is lost (including any components of other comprehensive income attributable to them);

(c)   recognises:

   (i)   the fair value of the consideration received, if any, from the transaction, event or circumstances that resulted in the loss of control; and

   (ii)   if the transaction that resulted in the loss of control involves a distribution of shares of the subsidiary to owners in their capacity as owners, that distribution;

(d)   recognises any investment retained in the former subsidiary at its fair value at the date when control is lost;

(e)   reclassifies to profit or loss, or transfers directly to retained earnings if required in accordance with other IFRSs, the amounts identified in paragraph 35 [of IAS 27 (as amended in 2008), which are discussed at C below]; and

(f)   recognises any resulting difference as a gain or loss in profit or loss attributable to the parent.'[28]

A   Distribution of subsidiary shares

As mentioned under (c)(ii) above, IAS 27 (as amended in 2008) only requires recognition of a distribution of shares of the subsidiary to owners in their capacity as owners, but does not describe how such transactions are to be accounted for as this was considered to be outside the scope of the business combinations project.[29] IFRIC 17 – *Distributions of Non-cash Assets to Owners*, which addresses distributions of subsidiary shares to shareholders, is discussed at 3.5 below.

B   Interest retained in the former subsidiary

On the loss of control of a subsidiary, any investment retained in the former subsidiary and any amounts owed by or to the former subsidiary should be accounted for in accordance with other IFRSs from the date when control is lost.[30] The fair value of any investment retained in the former subsidiary at the date when control is lost should be regarded as the fair value on initial recognition of a financial asset under IAS 39 or, if applicable, the cost on initial recognition of an investment in an associate or jointly controlled entity.[31]

The IASB considers that the loss of control of a subsidiary is a significant economic event that marks the end of the previous parent-subsidiary relationship and the start of a new investor-investee relationship. The Board rejected the argument made by some respondents to the exposure draft that 'the principles for revenue and gain recognition in the Framework would not be satisfied for the retained interest'.[32] Instead, the accounting under IAS 27 (as amended in 2008) is based on the premise that the investor-investee relationship differs significantly from the former parent-subsidiary relationship and that therefore 'any investment the parent has in the former subsidiary after control is lost should be measured at fair value at the date that control is lost and that any resulting gain or loss should be recognised in profit or loss'.[33]

Example 7.5:   Disposal of a subsidiary

A parent sells an 85% interest in a wholly-owned subsidiary as follows:

- after the sale the parent accounts for its remaining 15% interest as an available-for-sale investment;
- the subsidiary did not recognise any amounts in other comprehensive income;
- net assets of the subsidiary before the disposal are $500;
- cash proceeds from the sale of the 85% interests are $750; and
- the fair value of the 15% interest retained by the parent is $130.

The parent should account for the disposal of an 85% interest as follows:

	$	$
Available-for-sale investment	130	
Cash	750	
Net assets of the subsidiary		500
Gain on loss of control over subsidiary		380

The gain on the loss of control over the subsidiary comprises the following elements:

	$	$
Gain on interest disposed of		
Cash proceeds on disposal of 85% interest	750	
Carrying amount of 85% interest (85% × $500)	(425)	
		325
Gain on interest retained		
Carrying amount of 15% available-for-sale investment	130	
Carrying amount of 15% interest (15% × $500)	(75)	
		55
Gain on loss of control over subsidiary		380

C   Other comprehensive income

As mentioned under (e) above, if a parent loses control of a subsidiary IAS 27 (as amended in 2008) requires the parent to 'account for all amounts recognised in other comprehensive income in relation to that subsidiary on the same basis as would be required if the parent had directly disposed of the related assets or liabilities'.[34] Therefore, the parent should account for amounts recognised in other comprehensive income as follows (even if the parent only sells a part of its interest in a subsidiary):

(a)   'if a revaluation surplus previously recognised in other comprehensive income would be transferred directly to retained earnings on the disposal of the asset, the parent transfers the revaluation surplus directly to retained earnings when it loses control of the subsidiary';[35]

(b)   an actuarial gain or loss recognised in other comprehensive income would not be reclassified to profit or loss when the parent loses control of the subsidiary;[36] and

(c)   on disposal of a subsidiary that includes a foreign operation, the cumulative amount of the exchange differences relating to that foreign operation should be reclassified from equity to profit or loss, except for the amounts that have been attributed to the non-controlling interests. Those amounts should be derecognised, but should not be reclassified to profit or loss.[37]

What is less clear though is the treatment of other comprehensive income that would be reclassified to profit or loss on the disposal of the related assets or liabilities. The wording of paragraphs 34 and 35 of IAS 27 (as amended in 2008) lends itself to two different interpretations, that is, it requires reclassification of other comprehensive income related to the:

(1)   *Parent interest only* – Paragraph 34(b) of IAS 27 (as amended in 2008) requires derecognition of non-controlling interest (including any components of other comprehensive income attributable to them) at the date when control is lost, which implies derecognition of the non-controlling interest without reclassification. In addition, paragraph 34(f) of the standard requires recognition of a gain or loss in profit or loss that is attributable to the parent,

but does not require reclassification of other comprehensive income in respect of the non-controlling interest; and

(2)   *Parent and the non-controlling interest* – Paragraph 35 of IAS 27 (as amended in 2008) specifically requires that 'if a gain or loss previously recognised in other comprehensive income would be reclassified to profit or loss on the disposal of the related assets or liabilities, the parent reclassifies the gain or loss from equity to profit or loss (as a reclassification adjustment) when it loses control of the subsidiary. For example, if a subsidiary has available-for-sale financial assets and the parent loses control of the subsidiary, the parent shall reclassify to profit or loss the gain or loss previously recognised in other comprehensive income in relation to those assets'.[38] That would clearly require recycling of the entire other comprehensive income.

In our view, the approach under (1) above is preferable as it is consistent with the treatment of exchange differences relating to foreign operations as described under (c) above.

Example 7.6 below illustrates the application of the above requirements.

Example 7.6:   *Reclassification of other comprehensive income*

A parent sells a 70% interest in a 90%-owned subsidiary to a third party. The subsidiary had recognised, in its own financial statements, the following:

- a revaluation reserve in respect of property, plant and equipment of €2 million;
- a surplus on available-for-sale investments of €3 million;
- cumulative actuarial losses of €1.5 million; and
- cumulative translation differences of €4 million.

Under paragraph 35 of IAS 27 (as amended in 2008) the parent:

- reclassifies the entire revaluation surplus of €2 million related to property, plant and equipment within equity, 90% of the balance is attributable to the parent, while the remaining 10% is attributable to the non-controlling interest;
- accounts for the surplus on the available-for-sale investments using one of the following approaches:
  - approach (1): the parent reclassifies its €2.7 million interest in the surplus on available-for-sale investments to profit or loss for the period; and
  - approach (2): the entire €3 million surplus on available-for-sale investments is reclassified to profit or loss for the period. 90% of the balance (i.e. €2.7 million) is attributable to the parent, while the remaining 10% (i.e. €0.3 million) is attributable to the non-controlling interest; and
- is *not* permitted to reclassify the actuarial loss of €1.5 million to profit or loss.

Under paragraphs 48 to 48B of IAS 21 the parent is required to reclassify cumulative translation differences of €3.6 million (= 90% × €4 million) relating to the parent's interest to profit or loss, while the €0.4 million (= 10% × €4 million) relating to the non-controlling interest should be derecognised but not be reclassified to profit or loss.

The relative proportion of the shareholding disposed of is not relevant under IAS 27 (as amended in 2008) in determining the accounting for items within other comprehensive income.

D   Deemed disposal

A subsidiary may cease to be a subsidiary, or a group may reduce its interest in a subsidiary, other than by actual disposal. Such a reduction in interest is commonly referred to as a 'deemed disposal'. Deemed disposals may arise for a number of reasons, including:

- the group does not take up its full allocation in a rights issue by the subsidiary;
- the subsidiary declares scrip dividends which are not taken up by the parent so that its proportional interest is diminished;
- another party exercises its options or warrants issued by the subsidiary; or
- the subsidiary issues shares to third parties.

Under IAS 27 (as amended in 2008) a deemed disposal that results in the loss of control of a subsidiary should be accounted for as a regular disposal as is illustrated in Example 7.7 below.

Example 7.7:   Deemed disposal through share issue by subsidiary

A parent entity P owns 600,000 of the 1,000,000 shares issued by its subsidiary S, giving it a 60% interest. The carrying value of S's net identifiable assets in the consolidated financial statements of P is £120 million. In addition, goodwill of £15 million arose on the original acquisition of S, and has not subsequently been impaired. S issues 500,000 shares to a new investor for £80 million. As a result, P's 600,000 shares now represent 40% of the 1,500,000 shares issued by S in total and S becomes as associate of P. This transaction implies a fair value for S (excluding any control premium) of £240 million (the £80 million share issue proceeds give the new shareholder a one-third interest in S – £80m × 3 = £240m).

IAS 27 (as amended in 2008) requires the remaining interest in the former subsidiary to be recorded at fair value. Therefore, the profit or loss recognised on the loss of control of a subsidiary will take account of the fair value of new holding. As noted above, the implied fair value of S following the new share issue is £240 million, of which P's 40% share is £96 million. This would give rise to a profit of £9 million on disposal, recorded as follows:

	£m	£m
Interest in P	96	
Non-controlling interest *	48	
Profit on disposal		9
Net assets of S (previously consolidated)		120
Goodwill (previously shown separately)		15

* 40% of £120m = £48m, i.e. no goodwill was previously recognised under IFRS 3 (2007) in respect to the non-controlling interest.

3.2.2   Changes in ownership interest without a loss of control

An increase or decrease in a parent's ownership interest that does not result in a loss of control should be accounted for as an equity transaction under IAS 27 (as amended in 2008), i.e. a transaction with owners in their capacity as owners.[39] The carrying amounts of the controlling and non-controlling interests should be 'adjusted to reflect the changes in their relative interests in the subsidiary. Any difference between the amount by which the non-controlling interests are adjusted and the fair value of the consideration paid or received shall be recognised directly in equity and attributed to the owners of the parent'.[40]

In other words, no changes in a subsidiary's assets (including goodwill) and liabilities will be recognised in a transaction in which a parent company increases its interest in a subsidiary that it already controls.[41] It also means that reductions in the interest in a subsidiary will not result in the recognition of a gain or loss that is attributable to the controlling interest. This approach is consistent with the view of the Board that non-controlling interests should be treated as equity.

Transactions cost incurred (i.e. incremental costs directly attributable to the equity transaction that otherwise would have been avoided, but net of any related income tax benefits) in relation to an increase or a decrease in the non-controlling interest should be accounted for within equity, regardless of the form in which the consideration is paid. The standards are silent about where in equity the transaction costs should be recognised, in particular, whether they should be allocated to the parent or to the non-controlling interest. The parent may therefore choose where to allocate the transaction costs within equity, based on the facts and circumstances surrounding the change in ownership and any legal requirements. Even if the transactions costs are allocated to non-controlling interest, an entity needs to ensure that these costs are not subsequently reclassified to profit or loss in future periods.

A   Other comprehensive income

I   Partial disposals: Cumulative exchange gains and losses

IAS 21 requires that on the partial disposal without a loss of control of a subsidiary (i.e. any reduction in an entity's ownership interest) that includes a foreign operation, the proportionate share of the cumulative amount of exchange differences recognised in other comprehensive income should be reattributed to the non-controlling interests in that foreign operation.[42] If the entity subsequently disposes of the remainder of its interest in the subsidiary, the exchange differences reattributed to the non-controlling interests will not be reclassified to profit or loss (see Chapter 13 at 2.7.3).[43] In other words, upon loss of control only the exchange differences attributable to the controlling interest immediately before loss of control will be reclassified to profit or loss.

While IAS 21 deals with partial disposals without a loss of control of a subsidiary, it does not address the question of what happens when the controlling shareholder increases its interest. Intuitively it would make sense to apply a treatment that is symmetrical to the one applied to partial disposals without a loss of control. This issue is discussed in the context of other gains and losses recognised in other comprehensive income below.

II   Reattribution of other comprehensive income

IAS 27 (as amended in 2008) is silent on the issue of reattribution of other comprehensive income in transactions that do not result in the loss of control of a subsidiary. That leaves open the question of whether reattribution of other comprehensive income is required or at least permitted. Example 7.8 below illustrates the accounting issues that arise.

Example 7.8:   Reattribution of other comprehensive income

Increase in ownership

A parent holds an 80% interest in a subsidiary that has net assets of ¥4,000. The carrying amount of the 20% non-controlling interest is ¥800, which includes ¥200 that represents the non-controlling interests' share of total other comprehensive income of ¥1,000 related to gains on available-for-sale investments. The parent acquires an additional 10% interest in the subsidiary for ¥500, which increases its total interest to 90%. How should the parent account for this transaction?

Under the reattribution approach the parent would account for the transaction as follows:

	¥	¥
Non-controlling interest's share of other comprehensive income (¥1,000 × 10%)	100	
Non-controlling interests (excluding share of other comprehensive income) (¥800 × 10% / 20% − (¥1,000 × 10%))	300	
Parent's other reserves	200	
Parent's share of other comprehensive income (¥1,000 × 10%)		100
Cash		500

Alternatively, if the parent did not reattribute other comprehensive income, it would account for the same transaction as follows:

	¥	¥
Non-controlling interests (¥800 × 10% / 20%)	400	
Parent's other reserves	100	
Cash		500

Decrease in ownership

A parent holds a 100% interest in a subsidiary that has net assets of ¥4,000 and total other comprehensive income of ¥1,000. The parent sells a 10% interest in the subsidiary for ¥500. How should the parent account for this transaction?

Under the reattribution approach the parent would account for the transaction as follows:

	¥	¥
Cash	500	
Parent's share of other comprehensive income (¥1,000 × 10%)	100	
Parent's other reserves		200
Non-controlling interest's share of other comprehensive income (¥1,000 × 10%)		100
Non-controlling interests (excluding share of other comprehensive income) (¥4,000 × 10% − (¥1,000 × 10%))		300

Alternatively, if the parent did not reattribute other comprehensive income, it would account for the same transaction as follows:

	¥	¥
Cash	500	
Non-controlling interests (¥4,000 × 10%)		400
Parent's other reserves		100

The IASB requires the use of the reattribution approach. This was made clear in May 2009 when the IASB considered this issue in the context of its annual improvements project. The Board decided tentatively that 'there is no need to clarify the following points, because the relevant requirements are clear: ... When a change in ownership in a subsidiary occurs but does not result in the loss of control, the parent must reattribute other comprehensive income between the owners of the parent and the non-controlling interest'.[44]

A perceived drawback of the reattribution approach is that the proportion attributable to the parent upon subsequent reclassification of other comprehensive income into the profit or loss might include (exclude) gains or losses that arose at a time when the underlying shares were owned by the non-controlling interests (parent). However, the same would happen if a parent increased its interest in a subsidiary and then immediately sold one of that subsidiary's properties – that was previously carried at cost – at a profit.

There are a number of arguments in favour of applying a reattribution approach to other comprehensive income:

- if the parent in Example 7.8 above had instead acquired the entire 20% non-controlling interest for ¥1,000, the alternative approach would require that other comprehensive income of ¥200 remained attributed to a non-controlling interest that no longer existed. Subsequent reclassification in later years would then give rise to a rather counterintuitive profit or loss attributable to past non-controlling interests;

- in the case of a decrease in ownership interest the reattribution approach is identical to the approach required by IAS 21 in respect of cumulative translation differences; and

- a practical advantage of the reattribution approach is that it does not require a parent to keep track of past increases or decreases in its investment in subsidiaries for the purpose of determining the other comprehensive income attributable to non-controlling interests.

B   Goodwill attributable to non-controlling interests

Determining the goodwill attributable to non-controlling interests is necessary in accounting for transactions with non-controlling interests. Unfortunately IAS 27 (as amended in 2008) does not provide any guidance on the reallocation of goodwill between the controlling and non-controlling interests when their relative ownership interests change.

Under IFRS 3 (as revised in 2008) the proportion of goodwill that is attributable to the non-controlling interests is not necessarily equal to their ownership percentage.

Firstly, the parent may use the option in IFRS 3 (as revised in 2008) to recognise the non-controlling interest at its proportionate share of the acquiree's identifiable net assets, i.e. the parent does not recognise any goodwill in respect of the non-controlling interest. Secondly, even if the parent recognises the non-controlling interest at its fair value (and therefore recognises goodwill related to the non-controlling interest), the goodwill relating to the non-controlling interest is often relatively low compared to its ownership share if the parent paid a control premium upon acquisition.

Example 7.9 below illustrates the issue in more detail.

Example 7.9:   *Reallocation of goodwill to non-controlling interests*

A parent company pays €920 to acquire an 80% interest in a subsidiary that owns net assets with a fair value of €1,000. The fair value of the non-controlling interest at the acquisition date is €220.

	Share of net assets €m	Share of goodwill €m	Total €m
Parent	800	120	920
Non-controlling interests	200	20	220
	1,000	140	1,140

Decrease in ownership percentage

A year after the acquisition the parent sells a 20% interest in the subsidiary to a third party for €265. How should the parent account for this transaction?

The parent company's interest decreases to 60% and its share of net assets decreases to €600. Correspondingly the share of net assets attributable to the non-controlling interest increases from €200 to €400. It is not clear under IAS 27 (as amended in 2008) what happens to the non-controlling interests' share of goodwill. However, we believe that the parent should reallocate a proportion of the goodwill to the non-controlling interests. The parent company sold a 20% interest in its subsidiary. Therefore, one approach would be to allocate €30 (= 20%/80% × €120) of the parent's goodwill to the non-controlling interests. After the transaction the parent's share of goodwill is €90 (= €120 – €30).

In its consolidated financial statement the parent would account for this transaction as follows:

	€m	€m
Cash	265	
Non-controlling interest ((€400 – €200) + €30)		230
Equity of the parent		35

Increase in ownership percentage

Taking the initial fact pattern as a starting point, the parent acquires an additional 10% interest in the subsidiary for €115. How should the parent account for this transaction?

The parent company's interest increases to 90% and its share of net assets increases to €900. Correspondingly the share of net assets attributable to the non-controlling interest is reduced from €200 to €100. The parent company acquired half of the non-controlling interest. Using the proportionate allocation approach discussed above, the parent would allocate €10 (= 10%/20% × €20) of the non-controlling interests' goodwill to the parent.

In its consolidated financial statement the parent would account for this transaction as follows:

	€m	€m
Non-controlling interest ((€200 – €100) + €10)	110	
Equity of the parent	5	
Cash		115

The proportionate allocation approach described in Example 7.9 above is just one method that may result in relevant and reliable information. However, other approaches may also be appropriate depending on the circumstances. In developing its accounting policy on attributing goodwill an entity should consider the guidance in paragraphs 10 to 12 of IAS 8 – *Accounting Policies, Changes in Accounting Estimates and Errors* – and the guidance in IAS 36 – *Impairment of Assets* (and its Appendix C) on the allocation of goodwill and impairment losses.

3.2.3   Step-disposal of a subsidiary

IAS 27 (as amended in 2008) only permits recognition of a gain or loss upon disposal of a subsidiary when the parent loses control over the subsidiary. This requirement might present opportunities to structure the disposal in a way that achieves a particular accounting outcome. The Basis for Conclusions to the standard includes the following example that illustrates the potential problem.[45]

Example 7.10:   Step-disposal of a subsidiary (1)

A parent controls 70% of a subsidiary. The parent intends to sell all of its 70% controlling interest in the subsidiary. The parent could structure the disposal in two different ways:

- the parent could initially sell 19% of its ownership interest without loss of control and then, soon afterwards, sell the remaining 51% and lose control; or
- the parent could sell its entire 70% interest in one transaction.

In the first case, any difference between the amount by which the non-controlling interests are adjusted and the fair value of the consideration received upon sale of the 19% interest would be recognised directly in equity, while the gain or loss from the sale of the remaining 51% interest would be recognised in profit or loss. In the second case, however, a gain or loss on the sale of the whole 70% interest would be recognised in profit or loss.

While in practice few entities would be interested in concealing gains on a disposal of a subsidiary, the opportunities for hiding a loss on disposal appear to be fairly limited given the requirements of IAS 36 and IFRS 5. Those standards would usually require recognition of an impairment loss even before the completion of any sale (although they would not require reclassification of losses recognised in other comprehensive income). Nevertheless, the Board considered it important to prevent this potential abuse and 'decided that the possibility of such structuring could be overcome by requiring entities to consider whether multiple arrangements should be accounted for as a single transaction to ensure that the principle of faithful representation is adhered to. The Board believes that all of the terms and conditions of the arrangements and their economic effects should be considered in determining whether multiple arrangements should be accounted for as a single arrangement'.[46]

A parent should consider all of the terms and conditions of the arrangements and their economic effects in determining whether to treat that as a single transaction. The following circumstances may indicate that a parent should account for multiple arrangements as a single transaction:

'(a)   they are entered into at the same time or in contemplation of each other.

(b)   they form a single transaction designed to achieve an overall commercial effect.

(c)   the occurrence of one arrangement is dependent on the occurrence of at least one other arrangement.

(d)   one arrangement considered on its own is not economically justified, but it is economically justified when considered together with other arrangements. An example is when one disposal of shares is priced below market and is compensated for by a subsequent disposal priced above market.'[47]

These indicators make clear that arrangements that are somehow part of a package should be regarded as a single transaction. There is a risk, however, that by casting too wide a net an entity might end up accounting for a transaction that is truly separate as part of the loss of control.

IAS 27 (as amended in 2008) is silent on how an entity should account for multiple arrangements that are part of a single transaction. That leaves unanswered a number of questions that are of particular importance if some of the arrangements take place after the balance sheet date as can be seen in the example below.

Example 7.11:   Step-disposal of a subsidiary (2)

A parent initially controls 70% of a subsidiary that has net assets of $1,000 and a foreign currency translation loss in other comprehensive income of $100. In November 2009 the parent sells 19% of its ownership interest for $200. In February 2010, the parent sells the remaining 51% for $550 in an arrangement that is considered to be part of a single overall transaction. How should the parent account for this transaction?

The net assets of the subsidiary are not impaired under IAS 36, which is confirmed by the fact that the total sales price exceeds the parent's share in the net assets by $50. The total loss on disposal can be calculated as follows:

	$
Proceeds from the sale ($200 + $550 =)	750
Parent's interest in the net assets of the subsidiary	(700)
Parent's share of the loss in other comprehensive income	(70)
Parent's share of the loss on disposal of the subsidiary	(20)

What is less clear, however, is how the parent should account for the individual steps of the overall arrangement. Depending on the facts and circumstances the parent should account for these transactions in one of the following ways:

(a)   *Advance payment* – If the parent does not lose control over the investment and access to the benefits associated with ownership until February 2010 then the first transaction should be accounted for as a prepayment and the subsidiary continues to be consolidated until that date. Also, in most cases the parent's investment in the subsidiary will fall within the scope of IFRS 5; or

(b) *Immediate disposal* – If the parent loses control over the investment and access to the benefits associated with ownership in November 2009 then it should cease to consolidate the former subsidiary immediately, recognise a loss on disposal of $20 and account for deferred consideration.

The parent needs to consider the substance of the arrangement in deciding whether to apply the approach under (a) or (b) above. If the parent concluded that it should account for a partial disposal without a loss of control in November 2009 that would imply that the first and second transactions are not linked in the way required by paragraph 33 of IAS 27.

3.3   IAS 27 (2007)

3.3.1 *Accounting for a loss of control*

If a parent loses control of a subsidiary:

- the income and expenses of a subsidiary are included in the consolidated financial statements until the date on which the parent ceases to control the subsidiary;[48]

- a gain or loss on the disposal of the subsidiary is recognised in profit or loss that comprises:[49]

  - the difference between the proceeds from the disposal of the subsidiary and its carrying amount (i.e. net assets and recognised goodwill) as of the date of disposal; and

  - the cumulative amount of any exchange differences that relate to the subsidiary recognised in equity in accordance with IAS 21 (2007) – *The Effects of Changes in Foreign Exchange Rates* (see Chapter 13 at 2.7.3);[50]

- an investment in an entity should be accounted for in accordance with IAS 39 from the date that it ceases to be a subsidiary, provided that it does not become an associate as defined in IAS 28 or a jointly controlled entity as described in IAS 31;[51] and

- the carrying amount of the investment at the date that the entity ceases to be a subsidiary should be regarded as the cost on initial measurement of a financial asset under IAS 39.[52] The measurement rules in IAS 39 are complex and discussed in detail in Chapter 32. In brief, however, they will entail the former subsidiary being recorded initially at 'cost' (which is deemed to be its carrying amount on the date that it ceases to be a subsidiary)[53] and then classified as either a 'financial asset at fair value through profit or loss' or an 'available-for-sale' financial asset. In either case, the investment will be immediately remeasured at fair value, and continuously remeasured at fair value thereafter, with gains and losses arising on revaluation accounted for in profit or loss, in the case of as asset classified as a 'financial asset at fair value through profit or loss' or in equity, in the case of an 'available-for-sale' financial asset.

As drafted, IAS 27 (2007) could be literally construed as drawing a distinction between, on the one hand, the parent losing control of a subsidiary (at which point consolidation ceases) and the requirement to account for a gain or loss 'on disposal' of a subsidiary – the implication being that a gain or loss is recognised only on the outright disposal of a subsidiary and not, for example, when a holding is reduced below a controlling interest through a partial disposal or deemed disposal. In our view this is not the intention of IAS 27 (2007), and a gain or loss should be recognised on all reductions in the investor's interest, whether arising from disposal or deemed disposal (see the further discussion at A and 3.3.2 below).

A   Deemed disposals resulting in a loss of control

A subsidiary may cease to be subsidiary, or the group may reduce its interest in that subsidiary, other than by actual disposal. Such a reduction in interest is commonly referred to as a 'deemed disposal'. Deemed disposals may arise for a number of reasons, including:

- the group does not take up its full allocation in a rights issue by the subsidiary;

- the subsidiary declares scrip dividends which are not taken up by the parent so that its proportional interest is diminished;

- another party exercises its options or warrants issued by the subsidiary; or

- the subsidiary issues shares to third parties.

An illustration of such a transaction is given in Example 7.12 below. The more specialised case of a deemed disposal that reduces the parent's stake without resulting in a loss of overall control is discussed at 3.3.2 B below.

Example 7.12:   Deemed disposal through share issue by subsidiary

A parent entity P owns 600,000 of the 1,000,000 shares issued by its subsidiary S, giving it a 60% interest. The carrying value of S's net identifiable assets in the consolidated financial statements of P is £120 million. In addition, goodwill of £15 million arose on the original acquisition of S, and has not subsequently been impaired. S issues 500,000 shares to a new investor for £80 million. As a result, P's 600,000 shares now represent 40% of the 1,500,000 shares issued by S in total and S becomes as associate of P. This transaction implies a fair value for S (excluding any control premium) of £240 million (the £80 million share issue proceeds give the new shareholder a one-third interest in S – £80m × 3 = £240m).

In our view, a deemed disposal that results in a loss of control of a subsidiary gives rise to a gain or loss. Whilst IAS 27 (2007) does not prescribe how this should be calculated, in our view the most appropriate result is obtained by comparing the carrying value of P's effective interest in S before and after the transaction, as follows:

	£m
P's effective interest in S after S's share issue *	90
Less: P's effective interest in S before S's share issue †	(87)
Gain on deemed disposal	3

*   40% of £200m net identifiable assets (£120m original net identifiable assets + £80m cash raised by S's share issue) = £80m + £10m goodwill (40/60 ×£15m original goodwill) = £90m.

†   60% of £120m original net identifiable assets = £72m + £15m goodwill = £87m.

This gives rise to the following journal entry on the deemed disposal:

	£m	£m
Interest in P (see above)	90	
Minority interest *	48	
Profit on disposal (see above)		3
Net assets of S (previously consolidated)		120
Goodwill (previously shown separately)		15

* As previously recognised, 40% of £120m = £48m.

3.3.2 Decrease in ownership interest without loss of control

A   True disposals without loss of control

The reporting entity may dispose of part of its interest in a subsidiary, but still retain overall control of that subsidiary. IAS 27 (2007) is silent on this issue, as is IFRS 3 (2007) on the related issue of accounting for increases in a stake in a partly-owned subsidiary.

As discussed further in Example 7.15 at 3.3.3 below, we believe that there are three acceptable approaches to acquisitions of minority interests (the 'parent entity extension method', the 'entity concept method' and the 'hybrid entity concept/parent entity method'), but that an entity should apply one of these conceptual approaches consistently as a matter of accounting policy.

In our view, an entity should adopt an accounting policy for reductions in its interest in a subsidiary consistent with its policy for increases in its interest in a subsidiary. This will leave the entity with a broad choice between:

- calculating a gain or loss on disposal and reflecting it in profit or loss, where the 'parent entity extension method' is applied;

- treating the entire transaction as a transaction with other equity shareholders, where entity concept method is applied; or

- treating the difference between the cost of the additional interest in the subsidiary and the minority interest's share of the assets and liabilities partly as goodwill and partly as an equity transaction.

These broad approaches are illustrated in Example 7.13 below.

Example 7.13:   Partial disposal of subsidiary

As in Example 7.12 above, a parent entity P owns 600,000 of the 1,000,000 shares issued by its subsidiary S, giving it a 60% interest. The carrying value of S's net identifiable assets in the consolidated financial statements of P is £120 million. In addition, goodwill of £15 million arose on the original acquisition of S, and has not subsequently been impaired. P disposes of 50,000 of its shares for £10 million, leaving it with a 55% interest in S.

Parent entity extension method

If P accounts for acquisitions of minority interests using the parent entity extension method, it will recognise a gain on disposal in its consolidated financial statements calculated as follows:

	£m
Proceeds received	10.00
Share of identifiable net assets and goodwill disposed of *	7.25
Gain on disposal	2.75

*   £6m identifiable net assets (5% of £120m) + £1.25m goodwill (5/60 of £15m) = £7.25m.

This gives rise to the following journal entry to record the disposal in P's consolidated financial statements:

	£m	£m
Cash	10.00	
Minority interest *		6.00
Goodwill (as above)		1.25
Gain on disposal (as above)		2.75

*   Previously 40% of £120m = £48m, now 45% of £120m = £54m – increase of £6m.

Entity method

If P's policy is to recognise such disposals as transactions with shareholders, no gain or loss is recognised, nor is there any adjustment to goodwill, and the required journal entry in P's consolidated financial statements would be:

	£m	£m
Cash	10.00	
Minority interest (as above)		6.00
Equity		4.00

It is consistent with the underlying concept of the entity method that as this is a transaction with shareholders rather than a disposal not to adjust the carrying amount of goodwill. However, in some cases the effect might be that, since the goodwill relates only to the parent's interest in its subsidiary, it has become diluted to the extent that the goodwill relating to its original investment has effectively become impaired (e.g. because the control premium paid for a 100% interest is higher than that for a 55% interest). In such a case IAS 36 would require a charge to be recognised in the income statement (see Chapter 18).

Hybrid method

If P accounts for acquisitions of minority interests using the hybrid method, it will make the same adjustments to the carrying amounts of net assets, goodwill and minority interests as under the parent entity extension method above, but will record an adjustment to equity rather than a gain or loss on disposal, as follows:

	£m	£m
Cash	10.00	
Minority interest (as above)		6.00
Goodwill (as above)		1.25
Equity		2.75

An alternative analysis might be that in effect £1.25 million of goodwill has been transferred from the controlling shareholder to the minority interest, suggesting the accounting entry:

	£m	£m
Cash	10.00	
Minority interest *		7.25
Equity		2.75

*   £6m (as above) + £1.25m goodwill (as above) no longer attributed to controlling shareholder.

Some might question whether it is appropriate to attribute goodwill to the minority in this way, given that IAS 27 (2007) and IFRS 3 (2007) do not permit this on initial acquisition of a subsidiary. Those who support the approach above would presumably counter this by arguing that, in contrast to the initial acquisition of a subsidiary, in which the minority shareholders do not participate, in this case the minority shareholders are parties to the transaction, and it is therefore appropriate for some part of the goodwill to be allocated to them.

B   Deemed disposals without a loss of control

In our view, an entity applying IAS 27 (2007) should account for deemed disposals not resulting in a loss of control using the same policy as is used for actual disposals not resulting in a loss of control, as illustrated by Example 7.14 below.

Example 7.14:   Deemed partial disposal of subsidiary

As in Example 7.12 above, a parent entity P owns 600,000 of the 1,000,000 shares issued by its subsidiary S, giving it a 60% interest. The carrying value of S's net identifiable assets in the consolidated financial statements of P is £120 million. In addition, goodwill of £15 million arose on the original acquisition of S, and has not subsequently been impaired. However, in this case S issues 90,909 shares to parties other than P for £18.18 million, as a result of which P's 600,000 shares represent 55% of the 1,090,909 shares issued by S.

Parent entity extension method

If P accounts for acquisitions of minority interests using the parent entity extension method, it will recognise a gain on disposal in its consolidated financial statements calculated as follows:

	£m
P's effective interest in S after S's share issue *	89.75
Less: P's effective interest in S before S's share issue †	(87.00)
Gain on deemed disposal	2.75

* 55% of £138.18m net identifiable assets (£120m original net identifiable assets + £18.18m cash raised by S's share issue) = £76.00m + £13.75m goodwill (55/60 × £15m) =£89.75m.

† 60% of £120m net identifiable assets = £72m + £15m goodwill = £87m .

This gives rise to the following journal entry to record the disposal in P's consolidated financial statements:

	£m	£m
Cash	18.18	
Minority interest *		14.18
Goodwill †		1.25
Gain on deemed disposal (as above)		2.75

* Previously 40% of £120m = £48m, now 45% of £138.18m (£120m + £18.18m share issue proceeds) = £62.18m – increase of £14.18m.

† Originally £15m less amount retained £13.75m (see above) = £1.25m

Entity method

If P's policy is to recognise such disposals as transactions with shareholders, no gain or loss is recognised, nor is there any adjustment to goodwill, and the required journal entry in P's consolidated financial statements would be:

	£m	£m
Cash	18.18	
Minority interest (as above)		14.18
Equity		4.00

It is consistent with the underlying concept of the entity method that as this is a transaction with shareholders rather than a disposal not to adjust the carrying amount of goodwill. However, in some cases the effect might be that, since the goodwill is relates only to the parent's interest in its subsidiary, it has become diluted to the extent that the goodwill relating to its original investment has effectively become impaired (e.g. because the control premium paid for a 100% interest is higher than that for a 55% interest). In such a case IAS 36 would require a charge to be recognised in the income statement (see Chapter 18).

Hybrid method

If P accounts for acquisitions of minority interests using the hybrid method, it will make the same adjustments to the carrying amounts of net assets, goodwill and minority interests as under the parent entity extension method above, but will record an adjustment to equity rather than a gain or loss on disposal, as follows:

	£m	£m
Cash	18.18	
Minority interest (as above)		14.18
Goodwill (as above)		1.25
Equity		2.75

An alternative analysis might be that in effect £1.25 million of goodwill has been transferred from the controlling shareholder to the minority interest, suggesting the accounting entry:

	£m	£m
Cash	18.18	
Minority interest *		15.43
Equity		2.75

*   £14.18m (as above) + £1.25m goodwill (as above) no longer attributed to controlling shareholder.

Some might question whether it is appropriate to attribute goodwill to the minority in this way, given that IAS 27 (2007) and IFRS 3 (2007) do not permit this on initial acquisition of a subsidiary. Those who support the approach above would presumably counter this by arguing that, in contrast to the initial acquisition of a subsidiary, in which the minority shareholders do not participate, in this case the minority shareholders are parties to the transaction, and it is therefore appropriate for some part of the goodwill to be allocated to them.

3.3.3   Increase in ownership interest after obtaining control

The requirements in relation to step acquisitions discussed in Chapter 9 at 2.9 deal only with those situations where there have been earlier exchange transactions prior to the one that has resulted in a business combination, such as the acquisition of a subsidiary, whereby the acquirer now has control over that business. However, IAS 27 (2007) is silent on how later exchange transactions should be accounted for, such as the acquisition of some or all of the minority interest in a subsidiary.

Example 7.15:   Acquisition of minority interest

On 1 January 2010, Investor acquires the remaining 20% ownership interest in Investee that it does not already own for £6,500,000 cash. The total net assets of the Investee are £27,000,000, while their fair value is £31,000,000. The minority interest's share in the net assets of Investee is £5,400,000 (= 20% × £27,000,000), while their share in the fair value of the net assets is £6,200,000 (= 20% × £31,000,000). How should the acquisition of the remaining 20% be accounted for?

In accounting for the acquisition of the minority interest there are two main issues that need to be considered:

- are the acquiree's net assets restated – either in full or in part – to their fair values at the date the minority interest is acquired?

- how is any difference between the cost of acquisition and the minority interest acquired accounted for?

As far as the first issue is concerned, in our view the acquiree's net assets must not be restated, either in full or in part, to their fair value at the date the minority interest is acquired. Fair value adjustments are made only at the date of the business combination, and the acquisition of a minority interest is not considered a business combination under IFRS 3 (2007).

As far as the second issue is concerned, as the acquisition of a minority interest is not a business combination there is no specific accounting prescribed in IFRS for such a transaction. Therefore, Investor must apply the hierarchy in IAS 8 (see Chapter 3) to develop an appropriate accounting policy for such a transaction. Several conceptual approaches may be acceptable but the approach chosen should be consistently applied. In our view, the following are acceptable methods of accounting under IAS 27 (2007) for the difference between the cost of acquisition and the minority interest acquired:

(a) the entire difference may be reflected as goodwill (the 'Parent entity extension method' – see 1.2.2 above)

Under this method, the entire difference between the cost of the additional interest in the subsidiary and the minority interest's share of the assets and liabilities reflected in the consolidated balance sheet at the date of the acquisition of the minority interest is reflected as goodwill. The assets and liabilities of the subsidiary would not be remeasured to reflect their fair values at the date of the transaction. In this case, Investor would recognise additional goodwill of £1,100,000 being the difference between the cost of £6,500,000 and £5,400,000 (the minority interest's 20% share in the net assets of Investee). The drawback with this method is that it results in a figure for goodwill for that particular transaction that is not based on fair values at the date of that transaction.

(b) the entire difference may be reflected as an equity transaction (the 'Entity concept method' – see 1.2.1 above)

Under this method, the entire difference between the cost of the additional interest in the subsidiary and the minority interest's share of the assets and liabilities reflected in the consolidated balance sheet at the date of the acquisition of the minority interest is reflected as being a transaction between owners. In this case, Investor would recognise the £1,100,000 as an equity transaction. This method is supported by the fact IAS 27 (2007) requires minority interests to be presented in the consolidated balance sheet within equity, separately from the parent shareholders' equity (see 4 below). The drawback with this method is that the entity concept on which it is based, is not used under IFRS 3 (2007) for determining goodwill.

(c) the difference may be reflected partly as goodwill – measured using the principles of IFRS 3 (2007) – and partly as equity (effectively a 'Hybrid entity concept/parent entity method')

Under this method, the difference between the cost of the additional interest in the subsidiary and the minority interest's share of the assets and liabilities reflected in the consolidated balance sheet at the date of the acquisition of the minority interest is reflected partly as goodwill (measured using the principles of IFRS 3 (2007)) and partly as an equity transaction. In this case, the share of fair values of Investee at 1 January 2010 is £6,200,000, thus resulting in additional goodwill of £300,000 (£6,500,000 – £6,200,000), and the balance of £800,000 would be recognised directly in equity. As with the entity concept method, this approach is supported by the equity classification of minority interests and remains consistent with the purchased goodwill methodology required by IFRS 3 (2007). The drawback is that it does not consistently adopt one conceptual approach or the other.

As indicated above in respect of the first issue, we believe that the following methods that are sometimes advocated for dealing with this issue are not acceptable under IFRS:

- Full step-up

  This method would adopt the same treatment in IFRS 3 (2007), i.e. recording a full step up in values and using the cost of the transaction and fair value information at the date of this exchange transaction to determine the amount of any goodwill associated with this transaction. In this case the share of fair values at 1 January 2010 is £6,200,000, thus resulting in additional goodwill of £300,000. The net assets of Investee are included in the consolidated financial statements at their full fair value of £31,000,000 at 1 January 2010, resulting in a further asset revaluation surplus of £3,200,000 (= 80% × (£31,000,000 – £27,000,000)). The £800,000 attributable to the minority interest's share is eliminated as part of the calculation of goodwill relating to the acquisition of the minority interest. In our view, this method is unacceptable because this revaluation does not arise on the initial recognition by the acquirer of the acquiree's assets, and IFRS 3 (2007) only permits the remeasurement of existing assets and liabilities, including the recognition of identifiable intangible assets and contingent liabilities when there has been a business combination with a change in control. Further, there is no other IFRS that allows or requires recognition of contingent liabilities or the remeasurement of all internally generated intangible assets.

- Partial step-up (US GAAP)

  This method would adopt a similar approach to that in IFRS 3 (2007), but restricting the step-up in fair values to the amounts used for the purpose of determining the amount of any goodwill associated with that particular transaction. However, no adjustments are made to incorporate any revaluations in respect of the interest in the subsidiary that was already held. This is the treatment that was required by US GAAP under FAS 141 – *Business Combinations* – before the effective date of FAS 160 – *Noncontrolling Interests in Consolidated Financial Statements an amendment of ARB No. 51*.[54] In this case, Investor would still recognise goodwill of £300,000 but, in order to do so, it would need to reflect the net assets at £27,800,000. This would effectively represent £21,600,000 (being 80% of £27,000,000, the fair value at the date Investee became a subsidiary) and £6,200,000 (being 20% of £31,000,000, the fair value at the date of acquiring the minority interest). Although this method may result in a more meaningful figure for the goodwill arising on this transaction, in our view it is also unacceptable for the same reasons as for the full step-up method above. Whilst the method was permitted by US GAAP under FAS 141, IFRS only permits entities to look to another framework when IFRS is silent, and where the method does not conflict with the requirements of IFRS. As already noted, a step-up would conflict with the requirements of IFRS in several areas such as the recognition or remeasurements of certain intangible assets.

It is clear from the above example that the three methods that we regard as being acceptable have drawbacks and that none of them are ideal. However, whatever conceptual approach is adopted, it should be applied consistently. So, for example, the 'entity concept method' is acceptable but only if an entity follows that approach consistently, with any disposals of less than a controlling interest in a subsidiary by a parent to a minority shareholder also being recorded as an equity transaction.

An example of a company adopting the 'parent entity extension method' is Swisscom as shown in the following extract.

> **Extract 7.2: Swisscom AG (2006)**
>
> **Notes to the consolidated financial statements** [extract]
> **29   Repurchase of a share of 25% in Swisscom Mobile AG** [extract]
>
> On December 20, 2006, Swisscom bought back a minority share of 25% in Swisscom Mobile from Vodafone for CHF 4,258 million including transaction costs of CHF 8 million. On the date of acquisition the carrying amount of Vodafone's minority interest in Swisscom Mobile of CHF 565 million was removed from equity and offset against the purchasing price. The difference of CHF 3,693 million between the carrying amount of the minority interest and the purchase price was recorded as goodwill.

One company that states explicitly that it adopts such a method for both acquisitions and disposals in transactions with minority interests is Svenska Cellulosa as shown by the following extract from its accounting policies.

> **Extract 7.3: Svenska Cellulosa Aktiebolaget SCA (2006)**
>
> **Notes** [extract]
> **NOTE 1 Accounting principles** [extract]
> **Consolidated accounts** [extract]
> **Minority interests**
>
> Minority share in a subsidiary's net assets is reported as a separate item in the Group's equity. In the consolidated income statement, minority share is included in net profit. Transactions with minority interests are handled in the same way as transactions with external parties. Sale of participations to minority interests result in a gain or loss that is recognized in the consolidated income statement. Acquisition of minority shares can result in goodwill if the cost exceeds the carrying amount of the acquired net assets.

In February 2005, IFRIC discussed a potential agenda item regarding the accounting for the acquisition of a minority interest in an existing subsidiary by a reporting entity. Although IFRIC recognised this is an urgent issue and that there is wide divergence in current practice, it noted that it was being addressed by the IASB as part of phase II of its business combinations project. IFRIC concluded that it would monitor the progress of the Board's project, and reconsider whether to add the issue to the agenda later in 2005.[55] As discussed at 3.2.2 above, the Board has now dealt with this issue in IAS 27 (as amended in 2008), which requires increases in the ownership interest in a subsidiary after obtaining control to be accounted for as transactions between equity holders.[56] Accordingly, any premium or discount on subsequent purchases from minority interests ('non-controlling interests') is to be recognised directly in equity.

3.3.4   Cumulative gains and losses reflected in equity

A   Cumulative exchange gains and losses on full or partial disposal

IAS 27 (2007) requires cumulative foreign exchange differences relating to subsidiaries to be 'recycled' in profit or loss only on a disposal of the investment in the subsidiary. IAS 21 (2007) clarifies that disposal of a foreign operation may occur through sale, liquidation, repayment of share capital, abandonment or receipt of a dividend out of pre-acquisition profits. When a partial disposal occurs, only the proportionate share of the related accumulated exchange difference is included in profit or loss.[57]

IAS 21 (2007) further clarifies that a write-down of a foreign operation does not constitute a partial disposal, and accordingly no part of the deferred foreign exchange gain or loss is recognised in profit or loss at the time of the such a write-down,[58] unless of course the write-down is consequent upon an event of 'disposal' as described in the previous paragraph. Moreover, it is implicit in the requirement of IFRS 5 for separate disclosure of cumulative gains and losses recognised in equity relating to a disposal group (see Chapter 4) that the classification of a subsidiary as held for sale under IFRS 5 does not give rise to recycling of foreign exchange differences. Those cumulative gains and losses are only recognised in profit or loss on sale.

B   Cumulative exchange differences on interest retained in former subsidiaries

As noted above, IAS 27 (2007) requires the cost of an investment formerly a subsidiary to be treated as its 'carrying amount', which excludes, in the case of a foreign subsidiary, the cumulative amount of any exchange differences relating to the subsidiary that have previously been recognised in equity in accordance with IAS 21 (2007). This begs the question of how such differences are to be dealt with. The question is only one of time – it is clearly a fundamental principle of IAS 21 (2007), IAS 27 (2007) and IAS 39 that such differences must at some point be recognised in profit or loss.

In our view, the provisions of IAS 21 (2007) indicate that cumulative foreign exchange differences are reclassified only when the reporting entity's interest in the relevant investment is disposed of, not when its status changes (e.g. because of changes in the relative voting powers of the owners of the investment). However, this does create the slight anomaly in the case of a former subsidiary which is to be accounted for as 'at fair value through profit or loss' that some part of the gains or losses related to that subsidiary will have been accounted for in equity, and not in profit or loss, until ultimate disposal of the investment.

C   Other cumulative gains and losses previously recognised in other comprehensive income

IAS 27 (2007) does not specifically address the accounting treatment, on disposal of a subsidiary, of other cumulative gains and losses previously accounted for in other comprehensive income relating to assets and liabilities of the disposed subsidiary. Such cumulative gains and losses, which would be reclassified to profit or loss if those assets and liabilities had been disposed of separately, could include:

- accumulated hedging gains and losses accounted for under IAS 39 (see Chapter 33); and

- any other amounts previously recognised in equity that would have been recognised in profit or loss if the group had directly disposed of the assets to which they relate, such as gains or losses on available-for-sale financial assets accounted for under IAS 39 (see Chapter 32 at 3.4).

IAS 39 does not specifically address this issue either. However, in our view, reclassification to profit or loss is appropriate, because the disposal of a subsidiary results in derecognition of the separate assets and liabilities of that subsidiary just as if they had been disposed of separately.

When a partial disposal occurs not resulting in a loss of control, only the proportionate share of the other cumulative gains and losses recognised in other comprehensive income should be reclassified to profit or loss, which is consistent with the approach required by IAS 21 in the context of cumulative exchange gains and losses recognised in other comprehensive income. However, if the partial disposal does result in a loss of control the other cumulative gains and losses recognised in other comprehensive income could be reclassified to profit or loss in their entirety because the related assets and liability would be derecognised from the balance sheet of the parent.

3.4   Presentation of comparative information for a former subsidiary

In cases, such as that in Example 7.12 above, where a subsidiary becomes an associate accounted for under the equity method, the effect will be that the reporting entity's interest in the investee will be reported:

- under the equity method from the date on which control is lost in the current period; and
- for any earlier part of the current period, and of any earlier period, during which the investee was controlled using full consolidation.

There is no question of restating financial information for periods prior to the loss of control using the equity method so as to provide some form of comparability with the new presentation. IAS 27 (as amended in 2008) and IAS 27 (2007) are explicit that consolidation continues until control is lost (see 3.2 and 3.3 above, respectively), and IAS 28 is equally clear that equity accounting commences only from the date on which an entity becomes an associate (see Chapter 11).

3.5   Demergers

Groups may dispose of subsidiaries by way of a demerger. This typically involves the transfer of the subsidiaries to be disposed of, either:

- directly to shareholders, by way of a dividend in kind; or
- (more usually) to a newly formed company in exchange for the issue of shares by that company to the shareholders of the disposing entity.

This raises the question of how the disposing entity should account for the disposal of the demerged assets.

3.5.1   IFRIC 17

In November 2008, the IASB issued IFRIC 17 – *Distributions of Non-cash Assets to Owners* – because IFRSs did not 'address how an entity should measure distributions to owners acting in their capacity as owners' and significant diversity in practice existed in how entities measured distributions of non-cash assets.[59] The application of IFRIC 17 in the context of demergers is discussed at A to D below. The application of IFRIC 17 to assets in general is discussed in Chapter 8 at 2.3.2.

A   Scope

The interpretation applies to the following types of non-reciprocal distributions by an entity to its owners in their capacity as owners:[60]

(a)   distributions of non-cash assets such as items of property, plant and equipment, businesses, ownership interests in another entity or disposal groups as defined in IFRS 5 (see Chapter 4 at 2.1.1).; and

(b)   distributions that give owners a choice of receiving either non-cash assets or a cash alternative.

However, the scope of IFRIC 17 is limited in several respects:

- it only applies to distributions in which all owners of the same class of equity instruments are treated equally;[61]

- it does not apply to 'a distribution of a non-cash asset that is ultimately controlled by the same party or parties before and after the distribution',[62] which means that IFRIC 17 does not apply when:

  - a group of individual shareholders receiving the distribution, as a result of contractual arrangements, collectively have the power to govern financial and operating policies of the entity making the distribution so as to obtain benefits from its activities;[63]

  - 'an entity distributes some of its ownership interests in a subsidiary but retains control of the subsidiary. The entity making a distribution that results in the entity recognising a non-controlling interest in its subsidiary accounts for the distribution in accordance with IAS 27 (as amended in 2008)'; and[64]

  This exclusion applies to 'the separate, individual and consolidated financial statements of an entity that makes the distribution.'[65]

- it only address the accounting by an entity that makes a non-cash asset distribution. It does not address the accounting by shareholders who receive such a distribution.[66]

B   Recognition and measurement

An entity making a non-cash distribution to its owners should recognise a liability to pay a dividend when the dividend is appropriately authorised and is no longer at the discretion of the entity, which is the date:[67]

(a)   when declaration of the dividend (e.g. by management) is approved by the relevant authority (e.g. shareholders) if the jurisdiction requires such approval; or

(b)   when the dividend is declared (e.g. by management) if the jurisdiction does not require further approval.

An entity should 'measure a liability to distribute non-cash assets as a dividend to its owners at the fair value of the assets to be distributed'.[68] When the owners have a choice between receiving a non-cash asset or cash, the entity should estimate the dividend payable by considering both the fair value of each alternative and the associated probability of owners selecting each alternative.[69]

At the end of each reporting period and at the date of settlement, the entity should review and adjust the carrying amount of the dividend payable, with any changes in the carrying amount of the dividend payable recognised in equity as adjustments to the amount of the distribution.[70]

When an entity settles the dividend payable, it should recognise any difference between the carrying amount of the assets distributed and the carrying amount of the dividend payable in as a separate line item profit or loss.[71]

The non-cash assets that are to be distributed are measured in accordance with other applicable standards up to the time of settlement, i.e. IFRIC 17 does not override the recognition and measurement requirements of those standards. While the IFRIC recognised concerns about the potential 'accounting mismatch' in equity resulting from measuring the dividend payable and the related assets on a different basis,[72] it concluded that:

> '...there was no support in IFRSs for requiring a remeasurement of the assets because of a decision to distribute them. The IFRIC noted that the mismatch concerned arises only with respect to assets that are not carried at fair value already. The IFRIC also noted that the accounting mismatch is the inevitable consequence of IFRSs using different measurement attributes at different times with different triggers for the remeasurement of different assets and liabilities.'[73]

C   Presentation and disclosure

An entity should disclose the following information:

- the carrying amount of the dividend payable at the beginning and end of the period;[74]
- the increase or decrease in the carrying amount recognised in the period as result of a change in the fair value of the assets to be distributed; and[75]
- if, after the end of a reporting period but before the financial statements are authorised for issue, an entity declares a dividend to distribute a non-cash asset, it should disclose:[76]
  - the nature of the asset to be distributed;
  - the carrying amount of the asset to be distributed as of the end of the reporting period;
  - the estimated fair value of the asset to be distributed as of the end of the reporting period, if it is different from its carrying amount; and
  - information about the method used to determine that fair value required by paragraph 27(a) and (b) of IFRS 7 – *Financial Instruments: Disclosures*.

D   Effective date

While IFRIC 17 is effective for annual periods beginning on or after 1 July 2009, early adoption is encouraged. IFRIC 17 should not be applied retrospectively to comparative periods.[77]

3.5.2   Pre-IFRIC 17

As noted at 3.5.1 above, prior to the publication of IFRIC 17, significant diversity in practice existed in how entities measured distributions of non-cash assets. In practice this meant that entities would generally apply one of the following methods:

(a)   a demerger would be recorded as a distribution to shareholders at the carrying amount, in the consolidated financial statements, of the net assets and goodwill attributable to the demerged business. This was consistent with the treatment of cash dividends under IAS 32 – *Financial Instruments: Presentation* (see Chapter 31 at 5). Those who supported this approach argued that, as a demerger is not an exchange transaction, there is no need to measure it at the fair value of the net assets and goodwill transferred;

(b)   whilst essentially a distribution to shareholders, a demerger is an economic event of unusual significance, and it would be therefore most appropriately recorded at fair value, in order to show the true value returned to shareholders. Under this approach, it would be necessary to record an offsetting credit within equity (equivalent to a gain on revaluation of the net assets and goodwill disposed). The net of this gain and the demerger dividend at fair value would of course be the same as the amount shown as a distribution at carrying amount under the approach in (a) above; or

(c)   a demerger should be considered as the equivalent of two transactions – a cash dividend (of the fair value of the demerger dividend) to shareholders, who then use that cash to acquire the demerged net assets and goodwill, giving rise to a gain in profit or loss for the reporting entity.

Entities that currently apply methods (a) or (b) may want to consider adopting IFRIC 17 early.

4   NON-CONTROLLING (OR MINORITY) INTERESTS

4.1   The definition of non-controlling (or minority) interest

The definitions of non-controlling interest under IAS 27 (as amended in 2008) and minority interest under IAS 27 (2007) are not as clear as they may seem at first sight. Example 7.16 below illustrates the difficulties that currently exist in applying the definition of a non-controlling (or minority) interest.

Example 7.16:   Classification of equity instruments as non-controlling (or minority) interests

A parent owns 80% of the shares issued by a subsidiary, the remaining 20% of the shares are held by a third party that does not have control. At 1 January 2010 the value of the net assets of the subsidiary included in the consolidated financial statements is €1,000, of which €800 is attributable to its parent and €200 is attributable to the non-controlling (or minority) interest. On 1 January 2010 the subsidiary enters into a written call option over its own shares with an investor and receives €50 from the investor. How should the parent account for this transaction in its consolidated financial statements?

Two approaches present themselves:

(1) An increase of €40 in equity attributable to owners of the parent and an increase in non-controlling (or minority) interest of €10. While the written call option is an equity instrument, it does not give rise to a new non-controlling (or minority) interest. The increase in net assets of the subsidiary should therefore be apportioned between the existing 80% controlling and 20% non-controlling interest according to their respective ownership interests; or

(2) An increase in non-controlling (or minority) interest of €50. The written call option is an equity instrument that gives rise to a new non-controlling (or minority) interest with an initial value of €50. The option holder is not entitled to a share in the profit or loss of the subsidiary, therefore the new non-controlling interest remains €50 until the option either expires or is exercised.

Whether approaches (1) and (2) are valid interpretations of the requirements of IFRS is discussed at 4.1.1 and 4.1.2 below.

The definitions of a minority interest under IAS 27 (2007) and that of an non-controlling interest under IAS 27 (as amended in 2008) are discussed below at 4.1.1 and 4.1.2, respectively.

4.1.1   Definition of minority interest under IAS 27 (2007)

In 2003 the IASB issued an amended version of IAS 27 which introduced the definition of minority interests now found in IAS 27 (2007): 'minority interest is that portion of the profit or loss and net assets of a subsidiary attributable to *equity interests* [emphasis added] that are not owned, directly or indirectly through subsidiaries, by the parent'.[78] Though IAS 27 and other standards issued at the same time (e.g. IFRS 2 – *Share-based Payment* – and IFRS 3) mention 'equity interests', IFRS did not actually define the term.

While the natural meaning of the phrase 'equity interest' would suggest that it comprises all forms of equity issued by an entity (or subsidiary) the recognition and measurement requirements of IAS 27 (2007) are in fact more nuanced. An entity needs to distinguish between present ownership interests and potential voting rights. 'The existence and effect of potential voting rights that are currently exercisable or convertible, including potential voting rights held by another entity, are considered when assessing whether an entity has the power to govern the financial and operating policies of another entity.'[79] The standard describes potential voting rights as follows:

'An entity may own share warrants, share call options, debt or equity instruments that are convertible into ordinary shares, or other similar instruments that have the potential, if exercised or converted, to give the entity voting power or reduce another party's voting power over the financial and operating policies of another entity (potential voting rights).'[80]

According to paragraph 22(c) of IAS 27 (2007) the 'minority interests in the net assets consist of: (i) the amount of those minority interests at the date of the original combination calculated in accordance with IFRS 3; and (ii) the minority's share of changes in equity since the date of the combination'.[81] However, when potential voting rights exist, paragraph 23 of IAS 27 (2007) requires allocation (i.e. recognition and measurement) of proportions of profit or loss and changes in equity to the parent and minority interests on the basis of present ownership interests. An entity should not reflect the possible exercise or conversion of potential voting rights (such as share warrants, share call options, debt or equity instruments that are convertible into ordinary shares, or other similar instruments).[82] The implementation guidance to IAS 27 (2007), which accompanies the standard but is not part of it, blurs the distinction between present ownership interests and potential voting rights even further:

> 'The proportion allocated to the parent and minority interests in preparing consolidated financial statements in accordance with IAS 27 ... are determined solely on the basis of present ownership interests. The proportion allocated is determined taking into account the eventual exercise of potential voting rights and other derivatives that, in substance, give access at present to the economic benefits associated with an ownership interest.'[83]

> 'In some circumstances an entity has, in substance, a present ownership as a result of a transaction that gives it access to the economic benefits associated with an ownership interest. In such circumstances, the proportion allocated is determined taking into account the eventual exercise of those potential voting rights and other derivatives that give the entity access to the economic benefits at present.'[84]

It seems evident that, for example, sale-and-repurchase transactions, preference shares and options with a very low strike price give access to economic benefits associated with an ownership interest. Less clear is whether options with a relatively high strike price or unvested share-based payments give access to such economic benefits. At least outside business combinations it is accepted practice under IFRS to leave the issue of instruments giving rise to potential voting rights out of minority interest. In other words, entities would generally apply approach (1) in Example 7.16 above.

4.1.2 Definition of non-controlling interest under IAS 27 (as amended in 2008)

The 2008 amendments to IAS 27 changed the term 'minority interest' to 'non-controlling interest'. The term 'minority' was strictly a legacy from the 'ownership' model of consolidation. Under a 'legal and contractual' model or an 'economic control' model the owners of a minority of an entity's shares might still be able to control that entity. Conversely, it is quite possible for the 'minority' shareholders to own more than half the shares in a subsidiary. The IASB therefore concluded that 'non-controlling interest' is a more accurate description than 'minority interest' of the interests of those owners who do not have a controlling interest in an entity.[85]

The IASB also decided to reword the underlying definition. As noted at 4.1.1 above, IAS 27 (2007) used to define a minority interest as follows:[86]

> Minority interest is that portion of the profit or loss and net assets of a subsidiary attributable to equity interests that are not owned, directly or indirectly through subsidiaries, by the parent.

IAS 27 (as amended in 2008) defines a non-controlling interest differently:[87]

> Non-controlling interest is the equity in a subsidiary not attributable, directly or indirectly, to a parent.

IFRS 3 (as revised in 2008) provides the option to measure any non-controlling interest in the acquiree either at (1) fair value or (2) at the non-controlling interest's proportionate share of the acquiree's identifiable net assets.[88] This option suggests that non-controlling interest comprises all equity instruments issued by the subsidiary that are not owned by the parent and that the definition of a non-controlling interest is indeed different from that of a minority interest.

This is supported by the fact that IAS 32 defines equity instruments as contracts that evidence 'a residual interest in the assets of an entity after deducting all of its liabilities',[89] which is the same as the definition of 'equity' in the *Framework*.[90] Hence, the reference to 'equity' in the definition of a non-controlling interest should be read as a reference to those 'equity instruments' of a subsidiary that are not held, directly or indirectly, by its parent.

This has far reaching consequences because it means that any equity instruments in issue that are not owned by the parent would fall to be treated as non-controlling interests. Accordingly, the issuance of the following types of instruments by a wholly-owned subsidiary might give rise to non-controlling interests:

- convertible debt and other compound financial instruments;
- warrants;
- options over own shares; and
- options under share-based payment plans.

The issuance of such instruments results in a change in equity that is entirely attributable to the non-controlling interest.[91] Subsequently, a proportion of profit or loss is only attributed to these instruments if they give rise to a present ownership interest.[92] However, when the underlying instrument is exercised or expires, the amount originally recorded in non-controlling interest should be adjusted so that the carrying amounts of the controlling and non-controlling interest reflect the change in the relative interests in the subsidiary.

Considerable challenges remain in accounting for equity instruments that give third parties somewhat less than a present ownership interest in a consolidated subsidiary. Some of the accounting issues associated with such equity instruments are discussed at 4.1.3, 4.3, 4.5 and, in the context of call and put options over non-controlling (or minority) interests, at 5 below.

In summary, an entity should apply the following accounting policies:

- sale-and-repurchase transactions, preference shares and options with a very low strike price give access to economic benefits associated with an ownership interest should be accounted for as non-controlling interests under IAS 27 (as amended in 2008);

- we believe that even equity instruments issued by a subsidiary that do not give access to such economic benefits (e.g. options with a relatively high share price or unvested share payments) should be accounted for as non-controlling interest under IAS 27 (as amended in 2008). As discussed at A below, the IASB also reached this conclusion in July 2009 and tentatively decided to amend IFRSs to reflect this. However, we recognise that there is a tension between paragraphs 18 and 19 of IAS 27 (as amended in 2008) and the definition of non-controlling interests and accordingly until such time as IFRSs are amended there may be differences in practice; and

- an entity that recognises a non-controlling interest arising from a business combination at its proportionate share of identifiable net assets acquired would measure such equity interests at nil as illustrated at 4.1.3 below.

A   *Future developments*

In July 2009, the IFRIC and later the IASB discussed two issues in connection with the recognition and measurement of non-controlling interest:

- measurement of non-controlling interest in business combinations (see I below); and

- accounting for un-replaced and voluntarily replaced share-based payment transactions (see II below).

I   *Measurement of non-controlling interest in business combinations*

In July 2009, the IFRIC discussed whether 'an entity should apply the measurement choice in paragraph 19 of IFRS 3 (as revised in 2008) to all components of noncontrolling interest (NCI). Paragraph 19 states that, for each business combination, the acquirer shall measure any NCI in the acquiree either at fair value or at the non-controlling interest's proportionate share of the acquiree's identifiable net assets'.[93] The IFRIC agenda paper on the issue acknowledges that 'in phase II of the business combinations project, the Board amended the definition of minority interest (MI) in IAS 27 and changed its name from minority interest to non-controlling interest. The amendment has widened the scope of instruments to be included in NCI.'[94] That means that 'in addition to minority interests as defined in IFRS 3 (issued in 2004), the definition of NCI includes, for example, options or warrants over an entity's own shares that are classified as equity and the equity component of a convertible instrument'.[95]

Consequently 'some believe that if an entity chooses to measure NCI as a proportionate share of the acquiree's identifiable net assets, it should apply this measurement to all components of the acquiree's equity. The consequence would be that instruments other than those equivalent to minority interest would be measured at nil on acquisition.'[96]

The IFRIC concluded that the measurement choice in IFRS 3 'should apply only to instruments currently entitled to a proportionate share of the acquiree's net assets' and that other instruments should be recognised initially at fair value.[97] As IFRSs do not provide sufficient guidance to resolve this issue, the IFRIC tentatively decided to recommend that the Board amend IFRS 3 (as revised in 2008) as part of the annual improvements project.

In July 2009, the IASB discussed the IFRIC's conclusion in the context of its annual improvements project. The Board tentatively decided to clarify that the measurement option in IFRS 3 (as revised in 2008) applies 'only to instruments that are currently entitled to a proportionate share of the acquiree's net assets. Other equity instruments that are part of non-controlling interest should be measured at fair value or in accordance with applicable IFRSs.'[98] Consequently, in August 2009, the Board issued the exposure draft *Improvements to IFRSs* in which it proposes to amend paragraph 19 of IFRS 3 (as revised in 2008) to read as follows:

> 'For each business combination, the acquirer shall measure any non-controlling interest in the acquiree either at fair value or other measurement basis as required by IFRSs, except for the components of non-controlling interest that are present ownership instruments and entitle their holders to a pro rata share of the entity's net assets in the event of liquidation. The acquirer shall measure those components of non-controlling interest either at fair value or at the present ownership instruments' proportionate share of the acquiree's identifiable net assets.'[99]

The Board observed that 'without this amendment, if the acquirer chooses to measure NCI at its proportionate share of the acquiree's identifiable net assets, the acquirer might measure some equity instruments at nil. In the Board's view, this would result in not recognising economic interests that other parties have in the acquiree.'[100] The proposed improvement is illustrated in Example 7.17 below.

The detailed impact of the proposed change on business combinations is discussed in Chapter 9 at 3.9.

II   *Un-replaced and voluntarily replaced share-based payment transactions*

In July 2009, the IFRIC and later the IASB discussed the accounting for un-replaced and voluntarily replaced share-based payment transactions. The IASB staff's agenda paper on the issue states that:

> 'the staff considers that the unreplaced awards of the acquiree meet the definition of non-controlling interest. Equity-settled share-based payment awards are part of the equity of the acquiree. As they are not controlled by the owners of the acquirer after the acquisition, they meet the definition of NCI. Paragraph 4 of IAS 27 defines NCI as the equity in a subsidiary not attributable, directly or indirectly, to a parent.'[101]

'...the staff believes that NCI components other than [minority interest] should be measured at fair value or other measurement basis as required by the IFRS. That means the unreplaced awards that are stock options should be measured in accordance with the method in IFRS 2 *Share-based Payment*.'[102]

The IFRIC recommended that the Board amend IFRS 3 (as revised in 2008) to address the issues identified as a part of the annual improvements project.[103] Acting on this advice the Board tentatively decided to clarify that paragraphs B57-B62 of IFRS 3 (as revised in 2008) apply to all 'share-based payment transactions that are part of a business combination including share-based payment transactions of the acquiree that the acquirer chooses not to replace and those that the acquirer chooses to replace with its own share-based payment transactions, even though they would not expire as a consequence of the business combination'.[104] Consequently, in August 2009, the Board issued the exposure draft *Improvements to IFRSs* in which it proposes:

'...to amend the application guidance in IFRS 3 (to require the acquirer to apply paragraphs B57-B62 to all share-based payment transactions that are part of a business combination). Therefore, the application guidance would also apply to share-based payment transactions of the acquiree that the acquirer chooses not to replace and share-based payment transactions that the acquirer chooses to exchange for share-based payment transactions of the acquiree, even though they would not expire as a consequence of the business combination.'[105]

The detailed impact of the proposed change on business combinations and share-based payments is discussed in Chapter 9 at 5.4.3 and Chapter 27 at 11.2.2 A and 11.4, respectively.

4.1.3   Initial measurement of non-controlling interest

As discussed at 4.1.2 above, IFRS 3 (as revised in 2008) provides the option to measure any non-controlling interest in the acquiree either at:[106]

(a)   fair value; or

(b)   the non-controlling interest's proportionate share of the acquiree's identifiable net assets.

Application of these measurement requirements is, however, not as straight forward as it may seem at first sight. This is best illustrated by way of an example.

Example 7.17:   Initial recognition of non-controlling interest

Parent acquires 80% of the ordinary shares of Target for €950 in cash. The total fair value of the equity instruments issued by Target is €1,165 and the fair value of its identifiable net assets is €850. The market value of the 20% of the ordinary shares owned by non-controlling shareholders is €190. In addition, the subsidiary has also written gross settled call options over its own shares with a market value of €25, which are considered to be equity instruments under IAS 32. How should the parent account for the non-controlling interest under each of the options within IFRS 3 (as revised in 2008)?

Method (1) – Non-controlling interest at proportionate share of identifiable net assets

The parent measures the non-controlling interest at its proportionate share of the acquiree's identifiable net assets (as was previously required under IFRS 3 (2007) and permitted under IFRS 3 (as revised in 2008)) as follows:

	€	€
Fair value of identifiable net assets	850	
Goodwill (€950 – 80% × €850)	270	
Cash		950
Non-controlling interest (20% × €850)		170

Goodwill under this method represents the difference between the purchase consideration paid and the parent's share of the identifiable net assets. The non-controlling interest is measured at the non-controlling interest's proportionate share (determined on the basis of present ownership interests and not reflecting the possible exercise or conversion of potential voting rights) of the identifiable net assets of Target.[107]

Under the proposed amendments in the context of the IASB's annual improvements project (see 4.1.2 A I above), the non-controlling interest would be €195 (i.e. 20% × €850 + €25) and goodwill would be €295 (i.e. €950 – 80% × €850 + €25).

Method (2) – Non-controlling interest at fair value

The non-controlling interest is measured at the fair value of all equity instruments issued by Target that are not owned by the parent.

	€	€
Fair value of identifiable net assets	850	
Goodwill (€1,165 – €850)	315	
Cash		950
Non-controlling interest (€190 + €25)		215

However, under this method goodwill represents the difference between the fair value of Target and the fair value of its identifiable net assets. At the same time non-controlling interest is determined as the fair value of all equity instruments issued by Target that are not owned by the parent.

Reconciliation of goodwill

Goodwill as determined under the two methods can be reconciled as follows:

	€
Method (1): Goodwill (€950 – 80% × €850)	270
Fair value of call options	25
Goodwill related to the non-controlling interest in ordinary shares (€190 – 20% × €850)	20
Method (2): Goodwill (€1,165 – €850)	315

The above reconciliation makes clear that Method (1) effectively ignores the fair value of equity instruments that do not convey a present ownership interest. It also ignores the goodwill related to ordinary shares that are held by non-controlling shareholders, which is what would have happened if the parent had applied IFRS 3 (2007) and IAS 27 (2007) to the business combination.

4.2   Presentation of non-controlling (or minority) interests

IAS 27 (as amended in 2008) requires non-controlling interests to be presented in the consolidated statement of financial position within equity, separately from the equity of the owners of the parent.[108] 'Profit or loss and each component of other comprehensive income are attributed to the owners of the parent and to the non-controlling interests.'[109]

IAS 27 (2007) requires minority interests to be presented in the consolidated balance sheet within equity, separately from the parent shareholders' equity. Minority interests in the profit or loss of the group must also be separately disclosed.[110] The profit or loss is attributed to the parent shareholders and minority interests. Because the interest of parent shareholders and minority interests are both equity, the amount attributed to minority interests is not income or expense.[111]

4.3   Interaction with IAS 32

Notwithstanding the general requirement of IAS 27 (as amended in 2008) and IAS 27 (2007) to treat non-controlling (or minority) interests as equity, there are some circumstances – essentially where the non-controlling (or minority) interests have a claim on the group more akin to that of a creditor than that of an equity shareholder – where non-controlling (or minority) interests are required to be classified as financial liabilities (and payments to them as interest expense) by IAS 32. This is discussed further in Chapter 31 at 3.6.

However, where a non-controlling (or minority) interest is treated as equity in consolidated financial statements, in our view, it is subject to all the requirements of IAS 32 relating to own equity. For example, put or call options over non-controlling (or minority) interests accounted for as equity should be accounted for in consolidated financial statements as contracts over own equity instruments under IAS 32 (see Chapter 31 at 7).

In some cases, however, the effect of options over what are in law non-controlling (or minority) interests may be such that no non-controlling (or minority) interests is reflected in the financial statements, particularly when such options are put in place as part of a business combination transaction. This is discussed at 5 below.

4.4   Loss-making subsidiaries

4.4.1   *IAS 27 (2007)*

IAS 27 (2007) requires that where losses attributable to the minority in a consolidated subsidiary exceed the minority interest in the subsidiary's equity, the excess, and any further losses applicable to the minority, are allocated against the majority interest except to the extent that the minority has a binding obligation, and is able, to make an additional investment to cover the losses. If the subsidiary subsequently reports profits, such profits are allocated to the majority interest until the minority's share of losses previously absorbed by the majority has been recovered.[112]

This treatment under IAS 27 (2007), sometimes referred to as 'waterline accounting', is illustrated by Example 7.18 below.

Example 7.18:   Minority interest in loss-making subsidiary under IAS 27 (2007)

The reporting entity (P) sets up a subsidiary (S) with another party (M). P owns 70%, and M 30%, of the equity, and the terms of the arrangement are such that S is a subsidiary of P (rather than a joint venture of P and M), and M has no obligation to make additional investment to cover any losses.

The initial investment of the parties is €700,000 by P and €300,000 by M. Further finance is provided by way of a bank loan. The first five years' results of S are as follows:

Year	Profit/(loss) (€)	Shareholders' equity (€)
0		1,000,000
1	(700,000)	300,000
2	(800,000)	(500,000)
3	400,000	(100,000)
4	500,000	400,000
5	750,000	1,150,000

The allocation of each year's result between P and M would be as follows.

Year	Profit/(loss) (€)	P's share of result (€)	P's share of net equity (€)	M's share of result (€)	M's share of net equity (€)
0			700,000		300,000
1	(700,000)	(490,000)	210,000	(210,000)	90,000
2	(800,000)	(710,000)	(500,000)	(90,000)	–
3	400,000	400,000	(100,000)	–	–
4	500,000	380,000	280,000	120,000	120,000
5	750,000	525,000	805,000	225,000	345,000

In year 1 the loss does not reduce shareholders' equity to zero, and is therefore allocated 70/30 according the relative shareholdings of P and M. By year 2 the cumulative losses of €1,500,000 are greater than P's and M's initial investment, so that the share of the loss allocated to M is restricted to the amount needed to write its investment down to zero, with the balance of the loss being borne by P. In year 3, the profit is insufficient to return the shareholders' equity of S to more than zero, so that P takes credit for the full profit. At the end of year 4, shareholders' equity, though less than P's and M's initial investment, is €400,000, of which M's 30% share is €120,000. Accordingly, M's share of the year 4 profit is restricted to €120,000. In year 5, P and M once more participate in the result according to their relative shareholdings.

4.4.2   IAS 27 (as amended in 2008)

The requirements discussed at 4.4.1 above differ significantly from those under IAS 27 (as amended in 2008), which requires that total comprehensive income is 'attributed to the owners of the parent and to the non-controlling interests even if this results in the non-controlling interests having a deficit balance'.[113]

The IASB decided to change the requirements regarding loss-making subsidiaries because it considered the treatment under IAS 27 (2007) to be 'inconsistent with its conclusion that non-controlling interests are part of the equity of the group'.[114] The new approach is consistent with the fact that the controlling and the non-controlling interest participate proportionately in the risks and rewards of an investment in the subsidiary.[115]

Guarantees or other support arrangements by the parent often protect the non-controlling interests from losses of the subsidiary in excess of equity. Although the IASB considers that the parent ought to account for such arrangements separately, and that they should not affect the accounting for the non-controlling interest, it has so far resisted requests for further guidance.[116]

The Board believes that if a parent enters into an arrangement that places 'it under an obligation to the subsidiary or to the non-controlling interests, [it] should account for that arrangement separately and the arrangement should not affect the way the entity attributes comprehensive income to the controlling and non-controlling interests'.[117]

As mentioned in Chapter 6 at 6, the transitional provisions in IAS 27 (as amended in 2008) state that an entity 'shall not restate any profit or loss attribution for reporting periods before the amendment is applied'.[118] This transitional requirement gives rise to a number of issues that are illustrated in the example below.

Example 7.19:   *Accounting for the non-controlling interest's share of losses previously allocated to the parent*

Parent A has an 80% interest in subsidiary B, which it acquired in 2000. At 31 December 2009, the subsidiary had net negative equity of $100. Under IAS 27 (2007), the deficit of $20 attributable to the non-controlling interest was allocated to parent A. The parent adopts IAS 27 (as amended in 2008) on 1 January 2010.

How should parent A account for the following:

*   In the year ended 31 December 2010, subsidiary B earns profits of $150.

    Parent A's share of the profits is $120 (i.e. 80% of $150) and the non-controlling interest's share of the profits is $30 (i.e. 20% of $150). After adoption of IAS 27 (as amended in 2008), profits or losses and other comprehensive income are allocated to the parent and the non-controlling interest based on their present ownership interests. Any past losses that were absorbed by the parent will not be reversed.

*   On 1 January 2010, parent A pays $5 to acquire half of the 20% interest held by the non-controlling interest.

    Parent A does not reallocate any of the losses upon remeasuring the non-controlling interest for the change in relative ownership. When the non-controlling interest is remeasured following a decrease in relative ownership interest, it is remeasured based upon the 'change in their relative interest' and not by reference to a percentage share of net assets. Therefore, the non-controlling interest's existing interest is $nil and non-controlling interest is reduced by $nil (i.e. 10%/20% × $nil).

*   On 1 January 2010, parent A sells a 10% interest in subsidiary B for $5, i.e. its interest in subsidiary B is reduced from 80% to 70%.

    Parent A does not reallocate any of the losses upon remeasuring the non-controlling interest for the change in relative ownership. When non-controlling interest is remeasured following an increase in relative ownership interest, it is remeasured based upon the 'change in their relative interest' and not by reference to a percentage share of net assets. Therefore, the parent's existing interest is minus $100 and non-controlling interest takes up minus $12.5 (i.e. 10%/80% × minus $100). Accordingly, no catch-up adjustment for the non-controlling interest's unallocated share of previous losses is made at the remeasurement date.

The IASB confirmed in May 2009 that prospective application of the requirements of paragraph 28 of IAS 27 (as amended in 2008) means that it applies only to new transactions and events (in this case profits or losses incurred after the applicable date) and the old accounting policy for prior transactions and events remains (i.e. it is effectively grandfathered). Accordingly, the previous allocation of the non-controlling interest's share of losses to the parent remains and is not 'reversed' by any subsequent transaction.[119]

4.5 Cumulative preference shares held by non-controlling (or minority) interests

If a subsidiary has outstanding cumulative preference shares that are held by non-controlling (or minority) interests and classified as equity, the parent is required to compute its share of profits or losses after adjusting for the dividends on such shares, whether or not dividends have been declared.[120]

5 CALL AND PUT OPTIONS OVER NON-CONTROLLING (OR MINORITY) INTERESTS

In most business combinations where less than 100% of the equity shares have been acquired, the determination of the acquirer's share of the net assets of the acquiree (and, thus the amount of the non-controlling (or minority) interest) is relatively straightforward. Two approaches are permitted under IFRS 3 (as revised in 2008) (see 1.2.2 above):

(a) *Non-controlling interest at fair value* – All of the identifiable assets, liabilities and contingent liabilities of the acquiree are recognised in accordance with the standard at their fair values. Goodwill being the excess of the consideration transferred and fair value of the non-controlling interest recognised over the fair value of the net identifiable assets acquired. The non-controlling interest is recognised at fair value (see 4.1.3 above); or

(b) *Non-controlling interest at proportionate share of identifiable net assets* – The identifiable assets, liabilities and contingent liabilities of the acquiree recognised in accordance with the standard at their fair values. Goodwill is the excess of the consideration transferred over the acquirer's interest in those net assets. The non-controlling (or minority) interest in the acquiree reflects the minority's proportion of the net identifiable assets, liabilities and contingent liabilities of the acquiree at their attributed fair values; no amount is included for any goodwill relating to the non-controlling (or minority) interest (see 4.1.3 above).

IFRS 3 (2007) only permits the approach under (b) above.

In some business combinations where less than 100% of the equity shares are acquired, it may be that the transaction also involves options over some or all of the outstanding shares. It may be that the acquirer has a call option, i.e. a right to acquire the outstanding shares at a future date for cash at a particular price. Alternatively, it may be that the acquirer has granted a put option to the other shareholders whereby they have the right to sell their shares to the acquirer at a future date for cash at a particular price. Indeed in some cases, there may be a combination of such call and put options, the terms of which may be equivalent or may be different.

IFRS 3 (as revised in 2008) and IFRS 3 (2007) give no guidance as to how such options should impact on the accounting for a business combination. However, in determining the appropriate accounting in such situations, the implications of a number of other IFRSs need to be considered; these are IAS 27 (as amended in 2008), IAS 27 (2007), IAS 32 and IAS 39.

Although the discussion below deals with options, similar considerations to those discussed at 5.2 below will apply in situations where the transaction means that the acquirer has entered into a forward purchase contract in respect of the shares held by the other shareholders (see 5.3 below).

5.1   Call options only

As discussed in Chapter 6 at 2.1.2, IAS 27 (as amended in 2008) and IAS 27 (2007) require that where an entity has call options over shares in another entity that are currently exercisable, then the potential voting rights attaching to those shares are taken into account in determining whether the entity has control over that other entity. In the context of a business combination where an entity has acquired, say, a 60% interest in the shares of another entity, but also has a call option over the remaining shares, the option will be irrelevant in determining control, since the entity has obtained control through the acquisition of the 60% interest. However, where an interest of, say, only 40% has been acquired, but the entity also has a call option over a further 20%, then the existence of the call option may mean that it has acquired a subsidiary that needs to be accounted for as a business combination under IFRS 3 (as revised in 2008) or IFRS 3 (2007).

Although such call options are taken into account in determining whether the entity has obtained control, as discussed at 2.2 above, IAS 27 (as amended in 2008) and IAS 27 (2007) require that the proportions allocated to the parent and non-controlling (or minority) interests are determined on the basis of present ownership interests. However, the proportion allocated would be determined taking into account the eventual exercise of potential voting rights under the call option, if in substance the entity had access at present to the economic benefits associated with that ownership interest.[121]

5.1.1   Options giving the acquirer present access to benefits associated with ownership interest

Whether the call options, in substance, give the acquiring entity present access to such benefits will depend on the terms of the call option. This is likely to be the case if the option price is fixed (or determinable) and it is agreed between the parties that no dividends will be paid to the other shareholders, or the terms are set such that the other shareholders effectively receive only a lender's return. Accordingly, if the call option is over all of the other shares, then no non-controlling (or minority) interest would be reflected in equity. Thus, the business combination would be accounted for on the basis that a 100% interest had been acquired. Since the accounting reflects the 'eventual exercise' of the option, the cost of the business combination should include an amount representing the fair value of the 'liability' to the non-controlling (or minority) shareholders under the call option (effectively, the present value of the exercise price payable under the option). The unwinding of the discount will be reflected in profit or loss. In the event that the call option is not ultimately exercised, then the entity has effectively disposed of a partial interest in its subsidiary in return for the amount recognised as the 'liability' at the date of expiry and should account for the transaction as discussed in at 3.2.2 and 3.3.2 above.

5.1.2   *Options not giving the acquirer present access to benefits associated with ownership interest*

A call option may not give the acquiring entity present access to the benefits associated with the ownership interest because its terms contain one or more of the following features:

- the option price has not yet been determined or will be the fair value of the shares at the date of exercise;

- the option price is based on expected future results or net assets of the subsidiary at the date of exercise; or

- it has been agreed between the parties that, prior to the exercise of the option, all retained profits may be freely distributed to the existing shareholders according to their current shareholdings.

If the call option does not give access to the benefits associated with the ownership interest, the implementation guidance in IAS 27 (as amended in 2008) and IAS 27 (2007) requires that the 'instruments containing the potential voting rights are accounted for in accordance with IAS 39'.[122] This would appear to be based on paragraph 2(a) of IAS 39 which states that entities shall apply that standard 'to derivatives on an interest in a subsidiary ... unless the derivative meets the definition of an equity instrument of the entity in IAS 32'. Clearly, in the separate financial statements of the acquirer, this means that the call option over the shares in the subsidiary will be initially recognised as a financial asset at its fair value, with any subsequent changes in its fair value reflected in profit or loss. Such fair value may not be significant if the call option is exercisable at the fair value of the underlying shares at the date of exercise, or at an amount intended to be a surrogate for such a value.

Such a treatment would also apply in the consolidated financial statements of the acquirer if the call option does not meet the definition of an equity instrument of the entity. This would be the case if the terms of the option were such that it did not involve an exercise price that was a fixed amount. In the event that the call option is exercised, the fair value of the option at that date will be included as part of the cost of the acquisition of the non-controlling (or minority) interest (see 3.2.2 and 3.3.3 above). The accounting for acquisition of minority interests will depend on the acquirer's policy for such acquisitions. In the event that the option lapses unexercised, any carrying amount for the option will be expensed in profit or loss.

However, if the exercise price under the option was a fixed amount then as it is an option over the non-controlling (or minority) interest in the consolidated financial statements, and as indicated earlier IAS 27 (as amended in 2008) and IAS 27 (2007) regard the non-controlling (or minority) interest as 'equity' in those financial statements, it would seem that the call option should be accounted for in a similar fashion to that for a call option over an entity's own equity shares as discussed in Example 31.16 in Chapter 31. As the call option over the non-controlling (or minority) interest's shares will be gross-settled, this means that the initial fair value of the option is taken to equity. In the event that the call option is exercised, this initial fair value will be included as part of the cost of the acquisition of the non-controlling (or minority) interest (see 3.2.2 and 3.3.3 above). The accounting for acquisition of minority interests will depend on the acquirer's policy for such acquisitions.

5.2   Put options only

Suppose, in the context of a business combination where an entity has acquired, say, a 60% interest in the shares of another entity, the acquirer, rather than having a call option over the remaining shares, has granted a put option to the other shareholders whereby they have the right to sell their shares to the acquirer at a future date for cash at a particular price. As with call options discussed above, the price to be paid under the put option might be fixed, based on the fair value of the shares at the date of exercise, or determined by way of a formula based on expected future results or net assets of the subsidiary.

This is an area that IFRIC considered during 2006, not only in the context of put options negotiated at the time of the acquisition of the majority interest but also at a later date. In May 2006, it was reported that:

> 'IFRIC considered the treatment under IAS 32 and IFRS 3 of puts and forwards held by minority interests in response to a request to the IFRIC related to situations where a parent enters into a commitment through a written put or a forward purchase to acquire shares in a subsidiary held by a third party. The settlement amount might be fixed, based on fair value of the shares at the settlement date or based on a formula, such as a multiple of EBITDA or net income. This type of contract might be negotiated as part of the purchase of the majority interest or negotiated independently at a later date. Two issues that arise regularly in practice are whether the parent must recognise a liability for the amount potentially payable under the contract and whether the minority interest continues to be recognised for the minority's shares that are subject to the agreement.

> 'The IFRIC tentatively decided not to take the item onto its agenda but deferred publishing formal wording for this until the following meeting, when it intended to address the related issue, whether puts or forwards received by minority interests in a business combination are contingent consideration.'[123]

At the next meeting in July 2006, IFRIC considered this related issue and tentatively decided not to take it onto its agenda either, commenting that the 'accounting for these arrangements, including the circumstances considered by the

IFRIC, is being considered by the Board as part of the current redeliberations on the proposed revised IFRS 3 ... The IFRIC therefore believed that it could not develop guidance more quickly than is likely to be developed in the business combinations project and [decided] not to take a project on this issue onto its agenda.'[124]

At the same meeting, in relation to the original issue, IFRIC again tentatively decided not to take it onto its agenda, commenting that:

> 'Paragraph 23 of IAS 32 states that a parent must recognise a financial liability when it has an obligation to pay cash in the future to purchase the minority's shares, even if the payment of that cash is conditional on the option being exercised by the holder. After initial recognition any liability to which IFRS 3 is not being applied will be accounted for in accordance with IAS 39. The parent will reclassify the liability to equity if a put expires unexercised.
>
> 'The IFRIC agreed that there is likely to be divergence in practice in how the related equity is reclassified. However, the IFRIC did not believe that it could reach a consensus view on this matter on a timely basis.'[125]

In November 2006, IFRIC confirmed these decisions not to take these items onto its agenda.[126]

So, how should put options, granted to holders of non-controlling (or minority) interests at the date of acquiring control of a subsidiary, be accounted for?

Paragraph 23 of IAS 32 requires that a gross-settled written put option over an entity's own equity instruments (i.e. the entity pays cash in return for the counterparty delivering shares), whether for a fixed or variable amount, should be recognised as a financial liability at its fair value (see Chapter 31 at 3.3.3 and 7.3.2). As indicated earlier IAS 27 (as amended in 2008) and IAS 27 (2007) regard the non-controlling (or minority) interest as 'equity' for the purpose of the consolidated financial statements. Thus, any put options granted to non-controlling (or minority) interests give rise to a financial liability to be recognised initially at the present value of the amount payable upon exercise of the option. The liability is subsequently remeasured at each reporting date to the present value of the amount payable on exercise. The fact that such a financial liability should be recognised was confirmed by the IFRIC rejection notice quoted above.

However, we believe that the accounting for the remaining aspects of the put option depends in part upon an assessment of the terms of the transaction and may involve a choice of accounting policy, which once selected, must be applied consistently. These choices arise because of the lack of explicit guidance in IFRS and potential contradictions between the requirements of IAS 27 (as amended in 2008) and IAS 27 (2007) on the one hand and IAS 32 on the other hand, which is reinforced by the fact that IFRIC decided not to take the issue on to its agenda despite the fact that it agreed that there is likely to be divergence in practice. Phase II of the IASB's business combinations project has not resolved these issues as the Board decided not to reconsider the fundamental approach to consolidation of subsidiaries under IAS 27.

The various methods of accounting for put options over non-controlling interests under IAS 27 (as amended in 2008) and put options over minority interests under IAS 27 (2007) are discussed at 5.2.1 and 5.2.2 below, respectively.

5.2.1   Put options over non-controlling interests – IAS 27 (as amended in 2008)

An entity that applies IAS 27 (as amended in 2008), as with call options above, needs to consider whether or not the terms of the transaction give the acquirer present access to the economic benefits associated with the ownership interest that is the subject of the put option. In addition, key policy decisions that management must make in developing an accounting policy, are:

- given potential contradictions between IAS 32 and IAS 27 (as amended in 2008), which standard takes precedence;

- if non-controlling interest is recognised on initial acquisition – whether it continues to be recognised and, if so, how.

The following diagram summarises the analysis that we believe should be performed, the questions to be addressed and the alternatives that apply, which are discussed further below. 'Non-controlling interest' has been abbreviated in the diagram to 'NCI'.

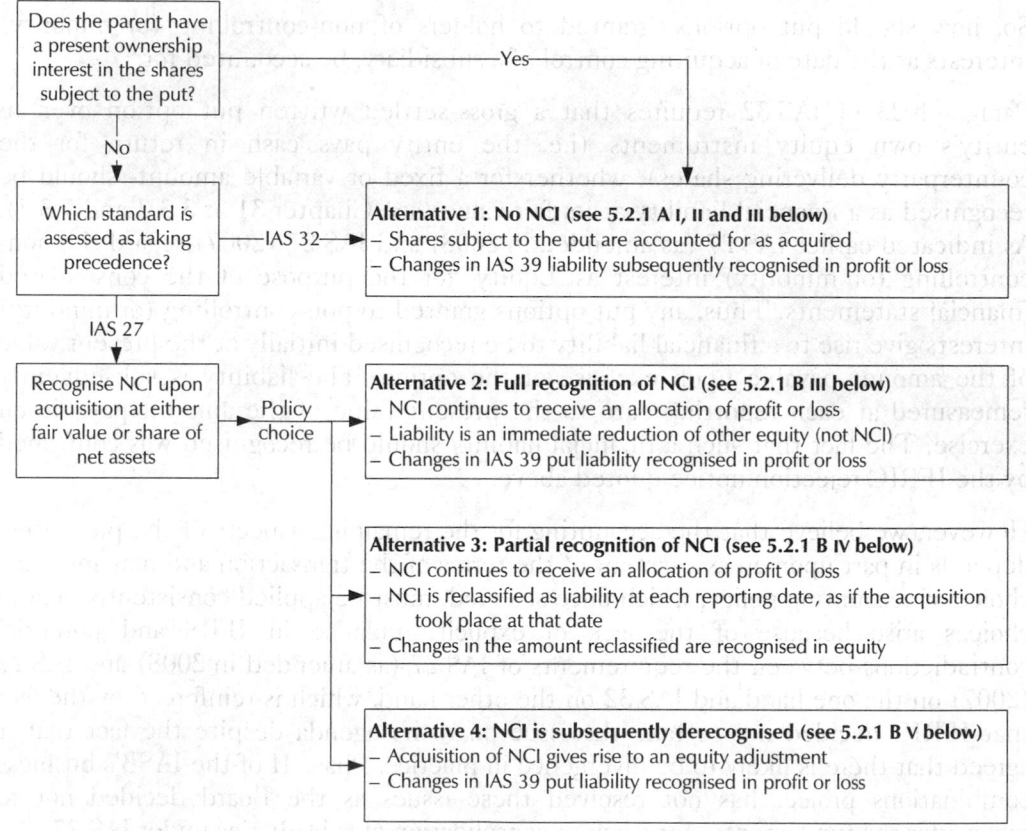

A   Options giving the acquirer present access to benefits associated with ownership interest

All of the terms and conditions of the option are analysed to assess whether these give the acquirer present access to the ownership interest in the shares concerned. Factors to consider in assessing whether or not a present ownership interest is granted to the acquirer include:

- pricing – to the extent that the price is fixed or determinable rather than being at fair value, it is an indicator that a present ownership interest has been granted;
- voting rights and decision-making – to the extent that the voting rights or decision-making connected to the shares concerned is restricted, it is an indicator that a present ownership interest has been granted;
- dividend rights – to the extent that the dividend rights attached to the shares concerned is restricted, it is an indicator that a present ownership interest has been granted; and
- issue of call options – combination of put and call options, with the same period of exercise and same/similar pricing are indicators that the arrangement is in the nature of a forward contract and therefore a present ownership interest has been granted.

I   No non-controlling interest

If it is concluded that the acquirer has a present ownership interest in the shares concerned, it is accounted for as an acquisition of those underlying shares, and no non-controlling interest will be recognised (see II below). Any dividends paid to the other shareholders are recognised as an expense of the group, unless they represent a repayment of the liability (e.g. where the exercise price is adjusted by the dividends paid). The put liability should be accounted for under IAS 39 (see III below).

II   Accounting for the business combination

The business combination is accounted for on the basis that the underlying shares subject to the put option have been acquired. Thus, if the acquirer has granted a put option over all of the remaining shares, the business combination is accounted for as if the acquirer has obtained a 100% interest in the acquiree. The consideration transferred for the business combination would include the fair value of the liability to the 'non-controlling interest' shareholders under the put option.

III   Accounting for a put liability under IAS 39

The liability under the put option should be accounted for as a financial instrument under IAS 39, even if it is regarded to be contingent consideration under IFRS 3 (as revised in 2008).[127] Changes in the fair value that are recognised during the measurement period because additional information was obtained after the acquisition date about facts and circumstances that existed at that date, should be recognised as part of the acquisition accounting. However, changes 'resulting from events after the acquisition date, such as meeting an earnings target, reaching a specified share price or reaching a milestone on a research and development project, are not measurement period adjustments'. Those changes should be measured at fair value, with any resulting gain or loss recognised in profit or loss under IAS 39.[128]

If the price under the option is based on the fair value of the underlying shares at the date of exercise, this means that the financial liability will be remeasured at each reporting date based on the fair value of the shares at that date, with any change in that value reflected in profit or loss, normally as a finance charge or credit. On the other hand, if the price is fixed, any unwinding of the discount will be reflected in profit or loss as a finance charge.

If the put option is ultimately exercised, the amount recognised as the financial liability at that date will be extinguished by the payment of the exercise price.

In the event that the put option is not ultimately exercised, then the entity has effectively disposed of a partial interest in its subsidiary, without loss of control, in return for the amount recognised as the 'liability' at the date of expiry and should account for the transaction as discussed at 3.2.2 above.

B   Options not giving the acquirer present access to benefits associated with ownership interest

If having considered the factors set out in A above, it is concluded that the acquirer does *not* have a present ownership interest in the shares concerned, we consider that there is a choice of policy available as to which standard takes precedence.

I   IAS 32 takes precedence over IAS 27 (as amended in 2008)

By recognising the liability in respect of the put option over the shares held by the non-controlling interest there is no non-controlling interest recognised at all. This is based on the requirements and guidance within IAS 32. In addition to the requirements of paragraph 23 of IAS 32 discussed above, paragraph AG29 of IAS 32 indicates that when a subsidiary in a group issues a financial instrument and a parent or other group entity agrees additional terms directly with the holders of the instrument, the group may not have discretion over distributions or redemption. Although the subsidiary may appropriately classify the instrument without regard to these additional terms in its individual financial statements, the effect of other agreements between members of the group and the holders of the instrument is considered in order to ensure that consolidated financial statements reflect the contracts and transactions entered into by the group as a whole. To the extent that there is such an obligation or settlement provision, the instrument (or the component of it that is subject to the obligation) is classified as a financial liability in the consolidated financial statements. Since this suggests that it is the financial instrument itself (i.e. the shares in the subsidiary) that is subject to the obligation that is classified as a financial liability, this means that the non-controlling interest shareholders' rights are represented by the financial liability. Accordingly, since their rights are not regarded as equity interests in the consolidated financial statements, there is no non-controlling interest that has to be accounted for under IAS 27.

The business combination and the liability in respect of the put option are accounted in the same way as discussed under A II and III above.

II   *IAS 27 (as amended in 2008) takes precedence over IAS 32*

A non-controlling interest in the acquiree is recognised as, having considered the terms of the put option in light of the guidance within IAS 27, it is determined that the non-controlling interest shareholders have a present ownership interest in the underlying shares. Consequently, in accounting for the business combination under IFRS 3 (as revised in 2008), the entity should measure any non-controlling interest in the acquiree either at fair value or at the non-controlling interest's proportionate share of the acquiree's identifiable net assets.[129] If the second option is chosen, the amounts recognised for the non-controlling interest and goodwill are likely to be lower than if the non-controlling interest was measured at its fair value.

As in the previous analysis, we believe that there is then a further choice of policy available as to whether the non-controlling interest that has initially been recognised should continue to be recognised or not. As a result, three alternatives exist depending on how the interaction between the requirements of IAS 27 (as amended in 2008) and IAS 32 is accounted for.

III   *Full recognition of non-controlling interest*

Alternative 2 takes the view that the requirements of IAS 27 (as amended in 2008) continue to take precedence and therefore non-controlling interest continues to be recognised in accordance with IAS 27 (as amended in 2008) until the put is exercised.

The financial liability in respect of the put option is accounted for under IAS 39 like any other written put option on equity instruments. On initial recognition of the financial liability the other side of the journal entry is reflected as a reduction in equity (see Chapter 31 at 3.3.3 and 7.3.2). However, since IAS 27 (as amended in 2008) requires the non-controlling interest to be presented separately within equity, the reduction needs to be reflected in another component of equity attributable to the parent.

The put option is accounted for as a liability under IAS 39 in the same way as discussed at A III above. The changes in the amount of the financial liability that are recognised in profit or loss are considered to be consolidation adjustments against the parent's income, so are not included as part of the non-controlling interest share of the income of the subsidiary.

If the put option is ultimately exercised, the entity will account for an increase in its ownership interest (see 3.2.2 above). At the same time, a credit entry equivalent to the financial liability will also need to be reflected in equity. If the put option expires unexercised, the financial liability will be transferred to equity. In both situations, it would seem appropriate to use the same component of equity that was previously reduced.

IV   *Partial recognition of non-controlling interest*

Alternative 3 takes the view that the requirements of IAS 27 (as amended in 2008) initially take precedence, such that the non-controlling interest is still attributed its share of profits and losses (and other changes in equity) of the acquiree after the business combination as required by IAS 27 (see 4 above). However, the impact of the put option is that paragraph AG29 of IAS 32 requires the amount attributable to the non-controlling interest to be reclassified as a financial liability. The reclassification of the non-controlling interest is deemed to be equivalent to a change in the non-controlling interest. Therefore, the accounting at the end of the reporting period should replicate the accounting that would be adopted as if the option had been exercised at that date.

Accordingly, any difference between the fair value of the liability under the put option at the end of the reporting period and the non-controlling interest reclassified is accounted for as a change in the non-controlling interest (see 3.2.2 above). No amount is recognised in profit or loss for the financial liability or separate accounting for the unwinding of any discount in respect of the liability.

While the put option remains unexercised the accounting at the end of each reporting period is as follows:

- the entity determines the amount that would have been recognised within equity for the non-controlling interest including an update to reflect its share of profits and losses (and other changes in equity) of the acquiree for the period; and

- the entity accounts for the difference between (1) the amount determined above and (2) the fair value of the liability under the put option, as a change in the non-controlling interest.

If the put option is ultimately exercised, the same treatment will be applied up to the date of exercise. The amount recognised as the financial liability at that date will be extinguished by the payment of the exercise price. If the put option expires unexercised, the position will be unwound such that the non-controlling interest at that date is reclassified back to equity and the financial liability is derecognised.

It should be noted though that whether this remains a valid option (which is based on alternative D as discussed at 5.2.2 B IV below) under IAS 27 (as amended in 2008) is still under discussion.

V   *Non-controlling interest is subsequently derecognised*

Alternative 4 takes the view that, based on the requirements of paragraphs 23 and AG29 of IAS 32, the recognition of the financial liability in respect of the put option results in derecognition of the non-controlling interest initially recognised. There are two ways this can be achieved, but the accounting effect is the same:

(a)   *Immediate acquisition of non-controlling interest* – The non-controlling interest that has initially been recognised as part of the business combination is treated as having been acquired. Any difference between the non-controlling interest and the initial liability recognised in respect of the put option is accounted as an acquisition of the non-controlling interests (see 3.2.2 above). That liability is subsequently accounted for under IAS 39 (see A III above).

(b)   *Non-controlling interest eliminated as part of equity deduction for financial liability* – The non-controlling interest is derecognised when the written put option is recognised. The written put is initially recognised and subsequently accounted for under IAS 39 (see A III above). On initial recognition of the financial liability the other side of the journal entry is reflected as a reduction in equity (see Chapter 31 at 3.3.3 and 7.3.2). However, the reduction in equity is reflected partially against non-controlling interest on the basis that paragraph AG29 of IAS 32 requires the financial instrument (i.e. the shares held by the non-controlling shareholder) to be reclassified from equity, with the remaining amount against another component of equity attributable to the parent. Such an amount will only be necessary if the non-controlling interest is initially measured at its proportionate share of the acquiree's identifiable net assets.

If the put option is ultimately exercised, the amount recognised as the financial liability at that date will be extinguished by the payment of the exercise price. If the put option expires unexercised, in accordance with paragraph 23 of IAS 32, the financial liability will be reclassified back to equity, by recognising the non-controlling interest in accordance with IAS 27 (as amended in 2008) (see 3.2.2 above), with any remaining amount taken to another component of equity. It would seem appropriate to use the same component of equity that was previously reduced.

5.2.2   Put options over minority interests – IAS 27 (2007)

An entity that applies IAS 27 (2007) needs to consider whether or not the terms of the transaction give the acquirer present access to the economic benefits associated with the ownership interest that is the subject of the put option. In addition, key policy decisions that management must make in developing an accounting policy, are:

- given potential contradictions between IAS 32 and IAS 27 (2007), which standard takes precedence;

- whether the liability arising from 'acquiring' shares held by the minority interest is to be an IFRS 3 (2007) liability (with elements of contingent consideration) or an IAS 39 financial liability;

- if minority interest is recognised on initial acquisition – whether it continues to be recognised or not;

- if minority interest is subsequently derecognised – whether it is to be accounted for as an acquisition of minority interest or not; and

- the accounting policy for acquisition of minority interest (see 3.3.3 above).

The following diagram summarises the analysis that we believe should be performed, the questions to be addressed and the alternatives that apply, which are discussed further below. 'Minority interest' has been abbreviated in the diagram to 'MI'.

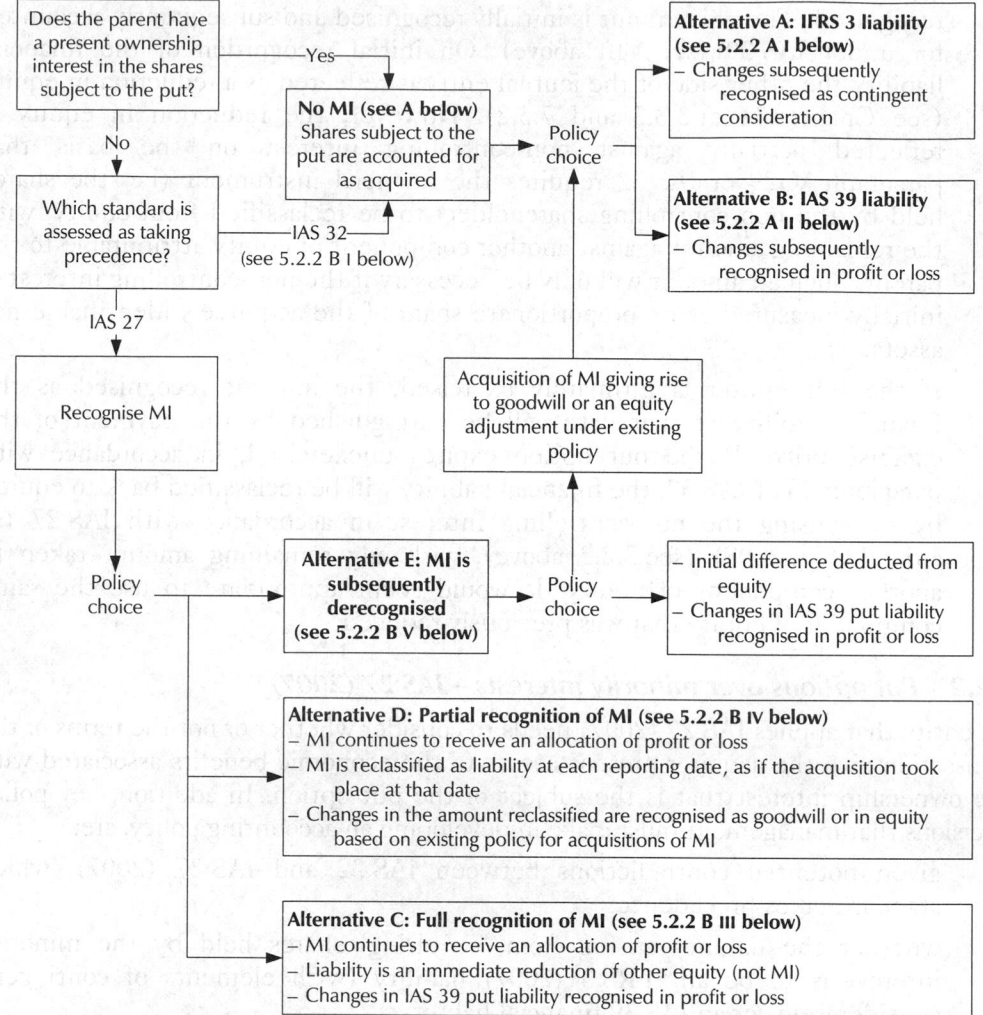

A   Options giving the acquirer present access to benefits associated with ownership interest

All of the terms and conditions of the option are analysed to assess whether these give the acquirer present access to the ownership interest in the shares concerned. Factors to consider in assessing whether or not a present ownership interest is granted to the acquirer include:

- pricing – to the extent that the price is fixed or determinable rather than being at fair value, it is an indicator that a present ownership interest has been granted;

- voting rights and decision-making – to the extent that the voting rights or decision-making connected to the shares concerned is restricted, it is an indicator that a present ownership interest has been granted;

- dividend rights – to the extent that the dividend rights attached to the shares concerned is restricted, it is an indicator that a present ownership interest has been granted; and

- issue of call options – combination of put and call options, with the same period of exercise and same/similar pricing are indicators that the arrangement is in the nature of a forward contract and therefore a present ownership interest has been granted.

If it is concluded that the acquirer has a present ownership interest in the shares concerned, it is accounted for as an acquisition of those underlying shares, and no minority interest will be recognised. Any dividends paid to the other shareholders are recognised as an expense of the group, unless they represent a repayment of the liability (e.g. where the exercise price is adjusted by the dividends paid).

The business combination is accounted for on the basis that the underlying shares subject to the put option have been acquired. Thus, if the acquirer has granted a put option over all of the remaining shares, the business combination is accounted for as if the acquirer has obtained a 100% interest in the acquiree. The cost of the business combination would include the fair value of the liability to the 'minority interest' shareholders under the put option (effectively, the present value of the exercise price under the option). Any difference between that cost, and the share of the net assets that would otherwise have been regarded as being attributable to the minority interest, will initially be reflected within goodwill.

In the event that the put option is not ultimately exercised, then the entity has effectively disposed of a partial interest in its subsidiary in return for the amount recognised as the 'liability' at the date of expiry and should account for the transaction as discussed at 3.3.2 above.

Having initially recognised a liability in respect of the put option, an accounting policy choice is then available as to the type of liability that exists, affecting how subsequent changes in the liability are accounted for.

I   Alternative A – IFRS 3 liability

The liability, in some form, relates to contingent consideration for the purchase of the shares subject to the put option, and can be accounted for as such under IFRS 3 (2007). As indicated earlier, IFRIC decided not to take this issue onto its agenda, but stated that after initial recognition of the financial liability for the put option any liability to which IFRS 3 (2007) is not being applied will be accounted for in accordance with IAS 39. Thus, it would appear that IFRIC does not preclude that some or all of the financial liability can be accounted for as contingent consideration under IFRS 3 (2007).

Under IFRS 3 (2007), changes in the liability relating to a business combination only affect the accounting for the combination if it is contingent on a future event. Paragraph 32 of IFRS 3 (2007) states that 'when a business combination agreement provides for an adjustment to the cost of the combination contingent on future events, the acquirer shall include the amount of that adjustment in the cost of the combination at the acquisition date if the adjustment is probable and can be measured reliably.' Paragraph 33 of IFRS 3 (2007) further states 'if the future events do not occur or the estimate needs to be revised, the cost of the business combination shall be adjusted accordingly.' The treatment of contingent consideration is discussed in Chapter 9 at 2.4.5.

However, it is not clear in the context of the liability for the put option, what element of the amount payable may be considered to be contingent on future events. Three possible views exist so, accordingly, we believe there is then a further choice as to which view to adopt to determine the amount of the liability that represents contingent consideration:

(a)   All of the liability is regarded as contingent consideration as the entire payment is conditional upon the put being exercised.

       This is based on the view that any eventual payment under the option is contingent on a future event, being the decision by the other shareholders to exercise their rights under the put option or not. In this case, all changes in the carrying amount of the liability are adjusted against goodwill, except for the unwinding of the discount due to the passage of time which is recognised in profit or loss.

(b)   All of the liability is regarded as contingent consideration only if exercise of the put is also conditional on certain criterion being met or there is a variable exercise price.

       This is based on the view that it is only if the terms of the put option are such that there are other future events that mean that there will be an adjustment to the amount of the cost of the business combination. On this basis, a put option that is merely exercisable at a fixed price would not qualify as contingent consideration; the liability for such a put option would be accounted for under Alternative B below. However, one with terms based on, say, achievement of a specified level of profits would qualify, as would put options exercisable at fair value at the date of exercise or at a price based on expected future results or net assets at the date of exercise. In this case, all changes in the carrying amount of the liability are adjusted against goodwill, except for the unwinding of the discount due to the passage of time which is recognised in profit or loss.

(c)   Contingent consideration exists only to the extent that the exercise price is *not* at fair value or is based on a formula that will not reflect fair value.

       This is based on the view that put options exercisable at fair value at the date of exercise, or at an exercise price based on a formula that is intended to be a proxy for such fair value, should not be regarded as contingent consideration. Changes in the value of the liability should be taken to profit or loss as this reflects the gain/loss of entering into the put option itself rather than being linked to a future event. Only to the extent that the exercise price was different from such fair value, such that it reflects an adjustment from market, would there be an element of contingent consideration.

Hence, any changes in the liability are adjusted against goodwill, except for the unwinding of the discount due to the passage of time. The unwinding of the discount is recognised in profit or loss. To the extent the liability does not qualify to be contingent consideration, it would be accounted for under Alternative B below.

II   Alternative B – IAS 39 liability

The liability under the put option is a financial liability that is to be accounted for under IAS 39. This is based on the view that future events that are a choice given to the other party, cannot be included in contingent consideration, as the future events being contemplated in paragraph 32 of IFRS 3 are events which change the amount of the consideration for an agreed purchase, rather than being contingent on whether or not the purchase actually occurs.

Accordingly, the financial liability is subsequently measured in accordance with the requirements of IAS 39. If the price under the option is based on the fair value of the underlying shares at the date of exercise, this means that the financial liability will be remeasured at each reporting date based on the fair value of the shares at that date, with any change in that value reflected in profit or loss, normally as a finance charge or credit. On the other hand, if the price is fixed, any unwinding of the discount will be reflected in profit or loss as a finance charge.

If the put option is ultimately exercised, the amount recognised as the financial liability at that date will be extinguished by the payment of the exercise price. If the put option expires unexercised, the entity has effectively disposed of a partial interest in its subsidiary in return for the amount recognised as the financial liability at the date of expiry and should account for the transaction as discussed at 3.3.2.

B   Options not giving the acquirer present access to benefits associated with ownership interest

If having considered the factors set out in A above, it is concluded that the acquirer does *not* have a present ownership interest in the shares concerned, we consider that there is a choice of policy available as to which standard takes precedence.

I   IAS 32 takes precedence over IAS 27

By recognising the liability in respect of the put option over the shares held by the minority shareholders there is no minority interest recognised at all. This is based on the requirements and guidance within IAS 32. In addition to the requirements of paragraph 23 of IAS 32 discussed above, paragraph AG29 of IAS 32 indicates that when a subsidiary in a group issues a financial instrument and a parent or other group entity agrees additional terms directly with the holders of the instrument, the group may not have discretion over distributions or redemption. Although the subsidiary may appropriately classify the instrument without regard to these additional terms in its individual financial statements, the effect of other agreements between members of the group and the holders of the instrument is considered in order to ensure that consolidated financial statements reflect the contracts and transactions entered into by the group as a whole. To the extent that there is such an obligation or settlement provision, the instrument (or the component of it that is subject to the obligation) is classified as a financial liability in the consolidated financial statements. Since this suggests that it is the financial instrument itself (i.e. the shares in the subsidiary) that is subject to the obligation that is classified as a financial liability, this means that the minority interest shareholders rights are represented by the financial liability. Accordingly, since their rights are not regarded as equity interests in the consolidated financial statements, there is no minority interest that has to be accounted for under IAS 27.

Consequently, the business combination is accounted for on the basis that the underlying shares subject to the put option have been acquired. Thus, if the acquirer has granted a put option over all of the remaining shares, the business combination is accounted for as if the acquirer has obtained a 100% interest in the acquiree. The cost of the business combination would include the fair value of the liability to the 'minority interest' shareholders under the put option (effectively, the present value of the exercise price under the option). Any difference between that cost, and the share of the net assets that would otherwise have been regarded as being attributable to the minority interest, will initially be reflected within goodwill.

In the event that the put option is not ultimately exercised, then the entity has effectively disposed of a partial interest in its subsidiary in return for the amount recognised as the 'liability' at the date of expiry and should account for the transaction as discussed at 3.3.2.

Having initially recognised a liability in respect of the put option, the same accounting policy choice as set out in A above (Alternative A or Alternative B) is then available as to the type of liability that exists, affecting how subsequent changes in the liability are accounted for.

II   IAS 27 (2007) takes precedence over IAS 32

A minority interest in the acquiree is recognised as, having considered the terms of the put option in light of the guidance within IAS 27, it is determined that the minority interest shareholders have a present ownership interest in the underlying shares. Consequently, the business combination is accounted for on the basis that the acquirer has obtained a less than 100% interest in the acquiree by reflecting the minority's proportion of the net identifiable assets, liabilities and contingent liabilities of the acquiree at their attributed fair values. No amount is included for any goodwill relating to the minority interest.

As in the previous analysis, we believe that there is then a further choice of policy available as to whether the minority interest that has initially been recognised should continue to be recognised or not. As a result, a number of alternatives exist depending on how the interaction between the requirements of IAS 27 (2007) and IAS 32 is accounted for.

III   Alternative C – Full recognition of minority interest

This takes the view that the requirements of IAS 27 (2007) continue to take precedence and therefore minority interest continues to be recognised in accordance with IAS 27 (2007) until the put is exercised.

The financial liability in respect of the put option is accounted for under IAS 39 like any other written put option on equity instruments. On initial recognition of the financial liability the other side of the journal entry is reflected as a reduction in equity (see Chapter 31 at 3.3.3 and 7.3.2). However, since IAS 27 (2007) requires the minority interest to be presented separately within equity, the reduction needs to be reflected in another component of equity.

Subsequently, the financial liability is measured in accordance with the requirements of IAS 39. If the price under the option is based on the fair value of the underlying shares at the date of exercise, this means that the financial liability will be remeasured at each reporting date based on the fair value of the shares at that date, with any change in that value reflected in profit or loss, normally as a finance charge or credit. On the other hand, if the price is fixed, any unwinding of the discount will be reflected in profit or loss as a finance charge. The changes in the amount of the financial liability that are recognised in profit or loss are considered to be consolidation adjustments against the parent's income, so are not included as part of the minority interest share of the income of the subsidiary.

If the put option is ultimately exercised, the entity will account for the acquisition of the minority interest in accordance with its chosen policy for such acquisitions (see 3.3.3 above). At the same time, a credit entry equivalent to the financial liability will also need to be reflected in equity. If the put option expires unexercised, the financial liability will be transferred to equity. In both situations, it would seem appropriate to use the same component of equity that was previously reduced.

IV   Alternative D – Partial recognition of minority interest

This takes the view that the requirements of IAS 27 (2007) initially take precedence, such that the minority interest is still attributed its share of profits and losses (and other changes in equity) of acquiree after the business combination as required by IAS 27 (see 4 above).

However, based on the requirements of paragraph AG29 of IAS 32 discussed earlier, the impact of the put option is that the amount of the minority interest that would have been included within equity at the end of the reporting period has to be reclassified as a financial liability. This means that the minority interest that has been reclassified is deemed to have been derecognised as it if had been acquired at the end of the reporting period. Effectively, the eventual acquisition of the minority interest is being anticipated, and therefore the accounting at the end of the reporting period should replicate the accounting that would be adopted as if the option had been exercised at that date.

Accordingly, any difference between the present value of the amount payable under the put option at the end of the reporting period and the minority interest reclassified and deemed to have been derecognised at that date is accounted for in accordance with the entity's chosen policy for acquisitions of minority interests. Where the entity's policy for such acquisitions is to use the 'parent entity extension method', then this means that the difference is taken to goodwill. Otherwise some or all of the difference between the initial fair value of the liability and the minority interest will be taken to equity.

While the put option remains unexercised the accounting at the end of each reporting period is as follows:

- the entity determines the amount that would have been recognised within equity for the minority interest including an update to reflect its share of profits and losses (and other changes in equity) of the acquiree for the period; and

- the entity accounts for the difference between (1) the amount determined above and (2) the present value of the amount payable under the put option, as an acquisition of a minority interest.

If the put option is ultimately exercised, the same treatment will be applied up to the date of exercise. The amount recognised as the financial liability at that date will be extinguished by the payment of the exercise price. If the put option expires unexercised, the position will be unwound such that the minority interest at that date is reclassified back to equity, the financial liability is derecognised, and any difference taken to goodwill or equity to negate the entries made under the policy for acquisitions of minority interests.

V   *Alternative E – Minority interest is subsequently derecognised*

This takes the view that, based on the requirements of paragraphs 23 and AG29 of IAS 32, the recognition of the financial liability in respect of the put option results in derecognition of the minority interest initially recognised. However, we consider that the entity has a choice of policy available as to how the derecognition of the minority interest is accounted for:

(a)   Immediate acquisition of minority interest

Under this view, the minority interest that has initially been recognised as part of the business combination is treated as having been acquired. Any difference between the minority interest and the initial liability recognised in respect of the put option is accounted for in accordance with the acquirer's chosen policy for the acquisition of the minority interests (see 3.3.3 above).

The same accounting policy choice as set out in A above (Alternative A or Alternative B) is then available as to the type of liability that exists, affecting how subsequent changes in the liability are accounted for.

If Alternative A is selected, any adjustments to the consideration will be recognised as an adjustment to goodwill or equity (depending on the entity's policy for accounting for the acquisition of minority interest).

(b)   Minority interest eliminated as part of equity deduction for financial liability

Under this view, the minority interest is derecognised when the written put option is recognised. The put option is accounted for as a liability under

IAS 39 the same way as discussed under Alternative B above. On initial recognition of the financial liability the other side of the journal entry is reflected as a reduction in equity (see Chapter 31 at 3.3.3 and 7.3.2). However, the reduction in equity is reflected partially against minority interest on the basis that paragraph AG29 of IAS 32 requires the financial instrument (i.e. the shares held by the minority shareholder) to be reclassified from equity, with the remaining amount against another component of equity.

Accordingly, as under Alternative B above, the financial liability is subsequently measured in accordance with the requirements of IAS 39. If the price under the option is based on the fair value of the underlying shares at the date of exercise, this means that the financial liability will be remeasured at each reporting date based on the fair value of the shares at that date, with any change in that value reflected in profit or loss, normally as a finance charge or credit. On the other hand, if the price is fixed, any unwinding of the discount will be reflected in profit or loss as a finance charge.

If the put option is ultimately exercised, the amount recognised as the financial liability at that date will be extinguished by the payment of the exercise price. If the put option expires unexercised, in accordance with paragraph 23 of IAS 32, the financial liability will be reclassified back to equity, partly by recognising the minority interest at an amount that reflects the minority's share of the net assets of the acquiree at that date, with any remaining amount taken to another component of equity. It would seem appropriate to use the same component of equity that was previously reduced.

5.3   Combination of call and put options

In some business combinations where an entity has acquired, say, a 60% interest in the shares of another entity, it may be that as part of the transaction there is a combination of call and put options, the terms of which may be equivalent or may be different.

The determination of the appropriate accounting for such options should be based on the discussions in 5.1 and 5.2 above. However, where there is a call and put option with equivalent terms, particularly at a fixed price, the combination of the options is more likely to mean that they give the acquirer present access to the economic benefits associated with the ownership interest that is the subject of the put option. In those cases the acquirer has effectively acquired a 100% interest in the subsidiary at the date of the business combination, and thus the accounting discussed at 5.1.1 above should be followed. In such situations, the entity may be in a similar position as if it had acquired a 100% interest in the subsidiary with either deferred consideration (where the exercise price is fixed) or contingent consideration (where the settlement amount is not fixed, but is dependent upon a future event).

5.4   Call and put options entered into in relation to existing non-controlling (or minority) interests

The discussion above has focused on call and put options entered into at the same time as the acquisition of the subsidiary. It may be that an entity enters into such options with the minority shareholders some time after the business combination. Again, the determination of the appropriate accounting for such options should be based on the discussions in 5.1 and 5.2 above.

The main difference in such situations, particularly in relation to put options, is where it is considered that the non-controlling (or minority) interest should no longer be recognised within equity, and the transaction is being accounted for as an acquisition of the non-controlling (or minority) interest. In this instance, such acquisitions are not business combinations under IFRS 3 (as revised in 2008) or IFRS 3 (2007). An entity that applies IAS 27 (as amended in 2008) should account for the acquisition of non-controlling interests as equity transactions (see 3.2.2 above). Whether an entity that applies IAS 27 (2007) recognises any goodwill is recognised on the acquisition of minority interests depends on its accounting policy for such transactions as discussed at 3.3.3 above.

6   TRANSITIONAL ISSUES

The transitional provisions of IAS 27 (as amended in 2008) and IAS 27 (2007) are discussed in Chapter 6 at 6.

References

1 IFRS 3, *Business Combinations*, IASB, para. 19.
2 IFRS 3, para. BC216.
3 IAS 27, *Consolidated and Separate Financial Statements*, IASB, para. 18 and IAS 27 (2007), *Consolidated and Separate Financial Statements*, IASB, 2007 Bound Volume, para. 22.
4 IAS 27, para. 4.
5 IAS 27 (2007), para. 4.
6 IAS 27, para. 18 and IAS 27 (2007), para. 22.
7 IFRS 3, para. 2(b) and IFRS 3 (2007), para. 4.
8 IAS 27, para. 19 and IAS 27 (2007), para. 23.
9 IAS 27, paras. IG1-IG8.
10 IAS 27, para. IG6.
11 IAS 27, para. IG7.
12 IFRIC 16, *Hedges of a Net Investment in a Foreign Operation*, IASB, footnote to para. 17.
13 IFRIC 16, para. BC36.
14 IFRIC 16, para. 17.
15 IAS 27, para. 20 and IAS 27 (2007), para. 24.

16 IAS 27, para. 21 and IAS 27 (2007), para. 25.
17 IAS 27, para. 21 and IAS 27 (2007), para. 25.
18 IAS 27, para. 21 and IAS 27 (2007), para. 25.
19 IAS 27, para. 22 and IAS 27 (2007), para. 26.
20 IAS 1, *Presentation of Financial Statements*, IASB, para. 7.
21 IAS 27, para. 23 and IAS 27 (2007), para. 27.
22 IAS 27, para. 24 and IAS 27 (2007), para. 28.
23 IAS 27, para. 25 and IAS 27 (2007), para. 29.
24 IAS 27, para. 2.
25 IAS 27, para. 26 and IAS 27 (2007), para. 30.
26 IAS 27, para. 26.
27 IAS 27, para. 32.
28 IAS 27, para. 34.
29 IAS 27, para. BC57.
30 IAS 27, para. 36.
31 IAS 27, para. 37.
32 IAS 27, para. BC55.
33 IAS 27, para. BC55.
34 IAS 27, para. 35.

35 IAS 27, para. 35.

36 IAS 19, *Employee Benefits*, IASB, para. 93D.

37 IAS 21, *The Effects of Changes in Foreign Exchange Rates*, IASB, paras. 48 and 48B.

38 IAS 27, para. 35.

39 IAS 27, para. 30.

40 IAS 27, para. 31.

41 IAS 27, para. BC41.

42 IAS 21, para. 48C.

43 IAS 21, para. 48B.

44 *IABS Update*, IASB, May 2009, p. 4.

45 IAS 27, para. BC58.

46 IAS 27, para. BC61.

47 IAS 27, para. 33.

48 IAS 27 (2007), para. 30.

49 IAS 27 (2007), para. 30.

50 IAS 21 (2007), *The Effects of Changes in Foreign Exchange Rates*, IASB, 2007 Bound Volume.

51 IAS 27 (2007), para. 31.

52 IAS 27 (2007), para. 32.

53 IAS 27 (2007), para. 32.

54 SFAS 141, *Business Combinations*, FASB, June 2001, para. 14 and Appendix A.

55 *IFRIC Update*, IASB, February 2005, p. 5.

56 IAS 27, para. 30.

57 IAS 27 (2007), para. 49.

58 IAS 21 (2007), para. 49.

59 IFRIC 17, *Distributions of Non-cash Assets to Owners*, IASB, para. BC2.

60 IFRIC 17, para. 3.

61 IFRIC 17, para. 4.

62 IFRIC 17, para. 5.

63 IFRIC 17, para. 6.

64 IFRIC 17, para. 7.

65 IFRIC 17, para. 5.

66 IFRIC 17, para. 8.

67 IFRIC 17, para. 10.

68 IFRIC 17, para. 11.

69 IFRIC 17, para. 12.

70 IFRIC 17, para. 13.

71 IFRIC 17, paras. 14 and 15.

72 IFRIC 17, para. BC55.

73 IFRIC 17, para. BC56.

74 IFRIC 17, para. 16.

75 IFRIC 17, para. 16.

76 IFRIC 17, para. 17.

77 IFRIC 17, para. 18.

78 IAS 27 (2007), para. 4.

79 IAS 27 (2007), para. 14.

80 IAS 27 (2007), para. 14.

81 IAS 27 (2007), para. 22(c).

82 IAS 27 (2007), para. 23.

83 IAS 27 (2007), para. IG5.

84 IAS 27 (2007), para. IG6.

85 IAS 27, para. BC28.

86 IAS 27 (2007), para. 4.

87 IAS 27, para. 4.

88 IFRS 3, para. 19.

89 IAS 32, *Financial Instruments: Presentation*, IASB, para. 11.

90 *Framework*, IASB, para. 49(c).

91 IAS 27, para. 18(c)(ii).

92 IAS 27, para. 19.

93 *IFRIC Update*, IASB, July 2009, p. 6.

94 IFRIC Agenda Paper 3C, *Amendments to IFRS 3 and IAS 27: Measurement of NCI*, IFRIC, July 2009, p. 1.

95 *IFRIC Update*, IASB, July 2009, p. 6.

96 *IFRIC Update*, IASB, July 2009, p. 6.

97 *IFRIC Update*, IASB, July 2009, p. 6.

98 *IASB Update*, IASB, July 2009, p. 4 and IASB Agenda Paper 3E, *Annual Improvements: IFRS 3 – Measurement of NCI*, IASB, July 2009.

99 *Exposure Draft – Improvements to IFRSs: Proposed amendments to IFRS 3 Business Combinations (as revised in 2008)*, IASB, August 2009, p. 17 (IFRS 3 (as revised in 2008), para. 19).

100 *Exposure Draft – Improvements to IFRSs: Proposed amendments to IFRS 3 Business Combinations (as revised in 2008)*, p. 23 (IFRS 3 (as revised in 2008), para. BC1).

101 IFRIC Agenda Paper 3D, *Amendments to IFRS 3 and IAS 27: Un-replaced and Voluntarily Replaced Share-based Payment Awards*, IFRIC, July 2009, p. 3 and IASB Agenda Paper 3D, *Annual Improvements: IFRS 3 – Unreplaced and Voluntarily Replaced Share-based Payment Awards*, IFRIC, July 2009, p. 3.

102 IFRIC Agenda Paper 3D, *Amendments to IFRS 3 and IAS 27: Un-replaced and Voluntarily Replaced Share-based Payment Awards*, IFRIC, July 2009, p. 3 and IASB Agenda Paper 3D, *Annual Improvements: IFRS 3 – Unreplaced and Voluntarily Replaced Share-based Payment Awards*, IFRIC, July 2009, p. 3.

103 *IFRIC Update*, IASB, July 2009, p. 6.

104 *IASB Update*, IASB, July 2009, p. 4.

105 *Exposure Draft – Improvements to IFRSs: Proposed amendments to IFRS 3 Business Combinations (as revised in 2008)*, p. 15.

106 IFRS 3, para. 19.

107 IAS 27, para. 19.

108 IAS 27, para. 27.

109 IAS 27, para. 28.

110 IAS 27 (2007), para. 33.

111 IAS 27 (2007), para. 34.

112 IAS 27 (2007), para. 35.

113 IAS 27, para. 28.

114 IAS 27, para. BC34.

115 IAS 27, para. BC38.

116 IAS 27, para. BC35.

117 IAS 27, paras. BC35 and BC39-BC40.

118 IAS 27, para. 45(a).

119 *IASB Update*, IASB, May 2009, p. 4.
120 IAS 27, para. 29 and IAS 27 (2007), para. 36.
121 IAS 27, paras. 19 and IG5-IG6 and IAS 27
     (2007), paras. 23 and IG5-IG6.
122 IAS 27, para. IG7 and IAS 27 (2007),
     para. IG7.
123 *IFRIC Update*, IFRIC, May 2006, p. 5.
124 *IFRIC Update*, IFRIC, July 2006, p. 6.
125 *IFRIC Update*, IFRIC, July 2006, p. 6.
126 *IFRIC Update*, IFRIC, November 2006, pp. 8
     and 10.
127 IFRS 3, para. 40 and IAS 39, *Financial
     Instruments: Recognition and Measurement*, IASB,
     para. 9.
128 IFRS 3, para. 58.
129 IFRS 3, para. 19.

Chapter 8   Separate and individual financial statements

1   SEPARATE AND INDIVIDUAL FINANCIAL STATEMENTS

This Chapter deals with two aspects of the preparation of financial statements for entities: their separate financial statements, which are defined by IFRS, and some of the consequences of intra-group transactions for their individual financial statements, where guidance in IFRS is limited and incomplete.

Under IFRS, 'separate financial statements' are not what might immediately be supposed. IAS 27 – *Consolidated and Separate Financial Statements* – defines 'separate financial statements' as those presented by a parent, an investor in an associate or a venturer in a jointly controlled entity, in which the investments are accounted for on the basis of the direct equity interest rather than on the basis of the reported results and net assets of the investees. In other words, they are the unconsolidated accounts of entities that would otherwise be within scope of IAS 27's consolidation requirements.

The IASB takes the view that the needs of users of financial statements are fully met by requiring entities to consolidate subsidiaries, equity account for associates, and proportionately consolidate or equity account for jointly controlled entities. It is recognised that entities with subsidiaries, associates or joint ventures may wish, or may be required by local law, to present financial statements in which their investments are accounted for simply as equity investments.[1]

Accordingly, IFRS does not require the preparation of separate financial statements. However, where an investor with subsidiaries, associates or joint ventures does prepare separate financial statements purporting to comply with IFRS, they must be prepared in accordance with IAS 27.[2]

It follows from this definition that the financial statements of an entity that does not have a subsidiary, associate or joint venture are not 'separate financial statements'.

This chapter also addresses matters that are not exclusive to separate financial statements but to any stand-alone financial statements prepared by any entity within a group. We have called these 'individual financial statements', although they may also be referred to (amongst other names) as 'stand-alone', 'solus' or 'single-entity' financial statements. Transactions often take place between a parent entity and its subsidiaries or between subsidiaries within a group that may or may not be carried out on an arm's length basis. As a result there may be uncertainty and ambiguity about how these transactions should be accounted for. IAS 24 – *Related Party Disclosures* – requires only that these transactions are disclosed and provides no accounting guidance.

Whilst such transactions do not influence the consolidated financial statements of the ultimate parent (as they are eliminated in the course of consolidation), they can have a significant impact on the individual financial statements of the entities concerned or on the consolidated financial statements prepared for a sub-group.

These issues are discussed at 4 below.

1.1   Consolidated financial statements and separate financial statements

A parent is a company that has one or more subsidiaries and any parent entity should present consolidated financial statements in which it consolidates its investments in subsidiaries in accordance with IAS 27.[3]

A parent need not present consolidated financial statements if and only if:[4]

(a)   the parent is itself a wholly-owned subsidiary, or is a partially-owned subsidiary of another entity and its other owners, including those not otherwise entitled to vote, have been informed about, and do not object to, the parent not presenting consolidated financial statements;

(b)   the parent's debt or equity instruments are not traded in a public market (a domestic or foreign stock exchange or an over-the-counter market, including local and regional markets);

(c)   the parent did not file, nor is it in the process of filing, its financial statements with a securities commission or other regulatory organisation for the purpose of issuing any class of instruments in a public market; and

(d)   the ultimate or any intermediate parent of the parent produces consolidated financial statements available for public use that comply with International Financial Reporting Standards.

An entity that avails itself of this exemption may, but is not required, to prepare separate financial statements as its only financial statements.[5] For example, most intermediate holding companies take advantage of this exemption. If such an entity prepares unconsolidated financial statements that are in accordance with IFRS, they must comply with the provisions of IAS 27 for such statements and they will then be separate financial statements as defined. The requirements for separate financial statements are dealt with in Section 2 below.

1.1.1 Separate financial statements and interests in associates and joint ventures

Separate financial statements are defined by IAS 28 – *Investments in Associates* – and IAS 31– *Interests in Joint Ventures* – consistent with IAS 27, as those presented by a parent, an investor in an associate or a venturer in a jointly controlled entity, in which the investments are accounted for on the basis of the direct equity interest rather than on the basis of the reported results and net assets of the investees.[6] Separate financial statements are financial statements presented in addition to:[7]

- consolidated financial statements;
- financial statements in which investments are accounted for using the equity method; and
- financial statements in which venturers' interests in joint ventures are proportionately consolidated.

There is no requirement for any entity to prepare separate financial statements, or for any separate financial statements that are voluntarily prepared to be appended to, or accompany, the 'main' financial statements.[8]

An entity may present separate financial statements as its only financial statements if it satisfies the conditions for exemption from:[9]

(a) preparing consolidated financial statements under paragraph 10 of IAS 27 (see 1.1. above);

(b) equity accounting for associates under paragraph 13(c) of IAS 28. (see Chapter 11 at 2.3); and

(c) proportionately consolidating (or equity accounting for) jointly controlled entities under paragraph 2 of IAS 31 (see Chapter 12 at 2.3).

As drafted, this exemption makes a curious distinction between an entity with associates and one with jointly controlled entities only.

An entity with associates may prepare separate financial statements as its only financial statements only if it satisfies the exemption in 'paragraph 13(c)' of IAS 28. In other words, if an entity has associates, but is exempt from equity accounting for all of them under paragraph 13(a) – i.e. because they are all accounted for under IFRS 5 – *Non-current Assets Held for Sale and Discontinued Operations* – it may apparently not present separate financial statements as its only financial statements. However, an entity with jointly controlled entities may prepare separate financial statements as its only financial statements if it satisfies the exemption in 'paragraph 2' of IAS 31, which includes jointly controlled entities accounted for under IFRS 5.

In our view, it can be assumed that this inconsistency was unintentional, but it is less obvious as to which exemption is correct and which incorrect. On balance, our view is that it is the exemption in relation to joint ventures which is incorrect. In other words, the IASB intended to give the exemption only to 'non-public interest' companies and should have referred to 'paragraph 2(c)' of IAS 31.

A parent cannot prepare financial statements in purported compliance with IFRS in which subsidiaries are consolidated, but associates and joint ventures are not accounted for under, respectively, IAS 28 and IAS 31 but on some other basis (e.g. at cost). Financial statements prepared on such a basis would be neither consolidated financial statements (because of the failure to apply IAS 28 and IAS 31) nor separate financial statements (because of the failure to account for subsidiaries on the basis of the direct equity interest).

The conditions for exemption in IAS 28 and IAS 31 in (b) and (c) above are the same as those in IAS 27. This means that:

- An entity that has subsidiaries and is exempt under IAS 27 from preparing consolidated accounts is automatically exempt in respect of its associates or jointly controlled entities as well, i.e. it does not have to account for them under IAS 28 and IAS 31;

- An entity that has associates or jointly controlled entities but no subsidiaries, and does not meet all the exemption criteria in 1.1 above, is required to apply equity accounting for its associates in its own (non-consolidated) financial statements. Such non-consolidated financial statements include the investment in the associate or joint venture on the basis of the reported results and net assets of the investment, and are thus *not* 'separate financial statements' as defined in IAS 27 (see definition above) and therefore do not have to meet the additional measurement and disclosure requirements required by IAS 27 for separate financial statements that are described at 3 below in order to comply with IFRS. Most of these disclosures would not be relevant to accounts that include the results of the associate or joint venture as they are based on providing information that is not otherwise given.

This is by contrast to some national GAAPs, under which investors that have no subsidiaries (and therefore do not prepare consolidated accounts) but do have associates or joint ventures, are not permitted to account for their share of the profits and net assets of associates or joint ventures in their individual financial statements.

1.1.2 *Publishing separate financial statements without consolidated financial statements*

IAS 27 does not directly address the publication requirements for separate financial statements. In some jurisdictions, an entity that prepares consolidated financial statements is prohibited from publishing its separate financial statements without also publishing its consolidated financial statements.

However, in our view, IAS 27 does not prohibit an entity that prepares consolidated financial statements from publishing its separate financial statements without also publishing its consolidated financial statements, provided that:

(a)   the separate financial statements give all the disclosures required by IAS 27 in respect of the consolidated financial statements;

(b)   the consolidated financial statements have been prepared no later than the date on which the separate financial statements have been approved. However, it is apparently not possible to publish the separate financial statements before the consolidated financial statements have been finalised; and

(c)   the separate financial statements include a note advising users how they can obtain a copy of the consolidated financial statements.

The requirement under (b) above that consolidated financial statements be published before the separate financial statements was explicitly considered by the IFRIC in March 2006. The IFRIC concluded that separate financial statements issued before consolidated financial statements could not comply with IFRS as issued by the IASB, because 'separate financial statements should identify the financial statements prepared in accordance with paragraph 9 of IAS 27 to which they relate (the consolidated financial statements), unless one of the exemptions provided by paragraph 10 is applicable.'[10] However, the situation may be different if the entity is incorporated in the European Union (EU), as described in 1.2 below.

1.2   Entities incorporated in the EU and consolidated and separate financial statements

The EU Regulation on International Accounting Standards requires IFRS to be applied by entities in their consolidated financial statements; because of the EU endorsement mechanism, IFRS as adopted in the EU may differ in some respects from the body of standards and Interpretations issued by the IASB (see Chapter 1 at 5.5). In some circumstances a difference between IFRS and IFRS as adopted by the European Union may affect separate financial statements.

1.2.1   *Issuing separate financial statements before consolidated statements*

As described above, the IFRIC has concluded that separate financial statements issued before consolidated financial statements cannot comply with IFRS as issued by the IASB. However, in January 2007 the European Commission stated that 'the Commission Services are of the opinion that, if a company chooses or is required to prepare its annual accounts in accordance with IFRS as adopted by the EU, it can prepare and file them independently from the preparation and filing of its consolidated accounts – and thus in advance, where the national law transposing the Directives requires or permits separate publication.'[11] In other words, under 'IFRS as adopted by the EU' it is possible to issue separate financial statements before the consolidated financial statements are issued.

1.2.2   *Differences between scope of consolidation under IAS 27 and European Union national legislation*

For entities incorporated in the European Union (EU), there may in some cases be a subtle interaction between the consolidation requirements of IAS 27 and IFRS as adopted by the EU. The determination of whether or not consolidated financial statements are required is made under the relevant national legislation based on the EU Seventh Directive and not IAS 27.[12]In the majority of cases this is a technicality with little practical effect. In some cases, however, there will be differences. For example, an entity may have an investment in a SPE that is not a subsidiary undertaking under the Seventh Directive. The entity is therefore not explicitly required to prepare consolidated financial statements under the Regulation, even though IAS 27 would oblige it to do so. This means that the entity cannot present separate financial statements in purported compliance with IFRS as issued by the IASB, unless it has prepared consolidated accounts as required by IAS 27.

However, in November 2006 the European Commission stated that in its opinion 'a parent company always has to prepare annual accounts as defined by the 4th Directive. Where, under the 7th Company Law Directive, a parent company is exempted from preparing consolidated accounts, but chooses or is required to prepare its annual accounts in accordance with IFRS as adopted by the EU, those provisions in IAS 27 setting out the requirement to prepare consolidated accounts do not apply. Such annual accounts are described as having been prepared in accordance with IFRS as adopted by the EU.'[13]

In member states where entities are required to apply IFRS as opposed to local GAAP in individual financial statements, an entity in this situation will either have to prepare consolidated financial statements under IAS 27 (if permitted to do so by local legislation) or individual financial statements in accordance with 'IFRS as adopted by the EU' rather than 'IFRS as issued by the IASB'.

2   REQUIREMENTS OF SEPARATE FINANCIAL STATEMENTS

In separate financial statements, investments in subsidiaries, associates and joint ventures that are classified as held for sale (or included in a disposal group that is classified as held for sale) in accordance with IFRS 5 are accounted for in accordance with IFRS 5,[14] i.e. at the lower of carrying amount and fair value less cost to sell (see Chapter 4).

All other investments are accounted for either at cost (see 2.1 below) or in accordance with IAS 39 – *Financial Instruments: Recognition and Measurement* (see 2.2 below). Each 'category' of investments must be accounted for consistently.[15] While 'category' is not defined, we take this to mean, for example, that, while all subsidiaries must be accounted for at cost or in accordance with IAS 39, it would be permissible (if perhaps rather strange) to account for all subsidiaries at cost and all associates under IAS 39.

Where an investment in an associate or jointly controlled entity is accounted for in accordance with IAS 39 in the consolidated financial statements, it must also be accounted for in accordance with IAS 39 in the separate financial statements.[16] The circumstances in which IAS 39 is applied in consolidated financial statements are discussed in, respectively, Chapter 11 at 2.1 and Chapter 12 at 2.1.

Whilst IAS 27 does not say so explicitly, it seems clear that not only must such investments be accounted for in accordance with IAS 39 in both the consolidated and separate financial statements, but they must also follow the same accounting model in IAS 39. In other words, the same investment cannot be treated as a 'financial asset at fair value through profit or loss' in one set of financial statements and as an 'available-for-sale financial asset' in the other.

2.1　Cost method

Until May 2008, IAS 27 described the cost method as 'a method of accounting for an investment whereby the investment is recognised at cost. The investor recognises income from the investment only to the extent that the investor receives distributions from accumulated profits of the investee arising after the date of acquisition. Distributions received in excess of such profits are regarded as a recovery of investment and are recognised as a reduction of the cost of the investment.'[17] This was consistent with the requirement of IAS 18 – *Revenue* – to treat dividends from pre-acquisition profits as a return of the initial investment.

This raised very significant issues of interpretation:

* the meaning of 'cost' and
* the meaning of 'profits … arising after the date of acquisition' in the context of the treatment of dividend income.

As a consequence, the IASB has amended IAS 27 ('IAS 27(revised)') by removing the definition of the cost method in its entirety and has deleted from IAS 18 its requirements regarding the treatment of dividends from subsidiaries. Instead, an entity is to recognise a dividend from a subsidiary, jointly controlled entity or associate in profit or loss in its separate financial statements when its right to receive the dividend is established.[18] Entities will be required to determine as a separate exercise whether or not the investment has been impaired as a result of the dividend. IAS 36 – *Impairment of Assets* – has been expanded to include specific triggers for impairment reviews on receipt of dividends.

In July 2007, the IASB noted that IFRS is being interpreted as always 'requiring a newly formed parent entity to measure its investment in the previous parent at fair value'.[19] The Board concluded that when a new holding company is established that becomes the parent of the existing parent in a one-for-one share exchange, there are no changes in substance resulting from such a revision of the organisation structure. IAS 27(revised) now includes additional explanation regarding the cost of an investment following various types of group reorganisation and IFRS 1 – *First-time Adoption of International Financial Reporting Standards* – has been amended so as to allow a 'deemed cost' transitional amendment for those applying IFRS for the first time in separate financial statements. These are described at 2.1.1D, 2.1.1 E and 2.1.2 below.

Finally, there is a change to IAS 21 – *The Effects of Changes in Foreign Exchange Rates* – which, before May 2008, referred in paragraph 49 to dividends out of pre-acquisition profits as a example of a part-disposal. This reference has been deleted. For a further discussion, see Chapter 13.

The amendments to IAS 21 and IAS 27 apply prospectively for annual periods beginning on or after 1 January 2009.

There is still no general definition or description of 'cost' and how the term applies in practice is described below.

2.1.1   Cost of investment

IAS 27 does not define what is meant by 'cost' except in the specific circumstances of certain types of group reorganisation and on first-time transition to IFRS, which are described below. As discussed further in Chapter 3 at 4.3, IAS 8 – *Accounting Policies, Changes in Estimates and Errors* – requires that, in the absence of specific guidance in IFRS, management should first refer to the requirements and guidance in IFRS dealing with similar and related issues.

A subsidiary may be acquired in an external transaction that is treated as a business combination (or part of a business combination) in the consolidated financial statements. Before the 2008 revision to IFRS 3 – *Business Combinations,* it was in our view appropriate for the cost of the subsidiary in the separate financial statements to be based on the cost attributed to the acquisition of the business (or the relevant part of it) in the consolidated financial statements.[20] However, IFRS 3 (as revised in 2008) no longer refers to the cost of an acquisition. The equivalent of 'cost' will now be based on the appropriate part of the 'consideration transferred', based on the definition of 'consideration' in paragraph 37 of the revised standard. The 'consideration transferred' in a business combination comprises the sum of the acquisition-date fair values of assets transferred by the acquirer, liabilities incurred by the acquirer to the former owners of the acquiree, and equity interests issued by the acquirer. The most significant difference as a consequence of this change is likely to be the measurement of contingent consideration as IFRS 3 (as revised in 2008) requires this to be measured and recognised at fair value at the acquisition date: see Chapter 9 at 3.8. This raises the question of the treatment of the costs of the acquisition as, under IFRS 3 (as revised in 2008) these costs are usually recognised as expenses in the consolidated accounts, rather than being included in goodwill. However, the IFRIC noted in July 2009 as a general rule under IFRS, 'cost' includes the purchase price and other costs directly attributable to the acquisition or issuance of the asset such as professional fees for legal services, transfer taxes and other transaction costs. As a result 'the cost of an investment in an associate at initial recognition determined in accordance with paragraph 11 of IAS 28 comprises its purchase price and any directly attributable expenditures necessary to obtain it'.[21] Therefore, it is reasonable to assume that the cost of the investment in a subsidiary may also include the costs of acquisition.

Another point of reference might be IAS 32 – *Financial Instruments: Presentation* – and IAS 39. Investments in subsidiaries, associates and joint ventures, while outside the scope of IAS 32 and IAS 39, are clearly financial assets (and therefore financial instruments) as defined in those standards. IAS 39 requires financial assets to be initially recognised at fair value together with directly attributable transaction costs (see Chapter 32 at 2).

In some jurisdictions, local law may permit investments acquired for an issue of shares to be recorded at a notional value (for example, the nominal value of the shares issued). In our view, this is not an appropriate measure of cost under IFRS.

A　　Investments acquired for own shares or other equity instruments

A transaction in which an investment in a subsidiary, associate or joint venture is acquired in exchange for an issue of shares or other equity instruments is not specifically addressed under IFRS, since it falls outside the scope of both IAS 39 (see above) and IFRS 2 – *Share-based Payment* (see Chapter 27 at 2.2.3).

Again, however, we believe that it would be appropriate, by analogy with IFRS on related areas, to account for such a transaction at the fair value of the investment acquired (together with directly attributable transaction costs).

B　　Common control transactions

When a subsidiary is acquired in a common control transaction, which is not accounted for as a business combination under IFRS 3 in consolidated financial statements (e.g. in a group reconstruction), the cost should be measured at the fair value of the consideration given (be it cash, other assets or additional shares) plus, where applicable any costs directly attributable to the acquisition, rather than at the cost in the books of the transferring entity or the acquired subsidiary's net book value. Common control transactions are discussed further at 4 below. This does not apply to certain arrangements involving the formation of a new parent or intermediate parent, for which there are now specific measurement requirements. These are described at D and E below.

C　　Cost of subsidiary acquired in stages

It may be that a subsidiary was acquired in stages so that, up to the date on which control was first achieved, the initial investment was accounted for at fair value under IAS 39. This raises the question of what the carrying amount should be in the separate financial statements when the cost method is applied.

In our view, if the business combination is being accounted for under IFRS 3(2007), there is only one acceptable method of accounting for the investment. The cost of the subsidiary is the sum of the actual amounts paid. Accordingly, any accumulated fair value changes relating to the investment should be reversed when control is obtained. The reversal will be an adjustment to the component of equity containing the cumulative valuation gains and losses, i.e. retained earnings, where the investment has been treated as at fair value through profit or loss, or the 'available-for-sale reserve' where the investment has been treated as available-for-sale. Any impairment recognised before control was obtained should not be reversed unless the conditions required for reversal under IAS 39 (see Chapter 32 at 6.2.5) have been satisfied.

IFRS 3(as revised in 2008) does not refer to the cost of individual acquisitions when there is a step acquisition, instead requiring the acquirer to remeasure its previously held equity interest in the acquiree at its acquisition-date fair value.[22] We do not consider that this affects the method applied in the investing company's own financial statements which remains as outlined above. The principles underlying the IFRIC's conclusions described in 2.1.1 above regarding the cost of investments in associates apply equally to the cost of investments in subsidiaries acquired in stages.

D   *Formation of a new parent: arrangements within scope of the IAS 27 amendment*

IAS 27 as revised in 2008 explains how to calculate the cost of the investment when a parent reorganises the structure of its group by establishing a new entity as its parent and meets the following criteria:

(a)   the new parent obtains control of the original parent by issuing equity instruments in exchange for existing equity instruments of the original parent;

(b)   the assets and liabilities of the new group and the original group are the same immediately before and after the reorganisation; and

(c)   the owners of the original parent before the reorganisation have the same absolute and relative interests in the net assets of the original group and the new group immediately before and after the reorganisation.

The new parent is to measure cost at the carrying amount of its share of the equity items shown in the separate financial statements of the original parent at the date of the reorganisation.[23]

This method also applies if the entity that puts a new parent between it and the shareholders is not itself a parent, i.e. it has no subsidiaries. In such cases, references in the three conditions are to be to 'original parent' and 'original group' are to the 'original entity'.[24]

The type of reorganisation to which the amendment applies involves an existing entity and its shareholders agreeing to create a new parent between them without changing either the composition of the group or their own absolute and relative interests. This is not a general rule that applies to all common control transactions. Transfers of subsidiaries from the ownership of one entity to another within a group are not within scope. The IASB has deliberately excluded extending the amendment to other types of reorganisations or to common control transactions more generally because they will be addressed in its project on common control transactions.[25] Entities will continue to account for such transactions in accordance with their accounting policies (see Chapter 10 at 3.1 and 4.4.2 below).

Arrangements that could meet the criteria include the following:

(a)   Reorganisations in which the new parent does not acquire all of the equity instruments issued by the original parent.

For example, the original parent may have preference shares that are classified as equity in addition to ordinary shares; the new parent does not have to acquire the preference shares in order for the transaction to be within scope.[26]

(b)   A new parent obtains control of the original parent without acquiring all of the ordinary shares of the original parent.[27] The absolute and relative holdings must be the same before and after the transaction

The amendment will apply, for example, if a controlling group of shareholders inserts a new entity between themselves and the original parent that holds all of their original shares in the same ratio as before.

Example 8.1:   New parent does not acquire all of original parent's ordinary shares

Shareholders A and B each hold 35% of the equity instruments of Original Parent. A and B transfer their shares to New Parent in a share-for-share exchange so that both now hold 50% of the shares in New Parent. The absolute and relative interests of A and B are unchanged and the arrangement is a reorganisation to which the cost method for reorganisations applies.

(c)   The establishment of an intermediate parent within a group[28]

The principle is exactly the same as inserting a new parent company over the top of a group. 'Original Parent' will be an intermediate company within a group, owned by another group company. If the transaction is within scope, the intermediate parent will acquire Original Parent from its parent (the Owner) in a share for share swap. The group structure before and after the transaction can be summarised as follows:

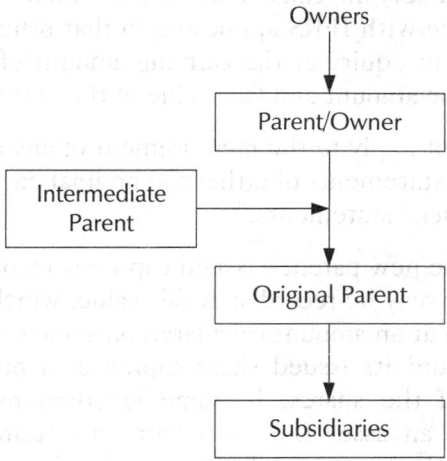

If the composition of the underlying group changes, perhaps because the intermediate parent acquires part only of that group or because it acquires another subsidiary as part consideration, then the arrangement will not be within scope.

E   Formation of a new parent: calculating the cost and measuring equity

IAS 27(revised) states that the new parent is to measure cost at the carrying amount of its share of the 'equity items' shown in the separate financial statements of the original parent at the date of the reorganisation.[29] It does not define 'equity items' but the term appears to mean the total equity in the original parent, i.e. its issued capital and reserves attributable to owners. This will be the equity as recorded in IFRS financial statements so it will exclude shares that are classified as liabilities and include, for example, the equity component of a convertible loan instrument.

It is important to stress that the new parent does not record its investment at the consideration given (the shares that it has issued) or at the consideration received (the fair value of the investments it has acquired or the book cost of those investments). Instead, it must look down, to the total of the equity in the original parent, which is the *acquired* entity. Even then, it does not record the investment at the amount of original parent's investments but, perhaps surprisingly, at the amount of its equity, that is to say its net assets.

It is possible for the original parent to have negative equity because its liabilities exceed its assets. IAS 27(revised) does not discuss this but we consider that in these circumstances the investment should be recorded at zero. There is no basis for recording an investment as if it were a liability.

The amendment applies only when the new parent issues equity instruments but it does not address the measurement of the equity. IFRS has no general requirements for accounting of the issue of equity instruments. Rather, consistent with the position taken by the *Framework* that equity is a residual rather than an item 'in its own right', the amount of an equity instrument is normally measured by reference to the item (expense or asset) in consideration for which the equity is issued, as determined in accordance with IFRS applicable to that other item. The new parent will record the increase in equity at the carrying amount of the investments it has acquired, regardless of the amount and face value of the equity issued.

The amendment does not apply to the measurement of any other assets or liabilities in the separate financial statements of either the original parent or the new parent or in the consolidated financial statements.[30]

The amount at which the new parent's issued capital is recorded will depend on the relevant law. The shares may be recorded at fair value, which is the fair value of the investments acquired, or at an amount calculated on some other basis. Local law may allow a company to record its issued share capital at a nominal amount, e.g. the nominal (face) value of the shares. In some jurisdictions, intermediate holding companies that acquire an asset from a parent (the 'transferor') for shares at a premium are required by law to record the share capital issued (its nominal value and share premium) at the carrying value in the transferor's books of the asset transferred; if the nominal value exceeds this book amount, the shares are recorded at their total nominal value.

Once the shares have been recorded, there will usually need to be an adjustment to equity so that it is equal to the carrying amount of the investments acquired. This adjustment may increase or decrease the acquirer's equity as it depends on the relative carrying amounts of the investment in the owner, original parent's equity and the number and value of the shares issued as consideration, as shown in the following example.

Example 8.2:   Adjustments to equity

Intermediate Parent A acquires the investments in Original Parent from Parent; the structure after the arrangement is as illustrated above. Parent carries its investment in Original Parent at £200 but it has a fair value of £750. Original Parent's equity in its separate financial statements is £650. Intermediate Parent A issues shares with a nominal value of £600 to Parent.

In accordance with IAS 27 paragraph 38B, Intermediate Company records its investment in Original Parent at £650. In accordance with local law*, it records its share capital at:

(i) £750, being the fair value of the consideration received for the shares. It records a negative adjustment of £100 elsewhere in equity; or

(ii) £600, as the nominal value of the shares issued is higher than the book value of the investment in Parent, so it records a credit adjustment of £50 elsewhere in equity

* the amount at which the share capital is recorded depends on other aspects of the arrangement that are not described here.

2.1.2 Deemed cost on transition to IFRS

There are a number of issues that have made IFRS an unattractive option for separate financial statements and have limited the extent to which it has been taken up in those areas where local law allows a choice. Two major stumbling blocks have been the carrying value of investments in subsidiaries, associates and jointly controlled entities at transition, dealt with in this section, and the related issue of the treatment of pre-acquisition dividends covered at 2.3 below; the former has been addressed by an amendment to IFRS 1.

Until the amendment to IFRS 1 in May 2008, there was no transitional relief from the requirement to measure investments in group entities at cost or in accordance with IAS 39. In order to apply IAS 27 retrospectively, an entity that applied the cost model would have had to be able to measure the fair value of the consideration given at the date of acquisition. The IASB has noted in the Basis of Conclusions of IFRS 1(revised) that establishing cost on an IFRS basis 'might be difficult, or even impossible, and perhaps costly'. Interestingly, as an example, it notes that 'in some jurisdictions, entities accounted for some previous acquisitions that were share-for-share exchanges using so-called "merger relief" or "group reconstruction relief". In this situation, the carrying amount of the investment in the parent's separate financial statements was based on the nominal value of the shares given rather than the value of the purchase consideration. This might make it difficult or impossible to measure the fair value of the shares given'.[31] This clarifies that recording the investment at the notional value allocated to the shares is not appropriate as cost under IFRS and is consistent with 2.1.1A and B above regarding the amount at which investments and equity instruments should be recorded in transactions that do not meet the 'new parent' requirements described in 2.1.1D above.

Accordingly, IFRS 1 now allows a first-time adopter an exemption with regard to its investments in subsidiaries, jointly controlled entities and associates in its separate financial statements.[32] If it elects to apply the cost method, it can either measure the investment in its separate opening IFRS balance sheet at cost determined in accordance with IAS 27 or at deemed cost. Deemed cost is either:

(i) fair value (determined in accordance with IAS 39) at the entity's date of transition to IFRSs in its separate financial statements; or

(ii) previous GAAP carrying amount at that date.

As with the other asset measurement exemptions, the first-time adopter may choose either (i) or (ii) above to measure each individual investment in subsidiaries, jointly controlled entities or associates that it elects to measure using a deemed cost.[33] It does not have to select one method as a policy choice.

2.2   IAS 39 method

The measurement rules in IAS 39 are complex and discussed in detail in Chapter 32. In brief, however, they will entail the subsidiary being recorded initially at cost and then classified as either a 'financial asset at fair value through profit or loss' or an 'available-for-sale financial asset'. In either case, the investment will be measured at fair value. However, the gains and losses arising on periodic remeasurement are accounted for:

- in the case of a financial asset at fair value through profit or loss, in profit or loss; and

- in the case of an available-for-sale financial asset, in equity.

Royal & Sun Alliance Insurance Group plc, which publishes its separate financial statements, accounts for its investments as available-for-sale financial assets. See Extract 8.2 below for an example of a company that classifies its investments as at fair value through profit or loss.

Extract 8.1: Royal & Sun Alliance Insurance Group plc (2007)

Notes to the separate financial statements

1   Significant accounting policies (extract)

Investment in subsidiaries [extract]

The Company accounts for its investments in directly owned subsidiaries as available for sale financial assets, which are included in the accounts at fair value.

Changes in the fair value of the investments in subsidiaries are recognised directly in equity in the statement of changes in equity. Where there is a decline in the fair value of a directly owned subsidiary below cost, and there is objective evidence that the investment is impaired, the cumulative loss that has been recognised in equity is removed from equity and recognised in the income statement

---

2.2.1   Proposals in the Improvements to IFRSs to apply IAS 39 to all investments in subsidiaries, associates and jointly controlled entities

The IASB proposes in the *Improvements to IFRSs* issued in August 2009 that in its separate financial statements the investor is to carry investments in subsidiaries, associates and jointly controlled entities at cost or at fair value through profit or loss, both in accordance with IAS 39 and to use that standard to test these investments for impairment.[34] At the same time it proposes removing investments in these investments from the scope of IAS 36, replacing that standard's requirements with the following:

> 'When an entity prepares separate financial statements, it shall apply the requirements of IAS 39 for the determination and measurement of impairment losses on investments in subsidiaries, jointly controlled entities and associates.'[35]

Testing investments in subsidiaries, jointly controlled entities and associates under IAS 36 is discussed in Chapter 18 at 5.5.2; testing financial assets for impairment is discussed in Chapter 32 at 6.

It is difficult to determine exactly what impact this might have as it appears to be linked to the IASB's proposals to replace IAS 39, at least in part as a response to the financial crisis; see in particular Chapter 29 at 1.6.

2.3   Dividends and other distributions

For annual periods beginning on or after 1 January 2009, IAS 27 contains a general principle for dividends received from subsidiaries, jointly controlled entities or associates that replaces the previous restrictions regarding 'pre-acquisition' dividends. This has been supplemented by specific indicators of impairment in IAS 36 – *Impairment* – that apply when a parent entity receives the dividend.

An Interpretation issued in November 2008, IFRIC 17 – *Distributions of Non-cash Assets to Owners*, applies to periods beginning on or after 1 July 2009 and considers in particular the treatment by the entity making the distribution. In certain circumstances, as discussed in 2.3.2 below, it will require gains or losses measured by reference to fair value of the assets distributed to be taken to profit or loss; amongst other restrictions, it excludes from its scope non-cash distributions made by wholly-owned group companies.

2.3.1   *Dividends from subsidiaries, jointly controlled entities or associates*

Until May 2008 IAS 27's cost method required distributions received in excess of profits arising after the date of acquisition (sometimes referred to as dividends out of 'pre-acquisition' profits) to be regarded as a recovery of the investment and therefore accounted for as a reduction of the cost of the investment. IAS 27(revised) removes all references to the cost method. Instead it states that an entity is to recognise dividends from subsidiaries, jointly controlled entities or associates in profit or loss in its separate financial statements when its right to receive the dividend is established.[36]

Dividends are recognised only when they are declared (i.e. the dividends are appropriately authorised and no longer at the discretion of the entity). IFRIC 17 expands on this point: the relevant authority may be the shareholders, if the jurisdiction requires such approval, or management or the board of directors, if the jurisdiction does not require further approval.[37] If the declaration is made after the balance sheet date but before the financial statements are authorised for issue, the dividends are not recognised as a liability at the end of the reporting period because no obligation exists at that time.[38] The parent cannot record income and recognise an asset until the dividend is a liability of its subsidiary, the paying company.

Instead of the cost method, entities are now obliged to apply a two-stage process. Once recognised, all dividends are taken to income and the parent must now determine whether or not the investment has been impaired as a result. The list of indicators in IAS 36 as amended includes the receipt of a dividend from a subsidiary, jointly controlled entity or associate where there is evidence that:

(i)   the dividend exceeds the total comprehensive income of the subsidiary, jointly controlled entity or associate in the period the dividend is declared; or

(ii)   the carrying amount of the investment in the separate financial statements exceeds the carrying amounts in the consolidated financial statements of the investee's net assets, including associated goodwill.[39]

IAS 36 requires the entity to assess at each balance sheet date whether there are any 'indications of impairment'. Only if indications of impairment are present will the impairment test itself have to be carried out.[40]

A   *The dividend exceeds the total comprehensive income*

Entities will have to be aware that there are many circumstances in which receipt of a dividend will trigger the second indicator, even if the dividend is payable entirely from the profit for the period.

First, as drafted, the indicator states that the test is by reference to the income in the period in which the declaration is made. Dividends are usually declared after the end of the period to which they relate; an entity whose accounting period ends on 31 December 2008 will not normally declare a dividend in respect of its earnings in that period until its financial statements have been drawn up, i.e. some months into the next period ended 31 December 2009. We assume that it is expected that the impairment review itself will take place at the end of the period, in line with the general requirements of IAS 36 referred to above, in which case the dividends received in the period will be compared to the income of the subsidiary for that period. This means that there may be a mismatch in that, say, dividends declared on the basis of 2008 profits will be compared to total comprehensive income in 2009, but at least the indicator of impairment will be by reference to a completed period. However, there may be a more significant mismatch for interim financial statements if these are drawn up for the separate financial statements of the parent.

Second, the test is by reference to total comprehensive income, not profit or loss for the period. The term is defined in IAS 1 – *Presentation of Financial Statements* – as 'the change in equity during a period resulting from transactions and other events, other than those changes resulting from transactions with owners in their capacity as owners'.[41] Total comprehensive income takes into account the components of 'other comprehensive income' that are not reflected in profit or loss that include[42]:

(a)   changes in revaluation surpluses of property, plant and equipment or intangible assets (see Chapters 15 and 16);

(b)   actuarial gains and losses on defined benefit plans taken to equity (see Chapter 36);

(c)   gains and losses arising from translating the financial statements of a foreign operation (see Chapter 13);

(d)   gains and losses on remeasuring available-for-sale financial assets (see Chapter 32);

(e)   the effective portion of gains and losses on hedging instruments in a cash flow hedge (see Chapter 24).

This means that all losses on remeasurement that are allowed by IFRS to bypass profit or loss and be taken directly to other components of equity are taken into account in determining whether a dividend is an indicator of impairment. If a subsidiary pays a dividend from its profit for the year that exceeds its total comprehensive income because there is a reduction in the fair value of its head office or a loss on remeasuring its hedging derivatives, then receipt of that dividend is an indicator of impairment to the parent.

The opposite must also be true – a dividend that exceeds profit for the period but does not exceed total comprehensive income (if, for example, the entity has a revaluation surplus on its property) is not an indicator of impairment.

It must be stressed that this test is solely to see whether a dividend triggers an impairment review. It has no effect on the amount of dividend that the subsidiary may pay, which remains governed by local law.

B   The carrying amount exceeds the consolidated net assets

It is an indicator of impairment if, after paying the dividend, the carrying amount of the investment in the separate financial statements exceeds the carrying amounts in the consolidated financial statements of the investee's net assets, including associated goodwill.

It will often be fairly clear in most cases of dividends paid out of profits for the period by subsidiaries, whether the consolidated net assets of the investee in question have declined below the carrying amount of the investment. Similar issues to those described above may arise, e.g. the subsidiary may have made losses or taken some sort of remeasurement to other comprehensive income in the period in which the dividend is paid. However, it is the net assets in the consolidated accounts that are relevant, not those in the subsidiary's own financial statements, which may be different if the parent acquired the subsidiary.

Testing assets for impairment is described in Chapter 18. There are particular problems in trying to assess the investments in subsidiaries for impairment because the asset (the investment) and the underlying CGU are not necessarily the same. These problems are discussed in Chapter 18 at 5.5.2.

C   Returns of capital

Returns of share capital are not usually considered to be dividends and hence they are not directly addressed by the amendment. They are an example of a 'distribution', the broader term applied when an entity gives away its assets to its members that was used by IAS 27 in its now-deleted cost method.

At first glance, a return of capital appears to be an obvious example of something that ought to reduce the carrying value of the investment in the parent. We do not think that is necessarily the case. Returns of capital cannot easily be distinguished from dividends. For example, depending on local law, entities may be able to:

• make repayments that directly reduce their share capital; or

• create reserves by transferring amounts from share capital into retained earnings and, at the same time or later, pay dividends from that reserve.

Returns of capital can be accounted for in the same away as dividends, i.e. by applying the two-stage process described above. However, the effect on an entity that makes an investment (whether on initial acquisition of a subsidiary or on a subsequent injection of capital) and immediately receives it back (whether as a dividend or return of capital) will be of a return of capital that reduces the carrying value of the parent's investment. In these circumstances there will be an impairment that is equal to the dividend that has been received. If there is a delay between the investment and the dividend or return of capital then the impairment (if any) will be a matter of judgement based on the criteria discussed above. It ought to make no difference precisely which reserve within equity the distribution has been charged to.

2.3.2   Distributions of Non-cash Assets to Owners (IFRIC 17)

Entities sometimes make distributions of assets other than cash, e.g. items of property, plant and equipment, businesses as defined in IFRS 3, ownership interests in another entity or disposal groups as defined in IFRS 5. There were concerns that entities were accounting differently in practice for non-cash distributions; many treated the distribution at the carrying value of the net assets, some grossed up the amount within equity to show the fair value of the assets distributed while yet others took the fair value surplus over the carrying amount to profit or loss. IFRIC 17 was issued in November 2008 to clarify the treatment. The Interpretation will have the effect that gains or losses relating to some non-cash distributions to shareholders (there are many exclusions) will be accounted for in profit or loss. IFRIC 17 addresses only the accounting by the entity that makes a non-cash asset distribution, not the accounting by recipients. It has mandatory application to financial statements beginning on or after 1 July 2009. The transitional arrangements are described below.

A   Scope

IFRIC 17 applies to any distribution of a non-cash asset, including one that gives the shareholder a choice of receiving either non-cash assets or a cash alternative[43] if it is within scope.

The IFRIC did not want the Interpretation to apply to exchange transactions with shareholders which can include an element of distribution, e.g. transactions at an undervalue include a distribution of a non-cash asset. Therefore, it applies only to distributions in which all owners of the same class of equity instruments are treated equally.[44]

It does not apply to distributions if the assets are ultimately controlled by the same party or parties before and after the distribution, whether in the separate, individual and consolidated financial statements of an entity that makes the distribution.[45] This means that it will not apply to distributions made by subsidiaries but only to distributions made by parent entities or individual entities that are not themselves parents. In order to avoid ambiguity regarding 'control' and to ensure that demergers achieved by way of distribution are dealt with, the Interpretation emphasises that 'control' is used in the same sense as in IFRS 3. A distribution to a group of individual shareholders will only be out of scope if those shareholders have ultimate collective power over the entity making the distribution as a result of contractual arrangements.[46]

There is a final exclusion. If the non-cash asset is an interest in a subsidiary over which the entity retains control, this is to be accounted for by recognising a non-controlling interest in the subsidiary in equity, as required by the IAS 27 (as amended in 2008) para. 30 (see Chapter 7 at 4).[47] Transitional rules in IFRIC 17 described below mean that entities are not able to adopt IFRIC 17 before applying IAS 27 (as amended in 2008).

B   Recognition, measurement and presentation

A dividend is not a liability until the entity is obliged to pay it to the shareholders.[48] The obligation arises when payment is no longer at the discretion of the entity, which will depend on the requirements of local law. In some jurisdictions, the UK for example, shareholder approval is required before there is a liability to pay. In other jurisdictions, declaration by management or the board of directors may suffice.[49]

The liability is to be measured at the fair value of the assets to be distributed.[50] If an entity gives its owners a choice of receiving either a non-cash asset or a cash alternative, the entity shall estimate the dividend payable by considering both the fair value of each alternative and the associated probability of owners selecting each alternative.[51] The Interpretation does not specify any method of assessing probability nor its effect on measurement.

Because the non-cash assets held for distribution are not a disposal group as defined, consequential changes have been made to IFRS 5 to bring them into scope of that standard's classification, presentation and measurement requirements. IFRS's requirements now apply also to a non-current asset (or disposal group) that is classified as held for distribution to owners acting in their capacity as owners (held for distribution to owners).[52] This means that assets or asset groups within scope of IFRS 5 will be carried at the lower of carrying amount and fair value less costs to distribute.[53]

Assets not within scope of IFRS 5 continue to be valued in accordance with the relevant standard. In practice, most non-cash distributions of assets out of scope of IFRS 5 will be of assets held at fair value in accordance with the relevant standard, e.g. financial instruments and investment property carried at fair value.[54] Accordingly there should be little difference between their carrying value and the amount of the distribution.

The liability is to be adjusted as at the end of any reporting period at which it remains outstanding and at the date of settlement with any adjustment being taken to equity.[55] When the liability is settled, the difference, if any, between its carrying amount and the carrying amount of the assets distributed is to be accounted for as a separate line item in profit or loss.[56] IFRIC 17 does not express any preference for particular line items or captions in the income statement.

It is rare for entities to distribute physical assets such as PP&E to shareholders, although these distributions are common within groups and hence out of scope of IFRIC 17. In practice, the Interpretation will have most effect on demergers by way of distribution, as illustrated in the following example. The parent's ownership interests will usually be carried at cost (see 2.1.1 above), sometimes in accordance with IAS 39 (see 2.2 above).

Example 8.3:   Non-cash asset distributed to shareholders

Conglomerate Plc has two divisions, electronics and music, each of which is in a separate subsidiary. On 17 December 2010 the shareholders approve a non-cash dividend of the electronics division, which means that the dividend is a liability when the annual financial statements are prepared as at 31 December 2010. The distribution is to be made on 17 January 2011.

In Conglomerate Plc's separate financial statements, the investment in Electronics Ltd, which holds the electronics division, is carried at €100 million; the division has consolidated net assets of €210 million. The electronics division's fair value at 17 December and 31 December is €375 million, so is the amount at which the liability to pay the dividend is recorded in Conglomerate Plc's separate financial statements and in its consolidated accounts, as follows:

Conglomerate Plc

Separate financial statements			Consolidated financial statements		
	€	€		€	€
Dr equity	375		Dr equity	375	
Cr liability		375	Cr liability		375

In Conglomerate's separate financial statements its investment in Electronics Ltd of €100 million is classified as held for sale. In the consolidated accounts, the net assets of €210 million are so classified.

If the value of Electronics Ltd had declined between the date of declaration of the dividend and the period end, say to €360 million (more likely if there had been a longer period between declaration and the period end) then the decline would be reflected in equity and the liability recorded at €360 million. Exactly the same entry would be made if the value were €375 million at the period end and €360 million on the date of settlement (dr liability €15 million, cr equity €15 million).

The dividend is paid on 17 January 2011 at which point the fair value of the division is €360 million. The difference between the assets distributed and the liability is recognised as a gain in profit or loss

Conglomerate Plc

Separate financial statements			Consolidated financial statements		
	€	€		€	€
Dr liability	360		Dr liability	360	
Cr profit or loss		260	Cr profit or loss		150
Cr asset held for sale		100	Cr disposal group		210

If the distribution is outstanding at a period end, the entity must disclose:

(a)   the carrying amount of the dividend payable at the beginning and end of the period: and

(b)   the increase or decrease in the carrying amount recognised in the period as result of a change in the fair value of the assets to be distributed.[57]

If an entity declares a dividend that will take the form of a non-cash asset after the end of a reporting period but before the financial statements are authorised the following disclosure should be made:

(a)   the nature of the asset to be distributed;

(b)   the carrying amount of the asset to be distributed as of the end of the reporting period; and

(c)   the estimated fair value of the asset to be distributed as of the end of the reporting period, if it is different from its carrying amount, and the information about the method used to determine that fair value required by IFRS 7 – *Financial Instruments: Disclosures* – paragraph 27(a) and (b).[58]

IFRIC 17 is to be applied prospectively for annual periods beginning on or after 1 July 2009. Retrospective application is not permitted. Earlier application is permitted but only if the entity also applies IFRS 3 (as revised in 2008), IAS 27 (as amended in May 2008) and IFRS 5 (as amended by IFRIC 17).[59]

3   DISCLOSURE

3.1   Separate financial statements prepared by parent electing not to prepare consolidated financial statements

When separate financial statements are prepared for a parent that, in accordance with the exemption discussed at 1.1 above, elects not to prepare consolidated financial statements, those separate financial statements shall disclose:[60]

(a)   the fact that the financial statements are separate financial statements;

(b)   that the exemption from consolidation has been used;

(c)   the name and country of incorporation or residence of the entity whose consolidated financial statements that comply with International Financial Reporting Standards have been produced for public use and the address where those consolidated financial statements are obtainable;

(d)   a list of significant investments in subsidiaries, jointly controlled entities and associates, including for each such investment its:

    (i)   name;

    (ii)   country of incorporation or residence; and

    (iii)   proportion of ownership interest and, if different, proportion of voting power held; and

(e)   a description of the method used to account for the investments listed under (d).

These disclosure requirements are illustrated in the extract below.

Extract 8.2: Lifetime Group Limited (2006)

Accounting policies [extract]

(A) Basis of presentation [extract]

As permitted under IAS 27, Consolidated and Separate Financial Statements, the Company has elected not to present consolidated financial statements. These financial statements present information about the Company as an individual undertaking and not about its Group. Information on the ultimate controlling parent and immediate parent can be found on page 23.

(F) Investments in subsidiaries

Investments in subsidiaries are stated at fair value through profit or loss. The fair value is based on net asset value.

8. Investment in subsidiaries

	2006 £'000	2005 £'000
Fair value		
At 1 January	1,685	–
Additions	6,750	2,250
Fair value losses	(3,130)	(565)
At 31 December	5,305	1,685

The Company's principal subsidiaries, which are wholly-owned, are shown below:

Name of company	Principal activity	Country of registration
Lifetime Marketing Services Limited	Financial services	England & Wales
Lifetime Online Solutions Pty Limited	IT development	Australia

21. Related party transactions [extract]

(d) Parent entity

The immediate holding entity is Norwich Union Life Holdings Limited, a company registered in England.

(e) Ultimate controlling entity

The ultimate controlling entity is Aviva plc, a company registered in England. Its Group financial statements are available on www.aviva.com or by application to the Group Company Secretary, Aviva plc, St Helen's, 1 Undershaft, London EC3P 3DQ.

These disclosures are given only where the parent has taken advantage of the exemption from preparing consolidated financial statements. Where the parent has not taken advantage of the exemption, and also prepares separate financial statements, it gives the disclosures at 3.2 below in respect of those separate financial statements.

3.2 Separate financial statements prepared by an entity other than a parent electing not to prepare consolidated financial statements

As drafted, IAS 27 requires these disclosures to be given by:

- a parent preparing separate financial statements in addition to consolidated financial statements (i.e. whether or not it is required to prepare consolidated financial statements – the disclosures in 3.1 apply only when the parent has actually taken advantage of the exemption, not merely when it is eligible to do so); and

- an entity (not being a parent) that is an investor in an associate or a venturer in joint venture in respect of any separate financial statements that it prepares, i.e. whether:

  (i)   as its only financial statements (if permitted by IAS 28 or IAS 31), or

  (ii)   in addition to financial statements in which the results and net assets of associates or joint ventures are included.

  However, the relevance of certain of these disclosures to financial statements falling within (i) above is not immediately obvious – see 3.2.1 below.

Where an entity is both a parent and either an investor in an associate or a venturer in a joint venture, it should follow the disclosure requirements governing parents – in other words, it complies with the disclosures in 3.1 above if electing not to prepare consolidated financial statements and otherwise with the disclosures below.

Separate financial statements prepared by an entity other than a parent electing not to prepare consolidated financial must disclose:[61]

(a)   the fact that the statements are separate financial statements and the reasons why those statements are prepared if not required by law;

(b)   a list of significant investments in subsidiaries, jointly controlled entities and associates, including for each such investment its:

  (i)   name;

  (ii)   country of incorporation or residence; and

  (iii) proportion of ownership interest and, if different, proportion of voting power held; and

(c)   a description of the method used to account for the investments listed under (b).

The separate financial statements must also identify the financial statements prepared in accordance with the requirements of paragraph 9 of IAS 27 (requirement to prepare consolidated financial statements), IAS 28 and IAS 31 to which they relate.[62] In other words, they must draw attention to the fact that the entity also prepares consolidated financial statements or, as the case may be, financial statements in which the results and net assets of associates or joint ventures are included.

The implication of this disclosure requirement is that an entity which publishes both separate and consolidated financial statements cannot issue the separate financial statements before the consolidated financial statements, since there would not be, at the date of issue of the separate financial statements, any consolidated financial statements 'to which they relate'. This is discussed at 1.1.2 above.

3.2.1   *Entities with no subsidiaries but exempt from applying IAS 28 or IAS 31*

Entities which have no subsidiaries, but which have investments in associates or jointly controlled entities are permitted by IAS 28 and IAS 31 to prepare separate financial statements as their only financial statements if they satisfy the conditions described at 1.1.1 above.

As drafted, IAS 27 requires such entities to make the disclosures in (a) to (c) above. In addition, the entity must identify the consolidated financial statements prepared in accordance with IAS 27 to which they (i.e. the separate financial statements) relate, or the relevant accounts prepared in accordance with IAS 28 and IAS 31.[63]

4   INDIVIDUAL FINANCIAL STATEMENTS

4.1   Introduction

Transactions often take place between a parent entity and its subsidiaries or between subsidiaries within a group that may, or may not, be carried out on an arm's length basis.

Whilst such transactions do not affect the consolidated financial statements of the parent as they are eliminated in the course of consolidation, they can have a significant impact on the separate financial statements of the parent and/or subsidiaries and/or a set of consolidated financial statements prepared for a sub-group. IAS 24 – *Related Party Disclosures* – requires only that these transactions are disclosed and provides no accounting guidance.

The IASB generally takes the view that the needs of users of financial statements are fully met by requiring entities to consolidate subsidiaries, equity account for associates, and proportionately consolidate or equity account for jointly controlled entities. Accounting issues within individual financial statements are not a priority issue and are usually only addressed when a standard affects consolidated and individual statements in different ways, for example accounting for pensions or employee benefits.

However, we consider that it is helpful to set out some general guidance in accounting for these transactions that enhances the consistency of application of IFRS whether for the separate financial statements of a parent, the individual financial statements of an entity that is not a parent or the consolidated financial statements of a sub-group. We have considered how to apply these principles to certain common types of arrangement between entities under common control, which are described in more detail at 4.4 below:

- Sales, exchanges and contributions of non-monetary assets
- Sales and exchanges of investments not within the scope of IAS 39 (i.e. subsidiaries, associates or joint ventures)
- Contributions of businesses in exchange for equity instruments
- Loans that bear interest at non-market rates or are interest free
- Early redemption of fixed rate loans
- Financial guarantee contracts given by a parent over its borrowings in the financial statements of a subsidiary
- Incurring costs and settling liabilities without recharge

Other arrangements that are subject to specific requirements in particular standards are dealt with in the relevant chapters. These include:

- Financial guarantee contracts over a subsidiary's borrowings in the accounts of the parent: see Chapter 32 at 2.2.4
- Share based payment plans of a parent: see Chapter 27 at 12
- Employee benefits: see Chapter 28 at 3.3.2

When considering how to account for any transactions between entities under common control, two points to consider are:

1   Is the transaction 'at arm's length'? IAS 39 and various other standards refer to 'the amount for which an asset could be exchanged between knowledgeable, willing parties in an arm's length transaction'.[64] It is necessary to consider whether the transaction is of a type that independent parties could or would enter into. It is also important to remember that an arm's length transaction includes the repayment terms that would be expected of independent parties and this is not the case in many intra-group transactions.

2   Is it a contractual arrangement and, if so, is the entity whose financial statements are being considered a party to the contract?

If the transaction is at fair value and the entity is a party to the contract, we believe that it should be accounted for in accordance with the terms of the contract. Other arrangements are discussed below.

There is often more than one acceptable way of accounting for many transactions and hence a choice of accounting policies. The entity must apply its chosen policy consistently to similar arrangements and disclose it if it is material. However, not all group entities need adopt the same accounting policy in their individual financial statements or sub-group consolidated financial statements. Nor is there a requirement for symmetrical accounting by the entities involved in the transaction.

4.2   Recognition

If an entity is a party to a contract under which it receives a right and incurs an obligation, then on the assumption that there is substance to the transaction, it will be recognised in the financial statements of the entity.

An entity may receive a right without incurring an obligation or *vice versa* without being a party to a contract. There are many different types of arrangement that contain this feature, either in whole or in part:

- Some arrangements are not contractual at all, such as capital contributions and distributions, that are in substance gifts made without consideration;
- Some standards require transactions to which the entity is not a party to be reflected in their financial statements. In effect, the accounting treatment is representing that the subsidiary has received a capital contribution from the parent, which the subsidiary has then spent on employee remuneration or *vice versa*. IFRS 2 – *Share-based Payments* – has such requirements (see Chapter 28 at 12);

- Some are contractual arrangements for the other party, e.g. a parent enters into a contract to engage an auditor for the subsidiary, and pays the audit fees without any recharge.

If an entity is not a party to a contractual relationship and there is no IFRS requiring recognition then the entity may choose not to recognise the transaction at all.

If it chooses to recognise the transaction then recognition will depend on whether the entity is a parent or a subsidiary, as well as the specific nature of the transaction. All such transactions will have an equal and opposite debit and credit. In some circumstances a parent may treat a debit as either an addition to its investment in its subsidiary or as an expense and the credit as a gain to profit or loss; gains to equity are unlikely as these are usually transactions with subsidiaries, not shareholders. A subsidiary can only treat the transaction as a credit or debit to income (a gain or expense) and an equal and opposite debit or credit to equity (a distribution or contribution of equity).

One example where a subsidiary is required by an IFRS to record an expense when it is not a party to a contractual arrangement is a share-based payment. If the employees of a subsidiary are granted options by the parent company over its shares in exchange for services to the subsidiary, the subsidiary must record a cost for that award within its own financial statements, even though it may not legally be a party to it. The parent must also record the share-based payment as an addition to the investment in the subsidiary (see Chapter 28 at 12). Other examples are described in 4.4 below.

The option to record the entry when not a party to it is only available where there is a real transfer of risks and benefits from one entity to the other. The choice is made independently by both entities involved in the transaction so there may not be a mirror treatment in the financial statements of each entity.

Note that this only applies to the entity that is not a party to a contractual arrangement and that has made no transfer of economic benefits. An entity that pays expenses on behalf of another group company without recharge may be required to expense the cost or may have a choice about whether to do so; sometimes a parent may be able to capitalise the cost as part of its investment in a subsidiary. However, in all cases the contracting entity is required to account for something (usually a net debit), unlike the non-contracting company that is grossing up something that has a net zero impact on its financial position.

The principles apply equally to transactions between a parent and its subsidiaries and transactions between subsidiaries in a group. If the transaction is between two subsidiaries, and both of the entities are either required or choose to recognise an equity element in the transaction, one subsidiary recognises a capital contribution from the parent, while the other subsidiary recognises a distribution to the parent. The parent may choose whether or not to recognise the equity transfer in its stand-alone financial statements.

4.3   Measurement

If a standard requires the transaction to be recognised initially at fair value, it must be measured at that fair value regardless of the actual consideration. A difference between the fair value and the consideration may mean that other goods or services are being provided, e.g. the transaction includes a management fee. This will be accounted for separately on one of the bases described below. If there is still a difference having taken account of all goods or services, it is accounted for as an equity transaction, i.e. as either a contribution or distribution of equity.

In all other cases, there is a choice available to the entity.

(a)   Recognise the transaction at fair value, irrespective of the actual consideration. Any difference between the fair value and the agreed consideration may reflect additional goods or services but once all of these have been identified and accounted for, any remaining difference will be a contribution or distribution of equity for a subsidiary, or an increase in the investment held or a distribution received by the parent.

(b)   Recognise the transaction at the actual consideration stated in any agreement related to the transaction.

This principle is demonstrated in the following flowchart:

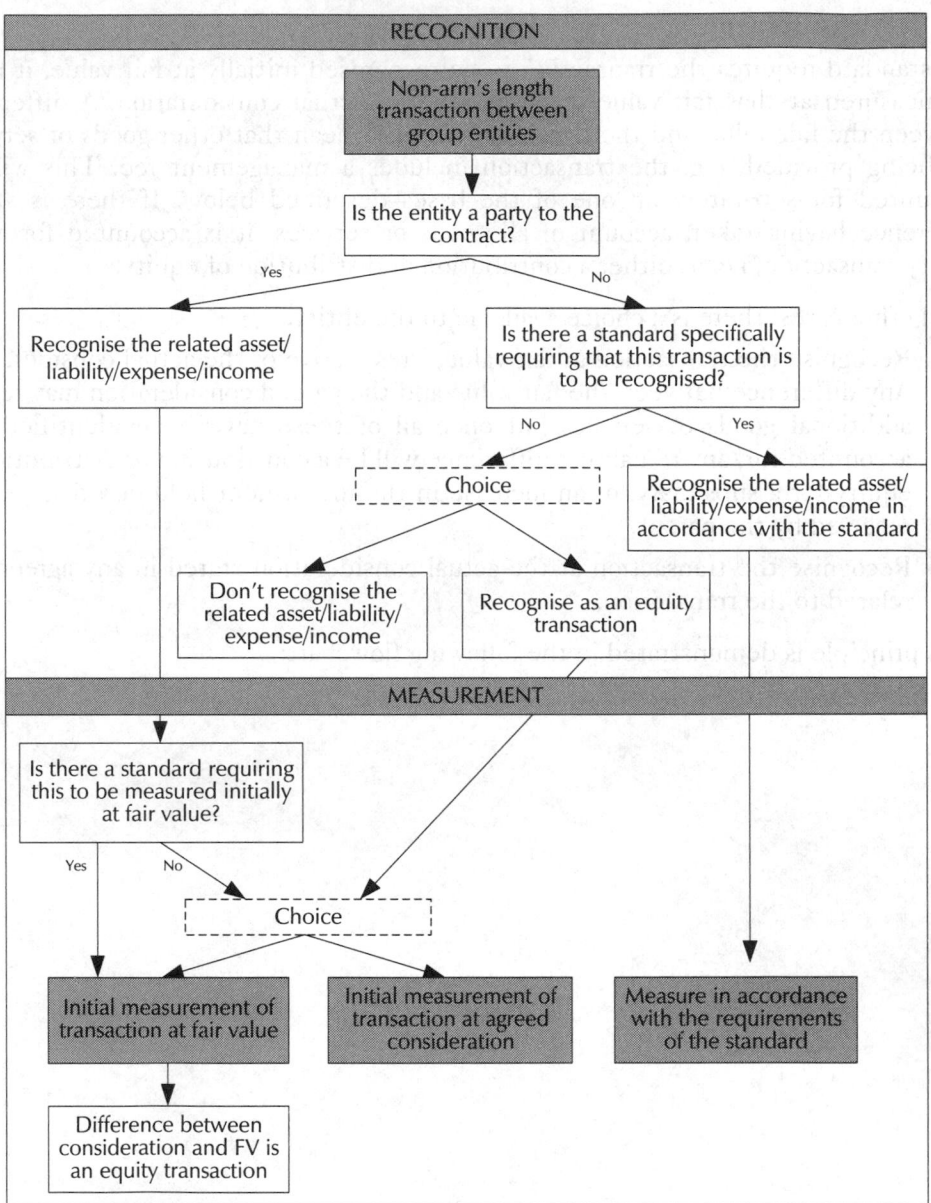

4.3.1   Fair value in intra-group transactions

Fair value can be extremely difficult to establish in intra-group transactions.

If there is more than one element to the transaction, this means in principle identifying all of the goods and services being provided and accounting for each element at fair value. This is not necessarily straightforward: a bundle of goods and services in an arm's length arrangement will usually be priced at a discount to the price of each of the elements acquired separately and this will have to be reflected in the fair value attributed to the transaction. It can be much harder to allocate fair values in intra-group arrangements where the transaction may not have a commercial equivalent.

As we have already noted, the transaction may be based on the fair value of an asset but the payment terms are not comparable to those in a transaction between independent parties. The purchase price often remains outstanding on intercompany account, whereas commercial arrangements always include agreed payment terms. Interest-free loans are common between group companies; these loans may have no formal settlement terms and, while this makes them technically repayable on demand, they too may remain outstanding for prolonged periods.

As a result, there is always a certain amount of estimation when applying fair values to group arrangements.

Some IFRSs are based on the assumption that one entity may not have the information available to the other party in a transaction, for example:

- a lessee under an operating lease may not know the lessor's internal rate of return, in which case IAS 17 – *Leases* – allows it to substitute its own incremental borrowing rate (see Chapter 22 at 3.1.5); and

- in exchanges of assets, IAS 16 – *Property, Plant and Equipment* – and IAS 38 – *Intangible Assets* – note that one party may not have information about the fair value of the asset it is receiving, the fair value of the asset it is giving up or it may be able to determine one of these values more easily than the other (see Chapter 16 at 3.2.4 and 4.4.1B below).

In an intra-group transaction it will be difficult to assume that one group company knows the fair value of the transaction but the other does not. The approximations allowed by these standards will probably not apply.

However, if a subsidiary is not wholly owned, it is to be assumed that such transactions are undertaken on arms' length terms. The reasons for, and implications of the non-arms' length terms within any such transaction must be assessed and carefully analysed.

4.4 Accounting for common control transactions

The following sections deal with common transactions that occur between entities under common control. While the scenarios depict transactions between a parent and its subsidiaries they apply equally to transactions between subsidiaries.

Deferred tax has been ignored for the purposes of the examples.

4.4.1 Transactions involving non-monetary assets

The same principles apply whether the asset that is acquired for a consideration different to its fair value is inventory (IAS 2 – *Inventories* – Chapter 20), property, plant and equipment ('PP&E') (IAS 16 – *Property, Plant and Equipment* – Chapter 16), an intangible asset (IAS 38 – *Intangible Assets* – Chapter 15) or investment property (IAS 40 – *Investment Property* – Chapter 17). These standards require assets to be recognised at cost.

A   *Sale of PP&E from the parent to the subsidiary for an amount of cash not representative of the value of the asset.*

The parent and subsidiary are both parties to the transaction and both must recognise it. As the asset is recognised by the acquiring entity at cost, and not necessarily at fair value, a choice exists as to how the cost is determined. Does the consideration comprise two elements, cash and equity, or cash alone?

In some jurisdictions, some entities are legally required to conduct such transactions at fair value.

Example 8.4:   Sale of PP&E at an undervalue

A parent entity sells PP&E that has a carrying amount of 50 and a fair value of 100 to its subsidiary for cash of 80.

Method (a)	*Method (b)*
Recognise the transaction at fair value, regardless of the values in any agreement, with any difference between that amount and fair value recognised as an equity transaction. (Note 1)	Recognise the transaction at the consideration agreed between the parties, being the amount of cash paid.

Subsidiary

	€	€		€	€
Dr PP&E	100		Dr PP&E	80	
Cr Cash		80	Cr Cash		80
Cr Equity		20			

Parent

	€	€		€	€
Dr Cash	80		Dr Cash	80	
Dr Investment	20		Cr PP&E		50
Cr PP&E		50	Cr Gain (profit or loss)		30
Cr Gain (profit or loss)		50			

Note 1   This may only be applied where fair value can be measured reliably

However, what if the asset is sold for more than fair value? What are the implications if, in the above example, the PP&E sold for 80 has a carrying value of 80 but its fair value is 75? There are a number of explanations that may affect the way in which the transaction is accounted for:

•   The excess reflects additional services or goods included in the transaction, e.g. future maintenance that will be accounted for separately;

•   The excess reflects the fact that the asset's value in use ('VIU') is at least 80. It is very common for PP&E to be carried at an amount in excess of fair value because its VIU, or the VIU of the cash-generating unit of which it is a part, is unaffected by falls in fair value. Plant and machinery often has a low resale value; vehicles lose much of their fair value soon after purchase; and falls in property values may not affect the VIU of the head office of a profitable entity (see Chapter 18). In such cases there is no reason why the subsidiary cannot record the asset it has acquired for the cash it has paid, which means that it effectively inherits the transferor's carrying value. An impairment test should not reveal any requirement to write down the asset, assuming of course that no other factors reduce the asset's VIU;

- The excess over fair value is a distribution by the subsidiary to the parent that will be accounted for in equity. This treatment is a legal requirement in some jurisdictions, which means that the overpayment must meet the legal requirements for dividends, principally that there be sufficient distributable profits to meet the cost; and

- The asset is impaired before transfer, i.e. both its fair value and VIU are lower than its carrying amount, in which case it must be written down by the transferor before the exchange takes place. If it is still sold for more than the impaired amount, the excess will be accounted for as a distribution received (by the parent) and a distribution made by the subsidiary (as above).

Purchases of assets at overvalue must always be treated with caution. Even if there are no legal constraints, the directors or officers of entities are usually obliged to act in the best interests of the entity, which may prevent them buying assets at an overvalue.

B　　The parent exchanges PP&E for a non-monetary asset of the subsidiary.

The parent and subsidiary are both parties to the transaction and both must recognise it. The exchange of an asset for another non-monetary asset is accounted for by recognising the received asset at fair value, unless the transaction lacks commercial substance (as defined by IAS 16) or the fair value of neither of the exchanged assets can be measured reliably.[65] The requirements of IAS 16 are explained in Chapter 16 at 3.2.4; the treatment required by IAS 38 and IAS 40 is the same.

The mere fact that an exchange transaction takes place between entities under common control does not of itself indicate that the transaction lacks commercial substance. However, in an exchange transaction between unrelated parties the fair value of the assets is usually the same but this does not necessarily hold true of transactions between entities under common control.

If the fair value of both assets can be measured reliably there may be a difference between the two. IAS 16 suggests that, if an entity is able to determine reliably the fair value of either the asset received or the asset given up, then the fair value of the asset given up is used to measure the cost of the asset received.[66] However, IAS 16 actually requires an entity to base its accounting for the exchange on the asset whose fair value is most clearly evident.[67] The reliability of asset valuations depends on the variability in the range of reasonable fair value estimates and the probabilities of the various estimates within the range. It is extremely unlikely in a group arrangement that both parties will have a different view of the reliability of the fair values. Both entities will use the same assumptions. If fair values are different it is much more likely that the group entities have entered into a non-reciprocal transaction. This means that the entity has the policy choice described at 4.3 above, which in this case means that there are three alternative treatments; it can recognise the transaction as follows:

- an exchange of assets at fair value with an equity transaction. Any difference between the fair value of the asset received and the fair value of the asset given up is an equity transaction, while the difference between the carrying value of the asset given up and its fair value is recognised in profit or loss;

- at fair value without recognising an equity element; or

- apply a 'cost' method based on IAS 16 (the fair value of the asset given up is used to measure the cost of the asset received) under which each entity records the asset at the fair value of the asset it has given up. This could result in one of the parties recording the asset it had received as an amount in excess of its fair value, in which case there is little alternative but to write down the asset. It would be consistent with the principles outlined at 4.3 above to treat the write down as an equity transaction, i.e. an addition to the carrying value of the subsidiary by the parent and a distribution by the subsidiary.

If the fair value of only one of the exchanged assets can be measured reliably, IAS 16 allows both parties to recognise the asset they have received at the fair value of the asset that can be measured reliably.[68] Underlying this requirement is a presumption that the fair value of both assets is the same, but one cannot assume this about common control transactions. It is to be hoped that the situation will rarely arise, as it is likely that the same degree of evidence will be available as to the fair value of both assets.

The difference between two reliable fair values may reflect additional goods and services, which will have to be identified and accounted for separately. A remaining difference will be an equity element.

If the fair value of neither of the exchanged assets can be measured reliably, or the transaction does not have commercial substance, both the parent and subsidiary recognise the received asset at the carrying amount of the asset they have given up.

Example 8.5:   Exchange of assets with dissimilar values

A parent entity transfers an item of PP&E to its subsidiary in exchange for an item of PPE of the subsidiary, with the following values:

Parent	Subsidiary
Carrying Value 50	Carrying Value 20
Fair Value 100	Fair Value 80

The fair value of both assets can be measured reliably.

Method (a)	Method (b)
Recognise the transaction as an exchange of assets at fair value with an equity transaction. Any difference between that value and the fair value of the asset given up is an equity transaction, while the difference between the carrying value of the asset given up and its fair value is recognised in profit or loss.	Recognise the transaction as an exchange of assets at fair value. Any difference between the fair value and the carrying value of the asset given up is recognised in profit or loss.

Parent

	€	€		€	€
Dr PP&E	80		Dr PP&E	80	
Dr Investment	20		Cr PP&E		50
Cr PP&E		50	Cr Gain (profit or loss)		30
Cr Gain (profit or loss)		50			

Subsidiary

	€	€		€	€
Dr PP&E	100		Dr PP&E	100	
Cr PP&E		20	Cr PP&E		20
Cr Gain (profit or loss)		60	Cr Gain (profit or loss)		80
Cr Gain (retained reserves)		20			

If the 'cost' method were applied, the transaction would be recorded as follows:

Parent			*Subsidiary*		
Dr PP&E (100 – 20)	80		Dr PP&E	80	
Dr Investment	20		Cr PP&E		50
Cr PP&E		50	Cr Gain (profit or loss)		30
Cr Gain (profit or loss)		50			

C *Acquisition of assets for shares*

These transactions include the transfer of inventory, property plant and equipment, intangible assets and investment property by one entity in return for shares of the other entity. These transactions are usually between parent and subsidiary.

(a) Accounting treatment by the subsidiary

The transaction is within the scope of IFRS 2, as goods have been received in exchange for shares. The asset is recognised at fair value, unless the fair value cannot be estimated reliably, and an increase in equity of the same amount is recognised. If the fair value of the asset cannot be estimated reliably, the fair value of the shares is used instead.[69]

(b) Accounting treatment by the parent

The parent has disposed of an asset in exchange for an increased investment in a wholly-owned subsidiary. As discussed in 2.1.1 above, a transaction in which an investment in a subsidiary, associate or joint venture is acquired is not specifically addressed under IFRS, as it falls outside the scope of both IAS 39 and IFRS 2 (see Chapter 31 at 2.2.3).

The asset's fair value may be lower than its carrying value but it is not impaired unless its VIU is insufficient to support that carrying value (see 4.4.1A above). If there is no impairment, the parent is not prevented from treating the carrying value of the asset as an addition to the investment in the subsidiary solely because the fair value is lower. If the asset is impaired then this should be recognised before reclassification, unless the reorganisation affects, and increases, the VIU.

If the fair value is higher than the carrying value, the transferring entity could recognise a gain if it decided, as a matter of policy, to record the exchange at fair value.

D   Contribution of assets

These transactions include transfers of inventory, property plant and equipment, intangible assets and investment property from one entity to another for no consideration. These arrangements are not contractual but are equity transactions: either specie capital contributions (an asset is gifted by a parent to a subsidiary) or non-cash distributions (an asset is given by a subsidiary to its parent). IFRIC 17 explicitly excludes intra-group non-cash distributions from its scope see 2.3.2 above.[70]

The relevant standards (IAS 2, IAS 16, IAS 38 and IAS 40) refer to assets being recognised at cost. Following the principles described at 4.3 above, the entity receiving the asset has a choice: recognise it at zero or at fair value. It is in practice more common for an entity that has received an asset in what is purely an equity transaction to recognise it at fair value.

The entity that gives away the asset must reflect the transaction. A parent that makes a specie capital contribution to its subsidiary will either recognise an increased investment in that subsidiary (in principle at fair value) or an expense. A subsidiary that makes a distribution in specie to its parent will account for the transaction in retained earnings. However, the subsidiary could account for the distribution at fair value, if this could be established reliably, potentially recognising a gain in profit or loss and a charge to equity of the fair value of the asset. This is consistent with IFRIC 17, although the distribution is not in scope.

E   Transfers between subsidiaries

As noted at 4.2 above, similar principles apply when the arrangement is between two subsidiaries rather than a subsidiary and parent. To illustrate this, assume that the transaction in Example 8.4 above takes place between two subsidiaries rather than parent and subsidiary.

Example 8.6:   Transactions between subsidiaries

The facts are as in Example 8.3 above except that Subsidiary A sells PP&E that has a carrying amount of 50 and a fair value of 100 to its fellow-subsidiary B for cash of 80. As before, it is assumed that fair value can be measured reliably

Method (a)	*Method (b)*
Recognise the transaction at fair value, regardless of the values in any agreement, with any difference between that amount and fair value recognised as an equity transaction. (Note 1)	Recognise the transaction at the consideration agreed between the parties, being the amount of cash paid.

Subsidiary A

	€	€		€	€
Dr Cash	80		Dr Cash	80	
Dr Equity (note 1)	20		Cr PP&E		50
Cr PP&E		50	Cr Gain (profit or loss)		30
Cr Gain (profit or loss)		50			

Subsidiary B

	€	€		€	€
Dr PP&E	100		Dr PP&E	80	
Cr Cash		80	Cr Cash		80
Cr Equity		20			

Parent(note 2)

	€	€	
Dr Investment in A	20		no entries made
Cr Investment in B		20	

Note 1   From subsidiary A's perspective there is an equity element to the transaction representing the difference between the fair value of the asset and the contractual consideration. This reflects the amount by which the transaction has reduced A's fair value and has been shown as a distribution by B to its parent.

Note 2   Parent can choose to reallocate the equity element of the transaction between its two subsidiaries so as to reflect the changes in value.

Transferring assets at less than fair value from one subsidiary to another may be subject to legal restrictions in some jurisdictions, e.g. the UK, where the transferring entity may be required to have sufficient distributable profits to meet the equity element in the arrangement.

In some circumstances the transfer of an asset from one subsidiary to another may affect the value of the transferor's assets to such an extent as to be an indicator of impairment in respect of the parent's investment in its shares. This can happen if the parent acquired the subsidiary for an amount that includes goodwill and the business or assets generating part or all of that goodwill have been transferred to another subsidiary. As a result, the carrying value of the shares in the parent may exceed the fair value or VIU of the remaining assets. This is discussed further in Chapter 18 at 5.5.2.

4.4.2   Acquiring and selling investments and businesses

The carrying value of investments in subsidiaries, associates and jointly controlled entities in the parent's separate financial statements is discussed at 2.1.1 above.

One group entity may sell, and another may purchase, the net assets of a business rather than the shares in the entity. The acquisition may be for cash or shares and both entities must record the transaction in their individual financial statements. There are a number of interrelated issues that must be addressed.

As this chapter only addresses transactions between entities under common control, any arrangement described in this section will be out of scope of IFRS 3(2007) or IFRS 3(as revised in 2008). IFRS 3(as revised in 2008) has essentially retained IFRS 3(2007)'s scope exclusion with some minor changes to the wording. IFRS 3(2007) refers to 'business combinations involving entities or businesses under common control,'[71] while IFRS 3(as revised in 2008) uses the description 'a combination of entities or businesses under common control'.[72] Both versions of the standard include application guidance.[73] The common control exemption is discussed in Chapter 10 at 2.

If the arrangement is a business combination for the acquiring entity it will not be within scope of IFRS 2[74].

There are a number of separate issues to be addressed and these are dealt with in Chapters 9 and 10.

A   Has a business been acquired?

The best guidance as to what comprises a business is in IFRS 3(as revised in 2008), which defines a business as 'an integrated set of activities and assets that is capable of being conducted and managed for the purpose of providing a return in the form of dividends, lower costs or other economic benefits directly to investors or other owners, members or participants'.[75] There is a change of emphasis from IFRS 3 (2007) – 'the integrated set of activities and assets must be capable of being conducted and managed for the purpose of providing a return in the form of dividends, lower costs or other economic benefits directly to investors or other owners, members or participants. Focusing on the capability to achieve the purposes of the business helps avoid the unduly restrictive interpretations that existed in accordance with the former guidance.'[76] See Chapter 9 at 3.2.2 (IFRS 3(as revised in 2008) and at 2.1.3A (IFRS 3(2007)) for descriptions of the features of a business.

B   If a business has been acquired, how should it be accounted for?

As described in Chapter 10 at 3.1, we believe that until such time as the IASB finalises its conclusions under its project on common control transactions entities should apply either:

(a)   the pooling of interest method; or

(b)   the purchase method (as in IFRS 3).

In our view, where the purchase method of accounting is selected, the transaction must have substance from the perspective of the reporting entity. This is because the purchase method results in a reassessment of the value of the net assets of one or more of the entities involved and/or the recognition of goodwill. Chapter 10 discusses the factors that will give substance to a transaction and although this is written primarily in the context of the acquisition of an entity by another entity, it applies equally to the acquisition of a business by an entity.

C   *Purchase and sale of a business for equity or cash not representative of the fair value of the business*

The principles are no different to those described at 4.4.1C above. The entity may:

- Recognise the transaction at fair value, regardless of the values in any agreement, with any difference between that amount and fair value recognised as an equity transaction; or

- Recognise the transaction at the consideration agreed between the parties, being the amount of cash paid

D   *If the net assets are not a business, how should the transactions be accounted for?*

Even though one entity acquires the net assets of another, this is not necessarily a business combination. IFRS 3(2007) and IFRS 3(as revised in 2008) both rule out of scope acquisitions of assets or net assets that are not businesses. IFRS 3(as revised in 2008) says:

> 'This IFRS does not apply to .... the acquisition of an asset or a group of assets that does not constitute a *business*. In such cases the acquirer shall identify and recognise the individual identifiable assets acquired (including those assets that meet the definition of, and recognition criteria for, *intangible assets* in IAS 38 – *Intangible Assets*) and liabilities assumed. The cost of the group shall be allocated to the individual identifiable assets and liabilities on the basis of their relative *fair values* at the date of purchase. Such a transaction or event does not give rise to goodwill.'[77]

This has the same effect as the requirement in IFRS 3(2007):

> 'When an entity acquires a group of assets or net assets that does not constitute a business, it shall allocate the cost of the group between the individual identifiable assets and liabilities in the group based on their relative fair values at the acquisition date.'[78]

If the acquisition is not a business combination, it will be an acquisition of assets for cash or shares: see 4.1.1A and 4.4.1C above.

4.4.3   *Transfers of businesses without consideration*

As well as making transfers for shares or cash, businesses can also be transferred from one group entity to another without any consideration. This section deals with the transfer of the entirety of the business from one group entity to another. Commonly the transfer is as a distribution by a subsidiary to its parent or a contribution, usually but not necessarily by a parent, to a subsidiary. The transfer can be a dividend but there are other legal arrangements that have similar effect that include reorganisations sanctioned by a court process or transfers after liquidation of the transferor entity. Some jurisdictions allow a legal merger between a parent and subsidiary to form a single entity. The general issues are discussed in A below, contributions of businesses in B while a summary of the special concerns raised by legal mergers are addressed in C.

A   *Distributions of businesses*

A feature that all distributions of businesses to parent entities have in common, whatever the legal form that they take, is that it is difficult to categorise them as business combinations. There is no acquirer whose actions result in it obtaining control of an acquired business; the parent already controls the business that has been transferred to it. From one perspective the transfer is a distribution and the model on which to base the accounting is that of receiving a dividend. Another view is that the parent has exchanged the investment in shares for the underlying assets and this is essentially a change in perspective from a direct equity interest to reflecting directly the net assets and results. Neither analogy is perfect (although both have their adherents) so it is no surprise that these two basic models do not deal with all of the issues that can arise when a business is transferred.

In all circumstances, there are two major features that will drive the decisions regarding the way in which the transfer is accounted for:

- whether the parent set up the subsidiary or acquired it; and
- whether the transfer is accounted for at fair value or at 'book value'.

Book value in turn may depend on whether the subsidiary has been acquired by the parent, in which case the relevant book values would be those reflected in the consolidated financial statements.

If the parent set up the subsidiary, all of its transactions have occurred while it has been under the parent's control. If it has acquired the subsidiary, its fair value and net assets may have changed in the period since acquisition. The acquired subsidiary's continuing ordinary activities will have generated returns from the assets, which may have been added to or sold and will have been depreciated or perhaps impaired. There may have been revaluations and other transactions directly affecting equity. These changes have not been reflected in the purchase price or the parent's individual financial statements but only in the consolidated accounts.

The two perspectives translate into two approaches to accounting by the parent:

(i)   Parent has received a distribution that it accounts for in its income statement at the fair value of the consideration received. It reflects the assets acquired at their fair value, including goodwill, which will be measured as at the date of the transfer. The existing investment is written off to the income statement.

- This treatment can be applied in all circumstances.
- This is the only appropriate method when the parent carries its investment in shares at fair value applying IAS 39.

(ii)   Parent has exchanged its investment for the underlying assets and liabilities of the subsidiary and accounts for them at book values. The values that are reported in the consolidated financial statements become the cost of these assets for the parent.

- This method is not appropriate if the investment in the parent is carried at fair value, in which case method (i) must be applied.

The two linked questions when using this approach are how to categorise the difference between the carrying value of the investment and the assets transferred and whether or not to reflect goodwill or an 'excess' (negative goodwill) in the parent's accounts. This will depend primarily on whether the subsidiary had been acquired by the parent (the only circumstances in which this approach allows post-transfer goodwill in the parent's financial statements) and how any remaining 'catch up' adjustment is classified.

These alternative treatments are summarised in the following table:

Subsidiary set up or acquired	Basis of accounting	Goodwill recognised	Effect on income statement
Subsidiary set up by parent	fair value	goodwill or negative goodwill at date of transfer	dividend recognised at fair value of net assets
	book value from underlying records	no goodwill or negative goodwill (note 1)	catch up adjustment recognised fully as income, except that the element relating to a transaction recorded directly in equity may be recognised in equity. (note 2)
Subsidiary acquired by parent	fair value	goodwill or negative goodwill at date of transfer	dividend recognised at fair value of net assets
	book value from consolidated accounts (note 3)	goodwill as at date of original acquisition (note 3)	catch up adjustment recognised fully as income, except that the element relating to a transaction recorded directly in equity may be recognised in equity. (note 2)

Notes

(1) If the parent established the subsidiary itself and its investment reflects only share capital it has injected then an excess of the carrying value over the net assets received will not be recognised as goodwill. This commonly arises because of losses and an excess of liabilities over assets in the transferred subsidiary.

If the subsidiary's net assets exceed the carrying value of the investment then this will be due to profits or gains taken to equity, e.g. revaluations.

(2) The catch up adjustment is not an equity transaction so all of it can be recognised in income. However, to the extent that it has arisen from a transaction that had occurred directly in equity, such as a revaluation, an entity can make a policy choice to recognise this element in equity. In this case the remaining amount is recognised in income.

(3) Because this was originally an acquisition, the values in the consolidated accounts (and not the subsidiary's underlying records) become 'cost' for the parent. The assets and liabilities will reflect fair value adjustments made at the time of the business combination. Goodwill or negative goodwill will be the amount as at the date of the original acquisition.

If the business of the acquired subsidiary is transferred to the parent company as a distribution shortly after acquisition, it will be accounted for solely as a return of capital. The parent eliminates its investment in the subsidiary, recognising instead all of the assets and liabilities acquired at their fair value including the goodwill that has arisen on the business combination. The effect is to reflect the substance of the arrangement which is that the parent acquired a business rather than a separate incorporated entity. It is clear that the parent can only reflect transactions that have arisen since it obtained control over the subsidiary.

B   Contributions of businesses

The principles that apply when an entity acquires the shares in another group entity, whether for cash or other consideration, apply equally to transfers of businesses without consideration. The consequences when an entity acquires the shares in another group entity for cash are discussed in Chapter 10 at 3.4.2.

While distributions of businesses to parents are not business combinations (see above), not all agree that the same is necessarily true of contributions of businesses to subsidiaries. These can be transferred from group entities other than parents and they also can be seen as common control transactions. The bases of accounting are described in 4.4.2B and C above. Depending on circumstances, the substance of the arrangement and the policy adopted by the receiving company, it may be able to apply pooling (and hence show comparative information in its financial statements) or use the acquisition method.

If the entity applies acquisition accounting then the aggregate fair value of the net assets acquired (including goodwill if appropriate) will be reflected as a capital contribution.

If the subsidiary applies pooling then, as described in Chapter 10 at 3.4.2, it can choose to apply either the carrying values reported in the consolidated financial statements or the carrying values reported in the transferor entity's own financial statements. Under the second approach, using the values as stated in the predecessor entity, the transaction is considered from the perspective of the reporting entity so the carrying value of the business before the transfer will be relevant. The financial statements of the entity that has acquired the business after the transfer will be effectively a combination of the financial statements of both entities. The parent shareholder is thus receiving the same financial information as before, but in one set of financial statements rather than two.

C   Legal merger of parent and subsidiary

In many jurisdictions it is possible to effect a 'legal merger' of a parent and its subsidiary whereby the two separate entities become a single entity without any issue of shares or other consideration.

a)   The parent is the surviving entity

In all instances the investment in the shares of the subsidiary is replaced by the net assets of the subsidiary, using one of the methods outlined below. The approaches and the underlying rationales are the same as those for distributions of businesses, described in A above:

(i)   the entity treats the business received as a distribution at fair value; or

(ii)   the entity uses book values, modified as appropriate if the subsidiary has itself been acquired which means that they will be adjusted for the effects of movements in the period after acquisition.

If the shares in the subsidiary were previously carried at fair value then only method (i) is applicable. Neither of these methods allow recognition of comparative information for the acquired business. The transferred business is reflected only from the date on which the transfer took place.

b)   The subsidiary is the surviving entity

If the subsidiary company is the surviving entity, then the combination can be treated as if it were analogous to a reverse acquisition, applying the principles in (i) and (ii) above. This will give the same results as when the parent is the surviving entity except that the financial statements will reflect the capital structure of the subsidiary. Any necessary adjustments will be made in equity. Again, the combination would be effected only from the date on which the merger took place and comparatives would not be presented.

This is based on the assumption that it is a matter of legal form whether the surviving entity is the parent or the subsidiary then accounting for the merger ought to be in substance the same whichever predecessor entity is the survivor.

4.4.4   *Incurring expenses and settling liabilities without recharges*

Entities frequently incur costs that provide a benefit to fellow group entities, e.g. audit, management or advertising fees, and do not recharge the costs. The beneficiary is not party to the transaction and does not directly incur an obligation to settle a liability. It may elect to recognise the cost, in which case it will charge profit or loss and credit retained earnings with equivalent amounts; there will be no change to its net assets. If the expense is incurred by the parent, it could elect to increase the investment in the subsidiary rather than expensing the amount. This would be extremely unusual and could lead to a carrying value that was impaired. Fellow subsidiaries will have no choice but to expense the cost. There is no policy choice if the expense relates to a share-based payment, in which case IFRS 2 mandates that expenses incurred for a subsidiary be added to the carrying amount of the investment in the parent and be recognised by the subsidiary (see Chapter 28 at 12).

Many groups recharge expenses indirectly, by making management charges or recoup the fund through intra-group dividends, and in these circumstances it would be inappropriate to recognise the transaction in any entity other than the one that makes the payment.

A parent or other group entity may settle a liability on behalf of a subsidiary. If this is not recharged, the liability will have been extinguished in the entity's accounts. This raises the question of whether the gain should be taken to profit or loss or to equity. IAS 18 defines revenue as a transaction giving rise to an inflow of benefits other than as contributions from owners.[79] Except in unusual circumstances, the forgiveness of debt will be a contribution from owners and therefore ought to be taken to equity.

It will usually be appropriate for a parent to add the payment to the investment in the subsidiary as a capital contribution, subject always to impairment of the investment but a parent may conclude that it is more appropriate to expense the cost. Fellow-subsidiaries will have to expense the cost of meeting the liability unless reimbursed by the parent.

4.4.5   Financial Instruments within the scope of IAS 39

IAS 39 requires that the initial recognition of financial assets and financial liabilities is at fair value,[80] so management has no policy choice. Financial instruments arising from group transactions are initially recognised at their fair value, with any difference between the fair value and the terms of the agreement recognised as an equity transaction.

A   Interest free or non-market interest rate loans

Parents commonly lend money to subsidiaries on an interest-free or low-interest basis and *vice versa*. A feature of many intra-group payables is that they have no specified repayment terms and are therefore repayable on demand. The fair value of a financial liability with a demand feature is not less than the amount payable on demand, discounted from the first date that the amount could be required to be paid.[81] This means that an intra-group loan payable on demand has a fair value that is the same as the cash consideration given.

Loans are recognised at fair value on initial recognition based on the market rate of interest for similar loans at the date of issue.[82] The party making the loan has a receivable recorded at fair value and must on initial recognition account for the difference between the fair value and the loan amount.

If the party making the non-market loan is a parent, it may add this to the carrying value of its investment. Subsidiary will initially record a capital contribution in equity. Subsequently, the parent will recognise interest income and the subsidiary income expense using the effective interest method so that the loan is stated at the amount receivable/repayable at the redemption date. When the loan is repaid, the overall effect in parent's accounts is of a capital contribution made to the subsidiary as it has increased its investment and recognised income to the same extent (assuming, of course, no impairment). By contrast, the subsidiary has initially recognised a gain in equity that has been reversed as interest has been charged.

If the subsidiary makes the non-market loan to its parent, the difference between the loan amount and its fair value is treated as a distribution by the subsidiary to the parent, while the parent reflects a gain. Again, interest is recognised so that the loan is stated at the amount receivable and payable at the redemption date. This has the effect of reversing the initial gain or loss taken to equity. Note that the effects in parent's financial statements are not symmetrical to those when it makes a loan at below market rates. The parent does not need to deduct the benefit it has received from the subsidiary from the carrying value of its investment.

The following example illustrates the accounting for a variety of intra-group loan arrangements.

Example 8.7: *Interest-free and below market rate loans within groups*

Entity S is a wholly owned subsidiary of Entity P. In each of the following scenarios one of the entities provides an interest free or below market rate loan to the other entity.

1 P provides an interest free loan in the amount of $100,000 to S. The loan is repayable on demand.

On initial recognition the receivable is measured at its fair value, which in this case is equal to the cash consideration given. The loan is classified as a current liability in the financial statements of the subsidiary. The classification in the financial statements of the parent depends upon management intention. If the parent had no intention of demanding repayment in the near term, the parent would classify the receivable as non-current in accordance with paragraph 57 (c) of IAS 1.

If S makes an interest-free loan to parent, the accounting is the mirror image of that for the parent.

2 P provides an interest free loan in the amount of $100,000 to S. The loan is repayable when funds are available.

Generally, a loan that is repayable when funds are available will be classified as a liability. The classification of such a loan as current or non-current and the measurement at origination date will depend on the expectations of the parent and subsidiary of the availability of funds to repay the loan. If the loan is expected to be repaid in three years, measurement of the loan would be same as in scenario 3.

If S makes an interest-free loan to parent, the accounting is the mirror image of that for the parent.

3 P provides an interest free loan in the amount of $100,000 to S. The loan is repayable in full after 3 years. The fair value of the loan (based on current market rates of 10%) is $75,131.

At origination, the difference between the loan amount and its fair value (present value using current market rates for similar instruments) is treated as an equity contribution to the subsidiary, which represents a further investment by the parent in the subsidiary.

Journal entries at origination:

	Parent	$	$
Dr	Loan receivable from subsidiary	75,131	
Dr	Investment in subsidiary	24,869	
Cr	Cash		100,000

	Subsidiary	$	$
Dr	Cash	100,000	
Cr	Loan payable to parent		75,131
Cr	Equity – capital contribution		24,869

Journal entries during the periods to repayment:

	Parent	$	$
Dr	Loan receivable from subsidiary (Note 1)	7,513	
Cr	Profit or loss – notional interest		7,513

	Subsidiary	$	$
Dr	Profit or loss – notional interest	7,513	
Cr	Loan payable to parent		7,513

Note 1 Amounts represent year one assuming no payments before maturity. Year 2 and 3 amounts would be $8,264 and $9,092 respectively i.e. accreted at 10%. At the end of year 3, the recorded balance of the loan will be $100,000.

4   S provides a below market rate loan in the amount of $100,000 to P. The loan bears interest at 4% and is repayable in full after 3 years (i.e. $112,000 at the end of year 3). The fair value of the loan (based on current market rates of 10%) is $84,147.

At origination, the difference between the loan amount and its fair value is treated as a distribution from the subsidiary to the parent.

Journal entries at origination:

		$	$
	Parent		
Dr	Cash	100,000	
Cr	Loan payable to subsidiary		84,147
Cr	Profit or loss – distribution from subsidiary		15,853

		$	$
	Subsidiary		
Dr	Loan receivable from parent	84,147	
Dr	Retained earnings – distribution	15,853	
Cr	Cash		100,000

Journal entries during the periods to repayment:

		$	$
	Parent		
Dr	Profit or loss – notional interest	8,415	
Cr	Loan payable to subsidiary		8,415

		$	$
	Subsidiary		
Dr	Loan receivable from parent (Note 1)	8,415	
Cr	Profit or loss – notional interest		8,415

Note 1   Amounts represent year one assuming no payments before maturity. Year 2 and 3 amounts would be $9,256 and $10,182, respectively i.e. accreted at 10% such that at the end of year 3 the recorded balance of the loan will be $112,000 being the principal of the loan ($100,000) plus the interest payable in cash ($12,000).

B   Financial guarantee contracts: Parent guarantee issued on behalf of subsidiary

Financial guarantees given by an entity that are within the scope of IAS 39 must be recognised initially at fair value.[83] If a parent or other group entity gives a guarantee on behalf of an entity, this must be recognised in its separate or individual financial statements. It is normally appropriate for a parent that gives a guarantee to treat the debit that arises on recognising the guarantee at fair value as an additional investment in its subsidiary. This is described in Chapter 32 at 2.2.4.

The situation is different for the subsidiary or fellow subsidiary. There will be no separate recognition of the financial guarantee unless it is provided to the lender separate and apart from the original borrowing, does not form part of the overall terms of the loan and would not transfer with the loan if it were to be assigned by the lender to a third party. This means that few guarantees will be reflected separately in the financial statements of the entities that benefit from the guarantees. In any event the amounts are unlikely to be significant.

Example 8.8:   Financial guarantee contracts

A group consists of two entities, H plc (the parent) and S Ltd (H's wholly owned subsidiary). Entity H has a stronger credit rating than S Ltd. S Ltd is looking to borrow €100, repayable in five years. A bank has indicated it will charge interest of 7.5% per annum. However, the bank has offered to lend S Ltd at a rate of 7.0% per annum if H plc provides a guarantee of S Ltd's debt to the bank and this is accepted by S Ltd. No charge was made by H plc to S Ltd in respect of the guarantee. The fair value of the guarantee is calculated at €2, which is the difference between the present value of the contractual payments discounted at 7.0% and 7.5%. If the bank were to assign the loan to S Ltd to a third party, the assignee would become party to both the contractual terms of the borrowing with S Ltd as well as the guarantee from H plc.

H plc will record the guarantee at its fair value of €2.

S Ltd will record its loan at fair value including the value of the guarantee provided by the parent. It will simply record the liability at €100 but will not recognise guarantee provided by the parent.

If the guarantee was separate, S Ltd would record the liability at its fair value without the guarantee of 98 with the difference recorded as a capital contribution.

4.5   Disclosures

Where there have been significant transactions between entities under common control that are not on arms' length terms, it will be necessary for the entity to disclose its accounting policy for recognising and measuring such transactions.

IAS 24 applies whether or not a price has been charged so gifts of assets or services and asset swaps are within scope. Details and terms of the transactions must be disclosed – see Chapter 38 at 2.4.

References

1 IAS 27, *Consolidated and Separate Financial Statements*, IASB, para. IN10.

2 IAS 27, para. 39.

3 IAS 27, para. 9.

4 IAS 27, para. 10.

5 IAS 27, para. 8.

6 IAS 28, *Investments in Associates*, IASB, para. 2.

7 IAS 28, para. 4.

8 IAS 28, para. 36.

9 IAS 28, para. 5.

10 *IFRIC Update*, IASB, March 2006, p. 7.

11 Agenda paper for the meeting of the Accounting Regulatory Committee on 2nd February 2007 (document ARC/08/2007), *Subject: Relationship between the IAS Regulation and the 4th and 7th Company Law Directives – Can a company preparing both individual and consolidated accounts in accordance with adopted IFRS issue the individual accounts before the consolidated accounts?*, European Commission: Internal Market and Services DG: Free movement of capital, company law and corporate governance: Accounting/PB D(2006), 15 January 2007, para. 3.1.

12 Regulation (EC) No. 1606/2002 of the European Parliament and of the Council of 19 July 2002 on the application of international accounting standards, preamble para. (3).

13 Agenda paper for the meeting of the Accounting Regulatory Committee on 24th November 2006 (document ARC/19/2006), *Subject: Relationship between the IAS Regulation and the 4th and 7th Company Law Directives – Meaning of 'Annual Accounts'*, European Commission: Internal Market and Services DG: Free movement of capital, company law

and corporate governance: Accounting/RC MX D(2006), 7 November 2006, para. 5.1.

14 IAS 27, para. 37.

15 IAS 27, para. 37.

16 IAS 27, para. 40.

17 IAS 27 (2007), *Consolidated and Separate Financial Statements*, IASB, 2007 Bound Volume, para. 4.

18 IAS 27, para. 38A.

19 IASB Agenda Paper 6, *IAS 27 – Accounting in the separate financial statements for the formation of a new parent*, IASB, 19 July 2007, para. 1.

20 IFRS 3 (2007), *Business Combinations*, IASB, 2007 Bound Volume, para. 24.

21 *IFRIC Update*, IASB, July 2009, p. 7.

22 IFRS 3, para. 42.

23 IAS 27, para. 38B.

24 IAS 27, para. 38C.

25 IAS 27, para. BC66Q.

26 IAS 27, para. BC66N.

27 IAS 27, para. BC66N.

28 IAS 27, para. BC66N.

29 IAS 27, para. 38B.

30 IAS 27, para. BC66O.

31 IFRS 1, *First-time adoption of International Financial Reporting Standards*, IASB, para. BC58C.

32 IFRS 1, para. D15.

33 IFRS 1, para. 31.

34 *Improvements to IFRSs*, August 2009, IASB, IAS 27, para. 38.

35 *Improvements to IFRSs*, August 2009, IASB, IAS 27, para. 38D.

36 IAS 27, para. 38A.

37 IFRIC 17, *Distributions of Non-cash Assets to Owners*, IASB, November 2008, para. 10.

38 IAS 10, *Events after the Reporting Period*, IASB, para. 13.

39 IAS 36, *Impairment*, IASB, para. 12(h).

40 IAS 36, paras. 8-9.

41 IAS 1, *Presentation of Financial Statements*, IASB, para. 7.

42 IAS 1, para. 7.

43 IFRIC 17, para. 3.

44 IFRIC 17, para. 4.

45 IFRIC 17, para. 5.

46 IFRIC 17, para. 6.

47 IFRIC 17, para. 7.

48 IFRIC 17, para. 9.

49 IFRIC 17, para. 10.

50 IFRIC 17, para. 11.

51 IFRIC 17, para. 12.

52 IFRS 5, *Non-current Assets Held for Sale and Discontinued Operations*, IASB, paras. 5A, 12A and 15A.

53 IFRS 5, paras. 15 and 15A.

54 IFRS 5, para. 5.

55 IFRIC 17, para. 13.

56 IFRIC 17, paras. 14 and 15.

57 IFRIC 17, para. 16.

58 IFRIC 17, para. 17.

59 IFRIC 17, para. 18.

60 IAS 27, para. 42.

61 IAS 27, para. 43.

62 IAS 27, para. 43.

63 IAS 27, para. 43.

64 IAS 39, *Financial Instruments: Recognition and Measurement*, IASB, para. 9.

65 IAS 16, *Property, Plant and Equipment*, IASB, para. 24.

66 IAS 16, para. 26.

67 IAS 16, para. 26.

68 IAS 16, para. 26.

69 IFRS 2, *Share-based Payment*, IASB, para. 10.

70 IFRIC 17, para. 6.

71 IFRS 3 (2007), para. 3(b).

72 IFRS 3, *Business Combinations*, IASB, para. 2.

73 IFRS 3 (2007), paras. 11-13 and IFRS 3, paras. B1-B4.

74 IFRS 2, para. 5.

75 IFRS 3, Appendix A.

76 IFRS 3, para. BC18.

77 IFRS 3 para. 2(b).

78 IFRS 3 (2007), para 4.

79 IAS 18, *Revenue*, IASB, para. 7.

80 IAS 39, para. 43.

81 IAS 39, para. 49.

82 IAS 39, para. AG64.

83 IAS 39, para. 43.

Chapter 9   Business combinations

1   INTRODUCTION

1.1   Background

Over the years, business combinations have been defined in different ways. Until recently, a business combination was defined by the IASB as 'the bringing together of separate entities or businesses into one reporting entity',[1] but this has since been revised to a 'transaction or other event in which an acquirer obtains control of one or more businesses'.[2] Whatever definition is applied, it includes not only when an entity becomes a subsidiary of a parent but also where an entity obtains control of an integrated set of activities and assets that constitute a business.

In accounting terms there have traditionally been two distinctly different forms of reporting the effects of a business combination; the purchase method of accounting (or acquisition method of accounting) and the pooling of interests method (or merger accounting).

The two methods of accounting look at business combinations through quite different eyes. An acquisition is seen as the absorption of the target into the clutches of the predator; there is continuity only of the acquiring entity, in the sense that only the post-acquisition results of the target are reported as earnings of the acquiring entity, and the comparative figures remain those of the acquiring entity. In contrast, a uniting of interests or merger is seen as the pooling together of two formerly distinct shareholder groups, and in order to present continuity of both entities there is retrospective restatement to show the enlarged entity as if the two entities had always been together, by combining the results of both entities pre- and post-combination and also by restatement of the comparatives. The difficulty for accountants has been how to translate this difference in philosophy into criteria which permit particular transactions to be categorised as being of one type or the other. However, during the last decade, the pooling of interests method has fallen out of favour with standard setters, including the IASB, as they consider virtually all business combinations as being acquisitions. The purchase method has become the established method of accounting for business combinations. Nevertheless, the pooling of interests method is still sometimes used for business combinations involving entities under common control where the transactions have been scoped out of the relevant standard dealing with business combinations generally (see Chapter 10).

The other main issues facing accountants have been in relation to accounting for an acquisition. In order to do so, the acquiring entity has generally had to determine the cost of its acquisition and then allocate that cost between the identifiable assets and liabilities of the target. Depending on what items are included within this allocation process and what values are placed on them, this will invariably result in a difference that has to be accounted for. Where the amounts allocated to the assets and liabilities are less than the overall cost, the difference is accounted for as goodwill. Over the years there have been different views on how goodwill should be accounted for, but the general method has been to deal with it as an asset. The question then has been: should it be amortised over its economic life (whatever that may be thought to be) or should it not be amortised at all, but subjected to some form of impairment test? Where the cost has been less than the values allocated to the identifiable assets and liabilities, then this has traditionally been treated as negative goodwill. The issue has then been whether and, if so, when such a credit should be taken to the income statement.

Having established the purchase method as the method to use in accounting for business combinations, the IASB and the FASB have published accounting standards dealing with the above issues, but in a recent joint project have looked to see how the method can be improved and give guidance on its application. As a result of that project, revised standards have been issued reflecting an approach whereby the various components of a business combination are measured at their acquisition-date fair values (albeit with a number of exceptions), rather than the previous cost-based approach, whereby the cost of the acquired entity is allocated to the assets acquired and liabilities (and contingent liabilities) assumed.

1.2   Development of an international standard

1.2.1   IAS 22 and related SIC Interpretations

Until a few years ago, the relevant international standard was IAS 22 – *Business Combinations*. The original standard was issued in November 1983, but had been revised and amended on a number of occasions since then.[3]

The SIC issued 3 interpretations relating to IAS 22: SIC-9 – *Business Combinations – Classification either as Acquisitions or Unitings of Interests*, SIC-22 – *Business Combinations – Subsequent Adjustment of Fair Values and Goodwill Initially Reported* – and SIC-28 – *Business Combinations – "Date of Exchange" and Fair Value of Equity Instruments*.

A summary of the requirements of these pronouncements can be found in section 1.2 of Chapter 6 of a previous edition of this book, *International GAAP 2005*.

1.2.2   IASB's project

In 2001 the IASB began a project to review IAS 22 as part of its initial agenda, with the objective of improving the quality of, and seeking international convergence on, the accounting for business combinations. The project on business combinations was originally considered to have two phases.

A   Phase I

As part of phase I, the IASB published in December 2002 ED 3 – *Business Combinations*, together with an exposure draft of proposed related amendments to IAS 38 – *Intangible Assets* – and IAS 36 – *Impairment of Assets*.[4] The Board's intention in developing an IFRS as part of the first phase of the project was not to reconsider all of the requirements in IAS 22. Instead, the Board's primary focus was on:

(a)   the method of accounting for business combinations;

(b)   the initial measurement of the identifiable assets acquired and liabilities and contingent liabilities assumed in a business combination;

(c)   the recognition of liabilities for terminating or reducing the activities of an acquiree;

(d)   the treatment of any excess of the acquirer's interest in the fair value of identifiable net assets acquired in a business combination over the cost of the combination; and

(e)   the accounting for goodwill and intangible assets acquired in a business combination.[5]

This phase of the IASB's project resulted in the Board issuing, simultaneously in March 2004, IFRS 3 – *Business Combinations* – and revised versions of IAS 36 and IAS 38.

B   Phase II

Phase II of the project was considered originally to have three aspects:[6]

- issues related to the application of the purchase method. This was to be conducted as a joint project with the FASB;

- the accounting for business combinations in which separate entities or operations of entities are brought together to form a joint venture, including possible applications for 'fresh start' accounting. 'Fresh-start' accounting derives from the view that a new entity emerges as a result of a business combination. Therefore, the assets and liabilities of each of the combining entities, including assets and liabilities not previously recognised, are recorded by the new entity at their fair values; and

- the accounting for business combinations excluded from phase I, i.e.:

  - business combination involving entities (or operations of entities) under common control;

  - business combinations involving two or more mutual entities (such as mutual insurance companies or mutual cooperative entities); and

- business combinations in which separate entities are brought together to form a reporting entity by contract only without the obtaining of an ownership interest (for example, business combinations in which separate entities are brought together by contract to form a dual listed company).

However, as the project has developed, what was regarded as being phase II is now being done as a number of separate phases.

Almost immediately after having issued IFRS 3, in April 2004, the IASB issued an exposure draft of proposed amendments to IFRS 3 to remove the scope exceptions for combinations by contract alone or involving mutual entities (see 2.1.3 B below). This was only an interim solution and proposed that in applying the purchase method of accounting, the acquirer measures the cost of such combinations in such a way that no goodwill would be recognised in the former type of combination and that goodwill would only be recognised in the latter situation to the extent that consideration was given by the acquirer in exchange for control of the acquiree. However, the accounting for such combinations has now been addressed as part of the joint project with the FASB in dealing with issues related to the application of the purchase method.[7]

This joint project involved a broad reconsideration of the requirements in IFRSs and US GAAP on applying the purchase method (which is now termed 'the acquisition method'), and resulted in the IASB publishing simultaneously in June 2005 a draft revised IFRS, which proposed to replace IFRS 3, together with exposure drafts proposing amendments to IAS 27 – *Consolidated and Separate Financial Statements* – and IAS 37 – *Provisions, Contingent Liabilities and Contingent Assets*.[8] The comment period for the exposure drafts ended in October 2005, and the Boards also held public round-table discussions on the IFRS 3/IAS 27 proposals in late October and early November of that year. In January 2006, the Boards began their redeliberations on the proposed requirements based on the comments received. These continued over the next 18 months or so, and during that time the IASB agreed to make some changes to the original proposals contained in the exposure drafts.

Eventually, in January 2008, the IASB issued revised versions of both IFRS 3 and IAS 27. In this Chapter, these revised versions of the standards are termed 'IFRS 3 (as revised in 2008)' and 'IAS 27 (as amended in 2008)' in order to distinguish them from the previous versions of the standards, which are termed 'IFRS 3 (2007)' and 'IAS 27 (2007)'.

IFRS 3 (as revised in 2008) is effective for business combinations where the acquisition date is on or after the beginning of annual periods starting on or after 1 July 2009, although earlier application is permitted. IAS 27 (as amended in 2008) has the same effective date.[9] For entities with calendar year ends they will not have to apply IFRS 3 (as revised in 2008) until their 31 December 2010 financial statements. Thus, at this time, many entities will still be applying the previous version of the standard, IFRS 3 (2007). The first entities that will have to apply IFRS 3 (as revised in 2008) will generally be those with 30 June 2010 year ends, although entities with shortened accounting periods may have to apply it earlier.

As a result of this delayed implementation date, this Chapter deals with the requirements of IFRS 3 (2007) and IFRS 3 (as revised in 2008) separately; IFRS 3 (2007) is principally dealt with at 2 below and IFRS 3 (as revised in 2008) at 3 below. Transitional arrangements relating to IFRS 3 (as revised in 2008) are dealt with at 4.2 below.

1.2.3 IFRS 3 (2007)

As mentioned above, the first phase of the IASB's project resulted in the Board issuing, simultaneously in March 2004, IFRS 3 (termed in this Chapter 'IFRS 3 (2007)') and revised versions of IAS 36 and IAS 38. The requirements of IFRS 3 (2007) are principally dealt with at 2 below. The requirements of IAS 36 are covered in Chapter 18, with those relating specifically to the impairment of goodwill dealt with at 3.4 of that Chapter. The specific requirements of IAS 38 relating to intangible assets acquired as part of a business combination accounted for under IFRS 3 (2007) are dealt with as part of the discussion of IFRS 3 (2007); the other requirements of IAS 38 are covered in Chapter 15.

The IASB's reasons for revising IAS 22, together with the main changes introduced by IFRS 3 (2007), are set out in the introduction to IFRS 3 (2007). A discussion of these reasons and changes can be found in section 1.2.3 of Chapter 7 of a previous edition of this book, *International GAAP 2008*.

1.2.4 IFRS 3 (as revised in 2008)

As mentioned at 1.2.2 B above, in January 2008, the IASB issued revised versions of both IFRS 3 and IAS 27. The requirements of IFRS 3 (as revised in 2008) are principally dealt with at 3 below. IFRS 3 (as revised in 2008) made some consequential amendments to other standards, including IAS 36 and IAS 38. The requirements of IAS 36 (as amended by this IFRS 3) are covered in Chapter 18, with those relating specifically to the impairment of goodwill dealt with at 3.4 of that Chapter. The specific requirements of IAS 38 (as amended by this IFRS 3) relating to intangible assets acquired as part of a business combination accounted for under IFRS 3 (as revised in 2008) are dealt with as part of the discussion of IFRS 3 (as revised in 2008); the other requirements of IAS 38 are covered in Chapter 15. The requirements of IAS 27 (as amended in 2008) are dealt with in Chapters 6, 7 and 8.

A Reasons for revising IFRS 3 (2007)

The IASB's reasons for revising IFRS 3 (2007) are set out in the introduction to IFRS 3 (as revised in 2008).

The IASB and the FASB had each decided to address the accounting for business combinations in two phases, but had deliberated the first phase separately. The standards that they issued as a result of their respective first phases were based on the conclusion that virtually all business combinations are acquisitions, and required the use of one method of accounting for business combinations – the acquisition method.[10] As mentioned at 1.2.2 A above, the IASB did not reconsider all of the requirements in IAS 22 when issuing IFRS 3 (2007), so there were a number of areas to be addressed in the second phase of the project.

The second phase of the project was to address the guidance for applying the acquisition method. The Boards decided that a significant improvement could be made to financial reporting if they had similar standards for accounting for business combinations. Thus, this phase was conducted as a joint effort with the objective of reaching the same conclusions.[11] Although this was achieved for most of the issues addressed in the project, they reached different conclusions on a few matters. Consequently, although the second phase has been concluded by the Boards issuing similar revised standards, differences remain. The substantive differences between IFRS 3 (as revised in 2008) and its US equivalent, SFAS 141R, are set out in IFRS 3 (as revised in 2008).[12]

B   *Main changes introduced by IFRS 3 (as revised in 2008)*

The current practice of accounting for business combinations under IFRS 3 (2007) is a cost-based approach, whereby the cost of the acquired entity is allocated to the assets acquired and liabilities (and contingent liabilities) assumed. In contrast, IFRS 3 (as revised in 2008) adopts an approach whereby the various components of a business combination are measured at their acquisition-date fair values (albeit with a number of exceptions including that relating to the measurement of any non-controlling interest). This represents a change from that originally proposed in the June 2005 exposure draft which was adopting an approach whereby the acquirer should recognise the fair value of the business acquired, regardless of the acquirer's percentage ownership, with any goodwill then being allocated between the acquirer and any non-controlling interest. The June 2005 exposure draft adopted the working principle that a business combination is an exchange of equal values and that the exchange should be measured based on the fair value of the consideration transferred or the fair value of the business (net assets) acquired, whichever is more reliably measurable.

The main changes introduced by IFRS 3 (as revised in 2008) are set out by the IASB as follows:[13]

- The scope was broadened to cover business combinations involving only mutual entities and business combinations achieved by contract alone;

- The definitions of a business and a business combination were amended and additional guidance was added for identifying when a group of assets constitutes a business;

- For each business combination, the acquirer must measure any non-controlling interest in the acquiree either at fair value or as the non-controlling interest's proportionate share of the acquiree's net identifiable assets. Previously, only the latter was permitted;

- The requirements for how the acquirer makes any classifications, designations or assessments for the identifiable assets acquired and liabilities assumed in a business combination were clarified;

- The period during which changes to deferred tax benefits acquired in a business combination can be adjusted against goodwill has been limited to the measurement period (through a consequential amendment to IAS 12 – *Income Taxes*);

- An acquirer is no longer permitted to recognise contingencies acquired in a business combination that do not meet the definition of a liability;

- Costs the acquirer incurs in connection with the business combination must be accounted for separately from the business combination, which usually means that they are recognised as expenses (rather than included in goodwill);

- Consideration transferred by the acquirer, including contingent consideration, must be measured and recognised at fair value at the acquisition date. Subsequent changes in the fair value of contingent consideration classified as liabilities are recognised in accordance with IAS 39 – *Financial Instruments: Recognition and Measurement*, IAS 37 or other IFRSs, as appropriate (rather than by adjusting goodwill). The disclosures required to be made in relation to contingent consideration were enhanced;

- Application guidance was added in relation to when the acquirer is obliged to replace the acquiree's share-based payment awards; measuring indemnification assets; rights sold previously that are reacquired in a business combination; operating leases; and valuation allowances related to financial assets such as receivables and loans;

- For business combinations achieved in stages, having the acquisition date as the single measurement date was extended to include the measurement of goodwill. An acquirer must remeasure any equity interest it holds in the acquiree immediately before achieving control at its acquisition-date fair value and recognise the resulting gain or loss, if any, in profit or loss.

It can be seen from the above that IFRS 3 (as revised in 2008) will change significantly the accounting for business combinations. The changes noted by the IASB principally relate to the accounting requirements, but there are a number of changes to the disclosures that are required to be made in relation to business combinations.

The main items for which new or specific information is now required by IFRS 3 (as revised in 2008) are listed below:

- contingent consideration (as mentioned above)[14]
- acquired receivables[15]
- transactions recognised separately from the business combination[16]
- acquisition-related costs[17]
- non-controlling interests[18]
- business combinations achieved in stages[19]
- revenue of the acquiree and of the combined entity[20]
- provisional amounts and measurement period adjustments[21]

One item of the previous disclosure requirements that has been deleted by IFRS 3 (as revised in 2008) is the disclosure of the acquiree's carrying amounts for each class of assets and liabilities immediately before the combination.[22]

1.2.5   Future developments

As discussed at 3.1.3 below, IFRS 3 (as revised in 2008) excludes from its scope the formation of a joint venture and a combination of entities or businesses under common control. In addition, proposals in the June 2005 exposure draft that preceded IFRS 3 (as revised in 2008) relating to contingencies and fair value guidance are not reflected in the final revised standard. Possible future developments on these issues are set out at 5.1 to 5.3 below.

Since the publication of the revised versions of IFRS 3 and IAS 27 a number of issues have arisen that have been raised with the IFRIC and the IASB. As a result, the IASB has decided to deal with some of the issues within the exposure draft of proposed *Improvements to IFRSs* issued in August 2009,[23] address some of the issues in other projects, but defer some of the other topics to the post-implementation review of the revised IFRSs to be conducted two years after their effective date.[24] To the extent that these relate to IFRS 3 (as revised in 2008), further discussion is set out at 5.4 to 5.6 below.

2   REQUIREMENTS OF THE ORIGINAL VERSION OF IFRS 3 'IFRS 3 (2007)'

2.1   Effective date, objective and scope

2.1.1   Effective date

IFRS 3 (2007) does not have an effective date in the sense that it is applicable for accounting periods commencing on or after a certain date. Instead, the standard applies to the accounting for business combinations for which the agreement date is on or after 31 March 2004 (the date of issue of the standard). It also applies to the accounting for:

(a)   goodwill arising from a business combination for which the agreement date is on or after 31 March 2004; or

(b)   any excess of the acquirer's interest in the net fair value of the acquiree's identifiable assets, liabilities and contingent liabilities over the cost of a business combination for which the agreement date is on or after 31 March 2004.[25]

As far as previously recognised goodwill, negative goodwill and intangibles in respect of business combinations for which the agreement date was before 31 March 2004 was concerned, the standard had transitional provisions that were to be applied from the beginning of the first annual period beginning on or after 31 March 2004.[26]

Entities, however, were permitted to apply the requirements of the standard to goodwill existing at or acquired after, and to business combinations occurring from, any date before the effective dates outlined above, provided certain conditions were met.[27]

These transitional arrangements for existing IFRS adopters are no longer relevant. A discussion of the arrangements can be found in section 4.1 of Chapter 7 of a previous edition of this book, *International GAAP 2007*.

2.1.2 Objective

IFRS 3 (2007) states that its objective 'is to specify the financial reporting by an entity when it undertakes a business combination. In particular, it specifies that all business combinations should be accounted for by applying the purchase method. Therefore, the acquirer recognises the acquiree's identifiable assets, liabilities and contingent liabilities at their fair values at the acquisition date, and also recognises goodwill, which is subsequently tested for impairment rather than amortised.'[28]

2.1.3 Scope

Entities are required to apply the provisions of IFRS 3 (2007) when accounting for all business combinations, except for those that are specifically excluded as set out at B below.[29] These types of business combination that are excluded are intended to be dealt with later as part of the IASB's ongoing project on business combinations.

A   Identifying a business combination

IFRS 3 (2007) defines a business combination as 'the bringing together of separate entities or businesses into one reporting entity'.[30] The standard then goes on to say that 'the result of nearly all business combinations is that one entity, the acquirer, obtains control of one or more other businesses, the acquiree'.[31]

For this purpose, IFRS 3 (2007) defines a 'business' as 'an integrated set of activities and assets conducted and managed for the purpose of providing:

(a)   a return to investors; or

(b)   lower costs or other economic benefits directly and proportionately to policyholders or participants'.[32]

It goes on to say that 'a business generally consists of inputs, processes applied to those inputs, and resulting outputs that are, or will be, used to generate revenues. If goodwill is present in a transferred set of activities and assets, the transferred set shall be presumed to be a business.'[33]

If an entity obtains control of one or more other entities that are not businesses, the bringing together of those entities is not a business combination.[34] Thus, it would seem that the requirements of IFRS 3 (2007) do not apply. However, the standard states that 'when an entity acquires a group of assets or net assets that does not constitute a business, it shall allocate the cost of the group between the individual identifiable assets and liabilities in the group based on their relative fair values at the acquisition date'.[35] Thus, existing book values or values in the acquisition agreement may not be appropriate, and no goodwill can be recognised in such an asset deal. Where an entity acquires a controlling interest in an entity that is not a business, but obtains less than 100% of the entity, after it has allocated its purchase consideration to the individual assets acquired, it notionally grosses up those assets and recognises the difference as minority interest (see Chapter 7 at 2.1.1).

In some situations, there may be difficulties in determining whether or not an acquisition of a group of assets constitutes a business, and judgement will be required to be exercised based on the particular circumstances.

IFRS 3 (2007) indicates that a business combination may be structured in a variety of ways for legal, taxation or other reasons. It may involve the purchase by an entity of the equity of another entity, the purchase of all the net assets of another entity, the assumption of the liabilities of another entity, or the purchase of some of the net assets of another entity that together form one or more businesses. It may be effected by the issue of equity instruments, the transfer of cash, cash equivalents or other assets, or a combination thereof. The transaction may be between the shareholders of the combining entities or between one entity and the shareholders of another entity. It may involve the establishment of a new entity to control the combining entities or net assets transferred, or the restructuring of one or more of the combining entities.[36] Whatever the legal structure, if it is a 'business combination' then the requirements of IFRS 3 (2007) apply (unless it is specifically excluded by the standard).

The standard notes that a business combination may result in a parent-subsidiary relationship in which the acquirer is the parent and the acquiree a subsidiary of the acquirer. In such circumstances, the acquirer applies IFRS 3 (2007) in its consolidated financial statements. It includes its interest in the acquiree in any separate financial statements it issues as an investment in a subsidiary under IAS 27 (2007) (see Chapter 8 at 2).[37]

As indicated above, a business combination may involve the purchase of the net assets, including any goodwill, of another entity rather than the purchase of the equity of the other entity. The standard notes that such a combination does not result in a parent-subsidiary relationship.[38] Nevertheless, the acquirer (even if it is a single entity) will account for such a business combination under the standard in its individual or separate financial statements and consequently in any consolidated financial statements.

The standard emphasises that, included within the definition of a business combination, and therefore the scope of IFRS 3 (2007), are business combinations in which one entity obtains control of another entity but for which the date of obtaining control (i.e. the acquisition date) does not coincide with the date or dates of acquiring an ownership interest (i.e. the date or dates of exchange). This situation may arise, for example, when an investee enters into share buy-back arrangements with some of its investors and, as a result, control of the investee changes.[39] Although not explicitly discussed in the standard, it would seem that the accounting for such a business combination would be done in a similar manner to that for business combinations achieved in stages (see 2.9 below).

B   Exclusions

The standard excludes the following types of business combinations from its scope:[40]

(a)   business combinations in which separate entities or businesses are brought together to form a joint venture;

(b)   business combinations involving entities or businesses under common control;

(c)   business combinations involving two or more mutual entities;

(d)   business combinations in which separate entities or businesses are brought together to form a reporting entity by contract alone without the obtaining of an ownership interest (for example, combinations in which separate entities are brought together by contract alone to form a dual listed corporation).

The exclusion in (b) above for business combinations involving entities or businesses under common control is discussed further in Chapter 10.

These exclusions were only intended to be a temporary measure while the IASB considered the issues relating to such combinations under the later phases of its business combinations project. As discussed at 3.1.3 below, combinations involving only mutual entities (e.g. mutual insurance companies, credit unions, cooperatives, etc.) and combinations in which separate entities are brought together by contract alone (e.g. dual listed corporations and stapled entity structures) are now within the scope of IFRS 3 (as revised in 2008).[41] However, the formation of a joint venture and combinations involving entities under common control are excluded from the scope of the revised standard.[42]

2.2   Purchase method of accounting

All business combinations (apart from those excluded from the scope of the standard) are accounted for by applying the purchase method.[43]

The purchase method views a business combination from the perspective of the combining entity that is identified as the acquirer. The acquirer purchases net assets and recognises the assets acquired and the liabilities and contingent liabilities assumed, including those not previously recognised by the acquiree. The measurement of the acquirer's assets and liabilities is not affected by the transaction, nor are any additional assets or liabilities of the acquirer recognised as a result of the transaction, because they are not the subjects of the transaction.[44] For example, if as a result of the business combination the acquirer is able to recognise a previously unrecognised tax asset of its own, this is not included as part of the accounting for the business combination and thus impact on the calculation of goodwill; the recognition of such an asset will be accounted for as income.

Application of the purchase method starts from the acquisition date, which is the date on which the acquirer effectively obtains control of the acquiree (see 2.3 below). Because control is the power to govern the financial and operating policies of an entity or business so as to obtain benefits from its activities, it is not necessary for a transaction to be closed or finalised at law before the acquirer obtains control. All pertinent facts and circumstances surrounding a business combination are considered in assessing when the acquirer has obtained control.[45]

No further guidance is given in IFRS 3 (2007) as to how to determine the acquisition date, but it is clearly a matter of fact. It cannot be artificially backdated or otherwise altered, for example, by the inclusion of terms in the agreement indicating that the acquisition is to be effective as of an earlier date, with the acquirer being entitled to profits arising after that date, even if the purchase price is based on the net asset position of the acquiree at that date.

The date control is obtained will be dependent on a number of factors, including whether the acquisition arises from a public offer or a private deal, is subject to approval by other parties, or is effected by the issue of shares.

For an acquisition by way of a public offer, the date of acquisition could be when the offer has become unconditional as a result of a sufficient number of acceptances being received or at the date that the offer closes. As noted at 2.1.1 above, IFRS 3 (2007) used the term 'agreement date' for the purposes of determining the date from which the standard was applicable, and in that context indicates that in the case of a hostile takeover, the earliest date this could be would be the date 'that a sufficient number of the acquiree's owners have accepted the acquirer's offer for the acquirer to obtain control of the acquiree'.[46] In a private deal, the date would generally be when an unconditional offer has been accepted by the vendors.

It can be seen from the above that one of the key factors is that the offer is 'unconditional'. Thus, where an offer is conditional on the approval of the acquiring entity's shareholders then until that has been received, it is unlikely that control will have been obtained. Where the offer is conditional upon receiving some form of regulatory approval, then it will depend on the nature of that approval. Where it is a substantive hurdle, such as obtaining the approval of a competition authority, it is unlikely that control could have been obtained prior to that approval. However, where the approval is merely a formality, or 'rubber-stamping' exercise, then this would not preclude control having been obtained at an earlier date.

Where the acquisition is effected by the issue of shares, then the date of control will generally be when the exchange of shares takes place.

However, as indicated above, whether control has been obtained by a certain date is a matter of fact, and all pertinent facts and circumstances surrounding a business combination need to be considered in assessing when the acquirer has obtained control.

Applying the purchase method involves the following steps:[47]

(a)   identifying an acquirer;

(b)   measuring the cost of the business combination; and

(c)   allocating, at the acquisition date, the cost of the business combination to the assets acquired and liabilities and contingent liabilities assumed.

These steps are discussed below.

2.3   Identifying the acquirer

Since the purchase method views a business combination from the acquirer's perspective, it assumes that one of the parties to the transaction can be identified as the acquirer.[48]

IFRS 3 (2007) therefore requires that an acquirer must be identified for all business combinations. The acquirer is the combining entity that obtains control of the other combining entities or businesses.[49]

Control is defined as 'the power to govern the financial and operating policies of an entity or business so as to obtain benefits from its activities'.[50] The standard states that 'a combining entity shall be presumed to have obtained control of another combining entity when it acquires more than one-half of that other entity's voting rights, unless it can be demonstrated that such ownership does not constitute control. Even if one of the combining entities does not acquire more than one-half of the voting rights of another combining entity, it might have obtained control of that other entity if, as a result of the combination, it obtains:

(a)   power over more than one-half of the voting rights of the other entity by virtue of an agreement with other investors; or

(b)   power to govern the financial and operating policies of the other entity under a statute or an agreement; or

(c)   power to appoint or remove the majority of the members of the board of directors or equivalent governing body of the other entity; or

(d)   power to cast the majority of votes at meetings of the board of directors or equivalent governing body of the other entity.'[51]

These provisions about 'control' are equivalent to those in IAS 27 (2007) with respect to the identification of subsidiaries for the purposes of consolidation. (See Chapter 6 at 2.1)

The standard notes that although sometimes it may be difficult to identify an acquirer, there are usually indications that one exists. For example:

(a)   if the fair value of one of the combining entities is significantly greater than that of the other combining entity, the entity with the greater fair value is likely to be the acquirer;

(b)   if the business combination is effected through an exchange of voting ordinary equity instruments for cash or other assets, the entity giving up cash or other assets is likely to be the acquirer; and

(c)   if the business combination results in the management of one of the combining entities being able to dominate the selection of the management team of the resulting combined entity, the entity whose management is able so to dominate is likely to be the acquirer.[52]

In a business combination effected through an exchange of equity interests, the standard takes the view that the entity that issues the equity interests is normally the acquirer. However, it emphasises that all pertinent facts and circumstances must be considered to determine which of the combining entities has the power to govern the financial and operating policies of the other entity (or entities) so as to obtain benefits from its (or their) activities. The standard recognises that in some business combinations, commonly referred to as reverse acquisitions, the acquirer is the entity whose equity interests have been acquired and the issuing entity is the acquiree. This might be the case when, for example, a private entity arranges to have itself 'acquired' by a smaller public entity as a means of obtaining a stock exchange listing[53] and, as part of the agreement, the directors of the public entity resign and are replaced with directors appointed by the private entity and its former owners.[54] Although legally the issuing public entity is regarded as the parent and the private entity is regarded as the subsidiary, the legal subsidiary is the acquirer if it has the power to govern the financial and operating policies of the legal parent so as to obtain benefits from its activities. Guidance on the accounting for reverse acquisitions is provided in Appendix B to IFRS 3 (2007) (see 2.10 below).[55]

Occasionally, a new entity is formed to issue equity instruments to effect a business combination between, for example, two other entities. In that situation, paragraph 22 of IFRS 3 (2007) requires that one of the combining entities that existed before the combination to be identified as the acquirer on the basis of the evidence available;[56] the new entity formed to effect the combination cannot be the acquirer.[57] In such a transaction, the combination between the new entity and the identified acquirer is effectively the same as if a new entity had been inserted above an existing entity. As discussed in Chapter 10 at 4.2, we believe that such a transaction should be accounted for under the pooling of interests method.

An example of such a business combination is illustrated in the 2005 financial statements of Group 4 Securicor as seen below.

Extract 9.1: Group 4 Securicor plc (2005)

Notes to the consolidated financial statements [extract]

1   General information [extract]

Group 4 Securicor plc is a company incorporated in the United Kingdom under the Companies Act 1985. As a result of a Scheme of Arrangement of Securicor plc, which became effective on 19 July 2004, Group 4 Securicor plc became the ultimate holding company of the Securicor plc group of companies and, on the same date, and as a result of a recommended offer for its shares, acquired Group 4 A/S, the holding company of the former security businesses of Group 4 Falck A/S. On the basis that the transaction was effected by using a new parent, Group 4 A/S was identified as the acquirer. The comparative results for the year to 31 December 2004 are therefore those of the full year of trading of the security businesses of the former Group 4 Falck A/S and the trading of the businesses of Securicor plc for the period from 20 July 2004 to 31 December 2004.

Similarly, when a business combination involves more than two combining entities, one of the combining entities that existed before the combination is identified as the acquirer on the basis of the evidence available. Determining the acquirer in such cases shall include a consideration of, amongst other things, which of the combining entities initiated the combination and whether the assets or revenues of one of the combining entities significantly exceed those of the others.[58]

An issue considered by IFRIC was whether a new entity formed to effect a business combination in which it pays cash as consideration for the business acquired could be identified as the acquirer. In March 2006, IFRIC decided that it is clear that paragraph 22 of IFRS 3 (2007) does not prohibit a newly formed entity that pays cash to effect a business combination from being identified as the acquirer; accordingly, it would not expect diversity in practice and did not take this item onto its agenda.[59]

One situation where we believe this would be appropriate is where the newly formed entity (hereafter referred to as 'Newco') is established and used on behalf of a group of investors or another entity to acquire a controlling interest in a 'target entity' in an arm's length transaction.

Example 9.1:   Business combination effected by a Newco for cash consideration (1)

Entity A intends to acquire the voting shares (and therefore obtain control) of Target Entity. Entity A incorporates Newco and uses this entity to effect the business combination. Entity A provides a loan at commercial interest rates to Newco. The loan funds are used by Newco to acquire 100% of the voting shares of Target Entity in an arm's length transaction.

The group structure post-transaction is as follows:

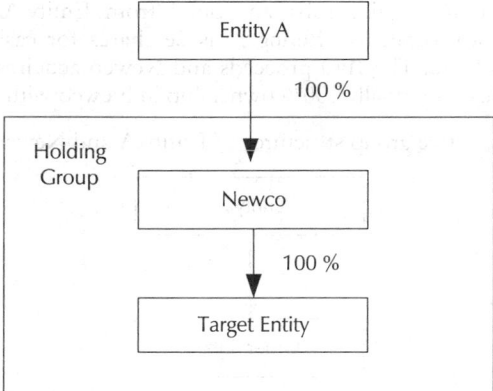

Under its local regulations, Newco is required to prepare IFRS-compliant consolidated financial statements for the Holding Group (the reporting entity). (In most situations like this, Newco would be exempt from preparing consolidated financial statements – see Chapter 6 at 3.1.)

As indicated above, under IFRS 3 (2007), the acquirer is 'the combining entity that obtains control of the other combining entities or businesses'. Whenever a new entity is formed to effect a business combination other than through the issue of shares, it is appropriate to consider that Newco as being an extension of one of the transacting parties. Where the Newco is considered to be an extension of the transacting party (or parties) that ultimately gain control of the other combining entities, the Newco would be identified as the acquirer.

In this situation, Entity A has obtained control of Target Entity in an arm's length transaction, using Newco to effect the acquisition. The transaction has resulted in a change in control of Target Entity and Newco is in effect an extension of Entity A acting at its direction to obtain control for Entity A. Accordingly, Newco would be identified as the acquirer at the Holding Group level.

If, rather than Entity A establishing Newco, a group of investors had established it as the acquiring vehicle through which they obtained control of Target Entity then again it would be appropriate for Newco to be regarded as the acquirer since it is an extension of the group of investors.

Another situation where we believe it is appropriate for a Newco to be identified as the acquirer is illustrated below.

Example 9.2:   Business combination effected by a Newco for cash consideration (2)

Entity A proposes to spin-off two of its existing businesses (currently housed in two separate entities, Sub1 and Sub2) as part of an initial public offering (IPO). The existing group structure is as follows:

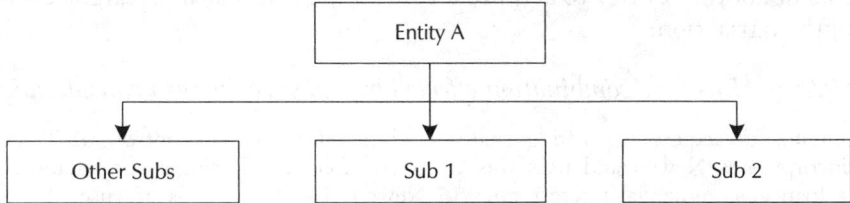

To facilitate the spin-off, Entity A incorporates a new company (Newco) with nominal equity and appoints independent directors to the Board of Newco.

Newco signs an agreement to acquire Sub1 and Sub2 from Entity A conditional on the IPO proceeding. Newco issues a prospectus offering to issue shares for cash to provide Newco with funds to acquire Sub1 and Sub2. The IPO proceeds and Newco acquires Sub1 and Sub2 for cash. Entity A's nominal equity leaves virtually 100% ownership in Newco with the new investors.

Following the IPO, the respective group structures of Entity A and Newco appear as follows:

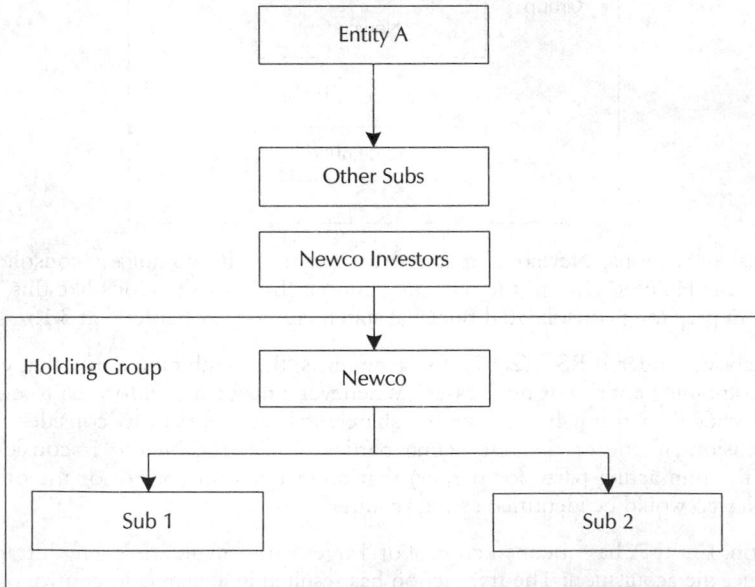

In this case, we believe it is appropriate that Newco should be identified as the acquirer. The Newco investors have obtained control and virtually 100% ownership of Sub1 and Sub2 in an arm's length transaction, using Newco to effect the acquisition. The transaction has resulted in a change in control of Sub1 and Sub2 (i.e. Entity A losing control and Newco investors, via Newco, obtaining control). Newco is in effect an extension of the Newco investors since:

- the acquisition of Sub1 and Sub2 was conditional on the IPO proceeding so that the IPO is an integral part of the transaction as a whole evidencing that Entity A did not have control of the transaction/entities; and

- there being a substantial change in the ownership of Sub1 and Sub2 by virtue of the IPO (i.e. Entity A only retains a negligible ownership interest in Newco).

Accordingly, Newco should be identified as the acquirer at the Holding Group level.

Whether a Newco formed to facilitate an IPO is capable of being identified as an acquirer depends on the facts and circumstances and ultimately requires judgement. Changes to the fact pattern could result in a different assessment. For example, where Entity A incorporates Newco and arranges for it to acquire Sub1 and Sub2 prior to the IPO proceeding (in other words, remove the conditionality element), it is likely that Newco would be viewed as an extension of Entity A or possibly an extension of Sub1 or Sub2. This is because the IPO and the reorganisation may not be seen as being part of the one integral transaction, and therefore the transaction would be a business combination involving entities under common control (see Chapter 10 at 3.1).

2.4 Cost of a business combination

Having identified the acquirer, the next step is for the acquirer to measure the cost of the business combination. IFRS 3 (2007) requires this to be the aggregate of:

(a) the fair values, at the date of exchange, of assets given, liabilities incurred or assumed, and equity instruments issued by the acquirer, in exchange for control of the acquiree; plus

(b) any costs directly attributable to the business combination.[60]

These requirements are essentially the same as those in IAS 22 and SIC-28, without reconsideration, but the IASB stated that it would be reconsidering these requirements as part of the second phase of its project.[61] As a result, the accounting treatment under IFRS 3 (as revised in 2008) for many of the items discussed below is significantly different under the revised standard (see 3 below).

2.4.1 Date of exchange

When a business combination is achieved in a single exchange transaction, the date of exchange coincides with the acquisition date (see 2.2 above). However, a business combination may involve more than one exchange transaction, for example when it is achieved in stages by successive share purchases. When this occurs:

(a) the cost of the combination is the aggregate cost of the individual transactions; and

(b) the date of exchange is the date of each exchange transaction (i.e. the date that each individual investment is recognised in the financial statements of the acquirer), whereas the acquisition date is the date on which the acquirer obtains control of the acquiree.[62]

The accounting for business combinations achieved in stages ('step acquisitions') is discussed at 2.9 below.

Accounting for step acquisitions is an area where the treatment under IFRS 3 (as revised in 2008) (see 3.10 below) is significantly different from that described at 2.9 below.

2.4.2 Assets given and liabilities incurred or assumed by the acquirer

Assets given and liabilities incurred or assumed by the acquirer in exchange for control of the acquiree are required by paragraph 24 of the standard to be measured at their fair values at the date of exchange. Fair value is defined as 'the amount for which an asset could be exchanged, or a liability settled, between knowledgeable, willing parties in an arm's length transaction'.[63] The standard gives no guidance as to how such fair values might be arrived at, other than to say that when settlement of all or any part of the cost of a business combination is deferred, the fair value of that deferred component is determined by discounting the amounts payable to their present value at the date of exchange, taking into account any premium or discount likely to be incurred in settlement.[64] No guidance is given as to what an appropriate discount rate would be. However, IAS 39 would suggest using a rate currently charged by others for similar debt instruments (i.e. similar remaining maturity, cash flow pattern, currency, credit risk, collateral and interest basis).[65] Where the assets given as consideration or the liabilities incurred or assumed by the acquirer are financial assets or financial liabilities under IAS 39, then it would seem appropriate that the guidance in determining the fair values of such financial instruments should be followed (see Chapter 32 at 4).

An example of a company giving an investment in another entity as part of the consideration for the acquisition of a business is Reuters as shown in the following extract.

Extract 9.2: Reuters Group plc (2005)

Notes to the financial statements [extract]

36   Acquisitions [extract]

On 3 June 2005, Reuters purchased the trade and assets of Telerate and 100% of the share capital of three of Telerate's subsidiaries in exchange for cash and the Group's 14% holding in Savvis convertible preference shares. In addition, on 6 June 2005, Reuters carried out a merger with Quick Telerate, the distributor of Telerate's products in Japan. All of these purchases have been accounted for as acquisitions. As a result of this acquisition, Reuters disposed of its 4.85% holding in Quick Corporation, the parent of Quick Telerate. The profit on disposal is detailed within note 37.

	Book value £m	Fair value adjustments £m	Provisional fair value £m
Non-current assets:			
Intangible assets	7	49	56
Property, plant and equipment	3	(1)	2
Current assets:			
Cash and cash equivalents	16	–	16
Other current assets	19	–	19
Current liabilities	(31)	1	(30)
Non-current liabilities	(3)	(2)	(5)
Net assets acquired	11	47	58
Goodwill			72
Total consideration			130

Consideration satisfied by:	
Cash (including £8 million of transaction fees)	99
Fair value of investment in Savvis convertible preference shares	31
Total consideration	**130**

The fair value adjustments in respect of intangible assets are due to the recognition of £2 million is respect of trademarks and £53 million in respect of customer relationships, which have been independently valued, partly offset by the write-off of £6 million of intangibles that were recorded on Telerate's balance sheet prior to the acquisition. Goodwill represents the value of synergies arising from the acquisition and the acquiree's assembled work force. The adjustments to property, plant and equipment, current assets, current liabilities and non-current liabilities relate to valuation adjustments and are provisional, based on management's best estimates. The fair values adjustments relating to the Telerate acquisition will be finalised in the 2006 financial statements.

The outflow of cash and cash equivalents on the acquisition can be calculated as follows:

	£m
Cash consideration	99
Cash acquired	(16)
Total outflow of cash and cash equivalents	**83**

From the date of acquisition to 31 December 2005, the acquisition contributed £74 million to turnover, £5 million loss before interest and amortisation of intangibles and £5 million loss before amortisation, but after interest.

If the acquisitions had been made at the beginning of the financial year, Telerate would have contributed £133 million to revenue and incurred a £21 million loss. This information takes into account the amortisation of acquired intangible assets, together with related income tax effects and should not be viewed as indicative of the results of operations that would have occurred if the acquisitions had been made at the beginning of the year.

In business combinations where some of the consideration is deferred, it may be that this will not be settled by cash, but by shares. IFRS 3 (2007) makes no explicit reference to such a situation, and IFRS 2 – *Share-based Payment* – explicitly scopes out from its provisions 'transactions in which an entity acquires goods as part of the net assets acquired in a business combination to which IFRS 3' applies. It also goes on to say that 'equity instruments issued in a business combination in exchange for control of the acquiree are not within the scope of' IFRS 2.[66] However, the contractual obligation will be a financial instrument within the scope of IAS 32 – *Financial Instruments: Presentation*. In relation to the acquirer in a business combination, IAS 32 (prior to its amendment by IFRS 3 (as revised in 2008)) only scoped out of its provisions 'contracts for contingent consideration' (see 2.4.5 below).[67]

Accordingly, the determination of the fair value of deferred consideration that is to be settled by shares will depend on whether it is an equity instrument or a financial liability under IAS 32 (see Chapter 31). In many situations, the consideration to be given will be fixed as a monetary amount, with the number of shares to be issued varying based on the share price at the date of their ultimate issue. In that case, the deferred consideration is a financial liability, and should be valued as outlined above, i.e. by discounting the amounts payable to their present value at the date of exchange. When the liability is ultimately settled by the issue of the shares, then the entity will derecognise the financial liability and credit equity with the then carrying amount of the liability. On the other hand, where the consideration will be settled by a fixed number of shares, then it will qualify as an equity instrument under IAS 32. In that case, the fair value of such deferred consideration should be based on the guidance in 2.4.3 below, rather than outlined above for deferred consideration. However, in this situation the fair value of the 'equity instrument' at the date of exchange would need to take into account, for example, an allowance for any estimated dividends on the shares that will not be payable during the deferral period. The amount attributed should be included within equity, possibly under a caption of 'shares to be issued'.

The cost of a business combination includes liabilities incurred or assumed by the acquirer in exchange for control of the acquiree. IFRS 3 (2007) states explicitly that future losses or other costs expected to be incurred as a result of a combination are not liabilities incurred or assumed by the acquirer in exchange for control of the acquiree, and are not, therefore, included as part of the cost of the combination.[68] The very restricted circumstances in which future losses or other costs may be recognised as part of the liabilities of the acquired entity are described at 2.5.1 below.

2.4.3   Equity instruments issued by the acquirer

Where equity instruments issued by the acquirer are given as consideration, IFRS 3 (2007) states that the published price at the date of exchange of a quoted equity instrument provides the best evidence of the instrument's fair value and is used, except in rare circumstances.[69] This value should be used even if a different share price was used in agreeing the terms of the business combination. Although IFRS 3 (2007) refers to the 'published price' it does not explicitly say whether this should be the 'bid' price, 'offer' price or 'mid' price at that date. However, as noted below, it does refer to the guidance on determining the fair value of equity instruments (held as investments) set out in IAS 39 which would indicate that the 'bid' price should be used. Other evidence and valuation methods are considered only in the rare circumstances when the acquirer can demonstrate that the published price at the date of exchange is an unreliable indicator of fair value, and that the other evidence and valuation methods provide a more reliable measure of the equity instrument's fair value. The standard takes the view that the published price at the date of exchange is an unreliable indicator only when it has been affected by the thinness of the market.[70] The fact that the price may have been affected by an undue price fluctuation is not considered by the IASB to be a justification for not using the published price at the date of exchange.[71] Also, the Basis for Conclusions indicates that 'estimates of premiums for large, and discounts for small, blocks of equity instruments issued in comparison to that exchanged in observable transactions are not considered'.[72]

If the published price at the date of exchange is an unreliable indicator or if a published price does not exist for equity instruments issued by the acquirer, the standard states that the fair value of those instruments could, for example, be estimated by reference to their proportional interest in the fair value of the acquirer or by reference to the proportional interest in the fair value of the acquiree obtained, whichever is the more clearly evident. The fair value at the date of exchange of monetary assets given to equity holders of the acquiree as an alternative to equity instruments may also provide evidence of the total fair value given by the acquirer in exchange for control of the acquiree. In any event, the standard requires that all aspects of the combination, including significant factors influencing the negotiations, are to be considered. Reference is also made to the further guidance on determining the fair value of equity instruments (held as investments) set out in IAS 39 (see Chapter 32 at 4).[73]

2.4.4 Costs directly attributable to the business combination

The cost of a business combination includes any costs directly attributable to the combination, such as professional fees paid to accountants, legal advisers, valuers and other consultants to effect the combination. General administrative costs, including the costs of maintaining an acquisitions department, and other costs that cannot be directly attributed to the particular combination being accounted for are not included in the cost of the combination: they are recognised as an expense when incurred.[74] Although not explicitly stated in IFRS 3 (2007), it would appear that it is only incremental costs that should be included.

It may be that an entity engages another party to investigate or assist in identifying a potential target. Whether any fee payable to such a party can be included as part of the cost of a business combination will depend on whether the work performed can be regarded as directly attributable to that particular business combination. Where the fee is payable only if the combination takes place then it should be included as part of the cost.

In some jurisdictions, tax relief may be given in respect of certain of the costs included as part of the cost of a business combination. In our view, any related taxes should not be netted against the costs in line with the 'no offsetting' principle in IAS 1 – *Presentation of Financial Statements*.[75] The implications for deferred taxation are discussed in Chapter 26 at 6.2.4.

IFRS 3 (2007) requires the costs of arranging and issuing financial liabilities to be an integral part of the liability issue transaction, even when the liabilities are issued to effect a business combination, rather than costs directly attributable to the combination. Therefore, entities shall not include such costs in the cost of a business combination. In accordance with IAS 39, such costs are to be included in the initial measurement of the liability (see Chapter 32 at 2.3).[76]

Similarly, the costs of issuing equity instruments are an integral part of the equity issue transaction, even when the equity instruments are issued to effect a business combination, rather than costs directly attributable to the combination. Therefore, entities shall not include such costs in the cost of a business combination. In accordance with IAS 32, such costs reduce the proceeds from the equity issue.[77] While these requirements will affect the amount at which the entity's liabilities and equity are recorded in the consolidated financial statements, they do not affect the measurement of goodwill in the business combination.

When professional advisors provide advice on all aspects of the business combination, including the arranging and issuing of financial liabilities and/or issuing equity instruments, it will be necessary for some allocation of the fees payable to be made, possibly by obtaining a breakdown from the relevant advisor.

It may be that an entity at the end of the reporting period is in the process of acquiring another business and has incurred costs that are considered to be directly attributable to that expected business combination. At that date, the entity has not yet obtained control over the business. In this situation how should the costs be accounted for? One view would be that the costs have to be expensed since at the end of the reporting period there has been no business combination. However, we believe that since directly attributable costs are to be included in the cost of a business combination, then the costs should be carried forward as an asset from the date that is considered probable that the business combination will be completed. Any costs incurred prior to the date that it is considered probable that the business combination will be completed should be expensed, and remain written off regardless of whether the acquisition takes place; they cannot be reinstated and capitalised at a later date. In the subsequent period when the business combination is completed, the costs carried forward will be reclassified as part of the cost of the business combination (and therefore into goodwill). If in the subsequent period it is no longer considered probable that the business combination will be completed, then the costs initially recognised as an asset will be expensed in the income statement.

Accounting for the costs directly attributable to a business combination is an area where the treatment under IFRS 3 (as revised in 2008) is significantly different from that described above. As discussed at 3.8.3 below, the revised standard requires that for business combinations to be accounted for under IFRS 3 (as revised in 2008), with the exception of the costs of registering and issuing debt and securities that continue to be recognised in accordance with IAS 32 and IAS 39 as described above, all acquisition-related costs are to be accounted for as expenses in the periods in which the costs are incurred and the related services are received.[78] This does raise the issue whether an entity in its final year of applying IFRS 3 (2007) can carry forward, at the end of the reporting period, the directly attributable costs relating to a probable business combination that will be accounted for under IFRS 3 (as revised in 2008). This is an issue that has been considered by the IFRIC. At its meeting in May 2009, and subsequently confirmed at its meeting in July 2009, the IFRIC noted that more than one interpretation of how the requirements of the two IFRSs interact is possible. Accordingly, the IFRIC concluded that an entity should disclose its accounting policy for such costs and the amount recognised in the financial statements. Because this is a transitional issue that will not arise for accounting periods beginning on after 1 July 2009, the IFRIC decided not to add the issue to its agenda.[79] Therefore an entity in this situation can either expense the costs or carry such costs forward as an asset, but should disclose the accounting policy adopted. Where the latter approach is adopted, this raises a further issue as to how they should be dealt with in the following year when IFRS 3 (as revised in 2008) has to be applied. This is discussed further at 4.2 3 below.

2.4.5 Adjustments to the cost of a business combination contingent on future events ('Contingent consideration')

IFRS 3 (2007) recognises that the terms of a business combination agreement may provide for an adjustment to the cost of the combination contingent on future events, such as a specified level of profit being maintained or achieved in future periods, or on the market price of the instruments issued being maintained.[80]

When a business combination agreement provides for an adjustment to the cost of the business combination contingent on future events, IFRS 3 (2007) requires the acquirer to include the amount of the adjustment in the cost of the combination at the acquisition date if the adjustment is probable and can be measured reliably.[81] If the future events do not occur or the estimate needs to be revised, the cost of the business combination is to be adjusted accordingly,[82] (unless the payment to the seller is compensation for a reduction in value of consideration received as discussed below).

The standard states that 'it is usually possible to estimate the amount of any such adjustment at the time of initially accounting for the combination without impairing the reliability of the information, even though some uncertainty exists'.[83] This is more likely to be the case in those situations where the contingent consideration is based on the acquiree maintaining a level of profits which it is currently earning (either for a particular period or as an average over a set period) or achieving profits which it is currently budgeting.

However, when a business combination agreement provides for such an adjustment, that adjustment is not included in the cost of the combination at the time of initially accounting for the combination if it either is not probable or cannot be measured reliably. If that adjustment subsequently becomes probable and can be measured reliably, the additional consideration shall be treated as an adjustment to the cost of the combination.[84]

Any subsequent adjustments in respect of such contingent consideration will consequently be reflected in the carrying amount of goodwill. However, if an impairment loss has already been recognised in respect of the goodwill (see Chapter 18 at 3.4), this is likely to require a further impairment loss to be recognised.

Where contingent consideration for a business combination does become probable after the date of acquisition, what amount should be recognised as the adjustment to the cost of acquisition and how should the adjustment be reflected in the financial statements?

Example 9.3:   Contingent consideration subsequently recognised

Entity A acquires Entity B on 31 December 2008 where consideration of $8 million is contingent on meeting a profit target by 31 December 2011.

At the date of acquisition it is not considered probable that the acquiree will meet the profit target. Accordingly, no amount is recognised as part of the cost of the acquisition in the financial statements for 31 December 2008. However, at 31 December 2009 it is considered probable that Entity B will meet the profit target.

Assuming a discount rate of 8% as at the date of acquisition (31 December 2008) and a discount rate of 7% as at the date of probability of meeting conditions (31 December 2009) the relevant present values are as follows:

	PV at 8%	PV at 7%
	$	$
31 December 2008	6,350,658	6,530,383
Interest for 2009	508,053	457,127
31 December 2009	6,858,711	6,987,510
Interest for 2010	548,696	489,126
31 December 2010	7,407,407	7,476,636
Interest for 2011	592,593	523,364
31 December 2011	8,000,000	8,000,000

What amount should be recognised as the adjustment to the cost of the combination at 31 December 2009 and how should it be reflected in the financial statements?

One view is that the adjustment should be calculated retrospectively, as if it had occurred as at the date of acquisition. Accordingly, the cost of the investment and goodwill would be adjusted by $6,350,658 (being the present value at the date of acquisition), with interest charged since the date of acquisition of $508,053.

However, we do not consider this view appropriate. The adjustment is due to a change in probability which is generally considered to be a change in estimate. As discussed in Chapter 3 at 4.5, changes in estimates are recognised prospectively from the date of change. Therefore at the date that the contingent event becomes probable it should be recognised as a change in estimate and measured at that date, taking into account the period in which the expected payment will be made. It is, therefore, discounted at the rate determined at the date that the contingent consideration is recognised to reflect the fair value of the consideration expected to be given. Accordingly, an adjustment of $6,987,510 to the purchase price and therefore goodwill is recognised at 31 December 2009. The unwinding of the discount will be reflected in the income statement in 2010 and 2011. However, the resulting liability should continue to be reassessed at the end of each reporting period thereafter for changes in estimated cash flows, including changes in discount rates, and any necessary adjustment made to the cost of the combination (and therefore goodwill).

Paragraph 35 of IFRS 3 (2007) also recognises that in some circumstances, the acquirer may be required to make a subsequent payment to the seller as compensation for a reduction in the value of the assets given, equity instruments issued or liabilities incurred or assumed by the acquirer in exchange for control of the acquiree. For example, the acquirer may guarantee the market price of equity or debt instruments issued as part of the cost of the business combination and is required to issue additional equity or debt instruments to restore the originally determined cost. In such cases, no increase in the cost of the business combination is recognised. In the case of equity instruments, the fair value of the additional payment is offset by an equal reduction in the value attributed to the instruments initially issued.[85] Thus, it would appear that any increase reflected in equity for the extra equity instruments issued is offset by a corresponding debit to equity. In the case of debt instruments, the additional payment is regarded as a reduction in the premium or an increase in the discount on the initial issue.[86] The extra payment will be taken to the income statement as part of an increased interest expense over the period of the debt instrument.

A   Distinguishing 'contingent consideration' from other arrangements

The requirements of IFRS 3 (2007) discussed above set out the accounting for 'contingent consideration' under the standard but the term is not defined. It is important to be able to identify those arrangements that represent contingent consideration and those that do not as contingent consideration generally results in some form of adjustment to the accounting for a business combination.

In our view, an arrangement that provides for additional payments to be made to the vendors of an acquiree should be accounted for as contingent consideration if the payment:

(a)   is made as consideration for the acquisition of a controlling interest in the acquiree (based on the substance of the arrangement); *and*

(b)   is contingent on future events that relate to either:

    (i)   the value of the acquiree (for example, an acquirer makes an additional cash payment if the acquiree achieves a profit target); *or*

    (ii)   the value of the purchase consideration (specifically in terms of the acquirer compensating the vendor for a reduction in the value of the consideration previously given, for example, an acquirer issues additional shares in order to compensate for a loss in value of the shares that were issued at the acquisition date).

These criteria are discussed below. However, as indicated earlier, accounting for contingencies of type (i) and (ii) is quite different. Contingencies that relate to the value of the acquiree result in an adjustment to the cost of the combination (and goodwill). However, where the contingency relates to the value of the purchase consideration, the fair value of the additional amount paid is offset by an equal reduction in the value of that initial consideration. Accordingly, there is no change in the total cost of the combination (nor to goodwill).

It is necessary to consider the substance of the arrangement to determine whether additional payments are made as consideration of the acquisition of a controlling interest in the acquiree (criterion (a) above). Where a vendor has a continuing relationship with the acquirer (for example, an on-going customer or supplier relationship) it is necessary to determine in what capacity payments are made to the vendor. As there is no specific guidance, the following factors may be considered in evaluating the substance of the arrangement:

•   whether the additional payments are linked to the on-going relationship;

•   what are the reasons for the contingent payments; and

•   the nature of the formula for determining the contingent payments.

A particular example of this type of situation is in an acquisition of an owner-managed business where the vendors continue to be key employees of the acquiree subsequent to the acquisition. This is discussed further at B below.

Criterion (b) above involves a consideration of whether the contingency relates to either the value of the acquiree or the value of the purchase consideration. Whilst contingent consideration is not defined in IFRS 3 (2007), the examples given in IFRS 3 (2007) are of contingencies relating to either the value of the business acquired or the value of the purchase consideration (the latter in terms of the acquirer being obliged to make additional payments to compensate the vendor for a reduction in the value of the consideration given). If it is not clear what the contingency relates to, it will be necessary to consider its nature carefully in order to determine whether it should be accounted for as contingent consideration or separately from the business combination.

I   *Examples of 'contingent consideration' relating to the value of the acquiree*

Arrangements that provide for additional payments to be made to the vendors of an acquiree that are contingent on future events relating to the value of the acquiree, and thus will result in adjustments to the cost of the business combination, can take a number of forms. Examples would include:

- an additional payment of €1m if the acquiree's profit in the year after acquisition exceeds €2m;
- an additional payment of $1m if a drug currently under development receives regulatory approval at a later date; and
- an additional payment of X% of actual EBITDA of the acquiree in the year after acquisition.

The first example of an 'earn-out' clause – whereby the acquirer agrees to pay additional amounts if the future earnings of the acquiree exceed specified amounts – is a typical example of contingent consideration relating to the value of the acquiree. The second example is where the contingency relates to a key business-related milestone that will have an impact on the value of the acquiree.

In both of these examples, there is uncertainty linked to a specific event as to whether an additional payment will be made (profit exceeding X or drug approval). In the third case, which also relates to the value of the acquiree, there will be an additional payment (on the assumption that a negative EBITDA is highly unlikely for that business) but there is uncertainty as to how much the payment will be.

In our view, IFRS 3 (2007) requires an adjustment to the cost of the business combination in all of these situations. 'Future events' should include events that affect the amount of the payment and not just those that affect whether a specified payment is required or not. Thus, any consideration for a business combination where the amount or the timing is unknown with certainty is contingent consideration.

II   Examples of 'contingent consideration' relating to the value of the purchase
           consideration

Arrangements that represent contingent consideration relating to the value of the
purchase consideration are illustrated below.

Example 9.4:   Acquirer guarantees the value of shares issued as consideration

Acquirer, a listed entity, acquires 100% of the issued shares of Target. The consideration is
10,000 shares of Acquirer that have a fair value of £100 each (i.e. a total value of £1m) at the date of
acquisition. Under the terms of the purchase agreement, Acquirer guarantees that the value of the
shares will not be less than £100 each one year after the acquisition date. If the share price is below
£100 at that time, Acquirer will issue sufficient additional shares so that the total value of all shares
given is £1m.

The guarantee satisfies the criteria for classification as contingent consideration. It is issued in
exchange for the ownership of Target and does not relate to any other arrangement with the
vendor. It relates specifically to the value of the 10,000 shares issued as consideration. Although the
guarantee meets the definition of a financial liability it is also contingent consideration and is,
therefore, accounted for under IFRS 3 (2007) rather than IAS 39.

In this case, no increase in the cost of the business combination is recognised – the contingent
payment is effectively regarded as an adjustment to the original consideration. So, if Acquirer's share
price has fallen to £80 one year after the acquisition date, then the 10,000 shares issued are now
only worth £800,000. Under the agreement, Acquirer is obliged to issue a further 2,500 shares
(worth £200,000 at the current price) so that a total of 12,500 shares have been issued that are now
worth £1m. The value of the new shares is offset by an equal reduction in the value attributed to the
shares originally issued i.e. the first 10,000 shares are now regarded as having been issued at a price
of £80, being £800,000. The total cost of the combination remains £1m.

Example 9.5:   Acquirer issues a put option on its shares that will be settled net in cash

Acquirer acquires 100% of the issued shares of Target. The consideration consists of 10,000 shares
of the Acquirer that have a fair value of £100 each (i.e. a total value of £1m) at the date of
acquisition. In addition, as part of the business combination agreement, Acquirer issues to the
vendor a put option on 10,000 of its shares that will be settled net in cash. That is, Acquirer gives
the vendor the right to receive and Acquirer the obligation to pay the shortfall of the fair value of
the 10,000 Acquirer's shares at the exercise date compared to a fixed amount (the 'exercise price')
representing the value of the shares at the date of the business combination, if vendor exercises that
right. The cash settled put option can be exercised one year after the acquisition date. Any payments
made by Acquirer under the put option are contingent on the vendor exercising its right under the
put option.

The put option satisfies the criteria for classification as contingent consideration. It is issued as part
of the consideration for a controlling interest in Target and does not relate to any other arrangement
with the vendor. It relates specifically to the value of the 10,000 shares issued as consideration.
Although the put option meets the definition of a financial liability it is also contingent
consideration and is, therefore, accounted for under IFRS 3 (2007) rather than IAS 39.

The contingent payment is effectively regarded as an adjustment to the original consideration and
no increase in the cost of the business combination is recognised. If Acquirer's share price has fallen
to £80 then the 10,000 shares issued are now worth £800,000. Vendor exercises the rights under the
put options and Acquirer is obliged to pay £200,000. The original consideration in shares is now
considered to have been only £800,000 rather than £1m. This is corrected by debiting equity and
crediting liability at £200,000. The total cost of the combination remains £1m.

III   Examples of arrangements that are not 'contingent consideration'

The following examples illustrate arrangements where the additional payments that may be made to the vendors under the business combination agreement should not be accounted for as 'contingent consideration' under IFRS 3 (2007).

Example 9.6:   *Business combination agreement commits acquirer to undertake capital expenditure*

Target is a State-owned organisation that is in the process of being privatised. Acquirer acquires 100% of the issued shares of Target. The privatisation agreement with the State commits Acquirer to undertake capital expenditure in connection with the activities of Target; otherwise, Acquirer has to pay a penalty to the state equivalent to the unfulfilled capital expenditure. However, Acquirer expects to carry out the capital expenditure and the obligation is not onerous.

The penalty arrangement does not satisfy the criteria for classification as contingent consideration.

Firstly, the contingent penalty payments are not made as consideration for the acquisition of an interest in Target. Acquirer will only be required to pay the penalty in the event that it fails to meet the capital expenditure commitments. The penalty arrangement is, in substance, an incentive to Acquirer to undertake the capital expenditure. Further, the formula for determining the contingent payment is by reference to the capital expenditure not undertaken, as opposed to the value of Target.

This is also consistent with paragraph 28 of IFRS 3 (2007) which states that 'future losses or other costs expected to be incurred *as a result of* a combination *are not liabilities incurred or assumed by the acquirer in exchange for control of the acquiree*, and are not, therefore, included as part of the cost of the combination.' [emphasis added] That is, whilst the payment of the penalty may arise as a result of Acquirer having acquired Target (and as a result of Acquirer failing to undertake the capital expenditure commitments), any such penalty payment is not made as consideration for the acquisition of a controlling interest in Target.

Secondly, the contingency relates neither to the value of the business acquired nor to the value of the consideration given (i.e. payment is contingent on Acquirer failing to undertake the capital expenditure commitments).

However, if Acquirer knew at the time of the acquisition that the capital expenditure would not be undertaken, or if the obligation to undertake the capital expenditure would have been onerous at the date of the business combination, then the Acquirer would have a liability at that time which would form part of the cost of the combination.

Example 9.7:   *Vendor retains a customer relationship with acquiree and is entitled to volume rebates on purchases it makes*

Target is a subsidiary of Vendor Entity. Target provides goods and services to Vendor Entity that represent a significant portion of Target's business. Acquirer acquires 100% of the issued shares of Target. The purchase price is considered to represent the fair value of Target.

As part of the business combination agreement, Acquirer agrees to pay Vendor Entity a volume rebate for the next 5 years if Vendor Entity's purchases from Target exceed a specified amount in each of those years). The volume rebate offered is consistent with terms offered to other customers.

The volume rebate arrangement with the Vendor should not be accounted for as contingent consideration as it does not satisfy the criteria.

Firstly, it is not consideration for the acquisition of a controlling interest in Target:

- The purchase price paid for the issued shares of Target is considered to represent fair value of Target; and

- Acquirer will only be required to pay the volume rebates in the event that Vendor Entity's purchases exceed a specified amount. The volume rebate arrangement is merely a means of securing Vendor Entity's custom for the next 5 years. Therefore, whilst the volume rebate arrangement arises by virtue of Acquirer having acquired Target, it does not represent additional consideration for the acquisition of a controlling interest in Target.

This is also consistent with paragraph 28 of IFRS 3 (2007) (see Example 9.6 above).

Secondly, the contingency relates neither to the value of the business acquired nor to the value of the consideration given because payment is contingent on Vendor Entity's future purchases exceeding a specified amount.

Example 9.8:   *Acquirer issues to the vendor a call option on its shares that will be settled net in cash*

Acquirer acquires 100% of the issued shares of Target. The consideration consists of 10,000 shares of the Acquirer. In addition, as part of the business combination agreement, Acquirer issues to the vendor call options on 1,000 of its shares exercisable at a fixed price that will be settled net in cash. That is, Acquirer gives the vendor the right to receive and Acquirer the obligation to pay the excess of the fair value of 1,000 of Acquirer's shares at the exercise date over the exercise price, if the vendor exercises that right. The cash settled call option can be exercised at anytime up until maturity date. Any payments made by Acquirer under the call option are contingent on the vendor exercising its right under the call option.

In this situation, the call option should not be accounted for as contingent consideration. Whilst it is granted as part of the consideration for acquisition of a controlling interest in Target (and therefore satisfies the first criterion for classification as contingent consideration) it does not satisfy the second criterion. This is because the contingency ultimately relates to the market price of Acquirer's own ordinary shares. As such, the contingency does not relate to the value of the acquiree (i.e. Target). Obviously since Target is now part of the Acquirer group, there will be some link between the value of Target and the value of the option issued by Acquirer. However, normally this indirect link would not justify treating the option as contingent consideration as the value of the option is likely to be much more directly affected by the performance of the Acquirer rather than the Target group.

Further, any payment made by Acquirer under the call option is not made to 'restore' the value of consideration previously given. Rather, the Acquirer's payments, if any, under the call option will increase as the value of its shares goes up and will decrease as the value of its shares goes down. Therefore, there is no element of compensation or restoration of value in the event that the value of the 10,000 shares issued as consideration goes down. As such, the contingency does not relate to the value of the share consideration given.

The call option represents a financial liability as at the acquisition date. It should therefore be accounted for consistent with all other liabilities incurred/assumed in exchange for control of the acquiree (see 2.4.2 above). That is, the fair value of the call option at the date of the business combination will be included in the cost of the combination. The call option obligation is a derivative that will be remeasured to fair value throughout its life, with fair value remeasurements recognised in profit or loss for the period.

B   *Contingent consideration relating to future services*

A particular example of a situation where vendors may have a continuing relationship with the acquirer is in an acquisition of an owner-managed business where the acquiree's former shareholders continue to be key employees of the acquiree subsequent to the acquisition, holding positions that may affect the financial results of the acquiree.

IFRS 3 (2007) does not distinguish between contingent consideration that, in substance, is additional purchase price and contingent consideration that, in substance, represents compensation for future services. However, consistent with the discussion at A above, we believe that an acquirer must make such a distinction and therefore identify contingent consideration that is, in substance, compensation for future services, and account for this separately from the cost of the combination. This is because the IASB's *Framework* requires that in order for the information to represent faithfully the transactions, they should be accounted for in accordance with their substance, rather than their legal form, which may not be consistent with the substance and economic reality.[87] Therefore, where a vendor is also a continuing employee it is necessary to determine whether payments are made to them in their capacity as vendor or as employee.

If, for example, the consideration takes the form of share-based payments, it is necessary to determine how much of the share-based payment relates to the acquisition of control (which forms part of the cost of combination, accounted for under IFRS 3 (2007)) and how much relates to the provision of future services (which is a post-combination operating expense accounted for under IFRS 2). This would be the case if, for example, the vendor of an acquired entity receives a share-based payment for transferring control of the entity and for remaining in continuing employment.

Prior to the application of IFRS 3 (as revised in 2008), there is no IFRS or interpretation containing guidance for evaluating the substance of the contingent consideration or determining an appropriate split (except for share-based payment transactions covered under IFRS 2). However, under the hierarchy set out in IAS 8 – *Accounting Policies, Changes in Accounting Estimates and Errors* (see Chapter 3 at 4.3) further guidance for making such an evaluation can be found in US GAAP. EITF 95-8 – *Accounting for Contingent Consideration Paid to the Shareholders for an Acquired Enterprise in a Purchase Business Combination* – includes a number of indicators to evaluate the substance of additional payments, which we believe are also applicable when implementing IFRS. These include:

(a)   the length of future service compared to the earn-out period;

(b)   whether payments made to vendors who are employees are comparable with payments made to vendors who are not employees or to employees who are not vendors;

(c)   what the reasons are for the contingent payments; and

(d)   the nature of the formula for determining contingent consideration.

In making such an evaluation, all terms of the agreement have a critical role in this assessment, and the reasons for structuring the terms of the transaction in a particular way, and the identity of the initiator, should be understood. Nevertheless, in general, when the agreement includes employment conditions such that the payments are forfeited upon termination of employment, all or a portion of, the additional payments will generally be classified as employment compensation.

This is consistent with the approach to be applied under IFRS 3 (as revised in 2008), the requirements of which are based on EITF 95-8. Indeed, as noted at 3.12.2 A below, IFRS 3 (as revised in 2008) categorically states that 'a contingent consideration arrangement in which the payments are automatically forfeited if employment terminates is remuneration for post-combination services'.

C   Contingent transaction costs

As indicated at A above, one of the examples of contingent consideration is where an additional payment is made if the acquiree's profits exceed a certain amount. In some business combinations an entity may agree to pay an adviser a fee for services relating to a business combination. If that fee is contingent on the acquiree achieving a specified profit hurdle can this be accounted for as contingent consideration arising on the business combination?

Example 9.9:   Contingent transaction costs

Entity A engages Entity X, which has specific technical knowledge, to assist in identifying an investment target. Entity X recommends that Entity A purchase Entity B. Entity A has agreed to pay Entity X a performance fee in the event that the return from its investment in Entity B exceeds a specified target. Can such a fee be regarded as 'contingent consideration' and therefore any reassessment of the fee payable accounted for as an adjustment to the cost of the business combination, and therefore adjusted against goodwill?

The contingent consideration requirements of IFRS 3 (2007) only apply 'when a business combination agreement provides for an adjustment to the cost of the combination'. By its nature, a business combination agreement is an agreement between the vendor and the purchaser – it does not include agreements between the purchaser and third parties unconnected with the vendor. Thus, in our view, the payment to Entity X is not contingent consideration as it is not part of the agreement between the vendor and the purchaser. It arises from a separate agreement with the third party adviser.

Accordingly, whilst the payment to Entity X is part of the cost of the combination it must be measured as at the date of acquisition. Any subsequent remeasurement cannot be adjusted against the cost of the combination except where it is an adjustment upon completion of the initial accounting (see 2.8.1 below). However, an adjustment to the initial accounting must reflect conditions as they existed at the date of the combination and does not take into account subsequent events.

D   Contingent consideration to be settled by equity instruments

In some business combination agreements involving contingent consideration, it may be that additional consideration will not be settled by cash, but by shares. IFRS 3 (2007) makes no explicit reference to such a situation, and IFRS 2 explicitly scopes out from its provisions 'transactions in which an entity acquires goods as part of the net assets acquired in a business combination to which IFRS 3' applies. It also goes on to say that 'equity instruments issued in a business combination in exchange for control of the acquiree are not within the scope of' IFRS 2.[88] In addition, IAS 32 (prior to its amendment by IFRS 3 (as revised in 2008)) also scopes out of its provisions 'contracts for contingent consideration'.[89]

In practice, there is a wide variety of share-settled contingent consideration arrangements, but they are generally based on one of two models:

- Arrangements whereby shares are issued to a particular value based on certain conditions being met, e.g. if profits are €A then additional consideration of €M will be given, to be satisfied by shares based on the share price at date of issue;

- Arrangements whereby a particular number of shares are issued if certain conditions are met, e.g. if profits are €A then X shares will be issued, but if profits are €B then Y shares will be issued.

The issues that need to be considered in accounting for such arrangements are:

- If the consideration is recognised, should it be classified as a liability or as equity?

- How should the consideration be valued, both on initial recognition and if re-assessed at a later date?

Example 9.10:   Share-settled contingent consideration (1)

Entity P acquires a 100% interest in Entity S on 31 December 2009. As part of the consideration arrangements, additional consideration will be payable on 1 January 2013, based on Entity S meeting certain profit targets over the 3 years ended 31 December 2012, as follows:

Profit target (average profits over 3 year period)	*Additional consideration*
€1m but less than €1.25m	€5m
€1.25m but less than €1.5m	€6m
€1.5m+	€7.5m

Any additional consideration will be satisfied by issuing the appropriate number of shares with a value equivalent to the additional consideration payable based on Entity P's share price at 1 January 2013.

At the date of acquisition, Entity P considers that it is probable that Entity S will meet the first profit target, but not the others.

How should Entity P classify the additional consideration in its financial statements for the year ended 31 December 2009, and what amount should be recognised in respect of it?

Contracts for contingent consideration are specifically scoped out of both IFRS 2 and IAS 32. IFRS 2 requires equity-settled share-based payment transactions to be reflected in equity (see Chapter 27 at 4). However, in our view the principles of IAS 32 appear more relevant than those of IFRS 2 in determining the appropriate classification of such arrangements. On that basis, the contingent consideration in this situation is of the type of arrangement considered in paragraph 21 of IAS 32 whereby an 'entity may have a contractual right or obligation to receive or deliver a number of its own shares or other equity instruments that varies so that the fair value of the entity's own equity instruments to be received or delivered equals the amount of the contractual right or obligation'. Accordingly, classification as a liability seems appropriate.

On the basis that the consideration is reflected as a liability then, as with contingent consideration payable in cash, the amount to be recognised at 31 December 2009 should be the present value of the €5m consideration expected to be payable on 1 January 2012.

If at 31 December 2010, Entity P considers that is it is probable that Entity S will now meet the second target, it should remeasure the liability at that date to the present value of the €6m that is now expected to be payable on 1 January 2013 with a corresponding adjustment to goodwill, having reflected the unwinding of the discount on the original €5m in the income statement (see Example 9.3 above).

In the above example, the arrangement was of the type where the shares issued to settle the consideration were equivalent to a particular value. However, what if the arrangement was of the type where a particular number of shares are to be issued to satisfy the consideration?

Example 9.11: Share-settled contingent consideration (2)

Assume the same facts as in Example 9.10 above, except that the additional consideration will be payable as follows:

Profit target (average profits over 3 year period)	*Additional consideration*
€1m but less than €1.25m	100,000 shares
€1.25m but less than €1.5m	150,000 shares
€1.5m+	200,000 shares

How should Entity P classify the additional consideration in its financial statements for the year ended 31 December 2009, and what amount should be recognised in respect of it?

Although in our view the principles of IAS 32 generally appear more relevant than those of IFRS 2 it is less clear whether the contingent consideration in this situation is the type of arrangement that ought to be classified as a liability. Paragraph 21 of IAS 32 does not consider a contract to be equity where an 'entity may have a contractual right or obligation to receive or deliver a number of its own shares or other equity instruments that varies so that the fair value of the entity's own equity instruments to be received or delivered equals the amount of the contractual right or obligation'. One view would be that on the basis that the number of shares to be issued does vary (depending on profit) and that the fair value of the shares to be issued does always equal the fair value of the obligation – by definition the two must always be the same – such an arrangement constitutes a liability. However this analysis does not seem entirely satisfactory when applied to contingent consideration.

In determining the contingent consideration to be recorded under IFRS 3 (2007), Entity P has to estimate what level of profit it anticipates Entity S will achieve and the relevant number of shares to be issued as a result. At 31 December 2009, Entity P has determined that it is probable that Entity S will meet the first target level, and as a result Entity P will issue 100,000 shares on 1 January 2013. Thereafter, if that level of profit is achieved there will no variation in the number of shares issued. Clearly Entity P may reassess the level of profit it expects to be achieved and revise the number of shares it expects to issue, but again once that determination is made if the revised estimate is achieved there is no variation in the number of shares to be issued.

Fundamentally, paragraph 21 of IAS 32 appears to be addressing situations where shares to be issued vary such that they are equal in value to a fixed or variable, but determinable, monetary amount. Unlike Example 9.10 above, that is not the case in this situation once the expected outcome of the contingency has been determined. Accordingly, we believe that it is appropriate that the consideration is classified as an equity instrument. Note that IFRS 3 (as revised in 2008) adopts a fundamentally different approach to contingent consideration and the classification is much more likely to be a liability as explained at 3.8.1 B below.

On the basis that the consideration is reflected as equity, we believe that the amount recognised for the consideration should be based on the requirements of IFRS 3 (2007) in respect of equity instruments issued as consideration (see 2.4.3 above), i.e. at the fair value at the date of exchange (31 December 2009). However, in this situation the fair value of the 'equity instrument' at the date of exchange would need to take into account, for example, an allowance for any estimated dividends on the shares that will not be payable during the period until they are issued on 1 January 2013.

One other issue that arises in this situation is whether adjustments should be made to the consideration, and thus goodwill, to reflect subsequent changes in the fair value of the shares such that the consideration is ultimately measured at Entity P's share price at the date the shares are finally issued. Although the requirements for contingent consideration would generally require subsequent changes in the estimate of the consideration that will ultimately be given to be recognised, we do not believe that this should reflect such changes in fair value. Since the consideration is regarded as equity, then consistent with the requirements of paragraph 22 of IAS 32, 'changes in the fair value of an equity instrument are not recognised in the financial statements'.

If at 31 December 2010, Entity P considers that is it is probable that Entity S will now meet the second target, then the financial statements at that date need to reflect that Entity P now expects to issue 150,000 shares. As discussed above, we do not believe that any change should be made to reflect changes in the value of Entity P's shares since the date of exchange (31 December 2009), and so the additional consideration of 50,000 shares should be valued using the same value per share as the original estimated consideration of 100,000 shares.

E   *Indemnities given by vendor to the acquirer in respect of contingencies of acquiree*

In some business combinations, it may be identified that the acquiree has a specific contingency for which no liability has been recognised as the acquiree did not consider that it was probable that any liability would crystallise. Consequently, the business combination agreement may provide for the vendor to indemnify the acquirer in the event that the acquiree has to make a payment in respect of the contingency by way of a refund of the consideration paid by the acquirer.

As discussed at 2.5.3 below, the acquirer will be required to recognise a liability for the contingency at its fair value, despite the fact that the acquiree has not recognised any liability for that contingency.

However, how should the acquirer account for the indemnity given by the vendor in relation to the contingency?

Example 9.12:   Indemnity given by vendor to the acquirer in respect of a contingent liability of the acquiree

Entity A intends to acquire Entity B. It is considered by both Entity A and the vendor of Entity B that the value of Entity B's business is $150m. As part of due diligence, Entity A identifies that Entity B has a contingent liability in respect of a claim by a third party that has not been recognised by Entity B as a liability on the basis that was not considered probable that any amount would be payable by Entity B. The maximum amount payable in respect of the claim is $60m, and the vendor is still of the view that no amount will ultimately be payable by Entity B.

Accordingly, the purchase agreement includes the following terms:
- $150m is to be paid upfront (being the value of Entity B excluding the contingent liability).
- The vendor agrees to pay an amount to the acquirer, Entity A, by way of a refund of the purchase price in the event that the contingent liability crystallises and is settled by Entity B.

The intention of these terms is that the impact of the contingent liability on the results reported in Entity A's consolidated financial statements should be the same, regardless of the outcome of the contingent liability.

The fair value of Entity B's net assets (excluding the contingent liability) is $50m, and the fair value of the contingent liability is determined to be $20m.

In the absence of the contingent liability, goodwill of $100m would be recognised, being the difference between the consideration paid ($150m) and the fair value of the net assets acquired ($50m). As indicated above, IFRS 3 (2007) requires the contingent liability to be recognised as a liability at its fair value of $20m; based on consideration of $150m this would mean that goodwill of $120m is recognised.

However, how should the indemnity be accounted for?

A literal application of IFRS 3 (2007) results in any reimbursement by the vendor being accounted for as 'negative' contingent consideration since the agreement provides for an adjustment to the cost of the combination contingent on a future event. On this basis, no adjustment would be made at the acquisition date (since it is not probable that any amount would be received), and thus goodwill of $120m would be recognised as indicated above. If at a later date, the contingent liability crystallised at its maximum amount of $60m, then the consolidated financial statements would recognise this increased liability of $60m, resulting in a loss of $40m in the income statement. The refund received by Entity A of $60m would be recognised as an adjustment to the consideration, resulting in a reduction of the goodwill by that amount. On the other hand, if at a later date, the uncertainty about the contingent liability was resolved such that no amount was payable by Entity B, then the consolidated financial statements would recognise the release of the original liability of $20m, resulting in a gain in the income statement. There would no adjustment to the goodwill. This does not seem a particularly sensible result.

Another approach might be to view the transaction as having two components – the business combination and the purchase of an indemnity asset. On this basis, therefore, the total price of $150m comprises two distinct elements: $130m representing the cost of the business combination, and the remaining $20m representing an additional payment to receive the indemnity from the vendor in relation to the contingent liability acquired. Therefore, based on the cost of the business combination of $130m, goodwill of $100m is recognised. A separate 'indemnity' asset of $20m is recognised (effectively Entity A has purchased a reimbursement right relating to the contingent liability). Any amount received under the indemnity is a realisation of that asset and is not adjusted against the cost of the business combination which remains $130m.

Proponents of this approach argue that contingent consideration is not defined in IFRS 3 (2007) and the examples given are for contingencies relating either to the value of the business acquired or the value of the consideration provided. For these contingencies there is a logical link to the combination accounting and, accordingly, these give rise to contingent consideration. In the case of the indemnity, it is argued that the contingency does not relate either to the value of the business (it only relates to one element) nor to the value of the consideration. In these circumstances, it is thought appropriate to consider the substance of the arrangement to determine whether or not it should be accounted for as contingent consideration.

In support of this approach, proponents would argue that in any event it would seem inappropriate to adjust any amount received against the cost of the combination (and goodwill). As noted earlier, paragraph 35 of IFRS 3 (2007) requires a different approach to accounting for contingencies when the acquirer guarantees the value of equity or debt instruments issued as consideration and must issue additional equity or debt instruments to restore the originally determined cost. In such cases, no increase in the cost of the business combination (or adjustment to goodwill) is recognised and the adjustment is reflected instead in the equity or debt instruments. Therefore, the accounting for the contingent consideration is determined by the nature of the contingency and the nature of the adjustment follows from this. This is thought to further support the view that the nature of the contingency needs to be considered to determine the appropriate accounting. For the indemnity, the contingency also does not relate to the value of the business acquired – rather it relates to the value of one of the specific liabilities acquired. Therefore, consistent with the approach in paragraph 35, it is argued that no adjustment should be made to the cost of the business combination as a result of any payment received under the indemnity. Subsequent movements in the value of the separate asset and contingent liability are adjusted for in the income statement.

We can see some merit in this 'indemnity asset' approach and consider it an acceptable way of accounting for such an indemnity. Under this approach, if at a later date, the contingent liability crystallised at its maximum amount of $60m, then the consolidated financial statements would recognise this increased liability of $60m, resulting in a loss of $40m in the income statement. However, this would be offset by an equivalent amount being the refund received by Entity A of $60m less the cost of 'indemnity' asset. On the other hand, if at a later date, the uncertainty about the contingent liability was resolved such that no amount was payable by Entity B, then the consolidated financial statements would recognise the release of the original liability of $20m, resulting in a gain in the income statement. This would then be offset by Entity A writing off its 'indemnity' asset.

Accounting for contingent consideration is an area where the treatment under IFRS 3 (as revised in 2008) (see 3.8.1 below) is significantly different from that described above. In addition, the revised standard also now deals explicitly with indemnification assets (see 3.6.6 D below) and whether or not arrangements should be accounted for as contingent consideration or as remuneration for services (see 3.12.2 below).

2.5   Allocating the cost to the assets acquired and liabilities and contingent liabilities assumed

Having determined the cost of the business combination, the next stage is to allocate that cost to the assets acquired and liabilities and contingent liabilities assumed.

IFRS 3 (2007) requires that the acquirer shall, at the acquisition date, allocate the cost of a business combination by recognising the acquiree's identifiable assets, liabilities and contingent liabilities that satisfy the recognition criteria in paragraph 37 of the standard at their fair values at that date, except for non-current assets (or disposal groups) that are classified as held for sale in accordance with IFRS 5 – *Non-current Assets Held for Sale and Discontinued Operations*, which are recognised at fair value less costs to sell. Any difference between the cost of the business combination and the acquirer's interest in the net fair value of the identifiable assets, liabilities and contingent liabilities so recognised is accounted for as goodwill or 'negative goodwill' (see 2.6 and 2.7 below respectively).[90]

Paragraph 37 of IFRS 3 (2007) states that the acquirer shall recognise separately the acquiree's identifiable assets, liabilities and contingent liabilities at the acquisition date only if they satisfy the following criteria at that date:

(a)   in the case of an asset other than an intangible asset, it is probable that any associated future economic benefits will flow to the acquirer, and its fair value can be measured reliably;

(b)   in the case of a liability other than a contingent liability, it is probable that an outflow of resources embodying economic benefits will be required to settle the obligation, and its fair value can be measured reliably;

(c)   in the case of an intangible asset or a contingent liability, its fair value can be measured reliably.[91]

It can be seen that the recognition criteria for intangible assets and contingent liabilities are different from those of other assets and liabilities. In the case of intangible assets, the IASB has taken the view that the probability recognition criterion is always considered to be satisfied for such assets acquired in a business combination. In developing the standard, the Board observed that the fair value of an intangible asset reflects market expectations about the probability that the future economic benefits associated with the intangible asset will flow to the acquirer. In other words, the effect of probability is reflected in the fair value measurement of an intangible asset. The IASB notes that this highlights a general inconsistency between the recognition criteria for assets and liabilities in its *Framework* (see Chapter 2 at 3.2.4) and the fair value measurements required in a business combination, but has concluded that the role of probability as a criterion for recognition in the *Framework* should be considered more generally as part of a forthcoming Concepts project.[92] The allocation of the cost of the business combination to intangible assets is discussed further at 2.5.2 below.

Similarly, in the case of contingent liabilities, the IASB takes the view that although a contingent liability of the acquiree is not recognised by the acquiree before the business combination, that contingent liability has a fair value, the amount of which reflects market expectations about any uncertainty surrounding the possibility that an outflow of resources embodying economic benefits will be required to settle the possible or present obligation. Again, the IASB notes that this highlights an inconsistency between the recognition criteria applying to liabilities and contingent liabilities in IAS 37 (see Chapter 24 at 3) and the *Framework* and the fair value measurement cost of a business combination, and that the role of probability should be considered more generally as part of a forthcoming Concepts project.[93] The allocation of the cost of the business combination to contingent liabilities is discussed further at 2.5.3 below.

The recognition criteria in paragraph 37 of the standard set out above makes no reference to contingent assets of the acquiree. We believe that, consistent with the treatment of contingent liabilities, IFRS 3 (2007) should have required an acquirer to recognise an acquiree's contingent assets at their fair value as part of allocating the cost of the business combination provided their fair values can be measured reliably. We see no conceptual justification to include only contingent liabilities but not contingent assets in the cost allocation process of a business combination, as both are likely to have had an impact on the purchase price and the contingent asset is as much an asset as the contingent liability is a liability. Arguably, a contingent asset that has not been recognised as an asset by the acquiree on the basis that the inflow of benefits is not virtually certain (see Chapter 24 at 3.2.2), but it is probable that the benefits will arise, is covered by criterion (a) above. However, it appears that this is not the case as at the time of issuing IFRS 3 (2007) the IASB indicated that it would consider as part of the second phase of its business combinations project whether items meeting the definition of contingent assets in IAS 37 should be recognised separately as part of allocating the cost of a business combination.[94]

The allocation of the cost of the business combination to the assets acquired and liabilities and contingent liabilities assumed is critical to the reporting of the post-acquisition performance relating to the business combination. As indicated in the standard, the acquirer's income statement shall incorporate the acquiree's profits and losses after the acquisition date by including the acquiree's income and expenses based on that allocation. For example, depreciation expense included after the acquisition date in the acquirer's income statement that relates to the acquiree's depreciable assets is based on the fair values of those depreciable assets at the acquisition date, i.e. their cost to the acquirer.[95] However, of more importance, is the fact that the subsequent accounting for the items that are being recognised separately will in most cases be different from that required for goodwill. For example, the requirement to recognise intangible assets with finite useful lives separately (rather than subsuming them within goodwill), will mean that the values attributed will be amortised over that useful life (see Chapter 15 at 2.5 and 2.6) whereas the goodwill will not be amortised, but subjected to an impairment test (see Chapter 18 at 3.4).

Further explanation as to how the recognition requirements for other assets and liabilities, principally liabilities, are to be applied is given in the standard. This is discussed at 2.5.1 below.

Guidance on determining the fair values of the acquiree's identifiable assets, liabilities and contingent liabilities for the purpose of allocating the cost of a business combination is discussed at 2.5.4 below.

As the acquirer recognises the acquiree's identifiable assets, liabilities and contingent liabilities that satisfy the recognition criteria in paragraph 37 at their fair values at the acquisition date, any minority interest in the acquiree is stated at the minority's proportion of the net fair value of those items.[96]

2.5.1   Acquiree's identifiable assets and liabilities

As indicated above, further explanation about how the recognition requirements for other assets and liabilities, principally liabilities, are to be applied is given in the standard.

Firstly, IFRS 3 (2007) makes it clear that the acquirer, when allocating the cost of the combination, shall not recognise liabilities for future losses or other costs expected to be incurred as a result of the business combination.[97]

Secondly, the standard severely restricts the ability of an acquirer to recognise a liability for reorganisation or restructuring costs resulting from the business combination. The standard states that 'the acquirer shall recognise liabilities for terminating or reducing the activities of the acquiree as part of allocating the cost of the combination only when the acquiree has, at the acquisition date, an existing liability for restructuring recognised in accordance with IAS 37'.[98] The requirements for the recognition of restructuring provisions under IAS 37 are discussed in Chapter 24 at 5.1.

The Basis for Conclusions accompanying IFRS 3 (2007) considers a number of ways that it might be thought possible to get around this requirement, for example, by the acquiree, on instructions of the acquirer, entering into obligations to restructure the business before the formal transfer of control.[99] It indicates that 'if the acquirer can compel the acquiree to incur obligations, then it is likely that the acquirer already controls the acquiree, given that control is the power to govern the financial and operating policies of an entity so as to obtain benefits from its activities'.[100] In that situation, the date of acquisition would be date the acquirer effectively obtained control, and at that time the acquiree would not have had an existing liability under IAS 37. However, the Basis for Conclusions does state that 'if, alternatively, the acquirer suggests that negotiations cannot proceed until the acquiree arranges, for example, to restructure its workforce, and the acquiree takes the steps necessary to satisfy the recognition criteria for restructuring provisions in IAS 37, then those obligations are pre-combination obligations of the acquiree and, in the Board's view, should be recognised as part of allocating the cost of the combination'.[101] In that situation, the acquiree has a liability for the restructuring irrespective of whether the business combination takes place or not, and is taking the risk that having made that commitment the acquirer may not complete the acquisition.

The IASB also considered the situation whereby the acquiree and the acquirer could agree for the acquiree to take the steps necessary to satisfy the recognition requirements of the standard, but to make the execution of the plan conditional on the acquiree being acquired in a business combination.[102] However, the standard clarifies that an acquiree's restructuring plan whose execution is conditional upon its being acquired in a business combination is not, immediately before the business combination, a present obligation of the acquiree.[103] The reason being that even if the main features of the plan were announced to those that would be affected by it, the entity has not raised the 'valid expectation' that it will be carried out since it is conditional on the entity being acquired in a business combination.[104] Nor is it a contingent liability of the acquiree immediately before the combination because it is not a possible obligation arising from a past event whose existence will be confirmed only by the occurrence or non-occurrence of one or more uncertain future events not wholly within the control of the acquiree.[105] The reason being that the uncertain future event (i.e. being acquired in a business combination) is generally within the acquiree's control.[106] Therefore, an acquirer shall not recognise a liability for such restructuring plans as part of allocating the cost of the combination.[107]

Thirdly, IFRS 3 (2007) states that a payment that an entity is contractually required to make, for example, to its employees or suppliers in the event that it is acquired in a business combination is a present obligation of the entity that is regarded as a contingent liability until it becomes probable that a business combination will take place. The contractual obligation is recognised as a liability by that entity in accordance with IAS 37 when a business combination becomes probable and the liability can be measured reliably. Therefore, when the business combination is effected, that liability of the acquiree is recognised by the acquirer as part of allocating the cost of the combination.[108]

Lastly, the standard states that the identifiable assets and liabilities that are recognised in accordance with paragraph 36 of the standard include all of the acquiree's assets and liabilities that the acquirer purchases or assumes, including all of its financial assets and financial liabilities. They might also include assets and liabilities not previously recognised in the acquiree's financial statements, e.g. because they did not qualify for recognition before the acquisition. For example, a tax benefit arising from the acquiree's tax losses that was not recognised by the acquiree before the business combination qualifies for recognition as an identifiable asset in accordance with paragraph 36 if it is probable that the acquirer will have future taxable profits against which the unrecognised tax benefit can be applied.[109]

2.5.2   Acquiree's intangible assets

As indicated at 2.5 above, the allocation of the cost of the business combination includes the separate recognition of the acquiree's intangible assets. This is irrespective of whether the asset had been recognised by the acquiree before the business combination.[110] IFRS 3 (2007) requires the acquirer to recognise separately an intangible asset of the acquiree at the acquisition date only if:

- it meets the definition of an intangible asset in IAS 38; and
- its fair value can be measured reliably.[111]

IAS 38 (prior to its amendment by IFRS 3 (as revised in 2008)) includes equivalent requirements, and also emphasises that the probability recognition criterion in paragraph 21(a) of IAS 38 (see Chapter 15 at 2.2.1) is always considered to be satisfied for an intangible asset acquired in a business combination, the effect of probability being taken into account in the determination of fair value.[112] In developing the revised IFRS 3, the IASB has now decided that in accounting for intangible assets acquired in a business combination under IFRS 3 (as revised in 2008), the reliable measurement criterion is always considered to be satisfied (see 3.6.5 B I below) and consequential amendments to IAS 38 were made. References to IAS 38 throughout the rest of this section below are to the version of the standard prior to its amendment by IFRS 3 (as revised in 2008).

IFRS 3 (2007) refers to the guidance provided within IAS 38 on determining whether the fair value of an intangible asset acquired in a business combination can be measured reliably.[113]

A   What is an intangible asset?

IAS 38 defines an 'intangible asset' as 'an identifiable non-monetary asset without physical substance'.[114] IFRS 3 (2007) states that in accordance with IAS 38, an asset meets the identifiability criterion in the definition of an intangible asset only if it:

(a)   is separable, i.e. capable of being separated or divided from the entity and sold, transferred, licensed, rented or exchanged, either individually or together with a related contract, asset or liability; or

(b)   arises from contractual or other legal rights, regardless of whether those rights are transferable or separable from the entity or from other rights and obligations.[115]

Both IFRS 3 (2007) and IAS 38 explicitly refer to the fact that this means that the acquirer recognises as an asset separately from goodwill an in-process research and development project of the acquiree (if the project meets the definition of an intangible asset and its fair value can be measured reliably).[116] This is discussed further below. IFRS 3 (2007) gives guidance in an Illustrative Example that provides a large list of examples of items acquired in a business combination that meet the definition of an intangible asset and are therefore to be recognised separately from goodwill, provided that their fair values can be measured reliably, whilst noting that they are not intended to be an exhaustive list of items acquired in a business combination that meet the definition of an intangible asset.[117] A non-monetary asset without physical substance acquired in a business combination might meet the identifiability criterion for identification as an intangible asset but not be included in the guidance.

The guidance designates the assets listed with symbols to identify those that meet part (a) of the definition and those that meet part (b) of the definition, whilst noting that those designated as meeting part (b) might also be separable. However, it emphasises that separability is not a necessary condition for an asset to meet the contractual-legal criterion.

The table below summarises the items included in the Illustrative Example that the IASB regard as meeting the definition of an intangible asset and are therefore to be recognised separately from goodwill, provided that their fair values can be measured reliably. Reference should be made to the Illustrative Example for any further explanation about some of these items.

Intangible assets arising from contractual or other legal rights (regardless of being separable)	Other intangible assets that are separable
Marketing-related	
– Trademarks, trade names, service marks, collective marks and certification marks – Internet domain names – Trade dress (unique colour, shape or package design) – Newspaper mastheads – Non-competition agreements	
Customer-related	
– Order or production backlogs – Customer contracts and the related customer relationships	– Customer lists – Non-contractual customer relationships
Artistic-related	
– Plays, operas and ballets – Books, magazines, newspapers and other literary works – Musical works such as compositions, song lyrics and advertising jingles – Pictures and photographs – Video and audiovisual material, including films, music videos and television programmes	
Contract-based	
– Licensing, royalty and standstill agreements – Advertising, construction, management, service or supply contracts – Lease agreements – Construction permits – Franchise agreements – Operating and broadcasting rights – Use rights such as drilling, water, air, mineral, timber-cutting and route authorities – Servicing contracts such as mortgage servicing contracts – Employment contracts that are beneficial contracts from the perspective of the employer because the pricing of those contracts is below their current market value	
Technology-based	
– Patented technology – Computer software and mask works – Trade secrets such as secret formulas, processes or recipes	– Unpatented technology – Databases

It can be seen from the table that customer relationships can potentially fall under either category. Where relationships are established with customers through contracts, those customer relationships arise from contractual rights, regardless of whether a contract exists, or there is any backlog of orders, at the date of acquisition. In such cases, it does not matter that the relationship is separable. It would only be if the relationship did not arise from a contract that the recognition depends on the separability criterion.

It is clear from the table above that the IASB envisages a wide range of items meeting the definition of an intangible asset, and therefore potentially being recognised separately from goodwill. Whether they are recognised separately or not will depend on whether their fair values can be measured reliably.

One company that has recognised numerous intangible assets as a result of business combinations is ITV as illustrated in the following extract.

Extract 9.3: ITV plc (2005)

Notes to the accounts [extract]
28   Acquisitions and disposals of business

Acquisition and disposals in 2005

SDN

On 27 April 2005, the Group acquired 50.1% of the shares in SDN Ltd and 100% of the shares in United Media & Information Ltd (which held the remaining shares in SDN Ltd) for a total consideration of £83 million in cash. As part of the acquisition, loan amounts due by these companies, totalling £53 million, were repaid bringing the total cash outflow of the Group to £136 million. SDN holds the licence to operate Multiplex A on digital terrestrial television.

In the period to 31 December 2005 SDN contributed £8 million to the consolidated operating profit of the Group (before additional amortisation of £4 million). Had the acquisition occurred on 1 January 2005, the estimated revenue for the Group would have been £7 million higher at £2,184 million and operating profit before amortisation and exceptional items £2 million higher at £462 million (additional amortisation is £2 million) for the year ended 31 December 2005. The acquired net assets of SDN are set out in the table below.

	Book value before acquisition £m	Fair value adjustments £m	Fair value to ITV plc £m
Intangible assets	–	82	82
Trade and other receivables	6	–	6
Borrowings	(53)	–	(53)
Trade and other payables	(7)	3	(4)
Deferred tax liability	–	(25)	(25)
Net assets and liabilities	(54)	60	6
Goodwill on acquisition			77
Consideration paid			83
Borrowings settled at date of acquisition			53
Total cash outflow			136

The intangible assets recognised at a fair value of £82 million include the Multiplex licence and customer contracts. A deferred tax liability of £25 million has been recognised in respect of these intangible assets.

The goodwill recognised represents the wider strategic benefits of the acquisition to ITV plc and the value of those assets not requiring valuation under IFRS 3 (Business combinations). The strategic benefits are principally the enhanced ability to promote Freeview as a platform, business relationships with the channels which are on Multiplex A and the additional capacity available from 2010. These, in combination with existing Group assets including the ITV brand and programming, generate the goodwill on acquisition.

Friends Reunited

On 6 December 2005, the Group agreed to acquire 100% of the shares in Friends Reunited Holdings Limited for a total initial consideration of £120 million and deferred consideration of up to £55 million payable in 2009 contingent upon the future performance of the acquired business. The initial consideration consisted of £75 million cash, £21 million loan notes and £24 million ITV plc shares. Of the initial consideration £94 million was paid in 2005 with the balance of £26 million paid in 2006 (being the 21 million (£24 million) ITV plc shares and £2 million loan notes).

The fair value of the consideration is £145 million. This takes into account the initial consideration, the present value of the expected deferred consideration and other costs associated with the acquisition.

Had the acquisition occurred on 1 January 2005, the estimated revenue for the Group would have been £12 million higher at £2,189 million and operating profit before amortisation and exceptional items £6 million higher at £466 million (additional amortisation would have been £4 million) for the year ended 31 December 2005.

The acquired net assets of Friends Reunited are set out in the table below.

	Book value before acquisition £m	Fair value adjustments £m	Fair value to ITV plc £m
Intangible assets	4	34	38
Cash and cash equivalents	3	–	3
Trade and other receivables	1	–	1
Borrowings	(2)	–	(2)
Trade and other payables	(5)	–	(5)
Current tax (liability)/asset	(1)	3	2
Deferred tax asset	–	8	8
Net assets and liabilities	–	45	45
Goodwill on acquisition			100
Fair value of consideration			145

The intangible assets recognised at fair value include the brands and customer relationships. A deferred tax liability of £10 million has been recognised in respect of these intangible assets. A current tax asset of £3 million and a deferred tax asset of £18 million has been recognised in respect of the exercise of share options.

The goodwill recognised represents the benefits of the acquisition across the Group when combined with existing Group assets and businesses and the value of those assets not requiring valuation under IFRS 3 (Business combinations).

Valuation of acquired intangible assets methodology

Valuation of acquired intangibles has been performed in accordance with industry standard practice. Methods applied are designed to isolate the value of each intangible asset separately from the other assets of the business. The value of brands are assessed by applying a royalty rate to the expected future revenues over the life of the brand. Licences are valued on a start-up basis. Customer relationships and controls are valued based on expected future cash flows from those existing at the date of acquisition. Contributory charges from other assets are taken as appropriate with post tax cash flows then being discounted back to their present value. Typical discount rates applied in the valuation of intangible assets acquired in the period are 8%-11%.

Disposal

During the year the Group disposed of Superhire Ltd for gross consideration of £2 million.

Acquisition and disposals in 2004

Summary of the effect of the acquisition of new businesses:

	Carlton		GMTV/GSkyB			
	Book value before acquisition £m	Fair value to ITV plc £m	Book value before acquisition £m	Fair value to ITV plc £m	Reclass-ifications* £m	Total £m
Intangible assets	87	583	–	31	–	614
Fixed assets	81	86	3	3	7	96
Investments	96	122	–	–	(36)	86
Distribution rights	13	13	–	–	–	13
Deferred tax	29	(106)	–	(9)	3	(112)
Programme rights and other inventory	106	96	7	1	6	103
Trade and other receivables	155	149	14	13	45	207
Current asset investments	182	178	–	–	–	178
Assets held for sale	–	59	–	–	–	59
Cash and cash equivalents	410	410	19	19	59	488
Trade and other payables, provisions and borrowings	(1,204)	(1,245)	(29)	(32)	(111)	(1,388)
Pensions	(129)	(129)	–	–	(9)	(138)
Current tax	(62)	(62)	–	–	–	(62)
	(236)	154	14	26	(36)	144

Share of net assets within equity accounted investments plus minority interest	(168)	(8)	(3)	(179)
Goodwill on acquisition	1,932	33	39	2,004
Revaluation reserve adjustment	–	(6)	–	(6)
	1,918	45	–	1,963
Fair value of consideration paid	1,897	45		1,942
Acquisition costs	21	–		21
	1,918	45		1,963

*Reclassification of ITV 2, LNN, ITFC, ITV News Channel and ITV Network Limited to subsidiaries on combination of Granada and Carlton. These were previously held within investments in joint ventures and associates.

The most material acquisition accounted for during 2004 results from acquisition accounting for the combination with Carlton Communications Plc on 2 February 2004. Consideration comprised 1,308 million ordinary shares and 124 million convertible shares in ITV plc. The fair value of the consideration at the date of merger was £1,897 million.

In the period to 31 December 2004 Carlton contributed £82 million to the consolidated operating profit of the Group (before additional amortisation of £101 million). Had the acquisition occurred on 1 January 2004, the estimated revenue for the Group would have been £30 million higher at £2,083 million and operating profit before amortisation and exceptional items £1 million higher at £325 million for the year ended 31 December 2004.

The principal fair value adjustments to the book values (under IFRS) of the acquired assets and liabilities are as follows:
- Recognition of acquired intangible assets at fair value. These are principally brands, customer contracts, customer relationships, licences and acquired film libraries.
- Acquired properties stated at market value.
- Revaluation of investments to estimated market value.
- Write down of inventories to estimated selling price less reasonable profit margin.
- Assets held for sale shown at expected net proceeds discounted back to their present value at the date of acquisition.
- Revaluation of financial instruments to market value.
- Deferred tax provided on acquisition accounting adjustments as appropriate.

Disposals

During 2004 the Group disposed of The Moving Picture Company Holdings Ltd and Carlton Books Ltd (which were classified as held for resale) for respective gross considerations of £59 million and £nil.

B Customer relationship intangible assets acquired in a business combination

Further guidance on customer relationships acquired in a business combination is provided by IFRS 3 (2007) in the Illustrative Examples (which forms the basis of the example below) that demonstrate how an entity should interpret the contractual-legal and separability criteria in the context of acquired customer relationships.[118]

Example 9.13: Customer relationship intangible assets acquired in a business combination

Supply agreement

Parent obtained control of Supplier in a business combination. Supplier has a five-year agreement to supply goods to Buyer. Both Supplier and Parent believe that Buyer will renew the supply agreement at the end of the current contract. The supply agreement is not separable.

The supply agreement (whether cancellable or not) meets the contractual-legal criterion for identification as an intangible asset, and therefore is recognised separately from goodwill, provided its fair value can be measured reliably. Additionally, because Supplier establishes its relationship with Buyer through a contract, the customer relationship with Buyer meets the contractual-legal criterion for identification as an intangible asset. Therefore, the customer relationship intangible asset is also recognised separately from goodwill provided its fair value can be measured reliably. In determining the fair value of the customer relationship, Parent considers assumptions such as the expected renewal of the supply agreement.

Sporting goods and electronics

Parent obtained control of Subsidiary in a business combination. Subsidiary manufactures goods in two distinct lines of business: sporting goods and electronics. Customer purchases from Subsidiary both sporting goods and electronics. Subsidiary has a contract with Customer to be its exclusive provider of sporting goods. However, there is no contract for the supply of electronics to Customer. Both Subsidiary and Parent believe that there is only one overall customer relationship between Subsidiary and Customer.

The contract to be Customer's exclusive supplier of sporting goods (whether cancellable or not) meets the contractual-legal criterion for identification as an intangible asset, and is therefore recognised separately from goodwill, provided its fair value can be measured reliably. Additionally, because Subsidiary establishes its relationship with Customer through a contract, the customer relationship with Customer meets the contractual-legal criterion for identification as an intangible asset. Therefore, the customer relationship intangible asset is also recognised separately from goodwill, provided its fair value can be measured reliably. Because there is only one customer relationship with Customer, the fair value of that relationship incorporates assumptions regarding Subsidiary's relationship with Customer related to both sporting goods and electronics.

However, if both Parent and Subsidiary believed there were separate customer relationships with Customer – one for sporting goods and another for electronics – the customer relationship with respect to electronics would be assessed by Parent to determine whether it meets the separability criterion for identification as an intangible asset.

Order backlog and recurring customers

Entity A obtained control of Entity B in a business combination on 31 December 2009. Entity B does business with its customers solely through purchase and sales orders. At 31 December 2009, Entity B has a backlog of customer purchase orders from 60 per cent of its customers, all of whom are recurring customers. The other 40 per cent of Entity B's customers are also recurring customers. However, as of 31 December 2009, Entity B does not have any open purchase orders or other contracts with those customers.

The purchase orders from 60 per cent of Entity B's customers (whether cancellable or not) meet the contractual-legal criterion for identification as intangible assets, and are therefore recognised separately from goodwill, provided their fair values can be measured reliably. Additionally, because Entity B has established its relationship with 60 per cent of its customers through contracts, those customer relationships meet the contractual-legal criterion for identification as an intangible asset. Therefore, the customer relationship intangible asset is also recognised separately from goodwill provided its fair value can be measured reliably.

Because Entity B has a practice of establishing contracts with the remaining 40 per cent of its customers, its relationship with those customers also arises through contractual rights, and therefore meets the contractual-legal criterion for identification as an intangible asset. Entity A recognises this customer relationship separately from goodwill, provided its fair value can be measured reliably, even though Entity B does not have contracts with those customers at 31 December 2009.

Motor insurance contracts

Parent obtained control of Insurer in a business combination. Insurer has a portfolio of one-year motor insurance contracts that are cancellable by policyholders. A reasonably predictable number of policyholders renew their insurance contracts each year.

Because Insurer establishes its relationships with policyholders through insurance contracts, the customer relationship with policyholders meets the contractual-legal criterion for identification as an intangible asset. Therefore, the customer relationship intangible asset is recognised separately from goodwill, provided its fair value can be measured reliably. In determining the fair value of the customer relationship intangible asset, Parent considers estimates of renewals and cross-selling. IAS 36 and IAS 38 apply to the customer relationship intangible asset.

In determining the fair value of the liability relating to the portfolio of insurance contracts, Parent considers estimates of cancellations by policyholders. IFRS 4 – *Insurance Contracts* – provides further guidance on accounting for the acquired contracts.

An example of a company recognising customer contracts and customer relationship intangible assets is ITV as illustrated in Extract 9.3 above. Another example is Reuters as shown in Extract 9.2 at 2.4.2 above.

One particular type of customer relationship intangible asset that should be recognised (as indicated by the last scenario in Example 9.13 above) is the value of the future profit of businesses acquired (VOBA) relating to insurance contracts or investment contracts, notwithstanding the fact that it is the customer or policyholder that decides on the continuation of the relationship. One company recognising such intangibles is Sanlam as shown below.

Extract 9.4: Sanlam Limited (2007)

Basis of Presentation and Accounting Policies [extract]
Valuation of insurance and investment business acquired

The value of insurance and investment management services contracts business acquired (VOBA) in a business combination is recognised as an intangible asset. VOBA, at initial recognition, is equal to the discounted value, using a risk-adjusted discount rate, of the projected stream of future after-tax profit that is expected to flow from the book of businesses acquired, after allowing for the cost of capital supporting the business, as applicable. The valuation is based on the Group's actuarial and valuation principles as well as assumptions in respect of future premium income, fee income, investment return, policy benefits, costs, taxation, mortality, morbidity and surrenders, as appropriate.

VOBA is amortised on a straight-line basis over the expected life of the client relationships underlying the book of business acquired. VOBA is tested for impairment on a bi-annual basis and written down for impairment where this is considered necessary. The gain or loss on disposal of a subsidiary or business includes the carrying amount of VOBA attributable to the entity or business sold. VOBA is derecognised when the related contracts are terminated, settled or disposed of.

C   Can fair value be measured reliably?

IFRS 3 (2007) itself provides no guidance on whether the fair value of an intangible asset can be measured reliably. Instead, it refers to the guidance contained in IAS 38.[119]

IAS 38 states that the fair value of intangible assets acquired in business combinations can normally be measured with sufficient reliability to be recognised separately from goodwill.[120] As noted earlier, IAS 38 indicates that the fair value of an intangible asset reflects market expectations about the probability that the future economic benefits embodied in the asset will flow to the entity. In other words, the effect of probability is reflected in the fair value measurement of the intangible asset.[121]

When, for the estimates used to measure an intangible asset's fair value, there is a range of possible outcomes with different probabilities, that uncertainty is factored into the measurement of the asset's fair value, rather than demonstrating an inability to measure fair value reliably.

If an intangible asset acquired in a business combination has a finite useful life, there is a rebuttable presumption in IAS 38 that its fair value can be measured reliably.[122]

In developing its proposals, the IASB had originally concluded that, except for an assembled workforce, sufficient information could reasonably be expected to exist to measure reliably the fair value of all intangible assets. However, after considering respondents' comments and the experiences of field visit and round-table participants, it concluded that, in some instances, there might not be sufficient information to measure reliably the fair value of an intangible asset separately from goodwill, notwithstanding that the asset is 'identifiable'.[123]

IAS 38 therefore states that 'the only circumstances in which it might not be possible to measure reliably the fair value of an intangible asset acquired in a business combination are when the intangible asset arises from legal or other contractual rights and either:

(a)   is not separable; or

(b)   is separable, but there is no history or evidence of exchange transactions for the same or similar assets, and otherwise estimating fair value would be dependent on immeasurable variables.'[124]

(As indicated at 2.5.2 above, in developing the revised IFRS 3, the IASB has now decided that in accounting for intangible assets acquired in a business combination under IFRS 3 (as revised in 2008), the reliable measurement criterion is always considered to be satisfied – see 3.6.5 B I below.)

It is clear that the IASB envisages that most intangible assets should be accounted for separately from goodwill. Possibly as an anti-avoidance measure, the IASB has introduced a specific disclosure requirement to give a description of each intangible asset that was not recognised separately from goodwill and an explanation of why the intangible asset's fair value could not be measured reliably (see item (h) at 2.13.1 A below).

The IASB has recognised that an intangible asset acquired in a business combination might be separable, but only together with a related tangible or intangible asset. For example, a magazine's publishing title might not be able to be sold separately from a related subscriber database, or a trademark for natural spring water might relate to a particular spring and could not be sold separately from the spring. In such cases IAS 38 requires the acquirer to recognise the group of assets as a single asset separately from goodwill if the individual fair values of the assets in the group are not reliably measurable.[125] In practice, where the other asset is a tangible asset it is likely that its fair value can be determined. (As indicated at 3.6.5 B IV below, for entities applying IFRS 3 (as revised in 2008), the IASB has made further amendments to IAS 38 that may limit the grouping of intangible assets with other intangible assets and the grouping of an intangible asset with a related tangible asset.)

IAS 38 notes that the terms 'brand' and 'brand name' are often used as synonyms for trademarks and other marks. However, the former are regarded as general marketing terms that are typically used to refer to a group of complementary assets such as a trademark (or service mark) and its related trade name, formulas, recipes and technological expertise. Accordingly, IAS 38 requires the acquirer to recognise as a single asset a group of complementary intangible assets comprising a brand if the individual fair values of the complementary assets are not reliably measurable. If the individual fair values of the complementary assets are reliably measurable, an acquirer may nevertheless still recognise them as a single asset provided the individual assets have similar useful lives.[126] Guidance on the determination of asset lives of intangible assets is discussed in Chapter 15 at 2.5.

Heineken, for example, combines the carrying amount of brands and customer bases acquired in business combinations, as shown below in Extract 9.5.

Extract 9.5: Heineken N.V. (2007)

Notes to the consolidated financial statements [extract]
3. Significant accounting policies [extract]
(g) Intangible assets [extract]
(ii) Brands

Brands acquired, separately, or as part of a business combination are capitalised as part of a brand portfolio if the portfolio meets the definition of an intangible asset and the recognition criteria are satisfied. Brand portfolios acquired as part of a business combination include the customer base related to the brand because it is assumed that brands have no value without customer base and vice versa. Brand portfolios acquired as part of a business combination are valued at fair value based on the royalty relief method. Brands and brand portfolios acquired separately are measured at cost. Brands and brand portfolios are amortised on a straight-line basis over their estimated useful life.

D   In-process research or development project expenditure

Both IFRS 3 (2007) and IAS 38 explicitly refer to the fact that the acquirer recognises as an asset separately from goodwill an in-process research and development project of the acquiree (if the project meets the definition of an intangible asset and its fair value can be measured reliably).[127] It is worth considering further the meaning of the words in parentheses.

An intangible asset meets the identifiability criterion under IAS 38 when it:

'(a)   is separable, i.e. is capable of being separated or divided from the entity and sold, transferred, licensed, rented or exchanged, either individually or together with a related contract, asset or liability; or

(b)   arises from contractual or other legal rights, regardless of whether those rights are transferable or separable from the entity or from other rights and obligations'.[128]

In-process research and development projects, whether or not recognised by the acquiree, are protected by legal rights and are on occasion bought and sold by entities without there being a business acquisition. Therefore, they are intangible assets as defined by IAS 38. Moreover, because they are separable and there is evidence of exchange transactions, the standard assumes that the fair value can be measured reliably. In addition, under IFRS 3 (2007) the probability criterion for recognition of an intangible asset is deemed to be met as long as its fair value can be measured reliably.

Therefore, the recognition of in-process research and development as an asset on acquisition applies different criteria to those that are required for internal projects. The research costs of internal projects may under no circumstances be capitalised.[129] Before capitalising development expenditure, entities must meet a series of exacting requirements. They must demonstrate the intangible assets' technical feasibility, their ability to complete the assets and use them or sell them and must be able to measure reliably the attributable expenditure.[130] The probable future economic benefits must be assessed using the principles in IAS 36 which means that they have to be calculated as the net present value of the cash flows generated by the asset or, if it can only generate cash flows in conjunction with other assets, of the cash-generating unit of which it is a part.[131] This process is described further in Chapter 18.

What this means is that entities will be required to recognise on acquisition some research and development expenditure that they would not have been able to recognise if it had been an internal project. The IASB was aware of this inconsistency but concluded that this did not provide a basis for subsuming in-process research and development within goodwill. It has considered the alternative (a reconsideration of the conditions for recognition of research and development costs) as being outwith the scope of the business combinations project.[132]

Although the amount attributed to the project is accounted for as an asset, IAS 38 goes on to require that any subsequent expenditure incurred after the acquisition of the project is to be accounted for in accordance with paragraphs 54-62 of IAS 38.[133] These requirements are discussed in Chapter 15 at 2.3.6.

In summary, this means that the subsequent expenditure is:

(a)   recognised as an expense when incurred if it is research expenditure;

(b)   recognised as an expense when incurred if it is development expenditure that does not satisfy the criteria for recognition as an intangible asset in paragraph 57; and

(c)   added to the carrying amount of the acquired in-process research or development project if it is development expenditure that satisfies the recognition criteria in paragraph 57.[134]

The inference is that the in-process research and development expenditure recognised as an asset on acquisition that never progresses to the stage of satisfying the recognition criteria for an internal project will ultimately be impaired, although it may be that this impairment will not arise until the entity is satisfied that the project will not continue. However, since it is an intangible asset not yet available for use, such an evaluation cannot be significantly delayed as it will need to be tested for impairment annually by comparing its carrying amount with its recoverable amount.[135] Any impairment loss will be reflected in the entity's income statement as a post-acquisition event.

E   Emission rights acquired in a business combination

If an acquiree has been granted emission rights or allowances under a cap and trade emission rights scheme (see Chapter 15 at 3.3), how should an acquirer recognise these rights and associated liabilities?

Emission rights meet the definition of an intangible asset and should therefore be recognised at the acquisition date at their fair value. Likewise, the acquirer is required to recognise a liability at fair value for the actual emissions made at the acquisition date.

As discussed in Chapter 15 at 3.3.2 B one approach that may be adopted in accounting for such rights is the 'net liability approach' whereby the emission rights are recorded at a nominal amount and the entity will only record a liability once the actual emissions exceed the emission rights granted and still held. Where the acquiree has adopted such an approach, it may be that at the date of acquisition it has not recognised an asset or liability. Nevertheless, the acquirer should recognise the emission rights as intangible assets at their fair value and a liability at fair value for the actual emissions made at the acquisition date. As discussed in Chapter 15 at 3.3.2 B, the net liability approach is not permitted for purchased emission rights and therefore is also not permitted to be applied to emission rights of the acquiree in a business combination.

Example 9.14:   *Emission rights acquired in a business combination under the 'net liability approach'*

Entity A acquires all of the shares in Entity B. Entity B had been granted emission rights for free and adopted the net liability approach for recognition of emission rights prior to the acquisition. At acquisition date the emission rights held exceed the actual emissions made and hence no asset or provision is recognised in the financial statements of Entity B in respect of emissions.

Entity A also adopts the net liability approach for emission rights granted.

In a business combination, the emission rights of the acquiree, regardless of how the acquiree received these rights, are considered to be rights purchased by the Entity A group. Accordingly, they should be treated in the same manner as emission rights purchased directly by the group.

At the acquisition date Entity A recognises the emission rights held by Entity B as intangible assets at fair value and recognises a provision for the actual emissions made up to that date at fair value.

One impact of this is that subsequent to the acquisition, the consolidated income statement will show an expense for the actual emissions made thereafter as a provision will have to be recognised on an ongoing basis. As discussed in Chapter 15 at 3.3.2 B II, there are different views of the impact that such 'purchased' emission rights have on the measurement of the provision.

The emission rights held by the acquiree will relate to specific items of property, plant and equipment. Therefore when determining the fair value of these assets, care needs to be taken to ensure that there is no double counting of the rights held.

2.5.3   *Acquiree's contingent liabilities*

As indicated at 2.5 above, the allocation of the cost of the business combination includes the separate recognition of the acquiree's contingent liabilities, if its fair value can be measured reliably, despite the fact that the acquiree has not recognised any liability for that contingency and that the recognition as a liability by the acquirer in accounting for the business combination is inconsistent with the recognition criteria in IAS 37. As indicated earlier, the IASB takes the view that the fair value of a contingent liability reflects market expectations about any uncertainty surrounding the possibility that an outflow of resources embodying economic benefits will be required to settle the possible or present obligation.

Since the recognition of this liability is not what would be required by IAS 37, IFRS 3 (2007) therefore includes requirements for the subsequent measurement of such liabilities. Accordingly, after their initial recognition, the acquirer shall measure contingent liabilities that are recognised separately in accordance with paragraph 36 of the standard at the higher of:

(a)   the amount that would be recognised in accordance with IAS 37, and

(b)   the amount initially recognised less, when appropriate, cumulative amortisation recognised in accordance with IAS 18 – *Revenue*.[136]

In developing the requirements the IASB had originally proposed that the amount should be remeasured at fair value, with any changes recognised in profit or loss until settled or the uncertain future event resolved. However, in considering respondents' comments, the IASB noted that the proposal was inconsistent with the accounting for financial guarantees and commitments to provide loans at below-market interest rates under IAS 39 (see Chapter 32 at 3.7 and Chapter 29 at 3.4 and 3.5) and so decided to amend its proposals for consistency with IAS 39.[137]

The implications of part (a) of the requirement are clear. If the acquiree has to recognise a provision in respect of the former contingent liability, and the best estimate of this liability is higher than the original fair value attributed by the acquirer, then the greater liability should now be recognised by the acquirer with the difference taken to the income statement. It would now be a provision to be measured and recognised in accordance with IAS 37. What is less clear is part (b) of the requirement. The reference to 'amortisation recognised in accordance with IAS 18' might relate to the recognition of income in respect of those loan commitments that are contingent liabilities of the acquiree, but have been recognised at fair value at date of acquisition. The implication of the requirement would appear to mean that the amount of the liability cannot be reduced below its originally attributed fair value except in restrictive circumstances. It would also seem to imply that the liability could not be derecognised even if the contingency were resolved without an outflow of economic benefits or the item has been settled at a lower amount, which clearly could not have been what was intended.

We consider that it is important to bear in mind that the contingent liabilities have not been recognised by the acquiree because they are either:

- possible obligations, as it has yet to be confirmed whether the entity has a present obligation that could lead to an outflow of resources embodying economic benefits; or

- present obligations that do not meet the recognition criteria in IAS 37 (because either it is not probable that an outflow of resources embodying economic benefits will be required to settle the obligation, or a sufficiently reliable estimate of the amount of the obligation cannot be made).[138]

In many instances, therefore, these contingent liabilities will never become liabilities under IAS 37 or be settled (in cash or other resources) by the entities. Therefore, it must be acceptable to write back the contingent liability if the uncertainty is resolved (whether by payment or otherwise) and it is clear that there is no remaining obligation on the part of the entity. Indeed, as indicated at 3.6.6 A II below, IFRS 3 (as revised in 2008) now clarifies that the subsequent measurement requirements apply until the liability is settled, cancelled or expires.

Despite the fact that the requirement for subsequent measurement discussed above was introduced for consistency with IAS 39, the standard makes it clear that the requirement does not apply to contracts accounted for in accordance with IAS 39. However, loan commitments excluded from the scope of IAS 39 (i.e. those other than those that are commitments to provide loans at below-market interest rates) will fall within the requirements of IFRS 3 (2007). Such loan commitments are to be regarded as contingent liabilities of the acquiree if, at the acquisition date, it is not probable that an outflow of resources embodying economic benefits will be required to settle the obligation or if the amount of the obligation cannot be measured with sufficient reliability. As with other contingent liabilities of the acquiree, such a loan commitment is recognised separately as part of allocating the cost of a combination only if its fair value can be measured reliably.[139]

IFRS 3 (2007) notes that contingent liabilities recognised separately as part of allocating the cost of a business combination are excluded from the scope of IAS 37. Nevertheless, the acquirer has to disclose for those contingent liabilities the information required to be disclosed by IAS 37 for each class of provision (see Chapter 24 at 6.1).[140]

If the fair value of a contingent liability cannot be measured reliably then the standard notes that this will affect the amount recognised as goodwill or 'negative goodwill' (see 2.6 and 2.7 below). In that case, the acquirer shall disclose the information about that contingent liability required to be disclosed by IAS 37 (see Chapter 24 at 6.2).[141]

2.5.4 Determining the fair values of the acquiree's identifiable assets, liabilities and contingent liabilities

IFRS 3 (2007) requires an acquirer to recognise the acquiree's identifiable assets, liabilities and contingent liabilities that satisfy the relevant recognition criteria at their fair values at the acquisition date (except for non-current assets (or disposal groups) that are classified as held for sale in accordance with IFRS 5 which are recognised at fair value less costs to sell). Fair value is defined as 'the amount for which an asset could be exchanged, or a liability settled, between knowledgeable, willing parties in an arm's length transaction'.[142] Appendix B to IFRS 3 (2007), which is an integral part of the standard, gives guidance on the measures that should be used in determining the fair values of various items. It also notes that if the guidance for a particular item does not refer to the use of present value techniques, such techniques may be used in estimating the fair value of that item.[143] Due to the IASB's project on fair value measurement, this detailed guidance is no longer included in IFRS 3 (as revised in 2008) (see 3.6.3 below).

In addition to the guidance in Appendix B to IFRS 3 (2007), IAS 38 contains specific guidance on measuring the fair values of intangible assets. The guidance for particular items is discussed below.

A   Financial instruments

Financial instruments traded in an active market should be valued at their current market values. For financial instruments not traded in an active market estimated values should be used taking into consideration features such as price-earnings ratios, dividend yields and expected growth rates of comparable instruments of entities with similar characteristics.[144] This guidance reflects the fact that its origin comes from IAS 22, which only referred to 'securities' rather than financial instruments. For other types of financial instruments that are not traded on an active market, fair values may need to be estimated using present value techniques. Further guidance on the fair values of financial instruments is discussed in Chapter 32 at 4.

Although investments in associates are scoped out of IAS 39 they meet the definition of a 'financial instrument'. Accordingly, where as part of a business combination one of the identified assets is an investment in an associate, then the fair value of the associate should be determined in accordance with the above guidance, rather than calculating a fair value based on the appropriate share of the fair values of the identifiable assets, liabilities and contingent liabilities of the associate. By doing so, any goodwill relating to the associate is subsumed within the carrying amount for the associate rather than within the goodwill arising on the overall business combination. Nevertheless, although this fair value is effectively the 'cost' to the group to which equity accounting is applied, the underlying fair values of the identifiable assets, liabilities and contingent liabilities also need to be determined to apply equity accounting (see Chapter 11 at 3.2).

If the fair value exercise results in an excess of assets over the fair value of the consideration (commonly referred to as 'negative goodwill'), in accordance with the requirements of IFRS 3 (2007) discussed at 2.7 below, the acquirer should challenge the fair value placed on the associate as it rechallenges the values place on all of the assets, liabilities and contingent liabilities of the acquiree to ensure that the value has not been overstated.

B　　　Receivables, beneficial contracts and other identifiable assets

Receivables, beneficial contracts and other identifiable assets should be valued based on the present values of the amounts to be received, determined at appropriate current interest rates, less allowances for uncollectibility and collection costs, if necessary. However, discounting is not required for short-term receivables, beneficial contracts and other identifiable assets when the difference between the nominal and discounted amounts is not material.[145]

C　　　Inventories

Finished goods and merchandise should be valued using selling prices less the costs of disposal and a reasonable profit allowance for the selling effort of the acquirer based on profit for similar finished goods and merchandise. Work in progress should be valued using selling prices of finished goods less the sum of the costs to complete, the costs of disposal and a reasonable profit allowance for the completing and selling effort based on profit for similar finished goods. Raw materials should be valued using current replacement costs.[146]

Example 9.15:　　Fair value of work in progress

Entity A acquires Entity B on 30 June 2009. Entity B operates a dairy business and included in its inventory at the date of acquisition was work in progress being inventory of cheddar cheese in the cellars of the dairy left to mature for a year. The carrying amount of this inventory, being the costs incurred to the date of acquisition, is €400,000.

The intention is to sell the cheese once it has matured. The sales price of fully-matured cheese of the same quality at 30 June 2009 is €900,000. Future storage, marketing and selling expenses required to complete the process and market the product to retailers are estimated at €185,000.

How should the fair value of the work in progress be determined?

The guidance in IFRS 3 (2007) requires that work in progress should be valued using the selling prices of finished goods less the sum of costs to complete, the cost of disposal and a reasonable profit allowance for completing and selling effort based on the profit for similar finished goods. This effectively means that the overall profit made as a result of manufacturing and selling the cheese is split between the pre-acquisition effort of the acquiree and the post-acquisition effort of the group. However, the standard does not define how to calculate the reasonable profit allowance to be related to the completing and selling efforts. Clearly, judgement will be required by entities in making such a determination.

Assuming that there are no significant inefficiencies in the business processes, one approach would be to use the cost structure of Entity B to determine the reasonable profit allowance for subsequent costs to be incurred. Accordingly, it may be concluded that if Entity B had not been acquired by Entity A, it would have incurred total costs of €585,000. Based on the estimated selling price of €900,000, this would result in an overall profit of €315,000. Consequently, the profit allowance to be made for the completing and selling effort would be €100,000 (being €315,000 × €185,000/€585,000). On this basis, the fair value of the work in progress would be €615,000 (being €900,000 − €185,000 − €100,000).

D　　　Land and buildings

These should be valued using market values.[147] Like plant and equipment below, these will probably need to be determined by appraisal. Also, in our view if there is no market-based evidence of fair value because of the specialised nature of the property, the fair value may need to be estimated using an income or a depreciated replacement cost approach.

E   Plant and equipment

Again, these should be valued using market values, normally determined by appraisal. If there is no market-based evidence of fair value because of the specialised nature of the item of plant and equipment and the item is rarely sold, except as part of a continuing business, an acquirer may need to estimate fair value using an income or a depreciated replacement cost approach.[148]

F   Intangible assets

Intangible assets should be valued by reference to an active market as defined in IAS 38 (see Chapter 15 at 2.3.2 A).[149] IAS 38 states that 'quoted market prices in an active market provide the most reliable estimate of the fair value of an intangible asset'. It goes on to say that 'the appropriate market price is usually the current bid price. If current bid prices are unavailable, the price of the most recent similar transaction may provide a basis from which to estimate fair value, provided that there has not been a significant change in economic circumstances between the transaction date and the date at which the asset's fair value is estimated.'[150]

However, IAS 38 also notes that it is uncommon for an active market to exist for intangible assets and that such a market cannot exist for brands, newspaper mastheads, music and publishing rights, patents or trademarks,[151] i.e. many of the intangible assets that IFRS 3 (2007) and IAS 38 require an acquirer to recognise as part of the allocation process. Accordingly, if no active market exists, the intangible assets should be valued on a basis that reflects the amounts the acquirer would have paid for the assets in arm's length transactions between knowledgeable willing parties, based on the best information available.[152] In determining this amount, an entity considers the outcome of recent transactions for similar assets.[153]

IAS 38 acknowledges that entities that are regularly involved in the purchase and sale of unique intangible assets may have developed techniques for estimating their fair values indirectly. Accordingly, it allows these techniques to be used for initial measurement of an intangible asset acquired in a business combination if their objective is to estimate fair value and if they reflect current transactions and practices in the industry to which the asset belongs. These techniques include, when appropriate:

(a)   applying multiples reflecting current market transactions to indicators that drive the profitability of the asset (such as revenue, market shares and operating profit) or to the royalty stream that could be obtained from licensing the intangible asset to another party in an arm's length transaction (as in the 'relief from royalty' approach); or

(b)   discounting estimated future net cash flows from the asset.[154]

However, as part of the annual improvement standard issued in April 2009, the IASB revised the above guidance in IAS 38 to clarify the description of valuation techniques commonly used by entities when measuring the fair value of intangible assets acquired in a business combination that are not traded in active markets, but decided that the amendments should be applied prospectively. This is because retrospective application might require some entities to remeasure fair values associated with previous transactions, and the Board did not think this was appropriate because the remeasurement might involve the use of hindsight in those circumstances.[155] The amended requirements below apply prospectively for annual periods beginning on or after 1 July 2009, with earlier application permitted. If an entity applies the amendments for an earlier period it should disclose that fact.[156]

Accordingly the amended guidance in IAS 38 continues to require that if no active market exists the intangible assets should be valued on a basis that reflects the amounts the acquirer would have paid for the assets in arm's length transactions between knowledgeable willing parties, based on the best information available. In determining this amount, an entity considers the outcome of recent transactions for similar assets. For example, an entity may apply multiples reflecting current market transactions to factors that drive the profitability of the asset (such as revenue, operating profit or earnings before interest, tax, depreciation and amortisation).[157]

The guidance continues to acknowledge that entities that are involved in the purchase and sale of intangible assets may have developed techniques for estimating their fair values indirectly. Accordingly, it allows these techniques to be used for initial measurement of an intangible asset acquired in a business combination if their objective is to estimate fair value and if they reflect current transactions and practices in the industry to which the asset belongs. However, it clarifies that these techniques include, for example:[158]

(a) discounting estimated future net cash flows from the asset; or

(b) estimating the costs the entity avoids by owning the intangible asset and not needing:

    (i) to license it from another party in an arm's length transaction (as in the 'relief from royalty' approach, using discounted net cash flows); or

    (ii) to recreate or replace it (as in the cost approach).

It is generally considered that there are three broad approaches to valuing intangible assets as shown in the diagram below.

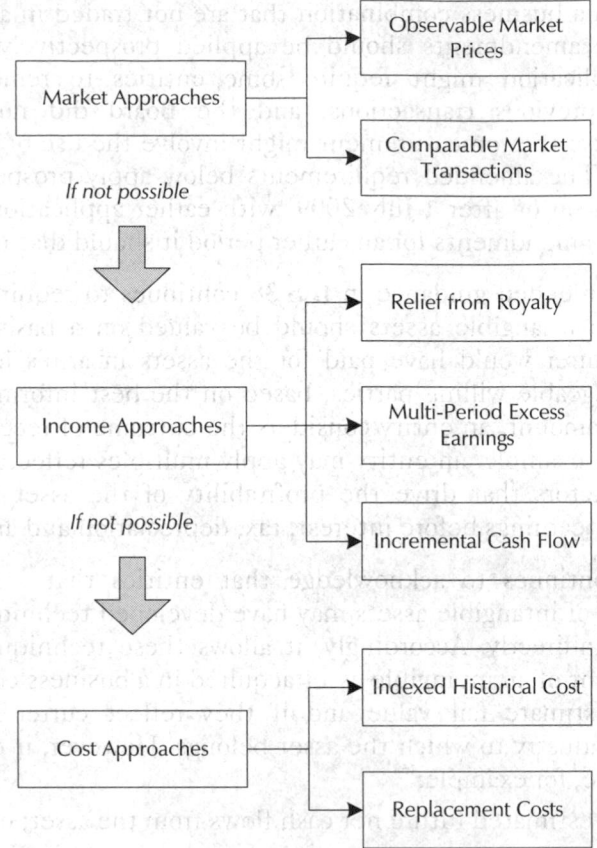

Under a market-based approach, if no actual market prices are available for the respective asset, the fair value of the intangible is derived by analysing similar intangible assets that have recently been sold or licensed, and then comparing these transactions to the intangible asset that needs to be valued. This approach is regarded as preferable where an active market for the assets exist. However, in practice, the ability to use such an approach is very limited. Intangible assets are generally unique, and there is rarely an active market to examine.

A cost-based approach is generally regarded as having limited application and difficult to use in many cases. The premise of the cost approach is that an investor would pay no more for an intangible asset than the cost to recreate it. However, for most intangibles, cost approaches are rarely consistent with the definition of 'fair value'.

Income-based approaches are much more commonly used. These involve identifying the expected economic benefits to be derived from the ownership of the particular intangible asset, and calculating the fair value of an intangible asset at the present value of those benefits. These are discussed further below.

For each asset, there are often several methodologies which can be applied. The choice will depend on the circumstances, in particular the nature of the value brought by the asset to the company (i.e. additional revenue, cost savings, replacement time and cost savings, etc.). In some cases, two methods may be used for the same asset – one as the primary approach to valuing the asset and the other as a check for reasonableness.

The two main income-based approaches that are used are:

- the Multi Period Excess Earnings Method ('MEEM')
- the Relief from Royalty method.

A discounted cash flow method may be used, for example, in determining the value of cost-savings that will be achieved as a result of having a supply contract with advantageous terms in relation to current market rates.

The MEEM approach will generally be used in valuing the most important intangible asset. This is because it is effectively a residual cash flow approach. The key issue in using this approach is how to determine the income/cash flow that is related to the intangible asset being valued, and the fact that it is not the full cash flow of the business that is used. As its name suggests, the value of an intangible asset determined under the MEEM approach is estimated through the sum of the discounted future excess earnings attributable to the intangible asset. The excess earnings is the difference between the after-tax operating cash flow attributable to the intangible asset and the required cost of invested capital on all other assets used in order to generate those cash flows. These contributory assets include property, plant and equipment, other identifiable intangible assets and net working capital. The allowance made for the cost of such capital is based on the value of such assets and a required rate of return reflecting the risks of the particular assets.

The Relief from Royalty method is used in many cases to calculate the value of a trademark or trade name. This approach is based on the concept that if an entity owns a trademark, it does not have to pay for the use of it and therefore is relieved from paying a royalty. The amount of that theoretical payment is used as a surrogate for income attributable to the trademark. The valuation is arrived at computing the present value of the after-tax royalty savings using an appropriate discount rate. The after-tax royalty savings are calculating by applying an appropriate royalty rate to the projected revenue, deducting the legal protection expenses relating to the trademark, and an allowance for tax at the appropriate rate.

Companies will generally use more than one of the above approaches in attributing fair values to intangible assets in a business combination as illustrated in the following extract:

Extract 9.6: Bayer AG (2005)

Notes to the Consolidated Financial Statements of the Bayer Group [extract]

5.   Critical accounting policies

Acquisition accounting [extract]

We account for the acquired businesses using the purchase method of accounting which requires that the assets acquired and the liabilities assumed be recorded at the date of acquisition at their respective fair values.

The application of the purchase method requires certain estimates and assumptions especially concerning the determination of the fair values of acquired intangible assets and property, plant and equipment as well as liabilities assumed at the date of the acquisition. Moreover the useful lives of the acquired intangible assets, property, plant and equipment have to be determined. The judgments made in the context of the purchase price allocation can materially impact our future results of operations. Accordingly, for significant acquisitions, we obtain assistance from third party valuation specialists. The valuations are based on information available at the acquisition date.

Significant judgments and assumptions made regarding the purchase price allocation in the course of the acquisition of Schering AG, Berlin, Germany, included the following:

For intangible assets associated with products, product related technology, and qualified in-process research and development (IPR&D) we base our valuation on the expected future cash flows using the Multi-Period Excess Earnings approach. This method employs a discounted cash flow analysis using the present value of the estimated after-tax cash flows expected to be generated from the purchased intangible asset using risk adjusted discount rates and revenue forecasts as appropriate. The period of expected cash flows was based on the individual patent protection, taking into account the term of the product's main patent protection and essential extension of patent protection, as well as market entry of generics, considering sales, volume, potential defense strategies and market development at patent expiry.

For the valuation of brands, the relief-from-royalty method was applied which includes estimating the cost savings that result from the company's ownership of trademarks and licenses on which it does not have to pay royalties to a licensor. The intangible asset is then recognized at the present value of these savings. The brand-specific royalty rates were calculated using a product-specific scoring model. The corporate brands "Schering" and "Medrad" were assumed to have an unlimited life. (Please note that the rights to the name "Schering" in the United States and Canada do not belong to us but to Schering-Plough Corporation, New Jersey. Schering-Plough Corporation and the company acquired by Bayer in June 2006, i.e. Bayer Schering Pharma AG (formerly named Schering AGI, Berlin, Germany, are unaffiliated companies that have been totally independent of each other for many years.) Product brands, however, were assumed to have limited lives depending on the respective products' life cycles. The expected amortization of these assets is determined on the basis of expected product-specific revenues.

Another example is ITV as shown in Extract 9.3 at 2.5.2 A above.

In some situations, it may be that the value of an intangible asset will reflect not only the present value of the future post-tax cash flows as indicated above, but also the value of any tax benefits (sometimes called 'tax amortisation benefits') that the owner might have obtained if the asset had been bought separately, i.e. not as part of a business combination. Whether such tax benefits are included will depend on the nature of the intangible asset and the relevant tax jurisdiction. Where such a value is included in the fair value of the intangible asset, an asset that has been purchased as part of a business combination may be one that is wholly or in part not actually tax-deductible by the entity. This therefore raises a potential impairment issue that is discussed in Chapter 18 at 5.2.2.

Another issue relating to the valuation of intangible assets is whether the acquirer's intention in relation to those assets should be taken into account in attributing a fair value, for example, where the acquirer does not intend to use an intangible asset of the acquiree.

Example 9.16:   *Impact of acquirer's intention on fair value of intangible asset*

Entity A acquires a competitor, Entity B. One of the identifiable intangible assets of Entity B is the trade name of one of Entity B's branded products. However, since Entity A has a similar product, it does not intend to use that trade name post-acquisition. Entity A will discontinue sales of Entity B's product, thereby eliminating competition and enhancing the value of its own branded product. The cash flows relating to the acquired trade name are therefore expected to be nil.

Given that the cash flows relating to that trade name will be nil, can Entity A attribute a fair value of nil to that trade name?

In our view, the answer is no. As indicated at 2.5.4 above, IFRS 3 (2007) defines fair value as 'the amount for which an asset could be exchanged, or a liability settled, between knowledgeable, willing parties in an arm's length transaction'. Accordingly, Entity A's future intentions about the asset should only be reflected in determining the fair value if that is what other knowledgeable willing buyers would do. In most situations, this will not be the case and therefore it is likely that the trade name does have a value. In fact, Entity A could probably have sold the trade name post-acquisition, but it has chosen not to do that to protect its own branded product. Accordingly, a fair value is attributed to that trade name. Only if it was not possible to reliably measure the fair value would no amount be recognised for the trade name (see 2.5.2 C above).

This does raise an issue as to whether an immediate impairment loss should be reflected in respect of the trade name since the expected cash flows relating to it are nil. Again, in our view the answer is no – there is no immediate impairment loss. As discussed at 3.3 of Chapter 18, for the purposes of the impairment test under IAS 36, the recoverable amount of an asset is the higher of its value in use (VIU) and its fair value less costs to sell (FV). The FV of the trade name will initially not be materially different from the fair value attributed to it, and therefore unlikely to be impaired.

However, since Entity A is not intending to use the trade name to generate cash flows, it is unlikely that it could be regarded as having an indefinite life for the purposes of IAS 38, and therefore it should be amortised over its expected useful life. The estimate of the life should reflect the use to which Entity A is putting the trade name, which is as a means of eliminating competition for its own product. This is likely to be a relatively short period as the impact of the absence of that particular trade name in the market will not last for long, and any value that it did have will quickly reduce.

Where the above situation arises, consideration should also be given as to whether all intangible assets of the acquiree have been identified, and an appropriate fair value attributed to them. For example, it may be that what is thought to be the value of a brand or trade name actually comprises of other rights connected to the business acquired such as customer relationships, distribution networks, etc. As indicated at 2.5.2 above, IFRS 3 (2007) requires such intangibles to be recognised separately.

G   *Defined benefit plans*

Net employee benefit assets or liabilities for defined benefit plans should be valued using the present value of the defined benefit obligation less the fair value of any plan assets. However, an asset is recognised only to the extent that it is probable it will be available to the acquirer in the form of refunds from the plan or a reduction in future contributions.[159] In computing the present value of the obligation, IAS 19 – *Employee Benefits* – states that any items such as actuarial gains and losses (whether or not within the 10% corridor allowed by IAS 19), past service costs and amounts not yet recognised by the acquiree under the transitional provisions of IAS 19 at the date of the acquisition should be included.[160] This means that there are no exemptions for the acquirer from recognising the full defined benefit obligation on acquisition.

H   Tax assets and liabilities

Tax assets and liabilities should be valued using the amount of the tax benefit arising from tax losses or the taxes payable in respect of profit or loss in accordance with IAS 12, assessed from the perspective of the combined entity. The tax asset or liability is determined after allowing for the tax effect of restating identifiable assets, liabilities and contingent liabilities to their fair values and is not discounted.[161] The deferred tax consequences of business combinations are discussed further in Chapter 26 at 6.2.

I   Payables

Accounts and notes payable, long-term debt, liabilities, accruals and other claims payable should be valued using the present values of amounts to be disbursed in settling the liabilities determined at appropriate current interest rates. However, discounting is not required for short-term liabilities when the difference between the nominal and discounted amounts is not material.[162]

J   Onerous contracts and other identifiable liabilities

Onerous contracts and other identifiable liabilities of the acquiree should be valued using the present values of amounts to be disbursed in settling the obligations determined at appropriate current interest rates.[163]

IFRS 3 (2007) contains no further reference to 'onerous contracts', nor does it give any examples. Clearly, any provisions for onerous contracts that would be recognised under IAS 37 will require to be recognised and measured at their fair value under IFRS 3 (2007). As discussed in Chapter 24 at 5.3, IAS 37 defines on onerous contract as 'a contract in which the unavoidable costs of meeting the obligations exceed the economic benefits expected to be received under it', i.e. one that is directly loss-making, not simply uneconomic by reference to current prices.

Accordingly, it might be thought that onerous contracts recognised under IFRS 3 (2007) should only encompass those that would be recognised under IAS 37, and therefore no liability should be recognised, for example, for leases at an unfavourable rental or for an excessive amount of space, or for contracts to provide services in an area of business which is uneconomic. However, as discussed at 2.5 above, IFRS 3 (2007) envisages liabilities being recognised at the date of acquisition that were not previously recognised by the acquiree before the acquisition. Also, much of the guidance in other areas in the standard require fair values to be based on market conditions at the acquisition date. Therefore, we believe that contracts that are 'onerous' by reference to market conditions at the date of acquisitions should be recognised as liabilities. This is consistent with the IFRS 3 (2007) requirements for intangible assets. As discussed at 2.5.2 A above, IFRS 3 (2007) includes within its list of examples of intangible assets that should be recognised, includes contract-based intangibles such as lease agreements. Thus, any leases that are 'favourable' by reference to market conditions would be recognised as assets at their fair value.

K   Contingent liabilities

Contingent liabilities of the acquiree should be valued using the amounts that a third party would charge to assume those contingent liabilities. Such an amount shall reflect all expectations about possible cash flows and not the single most likely or the expected maximum or minimum cash flow.[164] This is especially relevant given that many contingent liabilities are so defined as it is not probable that an outflow of resources embodying economic benefits will be required to settle the obligation[165] – even though the minimum cash flow may be zero, a third party would still charge a sum to assume the contingent liability.

2.5.5   Reassessment of the acquiree's classification of assets, liabilities, equity and relationships acquired in a business combination

As discussed at 2.5.1 above, IFRS 3 (2007) states that the identifiable assets and liabilities that are recognised in accordance with paragraph 36 of the standard include all of the acquiree's assets and liabilities that the acquirer purchases or assumes, including all of its financial assets and financial liabilities. They might also include assets and liabilities not previously recognised in the acquiree's financial statements, e.g. because they did not qualify for recognition before the acquisition.[166] It is irrelevant whether or not the acquiree had previously recognised those assets and liabilities; the acquirer makes a new assessment of what should be recognised based on conditions at the date of the business combination. The acquirer now controls the assets acquired and the liabilities assumed, and recognises them on this basis.

Although IFRS 3 (2007) is explicit on recognition, it is silent on classification. This issue was considered by the IFRIC in March 2007 when it was asked to provide guidance on whether, and in what circumstances, a business combination triggers reassessment of the acquiree's classification or designation of assets, liabilities, equity and relationships acquired in a business combination. Reassessment issues include, for instance, whether embedded derivatives should be separated from the host contract, the continuation or de-designation of hedge relationships and the classification of leases as operating or finance leases. The IFRIC noted that the IASB, at its meeting in February 2007, decided that the issue should be dealt with in Business Combinations phase II. Given that decision, the IFRIC decided not to take this item on to its agenda.[167]

In the meantime, since IFRS 3 (2007) does not contain a general principle regarding whether reassessment of the acquiree's classification of assets, liabilities and equity is allowed, required or prohibited in a business combination, we believe that the treatment should be based on the requirements of the particular IFRS relevant to the items concerned.

Example 9.17:   Reassessment of the acquiree's classification of assets, liabilities, equity and relationships acquired in a business combination

Entity A obtains control of Entity B in a business combination. Entity B is a party to a number of contracts such that included within the assets and liabilities of Entity B are the following:

(a) Lease contracts, some of which are classified as operating leases and some of which are classified as finance leases in accordance with paragraph 4 of IAS 17 – *Leases*;

(b) Some financial guarantee contracts are classified as insurance contracts and have been accounted for under IFRS 4;

(c) Certain hedge relationships have been designated at the inception of the hedges such that they qualify for hedge accounting in accordance with paragraph 88 of IAS 39;

(d) Financial assets and liabilities have been classified upon initial recognition in accordance with paragraph 9 of IAS 39, including items designated as at fair value through profit or loss and items as held-to-maturity; and

(e) Embedded derivatives, some of which have been separated from the host contract and some of which have not at the date of inception of the contracts in accordance with paragraph 11 of IAS 39.

Based on the requirements of the particular IFRS relevant to these items, whether Entity A is allowed or required to reassess the classification of such items is as follows:

(a) As discussed in Chapter 22 at 2.3.3, IAS 17 requires that lease classification is made at the inception of the lease. A change in classification only arises if the lessee and the lessor agree to change the provisions of the lease. Thus, in the absence of such changes, Entity A cannot reassess the classification of the leases.

(b) As discussed in Chapter 29 at 3.4.2, the election to classify financial guarantee contracts as insurance contracts and account for them under IFRS 4 is irrevocable. Also, paragraph B30 of IFRS 4 states that 'a contract that qualifies as an insurance contract remains an insurance contract until all rights and obligations are extinguished or expire'. Thus, Entity A cannot reassess the classification of these financial guarantee contracts.

(c) As discussed in Chapter 33 at 5, there are a number of conditions that need to be met for hedge relationships to qualify for hedge accounting, in particular formal documentation and an ongoing assessment of the designated hedge. As long as the documentation of Entity B is consistent with the risk management strategy of the Entity A group, the documentation can be carried over for both cash flow hedges and fair value hedges. However, we believe that there should exist some evidence of re-affirmation of the hedge relationship upon 'carry-over' of the hedge documentation. It should be noted that the documentation may differ depending upon the level of the entity (parent company, subsidiary, or consolidation) at which the hedge relationship exists.

Similar to the documentation requirements, the hedge effectiveness testing may also be carried forward. If effectiveness changes upon 'carry-over', the documentation will need to change.

However, if it is a cash flow hedge, the Entity A group does not inherit Entity B's existing cash flow hedge reserve, as this clearly represents cumulative pre-acquisition gains and losses. This has implications for the assessment of hedge effectiveness and the measurement of ineffectiveness because, so far as the Entity A group is concerned, it has started a new hedge relationship with a hedging instrument that is likely to have a non-zero fair value (see Chapter 33 at 4.2.4).

Thus, Entity A effectively needs to reassess the hedging relationships, even if in some situations it may only be reaffirming what Entity B has done.

(d) The requirements for the classification of financial assets and liabilities are discussed in Chapter 29 at 7. The classification is made upon initial recognition and the categories identified are: financial assets and liabilities at fair value through profit or loss, held-to-maturity investments, loans and receivables, available-for-sale financial assets, and other financial liabilities. As indicated at 7.5 in Chapter 29, financial assets and financial liabilities cannot be reclassified into or out of the fair value through profit or loss category. However, reclassifications are permitted, and in some situations required, between held-to-maturity investments and available-for-sale assets. Although IAS 39 would appear to prohibit the reclassification of items into or out of the fair value through profit or loss category, arguably this does not apply to the Entity A group, since from the perspective of Entity A, initial recognition only takes place at the date of the business combination. Also, if Entity A already has an accounting policy for like transactions, IAS 27 (2007) requires the Entity A consolidated financial statements to use uniform accounting policies. Thus, it would be appropriate for Entity A to reassess the designation of such financial assets and financial liabilities.

(e) The requirements for the reassessment of embedded derivatives are discussed in Chapter 29 at 5.4. Whereas IAS 39 requires an entity to assess whether an embedded derivative needs to be separated from the host contract and accounted for a derivative when it first becomes a party to that contract, IFRIC 9 – *Reassessment of Embedded Derivatives* – explains that during the life of the contract subsequent reassessment is prohibited. However, as indicated at 5.4.3 in Chapter 29, IFRIC makes it clear that it does not address the acquisition of contracts with embedded derivatives in a business combination nor their possible reassessment at the date of acquisition. Consequently, Entity A appears to have a choice of two accounting policies for such contracts: either reassess the contracts based on the terms of the contract and the economic circumstances at the date of the business combination or do not reassess the contracts and continue with the classification made by Entity B when it first became a party to the contracts. Whichever policy is adopted, it should be applied consistently.

As indicated above, in February 2007 the IASB decided to deal with this issue in its revision of IFRS 3. Accordingly, IFRS 3 (as revised in 2008) contains explicit requirements in this area (see 3.6.4 below).

2.5.6 *Pre-existing relationships with an acquiree*

In some business combinations an acquirer and an acquiree have a relationship that predates the business combination. Often the effect of consolidating the acquiree is that the pre-existing relationship is settled or extinguished. In such cases, should this be accounted for as part of the business combination or as a separate transaction?

Although IFRS currently has no specific guidance on accounting for pre-existing relationships between an acquirer and acquiree the fact that the business combination has two economic effects – the acquisition of a business and the effective settlement of the pre-existing arrangement – indicates that there are two components to be accounted for separately. This is consistent with existing guidance in US GAAP in EITF 04-1 – *Accounting for Pre-existing Relationships between the Parties to a Business Combination* – as well as the approach to be applied under IFRS 3 (as revised in 2008) (see 3.12.1 below).

In our view such pre-existing relationships should be accounted for separately from the business combination by:

(a) allocating the cost of the combination to all acquired assets and liabilities including those that reflect pre-existing relationships, and

(b) treating this as an effective settlement of the pre-existing relationship by applying the same accounting treatment that would have applied if the settlement had occurred as a stand alone transaction. This 'settlement' will generally result automatically through the application of normal consolidation elimination principles as required by IAS 27 (2007) (see Chapter 7 at 2.4).

The following table illustrates how the acquirer would account for the settlement of common pre-existing relationships in its consolidated financial statements:

Acquiree holds the following:	Acquirer accounts for as:
A receivable from / payable to the acquirer	Extinguishment of the acquirer's payable / receivable
Shares in the acquirer	Acquisition of treasury shares
Shares in a subsidiary of the acquirer	Acquisition of minority interest
Shares in an associate of the acquirer	Step acquisition of associate (or possibly a subsidiary)
A supply contract with the acquirer	Termination of the contract
Contractual rights to use an intangible asset of the acquirer (e.g. licence of trade name)	Repurchase of the contractual right

For financial assets and liabilities, such as receivables or payables, it can generally be presumed that they would be settled at fair value when undertaking an arms' length transaction. Accordingly, the allocated value would be equal to their fair value assessed by reference to the guidance in IAS 39 (see Chapter 32 at 4). Where this value is different from the acquirer's carrying value of the corresponding asset or liability, there is a resulting gain or loss on consolidation when the asset and liability are eliminated.

Similarly, the allocated value for shares in the acquirer, subsidiary of the acquirer or an associate of the acquirer would be equal to their fair value assessed by reference to the guidance in IAS 39. Where the asset held is shares in the acquirer, the effective settlement is accounted for as an acquisition of treasury shares, so the value attributed will be deducted from equity (see Chapter 31 at 6). Where the asset held is shares in a subsidiary of the acquirer, the value attributed will be treated as the cost of acquisition of a minority interest in that subsidiary (see Chapter 7 at 3.3.3 for guidance on the acquisition of minority interests). Where the asset held is shares in an associate of the acquirer, the value attributed will be treated as the cost in a step-acquisition of an associate (see Chapter 11 at 3.2.4 for guidance on such transactions) or possibly the cost in a step-acquisition of a subsidiary (if the additional shares together with the existing shares held now mean that the associate becomes a subsidiary) – see 2.9 below for guidance on such business combinations achieved in stages.

For supply and other executory contracts there is no explicit guidance in IFRS 3 (2007) regarding how to measure the effective settlement value. In our view it would be acceptable to measure this at either:

(a)   the least cost of exiting the contract i.e. the lesser of:

(i)   the amount by which the contract is favourable or unfavourable by reference to current market pricing for similar transactions; and

(ii)   any explicit settlement terms in the contract available to the party to which the contract is unfavourable; or

(b)   the total fair value of the contract which may also reflect the value associated with the selling effort in acquiring the contract and any related customer relationship.

This will result in a gain or loss on settlement equal to the settlement value less any amount that has already been recorded by the acquirer in relation to the contract.

Example 9.18:   Effective settlement of a supply contract with the acquirer

An acquirer pays €50m to acquire a business that has other identifiable net assets of €40m in addition to a supply contract. The contract is a fixed price contract for the acquiree to supply goods to the acquirer for a further three years. Current market prices are less than the contract price. The fair value of the contract is assessed as €6m comprising (i) €2m reflecting the value of an 'at market' three year contract (e.g. this could reflect the value of the selling effort in securing such a contract); and (ii) €4m reflecting the unfavourable pricing.

One approach is that the acquirer would assign a settlement value of €4m for the contract, being the amount reflecting the unfavourable pricing. Therefore, the acquirer would:

(a)   allocate the total cost of the combination (€50m) to (i) the contract (€4m); (ii) other identifiable net assets (€40m); and (iii) goodwill (€6m); and

(b)   eliminate the contract and thus recognise a settlement loss of €4m (less any amount that had already been recognised as a liability by the acquirer).

This approach reflects an expectation that if parties are acting rationally they ought to be prepared to settle based upon current market pricing (€4m in the example). However, if the contract contains explicit settlement terms then the party to whom the contract is unfavourable would be expected to exit on those terms where this is less than the 'off-market' value of the contract. So, if the acquirer was permitted to terminate the contract early upon payment of a penalty of, say, €3m then this value would be the settlement value. Thus, goodwill of €7m would be recognised.

As indicated above, the settlement value of a contract is not necessarily equal to its fair value since fair value will also reflect the value associated with the selling effort in acquiring the contract. Similarly, the settlement value does not include the value of any related customer relationship intangible that may arise from the contractual relationship between the parties. Since the consolidated entity cannot have a contractual relationship with itself no asset is recorded in relation to the contract or the relationship. This means that any such value is effectively subsumed within goodwill.

The alternative approach would be to measure the settlement value at the total fair value of the contract rather than just the off-market pricing. This is not the approach that is included in the guidance in the IASB's revised IFRS 3 (see 3.12.1 below). However, in the absence of explicit guidance in IFRS 3 (2007) this approach would also be considered acceptable since the amount attributed to the contract asset is its fair value. On this basis €6m would be allocated to the contract, thus resulting in a settlement loss of €6m and a correspondingly lower amount for goodwill of €4m.

Prior to the application of IFRS 3 (as revised in 2008), IFRS is silent on the accounting for the repurchase of contractual rights to use an intangible asset – such as the grant of a right to use a brand name or a franchise agreement. As with executory contracts, repurchased contractual rights may also give rise to a gain or loss on settlement due to any 'off-market' pricing value. For any remaining value of the repurchased right, i.e. the 'on-market' element, the accounting should be consistent with the accounting that would be adopted for the purchase of contractual rights outside of a business combination. Provided that the underlying intangible asset is capable of separate recognition as an asset any remaining value is accounted for by recognising a separate intangible asset for the repurchased right that is amortised over the original contract term. This is consistent with the approach to be applied under IFRS 3 (as revised in 2008) as discussed at 3.6.6 E below.

Note that the repurchase of a contractual right can be distinguished from executory contracts such as supply agreements. In the case of a supply agreement all of the rights and benefits are created by the agreement itself. In contrast, a contractual right to use an asset is the right to use an existing asset of the grantor i.e. a right that exists and is capable of being recognised independently of the contractual right to use. Accordingly, it is appropriate for the grantor in its consolidated financial statements to recognise an asset upon repurchase as it gives the grantor the ability to use those repurchased rights.

2.6   Goodwill

IFRS 3 (2007) defines 'goodwill' in terms of its nature, rather than in terms of its measurement.[168] It is defined as 'future economic benefits arising from assets that are not capable of being individually identified and separately recognised'.[169]

Accordingly, the standard requires an acquirer to recognise goodwill acquired in a business combination as an asset. However, rather than attributing a fair value to the goodwill directly, the standard requires that the initial measurement of goodwill is its cost, being the excess of the cost of the business combination (as determined in 2.4 above) over the acquirer's interest in the net fair value of the identifiable assets, liabilities and contingent liabilities recognised in accordance with the standard (as determined in 2.5 above).[170]

Thus, although any minority interest in the acquiree will reflect the minority's proportion of net fair value of those net assets, no amount is included for any goodwill relating to the minority interest.

IFRS 3 (2007) thus considers goodwill acquired in a business combination to represent a payment made by the acquirer in anticipation of future economic benefits from assets that are not capable of being individually identified and separately recognised.[171]

Since goodwill is measured as the residual cost of the business combination after recognising the acquiree's identifiable assets, liabilities and contingent liabilities, then to the extent that these do not satisfy the criteria in IFRS 3 (2007) for separate recognition at the acquisition date (see 2.5 above), there is a resulting effect on the amount recognised as goodwill.[172]

The IASB in developing the standard observed that 'when goodwill is measured as a residual it could comprise the following components:

(a)   the fair value of the "going concern" element of the acquiree. The going concern element represents the ability of the acquiree to earn a higher rate of return on an assembled collection of net assets than would be expected from those net assets operating separately. That value stems from the synergies of the net assets of the acquiree, as well as from other benefits such as factors related to market imperfections, including the ability to earn monopoly profits and barriers to market entry.

(b) the fair value of the expected synergies and other benefits from combining the acquiree's net assets with those of the acquirer. Those synergies and other benefits are unique to each business combination, and different combinations produce different synergies and, hence, different values.

(c) overpayments by the acquirer.

(d) errors in measuring and recognising the fair value of either the cost of the business combination or the acquiree's identifiable assets, liabilities or contingent liabilities, or a requirement in an accounting standard to measure those identifiable items at an amount that is not fair value.'[173]

The Board regards components (a) and (b) as being 'core goodwill' and conceptually part of goodwill that should be recognised as an asset, whereas components (c) and (d) are not. However, it took the view that it would not be feasible to determine the amount attributable to each component and, since the residual amount is likely to consist primarily of core goodwill, concluded it should be recognised as an asset.[174]

The main issue relating to the goodwill acquired in a business combination is how it should be subsequently accounted for. The requirements of IFRS 3 (2007) in this respect are straightforward; but that is only because the detailed requirements in relation to the subsequent accounting for goodwill are dealt with in IAS 36.

IFRS 3 (2007) requires that, after initial recognition, the acquirer measures goodwill acquired in a business combination at cost less any accumulated impairment losses.[175]

Goodwill acquired in a business combination is not to be amortised (as was the treatment under IAS 22). Instead, the acquirer has to test it for impairment annually, or more frequently if events or changes in circumstances indicate that it might be impaired, in accordance with IAS 36.[176] For the requirements of IAS 36 relating specifically to the impairment of goodwill, see Chapter 18 at 3.4.

2.7 Excess of acquirer's interest in the net fair value of acquiree's identifiable assets, liabilities and contingent liabilities over cost

IFRS 3 (2007) recognises that in some business combinations, the acquirer's interest in the net fair value of the acquiree's identifiable assets, liabilities and contingent liabilities exceeds the cost of the combination. Traditionally, that excess has been commonly referred to as 'negative goodwill' (although IFRS 3 (2007) does not use this term).

Where such an excess arises, IFRS 3 (2007) requires the acquirer to reassess the identification and measurement of the acquiree's identifiable assets, liabilities and contingent liabilities and the measurement of the cost of the combination.[177] This is because the existence of this excess might indicate that:

(a) the values attributed to the acquiree's identifiable assets have been overstated;

(b) identifiable liabilities and/or contingent liabilities of the acquiree have been omitted or the values attributed to those items have been understated; or

(c) the values assigned to the items comprising the cost of the business combination have been understated.[178]

The IASB considers that the excess cannot come about because there is an expectation of future losses and expenses. Instead, it considers that the expectation of such losses and expenses will depress the fair value of the acquiree's identifiable assets, liabilities and contingent liabilities.[179] As future losses and restructuring expenses are expressly prohibited from recognition as liabilities of the acquiree (see 2.5.1 above), there would appear to be many occasions where the acquirer will have to perform an impairment exercise of the assets or cash generating assets that it has acquired in order to reflect their fair values.

Having undertaken that reassessment, the standard then requires that any excess remaining after that reassessment is recognised immediately in profit or loss.[180]

The standard notes that a gain recognised in accordance with the above requirement could comprise one or more of the following components:

(a)   errors in measuring the fair value of either the cost of the combination or the acquiree's identifiable assets, liabilities or contingent liabilities, notwithstanding the reassessment. Possible future costs arising in respect of the acquiree that have not been reflected correctly in the fair value of the acquiree's identifiable assets, liabilities or contingent liabilities are a potential cause of such errors.

(b)   a requirement in an accounting standard to measure identifiable net assets acquired at an amount that is not fair value, but is treated as though it is fair value for the purpose of allocating the cost of the combination. For example, the guidance in Appendix B to the standard (see 2.5.4 H above) on determining the fair values of the acquiree's identifiable assets and liabilities requires the amount assigned to tax assets and liabilities to be undiscounted.

(c)   a bargain purchase.[181] This might occur, for example, when the seller of a business wishes to exit from that business for other than economic reasons and is prepared to accept less than its fair value as consideration;[182] this is particularly common if there is a distressed or 'fire' sale.

In developing the standard, the IASB considered whether the appropriate treatment for these components should be to recognise it as a reduction in the values attributed to the identifiable net asset, as a separate liability or immediately in profit or loss. However, the Board rejected the first two treatments and decided that the immediate recognition of a gain was the most faithful treatment of the part of the excess arising from a bargain purchase and that it would not be feasible to identify separately the amounts that are attributable to components (a) and (b) above.[183]

2.8   Subsequent adjustments to fair values

The initial accounting for a business combination under IFRS 3 (2007) involves identifying and determining the fair values to be assigned to the acquiree's identifiable assets, liabilities and contingent liabilities and the cost of the combination.[184]

The fact that the fair value process is inevitably, to some degree, a rationalisation of the price paid after the event means that an accounting issue arises: how much hindsight can the acquirer impute into the values assigned, or must the allocation be based solely on the information which it had at the time when it was making the bid?

There is a theoretical argument for the latter, which is that if the acquirer was unaware of a particular matter, such as the fact that there was a deficiency in the pension fund of the target, then it cannot have influenced the acquisition price and thus should not feature in any allocation of that price.

Whatever the merits of that view in theory, however, it cannot be used in practice. If the acquirer was only able to assign values to items that it knew about at the time of the acquisition, the exercise would in many cases be completely impossible, because most acquisitions are not primarily based on an assessment of the value of the assets and liabilities of the target entity, but on an assessment of future earnings and cash flows. It is therefore necessary to allow the acquirer a reasonable period of time in which to investigate the assets and liabilities that have been acquired and make a reasoned allocation of values to them. The remaining question is, how much time should be allowed?

IFRS 3 (2007) effectively requires the acquirer to complete the allocation of the cost of the business combination to the acquiree's assets, liabilities and contingent liabilities within a period of twelve months of the acquisition date.[185] The important practical point for an acquirer is that it will have to demonstrate that any subsequent adjustments were in fact made by this date and not at its subsequent period end date.

If the initial accounting for a business combination can be determined only provisionally by the end of the period in which the combination is effected because either the fair values to be assigned to the acquiree's identifiable assets, liabilities or contingent liabilities or the cost of the combination can be determined only provisionally, the acquirer shall account for the combination using those provisional values.[186] IFRS 3 (2007) requires disclosure of the fact that it has only been determined provisionally, with an explanation as to why that has been case (see 2.13 below).

2.8.1 *Adjustments upon completion of initial accounting*

Where as a result of completing the initial accounting within twelve months from the acquisition date adjustments to the provisional values have been found to be necessary, IFRS 3 (2007) requires them to be recognised from the acquisition date. This means, therefore, that:

(a)   the carrying amount of an identifiable asset, liability or contingent liability that is recognised or adjusted as a result of completing the initial accounting is calculated as if its fair value at the acquisition date had been recognised from that date;

(b)   goodwill or any gain recognised in accordance with paragraph 56 of the standard is adjusted from the acquisition date by an amount equal to the adjustment to the fair value at the acquisition date of the identifiable asset, liability or contingent liability being recognised or adjusted; and

(c)   comparative information presented for the periods before the initial accounting for the combination is complete is presented as if the initial accounting had been completed from the acquisition date. This includes any additional depreciation, amortisation or other profit or loss effect recognised as a result of completing the initial accounting.[187]

These requirements are illustrated in the following example, which is based on Example 7 included within the Illustrative Examples accompanying IFRS 3 (2007). The deferred tax implications have been ignored.

Example 9.19:   Finalisation of provisional values upon completion of initial accounting

Entity A prepares financial statements for annual periods ending on 31 December and does not prepare interim financial statements. The entity acquired another entity on 30 September 2008. Entity A sought an independent appraisal for an item of property, plant and equipment acquired in the combination. However, the appraisal was not finalised by the time the entity completed its 2008 annual financial statements. Entity A recognised in its 2008 annual financial statements a provisional fair value for the asset of €30,000, and a provisional value for acquired goodwill of €100,000. The item of property, plant and equipment had a remaining useful life at the acquisition date of five years.

Six months after the acquisition date, the entity received the independent appraisal, which estimated the asset's fair value at the acquisition date at €40,000.

In preparing its 2009 financial statements, Entity A is required to recognise any adjustments to provisional values as a result of completing the initial accounting from the acquisition date.

Part (a) of the requirement means that an adjustment is made to the carrying amount of the item of property, plant and equipment. That adjustment is measured as the fair value adjustment at the acquisition date of €10,000, less the additional depreciation that would have been recognised had the asset's fair value at the acquisition date been recognised from that date (€500 for three months' depreciation to 31 December 2008), i.e. an increase of €9,500. Part (b) requires the carrying amount of goodwill to be adjusted for the increase in value of the asset at the acquisition date of €10,000. Part (c) requires the 2008 comparative information to be restated to reflect these adjustments. Accordingly, the 2008 balance sheet is restated by increasing the carrying amount of property, plant and equipment by €9,500, reducing goodwill by €10,000 and retained earnings by €500. The 2008 income statement is restated to include additional depreciation of €500.

Entity A will disclose in its 2008 financial statements that the initial accounting for the business combination has been determined only provisionally, and explain why this is the case. In its 2009 financial statements it will disclose the amounts and explanations of the adjustments to the provisional values recognised during the current reporting period. Therefore, Entity A will disclose that:

- the fair value of the item of property, plant and equipment at the acquisition date has been increased by €10,000 with a corresponding decrease in goodwill; and

- the 2008 comparative information is restated to reflect this adjustment, including additional depreciation of €500 relating to the year ended 31 December 2008.

The above example illustrates a situation where a provisional value of an asset was finalised at a different amount as part of the completion of the initial accounting.

Example 9.20:   Identification of an asset upon completion of initial accounting

Entity C prepares financial statements for annual periods ending on 31 December and does not prepare interim financial statements. The entity acquired another entity on 30 November 2008. Entity C engaged an independent appraiser to assist with the identification and determination of fair values to be assigned to the acquiree's assets, liabilities and contingent liabilities and the cost of the business combination. However, the appraisal was not finalised by the time the entity completed its 2008 annual financial statements, and therefore the amounts recognised in its 2008 annual financial statements were on a provisional basis.

As part of the work carried out in finalising the initial accounting, it was identified by the independent appraiser that the acquiree had an intangible asset (meeting all of the IAS 38 recognition and identification criteria) with a fair value at the date of acquisition of €20,000. However, this had not been identified at the time when Entity C was preparing its 2008 annual financial statements. Thus, no value had been included for this intangible asset.

In preparing its 2009 financial statements, Entity C is required to recognise any adjustments to provisional values as a result of completing the initial accounting from the acquisition date. In this case, no value had been recognised, and indeed, the intangible asset had not even been identified at the time of preparing its 2008 financial statements. So, can an adjustment be made under these provisions of IFRS 3 (2007)?

In our view, an adjustment is appropriate. The requirements are not limited to measurement adjustments (although a literal reading of the first sentence of paragraph 62 could imply that to be the case). Adjustments to recognise subsequently identified assets or liabilities are permitted as a result of completing the initial accounting. The initial accounting involves the identification as well as the measurement of the acquiree's assets, liabilities and contingent liabilities, and it is clear from (a) above that adjustments are to be made for items that are *recognised* as a result of completing the exercise.

Although IFRS 3 (2007) allows this period of hindsight to be used, it is important that any adjustments to the provisional allocation reflect conditions as they existed at the date of the acquisition, rather than being affected by subsequent events; the objective is to determine the fair values of the items at the date of acquisition. There is a parallel to be drawn here with the accounting treatment of events after the end of the reporting period. Only those events which provide further evidence of conditions as they existed at the acquisition date should be taken into account.

2.8.2　*Adjustments after the initial accounting is complete*

With three exceptions (see 2.8.3 below), after the initial accounting is complete, IFRS 3 (2007) only allows adjustments to the initial accounting for a business combination to be made to correct an error in accordance with IAS 8 (see Chapter 3 at 4.6).[188] This would probably be the case only if the original allocation was based on a misinterpretation of the facts which were available at the time; it would not apply simply because new information had come to light which changed the acquiring management's view of the value of the item in question.

Adjustments to the initial accounting for a business combination after it is complete are not made for the effect of changes in estimates. In accordance with IAS 8, the effect of a change in estimates is recognised in the current and future periods (see Chapter 3 at 4.5).[189]

Where it is determined that an error has been made, IFRS 3 (2007) notes that IAS 8 requires an entity to account for an error correction retrospectively, and to present financial statements as if the error had never occurred by restating the comparative information for the prior period(s) in which the error occurred.[190] The accounting is similar to that outlined above for adjustments upon completion of initial accounting. The only difference being there is no time limit as to when such adjustments may be required.

These requirements are illustrated in Examples 9.21 and 9.22 below, which are based on Examples 8 and 9 included within the Illustrative Examples accompanying IFRS 3 (2007). The deferred tax implications have been ignored.

Example 9.21:   Error resulting in an increase in identifiable assets leading to a decrease in goodwill

Entity A prepares financial statements for annual periods ending on 31 December and does not prepare interim financial statements. The entity acquired another entity on 30 September 2008. As part of the initial accounting for that combination, Entity A recognised goodwill of €100,000 in its 2008 financial statements. No impairment was recognised for this goodwill, so the carrying amount of goodwill at 31 December 2008 was €100,000.

During 2009, Entity A becomes aware of an error relating to the amount initially allocated to property, plant and equipment assets acquired in the business combination. In particular, €20,000 of the €100,000 initially allocated to goodwill should have been allocated to property, plant and equipment assets that had a remaining useful life at the acquisition date of five years, with an assumed residual value of nil.

In preparing its 2009 financial statements, Entity A is required to account for the correction of the error retrospectively, and for the financial statements to be presented as if the error had never occurred by correcting the error in the comparative information for the prior period in which it occurred.

Therefore, in the 2009 financial statements, an adjustment is made to the carrying amount of property, plant and equipment assets at 31 December 2008. The adjustment is measured as the fair value adjustment at the acquisition date of €20,000 less the amount that would have been recognised as depreciation of the fair value adjustment (€1,000 for three months' depreciation to 31 December 2008); i.e. property, plant and equipment is increased by €19,000. The carrying amount of goodwill is also adjusted for the reduction in its value at the acquisition date of €20,000. Accordingly, retained earnings at 31 December 2008 are reduced by €1,000. The 2008 income statement is restated to include additional depreciation of €1,000.

In accordance with IAS 8, Entity A will disclose in its 2009 financial statements the nature of the error and that, as a result of correcting that error, an adjustment was made to the carrying amount of property, plant and equipment. It will also disclose that:

- the fair value of property, plant and equipment assets at the acquisition date has been increased by €20,000 with a corresponding decrease in goodwill; and
- the 2008 comparative information is restated to reflect this adjustment, including additional depreciation of €1,000 for the year ended 31 December 2008.

Example 9.22:   Error resulting in a decrease in identifiable assets leading to an increase in goodwill

This example assumes the same facts as in Example 9.21 above, except that the amount initially allocated to property, plant and equipment assets is decreased by €20,000 to correct the error, rather than increased by €20,000. This example also assumes that Entity A determines that the recoverable amount of the additional goodwill is only €17,000 at 31 December 2008.

Therefore, in the 2009 financial statements, an adjustment is made to the carrying amount of property, plant and equipment assets at 31 December 2008. The adjustment is measured as the fair value adjustment at the acquisition date of €20,000 less the amount that should not have been recognised as depreciation of the fair value adjustment (€1,000 for three months' depreciation to 31 December 2008); i.e. property, plant and equipment is reduced by €19,000. The carrying amount of goodwill is increased by €17,000, being the increase in value at the acquisition date of €20,000 less a €3,000 impairment loss to reflect that the carrying amount of the adjustment exceeds its recoverable amount. Accordingly, retained earnings at 31 December 2008 are reduced by €2,000.

The 2008 income statement is restated to reflect these adjustments; i.e. it includes the €3,000 impairment loss but excludes the €1,000 depreciation.

2.8.3 Recognition of deferred tax assets after the initial accounting is complete

IFRS 3 (2007) makes three exceptions to this requirement of only allowing adjustments for errors once the initial accounting is complete. The first two relate to adjustments to the cost of a business combination that was contingent on future events (see 2.4.5 above). The other exception relates to the recognition of deferred tax assets. This exception was carried forward from IAS 22 without reconsideration by the IASB, and has been reconsidered as part of phase II of its business combinations project in the development of IFRS 3 (as revised in 2008) (as have the other two exceptions) – see 3.6.6 B below.

If the potential benefit of the acquiree's income tax loss carry-forwards or other deferred tax assets did not satisfy the criteria in paragraph 37 of IFRS 3 (2007) for separate recognition when a business combination is initially accounted for but is subsequently realised, IFRS 3 (2007) states that the acquirer recognises that benefit as income in accordance with IAS 12. However, in addition, the acquirer:

(a) reduces the carrying amount of goodwill to the amount that would have been recognised if the deferred tax asset had been recognised as an identifiable asset from the acquisition date; and

(b) recognises the reduction in the carrying amount of the goodwill as an expense.

The standard goes on to say that this procedure is not to result in the creation of an excess as described in paragraph 56 of the standard (see 2.7 above), nor is it to increase the amount of any gain previously recognised in accordance with paragraph 56.[191]

These requirements are discussed further in Chapter 26 at 6.2.2 B II.

2.9 Business combinations achieved in stages ('step acquisitions')

So far, this chapter has discussed the application of the purchase method of accounting in the context of business combinations that result from a single exchange transaction. However, in practice some subsidiaries are acquired in a series of steps which can take place over an extended period, during which the underlying value of the subsidiary is likely to change, both because of the trading profits (or losses) which it retains and because of other movements in the fair values of its assets and liabilities. The accounting problems which this creates are therefore how to establish the cost of the business combination, the fair values of the net assets acquired, and therefore the amount of goodwill arising. It also has implications for the impact of the business combination on the post-acquisition reserves in the consolidated financial statements of the acquirer.

IFRS 3 (2007) recognises that a business combination may involve more than one exchange transaction, for example when it occurs in stages by successive share purchases. The requirements of the standard have principally been carried forward from IAS 22 and have been reconsidered as part of the second phase of the business combinations project in the development of IFRS 3 (as revised in 2008) (see 3.10 below).[192]

Where a business combination does involve more than one exchange transaction, the standard requires that each exchange transaction shall be treated separately by the acquirer; i.e. by using the cost of the transaction and fair value information at the date of each exchange transaction, to determine the amount of any goodwill associated with that transaction. This results in a step-by-step comparison of the cost of the individual investments with the acquirer's interest in the fair values of the acquiree's identifiable assets, liabilities and contingent liabilities at each step.[193] (It has to be said that this actually contradicts the requirement of paragraph 36 of the standard (see 2.5 above) which is to allocate the cost of the business combination (this is the same under both requirements) to the acquiree's identifiable assets, liabilities and contingent liabilities at their fair values at the date of acquisition (i.e. the date that it obtains control), with any difference between the cost and the acquirer's interest in those net fair values being accounted for as goodwill or a gain in profit or loss. This is because the methodology in paragraph 36 would otherwise result in the share of reserves and asset revaluation reserves relating to the interest in the associate being rolled into the calculation of goodwill, as can be seen in the following examples.)

Where a subsidiary has been acquired by successive share purchases, then theoretically the standard would require separate comparisons, even if the shares were purchased over a short period of time. However, it may that in such a situation that the fair values of the acquiree's identifiable assets, liabilities and contingent liabilities at the date of acquisition could be used, as long as the values are unlikely to have been materially different during the period the shares were being purchased.

The standard notes that when a business combination involves more than one exchange transaction, the fair values of the acquiree's identifiable assets, liabilities and contingent liabilities may be different at the date of each exchange transaction.[194] This is likely to be the case where the transactions have taken place over an extended period. The standard states that because:

(a)   the acquiree's identifiable assets, liabilities and contingent liabilities are notionally restated to their fair values at the date of each exchange transaction to determine the amount of any goodwill associated with each transaction; and

(b)   the acquiree's identifiable assets, liabilities and contingent liabilities must then be recognised by the acquirer at their fair values at the acquisition date,

any adjustment to those fair values relating to previously held interests of the acquirer is a revaluation to be accounted for as such. However, it goes on to say that because this revaluation arises on the initial recognition by the acquirer of the acquiree's assets, liabilities and contingent liabilities, it does not signify that the acquirer has elected to apply an accounting policy of revaluing those items after initial recognition in accordance with, for example, IAS 16 – *Property, Plant and Equipment*.[195]

Before qualifying as a business combination, a transaction may qualify as an investment in an associate and be accounted for in accordance with IAS 28 –

Investments in Associates – using the equity method. If so, the fair values of the investee's identifiable net assets at the date of each earlier exchange transaction will have been determined previously in applying the equity method to the investment (see Chapter 11 at 3.2).[196]

These requirements are illustrated in Examples 9.23 and 9.24 below which are based on Example 6 included within the Illustrative Examples accompanying IFRS 3 (2007), except that in Example 9.23 the acquirer has reflected the changes in value of its original investment as a component of other comprehensive income rather than in profit or loss.

Example 9.23:   Business combination achieved in stages – original investment treated as an available-for-sale investment under IAS 39

Investor acquires a 20 per cent ownership interest in Investee (a service company) on 1 January 2008 for £3,500,000 cash. At that date, the fair value of Investee's identifiable assets is £10,000,000, and the carrying amount of those assets is £8,000,000. Investee has no liabilities or contingent liabilities at that date. The following shows Investee's balance sheet at 1 January 2008 together with the fair values of the identifiable assets:

Investee's balance sheet at 1 January 2008	Carrying amounts £'000	Fair values £'000
Cash and receivables	2,000	2,000
Land	6,000	8,000
	8,000	10,000
Issued equity: 1,000,000 ordinary shares	5,000	
Retained earnings	3,000	
	8,000	

During the year ended 31 December 2008, Investee reports a profit of £6,000,000 but does not pay any dividends. In addition, the fair value of Investee's land increases by £3,000,000 to £11,000,000. However, the amount recognised by Investee in respect of the land remains unchanged at £6,000,000. The following shows Investee's balance sheet at 31 December 2008 together with the fair values of the identifiable assets:

Investee's balance sheet at 31 December 2008	Carrying amounts £'000	Fair values £'000
Cash and receivables	8,000	8,000
Land	6,000	11,000
	14,000	19,000
Issued equity: 1,000,000 ordinary shares	5,000	
Retained earnings	9,000	
	14,000	

On 1 January 2009, Investor acquires a further 60 per cent ownership interest in Investee for £22,000,000 cash, thereby obtaining control. Before obtaining control, Investor does not have significant influence over Investee, and accounts for its initial 20 per cent investment at fair value

with changes in value recognised as a component of other comprehensive income. Investee's ordinary shares have a quoted market price at 31 December 2008 of £30 per share.

Throughout the period 1 January 2008 to 1 January 2009, Investor's issued equity was £30,000,000. Investor's only asset apart from its investment in Investee is cash.

Accounting for the initial investment before obtaining control

Investor's initial 20 per cent investment in Investee is measured at its cost of £3,500,000. However, Investee's 1,000,000 ordinary shares have a quoted market price at 31 December 2008 of £30 per share. Therefore, the carrying amount of Investor's initial 20 per cent investment is remeasured in Investor's financial statements to £6,000,000 at 31 December 2008, with the £2,500,000 increase recognised as a component of other comprehensive income. Therefore, Investor's balance sheet at 31 December 2008, before the acquisition of the additional 60 per cent ownership interest, is as follows:

Investor's balance sheet at 31 December 2008	£'000
Cash	26,500
Investment in Investee	6,000
	32,500
Issued equity	30,000
Gain on available-for-sale investment	2,500
	32,500

Accounting for the business combination

Paragraph 25 of IFRS 3 (2007) (see 2.4.1 above) states that when a business combination involves more than one exchange transaction, the cost of the combination is the aggregate cost of the individual transactions, with the cost of each individual transaction determined at the date of each exchange transaction, i.e. the date that each individual investment is recognised in the acquirer's financial statements). This means that for this example, the cost to Investor of the business combination is the aggregate of the cost of the initial 20 per cent ownership interest (£3,500,000) plus the cost of the subsequent 60 per cent ownership interest (£22,000,000), irrespective of the fact that the carrying amount of the initial 20 per cent interest has changed.

In addition, and in accordance with paragraph 58 of IFRS 3 (2007), each transaction must be treated separately to determine the goodwill on that transaction, using cost and fair value information at the date of each exchange transaction. Therefore, Investor recognises the following amounts for goodwill in its consolidated financial statements:

	£'000	Goodwill £'000
Acquisition of 20% interest on 1 January 2008		
Cost	3,500	
Share of fair values at that date (20% × £10,000,000)	2,000	
		1,500
Acquisition of 60% interest on 1 January 2009		
Cost	22,000	
Share of fair values at that date (60% × £19,000,000)	11,400	
		10,600
		12,100

The following shows Investor's consolidation worksheet immediately after the acquisition of the additional 60 per cent ownership interest in Investee, together with consolidation adjustments and associated explanations:

	Investor	Investee	Consolidation adjustments Dr	Consolidation adjustments Cr		Consolidated	
	£'000	£'000	£'000	£'000		£'000	
Cash and receivables	4,500	8,000				12,500	
Investment in investee	28,000	–		2,500	(2)	–	
				3,500	(3)		
				22,000	(4)		
Land		6,000	5,000 (1)			11,000	(a)
Goodwill			1,500 (3)			12,100	(b)
			10,600 (4)				
	32,500	14,000				35,600	
Issued equity	30,000	5,000	1,000 (3)			30,000	(c)
			3,000 (4)				
			1,000 (5)				
Asset revaluation surplus			400 (3)	5,000 (1)		600	(d)
			3,000 (4)				
			1,000 (5)				
Gain on available-for-sale investment	2,500		2,500 (2)				
Retained earnings		9,000	600 (3)			1,200	(e)
			5,400 (4)				
			1,800 (5)				
Minority interest				3,800	(5)	3,800	(a)
	32,500	14,000				35,600	

Consolidation Adjustments

		£'000	£'000
(1)	Land	5,000	
	Asset revaluation surplus		5,000

To recognise Investee's identifiable assets at fair values at the acquisition date

		£'000	£'000
(2)	Gain on available-for-sale investment	2,500	
	Investment in Investee		2,500

To restate the initial 20 per cent investment in Investee to cost

		£'000	£'000
(3)	Issued equity [20% × 5,000,000]	1,000	
	Asset revaluation surplus [20% × 2,000,000]	400	
	Retained earnings [20% × 3,000,000]	600	
	Goodwill	1,500	
	Investment in investee		3,500

To recognise goodwill on the initial 20 per cent investment in Investee and record the elimination of that investment against associated equity balances

		£'000	£'000
(4)	Issued equity [60% × 5,000,000]	3,000	
	Asset revaluation surplus [60% × 5,000,000]	3,000	
	Retained earnings [60% × 9,000,000]	5,400	
	Goodwill	10,600	
	Investment in investee		22,000

To recognise goodwill on the subsequent 60 per cent investment in Investee and record elimination of that investment against associated equity balances

		£'000	£'000
(5)	Issued equity [20% × 5,000,000]	1,000	
	Asset revaluation surplus [20% × 5,000,000]	1,000	
	Retained earnings [20% × 9,000,000]	1,800	
	Minority interest (in issued equity)		1,000
	Minority interest (in asset revaluation surplus)		1,000
	Minority interest (in retained earnings)		1,800

To recognise the minority interest in the Investee

Notes

The above consolidation adjustments result in:

(a) investee's identifiable net assets being stated at their full fair values at the date Investor obtains control of Investee, i.e. £19,000,000. This means that the 20 per cent minority interest in Investee also is stated at the minority's 20 per cent share of the fair values of Investee's identifiable net assets.

(b) goodwill being recognised from the acquisition date at an amount based on treating each exchange transaction separately and using cost and fair value information at the date of each exchange transaction.

(c) issued equity of £30,000,000 comprising the issued equity of Investor of£30,000,000.

(d) an asset revaluation surplus of £600,000. This amount reflects that part of the increase in the fair value of Investee's identifiable net assets after the acquisition of the initial 20 per cent interest that is attributable to that initial 20 per cent interest [20% × £3,000,000].

(e) a retained earnings balance of £1,200,000. This amount reflects the changes in Investee's retained earnings after Investor acquired its initial 20 per cent interest that is attributable to that 20 per cent interest [20% × £6,000,000].

Therefore, the effect of applying the requirements in IFRS 3 (2007) to business combinations involving successive share purchases for which the investment was previously accounted for at fair value with changes in value taken to equity is to cause:

• changes in the fair value of previously held ownership interests to be reversed (so that the carrying amounts of those ownership interests are restated to cost).

• changes in the investee's retained earnings and other equity balances after each exchange transaction to be included in the post-combination consolidated financial statements to the extent that they relate to the previously held ownership interests.

The effect of these changes will need to be reflected in other comprehensive income in the statement of comprehensive income.

As noted earlier, these requirements contradict the requirements of paragraph 36 of the standard. If that paragraph had been applied literally, the goodwill would have been £10,300,000, being the total cost of investment of £25,500,000 less £15,200,000 (being Investor's interest of 80% of the fair value of Investee's assets of £19,000,000 at the date of acquisition). The difference of £1,800,000 between this figure and goodwill as calculated above on each exchange transaction is the asset revaluation surplus of £600,000 ((d) above) and the share of reserves of £1,200,000 ((e) above), both of which would be subsumed within goodwill calculated solely as at the date that Investee became a subsidiary.

If the investor in the above example had accounted for its original investment of 20% as an associate using the equity method under IAS 28, then the accounting would have been as follows:

Example 9.24:   *Business combination achieved in stages – original investment treated as an associate under IAS 28*

This example uses the same facts as in Example 9.23 above, except that Investor does have significant influence over Investee following its initial 20 per cent investment.

Accounting for the initial investment before obtaining control

Investor's initial 20 per cent investment in Investee is included in Investor's consolidated financial statements under the equity method (see Chapter 11 at 3). Accordingly, it is initially recognised at its cost of £3,500,000 and adjusted thereafter for its share of the profits of Investee after the date of acquisition of £1,200,000 (being 20% × £6,000,000). Investor's policy for property, plant and equipment is to use the cost model under IAS 16 (see Chapter 16 at 4), therefore in applying the equity method it does not include its share of the increased value of the land held by Investee. IAS 28 requires that on the acquisition of an associate, any difference between the cost of the acquisition and its share of the fair values of the associate's identifiable assets, liabilities and contingent liabilities is accounted for under IFRS 3 (2007), although any goodwill is included within the carrying amount of the investment in the associate. Accordingly, Investor has already calculated the goodwill of £1,500,000 arising on its original investment of 20%. Therefore, Investor's consolidated balance sheet at 31 December 2008, before the acquisition of the additional 60 per cent ownership interest, is as follows:

Investor's consolidated balance sheet at 31 December 2008	£'000
Cash	26,500
Investment in associate	4,700
	31,200
Issued equity	30,000
Retained earnings	1,200
	31,200

In its separate financial statements, Investor includes its investment in the associate at its cost of £3,500,000.

Accounting for the business combination

As in Example 9.23, the cost of the combination is the aggregate cost of the individual transactions, with the cost of each individual transaction determined at the date of each exchange transaction, i.e. the date that each individual investment is recognised in the acquirer's financial statements), and each transaction must be treated separately to determine the goodwill on that transaction, using cost and fair value information at the date of each exchange transaction. Therefore, Investor recognises the following amounts for goodwill in its consolidated financial statements:

	£'000	Goodwill £'000
Acquisition of 20% interest on 1 January 2008		
Cost	3,500	
Share of fair values at that date (20% × £10,000,000)	2,000	
		1,500
Acquisition of 60% interest on 1 January 2009		
Cost	22,000	
Share of fair values at that date (60% × £19,000,000)	11,400	
		10,600
		12,100

As indicated above, Investor will have already calculated the goodwill arising on its original investment, but not recognised it separately.

The following shows Investor's consolidation worksheet immediately after the acquisition of the additional 60 per cent ownership interest in Investee, together with consolidation adjustments and associated explanations.

| | Investor | Investee | Consolidation adjustments | | Consolidated | |
			Dr	Cr		
	£'000	£'000	£'000	£'000	£'000	
Cash and receivables	4,500	8,000			12,500	
Investment in investee	25,500	–		3,500 (3)	–	
				22,000 (4)		
Land		6,000	5,000 (1)		11,000	(a)
Goodwill			1,500 (3)		12,100	(b)
			10,600 (4)			
	30,000	14,000			35,600	
Issued equity	30,000	5,000	1,000 (3)		30,000	(c)
			3,000 (4)			
			1,000 (5)			
Asset revaluation surplus			400 (3)	5,000 (1)	600	(d)
			3,000 (4)			
			1,000 (5)			
Retained earnings		9,000	600 (3)		1,200	(e)
			5,400 (4)			
			1,800 (5)			
Minority interest				3,800 (5)	3,800	(a)
	30,000	14,000			35,600	

The consolidation adjustments are exactly the same as in Example 9.23, except that there was no need for adjustment (2) since the investment of 20% was already included at cost.

The notes in Example 9.23 also apply to this example. The only difference is that the retained earnings balance has already been reflected in the consolidated balance sheet of Investor at 31 December 2008.

Therefore, the effect of applying the requirements in IFRS 3 (2007) to business combinations involving successive share purchases for which the investment was previously accounted for under the equity method is to cause changes in the investee's equity balances after each exchange transaction that result from changes in fair values to be included in the post-combination consolidated financial statements to the extent that they relate to the previously held ownership interests (and have not already been recognised).

In this example, the £600,000 asset revaluation surplus will be recognised in other comprehensive income in the statement of comprehensive income in Investor's consolidated financial statements for 2007.

Overall, therefore, the effect of applying IFRS 3 (2007) to any business combination involving successive share purchases is to cause:

- any changes in the carrying amount of previously held ownership interests to be reversed (so that the carrying amounts of those ownership interests are restated to cost).

- changes in the investee's retained earnings and other equity balances after each exchange transaction to be included in the post-combination consolidated financial statements to the extent that they relate to the previously held ownership interests.

Consequently, the consolidated financial statements immediately after Investor acquires the additional 60 per cent ownership interest and obtains control of Investee would be the same irrespective of the method used to account for the initial 20 per cent investment in Investee before obtaining control.

In Examples 9.23 and 9.24 above, the changes in fair value related to a single asset, land, and resulted in a revaluation surplus being recognised in other comprehensive income in the statement of comprehensive income. However, in practice, the acquiree will have other identifiable assets and liabilities, some of which may not have been recognised previously, and there may be items that would not otherwise be revalued. In a business combination achieved in stages, are adjustments to the fair values of identifiable assets and liabilities relating to previously held interests of the acquirer always accounted for as a revaluation?

Example 9.25:   Business combination achieved in stages – accounting for fair value adjustments

In 2008, Entity A acquired a 25% ownership interest in Entity B and obtained significant influence. Entity A therefore accounted for this interest in Entity B under the equity method (see Chapter 11 at 3).

In 2009, Entity A acquired a further 40% ownership interest in Entity B, thereby obtaining control. When accounting for the business combination in 2009, how should Entity A account for the changes in the fair values of the following items between the date significant influence was acquired and the date control was obtained?:

(a) a newly identified contingent liability that did not exist in 2008 when the first tranche of 25% was acquired;

(b) a fixed interest rate loan liability measured at amortised cost in accordance with IAS 39 and for which the fair value has moved up or down due to movements in interest rates and/or the credit rating of the borrower;

(c) a provision for a legal claim that was recorded by Entity B in 2008 and whose value has changed prior to the date of control due to developments in the legal proceedings;

(d) a financial asset/liability measured at fair value through profit or loss for which the fair value has moved up or down; and

(e) an intangible asset identified in 2008 whose fair value has reduced significantly between 2008 and the date of control and the reduction is not attributable to the passage of time or normal use of the asset.

In a step acquisition, an acquirer generally accounts for adjustments to fair values relating to previously held interests as a revaluation in other comprehensive income in the statement of comprehensive income, even when they relate to items that are not normally revalued such as contingent liabilities and loan liabilities (items (a) and (b) above). IFRS 3 (2007) specifically acknowledges that the revaluation 'arises on the initial recognition of the acquiree's assets, liabilities and contingent liabilities.'[197] (An exception to this general principle, relates to a decline in fair value of an item of property, plant and equipment or intangible asset, as noted below.)

However, care needs to be taken to ensure that valuation movements that ought to be recognised outside of business combination accounting are recognised by the acquiree and included as part of the equity method results prior to the date control is obtained. For example, the acquiree recognises in its financial statements the changes in the amounts of the legal provision (item (c) above) and the financial instruments at fair value through profit or loss (item (d) above). Under IAS 28, the equity method of accounting is applied until the date an investor ceases to have significant influence over an associate.[198] Therefore, an investor records its share of the profit or loss of the investee until that date, i.e. the date of obtaining control, including any change in fair value, and impairment charges, that are included in the associate's results.

If the fair value of an item of property, plant and equipment or intangible asset declined significantly more than would be expected from the passage of time or normal use (item (e) above), then this is an impairment indicator.[199] An impairment test is conducted by both the acquiree – prior to the date of the acquisition – and by the acquirer – on the date of the acquisition. If necessary, an impairment loss is included as part of the equity accounted results prior to the date of control.

As an exception to the general principle of accounting for adjustments to fair values relating to previously held interests as a revaluation in other comprehensive income in the statement of comprehensive income set out above, we believe that any decline in fair value of an item of property, plant and equipment or intangible asset that does not give rise to an impairment loss may be accounted for in one of two ways:

- as part of the revaluation that is that is recognised in other comprehensive income in the statement of comprehensive income; or

- as an expense in profit or loss, consistent with the treatment of revaluation decreases in IAS 16 and IAS 38.

Some revaluation accounting can result in the recognition of expenses such as a revaluation decrease for property, plant and equipment or intangible asset in excess of existing revaluation credits.[200] However, Example 6 included within the Illustrative Examples accompanying IFRS 3 (2007) envisages that adjustments relating to step acquisition accounting are not recognised as part of the acquirer's profit or loss, but are recognised in other comprehensive income in the statement of comprehensive income. This is consistent with viewing these revaluations as capital maintenance adjustments, which the IASB's Framework notes are included in equity as adjustments or revaluation reserves.[201] In the light of this conflict between the requirements of IAS 16 and IAS 38 and IFRS 3 (2007), we believe that entities have a choice in accounting policy in accounting for any declines in fair value of an item of property, plant and equipment or intangible asset that does not give rise to an impairment loss. However, whichever policy is adopted must be applied consistently.

Accordingly, Entity A should account for the items listed above in the following manner:

(a) Contingent liability – as IAS 37 does not permit this to be recognised in the financial statements of Entity B, the contingent liability is not part of the equity accounted result. Therefore, the portion of the fair value that relates to the existing 25% ownership interest forms part of the step acquisition revaluation that is recognised in other comprehensive income in the statement of comprehensive income.

(b) Loan at fixed interest rate – as this is accounted for at amortised cost under IAS 39, any change in fair value is not part of the equity accounted result and results in a step acquisition revaluation (up or down). Therefore, the portion of the fair value adjustment that relates to the existing 25% ownership interest forms part of the step acquisition revaluation that is recognised in other comprehensive income in the statement of comprehensive income.

(c) Legal provision – as the change in the value of the provision is due to changes in estimated future cash flows, this must be reflected in the measurement of the provision. This is consistent with paragraph 59 of IAS 37, which requires the provision to be 'reviewed at the end of each reporting period and adjusted to reflect the current best estimate.' This change is part of the equity accounted result.

As the IAS 37 measurement is not necessarily equal to fair value, there may be some remaining difference between the remeasured provision and the fair value measurement performed when Entity A obtains control. The portion of the difference that relates to the existing 25% ownership interest forms part of the step acquisition revaluation that is recognised in other comprehensive income in the statement of comprehensive income.

(d) Financial instruments at fair value through profit or loss – again, the application of the equity method means that IAS 39 is applied to the underlying financial instruments until Entity A ceases to have significant influence and obtains control over Entity B. Accordingly, the revaluation to fair value will be included in the equity accounted results and there will be no need for a step acquisition revaluation.

(e) Intangible asset – a decline in fair value that is not attributable to the passage of time or normal use of the asset is an indicator of impairment under IAS 36. Therefore, even though Entity B may not conduct an impairment test at this time, Entity A must assess whether all or part of the decline in value is an impairment loss that is reflected in the equity accounting result.

To the extent that all or a part of the decline does not lead to an impairment loss being recognised, then two approaches are acceptable based on Entity A's choice of policy.

Consistent with the treatment of all other revaluations, the portion of the decline that relates to the existing 25% ownership interest forms part of the step acquisition revaluation that is recognised in other comprehensive income in the statement of comprehensive income.

Alternatively, the portion of the decline that relates to the existing 25% ownership interest is recorded as an expense in profit or loss. This is on the basis that IAS 38 states that a revaluation decrease for an intangible asset is recognised in profit or loss. The statement in IFRS 3 (2007) that the adjustment 'is a revaluation and shall be accounted for as such' can be interpreted as permitting the revaluation treatment specified in IAS 38. A similar approach could be applied to assets within the scope of IAS 16.

In the above example, Entity A accounted for its previous ownership interest under the equity method. If the interest had been accounted for at fair value (or cost), the impact of accounting for the various items on the consolidated financial statements, immediately after control was obtained, would be expected to be the same as in Example 9.25 above.

Example 6 included within the Illustrative Examples accompanying IFRS 3 (2007 clearly states that regardless of the method of accounting for the investment before gaining control, the cost of the investment and the goodwill calculated are the same, due to the adjustments made for any fair value adjustments and equity accounted results. It also clearly states that 'consolidated financial statements immediately after Investor acquires the additional 60 per cent ownership interest and obtains control of Investee would be the same irrespective of the method used to account for the initial 20 per cent investment in Investee before obtaining control.'

The step acquisition accounting has the effect that an adjustment is recognised in equity to effectively equity account for the existing ownership interest held, whether it was carried at cost or fair value. Therefore, the same approach is required for considering if an impairment is recognised. This may require management obtaining additional information to which they may not have previously had ready access, before gaining control.

As indicated earlier, IFRS 3 (2007) states that the adjustment to those fair values relating to previously held interests of the acquirer is a revaluation to be accounted for as such.[202] However, the standard is silent as to whether any such revaluation gain (or loss) can be reclassified into profit or loss at a later date. IAS 27 (2007) also does not make any reference to such items being taken into account in calculating the gain or loss on disposal of a subsidiary (see Chapter 7 at 3.3). Although in Examples 9.23 and 9.24 above the revaluation gain arose on land, in practice, and as illustrated in Example 9.25 above, any revaluation gain or loss is likely to arise on various assets or liabilities of the acquiree. It will therefore depend on the facts and circumstances whether revaluation amounts arising on business combinations achieved in stages are reclassified into profit or loss on subsequent disposal of the underlying assets (or liabilities) or businesses concerned. In many cases, the revaluation amounts are likely to arise on items such as intangible assets and property, plant and equipment, where under the relevant standard for such items, revaluations gains and losses are not reclassified into profit or loss upon disposal of the related asset, but may only be transferred to retained earnings. Accordingly, revaluation amounts in respect of such items that arise from a business combination involving successive share purchases should not be reclassified into profit or loss, either on disposal of the underlying assets or the business concerned. However, where the revaluation amounts relate specifically to items where the relevant accounting standard would require them to be reclassified into profit or loss, such as available-for-sale investments under IAS 39, then gains on such items should be treated no differently from any other subsequent gains or losses for such items that are taken to equity. Thus, they should be reclassified into the profit or loss, either on disposal of the underlying assets or the business concerned.

If the revaluation surplus in equity relates directly to an identifiable fixed asset, whether intangible or an item of property, plant and equipment, it may be transferred directly to retained earnings when the asset is derecognised, in whole on disposal or as the asset concerned is depreciated or amortised.[203] If, as may well be the case, the revaluation relates to fair value adjustments on a bundle of assets and liabilities, the reserve will only be transferred to retained earnings on derecognition of the interest in the subsidiary.

In situations such as that illustrated in Examples 9.24 and 9.25 above, where the equity method of accounting has been applied to the original investments, the requirements of IFRS 3 (2007) do not appear to create many additional practical difficulties over and above those that arose when the acquirer had to allocate the cost of the associate originally to the fair values of the acquiree's assets, liabilities and contingent liabilities. The main practical difficulty will be where equity accounting has not been applied to earlier stages of the business combination, such as in Example 9.23 above. In that case, the acquirer has to calculate goodwill based on fair values at the time of that original acquisition, yet will not have had to carry out such an exercise at that time. This situation is similar in many ways to that considered by the IASB in relation to the transitional provisions of IFRS 3 (2007) where it was decided that applying the standard retrospectively would be problematic, particularly in relation to the role of hindsight, and may even be impossible because the information needed may not exist or may no longer be obtainable. The IASB only allowed retrospective application of the standard where valuations and other information were obtained at the time the business combinations were initially accounted for.

Although the requirements discussed above, and Examples 9.24 and 9.25 above, deal with an associate becoming a subsidiary, the same accounting treatment applies when a jointly controlled entity becomes a subsidiary.

Example 9.26:   Business combination achieved in stages – jointly controlled entity becoming a subsidiary

Entity M and Entity P currently operate a joint venture, Entity J, with Entity M holding a 75% interest and Entity P a 25% interest, each party having joint control. Entity M accounts for Entity J's activities as a jointly controlled entity according to IAS 31 – *Interests in Joint Ventures* (see Chapter 12).

Entity M now buys out Entity P's 25% interest in Entity J and as a result, obtains control over Entity J's activities.

Consequently, the acquisition of the remaining 25% of Entity J gives rise to a business combination. Therefore, at the date control is obtained, Entity M accounts for the transaction as a step acquisition, and thus:

- determines goodwill for the newly acquired 25% interest using the cost of that transaction and the fair value of Entity J's identifiable net assets at the date control is obtained;
- recognises the assets and liabilities at 100% of their fair value at the date of control; and
- treats any adjustment to those fair values relating to previously held interests as a revaluation.

This applies irrespective of whether Entity M equity accounted for its 75% interest in the joint venture or dealt with it by way of proportionate consolidation.

The requirements discussed above deal only with those situations where there have been earlier exchange transactions prior to the one that has resulted in a business combination, such as the acquisition of a subsidiary, whereby the acquirer now has control over that business. However, the standard is silent on how later exchange transactions should be accounted for, such as the acquisition of some or all of the minority interest in a subsidiary. This is discussed in Chapter 7 at 3.3.3.

2.10   Reverse acquisitions

As discussed at 2.3 above, in some business combinations, commonly referred to as reverse acquisitions, the acquirer is the entity whose equity interests have been acquired and the issuing entity is the acquiree. This might be the case when, for example, a private entity arranges to have itself 'acquired' by a smaller public entity as a means of obtaining a stock exchange listing. Although legally the issuing public entity is regarded as the parent and the private entity is regarded as the subsidiary, the legal subsidiary is the acquirer if it has the power to govern the financial and operating policies of the legal parent so as to obtain benefits from its activities.

Appendix B to IFRS 3 (2007), which is an integral part of the standard, gives guidance on the accounting for reverse acquisitions. It notes that reverse acquisition accounting determines the allocation of the cost of the business combination as at the acquisition date and does not apply to transactions after the combination.[204]

2.10.1 Cost of the business combination

When equity instruments are issued as part of the cost of the business combination, paragraph 24 of the standard requires the cost of the combination to include the fair value of those equity instruments at the date of exchange (see 2.4 above). Paragraph 27 notes that, in the absence of a reliable published price, the fair value of the equity instruments can be estimated by reference to the fair value of the acquirer or the fair value of the acquiree, whichever is more clearly evident (see 2.4.3 above).[205]

In a reverse acquisition, the cost of the business combination is deemed to have been incurred by the legal subsidiary (i.e. the acquirer for accounting purposes) in the form of equity instruments issued to the owners of the legal parent (i.e. the acquiree for accounting purposes). If the published price of the equity instruments of the legal subsidiary is used to determine the cost of the combination, a calculation shall be made to determine the number of equity instruments the legal subsidiary would have had to issue to provide the same percentage ownership interest of the combined entity to the owners of the legal parent as they have in the combined entity as a result of the reverse acquisition. The fair value of the number of equity instruments so calculated shall be used as the cost of the combination.[206]

On the other hand, if the fair value of the equity instruments of the legal subsidiary is not otherwise clearly evident, the total fair value of all the issued equity instruments of the legal parent before the business combination is to be used as the basis for determining the cost of the combination.[207] The following example illustrates the application of this guidance. It is based on Example 5 within the Illustrative Examples accompanying IFRS 3 (2007).

Example 9.27:   Reverse acquisition – calculating the cost of the business combination using the fair value of the equity shares of the legal subsidiary

Entity A, the entity issuing equity instruments and therefore the legal parent, is acquired in a reverse acquisition by Entity B, the legal subsidiary, on 30 September 2009. The accounting for any income tax effects is ignored.

Balance sheets of Entity A and Entity B immediately before the business combination

	Entity A €	Entity B €
Current assets	500	700
Non-current assets	1,300	3,000
	1,800	3,700
Current liabilities	300	600
Non-current liabilities	400	1,100
	700	1,700
Owner's equity		
Issued equity		
100 ordinary shares	300	
60 Ordinary shares		600
Retained earnings	800	1,400
	1,100	2,000

Other information

(a) On 30 September 2009, Entity A issues 2½ shares in exchange for each ordinary share of Entity B. All of Entity B's shareholders exchange their shares in Entity B. Therefore, Entity A issues 150 ordinary shares in exchange for all 60 ordinary shares of Entity B.

(b) The fair value of each ordinary share of Entity B at 30 September 2009 is €40. The quoted market price of Entity A's ordinary shares at that date is €12.

(c) The fair values of Entity A's identifiable assets and liabilities at 30 September 2009 are the same as their carrying amounts, with the exception of non-current assets. The fair value of Entity A's non-current assets at 30 September 2009 is €1,500.

Calculating the cost of the business combination

As a result of the issue of 150 ordinary shares by Entity A, Entity B's shareholders own 60 per cent of the issued shares of the combined entity (i.e. 150 shares out of 250 issued shares). The remaining 40 per cent are owned by Entity A's shareholders. If the business combination had taken place in the form of Entity B issuing additional ordinary shares to Entity A's shareholders in exchange for their ordinary shares in Entity A, Entity B would have had to issue 40 shares for the ratio of ownership interest in the combined entity to be the same. Entity B's shareholders would then own 60 out of the 100 issued shares of Entity B and therefore 60 per cent of the combined entity.

As a result, the cost of the business combination is €1,600 (i.e. 40 shares each with a fair value of €40).

In the above example, the fair value of the ordinary shares was evident. However, in those situations where a private entity arranges to have itself 'acquired' by a smaller public entity as a means of obtaining a stock exchange listing, it may be that this will not be the case. In which case, the fair value of the shares of the legal parent should be used.

Example 9.28: Reverse acquisition – calculating the cost of the business combination using the fair value of the shares of the legal parent

If in the above example, the fair value of the ordinary shares of Entity B was not clearly evident, the total fair value of all the issued equity instruments of the Entity A before the business combination would be used as the basis for determining the cost of the combination.

The total fair value of all of Entity A's shares before the business combination was €1,200 (i.e. 100 shares each with a fair value of €12). Since Entity B is treated as having acquired a 100% interest in Entity A, then the cost of the business combination would be €1,200.

2.10.2 *Preparation and presentation of consolidated financial statements*

Since the legal parent is the acquiree for accounting purposes, the consolidated financial statements prepared following a reverse acquisition reflect the fair values of the assets, liabilities and contingent liabilities of the legal parent, not those of the legal subsidiary. Therefore, the cost of the business combination (as determined under 2.10.1 above) is allocated by measuring the identifiable assets, liabilities and contingent liabilities of the legal parent that satisfy the recognition criteria in paragraph 37 of the standard at their fair values at the acquisition date (see 2.5 above). Any excess of the cost of the combination over the acquirer's interest in the net fair value of those items is then accounted for as goodwill (see 2.6 above). Any excess of the acquirer's interest in the net fair value of those items over the cost of the combination is accounted for as an immediate gain in profit or loss (after having reassessed the fair value of those items and the measurement of the cost of the business combination) (see 2.7 above).[208]

Example 9.29:   Reverse acquisition – allocating the cost of the business combination to the assets acquired and liabilities and contingent liabilities assumed

Using the facts in Example 9.27 above, the acquirer, Entity B, has to allocate the cost of the business combination of €1,600 to the net fair value of Entity A's identifiable assets and liabilities. This results in goodwill of €300, measured as follows:

	€	€
Cost of the business combination		1,600
Net fair value of Entity A's identifiable assets and liabilities:		
Current assets	500	
Non-current assets	1,500	
Current liabilities	(300)	
Non-current liabilities	(400)	
		1,300
Goodwill		300

If the cost of the business combination had been determined as in Example 9.28 above, i.e. €1,200, then no goodwill would have arisen and, assuming no adjustments were required as a result of the re-assessment of that cost or of the net fair values of Entity A's net assets, a gain of €100 would be recognised immediately in profit or loss.

Although the accounting for the reverse acquisition reflects the legal subsidiary as being the acquirer, the consolidated financial statements prepared following a reverse acquisition are issued under the name of the legal parent. Consequently they have to be described in the notes as a continuation of the financial statements of the legal subsidiary, since it is the acquirer for accounting purposes. Because such consolidated financial statements represent a continuation of the financial statements of the legal subsidiary:

(a)   the assets and liabilities of the legal subsidiary are recognised and measured in those consolidated financial statements at their pre-combination carrying amounts; i.e. no fair value adjustments are made to the assets and liabilities of the legal subsidiary;

(b)   the retained earnings and other equity balances recognised in those
       consolidated financial statements are the retained earnings and other equity
       balances of the legal subsidiary immediately before the business combination,
       not those of the legal parent;

(c)   the amount recognised as issued equity instruments in those consolidated
       financial statements are determined by adding to the issued equity of the legal
       subsidiary immediately before the business combination the cost of the
       combination determined as discussed at 2.10.1 above. However, the equity
       structure appearing in those consolidated financial statements (i.e. the number
       and type of equity instruments issued) reflects the equity structure of the legal
       parent, including the equity instruments issued by the legal parent to effect
       the combination;

(d)   the comparative information presented in those consolidated financial
       statements is that of the legal subsidiary, not that originally presented in the
       previous financial statements of the legal parent;[209] and

(e)   the income statement for the current period reflects that of the legal
       subsidiary for the full period together with the post-acquisition results of the
       legal parent (based on the attributed fair values).

Continuing with Example 9.27 above, this results in the following consolidated
balance sheet.

Example 9.30:   Reverse acquisition – consolidated balance sheet

Using the facts in Example 9.27 above, this results in the following consolidated balance sheet at the
date of the business combination (the intermediate columns for Entity B and Entity A are included
to show the workings):

	Entity B Book values €	Entity A Fair values €	Consolidated €
Current assets	700	500	1,200
Non-current assets	3,000	1,500	4,500
Goodwill		300	300
	3,700	2,300	6,000
Current liabilities	600	300	900
Non-current liabilities	1,100	400	1,500
	1,700	700	2,400
Owner's equity			
Issued equity			
250 ordinary shares	600	1,600	2,200
Retained earnings	1,400	–	1,400
	2,000	1,600	3,600

Although reverse acquisition accounting is applied in the consolidated financial
statements, in the legal parent's separate financial statements, if any, the investment
in the legal subsidiary is accounted for in accordance with the requirements in
IAS 27 (2007) on accounting for investments in an investor's separate financial
statements.[210]

Example 9.31:   Reverse acquisition – legal parent's balance sheet in separate financial
statements

Using the facts in Example 9.27 above, the balance sheet of Entity A, the legal parent, in its separate
financial statements immediately following the business combination will be as follows:

	Entity A
	€
Current assets	500
Non-current assets	1,300
Investment in subsidiary (Entity B)	1,800
	3,600
Current liabilities	300
Non-current liabilities	400
	700
Owner's equity	
Issued equity	
250 ordinary shares	2,100
Retained earnings	800
	2,900

The investment in the subsidiary is included at its cost of €1,800, being the fair value of the shares
issued by Entity A (150 × €12). It can be seen that the issued equity is different from that in the
consolidated financial statements and its non-current assets remain at their carrying amounts before
the business combination.

2.10.3 Minority interest

In some reverse acquisitions, some of the owners of the legal subsidiary do not
exchange their equity instruments for equity instruments of the legal parent.
Although reverse acquisition accounting regards the entity in which those owners
hold equity instruments (the legal subsidiary) as having acquired another entity (the
legal parent), those owners are required to be treated as a minority interest in the
consolidated financial statements prepared after the reverse acquisition. This is
because the owners of the legal subsidiary that do not exchange their equity
instruments for equity instruments of the legal parent have an interest only in the
results and net assets of the legal subsidiary, and not in the results and net assets of
the combined entity. Conversely, all of the owners of the legal parent,
notwithstanding that the legal parent is regarded as the acquiree, have an interest in
the results and net assets of the combined entity.[211]

Because the assets and liabilities of the legal subsidiary are recognised and measured
in the consolidated financial statements at their pre-combination carrying amounts,
the minority interest shall reflect the minority shareholders' proportionate interest in
the pre-combination carrying amounts of the legal subsidiary's net assets.[212]

These requirements are illustrated in the following example (again based on
Example 5 within the Illustrative Examples accompanying IFRS 3 (2007)).

Example 9.32:   Reverse acquisition – minority interest

This example uses the same facts in Example 9.27 above, except that in this case only 56 of Entity B's ordinary shares are tendered for exchange rather than all 60. Because Entity A issues 2½ shares in exchange for each ordinary share of Entity B, Entity A issues only 140 (rather than 150) shares. As a result, Entity B's shareholders own 58.3 per cent of the issued shares of the combined entity (i.e. 140 shares out of 240 issued shares).

As in Example 9.27 above, the cost of the business combination is calculated by assuming that the combination had taken place in the form of Entity B issuing additional ordinary shares to the shareholders of Entity A in exchange for their ordinary shares in Entity A. In calculating the number of shares that would have to be issued by Entity B, the minority interest is ignored. The majority shareholders own 56 shares of Entity B. For this to represent a 58.3 per cent ownership interest, Entity B would have had to issue an additional 40 shares. The majority shareholders would then own 56 out of the 96 issued shares of Entity B and therefore 58.3 per cent of the combined entity.

As a result, the cost of the business combination is €1,600 (i.e. 40 shares each with a fair value of €40). This is the same amount as when all 60 of Entity B's ordinary shares are tendered for exchange (see Example 9.27 above). The cost of the combination does not change simply because some of Entity B's shareholders do not participate in the exchange.

The minority interest is represented by the 4 shares of the total 60 shares of Entity B that are not exchanged for shares of Entity A. Therefore, the minority interest is 6.7 per cent. The minority interest reflects the minority shareholders' proportionate interest in the pre-combination carrying amounts of the net assets of the legal subsidiary. Therefore, the consolidated balance sheet is adjusted to show a minority interest of 6.7 per cent of the pre-combination carrying amounts of Entity B's net assets (i.e. €134 or 6.7 per cent of €2,000).

The consolidated balance sheet at 30 September 2009 (the date of the business combination) reflecting the minority interest is as follows (the intermediate columns for Entity B, minority interest and Entity A are included to show the workings):

	Entity B Book values €	Minority interest €	Entity A Fair values €	Consolidated €
Current assets	700		500	1,200
Non-current assets	3,000		1,500	4,500
Goodwill			300	300
	3,700		2,300	6,000
Current liabilities	600		300	900
Non-current liabilities	1,100		400	1,500
	1,700		700	2,400
Owner's equity				
Issued equity				
240 ordinary shares	600	(40)	1,600	2,160
Retained earnings	1,400	(94)	–	1,306
Minority interest	–	134	–	134
	2,000	–	1,600	3,600

2.10.4 Earnings per share

As indicated at 2.10.2 above the equity structure appearing in the consolidated financial statements prepared following a reverse acquisition reflects the equity structure of the legal parent, including the equity instruments issued by the legal parent to effect the business combination.[213]

Where the legal parent is required by IAS 33 – *Earnings per Share* – to disclose earnings per share information (see Chapter 36), then for the purpose of calculating the weighted average number of ordinary shares outstanding (the denominator) during the period in which the reverse acquisition occurs:

(a)   the number of ordinary shares outstanding from the beginning of that period to the acquisition date is deemed to be the number of ordinary shares issued by the legal parent to the owners of the legal subsidiary (rather than the actual number of shares of the legal parent during that period); and

(b)   the number of ordinary shares outstanding from the acquisition date to the end of that period is the actual number of ordinary shares of the legal parent outstanding during that period.[214]

The basic earnings per share disclosed for each comparative period before the acquisition date that is presented in the consolidated financial statements following a reverse acquisition is calculated by dividing the profit or loss of the legal subsidiary attributable to ordinary shareholders in each of those periods by the number of ordinary shares issued by the legal parent to the owners of the legal subsidiary in the reverse acquisition.[215]

The calculations outlined above assume that there were no changes in the number of the legal subsidiary's issued ordinary shares during the comparative periods and during the period from the beginning of the period in which the reverse acquisition occurred to the acquisition date. The calculation of earnings per share is appropriately adjusted to take into account the effect of a change in the number of the legal subsidiary's issued ordinary shares during those periods.[216]

These requirements are illustrated in the following example (again based on Example 5 within the Illustrative Examples accompanying IFRS 3 (2007)).

Example 9.33:   Reverse acquisition – earnings per share

This example uses the same facts in Example 9.27 above. Assume that Entity B's profit for the annual period ending 31 December 2008 was €600, and that the consolidated profit for the annual period ending 31 December 2009 is €800. Assume also that there was no change in the number of ordinary shares issued by Entity B during the annual period ending 31 December 2008 and during the period from 1 January 2009 to the date of the reverse acquisition (30 September 2009).

Earnings per share for the annual period ending 31 December 2009 is calculated as follows:

Number of shares deemed to be outstanding for the period from 1 January 2009 to the acquisition date (30 September 2009), being the number of ordinary shares issued by Entity A in the reverse acquisition	150
Number of shares outstanding from the acquisition date to 31 December 2009	250
Weighted average number of shares outstanding $(150 \times 9/12) + (250 \times 3/12)$	175
Earnings per share €800/175	€4.57

The restated earnings per share for the annual period ending 31 December 2008 is €4.00 (being €600/150, i.e. the profit of Entity B for that period divided by the number of ordinary shares issued by Entity A in the reverse acquisition). Any earnings per share information for that period disclosed by either Entity A or Entity B is irrelevant.

2.10.5 Cash consideration

Typically, a reverse acquisition occurs where the legal acquirer (Entity A) issues new shares to 'acquire' shares in the legal acquiree (Entity B). However, in some circumstances the combination may be effected whereby some of the consideration given by Entity A to acquire the shares in Entity B is cash.

In such circumstances, can the combination be accounted for as a reverse acquisition of Entity A by Entity B despite some of the consideration being in the form of cash?

Normally, the entity issuing cash consideration would be considered to be the acquirer. However, despite the form of the consideration, the key determinant in identifying an acquirer remains the power of one party to control the other (see 2.3 above).

Therefore, where there is clear evidence demonstrating that the legal acquiree, Entity B, has obtained the power to govern the financial and operating policies of Entity A, for example, through domination of the selection of management (a control indicator under paragraph 20(c) of IFRS 3 (2007)), this will overcome the presumption that Entity A is the acquirer and the combination should be accounted for as a reverse acquisition.

In that case, how should any cash paid be accounted for?

One approach might be to treat the payment as a pre-acquisition transaction with a resulting reduction in the consideration and in net assets acquired (with no net impact on goodwill). However, we do not believe this to be appropriate. Any consideration, whether cash or shares, paid by Entity A cannot form part of the cost of the business combination as Entity A is the deemed acquiree. As discussed at 2.10.2 above, although the consolidated financial statements prepared following a reverse acquisition are issued under the name of the legal parent, they are to be described in the notes as a continuation of the financial statements of the legal subsidiary. Therefore, since the consolidated financial statements are a continuation of Entity B's financial statements, in our view the cash consideration paid from Entity A (the deemed acquiree) should be accounted for as a distribution from the consolidated group to the acquirer's (Entity B's) shareholders as at the combination date.

However, where a cash payment is made to effect the combination, then the requirements of Appendix B to IFRS 3 (2007) need to be applied with care as illustrated in the following example.

Example 9.34:   Reverse acquisition effected with cash consideration

Entity A has 100,000 ordinary shares in issue, with a market price of £2.00 per share, giving a market capitalisation of £200,000. It acquires all of the shares in Entity B for a consideration of £500,000 satisfied by the issue of 200,000 shares (with a value of £400,000) and a cash payment of £100,000 to Entity B's shareholders. Entity B has 200,000 shares in issue, with an estimated fair value of £2.50 per share.

After the combination Entity B's shareholders control the voting of Entity A and, as a result, have been able to appoint Entity B's directors and key executives to replace their Entity A counterparts. Accordingly, the combination must be accounted for as a reverse acquisition, i.e. Entity B is taken to have acquired Entity A since it has the power to govern the financial and operating policies of Entity A.

How should the cost of the combination be calculated?

Applying the requirements of paragraph B5 of IFRS 3 (2007) (discussed at A above) to the transaction might lead to the following conclusion. Entity A has had to issue 200,000 shares to Entity B's shareholders, resulting in Entity B's shareholders having 66.67% (200,000/300,000) of the equity and Entity A's shareholders 33.33% (100,000/300,000). If Entity B's share price is used to determine the cost of the acquisition, then under paragraph B5, Entity B would have had to issue 100,000 shares to Entity A's shareholders to result in the same % shareholdings (200,000/300,000 = 66.67%). This would apparently give a cost of 100,000 @ £2.50 = £250,000. This does not seem correct.

If there had been no cash consideration at all, then Entity A would have issued 250,000 shares to Entity B's shareholders, resulting in Entity B's shareholders having 71.43% (250,000/350,000) of the equity and Entity A's shareholders 28.57% (100,000/350,000). If Entity B's share price is used to determine the cost of the acquisition, then under paragraph B5, Entity B would have had to issue 80,000 shares to Entity A's shareholders to result in the same % shareholdings (200,000/280,000 = 71.43%). This would give a cost of 80,000 @ £2.50 = £200,000. If it is thought that the fair value of Entity B's shares is not otherwise clearly evident, paragraph B6 of IFRS 3 (2007) would require the total value of Entity A to be used instead. As Entity B has effectively acquired 100% of Entity A, the cost of the investment would be £200,000 (the same as under the revised paragraph B5 calculation above).

In our view, the proper analysis of the paragraph B5 calculation in this case is that of the 100,000 shares that Entity B is deemed to have issued, only 80,000 of them are to acquire Entity A's shares, resulting in a cost of £200,000. The extra 20,000 shares are to compensate Entity A's shareholders for the fact that Entity B's shareholders have received a cash distribution of £100,000, and is effectively a stock distribution to Entity A's shareholders of £50,000 (20,000 @ £2.50), being their share (33.33%) of a total distribution of £150,000. However, since the equity structure (i.e. the number and type of shares) appearing in the consolidated financial statements reflects that of the legal parent, Entity A, this 'stock distribution' will not actually be apparent. The only distribution that will be shown as a movement in equity is the £100,000 cash paid to Entity B's shareholders.

2.10.6 Reverse acquisitions involving a non-trading shell company

The requirements for reverse acquisitions in IFRS 3 (2007), and the guidance provided by the standard, discussed above are based on the premise that the legal parent (accounting acquiree) has a business which has been acquired by the legal subsidiary (accounting acquirer). In some situations, this may not be the case, for example where a private entity arranges to have itself 'acquired' by a non-trading public entity as a means of obtaining a stock exchange listing. As indicated at 2.1.3 above, the standard indicates that if an entity obtains control of an entity that is not a business, the bringing together of those entities is not a business combination.[217] In our view, a non-trading shell company will generally not be a business as defined in Appendix A to the standard (see 2.1.3 A above).

This is consistent with the position now taken by IFRS 3 (as revised in 2008). As indicated at 3.15 below, the revised standard notes that the accounting acquiree (legal acquirer) must meet the definition of a business (see 3.2.2 below) for the transaction to be accounted for as a reverse acquisition,[218] but does not say how the transaction should be accounted for where the accounting acquiree is not a business.

So, how should such a transaction be accounted for? It clearly cannot be accounted for as an acquisition of the legal acquiree by the legal acquirer under the standard either, if the legal acquirer has not been identified as the accounting acquirer based on the guidance in the standard.

In our view, such a transaction should be accounted for in the consolidated financial statements of the legal parent as a continuation of the financial statements of the private entity (the legal subsidiary), together with a deemed issue of shares, equivalent to the shares held by the former shareholders of the legal parent, and a re-capitalisation of the equity of the private entity. This deemed issue of shares is, in effect, an equity-settled share based payment transaction whereby the private entity has received the net assets of the legal parent, generally cash, together with the listing status of the legal parent.

Example 9.35:   Reverse acquisition of a non-trading shell company

Entity A is a non-trading public company with 10,000 ordinary shares in issue. On 31 December 2009, Entity A issues 190,000 ordinary shares in exchange for all of the ordinary share capital of Entity B, a private trading company, with 9,500 ordinary shares in issue.

At the date of the transaction, Entity A has $85,000 of cash and the quoted market price of Entity A's ordinary shares is $12.

The fair value of Entity B has been determined by an independent professional valuer as being $2,185,000, giving a value per share of $230.

Following the transaction, apart from one non-executive director, all of the directors of Entity A resign and four new directors from Entity B are appointed to the Board of Entity A.

As a result of Entity A issuing 190,000 ordinary shares, Entity B's shareholders own 95 per cent of the issued share capital of the combined entity (i.e. 190,000 of the 200,000 issued shares), with the remaining 5 per cent held by Entity A's existing shareholders.

How should this transaction be accounted for in the consolidated financial statements of Entity A?

As the shareholders of Entity A only retain a 5 per cent interest in the combined entity after the transaction, and the Board is dominated by appointees from Entity B, this cannot be accounted for as an acquisition of Entity B by Entity A. Also, as a result of Entity A being a non-trading cash shell company, and therefore not comprising a business (see 2.1.3 A above), it cannot be accounted for as a reverse acquisition of Entity A by Entity B either.

The consolidated financial statements should reflect the substance of the transaction which is that Entity B is the continuing entity, therefore the principles and guidance on the preparation and presentation of the consolidated financial statements in a reverse acquisition set out in IFRS 3 (2007) should be applied in this transaction by analogy.

However, as the transaction is not a business combination under IFRS 3 (2007), the transaction effectively involves a share-based payment transaction under IFRS 2 (see Chapter 27) whereby Entity B is deemed to have issued shares in exchange for the $85,000 cash held by Entity A together with the listing status of Entity A. However, the listing status does not qualify for recognition as an intangible asset, and therefore needs to be expensed in profit or loss. Under IFRS 2. for equity-settled share-based payments transactions, an entity measures the goods or services received, and the corresponding increase in equity, directly at the fair value of the goods or services received, unless that fair value cannot be estimated reliably. If the entity cannot estimate reliably the fair value of the goods and services received, the entity measures the amounts, indirectly, by reference to the fair value of the equity instruments issued.[219] For transactions with non-employees, IFRS 2 presumes that the fair value of the goods and services received is more readily determinable.[220] This would suggest that the increase in equity should be based on the fair value of the cash and the fair value of the listing status. However, it is unlikely that a fair value of the listing status can be reliably estimated, therefore the increase in equity should be measured by reference to the fair value of the shares that are deemed to have been issued. Indeed, even if a fair value could be attributed to the listing status, if the total identifiable consideration received is less than the fair value of the equity given as consideration, as a result of IFRIC 8, the transaction should be measured based on the fair value of the shares that are deemed to be issued.[221]

Given that the existing shareholders of Entity A have a 5 per cent interest in the combined entity, Entity B would have had to issue 500 shares for the ratio of ownership interest in the combined entity to be the same. Based on the fair value of an Entity B share of $230, the accounting for the deemed share-based payment transaction is:

	$	$
Cash received	85,000	
Listing expense (income statement)	30,000	
Issued equity (500 × $230)		115,000

As Entity B is a private entity, it may be that a more reliable basis for determining the fair value of the deemed shares issued would have been to use the quoted market price of Entity A's shares at the date of the transaction. On this basis, the issued equity would have been $120,000 (10,000 × $12), giving rise to a listing expense of $35,000.

In summary, the accounting for this transaction is similar in many respects to that which would have been the case if the transaction had been accounted for as a reverse acquisition; the main difference being that no goodwill arises on the transaction, and that any amount that would have been so recognised is accounted for as a listing expense. Indeed, if the transaction had been accounted for as a reverse acquisition, the overall effect may have been the same if an impairment loss on the 'goodwill' had been recognised.

2.11   Call and put options over minority interests

Where, in a business combination, the acquirer obtains less than a 100% interest in the acquiree, this will be accounted for by recognising at the date of acquisition:

- All of the identifiable assets, liabilities and contingent liabilities of the acquiree recognised in accordance with the standard at their fair values (as determined in 2.5 above);

- Goodwill being the excess of the cost of the business combination (as determined in 2.4 above) over the acquirer's interest in those net assets;

- A minority interest in the acquiree reflecting the minority's proportion of the net identifiable assets, liabilities and contingent liabilities of the acquiree at their attributed fair values; no amount is included for any goodwill relating to the minority interest.

Minority interest is defined in both IFRS 3 (2007) and IAS 27 (2007) as 'that portion of the profit or loss and net assets of a subsidiary attributable to equity interests that are not owned, directly or indirectly through subsidiaries, by the parent'.[222]

In most business combinations where less than 100% of the equity shares have been acquired, the determination of the acquirer's share of the net assets of the acquiree (and, thus the amount of the minority interest) is straightforward. If an entity acquires 60% of the equity shares of the acquiree then goodwill will be based on 60% of the net assets of the acquiree and a minority interest representing 40% of the net assets of the acquiree will be recognised. As discussed in Chapter 7 at 4.2, the minority interest will be presented in the consolidated balance sheet within equity, separately from the parent shareholders' equity.

However, in some business combinations where less than 100% of the equity shares are acquired, it may be that the transaction also involves options over some or all of the outstanding shares. It may that the acquirer has a call option, i.e. a right to acquire the outstanding shares at a future date for cash at a particular price. Alternatively, it may be that the acquirer has granted a put option to the other shareholders whereby they have the right to sell their shares to the acquirer at a future date for cash at a particular price. Indeed in some cases, there may be a combination of such call and put options, the terms of which may be equivalent or may be different.

IFRS 3 (2007) gives no guidance as to how such options should impact on the accounting for a business combination. This issue is discussed in Chapter 7 at 5.

2.12   Push down accounting

The term 'push down accounting' relates to the practice adopted in some jurisdictions of incorporating, or 'pushing down', the fair value adjustments which have been made by the acquirer into the financial statements of the acquiree, including the goodwill arising on the acquisition. It is argued that the acquisition, being an independently bargained transaction, provides better evidence of the values of the assets and liabilities of the acquiree than those previously contained within its financial statements, and therefore represents an improved basis of accounting. There are, however, contrary views, which hold that the transaction in question was one to which the reporting entity was not a party, and there is no reason why it should intrude into the entity's own accounting records.

Whatever the theoretical arguments, it is certainly true that push down accounting could be an expedient practice, because it obviates the need to make extensive consolidation adjustments in each subsequent year, based on parallel accounting records. Nevertheless, if the acquiree is preparing its financial statements under IFRS, in our view it cannot apply push down accounting and reflect the fair value adjustments made by the acquirer and the goodwill that arose on its acquisition.

All of the requirements of IFRS must be applied when an entity prepares its financial statements. IFRS requires assets and liabilities to be recognised initially at cost or fair value, depending on the nature of the assets and liabilities. The acquisition of an entity is not a transaction undertaken by that entity itself, hence it cannot be a transaction to determine cost.

Application of push down accounting would result in the recognition and measurement of assets and liabilities that are prohibited by some standards (such as internally generated intangibles and goodwill) and the recognition and measurement of assets and liabilities at amounts that are not permitted under IFRS. While some

IFRS standards include an option or requirement to revalue particular assets, this is undertaken as part of a process of determining accounting policies rather than as one-off revaluations. For example:

- IAS 2 – *Inventories* – requires that inventories are measured at the lower of cost and net realisable value (see Chapter 20 at 2.2);

- IAS 16 requires that items of property, plant and equipment are initially measured at cost. Subsequently, property, plant and equipment can be measured at cost or at revalued amount. However, revaluations must be applied consistently and must be performed on a regular basis. Therefore a one-off revaluation is not permitted (see Chapter 16 at 4.1);

- IAS 38 requires that intangible assets are initially measured at cost. Subsequently, they can be revalued only in rare circumstances where there is an active market. In addition, IAS 38 specifically prohibits the recognition of internally generated goodwill. Therefore a one-off revaluation is not permitted (see Chapter 15 at 2.3.5 and 2.4.2).

2.13   Disclosure requirements relating to business combinations

In developing the disclosure requirements of IFRS 3 (2007), the IASB identified three disclosure objectives that should be met.[223] Accordingly the standard sets out three principles of disclosure dealing with these objectives, and supplements them with specific disclosure requirements. The first two principles relate to business combinations generally, while the third deals with goodwill.

2.13.1 *Nature and financial effect of business combinations*

The first disclosure principle is that an acquirer discloses information that enables users of its financial statements to evaluate the nature and financial effect of business combinations that were effected:

(a)   during the period, or

(b)   after the reporting period but before the financial statements are authorised for issue.[224]

A   *Business combinations during the period*

To give effect to this principle, the acquirer is required to disclose the following information for *each* business combination that was effected during the period:

(a)   the names and descriptions of the combining entities or businesses;

(b)   the acquisition date;

(c)   the percentage of voting equity instruments acquired;

(d)   the cost of the combination and a description of the components of that cost, including any costs directly attributable to the combination.

When equity instruments are issued or issuable as part of the cost, the following shall also be disclosed:

(i)   the number of equity instruments issued or issuable; and

(ii)   the fair value of those instruments and the basis for determining that fair value.

If a published price does not exist for the instruments at the date of exchange, the significant assumptions used to determine fair value shall be disclosed.

If a published price exists at the date of exchange but was not used as the basis for determining the cost of the combination, that fact shall be disclosed together with:

- the reasons the published price was not used;
- the method and significant assumptions used to attribute a value to the equity instruments; and
- the aggregate amount of the difference between the value attributed to, and the published price of, the equity instruments;

(e)   details of any operations the entity has decided to dispose of as a result of the combination;

(f)   the amounts recognised at the acquisition date for each class of the acquiree's assets, liabilities and contingent liabilities, and, unless disclosure would be impracticable, the carrying amounts of each of those classes, determined in accordance with IFRSs, immediately before the combination.

If such disclosure about the carrying amounts would be impracticable, that fact shall be disclosed, together with an explanation of why this is the case;

(g)   the amount of any excess recognised in profit or loss in accordance with paragraph 56 of the standard (see 2.7 above), and the line item in the income statement in which the excess is recognised;

(h)   a description of the factors that contributed to a cost that results in the recognition of goodwill, including a description of each intangible asset that was not recognised separately from goodwill and an explanation of why the intangible asset's fair value could not be measured reliably – or a description of the nature of any excess recognised in profit or loss in accordance with paragraph 56 of the standard; and

(i)   the amount of the acquiree's profit or loss since the acquisition date included in the acquirer's profit or loss for the period, unless disclosure would be impracticable.

If such disclosure would be impracticable, that fact shall be disclosed, together with an explanation of why this is the case.[225]

The above information is required to be disclosed for each material business combination. For business combinations effected during the reporting period that are individually immaterial, the standard requires that the above information is disclosed in aggregate.[226]

If the initial accounting for a business combination that was effected during the period was determined only provisionally (see 2.8 above), that fact must be disclosed together with an explanation of why this is the case.[227]

To give effect to the principle, the acquirer discloses the following information, unless such disclosure would be impracticable:

(a)   the revenue of the combined entity for the period as though the acquisition date for all business combinations effected during the period had been the beginning of that period; and

(b)   the profit or loss of the combined entity for the period as though the acquisition date for all business combinations effected during the period had been the beginning of the period.

If disclosure of this information would be impracticable, that fact must be disclosed, together with an explanation of why this is the case.[228]

A number of the requirements allow the information not to be disclosed if disclosure would be impracticable. Whether an entity is justified to omit the disclosure on these grounds will depend on the particular circumstances. As discussed in Chapter 3 at 2.4 and 4.7, IAS 1 and IAS 8 both regard a requirement as being impracticable when the entity cannot apply it after making every reasonable effort to do so.

B   Business combinations effected after the reporting period

To give effect to the principle set out above, the acquirer is required to disclose the information under items (a) to (i) above for each business combination effected after the reporting period but before the financial statements are authorised for issue, unless such disclosure would be impracticable. If disclosure of any of that information would be impracticable, that fact must be disclosed, together with an explanation of why this is the case.[229]

2.13.2 Effects of gains, losses, error corrections and other adjustments recognised in the current period relating to business combinations

The second disclosure principle is that an acquirer discloses information that enables users of its financial statements to evaluate the financial effects of gains, losses, error corrections and other adjustments recognised in the current period that relate to business combinations that were effected in the current or in previous periods.[230]

To give effect to this principle, the acquirer is required to disclose the following information:

(a)   the amount and an explanation of any gain or loss recognised in the current period that:

(i)   relates to the identifiable assets acquired or liabilities or contingent liabilities assumed in a business combination that was effected in the current or a previous period; and

(ii)   is of such size, nature or incidence that disclosure is relevant to an understanding of the combined entity's financial performance;

(b)   if the initial accounting for a business combination that was effected in the immediately preceding period was determined only provisionally at the end of that period, the amounts and explanations of the adjustments to the provisional values recognised during the current period (see 2.8.1 above); and

(c)   the information about error corrections required to be disclosed by IAS 8 for any of the acquiree's identifiable assets, liabilities or contingent liabilities, or changes in the values assigned to those items, that the acquirer recognises during the current period (see 2.8.2 above).[231]

Item (a) has been included as an aid in meeting the objective of the second disclosure principle,[232] but does not really add anything to the requirement within IAS 1 to disclose the nature and amount of items of income and expenditure when they are material (see Chapter 3 at 3.2.6). Similarly, item (c) merely appears to repeat the requirements of IAS 8 (see Chapter 3 at 5.3).

2.13.3 Goodwill

The third disclosure principle is that an acquirer discloses information that enables users of its financial statements to evaluate changes in the carrying amount of goodwill during the period.[233]

To give effect to this principle, the entity is required to disclose a reconciliation of the carrying amount of goodwill at the beginning and end of the period, showing separately:

(a)   the gross amount and accumulated impairment losses at the beginning of the period;

(b)   additional goodwill recognised during the period (except goodwill included in a disposal group that, on acquisition, meets the criteria to be classified as held for sale in accordance with IFRS 5 – see Chapter 4 at 2.1);

(c)   adjustments resulting from the subsequent recognition of deferred tax assets during the period (see 2.8.3 above);

(d)   goodwill included in a disposal group classified as held for sale in accordance with IFRS 5 and goodwill derecognised during the period without having previously been included in a disposal group classified as held for sale;

(e)   impairment losses recognised during the period in accordance with IAS 36;

(f)   net exchange differences arising during the period in accordance with IAS 21 – *The Effects of Changes in Foreign Exchange Rates* (see Chapter 13 at 3.3.4);

(g)   any other changes in the carrying amount during the period; and

(h)   the gross amount and accumulated impairment losses at the end of the period.[234]

IFRS 3 (2007) emphasises that in addition to the information required by (e) above, the entity also discloses information about the recoverable amount and impairment of goodwill in accordance with IAS 36.[235] These requirements are dealt with in Chapter 18 at 4.2.

2.13.4 Other necessary information

The standard includes a catch-all disclosure requirement, that if in any situation the information required to be disclosed set out above does not satisfy the objectives of the disclosure principles, the entity shall disclose such additional information as is necessary to meet those objectives.[236] Possible disclosures under this requirement could be information relating to the cost of a business combination that is contingent on future events and any adjustments made thereto (see 2.4.5 above).

In addition to the disclosures required by IFRS 3 (2007) discussed above, IAS 7 – *Statement of Cash Flows* – requires disclosures in respect of obtaining control of subsidiaries and other businesses (see Chapter 39 at 2.4.2).[237]

3   REQUIREMENTS OF IFRS 3 (AS REVISED IN 2008)

3.1   Effective date, objective and scope

3.1.1   Effective date

IFRS 3 (as revised in 2008) is to be applied prospectively for business combinations where the acquisition date is on or after the beginning of annual periods starting on or after 1 July 2009. Earlier adoption is permitted, although it can only be applied as early as annual periods beginning on or after 30 June 2007. However, if IFRS 3 (as revised in 2008) is adopted early, that fact must be disclosed, and IAS 27 (as amended in 2008) must be applied at the same time.[238]

The revised standard contains a number of transitional provisions for existing IFRS reporters and these are discussed at 4.2 below.

As indicated above, the early adoption of IFRS 3 (as revised in 2008) comes as a package with IAS 27 (as amended in 2008), together with the various consequential amendments made to other IFRSs. Although IFRS 3 (as revised in 2008) says that it is to be applied prospectively for business combinations, this does not mean that an entity has to have a business combination in the period of adoption of the standard. If an entity wishes to adopt the package early in order to implement the requirements of one of the other IFRSs, it can do so irrespective of the fact that it has no business combination to be accounted for under IFRS 3 (as revised in 2008), but it does need to adopt all of the new requirements of the IFRSs in the package.

One issue relating to the early adoption of IFRS 3 (as revised in 2008) that has been considered by the IFRIC is whether it must be applied from the beginning of an annual period if it is adopted early. At its meeting in May 2009, and subsequently confirmed at its meeting in July 2009, the IFRIC noted that paragraph 64 of IFRS 3 (as revised in 2008) requires the revised IFRS to be applied for the whole annual period if it is applied early. The IFRIC also noted that the question of whether an entity can decide during a reporting period to apply a revised IFRS early is not unique to the revised IFRS 3. The IFRIC observed that this question should be answered in accordance with the general principles in IAS 8. Accordingly, if an entity chooses to apply the revised IFRS 3 early, it must apply it to all business combinations that occurred in the annual period in which the revised IFRS is first applied. The IFRIC concluded that relevant guidance on the early application of the revised IFRS 3 exists in IFRSs and it did not expect divergence in practice. Therefore, the IFRIC decided not to add the issue to its agenda.[239]

Although this statement by the IFRIC clarifies the position, practical problems can arise if the decision to early adopt is made some time after the beginning of the financial year and an acquisition has already occurred.

Example 9.36:   Early adoption of IFRS 3 (as revised in 2008)

Entity A has a financial year beginning on 1 January 2009. On 1 March 2009, it gains control of Entity B and, in preparing its interim financial statements for 30 June 2009, applies the previous version, IFRS 3 (2007). On 1 November 2009, Entity A gains control of Entity C, and decides to early adopt the revised accounting for business combinations in IFRS 3 (as revised in 2008).

IFRS 3 (as revised in 2008) is to be applied to acquisitions on or after the beginning of the financial year. Therefore, Entity A will need to restate its accounting for Entity B in accordance with the new requirements. This may mean obtaining fair values for some items that were not originally contemplated, for example, contingent consideration (see 3.8.1 below) and embedded derivatives (see 3.6.4 below). The longer the period between the acquisition and the decision to early adopt the revised standard, the more difficult it might be to obtain such values.

3.1.2   Objective

IFRS 3 (as revised in 2008) states that its objective 'is to improve the relevance, reliability and comparability of the information that a reporting entity provides in its financial statements about a business combination and its effects.' It goes on to say that to accomplish that, the standard 'establishes principles and requirements for how the acquirer:

(a)   recognises and measures in its financial statements the identifiable assets acquired, the liabilities assumed and any non-controlling interest in the acquiree;

(b)   recognises and measures the goodwill acquired in the business combination or a gain from a bargain purchase; and

(c)   determines what information to disclose to enable users of the financial statements to evaluate the nature and financial effects of the business combination.'[240]

3.1.3   Scope

Entities are required to apply the provisions of IFRS 3 (as revised in 2008) to transactions or other events that meet the definition of a business combination (see 3.2 below). The standard does not apply to:[241]

(a)   the formation of a joint venture;

(b)   the acquisition of an asset or a group of assets that does not constitute a business;

(c)   a combination of entities or businesses under common control.

The above exclusions from IFRS 3 (as revised in 2008) were also excluded from the previous version of IFRS 3 (see 2.1.3 above).

As far as (a) above is concerned, the Basis for Conclusions notes that in developing the previous version of IFRS 3, the IASB revised the definition of joint control in IAS 31 (see Chapter 12 at 2.2) to clarify that:[242]

- Unanimous consent on *all* financial and operating decisions is not necessary for an arrangement to satisfy the definition of a joint venture – unanimous consent on only strategic decisions is sufficient;

- In the absence of a contractual agreement requiring unanimous consent to strategic financial and operating decisions, a transaction in which the owners of multiple businesses agree to combine their businesses into a new entity (sometimes referred to as a roll-up transaction) should be accounted for by the acquisition method. Majority consent on such decisions is not sufficient.

As far as (b) above is concerned, although it would appear that the requirements of IFRS 3 (as revised in 2008) do not apply, the standard does go on to say that in such cases the acquirer is to identify and recognise the individual identifiable assets acquired (including those assets that meet the definition of, and recognition criteria for, intangible assets in IAS 38) and liabilities assumed. The cost of the group is to be allocated to the individual identifiable assets and liabilities on the basis of their relative fair values at the date of purchase. Such a transaction or event does not give rise to goodwill.[243] Thus, existing book values or values in the acquisition agreement may not be appropriate, and no goodwill can be recognised in such an asset deal. Where an entity acquires a controlling interest in an entity that is not a business, but obtains less than 100% of the entity, after it has allocated the cost to the individual assets acquired, it notionally grosses up those assets and recognises the difference as non-controlling interest (see Chapter 7 at 2.1.1).

In some situations, there may be difficulties in determining whether or not an acquired asset or a group of assets constitutes a business (see 3.2 below), and judgement will be required to be exercised based on the particular circumstances. The determination of a transaction as a business combination or an asset(s) acquisition can have a considerable impact on an entity's reported results and the presentation of its financial statements as the accounting for a business combination under IFRS 3 (as revised in 2008) differs from accounting for an asset(s) acquisition in a number of important respects:

- goodwill or a gain on bargain purchase only arise on business combinations;

- assets acquired and liabilities assumed are generally accounted for at fair value in a business combination, while they are assigned a carrying amount based on their relative fair values in an asset acquisition;

- directly attributable acquisition-related costs are expensed if they relate to a business combination, but are generally capitalised as part of the cost of the asset in an asset acquisition; and

- while deferred tax assets and liabilities must be recognised if the transaction is a business combination, they are not recognised under the current IAS 12 (see Chapter 26) if it is an asset acquisition.

All of these differences will impact future depreciation, possible impairment and other costs.

As far as (c) above is concerned, the Application guidance in Appendix B to IFRS 3 (as revised in 2008) gives some guidance about what constitutes business combinations involving entities or businesses under common control and therefore excluded from the requirements of the standard.[244] Such business combinations are discussed further in Chapter 10.

As indicated at 1.2.4 B above, the IASB has broadened the scope of IFRS 3 (as revised in 2008) such that the acquisition method of accounting applies to combinations involving only mutual entities (e.g. mutual insurance companies, credit unions, cooperatives, etc.) and combinations in which separate entities are brought together by contract alone (e.g. dual listed corporations and stapled entity structures).[245] Despite respondents' concerns, the Board considers that the attributes of mutual entities are not sufficiently different from those of investor-owned entities to justify a different method of accounting for business combinations between two mutual entities. It also considers that such combinations are economically similar to business combinations involving two investor-owned entities, and should be similarly reported.[246] Similarly, although the Board understands that difficulties may arise in applying the acquisition method to combinations achieved by contract alone, in particular the absence of the payment of any readily measurable consideration, it has concluded that the acquisition method should be applied for such transactions.[247] However, additional guidance is given in IFRS 3 (as revised in 2008) for applying the acquisition method to such business combinations (see 3.8.4 and 3.8.5 below).

3.2 Identifying a business combination

IFRS 3 (as revised in 2008) requires an entity to determine whether a transaction or event is a *business combination* by applying the definition in the standard, which requires that the assets acquired and liabilities assumed constitute a *business*. If the assets acquired and liabilities assumed do not constitute a business, the transaction is to be accounted for as an asset acquisition (see 3.1.3 above).[248]

Appendix B to IFRS 3 (as revised in 2008) gives the following application guidance on identifying a business combination and the definition of a business.

3.2.1 *Identifying a business combination*

Under the previous version of IFRS 3, a business combination was defined as 'the bringing together of separate entities or businesses into one reporting entity' (see 2.1.3 A above). This definition was considered to be too broad and that it could be read to include circumstances in which there may be no triggering economic event or transaction and thus no change in an economic entity, per se.[249] Therefore,

IFRS 3 (as revised in 2008) now defines a business combination as a 'transaction or other event in which an acquirer obtains control of one or more businesses'.[250]

By emphasising the obtaining of control, the IFRS 3 (as revised in 2008) apparently narrows the previous IFRS 3 definition of a business combination, which used the term 'bringing together' rather than 'obtaining control'. Notwithstanding this, the IASB states in the Basis for Conclusions accompanying IFRS 3 (as revised in 2008) that the revised definition includes all transactions and events initially included in the scope of the previous version of IFRS 3.[251]

IFRS 3 (as revised in 2008) notes that an acquirer might obtain control of an acquiree (i.e. the business or businesses over which the acquirer obtains control) in a variety of ways, for example:[252]

(a)   by transferring cash, cash equivalents or other assets (including net assets that constitute a business);

(b)   by incurring liabilities;

(c)   by issuing equity interests;

(d)   by providing more than one type of consideration; or

(e)   without transferring consideration – including by contract alone (see 3.8.4 below).

The standard also indicates that a business combination may be structured in a variety of ways for legal, taxation or other reasons, which include but are not limited to:[253]

(a)   one or more businesses become subsidiaries of an acquirer or the net assets of one or more businesses are legally merged into the acquirer;

(b)   one combining entity transfers its net assets, or its owners transfer their equity interests, to another combining entity or its owners;

(c)   all of the combining entities transfer their net assets, or the owners of those entities transfer their equity interests, to a newly formed entity (sometimes referred to as a roll-up or put-together transaction); or

(d)   a group of former owners of one of the combining entities obtains control of the combined entity.

Critical to the determination of whether a transaction or event is a 'business combination', and therefore required to be accounted for under IFRS 3 (as revised in 2008) is whether the assets acquired and liabilities assumed constitute a 'business' (an acquiree).

3.2.2   Definition of a business

IFRS 3 (as revised in 2008) defines a business as 'an integrated set of activities and assets that is capable of being conducted and managed for the purpose of providing a return in the form of dividends, lower costs or other economic benefits directly to investors or other owners, members or participants'.[254] This is similar to the definition in the previous version of IFRS 3 (see 2.1.3 A above); the Basis for Conclusions accompanying IFRS 3 (as revised in 2008) notes that the main modification being 'that the integrated set of activities and assets must be *capable* of being conducted and managed for the purpose of providing a return in the form of dividends, lower costs or other economic benefits directly to investors or other owners, members or participants. Focusing on the capability to achieve the purposes of the business helps avoid the unduly restrictive interpretations that existed in accordance with the former guidance.'[255]

The Application guidance to IFRS 3 (as revised in 2008) notes that a business consists of inputs and processes applied to those inputs that have the ability to create outputs. It goes on to say that although businesses usually have outputs, they do not need to be present for an integrated set of assets and activities to be a business. This is slightly different from that in the previous version of IFRS 3 which, as discussed at 2.1.3 A above, indicated that a business generally consists of three different elements – (1) inputs, (2) processes that are applied to those inputs, and (3) resulting outputs that are, or will be, used to generate revenues. The guidance in IFRS 3 (as revised in 2008) now provides definitions of each of these elements as follows:

- *Input*

    Any economic resource that creates, or has the ability to create, outputs when one or more processes are applied to it. Examples include non-current assets (including intangible assets or rights to use non-current assets), intellectual property, the ability to obtain access to necessary materials or rights and employees.

- *Process*

    Any system, standard, protocol, convention or rule that when applied to an input or inputs, creates or has the ability to create outputs. Examples include strategic management processes, operational processes and resource management processes. These processes typically are documented, but an organised workforce having the necessary skills and experience following rules and conventions may provide the necessary processes that are capable of being applied to inputs to create outputs. (Accounting, billing, payroll and other administrative systems typically are not processes used to create outputs.)

- *Output*

    The result of inputs and processes applied to those inputs that provide or have the ability to provide a return in the form of dividends, lower costs or other economic benefits directly to investors or other owners, members or participants.

The guidance in IFRS 3 (as revised in 2008) clarifies that a business is only required to have the first two of these three elements (i.e. inputs and processes), which together have the ability to create outputs.[256]

IFRS 3 (as revised in 2008) also clarifies that a transferred set of activities and assets need not be self-sustaining (i.e. contain all of the inputs and processes necessary for it to conduct normal operations after it is separated from the transferor) in order to be considered a business. The determination of whether a particular set of activities and assets is a business is to be based on whether others are capable of acquiring the business and continuing to produce outputs (e.g. by integrating the acquired business with their own inputs and processes). In evaluating whether a particular set of activities and assets is a business, it is not relevant whether the seller had historically operated the transferred set as a business or whether the acquirer intends to do so.

The guidance in IFRS 3 (as revised in 2008) also notes that the nature of the elements of a business varies by industry and by the structure of an entity's operations (activities), including the entity's stage of development. Established businesses often have many different types of inputs, processes and outputs, whereas new businesses often have few inputs and processes and sometimes only a single output (product). Nearly all businesses also have liabilities, but a business need not have liabilities.[257]

Additionally, IFRS 3 (as revised in 2008) contains guidance on assessing whether development stage entities are businesses. In these situations, various factors need to be assessed to determine whether the transferred set of assets and activities is a business, including whether the set has begun its planned principal activities, has employees, intellectual property, and other inputs and processes that can be applied to those inputs, is pursuing a plan to produce outputs, and has the ability to obtain access to customers that will purchase those outputs. Not all of these factors need to be present for a particular integrated set of activities and assets in the development stage to qualify as a business.[258]

IFRS 3 (as revised in 2008) retains the presumption in the previous version of IFRS 3 that if goodwill is present in a transferred set of activities and assets, the transferred set is presumed to be a business, but notes that a business need not have goodwill.[259]

As indicated at 3.1.3 above, in some situations, there may be difficulties in determining whether or not an acquired group of assets constitutes a business, and judgement will be required to be exercised based on the particular circumstances. The determination of a transaction as a business combination or an asset(s) acquisition can have a considerable impact on an entity's reported results and the presentation of its financial statements as the accounting for a business combination under IFRS 3 (as revised in 2008) differs from accounting for an asset(s) acquisition in a number of important respects.

At its meeting in May 2009, the IASB considered a number of issues brought by the IASB staff, but deferred them to the post-implementation review of IFRS 3 (as revised in 2008) and IAS 27 (as amended in 2008), to be conducted two years after their effective date. One of these issues related to the application of the definition of a business in particular situations.[260] It is not clear what these particular situations might have been as no details were included in the agenda papers available to the public.

3.3   Acquisition method of accounting

IFRS 3 (as revised in 2008) requires that a business combination is accounted for by applying the acquisition method.[261] The change in terminology from the purchase method (as used in the previous version of IFRS 3) is due to the fact that a business combination can arise in the absence of a purchase transaction.[262]

Applying the acquisition method involves the following steps:[263]

(a)   identifying an acquirer;

(b)   determining the acquisition date;

(c)   recognising and measuring the identifiable assets acquired, the liabilities assumed, and any non-controlling interest in the acquiree; and

(d)   recognising and measuring goodwill or a gain in a bargain purchase.

Steps (c) and (d) reflect the change in approach in IFRS 3 (as revised in 2008) from the cost-based approach used in the previous version of IFRS 3 (see 2.2 above), whereby the cost of the acquired entity was allocated to the assets acquired and liabilities (and contingent liabilities) assumed. They also represent a change from those in the June 2005 exposure draft whereby goodwill was to be measured by reference to the fair value of the acquiree, as a whole, including goodwill attributable to any non-controlling interest. As indicated at 1.2.4 B above, the reason for this change is due to the decision to focus on measuring the components of the business combination, including any non-controlling interest in the acquiree, rather than measuring the fair value of the acquiree as a whole.[264]

The above steps are discussed at 3.4, 3.5, 3.6 and 3.7 below.

3.4   Identifying the acquirer

The first step in applying the acquisition method is identifying the acquirer. IFRS 3 (as revised in 2008), as with the previous version of IFRS 3, requires one of the combining entities to be identified as the acquirer.[265] For this purpose the guidance in IAS 27 (as amended in 2008) is to be used, i.e. the acquirer is the entity that obtains control of the acquiree; control being defined as 'the power to govern the financial and operating policies of an entity so as to obtain benefits from its activities'.[266] The guidance in IAS 27 (as amended in 2008) for determining whether an entity has control over another is discussed in Chapter 6 at 2.1.

If a business combination has occurred, but applying that guidance in IAS 27 (as amended in 2008) does not clearly indicate which of the combining entities is the acquirer, additional guidance in IFRS 3 (as revised in 2008) includes various other factors that are to be considered in making the determination as to which entity is the acquirer.[267] Although changes have been made to the wording of the guidance that was included in the previous version of IFRS 3 (see 2.3 above) in order to clarify some of the intentions of the IASB, and to conform with that used in the equivalent US standard, the guidance in IFRS 3 (as revised in 2008) for identifying the acquirer is considered by the IASB to be, in substance, the same as that in the previous version of IFRS 3.[268]

The various other factors in IFRS 3 (as revised in 2008) that are to be considered in making the determination as to which entity is the acquirer are discussed below. These will require significant judgement, particularly when consideration is being given to as to whether the business combination is a 'reverse acquisition' or where the combination occurred by contract alone.

In a business combination effected primarily by transferring cash or other assets or by incurring liabilities, the acquirer is usually the entity that transfers the cash or other assets or incurs the liabilities.[269]

In a business combination effected primarily by exchanging equity interests, the acquirer is usually the entity that issues its equity interests, but in some business combinations, so-called 'reverse acquisitions', the issuing entity is the acquiree. Application guidance on the accounting for reverse acquisitions is provided in Appendix B to IFRS 3 (as revised in 2008) (see 3.15 below). In identifying the acquirer in a business combination effected by exchanging equity interests, IFRS 3 (as revised in 2008) requires that other pertinent facts and circumstances should also be considered, including:[270]

- the relative voting rights in the combined entity after the business combination. The acquirer is usually the combining entity whose owners as a group retain or receive the largest portion of the voting rights in the combined entity, after taking due account of any unusual or special voting arrangements and options, warrants or convertible securities;

- the existence of a large minority voting interest in the combined entity if no other owner or organised group of owners has a significant voting interest. The acquirer is usually the combining entity whose single owner or organised group of owners holds the largest minority voting interest in the combined entity;

- the composition of the governing body of the combined entity. The acquirer is usually the combining entity whose owners have the ability to elect or appoint or to remove a majority of the members of the governing body of the combined entity;

- the composition of the senior management of the combined entity. The acquirer is usually the combining entity whose (former) management dominates the management of the combined entity;

- the terms of the exchange of equity interests. The acquirer is usually the combining entity that pays a premium over the pre-combination fair value of the equity interests of the other combining entity or entities.

The guidance for identifying the acquirer also notes that the acquirer is usually the combining entity whose relative size (measured in, for example, assets, revenues or profit) is significantly greater than that of the other combining entity or entities.[271]

In a business combination involving more than two entities, determining the acquirer includes a consideration of, among other things, which of the combining entities initiated the combination, as well as the relative size of the combining entities.[272]

The guidance in IFRS 3 (as revised in 2008) emphasises that a new entity formed to effect a business combination is not necessarily the acquirer. If a new entity is formed to issue equity interests to effect a business combination, one of the combining entities that existed before the business combination is to be identified as the acquirer by applying the guidance described above.[273] In such a transaction, the combination between the new entity and the identified acquirer is effectively the same as if a new entity had been inserted above an existing entity. As discussed in Chapter 10 at 4.2, such a transaction should be accounted for under the pooling of interests method. The combination of the new entity with the identified acquirer cannot be accounted for as a 'reverse acquisition' because IFRS 3 (as revised in 2008) requires that the accounting acquiree must meet the definition of a business for a transaction to be accounted for as a reverse acquisition.[274]

In contrast, the guidance in IFRS 3 (as revised in 2008) notes that a new entity that transfers cash or other assets or incurs liabilities as consideration may be the acquirer. One situation where we believe this would be appropriate is where the newly formed entity (hereafter referred to as 'Newco') is established and used on behalf of a group of investors or another entity to acquire a controlling interest in a 'target entity' in an arm's length transaction.

Example 9.37: *Business combination effected by a Newco for cash consideration (1)*

Entity A intends to acquire the voting shares (and therefore obtain control) of Target Entity. Entity A incorporates Newco and uses this entity to effect the business combination. Entity A provides a loan at commercial interest rates to Newco. The loan funds are used by Newco to acquire 100% of the voting shares of Target Entity in an arm's length transaction.

The group structure post-transaction is as follows:

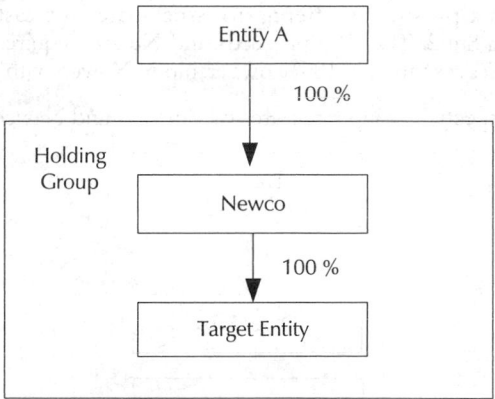

Under its local regulations, Newco is required to prepare IFRS-compliant consolidated financial statements for the Holding Group (the reporting entity). (In most situations like this, Newco would be exempt from preparing consolidated financial statements – see Chapter 6 at 3.1.)

As indicated above, under IFRS 3 (as revised in 2008), the acquirer is 'the entity that obtains control of the acquiree.' Whenever a new entity is formed to effect a business combination other than through the issue of shares, it is appropriate to consider that Newco as being an extension of one of the transacting parties. Where the Newco is considered to be an extension of the transacting party (or parties) that ultimately gain control of the other combining entities, the Newco would be identified as the acquirer.

In this situation, Entity A has obtained control of Target Entity in an arm's length transaction, using Newco to effect the acquisition. The transaction has resulted in a change in control of Target Entity and Newco is in effect an extension of Entity A acting at its direction to obtain control for Entity A. Accordingly, Newco would be identified as the acquirer at the Holding Group level.

If, rather than Entity A establishing Newco, a group of investors had established it as the acquiring vehicle through which they obtained control of Target Entity then again it would be appropriate for Newco to be regarded as the acquirer since it is an extension of the group of investors.

Another situation where we believe it is appropriate for a Newco to be identified as the acquirer is illustrated below.

Example 9.38:   Business combination effected by a Newco for cash consideration (2)

Entity A proposes to spin-off two of its existing businesses (currently housed in two separate entities, Sub1 and Sub2) as part of an initial public offering (IPO). The existing group structure is as follows:

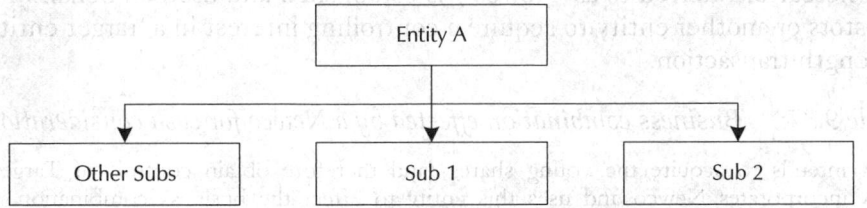

To facilitate the spin-off, Entity A incorporates a new company (Newco) with nominal equity and appoints independent directors to the Board of Newco.

Newco signs an agreement to acquire Sub1 and Sub2 from Entity A conditional on the IPO proceeding. Newco issues a prospectus offering to issue shares for cash to provide Newco with funds to acquire Sub1 and Sub2. The IPO proceeds and Newco acquires Sub1 and Sub2 for cash. Entity A's nominal equity leaves virtually 100% ownership in Newco with the new investors.

Following the IPO, the respective group structures of Entity A and Newco appear as follows:

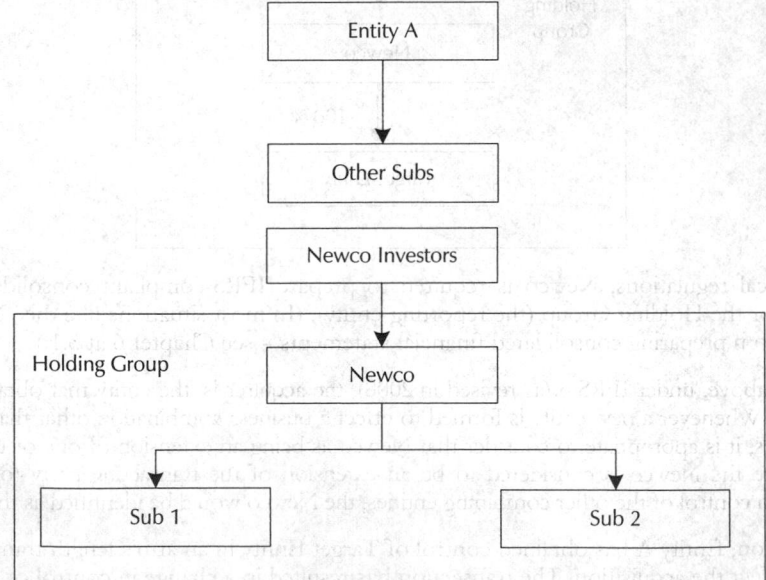

In this case, we believe it is appropriate that Newco should be identified as the acquirer. The Newco investors have obtained control and virtually 100% ownership of Sub1 and Sub2 in an arm's length transaction, using Newco to effect the acquisition. The transaction has resulted in a change in control of Sub1 and Sub2 (i.e. Entity A losing control and Newco investors, via Newco, obtaining control). Newco is in effect an extension of the Newco investors since:

- the acquisition of Sub1 and Sub2 was conditional on the IPO proceeding so that the IPO is an integral part of the transaction as a whole evidencing that Entity A did not have control of the transaction/entities; and
- there being a substantial change in the ownership of Sub1 and Sub2 by virtue of the IPO (i.e. Entity A only retains a negligible ownership interest in Newco).

Accordingly, Newco should be identified as the acquirer at the Holding Group level.

Whether a Newco formed to facilitate an IPO is capable of being identified as an acquirer depends on the facts and circumstances and ultimately requires judgement. Changes to the fact pattern could result in a different assessment. For example, where Entity A incorporates Newco and arranges for it to acquire Sub1 and Sub2 prior to the IPO proceeding (in other words, remove the conditionality element), it is likely that Newco would be viewed as an extension of Entity A or possibly an extension of Sub1 or Sub2. This is because the IPO and the reorganisation may not be seen as being part of the one integral transaction, and therefore the transaction would be a combination of entities under common control (see Chapter 10 at 3.1).

3.5   Determining the acquisition date

The next step in applying the acquisition method is determining the acquisition date. The acquirer has to identify the acquisition date which is defined in IFRS 3 (as revised in 2008) as 'the date on which the acquirer obtains control of the acquiree'.[275] This is essentially the same as in the previous version of IFRS 3 (see 2.2 above).

IFRS 3 (as revised in 2008) indicates that the acquisition date will generally be the 'closing date', i.e. the date on which the acquirer legally transfers the consideration, acquires the assets and assumes the liabilities of the acquiree.[276] Although the standard refers to the 'closing date', we do not believe that this necessarily means that the transaction has to be closed or finalised at law before the acquirer obtains control over the acquiree.

IFRS 3 (as revised in 2008) acknowledges that the acquirer might obtain control on a date that is either earlier or later than the closing date. The standard notes, for example, the acquisition date precedes the closing date if a written agreement provides that the acquirer obtains control of the acquiree on a date before the closing date.[277] That is not to say that the acquisition date can be artificially backdated or otherwise altered, for example, by the inclusion of terms in the agreement indicating that the acquisition is to be effective as of an earlier date, with the acquirer being entitled to profits arising after that date, even if the purchase price is based on the net asset position of the acquiree at that date.

Although the acquisition date cannot be artificially backdated or otherwise altered, the Basis for Conclusions to IFRS 3 (as revised in 2008) does acknowledge that, for convenience, an entity might wish to designate an acquisition date of the end (or the beginning) of a month, the date on which it closes its books, rather than the actual acquisition date during the month. Unless events between the 'convenience' date and the actual acquisition date result in material changes in the amounts recognised, that entity's practice would comply with the requirements of IFRS 3 (as revised in 2008).[278]

IFRS 3 (as revised in 2008) emphasises that all pertinent facts and circumstances in assessing the acquisition date must be considered.[279] No further guidance from that outlined above is given in the standard as to how to determine the acquisition date, but it is clearly a matter of fact.

The date control is obtained will be dependent on a number of factors, including whether the acquisition arises from a public offer or a private deal, is subject to approval by other parties, or is effected by the issue of shares.

For an acquisition by way of a public offer, the date of acquisition could be when the offer has become unconditional as a result of a sufficient number of acceptances being received or at the date that the offer closes. In a private deal, the date would generally be when an unconditional offer has been accepted by the vendors.

It can be seen from the above that one of the key factors is that the offer is 'unconditional'. Thus, where an offer is conditional on the approval of the acquiring entity's shareholders then until that has been received, it is unlikely that control will have been obtained. Where the offer is conditional upon receiving some form of regulatory approval, then it will depend on the nature of that approval. Where it is a substantive hurdle, such as obtaining the approval of a competition authority, it is unlikely that control could have been obtained prior to that approval. However, where the approval is merely a formality, or 'rubber-stamping' exercise, then this would not preclude control having been obtained at an earlier date.

Where the acquisition is effected by the issue of shares, then the date of control will generally be when the exchange of shares takes place.

However, as indicated above, whether control has been obtained by a certain date is a matter of fact, and all pertinent facts and circumstances surrounding a business combination need to be considered in assessing when the acquirer has obtained control.

3.6   Recognising and measuring the identifiable assets acquired, the liabilities assumed, and any non-controlling interest in the acquiree

The next step in applying the acquisition method involves recognising and measuring the identifiable assets acquired, the liabilities assumed, and any non-controlling interest in the acquiree.

3.6.1   General principles

The general principles of IFRS 3 (as revised in 2008) are that the identifiable assets acquired and liabilities assumed of the acquiree are recognised as of the acquisition date and measured at fair value as at that date, with certain limited exceptions.[280] Any non-controlling interest in the acquiree is to be recognised at the acquisition date, however, the acquirer can measure this either at fair value at that date or at the non-controlling interest's proportionate share of the acquiree's net identifiable assets as measured at the acquisition date.[281] The accounting for any non-controlling interest at the acquisition date is discussed further at 3.9 below.

3.6.2 Recognition conditions for identifiable assets acquired and liabilities assumed

To qualify for recognition as part of applying the acquisition method, an item acquired or assumed must be:[282]

(a)   an asset or liability at the acquisition date; and

(b)   part of the business acquired (the acquiree) rather than the result of a separate transaction.

The first condition requires that the identifiable assets acquired and liabilities assumed must meet the definitions of assets and liabilities in the IASB's *Framework* (see Chapter 2 at 3.2.3 A and B) at the acquisition date. This means, for example, costs the acquirer expects but is not obliged to incur in the future to effect its plan to exit an activity of an acquiree or to terminate the employment of or relocate an acquiree's employees are not liabilities at the acquisition date. Therefore, the acquirer does not recognise those costs as part of applying the acquisition method. Instead, the acquirer recognises those costs in its post-combination financial statements in accordance with other IFRSs.[283] Thus, an acquirer recognises liabilities for restructuring or exit activities acquired in a business combination only if they meet the definition of a liability at the acquisition date.[284] IFRS 3 (as revised in 2008) does not contain the same explicit requirements relating to restructuring plans that were in IFRS 3 (2007) discussed at 2.5.1 above, but the Basis for Conclusions accompanying IFRS 3 (as revised in 2008) clearly indicate that the requirements for recognising liabilities associated with restructuring or exit activities remain the same.[285] This is discussed further at 3.12.4 below.

This first condition for recognition makes no reference to reliability of measurement or probability as to the inflow or outflow of economic benefits as was the case under the previous version of IFRS 3 (see 2.5 above). This is because the IASB considers them to be unnecessary because reliability of measurement is a part of the overall recognition criteria in the *Framework* and that such recognition criteria includes the concept of 'probability' to refer to the degree of uncertainty that the future economic benefits associated with an asset or liability will flow to or from the entity.[286] Thus, identifiable assets and liabilities are recognised regardless of the degree of probability that there will be inflows or outflows of economic benefits. Nevertheless, in recognising a liability in respect of a contingent liability assumed in a business combination, IFRS 3 (as revised in 2008) still requires that its fair value can be measured reliably (see 3.6.6 A below).

The second condition requires that the identifiable assets acquired and liabilities assumed must be part of the exchange for the acquiree, rather than as a result of separate transactions.[287] Explicit guidance is given in the standard for making such an assessment as discussed at 3.12 below. The objective of this condition and the related guidance is to ensure that each component is accounted for in accordance with its economic substance.[288] One particular consequence of this condition is that acquisition-related costs are to be expensed, whereas under the previous version of IFRS 3 such costs were included as part of the cost of the business combination (see 2.4.4 above) and therefore recognised as part of goodwill. The IASB also considers that this meant such costs were being recognised *as if* they were an asset.[289]

IFRS 3 (as revised in 2008) emphasises that the acquirer's application of the recognition principle and conditions may result in recognising some assets and liabilities that the acquiree had not previously recognised as assets and liabilities in its financial statements. For example, the acquirer recognises the acquired identifiable intangible assets, such as a brand name, a patent or a customer relationship, that the acquiree did not recognise as assets in its financial statements because it developed them internally and charged the related costs to expense.[290]

Guidance is provided on recognising operating leases and intangible assets, as well as specifying types of identifiable assets and liabilities that include items for which IFRS 3 (as revised in 2008) provides limited exceptions to the recognition principle and conditions.[291] These are discussed at 3.6.5 and 3.6.6 below.

3.6.3   Acquisition-date fair values of identifiable assets acquired and liabilities assumed

The general measurement principle is that the recognised identifiable assets acquired and liabilities assumed are measured at their acquisition-date fair values. For this purpose, 'fair value' is defined as 'the amount for which an asset could be exchanged, or a liability settled, between knowledgeable, willing parties in an arm's length transaction'.[292] This is the same as the definition in the previous version of IFRS 3 as well in other IFRSs. On the other hand, the equivalent US standard, SFAS 141R, uses the definition in SFAS 157 which is 'the price that would be received to sell an asset or paid to transfer a liability in an orderly transaction between market participants at the measurement date'. The IASB considered also using the definition of fair value from SFAS 157 but decided that to do so would prejudge the outcome of its project on fair value measurement (see Chapter 2 at 6.3).[293] The Boards acknowledge that using the different definitions might result in measuring fair values differently but, based on consultations with valuation experts and the Boards' belief that the underlying concepts are essentially the same, understand that such differences are unlikely to occur often.[294] The Basis for Conclusions accompanying IFRS 3 (as revised in 2008) goes on to identify the following two particular areas where differences may occur as a result of applying the different definitions: (i) if an asset is acquired for its defensive value or (ii) if a liability is measured on the basis of settling it with the creditor rather than transferring it to a third party.[295]

Due to the IASB's current project on fair value measurement, much of the guidance relating to fair value that was contained in the previous version of IFRS 3 (see 2.5.4 above) is no longer included in IFRS 3 (as revised in 2008). In addition, the proposed guidance on how to measure fair value contained in Appendix E of the June 2005 exposure draft, including the 'fair value hierarchy', is not included in the revised standard.

Guidance is provided on measuring the fair value of particular identifiable assets, as well as specifying types of identifiable assets and liabilities that include items for which IFRS 3 (as revised in 2008) provides limited exceptions to the measurement principle.[296] These are discussed at 3.6.5 and 3.6.6 below.

In addition, although the objective of the second phase of the business combinations project was not focused on issues related to the 'day-two' accounting for assets acquired and liabilities assumed, IFRS 3 (as revised in 2008) provides guidance on the accounting for certain acquired assets and assumed liabilities subsequent to a business combination.[297] These are discussed at 3.14 below.

3.6.4 Classifying or designating identifiable assets acquired and liabilities assumed

As discussed at 2.5.5 above, the previous version of IFRS 3 was silent on whether, and in what circumstances, a business combination triggers reassessment of the acquiree's classification or designation of assets, liabilities, equity and relationships acquired in a business combination. The IFRIC considered this issue but decided not to take this item on to its agenda as it noted that the IASB, at its meeting in February 2007, decided that the issue should be dealt with in Business Combinations phase II.[298]

Accordingly, IFRS 3 (as revised in 2008) includes the principle that, at the acquisition date, the acquirer must classify or designate the identifiable assets and liabilities assumed as necessary in order to apply other IFRSs subsequently. Such classifications and designations made by the acquirer are to be based on the contractual terms, economic conditions, the operating and accounting policies of the acquirer, and any other pertinent conditions as they exist at the acquisition date.[299] However, the standard provides two exceptions to this principle:

- classification of leases in accordance with IAS 17;
- classification of a contract as an insurance contract in accordance with IFRS 4.

In both these situations, the acquirer classifies the contracts on the basis of the contractual terms and other factors at the inception of the contract or, if the terms of the contract have been modified in a manner that would change its classification, at the date of the modification (which might be the acquisition date).[300] Thus, if an acquiree is a lessee under a lease contract that has appropriately been classified as an operating lease under IAS 17, in the absence of any modification to the terms of the contract, the acquirer would continue to account for the lease as an operating lease. It would only be if, prior to or as at the acquisition date, the terms of the lease were modified in such a way that it would be reclassified as a finance lease under IAS 17 (see Chapter 22 at 2.3.3), that the acquirer would recognise the asset and the related finance lease liability.

As a result of this principle, examples of classifications or designations that the acquirer has to make on the basis of the pertinent conditions as they exist at the acquisition date include but are not limited to:[301]

(a) classification of particular financial assets and liabilities as a financial asset or liability at fair value through profit or loss, or as a financial asset available for sale or held to maturity, in accordance with IAS 39;

(b)   designation of a derivative instrument as a hedging instrument in accordance with IAS 39; and

(c)   assessment of whether an embedded derivative should be separated from the host contract in accordance with IAS 39 (which is a matter of 'classification' as IFRS 3 (as revised in 2008) uses that term).

The requirements for the classification of financial assets and liabilities under IAS 39 are discussed in Chapter 29 at 7. Although, as indicated at 7.5 in that Chapter, IAS 39 has particular requirements that would appear to prohibit the reclassification of items into or out of the fair value through profit or loss category, and permit, and in some situations require, reclassification between held-to-maturity investments and available-for-sale assets as far as the acquiree is concerned, the acquirer has to make its own classification at the acquisition date. If the acquirer has not had to consider the classification of such assets or liabilities before for the purposes of its financial statements, it could choose to continue to adopt the classification applied by the acquiree or adopt a different classification if appropriate. However, if the acquirer already has an accounting policy for like transactions, the classification should be consistent with that existing policy.

As discussed in Chapter 33 at 5, there are a number of conditions that need to be met for hedge relationships to qualify for hedge accounting, in particular formal designation and documentation, and an ongoing assessment of the designated hedge. If an acquiree has derivative or other financial instruments that have been used as hedging instruments in a hedge relationship, IFRS 3 (as revised in 2008) requires the acquirer to make its own designation about the hedging relationship that satisfy the conditions for hedge accounting, based on the conditions as they exist at the acquisition date. As long as the documentation of the acquiree is consistent with the risk management strategy of the acquirer, it may be possible for the documentation to be carried over for both cash flow hedges and fair value hedges, but there should exist some evidence of re-affirmation by the acquirer of the hedge relationship upon 'carry-over' of the hedge documentation. It should be noted that the documentation may differ depending upon the level of the entity (parent company, subsidiary, or consolidation) at which the hedge relationship exists.

Similar to the documentation requirements, the hedge effectiveness testing may also be carried forward. If effectiveness changes upon 'carry-over', the documentation will need to change. However, if the hedging relationship is being accounted for as a cash flow hedge by the acquiree, the acquirer does not inherit the acquiree's existing cash flow hedge reserve, as this clearly represents cumulative pre-acquisition gains and losses. This has implications for the assessment of hedge effectiveness and the measurement of ineffectiveness because, so far as the acquirer is concerned, it has started a new hedge relationship with a hedging instrument that is likely to have a non-zero fair value (see Chapter 33 at 4.2.4). This may mean that although the acquiree can continue to account for the relationship as a cash flow hedge, the acquirer is unable to account for it as a cash flow hedge in its financial statements.

In the situations discussed above, the effect of applying the principle in IFRS 3 (as revised in 2008) only affects the post-business combination accounting for the financial instruments concerned. The financial instruments that are recognised as at the acquisition date, and their measurement at their fair value at that date, do not change.

However, the requirement for the acquirer to assess whether an embedded derivative should be separated from the host contract based on pertinent conditions as they exist at the acquisition date could result in additional assets or liabilities being recognised (and measured at their acquisition-date fair value) different from those recognised by the acquiree. Embedded derivatives are discussed in Chapter 29 at 5.

3.6.5   Recognising and measuring particular assets acquired and liabilities assumed

As indicated earlier at 3.6.2 and 3.6.3 above, IFRS 3 (as revised in 2008) gives some application guidance on recognising and measuring particular assets acquired and liabilities assumed in a business combination, as discussed at A to F below.

A   Operating leases

As indicated at 3.6.4 above, although existing leases of the acquiree are new leases from the perspective of the acquirer, the classification of the leases between operating and finance is not revisited. If the acquiree is the lessee to an operating lease, the acquirer does not recognise the acquiree's rights under the operating lease separately from its obligations as part of the purchase price allocation (i.e. the asset and liability arising from the operating lease is not recognised on a gross basis). However, the acquirer is required to recognise operating leases in which the acquiree is the lessee as either intangible assets or liabilities if the terms of the lease are favourable (asset) or unfavourable (liability) relative to market terms and prices.[302]

IFRS 3 (as revised in 2008) also indicates that an identifiable intangible asset may be associated with an operating lease, even one that is at market terms. This may be evidenced by market participants' willingness to pay a price for the lease. For example, a lease of gates at an airport or of retail space in a prime shopping centre may provide entry into a market or other future economic benefits that qualify as identifiable intangible assets, for example, as a customer relationship. In that situation, the acquirer recognises the associated identifiable intangible asset(s) (see B below).[303]

However, where the acquiree is a lessor in an operating lease, the acquirer does not recognise separately an intangible asset or liability if the terms of the lease are favourable or unfavourable relative to market terms and prices. Instead, off-market terms are reflected in the acquisition-date fair value of the asset (such as a building or a patent) subject to the lease.[304] This is to avoid any inconsistency with the fair value model in IAS 40 – *Investment Property* – which requires the fair value of investment property to take into account rental income from current leases, and the IASB understands that practice is to measure the fair value of investment property taking into account the contractual terms of the leases and other contracts in place relating to the asset.[305] Although the reason for not separately recognising the favourable or unfavourable element is due to investment properties accounted for under the fair value model in IAS 40, the requirement to reflect the off-market terms in the fair value of the asset applies to any type of asset. The IASB notes that based on the requirements of IAS 16 and IAS 38, an entity would be required to adjust the depreciation or amortisation method for the leased asset so as to reflect the timing of the cash flows attributable to the underlying leases.[306]

B   Intangible assets

As indicated at 3.6.2 above, the acquirer's application of the recognition principle and conditions may result in recognising some assets and liabilities that the acquiree had not previously recognised as assets and liabilities in its financial statements. One of the main types of assets that an acquirer recognises, separately from goodwill, are identifiable intangible assets.[307] Both IFRS 3 (as revised in 2008) and IAS 38 give guidance on the recognition of intangible assets acquired in a business combination.

I   What is an identifiable intangible asset?

IFRS 3 (as revised in 2008) and IAS 38 both define an 'intangible asset' as 'an identifiable non-monetary asset without physical substance'.[308] The definition of an intangible asset requires an intangible asset to be identifiable to distinguish it from goodwill (see 3.7 below).[309] IFRS 3 (as revised in 2008) and IAS 38 both regard an asset as identifiable if it either:

(a)   is separable, i.e. capable of being separated or divided from the entity and sold, transferred, licensed, rented or exchanged, either individually or together with a related contract, identifiable asset or liability, regardless of whether it intends to do so; or

(b)   arises from contractual or other legal rights, regardless of whether those rights are transferable or separable from the entity or from other rights and obligations.[310]

Accordingly, IFRS 3 (as revised in 2008) regards an intangible asset as identifiable if it meets either the separability criterion or the contractual-legal criterion,[311] and provides the following Application guidance.

- *Separability criterion*

IFRS 3 (as revised in 2008) notes that the separability criterion means that an acquired intangible asset is capable of being separated or divided from the acquiree and sold, transferred, licensed, rented or exchanged, either individually or together with a related contract, identifiable asset or liability.

An intangible asset that the acquirer would be able to sell, license or otherwise exchange for something else of value meets the separability criterion even if the acquirer does not intend to sell, license or otherwise exchange it. An acquired intangible asset meets the separability criterion if there is evidence of exchange transactions for that type of asset or an asset of a similar type, even if those transactions are infrequent and regardless of whether the acquirer is involved in them. For example, customer and subscriber lists are frequently licensed and thus meet the separability criterion. Even if an acquiree believes its customer lists have characteristics different from other customer lists, the fact that customer lists are frequently licensed generally means that the acquired customer list meets the separability criterion. However, a customer list acquired in a business combination would not meet the separability criterion if the terms of confidentiality or other agreements prohibit an entity from selling, leasing or otherwise exchanging information about its customers.[312]

An intangible asset that is not individually separable from the acquiree or combined entity meets the separability criterion if it is separable in combination with a related contract, identifiable asset or liability. For example:[313]

(a)   market participants exchange deposit liabilities and related depositor relationship intangible assets in observable exchange transactions. Therefore, the acquirer should recognise the depositor relationship intangible asset separately from goodwill;

(b)   an acquiree owns a registered trademark and documented but unpatented technical expertise used to manufacture the trademarked product. To transfer ownership of a trademark, the owner is also required to transfer everything else necessary for the new owner to produce a product or service indistinguishable from that produced by the former owner. Because the unpatented technical expertise must be separated from the acquiree or combined entity and sold if the related trademark is sold, it meets the separability criterion.

* *Contractual-legal criterion*

An intangible asset that meets the contractual-legal criterion is identifiable even if the asset is not transferable or separable from the acquiree or from other rights and obligations. For example:[314]

(a)   an acquiree leases a manufacturing facility under an operating lease that has terms that are favourable relative to market terms. The lease terms explicitly prohibit transfer of the lease (through either sale or sublease). The amount by which the lease terms are favourable compared with the terms of current market transactions for the same or similar items is an intangible asset that meets the contractual-legal criterion for recognition separately from goodwill, even though the acquirer cannot sell or otherwise transfer the lease contract;

(b)   an acquiree owns and operates a nuclear power plant. The licence to operate that power plant is an intangible asset that meets the contractual-legal criterion for recognition separately from goodwill, even if the acquirer cannot sell or transfer it separately from the acquired power plant. However, IFRS 3 (as revised in 2008) goes on to say that an acquirer may recognise the fair value of the operating licence and the fair value of the power plant as a single asset for financial reporting purposes if the useful lives of those assets are similar;

(c)   an acquiree owns a technology patent. It has licensed that patent to others for their exclusive use outside the domestic market, receiving a specified percentage of future foreign revenue in exchange. Both the technology patent and the related licence agreement meet the contractual-legal criterion for recognition separately from goodwill even if selling or exchanging the patent and the related licence agreement separately from one another would not be practical.

- *Removal of reliability of measurement criterion*

As discussed at 2.5.2 above, the previous version of IFRS 3 included an additional criterion that had to be met for an identifiable intangible asset to be recognised separately from goodwill. This was that its fair value had to be measured reliably, although as discussed at 2.5.2 C above, the IASB within the guidance in IAS 38 made it clear that the IASB believed that there would only be limited circumstances when such a criterion would not have been met. The inclusion in the previous version of IFRS 3 of the reliability of measurement criterion was the result of extensive field tests conducted by the IASB on the proposals in the exposure draft preceding IFRS 3 (ED 3). Those field visits, which included discussions with accountants and valuation professionals, highlighted that there were certain circumstances in which an intangible asset acquired in a business combination might have a value that could not be measured reliably.

Despite this, and in the interest of convergence with US GAAP, the Board decided not to include an equivalent statement in IFRS 3 (as revised in 2008), with consequential amendments made to IAS 38 to remove the reliability of measurement criterion for intangible assets acquired in a business combination.[315] Although this was done, the IASB subsequently realised that IAS 38 still indicated that in some situations a group of intangible assets have to be recognised as a single asset separately from goodwill if the individual fair values of the assets within the group are not reliably measurable. The IASB considered that this did not clearly reflect its decisions about accounting for intangible assets acquired in a business, so as part of the annual improvement standard issued in April 2009, the IASB revised the requirements of IAS 38 to clarify what it meant to say in this regard when making the consequential amendments to IAS 38 as a result of IFRS 3 (as revised in 2008).[316] In doing so, it deleted all references to items not being reliably measurable. These amendments apply prospectively and take effect at the same as the original consequential amendments to IAS 38, i.e. at the same time when IFRS 3 (as revised in 2008) is applied.[317] This is discussed further at IV below.

Accordingly, under IFRS 3 (as revised in 2008), identifiable intangible assets are recognised separately from goodwill if they are either separable or arise from contractual or other legal rights.[318] It is no longer necessary that the intangible asset has to be capable of reliable measurement in order for it to be recognised, despite the reasons for including this criterion in the previous version of IFRS 3. Therefore, whenever an intangible asset can be separately identified it is now to be recognised and an acquisition-date fair value assigned to it.

II   Examples of identifiable intangible assets

The discussion above refers to a number of different types of identifiable intangible assets that IFRS 3 (as revised in 2008) requires to be separately recognised from goodwill, such as customer and subscriber lists, depositor relationships, registered trademarks, unpatented technical expertise, favourable operating leases, licences and technology patents.

IAS 38 also explicitly refers to the fact that the requirement in IFRS 3 (as revised in 2008) means that the acquirer recognises as an asset separately from goodwill an in-process research and development project of the acquiree (if the project meets the definition of an intangible asset).[319] IFRS 3 (as revised in 2008) itself only refers to this in its Basis for Conclusions, where it is made clear that the acquirer recognises all tangible and intangible research and development assets acquired in a business combination.[320] This is discussed further at V below.

IFRS 3 (as revised in 2008) gives further guidance in its Illustrative Examples that provides a large list of examples of items acquired in a business combination that are identifiable intangible assets and are therefore to be recognised separately from goodwill, whilst noting that the examples are not intended to be all-inclusive.[321] A non-monetary asset without physical substance acquired in a business combination might meet the identifiability criterion for identification as an intangible asset but not be included in the guidance.

The guidance designates the assets listed as being 'contractual', i.e. arising from contractual or other legal rights or 'non-contractual', i.e. not arising from contractual or other legal rights but are separable, whilst noting that those designated as 'contractual' might also be separable. However, it emphasises that separability is not a necessary condition for an asset to meet the contractual-legal criterion.

The table below summarises the items included in the Illustrative Examples that the IASB regard as meeting the definition of an intangible asset and are therefore to be recognised separately from goodwill. Reference should be made to the Illustrative Examples for any further explanation about some of these items.

Intangible assets arising from contractual or other legal rights (regardless of being separable)	Other intangible assets that are separable
Marketing-related	

− Trademarks, trade names, service marks, collective marks and certification marks
  − Trade dress (unique colour, shape or package design)
  − Newspaper mastheads
  − Internet domain names
  − Non-competition agreements	

Customer-related	
− Order or production backlog − Customer contracts and the related customer relationships	− Customer lists − Non-contractual customer relationships
Artistic-related	

− Plays, operas and ballets
  − Books, magazines, newspapers and other literary works
  − Musical works such as compositions, song lyrics and advertising jingles
  − Pictures and photographs
  − Video and audiovisual material, including motion pictures or films, music videos and television programmes	

Contract-based	

− Licensing, royalty and standstill agreements
  − Advertising, construction, management, service or supply contracts
  − Lease agreements
  − Construction permits
  − Franchise agreements
  − Operating and broadcast rights
  − Servicing contracts such as mortgage servicing contracts
  − Employment contracts
  − Use rights such as drilling, water, air, mineral, timber-cutting and route authorities	

Technology-based	

− Patented technology
  − Computer software and mask works
  − Trade secrets, such as secret formulas, processes or recipes
	− Unpatented technology
	− Databases, including title plants

In some situations, items have been designated as being 'contractual' due to legal protection, for example, trade marks and trade secrets. However, the guidance explains that even without that legal protection, they would normally meet the separability criterion so would still be recognised separately from goodwill.

It can be seen from the table that customer relationships can potentially fall under either category. Where relationships are established with customers through contracts, those customer relationships arise from contractual rights, regardless of whether a contract exists, or there is any backlog of orders, at the date of acquisition. In such cases, it does not matter that the relationship is separable. It would only be if the relationship did not arise from a contract that the recognition depends on the separability criterion.

It is clear from the table above that the IASB envisages a wide range of items meeting the definition of an intangible asset, and therefore potentially being recognised separately from goodwill.

One company that has recognised numerous intangible assets as a result of business combinations is ITV as illustrated in Extract 9.3 at 2.5.2 A above.

III   *Customer relationship intangible assets acquired in a business combination*

Further guidance on customer relationships acquired in a business combination is provided by IFRS 3 (as revised in 2008) in the Illustrative Examples (which forms the basis of the example below) that demonstrate how an entity should interpret the contractual-legal and separability criteria in the context of acquired customer relationships.[322]

Example 9.39:   Customer relationship intangible assets acquired in a business combination

Supply agreement

Acquirer Company (AC) acquires Target Company (TC) in a business combination on 31 December 2010. TC has a five-year agreement to supply goods to Customer. Both TC and AC believe that Customer will renew the agreement at the end of the current contract. The agreement is not separable.

The agreement, whether cancellable or not, meets the contractual-legal criterion. Additionally, because TC establishes its relationship with Customer through a contract, not only the agreement itself but also TC's customer relationship with Customer meet the contractual-legal criterion.

Sporting goods and electronics

AC acquires TC in a business combination on 31 December 2010. TC manufactures goods in two distinct lines of business: sporting goods and electronics. Customer purchases both sporting goods and electronics from TC. TC has a contract with Customer to be its exclusive provider of sporting goods but has no contract for the supply of electronics to Customer. Both TC and AC believe that only one overall customer relationship exists between TC and Customer.

The contract to be Customer's exclusive supplier of sporting goods, whether cancellable or not, meets the contractual-legal criterion. Additionally, because TC establishes its relationship with Customer through a contract, the customer relationship with Customer meets the contractual-legal criterion. Because TC has only one customer relationship with Customer, the fair value of that relationship incorporates assumptions about TC's relationship with Customer related to both sporting goods and electronics. However, if AC determines that the customer relationships with Customer for sporting goods and for electronics are separate from each other, AC would assess whether the customer relationship for electronics meets the separability criterion for identification as an intangible asset.

Order backlog and recurring customers

AC acquires TC in a business combination on 31 December 2010. TC does business with its customers solely through purchase and sales orders. At 31 December 2010, TC has a backlog of customer purchase orders from 60 per cent of its customers, all of whom are recurring customers. The other 40 per cent of TC's customers are also recurring customers. However, as of 31 December 2010, TC has no open purchase orders or other contracts with those customers.

Regardless of whether they are cancellable or not, the purchase orders from 60 per cent of TC's customers meet the contractual-legal criterion. Additionally, because TC has established its relationship with 60 per cent of its customers through contracts, not only the purchase orders but also TC's customer relationships meet the contractual-legal criterion. Because TC has a practice of establishing contracts with the remaining 40 per cent of its customers, its relationship with those customers also arises through contractual rights and therefore meets the contractual-legal criterion even though TC does not have contracts with those customers at 31 December 2010.

Motor insurance contracts

AC acquires TC, an insurer, in a business combination on 31 December 20X5. TC has a portfolio of one-year motor insurance contracts that are cancellable by policyholders.

Because TC establishes its relationships with policyholders through insurance contracts, the customer relationship with policyholders meets the contractual-legal criterion. IAS 36 and IAS 38 apply to the customer relationship intangible asset.

An example of a company recognising customer contracts and customer relationship intangible assets is ITV as illustrated in Extract 9.3 at 2.5.2 A above. Another example is Reuters as shown in Extract 9.2 at 2.4.2 above.

One particular type of customer relationship intangible asset that should be recognised (as indicated by the last scenario in Example 9.39 above) is the value of the future profit of businesses acquired (VOBA) relating to insurance contracts or investment contracts, notwithstanding the fact that it is the customer or policyholder that decides on the continuation of the relationship. One company recognising such intangibles is Sanlam as shown in Extract 9.4 at 2.5.2 A above.

Even with this guidance in IFRS 3 (as revised in 2008), the IFRIC received a request in 2008 to add to its agenda an item concerning the circumstances in which a non-contractual customer relationship arises in a business combination.

In considering this request, the IFRIC acknowledged that IFRS 3 (as revised in 2008) makes a distinction between contractual and non-contractual customer relationships. Contractual customer relationships are always recognised separately from goodwill as they meet the contractual-legal criterion. However, non-contractual customer relationships are recognised only if they meet the separability criterion. Consequently, determining whether a relationship is contractual is critical to identifying and measuring customer relationship intangible assets and different conclusions could result in substantially different accounting outcomes. The staff's survey of IFRIC members indicated that diversity exists in practice regarding which customer relationships have a contractual basis and which do not. In addition, valuation experts may be taking different views, which could also be contributing to diversity in this area.[323]

As it drew together the guidance already available, the IFRIC noted that the IFRS Glossary of Terms defines the term 'contract'[324] and that application guidance in IFRS 3 (as revised in 2008) considers the recognition of intangible assets and the different criteria related to whether they are established on the basis of a contract (see I above). The IFRIC also noted that paragraph IE28 in the Illustrative Examples accompanying IFRS 3 (as revised in 2008) highlights how a customer relationship is deemed to exist if on the one hand the entity has information about the customer and regular contact with it and on the other that the customer can make direct contact with the entity. Regardless of whether any contracts are in place at the acquisition date, the customer relationship meets the contractual-legal criterion for recognition as an intangible asset if an entity has a practice of establishing contracts with its customers. The paragraph also states that a customer relationship 'may also arise through means other than contracts, such as through regular contact by sales or service representatives.'[325]

The IFRIC concluded that whilst the manner in which a relationship is established is relevant to confirming the existence of a customer relationship, it should not be the primary basis for determining whether an intangible asset is recognised by the acquirer. What might be more relevant is whether the entity has a practice of establishing contracts with its customers or whether relationships arise through other means, such as through regular contact by sales and service representatives. The existence of contractual relationships and information about a customer's prior purchases would be important inputs in valuing a customer relationship intangible asset, but should not determine whether it is recognised.[326]

Having reviewed the explicit guidance in IFRS 3 (as revised in 2008), the IFRIC decided it was not possible to develop an Interpretation reflecting its conclusion. Nevertheless, given widespread confusion in practice on the issue, the IFRIC decided that the matter should be referred to the IASB and the FASB with a recommendation to review and amend IFRS 3 (as revised in 2008) by:[327]

- removing the distinction between 'contractual' and 'non-contractual' customer-related intangible assets recognised in a business combination; and

- reviewing the indicators that identify the existence of a customer relationship in paragraph IE28 of IFRS 3 (as revised in 2008) and including them in the standard.

At its meeting in December 2008, the IASB tentatively decided to consider a proposed amendment to IFRSs for possible inclusion in the next exposure draft of annual improvements to be published in August 2009.[328] At a subsequent meeting in May 2009, the IASB staff recommended that the Board defer the first issue but deal only with the second issue in the exposure draft, together with a proposal to relocate the depositor relationship example in paragraph B34(a) of the application guidance of IFRS 3 (as revised in 2008) from the section that illustrates 'separable' intangibles to a more appropriate location in that guidance.[329] However, as indicated at 5.6 below, the IASB deferred both of the IFRIC recommendations to the post-implementation review of IFRS 3 (as revised in 2008) and IAS 27 (as amended in 2008), to be conducted two years after their effective date, and it decided tentatively to retain the depositor relationship example in paragraph B34(a) of IFRS 3 (as revised in 2008), noting that this is a separable intangible asset (see I above).[330]

IV   *Combining an intangible asset with a related contract, identifiable asset or liability*

As indicated at I above, although IFRS 3 (as revised in 2008) made consequential amendments to IAS 38 to remove the reliability of measurement criterion for intangible assets acquired in a business combination, the IASB subsequently realised that paragraphs 36 and 37 of IAS 38 still indicated that that an intangible asset acquired in a business combination might be separable, but only together with a related tangible or intangible asset, or that a group of complementary intangible assets had to be recognised as a single asset separately from goodwill, if the individual fair values of the assets within the group are not reliably measurable.[331]

The IASB considered that this did not clearly reflect its decisions about accounting for intangible assets acquired in a business, so as part of the annual improvement standard issued in April 2009, the IASB revised the requirements of IAS 38 to clarify what it meant to say in this regard when making the consequential amendments to IAS 38 as a result of IFRS 3 (as revised in 2008).[332] Accordingly, paragraph 36 of IAS 38 now states that an intangible asset acquired in a business combination might be separable, but only together with a related contract, identifiable asset, or liability. In such cases, the acquirer recognises the intangible assets separately from goodwill, but together with the related item.

This paragraph is now consistent with what IFRS 3 (as revised in 2008) says about the 'separability criterion' in relation to an intangible asset that is not individually separable, but is separable in combination with a related contract, identifiable asset or liability at I above, and the examples included therein.

Similarly, paragraph 37 of IAS 38 now says that the acquirer may recognise a group of complementary intangible assets as a single asset provided the individual assets have similar useful lives. For example, 'the terms "brand" and "brand name" are often used as synonyms for trademarks and other marks. However, the former are general marketing terms that are typically used to refer to a group of complementary assets such as a trademark (or service mark) and its related trade name, formulas, recipes and technological expertise.'

Again, this is consistent with what IFRS 3 (as revised in 2008) says about brands in its Illustrative Examples, i.e. that an entity can recognise, as a single asset separately from goodwill, a group of complementary intangible assets commonly referred to as a brand if the assets that make up that group has similar lives.[333]

However, what is not clear from these requirements in IAS 38 is whether an intangible asset that is only separable in combination with a tangible asset can be recognised together as a single asset for financial reporting purposes in all circumstances. In its guidance about the 'contractual-legal criterion', IFRS 3 (as revised in 2008) gives an example of a licence to operate a nuclear power plant, and says that the fair value of the operating licence and the fair value of the power plant may be recognised as a single asset for financial reporting purposes, if the useful lives of those assets are similar (see I above), yet the requirements in IAS 38 only refers to similar useful lives in the context of a group of complimentary intangible assets.

These revised requirements apply prospectively and take effect at the same as the original consequential amendments to IAS 38, i.e. at the same time when IFRS 3 (as revised in 2008) is applied.[334]

Guidance on the determination of asset lives of intangible assets is discussed in Chapter 15 at 2.5.

V   *In-process research or development project expenditure*

As indicated at II above, IAS 38 explicitly refers to the fact that the requirements in IFRS 3 (as revised in 2008) mean that the acquirer recognises as an asset separately from goodwill an in-process research and development project of the acquiree (if the project meets the definition of an intangible asset).[335] IFRS 3 (as revised in 2008) itself only refers to in-process research and development in its Basis for Conclusions, where it is made clear that the acquirer recognises all tangible and intangible research and development assets acquired in a business combination.[336]

IAS 38 states that 'an acquiree's in-process research and development project meets the definition of an intangible asset when it:

(a)   meets the definition of an asset; and

(b)   is identifiable, i.e. is separable or arises from contractual or other legal rights.' [337]

In-process research and development projects, whether or not recognised by the acquiree, are protected by legal rights and are clearly separable as on occasion they are bought and sold by entities without there being a business acquisition. Therefore, they are intangible assets as defined by IAS 38. Moreover, IAS 38 takes the view that the fair value of an intangible asset will reflect expectation about the probability that the expected future economic benefits embodied in the asset will flow to the entity (despite the uncertainty about the timing or the amount of the inflow) and that sufficient information exists to measure reliably the fair value of the asset (even if there is a range of possible outcomes with different probabilities, that uncertainty enters into the measurement of the asset's fair value). Thus, the probability recognition criterion and the reliable measurement criterion in IAS 38 are always considered to be satisfied for in-process research and development projects acquired in a business combination.[338]

Therefore, the recognition of in-process research and development as an asset on acquisition applies different criteria to those that are required for internal projects. The research costs of internal projects may under no circumstances be capitalised.[339] Before capitalising development expenditure, entities must meet a series of exacting requirements. They must demonstrate the intangible assets' technical feasibility, their ability to complete the assets and use them or sell them and must be able to measure reliably the attributable expenditure.[340] The probable future economic benefits must be assessed using the principles in IAS 36 which means that they have to be calculated as the net present value of the cash flows generated by the asset or, if it can only generate cash flows in conjunction with other assets, of the cash-generating unit of which it is a part.[341] This process is described further in Chapter 18.

What this means is that entities will be required to recognise on acquisition some research and development expenditure that they would not have been able to recognise if it had been an internal project. The IASB was aware of this inconsistency when it developed the previous version of IFRS 3, but concluded that this did not provide a basis for subsuming in-process research and development within goodwill. It has considered the alternative (a reconsideration of the conditions for recognition of research and development costs) as being outwith the scope of the business combinations project.[342]

Although the amount attributed to the project is accounted for as an asset, IAS 38 goes on to require that any subsequent expenditure incurred after the acquisition of the project is to be accounted for in accordance with paragraphs 54-62 of IAS 38.[343] These requirements are discussed in Chapter 15 at 2.3.6.

In summary, this means that the subsequent expenditure is:

(a)   recognised as an expense when incurred if it is research expenditure;

(b)   recognised as an expense when incurred if it is development expenditure that does not satisfy the criteria for recognition as an intangible asset in paragraph 57; and

(c)   added to the carrying amount of the acquired in-process research or development project if it is development expenditure that satisfies the recognition criteria in paragraph 57.[344]

The inference is that the in-process research and development expenditure recognised as an asset on acquisition that never progresses to the stage of satisfying the recognition criteria for an internal project will ultimately be impaired, although it may be that this impairment will not arise until the entity is satisfied that the project will not continue. However, since it is an intangible asset not yet available for use, such an evaluation cannot be significantly delayed as it will need to be tested for impairment annually by comparing its carrying amount with its recoverable amount.[345]

VI   Emission rights acquired in a business combination

If an acquiree has been granted emission rights or allowances under a cap and trade emission rights scheme (see Chapter 15 at 3.3), how should an acquirer recognise these rights and associated liabilities?

Emission rights meet the definition of an intangible asset and should therefore be recognised at the acquisition date at their fair value. Likewise, the acquirer is required to recognise a liability at fair value for the actual emissions made at the acquisition date.

As discussed in Chapter 15 at 3.3.2 B one approach that may be adopted in accounting for such rights is the 'net liability approach' whereby the emission rights are recorded at a nominal amount and the entity will only record a liability once the actual emissions exceed the emission rights granted and still held. Where the acquiree has adopted such an approach, it may be that at the date of acquisition it has not recognised an asset or liability. Nevertheless, the acquirer should recognise the emission rights as intangible assets at their fair value and a liability at fair value for the actual emissions made at the acquisition date. As discussed in Chapter 15 at 3.3.2 B, the net liability approach is not permitted for purchased emission rights and therefore is also not permitted to be applied to emission rights of the acquiree in a business combination.

Example 9.40: Emission rights acquired in a business combination under the 'net liability approach'

Entity A acquires all of the shares in Entity B. Entity B had been granted emission rights for free and adopted the net liability approach for recognition of emission rights prior to the acquisition. At acquisition date the emission rights held exceed the actual emissions made and hence no asset or provision is recognised in the financial statements of Entity B in respect of emissions.

Entity A also adopts the net liability approach for emission rights granted.

In a business combination, the emission rights of the acquiree, regardless of how the acquiree received these rights, are considered to be rights purchased by the Entity A group. Accordingly, they should be treated in the same manner as emission rights purchased directly by the group.

At the acquisition date Entity A recognises the emission rights held by Entity B as intangible assets at fair value and recognises a provision for the actual emissions made up to that date at fair value.

One impact of this is that subsequent to the acquisition, the consolidated income statement will show an expense for the actual emissions made thereafter as a provision will have to be recognised on an ongoing basis. As discussed in Chapter 15 at 3.3.2 B II, there are different views of the impact that such 'purchased' emission rights have on the measurement of the provision.

The emission rights held by the acquiree will relate to specific items of property, plant and equipment. Therefore when determining the fair value of these assets, care needs to be taken to ensure that there is no double counting of the rights held.

VII   Determining the fair values of intangible assets

As indicated at 3.6.3 above, due to the IASB's current project on fair value measurement, much of the guidance relating to fair value that was contained in the previous version of IFRS 3 (see 2.5.4 above) is no longer included in IFRS 3 (as revised in 2008). Nevertheless, IAS 38 continues to have guidance relating to determining the acquisition-date fair value of an intangible asset acquired in a business combination. It states that the fair value of an intangible asset will reflect expectations about the probability that the expected future economic benefits embodied in the asset will flow to the entity.[346]

IAS 38 states that 'quoted market prices in an active market provide the most reliable estimate of the fair value of an intangible asset',[347] an active market being as defined in that standard (see Chapter 15 at 2.3.2 A). It goes on to say that 'the appropriate market price is usually the current bid price. If current bid prices are unavailable, the price of the most recent similar transaction may provide a basis from which to estimate fair value, provided that there has not been a significant change in economic circumstances between the transaction date and the date at which the asset's fair value is estimated.'[348]

However, IAS 38 also notes that it is uncommon for an active market to exist for intangible assets and that such a market cannot exist for brands, newspaper mastheads, music and film publishing rights, patents or trademarks,[349] i.e. many of the intangible assets that IFRS 3 (as revised in 2008) and IAS 38 require an acquirer to recognise in a business combination.

Although IFRS 3 (as revised in 2008) made some consequential amendments to IAS 38, the valuation guidance given in IAS 38 if no active market exists, did not change. Accordingly, the intangible assets should be valued on a basis that reflects the amounts the acquirer would have paid for the assets in arm's length transactions between knowledgeable willing parties, based on the best information available. In determining this amount, an entity considers the outcome of recent transactions for similar assets.[350]

Similarly, IAS 38 continued to acknowledge that entities that are regularly involved in the purchase and sale of unique intangible assets may have developed techniques for estimating their fair values indirectly. Accordingly, it allows these techniques to be used for initial measurement of an intangible asset acquired in a business combination if their objective is to estimate fair value and if they reflect current transactions and practices in the industry to which the asset belongs. These techniques include, when appropriate:

(a)   applying multiples reflecting current market transactions to indicators that drive the profitability of the asset (such as revenue, market shares and operating profit) or to the royalty stream that could be obtained from licensing the intangible asset to another party in an arm's length transaction (as in the 'relief from royalty' approach); or

(b)   discounting estimated future net cash flows from the asset.[351]

However, as part of the annual improvement standard issued in April 2009, the IASB revised the above guidance in IAS 38 to clarify the description of valuation techniques commonly used by entities when measuring the fair value of intangible assets acquired in a business combination that are not traded in active markets, but decided that the amendments should be applied prospectively. This is because retrospective application might require some entities to remeasure fair values associated with previous transactions, and the Board did not think this was appropriate because the remeasurement might involve the use of hindsight in those circumstances.[352] The amended requirements below apply prospectively for annual periods beginning on or after 1 July 2009, with earlier application permitted. If an entity applies the amendments for an earlier period it should disclose that fact.[353]

Accordingly the amended guidance in IAS 38 continues to require that if no active market exists the intangible assets should be valued on a basis that reflects the amounts the acquirer would have paid for the assets in arm's length transactions between knowledgeable willing parties, based on the best information available. In determining this amount, an entity considers the outcome of recent transactions for similar assets. For example, an entity may apply multiples reflecting current market transactions to factors that drive the profitability of the asset (such as revenue, operating profit or earnings before interest, tax, depreciation and amortisation).[354]

The guidance continues to acknowledge that entities that are involved in the purchase and sale of intangible assets may have developed techniques for estimating their fair values indirectly. Accordingly, it allows these techniques to be used for initial measurement of an intangible asset acquired in a business combination if their objective is to estimate fair value and if they reflect current transactions and practices in the industry to which the asset belongs. However, it clarifies that these techniques include, for example:[355]

(a)   discounting estimated future net cash flows from the asset; or

(b)   estimating the costs the entity avoids by owning the intangible asset and not needing:

     (i)   to license it from another party in an arm's length transaction (as in the 'relief from royalty' approach, using discounted net cash flows); or

     (ii)   to recreate or replace it (as in the cost approach).

It is generally considered that there are three broad approaches to valuing intangible assets as shown in the diagram below.

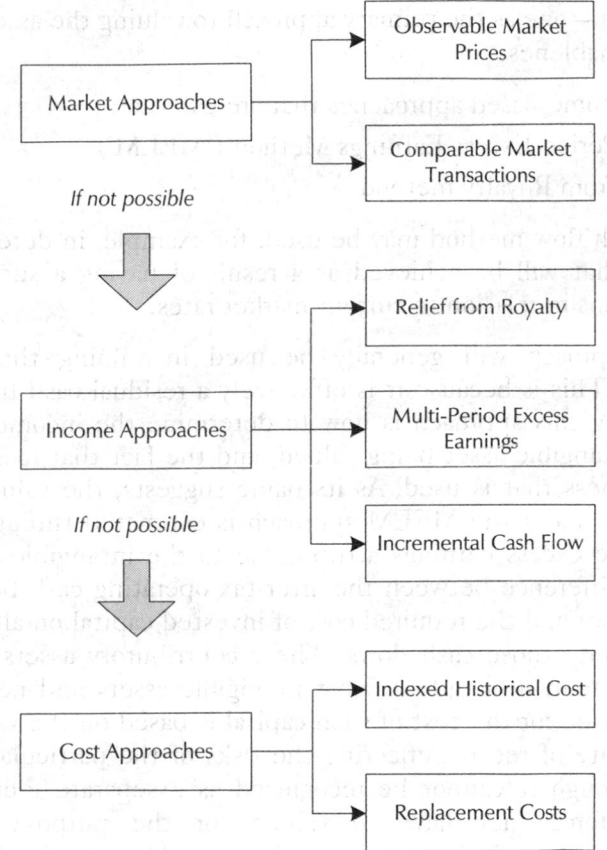

Under a market-based approach, if no actual market prices are available for the respective asset, the fair value of the intangible is derived by analysing similar intangible assets that have recently been sold or licensed, and then comparing these transactions to the intangible asset that needs to be valued. This approach is regarded as preferable where an active market for the assets exist. However, in practice, the ability to use such an approach is very limited. Intangible assets are generally unique, and there is rarely an active market to examine.

A cost-based approach is generally regarded as having limited application and difficult to use in many cases. The premise of the cost approach is that an investor would pay no more for an intangible asset than the cost to recreate it. However, for most intangibles, cost approaches are rarely consistent with the definition of 'fair value'.

Income-based approaches are much more commonly used. These involve identifying the expected economic benefits to be derived from the ownership of the particular intangible asset, and calculating the fair value of an intangible asset at the present value of those benefits. These are discussed further below.

For each asset, there are often several methodologies which can be applied. The choice will depend on the circumstances, in particular the nature of the value brought by the asset to the company (i.e. additional revenue, cost savings, replacement time and cost savings, etc.). In some cases, two methods may be used for the same asset – one as the primary approach to valuing the asset and the other as a check for reasonableness.

The two main income-based approaches that are used are:

- the Multi Period Excess Earnings Method ('MEEM')
- the Relief from Royalty method.

A discounted cash flow method may be used, for example, in determining the value of cost-savings that will be achieved as a result of having a supply contract with advantageous terms in relation to current market rates.

The MEEM approach will generally be used in valuing the most important intangible asset. This is because it is effectively a residual cash flow approach. The key issue in using this approach is how to determine the income/cash flow that is related to the intangible asset being valued, and the fact that it is not the full cash flow of the business that is used. As its name suggests, the value of an intangible asset determined under the MEEM approach is estimated through the sum of the discounted future excess earnings attributable to the intangible asset. The excess earnings is the difference between the after-tax operating cash flow attributable to the intangible asset and the required cost of invested capital on all other assets used in order to generate those cash flows. These contributory assets include property, plant and equipment, other identifiable intangible assets and net working capital. The allowance made for the cost of such capital is based on the value of such assets and a required rate of return reflecting the risks of the particular assets. As noted at D below, although it cannot be recognised as a separate identifiable asset, an assembled workforce may have to valued for the purpose of calculating a 'contributory asset charge' in determining the fair value of an intangible asset under the MEEM approach.

The Relief from Royalty method is used in many cases to calculate the value of a trademark or trade name. This approach is based on the concept that if an entity owns a trademark, it does not have to pay for the use of it and therefore is relieved from paying a royalty. The amount of that theoretical payment is used as a surrogate for income attributable to the trademark. The valuation is arrived at computing the present value of the after-tax royalty savings using an appropriate discount rate. The after-tax royalty savings are calculating by applying an appropriate royalty rate to the projected revenue, deducting the legal protection expenses relating to the trademark, and an allowance for tax at the appropriate rate.

Companies will generally use more than one of the above approaches in attributing fair values to intangible assets in a business combination as illustrated in Extract 9.6 at 2.5.4 F above.

Another example is ITV as shown in Extract 9.3 at 2.5.2 A above.

In some situations, it may be that the value of an intangible asset will reflect not only the present value of the future post-tax cash flows as indicated above, but also the value of any tax benefits (sometimes called 'tax amortisation benefits') that the owner might have obtained if the asset had been bought separately, i.e. not as part of a business combination. Whether such tax benefits are included will depend on the nature of the intangible asset and the relevant tax jurisdiction. Where such a value is included in the fair value of the intangible asset, an asset that has been purchased as part of a business combination may be one that is wholly or in part not actually tax-deductible by the entity. This therefore raises a potential impairment issue that is discussed in Chapter 18 at 5.2.2.

Another issue relating to the valuation of intangible assets is whether the acquirer's intention in relation to those assets should be taken into account in attributing a fair value, for example, where the acquirer does not intend to use an intangible asset of the acquiree. This is now explicitly addressed in IFRS 3 (as revised in 2008) as discussed at F below.

C   *Reacquired rights*

One particular identifiable intangible asset that IFRS 3 (as revised in 2008) requires an acquirer to recognise separately from goodwill is that of a reacquired right, that is a right previously granted to the acquiree to use one or more of the acquirer's recognised or unrecognised assets. For example, a right to use the acquirer's trade name under a franchise agreement or a right to use the acquirer's technology under a technology licensing agreement.[356]

The Basis for Conclusions accompanying IFRS 3 (as revised in 2008) notes that some commentators suggested recognising a reacquired right as the settlement of a pre-existing relationship; others said that a reacquired right should be recognised as part of goodwill. The IASB rejected the former because reacquisition of, for example, a franchise right does not terminate the right. After a business combination, the right to operate a franchised outlet in a particular region continues to exist. The difference is that the acquirer, rather than the acquiree by itself, now controls the franchise right. The IASB also rejected recognising a reacquired right as part of goodwill. Supporters of that alternative consider that such a right differs from other identifiable intangible assets recognised in a business combination because, from the perspective of the combined entity, a franchising relationship with an outside party no longer exists. As already noted, however, the reacquired right and the related cash flows continue to exist. The IASB concluded that recognising that right separately from goodwill provides users of the financial statements of the combined entity with more decision-useful information than subsuming the right into goodwill. The IASB also observed that a reacquired right meets the contractual-legal and the separability criteria and therefore qualifies as an identifiable intangible asset.[357]

Guidance on the valuation of such reacquired rights, and their subsequent accounting, is discussed at 3.6.6 E below.

Although the reacquired right itself is not treated as a termination of a pre-existing relationship, to the extent that the terms of the contract giving rise to the reacquired right are favourable or unfavourable relative to the terms of current market transactions for the same or similar items, IFRS 3 (as revised in 2008) regards this as the settlement of a pre-existing relationship and the acquirer has to recognise a settlement gain or loss.[358] Guidance on the measurement of any settlement gain or loss is discussed at 3.12.1 below.

D   Assembled workforce and other items that are not identifiable

The discussion at B above deals with the requirement in IFRS 3 (as revised in 2008) for an acquirer to recognise, separately from goodwill, the identifiable assets acquired in a business combination. The corollary, therefore, is that the acquirer subsumes into goodwill the value of an acquired intangible asset that is not identifiable as of the acquisition date.

I   Assembled workforce

A particular example of such an intangible asset is that of an assembled workforce, which IFRS 3 (as revised in 2008) regards as being an existing collection of employees that permits the acquirer to continue to operate an acquired business from the acquisition date.[359] Because an assembled workforce is a collection of employees rather than an individual employee, it does not arise from contractual or legal rights. Although individual employees might have employment contracts with the employer, the collection of employees, as a whole, does not have such a contract. In addition, an assembled workforce is not separable, either as individual employees or together with a related contract, identifiable asset or liability. An assembled workforce cannot be sold, transferred, licensed, rented or otherwise exchanged without causing disruption to the acquirer's business. In contrast, an entity could continue to operate after transferring an identifiable asset. Therefore, an assembled workforce is not an identifiable intangible asset to be recognised separately from goodwill.[360]

IFRS 3 (as revised in 2008) also states that an assembled workforce does not represent the intellectual capital of the skilled workforce – the (often specialised) knowledge and experience that employees of an acquiree bring to their jobs.[361] The IASB observed that the value of intellectual capital is, in effect, recognised because it is part of the fair value of the entity's other intangible assets, such as proprietary technologies and processes and customer contracts and relationships. In that situation, a process or methodology can be documented and followed to the extent that the business would not be materially affected if a particular employee left the entity. In most jurisdictions, the employer usually 'owns' the intellectual capital of an employee. Most employment contracts stipulate that the employer retains the rights to and ownership of any intellectual property created by the employee. For example, a software program created by a particular employee (or group of employees) would be documented and generally would be the property of the entity. The particular programmer who created the program could be replaced by another software programmer with equivalent expertise without significantly affecting the ability of the entity to continue to operate. But the intellectual property created in the form of a software program is part of the fair value of that program and is an identifiable intangible asset if it is separable from the entity. In other words, the prohibition of recognising an assembled workforce as an intangible asset does not apply to intellectual property; it applies only to the value of having a workforce in place on the acquisition date so that the acquirer can continue the acquiree's operations without having to hire and train a workforce.[362]

As indicated in the Basis for Conclusions accompanying IFRS 3 (as revised in 2008), some commentators said that an assembled workforce may be valued in many situations for the purpose of calculating a 'contributory asset charge' in determining the fair value of some intangible assets.[363] Nevertheless, because the assembled workforce is not an identifiable asset to be recognised separately from goodwill, any value that may be attributed to it by the acquirer is subsumed into goodwill.[364]

II   Items not qualifying as assets

The acquirer also subsumes into goodwill any value attributed to items that do not qualify as assets at the acquisition date.

- *Potential contracts with new customers*

IFRS 3 (as revised in 2008) notes, for example, that the acquirer might attribute value to potential contracts the acquiree is negotiating with prospective new customers at the acquisition date. Because those potential contracts are not themselves assets at the acquisition date, the acquirer does not recognise them separately from goodwill. In that case, the acquirer should not subsequently reclassify the value of those contracts from goodwill for events that occur after the acquisition date. However, IFRS 3 (as revised in 2008) goes on to say that the acquirer should assess the facts and circumstances surrounding events occurring shortly after the acquisition to determine whether a separately recognisable intangible asset existed at the acquisition date.[365]

- *Contingent assets*

Another example would be where the acquiree has a contingent asset. The IASB clarifies in the Basis for Conclusions accompanying IFRS 3 (as revised in 2008) that these should not be recognised unless they meet the definition of an asset in the IASB's *Framework*. This also appears to be the case even if it is virtually certain that they will become unconditional or non-contingent. It would only be if the entity determines that an asset exists at the acquisition date (that is, that it has an unconditional right at the acquisition date) that an asset is to be recognised.[366] This does appear to be inconsistent with the requirements of IAS 37 which states that, when the realisation of income is virtually certain, then the related asset is no longer regarded as contingent and recognition is appropriate (see Chapter 24 at 3.2.2).[367]

- *Future contract renewals*

One other situation discussed in IFRS 3 (as revised in 2008) is future contract renewals. Although the identifiability criteria determine whether an intangible asset is recognised separately from goodwill, IFRS 3 (as revised in 2008) notes that in measuring the fair value of an intangible asset, the acquirer would take into account assumptions that market participants would consider, such as expectations of future contract renewals, in measuring fair value of that intangible asset. It is not necessary for the renewals themselves to meet the identifiability criteria.[368] In this case any value attributable to the expected future renewal contracts is reflected in the value of, say, the customer relationship, rather than being subsumed within goodwill. As discussed at 3.6.6 E below, IFRS 3 (as revised in 2008) establishes an exception to the fair value measurement principle for reacquired rights recognised in a business combination. In that case, any potential contract renewals that market participants would consider in determining the fair value of those rights would be subsumed within goodwill.

E   Assets with uncertain cash flows (valuation allowances)

An acquiree may have financial assets, such as receivables and loans, against which it may have recognised a provision or valuation allowance for impairment or uncollectible amounts. However, an acquirer cannot 'carry over' any such valuation allowances nor create its own separate valuation allowances in respect of those financial assets. Under IFRS 3 (as revised in 2008), the acquirer may not recognise a separate provision or valuation allowance as of the acquisition date for assets acquired in a business combination that are initially recognised at fair value. For example, as receivables (including loans) that are acquired in a business combination are to be recognised and measured at fair value at the acquisition date, any uncertainty about collections and future cash flows are included in the fair value measure. Accordingly, the acquiring entity does not recognise a separate provision or valuation allowance for the contractual cash flows that are deemed to be uncollectible at the acquisition date.[369]

F   Assets that the acquirer intends not to use or to use in a way that is different from other market participants

For competitive or other reasons, the acquirer may intend not to use an acquired asset, for example, a research and development intangible asset, or it may intend to use the asset in a way that is different from the way in which other market participants would use it. Nevertheless, IFRS 3 (as revised in 2008) requires that the acquirer recognises all such identifiable assets, and measures the asset at its fair value determined in accordance with its use by other market participants.[370]

Example 9.41:   Acquirer's intention not to use an intangible asset

Entity A acquires a competitor, Entity B. One of the identifiable intangible assets of Entity B is the trade name of one of Entity B's branded products. However, since Entity A has a similar product, it does not intend to use that trade name post-acquisition. Entity A will discontinue sales of Entity B's product, thereby eliminating competition and enhancing the value of its own branded product. The cash flows relating to the acquired trade name are therefore expected to be nil.

Given that the cash flows relating to that trade name will be nil, can Entity A attribute a fair value of nil to that trade name?

As indicated above, the fair value of the asset has to be determined in accordance with its use by other market participants. Accordingly, Entity A's future intentions about the asset should only be reflected in determining the fair value if that is what other market participants would do. In most situations, this will not be the case as there are likely to be other market participants that would continue to sell the product and, on that basis, it is likely that the trade name does have a value. In fact, Entity A could probably have sold the trade name post-acquisition, but it has chosen not to do that to protect its own branded product. Accordingly, a fair value is attributed to that trade name. Indeed, even if all other market participants would do the same as Entity A, i.e. not sell the product in order to enhance the value of their own products, the trade name is still likely to have a value.

This does raise an issue as to whether an immediate impairment loss should be reflected in respect of the trade name since the expected cash flows relating to it are nil. IFRS 3 (as revised in 2008) does not address this particular issue. However, in our view there should be no immediate impairment loss. As discussed at 3.3 of Chapter 18, for the purposes of the impairment test under IAS 36, the recoverable amount of an asset is the higher of its value in use (VIU) and its fair value less costs to sell (FV). The FV of the trade name will initially not be materially different from the fair value attributed to it, and therefore unlikely to be impaired.

However, since Entity A is not intending to use the trade name to generate cash flows, it is unlikely that it could be regarded as having an indefinite life for the purposes of IAS 38, and therefore it should be amortised over its expected useful life. The estimate of the life should reflect the use to which Entity A is putting the trade name, which is as a means of eliminating competition for its own product. This is likely to be a relatively short period as the impact of the absence of that particular trade name in the market will not last for long, and any value that it did have will quickly reduce.

G   *Investments in equity-accounted entities*

It may be that one of the identifiable assets of an acquiree is an investment in an associate, which under IAS 28 is accounted for under the equity method (see Chapter 11 at 3). For the purposes of recognising and measuring this identifiable asset, there is no difference between an investment that is an associate or an investment that is a trade investment because the acquirer has acquired the investment not the underlying assets and liabilities of the associate. Accordingly, the fair value of the associate should be determined on the basis of the value of the shares of the associate rather than calculating a fair value based on the appropriate share of the fair values of the various identifiable assets and liabilities of the associate. By doing so, any goodwill relating to the associate is subsumed within the carrying amount for the associate rather than within the goodwill arising on the overall business combination. Nevertheless, although this fair value is effectively the 'cost' to the group to which equity accounting is applied, the underlying fair values of the various identifiable assets and liabilities also need to be determined to apply equity accounting (see Chapter 11 at 3.2).

If the fair value exercise for the business combination results in a gain on bargain purchase (commonly referred to as 'negative goodwill'), in accordance with the requirements of IFRS 3 (as revised in 2008) discussed at 3.11 below, the acquirer should challenge the fair value placed on the associate as it rechallenges the values place on all of the assets and liabilities of the acquiree to ensure that the value has not been overstated.

The above would also apply where one of the identifiable assets of an acquiree is an investment is a jointly controlled entity, which under IAS 31 is accounted for under the equity method (see Chapter 12 at 3.3.4).

3.6.6   Exceptions to the recognition and/or measurement principles

As indicated at 3.6.2 and 3.6.3 above, the IASB has made a number of exceptions to the principles in IFRS 3 (as revised in 2008) that all assets acquired and liabilities assumed should be recognised and measured at fair value.

For the particular items discussed below, IFRS 3 (as revised in 2008) requires the acquirer to account for those items by applying the requirements in paragraphs 22–31 of the standard, which will result in some items being:[371]

(a)   recognised either by applying recognition conditions in addition to those in paragraphs 11 and 12 of IFRS 3 (as revised in 2008) or by applying the requirements of other IFRSs, with results that differ from applying the recognition principle and conditions; and/or

(b)   measured at an amount other than their acquisition-date fair values.

A   Contingent liabilities

IAS 37 defines a contingent liability as:[372]

(a)   a possible obligation that arises from past events and whose existence will be confirmed only by the occurrence or non-occurrence of one or more uncertain future events not wholly within the control of the entity; or

(b)   a present obligation that arises from past events but is not recognised because:

   (i)   it is not probable that an outflow of resources embodying economic benefits will be required to settle the obligation; or

   (ii)   the amount of the obligation cannot be measured with sufficient reliability.

I   Initial recognition and measurement

Under IAS 37, contingent liabilities are only disclosed in financial statements, they are not recognised as liabilities. However, IFRS 3 (as revised in 2008) states that 'the requirements in IAS 37 do not apply in determining which contingent liabilities to recognise as of the acquisition date'. Instead, IFRS 3 (as revised in 2008) requires that for contingent liabilities assumed in a business combination, the acquirer recognises a liability at its fair value if there is a present obligation arising from a past event that can be reliably measured, even if it is not probable that an outflow of resources will be required to settle the obligation.[373] However, for a contingent liability that only represents a possible obligation that arises from a past event, whose existence will be confirmed only by the occurrence or non-occurrence of one or more uncertain future events not wholly within the control of the entity, no liability is to be recognised under IFRS 3 (as revised in 2008) (unlike the previous version of

IFRS 3 – see 2.5.3 above).[374] Similarly, no liability is recognised in respect of a contingent liability that represents a present obligation arising from a past event but whose acquisition-date fair value cannot be measured reliably.

As discussed at 3.6.5 D II above, the IASB clarifies in the Basis for Conclusions accompanying IFRS 3 (as revised in 2008) that contingent assets should not be recognised unless they meet the definition of an asset in the IASB's *Framework*.

These requirements of IFRS 3 (as revised in 2008) differ from those proposed in the June 2005 exposure draft which reflected proposed changes to the requirements of IAS 37 contained in another exposure draft issued at the same time (see Chapter 24 at 8.1 for a discussion of those proposals). At that time, the IASB expected that the effective date of the revised IAS 37 would be the same as the effective date for IFRS 3 (as revised in 2008), but the project on revising IAS 37 has been delayed. However, the IASB has indicated that it expects to reconsider the requirements within IFRS 3 (as revised in 2008) when it issues the revised IAS 37.[375] The IASB's latest work plan indicates that the Board is aiming to publish either a further exposure draft or the revised IAS 37 in the final quarter of 2009.[376]

II   Subsequent measurement and accounting

Where a liability is recognised for a contingent liability, since this is not what would be required under IAS 37, IFRS 3 (as revised in 2008) contains requirements for the subsequent measurement and accounting of such liabilities. These requirements retain the requirements for the subsequent measurement of such liabilities under the previous version of IFRS 3 – see 2.5.3 above.

Accordingly, IFRS 3 (as revised in 2008) requires that after initial recognition and until the liability is settled, cancelled or expires, the acquirer measures a contingent liability that is recognised in a business combination at the higher of:[377]

(a)   the amount that would be recognised in accordance with IAS 37, and

(b)   the amount initially recognised less, if appropriate, cumulative amortisation recognised in accordance with IAS 18.

The implications of part (a) of the requirement are clear. If the acquiree has to recognise a provision in respect of the former contingent liability, and the best estimate of this liability is higher than the original fair value attributed by the acquirer, then the greater liability should now be recognised by the acquirer with the difference taken to the income statement. It would now be a provision to be measured and recognised in accordance with IAS 37. What is less clear is part (b) of the requirement. The reference to 'amortisation recognised in accordance with IAS 18' might relate to the recognition of income in respect of those loan commitments that are contingent liabilities of the acquiree, but have been recognised at fair value at date of acquisition. The implication of the requirement would appear to mean that, unless amortisation under IAS 18 is appropriate, the amount of the liability cannot be reduced below its originally attributed fair value until the liability is settled, cancelled or expires.

Despite the fact that the requirement for subsequent measurement discussed above was originally introduced for consistency with IAS 39,[378] IFRS 3 (as revised in 2008) makes it clear that the requirement does not apply to contracts accounted for in accordance with IAS 39.[379] However, this would appear to mean that contracts that are excluded from the scope of IAS 39, but are accounted for by applying IAS 37, i.e. loan commitments other than those that are commitments to provide loans at below-market interest rates, will fall within the requirements of IFRS 3 (as revised in 2008) outlined above. It was explicitly stated in the previous version of IFRS 3 that such loan commitments were to be regarded as contingent liabilities of the acquiree.[380]

B   Income taxes

IFRS 3 (as revised in 2008) requires the acquirer to recognise and measure a deferred tax asset or liability arising from the assets acquired and liabilities assumed in a business combination in accordance with IAS 12.[381] The acquirer is also required to account for the potential tax effects of temporary differences and carryforwards of an acquiree that exist at the acquisition date or arise as a result of the acquisition in accordance with IAS 12.[382]

As most, if not all, of the requirements of IAS 12 are arguably consistent with the recognition principle in IFRS 3 (as revised in 2008), the IASB had considered identifying deferred tax assets and liabilities as an exception to only the measurement principle of using acquisition-date fair values. This is because deferred tax assets or liabilities generally are measured at undiscounted amounts in accordance with IAS 12, and it was decided not to require deferred tax assets or liabilities acquired in a business combination to be measured at fair value. However, the requirements are identified as being exceptions to both the recognition and measurement principles of IFRS 3 (as revised in 2008) to more clearly indicate that the acquirer should apply the recognition and measurement provisions of IAS 12.[383]

However, in order to address specific issues pertaining to the acquirer's income tax accounting in connection with a business combination, and to make the accounting more consistent with the principles in IFRS 3 (as revised in 2008), the requirements of IAS 12 have been amended. The first change relates to accounting for deferred tax benefits that do not meet the recognition criteria at the date of acquisition, but are subsequently recognised. IAS 12 now requires that:[384]

(a)   acquired deferred tax benefits recognised within the measurement period (see 3.13 below) that result from new information obtained about facts and circumstances existing at the acquisition date are to reduce the goodwill related to that acquisition. If the carrying amount of goodwill is zero, any remaining deferred tax benefits is to be recognised in profit or loss; and

(b)   all other acquired tax benefits realised are to be recognised in profit or loss.

It will therefore be necessary to carefully assess the reasons for changes in the assessment of deferred tax made during the measurement period to determine whether it relates to facts and circumstances at the acquisition date or if it is a change in facts and circumstances since acquisition date.

This differs from the treatment under the previous version of IFRS 3 of deferred tax benefits subsequently recognised, whereby the carrying amount of goodwill was reduced for the subsequent recognition of such deferred tax benefits without any time limit (see 2.8.3 above).

IAS 12 has also been amended so that tax benefits arising from the excess of tax-deductible goodwill over goodwill for financial reporting purposes is accounted for at the acquisition date as a deferred tax asset in the same way as other temporary differences.[385]

The requirements of IAS 12 relating to the deferred tax consequences of business combinations are discussed further in Chapter 26 at 6.2.

C   Employee benefits

IFRS 3 (as revised in 2008) requires the acquirer to recognise and measure a liability (or asset, if any) related to the acquiree's employee benefit arrangements in accordance with IAS 19.[386]

As with deferred tax assets and liabilities discussed at B above, the IASB considered identifying employee benefits as an exception only to the measurement principle, but in order to make it clear that the acquirer should apply the recognition and measurement requirements of IAS 19 without separately considering the extent to which those requirements are consistent with the principles of IFRS 3 (as revised in 2008), it exempts employee benefit obligations from both the recognition and measurement principles of IFRS 3 (as revised in 2008).[387]

Accordingly, the acquirer recognises assets and liabilities arising from post-employment benefits that are defined benefit plans at the present value of the defined benefit obligation less the fair value of any plan assets. In computing the present value of the obligation, IAS 19 requires that any items such as actuarial gains and losses (whether or not within the 10% corridor allowed by IAS 19), past service costs and amounts not yet recognised by the acquiree under the transitional provisions of IAS 19 at the date of the acquisition are included.[388] This means that there are no exemptions for the acquirer from recognising the full defined benefit obligation on acquisition. However, a net asset is recognised only to the extent that it is recoverable, based on the requirements of IAS 19 and IFRIC 14 (see Chapter 28 at 5.3.1 B). This is effectively the same as the treatment under the previous version of IFRS 3 as discussed at 2.5.4 G above.

Although IAS 19 only refers to business combinations in the context of defined benefit plans, IFRS 3 (as revised in 2008) requires liabilities (or assets, if any) related to all other types of employee benefit arrangements to be recognised and measured under IAS 19, rather than at their acquisition-date fair values.[389]

D   Indemnification assets

In certain situations, primarily those related to uncertainties as to the outcome of pre-acquisition contingencies (e.g. uncertain tax positions, environmental liabilities, or legal matters), the seller in a business combination may contractually indemnify the acquirer for the outcome of the contingency or uncertainty related to all or part of the specific asset or liability. The indemnification typically requires the acquiree's selling shareholders to reimburse the acquirer for some or all of the costs incurred by the acquirer in connection with the assumed pre-acquisition contingency. For example, the seller may indemnify the acquirer against losses above a specified amount on a liability arising from a particular contingency, in other words, the seller will guarantee that the acquirer's liability will not exceed a specified amount. As result, IFRS 3 (as revised in 2008) considers that the acquirer has obtained an indemnification asset.[390] As discussed at 2.4.5 E above, such indemnities were not explicitly addressed in the previous version of IFRS 3 but were either treated as 'negative' contingent consideration or as a separate 'indemnity asset'.

I   Initial recognition and measurement

From the acquirer's perspective, the indemnification is an acquired asset to be recognised at its acquisition-date fair value. However, in order to avoid 'recognition or measurement' anomalies for indemnifications related to items for which liabilities are either not recognised or are not required to be measured at fair value (e.g. uncertain tax positions), IFRS 3 (as revised in 2008) makes an exception to the general principles of recognising the indemnification asset at its acquisition-date fair values.[391]

Accordingly, under IFRS 3 (as revised in 2008), the acquirer recognises an indemnification asset at the same time that it recognises the indemnified item measured on the same basis as the indemnified item, subject to the need for a valuation allowance for uncollectible amounts. Therefore, if the indemnification relates to an asset or a liability that is recognised at the acquisition date and measured at its acquisition-date fair value, the acquirer recognises the indemnification asset at the acquisition date measured at its acquisition-date fair value. For an indemnification asset measured at fair value, the effects of uncertainty about future cash flows because of collectibility considerations are included in the fair value measure and a separate valuation allowance is not necessary (see 3.6.5 E above).[392]

However, in some circumstances, the indemnification relates to an asset or liability that is an exception to recognition or measurement principles of IFRS 3 (as revised in 2008). For example, an indemnification may relate to a contingent liability that is not recognised at the acquisition date because its fair value is not reliably measurable at that date[393] or it is only a possible obligation at that date (see A above). Alternatively, an indemnification may relate to an asset or a liability, for example, one that results from an employee benefit, that is measured on a basis other than acquisition-date fair value.[394] Another example would be an indemnification pertaining to a tax liability that is measured in accordance with IAS 12, rather than its acquisition-date fair value (see B above). If the indemnified item is recognised as a liability at the acquisition date, but is measured on a basis other than acquisition-date fair value, the indemnification asset is recognised and measured using assumptions consistent with those used to measure the indemnified item, subject to management's assessment of collectability of the indemnification asset and any contractual limitations on the indemnified amount.[395] However, if no liability is recognised for the indemnified item at the date of acquisition, the indemnification asset would also not be recognised.

II   Subsequent measurement and accounting

Subsequent to the business combination, the indemnification asset is measured using the same assumptions used to calculate the indemnified liability or asset, subject to any contractual limitations on its amount and, for an indemnification asset that is not subsequently measured at its fair value, management's assessment of collectability of the indemnification asset.[396] Thus, where the change in the value of the related indemnified liability or asset has to be recognised in profit or loss, this will be offset by any corresponding change in the value recognised for the indemnification asset. The acquirer derecognises the indemnification asset only when it collects the asset, sells it or otherwise loses the right to it.[397]

At its meeting in May 2009, the IASB considered a number of issues brought by the IASB staff, but deferred them to the post-implementation review of IFRS 3 (as revised in 2008) and IAS 27 (as amended in 2008), to be conducted two years after their effective date. One of these related to the treatment of indemnification assets, as part of the business combination transaction or as a separate transaction.[398] It is not clear what the particular issue was as no details were included in the agenda papers available to the public.

E   Reacquired rights

I   Initial recognition and measurement

As indicated earlier at 3.6.5 C above, if the assets of the acquiree include a right previously granted to it allowing use of the acquirer's assets (a reacquired right), IFRS 3 (as revised in 2008) requires it to be recognised as an identifiable intangible asset. For example, a right to use the acquirer's trade name under a franchise agreement or a right to use the acquirer's technology under a technology licensing agreement.[399] However, rather than valuing the intangible asset at its acquisition-date fair value, it is to be valued on the basis of the remaining contractual term of the related contract, regardless of whether market participants would consider potential contractual renewals in determining its fair value.[400]

The reason for departing from the assumptions that market participants would use in measuring the fair value of the reacquired right is that it would be inconsistent with the requirement for determining the useful life of the reacquired right (as discussed at II below). The IASB also noted that a contractual right transferred to a third party is not a *reacquired* right.[401]

As noted at 3.6.5 C above, to the extent that the terms of the contract giving rise to the reacquired right are favourable or unfavourable relative to the terms of current market transactions for the same or similar items, IFRS 3 (as revised in 2008) regards this as the settlement of a pre-existing relationship and the acquirer has to recognise a settlement gain or loss.[402] Guidance on the measurement of any settlement gain or loss is discussed at 3.12.1 below.

As discussed at 2.5.6 above, the previous version of IFRS 3 is silent in this area.

II   Subsequent measurement and accounting

After acquisition, the intangible asset is to be amortised over the remaining contractual period of the contract, without including any renewal periods.[403] The reason for excluding any renewal periods is that a reacquired right is no longer a contract with a third party; the acquirer who controls the reacquired right could assume indefinite renewals of its contractual term, effectively making the reacquired right an intangible asset with an indefinite life. The IASB considers that a right reacquired from an acquiree has in substance a finite life; a renewal of the contractual term after the business combination is not part of what was acquired in the business combination. Accordingly, the standard limits the period over which the intangible asset is amortised to the remaining contractual term of the contract from which the reacquired right stems.[404] If the acquirer subsequently sells a reacquired right to a third party, the carrying amount of the intangible asset is to be included in determining the gain or loss on the sale.[405]

F   Assets held for sale

IFRS 3 (as revised in 2008) requires that non-current assets (or disposal groups) classified as held for sale at the acquisition date in accordance with IFRS 5 are measured at fair value less costs to sell in accordance with paragraphs 15 to 18 of that IFRS (see Chapter 4 at 2.2).[406] This exception is to avoid the need to recognise a loss for the selling costs immediately after a business combination (a so-called Day 2 loss), if the assets had initially been measured at their fair value at the acquisition date.

Subsequent to the issue of the June 2005 exposure draft, the Board tentatively decided to remove the proposed exception and amend IFRS 5 by replacing the words 'fair value less costs to sell' with 'fair value'. However, this was not done, but the Basis for Conclusions accompanying IFRS 3 (as revised in 2008) indicated that the IASB intended that the eventual amendment to IFRS 5 would be effective at the same time as the revised IFRS 3,[407] at which time this temporary exception presumably would be removed. However, at its April 2008 Board meeting, the IASB has tentatively decided not to amend IFRS 5 for the measurement of non-current assets held for sale. Accordingly, the exception to the measurement principle of fair value related to non-current assets held for sale in IFRS 3 (as revised in 2008) will remain in force.[408]

G   Share-based payment awards

IFRS 3 (as revised in 2008) also provides an exception that, a liability or an equity instrument related to the replacement of an acquiree's share-based payment award is measured in accordance with IFRS 2 (referred to as the 'market-based measure'), rather than at fair value.[409] The reason for this exception is that application of measurement methods in IFRS 2 do not result in the amount at which market participants would exchange an award at a particular date (its fair value at that date), and the initial measurement of share-based payment awards at their acquisition-date fair values would cause difficulties with the subsequent accounting for those awards in accordance with IFRS 2.[410]

Additional guidance given in IFRS 3 (as revised in 2008) for accounting for replacement of share-based payment awards in a business combination is discussed at 3.12.2 below.

3.7   Recognising and measuring goodwill or a gain in a bargain purchase

The final step in applying the acquisition method is recognising and measuring goodwill or a gain in a bargain purchase.

IFRS 3 (as revised in 2008) defines 'goodwill' in terms of its nature, rather than in terms of its measurement. It is defined as 'an asset representing the future economic benefits arising from other assets acquired in a business combination that are not individually identified and separately recognised.'[411]

It is clear from the above definition that IFRS 3 (as revised in 2008) requires the acquirer to recognise goodwill as an asset. However, having concluded that the direct measurement of goodwill is not possible, the standard requires that goodwill is measured as a residual.[412]

Under IFRS 3 (as revised in 2008), the measurement of goodwill at the acquisition date is computed as the excess of (a) over (b) below:[413]

(a)   the aggregate of:

    (i)   the consideration transferred (generally measured at acquisition-date fair value);

    (ii)   the amount of any non-controlling interest in the acquiree; and

    (iii) the acquisition-date fair value of the acquirer's previously held equity interest in the acquiree.

(b)   the net of the acquisition-date fair values (or other amounts recognised in accordance with the requirements of the standard) of the identifiable assets acquired and the liabilities assumed.

Where (b) exceeds (a), IFRS 3 (as revised in 2008) regards this as giving rise to a gain on a bargain purchase.[414] Bargain purchase transactions are discussed further at 3.11 below.

The measurement of (b) has been discussed at 3.6 above. The items included within (a) are discussed at 3.8, 3.9 and 3.10 below.

The computation of goodwill outlined above differs from that in the previous version of IFRS 3, which also measured goodwill as a residual (see 2.6 above). This is due to the change in focus in IFRS 3 (as revised in 2008) on measuring the various components of the business combination at their acquisition-date fair values (albeit with a number of exceptions including that relating to the measurement of any non-controlling interest), whereas the previous version of IFRS 3 adopted a cost-based approach.

As indicated above, goodwill is to be recognised as an asset. This is because the IASB has concluded that 'core goodwill' (see below) meets the definition of an asset in its *Framework*.[415] The Basis for Conclusions accompanying IFRS 3 (as revised in 2008) contains a discussion of the following six components that, in practice, historically had been included in goodwill:[416]

- Component 1 – The excess of the fair values over the book values of the acquiree's net assets at the date of acquisition;

- Component 2 – The fair values of other net assets that the acquiree had not previously recognised. They may not have been recognised because they failed to meet the recognition criteria (perhaps because of measurement difficulties), because of a requirement that prohibited their recognition, or because the acquiree concluded that the costs of recognising them separately were not justified by the benefits;

- Component 3 – The fair value of the going concern element of the acquiree's existing business. The going concern element represents the ability of the established business to earn a higher rate of return on an assembled collection of net assets than would be expected if those net assets had to be acquired separately. That value stems from the synergies of the net assets of the business, as well as from other benefits (such as factors related to market imperfections, including the ability to earn monopoly profits and barriers to market entry – either legal or because of transaction costs – by potential competitors);

- Component 4 – The fair value of the expected synergies and other benefits from combining the acquirer's and acquiree's net assets and businesses. Those synergies and other benefits are unique to each combination, and different combinations would produce different synergies and, hence, different values;

- Component 5 – Overvaluation of the consideration paid by the acquirer stemming from errors in valuing the consideration tendered. Although the purchase price in an all-cash transaction would not be subject to measurement error, the same may not necessarily be said of a transaction involving the acquirer's equity interests. For example, the number of ordinary shares being traded daily may be small relative to the number of shares issued in the combination. If so, imputing the current market price to all of the shares issued to effect the combination may produce a higher value than those shares would command if they were sold for cash and the cash then used to effect the combination;

- Component 6 – Overpayment or underpayment by the acquirer. Overpayment might occur, for example, if the price is driven up in the course of bidding for the acquiree; underpayment may occur in a distress sale (sometimes termed a fire sale).

Components 3 and 4 are considered by the IASB to be part of goodwill. Component 3 relates to the acquiree and reflects the excess assembled value of the acquiree's net assets. It represents the pre-existing goodwill that was either internally generated by the acquiree or acquired by it in prior business combinations. Component 4 relates to the acquiree and the acquirer jointly and reflects the excess assembled value that is created by the combination – the synergies that are expected from combining those businesses. It is these components that are described collectively as 'core goodwill'.[417]

On the other hand, the IASB considers that the other components are conceptually not part of goodwill. Component 1 is not itself an asset; instead, it reflects gains that the acquiree had not recognised on its net assets. As such, that component is part of those assets rather than part of goodwill. Component 2 is also not part of goodwill conceptually; it primarily reflects intangible assets that might be recognised as individual assets. Component 5 is not an asset in and of itself or even part of an asset but, rather, is a measurement error. Component 6 is also not an asset; conceptually it represents a loss (in the case of overpayment) or a gain (in the case of underpayment) to the acquirer. Thus, neither of those components is conceptually part of goodwill.[418]

The Basis for Conclusions goes on to say that IFRS 3 (as revised in 2008) tries to avoid subsuming the first, second and fifth components of goodwill into the amount initially recognised as goodwill. Specifically, an acquirer is required to make every effort:[419]

(a)   to measure the consideration accurately (eliminating or reducing component 5);

(b)   to recognise the identifiable net assets acquired at their fair values rather than their carrying amounts (eliminating or reducing component 1); and

(c)   to recognise all acquired intangible assets meeting the criteria in the revised standard (paragraph B31 of IFRS 3 (as revised in 2008)) so that they are not subsumed into the amount initially recognised as goodwill (reducing component 2).

Despite these efforts, the amount of goodwill recognised as an asset may still represent more than what the IASB regards as 'core goodwill'. The fact that exceptions have been made such that certain assets and liabilities are not measured at their acquisition-date fair value, e.g. deferred tax assets and liabilities, will impact on the amount recognised for goodwill. As far as overpayments are concerned, it was concluded that in practice it is not possible to identify and reliably measure an overpayment at the acquisition date, and the accounting for overpayments is best addressed through subsequent impairment testing when evidence of a potential overpayment first arises.[420]

The main issue relating to the goodwill acquired in a business combination is how it should be subsequently accounted for. The requirements of IFRS 3 (as revised in 2008) in this respect are straightforward; but that is only because the detailed requirements in relation to the subsequent accounting for goodwill are dealt with in IAS 36.

IFRS 3 (as revised in 2008) merely states that the acquirer measures goodwill acquired in a business combination at the amount recognised at the acquisition date less any accumulated impairment losses.[421]

Goodwill acquired in a business combination is not to be amortised. Instead, the acquirer has to test it for impairment annually, or more frequently if events or changes in circumstances indicate that it might be impaired, in accordance with IAS 36. The requirements of IAS 36 relating specifically to the impairment of goodwill are dealt with in Chapter 18 at 3.4.

3.8   Consideration transferred

The first item in part (a) of the goodwill computation set out at 3.7 above is the consideration transferred.

IFRS 3 (as revised in 2008) requires that the consideration transferred in a business combination is to be measured at fair value, and comprises the sum of the acquisition-date fair values of assets transferred by the acquirer, liabilities incurred by the acquirer to the former owners of the acquiree, and equity interests issued by the acquirer. The consideration may take many forms, including cash, other assets, a business or subsidiary of the acquirer, and securities of the acquirer (e.g. ordinary shares, preferred shares, options, warrants, and debt instruments).

The consideration transferred also includes the fair value of any contingent consideration and may also include some or all of any acquirer's share-based payment awards exchanged for awards held by the acquiree's employees (these awards are measured using the 'market-based measure' under IFRS 2 rather than at fair value). These are discussed further at 3.8.1 and 3.8.2 below.[422]

When the consideration transferred includes assets or liabilities of the acquirer with carrying amounts that differ from the acquisition-date fair values, for example non-monetary assets or a business of the acquirer, the acquirer remeasures them at their acquisition-date fair values and recognise any resulting gains or losses in profit or loss. However, it may be that the transferred assets or liabilities remain within the combined entity after the acquisition date (for example, they were transferred to the acquiree rather than to its former owners), and therefore the acquirer retains control of them. In that case, they are measured at their existing carrying amounts immediately before the acquisition, and therefore no gain or loss is recognised.[423]

IFRS 3 (as revised in 2008) defines 'fair value' as 'the amount for which an asset could be exchanged, or a liability settled, between knowledgeable, willing parties in an arm's length transaction'.[424] This is the same as the definition in the previous version of IFRS 3 as well in other IFRSs. However, as is the case with measuring recognised identifiable assets acquired and liabilities assumed at their acquisition-date fair values, as discussed at 3.6.3 above, much of the guidance relating to the fair value of consideration given in the previous version of IFRS 3 (see 2.4.2 and 2.4.3 above) is no longer included in IFRS 3 (as revised in 2008).

Where the assets given as consideration or the liabilities incurred by the acquirer are financial assets or financial liabilities under IAS 39, then it would seem appropriate that the guidance in determining the fair values of such financial instruments should be followed (see Chapter 32 at 4).

Similarly, where equity interests are issued by the acquirer as consideration, it would seem appropriate that the guidance in IAS 39 on determining the fair value of equity instruments (held as investments) should be followed.

One aspect about measuring equity interests issued as consideration in a business combination that IFRS 3 (as revised in 2008) does clarify is that they are to be measured at their fair values at the acquisition date, rather than at an earlier agreement date (or on the basis of the market price of the securities for a short period before or after that date).[425] Some commentators cited one or more of the following as support for their view of using the agreement date:[426]

(a)   An acquirer and a target entity both consider the fair value of a target entity on the agreement date in negotiating the amount of consideration to be paid. Measuring equity securities issued as consideration at fair value on the agreement date reflects the values taken into account in negotiations;

(b)   Changes in the fair value of the acquirer's equity securities between the agreement date and the acquisition date may be caused by factors unrelated to the business combination;

(c)   Changes in the fair value of the acquirer's equity securities between the agreement date and the acquisition date may result in inappropriate recognition of either a bargain purchase or artificially inflated goodwill if the fair value of those securities is measured at the acquisition date.

Although it was considered that a valid conceptual argument could be made for the use of the agreement date, it was observed that the parties to a business combination are likely to take into account expected changes between the agreement date and the acquisition date in the fair value of the acquirer and the market price of the acquirer's securities issued as consideration. The argument against acquisition date measurement of equity securities noted in (a) above is mitigated if acquirers and targets generally consider their best estimates at the agreement date of the fair values of the amounts to be exchanged on the acquisition dates. In addition, measuring the equity securities on the acquisition date avoids the complexities of dealing with situations in which the number of shares or other consideration transferred can change between the agreement date and the acquisition date.

It was also noted that measuring the fair value of equity securities issued on the agreement date (or on the basis of the market price of the securities for a short period before and after that date) did not result in a consistent measure of the consideration transferred. The fair values of all other forms of consideration transferred are measured at the acquisition date. It was decided that all forms of consideration transferred should be valued on the same date, which should also be the same date as when the assets acquired and liabilities assumed are measured.[427]

Thus, it was concluded that equity instruments issued as consideration in a business combination should be measured at their fair values on the acquisition date.[428]

In a business combination in which the acquirer and the acquiree (or its former owners) exchange only equity interests, the acquisition-date fair value of the acquiree's equity interests may be more reliably measurable than that of the acquirer's equity interests. In that case, IFRS 3 (as revised in 2008) requires that the calculation of goodwill should use the acquisition-date fair value of the acquiree's equity interests rather than the acquisition-date fair value of the equity interests transferred.[429]

Where no consideration is transferred by the acquirer, IFRS 3 (as revised in 2008) gives additional guidance for such situations. This is discussed at 3.8.4 below.

3.8.1   Contingent consideration

The consideration the acquirer transfers in exchange for the acquiree includes any asset or liability resulting from a contingent consideration arrangement.

Contingent consideration is defined in IFRS 3 (as revised in 2008) as 'Usually, an obligation of the acquirer to transfer additional assets or equity interests to the former owners of an acquiree as part of the exchange for control of the acquiree if specified future events occur or conditions are met. However, contingent consideration also may give the acquirer the right to the return of previously transferred consideration if specified conditions are met.'[430]

As can be seen from the definition, contingent consideration generally arises where the acquirer agrees to transfer additional consideration to the former owners of the acquired business after the acquisition date if certain specified events occur or conditions are met in the future. Such arrangements are commonly used by buyers and sellers when there are differences in view as to the fair value of the acquired business.

One issue discussed by the IASB at its meeting in June 2009 was the treatment of contingent consideration arising from a prior business combination of an acquiree that an acquirer assumes in its subsequent acquisition of the acquiree ('pre-existing contingent consideration'). The IASB clarified that pre-existing contingent consideration does not meet the definition of contingent consideration in the acquirer's business combination. It is one of the identifiable liabilities assumed in the subsequent acquisition. Therefore, the Board decided tentatively not to add this topic to the annual improvements project.[431]

Nevertheless, as indicated in the IASB Staff Paper considered by the Board, in most situations it would not matter whether the pre-existing contingent consideration was treated as contingent consideration or as an identifiable liability. This is because most contingent consideration obligations are financial liabilities to be accounted for under IAS 39.[432] As discussed further below, they are initially recognised and measured at fair value at the date of acquisition, with any subsequent remeasurements to fair value recognised either in profit or loss or in other comprehensive income in accordance with IAS 39. The treatment of the pre-existing contingent consideration as an identifiable liability also results in the financial liability being measured at fair value at the date of acquisition, with any subsequent remeasurements to fair value recognised either in profit or loss or in other comprehensive income in accordance with IAS 39.

A   Initial recognition and measurement

Under IFRS 3 (as revised in 2008), the acquirer recognises the acquisition-date fair value of any contingent consideration as part of the consideration transferred in exchange for the acquiree.[433] This represents a significant change from the practice under the previous version of IFRS 3 of recognising contingent consideration obligations only when the contingency was probable and could be measured reliably (see 2.4.5 above).

The initial measurement of contingent consideration at the fair value of the obligation is to be based on an assessment of the facts and circumstances that exist at the acquisition date. The Basis for Conclusions accompanying IFRS 3 (as revised in 2008) acknowledges that measuring the fair value of some contingent payments may be difficult, but it was concluded that to delay recognition of, or otherwise ignore, assets or liabilities that are difficult to measure would cause financial reporting to be incomplete and thus diminish its usefulness in making economic decisions.[434]

The Basis for Conclusions goes on to say that a contingent consideration arrangement is inherently part of the economic considerations in the negotiations between the buyer and seller. Such arrangements are commonly used by buyers and sellers to reach an agreement by sharing particular specified economic risks related to uncertainties about future outcomes. Differences in the views of the buyer and seller about those uncertainties are often reconciled by their agreeing to share the risks in such ways that favourable future outcomes generally result in additional payments to the seller and unfavourable outcomes result in no or lower payments. It was observed that information used in those negotiations will often be helpful in estimating the fair value of the contingent obligation assumed by the acquirer.[435] It was also concluded that the requirements under IFRS 2 for awards of share-based payment subject to performance conditions should not determine the requirements for contingent (or conditional) consideration in a business combination. Again, it was concluded that the negotiations between buyer and seller inherent in a contingent consideration arrangement in a business combination provide better evidence of its fair value than is likely to be available for most share-based payment arrangements with performance conditions.[436]

It was also noted that most contingent consideration obligations are financial instruments, and many are derivative instruments. Reporting entities that use such instruments extensively, auditors and valuation professionals are familiar with the use of valuation techniques for estimating the fair values of financial instruments. It was concluded that acquirers should be able to use valuation techniques to develop estimates of the fair values of contingent consideration obligations that are sufficiently reliable for recognition. It was also observed that an effective estimate of zero for the acquisition-date fair value of contingent consideration, which was often the result under IFRS 3 (2007), was unreliable.[437]

It would also seem inappropriate to assume an effective estimate of 100% for the acquisition-date fair value of the obligation to make the payments under the contingent consideration arrangement. Given that the arrangement is generally designed to reflect uncertainties about future outcomes, it would seem that the fair value should reflect a weighted average probability of the potential future outcomes.

IFRS 3 (as revised in 2008) also recognises that, in some situations, the agreement may give the acquirer the right to the return of previously transferred consideration if specified future events occur or conditions are met. Such a right falls within the definition of 'contingent consideration', and is to be accounted for as such by recognising an asset at its acquisition-date fair value.[438]

B   Classification of a contingent consideration obligation

As indicated above, most contingent consideration obligations are financial instruments, and many are derivative instruments. Some contingent consideration arrangements oblige the acquirer to deliver equity securities if specified future events occur, rather than, say, making additional cash payments. As discussed at 2.4.5 D above, the previous version of IFRS 3 made no explicit reference to situations where contingent consideration was to be settled by equity instruments and they were also scoped out of IFRS 2 and IAS 32.

IFRS 3 (as revised in 2008) requires that the classification of a contingent consideration obligation as either a liability or equity is to be based on the definitions of an equity instrument and a financial liability in IAS 32 (see Chapter 31) or other applicable accounting standards.[439] Most contingent consideration obligations will be classified on the basis of IAS 32, and in many cases will meet the definition of a financial liability (including those arrangements where the acquirer is obliged to deliver equity securities). This is because IAS 32 defines a financial liability to include 'a contract that will or may be settled in the entity's own equity instruments' and is:[440]

- 'a non-derivative for which the entity is or may be obliged to deliver a variable number of the entity's own equity instruments'; or
- 'a derivative that will or may be settled other than by the exchange of a fixed amount of cash or another financial asset for a fixed number of the entity's own equity instruments'.

Most contingent consideration arrangements that are to be settled by delivering equity shares will involve a variable number of shares; for example, if the arrangement obliges the acquirer to issue between, say, zero and 1 million additional equity shares on a sliding scale based on the acquiree's post-combination earnings. Such arrangements will be classified as a financial liability. It is only likely to be in situations where the arrangement involves issuing, say, zero *or* 1 million shares depending on a specified event or target being achieved that the arrangement would be classified as equity. Where the arrangement involves a number of different discrete targets, which if met will result in additional equity shares being issued as further consideration, the classification of the obligation to provide such financial instruments in respect of each target is assessed separately in determining whether equity classification is appropriate. However, if the targets are interdependent, the classification of the obligation to provide such additional equity shares should be based on the overall arrangement, and as this is likely to mean that as a variable number of shares may be delivered, the arrangement would be classified as a financial liability.

Example 9.42:   Share-settled contingent consideration – financial liability or equity?

Entity P acquires a 100% interest in Entity S on 31 December 2010. As part of the consideration arrangements, additional consideration will be payable based on Entity S meeting certain profit targets over the 3 years ended 31 December 2012, as follows:

Profit target	*Additional consideration*
Year ended 31 December 2010 – €1m+	100,000 shares
Year ended 31 December 2011 – €1.25m+	150,000 shares
Year ended 31 December 2012 – €1.5m+	200,000 shares

Each target is non-cumulative. If the target for a particular year is met, the additional consideration will be payable, irrespective of whether the targets for the other years are met or not. If a target for a particular year is not met, no shares will be issued in respect of that year.

In this scenario, as each of the targets are independent of one another, we believe that this arrangement can be regarded as being three distinct contingent consideration arrangements that are assessed separately. As either zero or the requisite number of shares will be issued if each target is met, the obligation in respect of each arrangement is classified as equity.

On the other hand, if the targets were dependent on each other, for example, they were based on an average for the 3 year period, were based on a specified percentage increase on the previous year's profits the later targets were forfeited if the earlier targets were not met, or the total number of shares that would be provided was capped at, say, 300,000 shares, the classification would be assessed on the overall arrangement. As this would mean that a variable number of shares may be delivered, the obligation under such an arrangement would have to be classified as a financial liability.

IFRS 3 (as revised in 2008) does not indicate in what situations other applicable accounting standards would be relevant, but it would presumably relate to arrangements where the consideration was not a financial instrument, but was a non-monetary asset.

For those contingent consideration arrangements where the agreement gives the acquirer the right to the return of previously transferred consideration if specified future events occur or conditions are met, IFRS 3 (as revised in 2008) merely requires such a right is classified as an asset.[441]

At its meeting in May 2009, the IASB indicated that it will address 'contingent consideration: designation (categories of financial instruments) and classification (as equity or a liability)' in its projects on financial instruments.[442]

It is not entirely clear what aspect of the accounting for contingent consideration will be addressed as part of that project as no details were included in the agenda papers available to the public.

C   Subsequent measurement and accounting

As discussed at 2.4.5 above, the previous version of IFRS 3 required that subsequent changes in the amount recognised for any contingent consideration would generally be accounted for as adjustments to the consideration transferred in the business combination, resulting in changes to the goodwill until the final outcome was known.

This reflected the requirements of the previous standard, IAS 22, without reconsideration.

This has been reconsidered in developing IFRS 3 (as revised in 2008), and the IASB has concluded that subsequent changes in the fair value of a contingent consideration obligation generally do not affect the acquisition-date fair value of the consideration transferred to the acquiree. Instead, those subsequent changes in value are related to post-combination events and changes in circumstances of the combined entity. Thus, the Board believes that subsequent changes in value for post-combination events and circumstances should not affect the measurement of the consideration transferred or goodwill on the acquisition date.[443]

Accordingly, IFRS 3 (as revised in 2008) requires that after initial recognition, changes in the fair value of contingent consideration resulting from events after the acquisition date such as meeting an earnings target, reaching a specified share price, or meeting a milestone on a research and development project are accounted for as follows:[444]

- Contingent consideration classified as equity is not subsequently remeasured (consistent with the accounting for equity instruments generally), and its subsequent settlement is accounted for within equity;

- Contingent consideration classified as an asset or a liability that:

  - is a financial instrument and within the scope of IAS 39 is remeasured at fair value, with any resulting gain or loss recognised either in profit or loss or in other comprehensive income in accordance with IAS 39;

  - is not within the scope of IAS 39 is accounted for in accordance with IAS 37 or other standards as appropriate.

IFRS 3 (as revised in 2008) does not indicate in what situations contingent consideration classified as a liability would not be within the scope of IAS 39, and would therefore be accounted for under IAS 37 or another standard, although as noted at B above it would presumably relate to arrangements where the consideration was not a financial instrument, but was a non-monetary asset. Nevertheless, even where that is the case, any changes in the measurement of the liability would be recognised in profit or loss.

The Basis for Conclusions accompanying IFRS 3 (as revised in 2008) notes that many obligations for contingent consideration that qualify for classification as liabilities meet the definition of derivative instruments in IAS 39. To improve transparency in reporting particular instruments, it was concluded that all contracts that would otherwise be within the scope of that standard (if not issued in a business combination) should be subject to its requirements if issued in a business combination. Therefore, it was decided to eliminate the existing provisions (paragraph 2(f) of IAS 39) that excluded contingent consideration in a business combination from the scope of that standard. Accordingly, liabilities for payments of contingent consideration that are subject to the requirements of IAS 39 will be measured at fair value at the end of each reporting period, with changes in fair value recognised in accordance with IAS 39.[445] The equivalent scope exemptions in IAS 32 and IFRS 7 – *Financial Instruments: Disclosures* – have also been deleted.

In considering the subsequent accounting for contingent payments that are liabilities but are not derivatives, it was also concluded that, in concept, all liabilities for contingent payments should be accounted for similarly. Therefore, financial liabilities for contingent payments that are not derivative instruments should also be remeasured at fair value after the acquisition date.[446]

As indicated at B above, most contingent consideration obligations will be classified on the basis of IAS 32, and in many cases will meet the definition of a financial liability (including those arrangements where the acquirer is obliged to deliver a variable number of equity securities).

IFRS 3 (as revised in 2008) includes one exception to the above requirement for accounting for changes in the fair value of contingent consideration, and that is where the changes are the result of additional information about the facts and circumstances that existed at the acquisition date that the acquirer obtained after that date.[447] Such changes are measurement period adjustments and are to be accounted for as discussed at 3.13 below.

3.8.2 Share-based payment awards exchanged for awards held by the acquiree's employees

Acquirers often exchange share-based payment awards (i.e. replacement awards) for awards held by employees of the acquiree. These exchanges frequently occur because the acquirer wants to avoid the effect of having non-controlling interests in the acquiree represented by the shares that are ultimately held by employees, the acquirer's shares are often more liquid than the shares of the acquired business after the acquisition, and/or to motivate former employees of the acquiree toward the overall performance of the combined, post-acquisition business. Although such exchanges are accounted for in accordance with IFRS 2, as discussed in Chapter 27 at 11.1, until the issue of IFRS 3 (as revised in 2008), there was no specific guidance for the treatment of such replacement awards.

If the acquirer is obliged to replace any acquiree awards, as indicated at 3.8 above, the consideration transferred will include some or all of any acquirer's share-based payment awards exchanged for awards held by the acquiree's employees. In addition, as discussed at 3.12 below, IFRS 3 (as revised in 2008) requires that the acquirer recognises as part of applying the acquisition method only the consideration transferred for the acquiree and the assets and liabilities assumed in the exchange for the acquiree; separate transactions are accounted for in accordance with the relevant IFRSs. An example of a transaction that is not to be included in applying the acquisition method is one that remunerates employees or former owners for paying for future services.

IFRS 3 (as revised in 2008) includes Application Guidance dealing with the situation where an acquirer exchanges its share-based payment awards (replacement awards) for awards held by employees of the acquiree.[448] Such exchanges are modifications of share-based payment awards in accordance with IFRS 2. Discussion of this guidance, including illustrative examples that reflect the substance of the Illustrative Examples that accompany IFRS 3 (as revised in 2008),[449] is dealt with in Chapter 27 at 11.2.

That chapter also discusses issues relating to unreplaced share-based payment transactions of the acquiree and voluntary replacements of share-based payment transactions (see Chapter 27 at 11.4 and 11.2.2 respectively). As with the measurement of non-controlling interests in an acquiree (see 3.9.3 below), such share-based payment transactions were considered by the IFRIC at its meeting in July 2009. The IFRIC concluded that when an acquirer does not replace unexpired share-based payment awards of the acquiree or voluntarily issues share-based payment awards to replace such awards, at least some portion of the amount recognised for those awards should be regarded as part of the consideration transferred in the business combination. However, because IFRSs do not provide sufficient guidance to resolve this issue an amendment to IFRS 3 (as revised in 2008) is required.[450]

Consequently, the IASB has decided to deal with these issues within the exposure draft of proposed *Improvements to IFRSs* issued in August 2009.[451] The IASB proposes to amend the application guidance in IFRS 3 (as revised in 2008) so as to require the acquirer to apply paragraphs B57-B62 to all share-based payment transactions that are part of a business combination. Therefore, the application guidance would also apply to share-based payment transactions of the acquiree that the acquirer chooses not to replace and share-based payment transactions that the acquirer chooses to exchange for share-based payment transactions of the acquiree, even though they would not expire as a consequence of the business combination. Where the acquiree has outstanding share-based payment transactions that the acquirer does not exchange for its share-based payment transactions, the IASB proposes that those acquiree share-based payment transactions, if vested, are part of the non-controlling interest in the acquiree (see 3.9 3 below) and are measured at their fair value. If unvested, they are to be measured at their market-based measure as if the acquisition date were the grant date. The market-based measure of unvested share-based payment transactions is to be allocated to the non-controlling interest on the basis of the ratio of the portion of the vesting period completed to the total vesting period of the share-based payment transaction. The balance is to be allocated to post-combination service.[452] It is proposed that an entity applies the amendments for annual periods beginning on or after 1 July 2010. Earlier application is to be permitted, but if an entity applies the amendments for an earlier period it is to disclose that fact.[453]

3.8.3 Acquisition-related costs

An acquirer generally incurs various acquisition-related costs in connection with a business combination, including:

- direct costs of the transaction, such as (i) costs for the services of lawyers, investment bankers, accountants, and other third parties and (ii) costs to issue debt or equity instruments used to effect the business combination (i.e. issuance costs); and

- indirect costs of the transaction, such as recurring internal costs (e.g. the cost of maintaining an acquisition department).

Under the previous version of IFRS 3, payments made to third parties for services that were directly related to a business combination were included as part of the cost of the acquisition (see 2.4.4 above) and thus were included in the computation of goodwill. Debt issuance costs and the costs of registering and issuing equity securities were treated as a reduction of the proceeds of the debt or securities issued (see Chapter 31 at 5.1 and Chapter 32 at 2.3). The indirect costs of an acquisition were expensed in the period incurred.

In developing IFRS 3 (as revised in 2008), the IASB concluded that acquisition-related costs, whether for services performed by external parties or internal staff of the acquirer, are not part of the fair value exchange between the buyer and seller for the acquired business. Accordingly, they are not part of the consideration transferred for the acquiree. Rather, they are separate transactions in which the buyer makes payments in exchange for the services received. Consequently, under IFRS 3 (as revised in 2008), the acquirer accounts for acquisition-related costs separately from the business combination. The Board noted that acquisition-related costs generally do not represent assets of the acquirer at the acquisition date as they are consumed as the services are received.[454] Thus, with the exception of the costs of registering and issuing debt and securities that are recognised in accordance with IAS 32 and IAS 39, i.e. as a reduction of the proceeds of the debt or securities issued, IFRS 3 (as revised in 2008) requires that acquisition-related costs are to be accounted for as expenses in the periods in which the costs are incurred and the related services are received.[455]

In addition, in order to mitigate concerns about potential abuse, e.g. where a buyer might ask a seller to make payments to third parties on its behalf, but the consideration to be paid for the business is sufficient to reimburse the seller for making such payments, IFRS 3 (as revised in 2008) requires that a transaction that reimburses the acquiree or its former owners for paying the acquirer's acquisition-related costs is not to be included in applying the acquisition method (see 3.12.3 below).[456]

3.8.4 Business combinations achieved without the transfer of consideration

An acquirer sometimes obtains control of an acquiree without transferring consideration. IFRS 3 (as revised in 2008) indicates that such circumstances include:[457]

(a) the acquiree repurchases a sufficient number of its own shares for an existing investor (the acquirer) to obtain control;

(b) minority veto rights lapse that previously kept the acquirer from controlling an acquiree in which the acquirer held the majority voting rights; and

(c) the acquirer and the acquiree agree to combine their businesses by contract alone. In that case, the acquirer transfers no consideration in exchange for control of an acquiree and holds no equity interests in the acquiree, either on the acquisition date or previously. Examples of business combinations achieved by contract alone include bringing two businesses together in a stapling arrangement or forming a dual listed corporation.

The standard emphasises that the acquisition method applies to a business combination achieved without the transfer of consideration.[458] However, in computing the amount of goodwill in such a business combination, IFRS 3 (as revised in 2008) requires the acquirer to use the acquisition-date fair value of the acquirer's interest in the acquiree as the first item in part (a) of the goodwill computation set out at 3.7 above, instead of the acquisition-date fair value of the consideration transferred (which is nil).[459] The acquisition-date fair value of the acquirer's interest in the acquiree is to be determined using one or more valuation techniques that are appropriate in the circumstances and for which sufficient data is available. If more than one valuation technique is used, the acquirer should evaluate the results of the techniques, considering the relevance and reliability of the inputs used and the extent of the available data.[460]

In the first two circumstances described in (a) and (b) above, the acquirer has a previously-held equity interest in the acquiree. The computation of goodwill set out at 3.7 above would appear to suggest that the acquisition-date fair value of that previously-held interest would also be included as the third item in part (a) of the computation, but that would be clearly double-counting the value of the acquirer's interest in the acquiree. The acquisition-date fair value of the acquirer's interest in the acquiree should only be included once in the computation of goodwill. Nevertheless, it would appear that these two circumstances would also be examples of business combinations achieved in stages (see 3.10 below).

A   Business combinations by contract alone

In the third circumstance described above, that of a business combination achieved by contract alone, since the acquirer does not have an interest in the equity in the acquiree, it would appear that no amount is included for the first item in part (a) of the calculation of goodwill. However, in such a business combination, IFRS 3 (as revised in 2008) requires that the acquirer attributes to the owners of the acquiree the amount of the acquiree's net assets recognised under the standard (see 3.6 above). In other words, the equity interests in the acquiree held by parties other than the acquirer are a non-controlling interest in the acquirer's consolidated financial statements, even if it results in all of the equity interests in the acquiree being attributed to the non-controlling interest.[461] This might suggest that no goodwill is to be recognised in a business combination achieved by contract alone as the second item in part (a) will be equal to part (b) of the goodwill computation set out at 3.7 above. However, we believe that this requirement to attribute the equity interests in the acquiree to the non-controlling interest is emphasising the presentation within equity in the consolidated financial statements. Thus, where the option discussed at 3.9 below in measuring non-controlling interests in an acquiree at its acquisition-date fair value is chosen, goodwill would be recognised. If the option of measuring the non-controlling interest at its proportionate share of the value of net identifiable assets acquired is chosen, no goodwill would be recognised.

3.8.5   Combinations involving mutual entities

As indicated at 3.1.3 above, combinations involving mutual entities are within the scope of IFRS 3 (as revised in 2008) and the standard provides some guidance in applying its requirements when two mutual entities combine. A mutual entity is defined by IFRS 3 (as revised in 2008) as 'an entity, other than an investor-owned entity, that provides dividends, lower costs or other economic benefits directly to its owners, members or participants. For example, a mutual insurance company, a credit union and a co-operative entity are all mutual entities.'[462]

The standard notes that the fair value of the equity or member interests in the acquiree (or the fair value of the acquiree) may be more reliably measurable than the fair value of the member interests transferred by the acquirer. In that situation, the acquirer should determine the amount of goodwill by using the acquisition-date fair value of the acquiree's equity interests as the first item of part (a) of the goodwill computation set out at 3.7 above, instead of the acquirer's equity interests transferred as consideration.[463]

Some representatives of mutual entities suggested that the revised standard should permit an acquisition of a mutual entity to be reported as an increase in the retained earnings of the acquirer (combined entity) as had been previous practice. However, the IASB rejected this idea, concluding that business combinations of two investor-owned entities are economically similar to those of two mutual entities in which the acquirer issues members interests for all the member interests of the acquiree and should be similarly reported.[464] Accordingly, IFRS 3 (as revised in 2008) clarifies that the acquirer in a combination of mutual entities recognises the acquiree's net assets as a direct addition to capital or equity, not as an addition to retained earnings, which is consistent with the way other types of entity apply the acquisition method.[465]

IFRS 3 (as revised in 2008) recognises that mutual entities, although similar in many ways to other businesses, have distinct characteristics that arise primarily because their members are both customers and owners. Members of mutual entities generally expect to receive benefits for their membership, often in the form of reduced fees charged for goods and services or patronage dividends. The portion of such patronage dividends allocated to each member is often based on the amount of business the member did with the mutual entity during the year.[466]

The standard goes on to say that a fair value measurement of a mutual entity should include the assumptions that market participants would make about future member benefits as well as any other relevant assumptions market participants would make about the mutual entity. For example, where an estimated cash flow model is used to determine the fair value of the mutual entity, the cash flows used as inputs to the model should be based on the expected cash flows of the mutual entity, which are likely to reflect reductions for member benefits, such as reduced fees charged for goods and services.[467]

3.9　Recognising and measuring non-controlling interests in acquiree

The second item in part (a) of the goodwill computation set out at 3.7 above is the amount of any non-controlling interests in the acquiree.

IFRS 3 (as revised in 2008) requires any non-controlling interest in an acquiree to be recognised,[468] but provides a choice of two methods in measuring non-controlling interests arising in a business combination:

- Option 1, to measure the non-controlling interest at its acquisition-date fair value (consistent with the measurement principle for other components of the business combination)
- Option 2, to measure the non-controlling interest at the proportionate share of the value of net identifiable assets acquired (see 3.6 above).[469]

The choice of method is to be made for each business combination on a transaction-by-transaction basis, rather than being a policy choice, and will require management to carefully consider their future intentions about acquiring the non-controlling interest, as each option, combined with the revisions to accounting for changes in ownership interest of a subsidiary introduced in IAS 27 (as amended in 2008) (see Chapter 7 at 3.2.2) will potentially have a significant effect on the amount recognised for goodwill.

Under the previous version of IFRS 3, where the acquirer obtained less than a 100% interest in the acquiree, a minority interest in the acquiree was recognised reflecting the minority's proportion of the net identifiable assets, liabilities and contingent liabilities of the acquiree at their attributed fair values at the date of acquisition; no amount was included for any goodwill relating to the minority interest.

Under the June 2005 exposure draft, the IASB proposed that in a business combination in which the acquirer holds less than 100% of the equity interests in the acquiree at the acquisition date, the acquirer would recognise the acquiree, as a whole, and the assets acquired and liabilities assumed at the full amount of their fair values as of that date, regardless of the percentage ownership in the acquiree. The excess of the fair value of the business acquired over the net amount of the recognised identifiable assets acquired and liabilities assumed would be measured and recognised as goodwill. Thus, all of the goodwill of the acquired business, not only the acquirer's share, would be recognised under this 'full-goodwill' approach. The amount of goodwill would then be allocated to the controlling and non-controlling interests.[470]

In redeliberating the exposure draft, the Board observed that it had specified the mechanics of determining the reported amount of a non-controlling interest, but had not identified its measurement attribute. The result of those mechanics would have been that the non-controlling interest was effectively measured as the 'final residual' in a business combination. As goodwill is also measured as a residual, the Board concluded that it is undesirable to have two residual amounts in accounting for a business combination. Accordingly, it was concluded that, in principle, the non-controlling interest, like other components of the business combination, should be measured at fair value.[471] However, the IASB was unable to agree on a single measurement basis for non-controlling interests because neither of the alternatives (fair value or proportionate share of the acquiree's net identifiable assets) received sufficient Board support to enable a revised business combinations standard to be issued.[472]

3.9.1   Option 1 – Measuring non-controlling interest at acquisition-date fair value

Where this option is applied, IFRS 3 (as revised in 2008) states that an acquirer will sometimes be able to measure the acquisition-date fair value of a non-controlling interest on the basis of active market prices for equity shares not held by the acquirer. However, in other situations an active market price may not be available, so the acquirer will need to measure the fair value of the non-controlling interest by using other valuation techniques.[473]

The standard goes on to say that the fair value of the acquirer's interest in the acquiree and the non-controlling interest on a per-share basis might differ. This is likely to be because the consideration transferred by the acquirer will generally include a control premium, or conversely, the inclusion of a discount for lack of control (also referred to as a minority discount) in the per-share value of the non-controlling interest.[474] Therefore, it may not be appropriate to extrapolate the fair value of an acquirer's interest (i.e. the amount that the acquirer paid per share) to determine the fair value of the non-controlling interests.

3.9.2   Option 2 – Measuring non-controlling interest at the proportionate share of the value of net identifiable assets acquired

Under this option, the non-controlling interest is measured at the share of the value of the net assets acquired and liabilities assumed of the acquiree (see 3.6 above), consistent with the requirements of the previous version of IFRS 3. The result is that the amount recognised for goodwill is the equivalent of only the acquirer's share, as is the case under the previous version of IFRS 3. However, where the outstanding non-controlling interest is subsequently acquired, no additional goodwill is recorded since under IAS 27 (as amended in 2008) this is an equity transaction (see Chapter 7 at 3.2.2).

3.9.3   Implications of method chosen for measuring non-controlling interest

The following example illustrates the impact of these options.

Example 9.43:   Measurement of non-controlling interests

Entity B has 40% of its shares publicly traded on an exchange. Entity A purchases the 60% non-publicly traded shares in one transaction, paying €630. Based on the trading price of the shares of Entity B at the date of gaining control a value of €400 is assigned to the 40% non-controlling interest, indicating that Entity A has paid a control premium of €30. The fair value of Entity B's identifiable net assets is €700.

Option 1

Entity A accounts for the acquisition as follows:

	€	€
Fair value of identifiable net assets acquired	700	
Goodwill	330	
Cash		630
Non-controlling interest in entity B		400

Option 2

Entity A accounts for the acquisition as follows:

	€	€
Fair value of identifiable net assets acquired	700	
Goodwill	210	
Cash		630
Non-controlling interest in entity B (€700 × 40%)		280

The IASB has noted that there are likely to be three main differences arising from measuring the non-controlling interest at its proportionate share of the acquiree's net identifiable assets, rather than at fair value. First, the amounts recognised in a business combination for the non-controlling interest and goodwill are likely to be lower (as illustrated in the above example).

Second, if a cash generating unit to which the goodwill has been allocated is subsequently impaired, any resulting impairment of goodwill recognised through income is likely to be lower than it would have been if the non-controlling interest had been measured at fair value. The IASB states that it will not affect the impairment loss attributable to the controlling interest.[475]

The third difference noted by the IASB is that which arises if the acquirer subsequently purchases some or all of the shares held by the non-controlling shareholders. Under IAS 27 (as amended in 2008), such a transaction is to be accounted for as an equity transaction (see Chapter 7 at 3.2.2). By acquiring the non-controlling interest, presumably at fair value, the equity of the group is reduced by the non-controlling interest's share of any unrecognised changes in fair value of the net assets of the business, including goodwill. By measuring the non-controlling interest initially as a proportionate share of the acquiree's net identifiable assets, rather than at fair value, the reduction in the reported equity attributable to the acquirer is likely to be larger.[476] If in Example 9.43 above, Entity A were to subsequently acquire all of the non-controlling interest for, say, €500, then assuming that there had been no changes in the carrying amounts for the net identifiable assets and the goodwill, the equity attributable to the parent, Entity A, would be reduced by €220 (€500 – €280) if option 2 had been adopted, whereas the reduction would only be €100 (€500 – €400) if option 1 had been adopted.

IFRS 3 (as revised in 2008) defines non-controlling interest as 'the equity in a subsidiary not attributable, directly or indirectly, to a parent'.[477] This is the same as that in IAS 27 (as amended in 2008). As discussed in Chapter 7 at 4.1.2, this definition includes not only equity shares in the subsidiary held by other parties, but also other elements of 'equity' in the subsidiary that relates to, say, other equity instruments such as options or warrants, the equity element of convertible debt instruments, and the 'equity' related to share-based payment awards held by parties other than the parent. Where option 1 above is adopted, such non-controlling interests should be included at their acquisition-date fair value. However, where option 2 is adopted, to the extent that the rights held by these parties are not considered to represent present ownership rights, it would appear that they should be included at nil as they are not entitled to a 'share' of the acquiree's identifiable net assets.

At its meeting in June 2009, the IFRIC considered whether the option to measure non-controlling interests at the proportionate share of the value of net identifiable assets acquired is adopted should be applied to such other elements of 'equity' in the subsidiary. The IFRIC concluded that the measurement choice should apply only to instruments currently entitled to a proportionate share of the acquiree's net assets. However, because IFRSs do not provide sufficient guidance to resolve this issue an amendment to IFRS 3 (as revised in 2008) is required.[478]

Consequently, the IASB has decided to deal with this issue within the exposure draft of proposed *Improvements to IFRSs* issued in August 2009. The IASB proposes to amend paragraph 19 of IFRS 3 (as revised in 2008) to clarify that the choice of measuring non-controlling interest either at fair value or at the non-controlling interest's proportionate share of the acquiree's identifiable net assets applies only to instruments that are currently entitled to a proportionate share of the acquiree's net assets. Other instruments that meet the definition of non-controlling interest should be measured at fair value or in accordance with applicable IFRSs.[479] It is proposed that paragraph 19 is amended to say:

'For each business combination, the acquirer shall measure any non-controlling interest in the acquiree at either fair value or other measurement basis as required by IFRSs, except for the components of non-controlling interest that are present ownership instruments and entitle their holders to a pro rata share of the entity's net assets in the event of liquidation. The acquirer shall measure those components of non-controlling interest either at fair value or at the present ownership instruments' proportionate share of the acquiree's identifiable net assets.'[480]

It is proposed that an entity applies the amendments for annual periods beginning on or after 1 July 2010. Earlier application is to be permitted, but if an entity applies the amendments for an earlier period it is to disclose that fact.[481]

Example 7.17 in Chapter 7 at 4.1.3 illustrates the treatment of such other elements of 'equity' in a subsidiary under the existing options and that proposed by the IASB.

At an earlier meeting in May 2009, the IASB considered a number of issues brought by the IASB staff, but deferred them to the post-implementation review of IFRS 3 (as revised in 2008) and IAS 27 (as amended in 2008), to be conducted two years after their effective date. One of these issues related to the application of the definition of non-controlling interest to equity instruments other than shares (for example, share options) and the measurement of those instruments.[482] Although the IASB has stated that this issue has been deferred, this is presumably in relation to IAS 27 (as amended in 2008) generally. It is clear from the proposals in respect of such instruments in the context of IFRS 3 (as revised in 2008) that the IASB regards them as non-controlling interests that should be measured at their acquisition-date fair value (or at a market-based measure for unvested share-based payment transactions – see 3.8.2 above) in accounting for a business combination.

3.9.4   Call and put options over non-controlling interests

In some business combinations where less than 100% of the equity shares are acquired, it may be that the transaction also involves options over some or all of the outstanding shares held by the non-controlling shareholders. It may that the acquirer has a call option, i.e. a right to acquire the outstanding shares at a future date for cash at a particular price. Alternatively, it may be that the acquirer has granted a put option to the other shareholders whereby they have the right to sell their shares to the acquirer at a future date for cash at a particular price. Indeed in some cases, there may be a combination of such call and put options, the terms of which may be equivalent or may be different.

IFRS 3 (as revised in 2008) gives no guidance as to how such options should impact on the accounting for a business combination. This issue is discussed in Chapter 7 at 5.

3.10   Business combinations achieved in stages ('step acquisitions')

The third item in part (a) of the goodwill computation set out at 3.7 above is the acquisition-date fair value of the acquirer's previously held equity interest in the acquiree.

An acquirer sometimes obtains control of an acquiree in which it held an equity interest immediately before the acquisition date. For example, on 31 December 2010, Entity A holds a 35 per cent non-controlling equity interest in Entity B. On that date, Entity A purchases an additional 40 per cent interest in Entity B, which gives it control of Entity B. IFRS 3 (as revised in 2008) refers to such a transaction as a business combination achieved in stages, sometimes also referred to as a 'step acquisition'.[483]

Under the previous version of IFRS 3, an acquirer was required to treat each exchange transaction separately for the purpose of measuring goodwill. This resulted in a step-by-step comparison of the cost of the individual investments with the acquirer's interest in the net fair value of the acquiree's identifiable assets and liabilities at each step – see 2.9 above.

IFRS 3 (as revised in 2008) takes a completely different approach in accounting for step acquisitions. It requires that, if the acquirer holds a non-controlling equity investment in the acquiree immediately before obtaining control, the acquirer remeasures that previously held equity investment at its acquisition-date fair value and recognises any resulting gain or loss in profit or loss.[484] The Board has concluded that a change from holding a non-controlling equity investment in an entity to obtaining control of that entity is a significant change in the nature of and economic circumstances surrounding that investment. That change warrants a change in the investment's classification and measurement. Once it obtains control, the acquirer is no longer the owner of a non-controlling investment asset in the acquiree. In effect, the acquirer exchanges its status as an owner of an investment asset in an entity for a controlling financial interest in all of the underlying assets and liabilities of that entity (acquiree) and the right to direct how the acquiree and its management use those assets in its operations.[485]

In addition to recognising the above gain or loss, IFRS 3 (as revised in 2008) requires that if the acquirer had recognised changes in the value of its equity interest in the acquiree in other comprehensive income (i.e. the investment was classified as available-for-sale in accordance with IAS 39), the amount so recognised is to be recognised on the same basis that would be required if the acquirer had directly disposed of the previously held equity investment, i.e. the amount at the acquisition date is reclassified into profit or loss.[486]

The acquirer's non-controlling equity investment in the acquiree prior to obtaining control, after remeasurement to its acquisition-date fair value, would then be included as the third item of part (a) of the goodwill computation set out at 3.7 above.

These requirements are illustrated in the following examples. These are based on the same fact patterns as Examples 9.23 and 9.24 at 2.9 above that illustrate the requirements of the previous version of IFRS 3, thereby allowing comparison of the different treatments.

Example 9.44:   *Business combination achieved in stages – original investment treated as an available-for-sale investment under IAS 39*

Investor acquires a 20 per cent ownership interest in Investee (a service company) on 1 January 2008 for £3,500,000 cash. At that date, the fair value of Investee's identifiable assets is £10,000,000, and the carrying amount of those assets is £8,000,000. Investee has no liabilities or contingent liabilities at that date. The following shows Investee's balance sheet at 1 January 2008 together with the fair values of the identifiable assets:

Investee's balance sheet at 1 January 2008	Carrying amounts £'000	Fair values £'000
Cash and receivables	2,000	2,000
Land	6,000	8,000
	8,000	10,000
Issued equity: 1,000,000 ordinary shares	5,000	
Retained earnings	3,000	
	8,000	

During the year ended 31 December 2008, Investee reports a profit of £6,000,000 but does not pay any dividends. In addition, the fair value of Investee's land increases by £3,000,000 to £11,000,000. However, the amount recognised by Investee in respect of the land remains unchanged at £6,000,000. The following shows Investee's balance sheet at 31 December 2008 together with the fair values of the identifiable assets:

Investee's balance sheet at 31 December 2008	Carrying amounts £'000	Fair values £'000
Cash and receivables	8,000	8,000
Land	6,000	11,000
	14,000	19,000
Issued equity: 1,000,000 ordinary shares	5,000	
Retained earnings	9,000	
	14,000	

On 1 January 2009, Investor acquires a further 60 per cent ownership interest in Investee for £22,000,000 cash, thereby obtaining control. Before obtaining control, Investor does not have significant influence over Investee, and accounts for its initial 20 per cent investment at fair value with changes in value recognised as a component of other comprehensive income. Investee's ordinary shares have a quoted market price at 31 December 2008 of £30 per share.

Throughout the period 1 January 2008 to 1 January 2009, Investor's issued equity was £30,000,000. Investor's only asset apart from its investment in Investee is cash.

Accounting for the initial investment before obtaining control

Investor's initial 20 per cent investment in Investee is measured at its cost of £3,500,000. However, Investee's 1,000,000 ordinary shares have a quoted market price at 31 December 2008 of £30 per share. Therefore, the carrying amount of Investor's initial 20 per cent investment is remeasured in Investor's financial statements to £6,000,000 at 31 December 2008, with the £2,500,000 increase recognised as a component of other comprehensive income. Therefore, Investor's balance sheet at 31 December 2008, before the acquisition of the additional 60 per cent ownership interest, is as follows:

Investor's balance sheet at 31 December 2008	£'000
Cash	26,500
Investment in Investee	6,000
	32,500
Issued equity	30,000
Gain on available-for-sale investment	2,500
	32,500

Accounting for the business combination

Assuming Investor adopts option 2 for measuring the non-controlling interest in Investee, i.e. at the proportionate share of the value of the net identifiable assets acquired, it recognises the following amount for goodwill in its consolidated financial statements based on the computation set out at 3.7 above:

	£'000
Consideration transferred for 60% interest acquired on 1 January 2009	22,000
Non-controlling interest – share of fair values at that date (20% × £19,000,000)	3,800
Acquisition-date fair value of initial 20% interest	6,000
	31,800
Acquisition-date fair values of identifiable assets acquired	19,000
Goodwill	12,800

The following shows Investor's consolidation worksheet immediately after the acquisition of the additional 60 per cent ownership interest in Investee, together with consolidation adjustments and associated explanations:

	Investor	Investee	Consolidation adjustments		Consolidated	
			Dr	Cr		
	£'000	£'000	£'000	£'000	£'000	
Cash and receivables	4,500	8,000			12,500	
Investment in investee	28,000	–		28,000 (3)	–	
Land		6,000	5,000 (1)		11,000	(a)
Goodwill			12,800 (3)		12,800	(b)
	32,500	14,000			36,300	
Issued equity	30,000	5,000	4,000 (3)		30,000	(c)
			1,000 (4)			
Asset revaluation surplus			4,000 (3)	5,000 (1)	–	(d)
			1,000 (4)			
Gain on available-for-sale investment	2,500		2,500 (2)		–	(f)
Retained earnings		9,000	7,200 (3)		–	(e)
			1,800 (4)			(f)
Profit for 2009				2,500 (2)	2,500	(f)
Non-controlling interest				3,800 (4)	3,800	(a)
	32,500	14,000			36,300	

Consolidation Adjustments

		£'000	£'000
(1)	Land	5,000	
	Asset revaluation surplus		5,000

To recognise Investee's identifiable assets at fair values at the acquisition date

		£'000	£'000
(2)	Gain on available-for-sale investment	2,500	
	Profit for year		2,500

To reclassify to profit for year the existing gain in other comprehensive income relating to the previously held 20% interest in Investee.

		£'000	£'000
(3)	Issued equity [80% × 5,000,000]	4,000	
	Asset revaluation surplus [80% × 5,000,000]	4,000	
	Retained earnings [80% × 9,000,000]	7,200	
	Goodwill	12,800	
	Investment in investee		28,000

To recognise goodwill on obtaining control over Investee and record the elimination of Investor's investment against associated equity balances

		£'000	£'000
(4)	Issued equity [20% × 5,000,000]	1,000	
	Asset revaluation surplus [20% × 5,000,000]	1,000	
	Retained earnings [20% × 9,000,000]	1,800	
	Non-controlling interest (in issued equity)		1,000
	Non-controlling interest (in asset revaluation surplus)		1,000
	Non-controlling interest (in retained earnings)		1,800

To recognise the non-controlling interest in the Investee

Notes

The above consolidation adjustments result in:

(a) Investee's identifiable net assets being stated at their full fair values at the date Investor obtains control of Investee, i.e. £19,000,000. This means that the 20 per cent non-controlling interest in Investee also is stated at the non-controlling interest's 20 per cent share of the fair values of Investee's identifiable net assets.

(b) goodwill being recognised from the acquisition date based on the computation set out at 3.7 above.

(c) issued equity of £30,000,000 comprising the issued equity of Investor of£30,000,000.

(d) an asset revaluation surplus of £nil as Investor's share of the increase in the fair value of Investee's identifiable net assets at the acquisition date represents pre-acquisition profits.

(e) a retained earnings balance of £nil as Investor's share thereof represents pre-acquisition profits.

(f) profit of £2,500 being the amount reclassified from other comprehensive income relating to the previously held investment in Acquiree on the step acquisition. As a result, total retained earnings in the balance sheet are £2,500.

If the investor in the above example had accounted for its original investment of 20% as an associate using the equity method under IAS 28, then the accounting would have been as follows:

Example 9.45:   Business combination achieved in stages – original investment treated as an associate under IAS 28

This example uses the same facts as in Example 9.44 above, except that Investor does have significant influence over Investee following its initial 20 per cent investment.

Accounting for the initial investment before obtaining control

Investor's initial 20 per cent investment in Investee is included in Investor's consolidated financial statements under the equity method (see Chapter 11 at 3). Accordingly, it is initially recognised at its cost of £3,500,000 and adjusted thereafter for its share of the profits of Investee after the date of acquisition of £1,200,000 (being 20% × £6,000,000). Investor's policy for property, plant and equipment is to use the cost model under IAS 16 (see Chapter 16 at 4), therefore in applying the equity method it does not include its share of the increased value of the land held by Investee. IAS 28 requires that on the acquisition of an associate, any difference between the cost of the acquisition and its share of the fair values of the associate's identifiable assets and liabilities is accounted for as goodwill, but is included within the carrying amount of the investment in the associate. Accordingly, Investor has included goodwill of £1,500,000 arising on its original investment of 20%, being £3,500,000 less £2,000,000 (20% × £10,000,000). Therefore, Investor's consolidated balance sheet at 31 December 2008, before the acquisition of the additional 60 per cent ownership interest, is as follows:

Investor's consolidated balance sheet at 31 December 2008	£'000
Cash	26,500
Investment in associate	4,700
	31,200
Issued equity	30,000
Retained earnings	1,200
	31,200

In its separate financial statements, Investor includes its investment in the associate at its cost of £3,500,000.

Accounting for the business combination

Although Investor has previously equity accounted for its previously held 20% interest in Investee (and calculated goodwill on that acquisition), the computation of goodwill in its consolidated financial statements as a result of obtaining control over Investee is the same as that in Example 9.44 above:

	£'000
Consideration transferred for 60% interest acquired on 1 January 2009	22,000
Non-controlling interest – share of fair values at that date (20% × £19,000,000)	3,800
Acquisition-date fair value of initial 20% interest	6,000
	31,800
Acquisition-date fair values of identifiable assets acquired	19,000
Goodwill	12,800

The following shows Investor's consolidation worksheet immediately after the acquisition of the additional 60 per cent ownership interest in Investee, together with consolidation adjustments and associated explanations.

	Investor	Investee	Consolidation adjustments		Consolidated	
			Dr	Cr		
	£'000	£'000	£'000	£'000	£'000	
Cash and receivables	4,500	8,000			12,500	
Investment in investee	25,500	–	1,200 (2)	28,000 (3)	–	
			1,300 (2)			
Land		6,000	5,000 (1)		11,000	(a)
Goodwill			12,800 (4)		12,800	(b)
	30,000	14,000			36,300	
Issued equity	30,000	5,000	4,000 (3)		30,000	(c)
			1,000 (4)			
Asset revaluation surplus			4,000 (3)	5,000 (1)	–	(d)
			1,000 (4)			
Retained earnings		9,000	7,200 (3)	1,200 (2)	1,200	(f)
			1,800 (4)			
Profit for 2009				1,300 (2)	1,300	(f)
Non-controlling interest				3,800 (4)	3,800	(a)
	30,000	14,000			36,300	

The consolidation adjustments are exactly the same as in Example 9.44, except for adjustment (2) where 2 journals are required, being:

		£'000	£'000
(2)	Investment in investee	1,200	
	Retained earnings		1,200

To reflect the retained earnings balance that has already been reflected in the consolidated balance sheet of Investor at 31 December 2007 as a result of equity accounting for Investee while it was an associate.

	Investment in investee	1,300	
	Profit for year		1,300

To remeasure the investment in the associate from its equity-accounted amount of £4,700,000 to its acquisition-date fair value of £6,000,000 and recognising the resulting gain in profit for year.

The notes in Example 9.44 also apply to this example. The only difference is that the cumulative amount of retained earnings balance is made up of the 2 amounts in adjustment (2) above, rather than the reclassified amount of £2,500,000.

Although the Examples above illustrate the requirements of IFRS 3 (as revised in 2008) when the previously held investment has been accounted for as an available-for-sale investment or as an associate, the requirements in IFRS 3 (as revised in 2008) for step acquisitions apply to all previously held non-controlling equity investments in the acquiree, including those that were accounted for as jointly controlled entities under IAS 31.[487]

3.11   Bargain purchase transactions

The IASB considers bargain purchases anomalous transactions – business entities and their owners generally do not knowingly and willingly sell assets or businesses at prices below their fair values.[488] Nevertheless, occasionally, an acquirer will make a bargain purchase. As indicated at 3.7 above, IFRS 3 (as revised in 2008) regards a bargain purchase as being a business combination in which the amount specified in paragraph 32(b) exceeds the aggregate of the amounts specified in paragraph 32(a) of the standard, i.e.

- the net of the acquisition-date fair values (or other amounts recognised in accordance with the requirements of the standard) of the identifiable assets acquired and the liabilities assumed, exceeds

- the aggregate of:
  - the consideration transferred (generally measured at acquisition-date fair value);
  - the amount of any non-controlling interest in the acquiree; and
  - the acquisition-date fair value of the acquirer's previously held equity interest in the acquiree.[489]

A bargain purchase might happen, for example, in a business combination that is a forced sale in which the seller is acting under compulsion.[490] Circumstances in which they occur include a forced liquidation or distress sale (e.g. after the death of a founder or key manager) in which owners need to sell a business quickly. The IASB observed that an economic gain is inherent in a bargain purchase and concluded that, in concept, the acquirer should recognise that gain at the acquisition date. However, the Board acknowledged that sometimes there may not be clear evidence that a bargain purchase has taken place, and shared constituents' concerns about the potential for inappropriate gain recognition resulting from measurement bias or undetected measurement errors.[491]

Accordingly, IFRS 3 (as revised in 2008) requires that before recognising a gain on a bargain purchase, the acquirer should reassess all components of the computation. It should reassess whether it has correctly identified all of the assets acquired and all of the liabilities assumed and is to recognise any additional assets or liabilities that are identified in that review. The acquirer is then to review the procedures used to measure the amounts the standard requires to be recognised at the acquisition date for all of the following:

(a)   the identifiable assets acquired and liabilities assumed;

(b)   the non-controlling interest in the acquiree, if any;

(c)   for a business combination achieved in stages, the acquirer's previously held equity interest in the acquiree; and

(d)   the consideration transferred.

The objective of the review is to ensure that the measurements appropriately reflect consideration of all available information as of the acquisition date.[492]

Having undertaken that review (and made any necessary revisions), if an excess remains, a gain is to be recognised in profit or loss on the acquisition date. All of the gain is attributed to the acquirer.[493] The IASB has acknowledged that the required review might be insufficient to eliminate concerns about unintentional measurement bias, but considers that by limiting the measurement of the gain in the way that it is calculated will mitigate the potential for inappropriate gain recognition. The computation means that a gain on a bargain purchase and goodwill cannot both be recognised for the same business combination.[494]

IFRS 3 (as revised in 2008) acknowledges that the recognition and measurement exceptions for particular items (see 3.6.6 above), principally the requirements to measure particular assets acquired or liabilities assumed in accordance with other IFRSs, rather than their acquisition-date fair value, may result in recognising a gain (or change the amount of a recognised gain) on a bargain purchase this is not really a bargain purchase but a so-called negative goodwill result. However, it considers that in most situations this is a remote possibility.[495]

The computation of a gain on a bargain purchase is illustrated in the following example, which is based on one included within the Illustrative Examples accompanying IFRS 3 (as revised in 2008).[496]

Example 9.46:   Gain on a bargain purchase (1)

On 1 January 2010 Entity A acquires 80% of the equity interests of Entity B, a private entity, in exchange for cash of €150m. Because the former owners of Entity B needed to dispose of their investments in Entity B by a specified date, they did not have sufficient time to market Entity B to multiple potential buyers. The management of Entity A initially measures the separately recognisable identifiable assets acquired and the liabilities assumed as of the acquisition date in accordance with the requirements of IFRS 3 (as revised in 2008). The identifiable assets are measured at €250m and the liabilities assumed are measured at €50m. Entity A engages an independent consultant, who determines that the fair value of the 20% non-controlling interest in Entity B is €42m.

The amount of Entity B's identifiable net assets of €200m (being €250m – €50m) exceeds the fair value of the consideration transferred plus the fair value of the non-controlling interest in Entity B. Therefore, Entity A reviews the procedures it used to identify and measure the assets acquired and liabilities assumed and to measure the fair value of both the non-controlling interest in Entity B and the consideration transferred. After that review, Entity A decides that the procedures and resulting measures were appropriate. Entity A measures the gain on its purchase of the 80% interest as follows:

	€m	€m
Amount of the identifiable net assets acquired (€250m – €50m)		200
Less:		
Fair value of the consideration transferred for Entity A's 80% interest	150	
Fair value of non-controlling interest in Entity B	42	
		192
Gain on bargain purchase of 80% interest in Entity B		8

Entity A would record its acquisition of Entity B in its consolidated financial statements as follows:

	€m	€m
Identifiable assets acquired	250	
Cash		150
Liabilities assumed		50
Gain on bargain purchase		8
Equity – non-controlling interest in Entity B		42

If Entity A chose to measure the non-controlling interest in Entity B on the basis of its proportionate interest in the identifiable net assets of the acquiree, the gain on the purchase of the 80% interest would have been as follows:

	€m	€m
Amount of the identifiable net assets acquired (€250m – €50m)		200
Less:		
Fair value of the consideration transferred for Entity A's 80% interest	150	
Non-controlling interest in Entity B (20% × €200m)	40	
		190
Gain on bargain purchase of 80% interest in Entity B		10

On that basis, Entity A would record its acquisition of Entity B in its consolidated financial statements as follows:

	€m	€m
Identifiable assets acquired	250	
Cash		150
Liabilities assumed		50
Gain on bargain purchase		10
Equity – non-controlling interest in Entity B		40

It can be seen from the above example that the amount of the gain recognised is affected by the way in which the non-controlling interest is measured. Indeed, it might be that if the non-controlling interest is measured at its acquisition-date fair value, goodwill is recognised rather than a gain as shown below.

Example 9.47:   Gain on a bargain purchase (2)

This example uses the same facts as in Example 9.46 above, except that the independent consultant, determines that the fair value of the 20% non-controlling interest in Entity B is €52m.

In this situation, the fair value of the consideration transferred plus the fair value of the non-controlling interest in Entity B exceeds the amount of the identifiable net assets acquired, giving rise to goodwill on the acquisition as follows:

	€m
Fair value of the consideration transferred for Entity A's 80% interest	150
Fair value of non-controlling interest in Entity B	52
	202
Less: Amount of the identifiable net assets acquired (€250m – €50m)	200
Goodwill on acquisition of 80% interest in Entity B	2

So, although Entity A in the above example might have made a 'bargain purchase', the requirements of IFRS 3 (as revised in 2008) lead to no gain being recognised. If

Entity A wished to record a gain on the bargain purchase, it would need to choose the option to measure the non-controlling interest at its proportionate interest in the identifiable net assets of the acquiree, i.e. €40m, as shown in Example 9.46 above.

3.12 Assessing what is part of the exchange for the acquiree

The previous version of IFRS 3 had no specific guidance on accounting for pre-existing relationships between an acquirer and an acquiree (although, as discussed at 2.5.6 above, in our view such relationships should have been accounted for separately from the business combination). Similarly, the previous version of IFRS 3 did not distinguish between contingent consideration that, in substance, is part of the cost of the business combination and contingent consideration that, in substance represents compensation for future services (although as discussed at 2.4.5 B above, we believe that such a distinction should have been made). These are issues that are now explicitly addressed in IFRS 3 (as revised in 2008).

As indicated at 3.6.2 above, to be included in the accounting for the business combination, the identifiable assets acquired and liabilities assumed must be part of the exchange for the acquiree, rather than as a result of separate transactions.[497]

IFRS 3 (as revised in 2008) recognises that the acquirer and the acquiree may have a pre-existing relationship or other arrangement before the negotiations for the business combination, or they may enter into an arrangement during the negotiations that is separate from the business combination. In either situation, the acquirer is required to identify any amounts that are separate from the business combination and thus are not part of what the acquirer and the acquiree (or its former owners) exchanged in the business combination, that is, amounts that are not part of the exchange for the acquiree. Accordingly, the acquirer has to assess if any assets acquired, liabilities assumed, or portions of the consideration transferred for the acquiree are not part of the exchange for the acquiree to be included in applying the acquisition method, but should instead be accounted for as separate transactions in accordance with relevant IFRSs.[498] This requires the acquirer to evaluate the substance of transactions entered into by the parties to determine whether they were entered into by or on behalf of the acquirer or designed primarily for the economic benefit of the acquirer or the combined entity, rather than primarily for the economic benefit of the acquiree (or its former owners) before the transaction. The former are not part of the business combination transaction, and are likely to be accounted for as separate transactions.[499]

The standard requires that the acquirer should consider the following factors, which are neither mutually exclusive nor individually conclusive, to determine whether a transaction is part of the exchange for the acquiree or whether the transaction is separate from the business combination:[500]

- *The reasons for the transaction*

  Understanding the reasons why the parties to the combination (the acquirer and the acquiree and their owners, directors and managers – and their agents) entered into a particular transaction or arrangement may provide insight into whether it is part of the consideration transferred and the assets acquired or liabilities assumed. For example, if a transaction is arranged primarily for the benefit of the acquirer or the combined entity rather than primarily for the benefit of the acquiree or its former owners before the combination, that portion of the transaction price paid (and any related assets or liabilities) is less likely to be part of the exchange for the acquiree. Accordingly, the acquirer would account for that portion separately from the business combination;

- *Who initiated the transaction*

  Understanding who initiated the transaction may also provide insight into whether it is part of the exchange for the acquiree. For example, a transaction or other event that is initiated by the acquirer may be entered into for the purpose of providing future economic benefits to the acquirer or combined entity with little or no benefit received by the acquiree or its former owners before the combination. On the other hand, a transaction or arrangement initiated by the acquiree or its former owners is less likely to be for the benefit of the acquirer or the combined entity and more likely to be part of the business combination transaction;

- *The timing of the transaction*

  The timing of the transaction may also provide insight into whether it is part of the exchange for the acquiree. For example, a transaction between the acquirer and the acquiree that takes place during the negotiations of the terms of a business combination may have been entered into in contemplation of the business combination to provide future economic benefits to the acquirer or the combined entity. If so, the acquiree or its former owners before the business combination are likely to receive little or no benefit from the transaction except for benefits they receive as part of the combined entity.

Examples of transactions that IFRS 3 (as revised in 2008) regards as substantively separate that should not be considered part of the exchange for the acquiree are as follows:[501]

- A transaction that effectively settles pre-existing relationships between the acquirer and acquiree. For example, a lawsuit, supply contract, franchising or licensing arrangement;

- A transaction that remunerates employees or former owners of the acquiree for future services;

- A transaction that reimburses the acquiree or its former owners for paying the acquirer's acquisition-related costs.

Application guidance provided in IFRS 3 (as revised in 2008) in respect of these transactions is discussed at 3.12.1 to 3.12.3 below.

As indicated above, the acquirer and the acquiree may enter into an arrangement during the negotiations that is separate from the business combination, and which should be accounted for as a separate transaction in accordance with the relevant IFRS, rather than as part of the business combination transaction. One particular area that may be negotiated could be a restructuring plan relating to the activities of the acquiree. This is discussed at 3.12.4 below.

3.12.1 *Effective settlement of pre-existing relationships*

The first example is where the acquirer and acquiree may have a relationship that existed before they contemplated the business combination, referred to as a 'pre-existing relationship'. Such a relationship between the acquirer and acquiree may be contractual (for example, vendor and customer or licensor and licensee) or non-contractual (for example, plaintiff and defendant).[502]

The Basis for Conclusions accompanying IFRS 3 (as revised in 2008) explains that this first example is directed at ensuring that a transaction that in effect settles a pre-existing relationship between the acquirer and the acquiree is excluded from the accounting for the business combination. Assume, for example, that a potential acquiree has an asset (receivable) for an unresolved claim against the potential acquirer. The acquirer and the acquiree's owners agree to settle that claim as part of an agreement to sell the acquiree to the acquirer. It was concluded that if the acquirer makes a lump sum payment to the seller-owner, part of that payment is to settle the claim and is not part of the consideration transferred to acquire the business. Thus, the portion of the payment that relates to the claim settlement should be excluded from the accounting for the business combination and accounted for separately. In effect, the acquiree relinquished its claim (receivable) against the acquirer by transferring it (as a dividend) to the acquiree's owner. Thus, at the acquisition date the acquiree has no receivable (asset) to be acquired as part of the combination, and the acquirer would account for its settlement payment separately.[503]

IFRS 3 (as revised in 2008) requires that if the business combination results in the effective settlement of a pre-existing relationship, the acquirer is to recognise a gain or a loss, measured on the following bases.

For a pre-existing non-contractual relationship, such as a lawsuit, the gain or loss is measured at its fair value. For a pre-existing contractual relationship, such as a supply contract, the gain or loss is measured as the lesser of:

(a) the amount by which the contract is favourable or unfavourable from the perspective of the acquirer when compared with terms for current market transactions for the same or similar terms. (It is emphasised that an unfavourable contract is a contract that is unfavourable in terms of current market terms. It is not necessarily an onerous contract in which the unavoidable costs of meeting the obligations under the contract exceed the economic benefits expected to be received under it.); and

(b) the amount of any stated settlement provisions in the contract available to the counterparty to whom the contract is unfavourable.

If (b) is less than (a), the difference is included as part of the business combination accounting.

The Application guidance notes, however, that the amount of gain or loss recognised may depend in part on whether the acquirer had previously recognised a related asset or liability, and the reported gain or loss therefore may differ from the amount calculated by applying the above requirements.[504]

The requirements for contractual relationships are illustrated in the following example.[505]

Example 9.48:   Settlement of pre-existing contractual relationship

Entity A purchases electronic components from Entity B under a five-year supply contract at fixed rates. Currently, the fixed rates are higher than the rates at which Entity A could purchase similar electronic components from another supplier. The supply contract allows Entity A to terminate the contract before the end of the initial five-year term but only by paying a €6m penalty. With three years remaining under the supply contract, Entity A pays €50m to acquire Entity B, which is the fair value of Entity B based on what other market participants would be willing to pay.

Included in the total fair value of Entity B is €8m related to the fair value of the supply contract with Entity A. The €8m represents a €3m component that is 'at market' because the pricing is comparable to pricing for current market transactions for the same or similar items (selling effort, customer relationships and so on) and a €5 million component for pricing that is unfavourable to Entity A because it exceeds the price of current market transactions for similar items. Entity B has no other identifiable assets or liabilities related to the supply contract, and Entity A has not recognised any assets or liabilities related to the supply contract before the business combination.

In this example, Entity A calculates a loss of €5m (the lesser of the €6m stated settlement amount and the amount by which the contract is unfavourable to the acquirer) separately from the business combination. The €3m 'at-market' component of the contract is part of goodwill.

Whether Entity A had recognised previously an amount in its financial statements related to a pre-existing relationship will affect the amount recognised as a gain or loss for the effective settlement of the relationship. Suppose that IFRSs had required Entity A to recognise a €6m liability for the supply contract before the business combination. In that situation, Entity A recognises a €1m settlement gain on the contract in profit or loss at the acquisition date (the €5m measured loss on the contract less the €6m loss previously recognised). In other words, Entity A has in effect settled a recognised liability of €6m for €5m, resulting in a gain of €1m.

A pre-existing relationship may be a contract that the acquirer recognises as a reacquired right. As indicated at 3.6.6 E above, if the contract includes terms that are favourable or unfavourable when compared with pricing for current market transactions for the same or similar items, the acquirer recognises, separately from the business combination, a gain or loss for the effective settlement of the contract, measured in accordance with requirements described above.[506]

3.12.2 Remuneration for future services of employees or former owners of the acquiree

The second example is where a transaction remunerates employees or former owners of the acquiree for future services. The Basis for Conclusions accompanying IFRS 3 (as revised in 2008) explains that this example is directed at ensuring that payments that are not part of the consideration transferred for the acquiree are excluded from the business combination accounting. Instead, the payments should be accounted for separately.[507] Additional application guidance is given that deal with this aspect of the requirement in the standard.

A   Arrangements for contingent payments to employees (or selling shareholders)

The first area that is dealt with is arrangements for contingent payments to employees (or selling shareholders). Whether arrangement for contingent payments to employees (or selling shareholders) are contingent consideration to be included in the measure of the consideration transferred (see 3.8.1 above) or are separate transactions will depend on the nature of the arrangements. Understanding the reasons why the acquisition agreement includes a provision for contingent payments, who initiated the arrangement and when the parties entered into the arrangement may be helpful in assessing the nature of the arrangement.[508]

If it is not clear whether the arrangement for payments to employees (or selling shareholders) is part of the exchange for the acquiree or is a transaction separate from the business combination, the acquirer should consider the following indicators:[509]

- *Continuing employment*

  The terms of continuing employment by the selling shareholders who become key employees may be an indicator of the substance of a contingent consideration arrangement. The relevant terms of continuing employment may be included in an employment agreement, acquisition agreement or some other document. A contingent consideration arrangement in which the payments are automatically forfeited if employment terminates is remuneration for post-combination services. Arrangements in which the contingent payments are not affected by employment termination may indicate that the contingent payments are additional consideration rather than remuneration;

- *Duration of continuing employment*

  If the period of required employment coincides with or is longer than the contingent payment period, that fact may indicate that the contingent payments are, in substance, remuneration;

- *Level of remuneration*

  Situations in which employee remuneration other than the contingent payments is at a reasonable level in comparison with that of other key employees in the combined entity may indicate that the contingent payments are additional consideration rather than remuneration;

- *Incremental payments to employees*

  If selling shareholders who do not become employees receive lower contingent payments on a per-share basis than the selling shareholders who become employees of the combined entity, that fact may indicate that the incremental amount of contingent payments to the selling shareholders who become employees is remuneration;

- *Number of shares owned*

  The relative number of shares owned by the selling shareholders who remain as key employees may be an indicator of the substance of the contingent consideration arrangement. For example, if the selling shareholders who owned substantially all of the shares in the acquiree continue as key employees, that fact may indicate that the arrangement is, in substance, a profit-sharing arrangement intended to provide remuneration for post-combination services. Alternatively, if selling shareholders who continue as key employees owned only a small number of shares of the acquiree and all selling shareholders receive the same amount of contingent consideration on a per-share basis, that fact may indicate that the contingent payments are additional consideration. The pre-acquisition ownership interests held by parties related to selling shareholders who continue as key employees, such as family members, should also be considered;

- *Linkage to the valuation*

   If the initial consideration transferred at the acquisition date is based on the low end of a range established in the valuation of the acquiree and the contingent formula relates to that valuation approach, that fact may suggest that the contingent payments are additional consideration. Alternatively, if the contingent payment formula is consistent with prior profit-sharing arrangements, that fact may suggest that the substance of the arrangement is to provide remuneration;

- *Formula for determining consideration*

   The formula used to determine the contingent payment may be helpful in assessing the substance of the arrangement. For example, if a contingent payment is determined on the basis of a multiple of earnings, that might suggest that the obligation is contingent consideration in the business combination and that the formula is intended to establish or verify the fair value of the acquiree. In contrast, a contingent payment that is a specified percentage of earnings might suggest that the obligation to employees is a profit-sharing arrangement to remunerate employees for services rendered;

- *Other agreements and issues*

   The terms of other arrangements with selling shareholders (such as agreements not to compete, executory contracts, consulting contracts and property lease agreements) and the income tax treatment of contingent payments may indicate that contingent payments are attributable to something other than consideration for the acquiree. For example, in connection with the acquisition, the acquirer might enter into a property lease arrangement with a significant selling shareholder. If the lease payments specified in the lease contract are significantly below market, some or all of the contingent payments to the lessor (the selling shareholder) required by a separate arrangement for contingent payments might be, in substance, payments for the use of the leased property that the acquirer should recognise separately in its post-combination financial statements. In contrast, if the lease contract specifies lease payments that are consistent with market terms for the leased property, the arrangement for contingent payments to the selling shareholder may be contingent consideration in the business combination.

Although the guidance says that the acquirer should consider the above factors in determining whether the arrangement is part of the business combination or not, in the first bullet point dealing with 'continuing employment' it is categorically stated that 'a contingent consideration arrangement in which the payments are automatically forfeited if employment terminates is remuneration for post-combination services'.

The requirements for contingent payments to employees are illustrated in the following example.[510]

Example 9.49: *Contingent payments to employees*

Entity B appointed a candidate as its new CEO under a ten-year contract. The contract required Entity B to pay the candidate $5m if Entity B is acquired before the contract expires. Entity A acquires Entity B eight years later. The CEO was still employed at the acquisition date and will receive the additional payment under the existing contract.

In this example, Entity B entered into the employment agreement before the negotiations of the combination began, and the purpose of the agreement was to obtain the services of CEO. Thus, there is no evidence that the agreement was arranged primarily to provide benefits to Entity A or the combined entity. Therefore, the liability to pay $5m is included in the application of the acquisition method.

In other circumstances, Entity B might enter into a similar agreement with CEO at the suggestion of Entity A during the negotiations for the business combination. If so, the primary purpose of the agreement might be to provide severance pay to CEO, and the agreement may primarily benefit Entity A or the combined entity rather than Entity B or its former owners. In that situation, Entity A accounts for the liability to pay CEO in its post-combination financial statements separately from application of the acquisition method.

B Share-based payment awards exchanged for awards held by the acquiree's employees

The second area that is dealt with is arrangements whereby the acquirer exchanges share-based payment awards (i.e. replacement awards) for awards held by employees of the acquiree. As discussed at 3.8.2 above, if the acquirer is obliged to replace the acquiree awards, IFRS 3 (as revised in 2008) considers that the consideration transferred for the acquiree will include some or all of any acquirer's share-based payment awards exchanged for awards held by the acquiree's employees. To the extent that the market-based measure of those replacement awards is not included in the consideration transferred, it is treated as a post-combination remuneration expense.

IFRS 3 (as revised in 2008) includes Application guidance dealing with these arrangements.[511] Such exchanges are modifications of share-based payment awards in accordance with IFRS 2. Discussion of this guidance, including illustrative examples that reflect the substance of the Illustrative Examples that accompany IFRS 3 (as revised in 2008),[512] is dealt with in Chapter 27 at 11.2.

3.12.3 Reimbursement to the acquiree or its former owners for paying the acquirer's acquisition-related costs

The third example is where a transaction reimburses the acquiree or its former owners for paying the acquirer's acquisition-related costs (see 3.8.3 above). The Basis for Conclusions accompanying IFRS 3 (as revised in 2008) explains that this example is directed at ensuring that payments that are not part of the consideration transferred for the acquiree are excluded from the business combination accounting. Instead, the payments should be accounted for separately.[513]

As discussed at 3.8.3 above, IFRS 3 (as revised in 2008) requires that the acquirer expenses its acquisition-related costs – they are not included as part of the consideration transferred for the acquiree (and therefore included as part of the computation of goodwill as was the case under the previous version of IFRS 3). This third example is included in order to mitigate concerns about potential abuse with respect to the treatment of acquisition-related costs in IFRS 3 (as revised in 2008). If acquirers can no longer capitalise acquisition-related costs as part of the cost of the business acquired, they might modify transactions to avoid recognising those costs as expenses. For example, a buyer might ask a seller to make payments to third parties on its behalf. To facilitate the negotiations and sale of the business, the seller might agree to make those payments if the total amount to be paid to it upon closing of the business combination is sufficient to reimburse the seller for payments it made on the buyer's behalf. If the disguised reimbursements were treated as part of the consideration transferred for the business, the acquirer might not recognise those expenses.[514]

The same would also apply if the acquirer asks the acquiree to pay some or all of the acquisition-related costs on its behalf and the acquiree has paid those costs before the acquisition date, such that at the acquisition date the acquiree shows no liability for those costs.[515] This transaction has been entered into on behalf of the acquirer, or primarily for the benefit of the acquirer.

3.12.4 Restructuring plans

As indicated at 3.12 above, one particular area that may be negotiated between the acquirer and the acquiree (or its former owners) could be a restructuring plan relating to the activities of the acquiree.

Example 9.50:   Recognition or otherwise of a restructuring liability as part of a business combination

The acquirer and the acquiree (or the vendors of the acquiree) enter into an arrangement (before the acquisition) that requires the acquiree to restructure its workforce or activities (i.e. to develop the main features of a plan that involve terminating or reducing its activities and to announce the plan's main features to those affected by it so as to raise a valid expectation that the plan will be implemented). The combination is contingent on the plan being implemented.

Does such a restructuring plan that the acquiree puts in place simultaneously with the business combination (i.e. the plan is effective upon the change in control) but was implemented by or at the request of the acquirer qualify for inclusion as part of the liabilities assumed in accounting for the business combination?

Applying the guidance in paragraph B50 of IFRS 3 (as revised in 2008) set out at 3.12 above to the fact pattern:

(a)   *the reason:* a restructuring plan implemented at the request of the acquirer is presumably arranged primarily for the benefit of the acquirer or the combined entity because of the possible redundancy expected to arise from the combination of activities of the acquirer with activities of the acquiree (e.g. capacity redundancy that requires to close acquiree's facilities);

(b)   *who initiated:* if such a plan is the result of a request of the acquirer, it means that the acquirer is expecting future economic benefits from the arrangement and the decision to restructure;

(c)   *the timing;* the restructuring plan is usually discussed during the negotiations; therefore, it is contemplated in the perspective of the future combined entity.

Furthermore, as discussed at 3.6.2 above, an acquirer recognises liabilities for restructuring or exit activities acquired in a business combination only if they meet the definition of a liability at the acquisition date.[516] IFRS 3 (as revised in 2008) does not contain the same explicit requirements relating to restructuring plans that were in IFRS 3 (2007) discussed at 2.5.1 above, but the Basis for Conclusions accompanying IFRS 3 (as revised in 2008) clearly indicate that the requirements for recognising liabilities associated with restructuring or exit activities remain the same.[517]

Accordingly, such a restructuring plan that is implemented as a result of an arrangement between the acquirer and the acquiree is not a liability of the acquiree as at the date of acquisition and cannot be part of the accounting for the business combination under the acquisition method.

Does the answer differ if the combination is not contingent on the plan being implemented?

The answer applies regardless of whether the combination is contingent on the plan being implemented. A plan initiated by the acquirer will most likely not make commercial sense from the acquiree's perspective absent the business combination. For example, because there are retrenchments of staff whose position will only truly become redundant once the entities are combined. In that case, the guidance from paragraph B50 of to IFRS 3 (as revised in 2008) still indicates that this is an arrangement to be accounted for separately rather than as part of the business combination exchange.

A restructuring plan that is decided upon or put in place between the date the negotiations for the business combination started and the date the business combination is consummated is only likely to be accounted for as a pre-combination transaction of the acquiree if there is no evidence that the acquirer initiated the restructuring and the plan makes commercial sense even if the business combination does not proceed.

If a plan initiated by the acquirer is implemented without an explicit link to the combination this may indicate that control has already passed to the acquirer at this earlier date. Even if it does not, the conclusion remains the same when the combination is not contingent upon the plan being implemented. If the acquirer initiates the restructuring, then the restructuring will likely make no commercial sense from the acquiree's perspective absent the combination.

3.13 Measurement period

IFRS 3 (as revised in 2008) contains provisions in respect of a 'measurement period', which although quite similar to those in the previous version of IFRS 3 (see 2.8 above), are not identical.[518] The measurement period is to provide the acquirer with a reasonable time to obtain the information necessary to identify and measure all of the various components of the business combination as of the acquisition date in accordance with the standard, i.e.[519]

(a) the identifiable assets acquired, liabilities assumed and any non-controlling interest in the acquiree;

(b) the consideration transferred for the acquiree (or the other amount used in measuring goodwill);

(c) in a business combination achieved in stages, the equity interest in the acquiree previously held by the acquirer; and

(d) the resulting goodwill or gain on a bargain purchase.

For most business combinations, the main area where information will need to be obtained is in relation to the acquiree, i.e. the identifiable assets acquired and the liabilities assumed, particularly as these may include items that the acquiree had not previously recognised as assets and liabilities in its financial statements and, in most cases, need to be measured at their acquisition-date fair value (see 3.6 above).

Information may also need to be obtained in determining the fair value of any contingent consideration arrangements (see 3.8.1 above).

The measurement period ends as soon as the acquirer receives the information it was seeking about facts and circumstances that existed as of the acquisition date or learns that more information is not obtainable. However, the measurement period is not to exceed one year from the acquisition date.[520] The Basis for Conclusions accompanying IFRS 3 (as revised in 2008) notes that in placing this constraint it was 'concluded that allowing a measurement period longer than one year would not be especially helpful; obtaining reliable information about circumstances and conditions that existed more than a year ago is likely to become more difficult as time passes. Of course, the outcome of some contingencies and similar matters may not be known within a year. But the objective of the measurement period is to provide time to obtain the information necessary to measure the fair value of the item as of the acquisition date. Determining the ultimate settlement amount of a contingency or other item is not necessary. Uncertainties about the timing and amount of future cash flows are part of the measure of the fair value of an asset or liability.'[521]

Under IFRS 3 (as revised in 2008), if the initial accounting for a business combination is incomplete by the end of the reporting period in which the combination occurs, the acquirer reports in its financial statements provisional amounts for the items for which the accounting is incomplete.[522] It was concluded that acquirers should provide relevant information about the status of items that have been measured only provisionally, so IFRS 3 (as revised in 2008) specifies particular disclosures about those items (see 3.17.2 below).[523]

3.13.1 Adjustments made during measurement period to provisional amounts

During the measurement period, the acquirer retrospectively adjusts the provisional amounts recognised at the acquisition date to reflect new information obtained about facts and circumstances that existed as of the acquisition date and, if known, would have affected the measurement of the amounts recognised as of that date. Also, during the measurement period, the acquirer recognises additional assets or liabilities if new information is obtained about facts and circumstances that existed as of the acquisition date and, if known, would have resulted in the recognition of those assets and liabilities as of that date.[524]

IFRS 3 (as revised in 2008) requires the acquirer to consider all pertinent factors in determining whether information obtained after the acquisition date should result in an adjustment to the provisional amounts recognised or whether the information results from events that occurred after the acquisition date. Pertinent factors include the date when additional information is obtained and whether the acquirer can identify a reason for a change to provisional amounts. The standard states that information obtained shortly after the acquisition date is more likely to reflect circumstances that existed at the acquisition date than information obtained several months later. For example, the sale of an asset to a third party shortly after the acquisition date for an amount that differs significantly from its provisional fair value determined at that date is likely to indicate an 'error' in the provisional amount unless an intervening event that changes its fair value can be identified.[525]

Adjustments to provisional amounts that are made during the measurement period are recognised as if the accounting for the business combination had been completed at the acquisition date. Thus, the acquirer revises comparative information for prior periods presented in financial statements as needed, including making any change in depreciation, amortisation or other income effects recognised in completing the acquisition accounting.[526] These requirements are illustrated in the following example, which is based on one included within the Illustrative Examples accompanying IFRS 3 (as revised in 2008).[527] The deferred tax implications are ignored.

Example 9.51:   *Adjustments made during measurement period to provisional amounts*

Entity A acquired Entity B on 30 September 2010. Entity A sought an independent valuation for an item of property, plant and equipment acquired in the combination. However, the valuation was not complete by the time Entity A authorised for issue its financial statements for the year ended 31 December 2010. In its 2010 annual financial statements, Entity A recognised a provisional fair value for the asset of €30,000. At the acquisition date, the item of property, plant and equipment had a remaining useful life of five years. Five months after the acquisition date, Entity A received the independent valuation, which estimated the asset's acquisition-date fair value at €40,000.

In its financial statements for the year ended 31 December 2011 financial statements, Entity A retrospectively adjusts the 2010 prior year information as follows:

(a)   The carrying amount of property, plant and equipment as of 31 December 2010 is increased by €9,500. That adjustment is measured as the fair value adjustment at the acquisition date of €10,000 less the additional depreciation that would have been recognised if the asset's fair value at the acquisition date had been recognised from that date (€500 for three months' depreciation).

(b)   The carrying amount of goodwill as of 31 December 2010 is decreased by €10,000.

(c)   Depreciation expense for 2010 is increased by €500.

Entity A will disclose in its 2010 financial statements that the initial accounting for the business combination has not been completed because the valuation of property, plant and equipment has not yet been received.

In its 2011 financial statements, Entity A will disclose the amounts and explanations of the adjustments to the provisional values recognised during the current reporting period. Therefore, Entity A will disclose that the 2010 comparative information is adjusted retrospectively to increase the fair value of the item of property, plant and equipment at the acquisition date by €10,000, resulting in an increase to property, plant and equipment of €9,500, offset by a decrease to goodwill of €10,000 and an increase in depreciation expense of €500.

The above example illustrates a situation where a provisional value of an asset was finalised at a different amount as a result of receiving information during the measurement period about the asset's fair value as of the acquisition date. The example below illustrates that adjustments during the measurement period are also made where information is received about the existence of an asset as of the acquisition date:

Example 9.52:   *Identification of an asset during measurement period*

Entity C acquired Entity D on 30 November 2010. Entity C engaged an independent appraiser to assist with the identification and determination of fair values to be assigned to the acquiree's assets and liabilities. However, the appraisal was not finalised by the time Entity C authorised for issue its financial statements for the year ended 31 December 2010, and therefore the amounts recognised in its 2010 annual financial statements were on a provisional basis.

Six months after the acquisition date, Entity C received the independent appraiser's final report, in which it was identified by the independent appraiser that the acquiree had an intangible asset (meeting all of the IAS 38 recognition and identification criteria) with a fair value at the date of acquisition of €20,000. However, this had not been identified at the time when Entity C was preparing its 2010 annual financial statements. Thus, no value had been included for this intangible asset.

In its financial statements for the year ended 31 December 2011 financial statements, Entity C retrospectively adjusts the 2010 prior year information to reflect the recognition of this intangible asset.

Although in this case, no value had been recognised, and indeed, the intangible asset had not even been identified at the time of preparing its 2010 financial statements, IFRS 3 (as revised in 2008) requires that an acquirer recognises additional assets (or liabilities) if new information is obtained about facts and circumstances that existed *as of* the acquisition date and, if known, would have resulted in the recognition of those assets and liabilities *as of* that date.

Although an increase/(decrease) in the provisional amount recognised for an identifiable asset will usually mean a corresponding decrease/(increase) in goodwill, IFRS 3 (as revised in 2008) notes that the new information obtained may result in an adjustment to another identifiable asset or liability. For example, the acquirer might have assumed a liability to pay damages related to an accident in one of the acquiree's facilities, part or all of which are covered by the acquiree's liability insurance policy. If the acquirer obtains new information during the measurement period about the acquisition-date fair value of that liability, the adjustment to goodwill would be offset (in whole or in part) by a corresponding adjustment to goodwill resulting from a change to the provisional amount recognised for the claim receivable from the insurer.[528] Similarly, if there is a non-controlling interest in the acquiree, and this is measured based on the proportionate share of the net identifiable assets of the acquiree (see 3.9 above), any adjustments to those assets that had initially been determined on a provisional basis will be offset by the proportionate share attributable to the non-controlling interest.

3.13.2 Adjustments made after end of measurement period

Under IFRS 3 (as revised in 2008), after the measurement period ends, the acquirer can only revise the accounting for a business combination to correct an error in accordance with IAS 8.[529] This would probably be the case only if the original accounting was based on a misinterpretation of the facts which were available at the time; it would not apply simply because new information had come to light which changed the acquiring management's view of the value of the item in question.

Adjustments to the accounting for a business combination after the end of the measurement period are therefore not made for the effect of changes in estimates. In accordance with IAS 8, the effect of a change in estimates is recognised in the current and future periods (see Chapter 3 at 4.5).

3.14 Subsequent measurement and accounting

In general, an acquirer subsequently measures and accounts for assets acquired, liabilities assumed or incurred and equity instruments issued in a business combination in accordance with other applicable IFRSs for those items, depending on their nature. However, IFRS 3 (as revised in 2008) provides guidance on subsequently measuring and accounting for the following assets acquired, liabilities assumed or incurred and equity instruments issued in a business combination:[530]

(a) reacquired rights (see 3.6.6 E II above);

(b) contingent liabilities recognised as of the acquisition date (see 3.6.6 A II above);

(c) indemnification assets (see 3.6.6 D II above); and

(d) contingent consideration (see 3.8.1 C above).

The Application guidance in IFRS 3 (as revised in 2008) includes the following examples of other IFRSs that provide guidance on subsequently measuring and accounting for assets acquired and liabilities assumed or incurred in a business combination:[531]

(a) IAS 38 prescribes the accounting for identifiable intangible assets acquired in a business combination (see Chapter 15), although as noted elsewhere in the Application guidance 'as described in paragraph 3 of IAS 38, the accounting for some acquired intangible assets after initial recognition is prescribed by other IFRSs'[532] (see Chapter 15 at 2.1.1). The acquirer measures goodwill at the amount recognised at the acquisition date less any accumulated impairment losses. IAS 36 prescribes the accounting for impairment losses (see Chapter 18 at 3.4);

(b) IFRS 4 provides guidance on the subsequent accounting for an insurance contract acquired in a business combination (see Chapter 43);

(c) IAS 12 prescribes the subsequent accounting for deferred tax assets (including unrecognised deferred tax assets) and liabilities acquired in a business combination (see Chapter 26);

(d) IFRS 2 provides guidance on subsequent measurement and accounting for the portion of replacement share-based payment awards issued by an acquirer that is attributable to employees' future services (see Chapter 27);

(e) IAS 27 (as amended in 2008) provides guidance on accounting for changes in a parent's ownership interest in a subsidiary after control is obtained (see Chapter 7).

3.15 Reverse acquisitions

As discussed at 3.4 above, in a business combination effected primarily by exchanging equity interests, the standard takes the view that the acquirer is usually the entity that issues its equity interests, but recognises that in some business combinations, so-called 'reverse acquisitions', the issuing entity is the acquiree.

Under IFRS 3 (as revised in 2008), a reverse acquisition is stated to occur when the entity that issues securities (the legal acquirer) is identified as the acquiree for accounting purposes on the basis of the guidance in paragraphs B13-B18 of the standard discussed at 3.4 above. Or more accurately, the entity whose equity interests are acquired (the legal acquiree) must be identified as the acquirer for accounting purposes, based on that guidance, for the transaction to be considered a reverse acquisition. For example, reverse acquisitions sometimes occur when a private operating entity wants to become a public entity but does not want to register its equity shares. To accomplish that, the private entity will arrange for a public entity to acquire its equity interests in exchange for the equity interests of the public entity. In this example, the public entity is the legal acquirer because it issued its equity interests, and the private entity is the legal acquiree because its equity interests were acquired. However, application of the guidance results in identifying:

(a)   the public entity as the acquiree for accounting purposes (the accounting acquiree); and

(b)   the private entity as the acquirer for accounting purposes (the accounting acquirer).[533]

If the private entity is identified as the acquirer as a result of applying that guidance, the transaction should be accounted for as a reverse acquisition, i.e. as an acquisition by the private entity of the public entity, in which case, all of the recognition and measurement principles in IFRS 3 (as revised in 2008), including the requirement to recognise goodwill, apply. The standard also notes that the accounting acquiree (legal acquirer) must meet the definition of a business (see 3.2.2 above) for the transaction to be accounted for as a reverse acquisition,[534] but does not say how the transaction should be accounted for where the accounting acquiree is not a business. It clearly cannot be accounted for as an acquisition of the legal acquiree by the legal acquirer under the standard either, if the legal acquirer has not been identified as the accounting acquirer based on the guidance in the standard. This is discussed further at 3.15.8 below.

As indicated above, where a transaction is to be accounted for as a reverse acquisition, all of the recognition and measurement principles in IFRS 3 (as revised in 2008), including the requirement to recognise goodwill, apply, but treating the legal acquiree/subsidiary as the accounting acquirer and the legal acquirer/parent as the accounting acquiree. This means that the measurement of goodwill will not be as discussed at 3.7 above, but the amount of goodwill that is recognised in a reverse acquisition is generally measured as the excess of (a) over (b) below:[535]

(a)   the consideration transferred (generally measured at acquisition-date fair value) by the accounting acquirer, i.e. the legal acquiree/subsidiary;

(b)   the net of the acquisition-date fair values (or other amounts recognised in accordance with the requirements of the standard) of the identifiable assets acquired and the liabilities assumed of the accounting acquiree, i.e. the legal acquirer/parent.

There is no non-controlling interest in the accounting acquiree, i.e. the legal acquirer/parent, to be taken into account in the computation of goodwill, but there may be a non-controlling interest in the accounting acquirer, i.e. the legal acquiree/subsidiary, to be recognised in the consolidated financial statements (see 3.15.4 below).

IFRS 3 (as revised in 2008) gives the following guidance in the accounting for a reverse acquisition.

3.15.1 Measuring the consideration transferred

As indicated above, the first item to be included in the computation of goodwill in a reverse acquisition is the consideration transferred (generally measured at acquisition-date fair value) by the accounting acquirer, i.e. the legal acquiree/subsidiary.

However, in a reverse acquisition, the accounting acquirer usually issues no consideration for the acquiree. Instead, the accounting acquiree usually issues its equity shares to the owners of the accounting acquirer. Accordingly, the acquisition-date fair value of the consideration transferred by the accounting acquirer for its interest in the accounting acquiree is based on the number of equity interests the legal subsidiary would have had to issue to give the owners of the legal parent the same percentage equity interest in the combined entity that results from the reverse acquisition. The fair value of the number of equity interests calculated in that way can be used as the fair value of consideration transferred in exchange for the acquiree.[536]

These requirements are illustrated in the following example, which is based on one included within the Illustrative Examples accompanying IFRS 3 (as revised in 2008).[537]

Example 9.53:   *Reverse acquisition – calculating the fair value of the consideration transferred*

Entity A, the entity issuing equity instruments and therefore the legal parent, is acquired in a reverse acquisition by Entity B, the legal subsidiary, on 30 September 2010. The accounting for any income tax effects is ignored.

Balance sheets (Statements of financial position) of Entity A and Entity B immediately before the business combination are:

	Entity A €	Entity B €
Current assets	500	700
Non-current assets	1,300	3,000
Total assets	1,800	3,700
Current liabilities	300	600
Non-current liabilities	400	1,100
Total liabilities	700	1,700
Owner's equity		
Issued equity		
100 ordinary shares	300	
60 Ordinary shares		600
Retained earnings	800	1,400
Total shareholders' equity	1,100	2,000

Other information

(a) On 30 September 2010, Entity A issues 2.5 shares in exchange for each ordinary share of Entity B. All of Entity B's shareholders exchange their shares in Entity B. Therefore, Entity A issues 150 ordinary shares in exchange for all 60 ordinary shares of Entity B.

(b) The fair value of each ordinary share of Entity B at 30 September 2010 is €40. The quoted market price of Entity A's ordinary shares at that date is €16.

(c) The fair values of Entity A's identifiable assets and liabilities at 30 September 2010 are the same as their carrying amounts, except that the fair value of Entity A's non-current assets at 30 September 2010 is €1,500.

Calculating the fair value of the consideration transferred

As a result of Entity A (legal parent, accounting acquiree) issuing 150 ordinary shares, Entity B's shareholders own 60 per cent of the issued shares of the combined entity (i.e. 150 of 250 issued shares). The remaining 40 per cent are owned by Entity A's shareholders. If the business combination had taken the form of Entity B issuing additional ordinary shares to Entity A's shareholders in exchange for their ordinary shares in Entity A, Entity B would have had to issue 40 shares for the ratio of ownership interest in the combined entity to be the same. Entity B's shareholders would then own 60 out of the 100 issued shares of Entity B – 60 per cent of the combined entity.

As a result, the fair value of the consideration effectively transferred by Entity B and the group's interest in Entity A is €1,600 (i.e. 40 shares each with a fair value of €40).

The fair value of the consideration effectively transferred should be based on the most reliable measure. In this example, the quoted market price of Entity A's shares provides a more reliable basis for measuring the consideration effectively transferred than the estimated fair value of the shares in Entity B, and the consideration is measured using the market price of Entity A's shares – 100 shares with a fair value per share of €16, i.e. €1,600.

The final paragraph in the above example reflects that in the Illustrative Example accompanying IFRS 3 (as revised in 2008).[538] This would appear to based on the requirements of paragraph 33 of the standard, i.e. 'in a business combination in which the acquirer and the acquiree (or its former owners) exchange only equity interests, the acquisition-date fair value of the acquiree's equity interests may be more reliably measurable than the acquisition-date fair value of the acquirer's equity interests. If so, the acquirer shall determine the amount of goodwill by using the acquisition-date fair value of the acquiree's equity interests instead of the acquisition-date fair value of the equity interests transferred.' In the above example, this did not make any difference as the value of the consideration measured under both approaches was the same. However, it does suggest that as the quoted market price of Entity A's shares is a more reliable basis than the fair value of Entity B's shares, if the quoted market price of Entity A's shares had been, say, €14 per share, the fair value of the consideration effectively transferred would have been measured at €1,400.

3.15.2 Measuring goodwill

As there is no non-controlling interest in the accounting acquiree, and assuming that the accounting acquirer had no previously held equity interest in the accounting acquiree, goodwill is measured as the excess of (a) over (b) below:

(a)   the consideration effectively transferred (generally measured at acquisition-date fair value) by the accounting acquirer, i.e. the legal acquiree/subsidiary;

(b)   the net of the acquisition-date fair values (or other amounts recognised in accordance with the requirements of the standard) of the identifiable assets acquired and the liabilities assumed of the accounting acquiree, i.e. the legal acquirer/parent.

Example 9.54:   Reverse acquisition – measuring goodwill (1)[539]

Using the facts in Example 9.53 above, this results in goodwill of €300, measured as follows:

	€	€
Consideration effectively transferred by Entity B		1,600
Net recognised values of Entity A's identifiable assets and liabilities:		
Current assets	500	
Non-current assets	1,500	
Current liabilities	(300)	
Non-current liabilities	(400)	
		1,300
Goodwill		300

Example 9.55:   Reverse acquisition – measuring goodwill (2)

If Example 9.54 had been based on the same facts as Example 9.53, except that the quoted market price of Entity A's shares had been €14 per share, and this was considered to be a more reliable measure of the consideration transferred, this would have meant that the fair value of the consideration effectively transferred was €1,400, resulting in goodwill of €100.

Indeed, if the quoted market price of Entity A's shares had been €12 per share, such that the fair value of the consideration effectively transferred was €1,200, no goodwill would have arisen and, assuming no adjustments were required as a result of the re-assessment of the components of the computation (see 3.11 above), a gain on a bargain purchase of €100 would be recognised immediately in profit or loss.

3.15.3 *Preparation and presentation of consolidated financial statements*

Although the accounting for the reverse acquisition reflects the legal subsidiary as being the accounting acquirer, the consolidated financial statements prepared following a reverse acquisition are issued under the name of the legal parent (accounting acquiree). Consequently they have to be described in the notes as a continuation of the financial statements of the legal subsidiary (accounting acquirer), with one adjustment, which is to adjust retroactively the accounting acquirer's legal capital to reflect the legal capital of the accounting acquiree. Comparative information presented in those consolidated financial statements is therefore that of the legal subsidiary (accounting acquirer), not that originally presented in the previous financial statements of the legal parent (accounting acquiree), and also is retroactively adjusted to reflect the legal capital of the legal parent (accounting acquiree).[540]

Because such consolidated financial statements represent a continuation of the financial statements of the legal subsidiary (accounting acquirer) except for its capital structure, the consolidated financial statements reflect:

(a)   the assets and liabilities of the legal subsidiary (accounting acquirer) recognised and measured at their pre-combination carrying amounts, i.e. not at their acquisition-date fair values;

(b)   the assets and liabilities of the legal parent (accounting acquiree) recognised and measured in accordance with IFRS 3 (as revised in 2008), i.e. generally at their acquisition-date fair values;

(c)   the retained earnings and other equity balances of the legal subsidiary (accounting acquirer) *before* the business combination, i.e. not those of the legal parent (accounting acquiree);

(d)   the amount recognised as issued equity instruments in the consolidated financial statements determined by adding the issued equity of the legal subsidiary (accounting acquirer) outstanding immediately before the business combination to the fair value of the legal parent (accounting acquiree) determined in accordance with IFRS 3 (as revised in 2008). However, the equity structure (i.e. the number and type of equity instruments issued) reflects the equity structure of the legal parent (accounting acquiree), including the equity instruments issued by the legal parent to effect the combination. Accordingly, the equity structure of the legal subsidiary (accounting acquirer) is restated using the exchange ratio established in the acquisition agreement to reflect the number of shares of the legal parent (the accounting acquiree) issued in the reverse acquisition;

(e)   the non-controlling interest's proportionate share of the legal subsidiary's (accounting acquirer's) pre-combination carrying amounts of retained earnings and other equity interests (as discussed in 3.15.4 below);[541]

(f)   the income statement for the current period reflects that of the legal subsidiary (accounting acquirer) for the full period together with the post-acquisition results of the legal parent (accounting acquiree) (based on the attributed fair values).

It is unclear why the Application guidance in (d) above refers to using 'the fair value of the legal parent (accounting acquiree) determined in accordance with' IFRS 3 (as revised in 2008), when, as discussed previously at 3.15.1 above, the guidance for determining 'the fair value of the consideration effectively transferred' uses a different method of arriving at the value of the consideration given. We believe that the amount recognised as issued equity should reflect whichever value has been determined for the consideration effectively transferred.

Continuing with Example 9.53 above, the consolidated balance sheet immediately after the business combination will be as follows:

Example 9.56:   Reverse acquisition – consolidated balance sheet immediately after the business combination[542]

Using the facts in Example 9.53 above, the consolidated balance sheet immediately after the date of the business combination is as follows (the intermediate columns for Entity B (legal subsidiary, accounting acquirer) and Entity A (legal parent, accounting acquiree) are included to show the workings):

	Entity B Book values €	Entity A Fair values €	Consolidated €
Current assets	700	500	1,200
Non-current assets	3,000	1,500	4,500
Goodwill		300	300
Total assets	3,700	2,300	6,000
Current liabilities	600	300	900
Non-current liabilities	1,100	400	1,500
Total liabilities	1,700	700	2,400
Owner's equity			
Issued equity			
250 ordinary shares	600	1,600	2,200
Retained earnings	1,400	–	1,400
Total shareholders' equity	2,000	1,600	3,600

The amount recognised as issued equity interests in the consolidated financial statements (€2,200) is determined by adding the issued equity of the legal subsidiary immediately before the business combination (€600) and the fair value of the consideration effectively transferred (€1,600). However, the equity structure appearing in the consolidated financial statements (i.e. the number and type of equity interests issued) must reflect the equity structure of the legal parent, including the equity interests issued by the legal parent to effect the combination.

Interestingly, the final paragraph in the above example, which reflects that in the Illustrative Example accompanying IFRS 3 (as revised in 2008),[543] refers to the amount for issued equity instruments being determined by adding 'the fair value of the consideration effectively transferred' (see 3.15.1 above), rather than using 'the fair value of the legal parent (accounting acquiree) determined in accordance with' IFRS 3 (as revised in 2008) as discussed above. As noted above, we believe that the amount recognised as issued equity should reflect whichever value has been determined for the consideration effectively transferred.

The Application guidance in IFRS 3 (as revised in 2008) only deals with the reverse acquisition accounting in the consolidated financial statements; no mention is made as to what should happen in the separate financial statements of the legal parent (accounting acquiree), if any. However, the previous version of IFRS 3 indicated that reverse acquisition accounting applies only in the consolidated financial statements, and that in the legal parent's separate financial statements, the investment in the legal subsidiary is accounted for in accordance with the requirements in IAS 27 (2007) on accounting for investments in an investor's separate financial statements.[544]

Example 9.57:   Reverse acquisition – legal parent's balance sheet in separate financial statements

Using the facts in Example 9.53 above, the balance sheet of Entity A, the legal parent, in its separate financial statements immediately following the business combination will be as follows:

	Entity A
	€
Current assets	500
Non-current assets	1,300
Investment in subsidiary (Entity B)	2,400
Total assets	4,200
Current liabilities	300
Non-current liabilities	400
Total liabilities	700
Owner's equity	
Issued equity	
250 ordinary shares	2,700
Retained earnings	800
	3,500

The investment in the subsidiary is included at its cost of €2,400, being the fair value of the shares issued by Entity A (150 × €16). It can be seen that the issued equity is different from that in the consolidated financial statements and its non-current assets remain at their carrying amounts before the business combination.

3.15.4 Non-controlling interest

In a reverse acquisition, some of the owners of the legal subsidiary (accounting acquirer) might not exchange their equity instruments for equity instruments of the legal parent (accounting acquiree). Although reverse acquisition accounting regards the entity in which those owners hold equity instruments (the legal subsidiary) as having acquired the other entity (the legal parent), those owners are required to be treated as a non-controlling interest in the consolidated financial statements after the reverse acquisition. This is because the owners of the legal subsidiary that do not exchange their equity instruments for equity instruments of the legal parent have an interest only in the results and net assets of the legal subsidiary, and not in the results and net assets of the combined entity. Conversely, even though the legal parent is the acquiree for accounting purposes, the owners of the legal parent have an interest in the results and net assets of the combined entity.[545]

As indicated at 3.15.3 above, the assets and liabilities of the legal subsidiary (accounting acquirer) are recognised and measured in the consolidated financial statements at their pre-combination carrying amounts. Therefore, in a reverse acquisition the non-controlling interest reflects the non-controlling shareholders' proportionate interest in the pre-combination carrying amounts of the legal subsidiary's net assets even if the non-controlling interests in other acquisitions are measured at fair value at the acquisition date.[546]

These requirements are illustrated in the following example, which is based on one included within the Illustrative Examples accompanying IFRS 3 (as revised in 2008).[547]

Example 9.58:   Reverse acquisition – non-controlling interest

This example uses the same facts in Example 9.53 above, except that only 56 of Entity B's 60 ordinary shares are exchanged. Because Entity A issues 2.5 shares in exchange for each ordinary share of Entity B, Entity A issues only 140 (rather than 150) shares. As a result, Entity B's shareholders own 58.3 per cent of the issued shares of the combined entity (i.e. 140 shares out of 240 issued shares).

As in Example 9.53 above, the fair value of the consideration transferred for Entity A, the accounting acquiree) is calculated by assuming that the combination had had been effected by Entity B issuing additional ordinary shares to the shareholders of Entity A in exchange for their ordinary shares in Entity A. That is because Entity B is the accounting acquirer, and IFRS 3 (as revised in 2008) requires the acquirer to measure the consideration exchanged for the accounting acquiree (see 3.15.1 above).

In calculating the number of shares that Entity B would have had to issue, the non-controlling interest is excluded from the calculation. The majority shareholders own 56 shares of Entity B. For that to represent a 58.3 per cent ownership interest, Entity B would have had to issue an additional 40 shares. The majority shareholders would then own 56 out of the 96 issued shares of Entity B and therefore 58.3 per cent of the combined entity.

As a result, the fair value of the consideration transferred for Entity A, the accounting acquiree, is €1,600 (i.e. 40 shares, each with a fair value of €40). That is the same amount as when all 60 of Entity B's shareholders tender all 60 of its ordinary shares for exchange (see Example 9.53 above). The recognised amount of the group's interest in Entity A, the accounting acquiree, does not change if some of Entity B's shareholders do not participate in the exchange.

The non-controlling interest is represented by the 4 shares of the total 60 shares of Entity B that are not exchanged for shares of Entity A. Therefore, the non-controlling interest is 6.7 per cent. The non-controlling interest reflects the proportionate interest of the non-controlling shareholders in the pre-combination carrying amounts of the net assets of Entity B, the legal subsidiary. Therefore, the consolidated balance sheet is adjusted to show a non-controlling interest of 6.7 per cent of the pre-combination carrying amounts of Entity B's net assets (i.e. €134 or 6.7 per cent of €2,000).

The consolidated balance sheet at 30 September 2010 (the date of the business combination) reflecting the non-controlling interest is as follows (the intermediate columns for Entity B (legal subsidiary, accounting acquirer), non-controlling interest and Entity A (legal parent, accounting acquiree) are included to show the workings):

	Entity B Book values €	Non-controlling interest €	Entity A Fair values €	Consolidated €
Current assets	700		500	1,200
Non-current assets	3,000		1,500	4,500
Goodwill			300	300
Total assets	3,700		2,300	6,000
Current liabilities	600		300	900
Non-current liabilities	1,100		400	1,500
	1,700		700	2,400
Owner's equity				
Issued equity				
240 ordinary shares	600	(40)	1,600	2,160
Retained earnings	1,400	(94)	–	1,306
Non-controlling interest	–	134	–	134
	2,000	–	1,600	3,600

The non-controlling interest of €134 has two components. The first component is the reclassification of the non-controlling interest's share of the accounting acquirer's retained earnings immediately before the acquisition (€1,400 × 6.7 per cent or €93.80). The second component represents the reclassification of the non-controlling interest's share of the accounting acquirer's issued equity (€600 × 6.7 per cent or €40.20).

3.15.5 Earnings per share

As indicated at 3.15.3 above, the equity structure (i.e. the number and type of equity instruments issued) appearing in the consolidated financial statements following a reverse acquisition reflects the equity structure of the legal parent (accounting acquiree), including the equity instruments issued by the legal parent to effect the business combination.[548]

Where the legal parent is required by IAS 33 to disclose earnings per share information (see Chapter 36), then for the purpose of calculating the weighted average number of ordinary shares outstanding (the denominator of the earnings per share calculation) during the period in which the reverse acquisition occurs:

(a)   the number of ordinary shares outstanding from the beginning of that period to the acquisition date is computed on the basis of the weighted average number of ordinary shares of the legal subsidiary (accounting acquirer) outstanding during the period multiplied by the exchange ratio established in the acquisition agreement; and

(b)   the number of ordinary shares outstanding from the acquisition date to the end of that period is the actual number of ordinary shares of the legal parent (accounting acquiree) outstanding during that period.[549]

The basic earnings per share disclosed for each comparative period before the acquisition date presented in the consolidated financial statements following a reverse acquisition is calculated by dividing:

(a)   the profit or loss of the legal subsidiary (accounting acquirer) attributable to ordinary shareholders in each of those periods by

(b)   the legal subsidiary's historical weighted average number of ordinary shares outstanding multiplied by the exchange ratio established in the acquisition agreement.[550]

These requirements are illustrated in the following example, which is based on one included within the Illustrative Examples accompanying IFRS 3 (as revised in 2008).[551]

Example 9.59:   Reverse acquisition – earnings per share

This example uses the same facts in Example 9.53 above. Assume that Entity B's earnings for the annual period ended 31 December 2009 were €600, and that the consolidated earnings for the annual period ending 31 December 2010 were €800. Assume also that there was no change in the number of ordinary shares issued by Entity B (legal subsidiary, accounting acquirer) during the annual period ended 31 December 2009 and during the period from 1 January 2010 to the date of the reverse acquisition (30 September 2010), nor by Entity A (legal parent, accounting acquiree) after that date.

Earnings per share for the annual period ended 31 December 2010 is calculated as follows:

Number of shares deemed to be outstanding for the period from 1 January 2010 to the acquisition date	150
(i.e. the number of ordinary shares issued by Entity A (legal parent, accounting acquiree) in the reverse acquisition, or more accurately, the weighted average number of ordinary shares of Entity B (legal subsidiary, accounting acquirer) outstanding during the period multiplied by the exchange ratio established in the acquisition agreement, i.e. 60 × 2.5)	
Number of shares of Entity A (legal parent, accounting acquiree) outstanding from the acquisition date to 31 December 2010	250
Weighted average number of shares outstanding (150 × 9/12) + (250 × 3/12)	175
Earnings per share €800/175	€4.57

The restated earnings per share for the annual period ending 31 December 2009 is €4.00 (being €600/150, i.e. the earnings of Entity B (legal subsidiary, accounting acquirer) for that period divided by the number of ordinary shares Entity A issued in the reverse acquisition (or more accurately, by the weighted average number of ordinary shares of Entity B (legal subsidiary, accounting acquirer) outstanding during the period multiplied by the exchange ratio established in the acquisition agreement, i.e. 60 × 2.5). Any earnings per share information for that period previously disclosed by either Entity A or Entity B is irrelevant.

3.15.6 Cash consideration

Typically, a reverse acquisition occurs where the legal acquirer (Entity A) issues new shares to 'acquire' shares in the legal acquiree (Entity B), but on the basis of the guidance in paragraphs B13-B18 of the standard discussed at 3.4 above, Entity B is determined to be the accounting acquirer. However, in some circumstances the combination may be effected whereby some of the consideration given by Entity A to acquire the shares in Entity B is cash.

In such circumstances, can the combination be accounted for as a reverse acquisition of Entity A by Entity B despite some of the consideration being in the form of cash?

Normally, the entity issuing cash consideration would be considered to be the acquirer.[552] However, despite the form of the consideration, the key determinant in identifying an acquirer is whether it has control over the other (see 3.4 above).

Therefore, where having considered the guidance referred to above, including all the facts and circumstances relating to the business combination, there is evidence demonstrating that the legal acquiree, Entity B, has obtained the power to govern the financial and operating policies of Entity A so as to obtain benefits from its activities, this will overcome the presumption that Entity A is the acquirer and the combination should be accounted for as a reverse acquisition.

In that case, how should any cash paid be accounted for?

One approach might be to treat the payment as a pre-acquisition transaction with a resulting reduction in the consideration and in net assets acquired (with no net impact on goodwill). However, we do not believe this to be appropriate. Any consideration, whether cash or shares, transferred by Entity A cannot form part of the consideration transferred by the acquirer as Entity A is the accounting acquiree. As discussed at 3.15.3 above, although the consolidated financial statements following a reverse acquisition are issued under the name of the legal parent (Entity A), they are to be described in the notes as a continuation of the financial statements of the legal subsidiary (Entity B). Therefore, since the consolidated financial statements are a continuation of Entity B's financial statements, in our view the cash consideration paid from Entity A (the accounting acquiree) should be accounted for as a distribution from the consolidated group to the accounting acquirer's (Entity B's) shareholders as at the combination date.

However, where a cash payment is made to effect the combination, the requirements of the Application guidance in Appendix B to IFRS 3 (as revised in 2008) need to be applied with care as illustrated in the following example.

Example 9.60:   Reverse acquisition effected with cash consideration

Entity A has 100,000 ordinary shares in issue, with a market price of £2.00 per share, giving a market capitalisation of £200,000. It acquires all of the shares in Entity B for a consideration of £500,000 satisfied by the issue of 200,000 shares (with a value of £400,000) and a cash payment of £100,000 to Entity B's shareholders. Entity B has 200,000 shares in issue, with an estimated fair value of £2.50 per share. After the combination Entity B's shareholders control the voting of Entity A and, as a result, have been able to appoint Entity B's directors and key executives to replace their Entity A counterparts. Accordingly, as Entity B has the power to govern the financial and operating policies of Entity A so as to obtain benefits from its activities, Entity B is identified as the accounting acquirer. The combination must be accounted for as a reverse acquisition, i.e. an acquisition of Entity A (legal parent, accounting acquiree) by Entity B (legal subsidiary, accounting acquirer).

How should the consideration transferred by the accounting acquirer (Entity B) for its interest in the accounting acquiree (Entity A) be determined?

Applying the requirements of paragraph B20 of IFRS 3 (as revised in 2008) (discussed at 3.15.1 above) to the transaction might lead to the following conclusion. Entity A has had to issue 200,000 shares to Entity B's shareholders, resulting in Entity B's shareholders having 66.67% (200,000/300,000) of the equity and Entity A's shareholders 33.33% (100,000/300,000). If Entity B's share price is used to determine the fair value of the consideration transferred, then under paragraph B20, Entity B would have had to issue 100,000 shares to Entity A's shareholders to result in the same % shareholdings (200,000/300,000 = 66.67%). This would apparently give a value of the consideration transferred of 100,000 @ £2.50 = £250,000. This does not seem correct.

If there had been no cash consideration at all, Entity A would have issued 250,000 shares to Entity B's shareholders, resulting in Entity B's shareholders having 71.43% (250,000/350,000) of the equity and Entity A's shareholders 28.57% (100,000/350,000). If Entity B's share price is used to determine the value of the consideration transferred, then under paragraph B20, Entity B would have had to issue 80,000 shares to Entity A's shareholders to result in the same % shareholdings (200,000/280,000 = 71.43%). This would give a value for the consideration transferred of 80,000 @ £2.50 = £200,000. If it was thought that the fair value of Entity A's shares was more reliably measurable, paragraph 33 of IFRS 3 (as revised in 2008) would require the consideration to be measured using the market price of Entity A's shares. As Entity B has effectively acquired 100% of Entity A, the value of the consideration transferred would be £200,000 (the same as under the revised paragraph B20 calculation above).

In our view, the proper analysis of the paragraph B20 calculation in this case is that of the 100,000 shares that Entity B is deemed to have issued, only 80,000 of them are to acquire Entity A's shares, resulting in a cost of £200,000. The extra 20,000 shares are to compensate Entity A's shareholders for the fact that Entity B's shareholders have received a cash distribution of £100,000, and is effectively a stock distribution to Entity A's shareholders of £50,000 (20,000 @ £2.50), being their share (33.33%) of a total distribution of £150,000. However, since the equity structure (i.e. the number and type of shares) appearing in the consolidated financial statements reflects that of the legal parent, Entity A, this 'stock distribution' will not actually be apparent. The only distribution that will be shown as a movement in equity is the £100,000 cash paid to Entity B's shareholders.

3.15.7 Share-based payments

It may that in a reverse acquisition the legal acquirer (Entity A) has an existing share-based payment plan at the date of acquisition. In such a situation, how does the entity account for awards held by the employees of the accounting acquiree?

In a reverse acquisition, how does the entity account for awards held by the employees of the accounting acquiree?

Example 9.61:   *Share-based payments in a reverse acquisition*

Entity A legally acquires Entity B, but Entity B (the legal subsidiary) is the accounting acquirer under IFRS 3 (as revised in 2008). Entity A has an existing share-based payment plan at the date of acquisition. The terms of awards held by employees of Entity A are not changed. How are these share-based payment awards accounted for in the consolidated financial statements?

Under IFRS 3 (as revised in 2008), accounting for a reverse acquisition takes place from the perspective of the accounting acquirer, not the legal acquirer. Therefore, the accounting for the share-based payment plan of Entity A is based on what would have happened if Entity B rather than Entity A had issued such equity instruments. As indicated at 3.15.1 above, in a reverse acquisition, the acquisition-date fair value of the consideration transferred by the accounting acquirer for its interest in the accounting acquiree is based on the number of equity interests the legal subsidiary would have had to issue to give the owners of the legal parent the same percentage equity interest in the combined entity that results from the reverse acquisition. The fair value of the number of equity interests calculated in that way can be used as the fair value of consideration transferred in exchange for the acquiree. Therefore, although the legal form of awards made by the accounting acquiree (Entity A) does not change, from an accounting perspective, it is as if these awards have been exchanged for a share-based payment award of the accounting acquirer (Entity B).

As a result, absent any legal modification to the share-based payment awards in Entity A, the acquisition-date fair value of the legal parent's (accounting acquiree's, Entity A) share-based payments awards are included as part of the consideration transferred by the accounting acquirer (Entity B), based on the same principles as those described in paragraphs B56 to B62 of IFRS 3 (as revised in 2008) – see 3.8.2 above and Chapter 27 at 11.2. That is, the portion of the fair value attributed to the vesting period prior to the reverse acquisition is recognised as part of the consideration paid for the business combination and the portion that vests after the reverse acquisition is treated as post-combination expense.

3.15.8 Reverse acquisitions involving a non-trading shell company

The requirements for reverse acquisitions in IFRS 3 (as revised in 2008), and the guidance provided by the standard, discussed above are based on the premise that the legal parent (accounting acquiree) has a business which has been acquired by the legal subsidiary (accounting acquirer). In some situations, this may not be the case, for example where a private entity arranges to have itself 'acquired' by a non-trading public entity as a means of obtaining a stock exchange listing. As indicated at 3.15 above, the standard notes that the accounting acquiree (legal acquirer) must meet the definition of a business (see 3.2.2 above) for the transaction to be accounted for as a reverse acquisition,[553] but does not say how the transaction should be accounted for where the accounting acquiree is not a business. It clearly cannot be accounted for as an acquisition of the legal acquiree by the legal acquirer under the standard either, if the legal acquirer has not been identified as the accounting acquirer based on the guidance in the standard.

In our view, such a transaction should be accounted for in the consolidated financial statements of the legal parent as a continuation of the financial statements of the private entity (the legal subsidiary), together with a deemed issue of shares, equivalent to the shares held by the former shareholders of the legal parent, and a re-capitalisation of the equity of the private entity. This deemed issue of shares is, in effect, an equity-settled share based payment transaction whereby the private entity has received the net assets of the legal parent, generally cash, together with the listing status of the legal parent.

Example 9.62:   Reverse acquisition of a non-trading shell company

Entity A is a non-trading public company with 10,000 ordinary shares in issue. On 31 December 2010, Entity A issues 190,000 ordinary shares in exchange for all of the ordinary share capital of Entity B, a private trading company, with 9,500 ordinary shares in issue.

At the date of the transaction, Entity A has $85,000 of cash and the quoted market price of Entity A's ordinary shares is $12.

The fair value of Entity B has been determined by an independent professional valuer as being $2,185,000, giving a value per share of $230.

Following the transaction, apart from one non-executive director, all of the directors of Entity A resign and four new directors from Entity B are appointed to the Board of Entity A.

As a result of Entity A issuing 190,000 ordinary shares, Entity B's shareholders own 95 per cent of the issued share capital of the combined entity (i.e. 190,000 of the 200,000 issued shares), with the remaining 5 per cent held by Entity A's existing shareholders.

How should this transaction be accounted for in the consolidated financial statements of Entity A?

As the shareholders of Entity A only retain a 5 per cent interest in the combined entity after the transaction, and the Board is dominated by appointees from Entity B, this cannot be accounted for as an acquisition of Entity B by Entity A. Also, as a result of Entity A being a non-trading cash shell company, and therefore not comprising a business (see 3.2.2 above), it cannot be accounted for as a reverse acquisition of Entity A by Entity B either.

The consolidated financial statements should reflect the substance of the transaction which is that Entity B is the continuing entity, therefore the principles and guidance on the preparation and presentation of the consolidated financial statements in a reverse acquisition set out in IFRS 3 (as revised in 2008) should be applied in this transaction by analogy.

However, as the transaction is not a business combination under IFRS 3 (as revised in 2008), the transaction effectively involves a share-based payment transaction under IFRS 2 (see Chapter 27) whereby Entity B is deemed to have issued shares in exchange for the $85,000 cash held by Entity A together with the listing status of Entity A. However, the listing status does not qualify for recognition as an intangible asset, and therefore needs to be expensed in profit or loss. Under IFRS 2. for equity-settled share-based payments transactions, an entity measures the goods or services received, and the corresponding increase in equity, directly at the fair value of the goods or services received, unless that fair value cannot be estimated reliably. If the entity cannot estimate reliably the fair value of the goods and services received, the entity measures the amounts, indirectly, by reference to the fair value of the equity instruments issued.[554] For transactions with non-employees, IFRS 2 presumes that the fair value of the goods and services received is more readily determinable.[555] This would suggest that the increase in equity should be based on the fair value of the cash and the fair value of the listing status. However, it is unlikely that a fair value of the listing status can be reliably estimated, therefore the increase in equity should be measured by reference to the fair value of the shares that are deemed to have been issued. Indeed, even if a fair value could be attributed to the listing status, if the total identifiable consideration received is less than the fair value of the equity given as consideration, as a result of IFRIC 8, the transaction should be measured based on the fair value of the shares that are deemed to be issued.[556]

Given that the existing shareholders of Entity A have a 5 per cent interest in the combined entity, Entity B would have had to issue 500 shares for the ratio of ownership interest in the combined entity to be the same. Based on the fair value of an Entity B share of $230, the accounting for the deemed share-based payment transaction is:

	$	$
Cash received	85,000	
Listing expense (income statement)	30,000	
Issued equity (500 × $230)		115,000

As Entity B is a private entity, it may be that a more reliable basis for determining the fair value of the deemed shares issued would have been to use the quoted market price of Entity A's shares at the date of the transaction. On this basis, the issued equity would have been $120,000 (10,000 × $12), giving rise to a listing expense of $35,000.

In summary, the accounting for this transaction is similar in many respects to that which would have been the case if the transaction had been accounted for as a reverse acquisition; the main difference being that no goodwill arises on the transaction, and that any amount that would have been so recognised is accounted for as a listing expense. Indeed, if the transaction had been accounted for as a reverse acquisition, the overall effect may have been the same if an impairment loss on the 'goodwill' had been recognised.

3.16   Push down accounting

The term 'push down accounting' relates to the practice adopted in some jurisdictions of incorporating, or 'pushing down', the fair value adjustments which have been made by the acquirer into the financial statements of the acquiree, including the goodwill arising on the acquisition. It is argued that the acquisition, being an independently bargained transaction, provides better evidence of the values of the assets and liabilities of the acquiree than those previously contained within its financial statements, and therefore represents an improved basis of accounting. There are, however, contrary views, which hold that the transaction in question was one to which the reporting entity was not a party, and there is no reason why it should intrude into the entity's own accounting records.

Whatever the theoretical arguments, it is certainly true that push down accounting could be an expedient practice, because it obviates the need to make extensive consolidation adjustments in each subsequent year, based on parallel accounting records. Nevertheless, if the acquiree is preparing its financial statements under IFRS, in our view it cannot apply push down accounting and reflect the fair value adjustments made by the acquirer and the goodwill that arose on its acquisition.

All of the requirements of IFRS must be applied when an entity prepares its financial statements. IFRS requires assets and liabilities to be recognised initially at cost or fair value, depending on the nature of the assets and liabilities. The acquisition of an entity is not a transaction undertaken by that entity itself, hence it cannot be a transaction to determine cost.

Application of push down accounting would result in the recognition and measurement of assets and liabilities that are prohibited by some standards (such as internally generated intangibles and goodwill) and the recognition and measurement of assets and liabilities at amounts that are not permitted under IFRS. While some IFRS standards include an option or requirement to revalue particular assets, this is undertaken as part of a process of determining accounting policies rather than as one-off revaluations. For example:

- IAS 2 requires that inventories are measured at the lower of cost and net realisable value (see Chapter 20 at 2.2);

- IAS 16 requires that items of property, plant and equipment are initially measured at cost. Subsequently, property, plant and equipment can be measured at cost or at revalued amount. However, revaluations must be applied consistently and must be performed on a regular basis. Therefore a one-off revaluation is not permitted (see Chapter 16 at 4.1);

- IAS 38 requires that intangible assets are initially measured at cost. Subsequently, they can be revalued only in rare circumstances where there is an active market. In addition, IAS 38 specifically prohibits the recognition of internally generated goodwill. Therefore a one-off revaluation is not permitted (see Chapter 15 at 2.3.5 and 2.4.2).

3.17   Disclosures

IFRS 3 (as revised in 2008) identifies two disclosure objectives relating to business combinations and specifies particular disclosures that should be made to meet those objectives. These objectives are similar to those in the previous version of IFRS 3 (see 2.13 above), but IFRS 3 (as revised in 2008) incorporates the previously separate objective dealing with goodwill within the objective to provide information that enables users to evaluate the financial effects of adjustments recognised in the current period that relate to business combinations that occurred in the current or previous reporting periods.

Many of the specific disclosures required by the previous version of IFRS 3 are included within IFRS 3 (as revised in 2008), although some of them have been modified to reflect the acquisition-date fair value approach of IFRS 3 (as revised in 2008) rather than the cost-based approach of the previous version of IFRS 3. Some additional disclosures are now required (principally as a result of new explicit guidance for particular issues).[557]

The disclosure requirements of IFRS 3 (as revised in 2008) are dealt with below.

3.17.1 Nature and financial effect of business combinations

The first disclosure objective is that the acquirer discloses information that enables users of its financial statements to evaluate the nature and financial effect of a business combination that occurs either:[558]

(a)   during the current reporting period; or

(b)   after the end of the reporting period but before the financial statements are authorised for issue.

Information that is required to be disclosed by the acquirer to meet the above objective is specified in the Application guidance of the standard.[559]

A   *Business combinations during the current reporting period*

To meet the above objective, the acquirer is required to disclose the following information for *each* business combination that occurs during the reporting period:[560]

(a)   the name and a description of the acquiree;

(b)   the acquisition date;

(c)   the percentage of voting equity interests acquired;

(d)   the primary reasons for the business combination and a description of how the acquirer obtained control of the acquiree;

(e)   a qualitative description of the factors that make up the goodwill recognised, such as expected synergies from combining operations of the acquiree and the acquirer, intangible assets that do not qualify for separate recognition or other factors;

(f)   the acquisition-date fair value of the total consideration transferred and the acquisition-date fair value of each major class of consideration, such as:

     (i)   cash;

     (ii)   other tangible or intangible assets, including a business or subsidiary of the acquirer;

     (iii)   liabilities incurred, for example, a liability for contingent consideration; and

     (iv)   equity interests of the acquirer, including the number of instruments or interests issued or issuable and the method of determining the fair value of those instruments or interests;

(g)   for contingent consideration arrangements and indemnification assets:

     (i)   the amount recognised as of the acquisition date;

     (ii)   a description of the arrangement and the basis for determining the amount of the payment; and

     (iii)   an estimate of the range of outcomes (undiscounted) or, if a range cannot be estimated, that fact and the reasons why a range cannot be estimated. If the maximum amount of the payment is unlimited, the acquirer discloses that fact;

(h)   for acquired receivables:

     (i)   the fair value of the receivables;

     (ii)   the gross contractual amounts receivable; and

     (iii)   the best estimate at the acquisition date of the contractual cash flows not expected to be collected.

The disclosures are to be provided by major class of receivable, such as loans, direct finance leases and any other class of receivables;

(i)   the amounts recognised as of the acquisition date for each major class of assets acquired and liabilities assumed;

(j)   for each contingent liability recognised in accordance with paragraph 23 of the standard (see 3.6.6 A above), the information required in paragraph 85 of IAS 37 (see Chapter 24 at 6.1). If a contingent liability is not recognised because its fair value cannot be measured reliably, the acquirer discloses:

(i)   the information required by paragraph 86 of IAS 37 (see Chapter 24 at 6.2); and

(ii)   the reasons why the liability cannot be measured reliably;

(k)   the total amount of goodwill that is expected to be deductible for tax purposes;

(l)   for transactions that are recognised separately from the acquisition of assets and assumption of liabilities in the business combination in accordance with paragraph 51 of the standard (see 3.12 above):

(i)   a description of each transaction;

(ii)   how the acquirer accounted for each transaction;

(iii)   the amounts recognised for each transaction and the line item in the financial statements in which each amount is recognised; and

(iv)   if the transaction is the effective settlement of a pre-existing relationship, the method used to determine the settlement amount;

(m)   the disclosure of separately recognised transactions required by (l) includes the amount of acquisition-related costs and, separately, the amount of those costs recognised as an expense and the line item or items in the statement of comprehensive income in which those expenses are recognised. The amount of any issue costs not recognised as an expense and how they were recognised are also to be disclosed;

(n)   in a bargain purchase (see 3.11 above):

(i)   the amount of any gain recognised and the line item in the statement of comprehensive income in which the gain is recognised; and

(ii)   a description of the reasons why the transaction resulted in a gain;

(o)   for each business combination in which the acquirer holds less than 100 per cent of the equity interests in the acquiree at the acquisition date (see 3.9 above):

(i)   the amount of the non-controlling interest in the acquiree recognised at the acquisition date and the measurement basis for that amount; and

(ii)   for each non-controlling interest in an acquiree measured at fair value, the valuation techniques and key model inputs used for determining that value;

(p)   in a business combination achieved in stages (see 3.10 above):

(i)   the acquisition-date fair value of the equity interest in the acquiree held by the acquirer immediately before the acquisition date; and

(ii)   the amount of any gain or loss recognised as a result of remeasuring to fair value the equity interest in the acquiree held by the acquirer before the business combination and the line item in the statement of comprehensive income in which that gain or loss is recognised;

(q)   the following information:

(i)   the amounts of revenue and profit or loss of the acquiree since the acquisition date included in the consolidated statement of comprehensive income for the reporting period; and

(ii)   the revenue and profit or loss of the combined entity for the current reporting period as though the acquisition date for all business combinations that occurred during the year had been as of the beginning of the annual reporting period.

If disclosure of any of the information required by this subparagraph is impracticable, the acquirer shall disclose that fact and explain why the disclosure is impracticable. IFRS 3 (as revised in 2008) uses the term 'impracticable' with the same meaning as in IAS 8 (see Chapter 3 at 4.7).

The above information is required to be given for *each* material business combination. For individually immaterial business combinations occurring during the reporting period that are material collectively, the acquirer has to disclose, in aggregate, the information required by items (e) to (q) above.[561]

B   Business combinations effected after the end of the reporting period

If the acquisition date of a business combination is after the end of the reporting period but before the financial statements are authorised for issue, the acquirer is required to disclose the information set out in A above for that business combination, unless the initial accounting for the business combination is incomplete at the time the financial statements are authorised for issue. In that situation, the acquirer describes which disclosures could not be made and the reasons why they cannot be made.[562]

3.17.2 *Financial effects of adjustments recognised in the current reporting period relating to business combinations*

The second objective is that the acquirer discloses information that enables users of its financial statements to evaluate the financial effects of adjustments recognised in the current reporting period that relate to business combinations that occurred in the period or previous reporting periods.[563]

Information that is required to be disclosed by the acquirer to meet the above objective is specified in the Application guidance of the standard.[564]

To meet the above objective, the acquirer is required to disclose the following information for *each* material business combination or in the aggregate for individually immaterial business combinations that are material collectively:[565]

(a)   if the initial accounting for a business combination is incomplete (see 3.13 above) for particular assets, liabilities, non-controlling interests or items of consideration and the amounts recognised in the financial statements for the business combination thus have been determined only provisionally:

(i)   the reasons why the initial accounting for the business combination is incomplete;

(ii) the assets, liabilities, equity interests or items of consideration for which the initial accounting is incomplete; and

(iii) the nature and amount of any measurement period adjustments recognised during the reporting period in accordance with paragraph 49 of the standard (see 3.13.1 above);

(b) for each reporting period after the acquisition date until the entity collects, sells or otherwise loses the right to a contingent consideration asset, or until the entity settles a contingent consideration liability or the liability is cancelled or expires (see 3.8.1 above):

(i)   any changes in the recognised amounts, including any differences arising upon settlement;

(ii) any changes in the range of outcomes (undiscounted) and the reasons for those changes; and

(iii) the valuation techniques and key model inputs used to measure contingent consideration;

(c) for contingent liabilities recognised in a business combination, the acquirer shall disclose the information required by paragraphs 84 and 85 of IAS 37 for each class of provision (see Chapter 24 at 6.1);

(d) a reconciliation of the carrying amount of goodwill at the beginning and end of the reporting period showing separately:

(i)   the gross amount and accumulated impairment losses at the beginning of the reporting period;

(ii) additional goodwill recognised during the reporting period (except goodwill included in a disposal group that, on acquisition, meets the criteria to be classified as held for sale in accordance with IFRS 5 – see Chapter 4 at 2.1);

(iii) adjustments resulting from the subsequent recognition of deferred tax assets during the reporting period in accordance with paragraph 67 of the standard (see 4.2 1 below);

(iv) goodwill included in a disposal group classified as held for sale in accordance with IFRS 5 and goodwill derecognised during the reporting period without having previously been included in a disposal group classified as held for sale;

(v)   impairment losses recognised during the reporting period in accordance with IAS 36. (IAS 36 requires disclosure of information about the recoverable amount and impairment of goodwill in addition to this requirement –see Chapter 18 at 4.2);

(vi) net exchange rate differences arising during the reporting period in accordance with IAS 21 (see Chapter 13 at 3.3.4);

(vii) any other changes in the carrying amount during the reporting period; and

(viii) the gross amount and accumulated impairment losses at the end of the reporting period.

(e)   the amount and an explanation of any gain or loss recognised in the current reporting period that both:

(i)   relates to the identifiable assets acquired or liabilities assumed in a business combination that was effected in the current or previous reporting period; and

(ii)   is of such a size, nature or incidence that disclosure is relevant to understanding the combined entity's financial statements.

3.17.3 Other necessary information

IFRS 3 (as revised in 2008) includes a catch-all disclosure requirement, that if in any situation the information required to be disclosed set out above, or by other IFRSs, does not satisfy the objectives of IFRS 3 (as revised in 2008), the acquirer discloses whatever additional information is necessary to meet those objectives.[566]

In addition to the disclosures required by IFRS 3 (as revised in 2008) discussed above, IAS 7 requires disclosures in respect of obtaining control of subsidiaries and other businesses (see Chapter 39 at 2.4.2).[567]

3.17.4 Illustrative disclosures

An illustration of some of the disclosure requirements of IFRS 3 (as revised in 2008) is given by way of an example in the Illustrative Examples accompanying the standard. The example, which is reproduced below, assumes that the acquirer, AC, is a listed entity and that the acquiree, TC, is an unlisted entity. The illustration presents the disclosures in a tabular format that refers to the specific disclosure requirements illustrated. (The references to paragraph B64 correspond to the equivalent item at 3.17.1 A above and those to paragraph B67 correspond to the equivalent item at 3.17.2 above.) It is also emphasised that an actual footnote might present many of the disclosures illustrated in a simple narrative format.[568]

Example 9.63:   Footnote X: Acquisitions

Paragraph reference

B64(a-d)   On 30 June 20X0 AC acquired 15 per cent of the outstanding ordinary shares of TC. On 30 June 20X2 AC acquired 60 per cent of the outstanding ordinary shares of TC and obtained control of TC. TC is a provider of data networking products and services in Canada and Mexico. As a result of the acquisition, AC is expected to be the leading provider of data networking products and services in those markets. It also expects to reduce costs through economies of scale.

B64(e)   The goodwill of CU2,500 arising from the acquisition consists largely of the synergies and economies of scale expected from combining the operations of AC and TC.

B64(k)   None of the goodwill recognised is expected to be deductible for income tax purposes. The following table summarises the consideration paid for TC and the amounts of the assets acquired and liabilities assumed recognised at the acquisition date, as well as the fair value at the acquisition date of the non-controlling interest in TC.

At 30 June 20X2

	Consideration	**CU**
B64(f)(i)	Cash	5,000
B64(f)(iv)	Equity instruments (100,000 ordinary shares of AC)	4,000
B64(f)(iii); B64(g)(i)	Contingent consideration arrangement	1,000
B64(f)	**Total consideration transferred**	10,000
B64(p)(i)	**Fair value of AC's equity interest in TC held before the business combination**	2,000
		12,000
B64(m)	**Acquisition-related costs** (included in selling, general and administrative expenses in AC's statement of comprehensive income for the year ended 31 December 20X2)	1,250
B64(i)	**Recognised amounts of identifiable assets acquired and liabilities assumed**	
	Financial assets	3,500
	Inventory	1,000
	Property, plant and equipment	10,000
	Identifiable intangible assets	3,300
	Financial liabilities	–4,000
	Contingent liability	–1,000
	Total identifiable net assets	12,800
B64(o)(i)	Non-controlling interest in TC	–3,300
	Goodwill	2,500
		12,000

B64(f)(iv) The fair value of the 100,000 ordinary shares issued as part of the consideration paid for TC (CU4,000) was determined on the basis of the closing market price of AC's ordinary shares on the acquisition date.

B64(f)(iii) B64(g) B67(b)	The contingent consideration arrangement requires AC to pay the former owners of TC 5 per cent of the revenues of XC, an unconsolidated equity investment owned by TC, in excess of CU7,500 for 20X3, up to a maximum amount of CU2,500 (undiscounted).
	The potential undiscounted amount of all future payments that AC could be required to make under the contingent consideration arrangement is between CU0 and CU2,500.
	The fair value of the contingent consideration arrangement of CU1,000 was estimated by applying the income approach. The fair value estimates are based on an assumed discount rate range of 20-25 per cent and assumed probability-adjusted revenues in XC of CU10,000-20,000.
	As of 31 December 20X2, neither the amount recognised for the contingent consideration arrangement, nor the range of outcomes or the assumptions used to develop the estimates had changed.
B64(h)	The fair value of the financial assets acquired includes receivables under finance leases of data networking equipment with a fair value of CU2,375. The gross amount due under the contracts is CU3,100, of which CU450 is expected to be uncollectible.
B67(a)	The fair value of the acquired identifiable intangible assets of CU3,300 is provisional pending receipt of the final valuations for those assets.
B64(j) B67(c) IAS 37.84, 85	A contingent liability of CU1,000 has been recognised for expected warranty claims on products sold by TC during the last three years. We expect that the majority of this expenditure will be incurred in 20X3 and that all will be incurred by the end of 20X4. The potential undiscounted amount of all future payments that AC could be required to make under the warranty arrangements is estimated to be between CU500 and CU1,500. As of 31 December 20X2, there has been no change since 30 June 20X2 in the amount recognised for the liability or any change in the range of outcomes or assumptions used to develop the estimates.
B64(o)	The fair value of the non-controlling interest in TC, an unlisted company, was estimated by applying a market approach and an income approach. The fair value estimates are based on: (a) an assumed discount rate range of 20-25 per cent; (b) an assumed terminal value based on a range of terminal EBITDA multiples between 3 and 5 times (or, if appropriate, based on long term sustainable growth rates ranging from 3 to 6 per cent); (c) assumed financial multiples of companies deemed to be similar to TC; and (d) assumed adjustments because of the lack of control or lack of marketability that market participants would consider when estimating the fair value of the non-controlling interest in TC.
B64(p)(ii)	AC recognised a gain of CU500 as a result of measuring at fair value its 15 per cent equity interest in TC held before the business combination. The gain is included in other income in AC's statement of comprehensive income for the year ending 31 December 20X2.
B64(q)(i)	The revenue included in the consolidated statement of comprehensive income since 30 June 20X2 contributed by TC was CU4,090. TC also contributed profit of CU1,710 over the same period.
B64(q)(ii)	Had TC been consolidated from 1 January 20X2 the consolidated statement of comprehensive income would have included revenue of CU27,670 and profit of CU12,870.

4   TRANSITIONAL ARRANGEMENTS

4.1   Transitional arrangements under IFRS 3 (2007) for entities already reporting under IFRS

These transitional arrangements for existing IFRS adopters are no longer relevant. A discussion of the arrangements can be found in section 4.1 of Chapter 7 of a previous edition of this book, *International GAAP 2007*.

4.2   Transitional arrangements under IFRS 3 (as revised in 2008) for entities already reporting under IFRS

As indicated at 3.1.1 above, IFRS 3 (as revised in 2008) is to be applied prospectively to business combinations for which the acquisition date is on or after the beginning of the annual period in which the standard is adopted,[569] and contains a number of transitional provisions.

4.2.1   Business combinations accounted for under the previous version of IFRS 3

Assets and liabilities that arose from business combinations whose acquisition dates preceded the adoption of IFRS 3 (as revised in 2008) are not to be adjusted upon application of the standard.[570] As a result, with one exception relating to changes in deferred tax of the acquiree, the previous version of IFRS 3 (discussed at 2 above) will continue to apply to business combinations effected before the adoption date of IFRS 3 (as revised in 2008). In particular, the requirements relating to contingent consideration discussed at 2.4.5 above will continue to apply to those earlier business combinations, rather than those discussed at 3.8.1 above that apply to business combinations accounted for under IFRS 3 (as revised in 2008). Also, the requirements relating to subsequent adjustments to fair values discussed at 2.8 above will apply to those earlier business combinations (with one exception relating to deferred tax of the acquiree), rather than those discussed at 3.13 above.

As discussed at 3.6.6 B above, a consequential amendment to IAS 12 was made as a result of IFRS 3 (as revised in 2008) so as to change the accounting for deferred tax benefits that do not meet the recognition criteria at the date of acquisition, but are subsequently recognised. IAS 12 (as amended by IFRS 3 (as revised in 2008)) is to be applied prospectively. Therefore, for business combinations effected before the adoption date of IFRS 3 (as revised in 2008), goodwill is not to be adjusted for the subsequent recognition of deferred tax benefits that failed to satisfy the criteria for separate recognition as of the acquisition date,[571] unless the benefits subsequently recognised are within twelve months of the acquisition date and result from new information obtained about facts and circumstances existing at the acquisition date, in which case goodwill is adjusted until it is zero.[572] Where goodwill is adjusted due to the subsequent recognition of deferred tax assets, this needs to be disclosed as a separate reconciling item in the reconciliation of goodwill (see item (d) (iii) at 3.17.2 above). As discussed at 2.8.3 above, the previous version of IFRS 3 would have required an adjustment to goodwill no matter when the deferred tax benefits at the acquisition date were subsequently recognised.

4.2.2 *Entities previously outwith the scope of the previous version of IFRS 3*

As discussed at 3.1.3 above, business combinations involving only mutual entities and combinations in which separate entities are brought together by contract alone are now within the scope of IFRS 3 (as revised in 2008). As such business combinations were outwith the scope of the previous version of IFRS 3, an entity, such as a mutual entity, that had not applied the previous version of IFRS 3 and had one or more business combinations that were accounted for using the purchase method is to apply the following transitional provisions included in the Application guidance in IFRS 3 (as revised in 2008):[573]

- *Classification*

  The entity continues to classify the prior business combination in accordance with the entity's previous accounting policies for such combinations;

- *Previously recognised goodwill*

  At the beginning of the first annual period in which IFRS 3 (as revised in 2008) is applied, the carrying amount of goodwill arising from the prior business combination is its carrying amount at that date in accordance with the entity's previous accounting policies. In determining that amount, the entity shall eliminate the carrying amount of any accumulated amortisation of that goodwill and the corresponding decrease in goodwill. No other adjustments are to be made to the carrying amount of goodwill;

- *Goodwill previously recognised as a deduction from equity*

  The entity's previous accounting policies may have resulted in goodwill arising from the prior business combination being recognised as a deduction from equity. In that situation the entity is not to recognise that goodwill as an asset at the beginning of the first annual period in which IFRS 3 (as revised in 2008) is applied. Furthermore, the entity is not to recognise in profit or loss any part of that goodwill when it disposes of all or part of the business to which that goodwill relates or when a cash-generating unit to which the goodwill relates becomes impaired;

- *Subsequent accounting for goodwill*

  From the beginning of the first annual period in which IFRS 3 (as revised in 2008) is applied, the entity discontinues amortising goodwill arising from the prior business combination and tests goodwill for impairment in accordance with IAS 36;

- *Previously recognised negative goodwill*

  An entity that accounted for the prior business combination by applying the purchase method may have recognised a deferred credit for an excess of its interest in the net fair value of the acquiree's identifiable assets and liabilities over the cost of that interest (sometimes called negative goodwill). If so, the entity is to derecognise the carrying amount of that deferred credit at the beginning of the first annual period in which IFRS 3 (as revised in 2008) is applied with a corresponding adjustment to the opening balance of retained earnings at that date.

4.2.3 Asset brought forward relating to directly attributable costs of a probable business combination

As discussed at 2.4.4 above, an entity may have carried forward an asset in respect of the directly attributable costs relating to a probable business combination. If that business combination has now been completed, it has is be accounted for under IFRS 3 (as revised in 2008). The transitional arrangements in IFRS 3 (as revised in 2008) do not explicitly deal with this issue. Accordingly, in our view, the entity has a number of options available and can choose to recognise the carried forward costs as either:

- an expense in profit or loss for the current period

    As IFRS 3 (as revised in 2008) is to be applied prospectively to the business combination, any further acquisition-related costs have to be expensed in profit or loss for the period (see 3.8.3 above), so the carried forward costs should be expensed likewise;

- an immediate charge to retained earnings

    Again, IFRS 3 (as revised in 2008) is to be applied prospectively to the business combination. However, although any further acquisition-related costs have to be expensed in profit or loss for the period, the carried forward costs were not incurred in the current period and do not relate to services received in the period. Thus, they should be taken as an immediate charge to retained earnings;

- an expense in profit or loss of the prior period

    Although IFRS 3 (as revised in 2008) is to be applied prospectively to the business combination, the costs were incurred in the previous period and related to services received in that period. The transitional provisions in IFRS 3 (as revised in 2008) only deal with business combinations whose acquisition dates preceded the application of the revised standard. As there is no transitional provision within IFRS 3 (as revised in 2008) dealing specifically with this issue, under IAS 8 the entity's change in accounting policy for the treatment of acquisition-related costs should be applied retrospectively (see Chapter 3 at 4.4).

As discussed at 2.4.4 above, the treatment for such costs under IFRS 3 (2007) and IFRS 3 (as revised in 2008) has been considered by the IFRIC. At its meeting in May 2009, and subsequently confirmed at its meeting in July 2009, the IFRIC noted that more than one interpretation of how the requirements of the two IFRSs interact is possible. Accordingly, the IFRIC concluded that an entity should disclose its accounting policy for such costs and the amount recognised in the financial statements. Because this is a transitional issue, the IFRIC decided not to add the issue to its agenda.[574]

Each of the above treatments were included within the Staff Paper considered by the IFRIC at its meeting in May 2009,[575] so in the light of the IFRIC decision, an entity should disclose which treatment it has adopted and the amount of the expenses recognised in the financial statements.

5   FUTURE DEVELOPMENTS

As indicated at 1.2.5 above, IFRS 3 (as revised in 2008) excludes from its scope the formation of a joint venture and a combination of entities or businesses under common control. In addition, proposals in the June 2005 exposure draft that preceded IFRS 3 (as revised in 2008) relating to contingencies and fair value guidance are not reflected in the final revised standard. Possible future developments on these issues are discussed at 5.1 to 5.3 below.

Also, since the publication of the revised versions of IFRS 3 and IAS 27 a number of issues have arisen that have been raised with the IFRIC and the IASB. As a result, the IASB has decided to deal with some of the issues within the exposure draft of proposed *Improvements to IFRSs* issued in August 2009,[576] address some of the issues in other projects, but defer some of the other topics to the post-implementation review of the revised IFRSs to be conducted two years after their effective date.[577] To the extent that these relate to IFRS 3 (as revised in 2008), further discussion is set out at 5.4 to 5.6 below.

5.1   Formation of joint ventures and business combinations involving entities under common control

In the June 2005 exposure draft that preceded IFRS 3 (as revised in 2008), the IASB indicated that it would consider the following issues as part of future phases of its project on business combinations:[578]

(a)   the accounting for business combinations in which separate entities or businesses are brought together to form a joint venture, including possible applications of 'fresh start' accounting;

(b)   the accounting for business combinations involving entities under common control.

When IFRS 3 (as revised in 2008) was issued, it indicated that neither the FASB nor the IASB had on its agenda a project to consider the 'fresh start' method of accounting, although they might at some future date undertake a joint project to consider the issues.[579] At the time of writing, the IASB's latest work plan no longer includes a project on business combinations on its agenda.[580]

In December 2007, the IASB decided to add to its active agenda a project on common control transactions,[581] although at the time of writing, the project is currently paused. A comprehensive project outline will be presented to the Board when the project resumes after staff working on projects relating to the financial crisis become available.[582] This is discussed further in Chapter 10 at 1.4.

5.2   Contingencies

As indicated at 1.2.2 B above, the IASB had also issued an exposure draft proposing amendments to IAS 37 at the same as the June 2005 exposure draft that preceded IFRS 3 (as revised in 2008). At that time, the IASB expected that the effective date of the revised IAS 37 would be the same as the effective date of the revised IFRS 3. However, the IASB expects to issue a revised IAS 37 at a later date. Consequently, the IASB has not reflected in IFRS 3 (as revised in 2008) its original proposals for dealing with contingencies, but has indicated that it expects to reconsider the requirements within IFRS 3 (as revised in 2008) when it issues the revised IAS 37.[583] The IASB's latest work plan indicates that the Board is aiming to publish either a further exposure draft or the revised IAS 37 in the final quarter of 2009.[584] The IASB proposals for revising IAS 37 are discussed in Chapter 24 at 8.1.

5.3   Fair value measurement

As discussed at 3.6.3 above, for the purpose of determining acquisition-date fair values, 'fair value' is defined by IFRS 3 (as revised in 2008) as 'the amount for which an asset could be exchanged, or a liability settled, between knowledgeable, willing parties in an arm's length transaction'.[585] This is the same as the definition in the previous version of IFRS 3 as well in other IFRSs. On the other hand, the equivalent US standard, SFAS 141R, uses the definition in SFAS 157 which is 'the price that would be received to sell an asset or paid to transfer a liability in an orderly transaction between market participants at the measurement date'. The IASB considered also using the definition of fair value from SFAS 157 but decided that to do so would prejudge the outcome of its project on fair value measurement.[586] Consequently, much of the guidance relating to fair value that was contained in the previous version of IFRS 3 (see 2.5.4 above) is longer included in IFRS 3 (as revised in 2008). In addition, the proposed guidance on how to measure fair value contained in Appendix E of the June 2005 exposure draft, including the 'fair value hierarchy', is not included in the revised standard.

In May 2009, the IASB published an exposure draft – *Fair Value Measurement*. This proposes to clarify the definition of fair value, establish a framework for measuring fair value (including a fair value hierarchy) and enhance the disclosures where fair value is used (although it is unclear whether the disclosures would apply to fair values that are only attributed to assets and liabilities when initially recognised in a business combination). The guidance contained in other IFRSs will be removed. As a result, some consequential amendments to IFRS 3 (as revised in 2008) are to be made.[587] The exposure draft proposes to define fair value as 'the price that would be received to sell an asset or paid to transfer a liability in an orderly transaction between market participants at the measurement date',[588] i.e. the same as in SFAS 157. Fair value is therefore to be an exit price, rather than an entry price. Key aspects of the definition proposed in the exposure draft relate to the characteristics of the asset/liability, orderly transactions, most advantageous market, market participants, highest and best use, and the transfer of a liability. The proposals of the exposure draft, including these key aspects, are discussed further in Chapter 2 at 6.3. The IASB's latest work plan estimates that an IFRS on fair value measurement guidance is published in the second half of 2010.[589]

5.4   Improvements to IFRSs

As indicated at 5 above, since the publication of the revised versions of IFRS 3 and IAS 27 a number of issues have arisen that have been raised with the IFRIC and the IASB. As a result, the IASB has decided to deal with the following issues relating to

IFRS 3 (as revised in 2008) within the exposure draft of proposed *Improvements to IFRSs* issued in August 2009.[590] It is proposed that an entity applies the amendments for annual periods beginning on or after 1 July 2010. Earlier application is to be permitted, but if an entity applies the amendments for an earlier period it is to disclose that fact.[591]

5.4.1 Contingent consideration relating to business combinations originally accounted for under IFRS 3 (2007)

As indicated at 4.2.1 above, the requirements relating to contingent consideration discussed at 2.4.5 above will continue to apply to those earlier business combinations, rather than those discussed at 3.8.1 above that apply to business combinations accounted for under IFRS 3 (as revised in 2008). However, consequential amendments made to the financial instrument standards (IFRS 7, IAS 32 and IAS 39) by IFRS 3 (as revised in 2008) deleted the scope exemptions in those IFRSs relating to contingent consideration in a business combination. The IASB has noted that this is inconsistent with the requirement of paragraph 65 of IFRS 3 (as revised in 2008) that assets and liabilities that arose from business combinations whose acquisition dates preceded the application of the revised IFRS are not adjusted upon application of the revised IFRS.[592] Accordingly, the IASB is proposing to amend the effective date paragraph in the amendments made to IFRS 7, IAS 32 and IAS 39 to clarify that those standards do not apply to contingent consideration that arose from business combinations whose acquisition dates preceded the application of the revised IFRS 3,[593] thus reinstating the scope exemptions for such contingent consideration. The amendments also now explicitly state that such contingent consideration is accounted for in accordance with the requirements in paragraphs 32 to 35 of IFRS 3 (2007).[594]

5.4.2 Measurement of non-controlling interests in an acquiree

As discussed at 3.9 above, IFRS 3 (as revised in 2008) provides a choice for measuring non-controlling interests in an acquiree, and one issue that has been addressed by the IFRIC is whether the option to measure non-controlling interests at the proportionate share of the value of net identifiable assets acquired is adopted should be applied to other elements of 'equity' in the subsidiary that relates to, say, other equity instruments such as options or warrants, the equity element of convertible debt instruments, and the 'equity' related to share-based payment awards held by parties other than the parent. The IFRIC concluded that the measurement choice should apply only to instruments currently entitled to a proportionate share of the acquiree's net assets. However, because IFRSs do not provide sufficient guidance to resolve this issue an amendment to IFRS 3 (as revised in 2008) is required.[595]

Consequently, the IASB proposes to amend paragraph 19 of IFRS 3 (as revised in 2008) to clarify that the choice of measuring non-controlling interest either at fair value or at the non-controlling interest's proportionate share of the acquiree's identifiable net assets applies only to instruments that are currently entitled to a proportionate share of the acquiree's net assets. Other instruments that meet the definition of non-controlling interest should be measured at fair value or in accordance with applicable IFRSs.[596] It is proposed that paragraph 19 is amended to say:

'For each business combination, the acquirer shall measure any non-controlling interest in the acquiree at either fair value or other measurement basis as required by IFRSs, except for the components of non-controlling interest that are present ownership instruments and entitle their holders to a pro rata share of the entity's net assets in the event of liquidation. The acquirer shall measure those components of non-controlling interest either at fair value or at the present ownership instruments' proportionate share of the acquiree's identifiable net assets.'[597]

5.4.3   Unreplaced and voluntarily replaced share-based payment transactions

As discussed at 3.8.2 above, IFRS 3 (as issued in 2008) contains requirements for share-based payment transactions of the acquiree that the acquirer is obliged to replace or that expire as a consequence of the business combination. Those requirements are discussed further in Chapter 27 at 11.2. That chapter also discusses issues relating to unreplaced share-based payment transactions of the acquiree and voluntary replacements of share-based payment transactions (see Chapter 27 at 11.4 and 11.2.2 respectively). As with the measurement of non-controlling interests in an acquiree, such share-based payment transactions were considered by the IFRIC at its meeting in July 2009. The IFRIC concluded that when an acquirer does not replace unexpired share-based payment awards of the acquiree or voluntarily issues share-based payment awards to replace such awards, at least some portion of the amount recognised for those awards should be regarded as part of the consideration transferred in the business combination. However, because IFRSs do not provide sufficient guidance to resolve this issue an amendment to IFRS 3 (as revised in 2008) is required.[598]

Consequently, the IASB proposes to amend the application guidance in IFRS 3 (as revised in 2008) so as to require the acquirer to apply paragraphs B57-B62 to all share-based payment transactions that are part of a business combination. Therefore, the application guidance would also apply to share-based payment transactions of the acquiree that the acquirer chooses not to replace and share-based payment transactions that the acquirer chooses to exchange for share-based payment transactions of the acquiree, even though they would not expire as a consequence of the business combination. Where the acquiree has outstanding share-based payment transactions that the acquirer does not exchange for its share-based payment transactions, the IASB proposes that those acquiree share-based payment transactions, if vested, are part of the non-controlling interest in the acquiree (see 5.4.2 above) and are measured at their fair value. If unvested, they are to be measured at their market-based measure as if the acquisition date were the grant date. The market-based measure of unvested share-based payment transactions is to be allocated to the non-controlling interest on the basis of the ratio of the portion of the vesting period completed to the total vesting period of the share-based payment transaction. The balance is to be allocated to post-combination service.[599] It is proposed that an entity applies the amendments for annual periods beginning on or after 1 July 2010. Earlier application is to be permitted, but if an entity applies the amendments for an earlier period it is to disclose that fact.[600]

5.5   Other projects

Although the IASB has decided to deal with some of the issues that have arisen since the publication of the revised versions of IFRS 3 and IAS 27 within the exposure draft of proposed *Improvements to IFRSs*, it has also decided to address some of the issues in other projects. At its meeting in May 2009, the IASB indicated that it will address 'contingent consideration: designation (categories of financial instruments) and classification (as equity or a liability)' in its projects on financial instruments.[601]

The accounting for contingent consideration under IFRS 3 (as issued in 2008) is discussed at 3.8.1 above. It is not entirely clear what aspect of the accounting for such contingent consideration will be addressed as part of that project as no details were included in the agenda papers available to the public.

5.6   Post-implementation review of IFRS 3 (as revised in 2008) and IAS 27 (as amended in 2008)

At the same meeting in May 2009, the IASB deferred the following issues to the post-implementation review of IFRS 3 (as revised in 2008) and IAS 27 (as amended in 2008), to be conducted two years after their effective date:[602]

- The application of the definition of a business in particular situations (see 3.2.2 above);
- The application of the definition of non-controlling interest to equity instruments other than shares (for example, share options) and the measurement of those instruments;
- IFRIC recommendations on (a) removing the distinction between 'contractual' and 'non-contractual' customer-related intangible assets in a business combination and (b) including in the standard the indicators that identify the existence of a customer relationship. The Board decided tentatively to retain the depositor relationship example in paragraph B34(a) of IFRS 3, noting that this is a separable intangible asset (see 3.6.5 B above);
- the treatment of indemnification assets, as part of the business combination transaction or as a separate transaction (see 3.6.6 D above).

Although the IASB has stated that the issue in the second bullet point above has been deferred, this is presumably in relation to IAS 27 (as amended in 2008) generally. It is clear from the proposals in respect of such instruments in the context of IFRS 3 (as revised in 2008) that the IASB regards them as non-controlling interests that should be measured at their acquisition-date fair value (or in accordance with applicable IFRSs) in accounting for a business combination (see 5.4.2 above). The proposals relating to unreplaced share-based payment transactions (see 5.4.3 above) are consistent with that view.

6   CONCLUSION

The IASB clearly saw business combinations and goodwill as an area of considerable divergence across jurisdictions and one that was to be given priority in its initial agenda, but in splitting its project into two phases recognised that it would be a major task to deal with all of the issues.

The first phase of the project resulted in the publication in March 2004 of IFRS 3 (2007), together with revised versions of IAS 36 and IAS 38, which introduced a number of significant changes in accounting for business combinations and goodwill from that required by the previous standard, IAS 22.

One of the major implications of IFRS 3 (2007) has been the need for acquirers to recognise, separate from goodwill, the identifiable intangible assets of the acquiree and to attribute a fair value to them, assuming that the value can be measured reliably. The guidance for valuing intangibles is effectively contained in IAS 38, but in our view more detailed guidance is required. The fact that for most of the intangible assets that need to be valued there will be no quoted market price, means that entities have to determine the value 'based on the best information available'. Unless an entity has developed valuation techniques in valuing such assets, in many cases specialists are needed to assist in determining the appropriate fair values.

The other major change brought about by IFRS 3 (2007) has been the treatment of goodwill, whereby it is no longer amortised but is subject to an annual impairment test under IAS 36 (see Chapter 18).

However, the version of IFRS 3 introduced in 2004 has not been the IASB's last word on accounting for business combinations. In January 2008, the IASB issued a revised standard as part of phase II of its project in conjunction with the FASB in the US. By moving from a cost-based approach to one that is generally based on measuring the various components of a business combination at their acquisition-date fair values, IFRS 3 (as revised in 2008) changes significantly the accounting for business combinations to be accounted for under the revised standard, particularly in relation to transaction costs, contingent consideration and step-acquisitions.

As a result of the delayed implementation date for IFRS 3 (as revised in 2008), most entities have not yet had to apply its requirements, but as indicated at 5 above a number of issues have arisen that have been raised with the IFRIC and the IASB. Consequently, the IASB has decided to deal with some of the issues within the exposure draft of proposed *Improvements to IFRSs* issued in August 2009,[603] address some of the issues in other projects, but defer some of the other topics to the post-implementation review of the revised IFRSs to be conducted two years after their effective date.[604] In addition, the IASB's proposals on fair value measurement (see 5.3 above) could have implications on the determination of fair values. So, even IFRS 3 (as revised in 2008) is not the last word on accounting for business combinations!

References

1 IFRS 3 (2007), *Business Combinations*, IASB, 2007 Bound Volume, Appendix A.
2 IFRS 3, *Business Combinations*, IASB, Appendix A.
3 See the introductory pages of IAS 22, *Business Combinations*, IASC, September 1998 (superseded March 2004), for a summary of the changes.
4 IFRS 3 (2007), para. BC2.
5 IFRS 3 (2007), para. BC3.
6 Project Summary, *Business Combinations (Phase II) – Application of the Purchase Method*, IASB, 26 January 2004, pp. 1 and 2.
7 *Exposure Draft of Proposed Amendments to IFRS 3 Business Combinations* ('IFRS 3 ED'), IASB, June 2005, para. BC5.
8 IFRS 3 ED, para. BC7.
9 IFRS 3, para. 64; IAS 27, *Consolidated and Separate Financial Statements*, IASB, para. 45.
10 IFRS 3, para. IN1.
11 IFRS 3, para. IN2.
12 IFRS 3, *Comparison of IFRS 3 (as revised in 2008) and SFAS 141(R)*.
13 IFRS 3, *Table of Concordance*.
14 IFRS 3, paras. B64(g) and B67(b).
15 IFRS 3, para. B64(h).
16 IFRS 3, para. B64(l).
17 IFRS 3, para. B64(m).
18 IFRS 3, para. B64(o).
19 IFRS 3, para. B64(p).
20 IFRS 3, para. B64(q).
21 IFRS 3, para. B67(a).
22 IFRS 3, para. BC422(n).
23 Exposure Draft (ED 2009/11), IASB, August 2009, pp. 15-24 and 43-49.
24 *IASB Update*, IASB, May 2009, p. 5.
25 IFRS 3 (2007), para. 78.
26 IFRS 3 (2007), paras. 79-84.
27 IFRS 3 (2007), para. 85.
28 IFRS 3 (2007), para. 1.
29 IFRS 3 (2007), para. 2.
30 IFRS 3 (2007), para. 4.
31 IFRS 3 (2007), para. 4.
32 IFRS 3 (2007), Appendix A.
33 IFRS 3 (2007), Appendix A.
34 IFRS 3 (2007), para. 4.
35 IFRS 3 (2007), para. 4.
36 IFRS 3 (2007), para. 5.
37 IFRS 3 (2007), para. 6.
38 IFRS 3 (2007), para. 7.
39 IFRS 3 (2007), para. 8.
40 IFRS 3 (2007), para. 3.
41 IFRS 3, para. BC58.
42 IFRS 3, para. 2.
43 IFRS 3 (2007), para. 14.
44 IFRS 3 (2007), para. 15.
45 IFRS 3 (2007), para. 39.
46 IFRS 3 (2007), Appendix A.
47 IFRS 3 (2007), para. 16.
48 IFRS 3 (2007), para. 18.
49 IFRS 3 (2007), para. 17.
50 IFRS 3 (2007), Appendix A.
51 IFRS 3 (2007), para. 19.
52 IFRS 3 (2007), para. 20.
53 IFRS 3 (2007), para. 21.
54 IFRS 3 (2007), para. BC59.
55 IFRS 3 (2007), para. 21.
56 IFRS 3 (2007), para. 22.
57 IFRS 3 (2007), para. BC66.
58 IFRS 3 (2007), para. 23.
59 *IFRIC Update*, IASB, March 2006, p. 6.
60 IFRS 3 (2007), para. 24.
61 IFRS 3 (2007), para. BC67.
62 IFRS 3 (2007), para. 25.
63 IFRS 3 (2007), Appendix A.
64 IFRS 3 (2007), para. 26.
65 IAS 39, *Financial Instruments: Recognition and Measurement*, IASB, para. AG77.
66 IFRS 2, *Share-based Payment*, IASB, para. 5.
67 IAS 32 (2007), *Financial Instruments: Presentation*, IASB, 2007 Bound Volume, para. 4(c).
68 IFRS 3 (2007), para. 28.
69 IFRS 3 (2007), para. 27.
70 IFRS 3 (2007), para. 27.
71 IFRS 3 (2007), para. BC69.
72 IFRS 3 (2007), para. BC68.
73 IFRS 3 (2007), para. 27.
74 IFRS 3 (2007), para. 29.
75 IAS 1, *Presentation of Financial Statements*, IASB, para. 32.
76 IFRS 3 (2007), para. 30.
77 IFRS 3 (2007), para. 31.
78 IFRS 3, para. 53.
79 *IFRIC Update*, IASB, July 2009, p. 2.
80 IFRS 3 (2007), para. 33.
81 IFRS 3 (2007), para. 32.
82 IFRS 3 (2007), para. 33.
83 IFRS 3 (2007), para. 33.
84 IFRS 3 (2007), para. 34.
85 IFRS 3 (2007), para. 35.
86 IFRS 3 (2007), para. 35.
87 *Framework for the Preparation and Presentation of Financial Statements*, IASB, para. 35.
88 IFRS 2, para. 5.
89 IAS 32 (2007), para. 4(c).
90 IFRS 3 (2007), para. 36.
91 IFRS 3 (2007), para. 37.

92 IFRS 3 (2007), paras. BC95-BC96.
93 IFRS 3 (2007), paras. BC111-BC112.
94 IFRS 3 (2007), para. BC117.
95 IFRS 3 (2007), para. 38.
96 IFRS 3 (2007), para. 40.
97 IFRS 3 (2007), para. 41.
98 IFRS 3 (2007), para. 41.
99 IFRS 3 (2007), paras. BC83-87.
100 IFRS 3 (2007), para. BC85.
101 IFRS 3 (2007), para. BC85.
102 IFRS 3 (2007), paras. BC108-BC110.
103 IFRS 3 (2007), para. 43.
104 IFRS 3 (2007), para. BC109.
105 IFRS 3 (2007), para. 43.
106 IFRS 3 (2007), para. BC109.
107 IFRS 3 (2007), para. 43.
108 IFRS 3 (2007), para. 42.
109 IFRS 3 (2007), para. 44.
110 IAS 38 (2007), *Intangible Assets*, IASB, 2007 Bound Volume, para. 34.
111 IFRS 3 (2007), para. 45.
112 IAS 38 (2007), paras. 33-34.
113 IFRS 3 (2007), para. 45.
114 IAS 38 (2007), para. 8.
115 IFRS 3 (2007), para. 46 and IAS 38 (2007), para. 12.
116 IFRS 3 (2007), para. 45 and IAS 38 (2007), para. 34.
117 IFRS 3 (2007), Illustrative Examples, *Examples of items acquired in a business combination that meet the definition of an intangible asset*.
118 IFRS 3 (2007), Illustrative Examples, *Customer relationship intangible assets acquired in a business combination*.
119 IFRS 3 (2007), para. 45.
120 IAS 38 (2007), para. 35.
121 IAS 38 (2007), para. 33.
122 IAS 38 (2007), para. 35.
123 IFRS 3 (2007), paras. BC97-BC101.
124 IAS 38 (2007), para. 38.
125 IAS 38 (2007), para. 36.
126 IAS 38 (2007), para. 37.
127 IFRS 3 (2007), para. 45 and IAS 38 (2007), para. 34.
128 IAS 38 (2007), para. 12.
129 IAS 38 (2007), para. 54.
130 IAS 38 (2007), para. 57.
131 IAS 38 (2007), para. 60.
132 IFRS 3 (2007), BC106.
133 IAS 38 (2007), para. 42.
134 IAS 38 (2007), para. 43.
135 IAS 36, *Impairment of Assets*, IASB, para. 10.
136 IFRS 3 (2007), para. 48.
137 IFRS 3 (2007), paras. BC114-BC115.
138 IAS 37, *Provisions, Contingent Liabilities and Contingent Assets*, IASB, para. 13.
139 IFRS 3 (2007), para. 49.
140 IFRS 3 (2007), para. 50.
141 IFRS 3 (2007), para. 47.
142 IFRS 3 (2007), Appendix A.
143 IFRS 3 (2007), para. B17.
144 IFRS 3 (2007), para. B16.
145 IFRS 3 (2007), para. B16.
146 IFRS 3 (2007), para. B16.
147 IFRS 3 (2007), para. B16.
148 IFRS 3 (2007), para. B16.
149 IFRS 3 (2007), para. B16.
150 IAS 38 (2007), para. 39.
151 IAS 38 (2007), para. 78.
152 IFRS 3 (2007), para. B16 and IAS 38 (2007), para. 40.
153 IAS 38 (2007), para. 40.
154 IAS 38 (2007), para. 41.
155 *Improvements to IFRSs*, April 2009, IAS 38, para. BC19D.
156 *Improvements to IFRSs*, April 2009, IAS 38, para. 130E.
157 *Improvements to IFRSs*, April 2009, IAS 38, para. 40.
158 *Improvements to IFRSs*, April 2009, IAS 38, para. 41.
159 IFRS 3 (2007), para. B16.
160 IAS 19, *Employee Benefits*, IASB, para. 108.
161 IFRS 3 (2007), para. B16.
162 IFRS 3 (2007), para. B16.
163 IFRS 3 (2007), para. B16.
164 IFRS 3 (2007), para. B16.
165 IAS 37, para. 13.
166 IFRS 3 (2007), para. 44.
167 *IFRIC Update*, IASB, May 2007, p. 5.
168 IFRS 3 (2007), para. BC129.
169 IFRS 3 (2007), Appendix A.
170 IFRS 3 (2007), para. 51.
171 IFRS 3 (2007), para. 52.
172 IFRS 3 (2007), para. 53.
173 IFRS 3 (2007), para. BC130.
174 IFRS 3 (2007), paras. BC131-BC135.
175 IFRS 3 (2007), para. 54.
176 IFRS 3 (2007), para. 55.
177 IFRS 3 (2007), para. 56.
178 IFRS 3 (2007), para. BC146.
179 IFRS 3 (2007), para. BC149.
180 IFRS 3 (2007), para. 56.
181 IFRS 3 (2007), para. 57.
182 IFRS 3 (2007), para. BC148.
183 IFRS 3 (2007), paras. BC148-BC156.
184 IFRS 3 (2007), para. 61.
185 IFRS 3 (2007), para. 62.
186 IFRS 3 (2007), para. 62.
187 IFRS 3 (2007), para. 62.
188 IFRS 3 (2007), para. 63.
189 IFRS 3 (2007), para. 63.
190 IFRS 3 (2007), para. 64.

191 IFRS 3 (2007), para. 65.
192 IFRS 3 (2007), para. BC157.
193 IFRS 3 (2007), para. 58.
194 IFRS 3 (2007), para. 59.
195 IFRS 3 (2007), para. 59.
196 IFRS 3 (2007), para. 60.
197 IFRS 3 (2007), para. 59.
198 IAS 28, *Investments in Associates*, IASB, para. 18.
199 IAS 36, para. 12(a).
200 IAS 16, *Property, Plant and Equipment*, IASB, para. 40 and IAS 38 (2007), para 86.
201 *Framework for the Preparation and Presentation of Financial Statements*, IASB, para. 81.
202 IFRS 3 (2007), para. 59.
203 IAS 16, para. 41 and IAS 38 (2007), para. 87.
204 IFRS 3 (2007), paras. B1-B3.
205 IFRS 3 (2007), para. B4.
206 IFRS 3 (2007), para. B5.
207 IFRS 3 (2007), para. B6.
208 IFRS 3 (2007), para. B9.
209 IFRS 3 (2007), para. B7.
210 IFRS 3 (2007), para. B8.
211 IFRS 3 (2007), para. B10.
212 IFRS 3 (2007), para. B11.
213 IFRS 3 (2007), para. B12.
214 IFRS 3 (2007), para. B13.
215 IFRS 3 (2007), para. B14.
216 IFRS 3 (2007), para. B15.
217 IFRS 3 (2007), para. 4.
218 IFRS 3, para. B19.
219 IFRS 2, para. 10.
220 IFRS 2, para. 13.
221 IFRS 2, para. 13A (inserted by *Group Cash-settled Share-based Payment Transactions* IASB, June 2009); IFRIC 8, paras. 8-12.
222 IFRS 3 (2007), Appendix A and IAS 27 (2007), para. 4.
223 IFRS 3 (2007), para. BC170.
224 IFRS 3 (2007), para. 66.
225 IFRS 3 (2007), para. 67.
226 IFRS 3 (2007), para. 68.
227 IFRS 3 (2007), para. 69.
228 IFRS 3 (2007), para. 70.
229 IFRS 3 (2007), para. 71.
230 IFRS 3 (2007), para. 72.
231 IFRS 3 (2007), para. 73.
232 IFRS 3 (2007), para. BC175.
233 IFRS 3 (2007), para. 74.
234 IFRS 3 (2007), para. 75.
235 IFRS 3 (2007), para. 76.
236 IFRS 3 (2007), para. 77.
237 IAS 7, *Statement of Cash Flows*, IASB, paras. 39-42.
238 IFRS 3, para. 64.
239 *IFRIC Update*, IASB, July 2009, p. 3.
240 IFRS 3, para. 1.
241 IFRS 3, para. 2.
242 IFRS 3, para. BC60.
243 IFRS 3, para. 2.
244 IFRS 3, paras. B1-B4.
245 IFRS 3, para. BC58.
246 IFRS 3, paras. BC71-B72.
247 IFRS 3, para. BC79.
248 IFRS 3, para. 3.
249 IFRS 3, paras. BC8-BC10.
250 IFRS 3, Appendix A.
251 IFRS 3, para. BC11.
252 IFRS 3, para. B5.
253 IFRS 3, para. B6.
254 IFRS 3, Appendix A.
255 IFRS 3, para. BC18.
256 IFRS 3, para. B7.
257 IFRS 3, paras. B8-B11.
258 IFRS 3, para. B10.
259 IFRS 3, para. B12.
260 *IASB Update*, IASB, May 2009, p. 5.
261 IFRS 3, para. 4.
262 IFRS 3, para. BC14.
263 IFRS 3, para. 5.
264 IFRS 3, paras. BC80-BC81.
265 IFRS 3, para. 6.
266 IFRS 3, para. 7 and Appendix A.
267 IFRS 3, para. 7.
268 IFRS 3, para. BC102.
269 IFRS 3, para. B14.
270 IFRS 3, para. B15.
271 IFRS 3, para. B16.
272 IFRS 3, para. B17.
273 IFRS 3, para. B18.
274 IFRS 3, para. B19.
275 IFRS 3, para. 8 and Appendix A.
276 IFRS 3, para. 9.
277 IFRS 3, para. 9.
278 IFRS 3, para. BC110.
279 IFRS 3, paras. 8-9.
280 IFRS 3, paras. 10, 14, 18 and 20.
281 IFRS 3, paras. 10 and 19.
282 IFRS 3, para. BC112.
283 IFRS 3, para. 11.
284 IFRS 3, para. BC132.
285 IFRS 3, para. BC137.
286 IFRS 3, paras. BC125-BC130.
287 IFRS 3, para. 12.
288 IFRS 3, para. BC115.
289 IFRS 3, para. BC114.
290 IFRS 3, para. 13.
291 IFRS 3, para. 14.
292 IFRS 3, Appendix A.
293 IFRS 3, paras. BC246-247.
294 IFRS 3, paras. BC248-250.
295 IFRS 3, para. BC251.
296 IFRS 3, para. 20.
297 IFRS 3, paras. 54-57.

298 *IFRIC Update*, IASB, May 2007, p. 5.
299 IFRS 3, para. 15.
300 IFRS 3, para. 17.
301 IFRS 3, para. 16.
302 IFRS 3, paras. B28-29.
303 IFRS 3, para. B30.
304 IFRS 3, paras. B29 and B42.
305 IFRS 3, para. BC146.
306 IFRS 3, para. BC148.
307 IFRS 3, paras. B31.
308 IFRS 3, Appendix A and IAS 38, para. 8.
309 IAS 38, para. 11.
310 IFRS 3, Appendix A and IAS 38, para. 12.
311 IFRS 3, para. B31.
312 IFRS 3, para. B33.
313 IFRS 3, para. B34.
314 IFRS 3, para. B32.
315 IFRS 3, paras. BC172-BC174.
316 *Improvements to IFRSs*, April 2009, IASB, IAS 38, para. BC19C.
317 *Improvements to IFRSs*, April 2009, IAS 38, paras. 36, 37 and 130C.
318 IFRS 3, para. B31.
319 IAS 38, para. 34.
320 IFRS 3, paras, BC149-BC156.
321 IFRS 3, paras, IE16-IE44.
322 IFRS 3, paras, IE30.
323 *IFRIC Update*, IASB, September 2008, p. 2.
324 The Glossary of Terms defines a contract as 'An agreement between two or more parties that has clear economic consequences that the parties have little, if any, discretion to avoid, usually because the agreement is enforceable in law. Contracts may take a variety of forms and need not be in writing.'
325 IFRS 3, para. IE28.
326 *IFRIC Update*, IASB, March 2009, pages 2-3.
327 *IFRIC Update*, IASB, March 2009, p. 3.
328 *IASB Update*, IASB, December 2008, p. 4.
329 Staff Paper, IASB meeting, May 2009, Agenda reference 13E, *Annual Improvement Project, Amendments to IFRS 3 – Customer-related intangible assets*, pp. 2 and 3.
330 *IASB Update*, IASB, May 2009, p. 5.
331 IAS 38(2008), paras. 36 and 37.
332 *Improvements to IFRSs*, April 2009, IAS 38, para. BC19C.
333 IFRS 3, para. IE21.
334 *Improvements to IFRSs*, April 2009, IAS 38, para. 130C.
335 IAS 38, para. 34.
336 IFRS 3, paras, BC149-BC156.
337 IAS 38, para. 34.
338 IAS 38, paras. 34 and 35.
339 IAS 38, para. 54.
340 IAS 38, para. 57.
341 IAS 38, para. 60.
342 IFRS 3 (2007), para. BC106 and IAS 38, para. BC82.
343 IAS 38, para. 42.
344 IAS 38, para. 43.
345 IAS 36, para. 10.
346 IAS 38, para. 33.
347 IAS 38, para. 39.
348 IAS 38, para. 39.
349 IAS 38, para. 78.
350 IAS 38, para. 40.
351 IAS 38, para. 41.
352 *Improvements to IFRSs*, April 2009, IAS 38, para. BC19D.
353 *Improvements to IFRSs*, April 2009, IAS 38, para. 130E.
354 *Improvements to IFRSs*, April 2009, IAS 38, para. 40.
355 *Improvements to IFRSs*, April 2009, IAS 38, para. 41.
356 IFRS 3, para. B35.
357 IFRS 3, paras. BC182-BC184.
358 IFRS 3, para. B36
359 IFRS 3, para. B37.
360 IFRS 3, para. BC178.
361 IFRS 3, para. B37.
362 IFRS 3, para. BC180.
363 IFRS 3, para. BC177.
364 IFRS 3, para. B37.
365 IFRS 3, para. B38.
366 IFRS 3, para. BC276.
367 IAS 37, para. 33.
368 IFRS 3, para. B40.
369 IFRS 3, para. B41.
370 IFRS 3, para. B43.
371 IFRS 3, para. 21.
372 IFRS 3, para. 22 and IAS 37, para. 10.
373 IFRS 3, para. 23.
374 IFRS 3, para. BC275.
375 IFRS 3, para. BC272-BC273.
376 *IASB Work Plan – projected timetable as at 1 August 2009.*
377 IFRS 3, para. 56.
378 IFRS 3, para. BC245.
379 IFRS 3, para. 56.
380 IFRS 3 (2007), para. 49.
381 IFRS 3, para. 24.
382 IFRS 3, para. 25.
383 IFRS 3, paras. BC279-BC281.
384 IAS 12, *Income Taxes*, IASB, para. 68.
385 IAS 12, para. 32A.
386 IFRS 3, para. 26,
387 IFRS 3, paras. BC297-BC299.
388 IAS 19, para. 108.
389 IFRS 3, paras. 26 and BC296-B300.
390 IFRS 3, para. 27.
391 IFRS 3, paras. BC302-BC303.
392 IFRS 3, para. 27.

393 IFRS 3, para. 28.
394 IFRS 3, para. 28.
395 IFRS 3, paras. 27-28.
396 IFRS 3, para. 57.
397 IFRS 3, para. 57.
398 *IASB Update*, IASB, May 2009, p. 5.
399 IFRS 3, para. B35.
400 IFRS 3, para. 29.
401 IFRS 3, para. BC309.
402 IFRS 3, para. B36
403 IFRS 3, paras. 55 and BC308.
404 IFRS 3, para. BC308.
405 IFRS 3, paras. 55 and BC308.
406 IFRS 3, para. 31.
407 IFRS 3, paras. BC305-BC307.
408 *IASB Update*, IASB, April 2008, p.3.
409 IFRS 3, para. 30.
410 IFRS 3, para. BC311.
411 IFRS 3, Appendix A.
412 IFRS 3, para. BC328.
413 IFRS 3, para. 32.
414 IFRS 3, para. 34.
415 IFRS 3, paras. BC322-323.
416 IFRS 3, para. BC313.
417 IFRS 3, para. BC316.
418 IFRS 3, paras. BC314-BC315.
419 IFRS 3, para. BC317.
420 IFRS 3, para. BC382.
421 IFRS 3, para. B63.
422 IFRS 3, para. 37.
423 IFRS 3, para. 38.
424 IFRS 3, Appendix A.
425 IFRS 3, paras. BC341.
426 IFRS 3, paras. BC338-BC342.
427 IFRS 3, para. BC340.
428 IFRS 3, para. BC342.
429 IFRS 3, para. 33.
430 IFRS 3, Appendix A.
431 *IASB Update*, IASB, June 2009, p. 6.
432 Staff Paper, IASB meeting, June 2009, Agenda reference 13C, *Annual Improvements Process, Contingent consideration of an Acquiree ("pre-existing contingent consideration")*, p. 3.
433 IFRS 3, para. 39
434 IFRS 3, para. BC347.
435 IFRS 3, para. BC348.
436 IFRS 3, paras. BC350-BC351.
437 IFRS 3, para. BC349.
438 IFRS 3, paras. 39-40 and Appendix A.
439 IFRS 3, para. 40.
440 IAS 32, para. 11.
441 IFRS 3, para. 40.
442 *IASB Update*, IASB, May 2009, p. 5.
443 IFRS 3, para. BC357.
444 IFRS 3, para. 58.
445 IFRS 3, para. BC354.
446 IFRS 3, para. BC355.
447 IFRS 3, para. 58.
448 IFRS 3, paras. B56-B62.
449 IFRS 3, paras. IE61-IE71.
450 *IFRIC Update*, IASB, July 2009, p. 6.
451 ED 2009/11, pp. 15-24.
452 ED 2009/11, pp. 15, 19 and 20.
453 ED 2009/11, p. 18.
454 IFRS 3, paras. 53, BC365-BC367.
455 IFRS 3, para. 53.
456 IFRS 3, paras. 51-53 and BC370.
457 IFRS 3, para. 43.
458 IFRS 3, para. 43.
459 IFRS 3, para. 33.
460 IFRS 3, para. B46.
461 IFRS 3, para. 44.
462 IFRS 3, Appendix A.
463 IFRS 3, para. B47.
464 IFRS 3, para. BC72.
465 IFRS 3, para. B47.
466 IFRS 3, para. B48.
467 IFRS 3, para. B49.
468 IFRS 3, para. 10.
469 IFRS 3, para. 19.
470 IFRS 3 ED, paras. 49 and 58.
471 IFRS 3, paras. BC206-BC207.
472 IFRS 3, para. BC210.
473 IFRS 3, para. B44.
474 IFRS 3, para. B45.
475 IFRS 3, para. BC217.
476 IFRS 3, para. BC218.
477 IFRS 3, Appendix A.
478 *IFRIC Update*, IASB, July 2009, p. 6.
479 ED 2009/11, p. 15.
480 ED 2009/11, p. 17.
481 ED 2009/11, p. 18.
482 *IASB Update*, IASB, May 2009, p. 5.
483 IFRS 3, para. 41.
484 IFRS 3, para. 42.
485 IFRS 3, para. BC384.
486 IFRS 3, para. 42.
487 IAS 31, *Interests in Joint Ventures*, IASB, para. 45.
488 IFRS 3, para. BC371.
489 IFRS 3, para. 34.
490 IFRS 3, para. 35.
491 IFRS 3, paras. BC372-BC375.
492 IFRS 3, para. 36.
493 IFRS 3, para. 34.
494 IFRS 3, paras. BC376-BC377.
495 IFRS 3, paras. 35 and BC379.
496 IFRS 3, paras. IE45-IE49.
497 IFRS 3, para. 12.
498 IFRS 3, para. 51.
499 IFRS 3, para. 52.
500 IFRS 3, paras. B50-B51.
501 IFRS 3, para. 52.
502 IFRS 3, para. B51.
503 IFRS 3, para. BC122.

504 IFRS 3, para. B52.
505 IFRS 3, paras. IE54-IE57.
506 IFRS 3, para. B53.
507 IFRS 3, para. BC123.
508 IFRS 3, para. B54.
509 IFRS 3, para. B55.
510 IFRS 3, paras. IE58-IE60.
511 IFRS 3, paras. B56-B62.
512 IFRS 3, paras. IE61-IE71.
513 IFRS 3, para. BC123.
514 IFRS 3, para. BC370.
515 IFRS 3, para. BC120.
516 IFRS 3, para. BC132.
517 IFRS 3, para. BC137.
518 IFRS 3, para. BC394.
519 IFRS 3, para. 46.
520 IFRS 3, para. 45.
521 IFRS 3, para. BC392.
522 IFRS 3, para. 45.
523 IFRS 3, para. BC392.
524 IFRS 3, para. 45.
525 IFRS 3, para. 47.
526 IFRS 3, para. 49.
527 IFRS 3, paras. IE50-IE53.
528 IFRS 3, para. 48.
529 IFRS 3, para. 50.
530 IFRS 3, para. 54.
531 IFRS 3, para. B63.
532 IFRS 3, para. B39.
533 IFRS 3, para. B19.
534 IFRS 3, para. B19.
535 IFRS 3, para. IE6.
536 IFRS 3, para. B20.
537 IFRS 3, paras. IE1-IE5.
538 IFRS 3, para. IE5.
539 IFRS 3, para. IE6.
540 IFRS 3, para. B21.
541 IFRS 3, para. B22.
542 IFRS 3, paras. IE7-IE8.
543 IFRS 3, para. IE8.
544 IFRS 3 (2007), para. B8.
545 IFRS 3, para. B23.
546 IFRS 3, para. B24.
547 IFRS 3, paras. IE11-IE15.
548 IFRS 3, para. B25.
549 IFRS 3, para. B26.
550 IFRS 3, para. B27.
551 IFRS 3, paras. IE9-IE10.
552 IFRS 3, para. B14.
553 IFRS 3, para. B19.
554 IFRS 2, para. 10.
555 IFRS 2, para. 13.
556 IFRS 2, para. 13A (inserted by *Group Cash-settled Share-based Payment Transactions* IASB, June 2009); IFRIC 8, paras. 8-12.
557 IFRS 3, paras. BC419-BC422.
558 IFRS 3, para. 59.

559 IFRS 3, para. 60.
560 IFRS 3, para. B64.
561 IFRS 3, para. B65.
562 IFRS 3, para. B66.
563 IFRS 3, para. 61.
564 IFRS 3, para. 62.
565 IFRS 3, para. B67.
566 IFRS 3, para. 63.
567 IAS 7, paras. 39-42.
568 IFRS 3, para. IE72.
569 IFRS 3, para. 64.
570 IFRS 3, para. 65.
571 IFRS 3, para. 67.
572 IAS 12, para. 68.
573 IFRS 3, paras. 66 and B68-B69.
574 *IFRIC Update*, IASB, July 2009, p. 2.
575 Staff Paper, IFRIC meeting, May 2009, Agenda reference 6A, *Amendments to IFRS 3 and IAS 27 – Acquisition-related costs in a business combination*, pp. 2 and 3.
576 ED 2009/11, pp. 15-24 and 43-49.
577 *IASB Update*, IASB, May 2009, p. 5.
578 IFRS 3 ED, para. BC9.
579 IFRS 3, para. BC57.
580 *IASB Work Plan – projected timetable as at 1 August 2009*, IASB.
581 *IASB Update*, IASB, December 2007, p. 1.
582 *IASB Work Plan – projected timetable as at 1 August 2009*, IASB; Project Update Summary, *Common Control Transactions*, IASB, August 2009.
583 IFRS 3, paras. BC272-BC273.
584 *IASB Work Plan – projected timetable as at 1 August 2009*.
585 IFRS 3, Appendix A.
586 IFRS 3, paras. BC246-247.
587 Exposure Draft (ED 2009/05), *Fair Value Measurement*, IASB, paras. D6-D9.
588 ED 2009/05, para. 1.
589 *IASB Work Plan – projected timetable as at 1 August 2009*, IASB.
590 ED 2009/11, pp. 15-24.
591 ED 2009/11, pp. 18, 21 and 22.
592 ED 2009/11, p. 24.
593 ED 2009/11, pp. 16, 21 and 22.
594 ED 2009/11, pp. 21-22.
595 *IFRIC Update*, IASB, July 2009, p. 6.
596 ED 2009/11, p. 15.
597 ED 2009/11, p. 17.
598 *IFRIC Update*, IASB, July 2009, p. 6.
599 ED 2009/11, pp. 15, 19 and 20.
600 ED 2009/11, p. 18.
601 *IASB Update*, IASB, May 2009, p. 5.
602 *IASB Update*, IASB, May 2009, p. 5.
603 ED 2009/11, pp. 15-24 and 43-49.
604 *IASB Update*, IASB, May 2009, p. 5.

Chapter 10   Common control business combinations

1   INTRODUCTION

1.1   Background

Transactions between entities under common control are a normal feature of business. Many entities carry on their business activities through subsidiaries and there will inevitably be transactions between the entities comprising the group. It is also common for entities under common control, but not comprising a group for financial reporting purposes, to transact with each other. Transactions between entities under common control might include:

- the sale of goods, property and other assets;
- the provision of services (including those of employees);
- leasing and transfers under licence agreements; and
- financing transactions, including provisions of guarantees.

Where transactions such as these take place between entities under common control, it cannot always be assumed that they are undertaken on an arm's length basis or that equal values have been exchanged. As discussed in the introduction to Chapter 38, accounting-standard setters, including the IASB, have developed standards that require disclosures about related party transactions such as these, rather than requiring the transactions to be measured at fair value on an arm's length basis.

Nevertheless, entities that have entered into such transactions need to account for them in their financial statements in accordance with any relevant IFRS applicable to that transaction, as generally there are no exemptions within the standards for transactions between entities under common control.

However, one type of transaction between entities under common control for which an exemption is provided is that of a business combination involving such entities.

This chapter discusses the implications of that exemption and accounting treatments which may be adopted for such transactions.

1.2   IFRIC discussions on common control transactions

In 2002, the IFRIC discussed whether transactions between entities under common control that are not conducted on arm's length terms should be accounted for as a capital contribution from and/or distribution to the party having common control. To illustrate, assume that entity A has two subsidiaries, entities B and C. If entity C sells goods to entity B at a price below fair value the difference between fair value and the sales price of those goods could be seen as a distribution by entity C to entity A and a simultaneous contribution by entity A to entity B. However, the IFRIC did not reach a conclusion on this matter.[1]

General guidance in accounting for transactions between a parent and its subsidiaries, or between subsidiaries within a group, is given in Chapter 8 at 4.

1.3   Exemption for business combinations involving entities or businesses under common control

As indicated at 1.1 above, one type of transaction between entities under common control for which an exemption is provided in IFRS is that of a business combination involving such entities.

This has been a long-standing exemption under IFRS, having initially been included in IAS 22 – *Business Combinations*. In 2001, the IASB began a project to review IAS 22 as part of its initial agenda. As discussed more fully in Chapter 9 at 1.2.2, this project was split initially into 2 phases, with the accounting for business combination involving entities (or operations of entities) under common control being deferred until the second phase.

The first phase of the project resulted in the IASB issuing, in March 2004, IFRS 3 – *Business Combinations*. That version of IFRS 3 therefore retained a scope exclusion, but the Board concluded that the nature of the scope exclusion would be better expressed as 'business combinations involving entities or businesses under common control' rather than 'transactions among enterprises under common control' (the exclusion in IAS 22). In addition, authoritative guidance on the application of the exemption was included in the new standard.[2]

The second phase of the project was undertaken as a joint project with the FASB. This involved a broad reconsideration of the requirements in IFRS and US GAAP on applying the purchase method (which is now termed 'the acquisition method'), and resulted in the IASB publishing in June 2005 a draft revised IFRS, which proposed to replace the version of IFRS 3 issued in March 2004.[3] Eventually, this part of the project resulted in the IASB issuing, in January 2008, the revised version of IFRS 3.[4] In this chapter, this revised version of the standard is termed 'IFRS 3 (as revised in 2008)' in order to distinguish it from the previous version of the standard, which is termed 'IFRS 3 (2007)'.

However, there is no change to the position as regards common control business combination because IFRS 3 (as revised in 2008) has essentially retained the scope exclusion and application guidance that was in IFRS 3 (2007), albeit with some minor changes to the wording. The scope exclusion is expressed as 'a combination of entities or businesses under common control',[5] and the application guidance amended accordingly.[6] The Basis for Conclusions accompanying IFRS 3 (as revised in 2008) indicates that the IASB continues to believe that issues related to such combinations are appropriately excluded from the scope of this project and that it is aware of nothing that has happened since IFRS 3 (2007) was issued to suggest that the revised standard should be delayed to address the accounting for those events.[7]

Nevertheless, in the June 2005 exposure draft that preceded IFRS 3 (as revised in 2008), the IASB indicated that it would consider the accounting for business combinations involving entities under common control as part of future phases of its project on business combinations.[8]

1.4   Future developments: IASB project on common control transactions

At its meeting in December 2007, the IASB considered whether to add to its active agenda a project on common control transactions. In the relevant agenda paper it was noted that 'in September 2006, the European Roundtable on Consistent Application of IFRSs identified combinations between entities or businesses under common control as a problematic accounting issue where there is a general, widely shared sentiment that the risk of divergent application is both real and significant.' In response to discussions at the roundtable the European Commission submitted a formal agenda request to the IASB in October 2006. The agenda request states:

> 'Roundtable participants believe that the boundaries of the scope exclusion in IFRS 3 Business Combinations need further clarification. Furthermore, the basis of accounting to be used for common control transactions is currently not resolved in IFRSs and therefore needs to be developed urgently.
>
> ...
>
> In view of its scope and complexity the Roundtable further concluded that the issue should be dealt with by the IASB rather than IFRIC.
>
> IASB and IFRIC have made several attempts to deal with the issue in the past but none of them has resulted in the development of the principles urgently needed. The Roundtable participants took the view there remain compelling reasons for the IASB to take up this issue as it has widespread and practical relevance and divergent interpretations already exist.
>
> Therefore, the issue is of fundamental importance and quick resolution is required. In spite of IASB's constraints regarding staff resources and available Board time we believe that the issue should be taken on the IASB agenda as an active project as soon as possible in 2007.'[9]

The agenda paper adds that the IASB staff also sought the input of various national standard-setters on whether the IASB should add a project on common control to its technical agenda and many of them supported the request by the European Commission.[10]

Accordingly, in December 2007, the IASB decided to add to its active agenda a project on common control transactions. It noted that business combinations involving entities or businesses under common control are excluded from the scope of IFRS 3 and, as a consequence, practice diverges on the accounting for those transactions in the acquirer's consolidated and separate financial statements.

The project on common control transactions will examine:

(a)   the definition of a business combination involving entities or businesses under common control; and

(b)   the methods of accounting for those transactions in the acquirer's:

(i)   consolidated financial statements; and

(ii)   separate financial statements.

The Board observed that similar issues arise with respect to the accounting for demergers, such as the spin-off of a subsidiary or business. Therefore, the Board decided to also include demergers in the scope of the project.[11]

It is clear from the above that the IASB's project is limited in its scope and is not going to deal with the numerous other transactions that take place between entities under common control that some constituents believed should be included within the scope of the project.[12]

Although the IASB decided to undertake this project, not much has happened since. The project is currently an IASB-only project. However, the Board will discuss with the FASB and other national standard setters whether the project should be conducted as a joint project. The IASB staff had been undertaking preliminary research on the accounting for common control transactions and planned to present a comprehensive project outline to the Board in January 2009.[13] However, this did not happen and, at the time of writing this chapter, the project is currently paused. A comprehensive project outline will be presented to the Board when the project resumes after staff working on projects relating to the financial crisis become available. At that time, the IASB will consider whether it should establish a working group, and will decide whether the first due process document should be a discussion paper or an exposure draft.[14]

1.5   Scope of this chapter

This chapter deals with items (a) and (b)(i) of the IASB's project on common control transactions, i.e.

- The common control exemption in IFRS 3 (2007)/IFRS 3 (as revised in 2008) for business combinations involving or between entities under common control (see 2 below).
- The accounting for such business combinations in the acquirer's consolidated financial statements (see 3 below).

Although the discussion at 3 below (particularly the Examples contained therein) generally refers to business combinations involving 'entities' and 'consolidated financial statements', the accounting is equally applicable to individual financial statements of an entity that combines with the business of another entity under common control. It is unclear from the IASB's description of the project whether the accounting in individual financial statements of an entity that combines with a business of another entity under common control is within the scope of the project, but we would think it should be covered as it arises from the business combination exemption.

This chapter, however, does not deal with item (b)(ii) of the IASB's project, i.e. the accounting in the acquirer's separate financial statements. This is dealt with in Chapter 8 which discusses the IASB's requirements relating to separate financial statements. That chapter also deals with the accounting for other types of transactions between entities under common control, i.e. those that the IASB has decided not to include within the scope of its project.

This chapter also does not deal with the other area that the IASB is including in its project on common control, i.e. that of demergers, such as the spin off of a subsidiary or business. Demergers are discussed in Chapter 7 at 3.5 and in Chapter 8 at 2.3.2.

Business combinations involving entities or businesses under common control invariably arise as a result of a group reorganisation. Such reorganisations can take many forms. For some of the entities involved in the reorganisation, there may well be a business combination that needs to be accounted for. At 4 below, we consider this particular aspect of the transaction in the context of the forms of reorganisations that are illustrated, based on the discussions contained in 2 and 3 below with respect to the common control exemption in IFRS. Obviously, the transferors in the reorganisation will need to account for their part of the transaction in their own financial statements. In doing so, they will need to consider the requirements of other relevant IFRSs, in particular, the IAS 27 – *Consolidated and Separate Financial Statements* – requirements relating to disposals of/loss of control over subsidiaries (see Chapter 7 at 3.2.1 and 3.3.1) and the IFRS 5 – *Non-current Assets Held for Sale and Discontinued Operations* – requirements relating to disposal groups held for sale and discontinued operations (see Chapter 4). The discussion in Chapter 7 at 3.5 and in Chapter 8 at 2.3.2 relating to demergers may also be relevant. Chapter 8 will also be relevant to the accounting in the separate/individual financial statements of the entities involved in the reorganisation.

Obviously, any transaction between entities under common control is a related party transaction under IAS 24 – *Related Party Disclosures*, the requirements of which are dealt with in Chapter 38.

2 EXEMPTION FOR BUSINESS COMBINATIONS INVOLVING ENTITIES OR BUSINESSES UNDER COMMON CONTROL

As indicated at 1.3 above, the IASB's most recent standard on business combinations, IFRS 3 (as revised in 2008), excludes from its requirements 'a combination of entities or businesses under common control'.[15] On the other hand, IFRS 3 (2007) excludes 'business combinations involving entities or businesses under common control' from its scope. Despite the minor changes to the wording introduced by IFRS 3 (as revised in 2008), the authoritative application guidance is identical.[16]

IFRS 3 (as revised in 2008) is effective for business combinations where the acquisition date is on or after the beginning of annual periods starting on or after 1 July 2009, although earlier application is permitted.[17] For entities with calendar year ends they will not have to apply IFRS 3 (as revised in 2008) until their 31 December 2010 financial statements. Thus, at this time, many entities will still be applying the previous version of the standard, IFRS 3 (2007). The first entities that will have to apply IFRS 3 (as revised in 2008) will generally be those with 30 June 2010 year ends, although entities with shortened accounting periods may have to apply it earlier. Accordingly, the discussion of the authoritative application guidance below is written in the context of IFRS 3 (2007), but will also be applicable to those entities applying IFRS 3 (as revised in 2008). However, where it is considered necessary, additional commentary relating to IFRS 3 (as revised in 2008) is included.

Although there has been no change to the authoritative application guidance in the standard, the exemption under IFRS 3 (as revised in 2008) is likely to apply to more transactions involving entities or businesses under common control than before as a result of the revised definition of a 'business' under the revised standard (see Chapter 9 at 3.2.2).

If the transaction is not a business combination because the entity or assets being acquired do not meet the definition of a business, it is accounted for as an acquisition of assets. The accounting for such common control transactions is discussed in Chapter 8 at 4.4.2 D.

2.1   Common control exemption

For the purpose of the exemption, a business combination involving entities or businesses under common control 'is a business combination in which all of the combining entities or businesses are ultimately controlled by the same party or parties both before and after the business combination, and that control is not transitory'.[18] This will include transactions, such as the transfer of subsidiaries or businesses, between entities within a group.

The extent of minority interests (non-controlling interests) in each of the combining entities before and after the business combination is not relevant to determining whether the combination involves entities under common control.[19] This is because a partially-owned subsidiary is nevertheless under the control of the parent entity. Therefore transactions involving partially-owned subsidiaries would be outside the scope of the standard. Similarly, the fact that one of the combining entities is a subsidiary that has been excluded from the consolidated financial statements of the group in accordance with IAS 27 is not relevant to determining whether a combination involves entities under common control.[20]

2.1.1 Common control by an individual or group of individuals

The exclusion is not, however, restricted to transactions between entities within a group. The standard notes that an entity can be controlled by an individual, or by a group of individuals acting together under a contractual arrangement, and that individual or group of individuals may not be subject to the financial reporting requirements of IFRSs.[21] Thus a transaction involving entities controlled by the same individual, including one that results in a new parent entity, would be outwith the scope of the standard. It is not necessary for combining entities to be included as part of the same consolidated financial statements for a business combination to be regarded as one involving entities under common control.[22]

A group of individuals are regarded as controlling an entity when, as a result of contractual arrangements, they collectively have the power to govern its financial and operating policies so as to obtain benefits from its activities. Therefore, a business combination is outside the scope of IFRS 3 (2007) when the same group of individuals has, as a result of contractual arrangements, ultimate collective power to govern the financial and operating policies of each of the combining entities so as to obtain benefits from their activities, and that ultimate collective power is not transitory.[23]

It can be seen that for the exemption to apply when a group of individuals are involved there has to be a 'contractual arrangement' between them such that they have control over the entities involved in the transaction. IFRS 3 (2007) does not indicate what form such an arrangement should take. However, IAS 31 – *Interests in Joint Ventures* – in determining what is a 'joint venture' states that '... whatever its form, the contractual arrangement is usually in writing ...'.[24] Although it is acknowledged that a contractual arrangement is usually in writing, this also implies that it is possible for a contractual arrangement to be in non-written form. Clearly, where the arrangement is not in writing, consideration needs to be given to all of the facts and circumstances to determine whether it is appropriate to apply the exemption.

Example 10.1: Common control involving individuals

Entity A has 3 shareholders Mr W, Mr X, and Mr Y. Mr X and Mr Y are family members who each hold a 30% interest in Entity A. Mr X and Mr Y also each hold a 30% interest in Entity B. There is no written contractual arrangement between Mr X and Mr Y requiring them to act collectively as shareholders in Entity A and Entity B.

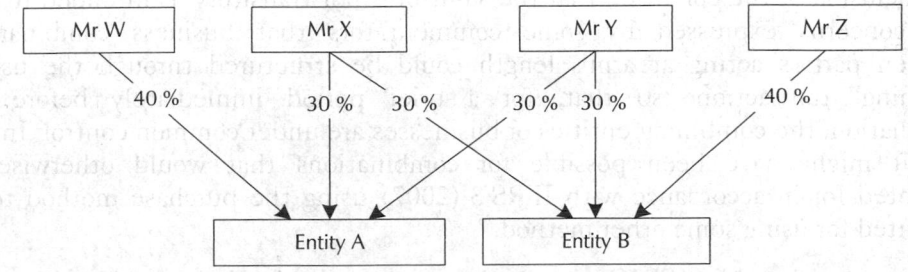

If Entity A acquires 100% of Entity B, is this a business combination involving entities under common control as a result of the joint holdings of Mr X and Mr Y, and therefore outside the scope of IFRS 3 (2007), where the nature of the family relationship is:

(a)   Mr X is the father and Mr Y is his young dependent son?; or

(b)   Mr X is a patriarchal father and, as a result of his highly influential standing, his adult son Mr Y has traditionally followed his father's decisions?; or

(c)   Mr X and Mr Y are adult siblings?

Whether common control exists between family members very much depends on the specific facts and circumstances. In the case of family members it is unlikely that there will be any written agreement between them. However, the influence that normally arises within relationships between 'close members of the family' as defined in IAS 24 (see Chapter 38 at 2.3.7) means that it is possible, but no means assured, that an unwritten arrangement may exist that they will act collectively such that there is common control, and thus the business combination can be considered to be outwith the scope of IFRS 3 (2007).

This may be the case in scenario (a), where the father, Mr X, may effectively control the voting of his dependent son (particularly a young dependant) by acting on his behalf and thus vote the entire 60% combined holding collectively. It may also be possible in scenario (b) as a highly influential parent may be able to ensure that the adult family members act collectively. However, there would need to be clear evidence that the family influence has resulted in a pattern of collective family decisions. Nevertheless, if there was any evidence to indicate that Mr X and Mr Y actually act independently (e.g. by voting differently at shareholder or board meetings), then the common control exemption would not apply since they have not been acting collectively to control the entities.

However, common control is unlikely to exist in scenario (c). Where the family members are not 'close members of the family', there is likely to be far less influence between them. Therefore, in scenario (c) where Mr X and Mr Y are adult siblings, it is far less likely that an unwritten agreement will exist as adult siblings generally would be expected to have less influence over each other and are more likely to act independently. Accordingly, we believe that there should be a presumption that common control does not exist between non-close family members and a high level of evidence that they act collectively, rather than independently, would need to exist to overcome this presumption.

If in the above example, Mr X and Mr Y had been unrelated, then in the absence of a written agreement, consideration would need to be given to all of the facts and circumstances to determine whether it is appropriate to apply the exemption. In our view, there would need to be a very high level of evidence of them acting together to control both entities in a collective manner in order to demonstrate that an unwritten contractual agreement really exists, and that such control is not transitory.

2.1.2   Transitory control

The inclusion of the condition that the 'control is not transitory' is intended to deal with concerns expressed by some commentators that business combinations between parties acting at arm's length could be structured through the use of 'grooming' transactions so that, for a brief period immediately before the combination, the combining entities or businesses are under common control. In this way, it might have been possible for combinations that would otherwise be accounted for in accordance with IFRS 3 (2007) using the purchase method to be accounted for using some other method.[25]

An issue considered by IFRIC was whether a reorganisation involving the formation of a new entity (Newco) to facilitate the sale of part of an organisation is a business combination within the scope of IFRS 3 (2007). It had been suggested to IFRIC that, because control of the new entity is transitory, a combination involving that newly formed entity would be within the scope of IFRS 3 (2007).

As discussed in Chapter 9 at 2.3, IFRS 3 (2007) states that when an entity is formed to issue equity instruments to effect a business combination, one of the combining entities that existed before the combination must be identified as the acquirer on the basis of the evidence available. IFRIC noted that, to be consistent, the question of whether the entities or businesses are under common control applies to the combining entities that existed before the combination, excluding the newly formed entity. Accordingly, IFRIC decided not to add this topic to its agenda.[26]

Example 10.2:   Formation of Newco to facilitate disposal of businesses

Entity A currently has two businesses operated through Entity X and Entity Y. The group structure (ignoring other entities within the group) is as follows:

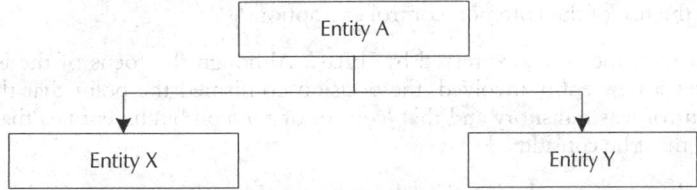

Entity A proposes to combine the two businesses (currently operated by Entity X and Entity Y) into the one entity and then spin-off the combined entity as part of an initial public offering (IPO). Both of the businesses have been owned by Entity A for several years. The internal reconstruction will be structured such that Entity A will establish a new entity (Newco) and transfer its interests in Entity X and Entity Y to Newco, resulting in the following group structure:

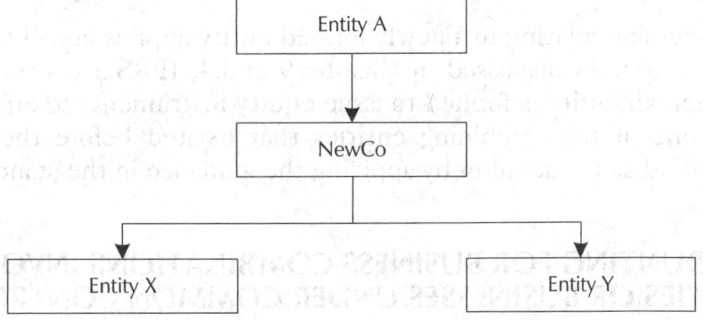

After the IPO, Newco will no longer be under the control of Entity A.

If Newco were to prepare consolidated financial statements, is it entitled to the 'common control' exemption?

As indicated by IFRIC, the question of whether the entities or businesses are under common control applies to the combining entities that existed before the combination, excluding the newly formed entity. In this situation, the combining entities that existed before the combination were Entity X and Entity Y, and these clearly are entities that have been under the common control of Entity A, and are still under the common control of Entity A after the transfer. Clearly, if Newco were preparing consolidated financial statements without there being an intended IPO, it would be entitled to the exemption. However, given that the purpose of the transaction was to facilitate the disposal of the businesses by way of the IPO, such that Entity A no longer has control over Entity X and Entity Y, does this mean that common control is 'transitory'?

In our view, the answer is 'no'. Common control is not considered to be transitory and therefore the reorganisation is excluded from the scope of IFRS 3 (2007). As indicated above, the reason for the requirement 'that control is not transitory' is intended as an anti-avoidance mechanism to prevent business combinations between parties acting at arm's length from being structured through the use of 'grooming' transactions so that, *for a brief period immediately before the combination*, the combining entities or businesses are under common control. Whether or not control is 'transitory' should be assessed by looking at the duration of control in the period both before and after the transaction – it is not limited to an assessment of the duration of control only after the transaction.

This is consistent with the ordinary meaning of 'transitory' being something which is fleeting, brief or temporary. The common control of Entity X and Entity Y was not fleeting in the fact pattern as both entities had been controlled by Entity A for several years. By contrast, if Entity Y had only recently come into the group, this may well indicate that control is transitory.

Therefore, an intention to sell the business or go to an IPO shortly after the restructure does not, by itself, prevent the use of the common control exemption.

This is consistent with the views expressed by IFRIC. Although the focus of the issue was on the fact that there was a new entity involved, the decision confirmed the point that the intended sale did not mean control was transitory and that 'control of the combining entities that existed before the combination' must be considered.

Although the above example involved a new entity, the same considerations apply regardless of the manner in which the internal reconstruction may have been structured prior to the IPO. For example, Entity X may have acquired Entity Y (or the net assets and trade of Entity Y), with Entity X then being the subject of an IPO. In such a situation, Entity X would be entitled to the common control exemption with respect to the business combination.

The above discussion relating to a newly formed entity applies equally under IFRS 3 (as revised in 2008). As discussed in Chapter 9 at 3.4, IFRS 3 (as revised in 2008) states that when an entity is formed to issue equity instruments to effect a business combination, one of the combining entities that existed before the combination must be identified as the acquirer by applying the guidance in the standard.

3   ACCOUNTING FOR BUSINESS COMBINATIONS INVOLVING ENTITIES OR BUSINESSES UNDER COMMON CONTROL

IFRIC also considered a request for guidance on how to apply IFRS 3 (2007) to reorganisations in which control remains within the original group. However, IFRIC decided not to add this topic to the agenda, since it was unlikely that it would reach agreement in a reasonable period, in the light of existing diversity in practice and the explicit exclusion of common control transactions from the scope of IFRS 3 (2007).[27]

As discussed at 1.4 above, the IASB's project on common control transactions will examine the methods of accounting for business combinations involving entities or businesses under common control in the acquirer's consolidated and separate financial statements.

In the meantime, both IFRS 3 (2007) and IFRS 3 (as revised in 2008) only prescribe the purchase method (acquisition method) for combinations that are within their scope and do not describe any other methods; they do not address at all the methods of accounting that may be appropriate when a business combination involves entities under common control.

As indicated at 2 above, IFRS 3 (as revised in 2008) is effective for business combinations where the acquisition date is on or after the beginning of annual periods starting on or after 1 July 2009, although earlier application is permitted.[28] For entities with calendar year ends they will not have to apply IFRS 3 (as revised in 2008) until their 31 December 2010 financial statements. Thus, at this time, many entities will still be applying the previous version of the standard, IFRS 3 (2007). The first entities that will have to apply IFRS 3 (as revised in 2008) will generally be those with 30 June 2010 year ends, although entities with shortened accounting periods may have to apply it earlier. Accordingly, the discussions in the sections below of the methods of accounting that we believe are available to entities in accounting for exempt business combinations involving entities or businesses under common control is written in the context of IFRS 3 (2007). In many cases, these will also be applicable to those entities applying IFRS 3 (as revised in 2008). However, where it is considered necessary, additional commentary relating to IFRS 3 (as revised in 2008) is included.

The discussions below are generally only relevant if the transaction is a business combination. As indicated at 2 above, if the transaction is not a business combination because the entity or assets being acquired do not meet the definition of a business, it is accounted for as an acquisition of assets. The accounting for such common control transactions is discussed in Chapter 8 at 4.4.2 D.

For some business combinations involving entities or entities under common control, it may be that the business is transferred without any consideration being given. Commonly the transfer is as a distribution by a subsidiary to its parent or contribution, usually but not necessarily by a parent, to a subsidiary. There can be legal arrangements that result in the distribution of a business to another group entity, including reorganisations sanctioned by a court process or transfers after liquidation of the transferor entity. In addition, some jurisdictions allow a legal merger between a parent and subsidiary to form a single entity. The accounting for such transactions is discussed in Chapter 8 at 4.4.3.

3.1   Pooling of interests method or purchase method (acquisition method)

As discussed further in Chapter 3 at 4.3, IAS 8 – *Accounting Policies, Changes in Accounting Estimates and Errors* – requires that in the absence of specific guidance in IFRS, management shall use its judgement in developing and applying an accounting policy that is relevant and reliable.[29] In making that judgement, in the absence of IFRS dealing with similar or related issues or guidance within the IASB *Framework*, management may also consider the most recent pronouncements of other standard-setting bodies that use a similar conceptual framework to develop accounting standards, to the extent that these do not conflict with the *Framework* or any other IFRS or Interpretation.[30] Several such bodies have issued guidance and some allow or require the pooling of interests method in accounting for business combinations involving entities under common control.

Accordingly, until such time as the IASB finalises its conclusions under its project on common control transactions, we believe that entities should apply either the:

(a)   pooling of interests method; or

(b)   purchase method (as in IFRS 3 (2007))

in accounting for business combinations involving entities or businesses under common control.

Although the pooling of interests method is not referred to in IFRS 3 (2007) (except in the context of eliminating it as a method for accounting for business combinations generally), since IFRS 3 (2007) scopes out common control business combinations it is therefore not prescriptive as to what method must be followed in such transactions. Therefore, an entity can choose either method for common control business combinations. The fact that IFRS 3 (2007) scopes out common control business combinations does not emanate from the fact that the Board felt either method was inappropriate, but that it wanted to address common control business combinations as a separate issue in the business combination project. The Board did not want to prescribe or ban either of these methods in the meantime. However, we do not consider that 'fresh start accounting', whereby all combining businesses are restated to fair value, is an appropriate method for accounting for combinations between entities under common control.

Whichever policy is adopted should be applied consistently. However, in our view, where the purchase method of accounting is selected, the transaction must have substance from the perspective of the reporting entity. This is because the purchase method results in a reassessment of the value of the net assets of one or more of the entities involved and/or the recognition of goodwill. IFRS contains limited circumstances when net assets may be restated to fair value and restricts the recognition of internally generated goodwill, and a common control transaction should not be used to circumvent these limitations. Careful consideration is required of all of the facts and circumstances from the perspective of each entity, before it is concluded that a transaction has substance. If there is no substance to the transaction, the pooling of interests method is the only method that may be applied to that transaction.

When evaluating whether the transaction has substance, the following factors should all be taken into account:

•   the purpose of the transaction;

•   the involvement of outside parties in the transaction, such as minority interests/non-controlling interests or other third parties;

•   whether or not the transaction is conducted at fair value;

•   the existing activities of the entities involved in the transaction;

- whether or not it is bringing entities together into a 'reporting entity' that did not exist before; and
- where a Newco is established, whether it is undertaken in connection with an IPO or spin-off or other change in control and significant change in ownership.

For entities where IFRS 3 (as revised in 2008) would otherwise be applicable, their policy choice should be between the:

(a)   pooling of interests method; or

(b)   acquisition method (as in IFRS 3 (as revised in 2008)).

As above, whichever policy is adopted should be applied consistently. However, in our view, where the acquisition method of accounting is selected, the transaction must have substance from the perspective of the reporting entity.

Example 10.3:   Accounting for common control business combinations (1)

Entity A currently has two businesses operated through two wholly-owned subsidiaries, Entity B and Entity C. The group structure (ignoring other entities within the group) is as follows:

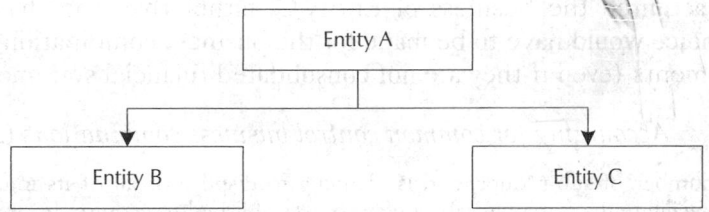

Entity A proposes to combine the two businesses (currently operated by Entity B and Entity C) into the one entity in anticipation of spinning-off the combined entity as part of an initial public offering (IPO). Both of the businesses have been owned by Entity A for several years. The internal reconstruction will be structured such that Entity B will acquire the shares of the much smaller Entity C from Entity A for cash at its fair value of £1,000. The carrying value of the net assets of Entity C is £200. This also represents the carrying amount of Entity C's net assets in the consolidated financial statements of Entity A. The fair values of Entity C's identifiable assets, liabilities and contingent liabilities are £600.

Assuming that the policy is to apply the purchase method of accounting to such transactions, how should this business combination be accounted for in the consolidated financial statements of both Entity B and Entity A?

Analysis under IFRS 3 (2007)

As far as Entity B is concerned, there does appear to be substance to this transaction from its perspective. There is a business purpose to the transaction; it has been conducted at fair value; both Entity B and Entity C have existing activities; and they have been brought together to create a reporting entity that did not exist before. Accordingly, since Entity B now controls Entity C, it can apply the purchase method of accounting (as discussed in Chapter 9 at 2.2) to its acquisition of its new subsidiary in its consolidated financial statements. In summary, this will mean that Entity C's identifiable assets, liabilities and contingent liabilities will be initially reflected at their fair values of £600, together with goodwill of £400 (£1,000 less £600), in the consolidated balance sheet, with only the post-acquisition results of Entity C reflected in the consolidated income statement.

As far as Entity A is concerned, from the perspective of the Entity A group, there has been no change in the reporting entity – all that has happened is that Entity C, rather than being directly held and controlled by Entity A, is now indirectly held and controlled through Entity B. Accordingly, there is no business combination that can be accounted for under the purchase method. In any event, the effects of applying purchase accounting would be eliminated on consolidation as required by IAS 27 (see Chapter 7 at 2.4). The transaction therefore has no impact on the consolidated financial statements of Entity A. Thus, the carrying amounts for Entity C's net assets included in those consolidated financial statements do not change.

Analysis under IFRS 3 (as revised in 2008)

Assuming that the policy is not to apply the pooling of interests method, but to apply the acquisition method of accounting to such transactions, the analysis is the same as above, except that Entity B applies the acquisition method of accounting in IFRS 3 (as revised in 2008) (as discussed in Chapter 9 at 3.3).

In the above example, Entity B had to account for its acquisition of its new subsidiary, Entity C, as it was preparing consolidated financial statements. This may only be required when the new Entity B group is being demerged or spun-off as part of an IPO as in the example. In some situations, Entity B would not need to account for the business combination at all, as it may be exempt from preparing consolidated financial statements – see Chapter 6 at 3.1. Nevertheless, if in Example 10.3 above, Entity B had acquired the business of Entity C, rather than the shares, then the same policy choice would have to be made for the business combination in Entity B's financial statements (even if they are not consolidated financial statements).

Example 10.4:   *Accounting for common control business combinations (2)*

Entity A has a number of sub-groups, and is planning to dispose of all of its interests in certain subsidiaries. To facilitate the potential sale, a Newco is established to acquire the entities to be sold – Subgroups C and E. Newco purchases the shares in Entity C from Entity A for cash from a bank loan. The group structure before and after this transaction is as follows:

Before

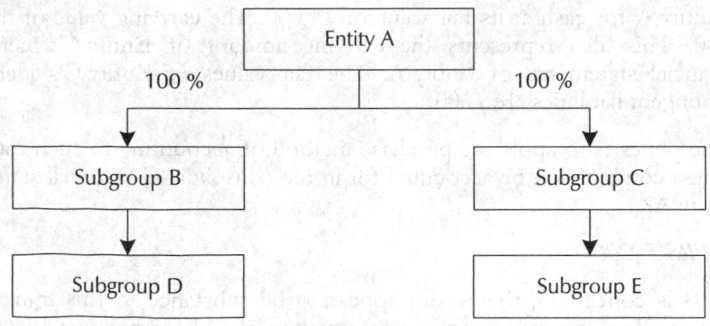

After

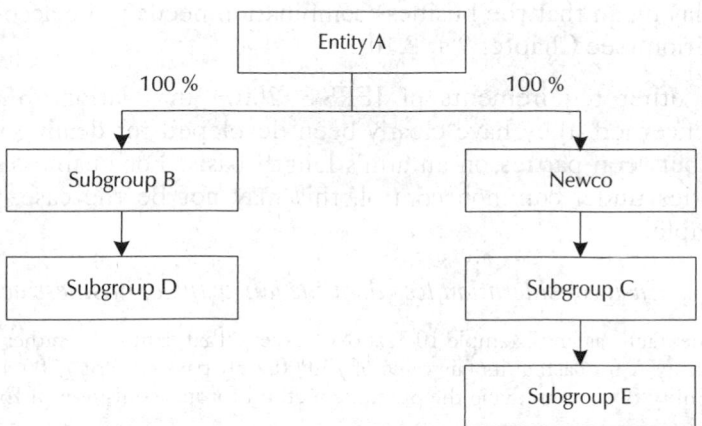

Analysis under IFRS 3 (2007)

In this situation, there is no substance to the transaction from Newco's perspective as the Newco group is simply a continuation of the existing subgroup comprising Subgroup C and Subgroup E's activities. Newco is essentially an extension of the parent as it does not have its own operations. The change in control is only planned, and it is not an integral part of the transaction. Thus, Newco cannot apply the purchase method of accounting in preparing its consolidated financial statements. It would have to apply the pooling of interests method. However, if such a restructuring was an integral part of another transaction such as a sale or disposal via an IPO, the circumstances may be such that Newco could be regarded as the acquirer if it is considered to be effectively an extension of the new owners (see Example 9.2 at 2.3 in Chapter 9).

Analysis under IFRS 3 (as revised in 2008)

The analysis is the same as above, except that the reference would be to Example 9.38 at 3.4 in Chapter 9.

3.2   Application of the purchase method under IFRS 3 (2007)

When the purchase method is being applied to business combinations involving entities under common control, then as indicated above entities need to follow the requirements of IFRS 3 (2007). As indicated in Chapter 9 at 2.2, applying the purchase method in IFRS 3 (2007) involves the following steps:[31]

(a)   identifying an acquirer (see 2.3 of that Chapter);

(b)   measuring the cost of the business combination (see 2.4 of that Chapter); and

(c)   allocating, at the acquisition date, the cost of the business combination to the assets acquired and liabilities and contingent liabilities assumed (see 2.5 of that Chapter).

Goodwill is recognised at its cost, being the excess of (b) over the acquirer's interest in (c) (see Chapter 9 at 2.6). If the acquirer's interest in (c) is greater than (b), the excess is recognised immediately in profit or loss (see Chapter 9 at 2.7).

As far as (a) is concerned, it may be that in some situations that the identification of the acquirer may mean that the business combination needs to be accounted for as a reverse acquisition (see Chapter 9 at 2.10).

As far as the other requirements of IFRS 3 (2007) in relation to the purchase method are concerned, they have clearly been developed for dealing with business combinations between parties on an arm's length basis. For business combinations involving entities under common control, this may not be the case. Consider the following example.

Example 10.5:   Cash consideration less than the fair value of business acquired

Assume the same facts as in Example 10.3 above, except that Entity B, rather than acquiring Entity C from Entity A for cash at its fair value of £1,000, only pays cash of £700. How should this be reflected by Entity B when applying the purchase method for its acquisition of Entity C?

In our view, there are two acceptable ways of accounting for this. Either:

(a) the cost of the business combination is the fair value of the cash given as consideration, i.e. £700. Accordingly, goodwill of only £100 (£700 less £600) is recognised; or

(b) the cost of the business combination is the fair value of the cash given as consideration (£700), together with a deemed capital contribution received from Entity A for the difference up to the fair value of the business of Entity C, i.e. £300 (£1,000 less £700), giving a total consideration of £1,000. Accordingly, goodwill of £400 is recognised. The capital contribution of £300 would be reflected in equity.

Whichever method is adopted should be applied on a consistent basis.

If Entity B only paid cash of £500, then the impact under (a) and (b) above would be:

(a) Since the cost is only £500, then no goodwill is recognised. However, £100 (being the excess of the fair values of the identifiable assets, liabilities and contingent liabilities (£600) over the cost of £500) is recognised immediately in profit or loss.

(b) As before, goodwill of £400 is recognised, but a capital contribution of £500 would be reflected in equity.

In Example 10.3 and Example 10.5 above, the consideration paid by Entity B was in cash. However, what if Entity B issued shares to Entity A to effect the business combination?

Where equity instruments are issued by an acquirer to effect a business combination, IFRS 3 (2007) requires the cost of the business combination to be based on the fair value of the equity instruments issued. As indicated in Chapter 9 at 2.4.3, for quoted equity instruments, IFRS 3 (2007) regards the published price at the date of exchange as providing the best estimate of the instrument's fair value. In situations such as this, where the business combination is between entities under common control, there is unlikely to be a published price for the acquirer's shares. Where this is the case, IFRS 3 (2007) states that 'if a published price does not exist for equity instruments issued by the acquirer, the fair value of those instruments could, for example, be estimated by reference to their proportional interest in the fair value of the acquirer or by reference to the proportional interest in the fair value of the acquiree obtained, whichever is the more clearly evident'.[32]

In Example 10.5 above, if Entity B issued shares to Entity A to acquire Entity C, and there is no quoted price for Entity B's shares, then the fair value of the shares issued would need to be based on either the fair value of Entity B or the fair value of Entity C, whichever is the more clearly evident. If the fair value of Entity B was more clearly evident, and the value of the shares issued as consideration was only £700, then as with cash consideration less than the fair value of the business acquired, Entity B would apply whichever method in Example 10.5 it has adopted for such transactions. However, in the absence of a 'more clearly evident' fair value for Entity B, the cost would be based on the fair value of Entity C, i.e. £1,000. Thus, goodwill of £400 would be recognised, with the £1,000 cost reflected in equity.

3.3 Application of the acquisition method under IFRS 3 (as revised in 2008)

For entities where IFRS 3 (as revised in 2008) would otherwise be applicable, entities need to follow the acquisition method in IFRS 3 (as revised in 2008). As indicated in Chapter 9 at 3.3, applying the acquisition method in IFRS 3 (as revised in 2008) involves the following steps:[33]

(a) identifying an acquirer (see 3.4 of that Chapter);

(b) determining the acquisition date (see 3.5 of that Chapter);

(c) recognising and measuring the identifiable assets acquired, the liabilities assumed, and any non-controlling interest in the acquiree (see 3.6 of that Chapter); and

(d) recognising and measuring goodwill or a gain on bargain purchase (see 3.7 of that Chapter).

As far as (a) is concerned, it may be that in some situations that the identification of the acquirer may mean that the business combination needs to be accounted for as a reverse acquisition (see Chapter 9 at 3.15).

Under (d) above, the measurement of goodwill at the acquisition date is computed as the excess of (a) over (b) below:[34]

(a) the aggregate of:

    (i) the consideration transferred (generally measured at acquisition-date fair value);

    (ii) the amount of any non-controlling interest in the acquiree; and

    (iii) the acquisition-date fair value of the acquirer's previously held equity interest in the acquiree.

(b) the net of the acquisition-date fair values (or other amounts recognised in accordance with the requirements of the standard) of the identifiable assets acquired and the liabilities assumed.

Where (b) exceeds (a), IFRS 3 (as revised in 2008) regards this as giving rise to a gain on a bargain purchase.[35]

Like IFRS 3 (2007) discussed at 3.2 above, the requirements of IFRS 3 (as revised in 2008) in relation to the acquisition method have clearly been developed for dealing with business combinations between parties on an arms' length basis. For business combinations involving entities under common control, this may not be the case. The example below is the same as Example 10.5 above, but the analysis is based on IFRS 3 (as revised in 2008) rather than on IFRS 3 (2007). As the example does not include any non-controlling interest in the acquiree nor any previously held interest in the acquiree by the acquirer, the computation of goodwill/gain on bargain purchase only involves the comparison between (a)(i) and (b) above.

Example 10.6:   Cash consideration less than the fair value of business acquired

Assume the same facts as in Example 10.3 above, except that Entity B, rather than acquiring Entity C from Entity A for cash at its fair value of £1,000, only pays cash of £700. How should this be reflected by Entity B when applying the acquisition method for its acquisition of Entity C?

In our view, there are two acceptable ways of accounting for this. Either:

(a) the consideration transferred is the fair value of the cash given as consideration, i.e. £700. Accordingly, goodwill of only £100 (£700 less £600) is recognised; or

(b) the consideration transferred is the fair value of the cash given as consideration (£700), together with a deemed capital contribution received from Entity A for the difference up to the fair value of the business of Entity C, i.e. £300 (£1,000 less £700), giving a total consideration of £1,000. Accordingly, goodwill of £400 is recognised. The capital contribution of £300 would be reflected in equity.

Whichever method is adopted should be applied on a consistent basis.

If Entity B only paid cash of £500, then the impact under (a) and (b) above would be:

(a) Since the consideration transferred is only £500, then no goodwill is recognised. However, a gain on bargain purchase of £100 (being the excess of the net acquisition-date fair values of the assets acquired less liabilities assumed (£600) over the consideration transferred of £500) is recognised immediately in profit or loss.

(b) As before, goodwill of £400 is recognised, but a capital contribution of £500 would be reflected in equity.

In Example 10.3 and Example 10.6 above, the consideration paid by Entity B was in cash. However, what if Entity B issued shares to Entity A to effect the business combination?

Where equity instruments are issued by an acquirer to effect a business combination, IFRS 3 (as revised in 2008) requires the consideration transferred to be based on the fair value of the equity instruments issued. As discussed in Chapter 9 at 3.8, IFRS 3 (as revised in 2008) states that in a business combination in which the acquirer and the acquiree (or its former owners) exchange only equity interests, the acquisition-date fair value of the acquiree's equity interests may be more reliably measurable than that of the acquirer's equity interests. In that case, IFRS 3 (as revised in 2008) requires that the calculation of goodwill should use the acquisition-date fair value of the acquiree's equity interests rather than the acquisition-date fair value of the equity interests transferred.[36] Apart from that, IFRS 3 (as revised in 2008) does not include any guidance on determining the fair value of such consideration. However, where equity interests are issued by the acquirer as consideration, it would seem appropriate that the guidance in IAS 39 – *Financial Instruments: Recognition and Measurement* – on determining the fair value of equity instruments (held as investments) should be followed. As discussed in Chapter 32 at 4.1, a quoted price in an active market is the best evidence of fair value, and if either the acquirer's or acquiree's equity shares are quoted, this would indicate which is the more reliably measurable. However, in situations such as this, where the business combination is between entities under common control, there is unlikely to be a quoted price for either the acquirer's or the acquiree's shares. Nevertheless, the consideration transferred should be measured at the acquisition-date fair value of either the acquirer's equity interests or the acquiree's equity instruments whichever is considered to be more reliably measurable.

In Example 10.6 above, if Entity B issued shares to Entity A to acquire Entity C, and there is no quoted price for either Entity B's or Entity C's equity shares, then the fair value of the consideration transferred would need to be based on whichever shares are considered to more reliably measurable. If the fair value of Entity B's shares were more reliably measurable, and the value of the shares issued as consideration was only £700, then as with cash consideration less than the fair value of the business acquired, Entity B would apply whichever method in Example 10.6 it has adopted for such transactions. However, if it is considered that the fair value of Entity B's equity shares is not more reliably measurable, the consideration transferred would be based on the fair value of Entity C, i.e. £1,000. Thus, goodwill of £400 would be recognised, with the £1,000 consideration transferred reflected in equity.

3.4 Application of the pooling of interests method

As indicated at 3.1 above, we believe that where entities do not adopt a policy of using the purchase method under IFRS 3 (2007), then they should apply the pooling of interests method when accounting for business combinations between entities under common control. Similarly, for entities where IFRS 3 (as revised in 2008) would otherwise be applicable, we believe that where entities do not adopt a policy of using the acquisition method under IFRS 3 (as revised in 2008), then they should apply the pooling of interests method when accounting for business combinations between entities under common control.

As indicated earlier, the discussion below is written in the context of IFRS 3 (2007). In many cases, this will also be applicable to those entities applying IFRS 3 (as revised in 2008). However, where it is considered necessary, additional commentary relating to IFRS 3 (as revised in 2008) is included.

3.4.1 *General*

IFRS 3 (2007) makes no reference to the pooling of interests method (except in the context of eliminating it as a method for accounting for business combinations generally). However, the pooling of interests method (or merger accounting as it is known in some jurisdictions) is generally considered to involve the following:[37]

- The assets and liabilities of the combining entities are reflected at their carrying amounts;

No adjustments are made to reflect fair values, or recognise any new assets or liabilities, that would otherwise be done under the purchase method. The only adjustments that are made are to harmonise accounting policies;

- No 'new' goodwill is recognised as a result of the combination;

  The only goodwill that is recognised is any existing goodwill relating to either of the combining entities. Any difference between the consideration paid/transferred and the equity 'acquired' is reflected within equity;

- The income statement reflects the results of the combining entities for the full year, irrespective of when the combination took place;

- Comparatives are presented as if the entities had always been combined.

In some jurisdictions, regulators take the view that comparatives cannot be restated as such a treatment is inconsistent with IAS 27. This appears to be on the basis that, even although IFRS 3 (2007) is not being applied to the business combination, IAS 27 requires that a parent's consolidated financial statements can only include the income and expenses of a subsidiary from the acquisition date as defined in IFRS 3 (2007), i.e. the date it obtains control of the subsidiary. Such a view would also appear to mean that, when applying the pooling of interests method, the pre-acquisition income and expenses of a subsidiary in the current year should also not be included. We believe that such a view is a narrow interpretation of IFRS, and that the general requirements outlined above should all be applied when using the pooling of interests method. Nevertheless, if a local regulator specifically prohibits restatement of comparatives then we believe that it is acceptable for the entity not to do so, but it should disclose the following:

- the comparatives on a pro forma basis. If the information is not available, that fact should be disclosed.

- an explanation of the fact that the regulator prohibits the entity from restating the comparatives.

- the fact that under IFRS comparatives are normally restated.

The application of the general requirements for the pooling of interests method in the context of business combinations involving entities under common control can sometimes raise particular issues as discussed below.

3.4.2   Carrying amounts of assets and liabilities

In general, no adjustments would be expected to be required to harmonise accounting policies of the entities involved in a business combination between entities under common control. This is because in the preparation of the consolidated financial statements of the ultimate parent entity under IFRS, uniform accounting policies should have been adopted by all members of the group. However, it may be necessary to make adjustments where the combining entities have used different accounting policies when preparing their own financial statements. Nevertheless, the main issue relating to the use of carrying amounts when applying the pooling of interests method for common control combinations is whether the amounts should be based on:

(a)   the carrying values reported in the consolidated financial statements of the parent; or

(b)   the carrying values reported in the standalone financial statements of the combining entities.

Consider the following example.

Example 10.7:   Carrying amounts of assets and liabilities

Entity A currently has two businesses operated through two wholly-owned subsidiaries, Entity B and Entity C. The group structure (ignoring other entities within the group) is as follows:

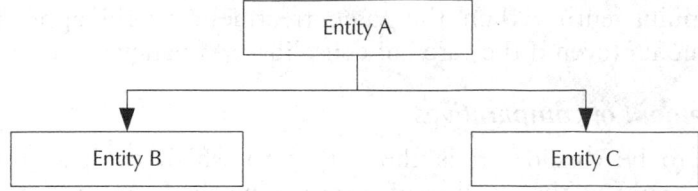

Both entities have been owned by Entity A for a number of years.

On 1 July 2009, Entity A restructures the group by transferring its investment in Entity C to Entity B, such that Entity C becomes a subsidiary of Entity B. The policy adopted for business combinations involving entities under common control is to apply the pooling of interests method.

In Entity B's consolidated financial statements for the year ended 31 December 2009, what values should be reflected in respect of Entity C?

Analysis under IFRS 3 (2007) and IFRS 3 (as revised in 2008)

In our view, Entity B can elect to use either:

(a)   the carrying values reported in Entity A's consolidated financial statements; or

(b)   the carrying values reported in Entity C's own financial statements.

Once an option is selected by an entity, the method should be applied consistently to all transactions of this type.

Under option (a) the value of the assets and liabilities of Entity C in Entity B's consolidated financial statements will be the carrying values that were used in Entity A's consolidated financial statements. Accordingly, they will be based on the fair value as at the date Entity C became part of the Entity A group and adjusted for subsequent transactions. Any goodwill relating to Entity C that was recognised in Entity A's consolidated financial statements will also be recognised. The carrying values of the assets of Entity B will remain as before.

The rationale for this approach is that the transaction is essentially a transfer of the assets and liabilities of Entity C from the consolidated financial statements of Entity A to the financial statements of Entity B. From a group perspective of Entity B's shareholder, nothing has changed except the location of those assets and liabilities. Entity B has effectively taken the group's ownership on. Therefore the values used in the consolidated financial statements are appropriate values to apply to the assets and liabilities, as they represent the carrying values to the Entity A group.

Under option (b) the carrying value of the assets and liabilities of Entity C in Entity B's consolidated financial statements will be the carrying values reported in Entity C's own financial statements. (Entity A will therefore still be required to make any necessary consolidation adjustments in preparing its own consolidated financial statements.)

Under this approach, the transaction is considered from the perspective of the reporting entity (Entity B sub-group), and the Entity A group's perspective is ignored in accounting for the transaction. Therefore the carrying value in Entity C's own financial statements will be relevant. The consolidated financial statements of Entity B after the transfer are effectively a combination of the financial statements of both entities. The shareholder, Entity A, is thus receiving the same financial information as before, but in one set of financial statements rather than two.

In our view, an entity should elect to apply either of the methods outlined in the above example when applying the pooling of interests method for common control business combinations – regardless of the legal form of the transaction. Therefore, if in Example 10.7 above, Entity B had 'acquired' the business of Entity C, rather than the shares, or the entities had been merged into one legal entity whereby Entity B was the continuing entity, then the same treatment would apply in Entity B's financial statements (even if they are not consolidated financial statements).

3.4.3   Restatement of comparatives

Another issue to be considered is the extent to which comparatives should be restated when applying the pooling of interests method. As indicated above, the pooling of interests method generally involves comparatives to be presented as if the entities had always been combined.

Example 10.8:   Restatement of comparatives (1)

Assume the same facts as in Example 10.7 above.

In preparing its consolidated financial statements for the year ended 31 December 2009, should Entity B restate the 2008 comparatives in its consolidated financial statements as if the business combination (and the investment in Entity C) took place as from 1 January 2008?

Analysis under IFRS 3 (2007) and IFRS 3 (as revised in 2008)

Since Entity C has been part of the Entity A group for a number of years, then Entity B should restate the 2008 comparatives in its consolidated financial statements for 2009. Restatement is required to reflect the combination as if it had occurred from the beginning of the earliest period presented in the financial statements, regardless of the actual date of the combination. In common control situations the logic of pooling is that there has been no change in the control the ultimate controlling party (in this case, Entity A) has had over the combined resources – it has merely changed the location of its resources. Accordingly, if the ultimate controlling party had control of these resources in the comparative period then the comparatives should be restated.

In the above example, Entity C had been part of the Entity A group for a number of years. What if this had not been the case?

Example 10.9:   Restatement of comparatives (2)

Assume the same facts as in Example 10.7 above, except that in this situation Entity A only acquired Entity C on 1 January 2009 (i.e. the transaction is still considered to be under common control at the date of Entity B's acquisition of Entity C, but Entity B and Entity C were not under common control during the comparative period).

In preparing its consolidated financial statements for the year ended 31 December 2009, should Entity B restate the 2008 comparatives in its consolidated financial statements as if the business combination (and the investment in Entity C) took place as from 1 January 2008?

Analysis under IFRS 3 (2007) and IFRS 3 (as revised in 2008)

In this situation, the pooling of interests method is applied from the date that the entities came under common control. Therefore, this would be 1 January 2009. In our view restatement of prior periods should not be made when adopting the pooling of interests method of accounting if the entities were not under common control during that comparative period.

As indicated above, in common control situations, the logic of pooling is that there has been no change in the control the ultimate controlling party has had over the combined resources – it has merely changed the location of its resources. Accordingly, if the ultimate controlling party had control of these resources in the comparative period then the comparatives should be restated. However, where there is a change in control, the ultimate controlling party has not always had control over these combined resources, and application of the pooling of interests method should reflect that – that is, it cannot be applied during the period that common control did not exist.

If Entity A had only acquired Entity C on 1 July 2008, such that Entity B and Entity C had come under common control as at that date, then Entity B would restate its comparatives but only to reflect the assets, liabilities and results of Entity C from 1 July 2008.

4   GROUP REORGANISATIONS

4.1   Introduction

Group reorganisations may be undertaken for a number of reasons, for example, to improve the co-ordination of diverse businesses possibly so that the different businesses are conducted through directly owned subsidiaries, or to create a tax grouping in a particular jurisdiction. In some cases, it may be to split up an existing group of companies into two or more separate groups of companies, in order to separate their different trades, possibly as a prelude to the disposal of part of the group either by way of sale or by way of an IPO. Similarly, the introduction of a new holding company may be undertaken as part of an IPO of the group.

Group reorganisations involve the restructuring of the relationships between companies in a group (or under common control) and can take many forms. For example, setting up a new holding company, changing the direct ownership of subsidiaries within the group (possibly involving the creation of a new intermediate holding company), or transferring businesses from one company to another. In principle, most such changes should have no impact on the consolidated financial statements of an existing group (provided there are no minority interests/non-controlling interests affected), because they are purely internal and cannot affect the group when it is being portrayed as a single entity. Some reorganisations may involve transferring businesses outwith the group (possibly involving the creation of a new holding company for those businesses).

For some of the entities involved in the reorganisation, there may well be a business combination that needs to be accounted for. In the sections below, we consider this particular aspect of the transaction in the context of the forms of reorganisations that are illustrated, based on the earlier discussions contained in 2 and 3 above with respect to the common control exemption in IFRS. Some other forms of reorganisation have already been considered in 2 and 3 above.

As indicated at 2 above, IFRS 3 (as revised in 2008) is effective for business combinations where the acquisition date is on or after the beginning of annual periods starting on or after 1 July 2009, although earlier application is permitted.[38] For entities with calendar year ends they will not have to apply IFRS 3 (as revised in 2008) until their 31 December 2010 financial statements. Thus, at this time, many entities will still be applying the previous version of the standard, IFRS 3 (2007). The first entities that will have to apply IFRS 3 (as revised in 2008) will generally be those with 30 June 2010 year ends, although entities with shortened accounting periods may have to apply it earlier. Accordingly, the discussions in the sections below are written in the context of IFRS 3 (2007). In many cases, these will also be applicable to those entities applying IFRS 3 (as revised in 2008). However, where it is considered necessary, additional commentary relating to IFRS 3 (as revised in 2008) is included.

Obviously, the transferors in the reorganisation will need to account for their part of the transaction in their own financial statements. In doing so, they will need to consider the requirements of other relevant IFRSs, in particular, the IAS 27 requirements relating to disposals of/loss of control over subsidiaries (see Chapter 7 at 3.2.1 and 3.3.1) and the IFRS 5 requirements relating to disposal groups held for sale and discontinued operations (see Chapter 4). The discussion in Chapter 7 at 3.5 and in Chapter 8 at 2.3.2 relating to demergers may also be relevant. Chapter 8 will also be relevant to the accounting in the separate/individual financial statements of the entities involved in the reorganisation.

The discussions below are generally only relevant if the reorganisation involves a business combination. As indicated at 2 above, if a transaction is not a business combination because the entity or assets being acquired do not meet the definition of a business, it is accounted for as an acquisition of assets. The accounting for such common control transactions is discussed in Chapter 8 at 4.4.2 D. In addition, in some of the situations where a new entity (Newco) is involved the transaction does not represent a business combination (e.g. Examples 10.10 and 10.13 at 4.2 and 4.4 below respectively).

For some business combinations involving entities or entities under common control, it may be that the business is transferred without any consideration being given. Commonly the transfer is as a distribution by a subsidiary to its parent or contribution, usually but not necessarily by a parent, to a subsidiary. There can be legal arrangements that result in the distribution of a business to another group entity, including reorganisations sanctioned by a court process or transfers after liquidation of the transferor entity. In addition, some jurisdictions allow a legal merger between a parent and subsidiary to form a single entity. The accounting for such transactions is discussed in Chapter 8 at 4.4.3.

All of the examples that follow at 4.2, 4.3 and 4.4 below involve a new entity (Newco) and assume that all entities are owned 100% by the entity at the top of the particular structure.

4.2   Setting up a new top holding company

Example 10.10:   Newco inserted at the top of an existing group

A Newco is incorporated and inserted at the top of an existing group. Newco issues shares to the existing shareholders of Entity A in exchange for the shares already held in that entity. There are no changes to the shareholder group. The group structure before and after this transaction is as follows:

Before

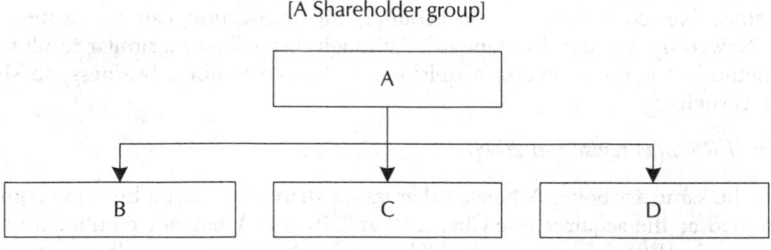

After

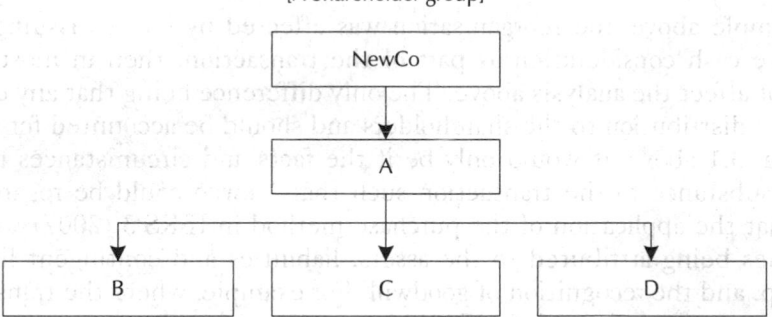

How should this reorganisation be accounted for in Newco's consolidated financial statements?

Analysis under IFRS 3 (2007)

In most situations this type of reorganisation will not qualify for the 'common control exemption' since there will be no contractual arrangement between the shareholders (see 2.1.1 above). However, even if it did qualify for the exemption because there is one individual, or a sub-group of the shareholders with a contractual arrangement, who controls Entity A and therefore the new Newco group, this is irrelevant.

This transaction does not represent a business combination, since a Newco that issues shares to effect a business combination can never be identified as the acquirer (see Chapter 9 at 2.3), and A has not combined with any other business. On this basis, the transaction is outside the scope of IFRS 3 (2007). Further, Newco cannot elect to apply the purchase method in IFRS 3 (2007) since there is no economic substance in terms of any real alteration to the composition or ownership of the group.

Accordingly, our view is that the consolidated financial statements should be presented as a continuation of the existing A group using the pooling of interests method (see 3.4 above).

Where the pooling of interests method is applied, as the consolidated financial statements are effectively presented as a continuation of the A group the previous reserves of the A group will continue to be reflected in the consolidated financial statements. The only difference is that the share capital will be that of Newco, and to the extent that this is different from that of A, then an adjustment needs to be made to equity. Where the share capital of Newco is greater than that of A, then this will require a debit adjustment to be made to equity. In our view, this should not be taken to any component of equity of the A group that may require to be reclassified from equity to profit or loss under IFRS at a later date. For example, reserves representing gains on available-for sale investments under IAS 39 or exchange gains on foreign operations under IAS 21 – *The Effects of Changes in Foreign Exchange Rates.*

It may be suggested that as Newco and the A group are separate entities that have been brought together, this is a 'business combination' as defined in paragraph 4 of IFRS 3 (2007), i.e. 'the bringing together of separate entities or businesses into one reporting entity'. On that basis, it is argued that, since Newco cannot be the acquirer, the transaction can be treated as a reverse acquisition of Newco by A under the standard. Although this will give a similar result to the pooling of interests method, it is not a reverse acquisition as Newco is not a business, so should not be accounted for as such.

Analysis under IFRS 3 (as revised in 2008)

The analysis is the same as above. A Newco that issues shares to effect a business combination can never be identified as the acquirer (see Chapter 9 at 3.4), and A has not combined with any other business. In addition, IFRS 3 (as revised in 2008) now explicitly states that 'the accounting acquiree must meet the definition of a business for the transaction to be accounted for as a reverse acquisition'.[39]

In the example above, the reorganisation was effected by Newco issuing shares. If Newco gave cash consideration as part of the transaction, then in most situations this will not affect the analysis above. The only difference being that any cash paid is effectively a distribution to the shareholders and should be accounted for as such. As discussed at 3.1 above, it would only be if the facts and circumstances meant that there was substance to the transaction such that Newco could be regarded as the acquirer that the application of the purchase method in IFRS 3 (2007) would result in fair values being attributed to the assets, liabilities and contingent liabilities of the A group, and the recognition of goodwill. For example, where the transaction was contingent on completion of an IPO that resulted in a change in control of the A group. For entities that would be applying IFRS 3 (as revised in 2008), the same conditions would need to be met for Newco to be the acquirer and for it to apply the acquisition method in IFRS 3 (as revised in 2008).

Example 10.11:   *Newco inserted at the top of entities owned by the same shareholders thereby creating a new reporting group*

A Newco is incorporated and inserted at the top of a number of entities owned by the same shareholders. Newco issues shares to the existing shareholders of entities B, C and D in exchange for the shares already held in those entities. The group structure before and after this transaction is as follows:

Before

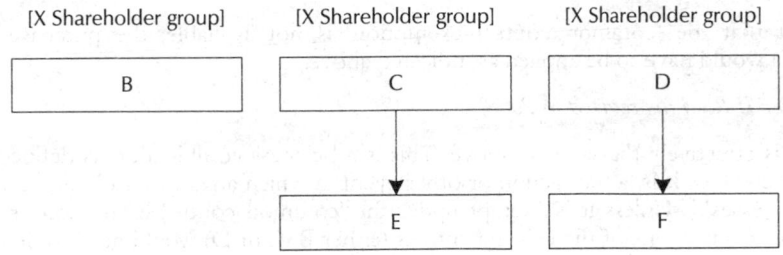

After

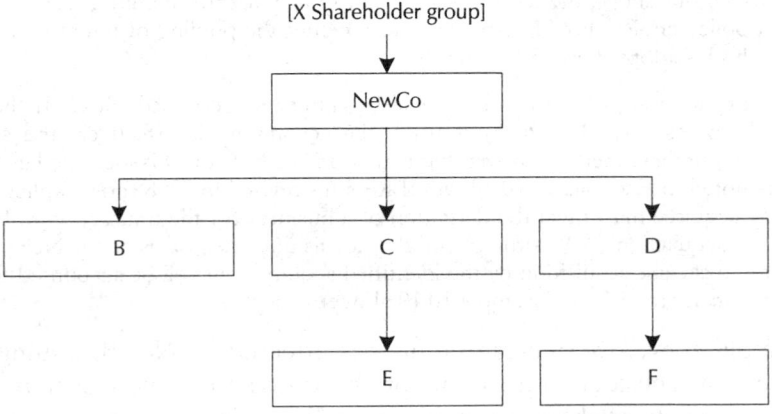

Analysis under IFRS 3 (2007)

Unlike the situation in Example 10.10 above, this is clearly a business combination as defined by IFRS 3 (2007) since B and sub-groups C and D have been brought together to form a new reporting entity under a new parent entity, Newco. Accordingly, it is within the scope of IFRS 3 (2007) unless otherwise exempt.

It may be that this type of reorganisation will qualify for the 'common control exemption' (see 2.1.1 above) since the number of shareholders will generally be relatively few. Accordingly, there may well be one individual, or a sub-group of the shareholders with a contractual arrangement, who controls entities B, C and D. The exemption will apply as long as the common control is not transitory (see 2.1.2 above). In that case, a policy choice should be made as to whether the pooling of interests method or the purchase method is adopted (see 3.1 above).

If the pooling of interests method is used, as discussed at 3.4 above, the consolidated financial statements will be presented as if the entities had always been combined, reflecting the carrying values of each of the entities (although since in this case the entities did not comprise a formal group before, it may be necessary to harmonise accounting policies) and including comparative figures for all of the entities 'acquired by Newco' (although this will depend on whether all of those entities were under common control for all of the periods presented).

If the purchase method in IFRS 3 (2007) is to be used, since Newco cannot be the acquirer, one of the existing entities (either B, C or D) will need to be identified as the acquirer (see Chapter 9 at 2.3), If, for example, B is identified as the acquirer, the consolidated financial statements will reflect book values for B, and comparative figures comprising those of B; fair values of the assets, liabilities and contingent liabilities, together with any resulting goodwill, for sub-groups C and D, whose results will be included only from the date of the combination. As Newco is not a business, it cannot be accounted for as a reverse acquisition by B; Newco will be accounted for under the pooling of interests method (as in Example 10.10 above).

In the event that the 'common control exemption' is not available, the purchase method in IFRS 3 (2007) would have to be applied as indicated above.

Analysis under IFRS 3 (as revised in 2008)

The analysis is effectively the same as above. This is a business combination as defined by IFRS 3 (as revised in 2008) as it is 'a transaction or other event in which an acquirer obtains control of one or more businesses'.[40] Unless it is exempt under the 'common control exemption', since Newco cannot be the acquirer, one of the existing entities (either B, C or D) would need to be identified as the acquirer obtaining control over the other businesses (see Chapter 9 at 3.4), and the acquisition method in IFRS 3 (as revised in 2008) applied.

For the reasons set out above, the reorganisation may qualify for the 'common control exemption'. In that case, a policy choice should be made as to whether the pooling of interests method or the acquisition method is adopted (see 3.1 above).

If the pooling of interests method is used, it will be applied as described above. If the acquisition method in IFRS 3 (as revised in 2008) is used, the accounting is effectively the same as that described for the purchase method above; that is that one of B, C or D is identified as the acquirer. In addition, as noted in Example 10.10 above, IFRS 3 (as revised in 2008) now explicitly states that 'the accounting acquiree must meet the definition of a business for the transaction to be accounted for as a reverse acquisition'.[41] Accordingly, if the acquisition method is used, Newco cannot be accounted for as a reverse acquisition by the identified acquirer, but will be accounted for under the pooling of interests method (as in Example 10.10 above).

In the example above, the reorganisation was effected by Newco issuing shares. If Newco gave cash consideration as part of the transaction, then in most situations this will not affect the analysis above. If the pooling of interests method was applied, any cash paid to the shareholders is effectively a distribution to the shareholders and should be accounted for as such. If the purchase method in IFRS 3 (2007) was applied, any cash paid to the shareholders in their capacity as owners of the identified acquirer is effectively a distribution to the shareholders and should be accounted for as such. Any cash paid to the shareholders as owners of the acquirees would form part of the cost of the acquisition of the entities acquired. As discussed at 3.1 above, it would only be if the facts and circumstances meant that there was substance to the transaction such that Newco could be regarded as the acquirer that the application of the purchase method in IFRS 3 (2007) would result in fair values being attributed to the assets, liabilities and contingent liabilities of all the existing businesses, and the recognition of goodwill relating to those businesses. For example, where the transaction was contingent on completion of an IPO that resulted in a change in control of the newly formed Newco group.

For entities that would be applying the acquisition method in IFRS 3 (as revised in 2008), the treatment of any cash paid would effectively be the same as above as any cash not treated as a distribution would form part of the consideration transferred for the entities acquired. The same conditions as described above would need to be met for Newco to be the acquirer and for it to apply the acquisition method in IFRS 3 (as revised in 2008).

4.3   Inserting a new intermediate parent within an existing group

Example 10.12:   Newco inserted as a new intermediate parent within an existing
                    group

A Newco is incorporated and inserted above a number of entities within an existing group so as to form a new sub-group. Newco issues shares to its parent A in return for the shares in entities C and D. The group structure before and after this transaction is as follows:

Before

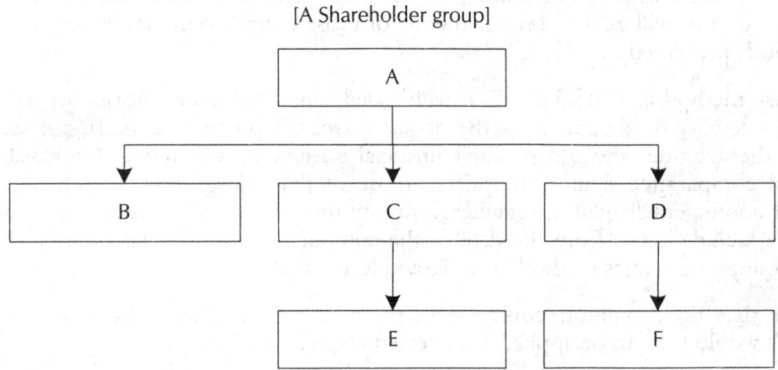

After

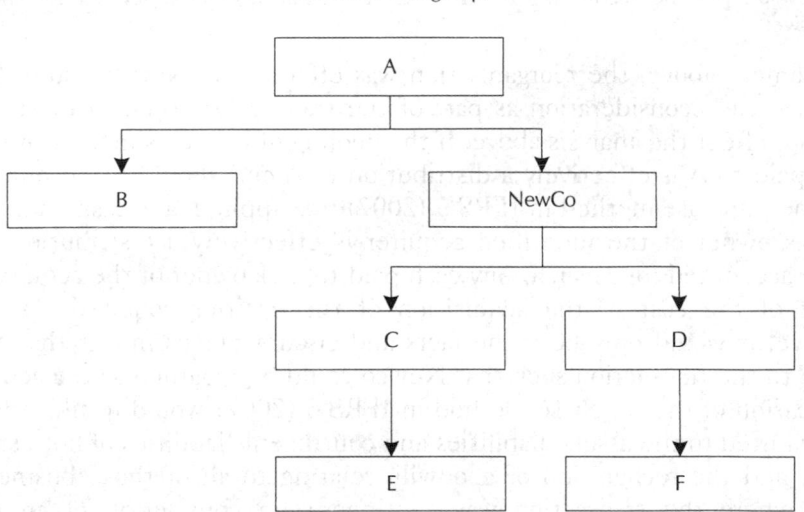

Analysis under IFRS 3 (2007)

In most situations, Newco will be exempt from preparing consolidated financial statements (see Chapter 6 at 3.1). However, if it chooses to prepare such financial statements, or loses the right to the exemption due to, say, an IPO of the Newco group, then the implications of IFRS 3 (2007) need to be considered.

This type of reorganisation will generally qualify for the 'common control exemption' in IFRS 3 (2007) since sub-group C and sub-group D are controlled by entity A. As discussed at 2.1.2 above, the exemption will apply as long as the common control is not transitory, and in making that assessment the newly formed entity Newco is excluded. It would only be if any of the entities within sub-group C and sub-group D had come into the A group recently, that this might indicate that control of that entity is transitory. Assuming that the exemption is available, a policy choice should be made as to whether the pooling of interests method or the purchase method is adopted (see 3.1 above).

If the pooling of interests method is used, as discussed at 3.4 above, the consolidated financial statements will be presented as if the entities had always been combined, reflecting the carrying values of each of the entities and including comparative figures for all of the entities 'acquired by Newco' (although this will depend on whether all of those entities were under common control for all of the periods presented).

If the purchase method in IFRS 3 (2007) is to be used, since Newco cannot be the acquirer, either C or D will need to be identified as the acquirer (see Chapter 9 at 2.3). If, for example, C is identified as the acquirer, the consolidated financial statements will reflect book values for sub-group C, and comparative figures comprising those of that sub-group; fair values of the assets, liabilities and contingent liabilities, together with any resulting goodwill, for sub-group D, whose results will be included only from the date of the combination; and Newco will be accounted for under the pooling of interests method (as in Example 10.10 above).

In the event that the 'common control exemption' is not available, the purchase method in IFRS 3 (2007) would have to be applied as indicated above.

Analysis under IFRS 3 (as revised in 2008)

The analysis is the same as above, except that if the acquisition method of accounting is to be applied, the identified acquirer (see Chapter 9 at 3.4) applies the acquisition method in IFRS 3 (as revised in 2008), but the accounting is effectively the same as that described for the purchase method above.

In the example above, the reorganisation was effected by Newco issuing shares. If Newco gave cash consideration as part of the transaction, then in most situations this will not affect the analysis above. If the pooling of interests method was applied, any cash paid to A is effectively a distribution to A and should be accounted for as such. If the purchase method in IFRS 3 (2007) was applied, any cash paid to A in its capacity as owner of the identified acquirer is effectively a distribution to A and should be accounted for as such. Any cash paid to A as owner of the acquirees would form part of the cost of the acquisition of the entities acquired. As discussed at 3.1 above, it would only be if the facts and circumstances meant that there was substance to the transaction such that Newco could be regarded as the acquirer that the application of the purchase method in IFRS 3 (2007) would result in fair values being attributed to the assets, liabilities and contingent liabilities of both sub-groups C and D, and the recognition of goodwill, relating to all of those businesses. For example, where the transaction was contingent on completion of an IPO that resulted in a change in control of the newly formed Newco group.

For entities that would be applying the acquisition method in IFRS 3 (as revised in 2008), the treatment of any cash paid would effectively be the same as above as any cash not treated as a distribution would form part of the consideration transferred for the entities acquired. The same conditions as described above would need to be met for Newco to be the acquirer and for it to apply the acquisition method in IFRS 3 (as revised in 2008).

4.4   Transferring businesses outwith an existing group using a Newco

In some cases, such a transfer involves using a Newco which is owned by the shareholders of the existing group as illustrated below.

Example 10.13:   Newco created to take over a business of an existing group

Entity C, a subsidiary of Parent A, transfers the shares held in its subsidiary, Entity E, to a newly formed entity, Newco. In return, Newco issues shares to the existing shareholders of Parent A. The group structure before and after this transaction is as follows:

Before

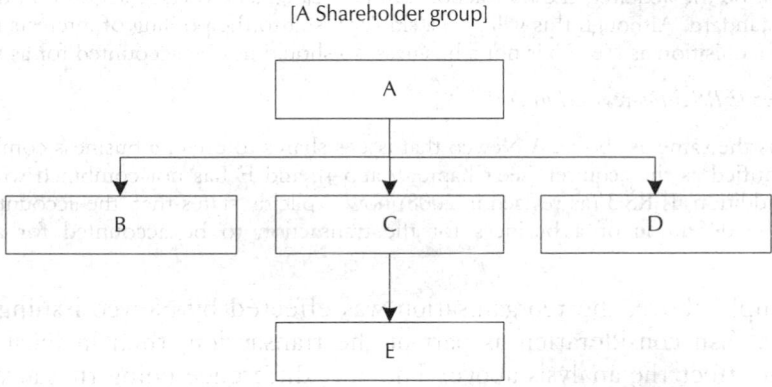

After

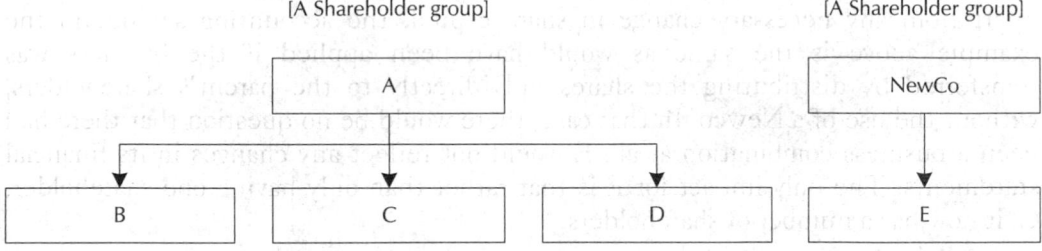

Analysis under IFRS 3 (2007)

In most situations this type of reorganisation will not qualify for the 'common control exemption' since there will be no contractual arrangement between the shareholders (see 2.1.1 above). However, even if it did qualify for the exemption because there is one individual, or a sub-group of the shareholders with a contractual arrangement, who controls entity A and the new Newco group, this is irrelevant.

This transaction does not represent a business combination, since a Newco that issues shares to effect a business combination can never be identified as the acquirer (see Chapter 9 at 2.3), and E has not combined with any other business. On this basis, the transaction is outside the scope of IFRS 3 (2007). Further, Newco cannot elect to apply the purchase method in IFRS 3 (2007) since there is no economic substance in terms of any real alteration to the composition or ownership of E.

Accordingly, our view is that the consolidated financial statements of Newco should be presented as a continuation of E using the pooling of interests method (see 3.4 above).

Where the pooling of interests method is applied, as the consolidated financial statements are effectively presented as a continuation of E the previous reserves of E will continue to be reflected in the consolidated financial statements. The only difference is that the share capital will be that of Newco, and to the extent that this is different from that of E, then an adjustment needs to be made to equity. Where the share capital of Newco is greater than that of E, then this will require a debit adjustment to be made to equity. In our view, this should not be taken to any component of equity of E that may require to be reclassified from equity to profit or loss under IFRS at a later date. For example, reserves representing gains on available-for sale investments under IAS 39 or exchange gains on foreign operations under IAS 21.

It may be suggested that as Newco and E are separate entities that have been brought together, this is a 'business combination' as defined in paragraph 4 of IFRS 3 (2007), i.e. 'the bringing together of separate entities or businesses into one reporting entity'. On that basis, it is argued that, since Newco cannot be the acquirer, the transaction can be treated as a reverse acquisition of Newco by E under the standard. Although this will give a similar result to the pooling of interests method, it is not a reverse acquisition as Newco is not a business, so should not be accounted for as such.

Analysis under IFRS 3 (as revised in 2008)

The analysis is the same as above. A Newco that issues shares to effect a business combination can never be identified as the acquirer (see Chapter 9 at 3.4), and E has not combined with any other business. In addition, IFRS 3 (as revised in 2008) now explicitly states that 'the accounting acquiree must meet the definition of a business for the transaction to be accounted for as a reverse acquisition'.[42]

In the example above, the reorganisation was effected by Newco issuing shares. If Newco gave cash consideration as part of the transaction, then in most situations this will not affect the analysis above. The only difference being that any cash paid to the shareholders is effectively a distribution to the shareholders and should be accounted for as such.

Apart from any necessary change in share capital, the accounting set out in the example above is the same as would have been applied if the business was transferred by distributing the shares in E directly to the parent's shareholders, without the use of a Newco. In that case, there would be no question that there had been a business combination at all. E would not reflect any changes in its financial statements. The only impact for E is that rather than only having one shareholder, C, it now has a number of shareholders.

As discussed at 3.1 above, it would only be if the facts and circumstances meant that there was substance to the transaction such that Newco could be regarded as the acquirer that the application of purchase method in IFRS 3 (2007) would result in fair values being attributed to the assets, liabilities and contingent liabilities of E, and the recognition of goodwill, with only the post-combination results being reported. For example, where the transaction was contingent on completion of an IPO that resulted in a change in control of the newly formed Newco group. For entities that would be applying IFRS 3 (as revised in 2008), the same conditions would need to be met for Newco to be the acquirer and for it to apply the acquisition method in IFRS 3 (as revised in 2008).

4.5　Transferring associates/jointly controlled entities within an existing group

It may be that a reorganisation involves the transfer of associates or jointly controlled entities within an existing group. As indicated at 2.1 above, for the purpose of the common control exemption, a business combination involving entities or businesses under common control 'is a business combination in which all of the combining entities or businesses are ultimately controlled by the same party or parties both before and after the business combination, and that control is not transitory'.[43] Although this will include transactions, such as the transfer of subsidiaries or businesses between entities within a group, the issue is whether it can be extended to an entity acquiring an associate or jointly controlled entity from another group entity.

Example 10.14:　Transfer of an associate within an existing group

Entities B and C are under common control of entity A. Entity C has an investment in an associate D which it sells to entity B for cash. The transaction can be illustrated as follows:

Before

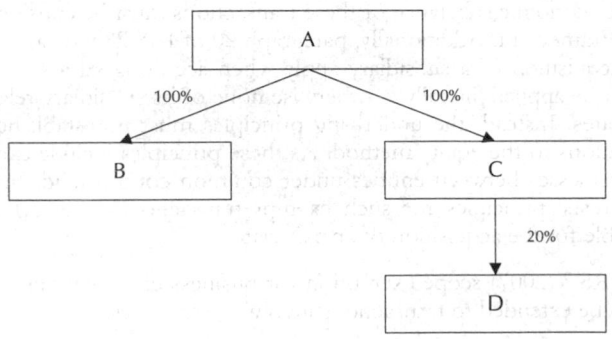

After

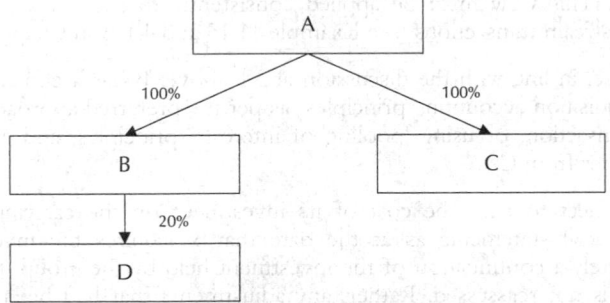

The equity accounted carrying value in C's financial statements of its 20% interest in D is £100, while the fair value of D's underlying assets and liabilities is £800. B pays C £190 for the 20% interest in D, which is considered to represent its fair value.

The consolidated financial statements prepared by A will not be impacted, as from the group's perspective there has been no change.

How should B account for this transaction when applying the equity accounting method in its own consolidated financial statements (or its stand-alone financial statements where the entity does not have any additional subsidiaries – see Chapter 11 at 2.3)?

We believe that there are two approaches that B can apply in accounting for this transaction.

Preferred approach

IAS 28 – *Investments in Associates*, unlike IFRS 3 (2007), does not exempt transactions that are between entities under common control. Furthermore, the IFRS 3 (2007) exemption is clearly for business combinations involving entities under common control – the acquisition of an associate is not a business combination. Therefore, IAS 28 applies as it would to any other acquisition of an associate (see Chapter 11) and the common control exemption given in IFRS 3 (2007) cannot be applied.

Accordingly, IAS 28 is applied by B when accounting for its acquisition of D, the consideration for which is the cash given up. B's share of the fair value of the underlying assets and liabilities of D is determined to identify any goodwill/gain to be recognised in profit or loss, and to consider any adjustments to the profit and loss when applying the equity accounting method.

Therefore, B recognises an investment in an associate with a cost of £190, inclusive of goodwill of £30 and its share of net assets of £160 (20% × £800).

Acceptable alternative approach

While IAS 28 does not specifically scope out transactions of this nature between entities under common control, the economic substance of these transactions must be considered as referred to in paragraph 35 of the Framework. Additionally, paragraph 20 of IAS 28 indicates that the concepts of accounting for the acquisition of a subsidiary apply when acquiring an associate. This means that IFRS 3 (2007) cannot be applied 'literally' – otherwise none of its subsidiary-related principles could be applied to associates. Instead, the underlying principles must be established and applied with appropriate modifications to the equity method. As these principles include exempting acquisitions of subsidiaries or businesses between entities under common control (and therefore the ability to use 'pooling of interests' principles for such exempt transactions – see 3.1 above), this option should also be available for the acquisition of an associate.

On this basis, the IFRS 3 (2007) scope exemption for business combinations among entities under common control can be extended to transactions involving associates.

However, we believe that this alternative may only be adopted, where equity accounting is seen by management as a form of consolidation rather than a valuation technique in aspects where IAS 28 is silent or ambiguous. This view must be applied consistently to such areas, for example, profit elimination on downstream transactions (see Example 11.15 at 3.4.1 A in Chapter 11).

Where this is the case, in line with the discussion at 3.1 above, B has a choice to account for the transaction using acquisition accounting principles (as per the preferred approach above), if there is substance to the transaction, or using 'pooling of interests' principles, and apply the carry over equity accounted values from C.

Accordingly, B can elect to base the cost of its investment on the carrying value of £100 as recorded in C's financial statements as at the date that B acquires the investment. As this is considered to be merely a continuation of the investment held by the group, the fair value of the assets and liabilities is not reassessed. Rather, any adjustments that had been made by C due to differences in fair values at the date it acquired its interest will continue to be applied by B. The excess of the consideration paid (£190) over the carrying value (£100) will be shown as a distribution of £90 by B.

Conclusion

Whichever approach is selected should be applied consistently, but the alternative acceptable approach can only be adopted where equity accounting is seen by management as a form of consolidation rather than a valuation technique in aspects where IAS 28 is silent or ambiguous.

Although the analysis in the example above is written in the context of IFRS 3 (2007) and IAS 28, we believe that it is also applicable to those entities applying IFRS 3 (as revised in 2008) and IAS 28 as amended by IFRS 3 (as revised in 2008) and IAS 27 (as amended in 2008).

Similarly, although Example 10.14 uses the transfer of an associate to illustrate the approaches that are available, these would also apply to transfers of jointly controlled entities within an existing group.

However, as indicated in Chapter 11 at 1.4, as a result of the revised versions of IFRS 3 and IAS 27, this has raised a number of new issues in the context of applying the equity method, and the extent to which the methodology and procedures under these revised standards should now be applied is open to further consideration. The position has been confused even further as a result of the publication of the IASB's annual improvement standard in April 2009 where in the context of an amendment to IAS 39 it is stated that the 'Board noted that paragraph 20 of IAS 28 explains only the methodology used to account for investments in associates. This should not be taken to imply that the principles for business combinations and consolidations can be applied by analogy to accounting for investments in associates and joint ventures.'[44] In May 2009, the IASB has indicated that it will address the interaction between the revised versions of IFRS 3 and IAS 27, and IAS 28 and IAS 31, as part of its project on joint ventures (see Chapter 12 at 7).[45]

At the time of writing, it is unclear exactly what changes may be introduced in the context of applying the equity method as a result of this project, but it may be that the changes the IASB introduces will mean that the alternative approach in Example 10.14 will no longer be acceptable.

5 CONCLUSION

The exemption under IFRS for business combinations involving entities or businesses under common control has been a long-standing one. In this chapter, we have discussed the implications of that exemption and accounting treatments which may be adopted for such transactions. Although IFRS 3 did introduce some authoritative guidance as to the circumstances in which the common control exemption may be applicable, it has meant that entities have had to develop their own policies for accounting for such transactions that are outwith the scope of IFRS 3. Inevitably, this has led to divergent practices on the accounting for such business combinations. Consequently, in December 2007, the IASB added to its agenda a project on common control transactions that will examine the definition of a business combination involving entities or businesses under common control and the methods of accounting for those transactions. The Board had been expected to consider a comprehensive project outline in January 2009. However, this did not happen and, at the time of writing this chapter, the project is currently paused. A comprehensive project outline will be presented to the Board when the project resumes after staff working on projects relating to the financial crisis become available.

References

1 Information for Observers (December 2007 IASB meeting), *Common Control Transactions (Agenda Paper 5C)*, para. 30.

2 IFRS 3 (2007), *Business Combinations*, IASB, 2007 Bound Volume, paras. BC24-26.

3 *Exposure Draft of Proposed Amendments to IFRS 3 Business Combinations* ('IFRS 3 ED'), IASB, June 2005, para. BC7.

4 IFRS 3, *Business Combinations*, IASB.

5 IFRS 3, para. 2.

6 IFRS 3, paras. B1-B4.

7 IFRS 3, para. BC59.

8 IFRS 3 ED, para. BC9.

9 Information for Observers (December 2007 IASB meeting), *Common Control Transactions (Agenda Paper 5C)*, para. 42.

10 Information for Observers (December 2007 IASB meeting), *Common Control Transactions (Agenda Paper 5C)*, para. 42.

11 *IASB Update*, IASB, December 2007, p. 1.

12 Information for Observers (December 2007 IASB meeting), *Common Control Transactions (Agenda Paper 5C)*, para. 30.

13 Project page, *Common Control Transactions*, IASB website, August 2008.

14 *IASB Work Plan – projected timetable as at 1 August 2009*, IASB; Project page, *Common Control Transactions*, IASB website, August 2009.

15 IFRS 3, para. 2.

16 IFRS 3 (2007), paras. 10-14; IFRS 3, paras. B1-B4.

17 IFRS 3, para. 64.

18 IFRS 3 (2007), para. 10; IFRS 3, para. B1.

19 IFRS 3 (2007), para. 13; IFRS 3, para. B4.

20 IFRS 3 (2007), para. 13; IFRS 3, para. B4.

21 IFRS 3 (2007), para. 12; IFRS 3, para. B3.

22 IFRS 3 (2007), para. 12.

23 IFRS 3 (2007), para. 11; IFRS 3, para. B2.

24 IAS 31, *Interests in Joint Ventures*, IASB, para. 10.

25 IFRS 3 (2007), para. BC28.

26 *IFRIC Update*, IFRIC, March 2006, p. 6.

27 *IFRIC Update*, IFRIC, March 2006, p. 6.

28 IFRS 3, para. 64.

29 IAS 8, *Accounting Policies, Changes in Accounting Estimates and Errors*, IASB, para. 10.

30 IAS 8, paras. 11-12.

31 IFRS 3 (2007), para. 16.

32 IFRS 3 (2007), para. 27.

33 IFRS 3, para. 5.

34 IFRS 3, para. 32.

35 IFRS 3, para. 34.

36 IFRS 3, para. 33.

37 For example, see SFAS 141R, *Business Combinations*, FASB, December 2007, paras. D11-14 and the previous version, SFAS 141, paras. D15-D17 and F1; and FRS 6, *Acquisitions and Mergers*, ASB, September 1994, paras. 16-19.

38 IFRS 3, para. 64.

39 IFRS 3, para. B19.

40 IFRS 3, Appendix A.

41 IFRS 3, para. B19.

42 IFRS 3, para. B19.

43 IFRS 3 (2007), para. 10; IFRS 3, para. B1.

44 *Improvements to IFRSs*, April 2009, IASB, IAS 39, para. BC24D.

45 *IASB Update*, IASB, May 2009, p. 5.

Chapter 11   Associates

1   INTRODUCTION

1.1   The origins of equity accounting

As noted in the introduction to Chapter 6, an entity may conduct its business not only directly but also through strategic investments in other entities. IFRS, and most national GAAPs, broadly distinguish three types of such strategic investment:

- entities controlled by the reporting entity (subsidiaries – see Chapter 6);

- entities jointly controlled by the reporting entity and one or more third parties (joint ventures – see Chapter 12); and

- entities that, while not controlled or jointly controlled by the reporting entity, are subject to significant influence by it (associates – the subject of this Chapter).

In the early days of consolidated financial statements, investments in entities which did not satisfy the criteria for classification as subsidiaries were carried at cost, and the revenue from them was recognised only on the basis of dividends received. However, during the 1960s it was recognised that there was a case for an intermediate form of accounting, since there was a growing tendency for groups to conduct part of their activities by taking substantial minority stakes in other entities and exercising a degree of influence over their business which, although falling short of complete control, was nevertheless significant. Mere recognition of dividends was seen to be an inadequate measure of the results of this activity (and one which could be manipulated by the investor, where it could influence the investee's distribution policy). Moreover, since it was unlikely that the investee would fully distribute its earnings, the cost of the investment would give an increasingly unrealistic indication of its underlying value.

This intermediate form of accounting, equity accounting, was first used by the Royal Dutch Shell group in 1964. It involves a modified form of consolidation of the results and assets of investees in the investor's financial statements when the investor exercises 'significant influence', but not control, over the management of the investee. The essence of equity accounting is that, rather than full scale consolidation on a line-by-line basis, it requires incorporation of the investor's share of net assets of the investee in one line in the investor's consolidated balance sheet and the share of its profit or loss at only one level of the income statement (although some national standards require equity accounting at more than one level of the income statement).

Another form of 'intermediate consolidation' used by some entities, particularly in certain industries, was proportional consolidation (now referred to under IFRS as 'proportionate' consolidation). As its name implies, this involves including the results and assets and liabilities of an investment on a line-by-line basis, but only to the extent of the investor's share, rather than, as under normal consolidation, in full with an apportionment to any non-controlling or minority interest. However, under IFRS currently, proportionate consolidation can be adopted only for certain types of joint venture, although the IASB has plans to eliminate the option of proportionate consolidation altogether (see Chapter 12 at 7.1).

1.2   Development of IAS 28

Under IFRS, accounting for associates is dealt with principally by IAS 28 – *Investments in Associates*. This was originally issued in April 1989 and has since been subject to a number of amendments, most significantly in December 2003 as part of the IASB's improvements project, when the previous version of IAS 28 was withdrawn and replaced by a significantly revised version that became effective for accounting periods beginning on or after 1 January 2005. IAS 28 has been subject to further amendment by IFRSs issued since December 2003.

1.3   Other applicable IFRSs

In addition to IAS 28, the following pronouncements are relevant to accounting for associates:

- IAS 1 – *Presentation of Financial Statements*;
- IAS 21 – *The Effects of Changes in Foreign Exchange Rates*;
- IAS 27 – *Consolidated and Separate Financial Statements*;
- IAS 36 – *Impairment of Assets*;
- IAS 39 – *Financial Instruments: Recognition and Measurement*;
- IFRS 1 – *First-time Adoption of International Financial Reporting Standards*;
- IFRS 3 – *Business Combinations*; and
- IFRS 5 – *Non-current Assets Held for Sale and Discontinued Operations*.

IAS 27 and IFRS 3 have both been substantially revised as a result of phase II of the Business Combinations project as explained in Chapter 9 at 1.2.2 and entities will need to be careful to ensure they are using the correct versions of each of these standards. IFRS 3 (as revised in 2008) is effective for business combinations for which the acquisition date is on or after the beginning of the first annual reporting period beginning on or after 1 July 2009 with early adoption possible as explained in Chapter 9 at 3.1.1. IAS 27 (as amended in 2008) has the same effective date.[1] Consequential amendments made to IAS 28 as a result of those revised standards also apply from the same date.

1.4 Future developments

As discussed later in 3 below, many procedures appropriate for the application of the equity method are similar to the consolidation procedures described in IAS 27 (see Chapter 7). Furthermore IAS 28 explains that the concepts underlying the procedures used in accounting for the acquisition of a subsidiary are also adopted in accounting for the acquisition of an investment in an associate.[2] This does raise a number of practical difficulties, and there has been an ongoing debate about whether the equity method of accounting is a consolidation method or a measurement method. Although IAS 28 generally adopts consolidation principles it nevertheless retains features of a valuation methodology.

As a result of the revised versions of IFRS 3 and IAS 27, this has raised a number of new issues in the context of applying the equity method, and the extent to which the methodology and procedures under these revised standards should now be applied is open to further consideration. The position has been confused even further as a result of the publication of the IASB's annual improvement standard in April 2009 where in the context of an amendment to IAS 39 regarding the application of the exemption in paragraph 2(g) of that standard (see Chapter 29 at 3.7.2) it is stated that the 'Board noted that paragraph 20 of IAS 28 explains only the methodology used to account for investments in associates. This should not be taken to imply that the principles for business combinations and consolidations can be applied by analogy to accounting for investments in associates and joint ventures.'[3] In May 2009, the IASB has indicated that it will address the interaction between the revised versions of IFRS 3 and IAS 27, and IAS 28 and IAS 31 – *Interests in Joint Ventures*, as part of its project on joint ventures (see Chapter 12 at 7).[4]

At the time of writing, it is unclear exactly what changes may be introduced in the context of applying the equity method as a result of this project. Hopefully it will resolve many of the issues that arise in practice. However, it may even go further than that. In the joint venture project, the IASB has proposed eliminating the option in IAS 31 of proportionate consolidation of jointly controlled entities, which means that joint venture entities will in the future all have to be accounted for under the equity method (after contractual rights and obligations to individual assets and individual liabilities have been identified and recognised – see Chapter 12 at 7.1). It is possible that in addressing the issues relating to the application of the equity method, the IASB may turn its attention to considering whether all investments in associates – and not just those held by venture capital organisations etc. (see 2.1.1 below) – should be accounted for at fair value under IAS 39, thereby leaving equity accounting as a method that applies solely to certain joint venture arrangements.

2   SCOPE OF IAS 28

2.1   General

IAS 28 must be applied in accounting for investments in associates (see 2.2 below). However, it does not apply to investments in associates held by:

(a)   venture capital organisations, or

(b)   mutual funds, unit trusts and similar entities including investment-linked insurance funds

that upon initial recognition are designated as financial assets 'at fair value through profit or loss' or are classified as financial assets held for trading and accounted for in accordance with IAS 39. Such investments are measured at fair value in accordance with IAS 39, with changes in fair value recognised in profit or loss in the period of the change (see Chapter 32).[5] This exemption is discussed further at 2.1.1 below.

A venturer with an interest in a jointly controlled entity within the scope of IAS 31 (see Chapter 12) that elects (as permitted by IAS 31) to account for that interest using the equity method should comply with the requirements of IAS 28 relating to the equity method of accounting (see 3 below).[6]

2.1.1   *Exemption for venture capital organisations and similar entities*

The exemption for venture capital organisations and other similar financial institutions raises a number of questions of interpretation. The first is exactly what entities comprise those described in (a) and (b) in 2.1 above, since they are not defined in IAS 28 – a deliberate decision by the IASB given the difficulty of crafting a definition.[7] The experience of similar exemptions in some national GAAPs has been that it can be difficult to limit precisely the entities to which they apply. The IASB no doubt hopes that preparers and their auditors can be relied upon not to abuse the scope of the exemption without the need for further intervention.

As discussed more fully in Chapter 6 at 4.1, IAS 27 does not exempt venture capital organisations and other similar financial institutions from consolidating investments in subsidiaries.

A   *Application of IAS 39 to associates exempt from IAS 28*

The reason for introducing the exemption was that the IASB considered that for venture capital organisations, mutual funds, unit trusts and similar entities the application of the equity method often produces information that is not relevant to their management and investors. As they often manage their investments on the basis of fair values, the application of IAS 39 would produce more relevant information. Furthermore, the financial statements would be less useful if changes in the level of ownership in an investment resulted in frequent changes in the method of accounting for the investment.[8] 3i Group plc applies this exemption as illustrated in the extract below.

Extract 11.1: 3i Group plc (2008)

Significant accounting policies [extract]

C Basis of consolidation [extract]

(ii) Associates

Associates are those entities in which the Group has significant influence, but not control, over the financial and operating policies. Investments that are held as part of the Group's investment portfolio are carried in the balance sheet at fair value even though the Group may have significant influence over those companies. This treatment is permitted by IAS 28 Investment in Associates, which requires investments held by venture capital organisations to be excluded from its scope where those investments are designated, upon initial recognition, as at fair value through profit or loss and accounted for in accordance with IAS 39, with changes in fair value recognised in the income statement in the period of the change. The Group has no interests in associates through which it carries on its business.

I   *Entities with a mix of activities*

The exemption clearly applies to venture capital organisations and other similar financial institutions whose main activities consist of managing an investment portfolio comprising investments unrelated to the investor's business. Although the exemption is not intended to apply to trading companies that hold investments in a number of associates, there are cases in which entities have significant venture capital activities as well as significant trading activities. In those cases, in our view the entity is permitted to use the exemption provided the venture capital activities are managed separately on the basis of fair values.

In making this assessment it is not relevant whether or not a venture capital activity is contained within a separate legal entity – it might only be a segment. In that case, the exemption can be used provided this is the way that management monitor the segment, and the venture capital activity is a substantive part of the business of the entity (rather than an isolated instance).

The entity should be able to demonstrate that it runs a proper venture capital business rather than merely undertaking, on an ad hoc basis, transactions which a venture capital business would undertake.

Example 11.1:   Entity owning a discrete venture capital organisation

Parent P operates a construction business and owns a venture capital organisation (subsidiary V) that invests in the telecommunications industry. V's business is monitored on the basis of the fair value of its investments. Even though P itself is not a venture capital organisation, subsidiary V would be able to apply the exemption and account for its investments at fair value under IAS 39. In the consolidated financial statements of P, the investments held by V would also be accounted for at fair value under IAS 39, with changes in fair value recognised in profit or loss in the period of change.

Example 11.2:   Entity owning an integrated venture capital organisation

Parent P is a software company and owns a venture capital organisation (subsidiary V) that invests in the software industry. Subsidiary V provides advisory services to some of its investees and it sometimes has significant involvement in management of the investees. As both P and V are active in the software industry, the activities of V may not be entirely separate from P. In addition, the activities of V in relation to its investments go beyond those of an ordinary investor. For those reasons the exemption from application of the equity method may not be available to V.

Example 11.3:   Entity with a venture capital organisation segment

Bank A has a number of separate activities. One segment's business is to acquire all the shares of companies which are then partially sold down to third-party investors. Bank A retains a portion of the shares as a co-investor and has significant influence, but not control, until the investment is exited.

Bank A considers these activities to be in the nature of venture capital (providing capital to a start up business or one which needs reorganising to optimise the full potential, which is at risk). The activities are a substantive part of Bank A's business and management monitors the activities of the segment on the basis of the fair value of the investments. Even though Bank A is itself not a venture capital organisation, it would be able to apply the exemption and account for its investments at fair value under IAS 39, with changes in fair value recognised in profit or loss in the period of change.

II   Designation of investments as 'at fair value through profit or loss'

As noted above, venture capital organisations and other similar financial institutions which use the exemption in IAS 28 for their investments in associates are required to apply IAS 39 to those investments. The exemption is available only where the associates are either (as defined under IAS 39) held for trading, or, if not, are designated upon initial recognition as investments to be accounted for 'at fair value through profit or loss' under IAS 39.[9] Designation at a later date is not possible. Whilst IAS 28 does not say so explicitly, we consider that such designation is irrevocable, as there is no provision in IAS 39 for investments that have been designated in this way to be subsequently de-designated.

IAS 28 does not explicitly require venture capital organisations and other similar financial institutions consistently to designate all their associates (other than those defined as held for trading) as 'at fair value through profit or loss' under IAS 39. However, such entities need to balance the free choice apparently given by IAS 28 with the requirement of IAS 8 – *Accounting Policies, Changes in Accounting Estimates and Errors* – for the adoption of consistent accounting policies for similar transactions. The freedom of choice may have been given so as to allow such entities to apply IAS 39 to their own portfolio investments but to apply IAS 28 to any strategic investments in similar entities which act as an extension of their own business.

The recognition, measurement and disclosure requirements of IAS 39 for items classified as held for trading or designated as at fair value through profit or loss are discussed in Chapters 30, 32 and 34.

III   Availability of fair value information

In the Basis for Conclusions of IAS 28 the IASB states that fair value information is often readily available because fair value measurement is a well-established practice in these industries including for investments in entities in the early stages of their development or in non-listed entities.[10] However, designation of investments as 'at fair value through profit or loss' is prohibited under IAS 39 for investments in equity instruments that (1) do not have a quoted market price in an active market and (2) for which the range of reasonable fair value estimates is significant and the probabilities of the various estimates cannot be reasonably assessed.[11] If reliable fair value information is not available the equity method should be applied.

IV Disclosure of interests in associates

Disclosures required for associates are detailed at 5.2 below. The IASB, as part of its Annual Improvements project, amended IAS 28 to clarify that where an associate is accounted for at fair value in accordance with IAS 39, as permitted under the standard for venture capital organisations, mutual funds, unit trusts and similar entities,[12] most of the IAS 28 disclosure requirements do not apply.[13] This is explained at 5.2.1 below.

B Venture capital consolidations and partial use of fair value through profit or loss

One issue that has been considered recently by the IFRIC and the IASB in relation to the scope of IAS 28 is situations in which a parent has an investment in an entity, one part of which is held by a subsidiary that is an investment-linked insurance fund (or mutual fund, unit trust or venture capital organisation) entitled to the scope exclusion in IAS 28, and the other part of the investment in the same entity is held by another group entity that accounts for its investment in accordance with IAS 28 using the equity method (or at cost, if certain conditions are met). The issue is whether both measurement bases can be used in the consolidated financial statements of the parent.[14] In deliberating the issue at its meeting in May 2009, the IFRIC considered 4 scenarios which are included in the following example:[15]

Example 11.4:   Venture capital consolidations and partial use of fair value through profit or loss

Parent company has two wholly-owned subsidiaries (A and B), each of which has an ownership interest in an 'associate', entity C. Subsidiary A, a life insurance business, holds its interest in an investment-linked fund backing its participating life insurance contracts. Subsidiary B is not in the insurance business. Neither of the investments held by subsidiaries A and B is held for trading.

Scenario 1: both investments in the associate result in significant influence on a stand-alone basis

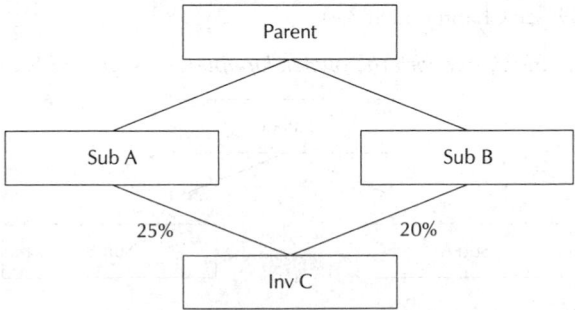

Subsidiary A accounts for its 25% share in the associate at fair value through profit or loss in accordance with IAS 39 (see Chapter 32 at 3.1).

Subsidiary B accounts for its 20% share in the associate using the equity method in accordance with IAS 28 (see 3 below).

Scenario 2: neither of the investments in the associate results in significant influence on a stand-alone basis

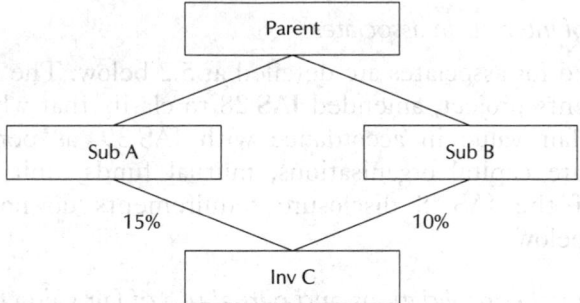

Subsidiary A accounts for its 15% share in the associate at fair value through profit or loss in accordance with IAS 39 (see Chapter 32 at 3.1)

Subsidiary B accounts for its 10% share in the associate as an available-for-sale investment in accordance with IAS 39 (see Chapter 32 at 3.4)

Scenario 3: one of the investments in the associate results in significant influence on a stand-alone basis and the other investment in the associate does not result in significant influence on a stand-alone basis

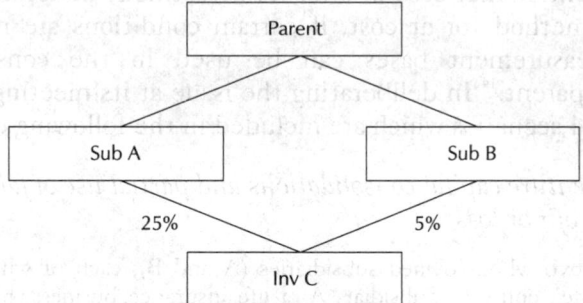

Subsidiary A accounts for its 25% share in the associate at fair value through profit or loss in accordance with IAS 39 (see Chapter 32 at 3.1)

Subsidiary B accounts for its 5% share in the associate as an available-for-sale investment in accordance with IAS 39 (see Chapter 32 at 3.4)

Scenario 4: same as scenario 3, but with the ownership interests switched between the subsidiaries

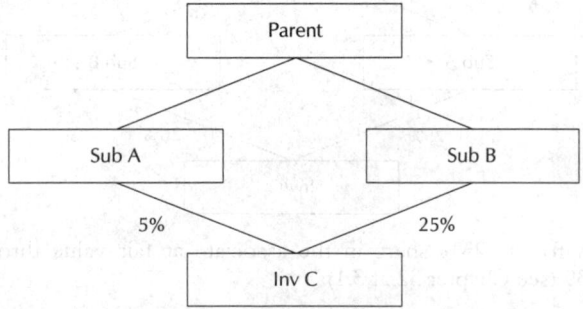

Subsidiary A accounts for its 5% share in the associate at fair value through profit or loss in accordance with IAS 39 (see Chapter 32 at 3.1)

Subsidiary B accounts for its 25% share in the associate using the equity method in accordance with IAS 28 (see 3 below).

How should the parent account for the associate in its consolidated financial statements?

One view would be that a parent identifies all direct and indirect interests held in the investee by either the parent or any of its subsidiaries and if it is determined that the group has an associate, it applies the equity method under IAS 28 to the entire investment in the associate. On that basis, Parent company would equity account for the entire ownership interest in entity C in its consolidated financial statements in each of the scenarios.

Another view would be that a parent identifies all direct and indirect interests held in the investee by either the parent or any of its subsidiaries and if it is determined that the group has an associate, it uses the scope criteria in IAS 28 to group the investment holdings into one of potentially two valuation models (equity method and fair value through profit or loss). On that basis, Parent company would equity account for the interest held by Subsidiary B and fair value through profit or loss the interest held by Subsidiary A in its consolidated financial statements in each of the scenarios.

At its meeting in May 2009, and subsequently confirmed at its meeting in July 2009, the IFRIC stated that 'Paragraph 6 of IAS 28 requires an entity to determine the existence of significant influence considering aggregate holdings, both direct and indirect. Paragraph 24 of IAS 27 – *Consolidated and Separate Financial Statements* (as amended in 2008) requires consolidated financial statements to be prepared using uniform accounting policies for like transactions and other events in similar circumstances. However, the IFRIC noted that some IFRSs allow different treatment of similar items when those items are used differently. For example, IAS 2 – *Inventories* – states that for inventories with a different nature or use, different cost formulas may be justified.

'The IFRIC noted that significant diversity exists in practice on this issue because of the apparently conflicting guidance within IAS 28 and between IAS 28 and other standards. Consequently, the IFRIC decided that it could be best resolved by referring it to the IASB. Therefore, the IFRIC decided not to add this issue to its agenda.'[16]

Consequently, the IASB has decided to deal with this issue within the exposure draft of proposed *Improvements to IFRSs* issued in August 2009.[17] The IASB is proposing to clarify that different measurement bases can be applied to portions of an investment in an associate when part of the investment is designated at initial recognition as at fair value through profit or loss in accordance with the scope exception in paragraph 1 of IAS 28.[18] It is proposed that an entity first determines in accordance with paragraphs 6-10 of IAS 28 whether it has significant influence over an associate. If a portion of the investment in the associate qualifies for the scope exemption, the entity applies the scope exemption to that portion (i.e. it measures that portion at fair value through profit or loss). The remaining investment in the associate is accounted for in accordance with the standard (i.e. under the equity method). It is proposed that an entity applies the amendment for annual periods beginning on or after 1 January 2011. Earlier application is to be permitted, but if an entity applies the amendment for an earlier period it is to disclose that fact.[19]

2.2   Definition of 'associate' and related terms

An *associate* is an entity, including an unincorporated entity such as a partnership, over which the investor has significant influence and that is neither a subsidiary nor an interest in a joint venture (see below).[20]

A *subsidiary* is an entity, including an unincorporated entity such as a partnership, that is controlled by another entity (known as the parent). *Control* is the power to govern the financial and operating policies of an entity so as to obtain benefits from its activities.[21] Although IFRS does not define what financial and operating policies are, these are generally presumed to include areas such as budgeting, capital expenditures, treasury management, dividend policy, production, marketing, sales and human resources. The definitions of 'subsidiary' and 'control' are the same as those in IAS 27 and are discussed in more detail in Chapter 6 at 2.

IAS 28 does not define *joint venture*, but the definition in IAS 31 is presumably intended to apply, namely a contractual arrangement whereby two or more parties undertake an economic activity that is subject to joint control.[22] *Joint control* is defined by IAS 28, albeit in the same terms as IAS 31, as contractually agreed sharing of control over an economic activity, which exists only when the strategic financial and operating decisions relating to the activity require the unanimous consent of the parties sharing control (the venturers).[23] The definitions of joint venture and joint control are discussed in more detail in Chapter 12 at 2.2.

Significant influence is the power to participate in the financial and operating policy decisions of the investee but is not control or joint control over those policies,[24] and is discussed further at 2.2.1 below.

2.2.1   *Significant influence*

Under IAS 28, a holding of 20% or more of the voting power of the investee is presumed to give rise to significant influence, unless it can be clearly demonstrated that this is not the case. Conversely, a holding of less than 20% of the voting power is presumed not to give rise to significant influence, unless it can be clearly demonstrated that there is in fact significant influence. The existence of a substantial or majority interest of another investor does not necessarily preclude the investor from having significant influence.[25] In calculating the interest of a group, account should be taken of shares held directly by the parent and those held indirectly through subsidiaries, but holdings by other associates or joint ventures of the group are ignored.[26] However, an entity should consider both ordinary shares and other categories of shares in determining its voting rights.

IAS 28 states that the exercise of significant influence will usually be evidenced in one or more of the following ways:

(a)   representation on the board of directors or equivalent governing body of the investee;

(b)   participation in policy-making processes, including participation in decisions about dividends and other distributions;

(c)   material transactions between the investor and the investee;

(d)   interchange of managerial personnel; or

(e)   provision of essential technical information.[27]

An entity loses significant influence over an investee when it loses the power to participate in the financial and operating policy decisions of that investee. The loss of significant influence can occur with or without a change in absolute or relative ownership levels. It could occur as a result of a contractual agreement. It could also occur, for example, when an associate becomes subject to the control of a government, court, administrator or regulator.[28] Loss of significant influence may therefore be an indicator of impairment also.

In some jurisdictions entities are able to seek protection from creditors without this resulting in the appointment of an administrator (e.g. under Chapter 11 of the Bankruptcy Code in the United States). Instead, existing management is given more time to reorganise the entity while enjoying protection from creditors. An investor in such an entity could still be able to exercise significant influence over the financial and operating policies.

Many of the factors relevant in assessing whether or not significant influence exists over another entity are also relevant to an assessment of whether control exists. Accordingly much of the implementation guidance to IAS 27 (discussed in Chapter 6 at 2.1) is also relevant to associates accounted for under IAS 28.[29]

In particular, IAS 27 notes that the reference to 'power' in the definition of 'significant influence' above means the ability to do or affect something. Consequently, an entity has significant influence over another entity when it currently has the ability to exercise that power, regardless of whether significant influence is actively demonstrated or is passive in nature.[30] Passive significant influence may be exercised over another entity through potential voting rights (see D below).

A   Lack of significant influence

The presumption of significant influence may sometimes be overcome in the following circumstances:

- the investor has failed to obtain representation on the investee's board of directors;

- the investee is opposing the investor's attempts to exercise significant influence;

- the investor is unable to obtain timely financial information or cannot obtain more information – required to apply the equity method – than shareholders that do not have significant influence; or

- a group of shareholders that holds the majority ownership of the investee operates without regard to the views of the investor.

Determining whether the presumption of significant influence has been overcome requires considerable judgement.

B   Holdings of less than 20% of the voting power

As noted above, there is a presumption that an investor that holds less than 20% of the voting power in an investee cannot exercise significant influence.[31] In our view, however, investments that give rise to only slightly less than 20% of the voting rights (e.g. 19.9% of the voting rights) should also generally be presumed to give rise to significant influence.

In some cases an investor may have an investment that gives rise to significantly less than 20% of the voting power. The investor may still be able to exercise significant influence in the following circumstances:

- the investor's voting power is much larger than that of any other shareholder of the investee;

- the corporate governance arrangements may be such that the investor is able to appoint members to the board, supervisory board or significant committees of the investee; or

- the investor has the power to veto significant financial and operating decisions. Determining which policies are significant requires considerable judgement.

Extract 11.2: GlaxoSmithKline plc (2007)

Notes to the financial statements [extract]

20 Investments in associates and joint ventures [extract]

The principal associated undertaking is Quest Diagnostics Inc. a US clinical laboratory business listed on the New York Stock Exchange. The investment had a book value at 31st December 2007 of £299 million (2006 – £262 million) and a market value of £970 million (2006 – £987 million).

At 31st December 2007, the Group owned 18.9% of Quest (2006 – 18.7%). Although the Group holds less than 20% of the ownership interest and voting control in Quest, the Group has the ability to exercise significant influence through both its significant shareholding and its nominated director's active participation on the Quest Board of Directors and Board sub-committees.

C   Holdings of more than 50% of the voting power

Control is presumed to exist under IAS 27 when the parent owns, directly or indirectly through subsidiaries, more than half of the voting power of an entity unless, in exceptional circumstances, it can be clearly demonstrated that such ownership does not constitute control (see Chapter 6 at 2.1.1).[32] An investor that does not have control despite holding more than 50% of the voting power, will typically be able to exercise significant influence and treat the investee as an associate.

D   Potential voting rights

An entity may own share warrants, share call options, debt or equity instruments that are convertible into ordinary shares, or other similar instruments that have the potential, if exercised or converted, to give the entity voting power or reduce another party's voting power over the financial and operating policies of another entity (potential voting rights).[33]

IAS 28 requires an entity to consider the existence and effect of potential voting rights that are currently exercisable or convertible, including potential voting rights held by another entity, when assessing whether an entity has significant influence over the financial and operating policies of another entity.[34]

Potential voting rights are not currently exercisable or convertible when they cannot be exercised or converted until a future date or until the occurrence of a future event.[35]

IAS 28 adds some further points of clarification. In assessing whether potential voting rights contribute to significant influence, an entity must examine all facts and circumstances (including the terms of exercise of the potential voting rights and any other contractual arrangements whether considered individually or in combination) that affect potential voting rights, except the intention of management and the financial ability to exercise or convert.[36]

The implementation guidance in IAS 27[37] elaborates on the above requirements in some detail, and reference should be made to the further discussion in Chapter 6 at 2.1.2.

E   Voting rights held in a fiduciary capacity

Voting rights on shares held as security remain the rights of the provider of the security, and are generally not taken into account if the rights are only exercisable in accordance with instructions from the provider of the security or in his interest. Similarly, voting rights that are held in a fiduciary capacity may not be those of the entity itself. However, if voting rights are held by a nominee on behalf of the entity, they should be taken into account.

F   Long-term restrictions over associate's ability to transfer funds to investor

Previous versions of IAS 28 contained an exemption from applying the equity method in accounting for an associate when severe long-term restrictions impaired an associate's ability to transfer funds to the investor. This exemption no longer applies.[38] The IASB indicates that it removed the exemption because such restrictions may not in fact affect the investor's significant influence over the associate. Whilst an investor should, when assessing its ability to exercise significant influence over an entity, consider restrictions on the transfer of funds from the associate to the investor, such restrictions do not in themselves preclude the exercise of significant influence.[39]

However, the nature and extent of any significant restrictions on the ability of associates to transfer funds to the investor in the form of cash dividends, or repayment of loans or advances should be disclosed (see 5.2.1 below).[40]

2.3   Requirement to apply the equity method

An investment in an associate must be accounted for using the equity method (see 3 below), except when:[41]

(a)   the investment is classified as held for sale in accordance with IFRS 5,[42] in which case it is accounted for under that standard (see 2.3.1 below);

(b)   the reporting entity is a parent (i.e. an entity with one or more subsidiaries)[43] exempt from preparing consolidated financial statements under IAS 27 (see Chapter 6 at 3.1); or

(c)   all of the following apply:

(i)   the investor is a wholly-owned subsidiary, or is a partially-owned subsidiary of another entity and its other owners, including those not otherwise entitled to vote, have been informed about, and do not object to, the investor not applying the equity method;

(ii)   the investor's debt or equity instruments are not traded in a public market (a domestic or foreign stock exchange or an over-the-counter market, including local and regional markets);

(iii)   the investor did not file, nor is it in the process of filing, its financial statements with a securities commission or other regulatory organisation, for the purpose of issuing any class of instruments in a public market; and

(iv)   the ultimate or any intermediate parent of the investor produces consolidated financial statements available for public use that comply with International Financial Reporting Standards.

Exemption (c) above will apply only where the investor in an associate is not also a parent. If it is a parent, it must look to the similar exemption from preparation of consolidated financial statements in IAS 27 (see Chapter 6 at 3.1). In fact, however, the conditions (i) to (iv) in (c) above are identical to the criteria that must be satisfied by a parent in order to be exempt from preparing consolidated financial statements under IAS 27. Further discussion of the meaning and interpretation of these conditions may be found in Chapter 6 at 3.1.

The exemption in (c) above is available only to entities that are themselves either wholly-owned subsidiaries or whose minority shareholders consent to the presentation of financial statements that do not include associates using the equity method. Some of these 'intermediate' entities will not be exempt, for example if none of their parent companies prepares consolidated financial statements in accordance with IFRS. A typical example is that of an entity that is a subsidiary of a US group that prepares consolidated accounts in accordance with US GAAP only. In addition, any entity that has publicly traded debt or equity, or is in the process of obtaining a listing for such instruments, will not satisfy the criteria for exemption.

The effect of the above requirements is that a reporting entity that has associates, but no subsidiaries, and does not meet all the criteria above, is required to apply equity accounting for its associates in its own (non-consolidated) financial statements (not to be confused with its 'separate financial statements' – see 2.4 below). This may be a significant change from many national GAAPs, where equity accounting for associates is required (or indeed permitted) only in consolidated financial statements.

As drafted, IAS 28 *requires*, rather than merely permits, an investor that meets the criteria in (b) or (c) above not to apply equity accounting. By contrast, the equivalent exemptions in IAS 27 (see Chapter 6 at 3.1) and IAS 31 (see Chapter 12 at 2.3) are drafted so as to be permissive rather than compulsory. We take the view that this was an unintentional drafting error, and that the exemption from equity accounting in IAS 28 is intended to be optional, not compulsory.

2.3.1   Associates held for sale

IAS 28 requires an investment in an associate to be accounted for under IFRS 5 and classified as held for sale if its carrying amount will be recovered principally through a sale transaction rather than through continuing use.[44] Although the introduction to IAS 28 still makes reference to disposals within twelve months of acquisition,[45] the corresponding guidance in the standard has been superseded by IFRS 5. The detailed IFRS requirements for classification as held for sale are discussed in Chapter 4 at 2.1.2.

From the date that an associate is classified as held for sale the investor ceases to apply the equity method, instead the associate is then measured at the lower of its carrying amount and fair value less cost to sell.[46] The measurement requirements as set out in IFRS 5 are discussed in detail in Chapter 4 at 2.2.

When an investment in an associate no longer meets the criteria to be classified as held for sale, it should be accounted for under the equity method from the date of its classification as held for sale. The financial statements of any prior periods since that classification must be restated.[47] The reason for requiring such restatement is not entirely clear (after all, the change in circumstances will often be the result of a non-adjusting event after the end of the reporting period), but it may well be intended to avoid abuse.

2.4   Separate financial statements

Separate financial statements are defined by IAS 28, consistent with IAS 27, as those presented by a parent, an investor in an associate or a venturer in a jointly controlled entity, in which the investments are accounted for on the basis of the direct equity interest rather than on the basis of the reported results and net assets of the investees.[48] IAS 27 requires that, in separate financial statements, investments in associates that are not classified as held for sale (or included in a disposal group that is classified as held for sale) in accordance with IFRS 5 should be accounted for either:[49]

* at cost; or
* in accordance with IAS 39.

IAS 27 has now been amended by deleting the definition of the 'cost method'. This is in response to difficulties raised in applying this cost method when a company adopts IFRS for the first time when, for example, the investments had been held for many years and an entity's previous GAAP did not require them to be accounted for at cost as applied by IFRS. Previously an investor applying the cost method in its separate financial statements would have been required to identify pre-acquisition profits of an associate and recognise dividends received out of these profits as a reduction of the cost of that associate. However the amendment requires the investor to recognise all dividends, whether relating to pre-acquisition or post acquisition profits of the investee, in profit or loss within its separate financial statements once the right to receive payments has been established.[50] The investor then needs to consider whether there are indicators of impairment as detailed within this amendment and as described in Chapter 8 at 2.3.1. The amendment is effective for annual periods beginning on or after 1 January 2009. Earlier application was permitted so long as this was disclosed and that related amendments to other standards were also applied.[51]

The detailed IFRS requirements for separate financial statements are set out in IAS 27[52] and are discussed more fully in Chapter 8.

It follows from the definition of separate financial statements above that financial statements (including non-consolidated financial statements) in which the equity method is applied are not separate financial statements; neither are the financial statements of an entity that does not have a subsidiary, associate or venturer's interest in a joint venture.[53]

Separate financial statements are financial statements presented in addition to:[54]

- consolidated financial statements;
- financial statements in which investments are accounted for using the equity method; and
- financial statements in which venturers' interests in joint ventures are proportionately consolidated.

There is no requirement for any entity to prepare separate financial statements, or for any separate financial statements that are voluntarily prepared to be appended to, or accompany, the 'main' financial statements.[55]

An entity may present separate financial statements as its only financial statements if it satisfies the conditions for exemption from:[56]

- preparing consolidated financial statements under paragraph 10 of IAS 27 (see Chapter 6 at 3.1);
- equity accounting for associates under paragraph 13(c) of IAS 28 (see (c) under 2.3 above); and
- proportionately consolidating (or equity accounting for) jointly controlled entities under paragraph 2 of IAS 31 (see Chapter 12 at 2.4).

As drafted, this exemption makes a curious distinction between an entity with associates and one with jointly controlled entities only.

An entity with associates may prepare separate financial statements as its only financial statements only if it satisfies the exemption in 'paragraph 13(c)' of IAS 28. In other words, if an entity has associates, but is exempt from equity accounting for all of them under paragraph 13(a) – i.e. because they are all accounted for under IFRS 5 – it may apparently not present separate financial statements as its only financial statements. However, an entity with jointly controlled entities may prepare separate financial statements as its only financial statements if it satisfies the exemption in 'paragraph 2' of IAS 31, which includes jointly controlled entities accounted for under IFRS 5.

In our view, it can be assumed that this inconsistency was unintentional, but it is less obvious as to which exemption is correct and which incorrect. On balance, our view is that it is the exemption in relation to joint ventures which is incorrect. In other words, the IASB intended to give the exemption only to 'non-public interest' companies and should have referred to 'paragraph 2(c)' of IAS 31.

2.4.1 Impairment of investments in associates in separate financial statements

One issue recently considered by the IFRIC and the IASB is how impairments of investments in associates should be determined in the separate financial statements of the investor. In our view, we believe that the requirements of IAS 36 and IAS 39 make it clear that IAS 36 applies to the impairment of associates measured at cost in the separate financial statements.[57]

However, at its meeting in May 2009, and subsequently confirmed at its meeting in July 2009, the IFRIC noted that 'IAS 36 – *Impairment of Assets* – provides clear guidance that its requirements apply to impairment losses of investments in associates when the associate is accounted for using the equity method. However, in its separate financial statements, the investor may account for its investment in an associate at cost. The IFRIC concluded that it is not clear whether in its separate financial statements the investor should determine impairment in accordance with IAS 36 or IAS 39 – *Financial Instruments: Recognition and Measurement*.

'In view of the existing guidance in IFRSs, the IFRIC concluded that significant diversity is likely to exist in practice on this issue. The IFRIC decided that it could be best resolved by referring it to the IASB. Therefore, the IFRIC decided not to add this issue to its agenda.'[58]

Consequently, the IASB has decided to deal with this issue within the exposure draft of proposed *Improvements to IFRSs* issued in August 2009.[59] The IASB is proposing that, as the purpose of separate financial statements is on the performance of the assets as investments,[60] when an entity prepares separate financial statements, it is to apply the requirements of IAS 39 rather than IAS 36 for the determination and measurement of impairment losses on investments in subsidiaries, jointly controlled entities and associates. It is proposed that an entity applies the amendments prospectively for annual periods beginning on or after 1 January 2011. Earlier application is to be permitted, but if an entity applies the amendments for an earlier period it is to disclose that fact.[61]

3   APPLICATION OF THE EQUITY METHOD

3.1   Overview

IAS 28 defines the equity method as 'a method of accounting whereby the investment is initially recorded at cost and adjusted thereafter for the post acquisition change in the investor's share of net assets of the investee. The profit or loss of the investor includes the investor's share of the profit or loss of the investee.'[62] Distributions received from an investee reduce the carrying amount of the investment. Adjustments to the carrying amount may also be necessary for changes in the investor's proportionate interest in the investee arising from changes in the investee's equity that have not been recognised in the investee's profit or loss, but in the investee's other comprehensive income. Such changes include those arising from the revaluation of property, plant and equipment and from foreign exchange translation differences. The investor's share of any such changes is recognised directly in other comprehensive income of the investor.[63]

Example 11.5:   Application of the equity method

On 1 January 2010 entity A acquires a 35% interest in entity B, over which it is able to exercise significant influence. Entity A paid €475,000 for its interest in B. At that date the book value of B's net assets was €900,000, and their fair value €1,100,000, the difference of €200,000 relates entirely to an item of property, plant and equipment with a remaining useful life of 10 years. During the year B made a profit of €80,000 and paid a dividend of €120,000 on 31 December 2010. Entity B also owned an investment in securities classified as available-for-sale that increased in value by €20,000 during the year.

Entity A accounts for its investment in B under the equity method as follows:

	€	€
Acquisition of investment in B		
Share in book value of B's net assets: 35% of €900,000	315,000	
Share in fair valuation of B's net assets: 35% of (€1,100,000 – €900,000) *	70,000	
Goodwill on investment in B: €475,000 – €315,000 – €70,000 *	90,000	
Cost of investment		475,000
Profit during the year		
Share in the profit reported by B: 35% of €80,000	28,000	
Adjustment to reflect effect of fair valuation *		
35% of ((€1,100,000 – €900,000) ÷ 10 years)	(7,000)	
Share of profit in B recognised in income by A		21,000
Revaluation of available-for-sale asset		
Share in revaluation recognised in other comprehensive income by A: 35% of €20,000		7,000
Dividend received by A during the year		(42,000)
Share in book value of B's net assets:		
€315,000 + 35% (€80,000 – €120,000 + €20,000)	308,000	
Share in fair valuation of B's net assets: €70,000 – €7,000 *	63,000	
Goodwill on investment in B *	90,000	
Closing balance of A's investment in B		461,000

*   These line items are normally not presented separately, but are combined with the ones immediately above.

IAS 28 explains that equity accounting is necessary because to recognise income simply on the basis of distributions received may not be an adequate measure of the income earned by an investor on an investment in an associate, since distributions received may bear little relation to the performance of the associate. Through its significant influence over the associate, the investor has an interest in the associate's performance and, as a result, the return on its investment. The investor accounts for this interest by extending the scope of its financial statements so as to include its share of profits or losses of such an associate. As a result, application of the equity method provides more informative reporting of the net assets and profit or loss of the investor.[64]

3.2 Similarities of equity accounting and consolidation

IAS 28 notes that many procedures appropriate for the application of the equity method, and described in more detail in 3.3 to 3.8 below, are similar to the consolidation procedures described in IAS 27 (see Chapter 7). Furthermore IAS 28 explains that the concepts underlying the procedures used in accounting for the acquisition of a subsidiary are also adopted in accounting for the acquisition of an investment in an associate.[65] However, it is unclear as to precisely what concepts this is meant to refer to. As a result of phase II of the Business Combinations project a substantially revised IFRS 3 – *Business Combinations* – and IAS 27 – *Consolidated and Separate Financial Statements* – were issued in January 2008. Consequential amendments were made to IAS 28, effective from the same date as application of the revised versions of IFRS 3 and IAS 27. However, an explicit reference to IFRS 3 that had existed, relating to the accounting for acquisitions of associates, in the previous version of IAS 28[66] was removed. Hence despite the completion of phase II of the Business Combinations project it is still difficult to ascertain what the accounting should be when, for example, an associate is acquired piecemeal (see 3.2.4 and 3.2.5 below). To what extent the methodology and procedures under IFRS 3 (as revised in 2008) should be applied is open to further consideration. The position has been confused even further as a result of the publication of the IASB's annual improvement standard in April 2009 where in the context of an amendment to IAS 39 regarding the application of the exemption in paragraph 2(g) of that standard (see Chapter 29 at 3.7.2) it is stated that the 'Board noted that paragraph 20 of IAS 28 explains only the methodology used to account for investments in associates. This should not be taken to imply that the principles for business combinations and consolidations can be applied by analogy to accounting for investments in associates and joint ventures.'[67] In May 2009, the IASB has indicated that it will address the interaction between the revised versions of IFRS 3 and IAS 27, and IAS 28 and IAS 31, as part of its project on joint ventures (see Chapter 12 at 7),[68] so hopefully the issue will be clarified in the near future. This ultimately may have implications for many of the issues discussed in 3.2 to 3.8 below.

The interaction between these IFRSs has also raised the more general issue as to how the initial carrying value of an equity method investment should be determined which has recently been considered by the IFRIC (see 3.2.2 and 3.2.3 below). Another issue in this context considered by the IFRIC is how an equity method investee's issue of shares should be accounted for (see 3.8.4 below).

IAS 28 states that on acquisition of an investment in an associate, any difference between the cost of the investment and the investor's share of the net fair value of the associate's identifiable assets, liabilities and contingent liabilities (or upon application of IFRS 3 (as revised in 2008) 'the associate's identifiable assets and liabilities') is accounted for as follows:[69]

- Goodwill relating to an associate is included in the carrying amount of the investment. Amortisation of that goodwill is not permitted;

- Any excess of the investor's share of the net fair value of the associate's identifiable assets, liabilities and contingent liabilities (or upon application of IFRS 3 (as revised in 2008) 'the associate's identifiable assets and liabilities') over the cost of the investment is included as income in the determination of the investor's share of the associate's profit or loss in the period in which the investment is acquired.

IAS 28 states that appropriate adjustments to the investor's share of the associate's profits or losses after acquisition are also made to account, for example, for depreciation of the depreciable assets based on their fair values at the acquisition date. Similarly, appropriate adjustments to the investor's share of the associate's profits or losses after acquisition are made for impairment losses recognised by the associate, such as for goodwill or property, plant and equipment (see 4.1 below).[70]

However, an investor will not necessarily simply recognise impairment losses in respect of an associate equivalent to its share of the impairment losses recognised by the associate itself (even after fair value and other consolidation adjustments). This is discussed further at 4 below.

Moreover, it may be necessary to make adjustments for transactions between the investor and its associates (see 3.4 below).

3.2.1 *Differences between equity accounting and consolidation*

An investor that controls a subsidiary has control over the assets and liabilities of that subsidiary. While an investor that has significant influence over an associate controls its holding in the shares of the associate, it does not control the assets and liabilities of that associate. Therefore, the investor does not account for the assets and the liabilities of the associate, but only accounts for its investment in the associate as a whole. This subtle difference means, for example, that an investor cannot capitalise its own borrowing costs in respect of an associate's assets under construction (an investment in an associate is not a qualifying asset under IAS 23 – *Borrowing Costs* – regardless of the associate's activities or assets). Similarly, difficulties would arise if an investor wanted to designate a financial instrument as a hedge of an associate's transactions, assets or liabilities (see Chapter 12 at 3.3.2 A III for more details).

3.2.2 *Initial carrying amount of an associate – prior to application of IAS 27 (as amended in 2008) and IFRS 3 (as revised in 2008)*

As indicated at 3.1 above, IAS 28 defines the equity method as 'a method of accounting whereby the investment is initially recorded at cost and adjusted thereafter … .'[71] However, no indication is given in the standard as to what is meant by 'cost'. As discussed further in Chapter 3 at 4.3, IAS 8 – *Accounting Policies, Changes in Estimates and Errors* – requires that, in the absence of specific guidance in IFRS, management should first refer to the requirements and guidance in IFRS dealing with similar and related issues.

As IAS 28, prior to its revision by IFRS 3 (as revised in 2008), included an explicit reference to previous version of the Business Combinations standard, 'IFRS 3 (2007)', in our view the requirements of that IFRS in determining the cost of a business combination would be the most appropriate point of reference. As discussed in Chapter 9 at 2.4, IFRS 3 (2007) requires the cost of a business combination to be the aggregate of:

(a)   the fair values, at the date of exchange, of assets given, liabilities incurred or assumed, and equity instruments issued by the acquirer, in exchange for control of the acquiree; plus

(b)   any costs directly attributable to the business combination.[72]

For most acquisitions of an associate, these requirements would effectively give the same answer as other various IFRSs that require assets to be measured at initial recognition at cost, where in general, cost includes the purchase price (being the amount cash or cash equivalents paid or the fair value of other consideration given), together with other costs directly attributable to the acquisition of the asset.[73]

However, one area where the requirements of IFRS 3 (2007) contain further guidance that may also be relevant in the context of the acquisition of an associate is that relating to business combinations achieved in stages ('step acquisitions') – see Chapter 9 at 2.9. The application of the IFRS 3 (2007) requirements for step acquisitions in the context of piecemeal acquisition of an associate is discussed further at 3.2.4 below.

3.2.3   Initial carrying amount of an associate – upon application of IAS 27 (as amended in 2008) and IFRS 3 (as revised in 2008)

IFRS 3 (as revised in 2008) is effective for business combinations for which the acquisition date is on or after the beginning of the first annual reporting period beginning on or after 1 July 2009 with early adoption possible as explained in Chapter 9 at 3.1.1. IAS 27 (as amended in 2008) has the same effective date.[74]

Whereas the accounting for a business combination under IFRS 3 (2007) was a cost-based approach, in contrast, IFRS 3 (as revised in 2008) adopts an approach whereby the various components of a business combination generally are measured at their acquisition date fair values (see Chapter 9 at 1.2.4 B). As noted at 3.2.2 above, under IFRS 3 (2007), any acquisition-related costs were included in arriving at the cost of the business combination, whereas under IFRS 3 (as revised in 2008) such acquisition-related costs are to be expensed (see Chapter 9 at 3.8.3). Also, the requirements for step-acquisitions under IFRS 3 (2007) meant that the cost of such a business combination was based on the value of the consideration given at the date of acquiring each tranche (see Chapter 9 at 2.9), whereas under IFRS 3 (as revised in 2008) any previously held interest is re-measured at its acquisition-date fair value in accounting for the business combination, with any resulting gain or loss being recognised in profit or loss (see Chapter 9 at 3.10).

As indicated at 3.2 above, although IAS 28 still explains that the concepts underlying the procedures used in accounting for the acquisition of a subsidiary are also adopted in accounting for the acquisition of an investment in an associate, a direct reference from IAS 28 to IFRS 3 has actually now been removed.[75] This has raised the issue as to what impact the new concepts inherent within IFRS 3 (as revised in 2008) should have on the accounting for associates particularly since, as indicated at 3.1 above, IAS 28 defines the equity method as 'a method of accounting whereby the investment is initially recorded at cost and adjusted thereafter ... .'[76]

The position has been confused even further as a result of the publication of the IASB's annual improvement standard in April 2009 where in the context of an amendment to IAS 39 it is stated that the 'Board noted that paragraph 20 of IAS 28 explains only the methodology used to account for investments in associates. This should not be taken to imply that the principles for business combinations and consolidations can be applied by analogy to accounting for investments in associates and joint ventures.'[77]

One potential effect of IFRS 3 (as revised in 2008) on the equity method of accounting that has recently been considered by the IFRIC is how the initial carrying value of an equity method investment should be determined.

At its meeting in May 2009, and subsequently confirmed at its meeting in July 2009, the IFRIC noted that IFRSs consistently require assets not measured at fair value through profit or loss to be measured at initial recognition at cost. Generally stated, cost includes the purchase price and other costs directly attributable to the acquisition or issuance of the asset such as professional fees for legal services, transfer taxes and other transaction costs. Therefore, the cost of an investment in an associate at initial recognition determined in accordance with paragraph 11 of IAS 28 comprises its purchase price and any directly attributable expenditures necessary to obtain it. The IFRIC decided not to add this issue to its agenda, having concluded that the agenda criteria were not met mainly because, given the guidance in IFRSs, it did not expect divergent interpretations in practice.[78]

This would appear to clarify that any acquisition-related costs should not be expensed, but should be included as part of the cost of the associate. The implications for the piecemeal acquisition of an associate are discussed further at 3.2.5 below.

A   *Retained interest in an associate following loss of control or joint control in an entity*

Circumstances where the cost of an investment in an associate at initial recognition will not comprise its purchase price and any directly attributable expenditures necessary to obtain it will be where an entity loses control or joint control of an entity, but retains an interest that is now to be accounted for as an associate. In such situations, the retained interest must be remeasured at its fair value,[79] and this fair value becomes the cost for applying the equity method.[80]

Example 11.6:　　*Accounting for retained interest in an associate following loss of control (or joint control) in an entity*

Entity A owns 100% of the shares of Entity B. The interest was originally purchased for £500,000 and £40,000 of directly attributable costs relating to the acquisition were incurred. On 30 June 2010, Entity A sells 60% of the shares to Entity C for £1,300,000. As a result of the sale, Entity C obtains control over Entity B, but by retaining a 40% interest, Entity A determines that it has significant influence over Entity B.

At the date of disposal, the carrying amount of the net assets of Entity B in Entity A's consolidated financial statements is £1,200,000 and there is also goodwill of £200,000 relating to the acquisition of Entity B. The fair value of the identifiable assets and liabilities of Entity B is £1,600,000. The fair value of Entity A's retained interest of 40% of the shares of Entity B is £800,000.

Upon Entity A's sale of 60% of the shares of Entity B, it deconsolidates Entity B and accounts for its investment in Entity B as an associate using the equity method of accounting.

Entity A's initial carrying amount of the associate has to be based on the fair value of the retained interest, i.e. £800,000. It is not based on 40% of the original cost of £540,000 (purchase price plus directly attributable costs) as might be suggested by the IFRIC statement, nor is it based on 40% of the carrying amount of the net assets and goodwill totalling £1,400,000 as would have generally been the treatment prior to changes made to IAS 27 and IFRS 3 as a result of phase II of the Business Combinations project.

Although it is clear that the initial carrying amount of the associate is the fair value of the retained interest, i.e. £800,000, does this mean that Entity A in applying the equity method under IAS 28 must:

(a)　remeasure the underlying assets and liabilities in Entity B at their fair values at the date Entity B becomes an associate i.e. effectively a new purchase price allocation is performed; and

(b)　reassess the classification and designation of assets and liabilities, e.g. the classification of financial instruments, embedded derivatives and hedge accounting, as required by IFRS 3 (revised 2008) – see Chapter 9 at 3.6.4?

In our view, as Entity A effectively accounts for the investment in Entity B as if it had acquired the retained investment at fair value as at the date control (or joint control) is lost, the answer to question (a) is 'yes'. Accordingly, in order to apply the equity method from the date control (or joint control) is lost, Entity A must remeasure *all* of the identifiable assets and liabilities underlying the investment at their fair values (or other measurement basis required by IFRS 3 (revised 2008) at that date). As far as question (b) is concerned, we also believe that Entity A should reassess the classification or designation of assets and liabilities in accordance with paragraph 15 of IFRS 3 (revised 2008), based on the circumstances that exist at that date. However, in doing so, there is no need to reassess whether an embedded derivative should be separated from a host contract. In the annual improvement standard issued in April 2009, the IASB, in clarifying the scope of IFRIC 9 – *Reassessment of Embedded Derivatives* – in relation to certain business combinations, noted in the context of an acquisition of an investment in an associate that 'reassessment of embedded derivatives in contracts held by an associate is not required by IFRIC 9 in any event. The investment in the associate is the asset the investor controls and recognises, not the underlying assets and liabilities of the associate.'[81] Despite this limited exception re embedded derivatives, we do not believe that it should be applied by analogy to other reassessments,

Paragraphs 20 and 23 of IAS 28 indicate that on initial recognition of an investment in an associate the concepts underlying the procedures used in accounting for the acquisition of a subsidiary are also adopted in accounting for the acquisition of an investment in an associate, and that fair values are applied to measure all of the identifiable assets and liabilities in calculating any goodwill or bargain purchase that exists.

Accordingly, based on the fair value of the identifiable assets and liabilities of Entity B of £1,600,000, Entity A's initial carrying amount of £800,000 will include goodwill of £160,000, being £800,000 – £640,000 (40% of £1,600,000).

It should be noted, however, that ED 9 – *Joint Arrangements* – proposes that there is not a revaluation to fair value when an entity loses joint control but retains significant influence and continues to use the equity method.[82]

3.2.4 Piecemeal acquisition of an associate – prior to application of IAS 27 (as amended in 2008) and IFRS 3 (as revised in 2008)

IFRS 3 (as revised in 2008) is effective for business combinations for which the acquisition date is on or after the beginning of the first annual reporting period beginning on or after 1 July 2009 with early adoption possible as explained in Chapter 9 at 3.1.1. For periods before adoption of this revised standard the previous version of the Business Combinations Standard, 'IFRS 3 (2007)', and the following guidance is applicable.

A   Step increase in an existing associate

Accounting for an increase of an interest in an associate that remains an associate after that increase is not specifically addressed by IAS 28. However, that standard does require the requirements of IFRS 3 (2007) to be applied in accounting for the acquisition of an investment in an associate.[83] IFRS 3 (2007) acknowledges that before qualifying as a business combination, a transaction may qualify as an investment in an associate and be accounted for in accordance with IAS 28, which means that the fair values of the investee's identifiable net assets at the date of each earlier exchange transaction should have been determined previously in applying the equity method to the investment.[84] This means that a step-by-step comparison of the cost of the individual investments with the acquirer's interest in the fair values of the acquiree's identifiable assets, liabilities and contingent liabilities at each step is required.[85] As discussed at 3.2.2 above, cost would be the aggregate consideration given plus any directly attributable costs in relation to each interest acquired. The requirement in IFRS 3 (2007) to revalue previously held interests of the investor to fair value only applies when the investor obtains control over the investment.[86] Therefore, in our view, when an additional interest is acquired in an associate that continues to be accounted for under the equity method, the existing interest in the associate should not be remeasured to take into account previously unrecognised changes in the fair value of the investor's share in the identifiable net assets.

The accounting for an increase in an associate that becomes a jointly controlled entity as a result is discussed in Chapter 12 at 3.3.8 A, and where it becomes a subsidiary is discussed in Chapter 9 at 2.9.

B   Financial instrument becoming an associate

A step acquisition also arises when an entity gains significant influence over an existing investment upon acquisition of a further interest or due to a change in circumstances. IAS 28 is unclear on how an investor should account for an existing investment, which is accounted for under IAS 39, that subsequently becomes an associate that should be accounted for under the equity method. In practice, there are two acceptable methods that are explained below. However, in our view Method A is most consistent with the principles underlying the equity method of accounting – namely, applying consolidation and business combination principles as well as accounting for the investor's share of associate's results after the date of acquisition. Nevertheless, there is also some support within IAS 28 for method B. The method that an entity selects should however be applied consistently.

I   Method A

Method A requires the investor to revert to its original cost and then recognise a 'catch up' equity method adjustment for its share of post acquisition profits and reserves since the original acquisition date. Dividend income continues to be recognised in profit or loss up to the date the entity becomes an associate.

IAS 28 notes that the concepts underlying the procedures used in accounting for the acquisition of a subsidiary should also be adopted in accounting for the acquisition of an associate.[87] Furthermore, the standard notes that 'on acquisition of the investment any difference between the cost of the investment and the investor's share of the net fair value of the associate's identifiable assets, liabilities and contingent liabilities is accounted for in accordance with IFRS 3'.[88] Although IFRS 3 (2007) only deals with business combinations that are achieved in stages, it does contain guidance that can be applied by analogy.[89] In particular, it notes that cost should be determined at the date of each exchange transaction irrespective of the fact that the carrying amount has changed. As discussed at 3.2.2 above, cost would be the aggregate consideration given plus any directly attributable costs in relation to each interest acquired. Example 6 in the IFRS 3 (2007) Illustrative Examples shows that the post-acquisition changes in *retained earnings* relating to each 'tranche' of a step acquisition should be included in retained earnings rather than being eliminated.[90] Therefore, on initial application of the equity method it is appropriate to recognise the investor's share of the investee's earnings on the existing tranches of its investment. This adjustment will, by necessity, be net of dividend income already recorded. This approach is consistent with the description of the equity method in paragraph 11 of IAS 28.

Example 6 in the IFRS 3 (2007) Illustrative Examples also shows that that the post-acquisition changes in *fair value* relating to each tranche are also included in equity rather than being eliminated.[91]

Similarly, goodwill is also calculated separately for each tranche in accordance with IFRS 3 (2007).[92] IAS 22 – *Business Combinations* – specifically required that when an investment 'did not qualify previously as an associate, the fair values of the identifiable assets and liabilities are determined as at the date of each significant step and goodwill or negative goodwill is recognised from the date of acquisition'.[93] Although an identical requirement does not appear in IFRS 3 (2007), its basis for conclusions indicates that the requirements of IAS 22 dealing with step acquisitions were not intended to be changed.[94] Therefore, we consider it appropriate to determine the fair values as at the date of each individual acquisition.

II   Method B

Method B requires the investor to revert to its original cost, but not to recognise a 'catch up' adjustment. Dividend income continues to be recognised in profit or loss up to the date the entity becomes an associate.

This method uses the same underlying logic as method A for determining cost and goodwill. However, IAS 28 states that 'an investment in an associate is accounted for using the equity method from the date on which it becomes an associate'.[95] To avoid contradicting this specific requirement in IAS 28, method B does not recognise a cumulative adjustment for prior periods.

However, it should be emphasised that if the ownership interest increases further and the investment becomes a subsidiary, and the full step acquisition guidance of IFRS 3 (2007) would apply at the time of that transaction, the cumulative results that are ignored by method B would need to be recognised at that point.

III   Practical example

The application of methods A and B is illustrated in the example below.

Example 11.7:   Accounting for existing financial instruments on the step-acquisition of an associate

In 2006, an investor acquired a 10% interest in an investee for $100. Three years later, in 2009, the investor acquired a further 15% interest in the investee for $225. The investor now holds a 25% interest and is able to exercise significant influence. For the purposes of the example, directly attributable costs have been ignored.

The investor had been accounting for its initial 10% interest at fair value in accordance with IAS 39. The financial information relating to the investee can be summarised as follows:

	2006		2009	
	100%	10%	100%	15%
	$	$	$	$
Purchase consideration			100	225
Change in fair value		50		
Fair value of shares in 2009		150		
Book value of net assets of investee	600		900	
Fair value of net assets of investee *)	800	80	1,200	180
Profit since acquisition in 2006	500	50		
Dividends declared between 2006 and 2009	−200	−20		
Increase in fair value of net assets of investee	100	10		
Cost plus post-acquisition changes in net assets		140		
Other changes in fair value of the investee		10		

*) The fair value uplift from $600 to $800 entirely relates to non-depreciable assets.

How should the investor account for the acquisition of the additional 15% interest?

Method A

Under this method, cost is the sum of the consideration paid for the two tranches. Therefore, the investor should account for the following:

- If the original investment had been fair valued through profit or loss, the change in fair value previously recognised through profit or loss (excluding dividend income) is reversed through retained earnings to bring the asset back to its original cost; or
- If the original investment had been fair valued through other comprehensive income, the change in fair value in other comprehensive income is reversed so as to bring the asset back to its original cost.

Goodwill is calculated as the difference between the cost of each tranche and the share of the fair value of the assets and liabilities acquired in each tranche. Dividend income continues to be recognised in profit or loss up to the date the entity becomes an associate. However, at that date an adjustment will also be made through retained earnings to recognise the investor's share of post acquisition profits or losses, net of (1) any dividends receivable and (2) any changes in fair value of the underlying assets since the acquisition of the first tranche.

Therefore, in the above example the total cost is $325. The change in the fair value of $50 relating to the initial 10% investment is reversed through retained earnings or the revaluation reserves as appropriate. The investor's share of the equity method retained profits of $30 earned on this investment and a share of the change in fair values of $10 is recognised. The overall effect of these adjustments, which reduce the carrying amount of the existing investment from $150 to $140, will be reflected in other comprehensive income in the statement of comprehensive income. The investment balance following the acquisition of the second tranche is therefore:

	First tranche $	Second tranche $	Total $
Cost	100	225	325
Profit since acquisition in 2006	50		
Dividends declared between 2006 and 2009	−20		
Increase in fair value of assets of investee	10		
Total investment	140	225	365
Goodwill included in the investment:			
– First tranche: $100 – $80 =			20
– Second tranche: $225 – $180 =			45
			65

Method B

Method B gives the same goodwill as method A, but there is no adjustment made to recognise the investor's share of profits or changes in fair value of underlying assets up to the date of gaining significant influence. In other words, the investment balance is the original cost of $325. The only adjustment reflected in other comprehensive income in the statement of comprehensive income is the $50 required to reduce the carrying amount of the existing investment from its fair value of $150 to its original cost of $100.

Finally, it should be noted that under both methods, the 'cost' in the separate financial statements of the investor would be $325 in each case.

3.2.5   Piecemeal acquisition of an associate – upon application of IAS 27 (as amended in 2008) and IFRS 3 (as revised in 2008)

IFRS 3 (as revised in 2008) is effective for business combinations for which the acquisition date is on or after the beginning of the first annual reporting period beginning on or after 1 July 2009 with early adoption possible as explained in Chapter 9 at 3.1.1. Upon this revision of IFRS 3 no additional guidance was introduced directly relating to piecemeal acquisitions of associates.

Indeed, as indicated at 3.2 above, although IAS 28 still explains that the concepts underlying the procedures used in accounting for the acquisition of a subsidiary are also adopted in accounting for the acquisition of an investment in an associate, a direct reference from IAS 28 to IFRS 3 has actually now been removed.[96] This has raised the issue as to what impact the new concepts inherent within IFRS 3 (as revised in 2008) should have on the accounting for associates.

As discussed at 3.2.3 above, one potential effect of IFRS 3 (as revised in 2008) on the equity method of accounting that has recently been considered by the IFRIC is how the initial carrying value of an equity method investment should be determined. At its meeting in May 2009, and subsequently confirmed at its meeting in July 2009, the IFRIC noted that the cost of an investment in an associate at initial recognition determined in accordance with paragraph 11 of IAS 28 comprises its purchase price and any directly attributable expenditures necessary to obtain it. The IFRIC decided not to add this issue to its agenda, having concluded that the agenda criteria were not met mainly because, given the guidance in IFRSs, it did not expect divergent interpretations in practice.[97]

Although the implications for the piecemeal acquisition of an associate are not explicitly addressed, it would appear that, as the IFRIC considers that the initial recognition of the associate is to be based on its cost, the accounting should reflect a cost-based approach.

A   Step increase in an existing associate

The explicit cross reference to IFRS 3 in the previous version of IAS 28 was the basis for the step-by-step methodology that is explained at 3.2.4 A above and that is applicable before adoption of IFRS 3 (as revised in 2008). This step-by-step methodology is not a feature of IFRS 3 (as revised in 2008). Revaluation of previously held interests in equity accounted for investments (with recognition of any gain or loss in profit or loss) is required when the investor acquires control of the investee.[98] At this point there is a significant change in the nature of and economic circumstances surrounding that investment and it is this that warrants a change in the classification and measurement of that investment.[99] In contrast a step increase in an existing associate that remains an associate after that increase is unlikely to significantly change the nature and economic circumstances of the investment, and hence there is little justification for any such remeasurement.

Although the IFRIC discussion referred to above relates to the *initial* recognition of an associate, given that the accounting should reflect a cost-based approach, in the absence of any additional guidance it seems most appropriate to follow the methodology explained at 3.2.4 A above. Accordingly, the purchase price and any directly attributable expenditures necessary to obtain the additional interest in the associate are added to the existing carrying amount for the associate. The alternative, to restate the investment to fair value through profit or loss every time there is a change in the investor's equity interest in an associate would be open to abuse and would in effect allow any investor to fair value interests in associates rather than limit this ability to venture capital organisations, mutual funds, unit trusts and similar entities that are specifically allowed this option under the scoping requirements of IAS 28.[100] We do not believe this can have been the intention of the IASB.

For the purposes of applying the equity method of accounting, the amount that has been added to the existing carrying amount for the associate still needs to be split between goodwill and the additional interest in the fair value of the assets and liabilities of the associate at the date of the increase in the associate.

The accounting for an increase in an associate that becomes a jointly controlled entity as a result is discussed in Chapter 12 at 3.3.9 A, and where it becomes a subsidiary is discussed in Chapter 9 at 3.10.

B   Financial instrument becoming an associate

A step acquisition also arises when an entity gains significant influence over an existing investment upon acquisition of a further interest or due to a change in circumstances. IAS 28 is unclear on how an investor should account for an existing investment, which is accounted for under IAS 39, that subsequently becomes an associate that should be accounted for under the equity method.

The methodologies that are believed appropriate before adoption of IFRS 3 (as revised in 2008) are all based upon guidance that was contained in IFRS 3 (2007). IFRS 3 (as revised in 2008) is clear that in a business combination where control over an acquiree is achieved in stages the previously held equity investment in that acquiree is required to be revalued to fair value through profit or loss.[101] If this equity investment was held at fair value through profit and loss this would have happened automatically. If the investment was classified as available-for-sale any previous remeasurement would be within other comprehensive income and on the date of the business combination any such amount would be reclassified to profit or loss as if that investment had been directly disposed of.[102]

It might be argued that a similar approach should be adopted when an associate is acquired in stages. At the date that significant influence is obtained the previously held interest would be revalued to fair value and the resulting gain or loss recognised in profit or loss.

Example 11.8:   Accounting for existing financial instruments on the step-acquisition of an associate

Using the same information as in Example 11.7 above the 10% existing interest would be revalued through profit and loss to $150. Any amount in other comprehensive income relating to this interest would be reclassified to profit or loss. Goodwill would then be calculated as the difference between $375 (the fair value of the existing 10% interest and the cost of the additional 15% interest) and $300 (25% of the fair value of net assets at the date significant influence is attained of $1,200).

This methodology would be consistent with the accounting that is required by IAS 28 in the reverse situation; i.e. when there is a loss of significant influence in an associate (see 3.8.2 below). Nevertheless, it is clear from the recent IFRIC discussion referred to above, that it does not expect such an approach be followed.

The IFRIC clearly expects a cost-based approach to be used as it states that the cost of an investment in an associate at initial recognition determined in accordance with paragraph 11 of IAS 28 comprises its purchase price and any directly attributable expenditures necessary to obtain it; i.e. the cumulative cost. However, as the implications for the piecemeal acquisition of an associate are not explicitly addressed by the IFRIC statement, it is unclear how such transactions should be accounted for. As illustrated in Example 11.9 below, we consider that, consistent with a cost-based approach, there are a number of possible methods that may be acceptable.

Example 11.9:   Accounting for existing financial instruments on the step-acquisition of an associate

Using the same information as in Example 11.7 above, how should the investor account for the acquisition of the additional 15% interest?

In accounting for the transaction there are two main issues that need to be considered:

- what should be the initial carrying amount of the associate?
- how should the goodwill (or gain on bargain purchase) be calculated?

In our view, any of the following cost-based methodologies would be acceptable.

(a)   Method 1

Based on the IFRIC statement, the initial amount recognised for the associate would be $325, being the original purchase price of $100 for the existing 10% interest plus the $225 paid for the additional 15% interest. The change in the fair value of $50 relating to the initial 10% investment is reversed through retained earnings or the revaluation reserves as appropriate. This will be reflected in other comprehensive income in the statement of comprehensive income.

Goodwill is calculated as required by paragraph 28 of IAS 28 at the date the investment becomes an associate. Accordingly, the goodwill is the difference between the cost of $325 and $300 (25% of the fair value of net assets at the date significant influence is attained of $1,200), resulting in goodwill of $25.

This method avoids some of the practical difficulties encountered when applying the other methods below, which reflect the methodology in IFRS 3 (2007) in having to determine fair values of the assets and liabilities of the associate at the dates of purchasing previous interests when no such exercise was required at the date of original purchase. The drawback with this method is that it involves comparing the cost of the first tranche with the relevant share of the assets and liabilities based on fair values at a later date.

(b)   Method 2

As with method 1, based on the IFRIC statement, the initial amount recognised for the associate would be $325, being the original purchase price of $100 for the existing 10% interest plus the $225 paid for the additional 15% interest. Again, the change in the fair value of $50 relating to the initial 10% investment is reversed through retained earnings or the revaluation reserves as appropriate. This will be reflected in other comprehensive income in the statement of comprehensive income.

However, rather than calculating goodwill in one step as in method 1, the goodwill is calculated as the difference between the cost of each tranche and the share of the fair value of the assets and liabilities acquired in each tranche, i.e. $65. This is based on the methodology in IFRS 3 (2007) and is the same as method B at 3.2.4 B above.

The drawbacks with this method is that the measurement of the assets and liabilities of the associate are based on fair values at different dates and it suffers from the practical difficulties encountered when applying the methodology in IFRS 3 (2007) in having to determine fair values of the assets and liabilities of the associate at the dates of purchasing previous interests when no such exercise was required at the date of original purchase.

(c) Method 3

Although the IFRIC statement requires a cost-based approach in applying the equity method under IAS 28, the methodology in IFRS 3 (2007) for such transactions whereby catch-up adjustments for the post-acquisition changes in both the retained profits and other comprehensive income and the fair values of the assets and liabilities relating to the original tranche are made was not considered to be inconsistent with such an approach, so is still a valid method. Accordingly, the initial carrying amount of the associate is $365 (as calculated under method A in Example 11.7 above). As in that Example, the change in the fair value of $50 relating to the initial 10% investment is reversed through retained earnings or the revaluation reserves as appropriate. The investor's share of the equity method retained profits of $30 earned on this investment and a share of the change in fair values of $10 is recognised. The overall effect of these adjustments, which reduce the carrying amount of the existing investment from $150 to $140, will be reflected in other comprehensive income in the statement of comprehensive income.

Goodwill is calculated as the difference between the cost of each tranche and the share of the fair value of the assets and liabilities acquired in each tranche, i.e. $65 (as calculated under method A in Example 11.7 above).

By requiring a catch-up adjustment for the post-acquisition changes in the fair values of the assets and liabilities relating to the original tranche, this method rectifies the mixed-measurement drawback of method 2, but still suffers from the same practical difficulties.

(d) Method 4

Although the IFRIC statement requires a cost-based approach in applying the equity method under IAS 28, the methodology in IFRS 3 (2007) for such transactions whereby a catch-up adjustment for the post-acquisition changes in the retained profits and other comprehensive income relating to the original tranche is made is consistent with such an approach, but reflecting a catch-up adjustment for the changes in the fair values of the assets and liabilities is not. Accordingly, the initial carrying amount of the associate is $355 (being the cumulative cost of $325 plus the share of post-acquisition retained profits of $30 relating to the original 10% interest). The change in the fair value of $50 relating to the initial 10% investment is reversed through retained earnings or the revaluation reserves as appropriate. The investor's share of the equity method retained profits of $30 earned on this investment is recognised. The overall effect of these adjustments, which reduce the carrying amount of the existing investment from $150 to $130, will be reflected in other comprehensive income in the statement of comprehensive income.

Goodwill is calculated as the difference between the cost of each tranche and the share of the fair value of the assets and liabilities acquired in each tranche, i.e. $65 (as calculated under method A in Example 11.7 above).

The drawbacks of this method are the same as for method 2.

3.3   Share accounted for

3.3.1   *Contingent voting rights*

As noted at 2.2.1 D above, an entity is required to consider currently exercisable potential voting rights in determining whether it has significant influence over an investee such that the investee is an associate. However, when applying the equity method, the investor determines its share of the profit or loss of the investee, and of changes in the investee's equity, by reference to its current ownership interest and does not reflect the possible exercise or conversion of potential voting rights.[103]

However, the implementation guidance on potential voting rights in IAS 27, which applies also to IAS 28, recognises that in some rare cases potential voting rights actually give rise to present access to the economic benefits inherent in those rights. An example might be a presently exercisable option over shares in the investee at a fixed price combined with the right to veto any distribution by the investee before the option is exercised. In these rare cases, it might be appropriate to equity account for the share that would be held if the option were exercised. This is discussed further in Chapter 6 at 2.1.2.

3.3.2   *Where the reporting entity or the associate is a group*

As noted at 2.2.1 above, a group's share in an associate is the aggregate of the holdings in that associate by the parent and its subsidiaries. The holdings of the group's other associates or joint ventures are ignored for this purpose. When an associate itself has subsidiaries, associates, or joint ventures, the profits or losses and net assets taken into account in applying the equity method are those recognised in the associate's financial statements (including the associate's share of the profits or losses and net assets of its associates and joint ventures), but after any adjustments necessary to give effect to uniform accounting policies (see 3.6 below).[104]

Example 11.10:   Share in an associate

Parent A holds a 95% investment in subsidiary B, which in turn holds a 25% investment in associate Z. In addition, parent A also holds a 30% investment in associate C and a 50% investment in joint venture D, each of which hold a 10% investment in associate Z.

In its consolidated financial statements parent A accounts for a 25% investment in associate Z under the equity method because:

- the investments in associate Z held by associate C and joint venture D should not be taken into account; and

- parent A fully consolidates the assets of subsidiary B, which include a 25% investment in associate Z.

3.3.3   *Cumulative preference shares held by parties other than the investor*

If an associate has outstanding cumulative preference shares that are held by parties other than the investor and that are classified as equity, the investor computes its share of profits or losses after adjusting for the dividends on such shares, whether or not the dividends have been declared.[105]

Example 11.11:   Cumulative preference shares issued by an associate

An entity holds an investment of 30% in the common shares of an associate that has net assets of £200,000 and net profit for the year of £24,500. The associate has issued 5,000 9% cumulative preference shares with a nominal value of £10. The cumulative preference shares are classified by the associate as equity in accordance with the requirements of IAS 32 – *Financial Instruments: Presentation*. The associate has not declared dividends on the cumulative preference shares in the past two years.

The investor calculates its share of the associate's net assets and net profit as follows:

	£
Net assets	200,000
9% Cumulative preference shares	(50,000)
Undeclared dividend on cumulative preference shares	
2 years × 9% × £50,000 =	(9,000)
Net assets value attributable to common shareholders	141,000
Investor's 30% share of the net assets	42,300
Net profit for the year	24,500
Share of profit of holders of cumulative preference shares	
9% of £50,000 =	(4,500)
Net profit attributable to common shareholders	20,000
Investor's 30% share of the net profit	6,000

If the investor also owned all of the cumulative preference shares then its share in the net assets of the associate would be £42,300 + £50,000 + £9,000 = £101,300. Its share in the net profit would be £6,000 + £4,500 = £10,500.

3.3.4   Several classes of equity

When an associate has a complicated equity structure with several classes of equity shares that have varying entitlements to net profits and equity, the investor needs to assess carefully the rights attaching to each class of equity share in determining the appropriate percentage of ownership interest.

Example 11.12:   Preference shares with a liquidation preference

Entity A has issued 10,000 preference shares with a nominal value of €0.10. The preference shareholders are entitled to a cumulative dividend equal to 25% of the net profits, 35% of the equity upon liquidation and have a liquidation preference in respect of the nominal value of the shares. Entity A has also issued ordinary shares that are entitled to the remainder of the net profits and equity upon liquidation.

An investor that holds 40% of the ordinary shares of Entity A will need to assess carefully what its appropriate share in the profits and equity of Entity A is. The investor would take the liquidation preference into account in calculating its interest in the associate to the extent that there is economic substance to that right.

3.4   Transactions between the reporting entity and associates

3.4.1   *Elimination of 'upstream' and 'downstream' transactions*

IAS 28 requires profits and losses resulting from what it refers to as 'upstream' and 'downstream' transactions between an investor (including its consolidated subsidiaries) and an associate to be recognised in the investor's financial statements only to the extent of unrelated investors' interests in the associate. 'Upstream' transactions are, for example, sales of assets from an associate to the investor. 'Downstream' transactions are, for example, sales of assets from the investor to an associate. The investor's share in the associate's profits and losses resulting from these transactions is eliminated.[106]

IAS 28 is not entirely clear as to how this very generally expressed requirement translates into accounting entries, but we suggest that an appropriate approach might be to proceed as follows:

- In the income statement, the adjustment should be taken against either the investor's profit or the share of the associate's profit, according to whether the investor or the associate recorded the profit on the transaction, respectively; and

- In the balance sheet, the adjustment should be made against the asset which was the subject of the transaction if it is held by the investor or against the carrying amount for the associate if the asset is held by the associate.

This is consistent with the approach required by SIC-13 – *Jointly Controlled Entities – Non-monetary Contributions by Venturers* in dealing with the related area of the contribution of assets by venturers to joint ventures (see Chapter 12 at 3.4.3).

Extract 11.3: Nokia Corporation (2007)

Notes to the Consolidated Financial Statements [extract]

1. Accounting principles [extract]

Principles of consolidation [extract]

Profits realized in connection with the sale of fixed assets between the Group and associated companies are eliminated in proportion to share ownership. Such profits are deducted from the Group's equity and fixed assets and released in the Group accounts over the same period as depreciation is charged.

Examples 11.13 and 11.14 below illustrate our suggested approach to this requirement of IAS 28. Both examples deal with the reporting entity H and its 40% associate A. The journal entries are based on the premise that H's financial statements are initially prepared as a simple aggregation of H and the relevant share of its associates. The entries below would then be applied to the numbers at that stage of the process.

Example 11.13:   Elimination of profit on sale by investor to associate

On 1 December 2009 H sells inventory costing £750,000 to A for £1 million. On 10 January 2010, A sells the inventory to a third party for £1.2 million. What adjustments are made in the group financial statements of H at 31 December 2009 and 31 December 2010?

In the year ended 31 December 2009, H has recorded revenue of £1 million and cost of sales of £750,000. However since, at the balance sheet date, the inventory is still held by A, only 60% of this transaction is regarded by IAS 28 as having taken place (in effect with the other shareholders of A). This is reflected by the consolidation entry:

	£	£
Revenue	400,000	
Cost of sales		300,000
Investment in A		100,000

This effectively defers recognition of 40% of the sale and offsets the deferred profit against the carrying amount of H's investment in A.

During 2010, when the inventory is sold on by A, this deferred profit can be released to group profit or loss, reflected by the following accounting entry.

	£	£
Opening reserves	100,000	
Cost of sales	300,000	
Revenue		400,000

Opening reserves are adjusted because the financial statement working papers (if prepared as assumed above) will already include this profit in opening reserves, since it forms part of H's opening reserves.

An alternative approach would be to eliminate the profit on 40% of the sale against the cost of sales, as follows:

	£	£
Cost of sales	100,000	
Investment in A		100,000

An argument in favour of this approach is that the revenue figures should not be adjusted because the sales to associates need to be disclosed as related party transactions. However, in our view, this is more than outweighed by the drawback of the approach, namely that it causes volatility in H's reported gross margin as revenue and the related net margin are not necessarily recognised in the same accounting period.

Example 11.14: *Elimination of profit on sale by associate to reporting entity*

This is the mirror image of the transaction in Example 11.13 above. On 1 December 2009 A sells inventory costing £750,000 to H for £1,000,000. On 10 January 2010, H sells the inventory to a third party for £1.2 million. What adjustments are made in the group financial statements of H at 31 December 2009 and 31 December 2010?

H's share of the profit of A as included on the financial statement working papers at 31 December 2009 will include a profit of £250,000 (£1,000,000 – £750,000), 40% of which (£100,000) is regarded under IAS 28 as unrealised by H, and is therefore deferred and offset against closing inventory:

	£	£
Share of A's result (income statement)	100,000	
Inventory		100,000

In the following period when the inventory is sold H's separate financial statements will record a profit of £200,000, which must be increased on consolidation by the £100,000 deferred from the previous period. The entry is:

	£	£
Opening reserves	100,000	
Share of A's result (income statement)		100,000

Again, opening reserves are adjusted because the financial statement working papers (if prepared as assumed above) will already include this profit in opening reserves, this time, however, as part of H's share of the opening reserves of A.

A slightly counter-intuitive consequence of this treatment is that at the end of 2009 the investment in A in H's consolidated balance sheet will have increased by £100,000 more than the share of profit of associates as reported in group profit or loss (and in 2010 by £100,000 less). This is because the balance sheet adjustment at the end of 2009 is made against inventory rather than the carrying value of the investment in A, which could be seen as reflecting the fact that A has, indeed, made a profit. It might therefore be necessary to indicate in the notes to the financial statements that part of the profit made by A is regarded as unrealised by the group in 2009 and has therefore been deferred until 2010 by offsetting it against inventory.

It may be that a transaction between an associate and its investor indicates an impairment of the asset that is the subject of the transaction. IAS 28 does not specifically address this issue. However, IAS 31 indicates that where a transaction between a venturer and a joint venture indicates an impairment of the asset that is the subject of the transaction, the venturer should recognise the full impairment loss and not merely its share.[107] In our view, this treatment should also be adopted when a transaction between and an investor its associate indicates an impairment of the investor's asset. Further discussion, and examples, of this treatment may be found in Chapter 12 at 3.4.2.

A   Elimination of 'downstream' unrealised gains in excess of the investment

Occasionally an investor's share of the unrealised profit on the sale of an asset to an associate exceeds the carrying value of the investment held, as illustrated in the following example.

Example 11.15:   Elimination of unrealised gains in excess of the investment

An investor has a 40% investment in an associate, which it carries in its balance sheet at €800,000. The investor sells a property to the associate in exchange for cash, which results in a profit of €3 million. After the sale, 40% of that profit (i.e. €1.2 million) is unrealised from the investor's perspective.

There are two approaches for determining to what extent a profit in excess of the carrying value of the investment should be eliminated.

Preferred approach

Our preferred approach is to apply the requirements in paragraph 22 of IAS 28 literally, which is also consistent with the general requirement to apply IAS 27 consolidation elimination principles.[108] Furthermore, the requirement in IAS 28 to discontinue application of the equity method when an investor's share of losses equals or exceeds it interest in the associate (see 3.7 below), should not apply as the elimination does not represent a real 'loss' to the investor but is simply the non-recognition of a gain as a result of normal consolidation principles. In other words, paragraph 29 of IAS 28 should not override the requirement to eliminate unrealised profits. Therefore, under the preferred approach the investor would eliminate the unrealised gain by reducing the investment in the associate to zero, with the excess deferred through the creation of a 'deferred income' or similar balance, as follows:

	€	€
Gain on sale of property	1,200,000	
Investment in associate		800,000
'Deferred income'		400,000

Acceptable alternative

There has been ongoing debate about whether the equity method of accounting is a consolidation method or a measurement method. Although IAS 28 generally adopts consolidation principles it nevertheless retains features of a valuation methodology – such as the one line nature of the profit or loss and balance sheet entries and the requirement to discontinue the equity method where losses would otherwise reduce the investment below zero (see 3.7 below). Therefore, it is considered an acceptable alternative to apply the principles of paragraph 29 of IAS 28 and not recognise elimination entries to the extent that the elimination exceeds the carrying amount of the investment in the associate, provided that the investor does not have any further legal or constructive obligations in relation to the asset or the associate. Under the alternative approach the investor would eliminate the unrealised gain as follows:

	€	€
Gain on sale of property	800,000	
Investment in associate		800,000

Future profits of the associate are not recognised until they exceed the unrecognised unrealised profits of €400,000.

Conclusion

An investor should apply its accounting policy choice consistently to all associates and should consistently treat the equity method as either a consolidation method or a measurement method. Furthermore, if an investor has any continuing involvement with a transferred asset caution needs to be exercised as this may indicate that no revenue or gain should be recognised in the first place.

B   Transactions between associates and/or joint ventures

When transactions take place between associates and/or joint ventures, which are accounted for under the equity method, the investor should apply the requirements of IAS 27 and IAS 28 by analogy and eliminate its share of the profits.[109] In practice it may be difficult though to determine whether such transactions have taken place.

3.4.2   Reciprocal interests

Reciprocal interests (or 'cross-holdings') arise when an associate itself holds an investment in the reporting entity. The reciprocal interests can give rise to a measure of double counting of profits and net assets between the investor and its associate. Paragraph 20 of IAS 28 states that many of the procedures appropriate for the application of the equity method are similar to the consolidation procedures described in IAS 27. Therefore, the requirement in paragraph 20 of IAS 27 to eliminate intragroup balances, transactions, income and expenses should be applied by analogy.

What is unfortunately not clear from either IAS 27 or IAS 28 is exactly how an entity should go about eliminating the double counting that arises from reciprocal holdings. In theory there are a number of methods that may seem attractive in dealing with reciprocal interests:

(1)   *Full gross up without elimination* – In this case the profit and net assets of both the investor and its associate are determined using a simultaneous equations method;

(2)   *Economic interest of 'outside' shareholders* – This method would take the outcome from the above method as its starting point and eliminate profits attributable to reciprocally held shares; and

(3)   *Direct holding only* – Under this method the profit of the investor is calculated by adding to its trading profits only its direct investment in the associate.

On balance we consider the 'direct holding only' method should be used for the reasons explained in the example below.

Example 11.16:   Elimination of reciprocal interests in profit or loss[110]

To effect a strategic alliance and profit sharing arrangement entity A has taken a 40% equity interest in entity B and conversely, entity B has taken a 30% interest in entity A. How should entity A and entity B account for their reciprocal investment?

The structure of the reciprocal holdings is shown in the diagram below:

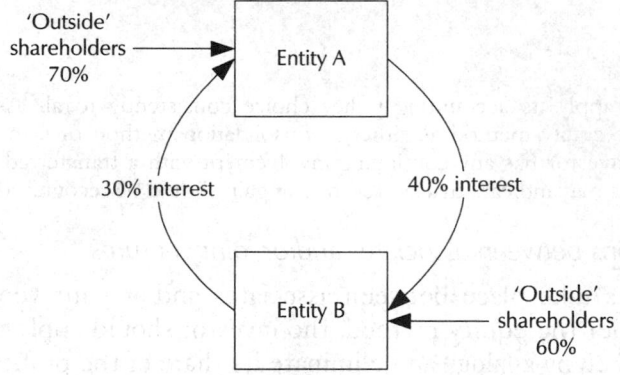

Entity A	
Share in equity of B	40%
Shares in A held by 'outside' shareholders	70%
Trading profit of A (before share in profit of B)	€60,000
Net assets of A (before share in net assets of B)	€600,000
Number of shares in issue	100,000

Entity B	
Share in equity of A	30%
Shares in B held by 'outside' shareholders	60%
Trading profit of B (before share in profit of A)	€110,000
Net assets of B (before share in net assets of A)	€1,100,000
Number of shares in issue	40,000

Method 1 – Full gross up without elimination

Income

The profit for the period is calculated by solving the simultaneous equations below:

Profit entity A = €60,000 + 40% × profit entity B

Profit entity B = €110,000 + 30% × profit entity A

by substitution:

Profit entity A = €60,000 + 40% × (€110,000 + 30% × profit entity A)

Profit entity B = €110,000 + 30% × (€60,000 + 40% × profit entity B)

this can be simplified to:

Profit entity A = (€60,000 + (40% × €110,000)) ÷ (1 – 40% × 30%) = €118,182

Profit entity B = (€110,000 + (30% × €60,000)) ÷ (1 – 40% × 30%) = €145,455

Balance sheet

A similar approach can be applied to calculate the net assets of A and B:

Net assets of entity A = €600,000 + 40% × net assets entity B

Net assets of entity B = €1,100,000 + 30% × net assets entity A

by substitution:

Net assets of entity A = €600,000 + 40% × (€1,100,000 + 30% × net assets entity A)

Net assets of entity B = €1,100,000 + 60% × (€600,000 + 40% × net assets entity B)

this can be simplified to:

Net assets of entity A = (€600,000 + (40% × €1,100,000)) ÷ (1 – 40% × 30%) = €1,181,818

Net assets of entity B = (€1,100,000 + (60% × €600,000)) ÷ (1 – 40% × 30%) = €1,454,545

Earnings per share

The earnings per share for the shareholders of A and B should be calculated as follows:

Earnings per share A = €118,182 ÷ 100,000 = €1.18

Earnings per share B = €145,455 ÷ 40,000 = €3.64

Under this method, it is not necessary to adjust the number of shares in issue as the net profit number relates to all shares in issue, rather than just those shares that are not held reciprocally.

It can be shown that, if both A and B were to distribute their entire profits – which would require a number of iterations because of their reciprocal interests – each share in A would, in fact, attract €1.18 in dividends, while each share in B would attract €3.64 in dividends.

Conclusion

It is questionable whether the 'full gross up without elimination' method complies with the spirit of the IAS 27 consolidation rules – or the IAS 32 rules on treasury shares – which would require elimination of an entity's holdings of its own shares.

It is worthwhile noting that the combined underlying trading profit of A and B is only €170,000 (i.e. €60,000 + €110,000), whereas their combined reported profit is €263,637 (i.e. €118,182 + €145,455). Similarly, the combined underlying net assets of A and B are only €1,700,000, whereas the combined reported net assets are €2,636,363.

Method 2 – Economic interest of 'outside' shareholders

Income

The profit for the period is calculated by taking the profit calculated under Method 1 above and eliminating the profits attributable to reciprocally held shares:

Profit entity A = (100% – 30%) × €118,182 = €82,727

Profit entity B = (100% – 40%) × €145,455 = €87,273

Balance sheet

A similar approach can be applied to calculate the net assets of A and B:

Net assets of A attributable to 'outside' shareholders = €827,272

Net assets of B attributable to 'outside' shareholders = €872,727

Earnings per share

The profit figure calculated above only related to the 'outside' shareholders in A and B and should therefore by divided by the number of 'outside' shares, as follows:

Earnings per share A = €82,727 ÷ 70,000 = €1.18

Earnings per share B = €87,273 ÷ 24,000 = €3.64

Conclusion

An advantage of this method is that the combined reported profit of A and B is €170,000 (= €82,727 + €87,273), which is equal to the combined underlying trading profit of A and B. In addition, the outcome of this method is very similar to that which would have arisen if A and B had entered into a regular profit sharing contract.

This method does, however, produce outcomes that, at first sight, seem somewhat counterintuitive, but do in fact reflect the economic reality that, in this example, the cross-holding is to A's advantage. For example, entity B's profit or loss would look as follows:

	€
Trading profit of B	110,000
Share in profit of associate A after elimination of reciprocal interests	(22,727)
Net profit for the period	87,273

The net profit for the period of €87,273 is actually less than its trading profit of €110,000, because the impact of the reciprocal interests is clearly not neutral. In this particular example the reciprocal relationship is disadvantageous for 'outside' shareholders of B which has a 30% interest in A which is not very profitable, while the 'outside' shareholders of A benefit from A's 40% interest in B which is very profitable. In other words, the profit sharing arrangement is unfavourable from B's point of view.

This method eliminates all shares that are not held by 'outside' shareholders, as it treats the combined reciprocal interests as if they were a single profit sharing arrangement. To achieve this, the method offsets (1) A's right to dividends from B against (2) A's obligation to pay dividends to B. This seems to go beyond the elimination requirements in IAS 27 in that it eliminates the interests that B shareholders have in A.

Method 3 – Direct holding only

Income

The profit for the period is calculated by adding the direct interest in the associate's profit:

Profit entity A = €60,000 + 40% × trading profit entity B = €60,000 + 40% × €110,000 = €104,000

Profit entity B = €110,000 + 30% × trading profit entity A = €110,000 + 30% × €60,000 = €128,000

Balance sheet

A similar approach can be applied to calculate the net assets of A and B:

    Net assets of A including share in B without eliminations = €1,040,000

    Net assets of B including share in A without eliminations = €1,280,000

Earnings per share

Under this method the profits related to the reciprocal interests have been ignored. Therefore, in calculating the earnings per share it is necessary to adjust the number of shares to eliminate the reciprocal holdings: For entity A it can be argued that it indirectly owns 40% of B's 30% interest, i.e. entity A indirectly owns 12% (= 40% × 30%) of its own shares. Those shares should therefore be treated as being equivalent to 'treasury shares' and be ignored for the purposes of the EPS calculation.

    Number of A shares after elimination of 'treasury shares' = 100,000 × (100% − 12%) = 88,000 shares

While entity B indirectly owns 30% of A's 40% interest, i.e. entity B indirectly owns 12% (= 30% × 40%) of its own shares.

    Number of B shares after elimination of 'treasury shares' = 40,000 × (100% − 12%) = 35,200 shares

The earnings per share for the shareholders of A and B should be calculated as follows:

    Earnings per share A = €104,000 ÷ 88,000 = €1.18

    Earnings per share B = €128,000 ÷ 35,200 = €3.64

As before, the earnings per share would be equivalent to the hypothetical dividend per share in the case of full distribution of all profits as discussed in Method 1 above.

Conclusion

Rather than treating the reciprocal holdings as a single profit sharing arrangement, this method only eliminates the effects of an entity's indirect investment in its own shares. The financial statements therefore reflect both the interests of the 'outside' shareholders and the interests that B shareholders have in A. On balance we believe that this method should be used.

It is worthwhile noting that the combined underlying trading profit of A and B is only €170,000 (i.e. €60,000 + €110,000), whereas their combined reported profit is €232,000 (i.e. €104,000 + €128,000). Similarly, the combined underlying net assets of A and B are only €1,700,000, whereas the combined reported net assets are €2,320,000.

From the above it seems that the elimination of reciprocal interests is somewhat more complicated than it might have appeared to the IFRIC in August 2002. The IFRIC agreed not to require publication of an Interpretation on this issue, but did state that 'like the consolidation procedures applied when a subsidiary is consolidated, the equity method requires reciprocal interests to be eliminated.'[111]

3.4.3 Loans and borrowings between the reporting entity and associates

IAS 28's requirement to eliminate partially unrealised profits or losses on transactions with associates is expressed in terms of transactions involving the transfer of assets. In our view, the requirement for partial elimination of profits does not apply to items such as interest paid on loans and borrowings between associates and the reporting entity, since such loans and borrowings do not involve the transfer of assets giving rise to gains or losses. Moreover, they are not normally regarded as part of the investor's share of the net assets of the associate, but as separate transactions, except in the case of loss-making associates, where interests in long-term loans and borrowings may be required to be accounted for as if they were part of the reporting entity's equity investment in determining the carrying value of the associate against which losses may be offset (see 3.7 below). Likewise, loans and borrowings between the reporting entity and associates should not be eliminated in the reporting entity's consolidated accounts because associates are not part of the group.

Finally, if the associate had a policy of capitalising borrowing costs then the investor would need to eliminate a relevant share of the profit, in the same way it would eliminate a share of the capitalised management or advisory fees charged to an associate.

3.4.4   Statement of cash flows

In the statement of cash flows (whether in the consolidated or separate financial statements) no adjustment is made in respect of the cash flows relating to transactions with associates, whereas in any consolidated statement of cash flows the cash flows between members of the group are eliminated in the same way as intragroup transactions are eliminated in the profit and loss account and balance sheet.

3.4.5   Contributions of non-monetary assets to an associate

It is fairly common for an entity to create or change its interest in an associate by contributing some of the entity's existing non-monetary assets to that associate. This raises a number of issues as to how such transactions should be accounted for, in particular whether they should be accounted for at book value or fair value. There is no explicit guidance on this issue in IFRS as regards the formation of associates. However, the SIC considered the issue in connection with the contribution of assets to joint ventures, and contributions of non-monetary assets are also addressed by IAS 16 – *Property, Plant and Equipment* – and IAS 38 – *Intangible Assets* (see Chapter 12 at 3.4.3). In our view, it would be appropriate to consider this guidance when accounting for contributions of assets to associates.

3.5   Non-coterminous accounting periods

In applying the equity method, the investor should use the most recent financial statements of the associate. Where the reporting dates of the investor and the associate are different, IAS 28 requires the associate to prepare, for the use of the investor, financial statements as of the same date as those of the investor unless it is impracticable to do so.[112]

When the financial statements of an associate used in applying the equity method are prepared as of a different reporting date from that of the investor, adjustments must be made for the effects of significant transactions or events, for example a sale of a significant asset or a major loss on a contract, that occurred between that date and the date of the investor's financial statements. In no case can the difference between the reporting date of the associate and that of the investor be more than three months.[113] There are no exemptions from this requirement despite the fact that it may be quite onerous in practice, for example, because:

- the associate might need to produce interim financial statements so that the investor can comply with this requirement; or

- the associate may be a listed company in its own right whose financial information is considered price-sensitive, which means that the associate may not be able to provide detailed financial information to one investor without providing equivalent information to all other investors at the same time.

The length of the reporting periods and any difference in the reporting dates must be the same from period to period.[114] This implies that where an associate previously equity accounted for on the basis of non-coterminous financial statements is equity accounted for using coterminous financial statements, it is necessary to restate comparative information so that financial information in respect of the associate is included in the investor's financial statements for an equivalent period in each period presented.

IAS 28 requires merely that a non-coterminous accounting period of an associate used for equity accounting purposes ends within three months of that of the investor. It is not necessary for such a non-coterminous period to end before that of the investor.

3.6   Consistent accounting policies

IAS 28 requires the investor's financial statements to be prepared using uniform accounting policies for like transactions and events in similar circumstances.[115] If an associate uses accounting policies different from those of the investor for like transactions and events in similar circumstances, adjustments must be made to conform the associate's accounting policies to those of the investor when the associate's financial statements are used by the investor in applying the equity method.[116]

In practice, this may be easier said than done, since an investor's influence over an associate, although significant, may still not be sufficient to secure access to the relevant underlying information in sufficient detail to make such adjustments with certainty. Restating the financial statements of an associate to IFRS may require, extensive detailed information that may simply not be required under the associate's local GAAP (for example, in respect of business combinations, share-based payments, financial instruments and revenue recognition).

3.7   Loss-making associates

An investor in an associate should recognise its share of the losses of an associate until its share of losses equals or exceeds its interest in the associate, at which point the investor discontinues recognising its share of further losses. For this purpose, the investor's interest in an associate is the carrying amount of the investment in the associate under the equity method together with any long-term interests that, in substance, form part of the investor's net investment in the associate. For example, an item for which settlement is neither planned nor likely to occur in the foreseeable future is, in substance, an extension of the entity's investment in that associate. The IASB argued that this requirement ensures that investors are not able to avoid recognising the loss of an associate by restructuring their investment to provide the majority of funding through non-equity investments.[117]

Such items include:

- preference shares; or
- long-term receivables or loans (unless supported by adequate collateral),

but do not include:

- trade receivables;
- trade payables; or
- any long-term receivables for which adequate collateral exists, such as secured loans.

Once the investor's share of losses recognised under the equity method has reduced the investor's investment in ordinary shares to zero, its share of any further losses is applied so as to reduce the other components of the investor's interest in an associate in the reverse order of their seniority (i.e. priority in liquidation).[118]

Once the investor's interest is reduced to zero, additional losses are provided for, and a liability is recognised, only to the extent that the investor has incurred legal or constructive obligations or made payments on behalf of the associate. The investor would account for such losses as a liability under IAS 37 – *Provisions, Contingent Liabilities and Contingent Assets*. If the associate subsequently reports profits, the investor resumes recognising its share of those profits only after its share of the profits equals the share of losses not recognised.[119] Whilst IAS 28 does not say so explicitly, it is presumably envisaged that, when profits begin to be recognised again, they are applied to write back the various components of the investor's interest in the associate (see previous paragraph) in the reverse order to that in which they were written down (i.e. in order of their priority in a liquidation).

This method of accounting, sometimes referred to as 'waterline accounting', is broadly equivalent to the requirements of IAS 27, before this practice was changed through the amendments made to IAS 27 in 2008, for the attribution of losses of partially-owned subsidiaries to the minority shareholders. An example of 'waterline accounting' may be found at Example 7.18 in Chapter 7 at 4.4.1. An investor in an associate would account for its share of the associate's losses in the same way that the losses of entity S in that example are allocated to the minority shareholder M.

In addition to the recognition of losses arising from application of the equity method, an investor in an associate must consider the additional requirements of IAS 28 in respect of impairment losses (see 4 below).

Example 11.17:   Accounting for a loss-making associate

At the beginning of the year entity H invests €5 million to acquire a 30% equity interest in an associate, entity A. In addition, H lends €9 million to the associate, but does not provide any guarantees or commit itself to provide further funding. How should H account for the €20 million loss that the associate made during the year?

H's share in A's loss is €20 million × 30% = €6 million. If H's loan to A is considered part of the net investment in the associate then the carrying amount of the associate is reduced by €6 million, from €14 million (= €5 million + €9 million) to €8 million. That is, the equity interest is reduced to nil and the loan is reduced to €8 million. However, if the loan is not part of the net investment in the associate then H accounts for the loss as follows:

— the equity interest in the associate is reduced from €5 million to zero;

— a loss of €1 million remains unrecognised because H did not provide any guarantees and has no commitments to provide further funding. If in the second year, however, A were to make a profit of €10 million then H would only recognise a profit of €2 million (= €10 million × 30% − €1 million). However, if in the second year H were to provide a €1.5 million guarantee to A and A's net profit were nil, then H would need to recognise an immediate loss of €1 million (i.e. the lower of the unrecognised loss of €1 million and the guarantee of €1.5 million) because it now has a legal obligation pay A's debts; and

— as there are a number of indicators of impairment, the loan from H to A should be tested for impairment in accordance with IAS 39.

3.8 Date of commencement and cessation of equity accounting

Under the general requirements for equity accounting discussed at 2.3 above, an investor will begin equity accounting for an associate from the date on which it has significant influence over it (and is not otherwise exempt from equity accounting for it).[120]

Where an investor has not been equity accounting for an associate on the basis that it is classified as held for sale under IFRS 5 (see 2.3.1 above), and the investment ceases to be so classified, the investor must apply equity accounting retrospectively as from the date on which the investment was originally classified as held for sale. The financial statements of any prior periods since that classification must be restated.[121]

An investor ceases to account for an investment using the equity method on the date that it ceases to have significant influence over it. If the investment becomes a subsidiary or joint venture, it will be accounted for in accordance with, respectively, IAS 27 (see Chapter 6) or IAS 31 (see Chapter 12). Otherwise it will be accounted for in accordance with IAS 39.[122]

3.8.1 Accounting for the cessation – prior to application of IAS 27 (as amended in 2008) and IFRS 3 (as revised in 2008)

IFRS 3 (as revised in 2008) is effective for business combinations for which the acquisition date is on or after the beginning of the first annual reporting period beginning on or after 1 July 2009 with early adoption possible as explained in Chapter 9 at 3.1.1. IAS 27 (as amended in 2008) has the same effective date.[123] For periods prior to adoption of these revised standards IAS 28 simply states that 'The carrying amount of the investment at the date that it ceases to be an associate shall be regarded as its cost on initial measurement as a financial asset in accordance with IAS 39'.[124]

The measurement rules in IAS 39 are complex and discussed in detail in Chapter 32. In brief, however, they will entail the former associate being recorded initially at fair value,[125] but its cost is deemed to be its carrying amount on the date that it ceases to be an associate.[126] Therefore, if the investment is subsequently accounted for as an 'available-for-sale' financial asset the difference between its cost and fair value should be accounted for within other comprehensive income. If the investment is subsequently accounted for as a 'financial asset at fair value through profit or loss' then the difference is recognised in net profit for the period. In either case, the investment will subsequently be measured at fair value – what differs is whether the gains and losses arising on revaluation are accounted for in profit or loss or in other comprehensive income.

A   Cumulative exchange differences

IAS 27 (2007) (see Chapter 7 at 3.3.4) specifically reinforces the requirement of IAS 21 – *The Effects of Foreign Exchange Rates* (see Chapter 13 at 2.7.3) that, when an investment in a foreign operation is disposed of, the gain or loss on disposal should include the 'recycling' of the cumulative exchange gains and losses that have, in accordance with IAS 21, been recognised in other comprehensive income in respect of that operation. Whilst there is no such explicit reinforcement of IAS 21 in the version of IAS 28 that is effective prior to adoption of IAS 27 (as amended in 2008) and IFRS 3 (as revised in 2008), it seems clear that the same principle should apply on disposal of an associate.

IAS 21 clarifies that disposal of a foreign operation may occur through sale, liquidation, repayment of share capital or abandonment. When a partial disposal occurs only the proportionate share of the related accumulated exchange difference is included in profit or loss. IAS 21 further clarifies that a write-down of a foreign operation does not constitute a partial disposal, and accordingly no part of the deferred foreign exchange gain or loss is recognised in profit or loss at the time of such a write-down,[127] unless the write-down is consequent upon an event of 'disposal' as just described. The amendments to IFRS 1 and IAS 27 published in May 2008 amended IAS 21 to clarify that a dividend made by a foreign operation and accounted for as revenue by its parent, investor or venturer in its separate financial statements (see Chapter 8 at 2.3.1) should not be treated as a disposal or partial disposal of a net investment.[128] This contrasts to the previous position where IAS 21 explained that the payment of a dividend was part of a disposal only when it constituted a return of the investment, e.g. when the dividend was paid out of pre-acquisition profits.[129]

This begs the further question of the appropriate treatment of any cumulative exchange gains and losses on a former associate which becomes subject to IAS 39 as described above. The issues here are very similar to those arising in respect of a former subsidiary which becomes subject to IAS 39, which are discussed in Chapter 7 at 3.3.1.

B   Other cumulative gains and losses previously recognised in other comprehensive income

Like IAS 27 (2007), the version of IAS 28 that is effective prior to adoption of IAS 27 (as amended in 2008) and IFRS 3 (as revised in 2008) does not specifically address the accounting treatment, on disposal of an associate, of the investor's share of other cumulative gains and losses previously accounted for in other comprehensive income relating to assets and liabilities of the disposed associate. Such cumulative gains and losses, which would be recycled in profit or loss if those assets and liabilities had been disposed of separately by the associate, could include:

- accumulated hedging gains and losses accounted for under IAS 39 (see Chapter 33); and

- any other amounts previously recognised in other comprehensive income that would have been recognised in profit or loss if the associate had directly disposed of the assets to which they relate, such as gains or losses on available-for-sale financial assets accounted for under IAS 39 (see Chapter 32 at 3.4).

IAS 39 does not specifically address this issue either. However, it would appear that recycling is appropriate, since the disposal of an associate does give rise to the derecognition of the investor's share of the separate assets and liabilities of that associate just as if they had been disposed of separately.

3.8.2 Accounting for the cessation – upon application of IAS 27 (as amended in 2008) and IFRS 3 (as revised in 2008)

IFRS 3 (as revised in 2008) is effective for business combinations for which the acquisition date is on or after the beginning of the first annual reporting period beginning on or after 1 July 2009 with early adoption possible as explained in Chapter 9 at 3.1.1. IAS 27 (as amended in 2008) has the same effective date.[130]

Phase II of the IASB's Business Combinations project, and the resulting revisions made to IAS 27 and IFRS 3, led to a number of changes in accounting for a loss of significant influence. Paragraph 18 of IAS 28 was amended to read as follows:

> 'An investor shall discontinue the use of the equity method from the date when it ceases to have significant influence over an associate and shall account for the investment in accordance with IAS 39 from that date, provided the associate does not become a subsidiary or a jointly controlled entity as defined in IAS 31. On loss of significant influence, the investor shall measure at fair value any investment the investor retains in the former associate. The investor shall recognise in profit or loss any difference between:
>
> (a) the fair value of any retained investment and any proceeds from disposing of the part interest in the associate; and
>
> (b) the carrying amount of the investment at the date when significant influence is lost.'

Therefore upon loss of significant influence there is a remeasurement to fair value of any remaining interest that is taken to profit or loss regardless of the prospective accounting for this interest under IAS 39.

Furthermore, IAS 28 has been amended to require that if an investor loses significant influence over an associate, all amounts recognised in other comprehensive income in relation to that associate should be recognised by the investor on the same basis that would be required if the associate had directly disposed of the related assets or liabilities.[131] Similarly, IAS 21 has been amended to require that upon loss of significant influence the cumulative amount of the exchange differences deferred in the separate component of equity relating to that associate be recognised in profit or loss.[132] In practice this means that a gain or loss should be recognised in profit or loss upon loss of significant influence, even if a former associate is subsequently accounted for as an available-for-sale financial asset.

It should be noted that if significant influence is lost but an interest is retained this reclassification adjustment from equity to profit or loss is for the full amount that is in other comprehensive income and not just a proportionate amount based upon the interest disposed of. The Basis of Conclusions to the amended version of IAS 21 explains that the loss of significant influence is a significant economic event that warrants accounting for the transaction as a disposal under IAS 21,[133] and hence the transfer of the full exchange difference rather than just the proportionate share that would be required if this was accounted for as a partial disposal under IAS 21.

However, when an investor's interest in an associate is reduced (but the investee remains an associate), then the investor should 'reclassify to profit or loss only a proportionate amount of the gain or loss previously recognised in other comprehensive income'[134] and 'reclassify to profit or loss only the proportionate share of the cumulative amount of the exchange differences recognised in other comprehensive income'.[135] That means that the investor should recognise in profit or loss a proportion of:

- foreign exchange differences recognised in other comprehensive income under IAS 21,

- accumulated hedging gains and losses recognised in other comprehensive income under IAS 39 (see Chapter 33), and

- any other amounts previously recognised in other comprehensive income that would have been recognised in profit or loss if the associate had directly disposed of the assets to which they relate, such as gains or losses on available-for-sale financial assets accounted for under IAS 39 (see Chapter 32 at 3.4),

in each case proportionate to the interest disposed of.

3.8.3   Deemed disposals – prior to application of IAS 27 (as amended in 2008) and IFRS 3 (as revised in 2008)

An investor's interest in an associate may be reduced other than by an actual disposal. Such a reduction in interest, which is commonly referred to as a 'deemed disposal', gives rise to a 'dilution' gain or loss. Deemed disposals may arise for a number of reasons, including:

- the investor does not take up its full allocation in a rights issue by the associate;

- the associate declares scrip dividends which are not taken up by the investor so that its proportional interest is diminished;

- another party exercises its options or warrants issued by the associate; or

- the associate issues shares to third parties.

An illustration of such a transaction is given in Example 11.18 below.

Example 11.18: Deemed disposal of an associate

On 1 January 2008 investor A acquired a 30% interest in entity B at a cost of £500,000. Investor A has significant influence over entity B and accounts for its investment in the associate under the equity method. The associate has net assets of £1,000,000 at the date of acquisition, which have a fair value of £1,200,000. During the year ended 31 December 2008 entity B recognised a post-tax profit of £200,000, and paid a dividend of £18,000. Entity B also recognised foreign exchange losses of £40,000 in other comprehensive income.

Entity B's net assets at 31 December 2008 can be determined as follows:

	£
Net assets 1 January 2008	1,000,000
Profit for year	200,000
Dividends paid	(18,000)
Foreign exchange losses	(40,000)
B's net assets at 31 December 2008	1,142,000

Investor A's interest in entity B at 31 December 2008 is calculated as follows:

	£
On acquisition (including goodwill of £500,000 – (30% × £1,200,000) = £140,000):	500,000
Share of after tax profit (30% × £200,000)	60,000
Elimination of dividend (30% of £18,000)	(5,400)
A's share of exchange differences (30% × £40,000)	(12,000)
A's interest in B at 31 December 2008 under the equity method	542,600

which can also be determined as follows:

	£
A's share of B's net assets (30% × £1,142,000)	342,600
Goodwill	140,000
A's share of fair value uplift (30% × £200,000) †	60,000
A's interest in B at 31 December 2008	542,600

† This assumes that none of the uplift related to depreciable assets, such that the £200,000 did not diminish after the acquisition.

On 1 January 2009, entity B has a rights issue that investor A does not participate in. The rights issue brings in an additional £150,000 in cash, and dilutes investor A's interest in entity B to 25%.

Consequently, entity B's net assets at 1 January 2009 are:

	£
Entity B's net assets at 31 December 2008	1,142,000
Additional cash	150,000
Entity B's net assets at 1 January 2009	1,292,000

Considering the facts above, how should investor A account for the dilution of its investment in entity B?

Method A

IAS 28 defines the equity method as 'a method of accounting whereby the investment is initially recognised at cost and adjusted thereafter for the post acquisition change in the investor's share of net assets of the investee. The profit or loss of the investor includes the investor's share of the profit or loss of the investee'.[136] A literal reading of this definition suggests that in calculating the loss on dilution, investor A should only take account of the change in its share of entity B's net assets but not account for a change in the notional goodwill component:

	£	£
Carrying amount of the investment before the deemed disposal		542,600
Cost of deemed disposal ([£542,600 − £140,000 †] × (30% − 25%) / 30%)	(67,100)	
Share of the contribution (£150,000 × 25%)	37,500	
Reduction in carrying amount of associate	(29,600)	(29,600)
Recycling of share in currency translation:		
(£40,000 × 30% × (25% − 30%) / 30%)	(2,000)	
Loss on deemed disposal	(31,600)	
Carrying amount of the investment after the deemed disposal		513,000

Whilst goodwill (†) is included in the carrying amount of the investment, it is not separately recognised nor tested separately for impairment. However, it could be argued that the dilution of the shareholding and the recognition of an initial loss of £31,600 provide objective evidence of impairment, requiring the carrying amount of £513,000 to be tested for impairment under IAS 36.

Method B

Others consider that deemed disposals should be accounted for in the same way as 'true' disposals. That is, the entire carrying amount of the equity investment – including goodwill – should be taken into account. Thus the loss on the deemed disposal is calculated as follows:

	£	£
Carrying amount of the investment before the deemed disposal		542,600
Cost of deemed disposal (£542,600 × (30% − 25%) / 30%)	(90,433)	
Share of the contribution (£150,000 × 25%)	37,500	
Reduction in carrying amount of associate	(52,933)	(52,933)
Recycling of share in currency translation:		
(£40,000 × 30% × (25% − 30%) / 30%)	(2,000)	
Loss on deemed disposal	(54,933)	
Carrying amount of the investment after the deemed disposal		489,667

Paragraph 33 of IAS 28 specifically states that goodwill included in the carrying amount of an investment in an associate is not separately recognised. Hence, there is a strong argument that it should not be excluded from the cost of a deemed disposal either.

Although the IASB did not explicitly consider accounting for deemed disposals of associates in drafting IAS 28, paragraph 20 of the standard refers to the concepts underlying the procedures used in accounting for the acquisition of a subsidiary in accounting for acquisitions of interests in associates. Therefore, rather than relying on a literal reading of the definition of the equity method, it is more appropriate to account for deemed disposals of associates in the same way as deemed disposals of subsidiaries.

Finally, in the absence of a Standard or an Interpretation that specifically applies to a transaction, other event or condition, IAS 8 requires management to consider pronouncements of other standard-setting bodies that use a similar conceptual framework to develop accounting standards. Several standard-setters (e.g. in the United Kingdom and United States) specifically require the goodwill component of an investment in an associate to be included in the calculation of any gain or loss of a deemed disposal.

Conclusion

In summary, on the strength of the above arguments, we believe that the method B is generally more appropriate than method A. However, it should be noted that when the SIC discussed accounting for dilution gains and losses on deemed disposals of subsidiaries, joint ventures and associates in 1997, it was unable to reach a consensus on both:

– how dilution gains and losses should be calculated; and
– whether dilution gains and losses should be recognised directly in profit or loss or in other comprehensive income.

3.8.4 Deemed disposals – upon application of IAS 27 (as amended in 2008) and IFRS 3 (as revised in 2008)

IAS 27 has been amended as part of phase II of the Business Combinations project so as to require that partial disposals of subsidiaries, where control is retained, are accounted for as equity transactions (see Chapter 7 at 3.2.2). We do not believe that this impacts on the accounting described in Example 11.18 above. Under equity accounting an investor only accounts for its own interest. Given that the other investors' ownership in the associate is not reflected in the accounts of an investor there is no basis for concluding that deemed disposals can only be treated as equity transactions. Therefore, the conclusion above remains valid.

As discussed at 3.8.2 above, the resulting revisions made to IAS 27 and IFRS 3 led to a number changes in the requirements of IAS 28 in relation to the accounting for the loss of significant influence and when an investor's interest in an associate is reduced (but the investee remains an associate)

One potential effect of these revised IFRSs on the equity method of accounting that has recently been considered by the IFRIC is how an equity method investee's issue of shares should be accounted for.

At its meeting in May 2009, and subsequently confirmed at its meeting in July 2009, the IFRIC noted that paragraph 19A of IAS 28 provides guidance on the accounting for amounts recognised in other comprehensive income when the investor's ownership interest is reduced, but the entity retains significant influence. The IFRIC noted that there is no specific guidance on the recognition of a gain or loss resulting from a reduction in the investor's ownership interest resulting from the issue of shares by the associate. However, the IFRIC also noted that reclassification of amounts to profit or loss from other comprehensive income is generally required as part of determining the gain or loss on a disposal. Paragraph 19A of IAS 28 applies to all reductions in the investor's ownership interest, no matter the cause.

The IFRIC concluded that the agenda criteria were not met mainly because, given the guidance in IFRSs, it did not expect divergent interpretations in practice. Therefore, the IFRIC decided not to add these issues to its agenda.[137]

Accordingly, it is clear that the IFRIC expects that gains or losses on deemed disposals are recognised in profit or loss, and these will include amounts reclassified from other comprehensive income.

3.9   Income taxes

Income taxes arising from investments in associates are accounted for in accordance with IAS 12 – *Income Taxes*. This will often lead to full provision for deferred tax on temporary differences relating to associates (see Chapter 26 at 4.2.6).

3.10   Distributions received in excess of the carrying amount

When an associate makes dividend distributions to the investor in excess of the investor's carrying amount it is not immediately clear how the excess should be accounted for. A liability under IAS 37 (see 3.7 above) should only be recognised if the investor is obliged to refund the dividend, has incurred a legal or constructive obligation or made payments on behalf of the associate. In the absence of such obligations, it would seem that the investor could recognise the excess in net profit for the period. When the associate subsequently makes profits, the investor should only start recognising profits when they exceed the excess cash distributions recognised in net profit plus any previously unrecognised losses (see 3.7 above).

4   IMPAIRMENT LOSSES

4.1   General

Determining whether an investment in an associate is impaired may be more complicated than is apparent at first sight, as it involves carrying out several separate impairment assessments:

- *Assets of the associate*

  It is generally not appropriate for the investor to simply multiply the amount of the impairment recognised in the investee's own books by the investor's percentage of ownership, because the investor should measure its interest in an associate's identifiable net assets at fair value at the date of acquisition of an associate (see 3.2 above). Therefore, if the value that the investor attributes to the associate's net assets differs from the carrying amount of those net assets in the associate's own books, the investor should restate any impairment losses recognised by the associate and also needs to consider whether it needs to recognise any impairments that the associate itself did not recognise in its own books.

  Any goodwill recognised by an associate needs to be separated into two elements. Goodwill that existed at the date the investor acquired its interest in the associate is not an identifiable asset of the associate from the perspective of the investor. That goodwill should be combined with the investor's goodwill on the acquisition of its interest in the associate. However, goodwill that arises on subsequent acquisitions by the associate should be accounted for as such in the books of the associate and is tested for impairment in accordance with IAS 36 – *Impairment of Assets* – by the associate. The investor should not make any adjustments to the associate's accounting for that goodwill.

- *Investment in the associate*

  As well as applying the equity method as summarised at 3 above, including the recognition of losses (see 3.7 above), IAS 28 requires an investor to apply the requirements of IAS 39 (which are discussed below and in Chapter 32 at 6) in order to determine whether it is necessary to recognise any additional impairment loss with respect to the investor's net investment in the associate.[138] Whilst IAS 39 is used to determine whether it is necessary to recognise any further impairment, the amount of any impairment is calculated in accordance with IAS 36 (see Chapter 18 and below);[139]

- *Loans that are not part of the net investment in the associate*

  The investor must also apply IAS 39 in order to determine whether it is necessary to recognise any additional impairment loss with respect to that part of the investor's interest in the associate that does not comprise its net investment in the associate. This would include, for example, trade receivables and payables, and collateralised long-term receivables (see 3.7 above). In this case, however, the impairment is calculated in accordance with IAS 39, and not IAS 36.[140]

This has the effect that it is extremely unlikely any impairment charge recognised in respect of an associate will simply be the investor's share of any impairment charge recognised by the associate itself, even when the associate complies with IFRS. This is illustrated in Example 11.20 at 4.3 below.

The requirement of IAS 28 to apply both IAS 36 and IAS 39 perhaps indicates ambivalence on the part of the IASB about whether associates are similar to subsidiaries (in which case information about goodwill and the cash generating units to which it is attributed ought to be available) or are, in fact, a type of financial asset.

IAS 28 requires the recoverable amount of an investment in an associate to be assessed individually, unless the associate does not generate cash inflows from continuing use that are largely independent of those from other assets of the entity.[141]

4.2 Goodwill

The requirements of IFRS 3 with respect to the fair value exercise mean that any goodwill that an associate may have recognised in its own financial statements at the date of its acquisition is not considered an identifiable asset from the investor's point of view. Rather, the investor recognises goodwill on its investment in the associate in accordance with IAS 28. Goodwill arising on the acquisition of an associate is not separately recognised, but is included in the carrying value of that associate (see 3.2 above).[142] Accordingly such goodwill, unlike that separately recognised, is not separately tested for impairment on an annual basis under IAS 36 – rather the entire carrying value of the investment in the associate is tested for impairment as a single asset.[143] Generally, impairment losses of goodwill recognised in the financial statements of an associate should be reversed when the investor applies the equity method. However, impairment losses that relate to goodwill on the associate's own business combinations, after the investor acquired its interest in that associate, should be taken into account in determining the investor's share of the associate's profits or losses (see 4.1 above).

Whenever application of the requirements in IAS 39 indicates that the investment may be impaired (see below), the entire carrying amount of the investment is tested under IAS 36 for impairment (for a description of impairment reviews under IAS 36 see Chapter 18), by comparing its recoverable amount (the higher of value in use and fair value less costs to sell) with its carrying amount. In determining the value in use of the investment, an entity estimates:[144]

- its share of the present value of the estimated future cash flows expected to be generated by the associate, including the cash flows from the operations of the associate and the proceeds on the ultimate disposal of the investment; or

- the present value of the estimated future cash flows expected to arise from dividends to be received from the investment and from its ultimate disposal.

IAS 28 notes that, under 'appropriate assumptions', both methods give the same result. In effect, IAS 28 requires the investor to regard its investment in an associate as a single cash-generating unit, rather than 'drilling down' into the separate cash-generating units determined by the associate itself for the purposes of its own financial statements. The IASB does not explain why it adopted this approach, although we imagine that it may have been for the very practical reason that an investor's influence over an associate, although significant, may still not be sufficient to secure access to the relevant underlying information. Furthermore, the standard requires the investment as a whole to be reviewed for impairment as if it were a financial asset.

IAS 39 states that financial assets are not impaired unless there is 'objective evidence' that one or more events occurring after the initial recognition of the asset ('loss events') have had an impact on the estimated future cash flows of the financial asset or group of financial assets that can be reliably estimated.

Such 'objective evidence' that a financial asset or group of assets is impaired includes observable data that comes to the attention of the holder of the asset about the following loss events:

(a)   significant financial difficulty of the issuer or obligor;

(b)   a breach of contract, such as a default or delinquency in interest or principal payments;

(c)   the lender, for economic or legal reasons relating to the borrower's financial difficulty, granting to the borrower a concession that the lender would not otherwise consider;

(d)   it becoming probable that the borrower will enter bankruptcy or other financial reorganisation;

(e)   the disappearance of an active market for that financial asset because of financial difficulties; or

(f)   observable data indicating that there is a measurable decrease in the estimated future cash flows from a group of financial assets since the initial recognition of those assets, although the decrease cannot yet be identified with the individual financial assets in the group, including:

(i)   adverse changes in the payment status of borrowers in the group (e.g. an increased number of delayed payments or an increased number of credit card borrowers who have reached their credit limit and are paying the minimum monthly amount); or

(ii)   national or local economic conditions that correlate with defaults on the assets in the group (e.g. an increase in the unemployment rate in the geographical area of the borrowers, a decrease in property prices for mortgages in the relevant area, a decrease in oil prices for loan assets to oil producers, or adverse changes in industry conditions that affect the borrowers in the group).[145]

Many of these considerations can only be applied with difficulty to an investment in an associate.

We consider that the only practical way in which entities can assess whether interests in associates need to be tested for impairment is by focusing on the cash flow assumptions, in the two bullets above, on which the value in use is to be based. IAS 28 appears to allow entities to estimate the present value of all cash flows that it expects to receive from the associate, no matter when it expects to get them. Only in that case could any entity expect the present value of its share of the cash flows generated by the associate to be equal to the dividends it expects to receive (in both cases aggregated with the proceeds of ultimate disposal). Such an approach is consistent with impairment reviews of financial assets under IAS 39.

In contrast to the requirement in IAS 36 for continuous annual testing of goodwill relating to subsidiaries, an entity will have to test its associate for impairment only if an event has occurred that indicates that it will not recover its carrying value. The most common of these events, trading losses, will (subject to the requirement to adopt 'waterline accounting' – see 3.7 above) have automatically been taken into account in determining the carrying value of the investment, leaving only the remaining net carrying amount (i.e. after deducting the share of trading losses) to be assessed for impairment.

4.3   Allocation and reversal of impairment

Whether or not impairment is allocated to the underlying assets or goodwill of the associate and whether such impairment can be reversed has been open to discussion.

Example 11.19:   Impairment and reversal of impairment

On 1 January 2008 an investor acquired a 25% interest in an associate for €1,000. The investor has identified goodwill of €125, which is included in the carrying amount of the associate.

During 2008 the associate makes a profit of €400, the investor's share in this profit is €100. In 2009 the associate reports a loss of €400, which reduces the carrying amount of the associate to €1,000 in the books of the investor. Based on its estimates of future cash flows to be received from the associate, the investor records an impairment of €200 and reduces the carrying amount of the associate to €800.

In 2010 the investor recalculates the value in use of the associate and determines that the recoverable amount has increased and is now in excess of €1,000. How should the investor account for the reversal of the impairment:

(a) reverse the entire €200 impairment;

(b) reverse €75, which is the amount by which the impairment exceeded the goodwill; or

(c) not reverse the impairment as this issue is not addressed by IAS 28?

Under IAS 28 an investor applies the requirements in IAS 39 to determine whether it is necessary to recognise impairment losses on its investment in associates.[146] However, other guidance on accounting for impairment of financial assets in IAS 39 does not apply to associates accounted for under the equity method.

In the above example the entity should reverse the entire €200 impairment. The goodwill included in the carrying amount of an investment in an associate is not separately tested for impairment under IAS 36 because it is not a separately recognised asset in the balance sheet.[147] Therefore if an investor concludes that the associate is impaired, the impairment should not be allocated to the underlying assets or goodwill of the associate. Consequently, the IAS 36 prohibition on the reversal of impairment losses on goodwill[148] would not apply. The previously recognised impairment of an investment in an associate is therefore fully reversible under IFRS.

This view is consistent with the conclusion of the IASB after they discussed this issue in May 2007. They noted that IAS 28 was 'unclear whether an impairment recognised against an investment in an associate should be allocated against the goodwill included in the investment, and thus whether the impairment can be reversed subsequently. The Board also noted that applying the equity method includes reflecting the impact of acquisition date fair values on the investor's share of impairment losses recognised by the associate against assets such as goodwill or property, plant and equipment.'[149] The Board decided that any further impairment recognised by an investor after applying the equity method should not be allocated against goodwill included in the carrying amount of the associate. In addition, such an impairment charge 'should therefore be reversed in a subsequent period to the extent that the recoverable amount of the associate increases'.[150] The Board amended the standard accordingly as part of the Annual Improvements project and this amendment is mandatory for annual periods beginning on or after 1 January 2009.[151]

As indicated at 4.1 above, the requirements of IAS 28 in respect of impairments has the effect that it is extremely unlikely any impairment charge recognised in respect of an associate will simply be the investor's share of any impairment charge recognised by the associate itself, even when the associate complies with IFRS.

Example 11.20: Impairment losses recognised by an associate

Entity A has a 40% interest in Entity B. Entity A has significant influence over Entity B and accounts for its investment under the equity method.

At 31 December 2010, Entity B, which prepares its financial statements under IFRS, has carried out impairment tests under IAS 36 and recognised an impairment loss of $140,000 calculated as follows:

	Carrying amount $'000	Recoverable amount $'000	Impairment loss $'000
CGU A	210	300	n/a
CGU B	250	450	n/a
CGU C	540	400	140
Total	1,000	1,150	140

In accounting for its associate, Entity B, in its consolidated financial statements for the year ended 31 December 2010, should Entity A reflect its 40% share of this impairment loss of $140,000?

As indicated earlier at 4.1 above, it is generally not appropriate for the investor to simply multiply the amount of the impairment recognised in the investee's own books by the investor's percentage of ownership, because the investor should initially measure its interest in an associate's identifiable net assets at fair value at the date of acquisition of an associate. Accordingly, appropriate adjustments based on those fair values are made for impairment losses recognised by the associate (see 3.2 above).

Prior to the recognition of the impairment loss by Entity B, the carrying amount of Entity A's 40% interest in the net assets of Entity B, after reflecting fair value adjustments made by Entity A at the date of acquisition, together with the goodwill arising on the acquisition is as follows:

	Carrying amount reflecting fair values made by Entity A $'000
CGU A	140
CGU B	100
CGU C	320
Net assets	560
Goodwill	40
Investment in associate	600

In applying the equity method, Entity A should compare its 40% share of the cash flows attributable to each of Entity B's CGUs to determine the impairment loss it should recognise in respect of Entity B. Accordingly, in equity accounting for its share of Entity B's profit or loss, Entity A should recognise an impairment loss of $180,000 calculated as follows:

	Carrying amount reflecting fair values made by Entity A $'000	Recoverable amount (40%) $'000	Impairment loss $'000
CGU A	140	120	20
CGU B	100	180	n/a
CGU C	320	160	160
Net assets	560	460	180

In addition, after applying the equity method, Entity A should calculate whether any further impairment loss is necessary in respect of its investment in its associate.

The carrying amount of Entity A's investment in Entity B under the equity method (after reflecting the impairment loss of $180,000 would be as follows:

	$'000
CGU A	120
CGU B	100
CGU C	160
Net assets	380
Goodwill	40
Investment in associate	420

Based on Entity A's 40% interest in the total recoverable amount of Entity B of $460,000, Entity A would not recognise any further impairment loss in respect of its investment in the associate.

It should be noted that the impairment loss recognised by Entity A of $180,000 is not the same as if it had calculated an impairment loss on its associate as a whole; i.e. by comparing its 40% share of the total recoverable amount of Entity B of $460,000 to its investment in the associate of $600,000 (prior to reflecting any impairment loss on its share of Entity B's net assets). Such an approach would only be appropriate if Entity B did not have more than one CGU. However, if in this example, the goodwill on the acquisition had been at least $80,000, the overall impairment loss recognised would have been the same, irrespective of whether the impairment loss had been calculated on an overall basis or as in the example.

5   PRESENTATION AND DISCLOSURE

5.1   Presentation

5.1.1   *Balance sheet*

In the balance sheet, the aggregate of investments in associates and joint ventures accounted for using the equity method are presented as a discrete line item[152] and classified as non-current assets.[153]

IAS 28 does not explicitly define what is meant by 'investment in an associate'. However, paragraph 29 states that 'the interest in an associate is the carrying amount of the investment in the associate under the equity method together with any long-term interests that, in substance, form part of the investor's net investment in the associate. ... Such items may include preference shares and long-term receivables or loans but do not include trade receivables, trade payables or any long-term receivables for which adequate collateral exists, such as secured loans.'[154] Some have interpreted this as a requirement to present the investment in ordinary shares and other long-term interests in associates within the same line item.

Yet, when associates are profitable, long-term interests such as loans are normally accounted for under IAS 39 rather than under the equity method. Therefore, it is generally considered acceptable to present the investment in ordinary shares and other long-term interests in associates in separate line items.

Goodwill relating to an associate is included in the carrying amount of the investment, as is illustrated by Anglo American below.[155]

Extract 11.4: Anglo American plc (2007)

Notes to financial statements [extract]

1. Accounting policies [extract]

Business combinations and goodwill arising thereon [extract]

Goodwill in respect of subsidiaries and joint ventures is included within intangible assets. Goodwill relating to associates is included within the carrying value of the associate.

5.1.2   Profit or loss

In the statement of comprehensive income or separate income statement, the aggregate of the investor's share of the profit or loss of associates and joint ventures accounted for using the equity method must be shown.[156] 'Profit or loss' in this context is interpreted in the implementation guidance to IAS 1 as meaning the 'profit attributable to owners of the associates', i.e. it is after tax.[157]

There is no requirement as to where in the statement of comprehensive income or separate income statement the investor's share of the profit or loss of associates and joint ventures accounted for using the equity method should be shown, and different approaches are therefore seen in practice. Nokia includes its share of the (post-tax) results of associates after operating profit, but before pre-tax profit:

Extract 11.5: Nokia Corporation (2007)

Consolidated profit and loss accounts, IFRS [extract]

		Financial year ended December 31		
		2007	2006	2005
Financial year ended Dec. 31	Notes	EURm	EURm	EURm
Net sales		51,058	41,121	34,191
Cost of sales		(33,754)	(27,742)	(22,209)
Gross profit		17,304	13,379	11,982
Research and development expenses		(5,647)	(3,897)	(3,825)
Selling and marketing expenses		(4,380)	(3,314)	(2,961)
Administrative and general expenses		(1,180)	(666)	(609)
Other income	6	2,312	522	285
Other expenses	6,7	(424)	(536)	(233)
Operating profit	2-9	7,985	5,488	4,639
Share of results of associated companies	14,31	44	28	10
Financial income and expenses	10	239	207	322
Profit before tax		8,268	5,723	4,971

By contrast, Nestlé includes its share of the post-tax results of associates below tax expense:

Extract 11.6: Nestlé S.A. (2007)

Consolidated income statement
For the year ended 31st December 2007 [extract]

In millions of CHF	Notes	2007	2006
Profit before taxes and associates		13,518	12,105
Taxes	5	(3,416)	(3,293)
Share of results of associates		1,280	963
Profit from continuing operations		11,382	9,775

A   Impairment of associates

It is unclear where impairments of associates should be presented in the statement of comprehensive income or separate income statement. IAS 28 requires an impairment test to be performed 'after application of the equity method',[158] which could be read as implying that impairment of an associate is not part of the investor's share of the profit or loss of an associate accounted for using the equity method. On the other hand, the guidance on accounting for impairment losses on associates is presented under the heading 'application of the equity method' in IAS 28, which suggests that accounting for impairments of associates is part of the equity method. In practice, both interpretations appear to have gained a degree of acceptance.

RWE reports impairment losses on associates within income from investments accounted for using the equity method.

Extract 11.7: RWE Aktiengesellschaft (2007)

Notes [extract]

Consolidation principles [extract]

These consolidation principles also apply to investments accounted for using the equity method. In relation to these investments, goodwill is not reported separately: it is included in the recognized value of the investment. Such goodwill is not amortized either. If necessary, impairment losses on the equity value are reported under income from investments accounted for using the equity method. The financial statements of investments accounted for using the equity method are also prepared using uniform accounting policies.

5.1.3   Other items of comprehensive income

The investor's share of items recognised in other comprehensive income by the associate is recognised by the investor in other comprehensive income.[159] In the statement of comprehensive income, the aggregate of the investor's share of the other comprehensive income of associates and joint ventures accounted for using the equity method must be shown as a separate line item.[160]

5.2 Disclosures

5.2.1 Requirements of IAS 28

As stated above, in the balance sheet the aggregate of investments in associates and joint ventures accounted for using the equity method are presented as a discrete line item[161] and classified as non-current assets.[162]

IAS 28 requires the following disclosures:

(a) the investor's share of the profits or losses of associates accounted for using the equity method;[163]

(b) the carrying amount of investments in associates accounted for using the equity method;[164]

(c) the investor's share of any discontinued operations of associates accounted for using the equity method;[165]

(d) the fair value of investments in associates for which there are published price quotations;[166]

(e) summarised financial information of associates, including the aggregated amounts of assets, liabilities, revenues and profit or loss (see A below);[167]

(f) if applicable, the reasons why the presumption that an investor does not have significant influence is overcome if the investor holds, directly or indirectly through subsidiaries, less than 20% of the voting or potential voting power of the investee but concludes that it has significant influence;[168]

(g) the reasons why the presumption that an investor has significant influence is overcome if the investor holds, directly or indirectly through subsidiaries, 20% or more of the voting or potential voting power of the investee but concludes that it does not have significant influence;[169]

(h) the end of the reporting period of the financial statements of an associate, when such financial statements are used in applying the equity method and are as of a date or for a period that is different from that of the investor, and the reason for using a different date or different period;[170]

(i) the nature and extent of any significant restrictions (e.g. resulting from borrowing arrangements or regulatory requirements) on the ability of associates to transfer funds to the investor in the form of cash dividends, or repayment of loans or advances;[171]

(j) the unrecognised share of losses of an associate, both for the period and cumulatively, if an investor has discontinued recognition of its share of losses of an associate;[172]

(k) the fact that an associate is not accounted for using the equity method in accordance with paragraph 13 of IAS 28 (i.e. the exemptions summarised at 2.3 above);[173] and

(l) summarised financial information of associates, either individually or in groups, that are not accounted for using the equity method, including the amounts of total assets, total liabilities, revenues and profit or loss.[174]

The information required under (a), (b) and (c) should be presented in the notes in the event that associates and jointly controlled entities are presented together on the face of the primary financial statements.

The IASB, as part of its Annual Improvements project, amended IAS 28 to clarify what disclosure is required by the standard in respect of an associate accounted for at fair value in accordance with IAS 39, as permitted under the standard for venture capital organisations, mutual funds, unit trusts and similar entities.[175] The only disclosure above that is required relating to that investment is of the nature and extent of any significant restrictions on the ability of the associate to transfer funds to the investor in the form of cash dividends, or repayment of loans or advances (see (i) above). This amendment applies for annual periods beginning on or after 1 January 2009 with earlier application permitted as long as this is disclosed and the related amendments to IFRS 7 – *Financial Instruments: Disclosures*, and IAS 31 – *Interests in Joint Ventures* – are also applied.[176]

Prior to application of this amendment an entity accounting for an interest in an associate using IAS 39 should still disclose all of the information required by IAS 28. This is because IFRS 7 specifically calls for the IAS 28 disclosures to be made in addition to the disclosures required by the standards themselves,[177] despite the fact that, as indicated at 2.1 above, IAS 28 does not apply to the investment.

Some of the disclosures required by IAS 28 can be seen in the financial statements of Barclays:

Extract 11.8: Barclays Bank PLC (2007)

19.   Investment in associates and joint ventures [extract]
Share of net assets

	Associates		Joint ventures		Total	
	2007	2006	2007	2006	2007	2006
The Group	£m	£m	£m	£m	£m	£m
At beginning of year	74	427	154	119	228	546
Share of results before tax	35	63	10	(6)	45	57
Share of tax	(2)	(10)	(1)	(1)	(3)	(11)
Share of post-tax results	33	53	9	(7)	42	46
Dividends paid	–	(17)	–	–	–	(17)
New investments	7	2	8	7	15	9
Acquisitions	56	51	150	102	206	153
Disposals	(47)	(404)	(72)	(72)	(119)	(476)
Exchange and other adjustments	(33)	(38)	38	5	5	(33)
At end of year	90	74	287	154	377	228

	Associates		Joint ventures		Total	
	2007	2006	2007	2006	2007	2006
The Bank	£m	£m	£m	£m	£m	£m
At beginning of year	7	326	90	84	97	410
New investments	7	–	16	6	23	6
Disposals	(7)	(319)	(1)	–	(8)	(319)
At end of year	7	7	105	90	112	97

The fair value of the Group's investments in Ambit Properties Limited, an associate listed on the Johannesburg Stock Exchange, is £42m.

Disposal of associates and joint ventures

On 29th June 2007 and 2nd July 2007, the Group disposed of its investment in Gabetti Property Solutions for cash consideration, net of transaction costs of £13m, which after deducting the Group's share of its net assets on the dates of disposal, resulted in a profit of £8m.

On 24th September 2007, the Group disposed of its investment in Intelenet Global Services for a cash consideration, net of transaction costs of £22m, which after deducting the Group's share of its net assets on the date of disposal, resulted in a profit of £13m.

Included within Barclays share of associates' and joint ventures' assets is goodwill as follows:

Goodwill

	The Group		The Bank	
	2007 £m	2006 £m	2007 £m	2006 £m
Cost				
At beginning of year	41	205	25	189
Disposals	(17)	(121)	(1)	(121)
Transfer	3	(43)	3	(43)
At end of year	27	41	27	25

Summarised financial information of the Group's associates and joint ventures is set out below:

	2007		2006	
	Associates £m	Joint ventures £m	Associates £m	Joint ventures £m
Property, plant and equipment	588	632	599	142
Financial investments	239	8	4	2
Trading portfolio assets	–	–	1	–
Loans to banks and customers	516	2,372	1,378	797
Other assets	1,387	314	541	199
Total assets	2,730	3,326	2,523	1,140
Deposits from banks and customers	1,515	2,189	1,421	769
Trading portfolio liabilities	–	–	1	–
Other liabilities	902	458	887	187
Shareholders' equity	313	679	214	184
Total liabilities	2,730	3,326	2,523	1,140
Net income	528	340	538	178
Operating expenses	(404)	(292)	(334)	(178)
Profit before tax	124	48	204	–
Profit/(loss) after tax	104	40	186	(2)

The amounts included above, which include the entire assets, liabilities and net income of the investees, not just the Group's share, are based on accounts made up to 31st December 2007 with the exception of certain undertakings for which the amounts are based on accounts made up to dates not earlier than three months before the balance sheet date.

Associates and join ventures in 2007 includes £1,728m (2006: £1,525m) of assets, £1,537m (2006: £1,380m) of liabilities and £18m (2006: £25m) of profit after tax in associates and joint ventures within the Absa Group.

The Group's share of commitments and contingencies of its associates and joint ventures is £6m (2006:£nil).

It is worth noting that Barclays' disclosure of summarised financial information of associates and joint ventures in which the Group has an interest is prepared on the basis of the relevant entities' entire financial position and results of operations, and not on the basis of Barclays' share thereof. Once again, the standard is unclear as to whether this information is to be shown on the basis of the associates' entire financial position and results of operations (as Barclays have done), or on the basis of the investor's share thereof. In our view, both approaches are acceptable, and we believe that it is more important that companies disclose which approach they have followed.

A   Summarised financial information of associates

IAS 28 is not clear about the basis on which the information required under (e) above should be presented. That is, it is not clear whether the information should:

- conform with IFRS as applied by the investor or should be based on the associate's own financial statements that may not even be prepared under IFRS;

- include the effects of the fair value exercise carried out by the investor; and

- be based on the investor's share of the associate or 100% of the associate's figures.

Two approaches, which both require the information to be presented in accordance with IFRS, are considered acceptable provided that they are applied consistently and are appropriately disclosed in the financial statements. The first approach is based on the view that the information disclosed should reflect the information that the investor uses in applying the equity method (i.e. reflecting the investor's accounting policies and its fair value exercise). If the information were to be measured on any other basis, its usefulness would be diminished considerably. The second approach is based on the argument that the whole purpose of the disclosure is for the reporting entity to present users with unadjusted summarised financial information of its associates. Nevertheless, we believe that this information would be most helpful to the user if it were to be presented based on the first approach. In fact, some may argue that only the first approach complies with the spirit of the requirements in IFRS, because:

- IAS 28 requires an associate to use the same accounting policies as the investor (see 3.6 above);[178]

- IAS 1 requires that financial statements and the notes thereto should be prepared on the same basis (see Chapter 3 at 2); and

- any references to assets, liabilities, revenues and profit or loss in IAS 28 must logically be references to those terms as defined under IFRS.

However, it needs to be made clear that our comments regarding this lack of clarity in the standard apply only to the disclosures required about summarised financial information under paragraph 37(b) of IAS 28. The standard is clear that, in the case of both recognition and measurement, investments in associates must be accounted for on the basis of the investor's uniform accounting policies and must reflect appropriate fair value adjustments on acquisition (see 3.2 and 3.6 above).

5.2.2   IAS 37 – Provisions, Contingent Liabilities and Contingent Assets

IAS 28 requires that in accordance with IAS 37[179] an investor must disclose:

- its share of the contingent liabilities of an associate incurred jointly with other investors; and

- those contingent liabilities that arise because the investor is severally liable for all or part of the liabilities of the associate.[180]

6   TRANSITIONAL ISSUES

6.1   General

As noted at 1.2 above, the December 2003 revised version of IAS 28 had to be applied for accounting periods beginning on or after 1 January 2005. Entities were encouraged to adopt this revised version of IAS 28 for earlier periods, but were required to disclose that they had done so.[181] There were no transitional provisions. Accordingly, an existing IFRS user had to apply the revised version of IAS 28 with full retrospective effect.

6.2   Upon application of IAS 27 (as amended in 2008) and IFRS 3 (as revised in 2008)

As explained at 3.2 and 3.8.2 above there have been a number of consequential amendments made to the standard as a result of phase II of the Business Combinations project and the substantial revisions made to IFRS 3 and IAS 27. There are no transitional requirements in respect of these consequential amendments made to IAS 28. Normally the lack of transitional requirements would mean the amendments should be applied retrospectively as required by IAS 8, although this would, in certain circumstances, be inconsistent with the transitional requirements in IAS 27 (as amended in 2008) and IFRS 3 (as revised in 2008).

For example the impact on profit or loss upon loss of significant influence in an associate may be very different if accounting for the transaction under the consequential amendments that have been made to IAS 28 and that are discussed at 3.8.2 above. IAS 27 (as amended in 2008) states that its requirements in respect of loss of control of a subsidiary should be applied prospectively so that any profit or loss recognised in the prior year should not be recalculated.[182] IFRS 3 (as revised in 2008) is to be applied prospectively to business combinations for which the acquisition date is on or after the beginning of the first annual reporting period beginning on or after 1 July 2009.[183] Given these prohibitions on restatement within these two standards it would seem inappropriate to recalculate the profit or loss upon a loss of significant influence that had occurred in the prior year.

The issue was considered by the IASB at its meeting in May 2009 as part of its Annual Improvements project. Consequently, in the exposure draft of proposed *Improvements to IFRSs* issued in August 2009, the IASB is proposing to clarify that the consequential amendments made by IAS 27 (as amended in 2008) to IAS 28 relating to the loss or reduction of significant influence over an associate should be applied prospectively. It is proposed that an entity applies the amendment for annual periods beginning on or after 1 July 2010. Earlier application is to be permitted, but if an entity applies the amendment for an earlier period it is to disclose that fact.[184] However, the IASB considered that there is no need to clarify the consequential amendments made by IFRS 3 (as revised in 2008) because that revised IFRS clearly requires prospective application.[185]

7   CONCLUSION

IAS 28 is a standard that was issued in its original form over 20 years ago; it applies to all investments in associates – except for investments held by a venture capital organisation, mutual fund, unit trust or similar entity that are accounted for as financial assets under IAS 39 at fair value, with changes in fair value recognised in profit or loss.

However, despite its prolonged existence as a method of accounting, equity accounting is not necessarily accepted by all as the most appropriate approach to accounting for investments in entities that are currently defined as associates. For example, there is still no general agreement as to whether equity accounting itself is a form of one-line consolidation, or whether it is a form of valuation methodology. Of those that take the view that it is a form of valuation methodology, there are some that believe that all associates should be accounted for as financial assets at fair value under IAS 39. Indeed, IAS 28's option that allows venture capital organisations, mutual funds, unit trusts and similar entity to elect to account for their associates under IAS 39 implies that the IASB may not be averse to this approach.

As a result of the revised versions of IFRS 3 and IAS 27, this has raised a number of new issues in the context of applying the equity method, and the extent to which the methodology and procedures under these revised standards should now be applied is open to further consideration. The IASB has cast doubt as to whether the principles for business combinations and consolidations can be applied by analogy to accounting for investments in associates and joint ventures, and in May 2009, it has indicated that it will address the interaction between these revised standards, and IAS 28 and IAS 31, as part of its project on joint ventures (see Chapter 12 at 7).

At the time of writing, it is unclear exactly what changes may be introduced in the context of applying the equity method as a result of this project. Hopefully it will resolve many of the issues that arise in practice. However, it may even go further than that. In the joint venture project, the IASB has proposed eliminating the option in IAS 31 of proportionate consolidation of jointly controlled entities, which means that joint venture entities will in the future all have to be accounted for under the equity method (after contractual rights and obligations to individual assets and individual liabilities have been identified and recognised – see Chapter 12 at 7.1). It is possible that in addressing the issues relating to the application of the equity method, the IASB may turn its attention to considering whether all investments in associates – and not just those held by venture capital organisations etc. (see 2.1.1

above) – should be accounted for at fair value under IAS 39, thereby leaving equity accounting as a method that applies solely to certain joint venture arrangements.

References

1 IFRS 3, *Business Combinations*, IASB, para. 64; IAS 27, *Consolidated and Separate Financial Statements*, IASB, para. 45.

2 IAS 28, *Investments in Associates*, IASB, para. 20.

3 *Improvements to IFRSs*, April 2009, IASB, IAS 39, para. BC24D.

4 *IASB Update*, IASB, May 2009, p. 5.

5 IAS 28, para. 1.

6 IAS 31, *Interests in Joint Ventures*, IASB, para. 38.

7 IAS 28, para. BC12.

8 IAS 28, paras. BC5-BC6.

9 IAS 28, paras. BC8-BC9.

10 IAS 28, para. BC7.

11 IAS 39, *Financial Instruments: Recognition and Measurement*, IASB, paras. 9 and AG80-AG81.

12 IAS 28, para. 1.

13 *Improvements to IFRSs*, IASB, May 2008, IAS 28, para. 1.

14 *IFRIC Update*, IFRIC, March 2009, p. 2; *IFRIC Update*, IFRIC, May 2009, p. 4.

15 Staff Paper, IFRIC meeting, May 2009, Agenda reference 3, *Venture capital consolidations and partial use of fair value through profit or loss.*

16 *IFRIC Update*, IFRIC, May 2009, p. 4; *IFRIC Update*, IFRIC, July 2009, p. 4.

17 Exposure Draft (ED 2009/11), IASB, August 2009, pp. 50-52.

18 ED 2009/11, p.48.

19 ED 2009/11, pp. 50-51.

20 IAS 28, para. 2.

21 IAS 28, para. 2.

22 IAS 31, para. 3.

23 IAS 28, para. 2.

24 IAS 28, para. 2.

25 IAS 28, para. 6.

26 IAS 28, para. 21.

27 IAS 28, para. 7.

28 IAS 28, para. 10.

29 IAS 27, paras. IG1-IG4.

30 IAS 27, para. IG2.

31 IAS 28, para. 6.

32 IAS 27, para. 13.

33 IAS 28, para. 8.

34 IAS 28, para. 8.

35 IAS 28, para. 8.

36 IAS 28, para. 9.

37 IAS 27, paras. IG1-IG4.

38 IAS 28, para. IN10.

39 IAS 28, para. BC15.

40 IAS 28, para. 37(f).

41 IAS 28, para. 13.

42 IAS 28, para. 14.

43 IAS 27, para. 4.

44 IAS 28, para. 14.

45 IAS 28, para. IN9.

46 IFRS 5, *Non-current Assets Held for Sale and Discontinued Operations*, IASB, para. 15.

47 IAS 28, para. 15.

48 IAS 28, para. 2.

49 IAS 27, para. 38.

50 IAS 27, para. 38A.

51 IAS 27, para. 45B.

52 IAS 28, para. 35 and IAS 27, paras. 38-43.

53 IAS 28, para. 3.

54 IAS 28, para. 4.

55 IAS 28, para. 36.

56 IAS 28, para. 5.

57 IAS 36, *Impairment of Assets*, IASB, paras. 2, 4 and 5; IAS 39, paras. 2(a) and 2(d).

58 *IFRIC Update*, IFRIC, May 2009, p. 4 and 5; *IFRIC Update*, IFRIC, July 2009, p. 4.

59 ED 2009/11, pp. 43-49.

60 ED 2009/11, p. 48.

61 ED 2009/11, pp. 44, 46 and 47.

62 IAS 28, para. 2.

63 IAS 28, para. 11.

64 IAS 28, para. 17.

65 IAS 28, para. 20.

66 IAS 28 (2007), *Investments in Associates*, IASB, 2007 Bound Volume, para 23.

67 *Improvements to IFRSs*, April 2009, IASB, IAS 39, para. BC24D.

68 *IASB Update*, IASB, May 2009, p. 5.

69 IAS 28, para. 23 and IAS 28 (2007), para 23.

70 IAS 28, para. 23 and IAS 28 (2007), para 23.

71 IAS 28, para. 2.

72 IFRS 3 (2007), *Business Combinations*, IASB, 2007 Bound Volume, para. 24.

73 For example, see IAS 2, *Inventories*, paras. 10 and 11; IAS 16, *Property, Plant and Equipment*,

paras. 6, 15-17; and IAS 40, *Investment Property*, paras. 5 and 21.

74 IFRS 3, para. 64; IAS 27, para. 45.

75 IAS 28, para. 20.

76 IAS 28, para. 2.

77 *Improvements to IFRSs*, April 2009, IASB, IAS 39, para. BC24D.

78 *IFRIC Update*, IFRIC, July 2009, p. 3.

79 IAS 27, para. 37; IAS 31, para. 45.

80 IAS 27, paras. 37 and BC56.

81 *Improvements to IFRSs*, April 2009, IASB, IFRIC 9, paras. BC5C and BC5D.

82 ED 9, paras. 30 and BC19.

83 IAS 28 (2007), para. 23.

84 IFRS 3 (2007), para. 60.

85 IFRS 3 (2007), para. 58.

86 IFRS 3 (2007), para. 59.

87 IAS 28 (2007), para. 20.

88 IAS 28 (2007), para. 23.

89 IFRS 3 (2007), paras. 58-60.

90 IFRS 3 (2007), I.E. Example 6.

91 IFRS 3 (2007), I.E. Example 6.

92 IFRS 3 (2007), para. 58.

93 IAS 22, *Business Combinations*, IASC, para. 38.

94 IFRS 3 (2007), paras. BC157-BC158.

95 IAS 28 (2007), para. 23.

96 IAS 28, para. 20.

97 *IFRIC Update*, IFRIC, July 2009, p. 3.

98 IFRS 3, paras. 41 and 42.

99 IFRS 3, para. BC384.

100 IAS 28, para 1.

101 IFRS 3, para 42.

102 IFRS 3, para 42.

103 IAS 28, para. 12.

104 IAS 28, para. 21.

105 IAS 28, para. 28.

106 IAS 28, para. 22.

107 There is a similar provision in IAS 27 (see Chapter 7 at 2.4).

108 IAS 28, para. 20.

109 IAS 27, para. 20 and IAS 28, paras. 20 and 22.

110 Detailed worked examples on the elimination cross-holdings in subsidiaries and associates can be found in *Bogie on group accounts*, John C. Shaw (editor), Bristol, 1973.

111 *IFRIC Update*, IFRIC, August 2002, p. 3.

112 IAS 28, para. 24.

113 IAS 28, paras. 25 and BC16.

114 IAS 28, para. 25.

115 IAS 28, para. 26.

116 IAS 28, para. 27.

117 IAS 28, paras. BC18-BC19.

118 IAS 28, para. 29.

119 IAS 28, para. 30.

120 IAS 28, para. 23.

121 IAS 28, para. 15.

122 IAS 28, para. 18.

123 IFRS 3, para. 64; IAS 27, para. 45.

124 IAS 28 (2007), para 19.

125 IAS 39, para. 43.

126 IAS 28 (2007), para. 19.

127 IAS 21 (2007), *The Effects of Changes in Foreign Exchange Rates*, IASB, 2007 Bound Volume, para. 49.

128 IAS 21, *The Effects of Changes in Foreign Exchange Rates*, IASB, para. BC35.

129 IAS 21 (2008), *The Effects of Changes in Foreign Exchange Rates*, IASB, 2008 Bound Volume, para. 49.

130 IFRS 3, para. 64; IAS 27, para. 45.

131 IAS 28, para. 19A.

132 IAS 21, para. 48A.

133 IAS 21, paras. BC33-34.

134 IAS 28, para. 19A.

135 IAS 21, para. 48C.

136 IAS 28, para. 2.

137 *IFRIC Update*, IFRIC, May 2009, p. 4; *IFRIC Update*, IFRIC, July 2009, p. 4.

138 IAS 28, para. 31.

139 IAS 28, para. 33.

140 IAS 28, para. 32.

141 IAS 28, para. 34.

142 IAS 28, para. 23.

143 IAS 28, para. 33.

144 IAS 28, para. 33.

145 IAS 39, para. 59.

146 IAS 28, para. 31.

147 IAS 28, para. 33.

148 IAS 36, paras. 124-125.

149 *IASB Update*, IASB, May 2007, p. 4.

150 *IASB Update*, IASB, May 2007, p. 4.

151 IAS 28, para. 41C.

152 IAS 1, *Presentation of Financial Statements*, IASB, para. 54(e).

153 IAS 28, para. 38.

154 IAS 28, para. 29.

155 IAS 28, para. 23.

156 IAS 1, para. 82(c).

157 IAS 1, para. IG6 'XYZ Group – Statement of comprehensive income for the year ended 31 December 20X7 (illustrating the classification of expenses within profit by function)'.

158 IAS 28, para. 31.

159 IAS 28, para. 39.

160 IAS 1, para. 82(h).

161 IAS 1, para. 54(e).

162 IAS 28, para. 38.

163 IAS 28, para. 38.

164 IAS 28, para. 38.

165 IAS 28, para. 38.

166 IAS 28, para. 37(a).

167 IAS 28, para. 37(b).

168 IAS 28, para. 37(c).

169 IAS 28, para. 37(d).
170 IAS 28, para. 37(e).
171 IAS 28, para. 37(f).
172 IAS 28, para. 37(g).
173 IAS 28, para. 37(h).
174 IAS 28, para. 37(i).
175 IAS 28, para. 1.
176 IAS 28, paras. 1 and 41C.
177 IFRS 7, *Financial Instruments: Disclosures*, IASB, para. 3(a).
178 IAS 28, para. 27.
179 The disclosure of contingent liabilities and contingent assets is dealt with in paragraphs 86 to 92 of IAS 37, *Provisions, Contingent Liabilities and Contingent Assets*, IASB.
180 IAS 28, para. 40.
181 IAS 28, para. 41.
182 IAS 27, para. 45(c).
183 IFRS 3, para. 64.
184 ED 2009/11, pp. 43 and 45.
185 *IASB Update*, IASB, May 2009, p. 4.

Chapter 12   Joint ventures

1   INTRODUCTION

1.1   The nature of joint ventures

As noted in the introduction to Chapter 6, an entity may conduct its business not only directly but also through strategic investments in other entities. IFRS, and most national GAAPs, broadly distinguish three types of such strategic investment:

- entities controlled by the reporting entity (subsidiaries – see Chapter 6);

- entities jointly controlled by the reporting entity and one or more third parties (joint ventures, the subject of this Chapter); and

- entities that, while not controlled or jointly controlled by the reporting entity, are subject to significant influence by it (associates – see Chapter 11).

There is a key distinction, both for the purposes of IFRS and commercially, between, on the one hand, subsidiaries and associates and, on the other hand, joint ventures. An interest in a subsidiary or an associate normally entails the acquisition or formation of a separate legal or economic entity. By contrast, a joint venture is essentially created by a legal or contractual relationship between the parties to the venture. Whilst many joint ventures do result in the creation of a separate legal entity to house the activities that are the subject of the venture, this is not a critical feature, and indeed many joint ventures result from direct joint ownership and control of assets, as opposed to joint ownership and control of an entity that in turn owns the assets.

Accounting for interests in joint ventures under IFRS is dealt with in IAS 31 – *Interests in Joint Ventures*. This is somewhat more complex than its 'sister' standards IAS 27 – *Consolidated and Separate Financial Statements* – and IAS 28 – *Investments in Associates* (which are discussed in Chapters 6, 7, 8 and 11) in two respects.

Firstly, IAS 31 distinguishes between three types of joint venture (jointly controlled operations, jointly controlled assets, and jointly controlled entities) and prescribes different accounting treatments for each. Secondly, it allows two rather different accounting treatments (proportionate consolidation and equity accounting) for accounting for jointly controlled entities.

This choice of accounting treatment is somewhat unusual, given the IASB's efforts during its improvements project to eliminate alternative accounting treatments within IFRS, but must be seen against the following background. Joint ventures comprise a major part – sometimes all – of the activities of entities in some sectors (particularly extractive industries, property and construction). Over the years, these sectors have developed generally accepted 'industry GAAPs' that result in similar arrangements being accounted for differently in different sectors. The IASB has however proposed to remove the option of proportionate consolidation for jointly controlled entities and has issued an exposure draft, ED 9 – *Joint Arrangements*, that is intended to replace IAS 31 (see 7.1 below). Since the publication of the exposure draft, the IASB has also tentatively decided that 'joint operations' and 'joint assets' should be merged into a single type of joint arrangement called 'joint operation' (see 7.2 below).[1]

1.2   Development of IAS 31

Under IFRS accounting for joint ventures is dealt with principally by IAS 31. This was originally issued in December 1990 and has since been subject to a number of amendments, most notably in December 2003 as part of the IASB's improvements project, when the previous version of IAS 31 was withdrawn and replaced by a significantly revised version that became effective for accounting periods beginning on or after 1 January 2005. IAS 31 has been subject to further amendment by IFRSs issued since December 2003.

The SIC has issued an interpretation of IAS 31, SIC-13 – *Jointly Controlled Entities – Non-monetary Contributions by Venturers*.

1.3   Other applicable IFRS

In addition to IAS 31 and SIC-13, the following pronouncements are relevant to accounting for joint ventures:

- IAS 1 – *Presentation of Financial Statements*;
- IAS 21 – *The Effects of Changes in Foreign Exchange Rates*;
- IAS 27 – *Consolidated and Separate Financial Statements*;
- IAS 28 – *Investments in Associates*;
- IAS 39 – *Financial Instruments: Recognition and Measurement*;
- IFRS 1 – *First-time Adoption of International Financial Reporting Standards*;
- IFRS 3 – *Business Combinations*; and
- IFRS 5 – *Non-current Assets Held for Sale and Discontinued Operations*.

IAS 27 and IFRS 3 have both been substantially revised as a result of phase II of the Business Combinations project as explained in Chapter 9 at 1.2.2 and entities will need to be careful to ensure they are using the correct versions of each of these standards. IFRS 3 (as revised in 2008) is effective for business combinations for which the acquisition date is on or after the beginning of the first annual reporting period beginning on or after 1 July 2009 with early adoption possible as explained in Chapter 9 at 3.1.1. IAS 27 (as amended in 2008) has the same effective date.[2]

Consequential amendments made to IAS 31 as a result of those revised standards also apply from the same date.

1.4   Future developments

As indicated at 1.1 above, the IASB has issued an exposure draft, ED 9 – *Joint Arrangements*, that is intended to replace IAS 31, and has proposed to remove the option of proportionate consolidation for jointly controlled entities, requiring such joint venture arrangements to be accounted for under the equity method. The proposals and subsequent developments since the publication of the exposure draft are discussed at 7.1 and 7.2 below.

As discussed in Chapter 11 at 3, many procedures appropriate for the application of the equity method are similar to the consolidation procedures described in IAS 27 (see Chapter 7). Furthermore IAS 28 explains that the concepts underlying the procedures used in accounting for the acquisition of a subsidiary are also adopted in accounting for the acquisition of an investment in an associate.[3] This does raise a number of practical difficulties, and there has been an ongoing debate about whether the equity method of accounting is a consolidation method or a measurement method. Although IAS 28 generally adopts consolidation principles it nevertheless retains features of a valuation methodology.

As a result of the revised versions of IFRS 3 and IAS 27, this has raised a number of new issues in the context of applying the equity method, and the extent to which the methodology and procedures under these revised standards should now be applied is open to further consideration. The position has been confused even further as a result of the publication of the IASB's annual improvement standard in April 2009 where in the context of an amendment to IAS 39 regarding the application of the exemption in paragraph 2(g) of that standard (see Chapter 29 at 3.7.2) it is stated that the 'Board noted that paragraph 20 of IAS 28 explains only the methodology used to account for investments in associates. This should not be taken to imply that the principles for business combinations and consolidations can be applied by analogy to accounting for investments in associates and joint ventures.'[4] In May 2009, the IASB has indicated that it will address the interaction between the revised versions of IFRS 3 and IAS 27, and IAS 28 and IAS 31, as part of its project on joint ventures.[5]

At the time of writing, it is unclear exactly what changes may be introduced in the context of applying the equity method as a result of this project. Hopefully it will resolve many of the issues that arise in practice.

2   SCOPE OF IAS 31

2.1   General

IAS 31 must be applied in accounting for interests in joint ventures (see 2.2 below) and the reporting of joint venture assets, liabilities, income and expenses in the financial statements of venturers and investors, regardless of the structures or forms under which the joint venture activities take place.

However, IAS 31 does not apply to venturers' interests (see 2.2.1 below) in jointly controlled entities (see 3.3.1 below) held by:

(a)   venture capital organisations, or

(b)   mutual funds, unit trusts and similar entities including investment-linked insurance funds

that upon initial recognition are designated as 'at fair value through profit or loss' or are classified as 'held for trading' and accounted for in accordance with IAS 39. Such investments are measured at fair value in accordance with IAS 39, with changes in fair value recognised in profit or loss in the period of the change.[6]

The exemption for venture capital organisations and other similar financial institutions raises the question of exactly what entities comprise those described in (a) and (b), since they are not defined. Essentially the same issues arise in respect of the equivalent exemption in IAS 28 for investments in associates held by such entities, which is discussed in Chapter 11 at 2.1.1.

2.1.1   Disclosures of venturers' interests

Disclosures required for joint ventures are detailed at 4.2 below. The IASB, as part of its Annual Improvements project, amended IAS 31 to clarify that where a joint venture is accounted for at fair value in accordance with IAS 39, as permitted under the standard for venture capital organisations, mutual funds, unit trusts and similar entities, some of the IAS 31 disclosure requirements do not apply.[7] This is explained at 4.2.4 below.

2.2   Definition of 'joint venture' and related terms

A *joint venture* is a contractual arrangement whereby two or more parties undertake an economic activity that is subject to joint control.[8]

Joint control is the contractually agreed sharing of control over an economic activity, and exists only when the strategic financial and operating decisions relating to the activity require the unanimous consent of the parties sharing control (the venturers).[9] Although IFRS does not define what financial and operating policies are, these are generally understood to include areas such as budgeting, capital expenditures, treasury management, dividend policy, production, marketing, sales and human resources.

An *investor* in a joint venture is a party to a joint venture and does not have joint control over that joint venture.[10]

A *venturer* is a party to a joint venture and has joint control over that joint venture.[11]

2.2.1   'Venturer' versus 'investor'

The definitions of 'investor' and 'venturer' above draw a distinction between participants in a joint venture who also participate in the joint control of that venture and more passive investors, as illustrated by Example 12.1.

Example 12.1:   'Venturer' versus 'investor'

A, B and C establish a fourth entity D, of which A owns 40%, B 11% and C 49%. A and B enter into a contractual arrangement whereby any financial and operating decisions taken by A and B relating to the activity of D require the unanimous consent of A and B. In the jurisdiction where D is incorporated a simple majority of shareholders only is required for all major decisions. IAS 31 would regard A and B as being 'venturers', and C as an 'investor', in D.

The interest of an 'investor' in a jointly controlled entity should be treated as:

(a)   an associate within the scope of IAS 28 if the investor has significant influence over the entity (see Chapter 11); or

(b)   otherwise as a financial asset within the scope of IAS 39 (see Chapter 29).[12]

2.2.2   *Joint control*

As noted in 1.1 above, joint ventures take many different forms and structures. However, IAS 31 identifies three broad types:

- jointly controlled operations (see 3.1 below);
- jointly controlled assets (see 3.2 below); and
- jointly controlled entities (see 3.3 below).

Under IAS 31, the following characteristics are common to all joint ventures:

(a)   two or more venturers are bound by a contractual arrangement (see A below); and

(b)   the contractual arrangement establishes joint control.[13]

A   *Contractual arrangement*

IAS 31 emphasises that it is the existence of a contractual arrangement that distinguishes interests that involve joint control from investments in associates in which the investor has significant influence[14] (i.e. the power to participate in the financial and operating policy decisions of the investee but not amounting to control or joint control over those policies).[15]

Activities that have no contractual arrangement to establish joint control are not joint ventures for the purposes of IAS 31.[16] In other words, if two entities A and B set up a third entity C in which A and B each hold 50% of the equity, C will not, by virtue of the relative shareholdings *alone*, be a joint venture of A and B for the purposes of IAS 31. There needs to be an agreement for unanimous decision making on key matters – although this might automatically flow from the general provisions of corporate law in the jurisdiction concerned.

A contractual arrangement between venturers may be evidenced in a number of ways. There might be a separate contract between the venturers or minutes of discussions between them. In some cases, the arrangement is incorporated in the articles or other by-laws of the joint venture. Whatever its form, the contractual arrangement is usually in writing and deals with such matters as:

(a)   the activity, duration and reporting obligations of the joint venture;

(b)   the appointment of the board of directors or equivalent governing body of the joint venture and the voting rights of the venturers;

(c)   capital contributions by the venturers; and

(d)   the sharing by the venturers of the output, income, expenses or results of the joint venture.[17]

The effect of a contractual arrangement is to establish joint control over the joint venture, ensuring that no single venturer is in a position to control the activity unilaterally.[18] That means, for example, that none of the parties to the contractual arrangement should have a casting vote that enables it to resolve a deadlock, as that would constitute a form of unilateral control.

A contractual arrangement may identify one venturer as the operator or manager of the joint venture. The operator does not control the joint venture but acts within the financial and operating policies agreed by the venturers in accordance with the contractual arrangement and delegated to the operator. If the operator does have the power to govern (i.e. not merely to execute) the financial and operating policies of the economic activity, the operator controls the venture and the venture is a subsidiary of the operator and not a joint venture.[19]

B   Legal and other restrictions on investee

IAS 31 notes that joint control may be precluded when an investee is in legal reorganisation or in bankruptcy, or operates under severe long-term restrictions on its ability to transfer funds to the venturer. However, if joint control continues, these events are not enough in themselves to justify not accounting for the investee as a joint venture in accordance with IAS 31.[20] This issue is discussed further (in the context of loss of control over subsidiaries) in Chapter 6 at 4.3.

C   Potential voting rights

An entity may own share warrants, share call options, debt or equity instruments that are convertible into ordinary shares, or other similar instruments that have the potential, if exercised or converted, to give the entity voting power or reduce another party's voting power over the financial and operating policies of another entity (potential voting rights).

Potential voting rights are not directly addressed in IAS 31. However, the application guidance on potential voting rights in IAS 27 (see Chapter 6 at 2.1.2) indicates that it may also be relevant to the determination of joint control under IAS 31, while at the same time acknowledging that a contractual arrangement giving rise to joint control will tend to over-ride relative ownership interests (see 3.3.1 below). This is an issue that will need to be addressed in the light of individual facts and circumstances.

2.3   Requirement to apply IAS 31 to jointly controlled entities

There are no exemptions from applying IAS 31 to jointly controlled operations (see 3.1 below) or jointly controlled assets (see 3.2 below). Nevertheless, IFRS 5 would apply to jointly controlled operations and jointly controlled assets that meet the definition of an asset held for sale (disposal group) or discontinued operation.

A venturer with an interest in a jointly controlled entity need not account for its interest using proportionate consolidation or equity accounting (see 3.3 below) if:[21]

(a)   the interest is classified as held for sale in accordance with IFRS 5, in which case it is accounted for under that standard (see Chapter 4 at 2);[22]

(b)   the venturer is a parent exempt from preparing consolidated financial statements under IAS 27 (see Chapter 6 at 3.1); or

(c)   all of the following apply:

(i)   the venturer is a wholly-owned subsidiary, or is a partially-owned subsidiary of another entity and its other owners, including those not otherwise entitled to vote, have been informed about, and do not object to, the investor not applying proportionate consolidation or the equity method;

(ii)   the venturer's debt or equity instruments are not traded in a public market (a domestic or foreign stock exchange or an over-the-counter market, including local and regional markets);

(iii)   the venturer did not file, nor is it in the process of filing, its financial statements with a securities commission or other regulatory organisation, for the purpose of issuing any class of instruments in a public market; and

(iv)   the ultimate or any intermediate parent of the venturer produces consolidated financial statements available for public use that comply with International Financial Reporting Standards.

Conditions (i) to (iv) in (c) above are identical to the criteria that must be satisfied by:

- a parent in order to be exempt from preparing consolidated financial statements under IAS 27; or

- an investor in an associate that is not a parent in order to be exempt from equity accounting for its investment under IAS 28.

Further discussion of the meaning and interpretation of these conditions may be found in Chapter 6 at 3.1 and Chapter 11 at 2.3.

Essentially, exemption (c) is only available to entities that are themselves either wholly-owned subsidiaries or whose minority shareholders approve the presentation of financial statements that do not include jointly controlled entities using proportionate consolidation or the equity method. Some of these 'intermediate' entities will not be exempt, for example if none of their parents prepares consolidated financial statements in accordance with IFRS. A typical example is that of an entity that is a subsidiary of a US group that prepares consolidated accounts in accordance with US GAAP only. In addition, any entity that has publicly traded debt or equity, or is in the process of obtaining a listing for such instruments, will not meet the exemptions.

The effect of the above requirements is that a reporting entity that has jointly controlled entities, but no subsidiaries, and does not meet all the criteria in (c), is required to apply proportionate consolidation or equity accounting to its jointly controlled entities in its own (non-consolidated) financial statements (not to be confused with its 'separate financial statements' – see 2.4 below). This is significantly different from the requirement of many national GAAPs, where proportionate consolidation or equity accounting for jointly controlled entities is required (or indeed permitted) only in consolidated financial statements.

2.4   Separate financial statements

Separate financial statements are defined by IAS 31, consistent with IAS 27, as those presented by a parent, an investor in an associate or a venturer in a jointly controlled entity, in which the investments are accounted for on the basis of the direct equity interest rather than on the basis of the reported results and net assets of the investees.[23] IAS 27 requires that, in separate financial statements, investments in jointly controlled entities that are not classified as held for sale (or included in a disposal group that is classified as held for sale) in accordance with IFRS 5 should be accounted for either:[24]

- at cost; or
- in accordance with IAS 39.

IAS 27 has now been amended by deleting the definition of the 'cost method'. This is in response to difficulties raised in applying this cost method when a company adopts IFRS for the first time when, for example, the investments had been held for many years and an entity's previous GAAP did not require them to be accounted for at cost as applied by IFRS. Previously an investor applying the cost method in its separate financial statements would have been required to identify pre-acquisition profits of a jointly controlled entity and recognise dividends received out of these profits as a reduction of the cost of that jointly controlled entity. However the amendment requires the investor to recognise all dividends, whether relating to pre-acquisition or post acquisition profits of the investee, in profit or loss within its separate financial statements once the right to receive payments has been established.[25] The investor then needs to consider whether there are indicators of impairment as detailed within this amendment and as described in Chapter 8 at 2.3.1. The amendment is effective for annual periods beginning on or after 1 January 2009. Earlier application was permitted so long as this was disclosed and that related amendments to other standards were also applied.[26]

The detailed IFRS requirements for separate financial statements are set out in IAS 27 and are discussed more fully in Chapter 8.[27]

It follows from the definition of separate financial statements above that financial statements (including non-consolidated financial statements) in which proportionate consolidation or the equity method is applied are not separate financial statements; neither are the financial statements of an entity that does not have a subsidiary, associate or venturer's interest in a joint venture.[28]

Separate financial statements are any financial statements presented in addition to:

- consolidated financial statements;
- financial statements in which investments are accounted for using the equity method; and
- financial statements in which venturers' interests in joint ventures are proportionately consolidated.

There is no requirement for an entity to prepare separate financial statements, or for any separate financial statements that are voluntarily prepared to be appended to, or accompany, the 'main' financial statements.[29]

An entity may present separate financial statements as its only financial statements if it satisfies the conditions for exemption from:[30]

- preparing consolidated financial statements under paragraph 10 of IAS 27 (see Chapter 6 at 3.1);

- equity accounting for associates under paragraph 13(c) of IAS 28 (see Chapter 11 at 2.3); and

- proportionately consolidating (or equity accounting for) jointly controlled entities under paragraph 2 of IAS 31 (see above).

As drafted this exemption makes a curious distinction between an entity with associates only and one with jointly controlled entities only.

An entity with associates may prepare separate financial statements as its only financial statements only if it satisfies the exemption in paragraph 13(c) of IAS 28. In other words, if an entity has associates, but is exempt from equity accounting for all of them under paragraph 13(a) – i.e. because they are all accounted for under IFRS 5 – it may apparently not present separate financial statements as its only financial statements. However, an entity with jointly controlled entities may prepare separate financial statements as its only financial statements if it satisfies the exemption in paragraph 2 of IAS 31, which includes jointly controlled entities accounted for under IFRS 5.

It can safely be assumed that this inconsistency was unintentional, but it is less obvious as to which exemption is correct and which incorrect. On balance, our view is that it is the exemption in relation to joint ventures which is incorrect. In other words, the IASB intended to give the exemption only to 'non-public interest' companies and should have referred to paragraph 2(c) of IAS 31. This view is also consistent with the exemption that has been proposed in ED 9,[31] the exposure draft that it is proposed will replace IAS 31 (see 7 below).

2.4.1 Impairment of interests in jointly controlled entities in a venturer's separate financial statements

As discussed more fully in Chapter 11 at 2.4.1, one issue recently considered by the IFRIC and the IASB is how impairments of investments in associates should be determined in the separate financial statements of the investor. In our view the requirements of IAS 36 – *Impairment of Assets* – and IAS 39 make it clear that IAS 36 applies to the impairment of associates measured at cost in the separate financial statements, and the same would apply to interests in jointly controlled entities.[32]

However, at its meeting in May 2009, and subsequently confirmed at its meeting in July 2009, the IFRIC concluded that it is not clear whether in its separate financial statements the investor in an associate should determine impairment in accordance with IAS 36 or IAS 39, but decided that the issue could be best resolved by referring it to the IASB. Therefore, the IFRIC decided not to add this issue to its agenda.[33]

Consequently, the IASB has decided to deal with this issue within the exposure draft of proposed *Improvements to IFRSs* issued in August 2009.[34] The IASB is proposing that, as the purpose of separate financial statements is on the performance of the assets as investments,[35] when an entity prepares separate financial statements, it is to apply the requirements of IAS 39 rather than IAS 36 for the determination and measurement of impairment losses on investments in subsidiaries, jointly controlled entities and associates. It is proposed that an entity applies the amendments prospectively for annual periods beginning on or after 1 January 2011. Earlier application is to be permitted, but if an entity applies the amendments for an earlier period it is to disclose that fact.[36]

2.5   'Pseudo' joint ventures

Some entities may have certain general characteristics of joint ventures, but not in fact be joint ventures. A particular example is the protected cell entity.

Example 12.2:   Is it a joint venture? – Protected cell entity

Some jurisdictions permit the formation of so called 'protected cell' entities. Essentially these are entities which have a number of 'cells', with the assets and liabilities of each cell being completely ring-fenced – in other words the creditors of a particular cell have recourse only to the assets of that cell. In addition to the cells, each one of which has its own capital, there is a so-called 'core', whose shareholders may manage the activities of the cells on behalf of their owners. Diagrammatically, the structure can be portrayed as follows:

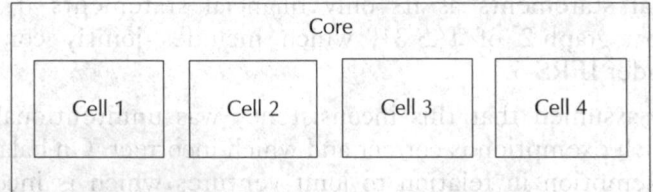

An original intention of this structure was to allow a fund-manager (who would hold the core shares) to run a number of independent funds (whose investors would hold the shares in the particular cell(s) concerned), with the incorporation of a single legal entity, as compared to the traditional position where each managed fund, and the management company, would be a separate legal entity, with all the attendant administrative costs and burdens.

Such a structure may give the superficial appearance of being a joint activity, but this is not the case. In most cases, it is extremely unlikely to be appropriate for an entity to regard an investment in a cell as a joint venture (or an associate). This is because the 'ring-fencing' of the assets and liabilities of each cell means that there is a direct linkage between the reporting entity and one or more particular cells, rather than that the reporting entity has some share of the profits or losses of the cell entity as a whole. The most likely conclusion is that each cell is a special purpose entity (SPE) of another entity (see Chapter 6 at 2.2).

3   ACCOUNTING REQUIREMENTS

3.1   Jointly controlled operations

A jointly controlled operation is one which involves the use of assets and other resources of the venturers, rather than the establishment of a corporation, partnership or other entity, or a financial structure, separate from the venturers themselves. Each venturer uses its own property, plant and equipment and carries its own inventories. It also incurs its own expenses and liabilities and raises its own finance, which represent its own obligations. The joint venture activities may be carried out by the venturer's employees alongside similar activities of the venturer. The joint venture agreement usually provides the basis for sharing among the venturers the revenue sales of the joint product and any common expenses incurred.[37]

An example of a jointly controlled operation might be that two or more venturers combine their operations, resources and expertise in order to jointly manufacture, market and distribute a particular product, such as an aircraft, with each venturer undertaking different parts of the manufacturing process. Each venturer bears its own costs and takes a share of the revenue from the sale of the aircraft, such share being determined in accordance with the contractual arrangement.[38]

In respect of its interest in a jointly controlled operation, IAS 31 requires a venturer to recognise in its financial statements:

- the assets that it controls and the liabilities that it incurs; and

- the expenses that it incurs and its share of the income that it earns from the sale of goods or services by the joint venture.[39]

IAS 31 notes that, because the assets, liabilities, income and expenses are already recognised in the financial statements of the venturer, no adjustments or other consolidation procedures are required in respect of these items when the venturer presents consolidated financial statements. Separate accounting records may not be required, nor financial statements prepared, for the joint venture itself, although the venturers may prepare management accounts so that they may assess the performance of the joint venture.[40]

When venturers are funding the operations of a jointly controlled operation they may need to account for a receivable or payable from other venturers, as illustrated in Example 12.3 below.

Example 12.3:   Loans to jointly controlled operations

Two entities – A and B – each own half of a jointly controlled operation. Entity A has lent €400 to the jointly controlled operation, while entity B has lent €300. How should entity A account for its loan?

The jointly controlled operation has total borrowings of €400 + €300 = €700. A's share in the borrowings of €350 (=50% of €700) should be offset against its receivable of €400. Entity A should, therefore, account for a net receivable from its joint venture partner of €50 (=€400 – €350).

The jointly controlled operation is not a separate legal entity and under the joint venture agreement A has a business relationship only with B. Gross presentation of a receivable of €200 (=€400 – 50% of €400) and a liability of €150 (=50% of €300) would therefore not be appropriate.

The extract below shows a typical accounting policy for jointly controlled operations.

Extract 12.1: Xstrata plc (2007)

Notes to the Financial Statements [extract]

6. Principal Accounting Policies [extract]

Jointly controlled operations

A jointly controlled operation involves the use of assets and other resources of the Group and other venturers rather than the establishment of a corporation, partnership or other entity. The Group accounts for the assets it controls and the liabilities it incurs, the expenses it incurs and the share of income that it earns from the sale of goods or services by the joint venture.

3.2   Jointly controlled assets

Some joint ventures involve the joint control, and often the joint ownership, of one or more assets contributed to, or acquired for, and dedicated to the purposes of, the joint venture. The assets are used to obtain benefits for the venturers, who may each take a share of the output from the assets and bear an agreed share of the expenses incurred. Such ventures do not involve the establishment of an entity or financial structure separate from the venturers themselves, so that each venturer has control over its share of future economic benefits through its share in the jointly controlled asset.[41]

IAS 31 notes that joint ventures of this type are particularly common in extractive industries. For example, a number of oil companies may jointly control and operate an oil pipeline. Each venturer uses the pipeline to transport its own product in return for which it bears an agreed proportion of the operating expenses of the pipeline. Another example of a jointly controlled asset could be that two entities jointly control a property, each taking a share of the rents received and bearing a share of the expenses.[42]

In respect of its interest in jointly controlled assets, IAS 31 requires a venturer to recognise in its financial statements:

- its share of the jointly controlled assets, classified according to the nature of the assets (i.e. a share in a jointly controlled pipeline should be shown within property, plant and equipment rather than as an investment);

- any liabilities which it has incurred;

- its share of any liabilities incurred jointly with the other venturers;

- any income from the sale or use of its share of the output of the joint venture;

- its share of any expenses incurred by the joint venture; and

- any expenses which it has incurred in respect of its interest in the joint venture (e.g. those relating to financing the venturer's interest in the assets and selling its share of the output).[43]

The IASB believes that this treatment reflects the substance and economic reality and, usually, the legal form of the joint venture.[44] However, it should be noted that, as Example 12.4 at 3.3.1 below illustrates, the classification of a joint venture as either a jointly controlled asset or a jointly controlled entity is largely form driven.

As in the case of jointly controlled operations (see 3.1 above), no adjustments or other consolidation procedures are required when the venturer presents consolidated financial statements, because the relevant assets, liabilities, income and expenses are already recognised in the financial statements of the venturer.[45]

IAS 31 notes that the accounting records of the joint venture itself may be limited to a record of the expenses incurred in common by the venturers, and ultimately borne by them according to their agreed shares. Financial statements may not be prepared for the joint venture, although the venturers may prepare management accounts so that they may assess the performance of the joint venture.[46]

Extract 12.2 below shows a typical accounting policy for jointly controlled assets.

Extract 12.2: Xstrata plc (2007)

Notes to the Financial Statements [extract]

6. Principal Accounting Policies [extract]

Jointly controlled assets

A jointly controlled asset involves joint control and ownership by the Group and other venturers of assets contributed to or acquired for the purpose of the joint venture, without the formation of a corporation, partnership or other entity. The Group accounts for its share of the jointly controlled assets, any liabilities it has incurred, its share of any liabilities jointly incurred with other ventures, income from the sale or use of its share of the joint venture's output, together with its share of the expenses incurred by the joint venture, and any expenses it incurs in relation to its interest in the joint venture.

Extract 12.3 below illustrates an example of a company contributing its own assets to joint ventures that are accounted for as jointly controlled assets.

Extract 12.3: Anglo Platinum Limited (2007)

NOTES TO THE CONSOLIDATED FINANCIAL STATEMENTS [extract]

17 Joint ventures [extract]

Jointly controlled assets

Bafokeng-Rasimone Platinum Mine (BRPM) Joint Venture

The Group and Royal Bafokeng Resources (Pty) Limited (RBR) have entered into a 50:50 joint venture. In terms of the agreement, the Group contributes the operating Bafokeng Rasimone Platinum Mine (BRPM) and the related mineral rights to the venture, while RBR contributes certain mineral rights and has to compensate the Group for the net cash spent on the development of BRPM, plus interest.

Mototolo Joint Venture

The Group and XK Platinum Partnership (a partnership between Xstrata South Africa (Pty) Limited and Kagiso Platinum Ventures (Pty) Limited) have entered into a 50:50 joint venture. In terms of the agreement, each party will contribute a similar amount of in situ PGM reserves and resources, from Xstrata's Thorncliffe farm, adjacent to its Thorncliffe chrome mine and the Group's bordering farm, part of its Der Brochen project area.

3.3   Jointly controlled entities

3.3.1   Definition

In contrast to a jointly controlled operation or jointly controlled asset, a jointly controlled entity is a joint venture that involves the establishment of a corporation, partnership or other entity in which each venturer has an interest. The entity operates in the same way as any other entity, except that a contractual arrangement between the venturers establishes joint control over the economic activity of the entity.[47]

A jointly controlled entity controls the assets of the joint venture, incurs liabilities and expenses and earns income. It may enter into contracts in its own name and raise finance for the purposes of the joint venture activity. IAS 31 notes that 'each venturer is entitled to a share of the results of the jointly controlled entity, although some jointly controlled entities also involve a sharing of output.'[48]

IAS 31's reference to the fact that a venturer's interest in a jointly controlled entity may be in its 'output' rather than its results, suggests that, once a separate legal entity is involved, one is dealing with a jointly controlled entity and not a jointly controlled asset, even if the economic substance appears very similar. Example 12.4 illustrates the point.

Example 12.4:   Jointly controlled asset or jointly controlled entity?

If three entities – A, B and C – each own one-third of a pipeline (and enter into a contractual agreement giving each party joint control), the venture is a jointly controlled asset. If, however, A, B and C each own one-third of a fourth entity D which owns the pipeline (and enter into a contractual agreement giving each party joint control), the venture is considered to be a jointly controlled entity.

This suggests that a venturer's share of the output of an asset may be accounted for differently depending on whether the share in the asset is held directly or through a separate legal entity, particularly when it is borne in mind that IAS 31 gives an exemption in respect of accounting for a jointly controlled entity (see 2.3 above), but not in respect of a jointly controlled asset.

However, it could be said that these different outcomes are no different to the fact that, if a company owns a property, it shows a property in its separate financial statements whereas, if it incorporates a subsidiary to hold the property, it shows an investment in subsidiary in its separate financial statements.

IAS 31 goes on to say that many jointly controlled entities are similar in substance to jointly controlled operations or jointly controlled assets. For example, the venturers may transfer a jointly controlled asset, such as an oil pipeline, into a jointly controlled entity, for tax or other reasons. Similarly, the venturers may contribute into a jointly controlled entity assets which will be operated jointly. Some jointly controlled operations also involve the establishment of a jointly controlled entity to deal with particular aspects of the activity, for example, the design, marketing, distribution or after-sales service of the product.[49]

This emphasises the fact that, whilst the economic substance of a jointly controlled asset and a jointly controlled entity may in fact be similar, the difference in form does matter in determining the accounting treatment. This is articulated in paragraph 32 of the standard (which deals with proportionate consolidation – see 3.3.3 below), as follows:[50]

> 'when recognising an interest in a jointly controlled entity, it is essential that a venturer reflects the substance and economic reality of the arrangement, rather than the joint venture's particular structure or form. In a jointly controlled entity, a venturer has control over its share of future economic benefits through its share of the assets and liabilities of the venture. This substance and economic reality are reflected in the consolidated financial statements of the venturer when the venturer recognises its interests in the assets, liabilities, income and expenses of the jointly controlled entity by using one of the two reporting formats for proportionate consolidation described [below].'

This indicates that, in the IASB's view (prior to ED 9), the substance of a joint venture is determined by its legal form and that, once joint ventures are enveloped in a separate legal entity, they become jointly controlled entities under IAS 31. Therefore a contractual arrangement that involves the establishment of a legal entity under joint control would be a jointly controlled entity, even if the entity does not carry on a trade or business of its own and merely owns a group of assets. However, as discussed at 7 below, the exposure draft that has been proposed to replace IAS 31

(ED 9) shifts the focus in accounting away from the legal form of the joint arrangement to the contractual rights and obligations within that joint arrangement.

IAS 31 notes that a common example of a jointly controlled entity is when two entities combine their activities in a particular line of business by transferring the relevant assets and liabilities into a jointly controlled entity. Another example might be that an entity, in order to commence a business in a foreign country in conjunction with the government or other agency in that country, establishes a separate entity which is jointly controlled by the entity and the government or a government agency.[51]

IAS 31 adds that another feature of a jointly controlled entity is that it maintains its own accounting records and prepares and presents financial statements in the same way as other entities in conformity with IFRS.[52] This again reinforces the message that the classification of joint ventures as jointly controlled entities is, in fact, rather form-based. Whether or not an entity keeps its own books is arguably more a reflection of local legal requirements than of the economic substance of its activities.

IAS 31 notes that each venturer usually contributes cash or other resources to the jointly controlled entity. These contributions are included in the accounting records of the venturer and recognised in its separate financial statements as an investment in the jointly controlled entity.[53]

3.3.2 Accounting treatment – summary

IAS 31 permits two methods of accounting for jointly controlled entities:

* proportionate consolidation (see 3.3.3 below), using one of two permitted formats; and
* the equity method (see 3.3.4 below).[54]

Subject to the exemption discussed at 2.3 above, the venturer must apply whichever method it selects irrespective of whether it also has investments in subsidiaries or whether it describes its financial statements as 'consolidated financial statements'.[55] This requirement in IAS 31 is intended to emphasise that proportionate consolidation (or equity accounting) for jointly controlled entities may be required even for an entity that is not preparing consolidated financial statements.

A   Difference between allowed treatments

In many cases the essential difference between the two methods is simply one of presentation – i.e. whether items are shown on a 'line-by-line' basis (in the case of proportionate consolidation) or a 'one line' basis (in the case of equity accounting). However, this is not always the case as is discussed at I to V below.

I   Loss-making joint ventures

The treatment of a loss-making jointly controlled entity may differ significantly under each method. Where proportionate consolidation is used, the venturer will simply pick up its share of all losses as they arise. Whereas under the equity method, the reporting entity will apply 'waterline accounting' (see Chapter 11 at 3.7), so that the carrying amount of its interest in the joint venture never falls below zero, except to the extent that the investor has incurred legal or constructive obligations or made payments on behalf of the joint venture. Of course, it is in the nature of joint ventures that a venturer in a joint venture is more likely to have such legal or constructive obligations than an investor in an associate. Therefore, in some cases there is no difference between equity accounting for, and proportionate consolidation of, loss-making jointly controlled entities.

II   Capitalisation of borrowing costs

A difference between proportionate consolidation and equity accounting may arise when the venturer capitalises borrowing costs that are directly attributable to the acquisition, construction or production of a qualifying asset. A qualifying asset is defined by IAS 23 – *Borrowing Costs* – as 'an asset that necessarily takes a substantial period of time to get ready for its intended use or sale.'[56]

If the jointly controlled entity itself did not incur any borrowing costs then the venturer would capitalise its own borrowing costs in respect of all qualifying assets of a proportionately consolidated jointly controlled entity. IAS 23 – *Borrowing Costs* – has recently been revised and the policy choice that existed under the previous version of the standard as to whether to capitalise or expense borrowing costs has been removed. Capitalisation of borrowing costs is mandatory, when certain criteria are met, under the revised standard which is effective for annual periods beginning on or after 1 January 2009.[57] Therefore, venturers that proportionately consolidate joint ventures will have to capitalise their own borrowing costs that relate to their share of qualifying assets where required to by IAS 23 (revised) when the jointly controlled entity itself does not incur borrowing costs (see Chapter 19 at 3.5.2). This will only be appropriate in accounts where proportionate consolidation is applied. A venturer applying the equity method to joint ventures is not able to capitalise its borrowing costs, under both the original and revised versions of IAS 23, because investments accounted for under the equity method are not qualifying assets.[58]

III   Hedging of the joint ventures

Another difference relates to the application of hedge accounting. A venturer that proportionately consolidates its investments in jointly controlled entities may be able to apply hedge accounting to assets, liabilities, firm commitments and highly probable forecast transactions of the joint venture. Whereas a venturer applying the equity method to similar joint ventures would only be able to apply hedge accounting to the equity accounted investment as a whole.

IV   Impairment of a jointly controlled entity

IAS 28 contains special impairment testing rules that apply to investments accounted for under the equity method (see Chapter 11 at 4). The equity method involves having to restate any impairment losses recognised by the investee as a result of appropriate adjustments to the fair values of the identifiable assets at the date of acquisition of the investee. However, as well as applying the equity method, an entity also has to apply the requirements of IAS 39 to determine whether an additional impairment exists, followed by an impairment test under IAS 36 of the investment as a whole. That is, the goodwill arising on the acquisition of the joint venture would not be tested separately for impairment under IAS 36. Consequently the IAS 36 prohibition on the reversal of impairment losses on goodwill would not apply either, and a previously recognised impairment of an investment that is accounted for under the equity method is fully reversible (see Chapter 11 at 4.3).

Venturers that proportionately consolidate their investments under IAS 31 would be required to test the cash generating units and goodwill of the joint venture separately for impairment under IAS 36, which means that impairment of goodwill is irreversible. However, it is not necessary to carry out an additional impairment test as envisaged under IAS 28.

V   *Acquisition of a jointly controlled entity – upon application of IAS 27 (as amended in 2008) and IFRS 3 (as revised in 2008)*

For venturers applying the equity method, it would appear that the IFRIC expects any acquisition-related costs should not be expensed, but should be included as part of the cost of the jointly controlled entity. However, for venturers applying proportionate consolidation, we believe that it would be more appropriate to apply the 'fair value' principles in IFRS 3 (as revised in 2008) – see Chapter 9 at 3, although a cost-based approach whereby the cost of the acquisition of the jointly controlled entity comprises its purchase price and any directly attributable expenditures necessary to obtain it would be acceptable in the light of the comments made by the IFRIC and the IASB. This is discussed further at 3.3.7 below.

As a consequence, similar differences may also apply in relation to piecemeal acquisitions of jointly controlled entities (see 3.3.9 below).

B   *Consistency of treatment*

As drafted, IAS 31 requires a venturer to apply either proportionate consolidation or equity accounting to its interest in 'a' jointly controlled entity.[59] This could be interpreted as suggesting that the venturer can make the choice of accounting treatment for each jointly controlled entity individually.

However, the disclosure provisions of IAS 31 (see 4.2.2 below) require a venturer to disclose 'the' method used to account for 'its interests in jointly controlled entities'.[60] In our view, this, together with:

- the use of similar wording in another disclosure requirement in IAS 31;

- the statement that IAS 8 – *Accounting Policies, Changes in Accounting Estimates and Errors* – incorporates the consensus in SIC-18 – *Consistency – Alternative Methods* – which specifically required consistent application of the option in IAS 31; and[61]

- the overall requirement of IAS 1 for the use of consistent accounting policies for similar transactions (see Chapter 3 at 4.1.4),

clearly indicates that the IASB expects a venturer to account for all jointly controlled entities on a consistent basis.

3.3.3 *Proportionate consolidation*

IAS 31 defines proportionate consolidation as 'a method of accounting whereby a venturer's share of each of the assets, liabilities, income and expenses of a jointly controlled entity is combined line by line with similar items in the venturer's financial statements or reported as separate line items in the venturer's financial statements.'[62]

As noted in the discussion at 3.3.1 above, IAS 31 asserts that this method of accounting is necessary in order to capture the substance and economic reality of a venturer's interest in a jointly controlled entity.[63]

The application of proportionate consolidation means that the balance sheet of the venturer includes its share of the assets that it controls jointly and its share of the liabilities for which it is jointly responsible. The income statement of the venturer includes its share of the income and expenses of the jointly controlled entity.[64] In effect, the end result is equivalent to accounting for a partly-owned subsidiary, but excluding the amounts attributable to the non-controlling or minority interest. IAS 31 notes that the procedures for consolidation of subsidiaries set out in IAS 27 (see Chapter 7) will generally be appropriate for the proportionate consolidation of joint ventures.[65]

Proportionate consolidation should be carried out using one of two permitted formats.

- *Line-by-line presentation*

    The jointly controlled entity is consolidated on an aggregated line-by-line basis (i.e. the venturer combines its share of the assets, liabilities, income and expenditure of the jointly controlled entity within the similar items in its own financial statements); or

- *Presentation as separate line items*

    The venturer includes separate line items for its share of the total assets, liabilities, income and expenditure of the jointly controlled entity in its own consolidated accounts. Thus for example the item 'debtors' in the venturer's own financial statements would include a sub-heading 'share of debtors of joint ventures'.

The difference between the formats is clearly one of presentation only. Both formats result in the reporting of identical amounts of profit or loss and of each major classification of assets, liabilities, income and expenses.[66] In practice though, few companies present their investment in jointly controlled entities as separate line items.

IAS 31 states that, whatever format is used to give effect to proportionate consolidation, it is inappropriate to offset any assets or liabilities by the deduction of other liabilities or assets or any income or expenses by the deduction of other expenses or income, unless a legal right of set-off exists and the offsetting represents the expectation as to the realisation of the asset or the settlement of the liability.[67] It is not entirely clear what IAS 31 means by this. It could be interpreted as prohibiting the partial elimination of balances between a venturer and its joint venture. However, on balance, we believe it is more appropriate to partially eliminate, i.e. eliminate to the extent of the venturer's interest, such balances. For example if a venturer had a 50% interest in a joint venture and was owed $2M from that joint venture then it would seem more appropriate when proportionately consolidating for this joint venture to show a net $1M receivable rather than show a $2M receivable and a $1M payable, the latter balance representing what would in effect be a payable to itself (the venturer). The same would apply to any transactions, income and expenses between the venturer and the jointly controlled entity (see 3.4.2 below).

IAS 31 does not explicitly state when an entity should commence proportionate consolidation of a jointly controlled entity, but it is evident that it should be from the date that the venturer begins to have joint control over the entity. The accounting for the acquisition of an interest in a jointly controlled entity is discussed at 3.3.6 and 3.3.7 below.

Proportionate consolidation of a jointly controlled entity should cease on the date that the venturer ceases to have joint control over the entity. This may occur either when the venturer disposes of its interest or when such external restrictions are placed on the jointly controlled entity that the venturer no longer has joint control.[68] The accounting for the loss of joint control is discussed at 3.3.10 and 3.3.11 below.

Under proportionate consolidation, the venturer simply accounts for its share of the jointly controlled entity. It does not, for example, treat the interests of any passive investors (see 2.2 above) as some form of non-controlling or minority interest.

Extract 12.4 below shows a typical accounting policy for the proportionate consolidation of jointly controlled entities.

Extract 12.4: Informa plc (2007)

Note 3. Accounting policies [extract]

Basis of consolidation [extract]

A joint venture is a contractual arrangement whereby the Group and other parties undertake an economic activity that is subject to joint control, which is when the strategic and operating policy decisions require the unanimous consent of the parties sharing control. The arrangements the Group has entered into involve the establishment of a separate entity in which each venturer has an interest. The Group reports its interests using proportionate consolidation and combines its share of the assets, liabilities, income and expense with the equivalent items in the consolidated financial statements on a line by line basis.

3.3.4 Equity method

The equity method is defined as in IAS 28 as a method of accounting whereby an interest in a jointly controlled entity is initially recorded at cost and adjusted thereafter for the post-acquisition change in the venturer's share of net assets of the jointly controlled entity. The profit or loss of the venturer includes the venturer's share of the profit or loss of the jointly controlled entity.[69]

Where a venturer accounts for its interest in jointly controlled entities using equity accounting, it follows the requirements of IAS 28 with regard to the application of the equity method (see Chapter 11 at 3).[70]

IAS 31 states that the use of the equity method is supported by:

(a) those who argue that it is inappropriate to combine controlled items with jointly controlled items; and

(b) those who believe that venturers have significant influence, rather than joint control, in a jointly controlled entity.[71]

Both these arguments are somewhat difficult to understand, at least as expressed here. The objection raised by the argument in (a) would be met by presenting the share of the jointly controlled entity's assets, liabilities, income and expenditure alongside, but not aggregated with, those of the venturer (see 'Presentation as separate line items' at 3.3.3 above).

The argument in (b) above makes little sense at all, since, as a matter of definition in IAS 28 and IAS 31, it is impossible for an entity over which the investor has only 'significant influence' to be a 'jointly controlled entity'. In effect, such an argument implies a belief that the definitions of 'significant influence' and 'joint control' are themselves wrong, and it therefore surprising that the IASB should permit an accounting treatment based on such a premise.

Rather curiously, IAS 31 does not acknowledge the real conceptual objection to proportionate consolidation, which is that in many cases 'joint control' is not the same as having an interest in part of the individual assets and liabilities; rather, it is a share in the venture as a whole. Indeed, those who hold this view often consider that there are circumstances in which it is appropriate to use equity accounting and others where proportionate consolidation may better represent the entity's interests in the underlying venture, so that it is not appropriate to prescribe a single accounting treatment for all joint ventures.

IAS 31 does not recommend the use of the equity method because, in its view, proportionate consolidation better reflects the substance and economic reality of a venturer's interest in a jointly controlled entity, that is to say, control over the venturer's share of the future economic benefits. Nevertheless, IAS 31 permits the use of the equity method, as an alternative treatment, when recognising interests in jointly controlled entities.[72] However, as discussed at 7.1 below, in the exposure draft ED 9 – *Joint Arrangements* – the IASB has taken the view that proportionate consolidation is not an appropriate method of accounting for jointly controlled entities and has proposed to remove this option when accounting for such entities.

As noted in 1.1 above, the choice of accounting treatment presently permitted by IAS 31 in all probability owes as much to 'political' as to technical considerations.

IAS 31 does not explicitly state when an entity should commence applying the equity method for a jointly controlled entity, but it is evident that it should be from the date that the venturer begins to have joint control over the entity. This is consistent with the requirements of IAS 28 (see Chapter 11 at 3.8). The accounting for the acquisition of an interest in a jointly controlled entity is discussed at 3.3.6 and 3.3.7 below.

A venturer that applies the equity method to its interest in a jointly controlled entity discontinues this accounting treatment from the date on which it ceases to have joint control over the entity, unless the entity becomes an associate under IAS 28, in which case the equity method is continued, but pursuant to IAS 28 rather than IAS 31.[73] The accounting for the loss of joint control is discussed at 3.3.10 and 3.3.11 below.

The extract below shows a detailed accounting policy for jointly controlled entities that are accounted for under the equity method.

Extract 12.5: BP p.l.c. (2007)

Notes on financial statements [extract]

1 Significant accounting policies [extract]

Interests in joint ventures

A joint venture is a contractual arrangement whereby two or more parties (venturers) undertake an economic activity that is subject to joint control. Joint control exists only when the strategic financial and operating decisions relating to the activity require the unanimous consent of the venturers. A jointly controlled entity is a joint venture that involves the establishment of a company, partnership or other entity to engage in economic activity that the group jointly controls with its fellow venturers.

The results, assets and liabilities of a jointly controlled entity are incorporated in these financial statements using the equity method of accounting. Under the equity method, the investment in a jointly controlled entity is carried in the balance sheet at cost plus post-acquisition changes in the group's share of net assets of the jointly controlled entity, less distributions received and less any impairment in value of the investment. Loans advanced to jointly controlled entities are also included in the investment on the group balance sheet. The group income statement reflects the group's share of the results after tax of the jointly controlled entity. The group statement of recognized income and expense reflects the group's share of any income and expense recognized by the jointly controlled entity outside profit and loss.

Financial statements of jointly controlled entities are prepared for the same reporting year as the group. Where necessary, adjustments are made to those financial statements to bring the accounting policies used into line with those of the group.

Unrealized gains on transactions between the group and its jointly controlled entities are eliminated to the extent of the group's interest in the jointly controlled entities. Unrealized losses are also eliminated unless the transaction provides evidence of an impairment of the asset transferred.

The group assesses investments in jointly controlled entities for impairment whenever events or changes in circumstances indicate that the carrying value may not be recoverable. If any such indication of impairment exists, the carrying amount of the investment is compared with its recoverable amount, being the higher of its fair value less costs to sell and value in use. Where the carrying amount exceeds the recoverable amount, the investment is written down to its recoverable amount.

The group ceases to use the equity method of accounting on the date from which it no longer has joint control over, or significant influence in the joint venture, or when the interest becomes held for sale.

Certain of the group's activities, particularly in the Exploration and Production segment, are conducted through joint ventures where the venturers have a direct ownership interest in and jointly control the assets of the venture. The income, expenses, assets and liabilities of these jointly controlled assets are included in the consolidated financial statements in proportion to the group's interest.

3.3.5 Jointly controlled entity previously accounted for under IFRS 5

Where an investor has not been proportionately consolidating, or equity accounting for, an interest in a jointly controlled entity on the basis that it is classified as held for sale under IFRS 5 (see 2.3 above), and the investment ceases to be so classified, the investor must apply proportionate consolidation or equity accounting retrospectively as from the date on which the investment was originally classified as held for sale. The financial statements of any prior periods since that classification must be restated.[74]

3.3.6   Accounting for the acquisition of an interest in a jointly controlled entity – prior to application of IAS 27 (as amended in 2008) and IFRS 3 (as revised in 2008)

IFRS 3 (as revised in 2008) is effective for business combinations for which the acquisition date is on or after the beginning of the first annual reporting period beginning on or after 1 July 2009 with early adoption possible as explained in Chapter 9 at 3.1.1. IAS 27 (as amended in 2008) has the same effective date.[75]

For periods prior to adoption of IFRS 3 (as revised in 2008) and IAS 27 (as amended in 2008), IAS 31 does not specifically provide any guidance on the accounting for the acquisition of an interest in a jointly controlled entity. Nevertheless, for venturers applying the equity method under IAS 28 appropriate guidance is given in that standard and this includes an explicit reference to the previous version of the Business Combinations standard, 'IFRS 3 (2007)' – see Chapter 11 at 3.2 and 3.2.2. Similarly, for venturers applying proportionate consolidation, it would be appropriate to apply the principles of IFRS 3 (2007) in measuring the cost of the acquisition of the interest in the jointly controlled entity, allocating that cost to the share of assets acquired and liabilities and contingent liabilities assumed and the recognition of the resulting goodwill/excess of net fair values of the share of those assets and liabilities over cost (see Chapter 9 at 2.4 to 2.7).

It may be that a venturer contributes non-monetary assets in exchange for an equity interest in a jointly controlled entity. Such transactions are discussed at 3.4.3 below.

Given that joint control is established by contractual arrangements, piecemeal acquisitions of jointly controlled entities are relatively uncommon. However they do occasionally occur. Such acquisitions are discussed at 3.3.8 below.

3.3.7   Accounting for the acquisition of an interest in a jointly controlled entity – upon application of IAS 27 (as amended in 2008) and IFRS 3 (as revised in 2008)

IFRS 3 (as revised in 2008) is effective for business combinations for which the acquisition date is on or after the beginning of the first annual reporting period beginning on or after 1 July 2009 with early adoption possible as explained in Chapter 9 at 3.1.1. IAS 27 (as amended in 2008) has the same effective date.[76]

Whereas the accounting for a business combination under IFRS 3 (2007) was a cost-based approach, in contrast, IFRS 3 (as revised in 2008) adopts an approach whereby the various components of a business combination generally are measured at their acquisition date fair values (see Chapter 9 at 1.2.4 B). Under IFRS 3 (2007), any acquisition-related costs were included in arriving at the cost of the business combination, whereas under IFRS 3 (as revised in 2008) such acquisition-related costs are to be expensed (see Chapter 9 at 3.8.3). Also, the requirements for step-acquisitions under IFRS 3 (2007) meant that the cost of such a business combination was based on the value of the consideration given at the date of acquiring each tranche (see Chapter 9 at 2.9), whereas under IFRS 3 (as revised in 2008) any previously held interest is re-measured at its acquisition-date fair value in accounting for the business combination, with any resulting gain or loss being recognised in profit or loss (see Chapter 9 at 3.10).

As before, IAS 31 still does not specifically provide any guidance on the accounting for the acquisition of an interest in a jointly controlled entity. Nevertheless, for venturers applying the equity method under IAS 28 appropriate guidance is given in that standard. However, as indicated in Chapter 11 at 3.2, although IAS 28 still explains that the concepts underlying the procedures used in accounting for the acquisition of a subsidiary are also adopted in accounting for the acquisition of an investment in an associate accounted for under the equity method, a direct reference from IAS 28 to IFRS 3 has actually now been removed.[77] This has raised the issue as to what impact the new concepts inherent within IFRS 3 (as revised in 2008) should have on the accounting for associates particularly since, as indicated in Chapter 11 at 3.1, IAS 28 defines the equity method as 'a method of accounting whereby the investment is initially recorded at cost and adjusted thereafter … .'[78]

The position has been confused even further as a result of the publication of the IASB's annual improvement standard in April 2009 where in the context of an amendment to IAS 39 it is stated that the 'Board noted that paragraph 20 of IAS 28 explains only the methodology used to account for investments in associates. This should not be taken to imply that the principles for business combinations and consolidations can be applied by analogy to accounting for investments in associates and joint ventures.'[79]

One potential effect of IFRS 3 (as revised in 2008) on the equity method of accounting that has recently been considered by the IFRIC is how the initial carrying value of an equity method investment should be determined.

At its meeting in May 2009, and subsequently confirmed at its meeting in July 2009, the IFRIC noted that IFRSs consistently require assets not measured at fair value through profit or loss to be measured at initial recognition at cost. Generally stated, cost includes the purchase price and other costs directly attributable to the acquisition or issuance of the asset such as professional fees for legal services, transfer taxes and other transaction costs. Therefore, the cost of an investment in an associate at initial recognition determined in accordance with paragraph 11 of IAS 28 comprises its purchase price and any directly attributable expenditures necessary to obtain it. The IFRIC decided not to add this issue to its agenda, having concluded that the agenda criteria were not met mainly because, given the guidance in IFRSs, it did not expect divergent interpretations in practice.[80]

This would appear to clarify that any acquisition-related costs should not be expensed, but should be included as part of the cost of the associate, and there is no reason that the same should not apply to the acquisition of a jointly controlled entity. The implications for piecemeal acquisitions are discussed further at 3.3.9 below.

For venturers applying proportionate consolidation, the decision by the IFRIC in the context of the equity method is not directly relevant and it is unclear whether the comment made by the IASB about whether the 'principles for business combinations and consolidations can be applied by analogy to accounting for investments in associates and joint ventures' relates only to accounting under the equity method or also to the accounting for joint ventures under proportionate consolidation. As noted at 1.4 above, in May 2009, the IASB has indicated that it will address the interaction between the revised versions of IFRS 3 and IAS 27, and IAS 28 and IAS 31, as part of its project on joint ventures.[81] Given that the project is proposing to eliminate the use of proportionate consolidation, this particular issue for venturers applying proportionate consolidation is likely to be only a short-term one, and as a result it may be that the IASB does not consider the issue. In the meantime, we believe that it would be more appropriate to apply the 'fair value' principles in IFRS 3 (as revised in 2008) – see Chapter 9 at 3, in accounting for the acquisition of a jointly controlled entity by a venturer applying proportionate consolidation. This is because the description of proportionate consolidation in IAS 31 does not refer to 'cost' as is done in IAS 28, and it involves the share of assets, liabilities, income and expenses being reflected in the venturer's financial statements, and any goodwill arising on the acquisition of the jointly controlled entity is included as goodwill. This accounting is similar to where an entity acquires control over a subsidiary or a business that is accounted for under IFRS 3 (as revised in 2008). Therefore in accounting for the acquisition of the jointly controlled entity that is not a piecemeal acquisition (see 3.3.9 below), in applying these 'fair value' principles, the goodwill or gain on bargain purchase arising will be measured by comparing:

(a)   the consideration transferred, including any contingent consideration, generally measured at acquisition-date fair value; and

(b)   the share of the acquisition-date fair values (or other amounts recognised in accordance with the requirements of IFRS 3 (as revised in 2008) of the identified assets acquired of any previously held interest and the liabilities assumed.

Under this fair-value approach, any acquisition-related costs are expensed. However, a cost-based approach whereby the cost of the acquisition of the jointly controlled entity comprises its purchase price and any directly attributable expenditures necessary to obtain it would be acceptable in the light of the comments made by the IFRIC and the IASB.

It may be that a venturer contributes non-monetary assets in exchange for an equity interest in a jointly controlled entity. Such transactions are discussed at 3.4.3 below.

Given that joint control is established by contractual arrangements, piecemeal acquisitions of jointly controlled entities are relatively uncommon. However they do occasionally occur. Such acquisitions are discussed at 3.3.9 below.

A   *Retained interest in a jointly controlled entity following loss of control in an entity*

One situation where a cost-based approach would not be acceptable will be where an entity loses control of an entity, but retains an interest that is now to be accounted for as a jointly controlled entity. In such situations, the retained interest must be remeasured at its fair value,[82] and this fair value becomes the cost on initial recognition of the jointly controlled entity.[83] This applies irrespective of whether the jointly controlled entity is proportionately consolidated or accounted for under the equity method.

Example 12.5:   *Accounting for retained interest in a jointly controlled entity following loss of control in an entity*

Entity A owns 100% of the shares of Entity B. The interest was originally purchased for £500,000 and £40,000 of directly attributable costs relating to the acquisition were incurred. On 30 June 2010, Entity A sells 50% of the shares to Entity C for £1,100,000. As a result of the sale, Entity A loses control over Entity B, but enters into a contractual arrangement with Entity C, such that it has joint control over Entity B.

At the date of disposal, the carrying amount of the net assets of Entity B in Entity A's consolidated financial statements is £1,200,000 and there is also goodwill of £200,000 relating to the acquisition of Entity B. The fair value of the identifiable assets and liabilities of Entity B is £1,600,000. The fair value of Entity A's retained interest of 50% of the shares of Entity B is £1,100,000.

Upon Entity A's sale of 50% of the shares of Entity B, it deconsolidates Entity B and accounts for its investment in Entity B as a jointly controlled entity using the equity method of accounting.

Entity A's initial carrying amount of the jointly controlled entity has to be based on the fair value of the retained interest, i.e. £1,100,000. It is not based on 50% of the original cost of £540,000 (purchase price plus directly attributable costs) as might be suggested by the IFRIC statement, nor is it based on 50% of the carrying amount of the net assets and goodwill totalling £1,400,000 as would have generally been the treatment prior to changes made to IAS 27 and IFRS 3 as a result of phase II of the Business Combinations project.

Although it is clear that the initial carrying amount of the associate is the fair value of the retained interest, i.e. £1,100,000, does this mean that Entity A in applying the equity method under IAS 28 must:

(a) remeasure the underlying assets and liabilities in Entity B at their fair values at the date Entity B becomes a jointly controlled entity i.e. effectively a new purchase price allocation is performed; and

(b) reassess the classification and designation of assets and liabilities, e.g. the classification of financial instruments, embedded derivatives and hedge accounting, as required by IFRS 3 (revised 2008) – see Chapter 9 at 3.6.4?

In our view, as Entity A effectively accounts for the investment in Entity B as if it had acquired the retained investment at fair value as at the date control is lost, the answer to question (a) is 'yes'. Accordingly, in order to apply the equity method from the date control is lost, Entity A must remeasure *all* of the identifiable assets and liabilities underlying the investment at their fair values (or other measurement basis required by IFRS 3 (revised 2008) at that date). As far as question (b) is concerned, we also believe that Entity A should reassess the classification or designation of assets and liabilities in accordance with paragraph 15 of IFRS 3 (revised 2008), based on the circumstances that exist at that date. However, in doing so, there is no need to reassess whether an embedded derivative should be separated from a host contract. In the annual improvement standard issued in April 2009, the IASB, in clarifying the scope of IFRIC 9 in relation to certain business combinations, noted in the context of an acquisition of an investment in an associate that 'reassessment of embedded derivatives in contracts held by an associate is not required by IFRIC 9 in any event. The investment in the associate is the asset the investor controls and recognises, not the underlying assets and liabilities of the associate.'[84] (Although this refers to an associate, we believe the same should apply to a jointly controlled entity that is accounted for under the equity method). Despite this limited exception re embedded derivatives, we do not believe that it should be applied by analogy to other reassessments,

Paragraphs 20 and 23 of IAS 28 indicate that on initial recognition of an investment in an associate the concepts underlying the procedures used in accounting for the acquisition of a subsidiary are also adopted in accounting for the acquisition of an investment in an associate, and that fair values are applied to measure all of the identifiable assets and liabilities in calculating any goodwill or bargain purchase that exists. The same procedures apply when equity accounting for a jointly controlled entity.

Accordingly, based on the fair value of the identifiable assets and liabilities of Entity B of £1,600,000, Entity A's initial carrying amount of £1,100,000 will include goodwill of £300,000, being £1,100,000 – £800,000 (50% of £1,600,000).

If Entity A were to account for its investment in Entity B using proportionate consolidation, the answers to questions (a) and (b) above would generally be the same; the only difference would be that we do not consider that the IFRIC 9 exception re embedded derivatives should apply. The principal difference of Entity A uses proportionate consolidation, however, will be that the goodwill and various assets and liabilities would be combined line by line with similar items or reported as separate line items.

3.3.8   Piecemeal acquisition of a jointly controlled entity – prior to application of IAS 27 (as amended in 2008) and IFRS 3 (as revised in 2008)

Given that joint control is established by contractual arrangements, piecemeal acquisitions of jointly controlled entities are relatively uncommon. However they do occasionally occur.

IFRS 3 (as revised in 2008) is effective for business combinations for which the acquisition date is on or after the beginning of the first annual reporting period beginning on or after 1 July 2009 with early adoption possible as explained in Chapter 9 at 3.1.1. For periods before adoption of this revised standard IFRS 3 (2007) and the following guidance is applicable.

A   Step acquisition from an associate to a jointly controlled entity

It is not clear under IFRS how an investor should account for a situation in which it obtains joint control over an associate because of an additional investment and new contractual arrangements. Example 12.6 below describes two methods of accounting for such transactions.

Example 12.6:   Associate becoming a joint venture after an increase in ownership

In 2006, Entity A acquired a 20% interest in Entity B. Entity A is able to exercise significant influence and accounts for its investment under the equity method. In 2009, A acquired an additional 30% interest in B, thereby increasing its total interest in B to 50%. At the time of the acquisition, A enters into a joint venture agreement that gives it joint control over B. Entity A accounts for its 50% interest in B using proportionate consolidation under IAS 31.

This raises the question whether A, in applying proportionate consolidation for the first time to its investment in B, should recognise its existing 20% interest in the net assets of B at (1) the amounts that it used in applying the equity method or (2) their fair value at the date that A obtained joint control. In our view the former approach is always acceptable but the latter, re-measurement of the existing 20% interest, is only appropriate when A applies proportionate consolidation in accounting for its interests in jointly controlled entities and there is:

- a change in the relationship between A and B, that is, from one in which A can exercise significant influence to one in which A has joint control; and
- a simultaneous change in the method of accounting for the investment from the equity method to proportionate consolidation.

Where these conditions apply, we consider it acceptable to view this as analogous to the initial application of the consolidation method so that the revaluation provisions of paragraph 59 of IFRS 3 (2007) could be applied. However, if Entity A's policy is to apply the equity method in accounting for its interests in joint ventures, the existing interest should not be re-measured. In addition, it would not be appropriate for the investor to change its policy from the equity method to proportionate consolidation to facilitate the re-measurement of its existing interest to fair value.

B *Step increase in an existing jointly controlled entity*

Accounting for an increase of an interest in a jointly controlled entity that remains a jointly controlled entity after that increase is not specifically addressed by IAS 31. The issues arising are similar to those when there is a step increase in an existing associate, therefore the discussion and guidance in Chapter 11 at 3.2.4 A are also relevant to the accounting for a step increase in an existing jointly controlled entity.

If the increase results from the venturer contributing non-monetary assets in exchange for an additional equity interest in a jointly controlled entity, the requirements of SIC-13 will be relevant (see 3.4.3 below).

The accounting for an increase in a jointly controlled entity that becomes a subsidiary is discussed in Chapter 9 at 2.9.

C *Financial instrument becoming a jointly controlled entity*

A step acquisition also arises when an entity gains joint control over an existing investment upon acquisition of a further interest or due to a change in circumstances. IAS 31 is unclear on how an investor should account for an existing investment, which is accounted for under IAS 39, that subsequently becomes a jointly controlled entity that should be accounted for under the equity method or proportionate consolidation. The issues arising are similar to those when a financial instrument becomes an associate, therefore the discussion and guidance in Chapter 11 at 3.2.4 B are also relevant to the accounting for a financial instrument becoming a jointly controlled entity.

3.3.9 Piecemeal acquisition of a jointly controlled entity – upon application of IAS 27 (as amended in 2008) and IFRS 3 (as revised in 2008)

IFRS 3 (as revised in 2008) is effective for business combinations for which the acquisition date is on or after the beginning of the first annual reporting period beginning on or after 1 July 2009 with early adoption possible as explained in Chapter 9 at 3.1.1. Upon this revision of IFRS 3 no additional guidance was introduced relating to piecemeal acquisitions of joint ventures. For venturers applying the equity method, as discussed in Chapter 11 at 3.2.5, there is similarly no guidance introduced in relation to piecemeal acquisitions of associates.

Indeed, as indicated at 3.3.7 above, although IAS 28 still explains that the concepts underlying the procedures used in accounting for the acquisition of a subsidiary are also adopted in accounting for the acquisition of an investment in an associate, a direct reference from IAS 28 to IFRS 3 has actually now been removed.[85] This has raised the issue as to what impact the new concepts inherent within IFRS 3 (as revised in 2008) should have on the accounting for associates.

As discussed at 3.3.7 above, one potential effect of IFRS 3 (as revised in 2008) on the equity method of accounting that has recently been considered by the IFRIC is how the initial carrying value of an equity method investment should be determined. At its meeting in May 2009, and subsequently confirmed at its meeting in July 2009, the IFRIC noted that the cost of an investment in an associate at initial recognition determined in accordance with paragraph 11 of IAS 28 comprises its purchase price and any directly attributable expenditures necessary to obtain it. The IFRIC decided not to add this issue to its agenda, having concluded that the agenda criteria were not met mainly because, given the guidance in IFRSs, it did not expect divergent interpretations in practice.[86]

Although the implications for the piecemeal acquisition of an associate are not explicitly addressed, it would appear that, as the IFRIC considers that the initial recognition of the associate accounted for under the equity method is to be based on its cost, the accounting should reflect a cost-based approach. This would equally be relevant for venturers applying the equity method for jointly controlled entities.

For venturers applying proportionate consolidation, the decision by the IFRIC in the context of the equity method is not directly relevant and it is unclear whether the comment made by the IASB about whether the 'principles for business combinations and consolidations can be applied by analogy to accounting for investments in associates and joint ventures' (see 3.3.7 above) relates only to accounting under the equity method or also to the accounting for joint ventures under proportionate consolidation. As noted at 1.4 above, in May 2009, the IASB has indicated that it will address the interaction between the revised versions of IFRS 3 and IAS 27, and IAS 28 and IAS 31, as part of its project on joint ventures.[87] Given that the project is proposing to eliminate the use of proportionate consolidation, this particular issue for venturers applying proportionate consolidation is likely to be only a short-term one, and as a result it may be that the IASB does not consider the issue. As indicated at 3.3.7 above, in the meantime, we believe that it would be more appropriate to apply the 'fair value' principles in IFRS 3 (as revised in 2008) – see Chapter 9 at 3, in accounting for the acquisition of a jointly controlled entity by a venturer applying proportionate consolidation. Under this fair-value approach, in accounting for a piecemeal acquisition of an entity that becomes a jointly controlled entity, the computation of goodwill or gain on bargain purchase outlined at 3.3.7 above also takes into account the acquisition-date fair value of the venturer's previously held interest in the entity. The remeasurement of that previously held interest results in a gain or loss being recognised in profit or loss. As before, under this fair-value approach, any acquisition-related costs are expensed. However, a cost-based approach whereby the cost of the acquisition of the jointly controlled entity comprises its purchase price and any directly attributable expenditures necessary to obtain it would be acceptable in the light of the comments made by the IFRIC and the IASB. Under such a cost-based approach, no gain or loss would be recognised in profit or loss on the piecemeal acquisition.

A   Step acquisition from an associate to a jointly controlled entity

Upon loss of significant influence IAS 28 now requires that there is a remeasurement of the retained interest in the investment to fair value and that this remeasurement is recognised in profit or loss (see Chapter 11 at 3.8.2).[88] In our view, this guidance is relevant to when significant influence is replaced by joint control and it is applicable regardless of whether the jointly controlled entity is subsequently accounted for under the equity method or by proportionate consolidation. In addition any amount in other comprehensive income relating to the previous associate would be reclassified to profit or loss.[89]

The accounting is also consistent with what is required by IFRS 3 (as revised in 2008) when an associate becomes a subsidiary where remeasurement of previously held interests in equity investments, with recognition of any gain or loss in profit or loss, is required at the time the investor acquires control of the investee.[90] The Basis of Conclusions to IFRS 3 (as revised in 2008) explains that there is a significant change in the nature of and economic circumstances surrounding that investment and it is this that warrants a change in the classification and measurement of that investment.[91]

Revaluation to fair value through profit or loss is also consistent with the accounting required upon loss of joint control (see 3.3.11 below). This remeasurement is justified on the basis that loss of control, loss of joint control and loss of significant influence are economically similar events that should therefore be accounted for similarly.[92] It seems logical that the reverse is also true; i.e. that the attainment of control, attainment of joint control and attainment of significant influence are also economically similar events that should be accounted for similarly. However ED 9 – *Joint Arrangements* – proposes that there is not a revaluation to fair value when an entity loses joint control but retains significant influence and continues to use the equity method[93] and therefore this justification to revalue in the reverse situation (i.e. when significant influence is replaced by joint control) will not exist if this exposure draft is finalised as it is presently drafted. In light of these proposals within the exposure draft, and the fact that the IASB has indicated that it will address the interaction between the revised versions of IFRS 3 and IAS 27, and IAS 28 and IAS 31, as part of its project on joint ventures, the IASB may reconsider this issue. In the meantime, and given the existing standards, we believe revaluation through profit or loss is the appropriate accounting when there is a step acquisition from an associate to a jointly controlled entity.

B   Step increase in an existing jointly controlled entity

Accounting for an increase of an interest in a jointly controlled entity that remains a jointly controlled entity after that increase is not specifically addressed by IAS 31. The issues arising are similar to those when there is a step increase in an existing associate. For venturers applying the equity method, the discussion and guidance in Chapter 11 at 3.2.5 A are also relevant to the accounting for a step increase in an existing jointly controlled entity.

For venturers applying proportionate consolidation, although IFRS 3 (as revised in 2008) requires revaluation of previously held interests in jointly controlled entities (with recognition of any gain or loss in profit or loss) when the investor acquires control of the investee,[94] at this point there is a significant change in the nature of and economic circumstances surrounding that investment and it is this that warrants a change in the classification and measurement of that investment.[95] In contrast a step increase in an existing jointly controlled entity is unlikely to significantly change the nature and economic circumstances of the investment, and hence there is little justification for any such remeasurement.

Restating the investment to fair value through profit or loss every time there is a change in the investor's equity interest in a jointly controlled entity would be open to abuse and would in effect allow any investor to fair value interests in jointly controlled entities rather than limit this ability to venture capital organisations, mutual funds, unit trusts and similar entities that are specifically allowed this option under the scoping requirements of IAS 31.[96] We do not believe this can have been the intention of the IASB.

As discussed at 3.3.9 above, for venturers applying proportionate consolidation in respect of an acquisition of a jointly controlled entity, we believe that it would be more appropriate to apply the 'fair value' principles in IFRS 3 (as revised in 2008) – see Chapter 9 at 3, in accounting for the acquisition of a jointly controlled entity by a venturer applying proportionate consolidation. Under this fair-value approach, the computation of the goodwill or gain on bargain purchase will be that outlined at 3.3.7. As indicated above, as there is no change in status of the jointly controlled entity, the previously held interest is not remeasured at its acquisition-date fair value. As before, under this fair-value approach, any acquisition-related costs are expensed. However, a cost-based approach whereby the cost of the acquisition of the jointly controlled entity comprises its purchase price and any directly attributable expenditures necessary to obtain it would be acceptable in the light of the comments made by the IFRIC and the IASB. Whichever approach is applied, the venturer should apply it in determining the amount of goodwill and the additional interest in the fair value of the assets and liabilities of the jointly controlled entity at the date of the increase in the jointly controlled entity. As noted at 1.4 above, in May 2009, the IASB has indicated that it will address the interaction between the revised versions of IFRS 3 and IAS 27, and IAS 28 and IAS 31, as part of its project on joint ventures.[97] Given that the project is proposing to eliminate the use of proportionate consolidation, this particular issue for venturers applying proportionate consolidation is likely to be only a short-term one, and as a result it may be that the IASB does not consider the issue.

If the increase results from the venturer contributing non-monetary assets in exchange for an additional equity interest in a jointly controlled entity, the requirements of SIC-13 will be relevant (see 3.4.3 below).

The accounting for an increase in a jointly controlled entity that becomes a subsidiary is discussed in Chapter 9 at 3.10.

C   *Financial instrument becoming a jointly controlled entity*

A step acquisition also arises when an entity gains joint control over an existing investment upon acquisition of a further interest or due to a change in circumstances. IAS 31 is unclear on how an investor should account for an existing investment, which is accounted for under IAS 39, that subsequently becomes a jointly controlled entity that should be accounted for under the equity method or proportionate consolidation. The issues arising are similar to those when a financial instrument becomes an associate. For venturers applying the equity method, the discussion and guidance in Chapter 11 at 3.2.5 B are also relevant to the accounting for a financial instrument becoming a jointly controlled entity.

As discussed at 3.3.9 above, for venturers applying proportionate consolidation in respect of an acquisition of a jointly controlled entity, we believe that it would be more appropriate to apply the 'fair value' principles in IFRS 3 (as revised in 2008) –

see Chapter 9 at 3, in accounting for the acquisition of a jointly controlled entity by a venturer applying proportionate consolidation. However, a cost-based approach whereby the cost of the acquisition of the jointly controlled entity comprises its purchase price and any directly attributable expenditures necessary to obtain it would be acceptable in the light of the comments made by the IFRIC and the IASB. Where a venturer applying proportionate consolidation uses a cost-based approach, the discussion and guidance in Chapter 11 at 3.2.5 B will also be relevant. However, where a venturer applies the 'fair value' principles in IFRS 3 (as revised in 2008) in respect of an acquisition of a jointly controlled entity, it would seem appropriate that the approach set out in Example 11.8 in Chapter 11 at 3.2.5 B should be applied for the reasons set out therein. The decision by the IFRIC in the context of the equity method is not directly relevant for an entity not using a cost-based approach. As noted at 1.4 above, in May 2009, the IASB has indicated that it will address the interaction between the revised versions of IFRS 3 and IAS 27, and IAS 28 and IAS 31, as part of its project on joint ventures.[98] Given that the project is proposing to eliminate the use of proportionate consolidation, this particular issue for venturers applying proportionate consolidation is likely to be only a short-term one, and as a result it may be that the IASB does not consider the issue.

3.3.10 Jointly controlled entity ceasing to be jointly controlled entity – prior to application of IAS 27 (as amended in 2008) and IFRS 3 (as revised in 2008)

IFRS 3 (as revised in 2008) is effective for business combinations for which the acquisition date is on or after the beginning of the first annual reporting period beginning on or after 1 July 2009 with early adoption possible as explained in Chapter 9 at 3.1.1. IAS 27 (as amended in 2008) has the same effective date.[99] Since amendments have been made to IAS 28 and IAS 31 alongside, and effective from the same date of, these revised standards, entities will need to ensure that they apply the appropriate rules for loss of joint control.

If a jointly controlled entity becomes a subsidiary, it should be accounted for, from the date that it does so, in accordance with IAS 27 (see Chapter 6). If a jointly controlled entity becomes an associate, it should be accounted for, from the date that it does so, in accordance with IAS 28 (see Chapter 11).[100]

For periods prior to adoption of IFRS 3 (as revised in 2008) and IAS 27 (as amended in 2008), IAS 31 does not specifically provide any guidance on the treatment of an interest in a jointly controlled entity that ceases to be so, and becomes neither a subsidiary nor an associate, but an investment. However, the clear inference is that:

- a former jointly controlled entity that has been accounted for using proportionate consolidation should be accounted for under the requirements of IAS 27 (2007) in respect of former subsidiaries that become investments (see Chapter 7 at 3); and
- a former jointly controlled entity that has been accounted for using equity accounting should be accounted for under the requirements of IAS 28 in respect of former associates that become investments (see Chapter 11 at 3.8.1).

In effect, the former jointly controlled entity will ultimately be accounted for in accordance with IAS 39. The measurement rules in IAS 39 are complex and are discussed in detail in Chapter 32. In brief, however, they will entail the former jointly controlled entity being recorded initially at 'fair value',[101] but its cost is deemed to be its carrying amount on the date that it ceases to be a jointly controlled entity.[102] Therefore, if the investment is subsequently accounted for as an 'available-for-sale' financial asset the difference between its cost and fair value should be accounted for within other comprehensive income. If the investment is subsequently accounted for as a 'financial asset at fair value through profit or loss' then the difference is recognised in net profit for the period. In either case, the investment will subsequently be measured at fair value – what differs is whether the gains and losses arising on revaluation are accounted for in the profit or loss or in other comprehensive income.

A   Cumulative exchange differences on jointly controlled entities

IAS 27 (2007) (see Chapter 7 at 3.3.4) specifically reinforces the requirement of IAS 21 – *The Effects of Foreign Exchange Rates* (see Chapter 13 at 2.7.3) that, when an investment in a foreign operation is disposed of, the gain or loss on disposal should include the 'recycling' of the cumulative exchange gains and losses that have, in accordance with IAS 21, been recognised in other comprehensive income in respect of that operation. Whilst there is no such explicit reinforcement of IAS 21 in the version of IAS 31 that is applicable before the adoption of IAS 27 (as amended in 2008) and IFRS 3 (as revised in 2008), it seems clear that the same principle should apply on disposal of a jointly controlled entity.

IAS 21 clarifies that disposal of a foreign operation may occur through sale, liquidation, repayment of share capital or abandonment. When a partial disposal occurs only the proportionate share of the related accumulated exchange difference is included in profit or loss. IAS 21 further clarifies that a write-down of a foreign operation does not constitute a partial disposal, and accordingly no part of the deferred foreign exchange gain or loss is recognised in profit or loss at the time of the such a write-down,[103] unless of course the write-down is consequent upon an event of 'disposal' as just described. The amendments to IFRS 1 and IAS 27 published in May 2008 amended IAS 21 to clarify that a dividend made by a foreign operation and accounted for as revenue by its parent, investor or venturer in its separate financial statements (see Chapter 8 at 2.3.1) should not be treated as a disposal or partial disposal of a net investment.[104] This contrasts to the previous position where IAS 21 explained that the payment of a dividend was part of a disposal only when it constituted a return of the investment, e.g. when the dividend was paid out of pre-acquisition profits.[105]

This begs the further question as to the appropriate treatment of any cumulative exchange gains and losses on a former jointly controlled entity which becomes subject to IAS 39, as described above. The issues here are very similar to those arising in respect of a former subsidiary which becomes subject to IAS 39, which are discussed in Chapter 7 at 3.3.1.

B   *Other cumulative gains and losses previously recognised in other
          comprehensive income*

Like IAS 27 (2007), the version of IAS 31 that is effective prior to adoption of IAS 27
(as amended in 2008) and IFRS 3 (as revised in 2008) does not specifically address
the accounting treatment, on disposal of a jointly controlled entity, of the venturer's
share of other cumulative gains and losses previously accounted for in other
comprehensive income relating to assets and liabilities of the disposed jointly
controlled entity. Such cumulative gains and losses, which would be recycled in
profit or loss if those assets and liabilities had been disposed of separately by the
jointly controlled entity, could include:

*   accumulated hedging gains and losses accounted for under IAS 39 (see
    Chapter 33), and

*   any other amounts previously recognised in other comprehensive income that
    would have been recognised in profit or loss if the jointly controlled entity had
    directly disposed of the assets to which they relate, such as gains or losses on
    available-for-sale financial assets accounted for under IAS 39 (see Chapter 32
    at 3.4).

IAS 39 does not specifically address this issue either. However, it would appear that
recycling is appropriate, since the disposal of a jointly controlled entity does give rise
to the derecognition of the venturer's share of the separate assets and liabilities of
that jointly controlled entity just as if they had been disposed of separately.

3.3.11 Jointly controlled entity ceasing to be jointly controlled entity – upon application of IAS 27 (as amended in 2008) and IFRS 3 (as revised in 2008)

IFRS 3 (as revised in 2008) is effective for business combinations for which the
acquisition date is on or after the beginning of the first annual reporting period
beginning on or after 1 July 2009 with early adoption possible as explained in
Chapter 9 at 3.1.1. IAS 27 (as amended in 2008) has the same effective date.[106]

Phase II of the IASB's Business Combinations project, and the resulting revisions
made to IAS 27 and IFRS 3, led to a number of changes in accounting for a loss of
joint control. Paragraph 45 of IAS 31 was amended to read as follows:

> 'When an investor ceases to have joint control over an entity, it shall account
> for any remaining investment in accordance with IAS 39 from that date,
> provided that the former jointly controlled entity does not become a subsidiary
> or associate. From the date when a jointly controlled entity becomes a
> subsidiary of an investor, the investor shall account for its interest in
> accordance with IAS 27 and IFRS 3 – *Business Combinations* (as revised in 2008).
> From the date when a jointly controlled entity becomes an associate of an
> investor, the investor shall account for its interest in accordance with IAS 28.
> On the loss of joint control, the investor shall measure at fair value any
> investment the investor retains in the former jointly controlled entity. The
> investor shall recognise in profit or loss any difference between:

     (a)   the fair value of any retained investment and any proceeds from disposing of the part interest in the jointly controlled entity; and

     (b)   the carrying amount of the investment at the date when joint control is lost.'

Therefore upon loss of joint control there is a remeasurement to fair value of any remaining interest that is taken to profit or loss regardless of the prospective accounting for this interest, be it under IAS 39 as a financial instrument, under IAS 27 as a subsidiary or under IAS 28 as an associate.

When a jointly controlled entity becomes a subsidiary this remeasurement through profit and loss is clearly required under the guidance on step acquisitions in IFRS 3 (as revised in 2008) – see Chapter 9 at 3.10.[107]

When a jointly controlled entity becomes an associate the requirement to remeasure through profit or loss is supported by the Basis of Conclusions to IAS 31 which explains that 'the loss of control of an investee and the loss of joint control of an investee are economically similar events; thus they should be accounted for similarly.'[108] As discussed in Chapter 7 at 3.2.1 this remeasurement is required by IAS 27 (as amended in 2008) upon loss of control of an investee. This remeasurement through profit or loss could be argued to be a little inconsistent with the cost methodology upon acquisition of an associate as described within IAS 28.[109] Nevertheless, it is clear from IAS 27 (as amended in 2008) that where an associate is 'acquired' upon loss of control of an entity, that the fair value of the retained interest becomes the cost for applying the equity method.[110] As the accounting for the loss of joint control should be accounted for similarly to the loss of control of an investee, the same should apply where an associate is 'acquired' upon loss of joint control of an entity. The accounting for a retained interest in an associate following loss of control or joint control in an entity is discussed further in Chapter 11 at 3.2.3 A. This remeasurement to fair value is inconsistent with proposals within ED 9 – *Joint Arrangements* (see 7.1 below), which is intended to replace IAS 31, which do not require any such remeasurement to fair value of a retained interest in an associate upon loss of joint control.[111]

Furthermore, IAS 31 has been amended to require that if an investor loses joint control of an entity, all amounts recognised in other comprehensive income and accumulated as a separate component of equity in relation to that entity should be recognised by the investor on the same basis that would be required if the jointly controlled entity had directly disposed of the related assets or liabilities.[112] Similarly, IAS 21 has been amended to require that upon loss of joint control the cumulative amount of the exchange differences deferred in the separate component of equity relating to that jointly controlled entity be recognised in profit or loss.[113] In practice this means that a gain or loss should be recognised in profit or loss upon loss of joint control, even if a former jointly controlled entity is subsequently accounted for as an available-for-sale financial asset.

It should be noted that if joint control is lost but an interest is retained this reclassification adjustment from equity to profit or loss is for the full amount that is in other comprehensive income and not just a proportionate amount based upon the interest disposed of. The Basis of Conclusions to the amended version of IAS 21 explains that the loss of joint control is a significant economic event that warrants accounting for the transaction as a disposal under IAS 21,[114] and hence the transfer of the full exchange difference rather than just the proportionate share that would be required if this was accounted for as a partial disposal under IAS 21.

However when an investor's interest in a jointly controlled entity is reduced (but the investee remains a jointly controlled entity), then the investor should 'reclassify to profit or loss only a proportionate amount of the gain or loss previously recognised in other comprehensive income'[115] and 'reclassify to profit or loss only the proportionate share of the cumulative amount of the exchange differences recognised in other comprehensive income'.[116] That means that the investor should recognise in profit or loss a proportion of:

- foreign exchange differences recognised in other comprehensive income under IAS 21,

- accumulated hedging gains and losses recognised in other comprehensive income under IAS 39 (see Chapter 33), and

- any other amounts previously recognised in other comprehensive income that would have been recognised in profit or loss if the jointly controlled entity had directly disposed of the assets to which they relate, such as gains or losses on available-for-sale financial assets accounted for under IAS 39 (see Chapter 32 at 3.4),

in each case proportionate to the interest disposed of.

3.4 Transactions between a venturer and a joint venture

3.4.1 Background

It is common for venturers to transact with the joint venture, in particular on the formation of the venture. Typical transactions include:

- The venturers contribute cash to the venture in proportion to their agreed relative shares. The venture then uses some or all of the cash to acquire assets from the venturers for use in the venture;

- The venturers contribute other assets (or a mixture of cash and other assets) to the joint venture with fair values, as agreed between the venturers, in proportion to the venturers' agreed relative shares in the venture;

- The venturers contribute other assets to the joint venture with fair values, as agreed between the venturers, not in proportion to the venturers' agreed relative shares. Cash 'equalisation' payments are then made between the venturers so that the overall financial position of the venturer does correspond to their agreed relative shares in the venture.

A further complication is that some of these assets that are the subject of such transactions may be intangible assets not recognised under IFRS in the financial statements of the contributing venturers (e.g. internally generated brands and know-how).

IAS 31, together with SIC-13, provides broad overall principles as to the treatment of such transactions, but no specific indication of the accounting entries required to give effect to those principles. Moreover, SIC-13 applies strictly only to transactions involving the transfer of assets to jointly controlled entities (and not to other types of joint venture).

3.4.2   IAS 31 requirements

When a venturer contributes or sells assets to a joint venture, IAS 31 requires that the recognition of any gain or loss should reflect the substance of the transaction. While the assets are retained by the joint venture, and provided that the venturer has transferred the significant risks and rewards of ownership, the venturer should recognise only that portion of the gain or loss which is attributable to the interests of the other venturers. However, the venturer should recognise the full amount of any loss when the contribution or sale provides evidence of a reduction in the net realisable value of current assets or an impairment loss. Where non-monetary assets are contributed to a jointly controlled entity, the additional guidance in SIC-13 must also be considered (see 3.4.3 below).[117]

When a venturer purchases assets from a joint venture, the venturer must not recognise its share of the profits of the joint venture from the transaction until it resells the assets to an unrelated third party. A venturer recognises its share of the losses resulting from these transactions in the same way as profits, except that (as in the case of sales to the joint venture) losses should be recognised immediately when they represent a reduction in the net realisable value of current assets or an impairment loss.[118]

The venturer should assess whether a transaction between itself and a joint venture provides evidence of impairment of any asset transferred in accordance with IAS 36 which is discussed in Chapter 18 at 3.[119]

The effect of these requirements is illustrated in Examples 12.7 to 12.10 below.

Example 12.7:   Sale of asset from venturer to joint venture at a profit

Two entities A and B establish a joint venture involving the creation of a jointly controlled entity C in which A and B each hold 50%. A and B each contribute €5 million in cash to the joint venture in exchange for equity shares. C then uses €8 million of its €10 million cash to acquire from A a property recorded in the financial statements of A at €6 million. It is agreed that €8 million is the fair market value of the property. How should A account for these transactions?

The required accounting entry if A accounts for its interest in C using proportionate consolidation is:

	€m	€m
Cash (1)	3	
Share of cash of C (2)	1	
Share of property of C (3)	3	
Property (4)		6
Gain on sale (5)		1

(1)   €8 million received from C less €5 million contributed to C.

(2)   50% of C's cash of €2 million [€10 million received from A and B less €8 million paid to A]

(3)   50% of €8 million (carrying value in books of C), less €1 million (share of profit eliminated – see (5) below). In effect, this treatment represents that A still holds 50% of the property at its original carrying value to A (50% of €6 million = €3 million).

(4)   Derecognition of A's original property.

(5)   Gain on sale of property €2 million (€8 million received from C less €6 million carrying value = €2 million), less 50% eliminated (so as to reflect only profit attributable to interest of other venturer B) = €1 million.

If A accounted for C using equity accounting the accounting would be identical, except that it would show simply 'Investment in C' of €4 million rather than the €1 million share of C's cash and €3 million share of C's property.

Example 12.8:   Sale of asset from venturer to joint venture at a loss

Two entities A and B establish a joint venture involving the creation of a jointly controlled entity C in which A and B each hold 50%. A and B each contribute €5 million in cash to the joint venture in exchange for equity shares. C then uses €8 million of its €10 million cash to acquire from A a property recorded in the financial statements of A at €10 million. €8 million is agreed to be the fair market value of the property. How should A account for these transactions?

The required accounting entry if A accounts for its interest in C using proportionate consolidation is:

	€m	€m
Cash (1)	3	
Share of cash of C (2)	1	
Share of property of C (3)	4	
Loss on sale (4)	2	
Property (5)		10

(1)   €8 million received from C less €5 million contributed to C.

(2)   50% of C's cash €2 million (€10 million from A and B minus €8 million to A)

(3)   50% of €8 million (carrying value in books of C), not adjusted since the transaction indicated an impairment of A's asset.

(4)   Loss on sale of property €2 million (€8 million received from C less €10 million carrying value = €2 million) not adjusted since the transaction indicated an impairment of the property. In effect, it is the result that would have been obtained if A had recognised an impairment charge immediately prior to the sale and then recognised no gain or loss on the sale.

(5)   Derecognition of A's original property.

If A accounted for C using equity accounting the accounting would be identical, except that it would show simply 'Investment in C' of €5 million rather than the €1 million share of C's cash and €4 million share of C's property.

Example 12.9:   Sale of asset from joint venture to venturer at a profit

Two entities A and B establish a joint venture involving the creation of a jointly controlled entity C in which A and B each hold 50%. A and B each contribute €5 million in cash to the joint venture in exchange for equity shares. C then uses €8 million of its €10 million cash to acquire a property from an independent third party D. The property is later sold to A for €12 million, which is agreed to be its market value. How should A account for these transactions?

The required accounting entry if A accounts for its interest in C using proportionate consolidation is:

	€m	€m
Property (1)	10	
Share of cash of C (2)	7	
Cash (3)		17

(1) €12 million paid to C less elimination of A's share of the profit made by C €2 million (50% of [€12 million sales proceeds less €8 million cost to C]).

(2) 50% of C's cash €14 million (€10 million from A and B minus €8 million to D plus €12 million from A).

(3) €5 million cash contributed to C plus €12 million consideration paid for property

If A accounted for C using equity accounting the accounting would be identical, except that it would show 'Investment in C' of €7 million rather than the €7 million share of C's cash.

Example 12.10: Sale of asset from joint venture to venturer at a loss

Two entities A and B establish a joint venture involving the creation of a jointly controlled entity C in which A and B each hold 50%. A and B each contribute €5 million in cash to the joint venture in exchange for equity shares. C then uses €8 million of its €10 million cash to acquire a property from an independent third party D. The property is then sold to A for €7 million, which is agreed to be its market value. How should A account for these transactions?

The required accounting entry if A accounts for its interest in C using proportionate consolidation is:

	€m	€m
Property (1)	7.0	
Share of cash of C (2)	4.5	
Share of loss of C (3)	0.5	
Cash (4)		12.0

(1) €7 million paid to C not adjusted since the transaction indicated an impairment of C's asset.

(2) 50% of C's cash €9 million (€10 million from A and B minus €8 million to D plus €7 million received from A).

(3) Loss in C's books is €1 million (€8 million cost of property less €7 million proceeds of sale). A recognises its 50% share because the transaction indicates an impairment of the asset. In effect, it is the result that would have been obtained if C had recognised an impairment charge immediately prior to the sale and then recognised no gain or loss on the sale.

(4) €5 million cash contributed to C plus €7 million consideration for property.

If A accounted for C using equity accounting the accounting would be identical, except that it would show 'Investment in C' of €4.5 million rather than the €4.5 million share of C's cash.

It may be that transactions occur between a venturer and a joint venture in assets, such as inventories, which are destined for onward sale in the normal course of business by the buying party. For venturers applying the equity method, the accounting adjustments required are the same as those for similar transactions between an investor and its associate – see Examples 11.13 and 11.14 in Chapter 11 at 3.4.1. However, for venturers using proportionate consolidation, the entries made in those examples against the investment/share of results of the equity accounted investee would be made against the particular line items affected, i.e. revenue, costs of sales, and inventory.

3.4.3 Non-monetary contributions to joint ventures

SIC-13 provides guidance on the application of these general principles to the specific situation of a transfer of non-monetary assets to a jointly controlled entity in exchange for equity. This states that the venturer should recognise in its income statement the portion of any gain or loss arising on the transfer attributable to the other venturers unless:

- significant risks and rewards of ownership of the contributed non-monetary asset(s) have not been transferred to the jointly controlled entity; or

- the gain or loss on the non-monetary contribution cannot be measured reliably; or

- the contribution lacks commercial substance, as that term is described in IAS 16 – *Property, Plant and Equipment* (see A below and Chapter 16 at 3.2.4).[120]

If any of the above conditions applies, the gain or loss arising would be considered 'unrealised' (and therefore not recognised in the income statement), unless in addition to receiving an equity interest in the entity, a venturer receives monetary or non-monetary assets, in which case an 'appropriate portion' of the gain or loss on the transaction should be recognised by the venturer. SIC-13 does not elaborate on what would constitute an appropriate portion of the gain or loss in such circumstances.[121]

Where the venturer accounts for the jointly controlled entity using proportionate consolidation, any unrealised gains or losses should be eliminated against the venturer's share of the underlying assets of the entity. Where equity accounting is used, the elimination should be against the carrying value of the investment in the entity. Unrealised gains or losses should not be accounted for as deferred income or expenditure.[122] Where 'unrealised' losses are eliminated in this way, the effect will be to apply what is sometimes referred to as 'asset swap' accounting. In other words, the carrying value of the investment in the jointly controlled entity will be the same as the carrying value of the non-monetary assets transferred in exchange for it, subject of course to any necessary provision for impairment uncovered by the transaction.

A   'Commercial substance'

As noted above, SIC-13 requires that a transaction should not be treated as realised when, inter alia, it lacks commercial substance as described in IAS 16. That standard states that an exchange of assets has 'commercial substance' when:

(a)   either:

   (i)   the configuration (risk, timing and amount) of the cash flows of the asset received differs from the configuration of the cash flows of the asset transferred; or

   (ii)   the entity-specific value of the portion of the entity's operations affected by the transaction changes as a result of the exchange; and

(b)   the difference in (i) or (ii) above is significant relative to the fair value of the assets exchanged.[123]

IAS 16's 'commercial substance' test is designed to enable an entity to measure, with reasonable objectivity, whether the asset that it has acquired in a non-monetary exchange is different to the asset it has given up.

The first stage is to determine the cash flows both of the asset given up and of the asset acquired (the latter being, of course, the interest in the jointly controlled entity). This determination may be sufficient by itself to satisfy (a) above, as it may be obvious that there are significant differences in the configuration of the cash flows. The type of income may have changed. For example, if the entity contributed a non-monetary asset such as a property or intangible asset to the jointly controlled entity, the reporting entity may now be receiving a rental or royalty stream from the jointly controlled entity, whereas previously the asset contributed to the cash flows of the cash-generating unit of which it was a part.

However, determining the cash flows may not result in a clear-cut conclusion, in which case the entity-specific value will have to be calculated. This is not the same as a value in use calculation under IAS 36, in that the entity is allowed to use a discount rate based on its own assessment of the risks specific to the operations, not those that reflect current market assessments[124] and post-tax cash flows.[125] The transaction will have commercial substance if these entity-specific values are not only different to one another but also significant compared to the fair values of the assets exchanged.

The calculation may not be highly sensitive to the discount rate as the same rate is used to calculate the entity-specific value of both the asset surrendered and the entity's interest in the jointly controlled entity. However, if the entity considers that a high discount rate is appropriate, this will have an impact on whether or not the difference is significant relative to the fair value of the assets exchanged. It is also necessary to consider the significance of:

(a)   the requirement above that the entity should recognise in its income statement the portion of any gain or loss arising on the transfer attributable to the other venturers;

(b)   the general requirements of IAS 31 in respect of transactions between venturers and their joint ventures; and

(c)   the general requirement of IFRS 3 – *Business Combinations* – to recognise assets acquired in a business combination at fair value (see Chapter 9).

As a result, we consider that it is likely that transactions entered into with genuine commercial purposes in mind are likely to pass the 'commercial substance' tests outlined above. However, these rules are designed to prevent the recognition of gains where an entity enters into an artificial transaction with the intention of manufacturing a gain by attributing inflated values to the assets exchanged.[126]

B   *Applying SIC-13 in practice – prior to application of IAS 27 (as amended in 2008) and IFRS 3 (as revised in 2008)*

SIC-13 does not give an example of the accounting treatment that it envisages when a gain is treated as 'realised'. However, we believe that the intended approach is that set out in Example 12.11 below. In essence, this approach reflects the fact that the reporting entity has:

(a)   acquired an interest in a jointly controlled entity that must be accounted for at fair value under IFRS 3; but

(b)   is required by SIC-13 to restrict any gain arising as a result of the exchange relating to its own assets to the extent that the gain is attributable to the other party to the joint venture. This leads to an adjustment of the carrying amount of the assets of the joint venture (as in Example 12.7 at 3.4.2 above).

In the example below, the non-monetary asset contributed is an interest in a subsidiary. Phase II of the IASB's Business Combinations project, and the resulting revisions made to IAS 27 and IFRS 3, has led to a number of changes in accounting for a loss of control of a subsidiary which are inconsistent with the accounting required by SIC-13. This is discussed further at C below.

Example 12.11:　Contribution of non-monetary assets to form joint venture

A and B are two major pharmaceutical companies, which agree to form a joint venture (JV Co) in respect of a particular part of each of their businesses. A will own 40% of the joint venture, and B 60%. The parties agree that the total value of the new business is £250 million.

A's contribution to the venture is one of its subsidiaries, in respect of which A's consolidated balance sheet reflects separable net assets of £50 million and goodwill of £10 million. The fair value of the separable net assets of the subsidiary contributed by A is considered to be £80 million. The implicit fair value of the business contributed is £100 million (40% of the total fair value of £250 million).

B also contributes a subsidiary, in respect of which B's consolidated balance sheet reflects separable net assets of £85 million and goodwill of £15 million. The fair value of the separable net assets is considered to be £120 million. The implicit fair value of the business contributed is £150 million (60% of total fair value of £250 million).

The book and fair values of the businesses contributed by A and B can therefore be summarised as follows:

(in £m)	A Book value	A Fair value	B Book value	B Fair value
Separable net assets	50	80	85	120
Goodwill	10	20	15	30
Total	60	100	100	150

How should A apply SIC-13 in accounting for the set-up of the joint venture?

The general principles of IFRS 3 require that A should account at fair value for the acquisition of its 40% interest in the new venture. However, as noted above, any gain or loss recognised by A must reflect only the extent to which it has disposed of the assets to the other partners in the venture (i.e. in this case, 60% – the extent to which A's former subsidiary is effectively transferred to B through B's 60% interest in the new venture).

This gives rise to the following accounting entry.

	£m	£m
Share of net assets of JV Co (1)	68	
Goodwill (2)	16	
Separable net assets and goodwill contributed to JV Co (3)		60
Gain on disposal (4)		24

(1)　40% of fair value of separable net assets of new entity £80 million (40% of [£80 million + £120 million] as in table above) less elimination of 40% of gain on disposal £12 million (40% of £30 million, being the difference between the book value [£50 million] and fair value [£80 million] of A's separable net assets, as in table above, contributed to JV Co) = £68 million.

　　This is equivalent to, and perhaps more easily calculated as, 40% of [book value of A's separable net assets + fair value of B's separable net assets], i.e. 40% × [£50 million + £120 million] = £68 million.

　　If A adopted proportionate consolidation, this £68 million would naturally be allocated to the relevant balance sheet headings.

(2) Fair value of consideration given £100 million (as in table above) less fair value of 40% share of separable net assets of JV Co acquired £80 million (see (1) above) = £20 million, less elimination of 40% gain on disposal £4 million (40% of £10 million, being the difference between the book value [£10 million] and fair value [£20 million] of A's goodwill, as in table above, contributed to JV Co) = £16 million.

This is equivalent to, and perhaps more easily calculated as, 40% of [book value of A's goodwill + fair value of B's goodwill], i.e. 40% × [£10 million + £30 million] = £16 million.

(3) Previous carrying amount of net assets contributed by A, now deconsolidated. In reality there would be a number of entries to deconsolidate these on a line-by-line basis.

(4) Fair value of business acquired £100 million (as in table above) less book value of assets disposed of £60 million (as in table above) = £40 million, less 40% of gain eliminated (£16 million) = £24 million. The £16 million eliminated reduces A's share of JV Co's separable net assets by £12 million (see (1) above) and its share of JV Co's goodwill by £4 million (see (2) above).

As noted in the introductory remarks above, it is common when joint ventures are set up in this way for the fair value of the assets contributed not to be exactly in proportion to the fair values venturers' agreed relative shares. Cash 'equalisation' payments are then made between the venturers so that the overall financial position of the venturer does correspond to their agreed relative shares in the venture (see Extract 12.6 below). Our suggested treatment of such payments in the context of a transaction within the scope of SIC-13 is illustrated in Example 12.12 below.

Example 12.12:   Contribution of non-monetary assets to form joint venture with cash equalisation payment between venturers

Suppose that the transaction in Example 12.11 was varied so that A is to have only a 36% interest in JV Co. However, as shown by the introductory table in Example 12.11, A is contributing a business worth 40% of the total fair value of JV Co. Accordingly, B makes good the shortfall by making a cash payment to A equivalent to 4% of the fair value of JV Co, i.e. £10 million (4% of £250 million).

This would require A to make the following accounting entries.

	£m	£m
Share of net assets of JV Co (1)	61.2	
Cash (equalisation payment from B)	10.0	
Goodwill (2)	14.4	
Separable net assets and goodwill contributed to JV Co (3)		60.0
Gain on disposal (4)		25.6

(1) 36% of fair value of separable net assets of new entity £72 million (36% of [£80 million + £120 million] as in table above) less elimination of 36% of gain on disposal £10.8 million (36% of £30 million, being the difference between the book value [£50 million] and fair value [£80 million] of A's separable net assets, as in table above, contributed to JV Co) = £61.2 million.

This is equivalent to, and perhaps more easily calculated as, 36% of [book value of A's separable net assets + fair value of B's separable net assets], i.e. 36% × [£50 million + £120 million] = £61.2 million.

If A adopted proportionate consolidation, this £61.2 million would naturally be allocated to the relevant balance sheet headings.

(2) Fair value of consideration given £100 million (as in table above), less cash equalisation payment received £10 million = £90 million less fair value of 36% share of separable net assets of JV Co acquired £72 million (see (1) above) = £18 million, less elimination of 36% gain on disposal £3.6 million (36% of £10 million, being the difference between the book value [£10 million] and fair value [£20 million] of A's goodwill, as in table above, contributed to JV Co) = £14.4 million.

This is equivalent to, and perhaps more easily calculated as, 36% of [book value of A's goodwill + fair value of B's goodwill], i.e. 36% × [£10 million + £30 million] = £14.4 million.

(3) Previous carrying amount of net assets (excluding goodwill) contributed by A, now deconsolidated. In reality there would be a number of entries to deconsolidate these on a line-by-line basis.

(4) Fair value of business acquired £90 million (36% of £250 million) plus cash equalisation payment £10 million = £100 million, less book value of assets disposed of £60 million (as in table above) = £40 million, less 36% of gain eliminated (£14.4 million) = £25.6 million. The £14.4 million eliminated reduces A's share of JV Co's separable net assets by £10.8 million (see (1) above) and its share of JV Co's goodwill by £3.6 million (see (2) above).

The extract below shows how a company might in practice want to disclose the effect of the application of SIC-13.

Extract 12.6: Alcatel-Lucent (2007)

Notes to consolidated financial statements [extract]

Note 3 – Changes in consolidated companies [extract]

On July 1, 2005, Alcatel and Finmeccanica announced the successful creation of two joint ventures that had been described in a memorandum of understanding signed by the parties on June 24, 2004: Alcatel Alenia Space (Alcatel-Lucent received 67% and Finmeccanica 33%) and Telespazio Holding (Finmeccanica received 67% and Alcatel 33%). These joint ventures are consolidated using the proportionate consolidation method starting July 1, 2005.

Alcatel analyzed this transaction as a sale to Finmeccanica of 33% of Alcatel Space's satellite industrial activity and 67% of its service activity and as an acquisition of 67% of Alenia Spazio (the industrial space systems of Finmeccanica) and of 33% of Telespazio (service activities for Finmeccanica's space systems).

The values assigned to this transaction were €1,530 million for Alenia Space and €215 million for Telespazio, resulting in a gain to Alcatel on the sale before tax of €129 million in 2005 and in goodwill not yet allocated of €143 million. Alcatel received from Finmeccanica an equalization payment of €109 million. Net cash resulting from the activities acquired and disposed of is €15 million at the transaction date. Due to the existence of price adjustment clauses in the agreement between Alcatel and Finmeccanica, adjustments to the above amounts were made during the third quarter 2006 (see above).

Proportionately consolidating the combined space activities of the two partners did not have a significant impact on Alcatel's revenues, operating margin and total balance sheet. However, this consolidation method resulted in recognizing a deferred tax charge of €38 million due to the removal from the French tax consolidation of the companies transferred to the joint ventures in the context of the transaction described above.

I   'Artificial' transactions

A concern with transactions such as this is that it is the relative, rather than the absolute, value of the transaction that is of concern to the parties. In other words, in Example 12.11 above, it could be argued that the only clear inference that can be drawn is that A and B have agreed that the ratio of the fair values of the businesses they have each contributed is 40:60, rather than that the business as a whole is worth £250 million. Thus it might be open to A and B, without altering the substance of the transaction, to assert that the value of the combined operations is £500 million (with a view to enlarging their balance sheets) or £200 million, (with a view to increasing future profitability).

Another way in which the valuation of the transaction might be distorted is through disaggregation of the consideration. Suppose that the £60 million net assets contributed by A in Example 12.11 above comprised:

	£m
Cash	12
Other net current assets	13
Property, plant and equipment	25
Goodwill	10
	60

Further suppose that, for tax reasons, the transaction was structured such that A was issued with 4% of the shares of JV Co in exchange for the cash and 36% in exchange for the remaining assets. This could lead to the suggestion that, as there can be no doubt as to the fair value of the cash, A's entire investment must be worth £120 million (i.e. £12 million × 40/4). Testing transactions for their commercial substance will require entities to focus on the fair value of the transaction as a whole and not to follow the strict legal form.

Of course, once cash equalisation payments are introduced, as in Example 12.12 above, the transaction terms provide evidence as to both the relative and absolute fair values of the assets contributed by each party.

II   *Accounts of JV Co*

IFRS 3 does not apply to business combinations in which separate entities or businesses are brought together to form a joint venture.[127] Therefore, it is not clear under IFRS how the acquisition of the former businesses of both A and B by JV Co should be accounted for. We consider that under the GAAP hierarchy in IAS 8 the pooling of interests method is still available when accounting for the formation of a joint venture and there may be other approaches (including the purchase method) that will be considered to give a fair presentation in particular circumstances.

If JV Co were to apply the purchase method, which it could justify under the GAAP hierarchy in paragraph 11 of IAS 8 (see Chapter 3 at 4.3), it would mean that the amounts taken up in the accounts of A and B may bear little relation to either party's share of the net assets of the joint venture as reported in the underlying financial statements of the investee. For example, A's share of any depreciation charge recorded by JV Co must be based on the carrying amount of A's share of JV Co's PPE, not as recorded in JV Co's books (i.e. at fair value) but as recorded in A's books, which will be based on book value as regards PPE contributed by A and at fair value as regards PPE contributed by B. Accordingly it may be necessary for both A and B to keep a 'memorandum' set of books for consolidation purposes reflecting their share of assets originally their own at book value and those originally of the other party at fair value.

Alternatively, if JV Co were to apply the pooling of interest method, both A and B would still need to keep a 'memorandum' set of books for consolidation purposes because their share of assets that were originally of the other party should be carried at fair value rather than carry-over cost.

In practice, however, keeping a set of 'memorandum' books may be easier said than done, and a fairly broad brush approach may be unavoidable.

C   *Applying SIC-13 in practice – upon application of IAS 27 (as amended in 2008) and IFRS 3 (as revised in 2008)*

IFRS 3 (as revised in 2008) is effective for business combinations for which the acquisition date is on or after the beginning of the first annual reporting period beginning on or after 1 July 2009 with early adoption possible as explained in Chapter 9 at 3.1.1. IAS 27 (as amended in 2008) has the same effective date.[128]

Phase II of the IASB's Business Combinations project, and the resulting revisions made to IAS 27 and IFRS 3, has led to a number of changes in accounting for a loss of control of a subsidiary which are inconsistent with the accounting required by SIC-13.

In Example 12.11 above, the non-monetary asset contributed is an interest in a subsidiary. Under SIC-13, the contributing venturer is required to restrict any gain arising as a result of the exchange relating to its own assets to the extent that the gain is attributable to the other party to the joint venture. This leads to an adjustment of the carrying amount of the assets of the joint venture. However, under IAS 27 (as amended in 2008) where an entity loses control of an entity, but retains an interest that is now to be accounted for as a jointly controlled entity, the retained interest must be remeasured at its fair value and is included in calculating the gain or loss on disposal of the subsidiary.[129] As discussed at 3.3.7 A above, this fair value becomes the cost on initial recognition of the jointly controlled entity.[130] This applies irrespective of whether the jointly controlled entity is proportionately consolidated or accounted for under the equity method. Consequently, under IAS 27 (as amended in 2008), the gain is not restricted to the extent that the gain is attributable to the other party to the joint venture, and there is no adjustment to reduce the fair values of the net assets contributed to the joint venture.

It would appear that the IASB did not consider the implications of the revisions made under Phase II of the Business Combinations project on the requirements of SIC-13. As noted at 1.4 above, in May 2009, the IASB has indicated that it will address the interaction between the revised versions of IFRS 3 and IAS 27, and IAS 28 and IAS 31, as part of its project on joint venture,[131] so hopefully it will be rectified then. In the meantime, we believe that, where the non-monetary asset contributed is an interest in a subsidiary, it is more appropriate that the requirements of IAS 27 (as amended in 2008) and IFRS 3 (as revised in 2008) are followed as IAS 27 (as amended in 2008) deals with the specific issue of loss of control, whereas the requirements of SIC-13 are more generic. However, where the requirements of IAS 27 (as amended in 2008) and IFRS 3 (as revised in 2008) are followed for transactions involving a contribution of an interest in a subsidiary, SIC-13 would continue to apply to other forms of non-monetary assets contributed, such as items of property, plant and equipment or intangible assets.

Example 12.13:   Contribution of subsidiary to form joint venture – upon application of IAS 27 (as amended in 2008) and IFRS 3 (as revised in 2008)

Based on Example 12.11 above, the application of IAS 27 (as amended in 2008) and IFRS 3 (as revised in 2008) to the transaction would result in A reflecting the following accounting entry.

	£m	£m
Share of net assets of JV Co (1)	80	
Goodwill (2)	20	
Separable net assets and goodwill contributed to JV Co (3)		60
Gain on disposal (4)		40

(1)   40% of fair value of separable net assets of new entity £80 million (40% of [£80 million + £120 million] as in table in Example 12.11 above). There is no elimination of 40% of the gain on disposal.

       If A adopted proportionate consolidation, this £80 million would naturally be allocated to the relevant balance sheet headings.

(2)   Fair value of consideration given of £60 million (being 60% of £100 million as in table in Example 12.11 above) plus fair value of retained interest of £40 million (being 40% of £100 million) less fair value of 40% share of separable net assets of JV Co acquired £80 million (see (1) above).

(3)   Previous carrying amount of net assets contributed by A as in table in Example 12.11 above, now deconsolidated. In reality there would be a number of entries to deconsolidate these on a line-by-line basis.

(4)   Fair value of consideration received of £60 million (being 40% of £150 million as in table in Example 12.11 above) plus fair value of retained interest of £40 million (being 40% of £100 million) less book value of assets disposed of £60 million (see (3) above) = £40 million.

3.4.4   Loans and borrowings between the reporting entity and joint ventures

IAS 31's requirement to eliminate partially unrealised profits or losses on transactions with joint ventures is expressed in terms of transactions involving the transfer of assets. This raises the question of whether this requirement is generally intended to items such as interest paid on loans between joint ventures and the reporting entity.

Where a jointly controlled entity is accounted for using proportionate consolidation, we believe that the requirement for partial elimination of profits is generally intended to be extended to loans and related items.

Where a jointly controlled entity is accounted for using equity accounting, however, we do not believe that the requirement for partial elimination of profits is generally intended to be extended to loans and related items, since such loans do not involve the transfer of assets giving rise to gains or losses. Moreover, they are not normally regarded as part of the investor's share of the net assets of the investee, but as separate transactions, except in the case of loss-making investees, where interests in long-term loans may be required to be accounted for as if they were part of the reporting entity's equity investment in determining the carrying value of the joint venture against which losses may be offset (see Chapter 11 at 3.7).

3.5   Income taxes

Income taxes arising from interests in joint ventures are accounted for in accordance with IAS 12 – *Income Taxes*. In cases where joint control does not give joint control over the distribution policy of the joint venture, the venturer may be required to provide in full for deferred tax on temporary differences relating to joint ventures.

Some might question whether the lack of joint control over distribution policy suggests that in fact the venturer does not exert joint control sufficient for the investment to be treated as a joint venture under IAS 31. However, IAS 12 notes that a joint venture agreement will 'usually' give joint control over distribution policy, but does not appear to regard it as an essential feature of such an agreement.[132] This is discussed further in Chapter 26 at 4.2.6.

3.6   Operators of joint ventures

One or more venturers may act as the operator or manager of a joint venture. Operators are usually paid a management fee for such duties. The fees are accounted for by the joint venture as an expense. IAS 31 requires the operators or managers of a joint venture to account for any such fees in accordance with IAS 18 – *Revenue* (see Chapter 25).[133]

An operator will often act as an agent and pay for specific costs on behalf of the joint venture (i.e. the principal). Such payments should not be accounted for as costs in the income statement of the operator and the reimbursement by the joint venture should not be presented as revenue. However, an operator that charges a management fee, which is intended to defray unspecified overhead costs, cannot be said to act as an agent. Therefore the operator should account for the management fee income and overhead costs in it income statement on a gross basis as it is not acting as an agent and does not meet the offset criteria in IAS 1.[134]

4   PRESENTATION AND DISCLOSURE

4.1   Presentation

4.1.1   *Jointly controlled operations and jointly controlled assets*

IFRS does not prescribe how jointly controlled operations and jointly controlled assets should be presented in the balance sheet or income statement of an entity. In practice few companies disclose details of those types of joint ventures on the face of their balance sheets or income statements.

4.1.2   Jointly controlled entities

An entity that proportionately consolidates its investments in jointly controlled entities can elect to use one of two permitted formats (see 3.3.3 above):

- *Line-by-line presentation* – The jointly controlled entity is consolidated on an aggregated line-by-line basis; or
- *Presentation as separate line items* – The venturer includes separate line items for its share of the total assets, liabilities, income and expenditure of the jointly controlled entity in its own consolidated accounts.

On the other hand, an entity that accounts for its investments in jointly controlled entities under the equity method is required to present:

- its aggregate share of the profit or loss of associates and joint ventures accounted for using the equity method on the face of its statement of comprehensive income (or separate income statement) (see Chapter 11 at 5.1.2);[135]
- its aggregate share of the other comprehensive income of associates and joint ventures accounted for using the equity method on the face of its statement of comprehensive income (see Chapter 11 at 5.1.3); and[136]
- its investments accounted for using the equity method as non-current assets[137] on the face of its balance sheet.[138] The entity would be permitted to combine its investments in jointly controlled entities and associates into one line item.

4.2   Disclosure

4.2.1   Interests in joint ventures

A venturer should disclose a listing and description of interests in significant joint ventures and the proportion of ownership interest held in jointly controlled entities.[139]

A venturer which reports its interests in jointly controlled entities using the line-by-line reporting format for proportionate consolidation or the equity method should disclose the aggregate amounts of each of:

- current assets;
- long-term assets;
- current liabilities;
- long-term liabilities;
- income; and
- expenses

related to its interests in joint ventures.[140] An example of this disclosure is found in the financial statements of Scottish & Newcastle.

Extract 12.7: Scottish & Newcastle plc (2007)

Notes to the accounts [extract]

18. Investment in joint ventures

The main joint venture investments are in the following brewers:

50% holding in Baltic Beverages Holding (BBH) which operates in Russia, Ukraine, the Baltic countries and Kazakhstan. 50% holding in Millennium Alcobev which operates in India. 37.5% holding in United Breweries Limited which operates in India. 45% holding in Serviced Dispense Equipment (Holdings) Limited which provides dispense equipment in the UK. 50% holding in Kuehne + Nagel Drinkflow Logistics Limited which provides logistical services in the UK.

The Group's share of joint ventures' assets and liabilities are as follows:

	2007 £m	2006 £m
Non current assets	2,100	1,798
Current assets	327	295
Current liabilities	(355)	(236)
Non current liabilities	(547)	(434)
Minority interest	(75)	(77)
Share of net assets of joint ventures	1,450	1,346

The Group's share of joint ventures' profits are as follows:

	2007			2006		
	Before exceptional items	Exceptional items	After exceptional items	Before exceptional items	Exceptional items	After exceptional items
Revenue	1,073	–	1,073	804	–	804
Net operating costs	(841)	2	(839)	(628)	14	(614)
Operating profit	232	2	234	176	14	190
Net finance costs	(25)	–	(25)	(18)	4	(14)
Profit before tax	207	2	209	158	18	176
Tax	(63)	–	(63)	(44)	–	(44)
Minorities	(20)	–	(20)	(21)	–	(21)
Share of profit of joint ventures	124	2	126	93	18	111

The Group's share of the capital commitments of joint ventures in respect of property, plant and equipment was £80m (2005 – £41m).

4.2.2   Accounting policy for jointly controlled entities

A venturer must disclose the method that it uses to recognise its interests in jointly controlled entities[141] (i.e. proportionate consolidation or the equity method – see 3.3.2 above).

4.2.3   Contingencies and commitments

IAS 31 requires a venturer to disclose the aggregate amount of the following contingent liabilities, unless the probability of loss is remote, separately from the amount of other contingent liabilities:

- any contingent liabilities that the venturer has incurred in relation to its interests in joint ventures and its share in each of the contingent liabilities that have been incurred jointly with other venturers;

- its share of the contingent liabilities of the joint ventures themselves for which it is contingently liable; and

- those contingent liabilities that arise because the venturer is contingently liable for the liabilities of the other venturers of a joint venture.[142]

A venturer must also disclose the aggregate amount of the following commitments in respect of its interests in joint ventures separately from other commitments:

- any capital commitments of the venturer in relation to its interests in joint ventures and its share in the capital commitments that have been incurred jointly with other venturers; and

- its share of the capital commitments of the joint ventures themselves.[143]

4.2.4 Disclosures required when accounting for an interest in a jointly controlled entity at fair value under IAS 39

The IASB, as part of its Annual Improvements project, amended IAS 31 to clarify that where a joint venture is accounted for at fair value in accordance with IAS 39, as permitted under the standard for venture capital organisations, mutual funds, unit trusts and similar entities, some of the above IAS 31 disclosure requirements – specifically those in respect of contingent liabilities – do not apply.[144] However the disclosures required by paragraphs 55 and 56 of the standard still apply (although the information about assets, liabilities, etc. for jointly controlled entities will not be necessary as the interests therein are not reported under proportionate consolidation or the equity method). This amendment applies for annual periods beginning on or after 1 January 2009 with earlier application permitted as long as this is disclosed and the related amendments to IFRS 7 – *Financial Instruments: Disclosures*, and IAS 28 – *Interests in Associates* – are also applied.[145]

Prior to application of this amendment an entity applying IAS 39 to an investment in a jointly controlled entity should still disclose all the information required by IAS 31. This is because IFRS 7 specifically calls for the IAS 31 disclosures to be made in addition to the IFRS 7 disclosures,[146] despite the fact that, as indicated at 2.1 above, IAS 31 does not apply to the entity.

5   PRACTICAL ISSUES

5.1   Variable profit share

Venturers may not always be entitled to a fixed proportion of the profit of a jointly controlled entity. Venturers that each have a 50% interest in a joint venture may, for example, agree that;

- in the initial three years of operation one of the venturers will be entitled to 75% of the profits in order to recover its investment quicker; or

- the venturers are entitled to a fixed proportion of cash flows 'as defined in the joint venture agreement'; or
- distribute the profit of the joint venture based on an alternative measure of profitability such as EBITDA.

It may not be appropriate in those cases for the venturers to account for 50% of the profit of the joint venture. Instead, they would need to take into account the substance of the profit sharing arrangements that apply in each reporting period, in determining their share of the profits and net assets of the joint venture. A venturer's profit share may therefore differ from its share in the net assets of the joint venture. This situation is not unlike the situation that arises in the case of an investment in an associate that has different classes of equity (see Chapter 11 at 3.3.4).

5.2   Related party disclosures

IAS 24 – *Related Party Disclosures* – treats joint ventures in which an entity is a venturer as related parties. Transactions with a jointly controlled entity would therefore need to be disclosed as related party transactions, at least to the extent that they are not eliminated as intercompany transactions under proportionate consolidation.

It is less obvious how this requirement should be applied in the case of jointly controlled operations and jointly controlled assets, because in those cases there is no separate legal entity that could be described as a related party. Since a venturer only has a contractual arrangement with the other venturers, one might argue that the other venturers should be treated as related parties. However, we believe that IAS 24 does not require respective venturers to be treated as related parties (see Chapter 38 at 2.3).

6   TRANSITIONAL ISSUES

6.1   General

The December 2003 revised version of IAS 31 had to be applied for accounting periods beginning on or after 1 January 2005. Entities were encouraged to adopt this revised version of IAS 31 for earlier periods, but were required to disclose that they had done so.[147] There were no transitional provisions. Accordingly, an existing IFRS user had to apply the revised version of IAS 31 with full retrospective effect.

6.2   Upon application of IAS 27 (as amended in 2008) and IFRS 3 (as revised in 2008)

As explained at various stages throughout the chapter, there have been a number of consequential amendments made to IAS 31, and to IAS 28 (see Chapter 11), as a result of phase II of the Business Combinations project and the substantial revisions made to IFRS 3 and IAS 27. There are no transitional requirements in respect of these consequential amendments made to IAS 28 and 31. Normally the lack of transitional requirements would mean the amendments should be applied retrospectively as required by IAS 8, although this would, in certain circumstances, be inconsistent with the transitional requirements in IAS 27 (as amended in 2008) and IFRS 3 (as revised in 2008).

For example the impact on profit or loss upon loss of joint control may be very different if accounting for the transaction under the consequential amendments that have been made to IAS 31 and that are discussed at 3.3.11 above. IAS 27 (as amended in 2008) states that its requirements in respect of loss of control of a subsidiary should be applied prospectively so that any profit or loss recognised in the prior year should not be recalculated.[148] IFRS 3 (as revised in 2008) is to be applied prospectively to business combinations for which the acquisition date is on or after the beginning of the first annual reporting period beginning on or after 1 July 2009.[149] Given these prohibitions on restatement within these two standards it would seem inappropriate to recalculate the profit or loss upon a loss of joint control that had occurred in the prior year.

The issue was considered by the IASB at its meeting in May 2009 as part of its Annual Improvements project. Consequently, in the exposure draft of proposed *Improvements to IFRSs* issued in August 2009, the IASB is proposing to clarify that the consequential amendments made by IAS 27 (as amended in 2008) to IAS 31 relating to the loss or reduction of joint control over a jointly controlled entity (and to IAS 28 relating to the loss or reduction of significant influence over an associate) should be applied prospectively. It is proposed that an entity applies the amendments for annual periods beginning on or after 1 July 2010. Earlier application is to be permitted, but if an entity applies the amendment for an earlier period it is to disclose that fact.[150] However, the IASB considered that there is no need to clarify the consequential amendments made by IFRS 3 (as revised in 2008) because that revised IFRS clearly requires prospective application.[151]

7   FUTURE DEVELOPMENTS IN JOINT VENTURE ACCOUNTING

7.1   Exposure Draft 9 (ED 9) – *Joint Arrangements*

In September 2007, the IASB issued Exposure Draft 9 (ED 9) – *Joint Arrangements*, which is intended to replace IAS 31 and SIC-13. ED 9 is another step in the short-term conversion project between the IASB and the Financial Accounting Standards Board (FASB).

The types of arrangement addressed by ED 9 are essentially the same as those covered by IAS 31, although some of the terminology has been changed. The principal change to IAS 31 is that proportionate consolidation of jointly controlled entities will no longer be allowed.[152] In this regard, the proposals in ED 9 would bring IFRS more in line, for most industries, with US GAAP. Under US GAAP, proportionate gross financial statement presentation (i.e. proportionate consolidation) is 'not appropriate for an investment in an unincorporated legal entity accounted for by the equity method of accounting unless the investee is in either the construction industry or an extractive industry where there is a longstanding practice of its use'.[153]

ED 9 defines a joint arrangement as a contractual arrangement whereby two or more parties undertake an economic activity together and share decision-making relating to that activity.[154] Joint arrangements are to be classified into three types (i.e. joint operations, joint assets and joint ventures) based on the rights and obligations that arise from the contractual arrangement:[155]

- 'Joint operation' will replace the term 'jointly controlled operation' used in IAS 31. A joint operation is one in which the parties to the arrangement use their own assets and other resources, and share revenues and expenses incurred in common in undertaking an activity.[156] As each party controls its own assets and incurs its own obligations, it accounts for those assets and liabilities in accordance with applicable IFRS, together with its share of revenue and expenses from the activities;[157]

- 'Joint asset' will replace the term 'jointly controlled asset' used in IAS 31. A joint asset is an asset to which each party has rights, often with joint ownership. Each party takes a share of the output from and shares the costs of operating the asset.[158] Each party recognises its share of the joint asset in accordance with applicable IFRS, any liabilities it incurs, together with its share of any liabilities incurred jointly with the other parties, revenue from the sale of its share of the output of the asset and expenses incurred in respect of its interest in the joint arrangement;[159] and

- 'Joint venture' will replace the term 'jointly controlled entity' used in IAS 31. A joint venture is an arrangement that is jointly controlled by the venturers.[160] In other words, a contractually agreed sharing of the power to govern the operating and financial policies of the venture to obtain benefits. In a joint venture, the venturers do not have direct rights to individual assets or direct obligations for expenses of the venture. Instead, each party shares in the outcome (e.g. profit or loss) of the activity. Such arrangements will be accounted for using the equity method[161] – proportionate consolidation will no longer be available.

Much of the terminology used in explaining each of these terms is very similar to that which presently exists within IAS 31. However there is a significant change in the application of these definitions when analysing and accounting for joint arrangements.

ED 9 establishes a core principle that parties in a joint arrangement are to recognise their contractual rights and obligations arising from the arrangement.[162] The objective of this broad principle is to shift the focus from how the form of a joint arrangement dictates the accounting to focus more on the contractual rights and obligations within the arrangement. Therefore, the structure of the arrangement is only one element in assessing these rights and obligations.

The most significant impact arising from the amendments is the possibility that, in any one structure, there may be a number of different arrangements, each of which would need to be separately accounted for. Consequently, the process of identifying the separate arrangements and then accounting for each of these adds to the complexity of accounting for joint ventures.

The exposure draft proposes that every joint arrangement is split between and/or classified into one of the three types defined above – a joint operation, a joint asset or a joint venture.[163] The concept behind this is that each party accounts for its own rights and obligations and records the assets it controls.[164] Many arrangements that exist within an entity structure may therefore comprise both a joint asset and a joint venture, or both a joint operation and a joint venture. In such cases, the balance sheet must be carefully analysed to determine which assets (and liabilities) are joint assets or are part of the joint operations that are to be accounted for 'in accordance with applicable IFRSs'.[165] The remaining or residual assets and liabilities then make up the 'joint venture', which is to be equity accounted.[166]

The exposure draft includes a flowchart to assist in determining how an arrangement should be accounted for:[167]

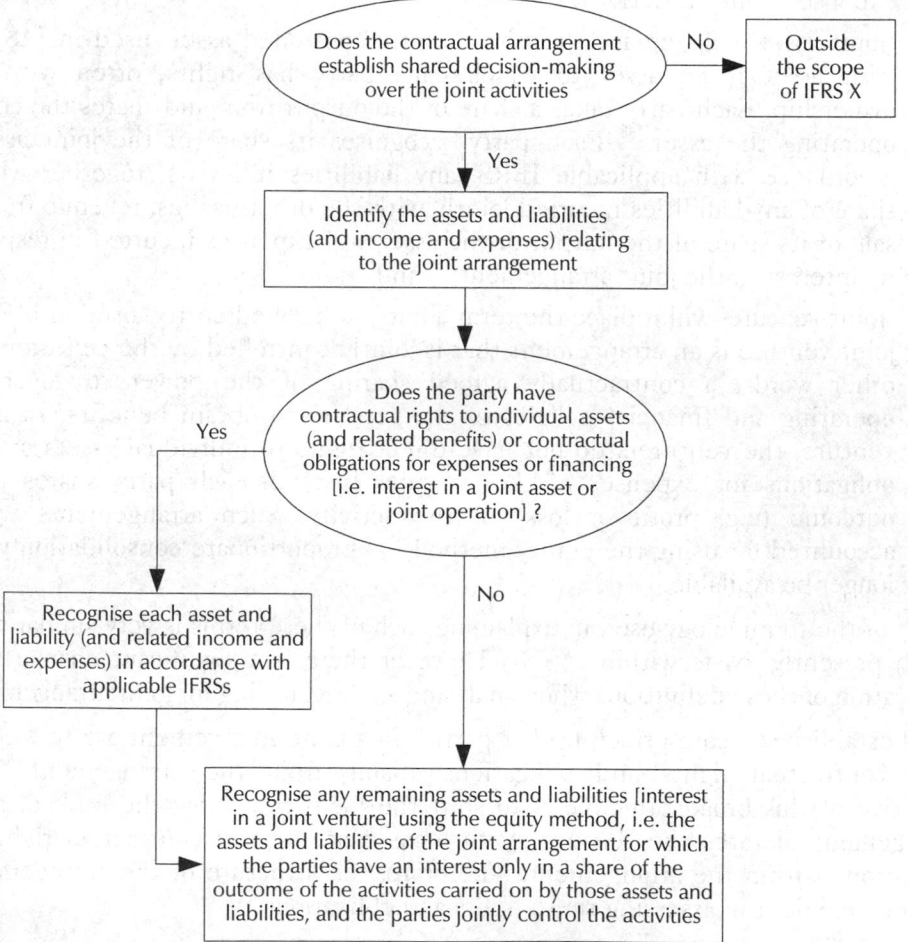

While the IASB did not intend that there would be a significant change to the accounting for joint assets and joint operations, the revisions made by ED 9 have unfortunately introduced doubt as to how such arrangements are accounted for. For example, if an arrangement or part of an arrangement is classified as a joint asset, ED 9 proposes that the share of the asset is accounted for in accordance with applicable IFRSs.[168] Which IFRS is then applicable? Is it 'the right of use' which then treats the asset as a lease, or is it a proportion of the asset itself to be recognised?

Example 12.14: Analysing an arrangement under ED 9[169]

Five advertising companies jointly buy an aircraft. They enter into an agreement whereby each party has the right to use the aircraft for its own purposes on some days of each year. They share decision-making regarding maintenance and disposal of the aircraft. The decisions require the agreement of all of the parties. The agreement covers the expected life of the aircraft and can be changed only if all of the parties agree. How should this arrangement be accounted for?

The aircraft is considered to be a joint asset. The joint arrangement is a way to share the costs of having access to an aircraft. Each party has a unilateral right to use the aircraft for some days. It is those rights that the parties control and recognise in accordance with the applicable IFRS.

However it is unclear what the applicable IFRS is. Should the venturer look to IAS 17 – *Leases*/IFRIC 4 – *Determining whether an Arrangement contains a Lease* – and therefore account for this as an operating lease? Or should the venturer look to IAS 16 – *Property, Plant and Equipment* – or IAS 38 – *Intangible Assets*? It may also be argued in this case, that if the right of use is the asset, it does not give rise to a joint asset at all.

When an arrangement is split between an element that is a joint asset and a residual that becomes the joint venture, the liabilities need also to be split. Only liabilities that are 'incurred jointly' with the other parties are recognised as part of the joint asset arrangement. In determining whether liabilities belong to the entity or are incurred jointly with the other party, any guarantees provided by the venturers are also taken into account. Often, when the joint arrangement is conducted through an entity structure, the liabilities will not be 'incurred jointly' (as the entity will enter into these in its own right), and these will remain in the joint venture, to be equity accounted. The Standard on equity accounting restricts the situations in which an equity accounted investment can be recognised below zero, hence, there may be some mismatch between the assets and liabilities ultimately recognised. This is illustrated by a variation of Example 12.14 above.

Example 12.15: Analysing an arrangement under ED 9[170]

Assume that the five advertising companies which jointly buy the aircraft in Example 12.14 above make the purchase in the name of a joint venture company and that it is this company that raises the finance itself by a combination of equity and third party borrowings, such that the borrowings are not guaranteed by any of the venturers . The venturers continue to have an operating agreement that gives them the same rights to the aircraft as in the original example. How would the arrangement now be accounted for?

Since there has been no change in the rights of each venturer in the aircraft, it is those rights that continue to be recognised, in a similar manner to previously, in accordance with applicable IFRS. The illustrative example in the exposure draft clarifies this point.

However it would now seem that there is a residual, the borrowings, that would now need to be accounted for as a joint venture. But if there was no legal or constructive obligation to make payments on behalf of the joint venture the ventures would be precluded from recognising any such liability,[171] hence the mismatch.

ED 9 also includes guidance on how the loss of control of an interest in a joint venture should be accounted for. Similar changes were made to IAS 31 after completion of phase II of the Business Combinations project and issuance of the resulting revised versions of IAS 27 and IFRS 3 and these are described at 3.3.11 above. However the exposure draft does introduce an inconsistency, compared to the revised version of IAS 27 and consequential amendments made to IAS 31, in the event that joint control of an entity is lost but replaced with significant influence and this is also highlighted at 3.3.11 above.

As in the case of IAS 31, ED 9 will not apply to interests in jointly controlled entities held by venture capital organisations and certain other investment vehicles that are measured at fair value through profit and loss.[172]

7.2   Subsequent developments since publication of ED 9

In April 2008, the IASB staff presented a summary of the comment letters received on ED 9. There has been widespread unfavourable reaction to the proposals within ED 9. Most respondents to the proposals agree that there should be a movement away from legal form being the most significant factor determining the accounting, but many of these respondents have differences of opinion on how best to achieve this and reservations about the proposals within the exposure draft. The IASB discussed the main issues raised and reaffirmed the principles in the exposure draft. However, the IASB recognised that many respondents had a different interpretation and assessment of the implications of the model proposed from those of the IASB and that the proposed IFRS will need to be improved to address this gap. The IASB asked the staff to seek the views of additional users and to contact some of the respondents in order to gain a better understanding of their concerns. The staff would bring the results of those enquiries to the IASB at a future meeting.[173]

It was not until May 2009 that the IASB continued its discussion of responses to ED 9 and decided tentatively:

- to replace the term 'shared decision-making' by 'joint control' for all types of joint arrangement;
- to merge 'joint operations' and 'joint assets' into a single type of joint arrangement called 'joint operation';
- that, for a joint arrangement established in a separate entity, it is necessary to consider all relevant facts and circumstances to assess whether the arrangement is a joint operation or a joint venture. There should not be a rebuttable presumption that the arrangement is a joint venture.

The IASB also had a preliminary discussion about how participants in a joint arrangement should account for their interest in the arrangement if they do not have joint control, but reached no decisions on this issue.[174]

This was discussed at the next meeting in June 2009 when the IASB decided tentatively:

- to introduce a term such as 'investor in a joint arrangement' to designate parties to joint arrangements that do not have joint control in the arrangement;
- that an investor in a joint arrangement that is a joint operation should account for its assets, liabilities, revenues and expenses, including its share of any assets, liabilities, revenues and expenses arising from the joint operation;
- that an investor in a joint arrangement that is a joint venture should account for its interest in accordance with IAS 39 or, if it has significant influence in the joint venture, in accordance with IAS 28;
- that parties with interests in a joint asset should directly recognise their share of the joint asset, classified according to the nature of the asset.

After the June meeting, the IASB indicated that will continue its discussion at future meetings, with the aim of publishing an IFRS in the third quarter of 2009.[175] However, it would appear that the timing has slipped yet again, as according to the latest Project Summary it is not expected to be published until the fourth quarter of 2009.[176]

Since the effective date of amendments or new standards is generally 6 to 18 months after publication it would seem that the earliest possible effective date would be for financial periods beginning 1 July 2010, with a later date being much more likely, especially given the significant changes to current accounting practice that may result from such a standard.

In addition, as indicated at 1.4 above, as a result of the revised versions of IFRS 3 and IAS 27, this has raised a number of new issues in the context of applying the equity method, and the extent to which the methodology and procedures under these revised standards should now be applied is open to further consideration. In May 2009, the IASB has indicated that it will address the interaction between the revised versions of IFRS 3 and IAS 27, and IAS 28 and IAS 31, as part of its project on joint ventures.[177]

References

1 *IASB Update*, IASB, May 2009, p. 3.
2 IFRS 3, *Business Combinations*, IASB, para. 64; IAS 27, *Consolidated and Separate Financial Statements*, IASB, para. 45.
3 IAS 28, *Investments in Associates*, IASB, para. 20.
4 *Improvements to IFRSs*, April 2009, IASB, IAS 39, para. BC24D.
5 *IASB Update*, IASB, May 2009, p. 5.
6 IAS 31, *Interests in Joint Ventures*, IASB, para. 1.
7 IAS 31, para. 1.
8 IAS 31, para. 3.
9 IAS 31, para. 3.
10 IAS 31, para. 3.
11 IAS 31, para. 3.
12 IAS 31, para. 51.
13 IAS 31, para. 7.
14 IAS 31, para. 9.
15 IAS 31, para. 3.
16 IAS 31, para. 9.
17 IAS 31, para. 10.
18 IAS 31, para. 11.
19 IAS 31, para. 12.
20 IAS 31, para. 8.
21 IAS 31, para. 2.
22 IAS 31, para. 42.
23 IAS 31, para. 3.
24 IAS 27, para. 38.
25 IAS 27, para. 38A.
26 IAS 27, para. 45B.
27 IAS 31, para. 46.
28 IAS 31, para. 4.
29 IAS 31, paras. 5 and 47.
30 IAS 31, para. 6.
31 ED 9, *Joint Arrangements*, IASB, para. 24.
32 IAS 36, *Impairment of Assets*, IASB, paras. 2, 4 and 5; IAS 39, *Financial Instruments: Recognition and Measurement*, IASB, paras. 2(a) and 2(d).
33 *IFRIC Update*, IFRIC, May 2009, p. 4 and 5; *IFRIC Update*, IFRIC, July 2009, p. 4.
34 Exposure Draft (ED 2009/11), IASB, August 2009, pp. 43-49.
35 ED 2009/11, p.48.
36 ED 2009/11, pp. 44, 46 and 47.
37 IAS 31, para. 13.
38 IAS 31, para. 14.
39 IAS 31, para. 15.
40 IAS 31, paras. 16-17.
41 IAS 31, paras. 18-19.
42 IAS 31, para. 20.
43 IAS 31, paras. 21-22.
44 IAS 31, para. 23.
45 IAS 31, para. 22.
46 IAS 31, para. 23.
47 IAS 31, para. 24.
48 IAS 31, para. 25.
49 IAS 31, para. 27.
50 IAS 31, para. 32.
51 IAS 31, para. 26.

52 IAS 31, para. 28.
53 IAS 31, para. 29.
54 IAS 31, paras. 30 and 38.
55 IAS 31, paras. 31 and 39.
56 IAS 23, *Borrowing Costs*, IASB, para. 5.
57 IAS 23, paras. 8 and 29.
58 IAS 23, paras. 7 and BC22(c).
59 IAS 31, paras. 30 and 38.
60 IAS 31, para. 57.
61 IAS 8, *Accounting Policies, Changes in Accounting Estimates and Errors*, IASB, para. IN16.
62 IAS 31, para. 3.
63 IAS 31, para. 32.
64 IAS 31, para. 33.
65 IAS 31, para. 33.
66 IAS 31, para. 34.
67 IAS 31, para. 35.
68 IAS 31, paras. 36-37.
69 IAS 31, para. 3.
70 IAS 31, para. 40.
71 IAS 31, para. 40.
72 IAS 31, para. 40.
73 IAS 31, para. 41.
74 IAS 31, para. 43.
75 IFRS 3, para. 64; IAS 27, para. 45.
76 IFRS 3, para. 64; IAS 27, para. 45.
77 IAS 28, para. 20.
78 IAS 28, para. 2.
79 *Improvements to IFRSs*, April 2009, IAS 39, para. BC24D.
80 *IFRIC Update*, IFRIC, July 2009, p. 3.
81 *IASB Update*, IASB, May 2009, p. 5.
82 IAS 27, para. 37.
83 IAS 27, paras. 37 and BC56.
84 *Improvements to IFRSs*, April 2009, IASB, IFRIC 9, paras. BC5C and BC5D.
85 IAS 28, para. 20.
86 *IFRIC Update*, IFRIC, July 2009, p. 3.
87 *IASB Update*, IASB, May 2009, p. 5.
88 IAS 28, para. 18.
89 IAS 28, para. 19A.
90 IFRS 3, para. 42.
91 IFRS 3, para. BC384.
92 IAS 28, para. BC21 and IAS 31, para. BC16.
93 ED 9, paras. 30 and BC19.
94 IFRS 3, paras. 41 and 42.
95 IFRS 3, para. BC384.
96 IAS 31, para 1.
97 *IASB Update*, IASB, May 2009, p. 5.
98 *IASB Update*, IASB, May 2009, p. 5.
99 IFRS 3, para. 64; IAS 27, para. 45.
100 IAS 31, para. 45.
101 IAS 39, para. 43.
102 IAS 27 (2007), *Consolidated and Separate Financial Statements*, IASB, 2007 Bound Volume, para. 32; IAS 28 (2007), *Investments in Associates*, IASB, 2007 Bound Volume, para. 19.
103 IAS 21 (2007), *The Effects of Changes in Foreign Exchange Rates*, IASB, 2007 Bound Volume, para. 49.
104 IAS 21, *The Effects of Changes in Foreign Exchange Rates*, IASB, para. BC35.
105 IAS 21 (2008), *The Effects of Changes in Foreign Exchange Rates*, IASB, 2008 Bound Volume, para. 49.
106 IFRS 3, para. 64; IAS 27, para. 45.
107 IFRS 3, para. 42.
108 IAS 31, para. BC16.
109 IAS 28, para. 23.
110 IAS 27, para. 37.
111 ED 9, para. BC19.
112 IAS 31, para. 45B.
113 IAS 21, para. 48A.
114 IAS 21, paras. BC33-34.
115 IAS 31, para. 45B.
116 IAS 21, para. 48C.
117 IAS 31, para. 48.
118 IAS 31, para. 49.
119 IAS 31, para. 50.
120 SIC-13, *Jointly Controlled Entities – Non-monetary Contributions by Venturers*, IASB, para. 5.
121 SIC-13, para. 6.
122 SIC-13, para. 7.
123 IAS 16, *Property, Plant and Equipment*, IASB para. 25.
124 IAS 16, para. BC22.
125 IAS 16, para. 25.
126 IAS 16, para. BC23.
127 IFRS 3, para. 2(a), and IFRS 3 (2007), *Business Combinations*, IASB, 2007 Bound Volume, para. 3(a).
128 IFRS 3, para. 64; IAS 27, para. 45.
129 IAS 27, para. 37.
130 IAS 27, paras. 37 and BC56.
131 *IASB Update*, IASB, May 2009, p. 5.
132 IAS 12, *Income Taxes*, IASB, para. 43.
133 IAS 31, paras. 52-53.
134 IAS 1, *Presentation of Financial Statements*, IASB, paras. 32-35.
135 IAS 1, para. 82(c).
136 IAS 1, para. 82(h).
137 IAS 28, para. 38.
138 IAS 1, para. 54(e).
139 IAS 31, para. 56.
140 IAS 31, para. 56.
141 IAS 31, para. 57.
142 IAS 31, para. 54.
143 IAS 31, para. 55.
144 IAS 31, para. 1.
145 IAS 31, para. 58B.
146 IFRS 7, *Financial Instruments: Disclosures*, IASB, para. 3(a).
147 IAS 31, para. 58.
148 IAS 27, para. 45(c).

149 IFRS 3, para. 64.
150 ED 2009/11, pp. 43, 45 and 46.
151 *IASB Update*, IASB, May 2009, p. 4.
152 ED 9, para. BC15.
153 EITF 00-1, *Investor Balance Sheet and Income Statement Display under the Equity Method for Investments in Certain Partnerships and Other Ventures*, EITF, July 2000, para. 4.
154 ED 9, Appendix A.
155 ED 9, paras. 1 and 5.
156 ED 9, para. 8
157 ED 9, para. 21.
158 ED 9, para. 11.
159 ED 9, para. 22.
160 ED 9, para. 15.
161 ED 9, para. 23.
162 ED 9, para. 1.
163 ED 9, paras. 1 and 5.
164 ED 9, para. 1.
165 ED 9, paras. 21-22.
166 ED 9, paras. 16 and 23.
167 ED 9, Appendix B.
168 ED 9, para. 22.
169 Based upon Example 2, I.E. ED 9.
170 Based upon Example 2, I.E. ED 9.
171 ED 9, para. 26.
172 ED 9, para. 2.
173 *IASB Update*, IASB, April 2008, p. 4; Information for Observers (April 2008 IASB meeting), *Joint Arrangements (Agenda Papers 10A and 10B)*.
174 *IASB Update*, IASB, May 2009, p. 3.
175 *IASB Update*, IASB, June 2009, p. 3.
176 Project Summary, *Joint Ventures*, IASB, July 2009.
177 *IASB Update*, IASB, May 2009, p. 5.

Chapter 13   Foreign exchange

1   INTRODUCTION

1.1   Background

An entity can engage in foreign currency activities in two ways. It may enter directly into transactions which are denominated in foreign currencies, the results of which need to be translated into the currency in which the company measures its results and financial position. Alternatively, it may conduct foreign operations through a foreign entity, such as a subsidiary, associate, joint venture or branch which keeps its accounting records in terms of its own currency. In this case it will need to translate the financial statements of the foreign entity for the purposes of inclusion in the consolidated financial statements.

Before an international standard was developed, there were four distinct methods which could be used in the translation process:

(a)   *current rate method* – all assets and liabilities are translated at the current rate of exchange, i.e. the exchange rate at the end of the reporting period;

(b)   *temporal method* – assets and liabilities carried at current prices (e.g. cash, receivables, payables, and investments at market value) are translated at the current rate of exchange. Assets and liabilities carried at past prices (e.g. property, investments at cost, prepayments) are translated at the rate of exchange in effect at the dates to which the prices pertain;

(c)   *current/non-current method* – all current assets and current liabilities are translated at the current rate of exchange. Non-current assets and liabilities are translated at historical rates, i.e. the exchange rate in effect at the time the asset was acquired or the liability incurred; and

(d)   *monetary/non-monetary method* – monetary assets and liabilities, i.e. items which represent the right to receive or the obligation to pay a fixed amount of money, are translated at the current rate of exchange. Non-monetary assets and liabilities are translated at the historical rate.

There was no consensus internationally on the best theoretical approach to adopt. In essence, the arguments surround the choice of exchange rates to be used in the translation process and the subsequent treatment of the exchange differences which arise.

1.2   Development of an international standard

1.2.1   IAS 21

The principal international standard dealing with this topic is IAS 21 – *The Effects of Changes in Foreign Exchange Rates*. The original standard was issued by the IASC in July 1983. Equivalent standards in the UK, US and Canada had already been issued following a long period of consultation between the ASC, the FASB and the CICA. The reason for the consultation was that it was considered that there was a need for international harmonisation in this field. IAS 21 followed the same general approach as its international counterparts in that it was based on a closing rate/net investment concept and an approach to translation which is related to the cash flow consequences of exchange movements. Exchange differences which give rise to cash flows, i.e. those resulting from business transactions, were to be reported as part of the profit or loss for the period. Other exchange differences which do not give rise to cash flows, because they result from retranslations of the holding company's long-term investment in the foreign subsidiary, were reported as reserve movements.

The standard therefore required that the procedures to be adopted when accounting for foreign operations should be considered in two stages, namely the preparation of the financial statements of the individual company and the preparation of the consolidated financial statements. The method used to translate the financial statements of a foreign operation for inclusion in consolidated financial statements depended on the way in which it was financed and operated in relation to the reporting entity. For this purpose, foreign operations were classified as either 'foreign entities' or 'foreign operations that are integral to the operations of the reporting enterprise'.[1] In the former case, the closing rate method of translation was used[2] and in the latter case the temporal method was used.[3] Although a revised version of IAS 21 was published in December 1993, it followed the same general approach as its predecessor.

1.2.2   IAS 21 (Revised 2003)

In December 2003, the IASB issued a revised version of IAS 21 to replace the earlier version issued by the IASC.

The IASB developed this revised IAS 21 as part of its project on Improvements to International Accounting Standards. The project was undertaken in the light of queries and criticisms raised in relation to the standards by securities regulators, professional accountants and other interested parties. The objectives of the project were to reduce or eliminate alternatives, redundancies and conflicts within the standards, to deal with some convergence issues and to make other improvements.[4]

For IAS 21 the Board's main objective was to provide additional guidance on the translation method and on determining the functional and presentation currencies.

Particularly, the requirements in the previous version of IAS 21 for distinguishing between foreign operations that are integral to the operations of the reporting entity and foreign entities were revised and they are now among the indicators of an entity's functional currency. As a result there is now no distinction between integral foreign operations and foreign entities. Instead an entity that was previously classified as an integral foreign operation will have the same functional currency as the reporting entity and will be subject to the same translation method as any other entity. The Board did not reconsider the fundamental approach to accounting for the effects of changes in foreign exchange rates contained in IAS 21.[5]

1.2.3 Subsequent amendments

After the revised version of IAS 21 was issued in December 2003, constituents raised a number of concerns with respect to the requirements for monetary items included as part of the net investment in a foreign operation. Following a proposal to deal with this issue by means of a 'Technical Correction',[6] the IASB published an Amendment to IAS 21 in December 2005 (see 3.4.1 B and D below).[7]

The publication of other standards and amendments to standards have resulted in consequential amendments to IAS 21, most notably IAS 27 – *Consolidated and Separate Financial Statements* – (as amended in 2008) and *Cost of an Investment in a Subsidiary, Jointly Controlled Entity or Associate* (amendments to IFRS 1 – *First-time Adoption of International Financial Reporting Standards* – and IAS 27). These amendments are discussed at 2.7.3 B and A below.

1.2.4 SIC and IFRIC pronouncements

The SIC had issued four interpretations of IAS 21 prior to its revision in 2003: SIC-7 – *Introduction of the Euro*; SIC-11 – *Foreign Exchange – Capitalisation of Losses Resulting from Severe Currency Devaluations*; SIC-19 – *Reporting Currency – Measurement and Presentation of Financial Statements under IAS 21 and IAS 29*; and SIC-30 – *Reporting Currency – Translation from Measurement Currency to Presentation Currency*.

SIC-7 deals with the application of IAS 21 to the changeover from the national currencies of participating Member States of the European Union to the euro and is covered at 3.6 below.

The other interpretations, SIC-11, SIC-19 and SIC-30, are no longer relevant following the revision to the standard in 2003.[8]

Whilst not actually an interpretation of IAS 21, IFRIC 16 – *Hedges of a Net Investment in a Foreign Operation* – which was published in July 2008, provides guidance on applying certain aspects of the standard. This is discussed at 3.3.5 and 3.3.6 below.

2   REQUIREMENTS OF IAS 21

2.1   Objective of the standard

As indicated at 1.1 above, an entity may carry on foreign activities in two ways. It may have transactions in foreign currencies or it may have foreign operations. In addition, an entity may present its financial statements in a foreign currency. IAS 21 does not set out what the objective of foreign currency translation should be, but just states that the objective of the standard is 'to prescribe how to include foreign currency transactions and foreign operations in the financial statements of an entity and how to translate financial statements into a presentation currency'.[9]

It also indicates that the principal issues to be addressed are 'which exchange rate(s) to use and how to report the effects of changes in exchange rates in the financial statements'.[10]

2.2   Scope

IAS 21 should be applied:[11]

(a)   in accounting for transactions and balances in foreign currencies, except for those derivative transactions and balances that are within the scope of IAS 39 – *Financial Instruments: Recognition and Measurement;*

(b)   in translating the results and financial position of foreign operations that are included in the financial statements of the entity by consolidation, proportionate consolidation or the equity method; and

(c)   in translating an entity's results and financial position into a presentation currency.

The standard explains that IAS 39 applies to many foreign currency derivatives and, accordingly, these are excluded from the scope of this standard. However, it goes on to say that those foreign currency derivatives that are not within the scope of IAS 39 (e.g. some foreign currency derivatives that are embedded in other contracts) are within the scope of IAS 21. In addition, it also states that IAS 21 applies when an entity translates amounts relating to derivatives from its functional currency to its presentation currency.[12]

IAS 21 also does not apply to hedge accounting for foreign currency items, including the hedging of a net investment in a foreign operation.[13] This is dealt with in IAS 39, which has detailed rules on hedging (see Chapter 33).

The standard explains that its requirements are applicable to an entity's statements that are to be described as complying with International Financial Reporting Standards. They do not apply to translations of financial information into a foreign currency that do not meet these requirements, although the standard does specify information to be disclosed in respect of such 'convenience translations'.[14]

IAS 21 does not apply to the presentation in a statement of cash flows of the cash flows arising from transactions in a foreign currency, or to the translation of cash flows of a foreign operation.[15] These are dealt with in IAS 7 – *Statement of Cash Flows* – (see Chapter 39 at 2.5.2).

2.3 Definitions of terms

The definitions of terms which are contained in IAS 21 are as follows:[16]

Closing rate is the spot exchange rate at the end of the reporting period.

Exchange difference is the difference resulting from translating a given number of units of one currency into another currency at different exchange rates.

Exchange rate is the ratio of exchange for two currencies.

Fair value is the amount for which an asset could be exchanged, or a liability settled, between knowledgeable, willing parties in an arm's length transaction.

Foreign currency is a currency other than the functional currency of the entity.

Foreign operation is an entity that is a subsidiary, associate, joint venture or branch of a reporting entity, the activities of which are based or conducted in a country or currency other than those of the reporting entity.

Functional currency is the currency of the primary economic environment in which the entity operates.

A *group* is a parent and all its subsidiaries.

Monetary items are units of currency held and assets and liabilities to be received or paid in a fixed or determinable number of units of currency.

Net investment in a foreign operation is the amount of the reporting entity's interest in the net assets of that operation.

Presentation currency is the currency in which the financial statements are presented.

Spot exchange rate is the exchange rate for immediate delivery.

The terms 'functional currency', 'monetary items' and 'net investment in a foreign operation' are elaborated on further within the standard. These are discussed at 2.5, 3.2.4 and 3.4.1 below.

2.4 Summary of the approach required by the standard

In preparing financial statements, each entity – whether a stand-alone entity, an entity with foreign operations (such as a parent) or a foreign operation (such as a subsidiary or branch) – determines its functional currency.[17] This is discussed at 2.5 below. In the case of group financial statements, it should be emphasised that there is not a 'group' functional currency; each entity included within the group financial statements, be it the parent, subsidiary, associate, joint venture or branch, has its own functional currency. Where an entity enters into a transaction denominated in a currency other than its functional currency, then it translates those foreign currency items into its functional currency and reports the effects of such translation in accordance with the provisions of IAS 21 discussed at 2.6 below.[18]

Many reporting entities comprise a number of individual entities (e.g. a group is made up of a parent and one or more subsidiaries). Various types of entities, whether members of a group or otherwise, may have investments in associates or joint ventures. They may also have branches. It is necessary for the results and financial position of each individual entity included in the reporting entity to be translated into the currency in which the reporting entity presents its financial statements (if this presentation currency is different from the individual entity's functional currency). The results and financial position of any individual entity within the reporting entity whose functional currency differs from the presentation currency are translated in accordance with the provisions of IAS 21 discussed at 2.7 below.[19] Since IAS 21 permits the presentation currency of a reporting entity to be any currency (or currencies), this translation process will also apply to the parent's figures if its functional currency is different from the presentation currency.

The standard also permits a stand-alone entity preparing financial statements or an entity preparing separate financial statements in accordance with IAS 27 to present its financial statements in any currency (or currencies). If the entity's presentation currency differs from its functional currency, its results and financial position are also translated into the presentation currency in accordance with the provisions of IAS 21 discussed at 2.7 below.[20]

2.5   Determination of an entity's functional currency

As indicated at 2.3 above, functional currency is defined as the currency of 'the primary economic environment in which the entity operates'. This will normally be the one in which it primarily generates and expends cash.[21]

IAS 21 sets out a number of factors or indicators that any entity should or may need to consider in determining its functional currency. When the factors or indicators are mixed and the functional currency is not obvious, the standard requires management to use its judgement to determine the functional currency that most faithfully represents the economic effects of the underlying transactions, events and conditions. As part of this approach, management gives priority to the following primary indicators before considering the other indicators set out in the standard, which are designed to provide additional supporting evidence to determine an entity's functional currency.[22]

The primary factors that IAS 21 requires an entity to consider in determining its functional currency are as follows:[23]

(a)   the currency:

    (i)   that mainly influences sales prices for goods and services (this will often be the currency in which sales prices for its goods and services are denominated and settled); and

(ii)   of the country whose competitive forces and regulations mainly determine the sales prices of its goods and services.

(b)   the currency that mainly influences labour, material and other costs of providing goods or services (this will often be the currency in which such costs are denominated and settled).

Where the functional currency of the entity is not obvious from the above, then the standard indicates that the following factors may also provide evidence of an entity's functional currency:[24]

(a)   the currency in which funds from financing activities (i.e. issuing debt and equity instruments) are generated;

(b)   the currency in which receipts from operating activities are usually retained.

The standard also says that the following additional factors are considered in determining the functional currency of a foreign operation, and whether its functional currency is the same as that of the reporting entity (the reporting entity, in this context, being the entity that has the foreign operation as its subsidiary, branch, associate or joint venture):[25]

(a)   whether the activities of the foreign operation are carried out as an extension of the reporting entity, rather than being carried out with a significant degree of autonomy. An example of the former is when the foreign operation only sells goods imported from the reporting entity and remits the proceeds to it. An example of the latter is when the operation accumulates cash and other monetary items, incurs expenses, generates income and arranges borrowings, all substantially in its local currency;

(b)   whether transactions with the reporting entity are a high or a low proportion of the foreign operation's activities;

(c)   whether cash flows from the activities of the foreign operation directly affect the cash flows of the reporting entity and are readily available for remittance to it;

(d)   whether cash flows from the activities of the foreign operation are sufficient to service existing and normally expected debt obligations without funds being made available by the reporting entity.

Although the standard says that these factors 'are' considered in determining the functional currency of a foreign operation, this contradicts the requirement in the standard that management gives priority to the primary indicators before considering the other indicators. If it is obvious from the primary indicators what the entity's functional currency is, then there is no need to consider any of the other factors.

Example 13.1:   Factors to be considered when determining the functional currency

A French entity (Parent A) has a US subsidiary (Subsidiary B) that produces and sells knitwear in the United States.

It is clear from the primary factors in paragraph 9 of IAS 21 described above that Subsidiary B's functional currency is the US dollar, because the US dollar mainly influences sales prices for goods, labour, material and other costs of providing goods, and the competitive forces and regulations that mainly determine the sales prices of the goods are located in the United States.

However, suppose Subsidiary B is financed by an inter-company loan denominated in euros granted from Parent A and the cash flows generated by Subsidiary B are transferred to Parent A on a regular basis. Should these additional factors be taken into account in determining the functional currency of Subsidiary B?

In our view, they should not. These additional factors only have to be considered when it is not obvious from the primary factors in paragraph 9 what Subsidiary B's functional currency is.

However, if Subsidiary B was not producing the knitwear itself, but purchasing it from sources in Europe (such that its operating costs were predominantly in euros, and this meant that it was no longer obvious based on the primary factors in paragraph 9 that its functional currency was the US dollar), then the additional factors would be taken into account in determining Subsidiary B's functional currency.

Since an entity's functional currency reflects the underlying transactions, events and conditions that are relevant to it, once it is determined, IAS 21 requires that the functional currency is not changed unless there is a change in those underlying transactions, events and conditions.[26] The implication of this is that management of an entity cannot decree what the functional currency is – it is a matter of fact, albeit subjectively determined fact based on management's judgement of all the circumstances.

For some entities the determination of functional currency may be relatively straightforward. However, for many entities, particularly entities within a group, this may not be the case. This is discussed further at 3.1 below.

2.6   Reporting foreign currency transactions in the functional currency of an entity

As indicated at 1.1 above, an entity may carry on foreign activities in two ways. It may have transactions in foreign currencies or it may have foreign operations. Where an entity enters into a transaction denominated in a currency other than its functional currency then it will have to translate those foreign currency items into its functional currency and report the effects of such translation.

The general requirements of IAS 21 are as follows.

2.6.1   Initial recognition

A foreign currency transaction is a transaction that is denominated or requires settlement in a foreign currency, including transactions arising when an entity:[27]

(a)   buys or sells goods or services whose price is denominated in a foreign currency;

(b)   borrows or lends funds when the amounts payable or receivable are denominated in a foreign currency; or

(c)   otherwise acquires or disposes of assets, or incurs or settles liabilities, denominated in a foreign currency.

On initial recognition, foreign currency transactions should be translated into the functional currency using the spot exchange rate between the foreign currency and the functional currency on the date of the transaction.[28] The date of a transaction is the date on which it first qualifies for recognition in accordance with IFRS. For convenience, an average rate for a week or month may be used for all foreign currency transactions occurring during that period, if the exchange rate does not fluctuate significantly.[29]

2.6.2 Reporting at the end of subsequent reporting periods

At the end of each reporting period:[30]

(a) foreign currency monetary items should be translated using the closing rate;

(b) non-monetary items that are measured in terms of historical cost in a foreign currency should be translated using the exchange rate at the date of the transaction; and

(c) non-monetary items that are measured at fair value in a foreign currency should be translated using the exchange rate at the date when the fair value was determined.

2.6.3 Treatment of exchange differences

A   Monetary items

The general rule in IAS 21 is that exchange differences on the settlement or retranslation of monetary items should be recognised in profit or loss in the period in which they arise.[31]

As the standard explains 'when monetary items arise from a foreign currency transaction and there is a change in the exchange rate between the transaction date and the date of settlement, an exchange difference results. When the transaction is settled within the same accounting period as that in which it occurred, all the exchange difference is recognised in that period. However, when the transaction is settled in a subsequent accounting period, the exchange difference recognised in each period up to the date of settlement is determined by the change in exchange rates during each period.'[32]

The above general requirements can be illustrated in the following examples:

Example 13.2:   *Reporting a foreign currency transaction in the functional currency*

A French entity purchases plant and equipment on credit from a Canadian supplier for C$328,000 in January 2010 when the exchange rate is €1=C$1.64. The entity records the asset at a cost of €200,000. At the French entity's year end at 31 March 2010 the account has not yet been settled. The closing rate is €1=C$1.61. The amount payable would be retranslated at €203,727 in the balance sheet and an exchange loss of €3,727 would be reported as part of the profit or loss for the period. The cost of the asset would remain as €200,000.

Example 13.3:   *Reporting a foreign currency transaction in the functional currency*

A UK entity sells goods to a German entity for €87,000 on 28 February 2010 when the exchange rate is £1=€1.45. It receives payment on 31 March 2010 when the exchange rate is £1=€1.50. On 28 February the UK entity will record a sale and corresponding receivable of £60,000. When payment is received on 31 March the actual amount received is only £58,000. The loss on exchange of £2,000 would be reported as part of the profit or loss for the period.

IAS 21 does not specify where any exchange differences on monetary items should be presented within the statement of comprehensive income. As indicated at 2.9.1 below, we recommend that entities in disclosing the amount of such exchange differences should indicate the line item(s) in which they are included. Further, the classification of exchange differences (both gains and losses) arising from transactions of a similar nature should be classified consistently throughout the periods presented.

However, there are situations where the above general rule will not be applied. The first exception to the general rule identified in IAS 21 relates to exchange differences arising on a monetary item that, in substance, forms part of an entity's net investment in a foreign operation (see 3.4.1 below). In this situation the exchange differences should be recognised initially in other comprehensive income until the disposal of the investment (see 2.7.3 below). However, this treatment only applies in the financial statements that include the foreign operation and the reporting entity (i.e. financial statements in which the foreign operation is consolidated, proportionately consolidated or accounted for using the equity method). It does not apply to the reporting entity's separate financial statements or the financial statements of the foreign operation; the exchange differences will be recognised in profit or loss in the period in which they arise in the financial statements of the entity that has the foreign currency exposure.[33] This is discussed further at 3.4.1 below.

The next exception relates to hedge accounting. As noted at 2.2 above, IAS 39 applies to hedge accounting for foreign currency items. The application of hedge accounting requires an entity to account for some exchange differences differently from the treatment of exchange differences required by IAS 21. For example, IAS 39 requires that exchange differences on monetary items that qualify as hedging instruments in a cash flow hedge or a hedge of a net investment in a foreign operation are recognised initially in other comprehensive income to the extent the hedge is effective (see Chapter 33).

In addition to the above exceptions identified in IAS 21, as discussed at 3.2.5 below, there can be other situations where exchange differences on monetary items are not recognised in profit or loss in the period they arise.

B   Non-monetary items

When non-monetary items that are measured at fair value in a foreign currency are translated using the exchange rate as at the date when the fair value was determined, any re-measurement gain or loss will include an element relating to the change on exchange rates. In this situation, the exchange differences are recognised as part of the gain or loss arising on the fair value re-measurement.

When a gain or loss on a non-monetary item is recognised in other comprehensive income, any exchange component of that gain or loss should also be recognised in other comprehensive income.[34] For example, IAS 16 – *Property, Plant and Equipment* – requires some gains and losses arising on a revaluation of property, plant and equipment to be recognised in other comprehensive income (see Chapter 16 at 4.1).

When such an asset is measured in a foreign currency, the revalued amount has to be translated using the rate at the date the value is determined, resulting in an exchange difference that is also recognised in other comprehensive income.[35]

Conversely, when a gain or loss on a non-monetary item is recognised in profit or loss (e.g. financial instruments that are measured at fair value through profit or loss in accordance with IAS 39, see Chapter 32 at 3.1), any exchange component of that gain or loss should be recognised in profit or loss.[36]

An example of an accounting policy dealing with the reporting of foreign currency transactions in the functional currency of an entity is illustrated below.

Extract 13.1: ING Groep N.V. (2007)

FOREIGN CURRENCY TRANSLATION [extract]

Functional and presentation currency

Items included in the financial statements of each of the Group's entities are measured using the currency of the primary economic environment in which the entity operates ('the functional currency'). The consolidated financial statements are presented in euros, which is the Company's functional and presentation currency.

Transactions and balances

Foreign currency transactions are translated into the functional currency using the exchange rates prevailing at the dates of the transactions. Foreign exchange gains and losses resulting from the settlement of such transactions and from the translation at year-end exchange rates of monetary assets and liabilities denominated in foreign currencies are recognised in the profit and loss account, except when deferred in equity as part of qualifying cash flow hedges or qualifying net investment hedges.

Translation differences on non-monetary items, measured at fair value through profit and loss, are reported as part of the fair value gain or loss. Non-monetary items are retranslated at the date fair value is determined. Translation differences on non-monetary items measured at fair value through the revaluation reserve are included in the revaluation reserve in equity.

2.6.4   *Change in functional currency*

As indicated at 2.5 above, IAS 21 requires management to use its judgment to determine the entity's functional currency such that it most faithfully represents the economic effects of the underlying transactions, events and conditions that are relevant to the entity. Accordingly, once the functional currency is determined, the standard only allows it to be changed if there is a change to those underlying transactions, events and conditions. For example, a change in the currency that mainly influences the sales prices of goods and services may lead to a change in an entity's functional currency.[37]

When there is a change in an entity's functional currency, the entity should apply the translation procedures applicable to the new functional currency prospectively from the date of the change.[38]

In other words, an entity translates all items into the new functional currency using the exchange rate at the date of the change. The resulting translated amounts for non-monetary items are treated as their historical cost. Exchange differences arising from the translation of a foreign operation recognised in other comprehensive income are not reclassified from equity to profit or loss until the disposal of the operation (see 2.7.3 below).[39]

Example 13.4:   Change in functional currency

The management of Entity A has considered the functional currency of the entity to be the euro. However, as a result of change in circumstances affecting the operations of the entity, management determines that on 1 January 2010 the functional currency of the entity is now the US dollar. The exchange rate at that date is €1=US$1.20. The balance sheet of Entity A at 1 January 2010 in its old functional currency is as follows:

	€
Property, plant and equipment	200,000
Current assets	
Inventories	10,000
Receivables	20,000
Cash	5,000
	35,000
Current liabilities	
Payables	15,000
Taxation	3,000
	18,000
Net current assets	17,000
	217,000
Long-term loans	120,000
	97,000

Included within the balance sheet at 1 January 2010 are the following items:

- Equipment with a cost of €33,000 and a net book value of €16,500. This equipment was originally purchased for £20,000 in 2006 and has been translated at the rate ruling at the date of purchase of £1=€1.65.

- Inventories with a cost of €6,000. These were purchased for US$6,000 and have been translated at the rate ruling at the date of purchase of €1=US$1.00.

- Payables of €5,000 representing the US$6,000 due in respect of the above inventories, translated at the rate ruling at 1 January 2010.

- Long-term loans of €15,000 representing the outstanding balance of £10,000 on a loan originally taken out to finance the acquisition of the above equipment, translated at £1=€1.50, the rate ruling at 1 January 2010.

Entity A applies the translational procedures applicable to its new functional currency prospectively from the date of change. Accordingly, all items in its balance sheet at 1 January 2010 are translated at the rate of €1=US$1.20 giving rise to the following amounts:

	$
Property, plant and equipment	240,000
Current assets	
Inventories	12,000
Receivables	24,000
Cash	6,000
	42,000
Current liabilities	
Payables	18,000
Taxation	3,600
	21,600
Net current assets	20,400
	260,400
Long-term loans	144,000
	116,400

As far as the equipment that was originally purchased for £20,000 is concerned, the cost and net book value in terms of Entity A's new functional currency are US$39,600 and US$19,800 respectively, being €33,000 and €16,500 translated at €1=US$1.20. Entity A does not go back and translate the £20,000 cost at whatever the £ sterling/US dollar exchange rate was at the date of purchase and calculate a revised net book value on that basis.

Similarly, the inventories purchased in US dollars are included at $7,200, being €6,000 translated at €1=US$1.20. This is despite the fact that Entity A knows that the original cost was $6,000.

As far as the payables in respect of the inventories are concerned, these are included at $6,000, being €5,000 translated at €1=US$1.20. This represents the original amount payable in US dollars. However, this is as it should be since the original payable had been translated into euros at the rate ruling at 1 January 2010 and has just been translated back into US dollars at the same rate. The impact of the change in functional currency is that whereas Entity A had recognised an exchange gain of €1,000 while the functional currency was the euro, no further exchange difference will be recognised in respect of this amount payable. Exchange differences will now arise from 1 January 2010 on those payables denominated in euros, whereas no such differences would have arisen on such items prior to that date.

Similarly, the £10,000 amount outstanding on the loan will be included at $18,000, being €15,000 translated at €1=US$1.20. This is equivalent to the translation of the £10,000 at a rate of £1=US$1.80, being the direct exchange rate between the two currencies at 1 January 2010. In this case, whereas previously exchange gains and losses would have been recognised on this loan balance based on movements of the £/€ exchange rate, as from 1 January 2010 the exchange gains and losses will be recognised based on the £/$ exchange rate.

2.7   Use of a presentation currency other than the functional currency

As indicated at 2.4 above, an entity may present its financial statements in any currency (or currencies). If the presentation currency differs from the entity's functional currency, it needs to translate its results and financial position into the presentation currency. For example, when a group contains individual entities with different functional currencies, the results and financial position of each entity are expressed in a common currency so that consolidated financial statements may be presented.[40] As noted earlier, there is no concept of a 'group' functional currency. Each entity within the group has its own functional currency, and the results and financial position of each entity have to be translated into the presentation currency that is used for the consolidated financial statements.[41]

The requirements of IAS 21 in respect of this translation process are discussed below. The procedures to be adopted apply not only to the inclusion of foreign subsidiaries in consolidated financial statements but also to the incorporation of the results of associates and joint ventures.[42] They also apply when the results of a foreign branch are to be incorporated into the financial statements of an individual entity or a stand-alone entity preparing financial statements or when an entity preparing separate financial statements in accordance with IAS 27 presents its financial statements in a currency other than its functional currency.

2.7.1   Translation to the presentation currency

Under IAS 21, the method of translation depends on whether the entity's functional currency is that of a hyperinflationary economy or not, and if it is, whether it is being translated into a presentation currency which is that of a hyperinflationary economy or not. A hyperinflationary economy is defined in IAS 29 – *Financial Reporting in Hyperinflationary Economies* (see Chapter 14 at 2.3.1). The requirements of IAS 21 discussed below can be summarised as follows:

	Presentation currency	
	Non-hyperinflationary	Hyperinflationary
Non-hyperinflationary functional currency		
Assets/liabilities		
– current period	Closing rate (current B/S date)	Closing rate (current B/S date)
– comparative period	Closing rate (comparative B/S date)	Closing rate (comparative B/S date)
Equity items		
– current period	Not specified	Not specified
– comparative period	Not specified	Not specified
Income/expenses (including those recognised in other comprehensive income)		
– current period	Actual rates (or appropriate average for current period)	Actual rates (or appropriate average for current period)
– comparative period	Actual rates (or appropriate average for comparative period)	Actual rates (or appropriate average for comparative period)
Exchange differences	Separate component of equity	Separate component of equity
Hyperinflationary functional currency		
Assets/liabilities		
– current period	Closing rate (current B/S date)	Closing rate (current B/S date)
– comparative period	Closing rate (comparative B/S date)	Closing rate (current B/S date)
Equity items		
– current period	Closing rate (current B/S date)	Closing rate (current B/S date)
– comparative period	Closing rate (comparative B/S date)	Closing rate (current B/S date)
Income/expenses (including those recognised in other comprehensive income)		
– current period	Closing rate (current B/S date)	Closing rate (current B/S date)
– comparative period	Closing rate (comparative B/S date)	Closing rate (current B/S date)
Exchange differences	Not specified	Not applicable

A   Functional currency is not that of a hyperinflationary economy

The results and financial position of an entity whose functional currency is not the currency of a hyperinflationary economy should be translated into a different presentation currency using the following procedures:[43]

(a)   assets and liabilities for each balance sheet presented (i.e. including comparatives) are translated at the closing rate at the date of that balance sheet;

(b)   income and expenses for each statement of comprehensive income or separate income statement presented (i.e. including comparatives) are translated at exchange rates at the dates of the transactions; and

(c)   all resulting exchange differences are recognised in other comprehensive income.

For practical reasons, the reporting entity may use a rate that approximates the actual exchange rate, e.g. an average rate for the period, to translate income and expense items. However, if exchange rates fluctuate significantly, the use of the average rate for a period is inappropriate.[44]

The translational process above makes only limited reference to the translation of equity items. The treatment of such items is discussed at 3.3.3 below.

IAS 21 indicates that the exchange differences referred to in item (c) above result from:[45]

- translating income and expenses at the exchange rates at the dates of the transactions and assets and liabilities at the closing rate. Such exchange differences arise both on income and expense items recognised in profit or loss and on those recognised in other comprehensive income; and

- translating the opening net assets at a closing rate that differs from the previous closing rate.

This is not in fact completely accurate since if the entity has had any transactions with equity holders that have resulted in a change in the net assets during the period there are likely to be further exchange differences that need to be recognised to the extent that the closing rate differs from the rate used to translate the transaction. This will particularly be the case where a parent has subscribed for further equity shares in a subsidiary.

The reason why these exchange differences are not recognised in profit or loss is because the changes in exchange rates have little or no direct effect on the present and future cash flows from operations.[46]

The application of these procedures is illustrated in the following example.

Example 13.5:   *Translation of a non-hyperinflationary functional currency to a non-hyperinflationary presentation currency*

An Australian entity owns 100% of the share capital of a foreign entity which was set up a number of years ago when the exchange rate was A\$1=FC2. It is consolidating the financial statements of the subsidiary in its consolidated financial statements for the year ended 31 December 2010. The exchange rate at the year-end is A\$1=FC4 (2009: A\$1=FC3). For the purposes of illustration, it is assumed that exchange rates have not fluctuated significantly and the appropriate weighted average rate for the year was A\$1=FC3.5, and that the currency of the foreign entity is not that of a hyperinflationary economy. The income statement of the subsidiary for that year and its balance sheet at the beginning and end of the year in its functional currency and translated into Australian dollars are as follows:

Income statement

	FC	A$
Sales	35,000	10,000
Cost of sales	(33,190)	(9,483)
Depreciation	(500)	(143)
Interest	(350)	(100)
Profit before taxation	960	274
Taxation	(460)	(131)
Profit after taxation	500	143

Balance sheets	2009	2010	2009	2010
	FC	FC	A$	A$
Property, plant and equipment	6,000	5,500	2,000	1,375
Current assets				
Inventories	2,700	3,000	900	750
Receivables	4,800	4,000	1,600	1,000
Cash	200	600	67	150
	7,700	7,600	2,567	1,900
Current liabilities				
Payables	4,530	3,840	1,510	960
Taxation	870	460	290	115
	5,400	4,300	1,800	1,075
Net current assets	2,300	3,300	767	825
	8,300	8,800	2,767	2,200
Long-term loans	3,600	3,600	1,200	900
	4,700	5,200	1,567	1,300
Share capital	1,000	1,000	500	500
Retained profits*	3,700	4,200	1,500	1,643
Exchange reserve*			(433)	(843)
	4,700	5,200	1,567	1,300

*   The opening balances for 2009 in A$ have been assumed and represent cumulative amounts since the foreign entity was set up.

The movement of A$(410) in the exchange reserve included as a separate component of equity is made up as follows:

(i)   the exchange loss of A$392 on the opening net investment in the subsidiary, calculated as follows:

Opening net assets at opening rate	– FC4,700 at FC3 = A$1 =	A$1,567
Opening net assets at closing rate	– FC4,700 at FC4 = A$1 =	A$1,175
Exchange loss on net assets		A$392

(ii) the exchange loss of A$18, being the difference between the income account translated at an average rate, i.e. A$143, and at the closing rate, i.e. A$125.

When the exchange differences relate to a foreign operation that is consolidated but not wholly-owned, accumulated exchange differences arising from translation and attributable to non-controlling interests are allocated to, and recognised as part of, non-controlling interests in the consolidated balance sheet.[47]

An example of an accounting policy dealing with the translation of entities whose functional currency is not that of a hyperinflationary economy is illustrated in the following extract.

Extract 13.2: Lloyds TSB Group plc (2007)

1   Accounting policies [extract]

(s)   Foreign currency translation

(1)   Functional and presentation currency

Items included in the financial statements of each of the Group's entities are measured using the currency of the primary economic environment in which the entity operates ('the functional currency'). The consolidated financial statements are presented in sterling, which is the Company's functional and presentation currency.

(2)   **Transactions and balances**

Foreign currency transactions are translated into the functional currency using the exchange rates prevailing at the dates of the transactions. Foreign exchange gains and losses resulting from the settlement of such transactions and from the translation at year end exchange rates of monetary assets and liabilities denominated in foreign currencies are recognised in the income statement, except when deferred in equity as qualifying cash flow or net investment hedges. Non-monetary assets that are measured at fair value are translated using the exchange rate at the date that the fair value was determined. Translation differences on equities and similar non-monetary items measured at fair value are recognised in profit or loss, except for differences on available-for-sale non-monetary financial assets such as equity shares, which are included in the fair value reserve in equity unless the asset is a hedged item in a fair value hedge.

(3)   **Group companies**

The results and financial position of all the Group entities (none of which has the currency of a hyperinflationary economy) that have a functional currency different from the presentation currency are translated into the presentation currency as follows:

(i)   assets and liabilities for each balance sheet presented are translated at the closing rate at the date of that balance sheet;

(ii)   income and expenses for each income statement are translated at average exchange rates (unless this average is not a reasonable approximation of the cumulative effect of the rates prevailing on the transaction dates, in which case income and expenses are translated at the dates of the transactions); and

(iii)   all resulting exchange differences are recognised as a separate component of equity.

On consolidation, exchange differences arising from the translation of the net investment in foreign entities are taken to shareholders' equity. When a foreign operation is sold, such exchange differences are recognised in the income statement as part of the gain or loss on sale.

Goodwill and fair value adjustments arising on the acquisition of a foreign entity are treated as assets and liabilities of the foreign entity and translated at the closing rate.

The IASB had considered an alternative translation method, which would have been to translate all amounts (including comparatives) at the most recent closing rate. This was considered to have several advantages: it is simple to apply; it does not generate any new gains and losses; and it does not change ratios such as return on assets. Supporters of this method believed that the process of merely expressing amounts in a different currency should preserve the same relationships among amounts as measured in the functional currency.[48] These views were probably based more on the IASB's proposals for allowing an entity to present its financial statements in a currency other than its functional currency, rather than the translation of foreign operations for inclusion in consolidated financial statements. Such an approach does have theoretical appeal. However, the major drawback is that it would require the comparatives to be restated from those previously reported.

The IASB rejected this alternative and decided to require the method that the previous version of IAS 21 required for translation the financial statements of a foreign operation.[49] It is asserted that this method results in the same amounts in the presentation currency regardless of whether the financial statements of a foreign operation are first translated into the functional currency of another group entity and then into the presentation currency or translated directly into the presentation currency.[50] We agree that it will result in the same amounts for the balance sheet, regardless of whether the translation process is a single or two-stage process. However, it does not necessarily hold true for income and expense items particularly if an indirectly held foreign operation is disposed of – this is discussed further at 3.3.5 and 3.3.6 below. Differences will also arise between the two methods if an average rate is used, although these are likely to be insignificant.

The IASB states that the method chosen avoids the need to decide the currency in which to express the financial statements of a multinational group before they are translated into the presentation currency. In addition, it produces the same amounts in the presentation currency for a stand-alone entity as for an identical subsidiary of a parent whose functional currency is the presentation currency.[51] For example, if a Swiss entity with the Swiss franc as its functional currency wishes to present its financial statements in euros, the translated amounts in euros should be the same as those for an identical entity with the Swiss franc as its functional currency that are included within the consolidated financial statements of its parent that presents its financial statements in euros.

B　　　*Functional currency is that of a hyperinflationary economy*

The results and financial position of an entity whose functional currency is the currency of a hyperinflationary economy should be translated into a different presentation currency using the following procedures:[52]

(a)　all amounts (i.e. assets, liabilities, equity items, income and expenses, including comparatives) are translated at the closing rate at the date of the most recent balance sheet, except that

(b)　when amounts are translated into the currency of a non-hyperinflationary economy, comparative amounts are those that were presented as current year amounts in the relevant prior year financial statements (i.e. not adjusted for subsequent changes in the price level or subsequent changes in exchange rates).

When an entity's functional currency is the currency of a hyperinflationary economy, the entity should restate its financial statements in accordance with IAS 29 before applying the translation method set out above, except for comparative amounts that are translated into a currency of a non-hyperinflationary economy (see (b) above).[53]

When the economy ceases to be hyperinflationary and the entity no longer restates its financial statements in accordance with IAS 29, it should use as the historical costs for translation into the presentation currency the amounts restated to the price level at the date the entity ceased restating its financial statements.[54]

Example 13.6:   *Translation of a hyperinflationary functional currency to a non-hyperinflationary presentation currency*

Using the same basic facts as Example 13.5 above, but assuming that the functional currency of the subsidiary is that of a hyperinflationary economy, the income account of the subsidiary for that year and its balance sheet at the beginning and end of the year in its functional currency and translated into Australian dollars are as shown below. For the purposes of illustration, any adjustments resulting from the restatement in accordance with IAS 29 have been ignored. See Chapter 14 for a discussion of such adjustments.

Income statement

	FC	A$
Sales	35,000	8,750
Cost of sales	(33,190)	(8,298)
Depreciation	(500)	(125)
Interest	(350)	(75)
Profit before taxation	960	240
Taxation	(460)	(115)
Profit after taxation	500	125

Balance sheets	2009 FC	2010 FC	2009 A$	2010 A$
Property, plant and equipment	6,000	5,500	2,000	1,375
Current assets				
Inventories	2,700	3,000	900	750
Receivables	4,800	4,000	1,600	1,000
Cash	200	600	67	150
	7,700	7,600	2,567	1,900
Current liabilities				
Payables	4,530	3,840	1,510	960
Taxation	870	460	290	115
	5,400	4,300	1,800	1,075
Net current assets	2,300	3,300	767	825
	8,300	8,800	2,767	2,200
Long-term loans	3,600	3,600	1,200	900
	4,700	5,200	1,567	1,300
Share capital	1,000	1,000	333	250
Retained profits*	3,700	4,200	1,234	1,050
	4,700	5,200	1,567	1,300

*The movement in retained profits is as follows:

	A$
Balance brought forward	1,234
Profit for year	125
Exchange difference	(309)
	1,050

The exchange loss of A$309 represents the reduction in retained profits due the movements in exchange, calculated as follows:

Opening balance at opening rate	– FC3,700 at FC3 = A$1 =	A$1,234
Opening balance at closing rate	– FC3,700 at FC4 = A$1 =	A$925
Exchange loss		A$(309)

It is unclear what should happen to such an exchange difference (and also the movement in share capital caused by the change in exchange rates) since paragraph 42 of IAS 21 makes no reference to any possible exchange differences arising from this process. However, in the absence of any requirement to recognise them in other comprehensive income (as in Example 13.5 above) or to profit or loss, it would seem that they are to be included as movements in the equity balances to which they relate.

An example of an accounting policy dealing with the translation of entities whose functional currency is that of a hyperinflationary economy is illustrated in the following extract.

Extract 13.3: France Telecom S.A. (2005)

2.1   SIGNIFICANT ACCOUNTING POLICIES [extract]

2.1.7   Effect of changes in foreign exchange rates [extract]

Translation of financial statements of foreign subsidiaries

The financial statements of foreign subsidiaries whose functional currency is not the euro or the currency of a hyperinflationary economy are translated into France Telecom's presentation currency (euros) as follows:

–   assets and liabilities are translated at the year-end rate;

–   items in the statement of income are translated at the average rate for the year;

–   the translation adjustment resulting from the use of these different rates is included as a separate component of shareholders' equity.

Hyperinflationary economies

The financial statements of subsidiaries whose functional currency is the currency of a hyperinflationary economy are adjusted for the effects of inflation prior to translation into euros as follows:

–   non-monetary balance sheet, statement of income and cash flow items are adjusted for inflation based on the change in a general price index from the date of acquisition to the balance sheet date;

–   the exchange gain or loss on the subsidiary's net monetary position during the period (determined based on the change in the general price index over the same period) is recognized in the income statement under exchange gains and losses;

–   the differences resulting from the application of the index of prices in force at the balance sheet date to monetary and non-monetary items reflected in the opening balance sheet are recorded as a separate component of shareholders' equity.

The financial statements of foreign subsidiaries previously adjusted for inflation as described above are subsequently translated into euros as follows:

–   assets, liabilities, statement of income and cash flow items are translated at the year-end rate;

–   the translation gains and losses resulting from the use of the year-end exchange rate to translate assets and liabilities presented in the opening balance sheet are recorded as a separate component of shareholders' equity.

2.7.2   Translation of a foreign operation

In addition to the procedures discussed at 2.7.1 above, IAS 21 has additional provisions that apply when the results and financial position of a foreign operation are translated into a presentation currency so that the foreign operation can be included in the financial statements of the reporting entity by consolidation, proportionate consolidation or the equity method.[55]

A   Exchange differences on intragroup balances

The standard states that 'the incorporation of the results and financial position of a foreign operation with those of the reporting entity follows normal consolidation procedures, such as the elimination of intragroup balances and intragroup transactions of a subsidiary'.[56] However, an intragroup monetary asset (or liability), whether short-term or long-term, cannot be eliminated against the corresponding intragroup liability (or asset) without the entity with the currency exposure recognising an exchange difference on the intragroup balance. As indicated at 2.6.3 A above this will be reflected in that entity's profit or loss for the period. Except as indicated below, IAS 21 requires this exchange difference to continue to be included in profit or loss in the consolidated financial statements. This is because the monetary item represents a commitment to convert one currency into another and exposes the reporting entity to a gain or loss through currency fluctuations. However, where the exchange difference arises on an intragroup balance that, in substance, forms part of an entity's net investment in a foreign operation (see 3.4.1 below), then the exchange difference is not to be recognised in profit or loss in the consolidated financial statements, but is recognised in other comprehensive income and accumulated in a separate component of equity until the disposal of the foreign operation (see 2.7.3 below).[57]

B   Non-coterminous period ends

IAS 21 recognises that in preparing consolidated financial statements it may be that a foreign operation is consolidated on the basis of financial statements made up to a different date from that of the reporting entity (see Chapter 7 at 2.5). In such a case, the standard initially states that the assets and liabilities of the foreign operation are to be translated at the exchange rate at the end of the reporting period of the foreign operation rather than that at the date of the consolidated financial statements. However, it then goes on to say that adjustments are made for significant changes in exchange rates up to the end of the reporting period of the reporting entity in accordance with IAS 27. The same approach is used in applying the equity method to associates and joint ventures and in applying proportionate consolidation to joint ventures in accordance with IAS 28 – *Investments in Associates* – and IAS 31 – *Interests in Joint Ventures* (see Chapters 11 and 12 respectively).[58]

The rationale for this approach is not explained in IAS 21. The initial treatment is that required by SFAS 52 – *Foreign Currency Translation* – and the reason given in that standard is that this presents the functional currency performance of the subsidiary during the subsidiary's financial year and its position at the end of that period in terms of the parent company's reporting (presentation) currency.[59] The subsidiary may have entered into transactions in other currencies, including the functional currency of the parent, and monetary items in these currencies will have been translated using rates ruling at the end of the subsidiary's reporting period. The income statement of the subsidiary will reflect the economic consequences of carrying out these transactions during the period ended on that date. In order that the effects of these transactions in the subsidiary's financial statements are not distorted, the financial statements should be translated using the closing rate at the end of the subsidiary's reporting period.

However, an alternative argument could have been advanced for using the closing rate ruling at the end of the parent's reporting period. All subsidiaries within a group should normally prepare financial statements up to the same date as the parent entity so that the parent can prepare consolidated financial statements that present fairly the financial performance and financial position about the group as that of a single entity. The use of financial statements of a subsidiary made up to a date earlier than that of the parent is only an administrative convenience and a surrogate for financial statements made up to the proper date. Arguably, therefore the closing rate that should have been used is that which would have been used if the financial statements were made up to the proper date, i.e. that ruling at the end of the reporting period of the parent. Another reason for using this rate is that there may be subsidiaries that have the same functional currency as the subsidiary with the non-coterminous year end that do make up their financial statements to the same date as the parent company and therefore in order to be consistent with them the same rate should be used.

C   Goodwill and fair value adjustments

Prior to its revision in 2003, IAS 21 allowed these items to be translated at historical rates.[60] In revising the standard, the IASB decided that the treatment of such items depends on whether they are part of:[61]

(a)   the assets and liabilities of the acquired entity (which would imply translating them at the closing rate); or

(b)   the assets and liabilities of the parent (which would imply translating them at the historical rate).

In the case of fair value adjustments these clearly relate to the acquired entity. However, in the case of goodwill there were different views expressed by commentators.

Example 13.7:   Translation of goodwill

A UK company acquires all of the share capital of an Australian company on 30 June 2010 at a cost of A$3m. The fair value of the net assets of the Australian company at that date was A$2.1m. In the consolidated financial statements at 31 December 2010 the goodwill is recognised as an asset in accordance with IFRS 3 – *Business Combinations*. The relevant exchange rates at 30 June 2010 and 31 December 2010 are £1=A$2.61 and £1=A$2.43 respectively. At what amount should the goodwill on consolidation be included in the balance sheet?

	A$	(i) £	(ii) £
Goodwill	900,000	344,828	370,370

(i)   This method regards goodwill as being an asset of the parent and therefore translated at the historical rate. Supporters of this view believe that, in economic terms, the goodwill is an asset of the parent because it is part of the acquisition price paid by the parent, particularly in situations where the parent acquires a multinational operation comprising businesses with many different functional currencies.[62]

(ii) This method regards goodwill as being part of the parent's net investment in the acquired entity and therefore translated at the closing rate. Supporters of this view believe that goodwill should be treated no differently from other assets of the acquired entity, in particular intangible assets, because a significant part of the goodwill is likely to comprise intangible assets that do not qualify for separate recognition; the goodwill arises only because of the investment in the foreign entity and has no existence apart from that entity; and the cash flows that support the continued recognition of the goodwill are generated in the entity's functional currency.[63]

The IASB was persuaded by the arguments set out in (ii) above.[64] Accordingly, IAS 21 requires that any goodwill arising on the acquisition of a foreign operation and any fair value adjustments to the carrying amounts of assets and liabilities arising on the acquisition of that foreign operation should be treated as assets and liabilities of the foreign operation. Thus they are expressed in the functional currency of the foreign operation and are translated at the closing rate in accordance with the requirements discussed at 2.7.1 above.[65] However, for entities affected by this change in requirement, transitional arrangements on implementation of the new standard were introduced as discussed at 4 below.

Clearly, if an entity acquires a single foreign entity this will be a straightforward exercise. Where, however, the acquisition is of a multinational operation comprising a number of businesses with different functional currencies this will not be the case. This is discussed at 3.3.4 below.

2.7.3   *Disposal or partial disposal of a foreign operation*

The requirements of IAS 21 relating to disposals and partial disposals of a foreign operation are different depending on whether or not IAS 27 (as amended in 2008) has been applied as it makes consequential amendments to IAS 21. These amendments are effective for annual periods beginning on or after 1 July 2009.[66]

The section discusses first the requirements of IAS 21 prior to application of the amendments and then the consequences of the amendments.

A   *IAS 21 prior to the application of IAS 27 (as amended in 2008)*

As discussed at 2.7.1 above, all resulting exchange differences on the translation of a foreign operation to a different presentation currency are to be recognised in other comprehensive income and accumulated within a separate component of equity.

On the disposal of a foreign operation, IAS 21 requires the exchange differences relating to that foreign operation that have been recognised in other comprehensive income and accumulated in the separate component of equity to be recognised in profit or loss when the gain or loss on disposal is recognised.[67] As indicated at 2.7.2 A above, this will include exchange differences arising on an intragroup balance that, in substance, forms part of an entity's net investment in a foreign operation.

Example 13.8:   Disposal of a foreign operation

A German entity has a Swiss subsidiary which was set up on 1 January 2006 with a share capital of CHF200,000 when the exchange rate was €1=CHF1.55. The subsidiary is included in the parent's separate financial statements at its original cost of €129,032. The profits of the subsidiary, all of which have been retained by the subsidiary, for each of the three years ended 31 December 2008 were CHF40,000, CHF50,000 and CHF60,000 respectively, so that the net assets at 31 December 2008 are CHF350,000. In the consolidated financial statements the results of the subsidiary have been translated at the respective average rates of €1=CHF1.60, €1=CHF1.68 and €1=CHF1.70 and the net assets at the respective closing rates of €1=CHF1.71, €1=CHF1.65 and €1=CHF1.66. All exchange differences have been recognised in other comprehensive income and accumulated in a separate exchange reserve. The consolidated reserves have therefore included the following amounts in respect of the subsidiary:

	Retained profit €	Exchange reserve €
1 January 2006	—	—
Movement during 2006	25,000	(13,681)
31 December 2006	25,000	(13,681)
Movement during 2007	29,762	5,645
31 December 2007	54,762	(8,036)
Movement during 2008	35,294	(209)
31 December 2008	90,056	(8,245)

The net assets at 31 December 2008 of CHF350,000 are included in the consolidated financial statements at €210,843.

On 1 January 2009 the subsidiary is sold for CHF400,000 (€240,964), thus resulting in a gain on disposal in the parent entity's books of €111,932, i.e. €240,964 less €129,032.

In the consolidated financial statements for 2009, IAS 21 requires the cumulative exchange losses of €8,245 to be recognised in profit or loss for that year. Indeed, IAS 27 (2007) requires them to be included as part of the gain on disposal which is reduced to €21,876, being €30,121 (the difference between the proceeds of €240,964 and net asset value of €210,843 at the date of disposal) together with the cumulative exchange losses of €8,245.[68]

In this example, this gain on disposal of €21,876 represents the parent's profit of €111,932 less the cumulative profits already recognised in group profit or loss of €90,056.

The following accounting policies of Pearson reflect these requirements as shown below.

Extract 13.4: Pearson plc (2007)

1   Accounting policies [extract]
c.   Foreign currency translation [extract]

(3) Group companies – The results and financial position of all Group companies that have a functional currency different from the presentation currency are translated into the presentation currency as follows:

i)   assets and liabilities are translated at the closing rate at the date of the balance sheet;

ii)   income and expenses are translated at average exchange rates;

iii)   all resulting exchange differences are recognised as a separate component of equity.

On consolidation, exchange differences arising from the translation of the net investment in foreign entities, and of borrowings and other currency instruments designated as hedges of such investments, are taken to shareholders' equity. The Group treats specific inter-company loan balances, which are not intended to be repaid in the foreseeable future, as part of its net investment. When a foreign entity is sold, such exchange differences are recognised in the income statement as part of the gain or loss on sale.

At the date of transition to IFRS the cumulative translation differences in respect of foreign operations have been deemed to be zero. Any gains and losses on disposals of foreign operations will exclude translation differences that arose prior to the transition date.

The principal overseas currency for the Group is the US Dollar. The average rate for the year against sterling was $2.00 (2006: $1.84) and the year end rate was $1.99 (2006: $1.96).

The treatment in IAS 21 is to be adopted not only when an entity sells an interest in a foreign entity, but also when it disposes of its interest through liquidation, repayment of share capital, or abandonment of that entity. It also applies for partial disposals, in which case, only the proportionate share of the related accumulated exchange differences is included in the gain or loss.[69]

The amendments to IFRS 1 and IAS 27 published in May 2008 amended IAS 21 to clarify that a dividend made by a foreign operation and accounted for as revenue by its parent, investor or venturer in its separate financial statements (see Chapter 8 at 2.3) should not be treated as a disposal or partial disposal of a net investment.[70] This contrasts to the previous position where IAS 21 explained that the payment of a dividend was part of a disposal only when it constituted a return of the investment, e.g. when the dividend was paid out of pre-acquisition profits.[71]

A write-down of the carrying amount of a foreign operation does not constitute a partial disposal, therefore no deferred exchange difference should be recognised in income at the time of the write-down.[72] Similarly, it is implicit in the requirement of IFRS 5 – *Non-current Assets Held for Sale and Discontinued Operations* – for separate disclosure of cumulative gains and losses recognised in equity relating to a disposal group (see Chapter 4 at 2.2.4) that the classification of a foreign operation as held for sale under IFRS 5 does not give rise to a reclassification of foreign exchange differences at that time.

There are a number of practical issues relating to the application of these requirements which are discussed at 3.3.6 and 3.4.1 F below.

B   IAS 27 (as amended in 2008)

In January 2008, the IASB concluded Phase II of its business combinations project by publishing revised versions of IFRS 3 and IAS 27. IAS 27 (as amended in 2008) contains a number of consequential amendments to IAS 21 that affect the way entities account for disposals and partial disposals of foreign operations.

I   Disposals

In addition to the disposal of an entity's entire interest in a foreign operation, the following are accounted for as disposals even if the entity retains an interest in the former subsidiary, associate or jointly controlled entity:[73]

(a)   the loss of control of a subsidiary that includes a foreign operation;

(b)   the loss of significant influence over an associate that includes a foreign operation; and

(c)   the loss of joint control over a jointly controlled entity that includes a foreign operation.

When a disposal (including situations (a) to (c) above) occurs, the exchange differences relating to that foreign operation recognised in other comprehensive income and accumulated in the separate component of equity should be reclassified from equity to profit or loss when the gain or loss on disposal is recognised.[74] This means that *all* exchange differences accumulated the separate component of equity relating to that foreign operation are reclassified on its disposal even if the disposal results from a sale of only part of the entity's interest in the operation, for example if a parent sold 60% of its shares in a wholly owned subsidiary which as a result became an associate. Prior to the application of IAS 27 (as amended in 2008), only the proportionate share of the exchange differences related to the interest disposed of would be reclassified to profit or loss.

Where it is a subsidiary that is disposed of, the related exchange differences that have been attributed to the non-controlling interests should be derecognised, but not reclassified to profit or loss.[75] This might seem a curious requirement given that (a) the exchange differences will have been recognised in their entirety in other comprehensive income (with an appropriate portion allocated to non-controlling interests) and (b) IAS 27 is unclear whether this treatment is required for other components of other comprehensive income, e.g. gains on available-for-sale investments. This is discussed further in Chapter 7 at 3.2.1 C.

II   Partial disposals

A partial disposal of an entity's interest in a foreign operation is any reduction in its ownership interest, except for those discussed at I above that are accounted for as disposals.[76]

The term 'ownership interest' is not defined within IFRS, although it is used in a number of standards,[77] normally to indicate an investor's proportionate interest in an entity. This seems to indicate that a partial disposal arises only when an investor reduces its proportionate interest in the foreign operation.

On the partial disposal of a subsidiary that includes a foreign operation, the proportionate share of the cumulative amount of exchange differences recognised in other comprehensive income should be reattributed to the non-controlling interests in that foreign operation.[78] As discussed at I above, if the entity subsequently disposes of the remainder of its interest in the subsidiary, the exchange differences reattributed will not be reclassified to profit or loss.

In any other partial disposal of a foreign operation, for example the sale of an ownership interest in an associate that does not result in the loss of significant influence, the proportionate share of the cumulative amount of exchange differences recognised in other comprehensive income should be reclassified from equity to profit or loss.[79] There are equivalent requirements in IAS 28 and IAS 31 applying to all gains and losses recognised in other comprehensive income that would be reclassified to profit or loss on disposal of the related assets or liabilities.[80] In this context, the IFRIC has concluded that this treatment applies however an investor's ownership interest is reduced, for example if an associate that is a foreign operation issues shares to third parties.[81]

2.8 Tax effects of all exchange differences

IAS 21 merely states that 'gains and losses on foreign currency transactions and exchange differences arising on translating the results and financial position of an entity (including a foreign operation) into a different currency may have tax effects' and that IAS 12 – *Income Taxes* – applies to these tax effects.[82] The requirements of IAS 12 are discussed in Chapter 26.

2.9 Disclosure requirements

2.9.1 Exchange differences

IAS 21 requires the amount of exchange differences recognised in profit or loss (except for those arising on financial instruments measured at fair value through profit or loss in accordance with IAS 39) to be disclosed.[83] Since IAS 21 does not specify where such exchange differences are presented in the income statement, we recommend that entities in disclosing the amount of such exchange differences indicate the line item(s) in which they are included. Further, the classification of exchange differences (both gains and losses) arising from transactions of a similar nature should be classified consistently throughout the periods presented.

The standard also requires disclosure of the net exchange differences recognised in other comprehensive income and accumulated in a separate component of equity, and a reconciliation of such amounts at the beginning and end of the period.[84]

2.9.2 Presentation and functional currency

When the presentation currency is different from the functional currency, that fact should be stated, together with disclosure of the functional currency and the reason for using a different presentation currency.[85] For this purpose, in the case of a group, the references to 'functional currency' are to that of the parent.[86]

When there is a change in the functional currency of either the reporting entity or a significant foreign operation, that fact and the reason for the change in functional currency should be disclosed.[87]

2.9.3 Convenience translations of financial statements or other financial information

Paragraph 55 of IAS 21 indicates that when an entity presents its financial statements in a currency that is different from its functional currency, it should describe the financial statements as complying with IFRS only if they comply with all the requirements of each applicable standard and interpretation of those standards, including the translation method set out in IAS 21 (see 2.7.1 above).[88]

However, the standard recognises that an entity sometimes presents its financial statements or other financial information in a currency that is not its functional currency without meeting the above requirements. Examples noted by IAS 21 are where an entity converts into another currency only selected items from its financial statements or where an entity whose functional currency is not the currency of a hyperinflationary economy converts the financial statements into another currency by translating all items at the most recent closing rate. Such conversions are not in accordance with IFRS; nevertheless IAS 21 requires disclosures to be made.[89]

The standard requires that when an entity displays its financial statements or other financial information in a currency that is different from either its functional currency or its presentation currency and the requirements of paragraph 55 are not met, it should:[90]

(a)   clearly identify the information as supplementary information to distinguish it from the information that complies with IFRS;

(b)   disclose the currency in which the supplementary information is displayed; and

(c)   disclose the entity's functional currency and the method of translation used to determine the supplementary information.

For the purpose of these requirements, in the case of a group, the references to 'functional currency' are to that of the parent.[91]

3   PRACTICAL ISSUES

3.1   Determination of functional currency

3.1.1   General

As indicated earlier, an entity is required to determine its functional currency using the guidance discussed at 2.5 above. For some entities that determination may be relatively straightforward. However, for many entities, particularly entities within a group, this may not be the case. As indicated earlier, when the factors or indicators set out at 2.5 above are mixed and the functional currency is not obvious, the standard requires management to use its judgement to determine the functional currency that most faithfully represents the economic effects of the underlying transactions, events and conditions.

Since the determination of an entity's functional currency is critical to the translation process under IAS 21, we believe that an entity should clearly document its decision about its functional currency, setting out the factors taken into account in making that determination, particularly where it is not obvious from the primary factors set out in paragraph 9 of the standard. We recommend that the ultimate parent entity of a group should do this for each entity within the group and agree that determination with the local management of those entities, particularly where those entities are presenting financial statements in accordance with IFRS. Although the determination of functional currency is a judgemental issue, it would be expected that within the group the same determination would be made as to the functional currency of a particular entity. If local management has come up with a different analysis of the facts from that of the parent, it should be discussed to ensure that both parties have considered all the relevant facts and circumstances and a final determination made.

By documenting the decision about the functional currency of each entity, and the factors taken into account in making that determination, the reporting entity will be better placed in the future to determine whether a change in the underlying transactions, events and conditions relating to that entity warrant a change in its functional currency.

3.1.2 Intermediate holding companies or finance subsidiaries

One particular difficulty is the determination of the functional currency of an intermediate holding company or finance subsidiary within an international group.

Example 13.9:   Functional currency of intermediate holding companies or finance subsidiaries

An international group is headquartered in the UK. The UK parent entity has a functional currency of pound sterling, which is also the group's presentation currency. The group has three international sub-operations, structured as follows:

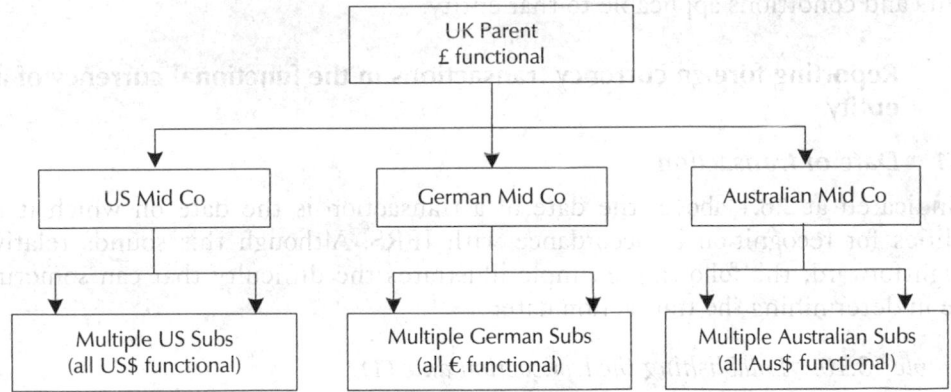

What is the functional currency of the three Mid Cos?

There are a variety of factors to be considered for intermediate holding companies or finance subsidiaries when deciding on the appropriate functional currency. Therefore, there will not be a single analysis applicable to all such entities.

As indicated at 2.3 above IAS 21 defines a 'foreign operation' as 'an entity that is a subsidiary...the activities of which are based or conducted in a country or currency other than those of the reporting entity'. This definition would seem to suggest that a foreign operation must have its own 'activities'.

Also, paragraph 9 of the standard states that the functional currency is 'the currency of the primary economic environment in which the entity operates'. However, as discussed at 2.5 above, under paragraph 9 this is determined by reference to the currency that mainly influences sales prices and the operation's costs, and is therefore not directly relevant to intermediate holding companies or finance subsidiaries. Paragraphs 10 and 11 set out a number of factors to consider in determining the functional currency of a foreign operation. The theme running through these factors is the extent to which the activities and cash flows of the foreign operation are independent of those of the reporting entity.

In the case of an intermediate holding company or finance subsidiary, the acid-test question to consider is whether it is an extension of the parent and performing the functions of the parent – i.e. whether its role is simply to hold the investment in, or provide finance to, the foreign operation on behalf of the parent company or whether its functions are essentially an extension of a local operation (e.g. performing selling, payroll or similar activities for that operation) or indeed it is undertaking activities on its own account.

This means that subsidiaries that do nothing but hold investments or borrow money on behalf of the parent will normally have the functional currency of the parent. The borrowings of such companies are frequently guaranteed by the parent, which is itself likely to be a relevant factor. In other words, on whose credit is the lender relying? If the lender is looking to the ultimate parent, then the functional currency is likely to be that of the ultimate parent. However, if the lender is looking to the sub-group, then the functional currency of the companies in the sub-group will be relevant. Accordingly, any analysis that such a company has a functional currency other than that of the parent will require careful consideration of the features of the entity which give rise to that conclusion. Complex situations are likely to require the application of careful management judgement as indicated by the standard.

As for other entities within a group, each entity should be reviewed for its particular circumstances against the indicators and factors set out in the standard. This review requires management to use its judgement in determining the functional currency that most faithfully represents the economic effects of the underlying transactions, events and conditions applicable to that entity.

3.2   Reporting foreign currency transactions in the functional currency of an entity

3.2.1   Date of transaction

As indicated at 2.6.1 above, the date of a transaction is the date on which it first qualifies for recognition in accordance with IFRS. Although this sounds relatively straightforward, the following example illustrates the difficulty that can sometimes arise in determining the transaction date:

Example 13.10:   Establishing the transaction date (1)

A Belgian entity buys an item of inventory from a Canadian supplier. The dates relating to the transaction, and the relevant exchange rates, are as follows:

Date	Event	€1=C$
14 April 2010	Goods are ordered	1.50
5 May 2010	Goods are shipped from Canada and invoice dated that day	1.53
7 May 2010	Invoice is received	1.51
10 May 2010	Goods are received	1.54
14 May 2010	Invoice is recorded	1.56
7 June 2010	Invoice is paid	1.60

IAS 2 – *Inventories* – does not make any reference to the date of initial recognition of inventory. However, IAS 39 deals with the initial recognition of financial liabilities. It requires the financial liability to be recognised when, and only when, the entity becomes a party to the contractual provisions of the instrument.[92] In discussing firm commitments to purchase goods, it indicates that an entity placing the order does not recognise the liability at the time of the commitment, but delays recognition until the ordered goods have been shipped or delivered,[93] i.e. the date that the risks and rewards of ownership have passed.

Accordingly, it is unlikely that the date the goods are ordered should be used as the date of the transaction.

If the goods are shipped free on board (f.o.b.) then as the risks and rewards of ownership pass on shipment then this date should be used.

If, however, the goods are not shipped f.o.b. then the risks and rewards of ownership normally pass on delivery and therefore the date the goods are received should be treated as the date of the transaction.

The dates on which the invoice is received and is recorded are irrelevant to when the risks and rewards of ownership pass and therefore should not in principle be considered to be the date of the transaction. In practice, it may be acceptable that as a matter of administrative convenience that the exchange rate at the date the invoice is recorded is used, particularly if there is no undue delay in processing the invoice. If this is done then care should be taken to ensure that the exchange rate used is not significantly different from that ruling on the 'true' date of the transaction.

It is clear from IAS 21 that the date the invoice is paid is not the date of the transaction because if it were then no exchange differences would arise on unsettled transactions.

The above example illustrated that the date that a transaction is recorded in an entity's books and records is not necessarily the same as the date at which it qualifies for recognition under IFRS. Other situations where this is likely to arise is where an entity is recording a transaction that relates to a period, rather than one being recognised at a single point in time, as illustrated below:

Example 13.11:   Establishing the transaction date (2)

On 30 September 2010 Company A, whose functional currency is the euro, acquires a US dollar bond for US$8,000. The bond carries fixed interest of 5% per annum paid quarterly, i.e. US$100 per quarter. The exchange rate at that date is US$1 to €1.50.

On 31 December 2010, the US dollar has appreciated and the exchange rate is US$1 to €2.00. Interest received on the bond on 31 December 2010 is US$100 (= €200).

Although the interest may only be being recorded at that date, the rate at 31 December 2010 is not the spot rate ruling at the date of the transaction. Since the interest has accrued over the 3 month period, it should be translated at the spot rates applicable to the accrual of interest during the 3 month period. Accordingly, a weighted average rate for the 3 month period should be used. Assuming that the appropriate average rate is US$1 to €1.75 the interest income is €175 (= US$100 × 1.75).

Accordingly, there is also an exchange gain on the interest receivable of €25 (= US$100 × [2.00 – 1.75]) to be reflected in profit or loss. The journal entry for recording the receipt of the interest on 31 December 2010 is therefore as follows:

	€	€
Cash	200	
Interest income (profit or loss)		175
Exchange gain (profit or loss)		25

3.2.2   *Use of average rate*

As indicated at 2.6.1 above, rather than using the actual rate ruling at the date of the transaction 'an average rate for a week or month may be used for all foreign currency transactions occurring during that period', if the exchange rate does not fluctuate significantly.[94] For entities which engage in a large number of foreign currency transactions it will be more convenient for them to use an average rate rather than using the exact rate for each transaction. If an average rate is to be used, what guidance can be given in choosing and using such a rate?

(a)   Length of period

As an average rate should only be used as an approximation of actual rates then care has to be taken that significant fluctuations in the day-to-day exchange rates do not arise in the period selected. For this reason the period chosen should not be too long. We believe that the period should be no longer than one month and where there is volatility of exchange rates it will be better to set rates on a more frequent basis, say, a weekly basis, especially where the value of transactions is significant;

(b)   Estimate of average rate relevant to date of transaction

The estimation of the appropriate average rate will depend on whether the rate is to be applied to transactions which have already occurred or to transactions which will occur after setting the rate. Obviously, if the transactions have already occurred then the average rate used should relate to the period during which those transactions occurred; e.g. purchase transactions for the previous week should be translated using the average rate for that week, not an average rate for the week the invoices are being recorded;

If the rate is being set for the following period the rate selected should be a reasonable estimate of the expected exchange rate during that period. This could be done by using the closing rate at the end of the previous period or by using the actual average rate for the previous period. We would suggest that the former be used. Whatever means is used to estimate the average rate, the actual rates during the period should be monitored and if there is a significant move in the exchange rate away from the average rate then the rate being applied should be revised;

(c)   Application of average rate to type of item

We believe that average rates should be used only as a matter of convenience where there are a large number of transactions. Even where an average rate is used, we recommend that the actual rate should be used for large one-off transactions such as the purchase of a fixed asset or an overseas investment or taking out a foreign loan. Where the number of foreign currency transactions is small it will probably not be worthwhile setting and monitoring average rates and therefore actual rates should be used.

3.2.3   *Dual rates or suspension of rates*

One practical difficulty in translating foreign currency amounts is where there is more than one exchange rate for that particular currency depending on the nature of the transaction. In some cases the difference between the exchange rates can be small and therefore it probably does not matter which rate is actually used. However, in other situations the difference can be quite significant. In these circumstances, what rate should be used? IAS 21 states that 'when several exchange rates are available, the rate used is that at which the future cash flows represented by the transaction or balance could have been settled if those cash flows had occurred at the measurement date'.[95] Companies should therefore look at the nature of the transaction and apply the appropriate exchange rate.

Another practical difficulty which could arise is where for some reason exchangeability between two currencies is temporarily lacking at the transaction date or subsequently at the end of the reporting period. In this case, IAS 21 requires that the rate to be used is 'the first subsequent rate at which exchanges could be made'.[96]

3.2.4   *Monetary or non-monetary?*

As indicated in 2.6.2 above, IAS 21 generally requires that monetary items denominated in foreign currencies be retranslated using closing rates at the end of the reporting period and non-monetary items should not be retranslated. Monetary items are defined as 'units of currency held and assets and liabilities to be received or paid in a fixed or determinable number of units of currency'.[97] The standard elaborates further on this by stating that 'the essential feature of a monetary item is a right to receive (or an obligation to deliver) a fixed or determinable number of units of currency'. Examples given by IAS 21 are pensions and other employee benefits to be paid in cash; provisions that are to be settled in cash; and cash dividends that are recognised as a liability.[98] More obvious examples are cash and bank balances; trade receivables and payables; and loan receivables and payables. IAS 39 also indicates that where a foreign currency bond is held as an available-for-sale financial asset, then it should first be accounted for at amortised cost in the underlying currency, thus effectively treating that amount as if it was a monetary item. This is discussed further in Chapter 32 at 7.1. This suggests that foreign currency bonds that are classified as held-to-maturity investments under IAS 39 are monetary items.

The following extract from Aviva's 2007 financial statements illustrates the IAS 39 treatment for monetary financial assets designated as available-for-sale.

Extract 13.5: Aviva plc (2007)

Accounting policies [extract]

(E)   Foreign currency translation

Income statements and cash flows of foreign entities are translated into the Group's presentation currency at average exchange rates for the year while their balance sheets are translated at the year end exchange rates. Exchange differences arising from the translation of the net investment in foreign subsidiaries, associates and joint ventures, and of borrowings and other currency instruments designated as hedges of such investments, are taken to the currency translation reserve within equity. On disposal of a foreign entity, such exchange differences are transferred out of this reserve and are recognised in the income statement as part of the gain or loss on sale. The cumulative translation differences were deemed to be zero at the transition date to IFRS.

> Foreign currency transactions are accounted for at the exchange rates prevailing at the date of the transactions. Gains and losses resulting from the settlement of such transactions, and from the translation of monetary assets and liabilities denominated in foreign currencies, are recognised in the income statement.
>
> Translation differences on debt securities and other monetary financial assets measured at fair value and designated as held at fair value through profit or loss (FV) (see policy S) are included in foreign exchange gains and losses in the income statement. For monetary financial assets designated as AFS, translation differences are calculated as if they were carried at amortised cost and so are recognised in the income statement, whilst foreign exchange differences arising from fair value gains and losses are included in the investment valuation reserve within equity. Translation differences on non-monetary items, such as equities which are designated as FV, are reported as part of the fair value gain or loss, whereas such differences on AFS equities are included in the investment valuation reserve.

IAS 21 also states that 'a contract to receive (or deliver) a variable number of the entity's own equity instruments or a variable amount of assets in which the fair value to be received (or delivered) equals a fixed or determinable number of units of currency is a monetary item'.[99] No examples of such contracts are given in IAS 21. However, it would seem to embrace those contracts settled in the entity's own equity shares that under IAS 32 – *Financial Instruments: Disclosure and Presentation* – would be presented as financial assets or liabilities (see Chapter 31 at 3.3.2 A).

Conversely, the essential feature of a non-monetary item is the absence of a right to receive (or an obligation to deliver) a fixed or determinable number of units of currency. Examples given by the standard are amounts prepaid for goods and services (e.g. prepaid rent); goodwill; intangible assets; inventories; property, plant and equipment; and provisions that are to be settled by the delivery of a non-monetary asset.[100] IAS 39 also indicates that equity instruments that are held as available-for-sale financial assets are non-monetary items.[101] This suggests that equity investments in subsidiaries, associates or joint ventures are non-monetary items.

Even with this guidance there will clearly be a number of situations where the distinction may not be altogether clear.

A   Deposits or progress payments

Entities may be required to pay deposits or progress payments when acquiring certain assets, such as property, plant and equipment or inventories, from foreign suppliers. The question then arises as to whether such payments should be retranslated as monetary items or not.

Example 13.12:   Deposits or progress payments

A Dutch entity contracts to purchase an item of plant and machinery for US$10,000 on the following terms:

Payable on signing contract (1 August 2010)	– 10%
Payable on delivery (19 December 2010)	– 40%
Payable on installation (7 January 2010)	– 50%

At 31 December 2010 the entity has paid the first two amounts on the due dates when the respective exchange rates were €1=US$1.25 and €1=US$1.20. The closing rate at the end of its reporting period, 31 December 2010, is €1=US$1.15.

		(i) €	(ii) €
First payment	– US$1,000	800	870
Second payment	– US$4,000	3,333	3,478
		4,133	4,348

(i)   If the payments made are regarded as prepayments or as progress payments then the amounts should be treated as non-monetary items and included in the balance sheet at €4,133. This would appear to be consistent with SFAS 52 which in defining 'transaction date' states: 'A long-term commitment may have more than one transaction date (for example, the due date of each progress payment under a construction contract is an anticipated transaction date).'[102]

(ii) If the payments made are regarded as deposits, and are refundable, then the amounts could possibly be treated as monetary items and included in the balance sheet at €4,348 and an exchange gain of €215 recognised in profit or loss. A variant of this would be to only treat the first payment as a deposit until the second payment is made, since once delivery is made it is less likely that the asset will be returned and a refund sought from the supplier.

In practice, it will often be necessary to consider the terms of the contract to ascertain the nature of the payments made in order to determine the appropriate accounting treatment.

B   Investments in preference shares

Entities may invest in preference shares of other entities. Whether such shares are monetary items or not will depend on the rights attaching to the shares. As noted at 3.2.4 above, IAS 39 indicates that equity instruments that are held as available-for-sale financial assets are non-monetary items.[103] Thus, it appears that if the terms of the preference shares are such that they are classified by the issuer as equity, rather than as a financial liability, then they are non-monetary items. However, if the terms of the preference shares are such that they are classified by the issuer as a financial liability (e.g. a preference share that provides for mandatory redemption by the issue for a fixed or determinable amount at a fixed or determinable future date), then it would appear that they should be treated as monetary items. Indeed, IAS 39 would allow such an instrument to be classified within loans and receivables by the holder provided the definition in IAS 39 is otherwise met (see Chapter 29 at 7.3). However, even where an investment in such redeemable preference shares is not classified within loans and receivables, but as a held-to-maturity investment or as an available-for-sale financial asset, then it would seem that it should be treated as a monetary item (in the latter case, to the extent that it would be measured at amortised cost, similar to an investment in a bond as discussed at 3.2.4 above).

C   Foreign currency share capital

Entities may issue share capital denominated in a currency that is not its functional currency or, due to changes in circumstances that result in a re-determination of its functional currency, may find that its share capital is no longer denominated in its functional currency. Neither IAS 21 nor IAS 39 addresses the treatment of translation of share capital denominated in a currency other than the functional currency. In theory two treatments are possible: the foreign currency share capital (and any related share premium or additional paid-in capital) could be maintained at a fixed amount by being translated at a historical rate of exchange, or it could be retranslated annually at the closing rate as if it were a monetary amount. In the latter case a second question would arise: whether to recognise the difference arising on translation in profit or loss or in other comprehensive income or to deal with it within equity.

Where the shares denominated in a foreign currency are ordinary shares, or are otherwise irredeemable and classified as equity instruments, our preferred view is that the shares should be translated at historical rates and not remeasured, because the effect of rate changes is not expected to have an impact on the entity's cash flows. Such capital items are included within the examples of non-monetary items listed in SFAS 52 as accounts to be remeasured using historical exchange rates when the temporal method is being applied.[104] As noted at 2.6.2 above, IAS 21 requires non-monetary items that are measured at historical cost in a foreign currency should be translated using the historical rate. This is also the treatment required by the equivalent Canadian standard.[105]

Where such share capital is retranslated at closing rate, we do not believe that it is appropriate for the exchange differences to be recognised in profit or loss, since they do not affect the cash flows of the entity. Further, because the retranslation of such items has no effect on assets or liabilities it is not an item of income or expense to be recognised in other comprehensive income. Instead, the exchange differences should be taken to equity. Consequently, whether such share capital is maintained at a historical rate, or is dealt with in this way, the treatment has no impact on the overall equity of the entity.

Where the shares are not classified as equity instruments, but as financial liabilities, under IAS 32, e.g. preference shares that provide for mandatory redemption by the issue for a fixed or determinable amount at a fixed or determinable future date, then, as with investments in such shares discussed at 3.2.4 B above, they should be treated as monetary items and translated at closing rate. Any exchange differences will be recognised in profit or loss, unless the shares form part of a hedging relationship and IAS 39 would account for the exchange differences differently (see Chapter 33).

D   Deferred tax

One of the examples of a monetary item included within the exposure draft that preceded IAS 21 was deferred tax.[106] However, this has been dropped from the list of examples in the final standard. No explanation is given in IAS 21 as to why this is the case. Nevertheless, IAS 12 (2007) suggested that any deferred foreign tax assets or liabilities are monetary items since it stated that 'where exchange differences on deferred foreign tax liabilities or assets are recognised in the income statement, such differences may be classified as deferred tax expense (income) if that presentation is considered to be the most useful to financial statement users'.[107] On the application of IAS 1 – *Presentation of Financial Statements* (as revised in 2007), the reference to 'income statement' was changed to 'statement of comprehensive income'. Nevertheless, the suggestion remains the same.

E   Post-employment benefit plans

As noted above, one of the examples of a monetary item given by IAS 21 is 'pensions and other employee benefits to be paid in cash'. For most entities, this will not be an issue because any pension benefits payable under a post-employment benefit plan that is a defined benefit plan will be payable in the functional currency of the entity. However, it may be that the plan has assets that are denominated in a foreign currency. Since IAS 19 – *Employee Benefits* – requires these to be measured at their fair value at the end of the reporting period, then IAS 21 requires such assets to be translated at closing rate. How should the entity deal with any exchange differences arising on such assets held by a defined benefit plan?

I   Foreign currency assets

One approach would be to follow the normal treatment within IAS 21. Accordingly, any exchange differences on non-monetary items such as investments in equity or property would be recognised in other comprehensive income since that is where the valuation gains and losses are normally recognised. For investments in currency bonds, as noted above, IAS 39 indicates these are first accounted for at 'amortised cost' i.e. as a monetary item with exchange differences on that amount recognised in profit or loss. Any further exchange differences due to being valued at fair value would be treated in the same way as those arising on the equity and property investments. However, the accounting for defined benefit schemes under IAS 19 requires an entity to reflect the expected return on any plan assets as part of the annual pension cost in profit or loss. As discussed in Chapter 28 at 5.4.3, this 'expected return' is a forward-looking expectation or estimate based on market expectations at the beginning of the period for returns over the entire life of the related obligation. Although IAS 19 is silent on the matter, it would seem that such an estimate should reflect the effect of any exchange risk relating to the assets that are in a foreign currency. On that basis, although the assets at the end of the reporting period would be translated at closing rate, the effect of doing so would be reflected as part of the actuarial gain or loss, being the difference between the actual return and the expected return, and accounted for in accordance with the entity's accounting policy for dealing with actuarial gains and losses (see Chapter 28 at 5.3.1 A).

II   Foreign currency plans?

For some entities it may be that the pension benefits payable under a post-employment benefit plan will not be payable in the functional currency of the entity. For example, a UK entity in the oil and gas industry may determine that its functional currency is the US dollar, but its employee costs including the pension benefits are payable in sterling. How should such an entity account for its post-employment benefit plan?

As noted above, one of the examples of a monetary item given by IAS 21 are 'pensions and other employee benefits to be paid in cash'. However, the standard does not expand on this, and does not appear to make any distinction between pensions provided by defined contribution plans or defined benefit plans. Clearly for pensions that are payable under a post-employment benefit plan that is a defined contribution plan (or is accounted for as such) this is straightforward. Any liability for outstanding contributions at the end of the reporting period is a monetary item that should be translated at closing rate, with any resulting exchange differences recognised in profit or loss. It would appear that IAS 21 envisages that the defined benefit obligation under a defined benefit plan at the end of the reporting period should also to be treated as a monetary item, and therefore translated at closing rate.

As far as the assets held by the plan are concerned, these will predominantly be non-monetary items, but since IAS 19 requires these to be measured at their fair value at the end of the reporting period, then IAS 21 requires such assets also to be translated at closing rate. However, as discussed at 2.6.3 above, exchange differences on monetary items are generally recognised in profit or loss, whereas the exchange differences on non-monetary assets are recognised in profit or loss only when valuation gains and losses are recognised in profit or loss. This clearly results in a mismatch since, under IAS 19, the valuation gains and losses will be actuarial gains and losses that are either immediately recognised in the statement of total recognised gains and losses or only recognised under the IAS 19 corridor approach (see Chapter 28 at 5.3.1 A). Is there any way in which this can be mitigated?

One approach would be to argue that the exchange differences relating to the defined benefit obligation are similar to actuarial gains and losses. The calculation of the obligation under IAS 19 will be based on actuarial assumptions that reflect the currency of the obligation to the employee (for example, the discount rate used 'shall be consistent with the currency and estimated term' of the obligation[108]). Any variations from those assumptions on both the obligation and the assets are dealt with in the same way under IAS 19. Actuarial assumptions are 'an entity's best estimates of the variables that will determine the ultimate cost of providing post-employment benefits' and include financial assumptions.[109] Although IAS 19 does not refer to exchange rates, it is clearly a variable that will determine the ultimate cost to the entity of providing the post-employment benefits. On that basis, it would seem reasonable for the effect of exchange rate differences on both the assets and the obligations of the fund to be accounted for in a similar manner to actuarial gains and losses, based on the entity's accounting policy for dealing with actuarial gains and losses (see Chapter 28 at 5.3.1 A).

It might be argued that the plan should be regarded as a 'foreign operation' under IAS 21 (see 2.3 above). However, in this situation it is very difficult to say that its 'functional currency' can be regarded as being different from that of the reporting entity given the relationship between the plan and the reporting entity (see 2.5 above). Thus, it would appear that the entity cannot treat the plan as a foreign operation with a different functional currency from its own.

3.2.5   Treatment of exchange differences

The general rule in IAS 21 is that exchange differences on the settlement or retranslation of monetary items should be recognised in profit or loss in the period in which they arise.[110] However, as noted at 2.6.3 A above, the standard identifies two exceptions to this rule – monetary items forming part of an entity's net investment in a foreign operation (see 3.4.1 below) and hedge accounting under IAS 39 (see Chapter 33). Apart from these, are there any other circumstances where it is possible for exchange differences not to be recognised in profit or loss in the period they arise?

One situation would be where an entity capitalises borrowing costs under IAS 23 – *Borrowing Costs* – since that standard allows exchange differences arising from foreign currency borrowings to be capitalised, but only to the extent that they are regarded as an adjustment to interest costs (see Chapter 19).[111]

As discussed at 3.2.4 E above, another situation might be in relation to the exchange differences on a defined benefit obligation where they are treated as being similar to the actuarial gains and losses on the obligation.

One example of a monetary item given by IAS 21 is 'provisions that are to be settled in cash'. In most cases it will be appropriate for the exchange differences arising on provisions to be recognised in profit or loss in the period they arise. However, it may be that an entity has recognised a decommissioning provision under IAS 37 – *Provisions, Contingent Liabilities and Contingent Assets*. One practical difficulty with such a provision is that due to the long timescale of when the actual cash outflows will arise, an entity may not be able to say with any certainty the currency in which the transaction will actually be settled. Nevertheless if it is determined that it is expected to be settled in a foreign currency it will be a monetary item. The main issue then is what should happen to any exchange differences. As discussed in Chapter 24 at 5.4.2 A, IFRIC 1 – *Changes in Existing Decommissioning, Restoration and Similar Liabilities* – applies to any decommissioning or similar liability that has been both included as part of an asset measured as a liability in accordance with IAS 37. IFRIC 1 requires, *inter alia*, that any adjustment to such a provision resulting from changes in the estimated outflow of resources embodying economic benefits (e.g. cash flows) required to settle the obligation should not be recognised in profit or loss as it occurs, but should be added to or deducted from the cost of the asset to which it relates. The requirement of IAS 21 to recognise the exchange differences arising on the provision in profit or loss in the period in which they arise conflicts with this requirement in IFRIC 1. Accordingly, we believe that it would be more logical for the exchange differences not to be recognised in profit or loss, but dealt with in accordance with IFRIC 1.

3.2.6 Books and records not kept in functional currency

Occasionally, an entity may keep its underlying books and records in a currency that is not its functional currency under IAS 21. For example, it could record its transactions in terms of the local currency of the country in which it is located, possibly as a result of local requirements.

When an entity keeps its books and records in a currency other than its functional currency, then IAS 21 requires that at the time the entity prepares its financial statements all amounts are translated into the functional currency in accordance with paragraphs 20-26 of the standard,[112] i.e. those discussed at 2.6.1, 2.6.2 and 3.2.1 to 3.2.4 above. The standard goes on to say that 'this produces the same amounts in the functional currency as would have occurred had the items been recorded initially in the functional currency. For example, monetary items are translated into the functional currency using the closing rate, and non-monetary items that are measured on a historical cost basis are translated using the exchange rate at the date of the transaction that resulted in their recognition.'[113] This presupposes that the initial recording of transactions in foreign currencies (including the entity's functional currency), and any subsequent retranslation of the resulting balance sheet items, have been translated into the recording currency in accordance with those paragraphs. For example, all foreign currency monetary items have been translated into the recording currency at the closing rate at the end of the reporting period. It is only if this has been done that the subsequent translation of those monetary items to the functional currency using the closing rate between the recording currency and the functional currency will result in the same amounts that would have occurred if the foreign currency amounts had been translated directly into the functional currency at their respective closing rates. However, if the foreign currency monetary items have been retained at their original historical rate in the books and records, then the subsequent translation of those monetary items to the functional currency using the closing rate between the recording currency and the functional currency will *not* result in the same amounts that would have occurred if the foreign currency amounts had been translated directly into the functional currency at their respective closing rates.

Accordingly, when an entity keeps its books and records in a currency other than its functional currency, it will be necessary to obtain an understanding about the underlying translation process before applying these requirements of the standard to ensure that the resulting amounts are the same amounts in the functional currency as would have occurred had the items been recorded initially in the functional currency.

As indicated above, IAS 21 only refers to the translation into the functional currency in accordance with paragraphs 20-26 of the standard. These paragraphs do not include those relating to the treatment of exchange differences arising from that translation process. However, we believe that any resulting exchange differences should be recognised as discussed at 2.6.3 above.

3.3   Translation to a different presentation currency

3.3.1   *Dual rates or suspension of rates*

The problems of dual rates and suspension of rates in relation to the translation of foreign currency transactions and balances into an entity's functional currency and the related requirements of IAS 21 dealing with such issues have already been discussed in 3.2.3 above. However, the standard makes no reference to them in the context of translating the results and financial position of an entity into a different presentation currency, particularly where the results and financial position of a foreign operation are being translated for inclusion in the financial statements of the reporting entity by consolidation, proportionate consolidation or the equity method.

Where the problem is one of suspension of rates, then we believe that the requirement in IAS 21 relating to transactions and balances should be followed; i.e. the rate to be used is 'the first subsequent rate at which exchanges could be made'.[114]

However, the requirement in IAS 21 relating to dual rates is not entirely relevant in this context. Again, guidance can be sought from SFAS 52 which states that the rate to be used to translate foreign financial statements should be, in the absence of unusual circumstances, the rate applicable to dividend remittances.[115] The reason for this is that the use of that rate is more meaningful than any other rate because cash flows to the parent company from the foreign entity can be converted only at that rate, and realisation of a net investment in the foreign entity will ultimately be in the form of cash flows from that entity.[116]

3.3.2   Calculation of average rate

As indicated at 2.7.1 A above, when translating the results of an entity whose functional currency is not that of a hyperinflationary economy, for practical reasons, the reporting entity may use a rate that approximates the actual exchange rate, e.g. an average rate for the period, to translate income and expense items.[117]

The standard does not give any guidance on the factors that should be taken into account in determining what may be an appropriate average rate for the period – it merely says that 'if exchange rates fluctuate significantly, the use of the average rate for the period is inappropriate'.[118] What methods are, therefore, available to entities to use in calculating an appropriate average rate? Possible methods might be:

(a)   mid-year rate;

(b)   average of opening and closing rates;

(c)   average of month end/quarter end rates;

(d)   average of monthly average rates;

(e)   monthly/quarterly results at month end/quarter end rates; or

(f)   monthly/quarterly results at monthly/quarterly averages.

Example 13.13:   Calculation of average rate

A Spanish entity has a foreign subsidiary and is preparing its consolidated financial statements for the year ended 30 April 2010. It intends to use an average rate for translating the results of the subsidiary. The relevant exchange rates for €1=FC are as follows:

Month	Month end	Average for month	Average for quarter	Average for year
April 2009	1.67			
May 2009	1.63	1.67		
June 2009	1.67	1.64		
July 2009	1.64	1.65	1.65	
August 2009	1.67	1.64		
September 2009	1.70	1.63		
October 2009	1.67	1.68	1.65	
November 2009	1.65	1.70		
December 2009	1.66	1.66		
January 2010	1.64	1.67	1.68	
February 2010	1.60	1.65		
March 2010	1.61	1.63		
April 2010	1.61	1.62	1.63	1.65

Average of month end rates – 1.65

Average of quarter end rates – 1.64

The results of the subsidiary for each of the 12 months to 30 April 2010 and the translation thereof under each of the above methods (using monthly figures where appropriate) are shown below:

Method (a)	FC31,050 @ 1.67 = €18,593
Method (b)	FC31,050 @ 1.64 = €18,933
Method (c) – monthly	FC31,050 @ 1.65 = €18,818
Method (c) – quarterly	FC31,050 @ 1.64 = €18,933
Method (d)	FC31,050 @ 1.65 = €18,818

		(e) quarterly	(e) monthly	(f) quarterly	(f) monthly
Month	FC	€	€	€	€
May 2009	1,000		613		599
June 2009	1,100		659		671
July 2009	1,200	2,012	732	2,000	727
August 2009	1,300		778		793
September 2009	1,300		765		798
October 2009	1,350	2,365	808	2,394	804
November 2009	1,400		848		824
December 2009	1,400		843		843
January 2010	2,000	2,927	1,220	2,857	1,198
February 2010	5,000		3,125		3,030
March 2010	10,000		6,211		6,135
April 2010	4,000	11,801	2,484	11,656	2,469
Total	31,050	19,105	19,086	18,907	18,891

It can be seen that by far the simplest methods to use are the methods (a) to (d).

In our view methods (a) and (b) should not normally be used as it is unlikely in times of volatile exchange rates that they will give appropriate weighting to the exchange rates which have been in existence throughout the period in question. They are only likely to give an acceptable answer if the exchange rate has been static or steadily increasing or decreasing throughout the period.

Method (c) based on quarter end rates has similar drawbacks and therefore should not normally be used.

Method (c) based on month end rates and method (d) are better than the previous methods as they do take into account more exchange rates which have applied throughout the year, with method (d) being preferable, as this will have taken account of daily exchange rates. Average monthly rates for most major currencies are likely to be given in publications issued by the government, banks and other sources and therefore it is unnecessary for entities to calculate their own. The work involved in calculating an average for the year, therefore, is not very onerous. Method (d) will normally give reasonable and acceptable results when there are no seasonal variations in items of income and expenditure.

Where there are seasonal variations in items of income and expenditure then this may not be the case. In these situations appropriate exchange rates should be applied to the appropriate items. This can be done by using either of methods (e) or (f) preferably using figures and rates for each month. Where such a method is being used care should be taken to ensure that the periodic accounts are accurate and that cut-off procedures have been adequate, otherwise significant items may be translated at the wrong average rate.

Where there are significant one-off items of income and expenses then it is likely that actual rates at the date of the transaction should be used to translate such items.

3.3.3   *Translation of equity items*

The method of translation of the results and financial position of an entity whose functional currency is not the currency of a hyperinflationary economy is discussed at 2.7.1 A above. The translation process makes only limited reference to the translation of equity items. The exposure draft that preceded the standard had proposed that '... equity items other than those resulting from income and expense recognised in the period ... shall be translated at the closing rate'. However, the IASB decided not to specify in the standard the translation rate for equity items,[119] but no explanation has been given in the Basis of Conclusions about this matter.

So how should entities deal with the translation of equity items?

A   *Share capital*

Where an entity is presenting its financial statements in a currency other than its functional currency, it would seem more appropriate that its share capital (whether they are ordinary shares, or are otherwise irredeemable and classified as equity instruments) should be translated at historical rates of exchange. As noted at 3.2.4 C above, such capital items are included within the examples of non-monetary items listed in SFAS 52 as accounts to be remeasured using historical exchange rates when the temporal method is being applied.[120] As noted at 2.6.2 above, IAS 21 requires non-monetary items that are measured at historical cost in a foreign currency to be translated using the historical rate. This is also the treatment required by the equivalent Canadian standard.[121] Translation at an historical rate would imply using the rate ruling at the date of the issue of the shares. However, where a subsidiary is presenting its financial statements in the currency of its parent, it may be that the more appropriate historical rate for share capital that was in issue at the date it became a subsidiary would be that ruling at the date it became a subsidiary of the parent, rather than at earlier dates of issue.

Where such share capital is retranslated at closing rate, we do not believe that it is appropriate for the exchange differences to be recognised in other comprehensive income nor for them to be taken to the separate component of equity required by IAS 21 (since to do so could result in them being reclassified from equity to profit or loss upon disposal of part of the entity's operations in the future), but should either be taken to retained earnings or some other reserve. Consequently, whether such share capital is maintained at a historical rate, or is dealt with in this way, the treatment has no impact on the overall equity of the entity.

B   *Other equity balances resulting from transactions with equity holders*

In addition to share capital, an entity may have other equity balances resulting from the issue of shares, such as a share premium account (additional paid-in capital). Like share capital, the translation of such balances could be done at either historical rates or at closing rate. However, we believe that whichever method is adopted it should be consistent with the treatment used for share capital. Again, where exchange differences arise through using the closing rate, we believe that it is not appropriate for them to be recognised in other comprehensive income or taken to the separate component of equity required by IAS 21.

A similar approach should be adopted where an entity has acquired its own equity shares and has deducted those 'treasury shares' from equity as required by IAS 32 (see Chapter 31 at 6).

C   *Other equity balances resulting from income and expenses being recognised in other comprehensive income*

Under IAS 21, income and expenses recognised in other comprehensive income are translated at the exchange rates ruling at the dates of the transaction.[122] Examples of such items are certain revaluation gains and losses on property, plant and equipment under IAS 16 (see Chapter 16 at 4.1) and on certain intangible assets under IAS 38 – *Intangible Assets* (see Chapter 15 at 2.4.2), gains and losses on available-for-sale financial assets under IAS 39 (see Chapter 32 at 3.4), gains and losses on cash flow hedges under IAS 39 (see Chapter 33 at 4.2.1), and any amounts of current and deferred tax recognised in other comprehensive income under IAS 12 (see Chapter 26 at 6.1). This would suggest that where these gains and losses are accumulated within a separate reserve or component of equity, then any period-end balance should represent the cumulative translated amounts of such gains and losses. However, as IAS 21 is silent on the matter it would seem that it would be acceptable to translate these equity balances at closing rate, as long as the exchange differences arising are not taken to the separate component of equity required by IAS 21. The differences would have to be taken to retained earnings or some other reserve, effectively as a transfer between the reserves. Consequently, whether such balances are maintained at the original translated rates, or are translated at closing rates, the treatment has no impact on the overall equity of the entity.

3.3.4   Goodwill

As discussed at 2.7.2 C above, IAS 21 requires that any goodwill arising on the acquisition of a foreign operation should be expressed in the functional currency of the foreign operation and be translated at the closing rate in accordance with the requirements discussed at 2.7.1 above.[123] Clearly, if an entity acquires a single foreign entity this will be a straightforward exercise. Where, however, the acquisition is of a multinational operation comprising a number of businesses with different functional currencies this will not be the case. The goodwill needs to be allocated to the level of each functional currency of the acquired operation. However, the standard gives no guidance on how this should be done.

In our view, the preferred basis of allocating goodwill to different functional currencies would be an economic value approach. This approach effectively calculates the goodwill relating to each different functional currency operation by allocating the cost of the acquisition to the different functional currency operations on the basis of the relative economic values of those businesses and then deducting the fair values that have been attributed to the net assets of those businesses as part of the fair value exercise in accounting for the business combination (see Chapter 9 at 2.5 and 3.6). We consider that any other basis for allocating goodwill to different functional currencies would need to be substantiated.

The Basis of Conclusions issued by the IASB notes that the level to which goodwill is allocated for foreign currency translation purpose may be different from the level at which the goodwill is tested for impairment under IAS 36 – *Impairment of Assets* (see Chapter 9 at 3.4.1).[124] In many cases the allocation under IAS 21 will be at a lower level. This will apply not only on the acquisition of a multinational operation but could also apply on the acquisition of a single operation where the goodwill is allocated to a larger cash generating unit under IAS 36 that is made up of businesses with different functional currencies.

As a consequence of this different level of allocation one particular difficulty that entities are likely to face is how to deal with an impairment loss that is recognised in respect of goodwill under IAS 36. If the impairment loss relates to a larger cash generating unit made up of businesses with different functional currencies, again some allocation of this impairment loss will be required to determine the amount of the remaining carrying amount of goodwill in each of the functional currencies for the purposes of translation under IAS 21.

3.3.5   Accounting for foreign operations where sub-groups exist

The method required by IAS 21 for the translation of a foreign operation whose functional currency is not that of a hyperinflationary economy to a different presentation currency was adopted by the IASB for reasons discussed at 2.7.1 A above. The discussion about the IASB's reasons for the choice of translation method suggests that the translation process can be a single or two-stage process and asserts in paragraph BC18 that both processes will result in the same amounts being reported in the presentation currency. However, as set out at 3.3.6 below, particularly in Example 13.16, this assertion is demonstrably untrue in certain situations.

The various requirements of the standard appear to indicate that a single stage process should be used when translating foreign operations for the purposes of consolidated financial statements.

Example 13.14:   Accounting for sub-groups

Parent A's functional currency is the US dollar and prepares its consolidated financial statements in US dollars. It has a 100% investment in Subsidiary A, the functional currency of which is the euro. Subsidiary A has a 100% investment in Subsidiary B, the functional currency of which is pound sterling.

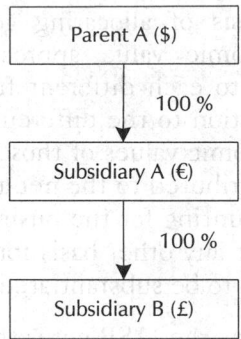

Should Parent A prepare consolidated financial statements by including the consolidated position of Subsidiary A (including Subsidiary B), or consolidate Subsidiary A and Subsidiary B as standalone entities?

It seems more consistent with various requirements of IAS 21 that each entity in a group should be consolidated individually, ignoring sub-groups and sub-consolidations. Under IAS 21, it makes no difference whether the reporting entity holds the foreign operation directly or whether there is an intermediate holding entity between the reporting entity and the foreign operation. This is made clear in paragraph 18 of the standard which states that 'it is necessary for the results and financial position of each individual entity included in the reporting entity to be translated into the currency in which the reporting entity presents its financial statements. ... The results and financial position of any individual entity within the reporting entity whose functional currency differs from the presentation currency are translated in accordance with paragraphs 38-50.'

Paragraph 38 states that 'An entity may present its financial statements in any currency (or currencies). If the presentation currency differs from the entity's functional currency, it translates its results and financial position into the presentation currency. For example, when a group contains individual entities with different functional currencies, the results and financial position of each entity are expressed in a common currency so that consolidated financial statements may be presented.'

Paragraph 45 continues by stating that 'The incorporation of the results and financial position of a foreign operation with those of the reporting entity follows normal consolidation procedures, such as the elimination of intragroup balances and intragroup transactions of a subsidiary (see IAS 27 and IAS 31). However, an intragroup monetary asset (or liability), whether short-term or long-term, cannot be eliminated against the corresponding intragroup liability (or asset) without showing the results of currency fluctuations in the consolidated financial statements. This is because the monetary item represents a commitment to convert one currency into another and exposes the reporting entity to a gain or loss through currency fluctuations. Accordingly, in the consolidated financial statements of the reporting entity, such an exchange difference continues to be recognised in profit or loss or, if it arises from the circumstances described in paragraph 32, it is recognised in other comprehensive income and accumulated within a separate component of equity until the disposal of the foreign operation.' Paragraph 32 is discussed at 3.4.1 below.

Furthermore paragraph 48 confirms that 'On the disposal of a foreign operation, the cumulative amount of the exchange differences relating to that foreign operation, recognised in other comprehensive income and accumulated in the separate component of equity, shall be reclassified from equity to profit or loss (as a reclassification adjustment) when the gain or loss on disposal is recognised'. This requirement is discussed further at 3.3.6 below.

The above-mentioned paragraphs refer to an *individual* entity being translated to the presentation currency, with the exchange differences arising from that process (i.e. between its functional currency and the presentation currency) being recognised in other comprehensive income, and for those cumulative exchange differences to be reclassified from equity to profit or loss upon the disposal of that foreign operation.

This is an aspect of IAS 21 that has been discussed by the IFRIC in developing IFRIC 16 (see Chapter 33 at 3.6.3 for a discussion of this interpretation). Initially the IFRIC noted that IAS 21 did not indicate a specific method of consolidation for foreign operations and referred to paragraph BC18 of the standard which, as noted above, states that the translation method in IAS 21 results in the same amounts in the presentation currency regardless of whether the direct or step-by-step method is used.[125] However, the IFRIC subsequently recognised that the two methods do not always result in the presentation of the same amounts and indicated that, although the direct method is conceptually correct, IAS 21 does not require an entity to use this method or to make adjustments to produce the same result.[126] IFRIC 16 simply says that an entity has an accounting policy choice as to which of the two methods it should use and that the method selected should be used consistently for all net investments.[127]

3.3.6   *Disposal of a foreign operation*

As discussed at 2.7.3 A above, on the disposal of a foreign operation, paragraph 48 of IAS 21 requires the related exchange differences recognised in other comprehensive income and accumulated in the separate component of equity to be reclassified from equity to profit or loss when the gain or loss on disposal is recognised.[128] This will include exchange differences arising on an intragroup balance that, in substance, forms part of an entity's net investment in a foreign operation. As set out at 2.7.3 B I above, following the application of IAS 27 (as amended in 2008) disposals include the loss of control of, significant influence over or joint control over a subsidiary, associate or jointly controlled entity respectively.[129]

Paragraph 49 of IAS 21 requires this reclassification of exchange differences from equity to profit or loss to be adopted not only when an entity sells an interest in a foreign entity, but also when it disposes of its interest through liquidation, repayment of share capital, or abandonment of that entity. Until IAS 27 (as amended in 2008) is applied (see 2.7.3 B II above) it also applies for all partial disposals, in which case only the proportionate share of the related accumulated exchange differences is included in the gain or loss. Following the application of IAS 27 (as amended in 2008) it only applies to partial disposals of foreign operations that are not subsidiaries.

The amendments to IFRS 1 and IAS 27 published in May 2008 amended IAS 21 to clarify that a dividend made by a foreign operation and accounted for as revenue by its parent, investor or venturer in its separate financial statements (see Chapter 8 at 2.3) should not be treated as a disposal or partial disposal of a net investment.[130] This contrasts to the previous position where IAS 21 explained that the payment of a dividend was part of a disposal only when it constituted a return of the investment, e.g. when the dividend was paid out of pre-acquisition profits.[131]

A write-down of the carrying amount of a foreign operation does not constitute a partial disposal, therefore no deferred exchange difference should be reclassified from equity to profit or loss at the time of the write-down.[132] Similarly, it is implicit in the requirement of IFRS 5 for separate disclosure of cumulative gains and losses recognised in equity relating to a disposal group (see Chapter 4 at 2.2.4) that the classification of a foreign operation as held for sale under IFRS 5 does not give rise to a reclassification of foreign exchange differences to profit or loss at that time.

There are a number of practical issues relating to the application of these requirements in IAS 21.

Whilst the reference to repayment of share capital might suggest that any such repayment could trigger a reclassification of exchange differences to profit or loss, we believe that there may be circumstances where this is not appropriate. The following example explores this issue further in the situation where IAS 27 (as amended in 2008) has not been adopted.

Example 13.15:   *Reclassification of exchange differences from equity to profit or loss on payments by a subsidiary to its parent*

The following scenarios consider a simple group as follows: Entity H, the parent, has the euro as its functional currency, presents its consolidated financial statements in euro and has not adopted IAS 27 (as amended in 2008) early. Entity S is Entity H's wholly owned subsidiary and has the US dollar as its functional currency. Both companies have substantive operations.

In each case the question addressed is whether or not any of the transactions identified should trigger a reclassification of exchange differences from equity to profit or loss in the consolidated financial statements.

Scenario 1

On 1 January 2006, Entity H establishes Entity S and subscribes US$100m for its entire share capital. During the next three years, Entity S makes profits of US$10m per year and retains them.

In 2009, it is decided that Entity S should repatriate US$30m (the amount of its retained profits) to Entity H which it can do in a number of ways including:

(a)   payment of a dividend of US$30m; or

(b)   partial redemption of share capital for US$30m.

Analysis

(a)   As indicated above, IAS 21 has been clarified so that a dividend recognised as revenue by Entity H should not be treated as a partial disposal and so this transaction should not result in any reclassification from equity to profit or loss.

(b)   Paragraph 49 of IAS 21 states that 'an entity may dispose of its interest in a foreign operation through sale, liquidation, repayment of share capital or abandonment of all, or part of, that entity.' Consequently, it appears that this transaction could trigger a reclassification of exchange differences from equity to profit or loss.

On the face of it, these two transactions appear to have very little to differentiate them, other than their legal form, particularly if Entity H is incorporated in a jurisdiction where the legal restrictions on companies repaying share capital are similar to those applying to dividend payments. Consequently, whilst the form of the payment will normally dictate the treatment to be adopted, there may be circumstances where it is appropriate, in accordance with Paragraph 35 of the *Framework*, to have regard to the substance of the transaction. In this case, the repayment of share capital appears, in substance, to be more akin to a dividend as it represents post-acquisition profits.

Scenario 2

On 1 January 2006, Entity H establishes Entity S and subscribes US$100m for its entire share capital. During the next three years, Entity S makes profits of US$10m per year and distributes them to Entity H at the end of each year.

In 2009, Entity S borrows US$40m from a third party and uses the proceeds to pay US$40m to Entity H, either by way of a dividend or by a partial repayment of share capital.

Analysis

For the same reasons as set out in Scenario 1 above, the distribution of profits in 2006 to 2008 do not trigger any reclassification from equity to profit or loss.

However, the transaction in 2009 clearly represents a significant reduction in the initial net investment in Entity S from US$100m to US$60m. Therefore, even if the legal form of the transaction is a dividend, it might be argued that it is more akin to a repayment of share capital and should trigger reclassification from equity to profit or loss.

The requirement to reclassify the cumulative exchange differences to profit or loss cannot be avoided, for example, by an entity merely disposing of the net assets and business of the foreign operation, rather than disposing of its interest in the legal entity that is the foreign operation. This is because paragraph 49 refers to the disposal of a foreign operation, and a foreign operation as defined by IAS 21 must have 'activities' (see 2.3 above). Following the disposal of the net assets and business, there no longer are 'activities'. Furthermore, a foreign operation need not be an incorporated entity but may be a branch, the disposal of which would necessarily take the form of an asset sale. The legal form of the entity should make no difference to the accounting treatment of exchange differences, including the reclassification of cumulative exchange differences from equity to profit or loss.

We illustrated the basic requirement to reclassify cumulative exchange differences from equity to profit or loss on the disposal of a foreign operation in Example 13.8 at 2.7.3 above where a parent sold a direct interest in a subsidiary. This requirement also applies on the sale of an indirect subsidiary. However, where the intermediate holding company and the subsidiary each have different functional currencies, the method of consolidation can have an impact on the amount of exchange differences reclassified from equity to profit or loss on the disposal of the subsidiary.

If the step-by-step method is used, this amount will have been measured based on the functional currencies of the intermediate holding company and the subsidiary. The translation of that amount into the presentation currency of the ultimate parent will not be the same as if the ultimate parent had consolidated the subsidiary individually. In this second case (the direct method), the exchange differences on translation of the subsidiary would have been measured based on the functional currency of the subsidiary and the presentation currency used by the ultimate parent. This is illustrated in the following example.

Example 13.16:   Disposal of an indirectly held foreign operation

On 1 January 2009, Entity A is incorporated in the UK with share capital of £300m. It sets up a wholly-owned Swiss subsidiary, Entity B, on the same day with share capital of CHF200m. Entity B in turn sets up a wholly-owned German subsidiary, Entity C, with share capital of €45m. All of the capital subscribed in each of the entities, to the extent that it has not been invested in a subsidiary, is used to acquire operating assets in their country of incorporation. The functional currency of each of the entities is therefore pound sterling, the Swiss franc and the euro respectively. The relevant exchange rates at 1 January 2009 are £1=CHF2.50=€1.50.

For the purposes of the example, it is assumed that in the year ended 31 December 2009 each of the entities made no profit or loss. The relevant exchange rates at that date were £1=CHF3.00=€1.25.

On 1 January 2010, the German subsidiary, Entity C, is sold by Entity B for €45m.

The exchange differences relating to Entity C that will be reclassified from equity to profit or loss in the consolidated financial statements of the Entity A group for the year ended 31 December 2010 on the basis that each of the subsidiaries are consolidated individually (the direct method) will be as follows:

Consolidating each subsidiary individually (the direct method)

The opening consolidated balance sheet of the Entity A group at 1 January 2009 is as follows:

	Entity A		Entity B		Entity C	Adjustments	Consolidated
Millions	£	CHF	£	€	£	£	£
Investment in B	80.0					(80.0)	
Investment in C		75.0	30.0			(30.0)	
Other net assets	220.0	125.0	50.0	45.0	30.0		300.0
	300.0	200.0	80.0	45.0	30.0		300.0
Share capital	300.0						300.0
Share capital		200.0	80.0			(80.0)	
Share capital				45.0	30.0	(30.0)	

The consolidated balance sheet of the Entity A group at 31 December 2009 is as follows:

	Entity A		Entity B		Entity C	Adjustments	Consolidated
Millions	£	CHF	£	€	£	£	£
Investment in B	80.0					(80.0)	
Investment in C		75.0	25.0			(25.0)	
Other net assets	220.0	125.0	41.7	45.0	36.0		297.7
	300.0	200.0	66.7	45.0	36.0		297.7
Share capital	300.0						300.0
Share capital		200.0	80.0			(80.0)	
Share capital				45.0	30.0	(30.0)	
Exchange – B			(13.3)			5.0	(8.3)
Exchange – C					6.0		6.0
	300.0	200.0	66.7	45.0	36.0		297.7

The exchange differences in respect of Entity B and Entity C are only shown for illustration purposes; the consolidated balance sheet would only show the net amount of £(2.3)m as a separate component of equity. The exchange difference of £6.0m in respect of Entity C is that arising on the translation of its opening net assets of €45m into the presentation currency of pound sterling based on the opening and closing exchange rates of £1=€1.50 and £1=€1.25 respectively, as required by paragraph 39 of IAS 21. Accordingly, it is this amount of £6.0m that will be reclassified from equity to profit or loss for the year ended 31 December 2010 upon the disposal of Entity C as required by paragraph 48 of IAS 21.

If the consolidated balance sheet for the Entity A group at 31 December 2009 had been prepared on the basis of a sub-consolidation of the Entity B sub-group incorporating Entity C, the position would have been as follows.

Consolidating using a sub-group consolidation (the step-by-step method)

The exchange rates at 1 January 2009 and 31 December 2009 are the equivalent of €1=CHF1.667 and €1=CHF2.400.

The sub-consolidation of Entity B and Entity C at 31 December 2009 is as follows:

Millions	Entity B CHF	Entity C €	CHF	Adjustments CHF	Consolidated CHF
Investment in C	75.0			(75.0)	
Other net assets	125.0	45.0	108.0		233.0
	200.0	45.0	108.0		233.0
Share capital	200.0				200.0
Share capital		45.0	75.0	(75.0)	
Exchange – C			33.0		33.0
	200.0	45.0	108.0		233.0

The exchange difference of CHF33.0m in respect of Entity C is that arising on the translation of its opening net assets of €45m into the functional currency of that of Entity B, the Swiss franc, based on the opening and closing exchange rates of €1=CHF1.667 and €1=CHF2.400 respectively.

In the consolidated financial statements of the Entity B sub-group for the year ended 31 December 2010, it is this amount of CHF33.0m that would be reclassified from equity to profit or loss upon the disposal of Entity C.

The consolidated balance sheet of the Entity A group at 31 December 2009 prepared using this sub-consolidation would be as follows:

Millions	Entity A £	Entity B sub-group CHF	£	Adjustments £	Consolidated £
Investment in B	80.0			(80.0)	
Other net assets	220.0	233.0	77.7		297.7
	300.0	233.0	77.7		297.7
Share capital	300.0				200.0
Share capital		200.0	80.0	(80.0)	
Exchange – C		33.0	11.0		11.0
Exchange – B group			(13.3)		(13.3)
	300.0	233.0	77.7		297.7

The exchange differences in respect of Entity C and that for the Entity B sub-group are only shown for illustration purposes; the consolidated balance sheet would only show the net amount of £(2.3)m as a separate component of equity. As can be seen, the consolidated position for the Entity A group is the same as that using the direct method. However, using the step-by-step method, the exchange difference of £11.0m in respect of Entity C is the exchange difference of CHF33.0 included in the Entity B sub-consolidation translated into the presentation currency used in the Entity A consolidated financial statements.

As indicated above, it is this amount of CHF33.0m that would be reclassified from equity to profit or loss upon the disposal of Entity C in the consolidated financial statements of the Entity B sub-group for the year ended 31 December 2010. In the consolidated financial statements of the Entity A group for the year ended 31 December 2010, it would be the translated amount of exchange differences of £11.0m that would be reclassified from equity to profit or loss on the disposal of Entity C.

In our view, the step-by-step method does not appear to result in the correct amount of exchange differences relating to the disposed entity being reclassified from equity to profit or loss which paragraph 39 of IAS 21 suggests should be measured by translating the functional currency figures for the entity into the presentation currency of the ultimate parent. Nevertheless, as noted at 3.3.5 above, IFRIC 16 permits the use of this approach as an accounting policy choice.

In certain situations, the methods of consolidation seem to result in more extreme differences. For example, consider the disposal of a US subsidiary by a US intermediate holding company (both of which have the US dollar as their functional currency) within a group headed by a UK parent (which has sterling as its functional and presentation currency). The US subsidiary that is disposed of is a foreign operation so exchange differences accumulated in the separate component of equity relating to it should be reclassified from equity to profit or loss on its disposal. Under the direct method of consolidation, this amount will represent exchange differences arising from translating the results and net assets of the US subsidiary directly into sterling. However, under the step-by-step method, these exchange differences will be entirely attributable to the intermediate parent undertaking and so there would be no reclassification from equity to profit or loss. This is a further reason why we believe it is more appropriate to use the direct method.

3.4   Intragroup transactions

The standard states that 'the incorporation of the results and financial position of a foreign operation with those of the reporting entity follows normal consolidation procedures, such as the elimination of intragroup balances and intragroup transactions of a subsidiary'.[133] On this basis, there is a tendency sometimes to assume that exchange differences on intragroup balances should not impact on the reported profit or loss for the group in the consolidated financial statements. However, as discussed at 2.7.2 A above, that is not the case. The general requirement of IAS 21 is that exchange differences arising on intragroup balances continue to be reflected in profit or loss in the consolidated financial statements, effectively treating them in the same way as exchange differences on monetary items resulting from transactions with third parties.

Nevertheless, the standard makes an exception to this requirement where the exchange difference arises on an intragroup balance that, in substance, forms part of an entity's net investment in a foreign operation. In that case, the exchange difference is not to be recognised in profit or loss in the consolidated financial statements, but is recognised in other comprehensive income and accumulated within a separate component of equity until the disposal of the foreign operation (see 2.7.3 above).[134]

3.4.1   *Monetary items included as part of the net investment in a foreign operation*

A   *General*

The 'net investment in a foreign operation' is defined as being 'the amount of the reporting entity's interest in the net assets of that operation'.[135] The standard elaborates on this by stating that 'an entity may have a monetary item that is receivable from or payable to a foreign operation. An item for which settlement is neither planned nor likely to occur in the foreseeable future is, in substance, a part of the entity's net investment in that foreign operation'. Such monetary items may include long-term receivables or loans. They do not include trade receivables or trade payables.[136]

Under what circumstances can receivables/payables be included as part of an entity's net investment in a foreign operation? Consider the following example:

Example 13.17:   Receivables/payables included as part of net investment in a foreign operation?

A UK entity, A, has a Belgian subsidiary, B. A has a receivable due from B amounting to £1,000,000.

In each of the following scenarios, could the receivable be included as part of A's net investment in B?

Scenario 1

The receivable arises from the sale of goods, together with interest payments and dividend payments which have not been paid in cash but have been accumulated in the inter-company account. A and B agree that A can claim at any time the repayment of this receivable. It is likely that there will be a settlement of the receivable in the foreseeable future.

Although the standard states that trade receivables and payables are not included, we do not believe that it necessarily precludes deferred trading balances from being included. In our view, such balances can be included as part of the net investment in the foreign operation, but only if cash settlement is not made or planned to be made in the foreseeable future.

In this scenario, the settlement of A's receivable due from B is not planned; however, it is likely that a settlement will occur in the foreseeable future. Accordingly, the receivable does not qualify to be treated as part of A's net investment in B. The term 'foreseeable future' is not defined and no specific time period is implied. It could be argued that the receivable should only be considered as part of the net investment if it will be repaid only when the reporting entity disinvests from the foreign operation. However, it is recognised that in most circumstances this would be unrealistic and therefore a shorter time span should be considered in determining the foreseeable future.

Scenario 2

The receivable represents a loan made by A to B and it is agreed that the receivable will be repaid in 20 years.

In this scenario, A's receivable due from B has a specified term for repayment. This suggests that settlement is planned. Accordingly, the receivable does not qualify to be treated as part of A's investment in B.

Scenario 3

A and B have previously agreed that the receivable under scenario 2 will be repaid in 20 years but A now decides that it will replace the loan on maturity either with a further inter-company loan or with an injection of equity. This approach is consistent with A's intention to maintain the strategic long-term investment in B.

In this scenario, the words from paragraph 15 of IAS 21 '... settlement is neither planned nor likely to occur in the foreseeable future ...' are potentially problematic, since a loan with a fixed maturity must, prima facie, have a planned settlement. However, from the date A decides that it will re-finance the inter-company debt upon maturity with a further long-term instrument, or replace it with equity, the substance of the inter-company loan is that it is part of the entity's net investment in the foreign operation, and there is no actual 'intent' to settle the investment without replacement. On this basis, loans with a stated maturity may qualify to be treated in accordance with paragraph 32 of IAS 21, with foreign currency gains and losses recognised in other comprehensive income and accumulated in a separate component of equity in the consolidated financial statements. However, in our view, management's intention to refinance the loan must be documented appropriately, for example in the form of a minute of a meeting of the management board or board of directors or letter of representation. In addition, there should not be any established historical pattern of the entity demanding repayment of such inter-company debt without replacement.

Consequently, when the purpose of the loan is to fund a long-term strategic investment then it is the entity's overall intention with regard to the investment and ultimate funding thereof, rather than the specific terms of the inter-company loan funding the investment, that should be considered.

Scenario 4

The receivable arises from the sale of goods, together with interest payments and dividend payments which have not been paid in cash but have been accumulated in the inter-company account. However, in this scenario, A and B agree that A can claim the repayment of this receivable only in the event that the subsidiary is disposed of. A has no plans to dispose of entity B.

In this scenario, the settlement of A's receivable due from B is not planned nor is it likely to occur in the foreseeable future. Although the term 'foreseeable future' is not defined, it will not go beyond a point of time after the disposal of a foreign operation. Accordingly, the receivable does qualify for being treated as part of a net investment in a foreign operation.

As indicated in scenario 1 in the above example, in our view trade receivables and payables can be included as part of the net investment in the foreign operation, but only if cash settlement is not made or planned to be made in the foreseeable future. However, if a subsidiary makes payment for purchases from its parent, but is continually indebted to the parent as a result of new purchases, then in these circumstances, since individual transactions are settled, no part of the inter-company balance should be regarded as part of the net investment in the subsidiary. Accordingly, exchange differences on such balances should be recognised in profit or loss.

B   Currency of the monetary item

When a monetary item is considered to form part of a reporting entity's net investment in a foreign operation and is denominated in the functional currency of the reporting entity, an exchange difference will be recognised in profit or loss for the period when it arises in the foreign operation's individual financial statements. If the item is denominated in the functional currency of the foreign operation, an exchange difference will be recognised in profit or loss for the period when it arises in the reporting entity's separate financial statements. Such exchange differences are only recognised in other comprehensive income and accumulated in a separate component of equity in the financial statements that include the foreign operation and the reporting entity (i.e. financial statements in which the foreign operation is consolidated, proportionately consolidated or accounted for using the equity method).[137]

Example 13.18: Monetary item in functional currency of either the reporting entity or the foreign operation

A UK entity has a Belgian subsidiary. On the last day of its financial year, 31 March 2009, the UK entity lends the subsidiary £1,000,000. Settlement of the loan is neither planned nor likely to occur in the foreseeable future, so the UK entity regards the loan as part of its net investment in the Belgian subsidiary. The exchange rate at 31 March 2009 was £1=€1.40. Since the loan was made on the last day of the year there are no exchange differences to recognise for that year. At 31 March 2010, the loan has not been repaid and is still regarded as part of the net investment in the Belgian subsidiary. The relevant exchange rate at that date was £1=€1.50. The average exchange rate for the year ended 31 March 2010 was £1=€1.45.

In the UK entity's separate financial statements no exchange difference is recognised since the loan is denominated in its functional currency of pound sterling. In the Belgian subsidiary's financial statements, the liability to the parent is translated into the subsidiary's functional currency of euros at the closing rate at €1,500,000, giving rise to an exchange loss of €100,000, i.e. €1,500,000 less €1,400,000 (£1,000,000 @ £1=€1.40). This exchange loss is reflected in the Belgian subsidiary's profit or loss for that year. In the UK entity's consolidated financial statements, this exchange loss included in the subsidiary's profit or loss for the year will be translated at the average rate for the year, giving rise a loss of £68,966 (€100,000@ £1=€1.45). This will be recognised in other comprehensive income and accumulated in the separate component of equity together with an exchange gain of £2,299, being the difference between the amount included in the Belgian subsidiary's income statement translated at average rate, i.e. £68,966, and at the closing rate, i.e. £66,667 (€100,000@ £1=€1.50). The overall exchange loss recognised in other comprehensive income is £66,667. This represents the exchange loss on the increased net investment of €1,400,000 in the subsidiary made at 31 March 2009, i.e. £1,000,000 (€1,400,000 @ £1=€1.40) less £933,333 (€1,400,000 @ £1=€1.50).

If, on the other hand, the loan made to the Belgian subsidiary had been denominated in the equivalent amount of euros at 31 March 2009, i.e. €1,400,000, the treatment would have been as follows:

In the UK entity's separate financial statements, the amount receivable from the Belgian subsidiary would be translated at the closing rate at £933,333 (€1,400,000 @ £1=€1.50), giving rise to an exchange loss of £66,667, i.e. £1,000,000 (€1,400,000 @ £1=€1.40) less £933,333, which is included in its profit or loss for the year. In the Belgian subsidiary's financial statements, no exchange difference is recognised since the loan is denominated in its functional currency of euros. In the UK entity's consolidated financial statements, the exchange loss included in its profit or loss for the year in its separate financial statements will be recognised in other comprehensive income and accumulated in the separate component of equity. As before, this represents the exchange loss on the increased net investment of €1,400,000 in the subsidiary made at 31 March 2009, i.e. £1,000,000 (€1,400,000 @ £1=€1.40) less £933,333 (€1,400,000 @ £1=€1.40).

In most situations, intragroup balances for which settlement is neither planned nor likely to occur in the foreseeable future will be denominated in the functional currency of either the reporting entity or the foreign operation. However, this will not always be the case. If a monetary item is denominated in a currency other than the functional currency of either the reporting entity or the foreign operation, the exchange difference arising in the reporting entity's separate financial statements and in the foreign operation's individual financial statements are also recognised in other comprehensive income and accumulated in the separate component of equity in the financial statements that include the foreign operation and the reporting entity (i.e. financial statements in which the foreign operation is consolidated, proportionately consolidated or accounted for using the equity method).[138] Prior to the December 2005 amendments (see 1.2.3 above), such a treatment was prohibited, i.e. the exchange differences arising on translating the monetary item into the functional currencies of the reporting entity and the foreign operation were to remain recognised in profit or loss.[139]

C   Treatment in the individual financial statements

It is emphasised that the exception for exchange differences on monetary items forming part of the net investment in a foreign operation applies only in the consolidated financial statements. In the individual financial statements of the entity (or entities) with the currency exposure the exchange differences have to be reflected in that entity's profit or loss for the period. It is unclear why this should be the case since the standard does not acknowledge that this represented a change from the version of IAS 21 prior to its revision in 2003.

We see no reason why such exchange differences should have to be recognised in profit or loss. When the Board amended IAS 21 in December 2005 it noted that the nature of the monetary item referred to in paragraph 15 is similar to an equity investment in a foreign operation, i.e. settlement of the monetary item is neither planned nor likely to occur in the foreseeable future. Therefore, the principle in paragraph 32 to recognise exchange differences arising on a monetary item initially in a separate component of equity effectively results in the monetary item being accounted for in the same way as an equity investment in the foreign operation when consolidated financial statements are prepared. Accordingly, the exchange differences are treated in the same way as the exchange differences on the net assets of the foreign operation. The stated reason within the standard as to why the exchange differences on the net assets of the foreign operation are not recognised in profit or loss is because the changes in exchange rates have little or no direct effect on the present and future cash flows from operations.[140] On that basis, the same would hold true for the separate financial statements of the reporting entity. Indeed, since the item is considered to be, in substance, part of the net investment, in our view it would have been more appropriate to treat it as such, and therefore consider it to be a 'non-monetary item' under the standard. Thus, either no exchange differences would have been recognised or they would have been reflected in equity.

D   Monetary items transacted by other members of the group

As illustrated in the examples above, the requirements of IAS 21 whereby exchange differences on a monetary item that forms part of the net investment in a foreign operation are recognised in other comprehensive income clearly apply where the monetary item is transacted between the parent preparing the consolidated financial statements and the subsidiary that is the foreign operation. However, loans from any entity (and in any currency) qualify for net investment treatment, so long as the conditions of paragraph 15 are met (this having been made clear by the December 2005 amendment of IAS 21).[141]

E   Monetary items becoming part of the net investment in a foreign operation

It may happen that a parent will decide that its subsidiary requires to be refinanced and instead of investing more equity capital in the subsidiary decides that an existing inter-company account, which has previously been regarded as a normal monetary item, should become a long-term deferred trading balance and no repayment of such amount will be requested within the foreseeable future. How should the parent treat the exchange differences relating to the inter-company account in the consolidated financial statements in the year it was so designated?

Example 13.19:   Monetary item becoming part of the net investment in a foreign operation

A UK entity has a wholly owned Canadian subsidiary whose net assets at 31 December 2009 were C\$2,000,000. These net assets were arrived at after taking account of a liability to the UK parent of £250,000. Using the closing exchange rate of £1=C\$2.35 this liability was included in the Canadian company's balance sheet at that date at C\$587,500. On 30 June 2010, when the exchange rate was £1=C\$2.45, the parent decided that in order to refinance the Canadian subsidiary it would regard the liability of £250,000 as a long-term liability which would not be called for repayment in the foreseeable future. Consequently, the parent thereafter regarded the loan as being part of its net investment in the subsidiary. In the year ended 31 December 2010 the Canadian company made no profit or loss other than any exchange difference to be recognised on its liability to its parent. The relevant exchange rate at that date was £1=C\$2.56. The average exchange rate for the year ended 31 December 2010 was £1=C\$2.50.

The financial statements of the subsidiary in C\$ and translated using the closing rate are as follows:

Balance sheet	31 December 2010		31 December 2009	
	C\$	£	C\$	£
Assets	2,587,500	1,010,742	2,587,500	1,101,064
Amount due to parent	640,000	250,000	587,500	250,000
Net assets	1,947,500	760,742	2,000,000	851,064
Income statement				
Exchange difference	(52,500)			

If the amount due to the parent is not part of the parent's net investment in the foreign operation, this exchange loss would be translated at the average rate and included in the consolidated profit and loss account as £21,000. As the net investment was C\$2,000,000 then there would have been an exchange loss recognised in other comprehensive income of £69,814, i.e. £851,064 less £781,250 (C\$2,000,000 @ £1=C\$2.56), together with an exchange gain of £492, being the difference between profit or loss translated at average rate, i.e. £21,000, and at the closing rate, i.e. £20,508.

However, the parent now regards the amount due as being part of the net investment in the subsidiary. The question then arises as to when this should be regarded as having happened and how the exchange difference on it should be calculated. No guidance is given in IAS 21.

In our view, the 'capital injection' should be regarded as having occurred at the time it is decided to redesignate the inter-company account. The exchange differences arising on the account up to that date should be recognised in profit or loss. Only the exchange difference arising thereafter would be recognised in other comprehensive income on consolidation. The inter-company account that was converted into a long-term loan becomes part of the entity's (UK parent's) net investment in the foreign operation (Canadian subsidiary) at the moment in time when the entity decides that settlement is neither planned nor likely to occur in the foreseeable future, i.e. 30 June 2010. Accordingly, exchange differences arising on the long-term loan are recognised in other comprehensive income and accumulated in a separate component of equity from that date. The same accounting treatment would have been applied if a capital injection had taken place at the date of redesignation.

At 30 June 2010 the subsidiary would have translated the inter-company account as C$612,500 (£250,000 @ £1=C$2.45) and therefore the exchange loss up to that date was C$25,000. Translated at the average rate this amount would be included in consolidated profit or loss as £10,000, with only an exchange gain of £234 recognised in other comprehensive income, being the difference between profit or loss translated at average rate, i.e. £10,000, and at the closing rate, i.e. £9,766. Accordingly, £11,000 (£21,000 less £10,000) offset by a reduction in the exchange gain on the translation of profit or loss of £258 (£492 less £234) would be recognised in other comprehensive income. This amount represents the exchange loss on the 'capital injection' of C$612,500. Translated at the closing rate this amounts to £239,258 which is £10,742 less than the original £250,000.

Some might argue that an approach of regarding the 'capital injection' as having occurred at the beginning of the accounting period would have the merit of treating all of the exchange differences for this year in the same way. However, for the reasons provided above we do not regard such an approach as being acceptable.

Suppose, instead of the inter-company account being £250,000, it was denominated in dollars at C$587,500. In this case the parent would be exposed to the exchange risk; what would be the position?

The subsidiary's net assets at both 31 December 2009 and 2010 would be:

Assets	C$2,587,500
Amount due to parent	587,500
Net assets	C$2,000,000

As the inter-company account is expressed in Canadian dollars, there will be no exchange difference thereon in the subsidiary's profit or loss.

There will, however, be an exchange loss in the parent as follows:

C$587,500	@ 2.35 =	£250,000
	@ 2.56 =	£229,492
		£20,508

Again, in the consolidated financial statements as the inter-company account is now regarded as part of the equity investment some of this amount should be recognised in other comprehensive income. For the reasons stated above, in our view it is only the exchange differences that have arisen after the date of redesignation, i.e. 30 June 2010, that should be recognised in other comprehensive income.

On this basis, the exchange loss would be split as follows:

C$587,500	@ 2.35 =	£250,000	
	@ 2.45 =	£239,796	
			£10,204
	@ 2.45 =	£239,796	
	@ 2.56 =	£229,492	
			£10,304

The exchange loss up to 30 June 2010 of £10,204 would be recognised in consolidated profit or loss and the exchange loss thereafter of £10,304 would be recognised in other comprehensive income. This is different from when the account was expressed in sterling because the 'capital injection' in this case is C$587,500 whereas before it was effectively C$612,500.

F   Monetary items ceasing to be part of the net investment in a foreign
         operation

I   *IAS 21 prior to the application of IAS 27 (as amended in 2008)*

The previous section dealt with the situation where a pre-existing monetary item was subsequently considered to form part of the net investment in a foreign operation. However, what happens where a monetary item ceases to be considered part of the net investment in a foreign operation, either because the circumstances have changed such that it is now planned or is likely to be settled in the foreseeable future or indeed that the monetary item is in fact settled?

Where the circumstances have changed such that the monetary item is now planned or is likely to be settled in the foreseeable future, then similar issues to those discussed at 3.4.1 A above apply; i.e. are the exchange differences on the intragroup balance to be recognised in profit or loss only from the date of change or from the beginning of the financial year? For the same reasons set out in Example 13.19 above, in our view, the monetary item ceases to form part of the net investment in the foreign operation at the moment in time when the entity decides that settlement is planned or is likely to occur in the foreseeable future. Accordingly, exchange differences arising on the monetary item up to that date are recognised in other comprehensive income and accumulated in a separate component of equity. The exchange differences that arise after that date are recognised in profit or loss.

Consideration also needs to be given as to the treatment of the cumulative exchange differences on the monetary item that have been recognised in other comprehensive income, including those that had been recognised in other comprehensive income in prior years. As indicated at 3.4 above, the treatment of these exchange differences is to recognise them in other comprehensive income and accumulate them in a separate component of equity until the disposal of the foreign operation (see 2.7.3 and 3.3.6 above).[142] In our view the change of circumstances does not represent a disposal or partial disposal and, accordingly, the exchange differences should remain in the separate component of equity.

However, where the intragroup balance is actually settled in cash, consideration needs to be given as to whether the cumulative exchange differences that relate to the amount repaid should be recognised in profit or loss at the time of the repayment, which will depend on whether the settlement constitutes a partial disposal of the net investment in the foreign operation. The repayment of the intragroup balance will be akin to the repayment of share capital if it constitutes a partial return of the investment, in which case a proportion of the cumulative exchange differences relating to the investment in the foreign operation should be reclassified from equity to profit or loss at the time of the repayment. However, as illustrated in Example 13.15 above, there are circumstances where the repayment of share capital are, in substance, much more like the payment of a dividend which do not result in a reclassification from equity to profit or loss. Also, the repayment of upstream intragroup loans, i.e. those made by a subsidiary to its parent, are more akin to a subscription for additional share capital rather than a repayment of share capital.

II   *IAS 27 (as amended in 2008)*

As noted at 2.7.3 B II above, once IAS 27 (as amended in 2008) has been applied, a partial disposal of an entity's interest in a foreign operation means any reduction in its ownership interest. Consequently, the repayment of an intragroup loan by a subsidiary, associate or joint venture would not result in a reclassification from equity to profit or loss unless it somehow represented a reduction in the reporting entity's ownership interest (perhaps, unusually, in the case of an investment in an associate or a joint venture).

3.4.2   *Other intragroup transactions*

As indicated in 3.4 above, exchange differences on intragroup transactions should normally be treated in the same way as if they arose on transactions with third parties. However, there are two further problem areas that arise when preparing the consolidated financial statements.

A   *Dividends*

The first area relates to dividends payable by a foreign subsidiary to its parent.

If a subsidiary pays a dividend to the parent during the year the parent should record the dividend at the rate ruling when the dividend was declared. An exchange difference will arise in the parent's own financial statements if the exchange rate moves between the declaration date and the date the dividend is actually received. This exchange difference is required to be recognised in profit or loss and will remain there on consolidation.

The same will apply if the subsidiary declares a dividend to its parent on the last day of its financial year and this is recorded at the year-end in both entities' financial statements. There is no problem in that year as both the intragroup balances and the dividends will eliminate on consolidation with no exchange differences arising. However, as the dividend will not be received until the following year an exchange difference will arise in the parent's financial statements in that year if exchange rates have moved in the meantime. Again, this exchange difference should remain in consolidated profit or loss as it is no different from any other exchange difference arising on intragroup balances resulting from other types of intragroup transactions. It should not be recognised in other comprehensive income.

It may seem odd that the consolidated results can be affected by exchange differences on inter-company dividends. However, once the dividend has been declared, the parent now effectively has a functional currency exposure to assets that were previously regarded as part of the net investment. In order to minimise the effect of exchange rate movements entities should, therefore, arrange for inter-company dividends to be paid on the same day the dividend is declared, or as soon after the dividend is declared as possible.

B   *Unrealised profits on intragroup transactions*

The other problem area is the elimination of unrealised profits resulting from intragroup transactions when one of the parties to the transaction is a foreign subsidiary.

Example 13.20:   Unrealised profits on intragroup transaction

An Italian parent has a wholly owned Swiss subsidiary. On 30 November 2010 the subsidiary sold goods to the parent for CHF1,000. The cost of the goods to the subsidiary was CHF700. The goods were recorded by the parent at €685 based on the exchange rate ruling on 30 November 2010 of €1=CHF1.46. All of the goods are unsold by the year-end, 31 December 2010. The exchange rate at that date was €1=CHF1.52. How should the intragroup profit be eliminated?

IAS 21 contains no specific guidance on this matter. However, SFAS 52 requires the rate ruling at the date of the transaction to be used.[143]

The profit shown by the subsidiary is CHF300 which translated at the rate ruling on the transaction of €1=CHF1.46 equals €205. Consequently, the goods will be included in the balance sheet at:

Per parent company balance sheet	€685
Less unrealised profit eliminated	205
	€480

It can be seen that the resulting figure for inventory is equivalent to the original euro cost translated at the rate ruling on the date of the transaction. Whereas if the subsidiary still held the inventory it would be included at €461 (CHF700 @ €1=CHF1.52).

If in the above example the goods had been sold by the Italian parent to the Swiss subsidiary then we believe the amount to be eliminated is the amount of profit shown in the Italian entity's financial statements. Again, this will not necessarily result in the goods being carried in the consolidated financial statements at their original cost to the group.

3.5   Change of presentation currency

IAS 21 does not address how an entity should approach presenting its financial statements if it changes its presentation currency. This is a situation that is commonly faced when the reporting entity determines that its functional currency has changed (the accounting implications of which are set out in IAS 21 and discussed at 2.6.4 above). However, because entities have a free choice of their presentation currency, it can occur in other situations too.

Changing presentation currency is, in our view, similar to a change in accounting policy, the requirements for which are set out in IAS 8 – *Accounting Policies, Changes in Accounting Estimates and Errors*. Therefore, when an entity changes its presentation currency, we consider it appropriate to follow the approach in IAS 8 which requires retrospective application except to the extent that this is impracticable (see Chapter 3 at 4.4).

It almost goes without saying that the comparatives should be restated and presented in the new presentation currency. Further, they should be prepared as if this had always been the entity's presentation currency (at least to the extent practicable). The main issue arising in practice is determining the amount of the different components of equity, particularly the exchange differences that IAS 21 requires to be accumulated in a separate component of equity, and how much of those differences relate to each operation within the group. The following example illustrates the impact of a change in presentation currency of a relatively simple group.

Example 13.21:   *Change of presentation currency*

A Canadian parent, P, was established on 1 January 2008 and issued new shares for C$20 million. On the same date it established two wholly owned subsidiaries, S1 and S2 incorporated in Canada and the UK respectively and subscribed C$10 million and £4.5 million for their entire share capital. The functional currency of each group company was determined to be its local currency, i.e. Canadian dollars for P and S1 and the pound sterling for S2.

During 2008, S1 made a profit of C$800,000, S2 made a profit of £350,000 and P made a loss of C$25,000. On 30 September 2008, P issued new shares for C$10 million of which £4 million was used immediately to subscribe for additional shares in S2.

During 2009, S1 made a profit of C$700,000, S2 made a profit of £750,000 and P made a loss of C$30,000 before dividends received from S2. On 30 June 2009, S2 paid dividends (out of profits then made) of £700,000 to P and on 30 September 2009 P paid dividends of C$1,000,000 to its shareholders.

The relevant exchange rates for C$1=£ were as follows:

1 January 2008	2.10
30 September 2008	2.28
31 December 2008	2.35
Average for 2008	2.24
30 June 2009	2.55
30 September 2009	2.63
31 December 2009	2.40
Average for 2009	2.52

Consequently, the statement of changes in equity in P's consolidated financial statements for 2008 and 2009 can be summarised as follows:

	Paid-in capital C$	Retained earnings C$	Foreign exchange C$	Total C$
1 January 2008	–	–	–	–
Issue of shares	30,000,000	–	–	30,000,000
Comprehensive income	–	1,559,000	1,443,500	3,002,500
31 December 2008	30,000,000	1,559,000	1,443,500	33,002,500
Comprehensive income	–	2,560,000	457,500	3,017,500
Dividends	–	(1,000,000)	–	(1,000,000)
31 December 2009	30,000,000	3,119,000	1,901,000	35,020,000

The comprehensive income reflected within retained earnings represents the profit for each year, calculated as follows:

2008: C$800,000 + (£350,000 × 2.24) – C$25,000 = C$1,559,000

2009: C$700,000 + (£750,000 × 2.52) – C$30,000 = C$2,560,000

The foreign exchange differences recognised in other comprehensive income, which are entirely attributable to S2, can be calculated as follows:

	2008			2009		
	£	Rate	C$	£	Rate	C$
Opening net assets*	4,500,000	2.10	9,450,000	8,850,000	2.35	20,797,500
		2.35	10,575,000		2.40	21,240,000
Exchange gain			1,125,000			442,500
Additional capital	4,000,000	2.28	9,120,000	–	–	–
		2.35	9,400,000	–		–
Exchange gain			280,000			–
Dividend	–	–	–	(700,000)	2.55	(1,785,000)
					2.40	(1,680,000)
Exchange gain			–			105,000
Profit	350,000	2.24	784,000	750,000	2.52	1,890,000
		2.35	822,500		2.40	1,800,000
Exchange gain/(loss)			38,500			(90,000)
	8,850,000		1,443,500	8,900,000		457,500

*for 2008, includes the proceeds received for issuing shares on 1 January.

For the year ended 31 December 2010, P decided to change its presentation currency to sterling. (This may or may not have coincided with a change of P's functional currency.) In P's consolidated financial statements for the year ended 31 December 2010, what amounts should be included in respect of the comparative period?

Direct method

If P's accounting policy was to use the direct method of consolidation (see 3.3.5 above), its financial statements for 2008 and 2009 would have been prepared by translating the financial statements of each entity within the group directly into sterling (where necessary). The revised statement of changes in equity in P's consolidated financial statements can be summarised as follows and these are the amounts that will be reflected as comparative amounts in P's consolidated financial statements for the year ended 31 December 2010:

	Paid-in capital £	Retained earnings £	Foreign exchange £	Total £
1 January 2008	–	–	–	–
Issue of shares	13,909,775	–	–	13,909,775
Comprehensive income	–	695,982	(562,140)	133,842
31 December 2008	13,909,775	695,982	(562,140)	14,043,617
Comprehensive income	–	1,015,873	(87,595)	928,278
Dividends	–	(380,228)	–	(380,228)
31 December 2009	13,909,775	1,331,627	(649,735)	14,591,667

The table above assumes that P will record its paid-in capital at historical exchange rates (£13,909,775 = C$20,000,000/2.10 + C$10,000,000/2.28). Alternatively, P could retranslate those amounts at year end rates although any difference arising would simply be recorded in another component of equity (but not the foreign exchange reserve) and this difference would not affect profit or loss or other comprehensive income in any period (see 3.3.3 A and B above).

The calculations showing how these amounts have been determined are shown below.

The comprehensive income reflected within retained earnings represents the profit for each year, calculated as follows:

$$2008: (C\$800,000/2.24) + £350,000 - (C\$25,000/2.24) = £695,982$$

$$2009: (C\$700,000/2.52) + £750,000 - (C\$30,000/2.52) = £1,015,873$$

In this case, the profit calculated in this way results in the same amount as translating the consolidated profit of C\$1,559,000 and C\$2,560,000 presented in Canadian dollars at the average rate for the period of C\$2.24=£1 and C\$2.52=£1 respectively. In practice minor differences can arise as a result of imperfections in the average rates used.

Similarly, the net assets presented above are the same as the amounts obtained by translating consolidated net assets of C\$33,002,500 and C\$35,020,000 at the closing rates at the end of the relevant period, C\$2.35=£1 and C\$2.40=£1 respectively. This should always be the case.

However, the foreign exchange reserve is fundamentally different to that in the financial statements presented in Canadian dollars. In this case it represents exchange differences arising from the translation of both P's and S1's financial statements into sterling whereas previously it represented exchange differences arising from the translation of S2's financial statements into Canadian dollars.

The foreign exchange differences recognised in other comprehensive income that are attributable to P can be calculated as follows:

		2008			*2009*	
	C$	Rate	£	C$	Rate	£
Opening net assets*	550,000	2.10	261,905	1,405,000	2.35	597,872
		2.35	234,042		2.40	585,417
Exchange loss			(27,863)			(12,455)
Additional capital**	880,000	2.28	385,965	–	–	–
		2.35	374,468	–		–
Exchange loss			(11,497)			–
Dividend received	–	–	–	1,785,000	2.55	700,000
	–		–		2.40	743,750
Exchange gain			–			43,750
Dividend paid	–	–	–	(1,000,000)	2.63	(380,228)
	–		–		2.40	(416,667)
Exchange loss			–			(36,439)
Loss	(25,000)	2.24	(11,161)	(30,000)	2.52	(11,905)
		2.35	(10,638)		2.40	(12,500)
Exchange gain/(loss)			523			(595)
	1,405,000		(38,837)	2,160,000		(5,739)

*for 2008, includes the proceeds received for issuing shares on 1 January (C\$20,000,000) less amounts invested in S1 (C\$10,000,000) and S2 (C\$9,450,000 = £4,500,000 × 2.10) on the same date.

**reduced by the amounts invested in S2 on the same date.

The foreign exchange differences recognised in other comprehensive income that are attributable to S1 can be calculated as follows:

	C$	2008 Rate	£	C$	2009 Rate	£
Opening net assets*	10,000,000	2.10	4,761,905	10,800,000	2.35	4,595,745
		2.35	4,255,319		2.40	4,500,000
Exchange loss			(506,586)			(95,745)
Profit	800,000	2.24	357,143	700,000	2.52	277,778
		2.35	340,426		2.40	291,667
Exchange (loss)/gain			(16,717)			13,889
	10,800,000		(523,303)	11,500,000		(81,856)

*for 2008, includes the proceeds received for issuing shares on 1 January.

Therefore the total foreign exchange loss arising in 2008 is £562,140 (£38,837 + £523,303) and in 2009 is £87,595 (£5,739 + £81,856).

Under this method amounts in the foreign exchange reserve would be reclassified to profit or loss on the subsequent disposal of S1, but not on the subsequent disposal of S2.

Step-by-step method

If P's accounting policy was to use the step-by-step method of consolidation (see 3.3.5 above), the first step in producing its consolidated financial statements for 2008 and 2009 would have been to translate the financial statements of S2 into Canadian dollars, the functional currency of P, to produce consolidated financial statements in Canadian dollars (effectively those that P had prepared historically). The second step involves translating these consolidated financial statements into sterling.

These financial statements (and hence the comparative amounts included in the financial statements for the year ended 31 December 2010) will appear to be the same as those produced under the direct method (assuming equity items are dealt with similarly, i.e. paid-in capital is translated at the relevant rate at the date of issue and that retained earnings represent each element translated at the relevant rates, being 2008 and 2009 profit at the average rate for the year, and dividends at the date of payment). However, the balance on the foreign exchange reserve will be attributable to different entities within the group (see 3.3.6 above). The calculations showing how these amounts have been determined are shown below.

The foreign exchange differences recognised in other comprehensive income in the financial statements presented in Canadian dollars that are attributable to S2 will remain attributable to S2, albeit that they are translated into sterling at the average rate:

   2008: C$1,443,500/2.24 = £644,420

   2009: C$457,500/2.52 = £181,548

The remaining exchange differences recognised in other comprehensive income, which arise from retranslating P's consolidated financial statements presented in Canadian dollars into sterling, are attributable to P. They can be calculated as follows:

	C$	2008 Rate	£	C$	2009 Rate	£
Opening net assets*	20,000,000	2.10	9,523,809	33,002,500	2.35	14,043,617
		2.35	8,510,638		2.40	13,751,042
Exchange loss			(1,013,171)			(292,575)
Additional capital	10,000,000	2.28	4,385,965	–		
		2.35	4,255,319			
Exchange loss			(130,646)			–
Dividend paid	–	2.24	–	(1,000,000)	2.63	(380,228)
		2.35	–		2.40	(416,667)
Exchange loss			–			(36,439)
Comprehensive income	3,002,500	2.24	1,340,402	3,017,500	2.52	1,197,421
		2.35	1,277,660		2.40	1,257,292
Exchange (loss)/gain			(62,742)			59,871
	33,002,500		(1,206,559)	35,020,000		(269,143)

*for 2008, includes the proceeds received for issuing shares on 1 January.

In contrast to the direct method, under this method amounts in the foreign exchange reserve would be reclassified to profit or loss on the subsequent disposal of S2, but not on the subsequent disposal of S1.

In the example above, it was reasonably straightforward to recreate the consolidated equity balances and identify the amounts of accumulated exchange differences related to each entity within the group using the new presentation currency. This is because the group had a very simple structure with operations having only two functional currencies, a short history and few (external and internal) equity transactions. Whilst entities should strive for a theoretically perfect restatement, in practice it is unlikely to be such an easy exercise.

As noted above, where an accounting policy is changed, IAS 8 requires retrospective application except to the extent that this is impracticable, in which case an entity should adjust the comparative information to apply the new accounting policy prospectively from the earliest practicable date. A similar approach is, in our view, appropriate when an entity changes its presentation currency. In this context the most important component of equity to determine correctly (or as near correctly as possible) is normally the foreign exchange reserve because that balance, or parts of it, has to be reclassified from equity to profit or loss in the event of any future disposal of the relevant foreign operation, and could therefore affect future earnings.

Where an entity applies the direct method of consolidation, it could be impracticable to determine precisely the amount of exchange differences accumulated within the separate component of equity relating to each individual entity within the group. In these circumstances, approximations will be necessary to determine the amounts at the beginning of the earliest comparative period presented, although all subsequent exchange differences should be accumulated in accordance with the requirements of IAS 21. For an entity that set its foreign exchange reserve to zero on transition to IFRS (see Chapter 5 at 4.3.1) it may be able to go back to that date and recompute the necessary components of equity. This should be less of an issue for entities applying the step-by-step method.

3.6 Introduction of the euro

From 1 January 1999, the effective start of Economic and Monetary Union (EMU), the euro became a currency in its own right and the conversion rates between the euro and the national currencies of those countries who were going to participate in the first phase were irrevocably fixed, such that the risk of subsequent exchange differences related to these currencies was eliminated from that date on.

In October 1997, the SIC issued SIC-7 which deals with the application of IAS 21 to the changeover from the national currencies of participating Member States of the European Union to the euro. Consequential amendments have been made to this interpretation as a result of the IASB's revised version of IAS 21.

Although the Interpretation is no longer relevant with respect to the national currencies of those countries that participated in the first phase, SIC-7 makes it clear that the same rationale applies to the fixing of exchange rates when countries join EMU at later stages.[144]

Under SIC-7, the requirements of IAS 21 regarding the translation of foreign currency transactions and financial statements of foreign operations should be strictly applied to the changeover.[145]

This means that, in particular:

(a)   Foreign currency monetary assets and liabilities resulting from transactions should continue to be translated into the functional currency at the closing rate. Any resultant exchange differences should be recognised as income or expense immediately, except that an entity should continue to apply its existing accounting policy for exchange gains and losses related to hedges of the currency risk of a forecast transaction.[146]

The effective start of the EMU after the reporting period does not change the application of these requirements at the end of the reporting period; in accordance with IAS 10 – *Events after the Reporting Period* – it is not relevant whether or not the closing rate can fluctuate after the reporting period.[147]

Like IAS 21, the Interpretation does not address how foreign currency hedges should be accounted for. The effective start of EMU, of itself, does not justify a change to an entity's established accounting policy related to hedges of forecast transactions because the changeover does not affect the economic rationale of such hedges. Therefore, the changeover should not alter the accounting policy where gains and losses on financial instruments used as hedges of forecast transactions are initially recognised in other comprehensive income and reclassified from equity to profit or loss to match with the related income or expense in a future period;[148]

(b)   Cumulative exchange differences relating to the translation of financial statements of foreign operations recognised in other comprehensive income should remain accumulated in a separate component of equity and be reclassified from equity to profit or loss only on the disposal (or partial disposal) of the net investment in the foreign operation.[149]

The fact that the cumulative amount of exchange differences will be fixed under EMU does not justify immediate recognition as income or expenses since the wording and the rationale of IAS 21 clearly preclude such a treatment.[150]

4   EFFECTIVE DATES AND TRANSITIONAL ARRANGEMENTS

This section contains information that is relevant for annual periods beginning on or after 1 January 2009. For earlier periods, equivalent requirements are dealt with in *International GAAP 2009* and other predecessors to this publication.

4.1   Effective dates

IAS 27 (as amended in 2008) and its consequential amendments to IAS 21 (see 2.7.3 B above) are effective for annual periods beginning on or after 1 July 2009. Entities are permitted to apply the revised standard earlier, provided it is for a period beginning on or after 30 June 2007 and provided IFRS 3 (as revised in 2008) is applied at the same time. Where the revised standard is applied early, this fact should be disclosed.[151]

The May 2008 amendments to IFRS 1 and IAS 27 and the consequential amendments to IAS 21 (see 2.7.3 A above) are effective for annual periods beginning on or after 1 January 2009. Entities were permitted to apply the amendments earlier, although if they did so, this fact was required to be disclosed.[152]

IFRIC 16 (see 3.3.5 and 3.3.6 above) was effective for annual periods beginning on or after 1 October 2008. Entities were permitted to apply the interpretation earlier, although if they did so, this fact was required to be disclosed.[153]

4.2   Transitional arrangements for entities already reporting under IFRS

As discussed in Chapter 6 at 6, IAS 27 (as amended in 2008) is generally required to be accounted for retrospectively, although there are certain exceptions. Unlike the consequential amendments made by IAS 27 (as amended in 2008) to a number of other standards, which are explicitly required to be applied retrospectively,[154] there is no such requirement for those made to IAS 21. In fact there are no transitional requirements at all. Normally the lack of transitional requirements would mean the amendments should be applied retrospectively as required by IAS 8, although this would, in certain circumstances, conflict with the transitional requirements in IAS 27 (as amended in 2008).

For example if, in the period prior to the adoption of IAS 27 (as amended in 2008), an entity had sold 10% of a wholly owned foreign subsidiary and had recognised a profit or loss on this partial disposal, the amount would have included the reclassification of 10% of the exchange gains or losses related to that subsidiary accumulated within equity (see 2.7.3 A above). IAS 27 (as amended in 2008) would treat such a disposal as an equity transaction, i.e. one which does not give rise to a gain or loss, and to make IAS 21 consistent with this, the consequential amendments would prohibit the related exchange gain or loss being reclassified from equity to profit or loss (see 2.7.3 B above). IAS 27 (as amended in 2008) states that its requirements in respect of changes in ownership interests in a subsidiary after control is obtained should be applied prospectively so that any profit or loss recognised in the prior year should not be reversed. In our view, it would be consistent with the more specific requirements in IAS 27 (as amended in 2008) not to reverse the reclassification of the foreign currency gain or loss from equity to profit or loss in these circumstances.

This conflict between the two standards is somewhat unsatisfactory and the IASB has tentatively decided to amend IAS 21 in its third annual improvements process to clarify that the consequential amendments made by IAS 27 (as amended in 2008) should be applied prospectively.[155]

The consequential amendments to IAS 21 arising from the amendments to IFRS 1 and IAS 27 should be applied prospectively.[156]

Whilst IAS 8 generally requires retrospective application of changes in accounting policy (see Chapter 3 at 4.4) entities are not required to follow the requirements of IAS 8 when IFRIC 16 is first applied.[157]

5 CONCLUSION

The issues relating to the accounting for foreign currency activities, whether through having transactions in another currency or through foreign operations, generally come down to two choices – the exchange rate to be used in the translation process and the subsequent treatment of the exchange differences that arise. The changes made by the IASB to IAS 21 in December 2003 (and in December 2005) have, in general, resulted in a better standard, and the revised version provides a workable basis for dealing with these issues.

The accounting for transactions in a currency other than the functional currency of an entity required by the standard is basically the same as that in the original standard, and as such, is well understood and does not give rise to too many difficulties. The critical issue is the determination of an entity's functional currency, since it is by reference to that currency that transactions and balances will be regarded as being 'foreign' and thus give rise to foreign exchange differences. The other main issue is that for certain items, the distinction as to whether it is a monetary item or not may not be clear cut; the importance being that it is only monetary items that are translated at closing rates and thus result in exchange differences being recognised in profit or loss.

As far as the translation of foreign operations is concerned, the standard deals with this as part of the process of an entity presenting its financial statements in a currency other than its functional currency or the functional currencies of the individual entities included in consolidated financial statements. However, for most situations, this translation process is effectively based on that in the previous version of the standard for translating foreign operations in consolidated financial statements, i.e. assets and liabilities translated at closing rates, income and expenses at actual rates (or an appropriate average rate), and resulting exchange differences recognised in other comprehensive income to be reclassified from equity to profit or loss upon disposal of the operation. Again, this process is well understood and does not give rise to too many difficulties that are not addressed by the standard. The main area that is not addressed is the translation of equity items where the IASB has deliberately remained silent.

One aspect of the revised standard that we consider was given inadequate attention by the IASB is that relating to monetary items forming part of the net investment in a foreign operation (see 3.4.1 above). As before, the standard allows exchange differences on such monetary items to be recognised in other comprehensive income in the consolidated financial statements. However, such a treatment cannot be adopted in the separate financial statements of the entity with the foreign currency exposure; it has to recognise the exchange differences in profit or loss, despite the fact that these are not expected to have any impact of the entity's cash flows and it is unclear what the rationale for this treatment is.

References

1 IAS 21 (revised 1993), *The Effects of Changes in Foreign Exchange Rates*, IASC, Revised 1993, para. 23.
2 IAS 21 (revised 1993), paras. 30-31.
3 IAS 21 (revised 1993), paras. 27-29.
4 IAS 21, *The Effects of Changes in Foreign Exchange Rates*, IASB, para. IN2.
5 IAS 21, paras. IN3 and IN9.
6 Draft Technical Correction 1, *Proposed Amendments to IAS 21 The Effects of Changes in Foreign Exchange Rates – Net Investment in a Foreign Operation*, IASB, October 2005.
7 Amendment to IAS 21, *The Effects of Changes in Foreign Exchange Rates – Net Investment in a Foreign Operation*, IASB, December 2005.
8 IAS 21, para. IN1.
9 IAS 21, para. 1.
10 IAS 21, para. 2.
11 IAS 21, para. 3.
12 IAS 21, para. 4.
13 IAS 21, para. 5.
14 IAS 21, para. 6.
15 IAS 21, para. 7.
16 IAS 21, para. 8.
17 IAS 21, para. 17.
18 IAS 21, para. 17.
19 IAS 21, para. 18.
20 IAS 21, para. 19.
21 IAS 21, para. 9.
22 IAS 21, para. 12.
23 IAS 21, para. 9.
24 IAS 21, para. 10.
25 IAS 21, para. 11.
26 IAS 21, para. 13.
27 IAS 21, para. 20.
28 IAS 21, para. 21.
29 IAS 21, para. 22.
30 IAS 21, para. 23.
31 IAS 21, para. 28.
32 IAS 21, para. 29.
33 IAS 21, para. 32.
34 IAS 21, para. 30.
35 IAS 21, para. 31.
36 IAS 21, para. 30.
37 IAS 21, para. 36.
38 IAS 21, para. 35.
39 IAS 21, para. 37.
40 IAS 21, para. 38.
41 IAS 21, para. 18.
42 IAS 21, para. 44.
43 IAS 21, para. 39.
44 IAS 21, para. 40.
45 IAS 21, para. 41.
46 IAS 21, para. 41.

47 IAS 21, para. 41.
48 IAS 21, para. BC17.
49 IAS 21, para. BC20.
50 IAS 21, para. BC18.
51 IAS 21, para. BC19.
52 IAS 21, para. 42.
53 IAS 21, para. 43.
54 IAS 21, para. 43.
55 IAS 21, para. 44.
56 IAS 21, para. 45.
57 IAS 21, para. 45.
58 IAS 21, para. 46.
59 SFAS 52, *Foreign Currency Translation*, FASB, December 1981, para. 139.
60 IAS 21 (revised 1993), para. 33.
61 IAS 21, para. BC27.
62 IAS 21, para. BC30.
63 IAS 21, para. BC31.
64 IAS 21, para. BC32.
65 IAS 21, para. 47.
66 IAS 21, para. 60B.
67 IAS 21, para. 48.
68 IAS 27 (2007), *Consolidated and Separate Financial Statements*, IASB, 2007 Bound Volume, para. 30.
69 IAS 21 (2007), para. 49.
70 IAS 21, para. BC35.
71 IAS 21 (2008), *The Effects of Changes in Foreign Exchange Rates*, IASB, 2008 Bound Volume, para. 49.
72 IAS 21, para. 49.
73 IAS 21, para. 48A.
74 IAS 21, para. 48.
75 IAS 21, para. 48B.
76 IAS 21, para. 48D.
77 For example, IAS 27, *Consolidated and Separate Financial Statements*, IASB, paras. 30, 41(e), 42(b) and 43(b) and IFRS 3, *Business Combinations*, IASB, para. B63(e).
78 IAS 21, para. 48C.
79 IAS 21, para. 48C.
80 IAS 28, *Investments in Associates*, IASB, para. 19A and IAS 31, *Interests in Joint Ventures*, IASB, para. 45B.
81 *IFRIC Update*, IASB, July 2009.
82 IAS 21, para. 50.
83 IAS 21, para. 52.
84 IAS 21, para. 52.
85 IAS 21, para. 53.
86 IAS 21, para. 51.
87 IAS 21, para. 54.
88 IAS 21, para. 55.
89 IAS 21, para. 56.
90 IAS 21, para. 57.
91 IAS 21, para. 51.
92 IAS 39, *Financial Instruments: Recognition and Measurement*, IASB, para. 14.
93 IAS 39, para. AG35.
94 IAS 21, para. 22.
95 IAS 21, para. 26.
96 IAS 21, para. 26.
97 IAS 21, para. 8.
98 IAS 21, para. 16.
99 IAS 21, para. 16.
100 IAS 21, para. 16.
101 IAS 39, para. AG83.
102 SFAS 52, para. 162.
103 IAS 39, para. AG83.
104 SFAS 52, para. 48.
105 CICA Handbook, Section 1651, Foreign currency translation, para. 47.
106 *Exposure Draft of Revised IAS 21*, IASB, May 2002, para. 14.
107 IAS 12 (2007), *Income Taxes*, 2007 Bound Volume, IASB, para. 78.
108 IAS 19, *Employee Benefits*, IASB, para. 78.
109 IAS 19, para. 73.
110 IAS 21, para. 28.
111 IAS 23, *Borrowing Costs*, IASB, para. 6.
112 IAS 21, para. 34.
113 IAS 21, para. 34.
114 IAS 21, para. 26.
115 SFAS 52, para. 27.
116 SFAS 52, para. 138.
117 IAS 21, para. 40.
118 IAS 21, para. 40.
119 *IASB Update*, IASB, February 2003, p.5.
120 SFAS 52, para. 48.
121 CICA 1651, para. 47.
122 IAS 21, paras. 39(b) and 41.
123 IAS 21, para. 47.
124 IAS 21, para. BC32.
125 IFRIC D22, *Hedges of a Net Investment in a Foreign Operation*, IASB, July 2007, para. BC7.
126 *IFRIC Update*, IASB, March 2008, p.2.
127 IFRIC 16, *Hedges of a Net Investment in a Foreign Operation*, IASB, July 2008, para. 17.
128 IAS 21, para. 48.
129 IAS 21, para. 48A.
130 IAS 21, para. BC35.
131 IAS 21 (2008), para. 49.
132 IAS 21, para. 49.
133 IAS 21, para. 45.
134 IAS 21, para. 45.
135 IAS 21, para. 8.
136 IAS 21, para. 15.
137 IAS 21, paras. 32-33.
138 IAS 21, para. 33.
139 IAS 21 (revised 2003), *The Effects of Changes in Foreign Exchange Rates*, IASB, December 2003, para. 33.
140 IAS 21, para. 41.
141 IAS 21, para. 15A.
142 IAS 21, para. 45.

143 SFAS 52, para. 25.
144 SIC-7, *Introduction of the Euro*, IASB, para. 3.
145 SIC-7, para. 3.
146 SIC-7, para. 4.
147 SIC-7, para. 5.
148 SIC-7, para. 6.
149 SIC-7, para. 4.
150 SIC-7, para. 7.
151 IAS 21, para. 60B; IAS 27, para. 45 and IFRS 3, para. 64.
152 IAS 27, para. 45B.
153 IFRIC 16, para. 18.
154 IAS 27, paras. A3 to A5.
155 *IASB Update*, IASB, May 2009.
156 IAS 27, para. 45B.
157 IFRIC 16, para. 19.

Chapter 14   Hyperinflation

1   INTRODUCTION

Accounting standards generally assume that the value of money (the unit of measurement) is constant over time, which normally is an acceptable practical assumption. However, when the effect of inflation on the value of money is no longer negligible, the usefulness of historical cost based financial reporting is often significantly reduced. High rates of inflation give rise to a number of problems for entities that prepare their financial statements on a historical cost basis, for example:

- historical cost figures expressed in terms of monetary units do not show the 'value to the business' of assets;

- holding gains on non-monetary assets that are reported as operating profits do not represent real economic gains;

- financial information presented for the current period is not comparable with that presented for the prior periods; and

- 'real' capital can be reduced because profits reported do not take account of the higher replacement costs of resources used in the period. Therefore, if calculating a nominal 'return on capital' based on profit, and not distinguishing this properly from a real 'return of capital', the erosion of capital may go unnoticed in the financial statements. This is the underlying point in the concept of capital maintenance.

Rates of inflation were well in excess of 10% during most of the 1970s and early 1980s in most of the world. This economic feature brought these and other shortcomings of historical cost based financial reporting in an inflationary environment to prominence. Though methods of inflation accounting were extensively debated, interest in the subject dissipated quickly in the late 1980s when inflation all but disappeared in the US and Western Europe. Moreover, the discussions about inflation accounting and concepts of capital maintenance, undeservingly, have left little traces in modern accounting standards.

The IASB's *Framework* mentions the existence of different concepts of capital maintenance[1] but is ultimately based on the financial capital maintenance concept (see Chapter 2 at 3.2.6). Under this concept, the capital of the entity will be maintained if the financial amount of net assets at the end of a period is at least equal to the financial amount of net assets at the beginning of that period, excluding contributions from and distributions to owners during the period. The IASB's Framework describes the concept of physical capital maintenance under which 'a profit is earned only if the physical productive capacity (or operating capability) of the entity (or the resources or funds needed to achieve that capacity) at the end of the period exceeds the physical productive capacity at the beginning of the period, after excluding any distributions to, and contributions from, owners during the period'.[2] However, the IASB did not further develop the physical capital maintenance concept in its Framework or any of its standards.[3] The financial capital maintenance concept on which International Financial Reporting Standards are based is only satisfactory under conditions of stable prices.

1.1   Hyperinflationary economies

For entities used to working in economies with low inflation it is easy to overlook that there are countries where inflation is still a major economic concern. In some of these countries, inflation has reached such levels – hyperinflation – that (1) the local currency is no longer a useful measure of value in the economy and (2) the general population may prefer not to hold its wealth in the local currency. Instead, they hold their wealth in a stable foreign currency or non-monetary assets. Under US accounting standards hyperinflation is deemed to exist when the cumulative rate of inflation over a three-year period exceeds 100%. As discussed at 2.3.1 below, there are several additional criteria that need to be taken into account under IFRS to determine whether hyperinflation exists.[4]

Countries that are generally considered hyperinflationary, because they have recently had three-year cumulative inflation of 100% or more, are Myanmar and Zimbabwe. Calculating the three-year cumulative inflation in Venezuela during 2009 requires judgement. The country reports a consumer price index limited to certain areas and a national price index (which has only been calculated since the beginning of 2008). Depending which rate (or blended rate) is considered, the country may have already met or be close to meeting a cumulative three-year 100% inflation threshold.[5] Countries that have currently high three-year cumulative inflation rates but would not be deemed to have met the 100% threshold are Ethiopia, Guinea, Iran, Iraq, São Tomé and Príncipe and Seychelles.[6]

1.2   Adjustment approaches

The historical cost based financial reporting problems reach such a magnitude under hyperinflationary circumstances that financial reporting in the hyperinflationary currency is all but meaningless. Therefore, a solution is needed to allow meaningful financial reporting by entities that operate in hyperinflationary economies. Two solutions to accounting for hyperinflation that have traditionally been applied can be summarised as follows:

- *Restatement approach* – Financial information recorded in the hyperinflationary currency is adjusted by applying a general price index and expressed in the measuring unit (the hyperinflationary currency) current at the end of the reporting period;

- *Stable foreign currency* – The entity uses a relatively stable currency, for example the presentation currency of its parent, as the currency in which it measures items in its financial statements. If the transactions of the operation are not recorded initially in that stable currency, then they are remeasured into the stable currency by applying the temporal method of translation (see Chapter 13 at 1.1 and 1.2.1).

IAS 29 – *Financial Reporting in Hyperinflationary Economies* – only permits the restatement approach. Entities operating in a hyperinflationary economy are prohibited under IFRS from selecting a stable currency as their unit of accounting if that currency is not its functional currency under IAS 21 – *The Effects of Changes in Foreign Exchange Rates*, i.e. 'the currency of the primary economic environment in which the entity operates' (see Chapter 13 at 2.5).[7]

2   REQUIREMENTS OF IAS 29

2.1   History

The (then) IASC adopted IAS 29 in April 1989 and has only since addressed the subject of hyperinflation to clarify the provisions of the standard. This is not surprising as memories of high inflation rapidly receded from the collective conscious of most of the IASC's more influential constituents in the 1990s.

In February 2000, SIC-19 – *Reporting Currency – Measurement and Presentation of Financial Statements under IAS 21 and IAS 29* – was adopted, which provided rules on the selection of a measurement currency. Before the adoption of SIC-19 it was possible for entities operating in hyperinflationary economies to use any measurement currency of their liking, which allowed them to avoid using a hyperinflationary measurement currency and thereby to sidestep the requirements of IAS 29. As a result of the IASB's Improvements Project, the rules in SIC-19 have now been incorporated in IAS 21, which specifically prohibits an entity from avoiding 'restatement in accordance with IAS 29 by, for example, adopting as its functional currency a currency other than the functional currency determined in accordance with this Standard'.[8] In November 2005, IFRIC issued IFRIC 7 – *Applying the Restatement Approach under IAS 29 Financial Reporting in Hyperinflationary Economies* – which provides certain specific guidance to facilitate the first time application of IAS 29.[9]

The IFRS literature defines the following currency related notions:

- *Functional currency* is defined in IAS 21 as the currency of the primary economic environment in which the entity operates;[10] and

- *Presentation currency* is defined in IAS 21 as the currency in which the financial statements are presented.[11]

In standards and interpretations that have since been superseded, other currency related notions were:

- *Measurement currency* was defined in SIC-19 as the currency in which the entity measures the items in the financial statements.[12] This notion has now been replaced by 'functional currency' (see above) which is more commonly used and, according to the IASB, has 'essentially the same meaning';[13] and

- *Reporting currency* was defined in IAS 21 (revised 1993) as the currency used in presenting the financial statements.[14] The standard did not specify the currency in which an entity presented its financial statements, although it noted that an entity would normally use the currency of the country in which it was domiciled.[15] However, the choice of reporting currency established that all other currencies were treated as foreign currencies for the purposes of IAS 21 (revised 1993) and therefore would affect the financial statements. IAS 21 (revised 2003) replaced the notion of 'reporting currency' with two notions 'functional currency' and 'presentation currency'.[16]

2.2   Objective

The underlying premise of IAS 29 is that 'reporting of operating results and financial position in the local [hyperinflationary] currency without restatement is not useful'.[17] The standard's approach is therefore to require that:[18]

(a)   the financial statements of an entity whose functional currency is the currency of a hyperinflationary economy, whether they are based on a historical cost approach or a current cost approach, should be stated in terms of the measuring unit current at the end of the reporting period;

(b)   the corresponding figures for the previous period required by IAS 1 – *Presentation of Financial Statements* – and any information in respect of earlier periods should also be stated in terms of the measuring unit current at the end of the reporting period; and

(c)   the gain or loss on the net monetary position should be included in profit or loss and separately disclosed.

IAS 29 requires balance sheet amounts not already expressed in terms of the measuring unit current at the end of the reporting period to be restated in terms of the measuring unit current at the end of the reporting period, by applying a general price index.[19] The example below illustrates how this would apply to the balance sheet of an entity (for a detailed discussion of IAS 29 and the restatement process see 2.4 below):

Example 14.1:   Accounting for hyperinflation under IAS 29

An entity that operates in a hyperinflationary economy is required under IAS 29 to restate all non-monetary items in its balance sheet to the measuring unit current at end of the reporting period by applying a general price index as follows:

	Before restatement (HC)	Historical general price index*	Year-end general price index	After restatement (HC)
Plant and equipment	225	150	600	900
Inventory	250	500	600	300
Cash	100			100
Total assets	575			1,300
Accounts payable	180			180
Long-term debt	250			250
Equity **	145			870
	575			1,300

*   General price index at the date of purchase
**   The restatement of equity is not illustrated here, but discussed at 2.4.2 G below.

The simplified example above already raises a number of questions, such as:

- Which balance sheet items are monetary and which are non-monetary?
- How does the entity select the appropriate general price index?
- What was the general price index when the assets were acquired?

The standard provides guidance on the restatement to the measuring unit current at the end of the reporting period, but concedes that the consistent application of these inflation accounting procedures and judgements from period to period is more important than the precise accuracy of the resulting amounts included in the restated financial statements.[20] The requirements of the standard look deceptively straightforward but their application may represent a considerable challenge. These difficulties and other aspects of the practical application of the IAS 29 method of accounting for hyperinflation are discussed at 2.4.2 and 4 below.

Apart from the more technical reservations that exist about IAS 29, the concept of restating financial information to the measuring units current at the end of the reporting period could have been articulated more clearly. Given the choice between (1) restating financial information for hyperinflation after the end of the reporting period or (2) financial statements expressed in a stable foreign currency, some users might prefer the latter. Nevertheless, even when translated to a stable foreign currency, difficulties remain because of the complexities of the economic phenomenon of hyperinflation. Additionally, expressing financial statements of entities operating in hyperinflationary economies in a stable currency might give users a false sense of security.

2.3 Scope

IAS 29 should be applied by all entities whose functional currency is the currency of a hyperinflationary economy because 'money loses purchasing power at such a rate that comparison of amounts from transactions and other events that have occurred at different times, even within the same accounting period, is misleading'.[21] The standard should be applied in an entity's separate financial statements and its consolidated financial statements, as well as by parents that include such an entity in their consolidated financial statements. Financial statements of entities whose functional currency is that of a hyperinflationary economy first have to be restated under IAS 29 and then, if their parent has a different presentation currency, translated under IAS 21 in order that they can be incorporated within the consolidated financial statements of the parent entity.

Almost all entities operating in hyperinflationary economies will be subject to the accounting regime of IAS 29, unless they can legitimately argue that the local hyperinflationary currency is not their functional currency as defined by IAS 21 (see Chapter 13 at 2.5).

2.3.1 Definition of hyperinflation

Determining whether an economy is hyperinflationary in accordance with IAS 29 requires judgement. The standard does not establish an absolute rate at which hyperinflation is deemed to arise. Instead, it considers the following characteristics of the economic environment of a country to be strong indicators of the existence of hyperinflation:[22]

(a)   the general population prefers to keep its wealth in non-monetary assets or in a relatively stable foreign currency. Amounts of local currency held are immediately invested to maintain purchasing power;

(b)   the general population regards monetary amounts not in terms of the local currency but in terms of a relatively stable foreign currency. Prices may be quoted in that currency;

(c)   sales and purchases on credit take place at prices that compensate for the expected loss of purchasing power during the credit period, even if the period is short;

(d)   interest rates, wages and prices are linked to a price index; and

(e)   the cumulative inflation rate over three years is approaching, or exceeds, 100%.

The above list is not exhaustive and there may be other indicators that an economy is hyperinflationary, such as the existence of price controls and restrictive exchange controls. In determining whether an economy is hyperinflationary, condition (e) is quantitatively measurable while the other indicators require reliance on more qualitative, often anecdotal, evidence. For the purposes of testing condition (e), reference should be made to authoritative sources such as the International Monetary Fund's international statistics publications, though too-mechanical an application of the 100% criterion is not necessarily advisable. Despite the fact that IAS 29 expresses a preference that all entities that report in the currency of the same hyperinflationary economy apply this Standard from the same date,[23] that is in practice often an unrealistic wish given the way it defines hyperinflation. In any event, once an entity has identified the existence of hyperinflation, it should apply IAS 29 from the beginning of the reporting period in which it identified the existence of hyperinflation.[24]

Identifying when a currency becomes hyperinflationary, and as importantly when it ceases to be so, is not easy in practice. The consideration of trends, and the application of common sense, is important in this judgement, as are consistency of measurement and of presentation (see 2.7 below).

2.4 The IAS 29 restatement process

Restatement of financial statements in accordance with IAS 29 can be seen as a process comprising the following steps:

(a)   selection of a general price index (see 2.4.1 below);

(b)   analysis and restatement of assets and liabilities (see 2.4.2 below);

(c)   restatement of income statements and statements of comprehensive income (see 2.4.3 below);

(d)   calculation of the gain or loss on the net monetary position (see 2.4.4 below);

(e)   restatement of the statement of cash flows (see 2.4.5 below); and

(f)   restatement of the corresponding figures (see 2.4.6 below).

These steps are discussed below.

2.4.1 Selection of a general price index

The standard requires entities to use a general price index that reflects changes in general purchasing power; preferably all entities that report in the same hyperinflationary currency should use the same price index (see 4.1 below).[25]

Sometimes the general price index chosen by the entity is not available for all periods for which the restatement of long-lived assets is required. In that case, the entity will need to make an estimate of the price index based, for example, on 'the movements in the exchange rate between the functional currency and a relatively stable foreign currency' (see 4.2 below).[26]

2.4.2 Analysis and restatement of balance sheet items

A broad outline of the process to restate assets and liabilities in accordance with the requirements of IAS 29 is shown in the diagram below:

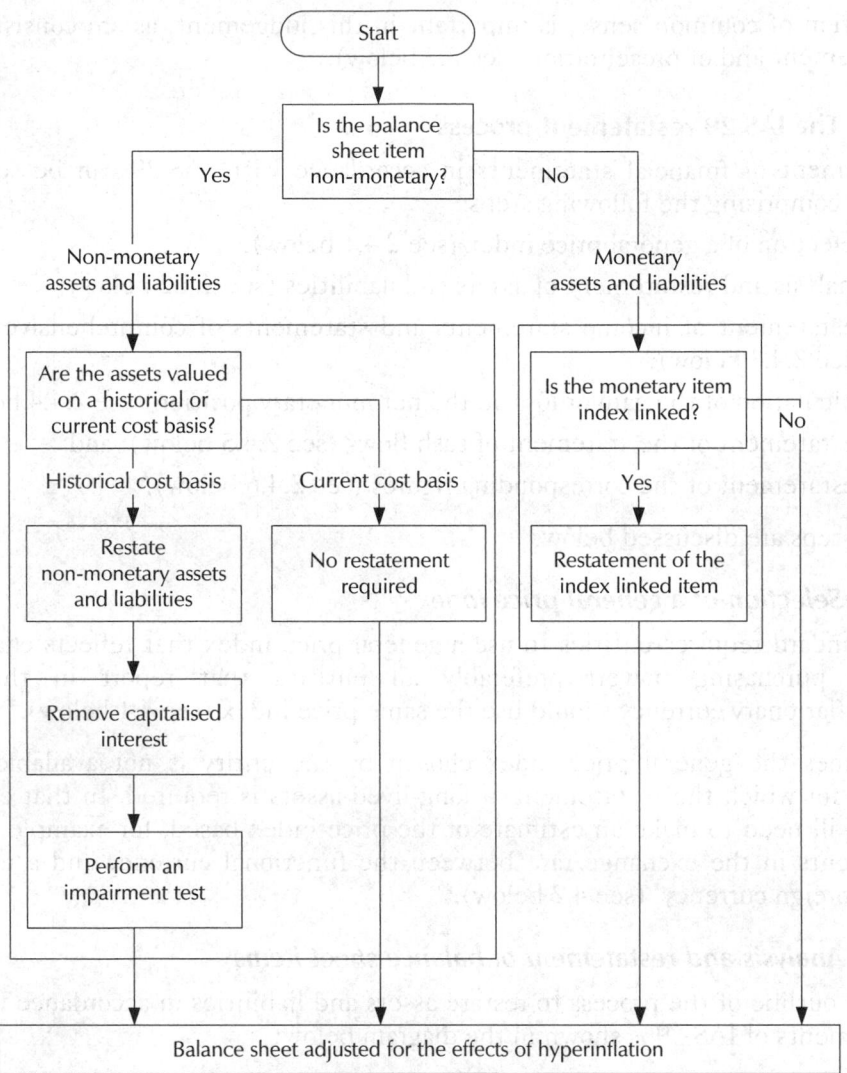

In many hyperinflationary economies, national legislation may require entities to adjust historical cost based financial information in a way that is not in accordance with IAS 29 (for example, national legislation may require entities to adjust the carrying amount of tangible fixed assets by applying a multiplier). Though financial information adjusted in accordance with national legislation is sometimes described as 'current cost' information, it will seldom meet the definition of current cost in accordance with the IASB's Framework (see C below).[27] Where this is the case, entities must first determine the carrying value on the historical cost basis for these assets and liabilities before applying the requirements of IAS 29.

The above flowchart does not illustrate the restatement of investees and subsidiaries (see E below), deferred taxation (see F below) and equity (see G below).

A   Monetary or non-monetary

Monetary items normally need not be restated as they are already expressed in the measurement unit current at the end of the reporting period. Therefore an entity needs to determine whether or not an item is monetary in nature. Most balance sheet items are readily classified as either monetary or non-monetary as is shown in the table below:

Monetary items	Non-monetary items
Assets	**Assets**
Cash and cash equivalents	Property, plant and equipment
Debt securities	Intangible assets
Loans	Investments in equity securities
Trade and other receivables	Assets held for sale
	Inventories
	Construction contract work-in-progress
	Prepaid costs
	Investment properties
Liabilities	**Liabilities**
Trade and other payables	Warranty provision
Borrowings	
Other liabilities	
Tax payable	

Classification of items as either monetary or non-monetary is not always straightforward. IAS 29 defines monetary items as 'money held and items to be received or paid in money'.[28] IAS 21 expands somewhat on this definition by defining monetary items as 'units of currency held and assets and liabilities to be received or paid in a fixed or determinable number of units of currency'.[29] It further states that the essential feature of a monetary item is a right to receive (or an obligation to deliver) a fixed or determinable number of units of currency. Examples given by IAS 21 are pensions and other employee benefits to be paid in cash, provisions that are to be settled in cash and cash dividends that are recognised as a liability.[30] More obvious examples are cash and bank balances, trade receivables and payables, and loan receivables and payables.

IAS 21 states that 'a contract to receive (or deliver) a variable number of the entity's own equity instruments or a variable amount of assets in which the fair value to be received (or delivered) equals a fixed or determinable number of units of currency is a monetary item.'[31] Although no examples of such contracts are given in IAS 21, it would seem to include those contracts settled in the entity's own equity shares that under IAS 32 – *Financial Instruments: Disclosure and Presentation* – would be presented as financial assets or liabilities.

Conversely, the essential feature of a non-monetary item is the absence of a right to receive (or an obligation to deliver) a fixed or determinable number of units of currency. Examples given by the standard are amounts prepaid for goods and services (e.g. prepaid rent); goodwill; intangible assets; inventories; property, plant and equipment; and provisions that are to be settled by the delivery of a non-monetary asset.[32] IAS 39 – *Financial Instruments: Recognition and Measurement* – indicates that equity instruments that are held as available-for-sale financial assets are non-monetary items.[33] This implies that equity investments in subsidiaries, associates or joint ventures are also non-monetary items.

Even with this guidance there will clearly be a number of situations where the distinction may not be altogether clear. Certain assets and liabilities may require careful analysis before they can be classified, and even then their classification is not entirely satisfactory. Examples of items that are not easily classified as either monetary or non-monetary include:

(a) *provisions for liabilities:* these can be monetary, non-monetary or partly monetary. For example, a warranty provision would be:

   (i)   entirely monetary when customers only have a right to return the product and obtain a cash refund equal to the amount they originally paid;

   (ii) non-monetary when customers have the right to have any defective product replaced; and

   (iii) partly monetary if customers can choose between a refund and a replacement of the defect product.

   Obviously, classification as either monetary or non-monetary is not very satisfactory in (iii) above. In the spirit of the IAS 29 requirements, part of the provision should be treated as a non-monetary item and the remainder as a monetary item;

(b) *deferred tax assets and liabilities:* characterising these as monetary or non-monetary is fraught with difficulties, which are explained in F below;

(c) *associates and joint ventures:* these are most likely to be at least partly monetary in nature, depending on the degree to which they themselves hold monetary items or non-monetary items. Whatever the case may be, IAS 29 provides separate rules on restatement of investees that do not rely on the distinction between monetary and non-monetary (see E below);

(d) *deposits or progress payments paid or received:* if the payments made are regarded as prepayments or as progress payments then the amounts should be treated as non-monetary items. However, if the payments made are in effect refundable deposits then the amounts should probably be treated as monetary items; and

(e) *index-linked assets and liabilities:* classification is particularly difficult when interest rates, lease payments or prices are linked to a price index.

In summary, the practical application of the monetary/non-monetary distinction is beset with difficulties and, after the classification of the more obvious items, judgement on the part of preparers of financial statements is required.[34] Further examples of problem areas in the application of the monetary/non-monetary distinction are discussed in Chapter 13 at 3.2.4.

B   Monetary items

Generally, monetary items need not be restated to reflect the effect of inflation. However, monetary assets and liabilities linked by agreement to changes in prices –

such as index-linked bonds and loans – should be adjusted in accordance with the underlying agreement to show the repayment obligation in accordance with the terms of the agreement at the end of the reporting period.[35] This adjustment should be offset against the gain or loss on the net monetary position (see 2.4.4 below). This type of restatement is in fact not an inflation accounting adjustment, but rather a gain or loss on a financial instrument. Accounting for inflation linked bonds and loans under IAS 39 may well lead to very complicated financial reporting. Depending on the specific wording of the inflation adjustment clause, such contracts may give rise to embedded derivatives and gains or losses will have to be recorded either in profit or loss or other comprehensive income depending on how the instrument is classified for IAS 39 purposes (see Chapter 29 at 5.1.2 C and 5.1.3 B).

C   Non-monetary items carried at current cost

Non-monetary items carried at current cost are not restated because they are already expressed in terms of the measuring unit current at the end of the reporting period.[36] Current cost is not defined by the standard, but the Framework provides the following definition: 'Assets are carried at the amount of cash or cash equivalents that would have to be paid if the same or an equivalent asset was acquired currently. Liabilities are carried at the undiscounted amount of cash or cash equivalents that would be required to settle the obligation currently'.[37] For the purposes of restating historical cost financial statements, IAS 29 expands this definition by including net realisable value and fair value into the concept of 'amounts current at the end of the reporting period'.[38]

It is important to note that non-monetary items that were revalued at some earlier date, are not necessarily carried at current cost and need to be restated from the date of their latest revaluation.[39]

D   Non-monetary items carried at historical cost

Non-monetary items carried at historical cost, or cost less depreciation, are stated at amounts that were current at the date of their acquisition. The restated cost, or cost less depreciation, of those items is calculated as follows:

$$\begin{array}{l}\text{net book value} \\ \text{restated for} \\ \text{hyperinflation}\end{array} = \text{historical cost} \times \dfrac{\text{general price index at the end of the reporting period}}{\text{general price index at the date of acquisition}}$$

Application of this formula to property, plant and equipment, inventories of raw materials and merchandise, goodwill, patents, trademarks and similar assets appears to be straightforward, but does require detailed records of their acquisition dates and accurate price indices at those dates.[40] It should be noted though that IAS 29 permits certain approximations as long as the procedures and judgements are consistent from period to period.[41] Where sufficiently detailed records are not available or capable of estimation, IAS 29 suggests that it may be necessary to obtain an 'independent professional assessment' of the value of the items as the basis for their restatement in the first period of application of the standard.[42]

Example 14.2:   Restatement of property, plant and equipment

The table below illustrates how the restatement of a non-monetary item (for example, property, plant and equipment) would be calculated in accordance with the requirements of IAS 29.

Net book value of property, plant and equipment	Historical movements	Conversion factor	Restated for hyperinflation	
Opening balance, 1 January	510	2.40	1,224	(a)
– Additions (May)	360	1.80	648	(b)
– Disposals (March)	(120)	2.10	(252)	(c)
– Depreciation	(200)		(448)	(d)
Closing balance, 31 December	550		1,172	(e)

(a) The opening balance is restated by adjusting the historical balance for the increase in the price index between the beginning and the end of the reporting period;

(b) The additions are restated for the increase in the price index from May to December;

(c) The disposals are restated for the increase in the price index between the beginning and the end of the reporting period;

(d) Depreciation has been recalculated using the cost balance restated for hyperinflation as a starting point. The alternative approach, to restate the depreciation charge by applying the appropriate conversion factor, could be easier to apply but may not be accurate enough when there is a significant level of additions and disposals during the reporting period;

(e) The closing balance is in practice determined by adding up items (a)-(d). Alternatively, the entity could calculate the closing balance by restating the acquisition cost of the individual assets for the change in the price index during the period of ownership.

The calculations described under (a)-(e) all require estimates regarding the general price index at given dates and are sometimes based on averages or best estimates of the actual date of the transaction.

Inventories of finished and partly finished goods should be restated from the dates on which the costs of purchase and of conversion were incurred.[43] This means that the individual components of finished goods should be restated from their respective purchase dates. Similarly, if assembly takes place in several distinct phases, the cost of each of those phases should be restated from the date that the cost was incurred.

When an entity purchases an asset and payment is deferred beyond normal credit terms, it would normally recognise the present value of the cash payment as its cost.[44] When it is impracticable to determine the amount of interest, IAS 29 provides relief by allowing such assets to be restated from the payment date rather than the date of purchase.[45]

In order to arrive at the restated cost of the non-monetary items, the provisional restated cost needs to be adjusted as follows:[46]

	net book value restated for hyperinflation	–	borrowing costs that compensate for inflation capitalised under IAS 23	–	adjustment to recoverable amount
restated costs =					

Capitalisation of all borrowing costs (see Chapter 19) is not considered appropriate under IAS 29 because of the risk of double counting as the entity would both restate the capital expenditure financed by borrowing and capitalise that part of the borrowing costs that compensates for the inflation during the same period.[47] Until recently, under IAS 23 – *Borrowing costs* – an entity could account for borrowing costs in one of two ways:

(a)   borrowing costs are capitalised; or

(b)   borrowing costs are expensed.[48]

In practice many entities operating in hyperinflationary economies preferred the simplicity of method (b). However, the revised version of IAS 23, that is effective for financial periods starting on or after 1 January 2009, requires method (a) to be used.[49] The detailed transitional provisions of that standard are discussed in Chapter 19 at 4.

The difficulty with method (a) is that IAS 29 only permits capitalisation of borrowing costs to the extent that those costs do not compensate for inflation. Unfortunately, the standard does not provide any guidance on how an entity should go about determining the component of borrowing costs that compensates for the effects of inflation.

It is possible that an IAS 29 inflation adjustment based on the general price index leads to non-monetary assets being stated above their recoverable amount. Therefore, IAS 29 requires that the restated amount of a non-monetary item is reduced, in accordance with the appropriate standard, when it exceeds its recoverable amount from the item's future use (including sale or other disposal).[50] This requirement should be taken to mean that overstated inventories should be written down to net realisable value under IAS 2 – *Inventories* – and that any overstatement of non-monetary assets not within the scope of IAS 39 should be calculated in accordance with IAS 36 – *Impairment of Assets*.

The example below, illustrates how, after it has restated the historical cost based carrying amount of property, plant and equipment by applying the general price index, an entity can adjust the net book value restated for hyperinflation:

Example 14.3:   Borrowing costs and net realisable value adjustments

After the entity has restated the historical cost based carrying amount of property, plant and equipment by applying the general price index, it needs to adjust the net book value restated for hyperinflation as follows:

Net book value restated for hyperinflation		1,725
Borrowing costs capitalised at historical cost under IAS 23	42	
Borrowing costs that compensated for inflation	(30)	
Borrowing costs permitted to be capitalised under IAS 29	12	
Borrowing costs that compensated for inflation	(30)	
Relevant conversion factor for the borrowing costs	2.10 ×	
		(63) (a)
Net book value restated for hyperinflation and after adjustment of capitalised borrowing costs		1,662
Net book value restated for hyperinflation and after adjustment of capitalised borrowing costs	1,662	
Amount recoverable from the item's future use	1,750	
	(88)	
Adjustment to lower recoverable amount		– (b)
Carrying amount restated under IAS 29		1,662

(a) The borrowing costs capitalised in the original historical cost financial statements are reversed, as they are not permitted under IAS 29;

(b) To the extent that the 'net book value restated for hyperinflation and after adjustment of capitalised borrowing costs' exceeds the 'amount recoverable from the item's future use', the restated amount should be reduced to the lower 'amount recoverable from the item's future use'.

E   Restatement of investees and subsidiaries

IAS 29 provides separate rules for the restatement of investees (i.e. associates and joint ventures) that are accounted for under the equity method. If the investee itself operates in the same currency, the entity should restate the balance sheet, income statement and the statement of comprehensive income of the investee in accordance with the requirements of IAS 29 in order to calculate its share of the investee's net assets and results of operations. If the restated financial statements of the investee are expressed in a foreign currency – that is either hyperinflationary or a non-hyperinflationary – they should be translated at the closing rate.[51] IAS 21 contains a similar provision that requires that all current year amounts related to an entity (i.e. investee), whose functional currency is the currency of a hyperinflationary economy, to be translated at the closing rate at the date of the most recent balance sheet (see Chapter 13 at 2.7.1 B).[52]

If a parent that reports in the currency of a hyperinflationary economy has a subsidiary that also reports in the currency of a hyperinflationary economy, then the financial statements of that subsidiary must first be restated by applying a general price index of the country in whose currency it reports before they are included in the consolidated financial statements issued by its parent.[53] IAS 21 further clarifies that all current year amounts related to an entity (i.e. subsidiary), whose functional currency is the currency of a hyperinflationary economy, should be translated at the closing rate at the date of the most recent balance sheet (see Chapter 13 at 2.7.1 B).[54]

If a parent that reports in the currency of a hyperinflationary economy has a subsidiary that reports in a currency that is not hyperinflationary, the financial statements of that subsidiary should be translated in accordance with paragraph 39 of IAS 21 (see Chapter 13 at 2.7.1 A).[55]

Finally, IAS 29 requires that when financial statements with different reporting dates are consolidated, all items, whether non-monetary or monetary be restated into the measuring unit current at the date of the consolidated financial statements.[56]

F   Calculation of deferred taxation

Determining whether deferred tax assets and liabilities are monetary or non-monetary is difficult because:

- deferred taxation could be seen as a valuation adjustment that is either monetary or non-monetary depending on the asset or liability it relates to, but

- it could also be argued that any deferred taxation payable or receivable in the very near future is almost identical to current tax payable and receivable. Therefore, at least the short-term portion of deferred taxation, if payable or receivable, should be treated as if it were monetary.

There continues to be a difference of opinion as to whether deferred taxation is monetary or non-monetary.[57] In any event, the debate has been settled for practical purposes because:

- IAS 12 – *Income Taxes* – requires deferred taxation in the closing balance sheet for the year to be calculated based on the difference between the carrying amount and the tax base of assets and liabilities, irrespective of the monetary/non-monetary distinction; and

- IFRIC 7 requires an entity to remeasure the deferred tax items in any comparative period in accordance with IAS 12 after it has restated the nominal carrying amounts of its non-monetary items at the date of the opening balance sheet of the reporting period by applying the measuring unit at that date. These remeasured deferred tax items are then restated for the change in the measuring unit between the beginning and the end of reporting period.[58]

The following example, which is based on the illustrative example in IFRIC 7, shows how an entity should restate its deferred taxation in the comparative period.[59]

Example 14.4:   Restatement of deferred taxation

Entity A owns a building that it acquired in December 2008. The carrying amount and tax base of the building, and the deferred tax liability are as follows:

Before IAS 29 restatement	2010	2009
Building (unrestated)	€300	€400
Tax base	€200	€333
Tax rate	30%	30%
Deferred tax liability:		
(€300 – €200) × 30% =	€30	
(€400 – €333) × 30% =		€20

Entity A has identified the existence of hyperinflation in 2010 and therefore applies IAS 29 from the beginning of 2010. Entity A will use the following general price index and conversion factors to restate its financial statements:

	General price index
December 2008	95
December 2009	135
December 2010	223

Before adoption of IFRIC 7 it was not clear from IAS 29 how deferred tax in the comparative period should be restated. A common method for restating deferred taxation, which is no longer allowed under IFRIC 7, was to treat it as a monetary item and adjust the balance for hyperinflation during the year, which would result in a restated balance of €20 × 223 ÷ 135 = €33.

The table below shows the method prescribed by IFRIC 7:

	2010	2009	
Building (unrestated)	€300	€400	
Building (restated in 2010 financial statements):			
€300×(223 ÷ 95) =	€704		
€400×(223 ÷ 95) =		€939	
Building (restated in 2009 financial statements):			
€400 × (135 ÷ 95) =		€568	(a)
Tax base	€200	€333	(b)
Tax rate	30%	30%	
Deferred tax liability (restated in 2010 financial statements):			
(€704 – €200) × 30% =	151		
(€568 – €333) × 30% × (223 ÷ 135) =		117	

Entity A measures the temporary difference at the end of 2009 by comparing (a) the restated carrying amount of the building in 2009 accounts to (b) its tax base at that date. The temporary difference calculated in that manner is then multiplied by the applicable tax rate and the resulting amount is then adjusted for the hyperinflation during 2010, resulting in a deferred tax liability of 117.

After entity A has restated its financial statements, all corresponding figures in the financial statements for a subsequent reporting period, including deferred tax items, are restated by applying the change in the measuring unit for that subsequent reporting period only to the restated financial statements for the previous reporting period.[60]

IAS 29 refers to IAS 12 for guidance on the calculation of deferred taxation by entities operating in hyperinflationary economies.[61] IAS 12 recognises that IAS 29 restatements of assets and liabilities may give rise to temporary differences when equivalent adjustments are not allowed for tax purposes.[62] Where IAS 29 adjustments give rise to temporary differences, IAS 12 requires the following accounting treatment:

'(1)   the deferred tax is recognised in profit or loss; and

(2)   if, in addition to the restatement, the non monetary assets are also revalued, the deferred tax relating to the revaluation is recognised in other comprehensive income and the deferred tax relating to the restatement is recognised in profit or loss.'[63]

For example, deferred taxation arising on *revaluation* of property, plant and equipment should be recognised in equity, just as it would be if the entity were not operating in a hyperinflationary economy. On the other hand, *restatement* in accordance with IAS 29 of property, plant and equipment that is measured at historical cost should be recognised in the profit or loss. Thus the treatment of deferred taxation related to non-monetary assets valued at historical cost and those that are revalued, is consistent with the general requirements of IAS 12.

G   *Restatement of equity*

At the beginning of the first period when an entity applies IAS 29, because the economy in which it is operating has become hyperinflationary, it should restate the components of owners' equity as follows:[64]

- the components of owners' equity, except retained earnings and any revaluation surplus, are restated by applying a general price index from the dates the components were contributed or otherwise arose;

- any revaluation surplus that arose in previous periods is eliminated; and

- restated retained earnings are derived from all the other amounts in the restated balance sheet.

At the end of the first period and in subsequent periods, all components of owners' equity are restated by applying a general price index from the beginning of the period or the date of contribution, if later.[65] It may seem anomalous that the restatement of a historical cost balance sheet for hyperinflationary conditions may possibly result in an increase in retained earnings. However, this may well be the effect of the transfer of revaluation reserve to retained earnings implicit in the second bullet point above. Finally, elimination of the revaluation surplus is only required when IAS 29 is first applied. Subsequent revaluations may therefore give rise to a revaluation surplus within equity.

Though IAS 29 provides guidance on the restatement of assets, liabilities and individual components of shareholders' equity, it should be noted that national laws and regulations with which the entity needs to comply might not permit such revaluations. This can mean that IAS 29 may require restatement of distributable reserves, but that from the legal point of view in the jurisdiction concerned, those same reserves remain unchanged. That is, it is possible that 'restated retained earnings' under IAS 29 will not all be legally distributable.

Example 14.5:   Restatement of equity

The table below shows the effect of a hypothetical IAS 29 restatement on individual components of equity. Issued share capital and share premium increase by applying the general price index, the revaluation reserve is eliminated as required, and retained earnings is the balancing figure derived from all other amounts in the restated balance sheet.

	Amounts before restatement	Amounts after IAS 29 restatement	Components of equity under national law
Issued capital and share premium	1,500	3,150	1,500
Revaluation reserve	800	–	800
Retained earnings	350	1,600	350
Total equity	2,650	4,750	2,650

A user of the financial statements of the entity might get the impression, based on the information restated in accordance with IAS 29, that distributable reserves have increased from 350 to 1,600. However, if national law does not permit revaluation of assets, liabilities and components of equity then distributable reserves remain unchanged.

Users of financial statements restated under IAS 29 may for that reason be misled about the extent to which components of equity are distributable. Entities reporting under IAS 29 should therefore disclose the extent to which components of equity are distributable where this is not obvious from the financial statements. In our view it is important for entities to give supplementary information in the circumstances where the IAS 29 adjustments have produced large apparently distributable reserves that are in fact not distributable.

Because of its global constituency, the IASB's standards cannot deal with specific national legal requirements relating to a legal entity's equity. Therefore, instead of prescribing an accounting treatment for individual components of equity, we consider that the IASB would be better advised to recognise the wide variety in national legislation, and prescribe disclosure requirements that ensure users of financial statements are not misled.

2.4.3   Restatement of statements of comprehensive income (and income statements if presented)

IAS 29 requires that all items in historical cost based statements of comprehensive income (and income statements if presented) be expressed in terms of the measuring unit current at the end of the reporting period.[66] The standard contains a similar requirement for current cost based statements of comprehensive income (and income statements if presented), because the underlying transactions or events are recorded at current cost at the time they occurred rather than in the measuring unit current at the end of the reporting period.[67] Therefore, all amounts in the statements of comprehensive income (and income statements if presented) need to be restated as follows:

$$\text{restated amount} = \text{amount before restatement} \times \frac{\text{general price index at the end of the reporting period}}{\text{general price index when the underlying income or expenses were initially recorded}}$$

Actually performing the above calculation on a real set of financial statements is often difficult because an entity would need to keep a very detailed record of when it entered into transactions and when it incurred expenses. Instead of using the exact price index for a transaction it may be more practical to use an average price index that approximates the actual rate at the date of the transaction. For example, an average rate for a week or a month might be used for all transactions occurring during that period. However, it must be stressed that if price indices fluctuate significantly, the use of an average for the period is inappropriate.

There may be items in statements of comprehensive income (and income statements if presented), e.g. interest income and expense, that comprise an element that is intended to compensate for the effect of hyperinflation. However, even those items need to be restated as IAS 29 specifically requires that 'all amounts need to be restated' (see 4.5 below).[68]

Example 14.6 illustrates how an entity might, for example, restate its revenue to the measuring unit current at the end of the reporting period. A similar calculation would work well for other items in statements of comprehensive income (and income statements if presented), with the exception of:

(a)   depreciation and amortisation charges which are often easier to restate by using the cost balance restated for hyperinflation as a starting point;

(b)   deferred taxation which should be based on the temporary differences between the carrying amount and tax base of assets and liabilities, the restated carrying amount of balance sheet items, and the underlying tax base of those items; and

(c)   the net monetary gain or loss which results from the IAS 29 restatements (see 2.4.4 below).

Example 14.6:   Restatement of historical cost income statement

An entity would restate its revenue for the period ending 31 December 2009, when the general price index was 2,880, as shown in the table below.

	General price index	Conversion factor	Revenue before restatement	Restated revenue
31 January 2009	1,315	(2,880 ÷ 1,315) = 2.19	40	87.6
28 February 2009	1,345	(2,880 ÷ 1,345) = 2.14	35	74.9
31 March 2009	1,371	etc. = 2.10	45	94.5
30 April 2009	1,490	1.93	45	87.0
31 May 2009	1,600	1.80	65	117.0
30 June 2009	1,846	1.56	70	109.2
31 July 2009	1,923	1.50	70	104.8
31 August 2009	2,071	1.39	65	90.4
30 September 2009	2,163	1.33	75	99.9
31 October 2009	2,511	1.15	75	86.0
30 November 2009	2,599	1.11	80	88.6
31 December 2009	2,880	1.00	80	80.0
			745	1,119.9

A similar calculation can be made for other items in statements of comprehensive income (and income statements if presented). Inevitably, in practice there is some approximation because of the assumptions that the entity is required to make, for example:

(a)   the use of weighted averages rather than more detailed calculations; and

(b)   assumptions as to the timing of the underlying transactions (e.g. the calculation above assumes the revenues for the month are earned on the final day of the month, which is not realistic).

2.4.4   Calculation of the gain or loss on the net monetary position

In theory, hyperinflation only affects the value of money and monetary items and does not affect the value, as distinct from the price, of non-monetary items. Therefore, any gain or loss because of hyperinflation will be the gain or loss on the net monetary position of the entity. By arranging the items in an ordinary balance sheet, it can be shown that the monetary position minus the non-monetary position is always equal to zero:

	Total	Monetary items	Non-monetary items
Monetary assets	280	280	
Non-monetary assets	170		170
Monetary liabilities	(200)	(200)	
Non-monetary liabilities	(110)		(110)
Assets minus liabilities	140		
Shareholders' equity	(140)		(140)
Net position	0	80	(80)

Theoretically, the gain or loss on the net monetary position can be calculated by applying the general price index to the entity's monetary assets and liabilities. This would require the entity to determine its net monetary position on a daily basis, which would be entirely impracticable given the difficulties in making the monetary/non-monetary distinction (see 2.4.2 A above). The standard therefore allows the gain or loss on the net monetary position to be estimated by applying the change in a general price index to the weighted average for the period of the difference between monetary assets and monetary liabilities.[69] Due care should be exercised in estimating the gain or loss on the net monetary position, as a calculation based on averages for the period (or monthly averages) can be unreliable if addressed without accurate consideration of the pattern of hyperinflation and the volatility of the net monetary position.

However, as shown in the above table, any restatement of the non-monetary items must be met by an equal restatement of the monetary items. Therefore, in preparing financial statements it is more practical to assume that the gain or loss on the net monetary position is exactly the reverse of the restatement of the non-monetary items. A stand-alone calculation of the net gain or loss can, however, be used to verify the reasonableness of the restatement of the non-monetary items.

The gain or loss on the net monetary position should be included in profit or loss and disclosed separately. It may be helpful to present it together with items that are also associated with the net monetary position such as interest income and expense, and foreign exchange differences related to invested or borrowed funds.[70]

2.4.5   Restatement of the statement of cash flows

The standard also requires that all items in the statement of cash flows be expressed in terms of the measuring unit current at the end of the reporting period.[71] This is a most difficult requirement to fulfil in practice.

An understanding of the complication inherent in this requirement of IAS 29 becomes apparent when the restatement of a cash flow is actually contemplated. IAS 7 – *Statement of Cash Flows* – requires the following information to be presented:[72]

(a)   cash flows from operating activities, which are the principal revenue-producing activities of the entity and other activities that are not investing or financing activities;

(b)   cash flows from investing activities, which are the acquisition and disposal of long-term assets and other investments not included in cash equivalents; and

(c)   cash flows from financing activities, which are activities that result in changes in the size and composition of the equity capital and borrowings of the entity.

In effect IAS 29 requires restatement of most items in a statement of cash flows, implying that therefore the actual cash flows at the time of the transactions will be different from the numbers presented in the statement of cash flows itself. However, not all items are restated using the same method and many of the restatements are based on estimates. For example, items in the income statement or statement of comprehensive income are to be restated using an estimate of the general price index at the time that the revenues were earned and the costs incurred. Unavoidably this will give rise to some inconsistencies. Similarly, the restatement of balance sheet items will give rise to discrepancies because some items are not easily classified as either monetary or non-monetary. This raises the question how an entity should classify the monetary gain or loss relating to a balance sheet item in its statement of cash flows.

It is not clear from IAS 29 how a monetary gain or loss should be presented in the statement of cash flows. In practice different approaches have been adopted such as:

(a)   presenting the effect of inflation on operating, investing and financing cash flows separately for each of these activities and present the net monetary gain or loss as a reconciling item in the cash and cash equivalents reconciliation;

(b)   presenting the monetary gain or loss on cash and cash equivalents and the effect of inflation on operating, investing and financing cash flows as one number; and

(c)   attributing the effect of inflation on operating, investing and financing cash flows to the underlying item and presenting the monetary gain or loss on cash and cash equivalents separately.

Irrespective of the method chosen, users of statements of cash flows prepared in the currency of a hyperinflationary economy should be mindful of the fact that figures presented in the statement of cash flows may have been restated in accordance with IAS 29 and may differ from the actual underlying cash flows. In our view it is important for entities that have a significant proportion of their activities in hyperinflationary economies to give supplementary information about this.

2.4.6   Restatement of the corresponding figures

The standard requires that all financial information be presented in terms of the measurement unit current at the end of the reporting period, therefore:[73]

*   corresponding figures for the previous reporting period, whether they were based on a historical cost approach or a current cost approach, are restated by applying a general price index; and

*   information that is disclosed in respect of earlier periods is also expressed in terms of the measuring unit current at the end of the reporting period.

2.5   Interim reporting

Appendix B to IAS 34 – *Interim Financial Reporting* – requires that interim financial reports in hyperinflationary economies are prepared by the same principles as at financial year end. This means that the financial statements must be stated in terms of the measuring unit current at the end of the interim period and that the gain or loss on the net monetary position is included in net income (profit or loss).[74] The comparative financial information reported for prior periods must also be restated to the current measuring unit.[75] An entity that reports quarterly information must restate the comparative balance sheets, income statements and other primary financial statements each quarter.

In restating its financial information an entity is not allowed to 'annualise' the recognition of the gain or loss on the net monetary position or to use an estimated annual inflation rate in preparing an interim financial report in a hyperinflationary economy.[76]

2.6   Economies becoming hyperinflationary

When the functional currency of an entity becomes hyperinflationary it must start applying IAS 29. The standard requires that the financial statements and any information in respect of earlier periods should be stated in terms of the measuring unit current at the end of the reporting period.[77] The standard does not explicitly state:[78]

(a)   whether restatement should be fully retrospective, i.e. items should be restated from the date of their acquisition or last revaluation; or

(b)   whether restatements should be prospective from the date that the economy became hyperinflationary.

IFRIC considered that the wording of paragraph 4 of IAS 29 was not sufficiently clear and that there was therefore 'uncertainty whether the opening balance sheet at the beginning of the reporting period should be restated to reflect changes in prices before that date'.[79] IFRIC 7 removes this ambiguity by requiring that items should be restated fully retrospectively. In the first year in which the entity identifies the existence of hyperinflation the requirements of IAS 29 should be applied as if the economy had always been hyperinflationary. The opening balance sheet at the beginning of the earliest period presented in the financial statements should be restated as follows:[80]

• non-monetary items measured at historical cost should be restated to reflect the effect of inflation from the date the assets were acquired and the liabilities were incurred or assumed; and

• non-monetary items carried at amounts current at dates other than those of acquisition or incurrence should be restated to reflect the effect of inflation from the dates those carrying amounts were determined.

What is less obvious is how an entity (a parent), which does not operate in a hyperinflationary economy, should account for the restatement of an entity (a subsidiary) that operates in an economy that became hyperinflationary in the current reporting period when incorporating it within its consolidated financial statements.

This issue has been clarified by paragraph 42(b) of IAS 21 which specifically prohibits restatement of comparative figures when the reporting currency is not hyperinflationary. This means that when the financial statements of a hyperinflationary subsidiary are translated into the non-hyperinflationary reporting currency of the parent, the comparative amounts are not adjusted.

2.7 Economies ceasing to be hyperinflationary

When an economy ceases to be hyperinflationary, entities should discontinue preparation and presentation of financial statements in accordance with IAS 29. The amounts expressed in the measuring unit current at the end of the previous reporting period will be treated as the deemed cost of the items in the balance sheet.[81]

Determining when a currency stops being hyperinflationary is not easy in practice. It is important to review trends, not just at the end of the reporting period but also subsequently. In addition, consistency demands that the financial statements do not unnecessarily 'yo-yo' in and out of a hyperinflationary presentation, where a more careful judgement would have avoided it.

It is possible or even likely that an economy becomes hyperinflationary sometime during an entity's financial year. Therefore, it would be reasonable and sensible that as soon as an entity determines that it is operating in hyperinflation it starts preparing its interim reports using the principles underlying IAS 29. The standard should be applied from the beginning of the reporting period in which the existence of hyperinflation is identified.[82] Equally, it is possible that an economy ceases to be hyperinflationary during the year. If an entity concludes that the economy ceases to be hyperinflationary during the year, the standard requires that the entity should stop applying IAS 29 at that point. It should be noted that, an amalgamation of interim periods during which IAS 29 was applied with those where it was not, may result in financial statements that are difficult to interpret.

2.8 Translation to a different presentation currency

An entity is permitted to present its financial statements in any presentation currency it chooses. However, a change in presentation currency will not alter the entity's functional currency or the requirement to apply IAS 29.

If an entity, whose functional currency is hyperinflationary, wants to translate its financial statements into a different presentation currency it must first restate its financial statements in accordance with IAS 29 and then apply the following procedures under IAS 21:

'(a) all amounts (i.e. assets, liabilities, equity items, income and expenses, including comparatives) shall be translated at the closing rate at the date of the most recent [balance sheet], except that

(b) when amounts are translated into the currency of a non-hyperinflationary economy, comparative amounts shall be those that were presented as current year amounts in the relevant prior year financial statements (i.e. not adjusted for subsequent changes in the price level or subsequent changes in exchange rates).'[83]

In other words, when an entity that applies IAS 29 translates its financial statements into a non-hyperinflationary presentation currency the comparative information should not be restated under IAS 29, instead IAS 21 should be applied (i.e. the comparative amounts should be those that were presented as current year amounts in the prior period). For a more detailed discussion of these requirements reference is made to Chapter 13 at 2.7.1 B.

When the economy ceases to be hyperinflationary, and restatement in accordance with IAS 29 is no longer required, an entity uses the amounts restated to the price level at the date it ceased restating its financial statements as the historical costs for translation into the presentation currency.[84]

2.9   Disclosures

IAS 29 requires that entities should disclose the following information when they apply the provisions of the standard:[85]

(a)   the fact that the financial statements and the corresponding figures for previous periods have been restated for the changes in the general purchasing power of the functional currency and, as a result, are stated in terms of the measuring unit current at the end of the reporting period;

(b)   whether the financial statements are based on a historical cost approach or a current cost approach; and

(c)   the identity and level of the price index at the end of the reporting period and the movement in the index during the current and the previous reporting period.

It should be noted that disclosure of financial information that is restated under IAS 29 as a supplement to unrestated financial information is not permitted. This is to prevent entities from giving the historical cost based financial information greater prominence than the information that is restated under IAS 29. The standard also discourages separate presentation of unrestated financial information, but does not explicitly prohibit it.[86] However, such unrestated financial statements would not be in accordance with IFRS and should be clearly identified as such.

An entity that is required (for example by local tax authorities or stock exchange regulators) to present unrestated financial statements needs to ensure that the IFRS financial statements are perceived to be the main financial statements rather than mere supplemental information. This means, for example, that an entity reporting under IAS 29 should refrain from presenting historical cost information on the face of the primary financial statements because this would not result in a fair presentation as required by paragraph 15 of IAS 1.

In its 2005 financial statements, Tofaş Türk Otomobil Fabrikası disclosed that it operated in a hyperinflationary economy and made the appropriate disclosures:

Extract 14.1: Tofaş Türk Otomobil Fabrikası A.Ş. (2005)
CONSOLIDATED CASH FLOW STATEMENT [extract]
For the year ended December 31, 2005
(Currency – Thousands of YTL in equivalent purchasing power at December 31, 2005, unless otherwise indicated)

...

Monetary loss on cash and cash equivalents	(14,761)	(14,574)
Net change in cash and cash equivalents	166,744	(19,675)
Cash and cash equivalents at the beginning of the year	291,982	311,657
Cash and cash equivalents at the end of the year	458,726	291,982

2. Summary of significant accounting policies [extract]

Measurement Currency and Reporting Currency

IAS 29 requires that financial statements prepared in the currency of a hyperinflationary economy be stated in terms of the measuring unit current at the balance sheet date and the corresponding figures for previous periods be restated in the same terms. Determining whether an economy is hyperinflationary in accordance with IAS 29 requires judgment as the standard does not establish an absolute rate, instead it considers the following characteristics of the economic environment of a country to be strong indicators of the existence of hyperinflation: (a) the general population prefers to keep its wealth in non monetary assets or in a relatively stable currency; amounts of local currency held are immediately invested to maintain purchasing power, (b) the general population regards monetary amounts not in terms of local currency but in terms of a relatively stable currency; prices may be quoted in that currency, (c) sales and purchases on credit take place at prices that compensate for the expected loss of purchasing power during the credit period, even if the period is short, (d) interest rates, wages and prices are linked to a price index and (e) the cumulative inflation rate over three years is approaching, or exceeds 100%. Although as of December 31, 2005, the three-year cumulative rate has been 35.6% (December 31, 2004 – 69.7%) based on the Turkish countrywide wholesale price index published by the State Institute of Statistics, considering the economic characteristics indicated above, IAS 29 is continued to be applied in the preparation of the current period financial statements. Such index and conversion factors as of the end of the three year period ended December 31, 2005 are given below:

Dates	Index	Conversion Factors
December 31, 2002	6,478.8	1.356
December 31, 2003	7,382.1	1.190
December 31, 2004	8,403.8	1.045
December 31, 2005	8,785.7	1.000

The main guidelines for the above mentioned restatement are as follows:

- The consolidated financial statements of prior year, including monetary assets and liabilities reported therein, which were previously reported in terms of the measuring unit current at the end of that year are restated in their entirety to the measuring unit current at December 31, 2005.

- Monetary assets and liabilities reported in the consolidated balance sheet as of December 31, 2005 are not restated because they are already expressed in terms of the monetary unit current at that balance sheet date.

- The inflation adjusted issued share capital was derived by indexing cash contributions, transfers from statutory retained earnings and income from sale of investments and property, transferred to issued share capital from the date they were contributed.

- Non-monetary assets and liabilities which are not carried at amounts current at the balance sheet date and other components of equity (except for the statutory revaluation adjustment which is eliminated) are restated by applying the relevant conversion factors.

- The effect of general inflation on the net monetary position is included in the income statement as monetary gain / (loss).

- All items in the income statement are restated by applying appropriate average conversion factors with the exception of depreciation, amortization, gain or loss on disposal of non-monetary assets.

Restatement of balance sheet and income statement items through the use of a general price index and relevant conversion factors does not necessarily mean that the Group could realize or settle the same values of assets and liabilities as indicated in the consolidated balance sheets. Similarly, it does not necessarily mean that the Group could return or settle the same values of equity to its shareholders.

10. Property, plant and equipment (PP&E), net [extract]

	Land, Land Improvements and Buildings
At January 1, 2005, net of accumulated depreciation	103,956
Additions	1,439
Disposals	(14,392)
Transfers	–
Depreciation charge for the period	(6,518)
Accumulated depreciation of disposals	14,376
At December 31, 2005, net of accumulated depreciation	**98,861**

15. Warranty provisions

Movements in the warranty provision for the years ended 2005 and 2004 are as follows:

	2005	2004
January 1	46,238	25,484
Amounts utilised	(20,934)	(15,674)
Current year provision	30,141	40,662
Monetary gain	(2,100)	(4,234)
December 31	53,345	46,238

Tofaş Türk Otomobil Fabrikası was required under IAS 29 to restate its comparative amounts of property, plant and equipment and therefore did not present the impact of the hyperinflation adjustments in the movement schedule. While Carlsberg, which had a number of subsidiaries that operated in countries with hyperinflationary economies, was not permitted to restate the comparative amounts and therefore reported a reconciling item for the effect of hyperinflation adjustments.

Extract 14.2: Carlsberg A/S (2005)

Accounting policies [extract]

Prior to translation of the financial statements of foreign entities in countries with hyperinflation, the statements (including comparative figures) are inflation-adjusted for changes in purchasing power in the local currency. Inflation adjustment is based on relevant price indexes at the balance sheet date.

Note 15 Property, plant and equipment [extract]

DKK million	2005 Land and buildings
Cost:	
Cost at 1 January 2005	13,187
Acquisition of subsidiaries	67
Divestment of subsidiaries	–
Additions during the year	167

Disposals during the year	−1,092
Currency translation adjustments etc.	315
Transfers to assets held for sale	−260
Transfers	221
Effect of hyperinflation adjustments	55
Cost at 31 December 2005	12,660

3 PRACTICAL PROBLEMS

3.1 Selecting a general price index

Selecting an appropriate general price index is fraught with difficulties in many cases. IAS 29 requires entities to use a general price index that reflects changes in general purchasing power.[87] It is generally accepted practice to use a Consumer Price Index (CPI) for this purpose, unless that index is clearly flawed. National statistical offices in most countries issue several price indices that potentially could be used for the purposes of IAS 29. Important characteristics of a good general price index include the following:

- a wide range of goods and services has been included in the price index;
- continuity and consistency of measurement techniques and underlying assumptions;
- free from bias;
- frequently updated; and
- available for a long period.

The entity should use the above criteria to choose the most reliable and most readily available general price index and use that index consistently. It is important that the index selected is representative of the real position of the hyperinflationary currency concerned.

3.2 General price index not available for all periods

IAS 29 requires an entity to make an estimate of the price index if the general price index is not available for all periods for which the restatement of long-lived assets is required. The entity could base the estimate, for example, on the movements in the exchange rate between the functional currency and a relatively stable foreign currency.[88] It should be noted that this method is only acceptable if the currency of the hyperinflationary economy is freely exchangeable, i.e. not subject to currency controls and 'official' exchange rates. Entities should be mindful that, especially in the short term, the exchange rate may fluctuate significantly in response to factors other than changes in the domestic price level.

Entities could use a similar approach when they cannot find a general price index that meets its minimum criteria for reliability (e.g. because the national statistical office in the hyperinflationary economy may be subject to significant political bias).

However, this would only be acceptable if all available general price indices are fatally flawed.

3.3   Inventories

To restate the balance sheet under IAS 29 an entity needs to exercise judgement and make assumptions regarding:

- whether balance sheet items are monetary or non-monetary in nature;
- the date of acquisition of items; and
- the level of the general price index at the date of acquisition.

Given the large number of transactions affecting an entity's inventory position, it is often a challenge to determine the date of acquisition of inventory. Therefore, entities commonly approximate the ageing of inventories by basing it on inventory turnover. In a similar vein, the level of the general price index at the date of acquisition is often determined at the average level for the month because an up-to-date price index is not available for each day of the month. Determining the appropriate level of the general price index can be particularly challenging when the price index is updated relatively infrequently and the entity's business is highly seasonal.

IAS 29 requires restatement of inventory by applying a general price index, which could result in an overvaluation when the price of inventory items increases at a different rate from the general price index. At the end of each period it is therefore essential to ensure that items of inventory are not valued in excess of their net realisable value.

3.4   Investees accounted for under the equity method

Restatement of such investees that also operate in hyperinflationary economies under IAS 29 is required in order to calculate the investor's share of its net assets and results of operations.[89] The standard specifically requires that the balance sheet, income statement and statement of comprehensive income of an investee is restated in accordance with IAS 29 in order to calculate the investor's share of the net assets and results of operations, i.e. the standard does not permit the investment in the investee to be treated as a single indivisible item for the purposes of the IAS 29 restatement.

Restating the financial statements of an associate before application of the equity method will often be difficult because the investor may not have access to the detailed information required. The fact that the investor can exercise significant influence or has joint control over an investee often does not mean that the investor has unrestricted access to the investee's books and records at all times.

3.5   Restatement of interest and exchange differences

A common question is whether an entity should restate exchange differences under IAS 29, because the standard considers that 'foreign exchange differences related to invested or borrowed funds ... are also associated with the net monetary position'.[90] Nevertheless, the standard requires that all items in the income statement and statement of comprehensive income are expressed in terms of the measuring unit current at the end of the reporting period. 'Therefore all amounts need to be restated by applying the change in the general price index from the dates when the items of income and expenses were initially recorded in the financial statements'.[91] Interest and exchange differences should therefore be restated for the effect of inflation as all the other items in the statement of comprehensive income (and income statements if presented) and be presented on a gross basis. However, though it may be helpful if they are presented together with the gain or loss on net monetary position in profit or loss.[92]

References

1 Framework, *Framework for the Preparation and Presentation of Financial Statements*, para. 100.
2 Framework, para. 104.
3 IAS 29, *Financial Reporting in Hyperinflationary Economies*, IASB, para. 6.
4 It should be noted that the definition of hyperinflation used in financial reporting does not have a solid theoretical basis. In fact, economists researching hyperinflation often use Cagan's definition which defines hyperinflation as consumer price increases of more than 50% per month. International Monetary Fund, *World Economic Outlook – Fiscal Policy and Macroeconomic Stability*, May 2001. Cagan, Phillip. *op. cit.*, 'The Monetary Dynamics of Hyperinflation.' In Studies in the Quantity Theory of Money, ed. by Milton Friedman, pp. 25-117. Chicago: University of Chicago Press.
5 *Highlights of the July 27, 2009 Joint Conference Call of the IPTF and the SEC Staff*, Center for Audit Quality, available at http://thecaq.org/iptf/pdfs/highlights/IPTF 7-27-09 Conference Call HLs – FINAL.pdf.
6 *Highlights of the May 14, 2009 Joint Meeting of the IPTF and the SEC Staff*, Center for Audit Quality, available at http://thecaq.org/iptf/pdfs/highlights/IPTF 5-14-09 Joint Meeting HLs – FINAL.pdf.
7 IAS 21, *The Effects of Changes in Foreign Exchange Rates*, IASB, paras. 8-14.
8 IAS 21, para. 14.
9 IFRIC 7, *Applying the Restatement Approach under IAS 29 Financial Reporting in Hyperinflationary Economies*.
10 IAS 21, para. 8.
11 IAS 21, para. 8.

12 SIC-19, *Reporting Currency – Measurement and Presentation of Financial Statements under IAS 21 and IAS 29*, SIC, November 2000 (superseded December 2003).
13 IAS 21, para. IN6.
14 IAS 21 (revised 1993), *The Effects of Changes in Foreign Exchange Rates*, IASB, December 1993, para. 7.
15 IAS 21 (revised 1993), para. 4.
16 IAS 21, para. IN6.
17 IAS 29, para. 2.
18 IAS 29, paras. 8-9.
19 IAS 29, para. 11.
20 IAS 29, para. 10.
21 IAS 29, paras. 1-2.
22 IAS 29, para. 3.
23 IAS 29, para. 4.
24 IAS 29, para. 4.
25 IAS 29, para. 37.
26 IAS 29, para. 17.
27 Framework, para. 100(b).
28 IAS 29, para. 12.
29 IAS 21, para. 8.
30 IAS 21, para. 16.
31 IAS 21, para. 16.
32 IAS 21, para. 16.
33 IAS 39, *Financial Instruments: Recognition and Measurement, IASB*, para. AG83.
34 *IFRIC Update*, IFRIC, October 2003, p. 2. IFRIC concluded in its October 2003 meeting that 'it is not clear how an entity should restate items that are neither monetary nor non-monetary in nature, e.g. deferred tax assets and deferred tax liabilities'.
35 IAS 29, para. 13.
36 IAS 29, para. 29.
37 Framework, para. 100(b).
38 IAS 29, para. 14.

39 IAS 29, para. 18.
40 IAS 29, para. 15.
41 IAS 29, para. 10.
42 IAS 29, para. 16.
43 IAS 29, para. 15.
44 IAS 16, *Property, Plant and Equipment*, IASB, para. 23.
45 IAS 29, para. 22.
46 IAS 29, paras. 19 and 21.
47 IAS 29, para. 21.
48 IAS 23 (2007), *Borrowing Costs*, IASB, 2007 Bound Volume, paras. 7 and 10.
49 IAS 23, *Borrowing Costs*, IASB, para. 8.
50 IAS 29, para. 19.
51 IAS 29, para. 20.
52 IAS 21, para. 42.
53 IAS 29, para. 35.
54 IAS 21, para. 42.
55 IAS 29, para. 35.
56 IAS 29, para. 36.
57 IFRIC 7, paras. BC21-BC22.
58 IFRIC 7, para. 4.
59 IFRIC 7, paras. IE1-IE6.
60 IFRIC 7, para. 5.
61 IAS 29, para. 32.
62 IAS 12, *Income Taxes*, IASB, Appendix A, para. 18.
63 IAS 12, Appendix A, para. 18.
64 IAS 29, para. 24.
65 IAS 29, para. 25.
66 IAS 29, para. 26.
67 IAS 29, para. 30.
68 IAS 29, paras. 26 and 30.
69 IAS 29, paras. 27 and 31.
70 IAS 29, para. 28.
71 IAS 29, para. 33.
72 IAS 7, *Statement of Cash Flows*, IASB, paras. 6 and 10.
73 IAS 29, para. 34.
74 IAS 34, *Interim Financial Reporting*, IASB, Appendix B, para. 33.
75 IAS 34, Appendix B, para. 32.
76 IAS 34, Appendix B, para. 34.
77 IAS 29, para. 8.
78 IAS 29, paras. 11-36.
79 IFRIC 7, para. BC2.
80 IFRIC 7, para. 3.
81 IAS 29, para. 38.
82 IAS 29, para. 4.
83 IAS 21, para. 42.
84 IAS 21, para. 43.
85 IAS 29, para. 39.
86 IAS 29, para. 7.
87 IAS 29, para. 37.
88 IAS 29, para. 17.
89 IAS 29, para. 20.
90 IAS 29, para. 28.
91 IAS 29, para. 26.
92 IAS 29, para. 28.

Chapter 15   Intangible assets

1   INTRODUCTION

1.1   The incidence of intangible assets

Today, businesses commonly invest substantial sums in ways that were unheard of twenty years ago. It is not unusual for the premium paid to acquire a business to be greater than the balance sheet value of net assets acquired. This trend has been fuelled in part by the cost and uncertainty of attempting to develop brands that are attractive to consumers from scratch. Equally, businesses that own successful brands spend large sums in maintaining consumer awareness of, and loyalty to them.

New types of business asset have come into being. Over the last fifteen years or so, entities had to consider how to account for software and related expenditure on computerised sales and marketing systems and website development. New businesses have emerged whose principal revenues come from the exchange of intangible rights, for example from acquiring and developing intellectual property rights. Governments have raised revenues from the sale of broadcasting rights and telecommunications licences. The question of how to account for such assets has become more important as the related costs become more significant for a larger number of businesses.

These relatively high levels of expenditure on intangible aspects of commerce have inevitably resulted in companies wanting to account for it in various different ways. As the incidence and magnitude of such expenditure increased, it became necessary for the IASB and the accounting profession generally, to develop common rules for its recognition and treatment in financial statements.

1.2   Background to accounting for intangible assets

In 2001 the IASB began a project to review its prescribed accounting for business combinations, pursued in two phases and obviously affecting the accounting treatment of intangible assets and goodwill.[1] The IASB's intention in the first phase was to clarify the following matters:

(a)   the treatment of any excess of the acquirer's interest in the fair value of identifiable net assets acquired in a business combination over the cost of the combination;[2]

(b)   the accounting for goodwill and intangible assets acquired in a business combination;[3]

(c)   the notion of 'identifiability' as it relates to intangible assets;[4]

(d)   the useful life and amortisation of intangible assets;[5] and

(e)   the accounting for in-process research and development projects acquired in business combinations.[6]

The first phase of the project resulted in the IASB issuing in March 2004 IFRS 3 – *Business Combinations* – and revised versions of IAS 36 – *Impairment of Assets* – and IAS 38 – *Intangible Assets*. This broadened significantly the range of intangible assets that an entity is required to recognise in accounting for business combinations.

The IASB revised IFRS 3 in January 2008. The consequential amendments to IAS 38, in particular to clarify the notion of 'identifiability' of intangible assets acquired in a business combination apply when an entity adopts IFRS 3, which is mandatory for annual reporting periods beginning on or after 1 July 2009.[7] In this chapter, the revised standard is referred to as IFRS 3 and the former version is referred to as IFRS 3 (2007), since it can be found in the IASB's 2007 Bound Volume of Standards.

The requirements of IFRS 3 (2007) are principally dealt with in Chapter 9 at 2 and those of IFRS 3 are discussed in Chapter 9 at 3; IAS 36 is covered in Chapter 18. The specific provisions of IAS 38 relating to intangible assets are dealt with at 2 below; while the requirements relating to intangible assets acquired as part of a business combination are covered both at 2.3.2 below and, for business combinations to which IFRS 3(2007) applies, in Chapter 9 at 2.5.2 and, for combinations accounted for under IFRS 3, in Chapter 9 at 3.6.5 B.

Other intangible assets are dealt with by specific accounting pronouncements. The late 1990s saw very large sums spent on the operation and development of websites and this led to the issue of SIC-32 (amended 2003) – *Intangible Assets – Web Site Costs* – that is discussed at 2.3.6 D below. Emissions trading schemes give rise to intangible rights and the attempts to devise a satisfactory accounting model for these and similar schemes are considered at 3.3 below.

2   THE REQUIREMENTS OF IAS 38

2.1   Scope and definitions

2.1.1   Scope

The objective of IAS 38 is to prescribe the accounting treatment for all intangible assets that are not specifically dealt with in another standard.[8] Hence, IAS 38 does not apply to accounting for:[9]

(a) intangible assets that are within the scope of another standard;

(b) financial assets, as defined in IAS 32 – *Financial Instruments: Presentation*;

(c) the recognition and measurement of exploration and evaluation assets within the scope of IFRS 6 – *Exploration for and Evaluation of Mineral Resources*; and

(d) expenditure on the development and extraction of, minerals, oil, natural gas and similar non-regenerative resources.

Examples of specific types of intangible asset that fall within the scope of another standard include:[10]

(a) intangible assets held by an entity for sale in the ordinary course of business, to which IAS 2 – *Inventories* – or IAS 11 – *Construction Contracts* – applies (see Chapters 20 and 21);

(b) deferred tax assets, which are governed by IAS 12 – *Income Taxes* (see Chapter 26);

(c) leases that are within the scope of IAS 17 – *Leases* (see Chapter 22). However, an entity that leases an intangible asset under a finance lease should apply IAS 38 to account for the underlying asset after its initial recognition.[11] Leases that are outside the scope of IAS 17 such as 'licensing agreements for such items as motion picture films, video recordings, plays, manuscripts, patents and copyrights'[12] are within the scope of IAS 38;[13]

(d) assets arising from employee benefits, for which IAS 19 – *Employee Benefits* – is relevant (see Chapter 28);

(e) financial assets as defined in IAS 32. The recognition and measurement of some financial assets are covered by IAS 27 – *Consolidated and Separate Financial Statements*, IAS 28 – *Investments in Associates* – and IAS 31 – *Interests in Joint Ventures* (see Chapters 6, 8, 11, 12 and 29 to 34);

(f) goodwill acquired in a business combination, which is determined under IFRS 3 (see Chapter 9);

(g) deferred acquisition costs, and intangible assets, arising from an insurer's contractual rights under insurance contracts within the scope of IFRS 4 – *Insurance Contracts*. IFRS 4 sets out specific disclosure requirements for those deferred acquisition costs but not for those intangible assets. Therefore, the disclosure requirements in this standard apply to those intangible assets (see Chapter 43); and

(h) non-current intangible assets classified as held for sale, or included in a disposal group that is classified as held for sale, in accordance with IFRS 5 – *Non-current Assets Held for Sale and Discontinued Operations* (see Chapter 4).

IAS 38 excludes insurance contracts and expenditure on the exploration for, or development and extraction of, oil, gas and mineral deposits in extractive industries from its scope because activities or transactions in these areas are so specialised that they give rise to accounting issues that need to be dealt with in a different way. However, the standard does apply 'to other intangible assets used (such as computer software), and other expenditure incurred (such as start-up costs), in extractive industries or by insurers'.[14]

Finally, the standard makes it clear that it does apply to expenditure on advertising, training, start-up and research and development activities.[15]

2.1.2   What is an intangible asset?

IAS 38 defines an asset as 'a resource controlled by an entity as a result of past events; and from which future economic benefits are expected to flow to the entity'.[16] Intangible assets form a sub-section of this group and are further defined as 'an identifiable non-monetary asset without physical substance'.[17] The IASB considers that the essential characteristics of intangible assets are that they are controlled by the entity; will give rise to future economic benefits for the entity; lack physical substance and are identifiable and that 'the purpose for which an entity holds an item with these characteristics is not relevant to its classification as an intangible asset, and that all such items should be within the scope of the Standard'.[18] However, there is one caveat, that intangible assets held for sale (either in the ordinary course of business or as part of a disposal group) and accounted for under IAS 2, IAS 11 or IFRS 5 are specifically excluded from the scope of IAS 38.[19]

Businesses frequently incur expenditure on all sorts of intangible resources such as scientific or technical knowledge, design and implementation of new processes or systems, licences, intellectual property, market knowledge, trademarks, brand names and publishing titles. Examples that fall under these headings include computer software, patents, copyrights, motion picture films, customer lists, licences, quotas, franchises, customer or supplier relationships, customer loyalty, market share and marketing rights.[20]

However, although these items are mentioned by the standard, not all of them will meet the standard's criteria for recognition as an intangible asset, which requires identifiability, control and the existence of future economic benefits. Expenditure on items that do not meet all three criteria will be expensed when incurred, unless they have arisen in the context of a business combination, where they will form part of the calculation of goodwill.[21]

A   Identifiability

An intangible asset needs to be identifiable to distinguish it from goodwill. IFRS 3 (2007) and IFRS 3 (as revised in 2008) define goodwill as 'representing the future economic benefits arising from other assets acquired in a business combination that are not individually identified and separately recognised.'[22] For example, the future economic benefits may result from synergy between the identifiable assets acquired or from assets that, individually, do not qualify for recognition in the financial statements.[23]

When the IASB was revising IAS 38 and first developing IFRS 3 it observed that intangible assets acquired in a business combination were often included in the amount recognised as goodwill, despite existing requirements for separate recognition.[24] The Board therefore concluded that it should provide a definitive basis for separating intangible assets from goodwill in a business combination and that, to achieve this, the concept of identifiability needed to be articulated more clearly.[25] Under the revised IAS 38 an intangible asset meets the identifiability criterion when it either:[26]

(a) is separable, meaning that it is capable of being separated or divided from the entity and sold, transferred, licensed, rented or exchanged, either individually or together with a related contract, identifiable asset or liability, regardless of whether the entity intends to do so; or

(b) arises from contractual or other legal rights, regardless of whether those rights are transferable or separable from the entity or from other rights and obligations.

This definition of identifiability requires preparers of financial statements to recognise more than those intangible resources that are obviously separable from the entity. Assets arising from contractual rights alone can qualify for recognition too. This definition is consistent with guidance from the previous version of the standard that separability is not the only indication of identifiability and confirms the IASB's position that the existence of contractual or legal rights is a characteristic that distinguishes an intangible asset from goodwill, even if those rights are not readily separable from the entity as a whole. The Board cites as an example of such an intangible asset a licence that, under local law, is not transferable except by sale of the entity as a whole.[27]

Equally, however, preparers should not restrict their search for intangible assets to those embodied in contractual or other legal rights, since the definition of identifiability merely requires such rights to be *capable* of separation. In considering the responses to ED 3 – *Business Combinations* – the Board observed that 'if an entity separately acquires a non-contractual customer relationship, the existence of an exchange transaction for that relationship provides evidence both that the item is separable, and that the entity is able to control the expected future economic benefits flowing from the relationship. Therefore, the relationship would meet the intangible asset definition and be recognised as such.' In the absence of exchange transactions for the same or similar non-contractual customer relationships, an entity would not be able to demonstrate that such relationships are separable or that it is able to control the expected future economic benefits flowing from those relationships[28] (see B below).

B   Control

Control is defined as the power to obtain the future economic benefits generated by the resource and the ability to restrict access of others to those benefits. Control normally results from legal rights, in the way that copyright, a restraint of trade agreement or a legal duty on employees to maintain confidentiality would protect the economic benefits arising from market and technical knowledge.[29] While it will be more difficult to demonstrate control in the absence of such rights, the standard is clear that legal enforceability of a right is not a necessary condition for control, because an entity may be able to control the future economic benefits in some other way.[30] As noted above, the existence of exchange transactions for similar non-contractual rights can provide sufficient evidence of control to require separate recognition as an asset.[31] Obviously, determining that this is the case in the absence of observable contractual or other legal rights requires the exercise of judgement based on an understanding of the specific facts and circumstances involved.

For example, the standard acknowledges that an entity usually has insufficient control over the future economic benefits arising from an assembled workforce (i.e. a team of skilled workers, or specific management or technical talent) or from training for these items to meet the definition of an intangible asset.[32] Therefore, if an entity acquires a pharmaceutical company, it is most unlikely that it will be able to recognise as an intangible asset the acquiree's team of research chemists. By contrast, it may be appropriate for the acquirer of a football club to recognise an intangible asset in respect of its squad of players because it is customary in that sector to see exchange transactions involving players' registrations. The payment to a player's previous club in connection with the transfer of the player's registration enables the acquiring club to negotiate a playing contract with the footballer that covers a number of seasons and prevents other clubs from using that player's services. This may give the entity sufficient control to enable it to recognise the cost of obtaining the registration as an intangible asset. In cases when the transfer fee is a stand-alone payment and not part of a business combination, i.e. when an entity separately acquires the intangible resource, it is much more likely that it can demonstrate that its purchase meets the definition of an asset (see 2.3.1 below).

Similarly, an entity 'may have a portfolio of customers or a market share and expect that, because of its efforts in building customer relationships and loyalty, the customers will continue to trade with the entity. However, in the absence of legal rights to protect, or other ways to control, the relationships with customers or the loyalty of the customers of the entity, the entity usually has insufficient control over the expected economic benefits from these items to meet the definition of intangible assets.'[33] Nevertheless, exchange transactions involving the same or similar non-contractual customer relationships may provide evidence that the entity is able to control the expected future economic benefits even in the absence of legal rights. Where this is the case, those customer relationships could meet the definition of an intangible asset.[34] IFRS 3 includes a number of examples of customer-related intangible assets acquired in business combinations that meet the definition of an intangible asset, which are discussed in more detail at 2.3.2 below.[35] It is worthwhile noting here that intangible assets should only be recognised when they meet both the definition of an intangible asset and the applicable recognition criteria in IAS 38,[36] which are discussed at 2.2.1 below. All that is established in the discussion above is whether the intangible right meets the definition of an asset.

The extract below illustrates the range of intangible assets that require recognition under IAS 38.

Extract 15.1: Reed Elsevier (2007)

Accounting policies [extract]
Intangible assets [extract]

Intangible assets acquired as part of business combinations comprise: market related assets (e.g. trade marks, imprints, brands); customer related assets (e.g. subscription bases, customer lists, customer relationships); editorial content; software and systems (e.g. application infrastructure, product delivery platforms, in-process research and development); contract based assets (e.g. publishing rights, exhibition rights, supply contracts); and other intangible assets. Internally generated intangible assets typically comprise software and systems development where an identifiable asset is created that is probable to generate future economic benefits.

C   Future economic benefits

Future economic benefits include not only future revenues from the sale of products or services but also cost savings or other benefits resulting from the use of the asset by the entity. For example, the use of intellectual property in a production process may reduce future production costs rather than increase future revenues.[37]

2.1.3   *Tangible and intangible assets*

Before the advent of IAS 38 many entities used to account for assets without physical substance in the same way as property, plant and equipment. Indeed, many intangible assets are 'contained in or on a physical substance such as a compact disc (in the case of computer software), legal documentation (in the case of a licence or patent) or film'.[38] An entity therefore needs to exercise judgement in determining whether an 'asset that incorporates both intangible and tangible elements should be treated under IAS 16 – *Property, Plant and Equipment* – or as an intangible asset' under IAS 38, for example:

- software that is embedded in computer-controlled equipment that cannot operate without that specific software is an integral part of the related hardware and is treated as property, plant and equipment;[39]

- application software that is being used on a computer is generally easily replaced and is not an integral part of the related hardware is treated as an intangible asset, whereas the operating system normally is integral to the computer and is included in property, plant and equipment;[40]

- a database that is stored on a compact disc is considered to be an intangible asset because the value of the physical medium is wholly insignificant compared to that of the data collection; and

- research and development expenditure may result in an asset with physical substance (e.g. a prototype), but as the physical element is secondary to its intangible component, the related knowledge, it is treated as an intangible asset.[41]

It is worthwhile noting that the 'parts approach' in IAS 16 requires an entity to account for significant parts of an asset separately because they have a different economic life or are often replaced[42] (see Chapter 16). This raises 'boundary' problems between IAS 16 and IAS 38 when software and similar expenditure is involved. We believe that where IAS 16 requires an entity to identify parts of an asset and account for them separately, the entity needs to evaluate whether any intangible-type part is actually integral to the larger asset or whether it is really a separate asset in its own right. The intangible part is more likely to be an asset in its own right if it was developed separately or if it can be used independently of the item of property, plant and equipment of which it apparently forms part.

This view is consistent with that taken in IFRS 3, when it asserts that related tangible and intangible components of an asset with similar useful lives (meaning that IAS 16 would not require separate accounting of parts of an asset) can be combined into a single asset for financial reporting purposes.[43]

2.2   Recognition and measurement

2.2.1   *Recognition*

Recognition of intangible assets under IAS 38 is based on a general principle that 'applies to costs incurred initially to acquire or internally generate an intangible asset and those incurred subsequently to add to, replace part of, or service it'.[44] An item that meets the definition of an intangible asset should only be recognised if:[45]

'(a)   it is probable that the expected future economic benefits that are attributable to the asset will flow to the entity; and

(b)   the cost of the asset can be measured reliably.'

Although IAS 38 does not define 'probable', it is defined in several other International Financial Reporting Standards as 'more likely than not'.[46] In measuring the probability of expected future economic benefits, the entity should use 'reasonable and supportable assumptions that represent management's best estimate of the set of economic conditions that will exist over the useful life of the asset'.[47] In making the above judgement the entity should assess the degree of certainty attached to the flow of future economic benefits based on the evidence available at the time of initial recognition, giving greater weight to external evidence.[48] The difficulties that may arise in applying these criteria when an entity enters into a contract to buy an intangible asset for delivery in some future period are discussed in detail at 3.4.2 below.

The guidance in IAS 38 on the recognition and initial measurement of intangible assets takes account of the way in which an entity obtained the asset. Separate rules for recognition and initial measurement apply for intangible assets depending on whether they were:[49]

- acquired separately (see 2.3.1 below);
- acquired as part of a business combination (see 2.3.2 below);
- acquired by way of government grant (see 2.3.3 below);
- obtained in an exchange of assets (see 2.3.4 below); and
- generated internally (see 2.3.6 below).

It is important to note here that for recognition purposes IAS 38 does not distinguish between an internally and an externally developed intangible asset (other than when considering the treatment of goodwill). When the definition of an intangible asset and the relevant recognition criteria are met, all such assets should be recognised.[50] Preparers do not have the option to decide, as a matter of policy, that costs relating to internally generated intangible assets are expensed.[51]

2.2.2 Measurement

Upon initial recognition an intangible asset should be measured at cost.[52] The standard defines this as 'the amount of cash or cash equivalents paid or the fair value of other consideration given to acquire an asset at the time of its acquisition or construction, or, when applicable, the amount attributed to that asset when initially recognised in accordance with the specific requirements of other IFRSs, e.g. IFRS 2 – *Share-based Payment*.'[53]

The components of the cost of an internally generated intangible asset are discussed in more detail at 2.3.7 below.

2.2.3 Subsequent expenditure

Although IAS 38 is based on a general recognition principle that applies to both initial acquisition and subsequent expenditures, the hurdle for the recognition of subsequent expenditure as an addition to an intangible asset is set higher, because it must first be confirmed that the expenditure is not associated with the replacement of an existing asset (see 2.9 below) or the creation of an internally generated intangible that would not be eligible for recognition under the standard (see 2.3.6 below). The standard argues that 'the nature of intangible assets is such that, in many cases, there are no additions to such an asset or replacements of part of it. Accordingly, most subsequent expenditures are likely to maintain the expected future economic benefits embodied in an existing intangible asset rather than meet the definition of an intangible asset and the recognition criteria in this Standard. In addition, it is often difficult to attribute subsequent expenditure directly to a particular intangible asset rather than to the business as a whole.'[54]

The standard therefore presumes that only rarely will subsequent expenditure, expenditure incurred after the initial recognition of an acquired intangible asset or after completion of an internally generated intangible asset, be recognised in the carrying amount of an asset.[55] Capitalisation of subsequent expenditure on brands, mastheads, publishing titles, customer lists and similar items is expressly forbidden even if they were initially acquired externally, which is consistent with the general prohibition on recognising them if internally generated. This is because the standard argues that such expenditure cannot be distinguished from the cost of developing the business of which they are a part.[56] Thus, at best such expenditure creates internally generated goodwill.

2.3   Specific recognition and measurement requirements

2.3.1   Separate acquisition

A   Recognition

Separately acquired intangible assets should normally be recognised as assets. IAS 38 assumes that the price paid to acquire an intangible asset separately usually will reflect expectations about the probability that the future economic benefits embodied in it will flow to the entity. In other words, the entity always expects there to be a flow of economic benefits, even if there is uncertainty about its timing or amount.[57] Therefore, when an entity separately acquires an intangible asset the standard:

- always considers future economic benefits to be probable;[58] and

- assumes that the cost of a separately acquired intangible asset can usually be measured reliably, especially in the case of a monetary purchase consideration.[59]

In its basis for conclusions on IAS 38, the IASB observed that 'this highlights a general inconsistency between the recognition criteria for assets and liabilities in the *Framework* (which states that an item meeting the definition of an element should be recognised only if it is probable that any future economic benefits associated with the item will flow to or from the entity, and the item can be measured reliably) and the fair value measurements required in, for example, a business combination. However, the Board concluded that the role of probability as a criterion for recognition in the *Framework* should be considered more generally as part of a forthcoming Concepts project.'[60] Indeed, in its work to determine new models for accounting for liabilities and for income taxes the IASB is proposing that uncertainty becomes a feature of measurement rather than of recognition.[61]

Not all external costs incurred to secure intangible rights automatically qualify for capitalisation as a separately acquired asset. An entity that subcontracts the development of intangible assets (e.g. development-and-supply contracts or R&D contracts) to other parties (its suppliers), must exercise judgement in determining whether it is acquiring an intangible asset or whether it is obtaining goods and services that are being used in the development of an intangible asset by the entity itself. For example, if the entity pays a supplier upfront or by milestone payments during the course of a project, it will not necessarily recognise an intangible asset on the basis of those payments. Only those costs that are incurred after it becomes probable that economic benefits are expected to flow to the entity will be part of the cost of an intangible asset. If a supplier is working on an internal project for the entity, costs can only be capitalised after the criteria have been met for recognising an internally developed intangible asset (see 2.3.6 below).

In determining whether a supplier is providing services to develop an internally generated intangible asset, it can be useful to consider the terms of the supply agreement, in particular whether the supplier is bearing a significant proportion of the risks associated with a failure of the project. For example, if the supplier is always compensated under a development-and-supply contract for development services and tool costs irrespective of the project's outcome, the entity on whose behalf the development is undertaken should account for those activities as its own.

B   Components of cost

The cost of a separately acquired intangible asset comprises:[62]

- its purchase price, including import duties and non-refundable purchase taxes, after deducting trade discounts and rebates; and
- any directly attributable cost of preparing the asset for its intended use, for example:[63]
  - costs of employee benefits arising directly from bringing the asset to its working condition;
  - professional fees arising directly from bringing the asset to its working condition; and
  - costs of testing whether the asset is functioning properly.

Capitalisation of expenditure ceases when the asset is in the condition necessary for it to be capable of operating in the manner intended by management.[64] This may well be before the date on which it is brought into use.

If payment for an intangible asset is deferred beyond normal credit terms, its cost is the cash price equivalent. The difference between this amount and the total payments is recognised as interest expense over the period of credit unless it is capitalised in accordance with IAS 23 – *Borrowing Costs*[65] (see Chapter 19).

C   Costs to be expensed

The following types of expenditure are not considered to be part of the cost of a separately acquired intangible asset:[66]

- costs of introducing a new product or service, including costs of advertising and promotional activities;
- costs of conducting business in a new location or with a new class of customer, including costs of staff training;
- administration and other general overhead costs;
- costs incurred in using or redeploying an intangible asset;
- costs incurred while an asset capable of operating in the manner intended by management has yet to be brought into use; and
- initial operating losses, such as those incurred while demand for the asset's output builds up.

Accordingly, start-up costs, training costs, advertising and promotional activities, and relocation or reorganisation costs should be expensed (see 2.3.8 below).

D   Incidental operations

When an entity generates income while it is developing or constructing an asset, the question arises as to whether this income should reduce the initial carrying value of the asset being developed or be recognised in profit or loss. IAS 38 states that when an entity engages in operations in connection with the development of an intangible asset that are 'not necessary to bring the asset to the condition necessary for it to be capable of operating in the manner intended by management', the entity should recognise the income and related expenses of incidental operations 'immediately in profit or loss ... in their respective classifications of income and expense'.[67] Such incidental operations can occur before or during the development activities. The example below illustrates these requirements.

Example 15.1:   Incidental operations

Entity A is pioneering a new process for the production of a certain type of chemical. Entity A will be able to patent the new production process. During the development phase, A is selling quantities of the chemical that are produced as a by-product of the development activities that are taking place. The expenditure incurred comprises labour, raw materials, assembly costs, costs of equipment and professional fees.

The revenues and costs associated with the production and sale of the chemical are accounted for in profit or loss for the period, while the development costs that meet the strict recognition criteria of IAS 38 are recognised as an intangible asset. Development costs that fail the IAS 38 recognition test are also expensed.

As the above example suggests, identifying the revenue from incidental operations will often be much easier than allocating costs to incidental operations. Furthermore, it will often be challenging to determine when exactly a project moves from the development phase into its start-up phase.

2.3.2   Acquisition as part of a business combination

For business combinations effected in financial periods commencing before 1 July 2009, the requirements of IFRS 3 (2007) apply. Chapter 9 at 2.5.2 discusses in detail the requirements of IFRS 3 (2007) regarding recognition and initial measurement of intangible assets acquired in a business combination. The requirements under IFRS 3, as revised in 2008, are discussed in Chapter 9 at 3.6.5. A summary of the requirements relating to intangible assets acquired in a business combination, including, where applicable, differences arising from the application of IFRS 3 (2007), is provided at A to E below.

The process of identifying intangible assets acquired in a business combination can be broken down into a number of steps as illustrated in the flow chart below, which reflects the recognition criteria in IAS 38 as discussed at 2.1.2 and 2.2.1 above.

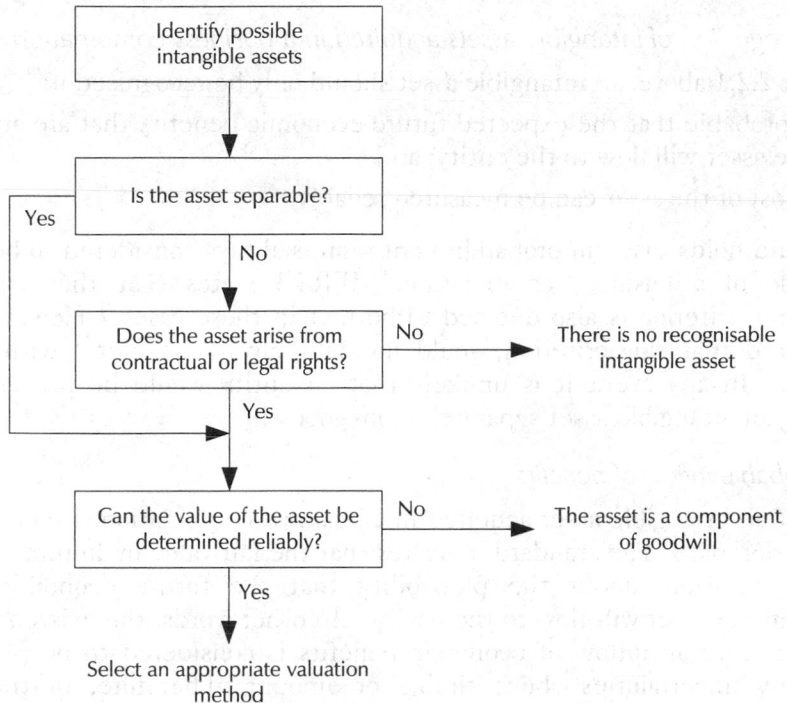

Identifying the intangible assets might involve, for example:

- reviewing the list of items acquired in a business combination that meet the definition of an intangible asset in IFRS 3 (see 2.3.2 B below);

- review of documents such as those related to the acquisition, other internal documents produced by the entity, public filings, press releases, analysts' reports, and other externally available documents; and

- comparing the acquired business to similar businesses and their intangible assets.

The intangible assets that are used will differ considerably between industries and between individual entities. Therefore, considerable expertise and careful judgement is required in determining whether there are intangible assets that need to be recognised and valued separately.

Both IFRS 3 (2007) and IFRS 3 give guidance in an Illustrative Example that provides a long (though not exhaustive) list of items acquired in a business combination that should be recognised separately from goodwill. This list includes, for example, the following types of intangible assets: trademarks, trade names, internet domain names, order or production backlog, customer lists, non-contractual customer relationships, films, music videos, television programmes, franchise agreements, unpatented technology and databases.[68]

A   Recognition of intangible assets acquired in a business combination

As noted at 2.2.1 above, an intangible asset should only be recognised if:[69]

'(a)   it is probable that the expected future economic benefits that are attributable to the asset will flow to the entity; and

(b)   the cost of the asset can be measured reliably.'

The standard holds that the probability criterion is always considered to be satisfied in the case of a business combination.[70] IFRS 3 states that the reliability of measurement criterion is also deemed to be met in these cases.[71] However IFRS 3 (2007) stated that this criterion would normally always be met,[72] with very few exceptions.[73] In any event it is unlikely that an entity would be prevented from recognising an intangible asset separately from goodwill.

I   Probable inflow of benefits

The cost of an intangible asset acquired in a business combination is its fair value at the acquisition date. The standard indicates that the fair value of an intangible asset reflects expectations about the probability that the future economic benefits embodied in the asset will flow to the entity.[74] In other words, the existence of a fair value means that an inflow of economic benefits is considered to be probable, in spite of any uncertainties about timing or amount. Therefore, in the case of intangible assets acquired in a business combination, the probability recognition criterion is always considered to be satisfied.[75]

II   Reliability of measurement

Under IFRS 3 the cost of the intangible asset acquired in a business combination can always be measured reliably. IFRS 3 (2007) allowed that there were a few circumstances in which this might not be the case.

In developing IAS 38, the IASB was presented with numerous examples of acquired intangible assets whose fair value could not be measured reliably.[76] These included many forms of permit allocated by local authorities. It is often a feature of such assets that the entity has legal rights, they are clearly valuable but they cannot legally be bought and sold other than as part of the business as a whole.[77] Nevertheless, the Board remained concerned that entities might avoid recognising intangible assets separately from goodwill by arguing that their cost could not be measured reliably.[78] Therefore, the standard as used in business combinations to which IFRS 3 (2007) applies is quite restrictive and states that 'the only circumstances in which it might not be possible to measure reliably the fair value of an intangible asset acquired in a business combination are when the intangible asset arises from legal or other contractual rights and either:[79]

(a)   is not separable; or

(b)   is separable, but there is no history or evidence of exchange transactions for the same or similar assets, and otherwise estimating fair value would be dependent on immeasurable variables.'

In developing IFRS 3, the Board concluded that the needs of users were better served by recognising intangible assets, on the basis of an estimate of fair value, rather than subsuming them in goodwill, even if a significant degree of judgement is required to estimate fair value.[80] Accordingly, if an asset acquired in a business combination is separable or arises from contractual or other legal rights, sufficient information exists to measure reliably the fair value of the asset. Thus, the requirement in 2.2.1 above for reliable measurement of cost is always considered to be satisfied for intangible assets acquired in business combinations.[81]

III   *Identifiability in relation to an intangible asset acquired in a business combination*

As noted at 2.1.2A above, an intangible asset needs to be identifiable to distinguish it from goodwill and the two elements of identifiability are the existence of contractual or other legal rights or separability. Separability means that the asset is capable of being sold, transferred, licensed, rented or exchanged, without having to dispose of the whole business. This includes transactions that could only be achieved by combining the intangible asset with a related contract, physical asset or liability. Also, an intangible is considered to be separable regardless of whether the entity intends to sell or otherwise transfer it.[82]

The IASB recognised that an intangible asset acquired in a business combination might be separable, but only together with a related contract, identifiable asset or liability. In such cases, IAS 38 requires the acquirer to recognise the intangible asset separately from goodwill, but together with the related contract, asset or liability.[83]

The standard notes that the acquirer may recognise a group of complementary intangible assets as a single asset provided the individual assets in the group have similar useful lives. For example, the terms 'brand' and 'brand name' are often used as synonyms for trademarks and other marks. However, 'brands' are regarded as general marketing terms that are typically used to refer to a group of complementary assets such as a trademark (or service mark) and its related trade name, formulas, recipes and technological expertise.[84] Heineken, for example, combines the carrying amount of brands and customer bases acquired in business combinations.

Extract 15.2: Heineken N.V. (2007)

Notes to the consolidated financial statements [extract]
3. Significant accounting policies [extract]
(g) Intangible assets [extract]
(ii) Brands

Brands acquired, separately, or as part of a business combination, are capitalised as part of a brand portfolio if the portfolio meets the definition of an intangible asset and the recognition criteria are satisfied. Brand portfolios acquired as part of a business combination include the customer base related to the brand because it is assumed that brands have no value without a customer base and vice versa. Brand portfolios acquired as part of a business combination are valued at fair value based on the royalty relief method. Brands and brand portfolios acquired separately are measured at cost. Brands and brand portfolios are amortised on a straight-line basis over their estimated useful life.

IFRS 3 contains additional guidance on the application of the contractual-legal and separability criteria which indicates how far the IASB expects entities to go to ensure that intangible assets acquired in a business combination are shown separately from goodwill.

- Contractual-legal criterion

An intangible asset that arises from contractual or other legal rights is recognised separately from goodwill even if it is not transferable or separable from the acquiree or from other rights and obligations. For example:[85]

(a)   an acquiree leases a manufacturing facility under an operating lease that has terms that are favourable relative to market terms. The lease terms explicitly prohibit transfer of the lease (through either sale or sublease). The amount by which the lease terms are favourable compared with the terms of current market transactions for the same or similar items is an intangible asset that meets the contractual-legal criterion for recognition separately from goodwill, even though the acquirer cannot sell or otherwise transfer the lease contract.

(b)   an acquiree owns and operates a nuclear power plant. The licence to operate that power plant is an intangible asset that meets the contractual-legal criterion for recognition separately from goodwill, even if the acquirer cannot sell or transfer it separately from the acquired power plant. However, IFRS 3 goes on to say that an acquirer may recognise the fair value of the operating licence and the fair value of the power plant as a single asset for financial reporting purposes if the useful lives of those assets are similar.

(c)   an acquiree owns a technology patent. It has licensed that patent to others for their exclusive use outside the domestic market, receiving a specified percentage of future foreign revenue in exchange. Both the technology patent and the related licence agreement meet the contractual-legal criterion for recognition separately from goodwill even if selling or exchanging the patent and the related licence agreement separately from one another would not be practical.

- Separability criterion

IFRS 3 emphasises that the separability criterion means that an acquired intangible asset is *capable* of being separated or divided from the acquiree, regardless of the intentions of the acquirer. It adds that an acquired intangible asset is recognised separately from goodwill if there is evidence of exchange transactions for that type of asset or an asset of a similar type, even if those transactions are infrequent and regardless of whether the acquirer is involved in them. For example, customer and subscriber lists are frequently licensed and thus merit recognition as an intangible asset. Even if an acquiree believes its customer lists have characteristics different from other lists, the fact that such customer lists are frequently licensed generally means that an asset should be recognised separately from goodwill. However, a customer list acquired in a business combination would not meet the separability criterion if the terms of confidentiality or other agreements prohibit an entity from selling, leasing or otherwise exchanging information about its customers.[86]

An intangible asset that is not individually separable from the acquiree or combined entity should still be recognised separately from goodwill if it could be separable in combination with a related contract, identifiable asset or liability. For example an acquiree owns a registered trademark and documented but unpatented technical expertise used to manufacture the trademarked product. The entity could not transfer ownership of the trademark without everything else necessary for the new owner to produce an identical product or service. Because the unpatented technical expertise must be transferred if the related trademark is sold, it is separable and not included in the carrying value of goodwill.[87]

Accordingly, the emphasis in IFRS 3 is that, in effect, it does not matter whether assets meeting the definition of an intangible asset have to be combined with other intangible assets, incorporated into the carrying value of a complementary item of property, plant and equipment with a similar useful life or included in the assessment of the fair value of a related liability. The important requirement is that the intangible asset is recognised separately from goodwill.

B   Examples of intangible assets acquired in a business combination

Both IFRS 3 and IFRS 3 (2007) provide a long list of examples of items acquired in a business combination that meet the definition of an intangible asset and should therefore be recognised separately from goodwill. The only material difference between the two standards is that, as noted above, under IFRS 3 (2007) recognition is dependent on their fair values being capable of reliable measurement. The list is not intended to be exhaustive and other items acquired in a business combination might still meet the definition of an intangible asset.[88]

The table below summarises the items included in the IASB's Illustrative Example. Reference should be made to the Illustrative Example itself for any further explanation about some of these items.

Intangible assets arising from contractual or other legal rights (regardless of being separable)	Other intangible assets that are separable
Marketing-related	
– Trademarks, trade names, service marks, collective marks and certification marks – Internet domain names – Trade dress (unique colour, shape or package design) – Newspaper mastheads – Non-competition agreements	
Customer-related	
– Order or production backlogs – Customer contracts and the related customer relationships	– Customer lists – Non-contractual customer relationships
Artistic-related	
– Plays, operas and ballets – Books, magazines, newspapers and other literary works – Musical works such as compositions, song lyrics and advertising jingles – Pictures and photographs – Video and audiovisual material, including films, music videos and television programmes	

Contract-based
- Licensing, royalty and standstill agreements
- Advertising, construction, management, service or supply contracts
- Lease agreements
- Construction permits
- Franchise agreements
- Operating and broadcast rights
- Use rights such as drilling, water, air, mineral, timber-cutting and route authorities
- Servicing contracts such as mortgage servicing contracts
- Employment contracts that are beneficial contracts from the perspective of the employer because the pricing of those contracts is below their current market value

Technology-based
- Patented technology
- Computer software and mask works
- Trade secrets such as secret formulas, processes or recipes
- Unpatented technology
- Databases

It is clear from the table above that the IASB envisages a wide range of items meeting the definition of an intangible asset, and therefore being recognised in a business combination separately from goodwill.

Further details on the requirements relating to intangible assets acquired as part of a business combination effected before 1 July 2009 are covered in Chapter 9 at 2.5.2. For business combinations to which IFRS 3 applies, see Chapter 9 at 3.6.5.

C   Measuring fair value of intangible assets acquired in a business combination

I   Reliability of measurement

As discussed at 2.3.2A above, IFRS 3 assumes that there will always be sufficient information to measure reliably the fair value of an intangible asset acquired in a business combination if it is separable or arises from contractual or other legal rights.[89] Under IFRS 3 (2007), there is a rebuttable presumption in the standard that the asset's fair value can be measured reliably if it has a finite useful life.[90]

II   Hierarchy of reliable sources of evidence of fair value

The standard sets out a hierarchy of sources for estimating fair value, stating that quoted market prices in an active market provide the most reliable estimate of the fair value of an intangible asset and that the appropriate market price is usually the current bid price. If current bid prices are unavailable, the price of the most recent similar transaction may provide a basis from which to estimate fair value, provided that there has not been a significant change in economic circumstances between the transaction date and the date at which the asset's fair value is estimated.[91]

As the standard itself notes, although intangible assets are bought and sold, it is uncommon for an active market to exist for intangible assets. The value of many intangible assets such as brands, newspaper mastheads, music and film publishing rights, patents or trademarks depends on the fact that they are unique. Sale and purchase contracts are negotiated between individual buyers and sellers and transactions are relatively infrequent. Accordingly an active market cannot exist for many of the intangible assets that IFRS 3 and IAS 38 require an acquirer to recognise as part of the allocation process.[92] Therefore the standard requires that in the absence of an active market, intangible assets are valued on a basis that reflects the amounts the acquirer would have paid for the assets in an arm's length transaction between knowledgeable willing parties, based on the best information available. In determining this amount, an entity should consider recent transactions for similar assets.[93] However, since many intangible assets are unique by nature, the objective in considering recent transactions for similar assets is to determine an appropriate valuation method for that type of asset rather than to apply the actual price agreed in the observed recent transaction. The IASB has clarified this point in an amendment to IAS 38 contained in its Improvements to IFRSs, issued in April 2009. The amendment adds an example in which an entity is looking to value an intangible asset by reference to multiples of revenue or profit and considers current market transactions for similar assets to determine an appropriate multiple to apply.[94]

IAS 38 acknowledges that entities that are involved in the purchase and sale of intangible assets may have developed techniques for estimating their fair values indirectly. Therefore, it allows these techniques to be used for initial measurement of an intangible asset acquired in a business combination if their objective is to estimate fair value and if they reflect current transactions and practices in the industry to which the asset belongs. These techniques include, when appropriate:[95]

(a)   applying multiples reflecting current market transactions to indicators that drive the profitability of the asset (such as revenue, market shares and operating profit) or to the royalty stream that could be obtained from licensing the intangible asset to another party in an arm's length transaction (as in the 'relief from royalty' approach); or

(b)   discounting estimated future net cash flows from the asset.

In its 2009 Improvements to IFRSs, the IASB replaced (a) above with 'estimating the costs the entity avoids by owning the intangible asset and not needing:[96]

(i)   to licence it from another party in an arm's length transaction (as in the "relief from royalty" approach, using discounted net cash flows); or

(ii)   to recreate or replace it (as in the cost approach)'.

Whilst these amendments apply prospectively for annual periods beginning on or after 1 July 2009,[97] their effect is to clarify rather than revise the treatment intended by the Board.

The issues underlying the initial measurement of these intangible assets are discussed further at 3.7.1 below.

D   *Customer relationship intangible assets acquired in a business combination*

Further guidance on customer relationships acquired in a business combination is provided by IFRS 3 (2007) and IFRS 3 in the Illustrative Examples (which form the basis of the example below). These demonstrate how the contractual-legal and separability criteria, discussed at 2.1.2 above, interact in the recognition of acquired customer relationships.[98] As noted above, where the examples are considered in the context of a business combination accounted for under IFRS 3 (2007), recognition of the intangible asset separately from goodwill also depends upon the acquirer being able to reliably measure its fair value.

Example 15.2:   Customer relationship intangible assets acquired in a business combination

Supply agreement

Acquirer Company (AC) acquires Target Company (TC) in a business combination. TC has a five-year agreement to supply goods to Customer. Both TC and AC believe that Customer will renew the supply agreement at the end of the current contract. The supply agreement is not separable.

The supply agreement (whether cancellable or not) meets the contractual-legal criterion for identification as an intangible asset, and therefore is recognised separately from goodwill. Additionally, because TC establishes its relationship with Customer through a contract, not only the agreement but also TC's customer relationship with Customer meets the contractual-legal criterion for identification as an intangible asset. Therefore, the customer relationship intangible asset is also recognised separately from goodwill.

Sporting goods and electronics

AC acquires TC in a business combination. TC manufactures goods in two distinct lines of business: sporting goods and electronics. Customer purchases both sporting goods and electronics from TC. TC has a contract with Customer to be its exclusive provider of sporting goods, but has no contract for the supply of electronics to Customer. Both TC and AC believe that there is only one overall customer relationship between TC and Customer.

The contract to be Customer's exclusive supplier of sporting goods (whether cancellable or not) meets the contractual-legal criterion for identification as an intangible asset, and is therefore recognised separately from goodwill. Additionally, because TC establishes its relationship with Customer through a contract, the customer relationship with Customer meets the contractual-legal criterion for identification as an intangible asset. Because TC has only one customer relationship with Customer, the fair value of that relationship incorporates assumptions regarding TC's relationship with Customer related to both sporting goods and electronics.

However, if AC determined that there were separate customer relationships with Customer – one for sporting goods and another for electronics – it would have to assess whether the customer relationship for electronics meets the separability criterion for identification as an intangible asset.

Order backlog and recurring customers

AC acquires TC in a business combination on 31 December 2010. TC does business with its customers solely through purchase and sales orders. At 31 December 2010, TC has a backlog of customer purchase orders from 60 per cent of its customers, all of whom are recurring customers. The other 40 per cent of TC's customers are also recurring customers. However, as of 31 December 2010, TC has no open purchase orders or other contracts with those customers.

The purchase orders from 60 per cent of TC's customers (whether cancellable or not) meet the contractual-legal criterion. Additionally, because TC has established its relationship with 60 per cent of its customers through contracts, not only the purchase orders but also TC's customer relationships also meet the contractual-legal criterion for identification as an intangible asset.

Because TC has a practice of establishing contracts with the remaining 40 per cent of its customers, its relationship with those customers also arises through contractual rights, and therefore meets the contractual-legal criterion for identification as an intangible asset, even though TC does not have contracts with those customers at 31 December 2010.

Motor insurance contracts

AC acquires TC, an Insurer, in a business combination. TC has a portfolio of one-year motor insurance contracts that are cancellable by policyholders.

Because TC establishes its relationships with policyholders through insurance contracts, the customer relationship with policyholders meets the contractual-legal criterion for identification as an intangible asset. IAS 36 and IAS 38 apply to the customer relationship intangible asset.

Even with this guidance, the IFRIC received a request in 2008 to add to its agenda an item concerning the circumstances in which a non-contractual customer relationship arises in a business combination.

In considering this request, the IFRIC acknowledged that IFRS 3 makes a distinction between contractual and non-contractual customer relationships. Contractual customer relationships such as those described above are always recognised separately from goodwill as they meet the contractual-legal criterion. However, non-contractual customer relationships (e.g. customer lists) are recognised only if they are separable. Consequently, determining whether a relationship is contractual is critical to identifying and measuring customer relationship intangible assets and different conclusions could result in substantially different accounting outcomes. The staff's survey of IFRIC members indicated that diversity exists in practice regarding which customer relationships have a contractual basis and which do not. In addition, valuation experts may be taking different views, which could also be contributing to diversity in this area.[99]

As it drew together the guidance already available, the IFRIC noted that the IFRS Glossary of Terms defines the term 'contract'[100] and that application guidance in IFRS 3 considers the recognition of intangible assets and the different criteria related to whether they are established on the basis of a contract (see 2.3.2 A above). The IFRIC also noted that paragraph IE28 in the illustrative examples accompanying IFRS 3 highlights how a customer relationship is deemed to exist if on the one hand the entity has information about the customer and regular contact with it and on the other that the customer can make direct contact with the entity. Regardless of whether any contracts are in place at the acquisition date, the customer relationship meets the contractual-legal criterion for recognition as an intangible asset if an entity has a practice of establishing contracts with its customers. The paragraph also states that a customer relationship 'may also arise through means other than contracts, such as through regular contact by sales or service representatives.'[101] The IFRIC concluded on the basis of the guidance set out above that the existence of contracts at the acquisition date and information about a customer's prior purchases are more important in valuing a customer relationship than in determining whether an intangible asset is recognised.[102]

Having reviewed the explicit guidance in IFRS 3, the IFRIC decided it was not possible to develop an Interpretation reflecting its conclusion. Nevertheless, given widespread confusion in practice on the issue, the IFRIC decided that the matter should be referred to the IASB and the FASB with a recommendation to review and amend IFRS 3 by:[103]

- removing the distinction between 'contractual' and 'non-contractual' customer-related intangible assets recognised in a business combination; and

- reviewing the indicators that identify the existence of a customer relationship in paragraph IE28 of IFRS 3 and including them in the standard.

E   In-process research and development

The term 'in-process research and development' (IPR&D) refers to those identifiable intangible assets resulting from research and development activities that are acquired in a business combination. An acquirer should recognise IPR&D separately from goodwill if the project meets the definition of an intangible asset and its fair value can be measured reliably. This is the case when the IPR&D project:

'(a)   meets the definition of an asset; and

(b)   is identifiable, i.e. is separable or arises from contractual or other legal rights.'[104]

Any subsequent expenditure incurred on the project after its acquisition should be accounted for in accordance with the general rules in IAS 38 on internally generated intangible assets which are discussed at 2.3.6 below.[105] In summary, this means that the subsequent expenditure is accounted for as follows:[106]

- research expenditure is recognised as an expense when incurred;
- development expenditure that does not satisfy the criteria for recognition as an intangible asset is recognised as an expense when incurred; and
- development expenditure that satisfies the recognition criteria is added to the carrying value of the acquired in-process research or development project.

Critics of the above approach have pointed out in the past that it results in some IPR&D projects acquired in business combinations being treated differently from similar projects started internally. The IASB acknowledged this criticism but decided that it could not support a treatment that allowed acquired IPR&D to be subsumed within goodwill and it would not extend the scope of its project to revise IAS 38 to reconsider the treatment of projects started internally.[107] Until the Board finds time to address this issue, users of financial statements will have to live with the problem that an asset can be recognised for acquired research and development projects despite the fact that the entity might recognise as an expense the costs of projects at a similar stage of development but started internally.

The implication is that if an acquired project never achieves the recognition criteria for an internal project, the asset recognised for in-process research and development expenditure will ultimately be impaired, although it may be that this impairment will not arise until the entity is satisfied that the project will not continue. However, since it is an intangible asset not yet available for use, such an evaluation cannot be significantly delayed as the entity will need to test the asset for impairment annually by comparing its carrying amount with its recoverable amount (see Chapter 18 at 3.5).[108] Any impairment loss will be reflected in the entity's income statement as a post-acquisition event.

2.3.3   Acquisition by way of government grant

An intangible asset may sometimes be acquired free of charge, or for nominal consideration, by way of a government grant. Examples of intangible assets that governments frequently allocate to entities include airport-landing rights, licences to operate radio or television stations, emission rights (see 3.3 below), import licences or quotas, or rights to access other restricted resources.[109]

Government grants should be accounted for under IAS 20 – *Accounting for Government Grants and Disclosure of Government Assistance* – which permits initial recognition of intangible assets received at either fair value or a nominal amount.[110]

This represents an accounting policy choice for an entity that should be applied consistently to all intangible assets acquired by way of government grant.

It is not possible to measure reliably the fair value of all of the permits allocated by governments because they may have been allocated for nil consideration, may not be transferable and may only be bought and sold as part of a business. Some of the issues surrounding the determining fair values in the absence of an active market were considered at 2.3.2 C above. On the other hand, other allocated permits such as milk quotas are freely traded and therefore do have a readily ascertainable fair value.

2.3.4   Exchanges of assets

Asset exchanges are transactions that have challenged standard-setters for a number of years. For example, an entity might swap certain intangible assets that it does not require or is no longer allowed to use for those of a counterparty that has other surplus assets. For example, it is not uncommon for airlines and media groups to exchange landing slots and newspaper titles, respectively, to meet demands of competition authorities. The question arises whether such transactions should be recorded at cost or fair value, which would give rise to a gain in the circumstances where the fair value of the incoming asset exceeds the carrying amount of the outgoing one. Equally, it is possible that a transaction could be arranged with no real commercial substance, solely to boost apparent profits.

Three separate international accounting standards contain virtually identical guidance on accounting for exchanges of assets: IAS 16 (see Chapter 16), IAS 40 – *Investment Property* (see Chapter 17) and IAS 38.

A   Measurement of assets exchanged

IAS 38 requires all acquisitions of intangible assets in exchange for non-monetary assets, or a combination of monetary and non-monetary assets, to be measured at fair value. The acquired intangible asset is measured at fair value unless:[111]

(a)   the exchange transaction lacks commercial substance; or

(b)   the fair value of neither the asset received nor the asset given up is reliably measurable.

The acquired asset is measured in this way even if an entity cannot immediately derecognise the asset given up. If an entity is able to determine reliably the fair value of either the asset received or the asset given up, then it uses the fair value of the asset given up to measure cost unless the fair value of the asset received is more clearly evident.[112] If the fair value of neither the asset given up, nor the asset received can be measured reliably the acquired intangible asset is measured at the carrying amount of the asset given up.[113]

B   Commercial substance

The commercial substance test for asset exchanges was put in place to prevent gains being recognised in income when the transaction had no 'discernable effect on the entity's economics'.[114] The commercial substance of an exchange is to be determined by forecasting and comparing the future cash flows budgeted to be generated by the incoming and outgoing assets. For commercial substance to be present there must be a significant difference between the two forecasts. The standard sets out this requirement as follows:[115]

> 'An entity determines whether an exchange transaction has commercial substance by considering the extent to which its future cash flows are expected to change as a result of the transaction. An exchange transaction has commercial substance if:
>
> (a)   the configuration (i.e. risk, timing and amount) of the cash flows of the asset received differs from the configuration of the cash flows of the asset transferred; or
>
> (b)   the entity-specific value of the portion of the entity's operations affected by the transaction changes as a result of the exchange; and
>
> (c)   the difference in (a) or (b) is significant relative to the fair value of the assets exchanged.'

IAS 38 defines the 'entity-specific value' of an intangible asset as 'the present value of the cash flows an entity expects to arise from the continuing use of an asset and from its disposal at the end of its useful life or expects to incur when settling a liability'.[116] In determining whether an exchange transaction has commercial substance, the entity-specific value of the portion of the entity's operations affected by the transaction should reflect post-tax cash flows.[117] This is somewhat different from the calculation of an asset's value in use under IAS 36 (see Chapter 18), as it uses a post-tax discount rate based on the entity's own risks rather than IAS 36's use of the pre-tax rate that the market would apply to a similar asset.

It should be noted that the above commercial substance test relies on a prediction of future cash flows in the determination of the carrying amount of some intangible assets. The standard states that 'the fair value of an intangible asset for which comparable market transactions do not exist is reliably measurable if (a) the variability in the range of reasonable fair value estimates is not significant for that asset or (b) the probabilities of the various estimates within the range can be reasonably assessed and used in estimating fair value.'[118] The standard allows an entity to forego the effort of performing these detailed calculations when the outcome would be clear in advance[119] – perhaps if it is obvious that there is no 'commercial substance' in this very restricted sense.

2.3.5   *Internally generated goodwill*

IAS 38 explicitly prohibits the recognition of internally generated goodwill as an asset,[120] because internally generated goodwill is neither separable nor does it arise from contractual or legal rights and, as such, is not an identifiable resource controlled by the entity that can be measured reliably at cost.[121] It therefore does not meet the definition of an intangible asset under the standard or that of an asset under the IASB's *Framework*. The standard maintains that the difference between the market value of an entity and the carrying amount of its identifiable net assets at any time may capture a range of factors that affect the value of the entity, but that such differences do not represent the cost of intangible assets controlled by the entity.[122]

2.3.6   *Internally generated intangible assets*

The IASB recognises that it may be difficult to decide whether an internally generated intangible asset qualifies for recognition because of problems in:[123]

(a)   confirming whether and when there is an identifiable asset that will generate expected future economic benefits; and

(b)   determining the cost of the asset reliably, especially in cases where the cost of generating an intangible asset internally cannot be distinguished from the cost of maintaining or enhancing the entity's internally generated goodwill or of running day-to-day operations.

To avoid the inappropriate recognition of an asset, IAS 38 requires that internally generated intangible assets are not only tested against the general requirements for recognition and initial measurement, but also meet criteria which confirm that the related internal development project is at a sufficiently advanced stage, is economically viable and includes only directly attributable costs.[124] Those criteria comprise detailed guidance on accounting for intangible assets in the research phase (see A below), the development phase (see B below) and on components of cost of an internally generated intangible asset (see 2.3.7 below).

If the general recognition and initial measurement requirements are met, the entity classifies the generation of the internally developed asset into a research phase and a development phase.[125] The standard defines research and development activities as follows:

Research is original and planned investigation undertaken with the prospect of gaining new scientific or technical knowledge and understanding.[126]

The standard gives the following examples of research activities:[127]

(a)   activities aimed at obtaining new knowledge;

(b)   the search for, evaluation and final selection of, applications of research findings or other knowledge;

(c)   the search for alternatives for materials, devices, products, processes, systems or services; and

(d)   the formulation, design, evaluation and final selection of possible alternatives for new or improved materials, devices, products, processes, systems or services.

Development is the application of research findings or other knowledge to a plan or design for the production of new or substantially improved materials, devices, products, processes, systems or services before the start of commercial production or use.[128]

The standard gives the following examples of development activities:[129]

(a)   the design, construction and testing of pre-production or pre-use prototypes and models;

(b)   the design of tools, jigs, moulds and dies involving new technology;

(c)   the design, construction and operation of a pilot plant that is not of a scale economically feasible for commercial production; and

(d)   the design, construction and testing of a chosen alternative for new or improved materials, devices, products, processes, systems or services.

A   Research phase

An entity cannot recognise an intangible asset arising from research or from the research phase of an internal project. Instead, any expenditure on research or the research phase of an internal project should be expensed as incurred because the entity cannot demonstrate that an intangible asset exists that will generate probable future economic benefits.[130]

B   Development phase

An intangible asset arising from development or from the development phase of an internal project should be recognised as an internally generated intangible if, and only if, an entity can demonstrate all of the following:[131]

(a)   the technical feasibility of completing the intangible asset so that it will be available for use or sale;

(b)   its intention to complete the intangible asset and use or sell it;

(c)   its ability to use or sell the intangible asset;

(d)   how the intangible asset will generate probable future economic benefits. Among other things, the entity can demonstrate the existence of a market for the output of the intangible asset or the intangible asset itself or, if it is to be used internally, the usefulness of the intangible asset;

(e)   the availability of adequate technical, financial and other resources to complete the development and to use or sell the intangible asset; and

(f)   its ability to measure reliably the expenditure attributable to the intangible asset during its development.

The standard requires recognition of a qualifying intangible asset in the development phase because the development phase of a project is further advanced than the research phase and an entity may be able to demonstrate that the asset will generate probable future economic benefits.[132]

It may be challenging to obtain objective evidence on each of the above conditions because:

- condition (b) relies on management intent;

- conditions (c), (e) and (f) are entity-specific, i.e. whether development expenditure meets any of these conditions depends both on the nature of the development activity itself and the financial position of the entity; and

- condition (d) above is more restrictive than is immediately apparent because the entity needs to assess the probable future economic benefits using the principles in IAS 36, i.e. using discounted cash flows. If the asset will generate economic benefits only in conjunction with other assets, the entity should apply the concept of cash-generating units.[133] The requirements of the IAS 36 are discussed in Chapter 18.

IAS 38 indicates that evidence may be available in the form of:

- a business plan showing the technical, financial and other resources needed and the entity's ability to secure those resources;[134]

- a lender's indication of its willingness to fund the plan confirming the availability of external finance;[135] and

- detailed project information demonstrating that an entity's costing systems can measure reliably the cost of generating an intangible asset internally, such as salary and other expenditure incurred in securing copyrights or licences or developing computer software.[136]

In any case, an entity should maintain books and records that allow it to prove whether it meets the conditions set out by IAS 38.

Certain types of product (e.g. pharmaceuticals, aircraft and electrical equipment) require regulatory approval before they can be sold. Regulatory approval is not one of the criteria for recognition under IAS 38. Therefore, when regulatory approval for a product under development has not yet been obtained, an entity would not necessarily be prohibited from capitalising its development costs. However, in the case of a totally new product, the absence of regulatory approval may indicate significant uncertainty around the possible future economic benefits. The practical impact of regulatory approval on pharmaceuticals is shown in Extract 15.4 below.

The standard does not define the terms 'research phase' and 'development phase' but explains that they should be interpreted more broadly than 'research' and 'development' which it does define.[137] The features characterising the research phase have less to do with what activities are performed, but relate more to an inability to demonstrate at that time that an intangible asset exists that will generate probable future benefits.[138] This means that the research phase may include activities that do not necessarily meet the definition of 'research'. For example, the research phase for IAS 38 purposes may extend to the whole period preceding a product launch, regardless of the fact that activities that would otherwise characterise development are taking place at the same time, because certain features that would mean the project has entered its development phase are still absent (such as confirming an ability to use or sell the asset; demonstrating sufficient market demand for a product; or uncertainty regarding the source of funds to complete the project). As a result, an entity might not be able to distinguish the research phase from the development phase of an internal project to create an intangible asset, in which case it should treat the expenditure on that project as if it were incurred in the research phase only and recognise an expense accordingly.[139] It also means that the development phase may include activities that do not necessarily meet the definition of 'development'. The example below explains how an entity would apply these rules in practice.

Example 15.3:   Research phase and development phase under IAS 38

Entity K is working on a project to create a database containing images and articles from newspapers around the world, which it intends to sell to customers over the internet. K has identified the following stages in its project:

(a)   Research stage – gaining the technical knowledge necessary to transfer images to customers and assessing whether the project is feasible from a technological point of view;

(b)   Development stage – performing market analysis to identify potential demand and customer requirements; developing the ability to exploit the image capture technology including configuration of the required database software and acquiring the required data to populate the database, designing the customer interface and testing a prototype of the system; and

(c)   Production stage – before and after the commercial launch of the service, debugging the system and improving functionality to service higher user volumes; updating and managing the database to ensure its currency.

The above can be summarised as follows:

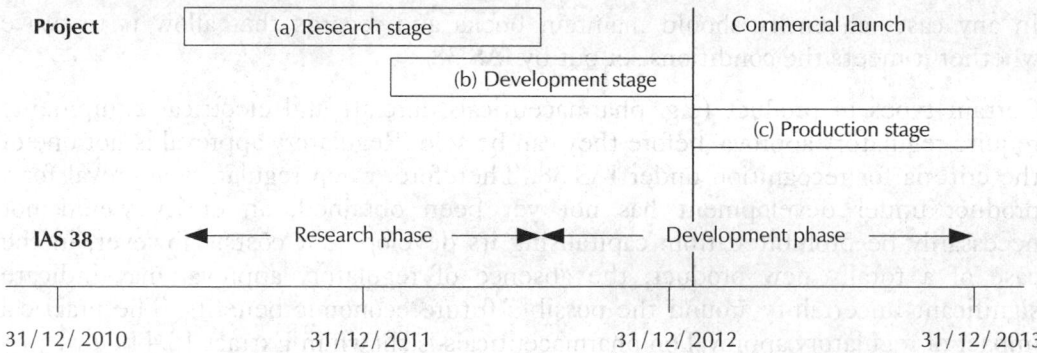

The activities in the research stage included under (a) meet the definition of research under IAS 38 and would be accounted for as part of the research phase of the project.

The activities in the development stage included under (b) meet the definition of development under IAS 38. However, whilst K has started to plan the commercial exploitation of its image and data capture technology, it will not be immediately apparent that the project is economically viable. Until this point is reached, for example when the entity has established there is demand for the database and it is likely that a working prototype of the system will be available, the development activities cannot be distinguished from the research activities taking place at the same time. Accordingly, the initial development activities are accounted for as if they were incurred in the research phase. Only once it becomes possible to demonstrate the existence of an intangible asset that will generate future income streams, can project expenditure be accounted for under IAS 38 as part of the development phase.

There may be a period after the commercial launch of the service that would still be accounted for as part of the development phase. For example, activities to improve functionality to deal with higher actual customer volumes could constitute development. This does not necessarily mean that K can capitalise all this expenditure because it needs pass the double hurdle of:

- the presumption in paragraph 20 of IAS 38 that 'there are no additions to such an asset or replacements of part of it' (see 2.2.3 above); and

- the six criteria in paragraph 57 for recognition of development costs (see above).

Activity to ensure that the database is up-to-date is a routine process that does not involve major innovations or new technologies. Therefore, these activities in the production stage do not meet the definition of 'research' or 'development' and the related costs are recognised as an expense.

As the above example illustrates, the guidance in IAS 38 seems to take a somewhat out-of-date view as to how internally generated intangible assets are created and managed in practice, as well as what types of internally generated intangible assets there can be. It requires activity to be classified into research and development phases, but this methodology does not easily fit with intangible assets that are created for use by the entity itself. The standard therefore ignores the everyday reality for software companies, television production companies, newspapers and data vendors that produce intangible assets in industrial-scale routine processes.

Many of the intangible assets produced in routine processes – e.g. software, television programmes, newspaper content and databases – meet the recognition criteria in the standard, but no specific guidance is available that could help an entity in dealing with the practical problems that arise when accounting for them.

On the one hand the standard requires recognition of an intangible asset arising from development (or the development phase of an internal project), while on the other hand it imposes stringent conditions that restrict recognition. For an entity that wants to recognise development expenditure as an intangible asset these tests create a sensible balance, ensuring that the entity does not recognise unrecoverable costs as an asset. It should be noted that the (then) IASC considered the argument that 'comparability of financial statements will not be achieved ... because the judgement involved in determining whether it is probable that future economic benefits will flow from internally generated intangible assets is too subjective to result in similar accounting under similar circumstances',[140] but ultimately decided that there 'should be no difference between the requirement for (a) intangible assets that are acquired externally and (b) internally generated intangible assets, whether they arise from development activities or other types of activities'.[141] They concluded that the recognition criteria are met implicitly for acquired intangible assets and, therefore, it is for the entity to demonstrate explicitly that they are met in the case of the internally generated assets.[142]

Extract 15.3 shows how Air Liquide navigates the distinction between the definitions of research and development and the broader interpretation applied for determining whether projects are classified as research phase or development phase activities in designing its accounting policies for research and development costs and for the treatment of other internally generated intangible assets.

Extract 15.3: L'Air Liquide S.A. (2007)

Accounting principles

Accounting policies [extract]

5.   Non-current assets [extract]

B.   RESEARCH AND DEVELOPMENT EXPENDITURES

Research and Development expenditures include all costs relating to the scientific and technical activities, patent work, education and training necessary to insure the development, manufacturing, start-up, and commercialization of new or improved products or processes.

According to IAS38, development costs shall be capitalized if and only if the Group can meet the following criteria:

- the intangible asset is clearly identified and the related costs are individualized and reliably monitored;
- the technical feasibility of completing the intangible asset so that it will be available for use or sale;
- there is a clear intention to complete the intangible asset and use or sell it;
- its ability to use or sell the intangible asset arising from the project;
- how the intangible asset will generate probable future economic benefits;
- the availability of adequate technical, financial and other resources to complete the development and to use or sell the intangible asset.

Research expenditures are recognized as an expense when incurred.

The Group did not capitalize development expenditures as it as it considers that the conditions required in IFRS for the capitalization of development costs were not met, since expenditures do not systematically result in the completion of an intangible asset that will be available for use or sale. As a result, the Development costs incurred by the Group in the course of its Research and Development projects are expensed.

C.   INTERNALLY GENERATED INTANGIBLE ASSETS

Internally generated intangible assets primarily include the development costs of information management systems. These costs are capitalized only if they satisfy the criteria defined by IAS38 and described above.

Internal and external development costs on management information systems arising from the development phase are capitalized. Significant maintenance and improvement costs are added to the initial cost of assets if they specifically meet the capitalization criteria.

Internally generated intangible assets are amortized over their useful lives.

The extract below illustrates some of the difficulty in applying the IAS 38 recognition criteria for development costs in the pharmaceutical industry. Typically, technical and economic feasibility are established very late in the process of developing a new product, which means that usually only a small proportion of the development costs is capitalised (see 3.2 below).

Extract 15.4: Merck KGaA (2007)

Accounting Policies [extract]

Research and development

The breakdown of research and development by divisions and regions is presented under "Segment Reporting". In addition to the costs of research departments and process development, this item also includes the cost of purchased services and the cost of clinical trials. The costs of research and development are expensed in full in the period in which they are incurred. Development expenses in the Pharmaceuticals business sector cannot be capitalized since the high level of risk up to the time that pharmaceutical products are marketed means that the requirements of IAS 38 are not satisfied in full. Costs incurred after regulatory approval are insignificant. In the same way, the risks involved until products are marketed means that

> development expenses in the Chemicals business sector cannot be capitalized. In addition to our own research and development, Merck is also a partner in collaborations aimed at developing marketable products. These collaborations typically involve payments for the achievements of certain milestones. With respect to this situation, an assessment is required as to whether these upfront or milestone payments represent ongoing research and development expense or whether these payments represent the acquisition of a right which has to be capitalized. Reimbursements for R&D are offset against research and development costs.

C   Internally generated brands, mastheads, publishing titles and customer lists

IAS 38 prohibits recognition of such items as intangible assets,[143] because it considers internally generated brands, mastheads, publishing titles, customer lists and items similar in substance to be indistinguishable from the cost of developing a business as a whole.[144] As discussed at 2.2.3 above, the same applies to subsequent expenditures incurred in connection with such intangible assets even when originally acquired externally.[145] For example, expenditure incurred in redesigning the layout of newspapers or magazines, which represent subsequent expenditure on publishing titles and mastheads, should not be capitalised.

The (then) IASC set out this explicit prohibition so as to remove any room for misunderstanding, but believed that in any event an entity would interpret the criteria in IAS 38 to determine that internally generated intangible items of this kind would rarely, and perhaps never, qualify for recognition.[146]

D   Website costs

In May 2001, the IASB issued SIC-32 in reaction to the very large sums that were being spent at the time on the operation and development of websites. An entity's own website that arises from development and is for internal or external access is an internally generated intangible asset that is subject to the requirements of IAS 38.[147] SIC-32 clarifies how IAS 38 applies to accounting for costs in relation to websites designed for use by the entity in its business, but does not apply to items that are accounted for under another standard, such as the development or operation of a website (or website software) for sale to another entity (IAS 2 and IAS 11); acquiring or developing hardware supporting a website (IAS 16); or in determining the initial recognition of an asset for a website subject to a leasing arrangement (IAS 17). However, SIC-32 should be applied by lessors providing a website under an operating lease and by lessees considering the treatment of subsequent expenditure relating to a website asset leased under a finance lease.[148]

The interpretation recognises that a website may be used for various purposes such as to promote and advertise an entity's own products and services, provide electronic services to customers, and sell products and services. A website may be used within the entity to give staff access to company policies and customer details, and allow them to search relevant information.[149]

Under SIC-32, an intangible asset should be recognised for website development costs if and only if, in addition to complying with the general recognition requirements in IAS 38 (see 2.2.1 above), the six conditions for the recognition of development costs are met in full (see 2.3.6 B above).[150] The interpretation deems that an entity is not able to demonstrate how a web site developed solely or primarily for promoting and advertising its own products and services will generate probable future economic benefits, and consequently all expenditure on developing such a web site should be recognised as an expense when incurred. Accordingly, it is unlikely that costs will be eligible for capitalisation unless an entity can demonstrate that the website is used directly in the income generating process, for example where customers can place orders on the entity's website.[151]

The following stages of a website's development are identified by the interpretation:[152]

(a)   *planning* includes undertaking feasibility studies, defining objectives and specifications, evaluating alternatives and selecting preferences. Expenditure incurred in this stage is similar in nature to the research phase and should be recognised as an expense when it is incurred;

(b)   *application and infrastructure development* includes obtaining a domain name, purchasing and developing hardware and operating software, installing developed applications and stress testing. The requirements of IAS 16 are applied to expenditure on physical assets. Other costs are recognised as an expense, unless they can be directly attributed, or allocated on a reasonable and consistent basis, to preparing the website for its intended use and the project to develop the website meets the SIC-32 criteria for recognition as an intangible asset;

(c)   *graphical design development* includes designing the appearance of web pages. Costs incurred at this stage should be accounted for in the same way as expenditure incurred in the 'application and infrastructure development' stage described under (b) above;

(d)   *content development* includes creating, purchasing, preparing and uploading information, either textual or graphical in nature, on the website before the completion of the website's development. An expense is always recognised for the costs of content that is developed to advertise and promote an entity's own products and services. Other costs incurred in this stage should be recognised as an expense unless the criteria for recognition as an asset described in (b) above are satisfied; and

(e)   the *operating stage*, which starts after completion of the development of a website, when an entity maintains and enhances the applications, infrastructure, graphical design and content of the website.[153] Expenditure incurred in this stage should be recognised as an expense when it is incurred unless it meets the asset recognition criteria in IAS 38.

In making the above assessments, the entity should evaluate the nature of each activity for which expenditure is incurred, independently of its consideration of the website's stage of development. Additional guidance is provided in the Appendix to SIC-32.[154] This means that even where a project has been determined to qualify for recognition as an intangible asset, not all costs incurred in relation to a qualifying stage of development are eligible for capitalisation. For example, whilst the direct costs of developing an online ordering system might qualify for recognition as an asset, the costs of training staff to operate that system should be expensed because training costs are not deemed necessary to creating, producing or preparing the website for it to be capable of operating (see 2.3.7 below).[155]

A website that is recognised as an intangible asset should be measured after initial recognition by applying the cost model or the revaluation model in IAS 38 as discussed at 2.4 and 2.5 below. The IASB requires an entity to be prudent in assessing the useful life of website assets, by stating it should be short.[156]

Extract 15.5: France Telecom S.A. (2007)

NOTE 2 Accounting policies [extract]

2.3 Methods used in the preparation of the consolidated financial statements [extract]

2.3.9 Intangible assets [extract]

Other development costs

Website development costs are capitalized when all of the following conditions are met:
- it is probable that the website will be successfully developed, the Group has adequate technical, financial and other resources to complete the development and has the intention of and ability to complete the site and use or sell it;
- the website will generate future economic benefits;
- the Group has the ability to reliably measure the expenditure attributable to the website during its development.

Website development costs are expensed as incurred or recognized as an intangible asset depending on the phase:
- initial design costs are expensed as incurred;
- qualifying development and graphic design costs are recognized as an intangible asset;
- expenditure incurred after the website has been completed is recorded as an expense, except where it enables the website to generate future additional economic benefits, and if it can be reliably estimated and attributed to the website.

2.3.7　Cost of an internally generated intangible asset

As discussed at 2.2 above, upon initial recognition an intangible asset should be measured at cost,[157] which the standard defines as 'the amount of cash or cash equivalents paid or the fair value of other consideration given to acquire an asset at the time of its acquisition or construction, or, when applicable, the amount attributed to that asset when initially recognised in accordance with the specific requirements of other IFRSs, e.g. IFRS 2.'[158] For internally generated intangible assets, it is important to ensure that cost includes only the expenditure incurred after the recognition criteria are met and to confirm that only costs directly related to the creation of the asset are capitalised.

A　　Establishing the time from which costs can be capitalised

The cost of an internally generated intangible asset is the sum of the expenditure incurred from the date when the intangible asset first meets the recognition criteria of the standard,[159] that is:

(a)　it is probable that the expected future economic benefits that are attributable to the asset will flow to the entity, using reasonable and supportable assumptions that represent management's best estimate of the set of economic conditions that will exist over the useful life of the asset;[160]

(b)   the cost of the asset can be measured reliably;[161] and

(c)   the asset meets the detailed conditions for recognition of development phase costs as an asset from paragraph 57 of the standard (see 2.3.6 B above).

Costs incurred before these criteria are met are recognised as an expense[162] and cannot be reinstated retrospectively,[163] because IAS 38 does not permit recognition of past expenses as an intangible asset at a later date.[164]

The following example, which is taken from IAS 38, illustrates how these above rules should be applied in practice.[165]

Example 15.4:   Recognition of internally generated intangible assets

An entity is developing a new production process. During 2010, expenditure incurred was €1,000, of which €900 was incurred before 1 December 2010 and €100 was incurred between 1 December 2010 and 31 December 2010. The entity is able to demonstrate that, at 1 December 2010, the production process met the criteria for recognition as an intangible asset. The recoverable amount of the know-how embodied in the process (including future cash outflows to complete the process before it is available for use) is estimated to be €500.

At the end of 2010, the production process is recognised as an intangible asset at a cost of €100 (expenditure incurred since the date when the recognition criteria were met, i.e. 1 December 2010). The €900 expenditure incurred before 1 December 2010 is recognised as an expense because the recognition criteria were not met until 1 December 2010. This expenditure does not form part of the cost of the production process recognised in the balance sheet.

During 2011, expenditure incurred is €2,000. At the end of 2011, the recoverable amount of the know-how embodied in the process (including future cash outflows to complete the process before it is available for use) is estimated to be €1,900.

At the end of 2011, the cost of the production process is €2,100 (€100 expenditure recognised at the end of 2010 plus €2,000 expenditure recognised in 2011). The entity recognises an impairment loss of €200 to adjust the carrying amount of the process before impairment loss (€2,100) to its recoverable amount (€1,900). This impairment loss will be reversed in a subsequent period if the requirements for the reversal of an impairment loss in IAS 36 are met.

B   Determining the costs eligible for capitalisation

The cost of an internally generated intangible asset comprises all directly attributable costs necessary to create, produce, and prepare the asset to be capable of operating in the manner intended by management. Examples of directly attributable costs are:[166]

●   costs of materials and services used or consumed in generating the intangible asset;

●   costs of employee benefits arising from the generation of the intangible asset;

●   fees to register a legal right;

●   amortisation of patents and licences that are used to generate the intangible asset; and

●   borrowing costs that meet the criteria under IAS 23 for recognition as an element of cost.

Indirect costs and general overheads, even if they can be allocated on a reasonable and consistent basis, cannot be recognised as part of the cost of the asset. The standard also specifically prohibits recognition of the following items as a component of cost:[167]

- selling, administrative and other general overhead expenditure unless this expenditure can be directly attributed to preparing the asset for use;

- identified inefficiencies and initial operating losses incurred before the asset achieves planned performance; and

- expenditure on training staff to operate the asset.

2.3.8   Recognition of an expense

Unless expenditure is incurred in connection with an intangible item that the standard requires to be recognised, and is an eligible component of cost, it should be expensed. The only exception is in connection with a business combination, where the costs associated with an intangible that cannot be recognised will form part of the carrying amount of goodwill.[168]

Some of the ineligible components of cost were identified in 2.3.7 above. Sometimes expenditure is incurred to provide future economic benefits to an entity, but no intangible asset or other asset is acquired or created that can be recognised. In these cases, the expenditure is recognised as an expense when it is incurred. IAS 38 provides other examples of expenditure that is recognised as an expense when incurred:[169]

(a)   start-up costs, unless they qualify for recognition as part of the cost of property, plant and equipment under IAS 16 (see Chapter 16 at 3.2.1) Start-up costs recognised as an expense may consist of establishment costs such as legal and secretarial costs incurred in establishing a legal entity, expenditure to open a new facility or business or expenditures for starting new operations or launching new products or processes;

(b)   training costs;

(c)   advertising and promotional activities; and

(d)   relocation or reorganisation costs.

The standard does not preclude an entity recognising a prepayment as an asset when payment for the delivery of goods or services has been made in advance of the delivery of goods or the rendering of services.[170] The wording of IAS 38 was amended by the Improvements to IFRSs, issued in May 2008, to clarify that in the case of the supply of goods, delivery is the point from which the entity obtains a right of access to those goods and in the case of the supply of services, an expense is recognised when the services are received.[171] Therefore, once an entity obtains a right of access to those goods or receives those services, it should recognise an expense if the related intangible asset does not meet the recognition criteria.

A   Catalogues and other advertising costs

The amendment noted above to the wording of IAS 38 is the result of deliberations started in September 2006 when the IFRIC discussed accounting for catalogues and other advertising costs. In March 2007, the IFRIC asked the IASB to consider the matter as part of its annual improvements process.[172]

The proposal submitted to the IASB was that a prepayment can be recognised only until the related goods and services are received by the entity, except in the case of advertising and promotional or training activities in which case deferral continues until the first time as the activities take place. The Board concluded that the question contained two elements, the treatment of the cost of developing content (advertising and training content or materials); and the treatment of costs relating to communication (delivery of that content, for example using television airtime).[173]

In May 2008, the Board published its first annual improvements standard, including an amendment to paragraphs 69-70 of IAS 38, such that the cost of advertising and promotional content and materials is expensed when the entity has a right to access those goods or receives the related services.[174]

The Board confirmed its view that advertising and promotional activities enhance or create brands or other customer relationships, which in turn generate revenues. The goods and services acquired for use in those activities have no other purpose and generate no additional benefits. In other words, the only benefit of those goods and services is to develop or create internally generated brands or customer relationships, which are not eligible under IAS 38 to be recognised as intangible assets.[175] The Board noted that an entity has a different asset, a prepayment, if it has paid for goods or services before they are provided and retained this provision in IAS 38. However, the Board did not believe this justified an asset being recognised beyond the point at which the entity gained the right of access to the related goods or received the related services.[176]

The IASB is deliberate in replacing references to 'the delivery of goods' with the phrase 'obtaining the right to access those goods' when it defines the point that an expense is recognised. This is because the date of physical delivery could be altered without affecting the substance of the commercial arrangement with the supplier.[177] Recognition is therefore determined by the point when the goods have been constructed by the supplier in accordance with the terms of the customer contract and the entity could demand delivery in return for payment.[178] Therefore an entity must recognise an expense for customer catalogues once they are ready for delivery from the printer, even if the entity has arranged for the printer to send catalogues directly to customers when advised by the entity's sales department. Similarly in the case of services, an expense is recognised when those services are received by the entity, and not deferred until the entity uses them in the delivery of another service, for example, to deliver an advertisement to its customers.[179]

Some respondents to the exposure draft sought to make a special case for mail order catalogues, arguing that they created a distribution network that could directly give rise to revenues and accordingly should be eligible for capitalisation in the same way as web site development costs in SIC-32. The board rejected this argument[180] and for the avoidance of doubt, the amended standard cites mail order catalogues as an example of expenditure on advertising and promotional activities that is recognised as an expense.[181]

2.4 Measurement after initial recognition

IAS 38, in common with a number of other standards, provides an entity the option to choose between two alternative treatments that may be summarised as follows:[182]

- the *cost model*, which requires measurement at cost less any accumulated amortisation and any accumulated impairment losses[183] (see 2.4.1 below); and

- the *revaluation model*, which requires measurement at a revalued amount (based on fair value) less any subsequent accumulated amortisation and any subsequent accumulated impairment losses[184] (see 2.4.2 below).

The revaluation option is only available if an active market exists for the intangible asset.[185] There are no provisions in IAS 38 allowing fair value in this situation to be determined indirectly, for example by using the techniques and financial models applied to estimate the fair value of intangible assets acquired in a business combination (see 2.3.2 above). When an entity chooses to measure an intangible asset at valuation, it must apply the revaluation model to all the assets in that class, unless there is no active market for those other assets.[186] A class of intangible assets is defined as 'a grouping of assets of a similar nature and use in an entity's operations'.[187] Examples of separate classes of intangible asset include:[188]

(a) brand names;

(b) mastheads and publishing titles;

(c) computer software;

(d) licences and franchises;

(e) copyrights, patents and other industrial property rights, service and operating rights;

(f) recipes, formulae, models, designs and prototypes; and

(g) intangible assets under development.

The standard requires assets in the same class to be revalued at the same time, 'to avoid selective revaluation of assets and the reporting of amounts in the financial statements representing a mixture of costs and values as at different dates'.[189]

2.4.1 Cost model

Under the cost model, after initial recognition the carrying amount of an intangible asset is its cost less any accumulated amortisation and accumulated impairment losses.[190] The rules on amortisation of intangible assets are discussed at 2.6 and 2.7 below; and impairment is discussed at 2.8 below.

2.4.2 Revaluation model

Under the revaluation model, after initial recognition an intangible asset should be carried at a revalued amount, which is its fair value at the date of the revaluation less any subsequent accumulated amortisation and any subsequent accumulated impairment losses.[191] An entity can only elect to apply the revaluation model if the fair value can be determined by reference to an active market for the intangible asset.[192] To prevent an entity from circumventing the recognition rules of the standard, the revaluation model does not allow:[193]

- the revaluation of intangible assets that have not previously been recognised as assets; or
- the initial recognition of intangible assets at amounts other than cost.

However, it is permitted to apply the revaluation model to the whole of an intangible asset even if only part of its cost is recognised as an asset because it did not meet the criteria for recognition until part of the way through the process.[194] These rules are designed to prevent an entity from recognising at a 'revalued' amount an intangible asset that was never recorded because its costs were expensed as they did not at the time meet the recognition rules. As these rules would also prohibit the revaluation of quotas and permits allocated by governments and similar bodies – which are amongst the few intangible assets that do have an active market – the standard specifically makes an exception and allows the revaluation model to be applied to 'an intangible asset that was received by way of a government grant and recognised at a nominal amount'.[195]

The example below illustrates how this would work in practice.

Example 15.5:   *Application of revaluation model to intangible assets that are partially recognised or received by way of government grant*

Entity C spent ¥12,000,000 in preparing its application for a number of taxi licenses, which it expensed because of the uncertain outcome of the process. The application was successful and C was granted a number of freely transferable taxi licenses and paid a nominal registration fee of ¥50,000, which it recognised as an asset. There is an active and liquid market in these taxi licenses.

C can apply the revaluation model under IAS 38 to these taxi licenses, because it previously recognised the license (even if it only recognised part of the costs as an asset) and there is an active market in these licenses.

Entity D obtained a number of freely transferable fishing quotas free of charge, which it recognised at a nominal amount as permitted under IAS 20. There is an active and liquid market in these quotas.

D can apply the revaluation model under IAS 38 to these fishing quotas, because it previously recognised the license (even if it only recognised it at a nominal amount) and there is an active market in these licenses.

A   Active market

As mentioned above, an entity can only elect to apply the revaluation model if the fair value can be determined by reference to an active market for the intangible asset.[196] IAS 38 defines an active market as one in which all the following conditions exist:[197]

(a)   the items traded in the market are homogeneous;

(b)   willing buyers and sellers can normally be found at any time; and

(c)   prices are available to the public.

The fact that all these criteria must be met means that few intangible assets will be eligible for revaluation and indeed the standard concedes that such an active market would be uncommon. Nevertheless it is possible for a class of intangible assets to be regarded as homogeneous. For example, in some jurisdictions, an active market may exist for freely transferable taxi licences, fishing licences or production quotas.[198] However, by their very nature most intangible assets are somehow unique or entity-specific. For example, the standard lists brands, newspaper mastheads, music and film publishing rights, patents or trademarks, as ineligible for revaluation because each such asset is unique.[199] In other words, 'homogeneous' in the definition of an active market is to be interpreted as meaning 'identical' or 'virtually identical'. It is not enough for intangible assets merely to be very similar in use or function.

The term 'homogeneous' in the definition applies not only to the nature of the asset, but also to the manner in which it is traded. Even if the intangible assets traded can be regarded as identical in nature, the existence of a previous sale and purchase transaction is not sufficient evidence for the market to be regarded as active. The standard notes that where contracts are negotiated between individual buyers and sellers or when transactions are relatively infrequent, the price of a previous transaction for *one* intangible asset may not provide sufficient evidence of the fair value of another. In addition, if prices are not available to the public, this is taken as evidence that an active market does *not* exist.[200]

B   Frequency of revaluations

If an active market exists for the intangible asset, IAS 38 requires revaluation to be performed 'with such regularity that at the end of the reporting period the carrying amount of the asset does not differ materially from its fair value'.[201] The standard lets entities judge for themselves the frequency of revaluations depending on the volatility of the fair values of the underlying intangible assets, though it does add that 'some intangible assets may experience significant and volatile movements in fair value, thus necessitating annual revaluation. Such frequent revaluations are unnecessary for intangible assets with only insignificant movements in fair value.'[202] Nevertheless, considering the narrow definition of an 'active market' and the definition of 'material' in IAS 1 – *Presentation of Financial Statements* – an entity should err on the side of caution and revalue frequently because there is normally no excuse for ignoring price information that the standard requires to be available to the public. As noted above, when an entity has a number of items in the same class of intangible assets, the standard requires that they are all valued at the same time.[203]

C   Accounting for revaluations

Increases in an intangible asset's carrying amount as a result of a revaluation should be credited to equity via other comprehensive income under the heading of revaluation surplus, except to the extent that the revaluation reverses a revaluation decrease of the same asset that was previously recognised in profit or loss.[204] Conversely, decreases in an intangible asset's carrying amount as a result of a revaluation should be recognised in profit or loss, unless the revaluation reverses an earlier revaluation increase, in which case the decrease should first be recognised in other comprehensive income to extinguish the revaluation surplus in respect of the asset.[205] The example below illustrates how this works.

Example 15.6:   Accounting for upward and downward revaluations

Entity E acquired an intangible asset that it accounts for under the revaluation model. The fair value of the asset changes as follows:

	£
Acquisition	530
A	550
B	520
C	510
D	555

The diagram below summarises this information (the impact of amortisation on the carrying amount and revaluation surplus has been ignored in this example for the sake of simplicity).

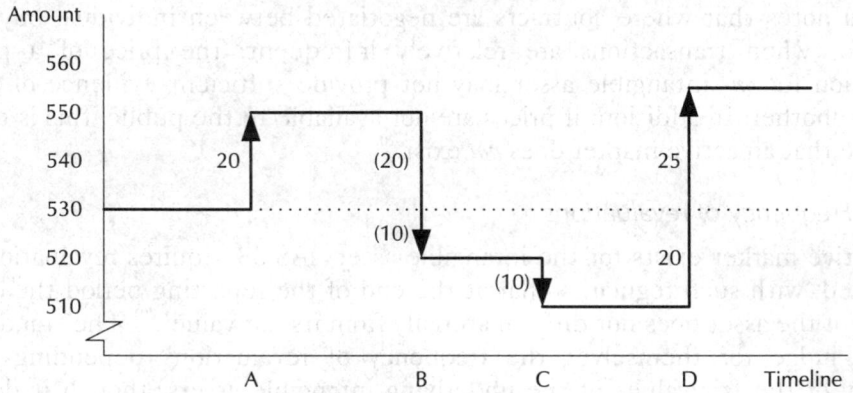

The table below shows how entity E should account for the upward and downward revaluations.

	Value of asset	Cumulative revaluation reserve	Revaluation recognised in other comprehensive income	Revaluation recognised in profit or loss
	£	£	£	£
Acquisition	530	–	–	–
A	550	20	20	–
B	520	–	(20)	(10)
C	510	–	–	(10)
D	555	25	25	20

The upward revaluation at A is accounted for in other comprehensive income. The downward revaluation at B first reduces the revaluation reserve for that asset to nil and the excess of £10 is recognised as a loss in the income statement. The second downward revaluation at C is recognised as a loss in income. The upward revaluation at D first reverses the cumulative loss recognised in income and the excess is accounted for in the revaluation reserve.

In the example above the impact of amortisation on the carrying amount of the assets and the revaluation surplus was ignored for the sake of simplicity. However, the cumulative revaluation surplus included in equity may be transferred directly to retained earnings when the surplus is realised, which happens either (1) on the retirement or disposal of the asset or (2) as the asset is used by the entity.[206] In the latter case, the 'amount of the surplus realised is the difference between amortisation based on the revalued carrying amount of the asset and amortisation that would have been recognised based on the asset's historical cost'.[207] In practice this means two things:

- an entity applying the revaluation model would need to track both the historical cost and revalued amount of an asset to determine how much of the revaluation surplus has been realised; and

- any revaluation surplus is amortised over the life of the related asset. Therefore, in the case of a significant downward revaluation there is a smaller revaluation surplus available against which the downward revaluation can be offset.

The transfer from revaluation surplus to retained earnings is not made through profit or loss.[208]

If an intangible asset is revalued, the standard allows an entity to account for the accumulated amortisation at the date of revaluation by either:[209]

(a) restating it proportionately with the change in the gross carrying amount of the asset so that the carrying amount of the asset after revaluation equals its revalued amount; or

(b) eliminating it against the gross carrying amount of the asset and the net amount restated to the revalued amount of the asset.

In practice the proportionate method is only used when the asset's net carrying amount is being revalued to depreciated replacement cost using an index, which will rarely be the case for an intangible asset.

Example 15.7:   Restatement of accumulated amortisation after a revaluation

Entity F revalued an intangible asset from its carrying amount of £120 to its fair value of £150. The proportionate restatement approach (in the middle column) leads to grossing up of both gross carrying amount and the accumulated amortisation. The elimination approach (in the right-hand column) results in elimination of the accumulated amortisation.

		After revaluation	
	Before *revaluation*	*Proportionate* *restatement*	*Eliminating* *amortisation*
	£	£	£
Gross carrying amount	300	375	150
Accumulated amortisation	(180)	(225)	–
Net carrying amount	120	150	150

D   No active market

The standard requires an entity to apply the revaluation model to entire classes of intangible assets,[210] but if there is no active market for an item in a class of revalued intangible assets, the asset is carried at its cost less any accumulated amortisation and impairment losses.[211]

Similarly, an entity should stop revaluing an asset if the market used to determine its fair value ceases to meet the criteria for an active market. The valuation is 'frozen' from that date, and reduced thereafter by subsequent amortisation and any subsequent impairment losses.[212] The IASB believes that such a disappearance of a previously active market may indicate that the asset needs to be tested for impairment in accordance with IAS 36.[213]

If an active market for the previously revalued asset emerges at a later date, the entity is required to apply the revaluation model from that date.[214]

2.5   Assessing the useful life of an intangible asset

IAS 38 defines the useful life of an intangible asset as:[215]

(a)   the period over which an asset is expected to be available for use by an entity; or

(b)   the number of production or similar units expected to be obtained from the asset by an entity.

Thus in some cases the useful life of an intangible asset should be expressed as a number of production or similar units rather than a period of time.

The standard requires an entity to assess whether the useful life of an intangible asset is finite or indefinite.[216] If an entity concludes that the useful life of an intangible asset is finite, it estimates the length of its useful life or the number of production units (or similar units) constituting that useful life.[217] An intangible asset with a finite useful life is amortised, whereas an intangible asset with an indefinite useful life is not.[218]

For this purpose the term 'indefinite' does not mean 'infinite'.[219] The standard requires an intangible asset to be classified as having an indefinite useful life 'when, based on an analysis of all of the relevant factors, there is no foreseeable limit to the period over which the asset is expected to generate net cash inflows for the entity'.[220]

The previous version of IAS 38 prescribed a presumptive maximum useful life for intangible assets of 20 years.[221] However, the IASB observed that 'some intangible assets are based on legal rights that are conveyed in perpetuity rather than for finite terms. ... The Board concluded that if the cash flows are expected to continue for a finite period, the useful life of the asset is limited to that finite period. However, if the cash flows are expected to continue indefinitely, the useful life is indefinite.'[222] The IASB decided to remove the presumptive maximum useful life for intangible assets, because it is 'inconsistent with the view that the amortisation period for an intangible asset should, to be representationally faithful, reflect its useful life and, by extension, the cash flow streams associated with the asset'.[223]

This means that under IAS 38 it is now possible to account for intangible assets without amortising them at all. However, an important underlying assumption in making the assessment of the useful life of an intangible asset is that it 'reflects only that level of future maintenance expenditure required to maintain the asset at its standard of performance assessed at the time of estimating the asset's useful life, and the entity's ability and intention to reach such a level. A conclusion that the useful life of an intangible asset is indefinite should not depend on planned future expenditure in excess of that required to maintain the asset at that standard of performance.'[224]

The standard identifies a number of factors that may affect the useful life of an intangible asset:[225]

(a)   the expected usage of the asset by the entity and whether the asset could be managed efficiently by another management team;

(b)   typical product life cycles for the asset and public information on estimates of useful lives of similar assets that are used in a similar way;

(c)   technical, technological, commercial or other types of obsolescence;

(d)   the stability of the industry in which the asset operates and changes in the market demand for the products or services output from the asset;

(e)   expected actions by competitors or potential competitors;

(f)   the level of maintenance expenditure required to obtain the expected future economic benefits from the asset and the entity's ability and intention to reach such a level;

(g)   the period of control over the asset and legal or similar limits on the use of the asset, such as the expiry dates of related leases; and

(h)   whether the useful life of the asset is dependent on the useful life of other assets of the entity.

Further guidance is provided by IAS 38 in the form of Illustrative Examples (which are reproduced in the example below) that demonstrate how an entity would go about determining the useful life for different intangible assets and the subsequent accounting for those assets based on the useful life determinations.[226]

Example 15.8:   Assessing the useful life of an intangible asset

Acquired customer list

A direct-mail marketing company acquires a customer list and expects that it will be able to derive benefit from the information on the list for at least one year, but no more than three years.

The customer list would be amortised over management's best estimate of its useful life, say 18 months. Although the direct-mail marketing company may intend to add customer names and other information to the list in the future, the expected benefits of the acquired customer list relate only to the customers on that list at the date it was acquired. The customer list also would be reviewed for impairment in accordance with IAS 36 by assessing at the end of each reporting period whether there is any indication that the customer list may be impaired.

An acquired patent that expires in 15 years

The product protected by the patented technology is expected to be a source of net cash inflows for at least 15 years. The entity has a commitment from a third party to purchase that patent in five years for 60 per cent of the fair value of the patent at the date it was acquired, and the entity intends to sell the patent in five years.

The patent would be amortised over its five-year useful life to the entity, with a residual value equal to the present value of 60 per cent of the patent's fair value at the date it was acquired. The patent would also be reviewed for impairment in accordance with IAS 36 by assessing at the end of each reporting period whether there is any indication that it may be impaired.

An acquired copyright that has a remaining legal life of 50 years

An analysis of consumer habits and market trends provides evidence that the copyrighted material will generate net cash inflows for only 30 more years.

The copyright would be amortised over its 30-year estimated useful life. The copyright also would be reviewed for impairment in accordance with IAS 36 by assessing at the end of each reporting period whether there is any indication that it may be impaired.

An acquired broadcasting licence that expires in five years

The broadcasting licence is renewable every 10 years if the entity provides at least an average level of service to its customers and complies with the relevant legislative requirements. The licence may be renewed indefinitely at little cost and has been renewed twice before the most recent acquisition. The acquiring entity intends to renew the licence indefinitely and evidence supports its ability to do so. Historically, there has been no compelling challenge to the licence renewal. The technology used in broadcasting is not expected to be replaced by another technology at any time in the foreseeable future. Therefore, the licence is expected to contribute to the entity's net cash inflows indefinitely.

The broadcasting licence would be treated as having an indefinite useful life because it is expected to contribute to the entity's net cash inflows indefinitely. Therefore, the licence would not be amortised until its useful life is determined to be finite. The licence would be tested for impairment in accordance with IAS 36 annually and whenever there is an indication that it may be impaired.

The broadcasting licence in the example above

The licensing authority subsequently decides that it will no longer renew broadcasting licences, but rather will auction the licences. At the time the licensing authority's decision is made, the entity's broadcasting licence has three years until it expires. The entity expects that the licence will continue to contribute to net cash inflows until the licence expires.

Because the broadcasting licence can no longer be renewed, its useful life is no longer indefinite. Thus, the acquired licence would be amortised over its remaining three-year useful life and immediately tested for impairment in accordance with IAS 36.

An acquired airline route authority between two European cities that expires in three years

The route authority may be renewed every five years, and the acquiring entity intends to comply with the applicable rules and regulations surrounding renewal. Route authority renewals are routinely granted at a minimal cost and historically have been renewed when the airline has complied with the applicable rules and regulations. The acquiring entity expects to provide service indefinitely between the two cities from its hub airports and expects that the related supporting infrastructure (airport gates, slots, and terminal facility leases) will remain in place at those airports for as long as it has the route authority. An analysis of demand and cash flows supports those assumptions.

Because the facts and circumstances support the acquiring entity's ability to continue providing air service indefinitely between the two cities, the intangible asset related to the route authority is treated as having an indefinite useful life. Therefore, the route authority would not be amortised until its useful life is determined to be finite. It would be tested for impairment in accordance with IAS 36 annually and whenever there is an indication that it may be impaired.

An acquired trademark used to identify and distinguish a leading consumer product that has been a market-share leader for the past eight years

The trademark has a remaining legal life of five years but is renewable every 10 years at little cost. The acquiring entity intends to renew the trademark continuously and evidence supports its ability to do so. An analysis of (1) product life cycle studies, (2) market, competitive and environmental trends, and (3) brand extension opportunities provides evidence that the trademarked product will generate net cash inflows for the acquiring entity for an indefinite period.

The trademark would be treated as having an indefinite useful life because it is expected to contribute to net cash inflows indefinitely. Therefore, the trademark would not be amortised until its useful life is determined to be finite. It would be tested for impairment in accordance with IAS 36 annually and whenever there is an indication that it may be impaired.

A trademark acquired 10 years ago that distinguishes a leading consumer product

The trademark was regarded as having an indefinite useful life when it was acquired because the trademarked product was expected to generate net cash inflows indefinitely. However, unexpected competition has recently entered the market and will reduce future sales of the product. Management estimates that net cash inflows generated by the product will be 20 per cent less for the foreseeable future. However, management expects that the product will continue to generate net cash inflows indefinitely at those reduced amounts.

As a result of the projected decrease in future net cash inflows, the entity determines that the estimated recoverable amount of the trademark is less than its carrying amount, and an impairment loss is recognised. Because it is still regarded as having an indefinite useful life, the trademark would continue not to be amortised but would be tested for impairment in accordance with IAS 36 annually and whenever there is an indication that it may be impaired.

A trademark for a line of products acquired several years ago in a business combination

At the time of the business combination the acquiree had been producing the line of products for 35 years with many new models developed under the trademark. At the acquisition date the acquirer expected to continue producing the line, and an analysis of various economic factors indicated there was no limit to the period the trademark would contribute to net cash inflows. Consequently, the trademark was not amortised by the acquirer. However, management has recently decided that production of the product line will be discontinued over the next four years.

Because the useful life of the acquired trademark is no longer regarded as indefinite, the carrying amount of the trademark would be tested for impairment in accordance with IAS 36 and amortised over its remaining four-year useful life.

The standard explicitly warns against both:

- overestimating the useful life of an intangible asset. For example, 'given the history of rapid changes in technology, computer software and many other intangible assets are susceptible to technological obsolescence. Therefore, it is likely that their useful life is short.';[227] and

- underestimating the useful life. For example, 'the useful life of an intangible asset may be very long or even indefinite. Uncertainty justifies estimating the useful life of an intangible asset on a prudent basis, but it does not justify choosing a life that is unrealistically short.'[228]

It may be clear from the above discussion that despite the fairly detailed guidance in the standard an entity will need to exercise judgement in estimating the useful life of intangible assets.

2.5.1   *Useful life of contractual or other legal rights*

Where an intangible asset arises from contractual or other legal rights, the standard requires an entity to take account of both economic and legal factors influencing its useful life and determine the useful life as the shorter of:[229]

- the period of the contractual or other legal rights; and
- the period (determined by economic factors) over which the entity expects to obtain economic benefits from the asset.

If the contractual or other legal rights are conveyed for a limited term that can be renewed, the useful life of the intangible asset should include the renewal period only if there is evidence to support renewal by the entity without significant cost.[230] The existence of the following factors may indicate that an entity is able to renew the contractual or other legal rights without significant cost:[231]

(a)   there is evidence, possibly based on experience, that the contractual or other legal rights will be renewed. If renewal is contingent upon the consent of a third party, this includes evidence that the third party will give its consent;

(b)   there is evidence that any conditions necessary to obtain renewal will be satisfied; and

(c)   the cost to the entity of renewal is not significant when compared with the future economic benefits expected to flow to the entity from renewal.

A renewal period is only added to the estimate of useful life if its cost is insignificant when compared with the future economic benefits expected to flow to the entity from renewal.[232] If this is not the case, then the original asset's useful life ends at the contracted renewal date and the renewal cost is treated as the cost to acquire a new intangible asset.[233] An entity needs to exercise judgement in assessing what it regards as a significant cost.

In the case of a reacquired contractual right, recognised as an intangible asset in a business combination accounted for under IFRS 3, its useful life is the remaining contractual period of the contract in which the right was granted, but excluding any renewal periods.[234]

2.6   Intangible assets with a finite useful life

2.6.1   *Amortisation period and method*

Amortisation is the systematic allocation of the depreciable amount of an intangible asset over its useful life. The depreciable amount is the cost of an asset, or other amount substituted for cost (e.g. revaluation), less its residual value.[235] The depreciable amount of an intangible asset with a finite useful life should be allocated on a systematic basis over its useful life in the following manner:[236]

- amortisation should begin when the asset is available for use, i.e. when it is in the location and condition necessary for it to be capable of operating in the manner intended by management. Therefore, even if an entity is not using the asset, it should still be amortised because it is available for use, although there may be exceptions from this general rule (see 2.6.2 below);

- amortisation should cease at the earlier of:
  - the date that the asset is classified as held for sale, or included in a disposal group that is classified as held for sale, in accordance with IFRS 5; and
  - the date that the asset is derecognised.
- the amortisation method should reflect the pattern of consumption of the economic benefits that the intangible asset provides. If that pattern cannot be reliably determined, a straight-line basis should be used.

Amortisation of an intangible asset with a finite useful life continues until the asset has been fully depreciated or is classified as held for sale, as noted above, or derecognised. Amortisation does not cease simply because an asset is not being used,[237] although this fact might give rise to an indicator of impairment.

The standard allows a variety of amortisation methods to be used to depreciate the asset on a systematic basis over its useful life (such as the straight-line method, the diminishing balance method and the unit of production method). It used to state that 'there is rarely, if ever, persuasive evidence to support an amortisation method for intangible assets with finite useful lives that results in a lower amount of accumulated amortisation than under the straight-line method'.[238] This was intended to require entities to seriously challenge the use of amortisation methods that indicate a pattern of consumption that is weighted towards the later period of an intangible asset's estimated useful life. However, this did not mean that such methods are prohibited when they would have been appropriate and to avoid that interpretation the IASB deleted this sentence as part of its annual improvements standard issued in May 2008.[239]

The amortisation charge for each period should be recognised in profit or loss unless IFRS specifically permits or requires it to be capitalised as part of the carrying amount of another asset (e.g. inventory or work in progress).[240]

2.6.2 Review of amortisation period and amortisation method

An entity should review the amortisation period and the amortisation method for an intangible asset with a finite useful life at least at each financial year-end. If the expected useful life of the asset has changed, the amortisation period should be changed accordingly.[241] An entity may, for example, consider its previous estimate of the useful life of an intangible asset inappropriate upon recognition of an impairment loss on the asset.[242]

If the expected pattern of consumption of the future economic benefits embodied in the asset has changed, the amortisation method should be changed to reflect the changed pattern.[243] The standard provides two examples of when this might happen:

- if it becomes apparent that a diminishing balance method of amortisation is appropriate rather than a straight-line method;[244] and
- if use of the rights represented by a licence is deferred pending action on other components of the business plan. In this case, economic benefits that flow from the asset may not be received until later periods.[245] This implies that circumstances may exist in which it is appropriate not to recognise an

amortisation charge in relation to an intangible asset, because the entity may not be ready to use the intangible asset e.g. as happened in the case of telecommunication companies that acquired Universal Mobile Telecommunications System (UMTS) licenses, but that had not completed the physical network to use the license. Note that an entity must perform an impairment test at least annually for any intangible asset that has not yet been brought into use: see 2.8 below.

Both changes in the amortisation period and the amortisation method should be accounted for as changes in accounting estimates in accordance with IAS 8 – *Accounting Policies, Changes in Accounting Estimates and Errors*[246] – which requires such changes to be recognised prospectively by revising the amortisation charge in the current period and for each future period during the asset's remaining useful life.[247]

2.6.3   *Residual value*

The residual value of an intangible asset is the estimated amount that an entity would currently obtain from disposal of the asset, after deducting the estimated costs of disposal, if the asset were already of the age and in the condition expected at the end of its useful life.[248]

IAS 38 requires entities to assume a residual value of zero for an intangible asset with a finite useful life, unless there is a commitment by a third party to purchase the asset at the end of its useful life *or* there is an active market for the asset from which to determine its residual value and it is probable that such a market will exist at the end of the asset's useful life.[249] The presumption that the residual value of an intangible asset is normally zero was included in the previous version of IAS 38 as an anti-abuse measure to prevent entities from circumventing the requirement to amortise all intangible assets. It was retained in the amended standard for similar anti-avoidance reasons,[250] but its effectiveness is much reduced as an entity can avoid amortisation altogether on intangible assets with an indefinite useful life.

Given the very restrictive definition of 'active market' (see 2.4.2 A above) it seems highly unlikely that – in the absence of a commitment by a third party to buy the asset – an entity will ever be able to prove that the residual value is other than zero. A residual value other than zero implies that the entity intends to dispose of the asset before the end of its economic life.[251]

If an entity can demonstrate a case for estimating a residual value other than zero, its estimate should be based on 'the amount recoverable from disposal using prices prevailing at the date of the estimate for the sale of a similar asset that has reached the end of its useful life and has operated under conditions similar to those in which the asset will be used'.[252] Contrary to what was required by the previous version of IAS 38, the standard now requires a review of the residual value at each financial year-end. This review can result in an upward or downward revision of the estimated residual value and thereby affect the depreciable amount of the asset; that change to depreciation should be accounted for as a change in an accounting estimate in accordance with IAS 8.[253]

The standard does not permit negative amortisation in the event that the residual value of an intangible asset increases to an amount greater than the asset's carrying amount. Instead, the asset's amortisation charge would be 'zero unless and until its residual value subsequently decreases to an amount below the asset's carrying amount'.[254]

2.7   Intangible assets with an indefinite useful life

IAS 38 prohibits amortisation of an intangible asset with an indefinite useful life.[255] Instead, such an intangible asset should be tested for impairment under IAS 36 by comparing its recoverable amount with its carrying amount annually and whenever there is an indication that the intangible asset may be impaired.[256]

In other words, intangible assets with an indefinite useful life should be tested for impairment annually, irrespective of whether there is an impairment trigger that warrants impairment testing (see Chapter 18).

An entity should review and validate at the end of each reporting period its decision to classify the useful life of an intangible asset as indefinite.[257] If events and circumstances no longer support an indefinite useful life, the change from indefinite to finite should be accounted for as a change in accounting estimate under IAS 8,[258] which requires such changes to be recognised prospectively.[259] Furthermore, reassessing the useful life of an intangible asset as finite rather than indefinite is an indicator that the asset may be impaired.[260]

2.8   Impairment losses

An impairment loss is the amount by which the carrying amount of an asset exceeds its recoverable amount.[261] An entity applies IAS 36 in determining whether an intangible asset is impaired (see Chapter 18 at 3).[262]

IAS 36 requires an entity to perform an annual impairment test on every intangible asset that has an indefinite useful life and every intangible asset that is not yet available for use (see Chapter 18 at 3.5).[263] The requirement for an annual impairment test of intangible assets that had a useful life of over twenty years was removed in 2004.

2.9   Retirements and disposals

An intangible asset should be derecognised on disposal *or* when no future economic benefits are expected from its use or disposal.[264] Although gains on disposal should not be classified as revenue,[265] an entity should apply the criteria for recognising revenue from the sale of goods in IAS 18 – *Revenue* – in determining the date of disposal of an intangible asset (see Chapter 25). In the case of a disposal by a sale and leaseback, an entity should apply IAS 17.[266]

The gain or loss on derecognition, which is determined as the difference between the net disposal proceeds and the carrying amount of the asset, should be accounted for in profit or loss unless IAS 17 requires otherwise on a sale and leaseback. Gains on disposal should not be presented as revenue,[267] because they are incidental to the entity's main revenue-generating activities.

The consideration receivable on disposal of an intangible asset is recognised initially at its fair value. This means that, if payment for the intangible asset is deferred, the consideration received is recognised initially at the cash price equivalent. The difference between the nominal amount of the consideration and the cash price equivalent is recognised as interest using the effective interest method under IAS 18.[268]

The standard requires an entity to recognise in the carrying amount of an asset the cost of a replacement for part of an intangible asset and to derecognise the carrying amount of the replaced part. 'If it is not practicable for an entity to determine the carrying amount of the replaced part, it may use the cost of the replacement as an indication of what the cost of the replaced part was at the time it was acquired or internally generated.'[269] However, as noted by the standard, the nature of intangible assets is such that that, in many cases, there are no additions or replacements that would meet its recognition criteria, so this should be an unlikely event (see 2.2.3 above).[270]

In the case of a reacquired contractual right, recognised as an intangible asset in a business combination accounted for under IFRS 3, if the right is subsequently reissued or sold to a third party, any gain or loss is determined using the remaining carrying amount of the reacquired right.[271]

2.10   Disclosure

The main requirements in IAS 38 are set out below, but it may be necessary to refer as well to the disclosure requirements of IFRS 5 in Chapter 4 and the disclosure requirements of IAS 36 in Chapter 18 in the event of a disposal or impairment.

2.10.1 General disclosures

IAS 38 requires certain disclosures to be presented by class of intangible assets. A class of intangible assets is defined as a grouping of assets of a similar nature and use in an entity's operations. The standard provides examples of classes of assets, which may be 'disaggregated (aggregated) into smaller (larger) classes if this results in more relevant information for the users of the financial statements' (see 2.4 above for examples of classes of intangible assets).[272] Although separate information is required for internally generated intangible assets and other intangible assets, these categories are not considered to be separate classes when they relate to intangible assets of a similar nature and use in an entity's operations. Hence the standard requires the following disclosures to be given for each class of intangible assets – distinguishing between internally generated intangible assets and other intangible assets:[273]

(a) whether the useful lives are indefinite or finite and, if finite, the useful lives or the amortisation rates used;

(b) the amortisation methods used for intangible assets with finite useful lives;

(c) the gross carrying amount and any accumulated amortisation (aggregated with accumulated impairment losses) at the beginning and end of the period;

(d) the line item(s) of the statement of comprehensive income in which any amortisation of intangible assets is included;

(e)   a reconciliation of the carrying amount at the beginning and end of the period showing:

     (i)   additions, indicating separately those from internal development, those acquired separately, and those acquired through business combinations;

     (ii)   assets classified as held for sale or included in a disposal group classified as held for sale in accordance with IFRS 5 and other disposals;

     (iii)   increases or decreases during the period resulting from revaluations under paragraphs 75, 85-86 and from impairment losses recognised or reversed in other comprehensive income in accordance with IAS 36 (if any);

     (iv)   impairment losses recognised in profit or loss during the period in accordance with IAS 36 (if any);

     (v)   impairment losses reversed in profit or loss during the period in accordance with IAS 36 (if any);

     (vi)   any amortisation recognised during the period;

     (vii)   net exchange differences arising on the translation of the financial statements into the presentation currency, and on the translation of a foreign operation into the presentation currency of the entity; and

     (viii)   other changes in the carrying amount during the period.

The standard permits an entity to present the reconciliation required under (e) above either for the net carrying amount or separately for (1) the gross carrying amount and (2) the accumulated amortisation and impairments (see Extract 15.6 below).

An entity may want to consider separate disclosure of intangible assets acquired by way of government grant or obtained in an exchange of assets, even though disclosure is not specifically required under (e)(i) above.

The current version of IAS 38 requires comparative information for the reconciliation in (e) above, the exemption in the earlier versions of the standard being withdrawn.

The extract below provides a typical example of the disclosures for goodwill and intangible assets, including the reconciliation, under IFRS.

Extract 15.6: Unilever Group (2007)

Notes to the consolidated accounts [extract]

9 Goodwill and intangible assets [extract]

Indefinite-lived intangible assets principally comprise those trademarks for which there is no foreseeable limit to the period over which they are expected to generate net cash inflows. These are considered to have an indefinite life, given the strength and durability of our brands and the level of marketing support. Brands that are classified as indefinite have been in the market for many years, and the nature of the industry we operate in is such that brand obsolescence is not common, if appropriately supported by advertising and marketing spend. Finite-lived intangible assets, which primarily comprise patented and non-patented technology, know-how, and software, are capitalised and amortised in operating profit on a straight-line basis over the period of their expected useful lives, none of which exceeds ten years. The level of amortisation for finite-lived intangible assets is not expected to change materially over the next five years.

At cost less amortisation and impairment	€ million 2007	€ million 2006
Goodwill	12 244	12 425
Intangible assets	4 511	4 781
Indefinite-lived intangible assets	3 921	4 174
Finite-lived intangible assets	273	343
Software	317	264
	16 755	17 206

Movements during 2007	€ million Goodwill	€ million Indefinite-lived intangible assets	€ million Finite-lived intangible assets	€ million Software	€ million Total
Cost					
1 January 2007	13 454	4 409	642	392	18 897
Acquisitions of group companies	334	–	–	–	334
Disposals of group companies	(4)	(1)	–	–	(5)
Change in useful life assumptions	–	(2)	2	–	–
Additions	–	–	3	133	136
Disposals	–	–	–	(16)	(16)
Currency retranslation	(602)	(272)	(26)	(8)	(908)
31 December 2007	13 182	4 134	621	501	18 438
Amortisation and impairment					
1 January 2007	(1 029)	(235)	(299)	(128)	(1 691)
Amortisation for the year	–	–	(64)	(76)	(140)
Disposals	–	–	–	16	16
Currency retranslation	91	22	15	4	132
31 December 2007	(938)	(213)	(348)	(184)	(1 683)
Net book value 31 December 2007	12 244	3 921	273	317	16 755

Movements during 2006	€ million Goodwill	€ million Indefinite-lived intangible assets	€ million Finite-lived intangible assets	€ million Software	€ million Total
Cost					
1 January 2006	14 080	4 713	631	291	19 715
Acquisitions of group companies	60	8	1	–	69
Disposals of group companies	(1)	–	–	–	(1)
Change in useful life assumptions	–	(32)	32	–	–
Additions	–	–	3	110	113
Currency retranslation	(685)	(280)	(25)	(9)	(999)
31 December 2006	13 454	4 409	642	392	18 897
Amortisation and impairment					
1 January 2006	(1 117)	(263)	(215)	(65)	(1 660)
Amortisation for the year	–	–	(94)	(63)	(157)
Impairment	(12)	–	–	(2)	(14)
Currency retranslation	100	28	10	2	140
31 December 2005	(1 029)	(235)	(299)	(128)	(1 691)
Net book value 31 December 2006	12 425	4 174	343	264	17 206

There are no significant carrying amounts of goodwill and intangible assets that are allocated across multiple cash generating units (CGUs).

In addition to the disclosures required above, any impairment of intangibles is to be disclosed in accordance with IAS 36, which is discussed in Chapter 18 at 4,[274] while the nature and amount of any change in useful life, amortisation method or residual value estimates should be disclosed in accordance with the provisions of IAS 8.[275]

There are a number of additional disclosure requirements, some of which only apply in certain circumstances:[276]

(a) for an intangible asset assessed as having an indefinite useful life, the carrying amount of that asset and the reasons supporting the assessment of an indefinite useful life. In giving these reasons, the entity shall describe the factor(s) that played a significant role in determining that the asset has an indefinite useful life;

(b) a description, the carrying amount and remaining amortisation period of any individual intangible asset that is material to the entity's financial statements;

(c) for intangible assets acquired by way of a government grant and initially recognised at fair value (see 2.3.3 above):

   (i)   the fair value initially recognised for these assets;

   (ii)   their carrying amount; and

   (iii) whether they are measured after recognition under the cost model or the revaluation model.

(d) the existence and carrying amounts of intangible assets whose title is restricted and the carrying amounts of intangible assets pledged as security for liabilities;

(e) the amount of contractual commitments for the acquisition of intangible assets.

In describing the factors (as required under (a) above) that played a significant role in determining that the useful life of an intangible asset is indefinite, an entity considers the list of factors in paragraph 90 of IAS 38 (see 2.5 above).[277]

Finally, an entity is encouraged to disclose the following information:[278]

(a) a description of any fully amortised intangible asset that is still in use; and

(b) a brief description of significant intangible assets controlled by the entity but not recognised as assets because they did not meet the recognition criteria in this Standard or because they were acquired or generated before the version of IAS 38 issued in 1998 was effective.

2.10.2 Balance sheet presentation

IAS 1 does not use the term fixed assets, which is used in accounting standards under many other GAAPs. Instead it draws a distinction between current and non-current assets. IAS 1 uses the term 'non-current' to include tangible, intangible and financial assets of a long-term nature, although it 'does not prohibit the use of alternative descriptions as long as the meaning is clear'.[279] Although most intangible assets are non-current, an intangible asset may meet the definition of a current asset (i.e. it has an economic life of less than 12 months) when it is acquired and should be classified accordingly.

IAS 1 requires intangible assets to be shown as a separate category of asset on the face of the balance sheet.[280] Intangible assets will, therefore, normally appear as a separate category of asset in the balance sheet at a suitable point within non-current assets, or at a point in an undifferentiated balance sheet that reflects their relative liquidity[281] – that is the time over which they are to be amortised or sold. An entity that holds a wide variety of different intangible assets may need to present these in separate line items on the face of the balance sheet if such presentation is relevant to an understanding of the entity's financial position.[282]

While the balance sheet figure for intangible assets may include goodwill, the relevant standards require more detailed disclosures of the constituent elements of the balance sheet figure to be included in the notes to the financial statements.

The extract below shows how GN Store Nord discloses no less than six different types of intangible asset on the face of its balance sheet.

Extract 15.7: GN Store Nord A/S (2007)		
BALANCE SHEET AT DECEMBER 31 – ASSETS [extract]	Consolidated	
(DKK millions)	2007	2006
Non-current assets		
Goodwill	2,525	455
Development projects, developed in-house	692	115
Software	97	66
Patents and rights	51	4
Telecommunications systems	19	27
Other intangible assets	268	79
Total intangible assets	3,652	746

In many cases though, entities will be able to aggregate the intangible assets into slightly broader categories in order to reduce the number of lines items on the face of their balance sheets.

2.10.3 Income statement presentation

Only limited guidance is available on the presentation of amortisation, impairment, and gains or losses related to intangible assets:

- Gains on the sale of intangible assets should not be presented within revenue;[283] and

- An entity should disclose the line item(s) of the statement of comprehensive income in which any amortisation of intangible assets is included.[284]

In the absence of detailed guidance on how to present such items in the income statement, it will in practice usually be appropriate to present them in a similar way as those related to property, plant and equipment.

2.10.4 Additional disclosures under the revaluation model

IAS 38 requires an entity, which accounts for intangible assets at revalued amounts, to disclose the following additional information:[285]

(a)   by class of intangible assets:

     (i)   the effective date of the revaluation;

     (ii)   the carrying amount of revalued intangible assets; and

     (iii)   the carrying amount that would have been recognised had the revalued class of intangible assets been measured after recognition using the cost model (see 2.4.1 above);

(b)   the amount of the revaluation surplus that relates to intangible assets at the beginning and end of the period, indicating the changes during the period and any restrictions on the distribution of the balance to shareholders; and

(c)   the methods and significant assumptions applied in estimating the assets' fair values.

Classes of revalued assets should only be aggregated for disclosure purposes to the extent that this does not result 'in the combination of a class of intangible assets that includes amounts measured under both the cost and revaluation models'.[286]

2.10.5   Research and development expenditure

An entity should disclose the aggregate total amount of all expenditure that is directly attributable to research or development activities that is recognised as an expense during the period.[287] Development expenditure that is capitalised during the period should be excluded for the purposes of this disclosure.

3   PRACTICAL ISSUES

3.1   Regulatory assets

In many countries the provision of utilities (e.g. water, natural gas or electricity) to consumers is regulated by the national government. Regulations differ between countries but often regulators operate a cost-plus system under which a utility is allowed to make a fixed return on investment. Similarly, a regulator may allow a utility to recoup its investment by increasing the prices over a defined period.

Consequently, the future price that a utility is allowed to charge its customers may be influenced by past cost levels and investment levels. Under a number of national GAAPs accounting practices have developed whereby an entity accounts for the effects of regulation by recognising a 'regulatory' asset (or liability) that reflects the increase (or decrease) in future prices approved by the regulator. Such 'regulatory assets' may have been classified as intangible assets under those national GAAPs.

During 2008 the IFRIC considered for a time whether regulated entities could or should recognise an asset or a liability as a result of regulation by regulatory bodies or governments. The IFRIC again decided not to add the issue to its agenda, coming to the same conclusion as before that whilst rate regulation is widespread and significantly affects the economic environment of regulated entities, there did not seem to be significant divergence in practice for entities that were already applying IFRS.[288] The current consensus among existing IFRS reporters was that no regulatory assets or liabilities are recognised, unless they meet the definition of a financial asset or a financial liability (these arise in few regulatory regimes).[289]

However, the IASB decided to add a project on rate-regulated activities to its agenda. The Board acknowledged that this was a matter of significant interest in a number of countries that would be adopting IFRS in the near future and where recognition of regulatory assets and liabilities was either permitted or required.[290] In July 2009, the IASB issued an exposure draft on rate-regulated activities, which is discussed at 5.1 below.

3.2   Research and development in the pharmaceutical industry

Entities in the pharmaceutical industry consider research and development to be of primary importance to their business. Consequently, these entities spend a considerable amount on research and development every year. Therefore, one would expect pharmaceutical companies to carry internally generated development intangible assets on their balance sheets. However, the financial statements of pharmaceutical companies reveal that they often consider the uncertainties in the development of pharmaceuticals to be too great to permit capitalisation of development costs.

Extracts 15.8 and 15.9 below illustrate this.

Extract 15.8: Bayer AG (2007)

Notes to the Consolidated Financial Statements of the Bayer Group [extract]
[4] Basic principles of the consolidated financial statements [extract]
Research and development expenses

A substantial proportion of the Bayer Group's financial resources is invested in research and development. In addition to in-house research and development activities, especially in the health care business, various research and development collaborations and alliances are maintained with third parties involving the provision of funding and/or payments for the achievement of performance milestones.

For accounting purposes, research expenses are defined as costs incurred for current or planned investigations undertaken with the prospect of gaining new scientific or technical knowledge and understanding. Development expenses are defined as costs incurred for the application of research findings or specialist knowledge to production, production methods, services or goods prior to the commencement of commercial production or use.

According to IAS 38 (Intangible Assets), research costs cannot be capitalized; development costs must be capitalized if, and only if, specific, narrowly defined conditions are fulfilled. Development costs must be capitalized if it is sufficiently certain that the future economic benefits to the company will also cover the respective development costs. Since development projects are often subject to regulatory approval procedures and other uncertainties, the conditions for the capitalization of costs incurred before approvals are received are not normally satisfied.

The following costs in particular, by their very nature, constitute research and development expenses: the appropriate allocations of direct personnel and material costs and related overheads for application technology, engineering and other departments; costs for experimental and pilot facilities; costs for clinical research; costs for the utilization of third parties' patents for research and development purposes; other taxes related to research facilities; and fees for the filing and registration of self-generated patents that are not capitalized.

Under IAS 38 (Intangible Assets), milestone payments must initially be capitalized to the extent that they are related to the acquisition of the related technology rights, even if uncertainties exist as the whether the research and development will ultimately be successful in producing a saleable product. Where research and development collaborations are embedded in contracts for a strategic alliance, it is necessary to assess whether milestone or advance payments constitute funding of research and development work or consideration for the acquisition of assets. Factors considered in reaching this determination are the reason for payment (for example, whether it is related to regulatory approval, the attainment of a sales target or outsourced research and development activities), and the ratio of the fair value of the planned research and development activities to the total amount of the payment.

Extract 15.9: Syngenta AG (2007)

2. Accounting policies [extract]

Research and development

Research and development expenses are charged to the income statement when incurred. Syngenta considers that the regulatory and other uncertainties inherent in the development of its key new products preclude it from capitalizing development costs.

Costs of purchasing patent rights are capitalized as intangible assets. Costs of applying for patents for internally developed products, costs of defending existing patents and costs of challenging patents held by third parties where these are considered invalid, are considered part of development expense and expensed as incurred.

One of the problems of course is that, in the case of true 'development' activities in the pharmaceutical industry, the technical and economic feasibility are typically established very late in the development phase, which means that only a small proportion of the development costs can ever be capitalised. In particular, many drugs require approval by a regulator such as the US Food and Drug Administration (FDA) before they can be put on the market and until that time the entity may be uncertain of their success. After approval, of course, there is little in the way of expenditure other than on advertising and entities are precluded from capitalising this as part of the asset.

In our opinion, in the pharmaceutical sector, the capitalisation of development costs for new drugs would in most cases begin at the date on which the product receives regulatory approval. In most cases that is when the IAS 38 criteria for recognition of intangible assets are met. It is unlikely that these criteria will have been met before the request for new drug approval is filed.

As noted at 2.3.2 E above, there is an inconsistency at the heart of IAS 38 that results in a different treatment of acquired versus internally generated intangible assets. Intangible assets acquired in a separate transaction or business combinations must be recognised while future economic benefits are deemed to be probable, whereas internally developed intangible assets can only be recognised when they meet the strict (and somewhat subjective) recognition criteria in IAS 38.

3.3 Emissions trading schemes

A number of countries around the world either have, or are in the process of developing, schemes to encourage reduced emissions of pollutants, in particular of greenhouse gases. These schemes comprise tradable emissions allowances or permits, an example of which is a 'cap and trade' model whereby participants are allocated emission rights or allowances equal to a cap (i.e. a maximum level of allowable emissions, usually less than the entity's current quantity) and are permitted to trade those allowances.

A cap and trade emission rights scheme typically has the following features:

- an entity participating in the scheme (participant) is set a target to reduce its emissions to a specified level (the cap). The participant is issued allowances equal in number to its cap by a government or government agency. Allowances may be issued free of charge, or participants may pay the government for them;

- the scheme operates for defined compliance periods;

- participants are free to buy and sell allowances at any time;

- if at the end of the compliance period a participant's actual emissions exceeded its emission rights, the participant will have to buy additional rights in the market or it will incur a penalty;

- in some schemes emission rights surpluses and deficits may be carried forward to future periods; and

- the scheme may provide for brokers – who are not themselves participants – to buy and sell emission rights.

3.3.1   Development and withdrawal of IFRIC 3

In December 2004 the IASB issued IFRIC 3 – *Emission Rights* – to address the accounting for emission permits that arise from cap and trade emission rights schemes. However, the interpretation met with significant resistance because application of IFRIC 3 (which is discussed in more detail at 3.3.2 A below) would result in a number of accounting mismatches:[291]

- a measurement mismatch between the assets and liabilities recognised in accordance with IFRIC 3;

- a mismatch in the location in which the gains and losses on those assets are reported; and

- a possible timing mismatch because allowances would be recognised when they are obtained – typically at the start of the year – whereas the emission liability would be recognised during the year as it is incurred.

Consequently, the IASB decided in June 2005 to withdraw IFRIC 3 despite the fact that it considered it to be 'an appropriate interpretation of existing IFRSs'.[292] The IASB activated its project on emission trading schemes in December 2007 in response to requests from several national standard setters to address the topic and the addition by the FASB of a project on emissions allowances to its agenda. The Board decided to limit the scope of the project to accounting issues relating to emissions trading schemes, rather than to consider more general issues regarding the accounting for government grants.[293] This project is discussed at 5.2 below.

3.3.2   Accounting for emission rights by participants in cap and trade schemes

Until the IASB completes its project on emissions trading schemes, an entity has the option either:

(a)   to apply IFRIC 3, which despite having been withdrawn, is considered to be an appropriate interpretation of existing IFRS (see A below); or

(b)   to develop its own accounting policy for cap and trade schemes based on the hierarchy of authoritative guidance in IAS 8 (see B below).

A   IFRIC 3

IFRIC 3 dealt with accounting for cap and trade schemes by entities that participated in them. It did not address accounting by entities that were not yet subject to a scheme (even if they expected to be subject to one in the future) and brokers that were not themselves participants.[294] The provisions of the interpretation were also considered to be relevant to other schemes designed to encourage reduced levels of emissions and share some of the features outlined above.[295]

IFRIC 3 took the view that a cap and trade scheme did not give rise to a net asset or liability, but that it gave rise to various items that were to be accounted for separately:[296]

(a)   *an asset for allowances held* – Allowances, whether allocated by government or purchased, were to be regarded as intangible assets and accounted for under IAS 38. Allowances issued for less than fair value were to be measured initially at their fair value;[297]

(b)   *a government grant* – When allowances are issued for less than fair value, the difference between the amount paid and fair value was a government grant that should be accounted for under IAS 20. Initially the grant was to be recognised as deferred income in the balance sheet and subsequently recognised as income on a systematic basis over the compliance period for which the allowances were issued, regardless of whether the allowances were held or sold;[298]

(c)   *a liability for the obligation to deliver allowances equal to emissions that have been made* – As emissions are made, a liability was to be recognised as a provision that falls within the scope of IAS 37 – *Provisions, Contingent Liabilities and Contingent Assets*. The liability was to be measured at the best estimate of the expenditure required to settle the present obligation at the balance sheet date. This would usually be the present market price of the number of allowances required to cover emissions made up to the balance sheet date.[299]

The interpretation also noted that 'the existence or requirements of an emission rights scheme may cause a reduction in the cash flows expected to be generated by certain assets. Such a reduction is an indication that those assets may be impaired and hence requires those assets to be tested for impairment in accordance with IAS 36.'[300]

B   Application of the IAS 8 hierarchy of authoritative guidance

In light of the accounting mismatches resulting from the application of IFRIC 3 (see 3.3.1 above), it is perhaps no surprise that in practice very few companies have applied IFRIC 3 on a voluntary basis. Instead companies have developed a range of different approaches in accounting for cap and trade emission rights schemes, which are discussed below:

- 'net liability' approaches (see I and II below);
- 'government grants' approach (see III below),

I   Net liability approach

Under the 'net liability' approach emission allowances received by way of grant are recorded at a nominal amount and the entity will only recognise a liability once the actual emissions exceed the emission rights granted and still held, thereby requiring the entity to purchase additional allowances in the market or incur a regulatory penalty.

We believe that an entity can apply a 'net liability' approach, because in the absence of specific guidance on the accounting for emission rights, IAS 20 allows non-monetary government grants and the related asset (in this case the emission rights) received to be measured at a nominal amount (i.e. nil).[301]

Under IAS 37, a provision can only be recognised if the recognition criteria in the standard are met, including that the entity has a present obligation as a result of a past event and it is probable that an outflow of economic resources will be required to settle the obligation[302] (see Chapter 24 at 3.1). As far as emissions are concerned, the 'obligating event' is the emission itself, therefore a provision is considered for recognition as emissions are made, but an outflow of resources is not probable until the reporting entity has made emissions in excess of any rights held. This means that an entity should not recognise a provision for any anticipated future shortfall of emission rights; nor should it accrete a provision over the period of the expected shortfall.

Under IAS 37 the entire obligation to deliver allowances should be measured at 'the best estimate of the expenditure required to settle the present obligation at the end of the reporting period' (see Chapter 24 at 4.1).[303] Accordingly any provision is based on the lower of the expected cost to purchase additional allowances in the market or the amount of any regulatory penalty.

Critics of the 'net liability' approach have noted that under IAS 20, recognition of the emission rights at their fair value or at a nominal amount constitute *alternative* treatments,[304] However, under a net liability approach, granted rights are recognised at nominal amount and purchased rights are carried at cost. Furthermore, they point out that IAS 37 requires that the best estimate of the expenditure required to settle the present obligation to be determined by reference to 'the amount that an entity would rationally pay to settle the obligation at the end of the reporting period or to transfer it to a third party at that time'.[305] Arguably that amount should be determined without reference to other assets held by the entity that could be exchanged as well. Therefore, these critics would consider it more appropriate to recognise the entire obligation at its present fair value (i.e. the approach under IFRIC 3). Nevertheless, the 'net liability' approach appears to have gained acceptance in practice.

Example 15.9:   Application of 'net liability' approach

Company A received allowances representing the right to produce 10,000 tons of CO_2 for the year to 31 December 2010. The expected emissions for the full year are 12,000 tons of CO_2. At the end of the third quarter, it has emitted 9,000 tons of CO_2. The market price of the allowances at the end of the each quarter is €10/ton, €12/ton, €14/ton and €16/ton respectively.

Under the 'net liability' approach, the provision at the end of the first, second and third quarters would be nil, because the company has not yet exceeded its emissions target. Only in the fourth quarter is a provision recognised, for the excess tonnage emitted, at 2,000 tons × €16/ton = €32,000.

The company cannot anticipate the future shortfall of 2,000 tons before the fourth quarter by accreting the provision over the year, nor can it recognise on day one the full provision for the 2,000 ton expected shortfall.

Some schemes cover a period of more than one year, such that the entity is unconditionally entitled to receive allowances for, say, a 3-year period, and it is possible to carry-over unused emission rights from one year to the next. In our view, these circumstances would justify application of the net liability approach for the entire period concerned, not just the reporting period for which emission rights have been transferred to the entity physically. Accordingly, when applying the net liability approach, an entity may choose a system that measures deficits on the basis of:

* an annual allocation of emission rights, or
* an allocation that covers the entire first 3-year period of the scheme (provided that the entity is unconditionally entitled to all the allowances for the first period concerned).

For such schemes, the entity must apply the chosen method consistently at every reporting date. If the entity chooses the annual allocation basis, a deficit is measured on that basis and there can be no carrying over of rights from one year to the next or back to the previous year.

II   *Impact of purchased emission rights on the 'net liability' approach*

In Example 15.9 above, the entity had an expected shortfall of 2,000 tons. Suppose that during the year it had purchased emission rights to cover some or all of the expected shortfall. How should these be accounted for?

Example 15.10:   Impact of purchased emission rights on the application of 'net liability' approach

In Example 15.9 above, Company A had an expected shortfall of 2,000 tons. The same facts apply, except that at the end of the second quarter, it purchases emission rights for 1,000 tons at €12/ton, i.e. a cost of €12,000. It records these as an intangible asset at cost. No impairment has been necessary.

In recognising the provision for its excess emissions of 2,000 tons at the end of the year, can the entity apply a method whereby the provision is based on the carrying amount of the emission rights it already owns (the 'carrying value method'), with the balance based on the market price at the year end? That is, can the entity recognise a provision of €28,000, being €12,000 (1,000 tons at €12/ton) plus €16,000 (1,000 tons at €16/ton)?

One view is that this 'net liability / carrying value' approach is indeed appropriate. As discussed in Chapter 24 at 4.1, IAS 37 requires the amount of a provision to be measured at 'the best estimate of the expenditure required to settle the present obligation at the end of the reporting period'. [306] The standard equates this estimate with 'the amount that an entity would rationally pay to settle the obligation at the balance sheet date or to transfer it to a third party at that time'.[307] Proponents of this view argue that this cannot be applied in measuring liabilities for emissions as an entity cannot settle the obligation other than by delivering allowances and is not permitted to pay someone to assume the obligation. For this reason, it is argued, the provision can be measured at the cost of settling the obligation, and that the cost to the entity is the current carrying value of the emission rights held.

Another view is that this in an incorrect interpretation of paragraph 37 of IAS 37 as the cost of settlement must be measured at the best estimate of the expenditure required to settle the obligation. The fact that assets that are currently being held may be used to settle the obligation is not relevant in measuring the provision. In accordance with this view, the provision has to be measured as in Example 15.9, i.e. at €32,000 (based on the market value of emission rights at the year end). However, although the measurement of the liability cannot be linked to the measurement of an asset, one could argue that the measurement of the asset could be linked to the measurement of the liability. In other words, IAS 37 allows for reimbursement rights to be measured based upon the measurement of the liability, and actually capped to that amount[308] (see Chapter 24 at 4.4).

Under this 'net liability / reimbursement rights' approach, the entity may consider the emission rights it has purchased as a reimbursement right in respect of the liability, which means it can re-measure to fair value the emission rights that are reimbursements against the liability caused by actual emissions that are measured at fair value. So although Company A has recognised a provision (and an expense) of €32,000, at the same time it would revalue its purchased emission rights, as a reimbursement right, from €12/ton to €16/ton. It would thus recognise a gain of 1,000 tons × €4/ton = €4,000. This leads to a net expense of €28,000 in the income statement. This is the same as the income statement effect of the method whereby the provision is partly measured based on the cost of the asset held.

We believe that both approaches are acceptable, although the reimbursement rights approach is, in our opinion, preferable to the carrying value method.

In practice both the 'net liability' approach and the 'net liability / reimbursement rights' approach have gained acceptance as is illustrated in Extracts 15.10 and 15.11 below.

Centrica applies a 'net liability' approach, i.e. emission rights granted free of charge are accounted for at their nominal value of zero and no government grant is recognised. A liability for the obligation to deliver allowances is only recognised when the level of emissions exceed the level of allowances granted. Centrica measures the liability at the cost of purchased allowances up to the level of purchased allowances held, and then at the market price of allowances ruling at the balance sheet date, with movements in the liability recognised in operating profit.

Extract 15.10: Centrica plc (2007)

Notes to the Financial Statements [extract]

2. Summary of significant accounting policies [extract]

EU Emissions Trading Scheme and renewable obligations certificates [extract]

Granted CO_2 emissions allowances received in a period are initially recognised at nominal value (nil value). Purchased CO_2 emissions allowances are initially recognised at cost (purchase price) within intangible assets. A liability is recognised when the level of emissions exceed the level of allowances granted. The liability is measured at the cost of purchased allowances up to the level of purchased allowances held, and then at the market price of allowances ruling at the balance sheet date, with movements in the liability recognised in operating profit. Forward contracts for the purchase or sale of CO_2 emissions allowances are measured at fair value with gains and losses arising from changes in fair value recognised in the Income Statement. The intangible asset is surrendered at the end of the compliance period reflecting the consumption of economic benefit. As a result no amortisation is recorded during the period.

EADS also applies a 'net liability' approach, but measures the entire liability for the obligation to deliver allowances in excess of those granted at fair value. By contrast, to Centrica, which treats all purchased emission rights as intangible assets, EADS adopts the 'net liability / reimbursement rights' approach whereby it considers purchased emission rights that are dedicated to offset a provision for in excess emission to be reimbursement rights that are accounted for at fair value.

Extract 15.11: European Aeronautic Defence and Space Company EADS N.V. (2007)

Notes to the Consolidated Financial Statements (IFRS) [extract]

Basis of Presentation [extract]

2. Summary of significant accounting policies [extract]

Emission Rights and Provisions for in-excess emission

Under the EU Emission Allowance Trading Scheme (EATS) national authorities have issued on 1st January 2005 permits (emission rights), free of charge, that entitle participating companies to emit a certain amount of greenhouse gas over the compliance period.

The participating companies are permitted to trade those emission rights. To avoid a penalty a participant is required to deliver emission rights at the end of the compliance period equal to its emission incurred.

EADS recognises a provision for emission in case it has caused emissions in excess of emission rights granted. The provision is measured at the fair value (market price) of emission rights necessary to compensate for that shortfall at each balance sheet date.

Emission rights held by EADS are generally accounted for as intangible assets, whereby

i)   Emission rights allocated for free by national authorities are accounted for as a non-monetary government grant at its nominal value of nil.

ii)   Emission rights purchased from other participants are accounted for at cost or the lower recoverable amount; if they are dedicated to offset a provision for in excess emission, they are deemed to be a reimbursement right and are accounted for at fair value.

By deeming the emission rights to be reimbursement rights, EADS can account for them at fair value (though not in excess of the amount of the provision) and to recognise changes in fair value in its income statement for the period. An entity that considers the emission rights to be intangible assets is allowed to account for them at fair value when an active market exists, but in that case would need to recognise the change in fair value in equity which would result in one of the mismatches discussed at 3.3.1 above.

III   Government grant approach

An alternative approach, which has gained acceptance in practice, is to recognise the emission rights granted by the government initially at their fair value and a corresponding government grant in the balance sheet. The government grant element is subsequently recognised in income in accordance with the requirements of IAS 20. To that extent, the approach follows that required by IFRIC 3. However, rather than measuring the liability for the obligation to deliver allowances at the present market price of those allowance, the liability is measured instead by reference to the amounts recorded for the emission rights held as assets that are used to settle the liability.

Although, as with the 'net liability' approach, critics have argued that this approach would not be in line with the requirement in IAS 37 that 'the best estimate of the expenditure required to settle the present obligation is the amount that an entity would rationally pay to settle the obligation at the balance sheet date or to transfer it to a third party at that time'.[309]

Both Stora Enso and Repsol initially recognise the emission rights at fair value as a government grant.

Extract 15.12: Stora Enso Oyj (2007)

Notes to the Consolidated Financial Statements [extract]

Note 1 Accounting Principles [extract]

Emission Rights & Trading

The Group's participation in the European Emissions Trading Scheme, in which it has been allocated allowances to emit a fixed tonnage of carbon dioxide in a fixed period of time, gives rise to an intangible asset for the allowances, a government grant and a liability for the obligation to deliver allowances equal to the emissions that have been made during the compliance period. Emissions Allowances recorded as intangible assets are recognised when the Group is able to exercise control and are measured at fair value at the date of initial recognition. If the market value of emission allowances falls significantly below the carrying amount, and the decrease is considered permanent, then an impairment charge is booked for allowances which the Group will not use internally. The liability to deliver allowances is recognised based on actual emissions; this liability will be settled using allowances on hand, measured at the carrying amount of those allowances, with any excess emissions being measured at the market value of the allowances at the period end.

In the Income Statement, the Group will expense, under Materials & Services, emissions made at the fair value of the rights at their grant date, together with purchased emission rights at their purchase price. Such costs will be offset under Other Operating Income by the income from the original grant of the rights used at their fair value at the grant date, together with income from the release or sale of surplus rights. The Income Statement will thus be neutral in respect of all rights consumed that were within the original grant, any net effect representing either the costs of purchasing additional rights to cover excess emissions, the sale of unused rights or the impairment of allowances not required for internal use.

Repsol applies a similar approach and illustrates even more clearly that the measurement of the liability follows that of the related emission rights. To the extent that emissions are not covered by emission rights, the liability is recognised at the fair value of such allowances at the balance sheet date. Similar to Stora Enso, the grant of emission rights is treated as government grant under IAS 20.

Extract 15.13: Repsol YPF, S.A. (2007)

Notes to the consolidated financial statements for 2007 [extract]

3. Accounting Policies [extract]

3.7. Other intangible assets [extract]

f) Emission allowances

Emission allowances are recognised as an intangible asset and are measured at acquisition cost.

Allowances received for no consideration under the National Emission Allowance Assignment Plan, are initially recognised at the market price prevailing at the beginning of the year in which they are issued, and a balancing item is recognised as a grant for the same amount under deferred income, which are charged against income as the corresponding tonnes of CO_2 emissions are consumed.

These allowances are not depreciated as their book value equals the residual value and, therefore, its depreciable basis is zero, as the allowances keep their value until delivery, and may be sold at any time. The rights of emissions are subject to an annual impairment analysis (see Note 3.9). The market value of the emisions allowances is measured according to the average price of the stock market of the European Union (European Union Allowances) provided by the ECX-European Climate Exchange (index used as benchmark price from 2007 as this is the most liquid market and provides the most stable price signal; until 2006 the benchmark price used was that provided by the LEBA-London Energy Brokers Association)

As the atmosphere emissions are made, the Group records an expense under the heading "Other Expenses" in the consolidated income statement acknowledging a provision based on the CO_2 tonnes emitted and measured (i) at its book value or (ii) by the quotation price at end-year in case Repsol YPF does not have sufficient emission allowances available for the period.

In 2007 the net effect on the income statement of the Group due to transactions related with emission allowances was under EUR 1 million, compared to a net expense of EUR 4 million in 2006.

When emissions allowances for CO_2 tonnes emitted are delivered to the authorities, the intangible assets as well as their corresponding provision are derecognised from the balance sheet without any effect on the income statement.

In determining the fair value upon initial recognition of emission rights that are accounted as intangible assets an entity should take account of the guidance in IAS 38.[310] However, if no active market in emission rights exists, an entity may want to refer to the application guidance in IAS 39 – *Financial Instruments: Recognition and Measurement* – which addresses the issue valuation in the absence of an active market.[311] In this latter case, whilst a fair value can assigned on initial recognition, the lack of an active market prohibits subsequent revaluation of the intangible asset.[312]

IV   Amortisation and impairment testing of emission rights

In principle it is possible to amortise emission rights that are accounted for as intangible assets, but their expected residual value, at least at inception, will be equal to their fair value. Subsequently, the residual value of emission rights is equal to their market value. In the case of cap and trade schemes, however, there is no consumption of economic benefit while the emission right is held. Instead, the economic benefits are realised by surrendering the rights to settle obligations under the scheme for emissions made, or by selling rights to another party. Therefore, the amount to be amortised will in many circumstances be nil. However, it is necessary to perform an IAS 36 impairment test whenever there is an indication of impairment. Nevertheless, when the market value of an emission right drops below its carrying amount, this does not automatically result in an impairment charge because emission rights are often tested for impairment as part of a larger cash generating unit.

V   Emission rights acquired in a business combination

Complications in accounting for emission rights also arise in the context of business combinations. At the date of acquisition of a business, an acquirer is required to recognise the acquiree's identifiable intangible assets (e.g. emission rights) at their fair values.[313] However, an acquirer should only recognise a provision for actual emissions that have occurred up to that date.

Accordingly, an acquirer cannot apply the 'net liability' approach to emission rights acquired in a business combination. Instead, such an acquirer should treat acquired emission rights in the same way as purchased emission rights (see II above). An acquirer that applies IFRIC 3 or the 'government grant' approach would recognise acquired emission rights at their fair value, but cannot recognise a deferred credit for a 'government grant' as it acquired the emission rights by way of a business combination.

Consequently, an acquirer may report a higher emission expense in its income statement in the compliance period in which it acquires a business.

VI   *Sale of emission rights*

The sale of emission rights that are accounted for as intangible assets should be recognised in accordance with IAS 38. This means that they should be derecognised on disposal or when no future economic benefits are expected from their use or disposal (see 2.9 above).[314] The gain or loss arising from derecognition of the emission rights should be determined as the difference between the net disposal proceeds and the carrying amount of emission rights.[315]

Prior to the sale the entity may not have recognised the obligation, to deliver allowances equal to the emissions caused, at its fair value at the date of derecognition. If that were the case then the entity would need to ensure that the liability in excess of the emission rights held by the company after the sale is recognised at the present fair value of the emission rights.

Both the gain or loss on the derecognition of the emission rights and the adjustment of the liability should be recognised when the emission rights are derecognised. Any gain should not be classified as revenue.[316]

If an entity that applies the 'net liability' approach were to sell all its emission rights at the start of the compliance period, it would not be permitted to defer the gain on that sale even if it was certain that the entity would need to repurchase emission rights later in the year to cover actual emissions. A gain is recognised immediately on the sale and a provision is recognised as gases are emitted.

VII   *Disclosure*

It is clear that the interpretation of the hierarchy of authoritative guidance in IAS 8 has led to a number of methods of accounting for emission rights, each with its own merits. In the absence of more detailed IFRS guidance, companies should disclose their accounting policies regarding grants of emission rights, the emission rights themselves, the liability for the obligation to deliver allowances equal to emissions that have been made and the presentation in the income statement.[317]

3.3.3 Accounting for emission rights by brokers and traders

As mentioned above, IFRIC 3 does not address accounting by brokers and traders that are not themselves participants in a cap and trade scheme. However, in their case emission rights are assets held for sale in the ordinary course of business, which means that they meet the definition of inventories in IAS 2.[318] Under that standard a broker-trader may choose between measuring emission rights at the lower of cost and net realisable value or at fair value less costs to sell. Commodity broker-traders who measure their inventories at fair value less costs to sell may recognise changes in fair value less costs in profit or loss in the period of the change.[319]

When a company trades derivatives based on the emission rights, they fall within the scope of IAS 39 and are accounted for at fair value through profit or loss unless they hedge the fair value of the emission rights granted to the company or qualify for the 'own use exemption'.[320]

When an entity holds emission rights for own use and also has a trading department trading in emission rights, the company should split the books between emission rights held for own use and those held for trading. The emission rights should be treated as intangible assets and inventory respectively.

3.4 Accounting for green certificates or renewable energy certificates

Some governments have launched schemes to promote power production from renewable sources, based on green certificates, also known as renewable energy certificates, green tags or tradable renewable certificates. There are similarities between green certificates and emission rights, except that whilst emission rights are granted to reflect a future limit on emissions, green certificates are awarded on the basis of the amount of green energy already produced.

In a typical scheme, producers of electricity are granted certificates by the government based on the power output (kWh) derived from renewable sources. Entities distributing electricity (produced from both renewable and traditional sources) are required to hand over to the government a number of certificates based on the total kWh of electricity sold to consumers during the year, or pay a penalty to the extent that an insufficient number of certificates is rendered. It is this requirement that creates a valuable market for the certificates, allowing producers to sell their certificates to distributors, using the income to subsidise in effect the higher cost of generation from renewable sources.

3.4.1 *Accounting by producers using renewable energy sources*

As in the case of emission rights, the award of green certificates is treated as a government grant by a producer. An intangible asset representing an entitlement to that grant is recognised at the point in time when the green electricity is produced. As with any government grant, the entitlement is initially measured at either fair value or a nominal amount, depending on the entity's chosen policy.

Where the entitlement asset is initially recognised at fair value, a credit entry is recorded in the income statement as either a reduction in production costs for the period (on the basis that the purpose of the grant is to compensate the producer for the higher cost of using renewable energy sources) or as other income. Subsequent revaluation of the intangible asset is only allowed if an active market exists for the green certificates, and the other requirements of IAS 38 are applied (see 2.4.2 above). The intangible is derecognised when the certificate is sold by the producer.

3.4.2 *Accounting by distributors of renewable energy*

When the distributor is also a producer of renewable energy, it has the option to use certificates granted to it or to sell them in the market. Accordingly, the permissible accounting treatments of green certificates are in principle the same as those discussed at 3.3.2 above for emission rights. The distributor is obliged to remit certificates and therefore recognises a provision as sales are recorded (in the same way that a provision for emission rights is recognised as emissions are made). As discussed at 3.3.2 above, the distributor might apply a 'net liability' approach, and only start to recognise a provision once it has achieved a level of sales exceeding that covered by certificates granted to the entity in its capacity as a producer.

Where a distributor is not also a producer of renewable energy, it recognises a provision as sales are made, measured at the fair value of green certificates to be remitted. A corresponding cost is included in cost of sales. The provision is remeasured to fair value at each reporting date. If such an entity purchases certificates in the market, they are recognised as an intangible asset and initially measured at cost. Subsequent revaluation is only allowed if an active market exists for the green certificates, and the other requirements of IAS 38 are applied (see 2.4.2 above).

Alternatively, as discussed in Example 15.10 above, the asset held may be designated by management as a reimbursement right in respect of the associated liability, allowing remeasurement to fair value. Similarly, although a less preferable approach in our view, the entity could apply a carrying value method, measuring the provision based on the value and extent of certificates already held and applying fair value only to the extent that it has an obligation to make further purchases in the market or to incur a penalty if it fails to do so.

3.4.3   Accounting by brokers and traders

As discussed at 3.3.3 above, brokers and traders should apply IAS 2 where green certificates are held for sale in the ordinary course of business; account for derivatives based on green certificates in accordance with IAS 39; and properly distinguish those held for own use (carried within intangible assets) from certificates held for trading (included in inventory).

3.5   Accounting for REACH costs

The European Regulation[321] concerning the Registration, Evaluation, Authorisation and Restriction of Chemicals (REACH) came into force from 1 June 2007 and raised questions as to whether the costs that will be incurred in connection with the Regulation could be capitalised under IAS 38 as intangible assets.

The regulation requires manufacturers or importers of substances to register them with a central European Chemicals Agency (ECHA). An entity will not be able to manufacture or supply unregistered substances. As a consequence, entities will incur different types of costs, such as:

- costs of identifying the substances that need to be registered;
- testing and other data collection costs, including outsourcing services from external laboratories, costs of tests in own laboratories – testing materials, labour costs and related overheads;
- registration fees payable to ECHA; and
- legal fees.

These costs may be part of the development of a new manufacturing process or product, or in the use of a new chemical in an existing manufacturing process or product. They might be incurred solely by an entity or shared with other entities (clients, partners or even competitors). Under the REACH legislation, cost sharing might be achieved by the submission of a joint registration (whereby testing and other data collection costs are shared before the registration is filed) or by reimbursement (whereby an entity pays an existing registrant for access to the registration and testing data used in its earlier application for registration). Accordingly, questions arise as to whether such costs should be capitalised or recognised as an expense and, if capitalised, on what basis the related intangible asset should be amortised.

In March and May 2009, the IFRIC considered whether to add the treatment of REACH costs to its agenda. The IFRIC noted that IAS 38 already included sufficient in the way of definitions and recognition criteria for intangible assets to enable entities to account for the costs of complying with the REACH regulation. All that it could add would be more in the nature of implementation guidance, so it decided not to add the issue to its agenda.[322]

In our opinion, a registration under the REACH regulation is an intangible asset as defined by IAS 38.[323] As it gives rise to a legal right, the registration is identifiable.[324] Because a registration cannot be arbitrarily withdrawn and also establishes intellectual property rights over the data used in the application for registration, a resource is controlled.[325] The future economic benefits relating to the registration arise from either the right to reimbursement for the use by others of data supporting the entity's earlier application; or from the revenues to be earned and cost savings to be achieved by the entity from the use of registered substances in its business activities.[326]

The appropriate accounting treatment under IAS 38 depends upon whether the required data is collected by the entity or acquired from an existing registrant and on whether the registration being completed is for a substance already used in an existing process or product (an existing substance) or intended to be used for the first time or in a new process or product (a new substance). The flow chart below demonstrates how these different features interact with the requirements of IAS 38.

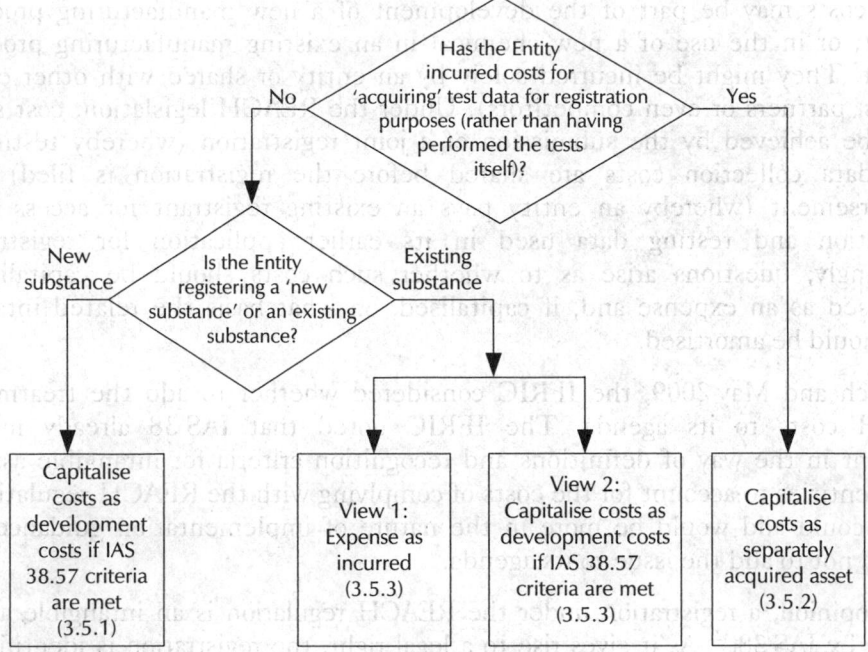

3.5.1   Costs of registering a new substance performed by the entity itself

If the entity itself incurs REACH costs (see 3.5 above), these activities meet the definition of development in IAS 38.[327] Accordingly, the entity must also meet the rigorous rules in the standard described in 2.3.6 B above which confirm that the related development project is at a sufficiently advanced stage, is economically viable and includes only directly attributable costs[328].

Costs of identifying the substances that need to be registered would have to be recognised as an expense when incurred, as this activity is regarded as research.[329]

3.5.2   Costs of acquiring test data from an existing registrant

An entity may acquire test data from an existing registrant that has already been used by it in its earlier application for registration. These costs should be capitalised as a separately acquired intangible asset (see 2.3.1 above).

3.5.3   Costs of registering an existing substance performed by the entity itself

In this case two alternative treatments are acceptable. If the costs of obtaining a REACH registration for existing substances used in existing processes are regarded as subsequent expenditure on an existing intangible asset, the related costs should be recognised as an expense as incurred[330] (see 2.2.3 above). As unregistered substances will no longer be available for use, this might indicate that the registration maintains the economic benefits associated with the related production process or product and does not improve it.

Alternatively, it could be argued that the cost of registering existing substances should be regarded as no different to the cost of registering a new product.

Accordingly, for the reasons noted at 3.5.1 above, such costs should be capitalised as an internally generated intangible asset.

3.5.4   Determining the basis for amortisation

The useful life of a registration reflects the entity's expectations as to how long it will benefit from the use of the registered substance, the related product life cycles and the effect of any legally imposed limit to the period over which the benefits of registration can be enjoyed[331] (see 2.6.1 above).

3.6   Television and programme rights

A number of accounting issues arise for television stations and other media companies that produce, own or broadcast programmes on television or otherwise:

- classification of programme rights (see 3.6.1 below);
- recognition of programme rights that have not been paid for (see 3.6.2 below);
- amortisation of programme rights (see 3.6.3 below).

3.6.1   Classification of programme rights

Programme rights meet the definition of intangible assets because they are identifiable non-monetary assets without physical substance. Earlier versions of IAS 38 required intangible assets to be 'held for use in the production or supply of goods or services, for rental to others, or for administrative purposes' in order to meet the definition of an intangible asset.[332] The amendment of IAS 38 in 2003 broadened the definition of an intangible asset and it now covers both programme rights that are 'held for use in the production or supply of goods or services, for rental to others, or for administrative purposes' and all other programme rights that are not specifically covered by another standard.

Programme rights that are held or developed for sale in the ordinary course of business also meet the definition of inventory and are therefore within the scope of IAS 2.[333] When an entity holds the rights to programmes exclusively with a view to selling those rights to other parties, they evidently meet the definition of inventory.

In the case of programmes held with a view to broadcasting them to an audience, it is possible to argue that they are comparable to 'materials or supplies to be consumed in the production process or in the rendering of services',[334] which would mean that they could also be treated as inventory. Equally, it can be argued that such programme rights are intangible assets as they are used in the production or supply of services.

Ultimately, the appropriate classification of programme rights will depend on the particular facts and circumstances as they apply to an entity. However, it is clearly possible for an entity to conclude that some of its programme rights are intangible assets while others should be treated as inventory.

In practice, companies either classify programme rights as intangible assets or as inventories. Vivendi accounts for its film and television rights catalogues as intangible assets (see Extract 15.15 below). ITV on the other hand, presents its programme rights as current assets under the caption 'Programme rights and other inventory'.

Extract 15.14: ITV plc (2007)

Notes to the accounts [extract]
1   **Accounting policies** [extract]
1.13)   **Programme rights** [extract]

Where programming, sports rights and film rights are acquired for the primary purpose of broadcasting, these are recognised within current assets. Assets are recognised when the Group controls, in substance, the respective assets and the risks and rewards associated with them. For acquired programme rights assets are recognised as payments are made and are recognised in full when the acquired programming is available for transmission. Programming produced internally either for the purpose of broadcasting or to be sold in the normal course of the Group's operating cycle is recognised within current assets at production cost.

Programme costs and rights, including those acquired under sale and leaseback arrangements, are written off to operating costs in full on first transmission except certain film rights which are written off over a number of transmissions. Programme costs and rights not yet written off at the balance sheet date are included on the balance sheet at the lower of cost and net realisable value.

17 Programme rights and other inventory

	2007 £m	2006 £m
Commissions	116	106
Sports rights	23	20
Acquired films	222	184
Production	55	48
Prepayments	22	41
Other	2	1
	440	400

Net programme rights and other inventory written off in the year, included within operating costs analysed in note 4, was £28 million (2006: £12 million).

3.6.2   Recognition of programme rights

Television stations frequently enter into contracts to buy programme rights related to long-running televisions series or future sports events that are not yet available for broadcast, which raises the question when those programme rights should be recognised in the balance sheet.

The IASB's Framework recognises that in practice 'obligations under contracts that are equally proportionately unperformed (for example, liabilities for inventory ordered but not yet received) are generally not recognised as liabilities in the financial statements'.[335] For example, liabilities in connection with non-cancellable orders of inventory or items of property, plant and equipment are generally not recognised in an entity's balance sheet until the goods have been delivered. The same approach can also be applied to programme rights as is illustrated in the extract from Vivendi below.

Extract 15.15: Vivendi S.A. (2007)

NOTES TO THE CONSOLIDATED FINANCIAL STATEMENTS [extract]
10.2. Contractual content commitments [extract]
Commitments given recorded in the Statement of Financial Position: content liabilities [extract]

	Minimum Future Payments as of December 31, 2007				Total as at December 31 2006
		Due in		After	
(in millions of euros)	Total	2008	2009-2012	2012	
Music royalties to artists and repertoire owners	1,485	1,436	49	–	1,334
Film and television rights (a)	182	182	–	–	116
Sport rights	473	464	9	–	500
Creative talent and employment agreements (b)	225	114	94	17	201
Total content liabilities	2,365	2,196	152	17	2,151

Off balance sheet commitments given/received [extract]

	Minimum Future Payments as of December 31, 2007				Total as at December 31 2006
		Due in		After	
(in millions of euros)	Total	2008	2009-2012	2012	
Film and television rights (a)	3,278	1,160	1,617	501	2,672
Sport rights					
Creative talent, employment agreements and others (b)	181	95	86	–	748
Total given	4,464	1,708	2,206	550	4,399
Film and television rights (a)	(87)	(67)	(20)	–	(118)
Sport rights	–	–	–	–	(29)
Creative talent, employment agreements and others(b)		not available			
Other	(9)	(8)	(1)	–	(19)
Total received	(96)	(75)	(21)	–	(166)
Total net	4,368	1,633	2,185	550	4,233

The amounts presented above for off balance sheet commitments given are the minimum amount guaranteed to third parties.

(a) Includes primarily contracts valid over several years relating to the broadcast of future film and TV productions (mainly exclusivity contracts with major US studios and pre-purchases in the French movie industry), StudioCanal film coproduction commitments (given and received) and broadcasting rights of CanalSat and Cyfra+ multichannel digital TV packages. They are recorded as content assets when the broadcast is available for initial release.

(b) UMG routinely commits to artists and other parties to pay agreed amounts upon delivery of content or other product ("Creative talent and employment agreements"). Until the artist or other party has delivered his or her content, UMG discloses its obligation as an off balance sheet commitment. While the artist or other party is also obligated to deliver his or her content or other product to UMG (these arrangements are generally exclusive), UMG does not report these obligations (or the likelihood of the other party's failure to meet its obligations) as an offset to its off balance sheet commitments.

As illustrated in Extract 15.14 above, ITV follows a similar type of approach for acquired programme rights under which an asset is recognised as payments are made and is recognised in full when the acquired programming is available for transmission.

3.6.3 Amortisation of programme rights

The value of programme rights diminishes because the programmes have been broadcast to the same audience before and as result of the passage of time (e.g. the right is for a limited period or audiences loose interest in old programmes). In accounting for this diminution in value, in practice, entities usually take into account how often a programme has been broadcast and, less frequently, the passage of time as such.

When an entity accounts for programme rights as inventory, the problem arises that IAS 2 requires valuation 'at the lower of cost and net realisable value' and does not appear to recognise the concept of amortisation of inventories.[336] However, it has been argued that a programme right embodies a series of identifiable components (i.e. first transmission, second transmission, etc.), which an entity should account for separately. This appears to be the approach that ITV applies in writing off its programme rights (see Extract 15.14 above).

An entity that accounts for programme rights as intangible assets would need to comply with the requirements of IAS 38, which requires that the amortisation method reflects the pattern in which the asset's future economic benefits are expected to be consumed by the entity.[337] As discussed at 2.6.1 above, the standard permits a range of amortisation methods (e.g. the straight-line method, the diminishing balance method and the unit of production method), provided that the chosen method reflects the pattern in which the asset's future economic benefits are expected to be consumed.[338]

The extract from Antena 3's financial statements below, illustrates a commonly used method of amortisation of programme rights that is based on the number of showings.

Extract 15.16: Antena 3 de Televisión, S.A. (2007)

NOTES TO THE 2006 AND 2005 CONSOLIDATED FINANCIAL STATEMENTS [extract]
3. Accounting policies [extract]
E) Inventories [extract]
Programme rights [extract]

Programme rights are valued, based on their nature, as follows:

1. Inventoriable in-house productions (programmes produced to be re-run, such as series) are measured at acquisition and/or production cost, which includes both external costs billed by third parties for programme production and for the acquisition of resources, and internal production costs, which are calculated by applying preset internal rates on the basis of the time during which operating resources are used in production. The costs incurred in producing the programmes are recognised, based on their nature, under the appropriate headings in the consolidated income statement and are included under "Programme Rights" in the consolidated balance sheet with a credit to "Inclusion in Inventories" under "Amortisation of Programmes and Other Rights" in the accompanying income statement.

    Amortisation of these programmes is recorded under "Amortisation of Programmes and Other Rights" in the income statement, on the basis of the number of showings, in accordance with the rates shown below:

	Amortisation Rate
1st showing	90%
2nd showing	10%

> The maximum period for amortisation of series is three years, after which the unamortised amount is written off.
>
> Given their special nature, the series which are broadcast daily are amortised in full when the first showing of each episode is broadcast.
>
> 2.　Non-inventoriable in-house productions (programmes produced to be shown only once) are valued by the same methods and procedures as those used to value inventoriable in-house productions. Programmes produced and not shown are recognised at year-end under "Programme Rights – In-House Productions and Productions in Process" in the balance sheet. Amortisation of rights is recorded under "Amortisation of Programmes and Other Rights" in the income statement at the time of the first showing.

Mediaset is an example of a company that amortises some of its programme rights on a straight line basis.

> *Extract 15.17: Mediaset S.p.A. (2007)*
>
> Explanatory notes [extract]
>
> 3. Summary of accounting standards and valuation criteria [extract]
>
> Intangible assets [extract]
>
> **Assets with defined useful life** are amortised on a straight-line basis starting from the moment when the asset is available for use for the period of their expected use; the possibility to recover their value is assessed according to the criteria envisaged by IAS 36, described in the next section *Impairment of assets*.
>
> This principle is also used for multi-year licences regarding **television rights**, which are generally amortised on a straight-line basis unless a different principle can be determined that can reasonably and reliably reflect the correlation between costs, audience and advertising revenues.
>
> In particular, for the library of television rights available for broadcasting on multiple networks, the straight-line amortisation method is generally adopted, calculated for ownership rights and rights with unlimited duration over a period of 60 months and for tights with limited duration over a period of the relevant contract and, in any case, a period not exceeding 120 months. This method reflects greater opportunities to exploit television rights, also considering the difficulty in identifying objective components for the correlation between advertising revenues and the amortisation of rights. Regardless of the amortisation already recognised, if all showings made available under the relevant television rights contracts have been used up, the residual value is fully discharged.

3.7　Intangible assets acquired in a business combination

3.7.1　*Valuing intangible assets*

Fair value is defined as 'the amount for which an asset could be exchanged, or a liability settled, between knowledgeable, willing parties in an arm's length transaction.'[339]

Currently IFRS does not offer detailed guidance on determining fair values. However, in May 2009, the IASB published an exposure draft – *Fair Value Measurement*, which proposes to clarify the definition of fair value, establish a framework for measurement including a fair value hierarchy and enhance disclosures where fair value is used. The proposed standard will replace guidance contained in other IFRSs and as a result, some consequential amendments to IAS 38 would be made.[340] The proposed fair value hierarchy is similar to that set out in the exposure draft issued in June 2005 out of the second phase of the business combinations project.[341] It groups into three broad categories (levels) the inputs used to estimate fair value, giving the highest priority to quoted prices in active markets for identical assets and liabilities and the lowest priority to unobservable inputs developed on the basis of assumptions that entities would use in the absence of market data.[342] The proposed levels of input in the fair value hierarchy are as follows:

(a)   Level 1 inputs are quoted prices (unadjusted) in active markets for identical assets or liabilities that the entity can access at the measurement date.[343]

(b)   Level 2 inputs are those other than quoted prices included in Level 1 that are either directly or indirectly observable for the asset or liability.[344]

(c)   Level 3 inputs are not based on observable market data. They reflect the assumptions that would be used by entities when pricing an asset or liability, including assumptions about risk.[345]

The practical reality is that a Level 3 assessment would be necessary for most intangible assets acquired in a business combination. 'Fair values' would be determined by estimating what the market price would be if there were a market.

The exposure draft describes a number of valuation techniques that could be used to estimate the market price of assets such as intangible assets:[346]

(a)   *Market approach* – The fair value of an intangible asset is derived by analysing market transactions for comparable intangible assets that have recently been sold or licensed, such as by applying market multiples.;

(b)   *Income approach* – The fair value of an intangible asset is calculated as the present value of the expected future cash flows or income and expenses. An example would be the multi-period excess earnings method used to measure the fair value of some intangible assets (see Chapter 9 at 2.5.4 F); and

(c)   *Cost approach* – The premise of the cost approach is that an investor would pay no more for an intangible asset than its replacement cost. Under IFRS, application of a cost approach may not always be appropriate for determining the recoverable amount of an asset as 'replacement cost measures the cost of an asset and not the future economic benefits recoverable from its use and/or disposal'.[347]

The extract below illustrates that many companies use more than one approach in calculating the fair value of intangible assets.

Extract 15.18: Bayer AG (2006)

Notes to the Consolidated Financial Statements of the Bayer Group [extract]

5.   Critical accounting policies

Acquisition accounting [extract]

For intangible assets associated with products, product related technology, and qualified in-process research and development (IPR&D) we base our valuation on the expected future cash flows using the Multi-Period Excess Earnings approach. This method employs a discounted cash flow analysis using the present value of the estimated after-tax cash flows expected to be generated from the purchased intangible asset using risk adjusted discount rates and revenue forecasts as appropriate. The period of expected cash flows was based on the individual patent protection, taking into account the term of the product's main patent protection and essential extension of patent protection, as well as market entry of generics, considering sales, volume, prices, potential defense strategies and market development at patent expiry.

For the valuation of brands, the relief-from-royalty method was applied which includes estimating the cost savings that result from the company's ownership of trademarks and licenses on which it does not have to pay royalties to a licensor. The intangible asset is then recognized at the present value of these savings. The brand-specific royalty rates were calculated using a product-specific scoring model. The corporate brands "Schering" and "Medrad" were assumed to have an unlimited life. (Please note that the rights to the name "Schering" in the United States and Canada do not belong to us but to Schering-Plough Corporation, New Jersey. Schering-Plough Corporation and the company acquired by Bayer in June 2006, i.e. Bayer Schering Pharma AG [formerly named Schering AG], Berlin, Germany, are unaffiliated companies that have been totally independent of each other for many years.) Product brands, however, were assumed to have limited lives depending on the respective products' life cycles. The expected amortization of these assets is determined on the basis of expected product-specific revenues.

The proposals in the exposure draft are discussed further in Chapter 2 at 6.3. At the time of writing, the IASB estimates that an IFRS on fair value measurement will be published in the second quarter of 2010.[348]

3.7.2   *Measurement of intangible assets acquired for contingent consideration*

Transactions involving contingent consideration are often very complex and payment is dependent on a number of factors. In the absence of specific guidance in IAS 38, entities trying to determine an appropriate accounting treatment are required not only to understand the commercial complexities of the transaction itself, but also to negotiate a variety of accounting principles and requirements.

Consider a relatively simple example where an entity acquires an intangible asset for consideration comprising a combination of up-front payment, guaranteed instalments for a number of years and additional amounts that vary according to future activity (revenue, profit or number of units output).

Does the contingent consideration relate solely to the acquisition of the asset (and thereby qualify as a component of cost[349]), or is an element related to its use (and accordingly recognised as an expense[350])? Should the obligation to pay contingent consideration be regarded as a financial liability (in respect of which subsequent changes are reflected in profit or loss[351]), or does the obligation give rise to a provision under IAS 37 and could the entity look to IFRIC 1 – *Changes in Existing Decommissioning, Restoration and Similar Liabilities* (see Chapter 16 at 3.2.3.), whereby changes in the provision are reflected in the carrying value of the related asset?[352]

We urge the IASB to consider these questions, in particular as it redeliberates its proposals to amend both IAS 39 and IAS 37.

4   TRANSITIONAL ARRANGEMENTS

The application of IAS 38 is linked to the implementation of IFRS 3 (2007) and IFRS 3, because of the common ground that exists between the standards on the matter of recognising intangible assets acquired in a business combination. Accordingly, IAS 38 (as revised in 2004) applied to 'the accounting for intangible assets acquired in business combinations for which the agreement date is on or after 31 March 2004' and to 'the accounting for all other intangible assets prospectively from the beginning of the first annual period beginning on or after 31 March 2004'.[353]

4.1 Adoption of IFRS 3 (as revised in 2008)

The amendments to IAS 38 that accompany the introduction of IFRS 3 are mandatory for annual periods beginning on or after 1 July 2009 and apply prospectively. If an entity adopts the revised version IFRS 3 early, it should also apply IAS 38 (as revised in 2008) prospectively from the same date. The entity should not adjust the carrying amount of intangible assets and goodwill in prior business combinations.[354]

4.2 Amendments arising from the 2008 improvements standard

As noted at 2.3.8 A above, the amendments to the standard arising from the Board's deliberations on advertising and catalogue costs take effect for annual periods beginning on or after 1 January 2009. Earlier application is permitted, provided that this is disclosed.[355]

4.3 Amendments arising from the 2009 improvements standard

The amendments to IAS 38 noted at 2.3.2 C above relating to the measurement, in the absence of an active market, of the fair value of intangible assets acquired in a business combination apply prospectively for annual periods beginning on or after 1 July 2009. Earlier application is permitted, provided that this is disclosed.[356]

5 FUTURE DEVELOPMENTS

5.1 Exposure draft on rate-regulated activities

As noted at 3.1 above, there are a number of countries adopting IFRS in the near future that currently allow or require the recognition of regulatory assets and liabilities, whereas existing IFRS reporters seem to do so rarely.[357] In July 2009, the IASB issued an exposure draft on certain types of rate-regulated activities, to secure what the board describes as 'a definitive conclusion on the question'.[358] The deadline for comments is 20 November 2009.

5.1.1 Scope of the proposals

The scope of the proposals is intended to be restrictive, applying only to entities whose operating activities meet the following criteria:[359]

(a) an authorised body (the 'regulator') establishes the price the entity must charge its customers for the goods or services that the entity provides and the customers are bound by that price; and

(b) the price established by regulation (the 'rate') is designed to recover the specific costs the entity incurs in providing the regulated goods or services and to earn a specified return (cost-of-service regulation). The specified return could be a minimum or range and need not be fixed or guaranteed.

Cost-of-service regulation is defined as 'a form of regulation for setting an entity's prices (rates) in which there is a cause-and-effect relationship between the entity's specific costs and its revenues.[360] Forms of regulation that establish different rates for different categories, such as different classes of customers or volumes purchased, are within this scope provided that the regulator approves the definition and the rate for each of those categories and that all customers of the same category are bound by the same rate.[361] For example, the rate-regulated activities of an entity would not be excluded from the proposals simply because the entity is also engaged in unregulated activities.[362] However, regulatory mechanisms applying targeted or assumed costs, such as industry averages, rather than an entity's specific costs, are outside the scope of the proposals.[363]

The scope of the proposals is limited to regulation based on an entity's actual costs because the Board has concluded that a regulatory asset can only be deemed to exist if the entity's rights under rate-regulation relates to identifiable future cash flows linked to costs it previously incurred, rather than relating to any expectation of future cash flows based on the existence of predictable demand. Such a 'cause-and-effect relationship' must be evident for an asset to exist.[364]

It is clear that a scope restriction would be required, because entities operating outside a regulatory environment might look for similar cause-and-effect relationships. For example, if a customer contractually agrees to suffer a future price increase on the basis of data demonstrating that its supplier had incurred higher than reasonable production costs in the past, the supplier might try to argue that there is just as compelling a case for recognising an intangible asset for the right to future price increases.

In addition, given the wide range of regulatory frameworks worldwide, it will be important that such a scope restriction clearly identifies which regimes would fall under the scope of the proposals and which would not. If drafted too loosely, the consequence may be that in meeting the conversion needs of, for example, North American power generators and distributors, the proposals bring into their scope entities previously unaffected by similar requirements under their local GAAP. Therefore, the IASB should confirm whether the proposals should be restricted to monopoly operators and to certain industries.

5.1.2 Recognition and measurement

The Exposure Draft proposes that when an entity falling within its scope has the right to increase or the obligation to decrease rates in future periods as a result of the actual or expected actions of the regulator, it shall recognise:[365]

(a)   a regulatory asset for its right to recover specific previously incurred costs and to earn a specified return; or

(b)   a regulatory liability for its obligation to refund previously collected amounts and to pay a specified return.

Accordingly a regulatory asset (or liability) is recognised to reflect amounts that would otherwise be recorded in that period in the statement of comprehensive income as an expense (or revenue).[366] That asset or liability should be carried initially and at the end of subsequent reporting periods at its expected present value.[367] Such an expected present value would comprise the following elements for a regulatory asset or a regulatory liability:[368]

(a)   an estimate of the future cash flows that will arise in a range of possible outcomes;

(b)   an estimate of the probability of each outcome occurring;

(c)   the time value of money, represented by the current market risk-free rate of interest; and

(d)   the price for bearing the uncertainty inherent in the regulatory asset or regulatory liability.

Changes in the estimate of the expected present value of the regulatory asset or regulatory liability after initial recognition are recorded as adjustments to the carrying value of the asset.[369] Where such assets are components of an item of property, plant and equipment or an internally generated intangible asset, it is proposed that entities could disregard the usual prohibition from capitalising costs after the asset is available for use,[370] but only if their inclusion by the regulator in the cost for rate-setting purposes is highly probable. Otherwise a separate regulatory asset is recognised.[371]

The proposals also require that regulatory assets are subject to a test of recoverability, whereby the entity considers the extent to which it will recover the previously incurred costs from its customers. This consideration should take into account the net effect that the imposed increase or decrease in prices is expected to have on the level of customer demand or competition during the period of cost recovery.[372] If an entity concludes that it is not reasonable to assume that it will be able to collect sufficient revenues from its customers to recover its costs, this is an indication that the cash-generating unit in which the regulatory assets and regulatory liabilities are included may be impaired and it will have to be tested for impairment in accordance with IAS 36.[373]

5.1.3   *Presentation and disclosure*

Regulatory assets and liabilities would be presented separately from other assets and liabilities on the face of the balance sheet, and classified as current and non-current items.[374] Offsetting would only be allowed for each category of asset or liability subject to the same regulator.[375]

The Exposure Draft proposes that entities would disclose the fact that some or all of its operating activities are subject to rate regulation, including a description of their nature and extent.[376] For each set of operating activities subject to a different regulator, an entity would disclose the following information:[377]

(a)   if the regulator is a related party;

(b)   an explanation of the approval process for the rate subject to regulation (including the rate of return), including information about how that process affects both the underlying operating activities and the specified rate of return;

(c)   the indicators that management considered in concluding that such operating activities have met the scope criteria (if that condition requires significant judgement);

(d)   significant assumptions used to measure the expected present value of a recognised regulatory asset or regulatory liability including:

   (i)   the supporting regulatory action, for example, the issue of a formal approval for costs to be recovered pending a final ruling at a later date and that date, when known, or

   (ii)   the entity's assessment of the expected future regulatory actions; and

(e)   the risks and uncertainties affecting the future recovery of the regulatory asset or final settlement of the regulatory liability, including the expected timing.

For each category of regulatory asset or regulatory liability recognised that is subject to a different regulator, it is proposed that the entity disclose:[378]

(a)   a reconciliation from the beginning to the end of the period, in tabular format unless another format is more appropriate, of the carrying amount in the balance sheet of the regulatory asset or regulatory liability, including at least the following elements:

   (i)   the amount recognised in the income statement/statement of comprehensive income relating to balances from prior periods collected or refunded in the current period;

   (ii)   the amount of costs incurred in the current period that were recognised in the balance sheet as regulatory assets or regulatory liabilities to be recovered or refunded in future periods; and

   (iii)   other amounts that affected the regulatory asset or regulatory liability, such as items acquired or assumed in business combinations or the effects of changes in foreign exchange rates, discount rates or estimated cash flows. If a single cause has a significant effect on the regulatory asset or regulatory liability, the entity shall disclose it separately.

(b)   the remaining period over which the entity expects to recover the carrying amount of the regulatory asset or to settle the regulatory liability; and

(c)   the amount of financing cost included in the cost of self-constructed property, plant and equipment and internally developed intangible assets in the current period that would not have been capitalised under IAS 23.

At the time of writing it is difficult to determine how this exposure draft will be received. Some might point to the way that a customer base acquired in a business combination is recognised as an intangible asset and regard the exposure draft as a logical extension of this thinking to assets and liabilities that arise in situations where a regulator is effectively negotiating on behalf of a whole customer base. Others might point to the current lack of diversity in practice and question the need for the proposed new standard. The challenge for the IASB will be twofold: to define clearly in what situations and regulatory environments it is appropriate to recognise regulatory assets and liabilities and to make the case for its proposals to current users of IFRS.

5.2   Emissions trading schemes

As noted at 3.3.1 above, the IASB resumed its project on emissions trading schemes in December 2007 in response to requests from several national standard setters to address the topic and the addition by the FASB of a project on emissions allowances to its agenda. The Board decided to limit the scope of the project to accounting issues relating to emissions trading schemes, rather than to consider more general issues regarding the accounting for government grants.[379]

In May 2008, the Board tentatively decided to address the accounting for all tradable emissions rights and obligations arising under emissions trading schemes and in addition to address the accounting of activities undertaken by entities contemplating the receipt of tradable rights in future periods, such as certified emissions reductions (CERs). At this time the Board confirmed that it would not be constrained by existing IFRSs, although the *Framework* would still be relevant.[380]

The objective of the project is to develop comprehensive guidance on the accounting for emissions trading schemes, including (but not limited to) the following issues:[381]

- Are emission allowances assets? Is this conclusion affected by how the allowance is acquired? What is the nature of the allowance (e.g. licence to emit or a form of emission currency)? If allowances are assets, should they be recognised and, if so, how should they be measured initially?

- What is the corresponding entry for an entity that receives allowances from government free of charge? Does a liability exist? If so, what is the nature of the liability and how should it be measured both initially and subsequently?

- How should allowances be accounted for subsequently? Is the existing model in IAS 38 or IAS 39 appropriate? If not, what is the appropriate accounting?

- When should an entity recognise its obligations in emissions trading schemes and how should they be measured? How does IAS 37 apply?

- What are the overall financial reporting effects of the above decisions?

In March 2009, the IASB tentatively decided that emission allowances received free of charge from government should be recognised as assets and initially measured at fair value. The Board also tentatively decided at that meeting that a liability should be recognised for the entity's obligation to reduce its emissions below the established cap level. This liability would be measured initially at the fair value of the allowances received.[382]

At the time of writing, the IASB expects to issue an exposure draft in the second quarter of 2010 and to publish a final standard in the first half of 2011.[383]

6   CONCLUSION

Throughout the last two decades there has been a gradual shift in the emphasis of what financial statements are meant to portray, from a transactions-based, performance-orientated model in which the income statement is most relevant towards a balance sheet-orientated model based on fair values.

This approach has not made the treatment of intangible assets in the balance sheet at the conceptual level any easier. Whilst the IASB has promulgated standards that have greatly reduced the scope for creative accounting as far as intangibles are concerned, it is also true that it remains for the Board to come up with a conceptually integrated or logically consistent treatment of intangible assets.

The current catalyst for the recognition of intangible assets lies in the accounting requirements for business combinations and the need to separate all other assets from goodwill. This is evident in the most recent revision to IFRS 3 in 2008, which in effect is ambivalent whether assets meeting the definition of an intangible asset are capable of being shown separately, or have to be combined with other intangible assets, incorporated into the carrying value of complementary item of property, plant and equipment with a similar useful life or included in the assessment of the fair value of a related liability. The important requirement is that the intangible asset is recognised separately from goodwill.

The virtual prohibition on the recognition of many internally generated intangibles outside a business combination is a tacit admission of the limits of our ability to deal with such items, rather than a deductive consequence of the reasons offered in the standards themselves. Thus it appears that accounting for intangible assets is at the stage of having a workable but imperfect set of rules which falls well short of consistency.

If the move towards an accounting model based on recording the entire balance sheet at fair values continues, the challenge will be to find an acceptable, logically consistent method that can value all intangibles that have worth, without arbitrarily scoping out those that present too many difficulties. The issue of rate-regulated assets is the most recent example of an area in which these challenges are pervasive.

References

1 IAS 38, *Intangible Assets*, IASB, para. IN2.
2 IAS 38, para. IN3.
3 IAS 38, para. IN3.
4 IAS 38, para. BC2.
5 IAS 38, para. BC2.
6 IAS 38, para. BC2.
7 IAS 38, para. IN4 and IFRS 3, *Business Combinations*, IASB, para. 64.
8 IAS 38, para. 1.
9 IAS 38, para. 2.
10 IAS 38, para. 3.
11 IAS 38, para. 6.
12 IAS 17, *Leases*, IASB, para. 2.
13 IAS 38, para. 6.
14 IAS 38, para. 7.
15 IAS 38, para. 5.
16 IAS 38, para. 8.
17 IAS 38, para. 8.
18 IAS 38, para. BC5.
19 IAS 38, para. 3.
20 IAS 38, para. 9.
21 IAS 38, para. 10.
22 IFRS 3, Appendix A and IFRS 3 (2007), *Business Combinations*, IASB, 2007 Bound Volume, Appendix A.
23 IAS 38, para. 11.
24 IAS 38, para. BC7.
25 IAS 38, para. BC8.
26 IAS 38, para. 12.
27 IAS 38, para. BC10.

28 IAS 38, para. BC13.
29 IAS 38, paras. 13-14.
30 IAS 38, para. 13.
31 IAS 38, para. 16.
32 IAS 38, para. 15.
33 IAS 38, para. 16.
34 IAS 38, para. 16.
35 IFRS 3, paras. IE23-IE31 and IFRS 3 (2007), Illustrative Examples, *Examples of items acquired in a business combination that meet the definition of an intangible asset.*
36 IAS 38, para. 18.
37 IAS 38, para. 17.
38 IAS 38, para. 4.
39 IAS 38, para. 4.
40 IAS 38, para. 4.
41 IAS 38, para. 5.
42 IAS 16, *Property, Plant and Equipment*, IASB, paras. 43-47.
43 IFRS 3, para. B32(b).
44 IAS 38, para. 18.
45 IAS 38, para. 21.
46 IFRS 3 (2007), Appendix A, IAS 37, *Provisions, Contingent Liabilities and Contingent Assets*, IASB, para. 23 and IFRS 5, *Non-current Assets Held for Sale and Discontinued Operations*, IASB, Appendix A.
47 IAS 38, para. 22.
48 IAS 38, para. 23.
49 IAS 38, para. 19.
50 IAS 38, paras. BCZ39-BCZ40.
51 IAS 38, para. BCZ41.
52 IAS 38, para. 24.
53 IAS 38, para. 8.
54 IAS 38, para. 20.
55 IAS 38, para. 20.
56 IAS 38, para. 20 and paras. 63-64.
57 IAS 38, para. 25.
58 IAS 38, para. 25.
59 IAS 38, para. 26.
60 IAS 38, para. BC18.
61 *Exposure Draft of Proposed Amendments to IAS 37 – Provisions, Contingent Liabilities and Contingent Assets*, IASB, June 2005, para. 1. and *Exposure Draft – Income Tax*, IASB, March 2009, para. 5.
62 IAS 38, para. 27.
63 IAS 38, para. 28.
64 IAS 38, para. 30.
65 IAS 38, para. 32.
66 IAS 38, paras. 29-30.
67 IAS 38, para. 31.
68 IFRS 3, paras. IE16-IE44 and IFRS 3 (2007), Illustrative Examples, *Examples of items acquired in a business combination that meet the definition of an intangible asset.*
69 IAS 38, para. 21.
70 IAS 38, para. 33.
71 IAS 38, para. 33.
72 IAS 38 (2007), para. 35.
73 IAS 38 (2007), para. 38.
74 IAS 38, para. 33.
75 IAS 38, para. 33.
76 IAS 38 (2007), para. BC21.
77 IAS 38 (2007), para. BC21.
78 IAS 38 (2007), para. BC23.
79 IAS 38 (2007), para. 38.
80 IAS 38, para. BC19B.
81 IAS 38, para. 33.
82 IAS 38, para. 12.
83 *Improvements to IFRSs*, April 2009, IASB, IAS 38, para. 36.
84 *Improvements to IFRSs*, April 2009, IASB, IAS 38, para. 37.
85 IFRS 3, para. B32.
86 IFRS 3, para. B33.
87 IFRS 3, para. B34.
88 IFRS 3, paras. IE16-IE44 and IFRS 3 (2007), Illustrative Examples, *Examples of items acquired in a business combination that meet the definition of an intangible asset.*
89 IAS 38, para. 35.
90 IAS 38 (2007), para. 35.
91 IAS 38, para. 39.
92 IAS 38, para. 78.
93 IAS 38, para. 40.
94 *Improvements to IFRSs*, April 2009, IASB, IAS 38, para. 40.
95 IAS 38, para. 41.
96 *Improvements to IFRSs*, April 2009, IASB, IAS 38, para. 41.
97 *Improvements to IFRSs*, April 2009, IASB, IAS 38, para. 130E.
98 IFRS 3, para. IE30 and IFRS 3 (2007), Illustrative Examples, *Customer relationship intangible assets acquired in a business combination.*
99 *IFRIC Update*, IFRIC, September 2008, p. 2.
100 The Glossary of Terms defines a contract as 'An agreement between two or more parties that has clear economic consequences that the parties have little, if any, discretion to avoid, usually because the agreement is enforceable in law. Contracts may take a variety of forms and need not be in writing.'
101 IFRS 3, para. IE28.
102 *IFRIC Update*, IFRIC, March 2009, pages 2-3.
103 *IFRIC Update*, IFRIC, March 2009, p. 3.
104 IAS 38, para. 34.
105 IAS 38, para. 42.
106 IAS 38, para. 43.
107 IAS 38, para. BC82.
108 IAS 36, *Impairment of Assets*, IASB, para. 10.
109 IAS 38, para. 44.

110 IAS 20, *Accounting for Government Grants and Disclosure of Government Assistance*, IASB, para. 23.
111 IAS 38, para. 45.
112 IAS 38, para. 47.
113 IAS 38, para. 45.
114 IAS 16, para. BC21.
115 IAS 38, para. 46.
116 IAS 38, para. 8.
117 IAS 38, para. 46.
118 IAS 38, para. 47.
119 IAS 38, para. 46.
120 IAS 38, para. 48.
121 IAS 38, para. 49.
122 IAS 38, para. 50.
123 IAS 38, para. 51.
124 IAS 38, para. 51.
125 IAS 38, para. 52.
126 IAS 38, para. 8.
127 IAS 38, para. 56.
128 IAS 38, para. 8.
129 IAS 38, para. 59.
130 IAS 38, paras. 54-55.
131 IAS 38, para. 57.
132 IAS 38, para. 58.
133 IAS 38, para. 60.
134 IAS 38, para. 61.
135 IAS 38, para. 61.
136 IAS 38, para. 62.
137 IAS 38, para. 52.
138 IAS 38, para. 55.
139 IAS 38, para. 53.
140 IAS 38, para. BCZ38.
141 IAS 38, para. BCZ40.
142 IAS 38, para. BCZ42.
143 IAS 38, para. 63.
144 IAS 38, para. 64.
145 IAS 38, para. 20.
146 IAS 38, para. BCZ45.
147 SIC-32, *Intangible Assets – Web Site Costs*, IASB, para. 7.
148 SIC-32, paras. 5-6.
149 SIC-32, para. 1.
150 SIC-32, para. 8.
151 SIC-32, para. 8.
152 SIC-32, paras. 2 and 9.
153 SIC-32, para. 3.
154 SIC-32, para. 9.
155 IAS 38, para. 67.
156 SIC-32, para. 10.
157 IAS 38, para. 24.
158 IAS 38, para. 8.
159 IAS 38, para. 65.
160 IAS 38, paras. 21-22.
161 IAS 38, para. 21.
162 IAS 38, para. 68.
163 IAS 38, para. 65.
164 IAS 38, para. 71.
165 IAS 38, Example Illustrating paragraph 65.
166 IAS 38, para. 66.
167 IAS 38, para. 67.
168 IAS 38, para. 68.
169 IAS 38, para. 69.
170 IAS 38, para. 70.
171 IAS 38, para. 69.
172 *IFRIC Update*, IFRIC, March 2007, p. 3.
173 *IASB Update*, IASB, April 2007, p. 4.
174 IAS 38, para. 69.
175 IAS 38, para. BC46B.
176 IAS 38, para. BC46D.
177 IAS 38, para. BC46E.
178 IAS 38, para. 69A.
179 IAS 38, para. 69A.
180 IAS 38, paras. BC46G-BC46H.
181 IAS 38, para. 69.
182 IAS 38, para. 72.
183 IAS 38, para. 74.
184 IAS 38, para. 75.
185 IAS 38, paras. 75, 81 and 82.
186 IAS 38, para. 72.
187 IAS 38, para. 73.
188 IAS 38, para. 119.
189 IAS 38, para. 73.
190 IAS 38, para. 74.
191 IAS 38, para. 75.
192 IAS 38, paras. 75, 81 and 82.
193 IAS 38, para. 76.
194 IAS 38, para. 77.
195 IAS 38, para. 77.
196 IAS 38, paras. 75, 81 and 82.
197 IAS 38, para. 8.
198 IAS 38, para. 78.
199 IAS 38, para. 78.
200 IAS 38, para. 78.
201 IAS 38, para. 75.
202 IAS 38, para. 79.
203 IAS 38, para. 73.
204 IAS 38, para. 85.
205 IAS 38, para. 86.
206 IAS 38, para. 87.
207 IAS 38, para. 87.
208 IAS 38, para. 87.
209 IAS 38, para. 80.
210 IAS 38, para. 72.
211 IAS 38, para. 81.
212 IAS 38, para. 82.
213 IAS 38, para. 83.
214 IAS 38, para. 84.
215 IAS 38, para. 8.
216 IAS 38, para. 88.
217 IAS 38, para. 88.
218 IAS 38, para. 89.
219 IAS 38, para. 91.
220 IAS 38, para. 88.

221 IAS 38, para. BC63.
222 IAS 38, para. BC62.
223 IAS 38, para. BC63.
224 IAS 38, para. 91.
225 IAS 38, para. 90.
226 IAS 38, para. 89 and Illustrative Examples.
227 IAS 38, para. 92.
228 IAS 38, para. 93.
229 IAS 38, paras. 94-95.
230 IAS 38, para. 94.
231 IAS 38, para. 96.
232 IAS 38, para. 94.
233 IAS 38, para. 96.
234 IAS 38, para. 94.
235 IAS 38, para. 8.
236 IAS 38, para. 97.
237 IAS 38, para. 117.
238 IAS 38 (2008), para. 98.
239 IAS 38, para. BC72A.
240 IAS 38, paras. 97 and 99.
241 IAS 38, para. 104.
242 IAS 38, para. 105.
243 IAS 38, para. 104.
244 IAS 38, para. 106.
245 IAS 38, para. 106.
246 IAS 38, para. 104.
247 IAS 8, *Accounting Policies, Changes in Accounting Estimates and Errors*, IASB, paras. 36 and 38.
248 IAS 38, para. 8.
249 IAS 38, para. 100.
250 IAS 38, para. BC59.
251 IAS 38, para. 101.
252 IAS 38, para. 102.
253 IAS 38, para. 102.
254 IAS 38, para. 103.
255 IAS 38, para. 107.
256 IAS 38, para. 108.
257 IAS 38, para. 109.
258 IAS 38, para. 109.
259 IAS 8, para. 36.
260 IAS 38, para. 110
261 IAS 38, para. 8.
262 IAS 38, para. 111.
263 IAS 36, para. 10.
264 IAS 38, para. 112.
265 IAS 38, para. 113.
266 IAS 38, para. 114.
267 IAS 38, para. 113.
268 IAS 38, para. 116.
269 IAS 38, para. 115.
270 IAS 38, para. 20.
271 IAS 38, para. 115A.
272 IAS 38, para. 119.
273 IAS 38, para. 118.
274 IAS 38, para. 120.
275 IAS 38, para. 121.
276 IAS 38, para. 122.
277 IAS 38, para. 123.
278 IAS 38, para. 128.
279 IAS 1, *Presentation of Financial Statements*, IASB, para. 67.
280 IAS 1, para. 54.
281 IAS 1, para. 60.
282 IAS 1, para. 55.
283 IAS 38, para. 113.
284 IAS 38, para. 118(d).
285 IAS 38, para. 124.
286 IAS 38, para. 125.
287 IAS 38, paras. 126-127.
288 *IFRIC Update*, IFRIC, November 2008, p. 4.
289 Information for Observers (December 2008 IASB Meeting), *Agenda proposal: rate-regulated activities (Agenda Paper 12)*, para. 14.
290 Exposure Draft (ED 2009/8), *Rate-regulated Activities*, IASB, July 2009, para. BC8.
291 *IASB Update*, IASB, June 2005, p. 1.
292 *IASB Update*, IASB, June 2005, p. 1.
293 *IASB Update*, IASB, December 2007, p. 1.
294 IFRIC 3, *Emission Rights*, 2005 Bound Volume, IASB, para. 2.
295 IFRIC 3, para. 3.
296 IFRIC 3, para. 5.
297 IFRIC 3, para. 6.
298 IFRIC 3, para. 7.
299 IFRIC 3, para. 8.
300 IFRIC 3, para. 9.
301 IAS 20, para. 23.
302 IAS 37, – *Provisions, Contingent Liabilities and Contingent Assets*, IASB, para. 14.
303 IAS 37, para. 36.
304 IAS 20, para. 23.
305 IAS 37, para. 37.
306 IAS 37, para. 36.
307 IAS 37, para. 37.
308 IAS 37, para. 53.
309 IAS 37, para. 37.
310 IAS 38, para. 75.
311 IAS 39, *Financial Instruments: Recognition and Measurement*, IASB, paras. AG74-AG79.
312 IAS 38, para. 75.
313 IFRS 3, para. B31 and IFRS 3(2007), paras. 36-37.
314 IAS 38, para. 112.
315 IAS 38, para. 113.
316 IAS 38, para. 113.
317 IAS 1, paras. 117 and 121.
318 IAS 2, *Inventories*, IASB, para. 6.
319 IAS 2, para. 3.
320 IAS 39, para. 5.
321 Regulation (EC) No. 1907/2006 of the European Parliament and of the Council of 18 December 2006 concerning the Registration, Evaluation, Authorisation and Restriction of Chemicals (REACH),

establishing a European Chemicals Agency, amending Directive 1999/45/EC and repealing Council Regulation (EEC) No. 793/93 and Commission Regulation (EC) No. 1488/94 as well as Council Directive 76/769/EEC and Commission Directives 91/155/EEC, 93/67/EEC, 93/105/EC and 2000/21/EC.

322 *IFRIC Update*, IFRIC, July 2009, p. 4.

323 IAS 38, para. 10.

324 IAS 38, para. 12(b).

325 IAS 38, para. 13.

326 IAS 38, para. 17.

327 IAS 38, para. 8.

328 IAS 38, para. 51.

329 IAS 38, para. 56.

330 IAS 38, para. 20.

331 IAS 38, para. 90.

332 IAS 38 (1998), *Intangible Assets*, IASB, September 1998, para. 7.

333 IAS 38, para. 3.

334 IAS 2, para. 6.

335 Framework, *Framework for the Preparation and Presentation of Financial Statements*, IASB, para. 91.

336 IAS 2, para. 9.

337 IAS 38, para. 97.

338 IAS 38, para. 97.

339 IAS 38, para. 8.

340 Exposure Draft (ED 2009/5), *Fair Value Measurement*, IASB, paras. D25-D26.

341 IFRS 3 (ED), *Exposure Draft of Amendments to IFRS 3 Business Combinations*, IASB, June 2005, paras. E11-E19.

342 ED 2009/05, para. 43.

343 ED 2009/05, para. 45.

344 ED 2009/05, para. 51.

345 ED 2009/05, para. 53.

346 ED 2009/05, para. 38.

347 IAS 36, para. BCZ29.

348 *IASB Work Plan – projected timetable as at 1 August 2009*, IASB.

349 IAS 38, para. 8.

350 IAS 38, para. 30.

351 IAS 39, para. 56.

352 IFRIC 1, *Changes in Existing Decommissioning, Restoration and Similar Liabilities*, paras. 4 and 7.

353 IAS 38, para. 130.

354 IAS 38, para. 130C.

355 IAS 38, para. 130D.

356 *Improvements to IFRSs*, April 2009, IASB, IAS 38, paras. 130C and 130E.

357 Information for Observers (December 2008 IASB Meeting), *Agenda proposal: rate-regulated activities (Agenda Paper 12)*, para. 14.

358 ED 2009/8, para. BC8.

359 ED 2009/8, para. 3.

360 ED 2009/8, Appendix A.

361 ED 2009/8, para. 4.

362 ED 2009/8, para. BC14.

363 ED 2009/8, para. 6.

364 ED 2009/8, para. BC17.

365 ED 2009/8, para. 8.

366 ED 2009/8, para. 10.

367 ED 2009/8, para. 12.

368 ED 2009/8, para. 13.

369 ED 2009/8, para. 12.

370 IAS 38, para. 30, IAS 16, *Property, Plant and Equipment*, IASB, para. 20 and IAS 23, *Borrowing Costs*, IASB, para. 22.

371 ED 2009/8, para. 16.

372 ED 2009/8, para. 18.

373 ED 2009/8, para. 19.

374 ED 2009/8, para. 22.

375 ED 2009/8, para. 23.

376 ED 2009/8, para. 25.

377 ED 2009/8, para. 26.

378 ED 2009/8, para. 27.

379 *IASB Update*, IASB, December 2007, p. 1.

380 *IASB Update*, IASB, May 2008, p. 4.

381 Project Update, *Emission Trading Schemes*, IASB, November 2008, para. 1.

382 *IASB Update*, IASB, March 2009, p. 2.

383 *IASB Work Plan – projected timetable as at 1 August 2009*, IASB.

Chapter 16

Property, plant and equipment

1   INTRODUCTION

One fundamental problem in financial reporting is how to account periodically for performance when many of the expenditures an entity incurs in the current period also contribute to future accounting periods. Expenditure on property, plant and equipment ('PP&E'), also known as fixed assets in many jurisdictions, is the best example of this difficulty. The accounting conventions permitted by the IASB to solve it are the subject of this chapter, although the underlying broad principles involved are among the first that accountants and business people learn in their business life. The cost of an item of PP&E is capitalised when acquired (i.e. recorded in the balance sheet as an asset); then subsequently a proportion of the cost is charged each year to profit or loss (i.e. the cost is spread out over the future accounting periods expected to benefit). Ideally, at the end of the item's working life the cost remaining in the balance sheet should be equal to the disposal proceeds of the item, or be zero if there are none.

Basic prudence dictates that during the life of the item any uncharged cost remaining in the balance sheet should be written down if it is not fully recoverable. Finally, when an item of PP&E is sold or scrapped, the difference between the written down value and any proceeds is recorded as the gain or loss on disposal.

There are inevitably some detailed rules required to apply these principles in practice, such as precisely when PP&E should initially be recognised, and how its cost should be measured. Additionally, it is not always obvious if an item is PP&E or not, nor, if a policy of revaluation is adopted, how the PP&E should be accounted for. Thus, although the basic principles are generally well understood, as in most other areas of financial reporting, the development of more detailed requirements has necessitated an accounting standard.

Under IFRS the main standard is IAS 16 – *Property, Plant and Equipment*. Impairment is covered by IAS 36 – *Impairment of Assets* – and dealt with as a separate topic in Chapter 18. Impairment is a major consideration in accounting for PP&E, as this procedure is intended to ensure PP&E costs that are not fully recoverable are immediately written down to a level that is. In addition, there is a separate standard, IAS 40 – *Investment Property* – that deals with that particular category of PP&E which is discussed in Chapter 17. Finally, IFRS 5 – *Non-current Assets Held for Sale and Discontinued Operations* – that deals with the accounting required when items of PP&E are held for sale, is discussed in Chapter 4.

The most recent version of IAS 16, published in March 2004 and which became effective for periods beginning on or after 1 January 2005, is discussed in this chapter.

2   THE REQUIREMENTS OF IAS 16

2.1   Introduction

IAS 16 retains two, very different, alternative accounting treatments that may be chosen to account for PP&E: items may be carried at either cost less accumulated depreciation, or at their fair value. Other than this, IAS 16 is a fairly straightforward standard that attempts to delineate the boundaries of what may, and may not, be considered part of the cost of an item of PP&E.

2.2   Scope

All PP&E is within the scope of IAS 16 except as follows:

- when another standard requires or permits a different accounting treatment (for example, IAS 40 for investment properties);

- PP&E classified as held for sale in accordance with IFRS 5;

- biological assets related to agricultural activity (covered by IAS 41 – *Agriculture*); and

- mineral rights and mineral reserves such as oil, gas, and similar 'non-regenerative' resources.[1] (see Chapter 42)

Although the standard scopes out biological assets and mineral resources, it includes any PP&E used in developing or maintaining such resources. Therefore, exploration PP&E is included in the scope of the standard, as is agricultural PP&E. It is also of note that prior to 1 January 2009 IAS 16 was applied to investment property during the time it was in the course of construction. However, from 1 January 2009 such investment property under construction is dealt with under IAS 40 (see Chapter 17 at 2.2.5).[2]

Other standards may require an item of PP&E to be recognised on a basis different from that required by IAS 16. For example IAS 17 – *Leases* – has its own rules regarding recognition and measurement; see Chapter 22 for a description of how an item of PP&E held under a finance lease is recognised and initially measured.

However, once an item of PP&E has been recognised as a finance lease under IAS 17, its treatment thereafter is in accordance with IAS 16.[3]

2.3   Definitions

IAS 16 defines the main terms it uses throughout the standard as follows:

Carrying amount is the amount at which an asset is recognised after deducting any accumulated depreciation and accumulated impairment losses.

Cost is the amount of cash or cash equivalents paid or the fair value of other consideration given to acquire an asset at the time of its acquisition or construction or, where applicable, the amount attributed to that asset when initially recognised in accordance with the specific requirements of other IFRSs, e.g. IFRS 2 – *Share-based Payment*.

Depreciable amount is the cost of an asset, or other amount substituted for cost, less its residual value.

Depreciation is the systematic allocation of the depreciable amount of an asset over its useful life.

Entity-specific value is the present value of the cash flows an entity expects to arise from the continuing use of an asset and from its disposal at the end of its useful life or expects to incur when settling a liability.

Fair value is the amount for which an asset could be exchanged between knowledgeable, willing parties in an arm's length transaction.

An *impairment loss* is the amount by which the carrying amount of an asset exceeds its recoverable amount.

Property, plant and equipment are tangible items that:

(a)   are held for use in the production or supply of goods or services, for rental to others, or for administrative purposes; and

(b)   are expected to be used during more than one period.

Recoverable amount is the higher of an asset's fair value less costs to sell and its value in use.

The *residual value* of an asset is the estimated amount that an entity would currently obtain from disposal of the asset, after deducting the estimated costs of disposal, if the asset were already of the age and in the condition expected at the end of its useful life.

Useful life is:

(a)   the period over which an asset is expected to be available for use by an entity; or

(b)   the number of production or similar units expected to be obtained from the asset by an entity.[4]

These definitions are discussed in the relevant sections below.

3   RECOGNITION

An item of PP&E should be recognised, i.e. its cost included in the balance sheet as an asset, only if its cost can be measured reliably and it is probable that future economic benefits associated with the item will flow to the entity.[5] This requirement for recognition is directly taken from the IASB's Framework, which is discussed in some detail in Chapter 2. It follows from the Framework's characterisation of an asset as future economic benefits, rather than the item of property itself, that to be recognised the economic benefits must be forthcoming, or at least probable.

Extract 16.1 below describes Skanska AB's criteria for the recognition of PP&E:

Extract 16.1: Skanska AB (2007)

Note 1   Accounting and Valuation principles [extract]
IAS 16, "Property, Plant and Equipment"

Property, plant and equipment are recognized as assets in the balance sheet if it is probable that the Group will derive future economic benefits from them and the cost of an asset can be reliably estimated. Property, plant and equipment are recognized at cost minus accumulated depreciation and any impairment losses. Cost includes purchase price plus expenses directly attributable to the asset in order to bring it to the location and condition to be operated in the intended manner. Examples of directly attributable expenses are delivery and handling costs, installation, ownership documents, consultant fees and legal services. Borrowing costs are included in the cost of self-constructed property, plant and equipment. Impairment losses are applied in compliance with IAS 36, "Impairment of assets."

The cost of self-constructed property, plant and equipment includes expenditures for materials and compensation to employees, plus other applicable manufacturing costs that are considered attributable to the asset.

Further expenditures are added to cost only if it is probable that the Group will enjoy future economic benefits associated with the asset and the cost can be reliably estimated. All other further expenditures are recognized as expenses in the period when they arise. What is decisive in determining when a further expenditure is added to cost is whether the expenditure is related to replacement of identified components, or their parts, at which time such expenditures are capitalized. In cases where a new component is created, this expenditure is also added to cost. Any undepreciated carrying amounts for replaced components, or their parts, are disposed of and recognized as an expense at the time of replacement. If the cost of the removed component cannot be determined directly, its cost is estimated as the cost of the new component adjusted by a suitable price index to take into account inflation. Repairs are recognized as expenses continuously.

Property, plant and equipment that consist of parts with different periods of service are treated as separate components of property, plant and equipment. Depreciation occurs on a straight-line basis during the estimated period of service, taking into account any residual value at the end of the period.

Office buildings are divided into foundation and frame, with a depreciation period of 50 years; installations, depreciation period 35 years; and non-weight-bearing parts, depreciation period 15 years. Generally speaking, industrial buildings are depreciated during a 20-year period without allocation into different parts. Stone crushing and asphalt plants as well as concrete mixing plants are depreciated over 10 to 25 years depending on their condition when acquired and without being divided into different parts. For other buildings and equipment, division into different components occurs only if major components with divergent useful lives can be identified. For other machinery and equipment, the depreciation period is normally between 5 and 10 years. Minor equipment is depreciated immediately. Gravel pits and stone quarries are depreciated as materials are removed. Land is not depreciated. Assessments of an asset's residual value and period of service are performed annually. The carrying amount of a property, plant and equipment item is removed from the balance sheet when it is disposed of or divested, or when no further economic benefits are expected from the use or disposal/divestment of the asset.

3.1   Aspects of recognition

3.1.1   Spare parts and minor items

There are materiality judgements to be considered when deciding how an item of PP&E should be accounted for. Major spare parts, for example, qualify as PP&E, while smaller spares would be carried as inventory, and as a practical matter many companies have a minimum value for capitalising assets (see Extract 16.2 below). However if a set of spares can only be used on one item of PP&E, then they should be accounted for as PP&E.[6]

Extract 16.2: BMW AG (2007)

Notes to the Group Financial Statements [extract]
Accounting Principles and Policies [extract]

Expenditure on low value non-current assets is written off in full in the year of acquisition.

Some types of business may have a very large number of minor items of PP&E such as spare parts, tools, pallets and returnable containers, which nevertheless are used in more than one accounting period. There are practical problems in recording them on an asset-by-asset basis in an asset register; they are difficult to control and frequently lost. The main consequence is that it becomes very difficult to provide depreciation on them. The standard notes that there are issues concerning what actually constitutes a single item of PP&E to be individually recognised. The 'unit of measurement for recognition' is not prescribed and entities have to apply judgement in defining PP&E in their individual circumstances. The standard suggests that some parts such as tools, moulds and dies should be aggregated and the standard applied to the aggregate amount (presumably without having to identify the individual assets).[7]

3.1.2   Environmental and safety equipment

The standard acknowledges that there may be expenditures forced upon an entity by legislation that require it to buy 'assets' that do not meet the recognition criteria because the expenditure does not directly increase the expected future benefits expected to flow from the asset.[8] Examples would be safety or environmental protection equipment. IAS 16 explains that these expenditures do qualify for recognition as they allow future benefits in excess of those that would flow if the expenditure had not been made; for example a plant might have to be closed down if the expenditures were not made.

In our view this approach is sensible (even if it is indicative of a deficiency in the recognition criteria) and has no more significance, and is in the same category as, the cost of fitting guards to machinery at original manufacture.

An entity may voluntarily invest in environmental equipment even though it is not required by law to do so. We consider that the entity should expense those investments in environmental and safety equipment as incurred, unless either it can demonstrate that the equipment is likely to increase the economic life of the related assets or that it can demonstrate all of the following:

- the entity can prove that a constructive obligation exists to invest in environmental and safety equipment (e.g. it is standard practice in the industry, environmental groups are likely to raise issues or employees demand certain equipment to be present);

- the expenditure is directly related to improvement of the asset's environmental and safety standards; and

- the expenditure is not related to repairs and maintenance or forms part of period costs or operational costs.

Whenever safety and environmental assets are capitalised, the standard requires the resulting carrying amount of the asset and any related asset to be reviewed in accordance with IAS 36 (see Chapter 18).[9]

3.1.3   Initial and subsequent expenditure

IAS 16 makes no distinction in principle between the initial costs of acquiring an asset and any subsequent expenditure upon it. In both cases any and all expenditure has to meet the recognition rules, and be expensed in profit or loss if it does not. IAS 16 states:

> 'An entity evaluates under this recognition principle all its property, plant and equipment costs at the time they are incurred. These costs include costs incurred initially to acquire or construct an item of property, plant and equipment and costs incurred subsequently to add to, replace part of, or service it.'[10]

The standard draws a distinction between servicing and more major expenditure. Day-to-day servicing, by which is meant the repair and maintenance of PP&E, and which largely comprises labour costs and minor parts, should be recognised in profit or loss as incurred.[11] However, if the expenditure involves replacing a significant part of the asset, this part should be recognised, i.e. capitalised as part of the fixed asset, if the recognition criteria are met. The carrying amount of the part that has been replaced should be derecognised, as described in 2.6 below. An example of this treatment of major maintenance expenditure is shown in Extract 16.3 below:

Extract 16.3: Akzo Nobel N.V. (2007)
Summary of significant accounting policies [extract]
Property, Plant and Equipment [extract]

Cost of major maintenance activities is capitalized as a separate component of property, plant, and equipment, and depreciated over the estimated useful life. Maintenance costs which cannot be separately defined as a component of property, plant, and equipment are expensed in the period in which they occur.

IAS 16 identifies two particular types of parts of assets. The first is an item that requires replacement at regular intervals during the life of the asset. For example a furnace may require relining after a specified number of hours of use, or aircraft interiors such as seats and galleys may require replacement several times during the life of the airframe. The second type involves less frequently recurring replacements, such as replacing the interior walls of a building. The standard proposes that under the recognition principle described above, an entity recognises in the carrying amount of an item of property, plant and equipment the cost of replacing part of such an item when that cost is incurred while derecognising the carrying amount of the parts that have been replaced.[12]

IAS 16 does not state that these expenditures necessarily qualify for recognition. Some of its examples, such as aircraft engines that require regular overhaul, are clearly best treated as separate assets as they have a useful life different from that of the asset of which they are part. With others, such as interior walls, it is less clear why they meet the recognition criteria. However, replacing internal walls or similar expenditure may extend the useful life of a building while upgrading machinery may increase its capacity, improve the quality of its output or reduce operating costs. Hence, this type of expenditure may give rise to future economic benefits.

This parts approach is illustrated by British Airways plc in Extract 16.4 below.

Extract 16.4: British Airways plc (2008)

Notes to the accounts [extract]
2   Accounting policies [extract]
Property, plant and equipment [extract]
b   Fleet

All aircraft are stated at the fair value of the consideration given after taking account of manufacturers' credits. Fleet assets owned, or held on finance lease or hire purchase arrangements, are depreciated at rates calculated to write down the cost to the estimated residual value at the end of their planned operational lives on a straight-line basis.

Cabin interior modifications, including those required for brand changes and relaunches, are depreciated over the lower of five years and the remaining life of the aircraft.

Aircraft and engine spares acquired on the introduction or expansion of a fleet, as well as rotable spares purchased separately, are carried as property, plant and equipment and generally depreciated in line with the fleet to which they relate.

Major overhaul expenditure, including replacement spares and labour costs, is capitalised and amortised over the average expected life between major overhauls. All other replacement spares and other costs relating to maintenance of fleet assets (including maintenance provided under 'power-by-the-hour' contracts) are charged to the income statement on consumption or as incurred respectively.

Accounting for parts of assets is also discussed in 4.2 below.

The standard also allows a separate part to be recognised if an entity is required to perform regular major inspections for faults, regardless of whether any physical parts of the asset are replaced.

The reason for this approach is to maintain a degree of consistency with IAS 37 – *Provisions, Contingent Liabilities and Contingent Assets* – which forbids an entity to make provisions that are not obligations. Therefore an entity is prohibited by IAS 37 from making a provision to overhaul (say) an aircraft engine by providing a quarter of the cost for four years and then utilising the provision when the engine is overhauled in year four. This had been a common practice in the airline and oil refining industries, although it had never been universally applied in either sector; some companies accounted for the expenditure when incurred, others capitalised the cost and depreciated it over the period until the next major overhaul. IAS 37 proposed that the entity's results could be largely insulated from the effects of any change in the policy of providing for repair costs over time by adjusting the asset's carrying value and depreciation charge.[13] IAS 16 now applies the same recognition criteria to the cost of major inspections. Inspection costs are added to the asset's cost and any amount remaining from the previous inspection is derecognised. This process of recognition and derecognition should take place regardless of whether the cost of the previous inspection was identified (and considered a separate part) when the asset was originally acquired or constructed. Therefore, if the element relating to the inspection had previously been identified, it would have been depreciated between that time and the current overhaul. However, if it had not previously been identified, the recognition and derecognition rules still apply, but the standard allows the estimated cost of a future similar inspection to be used as an indication of the cost of the existing inspection component that must be derecognised.[14] This appears to allow the entity to reconstruct the carrying amount of the previous inspection (i.e. to estimate the net depreciated carrying value of the previous inspection that will be derecognised) rather than simply using a depreciated replacement cost approach.

3.1.4   *Probable economic benefits*

The standard requires that PP&E only be recognised when it is probable that future economic benefits associated with the item will flow to the entity.

As set out in more detail in Chapter 17 at 2.3, in relation to property development, in many jurisdictions permissions are required prior to development whilst developers, including entities developing property for own use, typically incur significant costs prior to such permissions being granted.

In assessing whether such pre-permission expenditure falls to be capitalised – assuming it otherwise meets the criteria – a judgement must be made, at the date the expenditure is incurred, of whether it is sufficiently probable that the relevant permissions will be granted. Such expenditure does not fall to be part of the cost of the land, but to the extent it can be recognised, is a separate asset.

3.2   Measurement at recognition

IAS 16 draws a distinction between measurement at recognition (i.e. the initial recognition of an item of PP&E on acquisition) and measurement after recognition (i.e. the subsequent treatment of the item). Measurement after recognition is discussed at 4 below.

The standard states that 'An item of property, plant and equipment that qualifies for recognition as an asset shall be measured at its cost.'[15] Therefore the question arises as to what may be included in the cost of an item, and the standard contains considerable guidance on this matter, under the heading 'Elements of cost'.

3.2.1　*Elements of cost and cost measurement*

Paragraph 18 of IAS 16 sets out the constituents of the cost of an item of PP&E on its initial recognition, as follows:

'The cost of an item of property, plant and equipment comprises:

(a)　its purchase price, including import duties and non-refundable purchase taxes, after deducting trade discounts and rebates.

(b)　any costs directly attributable to bringing the asset to the location and condition necessary for it to be capable of operating in the manner intended by management.

(c)　the initial estimate of the costs of dismantling and removing the item and restoring the site on which it is located, the obligation for which an entity incurs either when the item is acquired or as a consequence of having used the item during a particular period for purposes other than to produce inventories during that period.'[16] The costs of obligations to dismantle, remove or restore an asset that is used to produce inventories are dealt with in accordance with IAS 2 – *Inventories* – as dealt with in Chapter 20.[17]

Note that all site restoration costs and other environmental restoration and similar costs must be estimated and capitalised at initial recognition, in order that such costs can be recovered over the life of the item of PP&E, even if the expenditure will only be incurred at the end of the item's life. The obligations are calculated in accordance with IAS 37.[18] This treatment is illustrated in Extract 16.5 below:

Extract 16.5: L'Air Liquide S.A (2007)

Accounting principles [extract]
4　　　Accounting policies [extract]
4.5　　Non current assets [extract]
e/　　Property, plant and equipment [extract]

Land, buildings and equipment are carried at cost less any accumulated depreciation and any accumulated impairment losses.

In the event of mandatory dismantling or asset removals, the related costs are added to the initial cost of the relevant assets and provisions are recognized to cover these costs.

A common instance of (c) above is dilapidation obligations in lease agreements, under which a lessee is obliged to return premises to the landlord in an agreed condition. Arguably, a provision is required whenever the 'damage' is incurred. Therefore, if a retailer rents two adjoining premises and knocks them into one and has an obligation to make good the party wall at the end of the lease term, he should immediately provide for the costs of so doing. The 'other side' of the provision entry is an asset that will be amortised over the lease term – notwithstanding the fact that some of the costs of modifying the premises may also have been capitalised as assets.

A　　*'Directly attributable' costs*

This is the key issue in the measurement of cost. The standard gives examples of types of expenditure that are, and are not, considered to be directly attributable.

The following examples are given of those types of expenditure that are considered to be directly attributable, and hence may be included in cost at initial recognition:

(a)   costs of employee benefits (as defined in IAS 19 – *Employee Benefits*) arising directly from the construction or acquisition of the item of property, plant and equipment. This means that the labour costs of an entity's own employees (e.g. site workers, in-house architects and surveyors) arising directly from the construction, or acquisition, of the specific item of PP&E may be recognised;

(b)   costs of site preparation;

(c)   initial delivery and handling costs;

(d)   installation and assembly costs;

(e)   costs of testing whether the asset is functioning properly, after deducting the net proceeds from selling any items produced while bringing the asset to that location and condition (such as samples produced when testing equipment); and

(f)   professional fees.[19]

Income received during the period of construction of PP&E is considered further in 3.2.2 below.

B   Borrowing costs

Capitalisation of borrowing costs in respect of certain qualifying assets – if those assets are measured at cost – is mandated for accounting periods beginning on or after 1 January 2009.

Entities are not required to capitalise borrowing costs in respect of assets that are measured at fair value. This includes assets measured at fair value through Other Comprehensive Income (see 4.1). However, to the extent that entities choose to capitalise borrowing costs in respect of such assets, in our view it is best practice to follow the methods allowed by IAS 23 – *Borrowing Costs*. The treatment of borrowing costs is discussed separately in Chapter 19.

C   Administration and other general overheads

Administration and other general overhead costs are not costs of an item of PP&E. This means that employee costs not related to a specific asset, such as site selection activities and general management time do not qualify for capitalisation. Entities are also not allowed to recognise so-called 'start up costs' as part of the item of PP&E. These include costs related to opening a new facility, introducing a new product or service (including costs of advertising and promotional activities), conducting business in a new territory or with a new class of customer (including costs of staff training) and similar items.[20] These costs should be accounted for (in general, expensed as incurred) in the same way as similar costs incurred as part of the entity's on-going activities.

D   Cessation of capitalisation

Once an item of PP&E is in the location and condition necessary for it to be capable of operating in the manner intended by management, which will usually be the date of practical completion of the physical asset, cost recognition ceases. IAS 16 therefore prohibits the recognition of relocation and reorganisation costs, costs incurred during the run up to full use once an item is ready to be used, and any initial operating losses.[21]An entity is not precluded from continuing to capitalise costs during an initial commissioning period that is necessary for running in machinery or testing equipment. By contrast no further costs should be capitalised if the asset is fully operational but is not yet achieving its targeted profitability because demand is still building up, for example in a new hotel that initially has high room vacancies or a partially let investment property. In these cases, the asset is clearly in the location and condition necessary for it to be capable of operating in the manner intended by management.

E   *Self-built assets*

If an asset is self-built by the entity, the same general principles apply as for an acquired asset. If the same type of asset is made for resale by the business, it should be recognised at cost of production, without including any profit element – this allows self-constructed assets to include attributable overheads in accordance with IAS 2 (see Chapter 20). Abnormal amounts of wasted resources, whether labour, materials or other resources, may not be included in the cost of self-built assets. IAS 23, discussed in Chapter 19, contains criteria relating to the recognition of any interest as a component of a self-built item of PP&E.[22] Kazakhmys PLC provides an example of an accounting policy for self-built assets:

Extract 16.6: Kazakhmys Plc (2007)

NOTES TO THE CONSOLIDATED FINANCIAL STATEMENTS [extract]
3.   SUMMARY OF SIGNIFICANT ACCOUNTING POLICIES [extract]
(d)   TANGIBLE ASSETS [extract]
(i)   **Property, plant and equipment** [extract]

Property, plant and equipment is stated at cost less accumulated depreciation and impairment losses. The cost of self-constructed assets includes the cost of materials, direct labour and an appropriate proportion of production overheads.

F   *Deferred payment*

IAS 16 specifically eliminates the capitalisation of 'hidden' credit charges as part of the cost of an item of PP&E, so the cost of an item of PP&E is its 'cash price equivalent' at the recognition date. This means that if payment is made in some other manner, the cost to be capitalised is the normal cash price. Thus, if the payment terms are extended beyond 'normal' credit terms, the cost to be recognised must be the cash price equivalent, and any difference must be treated as an interest expense.[23] Assets partly paid for by government grants, and those held under finance leases are discussed in Chapters 23 and 22, respectively.

G   *Land and buildings to be redeveloped*

It is common for property developers to acquire land with an existing building where the planned redevelopment necessitates the demolition of that building and its replacement with a new building that is to be held to earn rentals or will be owner occupied. Whilst IAS 16 requires that the building and land be classified as two separate items[24], in our view it is appropriate, if the existing building is unusable or likely to be demolished by any party acquiring it, that the entire purchase price be allocated to the land. Similarly, subsequent demolition costs should be treated as being attributable to the cost of the land.

Owner-occupiers may also replace existing buildings with new facilities for their own use or to rent to others. Here the consequences are different and the carrying of the existing building cannot be rolled into the costs of the new development. The existing building must be depreciated over its remaining useful life to reduce the carrying amount of the asset to its residual value (presumably nil) at the point at which it is demolished. Consideration will have to be given as to whether the asset is impaired in value in accordance with IAS 36. However, many properties do not directly generate independent cash inflows (i.e. they are part of a cash-generating unit) and reducing the useful life will not necessarily lead to an impairment of the cash-generating unit (see Chapter 18).

Developers or owner-occupiers replacing an existing building with a building to be sold in the ordinary course of their business will deal with the land and buildings under IAS 2 (see Chapter 20).

Section 3.2.2 B below discusses the treatment of income received during the development process.

H   Contributions of PP&E by customers

IFRIC 18 – *Transfers of Assets from Customers* – was issued by the IASB in January 2009 to provide guidance in situations in which entities receive contributions of PP&E from customers. These arrangements are widespread.

- A supplier may receive a contribution to the development costs of specific tooling equipment from another manufacturer to whom the supplier will sell parts using that specific tooling equipment under a supply agreement.

- Suppliers of utilities may receive items of PP&E from customers that are used to connect them to a network via which they will receive ongoing services (e.g. electricity, gas, water or telephone services). A typical arrangement is one in which a builder or individual householder must pay for power cables, pipes, or other connections.

- In outsourcing arrangements, the existing assets are often contributed to the service provider or the customer must pay for assets, or both.

This raises questions about recognising assets that the entity has not paid for. In what circumstances should the entity recognise these assets, at what carrying amount and how is the 'other side' of the entry dealt with? Is it revenue and if so, how and over what period is it recognised? There are a number of potential answers to this and, unsurprisingly, practice has differed. IFRIC 18 was developed to address them.

IFRIC 18 applies to all agreements under which an entity receives from a customer, or another party, an item of PP&E (or cash for the acquisition or construction of such items) that the entity must then use either to connect the customer to a network or to provide the customer with ongoing access to a supply of goods or services or both. Transfers that are government grants within the scope of IAS 20 – *Accounting for Government Grants and Disclosure of Government Assistance* – or assets used in a service concession within the scope of IFRIC 12 – *Service Concessions* – are out of scope of IFRIC 18.

If the item of PP&E meets the definition of an asset as set out in the *Framework*, as described at 3 above, then the transferred asset is measured at its fair value and this becomes its cost on initial recognition. This means that the entity has to demonstrate that it controls the asset. It does not have to own it but 'control' generally means that it can deal with that asset as it pleases – for example use it to produce goods and services, lease it to others, scrap it and replace it without the consent of others or sell it.

Control of assets is discussed in the following examples, extracted from IFRIC 18's illustrative examples 1 and 2. In both cases it is noteworthy that the utility receives the asset from another party (a builder) and not the customer.

Example 16.1:   IFRIC 18 and control of assets

Situation 1

A real estate company is building a residential development in an area that is not connected to the electricity network. In order to have access to the electricity network, the real estate company is required to construct an electricity substation that is then transferred to the network company responsible for the transmission of electricity. It is assumed in this example that the network company concludes that the transferred substation meets the definition of an asset. The network company then uses the substation to connect each house of the residential development to its electricity network. In this case, it is the homeowners that will eventually use the network to access the supply of electricity, although they did not initially transfer the substation.

Alternatively, the network company could have constructed the substation and received a transfer of an amount of cash from the real estate company that had to be used only for the construction of the substation. The amount of cash transferred would not necessarily equal the entire cost of the substation. It is assumed that the substation remains an asset of the network company

In this example, the Interpretation applies to the network company that receives the electricity substation from the real estate company. The network company recognises the substation as an item of PP&E and measures its cost on initial recognition at its fair value or at its construction cost in the circumstances described in the preceding paragraph.

Situation 2

A house builder constructs a house on a redeveloped site in a major city. As part of constructing the house, the house builder installs a pipe from the house to the water main in front of the house. Because the pipe is on the house's land, the owner of the house can restrict access to the pipe. The owner is also responsible for the maintenance of the pipe. In this example, the facts indicate that the definition of an asset is not met for the water company.

Alternatively, a house builder constructs multiple houses and installs a pipe on the commonly owned or public land to connect the houses to the water main. The house builder transfers ownership of the pipe to the water company that will be responsible for its maintenance. In this example, the facts indicate that the water company controls the pipe and should recognise it.

If the entity does control the asset then it is recognised as PP&E and accounted for thereafter in the same manner as any other item of PP&E.

The transaction is treated as an exchange transaction involving dissimilar goods and services under IAS 18 – *Revenue* (not an exchange of assets under IAS 16 as described at 3.2.4 below) and revenue is recognised. It will be necessary to identify the separate services that are to be provided in exchange for the item of PP&E.[25] This is in order to allocate revenue to these elements and to determine the manner in which that revenue should be recognised. If the only service is connection to the network, usually evidenced by the contributing customer paying the same as others who have not made contributions, then revenue will be recognised on connection. Allocation and recognition of revenue is described in more detail in Chapter 25 at 6.13.

IFRIC 18 provides examples of the services that can be provided in the arrangements and how this determines the recognition of revenue. These are reproduced below. For further illustrations from IFRIC 18, see Example 25.3 in Chapter 25.

Example 16.2:   IFRIC 18 and revenue recognition

The facts are as in Situation 2 in Example 16.1 above. By regulation, the network company has an obligation to provide ongoing access to the network to all users of the network at the same price, regardless of whether they transferred an asset. Therefore, users of the network that transfer an asset to the network company pay the same price for the use of the network as those that do not. Users of the network can choose to purchase their electricity from distributors other than the network company but must use the company's network to access the supply of electricity.

The fact that users of the network that transfer an asset to the network company pay the same price for the use of the electricity network as those that do not indicates that the obligation to provide ongoing access to the network is not a separately identifiable service of the transaction. Rather, connecting the house to the network is the only service to be delivered in exchange for the substation. Therefore, the network company should recognise revenue from the exchange transaction at the fair value of the substation or at the amount of the cash received from the real estate company when the houses are connected to the network in accordance with IAS 18.

In some circumstances, the customer is able to enjoy ongoing access to the supply of goods and services at a lower price than available to other customers. This would indicate that the ongoing access to future goods and services was, at least to some extent, in return for the contributed PP&E. This is particularly common in outsourcing arrangements where the price paid for the service may be lower if the customer contributes assets to the service provider. This is described in Chapter 25 at 6.13.

IFRIC 18 does not provide guidance on how the fair value of the PP&E should be allocated to any separately identifiable services, but the Basis of Conclusions refers to both IFRIC 12 and IFRIC 13 – *Customer Loyalty Programmes* – where it notes that such guidance (which is based upon fair values of the separate components) is provided. IFRIC 12 is discussed in Chapter 23 and IFRIC 13 in Chapter 25 at 6.14.

3.2.2   Incidental and non-incidental income

Under IAS 16, the cost of an item of PP&E includes any costs directly attributable to bringing the asset to the location and condition necessary for it to be capable of operating in the manner intended by management.[26] However, during the construction of an asset, an entity may enter into incidental operations that are not, in themselves, necessary to bring the asset itself into the location and condition necessary for it to be capable of operating in the manner intended by management.

The standard gives the example of income earned by using a building site as a car park prior to starting construction. Because incidental operations such as these are not necessary to bring an item to the location and condition necessary for it to be capable of operating in the manner intended by management, the income and related expenses of incidental operations are recognised in profit or loss and included in their respective classifications of income and expense.[27] Such incidental income is not offset against the cost of the asset.

If, however, some income is generated wholly and necessarily as a result of the process of bringing the asset into the location and condition for its intended use, for example from the sale of samples produced when testing the equipment concerned, then the income should be credited to the cost of the asset (see A below).

On the other hand, if the asset is *already in* the location and condition necessary for it to be capable of being used in the manner intended by management then IAS 16 requires capitalisation to cease and depreciation to start.[28] In these circumstances all income earned from using the asset must be recognised as revenue in profit or loss and the related costs of the activity should include an element of depreciation of the asset.

A   Proceeds from selling items produced while bringing the asset to the location and condition intended by management

As noted above at 3.2.1 A, the directly attributable costs of an item of PP&E include the costs of testing whether the asset is functioning properly, after deducting the net proceeds from selling any items produced while bringing the asset to that location and condition.[29] The standard gives the example of samples produced when testing equipment.

There are other situations in which income may be earned whilst bringing the asset to the intended location and condition. For example, the mining industry is highly capital intensive – particularly so in the case of deep level mining – and a mining operation may extract some saleable 'product' during the phase of its operation to sink mine shafts that reach the intended depth where the main ore-bearing rock is located. During the evaluation and construction phases, income can be earned by an entity in various ways. For example, during the evaluation phase – i.e. when the technical feasibility and commercial viability are being determined – an entity may 'trial mine', to determine which method would be the most profitable and efficient in the circumstances, and which metallurgical process is the most efficient. Ore mined through trial mining may be processed and sold during the evaluation phase. At the other end of the spectrum, income may be earned from the sale of product from 'ramping up' the mine to full production at commercial levels.

It will be a matter of judgement as to when the asset is in the location and condition intended by management, but as noted in 3.2.1 D above, capitalisation (including the recording of income as a credit to the cost of the mine) ceases when the asset is fully operational, regardless of whether or not it is yet achieving its targeted levels of production or profitability.

B   Income received during the construction of property

One issue that commonly arises is whether rental and similar income generated by existing tenants in a property development may be capitalised and offset against the cost of developing that property.

The relevant question is whether the leasing arrangements with the existing tenants are a necessary activity to bring the development property to the location and condition necessary for it to be capable of operating in the manner intended by management. Whilst the existence of the tenant may be a fact, it is not a necessary condition for the building to be developed to the condition intended by management – the building could have been developed in the absence of any existing tenants.

We therefore consider that rental and similar income from existing tenants are incidental to the development and should not be capitalised. Rather rental and similar income should be recognised in profit or loss in accordance with the requirements of IAS 17 together with related expenses.

C   Other forms of income

Income may arise in other ways, for example, liquidated damages received as a result of delays by a contractor constructing an asset. Normally such damages received should be set off against the asset cost. If however, the settlement specifically refers to damages as compensation for loss of revenue arising as a consequence of contract delays, and the basis is clearly related to income lost, then the damages received should be recognised in profit or loss.

Compensation for impairment (for example insurance proceeds) is dealt with at 4.3.1 below.

3.2.3   Accounting for changes in decommissioning and restoration costs

IAS 16 is unclear about the extent to which an item's carrying amount should be affected by changes in the estimated amount of dismantling and site restoration costs that occur *after* the estimate made upon initial measurement. This issue is the subject of IFRIC 1 – *Changes in Existing Decommissioning, Restoration and Similar Liabilities* – issued in May 2004.

IFRIC 1 applies to any decommissioning or similar liability that has both been included as part of an asset measured in accordance with IAS 16 and measured as a liability in accordance with IAS 37.[30] It deals with the impact of events that change the measurement of an existing liability. Such events include a change in the estimated cash flows, the discount rate and the unwinding of the discount.[31]

IFRIC 1 differentiates between the treatment required depending upon whether the items of PP&E concerned are valued under the cost or under the valuation model of IAS 16 (these models are discussed at 4 below). If the asset is carried at cost, changes in the liability are added to, or deducted from, the cost of the asset. This deduction may not exceed the carrying amount of the asset and any excess over the carrying value is taken immediately to profit or loss. If the change in estimate results in an addition to the carrying value, the entity is required to consider whether this is an indication of impairment of the asset as a whole and test for impairment in accordance with IAS 36 (see Chapter 18).[32]

If the related asset is carried at valuation and changes in the estimated liability alter the valuation surplus (i.e. the re-estimation takes place independently of the valuation of the asset), then a decrease in the liability is credited directly to the revaluation surplus, unless it reverses a revaluation deficit on the asset that was previously recognised in profit or loss, in which case it may be taken to profit or loss. Similarly, an increase in the liability is taken straight to profit or loss, unless there is a revaluation surplus existing in respect of that asset.[33]

If the liability decreases and the deduction exceeds the amount that the asset would have been carried at under the cost model (e.g. its depreciated cost), the amount by which the asset is reduced is capped at this amount. Any excess is taken immediately to profit or loss.[34] This means that the maximum amount by which an asset can be reduced is the same whether it is carried at cost or valuation.

This change in the revalued amount must be assessed against the requirements in IAS 16 regarding revalued assets, particularly the requirement that they must be carried at an amount that does not differ materially from fair value (see 4.1 below for the standard's rules regarding revaluations of assets). Such an adjustment is an indication that the carrying amount may differ from fair value and the asset may have to be revalued. Any such revaluation must, of course, take account of the adjustment of the estimated liability. If a revaluation is necessary, all assets of the same class must be revalued.[35]

Any changes in estimate taken to equity (or, as it is called in the revised IAS 1, effective for annual periods beginning on or after 1 January 2009, 'Other Comprehensive Income' or 'OCI') must be disclosed on the face of the statement of changes in equity in accordance with IAS 1 – *Presentation of Financial statements* – (see Chapter 3).[36] Depreciation of the 'decommissioning asset' and any changes thereto are covered by 4.2 below. The unwinding of the discount must be recognised in profit or loss as a finance cost as it occurs. Capitalisation under IAS 23 is not permitted.[37]

A first-time adopter of IFRIC 1 is not required to restate the carrying amount included in an asset in respect of decommissioning that occurred before the date of transition to IFRSs, e.g. those changes in respect of estimated cash outflows, discount rate and unwinding discount that are described in 3.1.3 above. Instead, the exemption allows the entity to estimate the liability by calculating it at the transition date in accordance with IAS 37 and adjusting this amount by discounting it at its best estimate of the historical risk-adjusted discount rate(s) that would have applied over the intervening period. Accumulated depreciation as at the transition date is then based on the current estimate of the useful life of the asset, using the depreciation policy adopted by the entity under IFRSs.[38] This is discussed in detail in Chapter 5 at 5.14.1.

3.2.4 Exchanges of assets

Asset exchanges are transactions that have been discussed intermittently by standard setters over a number of years. For example, an entity might swap a facility it does not require in a particular area, for one it does in another – the opposite being the case for the counterparty. Such exchanges are not uncommon in the hotel, retail and leisure businesses, particularly after an acquisition. Indeed, governmental competition rules may even require such exchanges in certain cases. The question arises whether such transactions give rise to a profit in circumstances where the carrying value of the outgoing facility is less than the incoming one. This can occur when carrying values are less than market values. Equally, it is possible that a transaction with no real commercial substance could be arranged solely to boost apparent profits.

IAS 16 requires all acquisitions of PP&E in exchange for non-monetary assets, or a combination of monetary and non-monetary assets, to be measured at fair value, subject to the following conditions:

'The cost of such an item of property, plant and equipment is measured at fair value unless (a) the exchange transaction lacks commercial substance or (b) the fair value of neither the asset received nor the asset given up is reliably measurable. The acquired item is measured in this way even if an entity cannot immediately derecognise the asset given up.'[39]

If the fair value of neither the asset given up nor the asset received can be measured reliably, the cost of the asset is measured at the carrying amount of the asset given up[40] and there is no gain on the transaction. That is, if at least one of the two fair values can be measured reliably, that value is used for measuring the exchange transaction; if not, then the exchange is measured at the carrying value of the asset the entity no longer owns. However, this relatively understandable requirement (leaving aside how straightforward determining a reliable fair value will actually be) is qualified by a 'commercial substance' test.[41] The commercial substance test was put in place as an anti-abuse provision to prevent gains in income being recognised when the transaction had no discernable effect on the entity's economics.[42] The commercial substance of an exchange is to be determined by forecasting and comparing the future cash flows budgeted to be generated by the incoming and outgoing assets. For commercial substance to be present, there must be a significant difference between the two forecasts. The standard sets out this requirement as follows:

'An entity determines whether an exchange transaction has commercial substance by considering the extent to which its future cash flows are expected to change as a result of the transaction. An exchange transaction has commercial substance if:

(a)   the configuration (risk, timing and amount) of the cash flows of the asset received differs from the configuration of the cash flows of the asset transferred; or

(b)   the entity-specific value of the portion of the entity's operations affected by the transaction changes as a result of the exchange; and

(c)   the difference in (a) or (b) is significant relative to the fair value of the assets exchanged.'[43]

As set out in the definitions of the standard, see 2.3 above, entity-specific value is the net present value of the future predicted cash flows from continuing use and disposal of the asset. Post-tax cash flows should be used for this calculation. The standard contains no guidance on the discount rate to be used for this exercise, nor on any of the other parameters involved, but it does suggest that the result of these analyses might be clear without having to perform detailed calculations.[44]

The IASB has concluded that the recognition of income from an exchange of assets does not depend on whether the assets exchanged are dissimilar.[45] Care will have to be taken to ensure that the transaction has commercial substance as defined in the standard if an entity receives a similar item of property, plant and equipment in exchange for a similar asset of its own. Commercial substance may be difficult to demonstrate if the entity is exchanging an asset for a similar one in a similar location. However, in the latter case, the risk, timing and amount of cash flows could differ if one asset were available for sale and the entity intended to sell it whereas the previous asset could not be realised by sale or only sold in a much longer timescale. It is feasible that such a transaction could meet conditions (a) and (c) above. Similarly, it would be unusual if the entity-specific values of similar assets differed enough in any arm's length exchange transaction to meet condition (c). However, many exchanges are more likely to pass the 'commercial substance' test, for example:

*   exchanging an interest in an investment property for one that the entity uses for its own purposes. The entity has exchanged a rental stream and instead has an asset that contributes to the cash flows of the cash-generating unit of which it is a part; or

*   exchanging a property for a stake in a jointly controlled entity. The entity will now receive a rental or royalty stream from an asset that was previously part of a cash-generating unit.

In both of these cases it is possible that the risk, timing and amount of the cash flows of the asset received would differ from the configuration of the cash flows of the asset transferred.

In the context of asset exchanges, the standard contains guidance on the reliable determination of fair values in the circumstances where market values do not exist:

'The fair value of an asset for which comparable market transactions do not exist is reliably measurable if (a) the variability in the range of reasonable fair value estimates is not significant for that asset or (b) the probabilities of the various estimates within the range can be reasonably assessed and used in estimating fair value. If an entity is able to determine reliably the fair value of either the asset received or the asset given up, then the fair value of the asset given up is used to measure the cost of the asset received unless the fair value of the asset received is more clearly evident.'[46]

No guidance is given on how to assemble a 'range of reasonable fair value estimates'. IAS 16 itself permits the estimation of the fair value using income or depreciated replacement cost bases (see 4.1 below) but the latter hardly seems relevant to an exchange transaction. Another way would be to base fair value on the 'entity-specific value' – i.e. on the discounted budgeted cash flows of the entity. This is a technique used for valuing investment properties in thin markets (see Chapter 17). However, if the fair value *is* the entity-specific value, how can the difference between it and the fair value be significant?

The term 'commercial substance' is used by the standard in a particular sense only, as in practice commercial substance can exist (in the sense that an entity has a good reason for the exchange) even if forecast cash flows are similar. If it is not possible to demonstrate that the transaction has commercial substance as defined by the standard, assets received in exchange transactions will be recorded at the carrying value of the asset given up.

If the transaction passes the 'commercial substance' test then IAS 16 requires the exchanged asset to be recorded at its fair value. As discussed in 5 below, the standard requires gains or losses on items that have been derecognised to be included in profit or loss in the period of derecognition but does not allow gains on derecognition to be classified as revenue.[47] It gives no further indication regarding their classification in profit or loss It should be noted that the exchange of goods and services is dealt with in IAS 18 which takes a different approach from IAS 16 with respect to exchanges of PP&E (see Chapter 25 at 3.10).

3.2.5   Assets held under finance leases

The cost at initial recognition of assets held under finance leases is determined in accordance with IAS 17,[48] as described in Chapter 22.

3.2.6   Assets acquired with the assistance of government grants

The carrying amount of an item of PP&E may be reduced by government grants in accordance with IAS 20 – *Accounting for Government Grants and Disclosure of Government Assistance.*[49] The requirements of that standard are discussed in Chapter 23.

4   MEASUREMENT AFTER RECOGNITION

IAS 16 allows one of two alternatives to be chosen as the accounting policy for measurement of PP&E after initial recognition. The choice made must be applied to an entire class of PP&E, but not all classes are required to have the same policy.[50]

The first alternative is the 'cost model' (the traditional way PP&E has been accounted for) whereby the item is carried at cost less accumulated depreciation and less any impairment losses.[51] The requirements of IAS 16 concerning depreciation are dealt with at 4.2 below. The second alternative, the revaluation model, is discussed below at 4.1.

4.1   Revaluation model

If the revaluation model is adopted, PP&E is to be carried at fair value less subsequent accumulated depreciation or impairment losses.[52] 'Fair value' will usually be the market value of the asset. In the case of land and buildings the standard states that this will be 'determined from market based evidence', which is normally to be determined by professional valuers, though there is no requirement for a professional external valuation or even for a professionally qualified valuer to perform the appraisal. The fair value of other items of PP&E is usually their appraised market value.[53] Although market value is not discussed further, fair value is defined as the amount at which an asset could be exchanged between knowledgeable, willing parties in an arm's length transaction.

If there is no market-based evidence of fair value because of the specialised nature of the items, or because they are rarely sold, a depreciated replacement cost approach or an 'income' approach is to be used.[54] Neither of these terms is explained further. These valuation issues are discussed further at 7.3.1 below.

Valuation frequency is not laid down precisely by IAS 16, which states that revaluations are to be made with sufficient regularity to ensure that the carrying amount does not differ materially from the fair value at the end of the reporting period.[55] When the fair value of a revalued asset differs materially from its carrying amount, a further revaluation is necessary. The standard suggests that some items of PP&E have frequent and volatile changes in fair value and these should be revalued annually. This is true of property assets in many jurisdictions, but even in such cases there may be quieter periods in which there is little movement in values. If there are only insignificant movements it may only be necessary to perform valuations at three or five year intervals.[56]

If the revaluation model is adopted, IAS 16 specifies that all items within a class of asset are to be revalued simultaneously to prevent selective revaluations. A class of PP&E is a grouping of assets of a similar nature and use in an entity's operations. This is not a precise definition. IAS 16 suggests that the following are examples of separate classes of asset:

(i)   land;

(ii)   land and buildings;

(iii)   machinery;

(iv)   ships;

(v)   aircraft;

(vi)   motor vehicles;

(vii)   furniture and fixtures; and

(viii) office equipment.[57]

These are very broad categories of asset and it is possible for them to be classified further into groupings of assets of a similar nature and use. Office buildings and factories or hotels and fitness centres, could be separate classes of asset. If the entity used the same type of asset in two different geographical locations, e.g. clothing manufacturing facilities for similar products or products with similar markets, say footwear in Sri Lanka and knitwear in Guatemala, it is likely that these would be seen as part of the same class of asset. However, if the entity manufactured pharmaceuticals and clothing, both in European facilities, then arguably these could be assets with a sufficiently different nature and use to be a separate class. Ultimately it must be a matter of judgement in the context of the specific operations of individual entities.

IAS 16 permits a rolling valuation of a class of assets, whereby the class is revalued over an (undefined) short period of time, 'provided the valuations are kept up to date'.[58] This final condition makes it difficult to see how rolling valuations can be performed unless the value of the assets changes very little (in which case the standard states that valuations need only be performed every three to five years) as, if a large change is revealed, then presumably a wholesale revaluation is required.

4.1.1 Accounting for valuation surpluses and deficits

Increases in a valuation should be credited to a revaluation surplus within Other Comprehensive Income ('OCI'). If a revaluation increase reverses a decrease that was recognised as an expense, it may be credited to income. Decreases in valuation should be charged to profit or loss, except to the extent that they reverse an existing revaluation surplus on the same asset.[59] This means that it is not permissible under the standard to carry a negative revaluation reserve in respect of any asset.

IAS 16 generally retains a model in which the revalued amount substitutes for cost in both balance sheet and income statement and there is no reclassification adjustment of amounts taken directly to OCI. This is unlike the treatment subsequently adopted by the IASB in relation to available for sale financial assets, in which gains and losses initially taken to OCI on remeasurement to fair value are taken to income when the asset is derecognised (see Chapter 30).

Different rules apply to impairment losses. An impairment loss on a revalued asset is first used to reduce the revaluation surplus for that asset. Only when the impairment loss exceeds the amount in the revaluation surplus for that same asset is any further impairment loss recognised in profit or loss (see Chapter 18 at 3.3.3).[60]

The revaluation surplus included in OCI may be transferred directly to retained earnings as the surplus is realised, and all of it may be transferred when the asset is disposed of.

The difference between depreciation based on the revalued carrying amount of the asset and depreciation based on its original cost may be transferred as the asset is used by the entity. This is illustrated in Example 16.3 below. This recognises that any depreciation on the revalued part of an asset's carrying value has been realised by being charged to income. Thus a transfer can be made of an equivalent amount from the revaluation surplus to retained profit. However any transfer is made directly from revaluation surplus to retained earnings and not through the income statement.[61]

Example 16.3:   Effect of depreciation on the revaluation reserve

On 1 January 2004 an entity acquired an asset for €1,000. The asset has an economic life of ten years and is depreciated on a straight-line basis. The residual value is assumed to be €nil. At 31 December 2008 (when the cost net of accumulated depreciation is €600) the asset is valued at €900. The entity accounts for the revaluation by debiting accumulated depreciation €300 and crediting €300 to the revaluation reserve. At 31 December 2008 the economic life of the asset is considered to be the remainder of its original life, i.e. six years, and its residual value is still considered to be €nil. In the year ended 31 December 2009 and in later years, the depreciation charged to profit or loss is €150.

The usual treatment thereafter for each of the remaining 6 years of the asset's life, is to transfer €50 each year from the revaluation reserve to retained earnings (not through profit or loss). This avoids the revaluation reserve being maintained indefinitely even after the asset ceases to exist, which does not seem sensible.

The effect on taxation, both current and deferred, of a policy of revaluing assets is dealt with in Chapter 26.

4.1.2   Adopting a policy of revaluation

Although the adoption of a policy of revaluation by an entity that has previously used the cost model is a change in accounting policy, it is not dealt with as a prior year adjustment in accordance with IAS 8 – *Accounting Policies, Changes in Accounting Estimates and Errors*, but instead is treated as a revaluation during the year.[62]

4.1.3   Assets held under finance leases

Once assets held under finance leases have been capitalised as items of PP&E, their subsequent accounting is the same as for any other asset. Therefore such assets may also be revalued using the revaluation model but, if the revaluation model is used, then the entire class of assets (both owned and those held under finance lease) must be revalued.

Whilst it is not explicit in IAS 16, in our view, to obtain the fair value of an asset held under a finance lease for financial reporting purposes, the assessed value must be adjusted to take account of any recognised finance lease liability. The mechanism for achieving this is set out in detail in Chapter 17 at 4.5.

PP&E acquired under a finance lease should be considered to be the same class of asset as those with a similar nature that are owned. Consequently, there is no need to provide separate reconciliations of movements in owned assets from assets held under finance leases (see 6.1 (e) below).

4.2   Depreciation

IAS 16 links its recognition concept of a 'part' of an asset, discussed at 3.1.3 above, with the analysis of assets for the purpose of depreciation. Each part of an asset with a cost that is significant in relation to the total cost of the item must be depreciated separately,[63] which means that the initial cost must be allocated between the significant parts by the entity. The standard's example again includes that of the airframe and engines of an aircraft but, effective for accounting periods beginning on or after 1 July 2009, also sets out that if an entity acquires PP&E subject to an operating lease in which it is the lessor, it may be appropriate to depreciate separately amounts reflected in the cost of that item that are attributable to favourable or unfavourable lease terms relative to market terms.[64] This amendment to the Standard results from the implementation of IFRS 3 – *Business Combinations* (as revised in 2008) that requires a similar treatment for PP&E purchased as part of a business combination.

A determination of the significant parts of office buildings can be seen in Extract 16.1 above from Skanska. In addition, Chapter 17 Extract 17.7 shows an example of the allocation for investment property, although favourable or unfavourable lease terms are not there identified as a separate part.

Because parts are identified by their significant cost rather than their effect on depreciation, they may have the same useful lives and depreciation method and the standard allows them to be grouped for depreciation purposes.[65] It also identifies other circumstances in which the significant parts do not correspond to the depreciable components within the asset. The remainder of an asset that has not separately been identified into parts may consist of other parts that are individually not significant and the entity may need to use approximation techniques to calculate an appropriate depreciation method for all of these parts.[66] The standard also allows an entity to depreciate separately parts that are not significant in relation to the whole.[67]

The depreciation charge is recognised in profit or loss unless it forms part of the cost of another asset, for example as part of the cost of finished manufactured goods held in inventory in accordance with IAS 2.[68]

Accounting for parts of assets is discussed further at 7.1 below.

4.2.1 Depreciable amount, useful life and residual values

As noted in 2.3 above, the depreciable amount of an item of PP&E is its cost or valuation less its estimated residual value. The standard states that an entity must review the residual values of all its items of PP&E, and therefore all parts of them, at least at each financial year-end. If the estimated residual value differs from previous estimates, changes must be accounted for prospectively as a change in accounting estimate in accordance with IAS 8.[69] Although not expressly stated, this passage in the standard applies only to material differences.

As the definition (see 2.3 above) implies, the residual value of an item of PP&E today is to be calculated by taking the price such an asset would fetch today, but assuming that it was already in the condition it will be in at the end of its useful life. Therefore IAS 16 contains an element of continuous updating of one component of an asset's carrying value.

As any change in the residual value directly affects the depreciable amount, it may also affect the depreciation charge. This is because the depreciable amount (i.e. the amount actually charged to profit or loss over the life of the asset) is calculated by deducting the residual value from the cost or valuation of the asset, although for these purposes the residual value is capped at the asset's carrying amount.[70] Although many items of PP&E have a negligible residual value because they are kept for significantly all of their useful lives, there are a number of types of asset where this requirement could have a significant effect, and conceivably cause noticeable volatility in the depreciation charge. The residual values, and hence depreciation charges, of ships, aircraft, hotels and other assets of this nature, could potentially be affected by this requirement.

In addition, the standard requires year-end reviews of an asset's useful life, and, if expectations differ from previous estimates, the depreciation charge should be adjusted prospectively.[71] Factors that may affect the useful life are discussed at 4.2.3 below.

The requirement concerning the residual values of assets highlights how important it is that residual values are considered and reviewed in conjunction with the review of useful lives. The useful life is the period over which the entity expects to use the asset, not the asset's economic life.

Residual values are of no relevance if the entity intends to keep the asset until it is of no use to anyone else. If an entity points to the prices fetched in the market by a type of asset that it holds, it must also demonstrate an intention to dispose of it before the end of its economic life.

4.2.2 Depreciation charge

The standard requires the depreciable amount of an asset to be allocated on a systematic basis over its useful life.[72]

The standard makes it clear that depreciation must be charged on all items of PP&E, including those carried under the revaluation model, even if the fair value of the asset at the year-end is higher than the carrying amount,[73] as long as the residual value of the item is lower than the carrying amount. If the residual value exceeds the carrying amount, no depreciation is charged until the residual value once again decreases to less than the carrying amount.[74] IAS 16 makes it clear that repair and maintenance of an asset does not of itself negate the need to depreciate it.[75] This is discussed further below.

There is no requirement in IAS 16 for an automatic impairment review if no depreciation is charged.

4.2.3 Useful lives

IAS 16 provides the following guidance about the factors to be considered when estimating the useful life of an asset:

'(a) expected usage of the asset. Usage is assessed by reference to the asset's expected capacity or physical output;

(b) expected physical wear and tear, which depends on operational factors such as the number of shifts for which the asset is to be used and the repair and maintenance programme, and the care and maintenance of the asset while idle;

(c)   technical or commercial obsolescence arising from changes or improvements in production, or from a change in the market demand for the product or service output of the asset;

(d)   legal or similar limits on the use of the asset, such as the expiry dates of related leases.'[76]

Arcelor is an example of an entity depreciating an asset over its expected usage by reference to the production period.

Extract 16.7: Arcelor SA (2006)

Notes to the Consolidated Financial Statements [extract]

Note 2   ACCOUNTING POLICIES [extract]

7)   Property, plant and equipment [extract]

The cost of the periodic relining of blast furnaces is capitalised and depreciated over the expected production period.

The initial assessment of the useful life of the asset will take account of the expected routine spending on repairs and expenditure necessary for it to achieve that life. Although (b) above implies that this refers to an item of plant and machinery, care and maintenance programmes are relevant to assessing the useful lives of many other types of asset. For example, an entity may assess the useful life of a railway engine at thirty-five years on the assumption that it has a major overhaul every seven years. Without this expenditure, the life of the engine would be much less certain and could be much shorter. Maintenance necessary to support the fabric of a building and its service potential will also be taken into account in assessing its useful life. Eventually, it will always become uneconomic for the entity to continue to maintain the asset so, while the expenditure may lengthen the useful life, it is unlikely to make it indefinite. However, as the maintenance spend may affect the residual value, it may indirectly reduce the depreciable amount to zero.

The useful life of an asset is defined in terms of its use to the business, not its economic life, so it is quite possible that an asset's useful life will be shorter than its economic life. Many entities have a policy of disposing of assets when they still have a residual value, which means that another user will benefit from the asset.[77] This is particularly common with property and motor vehicles, where there are effective second-hand markets, but less usual for plant and machinery.

The standard requires the land and the building elements of property to be accounted for as separate components. Land, which usually has an unlimited life, is not usually depreciated, while buildings are depreciable assets. IAS 16 states that the useful life of a building is not affected by an increase in the value of the land on which it stands.[78]

There are circumstances in which depreciation may be applied to land. In those instances in which land does have a finite life it will be either used for extractive purposes (a quarry or mine) or for some purpose such as landfill; it will be depreciated in an appropriate manner but it is highly unlikely that there will be any issue regarding separating the interest in land from any building element. However, the cost of such land may include an element for site dismantlement or restoration (see 3.1.3 above), in which case this element will have to be depreciated over an appropriate period. The standard describes this as 'the period of benefits obtained by incurring these costs';[79] which will often be the estimated useful life of the site for its purpose and function. So, for example, an entity engaged in landfill on a new site may make a provision for restoring it as soon as it starts preparation by removing the overburden. It will depreciate this 'restoration asset' over the landfill site's estimated useful life. If the land has an infinite useful life, an appropriate depreciation basis will have to be chosen that reflects the period of benefits obtained from the restoration asset.

If the estimated costs are revised in accordance with IFRIC 1, the adjusted depreciable amount of the asset is depreciated over its useful life. Therefore, once the related asset has reached the end of its useful life, all subsequent changes in the liability shall be recognised in profit or loss as they occur, irrespective of whether the entity applies the cost or revaluation model.[80]

4.2.4   When depreciation starts

The standard is clear on when depreciation should start and finish, and sets out the requirements succinctly as follows:

- depreciation of an asset begins when it is available for use, which is defined by the standard as occurring when the asset is in the location and condition necessary for it to be capable of operating in the manner intended by management. This is the point at which capitalisation of costs relating to the asset cease;

- depreciation of an asset ceases at the earlier of the date that the asset is classified as held for sale (or included in a disposal group that is classified as held for sale) in accordance with IFRS 5 and the date that the asset is derecognised.[81]

Therefore, an entity does not stop depreciating an asset merely because it has become idle or has been retired from active use (unless, of course, the asset is fully depreciated). However, if the entity is using a usage method of depreciation the charge can be zero while there is no production.[82] Of course, a prolonged period in which there is no production may raise questions as to whether the asset is impaired: an asset becoming idle is a specific example of an indication of impairment in IAS 36 (see Chapter 18).[83]

Assets held for sale under IFRS 5 are discussed below at 5.1.

4.2.5   Depreciation methods

The standard is not prescriptive about methods of depreciation, mentioning straight line, diminishing balance and units of production as possibilities. The overriding requirement is that the depreciation charge reflects the pattern of consumption of the benefits the asset brings over its useful life, and is applied consistently from period to period.[84] IAS 16 contains an explicit requirement that the depreciation method be reviewed at least at each period end to determine if there has been a significant change in the pattern of consumption of an asset's benefits. This would be unusual; it would mean, for example, concluding that the unit of production method was no longer appropriate and changing to a straight line or diminishing balance method. Nevertheless, if there has been such a change, the depreciation method should be changed to reflect it. However, under IAS 8, this change is a change in accounting estimate and not a change in accounting policy.[85] This means that the consequent depreciation adjustment should be made prospectively, i.e. the asset's depreciable amount should be written off over current and future periods.[86] See 7.6 below for a discussion of depreciation methods in practice.

4.3   Impairment

All items of PP&E accounted for under IAS 16 are subject to the impairment requirements of IAS 36. Impairment is discussed in Chapter 18.[87]

4.3.1   *Compensation for impairment*

The question has arisen about the treatment of any compensation an entity may be due to receive as a result of an asset being impaired. For example an asset that is insured might be destroyed in a fire, so repayment from an insurance company might be expected. IAS 16 states that these two events – the impairment and any compensation – are 'separate economic events' and should be accounted for separately as follows:

- impairments of PP&E are recognised in accordance with IAS 36 (see Chapter 18);

- derecognition of items retired or disposed of should be recognised in accordance with IAS 16 (derecognition is discussed below); and

- compensation from third parties for PP&E that is impaired lost or given up is included in profit and loss when it becomes receivable.[88]

Therefore any compensation is accounted for separately from any impairment. Although the question as to when 'compensation becomes receivable' is not discussed further in the standard, IAS 37 requires that reimbursements from third parties should be recognised as a separate asset when it is 'virtually certain' that the reimbursement will be received.[89]

5   DERECOGNITION AND DISPOSAL

Derecognition (i.e. removal of the carrying amount of the item from the financial statements of the entity) occurs when an item of PP&E is either disposed of, or when no further economic benefits are expected to flow from its use or disposal.[90] The actual date of disposal is determined in accordance with the criteria in IAS 18 for the recognition of revenue from the sale of goods[91] (revenue recognition is discussed in Chapter 25). All gains and losses on derecognition must be included in profit and loss for the period when the item is derecognised, unless another standard applies – for example under IAS 17 a sale and leaseback transaction might not give rise to a gain.

Gains are not to be classified as revenue, although in some limited circumstances presenting gross revenue on the sale of certain assets may be appropriate (see 5.2 below).[92] Gains and losses are to be calculated as the difference between any net disposal proceeds and the carrying value of the item of PP&E[93] – this means that any revaluation surplus relating to the asset disposed of is transferred directly to retained earnings when the asset is derecognised and not reflected in profit or loss.[94]

Replacement of 'parts' of an asset requires derecognition of the carrying value of the original part, even if that part was not being depreciated separately. Under these circumstances, the standard allows the cost of a replacement part to be a guide to the original cost of the replaced part, if that cannot be determined.[95]

Any consideration received on the disposal of an item should be recognised at its fair value. If deferred credit terms are given, the consideration for the sale is the cash price equivalent, and any surplus is treated as interest revenue using the effective yield method as required by IAS 18 (see Chapter 25 at 3.5).[96]

5.1   IFRS 5 – Non-current assets held for sale and discontinued operations

IFRS 5 introduced a category of asset, 'held for sale', and PP&E within this category is outside the scope of IAS 16, although IAS 16 requires certain disclosures about assets held for sale to be made, as set out at 6.1 below.

IFRS 5 requires that an item of PP&E should be classified as held for sale if its carrying amount will be recovered principally though a sale transaction rather then continuing use, though continuing use is not in itself precluded for assets classified as held for sale.[97] An asset can also be part of a 'disposal group' (that is a group of assets that are to be disposed of together), in which case the group can be treated as a whole. Once this classification has been made, depreciation ceases, even if the asset is still being used, but the assets must be carried at the lower of their previous carrying amount and fair value less costs to sell. For assets to be classified as held for sale, they must be available for immediate sale in their present condition, and the sale must be highly probable.[98]

Additionally, the sale should be completed within one year from the date of classification as held for sale, management at an 'appropriate level' must be committed to the plan, and an active programme of marketing the assets must have been started.[99]

The requirements of IFRS 5 are dealt with in Chapter 4.

5.2   Sale of assets held for rental

A number of entities sell assets that have previously been held for rental, for example, car rental companies that may acquire vehicles with the intention of holding them as rental cars for limited period and then selling them. The issue that arose was whether the sale of such assets (which arguably have a dual purpose of being rented out and then sold) should be presented gross (revenue and cost of sales) or net (gain or loss) in profit or loss.

The IFRIC, in considering this matter, noted that IAS 16 stated that disposals of PP&E should not be classified as revenue.[100] When it was referred to them by the IFRIC, the IASB took the view that the presentation of gross revenue, rather than a net gain or loss, would better reflect the ordinary activities of some such entities and amended IAS 16 accordingly. If an entity, in the course of its ordinary activities, routinely sells property, plant and equipment that it has held for rental to others, it should transfer such assets to inventories at their carrying amount when they cease to be rented and held for sale. The proceeds from the sale of such assets should be recognised as revenue.[101]

The IASB also made a consequential adjustment to IAS 7 – *Statement of Cash Flows* – to require that both (i) the cash payments to manufacture or acquire assets held for rental and subsequently held for sale; and (ii) the cash receipts from rentals and sales of such assets are presented as from operating activities.[102] This amendment to IAS 7 is intended to avoid initial expenditure on purchases of assets being classified as investing activities while inflows from sales are recorded within operating activities.

The amendments to IAS 16 and IAS 7 were approved by the IASB in May 2008, effective for periods beginning on or after 1 January 2009.

6   IAS 16 DISCLOSURE REQUIREMENTS

IAS 16 contains a well laid out disclosure section that is easy to understand. The main requirements are set out below, but note that the related disclosure requirements of IAS 36 are relevant also in the case of PP&E that is impaired. IAS 36 is dealt with in Chapter 18.

6.1   General disclosures

For each class of property plant and equipment the following should be disclosed in the financial statements:

(a)   the measurement bases used for determining the gross carrying amount (for example, cost, fair value). When more than one basis has been used, the gross carrying amount for that basis in each category should be disclosed (however the standard requires that if revaluation is adopted the entire class of assets must be revalued);

(b)   the depreciation methods used;

(c)   the useful lives or the depreciation rates used;

(d)   the gross carrying amount and the accumulated depreciation (aggregated with accumulated impairment losses) at the beginning and end of the period;

(e)   a reconciliation of the carrying amount at the beginning and end of the period showing:

(i)   additions;

(ii)   disposals,

(iii)   assets classified as held for sale, or included in a disposal group held for sale;

(iv)   acquisitions through business combinations;

(v)   increases or decreases during the period resulting from revaluations and from impairment losses recognised or reversed directly in equity under IAS 36 (if any);

(vi)   impairment losses recognised in profit or loss during the period under IAS 36 (if any);

(vii) impairment losses reversed in profit or loss during the period under IAS 36 (if any);

(viii) depreciation for the period;

(ix)   the net exchange differences arising on the translation of the financial statements from the functional currency into a different presentation currency, including the translation of a foreign operation into the presentation currency of the reporting entity; and

(x)   other changes.

Under the previous version of IAS 16, it was not required to provide comparative information for the reconciliation in (e) above, because the standard offered a specific exemption from the requirement in IAS 1 to disclose 'comparative information ... in respect of the previous period for all amounts reported in the financial statements'.[103] However, the current version of IAS 16 does not contain this exemption, thereby making it necessary to include comparative information for this reconciliation.

Extract 16.8 illustrates a PP&E accounting policy together with the movement and reconciliation note (a comparative is provided in the financial statements but is not reproduced here).

Extract 16.8: Volkswagen Aktiengesellschaft (2007)

Notes to the consolidated financial statements of the Volkswagen Group
for the Fiscal Year ended December 31, 2007 [extract]
PROPERTY, PLANT AND EQUIPMENT [extract]

Property, plant and equipment is carried at cost less depreciation and – where necessary – write-downs for impairment. Investment grants are generally deducted from cost. Cost is determined on the basis of the direct and indirect costs that are directly attributable. Borrowing costs are recorded as current expenses. Property, plant and equipment is depreciated using the straight-line method over its estimated useful life. The useful lives of items of property, plant and equipment are reviewed at each balance sheet date and adjusted if required.

Depreciation is based mainly on the following useful lives:

	Useful life
Buildings	25 to 50 years
Site improvements	10 to 18 years
Technical equipment and machinery	6 to 12 years
Other equipment, operating and office equipment, including special tools	3 to 15 years

[11]   PROPERTY, PLANT AND EQUIPMENT [extract]
CHANGES IN PROPERTY, PLANT AND EQUIPMENT
BETWEEN JANUARY 1 AND DECEMBER 31, 2007

€ million	Land, land rights and buildings, including buildings on third-party land	Technical equipment and machinery	Other equipment operating and office equipment	Payments on account and assets under construction	Total
Historical cost					
Balance at Jan. 1, 2007	14,141	24,538	31,311	1,518	71,508
Foreign exchange differences	2	– 69	– 48	– 3	– 118
Changes in consolidated Group	32	–	34	1	67
Additions	299	820	1,760	1,602	4,481
Transfers	120	563	532	– 1,240	– 25
Disposals	170	804	969	42	1,985
Balance at Dec. 31, 2007	14,424	25,048	32,620	1,836	73,928
Depreciation and impairment					
Balance at Jan. 1, 2007	7,214	18,801	25,146	7	51,168
Foreign exchange differences	– 7	– 29	– 28	1	63
Changes in consolidated Group	9	–	11	–	20
Additions to cumulative depreciation	472	1,730	2,628	–	4,830
Additions to cumulative impairment losses	2	24	414		440
Transfers	– 2	– 2	3		– 1
Disposals	143	784	877		1,804
Reversal of impairment losses	–	–	–		–
Balance at Dec. 31, 2007	7,545	19,740	27,297	8	54,590
Carrying amount at Dec. 31, 2007	6,879	5,308	5,323	1,828	19,338
Of which assets leased under finance lease contracts Carrying amount at Dec. 31, 2007	197	–	19	–	216

IAS 16 also requires the disclosure of the following information, which is useful to gain a fuller understanding of the entire position of the entity's holdings of and its commitments to purchase property plant and equipment:

(a)   the existence and amounts of restrictions on title, and property, plant and equipment pledged as security for liabilities;

(b)   the amount of expenditures recognised in the carrying amount of property, plant and equipment in the course of construction;

(c)   the amount of contractual commitments for the acquisition of property, plant and equipment; and

(d)   if it is not disclosed separately on the face of profit or loss, the amount of compensation from third parties for items of property, plant and equipment that were impaired, lost or given up that is included in profit or loss.[104]

In addition there is a reminder in the standard that, in accordance with IAS 8, any changes in accounting estimate (e.g. depreciation methods, useful lives, residual values) that have a material effect on the current or future periods must be disclosed.[105]

6.2   Additional disclosures for revalued assets

The IASB has gone to some lengths in IAS 16 to ensure that if the revaluation model is adopted, users of the financial statements should have enough information to clearly see its effects. The additional requirements if the revaluation basis is adopted are:

(a)   the effective date of the revaluation;

(b)   whether an independent valuer was involved;

(c)   the methods and significant assumptions applied in estimating the items' fair values;

(d)   the extent to which the items' fair values were determined directly by reference to observable prices in an active market or recent market transactions on arm's length terms or were estimated using other valuation techniques;

(e)   for each revalued class of property, plant and equipment, the carrying amount that would have been recognised had the assets been carried under the cost model; and

(f)   the revaluation surplus, indicating the change for the period and any restrictions on the distribution of the balance to shareholders.[106]

In particular the requirement under (e) is quite onerous for entities, as it entails their keeping asset register information in some detail in order to meet it.

Extract 16.9 below from AEGON NV shows disclosures relating to PP&E held at a valuation – in this case real estate held for own use.

Extract 16.9: AEGON N.V. (2007)

NOTES TO THE CONSOLIDATED FINANCIAL STATEMENTS OF
AEGON GROUP [extract]

6.2   REAL ESTATE HELD FOR OWN USE

Net book value		
At January 1, 2006		355
At December 31, 2006		313
AT DECEMBER 31, 2007		**329**

Cost	2007	2006
At January 1	341	377
Additions	75	90
Acquired through business combinations	4	18
Capitalized subsequent expenditure	3	5
Disposals	(2)	(3)
Unrealised gains/(losses) through equity	9	16
Realised gains/(losses) through income statement	3	(5)
Transfers to investments in real estate	(49)	(136)
Net exchange differences	(21)	(21)
AT DECEMBER 31	**363**	**341**

Accumulated depreciation and impairment losses	2007	2006
At January 1	28	22
Depreciation through income statement	8	8
Disposals	–	(1)
Net exchange differences	(2)	(1)
AT DECEMBER 31	34	28

General account real estate held for own use are mainly held by AEGON USA and AEGON The Netherlands, with relatively smaller holdings in Hungary and Spain and are carried at revalued amounts. The carrying value under a historical cost model amounts to EUR 213 million (2006: EUR 169 million).

61% of the real estate held for own use was last revalued in 2007, based on market value appraisals by qualified internal and external appraisers. All the appraisals in 2007 were performed by independent external appraisers.

Real estate held for own use has not been pledged as security for liabilities, nor are there any restrictions on title. Depreciation expenses are charged in 'Commissions and expenses' in the income statement. The useful lives of buildings range between 40 and 50 years.

Refer to note 46 for a summary of contractual commitments for the acquisition of real estate held for own use.

6.3   Other disclosures

The standard emphasises that entities are also required to disclose information about impairment in accordance with IAS 36, in addition to the disclosures on this matter required by IAS 16.

The standard encourages, but does not require, entities to disclose other additional information such as the carrying amount of any idle assets, the gross amount of any fully depreciated assets in use, and any held for disposal. For any property plant and equipment held at cost less depreciation, the disclosure of its fair value is also encouraged if it is materially different from the carrying amount.[107]

As set out in 8.1 below, in their May 2009 meeting, the IFRIC decided to recommend to the IASB that they undertake a review of all disclosures encouraged (but not required) by IFRSs with the objective of either confirming they are required or eliminating them.

7   PRACTICAL ISSUES

7.1   Accounting for parts ('components') of assets

IAS 16 has a single set of recognition criteria, which means that subsequent expenditure must also meet these criteria before it is recognised.

Parts of an asset are to be identified so that the cost of replacing a part may be recognised (i.e. capitalised as part of the asset) and the previous part derecognised. These parts are often referred to as 'components'. Parts' are distinguished from day-to-day servicing but they are not otherwise identified and defined; moreover, the unit of measurement to which the standard applies (i.e. what comprises an item of PP&E) is not itself defined.

IAS 16 requires 'significant parts' of an asset to be depreciated separately.[108] These are parts that have a cost that is significant in relation to the total cost of the asset. An entity will have to identify the significant parts of the asset on initial recognition in order for it to depreciate the asset properly. There is no requirement to identify all parts. IAS 16 requires entities to derecognise an existing part when it is replaced, regardless of whether it has been depreciated separately, and allows the carrying value of the part that has been replaced to be estimated if necessary:

'If it is not practicable for an entity to determine the carrying amount of the replaced part, it may use the cost of the replacement as an indication of what the cost of the replaced part was at the time it was acquired or constructed.'[109]

As a consequence, an entity may not actually identify the parts of an asset until it incurs the replacement expenditure, as in the following example.

Example 16.4:   Recognition and derecognition of parts

An entity buys a piece of machinery with an estimated useful life of ten years for €10 million. The asset contains two identical pumps, which are assumed to have the same useful life as the machine of which they are a part. After seven years one of the pumps fails and is replaced at a cost of €200,000. The entity had not identified the pumps as separate parts and does not know the original cost. It uses the cost of the replacement part to estimate the carrying value of the original pump. With the help of the supplier, it estimates that the cost would have been approximately €170,000 and that this would have a remaining carrying value after seven year's depreciation of €51,000. Accordingly it derecognises €51,000 and capitalises the cost of the replacement.

It may be that the entity has no better information than the cost of the replacement part, in which case it appears that the entity is permitted to use a depreciated replacement cost basis to calculate the amount derecognised in respect of the original asset.

7.2   Useful life

One of the critical assumptions on which the depreciation charge depends is the useful economic life of the asset. The useful economic life is the period over which the present owner will benefit and not the total potential life of the asset; the two will often not be the same. For example, an entity may have a policy of replacing all of its motor vehicles after three years, so this will be their estimated useful life for depreciation purposes. The entity will depreciate them over this period down to the estimated residual value. The residual values of motor vehicles are often easy to obtain and the entity will be able to reassess these residuals in line with the requirements of the standard.

The effects of technological change are often underestimated. It affects many assets, not only high technology plant and equipment such as computer systems. For example, many offices that have been purpose-built can become obsolete long before their fabric has physically deteriorated, for reasons such as the difficulty of introducing computer network infrastructures or air conditioning, poor environmental performance or an inability to meet new legislative requirements such as access for people with disabilities.

As explained above, the standard requires asset lives to be estimated on a realistic basis and reviewed at the end of each reporting period. The effects of changes in estimated life are to be recognised prospectively, over the remaining life of the asset. In practice, many entities have previously tended to use quite a 'broad brush' approach to estimating asset lives, often based on perceived norms (for example, 50 years for freehold buildings) rather than a close analysis of their own expectations. The requirements of IAS 16 will necessitate more attention being paid to asset lives and residual values.

7.3   The meaning of fair value

7.3.1   *Fair value or market value*

IAS 16 describes the process of determining fair value. For land and buildings, which are almost the only assets ever revalued, fair value should be 'determined from market-based evidence' (although income or depreciated replacement cost approaches are permitted if no such evidence is available).[110] The standard does not imply that fair value and market value are synonymous.

This allows a broader meaning of the term 'fair value'. The term can certainly be interpreted as encompassing the following two commonly used, market derived, valuation bases:

- market value in existing use, an entry value for property in continuing use in the business which is based on the concept of net current replacement cost; and
- open market value, which is an exit value and based on the amount that a property that is surplus to requirements could reach when sold.

Both of these bases are market derived, yet they can differ for a variety of reasons. A property may have a higher value on the open market if it could be redeployed to a more valuable use. On the other hand, the present owner may enjoy some benefits that could not be passed on in a sale, such as planning consents that are personal to the present occupier. Market valuation issues are further discussed in the context of Investment Property in Chapter 17 at 4.2.

The IASB has conceded that a lack of codified and consistent guidance has contributed to inconsistency in measuring fair value. In consequence a Fair Value Measurements project was added to their agenda in order to develop a single standard that provides guidance to entities on measuring the fair value of assets and liabilities when required by IFRS.

However, the IASB, noting that the Financial Accounting Standards Board (FASB) was nearing completion of its fair value measurements project, decided to issue the FASB's final fair value measurement standard as an IASB Exposure Draft. The FASB Statement of Financial Accounting Standard No. 157 – *Fair value measurements* (FAS 157) – was published in September 2006 and was issued by the IASB, in the form of a discussion paper, in the fourth quarter of 2006.

A subsequent Exposure Draft was issued in May 2009 which, the IASB say, would achieve 'overall' convergence with US GAAP. The guidance in this Exposure Draft would replace that currently included in IAS 16. The IASB has said it plans to hold round-table discussions during the fourth quarter of 2009 with the intention of publishing a final IFRS on fair value measurement guidance in 2010.

FASB Statement of Financial Accounting Standard No. 157 and the IASB Discussion Paper are further discussed in Chapter 2 at 6.2 and 6.3.

In the meantime, IAS 16 requires detailed disclosures regarding the methods and significant assumptions applied in estimating the items' fair values.[111] This means that the basis or bases that an entity has applied in valuing its assets will have to be disclosed in the accounts, including the extent to which it has applied either or both of the bases described above.

7.3.2   Other methods of calculating fair value

IAS 16 allows other methods of deriving the fair value of assets in the absence of market-based evidence. If there is no market-based evidence because of the specialised nature of the asset and because it is rarely sold except as part of a continuing business, the entity is allowed to base fair value on an income or a depreciated replacement cost (DRC) approach.[112]

A   Income approaches

The standard does not define what it means by an income approach. There are a number of techniques that may be used. The valuation may be based on transactions in an active market for dissimilar assets as adjusted to reflect the differences, or on transactions on less active markets if they have been adjusted to take account of subsequent changes in economic conditions. Both of these are allowed methods of calculating the fair value of investment property (see Chapter 17 at 4.2). Presumably income approaches could include use of discounted cash flow projections based on estimated future cash flows that will be generated by the asset. Care would have to be taken as the asset may not generate income by itself, being instead part of a cash generating unit (see Chapter 18); obviously, cash flows generated by other assets are not relevant to the valuation of the asset in question. Other methods that are encountered in practice include valuation methods based on factors such as notional rentals or multiples reflecting current transactions of indicators such as revenue or profits, which may be relevant for certain assets.

An entity must disclose the extent to which it has determined fair value using a valuation technique that is not based on observable process in an active market or recent market transactions.[113]

B   Depreciated replacement cost

IAS 16 states that the alternative basis for valuing assets when they are rarely sold except as part of a continuing business is a depreciated replacement cost (DRC) approach.[114] The basis underlying DRC is that the asset is so specialised that there is no market value for it. There are three main subsets of such assets: (a) those that are only ever sold as part of a business; (b) assets primarily used to provide services to the public (whether on a paying or non-paying basis); and (c) assets that are so specialised by nature of their size or location or similar features that there is no market for them.

Examples of specialised properties include:

- oil refineries and chemical works where, usually, the buildings are no more than housings or cladding for highly specialised plant;

- power stations and dock installations where the building and site engineering works are related directly to the business of the owner, it being highly unlikely that they would have a value to anyone other than a company acquiring the undertaking;

- schools, colleges, universities and research establishments where there is no competing market demand from other organisations using these types of property in the locality;

- hospitals, other specialised health care premises and leisure centres where there is no competing market demand from other organisations wishing to use these types of property in the locality; and

- museums, libraries, and other similar premises provided by the public sector.

In addition, there may be no market-based evidence for properties of such specialised construction, arrangement, size or specification that it is unlikely that there would be a single purchaser. The same may be the case even for standard properties in geographical areas remote from main business centres, perhaps originally located there for operational or business reasons that no longer exist. This could occur if the buildings were of such an abnormal size for the district that no market for them would exist.

DRC is considered to be the aggregate amount of the value of the land for the existing use or a notional replacement site in the same locality, and the gross replacement cost of the buildings and other site works, from which appropriate deductions may then be made to allow for the age, condition, economic or functional obsolescence and environmental factors. The objective of DRC is to make a realistic estimate of the current cost of constructing an asset that has the same service potential as the existing asset.

DRC is inevitably rather an unsatisfactory valuation basis at the theoretical level, as it is represented as a valuation of property, but in circumstances where, by definition, the asset has no market value. Moreover, because a DRC valuation is based on replacement cost, it is likely to give a higher valuation than one using market-based evidence that reflects the actual current condition of the asset. For this reason, it is necessary to ensure that the property really is so specialised that such evidence cannot be obtained. It is also necessary to be satisfied that the potential profitability of the business is adequate to support the value derived on a DRC basis.

DRC approaches are often applied to the valuation of plant and machinery, as distinct from property assets, where there is rarely a market from which to derive a fair value.

7.4   Reversals of downward valuations

IAS 16 requires that, if an asset's carrying amount is increased as a result of a revaluation, the increase should be credited directly to OCI under the heading of revaluation surplus. However, the increase should be recognised in profit or loss to the extent that it reverses a revaluation decrease of the same asset previously recognised in profit or loss.[115]

If the revalued asset is being depreciated, we consider that the full amount of any reversal should not be taken to profit or loss. Rather it should take account of the depreciation that would have been charged on the previously higher book value. This is required by IAS 36 when impairment losses are reversed, that standard stating:

> 'The increased carrying amount of an asset other than goodwill attributable to a reversal of an impairment loss shall not exceed the carrying amount that would have been determined for the asset in prior years'.[116]

The following example demonstrates a way in which this could be applied:

Example 16.5:   Reversal of a downward valuation

An asset has a cost of £1,000,000, a life of 10 years and a residual value of £nil. At the end of year 3, when the asset's NBV is £700,000, it is revalued to £350,000. This write down below cost of £350,000 is taken through profit or loss.

The entity then depreciated its asset by £50,000 per annum, so as to write off the carrying value of £350,000 over the remaining 7 years.

At the end of year 6, the asset is revalued to £500,000. The effect on the entity's asset is as follows:

	£000
Valuation	
At the beginning of year 6	350
Surplus on revaluation	150
At the end of the year	500
Accumulated depreciation	
At beginning of year 6*	100
Charge for the year	50
Accumulated depreciation written back on revaluation	(150)
At the end of the year	–
Net book value at the end of year 6	500
Net book value at the beginning of year 6	250

* Two year's depreciation (years 4 and 5) at £50,000 per annum.

Upon the revaluation in year 6 the total credit is £300,000. However, only £200,000 is taken through profit or loss. £100,000 represents depreciation that would otherwise have been charged to profit or loss in years 4 and 5. This will be taken directly to the revaluation surplus in OCI.

From the beginning of year 7 the asset will be written off over the remaining four years at £125,000 per annum.

In the example the amount of the revaluation that is credited to the revaluation surplus in OCI represents the difference between the net book value that would have resulted had the asset been held on a cost basis (£400,000) and the net book value on a revalued basis (£500,000).

Of course this is an extreme example. Most assets that are subject to a policy of revaluation would not show such marked changes in value and it would be expected that there would be valuation movements in the intervening years rather than dramatic losses and gains in years 3 and 6. However, we consider that in principle this is the way in which downward valuations should be effected.

There may be major practical difficulties for any entity that finds itself in the position of reversing revaluation deficits on depreciating assets, although whether in practice this eventuality often occurs is open to doubt. If there is any chance that it is likely to occur, the business would need to continue to maintain asset registers on the original, pre-write down basis.

7.5   Depreciation of infrastructure assets

In some jurisdictions, under their former national GAAPs, infrastructure assets such as electricity distribution networks have been dealt with on a renewals accounting basis. Under renewals accounting, the level of annual expenditure required to maintain the operating capacity of the infrastructure asset is treated as the depreciation charged for the period and is deducted from the carrying amount of the asset as part of accumulated depreciation. Actual expenditure is capitalised as part of the cost of the asset as incurred.

IAS 16 makes no mention of renewals accounting, which does not appear to be allowable under the standard.

7.6   Depreciation methods

There is little discussion of depreciation methods in IAS 16, which simply says that 'the depreciation method shall reflect the pattern in which the asset's future economic benefits are expected to be consumed by the entity'.[117]

IAS 16 mentions only three depreciation methods, straight line, diminishing (reducing) balance and units of production. The straight line and reducing balance methods are well known and understood. It may be appropriate to use other methods with particular assets and, for reference purposes, some are illustrated below.

7.6.1   Double declining balance

This method is sometimes applied in the US, where it has corresponded to tax allowances on assets. The method involves determining the asset's depreciation on a straight-line basis over its useful life. This annual amount is multiplied by an appropriate factor (it does not have to be doubled) to give the first year's charge and depreciation at the same percentage rate is charged on the reducing balance in subsequent years.

Example 16.6:   Double declining balance depreciation

An asset costs €6,000 and has a life of ten years, which means that, calculated on the straight-line basis, the annual depreciation charge would be €600. On the double declining balance method (assuming a factor of two), the depreciation charge for the first year would be €1,200 and depreciation would continue to be charged at 20% on the reducing balance thereafter.

7.6.2   Sum of the digits

This is another form of the reducing balance method, but one that is based on the estimated life of the asset and which can therefore easily be applied if the asset has a residual value. If an asset has an estimated useful life of four years then the digits 1, 2, 3, and 4 are added together, giving a total of 10. Depreciation of four-tenths, three-tenths and so on, of the cost of the asset, less any residual value, will be charged in the respective years. The method is sometimes called the 'rule of 78', 78 being the sum of the digits 1 to 12.

Example 16.7:   Sum of the digits depreciation

An asset costs €10,000 and is expected to be sold for €2,000 after four years. Depreciation is to be provided over four years using the sum of the digits method.

		€
		€
Year 1	Cost	10,000
	Depreciation at 4/10 of €8,000	3,200
	Net book value	6,800
Year 2	Depreciation at 3/10 of €8,000	2,400
	Net book value	4,400
Year 3	Depreciation at 2/10 of €8,000	1,600
	Net book value	2,800
Year 4	Depreciation at 1/10 of €8,000	800
	Net book value	2,000

7.6.3   Unit of production method

Under this method, the asset is written off in line with its estimated total output. By relating depreciation to the proportion of productive capacity utilised to date, it reflects the fact that the useful economic life of certain assets, principally machinery, is more closely linked to its usage and output than to time. This method is normally used in extractive industries, for example, to amortise the costs of development of productive oil and gas facilities.

The essence of choosing a fair depreciation method is to reflect the consumption of economic benefits provided by the asset concerned. In most cases the straight-line basis will give perfectly acceptable results, and the vast majority of entities use this method. Where there are instances, such as the extraction of a known proportion of a mineral resource, or the use of a certain amount of the total available number of working hours of a machine, it may be that a unit of production method will give fairer results.

7.7   New technology costs – PP&E or intangible assets?

The restrictions in IAS 38 – *Intangible Assets* – in respect of capitalising certain internally-generated intangible assets focused attention on the treatment of many internal costs. In practice, items such as computer software purchased by entities are frequently capitalised as part of a tangible asset, for example as part of an accounting or communications infrastructure. Equally, internally written software may be capitalised as part of a tangible production facility, and so on. Judgement must be exercised in deciding whether such items are to be accounted for under IAS 16 or IAS 38 and this distinction becomes increasingly important if the two standards would prescribe differing treatments in any particular case. IAS 16, unlike IAS 38, does not refer to this type of asset. IAS 38 states that an entity needs to exercise judgment in determining whether an asset that incorporates both intangible and tangible elements should be treated under IAS 16 or as an intangible asset under IAS 38, for example:

- computer software that is embedded in computer-controlled equipment that cannot operate without that specific software is an integral part of the related hardware and is treated as property, plant and equipment;

- application software that is being used on a computer is generally easily replaced and is not an integral part of the related hardware, whereas the operating system normally is; and

- a database that is stored on a compact disc is considered to be an intangible asset because the value of the physical medium is wholly insignificant compared to that of the data collection.[118]

It is worthwhile noting that as the 'parts approach' in IAS 16 requires an entity to account for significant parts of an asset separately, this raises 'boundary' problems between IAS 16 and IAS 38 when software and similar expenditure are involved. We believe that where IAS 16 requires an entity to identify significant parts of an asset and account for them separately, the entity needs to evaluate whether any software-type intangible part is actually integral to the larger asset or whether it is really a separate asset in its own right. The intangible part is more likely to be an asset in its own right if it was developed separately or if it can be used independently of the item of property, plant and equipment that it apparently forms part of.

7.8   Amounts charged under operating leases during the construction of an asset

In our view, amounts charged under operating leases during the construction period of an asset may be included as part of the cost of the PP&E if those lease costs are 'directly attributable to bringing the asset to the location and condition necessary for it to be capable of operating in the manner intended by management'.[119] This may be the case, for example, where a building is constructed on land that is leased under an operating lease. This approach must be applied consistently.

8   FUTURE DEVELOPMENTS

8.1   Disclosures encouraged but not required

As set out in 6.3 above the IFRIC received a request for more guidance on the extent of disclosures relating to PP&E temporarily idle or assets under construction when additional construction has been postponed. The IFRIC noted that disclosure regarding idle assets might be particularly relevant in the economic environment following the financial crisis and expected entities to provide information in addition to that specifically required by IAS 16.

As the IFRIC did not expect significant diversity in practice they decided not to add this issue to their agenda. However, in May 2009, the IFRIC recommended that the IASB should undertake a review of all disclosures encouraged but not required by IFRSs with the objective of either confirming that they are required or eliminating them.

8.2   The Fair Value Exposure Draft

In May 2009 the IASB issued an Exposure Draft 'Fair Value Measurement' that the IASB claim will achieve overall convergence with US GAAP.[120] The guidance in this Exposure Draft would replace that currently included in IAS 16.

The IASB has said it plans to hold round-table discussions during the fourth quarter of 2009 with the intention of publishing a final IFRS on fair value measurement guidance in 2010.

FAS 157 and the IASB discussion paper are discussed further in Chapter 2 at 6.2 and 6.3.

9   CONCLUSION

The essential purpose of accounting for PP&E is to allocate expenditure which provides enduring benefits against the revenues of the periods that enjoy those benefits, therefore reflecting the traditional accounting principle of cost matching. This is deeply rooted in the manufacturing tradition and the still works well for machinery assets that wear out reasonably predictably.

However the position is complicated by the option in IAS 16 to revalue assets which poses the fundamental question of what the balance sheet is meant to portray. The 'stretching' by the IASB of the meaning of fair value from a market price-based concept to include a mark-to-model valuation if a market price is not available has only added further complexity. How these matters might be resolved is the subject of much of the discussion concerning a new conceptual framework, a project currently being undertaken jointly by the FASB and the IASB, and fully discussed in Chapter 2 at 5.

References

1 IAS 16, *Property, Plant and Equipment*, IASB, paras. 2-3.
2 IAS 16, para. 5.
3 IAS 16, para. 4.
4 IAS 16, para. 6.
5 IAS 16, para. 7.
6 IAS 16, para. 8.
7 IAS 16, para. 9.
8 IAS 16, para. 11.
9 IAS 16, para. 11.
10 IAS 16, para. 10.
11 IAS 16, para. 12.
12 IAS 16, para. 13.
13 IAS 37, *Provisions, Contingent Liabilities and Contingent Assets*, IASB, Appendix C, Examples 11A and 11B.
14 IAS 16, para. 14.
15 IAS 16, para. 15.
16 IAS 16, para. 16.
17 IAS 16, para. 18.
18 IAS 16, para. 18.
19 IAS 16, para. 17.
20 IAS 16, para. 19.
21 IAS 16, para. 20.
22 IAS 16, para. 22.
23 IAS 16, para. 23.
24 IAS 16, para. 58.
25 IFRIC 18, *Transfers of Assets from Customers*, IFRIC, para. 14.
26 IAS 16, para. 16(b).
27 IAS 16, para. 21.
28 IAS 16, para. 20.
29 IAS 16, para. 17(e).
30 IFRIC 1, *Changes in Existing Decommissioning, Restoration and Similar Liabilities*, IFRIC, para. 2.
31 IFRIC 1, para. 3.
32 IFRIC 1, para. 5.
33 IFRIC 1, para. 6.
34 IFRIC 1, para. 7.
35 IFRIC 1, para. 7.
36 IFRIC 1, para. 6.
37 IFRIC 1, para. 8.
38 IFRS 1, para. 25E.
39 IAS 16, para. 24.
40 IAS 16, para. 24.
41 IAS 16, para. 24.
42 IAS 16, para. BC21.
43 IAS 16, para. 25.
44 IAS 16, para. 25.
45 IAS 16, para. BC19.
46 IAS 16, para. 26.
47 IAS 16, para. 68.
48 IAS 16, para. 27.
49 IAS 16, para. 28.
50 IAS 16, para. 29.
51 IAS 16, para. 30.
52 IAS 16, para. 31.
53 IAS 16, para. 32.
54 IAS 16, para. 33.
55 IAS 16, para. 31.
56 IAS 16, para. 34.
57 IAS 16, para. 37.
58 IAS 16, para. 38.
59 IAS 16, paras. 39-40.
60 IAS 36, *Impairment of Assets*, IASB, para. 61.
61 IAS 16, para. 41.
62 IAS 8, *Accounting Policies, Changes in Accounting Estimates and Errors*, IASB, para. 17.
63 IAS 16, para. 43.
64 IAS 16, para. 44.
65 IAS 16, para. 45.
66 IAS 16, para. 46.
67 IAS 16, para. 47.
68 IAS 16, paras. 48-49.
69 IAS 16, para. 51.
70 IAS 16, paras. 53-54.
71 IAS 16, para. 51.
72 IAS 16, para. 50.
73 IAS 16, para. 52.
74 IAS 16, para. 54.
75 IAS 16, para. 52.
76 IAS 16, para. 56.
77 IAS 16, para. 57.
78 IAS 16, para. 58.
79 IAS 36, para. 12(f).
80 IAS 36, para. 12(f).
81 IAS 16, para. 55.
82 IAS 16, para. 55.
83 IFRIC 1, para. 7.
84 IAS 16, paras. 60-62.
85 IAS 8, para. 32 (d).
86 IAS 8, para. 36.
87 IAS 16, para. 63.
88 IAS 16, paras. 65-66.
89 IAS 37, para 53.
90 IAS 16, para. 67.
91 IAS 16, para. 69.
92 IAS 16, para. 68.
93 IAS 16, para. 71.
94 IAS 16, para. 41.
95 IAS 16, para. 70.
96 IAS 16, para. 72.
97 IFRS 5, *Non-current Assets Held for Sale and Discontinued Operations*, IASB, para. 6.
98 IFRS 5, para. 7.
99 IFRS 5, para. 8.
100 IAS 16, para. 68.

101 IAS 16, para. 68A.
102 IAS 7, *Statement of Cash Flows*, IASB, para. 14.
103 IAS 1, *Presentation of Financial Statements*, IASB, para. 38.
104 IAS 16, para. 74.
105 IAS 16, para. 76.
106 IAS 16, para. 77.
107 IAS 16, para. 79.
108 IAS 16, paras. 43-44.
109 IAS 16, para. 70.
110 IAS 16, para. 32.
111 IAS 16, para. 77(c).
112 IAS 16, para. 33.
113 IAS 16, para. 77(d).
114 IAS 16, para. 33.
115 IAS 16, para. 39.
116 IAS 36, para. 117.
117 IAS 16, para. 60.
118 IAS 38, *Intangible Assets*, IASB, para. 4.
119 IAS 16, para. 16b.
120 Press release 'IASB publishes draft guidance on fair value measurement', IASB, 28 May 2009

Chapter 17   Investment property

1   INTRODUCTION

IAS 40 – *Investment property* – is a rare example of the particular commercial characteristics of an industry resulting in the special treatment of a certain category of property (investment properties), even though the assets themselves are not intrinsically different from those within the scope of IAS 16 – *Property Plant and Equipment*. Nevertheless, despite being focused on the needs of the investment property industry, the standard allows entities a free choice between two measurement models: historic cost and fair value. It should also be borne in mind that it is not only investment property companies that hold investment property; any property that meets the investment property definition is so classified, irrespective of the nature of the business of the reporting entity.

The original standard, which was approved in March 2000 by the Board of the former IASC, represented a major conceptual shift, as it was the first international standard to introduce the possibility of applying a full fair value model when accounting for non-financial assets. Under this option the asset is neither depreciated nor subject to impairment testing, rather all valuation changes (i.e. fair value changes) from one period to the next are treated as gains and losses and reported in profit or loss. Consequently, the fair value option of IAS 40 means that profit or loss will contain a mixture of realised gains and losses (for example rental income and maintenance costs) and unrealised fair value changes. This contrasts with the revaluation approach allowed under IAS 16 (see Chapter 16 at 4.1) where increases above cost, and their reversals, are recognised directly in equity – or 'Other Comprehensive Income' ('OCI') as this is now referred to in the revised version of IAS 1 – *Presentation of Financial Statements*, effective for annual periods beginning on or after 1 January 2009 (see Chapter 3 at 7). This latter description has been adopted in the rest of this chapter.

IAS 40 also allows investment property to be accounted for more conventionally, by being carried at cost less depreciation, under the cost model set out in IAS 16.

The exposure draft that preceded IAS 40 proposed that fair value should be the sole measurement model for investment property. However, in the light of comments received from respondents, several members of the Board of the former IASC were concerned that, in certain parts of the world, property markets were not sufficiently liquid to support fair value measurement for financial reporting purposes. Consequently, the cost option was introduced into the standard, together with the following explanation:

> 'This is the first time that the Board has proposed requiring a fair value accounting model for non-financial assets. The comment letters on E64 showed that although many support this step, many others still have significant conceptual and practical reservations about extending a fair value model to non-financial assets, particularly (but not exclusively) for entities whose main activity is not to hold property for capital appreciation. Also, some entities feel that certain property markets are not yet sufficiently mature for a fair value model to work satisfactorily. Furthermore, some believe that it is impossible to create a rigorous definition of investment property and that this makes it impracticable to require a fair value model at present.

> 'For those reasons the Board believes that it is impracticable, at this stage, to require a fair value model for all investment property. At the same time, the Board believes that it is desirable to permit a fair value model. This evolutionary step forward will allow preparers and users to gain greater experience working with a fair value model and will allow time for certain property markets to achieve greater maturity'.[1]

Despite this, IAS 40 actually sets out that only in exceptional cases will an entity not be able to reliably measure the fair value of an investment property (see section 9.3.2).

The question of the reliability of valuations is given greater focus following the change in scope of IAS 40 to include investment property under construction (see section 2.2.5).

2   DEFINITIONS AND SCOPE

An investment property is defined in IAS 40 as a:

> 'property (land or a building – or part of a building – or both) held (by the owner or by the lessee under a finance lease) to earn rentals or for capital appreciation or both, rather than for:
>
> (a)   use in the production or supply of goods or services or for administrative purposes; or
>
> (b)   sale in the ordinary course of business.'[2]

As stated above, this means that any entity, whatever the underlying nature of its business, can hold investment property assets.

In contrast, 'owner-occupied' property is defined as 'property held (by the owner or by the lessee under a finance lease) for use in the production or supply of goods or services or for administrative purposes'.[3] Such property falls outside the scope of IAS 40 and is accounted for under IAS 16, together with IAS 17 – *Leases*, if relevant.

IAS 40 does not apply to:[4]

    (a)   Biological assets related to agricultural activities. Under IAS 41 – *Agriculture* – biological assets that are physically attached to land (for example, trees in a plantation forest) are measured at their fair value less estimated point-of-sale costs separately from the land.[5] The land related to the agricultural activity is accounted for either as property under IAS 16 or investment property under IAS 40.[6]

    (b)   Mineral rights and mineral revenues such as oil, natural gas and similar non-regenerative resources.

2.1 Property interests held under operating leases

Entities are permitted to treat interests held under operating leases as investment properties – providing that they would otherwise meet the standard's investment property definition and that the fair value model is applied. This situation arises where, for example, an entity acquires an operating leasehold interest as an investment property by effectively prepaying a certain number of years' operating lease rentals. This classification alternative is available on a property-by-property basis so that the entity need not classify all property interests held under operating leases as investment property. However, IAS 40 requires that once one operating leasehold interest is classified as an investment property, all property classified as investment property must be accounted for under the fair value method. These leasehold interests are subject also to the same disclosure requirements as other investment properties (see 9 below).[7]

IAS 17 requires leases to be separated into land and building components, subject to this being possible or the land element being material (see Chapter 22). If the interest is to be an investment property carried at fair value in accordance with IAS 40, there is no requirement to separate the land and buildings elements of the lease.[8]

2.2 Identifying investment property

What primarily distinguishes investment property from other types of property interest is that its cash flows (from rental or sale) are largely independent of those from other assets held by the entity. By contrast, property used by an entity for administrative purposes or for the production or supply of goods or services do not generate cash flows themselves but do so only in conjunction with other assets.[9]

However, even with this distinction, it may not be easy to distinguish investment property from owner-occupied property to which IAS 16 applies. The standard therefore gives guidance to help determine whether or not an asset is an investment property.[10]

2.2.1 Land

Land is investment property if it is held either for long-term capital appreciation or for a currently undetermined future use. This is in contrast to land that is held for sale in the ordinary course of business (typically in the short term). If the entity has not determined whether it will use the land as owner-occupied property or for sale in the ordinary course of business, it is deemed to be held for capital appreciation and must be classified as investment property.[11]

2.2.2   Buildings leased to others

Buildings leased out under one or more operating leases are generally investment properties, whether they are owned by the reporting entity or held under a lease. This will also apply if the building is currently vacant while tenants are being sought.[12]

However, in our opinion, an exception should be made in those cases where, despite being leased out, properties are held for sale in the ordinary course of business. Leasing of properties prior to sale is a common practice in the real estate industry in order to minimise cash outflows and because prospective buyers may view the existence of lease contracts positively, especially those that wish to acquire property for investment purposes.

In those circumstances, and notwithstanding that they are leased to tenants under operating leases, the intention to hold property for short-term sale dictates that they should be accounted for as inventory under IAS 2 – *Inventories*.

Property that is leased to another entity under a finance lease is not an investment property but is accounted for under IAS 17 (see Chapter 22).[13]

2.2.3   *Property held for trading or being constructed for resale*

Property held for trading purposes or being constructed for resale is not investment property. This includes property held in the following circumstances:

(a)   property intended for sale in the ordinary course of business, including property in the process of construction or development. This includes property acquired exclusively for sale in the near future or for development and resale. These are accounted for as inventory under IAS 2 (see Chapter 20); and

(b)   property being built or developed under a construction contract for third parties. These are covered by IAS 11 – *Construction Contracts* – which is discussed in Chapter 21.[14]

In reality, the classification between investment property and property intended for sale in the ordinary course of business (which must be made on initial recognition of the property) is often a difficult judgement. There is only a fine line between:

•   a property held for capital appreciation, and therefore classified as investment property; and

•   a property intended for sale in the ordinary course of business (presumably because it is anticipated to grow in value), which would be classified as inventory.

As set out in 2.2.2, the receipt of rental income from a property would not necessarily be a relevant factor.

However, this judgement is important because whilst IAS 40 allows property held as inventory to be reclassified as investment property when an operating lease with a third party is entered into, it is much more difficult (and in the future may be almost impossible) to reclassify investment property as inventory (see section 10.1).

2.2.4 Owner occupation

As stated above, owner-occupied property, that is property held for use in the production or supply of goods or services or for administrative purposes,[15] is specifically excluded from being treated as investment property and is subject to the provisions of IAS 16. Owner-occupied property includes:

(a)   property that is going to be owner-occupied in the future (whether or not it has first to be redeveloped);

(b)   property occupied by employees, whether or not they pay rent at market rates; and

(c)   owner-occupied property awaiting disposal.[16]

Swiss Property Group discloses how it deals with owner occupied property below:

Extract 17.1: PSP Swiss Property Ltd (2008)

Notes to the Consolidated 2007 Financial Statements [extract]
Own-used properties [extract]

In accordance with IAS 16, properties used by the Company itself are stated at historical costs and depreciated over their economically useful life, divided according to their significant parts. Depreciable life (linear) is 40 years for buildings and 20 years for facilities (such as air-conditioning, elevators, ventilation, etc.). Land belonging to the property is not depreciated. Where the Company uses only part of a property it owns, utilisation of less than 25% is regarded as immaterial, which means that the whole property is stated at market value as an investment property.

Note that the treatment in the consolidated accounts does not necessarily determine the treatment by individual group entities. For example, it may be the case that a property is held by one group company for occupation by another group company. This will be owner-occupied from the perspective of the group as a whole but classified as an investment property in the accounts of the individual entity that owns it.[17] This classification in the individual entity's financial statements will apply even if the rental is not at arm's length and the individual entity is not in a position to benefit from capital appreciation. The IASB has concluded that it is more significant that the property itself will still generate largely independent cash flows.

Associates and joint ventures are not part of the group. Therefore properties owned by the group but occupied by associates and joint ventures would be accounted for as investment properties in the consolidated financial statements (provided, of course, they meet the investment property definition). This is the case, even if the property is occupied by a jointly controlled entity that is proportionately consolidated under paragraph 30 of IAS 31 – *Interests in Joint Ventures.*

2.2.5   *Property in the course of construction and redevelopment*

Prior to the 2008 annual improvement process, IAS 16 applied to property that was being constructed or developed for future use as investment property until construction or development was complete, at which time the property became investment property. This relaxation of the approach in the standard was primarily because, when IAS 40 was being developed, the IASB considered that fair values of incomplete investment properties were difficult to obtain.

In contrast, IAS 40 applied to existing investment property being redeveloped for continued future use as investment property. This meant that while entities applying IAS 40's fair value option did not have to reclassify such investment properties during redevelopment, they still had to revalue them to fair value during the redevelopment period.

In May 2008, as part of the annual improvement process, the IASB approved changes that brought investment property under construction into the scope of IAS 40.

However, because of the persistent concern that, in some situations, the fair value of investment property under construction cannot be measured reliably, the IASB concluded that it would, for those entities that chose the fair value model for completed investment property, allow investment property under construction to be measured at cost if fair value cannot be measured reliably until such time as the fair value becomes reliably measurable or construction is completed (whichever comes earlier).

It is worthy of note that the International Valuation Standard Board ('IVSB') were initially of the view that it will be rare for the fair value of investment property under construction to not be capable of reliable determination, although they are subsequently consider whether or not actually to opine on this(see 4.2.1).

The Standard also sets out that:
- The presumption that the fair value of investment property under construction can be determined reliably can be rebutted only on initial recognition. Therefore, an entity that has measured an item of investment property under construction at fair value may not subsequently conclude that the fair value of the completed investment property cannot be determined reliably. [18]
- Once construction of that property is complete, it is presumed that fair value can be measured reliably. [19] If this is not the case, and this will be only in exceptional situations, the property shall be accounted for using the principles in 4.7 below – that is, using the cost model in accordance with IAS 16.

Therefore entities who wish to measure their completed investment property at fair value will also need to measure their investment property under construction at fair value (subject to fair value being reliably determinable). IAS 40 does not allow an inconsistent application of its fair value model.

The IASB allowed that entities may apply these changes to IAS 40 prospectively for annual periods beginning on or after 1 January 2009. An entity is permitted to apply the amendments to investment property under construction from any date before 1 January 2009 provided that the fair values of investment properties under construction were determined at those dates. Earlier application is permitted if an entity discloses that fact.

2.2.6 Properties with dual uses

Often a property is used partly to derive rental income and partly as owner-occupied property. IAS 40 states that if a property has both investment property and non-investment property uses, providing the parts of the property could be sold or leased under a finance lease separately, they should be accounted for separately.[20]

However, to meet this requirement we consider that a property must actually be in a state and condition to enable it to be disposed of separately at the balance sheet date. The fact that a property could be divided in future periods if the owner so chose is insufficient to conclude that the portions can be accounted for separately. Consequently, if a property requires sub-division before the portions could be disposed of separately, then those parts should not, in our view, be accounted for as separate portions until such sub-divisions occur.

But it seems clear that 'separately' needs to be assessed both in terms of the physical separation (for example. mezzanine floors and partitioning walls) of the property and legal separation such as legally defined boundaries. Therefore judgement is required to determine whether legal separation is a substantive requirement that will restrict the property being currently separable or whether it is a non-substantive requirement where the property is currently separable.

In the event that no separation is possible, the property is an investment property only if an insignificant proportion is used for non-investment property purposes.[21]

2.2.7 Provision of services

If the owner supplies ancillary services to the user of the investment property, the property will not qualify as an investment property unless the value of these services is an insignificant component of the arrangement as a whole.[22]

Security and maintenance services are described by the standard as being insignificant.[23] It becomes more difficult to make the analysis when the building itself is used to generate the revenues. The crucial issue is the extent to which the owner retains significant exposure to the risks of running a business.[24] The standard uses the example of a hotel. An owner-managed hotel, for example, would be precluded from being an investment property as the services provided to guests are a significant component of the commercial arrangements.

Another common example is the incidence of turnover-related rents in retail leases. If the turnover-related element is a significant proportion of total rental then consideration must be given to whether the landlord is so exposed to the performance of the underlying retail business as to make classification of the property as investment property inappropriate.

The standard admits that this distinction can require judgements to be made, and specifies that businesses should develop consistent criteria for use in such instances that reflect the spirit of the provisions described above. These criteria must be disclosed in those cases where classification is difficult.[25]

One entity that does make such a distinction is Mapeley Limited as set out in their accounting policy below.

Extract 17.2: Mapeley Limited (2007)
2.3 Summary of significant accounting policies
Property, plant and equipment [extract]
Property [extract]

Where the Group provides significant levels of ancillary services to the occupiers of its property, this property is not classified as investment property. Such freehold property and property held under finance leases are revalued to fair value annually and depreciated in accordance with IAS 16 Property, Plant and Equipment.

2.2.8   *Group of assets leased out under a single operating lease*

It is sometimes the case in practice that a group of assets comprising land, buildings and 'other assets' is leased out by a lessor under a single operating lease contract in order to earn rentals. In such a case, the 'other assets' would generally comprise assets that relate to the manner in which the land and buildings are used under the lease. The issue that arises is under what circumstances should the 'other assets' be regarded by the lessor as part of an investment property rather than as a separate item of property, plant and equipment? This is illustrated in the following real-life example:

Example 17.1:   Definition of an investment property: a group of assets leased out under a single operating lease

A Lessor enters into the following two single contract leases in order to earn rentals. All the individual assets subject to the leases meet the test of being classified as an operating lease. The lessor applies the fair value measurement model for subsequent measurement of investment property.

Lease 1: Vineyard and winery

A vineyard including a winery is leased out under an operating lease. The vineyard comprises the following assets:

- Land
- Vineyard infrastructure (e.g. trellises)
- Winery building structures
- Winery plant and machinery (crushing equipment, distilling equipment)
- Vines (grapes are excluded, as they belong to the lessee).

Lease 2: Port

A port is leased out under an operating lease. The port comprises the following assets:

- Land
- Warehouses
- Transport infrastructure to and from the port (roads, rail tracks, bridges)

- Wharves
- Light towers (that enable the 24 hour operation of the port)
- Specialised container cranes.

To what extent can the 'other assets' included in the leases (but which are not considered to constitute a piece of land or a building) be included in the investment property definition under IAS 40?

This is an important issue, as the consequence of including plant and equipment in the definition of investment property is that if the investment property is accounted for at fair value, changes in the fair value of that plant and equipment will be recognised in profit or loss.

From a literal reading of the definition of an investment property as set out in paragraph 5 of IAS 40 it could be argued that an investment property can consist only of a building (or part of a building), a piece of land, or both and cannot include 'other assets'. However, such a reading of paragraph 5 of IAS 40 is inconsistent with paragraph 50 of IAS 40, which implies that a broader interpretation is more appropriate. Paragraphs 50(a) and (b) of IAS 40 read as follows:

'In determining the fair value of investment property, an entity does not double-count assets or liabilities that are recognised as separate assets or liabilities. For example:

(a) equipment such as lifts or air-conditioning is often an integral part of a building and is generally included in the fair value of the investment property, rather than recognised separately as property, plant and equipment.

(b) if an office is leased on a furnished basis, the fair value of the office generally includes the fair value of the furniture, because the rental income relates to the furnished office. When furniture is included in the fair value of investment property, an entity does not recognise that furniture as a separate asset.'[26]

Although paragraph 50 addresses the fair valuation of investment property, it nevertheless implies that other assets that are integral to the land and buildings should also be regarded as being part of the investment property.

Consequently, in our view, an item other than a piece of land or a building should be regarded by a lessor as being part of an investment property if this item is an integral part of it, that is, it is necessary for the land and buildings to be used by a lessee in the intended way and is leased to the lessee on the same basis (e.g. over the same lease term) as the land and buildings. The determination as to whether or not an item constitutes an integral part of an investment property requires judgement and will depend on the particular facts and circumstances. However, it is our view that in order for all the assets to be classified as investment property, the following conditions should be present:

- the land and buildings should be the 'dominant assets' that form the investment property;
- the 'other assets' are leased to the lessee together with the land and building as a whole; and
- the entire group of assets is generating the income stream from the lease contract.

This means that, in the case of Lease 1, the investment property comprises the land, the vineyard infrastructure, the winery building structures and the winery plant and machinery. Vines, which meet the definition of biological assets, are subject to the requirements of IAS 41 – *Agriculture*. This is because 'biological assets related to agricultural activity' are outside the scope of IAS 40.[27]

In the case of Lease 2, the investment property comprises all of the assets – i.e. the land, the warehouses, the transport infrastructure, the wharves, the light towers, and the specialised container cranes.

2.3   Recognition

An investment property should be recognised as an asset when it is probable that the future economic benefits that are associated with the investment property will flow to the entity and its cost can be measured reliably.[28]

These recognition criteria apply for any costs incurred, whether initially or subsequently. This means that all investment property costs, whether on initial recognition or thereafter (for example, to add to or replace part of a property) must meet the recognition criteria at the point at which the expenditure is incurred if they are to be capitalised.[29]

In many jurisdictions, permissions are required prior to development of new or existing investment property, and on these turn the success of the development. However, developers typically incur significant costs prior to such permissions being granted and of course, such permissions are rarely guaranteed. Therefore, in assessing whether such pre-permission expenditure falls to be capitalised – assuming it otherwise meets the criteria – a judgement must be made, at the date the expenditure is incurred, of whether there is sufficient certainty that the relevant permissions will be granted.

Day-to-day servicing, by which is meant the repairs and maintenance of the property which largely comprises labour costs and minor parts, should be recognised in profit or loss as incurred.[30] However, the treatment is different if larger parts of the building have been replaced – the standard cites the example of interior walls that are replacements of the original walls. In this case, the cost of replacing the part will be recognised, while the carrying amount of the original part is derecognised.[31] The inference is that by restoring the asset to its originally assessed standard of performance, the new part will meet the recognition criteria and future economic benefits will flow to the entity once the old part is replaced. The inference is also that replacement is needed for the total asset to be operative. This being the case, the new walls will therefore meet the recognition criteria and the cost will therefore be capitalised.

Other than interior walls, large parts that might have to be replaced include elements such as lifts, escalators, air conditioning equipment and the like.

IAS 40 does not explicitly require an analysis of investment properties into parts. However, this analysis is needed for the purposes of recognition and derecognition (see Chapter 16 at 5) of all expenditure after the asset has initially been recognised and (if the parts are significant) for depreciation of those parts. Some of this is not relevant to assets held under the fair value model that are not depreciated because the standard expects the necessary adjustments to the carrying value of the asset as a whole to be made via the fair value mechanism (see 4 below). However, entities that adopt the cost model are obliged to account for them after initial recognition in accordance with the requirements of IAS 16. The cost model is discussed further at 5 below.

2.4   Initial measurement

2.4.1   Costs

IAS 40 requires an investment property to be measured initially at cost, which includes transaction costs.[32] If a property is purchased, cost means purchase price and any directly attributable expenditure such as professional fees, property transfer taxes and other transaction costs.[33]

As noted in 2.2.5, prior to the implementation of the 2008 annual improvements, self-constructed investment property during construction was subject to IAS 16 until completed at which time it became investment property to which IAS 40 applies.[34] This meant that only those elements of cost that were allowed by IAS 16 could be capitalised and that capitalisation ceased when the asset has reached the condition necessary for it to be capable of operating in the manner intended by management (see also Chapter 16 at 3.2.1D).[35] Abnormal wastage of resources in constructing an investment property was not part of its cost.

The 2008 annual improvement process removed this specific reference to IAS 16. However, we consider that the principles in IAS 16 must still be applied to the recognition of costs in IAS 40. These principles are set out in detail in Chapter 16.

IAS 40 also specifies that start-up costs (unless necessary to bring the property into working condition) and operating losses before the investment property achieves the planned occupancy level, are not to be capitalised.[36] IAS 40 therefore prohibits the practice of capitalising costs until a particular level of occupation or rental income is achieved; this point normally would be reached considerably later than the date of physical completion – at which earlier time the asset would be *capable* of operating in the manner intended by management. This forestalls an argument, sometimes advanced in the past, that the asset being constructed was not simply the physical structure of the building but a fully tenanted investment property, and its cost correspondingly included not simply the construction period but also the letting period.

Finally, if payment for the property is deferred, the cost to be recognised is the cash price equivalent (which in practice must mean the present value of the payments due). Any difference between the cash price and the total payment to be made is recognised as interest over the credit period.[37]

2.4.2   Income from tenanted property during development

One issue that commonly arises is whether rental and similar income generated by existing tenants in a property development may be capitalised and offset against the cost of developing that property.

As more fully discussed in Chapter 16 at 3.2.2, IAS 16 requires that the income and related expenses of incidental operations are recognised in profit or loss and included in their respective classifications of income and expense. We consider that rental and similar income from existing tenants are incidental operations to the development.

In our view there should not be a measurement difference between the cost of a property development dealt with under IAS 40 and the cost of development dealt with under IAS 16. Therefore, rental and similar income generated by existing tenants in a property dealt with under IAS 40 and now intended for redevelopment should not be capitalised against the costs of the development. Rather rental and similar income should be recognised in profit or loss in accordance with the requirements of IAS 17 together with related expenses. For these purposes it is irrelevant whether the investment property is held at cost or fair value.

2.4.3   Reclassifications from Property, Plant and Equipment

Again as noted at 2.2.5 above, prior to the implementation of the 2008 annual improvements, the revaluation model in IAS 16 could be used for properties under development that were not previously investment properties. When completed, such properties were reclassified as investment properties. IAS 40 requires an entity to treat any difference between the fair value at the date of completion and the previous carrying amount to be recognised in profit and loss.[38] Although transfers on completion of construction of investment property are no longer relevant, the same principles should be applied when an entity otherwise reclassifies property, plant and equipment under IAS 16 to investment property (see 7 below).

IAS 40 is silent in respect of the treatment of any accumulated revaluation surplus in other comprehensive income in respect of such properties. In our view, it is appropriate, in order to be consistent with the treatment of revaluation surpluses under IAS 16 (see Chapter 16 at 4.1), for any surplus to be transferred directly to retained earnings (not through profit or loss) upon reclassification. Hammerson PLC described this approach (at that time for development properties) in their accounting policies, as follows:

Extract 17.3: Hammerson PLC (2008)

1. Significant Accounting Policies [extract]
Development properties [extract]

When development properties are completed, they are reclassified as investment properties and any accumulated revaluation surplus or deficit is transferred to retained earnings.

2.4.4   Initial measurement of property held under finance or operating leases

The same accounting is applied both to property acquired under finance leases and to operating leases where the property interests otherwise meet the definition of investment properties and have been classified as such. This means that a property interest that is held by a lessee under an operating lease and classified as an investment property must be accounted for as if it were a finance lease.

At the commencement of the lease term, the entity recognises the property asset and related liability in its balance sheet in accordance with IAS 17, at amounts equal at the inception of the lease to the fair value of the leased item or, if lower, at the present value of the minimum lease payments (see Chapter 22).[39] If the interest is held under an operating lease, then it must be recorded at the present value of the minimum lease payments. The entity's initial direct costs are added to the asset[40] – these might include similar costs to those described in 2.4 above such as professional fees for legal services.

If the entity pays a premium for the lease, this is part of the minimum lease payments and is included in the cost of the asset; however, it is, of course, excluded from the liability.[41]

The standard emphasises that the property interest, the fair value of which is to be determined, is the leasehold interest and not the underlying property. Guidance on fair values of property interests, which is also relevant for fair values used for initial recognition under the cost model, is described at 4.2 below.

2.4.5   *Initial measurement of assets acquired in exchange transactions*

The requirements of IAS 40 for investment properties acquired in exchange for non-monetary assets, or a combination or monetary and non-monetary assets, are the same as those of IAS 16.[42] These provisions are discussed in detail in Chapter 16 at 3.2.4.

2.4.6   *Initial measurement of leased investment property to be measured using the cost model*

As noted in Chapter 9 at 3.6.5A, during the development of the revised IFRS 3 – *Business Combinations* – effective for accounting periods after 1 July 2009, the IASB discussed whether it would be appropriate for any favourable or unfavourable lease aspect of an investment property to be recognised separately.

The IASB concluded that this was not necessary for investment property that will be measured at fair value because the fair value of investment property takes into account rental income from leases and therefore the contractual terms of leases and other contracts in place.

However, a different position has been taken for investment property to be measured using the cost model. In this case the IASB observed that the cost model requires:

- the use of a depreciation or amortisation method that reflects the pattern in which the entity expects to consume the asset's future economic benefits;
- each part of an item of property, plant and equipment that has a cost that is significant in relation to the total cost of the item to be depreciated separately.

Therefore, an acquirer of investment property in a business combination that is to be held using the cost model will need to adjust the depreciation method for the investment property to reflect the timing of cash flows attributable to the underlying leases.[43]

In effect, therefore, this requires that the favourable or unfavourable lease aspect of the investment property – measured with reference to market conditions at the date of the business combination – be separately identified in order that it may be subsequently depreciated or amortised, usually over the remaining lease term. Any such amount is not presented separately in the financial statements.

This approach has also been extended to purchase of property other than those acquired in a business combination (see 5.1.2).

2.4.7   Borrowing costs

As set out in Chapter 16 at 3.2.1B, in March 2007 the IASB issued a revised version of IAS 23 – *Borrowing Costs*, effective from 1 January 2009, that mandates capitalisation of borrowing costs. This also applies to investment property under construction.

The revision does not require entities to capitalise interest in respect of assets that are measured at fair value, but does not prohibit it Consequently, for investment property under construction that is now measured at fair value through profit or loss, there is an accounting policy choice that principally effects presentation in the income statement and not profit or net assets.

To the extent that entities choose to capitalise borrowing costs in respect of such assets, in our view it is best practice to follow the methods allowed by IAS 23. The treatment of borrowing costs is discussed separately in Chapter 19.

3   MEASUREMENT AFTER INITIAL RECOGNITION

Once recognised, IAS 40 allows entities to choose between one of two methods of accounting for investment property: the 'fair value model' or the 'cost model'. The standard does not identify a preferred alternative. There is, however, one exception to the choice of measurement: a property interest that is held by a lessee under an operating lease may be classified as an investment property – provided that the fair value model is applied for the asset recognised and, therefore, for all investment properties.

An entity has to choose one model or the other, and apply it to all its investment property (unless the entity is an insurer or similar, in which case there are exemptions that are described briefly below at 3.1).[44] The standard discourages changes from the fair value model to the cost model, stating that it is highly unlikely that this will result in a more relevant presentation, which is a requirement of IAS 8 – *Accounting Policies, Changes in Accounting Estimates and Errors* – for any change in accounting policy.[45]

All entities, regardless of which measurement option is chosen, are required to determine the fair value of their investment properties, because even those entities that use the cost model are required to disclose the fair value. Use of an independent valuer with a recognised qualification and recent experience is encouraged, but not required.[46]

3.1   Measurement by insurers and similar entities

The only exception to the requirement that an entity must apply either the fair value or the cost model to all its investment properties, is in respect of insurance companies and other entities that hold investment properties whose return is directly linked to the return paid on specific liabilities. These entities are permitted to choose either the fair value or the cost model for such properties without it affecting the choice available for any other investment properties that they may hold. However, all properties within a given fund must be held on the same basis and transfers between funds are to be made at fair value.[47]

4 THE FAIR VALUE MODEL

Under this model all investment property is included in the balance sheet at its fair value at the balance sheet date, and all changes in the fair value from one balance sheet to the next are included in profit or loss for the period.[48] However, as stated above, an entity must use the fair value model if it wishes to classify interests held under operating leases as investment properties.[49]

The standard defines fair value as 'the amount for which an asset could be exchanged between knowledgeable, willing parties in an arm's length transaction'.[50] Fair value specifically excludes an estimated price inflated or deflated by special terms or circumstances such as atypical financing, sale and leaseback arrangements that are not at market rates or special considerations or concessions granted by anyone associated with the sale.[51] Transaction costs which may be incurred by the vendor on sale are not deducted.[52]

4.1 Transaction costs incurred by the purchaser

An issue that arises in practice is whether transaction costs that have been incurred by the purchaser of an investment property should be taken into account in determining the subsequent fair value of the property when applying the fair value model. This is illustrated in the following example:

Example 17.2: The fair value model and transaction costs incurred at acquisition

On 1 January 2007 Entity A acquired an investment property for a purchase price of €10,000. In addition, A incurred legal costs of €200 in connection with the purchase and paid property transfer tax of €400. Accordingly, the investment property was initially recorded at €10,600. Company A applies the fair value model for subsequent measurement of investment property. At the next reporting date the following different scenarios are considered:

	Development of prices in property market	Appraised market value of property €	Cost of property initially recognised €	Difference €
Scenario 1	unchanged	10,000	10,600	(600)
Scenario 2	slightly increased	10,250	10,600	(350)
Scenario 3	significantly increased	11,000	10,600	400
Scenario 4	decreased	9,500	10,600	(1,100)

The issue that arises in practice is whether or not the purchase transaction costs that were incurred by Company A on 1 January 2007 can be considered in determining the fair value of the investment property at the next reporting date.

In our view, the purchase transaction costs incurred by Company A may not be considered separately in determining the fair value of an investment property. In the example above, on the next reporting date the carrying value to be recorded in the balance sheet is its fair value, which is the appraised market value at the reporting date. Changes from the initial carrying amount to the appraised market value at the subsequent reporting date (reflected in the 'Difference' column in the table) are recognised in profit or loss.

Although paragraph 21 of IAS 40 states that transaction costs incurred by a purchaser on the acquisition of an investment property are included in the cost of the investment property at initial recognition, if an entity applies the fair value model, the same investment property that was recorded at cost on initial recognition is subsequently measured at fair value. The fact that the cost of the investment property recorded on initial recognition included legal and other transaction costs is irrelevant to the subsequent fair valuation of the asset.

Professional valuers of investment property generally determine the *market value* of an investment property in an appraisal. International Valuation Standards state: '*The expression Market Value and the term Fair Value as it commonly appears in accounting standards are generally compatible, if not in every instance exactly equivalent concepts. Fair Value, an accounting concept, is defined in IFRS and other accounting standards as the amount for which an asset could be exchanged, or a liability settled, between knowledgeable, willing parties in an arm's-length transaction. Fair Value is generally used for both Market and Non-Market Values in financial statements. Where the Market Value of an asset can be established, this value will equate to Fair Value.*'[53]

Consequently, when the market value has been established for an investment property it is not, in our view, appropriate to add to this market value the transaction costs incurred by the purchaser, as these have no relevance to the market value of the property.

4.2   Determining fair value

Paragraphs 38 to 52 of IAS 40 contain a substantial amount of guidance on the methodology for valuing investment property in practice, necessitated by the number of jurisdictions to which the standard may apply. Fair value reflects market conditions as at the balance sheet date and is a valuation as at a specific moment in time. It assumes simultaneous exchange and completion, to avoid the variations in price that might otherwise take place.[54] The fair value of the property is driven, at least in part, by the rental income from tenants and, if appropriate, outflows such as rental payments. It is further assumed that the valuation is based on assumptions that would be considered to be reasonable and supportable by willing and knowledgeable parties.[55] For example, the buyer and seller must be 'knowledgeable', which means that they are reasonably informed about the property and the market at the date of the transaction; neither is under any compulsion to buy or sell; the buyer will not pay more than a knowledgeable, willing buyer; and the seller is not a forced seller.[56] The transaction is presumed to be at arm's length between unrelated parties.[57]

The standard states that the best evidence of fair value will be given by actual transactions in similar property in a similar location and condition.[58] However, it allows the fair value to be estimated by using other information when market values are not available. This means that gains and losses may be recorded in profit or loss where there is no market value for the property and its fair value has been constructed from a variety of other sources.

The other information that an entity may draw on includes:

(a)   transactions in an active market for dissimilar property (e.g. property of a different nature, condition or location, or subject to a different type of lease), as adjusted to reflect the differences;

(b)   transactions in less active markets if they have been adjusted to take account of subsequent changes in economic conditions; or

(c)   discounted cash flow projections based on estimated future cash flows (as long as these are reliable). These should be supported by existing leases and current market rents for similar properties in the same location and condition. The discount rate should reflect current market assessments of the uncertainty and timing of the cash flows.[59]

The technique suggested in (c) above is not dissimilar to a valuation using property yields (a basis on which properties commonly are bought and sold) except that yields already assume rental growth that would have to be separately factored into a discounted cash flow calculation.

The standard notes that in a lease negotiated at market rates, the fair value of an interest in a leased property at acquisition net of all expected lease payments should be zero ('acquisition' means the commencement of the lease as defined by IAS 17, which is before any lease payments are due or any other accounting entries are required to be made, see Chapter 22). This applies regardless of whether the asset is brought in at fair value (as is usually the case with a finance lease) or at the present value of the minimum lease payments (for an interest under an operating lease). Consequently, re-measuring an interest in a lease to fair value will only give rise to a gain or loss if the fair value model is applied, and only upon subsequent remeasurement after initial measurement.[60]

As these various bases may result in a range of valuations, the entity must consider the underlying reasons for the variation in order to determine the most reliable estimate, within a range of 'reasonable' estimates of fair value.[61] The fair value will not be determinable reliably on a continuing basis if the range is too wide and the probabilities of various outcomes are too difficult to assess.[62]

Fair value is based on a hypothetical transaction. It is not the same as 'value in use' as defined in IAS 36 – *Impairment of Assets*. In particular, it does not take account of additional value derived from holding a portfolio of assets, synergies between the investment properties and other assets or legal rights or tax benefits or burdens pertaining to the current owner.[63] Fair value is also not the same as net realisable value. It is a valuation as at a specific point in time rather than at a time at which the entity may realistically have expected to sell the property. It assumes circumstances that rarely apply in practice such as simultaneous exchange (i.e. contractual commitment) and completion.[64]

Finally, an entity must also take care, when determining the carrying amount of investment property under the fair value model, not to double count assets or liabilities that are recognised as separate assets or liabilities. Paragraph 50 of the standard describes a number of specific situations where this might otherwise happen. These are discussed in sections 4.3 to 4.5 below.

4.2.1   *The fair value of investment property under construction*

Because properties are rarely – if ever – identical, a comparison with the observed market prices in other property transactions can only be used as a guide to fair value. Valuation models are needed. However, a model used to determine the fair value of investment property under construction will inevitably be more complex and judgemental because:

- There is a much less active market for investment property under construction than for completed investment property. Where such assets are transacted, this is typically when it is in the very early stages of development or when it is nearly complete and substantially let; and

- Additional assumptions must be made about the risks and costs of any incomplete construction.

In January 2009, the International Valuation Standards Board ('IVSB') released an Interim Position Statement 'The Valuation of Investment Property under Construction under IAS 40'. This Position Statement acknowledged that few investment properties under construction are transferred between market participants except as part of a sale of the owning entity or where the seller is either insolvent or facing insolvency and therefore unable to complete the project.

Despite this the Position Statement set out that, since the property is being developed for either income or capital appreciation, the cash flows associated with its construction and completion should normally be readily identifiable and capable of reliable estimation. Consequently, the IVSB considered that it will be rare for the fair value of an investment property under construction not to be capable of reliable determination.

However, this latter comment is excluded from the subsequent Exposure Draft 'Proposed Guidance Note – The Valuation of Investment Property under Construction' issued by the IVSB in August 2009. The IVSB is now, on reflection, inviting views as to whether such a comment is outside of the scope of the Guidance Note.

4.2.2   *The fair value discussion paper*

The IASB believes that a lack of codified and consistent guidance across IFRS has contributed to inconsistency in measuring fair value. In consequence, in 2005 a Fair Value Measurements project was added to the Board's agenda in order to develop a single standard that provides guidance to entities on measuring the fair value of assets and liabilities when required by IFRS.

However, the IASB, noting that the Financial Accounting Standards Board (FASB) was nearing completion of its fair value measurements project, decided to issue the FASB's final fair value measurement standard as an IASB Exposure Draft. The FASB Statement of Financial Accounting Standard No. 157 – *Fair value measurements* (FAS 157) was subsequently published in September 2006 and was issued by the IASB, actually in the form of a discussion paper, in the fourth quarter of 2006.

A subsequent Exposure Draft was issued in May 2009 which, the IASB say, would achieve 'overall' convergence with US GAAP. The guidance in this Exposure Draft would replace that currently included in IAS 40.

The IASB has said it plans to hold round-table discussions during the fourth quarter of 2009 with the intention of publishing a final IFRS on fair value measurement guidance in 2010.

FAS 157 and the IASB discussion paper are discussed further in Chapter 2 at 6.2 and 6.3.

4.3   Assets and liabilities subsumed within fair value

Fixtures and fittings such as lifts or air conditioning units are usually reflected within the fair value of the investment property rather than being accounted for separately.[65] In other cases, additional assets may be necessary in order that the property can be used for its specific purposes. The standard refers to furniture within a property that is being let as furnished offices, and argues that this should not be recognised as a separate asset if it has been included in the fair value of the investment property.[66]

The entity may have other assets that have not been included within the valuation, in which case these will be recognised separately and accounted for in accordance with IAS 16.

4.4   Prepaid or accrued operating lease income

4.4.1   Accrued rental income

The requirement in IAS 40 not to double-count assets or liabilities recognised separately, is most commonly encountered when reducing the carrying value of an investment property below its fair value to the extent that an asset arises under SIC-15 – *Operating Leases – Incentives*. For example, when an entity offers an initial rent-free period to a lessee, it will build up an asset over the rent free period and amortise it over the remaining lease term, thereby spreading the reduction in rental income over the duration of the lease. The assessed fair value already includes this amount and, therefore, it should be deducted from the carrying value of the property in order to avoid double counting. This procedure is further described in Chapter 22.

One entity following this interpretation, The British Land Company PLC, explains the treatment in its accounting policies as shown below.

Extract 17.4: The British Land Company PLC (2008)

1. Basis of preparation
Net rental income [extract]

Rental income from fixed and minimum guaranteed rent reviews is recognised on a straight-line basis over the shorter of the entire lease term or the period to the first break option. Where such rental income is recognised ahead of the related cash flow, an adjustment is made to ensure the carrying value of the related property including the accrued rent does not exceed the external valuation.

This treatment can also be seen in Extracts 17.6 and 17.7 below.

4.4.2   *Prepaid rental income*

The same principles are applied when rental income arising from an operating lease is received in advance. This can be demonstrated in the example below:

Example 17.3:   Investment property and rent received in advance

A company owns land with an estimated value of £10m as at 1 January 2009 that is accounted for as investment property. The company applies the fair value option in IAS 40 and has a reporting period ended on 31 December 2009.

The land was unlet until, on 30 December 2009, a lease of 50 years was granted for consideration of £9.5m. The lease is considered to be an operating lease. No rental income was recognised in 2009 as it was considered immaterial. An external valuer estimated that, after the grant of the 50 year lease, the fair value of the company's interest in the land as at 31 December 2009 was £1m. As at 31 December 2010 the external valuer estimated the market value of the interest in the property was £1.2m.

The resultant accounting entries are summarised below:

Extracts from the ledgers for the year ended 31 December 2009

	As at 1 January 2009	Journal (1)	Journal (2)	Journal (3)	As at 31 December 2009
Investment property	10.0	–	(9.0)	9.5	10.5
Cash	–	9.5	–	–	9.5
Deferred Income	–	(9.5)	–	–	(9.5)
Net Assets	10.0	–	(9.0)		10.5
Equity	10.0	–	–	–	10
Retained profit	–	–	(9.0)	9.5	0.5
Total Equity	10.0	–	(9.0)	9.5	10.5

Journals:

(1) Issue of lease (£9.5m received on issue of lease)

(2) Write down investment property to £1m external valuation

(3) Write up book value of property by the amount of unamortised deferred revenue in the balance sheet

Extracts from the ledgers for the year ended 31 December 2010

	As at 1 January 2010	Journal (1)	Journal (2)	Journal (3)	As at 31 December 2010
Investment property	10.5	–	(9.3)	9.31	10.51
Cash	9.5	–	–	–	9.5
Deferred Income	(9.5)	0.19	–	–	(9.31)
	10.5	0.19	(9.3)	9.31	10.7
Equity	10.0	–	–	–	10.0
Retained profit	0.5	0.19	(9.3)	9.31	0.7
	10.5	0.19	(9.3)	9.31	10.7

Journals:
(1) Amortise rent (one year of the £9.5m received for 50 years)
(2) Write down investment property to £1.2m external valuation
(3) Write up the book value of property by the amount of unamortised deferred revenue in the balance sheet (£9.31m)

4.5   The fair value of properties held under a lease

The standard points out that the fair value of a lease interest takes account of all rental payments, including contingent rents, that an entity is expected to make. Therefore, if the entity obtains a property valuation net of the valuer's estimate of the present value of future lease obligations, which is usual practice, to the extent that the lease obligations have already been accounted for as a finance lease an amount is to be added back to arrive at the fair value of the investment property for the purposes of the financial statements.

The valuation adjustment referred to above is achieved by adjusting for the finance lease obligation recognised in the financial statements.

This is illustrated using the information in the following example:

Example 17.4:   Valuation of a property held under a finance lease

Company A pays €991,000 for a 50 year leasehold interest in a property which is classified as an investment property using the fair value model. In addition a ground rent of €10,000 is payable annually during the lease term, the present value of which is calculated at €99,000 using a discount rate of 10% which reflects the market required yield at that time. The company has initially recognised the investment property at the following amount:

	€'000
Amount paid	991
Present value of the ground rent obligation on acquisition	99
Cost recorded	1,090

At the next reporting date the leasehold interest in the property has been assessed to have a fair value of €1,006,000 calculated as follows:

	€'000
Present value of estimated future lease income	1,089
Less: Present value of the ground rent obligation at the reporting date *	(83)
Assessed fair value	1,006

*   at the next reporting date the market required yield has increased to 12%. Therefore the present value of the ground rent obligations of €10,000 per annum for the remaining 49 years is now €83,000. At the same time the ground rent finance lease liability has reduced to €98,000 as payments are made.

This would give the following results:

	€'000
Assessed fair value	1,006
Add recognised finance lease liability	98
	1,104

The effect of IAS 40 is therefore that the aggregate carrying value of investment property net of the related finance lease liability is the same as assessed fair value of the investment property.

Examples of this can be seen in the Extracts below:

Extract 17.5: Liberty International PLC (2005)

10   Investment and development properties [extract]

The group's interests in investment and development properties were valued as at 31 December 2005 by external valuers in accordance with the Appraisal and Valuation Manual of RICS, on the basis of Market Value. Market Value represents the figure that would appear in a hypothetical contract of sale between a willing buyer and a willing seller.

In the UK, properties were valued by either DTZ Debenham Tie Leung, Chartered Surveyors, Knight Frank LLP, CB Richard Ellis or Matthews & Goodman LLP. In the United States, properties were valued by Cushman and Wakefield California, Inc.

A reconciliation of investment and development property valuations to the balance sheet carrying value of property is shown below:

	2005 £m	2004 £m
Investment and development property at market value as determined by external valuers	6,936.3	5,309.7
Add minimum payment under head leases separately included as a creditor in the balance sheet	53.9	31.9
Less accrued incentives separately included as a debtor in the balance sheet	(52.4)	(44.0)
Balance sheet carrying value of investment and development property	6,937.8	5,297.6

Extract 17.6: Land Securities Group PLC (2008)

Notes to the Financial Statements [extract]
13.   Non-current assets [extract]

The following table reconciles the net book value of the investment properties (excluding those within Trillium) to the market value. Trillium's investment property have been excluded from this reconciliation as the net book value and the market value are not materially different. The components of the reconciliation are included within their relevant balance sheet headings.

	Property investment		
	Portfolio management £m	Development programme £m	Total investment properties £m
Net book value at 31 March 2007	10,607.4	2,284.3	12,891.7
Plus: amount included in prepayments in respect of lease incentives	93.6	37.4	131.0
Less: head leases capitalised (note 30)	(61.6)	(9.4)	(71.0)
Plus: properties treated as finance leases	163.1	–	163.1
Market value at 31 March 2007			
– Group	10,802.5	2,312.3	13,114.8
– Plus: share of joint ventures (note 19)			1,637.7
Market value at 31 March 2007			
– Group and share of joint ventures			14,752.5

Net book value at 31 March 2008	10,338.3	1,396.0	11,734.3
Plus: amount included in prepayments in respect of lease incentives	156.3	24.3	180.6
Less: head leases capitalised (note 30)	(65.3)	(2.0)	(67.3)
Plus: properties treated as finance leases	149.2	–	149.2
Market value at 31 March 2008			
– Group	10,578.5	1,418.3	11,996.8
– Plus: share of joint ventures (note 19)			1,589.9
Market value at 31 March 2008			
– Group and share of joint ventures			13,586.7

4.6   Future capital expenditure and development values

Future capital expenditure that will enhance the benefits may not be taken into account in determining the fair value, nor may the income that might arise from this expenditure.[67]

However, it is common for the value of land to reflect its potential future use and the value of land may increase in the event that the owner obtains any required permissions for a change in the use of that land. It may be, for example, that a permission to change from an industrial to residential use will increase the value of the property as a whole, not withstanding that the existing industrial buildings are still in place. This increase in value is typically attributable to the land, rather than the buildings.

If that value increase reflects the market value of the land, i.e. it is what every buyer of the land would incorporate in the price they are willing to pay, it would be appropriate to record any changes in value resulting from the receipt of such permissions in the fair value of the land.

But, if the increase in value is entity specific, for instance, if the benefit of the permission was only available to that owner and not the market generally, then no additional value can be recorded as part of the fair value of the land.

4.7   Inability to determine fair value of completed investment property

It is a rebuttable presumption that an entity can determine the fair value of a property reliably on a continuing basis, that is, on each subsequent occasion in which it records the investment property in its financial statements. The standard stresses that it is only in exceptional cases that the entity will be able to conclude, when it first recognises a particular investment property, that it will not be able to determine its fair value in the future. Additionally, entities are strongly discouraged from arguing that fair value cannot be reliably measured. It would only be an acceptable argument if there were infrequent market transactions and, either the entity was unable to construct a fair value using the alternative measures allowed by the standard, or the range of fair value estimates was too great to establish a reliable value. In such cases, the property should be treated under the cost model of IAS 16 and assumed to have a nil residual value.[68] This means that it has to be carried at cost and the building and its component parts depreciated over their useful lives. In these circumstances IAS 16's revaluation model, under which assets may be revalued to fair value, is specifically ruled out. If this situation occurs, the cost model of IAS 16 should continue to be applied until disposal. Even if an entity is 'compelled' to carry an individual property at cost, all other investment property must continue to be carried at fair value.[69]

In addition, once a property is initially recognised at its fair value, it must always be so recognised until disposed of or reclassified for owner-occupation or development, even if comparable market transactions become less frequent or market prices become less easily available.[70] This is to prevent a switch to the cost model if there were a property price collapse when there would be few transactions and the fair value could become uncomfortably low or volatile.

5   THE COST MODEL

The cost model requires that all investment property be measured after initial recognition under the cost model treatment of IAS 16. This means that the asset must be recognised at cost and depreciated systematically over its useful life.[71] The residual value and useful life of each investment property must be reviewed at least at each financial year-end and, if expectations differ from previous estimates, the changes must be accounted for as a change in accounting estimate in accordance with IAS 8.[72]

The revaluation model of IAS 16 is not available for investment property.

If an entity adopts the cost model, the fair value of its investment property must be disclosed (see section 9.2 below). Entities may have limited internal resources and consequently may need to obtain professional assistance in order to meet the disclosure requirements. In the past, such entities may have chosen the cost model in part to avoid the cost of an annual valuation. This benefit of using the cost model may no longer be so evident.

5.1   Initial recognition

5.1.1   Identification of tangible significant parts

The cost of the property has to be analysed into appropriate significant parts, each of which will have to be depreciated separately (see also Chapter 16 at 4.2).

The analysis into significant parts is not a straightforward exercise since properties typically contain a large number of components with varying useful lives. Klépierre, who adopted the cost model for investment property, disclose their approach to this exercise below:

Extract 17.7: Klépierre (2007)

2. Accounting principles and methods [extract]

2.5 Investment property [extract]

Components method [extract]

The components method is applied for the most part on the basis of recommendations by the *Fédération des Sociétés Immobiliéres et Fonciéres* (Federation of Property Companies – FSIF) on components and useful lives:

– for properties developed by the subsidiaries themselves, assets are classified by component type and measured at their realizable value;

– for properties held in the portfolio, sometimes for a long time, components are broken down into four categories: business premises, shopping centers, offices and residential properties.

Four components were identified for each of these asset types in addition to the land:

o Structure

o Facades, waterproofing and roofing;

o Mechanical/Electrical/Plumbing (MEP);

o Fittings

Component classification is based on the historic and technical features of each property

For the first-time adoption of the components method, the historic cost of property has been calculated based on the proportion of revalued amount used as presumed cost at January 1, 2003 that is assigned to each component.

	Office buildings		Shopping centers		Shops	
	Useful life	Share of Total	Useful life	Share of Total	Useful life	Share of Total
Structure	60 years	60%	35-50 years	50%	30-40 years	50%
Facades	30 years	15%	25 years	15%	15-25 years	15%
IGT	20 years	15%	20 years	25%	10-20 years	25%
Fittings	12 years	10%	10-15 years	10%	5-15 years	10%

All figures are based on an "as new" assumption. Klépierre has therefore calculated proportions for fittings, technical services and facades at January 1, 2003 using the useful lives shown in the above grid, calculated from the date of acquisition or latest general refurbishment of the property. The figure for structures is deduced from the figures for the other components and is amortized over the residual term set by the appraisers in 2003.

Purchase cost is divided up between land and buildings. The share allocated to buildings is amortized over the useful life of the structures.

Residual value is the current estimate of the amount the company would obtain (minus disposal costs) if the property were already of the age it will be and in the condition it will be in at the end of its useful life.

The entity is also required to recognise replacement parts and derecognise the replaced part as described in Chapter 16 at 5.

5.1.2 Identification of significant intangible parts

As set out in Chapter 16 at 4.2, IAS 16 links its recognition concept of a 'part' of an asset with the analysis of assets for the purpose of depreciation. Each part of an asset with a cost that is significant in relation to the total cost of the item must be depreciated separately, which means that the initial cost must be allocated between the significant parts by the entity.

Effective for accounting periods beginning on or after 1 July 2009, IAS 16 sets out that if an entity acquires PP&E subject to an operating lease in which it is the lessor, it may be appropriate to depreciate separately amounts reflected in the cost of that item that are attributable to favourable or unfavourable lease terms relative to market terms. This amendment to the Standard results from the implementation of IFRS 3 – *Business Combinations* (as revised in 2008) that requires a similar treatment for PP&E (see 2.4.6) purchased as part of a business combination.

5.2   Incidence of use of the cost model

It appears less common for entities to hold investment property using the cost model than the fair value model. For example, IVG Immobilien AG initially adopted the cost model and made the following statement in their 2005 financial statements:

Extract 17.8: IVG Immobilien AG (2005)

5.2   Investment properties [extract]

Investment properties are carried at depreciated cost (see 5.1) in accordance with IAS 40.56 and not at market value. As industry standards with regard to choice of accounting policy for investment property are still evolving, IVG opted to apply the cost model in its consolidated financial statements from 2004. This has the advantage that it is possible to change to the fair value model should this be adopted as best practice by the capital markets. A switch in the other direction from the fair value model to the cost model is not permitted.

But this policy choice was short lived as can be seen from the following statement in their 2007 financial statements:

Extract 17.9: IVG Immobilien AG (2007)

3.   Changes to accounting [extract]
Valuation of investment properties in accordance with fair value method

Pursuant to IAS 40 (Investment Property) property held as a financial investment is valued upon acquisition at cost. Until 31 December 2006, the IVG Group carried out subsequent valuations of its investment properties in accordance with the cost model, by which investment properties were valued at cost less scheduled or extraordinary depreciation.

As the fair value method has now been established on capital markets as best practice for the subsequent valuation of investment properties, IVG switched to the fair value method on 1 January 2007. Pursuant to this method, the IVG Group will value its investment properties with their fair value at balance sheet date and changes in the market value of properties will be recognised in the income statement. The IVG Group believes that using the fair value method will improve presentation of assets in the balance sheet, as it reveals hidden reserves or charges. It provides greater transparency in the financial statements, raises comparability with competitors and is in line with best practice recommendations of the European Public Real Estate Association (EPRA).

Whilst transferring over to the fair value model, a reclassification of acquired properties totalling €52.6 million was made in 2006 from investment properties to inventories. This had no effect on net profits.

However, anecdotal evidence suggests that the use of the cost model is being more widely considered by potential future adopters of IFRS. It may be that this is a result of the volatility in fair value of property caused by the 'credit crunch' of 2008 and consequent turbulence in global real estate markets.

The use of the cost model (rather than the fair value model) removes the need to report profits from increases in the fair value of property. However, it is unlikely to insulate an entity from reporting losses arising from falls in the fair value of investment property below the depreciated cost of the property – see 5.3 below.

5.3   Impairment and investment property

Investment property measured at cost is subject to the requirements of IAS 36 in respect of impairment. As set out in Chapter 18, IAS 36 requires a recoverable amount to determined either by (i) a value in use calculation; or (ii) by estimating fair value less costs to sell.

Both a value in use calculation and a fair value calculation (where there is no price quoted for identical assets on an active market) are based on discounted cash flow models. The former will typically use entity specific cash flows, whilst the latter would generally use market expected cash flows. Both would use a market determined discount rate.

For a rental generating asset such as an investment property, the future cash flows to be taken into account in any projection would, in simple terms, be (i) the rental stream under the existing lease arrangements; and (ii) an estimate of any rental stream thereafter.

The cash flows generated from the existing lease would be the same whether the basis was entity specific or market expected cash flows.

The estimate of any rental stream thereafter would also be the same unless the entity forecast it would outperform the market and achieve superior cash flows. This is unlikely to be an acceptable basis for a forecast as no entity can realistically expect to outperform the market for its whole portfolio or do so for more than the short term. Consequently, a forecast that cash flows from individual properties will outperform the market would have to be considered with scepticism.

Consequently, we would regard it as being a rare circumstance where the value in use of an individual investment property could be said to be higher than the fair value of that property. Indeed, in some circumstances – for example, where a fair value is partly dependant on a gain from future planned future development (see 4.6 above) but that expenditure is not be allowed to be considered in a value in use calculation – value in use may be lower than fair value.

6   IFRS 5 AND INVESTMENT PROPERTY

Under the cost model, investment properties that meet the criteria to be classified as held for sale, or that are included within a disposal group classified as held for sale, are measured in accordance with IFRS 5 – *Non-current Assets Held for Sale and Discontinued Operations*.[73] This means that they will be held at the lower of carrying amount and fair value less costs to sell, and depreciation of the asset will cease.

As set out in Chapter 4 at 2.2.1, investment property measured at fair value is not subject to the measurement requirements of IFRS 5. However, such property is subject to the presentation requirements of that standard. Consequently investment property that meets the definition of held for sale is required to be presented separately from other assets in the balance sheet. This does not mean that such property should be presented within current assets.

An example of an entity applying the presentation requirements of IFRS 5 to investment property measured at fair value is Development Securities plc in their 2006 financial statements.

Extract 17.10: Development Securities PLC (2006)

Financial Statements [extract]
Consolidated balance sheet [extract]=
As at 31 December 2006

	Notes	2006 £'000	£'000	2005 restated* £'000	£'000
Non-current assets					
Property, plant and equipment					
– Operating properties	10	8,090		9,000	
– Other property, plant and equipment	10	3,618		3,776	
Investment properties	11	139,461		159,568	
Financial assets	12	5,881		755	
Investments in joint ventures	12	20,464		–	
Investment in associates	12	673		1,165	
Trade and other receivables	14	1,468		1,420	
Deferred tax assets	17	6,215		4,387	
			185,870		180,071
Investment property – held for sale	11		5,299		–
Current assets					
Inventory – developments and trading properties	13	74,663		56,479	
Trade and other receivables	14	10,014		9,677	
Cash and short-term deposits		88,536		73,094	
			173,213		139,250
Total assets			364,382		319,321

Investment properties measured using the cost method are subject to both the measurement and presentation requirements of IFRS 5.

7   TRANSFER OF ASSETS INTO OR FROM INVESTMENT PROPERTY

The standard specifies the circumstances in which a property becomes, or ceases to be, an investment property. There must be a change in use, evidenced by:

(a)   the commencement or end of owner-occupation;

(b)   the commencement of development with a view to sale, at which point an investment property would be transferred to inventory (but see future developments at 10.1 where it is described how this requirement is likely to change). The standard allows a transfer to inventory only when there is a change of use evidenced by the start of a development with a view to subsequent sale; or

(c) entering into an operating lease to another party which would generally require a transfer from inventory to investment property (but see 2.2.2 above).

Extract 17.11 below describes how Land Securities deals with the requirements of (b) above.

Extract 17.11: Land Securities Group PLC (2008)
2.   **Significant accounting policies** [extract]
(d)   **Investment properties**

When the Group begins to redevelop an existing investment property with a view to sell, the property is transferred to trading properties and held as a current asset. The property is remeasured to fair value as at the date of the transfer with any gain or loss being taken to income statement. The remeasured amount becomes the deemed cost at which the property is then carried in trading properties.

An existing investment property that is being redeveloped for continued future use as an investment property by the entity must remain classified as an investment property and is not reclassified as owner-occupied property during the redevelopment.[74]

7.1 Transfers to inventory

As set out above, the standard allows a transfer to inventory only when there is a change of use evidenced by the start of a development with a view to subsequent sale. However, if an entity decides to dispose of an investment property without development with a view to sale, it may not be transferred to inventory.

This means that, unless there is such a development, it is not possible to reclassify investment property as inventory even if the entity holding that property changes its intentions and is no longer holding that property for rental or capital appreciation. Rather, IFRS 5 is applied to property held for sale to the extent that the requirements therein are met (see section 6).

As set out in 10.1 below, the IASB has tentatively decided to remove the requirement to transfer investment property to inventory when it will be developed before sale. Rather the Board will add a requirement for such investment property held for sale also to be disclosed consistent with IFRS 5.

7.2 Transfers from inventory

The question of when an inventory can be reclassified as investment property was, in fact, the subject of a restatement of financial statements required by the United Kingdom financial reporting regulator, the Financial Reporting Review Panel. (the 'Panel').

The Panel reviewed the report and accounts of Grainger Trust plc (now Grainger plc) for the year ended 30 September 2006. The Panel reported that during the period in question, the company transferred trading properties with a carrying amount, at cost, of £43.5m to a Jersey Property Unit Trust (the 'JPUT'), a wholly-owned subsidiary, at 30 September 2006. On transfer, the properties were reclassified as investment properties and a gain on revaluation to market value of £23.5m was recognised in the income statement.

As a result of discussion, the directors of Grainger agreed that the transfer did not comply with the requirements of IAS 40 as it did not provide evidence of the required change in use. However, the final outcome was that of a different type of prior year adjustment – the directors concluded that the properties transferred to the JPUT were originally acquired for the purpose of long term capital appreciation and rental growth and, consequently, should always have been shown as investment property rather than inventory.

This highlights the importance, as noted in section 1.1 above, of the classification of the property on initial recognition as either investment property or inventory.

7.3   Treatment of transfers

Transfers to and from the status of investment property under the fair value model are accounted for as follows:

- *Transfers to inventory or owner-occupation*: the cost for subsequent accounting under IAS 16 or IAS 2 should be its fair value at the date the use changed;[75]
- *Transfers from owner-occupation*: IAS 16 will be applied up to the time that the use changed. At that date any difference between the IAS 16 carrying amount and the fair value is to be treated in the same way as a revaluation under IAS 16.[76]

Up until the time that an owner occupied property becomes an investment property carried at fair value, depreciation under IAS 16 continues and any impairment losses up to the date of change of use must be recognised in accordance with IAS 36. The difference between the carrying value under IAS 16 and the fair value under IAS 40 is accounted for in the same way as a revaluation under IAS 16. If the owner occupied property had not previously been revalued, the transfer does not imply that the entity has now chosen a policy of revaluation for other property accounted for under IAS 16 in the same class. The treatment depends on whether it is a decrease or increase in value and whether the asset had previously been revalued or impaired in value (as described at 2.4). Paragraph 62 of the standard sets out the treatment as follows:[77]

'Up to the date when an owner-occupied property becomes an investment property carried at fair value, an entity depreciates the property and recognises any impairment losses that have occurred. The entity treats any difference at that date between the carrying amount of the property in accordance with IAS 16 and its fair value in the same way as a revaluation in accordance with IAS 16. In other words:

(a)   any resulting decrease in the carrying amount of the property is recognised in profit or loss. However, to the extent that an amount is included in revaluation surplus for that property, the decrease is charged against that revaluation surplus.

(b)   any resulting increase in the carrying amount is treated as follows:

(i) to the extent that the increase reverses a previous impairment loss for that property, the increase is recognised in profit or loss. The amount recognised in profit or loss does not exceed the amount needed to restore the carrying amount to the carrying amount that would have been determined (net of depreciation) had no impairment loss been recognised.

(ii) any remaining part of the increase is credited to revaluation surplus via OCI. On subsequent disposal of the investment property, the revaluation surplus may be transferred to retained earnings. The transfer from revaluation surplus to retained earnings is not made through profit or loss.'

When the business uses the cost model for investment property, transfers between investment property, inventory and owner occupation do not change the carrying amount of the property transferred.[78]

7.4 Transfers of investment property held under operating leases

An entity applying the fair value model is allowed to classify interests held under operating leases as investment properties in the same manner as if they were held under finance leases. In these circumstances, neither IAS 17 nor IAS 40 requires the entity to separate the land value from the value of the buildings. IAS 17 allows this treatment to continue even if the property interest ceases to be classified as an investment property by the lessee and gives two examples:

- the lessee occupies the property, in which case it is transferred to owner-occupied property at fair value at the date of change of use; or
- the lessee grants a sublease over substantially all of its property interest to an unrelated third party. It will treat the sublease as a finance lease to the third party even though the interest may well be accounted for as an operating lease by that party.[79]

Therefore, on transfer, the treatment of interests held under operating leases mirrors that of other ownership interests.

8 DISPOSAL OF INVESTMENT PROPERTY

IAS 40 requires that an investment property should be removed from the balance sheet ('derecognised') on disposal or when it is permanently withdrawn from use and no further economic benefits are expected from its disposal.[80]

A disposal of an investment property is achieved upon a sale or:

- when it becomes the subject of a finance lease (the owner becoming the lessor); or
- when it becomes the subject of a sale and leaseback deal (the original owner becoming the lessee).[81]

IAS 17 applies if a property is disposed of by the owner becoming a finance lessor, or if a property is the subject of a sale and leaseback transaction.[82]

These derecognition rules also apply to a part of the investment property that has been replaced, as discussed in 8.1 below.

IAS 18 – *Revenue* – applies on a sale.[83] IAS 18 allows that while revenue would normally be recognised when legal title passes, in some jurisdictions the risks and rewards of ownership may pass to the buyer before legal title has passed. In such cases, provided that the seller has no further substantial acts to complete under the contract, it may be appropriate to recognise revenue. Liberty International PLC has taken this approach.

Extract 17.12: Liberty International PLC (2007)
Principal accounting policies [extract]
Revenue recognition

Where revenue is obtained by the sale of properties, it is recognised when the significant risks and returns have been transferred to the buyer. This will normally take place on exchange of contracts unless there are conditions attached. For conditional exchanges sales are recognised when these conditions are satisfied.

An example given in IAS 18 of such a 'substantial act' is the completion of construction.[84] Another example of a 'substantial act' that has to be completed before a sale can be recognised is if formal shareholder approval is required before a property can be sold.

Gains and losses are calculated based on the difference between the net disposal proceeds and the carrying amount of the asset. This is recognised in profit or loss unless it is a sale and leaseback and IAS 17 requires a different treatment.[85] IAS 17 allows only the immediate recognition of profits and losses on a sale and operating leaseback if the transaction is established at fair value; no gains would be recognised if the transaction resulted in a finance leaseback. Refer to Chapter 22 for a discussion of sale and leaseback under IAS 17.

The proceeds of sale are recognised at their fair value. If the sale proceeds are deferred (deferral is not defined but it must mean beyond normal credit terms) the consideration recognised on the disposal will be the cash price equivalent (which in practice must mean the present value of the consideration). Any difference between the total payments received and this 'cash equivalent' will be treated as interest receivable under IAS 18 using the effective interest method.[86]

If an entity retains any liabilities after disposing of an investment property these are measured and accounted for in accordance with IAS 37 – *Provisions, Contingent Liabilities and Contingent Assets* – or other relevant standards.[87]

Finally, it is also of note that in July 2008 the IFRIC released Interpretation 15 – *Agreements for the Construction of Real Estate*, that deals with real estate sales in which an agreement for sale is reached before the construction of property is complete. The Interpretation addresses two issues:

- Is the agreement within the scope of IAS 11 or IAS 18?
- When should revenue from the construction of real estate be recognised?

But property that is subject to sale prior to completion of construction, if not previously classified as investment property, is likely to be property intended for sale in the ordinary course of business (see 2.2.3 above) and is therefore not investment property. IFRIC 15 is discussed in more detail in Chapter 25 at 6.11.2.

8.1   Replacement of parts of investment property

When an entity that applies the fair value model wishes to capitalise a replacement part, the question arises of how to deal with the cost of the new part and the carrying value of the original. The basic principle in IAS 40 is that the entity derecognises the carrying value of the replaced part. However the problem arises that even if the cost of the old part may be known, its carrying value – at fair value – is usually by no means clear. It is possible also that the fair value may already reflect the loss in value of the part to be replaced, because the valuation reflected the fact that an acquirer would reduce the price accordingly.

As all fair value changes are taken to profit or loss, the standard concludes that it is not necessary to identify separately the elements that relate to replacements from other fair value movements. Therefore, if it is not practical to identify the amount by which fair value should be reduced for the part replaced, the cost of the replacement is added to the carrying amount of the asset and the fair value of the investment property as a whole is reassessed. The standard notes that this is the treatment that would be applied to additions that did not involve replacing any existing part of the property.

If the investment property is carried under the cost model, then the entity should derecognise the carrying amount of the original part. A replaced part may not have been depreciated separately, in which case the standard allows the entity to use the cost of the replacement as an indication of an appropriate carrying value.[88] This does not mean that the entity has to apply depreciated replacement cost, rather that it can use the cost of the replacement as an indication of the original cost of the replaced part in order to reconstruct a suitable net present value for the replaced part.

8.2   Compensation from third parties

IAS 40 applies the same rules as IAS 16 to the treatment of compensation from third parties if property has been impaired, lost or given up. It stresses that impairments or losses of investment property, related claims for or payments of compensation from third parties and any subsequent purchase or construction of replacement parts are separate economic events that have to be accounted for separately.

Impairment of investment property will be recorded automatically if the fair value model is used; but if the property is accounted for using the cost model, it is to be calculated in accordance with IAS 36. If the entity no longer owns the asset, for example because it has been destroyed or subject to a compulsory purchase order, it will be derecognised as described in 8 above. Compensation (for example from an insurance company) is recognised in income when it is receivable. The cost of any replacement asset is accounted for wholly on its own merits according to the recognition rules covered in 2.3 above.[89]

9   THE DISCLOSURE REQUIREMENTS OF IAS 40

9.1   Introduction

For businesses that adopt the fair value option in IAS 40, attention will focus on the judgemental and subjective aspects of property valuations, because they will be reported in profit or loss. If a counter-intuitive failure were to occur (for instance a company that had reported large profits soon afterwards ran out of cash) this type of income statement could be discredited. Possibly as a consequence of these considerations, IAS 40 requires significant amounts of information to be disclosed about the judgements involved and the cash-related performance of the investment property, as set out below.

9.2   Disclosures under both fair value and cost models

Whichever model is chosen, fair value or cost, IAS 40 requires all companies to disclose the fair value of their investment property. Therefore the following disclosures are required in both instances:

(a)   whether the entity applies the cost model or the fair value model;

(b)   if it applies the fair value model, whether, and in what circumstances, property interests held under operating leases are classified and accounted for as investment property;

(c)   when classification is difficult (see 2.2 above), the criteria it uses to distinguish investment property from owner occupied property and from property held for sale in the ordinary course of business;

(d)   the methods and significant assumptions applied in determining the fair value of investment property, including a statement whether the determination of fair value was supported by market evidence or was more heavily based on other factors (which the entity shall disclose) because of the nature of the property and lack of comparable market data;

(e)   the extent to which the fair value of investment property (as measured or disclosed in the financial statements) is based on a valuation by an independent valuer who holds a recognised and relevant professional qualification and has recent experience in the location and category of the investment property being valued. If there has been no such valuation, that fact shall be disclosed;

(f)   the amounts recognised in profit or loss for:

  (i)   rental income from investment property;

  (ii)   direct operating expenses (including repairs and maintenance) arising from investment property that generated rental income during the period; and

  (iii)   direct operating expenses (including repairs and maintenance) arising from investment property that did not generate rental income during the period;

  (iv)   the cumulative change in fair value recognised in profit or loss on sale of an investment property from a pool of assets in which the cost model is used into a pool in which the fair value model is used (see 3.1 above).

(g)   the existence and amounts of restrictions on the realisability of investment property or the remittance of income and proceeds of disposal;

(h)   contractual obligations to purchase, construct or develop investment property or for repairs, maintenance or enhancements.[90]

Of immediate relevance is the impact of the 'credit crunch' in 2008, the resultant plunge in the volume of real estate transactions and the consequential difficulty of obtaining market evidence for the fair value of investment property. This heightened the importance of explaining the methods and significant assumptions. Rutley European Property Limited provided the following disclosures:

Extract 17.13: Rutley European Property Limited (2008)

Notes to the Consolidated Financial Statements [extract]

3.   Critical Accounting Estimates and Assumptions [extract]

The Group makes estimates and assumptions concerning the future and such accounting estimates may differ from the actual results. The estimates and assumptions that have a significant risk of causing material adjustments to the carrying amounts of assets and liabilities within the next financial year relate primarily to the valuation of investment properties.

The fair value of investment properties in the Consolidated Balance Sheet represents an estimate by independent professional valuers of the open market value of those properties as at 31 December 2008.

In assessing the open market value of investment properties, the professional valuers will consider lettings, tenant's profiles, future revenue streams, capital values of both fixtures and fittings and plant and machinery, any environmental matters and the overall repair and condition of the property in the context of the local market. Data regarding local market conditions is primarily historic in nature and provides a guide as to current letting values and yields.

The current volatility in the global financial system has created a significant degree of turbulence in commercial real estate markets across the world. There has been a significant reduction in transaction volumes with activity below the levels of recent years. Therefore, in arriving at their estimates of open market values as at 31 December 2008, the valuers have increasingly used their market knowledge and professional judgement and not only relied on historic transactional comparables. In these circumstances, there is a greater degree of uncertainty than that which exists in a more active market in estimating the open market values of investment property.

The lack of liquidity in capital markets also means that, if it was intended to dispose of the property, it may be difficult to achieve a successful sale of the investment property in the short term.

The significant methods and assumptions used by the valuers in estimating the fair value of investment property are set out in note 13.

13.   Investment Property [extract]

The investment properties were valued at 31 December 2008 at their open market value using an income capitalisation method in accordance with the Royal Institution of Chartered Surveyors Valuation Standards. The property valuations were carried out by CBRE and King Sturge, who are independent, professionally qualified valuers who have recent experience in the location and category of the investment properties being valued. Valuation of property is based on a number of factor including existing lease terms, estimates of market rents and estimates of capitalisation rates using comparable market evidence where available. As set out in note 3, due to a reduction in transaction volumes and therefore market evidence this year, the valuers have increasingly used their market knowledge and professional judgement and not only relied on historic transactional comparables.

The primary judgements made in arriving at the open market values are the yields. The table below sets out the weighted average yields for the initial (as at 31 December 2008) and equivalent yields applied on a country basis:

	2008 Equivalent Yield (%)	2008 Initial Yield (%)	2007 Equivalent Yield (%)	2007 Initial Yield (%)
Belgium	7.21	*0.95	6.62	6.29
Germany	6.30	6.44	5.80	5.84
The Netherlands	6.70	7.92	5.77	6.23

Describing the methods and significant assumptions applied in determining the fair value adequately can result in some lengthy disclosures, as shown in the Extract from Castellum AS below.

Extract 17.14: Castellum AB (publ) (2007)

Note 11 Investment properties [extract]

Valuation model

According to accepted theory, the value of an asset consists of the net present value of the future cash flows that the asset is expected to generate. This section aims to describe and illustrate Castellum's cash flow-based model for calculation of the value of the real estate portfolio. The value of the real estate portfolio is calculated in this model as the total present value of net operating income minus remaining investments on ongoing projects, during the next nine years and the present value of the estimated residual value in year ten. The residual value in year ten consists of the total present value of net operating income during the remaining economic life span. The estimated market value of undeveloped land is added to this.

The required yield and the assumption regarding future real growth are of crucial importance for the calculated value of the real estate portfolio, as they are the most important value-driving factors in the valuation model. The required yield is the weighted cost of borrowed capital and equity. The cost of borrowed capital is based on the market interest rate for loans. The cost of equity is based on a "risk-free interest rate" equivalent to the long-term government bond rate with the addition of a "risk premium". The risk premium is unique to each investment and depends on the investor's perception of future risk and potential.

To illustrate the model, the following example is provided. It should be noted that assumptions regarding cash flow growth and other assumptions included in the model are only intended to illustrate the model. The examples should thus not be regarded as a forecast of the company's expected earnings.

Assumptions in the example:

- The economic occupancy rate is assumed to increase in order to reach a long-term level of 95% in the year 2012.

- Net operating income for 2007 is based on the result for the investment properties, with an assumed cost of SEK 30/sq.m. for pure property administration.

- Growth in rental value and property costs has been assumed to 1% per annum during the calculation period.

- The average economic life of the real estate portfolio has been assumed to be 50 years.

- Projects and undeveloped land have been assumed to be SEKm 1111.

- The required yield is calculated according to the following assumptions:

	Required yield	Percentage of capital	Weighted required yield
Equity	7.0% - 20.5%	30%	2.1% - 6.1%
Borrowed capital	5.5%	70%	3.9%
Weighted required yield		100%	6.0% - 10.0%

Example – calculation of the value of the real estate portfolio

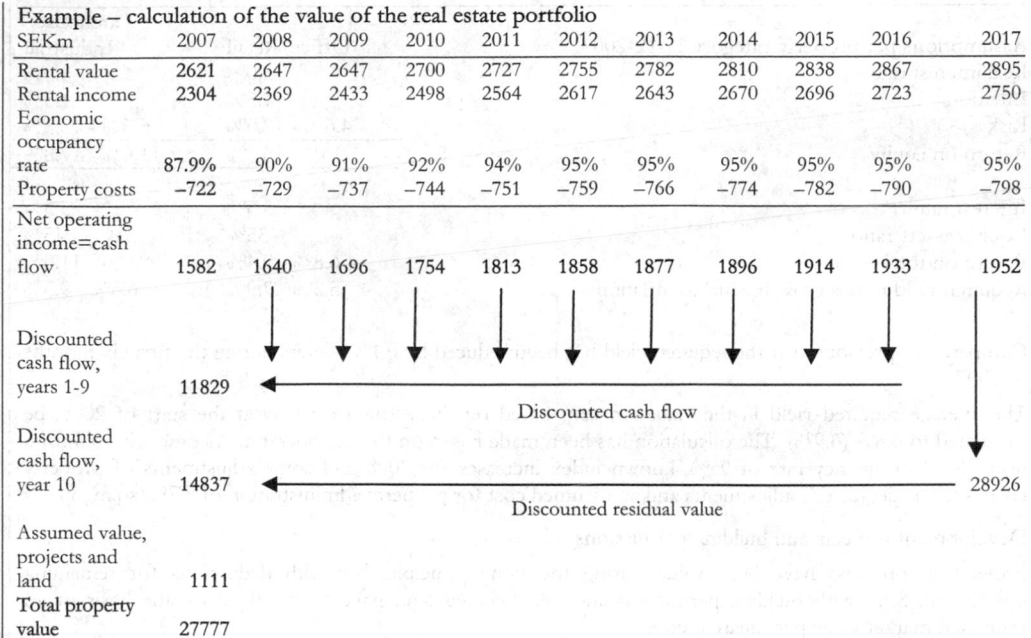

SEKm	2007	2008	2009	2010	2011	2012	2013	2014	2015	2016	2017
Rental value	2621	2647	2647	2700	2727	2755	2782	2810	2838	2867	2895
Rental income	2304	2369	2433	2498	2564	2617	2643	2670	2696	2723	2750
Economic occupancy rate	87.9%	90%	91%	92%	94%	95%	95%	95%	95%	95%	95%
Property costs	−722	−729	−737	−744	−751	−759	−766	−774	−782	−790	−798
Net operating income=cash flow	1582	1640	1696	1754	1813	1858	1877	1896	1914	1933	1952
Discounted cash flow, years 1-9	11829										
Discounted cash flow, year 10	14837										28926
Assumed value, projects and land	1111										
Total property value	27777										

Discounted cash flow

Discounted residual value

Internal Valuation

Castellum records the investment properties at fair value and has made an internal valuation of all properties as of December 31, 2007. The valuation was carried out in a uniform manner, and was based on a ten-year cash flow model, which was described in principle above. The internal valuation was based on an individual assessment for each property of both its future earnings capacity and its required yield. In assessing a property's future earnings capacity we took into account an assumed level of inflation of 1.5% and potential changes in rental levels from each contract's rent and expiry date compared with the estimated current market rent, as well as changes in occupancy rate and property costs. Included in property costs are operating expenses, maintenance, ground rent, real estate tax, and leasing and property administration. Possible premiums paid on portfolios have not been taken into account.

Assumptions on the required yield etc.

The required yield on equity is different for each property, and is based on assumptions regarding real interest rate, inflation and risk premium. The risk premium is different for each property and can be divided into two parts – general risk and individual risk. The general risk makes up for the fact that a real estate investment is not as liquid as a bond, and that the asset is affected by the general economic situation. The general risk was assumed to be 2.7%. The individual risk is specific to each property, and comprises a weighted assessment of; the property's category, the town/city in which the property is located, the property's location within the town/city with reference to the property's category, if the property has the right design, is appropriate and makes efficient use of space, the property's technical standard with regard to such criteria as the choice of materials, the quality of public installations, furnishing and equipment on the premises and apartments and the nature of the lease agreement, with regard to such issues as the length, size and number of agreements.

In order to calculate the required yield on total capital, an assumption has been made about the cost of borrowed capital of 5.5%. The required yield of borrowed capital comprises the real interest rate and inflation. The equity/assets ratio is assumed to be 35%-45%, depending on the property category.

The required yield on total capital is calculated by weighting the required yield on equity and the cost of borrowing capital depending on the equity/assets ratio. The required yield on total capital is used to discount the expected 10-year future cash flows, while the residual value is discounted by calculating the return on total capital minus growth which is set equal to the inflation.

The assumptions that form the basis for Castellum's valuation are shown in the table below.

Assumptions per property category 31-12-2007	Office/Retail	Warehouse/ Industrial
Real interest rate	3.0%	3.0%
Inflation	1.5%	1.5%
Risk	4.6% - 12.0%	6.5% - 13.3%
Return on equity	9.1% -16.5%	11.0% - 17.8%
Interest rate	5.5%	5.5%
Equity/assets ratio	35%	45%
Return on total capital	6.8% - 9.4%	8.0% - 11.0%
Required yield minus growth equal to inflation	5.3% - 7.9%	6.5% - 9.5%

Compared to previous year the required yield has been reduced by 0.1% – units during the first six months of 1007.

The average required yield in the valuation can, based on the earning capacity at the start of 2008, be calculated to 6.8% (6.9%). The calculation has been made based on the net operating income adjusted for a normalized occupancy rate of 95%, known index increases for 2008 and some adjustments of property costs such as degree day adjustments and an assumed cost for property administration of SEK/sq.m. 30.

Development projects and building permissions

Projects in progress have been valued using the same principle, but with deductions for remaining investment. Sites with building permission and undeveloped land have been valued on the basis of an estimated market value per square metre.

The value of the real estate portfolio and calculated net asset value

The internal valuation shows a fair value of SEKm 27,717 (24,238), which is an increase in value of approx. 3% (5%). The table below shows the fair value distributed by property category and region.

Property value, SEKm 31-12-2007	Office/ Retail	Warehouse/ Industrial	Projects and Land	Total
Greater Gothenburg	5127	3994	172	9293
Öresund Region	4854	1752	300	6906
Greater Stockholm	3603	1282	381	5266
Mälardalen	2324	819	135	3278
Eastern Götaland	2273	578	123	2974
Total	18181	8425	1111	27717

External valuation

In order to provide further assurance and validation of the valuation 111 properties, representing 50% of the value of the portfolio, were valued by NAI Svefa. The properties were selected on the basis of the largest properties in terms of value, but also in order to reflect the composition of the portfolio as a whole in terms of category and geographical location of the properties. NAI Svefa's valuation of the selected properties amounted to SEKm 13,976, within an uncertainty range of +/– 5%-10% on property level. The size of the uncertainty range varies depending on each property's category and location. Castellum's valuation of the same properties amounted to SEKm 13,909. It can be noted that, on portfolio level, the external and internal valuations correspond well, although there are individual differences.

Uncertainty range

A property's market value can only be confirmed when it is sold. Property valuations are calculations performed according to accepted principles and on the basis of certain assumptions. The value range of +/– 5-10% often used in property valuations should be seen as an indication of the uncertainty that exists in such assessments and calculations. For Castellum, an uncertainty range of +/– 5%, means a range in value of SEKm 26,331 – 29,103.

9.3 Additional disclosures for the fair value model

A reconciliation of the carrying amounts of investment property at the start and finish of the period must be given showing the following:

(a) additions, disclosing separately those additions resulting from acquisitions and those resulting from subsequent expenditure recognised in the carrying amount of an asset;

(b) additions resulting from acquisitions through business combinations;

(c) disposals;

(d) net gains or losses from fair value adjustments;

(e) the net exchange differences arising on the translation of the financial statements into a different presentation currency, and on translation of a foreign operation into the presentation currency of the reporting entity;

(f) transfers to and from inventories and owner-occupied property; and

(g) other changes.[91]

When a valuation obtained for investment property is adjusted significantly for the purpose of the financial statements, for example to avoid double-counting of assets or liabilities that are recognised separately as required by paragraph 50 of the standard, the entity must disclose a reconciliation between the valuation obtained and the adjusted valuation included in the financial statements, showing separately the aggregate amount of any recognised lease obligations that have been added back, and any other significant adjustments.[92] Extracts 17.6 and 17.7 above provide examples of such disclosure.

9.3.1 Presentation of changes in fair value

IAS 40 does not specify how changes in the fair value of investment property should be presented. The Extracts below show two different approaches. In Extract 17.15 the change in fair value (here referred to as a gain on revaluation) is presented together with the profit or loss on disposal of properties with an analysis of the components included in the notes to the accounts. By contrast, in Extract 17.16, the change in fair value is analysed and presented separately from the profit or loss on disposal of properties.

Both companies include the change in fair value within their definition of operating profit.

Extract 17.15: Liberty International plc (2007)

Consolidated Income Statement for the year ended 31 December 2007 [extract]

	Notes	2007 £m	2006 £m
Revenue	1	574.6	562.8
Rental income		546.7	493.1
Rental expenses		(172.4)	(152.5)
Net rental income	1	374.3	340.6
Other income		2.0	34.8
Gain on revaluation and sale of investment and development property	3	(279.1)	586.5
		97.2	961.9
Administration expenses		(45.2)	(34.2)
Operating profit		52.0	927.7

Extract 17.16: Rodamco Europe, NV (2006)

Consolidated Profit and Loss Account for the year ended December 31, 2006 [extract]

In €millions

	Notes	2006	2005
Gross rental income	4	652	594
Service charge income	5	98	83
Revenues		750	677
Service charge expenses	5	(103)	(89)
Property operating expenses	6	(84)	(85)
Net rental income		563	503
Valuation result investment property	7	1,270	965
Valuation result renovation projects	7	–	–
Valuation result pipeline projects	7	37	63
Valuation result		1,307	1,028
Result on disposal of investment property and pipeline	7	27	10
Administrative expenses	8	(52)	(44)
Other income and expenses	9	–	2
Operating profit		1,845	1,499

It is worth noting that as part of the 2008 annual improvement process, the IASB adapted IAS 16 to allow an entity that, in the course of its ordinary activities, routinely sells items of property, plant and equipment that it has held for rental to transfer such assets to inventories at their carrying amount when they cease to be rented and become held for sale. The proceeds from the sale of such assets are then recognised as revenue.

However, investment property, by definition, is held to earn rentals or for capital appreciation rather than for sale in the ordinary course of business. Consequently, we consider that the IAS 16 amendment may not be applied by analogy to IAS 40 and proceeds from the sale of investment property may not be presented as revenue.

9.3.2 *Extra disclosures where fair value cannot be determined reliably*

If fair value cannot be measured reliably and the asset is accounted for under the provisions of the cost model, the reconciliations described under 6.3 above should separately disclose the amounts for such investment property. In addition to this the following should be disclosed:

(a) a description of the investment property;

(b) an explanation of why fair value cannot be determined reliably;

(c) if possible, the range of estimates within which fair value is highly likely to lie; and

(d) on disposal of investment property not carried at fair value:

 (i) the fact that the entity has disposed of investment property not carried at fair value;

 (ii) the carrying amount of that investment property at the time of sale; and

 (iii) the amount of gain or loss recognised.[93]

The standard makes it clear that this situation, at least for completed investment property, would be exceptional (see 4.6 above). The situation for investment under construction is discussed in 4.2.1 above.

9.4 Additional disclosures for the cost model

In the event that investment property is carried at cost less depreciation, the following disclosures are required by IAS 40:

(a) the depreciation methods used;

(b) the useful lives or the depreciation rates used;

(c) the gross carrying amount and the accumulated depreciation (aggregated with accumulated impairment losses) at the beginning and end of the period;

(d) a reconciliation of the carrying amount of investment property at the beginning and end of the period, showing the following:

 (i) additions, disclosing separately those additions resulting from acquisitions and those resulting from subsequent expenditure recognised as an asset;

 (ii) additions resulting from acquisitions through business combinations;

 (iii) disposals;

 (iv) depreciation;

 (v) the amount of impairment losses recognised, and the amount of impairment losses reversed, during the period in accordance with IAS 36;

 (vi) the net exchange differences arising on the translation of the financial statements into a different presentation currency, and on translation of a foreign operation into the presentation currency of the reporting entity;

 (vii) transfers to and from inventories and owner-occupied property; and

 (viii) other changes; and

(e)   the fair value of investment property. In the exceptional cases when an entity cannot determine the fair value of the investment property reliably (see 4.6 above), it shall disclose:

(i)   a description of the investment property;

(ii)   an explanation of why fair value cannot be determined reliably; and

(iii) if possible, the range of estimates within which fair value is highly likely to lie.[94]

10   FUTURE DEVELOPMENTS

10.1   Transfers from investment property to inventory

In their December 2008 meeting the IASB discussed issues for possible inclusion in their next annual improvement exposure draft that is expected to be published in August 2009. One of the issues discussed was the apparent inconsistency within IAS 40 in respect of the decisions to develop or sell investment property previously measured at fair value.

The IASB noted that:

- an entity continues using the fair value model when a property is removed from active service while being renovated for continuing future use as an investment property.

- when there is 'commencement of development with a view to sale', an investment property is transferred to inventories and is within the scope of IAS 2 *Inventories*;

- when criteria in IFRS 5 *Non-current Assets Held for Sale and Discontinued Operations* are met, the entity continues to use the fair value model.

Consequently, in the exposure draft 'Improvements to IFRSs' issued in August 2009 the IASB proposes to:

- remove the requirement to transfer investment property to inventory when it will be developed for sale; and

- add a requirement for investment property held for sale to be displayed as a separate category in the statement of financial position and to require disclosures consistent with IFRS 5.

In fact, the requirement to provide disclosures in accordance with IFRS 5 already exists for all other investment property held for sale (see section 6) but if the amendment is approved then it will also need to be applied to investment property developed with a view to sell.

This amendment would also seem to eliminate entirely any possibility of reclassifying investment property as inventory after initial recognition.

10.2 The Fair Value Exposure Draft

As set out in 4.2 above, in May 2009 the IASB issued an Exposure Draft 'Fair Value Measurement' which, the IASB say, would achieve 'overall' convergence with US GAAP. The guidance in this Exposure Draft would replace that currently included in IAS 40.

The IASB has said it plans to hold round-table discussions during the fourth quarter of 2009 with the intention of publishing a final IFRS on fair value measurement guidance in 2010.

FAS 157 and the IASB discussion paper are discussed further in Chapter 2 at 6.2 and 6.3.

11 CONCLUSION

IAS 40 was the harbinger of a performance statement in which realised profits and unrealised gains are not distinguished. Consequently, it was inevitable that the volatility of reported assets and profits would increase.

It is therefore relevant to ask whether such fair values do provide the user of the financial statements with relevant, reliable and understandable information. Many would argue that the use of the fair value model for investment property does properly reflect the focus of the real estate sector on net asset performance. This view is reinforced by what appears to be the widespread, if not universal, use of the fair value model by investing entities. Perhaps, therefore, to the users of such financial statements it is of little consequence how the resulting fair value gain or loss is reported in the performance statements.

However, fair value accounting for such illiquid assets does require that users understand, both what mark-to-model asset valuations really are, and the implications in terms of liquidity and business performance of a fair value based profit or loss.

References

1 IAS 40, *Investment Property*, IASB, para. B4.
2 IAS 40, para. 5.
3 IAS 40, para. 5.
4 IAS 40, para. 4.
5 IAS 41, *Agriculture*, IASB, para. 12.
6 IAS 41, para. 2.
7 IAS 40, para. 6.
8 IAS 17, *Leases*, IASB, para. 18.
9 IAS 40, para. 7.
10 IAS 40, paras. 8-15.
11 IAS 40, para. 8.

12 IAS 40, para. 8.
13 IAS 40, para. 9.
14 IAS 40, para. 9.
15 IAS 40, para. 5.
16 IAS 40, para. 9.
17 IAS 40, para. 15.
18 IAS 40, para. 53B.
19 IAS 40, para. 53A.
20 IAS 40, para. 10.
21 IAS 40, para. 10.
22 IAS 40, para. 11.

23 IAS 40, para. 11.
24 IAS 40, paras. 12-13.
25 IAS 40, para. 14.
26 IAS 40, paras. 50(a) and (b).
27 IAS 40, para. 4(a).
28 IAS 40, para. 16.
29 IAS 40, para. 17.
30 IAS 40, para. 18.
31 IAS 40, para. 19.
32 IAS 40, para. 20.
33 IAS 40, para. 21.
34 IAS 40, para. 22.
35 IAS 16, *Property, Plant and Equipment*, IASB, para. 16(b).
36 IAS 40, para. 23.
37 IAS 40, para. 24.
38 IAS 40, para. 65.
39 IAS 40, para. 25.
40 IAS 17, para. 20.
41 IAS 40, para. 26.
42 IAS 40, para. 29.
43 IFRS 3, *Business Combinations*, IASB, para. BC148.
44 IAS 40, para. 30.
45 IAS 40, para. 31.
46 IAS 40, para. 32.
47 IAS 40, paras. 32A-32C.
48 IAS 40, paras. 33-35.
49 IAS 40, para. 34.
50 IAS 40, para. 5.
51 IAS 40, para. 36.
52 IAS 40, para. 37.
53 International Valuation Standards, General Valuation Concepts and Principles, Chapter 8.0.
54 IAS 40, paras. 38-39.
55 IAS 40, para. 40.
56 IAS 40, paras. 42-43.
57 IAS 40, para. 44.
58 IAS 40, para. 45.
59 IAS 40, para. 46.
60 IAS 40, para. 41.
61 IAS 40, para. 47.
62 IAS 40, para. 48.
63 IAS 40, para. 49.
64 IAS 40, para. 39.
65 IAS 40, para. 50.
66 IAS 40, para. 50.
67 IAS 40, para. 51.
68 IAS 40, para. 53.
69 IAS 40, para. 54.
70 IAS 40, para. 55.
71 IAS 40, para. 56.
72 IAS 16, para. 51.
73 IAS 40, para. 56.
74 IAS 40, para. 58.
75 IAS 40, para. 60.
76 IAS 40, para. 61.
77 IAS 40, para. 62.
78 IAS 40, para. 59.
79 IAS 17, para. 19.
80 IAS 40, paras. 66-67.
81 IAS 40, paras. 66-67.
82 IAS 40, para. 67.
83 IAS 40, para. 67.
84 IAS 18, *Revenue*, IASB, Appendix, para. 9.
85 IAS 40, para. 69.
86 IAS 40, para. 70.
87 IAS 40, para. 71.
88 IAS 40, para. 68.
89 IAS 40, para. 72.
90 IAS 40, para. 75.
91 IAS 40, para. 76.
92 IAS 40, para. 77.
93 IAS 40, para. 78.
94 IAS 40, para. 79.

Chapter 18   Impairment of fixed assets and goodwill

1   INTRODUCTION

In principle an asset is impaired when an entity will not be able to recover that asset's balance sheet carrying value, either through using it or selling it. The (then) IASC introduced IAS 36 – *Impairment of Assets* – in 1998 and it applied to periods beginning on or after 1 July 1999. At the time the point was made that writing down impaired assets is not in principle a new requirement, and prudence apart, in many jurisdictions provisions for diminution in value are required to be made for assets if a reduction in value is expected to be permanent.

The impairment provisions of IFRS are explicit and, to summarise, if circumstances arise which indicate assets might be impaired, a review should be undertaken of their cash generating abilities either through use or sale. This review will produce an amount which should be compared with the assets' carrying value, and if the carrying value is higher, the difference must be written off as an impairment adjustment in the income statement. The provisions within the standard that set out exactly how this is to be done, and how the figures involved are to be calculated, are detailed and quite complex. Therefore, as a preliminary introduction to the detail, the following section explains the theory underlying the type of impairment review adopted by the IASB in IAS 36.

2   THE THEORY BEHIND THE IMPAIRMENT REVIEW

The purpose of the review is to ensure that intangible and tangible assets, and goodwill are not carried at a figure greater than their *recoverable amount*. This recoverable amount is compared with the carrying value of the asset to determine if the asset is impaired. The definition of recoverable amount, therefore, is key. It is defined as the higher of *fair value less costs to sell* (FVLCS) and *value in use* (VIU); the underlying concept being that an asset should not be carried at more than the amount it will raise, either from selling it now or from using it in the future.

Fair value less costs to sell essentially means what the asset could be sold for, having deducted *costs of disposal* (incrementally incurred direct selling costs). *Value in use* is defined in terms of discounted future cash flows, as the present value of the cash flows expected from the future use and eventual sale of the asset at the end of its useful life. As the recoverable amount is to be expressed as a present value, not in actual terms, discounting is a central feature of the impairment test.

Diagrammatically, this comparison between carrying value and recoverable amount, and the definition of recoverable amount, can be portrayed as follows:

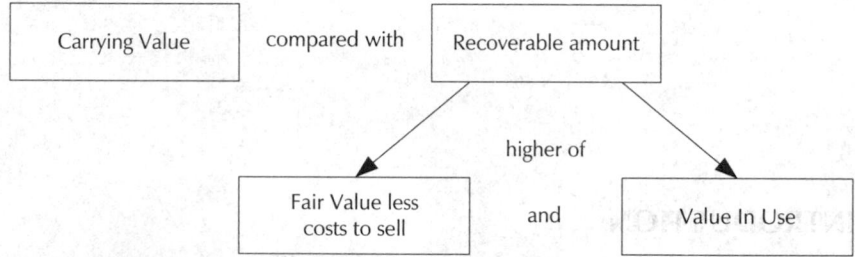

It may not always be necessary to identify both VIU and FVLCS, as if either of VIU or FVLCS is higher than the carrying amount then there is no impairment and no write-down is necessary. Thus, if FVLCS is greater than the carrying amount then no further consideration need be given to VIU, or to the need for an impairment write down. The more complex issues arise when the FVLCS is not greater than the carrying value, and so a VIU calculation is necessary. Typically for property plant and equipment used in manufacturing, this will be the case.

Although an impairment review might theoretically be conducted by looking at individual assets, this is likely to be a rare occurrence. It may not be possible to obtain reliable FVLCS estimates for all assets and some, such as goodwill or certain intangible assets, may not have a separate FVLCS at all. Even if FVLCSs can be obtained for individual items of property plant and equipment, estimates of VIUs usually cannot be. This is because the cash flows necessary for the VIU calculation are not usually generated by single assets, but by groups of assets being used together.

Often, therefore, the impairment review cannot be done at the level of the individual asset and it must be applied to a group of assets. IAS 36 uses the term *cash generating unit* (CGU) for the smallest identifiable group of assets that together have cash inflows that are largely independent of the cash inflows from other assets and that therefore can be the subject of a VIU calculation. CGU basically means a part of the business that generates income and which is largely independent of other parts of the business. This focus on the CGU is fundamental, as it has the effect of making the review essentially a business-value test, in as much as the assets of a business unit cannot usually be carried at an amount greater than the value of that business unit.

As it would be unduly onerous for all fixed assets and goodwill to be reviewed for impairment every year, IAS 36 in the main requires property, plant and equipment to be reviewed only if there is an indication that impairment may have occurred. If there are indications that the carrying amount of an asset may not be recoverable, a review for impairment should be carried out. The 'indications' of impairment may relate to either the assets themselves or to the economic environment in which they are operated. IAS 36 gives examples of indications of impairment, but makes it clear this is not an exhaustive list, and states explicitly that the entity may identify other indications that an asset is impaired, that would equally trigger an impairment review.[1]

The following section discusses in detail the individual provisions of IAS 36.

3   THE REQUIREMENTS OF IAS 36

3.1   Scope

IAS 36 was originally published in April 1998. A revised version of the standard was published in 2003 and amended variously in 2004, principally because of scope changes, as a result of the publication of IFRS 3 – *Business Combinations*, IFRS 4 – *Insurance Contracts*, IFRS 5 – *Non-current Assets Held for Sale and Discontinued Operations* – and as a result of the improvements project to existing standards, including IAS 38 – *Intangible Assets* – completed by the IASB in December 2003.

IAS 36 has since been amended, principally to take account of the following:

- The revised IFRS 3 ('IFRS 3 (as revised in 2008)'), which comes into force for accounting periods beginning on or after 1 July 2009 but may be applied early to accounting periods beginning on or after 30 June 2007. IFRS 3 (as revised in 2008) changes the way in which minority interests (now 'non-controlling interests') are calculated, with consequential effects on impairment testing in IAS 36 (see 3.4 below). Changes include a new Appendix C that describes the revised processes and replaces the paragraphs dealing with impairment and minority interests;

- The IASB has simultaneously revised IAS 27 – *Consolidated and Separate Financial Statements*[2]; changes affect the manner in which acquisitions of non-controlling interests are accounted for. It has also revised the 'cost' method that defined the carrying value of investments. The distinction between pre- and post-acquisition dividends has been removed. Instead there are circumstances in which receipt of a dividend from subsidiaries and jointly controlled entity triggers an impairment review. See further details in Chapter 8 and at 5.5.2 below;

- IFRS 8 – *Operating Segments* – issued by the IASB in November 2006, which replaces IAS 14 – *Segment Reporting* – and affects the allocation of goodwill. As from 1 January 2009 or such earlier date that the entity applies IFRS 8, goodwill to be tested for impairment cannot be allocated to a CGU or CGU group larger than an *operating* segment. This is dealt with at 5.6 below.

The objective of the standard is to ensure that assets are not carried at more than their recoverable amount (the principles underlying the term recoverable amount and other terms are explained in 2 above). If the carrying amount is higher than the amount estimated to be able to be recovered by use or sale of the asset, then the entity should recognise an impairment loss.[3]

The standard is a general impairment standard and its provisions are referred to in other standards, for example IAS 16 – *Property, Plant and Equipment*, IAS 38 and IFRS 3, where impairment is to be considered.

The standard has a general application to all assets, but the following are outside its scope: inventories, assets arising from construction contracts, deferred tax assets, assets arising from employee benefits, financial assets that are included in the scope of IAS 39 – *Financial Instruments: Recognition and Measurement,* investment property that is measured at fair value, biological assets under IAS 41 – *Agriculture* – deferred acquisition costs and intangible assets arising from an insurer's contractual rights under insurance contracts within the scope of IFRS 4, and non-current assets (or disposal groups) classified as held for sale in accordance with IFRS 5.[4] This, the standard states, is because these issues are subject to specific recognition and measurement rules.[5] The effect of these exclusions is to reduce the scope of IAS 36; however, it does not exempt investment properties not carried at fair value, oil and mineral exploration and evaluation assets or an entity's own shares held by a share trust. Investments in subsidiaries, jointly controlled entities and associates in the separate financial statements of the parent are within its scope[6], as are interests in jointly controlled entities and associates included in the consolidated accounts by way of the equity method.[7]

The standard applies to assets carried at revalued amounts, e.g. under IAS 16 (or rarely IAS 38) for two reasons. First, the only difference between fair value based on market value and fair value less costs to sell is the costs of disposal. Therefore, if these are not negligible, the entity may have to consider the asset's value in use. Second, in the absence of market values, the entity may have constructed a fair value using a technique acceptable under IAS 16 (see Chapter 16), in which case it would be quite possible for the asset to be impaired.[8] A specific example of a situation in which this might happen is if the asset is valued using depreciated replacement cost, a valuation method that often gives a higher valuation than one using market-based evidence.

3.2   When an impairment test is required

There is an important distinction in IAS 36 between assessing whether there are indications of impairment, and actually carrying out an impairment test. The standard has two different general requirements governing when an impairment test should be carried out:

- For all intangible assets with an indefinite life and goodwill (which as a result of the provisions of IFRS 3 will not be subject to systematic annual depreciation) the standard requires that an annual impairment test must be performed. The impairment test may be performed at any time in the annual reporting period, but it must be performed at the same time every year;[9]

    In addition, the carrying amount of an intangible asset that has not yet been brought into use must be tested at least annually. This, the standard argues, is because intangible assets are intrinsically subject to greater uncertainty before they are brought into use.[10]

- For all other classes of assets within the scope of IAS 36, the entity is required to assess at each balance sheet date whether there are any indications of impairment. Only if indications of impairment are present will the impairment test itself have to be carried out.[11]

The particular requirements of IAS 36 concerning the impairment testing of intangible assets with an indefinite life and goodwill are discussed separately at 3.4 and 3.5 below, however the methodology used is identical for all types of assets.

If indications of impairment exist, then an impairment test (i.e. a formal estimate of the asset's recoverable amount as set out in the standard) must be performed, unless there was sufficient headroom in a previous impairment calculation that would not have been eroded by subsequent events or the asset or CGU is not sensitive to a particular indicator; these exceptions are discussed further below.[12]

Normally however, if there are indications of impairment an impairment test must be undertaken.[13] Consequently the identification of indications of impairment becomes a crucial stage in the process.

IAS 36 lists examples of indicators but stresses that the examples represent the minimum indications that should be considered by the entity, and that the list is not exhaustive.[14] They are divided into external and internal indications as follows:

External sources of information:

(a)   a decline in an asset's market value during the period that is significantly more than would be expected from normal use;

(b)   significant adverse changes that have taken place during the period, or will take place in the near future, in the technological, market, economic or legal environment in which the entity operates or in the market to which an asset is dedicated;

(c)   an increase in the period in market interest rates or other market rates of return on investments if these increases are likely to affect the discount rate used in calculating an asset's value in use and decrease the asset's recoverable amount materially;

(d)   the carrying amount of the net assets of the entity exceeds its market capitalisation.

Internal sources of information:

(e)   evidence of obsolescence or physical damage of an asset;

(f)   significant changes in the extent to which, or manner in which, an asset is used or is expected to be used, that have taken place in the period or soon thereafter and that will have an adverse effect on it. These changes include the asset becoming idle, plans to dispose of an asset sooner than expected, reassessing its useful life as finite rather than indefinite or plans to restructure the operation to which the asset belongs;

(g)   internal reports that indicates that the economic performance of an asset is, or will be, worse than expected.[15]

The standard amplifies and explains what is relevant evidence from internal reporting that indicates that an asset may be impaired as follows:

(a)   cash flows for acquiring the asset, or subsequent cash needs for operating or maintaining it, are significantly higher than originally budgeted;

(b)   operating profit or loss or actual net cash flows are significantly worse than those budgeted;

(c)   a significant decline in budgeted net cash flows or operating profit, or a significant increase in budgeted loss; or

(d)   operating losses or net cash outflows for the asset, if current period amounts are aggregated with budgeted amounts for the future.[16]

The presence of indicators or impairment will not necessarily mean that the entity has to calculate the recoverable amount of the asset in accordance with IAS 36. A previous calculation may have shown that an asset's recoverable amount was significantly greater than its carrying amount and it may be clear that subsequent events have been insufficient to eliminate this headroom. Similarly, previous analysis may show that an asset's recoverable amount is not sensitive to one or more of these indicators.[17]

There are two particularly significant elements in this list of indications. The first is the inclusion of market capitalisation as an external indication of impairment. Market capitalisation is, potentially, a powerful indicator as, if it shows a lower figure than the book value of equity, it inescapably suggests the market considers that the business is overvalued. However, the market may have taken account of factors other than the return that the entity is generating on its assets. An individual entity may have a high level of debt that it is unable to service fully or a financial crisis may have led to a general collapse in market prices; a market capitalisation below equity will not necessarily be reflected in an equivalent impairment loss. What an entity has to do in response to this indicator depends very much on facts and circumstances. Most entities cannot avoid examining their CGUs in these circumstances and may have to test goodwill for impairment unless there was sufficient headroom in a previous impairment calculation that would not have been eroded by subsequent events or none of the assets or CGUs is sensitive to market capitalisation as an indicator.

The second significant element is an explicit reference in (b), (c) and (d) above to internal evidence that *future* performance will be worse than expected. Thus IAS 36 requires that an impairment review should be undertaken if performance is or will be significantly below that previously budgeted. In particular, there may be indicators of impairment even if the asset is profitable in the current period if budgeted results for the future indicate that there will be losses or net cash outflows when these are aggregated with the current period results.

Some of the indicators are aimed at individual fixed assets rather than the CGU of which they are a part, for example a decline in the market value of an asset or evidence that it is obsolete or damaged. However, they may also imply that a wider review of the business or CGU is required. For example, if there is a property slump and the market value of the entity's new head office falls below its carrying value this would constitute an indicator of impairment and trigger a review. At the level of the individual asset, as FVLCS is below carrying amount, this might indicate that a write-down is necessary. However, the building's recoverable amount may have to be considered in the context of a CGU of which it is a part and if it is, the recoverable amount will be based on VIU, not FVLCS. This is an example of a situation where it may not be necessary to re-estimate an asset's recoverable amount because it may be obvious that the CGU has suffered no impairment. In short, it may be irrelevant to the recoverable amount of the CGU that it contains a head office whose market value has fallen.

The inclusion of interest rates as an indicator of impairment could imply that assets are judged to be impaired if they are no longer expected to earn a market rate of return, even though they may generate the same cash flows as before. However, it may well be that an upward movement in general interest rates will not give rise to a write-down in assets because they may not affect the rate of return expected from the asset or CGU itself. The standard indicates that this may be another instance where the asset's recoverable amount is not sensitive to a particular indicator.

An entity is not required to make a formal estimate of an asset's recoverable amount if the discount rate used in calculating the asset's VIU is unlikely to be affected by the increase in market rates. The discount rate used in a VIU calculation should be based on the rate specific for the asset, and if the asset has a long remaining useful life this may not be materially affected by increases in short-term rates. Previous sensitivity analyses of the recoverable amount may show that it is unlikely that there will be a material decrease because future cash flows are also likely to increase to compensate. Consequently, the potential decrease in recoverable amount may simply be unlikely to be material.[18]

Events in the financial crisis of 2008/2009 demonstrated that the reverse may also be true. A substantial decline in short-term market interest rates did not lead to an equivalent decline in the market rates specific for the assets.

If there are indications that the asset is impaired, it may also be necessary to examine the remaining useful life of the asset, its residual value and the depreciation method used, as these may also need to be adjusted even if no impairment loss is recognised.[19]

3.3   The impairment test

IAS 36 defines VIU as the present value of the future cash flows expected to be derived from an asset or CGU and FVLCS as the amount obtainable from the sale of an asset or CGU in an arm's length transaction between knowledgeable, willing parties, less the costs of disposal.[20] The standard requires the carrying amount to be compared with the recoverable amount, which is the higher of VIU and FVLCS.[21] If either the FVLCS or the VIU is higher than the carrying amount, no further action is necessary as the asset is not impaired.[22]Recoverable amount is calculated for an individual asset, unless that asset does not generate cash inflows that are largely independent of those from other assets or groups of assets.[23]

Estimating the VIU of an asset involves estimating the future cash inflows and outflows that will be derived from the use of the asset and from its ultimate disposal, and discounting them at an appropriate rate.[24] There are complex issues involved in determining the cash flows and choosing a discount rate and often there is no agreed methodology to follow (refer to 3.3.2 below for a discussion of some of these difficulties).

It may be possible to estimate FVLCS even in the absence of an active market but if it cannot be estimated satisfactorily then the value of an asset must be based on its VIU.[25]

There are two practical points to emphasise. First, IAS 36 allows the use of estimates, averages and computational shortcuts to provide a reasonable approximation of FVLCS or VIU.[26] Second, if the FVLCS is greater than the asset's carrying value, no VIU calculation is necessary.

The standard describes circumstances in which it may be appropriate to use an asset or CGU's FVLCS without calculating its VIU, as the measure of its recoverable amount. There may be no significant difference between FVLCS and VIU, in which case the asset's FVLCS may be used as its recoverable amount. This is the case, for example, if management is intending to dispose of the asset or CGU, as apart from its disposal proceeds there will be few if any cash flows from further use.[27]

The asset may also be held for sale as defined by IFRS 5, by which stage it will be outside the scope of IAS 36, although IFRS 5 requires such assets to be measured immediately before their initial classification as held for sale 'in accordance with applicable IFRSs'.[28] A decision to sell is a triggering event for an impairment review, which means that any existing impairment will be recognised at the point of classification and not be rolled into the gain or loss on disposal of the asset. See Chapter 4 for a description of the subsequent measurement of the carrying amounts of the assets.

Clearly IFRS 5's requirement to test for impairment prior to redesignation is intended to avoid impairment losses being recognised as losses on disposal. However, one effect is that this rule may require the recognition of impairment losses on individual assets that form part of a single disposal group subsequently sold at a profit, as in the following example.

Example 18.1:   Impairment of assets held for sale

Entity A decided to sell a group of three assets in one transaction to the same acquirer. Each asset had been part of a different CGU. The decision to sell was made on 20 December 2009, just prior to Entity A's year end of 31 December. The assets met IFRS 5's requirements for classification as a disposal group on 10 January 2010.

The information about the carrying amounts and fair values less cost to sell of individual assets at 20 December 2009 and the disposal group on 10 January 2010 is summarised below. There was no change in the fair values of the assets between the two dates.

Asset	Carrying amount	FVLCS of separate assets	Aggregate of the lower of the carrying amount and FVLCS	Fair value of the group
	€	€	€	€
X	4,600	4,300	4,300	
Y	5,700	5,800	5,700	
Z	2,400	2,500	2,400	
Total	12,700	12,600	12,400	12,600

Although these assets were classified as held for sale subsequent to the year end, the decision to sell them was an indicator of impairment. Accordingly, it is necessary to determine whether the three assets together comprise a new CGU. If so, impairment would be assessed on the three assets together, prior to reclassification and remeasurement under IFRS 5.

If the three assets together do not comprise a CGU, they would have to be tested for impairment individually at the year end, which would result in an impairment loss on Asset X of €300. As there is no change in the recoverable amount between the year end and immediately before the classification under IFRS 5, the aggregate value of these assets prior to classification under IFRS 5 would be €12,400 (4,300 + 5,700 + 2,400). The fair value less costs to sell of the disposal group at the date of the first application of IFRS 5 (10 January 2005) is €12,600. Therefore according to the measurement criteria under IFRS 5 the carrying amount of the disposal group remains at €12,400 and the impairment loss previously recognised on Asset A would only be reversed, should the fair value less costs to sell of the disposal group exceed €12,600.

In different circumstances the requirement to take an impairment write down on reclassification may be far less clear-cut. Assets no longer form part of their original CGU once they have been designated for disposal. It is possible that a group of assets could comprise a new CGU if they are to be sold to a single purchaser as part of an arrangement. Their individual FVLCSs may be uncertain if they are sold as a parcel, as the seller receives aggregate proceeds for the group of assets (this could be the case whether the sale is of a CGU or a group of assets). There may be little separation in time between the decision to sell and designation as held for sale.

3.3.1   Fair value less costs to sell

The standard goes into detail regarding the estimation of an asset's FVLCS. The best evidence is the sales price of the asset in question, based on a binding sale agreement negotiated at arm's length, less incremental costs directly attributable to the sale.[29] If there is a binding sale agreement, the asset is either already classified as held for sale, in which case IFRS 5's measurement rules apply (see Chapter 4), or it is about to be reclassified and must be tested for impairment as described above.

If there is no binding sale agreement for the asset in question, but there is an active market for assets of this type, FVLCS may be estimated from current or recent bid prices. If there are no current bid prices, the price may be estimated from the most recent transaction provided there has been no significant change in economic circumstances in the intervening period.[30]

In reality there are few active markets for tangible and intangible assets, given that IFRSs define an active market as one in which all of the items traded are homogeneous, that has a constant supply of willing buyers and sellers and prices that are available to the public. Consequently, most estimates of fair value will be based on estimates of the market price of the asset in an arm's length transaction. This will involve consideration of the outcome of recent transactions for similar assets in the same industry. The entity will use the best information it has available at the balance sheet date to construct the price payable in an arm's length transaction between knowledgeable, willing parties.[31]

FVLCS does not reflect a forced sale unless the management is compelled to sell immediately.[32] In all cases, FVLCS should take account of estimated disposal costs. These include legal costs, stamp duty and other transaction taxes, costs of moving the asset and other direct incremental costs. Business reorganisation costs and employee termination costs (as defined in IAS 19 – *Employee Benefits* – see Chapter 28) may not be treated as costs of disposal.[33]

Although the approach to determining FVLCS is similar to that in the Exposure Draft – *Fair Value Measurement* – issued by the IASB in May 2009, it is not identical and it is not always clear how the analysis will apply to testing for impairment. These issues are described briefly at 5.4.2 below.

If the disposal of an asset would entail the buyer assuming a liability, then this liability should be deducted from the FVLCS in arriving at the relevant amount for determining the recoverable amount.[34] The obligation must also be taken into account in calculating the carrying value of the asset to enable a meaningful comparison.

3.3.2 Determining value in use (VIU)

IAS 36 requires the following elements to be reflected in the VIU calculation:

'(a) an estimate of the future cash flows the entity expects to derive from the asset;

(b) expectations about possible variations in the amount or timing of those future cash flows;

(c) the time value of money, represented by the current market risk-free rate of interest;

(d) the price for bearing the uncertainty inherent in the asset; and

(e) other factors, such as illiquidity, that market participants would reflect in pricing the future cash flows the entity expects to derive from the asset.'[35]

The calculation requires the entity to estimate the future cash flows and discount them at an appropriate rate.[36] It also requires uncertainty as to the timing of cash flows or the market's assessment of risk in those assets ((d) and (e) above) to be taken into account either by adjusting the cash flows or the discount rate. The intention is that the VIU should be the expected present value of those future cash flows.

If possible, recoverable amount is calculated for individual assets.[37]

If an impairment review has to be carried out then it will frequently be necessary to calculate the VIU of the CGU of which it is a part. This is because:

- the single asset may not generate sufficiently independent cash inflows[38], as is often the case; and

- in the case of the possible impairment of a single asset, FVLCS will frequently be lower than the carrying amount.

Where a CGU is being reviewed for impairment, this will involve calculation of the VIU of the CGU as a whole unless a reliable estimate of the CGU's FVLCS can be made. In general, the FVLCSs of CGUs are less reliable because CGUs are less homogeneous than individual assets and bought and sold far less often. If no such FVLCS is identifiable, or if it is below the total of the CGU's net assets, VIU will have to be calculated.

VIU calculations at the level of the CGU will thus be required when no satisfactory FVLCS is available or FVLCS is below the CGU's carrying amount and:

- goodwill is suspected of being impaired;

- a CGU itself is suspected of being impaired; or

- intangible assets or other fixed assets are suspected of being impaired and individual future cash flows cannot be identified for them.

The standard contains detailed requirements concerning the data to be assembled to calculate VIU that can best be explained and set out as a series of steps. These are set out in subsections 1 to 5 below that also contain a discussion of the practicalities and difficulties in determining the VIU of an asset. The steps in the process are:

Step 1: Dividing the entity into cash-generating units (CGUs)

Step 2: Identifying the carrying amount of CGU assets

Step 3: Estimating the future pre-tax cash flows of the CGU under review

Step 4: Identifying an appropriate discount rate and discounting the future cash flows

Step 5: Comparing carrying value with VIU and recognising impairment losses

Although this process describes the determination of the VIU of a CGU, steps 2 to 5 are the same as those that would be applied to an individual asset if it generated cash inflows independently of other assets.

Step 1   Dividing the entity into cash-generating units (CGUs)

If a calculation of VIU is required, one of the first tasks will be to identify the individual assets affected and if those assets do not have individually identifiable cash flows, divide the entity into CGUs i.e. groups of assets as defined at 3.3 above. The group of assets that is considered together should be as small as is reasonably practicable, i.e. the entity should be divided into as many CGUs as possible – an entity must identify the lowest aggregation of assets that generate largely independent cash inflows.[39]

Example 18.2:   Identification of CGUs and largely independent cash flows

An entity obtains a contract to deliver mail to all users within a region, for a price that depends solely on the weight of the item, regardless of the distance between sender and recipient. It makes a significant loss in deliveries to outlying regions. Because of the entity's service obligations, the CGU is the whole region covered by its mail services.

That said, the division should not go beyond the level at which each income stream is capable of being separately monitored and not beyond the point at which it would become necessary to start allocating direct costs between CGUs. For example, it may be difficult to identify a level below an individual factory as a CGU but of course an individual factory may or may not be a CGU. A practical approach to identifying CGUs involves two stages, the first being to work down to the smallest group of assets for which a stream of cash inflows can be identified. These groups of assets will be CGUs unless the performance of their cash inflow-generating assets are dependent on those generated by other assets, or *vice versa* their cash inflows are affected by those of other assets. If the cash inflows generated by the group of assets are not largely independent of those generated by other assets, the second stage is to add other assets to the group to form the smallest collection of assets that generates largely independent cash inflows. This approach might be characterised as a 'bottom-up' approach to identifying CGUs and is illustrated in Example 18.3 below. The existence of a degree of flexibility over what constitutes a CGU is obvious. Indeed, the standard acknowledges that the identification of CGUs involves judgement.[40] The key guidance offered by the standard is that CGU selection will be influenced by 'how management monitors the entity's operations (such as by product lines, businesses, individual locations, districts or regional areas) or how management makes decisions about continuing or disposing of the entity's assets and operations'.[41] While monitoring by management may help identify CGUs, it does not override the requirement that the identification of CGUs is based on largely independent cash *inflows*.

Example 18.3:   Identification of cash-generating units

Example A – newspapers

An entity publishes 10 suburban newspapers, each with a different mast-head, across 4 distinct regions within a major city. The price paid for a purchased mast-head is recognised as an intangible asset. The newspapers are distributed to residents free of charge. No newspaper is distributed outside its region. All of the revenue generated by each newspaper comes from advertising sales. An analysis of advertising sales shows that for each mast-head:

- Approximately 90% of sales come from advertisers purchasing 'bundled' advertisements that appear in all those newspapers published in one particular region of the city;

- Approximately 6% of sales come from advertisers purchasing 'bundled' advertisements that appear in all 10 newspapers in the major city; and

- Approximately 4% of sales come from advertisers purchasing advertisements that appear in one newspaper only.

What is the cash-generating unit for an individual mast-head?

Stage 1: Identify the smallest aggregation of assets for which a stream of cash inflows can be identified.

The fact that it is possible to use a pro-rata allocation basis to determine the cash inflows attributable to each newspaper means that each mast-head is likely to represent the smallest aggregation of assets for which a stream of cash inflows can be identified.

Stage 2: Are the cash inflows generated by an individual mast-head largely independent of those of other mast-heads and, conversely, is that individual mast-head affecting the cash inflows generated by other mast-heads?

As approximately 96% of cash inflows for each mast-head arise from 'bundled' advertising sales across multiple mast-heads, the cash inflows generated by an individual mast-head are not largely independent.

Therefore, the individual mast-heads would most likely need to be aggregated to form the smallest collection of assets that generates largely independent cash inflows. On the basis that approximately 90% of cash inflows for each mast-head arise from 'bundled' advertising sales across all of the newspapers published in a particular region, it is likely that those mast-heads published in one region will together form a cash-generating unit.

Example B – retail outlets

An entity has a chain of retail outlets located in the same country. The business model of the entity is highly integrated and the majority of the entity's revenue generating decisions, such as decisions about investments and monitoring of performance, are carried out at an entity level by the executive committee, with some decisions (such as product range and marketing) delegated to the regional or store levels. The majority of the operations, such as purchasing, are centralised. Management operates its business on a regional basis; but sales are monitored at the individual store level.

The outlets are usually bought and sold in packages of outlets that are subject to common economic characteristics e.g. outlets of similar size or location such as a shopping centre or city or region. Only in rare situations has the entity sold or closed down an individual outlet.

The determining factor for CGUs is the level at which largely independent cash inflows are generated, and not the manner in which the entity's operations are organised and monitored. The fact that operations and costs are managed centrally does not of itself affect the source and independence of the cash inflows. The interdependence of cash outflows is unlikely to be relevant to the identification of CGUs.

The key issue in deciding whether CGUs should be identified at the level of the individual store as opposed to a group of stores is whether, if a store is closed down, all the customers of that store would seek out another of the entity's stores such that there is no overall 'leakage' of custom from the store closure. In the highly likely event that all the customers would not do this, the individual stores are separate CGUs.

Example B above illustrates a very important point. Management may consider that the primary way in which they monitor their business is on a regional or segmental basis, but crucially, cash inflows are monitored at the level of an individual store and closure decisions are made at this level. In other cases it may be that the entity is capable of monitoring individual cash inflows from assets but this is not the most relevant feature in determining the composition of its CGUs.

Example 18.4:   Identification of cash-generating units – grouping of assets

A tour operator's hotels

A tour operator owns three hotels of a similar class near the beach at a large holiday resort. These hotels are advertised as alternatives in the operator's brochure, at the same price. Holidaymakers are frequently transferred from one to another and there is a central booking system for independent travellers. In this case, it may be that the hotels can be regarded as offering genuinely substitutable products by a sufficiently high proportion of potential guests and can be grouped together as a single cash-generating unit. Effectively, the hotels are being run as a single hotel on three sites. The entity will have to bear in mind that disposal decisions may still be made on a hotel-by-hotel basis and have to weight this appropriately in its determination of its CGUs.

The standard allows reasonable approximations and one way in which entities may apply this in practice is to group together assets that are separate CGUs, but which if considered individually for impairment would not be material. Retail outlets may be grouped on a geographical basis (e.g. all of the retail outlets in a city centre owned by a branded clothes retailer) because they are all subject to the same economic circumstances and individually will have an immaterial effect. However, the entity will still have to scrutinise the individual CGUs to ensure that those that it intends to sell or that have significantly underperformed the others with which they are grouped are identified and dealt with individually.

In practice different entities will inevitably have varying approaches to determining their CGUs. There is judgement to be exercised in determining an income stream and in determining whether it is largely independent of other streams. Given this, therefore, entities may tend towards larger rather than smaller CGUs, to keep the complexity of the process within reasonable bounds.

The standard stresses the significance of an active market for the output of an asset in identifying a CGU. An active market is a market in which the items traded within the market are homogeneous, willing buyers and sellers can normally be found at any time and prices are available to the public.[42] If there is an active market for the output produced by an asset or group of assets, the assets concerned are identified as a cash-generating unit, even if some or all of the output is used internally. If the cash inflows generated by the asset or CGU are based on internal transfer pricing, the best estimate of an external arm's length transaction price should be used in estimating the future cash flows to determine the asset's or CGU's VIU.[43] The reason given for this rule is that the existence of an active market means that the assets or CGU could generate cash inflows independently from the rest of the business by selling on the active market.[44]

There are active markets for many metals, energy products (various grades of oil product, natural gas) and other commodities that are freely traded.

Example A below, based on Example 1B in IAS 36's accompanying section of illustrative examples, illustrates the point. Example B describes circumstances in which the existence of an active market does not necessarily lead to the identification of a separate CGU.

Example 18.5:   *Identification of cash-generating units – internally-used products*

Example A – Plant for an Intermediate Step in a Production Process

A significant raw material used for plant Y's final production is an intermediate product bought from plant X of the same entity. X's products are sold to Y at a transfer price that passes all margins to X. 60 per cent of X's final production is sold to Y and the remaining 40 per cent is sold to customers outside of the entity. Y sells 80 per cent of its products to customers outside of the entity

If X can sell its products in an active market and generate cash inflows that are largely independent of the cash inflows from Y, it is likely that X is a CGU even though part of its production is used by Y. Therefore, its cash inflows can be regarded as being largely independent. It is likely that Y is also a separate CGU. However, internal transfer prices do not reflect market prices for X's output. Therefore, in determining value in use of both X and Y, the entity adjusts financial budgets/forecasts to reflect management's best estimate of future prices that could be achieved in arm's length transactions for those of X's products that are used internally.

If, on the other hand, there is no active market, it is likely that the recoverable amount of each plant cannot be assessed independently of the recoverable amount of the other plant. The majority of X's production is used internally and could not be sold in an active market. Cash inflows of X depend on demand for Y's products. Therefore, X cannot be considered to generate cash inflows that are largely independent of those of Y. In addition, the two plants are managed together. As a consequence, it is likely that X and Y together are the smallest group of assets that generates cash inflows that are largely independent.[45]

Example B – 'Market' for intermediate product not relevant to identification of a separate CGU

A vertically integrated operation located in Australia produces an intermediate product that is fully used internally to manufacture the end product. There is no active market for the intermediate product in Australia. The entity has only one other competitor in Australia, which is also vertically integrated and, likewise, uses the intermediate product internally. Both entities are, and have always been, very profitable when looking at their vertically integrated manufacturing processes to the end-stage product.

There is an active market for the intermediate product in China, but the prices at which the product can be sold are so low that a company based in Australia whose sole activity is to sell the intermediate product into China would never be profitable and a company would never set up manufacturing operations in Australia in order to sell into China.

Each of the Australian companies will occasionally sell small surpluses of their intermediate products into the active market in China, rather than make that product available to their competitor in Australia.

The existence of an active market for the intermediate product in China might suggest that the operations involved in it should be treated as a separate CGU. However, the mere existence of an active market somewhere in the world does not mean that the asset or CGU could realistically generate cash inflows independently from the rest of the business by selling on that active market. If such sales are a genuine incidental activity (i.e. if it is genuinely a case of obtaining some proceeds from excess product that would otherwise be scrapped), it may be appropriate not to regard that market as an active market for the intermediate product for IAS 36 purposes.

If the market is not regarded as an active market for IAS 36 purposes, the assets/operations involved in producing the intermediate product will not be treated as a separate CGU.

IAS 36 also requires that the identification of cash generating units shall be consistent from period to period unless the change is justified; if changes are made and the entity makes or reverses an impairment, disclosures are required.[46]

Assets held for resale cannot be subsumed within a larger CGU and their impairment should be judged solely by the cash flows expected to be generated by sale. Once they are classified as held for sale they will be accounted for in accordance with IFRS 5 and carried at an amount that may not exceed their FVLCS (see 3.3 above and Chapter 4 for a further discussion of IFRS 5's requirements).

Step 2   Identifying the carrying amount of CGU assets

The recoverable amount of a CGU is determined in the same way as for an individual asset and its carrying amount must be determined on a basis that is consistent with the way in which its recoverable amount is determined.[47]

The carrying amount of a CGU includes only those assets that can be attributed directly, or allocated on a reasonable and consistent basis. These must be the assets that will generate the future cash inflows used in determining the CGU's value in use. It does not include the carrying amount of any recognised liability, unless the recoverable amount of the cash-generating unit cannot be determined without taking it into account. Both FVLCS and VIU of a CGU are determined excluding cash flows that relate to assets that are not part of the cash-generating unit and liabilities that have been recognised.[48]

The standard emphasises the importance of completeness in the allocation of assets to CGUs. Every asset used in generating the cash flow being tested must be included in the CGU; otherwise an impaired CGU might appear to be unimpaired, as its carrying value would be understated by having missed out assets.[49]

There are exceptions allowed to the rule that recognised liabilities are not included in arriving at the CGU's carrying value or VIU. If the buyer would have to assume a liability if it acquired an asset, then this liability should be deducted from the CGU's carrying amount and VIU. This will enable a meaningful comparison between carrying amount and recoverable amount, whether the latter is based on FVLCS or VIU.[50]

For practical reasons the entity may determine the recoverable amount of a CGU after taking into account assets and liabilities such as receivables or other financial assets, trade payables, pensions and other provisions that are outside the scope of IAS 36.[51] If the cash flows of a CGU or its FVLCS are determined taking into account these sorts of items, then it is essential that cash flows and assets and liabilities within CGUs are prepared on a consistent basis. However, this frequently causes confusion in practice and it is discussed further at 5.7 below

Other assets such as goodwill and corporate assets may not be able to be attributed on a reasonable and consistent basis and the standard has separate rules regarding their treatment. Goodwill is dealt with separately at 3.4 below in detail.

I   Corporate assets

An entity may have assets that are inherently incapable of generating cash inflows independently, such as headquarters buildings or central IT facilities that contribute to more than one CGU. The characteristics that distinguish these corporate assets are that they do not generate cash inflows independently of other assets or groups of assets and their carrying amount cannot be fully attributed to the CGU under review.[52]

This presents a problem in the event of those assets showing indications of impairment. It also raises a question of what those indications might actually be, in the absence of cash inflows directly relating to this type of asset. Some, but not all, of these assets may have relatively easily determinable FVLCSs but while this is usually true of a headquarters building, it could not be said for a central IT facility. We have already noted in 3.2 above that a decline in market value of itself may not trigger a need for an impairment review if it is obvious that the CGUs of which corporate assets are a part are not showing any indications of impairment – unless, of course, management has decided to dispose of the asset. It is most likely that a corporate asset will show indications of impairment if the CGU or group of CGUs to which it relates are showing indications.

Therefore the corporate asset's carrying value has to be allocated to CGUs. This allocation allows the recoverable amount of all of the assets involved, both CGU and corporate ones, to be considered.[53]

If possible, the corporate assets are to be allocated to individual CGUs on a 'reasonable and consistent basis'.[54] This is not expanded upon and affords some flexibility, although plainly consistency is vital; the same criteria must be applied at all times. If the carrying value of a corporate asset can be allocated on a reasonable and consistent basis between individual CGUs, each CGU has its impairment test done separately and its carrying value includes its share of the corporate asset. If the corporate asset's carrying value cannot be allocated to an individual CGU, there are three steps. First the individual CGU is impairment tested and any impairment written off. Then a group of CGUs is identified to which, as a group, all or part of the carrying value of the corporate asset can be allocated. This group must include the individual CGU that was the subject of the first test. Finally, all CGUs in this group have to be tested to determine if the group's carrying value (including the allocation of the corporate asset's carrying value) is in excess of the group's VIU.[55] If it is not sufficient, the impairment loss will be allocated pro-rata to all assets in the group of CGUs and the allocated portion of the corporate asset, as described under 3.3.3 below.

In IAS 36's accompanying section of illustrative examples, Example 8 has a fully worked example of the allocation and calculation of a VIU involving corporate assets.[56] The table below is included in it, and serves to illustrate the allocation of the corporate asset to CGUs:

Example 18.6:   Allocation of corporate assets

An entity comprises three CGUs and a headquarters building. The carrying amount of the headquarters building of 150 is allocated to the carrying amount of each individual cash-generating unit. A weighted allocation basis is used because the estimated remaining useful life of A's cash-generating unit is 10 years, whereas the estimated remaining useful lives of B and C's cash-generating units are 20 years.

Schedule 1. Calculation of a weighted allocation of the carrying amount of the headquarter building

End of 20X0	A	B	C	Total
Carrying amount	100	150	200	450
Remaining useful life	10 years	20 years	20 years	
Weighting based on useful life	1	2	2	
Carrying amount after weighting	100	300	400	800
Pro-rata allocation of the building	(100/800)= 12%	(300/800)= 38%	(400/800)= 50%	100%
Allocation of the carrying amount of the building (based on pro-rata above)	19	56	75	(150)
Carrying amount (after allocation of the building)	119	206	275	600

The allocation need not be made on carrying value or financial measures such as turnover – employee numbers or a time basis might be a valid basis in certain circumstances.

One effect of this pro-rata process is that the amount of the head office allocated to each CGU will change as the useful lives and carrying values change. In the above example, the allocation of the head office to CGU A will be redistributed to CGUs B and C as A's remaining life shortens. The entity will have to ensure that B and C can support an increased head office allocation. Similar effects will be observed if the sizes of any other factor on which the allocation to the CGUs is made change relative to one another.

Step 3   Estimating the future pre-tax cash flows of the CGU under review

This step needs to be performed only if the CGU concerned either has no identifiable FVLCS, or a FVLCS that is lower than its carrying value. In order to calculate the VIU the entity needs to estimate the future cash flows that it will derive from its use and consider possible variations in their amount or timing.[57] In estimating future cash flows the entity must:

'(a)   base cash flow projections on reasonable and supportable assumptions that represent management's best estimate of the range of economic conditions that will exist over the remaining useful life of the asset. Greater weight shall be given to external evidence;

(b)   base cash flow projections on the most recent financial budgets/forecasts approved by management, but shall exclude any estimated future cash inflows or outflows expected to arise from future restructurings or from improving or enhancing the asset's performance. Projections based on these budgets/forecasts shall cover a maximum period of five years, unless a longer period can be justified;

(c)   estimate cash flow projections beyond the period covered by the most recent budgets/forecasts by extrapolating the projections based on the budgets/forecasts using a steady or declining growth rate for subsequent years, unless an increasing rate can be justified. This growth rate shall not exceed the long-term average growth rate for the products, industries, or country or countries in which the entity operates, or for the market in which the asset is used, unless a higher rate can be justified.'[58]

The standard describes in some detail the responsibilities of management towards the estimation of cash flows. Management are required to ensure that the assumptions on which its current cash flow projections are based are consistent with past actual outcomes by examining the causes of differences between past cash flow projections and actual cash flows. They can, of course, take account of the effects of subsequent events or circumstances that did not exist when those actual cash flows were generated.[59]

IAS 36 states that the cash flows should be based on the most recent budgets and forecasts for a maximum of five years because reliable forecasts are rarely available for a longer period. If management is confident that its projections are reliable and can demonstrate this from past experience, it may use a longer period.[60] In using budgets and forecasts, management is required to consider whether these really are the best estimate of economic conditions that will exist over the remaining useful life of the asset.[61] Cash flows for the period beyond that covered by the forecasts or budgets assume a steady, declining or even negative rate of growth. An increase in the rate may be used if it is supported by objective information.[62]

Therefore only in exceptional circumstances should an increasing growth rate be used, or should the period before a steady or declining growth rate is assumed extend to more than five years. This five year rule is based on general economic theory that postulates above-average growth rates will only be achievable in the short-term, because such above-average growth will lead to competitors entering the market. This increased competition will, over a period of time, lead to a reduction of the growth rate, towards the average for the economy as a whole. IAS 36 suggests that entities will find it difficult to exceed the average historical growth rate for the products, countries or markets over the long term, say twenty years.[63]

This stage of the impairment review illustrates the point that it is not only fixed assets that are being assessed. The future cash flow to be forecast is *all* cash flows – receipts from sales, purchases, administrative expenses, etc. It is akin to a free cash flow valuation of a business with the resulting valuation then being compared to the carrying value of the assets in the CGU.

The cash flow forecast should include three elements:

- cash inflows from the continuing use of the asset;
- the cash outflows necessary to generate these cash inflows, including cash outflows to prepare the asset for use, that can either be directly attributed, or allocated on a reasonable and consistent basis; and
- the net cash flows, if any, that the entity may receive or pay for the disposal of the asset at the end of its useful life.[64]

Cash flows can be estimated by taking into account general price changes caused by inflation, or on the basis of stable prices. If inflation is excluded from the cash flow then the discount rate selected must also be adjusted to remove the inflationary effect.[65] Generally entities will use whichever method is most convenient to them that is consistent with the method they use in their budgets and forecasts and it is, of course, fundamental that cash flows and discount rate are both estimated on a consistent basis.

To avoid the danger of double counting, the future cash flows exclude those relating to financial assets, including receivables and liabilities such as payables, pensions and provisions.[66] However, see Step 2 above: paragraph 79 allows the inclusion of such assets and liabilities for practical reasons in which case the cash flows must be reflected as well. See also 5.7 below for a discussion of some of the assets and liabilities that may or may not be reflected and the implications of so doing.

Projections in the cash flow should include costs of day-to-day servicing as well as overheads that can be reasonably attributed to the use of the asset.[67] Whilst a part-completed asset must have the costs to complete it included in the cash flow,[68] the general rule is that future cash flows should be forecast for CGUs or assets in their current condition. Forecasts should not include estimated future cash inflows or outflows that are expected to arise from improving or enhancing the asset's performance.[69]

While the restriction on enhanced performance may be understandable, it adds an element of unreality that is hard to reconcile with other assumptions made in the VIU process. For example, the underlying forecast cash flows that the standard makes the foundation of the procedure will obviously be based on the business as it is actually expected to develop in the future, growth, improvements and all. Producing a special forecast based on unrealistic assumptions, even for this limited purpose, may be difficult.

Nevertheless, paragraph 48 explicitly states that improvements to the current performance of an asset may not be included in the estimates of future cash flows until the expenditure that provides those improvements is incurred. The treatment of such expenditure is illustrated in Example 6 in the standard's accompanying section of illustrative examples.[70] The implication of this requirement is that if an asset is impaired, and even if the entity is going to make the future expenditure to reverse that impairment, the asset will still have to be written down. Subsequently, the asset's impairment can be reversed, to the degree appropriate, after the expenditure has taken place. Reversal of asset impairment is discussed at 3.6 below.

An assumption of new capital investment is in practice intrinsic to the VIU test. What has to be assessed is the future cash flows of a productive unit such as a factory or hotel. The cash flows, out into the far future, will include the sales of product, cost of sales, administrative expenses, etc. They must necessarily include capital expenditure as well, at least to the extent required to keep the CGU functioning as forecast. This is explicitly acknowledged as follows:

> 'Estimates of future cash flows include future cash outflows necessary to maintain the level of economic benefits expected to arise from the asset in its current condition. When a cash-generating unit consists of assets with different

estimated useful lives, all of which are essential to the ongoing operation of the unit, the replacement of assets with shorter lives is considered to be part of the day-to-day servicing of the unit when estimating the future cash flows associated with the unit. Similarly, when a single asset consists of components with different estimated useful lives, the replacement of components with shorter lives is considered to be part of the day-to-day servicing of the asset when estimating the future cash flows generated by the asset.'[71]

Accordingly, *some* capital expenditure cash flows must be built into the forecast cash flows. Whilst improving capital expenditure may not be recognised, routine or replacement capital expenditure necessary to maintain the function of the asset or assets in the CGU has to be included. This distinction may not be easy to draw in practice. Some of the practical difficulties in determining the amount of capital expenditure are described at 5.3 below.

The standard contains similar rules with regard to any future restructuring that may affect the VIU of the asset or CGU. The prohibition on including the results of restructuring applies only to those plans to which the entity is not committed. Again, this is because of the general rule that the cash flows must be based on the asset in its current condition and therefore future events that may change that condition are not to be taken into account.[72] When an entity becomes committed to a restructuring (as set out in IAS 37 – *Provisions, Contingent Assets and Contingent Liabilities* – see Chapter 24) IAS 36 then allows an entity's estimates of future cash inflows and outflows to reflect the cost savings and other benefits from the restructuring (based on the most recent financial budgets/forecasts approved by management).[73] Treatment of such a future restructuring is illustrated by Example 5 in the standard's accompanying section of illustrative examples. The standard specifically points out that the increase in cash inflows as a result of such a restructuring may not be taken into account until after the entity is committed to the restructuring.[74] Entities will sometimes be required to recognise impairment losses that will be reversed once the expenditure has been incurred and the restructuring completed.

The expected future cash flows of the CGU being assessed for impairment should not include cash inflows or outflows from financing activities or tax receipts or payments. This is because the discount rate used and the future cash flows are themselves determined on a pre-tax basis.[75]

In the case of long-lived assets, a large component of value attributable to an asset or CGU often arises from its terminal value, which is the net present value of all of the forecast free cash flows that are expected to be generated by the asset or CGU after the explicit forecast period. IAS 36 includes specific requirements if the asset is to be sold at the end of its useful life. The disposal proceeds and costs should be based on current prices and costs for similar assets, adjusted if necessary for price level changes if the entity has chosen to include this factor in its forecasts and selection of a discount rate. The entity must take care that its estimate is based on a proper assessment of the amount that would be received in an arm's length transaction.[76] However, CGUs usually have indefinite lives, as have some assets, and the terminal value is calculated by having regard to the forecast maintainable cash flows that are expected to be generated by the asset or CGU in the final year of the explicit forecast period ('the terminal year').

It is essential that the terminal year cash flows reflect maintainable cash flows as otherwise any material one-off or abnormal cash flows that are forecast for the terminal year will inappropriately increase or decrease the valuation.

The maintainable cash flow expected to be generated by the asset or CGU is then capitalised by a perpetuity factor based on either:

- the discount rate if cash flows are forecast to remain relatively constant; or
- the discount rate less the long term growth rate if cash flows are forecast to grow.

Care is required in assessing the growth rate to ensure consistency between the long term growth rate used and the assumptions used by the entity generally in its business planning.

Foreign currency cash flows should first be estimated in the currency in which they will be generated and then discounted using a discount rate appropriate for that currency. An entity should translate the present value calculated in the foreign currency using the spot exchange rate at the date of the value in use calculation.[77] This is to avoid the problems inherent in using forward exchange rates, which are based on differential interest rates. Using such a rate would result in double-counting the time value of money, first in the discount rate and then in the forward rate.[78] However, the method requires an entity to perform, in effect, separate impairment tests for cash flows generated in different currencies but make them consistent with one another so that the combined effect is meaningful, an extremely difficult exercise. Many different factors need to be taken into account including relative inflation rates and relative interest rates as well as appropriate discount rates for the currencies in question. Because of this, the possibility for error is great and the greatest danger is understating the present value of cash outflows by using too high a discount rate. In practice, valuers may assist entities to obtain a good enough result by assuming that cash flows are generated in a single currency even though they may be received or paid in another.

Significantly, this could well be a different rate from that used to translate the foreign currency assets, goodwill and liabilities of a subsidiary at the period end. For example, a non-monetary asset such as an item of property, plant and equipment may be carried at an amount based on exchange rates on the date on which it was acquired but generates foreign currency cash flows. In order to determine its carrying amount if there are indicators of impairment, IAS 21 – *The Effects of Changes in Foreign Exchange Rates* – states that the recoverable amount will be calculated in accordance with IAS 36, and the cash flows translated at the exchange rate at the date when that value was determined.[79] IAS 21 notes that this may be the rate at the balance sheet date. The VIU is then compared to the carrying value and the item is then carried forward at the lower of these two values. Similarly, different rates may be used if the impairment review is of goodwill or an intangible asset with indefinite life, where the review need not be carried out at the year-end.

Finally, although probably inherent in their identification, the forecast cash flows of the CGU have to be allocated to different periods for the purpose of the discounting step, discussed next.

Step 4   Identifying an appropriate discount rate and discounting the future cash flows

When the future cash flows have been estimated and allocated to different periods, the present value of these cash flows should then be calculated by discounting them. The discount rate is to be a pre-tax rate that reflects current market assessments of the time value of money and the risks specific to the asset for which the future cash flow estimates have not been adjusted.[80]

This means the discount rate to be applied should be an estimate of the rate that the market would expect on an equally risky investment. The standard states:

> 'A rate that reflects current market assessments of the time value of money and the risks specific to the asset is the return that investors would require if they were to choose an investment that would generate cash flows of amounts, timing and risk profile equivalent to those that the entity expects to derive from the asset.'[81]

Therefore, if at all possible, the rate is to be obtained from market transactions or market rates. It should be the rate implicit in current market transactions for similar assets or the weighted average cost of capital (WACC) of a listed entity that has a single asset (or a portfolio of assets) with similar service potential and risks to the asset under review.[82] If such a listed entity could be found, care would have to be taken in using its WACC as the standard specifies that the discount rate is independent of the entity's capital structure and the way it financed the purchase of the asset (see below). The effect of gearing and its effect on calculating an appropriate WACC are discussed further in Example 18.7 and there is more discussion on the use of the WACC in 5.1 below.

It is only in rare cases (e.g. property assets) that such market rates can be obtained. If an asset-specific rate not being available from the market, 'surrogates' should be used as set out in Appendix A of IAS 36. The discount rate that investors would require if they were to choose an investment that would generate cash flows of amounts, timing and risk profile equivalent to those that the entity expects to derive from the asset will not be easy to determine. IAS 36 suggests that, as a starting point, the entity may take into account the following rates:

(a)   the entity's weighted average cost of capital determined using techniques such as the Capital Asset Pricing Model;

(b)   the entity's incremental borrowing rate; and

(c)   other market borrowing rates.[83]

Appendix A also gives the following guidelines for selecting the appropriate discount rate:

- it should be adjusted to reflect the specific risks associated with the projected cash flows (such as country, currency, price and cash flow risks) and to exclude risks that are not relevant;[84]

- to avoid double counting, the discount rate does not reflect risks for which future cash flow estimates have been adjusted;[85]

- the discount rate is independent of the entity's capital structure and the way it financed the purchase of the asset;[86]

- if the basis for the rate is post-tax (such as a weighted average cost of capital), it is adjusted to reflect a pre-tax rate;[87] and

- normally the entity uses a single discount rate but it should use separate discount rates for different future periods if the VIU is sensitive to different risks for different periods or to the term structure of interest rates.[88]

The discount rate specific for the asset or CGU will take account of the period over which the asset or CGU is expected to generate cash inflows and it may not be sensitive to changes in short-term rates – this is discussed in 3.2 above.[89]

It is suggested that the incremental borrowing rate of the business is relevant to the selection of a discount rate. This could only be a starting point as the appropriate discount rate should be independent of the entity's capital structure or the way in which it financed the purchase of the asset. The incremental borrowing rate must be used with extreme caution as it might, for example, include an element of default risk for the entity as a whole, which is not relevant in assessing the return expected from the assets.

In practice many entities use the concept of the WACC to estimate the appropriate discount rate. The appropriate way to calculate WACC is an extremely technical subject, and one about which there is much academic literature and no general agreement. The selection of the rate is obviously a crucial part of the impairment testing process and in practice it will probably not be possible to obtain a theoretically perfect rate. The objective, therefore, must be to obtain a rate which is sensible and justifiable. There are probably a number of acceptable methods of arriving at the appropriate rate and one method is set out below. While this illustration may appear to be quite complex, it has been written at a fairly general level. In practice, the calculation of the appropriate discount rate may be extremely complex and specialist advice may be needed.[90]

Example 18.7:   Calculating a discount rate

This example is based on determining the WACC for a listed company with a similar risk profile to the CGU in question. Because it is highly unlikely that such a company will exist, it will usually have to be simulated by looking at a hypothetical company with a similar risk profile.

The following three elements need to be estimated for the hypothetical listed company with a similar risk profile:

- gearing, i.e. the ratio of market value of debt to market value of equity
- cost of debt; and
- cost of equity.

Gearing can best be obtained by reviewing quoted companies operating predominantly in the same industry as the CGU and identifying an average level of gearing for such companies. The companies need to be quoted so that the market value of equity can be readily determined.

Where companies in the sector typically have quoted debt, the cost of such debt can be determined directly. In order to calculate the cost of debt for bank loans and borrowings more generally, one method is to take the rate implicit in fixed interest government bonds – with a period to maturity similar to the expected life of the assets being reviewed for impairment – and to add to this rate a bank's margin, i.e. the commercial premium that would be added to the bond rate by a bank lending to the hypothetical listed company. In some cases, the margin being charged on existing borrowings to the company in question will provide evidence to help with establishing the bank's margin. Obviously, the appropriateness of this will depend upon the extent to which the risks facing the CGU being tested are similar to the risks facing the company or group as a whole.

If goodwill or intangible assets with an indefinite life were being included in a CGU reviewed for impairment (see 3.4 below) the appropriate Government bond rate to use might have to be adjusted towards that for irredeemable bonds. The additional bank's margin to add would be a matter for judgement but would vary according to the ease with which the sector under review was generally able to obtain bank finance and, as noted above, there might be evidence from the borrowings actually in place of the likely margin that would be chargeable. Sectors that invest significantly in tangible assets such as properties that are readily available as security for borrowings, would require a lower margin than other sectors where such security could not be found so easily.

Cost of equity is the hardest component of the cost of capital to determine. One technique referred to in the standard, frequently used in practice and written up in numerous textbooks is the 'Capital Asset Pricing Model' (CAPM). The theory underlying this model is that the cost of equity is equal to the risk-free rate plus a multiple, known as the beta, of the market risk premium. The risk-free rate is the same as that used to determine the nominal cost of debt and described above as being obtainable from government bond yields with an appropriate period to redemption. The market risk premium is the premium that investors require for investing in equities rather than government bonds. There are also reasons why this rate may be loaded in certain cases, for instance to take account of specific risks in the CGU in question that are not reflected in its market sector generally. Loadings are typically made when determining the cost of equity for a small company. The beta for a quoted company is a number that is greater or less than one according to whether market movements generally are reflected in a proportionately greater (beta more than one) or smaller (beta less than one) movement in the particular stock in question. Most betas fall into the range 0.4 to 1.5.

Various bodies, such as The London Business School, publish betas on a regular basis both for individual stocks and for industry sectors in general. Published betas are levered, i.e. they reflect the level of gearing in the company or sector concerned (although unlevered betas (based on risk as if financed with 100% equity) are also available and care must be taken not to confuse the two).

The cost of equity for the hypothetical company having a similar risk profile to the CGU is:

Cost of equity = risk-free rate + (levered beta × market risk premium)

Having determined the component costs of debt and equity and the appropriate level of gearing, the WACC for the hypothetical company having a similar risk profile to the CGU in question is:

$$\text{WACC} = (1 - t) \times D \times \frac{g}{(1 + g)} + E \times \left[1 - \frac{g}{(1 + g)} \right]$$

where:

D is the cost of debt;
E is the cost of equity
g is the gearing level (i.e. the ratio of debt to equity) for the sector; and
t is the rate of tax relief available on the debt servicing payments.

IAS 36 requires that the forecast cash flows are before tax and finance costs, though it is more common in discounted cash flow valuations to use cash flows after tax. However, as pre-tax cash flows are being used, the standard requires a pre-tax discount rate to be used.[91] This will theoretically involve discounting higher future cash flows (before deduction of tax) with a higher discount rate. This higher discount rate is the post-tax rate adjusted to reflect the specific amount and timing of the future tax flows. In other words, the pre-tax discount rate is the rate that gives the same present value when discounting the pre-tax cash flows as the post-tax cash flows discounted at the post-tax rate of return.[92]

Once the WACC has been calculated, the pre-tax WACC can be calculated. In those circumstances where a simple gross up is appropriate, it can be calculated by applying the fraction $1/(1-t)$. Thus, if the WACC comes out at, say, 10% the pre-tax WACC will be 10% divided by 0.7, if the relevant tax rate for the reporting entity is 30% , which will give a pre-tax rate of 14.3%.

However, the pre-tax discount rate may not be the post-tax rate grossed up by a standard rate of tax. It also depends on the timing of future tax cash flows and the useful life of the asset; these tax flows can be scheduled and an iterative process used to calculate the pre-tax discount rate.[93] The relationship between pre- and post-tax rates is discussed further in 5.1 below.

The selection of discount rates leaves considerable room for judgement in the absence of more specific guidance, and it is likely that many very different approaches will be applied in practice, even though this may not always be evident from the financial statements. However, once the discount rate has been chosen, the future cash flows are discounted in order to produce a present value figure representing the VIU of the CGU or individual asset that is the subject of the impairment test. The final step in the impairment review can now be taken.

Step 5 Comparing carrying value with VIU and recognising impairment losses

If the carrying value of an individual asset or of a CGU is less than (or equal to) its calculated VIU, there is no impairment. On the other hand, if the carrying value of the CGU is greater than its VIU and FVLCS, or the FVLCS cannot be calculated, an impairment write-down should be recognised. IAS 36 has rules on the allocation of impairment losses, depending upon whether an individual asset, an individual CGU, or a group of CGUs with goodwill or corporate assets allocated to the group as a whole, is involved. These aspects are discussed below.

3.3.3 *Recognition of impairment losses*

If the calculation of recoverable amount has produced an impairment loss, then IAS 36 sets out how such losses should be recognised. There are three scenarios, an impairment loss on an individual asset, an impairment loss on an individual CGU and an impairment loss on a group of CGUs. The last of these may occur where there are corporate assets (see 3.3.1 Step 2 above) or goodwill (see 3.4 below) that have been allocated to a group of CGUs rather than to individual ones.

A   *Impairment losses on individual assets*

For individual assets IAS 36 states:

> 'If, and only if, the recoverable amount of an asset is less than its carrying amount, the carrying amount of the asset shall be reduced to its recoverable amount. That reduction is an impairment loss.[94]
>
> An impairment loss shall be recognised immediately in profit or loss, unless the asset is carried at revalued amount in accordance with another Standard (for example, in accordance with the revaluation model in IAS 16). Any impairment loss of a revalued asset shall be treated as a revaluation decrease in accordance with that other Standard'[95]

If there is an impairment loss on a non-revalued asset it is recognised in profit or loss. However, an impairment loss on a revalued asset is first used to reduce the revaluation surplus for that asset. Only when the impairment loss exceeds the amount in the revaluation surplus for that same asset is any further impairment loss recognised in the profit and loss.[96] IAS 36 does not state a particular position in the income statement for impairment losses to be shown. Neither does it address whether any amounts written off a fixed asset should be treated as a deduction from the gross amount (cost or valuation) or as an increase in cumulative depreciation, in the reconciliation required by IAS 16 between the carrying amounts at the beginning and end of the year.[97] If the asset is carried at cost, we consider that it is more appropriate to carry an impairment write down within cumulative depreciation. If the asset is held at revalued amount then there is less of an issue and the impairment will be reflected in the revalued carrying amount.

An impairment loss greater than the carrying value of the asset does not give rise to a liability unless another standard requires it, presumably as this would be tantamount to providing for future losses.[98] An impairment loss will reduce the depreciable amount of an asset and the revised amount will be depreciated or amortised prospectively over the remaining life.[99] However, an entity ought also to review the useful life and residual value of its impaired asset, as both of these may need to be revised. The circumstances that give rise to impairments frequently affect these as well. Finally, an impairment loss will have implications for any deferred tax calculation involving the asset and in the standard's accompanying section of illustrative examples Example 3, on which the following is based, illustrates the possible effects.

Example 18.8:   Recognition of an impairment loss creates a deferred tax asset

An entity has an asset with a carrying amount of €2,000 whose recoverable amount is €1300. The tax rate is 30% and the tax base of the asset is €1,500. Impairment losses are not deductible for tax purposes. The effect of the impairment loss is as follows:

	Before impairment €	Effect of impairment €	After impairment €
Carrying amount	2,000	(700)	1,300
Tax base	1,500	–	1,500
Taxable (deductible) temporary difference	500	(700)	(200)
Deferred tax liability (asset) at 30%	150	(210)	(60)

The entity will recognise the deferred tax asset to the extent that it is probable that there will be available taxable profits against which the deductible temporary difference can be utilised.

B   Impairment losses and CGUs

Impairment losses in a CGU can occur in two ways:

(i)   an impairment loss is incurred in a CGU on its own, and that CGU may or may not have corporate assets or goodwill included in its carrying value;

(ii)   an impairment loss is identified that must be allocated across a group of CGUs because a corporate asset or goodwill is involved whose carrying value could only be allocated to a group of CGUs as a whole, rather than to individual ones (the allocation of corporate assets to CGUs is discussed in 3.3.1 Step 2 above, and goodwill is discussed at 3.4 below).

The relevant paragraphs from the standard deal with both instances but are readily understandable only if the above distinction is appreciated. The standard lays down that impairment losses in CGUs should be recognised to reduce the carrying amount of the assets of the unit (group of units) in the following order:

(a)   first, to reduce the carrying amount of any goodwill allocated to the CGU or group of units; and

(b)   if the goodwill has been written off, to reduce the other assets of the CGU (or group of CGUs) pro rata to their carrying amount.[100]

If there are indicators of impairment in connection with a CGU with which goodwill is associated, i.e. the CGU is part of a CGU group to which the goodwill is allocated, this CGU should be tested and any necessary impairment loss taken, before goodwill is tested for impairment (see 3.4.5 below).[101] These impairment losses and consequent reductions in carrying values are treated in exactly the same way as those for individual assets, in accordance with paragraph 60 of IAS 36, as explained above.

The important point is to be clear about the order set out above. Goodwill must be written down first, and if an impairment loss remains, the other assets in the CGU or group of CGUs are written down pro-rata to their carrying values. This pro-rating is in two stages if a group of CGUs is involved:

(i)   the loss is eliminated against goodwill (which by definition in this instance is unallocated to individual CGUs in the group);

(ii)   any remaining loss is pro-rated between the carrying values of the individual CGUs in the group; and

(iii) within each individual CGU the loss is again pro-rated between the individual assets' carrying values.

Unless it is possible to estimate the recoverable amount of each individual asset within a CGU, it is necessary to allocate impairment losses to individual assets in such a way that the revised carrying amounts of these assets correspond with the requirements of the standard. Therefore, the entity does not reduce the carrying amount of an individual asset below the highest of its FVLCS or VIU (if these can be established), or zero. The amount of the impairment loss that would otherwise have been allocated to the asset is then allocated pro-rata to the other assets of the CGU or CGU group.[102] The standard argues that this arbitrary allocation to individual assets when their recoverable amount cannot be individually assessed is appropriate because all assets of a CGU 'work together'.[103]

If corporate assets are allocated to a CGU or group of CGUs, then any remaining loss at (ii) above (i.e. after allocation to goodwill) is pro-rated against the allocated share of the corporate asset and the other assets in the CGU.

This process, then, writes down the carrying value attributed or allocated to a CGU until the carrying value of the net assets is equal to the computed VIU. It is logically possible, after all assets and goodwill are either written off or down to their FVLCS, for the carrying value of the CGU to be higher than the computed VIU. There is no suggestion that the net assets should be reduced any further because at this point the FVLCS would be the relevant impairment figure. The remaining amount will only be recognised as a liability if that is a requirement of another standard.[104]

IAS 36 includes in the standard's accompanying section of illustrative examples Example 2 which illustrates the calculation, recognition and allocation of an impairment loss across CGUs.

However, the standard stresses that no impairment loss should be reflected against an individual asset if the CGU to which it belongs has not been impaired, even if its carrying value exceeds its FVLCS. This is expanded in the following example, based on that in paragraph 107 of the standard:

Example 18.9:   Individually impaired assets within CGUs

A machine has suffered physical damage but is still working, although not as well as before it was damaged. The machine's FVLCS less costs to sell is less than its carrying amount. The machine does not generate independent cash inflows. The smallest identifiable group of assets that includes the machine and generates cash inflows that are largely independent of the cash inflows from other assets is the production line to which the machine belongs. The recoverable amount of the production line shows that the production line taken as a whole is not impaired.

Assumption 1: budgets/forecasts approved by management reflect no commitment of management to replace the machine.

The recoverable amount of the machine alone cannot be estimated because its VIU may be different from its FVLCS less costs to sell (because the entity is going to continue to use it) and can be determined only for the CGU to which it belongs (the production line).

As the production line is not impaired, no impairment loss is recognised for the machine. Nevertheless, the entity may need to reassess the depreciation period or the depreciation method for the machine. Perhaps a shorter depreciation period or a faster depreciation method is required to reflect the expected remaining useful life of the machine or the pattern in which economic benefits are expected to be consumed by the entity.

Assumption 2: budgets/forecasts approved by management reflect a commitment of management to replace the machine and sell it in the near future.

Cash flows from continuing use of the machine until its disposal are estimated to be negligible. The machine's VIU can be estimated to be close to its FVLCS less costs to sell. Therefore, the recoverable amount of the machine can be determined and no consideration is given to the CGU (the production line) to which it belongs. As the machine's carrying amount exceeds its FVLCS less costs to sell, an impairment loss is recognised to write it down to FVLCS less costs to sell.[105]

Note that it is assumed that the asset is still useable (otherwise it would not be contributing to the cash flows of the CGU and would have to be written off) and not held for sale as defined by IFRS 5, whose requirements are discussed further in Chapter 4.

3.4   Impairment of goodwill

With the publication of IFRS 3 came a change to the treatment of goodwill previously required by IFRS. Hitherto, entities were required to systematically depreciate goodwill, with a very strong presumption that its useful life would not exceed twenty years.

Since 1 January 2005, goodwill is subject to an annual impairment test instead of being systematically depreciated.[106] IAS 38 was amended at the same time so as to allow intangible assets to have indefinite useful lives. These are not depreciated, but, like goodwill, subject to an annual impairment test.[107] Intangible assets with finite useful lives must be depreciated systematically over their useful lives and are subject to impairment reviews when there are indications of impairment in the same way as any other asset within scope of IAS 36.

The impairment tests for goodwill and intangible assets with an indefinite life must be performed at least annually, but not necessarily at the end of the reporting period although an impairment test must be performed at the reporting date as well if there are indicators of impairment. This is in contrast to the impairment tests for other assets described in 3.2 and 3.3 above that are required only if there are indications of impairment, but which must be performed at the reporting date. The detailed requirements of IAS 36 concerning intangible assets with an indefinite life are discussed at 3.5 below.

3.4.1   Goodwill and its allocation to cash-generating units

The initial recognition and measurement of the goodwill acquired in a business combination is discussed in Chapter 9 at 2.6 (for business combinations accounted for under IFRS 3 (2007)) or at 3.7 (if the business combination falls under IFRS 3 (as revised in 2008)). (Note that a reference to 'IFRS 3' alone means that the requirement is the same in the standard's original or modified form.)

IFRS 3(2007) considers acquired goodwill to represent a payment made by an acquirer in anticipation of future economic benefits from assets that are not capable of being individually identified and separately recognised. IFRS 3(2007) requires that, after initial recognition, the acquirer measures acquired goodwill at cost less any accumulated impairment losses.[108] The acquirer has to test goodwill for impairment annually, or more frequently if events or changes in circumstances indicate that it might be impaired, in accordance with IAS 36.[109]

IFRS 3 (as revised in 2008) defines 'goodwill' in terms of its nature, rather than in terms of its measurement as 'an asset representing the future economic benefits arising from other assets acquired in a business combination that are not individually identified and separately recognised.'[110] The acquirer must recognise goodwill as an asset but as the direct measurement of goodwill is not possible, the standard requires that goodwill is measured as a residual.[111] IFRS 3 (as revised in 2008) merely states that the acquirer measures goodwill acquired in a business combination at the amount recognised at the acquisition date less any accumulated impairment losses and refers to IAS 36.[112]

An impairment test cannot be carried out on goodwill alone, as it does not generate cash flows independently of other assets. Testing goodwill for impairment necessitates its allocation to a cash-generating unit (CGU) of the acquirer or to a group of CGUs.

From the acquisition date acquired goodwill is to be allocated to each of the acquirer's CGUs, or to a group of CGUs, that are expected to benefit from the synergies of the combination. This is irrespective of whether other assets or liabilities of the acquiree are assigned to those CGUs or group of CGUs. The standard recognises that goodwill sometimes cannot be allocated on a non-arbitrary basis to an individual CGU, so permits it to be allocated to a group of CGUs. However, each CGU or group of CGUs to which the goodwill is so allocated must:

(a)   represent the lowest level within the entity at which the goodwill is monitored for internal management purposes; and

(b)   not be larger than an operating segment determined in accordance with IFRS 8.[113]

All CGUs or groups of CGUs to which goodwill has been allocated have to be tested for impairment on an annual basis.

The standard takes the view that applying the above requirements results in goodwill being tested for impairment at a level that reflects the way an entity manages its operations and with which the goodwill would naturally be associated. Therefore, the development of additional reporting systems is typically not necessary.[114] Only if an entity did not monitor goodwill at or below the segment level would it be necessary to develop new or additional reporting systems in order to comply with the standard.[115]

The replacement of IAS 14 by IFRS 8, issued by the IASB in November 2006, has changed the basis for identifying segments starting in financial statements from (at the latest) 1 January 2009 and may affect the allocation of goodwill. Under IAS 14 the segment level was based on either the entity's primary or secondary reporting under IAS 14 (see Chapter 35). Under IFRS 8 an 'operating segment' is identified on the basis of internal reports that are regularly reviewed by the entity's chief operating decision maker in order to allocate resources to the segment and assess its performance.[116] As a result, IAS 36 has been amended and as from 1 January 2009 (at the latest), goodwill to be tested for impairment cannot be allocated to a CGU or CGU group larger than an *operating* segment. IFRS 8 is discussed in Chapter 35.

As the adoption of IFRS 8 might result in a change in the identification of the entity's segments, some groups or entities will have to face the issue of validating the previous goodwill allocation to CGUs or group of CGUs or of reallocating goodwill to the new operating segments it has identified when performing the impairment test. This is discussed further at 5.6 below.

IAS 36 emphasises that a CGU to which goodwill is allocated for the purpose of impairment testing may not coincide with the level at which goodwill is allocated in accordance with IAS 21 for the purpose of measuring foreign currency gains and losses (see Chapter 13).[117] In many cases the allocation under IAS 21 will be at a lower level. This will apply not only on the acquisition of a multinational operation but could also apply on the acquisition of a single operation where the goodwill is allocated to a larger cash generating unit under IAS 36 that is made up of businesses with different functional currencies. However, IAS 36 clarifies that the entity is not required to test the goodwill for impairment at that same level unless it also monitors the goodwill at that level for internal management purposes.[118]

3.4.2   *Goodwill initially unallocated to cash-generating units*

IFRS 3 effectively requires the acquirer to complete the allocation of the cost of the business combination to the acquiree's assets, liabilities and contingent liabilities within a period of twelve months of the acquisition date.[119] See Chapter 9 at 2.8. Therefore, the initial accounting for a business combination may only been determined provisionally by the end of the period in which the combination is effected.

IFRS 3 (as revised in 2008) contains provisions in respect of a 'measurement period' which, although similar to those in IFRS 3(2007), are not identical. The measurement period is to provide the acquirer with a reasonable time to obtain the information necessary to identify and measure all of the various components of the business combination as of the acquisition date in accordance with the standard.[120]

The measurement period ends as soon as the acquirer receives the information it is seeking and is not to exceed one year from the acquisition date.[121]

IAS 36 recognises that in such circumstances, it might also not be possible to complete the initial allocation of the goodwill to a CGU or group of CGUs for impairment purposes before the end of the annual period in which the combination is effected.[122] Where this is the case, IAS 36 does not require a provisional allocation to be made, but the goodwill (or part of it) is left unallocated for that period. The standard requires disclosure of the amount of the unallocated goodwill together with an explanation as to why that is the case (see 4.2.2 below).

IFRS 3 allows an entity sufficient time to complete a fair value exercise and allocate goodwill to CGUs; this time may not exceed that required to obtain the information regarding circumstances as at the acquisition date. However, the entity may be able to make an allocation of goodwill as required by paragraph 81 on a provisional basis although it has not concluded its fair value exercise. While IAS 36 indicates that an entity might not be able to complete the initial allocation before the end of the annual period in which the combination is effect, it is quite possible that in some circumstances it may be able to do so. For example, in the following circumstances a provisional allocation of goodwill could be made:

- The entity might know that all goodwill relates to a single CGU or to a group of CGUs no larger than a single operating segment.

- The entity may know that the initial accounting for the combination is complete in all material respects, although some details remain to be finalised

If a provisional allocation can be make, that provisional goodwill is tested for impairment in accordance with IAS 36.

The initial allocation has to be completed before the end of the first annual period beginning after the acquisition date.[123] Note that this period differs from that allowed by IFRS 3 for finalisation of the allocation of the cost of the business combination and hence the initial measurement of goodwill, which is twelve months after the acquisition date. In the IASB's view, acquirers should be allowed time to complete the goodwill allocation after they have finished the initial accounting for the acquisition because that allocation might not be able to be performed until after the initial allocating is complete.[124] However, if an entity were to change its annual reporting date, it could mean that it is in fact a shorter period.

Example 18.10:   Impact of shortened accounting period

Entity A prepares its financial statements for annual periods ending on 31 December. It acquired Entity B on 30 September 2009. In accounting for this business combination in its financial statements for the year ended 31 December 2009, Entity A has only been able to determine the fair values to be assigned to Entity B's assets, liabilities and contingent liabilities on a provisional basis and has not allocated the resulting provisional amount of goodwill arising on the acquisition to any CGU (or group of CGUs). During 2010, Entity A changes its annual reporting date to June and is preparing its financial statements as at its new period end of 30 June 2010. IFRS 3 does not require the fair values assigned to Entity B's net assets (and therefore the initial amount of goodwill) to be finalised by that period end, since Entity A has until 30 September 2010 to finalise the values. However, IAS 36 would appear to require the allocation of the goodwill to CGUs for impairment purposes be completed by the date of those financial statements since these are for the first annual period beginning after the acquisition date, despite the fact that the initial accounting under IFRS 3 is not yet complete.

3.4.3   *Testing cash-generating units with goodwill for impairment*

IAS 36 requires a CGU or group of CGUs to which goodwill has been allocated to be tested for impairment annually by comparing the carrying amount of the CGU or group of CGUs, including the goodwill, with its recoverable amount.[125] The requirements of the standard in relation to the timing of such an annual impairment test (which need not be at the period end) are discussed at 3.4.4 below. This annual impairment test is not a substitute for management being aware of events occurring or circumstances changing between annual tests that might suggest that goodwill is impaired.[126] IAS 36 requires an entity to assess at each reporting date whether there is an indication that a CGU may be impaired.[127] So, whenever there is an indication that a CGU or group of CGUs to which goodwill has been allocated may be impaired it is to be tested for impairment by comparing the carrying amount, including the goodwill, with its recoverable amount.[128]

If the carrying amount of the CGU (or group of CGUs), including the goodwill, exceeds the recoverable amount of the CGU (or group of CGUs), then an impairment loss has to be recognised in accordance with paragraph 104 of the standard (see 3.3.3B above).[129]

3.4.4   *Timing of impairment tests*

IAS 36 requires an annual impairment test of CGUs or groups of CGUs to which goodwill has been allocated. The impairment test does not have to be carried out at the end of the reporting period. The standard permits the annual impairment test to be performed at any time during an annual period, provided the test is performed at the same time every year. Different CGUs may be tested for impairment at different times.

However, if some or all of the goodwill allocated to a CGU or group of CGUs was acquired in a business combination during the current annual period, that unit must be tested for impairment before the end of the current annual period.[130]

The IASB observed that acquirers can sometimes 'overpay' for an acquiree, so that the amount initially recognised for the business combination and the resulting goodwill exceeds the recoverable amount of the investment. The Board was concerned that without this requirement it might be possible for entities to delay recognising such an impairment loss until the annual period after the business combination.[131]

It has to be said that the wording of the requirement may not achieve that result, as the goodwill may not have been allocated to a CGU in the period in which the business combination occurs (see 3.4.1 above). Consider the following example.

Example 18.11:   Timing of annual impairment test of goodwill

Entity A prepares its financial statements for annual periods ending on 31 December. It carries out its annual impairment tests for all the CGUs to which it has allocated goodwill at the end of September. On 30 October 2009 Entity A acquires Entity B. In accounting for this business combination in its financial statements for the year ended 31 December 2009, Entity A has only been able to determine the fair values to be assigned to Entity B's assets, liabilities and contingent liabilities on a provisional basis because significant information is still outstanding and has not allocated the resulting provisional amount of goodwill arising on the acquisition to any CGU (or group of CGUs) as the synergies need to be considered carefully.

During 2010, as permitted by IFRS 3, Entity A does not finalise the fair values assigned to Entity B's net assets (and therefore the initial amount of goodwill) until 30 October 2010. Also, IAS 36 only requires Entity A to allocate the goodwill to CGUs by the end of the financial year. It does this in December.

In this case, at the time of carrying out its annual impairment tests at 30 September 2010, Entity A has not yet allocated the goodwill relating to Entity B, therefore no impairment test of that goodwill should be carried out at that time. When it does allocate the goodwill in December, the requirement to perform an impairment test for the CGUs to which this goodwill is allocated does not seem to be applicable since the goodwill does not relate to a business combination during the current annual period. It actually relates to a business combination in the previous period; it is just that it has only been allocated for impairment purposes in the current period. Nevertheless we believe that Entity A should perform an updated impairment test for the CGUs to which this goodwill is allocated for the purposes of its financial statements ended 31 December 2010 since this would seem to be the intention of the IASB. Not to do so, would mean that the impairment of this goodwill would not be tested until September 2011, nearly 2 years after the business combination.

3.4.5 Sequence of impairment tests for goodwill and other assets

When a CGU to which goodwill has been allocated is tested for impairment, there may also be an indication of impairment of an asset within the unit. IAS 36 requires the entity to test the asset for impairment first and recognise any impairment loss on it before carrying out the impairment test for the goodwill, although this is unlikely to have any practical impact as the assets within the CGU by definition will not generate separate cash flows. An entity will have to go through the same process if there is an indication of an impairment of a CGU within a group of CGUs containing the goodwill. The entity must test the CGU for impairment first, and recognise any impairment loss for that CGU, before testing the group of CGUs to which the goodwill is allocated.[132]

3.4.6 Carry forward of a previous impairment test calculation

IAS 36 permits the most recent detailed calculation of the recoverable amount of a CGU or group of CGUs to which goodwill has been allocated to be carried forward from a preceding period provided all of the following criteria are met:

(a) the assets and liabilities making up the CGU or group of CGUs have not changed significantly since the most recent recoverable amount calculation;

(b) the most recent recoverable amount calculation resulted in an amount that exceeded the carrying amount of the CGU or group of CGUs by a substantial margin; and

(c) based on an analysis of events that have occurred and circumstances that have changed since the most recent recoverable amount calculation, the likelihood that a current recoverable amount determination would be less than the current carrying amount of the CGU or group of CGUs is remote.[133]

The Basis for Conclusions indicates that the reason for this dispensation is to reduce the costs of applying the impairment test, without compromising its integrity.[134] However, clearly it is a matter of judgement as to whether each of the criteria is actually met.

3.4.7   *Reversal of impairment loss for goodwill prohibited*

Once an impairment loss has been recognised for goodwill, IAS 36 prohibits its reversal in a subsequent period.[135] The standard justifies this on the grounds that any reversal 'is likely to be an increase in internally generated goodwill, rather than a reversal of the impairment loss recognised for the acquired goodwill', and IAS 38 prohibits the recognition of internally generated goodwill.[136] The impairment test does not distinguish between purchased and internally generated goodwill,

3.4.8   *Non-controlling (minority) interests*

The amount of goodwill recorded by an entity when it acquires a controlling stake that is less than 100% of the equity in a subsidiary depends on whether the entity has accounted for the acquisition under IFRS 3 in its original form ('IFRS 3 (2007)') or IFRS 3 (as revised in 2008), which comes into force for accounting periods beginning on or after 1 July 2009 but may be applied early to accounting periods beginning on or after 30 June 2007.

Under the original standard, such goodwill represents only the goodwill acquired by a parent based on the parent's ownership interest, rather than the amount of goodwill controlled by the parent as a result of the business combination (see Chapter 9 at 2.6). Goodwill attributable to a minority interest is not recognised in the parent's consolidated financial statements as the minority interest is stated at its proportion of the net fair value of the acquiree. Accordingly, if there is a minority interest in a CGU to which goodwill has been allocated, the carrying amount of that CGU comprises:

(a)   both the parent's interest and the minority interest in the identifiable net assets of the CGU; and

(b)   the parent's interest in goodwill.

However, part of the recoverable amount of the CGU determined in accordance with IAS 36 is attributable to the minority interest in goodwill.[137]

IFRS 3(as revised in 2008) requires any non-controlling interest (as minority interests have been renamed) in an acquiree to be recognised,[138] but provides a choice of measurement methods; these are described in more detail in Chapter 9 at 3.9. The treatment under IFRS 3(2007) is retained but an entity may also choose to measure the non-controlling interest at its acquisition-date fair value, which means that its share of goodwill will also be recognised.[139]

The choice of method is to be made for each business combination, rather than being a policy choice, and could have a significant effect on the amount recognised for goodwill.

The IASB has noted that there are likely to be differences arising from measuring the non-controlling interest at its proportionate share of the acquiree's net identifiable assets, rather than at fair value. First, the amounts recognised in a business combination for the non-controlling interest and goodwill are likely to be lower (as illustrated in the example given in Chapter 9 at 3.9).

Second, if a CGU to which the goodwill has been allocated is subsequently impaired, any impairment of goodwill recognised through income is likely to be lower than it would have been if the non-controlling interest had been measured at fair value.

The IASB has amended IAS 36 to reflect the different treatments in IFRS 3 (as revised in 2008). Amendments have also been made to clarify the existing requirements of IAS 36 to reflect the fact that not all of the goodwill arising will necessarily be allocated to a CGU or group of CGUs which includes the subsidiary with the non-controlling interest[140] and guidance is given on the allocation of impairment losses:

(a)   If a subsidiary, or part of a subsidiary, with a non-controlling interest is itself a cash-generating unit, the impairment loss is allocated between the parent and the non-controlling interest on the same basis as that on which profit or loss is allocated;[141]

(b)   If it is part of a larger cash-generating unit, goodwill impairment losses are allocated to the parts of the cash-generating unit that have a non-controlling interest and the parts that do not. The impairment losses are allocated on the basis of:[142]

   (a)   to the extent that the impairment relates to goodwill in the cash-generating unit, the relative carrying values of the goodwill of the parts before the impairment; and

   (b)   to the extent that the impairment relates to identifiable assets in the cash-generating unit, the relative carrying values of the net identifiable assets of the parts before the impairment. Any such impairment is allocated to the assets of the parts of each unit pro-rata on the basis of the carrying amount of each asset in the part.

A   *Testing for impairment in entities with non-controlling (minority) interests measured at the proportionate share of net assets*

The same method applies whether the entity applies IFRS 3 in its original or modified form. To enable a like-for-like comparison, IAS 36 requires the carrying amount of a non-wholly-owned CGU to be notionally adjusted by grossing up the carrying amount of goodwill allocated to the CGU to include the amount attributable to the non-controlling (minority) interest. This notionally adjusted carrying amount is then compared with the recoverable amount. If there is an impairment, the entity allocates the impairment loss as usual, first reducing the carrying amount of goodwill allocated to the CGU (see 3.3.3B above).[143] However, because only the parent's goodwill is recognised, the impairment loss is apportioned between that attributable to the parent and that attributable to the non-controlling (minority) interest, with only the former being recognised.[144]

If any impairment loss remains, it is allocated in the usual way to the other assets of the CGU pro rata on the basis of the carrying amount of each asset in the CGU.[145]

These requirements are illustrated in the following example.[146]

Example 18.12:   A CGU with goodwill and non-controlling (minority) interest

Entity X acquires an 80 per cent ownership interest in Entity Y for €1,600 on 1 January 2009. At that date, Entity Y's identifiable net assets have a fair value of €1,500., Entity X recognises in its consolidated financial statements:

(a)   goodwill of €400, being the difference between the cost of the business combination of €1,600 and the non-controlling (minority) interest of €300 (20% of €1,500) and the identifiable net assets of Entity y of €1,500;

(b)   Entity Y's identifiable net assets at their fair value of €1,500; and

(c)   a non-controlling (minority) interest of €300.

At the end of 2009, the carrying amount of Entity Y's identifiable assets has reduced to €1,350 and Entity X determines that the recoverable amount of CGU Y is €1,000.

The carrying amount of CGU Y must be notionally adjusted to include goodwill attributable to the non-controlling interest, before being compared with the recoverable amount of €1,000. Goodwill attributable to Entity X's 80% interest in Entity Y at the acquisition date is €400. Therefore, goodwill notionally attributable to the 20% non-controlling (minority) interest in Entity Y at the acquisition date is €100, being €400 × 20/80.

Testing CGU Y for impairment at the end of 2009 gives rise to an impairment loss of €850 calculated as follows:

	Goodwill €	Identifiable net assets €	Total €
Carrying amount	400	1,350	1,750
Unrecognised non-controlling (minority) interest	100	–	100
Notionally adjusted carrying amount	500	1,350	1,850
Recoverable amount			1,000
Impairment loss			850

The impairment loss of €850 is allocated to the assets in the CGU by first reducing the carrying amount of goodwill to zero. Therefore, €500 of the €850 impairment loss for the CGU is allocated to the goodwill. However, because Entity X only recognises its 80% ownership interest in Entity Y, it recognises only 80 per cent of that goodwill impairment loss (i.e. €400). The remaining impairment loss of €350 is recognised by reducing the carrying amounts of Entity Y's identifiable assets, as follows:

	Goodwill €	Identifiable net assets €	Total €
Carrying amount	400	1,350	1,750
Impairment loss	(400)	(350)	(750)
Carrying amount after impairment loss	–	1,000	1,000

Of the impairment loss of €350 relating to Entity Y's identifiable assets, €70 (i.e. 20% thereof) would be attributed to the minority interest.

In this example the same result would have been achieved by just comparing the recoverable amount of €1,000 with the carrying amount of €1,750. However, what if the recoverable amount of the CGU had been greater than the carrying amount of the identifiable net assets prior to recognising the impairment loss?

Assume the same facts as above, except that at the end of 2009, Entity X determines that the recoverable amount of CGU Y is €1,400. In this case, testing CGU Y for impairment at the end of 2009 gives rise to an impairment loss of €450 calculated as follows:

	Goodwill €	Identifiable net assets €	Total €
Carrying amount	400	1,350	1,750
Unrecognised minority interest	100	–	100
Notionally adjusted carrying amount	500	1,350	1,850
Recoverable amount			1,400
Impairment loss			450

All of the impairment loss of €450 is allocated to the goodwill. However, Entity X recognises only 80 per cent of that goodwill impairment loss (i.e. €360). This allocation of the impairment loss results in the following carrying amounts for CGU Y in the financial statements of Entity X at the end of 2009.

	Goodwill €	Identifiable net assets €	Total €
Carrying amount	400	1,350	1,750
Impairment loss	(360)	–	(360)
Carrying amount after impairment loss	40	1,350	1,390

Of the impairment loss of €360, none of it is attributable to the non-controlling (minority) interest since it all relates to the majority shareholder's goodwill.

In this case the total carrying amount of the identifiable net assets and the goodwill has not been reduced to the recoverable amount of €1,400, but is actually less than the recoverable amount. This is because the recoverable amount of goodwill relating to the non-controlling (minority) interest (20% of [€500 – €450]) is not recognised in the consolidated financial statements.

B Testing for impairment in entities with non-controlling interests initially measured at fair value

The following example in which non-controlling interest is initially measured at fair value, is based on the new Examples 7B and 7C and illustrate the revised requirements.

Example 18.13: Non-controlling interests measured initially at fair value

Entity X acquires an 80 per cent ownership interest in Entity Y for €2,100 on 1 January 2009. At that date, Entity Y's identifiable net assets have a fair value of €1,500. Entity X chooses to measure the non-controlling interests at its fair value of €350. Goodwill is €950, which is the aggregate of the consideration transferred and the amount of the non-controlling interests (€2,100 + €350) and the net identifiable assets (€1,500).

(a) the acquired subsidiary is a stand-alone CGU

Entity Y is a CGU but part of the goodwill is allocated to other of Entity X's CGUs that are expected to benefit from the synergies of the combination. Goodwill of €450 is allocated to the Entity Y CGU and €500 to the other CGUs.

At the end of 2009, the carrying amount of Entity Y's identifiable assets excluding goodwill has reduced to €1,350 and Entity X determines that the recoverable amount of CGU Y is €1,650.

	Goodwill €	Identifiable net assets €	Total €
Carrying amount	450	1,350	1,800
Recoverable amount			1,650
Impairment loss			150

Of the goodwill impairment loss of €150, €30 (20%) will be allocated to the non-controlling interest because the goodwill is allocated to the controlling interest and non-controlling interest on the same basis as profit or loss.

(b) the acquired subsidiary is part of a larger CGU

Entity Y becomes part of a larger CGU, Z. As before, €500 of the goodwill is allocated to other of Entity X's CGUs that are expected to benefit from the synergies of the combination. Goodwill of €450 is allocated to Z. Z's goodwill related to previous business combinations is €800.

At the end of 2009, Parent determines that the recoverable amount of the Z CGU is €3,300. The carrying amount of its net assets excluding goodwill is €2,250.

	Goodwill €	Identifiable net assets €	Total €
Carrying amount	1,250	2,250	3,500
Recoverable amount			3,300
Impairment loss			200

All of the impairment loss of €200 is allocated to the goodwill. As the partially-owned subsidiary forms part of a larger CGU, the goodwill impairment loss must be allocated first to the parts of the cash-generating unit, Z, and then to the controlling and non-controlling interests of Entity Y.

The impairment loss is allocated on the basis of the relative carrying values of the goodwill of the parts before the impairment. Entity Y is allocated 36% of the impairment (450/1,250), in this case €72, of which €14.40 (20%) will be allocated to the non-controlling interest.

3.4.9 Disposal of operation within a cash-generating unit to which goodwill has been allocated

If goodwill has been allocated to a CGU (or a group of CGUs) and the entity disposes of an operation within that CGU, IAS 36 requires that the goodwill associated with the operation disposed of is included in the carrying amount of the operation when determining the gain or loss on disposal. For that purpose, the standard requires that the amount to be included is measured on the basis of the relative values of the operation disposed of and the portion of the CGU retained, unless the entity can demonstrate that some other method better reflects the goodwill associated with the operation disposed of.[147]

Example 18.14: Goodwill attributable to the disposal of an operation based on relative values

An entity sells for €100 an operation that was part of a CGU to which goodwill of €60 has been allocated. The goodwill allocated to the CGU cannot be identified or associated with an asset group at a level lower than that CGU, except arbitrarily. The recoverable amount of the portion of the CGU retained is €300. Because the goodwill allocated to the CGU cannot be non-arbitrarily identified or associated with an asset group at a level lower than that CGU, the goodwill associated with the operation disposed of is measured on the basis of the relative values of the operation disposed of and the portion of the CGU retained. Therefore, 25 per cent of the goodwill allocated to the CGU, i.e. €15 is included in the carrying amount of the operation that is sold.

The standard refers to the 'relative values' of the parts without specifying how these are to be calculated. The recoverable amount of the part that it has retained will be based on the principles of IAS 36, i.e. at the higher of FVLCS and VIU. This means that the VIU or FVLCS of the part retained may have to be calculated as part of the allocation exercise on disposal.

In addition, the VIU and FVLCS of the part disposed of will be materially the same. This is because the VIU will consist mainly of the net disposal proceeds; it cannot be based on the assumption that the sale would not take place.

It will not necessarily follow, for example, that the business disposed of generated 25% of the net cash flows of the combined CGU. Therefore, the method advocated by the standard to be applied in most circumstances may be based on a mismatch in the valuation bases used on the different parts of the business, reflecting the purchaser's assessment of the value of the part disposed of at the point of sale rather than that of the vendor at purchase.

The standard allows the use of some other method if it better reflects the goodwill associated with the part disposed of. The IASB had in mind a scenario in which an entity buys a business, integrates it with an existing CGU that does not include any goodwill in its carrying amount and immediately sells a loss-making part of the combined CGU. It is accepted that in these circumstances it may be reasonable to conclude that no part of the carrying amount of the goodwill has been disposed of.[148] The loss-making business being disposed of could, of course, have been owned by the entity before the acquisition or it could be part of the acquired business.

Where the operation disposed of is a foreign operation for the purposes of IAS 21, another possibility might be to use the goodwill allocated to that foreign operation for the purpose of measuring foreign currency gains and losses (see Chapter 13), particularly as the exchange gains and losses on that amount of goodwill will also be taken to profit or loss on disposal of that foreign operation (see Chapter 13). Even then, this might only be a better method if there has been no previous impairments recognised in respect of goodwill allocated to the CGU including that foreign operation since it was acquired.

One has to bear in mind that any basis of allocation of goodwill on disposal other than that recommended by the standard could be an indication that goodwill should have been allocated on a different basis on acquisition, i.e. there may have been some basis of allocating goodwill within a CGU group that was not arbitrary.

3.4.10 Changes in composition of cash-generating units

If an entity reorganises its reporting structure in a way that changes the composition of one or more CGUs to which goodwill has been allocated, IAS 36 requires that the goodwill be reallocated to the units affected. For this purpose, the standard requires the reallocation to be performed using a relative value approach similar to that discussed at 3.4.9 above when an entity disposes of an operation within a CGU, unless the entity can demonstrate that some other method better reflects the goodwill associated with the reorganised units.[149]

Example 18.15:   Reallocation of goodwill to CGUs based on relative values

Goodwill of €160 had previously been allocated to CGU A. A is to be divided and integrated into three other CGUs, B, C and D. Because the goodwill allocated to A cannot be non-arbitrarily identified or associated with an asset group at a level lower than A, it is reallocated to CGUs B, C and D on the basis of the relative values of the three portions of A before those portions are integrated with B, C and D. The recoverable amounts of these portions of A before integration with the other CGUs are €200, €300 and €500 respectively. Accordingly, the amounts of goodwill reallocated to CGUs B, C and D are €32, €48 and €80 respectively.

Again, the standard gives no indication as to what other methods might better reflect the goodwill associated with the reorganised units.

As in the case of a disposal, the recoverable amount of the CGUs will be based on the principles of IAS 36, so it will often be necessary to assess the VIU or FVLCS of all of the CGUs to which the goodwill is to be allocated.

In practice, situations may be considerably more complex than Examples 18.14 and 18.15 above. Elements of both may arise following an acquisition whereby there are disposals of acquired businesses, reorganisations and integrations. The entity may sell some parts of its acquired business immediately but may also use the acquisition in order to replace part of its existing capacity, disposing of existing elements. In addition, groups frequently undertake reorganisations of their statutory entities. It is often the case that CGUs do not correspond to these individual entities and the reorganisations may be undertaken for taxation reasons so the ownership structure within a group may not correspond to its CGUs. This makes it clear how important it is that entities identify their CGUs and the allocation of goodwill to them, so that they already have a basis for making any necessary allocations when an impairment issue arises or there is a disposal.

3.5 Impairment of intangible assets with an indefinite useful life

IAS 38 makes the point that 'indefinite' does not mean 'infinite', and unforeseeable factors may affect the entity's ability and intention to maintain the asset at its standard of performance assessed at the time of estimating the asset's useful life.[150] The requirements of IAS 36 for this type of asset can be summarised as follows:

1. All intangible assets with indefinite useful lives must be tested for impairment at least once per year and at the same time each year;[151]

2. Any intangible asset with an indefinite useful life recognised during the reporting period must be tested for impairment before the end of the period;[152]

3. Any intangible asset (regardless of whether it has an indefinite useful life or not) *that is not yet available for use* recognised during the reporting period must be tested for impairment before the end of the period;[153]

4. If an intangible asset that has an indefinite useful life or is not yet available for use can only be tested for impairment as part of a CGU, then that CGU must be tested for impairment at least annually;[154]

5. If there are indicators of impairment a period end test must also be performed;[155] and

6. For an intangible asset that has an indefinite useful life that is part of a CGU, there are specific concessions, discussed below, allowing an impairment test in a previous period to be used if that test showed sufficient headroom.[156]

Any intangible asset not yet ready for use must be tested annually because its ability to generate sufficient future economic benefits to recover its carrying amount is usually subject to greater uncertainty before the asset is available for use than after it is available for use.[157]

This will obviously have a major impact on any entity that capitalises development expenditure in accordance with IAS 38 where the period of development may straddle more than one accounting period.

An intangible asset with an indefinite useful life may generate independent cash inflows as an individual asset, in which case the impairment testing procedure for a single asset as set out in 3.2 and 3.3 above applies. Additionally an intangible asset may form part of the assets within a CGU, in which case the procedures relevant to testing a CGU as set out above apply. In particular IAS 36 makes it clear that if an intangible asset with an indefinite useful life, or any intangible asset not yet ready for use, is included in the assets of a CGU, then that CGU has to be tested for impairment annually.[158]

However, IAS 36 allows a concession that only applies to those intangible assets with an indefinite useful life that form part of a CGU. It allows the most recent detailed calculation of such an asset's recoverable amount made in a preceding period to be used in the impairment test in the current period if all of the following criteria are met:

(a) if the intangible asset is part of a CGU and the assets and liabilities making up that unit have not changed significantly since the most recent recoverable amount calculation;

(b) that calculation of the asset's recoverable amount exceeded its carrying amount by a substantial margin; and

(c) the likelihood that an updated calculation of the recoverable amount would be less than the asset's carrying amount is remote, based on an analysis of events and circumstances since the most recent calculation of the recoverable amount.[159]

Thus if there was sufficient headroom on the last calculation and little has changed in the CGU to which the asset belongs, it can be revisited and re-used rather than having to be entirely restarted from scratch, which considerably reduces the work involved in the annual test. The impairment test cannot be rolled forward forever, of course, and an entity will have to take a cautious approach to estimating when circumstances have changed sufficiently to require a new test.

Impairment losses experienced on intangible assets with an indefinite useful life are recognised exactly as set out above in 3.3.3, either as an individual asset or as part of a CGU, depending upon whether the intangible concerned is part of a CGU or not. Note that there is an important distinction concerning the allocation of losses in a CGU between the treatment of goodwill and intangible assets with an indefinite useful life. As set out above in 3.3.3, if goodwill forms part of the assets of a CGU, any impairment loss first reduces the goodwill and thereafter the remaining assets are reduced pro-rata. However, if an intangible asset is part of a CGU that is impaired, there is no requirement to write down the intangible before the other assets in the CGU, rather all assets are written down pro-rata.

3.6   Reversing impairment losses

IAS 36 does not permit an impairment loss on goodwill to be reversed under any circumstances.[160] The standard justifies this on the grounds that such a reversal would probably be an increase in internally generated goodwill, rather than a reversal of the impairment loss recognised for the acquired goodwill, and that internally generated goodwill is prohibited by IAS 38.[161]

Example 18.16:   Impairment of goodwill

Company A has a CGU that has a carrying value of $2,000,000 at 31 December 2009. This carrying value comprises $500,000 relating to goodwill and $1,500,000 relating to net tangible assets.

In 2010, as a result of losses, net tangible assets have decreased to $1,400,000 reducing the total carrying value of the unit to $1,900,000. Changes in the regulatory framework surrounding its business mean that the income-generating unit has a recoverable amount of $1,600,000 and has thus suffered an impairment loss of $300,000. This is charged to the profit and loss account. The carrying value of goodwill is reduced to $200,000.

In 2011 the company develops a new product with the result that the recoverable amount of the income-generating unit rises to $1,700,000. Net tangible assets have remained at $1,400,000. Despite the recoverable amount of the business unit now being $1,700,000 compared to its carrying value of $1,600,000, it is not possible to reverse $100,000 of the prior year's impairment loss of $300,000 since the reason for the increase in value of the business unit (the launch of the new product) is not the same as the reason for the original impairment loss (the change in the regulatory environment in which the business operates).

For all other assets, including intangible assets with an indefinite life, IAS 36 requires entities to assess at each reporting date whether there is any indication that an impairment loss may no longer exist or may have decreased. If there is any such indication, the entity has to recalculate the recoverable amount of the asset.[162]

Therefore if there are indications that a previously recognised impairment loss has disappeared or reduced, it is necessary to determine again the recoverable amount (i.e.

the higher of FVLCS or VIU) so that the reversal can be quantified. The standard sets out examples of what it notes are in effect 'reverse indications' of impairment.[163] These are the reverse of those set out in paragraph 12 of the standard as indications of impairment (see 3.2 above) and are, as in paragraph 12, in two categories:

External sources of information:

(a)   a significant increase in the asset's market value;

(b)   significant changes during the period or expected in the near future in the entity's technological, market, economic or legal environment that will have a favourable effect;

(c)   decreases in market interest rates or other market rates of return on investments and those decreases are likely to affect the discount rate used in calculating the asset's value in use and increase the asset's recoverable amount materially.

Internal sources of information:

(d)   significant changes during the period or expected in the near future that will affect the extent to which, or manner in which, the asset is used. These changes include costs incurred during the period to improve or enhance the asset's performance or restructure the operation to which the asset belongs;

(e)   evidence from internal reporting that the economic performance of the asset is, or will be, better than expected.[164]

Compared with paragraph 12, there are two notable omissions from this list of 'reverse indicators', one external and one internal.

The external indication not included is the mirror of the impairment indicator 'the carrying amount of the net assets of the reporting entity is more than its market capitalisation'. No explanation is provided as to why, if a market capitalisation below shareholders' funds is an indication of impairment, its reversal should not automatically be an indication of a reversal. However, the most likely reason is that all of the facts and circumstances need to be considered before assuming that an impairment has reversed. Deficits below market capitalisation may, in any event, affect goodwill so the impairment charge cannot be reversed.

The internal omission from the list of 'reverse indicators' is that evidence of obsolescence or physical deterioration has been reversed. Once again no reason is given. It may be that the standard-setters have assumed that no such reversal could take place without the entity incurring costs to improve or enhance the performance of the asset or the CGU so that this is, in effect, covered by indicator (d) above.

The standard also reminds preparers that a reversal, like an impairment, is evidence that the depreciation method or residual value of the asset should be reviewed and may need to be adjusted, whether or not the impairment loss is reversed.[165]

A further restriction is that impairment losses should be reversed only if there has been a change in the estimates used to determine the impairment loss, e.g. a change in cash flows or discount rate (for VIU) or a change in FVLCS. The 'unwinding' of the discount will increase the present value of future cash flows as they become closer but IAS 36 does not allow the mere passage of time to trigger the reversal of an impairment. In other words the 'service potential' of the asset must genuinely improve if a reversal is to be recognised.[166] However, this inability to recognise the rise in value can give rise to some seemingly illogical effects, as demonstrated by the following example:

Example 18.17:   Double counted losses

At the end of 2009, an entity with a single CGU is carrying out an impairment review. The discounted forecast cash flows for years 2011 and onwards would be just enough to support the carrying value of the firm's assets. However, 2010 is forecast to produce a loss and net cash outflow. The discounted value of this amount is accordingly written off the carrying value of the fixed assets in 2009 as an impairment loss. It is then suffered again in 2010 (at a slightly higher amount being now undiscounted) as the actual loss. Once that loss is past, the future cash flows are sufficient to support the original unimpaired value of the fixed assets. Nevertheless, the assets cannot be written back up through the profit and loss account to counter the double counting effect as the increase in value does not derive from a change in economic conditions or in the expected use of an asset. The entity will only 'benefit' as the assets are amortised.

If, on the other hand, the revival in cash flows is the result of expenditure by the entity to improve or enhance the performance of the asset or the CGU or on a restructuring of the CGU, there may be an obvious improvement in the service potential and the entity may be able to reverse some or all of the impairment write down.

In the event of an individual asset's impairment being reversed, the reversal may not raise the carrying value above the figure it would have stood at taking into account depreciation, if no impairment had originally been recognised.[167] Any increase above this figure would really be a revaluation, which would have to be accounted for in accordance with the standard relevant to the asset concerned.[168]

Example 18.18:   Reversal of impairment losses

At the beginning of 2007 an entity acquires an asset with a useful life of 10 years for $1000. The asset generates net cash inflows that are largely independent of the cash inflows of other assets or groups of assets. At the end of 2009, when the carrying amount after depreciation is $700, the entity recognises that there has been an impairment loss of $210. The entity writes the asset down to $490. As the useful life is not affected, the entity commences amortisation at $70 per annum which, if applied in each of the years 2010 – 2016, would amortise the carrying value over the remaining useful life, as follows:

Table 1	2007	2008	2009	2010	2011	2012	2013	2014	2015	2016
	$	$	$	$	$	$	$	$	$	$
NBV – beginning of the year	1000	900	800	490	420	350	280	210	140	70
Depreciation	100	100	100	70	70	70	70	70	70	70
Impairment			210							
NBV – end of the year	900	800	490	420	350	280	210	140	70	–
NBV without impairment	900	800	700	600	500	400	300	200	100	–

At the beginning of 2011, before depreciation for the year, the asset's carrying value is $420. Thanks to improvements in technology, the entity is able to increase the asset's VIU to $550 by spending $120 on parts that improve and enhance its performance.

However, this has taken no account of the previous impairment of $210 in 2009 or of the revised VIU at the end of 2011 of $550.Therefore, at the end of 2011, the asset can be written up to the *lower* of:

- $660, which is the net book value assuming that all of the impairment charge is reversed;
- $600, which the net book value of the asset after the additional expenditure, assuming that there had never been any impairment This is the balance brought forward at the beginning of 2011 of $600 (Table 1 bottom row) plus expenditure of $120 less depreciation for the year of (720/6) = $120; and
- $550, which is the VIU.

i.e. it can write the asset's net book value back up to $550. Therefore, the entity can reverse $100 of the impairment write down and amortise the remaining net book value of the asset of $550 to zero over the remaining five years, 2012 – 2016, at $110 per annum.

Table 2	2011	2012	2013	2014	2015	2016
	$	$	$	$	$	$
Cost	1000	1120	1120	1120	1120	1120
Expenditure in the year	120					
Cost carried forward	1120	1120	1120	1120	1120	1120
Accumulated depreciation brought forward	580	570	680	790	900	1010
Charge for the year (on opening balance – Table 2)	90	110	110	110	110	110
Reversal of impairment	(100)					
Accumulated depreciation carried forward	570	680	790	900	1010	1120
NBV	550	440	330	220	110	–

The Standard includes an illustration of the reversal of an impairment loss in the standard's accompanying section of illustrative examples, in Example 4.

All reversals are to be recognised in the income statement immediately, except for revalued assets which are dealt with below.[169]

If an impairment loss is reversed against an asset, its depreciation or amortisation is adjusted to allocate its revised carrying amount less residual value over its remaining useful life.[170]

A   Reversals of impairments – revalued assets

If an asset is recognised at a revalued amount under another standard any reversal of an impairment loss should be treated as a revaluation increase under that other standard. Thus a reversal of an impairment loss on a revalued asset is credited directly to equity under the heading revaluation surplus. However, to the extent that an impairment loss on the same revalued asset was previously recognised as an expense in the income statement, a reversal of that impairment loss is recognised as income in the income statement.[171]

As with assets carried at cost, after a reversal of an impairment loss is recognised on a revalued asset, the depreciation charge should be adjusted in future periods to allocate the asset's revised carrying amount, less any residual value, on a systematic basis over its remaining useful life.[172]

B   Reversals of impairments – cash-generating units

Where an entity recognises a reversal of an impairment loss on a CGU, the increase in the carrying amount of the assets of the unit should be allocated by increasing the carrying amount of the assets, other than goodwill, in the unit on a pro-rata basis. However, the carrying amount of an individual asset should not be increased above the lower of its recoverable amount and the carrying amount that would have resulted had no impairment loss been recognised in prior years. Any 'surplus' reversal is to be allocated to the remaining assets pro-rata, always remembering that goodwill, if allocated to an individual CGU, may not be increased under any circumstances.[173]

4   DISCLOSURES REQUIRED BY IAS 36

4.1   Introduction

This section sets out the principal disclosures required in financial statements complied under IFRS for impairment as set out in IAS 36. Any disclosures required relating to impairment by other standards are dealt with in the chapter concerned. Disclosures that may be required by other authorities such as national statutes or listing authorities are not included.

4.2   IAS 36 disclosures

The disclosures required fall into two broad categories:

(i)   disclosures concerning any actual impairment losses or reversals made in the period, that are obviously only required if such a loss or reversal has occurred, regardless of the type of asset involved; and

(ii)   yearly disclosures concerning the annual impairment tests required for goodwill and intangible assets with an indefinite useful life, that are required regardless of whether an impairment adjustment to these types of assets has occurred or not.

4.2.1   Disclosures required for impairment losses or reversals

IAS 36 defines a class of assets as 'a grouping of assets of similar nature and use in the entity's operations'.[174] For each class of assets the entity must disclose:

'(a)   the amount of impairment losses recognised in profit or loss during the period and the line item(s) in profit or loss in which those impairment losses are included;

(b)   the amount of reversals of impairment losses recognised in profit or loss during the period and the line item(s) in profit or loss in which those impairment losses are reversed;

(c)   the amount of impairment losses on revalued assets recognised directly in other comprehensive income during the period;

(d)   the amount of reversals of impairment losses on revalued assets recognised directly in other comprehensive income during the period.'[175]

These disclosures can be made as an integral part of the other disclosures, for example the property plant and equipment note reconciling the opening and closing values (as set out in Chapter 16 at 6.1) may contain the required information.[176]

Additionally, IAS 36 links disclosure of impairments with segment disclosures. Thus, if a business is subject to IFRS 8 after the implementation of that standard then any impairments or reversals must be disclosed by operating segment as follows:

(a)   the amount of impairment losses recognised in profit or loss and directly in other comprehensive income during the period;

(b)   the amount of reversals of impairment losses recognised in profit or loss and directly in other comprehensive income during the period.[177]

A   *Material impairments*

If an impairment loss for an individual asset or an individual cash-generating unit is recognised or reversed during the period and is material to the financial statements of the reporting entity as a whole, the following disclosures are required:

(a)   the events and circumstances that led to the recognition or reversal of the impairment loss;

(b)   the amount of the impairment loss recognised or reversed;

(c)   for an individual asset:

    (i)   the nature of the asset; and

    (ii)   if the entity reports segmental information in accordance with IFRS 8, the reportable segment to which the asset belongs.

(d)   for a cash-generating unit:

    (i)   a description of the cash-generating unit (such as whether it is a product line, a plant, a business operation, a geographical area, or a reportable segment as defined in IFRS 8;

    (ii)   the amount of the impairment loss recognised or reversed by class of assets and if the entity reports segmental information in accordance with IFRS 8, by reportable segment; and

    (iii) if the aggregation of assets for identifying the cash-generating unit has changed since the previous estimate of the cash-generating unit's recoverable amount (if any), a description of the current and former way of aggregating assets and the reasons for changing the way the cash-generating unit is identified.

(e)   whether the recoverable amount of the asset or cash-generating unit is its fair value less costs to sell (FVLCS) or its value in use (VIU);

(f)   if recoverable amount is FVLCS, the basis used to determine FVLCS (such as whether FVLCS was determined by reference to an active market); and

(g)   if recoverable amount is VIU, the discount rate used in the current estimate and previous estimate (if any) of VIU.[178]

It is logically possible for impairment adjustments *in aggregate* to be material, yet no single one material in itself, in which case the previous requirement that relates to individual assets or CGUs could theoretically be circumvented. Therefore the following 'catch all' requirement is added:

> 'An entity shall disclose the following information for the aggregate impairment losses and the aggregate reversals of impairment losses recognised during the period for which no information is disclosed in accordance with paragraph 130:
>
> (a)   the main classes of assets affected by impairment losses and the main classes of assets affected by reversals of impairment losses;
>
> (b)   the main events and circumstances that led to the recognition of these impairment losses and reversals of impairment losses.'[179]

If there are any cases of impairment adjustments where intangible assets with indefinite useful life and goodwill are not involved, IAS 36 encourages the disclosure of key assumptions made in the recoverable amount calculations used to determine any impairments recognised in the period.[180] However, as set out below, if there is any impairment of a CGU containing intangible assets with an indefinite useful life or goodwill, this type of disclosure is a requirement.

4.2.2   Annual impairment disclosures required for goodwill and intangible assets with an indefinite useful life.

Paragraph 84 of IAS 36 accepts that following a business combination it may not have been possible to allocate all the goodwill to individual CGUs or groups of CGUs by the end of the period in which the acquisition has been made. In these circumstances the standard requires that the amount of any such unallocated goodwill be disclosed, together with the reasons why it has not been allocated.[181]

The annual disclosures are intended to provide the user with information about the types of estimates that have been used in arriving at the recoverable amounts of goodwill and intangible assets with an indefinite useful life, that are included in the assets of the entity at the period end. They are divided into two broad categories:

(i)   those concerning individual CGUs or group of CGUs in which the carrying amount of goodwill or of intangible assets with an indefinite useful life is 'significant' in comparison with the entity's total carrying amount of these items. In this category disclosures are to be made separately for each significant CGU or group of CGUs; and

(ii)   those concerning CGUs or groups of CGUs in which the carrying amount of goodwill or of intangible assets with an indefinite useful life is *not* 'significant' individually in comparison with the entity's total carrying amount of these items. In this case the disclosures can be made in aggregate.

No definition of 'significant' is given; but in our view it must be taken to mean significant in relation to any or all of asset values, shareholders funds, and to profit for the year if a write off were to be required.

For each cash-generating unit or group of units for which the carrying amount of goodwill or intangible assets with indefinite useful lives allocated to that unit or group of units is significant, the following disclosures are required every year:

(a) the carrying amount of goodwill allocated to the CGU (group of CGUs);

(b) the carrying amount of intangible assets with indefinite useful lives allocated to the CGU (group of CGUs);

(c) the basis on which the CGU's or group of CGUs' recoverable amount has been determined (i.e. value in use or fair value less costs to sell);

(d) if the CGU's or group of CGUs' recoverable amount is based on value in use:

    (i) a description of each key assumption on which management has based its cash flow projections for the period covered by the most recent budgets/forecasts. Key assumptions are those to which the unit's (group of units') recoverable amount is most sensitive;

    (ii) a description of management's approach to determining the value(s) assigned to each key assumption, whether those value(s) reflect past experience or, if appropriate, are consistent with external sources of information, and, if not, how and why they differ from past experience or external sources of information;

    (iii) the period over which management has projected cash flows based on financial budgets/forecasts approved by management and, when a period greater than five years is used for a cash-generating unit (group of units), an explanation of why that longer period is justified;

    (iv) the growth rate used to extrapolate cash flow projections beyond the period covered by the most recent budgets/forecasts, and the justification for using any growth rate that exceeds the long-term average growth rate for the products, industries, or country or countries in which the entity operates, or for the market to which the unit (group of units) is dedicated;

    (v) the discount rate(s) applied to the cash flow projections.

(e) if the CGU's or group of CGUs' recoverable amount is based on fair value less costs to sell, the methodology used to determine fair value less costs to sell. If fair value less costs to sell is not determined using an observable market price for the unit (group of units), the following information shall also be disclosed:

    (i) a description of each key assumption on which management has based its determination of fair value less costs to sell. Key assumptions are those to which the unit's (group of units') recoverable amount is most sensitive;

    (ii) a description of management's approach to determining the value(s) assigned to each key assumption, whether those value(s) reflect past experience or, if appropriate, are consistent with external sources of information, and, if not, how and why they differ from past experience or external sources of information.

If fair value less costs to sell is determined using discounted cash flow projections, the following information shall also be disclosed:

    (iii) the period over which management has projected cash flows.

(iv)   the growth rate used to extrapolate cash flow projections.

(v)   the discount rate(s) applied to the cash flow projections.

(f)   if a reasonably possible change in a key assumption on which management has based its determination of the CGU's or group of CGUs' recoverable amount would cause the CGU's or group of CGUs' carrying amount to exceed its recoverable amount:

(i)   the amount by which the CGU's or group of CGUs' recoverable amount exceeds its carrying amount;

(ii)   the value assigned to the key assumption;

(iii) the amount by which the value assigned to the key assumption must change, after incorporating any consequential effects of that change on the other variables used to measure recoverable amount, in order for the CGU's or group of CGUs' recoverable amount to be equal to its carrying amount. [182]

As set out above, there are separate disclosure requirements for those CGUs or groups of CGUs that taken individually do not have significant amounts of goodwill in comparison with the total carrying value of goodwill or of intangible assets with an indefinite useful life within their carrying values. [183]

- First, an aggregate disclosure has to be made of the 'not significant' amounts of goodwill or of intangible assets with an indefinite useful life. If some or all of the carrying amount of goodwill or intangible assets with indefinite useful lives is allocated across multiple CGUs or group of CGUs, and the amount so allocated to each CGU or group of CGUs is not significant in comparison with the entity's total carrying amount of goodwill or intangible assets with indefinite useful lives, that fact shall be disclosed, together with the aggregate carrying amount of goodwill or intangible assets with indefinite useful lives allocated to those CGUs or group of CGUs.

- Second, if in aggregate these amounts are significant in relation to the entirety of the carrying amount of the entity's goodwill or intangible assets with an indefinite useful life, the following is required to be disclosed. If the recoverable amounts of any of those CGUs or group of CGUs are based on the same key assumption(s) and the aggregate carrying amount of goodwill or intangible assets with indefinite useful lives allocated to them is significant in comparison with the entity's total carrying amount of goodwill or intangible assets with indefinite useful lives, an entity shall disclose that fact, together with:

(a)   the aggregate carrying amount of goodwill allocated to those CGUs or group of CGUs);

(b)   the aggregate carrying amount of intangible assets with indefinite useful lives allocated to those CGUs or group of CGUs;

(c)   a description of the key assumption(s);

(d)   a description of management's approach to determining the value(s) assigned to the key assumption(s), whether those value(s) reflect past experience or, if appropriate, are consistent with external sources of information, and, if not, how and why they differ from past experience or external sources of information;

(e) if a reasonably possible change in the key assumption(s) would cause the aggregate of the CGU's or group of CGUs' carrying amounts to exceed the aggregate of their recoverable amounts:

  (i) the amount by which the aggregate of the CGU's or group of CGUs' recoverable amounts exceeds the aggregate of their carrying amounts;

  (ii) the value(s) assigned to the key assumption(s);

  (iii) the amount by which the value(s) assigned to the key assumption(s) must change, after incorporating any consequential effects of the change on the other variables used to measure recoverable amount, in order for the aggregate of the CGU's or group of CGUs' recoverable amounts to be equal to the aggregate of their carrying amounts.[184]

Example 9 in IAS 36's Illustrative Examples gives an indication of the types of assumptions and other relevant information the IASB envisages being disclosed under this requirement. The IASB expects disclosure of: budgeted gross margins, average gross margins, expected efficiency improvements., whether values assigned to key assumptions reflect past experience, what improvements management believes are reasonably achievable each year, forecast exchange rates during the budget period, forecast consumer price indices during the budget period for raw materials, market share and anticipated growth in market share.

An example of disclosures including key assumptions and sensitivities is given by Vodafone Group Plc.

Extract 18.1: Vodafone Group plc (2009)

Notes to the consolidated financial statements [extract]
10.   Impairment
Impairment losses

The impairment losses recognised in the consolidated income statement, as a separate line item within operating profit, in respect of goodwill and licences and spectrum fees are as follows:

Cash generating unit:	Reportable segment:	2009 £m	2008 £m	2007 £m
Spain	Spain	3,400	–	–
Turkey	Other Africa and Central Europe	2,250	–	–
Ghana	Other Africa and Central Europe	250	–	–
Germany	Germany	–	–	6,700
Italy	Italy	–	–	4,900
		5,900	–	11,600

Year ended 31 March 2009

The impairment losses were based on value in use calculations. The pre-tax adjusted discount rate used in the most recent value in use in the year ended 31 march 2009 calculation are as follows:

	Pre-tax adjusted discount rate
Spain	10.3%
Turkey [1]	19.5%
Ghana	26.9%

Note:

(1)   The pre-tax adjusted discount rate used in the value in use calculation at 30 September 2008 was 18.6%.

Spain

During the year ended 31 March 2009, the goodwill in relation to the Group's operation in Spain was impaired by £3,400 million following a fall in long term cash flow forecasts resulting from the economic downturn.

The pre-tax risk adjusted discount rate used in the previous value in use calculation at 31 January 2008 was 10.6%.

Turkey

During the year ended 31 March 2009, the goodwill and other intangible assets in relation to the Group's operations in Turkey was impaired by £2,250 million. At 30 September 2008, the goodwill was impaired by £1,700 million following adverse movements in the discount rate and adverse performance against previous plans. During the second half of the 2009 financial year, impairment losses of £300 million in relation to goodwill and £250 million in relation to licences and spectrum resulted from adverse changes in both the discount rate and a fall in the long term GDP growth rate. The cash flow projections within the business plans used for impairment testing were substantially unchanged from those used at 30 September 2008.

The pre-tax risk adjusted discount rate used in the previous value in use calculation at 31 January 2008 was 16.2%.

Ghana

During the year ended 31 March 2009, the goodwill in relation to the Group's operations in Ghana was impaired by £250 million following an increase in the discount rate. The cash flow projections within the business plan used for impairment testing was substantially unchanged from the acquisition business case.

Year ended 31 March 2007

Germany

During the year ended 31 March 2007, the goodwill in relation to the Group's mobile operation in Germany was impaired by £6,700 million following an increase in long term interest rates and increased price competition in the German market along with continued regulatory pressures.

The impairment loss was based on a value in use calculation using a pre-tax risk adjusted discount rate at 31 March 2007 of 10.6% (31 January 2008: 10.2%; 31 January 2007: 10.5%; 30 September 2006: 10.4%; 31 January 2006: 10.1%).

Italy

During the year ended 31 March 2007, the goodwill in relation to the Group's mobile joint venture in Italy was impaired by £4,900 million. During the second half of the 2007 financial year, £3,500 million of the impairment loss resulted from the estimated impact of legislation cancelling the fixed fees for the top up of prepaid cards and the related competitive response in the Italian market. At 30 September 2006, the goodwill was impaired by £1,400 million, following an increase in long term interest rates.

The impairment loss was based on a value in use calculation using a pre-tax risk adjusted discount rate at 31 March 2007 of 11.5% (31 January 2008: 11.5%; 31 January 2007: 11.2%; 30 September 2006: 10.9%; 31 January 2006: 10.1%).

Goodwill

The carrying value of goodwill at 31 March was as follows:

	2009 £m	2008 £m
Germany	12,786	10,984
Italy	15,361	13,205
Spain	10,561	12,168
	38,708	36,357
Other	15,250	14,979
	53,958	51,336

Key assumptions used in the value in use calculations

The key assumptions used in determining the value in use are:

Assumption	How determined
Budgeted EBITDA	Budgeted EBITDA has been based on past experience adjusted for the following: • voice and messaging revenue is expected to benefit from increased usage from new customers, the introduction of new services and traffic moving from fixed networks to mobile networks, though these factors will be partially offset by increased competitor activity, which may result in price declines, and the trend of falling termination rates; • non-messaging data revenue is expected to continue to grow strongly as the penetration of 3G enabled devices rises and new products and services are introduced; and • margins are expected to be impacted by negative factors such as an increase in the cost of acquiring and retaining customers in increasingly competitive markets and the expectation of further termination rate cuts by regulators and by positive factors such as the efficiencies expected from the implementation of Group initiatives.
Budgeted capital expenditure	The cash flow forecasts for capital expenditure are based on past experience and includes the ongoing capital expenditure required to roll out networks in emerging markets, to provide enhanced voice and data products and services and to meet the population coverage requirements of certain of the Group's licences. Capital expenditure includes cash outflows for the purchase of property, plant and equipment and computer software.
Long term growth rate	For businesses where five years of management plan data is used for the Group's value in use calculations, a long term growth rate into perpetuity has been determined as the lower of: • the nominal GDP rates for the country of operation; and • the long term compound annual growth rate in EBITDA in years six to ten estimated by management. For businesses where the ten years of management plan data is used for the Group's value in use calculations, a long term growth rate into perpetuity has been determined as the lower of: • the nominal GDP rates for the country of operation; and • the compound annual growth rate in EBITDA in years eight to ten of the management plan.

Pre-tax risk adjusted discount rate	The discount rate applied to the cash flows of each of the Group's operations is based on the risk free rate for ten year bonds issued by the government in the respective market, where possible adjusted for a risk premium to reflect both the increased risk of investing in equities and the systematic risk of the specific Group operating company. In making this adjustment, inputs required are the equity market risk premium (that is the required increased return required over and above a risk free rate by an investor who is investing in the market as a whole) and the risk adjustment, beta, applied to reflect the risk of the specific Group operating company relative to the market as a whole.

In determining the risk adjusted discount rate, management has applied an adjustment for the systematic risk to each of the Group's operations determined using an average of the betas of comparable listed mobile telecommunications companies and, where available and appropriate, across a specific territory. Management has used a forward looking equity market risk premium that takes into consideration both studies by independent economists, the average equity market risk premium over the past ten years and the market risk premiums typically used by investment banks in evaluating acquisition proposals.

Sensitivity to changes in assumptions

Other than as disclosed below, management believes that no reasonably possible change in any of the above key assumptions would cause the carrying value of any cash generating unit to exceed its recoverable amount.

31 March 2009

The estimated recoverable amount of the Group's operations in Spain, Turkey and Ghana equalled their respective carrying value and, consequently, any adverse change in key assumption would, in isolation, cause a further impairment loss to be recognised. The estimated recoverable amount of the Group's operations in the UK, Ireland, Romania, Germany and Italy exceeded their carrying value by approximately £900 million, £60 million, £300 million, £9,250 million and £2,200 million respectively. The tables below show the key assumptions used in the value in use calculation and, for the UK, Ireland, Romania, Germany and Italy, the amount by which each key assumption must change in isolation in order for the estimated recoverable amount to be equal to its carrying value in both cases.

Assumptions used in value in use calculation

	Spain	Turkey[(1)]	Ghana	UK	Ireland	Romania	Germany	Italy
	%	%	%	%	%	%	%	%
Pre-tax adjusted discount rate	10.3	19.5	26.9	8.6	10.2	14.8	8.5	11.8
Long term growth rate	1.1	7.5	7.3	1.0	–	1.1	1.1	–
Budgeted EBITDA[(2)]	(3.9)	22.3	37.2	(2.8)	(3.5)	(3.1)	n/a	2.2
Budgeted capital Expenditure[(3)]	9.1 to 11.8	8.2 to 69.8	7.7 to 91.6	n/a	n/a	n/a	5.5 to 9.7	7.7 to 9.9

Notes:

(1) The assumptions listed in the table were used in the value in use calculation at 31 March 2009. The pre-tax adjusted discount rate, long term growth rate, budgeted EBITDA and budgeted capital expenditure assumptions used in the value in use calculation at 30 September 2008 were 18.6%, 10.0%, 13.1% and 8.2% to 54.7%.

(2) Budgeted EBITDA is expressed as the compound annual growth rates in the initial ten years for Turkey and Ghana and the initial five years for all other cash generating units of the plans used for impairment testing.

(3) Budgeted capital expenditure is expressed as the range of capital expenditure as a percentage of revenue in the initial ten years for Turkey and Ghana and the initial five years for all other cash generating units of the plans used for impairment testing.

	UK	Ireland	Romania	Germany	Italy
			Change required for carrying value to equal the recoverable amount		
	pps	pps	pps	pps	pps
Pre-tax adjusted discount rate	0.9	0.2	2.2	3.3	1.4
Long term growth rate	(1.1)	(0.3)	(3.4)	(3.9)	(1.5)
Budgeted EBITDA [1]	(6.9)	(1.6)	(9.0)	n/a	(9.1)
Budgeted capital expenditure [2]	n/a	n/a	n/a	23.8	8.5

Notes:
(1)   Budgeted EBITDA is expressed as the compound annual growth rates in the initial five years of the plans used for impairment testing.
(2)   Budgeted capital expenditure is expressed as the range of capital expenditure as a percentage of revenue in the initial five years of the plans used for impairment testing.

The changes in the following table to assumptions used in the impairment review would, in isolation, lead to an (increase)/decrease to the aggregate impairment loss recognised in the year ended 31 March 2009:

	Spain		Turkey		Ghana		All other	
	Increase by 2%	Decrease by 2%	Increase by 2%	Decrease by 2%	Increase by 2%	Decrease by 2%	Increase by 2%	Decrease by 2%
	£bn	£bn	£bn	£bn	£bn	£bn	£bn	£bn
Pre-tax adjusted discount rate	(2.1)	3.3	(0.4)	0.6	(0.04)	0.05	(2.1)	–
Long term growth rate	3.4	(1.9)	0.3	(0.2)	0.01	(0.01)	–	(1.5)
Budgeted EBITDA [1]	0.4	(0.3)	0.1	(0.1)	0.02	(0.01)	–	–
Budgeted capital expenditure [2]	(0.4)	0.4	(0.1)	0.1	(0.02)	0.02	–	–

Notes:
(1)   Represents the compound annual growth rate for the initial ten years for Turkey and Ghana and the initial five years for all other cash generating units of the plans used for impairment testing.
(2)   Represents capital expenditure as a percentage of revenue in the initial ten years for Turkey and Ghana and the initial five years for all other cash generating units of the plans used for impairment testing.

31 March 2008

The estimated recoverable amount of the Group's operations in Germany and Italy exceeded their carrying value by approximately £2,700 million and £3,400 million respectively. The table below shows the key assumptions used in the value in use calculation and the amount by which each key assumption must change in isolation in order for the estimated recoverable amount to be equal to its carrying value in both cases.

	Assumptions used in value in use calculation		Change required for carrying value to equal the recoverable amount	
	Germany	Italy	Germany	Italy
	%	%	pps	pps
Pre-tax adjusted discount rate	10.2	11.5	1.6	2.7
Long term growth rate	1.2	0.1	(1.7)	(3.0)
Budgeted EBITDA [1]	(2.2)	1.4	(2.0)	(4.2)
Budgeted capital expenditure [2]	7.5 to 8.7	5.8 to 9.5	4.2	6.6

Notes:
(1)   Budgeted EBITDA is expressed as the compound annual growth rates in the initial five years of the plans used for impairment testing.
(2)   Budgeted capital expenditure is expressed as the range of capital expenditure as a percentage of revenue in the initial five years of the plans used for impairment testing.

5   PRACTICAL ISSUES

5.1   Discount rates and the weighted average cost of capital

One of the rates recommended as a starting point in calculating the appropriate discount rate for a VIU calculation is the entity's weighted average cost of capital ('WACC') determined using techniques such as the Capital Asset Pricing Model.[185] Example 18.7 above explains how it may be calculated. The WACC is often used in practice. It is usually acceptable to auditors as it is supported by valuation experts and is an accepted methodology based on a well-known formula and widely available information. In addition, many entities already know their own WACC. However, it can only be used as a starting point for determining an appropriate discount rate and some of the issues that must be taken into account are as follows:

a)   the WACC is a post-tax rate and IAS 36 requires VIU to be calculated using pre-tax cash flows and a pre-tax rate. Converting the former into the latter is not simply a question of grossing up the post-tax rate by the effective tax rate;

b)   other tax factors may need to be considered, whether or not these will result in tax cash flows in the period covered by budgets and cash flows;

c)   an entity's own WACC may not be suitable as a discount rate if there is anything atypical about the entity's capital structure compared with 'typical' market participants;

d)   the WACC must reflect the risks specific to the asset and not the risks relating to the entity as a whole, such as default risk; and

e)   the entity's WACC is an average rate derived from its existing business, yet entities frequently operate in more than one sector. Within a sector, different types of projects may have different levels of risk (e.g. a start-up as against an established product).

These are discussed further below.

One of the most difficult areas in practice is the effect of taxation on the WACC. In order to determine an appropriate pre-tax discount rate it is likely to be necessary to adjust the entity's actual tax cash flows.

Ultimately, the appropriate discount rate to select is one that reflects current market assessments of the time value of money and the risks specific to the asset in question, including taxation. Such a rate is one that reflects 'the return that investors would require if they were to choose an investment that would generate cash flows of amounts, timing and risk profile equivalent to those that the entity expects to derive from the asset.'[186] On the one hand, this will be a rate that takes account of some of the effects of taxation (see below); on the other, it will not necessarily be the entity's WACC.

5.1.1   *Pre-and post-tax discount rates*

As discussed in 3.3.2 step 4 above and explained in Example 18.7, the WACC is a post-tax rate and, when measuring VIU, IAS 36 requires pre-tax cash flows to be discounted using a pre-tax discount rate.

The basis of conclusions explains why this should be so. Future income tax cash flows may affect recoverable amount but they have two components:

(a)   temporary differences, which are the future tax cash flows that would result from any difference between the tax base of an asset (the amount attributed to it for tax purposes) and its carrying amount; and

(b)   the future tax cash flows that would result if the tax base of the asset were equal to its recoverable amount.[187]

In principle, VIU should include the present value of the future tax cash flows that would result if the tax base of the asset were equal to its value in use, as described in (b) above. To do so is not straightforward because:

(a)   to avoid double-counting, it is necessary to exclude the effect of temporary differences; and

(b)   VIU would need to be determined by 'an iterative and possibly complex computation so that value in use itself reflects a tax base equal to that value in use.'[188] This iterative process is described in Example 18.20 below.

For these reasons, IASC decided to require an enterprise to determine value in use by using pre-tax future cash flows and, hence, a pre-tax discount rate.

A pre-tax WACC is not necessarily a post-tax WACC grossed up for tax. IAS 36.BCZ85 recognises this problem and states that 'in theory, discounting post-tax cash flows at a post-tax discount rate and discounting pre-tax cash flows at a pre-tax discount rate should give the same result, as long as the pre-tax discount rate is the post-tax discount rate adjusted to reflect the specific amount and timing of the future tax cash flows. The pre-tax discount rate is not always the post-tax discount rate grossed up by a standard rate of tax.' Some may infer from this that it is appropriate to use entity's actual tax cash flows to calculate a pre-tax rate. We consider that this is not the intention of the standard. The discussion in the Basis for Conclusions referred to above makes it clear that only certain cash flows could be reflected if a post-tax rate were used (those that would result if the tax base of the asset were equal to its value in use). The reverse is also true in moving from a post-tax rate to a pre-tax rate. In addition, the entity's tax cash flows may be affected by matters unrelated to the asset or CGU that is being reviewed for impairment. Actual tax cash flows would not necessarily enable the calculation of either the pre-tax discount rate or the appropriate post-tax cash flows.

Grossing up the post-tax discount rate by the standard rate of tax can give the appropriate pre-tax discount rate, e.g. in the following conditions:

•   no growth in cash flows;

•   a perpetuity calculation; and

•   tax cash flows that are a constant percentage of total cash flows.

If these criteria are met (or there is a close approximation, which may be the case for some CGUs) a simple gross up may be materially correct. The criteria are unlikely to apply to the VIU of individual assets, not least because these are rarely perpetuity calculations. If it is inappropriate to make such a gross up, an iterative calculation may be necessary to compute the appropriate pre-tax discount rate.

The only way to calculate a pre-tax WACC accurately is to calculate the VIU by applying a post-tax rate to post-tax cash flows. The effective pre-tax rate is calculated by removing the tax cash flows and, by iteration, one can identify the pre-tax rate that makes the present value of the adjusted cash flows equal the post tax result.

IAS 36.BCZ85 includes an example that illustrates the calculation of a pre-tax discount rate in a specific case where the cost of the asset in question is wholly deductible for taxation in the first year. Discounting post-tax cash flows at a post-tax discount rate and discounting pre-tax cash flows at a pre-tax discount rate will only ever give the same result if the tax base of the asset equals its VIU and the VIU is wholly deductible for tax purposes; this is illustrated in Example 18.20 below. Therefore in order to use a post-tax discount rate or correctly calculate the pre-tax rate, an entity's actual tax cash flows may have to be replaced by notional tax cash flows reflecting this assumption.

It is relatively straightforward to make this calculation for a single asset, whether acquired separately or as part of a business combination. It would be much more difficult for CGUs or for goodwill impairment as there is no single asset on which to base the calculation and there are often additional complications, especially if the assets have been acquired as part of a business combination. This is discussed further at 5.2 below.

The illustrations in Example 18.20 are of course simplified, and in reality it is unlikely that entities will need to schedule all of the tax cash flows and tax consequences in order to calculate a pre-tax discount rate every time they perform an impairment review. In practice it will probably not be possible to obtain a rate that is theoretically perfect – the task is just too intractable for that. The objective, therefore, must be to obtain a rate which is sensible and justifiable. Some of the following may make the exercise somewhat easier.

An entity may calculate a pre-tax rate using adjusted tax cash flows based on the assumptions that we have described and apply that rate to discount pre-tax cash flows. This pre-tax rate will only need to be reassessed when relevant market rates change, i.e. those for instruments with a period to maturity similar to the expected life of the assets being reviewed for impairment, and will not necessarily need to be recalculated every time an impairment review is carried out. Short-term market rates may increase or decrease without affecting the rate of return that the market would require on long-term assets. The rate will not necessarily be affected if the entity ceases to make taxable profits.

Valuation practitioners often use approximations when computing tax cash flows that may also make the task more straightforward. It may often be a valid approximation to assume that the tax amortisation of assets equals their accounting depreciation. Tax cash flows will be based on the relevant corporate tax rate and the forecast earnings before interest and taxation to give post-tax 'cash flows' that can then be discounted using a post-tax discount rate. The circumstances in which this could lead to a material distortion (perhaps in the case of an impairment test for an individual asset) will probably be obvious. This approach is consistent with the overall requirement of IAS 36, which is that the appropriate discount rate to select is one that reflects current market assessments of the risks specific to the asset in question, including taxation.

As described above, some CGUs may approximate to the circumstances in which a standardised gross up will give an adequate discount rate (no growth in cash flows, a perpetuity calculation and tax cash flows that are a constant percentage of total cash flows). As long as these conditions remain unchanged, it will be straightforward to determine the discount rate for an impairment review at either the pre- or post-tax level. This does not mean that an entity can automatically use a post-tax rate. If it is appropriate for it to do so, it must be able to extrapolate from that to the relevant pre-tax rate, which is the explicit requirement of IAS 36. It must know the assumptions on which the post-tax rate is based in order to use it reliably.

Testing for impairment and tax losses is discussed at 5.1.2 below. A particular example when the specific tax consequences will have to be taken into account is testing assets and goodwill for impairment after an acquisition, as recognition of deferred tax, and the asset valuation methodology, may have consequences for the impairment test (see 5.2 below).

Example 18.20: Calculating the pre-tax weighted average cost of capital

Example A – Grossing up at standard rates of tax

Assume that an asset that has been acquired or constructed by the entity has a carrying value and tax base of €40,000. The tax rate is 25% and the asset is eligible for a 100% deduction in the first year. The entity's post-tax discount rate is 9%. If the cost is to be recovered in one year, the entity must generate taxable cash inflows of at least €44,800, i.e. a pre-tax rate of 12%, as follows:

	€	€
Cash inflows before taxation		44,800
Tax on income at 25%	(11,200)	
Tax credit at 25% of €40,000	10,000	
Tax charge		(1,200)
Post-tax cash inflow		43,600

In this case, discounting the pre-tax cash flows at 12% gives the same answer as discounting the post-tax cash flows at 9% – both give the same VIU for the asset of €40,000, which is equal to its tax base.

This is also the answer if this is a calculation of the VIU of a CGU and, instead of all cash flows arising in the first year, it is a perpetuity calculation with annual pre- and post-tax cash inflows of €4,800 and €3,600. In contrast to Example A, this would have to mean different tax assumptions, for example, a higher rate of tax on profits and a lower rate of deduction for the asset so that the net tax charge (tax on income less tax deduction for the asset) has a present value of €1,200; it also assumes that capital expenditure and tax amortisation remain the same in perpetuity. Each of these inflows extended in perpetuity has a present value of €40,000 at 12% and 9% respectively. In this case the calculation meets all of the criteria outlined above as this is a perpetuity calculation with no growth in cash flows and tax cash flows that are a constant percentage of total cash flows.

However, in the case of any asset with a finite life, it will not be a perpetuity calculation and the taxation may not be a constant percentage of the cash flows. In these cases it is necessary to calculate either a pre-tax rate or the appropriate tax assumptions to enable the post-tax rate to be used.

Example B – Calculation of pre-and post-tax discount rates

The facts are as in Example A above except that the asset's cost is expected to be recovered over its five year life. The carrying value of the asset is deductible for tax in equal instalments over the five year period.

Assuming that the income arises evenly over the period, the minimum annual income necessary if the entity is to apply a post-tax rate of 9% can be calculated as €11,045. The pre-and post-tax cash flows are as follows:

	€	€	€	€	€
Cash inflows before taxation	11,045	11,045	11,045	11,045	11,045
tax on income at 25%	(2,761)	(2,761)	(2,761)	(2,761)	(2,761)
tax credit at 25% of €40,000	2,000	2,000	2,000	2,000	2,000
tax charge	761	761	761	761	761
Post-tax cash inflow	10,284	10,284	10,284	10,284	10,284

PV of post-tax cash flows at 9%	€40,000
PV of pre-tax cash flows at 11.81%	€40,000

The VIU of the asset is still €40,000 but the pre-tax discount rate is 11.81%, rather than 12% as in Example A – this is not a calculation of the VIU using cash flows in perpetuity.

The tax credit of €10,000 arises because the VIU of the asset, which in this example is its cost, is fully deductible for taxation.

In Example B, the cash inflow has been calculated as the minimum amount necessary to recover the cost of the asset. The next step is to consider the calculation when the cash flows are insufficient.

Example C – Calculation of pre-and post-tax discount rates when the asset is impaired

The facts are as in Example A above except that the asset is only expected to generate pre-tax cash inflows of €8,500 per annum. If the minimum amount necessary to recover the cost of the asset is €11,045, as calculated in Example B above, then if all other factors remain the same, the carrying value of the impaired asset ought to be €30,783 (8,500/11,045 × 40,000), which is also the present value of the pre-tax cash flows using the discount rate calculated above. Assume that the impairment loss is not itself tax deductible.

In order to calculate its post-tax VIU at the same amount, the 'cash flows' are as follows:

	€	€	€	€	€
Cash inflows before taxation	8,500	8,500	8,500	8,500	8,500
tax on income at 25%	(2,125)	(2,125)	(2,125)	(2,125)	(2,125)
tax credit at 25% of €30,783	1,539	1,539	1,539	1,539	1,539
tax charge	586	586	586	586	586
Post-tax cash inflow	7,914	7,914	7,914	7,914	7,914

PV of post-tax cash flows at 9%	€30,783
PV of pre-tax cash flows at 11.81%	€30,783

In this case, it has been assumed that neither pre- nor post-tax discount rates are affected by the fact that the asset is now impaired. Therefore, if the pre-tax cash flows and pre- and post-tax discount rates are known, the only feature of the computation that can change in order to give the same answer at both pre- and post-tax levels is the assumed tax deduction for the asset. This figure has been calculated using an iterative process and, in the table above, the post-tax value for the asset using a 9% discount rate is also €30,783. The impairment will be reflected in the entity's income statement as an impairment of €9,217, on which there will be a deferred tax asset of €2,304.

If the calculation uses the actual tax base of the asset, the tax credit in each of the five years is €2,000 (as in Example B) the annual tax charge is €125 and the post-tax income is €8,375. The present value of the pre-tax cash flows at 11.81% is €30,783 but the post-tax present value at 9% is €32,576, i.e. a difference of €1,793 between pre- and post-tax calculations.

The difference is the present value of the difference in tax of €461 (€586 – €125) in each of the five years; this difference has a gross amount of €2,304 (after taking account of rounding) and a post-tax present value, discounted at 9%, of €1,793. In order to calculate impairment, the tax credit is based on its VIU (€30,783), not its tax base (which remains €40,000). In other words, using the actual tax deduction based on the asset's actual tax base overstates the VIU calculated on a post-tax basis by the present value of the deferred tax on the actual impairment loss.

Probably a more accurate way to describe the calculation is to assume the post-tax discount rate and uses an iterative process to arrive at the pre-tax rate and tax cash flows (both of which are unknown) that give the same present value at both pre- and post-tax level. The same result will be obtained.

The calculation would be based on the post-tax cash flows of €8,375, calculated using the actual tax base, and the post-tax discount rate of 9%. As we have seen above, the present value of these cash flows is €32,576. However, in order to obtain the same answer at pre- and post-tax levels, the pre-tax rate will be calculated at 11.81% and the deduction for tax will be based on a tax-deductible amount of €30,783 as above. The pre-tax VIU at 11.81% and the post-tax VIU at 9% will both be €30,783.

It will rarely be practicable to apply this methodology to calculate a discount rate for a CGU, as so many factors need to be taken into account. Even if all assets within the CGU are individually acquired or self-constructed, they may have a range of lives for depreciation and tax amortisation purposes, up to and including indefinite lives. There are additional issues if the CGU comprises or includes assets acquired in a business combination; the fair value may or may not reflect tax benefits and there may be complications caused by deferred tax (see 5.2 below). If goodwill is being tested it has an indefinite life whilst the underlying assets in the CGU or CGU group to which it has been allocated will usually have finite lives. It is likely that a reasonable approximation to the 'true' discount rate is the best that can be achieved.

5.1.2   Determining pre-tax rates taking account of tax losses

A common problem relates to the effect of tax losses on the impairment calculation, as they may reduce the total tax paid in the period under review or even eliminate it altogether. As noted in 5.1.1 above, however, a post-tax discount rate is based on certain assumptions about the tax-deductibility of the asset and not the actual tax cash flows. It is therefore unwarranted to assume that the post- and pre-tax discount rates will be the same if the entity pays no tax because of its own tax losses. The pre-tax rate should not include the benefit of available tax benefits and any deferred tax asset arising from tax losses carried forward at the reporting date must be excluded from the assets of the CGU if the impairment review is based on VIU.

In many circumstances the past history of tax losses affects the level of risk in the cash flows in the period under review, but one must take care not to increase the discount rate to reflect risks for which the estimated cash flows have been adjusted.[189] To do so would be to double count.

5.1.3   Entity-specific WACCs and different project risks within the entity

The entity's WACC is an average rate derived from its existing business, yet entities frequently operate in more than one sector. Within a sector, different types of projects may have different levels of risk, e.g. a start-up as against an established product. Therefore, entities must ensure that the different business risks pertaining to different CGUs are properly taken into account when determining the appropriate discount rates.

It must be noted that these areas of different risk will not always coincide with the assets or CGUs that are being tested for impairment as this is a test for impairment and not necessarily a determination of business value.

Example 18.21:   Different project risks and CGUs

An aircraft manufacturer makes both civilian and military aircraft. The risks for both sectors are markedly different as they are much lower for defence contractors than for the civilian market. The assembly plants for civilian and military aircraft are separate CGUs. In this sector there are entities that are based solely in one or other of these markets, i.e. they are purely defence or civilian contractors, so there will be a basis for identifying the different discount rates for the different activities. If the entity makes its own components then the defence CGU or CGUs could include the manufacturing activity if defence is vertically integrated and components are made solely for military aircraft. Manufacturing could be a separate CGU if components are used for both activities and there is an external market for the products.

A manufacturer of soft drinks uses the same plant to produce various flavours of carbonated and uncarbonated drinks. Because the market for traditional carbonated drinks is declining, it develops and markets a new uncarbonated 'health' drink, which is still produced using the same plant. The risks of the product are higher than those of the existing products but it is not a separate CGU.

Many sectors assume a high generation of new products and a high attrition rate (pharmaceuticals and biotechnology, for example) and this is likely built into industry WACCs. If the risk of failure is not reflected in the WACC because the entity is not typical of the industry then either the discount rate or the cash flows ought to be adjusted to reflect the risk (but not so as to double count).

5.1.4   Entity-specific WACCs and capital structure

The discount rate is a pre-tax rate that reflects current market assessments of the time value of money and the risks specific *to the asset* for which the future cash flow estimates have not been adjusted.[190] An entity's own WACC may not be suitable as a discount rate if there is anything atypical about the entity's capital structure compared with 'typical' market participants. In other words, would the market assess the cash flows from the asset or unit as being riskier or less risky than the entity-wide risks reflected in the entity-wide WACC? Some of the risks that need to be thought about are country risk, currency risks and price risk.

Country risk will reflect the area in which the assets are located. In some areas assets are frequently nationalised by governments or the area may be politically unstable and prone to violence. In addition, the potential impact of physical instability such as weather or earthquakes, and the effects of currency volatility on the expected return from the asset, must be considered.

Two elements of price risk are the gearing ratio of the entity in question (if, for example, it is much more or less geared than average) and any default risk built into its cost of debt. However, IAS 36 explicitly notes that the discount rate is independent of the entity's capital structure and the way the entity financed the purchase of the asset, because the future cash flows expected to arise from an asset do not depend on these features.[191]

Example 18.22:   Effect of entity default risk on its WACC

The formula for calculating the (post tax) WACC, as given in Example 18.7 above, is

$$\text{WACC} = (1 - t) \times D \times \frac{g}{(1 + g)} + E \times \left[1 - \frac{g}{(1 + g)} \right]$$

where:

   t is the rate of tax relief available on the debt servicing payments

   D is the pre-tax cost of debt;

   E is the cost of equity

   g is the gearing level (i.e. the ratio of debt to equity) for the sector

The cost of equity is calculated as follows:

   Cost of equity = risk-free rate + (levered beta (β*) × market risk premium)

Assume that the WACC of a typical sector participant is as follows:

Cost of equity	
risk free rate	4%
levered beta (β)	1.1
market risk premium	6%
cost of equity after tax (market risk premium × β + risk-free rate)	10.6%
Cost of debt	
risk free rate	4%
credit spread	3%
cost of debt (pre-tax)	7%
cost of debt (post-tax)	5.25%
Capital structure	
debt / (debt + equity)	25%
equity / (debt + equity)	75%
tax rate	25%
post-tax cost of equity (10.6 × 75%)	8%
post-tax cost of debt (5.25 × 25%)	1.3%
WACC (Post tax, nominal)	9.3%

* The beta is explained in Example 18.7 above.

However, the company has borrowed heavily and is in some financial difficulties. Its gearing ratio is 75% and its actual cost of debt, based on the market price of its listed bonds, is 18% (13.5% after taking account of tax at 25%). This makes its individual post-tax WACC 12.8% (10.6×25% + 13.5×75%). This is not an appropriate WACC for impairment purposes because it does not represent a market rate of return *on the assets*. Its entity WACC has been increased by default risk.

Ultimately it might be acceptable to use the entity's own WACC, but an entity cannot conclude on this without going through the exercise of assessing for risk each of the assets or units and concluding on whether or not they contain additional risks that are not reflected in the WACC.

5.1.5   Use of discount rates other than the WACC

IAS 36 allows an entity to use rates other than the WACC as a starting point in calculating the discount rate. These include:

    (a)   the entity's incremental borrowing rate; and

    (a)   other market borrowing rates.[192]

If borrowing rates (which are, of course, pre-tax) were used as a starting point, could this avoid some of the problems associated with adjusting the WACC for the effects of taxation? Unfortunately, this is unlikely. Debt rates reflect the entity's capital structure and do not reflect the risk inherent in the asset. A pure asset/business risk would be obtained from an entity funded solely by equity and equity risk premiums are always observed on a post-tax basis. Therefore the risk premium that must be added to reflect the required increased return required over and above a risk free rate by an investor will always have to be adjusted for the effects of taxation.

It must be stressed that the appropriate discount rate, which is the one that reflects current market assessments of the time value of money and the risks specific to the asset in question, ought to be the same whatever the starting point for the calculation of the rate.

Vodafone in its description of its pre-tax discount rate starts from the relevant bond (i.e. debt) rate (Extract 18.1 above). However, this describes many of the elements of the WACC calculation and how Vodafone has obtained these; it does not suggest that Vodafone has used anything other than an adjusted WACC as a discount rate for the purposes of the impairment test.

5.2   Impairment of assets and goodwill recognised on acquisition

There are a number of circumstances in which the fair value of assets or goodwill acquired as part of a business combination and as recorded in the consolidated accounts, may be measured at a higher amount through recognition of deferred tax or notional tax benefits. This raises the question of how to test for impairment and even whether there is, in fact, a 'day one' impairment in value. In other circumstances, deferred tax assets may or may not be recognised as part of the fair value exercise and this, too, may affect subsequent impairment tests of the assets and goodwill acquired as part of the business combination.

5.2.1   Testing goodwill 'created' by deferred tax for impairment

As described in Chapter 26 at 6.2, the requirement of IAS 12 – *Income Taxes* – to recognise deferred tax on all temporary differences arising on net assets acquired in a business combination may well lead to the recognition of goodwill and an increase in the net assets recognised in the consolidated accounts. This then begs the question of how to perform an impairment test on that goodwill. This is illustrated in the following example (also used to illustrate the point as Example 26.29 in Chapter 26):

Example 18.23:   Apparent 'day one' impairment arising from recognition of deferred tax in a business combination

Entity A, which is taxed at 40%, acquires Entity B for €100m in a transaction that is a business combination. The fair values and tax bases of the identifiable net assets of Entity B are as follows:

	Fair value	Tax base
	€m	€m
Brand name	60	nil
Other net assets	20	15

This will give rise to the following consolidation journal:

	€m	€m
Goodwill (balance)	46	
Brand name	60	
Other net assets	20	
Deferred tax[1]		26
Cost of investment		100

[1] 40% of (€[60m + 20m] – €15m)

The fair value of the consolidated assets of the subsidiary (excluding deferred tax) and goodwill is now €126m, but the cost of the subsidiary is only €100m. Clearly €26m of the goodwill arises solely from the recognition of deferred tax. However, IAS 36, paragraph 50, explicitly requires tax to be excluded from the estimate of future cash flows used to calculate any impairment. This raises the question of whether there should not be an immediate impairment write-down of the assets to €100m.

In our view, this cannot have been the intention of IAS 36, for the reasons described in 5.1 above. Adjustments need to be made to the post-tax discount rate in order to determine the appropriate pre-tax discount rate. This means, in effect, that as at the point of acquisition, the deferred tax liability can be offset against the CGU or CGU group in order to test that goodwill for impairment. As a result, the entity does not have to recognise an immediate loss.

This conclusion is consistent with the fact that the goodwill that is being recognised as part of this acquisition is a result of a measurement mismatch between two standards. The IASB is fully aware that this can happen. In the Basis of Conclusions to IFRS 3(2007), it is noted that goodwill, measured as a residual, could include 'errors in measuring and recognising the fair value of either the cost of the business combination or the acquiree's identifiable assets, liabilities or contingent liabilities, or *a requirement in an accounting standard to measure those identifiable items at an amount that is not fair value*' (our emphasis).[193]

This example assumes that the entity cannot get a deduction for tax purposes for the goodwill and brand name, as is often the case for assets that arise only on consolidation. It also assumes that the fair value of the brand name does not reflect the tax deductions that might have available had it not been acquired as part of a business combination (valuations that do reflect such assumptions are considered further below). Deferred tax is measured at its full and undiscounted value and not at fair value; had it been so, it is plausible that in this case its fair value would be negligible or zero. Note that despite this 'mismatch', goodwill still has to be recognised in the financial statements and is subject to all of IAS 36's requirements.

If it is assumed that the brand name is amortised over a finite useful life then the deferred tax relating to that asset (€24m in this example) will be released over that life with the effect that the net amount charged to the income statement of €36m (€60m – €24m) will be the same as if the amortisation charge were tax deductible. Although the deferred tax liability is diminishing in line with the amortisation of the brand, the total amount of goodwill is not amortised. This does not necessarily mean that the 'mismatch' goodwill will be impaired in line with the release of the deferred tax liability as this will depend on the individual circumstances of the entity and the manner in which purchased goodwill has been allocated to CGUs or CGU groups and their post-acquisition performance.

Only deferred tax that has arisen as described in Example 18.23 above may be taken into account in considering the impairment of the related goodwill; other unrelated deferred tax, whether it arises at the same time or subsequently, will be disregarded. Entities may, of course, find it difficult to track the relevant deferred tax an ongoing basis.

Xstrata plc discloses separately the amount of goodwill that has resulted from the recognition of deferred tax liabilities.

Extract 18.2: Xstrata plc (2008)

Notes to the Financial Statements [extract]
15.   Impairment
Goodwill

Goodwill has been allocated to a cash-generating unit (CGU) or groups of cash-generating units no larger than the reportable segment which are expected to benefit from the related acquisitions. The carrying values of goodwill by cash-generating unit are as follows:

US$m	2008	2007
Chrome – Africa	35	47
Copper – Americas	1,185	1,185
Zinc Lead	1,546	1,546
Zinc Lead – Europe	212	222
	2,978	3,000

The following goodwill balances result from the requirement to recognise a deferred tax liability, calculated as the difference between the tax effect of the fair value of the acquired assets and liabilities and their tax bases. For the purpose of testing this goodwill for impairment, any of the related deferred tax liabilities recognised on acquisition that remain at balance date are treated as part of the relevant CGU or group of CGUs.

US$m	2008	2007
Coal – Australia	233	125
Coal – Americas South	464	464
Copper – Americas South*	1,500	1,537
Copper – Australasia	151	151
Nickel – Americas North	856	856
Nickel – Americas South*	119	295
Nickel – Africa	78	78
Nickel – Australasia	79	34
Platinum – Africa	284	384
Zinc Lead – Americas North	244	244
Zinc Lead – Americas South	160	160
Zinc Lead – Australasia	–	8
	4,168	4,336
	7,146	7,336

* Net of 2008 impairment loss discussed below.

The Group performs goodwill impairment testing on an annual basis and at the reporting date if there are indicators of impairment. The most recent test was undertaken at 31 December 2008.

If the brand name is deemed to have an indefinite life it will not be amortised. It may be possible to continue to apply the short cut method of deducting the deferred tax liability from the CGU or CGU group of which the goodwill and brand name are part, unless the intangible asset is impaired or sold. It is still a requirement for the entity to be able to track the relevant deferred tax liability. The goodwill still has to be tested annually for impairment, even though in this case the goodwill itself ought to have no net effect on the net assets of the CGU or group of CGUs to which it is allocated. The standard's disclosure requirements including the pre-tax discount rate, principally described at 4.2.2 above, will apply.

5.2.2   Assets whose fair value reflects tax benefits

This is a related area to the one described in 5.2.1 that may also affect the post-acquisition impairment test. In order to determine the fair value in an acquisition of an asset (typically an intangible asset), its value on a post-tax basis may be grossed up to take account of the tax benefits (sometimes called 'tax amortisation benefits') that the owner might have obtained if the asset had been bought separately, i.e. not as part of a business combination. Yet the asset may be one that is wholly or in part not tax-deductible by the entity. This is demonstrated in the following example:

Example 18.24:   Impairment testing assets whose fair value reflects tax amortisation benefits

Assume that the entity in Example 18.23 above has acquired a brand that would be tax deductible if separately acquired but that also has a tax base of zero. The entity concludes that the fair value will reflect the tax benefit, whose gross amount is €40 (€60m × 40% / 60%) but in calculating the fair value this will be discounted to its present value – say €30m. The consolidation journal is now as follows:

	€m	€m
Goodwill (balance)	28	
Brand name (€(60 + 30))	90	
Other net assets	20	
Deferred tax[1]		38
Cost of investment		100

[1] 40% of (€[90m + 20m] − €15m)

Overall, the gross assets that cost €100m will now be recorded at €138m, as against the total of €126m in Example 18.23. This increase has come about because of recognition of deferred tax of €12m, which is 40% of €30m, the assumed tax amortisation benefit.

In this example, only €8m goodwill results from the recognition of deferred tax [€28m − (€100 − (€60m + €20m))] and its treatment is discussed above at 5.2.1.

Unlike goodwill, the intangible asset will only have to be tested for impairment if there are indicators of impairment, if it has an indefinite useful life or if it has not yet been brought into use.[194] Because its 'fair value' of €90m is much in excess of the amount that the entity considers that it paid to acquire the asset ,could this be considered an indicator of impairment? However, should, it be necessary to test it for impairment, the asset has been valued on the assumption that it will generate future tax inflows and it is only consistent that the impairment test takes account of the same assumptions. A discount rate is calculated using the assumptions about taxation described in 5.1.1 above (i.e. that VIU equals tax base). Whatever rate is selected, it will be one that reflects market assumptions about the availability of tax relief and the level of taxation. The implications are similar to those discussed in 5.1.1 above .

5.2.3   Deferred tax assets and losses of acquired businesses

Deferred tax assets arising from tax losses carried forward at the reporting date must be excluded from the assets of the CGU for the purpose of calculating its VIU. However, tax losses may not meet the criteria for recognition as deferred tax assets in a business combination, which means that their value is initially subsumed within goodwill. Under IFRS 3(2007) deferred tax assets recognised at a later date reduced the amount of goodwill which was written down to the extent of the deferred tax asset at the date of acquisition.[195] Under IFRS 3(as revised in 2008) and an amended IAS 12, only acquired deferred tax assets recognised within the 12 month measurement period are to reduce goodwill, with any excess once goodwill has been reduced to zero being taken to profit or loss.[196] This amendment applies to all accounting periods beginning on or after 1 July 2009 unless IFRS 3(as revised in 2008) has been applied from an earlier date.[197] Unlike other changes in IFRS 3(as amended in 2008) this applies to acquisitions originally accounted for under IFRS 3(2007). See also Chapter 26 at 6.2.2.

Unless and until the deferred tax asset is recognised (and this will be less likely to happen under the amended IFRS 3), this raises the same problems as in 5.2.1 and 5.2.2 above. Certain assumptions regarding future taxation are built into the carrying value of goodwill. In such situations it may be appropriate to recognise the benefits of this 'contingent asset' in the VIU calculation for the CGU or CGU group.

5.3   Future capital expenditure

IAS 36 requires an asset to be tested for impairment in its current condition, excluding estimated future cash flows that may arise from a future restructuring to which the entity is not committed or future expenditure on improving or enhancing the asset's performance.[198] At the same time, the entity is required to reflect appropriate maintenance and replacement expenditure[199] and, if the asset is incomplete, the costs necessary to make it ready for use or sale.[200]

Entities must therefore distinguish between maintenance, completion and enhancement expenditure. This is not always straightforward, as shown in the following example.

Example 18.25:   Distinguishing enhancement and maintenance expenditure

A telecommunications company provides fixed line, telephone, television and internet services. It must develop its basic transmission infrastructure (by overhead wires or cables along streets or railway lines etc) and in order to service a new customer it will have to connect the customer's home via cable and other equipment. It will extend its network to adjoining areas and perhaps acquire an entity with its own network. It will also reflect changes in technology, e.g. fibre optic cables replacing copper ones.

Obviously, when preparing the budgets which form the basis for testing the network for impairment, it will make assumptions regarding future revenue growth and will include the costs of connecting those customers. However, its infrastructure maintenance spend will inevitably include replacing equipment with the current technology. There is no option of continuing to replace equipment with something that has been technologically superseded. Once this technology exists it will be reflected in the entity's budgets and taken into account in its cash flows when carrying out impairment tests, even though this new equipment will enhance the performance of the transmission infrastructure.

This maintenance and replacement expenditure must be distinguished from step changes in services and the technology used to provide them. BT Group plc notes the following in its 2008 Operating and financial review.

Extract 18.3: BT Group plc (2008)

Operating and financial review
Technological advances

Our continued success depends on our ability to exploit new technology rapidly.

We operate in an industry with a recent history of rapid technological changes and we expect this to continue – new technologies and products will emerge, and existing technologies and products will develop further.

We need continually to exploit next-generation technologies in order to develop our existing and future services and products. However, we cannot predict the actual impact of these future technological changes on our business or our ability to provide competitive services. For example, there is evidence of substitution by customers using mobile phones for day-to-day voice calls in place of making such calls over the fixed network and of calls being routed over the internet in place of the traditional switched network. If these trends accelerate, our fixed-network assets may be used uneconomically and our investment in these assets may not be recovered through profits on fixed-line calls and line rentals.

The complexity of the 21CN programme, and the risk that our major suppliers fail to meet their obligations may result in delays to the delivery of expected benefits. Impairment write-downs may be incurred and margins may decline if fixed costs cannot be reduced in line with falling revenue.

Further examples indicate another problem area – the effects of future expenditure that the entity has identified but to which the entity is not yet committed. An entity may have acquired an asset with the intention of enhancing it in future and may, therefore, have paid for future synergies which will be reflected in the calculation of goodwill. Another entity may have plans for an asset that involve expenditure that will enhance its future performance and without which the asset may be impaired.

Examples could include:

- a TV transmission company that, in acquiring another, would expect to pay for the future right to migrate customers from analogue to digital services; or

- an aircraft manufacturer that expects to be able to use one of the acquired plants for a new model at a future point, a process that will involve replacing much of the current equipment.

In both cases the long-term plans reflect both the capital spent and the cash flows that will flow from it. There is no obvious alternative to recognising an impairment when calculating the CGU or CGU group's VIU as IAS 36 insists that the impairment test has to be performed for the asset in its current condition. This means that it is not permitted to include the benefit of improving or enhancing the asset's performance in calculating its VIU.

In the TV example above, it does not appear to matter whether the entity recognises goodwill or has a separable intangible right that it has not yet brought into use.

An entity in this situation may attempt to avoid an impairment write down by calculating the appropriate FVLCS, as this is not constrained by rules regarding future capital expenditure. As discussed further in 5.4 below, these cash flows can be included only to the extent that other market participants would consider them when evaluating the asset. It is not permissible to include assumptions about cash flows or benefits from the asset that would not be available to or considered by a typical market participant.

5.4   Use of FVLCS for the purposes of impairment testing

IAS 36 allows an entity to estimate FVLCS less costs to sell of an asset even if there is no active market for assets of this type[201] and there is no binding sale agreement for the asset in question.[202] Some of the issues that need to be taken into account are discussed below. However, the IASB in May 2009 issued an Exposure Draft about fair value measurement that would apply to all IFRSs; this is discussed in the context of the impairment test at 5.4.2 below.

5.4.1   Estimating FVLCS without an active market

Few assets are traded on an active market and there are no obvious examples of traded CGUs. However, it may be possible to determine fair value provided there is a basis for making a reliable estimate of the amount obtainable from the sale of the asset in an arm's length transaction between knowledgeable and willing parties.

IAS 36 permits entities to consider 'the outcome of recent transactions for similar assets within the same industry.'[203] If the entity has only recently acquired the asset or CGU in question then it may be able to demonstrate that its purchase price remains an appropriate measure of FVLCS, although it would have to make adjustments for material costs to sell.[204]

To rely on the outcome of a recent transaction for a similar asset by a third party, the following conditions must be met:

a) the transaction should be in the same industry, unless the asset is generic and its fair value would not be affected by the industry in which the purchaser operates;

b) the assets must be shown to be substantially the same as to their nature and condition;

c) the economic environment of the entity must be similar to the environment in which the previous sale occurred (e.g. no circumstances have arisen since the earlier transaction that affect the value of the asset). This means that previous transactions are particularly unreliable if markets are falling.

It would be unusual to be able to estimate FVLCS reliably from a single market transaction. It is much more likely that, if reliable market assumptions are known, as discussed below, a recent market transaction would be one of the factors taken into account in the calculation of FVLCS and used in conjunction with other valuation techniques.

If the entity cannot demonstrate that a recent transaction alone provides a reliable estimate of FVLCS, the transaction may be one of the sources of evidence used to validate an estimate of FVLCS using other valuation techniques. This is particularly likely to be the case if the impairment review is of a CGU or CGU group rather than an individual asset, as market transactions for individual assets are likely to be more relevant and reliable.

IAS 36 allows the use of cash flow valuation techniques such as discounted cash flows or other valuation techniques such as multiples. However, the use of these techniques and assumptions is only acceptable if it can be demonstrated that they would be used by the relevant 'market participants' i.e. other businesses in the same industry. When using a valuation technique to estimate FVLCS, all of the following conditions must be met:

a) a relevant model must be selected – this requires consideration of industry practice, for example, a multiple of EBITDA is often used in the hotel industry to estimate fair value, while discounted cash flows are used by many manufacturing entities;

b) assumptions used in the model must only be those that other market participants would use. They cannot be based on management's uncorroborated views or information that would not be known or considered by other market participants; and

c) there must be reliable evidence showing that these assumptions would be taken into account by market participants. For this purpose, it may be necessary for the entity to obtain external advice.

It is particularly important when markets are unstable to ensure that multiples remain valid. Entities cannot assume that the basis underlying the multiples remain unchanged.

If it is not possible to obtain reliable evidence regarding the assumptions and techniques that market participants would use, then fair value cannot be reliably estimated using valuation techniques and the recoverable amount of the asset must be based on its value in use.[205]

Therefore a discounted cash flow technique may be used if this is commonly used in that industry to estimate fair value. Cash flows used when applying the model may only reflect cash flows that market participants would take into account when assessing fair value. This includes the type of cash flows, for example future capital expenditure, as well as the estimated amount of cash flows. For example, an entity may wish to take into account cash flows relating to future capital expenditure, which would not be permitted for a VIU calculation (see 3.3.2 above). These cash flows can be included if, but only if, other market participants would consider them when evaluating the asset. It is not permissible to include assumptions about cash flows or benefits from the asset that would not be available to or considered by a typical market participant.

Obtaining reliable evidence of market assumptions is difficult, and unlikely to be achieved by many entities wishing to apply valuation techniques. However, Deutsche Telekom has calculated the FVLCS of one of its CGUs and has taken a third party transaction in the same sector and geographical area into account in its valuation model, as can be seen in the following extract:

Extract 18.4: Deutsche Telekom AG (2007)

Notes to the consolidated income statement [extract]

16.   Depreciation, amortization and impairment losses [extract]

In the 2005 financial year, Deutsche Telekom recognized an impairment loss of EUR 1.9 billion at the T-Mobile UK cash-generating unit. Telefónica announced its offer to acquire the UK group O2 at a price of 200 pence per share (approximately GBP 17.7 billion) on October 31, 2005. When determining the fair value less costs to sell, the purchase prices paid in comparable transactions must generally be given preference over internal DCF calculations. The fair value of the cash-generating unit T-Mobile UK was derived from the Telefónica offer in accordance with a valuation model based on multipliers.

5.4.2   *Exposure Draft – Fair Value Measurement – and IAS 36*

The IASB issued the Exposure Draft – *Fair Value Measurement* – in May 2009. The Exposure Draft proposes to clarify the definition of fair value that can be applied in all accounting standards and thereby to remove guidance in other standards. This will affect IAS 36's guidance on estimating FVLCS, described at 3.3.1 and discussed above. At present, it appears that the Exposure Draft is not intended to affect the concept of VIU in IAS 36.

The Exposure Draft defines fair value as 'the price that would be received to sell an asset or paid to transfer a liability in an orderly transaction between market participants at the measurement date'.[206] It is explicitly an exit price.

Much of the Exposure Draft is devoted to the terms in this definition and to the inputs into the measurement of fair value. It discusses the asset (or liability), the transaction, the market and participants and the price. As far as measurement is concerned, it applies a fair value hierarchy for inputs into the valuation with Level 1 being unadjusted quoted prices in an active market, Level 2 inputs that are directly or indirectly observable other than quoted prices and Level 3 inputs that are not based on observable market data but reflect assumptions used by market participants, including risk.

FVLCS in IAS 36 is already an exit value. IAS 36 has its own hierarchy for establishing FVLCS which, while not the same as that in the Exposure Draft, is similar in approach. As described in 3.3.1, if there is no binding sale agreement or active market from which to obtain a current bid price, the price may be estimated from the most recent transaction provided there has been no significant change in economic circumstances in the intervening period. If there is no active market, FVLCS will be based on estimates of the market price of the asset in an arm's length transaction.[207] Using the Exposure Draft's approach, estimating fair value will use Level 2 and Level 3 inputs. As these levels are tools for analysis and disclosure they will not of themselves change the measurement of fair value for the purposes of IAS 36. However, as the principles in the Exposure Draft do not address the issues relating to the fair value of businesses it is not yet clear that there will be no practical impact at all.

5.5 Testing for impairment: group issues

There are some challenging problems in testing for impairment when looking at part of a group. This section looks at a series of such issues:

- Associates and jointly controlled entities and testing goodwill for impairment (5.5.1)
- Testing investments in subsidiaries, jointly controlled entities and associates for impairment in separate financial statements (5.5.2)
- Testing for impairment in separate and individual financial statements (5.5.3)
- Acquisitions of non-controlling (minority) interests of a subsidiary and subsequent goodwill impairment tests (5.5.4)
- Acquisitions by subsidiaries and determining the level at which the group tests goodwill for impairment (5.5.5)

Some of these have been dealt with by the IASB or are in the process of being considered, as discussed in the sections below. However, two particular problem areas are:

(i)   testing the investments themselves for impairment, where the IASB has proposed improvements to IAS 27 and IAS 36, described at 5.5.2B below, and

(ii)   testing for impairment at the level of an individual group company, particularly a subsidiary, whether it prepares:

- separate financial statements in accordance with IAS 27 or individual financial statements (see Chapter 8 at 1 for an explanation of the difference); or
- consolidated financial statements for a subgroup that it heads.

The second case raises difficult issues, considered at 5.5.3 below, about the definition of the reporting entity and the CGU and how to apply the concepts to complex groups that may have reorganised their businesses to obtain fiscal or regulatory advantages.

The specific issue of dividends and their effect on investments in subsidiaries is dealt with in Chapter 8 at 2.3.

5.5.1   Associates and jointly controlled entities and testing goodwill for impairment

When calculating its share of an equity accounted investee's results, an investor makes adjustments to the associate's profit or loss to reflect depreciation and impairments of the associate's identifiable assets based on their fair values at the date the investor acquires its investment. This is covered in paragraph 23 of IAS 28 – *Investments in Associates* – which states that:

> 'Appropriate adjustments to the investor's share of the associate's profits or losses after acquisition are also made to account, for example, for depreciation of the depreciable assets, based on their fair values at the acquisition date. Similarly, appropriate adjustments to the investor's share of the associate's profits or losses after acquisition are made for impairment losses recognised by the associate, such as for goodwill or property, plant and equipment.'

Although this refers to 'appropriate adjustments' for goodwill impairment losses, this should not be interpreted as requiring the investor to recalculate the goodwill impairment on a similar basis to depreciation and impairment of tangible and intangible assets. The 'appropriate adjustment' is to reverse that goodwill impairment before calculating the investor's share of the investee's profit. After application of the equity method the entire equity-accounted carrying amount of the investor's investment, including the goodwill included in that carrying amount, is tested for impairment in accordance with paragraphs 31-34 of IAS 28. Note that there is no requirement to test investments in associates for impairment annually but only when there are indicators that the amount may not be recoverable. These requirements are described in detail in Chapter 11 at 4.

With jointly controlled entities, the treatment varies depending on whether the interest is included by way of proportionate consolidation or by equity accounting. If the investor uses proportionate consolidation then it accounts for its share of the underlying assets, including goodwill, and liabilities of the investee. Therefore, the investor's share of goodwill is tested for impairment annually as described in 3.4 above.

If, on the other hand, the investor uses the equity method then it applies the requirements of IAS 28 as described above.

Impairment provisions made against investments in associates or jointly controlled entities included by way of the equity method may be reversed if an impairment loss no longer exists or has decreased (see 3.6 above). IAS 36 does not allow impairments of goodwill to be reversed[208] but this is not a provision against goodwill so this prohibition does not apply. This was confirmed when IAS 28 was amended in 2008's

Annual Improvements, applicable to accounting periods beginning on or after 1 January 2009; paragraph 33 now states that 'an impairment loss recognised in those circumstances is not allocated to any asset, including goodwill, that forms part of the carrying amount of the investment in the associate. Accordingly, any reversal of that impairment loss is recognised in accordance with IAS 36 to the extent that the recoverable amount of the investment subsequently increases'.

Similarly, although IAS 39 restricts the circumstances in which impairments in investments in certain financial assets may be reversed (see Chapter 23) these do not apply to interests included in consolidated accounts using the equity method (or included in separate financial accounts if the entity applies the equity method).

5.5.2 Testing investments in subsidiaries, jointly controlled entities and associates for impairment in separate financial statements

Many entities within a group prepare separate financial statements in accordance with IAS 27 either through choice or legal obligation. Of these, most probably choose to carry their investments in subsidiaries, jointly controlled entities and associates at cost, which means that they are within scope of IAS 36.[209] Alternatively they may carry investments 'in accordance with IAS 39',[210] which means applying one of the classifications allowed by that standard (most likely at fair value through profit or loss or available for sale – see Chapter 29 at 7),

The IASB proposes in the *Improvements to IFRSs* issued by the IASB in August 2009 to 'clarify' that in its separate financial statements the investor is to carry these investments at cost or at fair value through profit or loss, both in accordance with IAS 39 and to use that standard to test these investments for impairment.[211] This is considered further at C below.

Unless and until the proposed amendment comes into effect, investments in subsidiaries, jointly controlled entities and associates carried at cost must be tested for impairment using IAS 36. This is a challenge as it is not clear how IAS 36's requirements are to be applied, as is discussed further below.

A   Applying an IAS 36 methodology

If an entity can demonstrate that a subsidiary contains one or more CGUs in their entirety then it will be able to use impairment tests of the underlying CGUs to test the investment for impairment. If the aggregate VIU or FVLCS of the CGU or CGUs is not less than the carrying value of the investment, then the investment will not be impaired.

However, it may not be so straightforward in practice. There are particular problems if the asset (the investment) and the underlying CGU are not the same. CGUs may overlap individual subsidiaries so, for example, a single CGU may contain more than one such subsidiary. There may be apparent indicators of impairment of the investment: the individual subsidiary may be loss-making or there may be little or no history of distributions. Even if the CGU and investment coincide, the shares may have been acquired in a business combination. It is quite possible that the synergies that gave rise to goodwill on acquisition are in another part of the group not controlled by the intermediate parent in question. Some of the matters that may be taken into account in testing subsidiaries for impairment are discussed at 5.5.3 below.

B   IAS 28's approach to impairment

IAS 28 includes guidance on establishing the VIU of an equity interest in an associate. It states that:

> 'In determining the value in use of the investment, an entity estimates:
>
> (a)   its share of the present value of the estimated future cash flows expected to be generated by the associate, including the cash flows from the operations of the associate and the proceeds on the ultimate disposal of the investment; or
>
> (b)   the present value of the estimated future cash flows expected to arise from dividends to be received from the investment and from its ultimate disposal.
>
> Under appropriate assumptions, both methods give the same result.[212]
>
> The recoverable amount of an investment in an associate is assessed for each associate, unless the associate does not generate cash inflows from continuing use that are largely independent of those from other assets of the entity.'[213]

This impairment approach resembles an IAS 39 methodology as it is based on all expected cash flows and it does not impose the restrictions on the cash flows required for a VIU calculation. For example, it does not restrict the cash flows, normally based on budgets and forecasts for a maximum of five years, nor does it impose restrictions on restructuring and reorganisation expenses.

Testing an investment in an associate or jointly controlled entity carried under the equity method in consolidated accounts using this method cannot always provide assurance about the cost of shares in the investor's separate financial statements. Accounting for the group's share of losses may take the equity interest below cost and an impairment test could reveal no need for an impairment provision. This might not provide any assurance about the (higher) carrying value of shares in the separate financial statements.

Some have taken the reasonable view that this approach can be applied to an investment in the shares of an associate carried at cost in the investor's accounts and, by analogy, to an investment in a subsidiary or jointly controlled entity. Applying the IAS 28 methodology may also run into problems if there have been group reorganisations. Entities may have reorganised the businesses within their subsidiaries in such a way that value (and future cash flows) have been transferred from one to another. One common example is discussed at 5.5.3A below.

However, the IFRIC considered that it is not clear whether the IAS 28 method of testing equity investments in associates is, in fact, appropriate in the separate financial statements and has gone further, questioning whether IAS 36 or IAS 39 applies in those statements to investments in subsidiaries, associates and jointly controlled entity. As a result, the IASB has proposed the amendments to IAS 27 and IAS 36 that are discussed at C below.

C   *The IASB's proposed approach to testing for impairment in separate financial statements*

In the IFRIC *Update*, May 2009, the IFRIC opined that it was not clear whether the IAS 28 method of testing equity investments in associates for impairment was appropriate in the separate financial statements. The IFRIC went further, questioning whether IAS 36 or IAS 39 applies in those statements. It noted that it had considered whether there was a need for further guidance:

> 'The IFRIC noted that IAS 36 *Impairment of Assets* provides clear guidance that its requirements apply to impairment losses of investments in associates when the associate is accounted for using the equity method. However, in its separate financial statements, the investor may account for its investment in an associate at cost. The IFRIC concluded that it is not clear whether in its separate financial statements the investor should determine impairment in accordance with IAS 36 or IAS 39 *Financial Instruments: Recognition and Measurement.*
>
> In view of the existing guidance in IFRSs, the IFRIC concluded that significant diversity is likely to exist in practice on this issue. The IFRIC decided that it could be best resolved by referring it to the IASB. Therefore, the IFRIC [decided] not to add this issue to its agenda.'

Note that IAS 28 acknowledges that the associate may be part of a larger CGU.

As a result, the IASB proposed in the *Improvements to IFRSs* issued in August 2009 to 'clarify' that in its separate financial statements the investor is to carry investments in subsidiaries, associates and jointly controlled entities at cost or at fair value through profit or loss, both in accordance with IAS 39 and to use that standard to test these investments for impairment.[214] At the same time it proposes removing investments in these investments from the scope of IAS 36, replacing that standard's requirements with the following:

> 'When an entity prepares separate financial statements, it shall apply the requirements of IAS 39 for the determination and measurement of impairment losses on investments in subsidiaries, jointly controlled entities and associates.'[215]

Testing financial assets for impairment is discussed in Chapter 32 at 6.

It is difficult to determine exactly what impact this might have as it appears to be linked to the IASB's proposals to replace IAS 39, under which there will be no 'cost' exemption for equity investments. The replacement is proposed, at least in part, as a response to the financial crisis; see in particular Chapter 29 at 1.6.

Unless and until the proposed amendment comes into effect, investments in subsidiaries, jointly controlled entities and associates carried at cost must be tested for impairment under IAS 36.

D   *Group reorganisations and the carrying value of investments in subsidiaries*

A common form of group reorganisation involves the transfer to another group company of the tangible assets and trade of a subsidiary. These transactions often take place at the book value of the transferor's assets rather than at fair value. If the original carrying value was a purchase price that included an element of goodwill, the remaining 'shell', i.e. an entity that no longer has any trade or activities, may have a carrying value in the parent company's balance sheet in excess of its net worth. It could be argued that as the subsidiary is now a shell with no possibility in its current state of generating sufficient profits to support its value, a provision should be made by the parent to reduce its investment in the shell company to its net worth. However, the transfer of part of the group's business from one controlled entity to another has no substance from the perspective of the group and will have no effect in the consolidated accounts. There has also been no loss overall to the parent as a result of this reorganisation.

This is, of course, a transaction between companies under common control as all of the combining entities or businesses are ultimately controlled by the same party or parties both before and after the business combination, and that control is not transitory.[216] This means that the treatment by the acquirer (the transferee) is out of the scope of IFRS 3.

From the transferor entity's perspective, the transaction combines a sale of its assets at an undervalue to the transferee, by reference to the fair value of the transferor's net assets, and a distribution of the shortfall in value to its parent. The fair value of those assets to the parent may well not be reflected in the transferor's own balance sheet because there is no push-down accounting under IFRS. The transferor is not obliged to record the 'distribution' to its parent at fair value. IFRIC 17 – *Distributions of Non-cash Assets to Owners* – issued in November 2008, will require gains or losses measured by reference to fair value of the assets distributed to be taken to profit or loss but, amongst other restrictions, excludes from its scope non-cash distributions made by wholly-owned group companies (see Chapter 8 at 2.3.2).

This interpretation of the transferor's transaction (as a sale at an undervalue and a deemed distribution to the parent) is wholly consistent with a legal analysis in some jurisdictions, for example the United Kingdom, where a company that does not have zero or positive distributable reserves is unable to sell its assets at an undervalue because it cannot make any sort of distribution.

The parent, in turn, could be seen as having made a capital contribution of the shortfall in value to the transferee. The parent may choose to record the distribution from the transferor (and consequent impairment in its carrying value) and the contribution to the transferee (and consequent increase in its carrying value). This is consistent with our analysis in Chapter 8 at 4.2 regarding intra-group transactions and the extent to which the arrangement affects the individual financial statements of the parent.

The transferee will not necessarily record the capital contribution even if this is an option available to it.

However, the underlying principles are not affected by whether or not the transferee makes this choice – there has been a transfer of value from one subsidiary to another.

This demonstrates why the business transfer alone does not necessarily result in an impairment charge in the parent entity.

If the above analysis is not supportable in a particular jurisdiction then an impairment write down may have to be taken.

Actual circumstances may be less straightforward. In particular, the transferor and transferee entities may not be held directly by the same parent. This may make it necessary to make a provision for impairment against the carrying value of the transferor ('shell') company in its intermediate parent to reflect its loss in value, which will be treated as an expense or as a distribution, depending on the policy adopted by the entity. See Chapter 8 at 4.4.1 for a discussion of the policy choices available to the entity. There may be another, higher level within the group at which the above arguments against impairment will apply.

Example 18.26:   Group reorganisations and impairment

Topco has two directly held subsidiaries, Tradeco and Shellco. It acquired Shellco for £30 million and immediately thereafter transferred all of its trade and assets to its fellow subsidiary Tradeco for book value of £10 million with the proceeds being left outstanding on intercompany account. Shellco now has net assets of £10 million (its intercompany receivable) but a carrying value in Topco of £30 million. On the other hand, the value of Tradeco has been enhanced by its purchase of the business at an undervalue.

In our view, there are two acceptable ways in which Tradeco may account for this. The cost of the business combination may be the fair value of the cash given as consideration, i.e. £10 million and Tradeco will recognise no goodwill. Alternatively, it is the fair value of the cash given as consideration (£10 million), together with a deemed capital contribution received from Topco for the difference up to the fair value of the business of Shellco of £20 million, which will be recognised in equity, giving a total consideration of £30 million. Tradeco will recognise goodwill of £20 million.

The capital contribution measured under the second method represents the value distributed by Shellco to its parent Topco and thence to Tradeco.

If there is an intermediate holding company between Topco and Shellco but all other facts remain the same, then it would appear that a provision for impairment ought to be made against the carrying value of Shellco in its immediate parent. The argument against impairment would still apply in Topco.

5.5.3   Testing for impairment in separate and individual financial statements

In many jurisdictions, subsidiary entities are not exempt from preparing financial statements and these may be required to comply with IFRSs. These may be accounts for the subsidiary on a stand-alone basis or may be consolidated accounts for the subgroup that it heads. Either way, there may be problems in testing its own assets or CGUs, or the assets or CGUs in its consolidated accounts, for impairment.

The first issue is whether CGUs are different from the perspective of the subsidiary entity compared with that of the parent's consolidated accounts. We consider that the answer is no; once CGUs have been properly established for the group as a whole, they cannot be subdivided or differently assessed. They are defined as the smallest identifiable group of assets that generates cash inflows that are largely independent of the cash inflows from other assets or groups of assets. Therefore, the first challenge is to ensure that the group has set its CGUs at an appropriate level and there are no smaller identifiable groups of assets that meet the definition. However, not all accept this analysis; some consider that the CGU must be considered from the perspective of the individual subsidiary, irrespective of the CGU in the consolidated accounts. Those that take this view may, therefore, take into account only those cash flows arising in the individual entity.

Regardless of which view is taken, it is necessary first of all to determine if the CGU itself is impaired in value, no matter how that CGU relates to individual entities within the group. Only then is it possible to see whether a reasonable allocation of the CGU's value can be made to the interests in subsidiaries in question. However, if one assumes that CGUs are set at the level of the consolidated accounts, it may still not be possible to use a test of a CGU under IAS 36 to provide sufficient assurance of the value of assets in an individual subsidiary. The issue that may have to be faced is how to test part of a CGU for impairment, if that is what is represented by the subsidiary's net assets and operations. In essence, the problems may be the same as whether one assumes that the CGU is set for the consolidated accounts or for the subsidiary.

It is necessary to establish whether there is an identifiable feature that has caused the apparent impairment as that will have an impact on how the investment in the subsidiary is tested. Issues relating to transfer pricing, on what basis intra-group charges are made or whether, indeed, they are made at all, may need to be considered.

A   Transfer pricing

A subsidiary's assets may appear to be impaired because internal transfer pricing is not based on market prices for the products or services in question. The VIU of the CGU of which the loss making subsidiary is a part could therefore be apportioned between the various subsidiaries, substituting the fair values of inputs and outputs of the subsidiaries in question for the internal transfer prices. This is similar to the requirement to substitute the value on an active market for the internal transfer price when determining the VIU of a CGU, as described in 3.3.2 above.[217] Obviously, calculating the VIU of the whole CGU and apportioning it in this manner will avoid the potential pitfall of taking account of a notional increase in income to one subsidiary but neglecting to reflect the notional increase in costs to another. Individual subsidiaries may be part of more than one CGU, for example group finance, property holding or service companies, in which case the value may need to be considered by reference to a larger group of CGUs, in a manner analogous with corporate assets (see 3.3.2 Step 2 above).

Few subsidiaries can be allowed to carry on making losses in the longer term. In particular, unless they return to profitability they will eventually need the parents' support in order to be able to pay their creditors. The requirement for parental support represents a crucial difference when compared with the 'shell company' situation described above, because a parent does not need to do anything if it wishes to support indefinitely a non-trading subsidiary. This reinforces the need to understand why the subsidiary is loss-making. Only a subsidiary that is genuinely part of a larger CGU can have its value supported in this manner. If the parent is unprepared to make such a commitment, this is evidence that the investment in the subsidiary is in fact impaired.

5.5.4 Acquisitions of non-controlling (minority) interests of a subsidiary and subsequent goodwill impairment tests

In addition to changes to IFRS 3(2007), the IASB has also updated IAS 27 – *Consolidated and Separate Financial Statements* – in a manner that affects the acquisition of non-controlling (minority) interests[218]. In this case, only one of the three treatments currently considered acceptable will be permitted. The revised standard must apply from 1 July 2009 but must be applied at the same time as IFRS 3(as revised in 2008).[219]

Until an entity adopts the revised standards, and as discussed in Chapter 7 at 3.3, we believe that there are three acceptable treatments for accounting for the difference between the cost of acquisition and the minority interest acquired when an entity acquires an existing minority interest in a subsidiary:

(a) the entire difference may be reflected as goodwill (the 'Parent entity extension method');

(b) the entire difference may be reflected as an equity transaction (the 'Entity concept method'); or

(c) the difference may be reflected partly as goodwill – measured using IFRS 3's principles – and partly as equity (the 'Hybrid entity concept/parent entity method').

Where an entity adopts either (b) or (c) in accounting for such a transaction, this raises the issue as to whether any notional adjustment needs to be made to gross up the carrying the amount of goodwill in carrying out the impairment test of goodwill, similar to that discussed at 3.4.8 above.

Under the revised IAS 27, any change in a parent's ownership interest in a subsidiary that does not result in a loss of control is accounted for as an equity transaction (i.e. a transaction with owners in their capacity as such).[220] This applies equally to purchases and sales of a non-controlling interest. Any difference between the amount by which the non-controlling interests are adjusted and the fair value of the consideration paid or received is to be recognised directly in equity and attributed to the equity share of the parent.[221] This means that once the revised standards are applied, only method (b) above may be used.

In our view, where all of the minority interest has been acquired such that the subsidiary is now wholly-owned, no notional adjustment should be made, whether the transaction has been accounted for under the original or revised IAS 27, and the carrying amount of the CGU to which the goodwill has been allocated only needs to reflect the amount of goodwill that has been recognised as an asset. A notional adjustment is only required where there is still a minority interest in the CGU.

5.5.5 Acquisitions by subsidiaries and determining the level at which the group tests goodwill for impairment

IAS 36 requires goodwill to be allocated to the lowest level within the entity at which the goodwill is monitored for internal management purposes. If a subsidiary undertakes acquisitions and recognises goodwill in its own financial statements, the level at which the subsidiary's management monitors the goodwill may differ from the level at which the parent's or group's management monitors goodwill from the group's perspective.

If a subsidiary's management monitors its goodwill at a lower level than the level at which the parent's or group's management monitors its goodwill, a key issue is whether that lower level should, from the group's perspective, be regarded as the 'lowest level within the entity at which the goodwill is monitored for internal management purposes'? The answer is no, as is demonstrated in the following example

Example 18.27: Monitoring goodwill arising from acquisitions by subsidiaries

A parent acquired 100% of the issued shares of a company that operates autonomously and is required to prepare IFRS-compliant financial statements. The subsidiary has acquired various businesses both before and after becoming part of the group. Those business combinations have included significant amounts of goodwill.

The subsidiary's management monitors its acquired goodwill at the level of the subsidiary's operating segments. The group has assessed that these will be operating segments for the purposes of IAS 14 (or IFRS 8 on transition to that standard – see Chapter 35). However, management of the parent/group monitors its acquired goodwill at the level of the group's operating segments, which is a higher level than the subsidiary's operating segments. The subsidiary's operations form part of two of the group's six operating segments.

The subsidiary's goodwill comprises goodwill arising on its acquisitions, some of which took place *before*, and some *after*, the subsidiary became part of the group.

In contrast, the goodwill recognised by the group comprises:

- Goodwill acquired by the parent in the acquisition of the subsidiary (some of which represents goodwill acquired and therefore recognised by the subsidiary and some of which was internally generated goodwill from the subsidiary's perspective and therefore not recognised by the subsidiary);
- Goodwill acquired by the subsidiary since becoming part of the group;
- Goodwill acquired by the parent in other operating combinations (i.e. goodwill that relates to other subsidiaries and businesses that make up the group).

The goodwill acquired in the acquisition of the subsidiary that is recognised by the parent in its consolidated financial statements is therefore different from the goodwill recognised by the subsidiary (which relates only to the acquisitions made by the subsidiary and was measured at the date of the acquisition concerned).

In such circumstances the actions of the subsidiary's management in deciding the level at which it tests its goodwill for impairment will *not* cause the group to be 'locked in' to testing goodwill at the same level in the consolidated financial statements.

Rather, the group should test its goodwill for impairment at the level at which management of the parent or group monitors its various investments in goodwill, namely, in this example, at the group's business segment level (or operating segment level after the group implements IFRS 8).

5.6   The effect of IFRS 8 – *Operating Segments* – on impairment tests

From 1 January 2009 entities must apply IFRS 8 in financial statements and goodwill to be tested for impairment cannot be allocated to a CGU or CGU group larger than an *operating* segment as defined by the new standard.[222] IFRS 8 is discussed in Chapter 35. In some circumstances implementing the new standard can affect testing for impairment of goodwill or assets and CGUs. A number of these issues are described below, including entities whose operating segments are redefined on applying the new standards and the impact on entities that have a matrix form of organisation.

5.6.1   *Implementation of IFRS 8 affects allocation of goodwill*

If the different basis of segmentation under IFRS 8 results in different segments being reported than were reported under IAS 14, it follows that there will be differences between the CGUs that make up an IFRS 8 segment and those that made up an IAS 14 segment. As a result, the CGUs supporting goodwill may no longer be in the same segment under IFRS 8 as under IAS 14. This could occur, in particular, where goodwill has been allocated to groups of CGUs at or close to the level of an IAS 14 segment or for an entity that has a matrix organisation (see below). Under IFRS 8, it may sometimes be necessary to reallocate goodwill. It is possible that this reallocation of goodwill could 'expose' CGUs for which the carrying amount, including the allocated goodwill exceeds the recoverable amount, thereby giving rise to an impairment loss.

Example 18.28:   Implementing IFRS 8 affects the allocation of goodwill to segments

An entity has a single segment under IAS 14, consisting of CGU A and CGU B. Goodwill of €100 is allocated at the segment level. Following the implementation of IFRS 8, the entity determines that CGU A and CGU B are separate operating segments and goodwill of €30 is allocable to CGU A and €70 to CGU B. An impairment loss is triggered on the implementation of IFRS 8, as follows:

	Single segment under IAS 14	CGU A under IFRS 8	CGU B under IFRS 8
Carrying amount (including goodwill)	230	100	130
Recoverable amount	280	80	200
Excess of recoverable amount over carrying amount of CGU	50	(20)	70
Impairment loss under IAS 14	nil	n/a	n/a
Impairment loss under IFRS 8	n/a	(20)	nil

There are no transitional rules for an entity that finds itself in this situation. In our view, the entity ought to be able to reallocate goodwill for the purposes of testing it for impairment but how, in the absence of guidance, ought it to go about the reallocation?

In two situations, the disposal of an operation within a CGU and a change in the composition of CGUs due to a reorganisation, which are described at 3.4.9 and 3.4.10 above, IAS 36 allows a reallocation based on relative values. A reallocation of goodwill driven by the identification of new operating segments has some similarities to a reorganisation of the reporting structure.

Additional difficulties may arise because it is difficult to reconstruct conditions that existed at the time of the past acquisition so it may no longer be clear what the acquired goodwill originally related to. The reallocation of the goodwill to the operating segment level will be more difficult and arbitrary when the acquired business has lost its separate identity as a result of post-acquisition integration with pre-existing operations or other reorganisations. Thus, when information relating to the goodwill allocation is not available, the entity will have no alternative to allocating goodwill based on the current segment reporting structure.

It will often be necessary in practice to assess the recoverable amount of all the operating segments to which goodwill is to be allocated. All segments ought to be valued on a similar basis, whether this be VIU or FVLCS.

IAS 36 allows the use of a method other than relative values if it better reflects the goodwill associated with the part disposed of or with the reorganised units, but it does not give any indication as to what such a method might be. Other possible methods are discussed further at 3.4.9 above.

Whatever allocation methodology is used, goodwill can be allocated only to operating segments that benefit from the synergies of the business combination concerned.

5.6.2 *Implementation of IFRS 8 affects impairment tests of CGUs*

It is no longer possible for organizations managed on a matrix basis to test goodwill for impairment at the level of internal reporting, if this level crosses more than one operating segment as defined in IFRS 8. In addition, the operating segments selected by the entities may not correspond with their CGUs.

These are entities that manage their businesses simultaneously on two different bases; for example, some managers may be responsible for different product and service lines while others are responsible for specific geographical areas. IFRS 8 notes that the characteristics that define an operating segment may apply to two or more overlapping sets of components for which managers are held responsible. Financial information is available for both and the chief operating decision maker may regularly review both sets of operating results of components. In spite of this, IFRS 8 requires the entity to characterise one of these bases as determining its operating segments.

An entity might have allocated goodwill to a geographical area under IAS 14 but concluded under IFRS 8 that its operating segments are the product or business lines within that area. As described in 5.6.1 above, in these circumstances the entity must reallocate goodwill to its operating segments in order to test for impairment.

However, the designation of business segments as IFRS 8 operating segments may have the effect that a single CGU contains more than one operating segment. The classification as a CGU (the smallest identifiable group of assets that generates largely independent cash inflows) is unaffected by the IFRS 8 operating segment analysis. Therefore, the CGU may contain operating segments to which goodwill relates. For example, a telecommunications business may designate its network in a particular country as its CGU but its operating segments may be identified by the type of service or type of clients (e.g. telephone, internet and television; individual clients, business clients, other operators, etc).

The network CGU will be tested for impairment in the same way as before. However, when the goodwill is tested for impairment, it is possible for an impairment charge to exceed the goodwill relating to that segment. IAS 36 requires an entity to allocate the remaining impairment charge to the other non-current assets of the CGU until they are reduced to zero or, if determinable, their individual recoverable amount. The assets in a CGU that crosses more than one operating segment cannot be written down to a value lower than their own recoverable amount.[223] Pro-rata allocation of impairment to all CGU non-current assets including assets in CGU that crosses more than one operating segment is not appropriate if the carrying value of such assets is lower than the recoverable amount determined in a separate test.

5.6.3 Aggregation of operating segments for disclosure purposes

IFRS 8 allows an entity to aggregate two or more operating segments into a single operating segment if this is 'consistent with the core principles' and, in particular, that the segments have similar economic characteristics.[224] Whilst this is specifically in the context of segmental reporting, it might also, in isolation, have suggested that individual operating segments could also be aggregated to form one operating segment that would also apply for impairment purposes. The IASB in its Annual Improvements project has clarified that the 'unit of accounting' for goodwill impairment is before any aggregation allowed by paragraph 12 of IFRS 8 and paragraph 80(b) has been amended accordingly. The required unit for goodwill impairment is not larger than the operating segment level as defined in paragraph 5 of IFRS 8 before any aggregation. This is because IAS 36 requires allocation of goodwill at the level monitored by management for internal purposes.[225] An operating segment under IFRS 8 is the component monitored by the chief operating decision maker to assess performance and allocate resources.[226] The monitoring will be at the same level in both standards.

Entities that have tested goodwill using aggregated segments should apply this amendment prospectively for annual periods beginning on or after 1 January 2010 because of the practical problems in using hindsight to determine the fair values of CGUs in respect of past reporting periods.[227]

5.7   Consistency and the impairment test

Consistency is a very important principle underlying IAS 36. In testing for impairment entities must ensure that the carrying amount of the CGU is consistent for VIU and FVLCS; in calculating VIU, or using a discounted cash flow methodology for FVLCS, entities must ensure that there is consistency between the assets and liabilities of the CGU and the cash flows taken into account, as there must also be between the cash flows and discount rate. The following reprises the requirements of IAS 36 but also expands on certain common problem areas.

In determining VIU (3.3.2 above) Step 2 describes the exceptions to the rule that recognised liabilities are not included in arriving at the CGU's carrying value or VIU. The first is straightforward. If the buyer would have to assume a liability if it acquired an asset or CGU, then this liability should be deducted from the CGU's carrying amount and recoverable amount in order to perform a meaningful comparison between VIU and FVLCS.

It is also accepted in IAS 36 that an entity might for practical reasons determine the recoverable amount of a CGU after taking into account assets and liabilities such as receivables or other financial assets, trade payables, pensions and other provisions that are outside the scope of IAS 36.

In all cases:

- the carrying amount of the CGU must be calculated on the same basis for VIU and FVLCS, i.e. including the same assets and liabilities; and

- it is essential that cash flows are prepared on a consistent basis to the assets and liabilities within CGUs.

In addition, some of these assets and liabilities have themselves been calculated using discounting techniques. There is a danger of distortion as the cash flows for impairment purposes will be discounted using a different rate to the rate used to calculate the item itself.

(a)   Environmental provisions and similar provisions and liabilities

IAS 36 illustrates liabilities that must be deducted form the carrying amount using an example of a mine in a country in which there is a legal obligation to restore the site by replacing the overburden. The restoration provision, which is the present value of the restoration costs, has been provided for and included as part of the carrying value of the asset. It will be taken into account in the estimation of FVLCS but must also be deducted in arriving at VIU so that both methods of estimating recoverable amount are calculated on a comparable basis. To calculate VIU, the cash flows essential to replace the overburden must be included whenever the restoration takes place. If the outflow does not take place within the period covered by budgets and forecasts then the costs must be built into the calculation of the terminal value.

There are other provisions for liabilities that would be taken over by the purchaser of a CGU, e.g. property dilapidations or similar contractual restoration provisions. These may relate to an off-balance sheet leasehold interest in property or equipment rather than a fixed asset. The provision will be accrued as the 'damage' is incurred and hence expensed over time rather than capitalised. If the provision is deducted from the assets of the CGU then the cash outflows must reflect the amount that will be paid to settle the contractual obligation.

Indeed, any IAS 37 provision may be reflected in the CGU's carrying amount as long as the relevant cash flows are reflected both as to their amount and timing. However, this class of liability will reflect a discount rate suitable for provisions, based on the time value of money and the risks relating to the provision. This is likely to be considerably lower than a suitable discount rate for an asset.

(b)   *Finance leases*

A CGU may include assets held under finance leases. IAS 17 – *Leases* – requires an entity to apply IAS 36 in determining whether leased assets have become impaired in value. An entity may exclude the finance lease liability from the carrying amount but then it must also exclude the rental payments under the lease. Alternatively, it can deduct the related liabilities from the assets of the CGU and include the rental payments in the cash outflows, even though finance lease costs are charged to profit or loss as depreciation and finance costs. The entity will have to ensure consistent treatment of the carrying value for FVLCS purposes as an acquirer of the CGU will take account of all payments under finance and operating leases.

(c)   *Trade debtors and creditors*

If an entity includes trade debtors and creditors in the assets of the CGU, it must avoid double counting the cash flows that will repay the receivable or pay those liabilities. This may be tricky because cash flows do not normally distinguish between cash flows that relate to working capital items and others. The same applies to the inclusion of any financial asset or financial liability: including the asset or deducting the liability has no significant effect as long as the relevant cash flows are included for the relevant period of time.

(d)   *Pensions*

Pensions are mentioned by IAS 36 as items that might be included in the recoverable amount of a CGU. In practice this could be fraught with difficulty, especially if it is a defined benefit scheme, as there can be so much difference between the measurement basis of the pension asset or (more likely) liability and the cash flows that relate to pensions. This can make it extremely difficult to distinguish between repayment of the liability and cash flows that relate to the CGU. A pragmatic solution in most cases may be to estimate a pension cost, perhaps based on an IAS 19 'regular cost' (see Chapter 28 at 5), that is included as part of the employee cost cash flows.

(e)   *Cash flow hedges*

In the examples considered until now, the basis for including or excluding various items has more to do with ease of preparation than any underlying principle. Indeed, it makes no significant difference if, in the case of a cash flow hedge, the hedging asset or liability and the hedging cash flows are included in the calculation of recoverable amount. The result is to gross up or net down the assets of the CGU and the relevant cash flows by an equivalent amount, except for the distorting effects of differing discount rates. However, some entities argue that they ought to be able to take into account cash flows from instruments hedging their sales that are designated as cash flow hedges under IAS 39 because not to do so misrepresents their economic position. In order to do this, they wish to include the cash flows but either exclude the derivative asset or liability from the CGU or alternatively reflect the related cash flow hedge reserve in the CGU as well (this latter treatment would not be a perfect offset to the extent of inefficiencies). They argue that the cash flow hedges protect the fair value of assets through their effect on price risk. They also note that this introduces a profit or loss mismatch by comparison with instruments that meet the 'normal purchase/normal sale' exemption under which the derivative remains off balance sheet until exercised.

Although logical from an income perspective, IAS 36 does not support these arguments. The derivative asset or liability can only be included in the CGU as a practical expediency and the hedge reserve is neither an asset nor liability to be reflected in the CGU. IAS 39 would not permit an entity to mitigate the effects of impairment by recycling the appropriate amount from the hedging reserve. Finally, entities must be aware that cash flow hedges may have negative values as well as positive ones.

6   EFFECTIVE DATE AND TRANSITIONAL PROVISIONS

6.1   Transitional provisions and effective date

The original transitional arrangements and effective date applied, at the latest, prospectively from the beginning of the first annual period beginning on or after 31 March 2004.[228]

7   CONCLUSION

Two developments have placed increased emphasis on the part to be played by impairment within financial reporting under International GAAP. First, the regime under which goodwill is not amortised means that impairment tests have to be applied at least annually by all entities that record goodwill in their consolidated accounts. Additionally, those entities that are adopting IFRSs for the first time will have to apply an impairment test to all goodwill carried forward at transition. Second, the policy of the IASB to extend fair value based accounting, especially fair values that are based on models and not on observable market transactions, will also increase the importance of testing for impairment.

Notwithstanding this central role, IAS 36 is not an easy standard for entities to apply in practice. To take discount rates as a case in point, an entity is required to arrive at an estimate of the rate that the market would expect on an equally risky investment.[229] This information is not readily obtainable. The standard allows a number of different methods to be used to estimate this rate; yet it gives little concrete guidance and allows as a starting point discount rates that are unlikely to be relevant, such as an entity's incremental borrowing rate. It is possible that the standard setters have attempted to deflect academic criticism by not specifying how a discount rate should be chosen; but this vagueness has left many entities unsure about how to proceed.

As a consequence, it becomes difficult to be convinced that the comparability requirement underlying IFRS is being met in practice, as entities interpret the standard's requirements in differing ways. Moreover, because assets (other than goodwill and intangible assets with an indefinite life) or CGUs are only tested for impairment if there are indicators of impairment, there must be comparability issues even within entities.

It is difficult to see how these issues can be resolved in the continuing absence of a clear underlying theoretical basis underpinning the carrying value of assets and liabilities. In the short term, it is likely that many entities will consult valuations experts in order to apply IAS 36. In the longer term it remains to be seen if the IASB will give entities the standard on impairment that they deserve, which is one that contains an unambiguous, comparable and useable impairment test.

References

1 IAS 36, *Impairment of Assets*, IASB, para. 13.
2 IAS 27, *Consolidated and Separate Financial Statements*, IASB, paras. 30 and 31.
3 IAS 36, para. 1.
4 IAS 36, para. 2.
5 IAS 36, para. 3.
6 IAS 36, para. 4.
7 IAS 28, *Investments in Associates*, IASB, para. 33.
8 IAS 36, para. 5.
9 IAS 36, para. 10.
10 IAS 36, para. 11.
11 IAS 36, paras. 8-9.
12 IAS 36, para. 15.
13 IAS 36, para. 9.
14 IAS 36, para. 13.
15 IAS 36, para. 12.
16 IAS 36, para. 14.
17 IAS 36, para. 15.
18 IAS 36, para. 16.
19 IAS 36, para. 17.
20 IAS 36, para. 6.
21 IAS 36, para. 18.
22 IAS 36, para. 19.
23 IAS 36, para. 22.
24 IAS 36, para. 31.
25 IAS 36, para. 20.
26 IAS 36, para. 23.
27 IAS 36, para. 21.
28 IFRS 5, *Non-current Assets Held for Sale and Discontinued Operations*, IASB, para. 18.
29 IAS 36, para. 25.
30 IAS 36, para. 26.
31 IAS 36, para. 27.
32 IAS 36, para. 27.
33 IAS 36, para. 28.
34 IAS 36, para. 29.

35 IAS 36, para. 30.
36 IAS 36, para. 31.
37 IAS 36, para. 66.
38 IAS 36, para. 67.
39 IAS 36, paras. 6 and 68.
40 IAS 36, para. 68.
41 IAS 36, para. 69.
42 IAS 36, para. 6.
43 IAS 36, para. 70.
44 IAS 36, para. 71.
45 IAS 36, I.E. Example 1B.
46 IAS 36, paras. 72-73.
47 IAS 36, paras. 74-75.
48 IAS 36, para. 76.
49 IAS 36, para. 77.
50 IAS 36, para. 78.
51 IAS 36, para. 79.
52 IAS 36, para. 100.
53 IAS 36, para. 101.
54 IAS 36, para. 102.
55 IAS 36, para. 102.
56 IAS 36, para. 103, I.E. Example 8.
57 IAS 36, para. 30.
58 IAS 36, para. 33.
59 IAS 36, para. 34.
60 IAS 36, para. 35.
61 IAS 36, para. 38.
62 IAS 36, para. 36.
63 IAS 36, para. 37.
64 IAS 36, para. 39.
65 IAS 36, para. 40.
66 IAS 36, para. 43.
67 IAS 36, para. 41.
68 IAS 36, para. 42.
69 IAS 36, para. 44.
70 IAS 36, para. 48.

71 IAS 36, para. 49.
72 IAS 36, paras. 44-45.
73 IAS 36, paras. 46-47.
74 IAS 36, para. 47.
75 IAS 36, paras. 50-51.
76 IAS 36, para. 52-53.
77 IAS 36, para. 54.
78 IAS 36, para. BCZ49.
79 IAS 21, *The Effects of Changes in Foreign Exchange Rates*, IASB, para. 25.
80 IAS 36, para. 55.
81 IAS 36, para. 56.
82 IAS 36, para. 56.
83 IAS 36, para. A17.
84 IAS 36, para. A18.
85 IAS 36, para. A18.
86 IAS 36, para. A19.
87 IAS 36, para. A20.
88 IAS 36, para. A21.
89 IAS 36, para. 16.
90 One source of reference which may prove useful is a Digest issued by the Corporate Finance Faculty of the ICAEW – *The Cost of Capital*, Simon Pallett, ICAEW, 1999.
91 IAS 36, para. 55.
92 IAS 36, para. BCZ85.
93 IAS 36, paras. BCZ85 and BCZ94.
94 IAS 36, para. 59.
95 IAS 36, para. 60.
96 IAS 36, para. 61.
97 IAS 16, *Property, Plant and Equipment*, IASB, para. 73(d).
98 IAS 36, para. 62.
99 IAS 36, para. 63.
100 IAS 36, para. 104.
101 IAS 36, para. 88.
102 IAS 36, para. 105.
103 IAS 36, para. 106.
104 IAS 36, para. 108.
105 IAS 36, para. 107.
106 IFRS 3 (2007), *Business Combinations*, IASB, 2007 Bound Volume, paras. 54-55.
107 IAS 38, *Intangible Assets*, IASB, paras. 89 and 107-108.
108 IFRS 3 (2007), para. 54.
109 IFRS 3 (2007), para. 55.
110 IFRS 3, *Business Combinations*, IASB, Appendix A.
111 IFRS 3, para. BC328.
112 IFRS 3, para. B63.
113 IAS 36, paras. 80-81.
114 IAS 36, para. 82.
115 IAS 36, para. BC140.
116 IFRS 8, *Operating Segments*, IASB, para. 5.
117 IAS 36, para. 83.
118 IAS 36, para. 83.
119 IFRS 3 (2007), para. 62.
120 IFRS 3, para. 46.
121 IFRS 3, para. 45.
122 IAS 36, para. 85.
123 IAS 36, para. 84.
124 IAS 36, para. BC152.
125 IAS 36, para. 90.
126 IAS 36, para. BC162.
127 IAS 36, para. 9.
128 IAS 36, para. 90.
129 IAS 36, para. 90.
130 IAS 36, para. 96.
131 IAS 36, para. BC173.
132 IAS 36, paras. 97-98.
133 IAS 36, para. 99.
134 IAS 36, para. BC177.
135 IAS 36, para. 124.
136 IAS 36, para. 125.
137 IAS 36, para. 91.
138 IFRS 3, para. 10.
139 IFRS 3, para. 19 and IAS 36 para. C1.
140 IAS 36, para. C2 and IFRS 3, para. C10 and IGA3.
141 IAS 36, para. C6.
142 IAS 36, para. C7.
143 IAS 36, paras. 92, C3 and C4.
144 IAS 36, paras. 93 and C6.
145 IAS 36, para. 94 and para. 104.
146 IAS 36, I.E. Example 7.
147 IAS 36, para. 86.
148 IAS 36, para. BC156.
149 IAS 36, para. 87.
150 IAS 38, para. 91.
151 IAS 36, para. 10.
152 IAS 36, para. 10.
153 IAS 36, paras. 10-11.
154 IAS 36, para. 89.
155 IAS 36, para. 9.
156 IAS 36, para. 24.
157 IAS 36, para. 11.
158 IAS 36, para. 89.
159 IAS 36, para. 24.
160 IAS 36, para. 124.
161 IAS 36, para. 125.
162 IAS 36, para. 110.
163 IAS 36, para. 111.
164 IAS 36, para. 111.
165 IAS 36, para. 113.
166 IAS 36, paras. 114-116.
167 IAS 36, para. 117.
168 IAS 36, para. 118.
169 IAS 36, para. 119.
170 IAS 36, para. 121.
171 IAS 36, paras. 119-120.
172 IAS 36, para. 121.
173 IAS 36, paras. 122-123.
174 IAS 36, para. 126.
175 IAS 36, para. 126.

Chapter 19

Capitalisation of borrowing costs

1   INTRODUCTION

A point of contention in determining the initial measurement of an asset is whether or not finance costs incurred during the period of its construction should be capitalised. There have always been a number of strong arguments in favour of the capitalisation of directly attributable finance costs. It is argued that they are just as much a cost as any other directly attributable cost, that expensing finance costs distorts the choice between purchasing and constructing an asset, that capitalising the costs leads to a carrying value that is far more akin to the market value of the asset and that the accounts are more likely to represent the true success or failure of the project. However, some proponents of this view have noted that there is a cost to all entities of constructing assets whether or not they have taken out borrowings for the purpose. Therefore if capitalisation is mandatory, in theory notional interest should also be capitalised. No standard-setter has yet taken this step.

In March 1984, the (then) IASC published IAS 23 – *Capitalisation of Borrowing Costs*. Under this original version of IAS 23, capitalisation was optional, but certain rules were laid down if a policy of capitalisation were to be adopted.[1] A new version of IAS 23 – *Borrowing Costs* – was issued in 1993, which did not go so far as to ban the capitalisation of borrowing costs but the benchmark treatment was that they should be recognised as an expense in the period in which they are incurred regardless of how the borrowings are applied.[2] Capitalisation of borrowing costs was an allowed alternative treatment.

However, the IASB has changed direction again. In March 2007, on the basis of eliminating some (but in fact by no means all) of the differences between IFRS and US GAAP in this area, it issued a revised version of IAS 23 this time mandating capitalisation of borrowing costs directly attributable to the acquisition, construction or production of a qualifying asset. The IASB made only minor changes to the rest of the standard, principally two amendments to the scope. It now takes account of those standards that allow assets to be measured at fair value, where capitalisation will continue to be a matter of accounting policy choice and exempts inventories that are routinely manufactured or otherwise produced in large quantities on a repetitive basis (see 2.1.2 below).

The revised standard applies to accounting periods commencing on or after 1 January 2009 although early implementation is permitted; this is discussed in more detail at 4.1 below. It is this revised standard that is the subject of this chapter.

The IASB noted that this latest revision eliminates the main difference between IAS 23 and FASB Statement No. 34 – *Capitalization of Interest Cost* (SFAS 34) although there remain many differences of detail that have not been addressed. The IASB has justified its change in stance by arguing that 'this will result in an improvement in financial reporting as well as achieving convergence in principle with US GAAP'.[3]

The revised standard is unlikely to have affected entities that have already adopted a policy of capitalisation as the requirements remain unchanged. The many entities that might otherwise have expensed all borrowing costs as incurred will have needed to introduce systems and processes to capture relevant information and calculate the amount of costs to be capitalised. They will also have needed to consider the impact of other finance costs such as hedging activities and exchange differences on foreign currency borrowings (see 3 below).

2   THE REQUIREMENTS OF IAS 23

2.1   Accounting policy

IAS 23 requires that borrowing costs must be capitalised if they are directly attributable to the acquisition, construction or production of a qualifying asset. These borrowing costs are included in the cost of the asset; all other borrowing costs are recognised as an expense in the period in which they are incurred.

2.2   Scope and definitions

2.2.1   Scope

IAS 23 deals with the treatment of borrowing costs in general, rather than focusing on capitalising borrowing costs as part of the carrying value of assets.

The standard does not deal with the actual or imputed costs of equity.[4] This means that any distributions or other payments made in respect of equity instruments, as defined by IAS 32 – *Financial Instruments: Presentation* – are not within the scope of IAS 23; conversely, interest and dividends payable on instruments classified as financial liabilities would appear to be within the scope of the standard. See Chapter 31 regarding the classification of instruments as debt or equity.

2.2.2   Qualifying assets

IAS 23 defines a qualifying asset as 'an asset that necessarily takes a substantial period of time to get ready for its intended use or sale'.[5] Assets that are ready for their intended use or sale when acquired are not qualifying assets.[6] Examples of qualifying assets in the standard are manufacturing plants, power generation facilities, investment properties and intangible assets[7], However, this should not be taken as evidence that intangible were not qualifying assets under the previous IAS 23. For instance, IFRIC 12 – *Service Concession Arrangements* – refers to an entity capitalising borrowing costs during the construction phase when the accumulating right to be paid for construction services and the ultimate asset are both accounted for as intangible assets (see Chapter 23 at 5.4.3).[8]

Inventories are within scope of IAS 23 as long as they meet the definition and require a substantial period of time to bring them to a saleable condition.[9] However, inventories that are routinely manufactured or otherwise produced in large quantities on a repetitive basis are not qualifying assets so capitalisation need not be applied.[10] There is no requirement that this production be only over a short period of time.

This exemption has been allowed because of the difficulty of calculating and monitoring the amount to be capitalised but it permits an entity that has chosen not to capitalise interest on such assets to continue with its existing policy. There are many examples of such inventories, including large manufactured or constructed items that take some time to complete but are basically sold as standard items, such as aircraft and large items of equipment or food and drink that takes a long time to mature, such as cheeses or alcohol that matures in bottle or cask.

IAS 23 does not require entities to capitalise interest in respect of assets that are measured at fair value that would otherwise be qualifying assets. If the assets are held under a full fair value model with all changes going to profit or loss then capitalisation does not affect measurement in the balance sheet and would be no more than a reallocation between finance costs and the fair value movement in profit or loss. However, IAS 23 does not restrict the exemption to assets where the fair value movement is taken to profit or loss. Other assets measured at fair value that fall under IAS 16's revaluation model, are also eligible for this scope exemption even though the revaluation goes to equity (or 'other comprehensive income' as it is referred to in the revised IAS 1 – *Presentation of Financial Statements* – see Chapter 3), not profit.[11]

IAS 11– *Construction Contracts* – permits borrowing costs to be capitalised when they can be attributable to contract activity and allocated to specific contracts.[12] Note that although the reference to IAS 23 in that paragraph was deleted with the revised IAS 23 by consequential amendment, borrowing costs will need to be capitalised, when they otherwise meet the criteria under the revised IAS 23. The IASB argued that it is unnecessary to refer to IAS 23 as attributing borrowing costs to contracts is really a matter of identifying the contract costs and does not affect the recognition of borrowing costs as specified in IAS 23.[13]

In the case of equity accounted investments, the (then) IASC considered whether or not the investor should look through to the investee's activities when applying the Standard. However, it decided that this could involve an element of double-counting borrowing costs, since the investee itself would also apply the Standard.[14] The revised IAS 23 has clarified this and now excludes all financial assets from the definition of qualifying assets.[15]

2.2.3   *Borrowing costs*

Borrowing costs are interest and other costs incurred by an entity in connection with the borrowing of funds.[16]

Borrowing costs are defined to include:

- interest expense calculated using the effective interest method as described in IAS 39 – *Financial Instruments: Recognition and Measurement*;

- finance charges in respect of finance leases recognised in accordance with IAS 17 – *Leases*; and

- exchange differences arising from foreign currency borrowings to the extent that they are regarded as an adjustment to interest costs.[17]

The identification and measurement of finance costs is not a matter for IAS 23 and this is an area that has changed considerably since the first version of the standard was issued in 1984. This is discussed further at 3.1 below.

2.3   Capitalisation of borrowing costs

2.3.1   *Directly attributable borrowing costs*

In determining which borrowing costs satisfy the 'directly attributable' criterion, the standard starts from the premise that directly attributable borrowing costs are those that would have been avoided if the expenditure on the qualifying asset had not been made.[18]

The standard notes that the borrowing costs that are directly related can be readily identified if an entity borrows funds specifically for the purpose.[19] In this case, the borrowing costs eligible for capitalisation are the actual borrowing costs incurred during the period.[20]

However, as entities frequently borrow funds in advance of expenditure on qualifying assets, investment income on the temporary investment of those borrowings should be deducted and only the net amount capitalised (see Example 19.5).[21] There is no restriction in IAS 23 as to the type of investments in which the funds can be invested, but in our view, to maintain the conclusion that the funds are specific borrowings, the investment must be of a nature that does not expose the principal amount to the risk of not being recovered. The more risky the investment, the greater is the likelihood that the borrowing is not specific to obtain the qualifying asset. If the investment returns a loss rather than income, such losses are not added to the borrowing costs to be capitalised.

In addition, as described in the next section, an entity that does not borrow specifically for the purpose may still be able to consider some of the borrowing costs on its general borrowings as directly attributable.

2.3.2   *Capitalisation rate*

IAS 23 concedes that there may be practical difficulties in identifying a direct relationship between particular borrowings and a qualifying asset and in determining the borrowings that could otherwise have been avoided. This could happen if the financing activity of an entity is co-ordinated centrally, by which the standard presumably means that the entity borrows to meet its requirements as a whole and the construction is being financed out of general borrowings. Other circumstances that may cause difficulties are identified by the standard as follows:

- an entity has a group treasury function that uses a range of debt instruments to borrow funds at varying rates of interest and lends those funds on various bases to other entities in the group; or

- loans are denominated in, or linked to, foreign currency, or the group operates in highly inflationary economies.

In any event, the standard makes allowance for the problems that arise in practice and concedes that the determination of attributable borrowing costs may be difficult and require the exercise of judgement.[22]

If funds are borrowed generally and used for the purpose of obtaining a qualifying asset, the amount of borrowing costs eligible for capitalisation should be determined by applying a capitalisation rate to the expenditures on that asset. The capitalisation rate should be the weighted average of the borrowing costs applicable to the borrowings of the entity that are outstanding during the period, other than borrowings made specifically for the purpose of obtaining a qualifying asset. The amount of borrowing costs capitalised during a period should not exceed the amount of borrowing costs incurred during that period.[23] Where funds are borrowed generally, the amount of borrowing costs capitalised cannot be reduced by interest income earned on those general funds. The standard allows that the average carrying amount of the asset during a period, including borrowing costs previously capitalised, is normally a reasonable approximation of the expenditures to which the capitalisation rate is applied in that period.[24]

In some circumstances all borrowings made by the group can be taken into account in determining the weighted average of the borrowing costs. In other circumstances only those borrowings made by individual subsidiaries may be taken into account.[25] It is likely that this will be largely determined by the extent to which borrowings are made centrally (and, perhaps, expenses met in the same way) and passed through to individual group companies via intercompany accounts and intra-group loans.

The capitalisation rate is discussed further at 3.2 below.

2.3.3 Impairment and capitalisation of borrowing costs

An entity continues to capitalise borrowing costs that are directly attributable to the acquisition, construction or production of a qualifying asset as part of the carrying amount of the asset, even if the capitalisation causes the carrying amount of the asset to exceed its recoverable amount.

If the carrying amount of the qualifying asset exceeds its recoverable amount or net realisable value, the asset must be written down in accordance with the relevant international standard. If the asset is incomplete, this assessment is performed by considering the assets expected ultimate cost.[26] The expected ultimate cost must include costs to complete and the estimated capitalised interest thereon.

IAS 36 – *Impairment of Assets* – will apply if the qualifying asset is property, plant and equipment accounted for in accordance with IAS 16 – *Property Plant and Equipment*[27] – or if the asset is otherwise within the scope of IAS 36. The following assets that could potentially be qualifying assets are outside the scope of IAS 36: inventories, assets arising from construction contracts, investment property that is measured at fair value and non-current assets (or disposal groups) classified as held for sale in accordance with IFRS 5 – *Non-current Assets Held for Sale and Discontinued Operations*.[28] Impairment is fully discussed in Chapter 18.

2.3.4   Capitalisation of borrowing costs in hyperinflationary economies

Paragraph 21 of IAS 29 – *Financial Reporting in Hyperinflationary Economies* – states that 'the impact of inflation is usually recognised in borrowing costs. It is not appropriate both to restate the capital expenditure financed by borrowing and to capitalise that part of the borrowing costs that compensates for the inflation during the same period. This part of the borrowing costs is recognised as an expense in the period in which the costs are incurred'.[29] IAS 23 specifies that when an entity applies IAS 29, the borrowing costs that can be capitalised should be restricted and the entity must expense the part of borrowing costs that compensate for inflation during the same period.

Issues relating to exchange differences that do not arise in hyperinflationary situations and their eligibility for capitalisation are dealt with at 3.1.1 below.

2.4   Commencement, suspension and cessation of capitalisation

2.4.1   Commencement of capitalisation

IAS 23 requires that capitalisation should commence when:

(a)   expenditures for the asset are being incurred;

(b)   borrowing costs are being incurred; and

(c)   activities that are necessary to prepare the asset for its intended use or sale are in progress.[30]

The standard makes it explicit that only those expenditures on a qualifying asset that have resulted in payments of cash, transfers of other assets or the assumption of interest-bearing liabilities, may be included in determining borrowing costs. Such expenditures must be reduced by any progress payments and grants received in connection with the asset.[31]

The activities necessary to prepare an asset for its intended use or sale extend to more than the physical construction of the asset. Necessary activities can start before the commencement of physical construction and include, for example, technical and administrative work such as obtaining permits. Note that this does not mean that borrowing costs can be capitalised if it is insufficiently certain that permits that are necessary for the construction will be obtained. No cost could be considered 'directly attributable' prior to this point. However, interest may not be capitalised during a period in which there are no activities that change the asset's condition. For example, borrowing costs incurred while land is under development are capitalised during the period in which activities related to the development are being undertaken. However, borrowing costs incurred while land acquired for building purposes is held without any associated development activity do not qualify for capitalisation.[32] For example a house-builder or property developer may not capitalise borrowing costs on its 'land bank' i.e. that land which is held for future development.

An entity may make a payment to third party contractor before that contractor commences construction activities. It is unlikely to be appropriate that capitalisation of borrowing costs should commence in the event of such a prepayment until that contractor commences activities that are necessary to prepare the asset for its intended use or sale.

Fortis's policy describes the period during which borrowing costs are capitalised, as well as noting that it uses either an actual rate or a weighted average cost of borrowings.

Extract 19.1: Fortis (2007)

Notes to the Group Financial Statements [extract]
2.37   **Borrowing costs** [extract]

Borrowing costs are generally expensed as incurred. Borrowing costs that are directly attributable to the acquisition or construction of an asset are capitalised while the asset is being constructed as part of the cost of that asset. Capitalisation of borrowing costs should commence when:

- expenditures for the asset and borrowing costs are being incurred
- activities necessary to prepare the asset for its intended use or sale are in progress.

Capitalisation ceases when the asset is substantially ready for its intended use or sale. If active development is interrupted for an extended period, capitalisation is suspended. When construction occurs piecemeal and use of each part is possible as construction continues, capitalisation for each part ceases upon substantial completion of that part.

For borrowing associated with a specific asset, the actual rate on that borrowing is used. Otherwise, a weighted average cost of borrowings is used.

2.4.2   *Suspension of capitalisation*

IAS 23 states that capitalisation should be suspended during extended periods in which active development is interrupted. However, the standard distinguishes between extended periods of interruption (when capitalisation would be suspended) and periods of temporary delay that are a necessary part of preparing the asset for its intended purpose (when capitalisation is not normally suspended). Capitalisation continues during periods when inventory is undergoing slow transformation – the example is given of inventories taking an extended time to mature (presumably such products as Scotch whisky or Cognac, although the relevance of this may be limited as these products are likely to meet the exemption for 'routinely manufactured' products – see 2.1.2 above). A bridge construction delayed by temporary adverse weather conditions, where such conditions are common in the region, would also not be a cause for suspension of capitalisation.[33]

2.4.3   Cessation of capitalisation

The standard requires capitalisation to cease when substantially all the activities necessary to prepare the qualifying asset for its intended use or sale are complete.[34] An asset is normally ready for its intended use or sale when the physical construction of the asset is complete even though routine administrative work might still continue. If minor modifications, such as the decoration of a property to the purchaser's specification, are all that are outstanding, this indicates that substantially all the activities are complete.[35] In some cases there may be a requirement for inspection (e.g. to ensure that the asset meets safety requirements) before the asset can be used. 'Substantially all the activities' must have been completed before this point is reached so capitalisation will cease prior to the inspection.

Furthermore, when the construction of a qualifying asset is completed in parts and each part is capable of being used while construction continues on other parts, capitalisation should cease when substantially all the activities necessary to prepare that part for its intended use or sale are completed.[36] An example of this might be a business park comprising several buildings, each of which is capable of being fully utilised while construction continues on other parts.[37]

2.5   Disclosure requirements

2.5.1   The requirements of IAS 23

An entity shall disclose:

* the amount of borrowing costs capitalised during the period; and
* the capitalisation rate used to determine the amount of borrowing costs eligible for capitalisation.[38]

AngloGold Ashanti discloses in its 'tangible assets' note its capitalisation rate used to determine its borrowing costs.

Extract 19.2: AngloGold Ashanti (2007)

Notes to the Group Financial Statements [extract]
16.   Tangible assets [extract]

The weighted average capitalisation rate used to determine the amount of borrowing costs eligible for capitalisation is 9.75% (2006: 8.23%).

The amount of borrowing costs capitalised during the period is disclosed within the table of movements in property, plant and equipment that precedes this narrative disclosure.

2.5.2   Other requirements

As noted in 3.1.1 below, the IFRIC has considered a request for guidance on the treatment of foreign exchange gains and losses and on the treatment of any derivatives used to hedge such foreign exchange exposures.

The IFRIC decided not to add the issue to their agenda but concluded both that (i) how an entity applies IAS 23 to foreign currency borrowings is a matter of accounting policy requiring the exercise of judgement and (ii) that IAS 1 – *Presentation of Financial Statements* – requires disclosure of significant accounting policies and judgements that are relevant to an understanding of the financial statements.

3 PRACTICAL ISSUES

3.1 Borrowing costs

The standard lists various costs that may comprise part of borrowing costs, together with finance charges in respect of finance leases recognised in accordance with IAS 17 (see 2.1.3 above). However, in the twenty years since the standard was originally issued, financial instruments have become considerably more complex.

Some of the practical issues that arise from such complex financing arrangements are discussed below. The treatment of lease liabilities is addressed further in Chapter 22.

3.1.1 *Exchange differences as a borrowing cost*

Borrowings in one currency may have been used to finance a development the costs of which are incurred primarily in another currency, e.g. a US dollar loan financing a rouble development. This may have been done on the basis that, over the period of the development, the cost, after allowing for exchange differences, was expected to be less than the interest cost of an equivalent rouble loan.

IAS 23 defines borrowing costs as including exchange differences arising from foreign currency borrowings to the extent that they are regarded as an adjustment to interest costs.[39] The standard does not expand on this point. Indeed, in their January 2008 meeting the IFRIC considered a request for guidance on the treatment of foreign exchange gains and losses and on the treatment of any derivatives used to hedge such foreign exchange exposures. The IFRIC decided not to add the issue to their agenda because:

- the standard acknowledges that judgement will be required in its application; and
- The IASB had considered this issue when developing IAS 23 (revised) and had decided not to provide any guidance.

We, however, consider that, as exchange rate movements are largely a function of differential interest rates, in most circumstances the foreign exchange differences on directly attributable borrowings will be an adjustment to interest costs that can meet the definition of borrowing costs. Care will have to be taken if there is a sudden fluctuation in exchange rates that cannot be attributed to changes in interest rates. In such cases we believe that a practical approach is to cap the exchange differences taken as borrowing costs at the amount of borrowing costs on functional currency equivalent borrowings.

If this approach is used and the construction of the qualifying asset takes more than one accounting period, there could be situations, where in one period, only a portion of foreign exchange differences could be capitalised. However, in subsequent years if the borrowings were assessed on a cumulative basis, the losses capitalised may meet the recognition criteria. The two methods are dealing with this are illustrated in Example 19.1 below:

Example 19.1:   Foreign exchange differences in more than one period

Method A – The discrete period approach

The amount of foreign exchange differences eligible for capitalisation is determined for each period separately. Foreign exchange differences losses that did not meet the criteria for capitalisation in previous years are not capitalised in subsequent years.

Method B – The cumulative approach

The borrowing costs to be capitalised are assessed on a cumulative basis based on the cumulative amount of interest expense that would have been incurred had the entity borrowed in its functional currency. The amount of foreign exchange differences capitalised cannot exceed the amount of foreign exchange losses incurred on a cumulative basis at the end of the reporting period. The cumulative approach looks at the construction project as a whole as the unit of account ignoring the occurrence of reporting dates. Consequently, the amount of the foreign exchange differences eligible for capitalisation as an adjustment to the borrowing cost in the period is an estimate, which can change as the exchange rates changes over the construction period.

An illustrative calculation of the amount of foreign exchange differences that may be capitalised under Method A and Method B is set out below.

	Year 1 CU	Year 2 CU	Total CU
Interest expense in foreign currency (A)	25,000	25,000	50,000
Hypothetical interest expense in functional currency (B)	30,000	30,000	60,000
Foreign exchange loss (C)	6,000	3,000	9,000
Method A – Discrete Approach			
Foreign exchange loss capitalised – lower of C and (B minus A)	5,000	3,000	8,000
Foreign exchange loss expensed	1,000	–	1,000
Method B – Cumulative Approach			
Foreign exchange loss capitalised	5,000 *	4,000 **	9,000
Foreign exchange loss expensed	1,000	(1,000)	–

* Lower of C and (B minus A) in Year 1

** Lower of C and (B minus A) in total across the two years. In this example this represents the sum of the foreign exchange loss of CU3,000 capitalised using the discrete approach plus the CU1,000 not capitalised in year 1.

In our view, it is a matter of accounting policy (which of course must be consistently applied) as to whether foreign exchange gains and losses are assessed on a discrete period basis or cumulatively over the construction period.

3.1.2 Other finance costs

IAS 23 does not address many of the ways in which an entity may finance its operations or other finance costs that it may incur. The standard does not, for example, address any of the following:

- the many derivative financial instruments such as interest rate swaps, floors, caps and collars that are commonly used to manage interest rate risk on borrowings;

- gains and losses on derecognition of borrowings, for example early settlement of directly attributable borrowings that have been renegotiated prior to completion of an asset in the course of construction;

- dividends payable on shares classified as financial liabilities (such as certain redeemable preference shares) that have been recognised as an expense in profit or loss; and

- the unwinding of discounts that may be included within the caption 'finance costs' in an entity's income statement.

These are simply a few of the most commonly encountered examples.

We consider that IAS 23 does not preclude the classification of costs other than those that it identifies as borrowing costs that may be eligible for capitalisation. However, they must meet the basic criterion in the standard, i.e. that they are costs that are directly attributable to the acquisition, construction or production of a qualifying asset, which would, therefore, preclude the classification of unwinding discounts as borrowing costs. In addition, as in the case of exchange differences (see 3.1.2 above), capitalisation of such costs should be permitted only 'to the extent that they are regarded as an adjustment to interest costs'.

A   Derivative financial instruments

The most straightforward and most commonly encountered derivative financial instrument used to manage interest rate risk is a floating to fixed interest rate swap, as in the following example.

Example 19.2:   Floating to fixed interest rate swaps

Entity A has borrowed €4 million for five years at a floating interest rate to fund the construction of a building. In order to hedge the cash flow interest rate risk arising from these borrowings, A has entered into a matching pay-fixed receive-floating interest rate swap, based on the same underlying nominal sum and duration as the original borrowing, that effectively converts the interest on the borrowings to fixed rate. The net effect of the periodic cash settlements resulting from the hedged and hedging instruments is as if A had borrowed €4 million at a fixed rate of interest. Prior to IAS 39, entities simply recognised, on an accruals basis, each periodic net cash settlement in profit or loss.

Although these instruments are not addressed in IAS 23, there is no doubt that prior to IAS 39 the net costs of such 'synthetic' fixed rate debt would have been treated as a borrowing cost and therefore eligible for capitalisation if it met the criteria in the standard.

IAS 39 has complicated the situation considerably by completely changing the basis on which such instruments are recognised and measured. Briefly, a derivative financial instrument is classified by IAS 39 as held for trading and recognised initially at its fair value with changes in the fair value being taken to profit or loss (see Chapter 29 at 7.1.) unless it is a designated effective hedging instrument (see Chapter 33), in which case the entity may be eligible to apply hedge accounting. IAS 39 describes hedge accounting as 'recognising the offsetting effects on net profit or loss of changes in the fair values of hedging instruments and related items being hedged';[40] for cash flow hedges this is achieved by taking fair value changes on hedging instruments to other comprehensive income and reclassifying the effective element to income to match the gain or loss on the hedged item. Those elements of the changes in value of designated effective hedging instruments that are not effective in offsetting the changes in fair value of the item being hedged (e.g. changes in the counterparties' creditworthiness) are always taken to profit or loss. See Chapter 33 at 4 regarding how to account for effective hedges and the conditions that these instruments must meet.

However, the net effect on income of an interest rate swap such as the above example 19.2 (referred to as a 'cash flow hedge' in IAS 39 because it is a hedge of the exposure to variability in cash flows) is very similar to the accruals accounting treatment under which the cash flows on the borrowing and the swap were recognised in income (see Chapter 33 at 4.2).

An entity may consider that a derivative financial instrument it has taken out, such as an interest rate swap, is directly attributable to the acquisition, construction or production of a qualifying asset. If the instrument does not meet the conditions for hedge accounting then the effects on income will be different from those if it does, and they will also be dissimilar from year to year. The question arises as to the impact of the derivative on borrowing costs eligible for capitalisation. In particular, does the accounting treatment of the derivative financial instrument affect the amount available for capitalisation? If hedge accounting is not adopted, does this affect the amount available for capitalisation?

The following examples illustrate the potential differences.

Example 19.3:   Cash flow hedge of variable-rate debt using an interest rate swap

Entity A is constructing a building and expects it to take 18 months to complete. To finance the construction, on 1 January 2008, the entity issues an eighteen month, €20,000,000 variable-rate note payable, due on 30 June 2009 at a floating rate of interest plus a margin of 1%. At that date the market rate of interest is 8%. Interest payment dates and interest rate reset dates occur on 1 January and 1 July until maturity. The principal is due at maturity. Also on 1 January 2008, the entity enters into an eighteen month interest rate swap with a notional amount of €10,000,000 from which it will receive periodic payments at the floating rate and make periodic payments at a fixed rate of 9%, with settlement and rate reset dates every 30 June and 31 December. The fair value of the swap is zero at inception.

On 1 January 2008, the debt is recorded at €20,000,000. No entry is required for the swap on that date because its fair value was zero at inception.

During the eighteen month period, floating interest rates change as follows:

	Cash payments	
	Floating rate on principal	Rate paid by Entity A
Period to 30 June 2008	8%	9%
Period to 31 Dec 2008	8.5%	9.5%
Period to 30 June 2009	9.75%	10.75%

Under the interest rate swap, Entity A receives interest at the market floating rate as above and pays at 9% on the nominal amount of €10,000,000 throughout the period.

At 31 December 2008 the swap has a fair value of €37,500, reflecting the fact that it is now in the money as Entity A is expected to receive a net cash inflow of this amount in the period until the instrument is terminated. There are no further changes in interest rates prior to the maturity of the swap and the fair value of the swap declines to zero at 30 June 2009. Note that this example excludes the effect of issue costs and discounting. In addition, it is assumed that, if Entity A is entitled to, and applies, hedge accounting, there will be no ineffectiveness.

The cash flows incurred by the entity on its borrowing and interest rate swap are as follows:

	Cash payments		
	Interest on principal	Interest rate swap (net)	Total
	€	€	€
30 June 2008	900,000	50,000	950,000
31 Dec 2008	950,000	25,000	975,000
30 June 2009	1,075,000	(37,500)	1,037,500
Total	2,925,000	37,500	2,962,500

There are a number of different ways in which Entity A could calculate the borrowing costs eligible for capitalisation, including the following.

(i) The interest rate swap meets the conditions for, and entity A applies, hedge accounting. The finance costs eligible for capitalisation as borrowing costs will be €1,925,000 in the year to 31 December 2008 and €1,037,500 in the period ended 30 June 2009.

(ii) Entity A does not apply hedge accounting. Therefore, it will reflect the fair value of the swap in income in the year ended 31 December 2008, reducing the net finance costs by €37,500 to €1,887,500 and increasing the finance costs by an equivalent amount in 2009 to €1,075,000. However, it considers that it is inappropriate to reflect the fair value of the swap in borrowing costs eligible for capitalisation so it capitalises costs based on the net cash cost on an accruals accounting basis. In this case this will give the same result as in (i) above.

(iii) Entity A does not apply hedge accounting and considers only the costs incurred on the borrowing, not the interest rate swap, as eligible for capitalisation. The borrowing costs eligible for capitalisation would be €1,850,000 in 2008 and €1,075,000 in 2009.

We consider that all these methods are valid interpretations of IAS 23, although the preparer will need to consider what method is more appropriate in the circumstances.

In particular, if using method (ii) it is necessary to demonstrate that the derivative financial instrument is directly attributable to the construction of a qualifying asset. In making this assessment it is clearly necessary to consider the term of the derivative and this method may not be practicable if the derivative has a different term to the underlying directly attributable borrowing.

Based on the facts in this example, method (iii) appears to be inconsistent with the underlying principles of IAS 23 – which is that the costs eligible for capitalisation are those costs that could have been avoided if the expenditure on the qualifying asset had not been made[41]. In other circumstances, however, it may not be possible to argue that specific derivative financial instruments are directly attributable to particular qualifying assets, rather than being used by the entity to manage its interest rate exposure on a more general basis. In such a case method (iii) may be a preferable treatment.

Note that these methods would not be permitted under US GAAP which prohibits the capitalisation of the gain or loss on the hedging instrument in a cash flow hedge. Instead, EITF 99-9 states that 'the amounts in accumulated comprehensive income related to a cash flow hedge of the variability of that interest should be reclassified into earnings over the depreciable life of the constructed asset, since that depreciable life coincides with the amortization period for the capitalized interest cost on the debt.'[42]

Whatever policy is chosen by the entity, it needs to be consistently applied in similar situations.

B   Gains and losses on derecognition of borrowings

If an entity repays borrowings early, in whole or in part, then it may recognise a gain or loss on the early settlement. This gain or loss includes amounts attributable to expected future interest rates; in other words it includes an estimated prepayment of the future cash flows under the instrument. The gain or loss is a function of relative interest rates and how the interest rate of the instrument differs from current and anticipated future interest rates. There may be circumstances in which a loan is repaid while the qualifying asset is still under construction. IAS 23 does not address the issue.

We consider that, generally, gains and losses on derecognition of borrowings are not eligible for capitalisation. It would be extremely difficult to determine an appropriate amount to capitalise and it would be inappropriate thereafter to capitalise any interest amounts (on specific or general borrowings) if to do so would amount to double counting. Decisions to repay borrowings are not usually directly attributable to the qualifying asset but to other circumstances of the entity.

C   Gains or losses on termination of derivative financial instruments

If an entity terminates an interest rate swap, for example, before the end of the term of the instrument, it will usually either have to make or receive a payment, depending on the fair value of the instrument at that time. This fair value is based on expected future interest rates; in other words it is an estimated prepayment of the future cash flows under the instrument.

The treatment of the gain or loss for the purposes of capitalisation will depend on the following:

- the basis on which the entity capitalises the gains and losses associated with derivative financial instruments, described in A above; and
- whether the derivative is associated with a borrowing that has also been terminated, whose treatment is described in B above.

Entities must adopt a treatment that is consistent with their policy for capitalising the gains and losses of derivative financial instruments.

The accounting under IAS 39 will differ depending on whether the instrument has been designated as a hedge or not; in the former case, and assuming that the borrowing has not also been repaid, the entity will usually continue to account for the cumulative gain or loss on the instrument as if the hedge were still in place (see Chapter 33 at 4.2). In such a case, the amounts that are reclassified from other comprehensive income will be eligible for capitalisation for the remainder of the period of construction.

If the entity is not hedge accounting for the derivative financial instrument but considers it to be directly attributable to the construction of the qualifying asset then it will have to consider whether part of the gain or loss relates to a period after construction is complete.

If the underlying borrowing is also terminated then the gain or loss will not be capitalised and the treatment will mirror that applied to the borrowing, as described in B above.

D   Dividends payable on shares classified as financial liabilities

An entity might finance its operations in whole or in part by the issue of preference shares and in some circumstances these will be classified as financial liabilities (see Chapter 31 at 3.2.1). In some circumstances these dividends would meet the definition of borrowing costs. For example, it is possible that an entity has issued redeemable preference shares that are redeemable at the option of the holder (and are classified as financial liabilities with the interest charge calculated using the effective interest method in IAS 39) to fund the development of a qualifying asset. In this case the dividends would meet the definition of borrowing costs. However, this would not apply to irredeemable shares as these would not be borrowings that could be avoided and hence could never be directly attributable to a qualifying asset.

E   Unwinding discounts on provisions classified as finance costs in profit or loss

Many unwinding discounts are treated as finance costs in profit or loss. These include discounts relating to various provisions such as those for onerous leases and decommissioning costs. These finance costs will not be borrowing costs under IAS 23 because they do not arise in respect of funds borrowed by the entity that can be attributed to a qualifying asset. Therefore, they cannot be capitalised.

3.2   Borrowings and capitalisation rate

IAS 23 requires that the borrowing costs capitalised are those costs that would have been avoided if the expenditure on the qualifying asset had not been made. If a project has been financed from the entity's general borrowings, the standard imposes a detailed calculation method as indicated at 2.3.2 above.

3.2.1   *Definition of general borrowings*

The standard acknowledges that determining general borrowings will not always be straightforward and that the determination of the amount of borrowing costs that are directly attributable to the acquisition of a qualifying asset is difficult and the exercise of judgement is required.

Indeed, in July 2009 the IFRIC received a request for guidance on what borrowings comprise 'general borrowings' for purposes of capitalising borrowing costs in accordance with IAS 23. The request asked for guidance on the treatment of general borrowings used to purchase a specific asset other than a qualifying asset.

The IFRIC noted that IAS 23 paragraph 14 states that 'To the extent that an entity borrows funds generally and uses them for the purpose of obtaining a qualifying asset, the entity shall determine the amount of borrowing costs eligible for capitalisation by applying a capitalisation rate to the expenditures on that asset. The capitalisation rate shall be the weighted average of the borrowing costs applicable to the borrowings of the entity that are outstanding during the period, other than borrowings made specifically for the purpose of obtaining a qualifying asset.'

The IFRIC also noted that because paragraph 14 refers only to qualifying assets:

*   some conclude that borrowings related to specific assets other than qualifying assets cannot be excluded from determining the capitalisation rate for general borrowings.
*   others note the general principle in paragraph 10 that the borrowing costs that are directly attributable to the acquisition, construction or production of a qualifying asset are borrowing costs that would have been avoided if the expenditure on the qualifying asset had not been made.

Consequently, the IFRIC concluded that any guidance it could provide would be in the nature of application guidance rather than an interpretation and because the IASB was due to consider whether to add this issue to the annual improvements project, therefore decided not to add the issue to its agenda.

The IASB did subsequently consider the issue of whether debt incurred specifically to acquire a non-qualifying asset could be excluded from general borrowings but as IAS 23 excludes only debt used to acquire qualifying assets from the determination of the capitalisation rate, decided not to include this issue in its annual improvements process.

Another question that arises is whether a specific borrowing undertaken to obtain a qualifying asset ever changes its nature into a general borrowing. Differing views exist as to whether or not borrowings change their nature throughout the period they are outstanding. Some consider that once the asset for which the borrowing was incurred has been completed, and the entity chooses to use its funds on constructing other assets rather than repaying the loan, this changes the nature of the loan into a general borrowing. However, to the extent that the contract linked the repayment of the loan to specific proceeds generated by the entity, its nature as a specific borrowing would be preserved. Others take the view that once the borrowing has been classified as specific, its nature does not change while it remains outstanding. Management will therefore need to exercise judgment in determining its policy and assessing the nature of the loans when construction activity is completed.

3.2.2 Calculation of capitalisation

As the standard acknowledges that determining general borrowings will not always be straightforward, it will be necessary to exercise judgement to meet the main objective – a reasonable measure of the directly attributable finance costs.[43]

The following example illustrates the practical application of the method of calculating the amount of finance costs to be capitalised:

Example 19.4:   *Calculation of capitalisation rate (no investment income)*

On 1 April 2008 a company engages in the development of a property, which is expected to take five years to complete, at a cost of €6,000,000. The balance sheets at 31 December 2007 and 31 December 2008, prior to capitalisation of interest, are as follows:

	31 December 2007 €	31 December 2008 €
Development property	–	1,200,000
Other assets	6,000,000	6,000,000
	6,000,000	7,200,000
Loans		
5.5% debenture stock	2,500,000	2,500,000
Bank loan at 6% p.a.	–	1,200,000
Bank loan at 7% p.a.	1,000,000	1,000,000
	3,500,000	4,700,000
Shareholders' equity	2,500,000	2,500,000

The bank loan with an effective interest rate at 6% was drawn down to match the development expenditure on 1 April 2008, 1 July 2008 and 1 October 2008.

Expenditure was incurred on the development as follows:

	€
1 April 2008	600,000
1 July 2008	400,000
1 October 2008	200,000
	1,200,000

(a) If the bank loan at 6% p.a. is a new borrowing specifically to finance the development then the amount of interest to be capitalised is:

	Weighted average borrowings €	Interest rate	Amount to be capitalised €
€600,000 × 9/12	450,000	× 6%	27,000
€400,000 × 6/12	200,000	× 6%	12,000
€200,000 × 3/12	50,000	× 6%	3,000
	700,000		42,000

(b) If all the borrowings were general (i.e. the bank loan at 6% was not specific to the development) and would have been avoided but for the development then the amount of interest to be capitalised is:

$$\frac{\text{Total interest expense for period}}{\text{Weighted average total borrowings}} \times \text{Development expenditure}$$

Total interest expense for the period

	€
€2,500,000 × 5.5%	137,500
€1,200,000 (as above)	42,000
€1,000,000 × 7%	70,000
	249,500

Therefore the capitalisation rate is calculated as:

$$\frac{249,500}{3,500,000 + 700,000} = 5.94\%$$

The capitalisation rate is then applied to the expenditure on the qualifying asset, resulting in an amount to be capitalised of €41,580 as follows:

	€
€600,000 × 5.94% × 9/12	26,730
€400,000 × 5.94% × 6/12	11,880
€200,000 × 5.94% × 3/12	2,970
	41,580

If the 5.5% debenture stock were irredeemable then it would be excluded from the above calculation as it could no longer be a borrowing that could have been avoided. The calculation would be done using the figures for the bank loans and their related interest costs only.

In this example, all borrowings are at fixed rates of interest and the period of construction extends beyond the end of the period. If borrowings are at floating rates then only the interest costs incurred during that period, and the weighted average borrowings for that period, will be taken into account.

Note that the company's share capital will not be taken into account and outstanding borrowings are presumed to finance the acquisition or construction of qualifying assets.

Example 19.4 also assumes that loans are drawn down to match expenditure on the qualifying asset. If, however, a loan is drawn down immediately and investment income is received on the unapplied funds, then the calculation is different. This is illustrated in Example 19.5.

Example 19.5:   *Calculation of amount to be capitalised – specific borrowings with investment income*

On 1 April 2008 a company engages in the development of a property, which is expected to take five years to complete, at a cost of €6,000,000. In this example, however, a bank loan of €6,000,000 with an effective interest rate at 6% was taken out on 31 March 2008 and fully drawn. The total interest charge for the year ended 31 December 2008 was consequently €270,000.

However, investment income was also earned at 3% on the unapplied funds during the period as follows:

	€
€5,400,000 × 3% × 3/12	40,500
€5,000,000 × 3% × 3/12	37,500
€4,800,000 × 3% × 3/12	36,000
	114,000

Consequently, the amount of interest to be capitalised is:

	€
Total interest charge	270,000
Less: investment income	(114,000)
	156,000

3.3   Accrued costs

IAS 23 states that expenditures on qualifying assets include only those that have resulted in the payments of cash, transfers of other assets or the assumption of interest-bearing liabilities.[44] Therefore, costs of a qualifying asset that have only been accrued but have not yet been paid in cash should be excluded from the amount on which interest is capitalised, as by definition no interest can have been incurred on an accrued payment. It should be noted that the effect of applying this principle is often merely to delay the capitalisation of interest since the costs will be included once they have been paid in cash. In most cases it is unlikely that the effect will be material as the time between accrual and payment of the cost will not be that great. However, the effect is potentially material where a significant part of the amount capitalised relates to costs that have been financed interest-free by third parties for a long period. An example of this is retention money that is not generally payable until the asset is completed.

3.4   Assets carried in the balance sheet below cost

An asset may be recognised in the financial statements during the period of production on a basis other than cost, i.e. it may have been written down below cost as a result of being impaired. As discussed in 2.3.3 above, an asset may be impaired when its expected ultimate cost, including costs to complete and the estimated capitalised interest thereon, exceed its estimated recoverable amount or net realisable value.

The question then arises whether the calculation of interest to be capitalised should be based on the asset's cost or its carrying amount. In this case, cost should be used, as this is the amount that the company or group has had to finance.

3.5   Group financial statements

3.5.1   Borrowings in one company and development in another

A question which often arises in practice is whether it is appropriate to capitalise interest in the group financial statements on borrowings that appear in the financial statements of a different group company from that carrying out the development. Based on the underlying philosophy of IAS 23, capitalisation in such circumstances would only be appropriate if the amount capitalised fairly reflected the interest cost of the group on borrowings from third parties which could have been avoided if the expenditure on the qualifying asset were not made.

Although it may be appropriate to capitalise interest in the group financial statements, the company carrying out the development should not capitalise any interest in its own financial statements as it has no borrowings. If, however, the company has intra-group borrowings then interest on such borrowings may be capitalised.

3.5.2   Qualifying assets held by joint ventures

A number of sectors carry out developments through the medium of joint ventures – this is particularly common with property developments. In such cases, the joint venture may be financed principally by equity and the joint venture partners may have financed their participating interests by borrowings. It is not appropriate to capitalise interest in the joint venture on the borrowings of the partners as the interest charge is not a cost of the joint venture. Neither would it be appropriate to capitalise interest in the individual (as opposed to group) financial statements of the venturers because the qualifying asset does not belong to them. The investing entities have an investment as an asset, which is excluded by IAS 23 from being a qualifying asset (see 2.1.2 above). If, however, the venturer is using proportionate consolidation and the jointly controlled entity itself does not incur borrowing costs, then the venturer should capitalise borrowing costs that relate to its share of the qualifying asset in its consolidated accounts.

4   TRANSITION

4.1   Effective date and transition to the revised IAS 23

The revised standard applies to accounting periods beginning on or after 1 January 2009. Applying the revised IAS 23 will be a change in accounting policy for those entities that currently expense borrowing costs.

The standard does not require full restatement. Instead, entities must begin to capitalise borrowing costs relating to qualifying assets for which the commencement date for capitalisation is on or after the effective date[45]. However, an entity may designate an earlier date and capitalise borrowing costs relating to all qualifying assets for which the commencement date for capitalisation is on or after that date.[46]

This means that an entity that has incomplete qualifying assets as at its effective date has a choice. It may continue not to capitalise borrowing costs on those assets already in the course of construction, manufacture or production and only start capitalising in respect of assets whose commencement date is after the effective date. Alternatively, it can select to capitalise borrowing costs as from an earlier date and apply the standard to all qualifying assets for which the commencement date for capitalisation is on or after that date – for example the date selected may be the date on which its incomplete construction projects commenced.

5   CONCLUSION

The capitalisation of finance costs is an important part of the wider issue of accounting for interest effects, about which there is no particular consensus.

Until recently, by neither banning it nor making it compulsory, the IASB had, in effect, adopted a holding position on the issue of capitalisation of borrowing costs. But the IASB has now thrown in its lot with the FASB and has decided to make capitalisation compulsory.

The decision on whether or not to capitalise interest should have been taken in the light of a discussion of the nature of finance costs and how they fit within the structure of financial reporting by a company to its stakeholders – in short, whether or not the capitalisation of finance costs is a conceptually sound basis of accounting. However, there was no sustained attempt to argue that capitalisation gives a conceptually 'better' result than expensing borrowing costs. Mandatory capitalisation is justified by the IASB solely on the basis of eliminating some, but by no means all, the differences between IFRS and US GAAP in this area.

In fact, at the conceptual level, there is a plausible argument for measuring the cost of financing the acquisition of qualifying assets on the basis of the entity's cost of capital, including imputed interest on equity capital as well as interest on borrowings. At the same time it must be recognised that the capitalisation of the cost of equity capital does not conform to the historical cost accounting framework, under which the cost of a resource is measured by reference to historical exchange prices. Nevertheless, to permit the capitalisation of interest only on borrowings is an incomplete approach.

Conversely, it may be argued that the capitalisation of borrowing costs in the context of, for example, most types of property development is an entirely logical and appropriate policy. Interest is a development cost, and is no different in this respect from the concrete and bricks. Unfortunately, the IASB decided that convergence with US GAAP is a greater priority than conducting a full debate on the issue of accounting for interest effects.

References

1 IAS 23 (1984), *Capitalisation of Borrowing Costs*, IASC, March 1984, paras. 21-27.
2 IAS 23, *Borrowing Costs*, IASB, 2007 Bound Volume, para. 8.
3 IAS 23, *Borrowing Costs*, IASB, para BC3.
4 IAS 23, para. 3.
5 IAS 23, para. 4 .
6 IAS 23, para. 6
7 IAS 23, para 7.
8 IFRIC 12, *Service Concession Arrangements*, IASB, para. IE15.
9 IAS 23, para. 6.
10 IAS 23, para 4.
11 IAS 16, *Property, Plant and Equipment*, IASB, December 2003, para. 31.
12 IAS 11, *Construction Contracts*, IASB, para. 18.
13 IAS 23, para. BC27.
14 *Insight*, IASC, October 1991, p. 10.
15 IAS 23, para. 7.
16 IAS 23, para. 4.
17 IAS 23, para. 5.
18 IAS 23, para. 13.
19 IAS 23, para. 13.
20 IAS 23, para. 15.
21 IAS 23, paras. 15-16.
22 IAS 23, para. 14.
23 IAS 23, para. 17.
24 IAS 23, para. 21.
25 IAS 23, para. 18.
26 IAS 23, para. 19.
27 IAS 16, *Property, Plant and Equipment*, IASB.
28 IAS 36, *Impairment of Assets*, IASB, para. 2.
29 IAS 29, *Financial Reporting in Hyperinflationary Economies*, IASB, para. 21.
30 IAS 23, para. 20.
31 IAS 23, para. 21.
32 IAS 23, para. 22.
33 IAS 23, paras. 23-24.
34 IAS 23, para. 25.
35 IAS 23, para. 26.
36 IAS 23, para. 27.
37 IAS 23, para. 28.
38 IAS 23, para. 29.
39 IAS 23, para. 5(e).
40 IAS 39, *Financial Instruments: Recognition and Measurement*, IASB, para. 85.
41 IAS 23, para. 13.
42 EITF 99-9, *Effect of derivative gains and losses on the capitalisation of interest*, FASB, July 1999, para. 6.
43 IAS 23, para. 14.
44 IAS 23, para. 21.
45 IAS 23, para. 27.
46 IAS 23, para. 28.

Chapter 20   Inventories

1   INTRODUCTION

Under IFRS the relevant standard for inventories is IAS 2 – *Inventories*. The term 'inventories' includes raw materials, work-in-progress, finished goods and goods for resale, although the standard does not include all instances of these categories; some are covered by other standards, for example growing crops are covered by IAS 41 – *Agriculture*. This chapter deals only with the inventories within the scope of IAS 2. Long-term contracts and the associated work in progress are the subject of a separate standard, IAS 11 – *Construction Contracts* – which is dealt with in Chapter 21.

1.1   Objectives of inventory measurement

Historically, the principal objective of inventory measurement within the historical cost accounting system has been the proper determination of income through the process of matching costs with related revenues. Under this system, costs of inventories comprise expenditure which has been incurred in the normal course of business in bringing the product or service to its present location and condition. All costs incurred in respect of inventories are charged as period costs, except for those which relate to those unconsumed inventories which are expected to be of future benefit to the entity. These are carried forward, to be matched with the revenues that they will generate in the future. A secondary objective of inventory measurement has been to provide a balance sheet entry. Under the historical cost system, inventories in the balance sheet have characteristics similar to those of prepaid expenses or property, plant and equipment – they are effectively deferred costs.

When IAS 2 was revised in 2003 all references to matching and to the historical cost system were deleted, even though historical cost was retained as the main measurement method for IAS 2 inventories. The IASB's measurement policy has meant that the secondary objective of inventory measurement – to define the basis on which inventory is presented in the balance sheet – has become increasingly important to the debate on whether a fair value measurement objective is suitable for use in financial statements. The principles underlying this controversial matter are discussed fully in Chapter 2.

2   THE REQUIREMENTS OF IAS 2

2.1   Scope and definitions

IAS 2 applies to inventories in all financial statements except work-in-progress arising under construction contracts including directly related service contracts (both of which are dealt with by IAS 11, see Chapter 21), financial instruments (see Chapters 29 to 34), and biological assets related to agricultural activity and agricultural produce at the point of harvest (see Chapter 41).[1]

The measurement provisions of the standard do not apply to the measurement of inventories held by:

(a)   producers of agricultural and forest products, agricultural produce after harvest, and minerals and mineral products, to the extent that they are measured at net realisable value in accordance with well-established practices in those industries.[2] When such inventories are measured at net realisable value, changes are recognised in profit or loss in the period of the change. This occurs, for example, when agricultural crops have been harvested or minerals have been extracted and sale is assured under a forward contract or a government guarantee, or when an active market exists and there is a negligible risk of failure to sell;[3]

(b)   commodity broker-traders who measure their inventories at fair value less costs to sell. If these inventories are measured at fair value less costs to sell, the changes are recognised in profit or loss in the period of the change.[4] Broker-traders are those who buy or sell commodities for others or on their own account and these inventories are principally acquired with the purpose of selling in the near future and generating a profit from fluctuations in price or broker traders' margin.[5]

In either case, the standard stresses that these inventories are scoped out only from the measurement requirements of IAS 2, i.e. not from the standard's other requirements such as disclosure.

Inventories are defined by IAS 2 as:

(a)   assets held for sale in the ordinary course of business;

(b)   assets in the process of production for such sale; or

(c)   materials or supplies to be consumed in the production process or in the rendering of services.[6]

Inventories can include all types of goods purchased and held for resale including, for example, merchandise purchased by a retailer and other tangible assets such as land and other property held for resale, although investment property accounted for under IAS 40 – *Investment Property* – is not treated as an inventory item. The term also encompasses finished goods produced, or work in progress being produced by the entity, and includes materials and supplies awaiting use in the production process. If the entity is a service provider, its inventories may be intangible (e.g. the costs of the service for which the entity has not yet recognised the related revenue).[7] The inventory of service providers will probably consist mainly of the labour costs of the people providing the service. There is a separate standard, IFRS 5 – *Non-current Assets Held for Sale and Discontinued Operations* – that governs the accounting treatment of non-current assets held for sale, for example a group of assets held for sale such as a business being disposed of. IFRS 5 is discussed in Chapter 4.

2.2 Measurement

The standard's basic rule is that inventories, apart from those inventories scoped out of the its measurement requirements as explained above, are measured at the lower of cost and net realisable value.[8] Net realisable value is 'the estimated selling price in the ordinary course of business less the estimated costs of completion and the estimated costs necessary to make the sale.'[9] Fair value is 'the amount for which an asset could be exchanged, or a liability settled, between knowledgeable, willing parties in an arm's length transaction.'[10] The standard points out that net realisable value is an entity-specific value – the amount that the entity actually expects to make from selling that particular inventory – while fair value is not. Therefore, net realisable value may not be the same as fair value less costs to sell.[11]

This basic measurement rule inevitably raises the question of what may be included in an inventory's cost.

2.2.1 What may be included in cost

The costs attributed to inventories under IAS 2 comprise all costs of purchase, costs of conversion and other costs incurred in bringing the inventories to their present location and condition.[12] These costs include import duties and other unrecoverable taxes, transport and other costs directly attributable to the inventories but trade discounts and similar rebates should be deducted from the costs attributed to inventories.[13] For example a supplier may pay to its customer an upfront cash incentive when entering into a contract. This is a form of rebate and the incentive should be accounted for as a liability by the customer until it receives the related inventory, which is then shown at cost net of this incentive.

Costs of conversion include direct costs such as direct labour, and also overheads. Overhead costs must be apportioned using a 'systematic allocation of fixed and variable production overheads that are incurred in converting materials into finished goods'.[14] The standard also suggests that there may be indirect materials and labour that vary with the volume of production.[15] Fixed production overheads are indirect costs that remain relatively constant over a wide range of production, such as building and equipment maintenance and depreciation, and factory management and administration expenses. The allocation of fixed production overheads is to be based on the normal capacity of the facilities. Normal capacity is defined as 'the production expected to be achieved on average over a number of periods or seasons under normal circumstances, taking into account the loss of capacity resulting from planned maintenance.'[16] While actual capacity may be used if it approximates to normal capacity, increased overheads may not be allocated to production as a result of low output or idle capacity. In these cases the unrecovered overheads must be expensed. The contrary situation is also considered; in periods of abnormally high production, the fixed overhead absorption must be reduced, as otherwise inventories would be recorded at an amount in excess of cost.[17]

Extract 20.1 below shows how Syngenta AG describes its inventory valuation policies.

Extract 20.1: Syngenta AG (2008)

Notes to the Syngenta Group Consolidated Financial Statements [extract]
2.   Accounting policies [extract]
Inventories

Purchased products are recorded at acquisition cost while own-manufactured products are recorded at manufacturing cost including related production expenses. In the balance sheet, inventory is valued at historical cost determined on a first-in-first-out basis, and this value is used for the cost of goods sold in the income statement. Allowances are made for inventories with a net realizable value less than cost, or which are slow moving. Unsalable inventory is fully written off. Inventories of biological assets, principally young plants and cuttings in the Seeds flowers business, are recorded at fair value less estimated point of sale costs.

IAS 2 mentions the treatment to be adopted when a production process results in the output of more than one product, for example a main product and a by-product. If the costs of converting each product are not separately identifiable, they should be allocated between the products on a rational and consistent basis; for example this might be the relative sales value of each of the products. If the value of the by-product is immaterial, it may be measured at net realisable value and this value deducted from the cost of the main product.[18]

Other costs are to be included in inventories only to the extent that they bring them into their present location and condition. An example is given in IAS 2 of design costs for a special order for a particular customer as being allowable,[19] and as a result other non-production overheads may possibly be appropriately included. However a number of examples are given of costs that are specifically disallowed. These include:

(a)   abnormal amounts of wasted materials, labour, or other production costs;

(b)   storage costs, unless those costs are necessary in the production process prior to a further production stage;

(c)   administrative overheads that do not contribute to bringing inventories to their present location and condition; and

(d)   selling costs.[20]

IAS 2 states that, in limited circumstances, borrowing costs are to be included in the costs of inventories.[21] IAS 23 – *Borrowing Costs* (revised 2007) – requires that borrowing costs be capitalised on qualifying assets but the scope of that standard exempts inventories that are manufactured in large quantities on a repetitive basis.[22] In addition the standard clarifies that inventories manufactured over a short period of time are not qualifying assets.[23] Given that the allowable alternative treatment to expense borrowing costs that existed under the previous version of IAS 23 has been removed any manufacturer that is now producing small quantities over a long time period has, for annual periods beginning on or after 1 January 2009, had to capitalise these borrowing costs. This is further discussed in Chapter 19.

The standard also states that on some occasions, an entity might purchase inventories on deferred settlement terms, accompanied by a price increase that effectively makes the arrangement a combined purchase and financing. Under these circumstances the price difference is to be recognised as an interest expense over the period of the financing.[24]

IAS 2 deals specifically with the inventories of service providers – effectively their work-in-progress. For this type of business, IAS 2 allows the labour and other costs of personnel directly engaged in providing the service, including supervisory personnel and attributable overheads, to be included in the cost of inventories. However, labour and other costs relating to sales and general administrative personnel must be expensed as incurred and inventories should not include profit margins or non-attributable overheads.[25]

Agricultural produce that has been harvested by the entity from its biological assets, is initially recognised at its fair value, less costs to sell at the point of harvest, as set out in IAS 41 (see Chapter 41). This figure becomes the cost of inventories at that date for the purposes of IAS 2.[26]

2.2.2 Cost measurement methods

IAS 2 specifically allows the use of standard costing methods or of the retail method (see 3.3 below) provided that the method gives a result which approximates to cost. Standard costs should take into account normal levels of materials and supplies, labour, efficiency and capacity utilisation. They must be regularly reviewed and revised where necessary.[27] Where the retail method is used, an appropriate gross margin may be applied, though adjustments must be made to take into account any inventory marked down for sale below its original selling price.[28]

Items that are not interchangeable and goods or services produced for specific projects should have their costs specifically identified,[29] and these costs will be matched with the goods physically sold. In practice this is a relatively unusual method of valuation, as the clerical effort required does not make it feasible unless there are relatively few high value items being bought or produced. Consequently, it would normally be used where the inventory comprised items such as antiques, jewellery and automobiles in the hands of dealers. However, this method is inappropriate where there are large numbers of items that are interchangeable; as specific identification of costs could distort the profit or loss arising from these inventories.[30]

Where it is necessary to use a cost-flow assumption (i.e. when there are large numbers of ordinarily interchangeable items) IAS 2 allows either a FIFO or a weighted average cost formula to be used.[31]

(a)   *FIFO (first-in, first-out)* – In the vast majority of businesses it will not be practicable to keep track of the cost of identical items of inventory on an individual unit basis; nevertheless, it is desirable to approximate to the actual physical flows as far as possible. The FIFO method probably gives the closest approximation to actual cost flows, since it is assumed that when inventories are sold or used in a production process, the oldest are sold or used first. Consequently the balance of inventory on hand at any point represents the most recent purchases or production.[32] This can best be illustrated in the context of a business which deals in perishable goods (e.g. food retailers) since clearly such a business will use the first goods received earliest. The FIFO method, by allocating the earliest costs incurred against revenue, matches actual cost flows with the physical flow of goods reasonably accurately. In any event, even in the case of businesses which do not deal in perishable goods, this would reflect what would probably be a sound management policy. Therefore, in practice where it is not possible to value inventory on an actual cost basis, the FIFO method is generally used since it is most likely to approximate the physical flow of goods sold, resulting in the most accurate measurement of cost flows;

(b)   *Weighted average* – This method, which like FIFO is suitable where inventory units are identical or nearly identical, involves the computation of an average unit cost by dividing the total cost of units by the number of units. The average unit cost then has to be revised with every receipt of inventory, or alternatively at the end of predetermined periods.[33] In practice, weighted average systems are widely used in packaged inventory systems that are computer controlled, although its results are not very different from FIFO in times of relatively low inflation, or where inventory turnover is relatively quick.

LIFO (last-in, first-out), as its name suggests, is the opposite of FIFO and assumes that the most recent purchases or production are used first. In certain cases this could represent the physical flow of inventory (e.g. if a store is filled and emptied from the top). However it is not an acceptable method under IAS 2. LIFO is an attempt to match current costs with current revenues so that the profit and loss account excludes the effects of holding gains. Essentially, therefore, LIFO is an attempt to achieve something closer to replacement cost accounting for the profit and loss account, whilst disregarding the balance sheet. Consequently, the period-end balance of inventory on hand represents the earliest purchases of the item, resulting in inventories being stated in the balance sheet at amounts which may bear little relationship to recent cost levels. LIFO is, perhaps surprisingly, allowable under US GAAP, and is popular in the US as the Internal Revenue Service officially recognises LIFO as an acceptable method for the computation of tax provided that it is used consistently for tax and financial reporting purposes.

The standard makes it clear that the same cost formula should be used for all inventories having a similar nature and use to the entity, although items with a different nature and use may justify the use of a different cost formula.[34] For example the standard allows that inventories used in one business segment may have a use to the entity different from the same type of inventories used in another business segment. However, a difference in geographical location of inventories (or in their respective tax rules) is not sufficient, by itself, to justify the use of different cost formulas.[35]

2.2.3   *Transfers of rental assets to inventory*

It is sometimes the case that an entity, in the course of its ordinary activities, routinely sells items that had previously been held for rental and classified as property, plant and equipment. For example, car rental companies may acquire vehicles with the intention of holding them as rental cars for a limited period and then selling them. An amendment has been made to IAS 16 – *Property, Plant and Equipment* – to require that when such items become held for sale rather than rental they be transferred to inventory at their carrying value.[36] Revenue from the subsequent sale is then recognised gross as discussed in Chapter 16 at 5.2.

2.2.4   *Net realisable value*

IAS 2 in paragraphs 28 to 33 carries substantial guidance on the identification of net realisable value, where this is below cost and therefore requires inventory to be written down.

The cost of inventory may have to be reduced to its net realisable value if it has become damaged, is wholly or partly obsolete, or if its selling price has declined. Additionally, the costs to complete, or the estimated selling costs, may have increased to levels such that the costs of inventory may not be recovered from sale.[37] However the costs to consider in making this assessment should only comprise direct and incremental costs to complete and sell the inventory and will not include any profit margin on these activities. They will also not include overheads or the costs of the distribution channel, such as shops, since these costs will be incurred regardless of whether or not any sale of this inventory actually takes place. The only situation in which the costs of a shop might be considered to be included in these selling costs is the exceptional case where one shop is entirely dedicated to selling impaired goods.

Writing inventory down to net realisable value should normally be done on an item-by-item basis, but it may be necessary to write down an entire product line or group of inventories in a given geographical area that cannot be practicably evaluated separately. IAS 2 specifically states that it is not appropriate to write down an entire class of inventory, such as finished goods, or all the inventory of a particular industry. Service contracts usually accumulate costs on a contract-by-contract basis and net realisable value must be considered on this basis.[38]

Estimates of net realisable value must be based on the most reliable evidence available and take into account fluctuations of price or cost after the end of the period if this is evidence of conditions at the end of the period.[39] A loss realised on a sale of a product after the end of the period may well provide evidence of the net realisable value of that product at the end of the period. However if this product is, for example, an exchange traded commodity and the loss realised can be attributed to a fall in prices on the exchange after the period end date then this loss would not, in itself, provide evidence of the net realisable value at the period end date.

Estimates of net realisable value must also take into account the purpose for which the inventory is held. Therefore inventory held for a particular contract has its net realisable value based on the contract price, and only any excess inventory held would be based on general selling prices. If there is a firm contract to sell and this is in excess of inventory quantities that the entity holds or is able to obtain under a firm purchase contract, this may give rise to a provision that should be recognised in accordance with IAS 37 – *Provisions, Contingent Liabilities and Contingent Assets* (see Chapter 24).[40]

IAS 2 explains that materials and other supplies held for use in the production of inventories are not written down below cost if the final product in which they are to be used is expected to be sold at or above cost. This is the case even if these materials in their present condition have a net realisable value that is below cost and therefore would otherwise require write down. The standard does also explain that where a decline in the price of materials indicates that the cost of the final product will exceed net realisable value then write down of these materials is necessary and that their replacement cost may be the best measure of their net realisable value.[41]

When the circumstances that previously caused inventories to be written down below cost no longer exist, or when there is clear evidence of an increase in net realisable value because of changed economic circumstances, the amount of the write-down is reversed. The reversal cannot be greater than the amount of the original write-down, so that the new carrying amount will always be the lower of the cost and the revised net realisable value.[42]

2.3   Recognition in profit or loss

IAS 2 specifies that when inventory is sold, the carrying amount of the inventory must be recognised as an expense in the period in which the revenue is recognised.[43] It is also clear that a failure to recognise revenue would not justify the non-recognition as an expense of inventory over which the entity no longer had control. Any writes-down or losses of inventory must be recognised as an expense when the write-down or loss occurs. Reversals of previous writes-down shall be recognised as a reduction in the inventory expense recognised in the period in which the reversal occurs.[44]

Judging when to recognise revenue (and therefore to charge the inventory expense) is one of the more complex accounting issues that can occasionally arise in some of those industries where extended payment arrangements, and manufacturer financing of sales to customers, are common. Aircraft manufacturing can provide an example under certain conditions; another one concerns the recognition of revenue in the mobile phone industry where handset costs are recovered over a number of months as part of a customer agreement. Revenue recognition is fully discussed in Chapter 25.

Inventory that goes into the creation of another asset, for instance into a self constructed item of property, plant or equipment, is expensed through the depreciation of that item during its useful life.[45]

2.4   Disclosure requirements of IAS 2

The financial statements should disclose:

(a)   the accounting policies adopted in measuring inventories, including the cost formula used;

(b)   the total carrying amount of inventories and the carrying amount in classifications appropriate to the entity;

(c)   the carrying amount of inventories carried at fair value less costs to sell;

(d)   the amount of inventories recognised as an expense during the period;

(e)   the amount of any write-down of inventories recognised as an expense in the period;

(f)   the amount of any reversal of any write-down that is recognised as a reduction in the amount of inventories recognised as expense in the period;

(g)   the circumstances or events that led to the reversal of a write-down of inventories; and

(h)   the carrying amount of inventories pledged as security for liabilities.[46]

IAS 2 does not specify the precise classifications that must be used to comply with (b) above. However it states that 'information about the carrying amounts held in different classifications of inventories and the extent of the changes in these assets is useful to financial statement users', and suggests suitable examples of common classifications such as merchandise, production supplies, materials, work-in-progress, and finished goods.[47]

Extract 20.2 below shows how the Unilever Group disclosed the relevant information.

Extract 20.2: Unilever N.V. (2007)

Notes to the consolidated accounts [extract]
13   Inventories

Inventories	€million 2007	€million 2006
Raw materials and consumables	1,406	1,360
Finished goods and goods for resale	2,488	2,436
	3,894	3,796

Inventories with a value of €101 million (2006: €96 million) are carried at net realisable value, this being lower than cost. During 2007, €177 million (2006: €160 million) was charged to the income statement for damaged, obsolete and lost inventories. In 2007, €25 million (2006: €34 million) was utilised or released to the income statement from inventory provisions taken in earlier years.

In 2007, inventories with a carrying amount of €4 million were pledged as security for certain of the Group's borrowings (2006: €6 million).

The amount of inventory recognised as an expense in the period is normally included in cost of sales; this category includes unallocated production overheads and abnormal costs as well as the costs of inventory that has been sold. However, the circumstances of the entity may warrant the inclusion of distribution costs into cost of sales.[48] Hence when a company presents its profit or loss based upon this function of expense or 'cost of sales' method it will normally be disclosing costs that are greater than those that have been previously classified as inventory, but this appears to be explicitly allowable by the standard.

Extract 20.3 below shows how Stora Enso Oyj classified their inventories in its 2008 financial statements.

Extract 20.3: Stora Enso Oyj (2008)

notes to the consolidated financial statements [extract]
Note 18   Inventories

EUR million	As at 31 December		
	2008	2007	2006
Materials and supplies	496.9	474.8	424.1
Work in progress	87.5	90.7	72.0
Finished goods	737.7	980.3	1,064.0
Spare parts and consumables	274.5	298.8	369.8
Other inventories	9.7	10.5	5.0
Advance payments & cutting rights	181.3	226.1	135.7
Obsolescence provision – spare parts	–68.2	–66.2	–28.1
Obsolescence provision – finished goods	–14.1	–16.4	–14.6
Net realisable value provision	–11.7	–6.0	–8.4
Total	1,693.6	1,992.6	2,019.5

Finally the disclosure requirements note that some entities adopt a format for profit or loss that results in amounts other than the cost of inventories being disclosed as an expense during the period. This will happen if an entity presents an analysis of expenses using a classification based on the nature of expenses. The entity then discloses the costs recognised as an expense for raw materials and consumables, labour costs and other costs together with the amount of the net change in inventories for the period.[49]

Formats for the presentation of profit or loss are discussed in Chapter 3.

3   PRACTICAL ISSUES

3.1   Constituents of cost

For the most part there are few problems over the inclusion of direct costs in inventories. Problems may arise over the inclusion of certain types of overheads, and over the allocation of overheads into the inventory valuation.

The costs of inventories include the cost of bringing them to their 'present location and condition'.[50] While the standard gives examples of costs that are excluded, there is little guidance regarding the identification of costs that should be included and it is therefore a matter of interpretation and judgement depending on the particular facts and circumstances surrounding the business in question. It must always be borne in mind that the inclusion of overheads is not voluntary. However, consistency must also mean that overheads should be allocated to the cost of inventory on a consistent basis from year to year, and should not be omitted in anticipation of a net realisable value difficulty. These points are discussed below.

3.1.1 Distribution and storage costs

Although distribution costs are obviously a cost of bringing an item to its present location, the question arises as to whether costs of transporting inventory from one location to another are eligible. If the condition of the inventory is not changed at either location, none of the warehousing costs may be included in inventory costs. Therefore it is not clear on what sensible basis transportation costs between two such locations could be included in inventory costs (unless they are an essential part of the production process as outlined below).

Storage costs are not allowed unless they are necessary in the production process. This appears to prohibit including the costs of the warehouse and the overheads of a retail outlet as part of inventory, as neither of these is a prelude to a further production stage. Costs of distribution to the customer are not allowed; they are selling costs and the standard prohibits their inclusion in the carrying value of inventory. It therefore seems probable that distribution costs of inventory whose production process is complete should not be included in its carrying value. A question arises about the meaning of 'production' in the context of large retailers, for example supermarkets. As the transport and logistics involved are essential to their ability to put goods on sale at a particular location in the correct condition, it seems reasonable to conclude that such costs are a part of the production process.

Where it is necessary to store raw materials or work in progress prior to a further processing or manufacturing stage, the costs of such storage should be included in production overheads. In addition, it would appear reasonable to allow the costs of storing maturing stocks, such as cheese, wine or whisky, in the cost of production.

3.1.2 General and administrative overheads

IAS 2 specifically disallows administrative overheads that do not contribute to bringing inventories to their present location and condition.[51] Other costs and overheads that do contribute are allowable as costs of production. There is a judgement to be made about such matters, as on a very wide interpretation any department could be considered to make a contribution. For example, the accounts department will normally support the following functions:

(a)   production – by paying direct and indirect production wages and salaries, by controlling purchases and related payments, and by preparing periodic financial statements for the production units;

(b)   marketing and distribution – by analysing sales and by controlling the sales ledger; and

(c)   general administration – by preparing management accounts and annual financial statements and budgets, by controlling cash resources and by planning investments.

Only those costs of the accounts department that can be allocated to the production function fall to be included in the cost of conversion. Part of the management and overhead costs of a large retailer's logistical department may be included in cost if it can be related to bringing the inventory to its present location and condition. These types of cost are unlikely to be material in the context of the inventory total held by organisations. In our view, an entity wishing to include a material amount of overhead of a borderline nature must ensure it can sensibly justify its inclusion under the provisions of IAS 2 by presenting an analysis of the function and its contribution to the production process similar to the above example.

3.1.3   *Allocation of overheads*

IAS 2 states that the allocation of fixed production overheads is to be based on the normal capacity of the production facilities, although the actual production level can be used if it approximates to normal circumstances.[52] However, it is important to bear in mind that the assumption of normal levels of activity relates to all costs including direct costs. In computing the costs to be allocated via the overhead recovery rate, costs such as distribution and selling must be excluded, together with cost of storing raw materials and work in progress, unless it is necessary that these latter costs be incurred prior to further processing, which may occasionally be the case.

Although determining the normal level of activity when allocating overheads is a judgemental area, it is relatively straightforward when dealing with the manufacturing and processing of physical inventory. It is far harder to establish what this can mean in the context of service industries where the 'inventory' is intangible and based on work performed for customers that has not yet been recognised as income. There really is no equivalent to the normal capacity of production facilities in these cases. However, the standard still requires the inclusion of attributable overheads, and entities must take care to establish an appropriate benchmark to avoid the distortions that could occur if overheads were attributed on the basis of actual 'output'.

3.2   Net realisable value

As already discussed, the basic rule of accounting for inventories under IAS 2 is that they are stated at the lower of their cost and net realisable value. The comparison of cost and net realisable value of finished goods is normally straightforward as long as there are established selling prices for the finished goods. The net realisable value of the raw materials, it is made clear in IAS 2, depends on the ultimate selling price of a completed product, rather than the current price of the raw materials involved.[53] Thus, a whisky distiller would not write down an inventory of grain because of a fall in the grain price, so long as it expected still to sell the whisky at a price which is sufficient to recover cost. Conversely though, where a write down is required in respect of finished goods, the carrying value of any related raw materials must also be reviewed to see if they too need to be written down.

Often raw materials are used to make a number of different products. In these cases it is normally not possible to arrive at a particular net realisable value for each item of raw material based on the selling price of any one type of finished item. If current replacement cost is less than historical cost, however, a provision is only required to be made if the finished goods into which they will be made are expected to be sold at a loss. No provision should be made just because the anticipated profit will be less than normal.

3.3   The valuation of high volumes of similar items of inventory

Practical problems in the valuation of inventory arise in the case of businesses with high volumes of various line items of inventory. This situation occurs extensively in the retail trade where similar mark-ups are applied to ranges of inventory items or groups of items, and the selling price is marked on each individual item of inventory (e.g. in the case of a supermarket). In such a situation, it may be unnecessarily time-consuming to determine the cost of the period-end inventory on a conventional basis. Consequently, the most practical method of determining period-end inventory may be to record inventory on hand at selling prices, and then convert it to cost by removing the normal mark-up. Not surprisingly, this method of inventory valuation is known as the 'retail method'.

A complication in applying the retail method is in determining the margin to be applied to the inventory at selling price to convert it back to cost. The percentage has to take account of circumstances in which inventories have been marked down to below original selling price. Adjustments have to be made to eliminate the effect of these markdowns so as to prevent any item of inventory being valued at less than both its cost and its net realisable value. In practice, however, entities that use the retail method apply a gross profit margin computed on an average basis appropriate for departments and/or ranges, rather than applying specific mark-up percentages. This practice is, in fact, acknowledged by IAS 2 that states: 'an average percentage for each retail department is often used'.[54]

3.4   Forward contracts to purchase inventory

The standard scopes out commodity broker-traders that measure inventory at fair value less costs to sell from its measurement requirements (see 2.1 above). If a broker-trader had a forward contract for purchase of inventory this contract would be accounted for as a derivative under IAS 39 – *Financial Instruments: Recognition and Measurement* – since it would not meet the normal purchase or sale exemption (see Chapter 29 at 3.9.2 B) and when the contract was physically settled the inventory would likewise be shown at fair value less costs to sell.[55] However, if such an entity was not measuring inventory at fair value less costs to sell it would be subject to the measurement requirements of IAS 2 and would therefore have to record the inventory at the lower of cost and net realisable value. This raises the question of what is cost when such an entity takes delivery of inventory that has been purchased with a forward contract? Upon delivery the cash paid (i.e. the fixed price agreed in the forward contract) is in substance made up of two elements:

(i)   an amount that settles the forward contract; and

(ii)   an amount that represents the 'cost of purchase', being the market price at the date of purchase.

This 'cost of purchase' represents the forward contract price adjusted for the derivative asset or liability. For example, assume that the broker-trader was purchasing oil and the forward contracted price was $140 per barrel of oil, but at the time of delivery the spot price of oil was $150 and the forward contract had a fair value of $10 at that date. The oil would be recorded at the fair value on what is deemed to be the purchase date of $150. The $140 cash payment would in substance consist of $150 payment for the inventory offset by a $10 receipt upon settlement of the derivative contract. This is exactly the same result as if the entity had been required to settle the derivative immediately prior to, and separate from, the physical delivery of the oil.

3.5   Manufacturer dealer transactions and goods on consignment

In some industries, for example automobile manufacturing and retailing, aircraft manufacturing, railway carriage manufacturing and maintenance, and mobile phone handset retailing, it is customary for the goods concerned to be subject to extended and complex delivery, sales and settlement arrangements. For these types of transactions, the accounting problem that arises principally concerns when to recognise revenue, the consequent derecognition of inventory being driven by the revenue recognition judgement, not vice-versa. The entire subject of revenue recognition is dealt with in Chapter 25, to which reference should be made in considering such issues.

3.6   Core inventories

In certain industries, for example the petrochemical industry, certain processes or storage arrangements require a core of inventory to be present in the system at all times. For example in order for a crude oil refining process to take place, the plant must contain a certain minimum quantity of oil. This can only be taken out once the plant is abandoned and could then only be sold as sludge. Similarly, underground gas storage caves are filled with gas; but a substantial part (perhaps say 25%) of that gas can never be sold as its function is to pressurise the cave, thereby allowing the remaining 75% to be extracted. Even though the gas will be turned around on a continuing basis, at any one time 25% of it will never be available to sell and cannot be recouped from the cave.

It is our view that if an item of inventory is not held for sale or consumed in a production process, but is necessary to the operation of a facility during more than one operating cycle, and its cost cannot be recouped through sale (or is significantly impaired), this item of inventory should be accounted for as an item of property, plant and equipment under IAS 16. This applies even if the part of inventory that is deemed to be an item of PP&E cannot be separated physically from the rest of inventory.

These matters will always involve the exercise of judgement, however, in the above instances, we consider that: (i) the deemed PP&E items do not meet the definition of inventories; (ii) although it is not possible to physically separate the chemicals involved into inventory and PP&E categories, there is no accounting reason why one cannot distinguish between identical assets with different uses and therefore account for them differently. Indeed, IAS 2 does envisage such a possibility in paragraph 25 when discussing different cost formulas; (iii) the deemed PP&E items are necessary to bring another item of PP&E to the condition necessary for it to be capable of operating in the manner intended by management. This meets the definition of the costs of PP&E in IAS 16.16(b) upon initial recognition; (iv) recognising these items as inventories would lead to an immediate loss because these items cannot be sold or consumed in a production process, or during the process of rendering services. This does not properly reflect the fact that the items are necessary to operate another asset over more than one operating cycle.

3.7 Real estate inventory

Quite often real estate businesses develop and construct residential properties for sale, often consisting of several units. The strategy is to make a profit from the development and construction of the property rather than to make a profit in the long term from general price increases in the property market. The intention is to sell the property units as soon as possible following their construction, and is therefore in the ordinary course of the entity's business. When construction is complete it is not uncommon for individual property units to be leased at market rates to earn revenues to partly cover expenses such as interest, management fees, and real estate taxes. In practice, the leasing of properties prior to sale is common in the real estate industry. Large-scale buyers of property, such as insurance companies, are often reluctant to buy unless tenants are *in situ*, as this assures immediate cash flows from the investment.

It is our view that if it is in the entity's ordinary course of business (supported by its strategy) to hold property for short-term sale rather than for long-term capital appreciation, the entire property (including the leased units) should be accounted for and presented as inventory. This will continue to be the case as long as it remains the intention to sell the property in the short term. Rent received should be included in other income as it does not represent a reduction in the cost of inventory.

Investment property is defined in paragraph 5 of IAS 40 as 'property ... held ... to earn rentals or for capital appreciation or both, rather than for ... use in the production or supply of goods or services or for administrative purposes; or ... for sale in the ordinary course of business.' Therefore in the case outlined above, the property does not meet the definition in IAS 40 of investment property. Properties intended for sale in the ordinary course of business – no matter whether leased out or not – are outside the scope of IAS 40. However, if a property is not intended for sale, IAS 40 requires it to be transferred from inventory to investment property when there is a change in use evidenced by the commencement of an operating lease to another party (see Chapter 17 at 7).

3.8   Property demolition and operating lease costs

During the course of a property redevelopment project, an existing property may need to be demolished in order for the new development to take place. The question arises, therefore, of how the cost of the existing building that will be demolished should be treated. Should it be capitalised as part of the construction cost for the new building to be erected on the same piece of land, or should the cost of the original building be derecognised and charged to profit or loss?

In all such cases judgement must be made on the basis of the particular facts involved, as the exact circumstances of the entity will bear upon the decision. There are three distinct scenarios to consider:

(a)   the entity is the owner-occupier, in which case the matter falls under IAS 16;

(b)   the entity holds the property to earn rentals, in which case the matter falls under IAS 40;

(c)   the entity sells such properties in its normal course of business.

If it is the strategy of the developer to sell the developed property after construction, the cost of the old building as well as demolition costs and costs of developing the new one would be treated as inventory, but must still be subjected to the normal 'lower of cost and net realisable value' requirements.

Paragraph 6 of IAS 2 defines inventories as assets (a) held for sale in the ordinary course of business; or (b) in the process of production for such sale; or (c) in the form of materials or supplies to be consumed in the production process or in the rendering of services. Paragraph 10 states that 'the cost of inventories shall comprise all costs of purchase, costs of conversion and other costs incurred in bringing the inventories to their present location and condition.' As the new development is to be held for sale in the normal course of business by the developer, it falls within the scope of IAS 2.

In our view a similar argument can be applied to operating lease costs for the land upon which a building is being constructed. If, for example, an entity enters into a 50 year operating lease for land on which it intends to construct a building for sale as part of its ordinary business activities then the operating lease expense during the time taken to construct the building may be regarded as part of the 'costs incurred in bringing the inventories to their present location and condition' referred to in paragraph 10 of the standard. However an alternative view could also be taken, that is that these operating lease costs are for the right to control the land during the 50 year period rather than costs in bringing this inventory to any particular condition, in which case expensing may be appropriate.

3.9   Drug production costs within the pharmaceutical industry

Pharmaceutical companies often commence production of drugs prior to obtaining the necessary regulatory approval to sell them. So long as the regulatory approval has been applied for and it is believed highly likely that this will be successfully obtained then it is appropriate to be recognising an asset and classifying this as inventory. Prior to this application for regulatory approval being made any costs would need to be classified as research and development costs rather than inventory and the criteria within IAS 38 – *Intangible Assets* – assessed to determine if capitalisation was appropriate (see Chapter 15).

3.10 Revaluation effects on inventory valuations

Paragraph 31 of IAS 16 provides the option of choosing a revaluation model for property, plant and equipment, rather than a cost model. Under that model 'after recognition as an asset, an item of property, plant and equipment whose fair value can be measured reliably shall be carried at a revalued amount, being its fair value at the date of the revaluation less any subsequent accumulated depreciation and subsequent accumulated impairment losses. Revaluations shall be made with sufficient regularity to ensure that the carrying amount does not differ materially from that which would be determined using fair value at the end of the reporting period'.

When the revaluation model in IAS 16 is applied, depreciation is based on the revalued amount, less the residual value of the asset.[56] When revaluation has occurred, the question therefore arises whether the 'revalued depreciation' should be used for inventory valuation purposes, or whether historical cost-based depreciation could also be permitted for inventory valuation purposes?

IAS 16 requires, when the revaluation model is adopted, that depreciation be recognised prospectively based on the revalued asset amount less its residual value. Although this issue is not specifically addressed by IAS 2, in our view consistency would indicate that when an entity adopts the revaluation model in IAS 16, the preferred approach would be to likewise use the 'revalued depreciation' for inventory valuation purposes under IAS 2.

4 CONCLUSION

This is one area of financial reporting that has hitherto been fairly uncontroversial. We had been a little concerned that, given the IASB's attempts to move to a system of financial reporting that recognises an ever-broadening range of assets and liabilities in the balance sheet at their fair values, there may have been calls for the measurement of inventories at fair value as well. However making the sale is the most difficult and unpredictable part of being in business, as anyone with commercial experience knows, and whether or not the sale is made represents the fundamental essence of business risk. If it was part of the agenda of the standard setters to value inventories at selling prices rather than cost (which is usually the effect of valuing inventories at fair value), it is our view that both the relevance and the reliability of financial statements would be noticeably diminished. It is therefore reassuring that the recently issued Discussion Paper – *Preliminary Views on Revenue Recognition in Contracts with Customers*[57] – indicates no such intention. The Discussion Paper simply refers to the need to consider whether, where inventory is presently recognised at fair value (e.g. as under IAS 41), changes in the value of inventory should be precluded from being presented within revenue. The proposed model within the Discussion Paper only applies when there is a contract with a customer. It therefore will have an impact on accounting for construction contracts presently accounted for under IAS 11 (see Chapter 21) but will not apply to inventory in the absence of a contract.[58]

References

1 IAS 2, *Inventories*, IASB, para. 2.

2 IAS 2, para. 3.

3 IAS 2, para. 4.

4 IAS 2, para. 3.

5 IAS 2, para. 5.

6 IAS 2, para. 6.

7 IAS 2, para. 8.

8 IAS 2, para. 9.

9 IAS 2, para. 6.

10 IAS 2, para. 6.

11 IAS 2, para. 7.

12 IAS 2, para. 10.

13 IAS 2, para. 11.

14 IAS 2, para. 12.

15 IAS 2, para. 12.

16 IAS 2, para. 13.

17 IAS 2, para. 13.

18 IAS 2, para. 14.

19 IAS 2, para. 15.

20 IAS 2, para. 16.

21 IAS 2, para. 17.

22 IAS 23, *Borrowing Costs*, IASB, paras. 4 and 8.

23 IAS 23, para. 7.

24 IAS 2, para. 18.

25 IAS 2, para. 19.

26 IAS 2, para. 20.

27 IAS 2, para. 21.

28 IAS 2, para. 22.

29 IAS 2, para. 23.

30 IAS 2, para. 24.

31 IAS 2, para. 25.

32 IAS 2, para. 27.

33 IAS 2, para. 27.

34 IAS 2, para. 25.

35 IAS 2, para. 26.

36 IAS 16, *Property, Plant and Equipment*, IASB, para. 68A.

37 IAS 2, para. 28.

38 IAS 2, para. 29.

39 IAS 2, para. 30.

40 IAS 2, para. 31.

41 IAS 2, para. 32.

42 IAS 2, para. 33.

43 IAS 2, para. 34.

44 IAS 2, para. 34.

45 IAS 2, para. 35.

46 IAS 2, para. 36.

47 IAS 2, para. 37.

48 IAS 2, para. 38.

49 IAS 2, para. 39.

50 IAS 2, para. 10.

51 IAS 2, para. 16.

52 IAS 2, para. 13.

53 IAS 2, para. 32.

54 IAS 2, para. 22.

55 IAS 2, para. 3(b).

56 IAS 16, para. 53.

57 Discussion Paper, *Preliminary Views on Revenue Recognition in Contracts with Customers*, IASB, December 2008.

58 Discussion Paper, *Preliminary Views on Revenue Recognition in Contracts with Customers*, IASB, December 2008, paras. 6.15-6.21.

Chapter 21   Construction contracts

1   INTRODUCTION

IAS 11 – *Construction Contracts* – is a standard designed under the historical cost system to deal with the accounting issues raised by its subject. Like a number of other older standards that have not yet been revised significantly by the IASB (IAS 11 was originally approved in 1978 and last revised in 1993), the focus is on the income statement and the basis on which income and expenditure should be recognised. IAS 11 identifies its principle purpose as the allocation of contract revenue and contract costs to the accounting periods in which contract work is performed, not on the identification of assets and liabilities as defined by the IASB Framework.

In the longer term, the IASB, in conjunction with the FASB, is developing a new revenue recognition standard. The Boards, in December 2008, issued a Discussion Paper entitled *Preliminary Views on Revenue Recognition in Contracts with Customers*.[1] This joint project and Discussion Paper are discussed in Chapter 25 and, as highlighted in that Chapter, the proposals could significantly impact the manner in which revenue is recognised under construction contracts. The proposals favour a revenue recognition model which focuses on when control of an asset is transferred to customers rather than, as under IAS 11 at present, when activity is performed. It is presently intended that any standard that results from this project will replace both IAS 18 – *Revenue*, and IAS 11.

1.1   Scope and definitions of IAS 11

IAS 11 applies to accounting for construction contracts in the financial statements of the contractor.[2]

A construction contract is defined as follows:

'a contract specifically negotiated for the construction of an asset or a combination of assets that are closely interrelated or interdependent in terms of their design, technology and function or their ultimate purpose or use.'[3]

The meaning of 'specifically negotiated for the construction of an asset' has recently been considered by the IFRIC. In July 2008 the IFRIC issued Interpretation 15 – *Agreements for the Construction of Real Estate* (IFRIC 15). Although IFRIC 15 has been written in the specific context of its title, it includes an analysis of the distinguishing features of construction contracts and it is, therefore, more generally relevant in determining whether any contract that involves the construction of an asset is within the scope of IAS 11 or is a sale of goods. See 4.1 below.

The problem is one of definition, as something that may be accounted for as a single construction contract can comprise a number of different elements. Single constructions could include a bridge, a building, a dam, a pipeline, a road, a ship or a tunnel. Other single contracts include groups of inter-related assets such as an oil refinery or complex pieces of plant and equipment.[4] Whether a contract is, in fact a single construction contract or one that should be separated into components, each of which is dealt with individually, is one of the more difficult and subjective areas of contract accounting and one that has also been considered by the IFRIC (see 4.2 below).

Contracts for services directly related to construction contracts are covered by IAS 11 and not by IAS 18. These include contracts for the services of project managers and architects. Contracts for the demolition and restoration of assets and restoration of the environment after an asset is demolished are also construction contracts.[5]

The standard identifies two specific types of construction contract:

> 'A *fixed price contract* is a construction contract in which the contractor agrees to a fixed contract price, or a fixed rate per unit of output, which in some cases is subject to cost escalation clauses;
>
> A *cost plus contract* is a construction contract in which the contractor is reimbursed for allowable or otherwise defined costs, plus a percentage of these costs or a fixed fee.'[6]

These types determine the basis on which income is recognised, as is discussed in 2.3.1 below.

Contracts that contain elements of both types, e.g. a cost plus contract that has an agreed maximum price, will have to be analysed in order to determine when to recognise contract revenue and expenses.[7]

1.2   Combination and segmentation of contracts

IAS 11 should be applied separately to each construction contract.[8] However, in order to reflect the substance of the transaction it may be necessary for a contract to be sub-divided and the standard to be applied individually to each component, or for a group of contracts to be treated as one.

IAS 11 provides guidance in three separate cases. The first is where a single contract covers the construction of a number of separate assets, each of which is in substance a separate contract, i.e.

(a)   separate proposals have been submitted for each asset;

(b)   the contractor and customer have negotiated separately for each asset and can accept or reject that part of the contract relating to each asset; and

(c)   the costs and revenues relating to each asset can be identified.[9]

The second case is effectively the reverse of the first and deals with situations where in substance there is only a single contract with a customer, or a group of customers. This group of contracts should be treated as a single contract where:

(a)   the group of contracts is negotiated as a single package;

(b)   the contracts are so closely interrelated that they are, in effect, part of a single project with an overall profit margin; and

(c)   the contracts are performed concurrently or in a continuous sequence.[10]

Finally it is possible that a contract may envisage the construction of a further asset at the customer's discretion. IAS 11 identifies two criteria, each of which would indicate that it should be accounted for as a separate contract:

(a)   the asset differs significantly in design, technology or function from the asset or assets covered by the original contract; or

(b)   the price of the asset is negotiated without regard to the original contract price.[11]

The issues connected with combining and segmenting contracts are considered at 4.2 below, while options to construct additional assets are discussed at 4.3 below.

2   CONTRACT REVENUE, COSTS AND EXPENSES

2.1   Contract revenue

Contract revenue comprises the amount of revenue initially agreed by the parties together with any variations, claims and incentive payments as long as it is probable that they will result in revenue and can be measured reliably.[12] The standard states that such revenue is to be measured at the fair value of the consideration received and receivable. In this context, 'fair value' appears to refer to the process whereby the consideration is to be revised as events occur and uncertainties are resolved. These may include contractual matters such as increases in revenue in a fixed price contract as a result of cost escalation clauses or, when a contract involves a fixed price per unit of output, contract revenue may increase as the number of units is increased. Penalties for delays may reduce revenue. In addition, variations and claims must be taken into account.[13] If deferred payments are due after completion of the contract, for example retention payments, such payments will be brought into account at their present value. Similarly if advance payments are received, and these constitute financing transactions, it may be appropriate to accrue interest on them (see Chapter 25 at 6.1.4).

Variations are instructions by the customer to change the scope of the work to be performed under the contract, including changes to the specification or design of the asset or of the duration of the contract. Variations may only be included in contract revenue when it is probable that the customer will approve the variation and the amount to be charged for it, and the amount can be measured reliably.[14]

Given the extended periods over which contracts are carried out and changes in circumstances prevailing whilst the work is in progress, it is quite normal for a contractor to submit claims for additional sums to a customer. Claims may be made for costs not included in the original contract or arising as an indirect consequence of approved variations, such as customer caused delays, errors in specifications or design and disputed variations. Because their settlement is by negotiation (which can in practice be very protracted), they are subject to a high level of uncertainty; consequently, no credit should be taken for them unless negotiations have reached an advanced stage such that:

- it is probable that the customer will accept the claim; and
- the amount that it is probable will be accepted by the customer can be measured reliably.[15]

This means that, as a minimum, the claims must have been agreed in principle and, in the absence of an agreed sum, the amount to be accrued must have been prudently assessed.

Contracts may provide for incentive payments, for example, for early completion or superior performance. They may only be included in contract revenue when the contract is at such a stage that it is probable the required performance will be achieved and the amount can be measured reliably.[16]

2.2   Contract costs

Contract costs are those that relate directly to the specific contract and to those that are attributable to contract activity in general that can be allocated to the contract. In addition, they include costs that are specifically chargeable to the customer under the terms of the contract.[17]

Directly related costs include:

(a)   direct labour costs, including site supervision;

(b)   costs of materials used in construction;

(c)   depreciation of plant and equipment used on the contract;

(d)   costs of moving plant, equipment and materials to and from the contract site;

(e)   costs of hiring plant and equipment;

(f)   costs of design and technical assistance that is directly related to the contract;

(g)   the estimated costs of rectification and guarantee work, including expected warranty costs; and

(h)   claims from third parties.[18]

If the contractor generates incidental income from any directly related cost, e.g. by selling surplus materials and disposing of equipment at the end of the contract, this is treated as a reduction in contract costs.[19]

The second category of costs comprises those attributable to contract activity in general that can be allocated to a particular contract. These include design and technical assistance not directly related to an individual contract, insurance, and construction overheads such as the costs of preparing and processing the payroll for the personnel actually working on the contract. These must be allocated using a systematic and rational method, consistently applied to all costs having similar characteristics. Allocation must be based on the normal level of construction activity.[20]

There are various costs that, in most circumstances, are specifically precluded by IAS 11 from being attributed to contract activity or allocated to a contract. These include general administration costs, selling costs, research and development costs and the depreciation of idle plant and equipment that is not used on a particular contract.[21] However, the entity is allowed to classify general administration costs and research and development as contract costs if they are specifically reimbursable under the terms of the contract.[22] An example is given by EADS, which discloses the following:

Extract 21.1: EADS N.V. (2008)

Notes to the Consolidated Financial Statements [extract]
2. Summary of Significant Accounting Policies
Research and Development Expenses [extract]
Research and Development Expenses – Research and development activities can be (i) contracted or (ii) self-initiated.
i)   Costs for contracted research and development activities, carried out in the scope of externally financed research and development contracts, are expensed when the related revenues are recorded.

Costs may be attributed to a contract from the date on which it is secured until its final completion. Additionally, costs relating directly to the contract, which have been incurred in gaining the business, may be included in contract costs if they have been incurred once it is probable the contract will be obtained. These costs must be separately identified and measured reliably.[23] This is not dissimilar to the general rules for recognition of an asset. An asset is defined in the IASB Framework as 'a resource controlled by the entity as a result of past events and from which future economic benefits are expected to flow to the entity'.[24] Therefore, we believe that this should be read restrictively and that these costs should not be recognised until they can themselves be seen as an asset of the entity through its control of the future economic benefits from the contract.

One entity that takes a prudent view of pre-contract costs is Balfour Beatty plc, which sets out that such costs are expensed until it is *virtually certain* that a contract will be awarded.

Extract 21.2: Balfour Beatty plc (2007)

Notes to the accounts [extract]
1.6   Construction and service contracts [extract]

Pre-contract costs are expensed as incurred until it is virtually certain that a contract will be awarded, from which time further pre-contract costs are recognised as an asset and charged as an expense over the period of the contract. Amounts recovered in respect of costs that have been written off are deferred and amortised over the life of the contract

---

Costs that have been written off cannot be reinstated if the contract is obtained in a subsequent period.[25]

Costs incurred in securing a contract include such things as the building of models (including computer modelling exercises) for tender purposes, travelling costs of technicians to survey sites, technical tendering costs, and similar expenses relating specifically to a given contract.

2.2.1   *Borrowing costs*

Borrowing costs may be specific to individual contracts or attributable to contract activity in general. From 1 January 2009 IAS 23 – *Borrowing Costs* – requires capitalisation of borrowing costs that are directly attributable to the acquisition, construction or production of qualifying assets.[26] The policy choice that previously allowed all borrowing costs to be expensed as incurred and that existed under the previous version of IAS 23 has been removed. See Chapter 19 for a detailed discussion of capitalisation of interest and of the revised standard; apart from the elimination of the previous benchmark treatment of expensing borrowing costs there are few other changes. This specific reference to IAS 23 that was previously included in paragraph 18 of IAS 11[27] was deleted as one of the consequential amendments made to the revised standard. The IASB argued that it was unnecessary, stating 'attributing borrowing costs to contracts is not a matter of capitalisation. Rather, it is a matter of identifying the contract costs'.[28] In other words, the inclusion of borrowing costs into construction contract costs means that the borrowing costs concerned will be expensed when the contract costs are expensed.

While it may appear initially that this change to the standard will require all companies to commence capitalising borrowing costs into their construction contracts, another decision, this time from the IFRIC, may have exactly the opposite effect and reduce capitalisation to an insignificant amount. During its debates on accounting for service concessions the IFRIC concluded that the 'amount due from customers' asset is a financial asset within the scope of IAS 32 – *Financial Instruments: Presentation.* This asset is not a qualifying asset for the purposes of capitalisation of borrowing costs because the treatment requires interest income to be imputed (see Chapter 23 at 5.4)[29]. Therefore, once revenue is recognised on work that has been performed, capitalisation of borrowing costs will cease. Only contract costs that related to future activity could be a qualifying asset and this will usually be an insignificant amount. In June 2005, the IFRIC decided not to prepare an Interpretation to this effect, stating that it 'was not aware of any evidence that the conclusion was of major importance outside the service concession sector'. The IFRIC indicated that it would reconsider this decision if the responses to the draft Interpretations on service concession arrangements indicated otherwise.[30] It did not do so. IFRIC 12 – *Service Concession Arrangements* – was issued in November 2006; the position taken with regard to amounts due from customers, i.e. that they are financial assets, remains unchanged and there has been no other comment on the matter.

IFRIC's interpretation is significant for all entities engaged in construction contracts if these are deemed to fall under IFRIC 12 and if, under this Interpretation, the operator has a financial asset rather than an intangible asset. Borrowing costs will only be capitalised under IFRIC 12 if the operator has an intangible asset.[31] Where the operator has a financial asset the borrowing costs will need to be expensed and, in addition, part of the contract revenue will be taken as finance income, as income is accreted on the carrying value of the financial asset.[32] This could also change the profile of income recognition although it is not yet clear how the percentage of completion method will be applied if the financial asset is one for which the effective interest method is mandated. The implications of this conclusion outside service concessions remain unclear.

2.3   The recognition of contract revenue and expenses

If the basic rule of accounting for inventories were applied to contracts, it would result in an annual income statement that reflected only the outcome of contracts completed during the year. In a contracting company this might bear no relation to the company's actual level of activity for that year. IAS 11 therefore requires revenue and expenses to be recognised on uncompleted contracts in order to present a consistent view of the results of the company's activities during the period and from one period to the next. The underlying principle in IAS 11 is that, once the outcome of a construction contract can be estimated reliably, revenue associated with the construction contract should be recognised by reference to the stage of completion of the contract activity at the end of the reporting period.[33] The standard does not define the attributable profit in a contract, which will therefore be the balancing figure once revenue and expenses are known.

If it is anticipated that the contract will be loss-making, the expected loss must be recognised immediately. This is described further in 2.3.6 below.

2.3.1   Types of construction contract

IAS 11 identifies two types of construction contract, fixed price and cost plus contracts.

A   Fixed price contracts

In the case of a fixed price contract, the standard states that the outcome of a construction contract can be estimated reliably when all the conditions discussed below are satisfied.

- First, it must be probable that the economic benefits associated with the contract will flow to the entity, which must be able to measure total contract revenue reliably. As discussed further below, these conditions will usually be satisfied when there are adequate contractual arrangements between the parties;

- Second, both the contract costs to complete the contract and the stage of contract completion at the end of the reporting period must be able to be measured reliably; and

- Third, the entity must be able to identify and measure reliably the contract costs attributable to the contract so that actual contract costs incurred can be compared with prior estimates.[34] This means that it must have adequate reporting and budgeting systems.

B   Cost plus contracts

Cost plus contracts are not subject to all of the same uncertainties as fixed price contracts. As with any transaction, it must be probable that the economic benefits associated with the contract will flow to the entity in order to recognise income at all. In most contracts this will be evidenced by the contract documentation. The fundamental criterion for a cost plus contract is the proper measurement of contract costs. Therefore, the contract costs attributable to the contract, whether or not specifically reimbursable, must be clearly identified and measured reliably.[35]

2.3.2   *The stage of completion method*

There are certain general principles that apply whether the contract is classified as fixed cost or as cost plus. Recognition of revenue is by reference to the 'stage of completion method', also known as the 'percentage of completion method'. Contract revenue and costs are recognised as revenue and expenses in profit or loss in the period in which the work is performed. Any anticipated excess of contract costs over contract income (i.e. a loss on the contract) is recognised as soon as it is anticipated.[36]

This does not mean that contract activity is necessarily based on the total costs that have been incurred by the entity. Contract costs that relate to future contract activity (i.e. that activity for which revenue has not yet been recognised) may be deferred and recognised as an asset as long as it is probable that they will be recovered. This point is made explicitly by Royal BAM Group nv in Extract 21.4 below. These costs are usually called contract work in progress.[37] An example of this may be materials purchased and stored for future use on a contract. Otherwise, contract costs are recognised in the profit or loss as they are incurred.

Importantly, neither does it mean that an entity can determine what it considers to be an appropriate profit margin for the whole contract and spread costs over the contract so as to achieve this margin, thereby classifying deferred costs as work in progress. As noted at 2.3 above, IAS 11 defines revenue and contract costs and not attributable profit. The standard does not seek to achieve a uniform profit margin throughout the contract, unless, of course, it is a cost plus contract.

An entity does not adjust the cumulative revenue it has recognised if it transpires in a subsequent period that there are doubts about the recoverability of an amount it has recognised as revenue and it consequently has to make provision against its debtor. Instead the amount that is no longer considered recoverable is written off as an expense.[38]

In order to be able to recognise revenue, the construction entity must be able to make reliable estimates of its income and costs. It is usually possible to do so once the parties have agreed to a contract that establishes both parties' enforceable rights, the contract consideration and the manner and terms of settlement. However, the entity must also be able to review and, where necessary revise, the estimates of contract revenue and contract costs as the contract progresses. This means that the entity must have an effective system of internal financial budgets and reporting systems.[39]

The standard allows the stage of completion of a contract to be determined in a number of ways, including:

- the proportion that contract costs incurred for work performed to date bear to the estimated total contract costs;

- surveys of work performed; or

- completion of a physical proportion of the contract work.[40]

These could, of course, give different answers regarding the stage of completion of a contract as demonstrated in the following example.

Example 21.1:   *Determination of revenue*

A company is engaged in a construction contract with an expected sales value of £10,000. It is the end of the accounting period during which the company commenced work on this contract and it needs to compute the amount of revenue to be reflected in the profit and loss account for this contract.

Scenario (i)   **Stage of completion is measured by the proportion that contract costs incurred for work performed to date bear to the estimated total contract costs**

The company has incurred and applied costs of £4,000. £3,000 is the best estimate of costs to complete. The company should therefore recognise revenue of £5,714, being the appropriate proportion of total contract value, and computed thus:

$$\frac{4,000}{7,000} \times 10,000 = 5,714$$

Scenario (ii)   **Stage of completion is measured by surveys of work performed**

An independent surveyor has certified that at the period-end the contract is 55% complete and that the company is entitled to apply for cumulative progress payments of £5,225 (after a 5% retention). In this case the company would record revenue of £5,500 being the sales value of the work done. (If it is anticipated that rectification work will have to be carried out to secure the release of the retention money then this should be taken into account in computing the stage of completion – but the fact that there is retention of an amount does not, in itself, directly impact the amount of revenue to be recorded.)

Scenario (iii)   **Stage of completion is measured by completion of a physical proportion of the contract work**

The company's best estimate of the physical proportion of the work it has completed is that it is 60% complete. The value of the work done and, therefore, the revenue to be recognised is £6,000.

Note that in each of the above scenarios the computation of the amount of revenue is quite independent of the question of how much (if any) profit should be taken. This is as it should be, because even if a contract is loss-making the sales price will be earned and this should be reflected by recording revenue as the contract progresses. In the final analysis, any loss arises because costs are greater than revenue, and costs should be reflected through cost of sales. Different methods of determining revenue will, as disclosed above, produce different results, which highlights the importance of disclosing the method adopted by the entity.

An entity that discloses that it uses a variety of methods to determine revenue is EADS, as shown in the following extract.

Extract 21.3: EADS N.V. (2008)

Notes to the Consolidated Financial Statements [extract]
2. Summary of Significant Accounting Policies
Revenue Recognition [extract]

For construction contracts, when the outcome can be estimated reliably, revenues are recognised by reference to the percentage of completion ("PoC") of the contract activity by applying the estimate at completion method. The stage of completion of a contract may be determined by a variety of ways. Depending on the nature of the contract, revenue is recognised as contractually agreed technical milestones are reached, as units are delivered or as the work progresses. Whenever the outcome of a construction contract cannot be estimated reliably – for example during the early stages of a contract or when this outcome can no longer be estimated reliably during the course of a contract's completion – all related contract costs that are incurred are immediately expensed and revenues are recognised only to the extent of those costs being recoverable ("early stage method of accounting"). In such specific situations, as soon as the outcome can (again) be estimated reliably, revenue is from that point in time onwards accounted for according to the estimate at completion method, without restating the revenues previously recorded under the early stage method of accounting. Changes in profit rates are reflected in current earnings as identified. Contracts are reviewed regularly and in case of probable losses, loss-at-completion provisions are recorded. These loss-at-completion provisions in connection with construction contracts are not discounted.

Conversely, many entities use just one principal method to calculate the percentage of completion.

The Royal BAM group considers contract costs incurred as a proportion of total costs.

Extract 21.4: Royal BAM Group nv (2007)

3.   Summary of significant accounting policies [extract]
3.10   Construction contracts

The Group uses the 'percentage of completion method' to determine the appropriate amount to be recognised in a given period. The stage of completion is measured by reference to the contract cost incurred as percentage of total actual or estimated project cost. Revenues and result are recognised in the income statement based on this progress. Costs incurred during the year that relate to future activity on a contract are excluded from the measurement.

On the balance sheet, projects are presented as receivables from or payables to customers for contract work. If the costs incurred (including the result recognised) exceed the invoiced instalments, the contract is presented as a receivable. If the invoiced instalments exceed the costs incurred (including the result recognised) the contract is presented as a liability.

Contracts containing the construction of a project and the possibility of subsequent long-term maintenance of that project as separate components, or for which these components could be negotiated individually in the market, are accounted for as two separate contracts. Revenue and results are recognised accordingly in the income statement as construction contracts for third parties and rendering services.

The Vitec Group relies on surveys of work completed.

> *Extract 21.5: Vitec Group plc (2008)*
> Notes to the Consolidated Accounts [extract]
> 2   Accounting Policies [extract]
> Long Term Contracts [extract]
>
> Contract revenue and expenses are recognised in the income statement in proportion to the stage of completion of the contract, to the extent that the contract outcome can be estimated reliably. The stage of completion is assessed by reference to surveys of work performed. An expected loss on a contract is recognised immediately in the income statement.

There are, of course, other ways of measuring work done, e.g. labour hours, which depending upon the exact circumstances might lead to a more appropriate basis for computing revenue.

The above examples apply only to fixed-price contracts. Where a contract is on a cost-plus basis, it is necessary to examine the costs incurred to ensure they are of the type and size envisaged in the terms of the contract. Only once this is done and the recoverable costs identified can the figure be grossed up to arrive at the appropriate revenue figure.

If the stage of completion is determined by reference to the contract costs incurred to date, it is fundamental that this figure includes only those contract costs that reflect work actually performed so far. Any contract costs that relate to future activity on the contract must be excluded. This includes the costs of materials that have been delivered to a contract site or set aside for use in a contract but not yet installed, used or applied during contract performance, unless the materials have been made especially for the contract. Payments made to subcontractors in advance of work performed under the subcontract would similarly not relate to work performed to date and have to be excluded.[41]

Example 21.2:   Determination of revenue – exclusion of unapplied costs

The circumstances are as in Scenario (i) of Example 21.1 above. The entity has incurred and applied costs of £4,000. £3,000 is the best estimate of costs to complete. If the costs incurred to date included, say, £500 in respect of unapplied raw materials, then the revenue to be recognised falls to £5,000 being:

$$\frac{\text{costs incurred and applied}}{\text{total costs}} = \frac{(4{,}000 - 500)}{7{,}000} \times 10{,}000 = 5{,}000$$

2.3.3   Changes in estimates

The percentage of completion method is applied on a cumulative basis in each accounting period to the current estimates of contract revenues and costs. The effect of any changes in estimates of revenue and costs, or the effect of any change in the estimate of the outcome of a contract, must be treated as a change in accounting estimate, in accordance with IAS 8 – *Accounting Policies, Changes in Accounting Estimates and Errors*. The revised estimates must be used in determining the amount of revenue and expenses recognised in profit or loss in the period in which the change is made, and in subsequent periods.[42]

2.3.4   The determination of contract revenue and expenses

It is now possible to see how these features of accounting for construction contracts are put together to calculate the timing and measurement of contract revenue and expenses throughout the term of a construction contract, as in the following example, based on that in the Appendix to IAS 11:

Example 21.3:   Cumulative example – the determination of contract revenue and expenses

The following example illustrates the determination of the stage of completion of a contract and the timing of the recognition of contract revenue and expenses, measured by the proportion that contract costs incurred for work performed to date bear to the estimated total contract costs.

A construction contractor has a fixed price contract to build a bridge. The initial amount of revenue agreed in the contract is €9,000. The contractor's initial estimate of contract costs is €8,000. It will take 3 years to build the bridge.

By the end of year 1, the contractor's estimate of contract costs has increased to €8,050.

In year 2, the customer approves a variation resulting in an increase in contract revenue of €200 and estimated additional contract costs of €150. At the end of year 2, costs incurred include €100 for standard materials stored at the site to be used in year 3 to complete the project.

The contractor determines the stage of completion of the contract by calculating the proportion that contract costs incurred for work performed to date bear to the latest estimated total contract costs. A summary of the financial data during the construction period is as follows:

	Year 1 €	Year 2 €	Year 3 €
Initial amount of revenue agreed in contract	9,000	9,000	9,000
Variation	–	200	200
Total contract revenue	9,000	9,200	9,200
Contract costs incurred to date	2,093	6,168	8,200
Contract costs to complete	5,957	2,023	–
Total estimated contract costs	8,050	8,200	8,200
Estimated profit	950	1,000	1,000
Stage of completion	26%	74%	100%

The constructor uses the percentages calculated as above to calculate the revenue, contract costs and profits over the term of the contract. The stage of completion for year 2 (74%) is determined by excluding from contract costs incurred for work performed to date the €100 of standard materials stored at the site for use in year 3.

The amounts of revenue, expenses and profit recognised in profit or loss in the three years are as follows:

	To date	Recognised in prior years	Recognised in current years
Year 1			
Revenue (9,000 × 26%)	2,340	–	2,340
Expenses	2,093	–	2,093
Profit	247	–	247
Year 2			
Revenue (9,200 × 74%)	6,808	2,340	4,468
Expenses (6,168 incurred less 100 of materials in storage)	6,068	2,093	3,975
Profit	740	247	493
Year 3			
Revenue (9,200 × 100%)	9,200	6,808	2,392
Expenses	8,200	6,068	2,132
Profit	1,000	740	260

2.3.5 Inability to estimate the outcome of a contract reliably

When the outcome of a construction contract cannot be estimated reliably, an entity will first of all have to determine whether it has incurred costs that it is probable will be recovered under the contract. It can then recognise revenue to the extent of these costs. Contract costs should be recognised as an expense in the period in which they are incurred,[43] unless, of course, they relate to future contract activity, such as materials purchased for future use on the contract as explained at 2.3.2 above.

It is often difficult to estimate the outcome of a contract reliably during its early stages. This means that it is not possible to recognise contract profit. However, the entity may be satisfied that some, at least, of the contract costs it has incurred will be recovered and it will be able to recognise revenue to this extent. If it is probable that total costs will exceed total revenues, even if the outcome of the contract cannot be estimated reliably, any expected excess of contract costs must be expensed immediately.[44]

If it is probable that contract costs cannot be recovered they must be recognised as expenses immediately. The standard identifies a number of situations that may give rise to irrecoverable contract costs. There may be deficiencies in the contract, which means that it is not fully enforceable. Other problems may be caused by the operation of law, such as the outcome of pending litigation or legislation or the expropriation of property. The customer or the contractor may no longer be able to meet their obligations or the contractor may be unable for some reason to complete the contract.[45]

If these uncertainties that prevent the outcome of the contract being estimated reliably are resolved, revenue and expenses are recognised by the stage of completion method.[46]

2.3.6   Loss-making contracts

As soon as the entity considers that it is probable that the contract costs will exceed contract revenue it must recognise immediately the expected loss as an expense. It is irrelevant whether work has commenced on the contract or the stage of completion of contract activity. In addition, the entity may not take into account any anticipated profits on other contracts with the same customer unless all of these contracts are treated as a single construction contract.[47]

2.3.7   Contract inefficiencies

IAS 2 – *Inventories* – explicitly excludes from the costs of inventories 'abnormal amounts of wasted materials, labour or other production costs'.[48] There is no such requirement in IAS 11 and this is reflected in a degree of uncertainty about how to account for inefficiencies and 'abnormal costs' incurred during the course of a construction contract. If such costs are simply added to the total contract costs, this may affect the stage of completion if contract activity is estimated based on the total costs that have been incurred (see 2.3.2 above).

It seems clear in principle that abnormal costs and inefficiencies that relate solely to a particular period ought to be expensed in that period as they are not 'costs that relate directly to the specific contract'.[49] The issue is often a practical one of how to distinguish such costs from revisions of estimates that can more reasonably be treated as contract costs.

Usually inefficiencies that result from an observable event can be identified and expensed. If a major supplier collapses and the materials from another source are more expensive, this may be an inefficiency that ought to be expensed, as well as being one where the costs ought to be identifiable without undue difficulty. On the other hand, an unexpected increase in costs of materials unrelated to such an event may be a revision to the estimate of costs. There are more marginal situations. A load of bricks may develop an off colour and not be suitable for their designated purpose. This is a natural, but intermittent defect that builders must face and here it is much less clear whether it is an inefficiency or change in estimate. In any particular case an assessment may have to be based on the significance to the project. It is relatively easy to distinguish cases at either extreme but much less so when the issues are marginal, where judgement will have to be exercised.

Note that this must be distinguished from cost increases that will result in the contract becoming loss-making, as these must be expensed immediately (see above).

3   DISCLOSURE REQUIREMENTS OF IAS 11

IAS 11 has detailed and onerous disclosure requirements. The following disclosures must be given by entities in respect of construction contracts:

(a)   the amount of contract revenue recognised as revenue in the period;

(b)   the methods used to determine the contract revenue recognised in the period; and

(c)   the methods used to determine the stage of completion of contracts in progress.[50]

The standard includes in its Appendix an example of accounting policy disclosures, shown below.

Example 21.4:   Disclosure of accounting policies

Revenue from fixed price construction contracts is recognised on the percentage of completion method, measured by reference to the percentage of labour hours incurred to date to estimated total labour hours for each contract.

Revenue from cost plus contracts is recognised by reference to the recoverable costs incurred during the period plus the fee earned, measured by the proportion that costs incurred to date bear to the estimated total costs of the contract.

The following is the accounting policy of Thales, which also refers to the treatment of the related balances in the balance sheet.

Extract 21.6: Thales (2007)

E. Notes to the Consolidated Financial Statements [extract]

i)   Construction Contracts

A construction contract is a contract specifically negotiated for the construction of an asset or of a group of assets which are interrelated in terms of their design, technology, function, purpose or use.

According to its characteristics, a notified construction contract can either be accounted for separately, be segmented into several components which are each accounted for separately, or be combined with another construction contract in progress in order to form a single construction contract for accounting purposes in respect of which revenues and expenses will be recognised.

Revenues and expenses on construction contracts are recognised in accordance with the technical percentage of completion method. However, where there is no significant timing difference between technical percentage of completion and contractual dates of transfer of ownership, the percentage of completion is determined according to the contractual transfer of ownership.

Revenues are measured at the fair value of the consideration received or receivable. In the case where the deferral of payment has a material effect on the determination of such fair value, the amount at which revenues are recognised is adjusted to take the financial impact of the deferral of payment into account.

Penalties for late payment or relating to improper performance of a contract are recognised as a deduction from revenues. In the balance sheet, provisions for penalties are deducted from assets related to the contract.

Expected losses on contracts, in progress or in the order backlog, are fully recognised as soon as they are identified.

Selling, administrative and interest expenses are directly charged to the profit and loss account in the financial year in which they are incurred.

Estimates of work remaining to be completed on loss-making contracts do not include revenues from claims made by the Group, except when it is highly probable that such claims will be accepted by the customer.

Progress payments received on construction contracts are deducted from contract assts as the contract is completed. Progress payments received before the corresponding work has been performed are classified in "Advances received from customers on contracts" in balance sheet liabilities.

The cumulative amount of costs incurred and profit recognised, reduced by recognised losses and progress billings, is determined on a contract-by-contract basis. If this amount is positive it is classified as "Construction contracts: assets" in balance sheet assets. If it is negative it is classified as "Construction contracts: liabilities" in balance sheet liabilities.

EADS identifies different features by which its contract revenue is recognised, as is disclosed in Extract 21.3 above.

In the case of contracts in progress at the end of the reporting period, an entity should disclose each of the following:

(a)   the aggregate amount of costs incurred and recognised profits (less recognised losses) to date;

(b)   the amount of advances received; and

(c)   the amount of retentions.[51]

Retentions, progress billings and advances are defined as follows:

'Retentions are amounts of progress billings which are not paid until the satisfaction of conditions specified in the contract for the payment of such amounts or until defects have been rectified. Progress billings are amounts billed for work performed on a contract whether or not they have been paid by the customer. Advances are amounts received by the contractor before the related work is performed.'[52]

In addition, an entity should present:

(a)   the gross amount due from customers for contract work as an asset for all contracts in progress for which costs incurred plus recognised profits (less recognised losses) exceed progress billings (i.e. the net amount of costs incurred plus recognised profits, less the sum of recognised losses and progress billings); and

(b)   the gross amount due to customers for contract work as a liability for all contracts in progress for which progress billings exceed costs incurred plus recognised profits (i.e. the net amount of costs incurred plus recognised profits, less the sum of recognised losses and progress billings).[53]

The following example is based on the Appendix to IAS 11, and serves to illustrate the financial statement disclosure requirements of the standard as they apply to the various circumstances that might arise concerning construction contracts. It is followed by an example of the disclosures in practice from the financial statements of Thales.

Example 21.5:   Disclosure of numerical information regarding construction contracts

A contractor has reached the end of its first year of operations. All its contract costs incurred have been paid for in cash and all its progress billings and advances have been received in cash. Contract costs incurred for contracts B, C and E include the cost of materials that have been purchased for the contract but which have not been used in contract performance to date.

For contracts B, C and E, the customers have made advances to the contractor for work not yet performed.

The status of the entity's five contracts in progress at the end of year 1 is as follows:

Contract	A	B	C	D	E	Total
Contract revenue recognised in accordance with IAS 11 paragraph 22 (see 2.3 above)	145	520	380	200	55	1,300
Contract expenses recognised in accordance with IAS 11 paragraph 22 (see 2.3 above)	110	450	350	250	55	1,215
Expected losses recognised in accordance with IAS 11 paragraph 36 (see 2.3.6 above)	–	–	–	40	30	70
Recognised profits less recognised losses	35	70	30	(90)	(30)	15
Contract costs incurred in the period	110	510	450	250	100	1,420
Contract costs incurred recognised as contract expenses in the period in accordance with IAS 11 paragraph 22	110	450	350	250	55	1,215
Contract costs that relate to future activity recognised as an asset in accordance with IAS 11 paragraph 27	–	60	100	–	45	205
Contract revenue	145	520	380	200	55	1,300
Progress billings (IAS 11 paragraph 41: see above)	100	520	380	180	55	1,235
Unbilled contract revenue	45	–	–	20	–	65
Advances (IAS 11 paragraph 41: see above)	–	80	20	–	25	125

The amounts to be disclosed in accordance with IAS 11 are as follows:

Contract revenue recognised as revenue in the period	1,300
Contract costs incurred and recognised profits (less recognised losses) to date	1,435
Advances received	125
Gross amount due from customers for contract work (presented as an asset)	220
Gross amount due to customers for contract work (presented as a liability)	(20)

These amounts are calculated as follows:

Contract	A	B	C	D	E	Total
Contract costs incurred	110	510	450	250	100	1,420
Recognised profits less recognised losses	35	70	30	(90)	(30)	15
	145	580	480	160	70	1,435
Progress billings	100	520	380	180	55	1,235
Due from customers	45	60	100	–	15	220
Due to customers	–	–	–	(20)	–	(20)

The amount disclosed in accordance with IAS 11 paragraph 40(a) (the aggregate amount of costs incurred and recognised profits (less recognised losses) to date) is the same as the amount for the current period because the disclosures relate to the first year of operation.

Thales discloses its contracts in progress at the year end as follows:

Extract 21.7: Thales (2007)

Notes to the Consolidated Financial Statements [extract]
14.   Construction contracts

The amounts shown in the balance sheet correspond, for each construction contract, to the aggregate amount of costs incurred plus recognised profits (less recognised losses), less progress billings.

---

	31 Dec. 07	31 Dec. 06	31 Dec. 05
Construction contracts: assets (a)	2,422.1	2,096.7	2,042.8
Construction contracts: liabilities	523.9	359.4	341.5
Construction contracts, net assets	1,898.2	1,737.3	1,701.3
This amount corresponds to:			
Aggregate amount of costs incurred plus recognised profits less (less recognised losses)	28,667.2	26,969.5	29,868.0
Less, progress billings	(26,769.0)	(25,232.2)	(28,166.7)

(a)   Includes work-in-progress for an amount of €1,029.2 million at 31 December 2007, €873.2 million at 31 December 2006 and €1,067.1 million at 31 December 2005.

Advances received from customers on construction contracts related to work not yet performed amount to €2,392.1 million at 31 December 2007 (€2,050.5 million at 31 December 2006 and €2,255.4 million at 31 December 2005). They partly cover work-in-progress relating to certain contracts.

Retentions on construction contracts amount to €25.3 million at 31 December 2007 (€21.9 million at 31 December 2006 and €18.2 million at 31 December 2005).

4   PRACTICAL ISSUES

4.1   Whether an arrangement is a construction contract and IFRIC 15 – *Agreements for the Construction of Real Estate*

In July 2008 the IFRIC issued IFRIC 15. The debate that led to the issue of the Interpretation was precipitated by the inconsistent accounting treatment of certain real estate sales. At issue was whether, or in what circumstances, residential or commercial real estate developments could be treated as construction contracts. This would require revenue to be recognised using the percentage of completion method. Otherwise these would be treated as sales of goods, governed by IAS 18, and revenue would not be recognised until the risks and rewards of ownership and control had passed. The Interpretation addresses the meaning of the term 'construction contract' as defined in IAS 11 and hence helps clarify the scope of this standard.

The specific accounting problem derived from the interpretation of the following example with regard to sales of property, that prior to IFRIC 15, was included in the Appendix to IAS 18:

'Revenue is normally recognised when legal title passes to the buyer. However, in some jurisdictions the equitable interest in a property may vest in the buyer before legal title passes and therefore the risks and rewards of ownership have been transferred at that stage. In such cases, provided that the seller has no further substantial acts to complete under the contract, it may be appropriate to recognise revenue. In either case, if the seller is obliged to perform any significant acts after the transfer of the equitable and/or legal title, revenue is recognised as the acts are performed. An example is a building or other facility on which construction has not been completed.'[54]

There is usually no issue when an entity sells a completed building in a jurisdiction where there is an enforceable right prior to legal completion, e.g. on exchange of contracts. The disposal may be subject to shareholder approval (the 'significant act') and revenue is recognised when this is obtained. If shareholder approval is not required, the entity may recognise a profit on exchange of contracts. These sales are quite clearly not within scope of IAS 11. However, there are many property sales, both residential and commercial real estate developments, where buyers enter binding 'pre-completion' agreements to purchase a specific unit that has not yet been completed (indeed, it may even be 'off plan', in which case the development has not even started). In this case, there was considerably more ambiguity about whether these are construction contracts in the first place and, if they are not, the meaning of 'significant acts' and the recognition of revenue as acts are performed.

Some developers had concluded that these arrangements were, indeed, contracts 'specifically negotiated for the construction of an asset or a combination of assets'[55] and within scope of IAS 11. Others argued that, although these were not construction contracts, the percentage of completion method provided the best proxy for 'as the acts are performed'. The IFRIC has, therefore, included within IFRIC 15 an analysis of the features of a construction contract and this is discussed below.

4.1.1   Scope of IAS 11 and features of a construction contract

IAS 11 defines a construction contract as 'a contract specifically negotiated for the construction of an asset or a combination of assets …'.[56] The IFRIC argued in Draft Interpretation D21 – *Real Estate Sales* (the draft Interpretation issued in July 2007 that preceded IFRIC 15) that a contract for 'construction' is a contract to provide 'construction services' to the buyer's specifications.[57] This phrase has previously been used in IFRIC 12 in the context of service concession arrangements.

The final IFRIC 15 provides more guidance in the particular context of real estate. Under the Interpretation:

- an agreement for the construction of real estate meets the definition of a construction contract when the buyer is able to specify the major structural elements of the design of the real estate before construction begins and/or specify major structural changes once construction is in progress (whether or not it exercises that ability). When IAS 11 applies, the construction contract also includes any contracts or components for the rendering of services that are directly related to the construction of the real estate;[58]

- an agreement for the construction of real estate in which buyers have only limited ability to influence the design of the real estate, for example to select a design from a range of options specified by the entity, or to specify only minor variations to the basic design, is an agreement for the sale of goods and therefore within the scope of IAS 18.[59]

Sometimes, at the early stage of a development, a real estate developer will lease the property to a lessee whilst an ultimate buyer is sought. It may be this lessee, rather than the ultimate buyer, who negotiates with the developer the major structural elements of the design. Consistent with IAS 17 – *Leases* –[60] so long as this lease is a finance lease then this lessee can be regarded as the buyer in determining whether they are able to specify the major structural elements of the design and hence concluding whether the contract falls under IAS 11. However if the lease is an operating lease then the lessee cannot be considered the buyer and revenue can only be recognised when an ultimate buyer is found and all of the conditions under IAS 18 are satisfied.

The Interpretation notes that within a single agreement, an entity may contract to deliver goods or services in addition to the construction of real estate (for example a sale of land or provision of property management services). Such an agreement may need to be split into separately identifiable components, which may include one for the construction of real estate. The fair value of the total consideration received or receivable for the agreement must be allocated to each component.[61] The Basis of Conclusions to the Interpretation points to IFRIC 12 – *Service Concession Arrangements* and IFRIC 13 – *Customer Loyalty Programmes* – for guidance on allocating the fair value;[62] in these Interpretations it is based on the fair values of the separate components. Segmenting of contracts is discussed below in 4.2.

The analysis within the Interpretation determining the appropriate revenue recognition policy assumes that there is revenue to be recognised, i.e. it assumes that the entity retains neither continuing managerial involvement to the degree usually associated with ownership nor effective control over the constructed real estate to an extent that would preclude recognition of some or all of the consideration as revenue.[63]

A feature not mentioned in IFRIC 15 but commonly the case where the agreement is for the sale of goods is that the item being sold is homogeneous and as a result can either be substituted or freely be used for another if the original purchaser does not complete the sale.

IFRIC 15 is discussed further in Chapter 25 at 6.11.2.

It can be seen from the above that, with these types of contracts in general, there is a range of contractual arrangements for similar products from, at one end sales of 'off the shelf' items through to large projects where a similar type of asset is constructed to a purchaser's specification.

An example of an entity whose activities cover this range is Vestas Wind Systems A/S whose revenue recognition policy is as follows:

Extract 21.8: Vestas Wind System A/S (2008)

Notes to the Consolidated Accounts
1. Group Accounting Policies [extract]
Income statement [extract]
Revenue [extract]

Contracts to deliver large wind power systems with a high degree of customisation are recognised in revenue as the systems are constructed based on the stage of completion of the individual contract (turnkey and supply-and-installation projects). Where the profit from a contract cannot be estimated reliably, revenue is only recognised equalling the expenses incurred to the extent that it is probable that the expenses will be recovered. Sale of individual wind turbines and small wind power systems based on standard solutions (supply-only projects) as well as spare parts sales are recognised in the income statement provided that the risk has been transferred to the buyer prior to the year end, and provided that the income can be measured reliably and is expected to be received.

4.2 Combining and segmenting of contracts: future developments and the convergence project

Contractors may provide different goods or services to their customers as part of a single contract or group of contracts. IAS 11 contains little guidance on the combining and segmenting of contracts. It really only considers the combining or otherwise of contracts in very clear-cut circumstances, i.e. where a number of contracts that purport to be separate have been negotiated as a single package or where a series of separate contracts have been subsumed within a single contract document but where the individual contracts should be dealt with separately (see 1.2 above). However, there is no further guidance in the standard on whether or how individual contracts or groups of contracts should be segmented or combined and contract revenue and costs recognised on the basis of the individual segments or combined contracts. These treatments can have a major effect on the recognition of income. Segmenting a contract can affect the profile of income recognition, perhaps allowing earlier recognition of revenue. If a series of contracts is negotiated as a package with the objective of achieving an overall profit margin, this will not be reflected if the individual contracts are accounted for separately, while inappropriate combining of the segments of a contract could result in the timing of profits or losses not being recognised on the basis required by the standard.

As part of its convergence project, the IASB has discussed whether some of the detailed guidance under US GAAP for combining and segmenting contracts as set out in AICPA Statement of Position (SOP) 81-1 – *Accounting for Performance of Construction-Type and Certain Production-Type Contracts* – should be incorporated into IAS 11.[64] At its meeting in February 2005, the IFRIC decided not to proceed with a draft Interpretation on combining and segmenting construction contracts. The IFRIC concluded that the matter was not a priority. In the Committee's view, an IFRS preparer with a US listing should be able to get to the same answer under both frameworks, as the conditions for combining and segmenting under IFRS and US GAAP were not inconsistent and IFRIC members were not aware of any significant divergence in practice. They also concluded that, because of differences between the two standards, full convergence of the conditions for combining and segmenting construction contracts could not be achieved simply through interpretation.[65]

We are not in agreement with applying SOP 81-1's criteria for combining contracts *verbatim*. We consider that SOP 81-1 is more restrictive than IAS 11 in allowing the combination of contracts and would allow contracts with more than one party to be combined only in very unusual circumstances.[66] Nevertheless, we do concur with the views expressed by the IFRIC referred to above; we would expect a SEC Registrant that applies SOP 81-1's more restrictive criteria in order to avoid a US GAAP reconciling item to be in compliance with IAS 11.

In the mean time and until the IFRIC issues an interpretation, segmentation and combination of construction contracts should be assessed in accordance with paragraphs 8 and 9 of IAS 11, as described above.

4.3   Options for the construction of an additional asset

Another area where it is necessary to consider whether contracts should be combined is in contract options and additions. Once again, combining of contracts is important because of its potential impact on the recognition of revenue and profits on transactions. If the optional asset is treated as part of the original contract, contract revenue will be recognised using the percentage of completion method over the combined contract.

As described in 1.2 above, IAS 11 considers the circumstances in which a contract gives a customer an option for an additional asset (or is amended in this manner) and concludes that this should be treated as a new contract if:

(a)   the asset differs significantly in design, technology or function from the asset or assets covered by the original contract; or

(b)   the price of the asset is negotiated without regard to the original contract price.[67]

This means, for example, that the contract for an additional, identical asset would be treated as a separate contract if its price was negotiated separately from the original contract price. Costs almost always decline with additional production, not only because of the effects of initial costs but also because of the 'learning curve' (the time taken by the workforce to perform activities decreases with practice and repetition). This could result in a much higher profit margin on the additional contract. If, for example, a Government department takes up its option with a defence contractor for five more aircraft, in addition to the original twenty-five that had been contracted for, but the option was unpriced and the new contract is priced afresh, then it cannot be combined with the original contract regardless of the difference in profit margins. Note that this conclusion appears consistent with SOP 81-1, which would only allow contracts not executed at the same time to be combined if they were negotiated as a package in the same economic environment. This means that the time period must be reasonably short.[68] Although 'short' is not defined, it is unlikely to cover a period of several years, as could happen in defence contracting.

The combining of contracts may also have unexpected results. If, for example, an entity has a contract with a government to build two satellites and a priced option to build a third, it may be obliged to combine the contracts as at the point at which the option is exercised. This could well be in a different accounting period to the commencement of the contract. Using the rules outlined in 2.3.3 above, there will be a cumulative catch-up of revenue, and probably also of profits. In subsequent periods results will be based on the combined contracts.

4.4   Service concession agreements

Service concession agreements commonly include the construction of an asset followed by a period in which the constructor maintains and services that asset; this secondary period may include asset replacement and refurbishment as well as service elements. Alternatively the contract might provide for the refurbishment of an existing infrastructure asset together with related services. These agreements provide particular accounting difficulties because they combine contract accounting issues and issues arising from a number of other accounting standards including IAS 11, IAS 17 and IAS 18. The accounting issues raised by IFRIC 12 are discussed further in Chapter 23 at 5.

4.5   Treatment of the land element of a construction contract

In some real estate markets an entity may enter into a contract to construct a building on land that the entity owns and then – after construction is complete – to deliver the entire property to a customer.

As noted above in 4.1.1, IFRIC 15 notes that a single agreement may contain a contract to deliver goods or services (for example a sale of land) in addition to the construction of real estate.

If the contract can be segmented into a construction contract and the sale of the land, the delivery of land follows the revenue recognition guidance of IAS 18 for sale of land whereas the construction of the building follows the revenue recognition guidance of IAS 11.

The effect of this can be seen in Example 21.6 below:

Example 21.6:   *Segmented construction contract*

On 1 January 2010, entity A entered into a contract to construct a building on a piece of land it has acquired and, when construction is complete, to deliver the entire property to a customer. A applies the percentage of completion method to account for contract revenues and expenses. The relative percentage of cost incurred is considered a reliable method for measuring the progress of the contract.

- Total cost of land: €2m
- Estimated total cost of construction: €8m
- Estimated total cost of contract: €10m
- Agreed sales price of the completed building: €11m

Construction has commenced and at the end of the reporting period (31 December 2010) total construction costs incurred amount to €2m.

Entity A considers that the amount of revenue in the contract attributable to the construction is €8.5m and the amount to the sale of land is €2.5m.

The percentage completion of the construction contract is 25% – calculated as €2m costs incurred as a proportion of the €8m estimated total cost of construction.

Accordingly, as at 31 December 2010 the following amounts are recorded:

Revenue	(€8.5m × 25%)	€2.13m
Contract expense	(Actual incurred on construction)	€2.00m
Gross amount due from customer	(Revenue of €2.13m)	€2.13m
Inventory	(Cost of the land)	€2.00m

The revenue and cost relating to the land will be recognised when the revenue recognition criteria of IAS 18 are met – this is often when legal title passes.

5   CONCLUSION

IAS 11 has not been amended or subjected to further interpretation in a long time and its principles are well understood. It is one of a number of older standards (another example is IAS 17 – see Chapter 22) that are based on principles different from those that underlie newer standards, such as those on financial instruments. The joint IASB/FASB Revenue Recognition Project that has now culminated in the issue of the Discussion Paper – *Preliminary Views on Revenue Recognition in Contracts with Customers*[69] – proposes a single revenue recognition model for contracts with customers and it is presently envisaged that any resulting final standard would replace both IAS 11 and IAS 18. This proposed model is discussed in Chapter 25 at 5 and the present proposals would have a significant impact on the accounting for many construction contracts with revenue recognition focusing on when control of assets is transferred to the customer rather than when activity is performed. This intention to replace IAS 11 may be why there has been no attempt to update the standard, even though there are obvious difficulties integrating its requirements with those of the newer standards; see, for example, the issues described in 2.2.1 above that arose during the service concession debate regarding the classification of contract assets, and the IFRIC's unwillingness to extrapolate from its conclusion to the generality of construction contracts.

References

1 Discussion Paper, *Preliminary Views on Revenue Recognition in Contracts with Customers*, IASB, December 2008.
2 IAS 11, *Construction Contracts*, IASB, para. 1.
3 IAS 11, para. 3.
4 IAS 11, para. 4.
5 IAS 11, para. 5.
6 IAS 11, para. 3.
7 IAS 11, para. 6.
8 IAS 11, para. 7.
9 IAS 11, para. 8.
10 IAS 11, para. 9.
11 IAS 11, para. 10.
12 IAS 11, para. 11.
13 IAS 11, para. 12.
14 IAS 11, para. 13.
15 IAS 11, para. 14.
16 IAS 11, para. 15.
17 IAS 11, para. 16.
18 IAS 11, para. 17.
19 IAS 11, para. 17.
20 IAS 11, para. 18.
21 IAS 11, para. 20.
22 IAS 11, paras. 19-20.
23 IAS 11, para. 21.
24 IASB Framework, IASC April 1989, adopted by the IASB April 2001, para. 49(a).
25 IAS 11, para. 21.
26 IAS 23, *Borrowing Costs*, IASB, paras. 8 and 29.
27 IAS 23 (2007), *Borrowing Costs*, IASB, 2007 Bound Volume, para. 18.
28 IAS 23, para. BC27.
29 IFRIC 12, *Service Concession Arrangements*, IFRIC, para. BC58.
30 *IFRIC Update*, IFRIC, June 2005, p.6.
31 IFRIC 12, para. 22.
32 IFRIC 12, para. BC58.
33 IAS 11, para. 22.
34 IAS 11, para. 23.
35 IAS 11, para. 24.
36 IAS 11, paras. 25-26.
37 IAS 11, para. 27.
38 IAS 11, para. 28.
39 IAS 11, para. 29.
40 IAS 11, para. 30.

41 IAS 11, para. 31.
42 IAS 11, para. 38.
43 IAS 11, para. 32.
44 IAS 11, para. 33.
45 IAS 11, para. 34.
46 IAS 11, para. 35.
47 IAS 11, paras. 36-37.
48 IAS 2, *Inventories*, IASB, para. 16(a).
49 IAS 11, para. 16(a).
50 IAS 11, para. 39.
51 IAS 11, para. 40.
52 IAS 11, para. 41.
53 IAS 11, paras. 42-44.
54 IAS 18 (2008), *Revenue*, IASB, 2008 Bound Volume, Appendix, para. 9.
55 IAS 11, para. 3.
56 IAS 11, para. 3.
57 IFRIC D21, para. 8.
58 IFRIC 15, *Agreements for the Construction of Real Estate*, para. 11.
59 IFRIC 15, para. 12.
60 IAS 17, *Leases*, IASB, paras. 42-44.
61 IFRIC 15, para. 8.
62 IFRIC 15, para. BC11.
63 IFRIC 15, para. 7.
64 *IFRIC Update*, IFRIC, March 2004, p.1.
65 *IFRIC Update*, IFRIC, February 2005, p.5.
66 SOP 81-1, *Accounting for Performance of Construction-Type and Certain Production-Type Contracts*, AICPA, July 1981, para. 37.
67 IAS 11, para. 10.
68 SOP 81-1, para. 37.
69 Discussion Paper, *Preliminary Views on Revenue Recognition in Contracts with Customers*, IASB, December 2008.

Chapter 22   Leases

1   INTRODUCTION

IAS 17 – *Accounting for Leases* – has been in place for many years, as have its equivalent standards around the world, SFAS 13 in the US and SSAP 21 in the UK.[1] These standards, all dealing with accounting for leases, were the first to apply the concept of 'substance over form' and the first to incorporate the present value basis of measurement into the historical cost model. In prescribed circumstances they required companies to capitalise assets in their balance sheets, together with the corresponding obligations, irrespective of the fact that legal title to those assets vested in another party.

The substance over form approach is based on the view that a lease that transfers substantially all of the risks and rewards of ownership to the lessee should be accounted for as an acquisition of an asset and the assumption of an obligation by the lessee and as a sale by the lessor. Such leases are termed 'finance leases' and are equivalent of 'capital leases' in the US. The lease accounting standards required relatively few changes for leases, now known as 'operating leases', that did not transfer substantially all the risks and rewards of ownership of an asset to the lessee. Operating leases are not capitalised in the lessee's balance sheet. Instead, operating lease rentals are charged to the profit and loss account of the lessee over the lease term, usually on a straight-line basis.

The IASB's requirements for lease accounting have remained essentially unchanged for more than twenty five years. Consequently, the accounting requirements are generally well understood and the distinction between finance and operating leases, and the related accounting consequences, are widely accepted internationally and applied in practice, even though much debate still takes place as to whether individual leases are financing or operating in nature. At the same time, though, conventional accounting in this area has been challenged. The IASB has been developing proposals under which the finance/operating distinction will be removed and all rights and obligations arising under lease contracts will be recognised at fair value in the balance sheets of lessees. Lease accounting is now recognised as one of the areas of current IFRS that must be improved to facilitate mandatory adoption of IFRS in all major capital markets. Lease accounting has always been a convergence project and the IASB and FASB have come to the conclusion that it would not be possible to draw up and have approved a comprehensive standard for all aspects of lease accounting based on new concepts by a target date of 2011. Accordingly, they have decided to adopt a simplified approach that only addresses lessee accounting. The Boards issued a joint discussion paper in March 2009. This proposed new approach is discussed at 1.2 below.

1.1   Background: the development of IAS 17

IAS 17 was issued in September 1982 for accounting periods beginning on or after 1 January 1984.[2] Although the standard has subsequently been updated, its definition of a finance lease as one that 'transfers substantially all the risks and rewards incident to ownership of an asset' to the lessee,[3] has remained unchanged. There have been no major changes to the standard since 1997. Amendments have been made to take account of IAS 40 – *Investment Property* – and IAS 41 – *Agriculture*. The two most recent changes, in November 2003 as part of the IASB's project *Improvements to International Accounting Standards*, and in April 2009 in *Improvements to IFRSs* both affect the classification of land and buildings and are dealt with in 2.3.4 below.

1.2   Updating lease accounting

Chapter 2 of this book discusses the IASB policy to move towards an asset/liability fair value approach to financial reporting. This approach could fundamentally change the way in which financial contracts such as leases are accounted for. In the case of lease accounting, assets and liabilities are the most relevant elements, and the IASB's *Framework for the Preparation and Presentation of Financial Statements* defines these particular elements as follows: an asset is 'a resource controlled by the entity as a result of past events and from which future economic benefits are expected to flow to the entity'; whilst a liability is 'a present obligation of the entity arising from past events, the settlement of which is expected to result in an outflow from the entity of resources embodying economic benefits'.[4]

An inescapable consequence of these two definitions is that most leases, including non-cancellable operating leases, will qualify for recognition as assets and liabilities. This is because, irrespective of whether the lease is finance or operating in nature, the lessee is likely both to control and enjoy the future economic benefits embodied in the leased asset, and will have an unavoidable legal obligation to transfer economic benefits to the lessor. Therefore the distinction between operating and finance leases is not supported at the conceptual level.

Following joint discussions on a revised Memorandum of Understanding in 2008, the IASB and FASB issued on 19 March 2009 a Discussion Paper *Leases: Preliminary Views*. As expected, the Boards propose that lease accounting should be based on the principle that all leases give rise to assets (the right to use the leased asset) and liabilities for future rental payments that should be recognised in an entity's statement of financial position. The Discussion Paper also includes a brief discussion of lessor and sub-lessor accounting issues.

The Boards have come to the preliminary view that a new standard should keep to the scope of the existing lease accounting standards[5] although there are differences between IAS 17 and SFAS 13 that will have to be resolved; in particular, IAS 17 has a wider scope that can include leases of intangible assets. The Boards are still considering whether some of the existing scope exemptions ought to be revisited e.g. both standards exclude lease agreements to explore for or use minerals, oil, natural gas and similar non-regenerative resources.[6] IAS 17's scope is discussed at 2.1 below and there is an analysis of some of the issues relating to leases and intangible assets at 2.1.1.

What is being proposed is not a comprehensive fair value approach. The model measures lease obligations and right-of-use assets at the present value of expected lease payments, not at their fair value. Unlike earlier approaches that would have required separate measurement and accounting for renewal or purchase options and residual value guarantees, the Boards have so far decided to base accounting on a single asset and liability.[7] This would reduce complexity, although the measurement and remeasurement requirements could mean that applying the model is not that straightforward. Lessees will have to apply judgment and make estimates that could be challenging about the lease term, contingent rentals and residual value guarantees and the appropriate incremental borrowing rate.

1.2.1 Lessee accounting

Briefly, the accounting model proposed by the Discussion Paper is as follows. The right-of-use asset would be measured at 'cost', which would be measured initially at the present value of the expected lease payments to be made over the term of the lease discounted at the lessee's incremental borrowing rate.[8] The lease obligation would be measured in the same way at the same amount.[9]

The lease term would represent the most likely term based on an assessment of all contractual, non-contractual and business factors and would consider the likelihood of exercise of renewal, termination and purchase options.[10] The lease payments would include rental payments required under the lease, as well as the lessee's estimate of payments expected to be made during the lease term including contingent rentals and residual value guarantees. The two Boards do not agree on the basis of measuring contingent rental payments and residual value guarantees. The IASB proposes the use of a probability-weighted approach to include contingent rentals and residual value guarantees in the lease measurement, whereas the FASB preferred an approach focusing on the most likely outcome.[11] The following example illustrates the difference in the approaches:

Example 22.1:   Probability weighting vs. most likely outcome in measuring contingent rentals

A lessee enters into a five-year non-cancellable lease of a retail store with no option to extend the lease. The lessee is required to make fixed annual payments of €100 and a 'turnover rent' of 1% of sales from the leased store. The lessee forecasts the following sales for the store and assigns each outcome a probability. Discounting has been ignored.

	€	€	€
Total forecast sales years 1-5	10,000	20,000	35,000
Probability that forecast sales will occur	10%	60%	30%
Total fixed rentals years 1-5 (CU)	500	500	500
Total contingent rentals 1% of forecast sales (CU)	100	200	350
Total estimated rentals years 1-5 (CU)	600	700	850

Probability-weighted estimate of the rentals payable (600 × 10% + 700 × 60% + 850 × 30%	€735
Most likely outcome, which has a 60% probability of occurrence	€700

In this example the contingent rentals are uncertain and both methods are reasonable approaches to estimating contingent rentals. The well known shortcoming of using probability weightings is that the outcome may be something that cannot happen in practice. If, for example, there are only two possible outcomes, then, unless the probability of one is zero, the result of a probability weighting will be an amount that will never actually be paid.

The present value of the expected lease payments would be calculated by discounting the expected lease payments using the lessee's incremental borrowing rate.[12]

The incremental borrowing rate is 'the rate of interest the lessee would have to pay on a similar lease or, if that is not determinable, the rate that, at the inception of the lease, the lessee would incur to borrow over a similar term, and with a similar security, the funds necessary to purchase the asset.' It takes account of the credit standing of the lessee, the length of the lease and the nature and quality of the security provided (i.e. the leased item).[13] This is not as easy to establish as first may appear and lessees may well underestimate the appropriate rate for short-term leases.

The right-of-use asset would be amortised over the shorter of the lease term or the economic life of the leased asset. The lease payments would be allocated between a reduction in the outstanding liability and interest expense under an effective yield method.

The assumptions underlying the lease obligation would be revisited at the end of each reporting period (including interim periods, of course). Changes in certain assumptions such as those relating to the lease term or expected lease payments, would require the lessee to remeasure the lease obligation. The crucial question is what then to do with the 'other side' of the entry. The Discussion Paper describes various approaches to recognising the effect of remeasuring lease obligations including immediate recognition of a gain or loss, adjusting the carrying amount of the right-of-use asset, or a combination of both. Both standard setters agree that changes to the lease term would lead to remeasurement of the asset.[14] This is appropriate as changes to terms clearly indicate that the rights under the lease have changed and the entity has a right to use more or less than before. However, there is no such unanimity about other changes to lease rentals where the significance to the right-of-use asset is much less clear, nor do they agree about presentation in the financial statements:

(i)   consistent with their views on initial measurement of the lease obligation, described above, the Boards disagree about the treatment on remeasurement of contingencies. The FASB concludes that that all changes should go to profit or loss; the IASB considers that they should be treated as adjustments to the right-of-use asset.[15] This is considered further below.

(ii)   the discount rate used to remeasure the lease obligation if assumptions change. The IASB's approach would require reassessment of the incremental borrowing rate while the FASB's preferred approach does not.[16]

(iii)   the presentation of right-of-use assets and lease obligations in the financial statements. The FASB's approach would require separate presentation of lease obligations from other liabilities, unlike the IASB's approach.[17] Furthermore, some FASB members consider that the decrease in value of the right-of-use asset should be described in the income statement as rental expense and support a view that assets obtained in leases that are, in substance, purchases should be presented separately from other right-of-use assets.[18]

Contingent rentals have proved a difficult and contentious area in attempts to revise lease accounting. The Discussion Paper identifies in Chapter 7 three main types of contingent rental:

(a)   contingent rentals based on price changes or an index, such as market interest rates or the consumer price index;

(b)   contingent rentals based on the lessee's performance derived from the leased item such as retail turnover rents; and

(c)   contingent rentals based on usage. For example, a car lease may require the lessee to pay additional rentals if the lessee exceeds a specified mileage.

It is much less clear what changes to these estimates represent and whether or not they should affect the right-of-use asset. If an entity acquires an item of property, plant and equipment it would not change the carrying value of the asset if, for example, interest rates change. The FASB has so far taken the view that complexity should be minimised; there should not be any revision to the asset and changes should be taken to the income statement. This would be simpler to prepare and easier for users to understand. By contrast, the IASB believes that the original asset has cost more or less than originally estimated and its carrying value should be adjusted. The IASB approach would result in changes in the carrying amount of the asset being written off prospectively through an ever-changing amortisation charge.

1.2.2   Lessor accounting

The joint project was originally expected to address both lessor and lessee accounting. However, the Boards consider that most current criticisms are about the limitations of lessee accounting. They were also concerned that the project would take considerably longer to complete if lessor accounting were included as well. Lessor accounting must take account of the revenue recognition project (see Chapter 25) and differences in accounting for investment property between US GAAP and IFRS. Many of those commenting on the Discussion Paper have been uncomfortable about the omission of lessor accounting, not only because many lessees are also lessors but also from a concern that lessee accounting might be modified if there was a subsequent lessor standard. However, the Discussion Paper includes a brief discussion of lessor accounting issues.

The Discussion Paper identifies in Chapter 10 two main approaches:

- derecognising part of the asset and recognising a receivable, i.e. a method comparable to current lessor accounting; and

- recognising a different right-of-use asset and a performance obligation to the lessee while retaining untouched the existing asset. This method follows the analysis underlying the Revenue Recognition Discussion Paper (see Chapter 25).

Under the second method, which the IASB and FASB have continued to develop at subsequent meetings,[19] a crucial accounting issue is whether to present the asset and liability gross or net. The Revenue Recognition Discussion Paper argues for a net presentation on the basis that only the net figure is an asset or liability as defined.

Lessor accounting will have to address the same issues that determine initial and subsequent measurement that are unresolved for lessee accounting, such as options, contingent rentals and residual value guarantees.

1.2.3   Subleases

An entity will sometimes act as both lessor and lessee of the same asset. This is common in the leasing industry where an entity may lease a piece of equipment from one party under a head lease and sublet the same piece of equipment to another party under a the sublease.[20] These are not straightforward under IAS 17 (see 4.5 below) but present particular difficulties to any revised lease accounting model. If the Discussion Paper continues to address only lessee accounting then something will have to be done to address the inconsistencies that would otherwise be introduced. The Discussion Paper considers developing an approach only for subleases, excluding them from scope or dealing with the inconsistencies through unspecified 'additional guidance'[21] or disclosure.

1.2.4   Next steps

It seems obvious that the Boards must settle their differences on scope and the measurement issues in order for the project to succeed as a standard that addresses lease accounting and deals with convergence issues between IFRS and US GAAP. Some areas of lessee accounting have not yet been addressed. They include the timing of initial recognition if the lease inception date differs from the commencement date; accounting for initial direct costs incurred to negotiate a lease (e.g. commissions and legal fees) and accounting for sale and leaseback transactions, including sale-leaseback transactions involving real estate.

One of the effects of bringing operating leases on balance sheet is to shift the critical focus from the distinction between finance and operating leases to that between operating leases and arrangements for services. Therefore the Boards also need to consider whether additional guidance is needed on separating payments for services from other lease payments and on how to distinguish contractual payments for services from arrangements that contain leases.

Proposals for those perennial problem areas, presentation, disclosure and transitional arrangements are yet to be fully developed.

Finally, the Boards must decide whether to focus only on lessee accounting or whether to address lessor and sublessor accounting as well.

The Boards are then expected to develop and expose for public comment an exposure draft of a new standard on accounting for leases, which the Boards currently plan to issue in the second quarter of 2010.

2   SCOPE AND CLASSIFICATION OF LEASES

2.1   Scope of IAS 17

The standard applies in accounting for all leases other than:

- lease agreements to explore for or use minerals, oil, natural gas and similar non-regenerative resources; and
- licensing agreements for such items as motion picture films, video recordings, plays, manuscripts, patents and copyrights.

Furthermore, the standard should not be applied to the measurement by:

- lessees of investment property held under finance leases; or
- lessors of investment property leased out under operating leases, as in these cases IAS 40 applies; (see Chapter 17); or
- lessees of biological assets held under finance leases; or
- lessors of biological assets leased out under operating leases, as in these cases IAS 41 applies (see Chapter 41).[22]

2.1.1   Leases and licences – IAS 17 and arrangements over intangible assets

IAS 17 does not define a licensing agreement so the distinction between 'leases' and 'licensing agreements' is not clear. This is not helped by the fact that the agreements may be economically similar. Further, while the examples of licensing agreements excluded from the scope of IAS 17 (motion picture films, video recordings, plays, manuscripts, patents and copyrights) are specific intangible assets, IAS 17 does not exclude leases of intangible assets from its scope. IAS 38 – *Intangible Assets* – by contrast, excludes from its scope 'lease agreements', stating 'this standard shall be applied in accounting for intangible assets, except intangible assets that are within the scope of another Standard.'[23] It emphasises that 'if another Standard prescribes the accounting for a specific type of intangible asset, an entity applies that Standard instead of this Standard. For example, this Standard does not apply to... leases that are within the scope of IAS 17, Leases.'[24]

IAS 17 does not apply to agreements that are contracts for services that do not transfer the right to use assets from one contracting party to the other. A conventional licence over an intangible asset (such as a film or video) commonly gives a non-exclusive right of 'access' to show or view the video simultaneously with many others but not a 'right of use' of the original film or video itself because the licensee does not control that asset. Arguably, this puts such a conventional licence outside the scope of IAS 17. There is a similar argument underlying IFRIC 4 – *Determining whether an Arrangement contains a Lease* – that is considered further in 2.2.1 below. Many licences of these intangible assets are paid for by way of royalties on some sort of 'per use' basis. Again, the relationship between these rights and the underlying asset is explored further by IFRIC 4.

On the other hand, there are arrangements involving intangible assets that could fall within IAS 17. Examples include the transfer of exclusive rights for a finite period (which may be a finance or operating lease over the right in question) and sale and leaseback transactions involving assets to which one party has legal title.

There are further issues to be considered because of some of the characteristics of intangible assets which means that there can be a variety of co-existing rights relating to the same underlying asset as well as different methods of paying for the rights. Many intangible rights can be purchased for an upfront sum, which will be accounted for as the acquisition of an intangible asset and capitalised at cost.[25] The right itself may have a finite life, e.g. a radio station may acquire a licence that gives it a right to broadcast over specified frequencies for a period of seven years. Yet the underlying asset on which the right depends exists both before and after the 'right' has been purchased. If, as an alternative to up-front purchase, an entity pays for the same right in a series of instalments over a period of time, does it become an operating lease (because it is only a short period out of the life of the underlying asset) or is it a finance lease over the *right* in question? Alternatively, is it the purchase of an intangible asset by instalments?

Whether it is a finance lease or an acquisition in instalments can be very significant because the arrangement may include contingent payments. IAS 17 excludes these from the measurement at inception of the asset and liability (see 3.1.3 below). IAS 38 requires an intangible asset to be measured initially at cost.[26] If the arrangement is seen as the acquisition of an asset on deferred payment terms, IAS 39 – *Financial Instruments: Recognition and Measurement* – principles would apply and the effective interest rate method is mandated. This will take account of estimated future cash payments or receipts through the expected life of the financial instrument that may include some of the 'contingent' payments (see 3.6 below).[27]

Therefore, there are arguments as to whether there are assets and liabilities to be recognised and, even if recognition is accepted, measurement depends on the view that is taken of the applicable standard. In the absence of a clear principle, there is bound to be diversity in practice.

2.2   What are leases?

IAS 17 defines a lease as 'an agreement whereby the lessor conveys to the lessee in return for a payment or series of payments the right to use an asset for an agreed period of time.'[28] The standard applies to agreements that transfer the right to use assets even though substantial services by the lessor may be called for in connection with the operation or maintenance of such assets. On the other hand, it does not apply to agreements that are contracts for services that do not transfer the right to use assets from one contracting party to the other. The definition of a lease includes contracts for the hire of an asset that contain a provision giving the hirer an option to acquire title to the asset when agreed conditions have been complied with (sometimes known as hire purchase contacts).[29]

In recent years new types of arrangements have arisen that do not take the legal form of leases. They take many forms, but essentially combine rights to use assets, and possibly the provision of services or outputs, for agreed periods of time in return for a payment or series of payments. As it was uncertain whether IAS 17 applied to such arrangements, the issues have been considered by the IFRIC and are dealt with in IFRIC 4 which is considered further in 2.2.1 below. Some of the arrangements under service concession arrangements give rise to further accounting issues that have been separately addressed by the IFRIC; these are discussed in 3.7 below and more fully in Chapter 23.

The SIC had previously considered whether all transactions in the legal form of a lease should be considered under IAS 17. The results of these deliberations, SIC-27 – *Evaluating the Substance of Transactions Involving the Legal Form of a Lease*, are covered in 2.2.2 below.

2.2.1 *Determining whether an arrangement contains a lease*

The IFRIC approved IFRIC 4 in October 2004. IFRIC 4 notes that arrangements have been developed in recent years that do not take the legal form of a lease but that nevertheless convey rights to use items for agreed periods of time in return for a payment or series of payments.[30] The Interpretation not only addresses this type of arrangement but also some more traditional forms of arrangement that are also within its scope.

The Interpretation focuses on the accounting implications of the following, in all of which an entity (the supplier) conveys a right to use an asset to another entity (the purchaser), together with related services or outputs:

- outsourcing arrangements, including outsourcing of the data processing functions of an entity;
- arrangements in the telecommunications industry, where suppliers of network capacity enter into contracts to provide purchasers with rights to capacity; and
- take-or-pay and similar contracts, in which purchasers must make specified payments regardless of whether they take delivery of the contracted products or services (e.g. where purchasers are committed to acquiring substantially all of the output of a supplier's power generator).[31]

Service concession arrangements, which were specifically referred to in the draft interpretation, are the subject of a separate IFRIC project on Service Concession Arrangements referred to at 3.7 below and in Chapter 23.

The IFRIC concluded that an arrangement of one of these types could be within the scope of IAS 17 if it met the definition of a lease, e.g. if it conveyed to the lessee the right to use an asset for an agreed period of time in return for a payment or series of payments.[32] IAS 17 applies to the lease element of the arrangement notwithstanding the related services or outputs because IAS 17 applies to 'agreements that transfer the right to use assets even though substantial services by the lessor may be called for in connection with the operation or maintenance of such assets.'[33] This is regardless of the fact that the arrangement is not described as a lease and is likely to grant rights that are significantly different from those in a formal lease agreement. The IFRIC therefore concluded that it should provide guidance to assist in determining whether an arrangement is, or contains, a lease.[34]

An example of an entity that applied IFRIC 4 and as a result identified an arrangement within scope of IAS 17 was Gaz de France, which, in its 2006 financial statements, identified a finance lease with the Group as lessor, as shown in the following extract.

Extract 22.1: Gaz de France (2006)

FINANCIAL INFORMATION FOR THE YEAR ENDED DECEMBER 31, 2006 [extract]
NOTES TO THE CONSOLIDATED FINANCIAL STATEMENTS [extract]
B –   Comparability between financial years [extract]
2 –   Changes in accounting policies and presentation [extract]
2.1.2   IFRIC 4 –Determining whether an Arrangement Contains a Lease [extract]

This interpretation deals with the method of identifying and recognizing service, purchase and sale contracts that do not take the legal form of a lease but convey a right to use an asset in return for a payment or series of payments. The lease element may constitute an operating lease or a finance lease. If a contract is assessed as containing a finance lease where the Group is lessor, a finance receivable should be recorded to reflect the financing provided to the customer.

IFRIC 4 applies to one of Gaz de France's contracts with an industrial customer, which provides for the operation by the Group of dedicated assets.

Application of IFRIC 4 led to the reclassification from "Property, plant and equipment" to "Other non-current assets" (long-term receivables) of 196 million euros at December 31, 2006, 233 million euros at December 31, 2005 and 200 million euros at December 31, 2004. The impact on equity and profit was not material.

IFRIC 4 has the objective only of dealing with the practical issues that arise when applying IAS 17 to arrangements that are not leases in form: how to identify an arrangement that is in substance a lease, when to make the assessment and how to measure the lease element.[35] The Interpretation does not provide any guidance for determining how such a lease should be classified under IAS 17[36] (in other words, it could be a finance lease or an operating lease under IAS 17), nor does it expect the guidance to extend the scope of that standard. If an arrangement turns out to contain a lease or licence of a type excluded from the scope of IAS 17 (see 2.1 above), the Interpretation does not apply. Service concession arrangements to which IFRIC 12 applies are also out of scope – see 3.7 below[37]

A   *How to determine whether an arrangement is, or contains, a lease*

IFRIC 4 sets down two criteria that must be met in order to determine whether an arrangement is, or contains a lease, as follows:[38]

(a)   fulfilment of the arrangement depends on a specific asset or assets; and

(b)   the arrangement conveys a right to use the asset.

These are discussed in B and C below.

B   *Identification of an asset*

IAS 17 applies only to an arrangement in which there is a 'right to use an asset', so an arrangement will not contain a lease unless it depends on a specific asset or assets. It provides the following additional guidance.

A specific asset that is explicitly identified by the arrangement will not be the subject of a lease if the arrangement is not dependent on the asset. If the seller is required under the arrangement to deliver a specified quantity of goods or services and has the right or ability to provide those goods using other assets not specified in the agreement, the arrangement will not contain a lease.[39]

On the other hand, an arrangement may still contain a lease if a specific asset is not explicitly identified but it would not be economically feasible or practical for the supplier to provide the use of alternative items. For example, the supplier may only own one suitable asset.[40]

Some arrangements may allow the supplier to replace the specified asset with a similar asset if the original asset is unavailable (e.g. because it is unexpectedly inoperable). The IFRIC takes the view as that such a requirement is in effect a warranty obligation it does not preclude lease treatment.[41]

To take a relatively simple example, an arrangement in which an entity (the purchaser) outsources its product delivery department to another organisation (the supplier) will not contain a lease if the supplier is obliged to make available a certain number of delivery vehicles of a certain standard specification and the supplier is a delivery organisation with many other vehicles available. However, if the supplier has to supply and maintain a specified number of specialist vehicles in the purchaser's livery, then this arrangement is more likely to contain a lease. The latter arrangement may be commercially more akin to outsourcing the purchaser's buying functions for delivery vehicles rather than its delivery functions. Similar issues would have to be taken into account if data processing functions are outsourced as these may require substantial investment by the supplier in computer hardware dedicated to the use of a single customer.

It is important to note that where the above examples are likely to contain leases (delivery vehicles in livery, dedicated hardware), the purchaser cannot be unaware that there are specific assets underlying the service. There would have been negotiations between supplier and purchaser that would probably be reflected in the contract documentation. By contrast, if the purchaser does not know what assets are used to provide the service (beyond the fact that they are trucks and computers, of course), and in the circumstances it is reasonable not to know, it is plausible that there is no underlying lease in the arrangement. This remains true even if the supplier has dedicated specific assets to the service being provided and expects their cost to be recouped during the course of the contractual relationship.

C   *Parts of assets and the unit of account*

IFRIC 4 notes that some arrangements transfer the right to use an asset that is a component of a larger asset but the issue of whether and when such rights should be accounted for as leases is not dealt with in the Interpretation. It states merely that 'arrangements in which the underlying asset would represent a unit of account in either IAS 16 – *Property, Plant and Equipment* – or IAS 38' are within the scope of the Interpretation.[42] 'Unit of account' presumably means an asset whose cost, replacement, impairment and depreciation is separately accounted for under one of these standards (see Chapters 15 and 16). However, the opposite is not necessarily the case. It does not mean that a component of one of these assets cannot be the underlying asset.

There are many arrangements in practice that demonstrate this issue. For example, a plant may contain more than one production unit or line that might be regarded as a single 'component' (because each makes the same product) or alternatively each of its units or lines might be regarded as separate 'components'. Depending on other aspects of the arrangement, a particular production line may be the asset that is the subject of a lease, if the supplier cannot transfer production to a different line to supply the goods. Similar examples from the telecommunications industry include communication satellites that contain dozens of identical transponders or fibre optical cables that contain more than 100 pairs of fibre. The fibre optical cable cannot be regarded as a separate 'portion', as the lease of a single fibre automatically requires the user to be able to use the rest of the asset. Therefore the payments under the arrangement are for the use of the whole asset, e.g. the satellite.

The Interpretation does not attempt to address whether there is any conceptual difference between, say, using a quarter of the capacity of a whole pipeline and all of the capacity of a pipeline a quarter of the size.

D   *The arrangement conveys a right to use the item*

An arrangement does not convey the right to use an asset unless the purchaser has the right to control the use of the underlying item, which depends on any one of the following conditions being met:[43]

(a)   The purchaser has the ability or right to operate the asset or direct others to operate the asset in a manner it determines while obtaining or controlling more than an insignificant amount of the output or other utility of the asset;

(b)   The purchaser has the ability or right to control physical access to the underlying asset while obtaining or controlling more than an insignificant amount of the output or other utility of the asset; or

(c)   Facts and circumstances indicate that it is remote that one or more parties other than the purchaser will take more than an insignificant amount of the output or other utility that will be produced or generated by the asset during the term of the arrangement, and the price that the purchaser will pay for the output is neither contractually fixed per unit of output nor equal to the current market price per unit of output as of the time of delivery of the output.

Therefore, control of the asset may be obtained in circumstances in which an entity obtains 'more than an insignificant amount of the output' but *only* if it has the ability or right to operate (or direct others to operate) in a manner that it determines or can control physical access to the asset.

On the other hand, a purchaser that pays market price at the date of transfer will not control the asset just because it takes almost all of the output. It would also have to be demonstrated that it controlled the asset by virtue of (a) or (b) above. The same applies if the price is contractually fixed, typically the case in take-or-pay contracts. Just because the price is fixed, it does not necessarily follow that the arrangement contains a lease. Control of the underlying asset must be demonstrated under (a) or (b).

When the arrangement involves a single purchaser in taking substantially all of the output from a specific asset other than at market price and the price varies other than in response to market price changes, the variability ('off-market' nature) is regarded by IFRIC 4 as indicating that payment is being made for the right to use the asset rather than for the actual use of or output from the asset.

The effects of this are demonstrated by the following examples.

E   Analysing the arrangements

The following examples of arrangements that may or may not contain a lease explain the identification of an asset and the application of the control criteria described above. Example 22.1 is based on an illustrative example in IFRIC 4.[44]

Example 22.2:   An arrangement that contains a lease

A production company (the purchaser) enters into an arrangement with a third party (the supplier) to supply a minimum quantity of gas needed in its production process for a specified period of time. The supplier designs and builds a facility near to the purchaser's plant to produce the needed gas and maintains ownership and control over all significant aspects of operating the facility. The agreement provides for the following:

- The facility is explicitly identified in the arrangement, and the supplier has the contractual right to supply gas from other sources. However, supplying gas from other sources is not economically feasible or practicable;

- The supplier has the right to provide gas to other customers and to remove and replace the facility's equipment and modify or expand the facility to enable the supplier to do so. However, at inception of the arrangement, the supplier has no plans to modify or expand the facility. The facility is designed to meet only the purchaser's needs;

- The supplier is responsible for repairs, maintenance and capital expenditures;

- The supplier must stand ready to deliver a minimum quantity of gas each month;

- On a monthly basis, the purchaser will pay a fixed capacity charge and a variable charge based on actual production taken. The purchaser must pay the fixed capacity charge irrespective of whether it takes any of the facility's production. The variable charge includes the facility's actual energy costs, which comprise approximately 90 per cent of the facility's total variable costs. The supplier is subject to increased costs resulting from the facility's inefficient operations;

- If the facility does not produce the stated minimum quantity, the supplier must return all or a portion of the fixed capacity charge.

The arrangement contains a lease within the scope of IAS 17. An asset (the facility) is explicitly identified in the arrangement and fulfilment of the arrangement is dependent on the facility. While the supplier has the right to supply gas from other sources, its ability to do so is not substantive. The purchaser has obtained the right to use the facility because, on the facts presented – in particular, that the facility is designed to meet only the purchaser's needs and the supplier has no plans to expand or modify the facility – it is remote that one or more parties other than the purchaser will take more than an insignificant amount of the facility's output and the price the purchaser will pay is neither contractually fixed per unit of output nor equal to the current market price per unit of output as of the time of delivery of the output.

Having concluded that the arrangement contains a lease, it is then necessary to classify it as an operating or a finance lease. Identifying the relevant lease payments is dealt with in G below.

The next two examples illustrate arrangements that do not contain a lease. The first, Example 22.3, illustrates two of the concepts in IFRIC 4. The first describes circumstances in which an arrangement does not contain a lease because no specific asset has been identified. The significance of the control concept is shown in the second example based on the second illustrative example in IFRIC 4.[45]

Example 22.3:   Arrangements that do not contain leases

(a)   Take-or-pay contract that does not depend on a specific asset

A purchaser enters into a take-or-pay contract to buy industrial gases from a supplier. The supplier is a large company operating similar plants at various locations. The amount of gas that the purchaser is committed to buy is roughly equivalent to the total output of one of the plants. Because a good distribution network is available, the supplier is able to provide gas from various locations to fulfil its supply obligation.

In this example, the arrangement does not depend upon a specific asset. This is because it is economically feasible and practical for the supplier to fulfil the arrangement by providing use of more than one plant. A specific asset has therefore not been identified either explicitly or implicitly.

Payments under the contract may be unavoidable (because it is a take-or-pay arrangement) and the purchaser may in fact take all of the output of a single plant but the arrangement does not convey a right to use the asset. The purchaser does not have the right to control the use of the underlying asset. It does not have the ability or right to operate the asset in a manner it determines (or to direct others to do so on its behalf), and it does not control physical access. The arrangement does not contain a lease.

(b)   The right to control the use of an underlying asset is not conveyed

A manufacturing company (the purchaser) enters into an arrangement with a third party (the supplier) to supply a specific component part of its manufactured product for a specified period of time. The supplier designs and constructs a plant next to the purchaser's factory to produce the component part. The designed capacity of the plant exceeds the purchaser's current needs, and the supplier maintains ownership and control over all significant aspects of operating the plant.

The supplier's plant is explicitly identified in the arrangement, but the supplier has the right to fulfil the arrangement by shipping the component parts from another plant owned by the supplier. However, to do so for any extended period of time would be uneconomical. The supplier must stand ready to deliver a minimum quantity. The purchaser is required to pay a fixed price per unit for the actual quantity taken. Even if the purchaser's needs are such that they do not need the stated minimum quantity, they still pay only for the actual quantity taken.

The supplier has the right to sell the component parts to other customers and has a history of doing so (by selling in the replacement parts market) so it is expected that parties other than the purchaser will take more than an insignificant amount of the component parts produced at the supplier's plant.

The supplier is responsible for repairs, maintenance, and capital expenditures of the plant.

This arrangement does not contain a lease. An asset (the plant) is explicitly identified in the arrangement and fulfilment of the arrangement is dependent on the facility. While the supplier has the right to supply component parts from other sources, the supplier would not have the ability to do so because it would be uneconomical. However, the purchaser has not obtained the right to use the plant because it does not control it, for the following reasons:

(a)   the purchaser does not have the ability or right to operate or direct others to operate the plant or control physical access to the plant; and

(b)   the likelihood that parties other than the purchaser will take more than an insignificant amount of the component parts produced at the plant is more than remote, based on the facts presented.

The fact that the price paid by the purchaser is fixed per unit of output taken is also mentioned in IFRIC 4 as a consideration.

F   Fixed or current market prices and control of the asset

The third control condition noted at D above states that an arrangement will not contain a lease notwithstanding that a purchaser takes all but an insignificant amount of the output or other utility if the price is contractually fixed per unit of output. By this the Interpretation means absolutely fixed, with no variance per unit based on underlying costs or volumes, whether discounts or stepped pricing.

In the manufacturing industry 'lifetime' agreements with step pricing between the supplier and the purchaser are not uncommon. The parties to the agreement agree in advance on progressive unit price reductions on achievement of specified production volume levels, reflecting the supplier's increasing efficiencies and economics of scale. These types of contracts should be closely analysed, especially to see whether one of the other two conditions, the 'right to operate the asset' or the 'right to control the physical access to the asset', is also met before concluding that the arrangement contains a lease.

'Current market price per unit of output' means that the cost is solely a market price for the output of the asset without any other pricing factors. A 'market price per KWH plus x per cent change in the price of natural gas' would not be the current market price per unit of the output of the asset. Price increases based on a general index such as a retail and prices index are unlikely to result in a current market price for the output in question.

Example 22.4:   Fixed prices per unit

Purchaser P and supplier S enter in a parts supply agreement for the lifetime of the finished product concerned. S uses tooling equipment that is specific to the needs of P. The tooling is explicitly identified in the agreement and S could not use an alternative asset. The estimated capacity of the tooling equipment is 500,000 units which corresponds to the total production of the finished product units over its life cycle. P takes substantially all of the output produced by S using the specific tooling.

Purchaser P and supplier S agree upon the following unit price reductions in the parts supply agreement to reflect S's increasing efficiencies and economics of scale:

- from 0 to 100,000 units, price per each unit €150;
- from 100,001 to 200,000, price per each unit €140;
- from 200,001 to 300,000, price per each unit €135;
- from 300,001 to 400,000, price per each unit €132;
- above 400,000 price per each unit €130.

The fulfilment of the arrangement depends on the use of a specific asset. the tooling. P has obtained the right to use the tooling because, on the facts presented, the likelihood is remote that one or more parties other than the P will take more than an insignificant amount of the tooling's output. As the estimated capacity of the tooling equipment corresponds to the total production of the finished product units produced by P, P takes substantially all of the output produced using that tooling.

However, stepped pricing does not mean price 'fixed per unit of output' and, particularly as the stepped pricing is agreed in advance, it is not equal to the current market price per unit as of the time of delivery of the output. The arrangement contains a lease within the scope of IAS 17.

G   When to assess the arrangements

IFRIC 4 states that the assessment described at A above, i.e. whether an arrangement contains a lease, should be made at the inception of the arrangement, being the earlier of the date of the arrangement and the date of commitment by the parties to the principle terms of the arrangement, and on the basis of all the facts and circumstances. A reassessment of whether the arrangement contains a lease should be made only if:[46]

(a)   there is a change in the terms of the contract, except for a renewal or extension of the arrangement;

(b)   a renewal option is exercised or an extension is agreed, unless these had been taken into account in the original assessment of the lease term in accordance with IAS 17;[47]

(c)   there is a change in whether or not the arrangement depends on specified item; or

(d)   there is a substantial physical change to the specified assets.

Changes to estimates, for example of the amount of output that would be taken by the purchaser, would not trigger a reassessment.[48]

If the arrangement is reassessed and found to contain a lease or vice versa then lease accounting will be applied or discontinued as from the time that the arrangement is reassessed, or renewal option exercised when this was not previously anticipated, as described in (b) above.[49]

H   Separation of leases from other payments within the arrangement

If an arrangement contains a lease, both parties to the arrangement are to apply IAS 17 to the lease element of the arrangement unless it is an arrangement that is not within IAS 17's scope. It must be stressed that this means that the lease element of the arrangement may be classified as an operating or finance lease. Other elements of the arrangement must be accounted for in accordance with the appropriate standards.[50]

Therefore, having identified the lease payments, the entity may still classify the arrangement as an operating lease if it does not transfer substantially all the risks and rewards incidental to ownership of an asset[51] (see 2.3 below).

In order to apply IAS 17, the payments and other consideration under the arrangement must be separated at inception or on reassessment between those for the lease of the asset and those for other services and outputs. IFRIC 4 requires this to be done on the basis of their relative fair values.[52] This may require the purchaser to use estimation techniques – this appears to be somewhat of an understatement as, unless the price to be paid for both elements is clear and they have both been negotiated at market value, it will always be necessary to use some form of estimation. The Interpretation suggests that it may be possible to estimate either the lease payments (by comparison with similar leases that do not contain other elements) or the other elements (using comparable arrangements) and then deduct the estimated amount from the total under the arrangement.[53]

This is not a straightforward exercise and the Interpretation does not go into any further detail as to how it would be carried out. There may be no market-based evidence of fair value of the underlying assets because of their specialised nature or because they are rarely sold, in which case it will be necessary to use valuation techniques. Discounted cash flow projections based on estimated future cash flows that will be generated by specialised assets may be difficult to obtain, although it should be possible to make some form of estimate, if need be with the assistance of valuation experts. The service elements within these agreements are by no means standardised and it may not be easy to identify comparable arrangements. The exercise will be complicated by the fact that the fair value of a bundle of services is not necessarily the same as the aggregation of their individual fair values and making such an assumption could lead to an overstatement of the service element and consequent understatement of the fair value of the lease element or *vice versa*. The discount rates should reflect current market assessments of the uncertainty and timing of the cash flows, i.e. the risk inherent in the separate elements of the transaction. There are usually very different risk profiles for the provision of services and for leasing assets. If, as suggested by the Interpretation, the entity estimates one of the elements under the arrangement and derives the other by deduction, it will always be necessary to carry out a 'sense check' on the derived payments.

IFRIC 4 suggests also that only in rare cases will a purchaser conclude that it is impracticable to separate the payments reliably. In the case of a finance lease, the entity should recognise an asset at an amount equal to the fair value of the underlying asset that it has identified as the subject of the lease, as described in B above. A liability should be set up at the same amount as the asset. The entity would impute a finance charge based on the purchaser's incremental borrowing rate of interest and, from this, compute the reduction in the liability as payments are made.[54] Presumably the IFRIC considers that the entity's incremental borrowing rate would have to be used because, if it were possible to determine the interest rate implicit in the lease, the arrangement would not be one in which it was impracticable to separate the payments reliably.

What this means, of course, is that an entity may be required to account for an asset held under a finance lease when it is, in fact, unable to identify the lease payments. It is to be hoped that the application of the control model means that this will not often happen in practice as control is more likely to result in an entity being able to identify the underlying payment streams.

If the lease is assessed as an operating lease, applying the Interpretation might affect the recognition of revenue over the term of the arrangement. IAS 17 requires lessors and lessees to recognise operating lease payments on a straight-line basis over the lease term (unless another systematic basis is more representative) and this may not be in line with the payments for the lease element so some adjustments might be required.[55]

There are disclosure implications if the arrangement is deemed to contain an operating lease and the purchaser concludes that it is impracticable to separate the payments reliably. These are discussed further below.

I   Disclosure requirements

IAS 17 required a general description of the lessee's material leasing arrangements,[56] which will require disclosure of the details of major transactions that have fallen within IFRIC 4.

There are no specific disclosure requirements if the arrangements are assessed as containing finance leases as these arrangements are deemed to be within the scope of IAS 17 and therefore within its disclosure requirements.

However, if it were considered to be an operating lease, the Interpretation may result in additional disclosures, because IAS 17 specifies that the lessor and lessee should disclose the future minimum lease payments. Although the arrangements discussed in the Interpretation typically represent significant future commitments, purchasers are not required to disclose them in the financial statements unless they fall within IAS 17. The IFRIC argues that bringing such arrangements within the scope of IAS 17 will provide users of financial statements with relevant information that is useful for assessing the purchaser's solvency, liquidity and adaptability.[57]

As long as the entity is able to distinguish the lease payments from other elements of the lease, then the disclosed information will relate only to the lease element of the arrangement. There appears to be no intention to require entities to disclose the service (executory) element of arrangements; the IFRIC agreed that it would consider addressing the disclosure of executory contracts more generally in a separate project.[58] However, if the arrangement is one of those in which it is impracticable to separate the payments reliably, the Interpretation requires disclosure of all payments under the arrangement separately from other minimum lease payments, together with a statement that the disclosed payments also include payments for non-lease elements in the arrangement.[59]

J   Effective date and transitional arrangements

IFRIC 4 applies to annual periods beginning on or after 1 January 2006.[60] The Interpretation is to be applied with retrospective effect in accordance with IAS 8 – *Accounting Policies, Changes in Accounting Estimates and Errors* (see Chapter 3). However, if a transaction has been entered into prior to the start of the earliest period for which comparative information is presented, it is only necessary to assess whether the arrangement contains a lease on the basis of the facts and circumstances existing at the start of that earliest period.[61] It is not necessary to go back to the inception of the arrangement.

2.2.2   Transactions that are not, in substance, leases

While there are some arrangements that contain leases that are not formally lease contracts, the reverse is also true: there are some 'lease agreements' that are not, in substance leases. These issues are addressed by SIC-27. The Interpretation became effective on 31 December 2001, with retrospective effect as a change in accounting policy in accordance with IAS 8.

Essentially, SIC-27 deals with the issue of how to evaluate the substance of transactions, or a series of linked transactions, in the legal form of a lease. The main purpose of the Interpretation is to reinforce the principle of substance over form, and to ensure that, where appropriate, a series of linked transactions should be accounted for as one transaction. If the transaction does not meet the definition of a lease under IAS 17, SIC-27 deals with the extent to which the arrangement gives rise to other assets and liabilities of the reporting entity, the reporting of any other obligations and the recognition of fee income.[62]

An entity may enter into a transaction or a series of structured transactions (an arrangement) with an unrelated party or parties (an investor) that involves the legal form of a lease. Although the details may vary considerably, a typical example involves an entity leasing or selling assets to an investor and leasing the same assets back. The lease and leaseback transactions are often entered into so that the investor may achieve a tax advantage.[63] The following example illustrates an arrangement that does not, in substance, involve a lease under IAS 17:

Example 22.5:   Substance of an arrangement

An entity (Company A) leases a specialised asset that it requires to conduct its business to an Investor and leases the same asset back for a shorter period of time under a sublease. At the end of the sublease period, Company A has the right to buy back the rights of the Investor under a purchase option. If Company A does not exercise its purchase option, the Investor has options available to it under each of which it receives a minimum return on its investment in the headlease – the Investor may put the underlying asset back to Company A, or require it to provide a return on the Investor's investment in the headlease.

The arrangement achieves a tax advantage for the Investor who pays a fee to Company A and prepays the lease payment obligations under the headlease. The agreement requires the amount prepaid to be invested in risk-free assets and, as a requirement of finalising the execution of the legally binding arrangement, placed into a separate investment account held by a Trustee outside of the control of the entity.

Over the term of the sublease, the sublease payment obligations are satisfied with funds of an equal amount withdrawn from the separate investment account. Company A guarantees the sublease payment obligations, and will be required to satisfy the guarantee should the separate investment account have insufficient funds. Company A, but not the Investor, has the right to terminate the sublease early under certain circumstances (e.g. a change in local or international tax law causes the Investor to lose part or all of the tax benefits, or Company A decides to dispose of (e.g. replace, sell or deplete) the underlying asset) and upon payment of a termination value to the Investor. If Company A chooses early termination, then it would pay the termination value from funds withdrawn from the separate investment account, and if the amount remaining in the separate investment account is insufficient, the difference would be paid by Company A.[64]

SIC-27 argues that a series of transactions that involve the legal form of a lease should be accounted for as one transaction when the overall economic effect cannot be understood without reference to the series of transactions as a whole. All aspects and implications of an arrangement should be evaluated to determine the substance of the arrangement, with greater weight given to those aspects and implications that will have an economic effect in practice. The accounting should reflect the substance of the arrangement.[65]

First, it must be part of a single 'arrangement'; a series of transactions may be closely interrelated, negotiated as a single transaction, and take place concurrently or in a continuous sequence.[66]

Second, there must be indicators that individually demonstrate that an arrangement may not, in substance, involve a lease under IAS 17. SIC-27 states that in the example above, these indicators are as follows:

(a)   the entity retains all the risks and rewards of ownership and there is no significant change in its rights to use the asset;

(b)   the primary reason for the arrangement is to achieve a particular tax result, and not to convey the right to use an asset; and

(c)   the options on which the arrangement depends are included on terms that make their exercise almost certain (e.g. a put option that is exercisable at a price sufficiently higher than the expected fair value when it becomes exercisable).[67]

In other words, the entity retains more rights than it would in a straightforward sale and finance leaseback. In the example, for instance, it retains all of the residual interests in the asset. The investor has no interest at all in the underlying asset while a lessor under a finance lease will often retain title and some residual value in the asset. The investor has only entered into the transaction to obtain a tax benefit.[68]

Third, the balances arising under the arrangement (in the example these comprise the separate investment account and the lease payment obligations under the sublease) must be assessed to see whether they represent assets and liabilities of the entity. SIC-27 refers to definitions of assets and liabilities and guidance in paragraphs 49-64 of the Framework. It argues that:

(a)   the investment account is not an asset of the entity because it cannot control it;

(b)   there is only a remote risk that the entity will have to pay out under the guarantee or reimburse the entire amount of any fee received; and

(c) once the arrangement has been set up and the initial payments have been made, no further cash flows will be made by Company A.

Company A cannot use the cash in the investment account for its own benefit, nor can it prevent it being used to make lease payments to the investor. The lease payments will be satisfied solely from funds withdrawn from the separate investment account established with the initial cash flows. In the example, the terms of the arrangement require that a prepaid amount is invested in risk-free assets that are expected to generate sufficient cash flows to satisfy the lease payment obligations.[69] This also demonstrates, *inter alia*, that Company A is not, in substance, entering into a financing arrangement, as it has no need of the funds.

However, other obligations of the entity, including any guarantees provided and obligations incurred upon early termination, should be accounted for under IFRIC 4, IAS 37 – *Provisions, Contingent Liabilities and Contingent Assets* – or IAS 39 depending on the terms of the arrangement.[70] Therefore, if Company A were to elect to terminate the arrangement, it would have to provide for its exposure in excess of the available funds in the investment account.

Fourth, SIC-27 addresses the recognition of fee income. There are many factors that could affect the economic substance and nature of the fee and it may not be appropriate to recognise it in its entirety at the inception of the agreement if the entity has significant future performance obligations, retained risks or a significant risk of repayment. Factors to be taken into account include:

(a) obligations that are conditions of earning the fee so that entering into the agreement is not the most significant act required by the arrangement;

(b) limitations are put on the use of the underlying asset that lead to significant changes in the entity's rights to use the asset, e.g. the entity's right to deplete or sell it or pledge it as collateral;

(c) the possibility of reimbursing any amount of the fee and possibly paying some additional amount is not remote. This occurs when, for example:

    (i) the underlying asset is essential for the entity's business, in which case there is a possibility that the entity may be prepared to pay to terminate the arrangement early (and thereby be required to repay all or part of the fee); or

    (ii) the possibility that there are insufficient assets in the investment account to meet the lease payment obligations is not remote, and therefore it is possible that the entity may be required to pay some additional amount. This may occur if the entity is required, or has some or total discretion, to invest in assets carrying more than an insignificant amount of risk (e.g. currency, interest rate or credit risk).[71]

Finally there are some specific presentation and disclosure requirements. The fee must be presented in the income statement based on its economic substance and nature.[72] The entity must disclose the following in each period that an arrangement exists:

An entity has to make the disclosures that are necessary to understand the arrangement and the accounting treatment adopted, including the following:

(a)   a description of the arrangement including:

      (i)   the underlying asset and any restrictions on its use;

      (ii)   the life and other significant terms of the arrangement;

      (iii) the transactions that are linked together, including any options; and

(b)   the accounting treatment of any fee received, the amount that has been recognised as income in the period, and the line item of the income statement in which it is included.

These disclosures should be provided individually for each arrangement or in aggregate for each class of arrangement. A class is a grouping of arrangements with underlying assets of a similar nature.[73] The following extract illustrates the disclosures.

Extract 22.2: Swisscom AG (2007)

Notes to the Consolidated Financial Statements [extract]
25   Financial liabilities [extract]
Financial liabilities from cross-border tax lease arrangements

Between 1996 and 2002, Swisscom entered into cross-border tax lease arrangements, under the terms of which parties of its fixed and mobile networks were to be sold or leased long-term to US Trusts and leased back with terms of up to 99 years. Swisscom has an early buyout option on these assets after a contractually agreed period.

The financial liabilities are based on lease and leaseback transactions from the years 1999, 2000, and 2002. The sale and leaseback from the year 1997 are presented as finance lease obligations.

Swisscom defeased a major part of the lease obligations through highly rated financial assets and payment undertaking agreements. The financial assets were irrevocably placed with trusts. The payment undertaking agreements were signed with financial institutions with a high credit standing. In accordance with Interpretation SIC-27 "Evaluating the substance of transactions involving the legal form of a lease", these financial assets or payment undertaking agreements and the liabilities in the same amount are offset and not presented in the balance sheet. One of the transactions entered into in 2000 does not meet the conditions of SIC-27 and is consequently reported in the balance sheet as a long-term financial asset and the corresponding lease obligation presented as a long-term financial liability.

As of December 31, 2007, the financial assets and liabilities resulting from these transactions including interest totalled USD 4,124 million (CHF 4,679 million) and USD 3,751 million (CHF 4,250 million), respectively. Of this amount USD 2,990 million (CHF 3,387 million) are not reported in the balance sheet in accordance with SIC-27. Of the liabilities reported in the amount of CHF 1,177 million (previous year CHF 1,459 million), CHF 862 million (previous year: CHF 1,125 million) are covered by financial assets.

The gains from the transactions were recorded as financial income in the period the transactions were closed.

Swisscom is exposed to market-related risks in connection with cross-border lease agreements. One particular risk lies in the credit standing of the counterparties in which investments were made. Swisscom must fulfill the agreed rating requirements for financial assets with a nominal value of USD 559 million (CHF 634 million) including interest incurred up to December 31, 2007. All the rating requirements are fulfilled. It is possible that the contractual rating requirements will no longer be fulfilled until the agreements expire. In such case the financial assets are to be replaced by assets with the required minimum rating. Swisscom would then incur costs amounting to the difference between the market value of the existing and the new financial assets.

Other market risks in connection with cross-border lease agreements are interest rate and foreign exchange risks, although most of these risks have been hedged through interest rate and currency swaps.

then it is unlikely that the lessor will look to any party other than the lessee to obtain its return from the lease.

Similarly, whilst (d) above refers to the present value of the minimum lease payments being at least 'substantially all of the fair value of the asset', it does so without putting a percentage to it. We have already speculated as to why this may be; nevertheless, we see no harm in practice in at least applying the '90% test' described above as a rule of thumb benchmark as part of the overall process in reaching a judgement as to the classification of a lease. Clearly, though, it cannot be applied as a hard and fast rule.

For an example of the 90% test, see Example 22.8 at 3.1.9 below. In that example, the present value of the minimum lease payments is calculated to be 92.74% of the asset's fair value; as this exceeds 90%, this would normally indicate that the lease is a finance lease. Nevertheless, the other criteria discussed above would need to be considered as well.

Consequently, we would stress that the 90% test is not an explicit requirement of the standard and should not be applied as a rule or in isolation, but it may be a useful tool to use in practice in attempting to determine the economic substance of a lease arrangement.

The standard then goes on to list the following indicators of situations that, individually or in combination, could also lead to a lease being classified as a finance lease:[81]

(a)   if the lessee can cancel the lease, the lessor's losses associated with the cancellation are borne by the lessee;

(b)   gains or losses from the fluctuation in the fair value of the residual fall to the lessee (for example, in the form of a rent rebate equalling most of the sale proceeds at the end of the lease); and

(c)   the lessee has the ability to continue the lease for a secondary period at a rent which is substantially lower than market rent.

In our view, other considerations that could be made in determining the economic substance of the lease arrangement include the following:

- are the lease rentals based on a market rate for use of the asset (which would indicate an operating lease) or a financing rate for use of the funds, which would be indicative of a finance lease?

- is the existence of put and call options a feature of the lease? If so, are they exercisable at a predetermined price or formula (indicating a finance lease) or are they exercisable at the market price at the time the option is exercised (indicating an operating lease)?

And finally, we have found the following to be a useful 'acid test' question to consider:

- does the lessor intend to earn his total return on this transaction alone or does he intend to rely on subsequent sales or lease revenue?[82] Clearly, if the lessor is looking to a return from a single lessee, then this would indicate that the lease is a finance lease.

2.3.3   *Changes to lease provisions*

Lease classification is made at the inception of the lease,[83] which is the earlier of the date of the lease agreement or of a commitment by the parties to the principal provisions of the lease.[84] Lease classification is only changed if, at any time during the lease, the lessee and the lessor agree to change the provisions of the lease (without renewing it) in such a way that it would have been classified differently at inception had the changed terms been in effect at that time. The revised agreement is considered as a new agreement and should be accounted for appropriately, prospectively over the remaining term of the lease. On the other hand, changes in estimates (for example, changes in estimates of the economic life or of the residual value of the leased item) or changes in circumstances (for example, default by the lessee) do not result in the lease being reclassified for accounting purposes.[85] This is of particular relevance given the requirement in IAS 16 that the residual value and useful life of an asset must be reviewed at least at each financial year-end.[86]

Example 22.6:   Lease classification

Consider the following two scenarios:

- Entity A leases a motor vehicle from Entity B for a non-cancellable three-year period. At the inception of the lease, the lease was assessed as an operating lease. The lease did not contain any explicit option in the lease contract to extend the term of the lease. After 2 years, Entity A applies to Entity B to extend the lease for a further two years after the initial three-year period is complete. This extension is granted by the leasing company on an arm's length basis.

- Entity C leases an asset from Entity D for 10 years. The lease includes a purchase option under which Entity C may purchase the asset from Entity D at the end of the lease. The exercise price is fair value. Entity C is required to give notice of its intention to purchase no later than the end of the eighth year of the lease (since this arrangement allows Entity D time to market the leased asset for sale). On inception, Entity C classifies the lease as an operating lease, believing there was a reasonable commercial possibility that it would not exercise the option. Near the end of the eighth year of the lease, Entity C serves notice that it will purchase the asset, thereby creating a binding purchase commitment.

In both of these cases, Entity A and Entity C will continue to classify the leases as operating leases. Changes in circumstances or intentions do not give rise to a new classification of a lease for accounting purposes, provided that the circumstances or intentions concerned do not indicate that the initial lease classification was not based on the substance of the lease arrangement at the time it was entered into, in which case the initial lease classification would be an error. A lease is reclassified only when its provisions are changed other than by renewing the lease, in such a way that the lease would have been classified differently if the changed terms had been in effect at the inception of the lease. The renewal of a lease or the execution of a purchase option, if these were not considered probable at the inception of the lease, does not require re-assessment of the classification of a lease.

IAS 17 does not, however, give any guidance on how to assess whether modified lease terms give rise to a new classification or on how to measure modifications of leases if changes affect the value of the assets and liabilities for both lessor and lessee. These issues are discussed at 4.2 below.

2.3.4   *Leases of land – finance or operating leases?*

Land normally has an indefinite economic life and, until IAS 17 was amended in 2009 as part of the Improvements Project, all leases over land were classified as operating leases unless title was expected to pass to the lessee by the end of the lease term. The special rules that related only to leases of land have now been significantly reduced in an amendment that comes into force on 1 January 2010. The standard will now require an entity to assess the classification of leases over land as finance or operating leases in accordance with the general rules in paragraphs 7-13 that are described above. Many leases include elements for both land and buildings and both parts must be considered separately as discussed in 2.3.5 below.

The revised standard includes a reminder that 'in determining whether the land element is an operating or a finance lease, an important consideration is that land normally has an indefinite economic life'.[87] A lease term for the major part of the economic life of the asset can indicate that a lease is a finance lease, even if title is not transferred,[88] and by repeating this in the amendment the IASB is stressing that this particular feature of finance leases is not likely to be met.

It is not clear exactly how the IASB expects the revised requirement to be applied in practice. It does appear that the Board expects the amendment to affect current lease classification, noting that it will be an improvement in accounting for leases and the significance of this issue in countries in which property rights are obtained under long-term leases.[89] In these jurisdictions these interests are frequently purchased for single lease premiums in a manner comparable to the purchase of a freehold, although there may also be a small annual rent payable (a 'ground rent' in the UK). The Basis for Conclusions suggests that the lessee in leases of this type 'will typically be in a position economically similar to an entity that purchased the land and buildings. The present value of the residual value of the property in a lease with a term of several decades would be negligible. The Board concluded that accounting for the land element as a finance lease in such circumstances would be consistent with the economic position of the lessee.'[90] Therefore, the fact that land has an indefinite life will be assessed alongside other features of finance leases, in particular whether the minimum lease payments amount to substantially all of the fair value.

An advantage of classifying certain land leases as finance leases is that they can then be presented in the financial statements as property, plant and equipment. Under the unamended standard, unless title to the land transfers to the lessee, premiums paid for a leasehold interest in land always represents pre-paid lease payments that are amortised over the lease term in accordance with the pattern of benefits provided.[91] Once the entity applies the amendment, this treatment will be reserved for pre-paid land rentals that are not classified as finance leases. An example would be a lease premium that comprises ten year's prepaid rentals, which is most unlikely to be classified as a finance lease.

A   *Lessors and land leases*

The requirement to treat all leases over land as operating leases probably had a more profound effect on lessors than lessees. The lessee could not classify its prepaid lease premium as 'property, plant and equipment' and could not revalue it, unless the interest met the definition of investment property (see 2.3.6 below) but it indubitably had acquired an asset that would be amortised over its useful life. Lessors selling a leasehold interest, no matter how long its term, were apparently unable to treat the element of the proceeds that related to the land as anything other than prepaid rent to be spread on a straight-line basis over the lease term. After applying the amendment, lessors ought to be able to treat leases over land as finance leases and recognise a profit on disposal when they conclude that the land lease element is a finance lease.

B   *Classification of leases over land – effective date and transition*

The classification of land elements of unexpired leases should be reassessed at the date the entity adopts the amendment, which is for annual periods beginning on or after 1 January 2010. Early adoption is permitted.[92]

The IASB was concerned that entities might not be able to apply full retrospective restatement because they might not have fair value information of the respective elements as at the inception of the lease.[93] Accordingly, if this information is not available, entities must instead base the lease assets and liabilities on the facts and circumstances existing on the date of adoption. The asset and liability relating to a land lease that has been newly classified as a finance lease will be recognised at their fair values on that date with any difference between those fair values being recognised in retained earnings.[94]

C   *Measurement and presentation – operating leases over land*

Prepayments that are classified as operating leases over land and buildings will continue to be disclosed as current or non-current assets, as appropriate, in the entity's balance sheet. If certain costs arise at the inception of the lease that are necessary to consummate the agreement and enable a lessee to exercise its rights under the lease agreement, these costs are incurred as a direct result of the lease. Therefore, it is appropriate to consider these as lease-related costs that should be subject to the same accounting treatment as prepaid lease payments.

The following is an example of presentation of pre-paid operating leases in the balance sheet, together with the supporting note.

Extract 22.3: VTech Holdings Ltd. (2008)

Consolidated Financial Statements [extract]
Consolidated Balance Sheet [extract]
As at 31st March 2008

	Note	2008 US$ million	2007 US$ million
Non-current assets			
Tangible assets	7	101.3	78.4
Leasehold land payments	8	3.8	3.7
Deferred tax assets	9	6.9	5.5
Investments	10	0.2	0.2
		112.2	87.8

Notes to the Financial Statements [extract]

Principal Accounting Policies [extract]
J   Leases [extract]

Leasehold land payments are up-front payments to acquire long-term leasehold interests in land. These payments are stated at cost and are amortised on a straight-line basis over the respective period of the leases.

8   Leasehold Land Payments

	Note	2008 US$ million	2007 US$ million
Net book value at 1st April		3.7	3.7
Amortisation	2	(0.1)	(0.1)
Effect of changes in exchange rates		0.2	0.1
Net book value at 31st March		3.8	3.7
Leasehold land payments in respect of:			
Owner-occupied properties		3.8	3.7

2.3.5   Separating land and buildings

A characteristic of property leases in some jurisdictions (such as the UK) is that it is not possible to lease a building without leasing the land on which it stands – under UK property law all such leases are leases of land. There is no separate fair value for the land and buildings elements as they cannot be disposed of separately. In substance such leases may differ little from buying a property.[95] They are classified as operating or finance leases in the same way as leases of other assets. The standard states explicitly that the land and buildings elements of leases are considered separately for the purposes of lease classification.[96]

Before applying the amendment to IAS 17 allowing land leases to be accounted for as finance leases, initial classification is based on whether or not title passes. Where title to the land does not pass and it has an indefinite economic life, the land will normally be classified as an operating lease while the buildings element will be an operating lease or finance lease according to the classification in the standard.[97] The initial classification will now depend on the individual assessment of both land and buildings parts of the lease.

Entities may need to make the allocation between the land and buildings elements even if both are clearly finance leases as there could be a difference in amortisation methods, although this would be very unusual[98] Much more common is a difference in useful economic life, where an entity takes out a lease for land and buildings where the term is longer than the useful life of any building on the land, e.g. a lease of 75 years over land on which there is a building that has a remaining useful life of 30 years.

If either or both parts of the lease might comprise a finance lease, the minimum lease payments need to be allocated between the land and buildings elements in proportion to the respective fair values of the leasehold interest in the land and buildings elements at the inception of the lease. The minimum lease payments must, of course, include any up-front payments, such as the payment for a lease premium.[99]

The allocation of the minimum lease payments should be weighted to reflect the fair value of the land and buildings components to the extent they are the subject of the lease. This means that the amount that is being allocated is the lessee's leasehold interest in the land and buildings and the compensation received by the lessor, not the relative fair values of the land and buildings. The amount for which the land could be purchased at the inception of the lease is not the same as the value of that interest to the lessee. As land has an indefinite life, the value to the lessor may not be significantly affected by the grant of the lease.[100]

The standard addresses the fact that it may not be possible to determine the fair values of the elements at inception and allows the following:

- if it is difficult or impossible to allocate the payments between the two elements, then the entire lease may be classified as a finance lease unless it is obvious that both the land and buildings elements are operating leases;[101]

- if the land element is immaterial, the lease may be treated as a single unit and classified as a finance or operating lease. The economic life of the entire leased asset will be the economic life of the buildings.[102]

Some examples of the ways in which these exemptions may operate in practice are as follows:

Example 22.7:   Leases of land and buildings

Consider the following scenarios:

- Company A leases a building (and the underlying land) for 10 years. The remaining economic life of the building when the lease is entered into is 30 years. The lease is for considerably less than the economic life of the building so it is clear that both the land and buildings elements are operating leases and no separation is necessary.

- Company B takes on a 30-year lease of a new building and the underlying land. It is on a retail park and almost all of the value is ascribed to the building as land values are low. Although the building has a fabric life of 60 years, its economic life is estimated to be 30 years, after which it is expected to be technologically obsolete. The lease is for most of the economic life of the buildings and the present value of the minimum lease payments amounts to substantially all of the fair value of the building. It is not legally possible to lease the building without leasing the underlying land or, therefore, to estimate the relative fair values reliably. In any event, the lessor retains the residual value in the land and the lessee's interest in the land alone must be insignificant. The entire lease is accounted for as a finance lease with an economic life of 30 years.

- Company C takes out a 25 year non-cancellable lease of premises in the centre of a major town where land values are high. There are upward-only rent reviews every 5 years. It is a modern building that may have a remaining economic life of 35 years (or perhaps more, as the building has a fabric life of 60 years) and the land is clearly valuable to the lessor, who will want a reasonable return from it over the lease term. In this case the interest in the building may or may not be a finance lease and the lessee's leasehold interest in the land is not insignificant. Company D will have to undertake a valuation exercise to determine the allocation of minimum lease payments between the land and building elements of the lease in order to determine whether or not it has finance or operating leases over the land and buildings.

There will be many circumstances in which it is unclear whether the lessee has a finance or operating lease over land and buildings. In such cases it will probably be necessary to obtain the help of a valuation expert.

In the UK, The Royal Institution of Chartered Surveyors has produced an information paper analysing the apportionments for lease classification under IFRSs.[103] This notes that there are four elements that need to be taken into account in the valuation (the value within the lease of the buildings and the land but also the residual value of both buildings and land) and proposes a method for apportioning the lease rentals based on these elements. The principal steps are as follows:

(a)   assess the freehold value of the land and buildings;

(b)   apportion the freehold value between the value within the lease and the residual (reversionary) value;

(c)   apportion the freehold value between land and buildings by calculating the value of one or other interest (usually, in practice, the building element) and deducting this from the value obtained in (b) to obtain the other;

(d)   apportion the value of the buildings element calculated at (c) between the residual and the value within the lease;

(e)   the value within the lease (b) can now be allocated between the buildings element (calculated at (d)) and the land element ((b) less (d)); and

(f)   apportion minimum lease payment between land and buildings in the ratio in (e) above.

Using this methodology it is now possible to calculate the implicit interest rate separately for the building as all elements needed for the calculation are known (fair value of the building, value of its residual and an appropriate proportion of the rentals paid).[104]

2.3.6 *Leases and investment properties*

Until both IAS 17 and IAS 40 were amended in 2003, it was not possible under IFRS for an interest in property held under an operating lease to be classified as an investment property. This was of great significance to the property industry in places such as the UK, where long leasehold interests in property are common, and to other jurisdictions such as Hong Kong where there are no freehold interests. In the UK these leasehold interests are normally acquired for an up-front premium that, if not recognised as an investment property asset, would have to be treated as a prepayment and gradually amortised. The amortisation of the prepayment would have effectively forced these entities to depreciate assets that had not previously been depreciated (investment properties are not depreciated under IAS 40). Under IAS 17, entities are allowed to treat interests under operating leases as investment properties as long as they apply the fair value model (see Chapter 17).

IAS 17 requires leases to be separated into land and building components, subject to this being possible or the land element being material (see 2.3.5 above). If the interest is an investment property carried at fair value in accordance with IAS 40, there is no requirement to separate the land and buildings elements of the lease.[105]

Once the lessee has classified an operating lease property interest as if it were held under a finance lease, it must apply the fair value model and it must continue to do so even if subsequent changes in circumstances mean that the property interest is no longer an investment property to the lessee. IAS 17 gives two examples:

(a)   the lessee occupies the property, in which case it is transferred to owner-occupied property at fair value at the date of change of use; or

(b)   the lessee grants a sublease over substantially all of its property interest to an unrelated third party. It will treat the sublease as a finance lease to the third party even though the interest may well be accounted for as an operating lease by that party.[106]

In some arrangements, a developer may acquire a headlease over land and sell its rights under that same headlease. In these circumstances the developer may apply an IAS 40 analysis and treat the transaction as a purchase and sale of the same investment property. However, this does depend on the disposal in substance of the same asset as the one that has been acquired.

3   ACCOUNTING FOR FINANCE AND OPERATING LEASES

3.1   Finance leases – summary of accounting by lessees and lessors

Lessees recognise finance leases as assets and liabilities in their balance sheets at the commencement of the lease term at amounts equal at the inception of the lease to the fair value of the leased item or, if lower, at the present value of the minimum lease payments. In calculating the present value of the minimum lease payments the discount factor is the interest rate implicit in the lease, if this is practicable to determine; if not, the lessee's incremental borrowing rate should be used. Any initial direct costs of the lessee are added to the asset.[107] 'Fair value' and 'minimum lease payments' are defined in 3.1.2 and 3.1.3 below.

The fair value and the present value of the lease payments are both determined as at the inception of the lease. At commencement, the asset and liability for the future lease payments are recognised in the balance sheet at the same amount.[108] The terms and calculations of initial recognition by lessees are discussed further in 3.1.1 to 3.1.7 below.

Lease payments made by the lessee are apportioned between the finance charge and the reduction of the outstanding liability. The finance charge should be allocated to periods during the lease term so as to produce a constant periodic rate of interest on the remaining balance of the liability for each period.[109] This is covered in 3.2 below.

Lessors recognise assets held under a finance lease as receivables in their balance sheets and present them as a receivable at an amount equal to the net investment in the lease.[110] Lessors who are not manufacturers or dealers include costs that they have incurred in connection with arranging and negotiating a lease as part of the initial measurement of the finance lease receivable. Initial recognition by lessors, which is in many respects a mirror image of lessee recognition, follows at 3.3 below. The recognition of finance income and other issues in connection with subsequent measurement of the lessor's assets arising from finance leases is dealt with in 3.3.1 to 3.3.3 below.

Manufacturer or dealer lessors have specific issues with regard to recognition of selling profit and finance income. These are dealt with under 3.3.5 below.

3.1.1   *Inception and commencement of the lease*

The standard now distinguishes between the inception of the lease (when leases are classified) and the commencement of the lease term (when recognition takes place). The *inception* of the lease is the earlier of the date of the lease agreement and the date of commitment of the parties to the principal terms of the lease. This is the date on which a lease is classified as a finance or operating lease and, for finance leases, the date at which the amounts to be recognised at commencement are recognised.[111] The *commencement* of the lease term is the date on which the lessee is entitled to exercise its right to use the leased asset and is the date of initial recognition of the assets, liabilities, income and expenses of the lease in the financial statements.[112] This means that the entity makes an initial calculation of the assets and liabilities under a finance lease at inception of the lease but does not recognise these in the financial statements until the commencement date, if this is later. These amounts may in some circumstances be revised; this is discussed below.

It is not uncommon for these two dates to be different, especially if the asset is under construction. Lease payments may be adjusted for changes in the lessor's costs during the period between inception and commencement. The lease may allow for changes in respect of costs of construction, acquisition costs, changes in the lessor's financing costs and any other factor, such as changes in general price levels, during the construction period. Changes to the lease payments as a result of such events are deemed to take place at inception of the lease, i.e. are taken into account in establishing, at inception, whether it is a finance or operating lease.[113] In other words, if the final cost of the asset, and hence its fair value, is not known until after the date of inception, hindsight is used to establish that fair value.

The fair value may be known at inception but payment delayed until commencement, which may happen with large but routinely constructed assets such as aircraft or railway locomotives. The lease liability will increase between the date of inception and the date of commencement, taking account of payments made and the interest rate implicit in the lease (see 3.1.5 below). Although IAS 17 does not address this, the lessee will add the increase in the liability until the commencement date to the asset. It is not a finance cost on the liability (no liability is recognised prior to commencement) and nor need it be an expense. It is not appropriate to recognise at commencement the liability that was calculated at inception as that would change the interest rate implicit in the lease.

The standard also considers what will happen if the lease terms are changed so radically (but without entering into a new lease agreement) that it would have been classified in a different way, e.g. it would have been a finance lease instead of an operating lease. Such changes could happen at any stage during the lease (see 2.3.3 above) but if they happen in the period between inception and commencement, the lease will be classified at inception in accordance with the revised terms as if they had existed as at that date. Modifications are discussed at 4.2 below.

3.1.2   Fair value

Fair value is defined, as elsewhere in IFRSs, as the amount for which an asset could be exchanged or a liability settled, between knowledgeable, willing parties in an arm's length transaction.[114] In practice, the transaction price, i.e. the purchase price of the asset that is the subject of the lease, will be its fair value, unless there is evidence to the contrary.

3.1.3   Minimum lease payments

The minimum lease payments are the payments over the lease term that the lessee is or can be required to make, excluding contingent rent, costs for services and taxes to be paid by and reimbursed to the lessor, together with:

(a)   for a lessee, any amounts guaranteed by the lessee or by a party related to the lessee;

(b)   for a lessor, any residual guaranteed to the lessor by:

(i)   the lessee or by a party related to the lessee; or

(ii)   a third party unrelated to the lessor who is financially capable of discharging the obligations under the guarantee.

The lessee may have an option to purchase the asset at a price that is expected to be sufficiently lower than the fair value at the date the option becomes exercisable so that, at the inception of the lease, it is reasonably certain to be exercised. In this case the minimum lease payments comprise the minimum payments payable over the lease term to the expected date of exercise of this purchase option and the payment required to exercise it.[115]

3.1.4   Lease term and non-cancellable period

The lease term is the non-cancellable period for which the lessee has contracted to lease the asset, together with any further terms for which the lessee has the option to continue to lease the asset, with or without further payment, if it is reasonably certain at the inception of the lease that the lessee will exercise the option.[116] A non-cancellable lease is either a lease that has no cancellation terms or one that has terms that effectively force the lessee to continue to use the asset for the period of the agreement. Therefore, a lease is considered to be non-cancellable if it can be cancelled only:

(a) on the occurrence of a remote contingency; or

(b) with the permission of the lessor; or

(c) if the lessee enters into a new lease with the same lessor for the same or an equivalent asset; or

(d) if the lessee is required to pay additional amounts that make it reasonably certain at inception that the lessee will continue the lease.[117]

An example of (d) is a requirement that the lessee pays a termination payment equivalent to the present value of the remaining lease payments.

3.1.5 Interest rate implicit in the lease and incremental borrowing rate

The interest rate implicit in the lease is the discount rate that, at the inception of the lease, causes the aggregate present value of

(a) the minimum lease payments; and

(b) the unguaranteed residual value

to be equal to the sum of the fair value of the leased asset and any initial direct costs of the lessor.

If it is not practicable to determine this then the lessee may use its incremental borrowing rate of interest, which it is the rate of interest the lessee would have to pay on a similar lease or, if that is not determinable, the rate that, at the inception of the lease, the lessee would have to pay to borrow over a similar term, and with a similar security, the funds necessary to purchase the asset.[118]

3.1.6 Residual value

The guaranteed residual value is:

(a) for a lessee, the part of the residual value that is guaranteed by itself or by one of its related parties. The amount of the guarantee is the maximum amount that could, in any event, become payable; and

(b) for a lessor, it is the part of the residual value that is guaranteed by the lessee or by a third party unrelated to the lessor who is financially capable of discharging the obligations under the guarantee.

The lessor's unguaranteed residual value is any part of the residual value of the leased asset, the realisation of which is not assured or is guaranteed solely by a party related to it.[119]

3.1.7 Contingent rents

Contingent rents (which are excluded from minimum lease payments) are defined in the standard as that portion of the lease payments that are not fixed in amount, but are based on a factor other than just the passage of time (for example, percentage of sales, amount of usage, price indices, market rates of interest).[120]

Contingent rents are embedded derivatives, as defined by IAS 39. This has not affected the accounting for the specific examples of contingent rents referred to above; IAS 39 specifically identifies them as being 'closely related' to the lease contract and hence not separately accounted for.[121] The issues are considered in 3.6 below.

A   Contingent rents and operating leases

IAS 17 specifies that lessees expense contingent rents relating to finance leases in the period in which they are incurred.[122] However, the Standard is not explicit in the treatment of contingent elements of operating lease rentals.

In its May 2006 meeting, the IFRIC considered whether an estimate of contingent rents should be included in the total operating lease payments or lease income to be recognised on a straight line basis over the lease term. It concluded that current practice was to exclude such amounts (which is consistent with our view of the issue) and did not, therefore, add the matter to its agenda for further consideration. Accordingly, lease payments or receipts under operating leases will exclude contingent amounts.

A clarification that would have achieved consistency in the treatment of contingent rent for finance and operating leases was proposed for the 2008 annual improvements but was not included in the final version of the *Improvements to IFRSs* issued in May 2008.[123] It has not been reintroduced in the August 2008 Exposure Draft of the *Improvements to IFRSs* either; it may be that it is being deferred because of the proposals to change the method of accounting for operating leases described at 1.2 above.

3.1.8   Initial direct costs

Initial direct costs are incremental costs that are directly attributable to negotiating and arranging a lease, except for such costs incurred by manufacturer or dealer lessors.[124]

If the lessee incurs costs that are directly attributable to activities it has performed to obtain a finance lease, these are added to the amount recognised as an asset.[125]

Initial direct costs of lessors include amounts such as commissions, legal fees and internal costs that are incremental and directly attributable to negotiating and arranging a lease. Internal costs must exclude general overheads such as those incurred by a sales or marketing team.[126] Lessors must add internal direct costs to the carrying value of leased assets under both finance and operating leases – see 3.3 and 3.4.4 below – unless they are manufacturer and dealer lessors, in which case they must be expensed – see 3.3.5 below.

3.1.9   Calculation of the implicit interest rate and present value of minimum lease payments

The following example illustrates the calculation of the implicit interest rate and present value of minimum lease payments:

Example 22.8:   Calculation of the implicit interest rate and present value of minimum lease payments

Details of a non-cancellable lease are as follows:

(i)   Fair value = €10,000

(ii)   Five annual rentals payable in advance of €2,100

(iii) Lessor's unguaranteed estimated residual value at end of five years = €1,000

The implicit interest rate in the lease is that which gives a present value of €10,000 for the five rentals plus the total estimated residual value at the end of year 5. This rate can be calculated as 6.62%, as follows:

Year	Capital sum at start of period €	Rental paid €	Capital sum during period €	Finance charge (6.62% per annum) €	Capital sum at end of period €
2010	10,000	2,100	7,900	523	8,423
2011	8,423	2,100	6,323	419	6,742
2012	6,742	2,100	4,642	307	4,949
2013	4,949	2,100	2,849	189	3,038
2014	3,038	2,100	938	62	1,000
		10,500		1,500	

In other words, 6.62% is the implicit interest rate that, at the inception of the lease, causes the aggregate present value of the minimum lease payments (€10,500) and the unguaranteed residual value (€1,000) to be equal to the fair value of the leased asset. Lessor's initial direct costs have been excluded for simplicity.

This implicit interest rate is then used to calculate the present value of the minimum lease payments, i.e. €10,500 discounted at 6.62%. This can be calculated at €9,274, which is 92.74% of the asset's fair value, indicating that the present value of the minimum lease payments is substantially all of the fair value of the leased asset and a finance lease is therefore indicated.

It would be appropriate for the lessee to record the asset at €9,274 as the present value of the minimum lease payments is lower than the fair value and this would take account of the lessor's residual interest in the asset.

The lessor will know all of the information in the above example, as it will have been used in the pricing decision for the lease. However, the lessee may not know either the fair value or the unguaranteed residual value and, therefore, not know the implicit interest rate. In such circumstances the lessee will substitute a rate from a similar lease or its incremental borrowing rate. The lessee is also unlikely to know the lessor's initial direct costs even if the other information is known, but this is unlikely to have more than a marginal effect on the implicit interest rate.

3.2   Accounting by lessees – finance leases

3.2.1   *Initial recognition*

At commencement of the lease, the asset and liability for the future lease payments are recorded in the balance sheet at the same amount, which is an amount equal to the fair value of the leased asset or the present value of the minimum lease payments, if lower, with initial direct costs of the lessee being added to the asset.[127] An example of the calculation is given in Example 22.8 above.

3.2.2   *Allocation of finance costs*

The standard requires that lease payments should be apportioned between the finance charge and the reduction of the outstanding liability. The finance charge should be allocated to periods during the lease term so as to produce a constant periodic rate of interest on the remaining balance of the liability for each period.[128]

Example 22.9:   Allocation of finance costs

In Example 22.8 above, the present value of the lessee's minimum lease payments was calculated at €9,274 by using the implicit interest rate of 6.62%. The total finance charges of €1,226 (total rentals paid of €10,500 less their present value of €9,274) are allocated over the lease term as follows:

Year	Liability at start of period €	Rental paid €	Liability during period €	Finance charge (6.62% per annum) €	Liability at end of period €
2010	9,274	2,100	7,174	475	7,649
2011	7,649	2,100	5,549	367	5,917
2012	5,917	2,100	3,817	253	4,070
2013	4,070	2,100	1,970	130	2,100
2014	2,100	2,100	–	–	–
		10,500		1,226	

The standard notes that, in practice, when allocating the finance charge to periods during the lease term some form of approximation may be used to simplify the calculation.[129] However, it provides no guidance as to the methodology that should be applied in allocating finance charges to accounting periods.

Two methods that are used as approximations are the 'sum of the digits' ('rule of 78') or simply taking the finance costs on a straight line basis over the lease term. These are progressively easier to apply but also give progressively less accurate answers. There is, therefore, a trade-off to be made between the costs versus benefits of achieving complete accuracy, but in making this trade-off, the question of materiality is important. If differences between allocated finance charges under each method are immaterial, the simplest method may be used for convenience. The converse also applies and, of course, a number of individually immaterial differences may in aggregate be material. The following example illustrates the implicit interest rate and sum of the digits methods of allocating finance charges to accounting periods.

Example 22.10:   Sum-of-digits allocation as compared to implicit interest rate

Continuing the lease example from Example 22.8 above, the sum of the digits method calculation is as follows:

Year	Number of rentals not yet due	×	total finance charge / sum of number of rentals	=	Finance charge per annum €
2010	4	×	€1,226 ÷ 10	=	490
2011	3	×	€1,226 ÷ 10	=	368
2012	2	×	€1,226 ÷ 10	=	245
2013	1	×	€1,226 ÷ 10	=	123
2014	–	×	€1,226 ÷ 10	=	
	10				1,226

We can now compare the finance charges in each of the five years under the implicit interest rate (IIR) as calculated in Example 22.8 and sum of the digits methods:

Year	Annual finance charge IIR €	Annual finance charge Sum of the digits €	Annual finance charge as % of total rentals IIR %	Annual finance charge as % of total rentals Sum of the digits %
2010	475	490	39	40
2011	368	368	30	30
2012	253	245	20	20
2013	130	123	11	10
2014	–	–	–	–
	1,226	1,226	100	100

As can be seen above, in situations where the lease term is not very long (typically not more than seven years) and interest rates are not very high, the sum of the digits method gives an allocation of finance charges that is close enough to that under the implicit interest rate method to allow the simpler approach to be used.

3.2.3   Recording the liability

The carrying amount of the liability will always be calculated in the same way, by adding the finance charge (however calculated) to the outstanding balance and deducting cash paid. The finance charge depends on the method used to apportion the finance costs. The liability in each of the years, as apportioned between the current and non-current liability, if the IIR method is used, is as follows:

Example 22.11:   Lessee's liabilities and interest expense

The entity entering into the lease in Example 22.8 will record the following liabilities and interest expense in its balance sheet:

Year	Liability at end of period €	Current liability at end of period €	Non-current liability at end of period €	Interest expense (at 6.62%) for the period €
2010	7,649	1,732	5,917	475
2011	5,917	1,847	4,070	368
2012	4,070	1,970	2,100	253
2013	2,100	2,100	–	130
2014	–	–	–	–
				1,226

3.2.4   Accounting for the leased asset

At commencement of the lease, the asset and liability for the future lease payments are recorded in the balance sheet at the same amount, with initial direct costs of the lessee being added to the asset.[130] These are costs that are directly attributable to the lease in question and are added to the carrying value[131] in an analogous way to the treatment of the acquisition costs of property, plant and equipment.

Accounting for the leased asset follows the general rules for accounting for property, plant and equipment or intangible fixed assets. A finance lease gives rise to a depreciation expense for depreciable assets as well as a finance expense for each accounting period. The depreciation policy for depreciable leased assets should be consistent with that for depreciable assets that are owned, and the depreciation recognised should be calculated in accordance with IAS 16 and IAS 38. If there is reasonable certainty that the lessee will obtain ownership by the end of the lease term, the period of expected use is the useful life of the asset. If there is no reasonable certainty, the asset is be depreciated fully over the shorter of the lease term or its useful life.[132] The useful life is the estimated remaining period, from the commencement of the lease term, over which the entity expects to consume the economic benefits embodied in the asset. This is different to the economic life which takes account of the period of time for which the asset is economically usable by one or more users and would therefore include additional lease terms with the same or different lessees.[133]

Because the lease expense and depreciation must be calculated separately and are unlikely to be the same it is not appropriate simply to treat the lease payments as an expense for the period.[134] This is demonstrated in the following example.

Example 22.12:   Lessee's depreciation and interest expense

The entity that has entered into the lease agreement described in Example 22.8 will depreciate the asset (whose initial carrying value, disregarding initial direct costs, is €9,274) on a straight-line basis over five years in accordance with its depreciation policy for owned assets, i.e. an amount of €1,855 per annum. The balances for asset and liability in the financial statements in each of the years 2010 – 2014 will be as follows:

Year	Carrying value of asset at end of period €	Total liability at end of period €	Total charged to income statement* €	Lease payments €
2010	7,419	7,649	2,330	2,100
2011	5,564	5,917	2,222	2,100
2012	3,709	4,070	2,108	2,100
2013	1,854	2,100	1,985	2,100
2014	–	–	1,855	2,100
			10,500	10,500

*   The total charge combines the annual depreciation of €1,855 and the interest calculated according to the IIR method in Example 22.9, which is in aggregate the initial carrying value of the asset of €9,274 and the total finance charge of €1,226, i.e. the total rent paid of €10,500. Note that this example assumes that the asset is being depreciated to a residual value of zero over the lease term, which is shorter than its useful life, so IAS 16's requirement to reconsider the residual value and useful life at least at each financial year end is unlikely to have an effect.[135]

An entity applies IAS 36 – *Impairment of Assets* – to determine whether the leased asset has become impaired in value (see Chapter 18).[136]

3.3   Accounting by lessors – finance leases

Under a finance lease, a lessor retains legal title to an asset but passes substantially all the risks and rewards of ownership to the lessee in return for a stream of rentals. In substance, therefore, the lessor provides finance and expects a return thereon.

The standard requires lessors to recognise assets held under a finance lease in their balance sheets as a receivable at an amount equal to the net investment in the lease.[137] The lease payments received from the lessee are treated as repayments of principal and finance income.[138] Initial direct costs may include commissions, legal fees and internal costs that are incremental and directly attributable to negotiating and arranging the lease. They are included in the measurement of the net investment in the lease at inception and reflected in the calculation of the implicit interest rate.[139]

The recognition of finance income should be based on a pattern reflecting a constant periodic rate of return on the lessor's net investment outstanding in respect of the finance lease.[140]

3.3.1   The lessor's net investment in the lease

The lessor's gross investment in the lease is the aggregate of the minimum lease payments receivable by the lessor under a finance lease and any guaranteed and unguaranteed residual value to which the lessor is entitled. The net investment in the lease is the gross investment discounted at the interest rate implicit in the lease,[141] i.e. at any point in time it comprises the gross investment after deducting gross earnings allocated to future periods.

The lessor's gross investment is, therefore, the same as the aggregate figures used to calculate the implicit interest rate and the net investment is the present value of those same figures – see 3.1.9 and Example 22.8 above.

Therefore, at inception, the lessor's net investment in the lease is the cost of the asset as increased by its initial direct costs. The difference between the net and gross investments is the gross finance income to be allocated over the lease term. Example 22.13 below illustrates this point.

3.3.2   Allocation of finance income

As noted above the lessor recognises finance income based on a pattern reflecting a constant periodic rate of return on the lessor's net investment outstanding in respect of the finance lease.[142] Lease payments, excluding costs for services, are applied against the gross investment in the lease to reduce both the principal and the unearned finance income.[143] The standard does not refer to the use of approximations by lessors and, accordingly, the methods noted at 3.2.2 should not be used unless the differences are clearly immaterial. Example 22.8 at 3.1.9 can be examined from the lessor's perspective:

Example 22.13:   The lessor's gross and net investment in the lease

The lease has the same facts as described in Example 22.8, i.e. the asset has a fair value of €10,000, the lessee is making five annual rentals payable in advance of €2,100 and the total unguaranteed estimated residual value at the end of five years is estimated to be €1,000. The lessor's direct costs have been excluded for simplicity.

The lessor's gross investment in the lease is the total rents receivable of €10,500 and the unguaranteed residual value of €1,000. The gross earnings are therefore €1,500. The initial carrying value of the receivable is its fair value of €10,000, which is also the present value of the gross investment discounted at the interest rate implicit in the lease of 6.62%.

Year	Receivable at start of period €	Rental received €	Finance income (6.62% per annum) €	Gross investment at end of period €	Gross earnings allocated to future periods €	Receivable at end of period €
2010	10,000	2,100	523	9,400	977	8,423
2011	8,423	2,100	419	7,300	558	6,742
2012	6,742	2,100	307	5,200	251	4,949
2013	4,949	2,100	189	3,100	62	3,038
2014	3,038	2,100	62	1,000	–	1,000
		10,500	1,500			

The gross investment in the lease at any point in time comprises the aggregate of the rentals receivable in future periods and the unguaranteed residual value, e.g. at the end of 2010, the gross investment of €7,300 is three years' rental of €2,100 plus the unguaranteed residual of €1,000. The net investment, which is the amount at which the debtor will be recorded in the balance sheet, is €7,300 less the earnings allocated to future periods of €558 = €6,742.

3.3.3   *Residual values*

Income recognition by lessors can be extremely sensitive to the amount recognised as the asset's residual value. This is because the amount of the residual directly affects the computation of the amount of finance income earned over the lease term – this is illustrated in Example 22.14 below. The standard gives no guidance regarding the estimation of unguaranteed residual values but it does require them to be reviewed regularly. If there has been a reduction in the estimated value, the income allocation over the lease term is revised and any reduction in respect of amounts accrued is recognised immediately.[144]

Example 22.14:   Reduction in residual value

Taking the same facts as used in Example 22.13 above, the lessor concludes at the end of 2011 that the residual value of the asset is only €500 and revises the income allocation over the lease term accordingly. It continues to apply the same implicit interest rate, 6.62%, as before.

Year	Receivable at start of period €	Rental received €	Finance income (6.62% per annum) €	Gross investment at end of period* €	Gross earnings allocated to future periods €	Receivable at end of period €
2011	8,423	2,100	419	6,800	471	6,329
2012	6,329	2,100	280	4,700	191	4,509
2013	4,509	2,100	160	2,600	31	2,569
2014	2,569	2,100	31	500	—	500

*   The gross investment in the lease now takes account of the revised unguaranteed residual of €500, rather than the original €1,000.

The lessor will have to write off €413, being the difference between the carrying amount of the receivable as previously calculated and the revised balance above (€6,742 – €6,329). This is the present value as at the end of 2010 of the part of the unguaranteed residual written off.

Impairment of lease receivables is within the scope of IAS 39[145] and this methodology is required by IAS 39 paragraph 63, described in 3.6.2 below.

3.3.4   *Disposals by lessors of assets held under finance leases*

If a lessor is to dispose of an asset under a finance lease that is classified as held for sale, or is included in a disposal group that is so classified, it is to apply the requirements of IFRS 5 – *Non-current Assets Held for Sale and Discontinued Operations* – to the disposal.[146] The 'asset under a finance lease' is the receivable from the lessee, which is not a financial asset under IAS 39; see 3.6 below for an analysis of the extent to which assets and liabilities under leases are within scope of that standard. This means that measurement as well as classification of the asset under the finance lease is within scope of IFRS 5, unlike financial assets within scope of IAS 39 that are subject only to its classification rules. Once classified as held for sale, it must be measured at the lower of carrying amount and fair value less costs to sell. Any residual interest in the leased asset, which is accounted for under IAS 16 or IAS 38, is clearly within scope of IFRS 5. IFRS 5's requirements are dealt with in Chapter 4.

3.3.5   *Manufacturer or dealer lessors*

Manufacturers or dealers often offer customers the choice of either buying or leasing an asset. A finance lease of an asset by a manufacturer or dealer lessor gives rise to two types of income:

(a)   the profit or loss equivalent to the profit or loss resulting from an outright sale of the asset being leased, at normal selling prices, reflecting any applicable volume or trade discounts; and

(b)   the finance income over the lease term.[147]

In those situations where the customer is offered the choice of paying the cash price for the asset immediately or paying for it on deferred credit terms then, as long as the credit terms are the manufacturer or dealer's normal terms, the cash price (after taking account of applicable or volume discounts) can be used for determining the selling profit.[148] However, in many cases such an approach should not be followed as the manufacturer or dealer's marketing considerations often influence the terms of the lease. For example, a car dealer may offer 0% finance deals instead of reducing the normal selling price of his cars. It would be wrong in this instance for the dealer to record a profit on the sale of the car and no finance income under the lease.

The standard, therefore, requires sales revenue to be based on the fair value of the asset (i.e. the cash price) or, if lower, the present value of the minimum lease payments computed at a market rate of interest. As a result, if artificially low rates of interest are quoted, selling profit is restricted to that which would apply if a commercial rate of interest were charged.[149] The cost of sales is reduced to the extent that the lessor retains an unguaranteed residual interest in the asset.[150]

Initial direct costs should be recognised as an expense in the income statement at the inception of the lease. This is not the same as the treatment when a lessor arranges a finance lease, where the costs are added to the finance lease receivable; the standard argues that this is because the costs are related mainly to earning the selling profit.[151] If the manufacturer or dealer is in the (relatively unlikely) position of incurring an overall loss because the total rentals receivable under the finance lease are less than the cost to it of the asset then this loss should be taken to the profit and loss account at the inception of the lease. IAS 17 assumes that the manufacturer or dealer will have a normal implicit interest rate based on its other leasing activity. However, in other situations where the manufacturer or dealer does not conduct other leasing business, an estimate will have to be made of the implicit rate for such leasing activity. A manufacturer or dealer lessor does not recognise any selling profit on entering into an operating lease because it is not the equivalent of a sale.[152]

3.4   Operating leases

3.4.1   *Operating leases in the financial statements of lessees*

IAS 17 requires that lease payments under an operating lease (excluding costs for services such as insurance and maintenance) should be recognised as an expense on a straight-line basis over the lease term unless another systematic basis is representative of the time pattern of the user's benefit, even if the payments are not on that basis.[153] Generally, the only other acceptable bases are where rentals are based on a unit of use or unit of production.

IAS 17 requires a straight line recognition of the lease expenses even when amounts are not payable on this basis. This does not require anticipation of contingent rental increases, such as those that will result from a periodic re-pricing to market rates or those that are based on some other index (see 3.1.7 above). However, lease payments may vary over time for other reasons that will have to be taken into account in calculating the annual charge. Described in more detail below are some examples, leases that are inclusive of services, leases with increments intended to substitute for inflation and security deposits made with lessors that attract low or no interest. Lease incentives are another feature that may affect the cash flows under a lease; they are dealt with in more detail in 3.4.2 (for lessees) and 3.4.5 (for lessors).

A   Leases that include payments for services

IAS 17 says that the costs of services should be excluded to arrive at the lease payments. This is straightforward enough if the payments are made by the lessor and quantified in the payments made by the lessee. It will be somewhat less so if, for example, the lessor makes all maintenance payments but does not specify the amounts; instead, payments are increased periodically to take account of changes in such costs. In such a case the lessee will have to estimate the amount paid for services and deduct them from the total. The remaining payments, which relate solely to the right to use the asset, will then be spread on a straight line basis over the non-cancellable term of the lease.

B   Straight-line recognition over the lease term

There are some leases that increase annually by fixed increments intended to compensate for expected annual inflation over the lease period. There has been debate as to whether such increases must also be taken on a straight-line basis over the non-cancellable lease term.

In considering the issue, the IFRIC noted that IAS 17 does not incorporate adjustments to operating lease payments to reflect the time value of money. Except in those cases where another basis is more appropriate, it requires all operating leases to be taken on a straight-line basis. They concluded that to allow recognition of these increases on an annual basis would be inconsistent with the treatment of other operating leases.[154]

Some leases allow for an annual increase in line with an index but with a fixed minimum increment. As discussed in 3.1.7 above, contingent rents are excluded from the lease payments but the fixed minimum increment will have to be spread so as to take the payments on a straight line basis over the lease term.

Example 22.15:   Operating lease expenses with fixed annual increment

Entity A leases a property at an initial rent of €1,000,000 per annum. The lease has a non-cancellable term of 30 years and rent increases annually in line with the Retail Prices Index (RPI) of the country in which the property is situated but with a minimum increase of 2.5% (the estimated long-term rate of inflation in the country in question) and a maximum of 5% per annum.

The annual increase of 2.5% must be taken into account in calculating the operating lease payment charged to profit or loss. On a straight-line basis this will be €1,463,000 per annum. Therefore, by the end of year 15 (at which point the amounts payable under the lease will exceed the straight-lined amount) the entity will have paid rentals of €15 million, charged €22 million to income and will be recording an accrual of €7 million.

If the increase in the RPI exceeds 2.5% these additional amounts will be charged to income as contingent rents.

C   *Notional or actual interest paid to lessors*

Lessees are sometimes required to place security deposits with lessors, on which they will receive either no or a reduced rate of interest. In accordance with IAS 39, the lessee initially measures the deposit at fair value and subsequently at amortised cost (assuming that the deposit is classified as a loan and receivable[155]) using the effective interest method; accordingly interest income is recognised through profit and loss over the useful life of the deposit.[156] At inception of an operating lease, the difference between the nominal value of the deposit and its fair value should be considered additional rent payable to the lessor. This will be expensed on a straight-line basis over the lease term.

Example 22.16:   Operating lease expenses reflecting interest payments to the lessor

A lessee makes an interest-free security deposit of €1,000 on entering into a five year lease. It assesses an appropriate rate of interest for the deposit to be 4% and accordingly the fair value of the deposit at inception is €822. On making the deposit, it will record it as follows:

Year		€	€
2010	Security deposit	822	
	Advance rentals	178	
	Cash		1,000

During the five years of the lease, it will record interest income and additional rental expense as follows:

Year	Interest income	Rental expense	Difference
2010	33	(36)	(3)
2011	34	(35)	(1)
2012	36	(36)	–
2013	37	(36)	1
2014	38	(35)	3
	178	(178)	

3.4.2   *Lease incentives – accounting by lessees*

On the matter of operating lease incentives, the SIC was asked to consider the accounting implications of a lessor providing incentives for a lessee to enter into a new or renewed operating lease agreement. Examples of such incentives are an up-front cash payment to the lessee or the reimbursement or assumption by the lessor of costs of the lessee (such as relocation costs, leasehold improvements and costs associated with a pre-existing lease commitment of the lessee). Alternatively, the lessor may grant the lessee rent-free or reduced rent initial lease periods.[157]

The consensus reached by the SIC in Interpretation SIC-15 – *Operating Leases – Incentives* – was that all incentives for the agreement of a new or renewed operating lease should be recognised as an integral part of the net consideration agreed for the use of the leased asset, irrespective of the incentive's nature or form or the timing of payments.[158] It was agreed further the lessee should recognise the aggregate benefit of incentives as a reduction of rental expense over the lease term, on a straight-line basis unless another systematic basis is representative of the time pattern of the lessee's benefit from the use of the leased asset.[159] Finally, SIC-15 requires that costs incurred by the lessee, including costs in connection with a pre-existing lease (for example, costs for termination, relocation or leasehold improvements), should be accounted for by the lessee in accordance with the IAS applicable to those costs, including costs which are effectively reimbursed through an incentive arrangement.[160] In an Appendix to SIC-15, the SIC has set out the following two examples that illustrate the application of the Interpretation:[161]

Example 22.17:   Application of SIC-15

Example 1

An entity agrees to enter into a new lease arrangement with a new lessor. The lessor agrees to pay the lessee's relocation costs as an incentive to the lessee for entering into the new lease. The lessee's moving costs are 1,000. The new lease has a term of 10 years, at a fixed rate of 2,000 per year.

The accounting is:

The lessee recognises relocation costs of 1,000 as an expense in Year 1. Net consideration of 19,000 consists of 2,000 for each of the 10 years in the lease term, less a 1,000 incentive for relocation costs. Both the lessor and lessee would recognise the net rental consideration of 19,000 over the 10 year lease term using a single amortisation method in accordance with paragraphs 4 and 5 of SIC-15.

Example 2

An entity agrees to enter into a new lease arrangement with a new lessor. The lessor agrees to a rent-free period for the first three years as incentive to the lessee for entering into the new lease. The new lease has a term of 20 years, at a fixed rate of 5,000 per annum for years 4 through 20.

The accounting is:

Net consideration of 85,000 consists of 5,000 for each of 17 years in the lease term. Both the lessor and lessee would recognise the net consideration of 85,000 over the 20-year lease term using a single amortisation method in accordance with paragraphs 4 and 5 of SIC-15.

One point about SIC 15 that has attracted considerable debate is its requirement to spread incentives over the lease term. The validity of this has been questioned if rentals are re-priced to market rates at periodic intervals – it is argued that in these circumstances the rent-free period is being given solely to compensate for an above-market rental in the primary period.

In its April 2005 meeting the IFRIC decided not undertake a project to modify SIC-15. It did not accept that the lease expense of a lessee after an operating lease is re-priced to market ought to be comparable with the lease expense of an entity entering into a new lease at that same time at market rates. Nor did it believe that the re-pricing itself would be reflective of a change in the time patterns of the lessee's benefit from the use of the leased asset.[162] In other words, incentives are seen in the context of the total cash flows under the lease and, except where the benefit of the lease is not directly related to the time during which the entity has the right to use the asset, IAS 17 requires these to be taken on a straight line basis.

There is a similar argument when lessees contend (as they often do) that they should not be obliged to spread rentals over a void period as they are not actually benefiting from the property during this time – it is a fit-out period or a start-up so activities are yet to increase to anticipated levels. However, the argument against this is really no different to the above: the lessee's period of benefit from the use of the asset is the lease term, so the incentive cannot be taken over the initial period. This was reinforced by the IFRIC in July 2008, when it noted that IAS 16 and IAS 38 require an entity to recognise the use of productive assets using the method that best reflects 'the pattern in which the asset's future economic benefits are expected to be consumed by the entity' but IAS 17 refers to the time pattern of the user's benefit.[163] Therefore, any alternative to the straight-line recognition of lease expense under an operating lease must reflect the time pattern of the use of the leased property rather than the amount of use or other factor related to economic benefits.[164] The IFRIC is not at present minded to accept economic arguments for other than straight-line treatment.

3.4.3   *Onerous contracts*

Although IAS 37 prohibits the recognition of provisions for future operating losses,[165] the standard does specifically address the issue of onerous contracts. It requires that if an entity has a contract that is onerous, the present obligation under the contract should be recognised and measured as a provision.[166]

The standard defines an onerous contract as 'a contract in which the unavoidable costs of meeting the obligations under it exceed the economic benefits expected to be received under it'.[167] This is taken to mean that the contract itself is onerous to the point of being directly loss-making, not simply uneconomic by reference to current prices. A common example of an onerous contract seen in practice relates to operating leases for the rent of property, and the standard includes the following example in Appendix C:

Example 22.18:   An onerous contract

An entity operates profitably from a factory that it has leased under an operating lease. During December 2010 the entity relocates its operations to a new factory. The lease on the old factory continues for the next four years, it cannot be cancelled and the factory cannot be re-let to another user.

Present obligation as a result of a past obligating event	The obligating event is the signing of the lease contract, which gives rise to a legal obligation.
Transfer of economic benefits in settlement	When the lease becomes onerous, a transfer of economic benefits is probable. (Until the lease becomes onerous, the entity accounts for the lease by applying IAS 17, Leases.)
Conclusion	A provision is recognised for the best estimate of the unavoidable lease payments (see IAS 37, paragraphs 5(c), 14 and 66).

Care must be taken to ensure that the lease itself is onerous. If an entity has a number of retail outlets and one of these is loss-making, this is not sufficient to make the lease onerous. However, if the entity vacates the premises and sub-lets them at an amount less than the rent it is paying, then the lease becomes onerous and the entity should provide for its best estimate of the unavoidable lease payments. This will include the difference between the lease and sub-lease payments, together with provision as appropriate for any period where there is no sub-tenant.

The accounting for onerous contracts is discussed in more detail in Chapter 24.

3.4.4   Operating leases in the financial statements of lessors

Lessors should present assets subject to operating leases in their balance sheets according to the nature of the asset. Lease income from operating leases should be recognised in income on a straight-line basis over the lease term, unless another systematic basis is more representative of the time pattern in which, the standard states, 'use benefit derived from the leased asset is diminished'.[168] Generally, the only other basis that is encountered is based on unit-of-production or service.

Lease income excludes receipts for services provided such as insurance and maintenance. IAS 18 – *Revenue* – provides guidance on how to recognise service revenue – see Chapter 25. Costs, including depreciation, incurred in earning the lease income are recognised as an expense.[169] Initial direct costs incurred specifically to earn revenues from an operating lease are added to the carrying amount of the leased asset and allocated to income over the lease term in proportion to the recognition of lease income.[170] This means that the costs will be depreciated on a straight-line basis if this is the method of recognising the lease income, regardless of the depreciation basis of the asset.

The depreciation policy for depreciable leased assets is to be consistent with the entity's policy for similar assets that are not subject to leasing arrangements and calculated in accordance with IAS 16 or IAS 38, as appropriate.[171] If the lessor does not use similar assets in its business then the depreciation policy must be set solely by reference to IASs 16 and 38. This also means that the lessor is obliged in accordance with IAS 16 to consider the residual value and economic life of the assets at least at each financial year-end.[172] There are similar requirements in the case of intangible assets, although IAS 38 notes that they rarely have a residual value.[173] These matters are discussed in Chapters 15 and 16. These assets are also tested for impairment in a manner consistent with other tangible and intangible fixed assets; IAS 17 refers to IAS 36 in providing guidance on the need to assess the possibility of an impairment of assets.[174]

3.4.5   *Lease incentives – accounting by lessors*

In negotiating a new or renewed operating lease, a lessor may provide incentives for the lessee to enter into the arrangement. For example, in the case of a property lease, the tenant may be given a rent-free period but other types of incentive may include up-front cash payments to the lessee or the reimbursement or assumption by the lessor of lessee costs such as relocation costs, leasehold improvements and costs associated with a pre-existing lease commitment of the lessee. This issue was addressed by the SIC in Interpretation SIC-15, which states that the lessor should recognise the aggregate cost of incentives as a reduction of rental income over the lease term, on a straight-line basis unless another systematic basis is representative of the time pattern over which the benefit of the leased asset is diminished.[175] The SIC rejected the argument that lease incentives for lessors are part of the initial direct costs of negotiating or arranging the contract; instead concluding that they are in substance, related to the amount of consideration received by the lessor for the use of the asset. This view was confirmed in the IASB's 2003 revision of IAS 17, which requires initial direct costs to be capitalised as part of the carrying value of the asset – see 3.1.8 above). Lessor accounting is, therefore, the mirror image of lessee accounting for the incentives, as described in 3.4.2 above.

3.5   **Sale and leaseback transactions**

These transactions involve the original owner of an asset selling it to a provider of finance and immediately leasing it back. These parties will be termed the seller/lessee (the original owner) and buyer/lessor (the finance provider) respectively. Sometimes, instead of selling the asset outright, the original owner will lease the asset to the other party under a finance lease and then lease it back. Such a transaction is known as a 'lease and leaseback' and has similar effects. The term 'sale and leaseback' is taken to include such a transaction.

Sale and leaseback transactions are a fairly common feature of a number of industries (such as the retail and hotel industries), where it is an accepted a form of financing as taking out a mortgage or a bank overdraft. Many parties are involved as buyer/lessors, not only finance houses and banks but also pension funds and property groups. From a commercial point of view, the important point of difference lies between an entity that decides that it is cheaper to rent than to own – and is willing to pass on the property risk to the landlord – and an entity which decides to use the property as a means of raising finance – and will therefore retain the property risk. However from the accounting point of view, a major consideration is whether a profit can be reported on such transactions.

The buyer/lessor will treat the lease in the same way as it would any other lease that was not part of a sale and leaseback transaction. The accounting treatment of the transaction by the seller/lessee depends on the type of lease involved, i.e. whether the leaseback is under a finance or an operating lease.[176]

3.5.1 Sale and finance leaseback

In order to assess whether the leaseback is under a finance lease, the seller/lessee will apply the qualitative tests in IAS 17 that are described at 2.3.2 above. If a sale and leaseback transaction results in a finance lease, any excess of sales proceeds over the carrying amount should not be recognised immediately as income by a seller-lessee. Instead, the excess is deferred and amortised over the lease term.[177] It is inappropriate to show a profit on disposal of an asset which has then, in substance, been reacquired by the entity under a finance lease as the lessor is providing finance to the lessee with the asset as security.[178] The asset will be restated to its fair value (or the present value of the minimum lease payments, if lower) in exactly the same way as any other asset acquired under a finance lease.

Example 22.19:   Sale and finance leaseback – accounting for the excess sale proceeds

An asset that has a carrying value of €700 and a remaining useful life of 7 years is sold for €1,200 and leased back on a finance lease. This is accounted for as a disposal of the original asset and the acquisition of an asset under a finance lease for €1,200. The excess of sales proceeds of €500 over the original carrying value should be deferred and amortised (i.e. credited to profit or loss) over the lease term.

The net impact on income of the charge for depreciation based on the carrying value of the asset held under the finance lease of €171 and the amortisation of the deferred income of €71 is the same as the annual depreciation of €100 based on the original carrying amount.

In 2007 the IFRIC considered the related area of sale and repurchase options, concluding that IAS 17 itself contains 'the more specific guidance with respect to sale and leaseback transactions'.[179] However, many still consider that there is an alternative treatment which is more consistent with the substance of the arrangement and with the approach in SIC-27 described at 2.2.2 above, which deals with transactions that have the form but not the substance of leases. It follows the standard's description of the transaction as 'a means whereby the lessor provides finance to the lessee, with the asset as security'.[180] The previous carrying value is left unchanged, with the sales proceeds being shown as a liability to be accounted for under IAS 39. The creditor balance represents the finance lease liability under the leaseback. This is consistent with IAS 18 which states that a transaction is not a sale and revenue is not recognised if the entity retains significant risks of ownership.[181] By definition the entity will have retained the significant risks and rewards, because it now holds the asset under a finance lease.

Both methods of accounting for sale and leaseback transactions are seen in practice and both have the same net effect on profit or loss. Therefore, an entity should select a treatment as a matter of accounting policy and apply it consistently.

If the sales value is less than the carrying amount then the apparent 'loss' need not be taken to income unless there has been an impairment under IAS 36.[182] There may be an obvious reason why the sales proceeds are less than the carrying value; for example, the fair value of a second-hand vehicle or item of plant and machinery is frequently lower than its book value, especially soon after the asset has been acquired by the entity. This fall in fair value after sale has no effect on the asset's value in use. What this means, of course, is that in the absence of impairment, a deficit (sales proceeds lower than carrying value) will be deferred in the same manner as a profit and spread over the lease term.

3.5.2   *Operating leaseback*

If a sale and leaseback transaction results in an operating lease, and it is clear that the transaction is established at fair value, any profit or loss should be recognised immediately. If the sale price is below fair value, any profit or loss should be recognised immediately unless the loss is compensated by future lease payments at below market price, in which case it should be deferred and amortised in proportion to the lease payments over the period for which the asset is expected to be used. If the sale price is above fair value, the excess over fair value should be deferred and amortised over the period for which the asset is expected to be used.[183]

The rationale behind the above treatments is that if the sales value is not based on fair values then it is likely that the normal market rents will have been adjusted to compensate. For example, a sale at above fair value followed by above-market rentals is similar to a loan of the excess proceeds by the lessor that is being repaid out of the rentals. Accordingly, the transaction should be recorded as if it had been based on fair value.

However, this will not always be the case. Where the sales value is less than fair value there may be legitimate reasons for this to be so, for example where the seller has had to raise cash quickly. In such situations, as the rentals under the lease have not been reduced to compensate, the profit or loss should be based on the sales value.

The standard includes an Appendix, which comprises the following table of the standard's requirements concerning sale and leaseback transactions, and is aimed at providing guidance in interpreting the various permutations of facts and circumstances that are set out in the requirements.

Sale price established at fair value (paragraph 61)	Carrying amount equal to fair value	Carrying amount less than fair value	Carrying amount above fair value
Profit	no profit	recognise profit immediately	not applicable
Loss	no loss	not applicable	recognise loss immediately

Sale price below fair value (paragraph 61)			
Profit	no profit	recognise profit immediately	no profit (note 1)
Loss *not* compensated by future lease payments at below market price	recognise loss immediately	recognise loss immediately	(note 1)
Loss compensated by future lease payments at below market price	defer and amortise loss	defer and amortise loss	(note 1)
Sale price above fair value (paragraph 61)			
Profit	defer and amortise profit	defer and amortise profit	defer and amortise profit (note 2)
Loss	no loss	no loss	(note 1)

Note 1   These parts of the table represent circumstances that would have been dealt with under paragraph 63 of the Standard. Paragraph 63 requires the carrying amount of an asset to be written down to fair value where it is subject to a sale and leaseback.

Note 2   The profit would be the difference between fair value and sale price as the carrying amount would have been written down to fair value in accordance with paragraph 63.

IAS 17's disclosure requirements for lessees and lessors apply equally to sale and leaseback transactions. The requirement in paragraph 35(d) of the standard for lessees to give a general description of their significant leasing arrangements will lead to the disclosure of unique or unusual provisions of the agreement or terms of the sale and leaseback transactions.[184] Furthermore, sale and leaseback transactions may meet the separate disclosure criteria for 'exceptional items' set out in IAS 1 – *Presentation of Financial Statements* (see Chapter 3).[185]

Sale and leaseback arrangements may also include features such as repurchase options. These are not addressed by IAS 17 and are discussed at 4.6 below.

3.6   Leases as financial instruments

In accordance with the accounting model in IAS 17, a finance lease is essentially regarded as an entitlement to receive, and an obligation to make, a stream of payments that are substantially the same as blended payments of principal and interest under a loan agreement. Consequently the lessor accounts for its investment in the amount receivable under the lease contract rather than for the leased asset itself. An operating lease, on the other hand, is regarded primarily as an uncompleted contract committing the lessor to provide the use of an asset in future periods in exchange for consideration similar to a fee for a service. The lessor continues to account for the leased asset itself rather than any amount receivable in the future under the contract.

Accordingly, a finance lease is regarded as a financial instrument and an operating lease is not regarded as a financial instrument (except as regards individual payments currently due and payable).[186]

In general the lease rights and obligations that come about as a result of IAS 17's recognition and measurement rules are not included within the scope of IAS 39. Finance lease assets and liabilities are not necessarily stated at the same amount as they would be if they were measured under IAS 39. The most obvious differences are those between the implicit interest rate (IIR) and the effective interest rate. The IIR (as described in 3.1.5 above) is the discount rate that, at the inception of the lease, causes the aggregate present value of the minimum lease payments (receivable during the non-cancellable lease term and any option periods that it is reasonably certain at inception the lessee will exercise) and the unguaranteed residual value to be equal to the sum of the fair value of the leased asset and any initial direct costs of the lessor.[187] The effective interest rate, by contrast, is the rate that exactly discounts estimated future cash payments or receipts through the expected life of the financial instrument.[188] The latter may include payments that would be considered contingent rentals, and hence excluded, from the calculation of the IIR and may take account of cash flows over a different period.

However, the following aspects of accounting for leases are within its scope:

(a)   lease receivables recognised by a lessor, which are subject to the derecognition and impairment provisions of IAS 39;

(b)   finance lease payables recognised by a lessee are subject to the derecognition provisions; and

(c)   derivatives that are embedded in leases are subject to IAS 39's embedded derivatives provisions.[189]

These matters are discussed further in 3.6.1 to 3.6.4 below.

IAS 39 will have little impact on traditional, straightforward leases. However, its requirements will have to be considered in many more complex situations.

3.6.1   Derecognition of lease receivables by lessors

A financial asset is derecognised when the contractual rights to the cash flows from that asset have expired.[190] This will apply to most leases at the end of the term when the lessor has no more right to cash flows from the lessee.

If the cash flows from the financial asset have not expired, it is derecognised when, and only when, the entity 'transfers' the asset within the specified meaning of the term in IAS 39, and the transfer has the effect that the entity has either:

(a)   transferred substantially all the risks and rewards of the asset; or

(b) neither transferred nor retained substantially all the risks and rewards of the asset and has not retained control of the asset.[191] If the rights to the cash are retained then there are other tests that must be met.[192]

An entity is regarded by IAS 39 as 'transferring' a financial asset if, and only if, it either:

(a) transfers the contractual rights to receive the cash flows of the financial asset; or

(b) retains the contractual rights to receive the cash flows of the financial asset, but assumes a contractual obligation to pay the cash flows to one or more recipients in an arrangement that meets the following conditions specified in the standard.[193]

>   (i) the entity has no obligation to pay amounts to the eventual recipients unless it collects equivalent amounts from the original asset. Short-term advances by the entity with the right of full recovery of the amount lent plus accrued interest at market rates do not violate this condition;
>
>   (ii) the entity is prohibited by the terms of the transfer contract from selling or pledging the original asset other than as security to the eventual recipients for the obligation to pay them cash flows; and
>
>   (iii) the entity has an obligation to remit any cash flows it collects on behalf of the eventual recipients without material delay. In addition, the entity is not entitled to reinvest such cash flows, except in cash or cash equivalents as defined in IAS 7 – *Cash Flow Statements* (see Chapter 39) during the short settlement period from the collection date to the date of required remittance to the eventual recipients, with any interest earned on such investments being passed to the eventual recipients.[194]

These requirements are relevant to common lease situations such as sub-leases and back-to-back leases, dealt with at 4.6 below. Derecognition of financial assets is a complex area discussed in particular in Chapter 30 at 4.

3.6.2 Impairment of lease receivables

If a lease receivable is impaired, for example, because the lessee is in default of lease payments, the amount of the impairment is measured as the difference between the carrying value of the receivable and the present value of the estimated future cash flows, discounted at the implicit interest rate used on initial recognition. Therefore, if the lessor makes an arrangement with the lessee and reschedules and/or reduces amounts due under the lease, the loss is by reference to the new carrying amount of the receivable, calculated by discounting the estimated future cash flows at the original implicit interest rate.[195] This methodology has been used in Example 22.14 at 3.3.3 above.

3.6.3 Derecognition of lease payables

IAS 39 requires an entity to derecognise (i.e. remove from its balance sheet) a financial liability (or a part of a financial liability) when, and only when, it is 'extinguished', that is, when the obligation specified in the contract is discharged, cancelled, or expires.[196] This will be achieved when the debtor either:

- discharges the liability (or part of it) by paying the creditor, normally with cash, other financial assets, goods or services; or

- is legally released from primary responsibility for the liability (or part of it) either by process of law or by the creditor.[197]

The difference between the carrying amount of a financial liability (or part of a financial liability) extinguished or transferred to another party and the consideration paid, including any non-cash assets transferred or liabilities assumed, is to be recognised in profit or loss.

In order to identify the part of a liability derecognised, it allocates the previous carrying amount of the financial liability between the part that continues to be recognised and the part that is derecognised based on the relative fair values of those parts on the date of the repurchase.[198]

The derecognition of financial liabilities is dealt with in Chapter 30 at 5.

3.6.4   *Embedded derivatives and contingent rentals*

It is a basic principle in IAS 39 that derivative instruments be recognised at fair value in the financial statements of entities (see Chapter 32). The same holds true of an embedded derivative, which is a component of a hybrid or combined instrument that also includes a non-derivative host contract; it has the effect that some of the cash flows of the combined instrument vary in a similar way to a stand-alone derivative. In other words it causes some or all of the cash flows that otherwise would be required by the contract to be modified according to a specified underlying.[199] IAS 39 does not require separation of the host contract and the derivative and separate recognition of the derivative in the financial statements of the entity if it is closely related to the economic characteristics and risks of the host contract.[200]

Common terms within leases that are embedded derivatives as defined by IAS 39 are:

- rental increases in line with a consumer price index;

- contingent rentals based on turnover or sales; or

- contingent rentals based on variable interest rates.

IAS 17 describes these lease terms as contingent rentals (see 3.1.7 above).

The Application Guidance to IAS 39 states that these embedded derivatives are closely related to the host lease contract; accordingly, they do not have to be separated from the lease contract as a whole, unless, for example, the lease is leveraged and the index relates to inflation in another economic environment.[201] This means that lessees continue to expense such contingent payments as they arise. In the case of more complex lease terms, reference should be made to IAS 39 paragraphs 10 to 13 and Section 5 of Chapter 29.

3.7   Service concessions and similar arrangements

'Service concession arrangements' have been developed as a new mechanism for procuring public services that give the public access to major economic and social facilities provided using private capital, although they are not necessarily arrangements solely between the public sector and private sector bodies.

The accounting challenge is to reflect the substance of these payments fairly in the financial statements of both of the contracting parties. It would be possible simply to take the contracts at fair value and account for the amounts paid and received as service payments; however, closer analysis may sometimes reveal that this is in reality a composite transaction whereby the public sector body is buying assets as well as services. In addition, there is the issue of how to account for the executory element of the contract, which may also include asset replacement and refurbishment as well as more obvious services.

The complex accounting issues raised by service concessions have been subject to prolonged debate by the IFRIC. Some service concessions may be deemed to be leases in substance under the terms of IFRIC 4 described at 2.2.1 above. However, these issues range across a number of other accounting standards, including IAS 11 – *Construction Contracts*, IAS 18 – *Revenue* and IAS 38 – *Intangible Assets*. Therefore accounting for service concessions is discussed separately in Chapter 23.

3.8   Disclosures required by IAS 17

This section deals only with the disclosure requirements of IAS 17 and those of other accounting standards to which it specifically refers. Disclosures required by SIC-27 are dealt with in 2.2.2 above.

3.8.1   Disclosures relating to financial assets and liabilities

Because finance lease assets and obligations and individual payments currently due and payable under operating leases are financial assets and liabilities, lessees and lessors have to meet the requirements of IFRS 7 – *Financial Instruments: Disclosures*, which came into effect for accounting periods beginning on or after 1 January 2007. This principally applies to the general requirements regarding classification and disclosure of financial assets and obligations in the balance sheet and disclosure of interest income and expense, together with other gains and losses arising from financial instruments, whether reflected in profit or loss or other comprehensive income. IFRS 7's disclosure requirements are covered in Chapter 34. However, if the lease arrangements contain more complex terms then there may be additional disclosure requirements, which are also summarised in Chapter 34.

3.8.2   Disclosure by lessees: finance leases

As well as meeting the IFRS7 disclosure requirements, IAS 17 requires lessees to make the following disclosures for finance leases:[202]

(a)   for each class of asset, the net carrying amount at the balance sheet date. Assets that are recognised under a finance lease will generally be considered to be the same class of assets with a similar nature that are owned, so there is no need to provide separate reconciliations of movements in owned assets from assets under finance leases;

(b)   a reconciliation between the total of future minimum lease payments at the balance sheet date, and their present value. The minimum lease payments will include adjustments that have been made following a rent review. In addition, an entity shall disclose the total of future minimum lease payments at the balance sheet date, and their present value, for each of the following periods:

(i)   not later than one year;

(ii)   later than one year and not later than five years;

(iii) later than five years.

(c)   contingent rents recognised as an expense in the period;

(d)   the total of future minimum sublease payments expected to be received under non-cancellable subleases at the balance sheet date;

(e)   a general description of the lessee's material leasing arrangements including, but not limited to, the following:

(i)   the basis on which contingent rent payable is determined;

(ii)   the existence and terms of renewal or purchase options and escalation clauses; and

(iii) restrictions imposed by lease arrangements, such as those concerning dividends, additional debt, and further leasing.

The following is an example of disclosures made in practice:

Extract 22.4: TeliaSonera AB (2007)

Notes to the Consolidated Financial Statements [extract]

29.   **Leasing agreements** [extract]

TeliaSonera as lessee [extract]

Finance leases

The Group's finance leases concerns computers and other IT equipment, production vehicles, company cars to employees, and other vehicles. There is no subleasing.

The carrying value of the leased assets as of the balance sheet date was as follows.

	December 31,	
SEK in millions	2007	2006
Cost	665	799
Less accumulated depreciation	−477	−545
Net carrying value of finance lease agreements	188	254

Deprecation and impairment losses totalled SEK 84 million and SEK 185 million for the years 2007 and 2006, respectively. Leasing fees paid in these years totalled SEK 82 million and SEK 185 million, respectively.

As of December 31, 2007, future minimum leasing fees and their present values as per finance lease agreements that could not be cancelled in advance and were longer than one year in duration were as follows.

Expected maturity, SEK in millions	Future minimum leasing fees	Present value of future minimum lease payments
2008	58	55
2009	35	32
2010	19	17
2011	12	10
2012	5	4
Later years	12	10
Total	141	128

As of balance sheet date, the present value of future minimum leasing fees under non-cancelable finance lease agreements was as follows.

SEK in millions	December 31, 2007	2006
Total future minimum leasing fees	141	208
Less interest charges	−13	−20
Present value of future minimum leasing fees	128	188

In addition, the leased asset is accounted for as property, plant and equipment of the reporting entity and the requirements for disclosure in accordance with IAS 16 (Chapter 16), IAS 36 (Chapter 18), IAS 38 (Chapter 15), IAS 40 (Chapter 17) and IAS 41 (Chapter 41) are applicable as appropriate.[203]

3.8.3   Disclosure by lessees: operating leases

In addition to meeting the requirements of IFRS 7, lessees must make the following disclosures for operating leases:[204]

(a)   the total of future minimum lease payments under non-cancellable operating leases for each of the following periods:

   (i)   not later than one year;

   (ii)   later than one year and not later than five years;

   (iii)   later than five years.

(b)   the total of future minimum sublease payments expected to be received under non-cancellable subleases at the balance sheet date;

(c)   lease and sublease payments recognised as an expense in the period, with separate amounts for minimum lease payments, contingent rents, and sublease payments;

(d)   a general description of the lessee's significant leasing arrangements including, but not limited to, the following:

   (i)   the basis on which contingent rent payable is determined;

   (ii)   the existence and terms of renewal or purchase options and escalation clauses; and

   (iii)   restrictions imposed by lease arrangements, such as those concerning dividends, additional debt and further leasing.

An example of the disclosures made by a lessee in respect of their obligations under operating leases is as follows.

Extract 22.5: TeliaSonera AB (2007)

Notes to the Consolidated Financial Statements [extract]
29.   Leasing agreements [extract]
TeliaSonera as lessee [extract]
Operating leases

TeliaSonera's operating lease agreements primarily concern office space, technical sites, land, computers and other equipment. Certain contracts include renewal options for various period of time. Subleasing consists mainly of office premises.

Future minimum leasing fees under operating lease agreements in effect as of December 31, 2007 that could not be canceled in advance and were in excess of one year were as follows.

Expected maturity, SEK in millions	Future minimum leasing fees	Minimum sublease payments
2008	1,797	27
2009	1,455	10
2010	1,111	6
2011	86	1
2012	794	–
Later years	2,033	–
Total	8,056	44

In 2007 and 2006, total rent and leasing fees paid were SEK 2,678 million and SEK 2,128 million, respectively. In these years, revenue for subleased items totaled SEK 27 million and SEK 46 million, respectively.

At the end of 2007 office space and technical site leases covered approximately 682,000 square meters, including approximately 5,000 square meters of office space for TeliaSonera's principal executive offices, located at Sturegatan 1 in Stockholm, Sweden. Apart from certain short-term leases, leasing terms range mainly between 3 and 21 years with an average term of approximately 6 years. All leases have been entered into on conventional commercial terms. Certain contracts include renewal options for various periods of time.

Rezidor Hotel Group AB makes the following disclosures with regard to its contingent rentals, first in respect of the amounts recognised as an expense in the period and second its commitments under such leases:

Extract 22.6: Rezidor Hotel Group AB (2007)

Notes to the group accounts [extract]
Note 12   RENTAL EXPENSE

TEUR	For the Year Ended December 31	
	2007	2006
Fixed rent [1]	161,120	144,139
Variable rent [2]	34,230	28,743
Guarantee payments [3]	4,902	10,210
Total rent	200,252	183,092

[1]   Fixed rent represent all fixed lease payments (or minimum lease payments) made to the owners of the leased hotels. This line item also includes rental costs of premises which are leased for administration purposes.

2)   Variable rent represent all variable lease payments (or contingent lease payments) made to the owners of the leased hotels (based on the underlying contract type) which are primarily based on the revenue of the leased hotels.

3)   Guarantee payments are payments (or shortfalls payments) made to the owners of the managed hotels (based on the underlying contract type) when Rezidor has guaranteed a certain annual result to the property owner. The guarantee payments represent the difference between the guaranteed and achieved result.

Notes to the group accounts [extract]

Note 38   MANAGEMENT CONTRACT COMMITMENTS

Under our management agreements, we provide management services to third-party hotel proprietors. We derive revenue primarily from base fees determined as a percentage of total hotel revenue and incentive management fees defined as a percentage of the gross operating profit or adjusted gross operating profit of the hotel operations.

In certain circumstances, we guarantee the hotel proprietor a minimum result measured by adjusted gross operating profit or some other financial measure (a "guarantee"). Under such contracts, in the event that the actual result of a hotel is less than the guaranteed amount, we compensate the hotel proprietor for the shortfall. However, in most agreements with such clauses, our obligation to compensate for such shortfall amount is typically limited to two or three times the annual guarantee (the "guarantee cap").

As at the end of the year, Rezidor had granted a certain level of financial commitment in 46 Management contracts in 2007, as compared to 41 in 2006. The management contracts containing such financial risk for the group will expire as presented in the table below:

	2007		2006
	Number of		
	management contracts		Number of leasing
Year	expiring	Year	agreements expiring
2007-2009	0	2006-2009	0
2010-2014	5	2010-2014	5
2015-2019	7	2015-2019	7
2020-2024	11	2020-2024	11
2025-2029	15	2025-2029	14
2030-2034	6	2030-2034	3
2035-2039	1	2035-2039	0
2040-2045	1	2040-2045	1

The following table presents the company's capped contractual obligations under all management contracts with financial guarantees and show the maximum capped financial exposure:

Total maximum future capped guarantee payments

TEUR	2007	2006
Within 1 year	81,239	69,612
1-5 years	139,555	147,949
After 5 years	34,121	42,692
Total	254,915	260,253

The capped guarantee payment includes the contingent liabilities as disclosed in note 36 (i.e. guarantees provided for management contracts). For the full fiscal year 2006, Rezidor paid TEUR 4,902 (10,210 in 2006) as shortfalls under its management agreements with guarantees (see Note 12).

3.8.4   Disclosure by lessors: finance leases

In addition to meeting the requirements in IFRS 7 (see 3.8.1 above), lessors must disclose the following for finance leases:

(a)   a reconciliation between the gross investment in the lease at the balance sheet date, and the present value of minimum lease payments receivable at the balance sheet date. In addition, an entity shall disclose the gross investment in the lease and the present value of minimum lease payments receivable at the balance sheet date, for each of the following periods:

(i)   not later than one year;

(ii)   later than one year and not later than five years;

(iii)   later than five years;

(b)   unearned finance income;

(c)   the unguaranteed residual values accruing to the benefit of the lessor;

(d)   the accumulated allowance for uncollectible minimum lease payments receivable;

(e)   contingent rents recognised as income in the period;

(f)   a general description of the lessor's material leasing arrangements.[205]

IAS 17 also recommends but does not require disclosure of the gross investment less unearned income in new business added during the period, after deducting the relevant amounts for cancelled leases as a useful indicator of growth.[206]

TeliaSonera discloses its activities as a finance lessor as follows:

Extract 22.7: TeliaSonera AB (2007)

Notes to the Consolidated Financial Statements [extract]

29.   **Leasing Agreements** [extract]

TeliaSonera as lessor [extract]

Finance leases

The leasing portfolio of TeliaSonera's customer financing operations in Sweden, Finland and Denmark comprises financing of products related to TeliaSonera's product offerings. The term of the contract stock is approximately 13 quarters. The term of new contracts signed in 2007 is 12 quarters. Of all contracts, 81 percent carry a fixed interest rate and 19 percent a floating rate. Most contracts include renewal options. In Finland, TeliaSonera under a finance lease agreement provides electricity meters with SIM cards for automated reading to a power company as part of TeliaSonera's service package. The term of the agreement is 15 years and carries a fixed interest rate.

As of the balance sheet date, the present value of future minimum lease payment receivables under non-cancelable finance lease agreements was as follows.

	December 31,	
SEK in millions	**2007**	**2006**
Gross investment in finance lease contracts	1,125	848
Less unearned finance revenues	−188	−129
Net investment in finance lease contracts	937	719
Less: Unguaranteed residual values of leased properties for the benefit of the lessor	−3	−0
Present value of future minimum lease payment receivables	934	719

As of December 31, 2007, the gross investment and present value of receivables relating to future minimum lease payments under non-cancelable finance lease agreements were distributed as follows.

Expected maturity, SEK in millions	Gross investment	Present value of receivables relating to future minimum lease payments
2008	270	257
2009	208	183
2010	130	110
2011	63	51
2012	47	36
Later years	407	297
Total	1,125	934

Reserve for doubtful receivables regarding minimum lease payments totaled SEK 6 million as of December 31, 2007. Credit losses on leasing receivables are reduced by gains from the sale of equipment returned.

3.8.5 Disclosure by lessors: operating leases

Lessors must, in addition to meeting the requirements of IFRS 7, disclose the following for operating leases:

(a)   the future minimum lease payments under non-cancellable operating leases in the aggregate and for each of the following periods:

   (i)   not later than one year;

   (ii)   later than one year and not later than five years;

   (iii) later than five years;

(b)   total contingent rents recognised as income in the period;

(c)   a general description of the lessor's leasing arrangements.[207]

TeliaSonera's lessor interests in operating leases are disclosed as follows.

Extract 22.8: TeliaSonera AB (2007)

Notes to the Consolidated Financial Statements [extract]
29.   Leasing agreements [extract]
TeliaSonera as lessor [extract]
Operating leases

The leasing portfolio refers to the international carrier business and includes some twenty agreements with other international operators and over 100 over contracts. Contract periods range between 10 and 25 years, with an average term of 20 years.

The carrying value of the leased assets as of the balance sheet date was as follows:

SEK in millions	December 31,	
	2007	2006
Cost	3,689	3,390
Less accumulated depreciation	−2,211	−1,799
Less accumulated impairment losses	−300	−300
Gross carrying value	1,178	1,291
Plus prepaid sales costs	2	2
Less prepaid lease payments	−800	−722
Net value of operating lease agreements	380	571

Depreciation and impairment losses totalled SEK 346 million in 2007 and SEK 330 million in 2006.

Future minimum lease payment receivables under operating lease agreements in effect as of December 31, 2007 that could not be cancelled in advance and were in excess of one year were as follows.

Expected maturity, SEK in millions	Future minimum lease payment
2008	242
2009	138
2010	117
2011	28
2012	18
Later years	21
Total	564

In addition, the leased asset is accounted for as a fixed asset of the reporting entity and the requirements for disclosure in accordance with IAS 16 (Chapter 15), IAS 36 (Chapter 18), IAS 38 (Chapter 14), IAS 40 (Chapter 17) and IAS 41 (Chapter 41) as appropriate.[208]

4   PRACTICAL ISSUES

4.1   Lease classification

It goes without saying that lessees and lessors often have different and incompatible goals when entering into leases. Many lessors have little desire to take the residual risk in an asset, as they are banks or other financial institutions and their prime business is to provide finance. Many lessees prefer not to capitalise leased assets because capitalisation adversely affects their debt/equity ratio and return on assets ratios. These differences underlie many of the problems with lease classification.

4.1.1   *The residual value of an asset*

If the net present value of the residual value of an asset is significant and is not guaranteed by the lessee or a party related to it, then the lease is likely to be classified as an operating lease. This is explained by the fact that the risks of recovering the significant residual value will be the lessor's, consequently it is unlikely that 'substantially all' of the risks and rewards of ownership will have passed to the lessee. There are frequently problems of interpretation regarding the significance of residual values in lease classification. Lessees may find it difficult to obtain information about the unguaranteed residual values. On the other hand, lessees may guarantee all or part of the residual value of the asset and this has to be taken into account in the lease classification.

A   Residual value guarantees by the lessee

Although a lessee may give a residual value guarantee in a lease, the lease itself may be structured so that the most likely outcome of events relating to the residual value indicates that no significant risk will attach to the lessee.

Example 22.20:   A lease structured such that the most likely outcome is that the lessee has no significant residual risk

Brief details of a motor vehicle lease are:

Fair value   –   €10,000
Rentals   –   20 monthly payments @ €300, followed by a final rental of
                  €2,000

At the end of the lease, the lessee sells vehicle as agent for the lessor and if sold for:

(i)   more than €3,000, 99% of the excess is repaid to the lessee; or

(ii)   less than €3,000, lessee pays the deficit to the lessor up to a maximum of 0.4 pence per mile above 25,000 miles p.a. on average that the leased vehicle has done.

The net present value of the minimum lease payments excluding the guarantee amounts to €7,365.

This lease involves a guarantee by the lessee of the residual value of the leased vehicle of €3,000, as a result of (ii) above. However, the guarantee will only be called upon if both:

(a)   the vehicle's actual residual value is less than €3,000; and

(b)   the vehicle has travelled more than 25,000 miles per year on average over the lease term.

Further, the lessee is only liable to pay a certain level of the residual; namely, €100 for each 2,500 miles above 25,000 miles that the vehicle has done.

One could argue that the guarantee should be assumed to apply only to the extent that experience or expectations of the sales price and/or the mileage that vehicles have done (and the inter-relationship between these) indicate that a residual payment by the lessee will be made and if this best estimate is that a zero or minimal payment will be made, this should be used for the purposes of lease classification. This would be applying the principles in IAS 37 to the calculation of the liability. However, IAS 17 states that the amount of the guarantee is 'the maximum amount that could, in any event, become payable'. Therefore, the standard appears to require the maximum guarantee of €3,000 to be taken into account.

By taking the maximum guarantee into account, the present value of the minimum lease payments could well equal the fair value of the asset. This does not necessarily mean that the lease will be automatically fall to be treated as a finance lease. This depends on the substance of the arrangement and the entity might take account of the residual it estimates it will actually pay in making this assessment.

B   Residual value guarantors

A lessee and lessor may legitimately classify the same lease differently because, for example, the lessor has received a residual value guarantee provided by a third party.[209] Residual value guarantors undertake to acquire the assets from the lessor at an agreed amount at the end of the lease term because they can dispose of the assets on a ready and reliable market. As a result, the lease is an operating lease for the lessee and a finance lease for the lessor. This is particularly common with vehicle leases where there is an efficient second-hand market, including price guides, many car dealers and car auctions. Residual value guarantors may be prepared to take the residual risk with many types of assets as long as there is a second-hand market.

4.1.2   Rental rebates

IAS 17 suggests that an indicator that the lease is a finance lease is that 'the gains or losses from the fluctuation in the fair value of the residual fall to the lessee (for example, in the form of a rent rebate equalling most of the sales proceeds at the end of the lease)'.[210] This is because a lessee that obtains most of the sales proceeds has received all of the risks and rewards of the residual value in the asset. This would indicate that the lessor has already been compensated for the transaction and hence that it is a finance lease.

Other leases require the asset to be sold at the end of the lease but the lessor receives the first tranche of proceeds and only those proceeds above a certain level are remitted to the lessee. These arrangements may have a different significance as the lessor may be taking the proceeds to meet its unguaranteed residual value. Lessors are prepared to take risks on residual values of such assets if there is an established and reliable market in which to sell them. This could mean that the gains or losses from the fluctuation in the fair value of the residual do not fall predominantly to the lessee and, in the absence of other factors, could indicate that it is an operating lease.

Example 22.21:   Rental rebates

The lease arrangements are as in Example 22.20, except that at end of the lease, the lessee sells the vehicle as agent for the lessor, and if it is sold for

(i)   up to £3,000, all of the proceeds are received by the lessor; or

(ii)   more than £3,000, 99% of excess is repaid to the lessee. The lessee does not have to make good any deficit, should one arise.

In this example, it appears that the lessor is using the sale proceeds to meet its unguaranteed residual value but it is also taking the first loss provision. Only thereafter does the lessee gain or lose from the fluctuations in the fair value. The lessee's minimum lease payments have a net present value of €7,365, it has not guaranteed the residual value at all and is not exposed to any risk of any fall in value, although it may benefit from increases in the fair value in excess of €3,000. On balance this indicates that the arrangement is an operating lease.

4.2   Modifying the terms of leases

Lessees may renegotiate lease terms for a variety of reasons. They may wish to extend the term over which they have a right to use the asset or to alter the number of assets that they have a right to use. They may consider that the lease is too expensive by comparison with current market terms. The renegotiations may deal with several such issues simultaneously. Lessors may also renegotiate leases, for example one lessor may sell the lease to another that offers to provide the lease service more cheaply to the lessee, usually because the new lessor's transactions have different tax consequences. Lease contracts may allow for changes in payments if specified contingencies occur, for example a change in taxation or interest rates.

The standard has little to say on the consequences such renegotiations. It states:

> 'If at any time the lessee and the lessor agree to change the provisions of the lease, other than by renewing the lease, in a manner that would have resulted in a different classification of the lease ... if the changed terms had been in effect at the inception of the lease, the revised agreement is regarded as a new agreement over its term.'[211]

As described at 2.3.3 above, the consequences of a different classification are clear. A revised agreement that is reclassified (e.g. an operating lease is reassessed as a finance lease or *vice versa*) is accounted for prospectively in accordance with the revised terms. However, IAS 17 leaves many questions of application unanswered. It provides no practical guidance on what to take into account to determine whether there would have been a different classification. It does not explain how to account for the consequences of modifications, whether or not they would lead to a different classification. These matters are described at 4.2.1 to 4.2.3 below.

Other changes to lease terms that do not lead to reclassification but that nevertheless need to be accounted for (for example variations due to changes in rates of taxation or interest rates) are discussed in 4.2.4 below.

As discussed at 2.3.3 above, changes in estimates (for example, changes in estimates of the economic life or of the residual value of the leased item) or changes in circumstances (for example, default by the lessee) do not result in a different classification.[212] Changes in estimates also include the renewal of a lease or the execution of a purchase option, if these were not considered probable at the inception of the lease.

4.2.1 Determining whether there is a different classification

Paragraph 13 of IAS 17 states that, if the terms of a lease are modified so that the revised terms would have resulted in a different classification of the lease had they been in effect at inception, the revised agreement is regarded as a new agreement over its term.

The modification must, therefore, be one that affects the risks and rewards incidental to ownership of the asset by changing the terms and cash flows of the existing lease, such as a renegotiation that changes the duration and/or the payments due under the lease.

One of the indicators used in practice is an assessment of the net present value of the minimum lease payments and whether or not these amount to substantially all of the fair value of the leased asset. An entity might use this test to help assess whether the revised lease is a finance or operating lease, in conjunction with a reassessment of the other factors described at 2.3.2 above. Therefore, the entity might use one of the following methods to calculate the net present value:

(a)   recalculate the net present value based on the revised lease term and cash flows (and revised residual value, if relevant), which will result in a different implicit interest rate to that used in the original calculation;

(b)   take into consideration the changes in the agreement but calculate the present value of the asset and liability using the interest rate implicit in the original lease. This approach, which is consistent with the remeasurement of the carrying value of financial instruments applying the effective interest rate method, as required by IAS 39,[213] will result in a 'catch up' adjustment as at the date of the reassessment; or

(c)   consider the revised agreement to be a new lease and assess the classification based on the terms of the new agreement and the fair value and useful life of the asset at the date of the revision. The inference of this method, unlike (a) and (b), is that the entity already considers that there is likely to be a new classification to the lease, based on an assessment of other factors.

A lessee under an operating lease will be able to apply methods (a) and (c) but (b) will not be available to it unless it has sufficient information to be able to calculate the IIR at the inception of the original lease. Lessees that are party to more complex leases or sale and leaseback arrangements are more likely to have the necessary information available to them.

Each of these three approaches is likely to lead to a different net present value for the minimum lease payments. They are compared in the following example.

Example 22.22:   Modifying the terms of leases

Details of a non-cancellable lease taken out on the first day of the year are as follows:

(i)   Fair value = €25,000

(ii)   Estimated useful life of asset = 8 years

(iii) Five annual rentals payable in advance of €4,200

(iv) At the end of year 5, the asset must be sold and all proceeds up to €8,292 taken by the lessor. If any amount in excess of €8,292 is received, 99% of the excess is repaid to the lessee.

The lease does not contain any renewal options.

The lessee assesses this as an operating lease because the terms suggest that substantially all of the risks and rewards of ownership have not been transferred to it – the lease term is only 62.5% of the useful life of the asset and there is clearly significant residual value.

At the end of year 2, the parties renegotiate the lease, with the changes coming into effect on the first day of year 3. The lease term is to be extended for a further two years, making the term seven years in total. Payments for the four years 2011-2014 have been reduced to €4,000 and €1,850 is payable for 2015. At the time of the renegotiation the estimated fair value of the asset is €17,500 and its residual value at the end of 2015 is €1,850.

The implicit interest rate in the original lease can be calculated because the maximum amount receivable by the lessor on the sale of the asset at the end of the lease term is the residual value (on the assumption that the lessor disregards any potential upside in its contingent 1%); the IIR is 5.92%, as follows:

Year	Capital sum at start of period €	Rental paid €	Capital sum during period €	Finance charge (5.92% per annum) €	Capital sum at end of period €
2009	25,000	4,200	20,800	1,231	22,031
2010	22,031	4,200	17,831	1,056	18,887
2011	18,887	4,200	14,687	869	15,556
2012	15,556	4,200	11,356	672	12,028
2013	12,028	4,200	7,828	464	8,292
		21,000		4,292	

This supports the lessee's assessment that this is an operating lease as the present value of the minimum lease payments is €18,588, which is 74.35% of the fair value of the asset.

If these revised terms had been in existence at inception then the implicit interest rate and NPV calculation would have been as follows. This corresponds to (a) above.

Year	Capital sum at start of period €	Rental paid €	Capital sum during period €	Finance charge (4.10% per annum) €	Capital sum at end of period €
2009	25,000	4,200	20,800	853	21,653
2010	21,653	4,200	17,453	715	18,168
2011	18,168	4,000	14,168	581	14,749
2012	14,749	4,000	10,749	441	11,190
2013	11,190	4,000	7,190	294	7,484
2014	7,484	4,000	3,484	143	3,627
2015	3,627	1,850	1,777	73	1,850
		26,250		3,100	

The NPV of the lessee's minimum lease payments is €23,603 which is 94.41% of the fair value of the asset. The lease would be classified as a finance lease .

Method (b) results in the following calculation:

Year	Capital sum at start of period €	Rental paid €	Capital sum during period €	Finance charge (5.92% per annum) €	Capital sum at end of period €
2009	25,000	4,200	20,800	1,231	22,031
2010	22,031	4,200	17,831	1,056	18,887
2011	17,566	4,000	13,566	803	14,369
2012	14,369	4,000	10,369	613	10,982
2013	10,982	4,000	6,982	414	7,396
2014	7,396	4,000	3,396	201	3,597
2015	3,597	1,850	1,747	103	1,850
		26,250		4,421	

The present value of the total payments over the revised lease term at the original discount rate is €22,585, which is 90.34% of the fair value of the asset at commencement of the lease. In order to make the computation, an adjustment is made to the capital amount as at the date that the lease is renegotiated. The outstanding amount is recomputed from €18,887 (the balance at the end of 2009 calculated using the original assumptions) to €17,566, the amount that corresponds to the new assumptions.

If method (c) is applied, the modified lease is considered as if it were a new five year lease. The IIR calculated prospectively over the remaining term is now 6.13%

Year	Capital sum at start of period €	Rental paid €	Capital sum during period €	Finance charge (6.13% per annum) €	Capital sum at end of period €
2011	17,500	4,000	13,500	827	14,327
2012	14,327	4,000	10,327	633	10,960
2013	10,960	4,000	6,960	426	7,386
2014	7,386	4,000	3,386	207	3,593
2015	3,593	1,850	1,743	107	1,850
		17,850		2,200	

The present value of the remaining payments is €16,126, which is 92.15% of the fair value of the asset (€17,500) at the date of entering into the new lease.

In this example, all three methods result in a present value of the minimum lease payments that exceeds 90% but this would not, of course, always be the case. It must be stressed that all features of the arrangement must be considered in order to assess whether or not the lease transfers substantially all of the risks and rewards of ownership.

4.2.2 Accounting for reclassified leases

IAS 17 states that the revised agreement is treated as a new agreement over its term.

If the original lease was a finance lease and the revised lease is an operating lease, then the balances relating to the finance lease must be derecognised. For the lessee, this involves derecognising both the asset (which will have been depreciated up to the point of derecognition over the shorter of the useful life or the lease term) and the finance lease liability. Finance lease derecognition is discussed further at 4.3 below.

If the original lease was an operating lease and the revised lease is a finance lease, then any balances resulting from recognising the lease cost on a straight line basis will be expensed and the balances relating to the finance lease must be recognised for the first time.

Although the standard says that 'the revised agreement is regarded as a new agreement over its term,'[214] this refers to classification; there is no consensus regarding the measurement of assets and liabilities as at this point.

The most obvious interpretation is that the revised lease is accounted for as a new lease as from the date on which the terms were changed, based on the fair value of the assets as at the date of revision. This is consistent with using either method (a) or method (c) in 4.2.1 above to help determine the revised classification. An example of the calculation is in Example 22.22 above – method (c) calculates the assets and liabilities as if the revised agreement were a new lease as from the date of reassessment.

However, some consider that the new lease can be accounted for using method (b) above, by taking into consideration the changes in the agreement but calculating the present value of the asset and liability by using the interest rate implicit in the original lease. This uses an accepted methodology and is consistent with the fact that there has, in fact, only been a change to the original terms and not a completely new lease; it also has the advantage that the revised fair value of the assets does not have to be known.

If the original lease agreement and the revised lease agreement are both finance leases, then the modification will have accounting consequences that are discussed in the following section.

4.2.3   Accounting for modifications to finance leases

If the rights under a finance lease have changed without a change in the classification, these changes to lease term and cash flows must be accounted for. Once again, the accounting consequences are not dealt with by IAS 17.

The two most obvious methods of calculating the impact of the changes are as follows:

(a)   Even though the classification has not changed, the revised agreement is accounted for as if it were a new lease. The calculation will be based on the fair value and useful life of the asset at the date of the revision.

(b)   Use the original IIR to discount the revised minimum lease payments and (for a lessee) adjust any change in lease liability to the carrying amount of the asset. Lessors will adjust the carrying value of the asset, taking gains or losses to income. As noted before, this approach is consistent with the requirements of IAS 39 when the effective interest rate method is applied and the cash flows change.[215]

These are described in 4.2.1 and example 22.22 above (method (c) and method (b)). For lessees, both of these methods will affect the carrying value of the asset and hence its future amortisation.

Another method that might be considered is to reflect changes prospectively over the remaining term of the lease; this is only likely to be appropriate if the cash flows are modified but all other rights remain unchanged. Some of the circumstances in which such changes can arise are considered at 4.2.4 below.

Example 22.23:   Accounting for lease modifications

The details of a lease are as in Example 22.22 above, except that the lease has an original duration of six years with an annual rent of €4,200, rather than five years. The present value of the minimum lease payments is €21,931, which is 87.72% of the fair value of the leased asset, calculated as follows:

Year	Capital sum at start of period	Rental paid	Capital sum during period	Finance charge (5.92% per annum)	Capital sum at end of period
	€	€	€	€	€
2009	21,931	4,200	17,731	1,050	18,780
2010	18,780	4,200	14,580	863	15,443
2011	15,443	4,200	11,243	666	11,909
2012	11,909	4,200	7,709	456	8,165
2013	8,165	4,200	3,965	235	4,200
2014	4,200	4,200	0	0	0
		25,200		3,270	

The directors of the entity assess this as a finance lease, taking account of all of the circumstances surrounding the agreement. The entity capitalise the asset at €21,931 at commencement of the lease and recognise an equivalent liability.

At the end of year 2, the lease term is extended for a further year, making the term seven years in total. Payments for the four years 2011-2014 are reduced to €4,000 and €1,850 is payable for 2015.

The asset (which has a useful life to the lessee of six years) has been depreciated on a straight line basis for two years and its carrying amount is €14,620, while the lessee's lease liability (as calculated above) is €15,443:

(a) If the modification is treated as a new lease, it will be accounted for as follows, using the revised fair value and IIR calculated at Example 22.22 above:

Year	Capital sum at start of period €	Rental paid €	Capital sum during period €	Finance charge (6.13% per annum) €	Capital sum at end of period €
2011	16,126	4,000	12,126	743	12,868
2012	12,868	4,000	8,868	543	9,412
2013	9,412	4,000	5,412	331	5,743
2014	5,743	4,000	1,743	107	1,850
2015	1,850	1,850	0	0	0
		17,850		1,724	

Therefore, the entity will derecognise both the leased asset of €14,620 and liability of €15,443, recognising a net gain of €823. The new asset of €16,126 will be depreciated prospectively over the remaining life of 5 years.

(b) If the modification is accounted for by restating the liability using the original IIR of 5.92%, the liability will be €16,178 calculated as follows:

Year	Capital sum at start of period €	Rental paid €	Capital sum during period €	Finance charge (5.92% per annum) €	Capital sum at end of period €
2011	16,178	4,000	12,178	721	12,899
2012	12,899	4,000	8,899	526	9,425
2013	9,425	4,000	5,425	322	5,747
2014	5,747	4,000	1,747	103	1,850
2015	1,850	1,850	0	0	0
		17,850		1,672	

The entity will increase the lease liability by €735 (from €15,443 to €16,178) but it will increase the asset's carrying mount by the same amount from €14,620 to €15,355 which will be depreciated prospectively over the asset's remaining life of 5 years.

4.2.4 Tax and interest variation clauses and similar modifications

The relationship between leasing and taxation is frequently complex. It depends on whether tax deductions or taxable income are based on amounts receivable or payable in accordance with the lease or on the amounts that are taken to the income statement. It further depends on the availability of tax deductions for the cost of leased assets and who is able to claim these deductions. Some lessors draw up leases that are based on a post-tax return that takes account of these factors. These leases include tax variation clauses that enable lessors to change the amounts receivable from the lessee so that their post-tax return remains constant. The rental could be adjusted in a number of different ways, e.g. a new fixed payment, an up-front sum or an adjustment on a rental-by-rental basis.

The variations are unlikely of themselves to change the lease classification because their potential impact will have been taken into account in making that original assessment. Nor are they likely to lead to an impairment of the lessor's finance lease asset (assuming that it is a finance lease) as the profitability of the lease (on a post-tax basis) is unaffected.

IAS 17 does not refer to variation clauses so the question is whether the change is a variety of contingent rent, defined by the standard as that portion of the lease payments that is not fixed in amount but is based on a factor that varies other than with the passage of time, such as percentage of sales, amount of usage, price indices or market rates of interest[216], or another type of event. Contingent rent is recognised when it is incurred. This means that a reduction in rentals because of a reduction in rates of taxation would be a negative contingent rent.

However, it is also argued that the effect of the change in tax rates is far more like the lease modifications described at 4.2.3 above and there is some merit in this argument. As a result, some lessors take the view that the most relevant method of accounting for the changes is to use the original IIR to discount the revised minimum lease payments, taking the change in value of the finance lease asset to income (this is method (b) as described in 4.2.3). If rental payments decrease because the revised rate of taxation is lower, lessors applying this approach will recognise a loss on remeasuring the asset.

Leases may also contain interest variation clauses which adjust the rental by reference to movements in bank base rates or similar. As market rates of interest are specific examples of contingent rent in the standard, they must be accounted for as such.

4.3   Derecognition of finance leases and termination payments

The expectations of lessors and lessees regarding the timing of termination of a lease may affect the classification of a lease as either operating or finance. This is because it will affect the expected lease term, level of payments under the lease and expected residual value of the lease assets.

Termination during the primary lease term will generally not be anticipated at the lease inception because the lessee can be assumed to be using the asset for at least that period. In addition, such an early termination will be unlikely because most leases are non-cancellable. A termination payment is usually required which will give the lessor an amount equivalent to most or all of the rental receipts which would have been received if no such termination had taken place, which means that it is reasonably certain at inception that the lease will continue to expiry.

However, there are consequences if the lease is terminated. The issues for finance lessees and lessors are discussed in the following sections.

4.3.1   Finance leases – lessee

Early termination of a finance lease (except as part of a renegotiation or business combination or similar larger arrangement) results in derecognition of the capitalised asset by the lessee, with any remaining balance of the capitalised asset being written off as a loss on disposal. Any payment made by the lessee will reduce the lease obligation that is being carried in the balance sheet. If either a part of this obligation is not eliminated or the termination payment exceeds the previously existing obligation, then the remainder or excess will be included as a gain or loss (respectively) on derecognition of a financial liability.

A similar accounting treatment is required where the lease terminates at the expected date and there is a residual at least partly guaranteed by the lessee. For the lessee, a payment made under such a guarantee will reduce the obligation to the lessor as the guaranteed residual would obviously be included in the lessee's finance lease obligation. If any part of the guaranteed residual is not called upon, then the lessee would treat this as a profit on derecognition of a financial liability.

The effect on the derecognition of the capitalised asset will depend on the extent to which the lessee expected to make the residual payment as this will have affected the level to which the capitalised asset has been depreciated. For example, if the total guaranteed residual was not expected to become payable by the lessee, then the depreciation charge may have been calculated to give a net book value at the end of the lease term equal to the residual element not expected to become payable. If this estimate was correct then the remaining obligation will equal the net book value of the relevant asset, so that the gain on derecognition of the liability will be equal to the loss on derecognition of the asset.

Example 22.24:   Early termination of finance leases by lessees

We can consider this in the context of Example 22.21 in 4.1.2 above, where there is effectively a guarantee of a residual of €3,000 dependent on the mileage done by the leased vehicle. Assuming that the lease is capitalised as a finance lease, if the lessee considers at the lease inception that the guarantee will not be called upon, then he will depreciate the vehicle to an estimated residual value of €3,000 over the lease term. In the event that his estimate is found to be correct, then the loss on disposal of the asset at its written down value will be equal and opposite to the gain on derecognition of the lease obligation of €3,000. However, if, for example, €1,000 of the guarantee was called upon, whereas the lessee had estimated that it would not be, then the net book value of €3,000 and the unused guarantee of €2,000 will both be derecognised and a loss of €1,000 will be shown on disposal of the vehicle.

4.3.2   Finance leases – lessor

Any termination payment received by a lessor upon an early termination will reduce the lessor's net investment in the lease shown as a receivable. If the termination payment is greater than the carrying amount of the net investment, the lessor will account for a gain on derecognition of the lease; conversely, if the termination payment is smaller than the net investment, a loss will be shown.

Losses on termination in the ordinary course of business are less likely to arise because a finance lease usually has termination terms so that the lessor is compensated fully for early termination and the lessor has legal title to the asset. The lessor can continue to include the asset in current assets as a receivable to the extent that sales proceeds or new finance lease receivables are expected to arise. If the asset is designated as held for sale then the requirements of IFRS 5 will apply (see Chapter 4). If the asset is then re-leased under an operating lease, the asset may be transferred to property, plant and equipment and depreciated over its remaining useful life.

To some extent, these two reasons (full compensation and legal title remaining with the lessor) that explain why losses on termination of a finance lease are unlikely to arise, are complementary. If the termination payment is intended to give full compensation, then the asset may be retained by the lessee and sold with any proceeds going to him. On the other hand, if the termination payment is not structured in this way then the lessor will repossess the asset and sell or re-lease it.

4.4   Payments made in connection with the termination of operating leases

Payments for terminating operating leases or payments between a lessee and a third party regarding a lease are extremely common but not all are directly addressed by either IAS 17 or SIC-15. In addition, neither statement addresses payments made between a lessee and a third party in connection with a lease. The following example addresses a variety of payments that might arise in connection with an operating lease over a property:

Example 22.25:   Payments made in connection with terminating an operating lease

Treatment in the financial statements of

Transaction	Lessor	Old tenant	New tenant
Lessor pays			
Old lessee – lessor intends to renovate the building.	Expense unless it meets the definition of an asset under IAS 16 (note 1)	Recognise income immediately (note 1)	
New tenant – an incentive to occupy	Prepayment amortised over the lease term on a straight line basis under SIC-15 (see 3.4.5 above)		Deferred lease incentive amortised over the lease term on a straight line basis under SIC-15 (see 3.4.2 above).

Building alterations specific to the lessee with no further value to the lessor after completion of the lease period.	Prepayment amortised over the lease term on a straight line basis under SIC-15 (see 3.4.5 above)		Leasehold improvements capitalised and depreciated or expensed as maintenance expenditure. Deferred lease incentive amortised over the lease term on a straight line basis under SIC-15 (see 3.4.2 above).

Old tenant pays

Lessor, to vacate the leased premises early	Recognised as income immediately to the extent not already recognised (note 2)	Recognised as expense immediately to the extent not already recognised (note 2)	
New tenant to take over the lease		Recognise as an expense immediately (note 3)	Recognise as income immediately, unless compensation for above market rentals, in which case amortise over expected lease term (note 3)

New tenant pays

	Lessor	*Old tenant*	*New tenant*
Lessor to secure the right to obtain a lease agreement	Recognise as deferred revenue under IAS 17 and amortise over the lease term on a straight line basis(see 3.4.4 above)		Recognise as a prepayment under IAS 17 and amortise over the lease term on a straight line basis (see 3.4.1 above).
Old tenant to buy out the lease agreement		Recognise as a gain immediately (note 4)	Recognised as an intangible asset with a finite economic life (note 4)

Note 1   A payment by a lessor to a lessee to terminate the lease is not dealt with under IAS 17 or SIC-15. If the lessor's payment meets the definition of a cost of an item of property, plant and equipment it must be capitalised.[217] If not, the payment will be expensed, as it does not meet the definition of an intangible asset in IAS 38.[218] As the lessee has no further performance obligation the receipt should be income.

Note 2   A payment made by the lessee to the lessor to get out of a lease agreement does not meet the appropriate definitions of an asset in IAS 16 or IAS 38 and does not fall within IAS 17 as there is no longer a lease – the payments are not for the use of the asset. Therefore it should be expensed. Similarly, from the lessor's perspective, income should be recorded.

Note 3   A payment made by an existing tenant to a new tenant to take over the lease would also not meet the definition of an asset under IAS 16 or IAS 38 (see above notes) and falls outside IAS 17 as the lease no longer exists. The old tenant must expense the cost. The new tenant will recognise the payment as income unless it is compensation for an above-market rental, in which case the treatment required by SIC-15 for a lease incentive must be applied and the payment will be amortised over the lease term (see 3.4.2 above)

Note 4   The new tenant has made a payment to an old tenant, and while it is in connection with the lease arrangements, it is not directly related to the actual lease as it was made to a party outside the lease contract. Therefore it cannot be accounted for under IAS 17. The old tenant will treat the receipt as a gain immediately. Any remaining balances of the lease will be removed and a net gain (or loss) recorded. The payment by the lessee will generally meet the definition of an intangible asset in IAS 38 and therefore will be amortised over the useful life, being the term of the lease. However, if other conditions and circumstances in the arrangement mean that this definition is not met, the payment will be expensed in the period in which it is incurred.

4.5   Sub-leases and back-to-back leases

4.5.1   Introduction

Situations arise where there are more parties to a lease arrangement than simply one lessor and one lessee. The discussion below relates to situations involving an original lessor, an intermediate party and an ultimate lessee. The intermediate party is unrelated to both lessor and lessee and may be acting either as both a lessee and lessor of the asset concerned or, alternatively, as an agent of the lessor in the transaction.

Both sub-leases and back-to-back leases involve the intermediate party acting as both lessor and lessee of the asset. The difference between the two arrangements is that, for a back-to-back lease, the terms of the two lease agreements match to a greater extent than would be the case for a sub-lease arrangement. This difference is really only one of degree, and the important decision to be made concerns whether the intermediate party is acting as both lessee and lessor in two related but independent transactions or whether the nature of the interest is such that it need not recognise the rights and obligations under the leases in its financial statements.

4.5.2   The original lessor and the ultimate lessee

The accounting treatment adopted by these parties will not be affected by the existence of sub-leases or back-to-back leases. The original lessor has an agreement with the intermediate party, which is not affected by any further leasing of the assets by the intermediate party unless the original lease agreement is thereby replaced.

Similarly, the ultimate lessee has a lease agreement with the intermediate party. The lessee will have use of the asset under that agreement and must make a decision, in the usual way, as to whether the lease is of a finance or operating type under the requirements of IAS 17.

4.5.3   The intermediate party

It is common for entities whose business is the leasing of assets to third parties to finance these assets themselves through leasing arrangements. There are also arrangements in which a party on-leases assets as an intermediary between a lessor and a lessee while taking a variable degree of risk in the transaction. The appropriate accounting treatment by the intermediate party depends on the substance of the series of transactions. Either the intermediate party will act as lessee to the original lessor and lessor to the ultimate lessee or, if in substance it has transferred the risks and rewards of ownership, it may be able to derecognise the assets and liabilities under its two lease arrangements and recognise only its own commission or fee income.

In order to analyse the issues that may arise, it is worth considering the various combinations of leases between lessor/intermediate and intermediate/lessee, which are summarised in the following table:

	Lessor	Intermediate party		Lessee
	Lease to Intermediate	Lease from Lessor	Lease to Lessee	Lease from Intermediate
(1)	Operating lease	Operating lease	Operating lease	Operating lease
(2)	Finance lease	Finance lease	Operating lease	Operating lease
(3)	Finance lease	Finance lease	Finance lease	Finance lease

Only in unusual circumstances could there be an operating lease from the lessor to the intermediate and a finance lease from the intermediate to the lessee. The intermediate would have to acquire an additional interest in the asset from a party other than the lessor in order to be in a position to transfer substantially all of the risks and rewards incidental to ownership of that asset to the lessee.

There are no significant accounting difficulties for the intermediate party regarding (1), an operating lease from the lessor to the intermediate and from the intermediate to the lessee. The intermediate may be liable to the lessor if the lessee defaults, in which case it would have to make an appropriate provision, but otherwise both contracts are executory and will be accounted for in the usual way.

In situation (2), the intermediate will record at inception an asset acquired under a finance lease and an obligation to the lessor of an equal and opposite amount. As it has granted an operating lease to the lessee, its risks and rewards incidental to ownership of the asset exceed those assumed by the lessee under the lease. It is appropriate for the intermediate party to record a fixed asset, which it will have to depreciate as set out in 3.2.4 above.

However, under scenario (3), the intermediate is the lessee under a finance lease with the lessor and lessor under a finance lease with the lessee. Its balance sheet, *prima facie*, records a finance lease receivable from the lessee and a finance lease obligation to the lessor. Both of these are treated as if they are financial instruments for derecognition purposes (see 3.6 above for the circumstances in which lease assets and liabilities are within scope of IAS 39).

The intermediate may be in a position to derecognise its financial asset and liability if it transfers to the lessor the contractual right to receive the cash flows of the lessee and thereby extinguishes its liability under the lease.[219] However, it is more likely that it retains the contractual right to receive the cash flow under the lease and a contractual obligation to pay the cash flows to the lessor. In accordance with the derecognition rules in IAS 39 it can derecognise its asset and liability if, and only if, it meets certain criteria, which are summarised in 3.6.1 above and described in detail in Chapter 30 at 4.4. In the context of leases, the most important is that the intermediate has no obligation to pay amounts to the lessor unless in collects equivalent amounts from the lessee.[220] If the ultimate lessee defaults on its lease obligations (for whatever reason), the original lessor must have no recourse against the intermediate party for the outstanding payments under the lease if derecognition is to be appropriate. Another important factor is what happens if the original lessor defaults, for example through insolvency. The analysis will also have to take account of the following conditions for derecognition of a financial asset in IAS 39:

(a) the entity is prohibited by the terms of the transfer contract from selling or pledging the original asset; and

(b) the entity has an obligation to remit any cash flows it collects without material delay. Investment in cash or cash equivalents is permitted, but interest earned must be passed to the eventual recipients.[221]

If these factors indicate that the intermediate party has derecognised its interest in the two leases, i.e. commercially it is acting merely as a broker or agent for the original lessor, it should not include any asset or obligation relating to the leased asset in its balance sheet. The income received by such an intermediary should be taken to profit and loss account on a systematic and rational basis – the discussion of the recognition of fee income in SIC-27, as discussed in 2.2.2 above, may be helpful. If, on the other hand, the intermediate party is taken to be acting as both lessee and lessor in two independent although related transactions, the assets and obligations under finance leases should be recognised in the normal way.

It should not be inferred from the above discussion that all situations encountered can be relatively easily analysed. In practice this is unlikely to be the case, as the risks and rewards will probably be spread between the parties involved. This is especially likely where more than the three parties discussed above are involved. Therefore, even if the arrangements meet the definition of a 'transfer' under IAS 39, the intermediate may have retained some of the risks and rewards of ownership or control of the asset and it may be necessary to recognise other assets and liabilities in this respect. The complex area concerning derecognition of financial assets is dealt with in Chapter 30 at 4.

4.6   Sale and leaseback arrangements including repurchase agreements and options

IAS 17 identifies a particular condition that may result in a lease being classified as a finance lease: where the lessee has a 'bargain purchase' option to acquire the asset. However, the standard does not deal explicitly with the function of options in the context of sale and leaseback arrangements, where circumstances are more complex and there may be a variety of options that may affect the overall assessment of the lease.

The IFRIC considered whether these arrangements would have to meet the derecognition criteria in IAS 18 in order to recognise the sale of the asset. If this were the case then it would be unlikely that the seller/lessee would ever achieve derecognition. Arguably the vendor would retain effective control through continuing managerial involvement to the degree usually associated with ownership. It might also retain the significant risks and rewards of ownership, e.g. through fixed price repurchase terms that allowed it to retain the rewards but not the risks of ownership.[222]

The IFRIC concluded that there was no such requirement as IAS 17 itself contained 'the more specific guidance with respect to sale and leaseback transactions'. However, these transactions may be outside the scope IAS 17 because they do not 'convey a right to use an asset' as defined by SIC-27 and IFRIC 4, whose requirements are described at 2.2 above. If the purchaser/lessor does not have a right of use, the transaction is outside the scope of IAS 17 and the sale and leaseback accounting in IAS 17 should not be applied.

The IFRIC considered that 'significantly divergent interpretations do not exist in practice on this issue and that it would not expect such divergent interpretations to emerge'. Consequently, the IFRIC decided not to take the issue onto its agenda.[223]

The IFRIC considers, therefore, that entities should use IFRIC 4 and SIC-27 to analyse whether or not the arrangement contains a lease and then apply IAS 18 to determine whether or not there is revenue relating to the transaction. SIC-27 is helpful in the analysis; it includes the following indicators that an arrangement is not in substance a lease:

(a)   the entity retains all the risks and rewards of ownership and there is no significant change in its rights to use the asset; and

(b)   the options on which the arrangement depends are included on terms that make their exercise almost certain (e.g. a put option that is exercisable at a price sufficiently higher than the expected fair value when it becomes exercisable).[224]

In practice entities may well have obtained the same answer by moving straight to IAS 18 and applying a 'risks and rewards' analysis, rather than considering whether the arrangement contains a lease, which could explain the lack of divergence in practice.

4.6.1 Sale and leaseback arrangements with put and call options

If a lease arrangement includes an option that can only be exercised by the seller/lessee at the then fair value of the asset in question, the risks and rewards inherent in the residual value of the asset have passed to the buyer/lessor. The option amounts to a right of first refusal to the seller/lessee.

Where there is both a put and a call option in force on equivalent terms at a determinable amount other than the fair value, it is clear that the asset will revert to the seller/lessee. It must be in the interests of one or other of the parties to exercise the option so as to secure a profit or avoid a loss, and therefore the likelihood of the asset remaining the property of the buyer/lessor rather than reverting to the seller must be remote. In such a case, this is a bargain purchase option and the seller/lessee has entered into a finance leaseback.

However, the position is less clear where there is only a put option or only a call option in force, rather than a combination of the two. Where there is only a put option by the buyer/lessor, the effect will be (in the absence of other factors) that the seller/lessee has disposed of the rewards of ownership to the buyer/lessor but retained the risks. This is because the buyer/lessor will only exercise his option to put the asset back to the seller/lessee if its value at the time is less than the repurchase price payable under the option. This means that if the asset continues to rise in value the buyer/lessor will keep it and reap the benefits of that enhanced value; conversely if the value of the asset falls, the option will be exercised and the downside on the asset will be borne by the seller/lessee.

This analysis does not of itself answer the question whether the deal should be treated as an operating or financing leaseback. The overall commercial effect will still have to be evaluated, taking account of all the terms of the arrangement and by considering the motivations of both of the parties in agreeing to the various terms of the deal; in particular it will need to be considered why they have each agreed to have this one-sided option.

Where there is only a call option exercisable by the seller/lessee, the position will be reversed. In this case, the seller/lessee has disposed of the risks, but retained the rewards to be attained if the value of the asset exceeds the repurchase price specified in the option. Once again, though, the overall commercial effect of the arrangement has to be evaluated in deciding how to account for the deal. Emphasis has to be given to what is likely to happen in practice, and it is instructive to look at the arrangement from the point of view of both parties to see what their expectations are and what has induced them to accept the deal on the terms that have been agreed. It may be obvious from the overall terms of the arrangement that the call option will be exercised, in which case the deal will again be a financing arrangement and should be accounted for as such. For example, the exercise price of the call option may be set at a significant discount to expected market value, the seller/lessee may need the asset to use on an ongoing basis in its business, or the asset may provide in effect the only source of the seller/lessee's future income. Equally, the financial effects of *not* exercising the option, such as continued exposure to escalating costs, may make it obvious that the option will have to be exercised (so-called 'economic compulsion').

The following is an example of a sale and leaseback deal where the seller has a call option to repurchase the asset but has no commitment to do so:

Example 22.26:   Sale and leaseback transaction involving escalating rentals and call options

Company S sells a property to Company B for £100,000,000 and leases it back on the following terms:

Rental for years 1 to 5	£3,900,000 per annum
Rental for years 6 to 10	£5,875,000 per annum
Rental for years 11 to 15	£8,830,000 per annum
Rental for years 16 to 20	£13,280,000 per annum
Rental for years 21 to 25	£19,970,000 per annum
Rental for years 26 to 30	£30,025,000 per annum
Rental for years 31 to 35	£45,150,000 per annum
Rental thereafter	open market rent

Rentals are payable annually in advance.

Company S has a call option to buy back the property at the following dates and prices:

At the end of year 5	£125,000,000
At the end of year 10	£150,000,000
At the end of year 15	£168,000,000
At the end of year 20	£160,000,000
At the end of year 25	£100,000,000

Company B has no right to put the property back to Company S.

An analysis of the economics of this deal suggests that whilst Company S has no legal obligation to repurchase the property, there is no genuine commercial possibility that the option will not be exercised. This is because the rentals and option prices are structured in such a way as to give the buyer of the property a lender's return whilst, at the same time, there is no commercial logic for the seller not to exercise the option at year 25, if not earlier. Exercising the option at the end of year 25 will mean that Company S will regain ownership of the property and will have had the use of the £100,000,000 at an effective rate of approximately 8.2% per annum; failure to exercise the option will mean additional lease obligations of £375,875,000 over the ten years from years 25 to 35, followed by the obligation to pay market rents thereafter.

5   EFFECTIVE DATE AND TRANSITIONAL PROVISIONS

5.1   Effective date and transitional provisions

The amendment relating to the reclassification of leases over land as finance leases, applies to annual periods beginning on or after 1 January 2010. Early adoption is permitted.[225]Transitional rules are given in 2.3.4 above.

6 CONCLUSION

IAS 17 has been in force for a long time and practice under it is well established. However, it is a standard that is showing its age. The distinction between operating and finance leases is not supported at the conceptual level, even if it is justifiable using a risks and rewards model. Inconsistencies between its rules and those of the standards with which it overlaps, in particular IAS 39, are increasingly causing problems. Although these problem areas should have meant that this was a standard with a relatively short remaining life, it has proved difficult to agree the way forward as many proposals have proved to be impractical. However, the issue of the Discussion Paper in March 2009 may mean that lessee accounting, at least, will finally change and all lease assets and liabilities will be reflected in entities' balance sheets.

References

1 IAS 17, *Accounting for Leases*, IASC, September 1982; SFAS 13, *Accounting for Leases*, FASB, November 1976 and SSAP 21, *Accounting for leases and hire purchase contracts*, ASC, 1984.
2 IAS 17 (1982).
3 IAS 17 (1982), para. 3.
4 *Framework for the Preparation and Presentation of Financial Statements*, IASB, September 1989, para. 49(a)-(b).
5 *Leases – Preliminary Views*, IASB, March 2009, para. 2.9.
6 *Leases – Preliminary Views*, para. 2.13.
7 *Leases – Preliminary Views*, para. 3.33.
8 *Leases – Preliminary Views*, para. 4.23.
9 *Leases – Preliminary Views*, para. 4.15.
10 *Leases – Preliminary Views*, paras. 6.36, 6.41 and 6.56
11 *Leases – Preliminary Views*, paras. 7.20, 7.21 and 7.46.
12 *Leases – Preliminary Views*, para. 4.15.
13 IAS 17, para. 4 and *Leases – Preliminary Views*, para. 4.10.
14 *Leases – Preliminary Views*, para. 6.54.
15 *Leases – Preliminary Views*, paras. 7.31 and 7.32
16 *Leases – Preliminary Views*, paras. 5.24 and 5.25
17 *Leases – Preliminary Views*, paras. 8.7 and 8.8
18 *Leases – Preliminary Views*, paras. 8.18 and 8.19
19 *IASB Update*, IASB, July 2009, p5.
20 *Leases – Preliminary Views*, para. 10.31
21 *Leases – Preliminary Views*, para. 10.37
22 IAS 17, *Leases*, IASB, para. 2.
23 IAS 38, *Intangible Assets*, IASB, para. 2.
24 IAS 38, para. 3.
25 IAS 38, para. 24.
26 IAS 38, para. 24.
27 IAS 39, *Financial Instruments : Recognition and Measurement*, IASB, para. 9.
28 IAS 17, para. 4.
29 IAS 17, para. 6.
30 IFRIC 4, *Determining whether an Arrangement contains a Lease*, IASB, para. 1.
31 IFRIC 4, para. 1.
32 IFRIC 4, para. BC2.
33 IAS 17, para. 3.
34 IFRIC 4, para. BC2.
35 IFRIC 4, para. 5.
36 IFRIC 4, para. 2.
37 IFRIC 4, para. 4.
38 IFRIC 4, para. 6.
39 IFRIC 4, para. 7.
40 IFRIC 4, para. 8.
41 IFRIC 4, para. 7.
42 IFRIC 4, para. 3.
43 IFRIC 4, para. 9.
44 IFRIC 4, paras. IE1-IE2.
45 IFRIC 4, paras. IE3-IE4.
46 IFRIC 4, para. 10.
47 IAS 17, para. 4.
48 IFRIC 4, para. 11.
49 IFRIC 4, para. 11.
50 IFRIC 4, para. 12.
51 IAS 17, paras. 4 and 8.
52 IFRIC 4, para. 13.

53 IFRIC 4, para. 14.
54 IFRIC 4, para. 15.
55 IFRIC 4, para. BC39.
56 IAS 17, para. 31(e).
57 IFRIC 4, para. BC39.
58 IFRIC 4, para. BC39.
59 IFRIC 4, para. 15.
60 IFRIC 4, para. 16.
61 IFRIC 4, para. 17.
62 SIC-27, *Evaluating the Substance of Transactions Involving the Legal Form of a Lease*, IASB, para. 2.
63 SIC-27, para. 1.
64 SIC-27, Appendix A.
65 SIC-27, paras. 3-4.
66 SIC-27, para. 3.
67 SIC-27, para. 5.
68 SIC-27, para. 5.
69 SIC-27, para. 6.
70 SIC-27, para. 7.
71 SIC-27, para. 8.
72 SIC-27, para. 9.
73 SIC-27, para. 10.
74 IAS 17, para. 4.
75 IAS 17, para. 9.
76 IAS 17, para. 7.
77 IAS 17, para. 10.
78 IAS 17, para. 4.
79 IAS 17, para. 4.
80 SFAS 13, para. 7(c).
81 IAS 17, para. 11.
82 For further discussion on determining the substance of a lease, see ICAEW Technical Release 664, *Implementation of SSAP 21* 'Accounting for leases and hire purchase contracts', July 1987.
83 IAS 17, para. 13.
84 IAS 17, para. 4.
85 IAS 17, para. 13.
86 IAS 16, *Property, Plant and Equipment*, IASB, para. 51.
87 *Improvements to IFRSs*, April 2009, IASB, IAS 17, para. 15A.
88 IAS 17, para. 10.
89 *Improvements to IFRSs*, IAS 17, para. BC8E.
90 *Improvements to IFRSs*, IAS 17, para. BC8C.
91 IAS 17, para. 14.
92 IAS 17, para. 69A.
93 *Improvements to IFRSs*, IAS 17, para. BC8F.
94 IAS 17, para. 68A.
95 IAS 17, para. BC5.
96 IAS 17, para. 15A.
97 IAS 17, para. 15.
98 IAS 17, paras. BC8F.
99 IAS 17, para. 16.
100 IAS 17, paras. BC9-BC11.
101 IAS 17, para. 16.
102 IAS 17, para. 17.
103 Valuation Information Paper No. 9, The Royal Institution of Chartered Surveyors, May 2006.
104 RICS Valuation Information Paper No. 9, paras. 4.7 and 4.8.
105 IAS 17, para. 18.
106 IAS 17, para. 19.
107 IAS 17, para. 20.
108 IAS 17, para. 22.
109 IAS 17, para. 25.
110 IAS 17, para. 36.
111 IAS 17, para. 4.
112 IAS 17, para. 4.
113 IAS 17, para. 5.
114 IAS 17, para. 4.
115 IAS 17, para. 4.
116 IAS 17, para. 4.
117 IAS 17, para. 4.
118 IAS 17, para. 4.
119 IAS 17, para. 4.
120 IAS 17, para. 4.
121 IAS 39, paras. 11 and AG33(f).
122 IAS 17, para. 25.
123 *Improvements to IFRSs*, IASB, May 2008.
124 IAS 17, para. 4.
125 IAS 17, para. 24.
126 IAS 17, para. 38.
127 IAS 17, para. 22.
128 IAS 17, para. 25.
129 IAS 17, para. 26.
130 IAS 17, para. 22.
131 IAS 17, para. 24.
132 IAS 17, paras. 27-28.
133 IAS 17, para. 4.
134 IAS 17, para. 29.
135 IAS 16, *Property, Plant and Equipment*, IASB, para. 51.
136 IAS 17, para. 30.
137 IAS 17, para. 36.
138 IAS 17, para. 37.
139 IAS 17, para. 38.
140 IAS 17, para. 39.
141 IAS 17, para. 4.
142 IAS 17, para. 39.
143 IAS 17, para. 40.
144 IAS 17, para. 41.
145 IAS 39, para. 2(b).
146 IAS 17, para. 41A.
147 IAS 17, para. 43.
148 IAS 17, para. 42.
149 IAS 17, paras. 44-45.
150 IAS 17, para. 44.
151 IAS 17, para. 46.
152 IAS 17, para. 55.
153 IAS 17, paras. 33-34.
154 *IFRIC Update*, IFRIC, September 2005.

155 IAS 39, para. 43.
156 IAS 39, para. 9.
157 SIC-15, *Operating Leases – Incentives*, IASB, para. 1.
158 SIC-15, para. 3.
159 SIC-15, para. 5.
160 SIC-15, para. 6.
161 SIC-15, Appendix, Examples 1-2.
162 *IFRIC Update*, IFRIC, April 2005.
163 IAS 16, para. 60, IAS 38, para. 97 and IAS 17, para. 33.
164 *IFRIC Update*, IFRIC, July 2008.
165 IAS 37, *Provisions, Contingent Liabilities and Contingent Assets*, IASB, para. 63.
166 IAS 37, para. 66.
167 IAS 37, para. 10.
168 IAS 17, paras. 49-50.
169 IAS 17, para. 51.
170 IAS 17, para. 52.
171 IAS 17, para. 53.
172 IAS 16, para. 51.
173 IAS 38, *Intangible Assets*, IASB, para. 100.
174 IAS 17, para. 54.
175 SIC-15, para. 4.
176 IAS 17, para. 58.
177 IAS 17, para. 59.
178 IAS 17, para. 60.
179 *IFRIC Update*, IFRIC, March 2007, page. 4.
180 IAS 17, para. 60.
181 IAS 18, *Revenue*, IASB, para. 16.
182 IAS 17, para. 64.
183 IAS 17, paras. 61-62.
184 IAS 17, para. 65.
185 IAS 17, para. 66.
186 IAS 32, *Financial Instruments: Presentation*, IASB, para. AG9.
187 IAS 17, para. 4.
188 IAS 39, para. 9.
189 IAS 39, para. 2(b).
190 IAS 39, para. 17.
191 IAS 39, para. 20.
192 IAS 39, para. 19.
193 IAS 39, para. 18.
194 IAS 39, para. 19.
195 IAS 39, para. 63.
196 IAS 39, para. 39.
197 IAS 39, para. AG57.
198 IAS 39, paras. 41-42.
199 IAS 39, para. 10.
200 IAS 39, para. 11.
201 IAS 39, para. AG33(f).
202 IAS 17, para. 31.
203 IAS 17, para. 32.
204 IAS 17, para. 35.
205 IAS 17, para. 47.
206 IAS 17, para. 48.
207 IAS 17, para. 56.
208 IAS 17, para. 57.
209 IAS 17, para. 9.
210 IAS 17, para. 11.
211 IAS 17, para. 13.
212 IAS 17, para. 13.
213 IAS 39, para. AG8.
214 IAS 17, para. 13.
215 IAS 39, para. AG8.
216 IAS 17, para. 4.
217 IAS 16, para. 7.
218 IAS 38, para. 8.
219 IAS 39, para. 18.
220 IAS 39, paras. 18-19.
221 IAS 39, para. 19.
222 IAS 18, para. 14.
223 *IFRIC Update*, IFRIC, March 2007, page. 4.
224 SIC-27, para. 5.
225 IAS 17, para. 69A.

Chapter 23   Transactions with governments: grants and service concession arrangements

1   INTRODUCTION

This chapter deals with two very different forms of transaction that most commonly (but not exclusively) take place between governments and the private sector. The first of these is government grants, where the accounting standard, IAS 20 – *Accounting for Government Grants and Disclosure of Government Assistance* – applied for the first time more than twenty-five years ago.[1] The application of IAS 20 After such a period of time it is perhaps not surprising that the standard is showing its age: it is arguably inconsistent with the IASB's *Framework*. Arguably, it results in the recognition in the balance sheet of deferred debits and credits that do not meet the Framework's definitions of assets and liabilities and can result in an understatement of assets controlled by an entity. It may well undergo fundamental revision in the near future. The discussion of government grants and other forms of assistance begins at 2 below.

The second form of transaction is service concession arrangements, where the accounting debate has a much shorter history. These are arrangements of great complexity, often devised to meet political as well as purely commercial ends. The issues cross the boundaries of a number of accounting standards, and this has made it extremely difficult to devise an adequate accounting model. IFRIC Interpretation 12 – *Service Concession Arrangements* – which took more than three years to develop, was finally approved by the IASB in November 2006. Service concession arrangements are discussed at 5 below.

2   GOVERNMENT GRANTS

Government grants are defined in IAS 20 as assistance by government in the form of transfers of resources to an entity in return for past or future compliance with certain conditions relating to the operating activities of the entity.[2] Such assistance has been available to commercial businesses for many years, although its form and extent will often have undergone various changes according to the shifting economic philosophies of the government of the day. The purpose of government grants (which may be called subsidies, subventions or premiums)[3] and other forms of government assistance is often to encourage a private sector entity to take a course of action that it would not normally have taken if the assistance had not been provided.[4] As the standard notes, the receipt of government assistance by an entity may be significant for the preparation of the financial statements for two reasons:[5]

- if resources have been transferred, an appropriate method of accounting for the transfer must be found; and

- it is desirable to give an indication of the extent to which an entity has benefited from such assistance during the reporting period, because this facilitates comparison of its financial statements with those of prior periods and with those of other entities.

The main accounting issue that arises from government grants is how to deal with the income that the grant represents. IAS 20 adopts a matching approach as its guiding principle, whereby grants of a capital nature, which are intended to subsidise the purchase of fixed assets, are credited to revenue over the life of the assets involved. The standard, in fact, pre-dates the IASB's Framework and the IASB itself notes that it is inconsistent with it.[6]

The standard recognises that an entity may receive other forms of government assistance, such as free technical or marketing advice and the provision of guarantees. However, rather than prescribe how these should be accounted for, it requires disclosure about such assistance.

The Board has discussed the replacement of IAS 20 intermittently for nearly six years without making any significant progress. During that time there has been one amendment to the standard; the *Improvements to IFRSs* in May 2008 removes a conflict with IAS 39 – *Financial Instruments: Recognition and Measurement* – over the measurement of loans with lower than market rates of interest (see 2.3.1A below). The project to update the standard remains deferred; the IASB's project summary has not been updated since May 2008 where it is noted that the timing is yet to be determined and has been deferred pending conclusion of work on other relevant projects. Work has recommenced on emission rights where the IASB expects to issue an exposure draft during 2010.[7] Accounting for emission rights is discussed in Chapter 15 at 3.3.

2.1   Requirements of IAS 20

The principal international accounting standard that deals with government grants is IAS 20, issued in 1983. In 1998, the SIC issued an interpretation dealing with certain forms of government assistance, SIC-10 – *Government Assistance – No Specific Relation to Operating Activities* (see 2.2 below). Government grants related to biological assets are excluded from the scope of IAS 20 and are dealt with in IAS 41 – *Agriculture* (see Chapter 41 at 2.4).

2.1.1 Nature of government grants and government assistance

IAS 20 is applied in accounting for, and in the disclosure of, government grants and in the disclosure of other forms of government assistance.[8] The distinction between government grants and other forms of government assistance is important because the standard's accounting requirements only apply to the former.

A   Government assistance

Government assistance is defined as action by government designed to provide an economic benefit to an entity or range of entities qualifying under certain criteria (see 2.6 below).[9] Government assistance takes many forms 'varying both in the nature of the assistance given and in the conditions which are usually attached to it'.[10] However, such assistance does not include benefits provided indirectly through action affecting general trading conditions, such as the provision of infrastructure in development areas or the imposition of trading constraints on competitors.[11]

B   Government grants

Government grants are a specific form of government assistance. Under IAS 20, *government grants* represent assistance by government in the form of transfers of resources to an entity in return for past or future compliance with certain conditions relating to the operating activities of the entity.[12] The standard identifies the following types of government grants:[13]

*   *grants related to assets* are government grants whose primary condition is that an entity qualifying for them should purchase, construct or otherwise acquire long-term assets. Subsidiary conditions may also be attached restricting the type or location of the assets or the periods during which they are to be acquired or held; and

*   *grants related to income* are government grants other than those related to assets.

The standard regards the term 'government' to include governmental agencies and similar bodies whether local, national or international.[14] Government grants exclude:

(a)   assistance to which no value can reasonably be assigned, e.g. free technical or marketing advice and the provision of guarantees;[15] and

(b)   transactions with government that cannot be distinguished from the normal trading transactions of the entity, e.g. where the entity is being favoured by a government's procurement policy.[16]

Such excluded items are to be treated as falling within the standard's disclosure requirements for government assistance (see A above and 2.7.2 below).

Loans at below market interest rates were also deemed to be a form of government assistance and the benefit was not quantified by the imputation of interest.

However, this has been deleted in the *Improvements to IFRSs* of May 2008 and replaced with a requirement to measure the benefit of the below-market rate of interest in accordance with IAS 39. The accounting consequences are discussed at 2.3.1 A below.

2.2   Scope

IAS 20 applies in accounting for, and in the disclosure of, government grants and in the disclosure of other forms of government assistance,[17] but the standard does not deal with:

(a)   accounting for government grants if the entity prepares financial information that reflect the effects of changing prices, whether as financial statements or in supplementary information;

(b)   government assistance in the form of benefits that are available in determining taxable income or are determined or limited on the basis of income tax liability, i.e. income tax holidays, investment tax credits, accelerated depreciation allowances and reduced income tax rates;

(c)   government participation in the ownership of the entity; and

(d)   government grants covered by IAS 41.[18]

The reason for exclusion (d) above is that the presentation permitted by IAS 20 of deducting government grants from the carrying amount of the asset (see 2.4.1 below) was considered inconsistent with a fair value model in which an asset is measured at its fair value.[19] The requirements of IAS 41 in relation to government grants are dealt with in Chapter 41 at 2.4.

There are no requirements for government grants in IAS 40– *Investment Property* – which adopts a similar fair value model (see Chapter 17), nor was IAS 20 revised to deal with the matter. This is probably because government grants in the investment property sector are relatively rare compared to the agricultural sector. However, governments do on occasion provide grants and subsidised loans to finance the acquisition of social housing that meets the definition of investment property; the discount on these subsidised loans is now considered to be a government grant, as described in 2.3.1A below.

One issue which has been considered by the SIC is the situation in some countries where government assistance is aimed at entities in certain regions or industry sectors, but without there being any conditions specifically relating to the operating activities of the entity concerned. In January 1998, the SIC determined that such forms of government assistance are to be treated as government grants.[20] This ruling was to avoid any suggestion that such forms of assistance were not governed by the standard and could be credited directly to equity.

In public-to-private service concession arrangements a government may give certain assets to the operator of the service concession. In those cases careful analysis is required to determine whether the entire arrangement is to be accounted for under IFRIC 12 – *Service Concession Arrangements* – or whether it contains a government grant.[21] Service concessions are discussed at 6 below.

While grants of emission rights and renewable energy certificates typically meet the definition of government grants under IAS 20, the rights and certificates themselves are intangible assets. Accounting for emission rights and renewable energy certificates is discussed in Chapter 15 at 3.3.

2.3   Accounting for government grants

2.3.1   Recognition and measurement

IAS 20 requires that government grants should be recognised only when there is reasonable assurance that:

(a)   the entity will comply with the conditions attaching to them; and

(b)   the grants will be received.[22]

The standard does not define 'reasonable assurance', which raises the question whether or not it means the same as 'probable'. When developing IAS 41 the Board believed that recognition of government grants when there is 'reasonable assurance' was different from both recognition when 'it is probable that the entity will meet the conditions attaching to the government grant' and 'the entity meets the conditions attaching to the government grant'.[23] The Board also noted that 'it would inevitably be a subjective decision as to when there is reasonable assurance that the conditions are met and that this subjectivity could lead to inconsistent income recognition.'[24] Nevertheless, in practice we would not expect an entity to recognise government grants before it was at least probable that the entity would comply with the conditions attached to them and the grants would be received.

The standard notes that receiving a grant does not of itself provide conclusive evidence that the conditions attaching to the grant have been or will be fulfilled.[25] After an entity has recognised a government grant, any related contingent liability or contingent asset should be accounted for under IAS 37 – *Provisions, Contingent Liabilities and Contingent Assets*.[26]

The accounting for government grants is not affected by the manner in which they are received, i.e. grants received in cash, as a non-monetary amount, or forgiveness of a government loan, are all accounted for in the same manner.[27] A forgivable loan from government, the repayment of which will be waived under certain prescribed conditions[28], is to be treated as a government grant when there is reasonable assurance that the entity will meet the terms for forgiveness of the loan.[29]

Example 23.1:   Repayment of government grant

An entity participates in a government sponsored research and development programme under which it is entitled to receive a government grant of up to 50% of the costs incurred. The government grant is interest-bearing and fully repayable based on a percentage ('royalty') of the sales revenue of any products developed. Although the repayment period is not limited, no repayment is required if there are no sales of the products.

The entity should account for this type of government grant as follows:

- initially recognise the government grant as a forgivable loan;
- apply the principles underlying the effective interest rate method in subsequent periods, which would involve estimating the amount and timing of future cash flows;
- review at each balance sheet date whether there is reasonable assurance that the entity will meet the terms for forgiveness of the loan. If this is the case then derecognise part or all of the liability initially recorded with a corresponding profit in the income statement; and
- if the entity subsequently revises its estimates of future sales upwards, it recognises a liability for any amounts previously included in profit and recognises a corresponding loss in the income statement.

A government grant in the form of a transfer of a non-monetary asset, such as land or other resources, which is intended for use by the entity, is usually recognised at the fair value of that asset. Fair value is 'the amount for which an asset could be exchanged between a knowledgeable, willing buyer and a knowledgeable, willing seller in an arm's length transactions.'[30]

However, the alternative of recognising such assets, and the related grant, at a nominal amount is permitted.[31] Under IAS 8 – *Accounting Policies, Changes in Accounting Estimates and Errors* – an entity should select an accounting policy and apply it consistently to all non-monetary government grants.[32]

A   Loans at less than market rates of interest

IAS 20 now requires government loans that have a below-market rate of interest to be recognised and measured in accordance with IAS 39, i.e. at their fair value.[33] The loans could be interest-free. The difference between the initial carrying value of the loan (its fair value), and the proceeds received is treated as a government grant. Subsequently, interest will be imputed to the loan using the effective interest method (see Chapter 32). Crucially, the grant will not necessarily be released on a basis that is consistent with the interest expense. The standard stresses that the entity has to consider the conditions and obligations that have been, or must be, met when 'identifying the costs for which the benefit of the loan is intended to compensate'.[34] This process of matching the benefit to costs is discussed at 2.3.2 below. This requirement is mandatory for new government loans received in accounting periods beginning on or after 1 January 2009.[35]

As well as routine subsidised lending to meet specific objectives, loans made as part of government rescue plans may now be caught if they are at a lower than market rates of interest. PSA Peugeot Citroën describes the treatment of one such loan in Extract 23.1 below.

Extract 23.1: PSA Peugeot Citroën (2009)

Half-Year Financial Report 2009 [extract]

17.2. REFINANCING TRANSACTIONS [extract]

– EIB loan

In April 2009, Peugeot Citroën Automobiles S.A. obtained a €400 million 4-year bullet loan from the European Investment Bank (EIB). Interest on the loan is based on the 3-month Euribor plus 179 bps. At June 30, 2009 the government bonds (OATs) given by Peugeot S.A. as collateral for all EIB loans to Group companies had a market value of €160 million. In addition, 4,695,000 Faurecia shares held by Peugeot S.A. were pledged to the EIB as security for the loans. The interest rate risk on the new EIB loan has not been specifically hedged.

This new loan is at a reduced rate of interest. The difference between the market rate of interest for an equivalent loan at the inception date and the rate granted by the EIB has been recognised as a government grant in accordance with IAS 20. The grant was originally valued at €38 million and was recorded as a deduction from the capitalized development costs financed by the loan. It is being amortised on a straight-line basis over the life of the underlying projects. The loan is measured at amortised cost, in the amount of €362 million at June 30, 2009. The effective interest rate is estimated at 5.90%.

This will also affect the manner in which arrangements that are similar in substance to loans are accounted for. Governments sometimes allow entities to retain sums that they collect on behalf of the government (e.g. value added taxes) to be retained until a future event, as in the following example:

Example 23.2:   Loan at less than market rates of interest

The local government of an underdeveloped region is trying to stimulate investment by allowing local companies to retain the value added tax (VAT) on their sales. An entity participating in this scheme is entitled to retain an amount up to 40% of its investment in fixed assets. The retained VAT must be paid to the local government after 5 years. The deferred VAT liability is comparable in nature to an interest free loan. The entity can reasonably place a value on the government assistance using the principles in IAS 39 and the benefit will be accounted for as government grants.

2.3.2   Matching grants against related costs

A   Income approach and capital approach

The 'capital approach', under which a grant is credited directly to equity,[36] was rejected despite the following arguments in its favour:

'(a)   government grants are a financing device and should be dealt with as such in the statement of financial position rather than be recognised in profit or loss to offset the items of expense which they finance. Since no repayment is expected, such grants should be recognised outside profit or loss; and

(b)   it is inappropriate to recognise government grants in profit or loss, since they are not earned but represent an incentive provided by government without related costs.'[37]

Instead the Board adopted the 'income approach', under which grants are taken to income over one or more periods,[38] because:[39]

(a)   government grants are receipts from a source other than shareholders, they should not be credited directly to shareholders' interests but should be recognised as income in appropriate periods;

(b)   government grants are rarely gratuitous. An entity earns them through compliance with their conditions and meeting the envisaged obligations. They should therefore be recognised as income and matched with the associated costs which the grant is intended to compensate; and

(c)   as income and other taxes are charges against income, it is logical to deal also with government grants, which are an extension of fiscal policies, in the income statement.

B   Application of the income approach

Grants should be recognised in income on a systematic basis that matches them with the related costs that they are intended to compensate.[40] They should not be credited directly to shareholders' funds. Income recognition on a receipts basis, which is not in accordance with the accruals accounting assumption, is only acceptable if no basis existed for allocating a grant to periods other than the one in which it was received.[41]

IAS 20 envisages that in most cases, the periods over which an entity recognises the costs or expenses related to the government grant are readily ascertainable and thus grants in recognition of specific expenses are recognised as income in the same period as the relevant expense.[42]

Grants related to depreciable assets are usually recognised as income over the periods, and in the proportions, in which depreciation on those assets is charged.[43] Grants related to non-depreciable assets may also require the fulfilment of certain obligations, in which case they would be recognised as income over the periods in which the costs of meeting the obligations are incurred. For example, a grant of land may be conditional upon the erection of a building on the site and it may be appropriate to recognise it as income over the life of the building.[44]

IAS 20 acknowledges that grants may be received as part of a package of financial or fiscal aids to which a number of conditions are attached. In such cases, the standard indicates that care is needed in identifying the conditions giving rise to the costs and expenses, which determine the periods over which the grant will be earned. It may also be appropriate to allocate part of the grant on one basis and part on another.[45]

Where a grant relates to expenses or losses already incurred, or for the purpose of giving immediate financial support to the entity with no future related costs, the grant should be recognised in income when it becomes receivable.[46] If such a grant is recognised as income of the period in which it becomes receivable, the entity should disclose its effects to ensure that these are clearly understood.[47]

Many of the problems in accounting for government grants relate to that of interpreting the requirement to match the grant with the related costs, particularly because of the international context in which IAS 20 is written. It does not address specific questions that relate to particular types of grant that are available in individual countries. The example below illustrates that the interpretation of the matching requirement in the standard is not always straightforward.

Example 23.3:   Grant associated with investment property

The government provides a grant to an entity that owns an investment property. The grant is intended to compensate the entity for the lower rent it will receive when the property is let as social housing at below market rates. That means that future rental income will be lower over the period of the lease which, at the same time, reduces the fair value of the investment property.

If the entity accounts for the investment property under the IAS 40 cost model then it could be argued that the government grant should be recognised over the term of the lease to offset the lower rental income.

Alternatively, if the entity applied the IAS 40 fair value model then the cost being compensated is the reduction in fair value of the investment property. In that case it is more appropriate to recognise the benefit of the government grant immediately.

If, instead of a grant, the government subsidises a loan used by the entity to acquire the property, then the loan will be brought in at its fair value. The difference between the face value and fair value will be a government grant and the arguments above will apply to its treatment.

If the government imposes conditions, e.g. that the building must be used for social housing for ten years, this does not necessarily mean that the grant should be taken to income over that period. Rather, it should apply a process similar to that in Example 23.1 above. The entity estimate whether there is reasonable assurance that it will meet the terms of the grant and, to that extent, treat an appropriate amount as a grant as above This should be reviewed at each balance sheet date and adjustments made if it appears that the conditions will not be met (see 2.5 below).

2.4   Presentation of grants

2.4.1   Presentation of grants related to assets

Grants that are related to assets (i.e. those whose primary condition is that an entity qualifying for them should purchase, construct or otherwise acquire long-term assets) should be presented in the balance sheet either:[48]

(a)   by setting up the grant as deferred income, which is recognised as income on a systematic and rational basis over the useful life of the asset;[49] or

(b)   by deducting the grant in arriving at the carrying amount of the asset, in which case the grant is recognised in income as a reduction of depreciation.[50]

IAS 20 regards both these methods of presenting grants in financial statements as acceptable alternatives.[51] It should be noted that these two methods could well result in the amounts and timing of government grants recognised in the income statement to be fundamentally different (see A and 2.5 below).

A company that adopted the former treatment is Electrolux, as shown below:

Extract 23.2: AB Electrolux (2006)

Notes to the financial statements [extract]

Note 1 Accounting and valuation principles [extract]

Government grants

Government grants relate to financial grants from governments, public authorities, and similar local, national, or international bodies. These are recognized when there is a reasonable assurance that the Group will comply with the conditions attaching to them, and that the grants will be received. Government grants related to assets are included in the balance sheet as deferred income and recognized as income over the useful life of the assets. In 2006, Government grants recognized in the balance sheet amounted to SEK 11m (40). Government grants that relate to expenses are recognized in the income statement as a deduction of the related expense. In 2006, these grants amounted to SEK 116m (16).

An example of a company adopting a policy of deducting grants related to assets from the cost of the assets is shown below:

Extract 23.3: Kazakhmys PLC (2006)

Notes to the consolidated financial statements [extract]

3. Summary of significant accounting policies [extract]

(d) Tangible assets [extract]

(v) Government grants

Government grants are recognised at their fair value where there is reasonable assurance that the grant will be received and all attaching conditions will be complied with. When the grant relates to an expense item, it is recognised as income over the periods necessary to match the grant on a systematic basis to the costs that it is intended to compensate. Where the grant relates to an asset, the fair value is credited to the cost of the asset and is released to the income statement over the expected useful life in a consistent manner with the depreciation method for the relevant asset.

A   Assets not being depreciated

The standard does not specifically address accounting for government grants related to depreciable assets for which no depreciation is being charged (e.g. a property whose residual value is equal to or in excess of its carrying amount). However, it appears that the accounting would be as follows:

(a)   if the grant is accounted for as deferred income, the entity would continue to recognise the grant as income on a systematic and rational basis over the useful life of the asset; and

(b)   if the grant is deducted from the carrying amount of the asset, the grant should be recognised 'over the life of a depreciable asset by way of a reduced depreciation charge'.[52] Therefore, in the absence of depreciation, no benefit from the government grant can be recognised in income until either the asset is disposed of or the asset has a depreciable amount through the subsequent revision of its estimated residual value.

Cash flows

The purchase of assets and the receipt of related grants can cause major movements in the cash flow of an entity. Therefore, such movements are often disclosed as separate items in the cash flow statement whether or not the grant is deducted from the related asset for the purpose of balance sheet presentation.[53]

2.4.2 Presentation of grants related to income

Grants related to income should be presented either as:[54]

(a)   a credit in the income statement, either separately or under a general heading such as 'other income'; or

(b)   a deduction in reporting the related expense.

The standard points out that supporters of method (a) consider it inappropriate to present income and expense items on a net basis and that 'separation of the grant from the expense facilitates comparison with other expenses not affected by a grant'. Furthermore, method (a) is consistent with the general prohibition of offsetting in IAS 1 – *Presentation of Financial Statements*.[55] However, supporters of method (b) would argue that 'the expenses might well not have been incurred by the entity if the grant had not been available and presentation of the expense without offsetting the grant may therefore be misleading'.[56] Although the arguments in favour of method (b) are not that convincing (it compares the accounting for the actual facts with that for a scenario that did not take place), the standard regards both methods as acceptable for the presentation of grants related to income.[57] In any case, the standard considers that disclosure of the grant may be necessary for a proper understanding of the financial statements. Furthermore, disclosure of the effect of grants on any item of income or expense, which should be disclosed separately, is usually appropriate.[58]

As illustrated below, InBev has adopted a policy of presenting grants within other operating income, although not separately on the face of the income statement, rather than as a deduction from the related expense.

Extract 23.4: InBev NV (2006)

3. Summary of significant accounting policies [extract]

(U) Income recognition [extract]

Government grants

A government grant is recognized in the balance sheet initially as deferred income when there is reasonable assurance that it will be received and that the company will comply with the conditions attached to it. Grants that compensate the company for expenses incurred are recognized as other operating income on a systematic basis in the same periods in which the expenses are incurred. Grants that compensate the company for the acquisition of an asset are presented by deducting them from the acquisition cost of the related asset in accordance with IAS 20 *Accounting for Government Grants and Disclosure of Government Assistance.*

Electrolux is an example of a company presenting the grant as a deduction from the related expense in the income statement, as illustrated in Extract 23.2 above.

2.5   Repayment of government grants

A government grant that becomes repayable should be accounted for as a revision of an accounting estimate. Repayment of a grant related to income should be charged against the related unamortised deferred credit and any excess should be recognised as an expense immediately.[59]

Repayment of a grant related to an asset should be recognised by increasing the carrying amount of the related asset or reducing the related unamortised deferred credit. The cumulative additional depreciation that would have been recognised to date as an expense in the absence of the grant should be charged immediately to income.[60]

IAS 20 emphasises that the circumstances giving rise to the repayment of a grant related to an asset may require that consideration be given to the possible impairment of the asset.[61]

2.6   Government assistance

As indicated above, IAS 20 excludes from the definition of government grants 'certain forms of government assistance which cannot reasonably have a value placed upon them and transactions with government which cannot be distinguished from the normal trading transactions of the entity'.[62] In many cases the 'existence of the benefit might be unquestioned but any attempt to segregate the trading activities from government assistance could well be arbitrary'.[63] The standard therefore requires disclosure of significant government assistance (see 2.7.2 below).

It should be noted that under IAS 20, 'government assistance does not include the provision of infrastructure by improvement to the general transport and communication network and the supply of improved facilities such as irrigation or water reticulation that is available on an ongoing indeterminate basis for the benefit of an entire local community.'[64]

2.7   Disclosures

2.7.1   General

IAS 20 requires that entities should disclose the following information regarding government grants:[65]

(a)   the accounting policy, including the method of presentation adopted in the financial statements;

(b)   a description of the nature and extent of the grants recognised and an indication of other forms of government assistance from which the entity has directly benefited; and

(c)   unfulfilled conditions or contingencies attaching to government assistance that has been recognised.

The extract below illustrates how companies typically disclose government grants under IFRS. It should be noted that disclosures concerning the nature and conditions of government grants are sometimes relatively minimal, possibly because the amounts involved are immaterial.

Extract 23.5: Danisco A/S (2006)

Note 1 – Accounting policies [extract]

Government grants

Government grants, which are disclosed in a note, include EU compensation for renouncing of sugar quotas as well as grants for research, development, CO2 allowances and investments. EU compensation for renouncing of sugar quotas and grants for research, development and CO2 allowances are recognised as income in the income statement on a systematic basis to match the related cost. Investment grants are set off against the cost of the subsidised assets.

28 Government grants

During the financial year ended, the Group received government grants for research and development of DKK 12 million (2004/05 DKK 3 million) and DKK 18 million (2004/05 DKK 6 million) for other purposes.

Further the Group was granted quotas of 655,326 tonnes of CO2 allowances. The value at grant date was DKK 69 million, and the quotas match the expected emission tax levied on the Group. For 2007 the Group will receive 655,326 tonnes.

In connection with the new EU sugar market regulation and Danisco's decision to close sugar factories and sell part of the sugar quotas in Sweden and Finland, DKK 506 million net was expensed in the financial year of which DKK 449 million is estimated income from the sale of sugar quotas.

Additional examples of accounting policies for government grants can be found in Extracts 23.2, 23.3 and 23.4 above.

2.7.2   Government assistance

In addition to the disclosures noted above, for those forms of government assistance that are excluded from the definition of government grants, the significance of such benefits may be such that the disclosure of the nature, extent and duration of the assistance is necessary to prevent the financial statements from being misleading.[66]

3   PRACTICAL ISSUES

3.1   Achieving the most appropriate matching

Most problems of accounting for grants fall into a single category: that of interpreting the requirement to match the grant against the costs that it is intended to compensate. This apparently simple principle can be extremely difficult to apply in practice, because it is sometimes far from clear what the essence of the grant was. Moreover, in practice, grants are sometimes given for a particular kind of expenditure that forms an element of a larger project, making the allocation a highly subjective matter. For example, government assistance that is in the form of a training grant might be:

(a)   matched against direct training costs; or

(b)   taken over a period of time against the salary costs of the employees being trained, for example over the estimated duration of the project; or

(c)   taken over the estimated period for which the company or the employees are expected to benefit from the training; or

(d)   not distinguished from other project grants received and therefore matched against total project costs; or

(e)   taken to income systematically over the life of the project, for example the total grant receivable may be allocated to revenue on a straight-line basis; or

(f)   as in (d) or (e) above, but using, instead of project life, the period over which the grant is paid; or

(g)   taken to income when received in cash.

Depending on the circumstances, any of these approaches might produce an acceptable result. However, our observations on these alternative methods are as follows:

Under method (a), the grant could be recognised as income considerably in advance of its receipt, since often the major part of the direct training costs will be incurred at the beginning of a project and payment is usually made retrospectively. As the total grant receivable may be subject to adjustment, this may not be prudent or may lead to a mismatch of costs and revenues.

Methods (b) to (e) all rely on different interpretations of the expenditure to which the grant is expected to contribute, and could all represent an appropriate form of matching.

Method (f) has less to commend it, but the period of payment of the grant might in fact give an indication (in the absence of better evidence) of the duration of the project for which the expenditure is to be subsidised.

Similarly, method (g) is unlikely to be the most appropriate method *per se*, but may approximate to one of the other methods, or may, in the absence of any conclusive indication as to the expenditure intended to be subsidised by the grant, be the only practicable method that can be adopted.

In some jurisdictions grants are taxed as income on receipt; consequently, this is often the argument advanced for taking grants to income when received in cash. However, it is clear that the treatment of an item for tax purposes does not necessarily determine its treatment for accounting purposes, and immediate recognition in the income statement may result in an unacceptable departure from the principle that government grants should be matched with the costs that they are intended to compensate. Consequently, the recognition of a grant in the income statement in a different period from that in which it is taxed, gives rise to a temporary difference that should be accounted for in accordance with IAS 12 – *Income Taxes* (see Chapter 26 at 4.2).

In the face of the problems described above of attributing a grant to related costs, it is difficult to offer definitive guidance; entities will have to make their own judgements as to how the matching principle is to be applied. The only overriding considerations are that the method should be systematically and consistently applied, and that the policy adopted in respect of both capital and revenue grants, if material, should adequately be disclosed. Nevertheless, we do offer the following points for consideration.

3.1.1   Should the grant be split into its elements?

The grant received may be part of a package, the elements of which have different costs and conditions. In such cases, it will often be appropriate to treat these different elements on different bases rather than accounting for the entire grant in one way. However, IAS 20 does caution that care is needed in identifying the conditions giving rise to the costs and expenses, which determine the periods over which the grant will be earned.[67]

3.1.2   What was the purpose of the grant?

The method by which the amount of grant receivable is calculated does not conclusively determine its accounting treatment. For example, the amount of the grant may be based on the creation of jobs but it may be intended to contribute towards the costs of acquiring long-term assets or other costs as well. It will be necessary to examine the full circumstances of the grant in order to determine its purpose.

3.1.3   What is the period to be benefited by the grant?

The qualifying conditions that have to be satisfied are not necessarily conclusive evidence of the period to be benefited by the grant. For example, certain grants may become repayable if assets cease to be used for a qualifying purpose within a certain period; notwithstanding this condition, the grant should be recognised over the whole life of the asset, not over the qualifying period.

3.1.4   Is a grant related to long-term assets or income?

In general, we recommend that grants should be regarded as linked to long-term assets where this is a possible interpretation and there is no clear indication to the contrary, particularly where the payment of the grant is based on the cost of acquisition of long-term assets. However, we believe that the most important consideration where there are significant questions over how the grant is to be recognised, and where the effect is material, is that the financial statements should explicitly state what treatment has been chosen and disclose the financial effect of adopting that treatment.

4   THE FUTURE OF IAS 20

The IASB has several legitimate concerns about IAS 20, particularly regarding the standard's inconsistency with the *Framework*, its numerous options and the fact that it is inconsistent with more recent pronouncements of other standard-setting bodies as well.[68] Consequently, as part of its short-term US GAAP convergence project, the IASB concluded that it should undertake a limited scope project to improve IAS 20. Initially the objective of the project was to amend IAS 20 by applying the accounting model for government grants contained in IAS 41 – *Agriculture* – to all government grants (see Chapter 41). At present, the model in IAS 41 applies only to biological assets measured at fair value less estimated point-of-sale costs and grants that require entities not to engage in specified agricultural activity. In contrast to IAS 20, recognition of a government grant as income in accordance with IAS 41 depends on whether the grant is conditional and, if so, when the conditions are satisfied. Hence, the objective in IAS 41 is to recognise the obligations the entity has until conditions are satisfied, rather than to match the grant with the expenses it is intended to compensate or the acquisition costs of assets that it is used to finance.

Nevertheless, the Board noted some concerns about the conceptual basis of the government grant model in IAS 41, particularly in its treatment of conditional grants. The Board noted also that its work in other projects, in particular its project to amend IAS 37 – *Provisions, Contingent Liabilities and Contingent Assets* – might yield insights into the appropriate treatment of obligations arising in conditional grants and enable it to develop a more robust model for accounting for government grants. Accordingly, the Board decided to defer work on the IAS 20 project until further progress is made on those projects; it has now concluded that progress in revenue recognition (Chapter 25), related parties (Chapter 28) and emissions trading schemes (Chapter 15) are also preconditions to updating IAS 20.

It is clear that IAS 20's income statement matching approach to the accounting for government grants has a limited remaining shelf life but it remains to be seen when the IASB will find the time to revise the standard.

5   SERVICE CONCESSION ARRANGEMENTS

5.1   Introduction

Service concession arrangements have been developed as a mechanism for procuring public services. Under a service concession arrangement ('SCA'), private capital is used to provide major economic and social facilities for public use, although such arrangements are not necessarily solely between the public sector and private sector bodies. The initial idea was that, rather than having bodies in the public sector taking on the entire responsibility for funding and building infrastructure assets such as roads, bridges, railways, hospitals, prisons and other infrastructure assets, some of these should be contracted out to private sector entities from which the public sector bodies would buy services. As time has passed, the types of services covered by such arrangements have changed and they no longer necessarily include the construction of a major asset. Many service concessions now require the private sector to bring an existing facility or service up to an agreed standard and continue to maintain it for a contracted period; this type of arrangement has covered a range of projects from the refurbishment of social housing and street lighting to major civil engineering projects to restore a city's underground rail system. In addition, similar arrangements have been developed between private sector bodies, thereby creating an indistinct boundary between service concession-type and outsourcing arrangements.

The accounting challenge is to reflect the substance of these arrangements fairly in the accounts of both of the contracting parties. It would be possible simply to take the contracts at fair value and account for the amounts received as revenue when due under the contract; however, closer analysis may sometimes reveal that this is, in reality, a composite transaction whereby the public sector body is paying for an asset to be constructed and operated at its direction as well as for services. There is the issue of how to account for the operations period of the contract, which may also include asset replacement and refurbishment as well as more obvious services.

The issues raised by service concessions range across a number of accounting standards and interpretations, including (at least) IAS 11 – *Construction Contracts*, IAS 16 – *Property, Plant and Equipment*, IAS 17 – *Leases*, IFRIC Interpretation 4 – *Determining whether an Arrangement contains a Lease*, IAS 18 – *Revenue*, IAS 20 – *Accounting for Government Grants and Disclosure of Government Assistance*, IAS 23 – *Borrowing Costs*, IAS 32 – *Financial Instruments: Presentation*, IAS 37 – *Provisions, Contingent Liabilities and Contingent Assets*, IAS 38 – *Intangible Assets*, and IAS 39 – *Financial Instruments: Recognition and Measurement*, which makes it extremely difficult to develop a coherent accounting model that deals with all of the features of service concessions simultaneously, and from the position of both the private sector (i.e. the 'operator') and public sector (i.e. the 'grantor'). Moreover, entrenched national positions had developed and differing accounting treatments had been widely adopted in various jurisdictions, with or without a basis in specific local accounting standards. For example, in the UK, where there is formal accounting guidance under UK GAAP, operators are required to analyse assets constructed for the concession as property, plant and equipment or as financial assets (receivables due from the public sector body).[69] Indeed, some jurisdictions accepted more than one treatment of broadly similar arrangements, some of which are associated with a taxation basis that has been agreed with the jurisdictional revenue authorities.

In May 2001, SIC-29 – *Disclosure – Service Concession Arrangements* – was issued. This did not attempt to address the accounting issues but considered the information that should be disclosed in the notes to the financial statements of an 'operator' and 'grantor' under a service concession arrangement . Its requirements are described further at 7 below.

Since then, the complex accounting issues raised by service concessions have been subject to prolonged debate. The IFRIC began its formal discussions in 2003 but it took until November 2006 to issue IFRIC Interpretation 12 – *Service Concession Arrangements*. The IFRIC discussions clearly demonstrate the complexity of the issues and the difficulty in fitting them into the existing accounting framework.

5.2   The IFRIC's approach to accounting for service concessions

The IFRIC views the primary accounting decision for the operator as being between:

- infrastructure assets where the grantor cedes control to the operator, or assets (whether constructed for the concession or otherwise) that remain within the operator's control; and

- infrastructure assets constructed for the concession or acquired from a third party that become those of the grantor because it controls them, or existing assets that remain under its control.

The IFRIC suggests that the first category (where the asset is either derecognised by the grantor or is an asset constructed for the concession that the grantor never controls) can be dealt with adequately by other accounting standards or interpretations. The interrelationship with other accounting standards is discussed further in 5.3 below.

The second category (infrastructure assets constructed for the concession that become those of the grantor because it controls them or existing assets that remain under its control) is the subject of IFRIC 12 relating to service concessions.[70]

'Control' is a central concept under the IFRIC approach and its definition and consequences are discussed further at 5.3.3 below.

Thus any infrastructure that remains under the control of the grantor will be accounted for using these two service concession models – the 'financial asset' model or the 'intangible asset' model. These are considered further in 5.4 below.

5.3   Scope of IFRIC 12

The IFRIC has concluded that the scope should be limited to the accounting by the operator in a public-to-private service concession that meets its control criteria.[71]

The grantor (including parties related to it) will be considered to control the property if the arrangement meets two conditions:

(a)   the grantor controls or regulates the services that the operator must provide using the infrastructure, to whom it must provide them, and at what price; and

(b)   the grantor controls any significant residual interest in the property at the end of the concession term through ownership, beneficial entitlement or otherwise. Infrastructure used for its entire useful life is within the scope if the arrangement meets the conditions in (a).[72]

Infrastructure assets within scope are those constructed or acquired for the purpose of the concession or existing infrastructure to which the operator is given access for these purposes (see 5.3.4 below).[73] Accounting is based on who controls the right to use the infrastructure. Crucially, control may be separated from ownership. Therefore, if the grantor controls the infrastructure assets, they should be accounted for according to one of the service concession models (see 5.3.3 below).

Arrangements within scope will be those that meet the following criteria:

1   the arrangement is a public-to-private service concession (5.3.1 below);

2   the grantor controls the services (5.3.3A below);

3   the grantor controls the residual interest (5.3.3B below);

4   infrastructure is constructed or acquired for the purpose of the service concession (5.3.4 below); and

5   The operator has a contract with the grantor under which there is a contractual right to receive cash from or at the direction of the grantor or a contractual right to charge users of the service (5.4 below).

If the answer to all of these is 'yes', then the arrangement is in scope of IFRIC 12. The last question also determines which of IFRIC 12's accounting models, financial asset or intangible asset, should be applied.

While the IFRIC expects IFRIC 12 to be applied to transactions that share the features of the public service obligation, it does not rule out the application of the principles to private-to-private arrangements. The Basis for Conclusions notes that this could be appropriate under the hierarchy in IAS 8 if the arrangement were of a similar type and met the control criteria quoted above.[74] The Interpretation does not expand on the features that could make an arrangement 'similar' to a transaction that is within scope.

The proposals apply only to accounting by the operator, not the grantor.[75] This seems reasonable as most grantors are governments who may have their own views about accounting and do not necessarily apply IFRS, to the extent that they prepare publicly available financial information at all.

The IFRIC's accounting framework is summarised in the following diagram from Information Note 1 in IFRIC 12. The diagram starts with the presumption that the arrangement has already been determined to be a service concession:

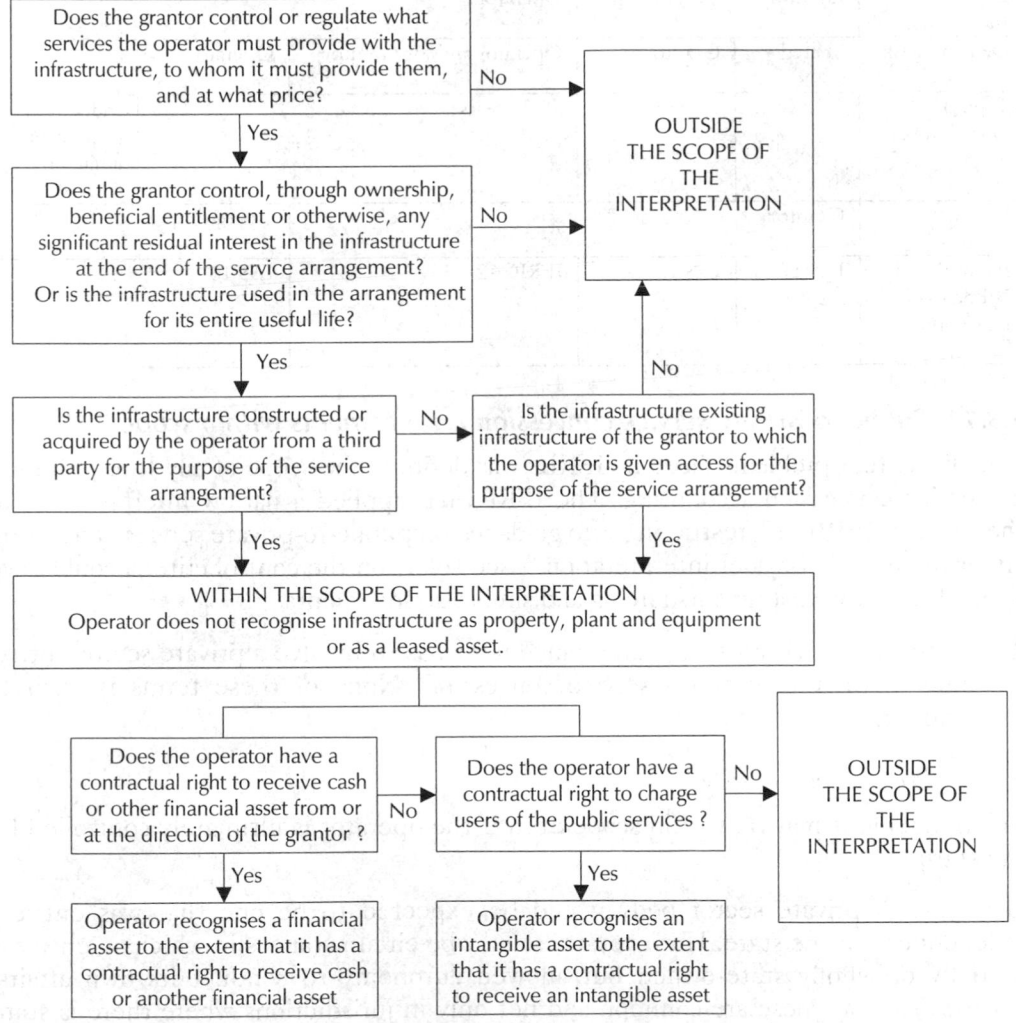

In an attempt to clarify the scope, the IFRIC has produced a table on which the following is based (included as Information Note 2 to IFRIC 12) and which shows the range of arrangements between the public and private sectors. The IFRIC's view is that it is interpreting IFRSs for the transactions in the middle of this range, where the application of standards is unclear.

Category	Lessee	Service Provider			Owner	
Typical Arrangement Types	Lease, e.g. Operator leases asset from grantor	Service and/or maintenance contract, e.g. specific tasks e.g. debt collection	Rehabilitate-operate-transfer	Build-operate-transfer	Build-own-operate	100% Divestment, privatisation, Corporation
Asset Ownership	Grantor				Operator	
Capital Investment	Grantor	Operator				
Demand Risk	Shared	Grantor	Operator and/or Grantor		Operator	
Typical Duration	8-20 years	1-5 years	25-30 years			Indefinite (or may be limited by license)
Residual Interest	Grantor				Operator	
Examples of IFRSs that may apply	IAS 17	IAS 18	IFRIC 12		IAS 16	

5.3.1   Public-to-private service concession arrangements within scope

One of the first problems faced by IFRIC was defining the scope of any Interpretation on service concession accounting. The IFRIC has applied a narrow interpretation to the scope of IFRIC 12, restricting it to guidance on public-to-private service concession arrangements.[76] A broader interpretation based solely on the control criteria could have applied to many existing outsourcing and similar arrangements.

Therefore, to be within scope, an arrangement has to involve a private sector entity, a public sector entity and a service concession. None of these terms is entirely self-evident.

A   Private sector body

An arrangement may be within scope even if the operator is ultimately controlled by the state.

Generally, a private sector body would be expected to be one that was entirely independent of the state. However, there may be circumstances in which an entity is partially or wholly state-owned but allowed autonomy to conduct its own affairs. Entities such as these are common and not only in jurisdictions where there is state ownership of all economic activity. Some governments allow utilities to control most of their own affairs while retaining ownership of the utility. Governments may take total or partial ownership of entities as a means of encouraging economic development but allow the entity control over its contractual arrangements.

If there is an arrangement that in all other respects appears to be the same as a service concession arrangement between a private body and the state, the state-owned entity may be considered as if it were a private sector body and IFRIC 12 will apply. If there is only a law regulating the activity of the 'service concession' rather than a contractual arrangement then the arrangement is not within scope.

B   Public sector body

IFRIC 12 notes that control over services and prices in paragraph 5(a), described above:

> '... includes circumstances in which the grantor buys all of the output as well as those in which some or all of the output is bought by other users. In applying this condition, the grantor and any related parties shall be considered together. If the grantor is a public sector entity, the public sector as a whole, together with any regulators acting in the public interest, shall be regarded as related to the grantor for the purposes of this Interpretation.'[77]

This means that the entire public may be considered as part of the 'public sector' if the grantor purchases all of the output and provides services for free, e.g. health services.

Not every related party of the grantor (as defined in paragraph 9 of IAS 24 – *Related Party Disclosure* – see Chapter 38) need be taken into account in determining whether the grantor controls the service concession. Some services may be provided simultaneously to more than one public sector body but they will only be taken into account together if they operate in concert to control the 'output'. For instance, an entity may provide similar information technology services to several government departments and local government bodies but each contract is negotiated separately; the departments and bodies are not necessarily 'related parties'. Regulators must be taken into account but may not be related parties of the grantor as defined by IAS 24 as they may be required to be independent to act in the public interest.

Control of prices is discussed further at 5.3.3 below.

C   Service concession arrangement ('SCA')

IFRIC 12 does not include the features of a service concession agreement within the scope paragraphs; instead they are included in 'background information' where they help define what is, and what is not, a public-private service arrangement. The main characteristic of a service concession is the public service nature of the obligation undertaken by the operator. The services related to the infrastructure are to be provided to the public as a matter of policy, irrespective of the identity of the party that operates the services. The service concession arrangement contractually obliges the operator to provide the services to the public on behalf of the public sector entity. IFRIC 12 states that 'other common features are:

(a)   the party that grants the service arrangement (the grantor) is a public sector entity, including a governmental body, or a private sector entity to which the responsibility for the service has been devolved.

(b)   the operator is responsible for at least some of the management of the infrastructure and related services and does not merely act as an agent on behalf of the grantor.

(c)   the contract sets the initial prices to be levied by the operator and regulates price revisions over the period of the service arrangement.

(d)   the operator is obliged to hand over the infrastructure to the grantor in a specified condition at the end of the period of the arrangement, for little or no incremental consideration, irrespective of which party initially financed it.'[78]

The meaning of the public service obligation remains somewhat elusive. SCAs fall into two broad categories where the public service obligation can be identified:

1   SCAs that provide services directly to the public (e.g. transport, water supply, sewage, landfills).

2   SCAs where the services 'related to the infrastructure' continue to be provided by the grantor, e.g. the services provided by hospitals, prisons or schools, all of which would usually be considered to be examples of service concession arrangements. However, the infrastructure that is the subject of the contractual arrangement is used to provide services directly to the public or a significant part of it.

In other cases, it is far less clear that there is a public service obligation. The services are those that need to be provided to the public as a matter of policy (e.g. the provision of electricity) but the contractual arrangement itself is unrelated to any public service obligation. The entity simply has to provide services to the grantor through an asset it has constructed. The arrangement is frequently the same as those that the operator has with private sector bodies.

These outsourcing-type arrangements are examples of perhaps the most problematic boundary, that between IFRIC 12 and IFRIC 4 –*Determining whether an Arrangement contains a Lease*. The IFRIC has attempted to deal with this, not wholly successfully, by introducing an amendment to IFRIC 4 specifically to exclude arrangements falling within the scope of IFRIC 12 from its scope.[79] This is discussed in 5.3.2 below.

D   Agent type arrangements

A feature of SCAs is that the operator is responsible for at least some of the management of the infrastructure and related services and does not merely act as an agent on behalf of the grantor.[80]

For example, an operator constructs and maintains for 25 years a building that will be used for administrative purposes by the Ministry of Defence. The building does not have any parts dedicated to the provision of services directly to the public although the service that is provided within the building may be provided to the public as a matter of policy. At the end of the concession term, the building reverts to the

Ministry for a nominal sum. In the interests of national security, all details of the services to be provided are predetermined.

This will always be a question of degree and is unlikely to be the crucial feature in making a decision but it may help distinguish SCAs within scope of IFRIC 12 from some of the 'outsourcing' type arrangements discussed in 5.3.2 below.

E   A contract with the grantor

An arrangement can only be a SCA if there is a contract with the grantor. If the operator obtains a licence but has no contractual obligation to the grantor to provide construction services in regards of any infrastructure, then, although the arrangement may be within scope of IFRIC 12, it will be in respect of post-construction services. Accounting for the post-contract period is described at 5.5.2 below.

Information Note 2 to IFRIC 12, reproduced in 5.3 above, indicates that there are certain contractual arrangements between grantor and operator that are not within scope of the Interpretation. These include arrangements in which there is a lease-type arrangement, e.g. the operator leases asset from grantor, in which case IAS 17 applies or a service and/or maintenance contract, e.g. to perform specific tasks, where IAS 18 is the relevant standard.

5.3.2   IFRIC 4 and IFRIC 12: outsourcing arrangements and SCAs

Many outsourcing-type arrangements may not necessarily be within scope of IFRIC 12. The IFRIC noted in September 2005 that it would not expect an information technology outsourcing arrangement for a government department to be dealt with under the Interpretation.[81] The IFRIC presumably concluded that as an outsourcing arrangement this more properly fell within IFRIC 4 – *Determining whether an Arrangement contains a Lease*; the infrastructure is used by the grantor in order that it can provide a public service but it is not used itself to provide the service.

The IFRIC has amended IFRIC 4 specifically to exclude arrangements falling within the scope of IFRIC 12 from its scope.[82] However, while this clarifies the treatment of arrangements that are clearly within scope of IFRIC 12, in which case that Interpretation takes priority, it does not help in the type of case where it is not clear that the arrangement falls within scope of IFRIC 12 in the first place.

In practice it may be hard to distinguish outsourcing arrangements accounted for under IFRIC 4 from arrangements in which the grantor controls the infrastructure and that are properly within scope of IFRIC 12. The control test alone does not seem to be adequate. There are numerous examples of arrangements in which the grantor controls the services in their entirety and controls the residual interest in the infrastructure asset but that would have been seen as containing leases under IAS 17 by applying an IFRIC 4 analysis. In other words, a grantor may have a 'right to control the use' of an infrastructure asset, under an IFRIC 4 analysis,[83] see Chapter 22 at 2.2.1, or an operator may have a 'right of access' of that same asset, if it is within the scope of IFRIC 12. This could make a significant difference to the manner in which the arrangement is accounted for. IFRIC 12's control model and IAS 17's risks and rewards tests could result in different assets being recognised in the financial statements of operator and grantor as an arrangement could be accounted for under the financial asset model under IFRIC 12 yet considered an operating lease under IAS 17.

The operator may have arrangements on the same terms with private sector bodies and with the public sector. In many parts of the world, governments have chosen to expand power generation by entering into contracts with operators. Some of these arrangements have the same features as power supply contracts to private sector purchasers to which IFRIC 4 applies. Commonly, the contract allows for a fixed charge that is payable irrespective of deliveries, which may or may not cover all of the capital expenditure, a variable charge related to the variable costs of generating power and a penalty regime under which part of the fixed cost is refundable. In other words, these are the features that are described in Chapter 22, Example 22.2, 'An arrangement that contains a lease'. Providing power is a public service yet the public service element may be irrelevant to the nature of the contract. The use to which the grantor puts the power need not affect the arrangement; for example, the power could be used solely by Government department buildings, by a government-owned industry, for naval dockyards or it could be put directly into the national electricity distribution network. Entities in these circumstances appear to have a choice. They may consider that IFRIC 12 is not mandatory because the contract is not a service concession containing any public service obligation on the basis that the way in which a transaction is accounted for should not be determined solely by the nature of the customer. Such an entity may adopt IFRIC 4 in accounting for the arrangement; alternatively, it may apply IFRIC 12.

The absence of services directly to the public may indicate that the arrangement is more of the nature of a government outsourcing. In the power supply case, there are no services in addition to those necessary to maintain the power supply, unlike the much more extensive services that are usually supplied as part of typical SCAs such as hospitals or prisons. By contrast, other SCAs that also have few associated services such as toll roads and bridges are clearly used directly by the public.

In the end, it is always likely to be a matter of judgement and there will be different views in practice. IFRIC 12 was developed because there are transactions that are so complex that it is very difficult to fit them into an existing accounting model and it is important not to lose sight of this. It appears that it was not the intention of the IFRIC to change the manner in which outsourcing arrangements were accounted for solely because the contracting party is a government body. If the arrangement closely resembles longstanding private-to-private arrangements that have always been analysed using other standards (e.g. IAS 16 and IFRIC 4), then it may not be necessary to consider them to be within scope of IFRIC 12.

If an arrangement is not clearly within scope then it is not possible to mandate the application of the Interpretation. Equally, there is nothing to prevent an entity applying IFRIC 12 to a particular outsourcing arrangement that meets the control criteria but has no obvious public service obligations. Entities that deal predominantly with the private sector but have arrangements of the same type with public sector grantors may find it more appropriate to apply the same accounting model to all contracts of similar nature and *vice versa*.

5.3.3   *The control model*

IFRIC 12 includes the following guidance that expands and explains its control criteria first described in 5.3 above:

(a)   the grantor controls or regulates the services that the operator must provide using the infrastructure, to whom it must provide them, and at what price; and

(b)   the grantor controls any significant residual interest in the property at the end of the concession term through ownership, beneficial entitlement or otherwise.[84]

The IFRIC considers that, taken together, these conditions identify when the infrastructure is controlled by the grantor for the whole of its economic life, in which case an operator is only managing the infrastructure on the grantor's behalf.[85] Crucially, it has concluded from this that an infrastructure asset controlled by the grantor cannot be the property, plant and equipment of the operator.[86]

A   *Regulation of services*

The control or regulation of services does not have to be by contract – it could include control via an industry regulator. Control also extends to circumstances in which the grantor buys all of the output as well as those in which it is bought by other users. The grantor and any related parties must be considered together. If the grantor is a public sector entity, the public sector as a whole, together with any independent regulators acting in the public interest, are to be regarded as related to the grantor.[87] 'Price' can mean the amount at which the grantor buys the service or the amount that the operator charges members of the public or a combination of both.

This means that many regulated public utilities (water, sewage, electricity supply etc.) will fall within (a). Other arrangements that fall within (a) include public health facilities that are free to users and subsidised transport facilities (rail, some toll roads and bridges) that are partly paid by public sector grant and partly by passenger fares. Of course, all of these will only be within scope of IFRIC 12 if any significant residual interest is also 'controlled' by the grantor under (b).

The IFRIC stresses that the grantor does not need to have complete control of the price. It is sufficient for the price to be regulated, which could be by way of a capping mechanism (regulated utilities are usually free to charge *lower* prices). Obviously, it is a requirement to look to the substance of the agreements so a cap that only applies in remote circumstances will be ignored. Other 'caps' may not be so apparent. A contract may give the operator freedom to set its prices but any excess is clawed back by the grantor (e.g. through setting a maximum return on an agreed investment in the infrastructure). In such a case, the operator's return is capped and the price element of the control test is substantively met.[88]

Some arrangements only allow the grantor to control prices for part of the life of the infrastructure, particularly if it is a lease-type arrangement. For example, an operator may construct clinical facilities that are used by a government health care provider (the grantor) for a five year contract term. At the end of the term, the grantor may extend the contract by renegotiation. If it does not do so, the operator can run the facilities for private health care. Although the prices are controlled for the first five years, this arrangement is unlikely to meet the control condition in (a) above.

B   *Control of the residual interest*

The grantor's control over any significant residual interest should restrict the operator's ability to sell or pledge the infrastructure. The grantor must have a right of use of the infrastructure throughout the concession term.[89]

The IFRIC has considered the impact of partial replacement on condition (b). If the operator has to replace part of an item of infrastructure during the life of the concession (for example, the top layer of a road or the roof of a building), the item of infrastructure is to be considered as a whole, so that condition (b) will be met for the whole of the infrastructure, including the part that is replaced, if the grantor has the residual interest in the final replacement of that part.[90]

IFRIC 12 pays little attention to the residual interest. It does not expand on 'significant' and how it should be measured. It does not explain whether there is a relationship between 'residual interest' and 'residual value' in IAS 16 (see Chapter 16). It may not be possible to base the assessment of 'significance' on the cash flows received by the operator on handing back the asset to the grantor as these may be nominal amounts; indeed, the grantor may pay nothing. The remaining useful life of the asset when it reverts may give a good indication, e.g. if a hospital is handed back to the public sector with a remaining useful life of twenty years, this residual interest is likely to be significant. Some infrastructure assets such as toll roads and bridges generate cash flows directly and it may be possible to use estimated future cash flows to calculate the significance of the residual value, whether or not the grantor will charge tolls after reversion of the asset.

In some arrangements the grantor only has an option to reacquire the asset at the end of the concession term. In the circumstances described above of an asset that still has a significant life or earnings potential at the end of the contract, the grantor will control the residual if the option is for a nominal sum. An option at fair value at the date of exercise may by itself be enough to give the grantor control over the residual under IFRIC 12. Other features may also indicate that the grantor controls the residual interest. There are usually several contractual alternatives: the operator is granted a second concession term, a new operator is allowed to acquire the assets or the grantor acquires the assets and brings the arrangement 'in house'. The grantor still controls the residual as it will determine which of these alternatives applies and the option exercise price (if it or a new operator acquires the infrastructure) is irrelevant. This is a clear difference between a 'risks and rewards' and a 'control' model as under the former, the operator would be seen as keeping the risks and rewards of ownership if another party had the right to acquire the asset at fair value. An arrangement in which the grantor only has an option to acquire at fair value may be evidence that the grantor does not control sufficient of the prices of the arrangement to be a SCA; see A above.

However, what if the arrangement is for the whole life of the infrastructure? Assets in service concession arrangements may revert to the grantor at the end of the concession term but they may not have much, if any, remaining useful life. Many modern buildings, for example, only have a useful life of thirty years or so and this is a common concession term. Consequently, infrastructure used in a service concession arrangement for the whole of its useful life ('whole of life infrastructure') is included within the scope of IFRIC 12.[91]

The IFRIC pointed out that one reason for including the 'significant residual interest' requirement was to differentiate between regulated industries and service concession arrangements, thereby seeming to confirm that it had not intended regulated industries to be in scope.[92] We assume that the IFRIC still considers that privatised regulated industries should generally be out of scope, perhaps because they are divestitures or privatisations where it is more appropriate to treat the infrastructure as the property, plant and equipment of the operator. In addition it is usually the case that the infrastructure only reverts to the grantor in the event of a major breach of the conditions of the concession and this may well mean that the grantor does not control it in the sense required by IFRIC 12.

GDF Suez discloses that some of its concessions are not considered to be within scope of IFRIC 12 as the infrastructure is not returned to the grantor at the end of the contract. These assets (for water and gas distribution) are likely to have a life in excess of the contract term.

Extract 23.6: GDF Suez SA (2008)

20.2   Notes to the Consolidated Financial Statements [extract]
Note 22   Service concession arrangements

The Group manages a large number of concessions are defined by SIC-29 covering drinking water distribution, water treatment, waste collection and treatment, and gas and electricity distribution.,

These concession arrangements set out rights and obligations relative to the infrastructure and to the public service, in particular the obligation to provide users with access to the public service. In certain concessions, a schedule is defined specifying the period over which udders should be provided access to the public service. The terms of the concession arrangements vary between 10 and 65 years, depending mainly on the level of capital expenditures to be made by the concession operator.

For the consideration of those obligations, GDF SUEZ is entitled to bill either the local authority, the grantor of the concession, (mainly incineration and BOT water treatment contracts) or the users (contracts for the distribution of drinking water or gas and electricity) for the services provided. This right to bill gives rise to an intangible asset, a tangible asset, or a financial asset, depending on the applicable accounting model (see note 1.4.7).

The tangible asset model is used when the concession grantor does not control the infrastructure. For example, this is the case of water distribution concessions in the United States, which do not provide for the return of the infrastructure to the grantor of the concession at the end of the contract (and the infrastructure therefore remains the property of GDF SUEZ), and gas distribution concessions in France, which all within the scope of law no. 46-628 of April 8, 1946.

A general obligation also exists to return the concession infrastructure to good working condition at the end of the concession. Where appropriate (see note 1.4.7), this obligation leads to the recognition of a capital renewal and replacement liability (see note 14.2.3).

5.3.4   Assets within scope

There are two groups of assets within scope of IFRIC 12:

(a)   the infrastructure that the operator constructs or acquires from a third party for the purpose of the concession; and

(b)   existing infrastructure to which the grantor gives the operator access for the purpose of the concession.[93]

The operator may use some of its existing assets for the purpose of the concession. These are out of scope. The IFRIC's view is that accounting for assets is already covered by existing accounting standards, principally IAS 16, and therefore it will not specify how the operator should account for its previously existing assets that now form part of the infrastructure. The suggestion in IFRIC D12 that it would be unusual for existing assets to be material[94] is, perhaps, based on the assumption that the assets in question would be equipment and other items used to construct the infrastructure and not a reflection of arrangements that happen in practice – there are examples of hospitals built by the private sector being taken over by the public sector as service concession arrangements. IFRIC 12 states that the service concession arrangement may convey a right of use of existing assets of the operator to the grantor, in which case the operator would apply the derecognition requirements of IAS 16 to determine whether it should derecognise them.[95] The implication is that losing control of the infrastructure asset by contractually giving control of its use to the grantor may in some circumstances be a deemed disposal of the asset under IAS 16 (see Chapter 16 at 5 where derecognition is discussed).

A   Partially regulated assets

IFRIC 12 notes that it is not uncommon for the use of infrastructure to be partly regulated and partly unregulated and gives examples while noting that these activities take a variety of forms:

'(a)   any infrastructure that is physically separable and capable of being operated independently and meets the definition of a cash generating unit as defined in IAS 36 [*Impairment of Assets*] shall be analysed separately if it is used wholly for unregulated purposes. For example this might apply to a private wing of a hospital, where the remainder of the hospital is used by the grantor to treat public patients.

(b)   where purely ancillary activities (such as a hospital shop) are unregulated, the control tests shall be applied as if those services did not exist, because in cases in which the grantor controls the services described in paragraph 5, the existence of ancillary activities does not detract from the grantor's control of the relevant infrastructure'[96]

In both of these cases, the operator may have a lease from the grantor that gives it a right to use the asset in question; if so, this is to be accounted for in accordance with IAS 17.[97] This would be likely to involve using IFRIC 4's principles to distinguish the lease payments from other parts of the arrangement (see Chapter 22 at 2.2.1).

There may be services that are neither purely ancillary nor delivered by using a physically separable portion of the total infrastructure, a situation not addressed by AG 7. For example, a grantor may control prices charged to children, pensioners and the unemployed who use a sports facility but the amounts charged to other adults are not controlled. The same swimming pool is being used by all, regardless of the amount that they pay. In such cases it will be a matter of judgement whether enough of the service is unregulated in order to demonstrate that the grantor is not considered to control the asset.

5.4 Accounting for the infrastructure asset: choosing between the financial asset and intangible asset models

The two models in the analysis utilise several decisions of principle, two of which we have already discussed:

- the control model applies as described in 5.3 and 5.3.3 above, which means that the operator will not recognise infrastructure assets as its property, plant and equipment;[98] and

- the operator is providing 'construction services' as described in 5.3.4 above and not, for example, constructing an item of property, plant and equipment for sale. Construction services are to be accounted for separately from 'operation services' in the operations phase of the contract.

There is a third important point of principle: the 'amounts due from customers' asset that arises from the application of the stage of completion method of revenue recognition required by IAS 11 (whose principles are used during the period of construction of the asset – see 5.4.2 and 5.4.3 below) is a financial asset as defined in IAS 32.

5.4.1 Consideration for services provided and the choice between the two models

Operators almost always negotiate a single contract with the grantor and, although the Interpretation does not refer to this, this will usually include a single payment mechanism throughout the concession term (sometimes called a 'unitary payment'). The operator is unlikely to be remunerated separately for its different activities. The payment mechanism often falls into one or other of the following models:

Example 23.4:   Payment mechanisms for service concessions

(a)   a hospital where the payment is based on the availability of the whole hospital

The unitary payment is based on the full provision of an overall accommodation requirement which is divided into different units, such as hospital wards, consulting rooms, operating theatres, common parts and reception. Availability is defined in terms of being usable and accessible and, includes some associated core services such as heating, power and (in the case of operating theatres) appropriate cleanliness. There is a payment deduction for failure to provide an available unit according to a contractual scale. There are no separate payment streams for any of the non-core services but substandard performance can result in payment deductions.

$P = (F \times I) - (D + E)$
P = unitary payment per day
F = price per day for overall accommodation requirement
I = Indexation increase based on the retail prices index
D = deductions for unavailability
E = performance deductions

The payments for both schemes are not immediately separable between amounts attributable to the construction or other services.

b)   a prison where payment is made based on the number of occupied places

The unitary payment is based on the number of occupied places. Occupied means not only that a prisoner is allocated a physical space but the associated core services and minimum requirements must be met in relation to services such as heating, mail delivery and food. No payment is made for unoccupied places. There are no separate payment streams for any of the non-core services (i.e. not associated with the definition of an occupied place) but deductions from the unitary payment can be made for substandard performance of these services.

The unitary payment is based on the following formula:

$P = (F \times I) - Z$
P = unitary payment per place
F = Fixed amount per occupied place per day
I = Indexation increase based on the retail prices index
Z = Performance deductions

Payments usually start only when the infrastructure asset has been completed and accepted as suitable for purpose by the grantor. Operators usually seek payment during the construction phase but whether or not they receive any is inevitably a result of negotiation between the parties.

IFRIC 12 clarifies the basis on which revenue is recognised in accordance with IAS 11 and IAS 18. It argues that if the operator provides separate services as part of its overall contractual arrangement it will allocate the consideration receivable by reference to their relative fair values. The exercise to separate the consideration receivable for the separate services (e.g. construction, upgrading or operating services) provided by the operator is expanded in A below. The nature of the consideration determines the accounting model, as described in B below.

A   Allocating the consideration

It is argued that it is in accordance with IAS 18 to separate the construction services that will be accounted for under IAS 11 from the remainder of the contract. Thereafter the separate services within this contract (for example 'upgrade services' or 'operations services') may also be disaggregated on the basis of their 'distinct skills, requirements and risks'.[99] IFRIC 12 argues that the operator might report different profit margins for its construction services within IAS 11 and the other services that are within IAS 18. The inference is that these different margins may also help allocate the total consideration.[100] One must be very cautious here as IAS 11 does not permit an entity to determine what it considers to be an appropriate profit margin for the contract and use this as the basis of recognising revenue and attributable contract costs (unless, of course, it is a cost plus contract) (see Chapter 21 at 2.3.2). The profit margin must be a consequence of the different fair values of the separate elements of the contract rather than driving the allocation of the consideration.

Although it is a single contract and a single payment mechanism, it is often straightforward in practice to identify the underlying revenue streams that relate to different activities. This may be on the basis of the original contract negotiations or because the contract contains terms allowing for subsequent price adjustments by 'market testing' or benchmarking. However, the revenue streams may not reflect the fair value of the underlying services so care will have to be taken. There will always be practical problems when it comes to apportioning the total contract consideration between the elements of the contract and the allocation will always be a matter of judgement.

B   Determining the accounting model

IFRIC 12 states that the operator may receive a financial asset or an intangible asset as consideration for its construction services and the asset that it receives determines the subsequent treatment.[101]

The operator will recognise a financial asset to the extent that it has a contractual right to receive cash or other financial assets from the grantor for the construction services, where the grantor has little, if any, discretion to avoid payment. This is usually because the agreement is legally enforceable.[102] The operator will recognise an intangible asset to the extent that it receives a licence to charge users of the public service.[103]

Sometimes it is necessary to 'bifurcate' the operator's right to cash flow into a financial asset and an intangible asset and account separately for each component of the operator's consideration. This, the IFRIC argues, is because the operator is paid for its services partly by a financial asset and partly by an intangible asset.[104]

As described in 5.4.2 and 5.4.3 below, IAS 11 will apply to the operator's activities ('construction or upgrade services') during the construction period.[105]

The IFRIC decided that the boundary between the financial and the intangible asset models should be based on the operator's contractual right to receive cash. The grantor does not need to pay the cash to the operator directly. If the grantor pays but the amounts are wholly based on usage of the infrastructure and there is no minimum guaranteed payment, the entity has no contractual right to receive cash. Therefore the intangible asset model will apply. Another consequence is so-called 'bifurcation', transactions in which the infrastructure asset is divided between a financial asset and an intangible asset.

The analysis between the different models can be seen in the following table:

	Arrangement	Applicable model
1	Grantor pays – fixed payments	Financial asset
2	Grantor pays – payments vary with demand	Intangible asset
3	Grantor retains demand risk – users pay but grantor guarantees amounts	Financial asset or bifurcated (part financial, part intangible)
4	Grantor retains demand risk – operator collects revenues from users until it achieves specified return	Intangible asset
5	Users pay – no grantor guarantees	Intangible asset

Of the two arrangements in Example 23.4 above, the hospital is an example of (1) above: the payments are contractually fixed if all obligations and services are provided. The prison, as described in Example 23.4 above, would fall within (2) and be accounted for as an intangible asset. However, the prison operator might be paid on a different basis, e.g. it might be paid for 1000 'available places' and receive this as long as heating and food were provided. In this case it would be no different to the hospital and be a financial asset. There are, of course, many potential variations and a combination of fixed and variable demand could lead to bifurcation.

The implications of service deductions are described at 5.4.2 below.

The IFRIC has concluded that what is important is that the operator has a contractual right to receive cash from, or at the direction of, the grantor. Fees or tolls received directly from users are viewed as essentially no more than collections on behalf of the grantor if they are part of an overall arrangement under which the grantor bears ultimate responsibility.

However, arrangements of the type in (4) above remain to be treated as intangible assets even if the overall risk to the operator of not obtaining a specified result is very low. This, it is argued, is not a contractual right to cash but a right to collect revenues from users and it is not relevant that the risk is low or that the operator will, in effect, get a fixed return. The following are examples of arrangements that will be accounted for using the intangible asset model:

(a)   A municipality grants the operator a contract to treat all of its waste collections for which it will be paid per unit processed. The arrangement does not provide for any guaranteed volume of waste to be treated by the operator (so it does not contain a take-or-pay arrangement) or any form of guarantee by the grantor. Historically, however, the annual volume of waste has never been less than

40,000 tons and the average annual volume over the last 20 years has been 75,000 tons.

(b)   An operator enters into a toll bridge concession. The operator is permitted to collect revenues from users or the grantor until it achieves a 6% return on its agreed infrastructure spend, at which point the arrangement comes to an end.

The toll bridge concession may be virtually commercially identical to a transaction that falls within (3), e.g. where the users pay tolls but the grantor guarantees a minimum 6% return. Somewhat ironically, this arrangement, which will contain a financial asset, is likely to leave more of the rewards of ownership with the operator than the intangible arrangement in (b) as the operator will be entitled to benefits in excess of the 6% return.

There are jurisdictions where public-to-private contract laws or the concession arrangements themselves allow an operator to ask the grantor for a revision of the tariffs for the public service when the operator's actual return is below initial expectations. Although this feature in the concession arrangement is included to reduce the operator's risk, it only gives the operator a right to re-negotiate and the outcome of that is not certain. As a result, the operator does not have an unconditional right to receive cash and, therefore, the operator may not apply the financial asset model.

5.4.2   *The financial asset model*

Under the financial asset model, which applies if the entity has a contractual right to receive cash or another financial asset,[106] the service element that relates to the construction of the infrastructure asset ('construction services') is accounted for in accordance with IAS 11. The consideration received by the operator for other services is addressed at 5.5 below.

As noted above, the IFRIC has argued that the 'amounts due from customers', i.e. those amounts recognised as revenue under IAS 11 from the point of initial recognition of the service concession, net of cash received, are deemed to be financial assets under IAS 32 because they represent contractual rights to receive cash or another financial asset from another entity.[107] This analysis is not affected by the fact that this contractual right may be contingent on performance standards, as in the example of a unitary charge for a hospital in Example 23.4 above. The IFRIC points out that this is no different from other circumstances and other financial assets where the payment depends on the subsequent performance of the asset.[108]

The financial asset will fall into one of the following three categories:

- a loan or receivable;
- an available-for-sale financial asset; or
- at fair value through profit or loss, if so designated on initial recognition.[109]

In the first two cases, interest income will be recognised, calculated using the effective interest method.[110]

The financial asset will not be classified as held-to-maturity.[111]

It is argued that the potential for variation that exists in any service concession arrangement does not comprise an embedded derivative because it is specific to the parties in the contract.[112]

The IFRIC also take the view, perhaps more surprisingly, that the financial asset may still be classified as a loan or receivable even if the amount to be received by the operator could vary either with the quality of subsequent services or performance or efficiency targets.[113] In other words, this would not prevent the amount to be received being 'determinable'.[114] Under IAS 39, amounts may only be classified as loans and receivables if the holder will receive 'substantially all of its initial investment, other than through credit deterioration'.[115] In this regard the IFRIC appears to have concluded that when the amount to be received by the operator could vary with the quality of services it provided or according to performance or efficiency targets, the arrangement does not contain an embedded derivative. These are non-financial measures and the remainder of the arrangement will meet the definition of a loan and receivable. If the contract is not classified as a loan and receivable it will most likely be classified as available-for-sale and be accounted for at fair value with changes in value taken to equity, unless it is designated as at fair value through profit or loss. These definitions are further described in Chapter 29.

The financial asset will be measured on initial recognition at its fair value, and interest will be calculated on the balance using the effective interest rate method.[116] Revenue will be recognised in accordance with IAS 11 when the contract work is performed using the percentage of completion method.[117] This means that the financial asset will be recognised from the beginning of contract activity.

How to measure this could represent a conundrum: it is necessary to recognise interest (using the effective interest rate method) on the financial asset simultaneously with revenue using the percentage of completion method. Part of what would otherwise have been recognised as construction revenue is now finance income. The Illustrative Example 1 in IFRIC 12, on which Example 23.5 below is based, avoids this problem by deeming the fair value of the consideration for construction services to be based on construction costs plus a margin. Potential issues with the use of a profit margin have previously been discussed at 5.4.1 above.

Borrowing costs cannot be capitalised under the financial asset model.[118]

Example 23.5:   *The Financial Asset Model – recording the construction asset*

Table 1 Concession terms

The terms of the arrangement require an operator to construct a road – completing construction within two years – and maintain and operate the road to a specified standard for eight years (i.e. years 3-10). The terms of the concession also require the operator to resurface the road at the end of year 8. At the end of year 10, the arrangement will end. The operator estimates that the costs it will incur to fulfil its obligations will be:

	Year	€
Construction Services	1	500
	2	500
Operation Services (per year)	3-10	10
Road resurfacing	8	100

The terms of the concession require the grantor to pay the operator €200 per year in years 3-10 for making the road available to the public.

For the purpose of this illustration, it is assumed that all cash flows take place at the end of the year.

Table 2 Contract revenue

The operator recognises contract revenue and costs in accordance with IAS 11 – *Construction Contracts*. The costs of each activity – construction, operation, maintenance and resurfacing – are recognised as expenses by reference to the stage of completion of that activity. Contract revenue – the fair value of the amount due from the grantor for the activity undertaken – is recognised at the same time.

The total consideration (€200 in each of years 3-8) reflects the fair values for each of the services, which are:

	Fair value		
Construction	Forecast cost	+	5%
Operation and maintenance	" "	+	20%
Road resurfacing	" "	+	10%
Lending rate to grantor	6.18% per year		

In year 1, for example, construction costs of €500, construction revenue of €525 (cost plus 5 per cent), and hence construction profit of €25 are recognised in the income statement.

Financial asset

The amount due from the grantor meets the definition of a receivable in IAS 39. The receivable is measured initially at fair value. It is subsequently measured at amortised cost, i.e. the amount initially recognised plus the cumulative interest on that amount calculated using the effective interest method minus repayments.

Table 3 Measurement of receivable

	€
Amount due for construction in year 1	525
Receivable at end of year 1*	525
Effective interest in year 2 on receivable at the end of year 1 (6.18% × €525)	32
Amount due for construction in year 2	525
Receivable at end of year 2	1,082
Effective interest in year 3 on receivable at the end of year 2 (6.18% × €1,082)	67
Amount due for operation in year 3 (€10 × (1 + 20%))	12
Cash receipts in year 3	(200)
Receivable at end of year 3	961

* No effective interest arises in year 1 because the cash flows are assumed to take place at the end of the year.

5.4.3   The intangible asset model

If the financial asset model does not apply, (if, for instance, the operator is paid directly by users and there is no contractual right to cash or other financial assets) it is proposed that the operator's consideration for its construction services will be an intangible asset.[119] As with the financial asset model, the operator cannot have an item of property, plant and equipment because the physical infrastructure is an asset of the grantor (see 5.3.4 above). Therefore, the IFRIC has concluded that the right of an operator to charge users of the public service, for example the right to collect tolls from a road or a bridge, meets the definition of an intangible asset, that should be accounted for in accordance with IAS 38. It is, in effect, a licence 'bought' in exchange for construction services.[120]

The IFRIC has concluded that an intangible asset will be recorded during the construction phase as activity progresses, representing the operator's right to receive the licence. On this assumption, the entity will account for the construction of the infrastructure asset as follows:

(i)   revenue will be measured at the fair value of the intangible asset received.[121]

(ii)   it will record this contract revenue in accordance with IAS 11 as it provides 'construction services' by constructing the asset.[122]

The IFRIC concluded that the intangible asset under the concession (the licence received in return for construction services) meets the definition of a qualifying asset of the operator because the licence would not be ready for use until the infrastructure was constructed. Therefore borrowing costs may be capitalised during the period of construction.[123] This contrasts with the treatment of borrowing costs under the financial asset model, where capitalisation is forbidden but financial income (the accretion of interest on the financial asset) is recognised. For accounting periods beginning after 1 January 2009, capitalisation of borrowing costs is mandatory (see Chapter 19).[124] Operators usually capitalise borrowing costs wherever permitted so this is unlikely to lead to a change in accounting policy.

Furthermore, it is proposed that an inevitable consequence of applying the intangible model is that there must be an exchange transaction in which the operator receives the intangible right in exchange for its construction services. As this is an asset exchange of dissimilar assets, revenue must be recognised in accordance with IAS 18, which requires the recognition of revenue and a profit (or loss) based on the fair value of the assets received (unless the fair value of the assets given up can be measured more reliably).[125] This means that the operator must establish the fair value of either the intangible asset it receives or the fair value of the services it has provided. The following example, based on Illustrative Example 2 in IFRIC 12, indicates how the IFRIC expects this to apply in practice. It assumes that the fair value can be based on the cost of the construction services plus a margin.

Example 23.6:   The Intangible Asset Model – recording the construction asset

Arrangement terms

The terms of a service arrangement require an operator to construct a road – completing construction within two years – and maintain and operate the road to a specified standard for eight years (i.e. years 3-10). The terms of the arrangement also require the operator to resurface the road when the original surface has deteriorated below a specified condition. The operator estimates that it will have to undertake the resurfacing at the end of the year 8. At the end of year 10, the service arrangement will end. The operator estimates that that costs it will incur to fulfil its obligations will be:

Table 1 Contract costs

	Year	€
Construction Services	1	500
	2	500
Operation services (per year)	3-10	10
Road resurfacing	8	100

The terms of the arrangement allow the operator to collect tolls from drivers using the road. The operator forecasts that vehicle numbers will remain constant over the duration of the contract and that it will receive tolls of €200 in each of years 3-10.

For the purpose of this illustration, it is assumed that all cash flows take place at the end of the year.

Intangible asset

The operator provides construction services to the grantor in exchange for an intangible asset, i.e. a right to collect tolls from road users in years 3-10. In accordance with IAS 38 – *Intangible Assets* – the operator recognises the intangible asset at cost, i.e. the fair value of consideration received or receivable.

During the construction phase of the arrangement the operator's asset (representing its accumulating right to be paid for providing construction services) is classified as an intangible asset (licence to charge users of the infrastructure). The operator estimates the fair value of its consideration received to be equal to the forecast construction costs plus 5 per cent margin. It is also assumed that the operator adopts the allowed alternative treatment in IAS 23 – *Borrowing*

Costs – and therefore capitalises the borrowing costs, estimated at 6.7 per cent, during the construction phase:

Table 2 Initial measurement of Intangible asset

	€
Construction services in year 1 (€500 × (1 + 5%))	525
Capitalisation of borrowing costs	34
Construction services in year 2 (€500 × (1 + 5%))	525
Intangible asset at end of year 2	1,084

In accordance with IAS 38, the intangible asset is amortised over the period in which it is expected to be available for use by the operator, i.e. years 3-10. The depreciable amount of the intangible asset (€1,084) is allocated using a straight-line method. The annual amortisation charge is therefore €1,084 divided by 8 years, i.e. €135 per year.

Construction costs and revenue

The operator recognises the revenue and costs in accordance with IAS 11 – *Construction Contracts* – i.e. by reference to the stage of completion of the construction. It measures contract revenue at the fair value of the consideration received or receivable. Thus in each of years 1 and 2 it recognises in its income statement construction costs of €500, construction revenue of €525 (cost plus 5 per cent) and, hence, construction profit of €25.

Toll revenue

The road users pay for the public services at the same time as they receive them, i.e. when they use the road. The operator therefore recognises toll revenue when it collects the tolls.

In practice, identifying the fair value of the construction revenue may prove difficult.

A   Amortisation

The intangible asset will subsequently be accounted for in accordance with IAS 38 (see Chapter 15), which means that the amount at which it is measured initially, i.e. after the exchange transaction, is its cost.[126] It will be amortised on a systematic basis over its useful life, which means that the methods permitted by IAS 38 (straight line, diminishing balance or unit-of-production) are available, should they be the most appropriate.[127] The IFRIC expressly considered unit-of-production methods to be appropriate in some circumstances; in March 2006, it was noted in *IFRIC Update* that the Basis of Conclusions had been redrafted to avoid the impression that these methods were not allowed.[128] Interest methods of amortisation are forbidden.[129]

There had been concern as a unit-of-production method could result in lower amortisation in the early years of the asset's operation and IAS 38 states that 'there is rarely, if ever, persuasive evidence to support an amortisation method for intangible assets with finite useful lives that results in a lower amount of accumulated amortisation than under the straight-line method.'[130] This might be regarded as discouraging, if not prohibiting, the use of the unit of production method in the case of many service concessions. Therefore, the IASB has deleted this sentence in IAS 38 in order to clarify that there is no prohibition when the method is the most appropriate.[131] Obviously the method may apply if there is a right to charge a specified number of users. This still leaves uncertain the circumstances in which the unit-of-production method is applicable; however, in all but unusual circumstances a straight line method of amortisation will be appropriate.

In the following extract from its accounting policies, GDF Suez (formerly Gaz de France) indicates that it amortises its intangible assets on a straight line basis over the concession term.

Extract 23.7: GDF Suez SA (2008)

20.2   Notes to the Consolidated Financial Statements [extract]

Other internally-generated or acquired intangible assets

Other intangible assets include mainly:

- amounts paid or payable as consideration for rights relating to concession contracts or public service contracts;
- customer portfolios acquired on business combinations;
- power station capacity rights: the Group helped finance the construction of certain nuclear power stations operated by third parties and in consideration received the right to purchase a share of the production rights are amortized over the useful life of the underlying assets, not to exceed 40 years;
- surface and underground water drawing rights, which are not amortized as they are granted indefinitely;
- concession assets;
- the GDF Gaz de France and gas supply contracts acquired as part of the business combination with Gaz de France in 2008.

Intangible assets are mortised on a straight-line basis over the following useful lives (in years):

	Useful life	
	Minimum	Maximum
Concession rights	10	65
Customer portfolios	10	40
Other intangible assets	1	40

Some intangible assets with an indefinite useful life such as trademarks and water drawing rights are not amortized.

B   Impairment

The operator will recognise an intangible right during the construction phase of the arrangement, which is before the asset has been brought into use. There may be other circumstances in which the operator will continue to recognise an intangible asset prior to the service being provided to users. IAS 36 – *Impairment of Assets* – requires any intangible asset that has not yet been brought into use to be tested for impairment annually, irrespective of whether there are any indications of impairment.[132]

5.4.4   *Revenue recognition implications of the two models*

The IFRIC considers that the consequences of its two models can be demonstrated by the following simple example:

Example 23.7:   Revenue under the financial asset and intangible models

An operator builds a road at a cost of 100. The construction profit is 10 and total cash inflows over the life of the concession are 200.

Under the financial asset model, the operator will recognise construction revenue of 110 and a receivable of 110. Of the future cash inflows of 200, 110 will be treated as repaying the receivable, with the remaining 90 being recognised as revenue over the life of the concession. Total revenue will be 200.

Under the intangible asset model, the operator will recognise construction revenue of 110, an intangible of 110, and a construction profit of 10. Over the life of the concession, the intangible asset of 110 would be amortised against revenues (which in this case would be from users) of 200. The net position is the same as in the financial asset case, but total revenues will be 310 rather than 200.

It is fair to say that this has proved highly controversial. In fact, the September 2004 IFRIC Update stated that 'the majority of the IFRIC strongly disliked this outcome.'[133] However, although some members are still 'uncomfortable' with this result, the IFRIC maintains that this is the appropriate application of accounting standards to the arrangements and is consistent with the treatment generally accorded to barter transactions.[134] It is hard to think of other sectors where barter transactions are fundamental to the arrangement. The possible implications for many other transactions with governmental grantors where licences are granted have also not been considered. Nevertheless, IFRIC 12 has been prepared on this basis.

5.4.5   'Bifurcation' – single arrangements that contain both financial and intangible assets

As part of its redeliberations, the IFRIC agreed that it may be necessary in certain circumstances to divide the operator's right to cash flows into a financial asset and an intangible asset.[135] The IFRIC Update (March 2006) reports that 'With this change, the proposed amendment would better reflect the economic reality of concession arrangements: to the extent that the operator is remunerated for its construction services by obtaining a contractual right to receive cash from, or at the direction of, the grantor, the operator would recognise a financial asset and, to the extent that the operator receives only a licence to charge users, it would recognise an intangible asset.'

The Basis for Conclusions to IFRIC 12 explains more of the reasoning and potential impact. In some arrangements both parties to the contract share the risk (demand risk) that the cash flows generated by the project will not be sufficient to recover the operator's capital investment. A common mechanism for achieving this is where the grantor pays partly by a financial asset (i.e. the grantor will pay cash for the services provided) but gives the operator the right to charge for services (i.e. the operator has an intangible asset). The operator's infrastructure asset is to be split into a financial asset component for any guaranteed amount of cash and an intangible asset for the remainder.[136]

These are common in transport concessions, e.g. a rail system paid for partly by grantor subsidy and partly by the payment of fares. There are clearly going to be difficult matters of interpretation. It may not be clear how much of the arrangement is a financial asset and, therefore, where to draw the boundary between the two assets. There may be minor amounts within a contract that fall within another model and entities may wish to conclude that these are *de minimis*. It remains to be seen how these will be applied in practice.

5.5 Revenue and expenditure during the operations phase of the concession agreement

So far, we have described the recognition and measurement of the infrastructure asset in the accounts of the operator under the two models. A significant issue in practice is that service concession arrangements are composite transactions. They usually have a long duration (twenty-five to thirty years is not uncommon) during which time the operator has a variety of obligations. These may be in connection with the infrastructure asset itself and include:

- enhancement of the infrastructure or construction of new infrastructure;
- infrastructure components that must be replaced in their entirety;
- infrastructure subject to major cyclical repairs; and
- regular repairs and maintenance.

In addition, many service concession arrangements involve the provision of services. In the case of a hospital, for example, this could include utilities (such as water and electricity) and a wide range of 'soft' services such as cleaning, laundry, meals, portering, security and grounds maintenance, amongst others. All of these might be paid for as a single unitary charge that would probably be adjusted according to performance as in Example 23.4 above. The accounting models for service concessions must be able to deal with all of these issues.

5.5.1 Additional construction services

The concession may include obligations to construct new infrastructure or to enhance either new or existing infrastructure to a condition better than at the start of the concession. IFRIC 12 does not deal in detail with the treatment to be adopted other than to say that revenue and costs relating to construction or upgrade services are recognised in accordance with IAS 11.[137] This means that all construction services are accounted for in accordance with the appropriate model, regardless of when they take place. It will often be a matter of judgement whether subsequent expenditure is operational maintenance or whether it is additional construction services that add to or enhance the infrastructure. In addition, under the intangible asset model, there are several issues – are the construction services part of the original asset or should they be accounted for as a new asset? If it is a new asset, when should it be recognised?

A   Subsequent construction services that are part of the initial infrastructure asset

In some circumstances, the 'enhancement' spend is part of the original intangible asset and should be recognised as part of the exchange transaction described in 5.4.3 above. An example of this is the common requirement in concession contracts that the operator replace certain items at the operator's cost, whether or not the items concerned have become unserviceable. For example, a water supply operator may be contractually required to replace all lead pipes for environmental and health reasons; similarly, a gas supply operator may be required to replace all cast-iron pipes for safety reasons.

Assuming that the intangible asset model is the relevant one, the first issue is whether these expenditures should be treated as operating costs (obligations to maintain or to restore the infrastructure) and treated as described in 5.5.2 below or as an additional cost of the intangible asset. They do not directly increase the future economic benefits of any particular infrastructure asset when the costs are incurred. However, IAS 16 explicitly allows such expenditure to be capitalised as part of an item of property, plant and equipment[138]and here the upgrade is a requirement of the contract so there seems little doubt that capitalisation is the appropriate treatment.

However, these features indicate that these expenditures should be included in the consideration given for the intangible asset and therefore recognised as part of its carrying value on initial recognition. This would require the recognition of a liability for the present value of the best estimate of the amount required to replace the underlying asset, such as the pipes.

The IFRIC did not, however, address the accounting treatment of subsequent variations in the amount of the liability for the operator's unfulfilled obligations that is recognised as part of the cost of the intangible asset (the licence) e.g. when the estimated amount of the expenditures to be incurred is revised. The situation may be regarded as analogous to the situation addressed by IFRIC 1 – *Changes in Existing Decommissioning, Restoration and Similar Liabilities*,[139] where a liability is recognised as a liability in accordance with IAS 37 and as part of the cost of an asset. Therefore, the principles set out in IFRIC 1 should be applied, i.e. a change in the measurement of the liability should be added to, or deducted from the cost of the intangible asset, subject to impairment testing and to the extent that the amount deducted from the cost of the asset does not exceed the carrying amount of the intangible asset. The periodic unwinding of the discount must be recognised in income.

B   Subsequent construction services that comprise a new infrastructure asset

An operator may be contractually entitled to add to or upgrade the infrastructure and from this generate additional revenues. The operator may have a right to extend a distribution network and, under its right to charge for the services, it will obtain revenues from newly connected users. There is an example of such a right in Extract 23.9 below, in which Telenor ASA discloses that it has a right 'to arrange, expand, operate and provide the cellular system radio communication services in various areas in Thailand'.

Revenues generated by the new infrastructure will be collected under the terms of the *original* licence granted to the operator. However, the cost of the extension work will only be recognised when the expenditure is made. That cost is not an additional cost of the original intangible asset but will be a new intangible asset recognised at cost using the same principles as the original as described at 5.4.3 above.

5.5.2   *Accounting for the operations phase*

Both models apply the same accounting in the operations phase. According to the September 2006 IFRIC Update, 'the nature of the asset recognised by the operator as consideration for providing construction services (a financial asset or an intangible asset) does not determine the accounting for the operation phase of the arrangement'.[140]

Revenue and costs for the operation services will be recognised in accordance with IAS 18.[141] This means that most operating and maintenance costs are likely to be executory and will be accounted for as incurred. Contractual obligations, including obligations to maintain, replace or restore infrastructure, are to be recognised and measured in accordance with IAS 37, i.e. at the best estimate of the expenditure required to settle the present obligation at the balance sheet date, as shown in Example 23.8 below. These include obligations to restore infrastructure to a specified condition before it is returned to the grantor at the end of the concession.[142] These do not include any upgrade element which is treated as an additional construction service (see 5.5.1 above).

Distinguishing between executory maintenance spend and contractual obligations is not always straightforward. A concession arrangement may provide for a specified total amount of expenditure to be incurred by the operator throughout the contract. Sometimes, the contract provides for mechanisms whereby at the end of the contract, any shortfall in the agreed amount is paid in cash to the grantor by the operator. Particularly in the case of older contracts, it is common for the maintenance and repair obligation to be expressed in very general terms such as keeping the infrastructure in 'good working condition' or 'state of the art' working condition. The obligation may include the requirement that the asset be handed over with a certain number of years' useful life remaining.

Local regulations or laws also change over time. Some operators are obliged to report annually to the grantor on the level of maintenance and renewal expenditure incurred during the year and on a cumulative basis from inception of the contract. Sometimes, the operator must report on expected expenditures over some future period of time (e.g. over the next 12 months or two years) as well. In these situations, more often than not the grantor compares the cumulative expenditure at any point in time with either the operator's prior estimates of expenditures or with the level of expenditure that had been anticipated at the outset of the arrangement and was factored into the level of usage charges. In such circumstances, judgment is required in deciding whether expenditure on renewals is an obligation or an executory contract.

Example 23.8:   *Executory and contractual obligations to maintain and restore the infrastructure*

The operator under a water supply service concession is required as part of the overall contractual arrangement to replace four water pumps as soon as their performance drops below certain quality levels. The operator expects this to be the case after 15 years of service. The expected cost of replacing the pumps is CU 1,000. The operator's best estimate is that the service potential of the pumps is consumed evenly over time and provision for the costs is made on this basis from inception of the service concession arrangement until the date of expected replacement. The provision is measured at the net present value of the amounts expected to be paid, using the operator's discount rate of 5%. The amount provided in the first year can be calculated as CU 33.67. Assuming no changes to estimates, in 15 years CU 1,000 would have been provided and would be utilised in replacing the pumps. The provision would be adjusted on a cumulative basis to take account of changes in estimates to the cost of replacement pumps, the manner in which they are wearing out or changes to the operator's discount rate.

The IFRIC has also provided an example in Illustrative Example 2, the intangible asset model, of how operational expenditure might be accounted for in practice (although, of course, the same accounting would be applied whatever the model). Major maintenance, in this case the requirement to resurface the road, will be recognised as the best estimate of the expenditure required to settle the present obligation at the balance sheet date and it is suggested that this might be proportional to the number of vehicles using the road, therefore increasing in measurable annual increments.[143] The basis for accounting for such obligations is discussed further in Chapter 24.

Example 23.9:   The Intangible Asset Model – recording the operations phase

Resurfacing obligations

The operator's resurfacing obligation arises as a consequence of use of the road during the operating phase. It is recognised and measured in accordance with IAS 37 – *Provisions, Contingent Liabilities and Contingent Assets* – i.e. at the best estimate of the expenditure required to settle the present obligation at the balance sheet date.

For the purpose of this illustration, it is assumed that the terms of the operator's contractual obligation are such that the best estimate of the expenditure required to settle the obligation at any date is proportional to the number of vehicles that have used the road by that date and increases by €17 (discounted to a current value) each year. The operator discounts the provision to its present value in accordance with IAS 37. The income statement charge each period is:

Table 3 Resurfacing obligation

Year	3 €	4 €	5 €	6 €	7 €	8 €	Total €
Obligation arising in year (€17 discounted at 6%)	12	13	14	15	16	17	87
Increase in earlier years' provision arising from passage of time	0	1	1	2	4	5	13
Total expense recognised in income statement	12	14	15	17	20	22	100

Overview of cash flows, income statement and balance sheet

For the purpose of this illustration, it is assumed that the operator finances the arrangement wholly with debt and retained profits. It pays interest at 6.7% a year on outstanding debt. If the cash flows and fair values remain the same as those forecast, the operator's cash flows, income statement and balance sheet over the duration of the arrangement will be:

Table 4 Cash flows

Year	1 €	2 €	3 €	4 €	5 €	6 €	7 €	8 €	9 €	10 €	Total €
Receipts	–	–	200	200	200	200	200	200	200	200	1,600
Contract costs	(500)	(500)	(10)	(10)	(10)	(10)	(10)	(110)	(10)	(10)	(1,180)
Borrowing costs†	–	(34)	(69)	(61)	(53)	(43)	(33)	(23)	(19)	(7)	(342)
Net inflow/ (outflow)	(500)	(534)	121	129	137	147	157	67	171	183	78

† Debt at start of year (table 6) × 6.7%

Table 5 Income statement

Year	1 €	2 €	3 €	4 €	5 €	6 €	7 €	8 €	9 €	10 €	Total €
Revenue	525	525	200	200	200	200	200	200	200	200	2,650
Amortisation	–	–	(135)	(135)	(136)	(136)	(136)	(136)	(135)	(135)	(1,084)
Resurfacing expense	–	–	(12)	(14)	(15)	(17)	(20)	(22)	–	–	(100)
Other operating costs†	(500)	(500)	(10)	(10)	(10)	(10)	(10)	(10)	(10)	(10)	(1,080)
Borrowing costs* (table 4)	–	–	(69)	(61)	(53)	(43)	(33)	(23)	(19)	(7)	(308)
Net profits	25	25	(20)	(20)	(14)	(6)	1	9	36	48	78

* Borrowing costs are capitalised during the construction phase   † Table 1

Table 6 Balance sheet

End of Year	1 €	2 €	3 €	4 €	5 €	6 €	7 €	8 €	9 €	10 €
Intangible asset	525	1,084	949	814	678	542	406	270	135	–
Cash/ (debt)*	(500)	(1,034)	(913)	(784)	(647)	(500)	(343)	(276)	(105)	78
Resurfacing obligation	–	–	(12)	(26)	(41)	(58)	(78)	–	–	–
Net assets	25	50	24	4	(10)	(16)	(15)	(6)	30	78

* Debt at start of year plus net cash flow in year (table 4)

To make this illustration as clear as possible, it has been assumed that the arrangement period is only ten years and that the operator's annual receipts are constant over the period. In practice, arrangement periods may be much longer and annual revenue may increase with time. In such circumstances, the changes in net profit from year to year could be greater.

5.6   Items provided to the operator by the grantor

Following the basic principles underlying the proposed accounting treatment and under both models, infrastructure items to which the operator is given access by the grantor for the purpose of the service concession are not recognised as its property, plant and equipment.[144] This is because they remain under the control of the grantor.

There is a different treatment for assets that are given to the operator as part of the consideration for the concession that can be kept or dealt with as the operator wishes. These assets are not to be treated as government grants as defined in IAS 20. Instead, they are brought into account by the operator at fair value, together with any unfulfilled obligations assumed in exchange for the assets.[145]

What this means is that an operator that has been given a licence or similar arrangement over a piece of land on which a hospital is to be built does not recognise the land as an asset. If, on the other hand, the operator has been given a piece of surplus land on which it can build private housing for sale, it will recognise an asset. The consideration, which is the fair value of that land, will be aggregated with the remainder of the consideration for the transaction and accounted for according to the model being used.

5.7   Effective date and transitional arrangements

IFRIC 12 applies to accounting periods beginning on or after 1 January 2008.[146] The transitional arrangements are the same for both models. They allow an exemption from full retrospective implementation if it is impracticable for the operator to do so. This is permitted on a contract-by-contract basis. Instead, the operator is permitted to recognise financial assets or intangible assets that existed at the start of the earliest period presented at their previous carrying amounts however they were previously classified. Financial and intangible assets should be tested for impairment as at that date, unless this is not practicable, in which case the impairment test should be performed as at the start of the current period.[147]

5.8   Accounting practice: applying IFRIC 12

The debate on how to account for service concessions has continued for several years. The Interpretations were not ready to meet the requirements of entities in their first IFRS accounts in 2005 and are only mandatory in accounting periods beginning on or after 1 January 2008, three years later. The European Commission requested the IFRIC to allow a temporary 'grandfathering' of existing treatments but was rebuffed on the grounds that these transactions were not scoped out of existing standards.[148] The European Commission itself finally endorsed IFRIC 12 in March 2009; to apply for the first accounting period beginning after the Interpretation entered force (the third day following that of its publication in the Official Journal on 26 March 2009). Although this means that there has been a difference between IFRS and IFRS as adopted by the European Union, many entities have voluntarily adopted IFRIC 12.

A number of entities implemented IFRIC 12 in 2006. Gaz de France's accounting policy for service concession arrangements has already been disclosed in Extract 23.5

above. The group also disclosed the impact of implementing IFRIC 4 and IFRIC 12 in its 2006 financial statements, as follows.

Extract 23.8: Gaz de France (2006)

FINANCIAL INFORMATION FOR THE YEAR ENDED DECEMBER 31, 2006 [extract]
NOTES TO THE CONSOLIDATED FINANCIAL STATEMENTS [extract]
B –   Comparability between financial years [extract]
2 –   Changes in accounting policies and presentation [extract]

In addition, the following changes in accounting methods and reclassifications have been applied

2.1.   Effect of changes in accounting methods in 2006

Condensed consolidated income statement

Millions of euros	2006	IFRIC 12	IFRIC 4	2006 after IFRIC 4 and IFRIC 12
Revenues	27,258	397	–13	27,642
Capitalized expenses	422	–198	–	224
Purchases and other external charges	–19,707	–493	–	–20,200
Personnel expenses	–2,851	–	–	–2,581
Other operating income and expenses	–237	7	–	–230
Amortization and provisions	–1,544	292	5	–1,247
Operating Income	3,611	5	–8	3,608
Net finance costs	–123	–	–	–123
Other financial income and expenses	–234	–	–	–234
Share in income of associates	176	–	–	176
Income before tax	3,430	5	–8	3,427
Corporate income tax	–1,104	–2	2	–1,104
Group's consolidated net income	2,326	3	–6	2,323
Group share	2,299	3	–4	2,298
Minority interests	27	–	–2	25

Condensed consolidated balance sheet

Millions of euros	2006	IFRIC 12	IFRIC 4	2006 after IFRIC 4 and IFRIC 12
Goodwill	1,649	–	–	1,649
Concession intangible assets	–	5,704	–	5,704
Other intangible assets	564	–	–	564
Concession assets	11,146	–11,114	–32	–
Non-concession tangible assets	16,807	–	–182	16,625
Other assets current and non-current	18,171	–	196	18,367
Total assets	48,337	–5,410	–18	42,909
Shareholders' equity – Group share	16,252	–47	–8	16,197
Minority interests	471	–	–5	466
Concession grantors' right	5,203	–5,203	–	–
Provision for replacement of concession assets	4,009	–135	–	3,874
Deferred tax liability	2,643	–30	–5	2,608
Other current and non-current liabilities	19,759	5	–	19,764
Total liabilities	48,337	–5,410	–18	42,909

6   CURRENT DISCLOSURE REQUIREMENTS: SIC-29

It is important to note that the scope of SIC-29 is much broader than IFRIC 12 described above. It applies to a type of transaction that is described although not really defined and which does not depend on the control criteria described in 5.3.3 above. It also applies to both sides of the transaction, whereas the IFRIC 12 applies only to the operator under the concession agreement.

SIC-29 describes service concessions as arrangements in which an entity (the Concession Operator) provides services on behalf of another entity (the Concession Provider, which may be a public or private sector entity, including a governmental body) that give the public access to major economic and social facilities. The examples of service concession arrangements given by SIC-29 include water treatment and supply facilities, motorways, car parks, tunnels, bridges, airports and telecommunication networks.[149]

SIC-29 states that the common characteristic of all service concession arrangements is that the Concession Operator both receives a right and incurs an obligation to provide public services.[150] It excludes from its scope an entity outsourcing the operation of its internal services (e.g. employee cafeteria, building maintenance, and accounting or information technology functions).[151] This means that some of the arrangements that do not include the construction of a major capital asset, as discussed above, may not be caught by the requirements of the SIC, although there is no hard-and-fast dividing line between service concessions and outsourcing arrangements. For example, if a major information technology project provides computer services for a government office that issues passports to the public, and that government office previously had little or nothing in the way of such support, it would appear to be more in the nature of a service concession and therefore fall to be included with SIC-29's requirements. On the other hand, a contract between a government department and an operator to maintain the existing computer system, including replacement of hardware and software as appropriate, may be outside the scope of SIC-29.

SIC-29 summarises the rights and obligations as follows:

For the period of the concession, the Concession Operator has received from the Concession Provider:

(a)   the right to provide services that give the public access to major economic and social facilities; and

(b)   in some cases, the right to use specified tangible assets, intangible assets, and/or financial assets,

in exchange for the Concession Operator:

(a)   committing to provide the services according to certain terms and conditions during the concession period; and

(b)   when applicable, committing to return at the end of the concession period the rights received at the beginning of the concession period and/or acquired during the concession period.[152]

The disclosure requirements in respect of such projects are as follows:

SIC-29 requires disclosure in addition to that required by other standards that may cover part of the transaction, such as IAS 16 (see Chapter 16), IAS 17 (see Chapter 22) and IAS 38 (see Chapter 15).[153] All aspects of a service concession arrangement should be considered in determining the appropriate disclosures in the notes to the financial statements.[154]

A Concession Operator and a Concession Provider should disclose the following in each period:

(a)   a description of the arrangement;

(b)   significant terms of the arrangement that may affect the amount, timing and certainty of future cash flows (e.g. the period of the concession, re-pricing dates and the basis upon which re-pricing or re-negotiation is determined);

(c)   the nature and extent (e.g. quantity, time period or amount as appropriate) of:

　　(i)   rights to use specified assets;

　　(ii)   obligations to provide or rights to expect provision of services;

　　(iii) obligations to acquire or build items of property, plant and equipment;

　　(iv) obligations to deliver or rights to receive specified assets at the end of the concession period;

　　(v)   renewal and termination options; and

　　(vi) other rights and obligations (e.g. major overhauls); and

(d)   changes in the arrangement occurring during the period.

These disclosures should be provided individually for each service concession arrangement or in aggregate for each class of service concession arrangements. A class is a grouping of service concession arrangements involving services of a similar nature (e.g. toll collections, telecommunications and water treatment services).[155]

IFRIC 12 has added a requirement to disclose 'the amount of revenue and profits or losses recognised in the period on exchanging construction services for a financial asset and an intangible asset'.[156]

An example of an entity that has made the disclosures for an arrangement accounted for under the IFRIC 12 is Telenor ASA, shown below.

Extract 23.9: Telenor ASA (2007)

Notes to the Consolidated Financial Statement [extract]

16.   Property, plant, equipment and intangible assets [extract]

DTAC's concession right

DTAC has a concession right to operate and deliver mobile services. The Communication Authority of Thailand (CAT) granted the concession to DTAC. CAT allows DTAC to arrange, expand, operate and provide the cellular system radio communication services in various areas in Thailand. The concession originally covered a 15 year period but the agreement was amended on 23 July 1993 and 22 November 1996, with the concession period being extended to 22 and 27 years, respectively. Accordingly, the concession period under the existing agreement expires in 2018.

The service rates and fees charged to customers are subject to approval by CAT. DTAC is obliged to pay fees in accordance with the concession. Fees are based on the greater of a minimum annual payment and a percentage of revenues from services. The percentages of revenues from services for each year and minimum annual payments are as follows:

Year[2]	Percentage of revenues per annum	Minimum annual payment (NOK in millions[1])	
		2007	2006
1 to 4	12	4 to 28	4 to 27
5	25	64	62
6 to 15	20	69 to 109	67 to 106
16 to 20	25	135 to 139	132 to 136
21 to 27	30	136 to 217	132 to 211

[1] Converted from Baht to NOK based on exchange rates as of 31 December 2007 in 2007 and based on exchange rates as of 31 December 2006 in 2006.

[2] DTAC commenced commercial operations on 16 September 1991 and the table above shows annual payments from that time.

DTAC shall provide, at its own expense, all devices and equipment which must be sufficient for provision of the services at all times. All such devices and equipment becomes the property of CAT when they are put into use. At the end of the concession period, or if the contract is terminated earlier DTAC must deliver all devices and equipment to CAT in a good working condition.

The service concession of DTAC is accounted for under the Intangible Asset Model according to IFRIC 12 Service Concession Arrangements. The intangible asset is amortized on a straight line basis over the concession period. Enhancements and extensions are capitalized as incurred. Repair, maintenance and replacements are expensed as incurred. The concession in DTAC was valued based on an income approach under the assumption that DTAC would sell its concession to a hypothetical operator.

7   CONCLUSION

This chapter deals with two distinct forms of government/private entity transactions. There is a need for an up-to-date standard on government grants because – whether companies like to admit to it or not – many industries receive significant government support. However, it is clear that this is not going to happen until a number of core standards, on revenue and provisions, have been developed. The growth and complexity of service concession arrangements provided a new set of accounting problems to be addressed by the IFRIC; the difficulty was manifest in the length of time to develop an interpretation and the length and complexity of the final product. The interpretation remains controversial. As IFRIC 12 has now been endorsed for use in the European Union, those who have no yet applied it voluntarily will now need to consider its problem areas and the effects these will have on their financial statements as a matter of urgency.

References

1 IAS 20, *Accounting for Government Grants and Disclosure of Government Assistance*, IASB, para. 41.
2 IAS 20, para. 3.
3 IAS 20, para. 6.
4 IAS 20, para. 4.
5 IAS 20, para. 5.
6 IASB website, *www.iasb.org*, May 2008.
7 IASB website, *www.iasb.org*, August 2009.
8 IAS 20, para. 1.
9 IAS 20, para. 3.
10 IAS 20, para. 4.
11 IAS 20, para. 3.
12 IAS 20, para. 3.
13 IAS 20, para. 3.
14 IAS 20, para. 3.
15 IAS 20, paras. 3 and 35.
16 IAS 20, paras. 3 and 35.
17 IAS 20, para. 1.
18 IAS 20, para. 2.
19 IAS 41, *Agriculture*, IASB, para. B66.
20 SIC-10, *Government Assistance – No Specific Relation to Operating Activities*, IASB, para. 3.
21 IFRIC 12, *Service Concession Arrangements*, IASB, para. 27.
22 IAS 20, para. 7.
23 IAS 41, para. B70.
24 IAS 41, para. B69.
25 IAS 20, para. 8.
26 IAS 20, para. 11.
27 IAS 20, para. 9.
28 IAS 20, para. 3.
29 IAS 20, para. 10.
30 IAS 20, para. 3.
31 IAS 20, para. 23.
32 IAS 8, *Accounting Policies, Changes in Accounting Estimates and Errors*, IASB, para. 13.
33 *Improvements to IFRSs*, IASB, May 2008, IAS 20, para. 10A and IAS 39, *Financial Instruments: Recognition and Measurement*, IASB, para. 43.
34 *Improvements to IFRSs*, May 2008, IAS 20, para. 10A.
35 *Improvements to IFRSs*, May 2008, IAS 20, para. 43.
36 IAS 20, para. 13.
37 IAS 20, para. 14.
38 IAS 20, para. 13.
39 IAS 20, para. 15.
40 IAS 20, para. 12.
41 IAS 20, para. 16.
42 IAS 20, para. 17.
43 IAS 20, para. 17.
44 IAS 20, para. 18.
45 IAS 20, para. 19.
46 IAS 20, paras. 20-22.
47 IAS 20, paras. 21-22.
48 IAS 20, para. 24.
49 IAS 20, para. 26.
50 IAS 20, para. 27.
51 IAS 20, para. 25.
52 IAS 20, para. 27.
53 IAS 20, para. 28.
54 IAS 20, para. 29.
55 IAS 1, *Presentation of Financial Statements*, IASB, paras. 32-33.
56 IAS 20, para. 30.
57 IAS 20, para. 31.
58 IAS 20, para. 31.
59 IAS 20, para. 32.
60 IAS 20, para. 32.
61 IAS 20, para. 33.
62 IAS 20, para. 34.
63 IAS 20, para. 35.
64 IAS 20, para. 38.
65 IAS 20, para. 39.
66 IAS 20, para. 36.
67 IAS 20, para. 19.
68 IASB website, *www.iasb.org*, May 2008.
69 FRS 5, *Reporting the substance of transactions*, ASB, April 1994 (with subsequent amendments), Application Note F, *Private finance initiative and similar contracts*.
70 IFRIC 12, para. 7.
71 IFRIC 12, paras. 4 and 5.
72 IFRIC 12, paras. 5 and 6.
73 IFRIC 12, para. 7.
74 IFRIC 12, para. BC14
75 IFRIC 12, para. 9.
76 IFRIC 12, para. 4.
77 IFRIC 12, para. AG2.
78 IFRIC 12, para. 3.
79 IFRIC 4, *Determining whether an Arrangement contains a Lease*, IASB, para. 4.
80 IFRIC 12, para. 3.
81 *IFRIC Update*, IFRIC, September 2005, pages. 1 to 3.
82 *IFRIC Update*, IFRIC, September 2006, page 1.
83 IFRIC 4, para. 9.
84 IFRIC 12, para. 5.
85 IFRIC 12, paras. AG4 and AG5.
86 IFRIC 12, paras. BC21 and BC22.
87 IFRIC 12, para. AG2.
88 IFRIC 12, para. AG3.
89 IFRIC 12, para. AG4.
90 IFRIC 12, para. AG6.
91 IFRIC 12, para. 6.

92 *IFRIC Update*, IFRIC, September 2005, pages. 1 to 3.
93 IFRIC 12, para. 7
94 IFRIC D12, para. BC21.
95 IFRIC 12, para. 8.
96 IFRIC 12, para. AG7.
97 IFRIC 12, para. AG8.
98 IFRIC 12, para. 11.
99 IFRIC 12, para. BC31.
100 IFRIC 12, para. BC31.
101 IFRIC 12, para. 13.
102 IFRIC 12, para. 16.
103 IFRIC 12, para. 17.
104 IFRIC 12, para. 18.
105 IFRIC 12, para. 14.
106 IFRIC 12, para. 16.
107 IAS 32, *Financial Instruments: Presentation*, IASB, para. 11.
108 IFRIC 12, para. BC44.
109 IFRIC 12, para. 24.
110 IFRIC 12, para. 25.
111 IFRIC 12, para. BC61.
112 IFRIC 12, para. BC62.
113 IFRIC 12, para. BC62.
114 IAS 39, para. 9.
115 IAS 39, para. 9.
116 IAS 39, para. 43.
117 IAS 11, *Construction Contracts*, IASB, para. 26.
118 IFRIC 12, para. 22.
119 IFRIC 12, para. 17.
120 IFRIC 12, para. 17.
121 IFRIC 12, para. 15.
122 IFRIC 12, para. 14.
123 IFRIC 12, para. 22.
124 IAS 23, *Borrowing Costs*, IASB, para. 1.
125 IFRIC 12, paras. BC32 to BC35.
126 IAS 38, *Intangible Assets*, IASB, para. 45.
127 IFRIC 12, para. BC64 and IAS 38, para. 98.
128 *IFRIC Update*, IFRIC, March 2006, pages. 2 and 3.
129 IFRIC 12, para. BC65.
130 IAS 38 (2007), *Intangible Assets*, IASB, 2007 Bound Volume, para. 98.
131 *Improvements to IFRSs*, May 2008, IAS 38, para. 98.
132 IAS 36, *Impairment of Assets*, IASB, para. 10.
133 *IFRIC Update*, IFRIC, September 2004, p. 2-3.
134 IFRIC 12, para. BC35.
135 IFRIC 12, para. 18.
136 IFRIC 12, para. BC53.
137 IFRIC 12, para. 14.
138 IAS 16, *Property, Plant and Equipment*, IASB, para. 1.
139 IFRIC 1, *Changes in Existing Decommissioning, Restoration and Similar Liabilities*, IASB, para. 1.
140 *IFRIC Update*, IFRIC, September 2006, pages 1 and 2.
141 IFRIC 12, para. 20.
142 IFRIC 12, para. 21.
143 IFRIC D14, paras. IE10 and 11.
144 IFRIC 12, para. 27.
145 IFRIC 12, para. 27.
146 IFRIC 12, para. 28.
147 IFRIC 12, para. 30.
148 *IFRIC Update*, IFRIC, Feb 2005, p. 2.
149 SIC-29, *Service Concession Arrangements: Disclosures*, IASB, para. 1.
150 SIC-29, para. 3.
151 SIC-29, para. 1.
152 SIC-29, para. 3.
153 SIC-29, para. 3.
154 SIC-29, para. 3.
155 SIC-29, paras. 6-7.
156 IFRIC 12, para. B12.

Chapter 24
Provisions, contingent liabilities and contingent assets

1   INTRODUCTION

1.1   Background

This chapter focuses only on those provisions that are the subject of IAS 37 – *Provisions, Contingent Liabilities and Contingent Assets*. Thus it only deals with provisions that are shown as liabilities in a balance sheet since the definition of a provision in IAS 37 is 'a liability of uncertain timing or amount'.[1] Like IAS 37, the chapter does not deal with items termed 'provisions' that reduce the carrying amount of assets.

Prior to the issue of IAS 37 in 1998, the accounting for provisions had traditionally been based on an approach that losses and expenses should be provided for on a prudent basis, both in terms of when provision was made and in terms of the amount. However, consistent with its *Framework*, the IASC was anxious to ensure that only those amounts that meet its definition of liabilities are reported as such in the balance sheet. A liability is defined as 'a present obligation of the entity arising from past events, the settlement of which is expected to result in an outflow from the entity of resources embodying economic benefits'.[2]

IAS 37 was developed in parallel with the equivalent UK standard, FRS 12 – *Provisions, Contingent Liabilities and Contingent Assets* – under a joint project between the IASC and the ASB. As a result, the two standards were published on the same day and, indeed, the text was mostly identical.

There is an area of overlap between provisions and contingent liabilities. Although contingent liabilities are clearly not as likely to give rise to outflows, similar judgments are made in assessing the nature of the uncertainties, the need for disclosures and ultimately the recognition of a liability in the financial statements.

Accordingly, the IASC addressed provisions and contingent liabilities in the same standard, and threw in contingent assets for good measure. Previously, contingent assets and liabilities were governed by IAS 10 – *Contingencies and Events Occurring After the Balance Sheet Date*.[3]

A further area of overlap exists between provisions and other liabilities, such as trade payables and accruals. In this case the standard seeks to separate the two and differentiates provisions on the basis that the uncertainty about the timing or amount of the future expenditure required in settlement is greater than that relating to trade payables and accruals.[4]

This is true, but the contrast with trade payables and their associated accruals is only the most straightforward example. In practice the difference between provisions and other liabilities is often far from clear-cut, and reclassification from one category to the other is not uncommon. (This is discussed further at 2.2.2 below.)

One reason why this distinction matters is that provisions are subject to disclosure requirements that do not apply to other payables, as discussed at 6.1 below. In fact, although questions of recognition and measurement are important, transparency of disclosure is also a very significant matter in relation to accounting for provisions. The issue is that, once a provision has been established, expenditure that is charged to it bypasses the statement of comprehensive income and to some extent therefore disappears from view. The original charge may well have been dealt with as an exceptional item in the statement of comprehensive income and glossed over by management in any discussion of their performance, and the subsequent application of the provision has no further impact on earnings – giving rise to a kind of 'off income statement' treatment. Also, in the early 1990s, prior to the issue of IAS 37 and its UK equivalent, FRS 12, some of the provisions that had been set up had been extremely large and wide-ranging. An example is to be found in the 1993 financial statements of what was then British Gas:

Extract 24.1: British Gas plc (1993)

Review of operating results [extract]

Operating costs [extract]

The results for 1993 include an exceptional charge of £1,650 million for the major restructuring of the UK Gas Business. This restructuring into five separate business streams will ensure that the Company's UK Gas Business will be leaner, more competitive and more commercially focused at a time when the gas market in Great Britain is undergoing radical change. The exceptional charge comprises severance and pension costs associated with the reduction in approximately 25,000 people and the related costs of restructuring the integrated UK Gas Business. The cash effect of this restructuring will be borne largely over the next three years.

The corresponding note to the profit and loss account (income statement) contained substantially the same information but added that the amount also included 'other incremental costs that will be required to implement the restructuring, such as training, property related costs and information technology costs'. The effect of this charge was to convert a pre-tax profit of approximately £1 billion into a loss of £613 million.

The need to restrict the creation of such 'big bath' provisions provided much of the impetus for the IASC's (and the ASB's) project on provisions, although some other important issues have been addressed as well, most notably how provisions should be measured.

1.2   Development of IAS 37

In November 1996, the IASC issued a Draft Statement of Principles – *Provisions and Contingencies* – proposing to take contingencies out of IAS 10 and to deal with them in the same standard as provisions, using the same recognition and measurement rules.[5] In July 1997, the IASC published an exposure draft on this basis, which was converted into a standard – IAS 37 – in September 1998.

As indicated at 1.1 above, IAS 37 was developed in parallel with the UK standard, FRS 12, under a joint project between the IASC and the ASB and the two standards were published on the same day. There were no differences of substance between the requirements of the two standards – indeed the text is still mostly identical despite the amendments to IAS 37 noted below – but FRS 12 includes slightly more guidance on two areas:

- recognition of an asset when a provision is recognised (see 3.3 below), and
- the discount rate to be used in the net present value calculation (see 4.2 below).

In December 2003, a number of minor consequential amendments were made to IAS 37 (principally relating to the scope of the standard) following the publication of some of the IASB's revised standards under its improvements project (IAS 8 – *Accounting Policies, Changes in Accounting Estimates and Errors*, IAS 10 and IAS 16 – *Property, Plant and Equipment*) and the revised IAS 39 – *Financial Instruments: Recognition and Measurement*. Further consequential amendments were made in March 2004 following the publication of IFRS 3 – *Business Combinations*, IFRS 4 – *Insurance Contracts* – and IFRS 5 – *Non-current Assets Held for Sale and Discontinued Operations*. In August 2005, another consequential amendment was made to the standard as a result of the IASB's amendments to IAS 39 and IFRS 4 relating to financial guarantee contracts.

Most recently the standard has been updated to reflect the requirements of IAS 1 – *Presentation of Financial Statements* (as revised in September 2007) and IFRS 3 – *Business Combinations* (as revised in January 2008). IAS 1 (as revised) is mandatory for annual periods beginning on or after 1 January 2009,[6] and the amendments arising from IFRS 3 (as revised) apply for annual periods beginning on or after 1 July 2009.[7] Earlier adoption is permitted, provided that this fact is disclosed.[8]

The requirements of IAS 37 are dealt with at 2 to 6 below.

1.3   IFRIC Interpretations

The IASB has issued a number of IFRIC Interpretations relating to the application of IAS 37 (although one of them was subsequently withdrawn).

1.3.1   IFRIC 1

In May 2004, the IASB issued IFRIC 1 – *Changes in Existing Decommissioning, Restoration and Similar Liabilities*. This interpretation provides guidance on how to account for the effect of changes in the measurement of existing provisions for obligations to dismantle, remove or restore items of property, plant and equipment, referred to as 'decommissioning, restoration and similar liabilities'. This is discussed at 4.2 and 5.4.2 A below.

1.3.2   IFRIC 3

Another issue considered by the IFRIC was how to account for a 'cap and trade' emission rights scheme. In December 2004, the IASB issued IFRIC 3 – *Emission Rights* – but this was later withdrawn in June 2005 with immediate effect. This interpretation, *inter alia*, required that as emissions are made, a liability was to be recognised for the obligation to deliver allowances equal to the emissions that had been made by the entity. Such liability was a provision within the scope of IAS 37, and was to be measured at the present market value of the number of allowances required to cover emissions made up to the end of the reporting period. This is discussed at 5.4.3 below.

The accounting for emission rights has now become an IASB project, but work has been deferred pending conclusion of work on other relevant projects.

1.3.3   IFRIC 5

In December 2004, the IASB issued IFRIC 5 – *Rights to Interests Arising from Decommissioning, Restoration and Environmental Rehabilitation Funds*. This deals with the accounting by an entity when it participates in a 'decommissioning fund', the purpose of which is to segregate assets to fund some or all of the costs of its decommissioning or environmental liabilities for which it has to make a provision under IAS 37 (see 5.4.1 and 5.4.2 below). This is discussed at 5.4.2 B below.

1.3.4   IFRIC 6

In September 2005, the IASB issued IFRIC 6 – *Liabilities arising from Participating in a Specific Market – Waste Electrical and Electronic Equipment* – giving guidance on the accounting for liabilities for waste management costs. This clarifies when certain producers of electrical goods will need to recognise a liability for the cost of waste management relating to the decommissioning of waste electrical and electronic equipment (historical waste) supplied to private households. This is discussed at 5.4.4 below.

The number of other Interpretations that refer to IAS 37 demonstrates just how pervasive the consideration of non-financial liabilities is in developing accounting practice. IAS 37 is also referred to in IFRIC 12 – *Service Concessions* (see Chapter 23 at 5); IFRIC 13 – *Customer Loyalty Programmes* (see Chapter 25 at 6.14); IFRIC 14 – *IAS 19 – The Limit on a defined benefit asset, Minimum Funding Requirements and their*

Interaction (see Chapter 28 at 5.3.1); and IFRIC 15 – *Agreements for the Construction of Real Estate* (see Chapter 21 at 4.1).

1.4   Future developments

In September 2002, the IASB agreed to add a short-term convergence project to its active agenda, the object being to reduce differences between IFRS and US GAAP. As a result of this project and Phase II of its business combinations project 1, in June 2005 the IASB issued an exposure draft proposing a number of amendments to IAS 37.

As part of these proposals, IAS 37 was to be re-named *Non-financial liabilities*, to reflect the elimination of the terms 'provision', 'contingent liability' and 'contingent asset'. However, these are not just cosmetic changes; they signal major modifications to IAS 37, including a fundamental change in approach to both the recognition and measurement of items that currently qualify for recognition as provisions.

Over the four years since the issue of the exposure draft, and in the light of comments received on it and round-table meetings held in November and December 2006, the Board has redeliberated its proposals and this has now become a 'Liabilities' project. At the time of writing, this process is coming to a conclusion with a view to either re-exposing the Board's revised proposals or publishing a final standard in the fourth quarter of 2009.[9]

An outline of the Board's proposals to revise IAS 37 (and IAS 19), derived from the original Exposure Draft and the Project Summary as issued in June 2009, is given at 8.1 below.

The IASB is engaged in two other projects related to liabilities, rate-regulated activities and emissions trading schemes. In July 2009, the IASB issued an exposure draft on rate-regulated activities, a project added to its agenda in December 2008. Rate regulation refers to the way a regulator imposes limits to prices charged by an entity to its customers, often based on an assessment of the returns made by the entity compared to its costs. The question arises as to whether an imposed price reduction relating to a past over recovery of costs should be recognised as a liability. Whilst, as discussed at 5.4.12 below, there is currently no evidence of divergence in practice, this is a matter of significant interest in a number of countries that plan to adopt IFRS in the near future and where recognition of regulatory liabilities (and assets) is either permitted or required. The Board's proposals are described at 8.4 below.

As regards its project on emissions trading schemes, the IASB currently expects to issue an exposure draft in the second quarter of 2010.[10] The Board's deliberations so far are described at 8.5 below. Current practice is discussed at 5.4.3 below and in Chapter 15 at 3.3.

2   OBJECTIVE AND SCOPE OF IAS 37

2.1   Objective

The objective of IAS 37 'is to ensure that appropriate recognition criteria and measurement bases are applied to provisions, contingent liabilities and contingent assets and that sufficient information is disclosed in the notes to enable users to understand their nature, timing and amount'.[11]

2.2   Scope

IAS 37 only deals with provisions that are liabilities. 'Provisions' for depreciation, impairment of assets and doubtful debts are not addressed in the standard, since these are adjustments to the carrying amounts of assets.[12] In addition, certain specific provisions, contingent liabilities and contingent assets are exempt.[13]

2.2.1   Exemptions

A   *Executory contracts, except where the contract is onerous*

The standard uses the term executory contracts to mean 'contracts under which neither party has performed any of its obligations, or both parties have partially performed their obligations to an equal extent'.[14] This means that contracts such as supplier purchase contracts and capital commitments, which would otherwise fall within the scope of the standard, are exempt.

This exemption prevents the balance sheet from being grossed up for all sorts of commitments that an entity has entered into, and is to be welcomed as a pragmatic measure. However, there is little theoretical justification for it, in that such items meet the definition of liabilities used by the standard, and of course give rise to corresponding assets. The need for this exemption arises because the liability framework on which this standard is based includes the concept of a constructive obligation (see 3.1.1 below) which, when applied to executory contracts would otherwise give rise to all sorts of contingent promises requiring recognition or disclosure.

An executory contract will still require provision if the contract becomes onerous.[15] Onerous contracts are dealt with at 5.3 below.

B   *Provisions, contingent liabilities or contingent assets covered by another standard*

Where another standard deals with a specific type of provision, contingent liability or contingent asset, it should be applied instead of IAS 37. Examples given in the standard are:[16]

* construction contracts (dealt with in IAS 11 – *Construction Contracts*);
* income taxes (dealt with in IAS 12 – *Income Taxes*);

- leases (dealt with in IAS 17 – *Leases*). However, the standard argues that if operating leases become onerous, there are no specific requirements within IAS 17 to address the issue and thus IAS 37 applies to such leases;

- employee benefits (dealt with in IAS 19 – *Employee Benefits*); and

- insurance contracts (dealt with in IFRS 4). However, IAS 37 requires an insurer to apply the standard to provisions, contingent liabilities and contingent assets, other than those arising from its contractual obligations and rights under insurance contracts within the scope of IFRS 4.

Before its amendment by IFRS 3 (as revised in 2008), IAS 37 also referred to the specific requirements in IFRS 3 (2007) – *Business Combinations* – relating to the recognition and measurement of contingent liabilities assumed in a business combination as superseding those in IAS 37[17] (see Chapter 9 at 2.4.5 and 2.5.3). Following its amendment, whilst IAS 37 contains no similar reference to IFRS 3 (as revised in 2008), the revised IFRS 3 states that the requirements in IAS 37 do not apply in determining which contingent liabilities to recognise as of the acquisition date[18] (see Chapter 9 at 3.6.6 A).

In addition, the standard does not apply to financial instruments (including guarantees) that are within the scope of IAS 39 (see Chapter 29).[19] This means that guarantees of third party borrowings (including those of subsidiaries, associates and joint ventures) are not covered by IAS 37 (see 3.2.1 below).

IAS 37 also notes that some amounts treated as provisions may relate to the recognition of revenue, for example where an entity gives guarantees in exchange for a fee, and states that the standard does not address the recognition of revenue. This is dealt with by IAS 18 – *Revenue* (see Chapter 25), and IAS 37 does not change the requirements of that standard.[20]

The standard applies to provisions for restructurings, including discontinued operations (see 5.1 below). However, it emphasises that when a restructuring meets the definition of a discontinued operation under IFRS 5, additional disclosures may be required under that standard (see Chapter 4 at 3).[21]

2.2.2 *Provisions and other liabilities*

IAS 37 states that the feature distinguishing provisions from other liabilities, such as trade payables and accruals, is the existence of 'uncertainty about the timing or amount of the future expenditure required in settlement. By contrast:

(a) trade payables are liabilities to pay for goods or services that have been received or supplied and have been invoiced or formally agreed with the supplier; and

(b) accruals are liabilities to pay for goods or services that have been received or supplied but have not been paid, invoiced or formally agreed with the supplier, including amounts due to employees (for example, amounts relating to accrued vacation pay). Although it is sometimes necessary to estimate the amount or timing of accruals, the uncertainty is generally much less than is the case for provisions.

Accruals are often reported as part of trade and other payables whereas provisions are reported separately.'[22]

This is true, but the contrast with trade payables and their associated accruals is only the most straightforward case. In practice the difference between provisions and other liabilities is often far from clear-cut, and reclassification from one category to the other is not uncommon.

One reason why this distinction matters is that provisions are subject to disclosure requirements that do not apply to other payables, as discussed at 6.1 below.

2.2.3   *Provisions and contingent liabilities*

As noted at 1.1 above, there is clearly an overlap between provisions and contingent liabilities and IAS 37 deals with both of them.

The standard notes that in a general sense, all provisions are contingent because they are uncertain in timing or amount. However, in IAS 37 the term 'contingent' is used for liabilities and assets that are not recognised because their existence will be confirmed only by the occurrence of one or more uncertain future events not wholly within the entity's control. In addition, the term 'contingent liability' is used for liabilities that do not meet the recognition criteria.[23]

Accordingly, the standard distinguishes between:

(a)   provisions – which are recognised as liabilities (assuming that a reliable estimate can be made) because they are present obligations and it is probable that an outflow of resources embodying economic benefits will be required to settle the obligations; and

(b)   contingent liabilities – which are not recognised as liabilities because they are either:

   (i)   possible obligations, as it has yet to be confirmed whether the entity has a present obligation that could lead to an outflow of resources embodying economic benefits; or

   (ii)   present obligations that do not meet the recognition criteria in the standard because either it is not probable that an outflow of resources embodying economic benefits will be required to settle the obligation, or a sufficiently reliable estimate of the amount of the obligation cannot be made.[24]

The recognition criteria are dealt with below.

3   RECOGNITION

3.1   Provisions

IAS 37 requires that a provision should be recognised when:

(a)   an entity has a present obligation (legal or constructive) as a result of a past event;

(b)   it is probable that an outflow of resources embodying economic benefits will be required to settle the obligation; and

(c)   a reliable estimate can be made of the amount of the obligation.

If these conditions are not met, no provision should be recognised.[25]

Each of these three conditions is discussed separately below.

3.1.1   'An entity has a present obligation (legal or constructive) as a result of a past event'

The standard defines both legal and constructive obligations. The definition of a legal obligation is fairly straightforward and uncontroversial; it refers to an obligation that derives from a contract (through its explicit or implicit terms), legislation or other operation of law.[26]

The definition of a constructive obligation, on the other hand, may give rise to more problems of interpretation. A constructive obligation is defined as 'an obligation that derives from an entity's actions where:

(a)   by an established pattern of past practice, published policies or a sufficiently specific current statement, the entity has indicated to other parties that it will accept certain responsibilities; and

(b)   as a result, the entity has created a valid expectation on the part of those other parties that it will discharge those responsibilities'.[27]

The essence of the idea is that the entity may be committed to certain expenditure because any alternative would be too unattractive to contemplate. The standard cites a generally known policy of giving refunds to customers, and a widely published policy to clean up all contamination it causes as examples of this.[28]

The standard states that in almost all cases it will be clear whether a past event has given rise to a present obligation. However, it notes that there will be some rare cases, such as a lawsuit against an entity, where this will not be so. In these cases, a past event is deemed to give rise to a present obligation if, taking account of all available evidence (including, for example, the opinion of experts), it is more likely than not that a present obligation exists at the end of the reporting period. The evidence to be considered includes any additional evidence provided by events after the end of the reporting period. Accordingly, if on the basis of the evidence it is concluded that a present obligation is more likely than not to exist, a provision will be required (assuming that the other recognition criteria are met).[29] Unfortunately, this is a direct contradiction of the standard's condition (a) for the recognition of a provision as set out at 3.1 above, which requires there to be a definite obligation, not just a probable one!

The second half of this condition uses the phrase 'as a result of a past event'. This is based on the concept of an obligating event, which the standard defines as 'an event that creates a legal or constructive obligation and that results in an entity having no realistic alternative to settling that obligation'.[30] The standard says that this will be the case only:

(a)   where the settlement of the obligation can be enforced by law; or

(b)   in the case of a constructive obligation, where the event (which may be an action of the entity) creates valid expectations in other parties that the entity will discharge the obligation.[31]

This concept of obligating event is used in the standard when discussing specific examples of recognition, which we discuss further at 5 below. However, it is worth mentioning here that this concept, like that of a constructive obligation, is open to interpretation, as the obligating event is not always easy to identify.

The standard notes that the financial statements deal with the financial position of an entity at the end of its reporting period, not its possible position in the future. Accordingly, no provision is to be recognised for costs that need to be incurred to operate in the future. The only liabilities to be recognised are those that exist at the end of the reporting period.[32]

IAS 37 disallows certain provisions that might otherwise qualify to be recognised by stating that it 'is only those obligations arising from past events existing independently of an entity's future actions (i.e. the future conduct of its business) that are recognised as provisions'.[33] It illustrates this restriction with an example of an entity required, because of commercial pressures or legal requirements, to fit smoke filters in a factory. It argues that the entity can avoid the expenditure by its future actions, for example by changing its method of operation, so there is no present obligation for the future expenditure.[34] Other kinds of provisions disallowed because the entity can avoid the future expenditure are refurbishment costs, and future staff training, both of which are illustrated in the examples.[35]

There is no requirement for an entity to know to whom an obligation is owed. The obligation may be to the public at large. It follows that the obligation could be to one party, but the amount ultimately payable will be to another party. For example, in the case of a constructive obligation for an environmental clean-up, the obligation is to the public, but the liability will be settled by making payment to the contractors engaged to carry out the clean-up. However, the principle is that there must be another party for the obligation to exist. It follows from this that a management or board decision will not give rise to a constructive obligation unless it is communicated in sufficient detail to those affected by it before the end of the reporting period.[36] The most significant application of this requirement relates to restructuring provisions, which is discussed further at 5.1 below.

The standard discusses the possibility that an event that does not give rise to an obligation immediately may do so at a later date, because of changes in the law or an act by the entity (such as a sufficiently specific public statement) which gives rise to a constructive obligation.[37] Changes in the law will be relatively straightforward to identify. The only issue that arises will be exactly when that change in the law should be recognised. IAS 37 states that an obligation arises only when the legislation is virtually certain to be enacted as drafted and suggests that in many cases, this will not be until it is enacted.[38]

The more subjective area is the possibility that an act by the entity will give rise to a constructive obligation. The example given is of an entity publicly accepting responsibility for rectification of previous environmental damage in a way that creates a constructive obligation.[39] This seems to introduce a certain amount of flexibility to management when reporting results. By bringing forward or delaying a public announcement of a commitment that management had always intended to honour, it can affect the reporting period in which a provision is recognised.

As the FASB in the US has also commented,[40] the critical event that creates a constructive obligation tends to be elusive, and this is demonstrated by the discussion of some of the examples at 5 below. That is not to say that we believe that only legal obligations should be recognised in the balance sheet, but we doubt if this particular approach is the best way of determining which additional items ought to be recognised. As with other aspects of the IASB's framework and its recognition criteria in particular, we think that the question is in reality one of expense recognition – in what reporting period should the cost be charged to the statement of comprehensive income – not liability recognition at all.

3.1.2   'It is probable that an outflow of resources embodying economic benefits will be required to settle the obligation'

This requirement has been included as a result of the standard's attempt to incorporate contingent liabilities within the definition of provisions. This is discussed in detail in 3.2 below.

The interpretation of *probable* in these circumstances is that the outflow of resources is more likely than not to occur; that is, it has a probability greater than 50%. The standard also makes it clear that where there are a number of similar obligations, the probability that an outflow will occur is based on the class of obligations as a whole. This is because in the case of certain obligations such as warranties, the possibility of an outflow for an individual item may be small (likely to be much less than 50%) whereas the possibility of at least some outflow of resources for the population as a whole will be much greater (almost certainly greater than 50%).[41]

3.1.3   'A reliable estimate can be made of the amount of the obligation'

The standard takes the view that a sufficiently reliable estimate can always be made for a provision where an entity can determine a range of possible outcomes. Hence, it will only be in extremely rare cases that a range of outcomes cannot be determined and so no provision is recognised. In these circumstances, the liability should be disclosed as a contingent liability (see disclosure requirements in 6.2 below).[42]

3.2   Contingencies

IAS 37 says that contingent liabilities and contingent assets should not be recognised, but only disclosed.[43]

As indicated at 2.2.1 B above, contingent liabilities that are recognised separately as part of allocating the cost of a business combination are covered by the requirements of IFRS 3.[44] The requirements in respect of business combinations accounted for under IFRS 3 (as revised in 2008) are discussed in Chapter 9 at 3.6.6 A and the accounting treatment under IFRS 3 (2007) are discussed in Chapter 9 at 2.5.3.

3.2.1   *Contingent liabilities*

At least for contingent liabilities, this treatment in IAS 37 may seem a surprising position to take and one which is different from that adopted previously. However, the explanation lies in the peculiar way in which a contingent liability has been defined. It is:

(a)   a possible obligation that arises from past events and whose existence will be confirmed only by the occurrence or non-occurrence of one or more uncertain future events not wholly within the control of the entity; or

(b)   a present obligation that arises from past events but is not recognised because:

    (i)   it is not probable that an outflow of resources embodying economic benefits will be required to settle the obligation; or

    (ii)   the amount of the obligation cannot be measured with sufficient reliability.[45]

What the IASC did was to define the category in a back to front way that depends on the recognition rule that it wanted to apply. Contingent liabilities as defined are now meant to be those that the IASC did not think should be recognised.

Even with that explanation, the above definition is not easy to understand. One problem with (a) is that the term 'possible' is not defined. Literally, it could mean any probability greater than 0% and less than 100%. However, in the context of the standard, a more sensible assumption is that since 'probable' is used within the standard as meaning 'more likely than not to occur' (see 3.1.2 above), i.e. a probability of greater than 50%, then 'possible' means a probability of 50% or less. Appendix A to IAS 37, in summarising the main requirements of the standard, uses the phrase 'a possible obligation ... that may, but probably will not, require an outflow of resources' which seems to support this argument. Assuming that this is what is meant, the definition restricts contingent liabilities to those where either the existence of the liability or the transfer of economic benefits arising is less than 50+% probable (or where the obligation cannot be measured at all, but as noted in 3.1.3 above, this would be relatively rare).

The standard's definition of a contingent liability is therefore tortuous and counter-intuitive. To say that a contingent liability is no longer contingent if it becomes more than 50% probable can cause a great deal of confusion. It is contrary to the natural meaning of the words, whereby a contingent liability is a liability that is contingent on a future event.

If the meaning of contingent liabilities is restricted in this way, the question obviously arises as to what happens to those items where the existence of the liability and the resulting transfer of economic benefits are greater than 50% probable. The answer is that the standard has attempted to catch these within provisions. As noted at 3.1 above, the recognition criteria for provisions include the requirement that it is probable that a transfer of economic benefits will be required to settle the obligation.

However, the uncertainty surrounding a liability is not always related only to whether an outflow of resources will arise, but may also relate to whether the liability exists at all. For example, take the case of litigation against an entity. The facts may suggest that the entity will probably be found at fault and required to pay appropriate damages, but it is still contesting the action and may win the case. In these circumstances, as well as uncertainty over any level of damages, there is currently uncertainty over whether the entity has a liability at all.

Nevertheless, as discussed at 3.1.1 above, the standard has attempted to deal with these uncertainties by stating that there will be some rare cases, such as a lawsuit against an entity, where it will not be clear that there is a 'present obligation'. In these cases, a past event is deemed to give rise to a present obligation if, taking account of all available evidence (including, for example, the opinion of experts), 'it is more likely than not that a present obligation exists at the end of the reporting period'. The evidence to be considered includes any additional evidence provided by events after the reporting period.[46] Indeed, IAS 10 includes 'the settlement after the reporting period of a court case that confirms that the entity had a present obligation at the end of the reporting period' as an example of an adjusting event.[47] Accordingly, if on the basis of the evidence it is concluded that a present obligation is more likely than not to exist, a provision will be required (assuming that the other recognition criteria are met). If it is considered that it is more likely that no present obligation exists, then the entity discloses a contingent liability (unless the possibility of a transfer of economic resources is remote).[48] The disclosure requirements are detailed at 6.2 below.

The standard requires that contingent liabilities are assessed continually to determine whether an outflow of resources embodying economic benefits has become probable. Where this becomes the case, then provision should be made in the period in which the change in probability occurs (except in the rare circumstances where no reliable estimate can be made).[49] To illustrate this, the Appendix to IAS 37 used to include an example of an entity guaranteeing the borrowings of another entity, the financial condition of which deteriorates from one year to the next such that provision then needs to be made for the obligation, rather than continuing to just disclose the contingent liability.[50] However, the example has been amended subsequently to reflect the fact that such a guarantee is an insurance contract under IFRS 4, within the scope of IAS 39. The example no longer indicates that there is disclosure of a contingent liability in the first year, but that the guarantee is recognised at its fair value, and that the guarantee is subsequently remeasured at the best estimate of the obligation under IAS 37 if this is higher then the amount initially recognised less, when appropriate, cumulative amortisation in accordance with IAS 18.[51]

3.2.2   Contingent assets

A contingent asset is defined in a more intuitive way. It is 'a possible asset that arises from past events and whose existence will be confirmed only by the occurrence or non-occurrence of one or more uncertain future events not wholly within the control of the entity'.[52] In this case, the word 'possible' is *not* confined to a level of probability of 50% or less, which may further increase the confusion over the different meaning of the word in the definition of contingent liabilities.

Contingent assets usually arise from unplanned or other unexpected events that give rise to the possibility of an inflow of economic benefits to the entity. An example is a claim that an entity is pursuing through legal process, where the outcome is uncertain.[53]

The standard states that a contingent asset should not be recognised, as this could give rise to recognition of income that may never be realised. However, when the realisation of income is virtually certain, then the related asset is no longer regarded as contingent and recognition is appropriate.[54] In practice this is interpreted as being between 95% and 100% probable.

The standard requires disclosure of the contingent asset when the inflow of economic benefits is probable.[55] As noted earlier, 'probable' is used within the standard as meaning 'more likely than not to occur' (see 3.1.2 above). The disclosure requirements are detailed at 6.3 below.

As with contingent liabilities, any contingent assets should be assessed continually. If it has become virtually certain that an inflow of economic benefits will arise, the asset and the related income should be recognised in the period in which the change occurs. If an inflow becomes probable, then the contingent asset should then be disclosed.[56]

As noted at 3.2.1 above, IAS 10 includes 'the settlement after the reporting period of a court case that confirms that the entity had a present obligation at the end of the reporting period' as an example of an adjusting event.[57] Does this mean that, if a court case initiated by an entity and unsettled at the end of the reporting period is subsequently settled favourably, an asset for the claim should be recognised at the end of the reporting period? In our view the answer is 'no', although disclosure would be required. As indicated above, IAS 37 only allows the asset and the related income to be recognised 'in the period in which the change occurs'.[58] In this instance, the period in which the change occurs is subsequent to the reporting period. There is also no suggestion that the example in IAS 10 is referring to anything but liabilities. The asset could only be recognised if, at the end of the reporting period, the entity could show that it was virtually certain to win the case.

3.2.3   Summary

The following matrix summarises the treatment of contingencies under IAS 37:

Likelihood of outcome	Accounting treatment: contingent liability	Accounting treatment: contingent asset
Virtually certain (say, >95% probable)	Not a contingent liability, therefore provide	Not a contingent asset, therefore accrue
Probable (say, 50-95% probable)	Not a contingent liability, therefore provide	Disclose
Possible but not probable (say, 5-50% probable)	Disclose	No disclosure permitted
Remote (say, <5% probable)	No disclosure required	No disclosure permitted

The standard does not put a numerical measure of probability on either 'virtually certain' or 'remote', which lie at the outer ends of the range, but we think it reasonable to regard them as falling above the 95th percentile and below the fifth percentile respectively. However, these are not definitive guides and each case must be decided on its merits. In any event, it is usually possible to assess the probability of the outcome of a particular event only very approximately.

3.3   Recognising an asset when recognising a provision

In most cases, the recognition of a provision results in an immediate charge to the statement of comprehensive income. Nevertheless, in some cases it may be appropriate to recognise an asset. As indicated at 1.2 above, this is not discussed in IAS 37, although it was dealt with explicitly in FRS 12, the UK equivalent standard. FRS 12 establishes a principle that when a provision is recognised or changed, an asset is also recognised when, and only when, the incurring of the present obligation recognised as a provision gives access to future economic benefits; otherwise the setting up of the provision should be charged immediately to the profit and loss account.[59] IAS 37 only says 'Other International Accounting Standards specify whether expenditures are treated as assets or as expenses. These issues are not addressed in this Standard. Accordingly, this Standard neither prohibits nor requires capitalisation of the costs recognised when a provision is made.'[60]

FRS 12 contains a specific reference to assets to deal with the treatment of provisions for decommissioning costs. However, IAS 16 requires the cost of an item of property, plant and equipment to include the initial estimate of the costs of dismantling and removing an asset and restoring the site on which it is located, the obligation for which an entity incurs either when the item is acquired or as a consequence of having used the item during a particular period for purposes other than to produce inventories during that period.[61] IAS 37 also includes an example in an appendix where such costs are included as part of the cost of an oil rig.[62] The treatment of decommissioning costs is discussed further at 5.4.2 below.

Extract 24.8 at 5.4.2 below illustrates an example of a company capitalising costs in respect of its provision for decommissioning costs.

4   MEASUREMENT

4.1   Best estimate of provision

A provision is to be measured before tax, as the tax consequences of the provision, and changes to it, are dealt with under IAS 12 (see Chapter 26).[63]

IAS 37 says that the amount provided should be the best estimate of the expenditure required to settle the present obligation at the end of the reporting period.[64] The standard equates this estimate with 'the amount that an entity would rationally pay to settle the obligation at the end of the reporting period or to transfer it to a third party at that time'.[65] It is interesting that a hypothetical transaction of this kind should be proposed as the conceptual basis of the measurement required, rather than putting the main emphasis upon the actual expenditure that is expected to be incurred in the future.

The standard does acknowledge that it would often be impossible or prohibitively expensive to settle or transfer the obligation at the end of the reporting period. However, it goes on to state that 'the estimate of the amount that an entity would rationally pay to settle or transfer the obligation gives the best estimate of the expenditure required to settle the present obligation at the end of the reporting period'.[66]

The estimates of outcome and financial effect are determined by the judgement of the entity's management, supplemented by experience of similar transactions and, in some cases, reports from independent experts. The evidence considered will include any additional evidence provided by events after the reporting period.[67]

Different methods of dealing with the uncertainties surrounding the amount to be recognised as a provision are detailed in the standard. Where a large population of items is being measured, such as warranty costs, the standard advances the use of 'expected values'. This is a statistical computation which weights the cost of all the various possible outcomes according to their probabilities, as illustrated in the following example taken from IAS 37.[68]

Example 24.1:   Calculation of expected value

An entity sells goods with a warranty under which customers are covered for the cost of repairs of any manufacturing defects that become apparent within the first six months after purchase. If minor defects were detected in all products sold, repair costs of £1 million would result. If major defects were detected in all products sold, repair costs of £4 million would result. The entity's past experience and future expectations indicate that, for the coming year, 75 per cent of the goods sold will have no defects, 20 per cent of the goods sold will have minor defects and 5 per cent of the goods sold will have major defects. In accordance with paragraph 24 of IAS 37 (see 3.1.2 above) an entity assesses the probability of a transfer for the warranty obligations as a whole.

The expected value of the cost of repairs is:

(75% of nil) + (20% of £1m) + (5% of £4m) = £400,000.

Another measurement approach described in the standard covers the situation where there is a continuous range of possible outcomes and each point in that range is as likely as any other. IAS 37 requires that, in this case, the mid-point of the range should be used.[69] This is not a particularly helpful example. It does not make it clear what the principle is meant to be, since the mid-point in this case represents the median as well as the expected value. The latter may have been what the IASC had in mind, but the median could be equally well justified on the basis that it is 50% probable that at least this amount will be payable, while anything in excess of that constitutes a possible but not a probable liability, that should be disclosed rather than accrued. Interestingly, US GAAP has a different approach to this issue in relation to contingencies. FASB Interpretation No. 14 states that where a contingent loss could fall within a range of amounts then, if there is a best estimate within the range, it should be accrued, with the remainder noted as a contingent liability. However, if there is no best estimate then the *lowest* figure within the range should be accrued, with the remainder up to the maximum potential loss noted as a contingent liability.[70]

Where the obligation being measured relates to a single item, the standard suggests that the best estimate of the liability may be the individual most likely outcome.[71] However, even in such a case, it notes that consideration should be given to other possible outcomes. It gives an example of an entity that has to rectify a fault in a major plant that it has constructed for a customer. The most likely outcome is that the repair will succeed at the first attempt. However, a provision should be made for a larger amount if there is a significant chance that further attempts will be necessary.[72] This again sounds like a vague leaning towards an expected value approach.

This example illustrates an inconsistency between these measurement rules and the recognition rules for contingent liabilities. Compare the above example with a case where the most likely outcome is that no repair will be required at all, but there is still a significant chance that a repair will be needed. In this scenario, there is a less than 50% probability that a cash outflow will arise, and so the item will fall within the definition of a contingent liability and no provision will be required. No account will have been taken of any other possible outcomes, unlike the first scenario.

It is also interesting to consider how the measurement rules detailed above should reflect prudence. The standard does not refer to prudence as such; however it does discuss the concept of risk. It refers to risk as being variability of outcome, and states that 'the risks and uncertainties that inevitably surround many events and circumstances shall be taken into account in reaching the best estimate of a provision'. It suggests that a risk adjustment may increase the amount at which a liability is measured, but gives no indication of how this may be done. It indicates that caution is needed in making judgements under conditions of uncertainty, so that expenses or liabilities are not understated. However, it says that uncertainty does not justify the creation of excessive provisions or a deliberate overstatement of liabilities. The paragraph goes on to warn against duplicating adjustments for risk, for example by estimating costs of an adverse outcome on a prudent basis and then overestimating its probability.[73] Any uncertainties surrounding the amount of the expenditure are to be disclosed (see 6.1 below).[74]

The overall result of all this is somewhat confusing. Whilst a best estimate based solely on the expected value approach or the mid-point of a range addresses the uncertainties relating to there being a range of possible outcomes, it does not fully reflect risk, because the actual outcome could still be higher or lower than the estimate. Therefore, the discussion on risk suggests that an additional adjustment should be made. However, apart from indicating that the result may be to increase the recognised liability and pointing out the need to avoid duplicating the effect of risk in estimates of either cash flows or probability,[75] quite how this might be achieved is unclear. This rather vague drafting leaves a certain amount of scope in the estimation of provisions and is further complicated when the concept of risk is combined with considerations relating to the time value of money (see 4.2.2 below).

4.2   Discounting to present value

The standard requires that where the effect of the time value of money is material, the amount of a provision should be the present value of the expenditures expected to be required to settle the obligation.[76] The discount rate (or rates) to be used in arriving at the present value should be 'a pre-tax rate (or rates) that reflect(s) current market assessments of the time value of money and the risks specific to the liability. The discount rate(s) shall not reflect risks for which the future cash flow estimates have been adjusted.'[77] However, it is worth noting that for many provisions, no discounting will be required as the cash flows will not be sufficiently far into the future for discounting to have a material impact.[78]

IAS 37 gives no guidance as to how these requirements are to be applied. On the other hand, FRS 12 in the UK gives some guidance on the discount rate to be used in the net present value calculation. The main types of provision where the impact of discounting will be significant are those relating to decommissioning and other environmental restoration liabilities. IFRIC 1 addresses some of the issues relating to the use of discounting (in the context of provisions for obligations to dismantle, remove or restore items of property, plant and equipment, referred to as 'decommissioning, restoration and similar liabilities') which are discussed at 5.4.2 A below.

4.2.1   Real v. nominal rate

IAS 37 does not indicate whether the discount rate should be a real discount rate or a nominal discount rate (although the example disclosure for decommissioning costs illustrates the use of a real discount rate).[79] FRS 12 in the UK notes that the discount rate used depends on whether:

(a)   the future cash flows are expressed in current prices, in which case a real discount rate (which excludes the effects of general inflation) should be used; or

(b)   the future cash flows are expressed in expected future prices, in which case a nominal discount rate (which includes a return to cover expected inflation) should be used.[80]

FRS 12 then allows either method to be used, and both these methods may produce the same figure for the initial present value of the provision. However, the effect of the unwinding of the discount will be different in each case (see 4.2.4 below). In Extract 24.7 at 5.4.1 below, BP discloses how its provision for the costs of decommissioning production facilities and pipelines is estimated using current prices and discounted using a real rate.

4.2.2   Adjusting for risk

As noted at 4.1 above, IAS 37 also requires that risk is taken into account in the calculation of a provision, but gives little guidance as to how this should be done. Where discounting is concerned, it merely says that the discount rate should not reflect risks for which the future cash flow estimates have been adjusted.[81] FRS 12 in the UK suggests that using a discount rate that reflects the risk associated with the liability (a risk-adjusted rate) may be the easiest method of reflecting risk.[82] It gives no indication of how to calculate such a risk adjusted rate, but a little more information can be obtained from the ASB's earlier Working Paper – *Discounting in Financial Reporting*[83] – on which the following example is based.

Example 24.2:   Calculation of a risk-adjusted rate[84]

A company has a provision for which the expected value of the cash outflow in three years' time is £150, and the risk-free rate (i.e. the rate unadjusted for risk) is 5%. However, the possible outcomes from which the expected value has been determined lie within a range between £100 and £200. The company is risk averse and would settle instead for a certain payment of, say, £160 in three years' time rather than be exposed to the risk of the actual outcome being as high as £200. The effect of risk in calculating the present value can be expressed as either:

(a)   discounting the risk-adjusted cash flow of £160 at the risk-free (unadjusted) rate of 5%, giving a present value of £138; or

(b)   discounting the expected cash flow (which is unadjusted for risk) of £150 at a risk-adjusted rate that will give the present value of £138, i.e. a rate of 2.8%.

As can be seen from this example, the risk-adjusted discount rate is a *lower* rate than the unadjusted (risk-free) discount rate. This may seem counter-intuitive initially, because the experience of most borrowers is that banks and other lenders will charge a higher rate of interest on loans that are assessed to be higher risk to the lender. However, in the case of a provision a risk premium is being suffered to eliminate the possibility of the actual cost being higher (thereby capping a liability), whereas in the case of a loan a premium is required to compensate the lender for taking on the risk of not recovering its full value (setting a floor for the value of the lender's financial asset). In both cases the actual cash flows incurred by the paying entity are higher to reflect a premium for risk. In other words, the discount rate for an asset is increased to reflect the risk of recovering less and the discount rate for a liability is reduced to reflect the risk of paying more.

A problem with changing the discount rate to account for risk is that this adjusted rate is a theoretical rate and has no obvious meaning in real life. However a lower discount rate is consistent with the premise that a risk-adjusted liability should be higher than a liability without risk.[85] It is also possible for the adjusted rate to be negative, although in practice the maximum amount a liability could increase to is the nominal amount of the expected future cash flow. It is also difficult to see how a risk-adjusted rate could be obtained in practice. In the above example, it was obtained only by reverse-engineering; it was already known that the net present value of a risk-adjusted liability was £138, so the risk-adjusted rate was just the discount rate applied to unadjusted cash flow of £150 to give that result.

FRS 12 does offer an alternative approach – instead of using a risk-adjusted discount rate, the cash flows themselves can be adjusted for risk and then discounted using a risk-free (unadjusted) rate.[86] This does of course present the problem of how to adjust the cash flows for risk. However, this may be easier than attempting to risk-adjust the discount rate.

FRS 12 suggests that an example of a risk-free rate would be a government bond rate.[87] Presumably, this government bond rate should strictly have a similar remaining term to the liability, although this is not specified in the standard. For the purposes of discounting post-employment benefit obligations, IAS 19 requires the discount rate to be determined by reference to market yields at the end of the reporting period on high quality corporate bonds (although in countries where there is no deep market in such bonds, the market yields on government bonds should be used).[88] Although IAS 19 indicates that this discount rate reflects the time value of money (but not the actuarial or investment risk),[89] we do not believe it is appropriate to use the yield on a high quality corporate bond for determining a risk-free rate to be used in discounting provisions under IAS 37. Accordingly, in our view, where an entity is using a risk-free discount rate for the purposes of calculating a provision under IAS 37, that rate should be based on a government bond rate with a similar currency and remaining term as the provision. It follows that because a risk-adjusted rate is always lower than the risk-free rate, an entity cannot justify the discounting of a provision at a rate that is higher than a government bond rate with a similar currency and term to the provision.

Whichever method of reflecting risk is adopted, IAS 37 emphasises that care must be taken that the effect of risk is not double-counted by inclusion in both the cash flows and the discount rate.[90]

4.2.3 Pre-tax discount rate

Since IAS 37 requires provisions to be measured before tax, it follows that cash flows should be discounted at a pre-tax discount rate. No further explanation of this is given in the standard. On the other hand, FRS 12 in the UK does have some discussion about pre- and post-tax rates in an appendix.[91]

However, it is unlikely that entities will need to compute a pre-tax rate from post-tax information. This is because, in reality, the discount rate will be calculated directly as a pre-tax discount rate. Supposing, for example, that the risk-free rate of return is being used, then the discount rate used will be a government bond rate. This rate will be obtained gross. Thus, the idea of obtaining a required post-tax rate of return and adjusting it for the tax consequences of different cash flows will seldom be relevant.

The calculation is illustrated in the following example.

Example 24.3:   Use of discounting and tax effect

It is estimated that the settlement of an environmental provision will give rise to a gross cash outflow of £500,000 in three years time. The gross interest rate on a government bond maturing in three years time is 6%. The tax rate is 30%.

The net present value of the provision is £419,810 (£500,000 × 1 ÷ $(1.06)^3$). Hence, a provision of £419,810 should be booked in the balance sheet. A corresponding deferred tax asset of £125,943 (30% of £419,810) would be set up if it met the criteria for recognition in IAS 12. (See Chapter 26 at 4.2.3).

4.2.4   Unwinding of the discount

As discussed at 4.6 below, IAS 37 indicates that where discounting is used, the carrying amount of a provision increases in each period to reflect the passage of time, and that this increase is recognised as a borrowing cost.[92] This is the only guidance that the standard gives on the unwinding of the discount. IFRIC 1 in relation to provisions for decommissioning, restoration and similar liabilities requires that the periodic unwinding of the discount is recognised in profit or loss as a finance cost as it occurs.[93] The IFRIC concluded that the unwinding of the discount is not a borrowing cost as defined in IAS 23 – *Borrowing Costs* – and thus cannot be capitalised under that standard (see Chapter 19).[94]

However, there is no discussion of the impact that the original selection of discount rate can have on its unwinding, that is the selection of real versus nominal rates, and risk-free versus risk-adjusted rates. The IASB (and the ASB for its part) appear to have overlooked the fact that these different discount rates will unwind differently. This is best illustrated by way of an example.

Example 24.4:   Effect of different bases of interest

A provision is required to be set up for an expected cash outflow of €100,000 (estimated at current prices), payable in three years' time. The appropriate nominal discount rate is 7.5%, and inflation is estimated at 5%. If the provision is discounted using the nominal rate, the expected cash outflow has to reflect future prices. Accordingly, if prices increase at the rate of inflation, the cash outflow will be €115,762 (€100,000 × 1.05^3). The net present value of €115,762, discounted at 7.5%, is €93,184 (€115,762 × 1 ÷ $(1.075)^3$). If all assumptions remain valid throughout the three-year period, the movement in the provision would be as follows:

	Undiscounted cash flows	Provision
	€	€
Year 0	115,762	93,184
Unwinding of discount (€93,184 × 0.075)		6,989
Revision to estimate		–
Year 1	115,762	100,173
Unwinding of discount (€100,173 × 0.075)		7,513
Revision to estimate		–
Year 2	115,762	107,686
Unwinding of discount (€107,686 × 0.075)		8,076
Revision to estimate		–
Year 3	115,762	115,762

If the provision is calculated based on the expected cash outflow of €100,000 (estimated at current prices), then it needs to be discounted using a real discount rate. This may be thought to be 2.5%, being the difference between the nominal rate of 7.5% and the inflation rate of 5%. However, it is more accurately calculated using the Fisher relation or formula as 2.381%, being $(1.075 \div 1.05) - 1$. Accordingly, the net present value of €100,000, discounted at 2.381%, is €93,184 ($€100,000 \times 1 \div (1.02381)^3$), the same as the calculation using future prices discounted at the nominal rate. If all assumptions remain valid throughout the three-year period, the movement in the provision would be as follows:

	Undiscounted cash flows	Provision
	€	€
Year 0	100,000	93,184
Unwinding of discount (€93,184 × 0.02381)		2,219
Revision to estimate (€100,000 × 0.05)	5,000	4,770
Year 1	105,000	100,173
Unwinding of discount (€100,173 × 0.02381)		2,385
Revision to estimate (€105,000 × 0.05)	5,250	5,128
Year 2	110,250	107,686
Unwinding of discount (€107,686 × 0.02381)		2,564
Revision to estimate (€110,250 × 0.05)	5,512	5,512
Year 3	115,762	115,762

It can be seen from the second table in the above example that using the real discount rate will give rise to a much lower finance charge each year. However, this does not lead to a lower provision in the balance sheet at the end of each year. Provisions have to be revised annually to reflect the current best estimate of the obligation (see 4.6 below). Thus, the provision in the above example at the end of each year needs to be adjusted to reflect current prices at that time (and any other adjustments that arise from changes in estimate of the provision), as well as being adjusted for the unwinding of the discount. For example, the revised provision at the end of Year 1 is €100,173, being €105,000 discounted for two years at 2.381%. After allowing for the unwinding of the discount, this required an additional provision of €4,770. Although the total expense in each year is the same under either method, what will be different under the two methods is the allocation of the change in provision between operating costs (assuming the original provision was treated as an operating expense) and finance charges. If the real discount rate is used, the finance charge each year will be lower and the operating costs higher than if the nominal rate is used.

A more significant difference will arise where the recognition of the original provision is included as part of the cost of property, plant or equipment, rather than an expense, such as when a decommissioning provision is recognised. In that case, using a real discount rate will result initially in a lower charge to the statement of comprehensive income, since under IFRIC 1 any revision to the estimate of the provision is not taken to the statement of comprehensive income but is treated as an adjustment of the related asset, which is then depreciated prospectively over the remaining life of the asset (see 5.4.2 A below).

A similar issue arises with the option of using the risk-free or the risk-adjusted discount rate. However, this is a more complex problem, because it is not clear what to do with the risk-adjustment built into the provision. This is illustrated in the following example, using the same facts as in Example 24.2 at 4.2.2 above:

Example 24.5:   Use of risk-free and risk-adjusted figures

As before, a company is required to make a provision for which the expected value of the cash outflow in three years' time is £150, when the risk-free rate (i.e. the rate unadjusted for risk) is 5%. However, the possible outcomes from which the expected value has been determined lie within a range between £100 and £200. The reporting entity is risk averse and would settle instead for a certain payment of, say, £160 in three years' time rather than be exposed to the risk of the actual outcome being as high as £200. The measurement options to account for risk can be expressed as either:

(a)   discounting the risk-adjusted cash flow of £160 is discounted at the risk-free (unadjusted) rate of 5%, giving a present value of £138; or

(b)   discounting the expected cash flow (which is unadjusted for risk) of £150 at a risk-adjusted rate that will give the present value of £138, i.e. a rate of 2.8%.

Assuming that there are no changes in estimate required to be made to the provision during the three-year period, alternative (a) will unwind to give an overall finance charge of £22 and a final provision of £160. Alternative (b) will unwind to give an overall finance charge of £12 and a final provision of £150.

In this example, the unwinding of different discount rates gives rise to different provisions. The difference of £10 relates to the risk adjustment that has been made to the provision. The standard gives no guidance as to how to treat this £10 if the provision is unwound at the risk-free rate. Given that the expected cash outflow is only £150, this additional £10 is likely to have to be released at some point, but it is unclear how to do this. Two alternatives are that it could be done gradually over the period in which the provision is unwound (perhaps as a reassessment of the required provision as it becomes less risky), or it could be taken in total once the provision has been settled. The lack of explicit guidance in the standard appears to give entities flexibility on this point.

4.2.5   Change in interest rates

The standard requires the discount rate to reflect current market assessments of the time value of money.[95] This appears to mean that where interest rates change, the provision should be recalculated on the basis of revised interest rates. This interpretation is reinforced by the disclosure requirement in the standard that entities should disclose the effect of any change in discount rate.[96]

This will give rise to an adjustment, but the standard does not explicitly say how this should be treated. Arguably, it could be treated in the same way as the unwinding of the discount and therefore included as a borrowing or finance cost in the year of change, which may be either a debit or a credit depending on which way interest rates move. However, we believe that the adjustment to the provision is a change in accounting estimate, as discussed in IAS 8 (see Chapter 3 at 4.5). Accordingly, it should be reflected in the financial statement classification in which the provision was originally recorded. Indeed, this latter approach is the one required by IFRIC 1 in relation to provisions for decommissioning, restoration and similar liabilities in relation to assets measured using the cost model (see 5.4.2 A below). However, in that case the adjustment is not taken to the statement of comprehensive income but added to or deducted from the cost of the asset to which it relates; the adjusted depreciable amount of the asset is then depreciated prospectively over its remaining useful life.[97] For other provisions, the adjustment would have to be taken to the appropriate expense category in the statement of comprehensive income.

Calculating this adjustment is not straightforward either, because the standard gives no guidance on how it should be done. For example, it is unclear whether the new discount rate should be applied during the year or just at the year-end, and whether the rate should be applied to the new estimate of the provision or the old estimate. Although IFRIC 1 requires that, where the related asset is measured using the cost model, changes in the provision resulting from a change in the discount rate is added to, or deducted from, the cost of the related asset in the current period,[98] it does not deal specifically with these points. However, since other changes affecting the estimate of a provision for decommissioning, restoration and similar liabilities are reflected as a change in the liability at the time the revised estimate is made, then it would appear that a change in the discount rate would also only be applied at that time, and thus the new estimate is discounted at the revised discount rate and applied from that point on. This is implied in Example 1 to IFRIC 1.[99]

4.3   Future events

The standard states that 'future events that may affect the amount required to settle an obligation shall be reflected in the amount of a provision where there is sufficient objective evidence that they will occur'.[100] The types of future events that the standard has in mind are advances in technology and changes in legislation.

This is intended to mean that a provision cannot be reduced simply on the basis of unspecified future developments in the intervening period before the liability is settled. There will need to be sufficient objective evidence that such future developments are possible. For example, an entity may believe that the cost of cleaning up a site at the end of its life will be reduced by future changes in technology. The amount recognised has to reflect a reasonable expectation of technically qualified, objective observers, taking account of all available evidence as to the technology that will be available at the time of the clean-up. Thus it is appropriate to include, for example, expected cost reductions associated with increased experience in applying existing technology or the expected cost of applying existing technology to a larger or more complex clean-up operation than has previously been carried out. However, an entity does not anticipate the development of a completely new technology for cleaning up unless it is supported by sufficient objective evidence.[101]

Similarly, if new legislation is to be anticipated, there will need to be evidence both of what the legislation will demand and whether it is virtually certain to be enacted and implemented. In many cases sufficient objective evidence will not exist until the new legislation is enacted.[102]

These requirements are most likely to impact provisions for liabilities that will be settled some distance in the future, such as decommissioning costs (see 5.4.2 below).

4.4   Recoveries from third parties

In some circumstances an entity is able to look to a third party to reimburse part of the costs required to settle a provision or to pay the amounts directly. Examples are insurance contracts, indemnity clauses and suppliers' warranties.[103]

In the majority of cases where a recovery is expected, the entity would remain liable for the whole costs if the third party failed to pay for any reason, for example as a result of the third party's insolvency. In such situations, the provision should be made gross and any reimbursement should be treated as a separate asset (but only when it is virtually certain that the reimbursement will be received if the entity settles the obligation). The amount recognised for the reimbursement should not exceed the amount of the provision.[104]

Although the provision and the reimbursement are shown as separate items in the balance sheet, in the statement of comprehensive income, the expense relating to the provision may be presented net of the amount recognised for the reimbursement.[105]

The above requirements will apply in most such cases. However, where the entity will not be liable for the costs in question if the third party fails to pay, then in such a case the entity has no liability for those costs and they are not included in the provision.[106]

Extract 24.6 at 5.4.1 below illustrates an example of a company treating amounts recoverable from third parties as separate assets.

One situation in which it might be thought appropriate to gross up for an expected recovery is a vacant leasehold property provision, where the calculation of the provision reflects cash flows that may arise from sub-letting the property. However, as discussed further at 5.3 below we believe that the most appropriate treatment for provisions for such onerous contracts is that they are shown at the net amount.

The main area of concern with these requirements is whether the 'virtually certain' criterion that needs to be applied to the corresponding asset might mean that some reimbursements will not be capable of recognition at all. For items such as insurance contracts, this may not be an issue, as entities will probably be able to argue that a recovery on an insurance contract is virtually certain if the entity is required to settle the obligation (although it may be more difficult for complex situations). For other types of reimbursement, however, recovery may be less certain.

It is interesting to contrast the approach to reimbursements with the case where an entity is jointly and severally liable for an obligation. In that case, the entity provides only for its own share and the remainder that is expected to be met by other parties is treated only as a contingent liability.[107] This means that a similar economic position is not always portrayed in the same way. If it were, then a liability would have to be set up for the whole amount for which the entity is jointly and severally liable, with a corresponding asset being recognised for the amount expected to be met by other parties.

4.5   Gains on disposals of related assets

IAS 37 states that gains from the expected disposal of assets should not be taken into account in measuring a provision, even if the expected disposal is closely linked to the event giving rise to the provision. Such gains should be recognised at the time specified by the Standard dealing with the assets concerned.[108] This is likely to be of particular relevance in relation to restructuring provisions (see 5.1.3 below). However, it may also apply in other situations. Extract 24.8 at 5.4.2 below illustrates an example of a company excluding gains from the expected disposal of assets in determining its provision for decommissioning costs.

The introduction of the equivalent requirement in FRS 12 in the UK led British Aerospace to write off the sum of £267 million, as shown in this extract:

Extract 24.2: British Aerospace Public Limited Company (1998)

24 Reserves [extract]

FRS 12 – Provisions, contingent liabilities and contingent assets

In previous years, expenditure on rationalisation schemes initiated before 1991 was included within development properties to the extent that it was recoverable from the estimated disposal proceeds. FRS 12 does not permit such expected gains to be taken into account when assessing the level of provision relating to such schemes. These rationalisation costs which amounted to £267 million at 31 December 1997 are now no longer included.

4.6   Changes and uses of provisions

IAS 37 requires that provisions should be reviewed at the end of each reporting period and adjusted to reflect the current best estimate. If it is no longer probable that an outflow of resources embodying economic benefits will be required to settle the obligation, the provision should be reversed.[109] Where discounting is used, the carrying amount of a provision increases in each period to reflect the passage of time. This increase is recognised as a borrowing cost.[110] This seems uncontroversial, other than in relation to changes in provisions for decommissioning, restoration and similar liabilities, including those arising from changes in discount rates, which are discussed at 4.2.5 above and 5.4.2 A below. As discussed at 4.2.4 above, IFRIC 1 in relation to provisions for decommissioning, restoration and similar liabilities requires that the periodic unwinding of the discount is recognised as a finance cost, and that it is not a borrowing cost capable of being capitalised under IAS 23.[111]

The standard emphasises that a provision should be used only for expenditures for which the provision was originally recognised, as to do otherwise would conceal the impact of two different events.[112] This means that the questionable practice of charging costs against a provision that was set up for a different purpose is specifically prohibited and the statement of comprehensive income will have to charge the new expenses separately from any release of an unused provision.

In a business combination, the acquirer recognises a liability at the acquisition date for those contingent liabilities of the acquiree that represent a present obligation arising as a result of a past event and in respect of which the fair value can be measured reliably.[113] After initial recognition, and until the liability is settled, cancelled or expires, the acquirer measures the contingent liability recognised in a business combination at the higher of:[114]

(a) the amount that would be recognised in accordance with IAS 37; and

(b) the amount initially recognised less, if appropriate, cumulative amortisation recognised in accordance with IAS 18 – *Revenue*.

This requirement does not apply to contracts accounted for in accordance with IAS 39.[115] For business combinations accounted for under IFRS 3 (as revised in 2008) see Chapter 9 at 3.6.6 A and, for business combinations accounted for under IFRS 3 (2007), Chapter 9 at 2.4.5 and 2.5.3).

5   APPLICATION OF THE RECOGNITION AND MEASUREMENT RULES

IAS 37 expands on the general recognition and measurement rules outlined at 3 and 4 above, by also including more specific requirements for particular situations, i.e. restructuring, future operating losses and onerous contracts. These are discussed at 5.1 to 5.3 below. In addition, IAS 37 contains a number of examples in an appendix which illustrate how the general recognition and measurement rules apply to other types of items where entities may or may not have made provision in the past. These are dealt with at 5.4 below.

5.1   Restructuring provisions

IAS 37 restricts both the freedom of entities to recognise restructuring provisions and the types of cost that are eligible for inclusion in such provisions, as discussed below.

5.1.1   *Definition*

IAS 37 defines a restructuring as 'a programme that is planned and controlled by management, and materially changes either:

(a) the scope of a business undertaken by an entity; or

(b) the manner in which that business is conducted'.[116]

This is said to include:

(a) the sale or termination of a line of business;

(b) the closure of business locations in a country or region or the relocation of business activities from one country or region to another;

(c) changes in management structure, for example, eliminating a layer of management; and

(d) fundamental reorganisations that have a material effect on the nature and focus of the entity's operations.[117]

This definition is very wide, and could encourage entities to classify all kinds of operating costs as restructuring costs, and thereby invite the reader to perceive them in a different light from the 'normal' costs of operating in a dynamic business environment. Even though IAS 37 prevents such costs being expensed too early (see the recognition rules below), their separate disclosure as restructuring costs may nonetheless cause users of financial statements to misinterpret the business's performance. 'Restructuring' is a term of art which can be, and is, used to cover a multitude of sins, and there is a risk that the standard perpetuates this. The reality is that change, and its consequent costs, has become a perennial feature of business and it is potentially misleading to afford it any special status in accounting terms. As such there can be a tension between the accounting for expected restructuring costs, which can be recognised if the recognition and measurement criteria below are met, and the general prohibition in IAS 37 against provision for future operating losses, which is discussed at 5.2 below.

IAS 37 emphasises that when a restructuring meets the definition of a discontinued operation under IFRS 5, additional disclosures may be required under that standard (see Chapter 4 at 3).[118]

5.1.2   Recognition

IAS 37 requires that restructuring costs are recognised only when the general recognition criteria in the standard are met (discussed at 3.1 above).[119] The interpretation of these criteria give rise to further specific requirements that 'a constructive obligation to restructure arises only when an entity:

(a)   has a detailed formal plan for the restructuring identifying at least:

    (i)   the business or part of a business concerned;

    (ii)   the principal locations affected;

    (iii)   the location, function, and approximate number of employees who will be compensated for terminating their services;

    (iv)   the expenditures that will be undertaken; and

    (v)   when the plan will be implemented; and

(b)   has raised a valid expectation in those affected that it will carry out the restructuring by starting to implement that plan or announcing its main features to those affected by it'.[120]

The standard gives examples of the entity's actions that may provide evidence that the entity has started to implement a plan, quoting the dismantling of plant or selling of assets, or the public announcement of the main features of the plan. However, it also emphasises that the public announcement of a detailed plan to restructure will not automatically create an obligation; the important principle is that the entity's actions give rise to valid expectations in other parties such as customers, suppliers and employees.[121]

The standard also suggests that for a plan to give rise to a constructive obligation, its implementation needs to be planned to begin as soon as possible and to be completed in a timeframe that makes significant changes to the plan unlikely. Any extended period before commencement of implementation, or if the restructuring will take an unreasonably long time, will mean that recognition of a provision is premature, because the entity is still likely to have a chance of changing the plan.[122]

In summary, these conditions require the plan to be detailed and specific, to have gone beyond the directors' powers of recall and to be put into operation without delay or significant alteration.

The criteria set out above for the recognition of provisions mean that a board decision, if it is the only relevant event arising before the end of the reporting period, is not sufficient. This message is reinforced specifically in the standard, the argument being made that a constructive obligation is not created by a management decision. There will only be a constructive obligation where the entity has, before the end of the reporting period:

(a)   started to implement the restructuring plan; or

(b)   announced the main features of the restructuring plan to those affected by it in a sufficiently specific manner to raise a valid expectation in them that the entity will carry out the restructuring.[123]

Examples are given in an appendix to IAS 37 illustrating the impact of these conditions.[124]

The standard acknowledges that there will be examples where a board decision does trigger recognition, but this would only be if earlier events such as negotiations with employee representatives for termination payments, or with purchasers for the sale of an operation, have been concluded subject only to board approval. In such circumstances, it is reasoned that when board approval has been obtained and communicated to the other parties, the entity is committed to restructure, assuming all other conditions are met.[125]

There is also discussion in the standard of the situation that may arise in some countries where, for example, employee representatives may sit on the board, so that a board decision effectively communicates the decision to them, which may result in a constructive obligation to restructure.[126]

When the ASB in the UK was developing its proposed FRS 12, a large number of commentators suggested that board decisions should act as a trigger for recognition of provisions, particularly if supported by subsequent events between the year end and approval of the financial statements which indicate that the board decision was a meaningful one. However, the ASB made no concessions to this view, and IAS 37 takes a similar approach. Under the standard, if an entity starts to implement a restructuring plan or announces its main features to those affected only after the reporting period, a provision cannot be made. However, disclosure may be required as a non-adjusting event after the reporting period under IAS 10 (see Chapter 37 at 2.1.2).[127]

We are not convinced that the change in recognition of reorganisation costs that IAS 37 has brought about is a beneficial one. We believe that it is misguided to ignore the effect of management intentions in portraying the financial performance and position of an entity, as this can often be highly relevant to an understanding of the entity's affairs. Although board decisions are capable of being reversed, this does not happen as a general rule.

Furthermore, the exclusion of the effect of management decisions is not a principle that has been applied consistently by the IASB. Take the example of a restructuring that is announced shortly after the reporting period involving the closure of plants and large scale redundancies. The reporting entity will be precluded from recognising the direct costs of the restructuring, as it does not have a constructive obligation at the end of the reporting period. However, the entity will be required to recognise any impairment in the carrying value of plant and other assets at the affected sites under IAS 36 – *Impairment of Assets* (see Chapter 18). Hence, board decisions would appear to be relevant when assessing impairment of assets but not when determining the reporting entity's liabilities, with the result that only some of the costs that result from the closure decision are recognised. Nevertheless, IAS 37 is clear that a provision for the direct cost of the restructuring can only be made if entity has a constructive obligation at the end of the reporting period.

It is also the case that the apparently robust tests of a constructive obligation set out in the standard are weaker than they seem. The determination of whether management actions 'raise a valid expectation in third parties' is extremely difficult and subjective. Even if a trigger point is easily identifiable, such as when an entity makes a detailed public announcement that meets all the specified criteria, it does not necessarily commit management to the 'restructuring' as such, but only to specific items of expenditure such as redundancy costs. Nevertheless, in practice, once a trigger point has been identified, an entity will presumably provide for all the costs of the reorganisation, assuming that they meet the eligibility criteria set out in 5.1.3 below.

Furthermore, the test is at least as manipulable as board decisions. Entities anxious to accelerate or postpone recognition of a liability could do so by advancing or deferring an event that signals such a commitment, such as a public announcement, without any change to the substance of their position.

IAS 37 has some further specific rules governing when to recognise the loss arising on the sale of an operation. It is unclear why this should have been the case, since such provisions are really adjustments to the carrying amounts of the assets concerned, not provisions as defined by the standard. Indeed, if the operation is a 'disposal group' classified as held for sale under IFRS 5, then there will be no need for a separate provision for the loss on sale since under that standard the disposal group is measured at the lower of its carrying amount and the fair value less costs to sell (see Chapter 4 at 2).

IAS 37 states that no obligation arises for the sale of an operation until the entity is committed to the sale, i.e. there is a binding sale agreement.[128] Thus a provision cannot be made for a loss on sale unless there is a binding sale agreement by the year-end. The standard says that this applies even when an entity has taken a decision to sell an operation and announced that decision publicly, it cannot be committed to the sale until a purchaser has been identified and there is a binding sale agreement. Until there is such an agreement, the entity will be able to change its mind and indeed will have to take another course of action if a purchaser cannot be found on acceptable terms.

Where it is considered that a provision for the loss on disposal cannot be recognised, then the standard emphasises that where the sale of the operation is envisaged as part of a larger restructuring, the assets of the operation must be reviewed for impairment under IAS 36. This may therefore mean that the statement of comprehensive income reflects effectively the same loss; it is just that the loss is presented as a reduction of the carrying amount of assets rather than as a liability. The standard also recognises that where a sale is only part of a restructuring, the entity could be committed to the other parts of restructuring before a binding sale agreement is in place.[129] Hence, the costs of the restructuring will be recognised over different reporting periods.

5.1.3 Costs that can be recognised within a restructuring provision

The recognition tests for reorganisation costs that are set out above are designed to establish whether or not there is a liability at the end of the reporting period, which is consistent with the conceptual approach of the standard and indeed with the IASB's *Framework*. It might therefore be rather surprising to find an additional paragraph in the standard that further limits the costs that can be provided for and which is founded on quite a different conceptual approach. It states that 'a restructuring provision should include only the direct expenditures arising from the restructuring, which are those that are both:

(a)   necessarily entailed by the restructuring; and

(b)   not associated with the ongoing activities of the entity'.[130]

While (a) is perhaps a further elaboration of the rules for defining the extent of the entity's obligations, the rationale for (b) is not so straightforward. The justification given for it ties in with the more general requirement in the standard that 'it is only those obligations arising from past events existing independently of an entity's future actions that should be recognised'.[131] Hence, these costs are recognised on the same basis as if they arose independently of the restructuring.[132]

In reality, this is an approach based on expense recognition, in that the costs associated with ongoing activities will produce future benefits, and thus should not be anticipated, whether or not a liability for them exists. Expense recognition is a concept not adequately acknowledged by the IASB's *Framework*, but one which the Board seems unable to do without.

The standard gives specific examples of those costs that may not be included within the provision. Such costs include:

(a)   retraining or relocating continuing staff;

(b)   marketing; or

(c)   investment in new systems and distribution networks.[133]

No examples of allowable costs are given within the standard. However, the exposure draft that preceded FRS 12 in the UK gave certain examples. These were the costs of:

(a)   making employees redundant;

(b)   terminating leases and other contracts whose termination results directly from the reorganisation; and

(c)   expenditures to be made in the course of the reorganisation, such as employees' remuneration while they are engaged in such tasks as dismantling plant, disposing of surplus stocks and fulfilling contractual obligations.[134]

Examples (a) and (b) would certainly be permitted under the rules in IAS 37. As far as (a) is concerned, IAS 19 has specific requirements about termination benefits (see Chapter 28 at 6.3). Although the criteria for recognising a liability for termination benefits in IAS 19 are expressed in different terms from that for restructuring provisions, we would not envisage any difference in practice in the timing of the recognition of a liability for the cost of redundancies.

Example (c) is slightly more contentious in relation to employee remuneration, in that unless an employee is being retained solely for the purpose of dismantling plant, etc, before being made redundant, it is questionable whether the remuneration costs meet the definition of being 'necessarily entailed by a restructuring'.

A further rule in IAS 37 is that the provision should not include identifiable future operating losses up to the date of the restructuring, unless they relate to an onerous contract.[135] This is consistent with the more general requirement in the standard that provision should not be made for future operating losses, discussed in 5.2 below.

The general requirement noted in 4.5 above that gains on the expected disposal of assets cannot be taken into account in the measurement of provisions is also particularly relevant to the measurement of restructuring provisions.[136] This has meant that larger restructuring provisions than before have been required as any corresponding expected gains on assets are no longer available for set off, as was the case with British Aerospace in the UK as shown in Extract 24.2 at 4.5 above. However, sometimes the impact of this rule will be mitigated by the fact that fewer costs will also be recognised within a provision, as some will not meet the criteria set out above.

5.2   Operating losses

IAS 37 explicitly states that 'provisions shall not be recognised for future operating losses'.[137] This is because such losses do not meet the definition of a liability and the general recognition criteria of the standard (see 3.1 above).[138] Such costs should be left to be reported in the future in the same way as future profits are.

However, it would be wrong to assume that this requirement has effectively prevented any future operating losses from being anticipated, because they are sometimes recognised as a result of requirements in another standard. For example:

- under IAS 2 – *Inventories* – inventories are written down to the extent that they will not be recovered from future revenues, rather than leaving the non-recovery to show up as future operating losses (see Chapter 20 at 2.2.4);

- under IAS 11 provision is made for losses expected on construction contracts (see Chapter 21 at 2.3.6); and

- under IAS 36, impairment of assets is measured on the basis of the present value of future operating cash flows, meaning that the effect of not only future operating losses but also sub-standard operating profits will be recognised (see Chapter 18 at 3.3.3 B). IAS 37 specifically makes reference to the fact that an expectation of future operating losses may be an indication that certain assets are impaired.[139]

This is therefore a rather more complex issue than IAS 37 acknowledges.

5.3   Onerous contracts

Although future operating losses in general cannot be provided for, IAS 37 requires that 'if an entity has a contract that is onerous, the present obligation under the contract shall be recognised and measured as a provision'.[140]

The standard notes that many contracts (for example, some routine purchase orders) can be cancelled without paying compensation to the other party, and therefore there is no obligation. However, other contracts establish both rights and obligations for each of the contracting parties. Where events make such a contract onerous, the contract falls within the scope of the standard and a liability exists which is recognised. As noted at 2.2.1 A above, executory contracts that are not onerous fall outside the scope of the standard.[141]

IAS 37 defines an onerous contract as 'a contract in which the unavoidable costs of meeting the obligations under the contract exceed the economic benefits expected to be received under it'.[142] This seems to require that the contract is onerous to the point of being directly loss-making, not simply uneconomic by reference to current prices.

IAS 37 considers that 'the unavoidable costs under a contract reflect the least net cost of exiting from the contract i.e. the lower of the cost of fulfilling it and any compensation or penalties arising from failure to fulfil it'.[143] An example of such a provision is BG Group's capacity contract provisions, which stood at £154 million at 31 December 2007, and are described in this extract.

Extract 24.3: BG Group plc (2007)

23 PROVISIONS FOR LIABILITIES AND CHARGES [extract]

OTHER [extract]

The balance as at 31 December 2007 includes … provisions for onerous contracts £154m (2006 £nil) … A provision for onerous contracts was recognised during the year in respect of capacity contracts in the Interconnector pipeline, retained following disposal of the Group's 25% equity interest in Interconnector (UK) Limited. The obligation associated with these contracts extends to 2018.

6 DISPOSALS, RE-MEASUREMENTS AND IMPAIRMENTS [extract]

DISPOSAL OF NON-CURRENT ASSETS [extract]

2007 [extract]

In June 2007, the Group sold its 25% interest in Interconnector (UK) Limited whilst retaining its throughput capacity contracts with this company … As part of this transaction, the Group reviewed the retained capacity contracts in the Interconnector pipeline and concluded that the obligations associated with these contracts exceed the benefit expected to be received from the Interconnector interest. Accordingly a pre-tax provision of £156m (post-tax £124m) was made to reflect the present obligation under these contracts.

The most common example of an onerous contract in practice probably relates to leasehold property. From time to time entities may hold vacant leasehold property (or property which is only partly occupied) which they have substantially ceased to use for the purpose of their business and where sub-letting is either unlikely, or would be at a significantly reduced rental from that being paid by the entity. This is reinforced by the inclusion of a specific example of a provision for a vacant leasehold property in an appendix to the standard.[144]

Entities have to make systematic provision when such properties become vacant, and on a discounted basis where the effect is sufficiently material. Indeed, it could be argued that it is not just when the properties become vacant that provision would be required, but that provision should be made at the time the expected economic benefits of using the property fall short of the unavoidable costs under the lease. As outlined at 8.1.6 below, the IASB as part of its convergence project with the FASB has proposed to amend IAS 37 so that when a contract becomes onerous as a result of an entity's own actions, the resulting provision should not be recognised until that action has occurred. In its discussions, the IASB had said that in the case of an operating lease on a property that will become vacant as a result of a restructuring, the provision for the unavoidable lease commitment should be recognised only when the entity vacates the property. However, the Board's discussion did not address the situation of an ongoing lease contract that might become onerous, before the entity has taken any specific action in respect of the lease. The IFRIC Agenda Committee recommended that the IFRIC take up this issue, because it was not clear when a provision for an onerous contract should be recognised or how it should be measured. Although the IFRIC had a preliminary discussion about the issue in December 2003, including whether it should be expanded to cover other types of executory contracts such as a take or pay contract, it agreed that the issue should not be taken onto its agenda at that time.[145] However, it is sometimes the case in practice that entities interpret the requirements of IAS 37 as meaning that they should only recognise a provision when the properties are vacated.

Nevertheless, where a provision is to be recognised a number of difficulties remain. The first is how the provision should be calculated. It is unlikely that the provision will simply be the net present value of the future rental obligation, because if a substantial period of the lease remains, the entity will probably be able either to agree a negotiated sum with the landlord to terminate the lease early, or to sub-lease the building at some point in the future. Hence, the entity will have to make a best estimate of its future cash flows taking all these factors into account.

Another issue that arises from this is whether the provision should be shown net of any cash flows that may arise from sub-leasing the property, or whether the provision must be shown gross, with a corresponding asset set up for expected cash flows from sub-leasing only if they meet the recognition criteria of being 'virtually certain' to be received. The strict offset criteria in the standard (see 4.4 above) would suggest the latter to be required, as the entity would normally retain liability for the full lease payments if the sub-lessee defaulted. However, the standard makes no explicit reference to this issue. We believe that a net approach is the most appropriate treatment for such onerous contracts under IAS 37. Indeed, it could be argued that the provision is only in respect of the loss-making element of the contract and therefore there is no corresponding asset to be recognised. In any event, as indicated at 8.1.6 below, the IASB has decided to specify that if an onerous contract is an operating lease, the provision should be reduced by the sublease rentals that could reasonably be obtained for the property.

In the past, some entities may have maintained that no provision is required for vacant properties, because if the property leases are looked at on a portfolio basis, the overall economic benefits from properties exceed the overall costs. However, this argument does not appear to be sustainable under IAS 37, as the definition of an onerous contract refers specifically to costs and economic benefits *under the contract*.

It is more difficult to apply the definition of onerous contracts to the lease on a head office which is not generating revenue specifically. If the definition were applied too literally, one might end up concluding that all head office leases should be provided against because no specific economic benefits are expected under them. It would be more sensible to conclude that the entity as a whole obtains economic benefits from its head office, which was presumably the reason for entering in to the lease to start with. However, this does not alter the fact that if circumstances change and the head office becomes vacant, a provision should then be made against the lease.

IAS 37 requires that any impairment loss that has occurred in respect of assets dedicated to an onerous contract is recognised before establishing a provision for the onerous contract.[146] For example, any leasehold improvements that have been capitalised should be written off before provision is made for excess future rental costs.

One company which has provided for onerous leases under IAS 37 is Jardine Matheson as indicated by the following extract.

Extract 24.4: *Jardine Matheson Holdings Limited* (2007)

Principal Accounting Policies [extract]

(n) Provisions [extract]

Provisions are recognized when the Group has present legal or constructive obligations as a result of past events, it is probable that an outflow of resources embodying economic benefits will be required to settle the obligations, and a reliable estimate of the amount of the obligations can be made.

32   Provisions

	Motor vehicle warranties US$m	Closure cost provisions US$m	Obligations under onerous leases US$m	Reinstatement and restoration costs US$m	Statutory employee entitlements US$m	Others US$m	Total US$m
2007							
At 1st January	22	15	8	18	22	19	104
Exchange differences	1	–	–	–	(1)	–	–
Additional provisions	4	7	2	8	5	4	30
Unused amounts reversed	–	–	–	(1)	(4)	(2)	(7)
Utilized	(6)	(7)	(2)	(2)	–	–	(17)
At 31st December	21	15	8	23	22	21	110
Non-current	–	1	2	20	19	–	42
Current	21	14	6	3	3	21	68
	21	15	8	23	22	21	110

2006							
At 1st January	19	12	7	8	12	20	78
Exchange differences	2	1	1	–	1	–	5
Additional provisions	7	8	1	11	9	7	43
Unused amounts reversed	–	(1)	–	–	–	(4)	(5)
Utilized	(6)	(5)	(1)	(1)	–	(4)	(17)
At 31st December	22	15	8	18	22	19	104
Non-current	–	–	4	14	16	–	34
Current	22	15	4	4	6	19	70
	22	15	8	18	22	19	104

Motor vehicle warranties are estimated liabilities that fall due under the warranty terms offered on sale of new and used vehicles beyond that which is reimbursed by the manufacturers.

Closure cost provisions are established when legal or constructive obligations arise on closure or disposal of businesses.

Provisions are made for obligations under onerous operating leases when the properties are not used by the Group and the net costs of exiting from the leases exceed the economic benefits expected to be received.

Other provisions comprise provisions in respect of indemnities on disposal of businesses, lease dilapidations, legal claims and statutory employee benefits.

The discussion above deals with situations where the leasehold property becomes vacant (or only partly occupied). However, what if the rentals payable by an entity increase due to market rates or are in excess of market rates. Does this mean that an entity has an onerous contract for which it should make a provision? Not necessarily. As noted above, IAS 37 defines an onerous contract as 'a contract in which the unavoidable costs of meeting the obligations under the contract exceed the economic benefits expected to be received under it'.[147] This seems to require that the contract is onerous to the point of being directly loss-making, not simply uneconomic by reference to current prices. Thus, if the entity still expects to operate profitably from the leased property over the remaining period of its use, despite these higher rental payments, no provision should be made. If the business operated out of the leased property has become loss-making, and the entity does not expect its operating results to improve such that the higher rental payments will not be fully recovered over the remaining period of its use, then a provision may be necessary. However, as indicated earlier, before a separate provision for an onerous contract is established, IAS 37 notes that an entity should first recognise any impairment loss that has occurred on assets dedicated to the contract.[148]

Tesco PLC includes in its property provisions an amount for the excess of future rents over market value on its loss-making stores.

Extract 24.5: Tesco PLC (2007)
Note 22 Provisions [extract]
Property provisions comprise future rents payable net of rents receivable on onerous and vacant property leases, provisions for terminal dilapidations and provisions for future rents above market value on unprofitable stores. The majority of the provision is expected to be utilised of the period to 2020.

Tesco also provides for dilapidation costs relating to leasehold properties, which are discussed at 5.4.6 below.

5.4   Other types of provisions

IAS 37 also deals with other types of situations where provisions may or may not have been made in the past. Although the standard does not include particular requirements about such items, it has either included an example in an appendix dealing with such situations or has mentioned them in passing while discussing the general recognition requirements of the standard. These, together with other situations discussed in FRS 12 in the UK and matters addressed by the IFRIC, are dealt with below.

5.4.1   *Environmental provisions*

The standard illustrates two examples of circumstances where environmental provisions would be required. The first deals with the situation where it is virtually certain that legislation will be enacted which will require the clean up of land already contaminated.[149] In these circumstances, a provision would obviously be required. However, in its discussion about what constitutes an obligating event, the standard notes that 'differences in circumstances surrounding enactment make it impossible to specify a single event that would make the enactment of a law virtually certain. In many cases, it will be impossible to be virtually certain of the enactment of a law until it is enacted.'[150] The second example deals with the situation where an entity has contaminated land, but is not legally required to clean it up.[151] In these circumstances, however, a provision is still required because the entity is deemed to have a constructive obligation to clean up the land. In the example given, a constructive obligation is said to exist because the entity has a widely publicised environmental policy undertaking to clean up all contamination that it causes, and has a record of honouring this policy.

These requirements are not particularly controversial, apart from the general difficulty in knowing exactly when a constructive obligation comes into existence.

One company which makes provision for environmental costs is Syngenta as shown below.

Extract 24.6: Syngenta AG (2007)

2.   Accounting policies [extract]
Provisions

A provision is recognized in the balance sheet when Syngenta has a legal or constructive obligation to third parties as a result of a past event and it is probable that an outflow of economic benefits will be required to settle the obligation. The amount recognized as a provision is the best estimate of the expenditure required to settle the obligation at the balance sheet date. If the effect of discounting is material, provisions are measured by discounting the expected value of future cash flows at a pre-tax rate that reflects current market assessments of the time value of money and, where appropriate, the risks specific to the liability. Where some or all of the expenditure required to settle a provision is expected to be reimbursed by another party, the reimbursement is recognized only when reimbursement is virtually certain. The amount to be reimbursed is recognized as a separate asset. Where Syngenta has a joint and several liability with one or more other parties, no provision is recognized to the extent that those other parties are expected to settle part or all of the obligation. Syngenta self-insures or uses a combination of insurance and self-insurance for certain risks. Provisions for these risks are estimated in part by considering historical claims experience and other actuarial assumptions.

Environmental provisions

Syngenta is exposed to environmental liabilities relating to its past operations, principally in respect of remediation costs. Provisions for non-recurring remediation costs are made when there is a present obligation, it is probable that expense on remediation work will be required within ten years (or a longer period if specified by a legal obligation) and the cost can be estimated within a reasonable range of possible outcomes. The costs are based on currently available facts; technology expected to be available at the time of the clean up, laws and regulations presently or virtually certain to be enacted and prior experience in remediation of contaminated sites. Environmental liabilities are recorded at the estimated amount at which the liability could be settled at the balance sheet date. Environmental liabilities are discounted if the impact is material and if cost estimates and timing are considered reasonably certain. Environmental costs are capitalized as part of property, plant and equipment where they are expected to increase the economic benefits flowing from the use or eventual disposal of the asset, or when they represent an obligation to remediate at the end of the asset's life and are recoverable from future economic benefits of using the asset. In all other cases, they are expensed. Environmental costs, unless related to restructuring, are included in cost of goods sold.

Additional environmental remediation costs and provisions may be required were Syngenta to decide to close certain of its sites. Syngenta's restructuring programs have involved closure of several sites to date. Remediation liabilities are accounted for as restructuring provisions and recognized when the site closure has been announced. In the opinion of Syngenta, it is not possible to estimate reliably the costs that would be incurred on eventual closure of its continuing sites, where there is no present obligation to remediate, because it is neither possible to determine a time limit beyond which the sites will no longer be operated, nor what remediation costs may be required on their eventual closure.

Restructuring provisions

A provision for restructuring is recognized when Syngenta has approved a detailed and formal restructuring plan and the restructuring has either commenced or been announced publicly.

Provision for severance payments and related employment costs is made in full when employees are given details of the termination benefits which will apply to individual employees should their contracts be terminated as a direct result of the restructuring plan. Costs relating to ongoing activities, such as relocation, training and information systems costs are recognized only when incurred.

22.   Provisions [extract]

(US$ million)	2007	2006	2005
Environmental provisions (Note 30)	450	412	386

The following table analyzes the movement in provisions during 2007: [extract]

(US$ million)	Balance at December 31, 2006	Charged to income	Release of provisions credited to income	Acquisitions	Payments	Reclass-ifications	Trans-lation effects	Balance at December 31, 2007
Environmental provisions (Note 30)	412	87	(4)	–	(64)	3	16	450

30.   Commitments and contingencies [extract]

Environmental Matters

Syngenta has environmental liabilities at some currently or formerly owned, leased and third party sites throughout the world.

In the USA, Syngenta, or its indemnities, has been named under federal legislation (the Comprehensive Environment Response, Compensation and Liability Act of 1980, as amended) as a potentially responsible party ("PRP") in respect of several sites. Syngenta expects to be indemnified against a proportion of the liabilities associated with a number of these sites by the seller of the businesses associated with such sites and, where appropriate, actively participates in or monitors the clean-up activities at the sites in respect of which it is a PRP.

Syngenta has provisions in respect of environmental remediation costs in accordance with the accounting policy described in Note 2 and as shown in Note 22, Provisions. Key assumptions and sources of estimation uncertainty are discussed in Note 2. The environmental provision is principally related to potential liabilities at various locations. The estimated provision takes into consideration the number of other PRPs at each site and the identity and financial positions of such parties in light of the joint and several nature of the liability.

The requirement in the future for Syngenta ultimately to take action to correct the effects on the environment of prior disposal or release of chemical substances by Syngenta or other parties, and its costs, pursuant to environment laws and regulations, is inherently difficult to estimate. The material components of the environmental provisions consist of a risk assessment based on investigation of the various sites. Syngenta's future remediation expenses are affected by a number of uncertainties which include, but are not limited to, the method and extent of remediation, the percentage of material attributable to Syngenta at the remediation sites relative to that attributable to other parties, and the financial capabilities of the other potentially responsible parties. It is often not possible to estimate the amounts expected to be recovered via reimbursement, indemnification or insurance due to the uncertainty inherent in this area.

Syngenta believes that its provisions are adequate based upon currently available information. However, given the inherent difficulties in estimating liabilities in this area, it cannot be guaranteed that additional costs will not be incurred beyond the amounts accrued. The effect of resolution of environmental matters on results of operations cannot be predicted due to uncertainty concerning both the amount and the timing of future expenditures and the results of future operations. Management believes that such additional amounts, if any, would not be material to Syngenta's financial condition but could be material to Syngenta's results of operations in a given period.

Potentially, a more significant effect of the standard is its requirement that provisions should be discounted, which will have a material impact if the expenditure is not expected to be incurred for some time. As a result of implementing FRS 12 in the UK, BP (then BP Amoco) changed its policy to reflect this, which had the effect of reducing its environmental provision by £350 million because of the discount factor, and its current policy is as shown in the following extract.

Extract 24.7: BP p.l.c. (2007)

1   **Significant accounting policies** [extract]

Environmental expenditures and liabilities

Environmental expenditures that relate to current or future revenues are expensed or capitalized as appropriate. Expenditures that relate to an existing condition caused by past operations and do not contribute to current or future earnings are expensed.

Liabilities for environmental costs are recognized when environmental assessments or clean-ups are probable and the associated costs can be reasonably estimated. Generally, the timing of recognition of these provisions coincides with the commitment to a formal plan of action or, if earlier, on divestment or on closure of inactive sites.

The amount recognized is the best estimate of the expenditure required. Where the liability will not be settled for a number of years, the amount recognized is the present value of the estimated future expenditure.

Decommissioning

Liabilities for decommissioning costs are recognized when the group has an obligation to dismantle and remove a facility or an item of plant and to restore the site on which it is located, and when a reasonable estimate of that liability can be made. Where an obligation exists for a new facility, such as oil and natural gas production or transportation facilities, this will be on construction or installation. An obligation for decommissioning may also crystallize during the period of operation of a facility through a change in legislation or through a decision to terminate operations. The amount recognized is the present value of the estimated future expenditure determined in accordance with local conditions and requirements.

A corresponding item of property, plant and equipment of an amount equivalent to the provision is also created. This is subsequently depreciated as part of the asset.

Other than the unwinding discount on the provision, any change in the present value of the estimated expenditure is reflected as an adjustment to the provision and the corresponding item of property, plant and equipment.

37   Provisions [extract]

	Decom-missioning	$ million Environ-mental
At 1 January 2007	8,365	2,127
Exchange adjustments	168	19
New or increased provisions	1,163	373
Write-back of unused provisions	–	(151)
Unwinding of discount	195	44
Utilization	(297)	(305)
Deletions	(93)	–
At 31 December 2007	9,501	2,107
Of which – expected to be incurred within 1 year	447	431
– expected to be incurred in more than 1 year	9,054	1,676

	Decom-missioning	$ million Environ-mental
At 1 January 2006	6,450	2,311
Exchange adjustments	13	31
New or increased provisions	2,142	423
Write-back of unused provisions	–	(355)
Unwinding of discount	153	45
Utilization	(179)	(324)
Deletions	(214)	(4)
At 31 December 2006	8,365	2,127
Of which – expected to be incurred within 1 year	324	444
– expected to be incurred in more than 1 year	8,041	1,683

The group makes full provision for the future cost of decommissioning oil and natural gas production facilities and related pipelines on a discounted basis on the installation of those facilities. The provision for the costs of decommissioning these production facilities and pipelines at the end of their economic lives has been estimated using existing technology, at current prices and discounted using a real discount rate of 2.0% (2006 2.0%). These costs are generally expected to be incurred over the next 30 years. While the provision is based on the best estimate of future costs and the economic lives of the facilities and pipelines, there is uncertainty regarding both the amount and timing of incurring these costs.

Provisions for environmental remediation are made when a clean-up is probable and the amount reliably determinable. Generally, this coincides with commitment to a formal plan of action or, if earlier, on divestment or closure of inactive sites. The provision for environmental liabilities has been estimated using existing technology, at current prices and discounted using a real discount rate of 2.0% (2006 2.0%). The majority of these costs are expected to be incurred over the next 10 years. The extent and cost of future remediation programmes are inherently difficult to estimate. They depend on the scale of any possible contamination, the timing and extent of corrective actions, and also the group's share of liability.

5.4.2   Decommissioning provisions

Decommissioning costs are those that arise, for example, when an oil rig or nuclear power station has to be dismantled at the end of its life.[152]

Practice prior to the issue of IAS 37 was to build up the required provision over the life of the facility by appropriate charges against revenues. IAS 37, on the other hand, requires that the liability is recognised as soon as the obligation exists, which will normally be at commencement of operations.

The accounting for decommissioning costs is dealt with in IAS 37 by way of an example, an offshore oilfield, in an appendix. The example discusses the situation where ninety per cent of the eventual costs relate to the removal of the rig and restoration of damage caused by building it, and ten per cent arises through the extraction of oil.[153] In these circumstances, a provision for ninety per cent of the total costs will be set up when the rig has been constructed, with the balance being recognised as the oil is extracted. This example requires that an entity should recognise a liability as soon as the decommissioning obligation is created, which is normally when the facility is constructed and the damage that needs to be restored is done. In this case, the ninety per cent represents the full liability at the date of constructing the rig. The total decommissioning cost is estimated, discounted to its present value and it is this amount which forms the initial provision and is added to the corresponding asset's cost. Thereafter, the asset is depreciated over its useful life, while the discounted provision is progressively unwound, with the unwinding charge showing as a finance cost.

Although we understand why the IASB's *Framework* pushes it towards recognition of the full liability, it seems that this can only be achieved by including a spurious asset on the other side of the balance sheet. In any case, if the principle that a liability should be recognised once costs have become unavoidable were really to be applied on a consistent basis, various other commitments (for example, expenditure commitments under licence agreements) would also be caught and there would be considerable grossing up of balance sheets.

Whilst discounting the estimated liability had been used for some time in the nuclear power plant industry, it was not commonly the previous accounting practice for oil companies. The effect of discounting on the statement of comprehensive income is to split the cost of the eventual decommissioning into two components: an operating cost based on the present value of the provision; and a finance element representing the unwinding of the discount. The overall effect is to produce a rising pattern of cost over the life of the facility, often with much of the total cost of the decommissioning recognised as a finance cost. In contrast, previous practice for oil companies was to show the whole amount in arriving at their operating results, and to aim to charge a level amount for each barrel of oil extracted, although the effects of changing estimates of costs, particularly inflation (which was not factored into the original estimates made), meant that this was not precisely achieved.

AngloGold Ashanti's accounting policies and provisions note in respect of decommissioning obligations and restoration obligations are shown in the following extract from its 2007 financial statements:

Extract 24.8: AngloGold Ashanti Limited (2007)

1.4   Summary of significant accounting policies [extract]

Provisions

Provisions are recognised when the group has a present obligation, whether legal or constructive, as a result of a past event for which it is probable that an outflow of resources embodying economic benefits will be required to settle the obligation and a reliable estimate can be made of the amount of the obligation. Where some or all of the expenditure required to settle a provision is expected to be reimbursed by another party, the reimbursement is recognised only when the reimbursement is virtually certain. The amount to be reimbursed is recognised as a separate asset. Where the group has a joint and several liability with one or more other parties, no provision is recognised to the extent that those other parties are expected to settle part or all of the obligation.

Provisions are measured at the present value of management's best estimate of the expenditure required to settle the obligation at the balance sheet date. The discount rate used to determine the present value reflects current market assessments of the time value of money and the risks specific to the liability.

Litigation and administrative proceedings are evaluated on a case-by-case basis considering the information available, including that of legal counsel, to assess potential outcomes. Where it is considered probable that an obligation will result in an outflow of resources, a provision is recorded for the present value of the expected cash outflows if these are reasonably measurable. These provisions cover the estimated payments to plaintiffs, court fees and the cost of potential settlements.

AngloGold Ashanti Limited does not recognise a contingent liability on its balance sheet except in a business combination. A contingent liability is disclosed when the possibility of an outflow of resources embodying economic benefits is not remote.

Environmental expenditure

The group has long-term remediation obligations comprising decommissioning and restoration liabilities relating to its past operations which are based on the group's environmental management plans, in compliance with the current environmental and regulatory requirements. Provisions for non-recurring remediation costs are made when there is a present obligation, it is probable that expense on remediation work will be required and the cost can be estimated within a reasonable range of possible outcomes. The costs are based on currently available facts, technology expected to be available at the time of the clean up, laws and regulations presently or virtually certain to be enacted and prior experience in remediation of contaminated sites.

Annual contributions for the South African operations are made to the Environmental Rehabilitation Trust Fund, created in accordance with local statutory requirements where applicable, to fund the estimated cost of rehabilitation during and at the end of the life of a mine. The amounts contributed to this trust fund are accounted for as non-current assets in the company. Interest earned on monies paid to rehabilitation trust funds is accrued on a time proportion basis and is recorded as interest income. For group purposes the trusts are consolidated.

AngloGold Ashanti is the sole contributor to the funds and exercises full control through the respective boards of trustees, hence the funds are consolidated.

Environmental rehabilitation obligations in respect of the non-South African operations are not funded through an established trust fund. Bank guarantees and reclamation bonds are provided for some of these liabilities.

Decommissioning costs

The provision for decommissioning represents the cost that will arise from rectifying damage caused before production commenced. Accordingly an asset is recognised and included within mine infrastructure.

Decommissioning costs are provided at the present value of the expenditures expected to settle the obligation, using estimated cash flows based on current prices. The unwinding of the decommissioning obligation is included in the income statement. Estimated future costs of decommissioning obligations are reviewed regularly and adjusted as appropriate for new circumstances or changes in law or technology. Changes in estimates are capitalised or reversed against the relevant asset. Estimates are discounted at a pre-tax rate that reflects current market assessments of the time value of money.

Gains or losses from the expected disposal of assets are not taken into account when determining the provision.

Restoration costs

The provision for restoration represents the costs of restoring site damage after the start of production. Increases in the provision are charged to the income statement as a cost of production.

Gross restoration costs are estimated at the present value of the expenditures expected to settle the obligation, using estimated cash flows based on current prices. The estimates are discounted at a pre-tax rate that reflects current market assessments of the time value of money and risks specific to the liability.

Figures in million	2007	2006
	US Dollars	
31 **Environmental rehabilitation and other provisions**		
Environmental rehabilitation obligations		
Provision for decommissioning		
Balance at beginning of year	175	143
Adjustments due to disposal of assets	–	(3)
Change in estimates[1]	13	36
Unwinding of decommissioning obligation (note 7)	12	6
Utilised during the year	(3)	–
Translation	6	(7)
Balance at end of year	203	175
Provision for restoration		
Balance at beginning of year	186	194
Adjustments due to disposal of assets	–	(2)
Charge to income statement	48	2
Change in estimates[1]	7	(5)
Unwinding of restoration obligation (note 7)	10	10
Utilised during the year	(15)	(10)
Translation	7	(3)
Balance at end of year	243	186

[1]   The change in estimates relates to changes in laws and regulations governing the protection of the environment and factors relative to rehabilitation estimates and a change in the quantities of material in reserves and a corresponding change in the life of mine plan. These provisions are anticipated to unwind beyond the end of the life of mine.

As noted at 4.6 above, the standard requires provisions to be revised annually to reflect the current best estimate of the provision. However, the standard gives no guidance on accounting for changes in the decommissioning provision. Similarly, IAS 16 is unclear about the extent to which an item's carrying amount should be affected by changes in the estimated amount of dismantling and site restoration costs that occur *after* the estimate made upon initial measurement. This was addressed by the IASB with the publication of IFRIC 1 in May 2004.

A   IFRIC 1

IFRIC 1 applies to any decommissioning, restoration or similar liability that has been both included as part of the cost of an asset measured in accordance with IAS 16 and recognised as a liability in accordance with IAS 37.[154] It addresses how the effect of the following events that change the measurement of an existing decommissioning, restoration or similar liability should be accounted for:[155]

(a)   a change in the estimated outflow of resources embodying economic benefits (e.g. cash flows) required to settle the obligation;

(b)   a change in the current market-based discount rate (this includes changes in the time value of money and the risks specific to the liability); and

(c)   an increase that reflects the passage of time (also referred to as the unwinding of the discount).

IFRIC 1 requires that (c) above, the periodic unwinding of the discount, is recognised in profit or loss as a finance cost as it occurs.[156] IFRIC concluded that the unwinding of the discount is not a borrowing cost as defined in IAS 23, and thus cannot be capitalised under that standard (see Chapter 19).[157]

For a change caused by (a) or (b) above, however, the adjustment is not taken to the income statement as it occurs, but is recognised in the carrying value of the related asset or in other comprehensive income, depending on whether the asset is measured at cost or using the revaluation model.[158]

If the related asset is measured using the cost model, the change in the liability should be added to or deducted from the cost of the asset to which it relates. Where the change gives rise to an addition to cost, the entity should consider the need to test the new carrying value for impairment. Reductions over and above the remaining carrying value of the asset are recognised immediately in profit or loss.[159] The adjusted depreciable amount of the asset is then depreciated prospectively over its remaining useful life.[160]

If the related asset is measured using the revaluation model, changes in the liability alter the revaluation surplus or deficit previously recognised for that asset. Changes to the provision are recognised in other comprehensive income and increase or decrease the value of the revaluation surplus in respect of the asset, except to the extent that:

(a)   a decrease in the provision reverses a previous revaluation deficit that was recognised in profit or loss;

(b)   a decrease in the provision exceeds the carrying amount of the asset that would have been recognised under the cost model; or

(c)   an increase in the provision exceeds the previous revaluation surplus relating to that asset,

in which case the change is recognised in profit or loss. Changes in the provision might also indicate the need for the asset to be revalued.[161]

These requirements are discussed further in Chapter 16 at 3.2.3.

As indicated at 4.2.5 above, IAS 37 is unclear whether a new discount rate should be applied during the year or just at the year-end, and whether the rate should be applied to the new estimate of the provision or the old estimate. Although IFRIC 1 requires that changes in the provision resulting from a change in the discount rate is added to, or deducted from, the cost of the related asset in the current period, it does not deal specifically with these points. However, Example 1 in the illustrative examples to IFRIC 1 indicates that a change in discount rate would be accounted for in the same way as other changes affecting the estimate of a provision for decommissioning, restoration and similar liabilities. That is, it is reflected as a change in the liability at the time the revised estimate is made and the new estimate is discounted at the revised discount rate from that point on.[162]

B   IFRIC 5

Some entities may participate in a decommissioning, restoration or environmental rehabilitation fund, the purpose of which is to segregate assets to fund some or all of the costs of its decommissioning or environmental liabilities for which the entity has to make a provision under IAS 37. IFRIC 5 was issued in December 2004 to address this issue.[163]

Contributions to these funds may be voluntary or required by regulation or law, and the funds may have one of the following common structures:[164]

- funds that are established by a single contributor to fund its own decommissioning obligations, whether for a particular site, or for a number of geographically dispersed sites;

- funds that are established with multiple contributors to fund their individual or joint decommissioning obligations, where contributors are entitled to reimbursement for decommissioning expenses to the extent of their fund contributions plus any actual earnings on those contributions less their share of the costs of administering the fund. In addition, contributors may have an obligation to make potential additional contributions, for example, in the event of the bankruptcy of another contributor;

- funds that are established with multiple contributors to fund their individual or joint decommissioning obligations when the required level of contributions is based on the current activity of a contributor, but the benefit obtained by that contributor is based on its past activity. Thus, there is a potential mismatch in the amount of contributions made by a contributor (based on current activity) and the value realisable from the fund (based on past activity).

Such funds generally have the following features:[165]

- the fund is separately administered by independent trustees;

- entities (contributors) make contributions to the fund, which are invested in a range of assets that may include both debt and equity investments, and are available to help pay the contributors' decommissioning costs. The trustees determine how contributions are invested, within the constraints set by the fund's governing documents and any applicable legislation or other regulations;

- the contributors retain the obligation to pay decommissioning costs. However, contributors are able to obtain reimbursement of decommissioning costs from the fund up to the lower of the decommissioning costs incurred and the entity's share of assets of the fund; and

- the contributors may have restricted or no access to any surplus of assets of the fund over those used to meet eligible decommissioning costs.

IFRIC 5 applies to accounting in the financial statements of a contributor for interests arising from decommissioning funds that have both the following features:[166]

- the assets are administered separately (either by being held in a separate legal entity or as segregated assets within another entity); and

- a contributor's right to access the assets is restricted.

A residual interest in a fund that extends beyond a right to reimbursement, such as a contractual right to distributions once all the decommissioning has been completed or on winding up the fund, may be an equity instrument within the scope of IAS 39 and is not within the scope of IFRIC 5.[167]

The issues addressed by IFRIC 5 are:[168]

(a)   How should a contributor account for its interest in a fund?

(b)   When a contributor has an obligation to make additional contributions, for example, in the event of the bankruptcy of another contributor, how should that obligation be accounted for?

I   Accounting for an interest in a fund

As far as issue (a) is concerned, IFRIC 5 requires the contributor to recognise its obligations to pay decommissioning costs as a liability and recognise its interest in the fund separately, unless the contributor is not liable to pay decommissioning costs even if the fund fails to pay.[169]

The contributor determines whether it has control, joint control or significant influence over the fund by reference to IAS 27 – *Consolidated and Separate Financial Statements*, IAS 31 – *Interests in Joint Ventures*, IAS 28 – *Investments in Associates* – and SIC-12 – *Consolidation – Special Purpose Entities*. If the contributor determines that it has such control, joint control or significant influence, it should account for its interest in the fund in accordance with the relevant standards (see Chapters 6, 11 and 12 respectively).[170]

One company that started to consolidate its interest in a decommissioning fund following the issue of IFRIC 5 is Anglo Platinum as shown below:

Extract 24.9: Anglo Platinum Limited (2005)

Principal Accounting Policies [extract]

IFRIC 5 – Rights to interests arising from Decommissioning, Restoration and Environmental Restoration Funds

On 1 January 2005, the Group adopted the requirements of IFRIC 5. The objective of the interpretation is to determine the accounting in the financial statements of a contributor for interests arising from decommissioning funds that have the following features:

(a)   the assets are administered separately (either by being held in a separate legal entity or as segregated assets within another entity).

(b)   A contributor's right to access the assets in restricted.

Adoption has the effect that the Platinum Producers' Environmental Trust is consolidated. The effect is that the balance previously included in originated loans is now reflected in non-current cash deposits held by Platinum Producers' Environmental Trust.

Otherwise, the contributor should recognise the right to receive reimbursement from the fund as a reimbursement in accordance with IAS 37 (see 4.4 above). This reimbursement should be measured at the lower of:[171]

- the amount of the decommissioning obligation recognised; and
- the contributor's share of the fair value of the net assets of the fund attributable to contributors.

This 'asset cap' means that the asset recognised in respect of the reimbursement rights can never exceed the recognised liability. Accordingly, rights to receive reimbursement to meet decommissioning liabilities that have yet to be recognised as a provision are not recognised.[172] Although many respondents expressed concern about this asset cap and argued that rights to benefit in excess of this amount give rise to an additional asset, separate from the reimbursement asset, the IFRIC, despite having sympathy with the concerns, concluded that to recognise such an asset would be inconsistent with the requirement in IAS 37 that 'the amount recognised for the reimbursement should not exceed the amount of the provision'.[173]

Changes in the carrying value of the right to receive reimbursement other than contributions to and payments from the fund should be recognised in profit or loss in the period in which these changes occur.[174]

The effect of this requirement is that the amount recognised in the statement of comprehensive income relating to the reimbursement bears no relation to the expense recognised in respect of the provision, particularly for decommissioning liabilities where most changes in the measurement of the provision are not taken to the profit or loss immediately, but are recognised prospectively over the remaining useful life of the related asset (see 5.4.2 A above).

One company that has been affected by the 'asset cap' is Fortum Corporation as shown below.

Extract 24.10: Fortum Corporation (2007)

1.   Accounting Policies [extract]
Assets and liabilities related to decommissioning of nuclear power plants and the disposal of spent fuel [extract]

Fortum owns Loviisa nuclear power plant in Finland. Fortum's part of the State Nuclear Waste Management Fund and the related nuclear provisions are both presented separately on the balance sheet. Fortum's share in the State Nuclear Waste Management Fund has been accounted for according to IFRIC 5, *Rights to interests arising from decommissioning, restoration and environmental rehabilitation funds* which states that the fund assets are measured at the lower of fair value or the value of the related liabilities since Fortum does not have control or joint control over the State Nuclear Waste Management Fund.

The fair values of the provisions are calculated by discounting the separate future cash flows, which are based on estimated future costs and actions already taken. The initial net present value of the provision for decommissioning (at the time of commissioning the nuclear power plant) has been included in the investment cost and depreciated over the estimated operating time of the nuclear power plant.

The provision for spent fuel covers the future disposal costs of fuel used until the end of the accounting period. Costs for disposal of spent fuel are expensed during the operating time based on fuel usage. The impact of the possible changes in the estimated future cash-flow for related costs is recognised immediately in the income statement based on fuel used until the end of the accounting period. The related interest costs due to unwinding of the provision, for the period during which the spent fuel provision has been accumulated and present point in time, are also recognised immediately in the income statement.

The timing factor is taken into account by recognising the interest expense related to discounting the nuclear provisions. The interest on the State Nuclear Waste Management Fund assets is presented as financial income.

Fortum's share of the State Nuclear Waste Management Fund, related to Loviisa nuclear power plant, is higher than the carrying value of the Fund in the balance sheet. The legal nuclear liability should, according to the Finnish Nuclear Energy Act, be fully covered by payments and guarantees to the State Nuclear Waste Management Fund. The legal liability is not discounted while the provisions are, and since the future cash-flow is spread over 100 years, the difference between the legal liability and the provisions are material.

The annual fee to the Fund is based on changes in the legal liability, the interest income generated in the State Nuclear Waste Management Fund and incurred costs of taken actions.

Fortum also has minority shareholdings in the associated nuclear power production companies Teollisuuden Voima Oy (TVO) in Finland and directly and indirectly OKG AB and Forsmarks Kraftgrupp AB in Sweden. Similar kinds of adjustments have been made through accounting of associates.

More information regarding nuclear related assets and liabilities, see Note 37 Nuclear Related Assets and Liabilities.

37.   Nuclear Related Assets and Liabilities

Fortum owns the Loviisa nuclear power plant in Finland. Based on the Nuclear Energy Act in Finland Fortum has a legal obligation to fully fund the legal liability, decided by the governmental authorities, for decommissioning of the power plant and disposal of spent fuel through the State Nuclear Waste Management Fund. The text below should be read in conjunction with information in Note 1 Accounting principles.

EUR million	2007	2006
Carrying values in the balance sheet		
Nuclear provisions	516	450
Share in the State Nuclear Waste Management Fund	516	450
Legal liability and actual share of the State Nuclear Waste Management Fund		
Liability for nuclear waste management according to the Nuclear Energy Act	816	685
Funding obligation target	698	649
Fortum's share in the State Nuclear Waste Management Fund	673	636

Nuclear related provisions

The nuclear provisions are related to future obligations for nuclear waste management including decommissioning of the power plant and disposal of spent fuel. The fair values of the provisions are calculated according to IAS 37 based on future cash-flows, regarding estimated future costs for each of the provisions separately. The cash-flows used are based on the cash-flows which are also the basis for the legal liability. Both provisions are included in Nuclear provisions in the balance sheet.

In September 2007 Fortum submitted the yearly proposal for the nuclear waste management legal liability regarding the Loviisa nuclear power plant to the Ministry of Employment and the Economy (previously Ministry of Trade and Industry). The legal liability is calculated according to the Nuclear Energy Act in Finland and is decided by the Ministry of Employment and the Economy in January every year. The proposal was based on an updated cost estimate, which is done every year, and on a new technical plan, which is made every third year. Based on the new plan, the future costs are estimated to increase mainly due to the new technical solution related to filling material for the tunnels in the final repository.

The updated legal liability at the end of 2007 amounted to EUR 816 million (2006: 685 million). The carrying value of the nuclear provisions in the balance sheet increased with EUR 66 million compared to 31 December 2006, totalling EUR 516 million as of 31 December 2007. The main reason for the difference between the carrying value of the provision and the legal liability is the fact that the legal liability is not discounted to net present value.

The increase of the provision for spent fuel caused a negative one-time effect of EUR 13 million in comparable operating profit in Q3 2007 due to higher nuclear waste management costs related to already spent fuel. The increase of the provision for spent fuel also caused negative one-time interest costs, due to unwinding of the provision for the period during which the spent fuel provision has been accumulated and present point in time, which are recognised immediately in the income statement.

The increase of the provision for decommissioning is added to the nuclear decommissioning cost and depreciated over the remaining estimated operating time of the nuclear power plant. See Note 22 Property, plant and equipment.

EUR million	2007	2006
Nuclear provisions		
At 1 January	450	418
Additional provisions	46	24
Used during the year	−15	−17
Unwinding of discount	35	24
At 31 December	516	450
Carrying value of Fortum's share in the State Nuclear Waste Management Fund	516	450

Carrying value of Fortum's share in the State Nuclear Waste Management Fund

Fortum contributes funds to the State Nuclear Waste Management Fund in Finland to cover future obligations based on the legal liability calculated according to the Finnish Nuclear Energy Act. The fund is managed by governmental authorities. The carrying value of the Fund in Fortum's balance sheet is calculated according to IFRIC 5 Rights to interests arising from Decommissioning, Restoration and Environmental Rehabilitation Funds.

According to the Nuclear Energy Act, Fortum is obligated to contribute the funds in full to the State Nuclear Waste Management Fund to cover the legal liability. Based on the law, Fortum applied for periodising of the payments to the Fund over six years, due to the proposed increase in the legal liability. The application was approved by Council of State in December 2007.

The periodisation of the payments to the State Nuclear Waste Management Fund has an impact on cash-flow, but also on operating profit since the carrying value of the Fund in the balance sheet cannot exceed the carrying value of the nuclear provisions according to IFRIC Interpretation 5. The Fund is from an IFRS perspective overfunded with EUR 157 million, since Fortum's share of the Fund as of 31 December 2007 is EUR 673 million and the carrying value in the balance sheet is EUR 516 million.

Operating profit for 2007 includes a positive cumulative adjustment of EUR 17 (0) million, due to the increase of the carrying value of the Fund in the balance sheet as a result of the increased provision. The positive effect on Q3 2007 was EUR 33 (−2) million. In Q4 the adjustment is negative, EUR −7 (−4) million, since the value of the Fund has increased more than the carrying value of the provision. These adjustments are included in "Other items effecting comparability" in the Power Generation segment, see Note 4 Primary segment information, and are not included in comparable operating profit. As long as the Fund stays overfunded from an IFRS perspective, positive accounting effects to Operating profit will always occur when the nuclear provision is increasing more than the net payments to the Fund. Negative accounting effects will occur when the net payments to the Fund are higher than the increase of the provision.

The funding obligation target

The funding obligation target for the each year is decided by the Ministry of Employment and the Economy retrospectively in January each year after the legal liability has been decided. The difference between the funding obligation target for Fortum and Fortum's actual share of the State Nuclear Waste Fund is paid in Q1 each year.

The funding obligation target corresponding to both the new legal liability and the new decision for periodisation to the Fund amounts EUR 698 (649) million. The difference between the legal liability at year end 2007 and the corresponding funding obligation target, EUR 25 million (2006: 13 million) is covered by a security which has been given in the end of June 2007. The real estate mortgages given also covers unexpected events according to the Nuclear Energy Act, see also Note 40 Pledged assets.

II   Accounting for obligations to make additional contributions

As far as issue (b) is concerned, IFRIC 5 requires that when a contributor has an obligation to make potential additional contributions, for example, in the event of the bankruptcy of another contributor or if the value of the investments held by the fund decreases to an extent that they are insufficient to fulfil the fund's reimbursement obligations, this obligation is a contingent liability that is within the scope of IAS 37. The contributor shall recognise a liability only if it is probable that additional contributions will be made.[175]

5.4.3   *Emission rights and green certificates*

A   Emission rights

A number of countries around the world either have, or are developing, schemes to encourage reduced emissions of pollutants, in particular of greenhouse gases. These schemes comprise tradable emissions allowances or permits, an example of which is a 'cap and trade' model whereby participants are allocated emission rights or allowances equal to a cap (i.e. a maximum level of allowable emissions) and are permitted to trade those allowances. A cap and trade emission rights scheme typically has the following features:[176]

- an entity participating in the scheme (participant) is set a target to reduce its emissions to a specified level (the cap). The participant is issued allowances equal in number to its cap by a government or government agency. Allowances may be issued free of charge, or participants may pay the government for them;

- the scheme operates for defined compliance periods;

- participants are free to buy and sell allowances;

- if at the end of the compliance period a participant's actual emissions exceeded its emission rights, the participant will incur a penalty;

- in some schemes emission rights may be carried forward to future periods; and

- the scheme may provide for brokers – who are not themselves participants – to buy and sell emission rights.

As there was no guidance on the accounting for cap and trade emission rights schemes and no consensus had emerged among market participants on what the accounting treatment should be, the IFRIC concluded that an interpretation should be issued to explain how IFRS should be applied to such schemes. Accordingly, in December 2004 the IASB issued IFRIC 3 – *Emission Rights* – to address the accounting for emission allowances that arise from cap and trade emission rights schemes.

IFRIC 3 took the view that a cap and trade scheme did not give rise to a net asset or liability, but that it gave rise to various items that were to be accounted for separately:[177]

(a)   *an asset for allowances held* – Allowances, whether allocated by government or purchased, were to be regarded as intangible assets and accounted for under

IAS 38 – *Intangible Assets*. Allowances issued for less than fair value were to be measured initially at their fair value;[178]

(b)   *a government grant* – When allowances are issued for less than fair value, the difference between the amount paid and fair value was a government grant that should be accounted for under IAS 20 – *Accounting for Government Grants and Disclosure of Government Assistance*. Initially the grant was to be recognised as deferred income in the balance sheet and subsequently recognised as income on a systematic basis over the compliance period for which the allowances were issued, regardless of whether the allowances were held or sold;[179]

(c)   *a liability for the obligation to deliver allowances equal to emissions that have been made* – As emissions are made, a liability was to be recognised as a provision that falls within the scope of IAS 37. The liability was to be measured at the best estimate of the expenditure required to settle the present obligation at the end of the reporting period. This would usually be the present market price of the number of allowances required to cover emissions made up to the end of the reporting period.[180]

However, the interpretation met with significant resistance because application of IFRIC 3 would result in a number of accounting mismatches:[181]

- a measurement mismatch between the assets and liabilities recognised in accordance with IFRIC 3;

- a mismatch in the location in which the gains and losses on those assets are reported; and

- a possible timing mismatch because allowances would be recognised when they are obtained – typically at the start of the year – whereas the emission liability would be recognised during the year as it is incurred.

Consequently, the IASB decided in June 2005 to withdraw IFRIC 3 despite the fact that it considered it to be 'an appropriate interpretation of existing IFRSs'.[182] The IASB also decided to reconsider the accounting for cap and trade emission right schemes itself rather than ask the IFRIC to continue its work, because developing a an approach that eliminates the mismatches will require the amendment of one or more standards. Work on emission rights and government grants had been deferred pending conclusion of work on other relevant projects, in particular the project to amend IAS 37.[183] However, in December 2007, the IASB decided that the continuing proliferation of such schemes, diversity in practice and requests to act by national standard setters required it to bring the issue back onto the IASB agenda. The Board decided to limit the scope of the project to accounting issues relating to emissions trading schemes, rather than to consider more general issues regarding the accounting for government grants[184] (see 8.5 below).

Given that IFRIC 3 has been withdrawn, and pending any substantive output from the IASB project on emission trading schemes, what can or should entities do in the absence of any precise guidance? As can be seen above, the topic cuts across a number of different areas of accounting, not just that of provisions. A fuller discussion of the issues and methods applied in practice are covered in Chapter 15 at 3.3.

B   Green certificates

Some countries have launched schemes to promote the production of power from renewable sources based on green certificates – also known as renewable energy certificates (RECs), green tags, or tradable renewable certificates.

In a green certificates system, a producer of electricity from renewable sources is granted certificates by the government based on the power output (kWh) of green electricity produced. These certificates may be used in the current and future compliance periods as defined by the particular scheme. The certificates can be sold separately. Generally the cost to produce green electricity is higher than the cost of producing an equivalent amount of electricity generated from non-renewable sources, although this is not always the case. Distributors of electricity sell green electricity at the same price as other electricity.

In a typical green certificates scheme, distributors of electricity to consumers (businesses, households etc.) are required to remit a number of green certificates based on the kWh of electricity sold on an annual basis. Distributors must therefore purchase green certificates in the market (such certificates having been sold by producers). If a distribution company does not have the number of required certificates, it is required to pay a penalty to the environmental agency. Once the penalty is paid, the entity is discharged of its obligations to remit certificates.

It is this requirement to remit certificates that creates a market in and gives value to green certificates (the value depends on many variables but primarily on the required number of certificates that have to be delivered relative to the amount of power that is produced from renewable sources, and the level of penalty payable if the required number of certificates are not remitted).

There are similarities between green certificates and emission rights. However, whereas emission rights are granted to producers as a means of settling future obligations, green certificates are granted on the basis of 'good' production achieved rather than 'bad' emissions in the future, irrespective of whether or not there is a subsequent sale of energy to an end consumer.

For a distributor of energy under a green certificate regime, a green certificate is similar in nature to an emission right except that a distributor of energy under a green certificate regime must acquire the certificates from the market (i.e. they are not granted to the distributor by the government). As with emission rights, the topic of green certificates cuts across a number of different areas of accounting, not just that of provisions. A fuller discussion of the issues and methods applied in practice are covered in Chapter 15 at 3.4.

5.4.4   EU Directive on 'Waste Electrical and Electronic Equipment'[185]

This Directive, which regulates the collection, treatment, recovery and environmentally sound disposal of waste equipment, has given rise to questions about when the liability for the decommissioning of WE&EE should be recognised. The Directive distinguishes between 'new' and 'historical' waste and between waste from private households and waste from sources other than private households. New waste relates to products sold after 13 August 2005. All household equipment sold before that date is deemed to give rise to historical waste for the purposes of the Directive.[186]

The Directive states that the cost of waste management for historical household equipment should be borne by producers of that type of equipment that are in the market during a period to be specified in the applicable legislation of each Member State (the measurement period). The Directive states that each Member State shall establish a mechanism to have producers contribute to costs proportionately 'e.g. in proportion to their respective share of the market by type of equipment.'[187]

The IFRIC was asked to determine in the context of the decommissioning of WE&EE what constitutes the obligating event in accordance with paragraph 14(a) of IAS 37 for the recognition of a provision for waste management costs:[188]

- the manufacture or sale of the historical household equipment?
- participation in the market during the measurement period?
- the incurrence of costs in the performance of waste management activities?

A   IFRIC 6

IFRIC 6 was issued in September 2005 and provides guidance on the recognition, in the financial statements of producers, of liabilities for waste management under the EU Directive on WE&EE in respect of sales of historical household equipment.[189] The interpretation addresses neither new waste nor historical waste from sources other than private households. The IFRIC considers that the liability for such waste management is adequately covered in IAS 37. However, if, in national legislation, new waste from private households is treated in a similar manner to historical waste from private households, the principles of IFRIC 6 are to apply by reference to the hierarchy set out in IAS 8 (see Chapter 3 at 4.3). The IAS 8 hierarchy is also stated to be relevant for other regulations that impose obligations in a way that is similar to the cost attribution model specified in the EU Directive.[190]

IFRIC 6 regards participation in the market during the measurement period as the obligating event in accordance with paragraph 14(a) of IAS 37. Consequently, a liability for waste management costs for historical household equipment does not arise as the products are manufactured or sold. Because the obligation for historical household equipment is linked to participation in the market during the measurement period, rather than to production or sale of the items to be disposed of, there is no obligation unless and until a market share exists during the measurement period. It is also noted that the timing of the obligating event may also be independent of the particular period in which the activities to perform the waste management are undertaken and the related costs incurred.[191]

The following example, which is based on one within the accompanying Basis for Conclusions on IFRIC 6, illustrates its requirements.[192]

Example 24.6:   Illustration of IFRIC 6 requirements

An entity selling electrical equipment in 2006 has a market share of 4 per cent for that calendar year. It subsequently discontinues operations and is thus no longer in the market when the waste management costs for its products are allocated to those entities with market share in 2009. With a market share of 0 per cent in 2009, the entity's obligation is zero. However, if another entity enters the market for electronic products in 2009 and achieves a market share of 3 per cent in that period, then that entity's obligation for the costs of waste management from earlier periods will be 3 per cent of the total costs of waste management allocated to 2009, even though the entity was not in the market in those earlier periods and has not produced any of the products for which waste management costs are allocated to 2009.

The IFRIC concluded that the effect of the cost attribution model specified in the Directive is that the making of sales during the measurement period is the 'past event' that requires recognition of a provision under IAS 37 over the measurement period. Aggregate sales for the period determine the entity's obligation for a proportion of the costs of waste management allocated to that period. The measurement period is independent of the period when the cost allocation is notified to market participants.[193]

Some constituents asked the IFRIC to consider the effect of the following possible national legislation: the waste management costs for which a producer is responsible because of its participation in the market during a specified period (for example 2009) are not based on the market share of the producer during that period but on the producer's participation in the market during a previous period (for example 2008). The IFRIC noted that this affects only the measurement of the liability and that the obligating event is still participation in the market during 2009.[194]

IFRIC 6 notes that terms used in the interpretation such as 'market share' and 'measurement period' may be defined very differently in the applicable legislation of individual Member States. For example, the length of the measurement period might be a year or only one month. Similarly, the measurement of market share and the formulae for computing the obligation may differ in the various national legislations. However, all of these examples affect only the measurement of the liability, which is not within the scope of the interpretation.[195]

5.4.5   Repairs and maintenance

Repairs and maintenance provisions in respect of owned assets are generally prohibited under IAS 37. Under the standard, the following principles apply:

(a)   provisions are recognised only for obligations existing independently of the entity's future actions (i.e. the future conduct of its business) and in cases where an entity can avoid future expenditure by its future actions, for example by changing its method of operation, it has no present obligation;[196]

(b)   financial statements deal with an entity's position at the end of the reporting period and not its possible position in the future. Therefore, no provision is recognised for costs that need to be incurred to operate in the future;[197] and

(c)   for an event to be an obligating event, the entity can have no realistic alternative to settling the obligation created by the event.[198]

These principles are applied strictly in the case of an obligation to incur repairs and maintenance costs in the future. This is illustrated by two examples in an appendix to the standard dealing with cyclical refurbishment costs. The first example relates to a furnace that has a lining requiring replacement every five years if it is to continue to function, and the second example relates to an aircraft that is required by law to be overhauled every three years.[199] Neither of these circumstances gives rise to a provision on the basis that there is no present obligation to incur the expenditure independently of the entity's future actions. This argument is used even in the case where there is a legal requirement for the asset in question to be repaired, since it is asserted that, even then, the entity could avoid the expenditure by, for example, selling the asset. (It is unclear why a similar argument has not been used in respect of decommissioning costs, where presumably an entity could also avoid such costs by selling, for example, its oil and gas assets).

Therefore the existence of plans by management to undertake future repairs and maintenance, even if approved by the entity's shareholders in general meeting, is insufficient to recognise a provision. The entity does not have an obligation to carry out the expenditure independently of its future actions. The mere act of approving a plan at a shareholders' meeting does not close the door to any alternative actions and by their nature the repairs and maintenance costs are only required to restore or improve future operating capability.

The effect of this prohibition on setting up provisions for repairs obviously has an impact on balance sheet presentation. It may not always, however, have as much impact on the statement of comprehensive income. This is because it is suggested in the examples that depreciation would be adjusted to take account of the repairs. For example, in the case of the furnace lining, the lining should be depreciated over five years in advance of its expected repair. Similarly, in the case of the aircraft overhaul, the example in the standard suggests that an amount equivalent to the expected maintenance costs is depreciated over three years.[200] The result of this is that the depreciation charge recognised in profit or loss over the life of the component of the asset requiring regular repair may be equivalent to that which would previously have arisen from the combination of depreciation and a provision for repair.

5.4.6 *Dilapidation and other provisions relating to leased assets*

The requirements discussed above relate to repairs and maintenance of owned assets (including assets held under finance leases). Operating leases often contain clauses which specify that the lessee should incur periodic charges for maintenance, make good dilapidations or other damage occurring during the rental period or return the asset to the configuration that existed as at inception of the lease. Hence, some entities in the past have built up a provision over the term of the lease for costs of repair and renovation of the leased asset.

IAS 37 is not clear as to whether such a provision meets the standard's recognition criteria. The issue, whilst not addressed in IAS 37 itself, is mentioned briefly in the appendix to FRS 12 in the UK in discussing the development of that standard. This notes that 'the principle illustrated in [the example on repairs] does not preclude the recognition of such liabilities once the event giving rise to the obligation under the lease has occurred'.[201] Since the repair examples in IAS 37 are the same as those in FRS 12, then we believe that the same comment is relevant in interpreting IAS 37.

This means that a provision for specific damage done to the asset would meet the criteria, as the event giving rise to the obligation under the lease has certainly occurred. For example, if an entity has erected partitioning or internal walls in a leasehold property and under the lease these have to be removed at the end of the term, then provision should be made for this cost (on a discounted basis, if material) at the time of putting up the partitioning or the walls. In this case, an equivalent asset would be recognised and depreciated over the term of the lease. This is similar to a decommissioning provision discussed at 5.4.2 above. Another example would be where an airline company leases aircraft under an operating lease, and upon delivery of the aircraft has made changes to the asset in the form of refitting and reconfiguration, but under the leasing arrangements has to return the asset to the configuration that existed as at inception of the lease.

What is less clear is whether a more general provision can be built up over time for maintenance charges and dilapidation costs. It might be argued that in this case, the event giving rise to the obligation under the lease is simply the passage of time, and so a provision can be built up over time. However, a stricter interpretation of the phrase 'the event giving rise to the obligation under the lease' may lead one to conclude that a more specific event has to occur; there has to be specific evidence of dilapidation etc. before any provision can be made.

One of the examples discussed in 5.4.5 above dealt with an owned aircraft that by law needs overhauling every three years, but no provision could be recognised for such costs. Instead, IAS 37 suggests that an amount equivalent to the expected maintenance costs is treated as a separate part of the asset and depreciated over three years. Airworthiness requirements for the airline industry are the same irrespective of whether the aircraft is owned or leased. So, if an airline company leases the aircraft under an operating lease, should a provision be made for the overhaul costs? The answer will depend on the terms of the lease.

If the lease requires the lessee to maintain the airworthiness of the aircraft and to return the aircraft at the end of the lease in the same condition as it was taken at inception of the lease, i.e. the aircraft has to be overhauled prior to its return, then the lessee should make provision. In this case the overhaul of the aircraft is a contractual obligation under the lease. The specific event that gives rise to the obligation is each flown hour or cycle completed by the aircraft as these determine the timing and nature of the overhaul that must be carried out. Provision should therefore be made for the costs of overhaul as the obligation towards the lessor arises (typically based upon the specific requirements of each aircraft type such as each flown hour or cycle), with a corresponding expense recognised in the statement of comprehensive income. For certain aircraft types and aircraft leases it is likely that the provision for the costs will be built up and then released, as the expenditure is incurred, a number of times during the term of the operating lease.

However, if the lease does not require the overhaul to be undertaken prior to the return of the aircraft (or require the lessee to make a contribution towards the next overhaul), then no provision should be made as the lessee does not have a contractual obligation to incur these costs that is independent of its own future actions.

The fact that a provision for repairs can be made at all in these circumstances might appear inconsistent with the case where the asset is owned by the entity. In that case, as discussed in 5.4.5 above, no provision for repairs could be made. There is, however, a difference between the two situations. Where the entity owns the asset, it has the choice of selling it rather than repairing it, and so the obligation is not independent of the entity's future actions. However, in the case of an entity leasing the asset, it can have a contractual obligation to repair any damage from which it cannot walk away.

Extract 24.4 at 5.3 above, shows an example of a company that has provided for dilapidation costs.

5.4.7   Warranty provisions

Warranty provisions are specifically addressed in one of the examples appended to IAS 37, which concludes that such provisions are appropriate.[202] The example deals with a manufacturer that gives warranties at the time of sale of its product. Under the terms of contract for sale the manufacturer undertakes to make good, by repair or replacement, manufacturing defects that become apparent within 3 years from the date of sale. On past experience, it is probable (i.e. more likely than not) that there will be some claims under the warranties. The past event giving rise to the legal obligation is the sale of the product on which the warranty is given. We concur with this view, although in practice considerations of materiality may sometimes permit it to be recognised on a pay-as-you-go basis.

As noted in 4.1 above, the standard makes it clear that where there are a number of similar obligations, the probability that an economic outflow will occur is based on the class of obligations as a whole. Hence, the probability of an economic outflow occurring for warranties as a whole will need to be evaluated. This is more likely to give rise to a provision, because the probability criterion is considered in terms of whether at least one item in the population will give rise to a payment. Recognition then becomes a matter of reliable measurement and entities calculate an expected value of the estimated warranty costs. IAS 37 discusses this method of 'expected value' and illustrates how it is calculated in an example of a warranty provision.[203] See Example 24.1 at 4.1 above.

An example of a company that makes a warranty provision is Nokia as shown below:

Extract 24.11: Nokia Oyj (2007)

1.   Accounting principles [extract]

Provisions [extract]

Provisions are recognized when the Group has a present legal or constructive obligation as a result of past events, it is probable that an outflow of resources will be required to settle the obligation and a reliable estimate of the amount can be made. Where the Group expects a provision to be reimbursed, the reimbursement would be recognized as an asset only when the reimbursement is virtually certain. At each balance sheet date, the Group assesses the adequacy of its pre-existing provisions and adjusts the amounts as necessary based on actual experience and changes in future estimates.

> **Warranty provisions**
>
> The Group provides for the estimated liability to repair or replace products under warranty at the time revenue is recognized. The provision is an estimate calculated based on historical experience of the level of repairs and replacements.
>
> **Use of estimates** [extract]
>
> The preparation of financial statements in conformity with IFRS requires the application of judgment by management in selecting appropriate assumptions for calculating financial estimates, which inherently contain some degree of uncertainty. Management bases its estimates on historical experience and various other assumptions that are believed to be reasonable under the circumstances, the results of which form the basis for making judgments about the reported carrying values of assets and liabilities and the reported amounts of revenues and expenses that may not be readily apparent from other sources. Actual results may differ from these estimates under different assumptions or conditions.
>
> Set forth below are areas requiring significant judgment and estimation that may have an impact on reported results and the financial position.
>
> **Warranty provisions**
>
> The Group provides for the estimated cost of product warranties at the time revenue is recognized. The Group's warranty provision is established based upon best estimates of the amounts necessary to settle future and existing claims on products sold as of each balance sheet date. As new products incorporating complex technologies are continuously introduced, and as local laws, regulations and practices may change, changes in these estimates could result in additional allowances or changes to recorded allowances being required in future periods.

5.4.8   Litigation and other legal claims

IAS 37 includes an example of a court case in its appendix to illustrate how its principles for recognising a provision should be applied in such situations.[204] However, the assessment of the particular case is clear-cut. In most situations, assessing the need to provide for legal claims is one of the most difficult tasks in the field of provisioning. This is due mainly to the inherent uncertainty in the judicial process itself, which may be very long and drawn out. Furthermore, this is an area where either provision or disclosure might risk prejudicing the outcome of the case, because they give an insight into the entity's own view on the strength of its defence that can assist the claimant. Similar considerations apply in other related areas, such as tax disputes.

In principle, whether a provision should be made will depend on whether the 3 conditions for recognising a provision are met, i.e.

(a)   there is a present obligation as a result of a past event;

(b)   it is probable that an outflow of resources embodying economic benefits will be required to settle the obligation; and

(c)   a reliable estimate can be made of the amount of the obligation.[205]

As noted at 3.1.1 above, in situations such as these, a past event is deemed to give rise to a present obligation if, taking account of all available evidence (including, for example, the opinion of experts), it is more likely than not that a present obligation exists at the end of the reporting period.[206] The evidence to be considered includes any additional evidence occurring after the end of the reporting period. Accordingly, if on the basis of the evidence it is concluded that a present obligation is more likely than not to exist, a provision will be required, assuming the other conditions are met.

Condition (b) will be met if the transfer of economic benefits is more likely than not to occur, that is, it has a probability greater than 50%. In making this assessment, it is likely that account should be taken of any expert advice.

As far as condition (c) is concerned, as noted at 3.1.3 above, the standard takes the view that a reasonable estimate can generally be made and it is only in extremely rare cases that this will not be the case.[207]

Clearly, whether an entity should make provision for the costs of settling a case or to meet any award given by a court will depend on a reasoned assessment of the particular circumstances, based on appropriate legal advice.

5.4.9   Refunds policy

An example is given in the appendix of IAS 37 of a retail store that has a policy of refunding goods returned by dissatisfied customers. There is no legal obligation to do so, but the company's policy of making refunds is generally known.[208]

The example argues that the conduct of the store has created a valid expectation on the part of its customers that it will refund purchases. The obligating event is the original sale of the item, and the probability of some economic outflow is greater than 50%, as there will nearly always be some customers demanding refunds. Hence, a provision should be made, presumably calculated on the 'expected value' basis (see 4.1 above).

This example is straightforward when the store has a very specific and highly publicised policy on refunds. However, some stores' policies on refunds might not be so clear cut. A store may offer refunds under certain conditions, but not widely publicise its policy. In these circumstances, there might be doubt as to whether the store has created a valid expectation on the part of its customers that it will honour all requests for a refund.

5.4.10 Staff training costs

In the normal course of business it is unlikely that provisions for staff training costs would be permissible. IAS 37 gives an example of the government introducing changes to the income tax system, such that an entity in the financial services sector needs to retrain a large proportion of its administrative and sales workforce in order to ensure continued compliance with financial services regulation. At the end of the reporting period no retraining has taken place.[209]

The standard argues that there is no present obligation because no training has taken place and so no provision should be recognised. We agree with this outcome, and presume that the IASB's justification in this case is that training represents a future operating cost that could be avoided by the entity, for example, if it withdrew from that market or hired new staff who were already appropriately qualified.

However, this example again seems to illustrate the subjectivity with which the concepts of 'constructive obligation' and 'obligating event' are invoked in the standard. An alternative interpretation of the above example could be that the entity has a constructive obligation to retrain its sales force, as it has built up a valid expectation in its employees and customers that the sales force will be up to date on changes to the income tax system which affect the products it sells, to enable it to adequately meet the needs of its customers. If this approach were taken, a provision would be required. This argument could be strengthened if the entity had published some sort of policy statement reassuring employees and customers that the sales force would receive adequate training on the income tax changes.

In other situations an obligating event could arise before the training has taken place, for example where a regulator has required staff retraining as part of the remedy for a breach of its regulations.

This all goes to show how sometimes it appears the standard is inconsistent. For example, the argument that no provision is made for future operating costs does not help in distinguishing staff training costs from provisions for refunds, which are required to be made. After all, the customer in the example on refunds has no legal right to a refund. The entity could refuse, but presumably would not because of the bad publicity and loss of goodwill that would be suffered. Similarly, in this example, the sales force could cease selling certain financial products, but would not do so because it would lose customers.

In reality, the distinction between the two examples comes down to when the benefits are obtained in each case, not whether the entity has a liability at the end of the reporting period. In the case of the refund policy, the revenue from the sale has already been booked, so any reversal of it should be recognised. However, in the case of staff training, the benefits of the training will be the impact on future sales, so it is not appropriate to provide for the costs of training in advance. This dimension of revenue and expense recognition is not acknowledged in the standard, presumably because it does not sit well within a framework centred on the balance sheet, but it does seem to underlie a number of the conclusions that are reached.

5.4.11 Self insurance

Another situation where entities have sometimes made provisions is self insurance which arises when an entity decides not to take out external insurance in respect of a certain category of risk because it would be uneconomic to do so. The same position may arise when a group insures its risks with a captive insurance subsidiary, the effects of which have to be eliminated on consolidation. In fact, the term 'self insurance' is potentially misleading, since it really means that the entity is not insured at all and will settle claims from third parties in the event that it is found to be liable. Accordingly, the recognition criteria in IAS 37 should be applied, with a provision being justified only if there is a present obligation as a result of a past event; if it is probable that an outflow of resources will occur; and a reliable estimate can be determined.[210]

Therefore, losses are recognised based on their actual incidence and any provisions that appear in the balance sheet should reflect only the amounts expected to be paid in respect of those incidents that have occurred by the end of the reporting period.

This is the conclusion of an example in FRS 12 in the UK for which there is no equivalent example in IAS 37.[211] Entities in the UK had previously sought to build up a provision from period to period by reference to a simulated insurance premium that it has not in fact paid.

In certain circumstances, a provision will often be needed not simply for known incidents, but also for those which insurance companies call IBNR – Incurred But Not Reported – representing an estimate of the latent liabilities at the year end that experience shows will come to the surface only gradually. We believe that it is entirely appropriate that provision for such expected claims is made.

5.4.12 Regulatory liabilities

Under certain national GAAPs, an entity can defer benefits that would otherwise be included in profit for the period (for example, revenues) as regulatory liabilities on the basis that the regulator requires it to reduce its tariffs so as to return the amounts concerned to customers. Under IFRS, should an entity recognise a liability (or a provision) when a regulator requires the entity to reduce its future prices/revenues so as to return to customers what the regulator regards as the excess amounts collected in the current period?

No reference is made within IAS 37, or any of its examples, to this type of situation. However, we believe that under IFRS no such liabilities can be recognised since there is no present obligation relating to a past transaction or event. A liability is defined in IAS 37 as 'a present obligation of the entity arising from past events, the settlement of which is expected to result in an outflow from the entity of resources embodying economic benefits'.[212]

The return to customers of amounts mandated by a regulator depends on future events including:

* future rendering of services;
* future volumes of output (generally consisting of utilities such as water or electricity) consumed by users; and
* the continuation of regulation.

Consequently, items described as 'regulatory liabilities' do not meet the definition of a liability cited above since there needs to be a present obligation at the end of the reporting period before a liability can be recognised. Entities, in general, would recognise a liability for those items only if an obligation to refund exists as a result of past events or transactions, and regardless of future events.

This conclusion is consistent with the position in the UK. In Appendix VII to FRS 12, which discusses the development of the standard, it is noted that by basing the recognition of a provision on the existence of a present obligation, the standard rules out the recognition of any provision made simply to allocate results over more than one period or otherwise to smooth the results reported. To illustrate this, it goes on to say 'For example, in a regulated industry the results achieved in the current period may cause the pricing structure in the next period to be adjusted, e.g. the higher the profits in this year the lower the prices permitted for next year. There is no justification under the FRS for a provision to be recognised in such circumstances. The purpose of such a provision would be to transfer some of the current year's profit to the following year, which would suffer from lower prices because of the current year's profits. However, there is no present obligation that requires the transfer of economic benefits to settle it and nothing to justify recognition of a provision.'[213]

As discussed in more detail at 3.1 in Chapter 15, the IFRIC has been asked a number of times to consider whether such regulatory liabilities should be recognised and on each occasion, the most recent being in November 2008, decided not to add the issue to its agenda, noting in particular that whilst rate regulation is widespread and significantly affects the economic environment of regulated entities, divergence did not seem to be significant in practice for entities that were already applying IFRS.[214] The current consensus among existing IFRS reporters is that no regulatory liabilities are recognised, unless in those rare cases where they meet the definition of a financial liability.[215]

However, in response to a request made to the November 2008 meeting of the Standards Advisory Council and discussions at its December 2008 meeting, the IASB decided to add a project on rate-regulated activities to its agenda. The Board acknowledged that while divergence in practice did not currently exist, this was a matter of significant interest in a number of countries that would be adopting IFRS in the near future and where recognition of regulatory liabilities (and assets) was either permitted or required. The approaching conversion of these jurisdictions to IFRS would increase pressure for a definitive conclusion on the question.[216] In July 2009, the IASB issued an exposure draft on rate-regulated activities (see 8.4 below).

6   DISCLOSURE REQUIREMENTS

The real distinction between the accounting treatment of provisions as opposed to other liabilities is the level of disclosure required.

6.1   Provisions

For each class of provision an entity should provide a reconciliation of the carrying amount of the provision at the beginning and end of the period showing:

(a)   additional provisions made in the period, including increases to existing provisions;

(b)   amounts used, i.e. incurred and charged against the provision, during the period;

(c)   unused amounts reversed during the period; and

(d)   the increase during the period in the discounted amount arising from the passage of time and the effect of any change in the discount rate.

Comparative information is not required.[217]

Disclosure (d) effectively requires the charge for discounting that is recognised in profit or loss to be split between the element that relates to the straightforward unwinding of the discount, and any further charge or credit that arises if discount rates have changed during the period. It is interesting that there is no specific requirement to disclose the discount rate used.

One of the important disclosures which is reinforced here is the requirement to disclose the release of provisions found to be unnecessary. This disclosure, along with the requirement in the standard that provisions should be used only for the purpose for which the provision was originally recognised,[218] is designed to prevent entities from concealing expenditure by charging it against a provision that was set up for another purpose.

In addition, for each class of provision an entity should disclose the following:

(a)   a brief description of the nature of the obligation and the expected timing of any resulting outflows of economic benefits;

(b)   an indication of the uncertainties about the amount or timing of those outflows. Where necessary to provide adequate information, an entity should disclose the major assumptions made concerning future events, as addressed in paragraph 48 of the standard (discussed at 4.3 above). This refers to future developments in technology and legislation and is of particular relevance to environmental liabilities; and

(c)   the amount of any expected reimbursement, stating the amount of any asset that has been recognised for that expected reimbursement.[219]

Appendix D to the standard provides examples of suitable disclosures in relation to warranties and decommissioning costs.

Most of the above disclosures are illustrated in the extract below.

Extract 24.12: Roche Group (2007)

25.   Provisions and contingent liabilities [extract]

Provisions: movements in recognised liabilities *in millions of CHF*

	Legal provisions	Environ-mental provisions	Restruct-uring provisions	Other provisions	Total
Year ended 31 December 2006					
At 1 January 2006	1,366	212	278	524	2,380
Additional provisions created	21	11	54	588	677
Unused amounts reversed	(4)	(25)	(62)	(95)	(186)
Utilised during the year	(35)	(9)	(98)	(331)	(473)
Unwinding of discount	62	4	2	6	74
Currency translation effects	(93)	(7)	–	(23)	(123)
At 31 December 2006	1,320	186	174	669	2,349
Of which					
– current portion	377	11	79	289	756
– non-current portion	943	175	95	380	1,593
Total provisions	1,320	186	174	669	2,349

Year ended 31 December 2007

	Legal provisions	Environmental provisions	Restructuring provisions	Other provisions	Total
At 1 January 2007	1,320	186	174	669	2,349
Additional provisions created	57	36	132	530	755
Unused amounts reversed	(92)	(1)	(28)	(40)	(161)
Utilised during the year	(288)	(11)	(82)	(315)	(696)
Unwinding of discount	60	3	–	6	69
Currency translation effects	(72)	(10)	(3)	(26)	(111)
At 31 December 2007	985	203	193	824	2,205
Of which					
— current portion	962	30	116	409	1,517
— non-current portion	23	173	77	415	688
Total provisions	985	203	193	824	2,205

	Legal provisions	Environ- mental provisions	Restruct- uring provisions	Other provisions	Total
Expected outflow of resources					
— within one year	962	30	116	409	1,517
— between one to two years	5	20	27	132	184
— between two to three years	2	15	18	38	73
— more than three years	16	138	32	245	431
Total provisions	985	203	193	824	2,205

Legal provisions

Legal provisions relate mainly to a number of major legal cases that are described below. The amounts, timing and uncertainties of any outflows are discussed below, as are the discount rates used. The remaining legal provisions, which account for less than 15% of the balance, consist of a number of other separate legal matters in various Group companies. The majority of any cash outflows for these other matters are expected to occur within the next one to three years, although these are dependent on the development of the various litigations. These provisions are not discounted as the time value of money is not material in these matters.

Environmental provisions

Provisions for environmental matters include various separate environmental issues in a number of countries. By their nature the amounts and timing of any outflows are difficult to predict. The estimated timings of these cash outflows are shown in the table above. Significant provisions are discounted by between 6% and 7% where the time value of money is material.

Restructuring provisions

These arise from planned programmes that materially change the scope of business undertaken by the Group or the manner in which business is conducted. Such provisions include only the costs necessarily entailed by the restructuring which are not associated with the recurring activities of the Group. The timings of these cash outflows are reasonably certain on a global basis and are shown in the table above. Significant provisions are discounted by 3% where the time value of money is material.

Other provisions

Other provisions consist mostly of claims arising from trade, sales returns, certain employee benefit obligations and various other provisions from Group companies that do not fit into the above categories. The timings of cash outflows are by their nature uncertain and the best estimates are shown in the table above. Significant provisions are discounted by between 4% and 6% where the time value of money is material.

> **Contingent liabilities**
>
> The operations and earnings of the Group continue, from time to time and in varying degrees, to be affected by political, legislative, fiscal and regulatory developments, including those relating to environmental protection, in the countries in which it operates. The industries in which the Group operates are also subject to other risks of various kinds. The nature and frequency of these developments and events, not all of which are covered by insurance, as well as their effect on future operations and earnings, are not predictable.
>
> The Group has entered into strategic alliances with various companies in order to gain access to potential new products or to utilise other companies to help develop the Group's own potential new products. Potential future payments may become due to certain collaboration partners achieving certain milestones as defined in the collaboration agreements. The Group's best estimates of future commitments for such payments are given in Note 14.

The standard states that in determining which provisions may be aggregated to form a class, it is necessary to consider whether the nature of the items is sufficiently similar for a single statement about them to fulfil the requirements of (a) and (b) above. An example is given of warranties: it is suggested that, while it may be appropriate to treat warranties of different products as a single class of provision, it would not be appropriate to aggregate normal warranties with amounts that are subject to legal proceedings.[220] This requirement could be interpreted to mean that in disclosing restructuring costs, the different components of the costs, such as redundancies, termination of leases, etc, should be disclosed separately. However, materiality will be an important consideration in judging how much analysis is required.

As indicated at 5.1.1 above, IAS 37 emphasises that when a restructuring meets the definition of a discontinued operation under IFRS 5, additional disclosures may be required under that standard (see Chapter 4 at 3).[221]

6.2   Contingent liabilities

Unless the possibility of any outflow in settlement is remote, IAS 37 requires the disclosure for each class of contingent liability at the end of the reporting period to include a brief description of the nature of the contingent liability, and where practicable:

(a)   an estimate of its financial effect, measured in accordance with paragraphs 36-52 of IAS 37 (discussed at 4 above);

(b)   an indication of the uncertainties relating to the amount or timing of any outflow; and

(c)   the possibility of any reimbursement.[222]

Where any of the information above is not disclosed because it is not practicable to do so, that fact should be stated.[223]

The guidance given in the standard on determining which provisions may be aggregated to form a class referred to in 6.1 above also applies to contingent liabilities.

A further point noted in the standard is that where a provision and a contingent liability arise from the same circumstances, an entity should ensure that the link between the provision and the contingent liability is clear.[224] This may arise, for instance, where there is a range of possible losses under a claim, for which part of the potential maximum has been provided. A further example of when this may arise would be where an entity is jointly and severally liable for an obligation. As noted in 4.4 above, in these circumstances the part that is expected to be met by other parties is treated as a contingent liability.

It is not absolutely clear what is meant by 'financial effect' in (a) above. Is it the *potential* amount of the loss or is it the *expected* amount of the loss? The explicit cross-reference to the measurement principles in paragraphs 36-52 might imply the latter, but in our view the former would be preferable.

6.3   Contingent assets

IAS 37 requires disclosure of contingent assets where an inflow of economic benefits is probable. The disclosures required are:

(a)   a brief description of the nature of the contingent assets at the end of the reporting period; and

(b)   where practicable, an estimate of their financial effect, measured using the principles set out for provisions in paragraphs 36-52 of IAS 37.[225]

Where any of the information above is not disclosed because it is not practicable to do so, that fact should be stated.[226] The standard goes on to emphasise that the disclosure must avoid giving misleading indications of the likelihood of income arising.[227]

One problem that arises with IAS 37 is that it requires the disclosure of an estimate of the potential financial effect for contingent assets to be measured in accordance with the measurement principles in the standard. Unfortunately, the measurement principles in the standard are all set out in terms of the settlement of obligations, and these principles cannot readily be applied to the measurement of contingent assets. Hence, judgement will have to be used as to how rigorously these principles should be applied.

6.4   Exemption from disclosure when seriously prejudicial

IAS 37 contains an exemption from disclosure of information in the following circumstances. It says that, 'in extremely rare cases, disclosure of some or all of the information required by [the disclosure requirements in 6.1 to 6.3 above] can be expected to prejudice seriously the position of the entity in a dispute with other parties on the subject matter of the provision, contingent liability or contingent asset'.[228]

In such circumstances, the information need not be disclosed. However, disclosure will still need to be made of the general nature of the dispute, together with the fact that, and the reason why, the required information has not been disclosed.[229]

7   TRANSITIONAL ARRANGEMENTS

7.1   Transitional arrangements for entities already reporting under IFRS

On first applying IAS 37 an entity was required to adjust the opening balance of retained earnings for the period of first adoption. Entities were encouraged but not required to restate comparatives. However if comparatives were not adjusted, that fact was required to be stated.[230]

Also, none of the related IFRIC Interpretations (IFRIC 1, IFRIC 5 and IFRIC 6) contained any transitional arrangements. Therefore any necessary changes in accounting policies resulting from their application needed to be accounted for in accordance with IAS 8 (see Chapter 3 at 4.4).

8   FUTURE DEVELOPMENTS

The IASB first agreed to add to its agenda a short-term convergence project on provisions, contingent liabilities and contingent assets in September 2002. As a result of this project and Phase II of its business combinations project, the Board issued an exposure draft proposing a number of amendments to IAS 37 and IAS 19 in June 2005.

In the years following the issue of the exposure draft, this has now become a 'Liabilities' project and IASB has determined to refer to 'Liabilities' in the title and in the text of the standard. In November and December 2006 the IASB held a number of round-table discussions to hear participants' views on the tentative conclusions reached after redeliberating issues associated with the recognition and measurement principles proposed in the exposure draft. In January 2007 the Board discussed the feedback received at the round-table meetings and agreed that the following issues require further research and debate:

- distinguishing between a liability and a business risk;
- uncertainty about the existence of a present obligation (including constructive obligations);
- whether all uncertainty about the outflow of economic benefits required to settle a liability can be reflected in measurement;
- guidance on the building blocks of an expected value calculation;
- lawsuits; and
- disclosure of items that do not satisfy the definition of a liability on the end of the reporting period (i.e. items currently described as 'possible obligations').

The IASB gave priority to these issues and, as a result, did not to start redeliberating other aspects of the exposure draft (contingent assets and reimbursement rights, restructuring provisions, termination benefits and onerous contracts) until 2008. The Board is now finalising its redeliberations on the Exposure Draft with a view to either re-exposing its revised proposals or publishing a final standard in the fourth quarter of 2009.[231]

The outline below of the Board's proposals to revise IAS 37 (and IAS 19) is derived from the original Exposure Draft and the Project Summary as issued in June 2009, to reflect the results of these redeliberations.

8.1   Overview of the proposals to amend IAS 37 and IAS 19

8.1.1   Scope and terminology

The IASB has determined that the proposed standard would apply to all liabilities not within the scope of other standards.[232] In particular, the Board intends to exclude financial liabilities as defined by IAS 32 – *Financial Instruments: Presentation* – from its scope.[233] The terms 'provision', 'contingent liability' and 'contingent asset' (see 3.1 and 3.2 above) would be eliminated. Instead, IAS 37 will refer simply to 'liabilities'. The only assets addressed by the exposure draft are reimbursement rights. For these, the current recognition requirement of 'virtual certainty' (see 4.4 above) is to be removed; such rights will be recognised unless they cannot be measured reliably. Entities will not be able to offset reimbursement rights against the related non-financial liability.[234] Items previously meeting the definition of contingent assets (and hence currently within the scope of IAS 37) will be brought within the scope of IAS 38.

In response to commentators' concerns about the relationship between IAS 18 and the proposed IAS 37, the IASB has decided to modify the proposed scope requirements in the exposure draft to clarify that performance obligations measured in accordance with IAS 18 on the basis of the consideration received (i.e. deferred revenue) would not be within the scope of the standard.[235]

8.1.2   Contingent liabilities

As stated above, the exposure draft proposes to eliminate the term 'contingent liability'. It argues that liabilities arise only from unconditional (or non-contingent) obligations, and hence that something that is a liability (an unconditional obligation) cannot be contingent or conditional.[236] Furthermore, the exposure draft asserts that an obligation that is contingent or conditional on the occurrence or non-occurrence of a future event does not by itself give rise to a liability.[237]

Some familiar items (like court cases and warranties) are the subject of a new theoretical concept: the 'stand ready' obligation.[238] This is discussed at 8.2.1 below.

Nevertheless, it is expected that the Board's revised proposals will retain the concept of a potential liability (where an entity is uncertain as to whether it has a present obligation but has judged that it does not) which is not recognised, but in respect of which information is disclosed (see 8.1.3 A below).

8.1.3   Recognition

Under the current version of IAS 37, a provision is recognised on (amongst other things) the basis of a probability criterion – i.e. it is probable that an outflow of resources embodying economic benefits will be required to settle the obligation[239] (see 3.1 above). Under the new proposals, this criterion will be omitted. Accordingly, amounts would be recognised if the definition of a liability has been satisfied and the amount can be measured reliably.[240] The Board's reasoning behind this omission is set out at length in the Basis for Conclusions.[241] The Board acknowledges that the omission of the probability criterion might give the impression of inconsistency with the *Framework*, but provides arguments as to why they do not believe this to be the case.[242] However, it is worth noting that one Board member disagreed with the omission of the probability recognition criterion and, as a result, voted against the publication of the exposure draft.[243]

In June 2006, the IASB noted that many respondents to the exposure draft disagreed with the proposal to omit this probability recognition criterion from IAS 37. Nevertheless, the Board has affirmed its previous conclusion that the probability recognition criterion should be omitted from the standard, but has acknowledged that measurement uncertainty may preclude recognition and, in due course, it will consider whether additional guidance about measurement uncertainty is required. The Board noted that its final conclusions about the probability recognition criterion would depend on affirming the measurement proposals and its continuing work on element uncertainty.[244]

At its previous meeting in May 2006, the Board noted that the definition of a liability in the *Framework* includes the phrase 'expected to result in an outflow from the entity of resources embodying economic benefits'. Some respondents to the exposure draft argued that this phrase implies that a particular degree of certainty about the outflow of resources associated with a present obligation is required before the obligation meets the definition of a liability. Hence, some argued that obligations with a remote or low likelihood of future settlement would not meet the definition of a liability. In the light of these comments, the Board decided to clarify that 'expected to' is not intended to imply that there must be a particular degree of certainty that an outflow of benefits will occur before an item meets the *Framework's* definition of a liability.[245]

The Board also noted that many respondents believed that the exposure draft provided insufficient guidance on determining whether a liability exists (and hence should be recognised), particularly in cases in which the existence of a present obligation is uncertain. The Board agreed with those respondents and decided to include additional guidance in any final standard.

A   Redeliberations following round-table discussions

Following the round-table discussions towards the end of 2006, the Board agreed that further research and debate is necessary in how to handle uncertainty about the existence of a liability. In July 2007, the Board tentatively concluded that uncertainty about the existence of a present obligation may arise when one or more of the following questions apply:[246]

(a)   did a transaction or event occur?

(b)   does a known transaction or event give rise to a present obligation?

(c)   how does authoritative guidance (for example, statute, law and regulations) apply to a known transaction or event?

(d)   in the absence of legal enforceability, can cumulative events and circumstances (in other words, items often described as constructive obligations – see 8.1.5 and 8.2.2 below) give rise to a present obligation?

The Board considered two forms of guidance that address uncertainty about the existence of a present obligation in the light of the views expressed at the IAS 37 round-tables:

*   indicators - for example, past experience with similar items; the experience of other entities with identical or similar items; the opinion of experts; and additional evidence provided after the end of the reporting period about conditions that existed on the end of the reporting period;

*   reinstating the 'more likely than not' criterion currently used in paragraph 15 of IAS 37.

The Board tentatively decided to use indicators to provide guidance on how to address uncertainty about the existence of a present obligation in any final standard. The Board acknowledged concerns that indicators could be perceived as a checklist of rules and therefore tentatively concluded that any final standard should emphasise that:

*   addressing uncertainty about the existence of a present obligation requires judgement;

*   when exercising judgement an entity should consider all of the available evidence; and

*   indicators should not be read as a minimum list of conditions that must be satisfied before concluding that a present obligation exists.

The Board also asked the staff to develop application guidance or illustrative examples to supplement the indicators included in the text of any final standard.

The Board also considered including an explicit 'more likely than not' criterion, in addition to indicators, in the text of any final standard. Whilst the Board was initially split on this issue,[247] it decided that a simple 'more likely than not' criterion failed to reflect its view that recognition is a matter of judgement based on all the available evidence.[248] Instead, entities would be required to disclose information about unrecognised liabilities (such as those relating to legal and other proceedings in process, pending or threatened against the entity) subject to uncertainty.[249] Unless the possibility of any outflow of economic benefits in settlement is remote, it is proposed that such disclosure would include:[250]

(a)   a description of the circumstances;

(b)   an indication of the financial effects;

(b)   an indication of the uncertainties relating to the amounts or timing of any outflow of economic benefits; and

(c)   the possibility of any reimbursement.

These requirements look remarkably similar to those currently applied for contingent liabilities (see 6.2 above).[251]

8.1.4   *Measurement*

Currently, the underlying measurement principle in IAS 37 is that a provision is measured at the best estimate of the expenditure required to settle the present obligation at the end of the reporting period[252] (see 4.1 above). This principle has been replaced by the requirement that 'an entity shall measure a non-financial liability at the amount that it would rationally pay to settle the present obligation or to transfer it to a third party' on the end of the reporting period.[253] This is sometimes known as 'legal lay-off amount' or 'relief value' (i.e. the amount an entity would pay a third party to relieve it of its obligation). The exposure draft proposes that this should be determined on the basis of an 'expected cash flow' approach, and asserts that this is an appropriate basis for measuring liabilities for both a class of similar obligations and a single obligation.[254] The current version of IAS 37 suggests that using such an approach is most appropriate for a large population of items, but that for a single item the best estimate of the liability may be the individual most likely outcome (see 4.1 above).

The Board contends that the existing measurement requirements in IAS 37 are not always consistent and can be interpreted in different ways. At the same time, the Board acknowledges that it would be awkward to apply some of the present measurement requirements to the new notion of a 'stand ready obligation'. Consequently, the amendments that are being proposed are designed both to remove the perceived inconsistencies in the existing standard as well as provide clarity to the approach to liability measurement.[255]

Many respondents to the exposure draft indicated that they understood the IAS 37 measurement principle to be an ultimate settlement notion, i.e. the amount estimated to be required to extinguish the obligation in the future. However, the Board affirmed its understanding that the principle is based on a current settlement notion, i.e. the amount an entity would pay to settle or transfer the present obligation *at the end of the reporting period*, not in the future.[256]

The Board also noted that some respondents perceive that the proposed measurement principle permits choice. This is because the principle includes two phrases - 'amount to settle' and 'amount to transfer'. The Board did not believe that more than one measurement attribute was intended. Indeed, the Board is of the opinion that where these two amounts are different, the 'amount that it would rationally pay' is the lower of the two.[257]

Where the obligation being measured is a requirement to undertake a service, such as an asset retirement obligation, it is proposed that the relevant cash flows are the amounts that an entity would rationally pay a contractor to undertake the service on its behalf. In the absence of an efficient market for those services, the entity could estimate the amount it would itself charge another party to carry out the service.[258] It is clear, therefore, that any estimate should not be based on the marginal cost of doing the work itself, but reflects the full cost including an element of a contractor's profit.

8.1.5   *Constructive obligations*

The threshold for recognising a constructive obligation will be raised, but will stop short of adopting the US doctrine of 'promissory estoppel', under which a constructive obligation is recognised in accordance with SFAS 143 only if that obligation is a legal obligation and could be enforced by a court. Consequently, the exposure draft emphasises that a constructive obligation involves an obligation to others by introducing into its definition the notion that the counterparty should reasonably be able to rely on the entity to discharge its responsibilities.[259] Currently, IAS 37 requires the creation of a 'valid expectation' amongst third parties that it will accept particular responsibilities, but without the additional requirement that the third parties must be able to 'reasonably rely' on the entity to discharge those responsibilities (see 3.1.1 above). However, the exposure draft does not provide examples of items that would fall to be constructive obligations under the current version of IAS 37, but not under the new proposals.

The proposals for constructive obligations are discussed further at 8.2.2 below.

8.1.6   *Onerous contracts*

IAS 37 currently provides little guidance as to when a provision for an onerous contract should be recognised. Consequently, the exposure draft is proposing to add some further guidance in this area. If a contract would become onerous as a result of an entity's own actions, the liability should be recognised only when that action is taken.[260] For example, costs of terminating a contract that was not previously considered onerous will only be recognised when the contract is terminated in accordance with its terms. Furthermore, the exposure draft proposes that if the onerous contract is an operating lease, the unavoidable cost of the contract is the remaining lease commitment reduced by the estimated rentals that the entity could reasonably obtain, regardless of whether or not the entity intends to enter into a sublease.[261]

In April 2008 the Board tentatively decided to make minor drafting changes to the proposed requirements to avoid any inference that a decline in the market price of products or services necessarily makes a contract for their purchase onerous and to clarify within the standard what is meant by 'actions' in the requirements for contracts that become onerous because of the entity's own actions.[262]

8.1.7   *Restructuring provisions*

The current version of IAS 37 states that an entity has a constructive obligation to restructure only when it has a detailed formal plan for the restructuring and has raised a valid expectation in those affected that it will carry out the restructuring[263] (see 5.1.2 above). Therefore, it recognises a provision for the direct expenditures arising from the restructuring[264] (see 5.1.3 above).

The exposure draft proposes that liabilities for costs associated with a restructuring should be recognised on the same basis as if they arose independently of a restructuring, namely when the entity has a liability for those costs. The exposure draft proposes guidance for applying this principle to two types of costs that are often associated with a restructuring: termination benefits and contract termination costs.[265] The former are to be dealt with in accordance with the proposals outlined at 8.1.10 below and the latter in accordance with the requirements for onerous contracts at 8.1.6 above.

8.1.8 Contingent assets

As a result of analysing items previously described as contingent assets into conditional and unconditional rights, the Board has decided to eliminate the term 'contingent asset'. The Board believes that the term is 'troublesome and confusing' since, in its view, assets arise only from unconditional (i.e. non-contingent) rights. Hence, the Board believes that an asset that embodies an unconditional right cannot be described as contingent or conditional. This line of argument leads to the conclusion that, because conditional or contingent rights do not by themselves give rise to assets, it is inconsistent with the *Framework* to recognise them, even if it is virtually certain that they will become unconditional or non-contingent.[266] Consequently, items that are currently described as contingent assets under IAS 37 that satisfy the definition of an asset will in future fall within the scope of IAS 38.[267]

8.1.9 Reimbursements

Under the current version of IAS 37, where some or all of the expenditure required to settle a provision is expected to be reimbursed by another party, the reimbursement should be recognised when, and only when, it is virtually certain that reimbursement will be received if the entity settles the obligation[268] (see 4.4 above). Having removed the notion of 'virtual certainty' the exposure draft is proposing to permit the recognition of a reimbursement right as an asset, provided that it can be measured reliably.[269]

IAS 37 presently does not provide any guidance on the measurement of reimbursement rights, and the exposure draft did not propose to so either. The IASB has tentatively decided not to specify a measurement objective for reimbursement rights but to state explicitly that the assumptions used to measure a reimbursement right should be consistent with those used to measure the related liability. The Board also determined that the amount to be recognised for any reimbursement right need not be limited to the amount recognised for the related liability.[270]

8.1.10 Proposed changes to IAS 19

The exposure draft proposes amending the definition of 'termination benefits' to clarify that benefits that are offered in exchange for an employee's decision to accept voluntary termination of employment are termination benefits only if they are offered for a short period.[271] In May 2008 the Board tentatively decided that the term 'short period' refers to a period between the offer for voluntary termination and the actual termination of the employment. The Board also determined that because the definition of voluntary termination benefits refers to a short period, voluntary termination benefits do not relate to future services.[272] Other employee benefits that are offered to encourage employees to leave service before normal retirement date are post-employment benefits.[273]

The Exposure Draft proposed that voluntary termination benefits will only be recognised upon employee acceptance, rather than (as at present) upon the demonstrable commitment of the employer.[274] However, in May 2008 the Board tentatively decided that if an entity offers voluntary termination benefits and cannot withdraw that offer, it should recognise a liability in the same way as for involuntary termination benefits.[275] Nevertheless, the inevitable result of this is that in many cases the costs of voluntary terminations will be recognised later and potentially (if the 'short' period of offer spans a year-end) in more than one reporting period.

Involuntary termination benefits will be recognised when the entity has communicated its plan of termination (which needs to meet the criteria set out below) to the affected employees, and actions required to complete the plan indicate that it is unlikely that significant changes to the plan will be made or that the plan will be withdrawn, unless the involuntary termination benefits are provided in exchange for employees' future services (i.e. in substance they are a 'stay bonus').[276] In such cases, the liability and expense would be recognised over the future service period to the date that employment is terminated.[277]

The plan of terminations needs to:

(a) identify the number of employees whose employment is to be terminated, their job classifications or functions and their locations, and the expected completion date; and

(b) establish the benefits that employees will receive upon termination of employment (including but not limited to cash payments) in sufficient detail to enable employees to determine the type and amount of benefits they will receive when their employment is terminated.[278]

In May 2008 the Board tentatively decided to add another criterion, being that before an obligation exists for involuntary termination benefits, employees need to know whether they are in the class of employees whose employment will be terminated.[279]

As for voluntary terminations, the costs of involuntary termination benefits will be recognised later and potentially in more than one period.

8.2   Explanation of the principal changes resulting from the proposals

8.2.1   'Stand ready' obligations

As indicated at 8.1.2 above, some familiar items (like court cases and warranties) are the subject of a new theoretical concept: the 'stand ready' obligation. This term has been drawn from US GAAP[280] and is used by the IASB to describe 'liabilities for which the amount that will be required in settlement is contingent on the occurrence or non-occurrence of a future event'. Such liabilities are termed stand ready obligations because the entity has an unconditional obligation to stand ready to fulfil the conditional obligation *if* the uncertain future event occurs (or fails to occur). The liability is the unconditional obligation to provide a service, which results in an outflow of economic benefits.[281]

This proposed new approach to provisions and contingencies is best illustrated by an example: Example 10A appended to the current IAS 37 describes legal proceedings against an entity arising from death due to food poisoning. The claimants blame the deaths on products sold by the entity and are claiming damages. The entity disputes this, and its lawyers advise that 'it is probable that the entity will not be found liable'.

The example explains that no provision is recognised because there is no 'present obligation'. This reflects the current requirement that for a provision to be *recognised* an outflow of economic benefits must be probable. The example concludes that there is a contingent liability, which requires disclosure unless the likelihood of loss is remote.[282]

This example is reproduced (almost, but not quite, exactly) as Example 1 appended to the proposed new standard. Here, reflecting a change in language used, the entity's lawyers advise that 'it is unlikely that the entity will be found liable'.

The analysis and conclusion in the exposure draft are quite different from the existing standard. The exposure draft concludes that from the start of legal proceedings the entity has an *unconditional* obligation to 'stand ready' to perform as the court directs. Hence, it has a present obligation and recognises a non-financial liability. In other words, likelihood of outcome no longer features in the test for *recognition* of the liability.

In June 2006, the Board continued the previous meeting's discussion of element uncertainty in the context of litigation. In particular, the Board reconsidered the conclusions in Example 1 (disputed lawsuit) and Example 2 (potential lawsuit) in the illustrative examples accompanying the exposure draft. It concluded that the examples are contradictory, and that the conclusion in Example 1 is incorrect. The start of legal proceedings, in itself, does not obligate an entity. Rather, the start of legal proceedings is another piece of evidence that may be relevant when an entity evaluates whether a liability exists.[283]

In measuring this liability, the entity must estimate what it would rationally pay to settle the case or transfer the liability at the end of the reporting period – what one might call a legal lay-off amount. Crucially, this will not be the single best estimate of the outcome (zero in this case). This is because, even though the entity expects to win, no other party would underwrite the outcome for nothing – an amount would be demanded in compensation of future costs and the risk of an adverse outcome.[284]

Other items are subjected to the same analysis. For example, a product warranty provides a further illustration of a stand ready obligation: the issuer of a product warranty has an unconditional obligation to stand ready to repair or replace the product (or, expressed another way, to provide warranty coverage over the term of the warranty) and a conditional obligation to repair or replace the product if it develops a fault. The issuer recognises its liability arising from its unconditional obligation to provide warranty coverage. Uncertainty about whether the product will require repair or replacement (i.e. the conditional obligation) is reflected in the measurement of the liability.[285]

Semantics aside, this amounts to a requirement to measure all 'non-financial liabilities' (that is, those not covered by IAS 39 or any other standard) at fair value – including items currently considered contingent liabilities. This is not surprising as the impetus for the change came from the IASB's business combinations project.

Currently, IFRS 3 (2007) requires an acquirer to recognise the acquiree's 'contingent liabilities' at fair value. The proposed 'stand ready obligation' approach allows the two standards to have the same recognition criteria for obligations whether or not they are acquired in a business combination.[286]

In May 2006, the Board noted that many respondents believed that the explanation of a stand ready obligation in the exposure draft was too broad and would lead to the recognition of an almost limitless number of items (including items currently regarded as general business risks, not liabilities). The Board began by confirming that a stand ready obligation must satisfy the *Framework's* definition of a liability to be recognised. The Board discussed some examples that had been developed to assist in distinguishing a liability from a general business risk, but agreed that further examples should be developed to clarify the exposure draft's explanation of a stand ready obligation and to distinguish between a stand ready obligation and a general business risk.[287]

A   Redeliberations following round-table discussions

Following the round-table discussions towards the end of 2006, the Board agreed that further research and debate is necessary in how to distinguish a liability from a business risk and how to handle uncertainty about the existence of a liability. In March 2007, the Board discussed a series of examples developed by the staff to assist in distinguishing a liability from a business risk. The Board noted that a present obligation is an essential characteristic of a liability, but not a business risk. Therefore, discussion focused on explaining when and why a present obligation exists. The Board tentatively concluded that a present obligation exists when (a) an entity is irrevocably committed to act in a particular way; and (b) an external party has an enforceable right to call upon the entity to act in that particular way. Consequently:

- an irrevocable action or event, by itself, does not give rise to a present obligation. A mechanism that establishes an external party's right to call upon the entity is also required;

- a law (including contract law) or regulation, by itself, does not give rise to a present obligation; an irrevocable action or event is also required. However, laws and regulations are examples of mechanisms that may establish an external party's right to call upon the entity to act in a particular way;

- a revocable (non-binding) action or event in a jurisdiction where there is a mechanism that establishes an external party's right to call upon the entity to act in a particular way does not give rise to a present obligation;

- planning a future irrevocable action or event in a jurisdiction where there is a mechanism that establishes an external party's right to call upon the entity to act in a particular way does not give rise to a present obligation.

As a result of working through the examples, the Board identified that a crucial point was to distinguish a stand ready obligation from a business risk.[288]

Also, at this meeting in March 2007, the Board went on to clarify that the notion of a stand ready obligation describes present obligations whereby an external party has a right to call upon the entity to act in a particular way in the future, but either the circumstances entitling the external party to exercise its right may not arise, or the external party may choose not to exercise its right. At the round table meetings on IAS 37 many participants were comfortable with applying the notion of a stand ready obligation to contracts. However, they were uncomfortable with extending the notion to non-contractual scenarios. The Board noted that because statutes and contracts are simply legal mechanisms that establish an external party's right to call upon the entity to act in a particular way, the form of the mechanism (i.e. statute or contract) should not influence whether a stand ready obligation exists. As a result, the Board tentatively affirmed that the notion of a stand ready obligation can apply to both contractual and non-contractual scenarios.

At the round-table meetings on IAS 37 some participants suggested that the Board should drop the label 'stand ready obligation' and simply focus on explaining when and why a present obligation exists. The Board acknowledged that, for some, the label 'stand ready obligation' was confusing, but believed that a short-hand term capturing the long-hand explanation was helpful. The Board tentatively decided to keep the term but consideration would be given to using other phrases or terms when drafting the standard.[289]

In May 2007, the Board continued discussing the issue of distinguishing uncertainty about the existence of a present obligation from a stand ready obligation based on the following simple facts:

- an entity sells hamburgers in a jurisdiction where the law states that the vendor must pay compensation of £100,000 to each customer that purchases a contaminated hamburger;
- at the end of the reporting period, the entity has sold one hamburger; and
- past experience indicates that one in a million hamburgers sold by the entity is contaminated. No other information is available.

The Board tentatively decided that these facts illustrate uncertainty about the existence of a present obligation because paying compensation is the potential consequence of past transactions. This is not an example of a stand ready obligation because there is no conditional future event that may or may not occur. However, the Board did not reach a consensus as to how to address such uncertainty about the existence of a present obligation.[290] Essentially the choice is whether the uncertainty is reflected as a recognition issue or as a measurement issue.

In July 2007, the Board tentatively affirmed that the existence of a present obligation distinguishes a liability from a business risk, emphasising that:

- an obligation exists when an entity has a duty or responsibility to an external party to act or perform in a particular way;
- a present obligation exists independently of future events;
- a potential outflow of economic benefits does not distinguish a liability from a business risk because both are capable of resulting in an outflow of economic benefits. A business risk is also capable of resulting in an inflow of economic benefits.

The Board went on to discuss the ambiguity caused by using the phrase 'little if any discretion' to describe when and why a present obligation exists. The Board acknowledged that this phrase comes from the *Framework*, but asked the staff to consider the use and positioning of this phrase when drafting revisions to the text proposed in the exposure draft.

The Board also tentatively affirmed that a stand ready obligation is a liability, not a business risk. It was therefore consistent with the Board's observations on distinguishing a business risk from a liability that a present obligation must exist before an item can be described as a stand ready obligation. The Board also affirmed that 'stand ready obligation' describes situations when there is uncertainty about the outflow of economic benefits required to settle a present obligation. Importantly, 'stand ready obligation' does not describe uncertainty about the existence of the present obligation.[291]

In October 2007, the Board revisited the hamburger example noted above and tentatively concluded that the supply of a hamburger was not sufficient to give rise to an obligation. There must also be evidence that the hamburger was contaminated. As noted at 8.1.3 A above, the Board tentatively decided not to specify a probability threshold (such as 'more likely than not') for judging whether a liability exists. In the Board's view the assessment of whether an entity had a present obligation should be a matter for judgement, taken on the basis of all the available evidence.[292]

8.2.2　*Constructive obligations*

As indicated at 8.1.5 above, the exposure draft proposes that the definition of constructive obligations be changed. The change is a subtle one and worth presenting here in full.

The current definition in IAS 37 is 'an obligation that derives from an entity's actions where:

(a)　by an established pattern of past practice, published policies or a sufficiently specific current statement, the entity has indicated to other parties that it will accept certain responsibilities; and

(b)　as a result, the entity has created a valid expectation on the part of those other parties that it will discharge those responsibilities.'[293]

The proposed new definition is 'a present obligation that arises from an entity's past actions when:

(a)   by an established pattern of past practice, published policies or a sufficiently specific current statement, the entity has indicated to other parties that it will accept particular responsibilities; and

(b)   as a result, the entity has created a valid expectation in those parties that they can reasonably rely on it to discharge those responsibilities.'[294]

This proposed change is the product of the IASB's convergence project. The Board observes that the notion of a constructive obligation is 'differently understood under US GAAP' which only recognises liabilities which a court would enforce. The IASB considered moving to this but concluded it would be premature in advance of reconsidering liabilities more generally.[295]

It is hard to divine quite what the IASB intends to achieve with this subtle change. However, the Basis for Conclusions indicates that the 'proposed amendment should not alter existing practice for well-understood examples of constructive obligations (for example, some environmental clean-up obligations and warranty obligations) ... However, items that were previously determined to be constructive obligations, but leave the entity discretion to avoid settling the item, will no longer be recognised as liabilities.'[296] Unfortunately, though, the IASB does not provide any examples of such items.

A   Redeliberations following round-table discussions

Following the round-table discussions towards the end of 2006, one of the issues that the Board agreed requires further research and debate is how to handle uncertainty about the existence of a liability, including constructive obligations. In May 2007, the Board started redeliberating issues associated with the proposed amendments to constructive obligations. In the light of the comment letters received and recent discussions on distinguishing a liability from a business risk, the Board tentatively affirmed its previous observation that the main issue is determining what makes a constructive obligation an obligation – i.e. something an entity cannot avoid because an external party has a right to call upon the entity to act in a particular way.

The Board instructed the staff to explore three options for discussion at a future meeting:[297]

(a)   limit the recognition of constructive obligations to those a court would enforce (effectively the US doctrine of 'promissory estoppel');

(b)   recognise constructive obligations that a court would enforce and constructive obligations that are enforceable 'by equivalent means' and explore the meaning of 'by equivalent means';

(c)   option (b), but using the explanatory text in paragraph 15 of the exposure draft as an explanation of 'by equivalent means'.

In July 2007, the Board tentatively affirmed that the main issue associated with constructive obligations is what makes a constructive obligation an obligation in the absence of legal enforceability. However, it stated that categorically answering this question goes beyond the scope of the IAS 37 project. Therefore the Board's redeliberations focused on the above three options that aim to encourage greater consistency in the accounting for constructive obligations.

As a result, the Board tentatively concluded that any final standard should emphasise that:

- a recognised constructive obligation is a liability, not a business risk. Therefore, consistently with the Board's observations on distinguishing a business risk from a liability, a present obligation must exist;

- a management decision or an intention to incur a future outflow of economic benefits by itself is not sufficient to justify recognising a liability.

The Board also tentatively affirmed that separately defining legal and constructive obligations in IAS 37 sometimes causes confusion. This is because many items described as constructive obligations are legally enforceable. Therefore, the Board asked the staff to incorporate the existing definitions of legal and constructive obligations into the text of any final standard.[298]

8.2.3 Contingent assets

The exposure draft proposes that the revised IAS 37 will not deal with contingent assets. Rather, these will be dealt with by IAS 38. A proposed amendment to IAS 38 will introduce a concept similar to the stand ready obligation, whereby a right is analysed into a conditional and unconditional right.

For example, benefits under a product warranty will be analysed as an unconditional right to warranty coverage and a conditional right to have a product repaired or replaced. An intangible asset arises from the unconditional right. As intangible assets are initially recognised at cost, the impact of this change is to re-characterise the familiar concept of a prepaid expense as an intangible asset. A similar analysis is applied to the pursuit of a legal claim. This clarifies that, whilst any receipts from the claim would not be anticipated the costs incurred in pursuing it represent an intangible asset.[299]

8.2.4 Liabilities for restructuring costs

In reviewing the current version of IAS 37, whereby the existence of a detailed formal plan together with its announcement gives rise to a liability by imposing on the entity a constructive obligation to restructure,[300] the Board noted the guidance in paragraph 17 of IAS 37 that an obligating event requires the entity to have 'no realistic alternative to settling the obligation' and, therefore, considered whether a restructuring plan and its announcement leave the entity in that position. The Board's conclusion is that, even if an entity has announced its restructuring plan in a general way, it has no obligation to others and is not bound by its plan to the extent that it cannot avoid an outflow of resources. As a result, the Board has decided that, because an entity can recall its restructuring plan once it has been announced, the restructuring guidance in the present version of IAS 37 is a misapplication of the Standard's notion of a constructive obligation.[301]

Accordingly, the Board has decided to withdraw the present guidance for the recognition of restructuring provisions in IAS 37 and, instead, state that liabilities arising from costs associated with a restructuring should be recognised on the same basis as if that cost arose independently of a restructuring – namely when the entity incurs a liability that can be measured reliably. Thus, instead of an entity recognising at a specified point a single liability for all of the costs associated with a restructuring, it will recognise liabilities for each cost associated with the restructuring as the liability for each cost is incurred.[302] Clearly, this represents a significant change from existing practice.

In April 2008, the Board considered and rejected arguments from some respondents to the Exposure Draft that a public announcement of a decision to restructure a business creates a constructive obligation because, from a commercial viewpoint, management has little if any discretion to reverse the decision. The Board also tentatively decided to add a requirement for entities to disclose details of restructuring activities, including a description of the restructuring, the segment affected, any impairment charges recognised, the total costs associated with the restructuring and the nature and timing of those costs.[303]

8.2.5   *Effective date and transition*

Whilst the originally proposed date for applying the revised standard has long passed (annual periods commencing on or after 1 January 2007),[304] it is still expected that the effective date will be set two or three years after publication and that both the restatement of comparative information and full retrospective application will be prohibited.[305] The Board's reasoning for this is that because the new standard will require the recognition of liabilities that previously failed to meet the probability criterion, existing users of IFRSs would, in many instances, find it impracticable to apply the amendments retrospectively without recourse to an inappropriate use of hindsight.[306] Earlier adoption will be encouraged – however, with the proviso that an entity will be able to apply the revised standard only from the beginning of an annual period commencing on or after the date that the standard is issued.[307]

At the time of writing, the Board expects either to re-expose its proposals or to publish a final standard in the fourth quarter of 2009.[308]

8.3   **Ernst & Young's concerns about the proposals**

Although we strongly support the long-term objective of convergence of International and U.S. accounting standards, in order to achieve convergence, the IASB needs to convince its constituents that proposals involving major changes in accounting practice will significantly improve the quality (i.e. the understandability, relevance, reliability and comparability) of the information provided in financial statements. In our view, the IASB has not yet made a sufficiently compelling case for the fundamental change in approach to accounting for non-financial liabilities and voluntary termination benefits that they are proposing.

Our main concerns with the proposals in the exposure draft relate to the following three areas.

8.3.1 *Recognition criteria for non-financial liabilities*

We disagree with the amendment of the recognition criteria for non-financial liabilities. We do not see how the deletion of the notion of probability from the recognition criteria can be reconciled with the definition of a liability in the *Framework* since that definition includes probability as an element. A liability is defined as 'a present obligation of the entity arising from past events, the settlement of which is expected to result in an outflow from the entity of resources embodying economic benefits'. To determine whether an outflow of resources is 'expected', it is necessary to assess whether such an outflow is probable. If an outflow of resources is not expected (or probable), there is no liability. We believe that the IASB should either retain the current recognition criteria for non-financial liabilities in IAS 37 or discuss a more fundamental re-consideration of the *Framework* definitions of the elements of financial statements. Such a re-consideration in our view would require a careful analysis of all other consequences, including the definition of an asset which is also based on 'expected' future economic benefits.

8.3.2 *Conditional versus unconditional non-financial liabilities*

Despite the examples given in the Illustrative Examples and the Basis for Conclusions in the exposure draft, we find it very hard to imagine how the distinction made between the conditional and the unconditional elements of an obligation might be applied in practice. On a more conceptual level, we do not understand why, when a conditional obligation does not meet the recognition criteria because it is not a present obligation, it must necessarily be included in the measurement of a non-financial liability in those cases in which it happens to be accompanied by an unconditional (or 'stand-ready') obligation.

If the IASB is to proceed along the lines of distinguishing conditional from unconditional obligations, it needs to clarify the notion of a 'past event triggering an unconditional obligation'. This notion is not defined in the proposed standard. Paragraph 13 states that 'For a past event to give rise to a present obligation, the entity must have little, if any, discretion to avoid settling it'. Paragraph 14 indicates that a liability arises, among others, from legal obligations, the settlement of which can be enforced by a court. We read that as meaning that a violation of the law or the violation of a contractual agreement is a past event that creates an unconditional obligation because it can be enforced by a court. If that is what the IASB means, it is not clear to us why in Example 1 (disputed lawsuit) the past event is the start of legal proceedings and not the fact that 10 people died as a result of an error made by the entity. A stand-ready obligation came into being when the entity violated the law or the contractual agreement with the customers. This being the case, the fact that the entity was not aware of the fact that it might have sold harmful food is irrelevant as there is an unconditional obligation (a stand-ready obligation towards those caused harm because it is enforceable by a court) and the entity would not be able to transfer this risk to a third party for no consideration, Taking this to the extreme, the thinking of the Board in its purest form would lead to the recognition of an infinite number of stand-ready obligations at end of the reporting period for all the laws and contractual arrangements that may potentially have been violated and for which the entity has a stand-ready obligation.

As indicated at 8.2.1 above, the Board has now acknowledged that the conclusion in Example 1 is incorrect. The start of legal proceedings, in itself, does not obligate an entity. The Board now regards the start of legal proceedings as being another piece of evidence that may be relevant when an entity evaluates whether a liability exists.

8.3.3   *Reliability of measurement*

We have serious concerns about the possibility of arriving at any kind of reliable measurement of the amount that the entity would rationally pay to settle the present obligation or to transfer a single liability to a third party. The number of cases where this assessment has to be made will increase under the proposed IAS 37 and will now include many cases where the probability of an actual outflow of resources is low, making it more difficult to measure. For example, lawsuits started against the entity with no basis whatsoever and where the likelihood of an outflow of resources other than legal fees is remote, would still be measured at a greater amount than the expected legal fees because a third party would not be willing to accept the risk at an amount that would only cover legal fees. As there are hardly any real transactions of risk transfer of non-financial liabilities, measurement of these liabilities is likely to be highly subjective and of questionable reliability.

8.4   **Exposure draft on rate-regulated activities**

Rate regulation refers to the way a regulator restricts the level of or movement in prices charged by an entity to its customers for its services or products. Whilst such regulation is common all over the world, the price control strategies applied can vary considerably. Where the price established by the regulator is, at least in part, derived from an objective to give an entity a fair return on its costs, the question arises as to whether an imposed price reduction in recognition of a past over recovery of costs should be recognised as a liability; and whether a future price increase in recognition of past costs incurred gives rise to an asset. As discussed at 5.4.12 above, the current consensus among existing IFRS reporters is that regulatory liabilities should be recognised only in those rare cases where they meet the definition of a financial liability in the *Framework*.[309]

The IASB issued an exposure draft on rate-regulated activities in July 2009, with the deadline for comments set for 20 November 2009. The Board acknowledged that while divergence in practice did not currently exist, this was a matter of significant interest in a number of countries that would be adopting IFRS in the near future and where recognition of regulatory assets and liabilities was either permitted or required. The approaching conversion of these jurisdictions to IFRS would increase pressure for what the Board describes as 'a definitive conclusion on the question'.[310]

At the time of writing it is difficult to determine how this exposure draft will be received, but it is clear that the challenge for the IASB will be twofold. To clearly define in what situations and regulatory environments it is appropriate to recognise regulatory liabilities and assets; and to make the case for its proposals to current users of IFRS, hopefully on the basis of the *Framework* and without recourse to the somewhat overplayed 'convergence card'. The IASB expects to issue a final standard based on these proposals in the second quarter of 2010.[311]

8.4.1   Scope of the proposals

The scope of the proposals is intended to be restrictive, applying only to entities with operating activities that meet the following criteria:[312]

(a)   an authorised body (the regulator) establishes the price the entity must charge its customers for the goods or services the entity provides, and that price binds the customers; and

(b)   the price established by regulation (the rate) is designed to recover the specific costs the entity incurs in providing the regulated goods or services and to earn a specified return (cost-of-service regulation). The specified return could be a minimum or range and need not be fixed or guaranteed.

Cost-of-service regulation is defined as 'a form of regulation for setting an entity's prices (rates) in which there is a cause-and-effect relationship between the entity's specific costs and its revenues.'[313] Forms of regulation that establish different rates for different categories, such as different classes of customers or volumes purchased, are within this scope provided that the regulator approves the definition and the rate for each of those categories and that all customers of the same category are bound by the same rate.[314] For example, the rate-regulated activities of an entity would not be excluded from the proposals simply because the entity is also engaged in unregulated activities.[315] However, regulatory mechanisms applying targeted or assumed costs, such as industry averages, rather than an entity's specific costs, are outside the scope of the proposals.[316]

The scope of the proposed standard and the detailed requirements are discussed further at 5.1 in Chapter 15. The proposals for recognition and measurement and for presentation and disclosure are summarised below.

8.4.2   Recognition and measurement

The Exposure Draft proposes that when an entity falling within its scope has the right to increase or the obligation to decrease rates in future periods as a result of the actual or expected actions of the regulator, it shall recognise:[317]

(a)   a regulatory asset for its right to recover specific previously incurred costs and to earn a specified return; or

(b)   a regulatory liability for its obligation to refund previously collected amounts and to pay a specified return.

Accordingly, where there is an obligation to lower prices in the future, a regulatory liability is recognised to reflect amounts that would otherwise be recorded in that period in the statement of comprehensive income as revenue.[318] That liability should be carried initially and at the end of subsequent reporting periods at its expected present value.[319] Such an expected present value would comprise the following elements for a regulatory liability:[320]

(a)   an estimate of the future cash flows that will arise in a range of possible outcomes;

(b)   an estimate of the probability of each outcome occurring;

(c)   the time value of money, represented by the current market risk-free rate of interest; and

(d)   the price for bearing the uncertainty inherent in the regulatory liability.

8.4.3   *Presentation and disclosure*

Regulatory assets and liabilities would be presented separately from other assets and liabilities on the face of the balance sheet, and classified as current and non-current items.[321] Offsetting would only be allowed for each category of asset or liability subject to the same regulator.[322]

The Exposure Draft proposes that entities would disclose the fact that some or all of its operating activities are subject to rate regulation, including a description of their nature and extent.[323] For each set of operating activities subject to a different regulator, an entity would disclose the following information:[324]

(a)   if the regulator is a related party;

(b)   an explanation of the approval process for the rate subject to regulation (including the rate of return), including information about how that process affects both the underlying operating activities and the specified rate of return;

(c)   the indicators that management considered in concluding that such operating activities have met the scope criteria (if that conclusion requires significant judgement);

(d)   significant assumptions used to measure the expected present value of a recognised regulatory asset or regulatory liability including:

   (i)   the supporting regulatory action, for example, the issue of a formal approval for costs to be recovered pending a final ruling at a later date and that date, when known, or

   (ii)   the entity's assessment of the expected future regulatory actions; and

(e)   the risks and uncertainties affecting the future recovery of the regulatory asset or final settlement of the regulatory liability, including the expected timing.

For each category of regulatory asset or regulatory liability recognised that is subject to a different regulator, it is proposed that the entity disclose:[325]

(a)   a reconciliation from the beginning to the end of the period, in tabular format unless another format is more appropriate, of the carrying amount in the balance sheet of the regulatory asset or regulatory liability, including at least the following elements:

   (i)   the amount recognised in the income statement / statement of comprehensive income relating to balances from prior periods collected or refunded in the current period;

(ii)   the amount of costs incurred in the current period that were recognised in the balance sheet as regulatory assets or regulatory liabilities to be recovered or refunded in future periods; and

(iii) other amounts that affected the regulatory asset or regulatory liability, such as items acquired or assumed in business combinations or the effects of changes in foreign exchange rates, discount rates or estimated cash flows. If a single cause has a significant effect on the regulatory asset or regulatory liability, the entity shall disclose it separately.

(b)   the remaining period over which the entity expects to recover the carrying amount of the regulatory asset or to settle the regulatory liability; and

(c)   the amount of financing cost included in the cost of self-constructed property, plant and equipment and internally developed intangible assets in the current period that would not have been capitalised under IAS 23.

8.5   Emissions trading schemes

As noted at 5.4.3 A above, the IASB resumed its project on emissions trading schemes in December 2007, deciding to limit the scope of the project to accounting issues relating to emissions trading schemes, rather than to consider more general issues regarding the accounting for government grants.[326]

In May 2008, the Board tentatively decided to address the accounting for all tradable emissions rights and obligations arising under emissions trading schemes and in addition to address the accounting of activities undertaken by entities contemplating the receipt of tradable rights in future periods, such as certified emissions reductions (CERs). At this time the Board confirmed that it would not be constrained by existing IFRSs, although the *Framework* would still be relevant.[327]

The objective of the project is to develop comprehensive guidance on the accounting for emissions trading schemes, including (but not limited to) the following issues:[328]

- Are emission allowances assets? Is this conclusion affected by how the allowance is acquired? What is the nature of the allowance (e.g. licence to emit or a form of emission currency)? If allowances are assets, should they be recognised and, if so, how should they be measured initially?

- What is the corresponding entry for an entity that receives allowances from government free of charge? Does a liability exist? If so, what is the nature of the liability and how should it be measured both initially and subsequently?

- How should allowances be accounted for subsequently? Is the existing model in IAS 38 or IAS 39 appropriate? If not, what is the appropriate accounting?

- When should an entity recognise its obligations in emissions trading schemes and how should they be measured? How does IAS 37 apply?

- What are the overall financial reporting effects of the above decisions?

In March 2009, the IASB tentatively decided that emission allowances received free of charge from government should be recognised as assets and initially measured at fair value. The Board also tentatively decided at that meeting that a liability should be recognised for the entity's obligation to reduce its emissions below the established cap level. This liability would be measured initially at the fair value of the allowances received.[329]

At the time of writing, the IASB expects to issue an exposure draft in the second quarter of 2010 and to publish a final standard in the first half of 2011.[330]

9   CONCLUSION

The subject of provisions and contingencies is a wide ranging one, but at its heart lie fundamental questions concerning the recognition and measurement of items in the financial statements. The IASB (and the ASB in the UK) see these issues straightforwardly in terms of balance sheet recognition, and have sought to apply their respective conceptual frameworks as a means of resolving them, but in many cases we think this does not work well and that it might be more fruitful to address the question from the point of view of expense recognition. In particular, we think the concepts of 'obligating events' and 'constructive obligations' are rather more nebulous than they are represented to be, and not always useful in identifying reliably when to include certain items in the financial statements. We would not be as dismissive as the standard setters about the relevance of management intent, since financial statements necessarily represent the report of management and it is futile to try to divorce them from that context. We are also concerned that the approach of IAS 37 means that the balance sheet will be inappropriately grossed up in some cases so as to include 'dubious' assets.

The measurement requirements also have their difficulties. We are concerned that they seem to be seeking to derive some form of theoretical market value for the obligations reported rather than focusing more directly on the actual expenditure that the entity is likely to make. We also think that the rules on discounting should have been given much deeper consideration. The use of discounting also means that the operating results of an entity are often heavily flattered at the expense of finance costs.

As a result, we do not think that IAS 37 is a very satisfactory standard. While the answers it gives rise to are usually acceptable, the reasoning that lies behind them is frequently suspect and is more likely to puzzle readers than enlighten them.

As far as the IASB's proposals to amend IAS 37 are concerned, we do not believe that the Board has made a sufficiently compelling case for the fundamental change in approach to accounting for non-financial liabilities. As discussed more fully at 8.3 above we:

- disagree with the amendment of the recognition for non-financial liabilities;
- find it very hard to operationalise the distinction made between the conditional and unconditional elements of an obligation; and
- have serious concerns about the possibility of arriving at any kind of reliable measurement of the amount that the entity would rationally pay to settle the present obligation or to transfer a single liability to a third party.

In light of these concerns, we believe that the IASB should not amend IAS 37 as proposed or, alternatively, should demonstrate more convincingly the practical deficiencies of the current IAS 37 that would require such a significant change in thinking and amendment of the definition of a liability in the current Framework.

References

1 IAS 37, *Provisions, Contingent Liabilities and Contingent Assets*, IASB, para. 10.
2 IAS 37, para. 10.
3 IAS 10 (1978), *Contingencies and Events Occurring After the Balance Sheet Date*, IASC, October 1978.
4 IAS 37, para. 11.
5 Draft Statement of Principles, *Provisions and Contingencies*, IASC, November 1996, paras. 89-95.
6 IAS 1, *Presentation of Financial Statements*, IASB, para. 139.
7 IAS 37, para. 95.
8 IAS 1, para. 139 and IAS 37, para. 95.
9 Project Summary, *Liabilities – Amendments to IAS 37 Provisions, Contingent Liabilities and Contingent Assets and IAS 19 Employee Benefits*, IASB, June 2009, para. 5.
10 *IASB Work Plan – projected timetable as at 1 August 2009*, IASB.
11 IAS 37, Objective.
12 IAS 37, para. 7.
13 IAS 37, para. 1.
14 IAS 37, para. 3.
15 IAS 37, para. 3.
16 IAS 37, para. 5.
17 IAS 37 (2007), *Provisions, Contingent Liabilities and Contingent Assets*, IASB, 2007 Bound Volume, para. 5.
18 IFRS 3, *Business Combinations*, IASB, para. 23.
19 IAS 37, para. 2.
20 IAS 37, para. 6.
21 IAS 37, para. 9.
22 IAS 37, para. 11.
23 IAS 37, para. 12.
24 IAS 37, para. 13.
25 IAS 37, para. 14.
26 IAS 37, para. 10.
27 IAS 37, para. 10.
28 IAS 37, Appendix C, Examples 4 and 2B.
29 IAS 37, paras. 15-16.
30 IAS 37, para. 10.
31 IAS 37, para. 17.
32 IAS 37, para. 18.
33 IAS 37, para. 19.
34 IAS 37, para. 19 and Appendix C, Example 6.
35 IAS 37, Appendix C, Examples 11A, 11B and 7.
36 IAS 37, para. 20.
37 IAS 37, para. 21.
38 IAS 37, para. 22.
39 IAS 37, para. 21.
40 *FASB Newsletter*, No. 310, 25 February 1999, p. 5.
41 IAS 37, paras. 23-24.
42 IAS 37, paras. 25-26.
43 IAS 37, paras. 27-28, 31 and 34.
44 IAS 37 (2007), para. 5 and IFRS 3, para. 23.
45 IAS 37, para. 10.
46 IAS 37, para. 16.
47 IAS 10, *Events After the Reporting Period*, IASB, para 9.
48 IAS 37, paras. 15-16.
49 IAS 37, para. 30.
50 IAS 37 (1998), *Provisions, Contingent Liabilities and Contingent Assets*, IASC, September 1998, Appendix C, Example 9.
51 IAS 37, Appendix C, Example 9.
52 IAS 37, para. 10.
53 IAS 37, para. 32.
54 IAS 37, para. 33.
55 IAS 37, paras. 34 and 89.
56 IAS 37, para. 35.
57 IAS 10, para 9.
58 IAS 37, para. 35.
59 FRS 12, *Provisions, Contingent Liabilities and Contingent Assets*, ASB, September 1998, para. 66.
60 IAS 37, para. 8.
61 IAS 16, *Property, Plant and Equipment*, IASB, para. 16.
62 IAS 37, Appendix C, Example 3.
63 IAS 37, para. 41.
64 IAS 37, para. 36.
65 IAS 37, para. 37.
66 IAS 37, para. 37.
67 IAS 37, para. 38.
68 IAS 37, para. 39.

69 IAS 37, para. 39.
70 FASB Interpretation No. 14, *Reasonable Estimation of the Amount of a Loss*, FASB, September 1976, para. 3.
71 IAS 37, para. 40.
72 IAS 37, para. 40.
73 IAS 37, paras. 42-43.
74 IAS 37, para. 44.
75 IAS 37, para. 43.
76 IAS 37, para. 45.
77 IAS 37, para. 47.
78 IAS 37, para. 46.
79 IAS 37, Appendix D, Example 2.
80 FRS 12, para. 50.
81 IAS 37, para. 47.
82 FRS 12, para. 49.
83 *Discounting in Financial Reporting*, ASB, April 1997.
84 *Discounting in Financial Reporting*, ASB, April 1997, para. 2.10.
85 IAS 37, para. 43.
86 FRS 12, para. 49.
87 FRS 12, para. 49.
88 IAS 19, *Employee benefits*, IASB, para. 78.
89 IAS 19, para. 79.
90 IAS 37, para. 47.
91 Paragraph 27 in Appendix VII to FRS 12 on the *Development of the FRS* states that 'the discount rate should be the rate of return that will, after tax has been deducted, give the required post-tax rate of return'. The paragraph goes on to explain that because the tax consequence of different cash flows may be different, the pre-tax rate of return is not always the post-tax rate of return grossed up by the standard rate of tax.
92 IAS 37, para. 60.
93 IFRIC 1, *Changes in Existing Decommissioning, Restoration and Similar Liabilities*, IASB, para. 8.
94 IFRIC 1, paras. 8 and BC26-BC27.
95 IAS 37, para. 47.
96 IAS 37, para. 84(e).
97 IFRIC 1, paras. 5 and 7.
98 IFRIC 1, para. 5.
99 IFRIC 1, para. IE5.
100 IAS 37, para. 48.
101 IAS 37, para. 49.
102 IAS 37, para. 50.
103 IAS 37, para. 55.
104 IAS 37, paras. 53 and 56.
105 IAS 37, para. 54.
106 IAS 37, para. 57.
107 IAS 37, paras. 29 and 58.
108 IAS 37, paras. 51-52.
109 IAS 37, para. 59.
110 IAS 37, para. 60.
111 IFRIC 1, paras. 8 and BC26-BC27.
112 IAS 37, paras. 61-62.
113 IFRS 3, para. 23 and IFRS 3 (2007), *Business Combinations*, IASB, 2007 Bound Volume, paras. 36 and 37.
114 IFRS 3, para. 56 and IFRS 3 (2007), paras. 48 and 49.
115 IFRS 3, para. 56 and IFRS 3 (2007), paras. 48 and 49.
116 IAS 37, para. 10.
117 IAS 37, para. 70.
118 IAS 37, para. 9.
119 IAS 37, para. 71.
120 IAS 37, para. 72.
121 IAS 37, para. 73.
122 IAS 37, para. 74.
123 IAS 37, para. 75.
124 IAS 37, Appendix C, Examples 5A-5B.
125 IAS 37, para. 76.
126 IAS 37, para. 77.
127 IAS 37, para. 75.
128 IAS 37, para. 78.
129 IAS 37, para. 79.
130 IAS 37, para. 80.
131 IAS 37, para. 19.
132 IAS 37, para. 81.
133 IAS 37, para. 81.
134 FRED 14, *Provisions and Contingencies*, ASB, June 1997, para. 61.
135 IAS 37, para. 82.
136 IAS 37, para. 83.
137 IAS 37, para. 63.
138 IAS 37, para. 64.
139 IAS 37, para. 65.
140 IAS 37, para. 66.
141 IAS 37, para. 67.
142 IAS 37, para. 10.
143 IAS 37, para. 68.
144 IAS 37, Appendix C, Example 8.
145 *IFRIC Update*, IFRIC, December 2003, pp. 4-5.
146 IAS 37, para. 69.
147 IAS 37, para. 10.
148 IAS 37, para. 69.
149 IAS 37, Appendix C, Example 2A.
150 IAS 37, para. 22.
151 IAS 37, Appendix C, Example 2B.
152 IAS 37, para. 19.
153 IAS 37, Appendix C, Example 3.
154 IFRIC 1, para. 2.
155 IFRIC 1, para. 3.
156 IFRIC 1, para. 8
157 IFRIC 1, paras. 8 and BC26-BC27.
158 IFRIC 1, paras. 4-7.
159 IFRIC 1, para. 5.
160 IFRIC 1, para. 7.
161 IFRIC 1, para. 6.
162 IFRIC 1, Appendix 1, para. IE5.

163 IFRIC 5, *Rights to Interests Arising from Decommissioning, Restoration and Environmental Rehabilitation Funds*, IASB, para. 1.

164 IFRIC 5, para. 2.

165 IFRIC 5, para. 3.

166 IFRIC 5, para. 4.

167 IFRIC 5, para. 5.

168 IFRIC 5, para. 6.

169 IFRIC 5, para. 7.

170 IFRIC 5, para. 8.

171 IFRIC 5, para. 9.

172 IFRIC 5, para. BC14.

173 IFRIC 5, paras. BC19-20.

174 IFRIC 5, para. 9.

175 IFRIC 5, para. 10.

176 IFRIC 3, *Emission Rights*, IASB, December 2004, para. 1.

177 IFRIC 3, para. 5.

178 IFRIC 3, para. 6.

179 IFRIC 3, para. 7.

180 IFRIC 3, para. 8.

181 *IASB Update*, IASB, June 2005, p. 1.

182 *IASB Update*, IASB, June 2005, p. 1.

183 *IASB Insight*, IASB, May 2006, p. 13.

184 *IASB Update*, IASB, December 2007, p. 1.

185 Directive 2002/96/EC of the European Parliament and of the Council of 27 January 2003 on waste electrical and electronic equipment and Directive 2003/108/EC of the European Parliament and of the Council of 8 December 2003 amending Directive 2002/96/EC on waste electrical and electronic equipment.

186 IFRIC 6, *Liabilities arising from Participating in a Specific Market – Waste Electrical and Electronic Equipment*, IASB, para. 3.

187 IFRIC 6, para. 4.

188 IFRIC 6, para. 8.

189 IFRIC 6, para. 6.

190 IFRIC 6, para. 7.

191 IFRIC 6, para. 9.

192 IFRIC 6, para. BC5.

193 IFRIC 6, para. BC6.

194 IFRIC 6, para. BC7.

195 IFRIC 6, para. 5.

196 IAS 37, para. 19.

197 IAS 37, para. 18.

198 IAS 37, para. 17.

199 IAS 37, Appendix C, Examples 11A-11B.

200 IAS 37, Appendix C, Examples 11A-11B.

201 FRS 12, Appendix VII, para. 39.

202 IAS 37, Appendix C, Example 1.

203 IAS 37, para. 39.

204 IAS 37, Appendix C, Example 10A.

205 IAS 37, para. 14.

206 IAS 37, para. 15.

207 IAS 37, para. 25.

208 IAS 37, Appendix C, Example 4.

209 IAS 37, Appendix C, Example 7.

210 IAS 37, para. 14.

211 FRS 12, Appendix III, Example 12.

212 IAS 37, para. 10.

213 FRS 12, Appendix VII, para. 16.

214 *IFRIC Update*, IFRIC, November 2008, p. 4.

215 Information for Observers (December 2008 IASB Meeting), *Agenda proposal: rate-regulated activities (Agenda Paper 12)*, para. 14.

216 Exposure Draft (ED 2009/8), *Rate-regulated Activities*, IASB, July 2009, para. BC8.

217 IAS 37, para. 84.

218 IAS 37, para. 61.

219 IAS 37, para. 85.

220 IAS 37, para. 87.

221 IAS 37, para. 9.

222 IAS 37, para. 86.

223 IAS 37, para. 91.

224 IAS 37, para. 88.

225 IAS 37, para. 89.

226 IAS 37, para. 91.

227 IAS 37, para. 90.

228 IAS 37, para. 92.

229 IAS 37, para. 92.

230 IAS 37, para. 93.

231 *IASB Work Plan – projected timetable as at 1 August 2009*, IASB.

232 *IASB Update*, IASB, March 2006, p. 6.

233 Project Summary, *Liabilities – Amendments to IAS 37 Provisions, Contingent Liabilities and Contingent Assets and IAS 19 Employee Benefits*, IASB, June 2009, Appendix A, para. 4.

234 *Exposure Draft of Proposed Amendments to IAS 37 Provisions, Contingent Liabilities and Contingent Assets* ('IAS 37 ED') *and IAS 19 Employee Benefits* ('IAS 19 ED'), IASB, June 2005, paras. 46-50.

235 *IASB Update*, IASB, March 2006, p. 6.

236 IAS 37 ED, para. BC11.

237 IAS 37 ED, para. BC30.

238 IAS 37 ED, paras. 24-26.

239 IAS 37, para. 14(b).

240 IAS 37 ED, para. 11.

241 IAS 37 ED, paras. BC36-48.

242 IAS 37 ED, para. BC48.

243 IAS 37 ED, paras. AV2-AV7.

244 *IASB Update*, IASB, June 2006, p. 3.

245 *IASB Update*, IASB, May 2006, p. 5.

246 *IASB Update*, IASB, July 2007, p. 4.

247 *IASB Update*, IASB, July 2007, p. 5.

248 *IASB Update*, IASB, October 2007, p. 3.

249 *IASB Update*, IASB, December 2008, p. 5.

250 *IASB Update*, IASB, June 2009, p. 4.

251 IAS 37, para. 86.

252 IAS 37, para. 36.

253 IAS 37 ED, para. 29.

254 IAS 37 ED, para. 31.
255 IAS 37 ED, para. BC78.
256 *IASB Update*, IASB, September 2006, p. 3.
257 *IASB Update*, IASB, February 2008, p. 3.
258 *IASB Update*, IASB, April 2009, p. 3.
259 IAS 37 ED, para. BC59.
260 IAS 37 ED, para. 55.
261 IAS 37 ED, para. 58.
262 *IASB Update*, IASB, April 2008, p. 2.
263 IAS 37, para. 72.
264 IAS 37, para. 80.
265 IAS 37 ED, paras. 61-64.
266 IAS 37 ED, para. BC17.
267 IAS 37 ED, paras. A22 and BC18.
268 IAS 37, para. 53.
269 IAS 37 ED, paras. 46-47.
270 *IASB Update*, IASB, June 2009, p. 4.
271 IAS 19 ED, para. 7.
272 *IASB Update*, IASB, May 2008, p. 4.
273 IAS 19 ED, para. 135.
274 IAS 19 ED, para. 137.
275 *IASB Update*, IASB, May 2008, p. 4.
276 IAS 19 ED, para. 138.
277 IAS 19 ED, para. 139.
278 IAS 19 ED, para. 138.
279 *IASB Update*, IASB, May 2008, p. 4.
280 IAS 37 ED, para. BC25.
281 IAS 37 ED, para. 24.
282 IAS 37, Appendix C, Example 10A.
283 *IASB Update*, IASB, June 2006, p. 3.
284 IAS 37 ED, Example 1.
285 IAS 37 ED, para. 25.
286 IAS 37 ED, para. BC22.
287 *IASB Update*, IASB, May 2006, p. 3.
288 *IASB Update*, IASB, March 2007, p. 5.
289 *IASB Update*, IASB, March 2007, p. 5.
290 *IASB Update*, IASB, May 2007, p. 3.
291 *IASB Update*, IASB, July 2007, p. 4.
292 *IASB Update*, IASB, October 2007, p. 2 and 3.
293 IAS 37, para. 10.
294 IAS 37 ED, para. 10.
295 IAS 37 ED, paras. BC54-59.
296 IAS 37 ED, para. BC60.
297 *IASB Update*, IASB, May 2007, p. 3.
298 *IASB Update*, IASB, July 2007, p. 5.
299 IAS 37 ED, para. A22.
300 IAS 37, para. 72.
301 IAS 37 ED, para. BC68.
302 IAS 37 ED, para. BC69.
303 *IASB Update*, IASB, April 2008, p. 2.
304 IAS 37 ED, para. 72.
305 IAS 37 ED, para. 72.
306 IAS 37 ED, para. BC92.
307 IAS 37 ED, para. 72.
308 *IASB Work Plan – projected timetable as at 1 August 2009*, IASB.
309 Information for Observers (December 2008 IASB Meeting), *Agenda proposal: rate-regulated activities (Agenda Paper 12)*, para. 14.
310 ED 2009/8, para. BC8.
311 *IASB Work Plan – projected timetable as at 1 August 2009*, IASB.
312 ED 2009/8, para. 3.
313 ED 2009/8, Appendix A.
314 ED 2009/8, para. 4.
315 ED 2009/8, para. BC14.
316 ED 2009/8, para. 6.
317 ED 2009/8, para. 8.
318 ED 2009/8, para. 10.
319 ED 2009/8, para. 12.
320 ED 2009/8, para. 13.
321 ED 2009/8, para. 22.
322 ED 2009/8, para. 23.
323 ED 2009/8, para. 25.
324 ED 2009/8, para. 26.
325 ED 2009/8, para. 27.
326 *IASB Update*, IASB, December 2007, p. 1.
327 *IASB Update*, IASB, May 2008, p. 4.
328 Project Update, *Emission Trading Schemes*, IASB, November 2008, para. 1.
329 *IASB Update*, IASB, March 2009, p. 2.
330 *IASB Work Plan – projected timetable as at 1 August 2009*, IASB.

Chapter 25   Revenue recognition

1   THE NATURE OF REVENUE

Revenue is generally discussed in accounting literature in terms of inflows of assets to an entity that occur as a result of outflows of goods and services from the entity. For this reason, the concept of revenue has normally been associated with specific accounting procedures that were primarily directed towards determining the timing and measurement of revenue and, until relatively recently, the revenue recognition debate has taken place in the context of the historical cost system. The original version of IAS 18 – *Revenue Recognition* – which was issued in 1982, defined revenue as the 'gross inflow of cash, receivables or other consideration arising in the course of the ordinary activities of an entity from the sale of goods, from the rendering of services, and from the use by others of entity resources yielding interest, royalties and dividends'.[1] The accounting principles that evolved focused on determining when transactions should be recognised in the financial statements, what amounts were involved in each transaction, how these amounts should be classified and how they should be allocated between accounting periods.

Historical cost accounting in its pure form avoids having to take a valuation approach to financial reporting by virtue of the fact that it is transactions-based; in other words, it relies on transactions to determine the recognition and measurement of assets, liabilities, revenues and expenses. Over the life of an entity, its total income will be represented by net cash flows generated; however, because of the requirement to prepare periodic financial statements, it is necessary to break up the entity's operating cycle into reporting periods. The effect of this is that at each reporting date the entity will have entered into a number of transactions that are incomplete; for example, it might have delivered a product or service to a customer for which payment has not been received, or it might have received payment in respect of a product or service yet to be delivered. Alternatively, it might have expended cash on costs that relate to future sales transactions, or it might have received goods and services that it has not yet paid for in cash.

Consequently, the most important accounting questions that have to be answered revolve around how to allocate the effects of these incomplete transactions between periods for reporting purposes, as opposed to simply letting them fall into the periods in which cash is either received or paid. Under historical cost accounting this allocation process is based on two, sometimes conflicting, fundamental accounting concepts: accruals (or matching), which attempts to allocate the costs associated with earning revenues to the periods in which the related revenues will be reported; and prudence (or conservatism), under which revenue and profits are not anticipated, whilst anticipated losses are provided for as soon as they are foreseen, with the result that costs are not deferred to the future if there is doubt as to their recoverability.

As a result, the pure historical cost balance sheet contains items of two types: cash (and similar monetary items), and debits and credits that arise as a result of allocating the effects of transactions between reporting periods by applying the accruals and prudence concepts; in other words, the balance sheet simply reflects the balances that result from the entity preparing an accruals-based profit and loss account rather than a receipts and payments account. A non-monetary asset under the historical cost system is purely a deferred cost that has been incurred before the balance sheet date and, by applying the accruals concept, is expected (provided it passes the prudence test) to give rise to economic benefits in periods beyond the balance sheet date, so as to justify it being carried forward. Similarly, the balance sheet incorporates non-monetary credit balances that are awaiting recognition in the profit and loss account but, as a result of the application of the prudence and/or matching concepts, have been deferred to future reporting periods.

However, financial reporting under IFRS is not a pure historical cost system; it incorporates a mixed model that embraces both historical costs and fair values. Moreover, the IASB's accounting model is based on fair values, meaning that gains and losses are determined by reference to the change in fair value that has occurred over the financial reporting period. This approach is evident in a number of standards, including IAS 39 – *Financial Instruments: Recognition and Measurement*, IAS 40 – *Investment Property*, IAS 41 – *Agriculture* – and IFRS 2 – *Share-based payment*. Other standards, such as IAS 16 – *Property, Plant and Equipment*, IAS 36 – *Impairment of Assets*, IAS 38 – *Intangible Assets*, IAS 37 – *Provisions, Contingent Liabilities and Contingent Assets* – and IFRS 5 – *Non-current Assets Held for Sale and Discontinued Operations* – contain elements of fair value measurement. It is clear also that as new standards are developed, greater emphasis will be placed on the balance sheet, with fair value as the relevant measurement attribute.

At the same time, though, the international standard that deals with revenue recognition, IAS 18 – *Revenue* – was issued in its original form in 1982 and received its last major revision in 1993. Consequently, it is a standard that is based on historical cost principles, not fair value. Thus, it is a standard that focuses on profit or loss, not assets and liabilities and therefore relies heavily on the concepts of prudence and matching.

This means that the traditional historical cost approach to revenue recognition remains in place for most practical purposes. For companies and their auditors, this is problematic: IAS 18 does not cope very well with a mixed model approach and does not address many of the complex transactions undertaken by modern business. In particular, transactions involving multiple deliverables – such as those found in the telecommunications and information technology sectors – present difficulties that are not addressed specifically in the literature.

The chapter discusses the subject drawing on both IASB and US pronouncements. For companies reporting under IFRS, IAS 18 is the main source of authoritative guidance on revenue recognition, but several other standards also address revenue recognition issues. These include IAS 11 – *Construction Contracts*, IAS 17 – *Leases*, IFRS 4 – *Insurance Contracts*, SIC-13 – *Jointly Controlled Entities – Non-Monetary Contributions by Venturers*, SIC-31 – *Revenue – Barter Transactions Involving Advertising Services*, IFRIC 13 – *Customer Loyalty Programmes*, IFRIC 15 – *Agreements for the Construction of Real Estate* – and IFRIC 18 – *Transfers of Assets from Customers*. In most cases, this revenue recognition guidance was developed in order to deal with specific issues on a piecemeal basis, rather than to follow any form of conceptual approach to revenue recognition.

The US in particular has a substantial body of literature on revenue recognition that can, on occasion, prove useful when there is no IFRS guidance available. Historically this was particularly relevant for IFRS-reporting companies registered with the US SEC, who wished to avoid as far as possible having IFRS/US GAAP differences. This is now less significant as reconciliation to US GAAP is no longer required (see 4.1 below). However, such differences are sometimes unavoidable, and it is not always the case that a revenue recognition policy under US GAAP is acceptable under IFRS, and vice versa.

The IASB and FASB have been working on a joint project to develop a new approach to revenue recognition for some years and this has recently become a much higher priority. The Boards see a revenue recognition standard as one of its chief areas of focus now that it expects the adoption of IFRS by all major markets. The revised proposals have now been issued in a discussion paper and these are outlined at 5 below.

2 THE TIMING OF REVENUE RECOGNITION

Under the historical cost system revenues are the inflows of assets to an entity as a result of the transfer of products and services by the entity to its customers during a period of time, and are recorded at the cash amount received or expected to be received (or, in the case of non-monetary exchanges, at their cash equivalent) as the result of these exchange transactions. However, because of the system of periodic financial reporting, it is necessary to determine the point (or points) in time when revenue should be measured and reported. This has traditionally been governed by what is known as the 'realisation principle', which acknowledges the fact that for revenue to be recognised it is not sufficient merely for a sale to have been made – there has to be a certain degree of performance by the vendor as well. Whilst there are many different (and sometime inconsistent) rules for different circumstances, the rules underlying revenue recognition have been developed from two broad approaches to the recognition of revenue: the critical event and the accretion approaches, each of which is appropriate under particular circumstances. These are discussed below.

2.1   The critical event approach

The fundamental approach to revenue recognition under both IFRS and US GAAP is still built on the foundation of critical event theory and the realisation principle.

The critical event approach is based on the belief that revenue is earned at the point in the operating cycle when the most critical decision is made or the most critical act is performed.[2] In theory, the critical event could occur at various stages during the operating cycle; for example, at the completion of production, at the time of sale, at the time of delivery or at the time of cash collection.

Revenue recognition is subject to a number of measurement uncertainties which could occur at any of these points. However, since these uncertainties fall away at various stages throughout the operating cycle, it is necessary to identify a point in the cycle at which the remaining uncertainties can be estimated with sufficient accuracy to enable revenue to be recognised. As discussed later in this chapter, the decision is often not straightforward; further complications arise in the case of transactions that involve multiple elements and/or significant post-delivery obligations.

2.1.1   The recognition of revenue at the completion of production

An entity may enter into a firm contract for the production and delivery of a product, where the sales price will have been determined and the selling costs will have already been incurred. Consequently, provided that both the delivery expenses and the bad debt risk can reasonably be assessed, it may be appropriate to report revenue on this basis, unless it is a transaction for which the percentage of completion method is mandated by IAS 11 or IAS 18. The completed contract method of recognising revenue on construction contracts is not common and is not permitted under IFRS (see Chapter 21).

The US FASB's Concepts Statement 5 – *Recognition and Measurement in Financial Statements of Business Enterprises* – allows a similar treatment. It acknowledges that revenue may be recognised on the completion of production of such assets, provided that they consist of interchangeable units and quoted prices are available in an active market that can rapidly absorb the quantity held by the entity without significantly affecting the price.[3]

2.1.2   The recognition of revenue at the time of sale

The point of sale is probably the most widely used basis of recognising revenue from transactions involving the sale of goods. The sale is usually the critical point in the earning process when most of the significant uncertainties are eliminated; the only uncertainties that are likely to remain are those of possible return of the goods (where the customer has the right to do so, thereby cancelling the sale), the failure to collect the sales price (in the case of a credit sale), and any future liabilities in terms of any express or implied customer warranties. Under normal circumstances, these uncertainties will be both minimal and estimable to a reasonable degree of accuracy, based, *inter alia*, on past experience.

However, should revenues be recognised at the time of sale if the sale takes place before production, or if delivery only takes place at some significantly distant time in the future? In practice, the time of sale is generally taken to be the point of delivery; among other reasons, this reflects the law in a large number of jurisdictions, under which title passes to the buyer upon delivery, whether or not payment has been made.

See 3.7 below for a discussion of the principles laid down in IAS 18 for determining when to recognise revenue from a transaction involving the sale of goods.

2.1.3 *The recognition of revenue subsequent to delivery*

The uncertainties that exist after delivery may be of such significance that recognition should be delayed beyond the normal recognition point.

If the principal uncertainty concerns collectibility, it might be appropriate to defer recognition of the whole sale (and not just the profit) until collection is reasonably assured – as is the requirement under US GAAP.

The entity may sell its product but give the customer the right to return the goods (for example, in the case of a mail order business where the customer is given an approval period of, say, 14 days). Revenue may be recognised on delivery if future returns can be predicted reasonably accurately; otherwise it should be recognised on receipt of payment for the goods, or on customer acceptance of the goods and express or implied acknowledgement of the liability for payment, or after the 14 days have elapsed – whichever is considered to be the most appropriate under the circumstances.

In fact, this is an area where practice has been somewhat inconsistent. A transaction with a right of return is usually accounted for as a sale, whereas revenue from a transaction with a 14-day acceptance period is usually deferred – despite the fact that the transactions are virtually identical in terms of the legal rights and obligations of the parties.

This area of uncertainty is dealt with in the US under SFAS 48 – *Revenue Recognition When Right of Return Exists* – which states that if an entity sells its product but gives the buyer the right to return the product, revenue from the sales transaction is recognised at time of sale only if *all* of the following conditions are met:[4]

(a)   the seller's price to the buyer is substantially fixed or determinable at the date of sale;

(b)   the buyer has paid the seller, or the buyer is obligated to pay the seller and the obligation is not contingent on resale of the product;

(c)   the buyer's obligation to the seller would not be changed in the event of theft or physical destruction or damage of the product;

(d)   the buyer acquiring the product for resale has economic substance apart from that provided by the seller (i.e. the buyer does not merely exist 'on paper' with little or no physical facilities, having been established by the seller primarily for the purpose of recognising revenue);

(e)   the seller does not have significant obligations for future performance to directly bring about resale of the product by the buyer; and

(f)   the amount of future returns can be reasonably estimated.

Revenue that was not recognised at the time of sale because these conditions were not met should be recognised either when the return privilege has 'substantially expired', or when all the above conditions are met, whichever occurs first.[5]

The ability to make a reasonable estimate of future returns depends on many factors and will vary from one case to the next. Furthermore, SFAS 48 lists the following factors as being those that might impair a seller's ability to make such an estimate:[6]

(a)   the susceptibility of the product to significant external factors, such as technological obsolescence or changes in demand;

(b)   relatively long periods in which a particular product may be returned;

(c)   absence of historical experience with similar types of sales of similar products, or inability to apply such experience because of changing circumstances; for example, changes in the selling entity's marketing policies or its relationships with its customers; and

(d)   absence of a large volume of relatively homogeneous transactions.

The right of return is, therefore, viewed as a significant uncertainty that would preclude recognition under circumstances when the level of returns cannot be estimated. This means, for example, that a 14-day acceptance period would not require deferral of a sale, provided that the 14-day period is normal and routine.

2.2   The accretion approach

The accretion approach involves the recognition of revenue during the process of production, rather than at the end of a contract or when production is complete. There are four broad areas of entity activity where the application of the accretion approach might be appropriate.

(a)   *The use by others of entity resources*

The traditional accrual basis of accounting recognises revenue as entity resources are used by others; this approach is followed, for example, in the case of rental or interest income. However, the question of uncertainty of collection should always be considered, in which case it might be appropriate to delay recognition until cash is received or ultimate collection is assured beyond all reasonable doubt.

(b)   *Long-term contracts*

The second accepted application of the accretion approach to revenue reporting may be found in the accounting practice for long-term construction contracts. For example, under IAS 11 the amount of revenue to be recognised on construction contracts is determined according to the 'percentage-of-completion method', whereby contract revenue is matched with the contract costs incurred in reaching the stage of completion, resulting in the reporting of revenue, expenses and profit that can be attributed to the proportion of work completed at each balance sheet date.[7] Normally, the main uncertainties in the application of this approach are the estimation of the total costs and the degree of completion attained at the balance sheet date, particularly in the early stages of the contract. However, the selling price is sometimes uncertain as well, owing to contract modifications that give rise to revenue from 'extras'. Accounting for construction contracts is dealt with in detail in Chapter 21 of this book.

(c)   *The rendering of services*

This is probably the most widespread example of the application of the accretion approach. For example, IAS 18 requires that when the outcome of a transaction involving the rendering of services can be estimated reliably, revenue is recognised 'by reference to the stage of completion of the transaction at the end of the reporting period'[8] (in other words, using the percentage-of-completion method). This is discussed further at 3.8 below.

(d)   *Natural growth and 'biological transformation'*

Where an entity's activity involves production through natural growth or ageing, the accretion approach suggests that revenue should be recognised at identifiable stages during this process. For example, in the case of livestock, there could be market prices available at the various stages of growth; revenue could, therefore, be recognised throughout the production process by making comparative stock valuations and reporting the accretions at each accounting date.

This is dealt with by IAS 41. The standard requires application of fair value accounting to all 'biological assets' (which are defined as being living animals and plants)[9] throughout their period of growth. Entities that undertake agricultural activity are required to measure all biological assets at fair value less costs to sell,[10] whilst all agricultural produce should be measured at fair value less costs to sell at the point of harvest, and thereafter inventory accounting (IAS 2 – *Inventory*) should be applied. Fair value at harvest becomes 'cost' for IAS 2 purposes at the date at which that standard first applies.[11]

The change in fair value of biological assets during a period is reported in net profit or loss for the period.[12] However, IAS 41 contains no guidance on revenue recognition. In fact, the term 'revenue' is not mentioned in the entire standard and in the illustration of the statement of comprehensive income set out in the Appendix to IAS 41, there is no revenue line. IAS 41 amended IAS 18 to exclude from the scope of IAS 18 changes in fair value and initial recognition at fair value of agricultural assets and produce before harvest. Fair value gains and revenue from the sale of biological assets and agricultural produce should not be aggregated as this may result in double counting.

IAS 41 is dealt with in detail in Chapter 41 and there is a discussion of the treatment of fair value movements in the statement of comprehensive income at 2.5.1.

3   THE REQUIREMENTS OF IAS 18

3.1   Scope

Income is defined in the *Framework* as increases in economic benefits during the accounting period in the form of inflows or enhancements of assets or decreases of liabilities that result in increases in equity, other than those relating to contributions from equity participants.[13] Consequently, the revised IAS 18 – *Revenue* – embraces in its objective the definition of income from the *Framework* and states that 'revenue is income that arises in the course of ordinary activities of an entity and is referred to by a variety of different names including sales, fees, interest, dividends and royalties'.[14] However, it is noteworthy that, having established the link between the *Framework's* definition of income and IAS 18's definition of revenue, the IASC Board then abandoned the *Framework's* implied asset/liability approach to revenue recognition. IAS 18 reverts to the transactions-based critical event approach for the recognition of revenues derived from the sale of goods.

The standard explains that its objective is to prescribe the accounting treatment of revenue arising from the following types of transactions and events:

(a)   the sale of goods;

(b)   the rendering of services; and

(c)   the use by others of entity assets yielding interest, royalties and dividends.[15]

The term 'goods' includes goods produced by the entity for the purpose of sale and goods purchased for resale, such as merchandise purchased by a retailer or land and other property held for resale.[16]

The rendering of services typically involves the performance by the entity of a contractually agreed task over an agreed period of time. The services may be rendered within a single period or over more than one period. However, some contracts for the rendering of services are directly related to construction contracts, for example, those for the services of project managers and architects. Consequently, revenue arising from these contracts is not dealt with in IAS 18, but is dealt with in accordance with the requirements for construction contracts as specified in IAS 11 (see Chapter 21).[17]

The use by others of entity assets gives rise to revenue in the form of:

(a)   interest – charges for the use of cash or cash equivalents or amounts due to the entity;

(b)   royalties – charges for the use of long-term assets of the entity, for example, patents, trademarks, copyrights and computer software; and

(c)   dividends – distributions of profits to holders of equity investments in proportion to their holdings of a particular class of capital.[18]

It is important to note that there are a number of matters that the standard expressly states that it does not deal with, because they are all dealt with in other standards. These are:[19]

(a) lease agreements (see IAS 17). However, IAS 17 itself does not apply to licensing agreements for such items as motion picture films, video recordings, plays, manuscripts, patents and copyrights,[20] thus leaving a substantial gap in the revenue recognition literature (see Chapter 22 at 2.1.1);

(b) dividends arising from investments that are accounted for under the equity method (see Chapter 11);

(c) insurance contracts within the scope of IFRS 4 (see Chapter 43);

(d) the changes in the fair value of financial assets and financial liabilities or their disposal (see Chapter 32);

(e) the changes in the value of other current assets;

(f) revenue arising from the initial recognition and from changes in the fair value of biological assets related to agricultural activity (see Chapter 41);

(g) the initial recognition of agricultural produce (see Chapter 41); and

(h) the extraction of mineral ores (see Chapter 42).

3.2 The distinction between income, revenue and gains

As stated above, the IASB's *Framework* defines income as 'increases in economic benefits during the accounting period in the form of inflows or enhancements of assets or decreases of liabilities that result in increases in equity, other than those relating to contributions from equity participants'.[21] The *Framework* explains that this definition of income encompasses both 'revenue' and 'gains'. Revenue arises in the course of the ordinary activities of an entity and is referred to by a variety of different names including sales, fees, interest, dividends, royalties and rent; gains represent other items that meet the definition of income and may, or may not, arise in the course of the ordinary activities of an entity. Gains include, for example, those arising on the disposal of non-current assets. The definition of income also includes unrealised gains; for example, those arising on the revaluation of marketable securities and those resulting from increases in the carrying amount of long-term assets.[22]

The rules on offset in IAS 1 – *Presentation of Financial Statements* – distinguish between revenue and gains. The standard states that an entity undertakes, in the course of its ordinary activities, other transactions that do not generate revenue but are incidental to the main revenue-generating activities. When this presentation reflects the substance of the transaction or other event, the results of such transactions are presented, by netting any income with related expenses arising on the same transaction. For example, gains and losses on the disposal of non-current assets, including investments and operating assets, are reported by deducting from the proceeds on disposal the carrying amount of the asset and related selling expenses.[23] IAS 16 has a general rule that 'gains shall not be classified as revenue'.[24] The only exception to this rule is where an entity routinely sells property, plant and equipment that it has held for rental to others. This results from an amendment to IAS 16, effective for annual periods beginning on or after 1 January 2009, which is discussed further at 6.11.1 below.

IAS 18 defines 'revenue' as the 'gross inflow of economic benefits during the period arising in the course of the ordinary activities of an entity when those inflows result in increases in equity, other than increases relating to contributions from equity participants'.[25] In setting down this definition, IAS 18 explains that revenue includes only the gross inflows of economic benefits received and receivable by the entity on its own account. In practice, the distinction between gross and net revenues is not always straightforward but there is now guidance regarding revenue and agency relationships that is discussed below.

Amounts collected on behalf of third parties such as sales taxes, goods and services taxes and value added taxes are not economic benefits that flow to the entity and do not result in increases in equity. Therefore, they are excluded from revenue. See 6.8 below for a discussion of some of the factors that need to be considered in determining whether gross or net revenue presentation is appropriate in relation to excise taxes and goods and services taxes.

3.3   Revenue and agency relationships

In an agency relationship, the gross inflows of economic benefits include amounts collected on behalf of the principal and which do not result in increases in equity for the entity. The amounts collected on behalf of the principal are not revenue; instead, revenue is the amount of commission.[26]

As part of its Annual Improvements project the IASB, in April 2009, added guidance to the Appendix of IAS 18 to help determine whether an entity is acting as a principal or as an agent.[27] Previously IFRS contained no guidance in making this determination. The Appendix to IAS 18 now starts by explaining that this is a subjective matter requiring consideration of all facts and circumstances and that an entity is acting as a principal when it has exposure to the significant risks and rewards associated with the sale of goods or rendering of services. This guidance then includes four criteria that, individually or in combination, indicate that an entity is acting as principal:[28]

- the entity has the primary responsibility for providing the goods or services to the customer or for fulfilling the order, for example by being responsible for the acceptability of the products or services ordered or purchased by the customer;

- the entity has inventory risk before or after the customer order, during shipping or on return;

- the entity has latitude in establishing prices, either directly or indirectly, for example by providing additional goods or services; and

- the entity bears the customer's credit risk on the receivable due from the customer.[29]

Conversely an entity is acting as agent when it does not have exposure to the significant risks and rewards associated with the sale of goods or rendering of services and this may be evidenced by the entity earning a predetermined amount, perhaps a fixed fee per transaction or a stated percentage of customer billings.[30]

This amendment is closely related to the more detailed US GAAP guidance contained in EITF 99-19 – *Reporting Revenue Gross as a Principal versus Net as an Agent*, which until now has been widely used as guidance on agency and gross versus net accounting.

Since this additional guidance is included within the Appendix to the standard there are no transitional provisions, any changes to accounting from consideration of this guidance will require restatement. However the guidance is both limited in detail and uncontroversial. Therefore, it is unlikely to change existing practices.

Sales to parties that are acting as agents are also addressed by IAS 18. In order to recognise revenue on the sale of goods the seller must have transferred the significant risks and rewards of ownership to the buyer and must not retain either continuing managerial involvement to the degree usually associated with ownership or effective control over the goods sold.[31] A specific example is given: revenue from sales to intermediate parties, such as distributors, dealers or others for resale is generally recognised when the risks and rewards of ownership have passed. However, when the buyer is acting, in substance, as an agent, the sale is treated as a consignment sale, i.e. no revenue is recognised until the goods are sold to a third party.[32]

3.4   Income and distributable profits

IFRS generally and IAS 18 specifically do not address the issue of profit distribution. Whether or not revenue and gains recognised in accordance with IFRS are distributable to shareholders of an entity will depend entirely on the national laws and regulations with which the entity needs to comply. Thus, income reported in accordance with IFRS does not necessarily imply that such income would either be realised or distributable under a reporting entity's applicable national legislation.

3.5   Measurement of revenue

Revenue should be measured at the fair value of the consideration received or receivable.[33] IAS 18 states that the amount of revenue arising on a transaction is usually determined by agreement between the entity and the buyer or user of the asset. This means that it is measured at the fair value of the consideration received or receivable taking into account the amount of any trade discounts and volume rebates allowed by the entity.[34] The standard defines fair value as 'the amount for which an asset could be exchanged, or a liability settled, between knowledgeable, willing parties in an arm's length transaction'.[35]

Usually, this will present little difficulty, as the consideration will normally be in the form of cash or cash equivalents and the amount of revenue will be the amount of cash or cash equivalents received or receivable. However, if the inflow is deferred, the fair value of the consideration will then be less than the nominal amount of cash received or receivable. IAS 18 attempts to deal with this by introducing a discounting requirement. Consequently, when an arrangement effectively constitutes a financing transaction, the fair value of the consideration is determined by discounting all future receipts using an imputed rate of interest. The imputed rate of interest is the more clearly determinable of either:

(a)   the prevailing rate for a similar instrument of an issuer with a similar credit rating; or

(b)   a rate of interest that discounts the nominal amount of the instrument to the current cash sales price of the goods or services.[36]

The difference between the fair value and the nominal amount of the consideration is recognised as interest revenue using the effective interest method as set out in IAS 39, paragraphs 9 and AG5 to AG8.[37] The application of the effective interest rate method is discussed in Chapter 32 at 5.

A further issue arises if a company offers prompt settlement discounts to its customers. An example of a prompt settlement discount is a reduction of 5% of the selling price for paying an invoice within 7 days instead of the usual 60 days. In such cases, in order to comply with IAS 18's requirement that revenue should be measured at the fair value of the consideration received or receivable,[38] prompt settlement discounts should be estimated at the time of sale and deducted from revenues.

3.6   Identification of the transaction

IAS 18 states that the recognition criteria of the standard are usually applied separately to each transaction. However, it goes on to say that, in certain circumstances, it is necessary to apply the recognition criteria to the separately identifiable components of a single transaction in order to reflect the substance of the transaction.[39] This means quite simply that transactions have to be analysed in accordance with their economic substance in order to determine whether they should be combined or segmented for revenue recognition purposes. For example, when the selling price of a product includes an identifiable amount for subsequent servicing, that amount is deferred and recognised as revenue over the period during which the service is performed.

Conversely, the recognition criteria are applied to two or more transactions together when they are linked in such a way that the commercial effect cannot be understood without reference to the series of transactions as a whole – as is the case, for example, with the sale of mobile phones combined with related service contracts (the issue of bundled offers in the telecommunications sector is discussed below at 6.7). A further example might be where an entity sells goods and, at the same time, enters into a separate agreement to repurchase the goods at a later date, thus negating the substantive effect of the transaction; in such a case, the two transactions are dealt with together.[40] The following extracts from the revenue recognition policies of Sandvik and Renault illustrate this point:

Extract 25.1: Sandvik AB (2008)

Accounting policies [extract]
REVENUE [extract]
Revenue from sales and services [extract]

Buy-back commitments may entail that sales revenue cannot be recognized if the agreement with the customer in reality implies that the customer has only rented the product for a certain period of time.

Extract 25.2: Renault SA (2007)

7.2.6.1 Accounting policies and scope of consolidation [extract]

2 – ACCOUNTING POLICIES [extract]

G – Revenues and margin [extract]

Sales of goods and services and margin recognition [extract]

Sales and margin recognition

Sales of goods are recognised when vehicles are made available to the distribution network in the case of non-Group dealers, or upon delivery to the end-user in the case of direct sales. The margin on sales is recognised immediately for normal sales by the Automobile division, including sales with associated financing contracts that can be considered as finance leases (long-term or with a purchase option). However, no sale is recognised when the vehicle is covered by an operating lease from a Group finance company or the Group has made a buy-back commitment, when the term of the contract covers an insufficient portion of the vehicle's useful life.

In such cases, the transactions are recorded as operating leases and included in sales of services. The difference between the price paid by the customer and the buy-back price is treated as rental income, and spread over the period the vehicle is at the customer's disposal. The production cost for the new vehicle concerned is recorded in inventories for contracts of less than one year, or included in property, plant and equipment under vehicles leased to customers when the contracts exceed one year. The sale of the vehicle as second-hand at the end of the lease gives rise to recognition of sales revenue and the related margin. As soon as a loss is expected on the resale, a provision (if the vehicle is in inventories) or additional depreciation (if the vehicle is included in property, plant and equipment) is recognised to cover the loss.

However, IAS 18 does not establish criteria for segmenting and combining revenue transactions. On the other hand, IAS 11 includes a requirement similar to that of IAS 18 in that it requires companies to apply the standard to separately identifiable components of a single construction contract, or to a group of contracts together, in order to reflect the substance of a contract or a group of contracts.[41] IAS 11 also sets down the following criteria to be used as guidance in determining whether construction contracts should be combined or segmented:[42]

When a contract covers a number of assets, the construction of each asset should be treated as a separate construction contract when:

(a) separate proposals have been submitted for each asset;

(b) each asset has been subject to separate negotiation and the contractor and customer have been able to accept or reject that part of the contract relating to each asset; and

(c) the costs and revenues of each asset can be identified.

A group of contracts, whether with a single customer or with several customers, should be treated as a single construction contract when:

(a) the group of contracts is negotiated as a single package;

(b) the contracts are so closely interrelated that they are, in effect, part of a single project with an overall profit margin; and

(c) the contracts are performed concurrently or in a continuous sequence.

A contract may provide for the construction of an additional asset at the option of the customer or may be amended to include the construction of an additional asset.

The construction of the additional asset should be treated as a separate construction contract when:

(a)   the asset differs significantly in design, technology or function from the asset or assets covered by the original contract; or

(b)   the price of the asset is negotiated without regard to the original contract price.

In the absence of any equivalent practical guidance in IAS 18, the above criteria set out in IAS 11 may be helpful in determining whether revenue transactions should be combined or segmented. However the underlying principle in paragraph 13 of IAS 18, which focuses on whether combination or segmentation is necessary to reflect the substance and understand the commercial effect, should remain the primary consideration in making this assessment. The practical issues in connection with combining and segmenting contracts (including IFRIC's discussion thereof) are considered further in Chapter 21 at 4.2. In the case of certain arrangements with multiple deliverables, it may also be helpful (but not required), under the hierarchy in IAS 8 – *Accounting Policies, Changes in Accounting Estimates and Errors*,[43] to refer to EITF 00-21 – *Revenue Arrangements with Multiple Deliverables* – which deals with the issue of separating elements of revenue (see 6.7.1 below for a discussion of how EITF 00-21 has been applied to recognising revenue on bundled offers in the telecommunications sector).

3.7   The sale of goods

IAS 18 lays down the following five criteria that must be satisfied in order to recognise revenue from the sale of goods:[44]

(a)   the entity has transferred to the buyer the significant risks and rewards of ownership of the goods;

(b)   the entity retains neither continuing managerial involvement to the degree usually associated with ownership nor effective control over the goods sold;

(c)   the amount of revenue can be measured reliably;

(d)   it is probable that the economic benefits associated with the transaction will flow to the entity; and

(e)   the costs incurred or to be incurred in respect of the transaction can be measured reliably.

If the costs incurred cannot be measured reliably, the standard requires that 'any consideration already received for the sale of the goods is recognised as a liability.'[45]

IAS 18 views the passing of risks and rewards as the most crucial of the five criteria, giving the following four examples of situations in which an entity may retain the significant risks and rewards of ownership:[46]

(a)   when the entity retains an obligation for unsatisfactory performance not covered by normal warranty provisions;

(b)   when the receipt of the revenue from a particular sale is contingent on the derivation of revenue by the buyer from its sale of the goods;

(c) when the goods are shipped subject to installation and the installation is a significant part of the contract which has not yet been completed by the entity; and

(d) when the buyer has the right to rescind the purchase for a reason specified in the sales contract and the entity is uncertain about the probability of return.

It is clear that the standard still advocates an earnings process-driven critical event approach to revenue recognition. It is, therefore, necessary to establish at which point in the earnings process both the significant risks and rewards of ownership are transferred from the seller to the buyer and any significant uncertainties (which would otherwise delay recognition) are removed. For example, the responsibilities of each party during the period between sale and delivery should be established, possibly by examination of the customer agreements. If the goods have merely to be uplifted by the buyer, and the seller has performed all his associated responsibilities, then the sale may be recognised immediately. However, if the substance of the sale is merely that an order has been placed, and the goods have still to be acquired or manufactured by the seller, then the sale should not be recognised.

The following extract from the accounting policies of Atlas Copco illustrates the deferral of revenue recognition until installation is completed in those cases where installation is a significant part of the contract:

Extract 25.3: Atlas Copco AB (2008)

Notes to the Consolidated Financial Statements [extract]

1. Significant accounting principles [extract]

Revenue recognition [extract]

Goods sold [extract]

Revenue from sale of goods is recognized when the significant risks and rewards of ownership have been transferred to the buyer, which in most cases occurs in connection with delivery. When the product requires installation and installation is a significant part of the contract, revenue is recognized when the installation is completed.

IAS 18 recognises also that, under certain circumstances, goods are sold subject to reservation of title in order to protect the collectibility of the amount due; in such circumstances, provided that the seller has transferred the significant risks and rewards of ownership, the transaction can be treated as a sale and revenue can be recognised.[47] The standard assumes that 'in most cases, the transfer of risks and rewards of ownership coincides with the transfer of legal title or the passing of possession to the buyer',[48] but acknowledges that this may not always be the case. Transfer of legal title is, therefore, not a condition for revenue recognition under IAS 18,[49] as the standard recognises that transactions occur where the transfer of risks and rewards of ownership occurs at a different time from the transfer of legal title or the passing of possession.[50]

This point is reinforced in the Appendix to IAS 18, which notes that laws in different countries may mean that the recognition criteria in the standard are met at different times. In particular, the law may determine the point in time at which an entity transfers the significant risks and rewards of ownership. Therefore, the examples in the Appendix need to be read in the context of the laws relating to the sale of goods in the country in which the transaction takes place.[51]

The following extracts from the financial statements of Smith & Nephew and Roche illustrate both the measurement principles of IAS 18 and the application of the critical event approach in determining the timing of revenue recognition:

Extract 25.4: Smith & Nephew plc (2007)

Notes to the Group Accounts [extract]

2.   **Accounting policies** [extract]

Revenue [extract]

Revenue comprises sales of products and services to third parties at amounts invoiced net of trade discounts and rebates, excluding taxes on revenue. Revenue from the sale of products is recognised upon transfer to the customer of the significant risks and rewards of ownership. This is generally when goods are despatched to customers except that sales of inventory located at customer premises and available for customers' immediate use are recognised when notification is received that the product has been implanted or used. Appropriate provisions for returns, trade discounts and rebates are deducted from revenue. Rebates comprise retrospective volume discounts granted to certain customers on attainment of certain levels of purchases from the Group. These are accrued over the course of the arrangement based on estimates of the level of business expected and adjusted at the end of the arrangement to reflect actual volumes.

Extract 25.5: Roche Holding Ltd (2008)

Notes to the Roche Group Consolidated Financial Statements [extract]

1.   **Summary of significant accounting policies** [extract]

Revenues

Sales represent amounts received and receivable for goods supplied to customers after deducting trade discounts, cash discounts and volume rebates, and exclude value added taxes and other taxes directly linked to sales. Revenues from the sale of products are recognised upon transfer to the customer of significant risks and rewards. Trade discounts, cash discounts and volume rebates are recorded on an accrual basis consistent with the recognition of the related sales. Estimates of expected sales returns, charge-backs and other rebates, including Medicaid in the United States and similar rebates in other countries, are also deducted from sales and recorded as accrued liabilities or provisions or as a deduction from accounts receivable. Such estimates are based on analyses of existing contractual or legislatively-mandated obligations, historical trends and the Group's experience. Other revenues are recorded as earned or as the services are performed. Where necessary, single transactions are split into separately identifiable components to reflect the substance of the transaction. Conversely, two or more transactions may be considered together for revenue recognition purposes, where the commercial effect cannot be understood without reference to the series of transactions as a whole.

3.8   The rendering of services

IAS 18 requires that when the outcome of a transaction involving the rendering of services can be estimated reliably, revenue is recognised 'by reference to the stage of completion of the transaction at the end of the reporting period'[52] (in other words, using the percentage-of-completion method). In applying the percentage-of-completion method, the requirements of IAS 11 are 'generally applicable to the recognition of revenue and the associated expenses for a transaction involving the rendering of services.'[53]

According to IAS 18, the outcome of a transaction can be estimated reliably when all the following conditions are satisfied:[54]

(a)   the amount of revenue can be measured reliably;

(b)   it is probable that the economic benefits associated with the transaction will flow to the entity;

(c)   the stage of completion of the transaction at the end of the reporting period can be measured reliably; and

(d)   the costs incurred for the transaction and the costs to complete the transaction can be measured reliably.

When the outcome cannot be estimated reliably, revenue is recognised only to the extent of the expenses recognised that are recoverable.[55] During the early stages of a transaction, it is often the case that the outcome of the transaction cannot be estimated reliably. Nevertheless, it may be probable that the enterprise will recover the transaction costs incurred. Therefore, revenue is recognised only to the extent of costs incurred that are expected to be recoverable. As the outcome of the transaction cannot be estimated reliably, no profit is recognised.[56] See an example of this in Nokia Corporation revenue recognition policy in Extract 25.7 below. When the outcome of a transaction cannot be estimated reliably and it is not probable that the costs incurred will be recovered, revenue is not recognised and the costs incurred are recognised as an expense. When the uncertainties that prevented the outcome of the contract being estimated reliably no longer exist, revenue is recognised by reference to the stage of completion of the transaction at the balance sheet date.[57]

The Appendix to IAS 18 provides several illustrative examples of transactions involving the rendering of services. All the examples are provided on the assumption that the amount of revenue can be measured reliably, it is probable that the economic benefits will flow to the entity and the costs incurred or to be incurred can be measured reliably. It is clear from these examples that, in the case of a transaction involving the rendering of services, the performance of the service is the critical event for revenue recognition.[58]

The standard claims that an entity is generally able to make reliable estimates after it has agreed to the following with the other parties to the transaction:[59]

(a)   each party's enforceable rights regarding the service to be provided and received by the parties;

(b)   the consideration to be exchanged; and

(c)   the manner and terms of settlement.

The standard suggests further that it is usually necessary for the entity to have an effective internal financial budgeting and reporting system. The entity reviews and, when necessary, revises the estimates of revenue as the service is performed. The need for such revisions does not necessarily indicate that the outcome of the transaction cannot be estimated reliably.[60]

When it comes to determining the stage of completion of a transaction, IAS 18 suggests three methods that may be used:[61]

(a)   surveys of work performed;

(b)   services performed to date as a percentage of total services to be performed; or

(c)   the proportion that costs incurred to date bear to the estimated total costs of the transaction. Only costs that reflect services performed to date are included in costs incurred to date. Only costs that reflect services performed or to be performed are included in the estimated total costs of the transaction.

For practical purposes, though, when services are performed by an indeterminate number of acts over a specified period, the standard states that revenue should be recognised on a straight-line basis over the specified period unless there is evidence that some other method better represents the stage of completion. However, when a specific act is much more significant than any other acts, the standard requires that the recognition of revenue be postponed until the significant act is executed.[62]

What this means in practice can be seen by considering outsourcing arrangements. These are contracts that require services to be provided on an ongoing basis, often for a number of years, rather than the provision of a single service or a number of services that constitute a single project. These arrangements are common across a wide range of services including processing, provision of telecommunications services, general professional advice, help desk support, accounting advice, maintenance or cleaning, The 'service' to which IAS 18's method applies is the individual act, whether it be the individual process, answering the telephone help line or cleaning the office each night. Clearly in most cases it would not be feasible to identify the costs and revenue for each of these acts so revenue is taken on a straight line over the contract term and costs are expensed as incurred.

The entities that provide outsourcing services frequently provide single services as well. The following revenue recognition policy for Cap Gemini illustrates both the treatment of revenue for outsourcing contracts and for its long-term contracts.

Extract 25.6: Cap Gemini S.A. (2007)

Notes to the consolidated financial statements [extract]

Note 1.   Accounting policies [extract]

F) Recognition of revenues and the cost of services rendered

The method for recognizing revenues and costs depends on the nature of the services rendered:

A. TIME AND MATERIALS CONTRACTS:

Revenues and costs relating to time and materials contracts are recognized as services are rendered.

B. LONG-TERM FIXED-PRICE CONTRACTS:

Revenues from long-term fixed-price contracts, including systems development and integration contracts, are recognized under the "percentage-of-completion" method. Costs related to long-term fixed price contracts are recognized as they are incurred.

> C. OUTSOURCING CONTRACTS:
>
> Revenues from outsourcing agreements are recognized over the life of the contract as the services are rendered. When the services are made up of different components which are not separately identifiable, the related revenues are recognized on a straight-line basis over the life of the contract.

Nokia provides an illustration of an accounting policy whereby revenue from contracts involving the modification of complex telecommunications equipment is recognised using the percentage-of-completion method:

> *Extract 25.7: Nokia Corporation (2008)*
>
> Notes to the consolidated financial statements [extract]
>
> 1.   Accounting principles [extract]
>
> Revenue recognition [extract]
>
> In addition, sales and cost of sales from contracts involving solutions achieved through modification of complex telecommunications equipment are recognized using the percentage of completion method when the outcome of the contract can be estimated reliably. A contract's outcome can be estimated reliably when total contract revenue and the costs to complete the contract can be estimated reliably, it is probable that the economic benefits associated with the contract will flow to the Group and the stage of contract completion can be measured reliably. When the Group is not able to meet those conditions, the policy is to recognize revenues only equal to costs incurred to date, to the extent that such costs are expected to be recovered.
>
> Progress towards completion is measured by reference to cost incurred to date as a percentage of estimated total project costs, the cost-to-cost method.

3.9   Exchanges of goods and services

Under IAS 18, when goods or services are exchanged or swapped for goods or services that are of a similar nature and value, the exchange is not regarded as a transaction that generates revenue. The standard notes exchanges of commodities like oil or milk, where suppliers exchange or swap inventories in various locations to fulfil demand on a timely basis in a particular location as examples of this. There are similar reasons behind exchanges of capacity in the telecommunications sector. When goods are sold or services are rendered in exchange for dissimilar goods or services, the exchange is regarded as a transaction that generates revenue. The revenue is measured at the fair value of the goods or services received, adjusted by the amount of any cash or cash equivalents transferred. When the fair value of the goods or services received cannot be measured reliably, the revenue is measured at the fair value of the goods or services given up, adjusted by the amount of any cash or cash equivalents transferred.[63]

IFRIC 18 – *Transfers of Assets from Customers* – provides guidance in situations where an entity receives an item of property, plant and equipment from a customer (or cash for the acquisition or construction of such items) that must then be used by the entity either to connect the customer to a network or to provide the customer ongoing access to a supply of goods or services.[64] These arrangements are relatively common in the utilities and automobile industries. The Interpretation is discussed at 6.13 below.

3.10   Exchanges of property plant and equipment

The accounting for exchanges of property, plant and equipment is dealt with in IAS 16, which takes a different approach to IAS 18's treatment of exchanges of goods and services. Following IAS 16's amendment in 2003, the IASB removed the distinction between similar and dissimilar assets that still remains in IAS 18 in respect of exchanges of goods and services. Instead, IAS 16 now requires property, plant and equipment acquired in exchange for a non-monetary asset or assets, or a combination of monetary and non-monetary assets to be accounted for at fair value, unless:

(a)   the exchange transaction lacks commercial substance, or

(b)   the fair value of neither the asset received nor the asset given up is reliably measurable.[65]

The acquired item is measured in this way even if an entity cannot immediately derecognise the asset given up.[66]

The standard notes further that the fair value of an asset for which comparable market transactions do not exist is reliably measurable if:

(a)   the variability in the range of reasonable fair value estimates is not significant for that asset, or

(b)   the probabilities of the various estimates within the range can be reasonably assessed and used in estimating fair value.[67]

If an entity is able to determine reliably the fair value of either the asset received or the asset given up, then the fair value of the asset given up is used to measure the cost of the asset received unless the fair value of the asset received is more clearly evident.[68] If the acquired item is not measured at fair value, its cost is measured at the carrying amount of the asset given up.[69] Exchanges of assets are discussed in Chapter 16 at 3.2.4.

BP p.l.c. is an example of a company that discloses an accounting policy for asset exchanges:

Extract 25.8: BP p.l.c. (2008)

Notes on financial statements [extract]

1   Significant accounting policies [extract]

Property, plant and equipment [extract]

Exchanges of assets are measured at fair value unless the exchange transaction lacks commercial substance or the fair value of neither the asset received nor the asset given up is reliably measurable. The cost of the acquired asset is measured at the fair value of the asset given up, unless the fair value of the asset received is more clearly evident. Where fair value is not used, the cost of the acquired asset is measured at the carrying amount of the asset given up. The gain or loss on derecognition of the asset given up is recognized in profit or loss.

IAS 16 stipulates that gains arising from the derecognition of property, plant and equipment may not be classified as revenue[70] and it is clear that this applies equally to derecognition by way of an exchange, sale and abandonment; this means that an exchange of property, plant and equipment does not result in the recognition of revenue.

IAS 38 – *Intangible Assets* – deals with exchanges of intangible assets, and includes the same requirements with respect to intangible assets as IAS 16 for exchanges of property, plant and equipment.[71]

IFRIC 18 – *Transfers of Assets from Customers* – provides guidance in situations where an entity receives an item of property, plant and equipment from a customer (or cash for the acquisition or construction of such items) that the entity must then use either to connect the customer to a network or to provide the customer ongoing access to a supply of goods or services.[72] These arrangements are relatively common in the utilities and automobile industries. The Interpretation is discussed at 6.13 below.

IFRS 5 – *Non-current Assets Held for Sale and Discontinued Operations* – lays down additional requirements for assets held for disposal; these requirements include measurement rules that affect the measurement of the amount of the gain on disposal to be recognised. These are discussed in Chapter 4 at 2.2.

3.11   Barter transactions involving advertising services

This is an issue that arose during the dotcom boom of the late 1990s and early 2000s, and is addressed in SIC-31. The issue arises where an entity (the Seller) enters into a barter transaction to provide advertising services in exchange for receiving advertising services from its customer (the Customer). Advertisements may be displayed on the Internet or poster sites, broadcast on television or radio, published in magazines or journals, or presented in another medium. In some cases, no cash or other consideration is exchanged between the entities. In some other cases, equal or approximately equal amounts of cash or other consideration are also exchanged.

It is clear that, under IAS 18, a seller that provides advertising services in the course of its ordinary activities recognises revenue from a barter transaction involving advertising when, amongst other criteria, the services exchanged are dissimilar,[73] and the amount of revenue can be measured reliably.[74] However, an exchange of similar advertising services is not a transaction that generates revenue under IAS 18.

The issue that the Standing Interpretations Committee (SIC) considered was under what circumstances can a Seller reliably measure revenue at the fair value of advertising services received or provided in a barter transaction involving dissimilar services?[75]

The SIC concluded that revenue from a barter transaction involving advertising cannot be measured reliably at the fair value of advertising services received. However, a Seller can reliably measure revenue at the fair value of the advertising services it provides in a barter transaction, by reference only to non-barter transactions that:

(a)   involve advertising similar to the advertising in the barter transaction;

(b)   occur frequently;

(c)   represent a predominant number of transactions and amount when compared to all transactions to provide advertising that is similar to the advertising in the barter transaction;

(d)   involve cash and/or another form of consideration (e.g. marketable securities, non-monetary assets, and other services) that has a reliably measurable fair value; and

(e)   do not involve the same counterparty as in the barter transaction.[76]

The conditions represent a relatively high hurdle for companies to overcome, and it would seem that in most instances they would find it difficult to be able to recognise any revenue. For example, a swap of cheques for equal or substantially equal amounts between the same entities that provide and receive advertising services does not provide reliable evidence of fair value. An exchange of advertising services that also includes only partial cash payment provides reliable evidence of the fair value of the transaction to the extent of the cash component (except when partial cash payments of equal or substantially equal amounts are swapped), but does not provide reliable evidence of the fair value of the entire transaction.[77]

Barter transaction involving services occur mainly in the media industry. German television corporation, ProSiebenSat.1 discloses the following accounting policy for barter transactions involving advertising:

Extract 25.9: ProSiebenSat.1 Media AG (2008)

Notes to the consolidated financial statements [extract]

[6]   ACCOUNTING POLICIES [extract]

Recognition of revenues [extract]

Revenues from barter transactions are considered realized when goods or services that are not of the same kind are exchanged, and the amount of the proceeds and costs, as well as the economic benefit, can be clearly measured. Revenues are recognized at the market value of the received bartered item or service, and may be adjusted with an additional cash payment. Barter transactions at the ProSiebenSat.1 Group are primarily trade-off transactions relating to the sale of advertising time.

In our view, SIC-31 was issued as a specific anti-abuse rule that does not have wider implications and should not be applied to other situations by analogy.

3.12   Interest, royalties and dividends

When it is probable that the economic benefits associated with the transaction will flow to the entity and that the amount of revenue can be measured reliably, IAS 18 requires that the revenue arising from the use by others of entity assets yielding interest, royalties and dividends should be recognised as follows:[78]

(a)   *interest:* using the effective interest method as set out in IAS 39, paragraphs 9 and AG5-AG8;

(b)   *royalties:* on an accrual basis in accordance with the substance of the relevant agreement; and

(c)   *dividends:* when the shareholder's right to receive payment is established.

When unpaid interest has accrued before the acquisition of an interest-bearing investment, the subsequent receipt of interest is allocated between pre-acquisition and post-acquisition periods; only the post-acquisition portion is recognised as revenue.

Until May 2008, IAS 18 required an entity to assess whether dividends on equity securities had been declared from pre-acquisition net income and, if so, those dividends were deducted from the cost of the securities.[79] This was consistent with the 'cost method' in IAS 27 – *Consolidated and Separate Financial Statements.* IAS 27 has been revised to remove all references to the cost method and instead states that an entity is to recognise dividends from subsidiaries, jointly controlled entities or associates in profit or loss in its separate financial statements when its right to receive the dividend is established.[80] Entities will now be required to determine as a separate exercise whether or not the investment has been impaired as a result of the dividend. IAS 36 has been expanded to include specific triggers for impairment reviews on receipt of dividends. IAS 18 has been modified in line with this; references to dividends from pre-acquisition profits being removed from paragraph 32. The amendments are mandatory from 1 January 2009. This change is discussed in Chapter 8 at 2.1.

Royalties accrue in accordance with the terms of the relevant agreement and are usually recognised on that basis unless, having regard to the substance of the agreement, it is more appropriate to recognise revenue on some other systematic and rational basis.[81]

Anglo Platinum provides a straightforward example of accounting policies for dividends, interest and royalties:

Extract 25.10: Anglo Platinum Limited (2007)

PRINCIPAL ACCOUNTING POLICIES [extract]

Revenue recognition [extract]

- Dividends are recognised when the right to receive payment is established.
- Interest is recognised on a time proportional basis, which takes into account the effective yield on the asset over the period it is expected to be held.
- Royalties are recognised when the right to receive payment is established.

3.13   Uncollectible revenue

Revenue is recognised only when it is probable that the economic benefits associated with the transaction will flow to the entity. In some cases, this may not be probable until the consideration is received or until an uncertainty is removed. However, when an uncertainty arises about the collectibility of an amount already included in revenue, the uncollectible amount or the amount in respect of which recovery has ceased to be probable is recognised as an expense, rather than as an adjustment of the amount of revenue originally recognised.[82]

3.14   Disclosure

IAS 18's disclosure requirements relate to both revenue recognition policies and amounts included in the financial statements under the different categories of revenue. They are set down in the standard as follows:[83]

(a)   the accounting policies adopted for the recognition of revenue including the methods adopted to determine the stage of completion of transactions involving the rendering of services;

(b)   the amount of each significant category of revenue recognised during the period including revenue arising from:

  (i)   the sale of goods;

  (ii)   the rendering of services;

  (iii)   interest;

  (iv)   royalties;

  (v)   dividends; and

(c)   the amount of revenue arising from exchanges of goods or services included in each significant category of revenue.

The disclosures required under (b) and (c) above may be provided in the notes to the financial statements, rather than on the face of the statement of comprehensive income or separate income statement (if presented).

3.15   What should be shown in the statement of comprehensive income within revenue?

IAS 1 contains minimum requirement for the contents of the statement of comprehensive income. A revised standard was issued in 2007, with an implementation date of 1 January 2009. This states that an entity is to present all items of income and expense recognised in a period either in a single 'statement of comprehensive income', or in two statements:

• a statement displaying components of profit or loss (separate income statement); and

• a second statement beginning with profit or loss and displaying components of other comprehensive income (the statement of comprehensive income).

If the second approach applies, the separate income statement will correspond to the income statement required by the previous version of the standard. There are minimum requirements for what must be disclosed on the face of the statement of comprehensive income or separate income statement (if presented). The formats and their requirements are described in Chapter 3. The following must be shown on the face of the statement of comprehensive income or separate income statement (if presented):[84]

(a)   revenue;

(b)   finance costs; and

(c)   share of the profit or loss of associates and joint ventures accounted for using the equity method.

IAS 1 goes on to state that additional line items, headings and subtotals are to be presented in the statement of comprehensive income and the separate income statement (if presented) when such presentation is relevant to an understanding of the entity's financial performance. Additional line items are included, and the descriptions used and the ordering of items are amended, when this is necessary to explain the elements of financial performance. Factors to be considered include materiality and the nature and function of the components of income and expenses.[85]

These requirements provide a company with a substantial amount of flexibility with regard to the presentation of its statement of comprehensive income and separate income statement (if presented). However, they also raise a number of practical questions about the presentation of revenue, such as:

* can the amount for 'finance costs' be shown net of interest and other finance income? and

* can gains on disposal of property, plant and equipment be shown within revenue?

3.15.1 Interest and other finance income

It used to be fairly widespread practice under a number of national GAAPs for companies to show finance costs net of interest and other finance income. However paragraphs 32 and 82 of IAS 1 preclude an entity presenting 'net finance costs' on the face of the statement of comprehensive income and separate income statement (if presented) without showing separately the finance costs and finance revenue included in the net amount. IAS 1 paragraph 32 requires that assets and liabilities, or income and expenses, shall not be offset unless required or permitted by a Standard or an Interpretation.[86] The standard goes on to explain that offsetting in the statement of comprehensive income, separate income statement (if presented) or balance sheet, except when offsetting reflects the substance of the transaction or other event, detracts from the ability of users both to understand the transactions, other events and conditions that have occurred and to assess the entity's future cash flows.[87] IAS 1 paragraph 82 lists 'finance costs' as one of the line items that must be included on the face of the statement of comprehensive income or separate income statement (if presented).[88] IAS 18 requires interest income to be disclosed as one of the categories of revenue.[89]

In *Improvements to IFRSs* issued in May 2008, the IASB amended IFRS 7 – *Financial Instruments: Disclosures* – paragraph IG13 and removed a reference to 'total interest income' as a component of finance costs. This amendment removed an inconsistency with paragraph 32 of IAS 1, which precludes the offsetting of income and expenses (except when required or permitted by an IFRS), thereby confirming the IASB's intention that finance income and finance expense be separately disclosed on the face of profit or loss. Of course, there is nothing to prevent an entity presenting gross interest income and gross interest expense on the face of the statement of comprehensive income or separate income statement (if presented), and then striking a sub-total that shows net interest.

IAS 1 permits some gains and losses arising from a group of similar transactions to be reported on a net basis, for example, foreign exchange gains and losses or gains and losses arising on financial instruments held for trading. Such gains and losses are, however, reported separately if they are material.[90]

Although there is no Standard or Interpretation that permits interest income to be offset against interest expense, we believe that net presentation is appropriate in the case of trading activities; in our view, the interest income on financial instruments (e.g. bonds) that are held as trading assets (e.g. by a financial institution) could be included within net trading income. UBS provide a good example of such an approach:

Extract 25.11: UBS AG (2007)

Notes to the Financial Statements [extract]

Income Statement

CHF million, except per share data	Note	31.12.07	31.12.06	31.12.05	% change from 31.12.06
Continuing operations					
Interest income	3	109,112	87,401	59,286	25
Interest expense	3	(103,775)	(80,880)	(49,758)	28
Net interest income	3	5,337	6,521	9,528	(18)
Credit loss (expense)/recovery		(238)	156	375	
Net interest income after credit loss expense		5,099	6,677	9,903	(24)
Net fee and commission income	4	30,634	25,456	21,184	20
Net trading income	3	(8,353)	13,743	8,248	
Other income	5	4,332	1,598	1,127	171
Revenues from industrial holdings		268	262	229	2
Total operating income		31,980	47,736	40,691	(33)

Note 3   Net Interest and Trading Income

Accounting standards require separate disclosure of net interest income and net trading income (see the tables on this and the next page). This required disclosure, however, does not take into account that net interest and trading income are generated by a range of different businesses. In many cases, a particular business can generate both net interest and trading income. Fixed income trading activity, for example, generates both trading profits and coupon income. UBS management therefore analyzes net interest and trading income according to the businesses that drive it.

The second table below (labeled Breakdown by businesses) provides information that corresponds to this management view. Net income from trading businesses includes both interest and trading income generated by the Group's trading businesses and the Investment Bank's lending activities. Net income from interest margin businesses comprises interest income from the Group's loan portfolio. Net income from treasury and other activities reflects all income from the Group's centralized treasury function.

Net interest and trading income

CHF million	31.12.07	31.12.06	31.12.05	% change from 31.12.06
Net interest income	5,337	6,521	9,528	(18)
Net trading income	(8,353)	13,743	8,248	
Total net interest and trading income	(3,016)	20,264	17,776	

Breakdown by businesses

CHF million	For the year ended			% change from
	31.12.07	31.12.06	31.12.05	31.12.06
Net income from trading businesses[1]	(10,658)	13,730	11,795	
Net income from interest margin businesses	6,230	5,718	5,292	9
Net income from treasury activities and other	1,412	816	689	73
Total net interest and trading income	(3,016)	20,264	17,776	

1 Includes lending activities of the Investment Bank.

Net interest income[1]

CHF million	For the year ended			% change from
	31.12.07	31.12.06	31.12.05	31.12.06
Interest income				
Interest earned on loans and advances[2]	21,263	15,266	11,678	39
Interest earned on securities borrowed and reverse repurchase agreements	48,274	39,771	23,362	21
Interest and dividend income from trading portfolio	39,101	32,211	24,134	21
Interest income on financial asses designated at fair value	298	25	26	
Interest and dividend income from financial investments available-for-sale	176	128	86	38
Total	109,112	87,401	59,286	25
Interest expense				
Interest on amounts due to banks and customers	29,318	20,024	11,226	46
Interest on securities lent and repurchase agreements	40,581	34,021	20,480	19
Interest and dividend expense from trading portfolio	15,812	14,533	10,736	9
Interest on financial liabilities designated at fair value	7,659	4,757	2,390	61
Interest on debt issued	10,405	7,545	4,926	38
Total	103,775	80,880	49,758	28
Net interest income	5,337	6,521	9,528	(18)

1 Interest includes forward points on foreign exchange swaps used to manage short-term interest rate risk on foreign currency loans and deposits.
2 Includes interest income on impaired loans and advances of CHF 110 million for 2007, CHF 158 million for 2006 and CHF 123 million for 2005.

Net trading income[1]

CHF million	For the year ended			% change from
	31.12.07	31.12.06	31.12.05	31.12.06
Equities	9,048	7,064	3,900	28
Fixed income	(20,949)	2,755	1,240	
Foreign exchange and other[2]	3,548	3,924	3,108	(10)
Net trading income	(8,353)	13,743	8,248	
thereof net gains/(losses) from financial assets designated at fair value	(30)	(397)	70	
thereof net gains/(losses) from financial liabilities designated at fair value	(3,779)	(3,659)	(4,024)	

1 Please refer to the table "Net Interest and Trading Income" on the previous page for the Net income from trading businesses (for an explanation, read the corresponding introductory comment).
2 Includes cash & collateral trading and commodities.

3.15.2 Gains on disposal of property, plant and equipment

As already discussed above, the IASB's *Framework* explains that income includes both 'revenue' and 'gains'. Revenue arises in the course of the ordinary activities of an entity and is referred to by a variety of different names including sales, fees, interest, dividends, royalties and rent; gains represent other items that meet the definition of income and may, or may not, arise in the course of the ordinary activities of an entity. Gains include, for example, those arising on the disposal of non-current assets. IAS 16 also makes it clear that 'gains shall not be classified as revenue'.[91]

Therefore, gains arising on the disposal of property, plant and equipment do not form part of revenue (aside from where an entity routinely sells property, plant and equipment that it has held for rental to others as discussed at 6.11.1 below). However, in our view, it is acceptable to show such gains net of any losses on disposal as part of income, whilst net losses on disposal should be shown within expenses.

4   REVENUE RECOGNITION UNDER US GAAP

4.1   Applicability of US literature

Although IAS 18 does lay down general principles of revenue recognition, there is a lack of specific guidance in relation to matters such as multiple-element revenue arrangements and industry-specific issues – for example, those relating to the software industry. Consequently, whilst the US literature does not override the specific requirements of IFRS, it may well be that companies might choose to avail themselves of the hierarchy set out in paragraph 11 of IAS 8 in order to use US GAAP as guidance to formulate appropriate accounting policies with respect to specific transactions. However, it needs to be made clear that, whilst US GAAP might provide useful guidance in certain instances – the IAS 8 hierarchy does not require companies to refer either to US GAAP or, indeed, any other national GAAP. It is crucial to bear in mind that not all industry practices under US GAAP are permissible under IFRS – for example, utility companies should not adopt a revenue recognition policy that gives rise to regulatory assets/liabilities (although this issue is once again being discussed by the IFRIC – see below at 6.12). It may also be the case that the application of the principles in IAS 18 could result in different accounting from that which would be achieved if the detailed rules in US GAAP were applied.

However, the important point to note is that the underlying approach to revenue recognition under US GAAP is closely aligned with that of IAS 18, in that it is based clearly on the earnings process and realisation principle. Therefore US revenue recognition guidance will in many instances be compatible with IAS 18. This used to be of particular relevance to those US foreign private issuer companies that report under IFRS but filed a Form 20-F with the US SEC and wished to avoid having IFRS/US GAAP reconciling items with respect to their revenue recognition policies. The reconciliation has become less significant as the SEC has now removed the reconciliation requirement, affecting statements for financial years ending on or after 15 November 2007, as long as IFRS as issued by the IASB has been used. Care always needs to be taken to ensure that the adoption of the more detailed US GAAP requirements results in IFRS compliance.

4.2 The general approach to revenue recognition under US GAAP

The accounting literature of US GAAP on revenue recognition includes both broad conceptual discussions and certain industry-specific guidance. If a transaction is within the scope of specific authoritative literature that provides revenue recognition guidance, that literature should be applied. However, in the absence of authoritative literature addressing a specific arrangement or a specific industry, the SEC staff will consider the existing authoritative accounting standards as well as the broad revenue recognition criteria specified in the FASB's conceptual framework that contain basic guidelines for revenue recognition.[92]

The FASB's Concepts Statement No. 5 – *Recognition and Measurement in Financial Statements of Business Enterprises* – deals with recognition issues primarily from the angle of providing reliability of measurement. However, the broad principle for revenue recognition laid down by Concepts Statement 5 is that revenues are not recognised until they are (a) realised or realisable and (b) earned.[93] Concepts Statement 5 states that 'an entity's revenue-earning activities involve delivering or producing goods, rendering services, or other activities that constitute its ongoing major or central operations, and revenues are considered to have been earned when the entity has substantially accomplished what it must do to be entitled to the benefits represented by the revenues'.[94] It goes on to state that 'the two conditions (being realized or realizable and being earned) are usually met by the time product or merchandise is delivered or services are rendered to customers, and revenues from manufacturing and selling activities and gains and losses from sales of other assets are commonly recognized at time of sale (usually meaning delivery).'[95] In addition, it states that 'if services are rendered or rights to use assets extend continuously over time (for example, interest or rent), reliable measures based on contractual prices established in advance are commonly available, and revenues may be recognized as earned as time passes.'[96]

As set out in SAB 104 (SEC Staff Accounting Bulletins, Topic 13: Revenue Recognition), the SEC staff believes that revenue generally is realised or realisable and earned when all of the following criteria are met:

- persuasive evidence of an arrangement exists;
- delivery has occurred or services have been rendered;
- the seller's price to the buyer is fixed or determinable; and
- collectability is reasonably assured.

Generally, the SEC staff believes that a sales price is not fixed or determinable when a customer has the unilateral right to terminate or cancel the contract and receive a cash refund. A sales price or fee that is variable until the occurrence of future events (other than product returns that are within the scope of SFAS 48) generally is not fixed or determinable until the future event occurs. The revenue from such transactions should not be recognised in earnings until the sales price or fee becomes fixed or determinable.[97] Note that IAS 18 states that revenue can be recognised at the time of sale if there is only an insignificant risk of ownership retained, the seller can estimate returns and provides for them, e.g. a retailer who offers refunds if the customer is not satisfied.[98]

4.3   US literature

There exists a number of FASB Statements and AICPA Statements of Position that deal with either the recognition of certain forms of revenue, or the recognition of revenue in certain specific industries. Set out below is a list of just some of the existing literature on revenue recognition:

SFAS 13:	Accounting for Leases
SFAS 45:	Accounting for Franchise Fee Revenue
SFAS 48:	Revenue Recognition When Right of Return Exists
SFAS 49:	Accounting for Product Financing Arrangements
SFAS 66:	Accounting for Sales of Real Estate
SFAS 91:	Accounting for Nonrefundable Fees and Costs Associated with Originating or Acquiring Loans and Initial Direct Costs of Leases
FTB 90-1:	Accounting for Separately Priced Extended Warranty and Product Maintenance
SOP 81-1:	Accounting for Performance of Construction-Type and Certain Production-Type Contracts
SOP 97-2:	Software Revenue Recognition
SOP 98-9:	Modification of SOP 97-2, Software Revenue Recognition, With Respect to Certain Transactions
EITF 99-19:	Reporting Revenue Gross as a Principal versus Net as an Agent
EITF 00-21:	Revenue Arrangements with Multiple Deliverables
EITF 00-22:	Accounting for 'Points' and Certain Other Time-Based or Volume-Based Sales Incentive Offers, and Offers for Free Products or Services to Be Delivered in the Future
EITF 01-9:	Accounting for Consideration Given by a Vendor to a Customer (Including a Reseller of the Vendor's Products)
SAB 104:	SEC Staff Accounting Bulletins, Topic 13: Revenue Recognition

SAB 104 supersedes SAB 101, but has not resulted in any notable new developments in revenue recognition literature in the US; instead, it serves to codify existing concepts in one place.[99]

5   THE IASB/FASB JOINT REVENUE RECOGNITION PROJECT

5.1   Project background

The IASB and FASB have been working since 2002 on a joint project on revenue recognition. This has culminated with them issuing, on 19 December 2008, a

Discussion Paper entitled *Preliminary Views on Revenue Recognition in Contracts with Customers*.[100] The Discussion Paper sought comments on the Boards' preliminary views on a single asset and liability based revenue recognition model that they believe will improve financial reporting under both IFRS and US GAAP by:

- providing clearer guidance on when an entity should recognise revenue;
- reducing the number of standards which entities have to refer to in determination of revenue; and
- establishing principles that will result in entities reporting revenue more consistently for similar contracts regardless of the industry in which an entity operates.

The Discussion Paper addresses the following specific areas:

- the perceived problems with the existing revenue recognition literature for both IFRS and US GAAP;
- an explanation of the focus on assets and liabilities for purposes of evaluating contractual arrangements and determining when revenue may be recognised;
- the rationale for proposing a single revenue recognition model;
- contractual rights and obligations, and changes thereto, and how changes in such rights and obligations affect revenue recognition;
- the proposed method of allocating consideration received or to be received from a customer to the performance obligations undertaken; and
- the effect of the proposed model on current revenue recognition practices.[101]

While the Discussion Paper is not a complete exposure draft of a revenue recognition standard, it describes the initial decisions made in the Boards' joint revenue recognition project, which have the potential to change how, and when, many entities recognise revenue. This may affect how an entity's management communicates with its key stakeholders. As such, it is important for entities to understand the Boards' preliminary views to be able to assess how the proposed model could affect their financial reporting.

Comments on the Discussion Paper were requested by June 2009. It is anticipated that based upon these comments and further deliberations by the Boards an exposure draft will be issued in 2010 and a final standard issued in 2011.[102] The Discussion Paper does not exclude any particular type of contract with customers from its scope but the Boards have specifically considered whether the proposed model would provide decision useful information in respect of financial instruments within scope of IAS 39, insurance contracts within scope of IFRS 4 and leasing contracts within scope of IAS 17 and it is presently unclear what the scope of the intended exposure draft and any final standard may be.[103] The Boards intend to consider the implications of the model on entities that recognise revenue in the absence of a contract, such as inventory under IAS 41 but there is no intention to change the way in which those entities measure inventory.[104]

5.2   Summary of the proposed model

The proposed model will apply to contracts with customers. A contract is defined as 'an agreement between two or more parties that creates enforceable obligations'.[105] A contract could be written, oral or evidenced in other ways – encompassing, for example, retail cash sales where the terms are implicit and exist regardless of any written or oral evidence. This definition is believed consistent with definitions that presently exist under IFRS and US GAAP.[106] A customer is defined as 'a party that has contracted with an entity to obtain an asset (such as a good or service) that represents an output of the entity's ordinary activities'.[107] Contractual promises to transfer goods or services that are outputs of the entity's operations with customers are referred to as performance obligations.[108]

When an entity becomes a party to a contract with a customer, the combination of the rights and the performance obligations in that contract gives rise to a net contract position. An entity's net contract position changes with either performance by the entity or the customer. In the proposed model, revenue is recognised when an entity's net position in a contract increases (i.e. either a net contract asset increases or a net contract liability decreases, or some combination of the two). This increase in the net position occurs as the entity satisfies the performance obligations in the contract by transferring a promised asset (goods or services) to the customer. An entity has transferred a promised asset when the customer controls the asset. Performance by the customer (typically, payment of consideration to the entity) does not lead to revenue recognition, but rather a decrease in the net position in a contract.[109]

Pursuant to the proposed model, entities will initially measure performance obligations at the transaction price – the consideration promised by the customer (the 'original transaction price approach'). Hence no revenue is recognised at contract inception. However, because there is no revenue, there may be a net loss at contract inception as any costs incurred in obtaining the contract are required to be expensed, unless they can be capitalised in accordance with another standard.[110]

An alternative model that the Boards had spent significant time debating had proposed measuring performance obligations at the amount that an entity would be required to pay to transfer those obligations to a third party, and to remeasure on this basis at each reporting date (the 'current exit price approach'). This alternative, and controversial, approach would have led to recognition of revenue at contract inception (and subsequently) independently of any performance by the entity. Many Board members felt this inappropriate. The associated model was considered too complex, with too much risk of error, and eventually this alternative approach was rejected.[111]

Under the proposed original transaction price approach if a contract comprises more than one performance obligation, an entity will allocate the transaction price to the different performance obligations based on the relative stand-alone selling prices of the goods and services comprising the various performance obligations.[112] The standalone selling price of a promised good or service is the price at which the entity would sell that good or service if it were sold separately (i.e. not as part of a multiple-element arrangement). The best evidence of such a price is the price of a good or service when the entity, or another entity, actually sells it separately. However, if neither the entity nor another entity sells the good or service separately, the entity will estimate the stand-alone selling price based on other evidence.[113]

As a performance obligation is satisfied, the amount of the transaction price allocated to that performance obligation at contract inception (based on its relative stand-alone selling price) is recognised as revenue. Consequently, the total amount of revenue that an entity recognises over the life of a contract, as it satisfies individual performance obligations, in aggregate is equal to the transaction price.[114]

A performance obligation is satisfied when, in the case of a good, the customer obtains control of it so that it becomes their asset. Similarly, in the case of a service, the performance obligation is satisfied when the service becomes the asset of the customer, i.e. when they receive that service.[115] The model focuses on this transfer of control of the asset even when the service is one that would not be recognised by a customer as an asset. For example legal services received are considered to be assets that are immediately consumed and expensed by the customer.[116]

After contract inception, a performance obligation is not remeasured unless it is deemed onerous. The Boards have tentatively concluded that a performance obligation is onerous when an entity's expected cost of satisfying the performance obligation exceeds its initial measurement. In such cases, the Boards have expressed a preliminary view that a performance obligation is remeasured to an amount equal to the entity's expected cost of satisfying the performance obligation.[117]

5.3 Issues not addressed by the proposed model

The discussion paper, although lengthy, fails to address many issues, and these are the ones that can cause most difficulty in practice. These include:

- the measurement of rights in a contract, including the effects of the time value of money, credit risk, contingent consideration and non-monetary consideration;
- the effect of contract cancellation (including return rights) and renewal provisions;
- the accounting for contract modifications and changes in terms after contract inception;
- when and how multiple contracts entered into (or contemplated) at the same time should be combined;
- the costs to be included in assessing and measuring whether a contract is onerous, as well as the unit of account to which the test should be applied (e.g. a single performance obligation, the remaining performance obligations in a contract or a portfolio of homogeneous performance obligations);
- presentational issues including gross versus net presentation of the rights and obligations in the balance sheet and gross versus net presentation in the statement of comprehensive income; and
- required disclosures.[118]

These issues are still under discussion by the Boards, as are the precise scope of the model, application guidance and the intended effective date.

5.4   Possible changes to current practice that may result from the proposed model

Given that this model will not lead to revenue at contract inception, does not require continual remeasurement to fair value of the performance obligations and is a performance based model it is currently envisaged that many revenue recognition practices and policies that exist under IFRS and US GAAP today will still be appropriate under this new model. However there still exist a number of areas that may be affected by this new model:

- revenue on construction contracts under IAS 11 is recognised in the period the work is performed.[119] The new model will only allow revenue to be recognised when a performance obligation is satisfied which will be when control of the asset has been transferred to the customer. Some construction contracts involve the continual transfer of such rights and work in progress to the customer but there are many that do not, which would lead to later revenue recognition on these;[120]

- the model requires an entity to estimate the stand-alone prices for each component in multiple-element contracts. This will have an impact on the timing of revenue recognition under US GAAP, which may also affect entities interpreting IFRS in a manner consistent with US GAAP, where previously vendor specific or other objective evidence of fair value was required in order to be able to recognise revenue on individual components;[121]

- the methodology by which all performance obligations under a contract are identified at contract inception will have an impact on the accounting for certain obligations, such as warranties that are not sold separately. The present practice is to recognise such warranty provisions under IAS 37 and recognise all revenue when the related good is sold, rather than allocating and recognising revenue on the warranty component;[122]

- at present some entities capitalise costs of obtaining contracts. The Discussion Paper requires that these costs will need to be expensed unless they can be capitalised in accordance with other standards. This would include any sales commissions paid upfront;[123] and

- performance obligations to transfer goods are satisfied when 'the enforceable rights or other access to the goods transfer from the entity to the customer' rather than when risks and rewards of ownership pass, which may affect the timing of recognition of revenue when a right to return exists. The Discussion Paper highlights that a right of return can either be considered a service that is transferred to the customer and therefore a performance obligation or alternatively represent a failed sale.[124] This latter belief may suggest that revenue would not be recognised until the right of return expires. The Boards have not concluded on this point.

Certain industries could be affected more significantly than others under the proposed model. For example in the telecommunications industry there are often multiple deliverables within a single product offering, such as provision of handsets, voice services and data services, and the consideration is often variable and contingent on the usage of future services, some of which are expected to be in secondary contract terms. There are often tripartite agreements between telecom suppliers, their customers and network operators and contracts are frequently subject to modification. Entities in such industries would face significant hurdles and costs in attempting to apply the proposed model, especially given the present lack of application guidance. There is significant development work still required in order for the model to cover these more complex arrangements.

6   PRACTICAL ISSUES

IAS 18 could be said to be one of the few truly principles-based standards in the IFRS literature. However, the broader the principles the more that judgement is required to apply them in practice, with the inevitable result that consistency is not always achieved. Nevertheless, consistency has tended to be achieved over time within specific industries on the basis of principles-based consensuses between the preparer, regulator and auditor communities.

The following table summarises the broad approaches to revenue reporting that would appear to have achieved general acceptance through existing reporting practice. The table indicates the circumstances under which it might be appropriate to apply each of the approaches; nevertheless, it is essential that each situation is considered on its individual merits, with particular attention being paid to the risks and uncertainties that remain at each stage of the earnings process and the extent to which the amount of revenue can be measured reliably.

The timing of recognition	*Criteria*	*Examples of practical application*
During production (accretion)	Revenues accrue over time, and no significant uncertainty exists as to measurability or collectibility. A contract of sale has been entered into and future costs can be estimated with reasonable accuracy.	Most services. The accrual of interest and dividend income. Accounting for construction contracts using the percentage-of-completion method.
At the completion of production	There is a ready market for the commodity that can rapidly absorb the quantity held by the entity; the commodity comprises interchangeable units; the market price should be determinable and stable; there should be insignificant marketing costs involved.	Certain precious metals and commodities.
At the time of sale (but before delivery)	Goods must have already been acquired or manufactured; goods must be capable of immediate delivery to the customer; selling price has been established; all material related expenses (including delivery) have been ascertained; no significant uncertainties remain (e.g. ultimate cash collection, returns).	Certain sales of goods (e.g. 'bill and hold' sales). Property sales where there is an irrevocable contract.
On delivery	Criteria for recognition before delivery were not satisfied and no significant uncertainties remain.	Most sales of goods and some services. Property sales where it is not certain that the sale will be completed.
Subsequent to delivery	Significant uncertainty regarding collectibility existed at the time of delivery; at the time of sale it was not possible to value the consideration with sufficient accuracy.	Certain sales of goods and services (e.g. where the right of return exists). Goods shipped subject to conditions (e.g. installation and inspection/performance).
On an apportionment basis (the revenue allocation approach)	Where revenue represents the supply of initial and subsequent goods/services.	Franchise fees. Sale of goods with after sales service.

All the same, because minimal implementation guidance is given in IFRS about the timing of revenue recognition, we have devoted the remainder of this Chapter to the examination of specific areas of revenue recognition in practice that might be open to inconsistent, controversial or varied accounting practices. Some of this comprises a discussion of the issues addressed in Appendix A to IAS 18, which expands on the principles in the standard. The IFRIC Interpretations that have a particular impact on revenue recognition (IFRIC 13 – *Customer Loyalty Programmes*, IFRIC 15 – *Agreements for the Construction of Real Estate* – and IFRIC 18 – *Transfers of Assets from Customers*) are also discussed below. Many of the issues discussed below relate to specific industries that pose particular revenue recognition problems.

6.1 Sale of goods

Appendix A identifies a number of different arrangements that may affect the point at which the risks and rewards of ownership pass to the buyer. The law governing the sale of goods in any particular jurisdiction must be taken into account.

6.1.1 'Bill and hold' sales

The term 'bill and hold' sales is used to describe a transaction where delivery is delayed at the buyer's request, but the buyer takes title and accepts billing.

Under the guidance provided in the Appendix to IAS 18, revenue is recognised when the buyer takes title, provided:

(a)   it is probable that delivery will be made;

(b)   the item is on hand, identified and ready for delivery to the buyer at the time the sale is recognised;

(c)   the buyer specifically acknowledges the deferred delivery instructions; and

(d)   the usual payment terms apply.

Revenue is not recognised when there is simply an intention to acquire or manufacture the goods in time for delivery.[125]

6.1.2 *Goods shipped subject to conditions*

The Appendix to IAS 18 identifies four scenarios where goods are shipped subject to various conditions:[126]

(a)   installation and inspection

Revenue is normally recognised when the buyer accepts delivery, and installation and inspection are complete. However, revenue is recognised immediately upon the buyer's acceptance of delivery when:

(i)   the installation process is simple in nature, for example the installation of a factory tested television receiver which only requires unpacking and connection of power and antennae; or

(ii)   the inspection is performed only for purposes of final determination of contract prices, for example, shipments of iron ore, sugar or soya beans.

(b)   on approval when the buyer has negotiated a limited right of return

If there is uncertainty about the possibility of return, revenue is recognised when the shipment has been formally accepted by the buyer or the goods have been delivered and the time period for rejection has elapsed. See the discussion at 2.1.3 above.

(c)   consignment sales under which the recipient (buyer) undertakes to sell the goods on behalf of the shipper (seller)

Revenue is recognised by the shipper when the goods are sold by the recipient to a third party.

(d)   cash on delivery sales

Revenue is recognised when delivery is made and cash is received by the seller or its agent.

The following extract from the financial statements of Sandvik illustrates a revenue recognition policy that reflects some of these requirements:

Extract 25.12: Sandvik AB (2008)

Accounting policies [extract]

Revenue [extract]

Revenue from sales and services [extract]

Revenue from the sale of goods is recognized in the income statement when the significant risks and rewards of ownership have been transferred to the buyer, that is, normally in connection with delivery. If the product requires installation at the buyer, and installation is a significant part of the contract, revenue is recognized when the installation is completed. Buy-back commitments may entail that sales revenue cannot be recognized if the agreement with the customer in reality implies that the customer has only rented the product for a certain period of time.

6.1.3   Layaway sales

The term 'layaway sales' applies to transactions where the goods are delivered only when the buyer makes the final payment in a series of instalments. This is fairly common in the retail sector – for example, clothing and household goods. Revenue from such sales is recognised when the goods are delivered. However, when experience indicates that most such sales are consummated, revenue may be recognised when a significant deposit is received provided the goods are on hand, identified and ready for delivery to the buyer.[127]

6.1.4   Payments in advance

In certain sectors (such as furniture and kitchen retail) payment or partial payment is received from the customer when he places his order for the goods. This is often well in advance of delivery for goods which are not presently held in inventory, if for example the goods are still to be manufactured or will be delivered directly to the customer by a third party. In such cases, revenue is recognised when the goods are delivered to the buyer.[128]

In other sectors – for example, utilities – companies receive advance payments from customers for services to be provided in the future. In some cases, these advance payments are long term in nature, and the issue that arises is whether or not interest should be accrued on these long term advances received for the delivery of such services and, if so, how revenue should be measured in these circumstances.

IAS 18 requires entities to measure revenue 'at the fair value of the consideration received or receivable'.[129] The standard elaborates on this requirement by referring to the situation in which an entity either provides interest-free credit to the buyer or accepts a note receivable bearing a below-market interest rate from the buyer as consideration for the sale of goods. If the arrangement effectively constitutes a financing transaction, IAS 18 requires that the entity determine the fair value of the consideration by discounting all future receipts using an imputed rate of interest.[130] Although IAS 18 does not address the reverse situation of the receipt of interest-free advances from customers, a similar rationale may be applied to justify the accruing of interest, i.e. there is a financing element to the transaction and this must be taken account of if revenue is to be measured at the fair value of the consideration at the time the good or service is provided.

However, in drafting IFRIC 18 the IFRIC considered the concept of accruing interest on advance payments received from customers but the majority of respondents commenting on the draft disagreed that this was necessary. The IFRIC subsequently agreed with this majority view and noted that 'paragraph 11 of IAS 18 requires taking the time value of money into account only when payments are deferred'.[131]

Given this lack of clarity we believe it is a policy choice of whether or not to accrue interest on advance payments received from customers. If interest is accrued it will be calculated based upon the incremental borrowing rate of the entity and revenue will ultimately be recognised based upon the nominal value of the advance payments received from customers plus this accrued interest. In fact accruing interest would seem to be more consistent with the principles of IAS 18 and hence it would be difficult to justify a change in accounting policy from accruing interest to not doing so. Whichever accounting policy is adopted should be applied consistently.

6.1.5 *Sale and repurchase agreements*

Sale and repurchase agreements take many forms: the seller concurrently agrees to repurchase the same goods at a later date, or the seller has a call option to repurchase, or the buyer has a put option to require the repurchase, by the seller, of the goods.

In a sale and repurchase agreement for an asset other than a financial asset, the terms of the agreement need to be analysed to ascertain whether, in substance, the seller has transferred the risks and rewards of ownership to the buyer and hence revenue is recognised. When the seller has retained the risks and rewards of ownership, even though legal title has been transferred, the transaction is a financing arrangement and does not give rise to revenue. Sale and leaseback arrangements including repurchase agreements and options are discussed in Chapter 22 at 4.6. For a sale and repurchase agreement on a financial asset, IAS 39 applies (see Chapter 30).[132]

6.1.6 *Instalment sales*

The term 'instalment sales' refers to sales where the goods are delivered to the customer, but payment is made by a number of instalments, which include a financing charge. In such cases, revenue attributable to the sale price, exclusive of interest, is recognised at the date of sale. The sale price is the present value of the consideration, determined by discounting the instalments receivable at the imputed rate of interest. The interest element is recognised as revenue as it is earned, using the effective interest method set out in IAS 39.[133] The application of the effective interest rate method is discussed in Chapter 32 at 5.

6.2   Receipt of initial fees

The practice that has developed in certain industries of charging an initial fee at the inception of a service, followed by subsequent service fees, can present revenue allocation problems. This is because it is not always altogether clear what the initial fee represents; consequently, it is necessary to determine what proportion (if any) of the initial fee has been earned on receipt, and how much relates to the provision of future services. In some cases, large initial fees are paid for the provision of a service, whilst continuing fees are relatively small in relation to future services to be provided; if it is probable that the continuing fees will not cover the cost of the continuing services to be provided plus a reasonable profit, then a portion of the initial fee should be deferred over the period of the service contract such that a reasonable profit is earned throughout the service period. Accounting for initial fees has proved problematic and the IFRIC has addressed the issue inconclusively – see 6.2.4 below.

6.2.1 *Franchise fees*

Franchise agreements between franchisors and franchisees can vary widely both in complexity and in the extent to which various rights, duties and obligations are explicitly addressed. There is no standard form of franchise agreement which would dictate standard accounting practice for the recognition of all franchise fee revenue. Only a full understanding of the franchise agreement will reveal the substance of a particular arrangement so that the most appropriate accounting treatment can be determined; nevertheless, the following are the more common areas which are likely to be addressed in any franchise agreement and which will be relevant to franchise fee revenue reporting:[134]

(a) *rights transferred by the franchisor:* the agreement gives the franchisee the right to use the trade name, processes, know-how of the franchisor for a specified period of time or in perpetuity.

(b) *the amount and terms of payment of initial fees:* payment of initial fees (where applicable) may be fully or partially due in cash, and may be payable immediately, over a specified period or on the fulfilment of certain obligations by the franchisor.

(c)   *amount and terms of payment of continuing franchise fees:* the franchisee will normally be required to pay a continuing fee to the franchisor – usually on the basis of a percentage of gross revenues.

(d)   *services to be provided by the franchisor initially and on a continuing basis:* the franchisor will usually agree to provide a variety of services and advice to the franchisee, such as:

- site selection;
- the procurement of fixed assets and equipment – these may be either purchased by the franchisee, leased from the franchisor or leased from a third party (possibly with the franchisor guaranteeing the lease payments);
- advertising;
- training of franchisee's personnel;
- inspecting, testing and other quality control programmes; and
- bookkeeping services.

(e)   *acquisition of equipment, stock and supplies*: the franchisee may be required to purchase these items either from the franchisor or from designated suppliers. Some franchisors manufacture products for sale to their franchisees, whilst others act as wholesalers.

The Appendix to IAS 18 includes a broad discussion of the receipt of franchise fees, stating that they are recognised as revenue on a basis that reflects the purpose for which the fees were charged.[135] The standard states that the following methods of franchise fee recognition are appropriate:[136]

Supplies of equipment and other tangible assets: the amount, based on the fair value of the assets sold, is recognised as revenue when the items are delivered or title passes.

Supplies of initial and subsequent services: fees for the provision of continuing services, whether part of the initial fee or a separate fee are recognised as revenue as the services are rendered. When the separate fee does not cover the cost of continuing services together with a reasonable profit, part of the initial fee, sufficient to cover the costs of continuing services and to provide a reasonable profit on those services, is deferred and recognised as revenue as the services are rendered.

The franchise agreement may provide for the franchisor to supply equipment, inventories, or other tangible assets, at a price lower than that charged to others or a price that does not provide a reasonable profit on those sales. In these circumstances, part of the initial fee, sufficient to cover estimated costs in excess of that price and to provide a reasonable profit on those sales, is deferred and recognised over the period the goods are likely to be sold to the franchisee. The balance of an initial fee is recognised as revenue when performance of all the initial services and other obligations required of the franchisor (such as assistance with site selection, staff training, financing and advertising) has been substantially accomplished.

The initial services and other obligations under an area franchise agreement may depend on the number of individual outlets established in the area. In this case, the fees attributable to the initial services are recognised as revenue in proportion to the number of outlets for which the initial services have been substantially completed.

If the initial fee is collectible over an extended period and there is a significant uncertainty that it will be collected in full, the fee is recognised as cash instalments are received.

Continuing Franchise Fees: fees charged for the use of continuing rights granted by the agreement, or for other services provided during the period of the agreement, are recognised as revenue as the services are provided or the rights used.

Agency Transactions: transactions may take place between the franchisor and the franchisee which, in substance, involve the franchisor acting as agent for the franchisee. For example, the franchisor may order supplies and arrange for their delivery to the franchisee at no profit. Such transactions do not give rise to revenue.

In summary, it is necessary to break down the initial fee into its various components, e.g. the fee for franchise rights, fee for initial services to be performed by the franchisor, fair value of tangible assets sold etc. The individual components may be recognised at different stages. The portion that relates to the franchise rights may be recognised in full immediately unless part of it has to be deferred because the continuing fee does not cover the cost of continuing services to be provided by the franchisor plus a reasonable profit. In this case a portion of the initial fee should be deferred and recognised as services are provided. The fee for initial services should only be recognised when the services have been 'substantially performed' (it is unlikely that substantial performance will have been completed before the franchisee opens for business). The portion of the fee which relates to tangible assets may be recognised when title passes. If the collection period for the initial fees is extended and there is doubt as to the ultimate collectibility, recognition of revenue should be deferred.

6.2.2   *Advance royalty or licence receipts*

The general guidance relating to licence fees and royalties states that 'fees and royalties paid for the use of an entity's assets (such as trademarks, patents, software, music copyright, record masters and motion picture films) are normally recognised in accordance with the substance of the agreement. As a practical matter, this may be on a straight line basis over the life of the agreement, for example, when a licensee has the right to use certain technology for a specified period of time.'[137]

Therefore, under normal circumstances, the accounting treatment of advance royalty or licence receipts is straightforward; under the accruals concept the advance should be treated as deferred income when received, and released to the profit and loss account when earned under the terms of the royalty/licence agreement. Bayer provides an example of such an approach:

> *Extract 25.13: Bayer AG (2007)*
>
> Notes [extract]
>
> 4.   Basic principles, methods and critical accounting policies [extract]
>
> Net sales and other operating income [extract]
>
> Some of the Bayer Group's revenues are generated on the basis of licensing agreements under which third parties are granted rights to its products and technologies. Payments relating to the sale or outlicensing of technologies or technological expertise – once the respective agreements have become effective – are immediately recognized in income if all rights relating to the technologies and all obligations resulting from them have been relinquished under the contract terms and Bayer has no continuing obligation to perform under the agreement. However, if rights to the technologies continue to exist or obligations resulting from them have yet to be fulfilled, the payments received are recorded in line with the actual circumstances. Upfront payments and similar non-refundable payments received under these agreements are recorded as other liabilities and recognized in income over the estimated performance period stipulated in the agreement. Revenues such as license fees or rentals are recognized according to the same principles.

However, in some industries the forms of agreement are such that advance receipts comprise a number of components, each requiring different accounting treatments. In the record and music industry, a record company will normally enter into a contractual arrangement with either a recording artist or a production company to deliver finished recording masters over a specified period of time. The albums are then manufactured and shipped to retailers for ultimate sale to the customer. The recording artist will normally be compensated through participating in the record company's sales and licence fee income (i.e. a royalty), but may also receive a non-returnable fixed fee on delivery of the master to the record company.

Example 25.1:   *Revenue recognition for licensors in the record and music industry*

For each recording master delivered by a pop group, THRAG, the group (which operates through a service company) receives a payment of €1,000,000. This amount comprises:

- a non-returnable, non-recoupable payment of €100,000;
- a non-returnable but recoupable advance of €600,000; and
- a returnable, recoupable advance of €300,000.

The recoupable advances of €900,000 can be recouped against royalties on net sales earned both on the album concerned and on earlier and subsequent albums. This is achieved by computing the total royalties on net sales on all albums delivered under THRAG's service company's agreement with its recording company, and applying against this total the advances and royalties previously paid on those albums.

It is clear that the non-recoupable advance of €100,000 should be recognised in income when received, since it is not related to any future performance; at the other end of the spectrum, recognition of the returnable advance should be deferred and recognised only when recouped. However, the question arises as to whether the non-returnable but recoupable advance on royalties should be recognised immediately or deferred. If one accepts that revenue may be recognised when it is absolutely assured, there is an argument to justify the immediate recognition of the recoupable advance, since it is non-returnable. Conversely, some might argue that although the advance is non-returnable, it is not earned until it is recouped; furthermore, immediate recognition of royalty advances is likely to lead to a significant distortion of reported income, resulting in there being little correlation between reported income and album sales.

However, in our view, from the perspective of THRAG, the earnings process on the non-returnable but recoupable advance of €600,000 is complete. This is because THRAG has no other service obligation to fulfil, and the fact that the advance is recoupable is a risk of the record company. Consequently, it should be recognised in revenue immediately on delivery of the master.

Similar recognition principles should be applied in the case of advance fees paid on the sale of film/TV rights.

6.2.3 *Financial service fees*

The Appendix to IAS 18 includes a series of illustrative examples that relate to financial service fees, pointing out that the recognition of revenue for financial service fees depends on the purposes for which the fees are assessed and the basis of accounting for any associated financial instrument.[138] The description of fees for financial services may not be indicative of the nature and substance of the services provided. Therefore, it is necessary to distinguish between fees that are an integral part of the effective interest rate of a financial instrument, fees that are earned as services are provided, and fees that are earned on the execution of a significant act. The Appendix to IAS 18 makes this distinction as follows:[139]

A   *Fees that are an integral part of the effective interest rate of a financial instrument*

Such fees are generally treated as an adjustment to the effective interest rate. However, when the financial instrument is measured at fair value with the change in fair value recognised in profit or loss the fees are recognised as revenue when the instrument is initially recognised.

- *Origination fees received by the entity relating to the creation or acquisition of a financial asset other than one that under IAS 39 is classified as a financial asset 'at fair value through profit or loss':* Such fees may include compensation for activities such as evaluating the borrower's financial condition, evaluating and recording guarantees, collateral and other security arrangements, negotiating the terms of the instrument, preparing and processing documents and closing the transaction. These fees are an integral part of generating an involvement with the resulting financial instrument and, together with the related transaction costs (as defined in IAS 39), are deferred and recognised as an adjustment to the effective interest rate.

ABN AMRO discloses a policy that reflects this requirement:

Extract 25.14: ABN AMRO Holding N.V. (2008)

Summary of significant accounting policies [extract]

Income statement [extract]

Fee and commission income [extract]

Fees and commissions are recognised as follows:

- Fees and commissions generated as an integral part of negotiating and arranging a funding transaction with customers, such as the issuance of loans are included in the calculation of the effective interest rate and are included in interest income and expense.

In the 2008 *Improvements to IFRSs,* an apparent inconsistency in the guidance on IAS 18 and in IAS 39 has been remedied. This relates to the identification of costs incurred in originating a financial asset that should be deferred and recognised as an adjustment to the effective interest rate. The IASB has concluded that the definition of transaction costs in IAS 39 as 'incremental costs that are directly attributable to the acquisition, issue…of a financial asset' is more appropriate than IAS 18's previous terminology of 'related direct costs'.[140] Therefore, the Appendix to IAS 18 now cross-refers to the definition of transaction costs as set out in IAS 39.[141]

- *Commitment fees received by the entity to originate a loan when the loan commitment is outside the scope of IAS 39:* If it is probable that the entity will enter into a specific lending arrangement and the loan commitment is not within the scope of IAS 39, the commitment fee received is regarded as compensation for an ongoing involvement with the acquisition of a financial instrument and, together with the related transaction costs (as defined in IAS 39), is deferred and recognised as an adjustment to the effective interest rate. If the commitment expires without the entity making the loan, the fee is recognised as revenue on expiry. Loan commitments that are within the scope of IAS 39 are accounted for as derivatives and measured at fair value.

- *Origination fees received on issuing financial liabilities measured at amortised cost:* These fees are an integral part of generating an involvement with a financial liability. When a financial liability is not classified as 'at fair value through profit or loss', the origination fees received are included, with the related transaction costs (as defined in IAS 39) incurred, in the initial carrying amount of the financial liability and recognised as an adjustment to the effective yield. An entity distinguishes fees and costs that are an integral part of the effective interest rate for the financial liability from origination fees and transaction costs relating to the right to provide services, such as investment management services.

B   Fees earned as services are provided

The following are examples of situations where revenue is recognised over the period of the related service:

- *Fees charged for servicing a loan:* These fees are recognised as revenue as the services are provided.

- *Commitment fees to originate a loan when the loan commitment is outside the scope of IAS 39:* If it is unlikely that a specific lending arrangement will be entered into and the loan commitment is outside the scope of IAS 39, the commitment fee is recognised as revenue on a time proportion basis over the commitment period. Loan commitments that are within the scope of IAS 39 are accounted for as derivatives and measured at fair value.

- *Investment management fees:* Fees charged for managing investments are recognised as revenue as the services are provided. Incremental costs that are directly attributable to securing an investment management contract are recognised as an asset if they can be identified separately and measured reliably and if it is probable that they will be recovered. As in IAS 39, an incremental cost is one that would not have been incurred if the entity had not secured the investment management contract. The asset represents the entity's contractual right to benefit from providing investment management services, and is amortised as the entity recognises the related revenue. If the entity has a portfolio of investment management contracts, it may assess their recoverability on a portfolio basis. Some financial services contracts involve both the origination of one or more financial instruments and the provision of investment management services. An example is a long-term monthly saving contract linked to the management of a pool of equity securities. The provider of the contract distinguishes the transaction costs relating to the origination of the financial instrument from the costs of securing the right to provide investment management services.

C   Fees that are earned on the execution of a significant act

The fees are recognised as revenue when the significant act has been completed, as in the examples below.

- *Commission on the allotment of shares to a client:* The commission is recognised as revenue when the shares have been allotted.

- *Placement fees for arranging a loan between a borrower and an investor:* The fee is recognised as revenue when the loan has been arranged.

- *Loan syndication fees:* A syndication fee received by an entity that arranges a loan and retains no part of the loan package for itself (or retains a part at the same effective interest rate for comparable risk as other participants) is compensation for the service of syndication. Such a fee is recognised as revenue when the syndication has been completed.

The following extracts from the financial statements of Barclays and HSBC illustrate the approach followed in practice:

Extract 25.15: Barclays PLC (2007)

Consolidated accounts Barclays PLC

Significant Accounting Policies [extract]

6.   Interest, fees and commissions [extract]

Fees and commissions

Unless included in the effective interest calculation, fees and commissions are recognised on an accruals basis as the service is provided. Fees and commissions not integral to effective interest arising from negotiating, or participating in the negotiation of a transaction from a third party, such as the acquisition of loans, shares or other securities or the purchase or sale of businesses, are recognised on completion of the underlying transaction. Portfolio and other management advisory and service fees are recognised based on the applicable service contracts. Asset management fees related to investment funds are recognised over the period the service is provided. The same principle is applied to the recognition of income from wealth management, financial planning and custody services that are continuously provided over an extended period of time.

Commitment fees, together with related direct costs, for loan facilities where draw down is probable are deferred and recognised as an adjustment to the effective interest on the loan once drawn. Commitment fees in relation to facilities where draw down is not probable are recognised over the term of the commitment.

Extract 25.16: HSBC Holdings plc (2008)

Notes on the Financial Statements [extract]

2   Summary of significant accounting policies [extract]

(b)   Non-interest income [extract]

Fee income is earned from a diverse range of services provided by HSBC to its customers. Fee income is accounted for as follows:

- income earned on the execution of a significant act is recognised as revenue when the act is completed (for example, fees arising from negotiating, or participating in the negotiation of, a transaction for a third party, such as the arrangement for the acquisition of shares or other securities);

- income earned from the provision of services is recognised as revenue as the services are provided (for example, asset management, portfolio and other management advisory and service fees); and

- income which forms an integral part of the effective interest rate of a financial instrument is recognised as an adjustment to the effective interest rate (for example, certain loan commitment fees) and recorded in 'Interest income' (Note 2a).

6.2.4   Initial and ongoing fees received by a fund manager

The IFRIC has considered on a number of occasions the appropriate accounting for commission arrangements that involve the payment and receipt of initial fees followed by further payments and receipts (so-called 'trail' or 'trailing' commissions) and failed to come to any conclusion, most recently in July 2008.[142] The IFRIC has focused on the accounting treatment by the party that receives the fee, usually the financial adviser to the investor.

These fees are typically paid by an investor who makes an investment in a fund, and they are non-refundable regardless of how long the investor chooses to remain invested. An investor may pay a non-refundable fee (for example 5% of the initial investment) on investing in a fund and ongoing fees (say 1% of the fund assets per annum) for continuing fund management. Units in the fund may be sold by an adviser from an in-house sales department of the same group as the fund manager or by a separate financial adviser. If they are sold by a separate financial adviser, that adviser will retain the 5 per cent upfront fee. There are considerable difficulties in determining the appropriate accounting and they demonstrate a tension between different accounting standards that can lead to different accounting treatments.

The upfront fee is a fixed sum receivable at the commencement of the arrangement. Various parties have argued that the initial fee should be recognised as revenue when receivable, or alternatively that it should be spread over the estimated life of the investment. Some members of the IFRIC viewed the fact that the upfront fee is the same, regardless of whether it is retained by a separate financial adviser (which is independent of the group that includes the fund manager and therefore has no further involvement with the transaction) or by an adviser from an in-house sales department of the same group as the fund manager, as evidence that upfront services were delivered and that the fair value of those services can be measured reliably. Other members noted that the receipt of a non refundable initial fee does not, in itself, give evidence that an up-front service has been provided or that the fair value of the consideration paid in respect of any upfront services is equal to the initial fee received.[143]

Trail commissions raise additional problems. They are paid periodically in arrears and the amounts payable vary with values (e.g. of funds under management). In July 2008 the IFRIC was again unable to determine whether there were future services but revenue recognition remains an issue even if it is assumed that there are no services provided during the arrangement. Some argue that IAS 18 should be used; revenue ought to be taken when the conditions are met as two of the basic criteria for revenue recognition cannot be demonstrated at inception (that the amount of revenue can be measured reliably and that is probable that the economic benefits associated with the transaction will flow to the entity).[144] Paragraph 20 of the Appendix notes, in the context of licence fees or royalty whose receipt is contingent on the occurrence of a future event, that revenue is recognised only when it is probable that the fee will be received, which is normally when the event has occurred. Others argue that the initial fee and trail commissions together comprise the revenue earned by the financial advisor. The fair value can be estimated and ought to be recognised at inception, using IAS 32 – *Financial Instruments: Presentation* – and IAS 39 as the relevant accounting standards.

Similar arrangements can be found in many industries, not all of which are financial services. For example, 'revenue share' arrangements in telecommunications share many features: an up-front commission is paid to the distributor, who receives further sums if the customer remains on the same network tariff. The corresponding treatment of the cost to the operator is also debated: is it an upfront cost under IAS 32, measured using IAS 39 principles or is it recognised when incurred under IAS 37? It is a widespread and complex problem and the arrangements create issues for the entity making the payment as well as the recipient. The accounting is likely to be affected by the project on revenue recognition (see 5 above). The IFRIC decided not to add this issue to its agenda. While industry practice varies, some asset management groups take the view that some front-end fees are earned over the period in which it is expected that services will be provided and other fees earned as conditions are met:

Extract 25.17: Henderson Group plc (2008)

2   Accounting policies [extract]

2.1   Significant accounting policies

Income recognition

Fee income and commission receivable

Fee income includes annual management charges, transaction fees and performance fees. Annual management charges and transaction fees are recognised in the accounting period in which the associated investment management or transaction services are provided. Performance fees are recognised when the prescribed performance hurdles have been achieved and it is probable that the fee will crystallise as a result. The Group's policy is to accrue 95% of the expected fee calculation on satisfaction of the recognition criteria it has established for performance fees, with the balance of 5% credited on cash settlement.

> Initial fees and commission receivable are deferred and amortised over the anticipated period in which services will be provided, determined by reference to the average term of investors in each product on which commissions are earned. Other income is recognised in the accounting period in which services are rendered.

6.2.5   *Insurance agency commissions*

The critical event for the recognition of insurance agency commissions is the commencement of the policy. Hence, the Appendix to IAS 18 states that insurance agency commissions received or receivable which do not require the agent to render further service are recognised as revenue by the agent on the effective commencement or renewal dates of the related policies. However, when it is probable that the agent will be required to render further services during the life of the policy, the commission, or part thereof, is deferred and recognised as revenue over the period during which the policy is in force.[145]

Some insurance agency commissions have similar features to the investment fund initial fee and 'trail commissions' noted above so there is a similar degree of uncertainty regarding the recognition and measurement of revenue.

6.2.6   *Credit card fees*

It is common practice in some countries for credit card companies to levy a charge, payable in advance, on its cardholders. Although such charges may be seen as commitment fees for the credit facilities offered by the card, they clearly cover the many other services available to cardholders as well. Accordingly, we would suggest that the fees that are periodically charged to cardholders should be deferred and recognised on a straight-line basis over the period the fee entitles the cardholder to use the card.[146]

6.2.7   *Entrance and membership fees*

The issue of entrance and membership fees is dealt with briefly in the Appendix to IAS 18, which states that revenue recognition depends on the nature of the services provided. If the fee permits only membership, and all other services or products are paid for separately, or if there is a separate annual subscription, the fee is recognised as revenue when no significant uncertainty as to its collectibility exists. If the fee entitles the member to services or publications to be provided during the membership period, or to purchase goods or services at prices lower than those charged to non-members, it is recognised on a basis that reflects the timing, nature and value of the benefits provided.[147]

6.3   Subscriptions to publications

Publication subscriptions are generally paid in advance and are non-refundable. As the publications will still have to be produced and delivered to the subscriber, the subscription revenue cannot be regarded as having been earned until production and delivery takes place. This is the approach adopted by IAS 18, which requires that revenue is recognised on a straight-line basis over the period in which the items are despatched when the items involved are of similar value in each time period. When the items vary in value from period to period, revenue is recognised on the basis of the sales value of the item despatched in relation to the total estimated sales value of all items covered by the subscription.[148]

Reed Elsevier discloses its policy for recognising revenue from subscriptions as follows:

Extract 25.18: Reed Elsevier (2007)

Combined financial statements [extract]

Accounting policies [extract]

Revenue

Revenue represents the invoiced value of sales less anticipated returns on transactions completed by performance, excluding customer sales taxes and sales between the combined businesses.

Revenues are recognised for the various categories of turnover as follows: subscriptions – on periodic despatch of subscribed product or rateably over the period of the subscription where performance is not measurable by despatch; circulation – on despatch; advertising – on publication or over the period of online display; exhibitions – on occurrence of the exhibition; educational testing contracts – over the term of the contract on percentage completed against contract milestones.

Where sales consist of two or more independent components whose value can be reliably measured, revenue is recognised on each component, as it is completed by performance, based on attribution of relative value.

6.4   Installation fees

Installation fees are recognised as revenue by reference to the stage of completion of the installation, unless they are incidental to the sale of a product in which case they are recognised when the goods are sold.[149] However, in certain circumstances where the installation fees are linked to a contract for future services (for example, in the telecommunications industry: see 6.7 below) it may be more appropriate to defer such fees over either the contract period or the average expected life of the customer relationship, depending on the circumstances.

6.5   Advertising revenue

The Appendix to IAS 18 adopts the performance of the service as the critical event for the recognition of revenue derived from the rendering of advertising services. Consequently, media commissions are recognised when the related advertisement or commercial appears before the public. Production commissions are recognised by reference to the stage of completion of the project.[150]

German television corporation ProSiebenSat.1's revenues are derived mainly from the sale of advertising time on television as disclosed in its accounting policy:

Extract 25.19: ProSiebenSat.1 Media AG (2008)

Notes to the consolidated financial statements [extract]

[6]   ACCOUNTING POLICIES [extract]

Recognition of revenues [extract]

The ProSiebenSat.1 Group's revenues are mainly advertising revenues derived from the sale of advertising time on television. Advertising revenues are net of volume discounts, agency commissions, cash discounts and value-added tax. Other revenues besides advertising revenues derive from cooperative media agreements and call revenues from transaction television, revenues from pay TV activities, revenues from the sale of print products, revenues from the sale of radio advertising, revenues from the marketing of rights and other merchandising services, revenues from the sale of Club articles, revenues from new media services (such as teletext, Internet, mobile telephony and added-value telephone services), and revenues from the sale of programming rights and ancillary programming rights.

Revenues are recognized when the principal risks and opportunities associated with ownership have been transferred to the buyer, the amount of the revenue can be determined reliably, an economic benefit from the sale is sufficiently probable, the costs associated with the sale can be determined reliably, and the selling company neither has the authority to decide the disposition of the sold items such as would normally be associated with ownership, nor has any lasting power of disposition over the items. Specifically, advertising revenues from both television and radio are considered realized when advertising spots are broadcast. Revenues from pay TV activities and from the sale of print products are considered realized when the service is provided. Revenues from the sale of merchandising licenses are realized at the agreed guarantee amount as of the inception of the license for the customer. Revenues from the sale of programming assets and ancillary programming rights are considered realized when the license term for the purchaser of the programming has begun and broadcast-ready materials have been delivered to the purchaser.

6.6   Software revenue recognition

The accounting problems in the software services industry relate to such issues as: when to recognise revenue from contracts to develop software, software licensing fees, customer support services and data services. However, these issues have not been addressed in the IFRS literature. IAS 18 provides only one sentence of guidance: fees from the development of customised software are recognised as revenue by reference to the stage of completion of the development, including completion of services provided for post delivery service support.[151] Because of the nature of the products and services involved, applying the general revenue recognition principles to software transactions can sometimes be difficult. As a result, software companies have used a variety of methods to recognise revenue, often producing significantly different financial results from similar transactions.

The problem of software revenue recognition was recognised in the US by the FASB and SEC who encouraged the AICPA to provide guidance on software revenue recognition methods. As a result of practical experiences, in 1997 the AICPA issued SOP 97-2 – *Software Revenue Recognition*.[152]

Whilst SOP 97-2 is not mandatory for companies reporting under IFRS, many of them benefit by using the hierarchy in IAS 8 to adopt the US requirements in the absence of an IFRS pronouncement of comparable detail. Set out below is a broad overview of SOP 97-2 but the detailed requirements are beyond the scope of this publication.

6.6.1   The basic principles of SOP 97-2

Software arrangements range from those that simply provide a licence for a single software product, to those that require significant production, modification or customisation of the software. Arrangements may also include multiple products or services. SOP 97-2 states that if the arrangement does not require significant production, modification or customisation of existing software (i.e. contract accounting does not apply – see below), revenue should be recognised when all of the following criteria are met:[153]

- persuasive evidence of an arrangement exists;

- delivery has occurred (and no future elements to be delivered are essential to the functionality of the delivered element);

- the vendor's fee is fixed or determinable (the 'determinable' criterion relates to the issue as to whether the fee is subject to factors such as acceptance, refund, extended payment terms); and

- collectability is probable (i.e. whether the customer has the ability to pay and will pay).

With respect to 'persuasive evidence of an arrangement', SOP 97-2 requires that if a vendor has a customary practice of obtaining written contracts, revenues should not be recognised until the contract is signed by both parties. Therefore, in the absence of a signed contract, revenue should not be recognised even if the software has been delivered and payment received.

The licence fee under an arrangement with multiple elements should be allocated to the elements according to 'vendor-specific objective evidence of fair value'. A portion of the licence fee should be allocated to elements that are deliverable on a when-and-if-available basis, whereby a vendor agrees to deliver software only when or if it becomes available while the agreement is in effect. However, absent such features and if all other criteria are met, this means that revenue may be recognised on entering into the arrangement in respect of a licence that allows the customer to use the software for a finite period.

6.6.2   Accounting for software arrangements with multiple elements

Software arrangements may provide licences for many products or services such as additional software products, upgrades/enhancements, rights to exchange or return software, post-contract customer support (PCS) or other services including elements deliverable only on a 'when-and-if-available' basis. These are referred to in SOP 97-2 as 'multiple elements'.

We have noted at 3.6 above that in certain circumstances it is necessary to apply the recognition criteria to the separately identifiable components of a single transaction in order to reflect the substance of the transaction.[154] However, IAS 18 does not establish more detailed criteria for segmenting and combining revenue transactions and in particular it contains little guidance on the allocation of revenue to those elements.

SOP 97-2 states that the fee should be allocated to the various elements based on vendor-specific objective evidence ('VSOE') of fair value, regardless of any separate prices stated within the contract for each element.[155] It requires deferral of all revenue from multiple-element arrangements that are not accounted for using long-term contract accounting if there is insufficient VSOE to allocate revenue to the various elements of the arrangement. However, if there is VSOE for the fair values of the undelivered elements in an arrangement, but not for one or more of the delivered elements in the arrangement, that fee can be recognised using the 'residual method'.[156] This means deducting the values for which there is VSOE from the total revenue and treating the remaining balance as the share of revenue for the element for which there is no VSOE.

If there is a discount, a proportionate amount must be applied to each element included in the arrangement based on relative fair values without regard to the discount. No portion of the discount should be allocated to any upgrade rights and the residual method attributes the discount entirely to the delivered elements.[157]

If there is insufficient VSOE, SOP 97-2 provides that all revenue from the arrangement should be deferred until the earlier of the date on which such sufficient VSOE is obtained or all elements of the arrangement have been delivered.[158]

VSOE is a complex area and there are many detailed rules and requirements that expand the basic points made above and deal with areas such as upgrades, post-contract customer support, extended payment terms, rights of return and services. It is not necessary under IFRS to demonstrate VSOE in order to allocate revenue on the basis of the fair value of individual components.

6.6.3 Accounting for arrangements which require significant production, modification or customisation of software

Where companies are running well-established computer installations with systems and configurations that they do not wish to change, off-the-shelf software packages are generally not suitable for their purposes. For this reason, some software companies will enter into a customer contract whereby they agree to customise a generalised software product to meet the customer's specific requirements. A simple form of customisation is to modify the system's output reports so that they integrate with the customer's existing management reporting system. However, customisation will often entail more involved obligations; for example, having to translate the software so that it is able to run on the customer's specific hardware configuration, data conversion, system integration, installation and testing.

The question that arises, therefore, is the basis on which a software company recognises revenue when it enters into a contract that involves significant obligations. It is our view that the principles laid down in IAS 11 should be applied in this situation.[159] This is supported by IAS 18, which states that the requirements of IAS 11 are generally applicable to the recognition of revenue and the associated expenses for a transaction involving the rendering of services.[160] Accounting under IAS 11 is described in Chapter 21.

Consequently, where the software company is able to make reliable estimates as to the extent of progress towards completion of a contract, the related revenues and the related costs, and where the outcome of the contract can be assessed with reasonable certainty, the percentage-of-completion method of profit recognition should be applied.

One company that follows this approach is SAP AG:

Extract 25.20: SAP AG (2007)

Notes to the Consolidated Financial Statements 2007 [extract]

3.   Summary of significant accounting policies [extract]

Revenue Recognition [extract]

Revenue for arrangements that involve significant production, modification, or customization of the software and those in which the services are not available from third-party vendors and are therefore deemed essential to the software, is recognized on a time-and-material basis or using the percentage of completion method of accounting, based on direct labor costs incurred to date as a percentage of total estimated project costs required to complete the project. If we do not have a sufficient basis to measure the progress of completion or to estimate the total contract revenues and costs, revenue is recognized only to the extent of contract cost incurred for which we believe recoverability to be probable.

Under SOP 97-2, if an arrangement to deliver software or a software system, either alone or together with other products or services, requires significant production, modification or customisation of software, the entire arrangement should be accounted for in accordance with Accounting Research Bulletin (ARB) No. 45 – *Long-Term Construction-Type Contracts* – and SOP 81-1 – *Accounting for Performance of Construction-Type and Certain Production-Type Contracts.*[161]

6.7   Revenue recognition issues in the telecommunications sector

There are significant revenue recognition complexities that affect the telecommunications sector, and about which IFRS is effectively silent. The complexities differ depending upon the type of telecommunications services being considered. For example fixed line (principally voice and data) services have recognition issues that may differ from wireless (principally mobile voice and data) services. It is the latter wireless services that currently provide many of the accounting challenges: wireless is a sector that is still developing rapidly; there is a wide range of offerings; and there are considerable differences between the regulatory frameworks in different jurisdictions. The wireless revenue recognition problems fall into two broad groupings:

- recording of revenue in respect of multiple service elements; and
- whether revenue should be recorded gross or net.

The difficulty of deciding whether to record revenue gross or net is pervasive in the telecommunications sector. The problem occurs because of the difficulty of deciding whether the parties involved in any particular agreement are acting as principal or agent. IAS 18 states that 'in an agency relationship, the gross inflows of economic benefits include amounts collected on behalf of the principal and which do not result in increases in equity for the entity. The amounts collected on behalf of the principal are not revenue. Instead, revenue is the amount of commission.'[162]

As part of its Annual Improvements project the IASB, in April 2009, added guidance to the Appendix of IAS 18 to help determine whether an entity is acting as a principal or as an agent.[163] This guidance is discussed at 3.3 above but does not necessarily help decide the matter in the following scenarios, all of which are common in the wireless sector:

- operators may sell handsets either directly to customers or via distribution channels;

- it can be difficult to identify the separate elements of the commission earned by a distribution channel. This is because part may relate to a possible discount on the handset, while part may relate to the commission earned on the payments the customer makes for the services provided by the distributor;

- often there is data content provided by third parties that is subject to a separate provider agreement; and

- there are issues of 'number portability', where the same customer telephone number is retained but the provider changes (this is also becoming an issue in the fixed line sector).

A number of general factors underlie the accounting issues. For example: local regulatory laws may dictate the way business is done by the operators; there may be restrictions on the discounting of handsets; handsets may be branded in some countries but not in others; both branded and unbranded handsets may co-exist in the same country; and, in addition, there may be varying degrees of price protection.

The sector is continuing to develop rapidly and it is likely that new business models being adopted by operators – in particular the convergence of fixed line voice services and broadband with wireless services – will give rise to new revenue recognition challenges.

6.7.1   Recording revenue for multiple service elements ('bundled offers')

IAS 18 refers specifically to situations where the selling price of a product includes an identifiable amount for subsequent servicing, in which case that amount is deferred and recognised as revenue over the period during which the service is performed.[164] This is directly relevant to some aspects of multiple service offerings, where customers are offered a 'bundle' of assets and services.

Usually, when a consumer enters into a mobile phone contract with a provider, he is provided with a package that may include a handset, free minutes of talktime (either voice or video) and other services such as data downloads, SMS (short message service, i.e. text messages), other MMS (multimedia message service) etc. It is also possible that the 'bundle' will include talktime and data (content, MMS, SMS etc), and certain operators have started offering a bundle of fixed line broadband and mobile services. The wireless provider's systems may not be able to track the usage of such bundled services.

Consumers may pay for their bundle of assets and services in a number of different ways: a payment for the handset (which may be discounted); connection charges related to the costs of connection (or market-based initial fees that are not directly related to connection costs); contracts that provide for monthly payments; non-binding contracts that provide for prepayments by credit card or by voucher, and which may or may not be discounted at the point of sale. None of these payments may relate directly to the cost of the services being provided by the operator, and operators also may be involved in loyalty programs that entail the provision of future free services.

As there is no specific guidance within IFRS on the subject of multiple deliverables beyond this general principle, many companies use the hierarchy in IAS 8 to consider any relevant US requirements in the absence of a comparable IFRS pronouncement, particularly if they either have a US listing or have ambitions of a US listing. However, it needs to be made clear that – whilst US GAAP might provide useful guidance in this area – the IAS 8 hierarchy does not require companies to refer to it.

Telkom SA is an example of a company that discloses in its financial statements that, in order to formulate its accounting policies for multiple element revenue arrangements, it has considered the guidance contained in EITF 00-21 – *Revenue Arrangements with Multiple Deliverables*:

Extract 25.21: Telkom SA Limited (2008)

Notes to the consolidated annual financial statements

for the three years ended March 31, 2008 [extract]

2.   Significant accounting policies [extract]

Significant accounting judgements and estimates [extract]

Revenue recognition

To reflect the substance of each transaction, revenue recognition criteria are applied to each separately identifiable component of a transaction. In order to account for multiple-element revenue arrangements in developing its accounting policies, the Group considered the guidance contained in the United States Financial Accounting Standards Board ('FASB') Emerging Issues Task Force No 00-21 Revenue Arrangements with Multiple Deliverables. Judgement is required to separate those revenue arrangements that contain the delivery of bundled products or services into individual units of accounting, each with its own earnings process, when the delivered item has stand-alone value and the undelivered item has fair value. Further judgement is required to determine the relative fair values of each separate unit of accounting to be allocated to the total arrangement consideration. Changes in the relative fair values could affect the allocation of arrangement consideration between the various revenue streams.

Judgement is also required to determine the expected customer relationship period. Any changes in these assessments may have a significant impact on revenue and deferred revenue.

A   Accounting for handsets and airtime

Most mobile operators provide telephone handsets free of charge or at reduced prices to customers who subscribe to service contracts. In March 2006, the IFRIC was asked whether:

- the contracts should be treated as comprising two separately identifiable components, i.e. the sale of a telephone and the rendering of telecommunication services, as discussed in paragraph 13 of IAS 18 (under which revenue would be attributed to each component); or

- the telephones should be treated as a cost of acquiring the new customer, with no revenue being attributed to them.

The IFRIC did not take this issue on to its agenda; instead, it published the following 'rejection notice' in the March 2006 issue of IFRIC Update:

'The IFRIC acknowledged that the question is of widespread relevance, both across the telecommunications industry and, more generally, in other sectors. IAS 18 does not give guidance on what it means by "separately identifiable components" and practices diverge.

'However, the IFRIC noted that the terms of subscriber contracts vary widely. Any guidance on accounting for discounted handsets would need to be principles-based to accommodate the diverse range of contract terms that arise in practice. The IASB is at present developing principles for identifying separable components within revenue contracts. In these circumstances, the IFRIC does not believe it could reach a consensus on a timely basis. The IFRIC, therefore, decided not to take the topic onto its agenda.'[165]

The IFRIC did not publish its views on how (or whether) revenue ought to be attributed to each element if the transaction is treated as falling under paragraph 13. Usually, an allocation of revenue based on relative fair values would be considered an appropriate basis.

Most telecommunications operators have an accounting policy under which handsets and airtime are separately identifiable components but they apply a form of 'residual method' to the amount of revenue taken for the sale of the handset, recognising no more than the amount contractually payable for it. This assumes that the amount payable for airtime is the fair value attributable to the service. However, at the same time as they recognise minimal (if any) revenue, the operators expense the cost of the handsets, together with other costs such as commissions that comprise 'subscriber acquisition costs' or 'SACs'. An example of this is France Télécom's policy with respect to bundled offers:

Extract 25.22: France Télécom (2007)

CONSOLIDATED FINANCIAL STATEMENTS [extract]

NOTE 2 – Accounting policies [extract]

2.3.4 Revenues [extract]

Separable components of packaged and bundled offers

Numerous service offers on the Group's main markets include two components: an equipment (e.g. a mobile handset) and a service (e.g. a talk plan).

For the sale of multiple products or services, the Group evaluates all deliverables in the arrangement to determine whether they represent separate units of accounting. A delivered item is considered a separate unit of accounting if (i) it has value to the customer on a standalone basis and (ii) there is objective and reliable evidence of the fair value of the undelivered item(s). The total fixed or determinable amount of the arrangement is allocated to the separate units of accounting based on their relative fair value. However, when an amount allocated to a delivered item is contingent upon the delivery of additional items or meeting specified performance conditions, the amount allocated to that delivered item is limited to the non contingent amount. The case arises in the mobile business for sales of bundled offers including a handset and a telecommunications service contract. The handset is considered to have value on a standalone basis to the customer, and there is objective and reliable evidence of fair value for the telecommunications service to be delivered. As the amount allocable to the handset generally exceeds the amount received from the customer at the date the handset is delivered, revenue recognized for the handset sale is generally limited to the amount of the arrangement that is not contingent upon the rendering of telecommunication services, i.e. the amount paid by the customer for the handset.

B   'Free' services

'Free' services are often included in the monthly fee for contract subscribers as an additional incentive to encourage subscribers to sign up for a fixed contract period, typically twelve months.

'Free' services can either be provided up-front as inclusive services for a fixed monthly fee, or as an incentive after a specific threshold has been exceeded to encourage subscribers to spend more than a specified amount.

These 'free' services may be provided to subscribers either in the form of 'free' talktime (e.g. 300 free minutes each month) or free credit (e.g. €50 to spend on any of the services offered each month). The matter is further complicated as increasing competition has led to the bundling of 'free' services, including talktime (voice and video), MMS, SMS and content downloads (wallpapers, ringtones, games etc.).

As a result, one of the challenges that mobile operators will increasingly face is the allocation of the monthly fee between each element within the bundle. This analysis is a key requirement of investment analysts and may also be necessary for segmental disclosure purposes, and will probably have to be based on the fair value of each element of the free services provided. A significant degree of estimation is involved, as the usage profile for an operator's subscribers has to be determined before the monthly revenue can be allocated.

The following example illustrates the accounting for free minutes granted at subscription date by a mobile operator to a subscriber:

Example 25.2:   Accounting for free minutes

An operator enters into a service contract with a customer for a period of 12 months. Under the contract specifications, the customer is offered for the first 2 months 60 free minutes per month of communication, and for the remaining 10 months of the contract the customer will pay a fixed fee of €30 per month for 60 minutes of communication per month. The operator considers the recoverability of the amounts due under the contract from the customer to be probable.

In our view, since the free minute offer is linked to the non-cancellable contract, the fee received for the non-cancellable contract is spread over the entire contract term.

Consequently, the fixed fee of €300 (€30 × 10 months) to be received from the subscriber would be recognised on a straight line basis over the 12 month contract period, being the stage of completion of the contract. The operator therefore would recognise €25 each month over the twelve month period (€30 × 10/12 = €25).

C   Connection and up-front fees

When the mobile telecoms industry was in its infancy, up-front costs such as connection fees, contract handling fees, registration fees, fees for changing plans etc., were commonly charged by operators to cover their administrative costs. Such charges have been phased out over the years and are no longer a common feature in a number of markets.

Nevertheless, there are still occasions in which a telecommunications operator charges its subscribers a one-time non-refundable fee for connection to its network.

Chapter 25: Revenue recognition · Ch 25: s6.7   1679

The contract for telecommunications services between the operator and the subscriber has either a finite or an indefinite life and includes the provision of the network connection and ongoing telecommunications services. The direct/incremental costs incurred by the operator in providing the connection service are primarily the technician's salary and related benefits; this technician provides both connection and physical installation services at the same time.

In such cases, the connection service and the telecommunications services have to be analysed in accordance with their economic substance in order to determine whether they should be combined or segmented for revenue recognition purposes. When the connection transaction is bundled with the service arrangement in such a way that the commercial effect cannot be understood without reference to the two transactions as a whole, the connection fee revenue should be recognised over the expected term of the customer relationship under the arrangement which generated the connection. In our view, the expected term of the customer relationship may not necessarily be the contract period, but may be the estimated average life of the customer relationship, provided that this can be estimated reliably.

Up-front recognition of the non-refundable fee may be possible if there is a clearly demonstrable separate service and it is provided at the inception of the contract.

Vodafone is an example of a company that defers customer connection fees over the expected life of the customer relationship.

Extract 25.23: Vodafone Group Plc (2008)

Critical Accounting Estimates [extract]

Revenue recognition and presentation [extract]

Customer connection fees, when combined with related equipment revenue, in excess of the fair value of the equipment are deferred and recognised over the expected life of the customer relationship. The life is determined by reference to historical customer churn rates. An increase in churn rates would reduce the expected customer relationship life and accelerate revenue recognition. Historically, changes to the expected customer relationship lives have not had a significant impact on the Group's results and financial position.

6.7.2   Other 'gross versus net' issues

A   Third party content providers

Content, such as ringtones, wallpapers, games and traffic updates, are increasingly used by operators. These products/services can either be included in the monthly price plan, or purchased separately on an *ad hoc* basis. Operators can either develop the content in-house, or use third party providers to offer a range of services to their subscribers, with charges based either on duration (news, traffic updates etc.) or on quantity (number of ringtones, games etc.).

The issue is whether the operator should report the content revenue based on the gross amount billed to the subscriber because it has earned revenue from the sale of the services or the net amount retained (that is, the amount billed to the subscriber less the amount paid to a supplier) because it has only earned a commission or fee. Is the substance of the transaction with the supplier one of buying and on-selling goods or selling goods on consignment (i.e. an agency relationship)? As described at 3.3 above, the IASB has recently included guidance in the Appendix to IAS 18 as part of its Annual Improvements project. The two most important are whether the operator has the primary responsibility for providing the services to the customer or for fulfilling the order, for example by being responsible for the acceptability of the services ordered or purchased by the customer, and whether it has discretion in establishing prices, either directly or indirectly, for example by providing additional goods or services. Inventory risk is unlikely to be relevant for a service provision.

Therefore, if the content is an own-brand product or service then the revenue receivable from subscribers should be recorded as revenue by the operator, and the amounts payable to the third party content providers should be recorded as costs.

On the other hand, if the content is a non-branded product/service that is merely using the mobile operator's network as a medium to access its subscriber base, then the income receivable from subscribers should not be recorded as revenue. The operator's revenue will comprise only the commissions receivable from the content providers for the use of the operator's network.

Vivendi discloses that it bases the decision on whether it is an agent or principal status on who has responsibility for content and setting the price to subscribers, as follows:

Extract 25.24: Vivendi SA (2007)

Notes to the Consolidated Financial Statements [extract]

Note 1. Accounting Policies and Valuation Methods [extract]

1.3. Principles Governing the Preparation of the Consolidated Financial Statements [extract]

1.3.4. Revenues from operations and associated costs [extract]

1.3.4.3. SFR and Maroc Telecom [extract]

Sales of services provided to customers managed by SFR and Maroc Telecom on behalf of content providers (mainly toll numbers) are accounted for gross, or net of content providers' fees when the provider is responsible for the content and for setting the price to be paid by subscribers.

B   Number portability

Number portability refers to the service that will allow a subscriber, who was previously with another operator, to keep his existing phone number when transferring to a new operator. Operators are obliged to provide number portability in certain jurisdictions.

When a consumer switches from Operator A to Operator B and keeps his number, in most jurisdictions the phone number remains an Operator A phone number and will be recognised as such by the other network operators.

When a subscriber (S) makes a phone call, the mobile operator (A) incurs a cost in terms of network traffic, but charges S for the phone call. If S's number has been transferred via number portability to another operator (B), there are no apparent changes to S when a phone call is made, as S still gets billed for the call (by B instead of A). However, the additional operations behind the scenes are as follows.

The call still goes through A's network, as it still owns the number. A then transfers the call to B's network and charges B a 'termination' (pass-through) fee. B then connects the call to the intended recipient with no discernible time lag to S.

In our view, the termination fee received by A from B should not be recognised as revenue by A, and should be netted off against cost of sales in A's financial statements. This is because the pass-through of the call by A to B's network is not a value-added or revenue generating activity. The fee received by A is merely a contribution by B to A for reimbursement of A's costs in passing the call on.

6.7.3 Accounting for roll-over minutes

Where an operator offers a subscriber a finite number of call minutes for a fixed amount per period with the option of rolling over any unused minutes, the question arises as to how the operator should account for the unused minutes that the subscriber holds. The operator is not obliged to reimburse the subscriber for unused minutes, but is obliged (normally subject to a ceiling) to provide the accumulated unused call minutes to the subscriber until the end of the contract, after which they expire.

In such cases, revenue is recognised at the time the minutes are used. Any minutes unused at the end of each month should be recognised as deferred revenue.

However, in some instances, the operator has relevant and reliable evidence that shows that a portion of those unused minutes will not be used before the expiration of the validity period. In that case, the operator could consider an alternative revenue recognition policy that would take account of the probability of unused minutes at the end of the validity period in the computation of the revenue per minute used by the subscriber. This would result in allocating a higher amount of revenue per minute used.

When the validity period expires, any remaining balance of unused minutes would be recognised as revenue immediately, since the obligation of the operator to provide the contractual call minutes is extinguished.

6.7.4 Accounting for the sale of pre-paid calling cards

Prepaid cards are normally sold by an operator either through its own sales outlet or through distributors. The communication credit sold with the cards has an expiry date that varies from one operator to another, although, in certain limited jurisdictions, there is no expiry date. For example: prepaid cards may be sold with an initial credit of €50 covering 50 minutes of communication and the credit has a validity period of 90 days from the date of activation. If not used within this period, the credit is lost.

When the cards are sold through distributors, the distributor is usually obliged to sell the cards to the customers at the face value of the card. On sale of the card, the distributor pays the operator the face value less a commission. The distributor has a right to return unsold cards to the operator. Once the distributor has sold the cards, it has no further obligation to the operator.

In our view, when an operator sells calling cards directly, revenue is recognised at the time the minutes are used. Any minutes unused at the end of each month should be recognised as deferred revenue. However, in some instances, the operator has relevant and reliable evidence that shows that a portion of those unused minutes will not be used before the expiration of the validity period. In such cases, the operator could consider an alternative revenue recognition policy that would take account of the probability of unused minutes at the end of the validity period in the computation of the revenue per minute used by the subscriber.

When the validity period expires, any remaining balance of unused minutes would be recognised as revenue immediately, since the obligation of the operator to provide the contractual call minutes is extinguished.

When an operator sells calling cards through a distributor, the revenue is required to be recognised based on the substance of the arrangement with the distributor.

If as is usually the case, the distributor is in substance acting as an agent for the operator, the revenue associated with the sale of the calling card by the distributor to the subscriber is accounted for on a gross basis as set out above (i.e. as and when the subscriber uses the minutes). In our view, unless the distributor is also an operator or the calling card could be used on any operator's network (which is rare), it would be difficult to conclude that the distributor is the principal in the arrangement with the subscriber, because the distributor would not have the capacity to act as the principal under the terms of the service provided by the calling card to the subscriber (see 3.3 and 6.7.2 above).

6.8   Excise taxes and goods and services taxes: Recognition of gross versus net revenues

Many jurisdictions around the world raise taxes that are based on components of sales or production. These include excise taxes and goods and services or valued added taxes. In some cases these taxes are in effect collected by the entity from customers on behalf of the taxing authority. In other cases the taxpayer's role is more in the nature of principal than agent. The regulations (for example, excise taxes in the tobacco and drinks industries) differ significantly from one country to another. The practical accounting issue that arises concerns the interpretation of paragraph 8 of IAS 18: should excise taxes and goods and services taxes be deducted from revenue (net presentation) or included in the cost of sales and therefore, revenue (gross presentation)?

Clearly, the appropriate accounting treatment will depend on the particular circumstances. In determining whether gross or net presentation is appropriate, the entity needs to consider whether it is acting in a manner similar to that of an agent or principal. Until recently there has been little IFRS guidance in this area and entities have tended to look to EITF 99-19 – *Reporting Revenue Gross as a Principal versus Net as an Agent*. However, as described at 3.3 above, the IASB has now added very similar guidance to IAS 18 as part of its Annual Improvements project.

Whether an entity is acting as principal or agent is a matter of judgement that depends on the relevant facts and circumstances of the particular tax in the country concerned. The factors that should be taken into account in determining gross or net treatment are summarised in the following table:

Example 25.3:　　*Excise taxes and goods and services taxes: recognition of gross versus net revenues*

Several national jurisdictions raise 'taxes' that are based on components of sales or production. These include excise taxes and goods and services or valued added taxes. The regulations (for example excise taxes in the tobacco and drinks industries) differ significantly from one country to another.

In such circumstances, the issues that arise in practice are as follows:

- Should excise taxes and goods and services taxes be deducted from revenue (net presentation) or included in the cost of sales and therefore, revenue (gross presentation)?

- What indicators are relevant in determining whether net or gross presentation should be used?

We believe that there are two main indicators that should be considered when determining whether the entity is acting as principal or agent. An additional two indicators relating to the nature of the tax itself should also be considered to determine whether a net or gross presentation is applicable. No one indicator is considered to be conclusive on its own. These indicators are:

Acting as Principal or Agent:

A　whether the entity is exposed to financial risk in relation to the tax (e.g. non-recovery of the tax from the customers); and

B　whether the entity has an obligation to change prices in line with changes in the rate or amount of the tax.

Nature of Taxes:

C　basis of calculation – whether the tax is levied on sales proceeds or on units of production; and

D　point of payment – whether the entity becomes liable to pay the tax at the point of sale or at the time of production.

Indicator	Circumstances indicating:	
	<u>net</u> revenue recognition	<u>gross</u> revenue recognition
A Whether the entity is exposed to financial risk in relation to the tax (e.g. non-recovery of the tax from the customers) (i) who benefits from any short term fluctuations? (ii) who bears the inventory risk? (iii) who bears the credit risk?	• The tax is refundable in the event that stock becomes damaged or obsolete, or receivables are not collectible.	• The entity will not be refunded for the tax paid if the stock is not sold or the receivables are not collected.
B Whether the entity has an obligation to change prices in line with changes in the rate or amount of the tax.	• The tax is included in the selling price and the selling price can never fall below taxes paid. • The entity will change or is required (by law) to change the price of the product to reflect the tax increases but is unable to increase the price above tax increases. • The entity will reduce or is required (by law) to reduce the price of the product to reflect tax decreases.	• The entity has the discretion to determine the final selling price of the products. It bears the tax and makes the decision whether to pass the tax (entire/a portion of it) to the consumer.
C Basis of calculation – Whether the tax is levied on sales proceeds or on units of production.	• The tax is computed based on the sales price or units sold rather than producing activities.	• The tax is computed based on the number of units produced rather than sold. This suggests that it is a type of production tax.
D Point of payment – Whether the entity becomes liable to pay the tax at the point of sale or at the time of production. (This is likely to be a weak indicator that should not be considered without additional factors.)	• The tax is payable to the government only when the sale has occurred or the entity is required to make payment to the government at a date relatively close to the point of sale. The closer the payment is to the point of sale the more likely it is that the tax is similar to a sales tax.	• The tax is payable to the government when the unit is produced or the entity is required to make payment to the government at a date relatively close to the point of production. The closer the payment is to the point of production the more likely it is that the tax is a production tax.

Clearly, it is important that companies disclose the policies that they have adopted in accounting for duty. BP is an example of a company that provides clear disclosure in this area:

Extract 25.25: BP p.l.c. (2008)

Notes on financial statements [extract]

1   Significant accounting policies [extract]

Customs duties and sales taxes

Revenues, expenses and assets are recognized net of the amount of customs duties or sales tax except:

- Where the customs duty or sales tax incurred on a purchase of goods and services is not recoverable from the taxation authority, in which case the customs duty or sales tax is recognized as part of the cost of acquisition of the asset or as part of the expense item as applicable.
- Receivables and payables are stated with the amount of customs duty or sales tax included.

  The net amount of sales tax recoverable from, or payable to, the taxation authority is included as part of receivables or payables in the balance sheet.

6.9   Sales incentives

Paragraph 10 of IAS 18 states that 'the amount of revenue arising on a transaction is usually determined by agreement between the entity and the buyer or user of the asset. It is measured at the fair value of the consideration received or receivable taking into account the amount of any trade discounts and volume rebates allowed by the entity.'[166] Consequently, where an entity provides sales incentives to a customer when entering into a contract these are usually treated as rebates and will be included in the measurement of (i.e. deducted from) revenue when the goods are delivered or services provided. This applies to incentives that have a cost to the seller, such as cash payments it has made itself or liabilities to third parties that have provided goods or services to the purchaser. The seller can carry forward the expense as an asset until the customer pays in accordance with the contract. Revenue will be recognised at a reduced amount taking into account the rebate factor from the cash incentive.

Non-cash incentives, such as 'free postage' or gifts from third parties, will not affect the measurement of revenue unless it is part of the seller's business to sell such items. Amounts paid by the seller to procure such items are expensed unless another IFRS requires capitalisation. Prompt settlement discounts (for example, customers are offered a reduction of 5% of the selling price for paying an invoice within 7 days instead of the usual 60 days) should be estimated at the time of sale and deducted from revenues. The entity will have to ensure that these are discounts on the current (and only) sale and not incentives to enter into a future transaction, in which case IFRIC 13 will apply (see 6.14 below).

From the perspective of the buyer, cash incentives are accounted for as a liability when received until the buyer receives the goods, pays for the inventory (thereby reducing the cost of goods sold) and meets any additional obligations that might be attached to the incentives. Non-cash incentives, such as gifts, would only be considered part of inventories if they meet the definition of inventories.

Sanofi-aventis is an example of a company that provides various forms of sales incentives to its customers:

Extract 25.26: Sanofi-aventis SA (2007)

NOTES TO THE CONSOLIDATED FINANICIAL STATEMENTS

Year ended December 31, 2007 [extract]

B.   SUMMARY OF SIGNIFICANT ACCOUNTING POLICIES [extract]

B.14.   Revenue recognition

Revenue arising from the sale of goods is presented in the income statement under *net sales.* Net sales comprise revenue from sales of pharmaceutical products, vaccines, and active ingredients, net of sales returns, of customer incentives and discounts, and of certain sales-based payments paid or payable to the healthcare authorities.

Revenue is recognised when all of the following conditions have been met: the risks and rewards of ownership have been transferred to the customer; the Group no longer has effective control over the goods sold; the amount of revenue and costs associated with the transaction can be measured reliably; and it is probable that the economic benefits associated with the transaction will flow to the Group, in accordance with IAS 18 (Revenue).

Sanofi-aventis offers various types of price reductions on its products. In particular, products sold in the United States of America are covered by various programs (such as Medicare and Medicaid) under which products are sold at a discount. Rebates are granted to healthcare authorities, and under contractual arrangements with certain customers. Some wholesalers are entitled to chargeback incentives based on the selling price to the end customer, under specific contractual arrangements. Cash discounts may also be granted for prompt payment.

Returns, discounts, incentives and rebates as described above are recognized in the period in which the underlying sales are recognized, as a reduction of sales revenue.

These amounts are calculated as follows:

- Provisions for chargeback incentives are estimated on the basis of the relevant subsidiary's standard sales terms and conditions, and in certain cases on the basis of specific contractual arrangements with the customer. They represent management's best estimate of the ultimate amount of chargeback incentives that will eventually be claimed by the customer.

- Provisions for rebates based on attainment of sales targets are estimated and accrued as each of the underlying sales transactions is recognized.

- Provisions for price reductions under Government and State programs, largely in the United States, are estimated on the basis of the specific terms of the relevant regulations and/or agreements, and accrued as each of the underlying sales transactions is recognized.

- Provisions for sales returns are calculated on the basis of management's best estimate of the amount of product that will ultimately be returned by customers.

In each case, the provisions are subject to continuous review and adjustment as appropriate based on the most recent information available to management.

The Group believes that it has the ability to measure each of the above provisions reliably, using the following factors in developing its estimates:

- the nature and patient profile of the underlying product;

- the applicable regulations and/or the specific terms and conditions of contracts with governmental authorities, wholesalers and other customers;

- historical data relating to similar contracts, in the case of qualitative and quantitative rebates and chargeback incentives;

- past experience and sales growth trends for the same or similar products;

- actual inventory levels in distribution channels, monitored by the Group using internal sales data and externally provided data;

- the shelf life of the Group's products;

- market trends including competition, pricing and demand;
- the possibility of reusing returned goods.

Non-product revenues, mainly comprising royalty income from licence arrangements that constitute ongoing operations of the Group (see Note C), are presented in *Other revenues*.

6.10   Film exhibition and television broadcast rights

Revenue received from the licensing of films for exhibition at cinemas and on television should be recognised in accordance with the general recognition principles discussed in this chapter.

Contracts for the television broadcast rights of films normally allow for multiple showings within a specific period; these contracts usually expire either on the date of the last authorised telecast, or on a specified date, whichever occurs first. Rights for the exhibition of films at cinemas are generally sold either on the basis of a percentage of the box office receipts or for a flat fee.

The Appendix to IAS 18 states that an assignment of rights for a fixed fee or non refundable guarantee under a non cancellable contract which permits the licensee to exploit those rights freely and the licensor has no remaining obligations to perform is, in substance, a sale. When a licensor grants rights to exhibit a motion picture film in markets where it has no control over the distributor and expects to receive no further revenues from the box office receipts, revenue is recognised at the time of sale.[167]

Therefore, it is our view that the revenue from the sale of broadcast, film or exhibition rights may be recognised in full upon commencement of the licence period provided the following conditions are met:

(a)   a contract has been entered into;

(b)   the film is complete and available for delivery;

(c)   there are no outstanding performance obligations, other than having to make a copy of the film and deliver it to the licensee; and

(d)   collectibility is reasonably assured.

This applies even if the rights allow for multiple showings within a specific period for a non-refundable flat fee and the contract expires either on the date of the last authorised telecast, or on a specified date, whichever occurs first. The sale can be recognised even though the rights have not yet been used by the purchaser. We do not believe it appropriate to recognise revenue prior to the date of commencement of the licence period since it is only from this date that the licensee is able to freely exploit the rights of the licence and hence has the rewards of ownership as required by paragraph 14(a) of IAS 18.

When the licensor is obliged to perform any significant acts or provide any significant services subsequent to delivery of the film to the licensee – for example to promote the film – it would be appropriate to recognise revenue as the acts or services are performed (or, as a practical matter, on a straight-line basis over the period of the licence).

Rights for the exhibition of a film at cinemas may be granted on the basis of a percentage of the box office receipts, in which case revenue should be recognised as the entitlement to revenue arises based on box office receipts.

If the fees only become payable when the box office receipts have exceeded a minimum level, IAS 18 suggests that revenue should not be recognised until the minimum level has been achieved. In the Appendix, it states that revenue that is contingent on the occurrence of a future event is recognised only when it is probable that the fee or royalty will be received, which is normally when the event has occurred.[168]

In this instance the guidance in IAS 18 supports deferral until the contingency has occurred. This differs from the arguments based on IAS 32 described in 6.2.4 in the context of initial and ongoing fees, in which the full amount can be recognised at inception and the contingency affects measurement.

6.11   The disposal of property, plant and equipment

IAS 16 requires that the gain or loss arising from the derecognition of an item of property, plant and equipment be included in profit or loss when the item is derecognised unless IAS 17 requires otherwise on a sale and leaseback. IAS 16 prohibits recognition of any such gain as revenue[169] except in the case of entities that are in the business of renting and selling the same asset (see below).

An item is disposed of when the criteria in IAS 18 for recognising revenue from the sale of goods are met (see 3.7 above). IAS 17 applies to disposal by a sale and leaseback.[170] IAS 18's criteria are essentially built around the transfer of significant risks and rewards of ownership.[171] Although IAS 18 states that in most cases the transfer of the risks and rewards of ownership coincide with the transfer of legal title, it acknowledges that legal title sometimes passes at a different time.[172]

Consequently, the general principles of revenue recognition should be applied. There are two significant points in the earning process that could, depending on the circumstances of the sale, be considered to be the critical event for recognition. The first point is on exchange of contracts, at which time the vendor and purchaser are both bound by a legally enforceable contract of sale, whilst the second possible point of recognition is on completion of the contract.

Although legal title and beneficial ownership do not pass until the contract is completed and the transfer is registered, it is possible that the earnings process is sufficiently complete to permit recognition to take place on exchange of contracts. This is because the selling price would have been established, all material related expenses would have been ascertained and, usually, no significant uncertainties would remain. If, however, on exchange of contracts there are doubts that the sale will ultimately be completed, recognition should take place on the receipt of the sales proceeds at legal completion.

The evidence is that some companies delay profit recognition until legal completion, whilst others recognise profit before completion when the significant risks and returns have been transferred to the buyer. In our view, both approaches are acceptable. The two approaches had previously been supported by the Appendix to IAS 18, which stated that, in the case of real estate sales, revenue is normally recognised when legal title passes to the buyer; however, at the same time, it acknowledged that recognition might take place before legal title passes, provided that the seller has no further substantial acts to complete under the contract.[173] However, as from 1 January 2009 or on earlier adoption of IFRC 15 – *Agreements for the Construction of Real Estate* (see 6.11.2 below) this paragraph was deleted. We do not believe this affects the principles or the availability of the two approaches but reinforces that care must be taken before recognising profits before completion and it may be that in many cases, legal completion is the more appropriate point at which to recognise revenue. However, whichever policy is adopted, it is important to ensure that all of the general conditions in IAS 18 have been met (see 3.7 above),

The two approaches are illustrated in the following extracts:

Extract 25.27: Hammerson plc (2008)

NOTES TO THE ACCOUNTS [extract]

1. SIGNIFICANT ACCOUNTING POLICIES [extract]

PROFITS ON SALE OF PROPERTIES

Profits on sale of properties are taken into account on the completion of contract, and are calculated by reference to the carrying value at the end of the previous year, adjusted for subsequent capital expenditure.

Extract 25.28: Liberty International PLC (2008)

2 Accounting policies – group and company [extract]

Revenue recognition [extract]

Where revenue is obtained by the sale of properties, it is recognised when the significant risks and returns have been transferred to the buyer. This will normally take place on exchange of contracts unless there are conditions attached. For conditional exchanges sales are recognised when these conditions are satisfied.

The gain or loss on derecognition of an item of property, plant and equipment is the difference between the net disposal proceeds, if any, and the carrying amount of the item.[174] This means that any revaluation surplus relating to the asset disposed of is transferred within equity to retained earnings when the asset is derecognised and not reflected in profit or loss.

The consideration receivable on disposal of an item of property, plant and equipment is recognised initially at its fair value. If payment for the item is deferred, the consideration received is recognised initially at the cash price equivalent. The difference between the nominal amount of the consideration and the cash price equivalent is recognised as interest revenue in accordance with IAS 18 reflecting the effective yield on the receivable (see 3.5 above).[175]

IFRS 5 – *Non-current Assets Held for Sale and Discontinued Operations* – lays down additional requirements for assets held for disposal; these requirements include measurement rules, which affect the measurement of the amount of the gain on disposal to be recognised. These are discussed in Chapter 4 at 2.2.

6.11.1 Sale of assets held for rental

Until 2008, IAS 16 prohibited classification as revenue any gains arising from the derecognition of items of property, plant and equipment.[176] However, some entities are in the business of renting and subsequently selling the same asset. The IASB has agreed that the presentation of gross selling revenue, rather than a net gain or loss on the sale of the assets, would better reflect the ordinary activities of such entities.[177]

A new paragraph 68A has been added to IAS 16 that requires an entity that, in the course of its ordinary activities, routinely sells items of property, plant and equipment that it has held for rental to others to transfer the assets to inventories at their carrying amount when they cease to be rented and are held for sale. The proceeds from the sale of such assets are to be recognised as revenue in accordance with IAS 18. IFRS 5 does not apply when assets that are held for sale in the ordinary course of business are transferred to inventories.[178]

Paragraph 14 of IAS 7 – *Statement of Cash Flows* – has been amended to require presentation within operating activities cash payments to manufacture or acquire such assets and cash receipts from rents and sales of such assets.[179]

These amendments apply to annual periods beginning on or after 1 January 2009.[180] The amendments are likely to have quite a significant impact on the way that performance is measured and reported in a number of industries, including the hotel and equipment and car rental industries.

6.11.2 Pre-completion contracts

The recognition of revenue on real estate sales becomes more complex in the case of real estate developments where there are agreements for sale to the ultimate buyer prior to the completion of construction. Such 'forward sale' contracts are common in areas such as multiple-unit real estate developments (for example, residential apartment blocks) and commercial property developments that the developer has decided not to build speculatively and where agreements for sale are reached before construction is complete. In these situations, the developers start marketing the development before construction is complete (perhaps even before construction has started) and buyers enter into agreements to acquire either the entire building or a specific unit within the building development on completion of the construction. The contracts may require the buyer to pay a deposit and progress payments, which are refundable only if the developer fails to complete and deliver the unit. The balance of the purchase price may be payable only when the buyer gains possession, which often coincides with the point at which legal title is transferred to the buyer. However, legal title may transfer at different times, depending on national laws and practices.

The first issue that needs to be resolved is which standard is the relevant standard to apply: IAS 18 or IAS 11? IFRIC 15 was issued in July 2008 and applies to the accounting for revenue and associated expenses by entities that undertake the construction of real estate directly or through subcontractors.[181] In substance the Interpretation argues that pre-completion sales contracts typically do not meet the IAS 11 definition of, and are distinguishable from, construction contracts. They are instead generally sales of goods for which IAS 18 is the applicable standard. This means that revenue is recognised only when the IAS 18 conditions are met. Such contracts may span more than one accounting period but this does not, by itself, justify the use of the percentage of completion method. Consequently there will be differences between IFRS and US GAAP, which requires a percentage of completion method for recognising profit from sales of units in condominium projects or time-sharing interests (provided specified criteria are met), but the IFRIC considers that these differences should be resolved by harmonising standards.

The scope of the Interpretation includes agreements for the construction of real estate. Such agreements may include the delivery of other goods or services.[182] As well as guidance as to the applicable standard, the Interpretation addresses when revenue from the construction of real estate should be recognised.[183]

The IFRIC has focused on IAS 11's definition of a construction contract as 'a contract specifically negotiated for the construction of an asset or a combination of assets...'.[184] An agreement for the construction of real estate meets the definition of a construction contract when the buyer is able to specify the major structural elements of the design of the real estate before construction begins and/or specify major structural changes once construction is in progress (whether or not it exercises that ability).[185] By contrast, the buyer may only have limited ability to influence the design of the real estate, for example to select a design from a range of options specified by the entity, or to specify only minor variations to the basic design. In practice many agreements only give the buyer the right of choice over a few options, such as types of flooring or kitchen fittings. In this case the agreement is for the sale of goods and is within the scope of IAS 18 rather than IAS 11.[186]

The analysis assumes that there is revenue to be recognised, i.e. it assumes that the entity retains neither continuing managerial involvement to the degree usually associated with ownership nor effective control over the constructed real estate to an extent that would preclude recognition of some or all of the consideration as revenue.[187] Examples are agreements in which the entity guarantees occupancy of the property for a specified period, or guarantees a return on the buyer's investment for a specified period. In such circumstances, recognition of revenue may be delayed or precluded altogether.[188]

A feature of many of these agreements is that an entity may contract to deliver goods or services in addition to the construction of real estate, for example the sale of land or provision of property management services – and these may need to be split into their separate components.[189] The fair value of the total consideration received or receivable for the agreement is allocated to each component. The entity will apply IFRIC 15 to the component for the construction of real estate in order to determine the appropriate accounting,[190] as illustrated in the following flowchart:

Analysis of a single agreement for the construction of real estate

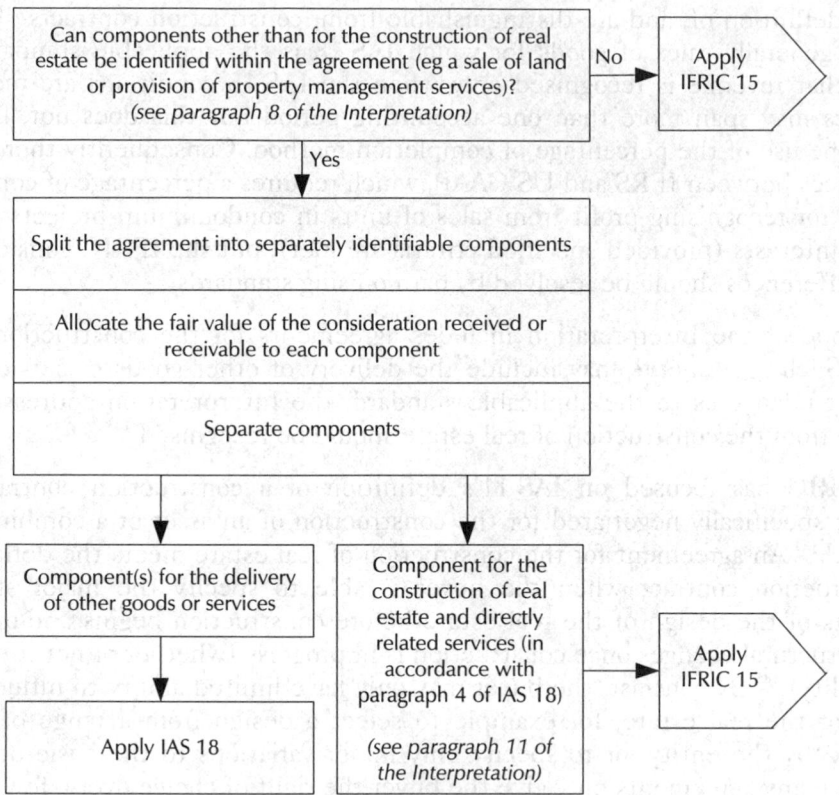

Analysis of the agreement, or components within it, will determine whether it is a construction contract, a contract for services or a contract for the sale of goods:

(a)   if the agreement is a construction contract and its outcome can be estimated reliably, the entity should recognise revenue by reference to the stage of completion of the contract activity in accordance with IAS 11;[191]

(b)   if the entity does not have to acquire and supply construction materials, the agreement may be for services and IAS 18 requires revenue to be recognised by reference to the stage of completion using IAS 11 principles;[192] (see 3.8 above) or

(c)   if the entity has to provide services and construction materials as part of its contractual obligation to deliver the real estate to the buyer, the agreement is an agreement for the sale of goods – see 3.7 above.[193] Under the agreement:

(i)   the entity may transfer to the buyer control and the significant risks and rewards of ownership of the work in progress in its current state as construction progresses, i.e. in a process of continuous transfer, and the percentage of completion method will apply;[194] or

(ii)   the entity may transfer to the buyer control and the significant risks and rewards of ownership of the real estate in its entirety at a single time (whether this be at completion, on or after delivery). In this case, the entity can recognise revenue only when all the criteria in paragraph 14 of IAS 18 are satisfied.[195]

To meet the criteria in paragraph 14, as discussed at 3.7 above, means that, in addition to transferring significant risks and rewards of ownership, the entity retains neither continuing managerial involvement to the degree usually associated with ownership nor effective control over the goods sold. In addition, the amount of revenue can be measured reliably, it is probable that the economic benefits associated with the transaction will flow to the entity and the costs incurred or to be incurred in respect of the transaction can be measured reliably.

If the entity has to carry out any further work on the real estate itself that has already been delivered to the buyer, it should recognise a liability measured in accordance with IAS 37 and an expense for this work. Additional separately identifiable goods or services would already have been identified as a separate component and revenue allocated accordingly (see flowchart above).[196]

When this Interpretation was in draft form the IFRIC believed that the 'continuous transfer' of work in progress envisaged in (c)(i) above indicated that the contract was a construction contract and hence should be accounted for under IAS 11. However, in response to comments received, the IFRIC accepted that these were not construction contracts but still argued that when the criteria for recognising revenue from the sale of goods are met continuously, it is appropriate to recognise revenue as the criteria are met.[197] The Interpretation states that the requirements of IAS 11 are generally applicable to the recognition of revenue and the associated expenses for such a transaction,[198] i.e. they will give the best approximations in this type of arrangement.

Features of 'continuous transfer' include circumstances in which the buyer has a right to take over the work in progress during construction (albeit with a penalty) and to engage a different entity to complete it. During this process the builder will have access to the land and the work in progress in order to perform its contractual obligations. However, this access does not necessarily imply that the builder retains continuing managerial involvement to the degree usually associated with ownership to an extent that would preclude recognition of some or all of the consideration as revenue. The builder may have control over the activities related to the performance of its contractual obligation but not over the real estate itself.[199]

The IFRIC believe that arrangements involving this 'continuous transfer' of work in progress (in (c)(i) above) are uncommon. If a builder/developer 'pre-sells' a development to an institutional investor, this contractual arrangement is usually, in substance, a financing arrangement and the purchaser will not have the right to assume the work in progress. Revenue recognition will normally be deferred until a single point of time (as in (c)(ii) above), such as on completion.[200]

The following, based on the illustrative examples that accompany IFRIC 15, helps identify the different elements within these arrangements.

Example 25.4:   Applying IFRIC 15 to commercial real estate[201]

An entity buys a plot of land for the construction of commercial real estate. It designs an office block and applies for building permission. The entity markets the office block to potential tenants and signs conditional lease agreements.

(a) It then markets the office block itself to potential buyers and signs with one of them a conditional agreement for the sale of land and the construction of the office block. The buyer cannot put the land or the incomplete office block back to the entity. When the entity receives the building permission and all agreements become unconditional, it constructs the office block.

The agreement should be separated into a component for the sale of land and a component for the construction of the office block. The component for the sale of land is a sale of goods within the scope of IAS 18.

Because all the major structural decisions were made by the entity and were included in the designs submitted to the planning authorities before the buyer signed the conditional agreement, it is assumed that there will be no major change in the designs after the construction has begun. Consequently, the construction of the office block is not a construction contract and is within the scope of IAS 18. Construction takes place on land the buyer owns before construction begins and the buyer cannot put the incomplete office block back to the entity. This indicates that the entity transfers to the buyer control and the significant risks and rewards of ownership of the work in progress in its current state as construction progresses. Therefore, the entity recognises revenue from the construction of the office block by reference to the stage of completion using the percentage of completion method.

(b) Alternatively, assume that the construction of the office block started before the entity signed the agreement with the buyer. In that event, the agreement should be separated into three components: a component for the sale of land, a component for the partially constructed office block and a component for the construction of the office block. The entity should apply the recognition criteria separately to each component. Assuming that the other facts remain unchanged, the entity recognises revenue from the component for the construction of the office block by reference to the stage of completion using the percentage of completion method.

In this example, the sale of land is a separately identifiable component but this will not always be the case. IFRIC 15 notes that in some jurisdictions, a condominium is legally defined as the absolute ownership of a unit based on a legal description of the airspace the unit actually occupies, plus an undivided interest in the ownership of the common elements (that includes the land and actual building itself, all the driveways, parking, lifts, outside hallways, recreation and landscaped areas) that are owned jointly with the other condominium unit owners. In this case, the undivided interest in the ownership of the common elements does not give the buyer control over the significant risks and rewards of the land itself. The right to the unit itself and the interest in the common elements are not separable.[202]

Example 25.5:   Applying IFRIC 15 to residential real estate[203]

An entity is developing residential real estate and starts marketing individual units (apartments) while construction is still in progress. Buyers enter into a binding sale agreement that gives them the right to acquire a specified unit when it is ready for occupation. They pay a deposit that is refundable only if the entity fails to deliver the completed unit in accordance with the contracted terms. Buyers are also required to make progress payments between the time of the initial agreement and contractual completion. The balance of the purchase price is paid only on contractual completion, when buyers obtain possession of their unit. Buyers are able to specify only minor variations to the basic design but they cannot specify or alter major structural elements of the design of their unit.

(a) In Country A, no rights to the underlying real estate asset transfer to the buyer other than through the agreement. Consequently, the construction takes place regardless of whether sale agreements exist. The terms of the agreement and other facts and circumstances indicate that the agreement is not a construction contract. It is a forward contract that gives the buyer an asset in the form of a right to acquire, use and sell the completed real estate at a later date and an obligation to pay the purchase price in accordance with its terms. Although the buyer might be able to transfer its interest in the forward contract to another party, the entity retains control and the significant risks and rewards of ownership of the work in progress in its current state until the completed real estate is transferred. Therefore, revenue should be recognised at completion as it is only at this point that all of IAS 18's criteria are met.

(b) In Country B, the law requires the entity to transfer immediately to the buyer ownership of the real estate in its current state of completion and that any additional construction becomes the responsibility and property of the buyer as construction progresses. In this case it is possible that the entity transfers to the buyer control and the significant risks and rewards of ownership of the work in progress in its current state as construction progresses. For example, if the agreement is terminated before construction is complete, the buyer retains the work in progress and the entity has the right to be paid for the work performed. This might indicate that control is transferred along with ownership. If it does, the entity recognises revenue using the percentage of completion method taking into account the stage of completion of the whole building and the agreements signed with individual buyers.

As mentioned earlier, the situation (b) in this illustrative example involving the continuous transfer of work in progress, is believed by the IFRIC to be uncommon. However in certain jurisdictions, such as France and Belgium, there are agreements defined by law (Vente en l'Etat Final d'Achèvement – otherwise known as 'VEFA' agreements) under which the seller of real estate does immediately transfer the rights of ownership of the floor area and existing work to the buyer, and additional construction work becomes the property of the buyer as it is performed.[204] These specific agreements were discussed by the IFRIC in developing the Interpretation and may be an example of this continuous transfer.

IAS 18 has fewer disclosure requirements than IAS 11 and therefore the IFRIC Board have inserted a number of specific disclosures in IFRIC 15 that are required when these agreements are deemed to be 'continuous transfer' arrangements that are accounted for under IAS 18:[205]

(a) When an entity recognises revenue using the percentage of completion method for agreements that meet all the criteria in paragraph 14 of IAS 18 continuously as construction progresses it should disclose:

   (i) how it determines which agreements meet all the criteria in paragraph 14 of IAS 18 continuously as construction progresses;

   (ii) the amount of revenue arising from such agreements in the period; and

   (iii) the methods used to determine the stage of completion of agreements in progress.

(b) For the agreements described in the paragraph above that are in progress at the reporting date, the entity shall also disclose:

   (i) the aggregate amount of costs incurred and recognised profits (less recognised losses) to date; and

   (ii) the amount of advances received.

The guidance in IFRIC 15 replaces the guidance on real estate sales that was previously included in the Appendix to IAS 18. The reference to revenue generally being recognised on the passing of legal title has been deleted[206] but of course the general criteria of IAS 18 applicable to the sale of goods (see 3.7 above) will still be applicable.

IFRIC 15 was issued in July 2008 and is effective for annual periods commencing on or after 1 January 2009 with earlier application permitted.[207] There are no transitional exemptions, so changes in accounting policy are to be applied retrospectively.[208]

6.12   Regulatory liabilities

In many countries the provision of utilities (e.g. water, natural gas or electricity) to consumers is regulated by a government agency. Regulations differ between countries but often regulators operate a cost-plus system under which a utility is allowed to make a fixed return on investment. Consequently, the future price that a utility is allowed to charge its customers may be influenced by past cost levels and investment levels.

Under many national GAAPs (including US GAAP – see FAS 71 – *Accounting for the Effects of Certain Types of Regulation*) accounting practices have been developed that allow an entity to account for the effects of regulation by deferring revenue and recognising a 'regulatory liability' that reflects the decrease in future prices required by the regulator.

The issue of regulatory assets and liabilities has been discussed by the IFRIC on numerous occasions, most recently at its meetings in September and November of 2008 where it concluded that it would not take this matter onto its agenda on the grounds that it thought divergence in practice was not significant under IFRS,[209] where such items are only rarely recognised.

However in December 2008 the IASB agreed to add this project to its agenda. In July 2009 it issued an exposure draft – *Rate-regulated Activities*.[210] This exposure draft favours the US GAAP approach, requiring an entity to:[211]

(a)   recognise a regulatory asset or regulatory liability if the regulator permits the entity to recover specific previously incurred costs or requires it to refund previously collected amounts and to earn a specified return on its regulated activities by adjusting the prices it charges its customers; and

(b)   measure a regulatory asset or regulatory liability at the expected present value of the cash flows to be recovered or refunded as a result of regulation, both on initial recognition and at the end of each subsequent reporting period. This net present value will be an estimated probability-weighted average of the present value of the expected cash flows.

The proposals within the exposure draft would apply to the activities of an entity that meet both of the following criteria:[212]

(a)   an authorised body (the regulator) establishes the price the entity must charge its customers for the goods or services the entity provides, and that price binds the customers; and

(b)   the price established by regulation (the rate) is designed to recover the specific costs the entity incurs in providing the regulated goods or services and to earn a specified return (cost-of-service regulation). The specified return could be a minimum or range and need not be a fixed or guaranteed return.

If finalised as drafted this exposure draft would have a significant impact on rate regulated entities within its scope. For further details, including our opinion of the proposals within the exposure draft, see Chapter 15 at 3.1 and Chapter 24 at 5.4.12.

6.13   Transfers of Assets from Customers

It is quite common for utilities, in particular, to receive contributions of assets from customers so that they can be connected to networks or receive services from them. IFRIC 18 was issued by the IASB in January 2009 to provide guidance in these situations.[213]

This Interpretation applies to all agreements under which an entity receives from a customer, or another party, an item of property, plant and equipment (or cash to acquire or construct such an asset) that the entity must then use either to connect the customer to a network or to provide the customer ongoing access to a supply of goods or services or both.[214] The Interpretation does not apply if this transfer is a government grant within the scope of IAS 20 – *Accounting for Government Grants and Disclosure of Government Assistance* – or the asset is used in a service concession within the scope of IFRIC 12 – *Service Concession Arrangements*;[215] see Chapter 23.

A typical arrangement is one in which a builder or individual householder must pay for power cables, pipes, or other connections for water, electricity or other supplies. However, the Interpretation will also apply to many outsourcing arrangements where the existing assets are contributed to the service provider or the customer must pay for assets or both. For example, in an arrangement under which an entity outsources its telephony, it is very common for it to transfer its existing assets to the service provider and for this to be reflected in the contract price.

The first step is to assess whether the item of property, plant and equipment received meets the definition of an asset as set out in the *Framework*.[216] In other words, whose asset is it? Something can only be an asset of the reporting entity if that entity controls it. The water pipes put in to connect the new house may be controlled by the householder from the house to the boundary of the property and the utility will control everything from the boundary. Note that a third party that has no direct connection to the ongoing service may have constructed and contributed the asset, e.g. the builder; this does not prevent the arrangement being within scope. In an outsourcing arrangement, the service provider may operate the equipment but may or may not have rights over its maintenance and replacement which will indicate who controls the asset.

If the reporting entity does control the asset, the transferred asset must be recognised and is initially measured at its fair value, which becomes its cost on initial recognition.[217] This is discussed in more detail in Chapter 16 at 3.2.1 H. It is an exchange transaction involving dissimilar goods and services[218](see 3.9 above), therefore it will be necessary to identify the separate services that are to be provided in exchange for the item of property, plant and equipment.[219] This is in order to allocate revenue to these elements and to determine the manner in which that revenue should be recognised.

The service may simply be connection of the customer to the network if this represents stand-alone value to the customer and has a fair value that is reliably measurable.[220] Would the customer who made the contribution pay the same amount for the ongoing goods and services as others who have not done so?, If so, this suggests that connection is the only service provided in exchange for the contributed asset.[221] On the other hand, a lower price for ongoing goods and services than is available to other customers suggests that the future goods and services are, at least to some extent, provided in return for the contributed asset.[222]

The fair value of the total consideration received or receivable under the agreement, i.e. including the fair value of the contributed asset, is allocated to each service and each must be separately assessed using IAS 18's general recognition criteria, described at 3.7 above.[223] This enables the entity to determine the period over which the revenue is recognised. If there are no ongoing goods and services provided in exchange, then revenue is recognised as soon as the connection is complete. The revenue for ongoing access to the supply of goods and services will be recognised in accordance with the terms of the agreement if it has a specified term. If there is no specified period in the agreement the related revenue will be recognised over a period not exceeding the useful life of the contributed item of property, plant and equipment.[224] The following example based on Illustrative Example 3 in IFRIC 18 illustrates issues concerning revenue recognition (rather than asset recognition):

Example 25.6:   Analysing an agreement under IFRIC 18[225]

An entity enters into an agreement with a customer involving the outsourcing of the customer's information technology (IT) functions. As part of the agreement, the customer transfers ownership of its existing IT equipment to the entity. Initially, the entity must use the equipment to provide the service required by the outsourcing agreement. The entity is responsible for maintaining the equipment and for replacing it when it decides to do so. The useful life of the equipment is estimated to be three years. The outsourcing agreement requires service to be provided for ten years for a fixed price that is lower than the price the entity would have charged if the IT equipment had not been transferred.

These facts indicate that the IT equipment is an asset of the entity, who will recognise the equipment and measure its cost on initial recognition at its fair value. Because the price charged for the service is lower than the price the entity would charge without the transfer of the IT equipment, this service is a separately identifiable service included in the agreement. The facts also indicate that it is the only service to be provided in exchange for the transfer of the IT equipment. Therefore, the entity should recognise revenue arising from the exchange transaction when the service is performed, i.e. over the ten-year term of the outsourcing agreement.

Alternatively, assume that after the first three years, the price the entity charges under the outsourcing agreement increases to reflect the fact that it will then be replacing the equipment the customer transferred. In this case, the reduced price for the services provided under the outsourcing agreement reflects the useful life of the transferred equipment. For this reason, the entity should recognise revenue from the exchange transaction over the first three years of the agreement.

The Basis of Conclusions to the Interpretation points to IFRIC 12 and IFRIC 13 for guidance on allocating the fair value; in these Interpretations it is based on the fair values of the separate components.[226] IFRIC 12 is discussed in Chapter 23 and IFRIC 13 at 6.14 below.

The following flowchart illustrates the analysis and accounting to be applied under the Interpretation:

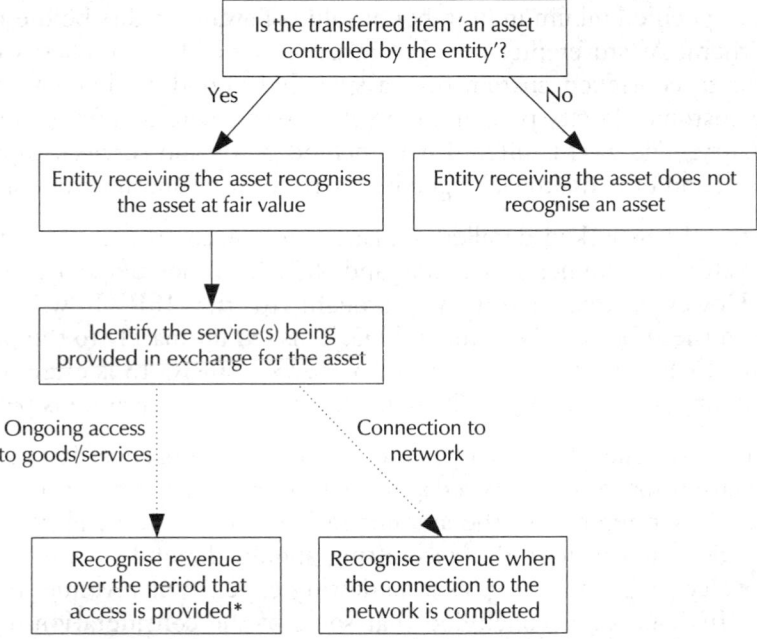

* If the agreement is silent, this is no longer than the life of the related asset.

The analysis and accounting to be applied when the entity receives cash that it must use to construct or acquire the assets is similar to the above. The entity needs to assess whether the agreement is within scope of the Interpretation and, if so, it will need to assess whether an asset is required to be recognised. The property, plant and equipment acquired or constructed will be recognised in accordance with IAS 16 and revenue, at the amount of cash received, will be recognised according to each separately identifiable service provided, as explained above.[227]

This Interpretation is prospectively applied to transfers of assets from customers received on or after 1 July 2009. Given that this effective date is based upon when transactions occur rather than when an entity's accounting period commences it is very possible that two different accounting policies will be applied in the year of adoption (and subsequently). Earlier application is allowed, provided the valuations and other information necessary to apply the Interpretation were obtained at the time of those transfers.[228]

6.14   Customer loyalty programmes

Customer loyalty programmes are now an integral element of a wide range of businesses – from airlines to retail, and from consumer credit to mobile telecommunications. Customer loyalty programmes are used by companies to provide incentives to their customers to buy their products or use their services. Customer loyalty is recognised through the grant of award credits, such as 'points' or 'airmiles'; customers can then redeem the award credits for free or discounted goods or services.

The programmes operate in a variety of ways. Customers may be required to accumulate a specified minimum number or value of award credits before they are able to redeem them. Award credits may be linked to individual purchases or groups of purchases, or to continued custom over a specified period of time. A company may operate the customer loyalty programme itself or participate in a programme operated by a third party. The awards offered may include goods and services supplied by the company itself and/or rights to claim goods or services from another vendor.[229]

Until recently, IFRSs lacked detailed guidance on how companies should account for customer loyalty programmes in general, and their liabilities under these schemes in particular. However, the matter was brought to the IFRIC, who commenced discussions on the subject in November 2005. This led ultimately to the publication in June 2007 of IFRIC 13 – *Customer Loyalty Programmes*. IFRIC 13 is effective for annual periods beginning on or after 1 July 2008; however, earlier application is permitted.

In addressing the issue, the IFRIC has rejected two approaches. It does not accept that an obligation for expenses is recognised as an expense at the time of the initial sale, measured by reference to the amount required to settle it, in accordance with IAS 37. Nor does it consider the accounting should depend on the nature of the customer loyalty programme, e.g. as a marketing expense or revenue, depending on significance. Instead it has concluded that some of the consideration received from the customer should be allocated to the award credits and deferred as a liability until the entity fulfils its obligations to deliver awards to customers. The liability is measured by reference to the value of the award credits to the customer (not their cost to the entity) and recognised as a deferral of revenue (not an expense). In support of this approach, it is argued that:

(a)   award credits are an element of the market exchange of economic benefits between the entity and the customer. They represent rights granted to a customer, for which the customer is implicitly paying. They can be distinguished from marketing expenses because they are granted to the customer as part of a sales transaction; and

(b)   award credits are separately identifiable from the other goods or services sold as part of the initial sale,

In the IFRIC's view, paragraph 13 of IAS 18 applies if a single transaction requires two or more separate goods or services to be delivered at different times; it ensures that revenue for each item is recognised only when that item is delivered. In contrast, paragraph 19 of IAS 18 applies only if the entity has to incur further costs directly related to items already delivered – for example, to meet warranty claims. In the IFRIC's view, loyalty awards are not costs that directly relate to the goods and services already delivered – rather, they are separate goods or services delivered at a later date.[230]

Although the issue of customer loyalty programmes was discussed by the US Emerging Issues Task Force (EITF), no conclusion was reached. As a result, under US GAAP there is no specific authoritative accounting guidance on accounting for the issue of award credits, and in practice entities commonly recognise an expense on original sale or when the obligation is fulfilled. In the airline sector – where such arrangements are pervasive – the majority of airlines have historically used the first approach.

6.14.1 The scope of IFRIC 13

According to the IFRIC, the main area of accounting diversity concerns award credits that entities grant to their customers as part of a sales transaction, and that the customers can redeem in the future for free or discounted goods or services.[231] Consequently, the scope of IFRIC 13 is somewhat limited, in that it applies only to transactions whereby an entity grants award credits to its customers as part of a sales transaction and, subject to meeting any further qualifying conditions, those customers can redeem the credits for free or discounted goods and services.[232]

The Interpretation states clearly that it applies to customer loyalty award credits that an entity grants to its customers as part of a sales transaction – i.e. a sale of goods, rendering of services or use by a customer of entity assets.[233] In other words, it applies to schemes whereby the award credits offered to customers derive from a past transaction. This means that it does not apply to the distribution of 'money off' vouchers or other schemes that do not involve an initial sales transaction.

IFRIC 13 does not specifically address the situation where an operator of a loyalty programme (e.g. an airline) sells award credits to another entity (e.g. a credit card company) and that other entity grants the purchased award credits to its own customers who are also members of the loyalty programme. This type of transaction is a direct sale of the award credits to a third party and therefore is within the scope of IAS 18, as opposed to IFRIC 13. Consequently, since the cardholders / members can redeem the awards directly with the programme operator, it is our view that the programme operator still has an obligation that should be recognised through the deferral of some or all of the sales proceeds. Furthermore, the award credits granted to programme members directly by the programme operator versus those granted by third parties will, in both cases, have the same rights attaching to them and are indistinguishable from one another in the members' accounts.

However, where a programme operator sells its award credits to a third party, it is likely that the sale will involve a number of components. For example, an airline selling its airmiles to a credit card company is likely to be selling both a travel component (for redemption by the third party's customers) and a marketing component for allowing the third party access to its loyalty program and customer base. Consequently, in determining how much revenue should be recognised on the sale of the airmiles to the third party, the airline should determine how much of the consideration should be attributed to these components, since it is likely that the consideration related to marketing component may not require deferral. This is discussed in more detail in section 6.14.3 below.

6.14.2 The requirements of IFRIC 13

Under IFRIC 13, an entity must apply paragraph 13 of IAS 18 and account for award credits as a separately identifiable component of the sales transaction(s) in which they are granted (the 'initial sale'). The fair value of the consideration received or receivable in respect of the initial sale must be allocated between the award credits and the other components of the sale.[234]

However, IAS 18 does not prescribe an allocation method for multiple-component sales. Its overall objective is to determine the amount the customer is paying for each component, which can be estimated by drawing on the entity's experience of transactions with similar customers. Hence, the Interpretation requires the consideration allocated to award credits to be measured by reference to their fair value.

The Interpretation does not specify whether the amount allocated to the award credits should be:

(a)   equal to their fair value (irrespective of the fair values of the other elements); or

(b)   a proportion of the total consideration based on the fair value of the award credits relative to the fair values of the other elements of the sale.

The IFRIC noted that IAS 18 does not specify which of these methods should be applied, or in what circumstances and decided that the Interpretation should not be more prescriptive than IAS 18. The selection of one or other method is therefore left to management's judgement.

The measurement of fair value is discussed in more detail in 6.14.3 below.

However, since not all award credits will ultimately be redeemed, IFRIC 13 specifies the basis on which revenue should be recognised, depending on whether the awards are supplied by the entity itself or by a third party. If the entity supplies the awards itself, it should recognise the consideration allocated to award credits as revenue when award credits are redeemed and it fulfils its obligations to supply awards. The amount of revenue recognised should be based on the number of award credits that have been redeemed in exchange for awards, relative to the total number expected to be redeemed.[235]

The practical application of this approach is illustrated in Example 1 of the illustrative examples appended to IFRIC 13, as follows:[236]

Example 25.7:   Awards supplied by the entity

A grocery retailer operates a customer loyalty programme. It grants programme members loyalty points when they spend a specified amount on groceries. Programme members can redeem the points for further groceries. The points have no expiry date. In one period, the entity grants 100 points. Management expects 80 of these points to be redeemed. Management estimates the fair value of each loyalty point to be $1, and defers revenue of $100.

Year 1

At the end of the first year, 40 of the points have been redeemed in exchange for groceries, i.e. half of those expected to be redeemed. The entity recognises revenue of (40 points / 80 points) × $100 = $50.

Year 2

In the second year, management revises its expectations. It now expects 90 points to be redeemed altogether.

During the second year, 41 points are redeemed, bringing the total number redeemed to 40 + 41 = 81 points. The cumulative revenue that the entity recognises is (81 points / 90 points) × $100 = $90. The entity has already recognised revenue of $50 in the first year, so it recognises $40 in the second year.

Year 3

In the third year, a further nine points are redeemed, taking the total number of points redeemed to 81 + 9 = 90. Management continues to expect that only 90 points will ever be redeemed, i.e. that no more points will be redeemed after the third year. So the cumulative revenue to date is (90 points / 90 points) × $100 = $100. The entity has already recognised $90 of revenue ($50 in the first year and $40 in the second year), so it recognises the remaining $10 in the third year. All of the revenue initially deferred has now been recognised.

In August 2009, as part of its Annual Improvements project, the IASB issued an exposure draft clarifying that when the fair value of the award credit is calculated by reference to the value of the awards for which they could be redeemed, the value of the awards for which they could be redeemed must be adjusted to reflect expected forfeitures. In the exposure draft the opening paragraph of the above example is amended to explain that each loyalty point issued could be redeemed for groceries valued at $1.25 but that the fair value of the award credits is calculated at $100 being the 100 points issued multiplied by 80% (given the 20% forfeiture rate) of $1.25.[237] It is proposed that this amendment be effective for annual periods commencing on or after 1 January 2011 with earlier application permitted.[238]

If a third party supplies the awards, the entity must assess whether it is collecting the consideration allocated to the award credits on its own account (i.e. as the principal in the transaction) or on behalf of the third party (i.e. as an agent for the third party).

(a)   If the entity is collecting the consideration on behalf of the third party, it must:

   (i)   measure its revenue as the net amount retained on its own account, i.e. the difference between the consideration allocated to the award credits and the amount payable to the third party for supplying the awards; and

   (ii)   recognise this net amount as revenue when the third party becomes obliged to supply the awards and entitled to receive consideration for doing so. These events may occur as soon as the award credits are granted. Alternatively, if the customer can choose to claim awards from either the entity or a third party, these events may occur only when the customer chooses to claim awards from the third party.

(b)   If the entity is collecting the consideration on its own account, it must measure its revenue as the gross consideration allocated to the award credits and recognise the revenue when it fulfils its obligations in respect of the awards.[239]

The practical application of this approach is illustrated in Example 2 of the illustrative examples appended to IFRIC 13, as follows:[240]

Example 25.8:   Awards supplied by a third party

A retailer of electrical goods participates in a customer loyalty programme operated by an airline. It grants programme members one airmile with each $1 they spend on electrical goods. Programme members can redeem the airmiles for air travel with the airline, subject to availability. The retailer pays the airline $0.009 for each airmile.

In one period, the retailer sells electrical goods for consideration totalling $1 million and grants 1 million airmiles.

Allocation of consideration to airmiles

The retailer estimates that the fair value of an airmile is $0.01. It allocates to the airmiles 1 million × $0.01 = $10,000 of the consideration it has received from the sales of its electrical goods.

Revenue recognition

Having granted the airmiles, the retailer has fulfilled its obligations to the customer. The airline is obliged to supply the awards and entitled to receive consideration for doing so. Therefore the retailer recognises revenue from the airmiles when it sells the electrical goods.

Revenue measurement

If the retailer has collected the consideration allocated to the airmiles on its own account, it measures its revenue as the gross $10,000 allocated to them. It separately recognises the $9,000 paid or payable to the airline as an expense. If the retailer has collected the consideration on behalf of the airline, i.e. as an agent for the airline, it measures its revenue as the net amount it retains on its own account. This amount of revenue is the difference between the $10,000 consideration allocated to the airmiles and the $9,000 passed on to the airline.

Normally, the deferred consideration will exceed the unavoidable costs of meeting the obligation to supply the awards. However, if at any time the unavoidable costs of meeting the obligations to supply the awards are expected to exceed the consideration received and receivable for them (i.e. the consideration allocated to the award credits at the time of the initial sale that has not yet been recognised as revenue plus any further consideration receivable when the customer redeems the award credits), the entity has onerous contracts. A liability must be recognised for the excess in accordance with IAS 37. The need to recognise such a liability could arise if the expected costs of supplying awards increase, for example if the entity revises its expectations about the number of award credits that will be redeemed.[241]

6.14.3 *Measuring the fair value of award credits*

IAS 18 requires revenue to be measured at the fair value of the consideration received or receivable.[242] Hence the amount of revenue attributed to award credits should be the fair value of the consideration received for them.

IFRIC 13 requires also that the consideration allocated to the award credits must be measured by reference to their fair value but goes further and explains it as ', *i.e. the amount for which the award credits could be sold separately*'.[243] The brief Application Guidance set out in the Appendix to IFRIC 13 notes that this amount is often not directly observable and in such circumstances, it must be estimated.[244]

This can lead to some confusion as, for example, airlines also sell airmiles/award credits to third parties to use in their marketing programs. However, airlines would not consider the amount for which the credits are sold separately to be the same as the fair value of airmiles issued as part of sale of a ticket. The reason is that when airlines sell airmiles to third parties they are selling both a travel component (for redemption by the third party's customers) and a marketing component for allowing the third party access to their loyalty program and customer base. In such cases these sales would themselves be required to be accounted for under IFRIC 13 with an estimation required for the two components.

It is expected that in the majority of cases the fair value will need to be estimated. IFRIC 13 sets out in the application guidance that an entity may estimate the fair value of award credits by reference to the fair value of the awards for which they could be redeemed. It goes further and notes that if customers can choose from a range of different awards, the fair value of the award credits will reflect the fair values of the range of available awards, weighted in proportion to the frequency with which each award is expected to be selected.[245]

This means, for example, that airlines may be required to estimate the fair value of an airmile by reference to a weighted average ticket value using an equivalent restricted fare as a proxy for tickets representing the profile of actual redemptions. These would depend on which routes, classes of travel, and the time of flights for which the miles are redeemed. Therefore an airline would be expected to determine the fair value of the airmiles on a basis that is 'weighted in proportion to the frequency with which each award is expected to be selected'. In our view, companies will be required in a number of cases to maintain comprehensive redemption data covering all variables subject to estimation, and that this is likely to place an onerous burden on many companies that grant loyalty awards.

However, the Application Guidance goes on to state that, in some circumstances, other estimation techniques may be available.[246] For example, if a third party will supply the awards and the entity pays the third party for each award credit it grants, it could estimate the fair value of the award credits by reference to the amount it pays the third party, adding a reasonable profit margin. The Application Guidance then ends off merely by stating that 'Judgement is required to select and apply the estimation technique that satisfies the requirements of paragraph 6 of the consensus and is most appropriate in the circumstances.'[247] Clearly, this provides preparers with substantial flexibility in choosing the estimation techniques that they apply in practice. At the same time, though, it needs to be recognised that in most cases the amount of revenue that is attributable to the award credits is not directly observable because the award credits are granted as part of a larger sale.

6.14.4 *Effective date and transition*

IFRIC 13 is effective for annual periods beginning on or after 1 July 2008. Earlier application is permitted, although if an entity applies the Interpretation for a period beginning before 1 July 2008, it must disclose that fact.[248]

No specific transitional provisions are specified in IFRIC 13. This means in practice that IAS 8 applies. This requires that any changes be recognised retrospectively, where practicable. If an entity has previously applied paragraph 19 of IAS 18 and provided for the future incremental cost of providing the awards it should, in our view, treat the adoption of IFRIC 13 as a change in accounting policy. If an entity has previously used the deferred revenue model, but based on an allocation method other than fair value, the adoption of the Interpretation should be treated as a change in an accounting estimate.

7   CONCLUSION

The growing complexity and diversity of business activity have given rise to a variety of forms of revenue-earning transactions which were never contemplated when the point of sale was established several decades ago as the general rule for revenue recognition. Added to this, as generally accepted accounting practice for the recognition of revenue has gradually moved away from strict adherence to the realisation concept, it has become haphazard. There is clear tension between a growing practice of recognising revenue during the course of productive activity with an approach based on taking revenue and expenses at inception, using an argument based on accounting for financial instruments, an example being fund managers' fees and trail commissions described at 6.2.4 above. This is occurring and is rationalised on a case-by-case basis, rather than in terms of an established principle.

Now that the lengthy IASB/FASB joint project on revenue recognition has at last culminated in the issue of a Discussion Paper it is clear that the favoured model represents less of a fundamental change in approach to revenue recognition than other methods discussed during its development. However, the project has so far avoided many of the more complex and contentious issues surrounding revenue recognition. Until significant further work is completed, it is unclear as to what the extent of its impact may be. The IASB has set itself a challenging timetable for a new standard and it is to be hoped that the final result helps address some of the current inconsistencies as well as providing a more coherent general approach.

References

1 IAS 18 (Original), *Revenue Recognition*, IASC, December 1982, para. 4.
2 John H. Myers, *'The Critical Event and Recognition of Net Profit'*, Accounting Review 34, October 1959, pp. 528-532.
3 SFAC No. 5, *Recognition and Measurement in Financial Statements of Business Enterprises*, FASB, December 1984, paras. 83-84.
4 SFAS 48, *Revenue Recognition When Right of Return Exists*, FASB, June 1981, para. 6.
5 SFAS 48, para. 6.
6 SFAS 48, para. 8.
7 IAS 11, *Construction Contracts*, IASB, para. 25.
8 IAS 18, *Revenue*, IASB, para. 20.
9 IAS 41, *Agriculture*, IASB, para. 5.
10 IAS 41, para. 12.
11 IAS 41, para. 13.
12 IAS 41, para. 26.
13 *Framework for the Preparation and Presentation of Financial Statements*, IASB, September 1989, para. 70(a).
14 IAS 18, Objective.
15 IAS 18, para. 1.
16 IAS 18, para. 3.
17 IAS 18, para. 4.
18 IAS 18, para. 5.
19 IAS 18, para. 6.
20 IAS 17, *Leases*, IASB, para. 2.
21 *Framework*, para. 70(a).
22 *Framework*, paras. 74-76.
23 IAS 1, *Presentation of Financial Statements*, IASB, para. 34.
24 IAS 16, *Property, Plant and Equipment*, IASB, para. 68.
25 IAS 18, para. 7.
26 IAS 18, para. 8.
27 *Improvements to IFRSs*, April 2009, IASB, IAS 18, Appendix, para. 21.
28 *Improvements to IFRSs*, April 2009, IASB, IAS 18, Appendix, para. 21.
29 *Improvements to IFRSs*, April 2009, IASB, IAS 18, Appendix, para. 21.
30 *Improvements to IFRSs*, April 2009, IASB, IAS 18, Appendix, para. 21.
31 IAS 18, paras. 14(a) and (b).
32 IAS 18, Appendix, paras. 6 and 2(c).
33 IAS 18, para. 9.
34 IAS 18, para. 10.
35 IAS 18, para. 7.
36 IAS 18, para. 11.
37 IAS 18, paras. 11 and 30(a).
38 IAS 18, para. 9.
39 IAS 18, para. 13.
40 IAS 18, para. 13.
41 IAS 11, para. 7.
42 IAS 11, paras. 8-10.
43 IAS 8, *Accounting Policies, Changes in Accounting Estimates and Errors*, IASB, para. 12. This provides that, in the selection and application of accounting policies, management *may*, in certain circumstances, also consider the most recent pronouncements of other standard-setting bodies that use a similar conceptual framework.
44 IAS 18, para. 14.
45 IAS 18, para. 19.
46 IAS 18, para. 16.
47 IAS 18, para. 17.
48 IAS 18, para. 15.
49 IAS 18, para. 14.
50 IAS 18, para. 15.
51 IAS 18, Appendix, Sale of Goods.
52 IAS 18, para. 20.
53 IAS 18, para. 21.
54 IAS 18, para. 20.
55 IAS 18, para. 26.
56 IAS 18, para. 27.
57 IAS 18, para. 28.
58 IAS 18, Appendix, paras. 10-19.
59 IAS 18, para. 23.
60 IAS 18, para. 23.
61 IAS 18, para. 24.
62 IAS 18, para. 25.
63 IAS 18, para. 12.
64 IFRIC 18, *Transfers of Assets from Customers*, IFRIC, paras. 4-6.
65 IAS 16, para. 24.
66 IAS 16, para. 24.
67 IAS 16, para. 26.
68 IAS 16, para. 26.
69 IAS 16, para. 24.
70 IAS 16, para. 68.
71 IAS 38, *Intangible Assets*, IASB, paras. 45-47.
72 IFRIC 18, paras. 4-6.
73 IAS 18, para. 12.
74 IAS 18, para. 20(a).
75 SIC-31, *Revenue – Barter Transactions Involving Advertising Services*, IASB, para. 4.
76 SIC-31, para. 5.
77 SIC-31, para. 9.
78 IAS 18, paras. 29-30.
79 IAS 18, para. 32.
80 IAS 27, *Consolidated and Separate Financial Statements*, IASB, para. 38A.
81 IAS 18, para. 33.
82 IAS 18, paras. 18, 22 and 34.
83 IAS 18, para. 35.
84 IAS 1, paras. 81-82.

85 IAS 1, paras. 85-86.

86 IAS 1, para. 32.

87 IAS 1, para. 33.

88 IAS 1, para. 82(b).

89 IAS 18, para. 35(b).

90 IAS 1, para. 35.

91 IAS 16, para. 68.

92 SEC, Staff Accounting Bulletins, Topic 13: Revenue Recognition, *1. Revenue Recognition – general*.

93 SFAC No. 5, para. 83.

94 SFAC No. 5, para. 83(b).

95 SFAC No. 5, para. 84(a).

96 SFAC No. 5, para. 84(d).

97 SEC, Staff Accounting Bulletins, Topic 13: Revenue Recognition, *4. Fixed or determinable sales price*.

98 IAS 18, para. 17.

99 SEC, Staff Accounting Bulletins, Topic 13: Revenue Recognition.

100 Discussion Paper, *Preliminary Views on Revenue Recognition in Contracts with Customers*, IASB, December 2008.

101 This information has been summarised from the Discussion Paper – *Preliminary Views on Revenue Recognition in Contracts with Customers*.

102 IASB Work Plan as at 3 June 2009 available on the IASB website at http://www.iasb.org.

103 Discussion Paper – *Preliminary Views on Revenue Recognition in Contracts with Customers*, IASB, December 2008, para. S11.

104 Discussion Paper, para. S12.

105 Discussion Paper, para. 2.11.

106 Discussion Paper, paras. 2.12-2.18.

107 Discussion Paper, para. 2.21.

108 Discussion Paper, para. 3.2.

109 Discussion Paper, paras. 2.28-2.34.

110 Discussion Paper, paras. 5.28 and 5.31.

111 Discussion Paper, paras. 5.15-5.24.

112 Discussion Paper, para. 5.46.

113 Discussion Paper, para. 5.46.

114 Discussion Paper, paras. 5.103-5.104.

115 Discussion Paper, paras. S20-S22.

116 Discussion Paper, paras. 3.14-3.15.

117 Discussion Paper, para. 5.105.

118 Discussion Paper, Appendix C.

119 IAS 11, para. 26.

120 Discussion Paper – *Preliminary Views on Revenue Recognition in Contracts with Customers*, IASB, December 2008, paras. 6.17-6.21.

121 Discussion Paper, paras. 6.36-6.42.

122 Discussion Paper, paras. 6.26-6.29.

123 Discussion Paper, paras. 6.43-6.46.

124 Discussion Paper, paras. 3.34-3.42.

125 IAS 18, Appendix, para. 1.

126 IAS 18, Appendix, para. 2.

127 IAS 18, Appendix, para. 3.

128 IAS 18, Appendix, para. 4.

129 IAS 18, para. 9.

130 IAS 18, para. 11.

131 IFRIC 18, para. BC22.

132 IAS 18, Appendix, para. 5.

133 IAS 18, Appendix, para. 8.

134 Based on the AICPA Industry Accounting Guide, *Accounting for Franchise Fee Revenue*, AICPA, 1973.

135 IAS 18, Appendix, para. 18.

136 IAS 18, Appendix, para. 18.

137 IAS 18, Appendix, para. 20.

138 IAS 18, Appendix, para. 14.

139 IAS 18, Appendix, para. 14.

140 *Improvements to IFRSs*, May 2008, IAS 18, Appendix, para. 14.

141 IAS 18, Appendix, para. 14.

142 *IFRIC Update*, IFRIC, July 2008.

143 *IFRIC Update*, IFRIC, January 2007.

144 IAS 18, para. 14.

145 IAS 18, Appendix, para. 13.

146 This is also the view taken under US GAAP; see SFAS 91 at para. 10.

147 IAS 18, Appendix, para. 17.

148 IAS 18, Appendix, para. 7.

149 IAS 18, Appendix, para. 10.

150 IAS 18, Appendix, para. 12.

151 IAS 18, Appendix, para. 19.

152 Statement of Position 97-2, *Software Revenue Recognition*, Accounting Standards Executive Committee, AICPA, October 27, 1997.

153 SOP 97-2, para. 8.

154 IAS 18, para. 13.

155 SOP 97-2, para. 10.

156 SOP 97-2, para. 12, as amended by SOP 98-9, para. 6(b).

157 SOP 97-2, para. 11, as amended by SOP 98-9, para. 6(a).

158 SOP 97-2, para. 12.

159 Companies reporting under US GAAP would apply Accounting Research Bulletin (ARB) No. 45, *Long-Term Construction-Type Contracts*, and SOP 81-1, *Accounting for Performance of Construction-Type and Certain Production-Type Contracts*.

160 IAS 18, para. 21.

161 SOP 97-2, para. 7.

162 IAS 18, para. 8.

163 *Improvements to IFRSs*, April 2009, IASB, IAS 18, Appendix, para. 21.

164 IAS 18, para. 13.

165 *IFRIC Update*, IFRIC, March 2006, Page 7.

166 IAS 18, para. 10.

167 IAS 18, Appendix, para. 20.

168 IAS 18, Appendix, para. 20.

169 IAS 16, para. 68.

170 IAS 16, para. 69.

171 IAS 18, paras. 14-16.
172 IAS 18, para. 15.
173 IAS 18, Appendix, para. 9.
174 IAS 16, para. 71.
175 IAS 16, para. 72.
176 IAS 16, para. 68.
177 IAS 16, para. BC35C.
178 IAS 16, para. 68A.
179 IAS 7, *Statement of Cash Flows*, IASB, para. 14.
180 IAS 16, para. 81D.
181 IFRIC 15, *Agreements for the Construction of Real Estate*, IASB, para. 4.
182 IFRIC 15, para. 5.
183 IFRIC 15, para. 6.
184 IAS 11, para. 3.
185 IFRIC 15, para. 11.
186 IFRIC 15, para. 12.
187 IFRIC 15, para. 7.
188 IFRIC 15, paras. IE9-IE10.
189 IAS 18, para. 13.
190 IFRIC 15, para. 8.
191 IFRIC 15, para. 13.
192 IFRIC 15, para. 15.
193 IFRIC 15, para. 16.
194 IFRIC 15, para, 17.
195 IFRIC 15, para. 18.
196 IFRIC 15, para. 19.
197 IFRIC 15, para. BC35(c).
198 IFRIC 15, para. 17.
199 IFRIC 15, para. IE11.
200 *IFRIC Update*, IFRIC, May 2008.
201 IFRIC 15, paras. IE1-IE4.
202 IFRIC 15, para. IE5.
203 IFRIC 15, paras. IE6-IE8.
204 Agenda Paper 2B to the May 2008 IFRIC meeting, para. 12.
205 IFRIC 15, paras. 20-21.
206 IAS 18, Appendix, para. 9.
207 IFRIC 15, para. 24.
208 IFRIC 15, para. 25.
209 *IFRIC Update*, IFRIC, November 2008, page 4.
210 Exposure Draft, *Rate-regulated Activities*, IASB, July 2009.
211 Exposure Draft, *Rate-regulated Activities*, para. 2.
212 Exposure Draft, *Rate-regulated Activities*, para. 3.
213 IFRIC 18.
214 IFRIC 18, paras. 3-6.
215 IFRIC 18, para. 7.
216 IFRIC 18, para. 9.
217 IAS 18, para. 12 and IFRIC 18, para. 11.
218 IFRIC 18, para. 13.
219 IFRIC 18, para. 14.
220 IFRIC 18, para. 15.
221 IFRIC 18, para. 17.
222 IFRIC 18, para. 16.
223 IFRIC 18, para. 19.

224 IFRIC 18, para. 20.
225 IFRIC 18, Illustrative examples, Example 3.
226 IFRIC 18, para. BC19.
227 IFRIC 18, para. 21.
228 IFRIC 18, para. 22.
229 IFRIC 13, *Customer Loyalty Programmes*, IASB, para. 2.
230 IFRIC 13, para. BC9(a).
231 IFRIC 13, para. BC3.
232 IFRIC 13, para. 3.
233 IFRIC 13, para. 3(a).
234 IFRIC 13, para. 5.
235 IFRIC 13, para. 7.
236 IFRIC 13, Illustrative examples, Example 1.
237 *Proposed amendments to International Financial Reporting Standards*, IASB, August 2009, IFRIC 13, paras. AG2 and IE1.
238 *Proposed amendments to International Financial Reporting Standards*, IASB, August 2009, IFRIC 13, para. 10A.
239 IFRIC 13, para. 8.
240 IFRIC 13, Illustrative examples, Example 2.
241 IFRIC 13, para. 9.
242 IAS 18, para. 9.
243 IFRIC 13, para. 6.
244 IFRIC 13, Appendix – Application guidance, AG1.
245 IFRIC 13, Appendix – Application guidance, AG2.
246 IFRIC 13, Appendix – Application guidance, AG3.
247 IFRIC 13, Appendix – Application guidance, AG3.
248 IFRIC 13, para. 10.

Index of extracts from financial statements

Index of standards

Unless otherwise indicated, all references in the index below are to the versions of those pronouncements as approved and included in the Bound Volume of International Financial Reporting Standards at 1 January 2009 published by the IASB (ISBN 978-1-905590-90-2).

IFRS 1 – First-time Adoption of International Financial Reporting Standards

IFRS 2 – Share-based Payment

IFRS 2 (2009) – IFRS 2 as amended in April and June 2009

IFRS 3 – Business Combinations

IFRS 3 (2007) – IFRS 3 as per the 2007 Bound Volume of Standards

IFRS 5 – Non-current Assets Held for Sale and Discontinued Operations

IFRS 6 – Exploration for and Evaluation of Mineral Resources

IFRS 7 – Financial Instruments: Disclosures

IFRS 8 – Operating Segments

IAS 1 – Presentation of Financial Statements

IAS 2 – Inventories

IAS 8 – Accounting Policies, Changes in Accounting Estimates and Errors

IAS 17 – Leases

IAS 19 – Employee Benefits

IAS 20 – Accounting for Government Grants and Disclosure of Government Assistance

IAS 21 – The Effects of Changes in Foreign Exchange Rates

IAS 23 – Borrowing Costs

IAS 24 – Related Party Disclosures

IAS 27 (2007) – IAS 27 as per the 2007 Bound Volume of Standards

IAS 28 – Investments in Associates

IAS 29 – Financial Reporting in Hyperinflationary Economies

IAS 31 – Interests in Joint Ventures

IAS 32 – Financial Instruments: Presentation

IAS 33 – Earnings per Share

IAS 37 – Provisions, Contingent Liabilities and
Contingent Assets

IAS 38 – Intangible Assets

IAS 39 – Financial Instruments: Recognition and Measurement

IAS 40 – Investment Property

IAS 41 – Agriculture

Index